HAVE YO
THE FREE

TRACKER

Create your own horses to follow list with the **My Timeform Tracker**. Make notes about your eyecatchers on race and results screens, save and sort your lists of horses then choose from multiple alert options!

Unlimited horses, any time and free.
At timeform.com and on the App

AGE, WEIGHT & DISTANCE TABLE
For use with Chase and Hurdle races

Distance	Age	Jan	Feb	Mar	Apr	May	June
2m	5	12—7	12—7	12—7	12—7	12—7	12—7
	4	11—13	12—0	12—1	12—2	12—3	12—4
2¼m	5	12—7	12—7	12—7	12—7	12—7	12—7
	4	11—12	11—13	12—0	12—1	12—2	12—3
2½m	5	12—7	12—7	12—7	12—7	12—7	12—7
	4	11—11	11—12	11—13	12—0	12—1	12—2
2¾m	5	12—6	12—7	12—7	12—7	12—7	12—7
	4	11—10	11—11	11—12	11—13	12—0	12—1
3m	5	12—6	12—6	12—7	12—7	12—7	12—7
	4	11—8	11—10	11—11	11—12	11—13	12—0

Distance	Age	July	Aug	Sep	Oct	Nov	Dec
2m	5	12—7	12—7	12—7	12—7	12—7	12—7
	4	12—4	12—5	12—5	12—6	12—6	12—7
	3	11—5	11—6	11—8	11—9	11—11	11—12
2¼m	5	12—7	12—7	12—7	12—7	12—7	12—7
	4	12—3	12—4	12—5	12—5	12—6	12—6
	3	11—4	11—5	11—7	11—8	11—9	11—10
2½m	5	12—7	12—7	12—7	12—7	12—7	12—7
	4	12—2	12—3	12—4	12—5	12—6	12—6
	3		11—4	11—6	11—7	11—8	11—9
2¾m	5	12—7	12—7	12—7	12—7	12—7	12—7
	4	12—2	12—3	12—4	12—5	12—5	12—6
	3					11—7	11—8
3m	5	12—7	12—7	12—7	12—7	12—7	12—7
	4	12—1	12—2	12—3	12—4	12—5	12—5
	3				11—5	11—6	11—7

For 6-y-o's and older, use 12-7 in all cases

Note Race distances in the above tables are shown only at ¼-mile intervals. For races of 2m1f use the 2¼-mile table weights; for races of 2m3f use 2½ miles; and so forth. For races over odd distances, the nearest distance shown in the table should be used. Races over distances longer than 3 miles should be treated as 3-mile races.

National Hunt Flat races A separate age, weight & distance table is used for NH Flat races but there is no weight-for-age allowance for 5-y-o's; over 2 miles from January to November the allowance for 4-y-o's is 1 lb less than it is over jumps.

CHASERS & HURDLERS 2017/18

Price £75.00

A TIMEFORM PUBLICATION

A Timeform Publication

Compiled and produced by

Geoff Greetham (Publishing Editor), Paul Muncaster (Managing Editor), John Ingles (Senior Editor, 'Top Horses In France' & Editor for pedigrees), Phil Turner (Handicapper and Consultant Editor), Dan Barber (Handicapper and noteforms), Martin Rigg, Paul Goodenough (Handicappers), Nic Doggett, Ben Fearnley, Adam Houghton (Essays), Kris Hilliam, Jake Price (noteforms), Thomas Heslop (Research), David Holdsworth, Wendy Muncaster, Rachel Todd, Chris Wright, Ivan Gardiner, Michael Williamson (Production)

COPYRIGHT AND LIABILITY

Copyright in all Timeform Publications is strictly reserved by the Publishers and no material therein may be reproduced stored in a retrieval system or transmitted in any form or by any means electronic mechanical photocopying recording or otherwise without written permission of Timeform Limited.

The annual volume of 'Chasers & Hurdlers' registered at Stationers Hall is published by Timeform Limited, Halifax, West Yorkshire HX1 1XF (Tel: 01422 330330 Fax: 01422 398017 E-Mail: timeform@timeform.com) and printed and bound by Charlesworth Press, Wakefield, West Yorkshire WF2 9LP. It is supplied to the purchaser for his personal use and on the understanding that its contents are not disclosed. Except where the purchaser is dealing as a consumer (as defined in the Unfair Contract Terms Act 1977 Section 12) all conditions warranties or terms relating to fitness for purpose merchantability or condition of the goods and whether implied by Statute Common Law or otherwise are excluded and no responsibility is accepted by the Publishers for any loss whatsoever caused by any acts errors or omissions whether negligent or otherwise of the Publishers their Servants Agents or otherwise.

© **Timeform Limited 2018** ISBN 978-1-9997783-1-6

CONTENTS

4	Introduction
21	Highest Timeform Ratings
22	Timeform Champion Jumpers 2017/18
24	The Timeform 'Top 100'
26	2017/18 Statistics
29	Explanatory Notes
32	The Form Summaries and Rating Symbols
33	Chasers & Hurdlers 2017/18
910	Promising Horses
914	2017/18 Irish Statistics
916	Selected Big Races 2017/18
981	Errata & Addenda
982	Timeform 'Top Horses In France'
990	Index to Photographs
995	Horse of The Year and Champions from the 'Chasers & Hurdlers' series
1000	Big Race Winners

The age, weight and distance table, for use in applying the ratings in races involving horses of different ages, appears on the end paper at the front of the book

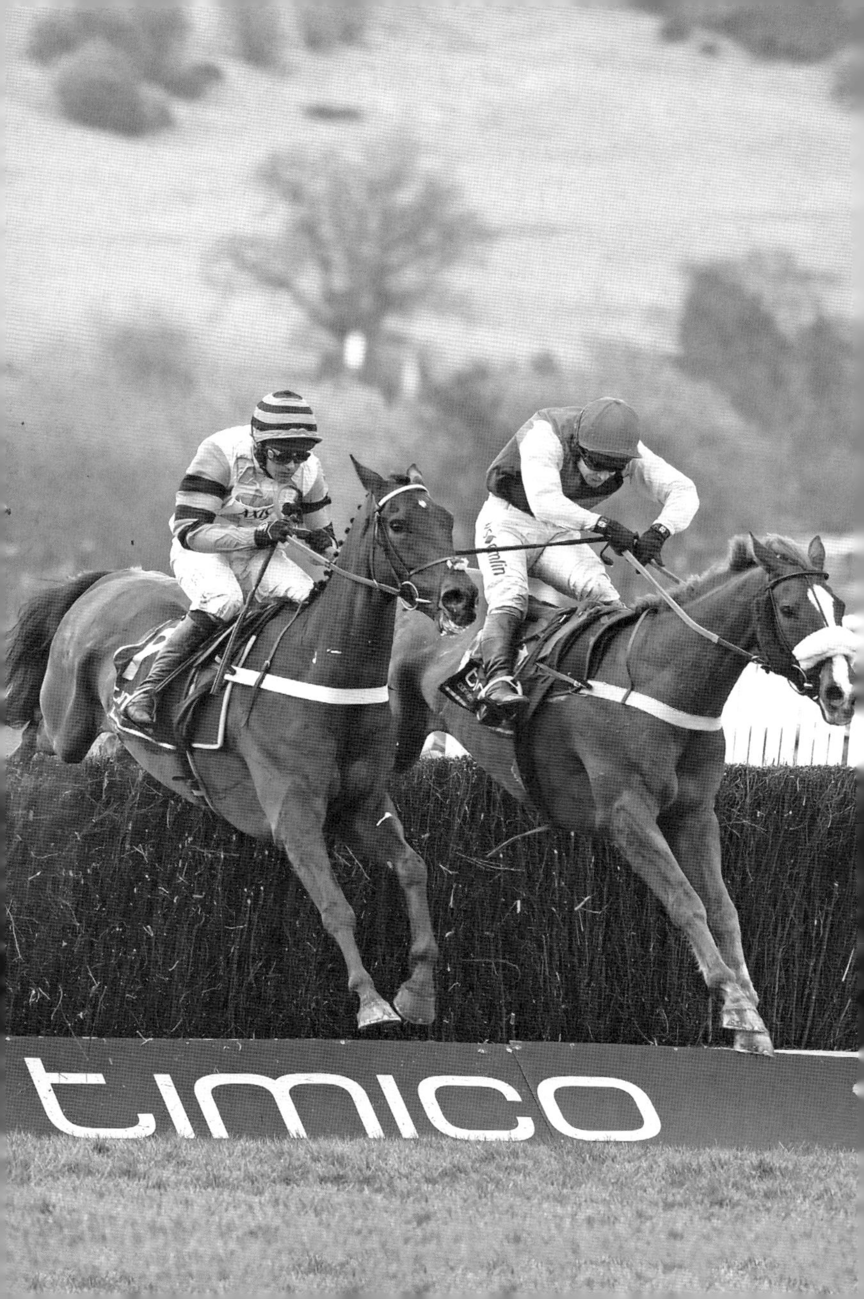
timico

Chasers & Hurdlers 2017/18

Introduction

'Leprechaun economics'. The phrase was coined by *New York Times* columnist and Nobel Prize-winning economist Paul Krugman in 2016 after Ireland's Central Statistics Office announced that the country had achieved 26% economic growth in 2015. Krugman wasn't alone in finding the figures hard to swallow, but the CSO hadn't got its sums wrong. Rather, something had artificially inflated Ireland's GDP to the point where the standard measure of an economy's health was about as credible as the mythical pot of gold at the end of the rainbow. Ireland has one of the lowest rates of corporation tax in Europe and has become a highly attractive base for multinational companies, particularly for United States 'tech giants' whose assets are based largely on intellectual property. According to the CSO, Ireland's top ten companies alone account for almost half of the country's GDP. Among them are 'Silicon Valley' household names such as Google, Microsoft and Facebook, but by far the largest is Apple whose European headquarters is in Cork. Confirmation finally came early in 2018 that it was Apple which had been responsible for distorting Ireland's GDP three years earlier when, as part of a 'restructuring' (prompted by the closure of a loophole in Irish tax legislation that allowed companies a nominal base in an offshore tax haven), it had apparently moved almost 300 billion dollars of intellectual property to Ireland, which naturally had a massive impact on such a modest-sized economy. At the same time, Apple was the subject of a two-year investigation by the EU which resulted in 2016 in the Commission ordering the company to pay €13 billion, plus interest, in unpaid Irish taxes—the biggest tax fine in history—for the period 2004-2014 when it was deemed to be, in effect, receiving illegal state aid. Apple began paying the fine in 2018, though both they and the Irish state are appealing against the decision.

It is now ten years since Ireland became the first country in the Eurozone to go into recession during the global financial crisis, 'the worst crisis since the potato famine' in the words of Ireland's former Finance Minister Michael Noonan. Ireland was also the first member state to be able to exit the Eurozone bailout programme in December 2013, having received €85 million from the European Central Bank and International Monetary Fund three years earlier when the country was in dire financial straits. The Irish economy, boosted by the activities of the multinationals (employers of a quarter of Ireland's private sector workforce), is considerably healthier now, so much so that it is the fastest-growing country in the Eurozone according to EU figures published in February, while in July the Bank of Ireland significantly raised its growth forecast. The EU warns, however, that the activities of the multinationals are 'subject to high uncertainty', while the impending consequences of Brexit—further uncertainty—will affect Ireland more than any other EU member. The future of the border between the Republic and Northern Ireland is proving one

British stables received a thrashing—seventeen wins to eleven—at the hands of their Irish counterparts at the Cheltenham Festival, but the successes of Buveur d'Air (Champion Hurdle), Altior (Queen Mother Champion Chase) and Native River (Gold Cup) did mean that the three most valuable and prestigious races stayed at home; the drawn-out duel between Native River and Might Bite in the blue riband event, pictured (Native River, right), was an enthralling encounter that produced one of the finest sights in modern racing as the pair turned for home together, clear of their field, and fought out a thrilling climax

Patrick, Jackie and Willie Mullins at Ireland's end-of-season champions presentations after a sparkling Punchestown Festival for the Closutton stable; Willie Mullins won the trainers' title for the eleventh season in a row after overturning a big deficit in his season-long battle with Gordon Elliott; son Patrick was Ireland's leading amateur for the eleventh time, equalling the achievement of Mr Ted Walsh, whose record number of wins for an amateur under Rules (545) he went on to pass in the summer of 2018

of the main talking points in the whole Brexit process, while concerns relating specifically to racing are touched on in the essay on **Top Notch**. The clock is ticking, though, with the UK due to leave the EU on March 29th 2019—a fortnight after the Cheltenham Gold Cup and a week before the Grand National.

A prospering Irish economy has been good news for jumps racing in particular. A study by the University of Gloucestershire on behalf of Cheltenham found that Irish racegoers spent more than €22m attending the 2016 Festival, while Irish attendance at the Festival had risen by 22% since 2010. It may be too simplistic to use Irish success at the Cheltenham Festival as a barometer of the wider economy but is it really a coincidence that there were a record nineteen Irish winners at Cheltenham in 2017 and seventeen more at the latest Festival? In the aftermath of the financial crisis, the visitors' total had dipped to just five in 2012. This Annual is first and foremost a record of Britain's jumpers, with over 8,500 horses treated individually, but the majority of those dealt with in essay form, those highlighted in bold in the following pages, are trained in Ireland, as good a reflection as any of where the balance of power currently lies. Whichever side of the Irish Sea you happened to be, the latest season in Ireland was a most compelling one. Former Champion Hurdle winner **Faugheen** provided an early highlight when returning from a lengthy absence with an impressive win in the Morgiana Hurdle at Punchestown in November, and there was little let-up from then on in memorable moments. Leopardstown's Christmas meeting featured some unexpected results (Faugheen's defeat chief among them); the track's new two-day Dublin Racing Festival in early-February provided a welcome addition to the season (discussed in **Monalee**'s essay); little more than a length covered the first five home in a desperate finish to the Irish Grand National, Ireland's richest race over jumps, won by **General Principle**; while the Irish season climaxed in a dramatic and at times extraordinary Punchestown Festival at which, for the second year running, there was a dramatic late change in the lead in the trainers' championship.

Just as a small number of multi-billion-dollar firms dominate the Irish economy, so Willie Mullins and Gordon Elliott tower over all others among Ireland's jumps trainers. Combined, the two stables ran more than five hundred and fifty individual horses in the course of the season and between them won over €11m in prize money, more than the total haul of the next thirty trainers in the table! Elliott became the first trainer to win two hundred races in an Irish jumps season, reaching that total at Cork on the same day that General Principle won him his first Irish National (in which he saddled a record thirteen runners). The mob-handed approach of the two stables is covered in General Principle's essay, while Mullins' all-out assault at Punchestown to retain his title (he saddled thirteen in a handicap hurdle on the final day—'If we had a race for the stable cat I'm sure that would be up there too') is reviewed in **Kemboy**'s entry. Mullins also reached the two hundred winner mark for the season, doing so at Punchestown, and ended with a record total of 212 to Elliott's 210. The top two won 75% of the Grade 1s in Ireland (26 out of 35) and around 30% of all the races there over jumps.

Mullins clinched his eleventh title in a row after Elliott went into the final week of the season with an even bigger lead than the year before. More than €500,000 behind at the start of the week, Mullins saddled a record eighteen winners at Punchestown, half of them in the meeting's Grade 1s. A remarkable statistic was that he would still have finished second in the season's overall standings solely on prize money won over those five days. The essays on Punchestown winners **Bellshill** and **Draconien** highlight respectively the variety of owners and jockeys who shared in the yard's success at the meeting. The second day proved the turning point when Mullins wiped out Elliott's lead with a six-timer which included **Next Destination**, part of a redemptive treble on the day for jockey Paul Townend who had thrown away near-certain victory in bizarre circumstances on **Al Boum Photo** (**Finian's Oscar** a victim of the same incident) in the three-mile Champion Novices' Chase the day before. Townend enjoyed a higher profile as a result of the stable's number one jockey Ruby Walsh missing much of the season through injury. Walsh's return for Cheltenham proved all too brief after a fall on Al Boum Photo in the RSA Chase put him on the sidelines again for the rest of the campaign. Faugheen returned to winning form when stepped up to three miles at Punchestown and was one of four winners at the Festival for Mullins' main patrons Rich and Susannah Ricci in a mixed season for the owners reviewed in the entry on **Saldier**, winner of the Champion Four Year Old Hurdle in which Mullins trained the first four home.

The rivalry between Mullins and Elliott wasn't confined to their home turf; 'offshore' earnings put them sixth and seventh respectively in the British table. The pair were responsible for the majority of the Irish winners at Cheltenham, winning more than half of the Festival's twenty-eight races in fact, and it was Elliott who came out on top for the second year, by eight wins to seven, to equal the record total Mullins had set in 2015. Elliott's Cheltenham winners were headed by the Baring Bingham winner **Samcro**, currently jumping's most exciting prospect who has the potential to go right to the top even though his first meeting with seasoned hurdlers ended in a fall at Punchestown. His essay recalls the brilliant but ill-fated career forty years earlier of another immensely promising Irish novice, Golden Cygnet. Samcro was among a record seven Festival winners for Gigginstown House Stud, champion owner in Ireland for the fourth season running. Elliott supplied Gigginstown with all bar one of their Festival winners, among them the mare **Shattered Love** in the Golden Miller, **Delta Work** (whose entry will provide food for thought for racing's TV pundits) in the Pertemps Final and **Farclas**, who turned Irish form around with the Mullins-trained **Mr Adjudicator** to win the Triumph Hurdle. **Apple's Jade** disappointed in her bid to win the David Nicholson Mares' Hurdle for the second year, the write-up on her advocating extending forty-eight-hour declarations beyond the Festival. Gigginstown's other Cheltenham winner was the Henry de Bromhead-trained **Balko des Flos** who provided owner Michael O'Leary with a long-awaited first win in the race he sponsors, the Ryanair Chase, which has become the most valuable event, ahead of the Stayers' Hurdle, on the third day of the Festival. The addition of a fifth day, still being mooted in some quarters, is again given a firm 'no' in the Ryanair winner's essay. O'Leary won more of his own sponsorship money when Balko des Flos' stable-companion **Identity Thief** won the Liverpool Hurdle (run as the Ryanair Stayers') at Aintree.

Mullins might have lost out to Elliott again at the latest Festival, but the last of his six winners during the week, **Laurina** in the Dawn Run Mares' Novices' Hurdle, made him the most successful trainer in Cheltenham Festival history with sixty-one wins. Laurina's essay looks at other Irish trainers who have made their mark at the Festival in the past and reviews the contribution mares have made to Mullins' success at the meeting over the years; both Laurina and his latest David Nicholson winner **Benie des Dieux** have the potential to add to Closutton's reputation for housing 'jumping's greatest ever pool of female talent.' Another mare, **Relegate**, provided Mullins with his ninth win in the Champion Bumper in which he saddled the first three home. **Penhill**'s win on his seasonal reappearance in the Stayers' Hurdle was another fine training feat (though the credit was due elsewhere according to Mullins, as the essay reveals, with a story on the same theme also recounted in Top Notch's entry), while **Footpad** looks another tip-top Arkle winner for the stable, in the mould of its past winners **Un de Sceaux** and Douvan, that pair finishing first and second in the latest Champion Chase at Punchestown. The essays

As a consequence of the battle for the trainers' championship in Ireland, Punchestown Festival racegoers and armchair viewers were treated to some tremendous races as the stables of Willie Mullins and Gordon Elliott fielded multiple entries in an attempt to pick up prize money in the championship events and the valuable handicaps; the pair were responsible for four runners apiece in the nine-runner Boylesports Champion Chase in which Un de Sceaux, Douvan and Min, three of the Closutton stable stars, took each other on, Un de Sceaux jumping superbly and overturning the odds laid on Douvan

on Footpad and another of the stable's top-class two-mile chasers **Min** cover Timeform's introduction of jumps timefigures in the latest season. Min was demoted at Leopardstown's Christmas meeting—giving British stables their only winner of an Irish Grade 1 with promoted Simply Ned—where **Nichols Canyon** was fatally injured to add to the mixed set of results for Mullins at that fixture; the essay on the 2017 Stayers' Hurdle winner rounds up some of the season's other equine losses.

Irish success at recent Cheltenham Festivals can be put down to the racing programme according to Mullins. 'We have a good environment for people to spend money on nice young horses and there is prize money to run them for. English racing is a diet of handicaps and there is no incentive. Nobody sets out to buy a handicapper, you set out to buy a good horse, and we [in Ireland] have a better system to educate and bring on good horses.' Irish jumping has a bloated programme of pattern races (there will be 36 Grade 1s in the next season, only four fewer than in Britain which has a 40% bigger horse population). Graded races may provide easier pickings in Ireland, especially for the two superpower stables and their owners, but it probably matters little to British followers of jumping which side of the Irish Sea a Cheltenham winner happens to be trained. Irish-bred horses, as well as Irish-born jockeys, are such an integral part of the sport in Britain, and have been for decades, that partisanship is meaningless in any case. The close ties which unite the sport in Britain and Ireland easily outweigh any differences between the two countries, which partly accounts for the fears over what Brexit might mean for the closeness of the relationship. It was surprising, therefore, that *The Guardian* ran a story on Gold Cup day under the headline 'British Horseracing Authority may use barriers to keep Irish raiders in check', with the sub-headline 'Measures planned as Irish dominate Cheltenham Festival.'

It was much less clear what form of protectionism the BHA supposedly had in mind. For the first time, however, the BHA undertook unannounced drug testing at Irish stables, specifically those of both Mullins and Elliott, in the run-up to the Festival. The BHA rejected claims that it reflected a lack of faith in the Irish Horseracing Regulatory Board's own anti-doping measures and insisted it was part of a new BHA strategy to increase testing on horses from abroad running at Britain's major meetings. BHA spokesman Robin Mounsey explained 'With Cheltenham it wouldn't make a lot of sense to encourage out of competition testing and not apply that strategy to half the population of horses at that Festival.' Some, though, interpreted it as a case of sour grapes, Irish Flat trainer Ger Lyons tweeting 'Implies that Irish horses are cheating and that our authorities are turning a blind eye to it!' Mullins, for one, was more phlegmatic about the testing procedure, having been subject to the process when sending runners to Hong Kong and Australia—'We just let them get on with it. It's part and parcel of racing. To me it's just normal.'

All the samples taken by the BHA before the Festival proved negative. Protecting the sport in Britain from cheats, regardless of where they come from—which is a different thing entirely from protectionism—is one of the BHA's main roles and the essay on **Pacha du Polder**, who won the Foxhunter Chase for the second year running, explains the circumstances leading to the withdrawal of Irish hunter Anseanachai Cliste from the 2017 Foxhunter. That counted as a success for the BHA's vigilance but British racing's administrators seldom enjoy a year when everything goes smoothly and the much needed reforming of the BHA's disciplinary panels produced some awkward judgements for the sport's regulator in the first year or so. A report in 2016 by Christopher Quinlan QC, commissioned by the BHA itself, concluded that there was an 'urgent need' for reform to restore trust in the fairness of some of British racing's disciplinary processes. One of the changes has involved recruiting members of the disciplinary panels from a broader background within the sport (they had previously consisted almost entirely of stewards). The long-standing zero-tolerance stance against doping has traditionally meant that a trainer is held responsible for illegal substances found in his or her horses unless a probable source can be established. However, in two cases in 2017, one of them involving top jumps trainer Philip Hobbs, the trainers were effectively exonerated by a disciplinary panel which ruled that 'on the balance of probabilities' neither had been involved in administering the substance which was deemed to be the work of 'person or persons unknown'.

The burden of proof has never been so great at a disciplinary hearing as it has to be in a court of law, and the fact that defendants have not always had appropriate legal support or representation has, on occasions, resulted in proceedings and verdicts that have looked unsafe and sometimes plain unjust. Society in general seems nowadays to regard it as worse to put an innocent man behind bars than to allow a guilty one to walk free, with 'beyond reasonable doubt' the guiding principle for conviction in a British court of law. Since the reforms were implemented, racing's disciplinary panels also seem to require more proof, a change which has to be welcomed. Not all allegations are true, as the BHA has found.

A recent embarrassing case for the administrators involved Irish vet Tim Brennan who appeared before a disciplinary panel charged with passing confidential information about the impending withdrawal of the favourite Faugheen from the 2016 Champion Hurdle. Brennan's brother, who had been excluded from racing in Britain for failing to co-operate with the BHA's investigators, was said to have used the information to lay Faugheen on the Betfair Exchange before the news became public. Tim Brennan's defence team dismissed the BHA's case as 'complete fantasy', saying that, on the day he was supposed to be conspiring with his brother, the defendant was preoccupied with his daughter who was taken seriously ill. While no evidence was produced to prove that Faugheen was actually lame when Brennan's brother began placing his bets, the defence also showed that it was 'overwhelmingly likely that there were other sources of information' available (a bookmaker had placed similar bets at the same time as Brennan's brother and the Irish Turf Club knew of another individual with connections to the Willie Mullins stable who had been involved in the suspicious betting activity around Faugheen).

The more that came out about the Brennan case, the more it seemed that the BHA's prosecutors had relied too much on supposition. There was no hard evidence of wrongdoing and the issue was further complicated by a defence submission that the BHA did not have the authority to bring the case (the Champion Hurdle on which the bets were placed may have taken place in Britain but the two people involved were Irish citizens, neither of whom was bound by the rules of racing, and the betting transactions took place online). Tim Brennan was cleared after a two-day inquiry held in July 2018, the disciplinary panel concluding that it had 'not been proved to the appropriate standard that Timothy Brennan was the source of any confidential information to his brother.' The panel also found that, as a self-employed vet, Brennan was not subject to the rules of racing.

The verdict was an overwhelming victory for Brennan who had employed a high-powered legal team at considerable expense to defend himself against charges that could effectively have destroyed his professional career. Many reading the basic outline of the case as it was presented beforehand could easily have been misled into assuming Tim Brennan's guilt. However, the BHA's case fell apart under scrutiny and Brennan emerged from a stressful situation for himself and his family to win a battle that needed to be fought. Racing should trust that his efforts have not been wasted and that lessons have been learned by the BHA. The BHA is sure to move to close the loophole that was used to argue that Brennan was not bound by the rules of racing; the panel itself recommended that the relevant rule should be amended to include 'self-employed vets, farriers or equine physiotherapists and suchlike.' The BHA had also announced, after the conclusion of the two earlier doping cases, that it would be amending the rules to clarify its interpretation of strict liability in doping cases. Nick Rust, the BHA's chief executive, justified the bringing of the Brennan case, saying 'We're not the judge and jury, it is not for us to decide whether individuals are in breach of the rules or not.'

It is, of course, vital for the governing body of the sport—which is also revamping its raceday officiating—to investigate breaches of the rules of racing in the interests of protecting racing's integrity, but, for the sake of the BHA's own credibility, cases that are pursued must be more watertight than the slipshod one brought against Tim Brennan who had his reputation unfairly besmirched, as had happened before in some of the unfortunate cases in recent years that eventually led to the commissioning of the Quinlan Report.

Behind Ireland's two powerhouse stables, the quartet of Joseph O'Brien, Henry de Bromhead, Jessica Harrington and Noel Meade, were the other trainers with Irish earnings of more than €1m. Henry de Bromhead was the only one of those to have a winner at Cheltenham, as already mentioned, but the three other stables all housed legitimate Gold Cup contenders. Harrington began the season with two of the ante-post favourites, though **Sizing John** became the third consecutive Gold Cup winner denied a chance to defend his title due to injury, while ill-fated former Irish National winner Our Duke was let down by his jumping in the Gold Cup. Instead, the previous season's versatile Coral Cup winner **Supasundae** proved the flagship horse for Harrington, winning both the Irish Champion and Punchestown Champion Hurdles, and

Tiger Roll was almost overhauled on the Grand National's famous 494-yard run-in, which has been the scene of some heartbreaking incidents in jumping's biggest race, his fast-diminishing lead over the Mullins-trained Pleasant Company in keeping with the season-long storyline of the close encounters between the Elliott and Mullins teams; Gordon Elliott, Anita O'Leary, Davy Russell and Michael O'Leary are pictured after Tiger Roll's win (O'Leary's Gigginstown House Stud farmed Ireland's big races and also set a new record for an owner with seven wins at the Cheltenham Festival)

Nicky Henderson, champion trainer in Britain for the fifth time, won almost a third of Britain's forty Grade 1 events, but unusually had no runners at Ireland's prestigious end-of-season Punchestown Festival, famously saying he 'wasn't keen on coming over for a drubbing'

finishing second in the Stayers' Hurdle and Aintree Hurdle in between. **Road To Respect** (Meade) and **Edwulf** (O'Brien) earned their places in the Gold Cup field with wins in the Leopardstown Christmas Chase (formerly the Lexus) and Irish Gold Cup respectively. Road To Respect fared the better of that pair when fourth at Cheltenham but Edwulf provided one of the season's heartwarming stories as his essay relates. Ireland's best hopes of a Gold Cup win in 2019 could well lie with **Presenting Percy**, the former Pertemps Final winner adding the RSA Insurance Chase to his Cheltenham record in the latest season for the small yard of Pat Kelly who has now been successful at each of the last three Festivals.

No fewer than nine of the fifteen runners in the Gold Cup were trained in Ireland, 33/1-shot **Anibale Fly**, the Paddy Power Chase winner, faring best of them in third before going on to finish in the frame in the Grand National as well. Indeed, the Grand National result was yet another Irish show of strength, the first four home all Irish-trained, prompting winning owner Michael O'Leary to declare 'We are in a golden age in Ireland, keeping our best horses.' **Tiger Roll**'s narrow victory over Pleasant Company was also another occasion during the season when Elliott and Mullins locked horns. The result could easily have gone the other way (after all, the winner had a 'squiggle'—a topic in his essay—as has **Ultragold** who won his second Topham Trophy over the National fences). Tiger Roll's extended entry begins by recalling past Grand Nationals which have been won and lost on the long run-in. Tiger Roll had been another Festival winner for Elliott and Gigginstown, in the Cross Country Chase, and he provided both trainer and owner with their second National victories, Elliott having come a long way since Silver Birch's win in 2007 when he had still to train a winner on Irish soil. Tiger Roll was a first Grand National winner for the oldest jockey with a ride in the race, Davy Russell, who was Irish champion for a third time as well as leading rider at Cheltenham where he maintained his record of having at least one winner at the Festival each year since 2006. While losing out narrowly at Aintree, Mullins won Britain's second most valuable handicap chase, the first running of the Ladbrokes Trophy at Newbury, with **Total Recall** whose jumping let him down later in both the Gold Cup and Grand National for which he started favourite. Short of putting their branding on every blade of grass on the track, the new sponsors couldn't have done much more to hammer home the message that the Newbury race was no longer 'the Hennessy', though for many it will surely be a case of old habits dying hard when referring to the race!

With Mullins and Elliott keeping most of their powder dry for Punchestown, the Grand National meeting belonged to Nicky Henderson who made hay with five Grade 1 winners. As for taking on the Irish superpowers on their home turf, Henderson had no runners at all at Punchestown, freely admitting he 'wasn't keen on coming over for a drubbing'. Top juvenile **We Have A Dream** had to miss Cheltenham but Henderson's four other big winners at Aintree had all been beaten at Cheltenham. We Have A Dream, along with **L'Ami Serge** (Aintree Hurdle) and **Terrefort** (Mildmay Novices'), also made it a good meeting for one of Henderson's main supporters, the partnership of Simon Munir and Isaac Souede, whose Top Notch also enjoyed a lucrative campaign for the same stable, despite missing the spring festivals, and was one of four winners for his stable at Sandown's Finale meeting when winning the Oaksey Chase. There is more on the owners' string, which is spread among some of the top stables, in the essay on novice chaser **Sceau Royal**, while their biggest win came when **Bristol de Mai** ran away with the Betfair Chase under extreme conditions at Haydock.

Henderson won almost a third of Britain's forty Grade 1 races, with the top-class trio of **Altior**, **Buveur d'Air** and **Might Bite** doing most to help their trainer comfortably retain his title and become champion for the fifth time in all. All three members of the 'A-team' at Seven Barrows were unbeaten for the season going to Cheltenham, but Altior had managed only one run beforehand after needing a breathing operation, which it became mandatory for trainers to declare in January, a requirement which generated plenty of debate (the issue is discussed in the essay on Altior). Altior maintained his unbeaten record over jumps to win the Queen Mother Champion Chase and subsequently the Celebration Chase at Sandown for the second year to join a select list of jumpers who have been Timeform Horse of the Year more than once, namely

The Nicky Henderson-trained Altior maintained his unbeaten record over jumps, warding off the Mullins challenge in the Queen Mother Champion Chase (pictured jumping the last with Min, far side); Altior was named Timeform Horse of the Year for the second successive season

Night Nurse, Monksfield, Dawn Run, Desert Orchid, Istabraq, Moscow Flyer, Kauto Star and Don Cossack. Buveur d'Air, whose only defeat over jumps remains his third place behind Altior in the 2016 Supreme Novices', enjoyed an altogether more straightforward campaign, taking the 'Fighting Fifth' and Christmas Hurdles on his way to retaining his Champion Hurdle crown for J. P. McManus who also retained his title as champion owner. Champion Hurdle-standard horses remain in short supply, at least in Britain, and it was **Melon** and **Mick Jazz**, trained respectively by Mullins and Elliott, who took the places behind Buveur d'Air.

After Altior and Buveur d'Air had landed the odds in their races, King George winner Might Bite lined up for the Gold Cup in a bid to complete what would have been a unique treble for Seven Barrows. But as Might Bite's essay recalls, Henderson's then boss Fred Winter had odds-on shots beaten in the same three races at the 1973 Festival. Might Bite was outstayed in the end by doughty front runner **Native River** but the pair of them served up an enthralling highlight to the Festival (which drew a record total attendance of 262,637), prompting Native River's essay to ask which was the greatest Gold Cup? Might Bite went on to be another of his stable's Aintree winners when beating Bristol de Mai in the Bowl, while the Gold Cup (despite a whip ban and hefty fine, prompting the whip rules to be discussed in the essay) provided the highlight of the season for Richard Johnson who retained his jockeys' title (he has yet to win a Grand National, a point discussed in the entry on **Thomas Patrick**). Native River had been 'one that got away' from Irish trainers. He unseated in a point in Ireland before joining Colin Tizzard—the stable's other Gold Cup day winner **Kilbricken Storm** had been a winner in that sphere—and succeeded at his second Gold Cup attempt (third in 2017) for a yard whose great servant **Cue Card** had fallen on both his appearances in the race. The tremendously popular Cue Card, retired at the age of twelve, was pulled up in the Ryanair Chase in what proved the final start of his

Snow swept across the country in late-February and the beginning of March (there were also abandonments for snow in December with Huntingdon pictured on the morning of the Peterborough Chase which had to be rescheduled and was run at Taunton); one of the worst and most dismal winters for years had already seen jumping in Britain largely come off second best in its battle with the weather, even before the arrival of the 'beast from the east' in the run up to Cheltenham

Champion jockey Richard Johnson presents the trophy for champion conditional to the very promising James Bowen who was only three years older than his mount Raz de Maree when the pair teamed up to win the Welsh Grand National at Chepstow

lengthy career which included a win in the same race in 2013 and victory in the Champion Bumper as a four-year-old, before Native River had even been foaled.

Native River, like several Gold Cup winners before him—Burrough Hill Lad, Cool Ground, Master Oats and Synchronised—was a former Welsh Grand National winner, and it was stamina which won the day in unusually testing conditions for a modern-day Gold Cup. Indeed, the Festival had been fortunate to miss the worst of the weather in March, a month which began in the grip of biting winds and sub-zero daytime temperatures as the so-called 'beast from the east' swept snow across the country, at one point wiping out all jumping cards in both Britain and Ireland (even some all-weather Flat meetings succumbed) for six consecutive days. Racing resumed only eight days before the Festival but the snow returned the weekend after Cheltenham. The Festival began on officially 'heavy' ground ('soft in places') for the first time since 1982, while it was officially 'soft, heavy in places' on Gold Cup day; the last heavy ground Gold Cup had been Desert Orchid's year, 1989. Timeform returned the going as 'soft' for the first three days and 'heavy' on Gold Cup day. Before the late cold snap, a generally wet winter affected other major meetings, and conditions remained on the testing side for Aintree. **Elgin**'s essay refers to controversy over the going at Cheltenham's November meeting (and explains that fixture's name change from The Open), while the

The trainer/jockey partnership of Dan and Harry Skelton continued to put the family's Lodge Hill stable on the map, both recording seasonal-best scores; Dan brought up his century for the season before the end of November and went on to saddle more winners in Britain over the season than any other trainer, while Harry made it to three figures in December, all his wins up to that point coming on horses trained by his brother

latest Welsh Grand National was the fourth in the last eight seasons to be postponed from just after Christmas until the New Year—a consequence of which meant that the winner **Raz de Maree** had just turned thirteen, while his jockey, conditional champion James Bowen, was only three years older! On the same day as the rearranged Welsh National, the often frustrating **Buywise**, a relative youngster at eleven, finally landed a big prize in the final of the Veterans' Handicap Chase series at Sandown.

Nicky Henderson is the leading trainer at many of the courses at which he has runners—including Towcester whose future was called into doubt when it was placed in administration in the summer of 2018—and he will be hard to dislodge as champion in the near future as Seven Barrows is home to plenty of promising young horses as well as an established championship team. Sefton winner **Santini** was just about the pick of the stable's novice hurdlers and looks a top novice chasing prospect. A number of the top stables had unusually quiet seasons, with Philip Hobbs, Jonjo O'Neill, David Pipe and Venetia Williams among those to finish outside the top dozen. Former champion Paul Nicholls was runner-up to Henderson for the second season running while still seeking to unearth another champion in the mould of previous stable stars. Even so, Nicholls got the most out of his yard's best performers, with **Politologue** capitalising on Altior's absence from races like the Tingle Creek and the Melling Chase, while novice chaser **Black Corton**, who learned his trade at the likes of Worcester (the track is profiled in his essay) and Fontwell over the summer, enjoyed a prolific season that took him and regular conditional partner Bryony Frost, the season's most successful female jockey, to Grade 1 success in the Kauto Star at Kempton. Frost's profile was also raised by big Saturday handicap wins on Frodon at Cheltenham and Milansbar at Warwick (Classic Chase) and she rode the latter into fifth in the

Grand National. Mohaayed gave Nicholls' former assistant Dan Skelton a second win in three years in the County Hurdle at the Festival but the stable made its mark principally through the quantity of its winners. Although fifth by prize money, Dan Skelton trained more winners than anyone else for the first time in his burgeoning career, while brother Harry finished third in the jockeys' table, only three of his one hundred and thirty-one wins coming for other yards. Tom George retained his place among the top dozen trainers and has plenty to look forward to with the promising novice hurdlers **Summerville Boy** and **Black Op**, Grade 1 winners in the Supreme at Cheltenham and Mersey at Aintree respectively. Between them, the pair also transformed the fortunes of their hitherto barely-used sire Sandmason.

For smaller yards, one good horse can make all the difference. Olly Murphy and Amy Murphy (no relation) each had big boosts to their fledgling training careers when landing two of the season's big handicap hurdles with **Hunters Call** (Racing Welfare Handicap at Ascot) and **Kalashnikov** (Betfair Hurdle) respectively. The Long Walk Hurdle winner **Sam Spinner** was one of only three winning horses during the season for his trainer Jedd O'Keeffe, while **Joe Farrell** was a particularly welcome winner for Rebecca Curtis in the Scottish Grand National. **Step Back**, another novice, like the Scottish National winner, routed his field in the bet365 Gold Cup at Sandown and looks a ready successor to former Gold Cup winner Coneygree as star of the Bradstock stable. Two other smaller stables which would otherwise have had much to celebrate in the latest season had sorrow to deal with as well. Malton trainer Malcolm Jefferson died at the age of seventy-one in February, his funeral taking place just a day before daughter Ruth saddled **Waiting Patiently** to keep his unbeaten record over fences in the Ascot Chase. Waiting Patiently's essay (which also remembers dual-purpose trainer Mary Reveley) paints a brighter picture of jumping in the North where his jockey Brian Hughes was again the leading rider, as well as finishing runner-up in the championship. There was also the tragic loss of Devon trainer Richard Woollacott at the age

The Betfair Ascot Chase in February turned into one of the races of the season, with the North's top chaser Waiting Patiently (right) fighting out a splendid finish with the veteran Cue Card to maintain his unbeaten record over fences

of just forty after he had enjoyed the limelight with a big winner at Newbury in December with Beer Goggles; he sadly didn't live to see **Lalor** win for the second year running at the Grand National meeting.

Among the ranks of owners, Alan Potts died aged eighty in November just months after his wife Ann, as related in the essay on their Gold Cup winner Sizing John who, like Supasundae and the rest of their string, will see out the remainder of their careers in the couple's colours. An owner with a much longer history in the sport was Maria de la Soledad Cabeza de Vaca y Leighton, better known in racing under her Spanish title the Marquesa de Moratalla, who died at the age of eighty-seven in November. Raz de Maree's essay reminds readers of some of the Marquesa's best horses, the Welsh National winner being related to one of her 'three musketeers' Ucello II. Irish racing was saddened by the death in the summer of 2018 of one of its Cheltenham Gold Cup-winning trainers Mick O'Toole (Davy Lad 1977), a popular character who died at the age of eighty-six; in recent years he was connected in an informal role with the horses owned by Marie Donnelly and her husband former bookie Joe Donnelly, among which were Melon and Al Boum Photo. Further sad news was the death in December, at the age of fifty-seven, of Noel O'Brien who had held the role of senior jumps handicapper in Ireland since 1995. O'Brien founded the Anglo-Irish Jumps Classifications along with Phil Smith who retired as Head of Handicapping in June after almost twenty-three years at the BHA. Smith had a higher profile (and had probably developed a thicker skin) than most in his profession, largely due to being responsible for framing the Grand National weights every year.

A couple of Grand National-winning jockeys featured among those who retired, Liam Treadwell who partnered 100/1 winner Mon Mome in 2009, and Timmy Murphy who won the race a year earlier on Comply Or Die. Murphy had switched successfully to the Flat in recent seasons but found it increasingly difficult to do the lighter weights. Forty-five-year-old Andrew Thornton, whose achievement of reaching a thousand winners was covered in the Introduction to last year's Annual, called it a day at Uttoxeter in June when one of his last four mounts was successful. Ian Popham (see Annacotty's essay in *Chasers & Hurdlers 2015/16*) and Willy Twiston-Davies, who hadn't ridden since a bad fall at the 2017 Festival, were others to retire from the saddle, Popham to become a jockeys' agent, with Twiston-Davies having ambitions to take over

Two jockeys who made the headlines: Paul Townend was involved in a bizarre incident on Al Boum Photo towards the end of the Growise Champion Novices' Chase at Punchestown's end-of-season festival meeting, while evergreen Andrew Thornton finally hung up his saddle at the age of forty-five (he had reached the landmark of a thousand winners the previous season)

Irish amateurs Nina Carberry (left) and Katie Walsh, who both announced their retirement at the Punchestown Festival, played their part in raising the profile of female jockeys; Ms Walsh was one of four winning female jockeys at the latest Cheltenham Festival where 3-lb claimers Lizzie Kelly and Bridget Andrews became the first female professionals to win races at the Festival

his father Nigel's yard in the longer term (another of the jockeys to ride for the yard, Ryan Hatch, retired on medical advice, having not ridden since a bad fall at Cheltenham in December 2016). Sisters-in-law Nina Carberry and Katie Walsh each announced they were quitting the saddle after riding winners at the Punchestown Festival. Walsh rode her third Cheltenham Festival winner on Relegate (whose essay recounts the careers of Walsh and Carberry), while her final Grand National ride, **Baie des Iles**, trained by husband Ross O'Sullivan, went on to gain a rare success over fences at Auteuil for a horse trained outside France (The 'Top Horses In France' section gives a full account of the French season as usual at the end of this Annual). Carberry, with seven Festival winners (her first ride at the meeting in 2005 had been a winning one on Dabiroun in the Fred Winter), is the most successful of the fourteen women to have ridden a winner at the meeting, beginning with Caroline Beasley who won the 1983 Foxhunter on Eliogarty. Lizzie Kelly made history when becoming the first female professional to win at the Festival on Coo Star Sivola in the Ultima Handicap Chase, Mohaayed's rider Bridget Andrews quickly became the second, and together with Katie Walsh and Harriet Tucker, who won the Foxhunter on Pacha du Polder, they made it the most successful Festival yet for female jockeys.

This is the first *Chasers & Hurdlers* without photographs by Alec Russell who died in February at the age of eighty-five. The first pictures credited to 'A. Russell' appeared in *Racehorses of 1965*, Timeform's Flat annual, and they covered races at the St Leger meeting, with the odd picture from Redcar, Ripon, Thirsk and Alec's local track York. It wasn't long before Alec moved

Alec Russell's photographs appeared in fifty-three consecutive editions of the Timeform Racehorses annual and in the first forty-two editions of Chasers & Hurdlers

into photography full time, attending all the big meetings and becoming one of the main contributors to the Timeform Annual, as well as supplying pictures to *The Sporting Life* and *Horse & Hound*. This was long before the digital era when supplying pictures for a national daily was far from straightforward. Alec's phlegmatic temperament was ideal and he was inventive and adapted smoothly to change, which helps to explain why he continued to produce work of the highest standard and remained at the top of his profession for so long. He was taking action photographs for Timeform up to York's Dante meeting in 2017 and continued to take posed shots of the best horses right up to the end of that season, the last of them at Karl Burke's and Kevin Ryan's which appeared in *Racehorses of 2017*, the sad news of Alec's passing coming too late to be recorded in those pages. That was the fifty-third consecutive edition of *Racehorses* in which Alec's pictures featured and he also contributed to the first forty-two editions of *Chasers & Hurdlers*. His work was acknowledged by the Horserace Writers' and Photographers' Association with both a photographer of the year award and another for outstanding achievement. The images Alec took have become an important part of the history of the sport and will stand as a lasting legacy to him.

October 2018

HIGHEST TIMEFORM RATINGS

Chasers & Hurdlers 1975/76 was the first in the Timeform annual series but the jumping edition of the weekly Timeform Black Book has been published since 1962/3. The following 'annual' ratings are the highest achieved in Britain and Ireland since that time.

Chasers
- 212 Arkle
- 210 Flyingbolt
- 192p Sprinter Sacre
- 191 Kauto Star
- 191 Mill House
- 187 Desert Orchid
- 186 Dunkirk
- 184+ Moscow Flyer
- 184 Burrough Hill Lad, Long Run
- 183 Don Cossack, Master Oats
- 182 Azertyuiop, Best Mate, Captain Christy, Carvill's Hill, Douvan, Imperial Commander, Kicking King, See More Business, Well Chief
- 181 Cue Card, Denman
- 180 First Gold, Vautour
- 179p Altior
- 179 Badsworth Boy, Bobs Worth, Fortria, Master Minded, One Man
- 178 Imperial Call, Pendil
- 177 Bregawn, Kinloch Brae, Klairon Davis, Martha's Son, The Dikler
- 176 Buona notte, Little Owl, Looks Like Trouble, Silviniaco Conti, Suny Bay, Titus Oates
- 175+ Exotic Dancer
- 175 Brown Lad, Captain Chris, Djakadam, Flagship Uberalles, Kingscliff, L'Escargot, Night Nurse, Rough Quest, Silver Buck, Wayward Lad
- 174p Footpad
- 174 Barnbrook Again, Beef Or Salmon, Bula, Finian's Rainbow, Flemenstar, Jodami, Pearlyman, Thistlecrack, Tidal Bay, Un de Sceaux
- 173 Blazing Walker, Captain John, Cool Dawn, Cyfor Malta, Florida Pearl, Remittance Man, Sir des Champs, Teeton Mill

Hurdlers
- 182 Night Nurse
- 180 Istabraq, Monksfield
- 179 Persian War
- 178 Comedy of Errors
- 177 Lanzarote, Limestone Lad
- 176+ Big Buck's
- 176 Bird's Nest, Bula, Faugheen, Golden Cygnet
- 175 Baracouda, Deano's Beeno, Gaye Brief, Salmon Spray, Sea Pigeon
- 174p Thistlecrack
- 174 Alderbrook, Dramatist, For Auction, Magic Court, Morley Street
- 173p More of That
- 173 Dato Star, Dawn Run, Hurricane Fly, See You Then
- 172 Anzio, Bannow Rambler, Beech Road, Boreen Prince, Browne's Gazette, Danoli, Flatterer, Iris's Gift, Mighty Man, Prideaux Boy
- 171 Barnbrook Again, Canasta Lad, Captain Christy, Celtic Gold, Chorus, Daring Run, Grands Crus, Jezki, Le Coudray, Moyne Royal, Pollardstown, Punchestowns, Rock On Ruby

The following ratings for horses in the pre-Timeform era, compiled by Randall and Morris for 'A Century of Champions', were used by Timeform for an exhibit in Cheltenham's Hall of Fame:

- 190 Easter Hero
- 188 Golden Miller
- 183 Pas Seul, Prince Regent
- 176 Sir Ken

TIMEFORM CHAMPIONS OF 2017/18

Altior joins a select list of jumpers who have been Timeform Horse of the Year more than once; the others are Night Nurse, Monksfield, Dawn Run, Desert Orchid, Istabraq, Moscow Flyer, Kauto Star and Don Cossack

HORSE OF THE YEAR
& BEST TWO-MILE CHASER
RATED AT 179p

ALTIOR

8 b.g High Chaparral – Monte Solaro (Key of Luck)

Owner Mrs Patricia Pugh   Trainer Nicky Henderson

BEST STAYING CHASER – RATED AT 172
NATIVE RIVER
8 ch.g Indian River – Native Mo (Be My Native)
Owner Brocade Racing   Trainer Colin Tizzard

BEST NOVICE CHASER – RATED AT 174p
FOOTPAD
6 b.g Creachadoir – Willamina (Sadler's Wells)
Owner Mr Simon Munir/Mr Isaac Souede   Trainer W. P. Mullins

BEST HUNTER CHASERS – RATED AT 134
GILGAMBOA
10 b.g Westerner – Hi Native (Be My Native)
Owner John P. McManus   Trainer Enda Bolger

PACHA DU POLDER
11 b.g Muhtathir – Ambri Piotta (Caerwent)
Owner The Stewart Family   Trainer Paul Nicholls

BEST TWO-MILE HURDLER – RATED AT 167
BUVEUR D'AIR
7 b.g Crillon – History (Alesso)
Owner Mr John P. McManus   Trainer Nicky Henderson

BEST STAYING HURDLER – RATED AT 165
FAUGHEEN
10 b.g Germany – Miss Pickering (Accordion)
Owner Mrs S. Ricci   Trainer W. P. Mullins

BEST NOVICE HURDLER – RATED AT 163p
SAMCRO
6 ch.g Germany – Dun Dun (Saddlers' Hall)
Owner Gigginstown House Stud   Trainer Gordon Elliott

BEST JUVENILE HURDLER – RATED AT 150p
WE HAVE A DREAM
4 b.g Martaline – Sweet Dance (Kingsalsa)
Owner Mr Simon Munir/Mr Isaac Souede   Trainer Nicky Henderson

BEST BUMPER PERFORMER – RATED AT 125
TORNADO FLYER
5 b.g Flemensfirth – Mucho Macabi (Exceed And Excel)
Owner T. F. P. Partnership   Trainer W. P. Mullins

THE TIMEFORM 'TOP 100' CHASERS AND HURDLERS

Hurdlers
167 Buveur d'Air
166 Melon
165 Faugheen
164 Penhill
163p Samcro
163 L'Ami Serge
162 Bapaume
162 Supasundae
161 Identity Thief
161 Mick Jazz
161§ Wicklow Brave
160 Agrapart
159 My Tent Or Yours
159 Wholestone
158 Sam Spinner
157 Cilaos Emery
157 Elgin
157 The New One
156p Summerville Boy
156 Apple's Jade (f)
156 Beer Goggles
156 Nichols Canyon
156 The Last Samuri
155 Bacardys
154 Call Me Lord
154 Shaneshill
154 Topofthegame
154 Unowhatimeanharry
153 Coquin Mans
153 The Worlds End
153 Yanworth
152p Kalashnikov
152 Black Op
152 Lil Rockerfeller
152 Presenting Percy
152 Swamp Fox
151p Benie des Dieux (f)
151p Next Destination
151 Bleu Et Rouge
151 Campeador
151 Diamond Cauchois
151 Kilbricken Storm
151 Old Guard
150p Cracking Smart
150p Laurina (f)
150p We Have A Dream
150 Ch'tibello
150 Colin's Sister (f)
150 Delta Work
150 John Constable
150 Santini
150 William Henry
149p If The Cap Fits
149 Blow By Blow
149 Draconien
149 Farclas
149 Mengli Khan
149 Thomas Campbell
148 Augusta Kate (f)
148 Cyrus Darius
148 Jezki
148 Ok Corral
148 Paloma Blue
147+ Ballyoptic
147 Bleu Berry
147 Claimantakinforgan
147 Desert Cry
147 Lalor
147 Lostintranslation
147 Mr Adjudicator
147 Remiluc
146p Soul Emotion
146p Vinndication
146 Dortmund Park
146 Mohaayed
146 On The Blind Side
146 Scarpeta
146 Vision des Flos
146 Who Dares Wins
145 Ballyward
145 Bunk Off Early
145 Duc des Genievres
145 La Bague Au Roi (f)
145 Meri Devie (f)
145 Saldier
145 Wakea
145 Western Ryder
145x Clyne
144 Air Horse One
144 Bedrock
144 Court Minstrel
144 Donna's Diamond
144 Getabird
144 Glenloe
144 Izzo
144 Jenkins
144 Lagostovegas (f)
144 Minella Awards
144 Pallasator
144 Rashaan
144 Taquin du Seuil
144 Tigris River

Chasers
179p Altior
174p Footpad
172 Native River
171 Might Bite
171 Sizing John
170p Great Field
169 Min
169 Un de Sceaux
168p Waiting Patiently
168 Bellshill
167 Fox Norton
167 Road To Respect
167x Our Duke
166 Balko des Flos
166 Politologue
166 Top Notch
165+ Douvan
165 Cue Card
165 Djakadam
165 Whisper
165x Bristol de Mai
164p Presenting Percy
164+ Disko
164 Anibale Fly
164 Definitly Red
164§ Outlander
163+ Total Recall
163x Killultagh Vic
162 Clan des Obeaux
162 Doctor Phoenix
162? Double Shuffle
161+ Al Boum Photo
161 Edwulf
161 Smad Place
160 Ballyoisin
160 Blaklion
160 Coney Island
160 Frodon
160 Tea For Two
160? Sizing Codelco
159p Bachasson
159+ Petit Mouchoir
159 Kylemore Lough
159 Sub Lieutenant
159 The Last Samuri
159x Minella Rocco
158+ Thistlecrack
158 San Benedeto
158 Sir Valentino
157p Kemboy
157p Monalee
157+ Saint Calvados
157 A Toi Phil
157 Ar Mad
157 Ball d'Arc
157 Charbel
157 Cloudy Dream
157 Sceau Royal
157 Simply Ned
157 Sizing Granite
156p Terrefort
156 Alpha des Obeaux
156 Cyrname
156 Finian's Oscar
156 Starchitect
156x Le Prezien
155p Diego du Charmil
155 Art Mauresque
155 Gold Present
155 Mala Beach
155 Ordinary World
155 Sandymount Duke
155 Shantou Flyer

155	Special Tiara	154	Hammersly Lake	153	Fountains Windfall
155	Tiger Roll	154	Invitation Only	153	Gino Trail
154+	Death Duty	154	Shattered Love (f)	153	Perfect Candidate
154+	God's Own	154	Valseur Lido	153	Rathvinden
154	Ballyoptic	153+	American	153	Speredek
154	Brain Power	153+	L'Ami Serge	153	The Storyteller
154	Devils Bride	153	Ballycasey	152p	Rather Be
154	Forest Bihan	153	Dounikos		

THE TIMEFORM TOP JUVENILES, NOVICES, HUNTER CHASERS AND NH FLAT HORSES

Juvenile Hurdlers
150p We Have A Dream
149 Farclas
147 Mr Adjudicator
145 Saldier
142 Espoir d'Allen
142 Sayo
141 Redicean
140 Gumball
138 Mitchouka
138 Saglawy
137 Apple's Shakira (f)
137 Stormy Ireland (f)
136 Beau Gosse
136 Msassa
134 Style de Garde
133 Malaya (f)
132 Act of Valour
131 Nube Negra
131 Sussex Ranger
130 Veneer of Charm
129 Casa Tall
128p Albert's Back
127p The Statesman
127 City Dreamer
127 Crucial Moment
127 Doctor Bartolo
127 Look My Way
127 Taxmeifyoucan
126 Mercenaire
126 Oistrakh Le Noir

Novice Hurdlers
163p Samcro
156p Summerville Boy
152p Kalashnikov
152 Black Op
151p Next Destination
151 Kilbricken Storm
150p Cracking Smart
150p Laurina (f)
150 Delta Work
150 Santini
149p If The Cap Fits
149 Blow By Blow
149 Draconien
149 Mengli Khan
148 Ok Corral
148 Paloma Blue
147 Claimantakinforgan
147 Lalor

147 Lostintranslation
146p Vinndication
146 Dortmund Park
146 On The Blind Side
146 Scarpeta
146 Vision des Flos
145 Ballyward
145 Duc des Genievres
145 Western Ryder
144 Bedrock
144 Getabird
144 Pallasator

Novice Chasers
174p Footpad
164p Presenting Percy
161+ Al Boum Photo
159+ Petit Mouchoir
157p Kemboy
157p Monalee
157+ Saint Calvados
157 Sceau Royal
156p Terrefort
156 Cyrname
156 Finian's Oscar
155p Diego du Charmil
154+ Death Duty
154 Ballyoptic
154 Brain Power
154 Invitation Only
154 Shattered Love (f)
153 Dounikos
153 Fountains Windfall
153 Rathvinden
153 The Storyteller
152p Rather Be
151+ Bamako Moriviere
151 Black Corton
151 Elegant Escape
150p Benatar
150+ Jury Duty
150+ Ozzie The Oscar
150+ Yanworth
150 Dolos

National Hunt Flat Horses
125 Tornado Flyer
123 Blackbow
123 Carefully Selected
119 Rhinestone
118 Acey Milan

116 Relegate (f)
115 Getaway John
115 Hollowgraphic
114 Downtown Getaway
113 Brace Yourself
113 Good Boy Bobby
113 Rapid Escape
112p Brewin'upastorm
112 Caribert
112 Felix Desjy
112 Minella Encore
112 Portrush Ted
111+ Didtheyleaveuoutto
110 Voix des Tiep
109 Mercy Mercy Me
108 Bullionaire
108 Getaway Katie Mai (f)
108 Harambe
108 Kalum River
108 Kateson
108 Two For Gold
107p Commander of Fleet
107p Dream Conti
107p Seddon
107p Time To Move On
107 Black Pirate
107 Clinton Hill
107 Colreevy (f)
107 Crooks Peak
107 Gallahers Cross
107 Posh Trish (f)
107 Queenohearts (f)
107 Queens Cave (f)
107 The Big Bite
107 The Flying Sofa

Hunter Chasers
134+ Gilgamboa
134 Pacha du Polder
133 Creevytennant
132p Burning Ambition
131 Marinero
130 Galway Jack
130 Unioniste
129 Barel of Laughs
129 Cousin Pete
129 Mendip Express
129 Shotavodka
129 Wells de Lune
128 Balnaslow
127 Full Trottle

2017/18 STATISTICS

The following tables show the leading owners, trainers, jockeys, sires of winners and horses over jumps in Britain during 2017/18. The prize-money statistics, compiled by *Timeform*, relate to win-money and to first-three prize money. Win money has traditionally been used to decide the trainers' championship, though since 1994 the BHB (now the BHA) and the National Trainers' Federation have recognised championships decided by total prize money as determined by the *Racing Post*. The jockeys' championship has traditionally been decided by the number of wins.

	OWNERS (1,2,3 earnings)	Horses	Wnrs	Indiv'l Races Won	Runs	%	Stakes £
1	Mr John P. McManus	152	56	85	507	16.8	1,678,058
2	Mr Simon Munir & Mr Isaac Souede	36	22	43	134	32.0	1,484,998
3	Gigginstown House Stud	35	8	9	47	19.1	1,283,609
4	Paul & Clare Rooney	81	33	59	261	22.6	679,210
5	Ann & Alan Potts Limited	22	9	11	94	11.7	527,459
6	Brocade Racing	17	7	10	69	14.5	463,574
7	The Knot Again Partnership	1	1	3	4	75.0	393,103
8	Mr Trevor Hemmings	46	15	24	172	14.0	346,991
9	S Such & CG Paletta	5	5	8	35	22.9	345,470
10	Mr J. Hales	3	1	4	13	30.8	343,608
11	Mrs Patricia Pugh	2	1	3	5	60.0	343,003
12	Mrs Johnny de la Hey	15	10	18	72	25.0	335,037

	OWNERS (win money)	Horses	Wnrs	Indiv'l Races Won	Runs	%	Stakes £
1	Mr John P. McManus	152	56	85	507	16.8	1,230,722
2	Gigginstown House Stud	35	8	9	47	19.1	1,175,197
3	Mr Simon Munir & Mr Isaac Souede	31	21	42	129	32.6	1,044,213
4	Paul & Clare Rooney	81	33	59	261	22.6	446,085
5	Brocade Racing	17	7	10	69	14.5	435,289
6	Mrs Patricia Pugh	2	1	3	5	60.0	342,087
7	Mr J. Hales	3	1	4	13	30.8	331,969
8	The Knot Again Partnership	1	1	3	4	75.0	254,330
9	S Such & CG Paletta	5	5	8	35	22.9	242,493
10	Mrs Johnny de la Hey	15	10	18	72	25.0	226,808

	TRAINERS (1,2,3 earnings)	Horses	Wnrs	Indiv'l Races Won	Runs	%	Stakes £
1	Nicky Henderson	154	85	141	524	26.9	3,376,169
2	Paul Nicholls	150	68	127	576	22.0	2,371,072
3	Colin Tizzard	111	50	79	536	14.7	1,903,524
4	Nigel Twiston-Davies	128	56	80	527	15.2	1,807,755
5	Dan Skelton	215	90	156	801	19.5	1,643,967
6	W. P. Mullins, Ireland	66	9	10	74	13.5	1,487,238
7	Gordon Elliott, Ireland	72	19	21	106	19.8	1,317,008
8	Tom George	105	34	47	356	13.2	912,070
9	Alan King	125	36	58	389	14.9	855,241
10	Donald McCain	113	58	98	539	18.2	785,839
11	Harry Fry	71	34	53	245	21.6	766,911
12	Evan Williams	103	37	52	461	11.3	730,488

	TRAINERS (by win money)	Horses	*Indiv'l* Wnrs	*Races* Won	Runs	%	*Stakes* £
1	Nicky Henderson	154	85	141	524	26.9	2,652,750
2	Paul Nicholls	150	68	127	576	22.0	1,678,614
3	Colin Tizzard	111	50	79	536	14.7	1,309,071
4	Nigel Twiston-Davies	128	56	80	527	15.2	1,226,946
5	Dan Skelton	215	90	156	801	19.5	1,085,488
6	Gordon Elliott, Ireland	72	19	21	106	19.8	1,055,844
7	W. P. Mullins, Ireland	66	9	10	74	13.5	840,634
8	Donald McCain	113	58	98	539	18.2	578,064
9	Alan King	125	36	58	389	14.9	566,484
10	Tom George	105	34	47	356	13.2	539,767
11	Harry Fry	71	34	53	245	21.6	513,036
12	Fergal O'Brien	106	43	60	338	17.8	469,854

	TRAINERS (with 100+ winners)	Horses	*Indiv'l* Wnrs	*Races* Won	2nd	3rd	Runs	%
1	Dan Skelton	215	90	156	121	124	801	19.5
2	Nicky Henderson	154	85	141	82	49	524	26.9
3	Paul Nicholls	150	68	127	94	74	576	22.0

	JOCKEYS (by wins)	1st	2nd	3rd	Unpl	Mts	%
1	Richard Johnson	176	156	118	451	901	19.5
2	Brian Hughes	142	131	112	425	810	17.5
3	Harry Skelton	131	107	104	270	612	21.4
4	Noel Fehily	110	82	62	278	532	20.7
5	Sam Twiston-Davies	108	90	83	287	568	19.0
6	Aidan Coleman	104	73	84	409	670	15.5
7	Sean Bowen	82	64	55	281	482	17.0
8	Nico de Boinville	77	54	44	192	367	21.0
9	Harry Cobden	76	71	67	226	440	17.3
10	Tom Scudamore	74	82	79	375	610	12.1
11	Paddy Brennan	70	57	72	242	441	15.9
12	Daryl Jacob	63	53	38	206	360	17.5

	JOCKEYS (1,2,3 earnings)	Races Won	Rides	%	*Stakes* £
1	Richard Johnson	176	901	19.5	1,845,670
2	Nico de Boinville	77	367	21.0	1,733,066
3	Sam Twiston-Davies	108	568	19.0	1,617,622
4	Daryl Jacob	63	360	17.5	1,465,437
5	Brian Hughes	142	810	17.5	1,366,261
6	Harry Cobden	76	440	17.3	1,360,723
7	Harry Skelton	131	612	21.4	1,324,401
8	Noel Fehily	110	532	20.7	1,319,266
9	Davy Russell	12	63	19.0	1,319,266
10	Barry Geraghty	31	137	22.6	1,163,634

	JOCKEYS (by win money)	Races Won	Rides	%	*Stakes* £
1	Richard Johnson	176	901	19.5	1,406,149
2	Nico de Boinville	77	367	21.0	1,298,343
3	Sam Twiston-Davies	108	568	19.0	1,171,448
4	Daryl Jacob	63	360	17.5	1,114,523

CONDITIONAL JOCKEYS	1st	2nd	3rd	Unpl	Mts	%
1 James Bowen	58	37	40	213	348	16.7
2 Bryony Frost	38	21	24	121	204	18.6
3 Ross Chapman	37	29	33	140	239	15.5

AMATEUR RIDERS	1st	2nd	3rd	Unpl	Mts	%
1 Miss Page Fuller	14	12	8	57	91	15.4

Mr Alex Edwards, Miss Becky Smith, Mr Zac Baker and Mr Lorcan Williams all rode 11 winners

SIRES OF WINNERS (1,2,3 earnings)	Races Won	Runs	%	Stakes £
1 King's Theatre (by Sadler's Wells)	87	697	12.5	1,675,857
2 Presenting (by Mtoto)	110	845	13.0	1,547,559
3 Kayf Tara (by Sadler's Wells)	109	885	12.3	1,436,250
4 Flemensfirth (by Alleged)	102	698	14.6	1,271,108
5 Oscar (by Sadler's Wells)	97	675	14.4	1,205,907
6 Milan (by Sadler's Wells)	107	747	14.3	1,109,135
7 Midnight Legend (by Night Shift)	101	738	13.7	1,026,603
8 Westerner (by Danehill)	98	674	14.5	1,024,539
9 Beneficial (by Top Ville)	82	645	12.7	840,544
10 Scorpion (by Montjeu)	56	428	13.1	768,609
11 Authorized (by Montjeu)	25	156	16.0	761,703
12 Indian River (by Cadoudal)	27	150	18.0	696,938
13 Martaline (by Linamix)	37	192	19.3	628,245
14 Poliglote (by Sadler's Wells)	18	76	23.7	610,489
15 Kapgarde (by Garde Royale)	27	176	15.3	519,319

SIRES OF WINNERS (by win money)	Horses	Indiv'l Wnrs	Races Won	Stakes £
1 King's Theatre (by Sadler's Wells)	157	64	87	1,032,822
2 Presenting (by Mtoto)	225	74	110	927,517
3 Flemensfirth (by Alleged)	190	71	102	926,153
4 Kayf Tara (by Sadler's Wells)	227	75	109	923,403
5 Oscar (by Sadler's Wells)	185	61	97	874,827
6 Westerner (by Danehill)	150	61	98	765,124

LEADING HORSES (1,2,3 earnings)	Won	Runs	£
1 Tiger Roll 8 b.g Authorized–Swiss Roll	2	3	540,417
2 Buveur d'Air 7 b.g Crillon–History	4	4	413,789
3 Native River 8 ch.g Indian River–Native Mo	2	2	402,972
4 Might Bite 9 b.g Scorpion–Knotted Midge	3	4	393,103
5 Politologue 7 gr.g Poliglote–Scarlet Row	4	6	342,654
6 Altior 8 b.g High Chaparral–Monte Solaro	3	3	342,087
7 Bristol de Mai 7 gr.g Saddler Maker–La Bole Night	2	5	226,299
8 Balko des Flos 7 ch.g Balko–Royale Marie	1	2	204,015
9 Pleasant Company 10 b.g Presenting–Katie Flame	0	1	200,000
10 L'Ami Serge 8 b.g King's Theatre–La Zingarella	1	5	193,275

EXPLANATORY NOTES

'Chasers & Hurdlers 2017/18' deals individually, in alphabetical sequence, with every horse that ran over jumps or in National Hunt Flat races in Britain during the 2017/18 season, plus a number of foreign-trained horses that did not race here. For each of these horses is given (1) its age, colour and sex, (2) its breeding and, where this information has not been given in a previous Chasers & Hurdlers or Racehorses Annual, usually a family outline, (3) a form summary giving its Timeform rating—or ratings—at the end of the previous season, followed by the details of all its performances during the past season, (4) a Timeform rating—or ratings—of its merit (which appears in the margin), (5) a Timeform commentary on its racing or general characteristics as a racehorse, with some suggestions, perhaps, regarding its prospects for 2018/19 and (6) the name of the trainer in whose charge it was on the last occasion it ran.

The book is published with a twofold purpose. Firstly, it is intended to have permanent value as a review of the exploits and achievements of the more notable of our chasers and hurdlers in the 2017/18 season. Thus, while the commentaries upon the vast majority of the horses are, of necessity, in note form, the best horses are more critically examined. The text is illustrated by posed portraits of the most notable horses (where these are available) and photographs of the major races. Secondly, the book is designed to help the punter to analyse races, and the notes which follow contain instructions for using the data.

TIMEFORM RATINGS

The Timeform Rating of a horse is simply the merit of the horse expressed in pounds and is arrived at by careful examination of its running against other horses using a scale of weight for distance beaten. Timeform maintains a 'running' handicap of all horses in training throughout the season.

THE LEVEL OF THE RATINGS

At the close of each season the ratings of all the horses that have raced are re-examined which explains why some of the ratings may be different from those in the final issue of the 2017/18 Timeform Chasing Black Book series. The 'Chasers & Hurdlers' figure is the definitive Timeform Rating.

RATINGS AND WEIGHT-FOR-AGE

The reader has, in the ratings in this book, a universal handicap embracing all the horses in training it is possible to weigh up, ranging from tip-top performers, with ratings from 170 upwards, down to those rated around the 60 mark. All the ratings are at weight-for-age, so that equal ratings mean horses of equal merit. In using Timeform to assess the prospects of various runners, allowance should be made for any difference specified by the Age, Weight and Distance Table at the front.

Steeplechase ratings, preceded by c, should not be confused with hurdle ratings, preceded by h. Where a horse has raced over fences and also over hurdles its ratings as a chaser and hurdler are printed one above the other, the steeplechase rating (c) being placed above the hurdle rating (h).

Thus with REGALITY c157
h143

the top figure, 157, is the rating to be used in steeplechases, and the one below, 143, is for use only in hurdle races. Where a horse has a rating based on its performance in a bumper it is preceded by 'b'. The procedure for making age and weight adjustments to the ratings (i.e. for the calculation of Race Ratings) is as follows:

A. Horses of the Same Age

If the horses all carry the same weight there are no adjustments to be made, and the horses with the highest ratings have the best chances. If the horses carry different weights, jot down their ratings, and to the rating of each horse add one point for every pound the horse is set to carry less than 12st 7lb, or subtract one point for every pound it has to carry more than 12st 7lb. When the ratings have been adjusted in this way the highest resultant figure indicates the horse with the best chance at the weights.

Example (any distance: any month of the season)

Teucer	5 yrs (11-0) ..	Rating 140 ..	add 21	 161
Kiowa	5 yrs (10-7) ..	Rating 125 ..	add 28	 153
Golden Age	5 yrs (10-4) ..	Rating 120 ..	add 31	 151

Teucer has the best chance, and Golden Age the worst

B. Horses of Different Ages

In this case, reference must be made to the Age, Weight and Distance Table at the front. Use the Table for steeplechasers and hurdlers alike. Treat each horse separately, and compare the weight it has to carry with the weight prescribed for it in the table, according to the age of the horse, the distance of the race and the month of the year. Then, add one point to the rating for each pound the horse has to carry less than the weight given in the table: or, subtract one point from the rating for every pound it has to carry more than the weight prescribed by the table. The highest resultant figure indicates the horse most favoured by the weights.

Example (2¾m steeplechase in January)

(Table Weights: 8-y-o 12-7; 7-y-o 12-7; 5-y-o 12-6)

Black Book	8 yrs (12-8) ..	Rating 140 ..	subtract 1	 139
Pressman	7 yrs (12-3) ..	Rating 132 ..	add 4	 136
Copyright	5 yrs (12-7) ..	Rating 150 ..	subtract 1	 149

Copyright has the best chance, and Pressman the worst

Example (3m hurdle race in March)

(Table Weights: 9-y-o 12-7; 5-y-o 12-7; 4-y-o 11-11)

Oxer	9 yrs (10-12) ..	Rating 110 ..	add 23	 133
Clairval	5 yrs (10-7) ..	Rating 119 ..	add 28	 147
Gallette	4 yrs (10-7) ..	Rating 128 ..	add 18	 146

Clairval has the best chance, and Oxer the worst

C. Horses in bumpers

The procedure for calculating Race Ratings in bumpers is precisely the same as in (A) or (B).

Example (2m bumper in February)

(Table Weights: 6-y-o 12-7; 5-y-o 12-7; 4-y-o 12-1)

Squall	6 yrs (10-12) ..	Rating 88 ..	add 23	 111
Lupin	5 yrs (11-3) ..	Rating 97 ..	add 18	 115
Chariot	4 yrs (10-9) ..	Rating 84 ..	add 20	 104

Lupin has the best chance, and Chariot the worst

The bumper ratings can be used not only within the context of bumper races themselves, but also as an indication of the potential form of such horses in their first few starts over jumps.

JOCKEYSHIP AND RIDERS' ALLOWANCES

For the purposes of rating calculations it should, in general, be assumed that the allowance the rider is able to claim (3 lb, 5 lb, or 7 lb) is nullified by his or her inexperience. Therefore, the weight adju*stments to the ratings should be calculated on the weight allotted by the handicapper, or determined by the conditions of the race*, and no extra addition should be made to a rating because the horse's rider claims an allowance. This is the general routine procedure; but, of course, after the usual adjustments have been made the quality of jockeyship is still an important factor to be considered when deciding between horses with similar chances.

WEIGHING UP A RACE

The ratings tell which horses in a particular race are most favoured by the weights; but complete analysis demands that the racing character of each horse is also studied carefully to see if there is any reason why the horse might be expected not to run up to its rating. It counts for little that a horse is thrown in at the weights if it has no pretensions whatever to staying the distance, or is unable to act on the prevailing going. Suitability of distance and going are no doubt the most important points to be considered, but there are others. For example, the ability of a horse to accommodate itself to the conformation of the track. There is also the matter of a horse's ability and dependability as a jumper and of its temperament: nobody would be in a hurry to take a short price about a horse with whom it is always an even chance whether it will get round or not, or whether it will consent to race.

A few minutes spent checking up on these matters in the commentaries upon the horses concerned will sometimes put a very different complexion on a race from that which is put upon it by the ratings alone. We repeat, therefore, that the correct way to use Timeform, or this annual volume, in the analysis of individual races is, first to use the ratings to discover which horses are most favoured by the weights, and second, to check through the comments on the horses to see what factors other than weight might also affect the outcome of the race.

THE FORM SUMMARIES

The form summaries enclosed in the brackets list each horse's performances in the last season in sequence, showing, for each race, its distance in furlongs, the state of the going and the horse's placing at the finish. Steeplechase form figures are prefixed by the letter 'c', hurdle form figures by the letter 'h' and bumper form figures by the letter 'b'.

The going is symbolised as follows: f–firm, m–good to firm, g–good, d–good to soft/dead, s–soft, v–heavy.

Placings are indicated up to sixth place, by superior figures, an asterisk denoting a win; and superior letters are used to convey what happened to the horse during the race: F–fell (F^3 denotes remounted and finished third); pu–pulled up; ur–unseated rider; bd–brought down; R–refused; rr–refused to race; su–slipped up; ro–ran out; co–carried out; d–disqualified

Thus, [2017/18 h82, b80: h16g h16s* c18g^{pu} h16f^2 c20v^F Apr 10] states that the horse was rated 82 over hurdles and 80 in bumpers at the end of the previous season. In the 2017/18 jumping season the horse ran five times; unplaced in a 2m hurdle race on good going, winning a 2m hurdle race on soft going, being pulled up in a 2¼m steeplechase on good going, running second in a 2m hurdle race on firm going and falling in a 2½m steeplechase on heavy going. Its last race was on April 10th.

Where sale prices are given they are in guineas unless otherwise stated. The prefix $ refers to American dollars and € indicates the euro. Any other currencies are converted into pounds sterling at the prevailing exchange rate.

THE RATING SYMBOLS

The following symbols, attached to the ratings, are to be interpreted as stated:-

p   likely to improve.
P   capable of *much* better form.
\+   the horse may be better than we have rated it.
d   the horse appears to have deteriorated, and might no longer be capable of running to the rating given.
§   unreliable (for temperamental or other reasons).
§§   so temperamentally unsatisfactory as to be not worth a rating.
x   poor jumper.
xx   a very bad jumper, so bad as to be not worth a rating.
?   the horse's rating is suspect or, used without a rating, the horse can't be assessed with confidence or, if used in the in-season Timeform publications, that the horse is out of form.

CHASERS & HURDLERS 2017/18

Horse   *Commentary*   *Rating*

AACHEN 14 b.g. Rainbow Quest (USA) – Anna of Saxony (Ela-Mana-Mou) [2017/18 c–, h–: c24d^{pu} May 20] useful-looking gelding: winning hurdler: smart chaser at best, no form since 2015/16: tried in headgear. *Venetia Williams*   **c–** **h–**

AAMAN (IRE) 12 gr.g. Dubai Destination (USA) – Amellnaa (IRE) (Sadler's Wells (USA)) [2017/18 h81: h15.8d h15.8g^5 h21.6g^3 Sep 2] poor handicap hurdler: stays 2¾m: acts on good to soft going: has worn tongue tie. *Bernard Llewellyn*   **h71**

AARDWOLF (USA) 4 b.g. Cape Cross (IRE) – Desert Gazelle (USA) (Smart Strike (CAN)) [2017/18 h15.3v^4 h15.5s^{ur} h16.2s^3 h16.2v^2 Apr 10] fairly useful on Flat, stays 1¼m: fair form over hurdles. *Warren Greatrex*   **h102**

AARON LAD (IRE) 7 b.g. Daylami (IRE) – Borntobepampered (Entrepreneur) [2017/18 h21g^F h20v^{pu} h20.8s^3 h19.9v^2 h19.3s^2 h19.9v* h23.1v* h22.8v^{pu} Mar 31] €1,600 4-y-o: fifth foal: half-brother to a winning sprinter in Italy by Modigliani: dam unraced half-sister to fairly useful hurdler (stayed 25f) Mith Hill (by Daylami): fairly useful hurdler: trained in 2016/17 by Kieran Purcell: won handicaps at Sedgefield in February and Market Rasen in March: stays 23f: acts on heavy going. *Dr Richard Newland*   **h117**

AARYAM (FR) 6 b.g. Dylan Thomas (IRE) – Selinea (FR) (Keltos (FR)) [2017/18 h77, b–: h15.8v Feb 18] maiden hurdler: in blinkers last 2 starts: in tongue tie last 3. *John Flint*   **h–**

ABBEYGREY (IRE) 9 b.g. Generous (IRE) – Garw Valley (Mtoto) [2017/18 c108, h102: c23.8g^5 c25.8d* c23g^4 c20.9s^{pu} c25.6g^{pu} h23.1v h23.6v Mar 21] winning hurdler: fair handicap chaser: won at Newton Abbot (conditional) in September: lost form after next start: stays 3¼m: acts on heavy going: in headgear last 3 starts: tried in tongue tie: often races towards rear. *Evan Williams*   **c104 h–**

ABBEY LANE (IRE) 13 b.g. Flemensfirth (USA) – Hazel Sylph (IRE) (Executive Perk) [2017/18 c109, h–: c23.6m^4 May 23] strong gelding: multiple winning pointer: winning hurdler/maiden chaser, useful at best: stays 3m: acts on good to firm and heavy going. *A. Pennock*   **c75 h–**

ABBEY STREET (IRE) 7 b.g. Asian Heights – Cnocbui Cailin (IRE) (Moscow Society (USA)) [2017/18 h19.5s h16.3d h15.9v h19.6s^2 h24v^5 h19.5v Apr 14] compact gelding: fifth foal: brother to a winning pointer: dam unraced: placed both completed starts in Irish points: modest form over hurdles: best effort at 2½m: acts on soft going: usually races in rear. *Paul Henderson*   **h98**

ABBEYVIEW (IRE) 11 b.g. Misternando – Castle Spirit (IRE) (Clearly Bust) [2017/18 c103: c24.5g* c25.5d^6 May 31] multiple point winner, including in 2018: fair form in chases: won hunter at Towcester in May: stays 3m: acts on good to firm going. *Mrs Sheila Crow*   **c103**

ABBOTSWOOD (IRE) 7 b.g. Stowaway – Grove Juliet (IRE) (Moscow Society (USA)) [2017/18 h109: c24.1d^4 Oct 4] winning pointer: fair hurdle winner: 14/1, fourth in novice handicap at Bangor (15½ lengths behind Cuirassier Dempire) on chasing debut: probably stays 3m: wears tongue tie: sold £4,000 in November. *Charlie Longsdon*   **c112 h–**

ABBREVIATE (GER) 7 b.g. Authorized (IRE) – Azalee (GER) (Lando (GER)) [2017/18 h125: c22.6s^4 c23.6g^3 c23.8d^6 c23.4s^5 c23.6s^2 c24.5v^3 Mar 15] good-topped gelding: fairly useful hurdler: similar form over fences: third in novice handicap at Huntingdon in October, bad mistake 2 out: stays 3m: acts on soft going: in cheekpieces last 5 starts: front runner/races prominently. *Kim Bailey*   **c128 h–**

ABBYSSIAL (IRE) 8 ch.g. Beneficial – Mega d'Estruval (FR) (Garde Royale) [2017/18 h16v^4 h21.1s^{pu} h16s h20s Apr 28] good-topped gelding: very smart hurdler at one time, well below best in 2017/18 after 3-year absence: unproven beyond 2m: acts on heavy going. *W. P. Mullins, Ireland*   **h132**

ABE

ABERTILLERY 6 b.g. Shamardal (USA) – Nantyglo (Mark of Esteem (IRE)) [2017/18 h–: h16.8g May 10] sturdy gelding: poor maiden on Flat: lightly raced over hurdles, no form since debut in 2015/16. *Michael Blanshard* — h–

ABIDJAN (FR) 8 b.g. Alberto Giacometti (IRE) – Kundera (FR) (Kadalko (FR)) [2017/18 c127, h–: c16.2g* h18.6g³ c16m³ c16.5g³ c16.5g* Aug 23] fairly useful handicap hurdler: useful handicap chaser: won at Warwick in May and Worcester in August: stays 19f: acts on good to firm and good to soft going: has worn tongue tie, including last 3 starts: races towards rear, often travels strongly. *Dan Skelton* — c138 h120

ABLAZING (IRE) 7 b.g. Mastercraftsman (IRE) – Moore's Melody (IRE) (Marju (IRE)) [2017/18 h116: h20g^F Jun 3] fairly useful handicap hurdler: beaten when fell last only start in 2017/18: stays 2½m: acts on good to soft going: wears blinkers: usually travels strongly. *Johnny Farrelly* — h–

A BOLD MOVE (IRE) 8 b.g. Shantou (USA) – Sprint For Gold (USA) (Slew O' Gold (USA)) [2017/18 h114: h20g² h23d³ c20.9v^{pu} Nov 24] dual point winner: fair maiden hurdler: pulled up in novice handicap on chasing debut: stays 2½m: acts on soft going: in cheekpieces last 4 starts. *Christian Williams* — c– h108

A BOOK OF INTRIGUE 5 b.g. Alflora (IRE) – Kahlua Cove (Karinga Bay) [2017/18 b15.8v³ Dec 18] 2/1, third in maiden bumper at Ffos Las (11¾ lengths behind Echo Watt). *Fergal O'Brien* — b78

ABOUT GLORY 4 b.g. Nayef (USA) – Lemon Rock (Green Desert (USA)) [2017/18 h16s⁶ h15.7s h16v⁶ Jan 23] fair on Flat, stays 1¾m: no form over hurdles. *John David Riches* — h–

ABOVE BOARD (IRE) 7 b.g. Mahler – Blackwater Babe (IRE) (Arctic Lord) [2017/18 h119: c23g* c24.2v^{pu} Nov 7] rangy gelding: fairly useful hurdle winner: similar form over fences: won maiden at Worcester in October, plenty in hand: lame next time: stays 23f: acts on soft going: often races prominently/travels strongly. *Jonjo O'Neill* — c124 h–

A BOY NAMED SUZI 10 b.g. Medecis – Classic Coral (USA) (Seattle Dancer (USA)) [2017/18 h116: h21m⁴ h20.6g h20.3g⁴ h23g² h23g⁴ h23g³ Aug 1] sturdy gelding: fair handicap hurdler nowadays: barely stays 23f: acts on heavy going: has worn cheekpieces, including last 4 starts: front runner/races prominently. *Lucy Wadham* — h111

ABRACADABRA SIVOLA (FR) 8 br.g. Le Fou (IRE) – Pierrebrune (FR) (Cadoudal (FR)) [2017/18 c128, h–: c24d³ c23.8g c26.2d c25.6g c26s⁵ c25.1v⁴ c25.6s⁵ c24s* c25.6v⁴ Mar 31] useful-looking gelding: winning hurdler: fairly useful handicap chaser: down in weights when won at Kempton in March: stays 3½m: acts on heavy going: wears headgear, in tongue tie last 5 starts: temperamental. *David Pipe* — c124 § h–

ABRICOT DE L'OASIS (FR) 8 b.g. Al Namix (FR) – La Normandie (FR) (Beyssac (FR)) [2017/18 c136, h126: h23.1m⁴ c22.6d* Apr 22] fairly useful handicap hurdler: useful chaser at best: won hunter at Stratford in April: left Dan Skelton after first start: stays 3m: acts on soft and good to firm going: has worn headgear, including last 4 starts: front runner/races prominently. *J. H. Henderson* — c110 h108

ABSOLUTE (IRE) 7 b.g. Danehill Dancer (IRE) – Beyond Belief (IRE) (Sadler's Wells (USA)) [2017/18 h72: h16.8g h16.2g⁴ h17.2g Jun 30] rather lightly-made gelding: poor maiden hurdler: unproven beyond 17f: acted on heavy going: dead. *Sue Smith* — h74

ABSOLUTELY DYLAN (IRE) 5 b.g. Scorpion (IRE) – Cash Customer (IRE) (Bob Back (USA)) [2017/18 b164.g⁶ h18.6d³ h18.6v² h16.4v* h18.9s h20.1d Apr 23] €20,000 3-y-o, £15,000 4-y-o: third foal: half-brother to bumper winner/fairly useful hurdler Round Tower (21f winner, by Presenting), stays 25f, and modest chaser The Purchaser (2¾m winner, by Definite Article): dam unraced sister to fairly useful hurdler/fair chaser (stayed 3m) Dead Sound and half-sister to smart chaser (winner up to 21f) Go Roger Go: unplaced in Irish points: sixth in bumper at Newcastle: fair form over hurdles: won novice at Newcastle in February: should stay at least 2½m: acts on heavy going: usually races prominently: signs of temperament. *Sue Smith* — h107 b83

ABSOLUTELY FRANKIE 8 ch.g. Zaha (CAN) – La Piazza (IRE) (Polish Patriot (USA)) [2017/18 h–, b–: h16s Nov 22] no form in bumper/over hurdles. *Martin Bosley* — h–

ACE

ABSOLUTE POWER 7 b.g. Flemensfirth (USA) – Crystal Ballerina (IRE) (Sadler's Wells (USA)) [2017/18 b97: h19.3s² h20v⁶ Nov 12] placed in bumpers: fair form over hurdles: better effort when second in novice at Carlisle in October: should stay 2½m+. *Rebecca Curtis* **h107**

ACADEMY GENERAL (IRE) 12 b.g. Beneficial – Discerning Air (Ezzoud (IRE)) [2017/18 c63, h55: c22.6g⁵ c25.8m⁶ c16.3m³ c25.8g c20m Jul 5] winning hurdler/maiden chaser, retains little ability (failed to complete in points after final chase start): stays 23f: acts on good to firm and acts on good to soft going: wears headgear: has worn tongue tie, including in 2017/18. *Jackie du Plessis* **c56 h–**

ACAPELLA BOURGEOIS (FR) 8 ch.g. Network (GER) – Jasmine (FR) (Valanjou (FR)) [2017/18 c148+, h–: c24vᶠ c20s² c17sᵖᵘ Jan 14] lengthy gelding: winning hurdler: smart handicap chaser: second at Navan (9 lengths behind Polidam) in December: reportedly bled final start: stays 3m: acts on heavy going: often wears hood: tried in tongue tie. *W. P. Mullins, Ireland* **c150 h–**

ACARO (FR) 4 b.g. Sinndar (IRE) – Accusation (IRE) (Barathea (IRE)) [2017/18 h17.7d⁶ h17.7v² h16.3v³ h15.3v Jan 18] good-topped gelding: dam, maiden on Flat, sister to useful hurdler (2m-2½m winner) Silk Affair and half-sister to useful hurdler/chaser (2m-19f winner) Direct Bearing: ran once on Flat for Rodolphe Collet: fair form over hurdles: in tongue tie last 2 starts. *Robert Walford* **h103**

ACCESSALLAREAS (IRE) 13 ch.g. Swift Gulliver (IRE) – Arushofgold (IRE) (Alphabatim (USA)) [2017/18 c83§, h–: c16.5mᵖᵘ c16.1g⁴ c19.2g² c19.4g⁵ c17.3g⁴ c19.4m c17.4g³ c16.3m* c17g⁶ c15.7d c20gᵘʳ c21.7mᵖᵘ Apr 25] workmanlike gelding: very lightly raced over hurdles: poor handicap chaser: won at Newton Abbot in August: stays 21f: acts on soft and good to firm going: wears headgear: has worn tongue tie: front runner/races prominently: unreliable. *Sarah-Jayne Davies* **c82 § h–**

ACCORDING TO HARRY (IRE) 9 b.g. Old Vic – Cassilis (IRE) (Persian Bold) [2017/18 c126, h117: c25g h24g⁵ c25.6g⁵ c23.8d⁴ c23.8d Apr 24] fairly useful hurdler/chaser, below best in 2017/18: stays 3m: acts on soft and good to firm going. *Nicky Martin* **c102 h–**

ACCORDING TO TREV (IRE) 12 ch.g. Accordion – Autumn Sky (IRE) (Roselier (FR)) [2017/18 c–, h–: c25.8m⁴ c25.5m⁵ c23g⁶ Jul 10] good-topped gelding: winning hurdler: useful chaser at best, retains little ability: has worn headgear/tongue tie: often races lazily. *Lawney Hill* **c– § h–**

ACCORD (IRE) 8 b.g. Arcadio (GER) – Detente (Medicean) [2017/18 h113: c19.5g* c19.7d⁴ c20s c15.5d⁶ c19.9s⁶ Jan 12] sturdy, workmanlike gelding: maiden hurdler: fairly useful form over fences: won novice handicap at Fontwell in October: stays 19f: best form on good going: tried in cheekpieces: often races prominently. *David Bridgwater* **c120 h–**

ACCOST (IRE) 5 b.m. Ask – Minora (IRE) (Cataldi) [2017/18 ab16.3g b16.2s Apr 27] closely related to fair hurdler Buffalo Ballet (2½m winner, by Kayf Tara), stays 3m: dam unraced half-sister to high-class chaser Observe and very smart hurdler Minorettes Girl, herself dam of staying chasers Shotgun Willy (high class) and Mini Sensation (smart): no form in bumpers: tried in tongue tie. *N. W. Alexander* **b–**

ACDC (IRE) 8 b.g. King's Theatre (IRE) – Always Alert (IRE) (Slip Anchor) [2017/18 h109, b84: c23.4g² c24.3v* c23.4v⁴ c24.1v⁴ c21.6v* c20.1sᵘʳ c21.5v² c23.4v* c24.1g³ Apr 21] fair hurdler: fairly useful chaser: won handicap at Ayr in November, and novices at Kelso in January and April (handicap): stays 3m: acts on heavy going: wears hood/tongue tie. *Chris Grant* **c127 h–**

ACE CHEETAH (USA) 4 b.g. Kitten's Joy (USA) – Imagistic (USA) (Deputy Minister (CAN)) [2017/18 ab16g⁵ Mar 5] 12/1, fifth in bumper at Lingfield (9¾ lengths behind Dazibao). *J. R. Jenkins* **b74**

ACERTAIN CIRCUS 8 ch.g. Definite Article – Circus Rose (Most Welcome) [2017/18 h21g⁴ Nov 30] well-made gelding: fairly useful hurdler at best, very lightly raced since 2014/15: stays 2½m: acts on soft going: has worn tongue tie. *Pam Sly* **h104**

ACES OVER EIGHTS (IRE) 9 b.m. Old Vic – Conjure Up (IRE) (Jurado (USA)) [2017/18 c104, h–: c20.3dᵖᵘ c20gᵖᵘ c15.7gᵖᵘ Jul 16] workmanlike mare: winning hurdler: fair handicap chaser: pulled up all starts in early-2017/18: stays 21f: acts on soft going: usually wears cheekpieces. *Kerry Lee* **c– h–**

Owner For Owners: Acey Milan's "Acey Milan"

ACEY MILAN (IRE) 4 b.g. Milan – Strong Wishes (IRE) (Strong Gale) [2017/18 b13.2s² b15.3v* b14s* b16.3v* b16.4s⁴ Mar 14] rather unfurnished gelding: brother to useful hurdler/fairly useful chaser Lord Wishes (19f-2¾m winner), closely related to 2 winners by Oscar, including useful hurdler/smart chaser William's Wishes (2m-2½m winner), and half-brother to fair 17f hurdle winner Scorpions Sting (by Scorpion): dam (h97) in frame in bumpers/over hurdles: smart bumper performer: won junior event at Wincanton in December, and listed events at Cheltenham (by 3¾ lengths from Malinas Jack) in January and Newbury (by 11 lengths from Woulduadamandeveit) in February: fourth in Champion Bumper at Cheltenham (5¼ lengths behind Relegate) in March: in tongue tie last 4 starts: front runner/races prominently, usually travels strongly. *Anthony Honeyball* **b118**

ACHILLE (FR) 8 gr.g. Dom Alco (FR) – Hase (FR) (Video Rock (FR)) [2017/18 c20.2s⁵ c20.9s⁵ h25v c25.1v² Mar 28] lengthy gelding: winning hurdler: fair chaser nowadays: stays 25f: acts on heavy going: often wears cheekpieces. *Venetia Williams* **c113 h–**

ACHILL ROAD BOY (IRE) 9 b.g. Morozov (USA) – Presenting Katie (IRE) (Presenting) [2017/18 c103, h103: c15.6v c23.4g² c20d³ h22.8v⁵ c24.1v⁵ c24.1v c21.2v² c23.8d⁵ c20.1v⁶ c26.2d* c26.2v⁴ Apr 17] fair handicap hurdler/chaser: won over fences at Carlisle in March: stays 3¼m: acts on heavy going: usually races nearer last than first. *Stuart Coltherd* **c98 h91**

ACTING LASS (IRE) 7 b.g. King's Theatre (IRE) – Darrens Lass (IRE) (Montelimar (USA)) [2017/18 h133: c21.4d* c20.2s* c21v* c24g Feb 24] lengthy gelding: useful hurdle winner: smart form over fences: won novice handicaps at Market Rasen in November and Leicester (by 1¼ lengths from Ballyarthur) in January, and bet365 Handicap Chase at Ascot (by 2¼ lengths from Kilcrea Vale) in January: should stay 3m: acts on heavy going: wears tongue tie: remains with potential over fences. *Harry Fry* **c149 p h–**

ADA

ACTINPIECES 7 gr.m. Act One – Bonnet's Pieces (Alderbrook) [2017/18 c133, h–: c24.2d* c24.1s² h24.2d c24.2s⁴ c23.8s* c26s⁵ Mar 15] workmanlike mare: winning hurdler: useful handicap chaser: won at Fakenham in October and Ludlow in January: stays 25f: acts on soft going: often races towards rear. *Pam Sly* **c143 h–**

ACTION REPLAY (IRE) 7 b.g. Milan – Mary Connors (IRE) (Mandalus) [2017/18 h115p: h15.9d⁵ c15.7s^ur Nov 23] maiden hurdler, fairly useful form at best: yet to be asked for effort when unseated 5 out in novice handicap won by Drumcliff at Wincanton on chasing debut: raced around 2m: acts on heavy going. *Philip Hobbs* **c– p h96**

ACTIVIAL (FR) 8 g.g. Lord du Sud (FR) – Kissmirial (FR) (Smadoun (FR)) [2017/18 c–, h–: h20.3g Apr 18] angular gelding: smart hurdler at best, below form only start (hood) in 2017/18: winning chaser: stays 21f: acts on heavy going: has worn tongue tie. *Neil Mulholland* **c– h–**

ACT NOW 9 br.m. Act One – Lady Turk (FR) (Baby Turk) [2017/18 h106: h23.9v⁵ h25d² c20.2v⁵ c25.7v² c30.7s^pu h25.5s⁶ Mar 27] fair handicap hurdler: fairly useful form over fences: best effort when second in handicap at Plumpton in January: stays 3¼m: acts on heavy going: in headgear last 2 starts: wears tongue tie. *Anthony Honeyball* **c115 h108**

ACT OF VALOUR 4 b.g. Harbour Watch (IRE) – B Berry Brandy (USA) (Event of The Year (USA)) [2017/18 h16.4v* h16.6d⁵ h15.6s² h16.4s h16d* h16s⁵ Apr 28] strong gelding: useful on Flat, stays 1½m: useful form over hurdles: won juvenile at Newcastle in December and novice at Fakenham in April: second in listed juvenile at Musselburgh (4½ lengths behind We Have A Dream) in February and fifth in novice handicap at Sandown (3½ lengths behind Ballymoy) in April: raced around 2m: acts on heavy going: often travels strongly. *Paul Nicholls* **h132**

ACTONETAKETWO 8 b.m. Act One – Temple Dancer (Magic Ring (IRE)) [2017/18 h–: h21.6g^pu h18.5m h21.6m h18.5g^pu Jun 27] sturdy mare: no form over hurdles: in cheekpieces last 4 starts: temperamental. *Derrick Scott* **h– §**

ADAM DU BRETEAU (FR) 8 ch.g. Network (GER) – Odelie de Fric (FR) (April Night (FR)) [2017/18 c128, h–: c25.5d³ c27.5g c25.5g⁶ c26.7g⁶ c30.2g⁵ Nov 17] maiden hurdler: fairly useful handicap chaser: stays 3¾m: acts on good to firm and good to soft going: usually wears headgear: usually races close up: unreliable. *Jonjo O'Neill* **c125 § h–**

bet365 Handicap Chase, Ascot—the novice Acting Lass is more fluent at the last than runner-up Kilcrea Vale as he lands a weak race for the money

ADA

ADARENNA (IRE) 6 b.m. Nayef (USA) – Adelfia (IRE) (Sinndar (IRE)) [2017/18 c101, h88: c19.8m³ c19.5g⁵ c20.6s^pu h24.8d c17.3s^pu h19.8g c26g^pu c21.6g^pu Oct 7] maiden hurdler: fair handicap chaser at best, little form in 2017/18: unproven beyond 17f: acts on good to soft going: wears headgear: has worn tongue tie: temperamental. *John Joseph Hanlon, Ireland* — **c81 §** **h69 §**

ADELPHI PRINCE 5 b.g. Schiaparelli (GER) – Cailin Na Ri (IRE) (King's Theatre (IRE)) [2017/18 b15.7s⁵ Feb 12] 8/1, fifth in conditional/amateur maiden bumper at Catterick (17½ lengths behind The Some Dance Kid). *Martin Todhunter* — **b70**

ADHERENCE 5 b.g. Sir Percy – Straight Laced (Refuse To Bend (USA)) [2017/18 h–: h16.8s h16.8s h15.7s h19.9v³ Mar 23] fair on Flat, stays 1¾m: modest form over hurdles: stays 2½m: acts on heavy going: sometimes in cheekpieces. *Kenneth Slack* — **h96**

ADMAN SAM (IRE) 7 b.g. Black Sam Bellamy (IRE) – Koral Bay (FR) (Cadoudal (FR)) [2017/18 h20.3g* May 24] in frame in bumpers: fair form over hurdles: won novice at Southwell on sole outing since 2015/16: stays 2½m. *Ian Williams* — **h111**

ADMIRAL ANSON 4 br.c. Bahri (USA) – Bromeigan (Mtoto) [2017/18 b16d^pu Apr 26] compact gelding: pulled up in bumper. *Michael Appleby* — **b–**

ADMIRAL BARRATRY (IRE) 5 b.g. Soldier of Fortune (IRE) – Haskilclara (FR) (Green Tune (USA)) [2017/18 h115: h19.2g⁵ h16.3d² Dec 1] useful-looking gelding: fairly useful form over hurdles: second in maiden at Newbury in December. *Nick Williams* — **h116**

ADMIRAL BLAKE 11 b.g. Witness Box (USA) – Brenda Bella (FR) (Linamix (FR)) [2017/18 c79, h65: h19.5d h21.6v⁵ h21.6v⁵ h23.3v⁴ c25.2s⁵ c23.6v h23.9v² h23.9s^F h23.1d⁵ Apr 24] poor handicap hurdler: maiden chaser: stays 3m: raced mostly on soft/heavy going: tried in blinkers: wore tongue tie last 3 starts. *Laura Young* — **c–** **h79**

ADMIRAL KID (IRE) 7 b.g. Mythical Kid (USA) – English Clover (Tina's Pet) [2017/18 h105: h16s^pu h19.8s Mar 9] lengthy gelding: third in Irish point: bumper winner: maiden hurdler, no form in 2017/18: should be suited by further than 2m. *Neil Mulholland* — **h–**

ADMIRAL'S SECRET 7 b.g. Kayf Tara – Bobs Bay (IRE) (Bob's Return (IRE)) [2017/18 h107: c16s^pu c18d⁵ c19.2v^pu c16d* c17.4d* Apr 21] lightly-raced maiden hurdler: fairly useful form over fences: won handicaps at Ludlow (novice) in February and Bangor in April: bred to be suited by further than 2m: acts on heavy going: wears tongue tie. *Victor Dartnall* — **c118** **h–**

ADRIEN DU PONT (FR) 6 b.g. Califet (FR) – Santariyka (FR) (Saint des Saints (FR)) [2017/18 h145: c21.6g* c19.9g³ c21d² c16.4s³ c21s² c20.5g^F Apr 21] well-made gelding: smart hurdler: useful form over fences: won novice at Fontwell in October: stays 2¾m: acts on heavy going: ran well in hood: wears tongue tie: reportedly bled fifth outing. *Paul Nicholls* — **c143** **h–**

ADRRASTOS (IRE) 6 b.g. Areion (GER) – Laren (GER) (Monsun (GER)) [2017/18 h115, b80: h16.8g³ h16g³ c16.5g* c17m* c16.5g³ c19.7d^pu Oct 23] lengthy gelding: fairly useful hurdler: useful form over fences: won novice handicaps at Worcester in July and Stratford in August: unproven beyond 17f: acts on good to firm and heavy going: has worn hood: front runner. *Jamie Snowden* — **c131** **h115**

ADSUP (IRE) 7 b.g. Ad Valorem (USA) – Headborough Lass (IRE) (Invincible Spirit (IRE)) [2017/18 h16.2g^pu May 18] pulled up in 2 points and maiden hurdle (tongue tied). *Stuart Crawford, Ireland* — **h–**

AENGUS (IRE) 8 b.g. Robin des Champs (FR) – Which Thistle (IRE) (Saddlers' Hall (IRE)) [2017/18 c–, h121: h23.3s h23.6v h24.3v³ h22.7v⁶ h23.1v h25s³ h26.6s⁶ Apr 26] fairly useful handicap hurdler: all but fell only start over fences: stays 25f: acts on heavy going: usually wears cheekpieces. *Jennie Candlish* — **c–** **h121**

AERLITE SUPREME (IRE) 11 b.g. Gold Well – Supreme Evening (IRE) (Supreme Leader) [2017/18 c124, h–: c20g* c23.8m² c26.1m c20s⁴ Jul 30] rangy gelding: winning hurdler: fairly useful handicap chaser: won at Warwick in May: barely stays 3¼m: acts on good to firm and heavy going: has worn headgear, including last 4 starts: wears tongue tie: irresolute. *Evan Williams* — **c122 §** **h–**

AERO MAJESTIC (IRE) 5 b.g. Arcadio (GER) – So Pretty (IRE) (Presenting) [2017/18 b16.8g³ h24g³ h20d⁴ h18.5d⁵ h15.3g h23.1s c15.9v c21s Mar 25] €16,000 3-y-o, £28,000 4-y-o: angular gelding: fifth foal: half-brother to useful chaser Monbeg River (2m-19f winner, by Indian River) and fair hurdler Pretty Miss Mahler (2½m-25f winner, by Mahler): dam runner-up in point: maiden pointer: third in bumper: fair form over hurdles: well held in hunter chases: left David Pipe after sixth start: should be suited by further than 2½m: acts on good to soft going: usually wears cheekpieces: often races towards rear: temperamental. *Sean Conway* — **c–** **h100 §** **b85 §**

38

AGE

AFFAIRE D'HONNEUR (FR) 7 ch.g. Shirocco (GER) – Affaire de Moeurs (FR) (Kaldounevees (FR)) [2017/18 h118: c19.9g⁵ h19d Apr 26] leggy gelding: fairly useful hurdler at best: 15/8, last of 5 finishers in novice handicap at Musselburgh on chasing debut: left Harry Whittington after that: stays 19f: acts on soft going: tried in cheekpieces. *Kevin Frost* — c–, h88

AFICIONADO 8 ch.g. Halling (USA) – Prithee (Baratheon (IRE)) [2017/18 h18.7g⁶ c18d Nov 13] fairly useful hurdler at best, below form on return in 2017/18 after long absence: well beaten in novice handicap on chasing debut: stays 2½m: acts on good to firm and heavy going: wears headgear. *Dr Richard Newland* — c–, h–

AFTER ASPEN (IRE) 8 b.g. Mountain High (IRE) – None The Wiser (IRE) (Dr Massini (IRE)) [2017/18 c20.3s⁶ h24s⁴ h24v h23v* c21.2s³ h24v⁴ Apr 27] fairly useful handicap hurdler: won at Lingfield in February: fair chaser: left Miss Elizabeth Doyle after third start: stays 3m: acts on heavy going: usually wears headgear nowadays: tried in tongue tie. *Olly Murphy* — c111, h115

AFTER EIGHT SIVOLA (FR) 8 b.g. Shaanmer (IRE) – Eva de Chalamont (FR) (Iron Duke (FR)) [2017/18 c108, h117: h20.6g⁴ h20g⁶ h23.3g h18.5d Oct 12] sturdy gelding: fair handicap hurdler nowadays: winning chaser: stays 21f: acts on heavy going: usually wears hood: often races towards rear. *Nick Williams* — c–, h111

AFTER HOURS (IRE) 9 b.g. Milan – Supreme Singer (IRE) (Supreme Leader) [2017/18 c125, h–: c19.4d⁵ c25.6g⁶ Nov 16] workmanlike gelding: winning Irish pointer: winning hurdler: maiden chaser, well below best in 2017/18: stays 3m: acts on heavy going: in cheekpieces last 5 starts. *Henry Oliver* — c96, h–

AGAINN DUL AGHAIDH 7 b.g. Black Sam Bellamy (IRE) – Star Ar Aghaidh (IRE) (Soviet Star (USA)) [2017/18 c24.2g⁴ May 6] first foal: dam (b81), lightly raced in bumpers, half-sister to fairly useful hurdler/fair chaser (stayed 3m) King Ar Aghaidh out of Stayers' Hurdle winner Shuil Ar Aghaidh: multiple point winner: 3/1, fourth in maiden hunter at Hexham (14 lengths behind Tallow Fair) on chasing debut: may do better. *J. J. O'Shea* — c85

AGAMEMNON (IRE) 6 b.g. Getaway (GER) – Oscar Road (IRE) (Oscar (IRE)) [2017/18 h114, b99: c19.9g² c20.3s⁵ Nov 15] rather unfurnished gelding: point/bumper winner: fairly useful from over hurdles: fair form over fences: better effort when second in novice handicap at Huntingdon: stays 21f: acts on soft going: tried in blinkers: front runner/races prominently. *Tom George* — c113, h–

AGATHE ROSALIE (IRE) 5 b.m. Presenting – Agathe du Berlais (FR) (Poliglote) [2017/18 b–: ab16g² Nov 14] modest form in bumpers: second in mares event at Lingfield on sole start in 2017/18: in hood last 2 starts. *Lucy Wadham* — b82

A GENIE IN ABOTTLE (IRE) 7 b.g. Beneficial – Erkindale Miss (IRE) (Supreme Leader) [2017/18 c150, h–: c22.5v* c23s* c26g c25v c25s² Feb 24] rangy gelding: winning hurdler: smart chaser: won minor event at Galway (by 2½ lengths from Mala Beach) and listed event at Wexford (by 1½ lengths from Tiger Roll) in October: second in Bobbyjo Chase at Fairyhouse (4¾ lengths behind Bellshill) in February: should stay long distances: acts on heavy going: tried in cheekpieces: front runner/races prominently. *Noel Meade, Ireland* — c147, h–

AGENTLEMAN (IRE) 8 b.g. Trans Island – Silvine (IRE) (Shernazar) [2017/18 c89, h83: c15.7g³ c16.3d⁴ c15.6g⁶ Aug 21] point winner, failed to complete all starts in 2018: maiden hurdler: poor maiden chaser: stays 21f: acts on heavy going: wears cheekpieces nowadays: tried in tongue tie: usually travels strongly, tends to find little: temperamental. *Evan Williams* — c82 §, h–

AGENT LOUISE 10 b.m. Alflora (IRE) – Oso Special (Teenoso (USA)) [2017/18 h73§: h24gpu h24vpu h25.3s⁵ h23.3v* h27v² Mar 23] poor handicap hurdler: won mares event at Uttoxeter in March: stays 27f: acts on good to firm and heavy going: usually wears headgear: unreliable. *Mike Sowersby* — h80 §

AGENT MEMPHIS (IRE) 6 b.m. Scorpion (IRE) – Forces of Destiny (IRE) (Luso) [2017/18 h20.7d h23.1d Apr 21] €6,700 3-y-o, £42,000 5-y-o: first foal: dam unraced half-sister to smart hurdler/useful chaser (stayed 3m) Emotional Moment: runner-up both starts in Irish points: limited impact in 2 starts over hurdles: should be suited by 2¾m+. *Kim Bailey* — h–

AGE OF GLORY 9 b.g. Zamindar (USA) – Fleeting Moon (Fleetwood (IRE)) [2017/18 h92: h16.4s⁵ h19.7v* Jan 23] fair handicap hurdler: won at Wetherby in January: stays 2½m: acts on heavy going. *Barbara Butterworth* — h100

galliardhomes.com Cleeve Hurdle, Cheltenham—proven mudlark Agrapart (left) relishes the testing conditions as he reverses placings with Wholestone from earlier in the month

AGE OF WISDOM (IRE) 5 ch.g. Pivotal – Learned Friend (GER) (Seeking The Gold (USA)) [2017/18 h15.9v Jan 7] fairly useful on Flat, stays 2m: in cheekpieces, 20/1, seventh in novice at Plumpton on hurdling debut: open to improvement. *Gary Moore* — **h66 p**

AGHA DES MOTTES (FR) 8 b.g. Mister Sacha (FR) – Java des Mottes (FR) (Passing Sale (FR)) [2017/18 h–: h16d Sep 3] bumper winner: maiden hurdler, not knocked about only start in 2017/18: raced around 2m. *Ian Williams* — **h–**

AGINCOURT REEF (IRE) 9 b.g. Gold Well – Hillside Native (IRE) (Be My Native (USA)) [2017/18 c122§, h115§: h21g^6 c20.3g^5 ab18d^4 h19.5v^6 h21.4v Apr 9] good-topped gelding: fairly useful hurdler/chaser at best, well below that in 2017/18: stays 21f: acts on soft and good to firm going: wears headgear: usually races prominently: moody. *Roger Teal* — **c– §**, **h91 §**

A GOOD SKIN (IRE) 9 b.g. Presenting – Trixskin (IRE) (Buckskin (FR)) [2017/18 c136, h–: h23.3d^2 c23g^4 c26.2d c19.9d^2 c26d^{pu} Dec 15] lengthy gelding: lightly-raced maiden hurdler: useful handicap chaser at best: stayed 3¼m: acted on soft going: tried in headgear: dead. *Tom George* — **c119**, **h110**

AGRAPART (FR) 7 b.g. Martaline – Afragha (IRE) (Darshaan) [2017/18 h154: h19.4s h23.9s h20.3s^2 h24v* h22.8v^2 Feb 17] good-topped gelding: high-class hurdler: won Cleeve Hurdle at Cheltenham (by 3 lengths from Wholestone) in January: second in Relkeel Hurdle there (3¼ lengths behind same rival) earlier in month: stays 3m: best form on soft/heavy going. *Nick Williams* — **h160**

A GREAT VIEW (IRE) 7 b.g. Kayf Tara – Liss A Chroi (IRE) (Exit To Nowhere (USA)) [2017/18 h20v^6 h20s^4 h24s^2 h24s^5 h24s^6 h24d* Apr 26] workmanlike gelding: useful handicap hurdler: won at Punchestown (by short head from Ainsi Va La Vie) in April: winning chaser: stays 3m: acts on heavy going: in cheekpieces last 3 starts: usually races towards rear. *Denis W. Cullen, Ireland* — **c–**, **h139**

AGREEMENT (IRE) 8 b.g. Galileo (IRE) – Cozzene's Angel (USA) (Cozzene (USA)) [2017/18 c–, h–: c20g^4 c22.6g^2 c22.7m^5 c23.8v^{pu} Jan 3] lengthy gelding: winning hurdler: poor form over fences: probably stays 23f: acts on soft going: often wears headgear. *Nikki Evans* — **c83**, **h–**

AGRICULTURAL 12 b.g. Daylami (IRE) – Rustic (IRE) (Grand Lodge (USA)) [2017/18 c–§, h–§: h20.2g^{pu} h20.2d^{pu} Aug 2] winning hurdler/maiden chaser, no form since 2013/14: temperamental. *Lucy Normile* — **c– §**, **h– §**

AIN

A HARE BREATH (IRE) 10 b.g. Alkaadhem – Lady Willmurt (IRE) (Mandalus) [2017/18 c139, h136: h16s* h16.8v h16g Apr 21] well-made gelding: useful handicap hurdler: won listed event at Sandown (by ½ length from Caid du Lin) in December: useful chase winner: stays 21f: acts on soft going. *Ben Pauling*   c– h138

AHEAD OF THE CURVE (IRE) 6 b.g. Ballingarry (IRE) – Jasla (FR) (Highest Honor (FR)) [2017/18 h23.3g² h22.2d* h20g² h20.2s* h23.9v² h21.1s^{pu} h19.4d³ h23.8d⁴ h21.1s^{pu} h17d⁴ Mar 25] £18,000 3-y-o, £24,000 5-y-o: sturdy gelding: seventh foal: brother to French 17f/2¼m hurdle winner Jaslinga and half-brother to French 3m/25f cross-country chase winner Quick Solitaire (by Loup Solitaire): dam French 11f winner: off mark in Irish maiden hurdle at fourth attempt: useful hurdler: won maiden at Uttoxeter in July and handicap at Perth in August: second at Perth (2¼ lengths behind Sun Cloud) in September and fourth at Musselburgh (3¾ lengths behind Cresswell Legend) in January, both handicaps: stays 3m: acts on heavy going: usually wears headgear: wears tongue tie. *Susan Corbett*   h133

AH LITTLELUCK (IRE) 8 b.g. Mahler – Star of Hope (IRE) (Turtle Island (IRE)) [2017/18 h132: h22s⁵ h20m⁶ h22.8s⁵ h22g h20s h22v* h24.7s³ h24d Apr 26] compact gelding: maiden pointer: useful handicap hurdler: won at Fairyhouse by 5½ lengths from Miles To Memphis) in April: stays 25f: acts on heavy going: usually wears tongue tie nowadays: front runner/races prominently. *T. Gibney, Ireland*   h132

AIAAM AL NAMOOS 9 b.g. Teofilo (IRE) – Deveron (USA) (Cozzene (USA)) [2017/18 c–, h–: h20.1g^{pu} Jun 17] fair hurdler at best, very lightly raced, no show only start in 2017/18: unseated early sole start over fences: stays 3m: acts on good to soft going (won bumper on good to firm). *Chris Grant*   c– h–

AIGUILLE ROUGE (FR) 4 ch.f. Falco (USA) – Avanguardia (GER) (Choisir (AUS)) [2017/18 h119: h17.7v* h17.7v* h15.8s³ Jan 12] half-sister to high-class hurdler Labaik (2m winner, by Montmartre): fairly useful maiden on Flat, stays 1¼m: fairly useful form over hurdles: won juveniles at Fontwell (twice) in December. *Gary Moore*   h119

AIMEE DE SIVOLA (FR) 4 ch.f. Network (GER) – Neva de Sivola (FR) (Blushing Flame (USA)) [2017/18 b14s⁴ b12.6s* b16.7v² b16v⁴ Mar 10] rather unfurnished filly: half-sister to several winners, including useful hurdler Urbain de Sivola (2m-2¼m winner, by Le Fou), stayed 2½m, and fairly useful hurdler Culture de Sivola (2m-3m winner, by Assessor): dam, French 15f hurdle winner, half-sister to high-class hurdler/useful chaser (stayed 25f) Reve de Sivola: fairly useful form in bumpers: won fillies junior race at Newbury in December: second in listed mares event at Market Rasen (2½ lengths behind Dissavril) in January and fourth in similar event at Sandown (4¾ lengths behind Queenohearts) in March: will stay at least 2½m. *Nick Williams*   b98

AINCHEA (IRE) 5 b.g. Flemensfirth (USA) – Lady Petit (IRE) (Beneficial) [2017/18 b16.4g² h16s* h20.3s² h16v^F Feb 3] €155,000 3-y-o: well-made gelding: fourth foal: brother to bumper winner/high-class hurdler One Track Mind (2½m-3m winner): dam unraced sister to fairly useful hurdler/useful chaser (stays 2½m) One Term): shaped well when second in bumper at Cheltenham (1¼ lengths behind Herecomestheboom): useful form over hurdles: won novice at Sandown in December: best effort when second in listed novice at Cheltenham (1¼ lengths behind Tikkanbar) in January: remains open to improvement. *Colin Tizzard*   h136 p b104

AINSI VA LA VIE (FR) 8 gr.m. Lavirco (GER) – Joie de La Vie (FR) (Quart de Vin (FR)) [2017/18 b20g* b16s* b16v* h16s* h22.8v* h24v* h18v⁶ h24d² Apr 26] sixth foal: half-sister to 3 winners, including useful hurdler Sous Les Cieux (2m-2½m winner, by Robin des Champs): dam useful form in bumpers: won at Limerick (mares maiden) in July, Galway in August and Gowran (listed mares event, by 2 lengths from Glens Harmony) in September: useful form over hurdles: won mares maiden at Thurles in November: best effort when second in handicap at Punchestown (short head behind A Great View) in April: stays 3m: acts on heavy going: often travels strongly. *W. P. Mullins, Ireland*   h134 b113

AIN'T NO LIMITS (FR) 6 b.g. Kapgarde (FR) – Elitiste (FR) (Arctic Tern (USA)) [2017/18 h98, b90: h24g³ May 16] good-topped gelding: fair maiden hurdler: won maiden point in March: stays 3m: acts on good to soft going. *Charlie Longsdon*   h103

AINTREE MY DREAM (FR) 8 b.g. Saint des Saints (FR) – Pretty Melodie (FR) (Lesotho (USA)) [2017/18 h139: c19.4d³ Oct 14] lengthy gelding: winning pointer: useful hurdler: 10/1, third in handicap hurdle at Chepstow (14¾ lengths behind Finian's Oscar) on chasing debut, going off too hard: barely stays 23f: acts on heavy going: wears tongue tie: front runner, strong traveller: should improve over fences. *Dan Skelton*   c132 p h–

AIR

AIR APPROACH 6 b.g. New Approach (IRE) – Grecian Air (FR) (King's Best (USA)) [2017/18 h98, b–: h18.7g^F Aug 3] well held in bumpers: second in maiden on completed start over hurdles: in tongue tie last 2 starts: dead. *Tim Vaughan* — h–

AIR DE ROCK (FR) 6 b.g. High Rock (IRE) – Onciale (FR) (Ultimately Lucky (IRE)) [2017/18 h99: c16s^5 Nov 8] maiden hurdler: 9/1, fifth in novice handicap at Chepstow (12½ lengths behind Itshard To No) on chasing debut: unproven beyond 17f: acts on heavy going: tried in cheekpieces. *Venetia Williams* — c90 / h–

AIRDRIGH (IRE) 6 b.g. Winged Love (IRE) – Maolisa (IRE) (Jamesmead) [2017/18 h20.2m^{ur} h20.5d h20.2g h17.2s^6 h16.7g h16g^{pu} h20.5s^4 Oct 30] poor maiden hurdler: bred to be suited by 2¾m+: tried in cheekpieces: sketchy jumper. *Stuart Crawford, Ireland* — h74 x

AIR HORSE ONE 7 gr.g. Mountain High (IRE) – Whisky Rose (IRE) (Old Vic) [2017/18 h142: h15.7g^4 h20.5d^3 h15.7d h19.3v^2 h19.2d^3 h20s^{pu} Apr 12] smart handicap hurdler: second in Holloway's Handicap Hurdle at Ascot (2¼ lengths behind Jenkins) in January: stays 21f: acts on heavy going: often races towards rear. *Harry Fry* — h144

AIRLIE BEACH (IRE) 8 b.m. Shantou (USA) – Screaming Witness (IRE) (Shernazar) [2017/18 h140: h16d^3 Aug 3] sturdy mare: useful hurdler: third in Galway Hurdle (5¼ lengths behind Tigris River) on handicap debut: won twice on Flat after, including listed event: stayed 21f: acted on soft going: usually led: retired. *W. P. Mullins, Ireland* — h138

AIR NAVIGATOR 7 b.g. Yeats (IRE) – Lox Lane (IRE) (Presenting) [2017/18 b101: b16.4s^2 b15.7v* h16.3v^{ur} h16.6s^4 h16v^5 h16s^3 Apr 27] big, rangy gelding: useful form in bumpers: won at Haydock (by 9 lengths from Informateur) in December: second in listed event at Cheltenham (1½ lengths behind Crooks Peak) previous month: fair form over hurdles: will be suited by 2¼m+. *Tom George* — h107 / b105

AIRPUR DESBOIS (FR) 8 b.g. Canyon Creek (IRE) – Hero's Dancer (FR) (Hero's Honor (USA)) [2017/18 c–, h92: h23.3d May 6] maiden hurdler: pulled up only start over fences: stays 3m: acts on heavy going: wears headgear: in tongue tie last 4 starts. *Oliver Greenall* — c– / h–

AIR SQUADRON 8 b.g. Rail Link – Countess Sybil (IRE) (Dr Devious (IRE)) [2017/18 h16.8m^2 h20.2m^3 h20.6g^2 h23.9d^2 h24g* h25g Oct 5] fairly useful on Flat, stays 2m: fair form over hurdles: won novice at Southwell in September: should stay beyond 3m: acts on good to firm and good to soft going: in cheekpieces last 2 starts: usually races prominently. *Tom George* — h110

AIRTIGHT 5 b.g. Proclamation (IRE) – Megasue (Kayf Tara) [2017/18 b13.6g^2 b15.7g^6 h16d h17.7v^3 h16v^4 h15.9v^6 Apr 1] big, strong gelding: second foal: dam (h108), bumper/2m hurdle winner, sister to Champion Bumper/Betfair Hurdle winner Ballyandy: fair form in bumpers: modest form over hurdles: often races towards rear: headstrong. *Gary Moore* — h97 / b88

AJABINDEJAW (IRE) 8 b.g. Mahler – Laampagne (Overbury (IRE)) [2017/18 h16g^4 h18.8g h24g^{pu} h16.4g h16.8v h20.6s h21.2g Apr 23] modest maiden hurdler: standout effort on return: left T. Gibney after fourth start: tried in tongue tie. *Micky Hammond* — h90

AKARITA LIGHTS (IRE) 4 b.g. Arctic Cosmos (USA) – Akarita (IRE) (Akarad (FR)) [2017/18 ab16.3g^2 b16.7v^2 Apr 11] half-brother to several winners on Flat, including winner around 1½m Chant (by Oratorio): dam 7.6f winner who stayed 1¼m: fair form when second in bumpers at Newcastle and Market Rasen. *John Quinn* — b91

AKKADIAN EMPIRE 4 b.g. Arabian Gleam – Floral Beauty (Shamardal (USA)) [2017/18 h16.2v^4 h16.8g h16.2s Apr 26] fair on Flat, stays 1½m: no form over hurdles: has worn hood. *Iain Jardine* — h–

AKKAPENKO (FR) 4 b.g. Archipenko (USA) – Akka (Hernando (FR)) [2017/18 h16.5s h16.5v h16.8s Apr 23] fair on Flat in France, stays 12.5f: no form over hurdles. *Tim Vaughan* — h–

AKULA (IRE) 11 ch.g. Soviet Star (USA) – Danielli (IRE) (Danehill (USA)) [2017/18 c–, c88, h103: h15.8g^5 c17.4s^{ur} h16.7s^2 h15.7s h15.7v^3 h15.8v^3 h16s^6 h15.7v^4 h15.8v^6 Apr 7] angular gelding: modest handicap hurdler: maiden chaser: unproven beyond 17f: acts on good to firm and heavy going: wears headgear: has worn tongue tie, including last 2 starts: usually leads. *Barry Leavy* — c– / h95

ALADDIN SANE (IRE) 4 b.g. Teofilo (IRE) – Aqua Aura (USA) (Distorted Humor (USA)) [2017/18 h16.2v^{pu} h16d^{pu} Mar 29] has had breathing operation: limited impact in maidens/handicap on Flat: pulled up both starts in juvenile hurdles: tried in hood. *Henry Hogarth* — h–

ALB

AL ALFA 11 ch.g. Alflora (IRE) – Two For Joy (IRE) (Mandalus) [2017/18 c131, h–: c24m² c24d⁵ c23g⁶ Jun 28] workmanlike gelding: winning hurdler: fairly useful handicap chaser: second at Kempton in May: little show after, including in points: stays easy 3m: acts on good to firm and heavy going: tried in tongue tie: usually leads. *Philip Hobbs* — **c127 h–**

ALAMEDA 7 b.m. Indian Danehill (IRE) – Madge Carroll (IRE) (Hollow Hand) [2017/18 h88, b75: h20m⁶ h23.3d h22g^pu Jul 4] maiden hurdler, no form in 2017/18: tried in visor. *Henry Daly* — **h–**

ALAMEIN (IRE) 8 b.g. Beneficial – Lady of Appeal (IRE) (Lord of Appeal) [2017/18 c134, h119: c19.9s c16g⁶ c19.9g^pu c20.5g^F c17.1d^pu h16d h18.7g⁶ Nov 2] fairly useful hurdler/chaser: left M. F. Morris/no form after fourth start: unproven beyond 17f: acts on heavy going: usually wears headgear/tongue tie: often leads. *Richard Hobson* — **c126 h–**

ALARY (FR) 8 ch.g. Dream Well (FR) – Cate Bleue (FR) (Katowice (FR)) [2017/18 c161?, h–: h19.5d h21.4s c21.9s⁶ Apr 12] maiden hurdler: high-class chaser at best: no form in 2017/18: left Colin Tizzard after first start: has worn tongue tie, including in 2017/18. *J. Bertran de Balanda, France* — **c– h–**

A L'ASSEAU (FR) 8 b.g. Assessor (IRE) – En Piste (FR) (Pistolet Bleu (IRE)) [2017/18 h–, b–: h16.3s Oct 2] little form: in tongue tie last 2 starts: dead. *Evan Williams* — **h–**

ALBATROS DE GUYE (FR) 8 ch.g. Maille Pistol (FR) – Balibirds (FR) (Bricassar (USA)) [2017/18 c60, h–: h20.5d c20d⁶ c21.7g c25.6s^pu c17.8v⁵ Dec 26] sturdy gelding: maiden hurdler/winning chaser, no longer of any account: has worn headgear, including last 2 starts: wears tongue tie: temperamental. *Anna Newton-Smith* — **c– § h– §**

ALBEROBELLO (IRE) 10 b.g. Old Vic – Tourist Attraction (IRE) (Pollerton) [2017/18 c122, h–: c23.8g³ c24g⁵ c23g⁶ c23.6v^pu Jan 19] stocky gelding: has had breathing operation: winning hurdler: fairly useful handicap chaser: stays 3½m: acts on good to firm and heavy going: wears tongue tie: front runner/races prominently. *Nicky Martin* — **c118 h–**

ALBERTA (IRE) 9 ch.g. Choisir (AUS) – Akita (IRE) (Foxhound (USA)) [2017/18 h113: h16s* h15.8s⁴ h15.9v³ h16m Apr 26] fair handicap hurdler: won at Kempton (conditionals) in February: should stay beyond 2m: acts on soft going: wears visor: often races towards rear. *Suzi Best* — **h113**

ALBERT D'OLIVATE (FR) 8 b.g. Alberto Giacometti (IRE) – Komunion (FR) (Luchiroverte (IRE)) [2017/18 c112, h95: h23.1s⁴ h21.6v⁶ h26v² h23.1v^pu Apr 17] good-topped gelding: fair handicap hurdler: maiden chaser: left Robert Walford after second start: stays 3¼m: best form on soft/heavy going: usually wears headgear: in tongue tie last 4 starts: often races prominently: temperamental. *Neil Mulholland* — **c– h110 §**

ALBERTO'S DREAM 9 b.g. Fantastic Spain (USA) – Molly's Folly (My Lamb) [2017/18 c79, h85: h19.5d^pu c23.8v^pu c20v⁵ c26v⁵ c23.5v* c22.7v* c23.6s* c29.2v* c24.2v² Apr 8] winning hurdler: fairly useful handicap chaser: won at Lingfield, Leicester, Huntingdon and Warwick, all in March: left Tom Symonds after fourth start: stays 29f: acts on heavy going: has worn headgear: often races prominently, usually travels strongly. *Tom Lacey* — **c117 h–**

ALBERT'S BACK 4 b.g. Champs Elysees – Neath (Rainbow Quest (USA)) [2017/18 h16s* h16s* Dec 27] fair maiden on Flat: fairly useful form over hurdles: won juveniles at Wetherby in November (maiden) and December, impressively by 11 lengths from Turning Gold on latter occasion: will go on improving. *Michael Easterby* — **h128 p**

AL BOUM PHOTO (FR) 6 b.g. Buck's Boum (FR) – Al Gane (FR) (Dom Alco (FR)) [2017/18 h142: c17v* c19.5v^F c21s² c24.4s^F c20v* c24.5s^ro Apr 24] — **c161 + h–**

Live televised stewards' inquiries have been available in Britain via the sport's main terrestrial broadcaster since 2010 (an inquiry into interference in the Nassau Stakes at Goodwood that year was the first). Jockeys are shown giving evidence, although subsequent discussion among the stewards still takes place in private. Microphones and cameras are not admitted to stewards' inquiries in Ireland, however, where the jockeys succeeded in blocking such requests from broadcaster RTE (the Irish turf authorities are said to have no objection to following Britain's example). Had the latest, very controversial Grade 1 Growise Champion Novices' Chase taken place in Britain, instead of at Punchestown on the opening day of its big five-day meeting in April, there would have been live coverage of the jockeys' evidence. Such coverage would have given the betting public an insight into a calamitous 'human error' made by Al Boum Photo's jockey Paul Townend who, looking over his right shoulder, suddenly seemed to start easing his mount before then steering

Ryanair Gold Cup Novices' Chase, Fairyhouse—Al Boum Photo (checks) stays on strongly under David Mullins to win after the leader Shattered Love loses momentum at the last

sharply to the right on the approach to the final fence, after he had seemingly looked in command of the race. Al Boum Photo crashed through the wing, parting company with Townend, and, at the same time, carried the challenging Finian's Oscar out of the race. Al Boum Photo and Finian's Oscar would both have beaten the eventual winner 16/1-shot The Storyteller, with Al Boum Photo looking the much more likely of the pair to have come out on top, despite the protestations by Finian's Oscar's jockey that his mount was 'just starting to rally' and would have won.

The Punchestown stewards held a lengthy inquiry into the race which resulted in Paul Townend being banned for twenty-one days for dangerous riding and being ordered to forfeit his riding fee. The report issued by the stewards was perfunctory, offering nothing beyond the fact that the stewards had 'viewed the recording of the race and considered the evidence and were of the opinion that P. Townend was in breach of rule 214 in that he had ridden dangerously.' There were no details of any of the evidence given, most notably that by Townend himself, who avoided the media altogether after the race, as did Al Boum Photo's trainer Willie Mullins who was reported to have left the track straight after viewing the race from the owners' and trainers' stand (Al Boum Photo's front-running stablemate Invitation Only, still with the leaders and in the process of running creditably, had been brought down at the second last). The principal beneficiary of the bizarre closing stages of the Champion Novices' Chase was the stable of Mullins' great rival Gordon Elliott which ended up having the first three home in a race that seemed, at the time, likely to prove very costly for Mullins in his attempt to retain the Irish trainers' championship

(Elliott finished the day with a lead of over €400,000, though, in the end, Mullins saddled a record eighteen winners at the meeting, landing nine of the Grade 1s, and comfortably overturned the large prize money deficit).

In the absence of any official account of why the vastly experienced Townend acted in the way he did, it was left to media, racegoers and punters to fill the vacuum with speculation. The most charitable explanation—that Townend had first started to ease down because he perhaps believed his mount had been injured—was undermined by the fact that Al Boum Photo returned completely sound and that the penalty imposed by the stewards on Townend was so serious. What else could have caused Townend to try to avoid the final obstacle? Had he heard a shout that could have been interpreted as a signal to bypass the fence (though there were no signs of markers on the fence to indicate a requirement to do so)? Had he simply suffered a momentary brainstorm? The most widely-held reaction—'I just don't know what happened'—was that shared by Gordon Elliott who had watched from the final fence and had a close-up view. Social media—which can quickly get out of control—stoked some wild speculation, which was prejudicial to the reputation of the sport and particularly damaging to its integrity, and there is no doubt that the Punchestown stewards could have helped matters considerably by publishing more detail. The Irish Horseracing Regulatory Board did so the following day when issuing a second statement after suggesting that the stewards had withheld information the previous day because they had been concerned about Townend's 'well-being and state of mind' after the inquiry. In the second statement, it was reported that Townend had told the stewards he was 'riding with his head down between the last two fences and heard roaring on his left ... He thought he had to bypass the fence but didn't know which side to bypass on. He panicked and commenced his move to bypass the fence on the right side but then realised there was nothing on the fence to indicate a bypass was needed and tried to correct his actions but it was too late.' Townend told the stewards he made a genuine mistake and apologised for what had occurred.

That, it seemed, closed the affair from an official viewpoint, though the seriousness of the case arguably merited a full and much more detailed investigation, certainly involving the other jockeys in the race, in addition to Paul Townend and Robbie Power (who passed it off as 'just one of those unfortunate incidents' in his blog for bookmakers Boylesports). In view of Townend's claim that he heard shouting, should racecourse staff and others nearby have perhaps been asked for an account of anything they might have heard? None of the other jockeys around Al Boum Photo at the time of the incident reported hearing a call, incidentally. Paul Townend confirmed to the media the next day that he thought he had heard a shout and that the last fence was being bypassed. 'It was a split-second reaction and I wish to apologise to connections and to punters, but I have a job to do and would like to leave this behind me and move on with today's rides'. Townend went on to have three winners for Mullins on the second day of the meeting, which must have taken some of the weight off his shoulders after the trainer had described the defeat of Al Boum Photo as 'most unfortunate, but it happened; we got plenty of slagging into Paul this morning and we have forgotten about it.' It should be said that the general betting public, especially those who backed Al Boum Photo and Finian's Oscar (the third and fourth favourites for the race), were probably much less forgiving of Townend than his fellow professionals appeared to be, although he got a genuinely warm reception from the Punchestown crowd when returning on Next Destination, the first of his three second-day winners.

Al Boum Photo showed useful form over hurdles in his first season with the Mullins stable, winning a Grade 2 novice at Fairyhouse over two and a half miles in which he was ridden by Paul Townend (Invitation Only, the 11/10 favourite ridden by Ruby Walsh, finished only sixth). Townend, second jockey at Closutton, enjoyed more of the limelight in the latest season with Walsh on the sidelines for much of the time because of injury. Townend rode Al Boum Photo when he made a successful debut over fences in a maiden chase at Navan in November, landing the odds by seven lengths from Tycoon Prince. Recent winners of the same race had included Mullins stars such as Vautour, Douvan and Min, and Al Boum Photo also found

Growise Champion Novices' Chase, Punchestown—David Mullins is sitting up in the background this time (following a luckless unseat from Invitation Only) as he gets a distant view of the bizarre events about to unfold at the last fence ...

himself quickly promoted to a higher grade. He would have followed up his Navan success in a Grade 2 at Limerick on Boxing Day but for coming down when a length in front of Dounikos at the last (David Mullins rode him that day, with Townend otherwise engaged at Leopardstown).

Townend rode the shorter-priced Invitation Only when Al Boum Photo ran in the Flogas Novices' Chase at Leopardstown in February and in the Ryanair Gold Cup at Fairyhouse in April (Al Boum Photo had taken a heavy fall in the interim at the second last, when held in third, in the RSA Chase, a fall that ended Ruby Walsh's brief comeback, leading to his missing the rest of the season). With David Mullins again in the saddle, Al Boum Photo finished ahead of Invitation Only at both Leopardstown and Fairyhouse, the pair finishing a close second and third to Monalee in the Flogas Novices' Chase (a race registered as the Scalp) and Al Boum Photo having Invitation Only back in third when winning the Ryanair Gold Cup (in which Willie Mullins, winning the race for the first time, and Gordon Elliott supplied all nine runners) by a length from Shattered Love, wearing down that rival to lead in the final hundred yards. The Growise Champion Novices' (registered as the Ellier) drew a cracking line-up, although Finian's Oscar was the only British-trained challenger in a field in which the betting was headed by Monalee and Shattered Love, who had both run very well at the Cheltenham Festival (Monalee runner-up to Presenting

... which sees Al Boum Photo crash out in spectacular fashion after being steered right in a moment of panic by Paul Townend, carrying out a bemused Robbie Power aboard Finian's Oscar (left) in the process; fortunate winner The Storyteller (right) is left to pick up the pieces

Percy in the RSA and Shattered Love winning the Golden Miller before her second to Al Boum Photo at Fairyhouse). Al Boum Photo and Invitation Only were part of a three-strong challenge from Willie Mullins, the trio completed by the National Hunt Chase winner Rathvinden, while Gordon Elliott saddled five of the eleven runners, Shattered Love joined by The Storyteller (also a Cheltenham Festival winner), Jury Duty, Monbeg Notorious and Dounikos. As well as suffering that unfortunate fall in the race won by Dounikos, Al Boum Photo's jumping had also let him down in the Flogas Novices', in which he might well have beaten Monalee had he put in a more fluent round (after another untidy jump at the last, where he was also slightly hampered, he kept on well to take second close home, only three quarters of a length down on Monalee).

Al Boum Photo gave a most polished display of jumping in the Growise Champion Novices' until his bizarre exit, making smooth headway from five out, after being waited with, and going best when left in front by the departure of Monalee and Invitation Only at the second last. The eventual winner The Storyteller was extremely fortunate and would probably have finished only fifth but for events at the last two fences. As for the luckless Al Boum Photo, he is still only six and, hopefully, there will be other days for him. Judged on his improved display of jumping at Punchestown, he probably has the potential to do better still and a race like the Ladbrokes Trophy at Newbury (won by the Mullins-trained Total Recall in the latest season) appeals as an autumn target in 2018/19.

Al Boum Photo (FR) (b.g. 2012)	Buck's Boum (FR) (b 2005)	Cadoudal (br 1979)	Green Dancer / Come To Sea
		Buck's (b 1993)	Le Glorieux / Buckleby
	Al Gane (FR) (b 2005)	Dom Alco (gr 1987)	Dom Pasquini / Alconaca
		Magic Spring (b 1997)	True Brave / Carama

Al Boum Photo, a tall gelding, is from the first crop of Buck's Boum, a brother to Big Buck's who won his historic fourth World [Stayers'] Hurdle in the same year that Al Boum Photo was foaled. Buck's Boum was no slouch himself, being one of the leading juvenile hurdlers of his year at Auteuil (runner-up to another son of Cadoudal, none other than Long Run, in the top autumn hurdle race for three-year-olds in France, the Prix Cambaceres). Buck's Boum had to be retired after suffering an injury at four and, still being an entire, was found a home at the Haras d'Enki near Vichy where he has stood ever since (current fee €3,000). He was also represented in Ireland in the latest season by Duc des Genievres, runner-up to Samcro in the Deloitte Novices' Hurdle and fifth to him in the Baring Bingham at Cheltenham. Al Boum Photo, a first foal, is one of two winners produced so far by the unraced Dom Alco mare Al Gane whose second foal Diteou, a sister to Al Boum Photo, is a winning chaser over two and a quarter miles in France. Al Gane also has a 2017 colt by Buck's Boum. Al Boum Photo's great grandam Carama, a winner at around two miles over hurdles in the French Provinces, produced several winners over jumps including the Scottish Grand National winner Al Co and his sister Al Tip who was a useful hurdler (successful in listed company), and a winning chaser at up to two and a half miles. A half-sister to Al Co and Al Tip, the unraced Fee Magic, is the dam of Grands Crus, a top-class hurdler and a high-class chaser at his best, and of the smart Gevrey Chambertin, both of whom, like Al Co and Al Tip, are also by Dom Alco (Grands Crus and Gevrey Chambertin, like Al Co, both stayed well). Al Boum Photo, who often travels strongly in his races, hasn't yet won beyond two and a half miles but will prove equally effective at around three miles (which distance he tackled in the RSA—in which he wore ear plugs—and the Growise Champion Novices', two of the races in which he failed to complete). He acts on heavy going, and the less testing conditions (good to soft) he encountered when below form in the War of Attrition Novices' Hurdle at Punchestown in 2016/17 may have been more of a factor in that performance than the three-mile trip. He hasn't encountered going less yielding than soft so far over fences. *W. P. Mullins, Ireland*

*Betfred Summer Plate Handicap Chase, Market Rasen—
the grey Alcala edges out Wadswick Court to land this valuable prize, which formed the centre-piece
of a five-timer for the winner during the early months of 2017/18*

ALCALA (FR) 8 gr.g. Turgeon (USA) – Pail Mel (FR) (Sleeping Car (FR)) [2017/18 c134, h115: c21s* c21m* c21.4g* c25.8g* c21m* c19.4d^{su} c19.8g^4 c22.7d^5 Apr 28] tall gelding: winning hurdler: smart chaser: won handicaps at Newton Abbot (twice, 2-runner novice event on first occasion) in June, Summer Plate at Market Rasen (by ¾ length from Wadswick Court) in July, and small-field novices at Newton Abbot (twice) in August: stays 3¼m: acts on good to firm and heavy going: has worn hood: wears tongue tie: often travels strongly. *Paul Nicholls* — **c151 h–**

ALCHIMIX (FR) 8 b.g. Al Namix (FR) – Julie Noire (FR) (Agent Bleu (FR)) [2017/18 c82, h87: c17.3d c21.2g^5 c21.2d^5 c15.6v^4 c15.6v^5 Oct 14] maiden hurdler: poor maiden chaser: barely stays 21f: acts on good and good to soft going: wears cheekpieces: tried in tongue tie: temperamental. *Micky Hammond* — **c75 § h–**

ALCOCK AND BROWN (IRE) 6 b.g. Oasis Dream – Heart Stopping (USA) (Chester House (USA)) [2017/18 h119: h15.8d Mar 26] fairly useful hurdler: shaped as if better for run only start in 2017/18: stays 2½m: acts on soft and good to firm going. *Dan Skelton* — **h–**

AL CO (FR) 13 ch.g. Dom Alco (FR) – Carama (FR) (Tip Moss (FR)) [2017/18 c137d, h–: c25g c23.4s* c23.4v^4 c23.6s^5 Mar 22] smallish, angular gelding: winning hurdler: fairly useful chaser: won hunter at Kelso in January: stays 4m: acts on any going: has worn headgear. *Mickey Bowen* — **c123 h–**

AL DANCER (FR) 5 gr.g. Al Namix (FR) – Steel Dancer (FR) (Kaldounevees (FR)) [2017/18 b15.8s^2 b15.8v^3 b16.7s* b17s^4 Apr 13] well-made gelding: fourth foal: half-brother to 3 winners in France, including fairly useful hurdler/smart chaser Tzar's Dancer (17f-3¼m winner, by Tzar Rodney): dam unraced: useful form in bumpers: won maiden at Bangor in March: fourth in Grade 2 at Aintree (in hood, 7¼ lengths behind Portrush Ted) 3 weeks later: left Christian Williams after second start. *Nigel Twiston-Davies* — **b105**

ALDEBURGH 9 b.g. Oasis Dream – Orford Ness (Selkirk (USA)) [2017/18 h–: h15.8g^{pu} May 28] compact gelding: maiden hurdler, fair form at best: dead. *Nigel Twiston-Davies* — **h–**

ALDERBROOK LAD (IRE) 12 ch.g. Alderbrook – Alone Tabankulu (IRE) (Phardante (FR)) [2017/18 c132, h–: c21.2d^2 c21.2g* c25.5s^2 c21.2g^{pu} c24.5s^R c25d^{pu} c20.1g^{pu} c19.3g^5 Apr 23] winning hurdler: fairly useful handicap chaser: won at Cartmel in July: stays 25f: acts on good to firm and heavy going: tried in hood/tongue tie: front runner/races prominently: often let down by jumping. *Micky Hammond* — **c121 x h–**

ALDERSON 5 b.g. Zamindar (USA) – Claradotnet (Sri Pekan (USA)) [2017/18 b16.7v^3 h15.8v Feb 10] sixth foal: dam, 11.6f winner who stayed 2m on Flat, half-sister to fairly useful hurdler (stayed 2½m) Tokala: third of 4 in bumper at Bangor: well held in maiden on hurdling debut. *Oliver Greenall* — **h– b83**

AL DESTOOR 8 ch.g. Teofilo (IRE) – In A Silent Way (IRE) (Desert Prince (IRE)) [2017/18 h104: h19.9v² Nov 26] close-coupled gelding: useful on Flat, stays 1½m: fair maiden hurdler: stays 2½m: acts on heavy going: has worn hood/tongue tie. *Jennie Candlish* **h110**

ALDRIN (FR) 5 b.g. New Approach (IRE) – Trip To The Moon (Fasliyev (USA)) [2017/18 h15.8g³ h16.7g* h16.8m⁵ Aug 29] fair form in Flat maidens: fair form over hurdles: won maiden at Bangor in August: likely to prove best at around 2m: wears tongue tie. *David Pipe* **h103**

A LEGAL BEAUTY (IRE) 6 b.m. Robin des Champs (FR) – Afreen (IRE) (Entrepreneur) [2017/18 b16.3g Jul 23] sixth foal: half-sister to fair hurdler Underdefloorboards (2½m winner, by Deploy) and a winning pointer by Exit To Nowhere: dam, 11f winner, half-sister to temperamental but very smart hurdler/fairly useful chaser (2m/17f winner) Afsoun and high-class hurdler up to 3m Agrapart: runner-up on completed start in Irish maiden points: tailed off in mares bumper (tongue tied). *Fergal O'Brien* **b–**

ALEXANDER THE GREY 7 gr.g. Fair Mix (IRE) – Cadourova (FR) (Cadoudal (FR)) [2017/18 h104, b–: h18.7g⁵ h19.9m⁵ h16.8d⁴ h16d² h16g³ h18.6s Dec 26] fair maiden hurdler: unproven beyond 2m: acts on good to soft going: usually wears hood: in tongue tie last 4 starts. *Graeme McPherson* **h101**

ALEX THE LION (IRE) 5 b.g. Let The Lion Roar – Belle Dame (IRE) (Executive Perk) [2017/18 h16.7d Apr 21] tailed off in bumper. *Adrian Wintle* **b–**

ALF 'N' DOR (IRE) 7 ch.g. Flemensfirth (USA) – Greenflag Princess (IRE) (Executive Perk) [2017/18 h115: c23.8g⁴ h24d³ c23g^ur c23.6s³ c20.9v³ c24.1v^pu c23.6v³ c20v² c21.4s⁵ c19.4v* Apr 15] winning hurdler: fair chaser: won seller at Ffos Las in April: stays 3m: acts on heavy going: usually wears headgear/tongue tie: temperamental. *Peter Bowen* **c108 §**
h90

ALFIBOY 8 b.g. Alflora (IRE) – Cloudy Pearl (Cloudings (IRE)) [2017/18 c–, h–: h19.7d^F h16s^pu h16s h16.4v² h16.8g Apr 23] workmanlike gelding: modest maiden hurdler: pulled up only start over fences: should stay beyond 2m: acts on heavy going: has worn hood. *Sue Smith* **c–**
h94

ALFIE'S CHOICE (IRE) 6 b.g. Shantou (USA) – Bally Bolshoi (IRE) (Bob Back (USA)) [2017/18 h108: h21.3s² h23.6v h23.1v⁵ Jan 17] fair maiden hurdler: stays 23f: acts on soft going: in cheekpieces last 3 starts: races prominently: has joined Keith Dalgleish. *Kim Bailey* **h112**

ALFIE SPINNER (IRE) 13 b.g. Alflora (IRE) – Little Red Spider (Bustino) [2017/18 c131, h–: c25.1s^pu c23.6v² c29.5v² c34v⁵ c23.8v² Apr 15] good-topped gelding: winning hurdler: useful handicap chaser: second at Chepstow (beaten 6 lengths by Raz de Maree in Welsh Grand National) in January and Ffos Las (2 lengths behind Ballycross) in April: stays 4m: acts on heavy going: wears cheekpieces/tongue tie: front runner/races prominently. *Kerry Lee* **c134**
h–

ALFRED OATS 14 b.g. Alflora (IRE) – Easter Oats (Oats) [2017/18 c85: c24.3v c24.1v⁶ c20.5v^pu Jan 31] poor maiden chaser nowadays: stays 25f: best form on soft/heavy going: wears tongue tie: usually races towards rear. *Robert Goldie* **c83**

ALFRED ROLLER (IRE) 6 b.g. Mahler – Cointessa (IRE) (Nordico (USA)) [2017/18 h94, b–: h20.3g^pu Sep 6] placed in Irish maiden point: maiden hurdler, pulled up only start in 2017/18: unproven beyond 2m: acts on soft going. *Jonjo O'Neill* **h–**

ALFSTAR 10 b.g. Alflora (IRE) – Starboard Tack (FR) (Saddlers' Hall (IRE)) [2017/18 c26d^pu c20.3v³ c23.4s^pu Mar 23] has had breathing operation: won 3 times in points: fair form when third at Bangor in February on completed start in hunter chases. *Joanne Priest* **c113**

ALIANDY (IRE) 7 b.g. Presenting – Water Rock (El Conquistador) [2017/18 h114: h21v^pu Mar 28] good-topped gelding: fair hurdler at best, little show only start in 2017/18: stays 3m: acts on soft going: usually races nearer last than first. *Kim Bailey* **h–**

ALI BIN NAYEF 6 b.g. Nayef (USA) – Maimoona (IRE) (Pivotal) [2017/18 h92: h16g h21.3g⁵ h16d⁴ h17.3s³ h21g² h20g h20v h25.8g h16d h20s* h21v² h19.3v⁵ h21v^pu Dec 28] modest handicap hurdler: won at Fairyhouse in November: stays 21f: acts on heavy going: has worn cheekpieces, including last 4 starts. *John Joseph Hanlon, Ireland* **h94**

ALICE LISLE 4 ch.f. Flemensfirth (USA) – Twilight Affair (Dansili) [2017/18 b16.6s b16v⁴ b15.7s⁶ h16.8v^pu Mar 23] first foal: dam, ran twice in bumpers, sister to useful hurdler/smart chaser (stayed 2½m) Perce Rock: poor form in bumpers: pulled up in mares novice on hurdling debut: bred to stay 2½m+. *Tim Easterby* **h–**
b60

ALICE PINK (IRE) 8 b.m. Milan – That's The Goose (IRE) (Be My Native (USA)) [2017/18 h19.5s⁶ h16.3s h16.3s Jan 17] lengthy mare: bumper winner: no form over hurdles. *Paul Henderson* **h–**

ALI

ALICES MAN (IRE) 8 b.g. Golan (IRE) – Awbeg Flower (IRE) (Alphabatim (USA)) [2017/18 h24d[5] c16.8s c19.2g c15.7g h15.8d h18.6g[6] h23.3s* c24.2s[4] h19.3v[pu] c21v[pu] c19.7v[pu] Dec 26] workmanlike gelding: poor handicap hurdler: won at Hexham in October: poor form over fences: left Miss Elizabeth Doyle after first start: stays 3m: acts on soft going: has worn blinkers, including last 5 starts: has worn tongue tie, including in 2017/18. *John Patrick Ryan, Ireland* — **c73 h80**

ALISIER D'IRLANDE (FR) 8 br.g. Kapgarde (FR) – Isati's (FR) (Chamberlin (FR)) [2017/18 c149, h–: c16v[2] c16.7v[3] c17s c16s[2] c16v[3] Mar 23] good sort: winning hurdler: useful chaser: second in Fortria Chase at Navan in November and Grade 3 event at Naas (13 lengths behind Doctor Phoenix) in February: unproven beyond 17f: acts on heavy going: has worn headgear: wears tongue tie: front runner/races prominently. *Henry de Bromhead, Ireland* — **c144 h–**

ALI THE HUNTER (IRE) 5 ch.m. Papal Bull – Polish Spring (IRE) (Polish Precedent (USA)) [2017/18 b16.3g[4] b17.7g[3] Aug 24] eighth foal: dam useful 6f-1m winner: poor form in bumpers: well held in Flat maiden: temperament under suspicion. *Johnny Farrelly* — **b72**

A LITTLE MAGIC (IRE) 7 b.g. Kayf Tara – Debut (IRE) (Presenting) [2017/18 c135, h103: c18m* c20g[F] May 28] winning hurdler: useful handicap chaser: won at Kempton in May: stays 21f: acts on good to firm and good to soft going: wears hood: in tongue tie last 4 starts: front runner/races prominently. *Jonjo O'Neill* — **c139 h–**

ALIZEE DE JANEIRO (FR) 8 b.m. Network (GER) – Katana (GER) (Funambule (USA)) [2017/18 c99, h105: h16.2g[2] h16.2g[3] h19.4s[6] h19.4d[4] Mar 16] fair handicap hurdler: lightly raced over fences: stays 19f: acts on heavy going: wears cheekpieces: often races prominently. *Lucinda Russell* — **c– h107**

ALIZEE JAVILEX (FR) 8 b.m. Le Fou (IRE) – Etoile du Lion (FR) (New Target) [2017/18 h96: h20.7s h20.5v[6] h15.8s[4] Mar 14] bumper winner: maiden hurdler, well below best in 2017/18: stays 21f: acts on soft and good to firm going: tried in cheekpieces: often races towards rear. *Lucy Wadham* — **h71**

ALKA STEP (IRE) 7 gr.g. Alkaadhem – D'bibbys Step (IRE) (Step Together (USA)) [2017/18 h16.8s h17.7g[5] h15.9d h19.2v Dec 26] off mark in Irish points at second attempt: no form over hurdles. *Nick Gifford* — **h–**

ALLBARNONE 10 b.g. Alflora (IRE) – What A Gem (Karinga Bay) [2017/18 c120, h116: h25.4d[5] h21.2g h24.1d[5] h23.8s Jan 18] good-topped gelding: fair handicap hurdler: lightly raced over fences: left William Kinsey after first start: probably stays 3m: acts on soft and good to firm going. *Gary Hanmer* — **c– h108**

ALL BUT GREY 12 gr.g. Baryshnikov (AUS) – Butleigh Rose (Nicholas Bill) [2017/18 c79, h70: c20.9d[4] h23g May 26] compact gelding: modest hurdler/fair chaser at best, little form after 2015/16: stayed 21f: acted on good to firm and heavy going: wore tongue tie: dead. *Carroll Gray* — **c54 h–**

ALL CHANGE 5 b.m. Motivator – Polly Flinders (Polar Falcon (USA)) [2017/18 b15.7s b16.6s Jan 27] fourth foal: dam maiden (stayed 1¼m): modest form in bumpers: better effort when seventh in mares event at Doncaster, very much having run of race. *Paul Webber* — **b80**

ALLCHILLEDOUT 9 b.g. Alflora (IRE) – Miss Chinchilla (Perpendicular) [2017/18 c112, h–: c23.6s c23.5s[pu] c26v[3] c23.6v[pu] Apr 14] sturdy gelding: winning hurdler: fair handicap chaser: stays 3¼m: best form on soft/heavy going: wears blinkers nowadays: usually in tongue tie: unreliable. *Colin Tizzard* — **c104 § h–**

ALL CURRENCIES (IRE) 6 b.m. Getaway (GER) – Splendid Presence (IRE) (Presenting) [2017/18 b87: h16g[4] h16.3d[3] h16.5s[4] h20.5s* h19.8v Feb 16] rather unfurnished mare: won Irish maiden point on debut: fairly useful form over hurdles: won mares novices at Worcester in October and Newbury in January: third in listed mares novice at Newbury (9¾ lengths behind Dame Rose) in between: stays 21f: acts on soft going: tried in hood: often races towards rear. *Gary Moore* — **h120**

ALL DOLLED UP (IRE) 6 b.m. Aussie Rules (USA) – All On Sugar (GER) (Red Ransom (USA)) [2017/18 h–: h15.8m[4] h16.7d Jun 8] maiden on Flat: no form over hurdles. *Sarah-Jayne Davies* — **h–**

ALLEE BLEUE (IRE) 8 ch.g. Mount Nelson – Murrieta (Docksider (USA)) [2017/18 h131: c20d c16d c19.2v[3] c19.9s[3] c20.2s[2] c24s[6] Mar 17] well-made gelding: useful hurdler at one time: fair form over fences: stays 2½m: best form on soft/heavy going. *Philip Hobbs* — **c114 h–**

ALLELU ALLELUIA (GER) 7 b.g. Doyen (IRE) – Anna Spectra (IRE) (Spectrum (IRE)) [2017/18 h12p h20g[3] h19.9g[4] May 28] fairly useful form over hurdles, lightly raced: third in handicap at Ffos Las in May: will be suited by further than 2½m: acts on good to soft going. *Jonjo O'Neill* — **h116**

50

ALL

ALLEZ COOL (IRE) 9 ch.g. Flemensfirth (USA) – La Fisarmonica (IRE) (Accordion) [2017/18 c105, h–: c24.2v³ c23.4g⁶ Oct 28] winning hurdler: fair handicap chaser, well below best in 2017/18: stays 25f: acts on heavy going: wears headgear: front runner/races prominently. *George Bewley* — c80 h–

ALLEZ JACQUES (IRE) 6 b.g. Robin des Champs (FR) – Crystal Stream (IRE) (Dr Massini (IRE)) [2017/18 h92, b86: h21.4s⁵ h19.9d² h21.4v³ h24.4s h21.2s³ Feb 21] compact gelding: fair form over hurdles: stays 21f: acts on heavy going: usually races towards rear. *Emma Lavelle* — h109

ALL FOR JOY (IRE) 6 b.g. Robin des Pres (FR) – Mountain Empress (IRE) (Accordion) [2017/18 b16v² h16d⁴ b16v² b16v² b18s² Apr 27] third foal: dam little form in bumpers/ over hurdles: winning pointer: useful form in bumpers: second in maiden at Punchestown (head behind Lone Wolf) in April: 25/1, shaped well when fourth in maiden at Leopardstown (21¼ lengths behind Paloma Blue) on hurdling debut: usually leads: should do better. *Oliver McKiernan, Ireland* — h109 p b106

ALL FOR THE BEST (IRE) 6 b.g. Rip Van Winkle (IRE) – Alleluia (Caerleon (USA)) [2017/18 h116: h20m³ h24.4s Feb 21] fairly useful handicap hurdler: stays 2½m: acts on good to firm and good to soft going: has worn cheekpieces: in tongue tie last 3 starts. *Robert Stephens* — h117

ALLFREDANDNOBELL (IRE) 5 b.g. Alfred Nobel (IRE) – Its In The Air (IRE) (Whipper (USA)) [2017/18 h107: h19.3d³ h19.9s⁶ h19.7v⁴ h21.3d* h21.2g Apr 23] has had breathing operation: fair handicap hurdler: won at Wetherby in March: stays 21f: acts on soft going: in visor last 2 starts. *Micky Hammond* — h101

ALL HAIL CAESAR (IRE) 4 b.g. Nathaniel (IRE) – Ragiam (ITY) (Martino Alonso (IRE)) [2017/18 b16g Apr 21] 29,000 3-y-o: third foal: dam useful Italian 9f-11f winner: 33/1, some encouragement when eighth in bumper at Ayr (11 lengths behind Sebastopol): open to improvement. *Rebecca Menzies* — b86 p

ALL HANDS ON DECK (IRE) 5 b.m. Flemensfirth (USA) – On Galley Head (IRE) (Zaffaran (USA)) [2017/18 b16s⁵ b16.5m⁵ Apr 25] £4,500 3-y-o: fourth foal: dam (6½), 2¼m bumper winner, half-sister to useful hurdler/smart chaser (stayed 21f) Dare Me: modest form in bumpers: in hood second start. *Harry Fry* — b82

ALL IS GOOD (IRE) 6 b.g. Scorpion (IRE) – Peinture Rose (IRE) (Marathon (USA)) [2017/18 h107: h19.3g h16s⁵ h16.2s* h15.8d⁴ h16m⁶ Apr 26] sturdy gelding: fell in Irish maiden point: fair handicap hurdler: won novice event at Hereford in January: unproven beyond 17f: acts on soft going: has worn hood: front runner/races prominently, usually travels strongly. *Robin Dickin* — h110

ALL KINGS (IRE) 9 b.g. Milan – Rilmount (IRE) (Roselier (FR)) [2017/18 h–§: h23.1v³ h23.1v c23s² c23.6v⁶ c30.7s⁶ c31.8s^pu Mar 13] lengthy gelding: fair handicap hurdler: similar form over fences: stays 23f: acts on heavy going: tried in tongue tie: temperamental. *Bob Buckler* — c109 § h105 §

ALL MY FRIENDS SAY (IRE) 7 b.g. Scorpion (IRE) – Sounds Attractive (IRE) (Rudimentary (USA)) [2017/18 h23.3g^pu h22.1s^pu Jul 22] little show in Irish maiden points: pulled up in novice hurdles: in tongue tie second start. *Sheena Walton* — h–

ALL MY LOVE (IRE) 6 b.m. Lord Shanakill (USA) – Afilla (Dansili) [2017/18 h115: h19.8s³ h19.4s h16s² h18.9v h16.3d⁴ Apr 22] fairly useful handicap hurdler: second at Fakenham in March: likely to prove best at around 2m: acts on soft going: usually races towards rear, often travels strongly. *Pam Sly* — h117

ALLMYOWN (IRE) 7 b.g. Mr Combustible (IRE) – Cappard Ridge (IRE) (Executive Perk) [2017/18 h20.1v^pu h24d³ h21.3s h19.3s⁵ c25.2s³ h25.3s⁴ c21.3v* c24.5d^pu Mar 25] modest form over hurdles: fair form over fences: won handicap at Wetherby in March: stayed 25f: acted on heavy going: dead. *Philip Kirby* — c103 h90

ALLOW DALLOW (IRE) 11 b.g. Gold Well – Russland (GER) (Surumu (GER)) [2017/18 c118, h–: c20d c19.4v^pu Dec 9] maiden hurdler: fairly useful chaser at best, no form in 2017/18: stays 3m: acts on heavy going: wears headgear: has worn tongue tie. *Nikki Evans* — c– h–

ALL SET TO GO (IRE) 7 gr.g. Verglas (IRE) – Firecrest (IRE) (Darshaan) [2017/18 h142: h16.8v h16.5s⁴ Apr 14] angular gelding: useful handicap hurdler: below best in 2017/18 after long absence/change of yards: raced around 2m: acts on good to firm and heavy going: has worn tongue tie, not in 2017/18. *Kevin Frost* — h124

ALL THE COLOURS 7 b.g. Rainbow High – Stephanie (Shernazar) [2017/18 b16.3d b17.7g Nov 10] no form in bumpers. *Phil York* — b–

ALL

ALLTHEGEAR NO IDEA (IRE) 11 b.g. Sayarshan (FR) – All The Gear (IRE) (Nashamaa) [2017/18 c116, h–: c23.9g^3 c20s^5 c24v^2 h26s^6 h23v^2 h24v^5 h23.3v^4 h26.6s* Apr 26] fair handicap hurdler: won at Perth (conditionals) in April: fair maiden chaser: stays 27f: acts on heavy going: has worn headgear, including last 3 starts: often let down by jumping over fences. *Nigel Twiston-Davies* — c111 x / h110

ALLTHEKINGSHORSES (IRE) 12 b.g. King's Theatre (IRE) – Penny Brae (IRE) (Montelimar (USA)) [2017/18 c23.8g^{pu} c25.5d^5 May 31] sturdy gelding: multiple point winner: winning hurdler: fairly useful chaser at best, no form in hunters in 2017/18: stays 3¾m: acts on good to firm and heavy going: wears cheekpieces/tongue tie: often let down by jumping over fences. *N. W. Alexander* — c– x / h–

ALLTIMEGOLD (IRE) 5 b.g. Gold Well – Carryonharriet (IRE) (Norwich) [2017/18 b17.7g h19.5d h16v^4 h16v^6 h19.6d Apr 21] well beaten in bumper: poor form over hurdles. *Tim Vaughan* — h75 / b–

ALL TOGETHER (FR) 7 ch.g. Zambezi Sun – Mareha (IRE) (Cadeaux Genereux) [2017/18 c131, h114: h19.5s^2 Apr 27] compact gelding: fair maiden hurdler: useful chaser: stays 2½m: acts on heavy going: often races prominently. *Johnny Farrelly* — c– / h112

ALLYSSON MONTERG (FR) 8 b.g. Network (GER) – Mellyssa (FR) (Panoramic) [2017/18 h110: c19.2v* c24.4s^{pu} c20v^3 c23.8s* Apr 25] strong gelding: useful hurdler: useful form over fences: won novice at Exeter in February and handicap at Perth (by 4½ lengths from As de Pique) in April: stays 3m: best form on soft/heavy going: in tongue tie last 4 starts: front runner/races prominently. *Richard Hobson* — c142 / h–

ALMAHOY 7 b.m. Martaline – Tokahy (FR) (Kahyasi) [2017/18 b16.8s Dec 26] no form in bumpers over 2 years apart. *Julia Brooke* — b–

ALMINAR (IRE) 5 b.g. Arakan (USA) – Classic Magic (IRE) (Classic Cliche (IRE)) [2017/18 h15.8v^5 h18.5v^5 h19.5v^6 h16.8v Apr 17] £10,000 3-y-o: first foal: dam (b74) fourth only start in bumper/second on completed outing in points: tailed off in bumper: modest form over hurdles: best effort when fifth in novice at Exeter in February. *Nigel Hawke* — h93 / b–

ALMOST GEMINI (IRE) 9 gr.g. Dylan Thomas (IRE) – Streetcar (IRE) (In The Wings) [2017/18 c–, h106: h19.9g^4 h24.7d^4 Oct 29] fair handicap hurdler: well held only start over fences: stays 25f: acts on soft going: wears headgear. *Kenneth Slack* — c– / h108

ALMOST GOLD (IRE) 5 b.g. Gold Well – Shining Lights (IRE) (Moscow Society (USA)) [2017/18 h20d h20.5s h19.4s h21.2d^4 Mar 22] €36,000 3-y-o: good-topped gelding: fifth foal: closely related to fairly useful chaser Oscar O'Scar (19f-23f winner, by Oscar): dam (c107/h114) moody 2½m-3m hurdle/chase winner: modest form over hurdles: remains with potential. *Ian Williams* — h87 p

ALMUNTHER (IRE) 5 b.g. Invincible Spirit (IRE) – Adaala (USA) (Sahm (USA)) [2017/18 h15.7d h16.8s^{pu} Dec 8] fair maiden on Flat, stays 1¼m: no form over hurdles: wears tongue tie. *Micky Hammond* — h–

ALOHAMORA (IRE) 4 ch.f. English Channel (USA) – America Alone (Dalakhani (IRE)) [2017/18 h15.7d* h16s^4 h15.7s^3 Mar 7] modest maiden on Flat, stays 1½m: fair form over hurdles: won fillies juvenile at Catterick in February. *James A. Nash, Ireland* — h107

ALONG CAME THEO (IRE) 8 b.g. Vertical Speed (FR) – Kachina (IRE) (Mandalus) [2017/18 h80: h20.1v^2 h19.7s^2 h19.7v^2 h20.3v^{pu} Mar 5] modest maiden hurdler: stays 2½m: acts on heavy going: temperamental. *Andrew Crook* — h98 §

ALOOMOMO (FR) 8 b.g. Tirwanako (FR) – Kayola (FR) (Royal Charter (FR)) [2017/18 c–, h119: h20d^3 h24d^2 c24.2s^{pu} c24.2v^{pu} c20v^2 c19.9s h24.3g Apr 20] well-made gelding: fairly useful maiden hurdler: useful chaser at best, out of sorts over fences in 2017/18: stays 3¼m: acts on heavy going: has worn headgear, including last 3 starts. *Warren Greatrex* — c109 / h122

ALOTTARAIN (IRE) 8 b.m. Zerpour (IRE) – Alottalady (IRE) (Mandalus) [2017/18 c72, h83: h15.7g^3 c16.5g^4 c19.4m^4 c16.3d^5 c20g c17.8d^6 h16.3s^{pu} Oct 2] close-coupled mare: poor handicap hurdler/maiden chaser nowadays: stays 19f: acts on good to firm going: wears cheekpieces. *Seamus Mullins* — c71 / h60

ALPHABET BAY (IRE) 8 b.g. Kalanisi (IRE) – A And Bs Gift (IRE) (Mr Combustible (IRE)) [2017/18 h21.4g Oct 29] rangy gelding: bumper winner: maiden hurdler, well beaten only start (tongue tied) in 2017/18: unproven beyond 2m: acts on soft going. *Warren Greatrex* — h–

ALPHABETICAL ORDER 10 b.g. Alflora (IRE) – Lady Turk (FR) (Baby Turk) [2017/18 h16.2d^3 h16v^2 h20v^3 Dec 9] fairly useful handicap hurdler: second at Ayr in November: stays 21f: acts on heavy going. *R. Mike Smith* — h115

ALT

ALPHA DES OBEAUX (FR) 8 b.g. Saddler Maker (IRE) – Omega des Obeaux (FR) (Saint Preuil (FR)) [2017/18 c147, h–: c24s² c24s⁴ c20.6v* c25v⁴ c24d⁶ h24v⁴ c24s⁶ c34.3s^F Apr 14] lengthy gelding: high-class hurdler at best: very smart chaser: won Clonmel Oil Chase (by 5½ lengths from A Toi Phil) in November: second in Munster National Handicap Chase at Limerick (7 lengths behind Total Recall) on return: close up when fell heavily at the Chair in Grand National at Aintree: stays 3m: acts on heavy going: usually wears headgear nowadays: has worn tongue tie: usually races prominently. *M. F. Morris, Ireland* **c156 h143**

ALPHA INDI (IRE) 7 b.g. Oscar (IRE) – High Park Lady (IRE) (Phardante (FR)) [2017/18 h100p: h19.2g³ h20.3d⁴ h19.4d h19.2v⁶ h24v⁴ c21.2s³ Mar 16] in frame in Irish maiden points: fair maiden hurdler: 9/4, third of 4 in novice handicap at Fakenham (23¼ lengths behind Heresmynumber) on chasing debut: stays 19f: best form on good going. *James Evans* **c77 h102**

ALPHIE 6 b.g. Alflora (IRE) – Clever Liz (Glacial Storm (USA)) [2017/18 h19.3v h20.1s^pu Nov 10] strong gelding: no show in novice hurdles. *Sue Smith* **h–**

ALPINE SECRET (IRE) 6 br.g. Stowaway – Squaw Valley (IRE) (Saddlers' Hall (IRE)) [2017/18 h102: c20.1v^pu c17.4g² c15.9d⁵ Dec 7] maiden hurdler: modest form over fences: best effort when second in handicap at Bangor in October: stays 21f: acts on heavy going. *Ben Pauling* **c97 h–**

ALRIGHTJACK (IRE) 4 b.g. Stowaway – Brogella (IRE) (King's Theatre (IRE)) [2017/18 b15.3d³ Apr 22] €50,000 3-y-o: seventh foal: half-brother to smart hurdler Swamp Fox (2m-2½m winner, by Windsor Knot) and fairly useful hurdler/useful chaser Rene's Girl (2½m-3m winner, by Presenting): dam (h131), 2m/2¼m hurdle winner (stayed 2½m), also 9f-1½m winner on Flat: 7/1, shaped well when third in bumper at Wincanton (1½ lengths behind Ebony Gale): sure to progress. *Jamie Snowden* **b95 p**

AL SHAHIR 6 b.g. Robin des Champs (FR) – Sarah Massini (IRE) (Dr Massini (IRE)) [2017/18 b104: h16.8g² h16s² h16s² h15.7s* h19.8v^pu Mar 10] useful-looking gelding: bumper winner: fairly useful form over hurdles: won maiden at Towcester in December: bred to stay beyond 17f: acts on soft going: usually races close up. *Dan Skelton* **h122**

ALSKAMATIC 12 b.g. Systematic – Alska (FR) (Leading Counsel (USA)) [2017/18 c25.3d^pu May 5] multiple winning pointer: fairly useful chaser at best, pulled up in hunter only start in 2017/18: stays 33f: acts on heavy going: wears cheekpieces. *Richard J. Bandey* **c–**

ALTAAYIL (IRE) 7 br.g. Sea The Stars (IRE) – Alleluia (Caerleon (USA)) [2017/18 h–p: h17.7g³ Aug 24] good-topped gelding: useful on Flat (stays 2m, lightly raced): poor form over hurdles: open to further improvement. *Gary Moore* **h83 p**

ALTESSE DE GUYE (FR) 8 ch.m. Dom Alco (FR) – Mascotte de Guye (FR) (Video Rock (FR)) [2017/18 c116, h111: h23g⁶ h23g^pu Sep 18] angular mare: fair handicap hurdler: lightly-raced chaser: stayed 3m: acted on soft going: often wore hood: dead. *Martin Keighley* **c– h106**

ALTIEPIX (FR) 8 ch.g. Fragrant Mix (IRE) – Naltiepy (FR) (Dom Alco (FR)) [2017/18 c120, h–: c17d* c19.4g³ c19.4g^pu c16.5g c16.3g^pu Nov 1] winning hurdler: fairly useful handicap chaser: won at Stratford in May: has won over 3m, just as effective around 2m: acts on heavy going: has worn headgear: wears tongue tie nowadays. *Kerry Lee* **c125 h–**

ALTIOR (IRE) 8 b.g. High Chaparral (IRE) – Monte Solaro (IRE) (Key of Luck (USA)) [2017/18 c175p, h–: c16.4s* c15.9s* c15.5d* Apr 28] **c179 p h–**

Altior's achievements and performances in an abbreviated second season over fences, in which he wasn't seen out until mid-February and ran only three times, earned him the distinction of being the highest-rated horse in this Annual. He was Timeform Horse of the Year for the second time, having also been awarded that title after recording an exceptionally high rating for a novice (175p) in 2016/17 which had produced some outstanding novice chasers, no fewer than five of whom—a record for any one season—had ended the campaign rated higher than 165, a mark bettered in the *Chasers & Hurdlers* era by just fourteen novice chasers in all before 2016/17. Among the unique quintet of 'super novices' was Altior's stablemate Might Bite who, kept to the novice ranks, crowned his 2016/17 campaign by winning the RSA Chase at Cheltenham (known as the 'novices' Gold Cup') and the Mildmay Chase at Aintree. Had he not fallen when well clear at the last in the Kauto Star Novices' Chase at Kempton's Christmas meeting, Might Bite would have won that

53

*Betfair Exchange Chase (Game Spirit), Newbury—
no rustiness in the jumping department for Altior, who is poised to brush aside the grey Politologue
in a steadily-run race; outsider Valdez (hoops) is about to drop away*

race in a faster time than the one recorded by another of the season's brilliant novices Thistlecrack who beat established chasers over the same course and distance in the King George just over an hour later.

Thistlecrack was the first novice to win the race acknowledged as the mid-season championship for the staying chasers, and he did so on just his fourth start over fences. A tendon tear, suffered on the gallops towards the end of February that season, put paid to plans for Thistlecrack to try to emulate Red Splash, Golden Miller, Mont Tremblant, Captain Christy and Coneygree by winning the Cheltenham Gold Cup in the same season as his first victory over fences. It was one of the biggest disappointments of the latest season that Thistlecrack appeared only twice and wasn't seen again after managing only fourth behind Might Bite when attempting a second win in the King George VI Chase. The star novice quintet from 2016/17 had been completed by two Irish-trained chasers, Our Duke, a brilliant winner of the Irish Grand National, and the two-miler Great Field, who won all four of his starts (like Might Bite kept to novice events) in increasingly impressive pillar-to-post fashion, stepped up in class with each race. Readers won't need reminding, however, that injury, illness and loss of form deplete the ranks of the top jumpers each season and, sadly, both Great Field and the ill-fated Our Duke (who died from a heart attack in his stable in April) also had training troubles in the latest season which restricted their appearances. In fact, Might Bite was the only one of the five to enjoy anything like a clear run, just coming up short, after his King George success, against a stronger stayer Native River in a heavy-ground Gold Cup before regaining the winning thread at Aintree's Grand National meeting with a decisive victory in the Bowl Chase.

There were fears for Altior's future when his trainer Nicky Henderson announced out of the blue in November that he would have to miss the Tingle Creek Chase at Sandown, his first target in the new season, because he needed a breathing operation. The principal concern was for Altior's welfare, although there was some attendant controversy about the fact that the announcement was made through an exclusive blog which Henderson writes for bookmakers Unibet (wouldn't it be more transparent to have central reporting of such sensitive issues to the BHA in the first instance?). Altior's achievements as a novice, and the fact that he was still unbeaten over jumps, had raised expectations that his stable might have a true heir to Sprinter Sacre who recorded a rating of 192p in 2012/13, the highest over jumps in the forty-three years of *Chasers & Hurdlers*, just ahead of that achieved by Kauto Star at his peak. Sprinter Sacre, who won the Queen Mother Champion Chase twice (the first edition by nineteen lengths) in a career that was interrupted for a time by the effects of a heart condition, emulated another great champion, Istabraq, when he won major championship races in the same season at the three major spring festivals at Cheltenham, Aintree and Punchestown (a feat subsequently also achieved by Douvan, though he did it in championship events restricted to novices). In common with Sprinter Sacre and Douvan, both of whom were also unbeaten in their novice chasing seasons and earned exceptionally high ratings (175p and 180p respectively), Altior won the top race for two-mile novice chasers, the Arkle Trophy at the Cheltenham Festival. His six wins also included two in open company, the Game Spirit Chase at Newbury (by thirteen lengths from Fox Norton who went on to finish a close second in the Queen Mother Champion Chase before winning the Melling Chase at Aintree and the Champion Chase at Punchestown) and in the Celebration Chase at Sandown (with an eight-length victory over the Queen Mother Champion Chase winner Special Tiara).

Exactly how serious Altior's breathing problem might be, and the prospects for a successful outcome to the operation, were the subject of fevered speculation, which continued, on and off, until he reappeared on the track. Here, after all, was the sport's top prospect, a seven-year-old who had looked set to make an indelible mark on the game in the years to come. His trainer explained that Altior's breathing problem had been discovered while he was 'showing brilliant form, though we never got as far as galloping before we had to stop.' Henderson explained that 'In terms of timing, I'd far prefer if this had cropped up a month ago because we have to try to get a run into him before the Festival, which is not guaranteed now.' Wind surgery varies from minor procedures to complex operations and Altior's problems were reportedly treated by hobdaying which, coincidentally, along with 'tie-back' 'tie-forward' and 'soft palate' operations and surgery on the epiglottis, comprised the 'breathing' operations that, from January 19th 2018, have had to be publicly declared before a horse's next start. The efficacy of breathing operations has long been a subject for debate. They clearly work for some horses and not for others, but concrete claims for their success and benefits are hard to find, even among vets who perform them. However, the call for greater data provision, skilfully articulated by the Horseracing Bettors Forum, convinced the BHA that any breathing operation since a horse's last start should be added to items such as various types of headgear and tongue-ties that are already carried on race cards. The decision was not met with unanimous approval among the sport's professionals. While there was support for the proposals on the grounds of transparency—'At least we are giving the information, rather than everyone finding out in the winner's enclosure'—there were those anxious to warn punters against believing they were being given a magic formula for profit.

Betway Queen Mother Champion Chase, Cheltenham—Altior's trademark strong late surge is about to kick in as he challenges old rival Min (No.6); outsider God's Own (checks) takes third

bet365 Celebration Chase, Sandown—a rather workmanlike display but the 100% record over fences is never seriously in doubt as Altior (left) repeats his 2017 success; 2017 third San Benedeto finishes one place better this time

Leading Flat trainer Mark Johnston was among the most vociferous opponents of the move, rightly pointing to the difficulty of policing the rule. 'Voluntary declaration isn't always guaranteed to be accurate [examples soon arose of trainers having forgotten to declare breathing ops] and while racecourse vets can usually verify whether a horse has been gelded [which has to be notified], for example, they most certainly can't tell that it has had wind surgery,' Johnston said. It is not always possible even with an endoscopy to tell exactly what has been done. Whether the declaration of breathing operations will eventually provide enough data to prove the success or otherwise of the procedures is a moot point. Attributing a racehorse's improvement to a particular piece of headgear or to breathing surgery, for example, is not always valid if further options, such as other medical treatment or changes in training routine, are being tried at the same time. Assessment of the severity of breathing problems before surgery differ too and are not collated, and a good proportion of jumpers are believed to have 'precautionary' surgery simply because it is thought to be worthwhile, given that the horse's commercial value—unlike that of its Flat counterpart with breeding potential—is not affected by its having surgery. There is no way of knowing whether the jumpers who go on to show improved form might have shown similar improvement without surgery. Furthermore, the data will also be limited by the fact that there will be no information about any operations or procedures conducted before a horse goes into training, or similar information for animals that come from abroad. Mark Johnston expressed concern that the new ruling might result in more Flat horses undergoing 'precautionary' surgery before they go into training, reflecting the fact that the values of potential stallions and broodmares are affected if it becomes known that they have a breathing problem. Johnston called the possibility of that particular development 'a tragedy for the breed', a phrase that was given undue prominence, and rather taken out of context, in reports of his reaction to the declaration of breathing operations in general. Greater data provision, incidentally, is reportedly seen by the BHA as something that will 'grow interest in betting on British racing'. Educating racegoers in interpreting the usefulness or otherwise of some of the information that is put in front of them is far from straightforward, however, especially when data is incomplete and there are anomalies in the way information is collated and presented.

The moment of truth, as some labelled it, came for Altior in the Game Spirit (branded as the Betfair Exchange Chase) at Newbury in February. Altior's hobday operation had been carried out without a general anaesthetic and he had been confined to his box for around just two weeks before resuming walking exercise again. In mid-January he was reported by his trainer to be ready for 'stepping up his work to the point I suspect where we would hear the noise that we had heard in November, he wouldn't be making a noise with the work he has been doing up to now.' Altior showed no ill-effects when his work was intensified and the bulletins from Seven Barrows continued to be upbeat in the run up to the Game Spirit in which Altior faced two opponents. One of them was the Tingle Creek winner Politologue who had won all three of his races in the latest season, the most recent of them the Desert Orchid Chase at Kempton's Christmas meeting. Altior had been off the course for ten months but he was sent off at 3/1-on, with Politologue at 5/2 and the other runner, the one-time high-class Valdez, who had been off the course for the best part of three seasons after suffering a tendon injury, virtually friendless at 25/1. To the palpable relief of his trainer, and probably nearly all of those watching at Newbury or on TV, Altior turned in a performance that seemed to confirm that he was every bit as good as ever. Politologue made the running before Altior, who jumped well all the way, taking a keen hold, swept him aside with ease. Stalking Politologue from before the second last, Altior was just nudged along early on the run-in and quickened four lengths clear for an impressive victory (Valdez was left behind from the second last and finished thirteen lengths behind Politologue). As a preparatory race for Cheltenham, it could hardly have gone better for Altior, of whom Nicky Henderson said 'If you could dream what would happen, that was just about perfection.' Altior's performance, along with the successful return of leading Cheltenham Gold Cup contender Native River in the Denman Chase on the same card (Kalashnikov won the featured Betfair Hurdle), provided a low-key jumps season in Britain with a much needed shot in the arm in the lead up to the Cheltenham Festival.

One of the worst and most dismal winters for years had seen jumping in Britain largely come off second best in its battle with the weather, especially after Christmas when the rain only relented to be followed by snow and freezing temperatures in late-February. The word 'heavy' featured in the official going description on the opening day at the Cheltenham Festival for the first time since 1982 with two hundred tons of snow having to be moved from the course when the thaw began in the week before the meeting (the snow returned to Cheltenham in the days after the Festival). The going was still very soft on the second day when Altior lined up at even money in the Betway Queen Mother Champion Chase against eight opponents, headed by a two-pronged challenge from the Mullins stable with the top-class pair Min (warmed up with a twelve-length victory in the newly-instituted Dublin Chase at Leopardstown's revamped two-day festival in February) and Douvan (who hadn't been seen since flopping in the Queen Mother twelve months earlier). Min and Douvan, the latter due to be ridden by Ruby Walsh in preference to Min before Walsh was injured earlier in the afternoon, were the only opponents who started at single-figure odds, with Politologue fourth favourite at 12/1, reigning champion Special Tiara (running in the race for the fifth time) at 25/1 and the rest at odds ranging from 28/1 to 50/1.

Notwithstanding the strength of the field, Altior would almost certainly have been odds on for the Queen Mother Champion Chase but for the publicity given to a scare when he was found to be lame two days before the race and pus had to be drained from his near-fore hoof (Altior had to pass an examination on the day by one of the racecourse vets before being deemed fit to run). Altior and Douvan had never met, but Altior and Min had met in a very strong edition of the Supreme Novices' Hurdle in 2016 when Altior was a clear-cut winner by seven lengths from Min, with Altior's stablemate Buveur d'Air, who won his second Champion Hurdle the day before the latest Queen Mother Champion Chase, in third place, ahead of a host of other big-race winners who have subsequently emerged from the race. A 'little stress fracture' had ruled out Min from a rematch with Altior twelve months later in the Arkle Trophy (which 4/1-on Altior won by six lengths and nine lengths

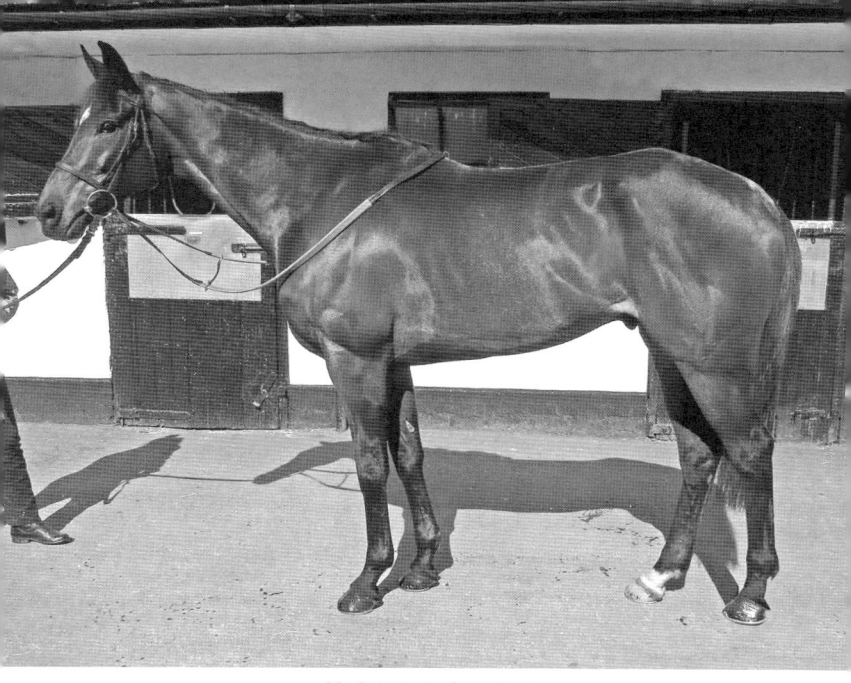

Mrs Patricia Pugh's "Altior"

from Cloudy Dream and Ordinary World); Min's trainer—who described the horse's absence from the 2017 Festival as the most disappointing among his stable's various absentees through injury—had expected Min to close the gap ('He has improved hugely from last year'). In the end, Min didn't manage to close the gap at all on Altior when they met in the Queen Mother Champion Chase. Altior again beat him into second by seven lengths but Min looked a real danger to Altior and the rest when clearly travelling best at the third last, before being overpowered by Altior in the home straight.

The 40/1-shot God's Own, a three-times Grade 1 winner who would have finished third in the race the previous year but for late jumping errors, and Politologue were in front on the short run to the second last after the runners straightened up, but God's Own forfeited the lead to Min with a mistake there. The chasing Altior, who had had to be pushed along before three out, was steered off the running rail to give him plenty of daylight and stayed on very strongly up the hill, after taking the lead soon after jumping the last fence with Min. The ability to produce a storming finish has been a feature of Altior's career and, in the final analysis, there was no denying his complete dominance over a good field on the day. God's Own came eleven lengths behind Min in third, and was, in turn, a further five lengths and twelve lengths ahead of Politologue and Ordinary World (the only other finishers after strong-travelling Douvan fell four out). Min finished the race well and his own performance would have been good enough to have won several recent editions of the Queen Mother Champion Chase. Altior's top drawer performance—Douvan would have needed to be at least as good as ever to have given him a race—was one of the best in the race in the modern era. While not matching Sprinter Sacre's performance in 2013, it was certainly on a par with those of Moscow Flyer in 2005 and Master Minded in 2008, the two best winning performances recorded in the race this century before Sprinter Sacre's and both brilliant displays by any standards. One final point before leaving the Queen Mother Champion Chase: there was mention in some quarters about Altior's winning time being 'slow' compared to the previous day's Arkle (won by the outstanding Footpad) which, apart from the dubious practice of drawing comparisons from raw times from two different days, ignored the fact that the Arkle was the first race on the chase track which had since been churned up by three large fields before the Champion Chase was run. Time analysis needs to take into account the prevailing conditions (it was also windier on the second day at Cheltenham, for example) and, taking all such variables into account, Altior recorded a Timeform timefigure equivalent to a timerating of 180, the best recorded all season by any jumper over any distance in Britain and Ireland (just having the edge over Footpad's in the Arkle).

The effort required to produce the level of performance reached by Altior at Cheltenham—especially in very testing conditions—is hard to quantify but all too easy to underestimate. It seemed to be generally assumed that he would go on to Aintree for the Melling Chase over two and a half miles, a distance over which he is still untried (Sprinter Sacre had won both races in 2013, as had Finian's Rainbow, another of his trainer's five Champion Chase winners, in 2012 and Moscow Flyer in 2005, as well as others before them). However, Altior soon showed on his return to Seven Barrows that Cheltenham had taken plenty out of him and connections decided to skip Aintree—as they had the previous season—and aim him for a second Celebration Chase at Sandown's Finale meeting. God's Own, Special Tiara and Ar Mad (50/1 rank outsider at Cheltenham) took him on again from the Queen Mother Champion Chase field, joined by two younger chasers trained by Paul Nicholls, San Benedeto and the smart novice (winner of the Maghull Chase at Aintree) Diego du Charmil. Altior started at 11/2-on and didn't need to run anywhere near his Queen Mother Champion Chase form to complete his short campaign in style, jumping well in the main and taking the lead before the second last, after being shaken up, to win by three and a quarter lengths and three and three quarters from San Benedeto and God's Own, with Special Tiara and Diego du Charmil fourth and fifth (front-running Ar Mad suffered a fatal fall at the eighth).

Buveur d'Air, Might Bite and Altior were among the top half dozen earners in the end-of-season jumps prize money table in Britain and they were the mainstays in Nicky Henderson's successful pursuit of a fifth trainers' championship, which he won by a wide margin from Paul Nicholls. Henderson's first-three earnings of £3,376,169 were the second highest recorded for a season in Britain over jumps, his total edging close to the long-standing record of Paul Nicholls whose stable won £3,507,643 in 2007/8 when the team of chasers at Manor Farm Stables included Kauto Star, Denman, Master Minded and Neptune Collonges. Henderson won thirteen of Britain's forty Grade 1s, those of Buveur d'Air and Altior at the Cheltenham Festival taking his career total at that meeting to sixty (though the seven for Willie Mullins saw him supplant Henderson as the most successful trainer in Cheltenham Festival history). Henderson won five of the eleven Grade 1s at Aintree's Grand National meeting which was weakened by Ireland's juggernaut stables of Mullins and Elliott keeping most of their big guns in reserve for Punchestown (Henderson himself didn't have a single runner at Ireland's five-day end-of-season festival, saying he 'wasn't keen on coming over for a drubbing').

Altior joins a select list who have been Timeform Horse of the Year over jumps more than once (he was only the third novice to take the title when winning it for the first time). If he wins a third Horse of the Year title he will join iconic performers Istabraq and Kauto Star and stand just one short of equalling Desert Orchid's four titles. Longevity and enduring brilliance contributed to that trio making names for themselves outside the normal boundaries of the sport. Desert Orchid's career spanned ten seasons and he had nine essays in *Chasers & Hurdlers* over the years, one more than Kauto Star who, like Desert Orchid, had his death in retirement reported in the National TV and radio news bulletins, a rare occurrence for a racehorse. Desert Orchid and Kauto Star are remembered with life-sized statues at Kempton where they won nine editions of the King George VI Chase between

ALT

them, Kauto Star's five victories equalling the great Golden Miller's five wins in the Cheltenham Gold Cup in the 'thirties (no other horses have won the same top-level open championship race over jumps in Britain five times). Istabraq, the first British or Irish jumper to win over £1m in prize money, was pre-eminent among the hurdlers of his time and won three Champion Hurdles and four Champion Hurdles at Leopardstown (a fourth victory in Cheltenham's championship looked a formality before a foot and mouth outbreak put paid to the 2001 Festival). Desert Orchid, Kauto Star and Istabraq were symbols of so much that is good about National Hunt racing. As well as being champions, they were tough, versatile and a joy to watch. Altior has some way to go before he earns wider recognition outside the confines of the racing world. He is an exceptional two-mile chaser but perhaps lacks the charisma of his erstwhile stablemate Sprinter Sacre, who travelled majestically in his races and really caught the imagination of his host of followers. Still only eight, Altior has time on his side, however, and might well eventually earn wider appreciation, especially if he is stepped up in trip. Given the way he finishes his races, he is clearly capable of winning top events beyond two miles, perhaps even a King George VI Chase, though his stable has other candidates for that race, most notably Might Bite. The top two-mile chasers, however, often do not gain the recognition they deserve and it is worth recalling that both Desert Orchid and Kauto Star were champions at two miles but made even bigger names for themselves at three miles plus (Desert Orchid was champion two-miler and champion staying chaser for three years concurrently).

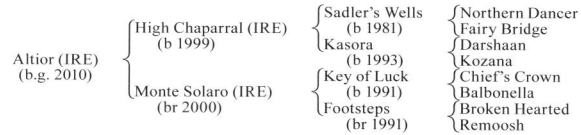

Altior (IRE) (b.g. 2010)	High Chaparral (IRE) (b 1999)	Sadler's Wells (b 1981)	Northern Dancer / Fairy Bridge
		Kasora (b 1993)	Darshaan / Kozana
	Monte Solaro (IRE) (br 2000)	Key of Luck (b 1991)	Chief's Crown / Balbonella
		Footsteps (br 1991)	Broken Hearted / Remoosh

Altior might not fill the eye before his races in the same way as the imposing Sprinter Sacre used to do, but he is a good-topped individual who always possessed the size and scope to make a chaser. Altior's sire, the now-deceased High Chaparral, was one of the best sons of Sadler's Wells and was by no means a failure as a Flat stallion. However, towards the end of his career, when his fee had fallen to €10,000, he began to attract patronage from National Hunt breeders and has made an impact on the jumping game, his other winners including the Sandown Gold Cup winner Hadrian's Approach, the Grade 1-winning novice hurdler Tower Bridge, the runner-up in Punchestown's Champion Four Year Old Hurdle Landofhopeandglory and the Fred Winter Juvenile Hurdle winner Hawk High. The distaff side of Altior's pedigree has been discussed in the two previous essays on him. His dam Monte Solaro was a fair winning hurdler at two miles and Altior is the third of four winners she has produced so far, the best of the others being a year-older half-sister Princess Leya (by Old Vic), who was a useful two-mile hurdler, and a year-younger half-brother Silverhow (by another stamina influence, Yeats), a fairly useful novice chaser in the latest season who won twice at two and a half miles, in a handicap at Wincanton and a novice handicap at Sandown. Altior's closely-related three-year-old sibling (by the Sadler's Wells stallion Milan) set a new record for the Derby Sale in June 2018 when knocked down for €365,000 to Aiden Murphy and M. V. Magnier. The sound-jumping Altior stays two and a quarter miles and will get further. He acts on soft going and usually races prominently. He has worn ear plugs and did so for the Queen Mother Champion Chase. His unbeaten run over hurdles and fences, which includes three successive victories at the Cheltenham Festival, now stretches to fourteen (he needs one more to match Sprinter Sacre's ten-race unbeaten start over fences). *Nicky Henderson*

ALTO DES MOTTES (FR) 8 b.g. Dream Well (FR) – Omance (FR) (Video Rock (FR)) [2017/18 c122, h–: h20.3g⁵ c20.1spu c30spu c23.4v⁵ c24.2vpu c23.4v³ Apr 14] rather sparely-made gelding: fair hurdler/fairly useful chaser at best, no form in 2017/18: stays 3¾m: acts on heavy going: wears headgear: tried in tongue tie. *Henry Hogarth*   c– h–

ALY

ALTRUISM (IRE) 8 b.g. Authorized (IRE) – Bold Assumption (Observatory (USA)) [2017/18 c135, h135: h17.3d^{pu} h17.2g h22.1s* Jul 22] workmanlike gelding: useful handicap hurdler: won at Cartmel (fifth course success, by 8 lengths from Gran Maestro) in July: similar form over fences: stays 2¾m: acts on soft and good to firm going: has worn headgear: usually races close up. *James Moffatt*   c–
h135

ALVARADO (IRE) 13 ch.g. Goldmark (USA) – Mrs Jones (IRE) (Roselier (FR)) [2017/18 c132§, h–: c24.2s^3 c26d^2 Dec 15] tall gelding: winning hurdler: useful handicap chaser: placed at Exeter in October and Doncaster in December: thorough stayer (twice in frame in Grand National/Scottish National): acts on good to firm and heavy going: has refused twice. *Fergal O'Brien*   c129 §
h–

ALWAYS ARCHIE 11 b.g. Silver Patriarch (IRE) – Angel Dust (FR) (Cadoudal (FR)) [2017/18 c120, h–: c25.3d^2 c23.6m^2 c22.6g^2 c24.2d^3 Sep 5] winning hurdler: fairly useful chaser: finished alone in point in February: stays 3m: acts on heavy going: tried in tongue tie: often travels strongly. *Tim Vaughan*   c115
h–

ALWAYS DU CERISIER (FR) 5 b.g. Apsis – Tyr Elissa (FR) (Smadoun (FR)) [2017/18 b16.7d^3 Apr 21] €26,000 3-y-o, £15,000 4-y-o: first foal: dam French 1½m winner: third both starts in Irish points: 8/1, also third in conditionals/amateur bumper at Bangor (5½ lengths behind Norman Stanley). *Donald McCain*   b90

ALWAYS LION (IRE) 8 b.g. Let The Lion Roar – Addie's Choice (IRE) (Norwich) [2017/18 c23.9g* May 21] lightly-raced winning hurdler: off 19 months, 7/4, won novice handicap at Market Rasen (by 1½ lengths from Beneficial Joe) on chasing debut: stays 3m. *Ben Pauling*   c122
h–

ALWAYS MANAGING 9 b.m. Oscar (IRE) – Sunshine Rays (Alflora (IRE)) [2017/18 h20.4g^4 h20.5g^5 Jul 27] modest handicap hurdler: likely to stay 3m: acts on good to firm going: tried in cheekpieces: usually wears tongue tie. *Oliver Sherwood*   h87

ALWAYS ON THE BALL (FR) 5 ch.g. Kapgarde (FR) – Etoile des Iles (FR) (Starborough) [2017/18 h19.9v^4 Apr 7] €35,000 3-y-o, £40,000 5-y-o: sixth foal: half-brother to French 17f chase winner South Pacific (by Martaline) and French 17f hurdle winner Turtle Bay (by Turtle Bowl): dam, French 17f hurdle winner, also 7f winner on Flat: runner-up twice in Irish points: 8/1, fourth in maiden at Uttoxeter (16¾ lengths behind Secret Legacy) on hurdling debut. *Charlie Longsdon*   h96

ALWAYS ON THE RUN (IRE) 8 br.g. Robin des Pres (FR) – Kerrys Cottage (IRE) (Leading Counsel (USA)) [2017/18 c134, h–: c19.4g^3 c20.1m^3 c23.8g^2 c22.6g^3 c23.8m Oct 11] winning hurdler: useful handicap chaser: barely stays 3m: acts on soft and good to firm going: usually wears hood: front runner/races prominently, often travels strongly. *Tom George*   c133
h–

ALWAYS RESOLUTE 7 b.g. Refuse To Bend (IRE) – Mad Annie (USA) (Anabaa (USA)) [2017/18 h16.6d^6 h21.3s^6 h19.3v h16.7s^4 h17d^5 h20.5g Apr 21] strong, close-coupled gelding: fair handicap hurdler: unproven beyond 2m: acts on soft going: tried in blinkers. *Brian Ellison*   h106

ALWAYS TIPSY 9 b.g. Dushyantor (USA) – French Pick (USA) (Johannesburg (USA)) [2017/18 c102, h111: c20d^{pu} c21.6v* Apr 16] smallish, lengthy gelding: multiple point winner: fair hurdler: fair form over fences: won handicap at Kelso in April: should stay 3m: acts on good to firm and heavy going. *N. W. Alexander*   c107
h–

ALYASAN (IRE) 7 ch.g. Sea The Stars (IRE) – Alaya (IRE) (Ela-Mana-Mou) [2017/18 h105: h16.2g^6 h20.3g h20.g^{pu} Jun 14] sturdy gelding: fair hurdler at best, no form in 2017/18: has worn headgear, including in 2017/18: has worn tongue tie: usually races towards rear. *David Thompson*   h–

ALYS KEYS (IRE) 6 b.m. Beneficial – African Keys (IRE) (Quws) [2017/18 h15.8d^F h16.2g^4 c16g^4 Aug 1] €10,000 3-y-o: third foal: half-sister to fair chaser Flash Tommie (2½m winner, by City Honours): dam unraced half-sister to smart hurdler/top-class chaser (stayed 25f) China Rock: little form over hurdles: tailed off in novice on chasing debut: tried in hood/tongue tie. *Patrick Griffin, Ireland*   c–
h–

ALYS ROCK (IRE) 9 gr.m. Medaaly – Rock Slide (IRE) (Bob Back (USA)) [2017/18 c97p, h77: c16.4g^5 h15.7g h18.7g Jun 20] rather sparely-made mare: modest handicap hurdler/winning chaser, below form in 2017/18: stays 21f, effective at shorter: acts on soft and good to firm going: tried in tongue tie: usually travels strongly/finds little. *Michael Appleby*   c71
h69

ALZ

ALZAMMAAR (USA) 7 b.g. Birdstone (USA) – Alma Mater (Sadler's Wells (USA)) [2017/18 h133: c20d^2 c19.2d^2 c25.2d* c19.9s^2 c20d^4 c31.8g Apr 21] good-topped gelding: useful hurdler: fairly useful form over fences: finished alone in maiden at Catterick in December: stays 25f: acts on good to firm and heavy going: has worn headgear/tongue tie: front runner/races prominently. *Sam England* c129 h–

AMADEUS ROX (FR) 4 b.g. Falco (USA) – Vittoria Vetra (Danehill Dancer (IRE)) [2017/18 h16.8d^2 h16.7g^4 h16d^2 h15.8g^4 h16d^3 h19.4s Jan 27] small gelding: modest maiden on Flat, stays 1¾m: fair form over hurdles: unproven beyond 17f: acts on good to soft going: in cheekpieces last 4 starts: has joined Alexandra Dunn. *Alan King* h103

AMADOUE (FR) 5 b.g. Smadoun (FR) – Aimessa du Berlais (FR) (Nikos) [2017/18 h16g^4 h16g^3 h17.7d^3 h19.8s^5 h16d h16.8v^{pu} Feb 22] €20,000 3-y-o: half-brother to French 17f-21f hurdle/chase winner Adieu Uat (by Lost World): dam, placed around 2m over hurdles in France, half-sister to dams of useful French chaser (stays 3¼m) Caid du Berlais and high-class French hurdler/useful chaser (stayed 2¾m) Bonito du Berlais: fair form over hurdles: may prove best short of 2½m: acts on soft going: often in hood: often races freely. *Tom Lacey* h103

AMALFI DOUG (FR) 8 gr.g. Network (GER) – Queissa (FR) (Saint Preuil (FR)) [2017/18 h98, b–: h16g^4 c17v^{pu} c19.4d Apr 22] modest form over hurdles: no promise over fences: left Tom Lacey after first start: unproven beyond 2m: acts on good to firm going: tried in hood: in tongue tie last 2 starts: front runner/races prominently: has joined Dan Skelton. *Sam Thomas* c– h95

AMANDA'S TEDDY 4 b.g. Dick Turpin (IRE) – Molly Pitcher (IRE) (Halling (USA)) [2017/18 b13.7g ab16g Feb 19] angular gelding: behind in bumpers/on Flat. *Pat Phelan* b–

AMANTO (GER) 8 b.g. Medicean – Amore (GER) (Lando (GER)) [2017/18 c122, h117: h16g^2 h18.5m^2 h16g^3 h19.6g^3 Oct 17] good-topped gelding: fair maiden hurdler nowadays: lightly-raced chaser: stays 19f: acts on soft going: usually wears headgear: has worn tongue tie, including in 2017/18. *Ali Stronge* c– h108

AMARANTH (IRE) 5 b.g. New Approach (IRE) – Kitty Kiernan (Pivotal) [2017/18 b16.4d Mar 16] has reportedly had breathing operation: tailed off in bumper (tongue tied): showed more in minor events on Flat. *Michael Scudamore* b–

AMARILLO ROSE (IRE) 6 ch.m. Flemensfirth (USA) – Compton Fair (Compton Place) [2017/18 h–, b77: b17.3g b16.5s h16.5m^4 h16g^4 h16d^{ur} h18.8g^3 h16s^2 h16g h18.8v^5 h20.2v^2 h19.5v Mar 19] modest bumper performer: modest maiden hurdler: stays 2½m: acts on heavy going: usually races close up. *Liam Lennon, Ireland* h92 b67

AMARONE GENTLEMAN (IRE) 6 b.g. Oscar (IRE) – Tigrera (IRE) (Helissio (FR)) [2017/18 b17v^3 b16.2s^6 Apr 27] has had breathing operation: no form in bumpers: wears tongue tie. *Susan Corbett* b–

AMBER FLUSH 9 b.m. Sir Harry Lewis (USA) – Sari Rose (FR) (Vertical Speed (FR)) [2017/18 c–, h86: h19.2g^{pu} h23m* h24g^6 h23.1s^{pu} Dec 2] poor handicap hurdler nowadays: won at Worcester in July: maiden chaser: stays 25f: acts on good to firm and good to soft going: has worn cheekpieces, including last 4 starts: tried in tongue tie: often races towards rear. *Clare Ellam* c– h81

AMBER GAMBLER (GER) 8 b.g. Doyen (IRE) – Auenglocke (GER) (Surumu (GER)) [2017/18 c113, h96: c22.6g^6 c20s^4 c24s^5 c19.9s* c20.2d^4 Apr 22] workmanlike gelding: winning hurdler: fairly useful handicap chaser: won at Haydock in March: stays 3m, stays at much shorter: acts on soft going. *Ian Williams* c116 h–

AMBERJAM (IRE) 8 b.g. Duke of Marmalade (IRE) – Makarova (IRE) (Sadler's Wells (USA)) [2017/18 c102, h99: c25.7d^2 c27.6s^{pu} h24.4s^2 h24.4s^2 h25s* h25v^5 h25d Apr 24] workmanlike gelding: fair handicap hurdler: won at Huntingdon in February: modest chaser: stays 27f: acts on heavy going: in cheekpieces last 5 starts: has worn tongue tie. *Lucy Wadham* c97 h109

AMBION LANE (IRE) 8 b.g. Scorpion (IRE) – Thrilling Prospect (IRE) (King's Ride) [2017/18 c–, h103: h23.1s h21.6v^5 c25.1v^{pu} c24.5v h26v^{pu} h23.1d Apr 24] modest maiden hurdler: no form over fences: stays 3m: best form on heavy going: wears headgear/tongue tie. *Victor Dartnall* c– h95

AMBIVALENT ABOUT 7 b.g. Josr Algarhoud (IRE) – Peppermint Plod (Kinglet) [2017/18 h59: h15.7m^5 h15.7g^{pu} May 22] no form over hurdles. *David Arbuthnot* h–

AMBLE INN 6 b.m. Sulamani (IRE) – Distant Florin (Medicean) [2017/18 h76, b67: h19.9g^5 h15.8d^6 h21v^{ur} Apr 27] poor form in bumpers/over hurdles. *Anthony Carson* h82

62

AMBRE DES MARAIS (FR) 8 ch.m. Network (GER) – Fee des Marais (FR) (Chamberlin (FR)) [2017/18 h16.8d* h19.6g* h16.8d* h16.5g² h16.3s^{pu} Jan 17] fair handicap hurdler: won at Newton Abbot (mares) in August, and Bangor and Worcester in September: stays 2½m: acts on heavy going: tried in hood: usually races in rear. *Johnny Farrelly* — **h108**

AMERICAN CRAFTSMAN (IRE) 4 gr.g. Mastercraftsman (IRE) – Quiet Mouse (USA) (Quiet American (USA)) [2017/18 h16d* h16s² h16s⁴ h19.3d Mar 25] half-brother to fairly useful hurdler/chaser Houston Dynimo (2m-23f winner, by Rock of Gibraltar) and fairly useful hurdler Bohemian Rhapsody (19f/2½m winner, by Galileo): fair on Flat, stays 1½m: fair form over hurdles: won juvenile at Wetherby in October: should stay 2½m: tried in cheekpieces: has joined Henry Oliver. *Jedd O'Keeffe* — **h112**

AMERICAN (FR) 8 b.g. Malinas (GER) – Grande Sultane (FR) (Garde Royale) [2017/18 c156p, h–: c26g^{pu} c25.3v² c26.3v Mar 16] tall, useful-looking gelding: winning hurdler: smart chaser: second in Cotswold Chase at Cheltenham (8 lengths behind Definitly Red) in January: stays 3m: acts on heavy going: usually travels strongly/jumps fluently. *Harry Fry* — **c153 + h–**

AMERICAN GIGOLO 6 b.g. Azamour (IRE) – Sadie Thompson (IRE) (King's Best (USA)) [2017/18 h109, b90: h16m* h15.7g² Nov 4] rather unfurnished gelding: bumper winner: fairly useful form over hurdles: won novice at Kempton in May: left Charlie Mann after that: raced around 2m: acts on good to firm going: in hood last 2 starts: tried in tongue tie: useful on Flat, stays 16.5f, completed hat-trick in 2018. *Harry Fry* — **h120**

AMERICAN HUSTLE (IRE) 6 b.m. Jeremy (USA) – Love In May (IRE) (City On A Hill (USA)) [2017/18 h16.8g^{pu} Aug 31] fair maiden on Flat, stays 1m: pulled up in novice on hurdling debut. *Brian Ellison* — **h–**

AMERICAN LIFE (FR) 11 b.g. American Post – Poplife (FR) (Zino) [2017/18 h93§: h23.1d² h25.3d² h23.1v³ h24v³ h26s⁴ h24v⁴ Mar 15] close-coupled gelding: modest handicap hurdler: stays 27f: acts on heavy going: wears headgear/tongue tie: often races towards rear: temperamental. *Oliver Greenall* — **h98 §**

AMERICAN TOM (FR) 7 b.g. American Post – Kirkla (FR) (Bikala) [2017/18 c140p, h–: c16v³ c20v² c16s³ c16v⁶ c16d Apr 26] winning hurdler: useful chaser: third in Poplar Square Chase at Naas (6½ lengths behind Ball d'Arc) in November and second in Kinloch Brae Chase at Thurles (9½ lengths behind A Toi Phil) in January: stays 2½m: acts on heavy going: in tongue tie last 3 starts. *W. P. Mullins, Ireland* — **c139 h–**

AMERTON LANE 6 b.g. Multiplex – Sunisa (IRE) (Daggers Drawn (USA)) [2017/18 h–, b–: h16.7v h15.8v h19.5s^{pu} c24.1d^{pu} Apr 21] sturdy gelding: no sign of ability. *Evan Williams* — **c– h–**

AM I APPROPRIATE 5 b.m. Kadastrof (FR) – Shuil Do (IRE) (Be My Native (USA)) [2017/18 b15.7d² b20.5d⁶ h21s^{pu} h16.6d h15.8s h20.7s h21s⁵ h19.6d^{pu} Apr 21] half-sister to modest hurdler/fairly useful chaser Time To Think (17f-2¾m winner) and modest 2½m chase winner Seventh Hussar (both by Alflora): dam (b68), ran once in bumper, half-sister to fair hurdler/useful chaser (19f-3m winner) The Outlier: second in mares bumper at Southwell: poor maiden hurdler: in cheekpieces last 2 starts. *Ben Pauling* — **h77 b87**

AMI DESBOIS (FR) 8 b.g. Dream Well (FR) – Baroya (FR) (Garde Royale) [2017/18 h142: c15.2d² c19.4s* c20.8m² c24.2v^{pu} Feb 3] good-topped gelding: useful hurdler: similar form over fences: won novices at Wetherby in November and December (2 ran): poor efforts last 2 starts: stays 3m: acts on heavy going: wears tongue tie: usually races close up. *Graeme McPherson* — **c136 h–**

AMIGO (FR) 11 b.g. Ballingarry (IRE) – Allez Y (FR) (Pistolet Bleu (IRE)) [2017/18 c111§, h–: c21.1s³ May 18] winning hurdler: useful chaser at best, has deteriorated considerably (ran mostly in points in 2017/18): stays 4m: acts on good to firm and heavy going: usually wears headgear/tongue tie: unreliable. *Mrs L. Braithwaite* — **c87 § h–**

AMILLIONTIMES (IRE) 10 b.g. Olden Times – Miss Million (IRE) (Roselier (FR)) [2017/18 c116, h–: c20.1g² c20.1g⁶ c23.8d⁴ c21.6g⁴ Nov 11] winning hurdler: fairly useful handicap chaser: stays 2¾m: acts on good to firm and good to soft going: wears tongue tie: usually races towards rear. *Jackie Stephen* — **c116 h–**

AMINABAD (FR) 8 b.g. Singspiel (IRE) – Amenapinga (FR) (Spinning World (USA)) [2017/18 c121, h–: c15.8g⁴ c20.1g Jul 6] winning hurdler: fairly useful chaser: stays 21f: acts on heavy going: tried in cheekpieces: wears tongue tie: usually races nearer last than first. *Patrick Griffin, Ireland* — **c113 h–**

AMIRAL COLLONGES (FR) 8 ch.g. Dom Alco (FR) – Idole Collonges (FR) (Brezzo (FR)) [2017/18 c107§, h–: c29.1m* c24.2g^{pu} c25g^{pu} c23.9d² c27.6s² c24d^{ur} Feb 8] sturdy gelding: winning hurdler: fair handicap chaser: won at Fakenham in May: stays 29f: acts on soft and good to firm going: wears cheekpieces: temperamental. *James Evans* — **c114 § h–**

AMI

AMIRR (IRE) 8 b.g. New Approach (IRE) – Dress Uniform (USA) (Red Ransom (USA)) [2017/18 h16g² h15.7g³ h16g h20g h25.5g^{pu} h15.7s Dec 17] dual money winner: fair form over hurdles: unproven beyond 2m: acts on good to firm and good to soft going: often races prominently. *Seamus Mullins* — **h102**

AMLOVI (IRE) 5 b.m. Court Cave (IRE) – Portanob (IRE) (Be My Native (USA)) [2017/18 b16.2s^{pu} Jan 29] €2,700 3-y-o: sister to a winning pointer, and closely related to fairly useful hurdler/useful chaser Risk A Fine (17f-21f winner, by Saffron Walden) and a winning pointer by Accordion: dam unraced: pulled up in bumper. *Adrian Wintle* — **b–**

A MONTMARTRE (FR) 6 b.m. Montmartre (FR) – Stefania (IRE) (Monsun (GER)) [2017/18 h104: h16.2g^F h16g Jul 10] fair hurdler at best, well held completed start in 2017/18: stays 2¼m: acts on soft and good to firm going. *Nick Mitchell* — **h–**

AMOOLA GOLD (GER) 5 b.g. Mamool (IRE) – Aughamore Beauty (IRE) (Dara Monarch) [2017/18 b93: b17s Apr 13] rangy gelding: fair form when runner-up on first of 2 starts in bumpers 14 months apart. *Dan Skelton* — **b–**

AMORE ALATO 9 b.g. Winged Love (IRE) – Sardagna (FR) (Medaaly) [2017/18 c135, h–: c26s⁴ Mar 24] strong gelding: winning hurdler: useful handicap chaser: not disgraced after long absence/change of stables only start in 2017/18: stays 3m: acts on soft going: tried in cheekpieces. *Dan Skelton* — **c125 h–**

AMOUR DE NUIT (IRE) 6 b.g. Azamour (IRE) – Umthoulah (IRE) (Unfuwain (USA)) [2017/18 h124: h16.8g² h16.8d⁴ h19.5d² h16g* h16.3d⁵ h16.6d³ h15.6s³ h16.8g^F Apr 18] good-bodied gelding: useful hurdler: won novices at Newton Abbot in September and Kempton (listed event, by 2¾ lengths from Listen To The Man) in October: second in Persian War Novices' Hurdle at Chepstow (1¼ lengths behind Poetic Rhythm) in between: stays 19f: acts on good to firm and good to soft going: in hood last 2 starts: often races prominently. *Paul Nicholls* — **h137**

AMOUR D'OR 7 b.m. Winged Love (IRE) – Diletia (Dilum (USA)) [2017/18 h–: h16.5s h16.5v³ h19.5s⁴ Apr 27] sturdy mare: modest handicap hurdler nowadays: stays 2¾m: acts on heavy going: in tongue tie last 5 starts. *Gail Haywood* — **h90**

AMRON KALI (IRE) 8 b.m. Kalanisi (IRE) – Glacial Snowboard (IRE) (Glacial Storm (USA)) [2017/18 h100: h20m* h23s* h19.1m³ h26.5m h25.8g⁵ h21.4g h21.6d h21s^{pu} h24.6s Apr 9] sturdy mare: has had breathing operation: fair handicap hurdler: won at Fakenham and Worcester (mares) in May: stays 23f: acts on good to firm and heavy going: tried in cheekpieces: wears tongue tie: waited with. *Paul Henderson* — **h104**

AMUSE ME 12 gr.g. Daylami (IRE) – Have Fun (Indian Ridge) [2017/18 c106, h111: c21.1g c20s⁶ c19.2d c19.9d⁶ c21.4d² Apr 22] sturdy gelding: winning hurdler: poor handicap chaser nowadays: left James Moffatt after third start: stays 2¾m: acts on good to firm and heavy going: has worn cheekpieces/tongue tie, including in 2017/18: often races in rear. *Lucinda Egerton* — **c77 h–**

AMYBELL 6 ch.m. Black Sam Bellamy (IRE) – Ninna Nanna (FR) (Garde Royale) [2017/18 h16v h18v h16v Feb 26] €18,000 3-y-o: fourth foal: closely related to 3 winners, including fairly useful hurdler/useful chaser Ballycross (21f-3m winner) and bumper winner/useful hurdler Jacks Last Hope (2m-3m winner) (both by King's Theatre): dam second at 1¼m in France: little show in bumpers/over hurdles. *S. Wilson, Ireland* — **h–**

AMZAC MAGIC 6 b.g. Milan – Queen's Banquet (Glacial Storm (USA)) [2017/18 h19s⁵ h18.5d³ Apr 24] €16,000 3-y-o: sixth foal: brother to bumper winner Flame of Desire, and half-brother to fair hurdler Sara's Smile (2m/17f winner, by Presenting) and fair hurdler/chaser Stormyisland Ahead (2m-3m winner, by Turtle Island): dam (b85), temperamental, lightly raced in bumpers/over hurdles: point winner: poor form in maiden hurdles: in hood second start. *Jack R. Barber* — **h84**

ANDHAAR 12 b.g. Bahri (USA) – Deraasaat (Nashwan (USA)) [2017/18 h85§: h23.3g⁶ h22.7g^{pu} h23.9s Apr 25] rather leggy gelding: poor handicap hurdler nowadays: stays 3m: acts on soft going: has worn headgear, including in 2017/18: tried in tongue tie: often races towards rear: ungenuine. *N. W. Alexander* — **h73 §**

AND THE NEW (IRE) 7 b.g. Kalanisi (IRE) – Wheredidthemoneygo (IRE) (Anshan) [2017/18 b112: h16.3d³ h16.6s* h16.6d³ Feb 8] useful bumper performer: fairly useful form over hurdles: won novice at Doncaster in January: improved again when third in similar event there month later: will stay at least 2¼m: in hood last 2 starts. *Johnny Farrelly* — **h128**

ANEMOI (FR) 4 b.g. Manduro (GER) – Recambe (IRE) (Cape Cross (IRE)) [2017/18 b13.7s⁴ b16g⁵ Apr 21] third foal: half-brother to fairly useful French hurdler Autignac (2¼m winner, by Solon): dam French 1¼m-14.5f winner: fairly useful form in bumpers: won at Huntingdon in January. *Harry Whittington* — **b95**

ANI

AN FEAR CIUIN (IRE) 7 b.g. Galileo (IRE) – Potion (Pivotal) [2017/18 h92: h20.2g² h20.2m² h16.2g² h20.2g⁴ h16.2d² h16.2d h16.2g Oct 28] fair maiden hurdler: stays 2½m: acts on good to firm going: tried in cheekpieces: front runner/races prominently. *R. Mike Smith* — **h105**

ANGE DES MALBERAUX (FR) 8 b.g. Michel Georges – Petite Baie (FR) (Alamo Bay (USA)) [2017/18 h90: h16.2g h17.2s* h17.2d⁴ h21.2g³ h16.2s h23.8g³ h19.9s h25.8s h23.8d³ h19.9v² h20.6v^pu Apr 14] modest handicap hurdler: won at Cartmel in July: stays 3m: acts on heavy going: wears headgear. *James Ewart* — **h95**

ANGEL MOON 5 gr.m. Fair Mix (IRE) – Pougatcheva (FR) (Epervier Bleu) [2017/18 b15.8v⁵ Jan 3] seventh foal: half-sister to fair hurdler The Big Dipper (3m winner, by Alflora): dam (c86/h102), 2m-19f hurdle winner, half-sister to fair hurdler/useful chaser (stayed 2¾m) Noisetine: 11/1, fifth in mares bumper at Ludlow (20½ lengths behind Sea Story). *Fergal O'Brien* — **b68**

ANGEL OF HARLEM 5 b.m. Presenting – Whoops A Daisy (Definite Article) [2017/18 b–: h20.5s⁴ h17.7v² h19.9v⁵ h20.5v⁵ Apr 1] modest form over hurdles: usually leads. *Mark Bradstock* — **h96**

ANGEL OF ROME (IRE) 4 gr.f. Mastercraftsman (IRE) – Bright Sapphire (IRE) (Galileo (IRE)) [2017/18 h17.7d⁶ Sep 10] fair maiden on Flat, stays 8.5f: 20/1, sixth in juvenile at Fontwell (19½ lengths behind Lord E) on hurdling debut. *Richard Hughes* — **h76**

ANGELS ANTICS 5 b.m. Schiaparelli (GER) – Safari Run (IRE) (Supreme Leader) [2017/18 b15.8g² h15.8s³ h15.8v* h16.3d⁴ h18.9v² h19.8s⁴ h16.8s^pu h20.3g⁶ Apr 19] strong mare: third foal: half-sister to bumper winner Angel Face (by Kayf Tara): dam (c118/h128) 2m-2½m hurdle/chase winner: green when second in maiden bumper at Ffos Las: fairly useful hurdler: won novice at same course in November: second in listed mares novice at Haydock (neck behind Cap Soleil) in December: should stay 2½m: acts on heavy going: often races prominently. *Nigel Twiston-Davies* — **h122 b78**

ANGEL'S ENVY 6 b.m. Yeats (IRE) – Caoba (Hernando (FR)) [2017/18 h–, b64: h19.9g^pu h20.6g⁶ h23.8g⁶ h23.8g⁶ h17d⁶ Mar 31] poor maiden hurdler: stays 3m: tried in hood/tongue tie. *Iain Jardine* — **h80**

ANGINOLA (IRE) 9 b.m. Kodiac – Lady Montekin (Montekin) [2017/18 h17.2d⁴ h16.2g h17.2s⁶ h22.1d⁶ h19.9g⁴ h16d⁴ h19.9d^pu Nov 18] poor handicap hurdler: stays 2¼m: acts on soft going: usually wears headgear. *Julia Brooke* — **h60**

ANGUINO (FR) 5 b.g. Lucarno (USA) – Anguilla (GER) (Trempolino (USA)) [2017/18 h16v⁶ h16.9s h16g⁵ h19.7s^pu h15.6s Feb 3] once-raced on Flat: modest form over hurdles: well held only start over fences: left Thomas Cooper after third start: best effort at 2m: usually races towards rear. *Patrick Holmes* — **c– h98**

ANGUS MILAN (IRE) 9 b.g. Milan – Lasado (IRE) (Jurado (USA)) [2017/18 c124, h–: c24s c25d c17v c20v³ c21.5v* c20.4s² c21.2v⁵ Apr 15] winning hurdler: fairly useful handicap chaser: won at Ayr in March: stays 2¾m: acts on heavy going: tried in cheekpieces: wears tongue tie: often races prominently. *Noel C. Kelly, Ireland* — **c121 h–**

ANIBALE FLY (FR) 8 b.g. Assessor (IRE) – Nouba Fly (FR) (Chamberlin (FR)) [2017/18 c151, h–: c19.5s⁵ c16.5s c24.5d* c24s^F c26.3v³ c34.3s⁴ Apr 14] — **c164 h–**

'It's Aldaniti in the lead but being pressed now by Spartan Missile. It's Aldaniti from Spartan Missile and here comes John Thorne, fifty-four-year-old John Thorne putting in a storming finish. It's Aldaniti from Spartan Missile. Aldaniti is gonna win it ... at the line, Aldaniti wins the National!'

The 1981 renewal—one of the best illustrations of what the Grand National can produce by way of entertainment, drama and stories of courage—has rightly entered racing folklore. Winning jockey Bob Champion made a triumphant return, after overcoming testicular cancer, on an injury-plagued Aldaniti, but the race was also notable for the performance of John Thorne, a fifty-four-year-old amateur rider, and a grandfather, on Spartan Missile, a horse he also bred, owned and trained. Having a long-held dream of riding the winner of the Grand National, Thorne declined an offer from then-champion jockey John Francome to ride big-race favourite Spartan Missile, on whom he put up 3 lb overweight which, coupled with a serious error jumping the eighteenth, and the second fence on the final circuit, probably cost him the race. Spartan Missile made ground relentlessly in the straight, but four lengths separated him from Aldaniti at the line. Just a month earlier, Spartan

Paddy Power Chase, Leopardstown—another very valuable handicap goes to Anibale Fly, who is already in command at the last; 2015 runner-up Ucello Conti (No.6) fills that spot again

Missile had finished fourth in the Cheltenham Gold Cup, one of only nine horses to have made the frame in both the Gold Cup and Grand National in the same season during the *Chasers & Hurdlers* era. Others to have done so are West Tip, Garrison Savannah, Docklands Express, Dubacilla, Rough Quest, Royal Auclair and Hedgehunter. The latest to join this select group is the Tony Martin-trained Anibale Fly, who achieved the feat in the most recent season—though with nothing like the attendant publicity—when finishing third at Cheltenham and fourth at Aintree.

The *Chasers & Hurdlers 2015/16* essay on Anibale Fly detailed his eye-catching novice hurdle campaign and his well-backed win in the Coral Handicap Hurdle at the Punchestown Festival. After adding a maiden chase at Navan and a Grade 3 novices' chase at Naas to his tally the following season, Anibale Fly began the latest one at Down Royal in early-November when he was sent off at 10/1 in a seven-runner field for a Grade 2 contest for second-season chasers which included Disko, who had beaten Anibale Fly in the previous season's Champion Novices' Chase at Punchestown, and the PWC Champion Chase winner A Toi Phil. A rusty Anibale Fly could finish only a well-held fifth, with the Timeform report describing Anibale Fly as a horse that 'remains low-mileage and starts this season on an attractive mark based on last season's novice efforts, one to note should his shrewd connections tackle a top-end handicap at some stage'. Following another modest run over two miles at Fairyhouse, it was in just such a race that Anibale Fly produced his first meaningful effort of the campaign. Stepped up a mile in trip, Anibale Fly turned in a career-best effort to run out a most convincing winner of the Paddy Power Chase at Leopardstown, one of the top handicap chases in the Irish calendar. It is a race in which his trainer has done well, having won it with Newbay Prop in 2007 and Living Next Door in 2014, and in the year of its twenty-first anniversary it was worth a record €200,000. After racing in mid-division, Anibale Fly made headway under Donagh Meyler from three out and was produced to lead early in the straight to win in good style, staying on well. The winning jockey, who had also ridden the horse on two of his three bumper starts in the 2014/15 season, was replaced by Barry Geraghty for Anibale Fly's next start, in the Irish Gold Cup. The race reached a dramatic conclusion, with Edwulf prevailing from Outlander in a tight finish following the late departure of Killultagh Vic, the last-named having made smooth headway and seemingly in command when falling at the last. Anibale Fly and Geraghty also failed to complete, though that pair were making little impression on the leaders when departing in spectacular fashion two out.

Anibale Fly's next start came in the Cheltenham Gold Cup nearly six weeks later, a race that had hints of the Denman against Kauto Star duel of ten years earlier, with Native River and Might Bite dominating much of the pre-race coverage and, in this case, the post-race analysis, too. That pair had the contest to themselves from the top of the hill, but very much catching the eye in third was Anibale Fly. He proved well suited by the thorough stamina test, tackling a longer trip than any he had faced before, and he might have got closer still but for a couple of minor jumping errors coming down the hill for the last time. Anibale Fly looked as if he would be an interesting runner if taking his chance in the Grand National from a BHA mark of 159, which looked lenient on his Gold Cup form, especially as he had shaped as if he would stay extreme distances. Having also had his chance highlighted by outgoing BHA head of handicapping Phil Smith ('If I could re-handicap Anibale Fly I'd have him 9 lb higher'), Anibale Fly was well backed in the run up to the race, eventually sent off the 10/1 co-second favourite.

Taking a circuitous route around the Grand National course didn't appear to hinder the J.P. McManus-owned 2012 runner-up Sunnyhillboy—who was only collared in the closing strides by Neptune Collonges after breaking down late on—but Barry Geraghty's similar, round-the-houses approach to the most recent renewal seemed detrimental to Anibale Fly's chance. Whereas Sunnyhillboy—who raced in the same emerald green and yellow hoops—jumped exuberantly when given a clear sight of his fences by Richie McLernon, Anibale Fly's generally sound jumping technique did not appear to warrant the tactics adopted. When he made a mistake at the fifth-last, which left him with plenty to do, he was up against it. With Geraghty keeping his mount well away from most of his rivals down the back straight on both circuits, he added as much as a hundred yards to the race distance that Anibale Fly covered, according to Timeform calculations. Anibale Fly did very well to finish as close as he did in fourth, eleven and a quarter lengths behind Tiger Roll and Pleasant Company. Of the last ten Grand National winners, only Pineau de Re was steered noticeably wide, with Ballabriggs (2011), Many Clouds (2015) and One For Arthur (2017) all recent examples of winners whose connections plotted a path towards the inside. Geraghty himself knows what it takes to win the Grand National, having guided Monty's Pass round the inner to win the 2003 renewal. However, his record has been inconsistent since; he was placed on four of his seven rides between 2004 and 2010, but ninth (twice) had been his best finish between 2011 and 2017.

Anibale Fly (FR) (b.g. 2010)
- Assessor (IRE) (b 1989)
  - Niniski (b 1976)
    - Nijinsky
    - Virginia Hills
  - Dingle Bay (b 1976)
    - Petingo
    - Border Bounty
- Nouba Fly (FR) (b 2001)
  - Chamberlin (b 1978)
    - Green Dancer
    - On The Wing
  - Joie de Cotte (b 1997)
    - Lute Antique
    - Vanille de Cotte

Anibale Fly's pedigree was covered in *Chasers & Hurdlers 2015/16*. Since then, his year-younger half-brother Boubafly (by Le Balafre) has had three runs for the Martin yard but has yet to show much form. Their unraced dam Nouba Fly is now also dam of a winner in France at up to twenty-one furlongs, Calgary Fly (by Great Pretender), successful over both hurdles and fences for Guillaume Macaire. The rating achieved by Anibale Fly in the Gold Cup drew him level with My Way de Solzen at the head of the rankings of Assessor's progeny, with Reve de Sivola just behind, that trio some way clear. Coo Star Sivola—winner of the Ultima Handicap Chase at the Cheltenham Festival, and two years younger than Anibale Fly—is one candidate who might bridge the gap over the coming seasons. Anibale Fly stays four and a quarter miles and acts on heavy going. *A. J. Martin, Ireland*

ANIF (IRE) 4 b.g. Cape Cross (IRE) – Cadenza (FR) (Dansili) [2017/18 h16d^{pu} Nov 10] **h–** fair on Flat, stays 9.5f: pulled up in juvenile on hurdling debut (tongue tied). *Jean-Rene Auvray*

ANIKNAM (FR) 8 b.g. Nickname (FR) – Kelle Home (FR) (Useful (FR)) [2017/18 **h80** h16s^{pu} h16.2v^{pu} h18.9v^6 h16v h19.9v^F h23.3v^{pu} h19.3v Apr 17] fairly useful hurdler at best, little show in 2017/18 after 2-year absence: stays 2½m: best form on soft/heavy going: has worn hood: usually races towards rear. *Philip Kirby*

ANI

ANIMATED HERO 5 b.g. Sakhee's Secret – Society (IRE) (Barathea (IRE)) [2017/18 b16.8g⁵ b16.4g⁴ ab16.3g⁶ h16.8vᵖᵘ Apr 13] fifth foal: half-brother to 1m-11f winner Hurlingham (by Halling): dam 1¼m winner: fair form in bumpers: best effort when fourth at Newcastle in November: pulled up in novice on hurdling debut: in tongue tie last 3 starts. *Rebecca Menzies* — h– b85

AN LAOCH (IRE) 6 b.g. Flemensfirth (USA) – Petite Ballerina (IRE) (Oscar (IRE)) [2017/18 h97: h19.9g⁵ c23.4d² c26.3g² c16.3g² c23.8gᵖᵘ c16.9d³ c23.9d Apr 22] point winner: maiden hurdler: fair form in chases: stays 3¼m: acts on good to soft going: tried in cheekpieces: wears tongue tie. *Chris Grant* — c108 h–

ANNDARROW (IRE) 5 b.m. Beat Hollow – Kim Hong (IRE) (Charnwood Forest (IRE)) [2017/18 h16g h18.5sᵖᵘ h16.5g³ h15.3v⁵ h23.9m² Apr 25] fifth foal: closely related to useful hurdler Minella Charmer (2½m winner, by King's Theatre): dam unraced half-sister to smart hurdler (2m-21f winner) William Henry and useful hurdler (2½m-3m winner) Electric Concorde: modest form over hurdles: best effort at 3m: acts on good to firm going. *Philip Hobbs* — h88

ANNIE ANGEL (IRE) 7 b.m. King's Theatre (IRE) – Lady Rene (IRE) (Leading Counsel (USA)) [2017/18 b16s² b17.7d³ h19.5d⁵ h21v⁶ h20.5s Jan 17] £75,000 6-y-o: second foal: closely related to bumper winner/fairly useful hurdler Myztique (2¼m winner, by High Chaparral), stayed 2¾m: dam unraced sister to fair hurdler/useful chaser (2½m-3¼m winner) Dun Doire and fairly useful staying hurdler Elbow High: won Irish mares maiden point on debut: fair form in bumpers: better effort when second in mares event at Worcester: fair form over hurdles: best effort when fifth in mares novice at Chepstow in October. *Amanda Perrett* — h102 b89

ANNIE PROBUS 5 ch.m. Geordieland (FR) – Probus Lady (Good Times (ITY)) [2017/18 b16d b16.8v Dec 8] third foal: dam little sign of ability: no form in bumpers: tried in hood. *Chris Down* — b–

ANNIE'SBOYDAVE 8 b.g. Passing Glance – Earcomesannie (IRE) (Anshan) [2017/18 h–: h23.3dᵖᵘ h22g⁴ h23gᵖᵘ h23.9mᵖᵘ h25.5gᵖᵘ h24s³ h26sᶠ Feb 23] angular gelding: poor maiden hurdler: in headgear last 3 starts: wore tongue tie: dead. *Peter Pritchard* — h65

ANN MARIES REJECT (IRE) 9 br.m. Sendawar (IRE) – Charlestown Lass (Bob Back (USA)) [2017/18 h74: h21.6g h18.5v⁴ h23.9m⁶ Nov 1] failed to complete both starts in points: poor maiden hurdler: stays 23f: acts on good to firm going: tried in cheekpieces. *Carroll Gray* — h59

ANN SCOTT (IRE) 7 b.m. Mr Dinos (IRE) – Jinxies Girl (IRE) (Beckett (IRE)) [2017/18 c23.6sᵖᵘ Apr 27] €300 3-y-o, £2,400 4-y-o: first foal: dam unraced half-sister to useful hurdler/chaser (2½m-3m winner) Uimhiraceathair: winning pointer: pulled up in novice hunter on chasing debut (tongue tied). *Mrs Sherree Lean* — c–

ANOTHER BILL (IRE) 8 ch.g. Beneficial – Glacier Lilly (IRE) (Glacial Storm (USA)) [2017/18 h124: c20d h22.8v⁶ h24.4d Feb 8] fairly useful hurdler at best, no form in 2017/18 (including on chasing debut): stays 23f: acts on soft going: tried in cheekpieces: often races towards rear. *Nicky Richards* — c– h–

ANOTHER CRICK 5 b.g. Arcadio (GER) – Suetsu (IRE) (Toulon) [2017/18 b88: b16.7g⁵ b15.8g⁶ ab16g² h16.8v⁴ h16.5s² h16.3v³ h15.3v⁵ Mar 8] fair form in bumpers/over hurdles: wears hood: often races in rear. *Noel Williams* — h109 b88

ANOTHER DAY DONE (IRE) 7 b.g. Davorin (JPN) – Perfect Memory (IRE) (Nashwan (USA)) [2017/18 b16m⁵ b16g⁵ b16.2g⁴ Jul 6] maiden pointer: poor form in bumpers: has worn hood. *Stuart Crawford, Ireland* — b73

ANOTHER EMOTION (FR) 6 gr.g. Turgeon (USA) – Line Perle (FR) (Gold And Steel (FR)) [2017/18 h16v² h20v* Apr 15] £55,000 4-y-o: sixth foal: half-brother to fairly useful French hurdler/chaser Linodargent (19f/2½m winner, by Kendargent): dam, French 19f hurdle winner, half-sister to very smart French chaser Grey Jack and useful chaser Mondial Jack, both stayed 25f: runner-up on second start in Irish points: fair form over hurdles: won novice at Ffos Las in April: will stay beyond 2½m: likely to progress further. *Warren Greatrex* — h113 p

ANOTHER FRONTIER (IRE) 7 b.g. Darsi (FR) – Scent With Love (IRE) (Winged Love (IRE)) [2017/18 h118: h24.7d⁵ h21.1sᵖᵘ c21.7s c24d* c23.4s² Mar 23] sturdy gelding: fairly useful handicap hurdler: similar form over fences: won handicap at Doncaster in February: stays 25f: acts on heavy going: has worn headgear, including last 4 starts: usually races prominently. *Nigel Twiston-Davies* — c116 h114

ANOTHER GO (IRE) 5 gr.g. Strategic Prince – Golden Rose (GER) (Winged Love (IRE)) [2017/18 h16.8v³ Apr 13] fairly useful at one time on Flat, stays 1¼m: well beaten in novice on hurdling debut. *Sally Haynes* — **h68**

ANOTHER HERO (IRE) 9 b.g. Kalanisi (IRE) – Storm Front (IRE) (Strong Gale) [2017/18 c135, h–: c26g* Apr 18] workmanlike gelding: winning hurdler: useful handicap chaser: won at Cheltenham (by short head from Singlefarmpayment) in April after 12-month absence: stays 3¼m: acts on good to firm and heavy going: tried in cheekpieces/tongue tie. *Jonjo O'Neill* — **c136 h–**

ANOTHER JOURNEY 9 b.g. Rail Link – Singasongosixpence (Singspiel (IRE)) [2017/18 c–, h–: h16.7s⁶ h16.8s h15.8d h16.7g⁶ h19.6g⁵ c16dpu h16.3gpu Oct 21] big gelding: fairly useful handicap hurdler, out of form in 2017/18: maiden chaser: in headgear last 4 starts: front runner/races prominently. *Sarah-Jayne Davies* — **c– h76**

ANOTHER MATTIE (IRE) 11 b.g. Zagreb (USA) – Silver Tassie (FR) (Kaldounevees (FR)) [2017/18, h115: h24.3vpu h24.3v⁴ h24.6spu h24.3v h22.7v⁴ h24.3v³ h20.9v³ Apr 7] workmanlike gelding: fair handicap hurdler: maiden chaser: stays 3m: acts on heavy going: tried in cheekpieces: wears tongue tie. *N. W. Alexander* — **c– h109**

ANOTHER RATTLER (IRE) 9 br.g. Mountain High (IRE) – Heather's Perk (IRE) (Executive Perk) [2017/18 h16.4d h15.8d⁶ Jul 30] modest hurdler, no form in 2017/18: left P. J. Rothwell after first start: unproven beyond 17f: best form on heavy going: has worn headgear, including in 2017/18. *Joanne Foster* — **h–**

ANOTHER STOWAWAY (IRE) 6 b.g. Stowaway – Another Pet (IRE) (Un Desperado (FR)) [2017/18 b92: h20gur h20d² h24d² h19.4s² h24.7spu Apr 13] well-made gelding: will make a chaser: third in Irish maiden point: fairly useful form over hurdles, second in maidens/novice: stays 3m: acts on soft going: in tongue tie last 2 starts: often races prominently. *Tom George* — **h122**

ANOTHER SUNSHINE 7 b.m. Kayf Tara – Sunshine Rays (Alflora (IRE)) [2017/18 b78: b16spu May 17] mid-division at best in bumpers: in hood last 2 starts. *Nick Mitchell* — **b–**

ANOTHER VENTURE (IRE) 7 ch.g. Stowaway – Hard Luck (IRE) (Old Vic) [2017/18 h120: c22.5s⁵ c24.2s² c30.7v⁶ c23.6v* c25.2s³ c23.8s³ c24v⁴ Mar 17] tall, strong gelding: fairly useful hurdler: useful handicap chaser: won at Chepstow (novice) and Hereford in January, idling both times: stays 25f: acts on heavy going: in cheekpieces last 2 starts: front runner/races prominently. *Kim Bailey* — **c132 h–**

ANSEANACHAI CLISTE (IRE) 10 b.g. Bach (IRE) – Susies Benefit (IRE) (Beneficial) [2017/18 c26.2g⁶ c23.5g⁵ c24s³ c29s c24.1v c28.5sur c24.7v² c30s Apr 28] fair handicap chaser: left S. McConville after second start, Ronan M. P. McNally after fifth: stays 29f: acts on heavy going: wears headgear. *Alan A. H. Wells, Ireland* — **c110**

ANTARTICA DE THAIX (FR) 8 gr.m. Dom Alco (FR) – Nouca de Thaix (FR) (Subotica (FR)) [2017/18 c145, h123+: c23.9g² c20.2vF c22.7s² c19.9spu Feb 22] good-topped mare: fairly useful hurdler: useful chaser: second in listed mares events at Market Rasen and Leicester: stays 23f: acts on good to firm and heavy going: has worn hood, including on return in 2017/18: wears tongue tie: front runner/races prominently. *Paul Nicholls* — **c141 h–**

ANTEROS (IRE) 10 b.g. Milan – Sovereign Star (IRE) (Taufan (USA)) [2017/18 c120§, h127§: c21.2d³ c24.1d² h23.9gF h25.3s² h24s⁵ h20.3s⁶ Jan 1] lengthy gelding: fairly useful handicap hurdler: second in listed event won by Thomas Campbell at Cheltenham in November: maiden chaser: stays 25f: acts on heavy going: usually wears headgear: wears tongue tie: often races in rear: unreliable. *Sophie Leech* — **c111 § h127 §**

ANTEY (GER) 5 b.g. Lord of England (GER) – Achinora (Sleeping Indian) [2017/18 h16d³ h20v⁶ h16v² h20v* h16s* Apr 27] fairly useful form on Flat in France, won 13.5f maiden: useful form over hurdles: won maiden at Cork in March and novice at Punchestown (by nose from Shady Operator) in April: stays 2½m: acts on heavy going. *W. P. Mullins, Ireland* — **h135**

ANTIPHONY (IRE) 7 b.g. Royal Anthem (USA) – Hazel's Glory (IRE) (Mister Lord (USA)) [2017/18 c100, h100: c16.5g³ c16.5g⁵ c19.4mpu Jul 16] rangy gelding: point winner: maiden hurdler/chaser: fair at best: stays 2¼m: acts on heavy going: usually wears hood: in tongue tie last 3 starts. *Tom Weston* — **c89 h–**

ANTON CHIGURH 9 b.g. Oasis Dream – Barathiki (Barathea (IRE)) [2017/18 h16.7spu May 20] modest on Flat nowadays, stays 9.5f: maiden hurdler, too free only outing in 2017/18. *Nikki Evans* — **h–**

ANT

ANTON DOLIN (IRE) 10 ch.g. Danehill Dancer (IRE) – Ski For Gold (Shirley Heights) [2017/18 h91§: h16.7g h15.7g⁶ h16.7³ h18.7g² h16g⁴ h15.8d³ h18.7m⁵ h16.7g⁴ h19.6g³ h19.6g³ h19.6g⁵ h19.9s^pu Oct 19] modest handicap hurdler: stays 2½m: acts on soft and good to firm going: has worn headgear: unreliable. *Michael Mullineaux* — **h89 §**

ANTONY (FR) 8 b.g. Walk In The Park (IRE) – Melanie du Chenet (FR) (Nikos) [2017/18 c131, h–: c21.6g³ c23.8g⁵ c23.8d^pu h25.8v⁴ c21.6g* Apr 20] good-topped gelding: winning hurdler: useful handicap chaser: won at Fontwell (by 13 lengths from Bishops Court) in April: stays 3m: acts on soft and good to firm going: tried in cheekpieces. *Gary Moore* — **c131 h–**

ANTUNES 4 b.g. Nathaniel (IRE) – Aigrette Garzette (IRE) (Peintre Celebre (USA)) [2017/18 h16.7s² h16.3s³ Mar 24] well-made gelding: fair maiden on Flat, stays 11f: fair form over hurdles: better effort when second in juvenile at Market Rasen in February. *Dan Skelton* — **h107**

ANY MINUTE NOW (IRE) 4 br.g. Getaway (GER) – Third Wish (IRE) (Second Empire (IRE)) [2017/18 b16.7v h15.7v⁶ Apr 27] well held in bumper/novice hurdle. *Charlie Longsdon* — **h– b–**

ANY SECOND NOW (IRE) 6 b.g. Oscar (IRE) – Pretty Neat (IRE) (Topanoora) [2017/18 h138p: c20s² c20s² c17d² c17s³ c20.4s Mar 13] rangy gelding: useful hurdle winner: useful form over fences: second in maiden at Navan (4¼ lengths behind Invitation Only) and Racing Post Novices' Chase at Leopardstown (11 lengths behind Footpad) in December: stays 2½m: acts on heavy going. *T. M. Walsh, Ireland* — **c144 h–**

ANYTHINGMAYHAPPEN (IRE) 7 b.g. Publisher (USA) – Wild Coast (IRE) (Gothland (FR)) [2017/18 h89, b64: h22g^pu h23.3d^pu Sep 24] modest hurdler at best, no form in 2017/18: should stay 2¾m+: acts on good to soft going: front runner/races prominently. *Jeremy Scott* — **h–**

ANYTIME WILL DO (IRE) 5 b.g. Scorpion (IRE) – Pellerossa (IRE) (Good Thyne (USA)) [2017/18 b16.5m* Apr 25] £10,000 3-y-o: fifth foal: half-brother to fair hurdler Roving Lad (2¼m-21f winner) and a winning pointer (both by Vinnie Roe): dam, winning pointer, half-sister to fair hurdler/fairly useful chaser (stayed 25f) Presentandcorrect: second when fell 2 out in point: 7/2, looked good prospect when won bumper at Taunton by 3 lengths from Newtown Boy, storming clear. *Dan Skelton* — **b103 p**

APACHEE PRINCE (IRE) 9 b.g. Indian Danehill (IRE) – Wheredidthemoneygo (IRE) (Anshan) [2017/18 c98, h–: h20g h22.4g⁴ h23.9d⁵ h20.1d² h20.2d* h19.9g⁵ h22.7g⁴ h24.1d⁶ h23.8g² h23.8g⁴ c23.8d^ur Jan 1] modest handicap hurdler: won at Perth (conditional) in September: maiden chaser: stays 3m: acts on good to soft going: has worn headgear: wears tongue tie. *Alistair Whillans* — **c– h88**

APACHE JACK (IRE) 10 b.g. Oscar (IRE) – Cailin Supreme (IRE) (Supreme Leader) [2017/18 c98, h–: c21.2s³ c23.8s^pu h16.2s h24v h23v⁴ h24s⁴ h19.5v h19.3d* Mar 25] fairly useful handicap hurdler: won at Carlisle in March: fair handicap chaser: stays 3m: acts on heavy going: has worn headgear, including last 4 starts. *Stuart Crawford, Ireland* — **c111 h126**

APACHE PILOT 10 br.g. Indian Danehill (IRE) – Anniejo (Presenting) [2017/18 c86, h–: c24.2g² c24.2g⁴ c24.2g³ c21.4d^ro Apr 22] maiden hurdler: modest handicap chaser: stays 25f: acts on soft going: usually wears headgear: wears tongue tie: usually responds generously to pressure. *Maurice Barnes* — **c88 h–**

APACHE SONG 5 ch.m. Mount Nelson – Pantita (Polish Precedent (USA)) [2017/18 h106: h16.7g* h16.2g² h16v⁶ h15.7v^bd h15.3v* h20.3g Apr 19] sturdy mare: fairly useful hurdler: won mares novice at Market Rasen in September and mares handicap at Wincanton in March: unproven beyond 2m: acts on heavy going: often races prominently. *James Eustace* — **h124**

APASIONADO (GER) 7 ch.g. Mamool (IRE) – Api Sa (IRE) (Zinaad) [2017/18 h130, b97: h16.7s^pu Feb 18] sturdy gelding: bumper winner: useful hurdler: ran poorly only start in 2017/18: best form at 2m: acted on good to soft going: dead. *Stuart Edmunds* — **h–**

APOLLO CREED (IRE) 6 b.g. Vinnie Roe (IRE) – Just Cassandra (IRE) (Eurobus) [2017/18 h98: h19.3s³ h23.9v* h22.8v⁶ h25s Apr 8] fairly useful form over hurdles: won novice at Ffos Las in November. *Evan Williams* — **h115**

APPARITION (IRE) 4 br.g. Dream Ahead (USA) – Bluebell Park (USA) (Gulch (USA)) [2017/18 h16v¹ h16g* h16s³ h16.4s⁶ h16v h16.2d Apr 26] useful-looking gelding: half-brother to useful hurdler Manhattan Swing (winner around 2m, by Invincible Spirit), stays 21f, and fair hurdler/chaser Solar Heat (17f/2¼m winner, by Jeremy): useful on Flat, stays 1½m: fair form over hurdles: won juvenile maiden at Thurles in October: raced only at 2m: acts on soft going. *Joseph Patrick O'Brien, Ireland* — **h110**

APPLAUS (GER) 6 b.g. Tiger Hill (IRE) – All About Love (GER) (Winged Love (IRE)) **c119**
[2017/18 h108: c15.9v^{pu} c16.3s^2 c15.7v^3 c16.3s^4 c15.2d* h16.4v^3 Apr 14] fair handicap **h99**
hurdler: fairly useful form over fences: won handicap at Wetherby in March: unproven
beyond 2m: acts on heavy going: has worn headgear, including last 5 starts: tried in tongue
tie: often races prominently. *Micky Hammond*

APPLE OF OUR EYE 8 b.g. Passing Glance – Apple Anthem (True Song) [2017/18 **c118**
h119: h20d^3 c19.7d^F c19.1d^3 h23.1s^5 h23.8d Apr 24] fairly useful handicap hurdler: **h121**
running to similar level (in third) when fell 2 out in novice handicap at Plumpton on
chasing debut: jumped with no conviction next time: stays 21f: acts on soft going: tried in
blinkers. *Charlie Longsdon*

APPLESANDPIERRES (IRE) 10 b.g. Pierre – Cluain Chaoin (IRE) (Phardante (FR)) **c–**
[2017/18 c–p, h129: h20.6d^5 h21.3s^5 h19.7s h19.9v^2 h16s^2 h19.9v^3 h15.7s Mar 31] won 2 **h125**
of 4 starts in Irish points: fairly useful handicap hurdler: fell only chase outing: stays 2½m:
acts on good to firm and heavy going: has worn headgear, including in 2017/18: usually
races towards rear. *Dan Skelton*

APPLE'S JADE (FR) 6 b.m. Saddler Maker (IRE) – Apple's For Ever (FR) (Nikos) **h156**
[2017/18 h158: h20v* h20s* h24s* h19.9s^3 Apr 28]

The move to a fourth day at the Cheltenham Festival in 2005 necessitated the
expansion of the programme of races. However, while some of the newly-created
events slotted in smoothly, others simply provided more choice for the connections
of good horses. As well as creating opportunities for the best horses to avoid each
other, the additional races had another unfortunate consequence in that they made
it harder for racegoers and punters to pin down running plans, with the final make-
up of the fields too often shrouded in uncertainty until the last minute as the big
stables, in particular, pondered their options. Notwithstanding the frustration caused
to racegoers and punters, Cheltenham began to miss out on valuable opportunities to
promote the meeting to full effect. The strong resistance among jumping's trainers to
pushing back the declaration time for runners has held back jumping over the years,
but, at least now, the jump meeting with the most popular appeal has forty-eight-
hour declarations for all its races (which had applied previously only to the Grade 1
non-novice events).

The British Horseracing Authority's decision to introduce forty-eight-hour
declarations for the four days of Cheltenham in March was a victory for popular
opinion and was long overdue. The racing public now has an extra day to study the
fields for the sport's most important four days and, with the prosperity of racing
directly linked to bookmakers' profits, anything that might stimulate higher betting
turnover can only be welcomed. The additional publicity that can now be generated
is most welcome too, as jumping becomes increasingly squeezed in a crowded
winter sporting calendar, where it also faces a serious threat throughout its core
season from the much improved quality of the all-weather Flat racing that is now put
before punters over the winter (there have been forty-eight-hour declarations for all
Flat racing in Britain since 2006 which enables the all-weather meetings to steal a
march on their jumping competition).

The next step for jumping—at a time when the global market for British
racing has never been more important—ought to be to extend forty-eight-hour
declarations to all fixtures in order to bring British racing, as a whole, more into line
with the international standard (no other major racing country outside the British
Isles operates with overnight declarations). If nothing else, the BHA must build on
the popularity of its innovation at the Cheltenham Festival by widening the scope
of forty-eight-hour declarations to jumping's other big meetings, starting with the
Grand National meeting at Aintree and, perhaps, all Saturday fixtures (the day of
the week when racing usually faces its stiffest competition from other sports). The
latest jumps season—which was not well served by dismal winter weather after
Christmas—emphasised the importance of the sport having a vibrant structure to
combat abandonments and small field sizes. Unless it can sustain a programme of
more generally competitive racing all the year round, jumping could face a challenge
to its finances from bookmaker-led calls for more all-weather flat fixtures in the
middle of winter. The question of how to help jump racing in the long term is a much
bigger one, but there is absolutely no reason why the sport should have one hand

Bar One Racing Hatton's Grace Hurdle, Fairyhouse—Apple's Jade repeats her 2016 win in much more emphatic fashion with a nine-length beating of Nichols Canyon (right)

tied behind its back with outmoded overnight declarations. Racing has to fight for its share of the betting market and jumping, in particular, needs to make the most of every opportunity it can get to promote itself.

Forty-eight-hour declarations worked well at the latest Cheltenham Festival, though there was a 'will-he-won't-he' moment when late uncertainty was created over which race Douvan would run in. There was talk that he might be switched from the Queen Mother Champion Chase on the Wednesday to the Ryanair Chase on the following day, and he was declared for both races before finally contesting the Champion Chase. Another leading Irish contender, the mare Apple's Jade, was also doubly declared, for the David Nicholson Mares' Hurdle on Tuesday and the Stayers' Hurdle on Thursday. The Cheltenham stewards took a dim view of the actions of both sets of connections, telling them they were not accepting the self-certificates that had been lodged and instead imposing the fixed penalty of £500 on the horses' respective trainers, Willie Mullins and Gordon Elliott. While the uncertainty lasted, Douvan and Apple's Jade were still in the betting on both races.

The situation was more puzzling with Apple's Jade who, it seemed, had virtually always been bound for the Mares' Hurdle, a race she had won the previous year. Apple's Jade's trainer had been thought, at the start of the campaign, to favour a bolder policy, involving Apple's Jade being stepped up in trip and being aimed at the Stayers' Hurdle, but owner Michael O'Leary never wavered from his view that the Mares' Hurdle was the right race for her at Cheltenham. Gordon Elliott was soon converted and, after Apple's Jade had followed up a reappearance win in the Lismullen Hurdle at Navan with an even more clear-cut one in the Grade 1 Bar One Racing Hatton's Grace Hurdle at Fairyhouse, Elliott told the media that 'she is stronger and better this year but the mares race will be her target.' The Hatton's Grace is one of three Grade 1s on the same day at Fairyhouse in early-December and the Elliott stable won all three, with Mengli Khan landing the Royal Bond Novices' Hurdle and Death Duty the Drinmore Novices' Chase. It was Apple's Jade's second victory in the Hatton's Grace and, while she had scraped home by a short head from Vroum Vroum Mag twelve months earlier, she won the latest running by nine lengths from the reigning Stayers' Hurdle winner Nichols Canyon, with the Coral Cup winner Supasundae (runner-up in the Stayers' Liverpool Hurdle) a length and three quarters further back in third. Neither Nichols Canyon nor Supasundae had had a preparatory race for the Hatton's Grace but Apple's Jade, who made all, jumping fluently, stormed right away in the closing stages and could hardly have been more impressive.

The first three in the Hatton's Grace met again in the Squared Financial Christmas Hurdle at Leopardstown where Apple's Jade was tried over three miles for the first time. The race was marred by the fatal fall of Nichols Canyon at the fifth which left Apple's Jade and Supasundae to fight out the finish, odds-on Apple's Jade prevailing by half a length, wearing down her rival close home, after the pair had contested the lead throughout. Bapaume kept on for third, four and three quarter lengths behind Supasundae, in a truly-run race that looked likely to prove solid form. Supasundae went on to win both the Irish Champion Hurdle and the Punchestown Champion Hurdle at two miles, also finishing runner-up in the Stayers' Hurdle at

Squared Financial Christmas Hurdle, Leopardstown—a seventh Grade 1 win for Apple's Jade, who copes well with the longer trip as she edges out Supasundae (right) and Bapaume (No.5)

Cheltenham and the Aintree Hurdle in between; Bapaume ended his campaign with a victory, after the end of the British and Irish seasons, in the Prix La Barka at Auteuil after finishing second in the Grande Course de Haies.

For Apple's Jade, however, the Christmas Hurdle turned out to be her final win of the campaign. She wasn't seen out between Christmas and the Cheltenham Festival and was surprisingly beaten at 2/1-on in the OLBG-sponsored David Nicholson Mares' Hurdle in which she seemed too fresh for her own good (taking a strong hold after eleven weeks off). Prominent all the way, Apple's Jade still had every chance at the last at Cheltenham but was outpointed on the run-in by second favourite Benie des Dieux, who was being switched back to hurdling after showing smart form over fences, and, even more surprisingly, by 33/1-shot Midnight Tour. Apple's Jade was beaten again by Benie des Dieux when only third in the Annie Power Mares Champion Hurdle at Punchestown, a race Apple's Jade had also won the previous year (Augusta Kate, fifth behind Apple's Jade that day, and also decisively beaten by her in the Hatton's Grace and the Christmas Hurdle, split Benie des Dieux and Apple's Jade, who started odds-on again). Apple's Jade's performance at Punchestown was disappointing on the face of it, but she wasn't the only high-profile runner from her stable to run below form at the meeting and, given the subsequent patchy form of the string in the weeks that followed, it is well worth forgiving Apple's Jade that lapse.

Apple's Jade (FR) (b.m. 2012)	Saddler Maker (IRE) (b 1998)	Sadler's Wells (b 1981)	Northern Dancer Fairy Bridge
		Animatrice (b 1985)	Alleged Alexandrie
	Apple's For Ever (FR) (b 2000)	Nikos (b or br 1981)	Nonoalco No No Nanette
		Apple's Girl (b 1989)	Le Pontet Silver Girl

The tall, unfurnished Apple's Jade, whose build certainly does not preclude her connections from trying her over fences should they wish to do so, is by the now-deceased French stallion Saddler Maker, about whom there is more in the essay

APP

on Bristol de Mai. Apple's Jade's dam Apple's For Ever, a daughter of a Prix La Barka winner in Apple's Girl, was successful five times over hurdles and fences at up to around two and a half miles. Apple's Forever was a regular visitor to Saddler Maker after she was retired to the paddocks and four of her first five offspring by him have won over jumps, two of them in France before Apple's Jade put her dam on the map. Apple's Jade was followed in the latest season by the juvenile hurdler Apple's Shakira who won her first four races before finishing in the frame in both the Triumph Hurdle and the Anniversary at Aintree. Apple's Jade, who wears a tongue tie, stays three miles and acts on heavy going, though she doesn't need the mud. She usually makes the running and is a fluent jumper. *Gordon Elliott, Ireland*

APPLESOLUTELY 7 b.m. Apple Tree (FR) – Allerford Annie (IRE) (Oscar (IRE)) [2017/18 b–: h23.9s* h23.1v² h25.5v² Mar 10] point winner: fairly useful form over hurdles: won maiden at Taunton in January: stays 3m: tried in hood. *Richard Mitford-Slade* **h122**

APPLE'S QUEEN (FR) 8 gr.g. Saddler Maker (IRE) – Queenhood (FR) (Linamix (FR)) [2017/18 c58, h–: c25.5s^{pu} May 18] multiple point winner: lightly raced over hurdles: maiden chaser: has worn cheekpieces. *Mrs S. Alner* **c–**
h–

APPLE'S SHAKIRA (FR) 4 b.f. Saddler Maker (IRE) – Apple's For Ever (FR) (Nikos) [2017/18 h16.4s* h16.4s* h16.8s* h16.8v⁴ h17s³ Apr 12] lengthy filly: fifth foal: sister to 3 winners, notably very smart hurdler Apple's Jade (2m-3m winner): dam French 17f-2½m hurdle/chase winner: useful form over hurdles: won juvenile at Vichy in May, Prestbury Juvenile Hurdle (by 17 lengths from Gumball) in November, another juvenile in December and Triumph Trial (Finesse) (by 8 lengths from Look My Way) in January, all 3 British successes at Cheltenham: looked short of pace when in frame in Triumph Hurdle and Anniversary at Aintree last 2 starts: left Emmanuel Clayeux after first start: will be suited by 2½m: raced only on soft/heavy going: tried in hood. *Nicky Henderson* **h137**

APPLETREE LANE 8 b.m. Croco Rouge (IRE) – Emmasflora (Alflora (IRE)) [2017/18 h92: h21g⁴ c19.9s³ c19.2s⁵ c19.9s^{pu} h20.6v^{pu} Apr 14] modest maiden hurdler: poor form over fences: stays 2½m: acts on heavy going: tried in cheekpieces. *Tom Gretton* **c80**
h83

APPROACHING STAR (FR) 7 ch.m. New Approach (IRE) – Madame Arcati (IRE) (Sinndar (IRE)) [2017/18 h68: h16.3d⁵ May 21] sparely-made mare: maiden on Flat: poor form over hurdles. *Dai Burchell* **h–**

APRES LE DELUGE (FR) 4 gr.g. Stormy River (FR) – Ms Cordelia (USA) (Anabaa (USA)) [2017/18 b16.2s* Dec 16] first foal: dam (h91), ran twice over hurdles, French 1m-10.5f winner on Flat: 7/1, won junior bumper at Hereford by 3¾ lengths from Topofthecotswolds: open to improvement. *Hughie Morrison* **b91 p**

JCB Triumph Trial Juvenile Hurdle (Finesse), Cheltenham—
Apple's Shakira (right) cements her position at the head of the ante-post Triumph betting as she overhauls long-time leader Look My Way to claim a third straight win at Cheltenham

ARC

APTERIX (FR) 8 b.g. Day Flight – Ohe Les Aulmes (FR) (Lute Antique (FR)) [2017/18 c142, h122: h16.7g h19.9g³ h16v⁶ h15.6d^pu h19.3v⁴ h16.8v⁵ Feb 22] workmanlike gelding: fairly useful handicap hurdler, regressed in 2017/18: useful chaser: stays 19f: acts on soft going. *Brian Ellison* — c–, h113

APTLY PUT (IRE) 6 b.g. Yeats (IRE) – Versatile Approach (IRE) (Topanoora) [2017/18 b17g² h21.7s⁶ h20s³ h19.2d⁵ Feb 25] first foal: dam, pulled up sole start in points, half-sister to useful hurdler/smart chaser (stayed 3m) Apt Approach: won maiden point at second attempt: second in bumper at Aintree: fair form over hurdles: best effort when third in novice at Fakenham in February. *Richard Spencer* — h110, b81

AQUA DUDE (IRE) 8 br.g. Flemensfirth (USA) – Miss Cozzene (FR) (Solid Illusion (USA)) [2017/18 c138, h–: c20d* c20.4s^pu Nov 18] well-made gelding: winning hurdler: useful chaser: won maiden at Uttoxeter (by 3 lengths from Qualando) in October: stays 2½m: acts on soft going. *Evan Williams* — c137, h–

ARABIAN OASIS 6 b.g. Oasis Dream – Love Divine (Diesis) [2017/18 h95: h19.3m² h18.6g⁵ h16.8g Aug 31] fair on Flat, stays 1½m: modest handicap hurdler: stays 2½m: acts on good to firm going: has worn cheekpieces, including last 5 starts: untrustworthy. *Philip Kirby* — h92 §

ARAMIST (IRE) 8 gr.g. Aussie Rules (USA) – Mistic Sun (Dashing Blade) [2017/18 h89p: h19.7d⁴ h25.3d⁵ h25.3s^F Jan 11] fair on Flat nowadays, stays 16.5f: modest form over hurdles: should stay at least 2¾m. *Sally Haynes* — h90

ARANTES 7 b.g. Sixties Icon – Black Opal (Machiavellian (USA)) [2017/18 c67, h84: c20.1g⁴ c23.8g⁵ May 18] maiden hurdler: poor maiden chaser: unproven beyond 2¼m: acts on heavy going: has worn headgear: usually leads. *Andrew Hamilton* — c64, h–

A RATED (IRE) 7 b.g. Flemensfirth (USA) – Dawn Court (Rakaposhi King) [2017/18 c22.5d^ur c19.9g* c16g* c18d⁴ c21s² Apr 27] €57,000 3-y-o: brother to fair hurdler/fairly useful chaser Our Girl Lucy (2½m-2¾m winner) and half-brother to 2 winners, including fair hurdler/fairly useful chaser Royal Boru (2m winner, by Brian Boru): dam lightly-raced half-sister to useful hurdler/very smart chaser (stayed 3¼m) Planet of Sound: winning pointer: maiden hurdler: useful form over fences: won maiden at Kilbeggan in August and novice at Wexford in September: second in novice handicap at Punchestown (5 lengths behind Kemboy) in April: left Liam Kenny after fourth start: stays 23f: acts on heavy going: front runner/races prominently. *Henry de Bromhead, Ireland* — c141, h–

ARBEO (IRE) 12 b.g. Brian Boru – Don't Waste It (IRE) (Mister Lord (USA)) [2017/18 c95§, h–: c24.2s Mar 9] useful-looking gelding: maiden hurdler: fairly useful chaser at best, has deteriorated considerably: stays 29f: acts on heavy going: tried in blinkers: usually races close up: temperamental. *Miss Rose Grissell* — c– §, h–

ARBORETUM 10 b.g. Kayf Tara – Step Lively (Dunbeath (USA)) [2017/18 c80, h–: h20.3g* h20.6g* h19.9g³ h24g³ Jul 16] point winner: modest form over hurdles: won handicaps at Southwell in May and Market Rasen (novice) in June: maiden chaser: barely stays 3m: best form on good going: has worn tongue tie: often races towards rear/travels strongly. *Mike Sowersby* — c–, h89

ARBRE DE VIE (FR) 8 b.g. Antarctique (IRE) – Nouvelle Recrue (FR) (Ragmar (FR)) [2017/18 c149, h–: h20s c22.5g⁶ c22.5s* c24v c22.5v⁴ c22.6s⁴ c19.5v³ c20v⁶ c21s^pu Feb 4] angular gelding: winning hurdler: smart chaser: won minor event at Galway (by 6 lengths from Shaneshill) in August: stays 3m: acts on heavy going: tried in hood. *W. P. Mullins, Ireland* — c146, h–

ARCHANGEL RAPHAEL (IRE) 6 b.g. Montjeu (IRE) – La Sylvia (IRE) (Oasis Dream) [2017/18 h107: h15.8g⁴ May 29] good-bodied gelding: fair on Flat nowadays, stays 2m: lightly raced over hurdles, fair form at best: in cheekpieces last 3 starts. *Amanda Perrett* — h95

ARCHIE RICE (USA) 12 b.g. Arch (USA) – Gold Bowl (USA) (Seeking The Gold (USA)) [2017/18 c–, h98: h26.5g³ h26.5d⁶ h21.6v^pu Oct 2] good-topped gelding: multiple point winner: modest handicap hurdler: well held only chase start: stays 3¼m: acts on soft and good to firm going: often races prominently. *Jimmy Frost* — c–, h94

ARCHIES BET (IRE) 7 b.g. Kheleyf (USA) – Royal Crescent (IRE) (Spectrum (IRE)) [2017/18 b16.2m b16.2g^u b16.2g Jul 6] no form in bumpers: wears tongue tie. *Katie Scott* — b–

ARCHIMENTO 5 ch.g. Archipenko (USA) – Caribana (Hernando (FR)) [2017/18 h16.3d⁵ Nov 9] fair on Flat, stays 11f: in tongue tie, 40/1, fifth in novice at Newbury (23 lengths behind Claimantakinforgan) on hurdling debut. *Philip Hide* — h98

ARC

ARCHIVE (FR) 8 b.g. Sulamani (IRE) – Royale Dorothy (FR) (Smadoun (FR)) [2017/18 c16g* c17g⁴ c19.9g⁵ c16.5v* c15.2s⁵ c15.8s⁵ h16.8v³ Feb 22] one-time useful hurdler: fairly useful handicap chaser: won at Wexford in June and Ayr in November: left Henry de Bromhead after third start: best at 2m: acts on heavy going: has worn tongue tie: usually races nearer last than first. *Brian Ellison* — **c129 h106**

ARCH MY BOY 4 b.g. Archipenko (USA) – Fairy Slipper (Singspiel (IRE)) [2017/18 b14s b13.7s³ b16s² b16.4s Mar 14] sturdy gelding: third foal: dam little form on Flat: fair form when placed in bumpers. *Martin Smith* — **b92**

ARCTIC CHIEF 8 b.g. Sleeping Indian – Neiges Eternelles (FR) (Exit To Nowhere (USA)) [2017/18 h–: h15.8g⁶ h16.3g Oct 21] placed in bumpers: poor form over hurdles: tried in tongue tie. *Richard Phillips* — **h78**

ARCTIC GOLD (IRE) 7 b.g. Gold Well – Arctic Warrior (IRE) (Arctic Lord) [2017/18 c134, h132: h22.8m c23.8v² c20.5v² c21.1v^F c20v² c20.8v c26s^F Mar 15] good-topped gelding: useful handicap hurdler: useful maiden chaser: stays 3m: acts on heavy going: front runner/races prominently: often let down by jumping over fences. *Nigel Twiston-Davies* — **c133 x h123**

ARCTIC LADY (IRE) 7 b.m. Milan – Arctic Rose (IRE) (Jamesmead) [2017/18 c–, h96, b84: c22.6g⁴ May 8] won Irish mares maiden point on debut: placed over hurdles: poor form over fences: stays 2¾m: acts on heavy going: wears tongue tie: front runner/races prominently. *Tom George* — **c75 h–**

ARCTIC SWORD 5 b.g. Schiaparelli (GER) – Malindi Bay (Alflora (IRE)) [2017/18 b16g⁶ b16g Jun 14] pulled up in points: showed a bit on first of 2 starts in bumpers. *Tom Lacey* — **b75**

ARCTIC VODKA 6 gr.g. Black Sam Bellamy (IRE) – Auntie Kathleen (Terimon) [2017/18 h–, b73: h20.9d h19.3v² h20.5v³ h19v² h21.4v^pu h20.1v* h20.6v² Apr 15] fairly useful hurdler: won maiden at Hexham in March: second in handicap at Newcastle month later: stays 21f: acts on heavy going: front runner/races prominently. *Sharon Watt* — **h122**

ARDAMIR (FR) 6 b.g. Deportivo – Kiss And Cry (FR) (Nikos) [2017/18 h90: h17.7d Nov 19] good-topped gelding: fair maiden on Flat nowadays, stays 16.5f: fairly useful hurdler at best, well held only 2 starts since 2015/16: raced around 2m: acts on good to firm going. *Laura Mongan* — **h–**

ARDEA (IRE) 10 b.g. Millenary – Dark Dame (IRE) (Norwich) [2017/18 c123: c26s² Feb 21] multiple point winner: fairly useful chaser: second in hunter at Doncaster in February: stays 3¼m: acts on soft going. *Justin Landy* — **c122**

ARDEAN LASS (IRE) 7 b.m. Winged Love (IRE) – Scathach (IRE) (Nestor) [2017/18 h16v⁴ h20.5v² h21.4v³ h21.6v³ h20.1d³ Apr 23] sixth foal: sister to useful 2m hurdle winner Flycorn, stayed 2½m, and half-sister to 2 winners, including fair hurdler/chaser Dun Scaith (2½m/21f winner, by Vinnie Roe): dam, poor maiden hurdler/chaser (stayed 3m), sister to top-class staying chaser Grey Abbey: off mark in points at fourth attempt: fair maiden hurdler: stays 2¾m: raced mainly on heavy going: tried in hood: wears tongue tie. *Stuart Crawford, Ireland* — **h106**

ARDEN DENIS (IRE) 9 ch.g. Generous (IRE) – Christian Lady (IRE) (Mandalus) [2017/18 h99: c20d^pu h23.1v² h19.9v h21.7v³ h23.3v^pu Apr 7] good-topped gelding: winning pointer: fair handicap hurdler: pulled up in novice handicap on chasing debut: stays 23f: acts on heavy going. *Neil Mulholland* — **c– h101**

ARDMAYLE (IRE) 6 ch.g. Whitmore's Conn (USA) – Welsh Connection (IRE) (Welsh Term) [2017/18 c120, h102p, b–: h19.3g h19.5s⁴ h16s h15.5v* h20.3v³ h16v* Apr 14] compact gelding: fairly useful handicap hurdler: won at Leicester in January and Chepstow in April: similar form over fences: stays 2½m, effective at shorter: best form on soft/heavy going. *Ali Stronge* — **c– h116**

ARDMILLAN (IRE) 10 b.g. Golan (IRE) – Black Gayle (IRE) (Strong Gale) [2017/18 c88, h103: c23.5d c24s⁶ h20s h19v³ c20v² h16v³ c19.2s⁴ h20.2s⁵ Apr 27] modest maiden hurdler: modest handicap chaser: stays 3m: acts on heavy going: tried in cheekpieces/tongue tie: usually races towards rear. *Stuart Crawford, Ireland* — **c93 h96**

ARDVIEW BOY (IRE) 9 b.g. Tamayaz (CAN) – Cill Uird (IRE) (Phardante (FR)) [2017/18 h93: h16m⁴ h16m² h17.3g h16.2g⁴ h17.3s h16g h16.8s³ Dec 8] modest maiden hurdler: left Anthony Mulholland after sixth start: unproven beyond 17f: acts on soft and good to firm going: front runner/races prominently. *Ronan M. P. McNally, Ireland* — **h91**

AREGRA (FR) 8 gr.g. Fragrant Mix (IRE) – Elisa de Mai (FR) (Video Rock (FR)) [2017/18 c74§, h61: c19.4g c20g² c15.6v^ur c19.3d c15.6v Oct 14] maiden hurdler: poor handicap chaser: stays 2½m: acts on good to soft going: wears headgear: front runner/races prominently: temperamental. *Peter Niven* — c75 § h–

ARE THEY YOUR OWN (IRE) 10 b.g. Exit To Nowhere (USA) – Carioca Dream (USA) (Diesis) [2017/18 c116, h–: c16.3d* c16g² c17.2g^pu Jul 22] sturdy gelding: winning hurdler: fairly useful form over fences: won hunter at Cheltenham in May: unproven beyond 2m: acts on good to firm and good to soft going: has worn tongue tie, including in 2017/18. *Fergal O'Brien* — c123 h–

ARGANTE (FR) 9 b.g. Singspiel (IRE) – Abyaan (IRE) (Ela-Mana-Mou) [2017/18 h114: h21g h20v^pu Jan 1] sturdy gelding: fair on Flat, stays 2m: fair hurdle winner for Nicky Henderson, no form in handicaps in 2017/18: stays 2½m. *Henry Spiller* — h–

ARGENTIX (FR) 8 gr.g. Fragrant Mix (IRE) – Fleche Noir II (FR) (Quart de Vin (FR)) [2017/18 c20.1g² c20d c17.2s⁴ Dec 26] runner-up both starts over hurdles: fair chaser: won minor event at Le Lion-d'Angers in 2016/17 for Mlle Louisa Carberry: stays 2½m. *Lucinda Russell* — c108 h–

ARGENT KNIGHT 8 gr.g. Sir Percy – Tussah (Daylami (IRE)) [2017/18 h16.4d h19.4d h25s⁴ Mar 14] compact gelding: fair maiden hurdler, below best in 2017/18: stays 19f: acts on good to soft going: tried in blinkers. *Christopher Kellett* — h101

ARGOCAT (IRE) 10 b.g. Montjeu (IRE) – Spirit of South (AUS) (Giant's Causeway (USA)) [2017/18 c22.2v^pu Feb 17] smallish, well-made gelding: easy winner on completed start in points in February: winning hurdler: high-class chaser at best: stayed 25f: acted on heavy going: tried in tongue tie: dead. *Miss Sarah Rippon* — c– h–

ARGOT 7 b.g. Three Valleys (USA) – Tarot Card (Fasliyev (USA)) [2017/18 c118, h–: c15.9v* c20d⁵ c20.3g⁴ Apr 20] lengthy gelding: winning hurdler: fair chaser: won hunter at Leicester in March: also won point shortly after end of season: stays 21f: acts on heavy going: usually wears headgear. *J. R. Barlow* — c114 h–

ARGUS (IRE) 6 b.g. Rip Van Winkle (IRE) – Steel Princess (IRE) (Danehill (USA)) [2017/18 h81p: h16d* h16.7d Oct 4] rather leggy gelding: fairly useful on Flat, stays 2m, won twice in 2018: fair form over hurdles: won novice at Warwick in May: in hood last 3 starts. *Alexandra Dunn* — h105

ARGYLE (IRE) 5 gr.g. Lawman (FR) – All Hallows (IRE) (Dalakhani (IRE)) [2017/18 h97: h16d² h17.7v⁴ h15.9v* h15.3v⁵ Apr 9] fair handicap hurdler: won at Plumpton in January: unproven beyond 2m: acts on heavy going: in visor last 5 starts. *Gary Moore* — h108

ARIAN (IRE) 6 b.m. King's Theatre (IRE) – Brave Betsy (IRE) (Pistolet Bleu (IRE)) [2017/18 h103, b93: h15.8s² h15.8v² h15.5v² h16s* Apr 27] bumper winner: fair form over hurdles: won maiden at Chepstow in April: stays 19f: acts on heavy going: tried in cheekpieces: usually races close up. *John Flint* — h109

ARISTOCLES (IRE) 5 b.g. High Chaparral (IRE) – Amathusia (Selkirk (USA)) [2017/18 h85: h20.5d^pu h19g^pu Nov 30] maiden hurdler, no form in 2017/18: in cheekpieces last 5 starts. *Nikki Evans* — h–

ARISTOCRACY 7 b.g. Royal Applause – Pure Speculation (Salse (USA)) [2017/18 h23.1g² h27g³ h23.3d* Sep 24] good-topped gelding: modest handicap hurdler: won at Uttoxeter in September: stays 27f: acts on good to firm and good to soft going: tried in headgear/tongue tie. *Fergal O'Brien* — h87

ARISTO DU PLESSIS (FR) 8 b.g. Voix du Nord (FR) – J'aime (FR) (Royal Charter (FR)) [2017/18 c–, h121: h16s* h16s* Dec 9] angular gelding: useful handicap hurdler: won at Wetherby in November and December (3-runner event, by 6 lengths from Sakhee's City): well held only start over fences: stays 2½m: acts on soft going: has worn headgear: front runner/races prominently. *James Ewart* — c– h138

ARIZONA BOUND (IRE) 6 b.g. Presenting – Loyal Gesture (IRE) (Darazari (IRE)) [2017/18 b16.2m² b16.2g² b15.8g* h20.9g h15.6s h23.8s⁵ ab16.3g⁵ h21.4v² h20.6v^ur Apr 14] sixth foal: brother to 3 winners, including bumper winner/fairly useful hurdler Listen And Learn (2¾m-25f winner) and fair hurdler/chaser Lilywhite Gesture (2½m-27f winner): dam, unraced, out of half-sister to top-class hurdler Rhinestone Cowboy and smart hurdler/chaser Wichita Lineman, both up to 3m: twice-raced in points: fair form in bumpers: won at Uttoxeter in July: modest form over hurdles: left Gordon Elliott after third start, Jim Goldie after seventh: stays 21f: acts on heavy going: tried in cheekpieces. *Lucinda Russell* — h93 b94

ARK

ARKADIOS (FR) 7 b.g. Elusive City (USA) – Blue Card (FR) (Trempolino (USA)) [2017/18 h97: h21m^{pu} h18.5m^5 h23.1d^{pu} Jun 8] 1½m winner on Flat: modest maiden hurdler: tried in headgear: wears tongue tie: ungenuine. *David Pipe* — **h91 §**

ARKOSE (IRE) 14 b.g. Luso – Endless Patience (IRE) (Miner's Lamp) [2017/18 c79, h–: c26.3d May 5] well-made gelding: multiple point winner: winning hurdler/chaser: stays 3¾m: acts on soft and good to firm going: wears headgear. *Tim Thirlby* — **c61 h–**

ARKWRISHT (FR) 8 b.g. Lavirco (GER) – Latitude (FR) (Kadalko (FR)) [2017/18 h24^{dur} c19.9g^2 c19.9d* c24v^2 c24s^F c28s^4 c24v c20s c29v^6 Apr 2] well-made gelding: fairly useful hurdler: useful chaser: won maiden at Kilbeggan in August: better than result when sixth in Irish Grand National Chase at Fairyhouse final start, challenging when badly hampered last: stays 29f: acts on heavy going: tried in cheekpieces: wears tongue tie. *Joseph Patrick O'Brien, Ireland* — **c141 h–**

AR MAD (FR) 8 b.g. Tiger Groom – Omelia (FR) (April Night (FR)) [2017/18 c161+, h–: c17.5v^{pu} c15.5d^3 c15.9s^{pu} c15.5d^F Apr 28] lengthy gelding: winning hurdler: very smart chaser: third in Tingle Creek Chase at Sandown (5½ lengths behind Politologue) in December: stayed 21f: acted on heavy going: tried in headgear: front runner/raced prominently: dead. *Gary Moore* — **c157 h–**

ARMEDANDBEAUTIFUL 10 b.m. Oscar (IRE) – Grey Mistral (Terimon) [2017/18 c–, h–: h23.3g^2 c24.2s^2 c26.7v^{pu} c20.9s^{pu} Mar 27] angular mare: modest maiden hurdler/chaser: stays 3m: acts on soft going: in cheekpieces last 4 starts. *Tom Gretton* — **c84 h90**

AR MEST (FR) 5 bl.g. Diamond Boy (FR) – Shabada (FR) (Cadoudal (FR)) [2017/18 b15.7d^5 ab16g^3 h16d^5 h15.8s^3 h16v* h16s^F h16s Apr 28] close-coupled gelding: fifth foal: dam French 17f hurdle winner: fair form in bumpers: fair form over hurdles: won maiden at Lingfield in February: raced only at 2m: acts on heavy going: front runner/races prominently. *Gary Moore* — **h113 b91**

ARMOROUS 7 b.g. Generous (IRE) – Armorine (FR) (Jeune Homme (USA)) [2017/18 h77: h19.3d h19.7v Jan 23] maiden hurdler: no form in 2017/18, including in points: best effort at 2m: acts on good to soft going: has worn hood. *Joanne Foster* — **h–**

AROUSAL 6 b.m. Stimulation (IRE) – Midnight Mover (IRE) (Bahamian Bounty) [2017/18 h–: h23.3g^{pu} h23.3g^{pu} Jun 25] of no account: tried in cheekpieces. *Tina Jackson* — **h–**

ARQUEBUSIER (FR) 8 br.g. Discover d'Auteuil (FR) – Djurjura (FR) (Akarad (FR)) [2017/18 c99, h–: c19.2d^6 c20v^3 c20v^4 c19.4v^2 c16v^{pu} c19.4v^6 c21s^{pu} Apr 23] sturdy gelding: winning hurdler: modest handicap chaser: stays 21f: acts on heavy going: wears headgear/tongue tie: often races prominently. *Emma-Jane Bishop* — **c94 h–**

ARTHINGTON 5 b.g. Haafhd – Pequenita (Rudimentary (USA)) [2017/18 b83: h16.3d* h17.7m* h16f^2 h16.4g^2 h15.5d* h16v^2 h20.3v h16g^3 Apr 20] compact gelding: fairly useful hurdler: won novices at Stratford in May, Plumpton in September and Leicester in December: stays 2¼m: acts on good to firm and heavy going: often races towards rear. *Seamus Mullins* — **h127**

ARTHUR BURRELL 9 ch.g. With The Flow (USA) – Kingsmill Quay (Noble Imp) [2017/18 h99: h21.6v^3 c24.2d^3 c19.4v^6 c23s^{pu} h19s^2 Dec 30] bumper winner: modest form over hurdles/fences: stays 2¾m: acts on good to firm and heavy going: in tongue tie last 3 starts: usually races nearer last than first. *Jackie du Plessis* — **c86 h99**

ARTHUR MAC (IRE) 5 ch.g. Getaway (GER) – Orchardstown Moss (IRE) (Lord of Appeal) [2017/18 b16.2s* b17s Apr 13] sturdy gelding: sixth foal: dam, unraced, closely related to fairly useful hurdler (stayed 2½m) Tarn Hows and half-sister to fairly useful hurdler/chaser (stayed 25f) Kings Orchard: fairly useful form in bumpers: won at Hereford in January, digging deep. *Philip Hobbs* — **b101**

ARTHUR MC BRIDE (IRE) 9 b.g. Royal Anthem (USA) – Lucky Diverse (IRE) (Lucky Guest) [2017/18 c–, h109x: h23.1v^5 Nov 7] useful-looking gelding: fair handicap hurdler: pulled up only start over fences: stays 3m: acts on good to firm and heavy going: in tongue tie last 2 starts: often let down by jumping. *Nigel Twiston-Davies* — **c– x h99 x**

ARTHUR'S GIFT (IRE) 7 b.g. Presenting – Uncertain Affair (IRE) (Darshaan) [2017/18 h15.7d^4 h20g^2 h20s* h20.6d* h24s* h24s^4 h25s^4 h22.8v^4 h21s Mar 17] rangy gelding: will make a chaser: useful handicap hurdler: completed hat-trick at Worcester, Market Rasen and Cheltenham (by 1¾ lengths from Sykes) in November/December: stays 3m: acts on soft and good to firm going. *Nigel Twiston-Davies* — **h130**

ARTHUR'S OAK 10 b.g. Kayf Tara – Myumi (Charmer) [2017/18 c131, h–: c19.4d^F Oct 15] strong gelding: winning hurdler: smart chaser at best: stayed 2½m: acted on heavy going: dead. *Dan Skelton* — **c– h–**

ART

ARTHUR'S QUEEN (FR) 7 b.m. Soldier of Fortune (IRE) – Tintagel (Oasis Dream) [2017/18 h21.6g May 10] little form over hurdles. *Carroll Gray*   **h–**

ARTHUR'S REUBEN 5 b.g. Malinas (GER) – Ambitious Annie (Most Welcome) [2017/18 h60: h16g h19.9d h20s⁶ h15.8s h19.9vᵖᵘ h20.7s⁴ h25d⁵ Apr 24] lengthy gelding: modest maiden hurdler: stays 25f: acts on soft going: in cheekpieces/tongue tie last 2 starts: often races prominently. *Jennie Candlish*   **h89**

ARTHURS SECRET 8 ch.g. Sakhee's Secret – Angry Bark (USA) (Woodman (USA)) [2017/18 h119: h23.8d h26.1s ab16.3g² h19.4d² h25.8v⁴ Apr 7] fairly useful handicap hurdler: second at Musselburgh in March: stays easy 3¼m: acts on good to firm and good to soft going: has worn headgear, including in 2017/18. *Sandy Thomson*   **h116**

ARTICLE FIFTY (IRE) 5 b.g. Doyen (IRE) – Annie Go (IRE) (Golan (IRE)) [2017/18 b15.8d* h15.7s³ h16.7v⁶ ab16d⁶ h16.3s² Mar 24] €22,000 3-y-o, £115,000 4-y-o: sturdy gelding: first foal: dam (h87), bumper winner, also 13f winner on Flat, half-sister to fair hurdler/fairly useful chaser (2m-21f winner) Saafend Rocket: winning pointer: fairly useful form in bumpers: won at Uttoxeter in November: placed in maiden at Southwell and novice at Newbury: front runner/races prominently. *Warren Greatrex*   **h111 b96**

ARTIC MILAN (IRE) 6 b.g. Milan – Arctic Rose (IRE) (Jamesmead) [2017/18 c20m h20.6s h15.7s Jan 11] unplaced both starts in points: maiden hurdler: no form in 2017/18, including on chasing debut: left Liam Lennon after first start: tried in cheekpieces. *Steve Gollings*   **c– h–**

ARTICULUM (IRE) 8 b.g. Definite Article – Lugante (IRE) (Luso) [2017/18 h16v* h22.3vᵖᵘ h20s⁴ h16v² h19v⁴ h16.5d Apr 24] point/bumper winner: useful form over hurdles: won bumper at Cork (by 35 lengths from Itsonlyrocknroll) in November after 19-month absence: second in listed novice at Navan (½ length behind Cartwright) in March: unproven beyond 2m: acts on heavy going: in tongue tie last 4 starts: often races prominently. *Terence O'Brien, Ireland*   **h132**

ARTIFICE SIVOLA (FR) 8 gr.g. Dom Alco (FR) – Kerrana (FR) (Cadoudal (FR)) [2017/18 c124, h121: c18m² c16.2g² c16.3gᶠ h20v* Jan 1] compact gelding: fairly useful handicap hurdler: won at Fakenham in January: fairly useful handicap chaser: second at Kempton in May: stays 2½m: acts on good to firm and heavy going: wears hood. *Lucy Wadham*   **c124 h122**

ARTISTE CELEBRE (IRE) 6 ch.g. Peintre Celebre (USA) – Penlova (IRE) (Orpen (USA)) [2017/18 h16⁶ h16g h16g² h17.6d³ h16s h16.5g⁶ h19.8s Oct 20] modest maiden on Flat, stays 10.5f: modest maiden hurdler: left Garrett James Power after second start, Eoin Doyle after sixth: unproven beyond 2m: best form on good going: tried in tongue tie: often races towards rear. *Carroll Gray*   **h96**

ART LOOKER (IRE) 6 b.g. Excellent Art – Looker (Barathea (IRE)) [2017/18 h87: h16m⁵ h18.5m h16g h20g⁶ h18.7g⁶ Jul 23] maiden hurdler, no form in 2017/18: tried in blinkers: wears tongue tie. *Tracey Barfoot-Saunt*   **h–**

ART MAURESQUE (FR) 8 b.g. Policy Maker (IRE) – Modeva (FR) (Valanour (IRE)) [2017/18 c149, h–: c23.8gᶠ c20.5d² c24gᵘ⁴ c22.7d² Apr 28] rangy gelding: has reportedly had breathing operation: winning hurdler: very smart chaser: second in listed event at Kempton (8 lengths behind Waiting Patiently) in January and Oaksey Chase at Sandown (2¾ lengths behind Top Notch) in April: barely stays 3m: acts on good to firm and heavy going: has worn headgear. *Paul Nicholls*   **c155 h–**

ART OF PAYROLL (GER) 9 b.g. Shirocco (GER) – Anna Maria (GER) (Night Shift (USA)) [2017/18 c133, h–: c20m⁵ c20.3g* c24gᵖᵘ c20.8g² Apr 18] winning hurdler: smart chaser: won maiden at Down Royal (by 2 lengths from Winter Lion) in May and handicap at Southwell (by ½ length from Hammersly Lake) in August: second in Silver Trophy Chase (Limited Handicap) at Cheltenham (1½ lengths behind Traffic Fluide) in April: left Ms Sandra Hughes after first start: stays 2¾m: acts on good to firm and heavy going: wears tongue tie: often travels strongly. *Harry Fry*   **c145 h–**

ART OF SUPREMACY (IRE) 6 b.g. Milan – Marble Desire (IRE) (Un Desperado (FR)) [2017/18 h24g c20dᵖᵘ h19.7s⁴ h21.2vᵖᵘ Jan 28] €31,000 3-y-o: sixth foal: half-brother to fairly useful chaser Cango (2m winner, by Presenting) and bumper winner Marble Article (by Definite Article): dam unraced sister to smart chaser up to 25f El Vaquero: fair form over hurdles: pulled up in maiden on chasing debut: left Noel Meade after second start: stays 2½m: acts on soft going: usually races nearer last than first. *Micky Hammond*   **c– h103**

ART

ARTY CAMPBELL (IRE) 8 b.g. Dylan Thomas (IRE) – Kincob (USA) (Kingmambo (USA)) [2017/18 h99: h16.8s^{pu} h19.9m^3 h16.8d^2 h19.8s* h16.4d^6 Nov 17] workmanlike gelding: fairly useful on Flat, stays 17f: fair handicap hurdler: won novice event at Wincanton in October: stays 2½m: acts on soft going: wears cheekpieces. *Bernard Llewellyn* **h100**

ASCENDANT 12 ch.g. Medicean – Ascendancy (Sadler's Wells (USA)) [2017/18 c–, h119: h20g* h20g* h15.8g* h15.8d^3 h20v* h19.9v* h16s* Mar 16] well-made gelding: fairly useful hurdler: won seller at Ffos Las in June, claimers at Worcester later in June and Huntingdon in November, and more sellers at Fakenham and Sedgefield in January and Fakenham again in March: unseated early only outing over fences: stays 21f: acts on good to firm and heavy going: has worn blinkers/tongue tie. *Johnny Farrelly* **c– h118**

ASCOT DE BRUYERE (FR) 8 b.g. Kapgarde (FR) – Quid de Neuville (FR) (Le Balafre (FR)) [2017/18 c113, h–: c23.4v* Apr 14] winning hurdler: fair handicap chaser: won at Newcastle in April after 13-month absence: stays 23f: acts on heavy going: wears headgear: usually leads. *James Ewart* **c114 h–**

AS DE MEE (FR) 8 b.g. Kapgarde (FR) – Koeur de Mee (FR) (Video Rock (FR)) [2017/18 c143, h–: c21.6g^2 c26.2g* c24.2s^4 c25.9v^{ur} c24g Feb 24] rangy gelding: winning hurdler: smart handicap chaser: won at Kelso (by 7 lengths from Wakanda) in October: stays 3¼m, effective at fair bit shorter: acts on heavy going: has worn headgear. *Paul Nicholls* **c147 h–**

AS DE PIQUE (IRE) 13 b.g. Woods of Windsor (USA) – Casheral (Le Soleil) [2017/18 c22.6s^F c25d^{ur} c24v^{pu} c25v^F c23.5v^4 c23.8s^2 c30.6s^5 Apr 27] lightly raced over hurdles: fairly useful handicap chaser: back to form when second at Perth in April: stays 31f: acts on soft going: has worn headgear: wears tongue tie nowadays: usually races nearer last than first: often let down by jumping. *Gavin Patrick Cromwell, Ireland* **c124 x h–**

ASHCOTT BOY 10 ch.g. Lahib (USA) – Last Ambition (IRE) (Cadeaux Genereux) [2017/18 c124, h–: c19.9g^2 c19.4g^4 c21.2g^5 h19.9d^5 h21.7g^4 c23.6g Sep 2] lengthy gelding: fair handicap hurdler: fairly useful handicap chaser: second at Aintree in May: stays 2¾m: acts on good to firm and heavy going: has worn headgear. *Neil Mulholland* **c118 h103**

ASHFORD ISLAND 5 b.g. Munnings (USA) – Falling Angel (Kylian (USA)) [2017/18 h17.7m^6 h20.3g h17.7m h16s^{pu} Nov 28] modest at one time on Flat, stays 1m: no form over hurdles. *Adam West* **h–**

ASHKOUL (FR) 5 b.g. Tamayuz – Asharna (IRE) (Darshaan) [2017/18 h16d^2 h15.7d^2 h16.7s* h15.7v^5 h16d* Apr 7] half-brother to 3 winning jumpers, notably very smart hurdler/useful chaser Ashkazar (2m-25f winner, by Sadler's Wells): useful on Flat, stays 1½m: fairly useful form over hurdles: won novice at Market Rasen in December and handicap at Fakenham in April: raced around 2m: acts on soft going: in tongue tie last 4 starts: usually travels strongly. *Dan Skelton* **h125**

ASHKOUN (FR) 7 b.g. Sinndar (IRE) – Ashalina (FR) (Linamix (FR)) [2017/18 h74: h15.8g^2 h18.5g^4 h16.2d Sep 5] modest maiden hurdler: should stay 2½m: acts on good to firm and heavy going: wears hood/tongue tie: front runner/races prominently, often freely: has returned to France. *Tim Vaughan* **h87**

ASHOKA (IRE) 6 gr.g. Azamour (IRE) – Jinskys Gift (IRE) (Cadeaux Genereux) [2017/18 h116: h16d^3 h16.5g^6 h16g c16.4g* c17.8g^3 c16.3g^{pu} c16d^4 c16.8s* c16.5g^4 Apr 21] well-made gelding: fairly useful handicap hurdler: similar form over fences: won novice handicaps at Sedgefield in August and Ascot in March: stays 19f: acts on good to firm and heavy going: usually wears cheekpieces: wears tongue tie. *Dan Skelton* **c122 h107**

ASH PARK (IRE) 10 b.g. Milan – Distant Gale (IRE) (Strong Gale) [2017/18 c133, h118: c21.3m^5 c26.2g^2 c26.2g^3 Oct 28] fairly useful hurdler: fairly useful handicap chaser: second at Kelso in May: barely stays 3¼m: acts on soft and good to firm going. *Stuart Coltherd* **c125 h–**

AS I SEE IT 6 b.g. King's Theatre (IRE) – Chomba Womba (IRE) (Fourstars Allstar (USA)) [2017/18 h16d^5 h21.4s^4 h23.9s^2 h23.9s^3 h25s* h24g Apr 18] £50,000 5-y-o: third foal: closely related to bumper winner/fair hurdler Chocca Wocca (17f winner, by Kayf Tara): dam (h145), bumper/2m-21f hurdle winner, half-sister to fairly useful hurdler/smart chaser (stayed 2½m) Down In Neworleans: off mark on second attempt: fifth in bumper at Chepstow: fairly useful form over hurdles: won maiden at Huntingdon in March: stays 25f: acts on soft going: front runner/races prominently. *Harry Fry* **h123 b81**

A SIZING NETWORK (FR) 8 ch.g. Network (GER) – Gemma (FR) (Djarvis (FR)) [2017/18 c22g^4 c25.5d^4 c19.9g^2 c19.9d^2 c20s^2 c24s* c22.6s* c28s^{pu} c21s^4 Apr 27] winning hurdler: useful chaser: won novice at Clonmel in September and handicap at Punchestown (by 9½ lengths from Static Jack) in October: stays 3m: acts on soft going: has worn cheekpieces: usually leads. *Mrs J. Harrington, Ireland* **c136 h–**

80

ASO

ASK ALICE 5 b.m. Robin des Champs (FR) – Viva Victoria (Old Vic) [2017/18 b–: b15.8g⁴ b15.7g⁶ h16.7g h15.7g h21v^{pu} Dec 31] poor form in bumpers: no form over hurdles: tried in hood. *Martin Keighley* — h– b72

ASKAMORE DARSI (IRE) 9 b.g. Darsi (FR) – Galamear (Strong Gale) [2017/18 c113§, h115§: h27g⁴ h24.4d⁴ h25.3d^F h24.3v^{pu} Mar 9] good-bodied gelding: fair handicap hurdler/chaser: stays 27f: acts on heavy going: wears headgear: front runner/races prominently: temperamental. *Donald McCain* — c– § h111 §

ASK CATKIN (IRE) 6 b.m. Ask – Simple Reason (IRE) (Snurge) [2017/18 h20.3g^{pu} h15.7g⁵ h21.2d⁴ h21.2s⁴ h25s⁵ h21.2d Apr 9] second foal: dam unraced half-sister to fairly useful hurdler/useful chaser (stays 3m) Jet Master: modest form over hurdles: should stay 25f: acts on soft going: tried in hood: usually races in rear. *Tom Symonds* — h95

ASKING QUESTIONS (IRE) 6 b.g. Ask – Just Sara (IRE) (Insan (USA)) [2017/18 b84: h21.2m⁴ h19.9d h19.6s h20v² h21.7s⁶ h24.1v³ h26s⁶ c20.9v* c20.9s* c20.1v² Apr 15] modest maiden hurdler: fair form over fences: won novice handicaps at Carlisle in March and April: stays 3m: best form on soft/heavy going: wears headgear/tongue tie: usually races close up. *Oliver Greenall* — c113 h96

ASK JD (IRE) 5 b.g. Ask – Sara Cara (IRE) (Dilshaan) [2017/18 h19.9v³ h18.1v^F Apr 16] maiden pointer: poor form on completed start over hurdles. *Alison Hamilton* — h72

ASK NELLIE (IRE) 6 b.m. Ask – Lady Shackleton (IRE) (Zaffaran (USA)) [2017/18 b15.8d h19.6s^{pu} Dec 26] €18,000 3-y-o: half-sister to useful hurdlers/chasers Los Amigos (21f/2¾m winner, by Overbury), stays 5f, and Tom Horn (2½m-25f winner, by Beneficial): dam unraced: no show in bumper/novice hurdle: tried in tongue tie. *Mark Bradstock* — h– b–

ASK NILE (IRE) 6 b.g. Ask – Spirit of The Nile (FR) (Generous (IRE)) [2017/18 c17g* c22.5s³ c16g³ c20v² h24v c17d c16.7v c21s^F Apr 27] €12,500 3-y-o: half-brother to several winners, including fairly useful hurdlers Man On The Nile (2m-3m winner, by Snurge) and Cler (17f winner, by Second Empire): dam 13f winner who stayed 2m: fairly useful hurdler: useful chaser: won maiden at Killarney (by 4¾ lengths from Gwencily Berbas) in May: second in Grade 3 novice at Tipperary (18 lengths behind Rathvinden) in October: stays 2½m: acts on heavy going. *Seamus Neville, Ireland* — c131 h95

ASK PADDINGTON (IRE) 4 ch.g. Ask – Dual Obsession (Saddlers' Hall (IRE)) [2017/18 b16.6s Feb 21] tailed off in bumper. *Micky Hammond* — b–

ASK PADDY (IRE) 6 ch.g. Ask – Dalzenia (FR) (Cadoudal (FR)) [2017/18 h101: c26.3s³ Dec 8] sturdy gelding: fair hurdler: 16/1, third in novice handicap at Sedgefield (6¼ lengths behind Kings Eclipse) on chasing debut: stays 3¼m: acts on soft going: tried in tongue tie: usually leads, often travels strongly: open to improvement over fences. *Sam England* — c103 p h–

ASKPHILMOR (IRE) 5 b.m. Ask – Barchetta (IRE) (Flemensfirth (USA)) [2017/18 b16.3d² Jun 9] €6,000 3-y-o: first foal: dam unraced half-sister to smart hurdler William Henry (2m-21f winner) and useful hurdlers Sesenta (stayed 2½m) and Electric Concorde (stayed 3m): runner-up on completed start in points: 14/1, second in conditional/amateur bumper at Stratford (head behind Pistol Shoot). *Mrs Sherree Lean* — b78

ASK SHANROE (IRE) 6 b.g. Ask – Lady Quesada (IRE) (Alflora (IRE)) [2017/18 b16.2m h16.7g h23.3d⁶ h19.9g⁶ h23.3s^{pu} Nov 10] compact gelding: maiden Irish pointer: no form in bumper/over hurdles. *Mark Campion* — h– b–

ASK THE DIVINER (IRE) 6 ch.m. Ask – Well Water (IRE) (Old Vic) [2017/18 b16d h16.5g h19g h21g h16g h19.5d Oct 14] second foal: half-sister to bumper winner/fairly useful 2m hurdle winner Collen Beag (by Mountain High), stayed 2½m: dam, unraced, out of half-sister to Scottish Grand National winner Moorcroft Boy: modest form in bumpers: no form over hurdles: left David M. O'Brien after fourth start: usually wears tongue tie. *Tim Vaughan* — h– b75

ASK THE TYCOON (IRE) 5 b.g. Ask – Mountainviewqueen (IRE) (Norwich) [2017/18 b16v* h16.4v³ h20.5v⁴ h15.6d⁵ Feb 1] €5,000 3-y-o: first foal: dam unraced: off mark in Irish points at third attempt: won maiden bumper at Ayr (by 4 lengths from Calach) in November: fair form over hurdles: will prove suited by 2½m+. *Lucinda Russell* — h102 b90

ASK THE WEATHERMAN 9 b.g. Tamure (IRE) – Whatagale (Strong Gale) [2017/18 c127p: c24.2v* c29.5v^{pu} c24s^{pu} c28.4v^{pu} Mar 12] sturdy gelding: prolific winning pointer: useful form over fences: won handicap at Exeter in November: disappointing after: stays 3¼m: acts on heavy going: wears headgear: usually races prominently. *Jack R. Barber* — c134

ASOCKASTAR (IRE) 10 b.g. Milan – Baie Barbara (IRE) (Heron Island (IRE)) [2017/18 c90§, h96§: h15.8m⁴ c19.4g Aug 3] winning hurdler/maiden chaser: won point in January: stays 23f: acts on soft and good to firm going: has worn headgear, including last 2 starts: tried in tongue tie: unreliable. *Tim Vaughan* — c– § h72 §

ASO

ASO (FR) 8 b.g. Goldneyev (USA) – Odyssee du Cellier (FR) (Dear Doctor (FR)) [2017/18 c160, h–: c19.9d⁵ Oct 29] useful-looking gelding: winning hurdler: high-class chaser: below form only start in 2017/18: stays 3m: acts on heavy going: has worn cheekpieces: often races towards rear. *Venetia Williams* — c137 h–

ASPECIALPRESENT (IRE) 8 br.g. Presenting – Escrea (IRE) (Oscar (IRE)) [2017/18 h–: h19d h21.9d⁵ h22g^{pu} Jul 4] poor form in bumpers, none over hurdles: tried in tongue tie. *Adrian Wintle* — h–

ASTAROLAND (FR) 8 b.g. Astarabad (USA) – Orlandaise (FR) (Goldneyev (USA)) [2017/18 h109: h17d h16s⁴ h19.3s³ h19.4s h17s³ Apr 8] modest handicap hurdler: stays 2½m: acts on good to firm and heavy going: tried in cheekpieces: has worn tongue tie, including last 3 starts: often races towards rear. *Jennie Candlish* — h98

ASTHURIA (FR) 7 b.m. Sagacity (FR) – Baturia (FR) (Turgeon (USA)) [2017/18 h138: h17g* c18v² c16v³ c16v² c20s² c16d³ Apr 26] smallish mare: useful hurdler: won listed mares event at Killarney (by 4 lengths from Good Thyne Tara) in May: useful form over fences: won mares maiden at Naas in January: second after in listed mares event at Naas (2½ lengths behind Benie des Dieux) and Grade 3 mares event at Fairyhouse (6 lengths behind Youcantcallherthat), and third in Ryanair Novices' Chase at Punchestown (17 lengths behind Footpad): stays 2½m: acts on heavy going: wears hood: usually leads. *W. P. Mullins, Ireland* — c138 h131

ASTIGOS (FR) 11 b.g. Trempolino (USA) – Astonishing (BRZ) (Vacilante (ARG)) [2017/18 c66§, h–§: c17.4g⁶ c20.3s c25.3v² c24v³ c23.6v⁵ c29.6v⁵ c25.5s⁵ c24.1s⁶ c19.4v³ c26.2s* Apr 27] sturdy gelding: winning hurdler: modest handicap chaser: won at Chepstow in April: stays 3¼m: best form on soft/heavy going: has worn headgear: tried in tongue tie: often races prominently: ungenuine. *Lady Susan Brooke* — c88 § h– §

ASTRACAD (FR) 12 b.g. Cadoudal (FR) – Astre Eria (Garde Royale) [2017/18 c133, h–: c19m^{pu} c25d³ c22.7g³ c19.4s³ c24s c20.5s Apr 9] sturdy gelding: winning hurdler: useful handicap chaser: largely below form in 2017/18: stays 21f: acts on soft going: has worn headgear/tongue tie. *Nigel Twiston-Davies* — c120 h–

ASTROSECRET 5 b.m. Halling (USA) – Optimistic (Reprimand) [2017/18 h19.6g^{ur} Aug 4] sister to useful hurdler/chaser Rayvin Black (15f-2½m winner) and half-sister to 2 winners, including fairly useful hurdler Rajayoga (2m/17f winner, by Kris), stayed 27f: fair maiden at best on Flat, stays 1½m: struggling when hampered and unseated 3 out in mares maiden at Bangor on hurdling debut. *Mark H. Tompkins* — h–

ASTRUM 8 gr.g. Haafhd – Vax Star (Petong) [2017/18 h105§: h16g³ h16g h16g h16.3m⁶ h16.2d² h18.7g* h16.3s² h16.3g⁵ h15.7d³ h20.5s⁵ h20s² h20v⁵ Jan 22] angular gelding: modest handicap hurdler: won conditionals selling event at Stratford in September: stays 2½m: acts on heavy going: wears headgear/tongue tie: temperamental. *Phil Middleton* — h96 §

ASUM 7 b.g. Kayf Tara – Candy Creek (IRE) (Definite Article) [2017/18 h118: h16.7s⁵ h16.2d h16s* h15.6s² Jan 19] fairly useful handicap hurdler: won at Wetherby in December: left Dan Skelton after first start, Jackie Stephen after second: unproven beyond 2m: acts on soft going: often in hood: has worn tongue tie, including in 2017/18. *Philip Kirby* — h120

ASUNCION (FR) 8 b.m. Antarctique (IRE) – Liesse de Marbeuf (FR) (Cyborg (FR)) [2017/18 c81§, h–: c22.5d^{pu} May 20] maiden hurdler: poor handicap chaser: stays 2½m: best form on soft/heavy going: wears headgear: front runner/races prominently: unreliable. *Rebecca Menzies* — c– § h–

ASYLO (IRE) 6 b.g. Flemensfirth (USA) – Escrea (IRE) (Oscar (IRE)) [2017/18 h87: b15.6s⁶ h16.6d h16.2s* Apr 26] bumper winner: fair form over hurdles: won novice at Perth in April: left Patrick Holmes after second start: signs of temperament. *Julia Brooke* — h108 b–

AS YOU LIKE (IRE) 7 b.g. Beneficial – Rubys Shadow (IRE) (Supreme Leader) [2017/18 h101p: h21d* h20g h25.4s h19.9d c19.9g⁵ c24.2s^{pu} c19.9s Dec 26] fair handicap hurdler: won at Warwick in May: poor form over fences: stays 21f: acts on good to soft going: often races towards rear/travels strongly, tends to find little. *Jonjo O'Neill* — c84 h110

AS YOU WERE (FR) 6 br.g. Azamour (IRE) – Princess Skippie (Skip Away (USA)) [2017/18 b109: h18s⁴ h23v² h19v² h21.1s^{pu} Mar 14] bumper winner: fairly useful form over hurdles: second in maidens at Navan/Naas: in cheekpieces/tongue tie last 3 starts. *Alan Fleming, Ireland* — h126

ATAGUISEAMIX (FR) 5 b.g. Al Namix (FR) – Olafane (FR) (Le Balafre (FR)) [2017/18 h16.8v^{pu} h20.6s^{pu} Apr 11] runner-up sole start in Irish points: pulled up in novice/maiden hurdles (had breathing operation between starts): wears hood: in tongue tie second start. *Paul Nicholls* — h–

ATO

A TAIL OF INTRIGUE (IRE) 10 b.g. Tillerman – Princess Commanche (IRE) (Commanche Run) [2017/18 c113, h–: c23g³ c25.8d^F c23.9g^pu c30.7v^pu h25s^pu Dec 26] workmanlike gelding: winning hurdler: fairly useful chaser at one time: no form in 2017/18 after return: left Nicky Henderson after third start: stays 3m: acts on good to firm and heavy going: has worn headgear: often let down by jumping over fences. *Fergal O'Brien* c107 x h–

ATALANTA'S GOLD (IRE) 5 b.m. Arcadio (GER) – Sandy Desert (Selkirk (USA)) [2017/18 h19.5d h15.9v^pu h15.9s⁶ Apr 15] half-sister to fair hurdler Nemean Lion (2½m-3m winner, by Mahler): dam unraced half-sister to fairly useful hurdler/fair chaser (2m winner) Dealing River: poor form over hurdles: best effort when sixth in maiden at Plumpton. *Gary Moore* h82

ATAMAN (IRE) 6 b.g. Sholokhov (IRE) – Diora (IRE) (Dashing Blade) [2017/18 h16d⁵ h16.5m h17.7g⁶ h15.7d h16s^pu h16.v⁴ Jan 22] sturdy gelding: fair maiden on Flat, stays 1¼m: poor form over hurdles: likely to prove best around 2m: acts on heavy going: sometimes in tongue tie: often races towards rear. *Olly Murphy* h79

AT FIRST LIGHT 9 b.m. Echo of Light – Bisaat (USA) (Bahri (USA)) [2017/18 h105§: h17.7v⁴ h19.5s Apr 27] lengthy mare: fair handicap hurdler, well held both starts in 2017/18 after long absence: stays 3m: acts on heavy going: temperamental. *David Weston* h59 §

A THREE EIGHTY (FR) 5 b.m. Slickly (FR) – Fleche Rose (USA) (Elusive Quality (USA)) [2017/18 b16s* May 17] second foal: half-sister to French 1m-1½m winner Queen of Holy (by Holy Roman Emperor): dam unraced: fair form in bumpers: won mares event at Worcester in May. *T. Hogan, Ireland* b88

ATHREEOTHREE (IRE) 7 b.g. Presenting – Lucina (GER) (Groom Dancer (USA)) [2017/18 h19.8v⁵ Apr 9] multiple point winner: well beaten in maiden on hurdling debut (wore blinkers). *Jack R. Barber* h–

ATLANTA ABLAZE 7 b.m. Kayf Tara – Rocheflamme (FR) (Snurge) [2017/18 h113: c19.8v^F Apr 27] well-made mare: fair hurdler: fell fifth on chasing debut: likely to stay further than 21f: acts on soft and good to firm going. *Henry Daly* c– h–

ATLANTIC GREY (IRE) 5 gr.g. Acambaro (GER) – Clooney Eile (IRE) (Definite Article) [2017/18 b79: h19.7d³ h16g² h21.1s h19.7s^pu Dec 26] smallish, lengthy gelding: fair form over hurdles: should stay beyond 2½m: tried in tongue tie. *Nigel Twiston-Davies* h108

ATLANTIC KING (GER) 5 b.g. King's Best (USA) – Atlantic High (Nashwan (USA)) [2017/18 h82: h21.6s^pu h15.8g³ h21.6m h20g^rr c17.4g² c21.6g³ c20.3d³ c24.2s^pu c23.8v⁴ Nov 24] modest maiden hurdler: poor form over fences: stays 3m: acts on heavy going: has worn headgear/tongue tie: unreliable. *Nigel Hawke* c84 § h89 §

ATLANTIC ROLLER (IRE) 11 b.g. Old Vic – Tourist Attraction (IRE) (Pollerton) [2017/18 c110§, h–: c17.8v⁴ c17.8v* c17.8s² c19.4v² Apr 15] well-made gelding: winning hurdler: fair handicap chaser: won at Fontwell in January: stays 3m: acts on heavy going: wears cheekpieces: has worn tongue tie, including last 4 starts: front runner/races prominently: ungenuine. *Chris Gordon* c111 § h–

ATLANTIC STORM (IRE) 6 b.g. September Storm (GER) – Double Dream (IRE) (Double Eclipse (IRE)) [2017/18 h118, b–: h16s⁶ c21.7s^F h19s h15.9v⁵ h15.7v Jan 20] good-topped gelding: fair handicap hurdler, below best in 2017/18: fell heavily tenth in novice handicap at Towcester on chasing debut: unproven beyond 17f: acts on soft going: has worn hood: in tongue tie last 4 starts. *Dan Skelton* c– p h95

ATLAS PEAK (IRE) 13 b.g. Namid – My Delilah (IRE) (Last Tycoon) [2017/18 h15.7v^pu h19.9v h16.4v h15.7s⁴ h24v⁶ Apr 14] good-topped gelding: maiden hurdler, no form in 2017/18: has worn headgear. *Victor Thompson* h–

A TOI PHIL (FR) 8 b.g. Day Flight – Lucidrile (FR) (Beyssac (FR)) [2017/18 c148, h–: c22.5g⁴ c24v⁵ c20v* c19.5s⁴ c20.6v² c20.2v⁴ c21v² c20v* c20v* c20v² c16s³ Apr 24] sturdy gelding: winning hurdler: very smart chaser: won PWC Champion Chase at Gowran (by 6½ lengths from Balko des Flos) in September and Kinloch Brae Chase at Thurles (by 9½ lengths from American Tom) in January: third in Boylesports Champion Chase at Punchestown (9¾ lengths behind Un de Sceaux) in April: stays 25f, effective at much shorter: acts on heavy going: wears tongue tie nowadays: usually races towards rear. *Gordon Elliott, Ireland* c157 h–

ATOMIC RUMBLE (IRE) 5 b.g. Oscar (IRE) – Atomic Betty (IRE) (Anshan) [2017/18 b77: b17.7g⁵ b17s³ h19.6s h15.8v⁴ h19.5v h22d Apr 22] fair form in bumpers: modest form over hurdles: will prove suited by 2½m+: in tongue tie last 5 starts. *Peter Bowen* h95 b86

ATO

ATOMIX (GER) 7 b.g. Doyen (IRE) – Aloe (GER) (Lomitas) [2017/18 h105: h16.2g* c17.2g[6] Oct 21] leggy gelding: fair handicap hurdler: won at Hexham in May: 22/1, sixth in novice at Market Rasen (26½ lengths behind Capitaine) on chasing debut: may prove best around 2m: acts on good to firm and good to soft going. *Peter Niven* — **c108 h106**

A TOUCH OF SASS (IRE) 8 b.m. Mahler – Lwitikila (Denel (FR)) [2017/18 h–: h20g[rr] Jul 18] winning pointer: maiden hurdler, refused to race only start in 2017/18: tried in hood: one to avoid. *John Spearing* — **h– §**

A TOUCH OF SPARKLE (IRE) 8 gr.m. Golan (IRE) – Another Sparkle (Bustino) [2017/18 h22.1d[4] h18.8g[4] h20.2g[5] h17.2s* h15.7g[F] h22.1d[2] c19.2v[3] c21d[3] Oct 7] sixth foal: half-sister to modest 2m hurdle winner/winning pointer Indy Island (by Indian Danehill) and a winning pointer by Pilsudski: dam (b64) ran twice in bumpers: maiden pointer: fair hurdler: won mares handicap at Cartmel in July: modest form over fences: stays 2¾m: acts on heavy going. *Stuart Crawford, Ireland* — **c92 h103**

ATTENTION PLEASE (IRE) 8 b.g. Kalanisi (IRE) – Dangerous Dolly (IRE) (Jurado (USA)) [2017/18 c81, h–: c23.4g c24.2d c26d* c25.2d* c23.8s[F] c26.6s* c23.8d[3] c26.2v[pu] Apr 17] maiden hurdler: modest handicap chaser: won at Doncaster (conditional) and Catterick in December, and Musselburgh in February: stays 27f: acts on soft and good to firm going: wears headgear. *Rose Dobbin* — **c97 h–**

ATTENTION SEEKER 8 b.m. Bollin Eric – Pay Attention (Revoque (IRE)) [2017/18 h22.1g h20.5v* Nov 15] fairly useful handicap hurdler: won mares event at Ayr (tongue tied) in November: stays 2½m: best form on soft/heavy going. *Tim Easterby* — **h116**

ATTEST 5 b.g. Cacique (IRE) – Change Course (Sadler's Wells (USA)) [2017/18 h104: h16d* h16.2m* h15.8m[2] h15.7g[5] h16.8s[5] h15.5s* h16g Apr 21] lengthy gelding: fairly useful handicap hurdler: won at Warwick in May, Perth in June and Taunton in December: stays 19f: acts on soft and good to firm going: in cheekpieces last 2 starts: often races prominently. *Warren Greatrex* — **h126**

ATTIMO (GER) 9 ch.g. Nayef (USA) – Alanda (GER) (Lando (GER)) [2017/18 c112, h–: c19.3g[4] May 16] big gelding: lightly-raced hurdler: fair chaser at best, has lost his way (pulled up in points in 2018): stays 3m: acts on soft going: wears headgear/tongue tie: often races towards rear. *Sam England* — **c– h–**

ATTRACTIVE LIASON (IRE) 8 b.m. Scorpion (IRE) – Sounds Attractive (IRE) (Rudimentary (USA)) [2017/18 h15.8g[pu] h16.8v[pu] h15.3v[pu] Feb 1] useful-looking mare: winning pointer: no form over hurdles: tried in tongue tie. *Neil Mulholland* — **h–**

ATTRIBUTION 8 ch.g. Alhaarth (IRE) – Competa (Hernando (FR)) [2017/18 c143, h–: c18g* c18.2s[3] c19.5s* c20s[5] Dec 9] winning hurdler: useful chaser: won minor events at Limerick in July and October (by ½ length from Childrens List): stays 2½m: acts on heavy going: tried in cheekpieces: races prominently. *Henry de Bromhead, Ireland* — **c142 h–**

AUBUSSON (FR) 9 b.g. Ballingarry (IRE) – Katioucha (FR) (Mansonnien (FR)) [2017/18 c136+, h145+: c22.9s[3] c30.2g c23.8s[2] c24.2v[2] c26s Mar 15] tall, good-topped gelding: smart hurdler: useful handicap chaser: second at Ludlow (4 lengths behind Actinpieces) in January and Sandown (3 lengths behind Tanit River) in February: stays 3¼m: acts on heavy going: tried in cheekpieces. *Nick Williams* — **c134 h–**

AUDACIOUS PLAN (IRE) 9 b.g. Old Vic – North Star Poly (IRE) (Presenting) [2017/18 c120, h108: c24d[2] h25g* c29.2g* c25.6g* Dec 6] good-topped gelding: fairly useful handicap hurdler: won at Huntingdon in October: useful handicap chaser: won at Sedgefield in November and Ludlow in December: stays 3¾m: acts on soft going: wears headgear: usually travels strongly. *Dr Richard Newland* — **c137 h121**

AUDORA 7 b.m. Alflora (IRE) – Vixen Run (IRE) (Presenting) [2017/18 b16.3s b16.8v[6] h16.5m Apr 25] first foal: dam (b78) ran twice in bumpers: well held in bumpers/mares novice hurdle. *Martin Hill* — **h– b–**

AUENWIRBEL (GER) 7 b.g. Sholokhov (IRE) – Auentime (GER) (Dashing Blade) [2017/18 c–, h96: h19.9d c19.4v[3] c19.2v[ur] c16.1s[3] c19.4v[4] c19.4v[5] c18.2s[bd] c16s[6] Feb 24] angular gelding: winning hurdler: modest handicap chaser: stays 19f: acts on heavy going: tried in blinkers: wears tongue tie. *Laura Young* — **c92 h–**

AUGUSTA KATE 7 b.m. Yeats (IRE) – Feathard Lady (IRE) (Accordion) [2017/18 h142, b–: h20s[6] h24s[4] h24v[2] h24s h20v[5] h20s[2] Apr 28] neat mare: bumper winner: smart hurdler: second in John Mulhern Galmoy Hurdle at Gowran (5½ lengths behind Presenting Percy) in January and Mares Champion Hurdle at Punchestown (3 lengths behind Benie des Dieux) in April: stays 3m: acts on heavy going: usually races towards rear. *W. P. Mullins, Ireland* — **h148**

AVO

AULDTHUNDER (IRE) 11 b.g. Oscar (IRE) – Jill's Girl (IRE) (Be My Native (USA)) [2017/18 c23.8g[6] h23.3g[5] c24.2v[2] h24v[5] h23.9s Apr 25] has had breathing operation: point winner: poor hurdler/chaser nowadays: stays 3¼m: acts on heavy going. *Tim Reed* — **c75 h–**

AUNTY ANN (IRE) 7 b.m. Vinnie Roe (IRE) – On Good Advise (IRE) (Taipan (IRE)) [2017/18 h111: h19.6g h21.7g[2] c20g[3] c20.9s[3] c23g* c25.6g[3] c20.8g[5] Apr 19] fair handicap hurdler: fairly useful form over fences: won handicap at Worcester in October: stays 23f: acts on soft and good to firm going: tried in tongue tie: front runner/races prominently: temperamental. *Charlie Longsdon* — **c115 § h109 §**

AUTHORIZED TOO 7 b.g. Authorized (IRE) – Audaz (Oasis Dream) [2017/18 c121, h119: h16.3g[2] Aug 3] rather leggy gelding: fairly useful hurdler/chaser: similar standard on Flat, won twice in 2017: stays 21f: acts on good to firm and heavy going: wears cheekpieces. *Noel Williams* — **c– h113**

AUTUMN SURPRISE (IRE) 5 b.m. Yeats (IRE) – Septembers Hawk (IRE) (Machiavellian (USA)) [2017/18 h16d[3] h19.7s[5] h15.6s[4] Jan 19] closely related to useful hurdler Hawk High (2m/17f winner, by High Chaparral) and half-sister to fair hurdler Dactik (2½m winner, by Diktat): fair form on Flat, stays 11f: modest form in mares novice hurdles. *Tim Easterby* — **h88**

AUTUM RAIN (IRE) 6 b.m. Arcadio (GER) – Liberty Miss (IRE) (Flemensfirth (USA)) [2017/18 h70: h23.3d[pu] Sep 24] runner-up on second of 2 starts in Irish maiden points: maiden hurdler, lame only start (hooded) in 2017/18. *Tom Weston* — **h–**

AUVERGNAT (FR) 8 b.g. Della Francesca (USA) – Hesmeralda (FR) (Royal Charter (FR)) [2017/18 c143, h–: c26s* c24.9s[2] c24s[bd] h21.6s[3] c30.2g[F] c24v* c30.2s[4] c33.5d* Apr 26] workmanlike gelding: fairly useful handicap hurdler: third at Galway in October: smart chaser: won handicap at Killarney in May, and cross-country events at Punchestown in February and April (La Touche Cup), narrowly from Josies Orders on both occasions: stays 33f: acts on heavy going: tried in cheekpieces/tongue tie. *Enda Bolger, Ireland* — **c150 h119**

AUXILIARY 5 b.g. Fast Company (IRE) – Lady Xara (IRE) (Xaar) [2017/18 h15.7d h15.6g[3] h16.2s Jan 14] fair on Flat, stays 1¼m: modest form over hurdles: best effort when third in novice at Musselburgh in December. *Patrick Holmes* — **h91**

AVARCHIE (FR) 4 b.g. Kentucky Dynamite (USA) – Teatime (FR) (Loup Solitaire (USA)) [2017/18 b13.7g[6] b13.7g Nov 30] tall gelding: poor form in bumpers: left Giles Bravery after first start. *Michael Wigham* — **b71**

AVENIR D'UNE VIE (FR) 8 gr.g. Lavirco (GER) – Par Bonheur (FR) (Robin des Champs (FR)) [2017/18 c19v[6] c16.1s[F] c16v* c17d[ur] c16v[2] Jan 7] workmanlike gelding: winning hurdler: useful form over fences: won maiden at Punchestown in December: second in novice at Naas (1¼ lengths behind Demi Sang) in January: unproven beyond 2m: best form on soft/heavy going: front runner, often travels strongly. *Henry de Bromhead, Ireland* — **c140 h–**

AVENUE OF STARS 5 b.g. Makfi – Clifton Dancer (Fraam) [2017/18 h15.6g[5] Dec 18] fair on Flat, stays 6f: well held in novice on hurdling debut. *Karen McLintock* — **h–**

AVIATOR (GER) 10 br.g. Motivator – Amore (GER) (Lando (GER)) [2017/18 h21g[6] h20.6d[6] Dec 7] fairly useful hurdler at best, little show in handicaps in 2017/18: stays 21f: acts on good to firm and good to soft going. *James Eustace* — **h–**

AVIDITY 9 b.g. Passing Glance – Epicurean (Pursuit of Love) [2017/18 c128, h–: c17.1g[2] c15.8g[pu] c17.4g h16.8g[6] Sep 7] rather leggy, workmanlike gelding: fairly useful hurdler/chaser at best, little form in 2017/18: stays 2½m: acts on good to firm and heavy going: often in cheekpieces nowadays: has worn tongue tie: often races towards rear. *James Ewart* — **c101 h–**

AVISPA 9 b.m. Kayf Tara – Ladylliat (FR) (Simon du Desert (FR)) [2017/18 h118: h16.3g[4] c16.5g[5] Jul 18] lengthy, rather sparely-made mare: fairly useful hurdler: well held in novice handicap on belated chasing debut: stays 19f: acts on soft and good to firm going: tried in hood: usually travels strongly. *Alan King* — **c– h–**

AVITHOS 8 b.m. Kayf Tara – Digyourheelsin (IRE) (Mister Lord (USA)) [2017/18 h92, b–: h21.6s h21.6m[pu] h16.8d Aug 22] modest hurdler at best, no form in 2017/18: tried in blinkers. *Mark Gillard* — **h–**

AVONDHU PEARL (IRE) 7 ch.m. Beneficial – Ballinapierce Lady (IRE) (Glacial Storm (USA)) [2017/18 c25.5g[6] h20.1v[pu] h20.6g h23.8g h17d[3] c21.1v[3] Apr 13] €8,500 3-y-o: sixth foal: half-sister to winning pointers by Milan and Oscar: dam, unraced, out of sister to very smart chaser (stayed 3m) Nick Dundee and half-sister to high-class 2m hurdler Ned Kelly: winning pointer: poor form over hurdles: maiden chaser: left David Fenton after first start: unproven beyond 17f: acts on good to soft going: tried in cheekpieces. *Stuart Coltherd* — **c– h82**

AVO

A VOS GARDES (FR) 8 br.g. Kapgarde (FR) – Miscia Nera (FR) (Panoramic) [2017/18 c19.4s² c22.4v^F c19.9v^F h24v^pu c23.6v³ Apr 14] lengthy gelding: useful hurdler at best: fairly useful form over fences, fell on 2 of 4 starts: stays 23f: acts on heavy going: wears tongue tie: races prominently. *Charlie Longsdon* — **c122 h–**

AWAKE AT MIDNIGHT 6 b.g. Midnight Legend – Wakeful (Kayf Tara) [2017/18 b70: h15.8d² h15.7s³ h15.8s² h15.8d³ h19d Apr 26] useful-looking gelding: fair form over hurdles: should be suited by 19f+: acts on soft going: usually races prominently. *Philip Hobbs* — **h113**

AWAY DOWN WEST (IRE) 8 b.g. Stowaway – Western Starlight (IRE) (Shahanndeh) [2017/18 c–, h–,: c24.2g h23g c25.8d⁵ Aug 22] little form over hurdles/fences: usually in headgear: tried in tongue tie. *Johnny Farrelly* — **c– h–**

AWAY FOR SLATES (IRE) 8 b.g. Arcadio (GER) – Rumi (Nishapour (FR)) [2017/18 h19.5d⁴ h19.7s² h22.8v⁶ h19.7s h16v³ h21v^pu h19.7d³ h16m^pu Apr 26] maiden pointer: fairly useful handicap hurdler, became disappointing in 2017/18: stays 2½m: acts on heavy going: has worn headgear, including last 4 starts: tried in tongue tie. *Dan Skelton* — **h114 d**

AWAYWITHTHEBLUES (IRE) 6 ch.g. Stowaway – Rhythm 'N' Blues (IRE) (Sinndar (IRE)) [2017/18 b15.8d⁵ h21.6m^ur h20g h21d h19.7s Dec 16] no form in bumper/over hurdles. *Robert Stephens* — **h– b–**

AWAYWITHTHEGREYS (IRE) 11 gr.g. Whipper (USA) – Silver Sash (GER) (Mark of Esteem (IRE)) [2017/18 c–§, h116§: h20g² h23.9g* h26.5m⁵ h23.9v Nov 12] angular gelding: fairly useful handicap hurdler: won at Ffos Las in June: maiden chaser: stays 3¼m: acts on good to firm and heavy going: wears headgear: tried in tongue tie: usually leads: unreliable. *Peter Bowen* — **c– § h120 §**

AWEEMINIT (IRE) 4 b.f. Arcadio (GER) – Campanella (GER) (Lomitas) [2017/18 b12.6s⁶ b12.4s⁵ Jan 13] seventh foal: half-sister to smart hurdler Caracci Apache (2m-3m winner, by High Chaparral): dam (h111), 2m hurdle winner, also 8.5f-11f winner on Flat, half-sister to useful hurdler/smart chaser (stayed 21f) Caracciola: little form in bumpers. *Fergal O'Brien* — **b56**

AWESOME ROSIE 7 b.m. Midnight Legend – Awesome Aunt (IRE) (Vestris Abu) [2017/18 h117: h20.3g³ h19.8s* h21g⁶ h18.9v⁴ Mar 31] compact mare: fairly useful handicap hurdler: won mares event at Sandown in December: will prove best up to 21f: acts on heavy going: often travels strongly. *Alan King* — **h117**

AWESOME TUNES (IRE) 8 b.g. Milan – Europet (IRE) (Fourstars Allstar (USA)) [2017/18 c84, h87: c22.6d^pu Jun 9] multiple point winner: maiden hurdler/chaser, modest form at best: tried in hood: usually in tongue tie. *E. Walker* — **c– h–**

AYE AYE CHARLIE 6 b.g. Midnight Legend – Trial Trip (Le Moss) [2017/18 h97: h20d³ h21.1d^F h20.3s⁴ h20.3v³ h21.1s h20s⁴ Apr 14] rather unfurnished gelding: bumper winner: useful form over hurdles: best effort when 4½ lengths fourth of 12 to Black Op in Mersey Novices' Hurdle at Aintree final start: will stay beyond 21f: acts on soft going: often races towards rear. *Fergal O'Brien* — **h137**

AYE AYE ENYA 5 b.g. Sixties Icon – Ishka Baha (IRE) (Shernazar) [2017/18 b16.7d⁵ b15.8g⁵ b16.7g⁶ b16.3d⁴ h16.8g h16.8s⁶ Dec 26] poor form in bumpers: well beaten over hurdles: in tongue tie last 5 starts. *John Norton* — **h– b73**

AYE RIGHT (IRE) 5 b.g. Yeats (IRE) – Gaybric (IRE) (Presenting) [2017/18 b16.2g³ b17d* h16.2s² h17d² Mar 25] third foal: dam (b82), third in bumper on only start, half-sister to dam of smart 2m chaser Ordinary World: fairly useful form in bumpers: won at Carlisle in November: fairly useful form over hurdles: second in novices at Kelso and Carlisle: bred to stay at least 2½m. *Harriet Graham* — **h117 b99**

AYLA'S EMPEROR 9 b.m. Holy Roman Emperor (IRE) – Ayla (IRE) (Daylami (IRE)) [2017/18 h99: h20d* h19.6d⁶ h21.7d³ h22s³ h21.6g h23.1v^pu Nov 26] sturdy mare: fair handicap hurdler: won at Ffos Las in May: stays 2¾m: acts on soft going: wears cheekpieces: often races towards rear. *John Flint* — **h100**

AZAMESSE (IRE) 6 b.m. Azamour (IRE) – Jeunesse Doree (IRE) (Rock of Gibraltar (IRE)) [2017/18 h20g⁴ h21.6m⁶ h19.9d³ Jul 28] modest on Flat, stays 1¾m: modest maiden hurdler: stays 2½m: acts on soft going: has worn cheekpieces/tongue tie. *J. R. Jenkins* — **h89**

AZA RUN (IRE) 8 b.g. Hurricane Run (IRE) – Aza Wish (IRE) (Mujadil (USA)) [2017/18 h90: h20.6g h15.8d* h15.8v⁶ h15.7v³ h16.7s⁵ c15.7g⁴ Apr 20] modest handicap hurdler: won at Uttoxeter in November: 16/1, fourth in novice at Southwell (24¼ lengths behind Peter The Mayo Man) on chasing debut: unproven beyond 2m: acts on heavy going: tried in tongue tie: often races towards rear: unreliable. *Shaun Harris* — **c93 § h89 §**

AZERT DE COEUR (FR) 8 b.g. Tiger Groom – Eden de Coeur (FR) (Lampon (FR)) [2017/18 c112, h–: c17.1g^5 c19.3s^{pu} h21.2v ab16.3g^4 Mar 3] good-topped gelding: fair hurdler/chaser at one time, retains little ability: stays 19f: acts on heavy going: tried in blinkers. *Rebecca Menzies*   **c74 h–**

AZUMINI (FR) 4 gr.g. Stormy River (FR) – Lunaba (FR) (Anabaa (USA)) [2017/18 b13.7g^{ur} b16.2s Dec 16] behind on completed start in bumpers. *Charlie Longsdon*   **b–**

AZURE FLY (IRE) 10 br.g. Blueprint (IRE) – Lady Delight (IRE) (Be My Native (USA)) [2017/18 c123, h–: c25.8d* c25g^6 c27.7d^{pu} c32.8s^{pu} Feb 3] good-topped gelding: winning hurdler: fairly useful handicap chaser: won at Newton Abbot in September: stays 33f: acts on good to firm and heavy going: wears headgear/tongue tie: front runner/races prominently: temperamental. *Charlie Longsdon*   **c121 § h– §**

AZZERTI (FR) 6 b.g. Voix du Nord (FR) – Zalagarry (FR) (Ballingarry (IRE)) [2017/18 h127: h19.2g h16.8s^4 h16v^3 h19.6s* h21s h20.3g^2 Apr 18] rather leggy gelding: useful handicap hurdler: won at Huntingdon in February: second at Cheltenham (1¼ lengths behind Champagne Express) in April: stays 2½m: acts on soft going: has worn hood: often races towards rear/travels strongly. *Alan King*   **h137**

AZZURI 6 b.g. Azamour (IRE) – Folly Lodge (Grand Lodge (USA)) [2017/18 h126: h15.8m* h16.7g^2 c15.7g* c15.7g* c16.5g^3 c16.2s^6 c16.3v^4 c20.2v^3 c16.5g* Apr 20] sturdy gelding: fairly useful hurdler: won novice at Ludlow in May: useful chaser: won novices at Southwell in July and August, and novice handicap at Ayr (by 15 lengths from Lofgren) in April: will prove best up to 2½m: acts on good to firm and heavy going: wears tongue tie: often leads/travels strongly. *Dan Skelton*   **c133 h121**

B

BAB EL MANDEB (USA) 4 b.g. Blame (USA) – April Pride (Falbrav (IRE)) [2017/18 h16.3m^{pu} h16.2d^4 Aug 21] £21,000 3-y-o: second foal: half-brother to 6f/7f winner Henrytheaeroplane (by Henrythenavigator): dam scaled 5f-1m winner: modest form over hurdles: better effort when fourth in juvenile at Hexham: has joined Michael Scudamore. *Lucinda Russell*   **h90**

BABY BACH (IRE) 8 gr.g. Bach (IRE) – Anns Island (IRE) (Turtle Island (IRE)) [2017/18 c121, h–: c23.8g* c23.8g^{pu} Jul 5] winning hurdler: fairly useful chaser: won novice at Perth in May: reportedly lame next time: stays 3m: acts on heavy going: tried in cheekpieces: often races towards rear. *Stuart Crawford, Ireland*   **c123 h–**

BABY JAKE (IRE) 9 b.g. Morozov (USA) – Potters Dawn (IRE) (Talkin Man (CAN)) [2017/18 c114, h124: c17m^3 c16g^5 h17.2s^3 c17.8g^4 c16.3g^2 h15.8d^2 h16s Dec 27] fairly useful handicap hurdler: second in lady riders event at Huntingdon in November: fairly useful form over fences: second in handicap at Fakenham earlier in November: stays 2½m: acts on good to firm and good to soft going: tried in hood. *John Joseph Hanlon, Ireland*   **c123 h124**

BABY KING (IRE) 9 b.g. Ivan Denisovich (IRE) – Burn Baby Burn (IRE) (King's Theatre (IRE)) [2017/18 c135, h124: c19.2g^F c15.8s* c16.4g c15.8s^2 c16s^5 c15.8s^{pu} c16.8s* Apr 26] good-topped gelding: has had breathing operation: fairly useful hurdler: useful handicap chaser: won at Aintree in November and Perth (by head from Mixboy) in April: best at 2m: acts on heavy going: wears tongue tie. *Tom George*   **c136 h–**

BABY SHERLOCK 7 ch.g. Shirocco (GER) – Lady Cricket (FR) (Cricket Ball (USA)) [2017/18 h66p: h23g^{pu} Jun 14] placed in points: no form over hurdles: tried in blinkers. *David Pipe*   **h–**

BABYTAGGLE (IRE) 7 b.g. Brian Boru – Ardnataggle (IRE) (Aristocracy) [2017/18 h23.6v^{ur} h23.1v^{pu} h19.2v^5 h15.7v^F h16v h19.5v^5 Apr 14] winning pointer: maiden hurdler, little form since debut in Ireland in 2016/17: stays 19f: raced only on soft/heavy going: often wears hood. *Dai Williams*   **h80**

BABY TED 5 ch.g. Pasternak – Dd's Glenalla (IRE) (Be My Native (USA)) [2017/18 b16s^3 b16.7v^3 h19.6s^5 Mar 24] strong, compact gelding: sixth foal: half-brother to 3 winners, including smart hurdler Colin's Sister (19f-3m winner, by Central Park) and fairly useful hurdler/useful chaser Colin's Brother (2m-2½m winner, by Overbury): dam (h96) 25f hurdle winner: modest form when third in bumpers: 12/1, fifth in novice at Bangor (29½ lengths behind Knockrobin) on hurdling debut: bred to be suited by 2¼m+. *Nigel Twiston-Davies*   **h92 b81**

BAB

BABY TICKER 9 ch.m. Endoli (USA) – Baby Gee (King Among Kings) [2017/18 h95: h16.4s² h16v* h19.5v² h18.9v⁵ h24.3g Apr 20] fair handicap hurdler: won mares event at Ayr in January: stays 19f: best form on soft/heavy going: often races towards rear. *Donald Whillans* — **h112**

BACARDYS (FR) 7 b.g. Coastal Path – Oasice (FR) (Robin des Champs (FR)) [2017/18 h155p, b–: c19v³ c21d^F h24s^F h24d Apr 26] angular gelding: point winner: very smart hurdler: running well when falling last in Stayers' Hurdle at Cheltenham, left poorly placed but making headway and likely to have finished third: useful form over fences: third in maiden at Naas (10 lengths behind Mossback) on completed start: should prove suited by 3m: acts on heavy going: should do better over fences. *W. P. Mullins, Ireland* — **c136 p / h155**

BACCALAUREATE (FR) 12 b.g. High Chaparral (IRE) – Rose d'Or (IRE) (Polish Precedent (USA)) [2017/18 c–, h90: h20g⁵ h21.6m⁵ h23g⁵ h23.9g Nov 16] rather leggy gelding: modest handicap hurdler: maiden chaser: stays 3m: acts on firm and soft going: wears headgear: has worn tongue tie, including last 2 starts. *Jimmy Frost* — **c– / h85**

BACCHANEL (FR) 7 b.g. Vendangeur (IRE) – Pardielle (FR) (Robin des Champs (FR)) [2017/18 c111, h76: c23.6d c24.2vpu Jan 23] rangy gelding: modest form over hurdles: fair form over fences: folded tamely both starts in 2017/18: stays 3m: acts on heavy going: tried in cheekpieces: temperamental. *Philip Hobbs* — **c– § / h–**

BACHASSON (FR) 7 gr.g. Voix du Nord (FR) – Belledonne (FR) (Shafoun (FR)) [2017/18 c147p, h–: c22v* c21v* c26.3v^F Mar 16] smallish gelding: winning hurdler: very smart form over fences: won listed events at Thurles (by 24 lengths from Val de Ferbet) in November and Tramore (by 13 lengths from A Toi Phil) in January: fell second in Cheltenham Gold Cup: should stay 3m: acts on heavy going: usually travels strongly: remains open to improvement as a chaser. *W. P. Mullins, Ireland* — **c159 p / h–**

BACH DE CLERMONT (FR) 7 b.g. Della Francesca (USA) – Fleur de Princesse (FR) (Passing Sale (FR)) [2017/18 h116: h15.7g⁴ h16.8g³ h15.7d² c18g⁴ c16.3s² c20d³ Dec 22] well-made gelding: Irish point winner: fairly useful hurdler: won maiden at Southwell in May: second in novice at same course in October: similar form over fences: second in handicap at Fakenham in November: stays 2½m: acts on soft going: front runner/races prominently. *Evan Williams* — **c119 / h116**

BACHY BABY 6 b.g. Bach (IRE) – Bathwick Annie (Sula Bula) [2017/18 b15.8vsu b16.5m Apr 25] modest form in bumpers: likely to have finished fourth but for slipping up over 1f out at Ffos Las on debut: left Neil Mulholland after that. *Michael Blake* — **b77**

BACK BY MIDNIGHT 9 ch.g. Midnight Legend – Roberta Back (IRE) (Bob Back (USA)) [2017/18 c115, h–: c18g⁴ Oct 22] sturdy gelding: winning hurdler: fairly useful handicap chaser: stayed 2½m: acted on heavy going: tried in hood: wore tongue tie: front runner/raced prominently: dead. *Emma-Jane Bishop* — **c110 / h–**

BACK IN BLACK (IRE) 9 b.g. Strategic Prince – Leopardess (IRE) (Ela-Mana-Mou) [2017/18 h24g h20d h18.7mpu Aug 24] modest form over hurdles: left Michael G. Cleary after second start: best effort at 2m: acted on soft going: dead. *Katy Price* — **h77**

BACK IN JUNE 10 b.g. Bach (IRE) – Bathwick June (IRE) (Supreme Leader) [2017/18 c16.3d⁴ c25.8m² c27.5dpu Jun 9] lengthy gelding: multiple point winner, pulled up in December: maiden hurdler: modest maiden hunter chaser nowadays: stays 3¼m: acts on soft and good to firm going: often wears headgear. *Mrs K. Heard* — **c93 / h–**

BACKINTHESADDLE (IRE) 10 ch.g. Rudimentary (USA) – Grangeclare Lodge (IRE) (Top of The World) [2017/18 h95: c16v³ c20.5s⁶ h24s h20v⁵ h16v⁵ Dec 22] modest handicap hurdler: similar form over fences: stays 2½m: acts on soft going: tried in hood: wears tongue tie: front runner/races prominently: has joined Daniel Steele. *Stuart Crawford, Ireland* — **c85 / h88**

BACKOFTHEROCK 9 b.g. Scorpion (IRE) – Oscars Vision (IRE) (Oscar Schindler (IRE)) [2017/18 h20g h19.9m h26.5d⁵ h23.1g^F c25.8g⁴ c23g⁵ c22.5d² h23.6s⁴ c25.5s³ c26.7v^F Dec 7] raw-boned gelding: winning pointer: poor form over hurdles/fences: stays 3¼m: acts on good to soft going: often wears hood: wears tongue tie: often races in rear. *David Rees* — **c78 / h81**

BACK TO BALLOO (IRE) 12 gr.g. Jimble (FR) – Fleur du Chenet (FR) (Northern Fashion (USA)) [2017/18 c–, h97: h16m* h16.2g² h15.8g² h16.2g* h17.2g⁵ h16.3m⁴ h15.7g⁶ h15.8m h15.7d h16.6d ab16g² Mar 2] fair handicap hurdler: won at Fakenham (seller) in May and Hexham in June: winning chaser: stays 2¼m: acts on good to firm and heavy going: has worn headgear: tried in tongue tie. *Peter Winks* — **c– / h104**

BAH

BACK TO THE THATCH (IRE) 6 b.g. Westerner – Melville Rose (IRE) (Phardante (FR)) [2017/18 h120: c23.8v^F c22.9v^2 c20v^3 c23.6v* c32.6s^F c34v^{pu} Mar 17] fairly useful hurdler: fairly useful form over fences: won handicap at Chepstow in January: may prove best at around 3m: best form on soft/heavy going: often races towards rear: still unexposed as a chaser. *Henry Daly*   **c127 p** / **h–**

BACT TO BLACK 6 b.g. Black Sam Bellamy (IRE) – Linagram (Classic Cliche (IRE)) [2017/18 h76: h21.6v^{ur} h16v h21.6v h20.5v^5 h23.1v^2 h23.1v^6 Apr 17] modest maiden hurdler: stays 23f: best form on heavy going: tried in cheekpieces: often races prominently. *Robert Walford*   **h97**

BAD BOY DU POULDU (FR) 7 b.g. Loup Solitaire (USA) – Wild Flush (USA) (Pine Bluff (USA)) [2017/18 h110: c18g^5 c18d^2 c15.7d^2 c20.5d^{pu} c19.9s c19.9d^5 Mar 26] good-topped gelding: fair hurdler: similar form over fences: stays 2½m: acts on soft going: often wears headgear: tried in tongue tie. *Gary Moore*   **c114** / **h–**

BADDESLEY KNIGHT (IRE) 5 b.g. Doyen (IRE) – Grangeclare Rhythm (IRE) (Lord Americo) [2017/18 b17.7g^3 b16.3s^2 b17.7s* Apr 15] second foal: dam (h97), maiden hurdler (best effort at 2m), half-sister to smart hurdler/chaser (stayed 2½m) Real Steel: fairly useful form in bumpers: won at Plumpton in April. *Chris Gordon*   **b104**

BADEN (FR) 7 gr.g. Martaline – Ma Sonate (USA) (Val de L'Orne (FR)) [2017/18 h122: c20s^4 c23.4s^2 c24d^2 c24.2s* c25.3g^4 Apr 18] deep-girthed, well-made gelding: fairly useful hurdler: similar form over fences: won Grand Military Gold Cup (Amateur Riders) at Sandown in March: stays 25f: acts on soft going: in cheekpieces last 2 starts: front runner/races prominently. *Nicky Henderson*   **c129** / **h–**

BADGERFORT (IRE) 9 b.g. Fruits of Love (USA) – Ding Dong Belle (Minster Son) [2017/18 h20.2m c25.8m^{pu} h23.3g^{pu} Jul 19] lengthy, leggy gelding: fair maiden hurdler: similar form at best over fences: left N. Madden after first start: stays 3m: acts on soft going: tried in cheekpieces: often races towards rear: often let down by jumping over fences. *Jonjo O'Neill*   **c– x** / **h97**

BADILOU (FR) 7 b.g. Ballingarry (IRE) – Doumia (FR) (Dounba (FR)) [2017/18 h70: h21.6s c25.8g^6 c23g^3 c20g^{pu} h21.6v c19.4v^3 c21.7v^{pu} c18.2m Apr 25] angular gelding: fair hurdler at best, well held both starts in 2017/18: poor form over fences: stays 23f: best form on good going: wears headgear: often travels strongly. *Martin Hill*   **c83** / **h–**

BAFANA BLUE 7 b.g. Blueprint (IRE) – Anniejo (Presenting) [2017/18 h–, b–: h19.9g^3 h20.1v^4 h19.9g^6 h20.5s^3 h20.1s^2 h19.5s^1 h21.4v^{pu} h19.9v^4 h16.8g Apr 23] compact gelding: modest maiden hurdler: stays 2½m: acts on heavy going: wears tongue tie. *Maurice Barnes*   **h95**

BAFANA CHOICE 12 b.g. Bollin Eric – Lorna's Choice (Oats) [2017/18 c93: c24.2g^2 c21.2d^6 c24.2g^5 c25.5g^3 c25.5s^2 Jul 22] multiple point winner: modest maiden chaser: stays 3¼m: acts on soft going: has worn cheekpieces: usually races close up. *Chris Grant*   **c99**

BAGAD BIHOUE (FR) 7 b.g. Nickname (FR) – Lann Bihouee (FR) (Video Rock (FR)) [2017/18 h129, b102: c20.5m* c20g^{pu} c16.3m* c16.3d^2 c17.3g^6 c16.3d^2 c24.2d^{ur} c18.8g^6 Nov 4] useful-looking gelding: fairly useful hurdler: useful chaser: won novices at Kempton and Warwick in May, and Newton Abbot in June (by 30 lengths from Kayf Blanco) and July: stays 2¾m, effective at much shorter: acts on good to firm and good to soft going: usually leads. *Paul Nicholls*   **c141** / **h–**

BAGGING TURF (IRE) 8 b.m. Scorpion (IRE) – Monica's Story (Arzanni) [2017/18 c116, h–: c16.4s^5 c19.5v^4 c16v^5 Mar 5] lengthy mare: winning hurdler: fair handicap chaser, well below form in 2017/18: stays 21f: acts on heavy going: often in cheekpieces. *Gary Moore*   **c89** / **h–**

BAGS GROOVE (IRE) 7 b.g. Oscar (IRE) – Golden Moment (IRE) (Roselier (FR)) [2017/18 h128: h19.5d h20d* h21d* h21s Jan 13] good-topped gelding: useful handicap hurdler: won at Aintree in October and Kempton (by 1¼ lengths from The Last Samuri) in November: stays 21f: acts on good to soft going: tried in cheekpieces: wears tongue tie. *Harry Fry*   **h141**

BAHAMA MOON (IRE) 6 b.g. Lope de Vega (IRE) – Bahama Bay (GER) (Dansili) [2017/18 h15.8s^6 h15.8v h16v^{pu} h15.8d Mar 26] fairly useful on Flat, stays 10.5f: modest form over hurdles, standout effort on debut: will prove best at easy 2m. *Jonjo O'Neill*   **h97**

BAH LAMB 7 ch.m. Sakhee (USA) – Lucinda Lamb (Kayf Tara) [2017/18 b–: b16.8g^6 May 4] no form in bumpers. *Andrew Crook*   **b–**

BAHRIKATE 5 b.m. Bahri (USA) – Dispol Katie (Komaite (USA)) [2017/18 h91: h16.2g^3 h16.2g^6 h16.2g^4 h17d^3 h16.8s^4 h16s^2 h16.2s^{ur} Apr 26] modest handicap hurdler: likely to prove best at sharp 2m: acts on soft going: wears tongue tie. *Susan Corbett*   **h96**

89

BAHUMBUG 8 b.g. Bahamian Bounty – Stan's Smarty Girl (USA) (Smarty Jones (USA))   **c59**
[2017/18 c–, h–: c25.5g^{pu} c17.4d^3 h18.5v^{pu} h19.8s^{pu} Nov 23] sturdy gelding: little form   **h–**
over hurdles/fences: left Seamus Mullins after second start: often wears headgear
nowadays: tried in tongue tie. *Jackie du Plessis*

BAIE DES ILES (FR) 7 gr.m. Barastraight – Malownia (FR) (Smadoun (FR))   **c144**
[2017/18 c143, h–: h22.6v^6 c19.5v^6 c28.7v^3 c34.3s Apr 14]   **h117**

    Successes for British- or Irish-trained jumpers in the top French races over hurdles are no longer the rarity they once were. Three consecutive editions of the top French hurdle, the Grande Course de Haies d'Auteuil, fell to British stables between 2015 and 2017 and it is a race that had been won four times earlier this century by Willie Mullins. Mullins had the runner-up, Bapaume, in the latest edition after the end of the British and Irish seasons at the end of May, and three weeks later Bapaume went one better in the Prix La Barka to become his trainer's third consecutive winner of a contest which has now swapped places in the calendar with the Grande Course de Haies, having formerly served as the main preparatory race. The last seven editions of the La Barka have been won by the visitors, five of them by Mullins. Auteuil's chases, on the other hand, are a very different matter. Considerably fewer British or Irish chasers take on the varied and sometimes daunting obstacles of Auteuil's steeplechase course and major successes are extremely rare. Which is why the victory of the seven-year-old Irish-trained mare Baie des Iles in the Prix des Drags, a contest worth €99,000 to the winner on the same card as the La Barka, deserved more publicity than it received on a day when international focus was on Justify's completion of the American Triple Crown.

    It has been a long time since Mandarin's famous victory in the 1962 Grand Steeple-Chase de Paris for trainer Fulke Walwyn and jockey Fred Winter. The only chaser since then from outside France to go close to winning the top French steeplechase was the Pat Taaffe-trained Captain Christy who was runner-up in 1975. The outstanding Captain Christy won a Cheltenham Gold Cup and two editions of the King George, as did Long Run who finished well held in his attempt to win the Grand Steeple-Chase in 2014. The Mullins-trained Djakadam became the latest foreign challenger in the Grand Steeple-Chase de Paris but the dual Cheltenham Gold Cup runner-up sustained a career-ending injury when a tailed-off last of eight finishers in May. In winning the Group 2 Prix des Drags, Baie des Iles became only the third chaser trained outside France to win a major prize over fences since the top French jumps races were given pattern status in 1999; Batman Senora won the 2003 Prix La Haye Jousselin for Ian Williams and Halley the 2011 Prix Maurice Gillois for four-year-olds for Tom George. Baie des Iles was not the first Irish-trained winner of the Prix des Drags, however. The race was won in 1970 by Herring Gull, winner of the Irish Grand National two years earlier. He was trained by Willie Mullins' father Paddy who went on to win both the Grande Course de Haies and La Barka with Dawn Run, though it was Chantilly trainer John Ciechanowski whose name appeared on the programme next to Herring Gull, seemingly to avoid some infamous French red tape. 'All I can remember is that it avoided the horse having to cross the Belgian border twice!' recalled Willie Mullins when asked about the venture after Baie des Iles' success. The main reason for Herring Gull's trip across the Channel had been to contest the Grand Steeple-Chase de Paris but he fell in that race and was

Prix des Drags Chase, Auteuil—Baie des Iles takes full advantage of her light weight to claim a rare big chase win for a foreign raider on French soil

turned out again for the Prix des Drags (then a handicap) three days later, ridden in both races by former British champion Stan Mellor. A more recent Irish challenger in the Drags was the Ted Walsh-trained Seabass who finished a respectable sixth on his Auteuil debut in 2013 for Ruby Walsh.

Seabass was best known for finishing third in the previous year's Grand National under Katie Walsh, the best placing in the race by a female jockey. There was plenty of support for Katie Walsh in her attempt to better that effort in the latest Grand National on Baie des Iles, who is trained by her husband Ross O'Sullivan. Sent off at 16/1 for what proved to be Walsh's final ride in the race (she announced her retirement from the saddle at the Punchestown Festival), Baie des Iles trailed home last of the dozen finishers after never getting into the race (she has often been ridden more prominently) and was still towards the rear when hampered by a loose horse at Valentine's on the second circuit. Although young by Grand National standards, Baie des Iles had plenty of chasing experience, proven as a thorough stayer who goes well in the mud. Both her Irish wins had come in staying handicap chases at Punchestown, notably when making all in the Grand National Trial over three and a half miles in 2017. In a light campaign building up to Aintree in the latest season, which had begun over hurdles, Baie des Iles ran her best race when third to Folsom Blue in the same race in February, having also finished runner-up in 2016. She had also finished sixth in the Irish Grand National and fifth in the Welsh National (won by Native River) when still only a five-year-old.

For her tilt at the Prix des Drags, Baie des Iles had previous experience around Auteuil to call on. She was trained in France as a three-year-old by Arnaud Chaille-Chaille and had won at the track over both hurdles and fences. On her final start for her French stable she finished third in the Group 2 Prix Congress, the top chase for three-year-olds. It was won by Kobrouk whom Baie des Iles had beaten into third on her previous start and who went on to be one of the leading four-year-old chasers of his crop, finishing second to So French in the Prix Maurice Gillois the following autumn. So French went on to win two editions of the Grand Steeple-Chase de Paris but his hopes of a hat-trick in the latest renewal were ended quickly when he was brought down in a three-horse pile-up at the very first obstacle, caused by the fall of the Prix La Haye Jousselin winner Bipolaire. Bipolaire and So French headed the betting in the Prix des Drags, with Baie des Iles one of the outsiders in the field of nine at odds of 27/1. Baie des Iles showed prominently in the early stages but by the time they came to the big water jump in front of the stands, the riviere des tribunes, she had drifted back and had just one behind her. Meanwhile, So French cut out the running but showed little conviction in his jumping and, while the leader was hesitant at the formidable 'rail ditch and fence' five out, Baie des Iles gained several places with a good jump on the outside that put her right back into contention. Once in line for home, Baie des Iles asserted from So French at the second last and stayed on well on the run-in to beat Bipolaire, from whom she was getting almost a stone, by a length and a quarter, while So French faded into sixth. Paul Townend, who had earlier partnered Bapaume in the La Barka, thus won both the big races on the card, that despite being in the middle of serving the lengthy ban he had picked up at the Punchestown Festival. Irish suspensions only apply on days when there is jump racing in Ireland and, being a blank day at home, Townend was free to ride abroad.

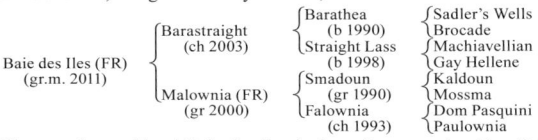

Baie des Iles (FR) (gr.m. 2011)	Barastraight (ch 2003)	Barathea (b 1990)	Sadler's Wells
			Brocade
		Straight Lass (b 1998)	Machiavellian
			Gay Hellene
	Malownia (FR) (gr 2000)	Smadoun (gr 1990)	Kaldoun
			Mossma
		Falownia (ch 1993)	Dom Pasquini
			Paulownia

The non-thoroughbred Baie des Iles is the only runner in either Britain or Ireland to date for her sire Barastraight whose biggest win came in the Group 3 Prix La Force over a mile and a quarter. Barastraight's dam was a half-sister to the high-class hurdler and Cesarewitch winner Landing Light. Baie des Iles' dam Malownia raced only on the Flat, winning a couple of 'French bumpers' or AQPS races, over eleven furlongs, and she has produced one other winner so far, Valownia

BAI

(by Ballingarry), successful in a similar event, and a chase over seventeen furlongs. Otherwise, the family has had most success with a couple of its exports to Britain. Harlov, out of Baie des Iles' great grandam Paulownia, a cross-country chaser, was also a thorough stayer whose wins included the North Yorkshire Grand National at Catterick and the Champion Hunters' Chase at Stratford. Camitrov, a half-brother to Paulownia, finished third in the Arkle and the Peterborough Chase and went on to win a Grand Military Gold Cup. The angular Baie des Iles, who wears cheekpieces, stays really well—she coped surprisingly well with the shorter trip in the Prix des Drags which is run over two and three quarter miles—and she should have no problems with the extra mile or so of the Grand Steeple-Chase de Paris at which she will be aimed in 2019. It will be interesting to see if the enterprise shown by her small stable, which was so well rewarded, prompts more frequent raids on Auteuil's chases by other British and Irish yards. The prize money is excellent, but some course experience is almost certainly a must. *Ross O'Sullivan, Ireland*

BAIHAS 8 b.g. Nayef (USA) – Allegretto (IRE) (Galileo (IRE)) [2017/18 h20v h19.5v h16.8v h19.2d^{pu} Feb 25] useful 1¾m winner on Flat at 3 yrs: no form over hurdles in 2017/18 after long absence: tried in tongue tie. *Neil Mulholland* h–

BAILEYS CONCERTO (IRE) 12 b.g. Bach (IRE) – None The Wiser (IRE) (Dr Massini (IRE)) [2017/18 c125, h–: c19.9g^4 c23.8g^4 c23.8g^2 c23.8d^3 c25d c20.1g^5 c19.1d c24s^{pu} Jan 26] winning hurdler: fairly useful handicap chaser: stayed 3m: acted on heavy going: usually wore headgear: sometimes wore tongue tie: usually raced prominently: dead. *Dianne Sayer* c117 h–

BAILEYS GALAXY (FR) 5 b.g. Elusive City (USA) – Kosmic View (USA) (Distant View (USA)) [2017/18 h16.7m h16.7g h16.3s^{pu} Dec 20] modest maiden on Flat: no form over hurdles: dead. *Sarah-Jayne Davies* h–

BAJARDO (IRE) 10 b.g. Jammaal – Bit of Peace (IRE) (Le Bavard (FR)) [2017/18 c97, h–: c15.7g^4 c16.3s* c17.8v^3 c18.2s^{bd} c15.9v^3 Mar 9] raw-boned gelding: maiden hurdler: modest handicap chaser: won at Fakenham in December: stays 2¼m: acts on heavy going: wears tongue tie nowadays. *Emma-Jane Bishop* c99 h–

BAKO DE LA SAULAIE (FR) 7 b.g. Balko (FR) – Krickette (FR) (Passing Sale (FR)) [2017/18 h116: c23.4s^4 c24s^2 c24.5v^2 c20.6s* Mar 21] fairly useful hurdler: similar form over fences: second in handicap at Doncaster in January: stays 3m: acts on soft going: usually travels strongly. *Rose Dobbin* c122 h–

BALACH MOR (IRE) 6 b.g. Robin des Champs (FR) – Silver Skirt (IRE) (Silver Patriarch (IRE)) [2017/18 b–: h19.5d^{pu} Oct 31] no show in bumper/maiden hurdle. *Michael Scudamore* h–

BALANCING TIME 5 b.g. Pivotal – Time On (Sadler's Wells (USA)) [2017/18 h17.7m* Aug 17] fairly useful on Flat, stays 2m: 8/1, won novice at Fontwell (dictated, by nose from Psychedelic Rock) on hurdling debut. *Amanda Perrett* h108

BAL DE RIO (FR) 5 b.g. Vertigineux (FR) – Baldoranic (FR) (Panoramic (FR)) [2017/18 h19.9g^2 h16.2d^3 h17s^2 h19.9s^2 h16.8v^2 Feb 22] fairly useful on Flat, stays 16.5f: fair form over hurdles: stays 2½m: acts on soft going: in headgear last 2 starts: often races prominently. *Brian Ellison* h112

BALGEMMOIS (FR) 5 ch.g. Balko (FR) – Venise Doree (FR) (Starborough) [2017/18 h99, b73: h19.8s h15.5s* h15.5v^4 h16v^5 h20.5s Apr 15] rather unfurnished gelding: fair handicap hurdler: won at Leicester in December: should stay further than 2m: acts on heavy going: front runner/races prominently. *Ali Stronge* h110

BALIBOUR (FR) 6 b.g. Policy Maker (IRE) – Saintheze (FR) (Saint des Saints (FR)) [2017/18 b–: b16g^4 h19.9d^6 h22g^5 h21.4s^3 h19.6s^3 h16v^2 h19v Mar 12] poor form in bumpers: fair form over hurdles: stays 2¾m: acts on heavy going: tried in tongue tie. *Emma Lavelle* h113 b70

BALKATO DES BOIS (FR) 7 b.g. Balko (FR) – Equatoriale (FR) (Saint Estephe (FR)) [2017/18 h20.6s^{pu} Apr 11] failed to complete all 5 starts in points: well held in bumper: pulled up in maiden on hurdling debut. *Robyn Brisland* h–

BALKINSTOWN (IRE) 8 b.g. Westerner – Graffogue (IRE) (Red Sunset) [2017/18 h23m^6 h23g* h24g^4 h23.6s^3 h25d^3 h21.6v^3 h23.8s^6 h21s Feb 9] point winner: modest handicap hurdler: won at Worcester (amateur) in July: stays 23f: acts on heavy going: wears headgear/tongue tie. *Robert Stephens* h91

BALKO DES FLOS (FR) 7 ch.g. Balko (FR) – Royale Marie (FR) (Garde Royale)   c166
[2017/18 c149, h–: c22.5g* c20v^2 c20.6v^3 c24d^2 c20.8s* c19.9s^4 Apr 13]   h–

A fifth day? Speculation continues that the Cheltenham Festival might be about to be expanded again—though Cheltenham says such a move is 'not on the table'. If commercial forces eventually win the argument, Cheltenham will forfeit any shred of integrity as jumping's major championships. The Festival has made its name by bringing the best horses of each type to race against each other, with the aim of identifying the season's champions. The creation of a fourth day in 2005 and the addition of further races since then has already resulted in too much watering down—there are now twenty-eight races, compared to the eighteen, and then nineteen (the Champion Bumper), when the Festival was three days. Sir Anthony McCoy, now the star pundit for Cheltenham's terrestrial rights holder ITV, is one of the most vehement critics of further expansion. 'I worry about how diluted it has become already and there are still talks about five days,' he said in a *Racing Post* interview in the latest season. 'The whole game's gone if that happens. There are races at the Festival that are a waste of space as it is and it will end up like a lot of the festivals in Ireland with one or two decent races a day. The rest won't be worth watching. Is that good for the sport?' A fifth day at Cheltenham would only lead to the good horses being spread even more thinly to make the most of the increased opportunities. There are already five races restricted to novice chasers, for example, with the Golden Miller, which was only added to the Festival in 2011, being fast-tracked after only three runnings to join the two long-standing Grade 1s, the Arkle Trophy and the RSA Chase.

The advent of a four-day Festival did not result in wholesale amendments to the running order, with Cheltenham being careful to retain, where possible, sequences of races that racegoers and punters were familiar with. The Champion Hurdle, preceded by the Supreme Novices' and the Arkle, remained on the first day, with the Queen Mother Champion Chase and the RSA among the retained second-day highlights and the Gold Cup and the Triumph Hurdle heading the final day as usual. The fourth day—which chronologically became the third day—saw the Stayers' Hurdle plucked from its supporting role on Gold Cup day (until the early-'nineties it was run on Champion Hurdle day) to head the programme, supported by a new race, the Festival Trophy, which replaced the Cathcart which used to be run on the final card of the three-day Festival, with its entry restricted to novices and second-season chasers. The new fourth—or rather third—day has sometimes struggled to live up to its billing, though the Stayers' [World] Hurdle has had some notable winners since its 'promotion', among them three-times winner Inglis Drever and four-times winner Big Buck's. The Festival Trophy, sponsored since its second

thetote.com Galway Plate, Galway—a second Galway Plate win in three years for trainer Henry de Bromhead as Balko des Flos forges clear under Davy Russell; the favourite Shaneshill (centre), Slowmotion (right) and A Toi Phil (star on cap) complete the frame

Ryanair Chase (Festival Trophy), Cheltenham—
Balko des Flos already has the measure of 2017 winner Un de Sceaux two out as the sponsors finally land their own race after numerous near-misses

running by Ryanair, has had its moments too, with Cue Card and Vautour its best winners, but the creation of this open championship race, over an intermediate distance, has sometimes been a distraction for potential contenders for the Queen Mother Champion Chase and the Gold Cup. Cheltenham's determination, however, to build the Ryanair Chase into a genuine championship event in its own right finally resulted in its overtaking the Stayers' Hurdle in value in the latest season when the third day became known—and recognised on the front cover of the official race card—as Ryanair Chase day, rather than Stayers' [World] Hurdle day, as it had been labelled since the expansion of the Festival to four days.

Field sizes aren't always a fair barometer of a race's standing but the six-strong field for the latest Ryanair Chase was the smallest for the race since it replaced the Cathcart. The contest was rendered even more disappointing by the below-par performances on the day of the two previous winners in the line-up, odds-on Un de Sceaux and the second favourite Cue Card, the last-named pulled up on what turned out to be his swansong at the age of twelve. The previous year's runner-up Sub Lieutenant wasn't in the same form this time around either, managing to beat only the equally disappointing Frodon. Sub Lieutenant's second to Un de Sceaux in 2017 had made him the latest of four runners-up in the race to carry the Gigginstown House Stud colours. Gigginstown House Stud is the name under which Ryanair supremo Michael O'Leary runs his horses and an elusive victory in the race he sponsors was finally achieved in the latest edition by the other runner to carry the maroon, white star and armlets, seven-year-old Balko des Flos who gained his first Grade 1 success after finishing second at 66/1—splitting two other Gigginstown runners Road To Respect and Outlander—in the Leopardstown Christmas Chase on his previous outing, seeming to excel himself on that occasion but going on to repeat his much improved form at Cheltenham.

Balko des Flos was among the sixty horses famously removed by his owners from Willie Mullins in September 2016 over a reported disagreement about an increase in training fees. Mullins' biggest rival Gordon Elliott was the chief beneficiary as the horses were dispersed among Gigginstown's other trainers, but useful hurdler Balko des Flos was among a smaller group sent to Henry de Bromhead. Balko des Flos had finished fifth in the Spa Novices' at Cheltenham and fourth in the Sefton at Aintree on his last two outings for Mullins but, like nearly all the Gigginstown recruits, he had been bought as a long-term chasing prospect and he made his debut over fences for de Bromhead in November 2016, after seven months off. Bellshill and Don't Touch It, both winners of Grade 1 novice hurdles, made their eagerly anticipated debuts over fences in the same maiden chase at Gowran and Balko des Flos split them at the finish, making an encouraging start to his new career and looking sure to progress. He won only once that season, however, in a maiden chase at Fairyhouse but finished third to Disko and Our Duke in the Grade 1 Flogas Novices' Chase at Leopardstown and was running well in the Golden Miller at Cheltenham, yet to be asked for his effort, when falling heavily at the fourth last.

Balko des Flos returned to winning ways on his first outing of the latest season in a typically competitive renewal of thetote.com Galway Plate in early-August, landing Ireland's second richest handicap chase (behind only the Irish National) in good style by four and three quarter lengths from Shaneshill, from whom he received 7 lb. The finish was dominated largely by second-season chasers and it was only the seventh start over fences for Balko des Flos who produced a career-best effort, up to that time. He couldn't repeat the form, however, with the Galway Chase fourth A Toi Phil when runner-up next time in the Grade 2 Champion Chase at Gowran and he finished behind A Toi Phil again when the pair filled the minor places behind Alpha des Obeaux in another Grade 2 the Clonmel Oil Chase, jumping mistakes not helping his cause on either occasion. Both Alpha des Obeaux and Balko des Flos were sent off at 66/1 in the Leopardstown Christmas Chase, the Grade 1 (sponsored by Lexus from 2004/5 until the latest season) that is Ireland's closest equivalent to the King George VI Chase and regarded as the mid-season championship chase in Ireland for stayers. Balko des Flos jumped much better than he had at Gowran and Clonmel which, together with the step back up in trip—it was his first run at three miles since his third in the Flogas Novices'—and the return to a sounder surface, offered the most plausible explanation for his improved effort in running Road To Respect to a length and a quarter, seeing the race out well after being prominent all the way and only being collared by the winner at the last.

If Balko des Flos had benefited from the combination of being put back to three miles and encountering a sounder surface, he didn't have either at Cheltenham, finding himself down in trip again to two miles five furlongs in the Ryanair for which the going was very soft. With the exuberant Un de Sceaux in the line-up, Balko des Flos was ridden more patiently than usual, given a fine ride by Davy Russell whose prowess was highlighted in Cheltenham week by four winners (pipping Jack Kennedy to the meeting's top jockey title by virtue of more second places). Russell sent Balko des Flos in pursuit of Un de Sceaux coming down the hill on the approach to the home straight. In front on the bridle at the third last, and cementing his advantage rounding the final turn, with Russell kicking him on, Balko des Flos never looked like being caught. Despite not being fluent at the last (his jumping was good otherwise), he went on to beat Un de Sceaux, ridden out, by four and a half lengths, with Cloudy Dream a further eight lengths back in third and Sub Lieutenant another fifteen behind in fourth. The placed horses might not have produced their best on the day, but Balko des Flos almost certainly did and, in hindsight, the race probably took plenty out of him. He showed nothing like the same form when fourth in the Melling Chase at Aintree on his only subsequent outing, finishing over thirty lengths behind as the finish was fought out by Politologue and Min who had been in the frame behind Altior in the Queen Mother Champion Chase, which turned out to be a much stronger Grade 1 than the Ryanair in the latest season.

Balko des Flos (FR) (ch.g. 2011)	Balko (FR) (b 2001)	Pistolet Bleu (b 1988)	Top Ville
			Pampa Bella
		Ella Royale (gr 1994)	Royal Charter
			La Main Heureuse
	Royale Marie (FR) (b 1997)	Garde Royale (br 1980)	Mill Reef
			Royal Way
		Marie des Epeires (b 1990)	Rose Laurel
			Marie de Bethisy

The good-topped Balko des Flos is by Balko who stands at Haras du Lion in France at a fee of €6,000. Balko was trained by Guillaume Macaire, who handled several other popular jumps stallions in their racing days, among them Saint des Saints and Robin des Champs. Balko won nine times over jumps for Macaire and

BAL

was successful in Group 2 company over both hurdles and fences. Balko's stock have been quite well represented in recent seasons in Britain and Ireland, with Gitane du Berlais among the first to put him on the map on this side of the Channel when she won the Scilly Isles Novices' Chase at Sandown in 2015 as a five-year-old. A close relation to Balko des Flos and by the same sire, the Colin Tizzard-trained Vision des Flos (a €270,000 purchase as a four-year-old) was second to Draconien in the Champion Novices' Hurdle at the latest Punchestown Festival. Marie Royale (by Turgeon), the dam of Vision des Flos, is a daughter of Balko des Flos' dam Royale Marie who was successful at two and a quarter miles over hurdles in France. Royale Marie has now bred two Cheltenham Festival winners, also being the dam of the ill-fated Salut Flo (by Saint des Saints) who won the Plate, the handicap chase over the Ryanair Chase distance, in 2012. Royale Marie has since had a third winner in Flot des Flos, a five-year-old sister to Balko des Flos, who has been successful over jumps in France. Marie des Epeires, the grandam of Balko des Flos, won on the Flat, over hurdles and over fences in France and is a half-sister to Marie de Beaujeu, the dam of Deutches Derby winner All My Dreams and the grandam of the Beverly D Stakes winner I'm A Dreamer. Balko des Flos, who stays twenty-five furlongs and is effective at shorter, is regarded by connections as best suited by ground no softer than good to soft, but he handled the testing conditions at the Cheltenham Festival well enough. He usually races close up but was waited with at Cheltenham. *Henry de Bromhead, Ireland*

BALLASALLA (IRE) 6 br.g. Presenting – Papoose (IRE) (Little Bighorn) [2017/18 b–: b16.7s h19.3s⁶ h19.4s h19.9v Mar 23] behind in bumpers: modest form over hurdles: tried in tongue tie: often races prominently. *Donald McCain* — **h88 b–**

BALL D'ARC (FR) 7 b.g. Network (GER) – Pretty Moon (FR) (Moon Madness) [2017/18 c154, h–: c19.5s³ c16v* c17dᵘʳ c16s⁵ Feb 25] sturdy gelding: winning hurdler: very smart chaser: won Poplar Square Chase at Naas (by 5 lengths from Ordinary World) in November: reportedly lame final start: stays 2½m: acts on heavy going: has worn hood: often races towards rear: consistent. *Gordon Elliott, Ireland* — **c157 h–**

BALLET MARBLELESS 12 b.g. Baryshnikov (AUS) – Lost Your Marbles (IRE) (Mandalus) [2017/18 c–: c21.1s⁶ c17d Jun 9] long-standing maiden pointer: little impact in hunter chases: in cheekpieces/tongue tie last 2 starts. *John Mead* — **c–**

BALLI MARTINE (FR) 5 b.g. Ballingarry (IRE) – Miss Martine (FR) (Waki River (FR)) [2017/18 b15.8d³ b16s ab16g² Mar 5] €7,500 3-y-o: closely related to 2 winners in France by French Glory, including 2¼m hurdle winner Frenchtine, and half-brother to fairly useful hurdler/useful chaser Solighoster (2m-3m winner, by Loup Solitaire): dam unraced: fair form in bumpers: best effort when second at Lingfield in March: wears hood. *Noel Williams* — **b90**

BALLINACLASHA LAD (IRE) 12 b.g. Snurge – Best Trump (Le Bavard (FR)) [2017/18 c24.2mᵖᵘ May 9] point winner: in tongue tie, pulled up in hunter on chasing debut: dead. *L. Jefford* — **c–**

BALLINAHINCH (IRE) 6 b.g. Oscar (IRE) – Before (IRE) (Ore) [2017/18 ab16g⁴ b15.8d² Mar 22] €25,000 3-y-o: sixth foal: brother to 9.5f-1½m winner Mongoose Alert and to a winning pointer: dam unraced half-sister to fairly useful chaser (stayed 21f) Cool Spot: fairly useful form in bumpers: second at Ludlow in March. *Seamus Durack* — **b95**

BALLINA LADY (IRE) 7 b.m. Royal Storm (IRE) – Tinas Friend (Environment Friend) [2017/18 h21.3s h19.6sᵖᵘ h16.5sᵖᵘ c19.4d⁴ Apr 22] £6,500 6-y-o: third foal: dam unraced: in frame last 3 starts in Irish points: no form over hurdles: 16/1, fourth in novice handicap at Stratford (tongue tied, 15¼ lengths behind Zamparelli) on chasing debut. *Graeme McPherson* — **c69 h–**

BALLINISKA BAND (IRE) 4 b.g. Vinnie Roe (IRE) – Maryiver (IRE) (Runyon (IRE)) [2017/18 b16v* b16v* Apr 12] third foal: half-brother to useful hurdler Gowiththeflow (21f winner, by Westerner) and fairly useful hurdler Lough Derg Farmer (21f-2¾m winner, by Presenting), both winning pointers: dam (c112/h114) 2m-21f hurdle/chase winner: useful form in bumpers: won maiden at Naas (by 2¼ lengths from Eagle Roque) in February and listed event at Limerick (by 6 lengths from Barrington Court) in April. *Charles Byrnes, Ireland* — **b106**

BALLINSLEA BRIDGE (IRE) 6 b.g. Pierre – Feelin' Looser (IRE) (Mazaad) [2017/18 b16g² b16.4g² h20s² h16.7s² h18.6v* h19.3v* Feb 19] £25,000 5-y-o: fourth foal: dam, (h78) 2m hurdle winner, also 1¼m-13f winner on Flat: off mark at fourth attempt in Irish — **h125 p b94**

points: fair form in bumpers: runner-up both starts in November: fairly useful form over hurdles: won novices at Market Rasen in January and Carlisle in February: should be suited by 2½m+: front runner/races prominently: remains open to improvement. *Olly Murphy*

BALLINTARA (IRE) 6 b.g. Getaway (GER) – Miltara (IRE) (Milan) [2017/18 b87: h19.5d h20.5v^4 h21s h25d^6 Apr 24] workmanlike gelding: fell in point: fair form over hurdles. *Diana Grissell*   h105

BALLINURE (IRE) 8 b.g. Alkaadhem – Christy's Pride (IRE) (Kambalda) [2017/18 h119: c21.4g* c23g^{pu} c22.6m* h21.6g c18.8g Nov 4] compact gelding: fairly useful hurdler: similar form over fences: won maiden at Market Rasen in June and novice at Stratford in August: stays 3m: acts on good to firm and good to soft going: tried in cheekpieces. *Nicky Henderson*   c128 h–

BALLINVARRIG (IRE) 11 b.g. Beneficial – Leos Holiday (IRE) (Commanche Run) [2017/18 c132§, h–: c19.4v^{pu} c20.2v^{pu} Feb 1] big, strong gelding: maiden hurdler: useful chaser at best, pulled up both starts in 2017/18: stays 3m: acts on heavy going: wears headgear: usually races prominently, often travels strongly. *Tom George*   c– h–

BALLOTIN (FR) 7 b.g. Enrique – Orphee de Vonnas (FR) (Jimble (FR)) [2017/18 c21.9s^3 c19.4d^4 c17.4s^5 c21d^2 h19.8s^{pu} Apr 28] fourth foal: brother to bumper winner/fairly useful hurdler Voluptueux (2m winner): dam French 2m-19f hurdle/chase winner: bumper winner: useful hurdler, pulled up final start in 2017/18: smart chaser: won handicap at Wetherby (by neck from Monbeg River) in October: left Guillaume Macaire after first start: stays 3m: acts on heavy going: wears headgear. *Philip Hobbs*   c146 h–

BALLYALTON (IRE) 11 b.g. Pierre – Almilto (IRE) (Mandalus) [2017/18 h20d^6 c20.4s^4 c20.8s^4 c24d^{pu} c20.8s^4 c21.1s^5 Apr 13] tall, good sort: smart hurdler at best: useful handicap chaser: fourth in BetVictor Gold Cup at Cheltenham (6½ lengths behind Splash of Ginge) in November: stays 2¾m: acts on good to firm and heavy going: usually wears cheekpieces: strong traveller. *Ian Williams*   c139 h128

BALLYANDREW (IRE) 7 b.g. Westerner – Royale Acadou (FR) (Cadoudal (FR)) [2017/18 h–: h20g^3 h22g h20g^{pu} h15.8d^3 c17.4g^6 Aug 16] modest form over hurdles: 9/1, sixth in novice handicap at Bangor (17¼ lengths behind Sage Monkey) on chasing debut: best effort at 2m: acts on good to soft going: tried in hood. *Nigel Twiston-Davies*   c81 h85

BALLYANDY 7 b.g. Kayf Tara – Megalex (Karinga Bay) [2017/18 h145: c20.1v* c20.8s^4 c20.8v^{pu} Jan 27] well-made gelding: smart hurdler: useful form over fences: won novice at Perth in September, digging deep: will stay beyond 2½m: acts on heavy going. *Nigel Twiston-Davies*   c139 h–

BALLYANTICS (IRE) 7 b.g. Marienbard (IRE) – Ballindante (IRE) (Phardante (FR)) [2017/18 h–: h16.8g^6 h16g h20g h21.7d h23.9s^3 h24.1v^5 h23.9v^4 h21.7g^6 Apr 20] modest maiden hurdler: stays 3m: acts on heavy going: usually races prominently. *Neil Mulholland*   h88

BALLYARTHUR (IRE) 8 b.g. Kayf Tara – Ariels Serenade (IRE) (Presenting) [2017/18 h126: c25d^3 c19.8g^{pu} c20.2s^2 c22.7v^3 c20v* c20.1s* Apr 26] tall gelding: fairly useful hurdler: useful form over fences: won novice handicaps at Uttoxeter and Perth (by 8 lengths from Bollin Ace) in April: stays 21f: acts on heavy going: often wears tongue tie: races prominently. *Nigel Twiston-Davies*   c137 h–

BALLYBEN (IRE) 10 ch.g. Beneficial – I'm Maggy (NZ) (Danseur Etoile (FR)) [2017/18 c127, h–: c23.8v* c24.5s h24.4s c23.8s Apr 25] fair hurdler at best: fairly useful chaser: won at Perth in September: stays 3¼m: acts on heavy going: has worn cheekpieces, including final start: usually races close up. *Ruth Jefferson*   c129 h–

BALLYBOLLEY (IRE) 9 b.g. Kayf Tara – Gales Hill (IRE) (Beau Sher) [2017/18 c148, h–: c21g^3 c20g^F c22.5g c21.4g* c19.9s^3 c24d^5 c20.5d^6 c20.8s Mar 15] tall gelding: winning hurdler: smart handicap chaser: won listed event at Market Rasen (by 4 lengths from Guitar Pete) in September: stays 21f: acts on good to firm and heavy going: has worn hood: wears tongue tie: often races in rear. *Nigel Twiston-Davies*   c147 h–

BALLYBROWNEYBRIDGE (IRE) 8 b.m. Kalanisi (IRE) – Ballybrowney Hall (IRE) (Saddlers' Hall (IRE)) [2017/18 h74: h19.9s c20s h23.1s^5 Dec 2] poor maiden hurdler: well held in novice handicap on chasing debut: bred to stay 3m+: acts on heavy going. *Venetia Williams*   c– h55

BALLYCAMP (IRE) 9 br.g. Kayf Tara – All Our Blessings (IRE) (Statoblest) [2017/18 c117, h111: c16.4s^4 c17.2v^2 c16.5g^3 Apr 24] lengthy gelding: maiden hurdler: fair maiden chaser: stays 21f: acts on good to soft going: often wears tongue tie: usually races close up. *Charles Pogson*   c107 h–

BAL

BALLYCASEY (IRE) 11 gr.g. Presenting – Pink Mist (IRE) (Montelimar (USA)) [2017/18 c159, h–: c20.5s* c22.5g h16v² c20v³ c17s⁵ c20v³ c20v³ c16s⁶ Apr 24] good-topped gelding: useful hurdler: second in minor event at Listowel (head behind The Game Changer) in September: smart chaser: won Grade 3 event at Killarney (by 14 lengths from Rock The World) in May: placed on 3 other occasions: stays 25f: acts on heavy going: has worn cheekpieces. *W. P. Mullins, Ireland* **c153 d h134**

BALLYCASH (IRE) 7 b.g. Kalanisi (IRE) – Waterlily (IRE) (Revoque (IRE)) [2017/18 c–, h103: h16m³ h20g⁴ Jun 1] good-topped gelding: point winner: fair maiden hurdler, below form in selling events in 2017/18: pulled up on chasing debut: stays 21f: acts on soft going: tried in hood: usually races towards rear: temperamental. *Nigel Twiston-Davies* **c– h83 §**

BALLYCOE 9 b.g. Norse Dancer (IRE) – Lizzy Lamb (Bustino) [2017/18 c112, h–: h21.4d^F Apr 22] tall gelding: winning hurdler, beaten when fell sole start in 2017/18: fair chaser: stays 23f: acts on soft going: wears tongue tie. *Chris Gordon* **c– h–**

BALLYCOOL (IRE) 11 b.g. Helissio (FR) – Carnoustie (USA) (Ezzoud (IRE)) [2017/18 c100§, h–: c15.6g⁴ c15.6g⁶ c19.4m⁵ c20.3g² c17.4g⁴ c16.3v^ur c15.6d⁵ Apr 23] maiden hurdler: modest handicap chaser: stays 2½m: acts on heavy going: wears tongue tie: unreliable. *Lucinda Russell* **c88 § h–**

BALLYCROSS 7 b.g. King's Theatre (IRE) – Ninna Nanna (FR) (Garde Royale) [2017/18 c132, h–: c24g³ c23.8g^pu c23.6v⁴ c29.2s^pu c28.4v⁴ c23.8v* Apr 15] sturdy gelding: winning hurdler: useful handicap chaser: won at Ffos Las (by 2 lengths from Alfie Spinner) in April: third at Warwick in October: stays 3m: acts on heavy going: in cheekpieces last 3 starts: unreliable. *Nigel Twiston-Davies* **c132 § h–**

BALLYCRYSTAL COURT (IRE) 6 b.g. Court Cave (IRE) – Monavale (IRE) (Strong Gale) [2017/18 h19.4g⁴ h19.4g* h24.4s^pu h19.4d⁴ Mar 16] €28,000 3-y-o, £11,000 5-y-o: half-brother to fair hurdler Geton (17f winner, by Glacial Storm) and fair further/fairly useful chaser Any Bets (2m-2½m winner, by Beneficial): dam, maiden hurdler, out of half-sister to Champion Hurdle winners Granville Again and Morley Street: placed in Irish points: fair form over hurdles: won novice at Musselburgh in December. *Sandy Thomson* **h107**

BALLYCRYSTAL (IRE) 7 b.g. Oscar (IRE) – Musical Madam (IRE) (Musical Pursuit) [2017/18 h121: c19.3g² c24d³ ab16.3g² c20d* c24.1g^pu Apr 21] useful-looking gelding: fairly useful form over hurdles: similar form over fences: won novice at Carlisle in March: third in December Novices' Chase at Doncaster (9¾ lengths behind Keeper Hill): stays 3m: acts on soft going. *Brian Ellison* **c127 h–**

BALLYDINE (IRE) 8 ch.g. Stowaway – Bealaha Essie (IRE) (Denel (FR)) [2017/18 c20.6v² c20.2s³ c24.2s* Feb 3] winning hurdler: useful form over fences: won Masters Handicap Chase at Sandown in February: best effort when second in novice at Haydock (neck behind Eamon An Cnoic) in December: will stay long distances: acts on heavy going: remains open to improvement. *Charlie Longsdon* **c133 p h–**

BALLYEGAN (IRE) 13 b.g. Saddlers' Hall (IRE) – Knapping Princess (IRE) (Prince of Birds (USA)) [2017/18 c80x, h–: c21.7m⁵ c20.9g³ c23g⁴ c19.8s* c19.4v⁵ c18.2s⁴ Feb 20] workmanlike gelding: maiden hurdler: poor handicap chaser: won at Towcester in December: stays 3¾m: acts on heavy going: has worn tongue tie: front runner/races prominently: often let down by jumping. *Bob Buckler* **c79 x h–**

BALLYEGAN WARRIOR (IRE) 6 b.g. Getaway (GER) – Sweet Empire (IRE) (Second Empire (IRE)) [2017/18 h20d h24g^pu c20.3v⁶ Jan 4] maiden pointer: little impact over hurdles: well beaten in novice handicap on chasing debut: left Robert Tyner after second start: often races towards rear. *David Dennis* **c– h–**

BALLYELLIS (IRE) 5 b.g. Shantou (USA) – Chalice Wells (Sadler's Wells (USA)) [2017/18 b16.7v Apr 11] well beaten in bumper. *Nigel Twiston-Davies* **b–**

BALLY GILBERT (IRE) 7 ch.g. Stowaway – Reedsbuck (FR) (Cyborg (FR)) [2017/18 h112: c20s c15.5d³ c16.4s⁴ c19.9s² c19.9d^pu Mar 26] tall, good sort: fair form over hurdles: fairly useful form over fences: placed in handicaps at Sandown in December and Huntingdon in February: stayed 2½m: acted on soft going: sometimes wore tongue tie: dead. *Ben Pauling* **c116 h–**

BALLYGOMARTIN (IRE) 5 br.g. Scorpion (IRE) – Moll Bawn (IRE) (Presenting) [2017/18 b16.7g* b16.4s⁴ h20.3s^pu Dec 17] rangy gelding: pulled up in Irish point: fairly useful form in bumpers: won at Bangor in October: fatally injured on hurdling debut. *Nigel Twiston-Davies* **h– b101**

BAL

BALLYGOWN BAY (IRE) 5 b.g. Flemensfirth (USA) – Star Shuil (IRE) (Soviet Star (USA)) [2017/18 b87: h16g³ h19.5d³ h20.5s^pu Apr 15] fair form over hurdles: best effort when third in maiden at Chepstow in October: often races freely. *Philip Hobbs* **h108**

BALLYGROOBY BERTIE (IRE) 10 b.g. King's Theatre (IRE) – Vigna Maggio (FR) (Starborough) [2017/18 c96, h78: c24.2g⁴ c20.1g c24g^pu c20d^F Jul 28] winning hurdler: modest maiden chaser: barely stays 3m: acts on good to firm and good to soft going: has worn headgear, including final start: has worn tongue tie: usually races prominently. *R. A. Curran, Ireland* **c92 h–**

BALLYHEIGUE BAY (IRE) 11 b.g. Rudimentary (USA) – Terinka (IRE) (Erins Isle) [2017/18 c123, h110: h25m h19.5s³ h21.4v^F h25v* h23.5s⁵ h25v² h23.5s³ c30.7v² Apr 17] good-topped gelding: fairly useful handicap hurdler: won at Plumpton (conditional) in January and Ascot in February: fairly useful handicap chaser: second at Exeter in April: stays 31f: acts on heavy going: usually wears headgear: wears tongue tie: usually leads, often travels strongly. *Chris Gordon* **c123 h123**

BALLYHILL (FR) 7 b.g. Al Namix (FR) – Laly Light (FR) (Start Fast (FR)) [2017/18 h126, b82: c16.2g² c15.9g³ c15.8s⁵ c19.9v^F c20.8s* c20.8v c20.4s c20.5g^pu Apr 20] good-topped gelding: fairly useful hurdler: useful handicap chaser: won Grade 3 at Cheltenham (by 1¾ lengths from Shantou Flyer) in January: placed in novices at Warwick and Cheltenham in October: stays 21f: acts on heavy going: often races towards rear: often let down by jumping over fences. *Nigel Twiston-Davies* **c137 x h–**

BALLYHOME (IRE) 7 b.g. Westerner – Nostra (FR) (Limnos (JPN)) [2017/18 h15.7v⁵ h19.2d h16v⁶ h21s² Apr 9] £60,000 5-y-o: fourth foal: dam, French 15f-17f hurdle/chase winner, also 10.5f winner on Flat: point winner: fair form over hurdles: often races towards rear: open to further improvement. *Brendan Powell* **h104 p**

BALLYHOWNE (IRE) 8 b.g. Generous (IRE) – Izzy Saddler (IRE) (Saddlers' Hall (IRE)) [2017/18 h18.8g h16.2g⁵ May 18] winning pointer: modest form at best over hurdles: tried in hood: often wears tongue tie. *Stuart Crawford, Ireland* **h66**

BALLYKAN 8 b.g. Presenting – La Marianne (Supreme Leader) [2017/18 c138, h–: c23.8m^pu c23.6d³ c23.8g c23.8d⁴ c24d² c24g² Feb 24] lengthy, useful-looking gelding: winning hurdler: useful handicap chaser: second in Betdaq Chase at Kempton (3¾ lengths behind Master Dee) in February: stays 3m: acts on soft and good to firm going: usually wears cheekpieces: wears tongue tie. *Nigel Twiston-Davies* **c136 h–**

BALLYKNOCK CLOUD (IRE) 7 gr.g. Cloudings (IRE) – Ballyknock Present (IRE) (Presenting) [2017/18 h24g* h23.9s^pu h19.8d Apr 22] £15,000 5-y-o: second foal: dam, pulled up both starts over hurdles, half-sister to useful hurdler/chaser (stayed 19f) Far Away So Close: multiple point winner: fair form over hurdles: won novice at Southwell in October: wears cheekpieces/tongue tie. *Jack R. Barber* **h110**

*BetBright Best For Festival Betting Handicap Chase, Cheltenham—
the novice Ballyhill holds off 2017 winner Shantou Flyer (cheekpieces)*

totesport.com Towton Novices' Chase, Wetherby—Tom Bellamy produces Ballyoptic to beat the grey Vintage Clouds and claim a third win in the race for trainer Nigel Twiston-Davies

BALLY LAGAN (IRE) 10 gr.g. Kalanisi (IRE) – Rose Palma (FR) (Great Palm (USA)) [2017/18 c98, h–: c16.1g[6] c20g[2] c20g[5] c20.2g c15.9v[4] c21.7m[2] Apr 25] stocky gelding: maiden hurdler: modest handicap chaser: stays 2¾m: acts on soft and good to firm going: wears headgear: has worn tongue tie: unreliable. *Robin Dickin*   **c99 §**
h–

BALLY LONGFORD (IRE) 10 b.g. Gold Well – Stay On Line (IRE) (Over The River (FR)) [2017/18 c134, h–: c26.7g[4] c23.8d[3] c20.8vpu c24.2vpu c22.4s* Mar 23] lengthy gelding: winning hurdler: useful handicap chaser: won at Newbury in March: third at Ascot in November: best up to 3m: acts on soft and good to firm going: usually wears tongue tie: often races prominently. *Colin Tizzard*   **c136**
h–

BALLYMAGROARTY BOY (IRE) 5 b.g. Milan – Glazed Storm (IRE) (Vinnie Roe (IRE)) [2017/18 b16d h16.8vpu h20vpu h19.5s h19.5v[5] h16.8v Apr 17] £5,500 3-y-o: first foal: dam unraced half-sister to useful hurdler (2½m-23f winner) Tornado Bob: well beaten in bumper: modest form over hurdles: best effort at 19f: acts on heavy going: tried in cheekpieces: usually races in rear. *Nigel Hawke*   **h97**
b–

BALLYMALIN (IRE) 8 b.g. Presenting – Murrurundi (IRE) (Old Vic) [2017/18 h136: c23d* c24.4g[3] c25.6vR c26.3s[3] c32.8sF c34v[3] c30.6s Apr 27] lengthy gelding: useful hurdler: useful chaser: won novice at Worcester in September: stays 4¼m: acts on heavy going: tried in visor. *Nigel Twiston-Davies*   **c133**
h–

BALLYMILLEN (IRE) 6 ch.g. Mahler – Tigger Dream (IRE) (Double Trigger (IRE)) [2017/18 h21.2d[5] Mar 22] first foal: dam lightly raced in points: Irish point winner: hinted at better when well beaten in novice on hurdling debut. *Nigel Twiston-Davies*   **h– p**

BAL

BALLYMOUNTAIN BOY (IRE) 7 b.g. Mountain High (IRE) – Minoras Return (IRE) (Bob's Return (IRE)) [2017/18 h111, b100: h21m* h19.9d* h19.5d⁶ h23.9g³ h20.3g Apr 18] useful-looking gelding: Irish point winner: bumper winner: fairly useful hurdler: won handicap at Kempton in May and novice at Uttoxeter in September: third in novice at Cheltenham in October: stays 3m: acts on soft and good to firm going: often in cheekpieces: tried in tongue tie: front runner/races prominently, often races freely. *Martin Keighley* — h123

BALLYMOY (IRE) 5 b.g. Flemensfirth (USA) – John's Eliza (IRE) (Dr Massini (IRE)) [2017/18 b16.7g³ h16s⁵ h15.8v* h16.7s* h16s*] Apr 28] £75,000 4-y-o: sturdy gelding: fourth foal: half-brother to modest hurdler Sierra Oscar (21f winner, by Robin des Champs): dam (h108), 19f bumper/2½m hurdle winner, half-sister to fairly useful hurdler/smart chaser (stayed 3m) Invictus (by Flemensfirth): placed in Irish points: fair form only start in bumpers: useful form over hurdles: won maiden at Uttoxeter in February, novice at Bangor in March and novice handicap at Sandown (by 1¼ lengths from Highway One O One) in April: will prove suited by 2½m+: usually races prominently: smart prospect. *Nigel Twiston-Davies* — h136 p b92

BALLYNAGOUR (IRE) 12 b.g. Shantou (USA) – Simply Deep (IRE) (Simply Great (FR)) [2017/18 c155d, h–: c20gᵘʳ c24sᵖᵘ Feb 21] sturdy gelding: winning hurdler: high-class chaser at best, failed to complete in 2017/18: left David Pipe after first start: stays 3¼m: acts on heavy going: wears hood: usually wears tongue tie: waited with: not one to trust (has bled). *Ian Williams* — c– § h–

BALLYOISIN (IRE) 7 b.g. Presenting – Regal Force (IRE) (King's Ride) [2017/18 c147, h–: h16.5g³ c17g* c18g² c17d* c19.5s² c16.7vᶠ h16.5d Apr 24] fairly useful form over hurdles: fairly useful form at Punchestown in May: high-class chaser: won handicaps at Killarney (by 4¾ lengths from Devils Bride) in July and Cork (by 3¾ lengths from Doctor Phoenix) in October: second in Grade 2 at Down Royal in November: stays 2½m: acts on soft going. *Enda Bolger, Ireland* — c160 h129

BALLYOPTIC (IRE) 8 b.g. Old Vic – Lambourne Lace (IRE) (Un Desperado (FR)) [2017/18 h151: h26.5g⁵ c24.2v* c24.4s² c24d⁴ c24.2v* c24.4s⁴ c31.8g² Apr 21] well-made gelding: smart handicap hurdler: smart form over fences: won novice at Exeter (by 13 lengths from Elegant Escape) in November and Towton Novices' Chase at Wetherby (by 2¾ lengths from Vintage Clouds) in February: second in Scottish Grand National at Ayr (nose behind Joe Farrell) in April: stays 4m: acts on heavy going: has worn tongue tie. *Nigel Twiston-Davies* — c154 h147 +

BALLYPOINT (IRE) 7 b.g. Mahler – Angel Trix (IRE) (Un Desperado (FR)) [2017/18 c116, h–: c24d⁵ c22.6g² c23g² c23.8v³ c23.6gᵖᵘ h23.3dᵖᵘ Nov 3] tall gelding: fairly useful hurdler at best, pulled up final start in 2017/18: fair maiden chaser: stays 23f: acts on heavy going: usually wears tongue tie: often races prominently: often let down by jumping over fences. *Nigel Twiston-Davies* — c105 x h–

BALLYROCK (IRE) 12 b.g. Milan – Ardent Love (IRE) (Ardross) [2017/18 c119§, h109§, h20g² h23.3g* h20.5v⁵ h25.5vᵖᵘ Mar 10] useful-looking gelding: fair hurdler: won conditional seller at Hexham in June: fairly useful form over fences: stays 3m: acts on heavy going: wears headgear/tongue tie: front runner/races prominently: one to be wary of. *Tim Vaughan* — c– § h111 §

BALLY SANDS (IRE) 14 b.g. Luso – Sandwell Old Rose (IRE) (Roselier (FR)) [2017/18 c–, h82: h19.9mᵖᵘ c25.8dᵖᵘ Jul 31] tall, good-topped gelding: fair hurdler/chaser at best, no form in 2017/18: stays 29f: acts on heavy going: usually wears headgear: often leads. *Robin Mathew* — c– h–

BALLYTHOMAS 11 b.g. Kayf Tara – Gregale (Gildoran) [2017/18 c102, h–: h24sᵖᵘ c25.2dᵖᵘ c24dᵖᵘ c20.3vᵖᵘ Mar 5] fair hurdler/chaser at best, no form in 2017/18: has worn cheekpieces: often leads. *David Thompson* — c– h–

BALLYTOBER 12 b.g. Kahyasi – Full of Birds (FR) (Epervier Bleu) [2017/18 c114, h–: c32.5dᵖᵘ May 5] tall gelding: has had breathing operation: winning hurdler: fair hunter chaser, pulled up sole start in 2017/18: stays 25f: acts on good to firm and heavy going: usually wears headgear: wears tongue tie. *Ian Prichard* — c– h–

BALLYVIC BORU (IRE) 6 b.g. Brian Boru – Thedoublede (IRE) (Deploy) [2017/18 b99: h16.2m* h15.6s⁵ ab16.3g* h16.7v³ h20.5g Apr 21] placed in Irish maiden points at second attempt: fairly useful form over hurdles: won maiden at Perth in July: won jumpers bumper at Newcastle in March: tried in tongue tie. *Brian Ellison* — h119

BAL

BALLYWARD (IRE) 6 b.g. Flemensfirth (USA) – Ifyoucouldseemenow (IRE) (Saddlers' Hall (IRE)) [2017/18 b111p: h20s⁴ h19v* h24v⁴ h24s⁴ Apr 25] sturdy gelding: runner-up in point: smart form over hurdles: won maiden at Naas (by ½ length from As You Were) in January: fourth in Albert Bartlett Novices' Hurdle (Spa) at Cheltenham in March: will stay long distances: acts on heavy ground. *W. P. Mullins, Ireland* — **h145**

BALLYWOOD (FR) 4 b.g. Ballingarry (IRE) – Miss Hollywood (FR) (True Brave (USA)) [2017/18 h17.4g³ h16.9s* h16.9s* c17.9s² h16g Feb 24] fifth foal: half-brother to winning hurdler/smart chaser As de Fer (17f-25f winner, by Passing Sale) and French 2¼m hurdle/chase winner Prince Angevin (by Sleeping Car): dam unraced: fairly useful form over hurdles: won juveniles at Dieppe and Clairefontaine in June: 2/1, second in minor event at Fontainebleau (neck behind Nadia Has) on chasing debut: left Francois Nicolle after fourth start: stays 2¼m: acts on soft going: should do better over fences. *Alan King* — **c117 p / h121**

BALMONT BELLE (IRE) 8 b.m. Balmont (USA) – Social Set (IRE) (Key of Luck (USA)) [2017/18 h16gᵘʳ Sep 26] temperamental/modest on Flat, stays 10.5f: unseated first on hurdling debut. *Barry Leavy* — **h–**

BALNASLOW (IRE) 11 b.g. Presenting – Noble Choice (Dahar (USA)) [2017/18 c135, h–: c27.5d² c26.3v c21.1s* c24.5sᵖᵘ Apr 27] tall gelding: winning hurdler: fairly useful hunter chaser: won Foxhunters' Chase at Aintree (by 2½ lengths from Bear's Affair) in April: stays 3½m: acts on soft and good to firm going: has worn tongue tie. *Graham McKeever, Ireland* — **c128 / h–**

BAMAKO MORIVIERE (FR) 7 b.g. Califet (FR) – Halladine (FR) (Passing Sale (FR)) [2017/18 h145: c19.9gᶠ c18.2g² c17g³ c17vᶠ c16d* c20s* Nov 5] smart gelding: similar form over fences: won maiden at Fairyhouse (by 2¼ lengths from Tombstone) in October and Grade 3 novice at Cork (by 16 lengths from Jury Duty) in November: stays 2½m: acts on heavy going: wears tongue tie: front runner/races prominently, often travels strongly. *W. P. Mullins, Ireland* — **c151 + / h–**

BAMBI DU NOYER (FR) 7 b.g. Sageburg (IRE) – Zouk Wood (USA) (Woodman (USA)) [2017/18 c–, h97: h19.9d⁴ h20d² h20g⁴ h18.5d h16.8d* h19.9s⁴ h19m h21.2d⁵ c20.9v³ c20.9v⁴ c23.4s⁵ c20.3g⁶ Apr 20] sturdy gelding: fair handicap hurdler: won at Exeter (conditional) in October: fair chaser: left David Pipe after eighth start: stays 2½m: acts on soft going: often in headgear/tongue tie in 2017/18. *Sean Conway* — **c106 / h108**

BAMBYS BOY 7 b.g. Lucarno (USA) – Bamby (IRE) (Glacial Storm (USA)) [2017/18 b15.7d⁵ h16.6s Jan 26] bumper winner: well beaten in novice on hurdling debut. *Micky Hammond* — **h– / b94**

BANCO DE LOGOS (FR) 7 b.g. Laverock (IRE) – Funkia (FR) (Royal Charter (FR)) [2017/18 h102, b33: h23.1s h16s⁴ h22vᵖᵘ Mar 15] workmanlike gelding: fair form over hurdles: left Charles Whittaker after first start: stays 3m: acts on heavy going: tried in cheekpieces. *Seamus Mullins* — **h110**

BANDITRY (IRE) 6 b.g. Iffraaj – Badalona (Cape Cross (IRE)) [2017/18 h108p: h16g² h15.7d* h15.8g² h16.4d Nov 17] sturdy gelding: fairly useful form over hurdles: won novice at Southwell in October: second in handicap at Ludlow in October: may prove best at sharp 2m: acts on good to soft going: often in hood: often races towards rear. *Ian Williams* — **h117**

BAND OF BLOOD (IRE) 10 b.g. King's Theatre (IRE) – Cherry Falls (IRE) (Ali-Royal (IRE)) [2017/18 c24.2v* c24s* c26s c23.8s⁶ c28.8d Apr 28] sturdy gelding: winning hurdler: useful handicap chaser: won veterans events at Exeter and Doncaster in February: probably best around 3m: acts on heavy going: wears blinkers: has worn tongue tie. *Dr Richard Newland* — **c131 / h–**

BANDOL (IRE) 10 b.g. Zagreb (USA) – Formal Affair (Rousillon (USA)) [2017/18 c92, h73: h20.3g⁶ c16d⁵ h16.2s⁴ c16.4s⁶ h19.7v c16.4vᵖᵘ Mar 13] rather lightly-built gelding: poor maiden hurdler: poor handicap chaser: stays 19f: acts on heavy going: often races prominently. *Simon West* — **c71 / h69**

BANDON ROC 7 b.g. Shirocco (GER) – Azur (IRE) (Brief Truce (USA)) [2017/18 h116: c26.2dᵖᵘ c21.7s c25.6sᵖᵘ c24.2v² c21.3v⁴ h24v* Apr 27] fairly useful handicap hurdler: won at Towcester in April: little enthusiasm for chasing: stays 25f: acts on heavy going: often in headgear: usually races prominently. *Kim Bailey* — **c110 § / h116**

BANDSMAN 7 b.g. Bandmaster (USA) – Soleil Sauvage (Loup Sauvage (USA)) [2017/18 h125, b96: h16.5s⁵ h19s h19.4s Jan 27] good-topped gelding: fairly useful hurdler, below form in 2017/18. *Dan Skelton* — **h–**

BANFF (IRE) 5 b.g. Papal Bull – Hugs 'N Kisses (IRE) (Noverre (USA)) [2017/18 h–: h16.7g² h20.1d⁴ Aug 21] modest form over hurdles: stays 2½m: acts on good to soft going: in cheekpieces both starts in 2017/18: often races towards rear. *Olly Murphy* — **h98**

102

Randox Health Foxhunters' Chase, Aintree—
crack Irish amateur Mr Derek O'Connor registers his first win in the race as Balnaslow (left) goes one place better than in 2017; outsiders Bear's Affair (centre) and Greensalt (second left) fill the places; the other horse pictured, 100/1-shot Bound For Glory, fades into sixth

BANG ON FRANKIE (IRE) 6 br.g. Kalanisi (IRE) – Shuil Abbey (IRE) (Saddlers' Hall (IRE)) [2017/18 b101: h20d⁶ h16v² Nov 22] strong gelding: fairly useful form in bumpers: similar form over hurdles: better effort when second in novice at Chepstow in November: has joined Nicky Martin. *Colin Tizzard* **h117**

BANG ON (IRE) 5 ch.g. Fracas (IRE) – Carramanagh Lady (IRE) (Anshan) [2017/18 b13.7v² b16.8v² b15.3d⁵ Apr 22] €15,000 3-y-o: second foal: half-brother to fairly useful hurdler/chaser Court Dismissed (17f-25f winner, by Court Cave): dam (b88) ran twice in bumpers: fair form in bumpers: best effort when second at Fontwell on debut: tried in hood. *Jeremy Scott* **b92**

BANJO GIRL (IRE) 6 ch.m. Presenting – Oh Susannah (FR) (Turgeon (USA)) [2017/18 h112: h15.7d* h16.3d⁵ h16s* h15.5v² h19.8v⁴ h17.7v* h20.3g³ Apr 19] good-topped mare: fairly useful hurdler: won novice at Southwell in November, mares novice at Fakenham in December and mares handicap at Fontwell in March: may prove best short of 2½m: acts on heavy going: has worn hood: tried in tongue tie: front runner/races prominently, often travels strongly. *Lucy Wadham* **h124**

BANKHALL (IRE) 7 b.g. Trans Island – Agena d'Auteuil (FR) (Persian Combat (USA)) [2017/18 c93§, h97§: h22.7g⁴ c25.8spu c21.2gpu h26.5d h24g Aug 20] close-coupled gelding: modest hurdler/chaser, little show in 2017/18: left Mark Walford after first start: stays 25f: acts on soft and heavy going: wears headgear: temperamental. *Kevin Bishop* **c– §** **h81 §**

BANNY'S LAD 9 ch.g. Osorio (GER) – Skytrial (USA) (Sky Classic (CAN)) [2017/18 c105x, h109: c19.3g* c19.2g³ c19.2spu h21.2vpu h20.3v Feb 5] fair hurdler, no form in 2017/18: fair handicap chaser: won at Sedgefield in May: stays 25f: acts on good to firm and heavy going: often in cheekpieces: often races prominently: often let down by jumping over fences. *Michael Easterby* **c109 x** **h–**

BANRION SCAIRP (IRE) 5 b.m. Scorpion (IRE) – Pairtree (Double Trigger (IRE)) [2017/18 h15.7s³ h19.9v⁴ h23.1d⁵ Apr 21] £6,000 4-y-o: sixth foal: half-sister to 3 winners, including useful hurdler Provo (2¾m winner, by Presenting) and fair but unreliable chaser Clubs Are Trumps (23f/3m winner, by Flemensfirth): dam (b86), bumper winner, half-sister to useful hurdler/very smart chaser (stayed 3m) Our Ben: runner-up in Irish point: fair form over hurdles: best effort when third in mares novice at Catterick in January. *Donald McCain* **h103**

Prix La Barka Hurdle, Auteuil—a sweet moment for Paul Townend as Bapaume initiates a big-race double on French soil completed by Baie des Isles in the Prix des Drags

BAPAUME (FR) 5 b.g. Turtle Bowl (IRE) – Brouhaha (FR) (American Post) [2017/18 h146: h19.4s² h24s³ h16s h21v³ h20v^{pu} h24d⁵ Apr 26] useful-looking gelding: high-class hurdler: improved on 2 starts at Auteuil soon after end of season, 16 lengths second to De Bon Coeur in Grande Course de Haies d'Auteuil then won 12-runner Prix La Barka by 6 lengths from Le Grand Luce: stays 25f: acts on soft going: usually races towards rear. *W. P. Mullins, Ireland* **h162**

BARABOY (IRE) 8 b.g. Barathea (IRE) – Irina (IRE) (Polar Falcon (USA)) [2017/18 c96, h100: h15.8d h16.2g h17.2s h17.2d* h16.8g³ h18.1g^{ur} h15.8d⁴ h16.8g² h15.8d⁴ Nov 18] modest handicap hurdler: won conditional/amateur event at Cartmel in August: modest form over fences: best around 2m: acts on heavy going: wears headgear: has worn tongue tie: often races towards rear. *Barry Murtagh* **c– h93**

BARACALU (FR) 7 gr.g. Califet (FR) – Myragentry (FR) (Myrakalu (FR)) [2017/18 b105: h20.1s⁴ h16.8s² Dec 8] good-topped gelding: placed in Irish points: useful bumper performer: fair form over hurdles: better effort when second in maiden at Sedgefield in December. *Philip Kirby* **h109**

BARATINEUR (FR) 7 ch.g. Vendangeur (IRE) – Olmantina (FR) (Ragmar (FR)) [2017/18 h119§: h20.5g⁶ h19.2m h16.8g h15.8s⁶ h19v^{pu} Mar 12] fairly useful hurdler, no form in 2017/18: left Nicky Henderson after first start, Richard Hawker after third: usually races nearer last than first: unreliable. *Kevin Bishop* **h– §**

BARAYMI (FR) 6 b.g. Makfi – Brusca (USA) (Grindstone (USA)) [2017/18 h105§: h19.2g⁵ h21.5d⁴ Jun 7] sturdy gelding: placed in points: fair maiden hurdler, well held both starts in 2017/18: stays 2½m: probably acts on any going: usually wears headgear: temperamental. *Jamie Snowden* **h– §**

BARAZA (FR) 7 gr.g. Smadoun (FR) – Gerbora (FR) (Art Bleu) [2017/18 c113, h99: c16.5g Oct 25] good-topped gelding: modest form over hurdles: fair form over fences, shaped as if amiss sole start in 2017/18: should stay 2½m: acts on good to firm going: in blinkers last 2 starts: usually wears tongue tie: front runner/races prominently. *Tom George* **c– h–**

BARBROOK STAR (IRE) 6 b.g. Getaway (GER) – Fille de Robin (FR) (Robin des Champs (FR)) [2017/18 h–, b82: h21g³ h19.5s h21.2v h21.4d⁶ Apr 22] useful-looking gelding: fair form over hurdles: best effort at 21f: acts on good to soft going. *Philip Hobbs* **h110**

BARCALONA 6 gr.m. Sulamani (IRE) – Ruby Isabel (IRE) (Great Palm (USA)) [2017/18 b16g b17.7g⁴ b17.7s b16s Mar 22] £2,200 3-y-o: first foal: dam (c99/h89), 2m chase winner (stayed 2½m), half-sister to useful hurdler/fairly useful chaser (stayed 3½m) Valley Ride: poor form in bumpers: left Chris Gordon after third start. *Colin Tizzard* **b68**

BARDD (IRE) 6 b.g. Dylan Thomas (IRE) – Zarawa (IRE) (Kahyasi) [2017/18 h113, b94: h16d³ h19.3g⁴ h16s³ Nov 21] compact gelding: bumper winner: fair maiden hurdler: stays 2½m: acts on soft going: temperamental. *Nicky Henderson* **h104 §**

BARDISTA (IRE) 6 b.g. Marienbard (IRE) – Rapsan (IRE) (Insan (USA)) [2017/18 h21.6v^{pu} h23.1s⁴ h20.8d h20.5s⁶ h24.4s h20.3v⁶ h20.3g^{pu} Apr 20] €7,000 3-y-o, £10,000 5-y-o: good-topped gelding: sixth foal: half-brother to fair chaser Shanty Town (21f winner, by Zagreb) and winning pointers by Zagreb and Bishop of Cashel: dam (h111) 2½m bumper/2¾m hurdle winner: third on Irish point debut: fair maiden hurdler: stays 23f: acts on soft going: tried in tongue tie: usually races close up. *Ben Pauling* **h106**

BAR

BARD OF BRITTANY 4 b.g. Sayif (IRE) – Lily Le Braz (Montjeu (IRE)) [2017/18 b15.3v⁶ ab16g h16.7s^bd Mar 26] angular gelding: little impact in bumpers: brought down first on hurdling debut: tried in hood. *Mick Channon*   h– b–

BAREL OF LAUGHS (IRE) 12 b.g. Milan – Danette (GER) (Exit To Nowhere (USA)) [2017/18 c131, h–: c26.3d* c26.3v³ Mar 16] workmanlike gelding: multiple point winner: maiden hurdler: fairly useful chaser: won hunter at Cheltenham in May: third in Foxhunter Chase at same course in March: stays 3¼m: acts on heavy going: wears cheekpieces: tried in tongue tie: usually responds generously to pressure. *Philip Rowley*   c129 h–

BARELY BLACK (IRE) 6 b.m. Urban Poet (USA) – Downtown Rosie (IRE) (Good Thyne (USA)) [2017/18 b–: h22.1d⁶ h20.3g² h22.1g⁴ h20.3g² h20.6s h16.8v Jan 28] poor form over hurdles: best effort at 2½m: best form on good going: tried in cheekpieces. *Julia Brooke*   h84

BARE NECESSITIES (IRE) 8 b.g. Sandmason – Marquante (IRE) (Brief Truce (USA)) [2017/18 h–: h19.6m^pu May 23] Irish point winner: fair hurdler at best, lightly raced and no form since 2015/16. *Shaun Lycett*   h–

BARIZAN (IRE) 12 b.g. Kalanisi (IRE) – Behra (USA) (Grand Lodge (USA)) [2017/18 c–, h119§: h16g⁴ h17.7g⁵ h20g⁶ Sep 3] sturdy gelding: useful hurdler at best, on downgrade nowadays: winning chaser: stays easy 3m, effective at much shorter: acts on good to firm and heavy going: wears headgear: usually wears tongue tie: temperamental. *Brendan Powell*   c– h98 §

BARKIS 9 ch.g. Selkirk (USA) – Batik (IRE) (Peintre Celebre (USA)) [2017/18 h104: h20.3g² h23.9g Jul 5] fair form over hurdles: stays 2½m: best form on good going. *Nicky Henderson*   h106

BARLEY HILL (IRE) 5 ch.g. Stowaway – Saysi (IRE) (Scribano) [2017/18 b15.7d⁶ b16v² b16.7v⁴ Feb 9] €42,000 3-y-o: third foal: dam (h77), lightly raced in bumpers/over hurdles, half-sister to dam of high-class 2m chaser Dempsey and useful chaser up to 3m Puget Blue: fair form in bumpers: best effort when second at Warwick in December. *Ben Pauling*   b86

BARLOW (IRE) 11 br.g. Beneficial – Carrigeen Kerria (IRE) (Kemal (FR)) [2017/18 c82, h–: c23.8g³ c26d⁴ Dec 2] sturdy gelding: winning hurdler: fairly useful chaser at best, nothing like force of old: stays 3¼m: acts on soft going: sometimes wears cheekpieces: tried in tongue tie. *Emma Lavelle*   c87 h–

BARMAN (FR) 7 b.g. Racinger (FR) – Koscina (FR) (Dress Parade) [2017/18 h120: h16.3g⁴ h20m⁵ h16.8d h16.7d² h15.3s³ h16.5m* h16.3d⁵ Nov 9] sturdy gelding: fairly useful handicap hurdler: won confined event at Taunton in November: best form at 2m: acts on good to firm and good to soft going: has worn headgear, including last 3 starts. *Nicky Henderson*   h121

BARNEY BOY 10 b.g. Septieme Ciel (USA) – Keysmith (Greensmith) [2017/18 h–: c20g⁴ May 13] placed once in points: no form under Rules. *Nick Lampard*   c– h–

BARNEY DWAN (IRE) 8 b.g. Vinnie Roe (IRE) – Kapricia Speed (FR) (Vertical Speed (FR)) [2017/18 c138p, h146: c24.2v³ c23.9d* c19.9s* c20.4s⁴ c24.1g^F Apr 21] sturdy gelding: smart hurdler: smart chaser: won novices at Market Rasen (by 15 lengths from Clondaw Cian) in December and Musselburgh (by 5 lengths from Alzammaar) in February: fourth in Close Brothers Novices' Handicap Chase at Cheltenham in March: stays 3m: acts on heavy going: often races prominently/travels strongly. *Fergal O'Brien*   c145 h–

BARNEY FROM TYANEE (IRE) 7 b.g. Milan – Miss Opera (Alflora (IRE)) [2017/18 h94: h18.5d⁶ c17d² c17.8g⁴ c16.1v⁶ c16v⁴ h19.8v* Mar 8] placed in Irish points: modest handicap hurdler: won at Wincanton in March: similar form over fences: stays 2½m: acts on heavy going: tried in cheekpieces/tongue tie. *Michael Blake*   c94 h92

BARNEY RUBBLE 9 b.g. Medicean – Jade Chequer (Green Desert (USA)) [2017/18 h20d⁶ h23.3g^pu Jun 21] point winner: little form over hurdles: tried in visor. *Debra Hamer*   h57

BARNEY'S CAULKER 7 b.g. Captain Gerrard (IRE) – Little Cascade (Forzando) [2017/18 b73: h16.2g⁴ h16.2m⁵ h16.8v^pu Apr 13] little impact in bumpers/over hurdles: in tongue tie last 3 starts: often races towards rear. *Maurice Barnes*   h64

BARN HILL 6 b.g. Kayf Tara – Shuil Mavourneen (IRE) (Welsh Term) [2017/18 h16.5g^F Nov 30] behind when fell 3 out in novice hurdle at Taunton. *Philip Hobbs*   h–

BAR

BARON DU PLESSIS (FR) 7 b.g. Network (GER) – Larme A L'Oeil (FR) (Luchiroverte (IRE)) [2017/18 h100: c26.2d⁵ c23.6v² c19.1d³ c25.2s³ c23.6d Apr 24] placed in Irish points: fair hurdler: similar form over fences: stays 3m: acts on heavy going: often races prominently. *Ian Williams*   c103 h–

BARRA (FR) 7 b.m. Vendangeur (IRE) – Oasaka (FR) (Robin des Champs (FR)) [2017/18 h133: h20s² h18.2s³ h16s⁴ h18s² h21.1s³ h20v⁶ h20s⁵ Apr 28] lengthy mare: useful hurdler: third in Coral Cup at Cheltenham (1½ lengths behind Bleu Berry) in March: stays 21f: acts on soft going: has worn cheekpieces: wears tongue tie: usually races nearer last than first. *Gordon Elliott, Ireland*   h139

BARRAKILLA (IRE) 11 b.g. Milan – Kigali (IRE) (Torus) [2017/18 c20.3v* c20v² c21.1s⁴ Apr 12] good-topped gelding: winning hunter: fairly useful hunter chaser: won at Bangor in February: stays 2½m: acts on heavy going. *Fergal O'Brien*   c126 h–

BARRISTER 4 b.f. Lawman (FR) – Ella (Pivotal) [2017/18 b12.4s Jan 13] second foal: dam useful 1¼m-1½m winner: tailed off in bumper. *Tracy Waggott*   b–

BARRSBROOK 4 b.g. Doyen (IRE) – Sayrianna (Sayaarr (USA)) [2017/18 b13.7g b15.3v Dec 7] good-topped gelding: no form in bumpers: fair maiden on Flat. *Gary Moore*   b–

BARRYS JACK (IRE) 8 b.g. Well Chosen – Theatre Fool (IRE) (King's Theatre (IRE)) [2017/18 h101: h21d⁴ h19.6d² c16v* h17s* h17v* c16.4sᵘʳ c19.9v⁴ c16.3sᶠ h18.6vᵖᵘ h17v⁶ h20.9vᵖᵘ h20.6v⁵ Apr 15] fair handicap hurdler: won conditional event and intermediate event, both at Carlisle in October: fairly useful form over fences: won novice handicap at Perth in September: stays 21f: acts on heavy going. *Brian Ellison*   c115 h107

BARTERS HILL (IRE) 8 b.g. Kalanisi (IRE) – Circle The Wagons (IRE) (Commanche Run) [2017/18 c–p, h–: h24.2v⁶ Feb 10] strong, lengthy gelding: smart form over hurdles at best, well held sole start in 2017/18: pulled up on chasing debut: stays 3m: acts on soft going. *Ben Pauling*   c– h–

BARTON GIFT 11 b.g. Alflora (IRE) – Marina Bird (Julio Mariner) [2017/18 c122§, h–: c26.1d⁴ c30.7vᵖᵘ c26.7vᵖᵘ c29.6vᵖᵘ Feb 9] strong gelding: winning hurdler: fairly useful handicap chaser: fourth at Uttoxeter in November: stays 31f: acts on heavy going: wears headgear: usually races close up: unreliable. *John Spearing*   c121 § h–

BARTON KNOLL 6 b.g. Midnight Legend – Barton Flower (Danzero (AUS)) [2017/18 h104, b–: h19.2g² h19.7d* h20s⁵ h19.4dʳᵒ Dec 1] fair form over hurdles: won novice at Wetherby in October: stays 2½m: acts on soft going: usually races prominently, often travels strongly. *John Mackie*   h110

BARTON ROSE 9 b.m. Midnight Legend – Barton Flower (Danzero (AUS)) [2017/18 c106, h100: c19.8m² c20g* c19.2d³ c20.3s c20.3s⁴ c16.3g² Apr 19] rather leggy mare: fair hurdler: fair handicap chaser: won at Uttoxeter in September: stays 3m: acts on good to firm and heavy going: has worn cheekpieces. *Charlie Longsdon*   c107 h–

BASFORD BEN 10 b.g. Trade Fair – Moly (FR) (Anabaa (USA)) [2017/18 c106§, h–: c24.5g⁵ c26.1d⁵ c26.1gᵖᵘ c24.2s⁶ c24.5s c23.6s* c24.5vᴿ h24s⁵ c22.7vᴿ Mar 9] smallish, well-made gelding: maiden hurdler: modest handicap chaser: won at Huntingdon in December: stays 3¼m: acts on good to firm and heavy going: wears headgear: tried in tongue tie: front runner: temperamental (refused twice in 2017/18). *Jennie Candlish*   c92 h– §

BASIL BERRY 7 b.g. Tobougg (IRE) – Dolly Coughdrop (IRE) (Titus Livius (FR)) [2017/18 h16gᶠ Jun 4] useful on Flat, stays 1¼m: yet to be asked for effort when fell 3 out in maiden won by Gannicus at Fakenham on hurdling debut. *Chris Dwyer*   h–

BASSARABAD (FR) 7 b.g. Astarabad (USA) – Grivette (FR) (Antarctique (IRE)) [2017/18 c107, h100: c23.6dᵖᵘ c23.8v⁴ c24.2v* c28.4vᵖᵘ Mar 31] tall, useful-looking gelding: fair hurdler: fair handicap chaser: won at Wetherby in January: stays 3m: acts on heavy going: often wears visor: in tongue tie last 2 starts: temperamental. *Tim Vaughan*   c107 § h–

BASTIEN (FR) 7 b.g. Panoramic – Que du Charmil (FR) (Grand Seigneur (FR)) [2017/18 h126, b87: h19.8s³ h21g⁴ h21.4vᶠ h24.2v⁵ h21.1s Mar 14] sturdy gelding: useful handicap hurdler: won at Towcester (by 4½ lengths from Who's My Jockey) in November: stays 21f: acts on heavy going: often races towards rear. *Alan King*   h131

BATHWICK SCANNO (IRE) 10 b.g. Aptitude (USA) – Hundred Year Flood (USA) (Giant's Causeway (USA)) [2017/18 c24.2dᵖᵘ Apr 24] multiple point winner: maiden hurdler: no form in hunter chases: has worn headgear, including in 2017/18: in tongue tie last 3 starts: none too genuine. *Mrs Teresa Clark*   c– § h– §

BEA

BATTALION (IRE) 8 b.g. Authorized (IRE) – Zigarra (Halling (USA)) [2017/18 h15.7v^F Feb 25] useful on Flat, stays 1½m: fell heavily last in novice won by Contre Tous at Southwell on hurdling debut, looking sure to be placed: open to improvement. *Jamie Osborne* — **h114 p**

BATTLE ANTHEM (IRE) 7 b.g. Royal Anthem (USA) – Chika Boom (IRE) (Kalanisi (IRE)) [2017/18 c19.9g^{pu} Dec 1] workmanlike gelding: multiple Irish point winner: pulled up in Berkshire Novices' Chase at Newbury on chasing debut. *Richard Rowe* — **c–**

BATTLEBRAVE (IRE) 5 b.g. Fracas (IRE) – Silly Mille (IRE) (Luso) [2017/18 b15.8g Nov 9] last in bumper. *John Groucott* — **b–**

BATTLE DUST (IRE) 9 b.g. Portrait Gallery (IRE) – Katie O'Toole (IRE) (Commanche Run) [2017/18 c107§, h–§: c25.2s^2 c23.6s* Mar 22] multiple point winner: winning hurdler: fairly useful form over fences: won hunter at Chepstow in March: stays 3¼m: best form on soft/heavy going: wears headgear: temperamental. *Philip Rowley* — **c118 § h– §**

BATTLE OF IDEAS (IRE) 5 ch.g. Fracas (IRE) – Haven't A Notion (Definite Article) [2017/18 b82: h19.2g h16.8v^3 h20.5d* h23.6v^{pu} h21s^6 h19.2s^3 h21.2d^4 Apr 9] fairly useful hurdler: won maiden at Plumpton in December: stays 21f: acts on heavy going: usually races prominently. *Colin Tizzard* — **h115**

BATTLE OF SHILOH (IRE) 9 b.g. Shantou (USA) – Realt Na Ruise (IRE) (Soviet Star (USA)) [2017/18 c139, h116p: c24.1s^3 c23.8d^{pu} Dec 20] fairly useful hurdle winner: useful chaser: third in handicap at Bangor (3¼ lengths behind Sir Mangan) in November: bled next time: stays 3m: acts on heavy going: tried in cheekpieces. *Tom George* — **c136 h–**

BATTLINGBETTY 9 br.m. Guest Right – Durness Duchess (Duke of Durness) [2017/18 h16.2g^{pu} May 13] second foal: dam unraced: pulled up in novice hurdle. *R. Mike Smith* — **h–**

BAY FORTUNA 9 b.g. Old Vic – East Rose (Keen) [2017/18 h80: h19.9g* h15.8d Apr 24] sturdy gelding: modest handicap hurdler: won at Uttoxeter in June: stays 2½m: best form on good going: tried in cheekpieces. *Mark Usher* — **h89**

BAYMORE ROAD 4 b.g. Josr Algarhoud (IRE) – Animal Cracker (Primo Dominie) [2017/18 b17v^{pu} Apr 17] pulled up in bumper. *Barry Murtagh* — **b–**

BAY OF FREEDOM (IRE) 9 b.g. Heron Island (IRE) – Kate Gale (IRE) (Strong Gale) [2017/18 c131, h106: h24d^4 c24v^3 c23s^3 c24.5d c23.5v^{pu} Feb 7] angular gelding: fair hurdler: useful chaser: third in Kerry National Handicap Chase at Listowel in September and listed event at Wexford (2¾ lengths behind A Genie In Abottle) in October: stays 3m: acts on heavy going. *Peter Fahey, Ireland* — **c138 h107**

BAY SLY (IRE) 11 b.g. Stowaway – On A Mission (IRE) (Dolphin Street (FR)) [2017/18 c22.6d* c20d c23.8d^{pu} Apr 24] point winner: maiden hurdler: fairly useful form in hunter chases: won novice at Stratford in June: stays 23f: acts on heavy going: often wears hood. *Miss H. Brookshaw* — **c115 h–**

BAYWING (IRE) 9 br.g. Winged Love (IRE) – Cerise de Totes (FR) (Champ Libre (FR)) [2017/18 c145, h–: c20d^3 c25.6v^F c24.2s^5 c23.4v^3 c32.6s* c26.2v^2 Apr 7] winning hurdler: smart handicap chaser: won Betfred Eider (Handicap Chase) at Newcastle (by 4 lengths from West of The Edge) in February: stays 33f: best form on soft/heavy going: usually races nearer last than first: often let down by jumping. *Nicky Richards* — **c149 x h–**

BAZOOKA (IRE) 7 b.g. Camacho – Janadam (IRE) (Mukaddamah (USA)) [2017/18 h106: h16s^3 h18.9v^5 h16v Feb 16] angular gelding: fair form over hurdles: unproven beyond 2m: best form on soft/heavy going: tried in cheekpieces: often races towards rear. *David Flood* — **h111**

BEACH BREAK 4 b.g. Cacique (IRE) – Wemyss Bay (Sadler's Wells (USA)) [2017/18 h16.7s^2 h15.7d^4 h15.6d^4 Jan 1] closely related to fairly useful hurdler Wemyss Point (2½m winner, by Champs Elysees): fairly useful on Flat, stays 1½m: modest form over hurdles: best effort when fourth in juvenile at Musselburgh in January. *Donald McCain* — **h99**

BEAKSTOWN (IRE) 5 b.g. Stowaway – Midnight Reel (IRE) (Accordion) [2017/18 b16s^2 Feb 9] third foal: half-brother to bumper winner/winning pointer Minutestomidnight (by Vinnie Roe): dam unraced half-sister to useful 21f hurdle winner My Wigwam Or Yours: won Irish point on debut: in tongue tie. 10/3, second in maiden bumper at Kempton (5 lengths behind Commanche Red): likely to improve. *Dan Skelton* — **b95 p**

BEA

BEALLANDENDALL (IRE) 10 b.g. Beneficial – Railstown Lady (IRE) (Supreme Leader) [2017/18 c–, h109: h18.5g⁴ h16d h15.8m h19.5d⁵ c20g² c16s* c16v* c19.4v² c19.4s² Apr 27] compact gelding: modest handicap hurdler: fair handicap chaser: won at Chepstow in February and March: stays 19f: acts on heavy going: has worn headgear: front runner/races prominently. *Deborah Faulkner* **c107 h94**

BEAN LIATH (IRE) 7 gr.m. Portrait Gallery (IRE) – Coolnasmear (IRE) (Flemensfirth (USA)) [2017/18 h15.7v³ h21.6v⁵ Apr 17] first foal: dam lightly-raced half-sister to fairly useful but temperamental chaser (2¾m-3m winner) Coljon: point winner: poor form over hurdles. *Dai Williams* **h75**

BEARLY LEGAL (IRE) 12 b.g. Court Cave (IRE) – Fair Size (IRE) (Jurado (USA)) [2017/18 c125, h111: c24.9sᵖᵘ h24g h22g c25vᶠ c24s c24.7vᵖᵘ c25s Apr 14] medium-sized gelding: fair handicap hurdler/fairly useful chaser, below form in 2017/18: stays 29f: acts on heavy going: wears tongue tie. *Karl Thornton, Ireland* **c– h99**

BEAR'S AFFAIR (IRE) 12 br.g. Presenting – Gladtogetit (Green Shoon) [2017/18 c123, h–: c24.5gᶠ c27.5d⁶ c23s³ c21.1s² Apr 12] sturdy gelding: point winner: winning hurdler: fairly useful chaser: second in Foxhunters' Chase at Aintree in April: stays 25f: acts on heavy going. *Philip Rowley* **c126 h–**

BEAR SPIRIT (IRE) 5 b.g. Oscar (IRE) – Toulon Pass (IRE) (Toulon) [2017/18 h25.5g⁵ Nov 29] well beaten in maiden hurdle (tongue tied). *David Pipe* **h–**

BEARS RAILS 8 b.g. Flemensfirth (USA) – Clandestine (Saddlers' Hall (IRE)) [2017/18 c114§, h–: c24.2sᵖᵘ c26.1v² c25.7s² c28.5v c28.8v⁵ c23.6s⁶ c26s⁴ c25.1d* Apr 22] big, workmanlike gelding: maiden hurdler: fairly useful handicap chaser: won at Wincanton in April: second at Uttoxeter in November: stays 3¼m: acts on heavy going: wears blinkers: tried in tongue tie: temperamental. *Colin Tizzard* **c116 § h–**

BEAST OF BURDEN (IRE) 9 ch.g. Flemensfirth (USA) – Nuit des Chartreux (FR) (Villez (USA)) [2017/18 c82, h–: h23.3v³ Nov 26] fairly useful handicap hurdler: third at Uttoxeter on sole start in 2017/18: maiden chaser: stayed 3m: acted on heavy going: tried in hood/tongue tie: dead. *Dan Skelton* **c– h124**

BEAT THAT (IRE) 10 b.g. Milan – Knotted Midge (IRE) (Presenting) [2017/18 h136+: c20g² c23.8gᶠ c24.4gᶠ c20g⁵ h23.4s³ h23.4v Feb 3] tall gelding: useful handicap hurdler: third at Sandown (9¼ lengths behind Holly Bush Henry) in December: similar form over fences: second in maiden at Uttoxeter in May: stays 3m: acts on soft going. *Nicky Henderson* **c136 h138**

BEAU BAY (FR) 7 b.g. Bernebeau (FR) – Slew Bay (FR) (Beaudelaire (USA)) [2017/18 h–: h16.8g h17.2d h20g⁵ h15.8g⁴ h15.8d² h18.6g² c20.1s* c21g³ c20d³ c20.1s² c15.9s² c16.4v³ c16v* c15.7s³ c16v* c16.8s² c21.1sᵘʳ Apr 13] lengthy gelding: fair handicap hurdler: useful handicap chaser: won at Perth (novice) in August, Uttoxeter in February and Hereford (awarded race) in March: left Alan Jones after third start: stays 2½m: acts on heavy going: wears hood/tongue tie: usually leads. *Dr Richard Newland* **c130 h100**

BEAU DU BRIZAIS (FR) 6 gr.g. Kapgarde (FR) – Belle du Brizais (FR) (Turgeon (USA)) [2017/18 h117: h21.2mᶠ h20g h19.9g⁴ h22s² c23.6gᶠ c22.6g² c23gᶠ c25.1vᵖᵘ Dec 26] compact gelding: fairly useful handicap hurdler: similar form over fences: second in novice handicap at Taunton in November: stays 23f: acts on soft and good to firm going. *Philip Hobbs* **c123 h116**

BEAU GOSSE (FR) 4 b.g. Falco (USA) – Mazaya (IRE) (Sadler's Wells (USA)) [2017/18 h16.9s* h16.9s² h17.9s* h17.9s* h17.9sᶠ h17.9s h16g³ h17s Apr 12] leggy gelding: half-brother to several winners on Flat, including smart 9f-13f winner Munsef (by Zafonic): dam useful 1½m winner: useful hurdler: won newcomers race at Clairefontaine in July, juvenile there in August and listed event at Auteuil (by short head from Tunis) in September: below best in Britain last 2 starts: stays 2¼m: acts on soft going: has had tongue tied. *Guillaume Macaire, France* **h136**

BEAU KNIGHT 6 b.g. Sir Percy – Nicola Bella (IRE) (Sadler's Wells (USA)) [2017/18 h–: h15.8d⁵ Nov 18] no form over hurdles. *Alexandra Dunn* **h61**

BEAUMONT'S PARTY (IRE) 11 b.g. High Chaparral (IRE) – Miss Champagne (FR) (Bering) [2017/18 h91: h20.6g h20g* h23g h20.5dᵖᵘ Oct 23] good-topped gelding: poor handicap hurdler: won lady amateur event at Fakenham in June: stays 2½m: acts on heavy going: has worn headgear. *Laura Morgan* **h76**

BEE

BEAU PHIL (FR) 7 ch.g. Cachet Noir (USA) – Neyrianne (FR) (Sheyrann) [2017/18 **h–** h111: h21.4v^{pu} h21.6s^{pu} Apr 23] fair hurdler at best, pulled up both starts in 2017/18: stays 2¾m: acts on soft and good to firm going: has worn hood, including last 3 starts: wears tongue tie: temperament under suspicion. *Jeremy Scott*

BEAU SANCY (FR) 6 b.g. Blue Bresil (FR) – Touquette (FR) (Phantom Breeze) **c86** [2017/18 b–: b16.2v b16.7d h20s^6 h19.9s^4 h22v h17v h16.8v^6 h21.3v^6 c20d^6 c21.6v^2 **h90** c24.2d Apr 23] no form in bumpers: modest form over hurdles: similar form over fences: **b–** best effort when second in handicap at Kelso in April: stays 2¾m: best form on soft/heavy going: sometimes in headgear: has worn tongue tie: usually races in rear: claimer ridden: has joined Olly Murphy. *Kenny Johnson*

BEAUTIFUL PEOPLE (FR) 7 b.m. Early March – Night Fever (FR) (Garde Royale) **h75** [2017/18 h88: h23.3d h25g^3 h23.3g h22g^3 h24g^5 h25.8g^6 h23.9m^5 Nov 1] lengthy mare: poor maiden hurdler: stays 3m: acts on good to firm going: often wears tongue tie: often races towards rear. *Richard Phillips*

BECAUSESHESAIDSO (IRE) 10 b.g. Winged Love (IRE) – Huit de Coeur (FR) **c114** (Cadoudal (FR)) [2017/18 h105: h26.4d^{pu} c20.3d^3 c26.2d^6 c20s^2 c23.6s^4 c19.4v* c20.9s^{pu} **h–** Jan 29] fair hurdler: similar form over fences: won handicap at Chepstow in January: stayed 2½m: acted on heavy going: tried in hood: front runner/raced prominently: dead. *Venetia Williams*

BECKY THE THATCHER 5 b.m. Mastercraftsman (IRE) – Fairmont (IRE) (Kingmambo **h121** (USA)) [2017/18 h115: h19.7s* h22.8v^4 h19.7s h20.5v^{pu} Mar 10] close-coupled, rather lightly-built mare: fairly useful handicap hurdler: won at Wetherby in November: stays 23f: acts on heavy going: often races prominently. *Micky Hammond*

BE DARING (FR) 7 gr.g. Dom Alco (FR) – Quinine (FR) (Network (GER)) [2017/18 **h91** h105: h17.7d^4 h20.5d h19.2d^4 h15.9d^{ur} h19.2v^5 h17.7v^2 h15.9v^{ur} h15.9v^2 h19.2v^4 h17.7s^2 Apr 6] good-topped gelding: modest maiden hurdler: likely to prove best up to 2¼m: best form on soft/heavy going: usually wears hood: often races towards rear. *Chris Gordon*

BEDFORD FORREST (IRE) 9 br.g. Desert King (IRE) – Nadisha (IRE) (Rainbows **c108** For Life (CAN)) [2017/18 c21.2d^2 c27.5d^F c21.2g^2 c21.2s^6 Jul 24] point winner: fair form over fences: left Andrew Nicholls after second start. *Mike Sowersby*

BEDROCK 5 b.g. Fastnet Rock (AUS) – Gemstone (IRE) (Galileo (IRE)) [2017/18 **h144** h134p: h19d^4 h16.7d^4 h16.4g^3 h16.4s^4 h19.4d* h16.5s^3 Apr 13] sturdy gelding: useful hurdler: won novices at Warwick in May, Bangor in October and Musselburgh in March: third in Top Novices' Hurdle at Aintree (3¼ lengths behind Lalor) in April: left Dan Skelton after fourth start: stays 19f: acts on soft going: wears tongue tie: front runner/races prominently. *Iain Jardine*

BEDROCK BOY 8 ch.g. Trade Fair – Lady Sunrize (Whittingham (IRE)) [2017/18 **h–** h20g^{pu} Jun 14] pulled up in maiden hurdle. *Deborah Faulkner*

BEE AN ARISTOCRAT (IRE) 9 b.m. Flemensfirth (USA) – Windy Bee (IRE) **h87** (Aristocracy) [2017/18 h24g^4 h22d h17.7s h16.5m^2 Apr 25] little impact in points: modest maiden hurdler: left Paul W. Flynn after second start: best effort at 2m: acts on good to firm going: tried in tongue tie. *Jimmy Frost*

BEECH HILL (IRE) 10 b.m. Craigsteel – Glacial Shoon (IRE) (Glacial Storm (USA)) **c–** [2017/18 c21.2d^4 h18.8g Jul 13] fifth foal: dam unraced: placed in points: tailed off in **h–** maiden hurdle/chase. *Mrs Sarah Dawson, Ireland*

BEE CROSSING 7 b.m. Fair Mix (IRE) – Indeed To Goodness (IRE) (Welsh Term) **h109** [2017/18 h15.3v^2 h17.7v^2 h18.5s^3 h21v^2 h20.5s Mar 24] £15,000 3-y-o, £2,800 4-y-o: lengthy mare: fourth foal: half-sister to useful hurdler/top-class chaser Harry Topper (2½m-25f winner, by Sir Harry Lewis): dam (c113/h102) 21f-3¼m hurdle/chase winner: point winner: fair form over hurdles: stays 21f: raced only on soft/heavy going. *Seamus Mullins*

BEENO (IRE) 9 b.g. Exit To Nowhere (USA) – Kay Theatre (IRE) (King's Theatre (IRE)) **h131** [2017/18 h104, b–: h17.2d^4 h17.2g* h17.2s* h17.2d* h16.2g^2 h15.6d^5 h19.3v^3 h16.8v* h17d Mar 25] useful handicap hurdler: completed hat-trick at Cartmel in June (novice event), July (lady riders event) and August, and also won at Sedgefield (by 12 lengths from Ninepointsixthree) in February: unproven beyond 17f: acts on heavy going: wears hood: usually races close up, often freely: has joined Dianne Sayer. *Kenneth Slack*

Ladbrokes Long Distance Hurdle, Newbury—the longest-priced winner in the race's 28-year history as 40/1-shot Beer Goggles makes all under Richard Johnson to hold off 2016 winner Unowhatimeanharry

BEER GOGGLES (IRE) 7 br.g. Oscar (IRE) – Tynelucy (IRE) (Good Thyne (USA)) [2017/18 c101, h129: h24.7g² h26.5g* h24.7s³ h24.2d* h24v⁵ Jan 27] sturdy gelding: smart hurdler: won handicap at Newton Abbot (by ¾ length from Sir Mangan) in October and Long Distance Hurdle at Newbury (by 2¼ lengths from Unowhatimeanharry) in December: also placed in handicaps at Aintree in May and November: maiden chaser: stays 27f: acts on heavy going: often wears tongue tie: front runner/races prominently, often travels strongly: has joined Nicky Martin. *Kayley Woollacott* — c–, h156

BEEVES (IRE) 11 b.g. Portrait Gallery (IRE) – Camas North (IRE) (Muharib (USA)) [2017/18 c143, h–: c23.8m* h26.1s c30.2s Mar 14] lengthy gelding: useful hurdler at best, well held sole start in 2017/18: useful chaser: won handicap at Perth (by neck from Aerlite Supreme) in June: stays 33f: acts on good to firm and heavy going: wears headgear: usually leads. *Jennie Candlish* — c143, h–

BEFORE MIDNIGHT 5 ch.g. Midnight Legend – Lady Samantha (Fraam) [2017/18 b16.7v* b16.6s³ b16d* Apr 7] €55,000 3-y-o: third foal: dam (h76), 3m hurdle winner, half-sister to useful hurdler (stayed 25f) Lord Generous out of top-class 2½m-3m hurdle winner Lady Rebecca: fairly useful form in bumpers: won at Bangor in January and Fakenham in April. *Nicky Henderson* — b103

BEGBIE (IRE) 5 b.g. Scorpion (IRE) – Ben's Pride (Bollin Eric) [2017/18 b17.7d³ b15.3v² Dec 26] €25,000 3-y-o: fourth foal: half-brother to useful hurdler Copy That (2m winner, by Milan): dam unraced half-sister to useful hurdler/very smart chaser (stayed 3m) Our Ben: fair form in bumpers: better effort when third at Plumpton in December. *Warren Greatrex* — b92

BEGGARS CROSS (IRE) 8 b.g. Presenting – Ballygill Heights (IRE) (Symboli Heights (FR)) [2017/18 c118, h112: c24g* c26.2d c23.8d⁴ c23.8d^pu Apr 24] sturdy gelding: winning hurdler: fairly useful handicap chaser: won at Warwick in October: stays 3m: acts on soft going: sometimes in cheekpieces: tried in tongue tie. *Jonjo O'Neill* — c120, h–

BEGGAR'S VELVET (IRE) 12 b.g. Dr Massini (IRE) – Lakelough (IRE) (Mandalus) [2017/18 c101, h–: c26.3d^pu c22.6d⁴ Jun 9] sturdy gelding: multiple point winner: winning hurdler: modest hunter chaser: stays 3¼m: acts on good to firm and heavy going: wears cheekpieces. *Mrs Amy Cox* — c93, h–

BEGGAR'S WISHES (IRE) 7 b.g. Oscar (IRE) – Strong Wishes (IRE) (Strong Gale) [2017/18 h112, b77: c16.4g* c15.5d⁵ c20.5d⁴ c20.2v² c21.4v* Apr 11] sturdy gelding: fair hurdler: fairly useful form over fences: won novice handicaps at Sedgefield in November and Market Rasen in April: stays 21f: acts on heavy going: usually wears headgear: wears tongue tie. *Peter Bowen* — c128, h–

BEL

BE HAPPY TWO 4 b.f. Delegator – There's Two (IRE) (Ashkalani (IRE)) [2017/18 ab16g Jan 30] half-sister to several winners on Flat, including 1¼m-17f winner Sula Two (by Sulamani): dam 2-y-o 6f winner: 25/1, eighth of 9 in mares bumper at Lingfield. *Ron Hodges*   **b–**

BEHINDTHELINES (IRE) 6 b.g. Milan – Sunset Leader (IRE) (Supreme Leader) [2017/18 h22.7s³ h21.4v² h20.1v² h24v* Apr 15] closely related to useful hurdler Pere Blanc (2½m/21f winner, by King's Theatre): dam unraced half-sister to useful hurdler Glacial Sunset (stayed 3¼m): runner-up on completed start in Irish points: fairly useful form over hurdles: won novice at Newcastle in April: stays 3m: wears tongue tie. *Lucinda Russell*   **h115**

BEHIND TIME (IRE) 7 b.g. Stowaway – She's Got To Go (IRE) (Glacial Storm (USA)) [2017/18 h129: c17.5s⁵ c16.5s³ c17d⁴ c20.2v² c23.8v³ c24v* c25.6v^{pu} c23.8v^{pu} Apr 15] good-topped gelding: fairly useful hurdler: fairly useful handicap chaser: won novice event at Uttoxeter in March: stays 3m: best form on soft/heavy going: in cheekpieces last 3 starts: often races towards rear: temperamental. *Harry Fry*   **c124 §**   **h–**

BEHRANELL 4 b.f. Paco Boy (IRE) – Behra (IRE) (Grand Lodge (USA)) [2017/18 b12.4s ab16g⁶ b16.7s Mar 26] half-sister to several winners, including smart hurdler Baradari (2m-23f winner, by Manduro) and useful hurdler/chaser Barizan (2m-2¼m winner, by Kalanisi): dam, useful 1¼m winner, half-sister to very smart hurdler/top-class chaser (winner up to 25f) Behrajan: poor form in bumpers. *David Dennis*   **b70**

BEKKENSFIRTH 9 b.g. Flemensfirth (USA) – Bekkaria (FR) (Clafouti (FR)) [2017/18 h20.5d⁶ c20s⁶ c20.2v⁴ Jan 31] well-made gelding: modest form over hurdles: fairly useful form over fences: fourth in handicap at Leicester in January: stays 2½m: acts on heavy going. *Dan Skelton*   **c116**   **h91**

BEL AMI DE SIVOLA (FR) 7 b.g. Network (GER) – Notting Hill (FR) (Garde Royale) [2017/18 h127, b103: h22m² c20s³ c18.2v⁵ c17v³ c16.5s⁴ c17d² c17s c16.7v* c21s³ Apr 27] well-made gelding: bumper winner: fairly useful hurdler: useful handicap chaser: won novice event at Fairyhouse (by 1½ lengths from Bon Papa) in April: third in similar event at Punchestown next time: stays 21f: acts on heavy going: tried in hood: often races prominently. *Noel Meade, Ireland*   **c136**   **h112**

BELAMI DES PICTONS (FR) 7 b.g. Khalkevi (IRE) – Nina des Pictons (FR) (Denham Red (FR)) [2017/18 c148p, h–: c20d² Nov 5] strong, compact gelding: winning hurdler: smart form over fences: completed hat-trick in 2016/17: second in intermediate event at Carlisle (2½ lengths behind Waiting Patiently) on sole start in 2017/18: stays 3m: acts on heavy going: usually races close up/travels strongly: open to further improvement as a chaser. *Venetia Williams*   **c150 p**   **h– p**

BELAMIX DOR (FR) 7 b.m. Al Namix (FR) – Paladoune (FR) (Dounba (FR)) [2017/18 c20.9s^F c18.4s⁶ c18.9s³ c22.9s³ c19.9v² c19.9v c30.2s^{pu} Mar 14] tall, leggy mare: first foal: dam French 1½m winner: winning useful maiden chaser: second in handicap at Pau in January: always behind in cross-country event at Cheltenham final start: stays 2½m: acts on heavy going: has had tongue tied. *Patrice Quinton, France*   **c118**   **h–**

BELEAVE 5 gr.m. Avonbridge – Grezie (Mark of Esteem (IRE)) [2017/18 h16v⁶ Jan 30] fairly useful on Flat, stays 1m: in hood, well held in mares novice on hurdling debut. *Luke Dace*   **h–**

BEL ESPRIT (IRE) 9 b.m. Presenting – D Judge (IRE) (Strong Gale) [2017/18 h88: h23.3d³ May 6] modest maiden hurdler: stays 23f: acts on good to soft going. *Robert Stephens*   **h78**

BELLAMY'S GREY 6 gr.g. Black Sam Bellamy (IRE) – Lambrini Queen (Environment Friend) [2017/18 b15.3v³ b15.3v⁴ h21.4v³ h16.8v² Apr 17] £1,000 3-y-o, £4,500 5-y-o: third foal: dam winning pointer: unplaced in points: modest form in bumpers: similar form over hurdles: better effort when third in novice at Wincanton in March: remains with potential. *Carroll Gray*   **h96 p**   **b75**

BELLANEY KNIGHT (IRE) 8 bl.g. Marienbard (IRE) – Bellaney Jewel (IRE) (Roselier (FR)) [2017/18 h113: h23.1g⁴ h23.3v⁵ Oct 14] chasing sort: fair handicap hurdler: will be suited by 3m+: acts on good to soft going: tried in tongue tie. *John Quinn*   **h99**

BELLA'S VISION (FR) 5 ch.m. Vision d'Etat (FR) – Dalina (FR) (Trempolino (USA)) [2017/18 b16d b15.8g h16.8s Feb 23] second foal: half-sister to useful hurdler Mon Lino (2¾m winner, by Martaline), stays 3m: dam (h122), French 2¼m/19f hurdle winner, also 10.5f-15f winner on Flat: well held in bumpers/novice hurdle. *Richard Phillips*   **h–**   **b–**

BEL

BELLE AMIS 5 ch.m. Black Sam Bellamy (IRE) – Amaretto Rose (Alflora (IRE)) [2017/18 b16s* b16.7v³ b16v⁶ Mar 10] fifth foal: dam (h141) bumper/2m hurdle winner: fair form in bumpers: won mares event at Wetherby in November. *Fergal O'Brien* **b93**

BELLE BANJO (FR) 7 gr.m. Smadoun (FR) – Calingyou (FR) (Homme de Loi (IRE)) [2017/18 b16.8g⁵ b16.8m Aug 29] £4,000 5-y-o: third foal: dam unraced half-sister to fairly useful hurdler (stayed 25f) Canalturn: poor form in bumpers. *William Reed* **b62**

BELLE EMPRESS 7 b.m. Black Sam Bellamy (IRE) – Empress of Light (Emperor Jones (USA)) [2017/18 h20.5s⁵ h19.5v³ h21.7v* Mar 17] £65,000 4-y-o: closely related to 2 winners, including useful hurdler/chaser Rons Dream (2m-25f winner, by Kayf Tara), and half-sister to 2 winners by Definite Article, including fairly useful hurdler/useful chaser Fistral Beach (2½m/21f winner, stayed 3m): dam, lightly raced on Flat, half-sister to high-class hurdler/very smart chaser (winner up to 2½m) Wahiba Sands: point winner: fair form over hurdles: won mares novice at Fontwell (by 12 lengths from Illtellmema) in March. *Emma Lavelle* **h106**

BELLE EN NOIR 6 b.m. Black Sam Bellamy (IRE) – Miss Holly (Makbul) [2017/18 b–: b16s⁵ b16s h21v⁵ Mar 15] poor form in bumpers: well beaten in mares novice on hurdling debut: tried in tongue tie. *Steph Hollinshead* **h–** **b64**

BELLE OF YORK (IRE) 5 b.m. Vale of York (IRE) – Belle Rebelle (IRE) (In The Wings) [2017/18 b16sᵖᵘ b17d Mar 31] €5,200 3-y-o: sixth foal: half-sister to 3 winners, including useful hurdler/fairly useful chaser King of The Picts (2m/17f winner, by Rock of Gibraltar): dam unraced: no form in bumpers. *Martin Todhunter* **b–**

BELLE'S SPIRIT 5 b.m. Kutub (IRE) – Dickies Girl (Saxon Farm) [2017/18 b15.7s h15.7sᵖᵘ h15.8s h15.8s h15.8d Apr 9] half-sister to several winners, including fair chaser Autumm Spirit (2m-2½m winner, by Kadastrof) and fair hurdler/chaser Arctic Shadow (2¾m-3m winner, by Bonny Scot): dam poor maiden hurdler: no form in bumper/over hurdles. *Robin Dickin* **h–** **b–**

BELLE'S THEATRE 5 b.m. Black Sam Bellamy (IRE) – Falcons Theatre (IRE) (King's Theatre (IRE)) [2017/18 b16.6s h19.5sᵖᵘ Feb 24] second foal: dam (h69) maiden hurdler (stayed 2½m): no show in bumper/maiden hurdle. *Venetia Williams* **h–** **b–**

BELL OFTHE BONGATE (IRE) 4 b.f. Sakhee (USA) – Peace Lily (Dansili) [2017/18 b16.2v⁶ b17d Mar 25] fifth foal: half-sister to 7f/1m winner Golden Wedding (by Archipenko): dam 7f winner: no form in bumpers. *Harriet Graham* **b–**

BELLSHILL (IRE) 8 b.g. King's Theatre (IRE) – Fairy Native (IRE) (Be My Native (USA)) [2017/18 c151, h–: c25s* c29v⁵ c24.5s* Apr 25] **c168** **h–**

The record-breaking eighteen winners saddled by Willie Mullins at the Punchestown Festival belonged to thirteen different sets of owners including two of the stable's biggest patrons in recent years, Mrs Susannah Ricci (and American husband Rich Ricci) and Andrea and Graham Wylie. The Riccis and Wylies live in Britain but have nearly all their horses with Mullins (the Wylies used to have their string with Howard Johnson before he gave up training, and then also had horses with Paul Nicholls, but now base them exclusively in Ireland). The Mullins connection has been a highly successful one for both couples over the years but both must have been relieved by the last-gasp upturn in their fortunes at Punchestown after a largely frustrating 2017/18 campaign. Faugheen's victory in the Champion Stayers' Hurdle boosted the end-of-season statistics for the Riccis, while Bellshill's triumph in the Punchestown Gold Cup did the same for the Wylies. The Wylies had had the misfortune to see their reigning Stayers' Hurdle winner Nichols Canyon killed in the Christmas Hurdle at Leopardstown, while another of their great hopes for the latest season, the high-class but enigmatic Yorkhill, had an abject campaign, failing to reach a place on any of his starts, tried at two miles and three miles over both hurdles and fences, and leaving his connections to ponder limited options for a resurrection in the next season. Shaneshill, another of the Wylie horses with 'hill' in their name (all of whom started out in Irish points), had won the Prix La Barka over hurdles at Auteuil shortly after the end of the 2016/17 British and Irish seasons but he didn't win again, though picking up good place money over fences in races like the Galway Plate and also finishing third to Faugheen in the Champion Stayers' Hurdle. 'Horses aren't robots and you get these seasons, you get ups and downs and you just have to live through it,' was how Graham Wylie summed it up.

Coral Punchestown Gold Cup Chase, Punchestown—
Bellshill (left) makes amends for his Irish National aberration; stable-companion Djakadam
(second left) fills the runner-up spot for the fourth year running

Bellshill's season also had its ups and downs after he returned in the spring for the first time since finishing a respectable third to Might Bite and Whisper in the RSA Chase at the previous year's Cheltenham Festival. The RSA Chase was Bellshill's third successive appearance at the Cheltenham Festival. He had finished tenth in the Champion Bumper (before following in the hoofprints of Shaneshill to win the Champion INH Flat Race at the Punchestown Festival) and then managed only thirteenth of fourteen in the Supreme Novices' Hurdle. Bellshill had shaped like a stayer from an early stage in his career and he would clearly have been better suited by one of the longer novice hurdles at the Festival, but his owners had Yorkhill for the Baring Bingham and the already proven stayer Up For Review for the Spa. Yorkhill won a strong renewal of the Baring Bingham, looking very much one to follow, while Up For Review was pulled up in the Spa after making most of the running and missed the following season before returning in the latest one to show himself a useful novice chaser in a fairly light campaign; Bellshill went on to finish second in the Sefton at Aintree and win the War of Attrition at Punchestown when stepped up markedly in trip after the Supreme.

Bellshill's lengthy absence—he had nearly a year off after the RSA Chase—didn't prevent him from making an impressive reappearance in the five-runner At The Races Bobbyjo Chase at Fairyhouse in late-February when he won readily from the two other finishers A Genie In Abottle and Val de Ferbet. Connections announced that the next target would be either the Grand National or the Irish Grand National. Bellshill had also been entered in the Ryanair Chase at the Cheltenham Festival but his trainer said he was looking 'more at the big handicaps with him and Fairyhouse might be the thing to do as he is at home on the track.' Bellshill had been allotted 10-8 in Ireland's richest jumps race and he eventually carried second top weight of 11-5 behind Outlander in a field of thirty, having picked up a discretionary 8-lb penalty from the Irish handicapper for his victory in the Bobbyjo. For most of the Irish National, Bellshill looked like making light of the penalty—and of the atrocious conditions—but he suddenly slowed when in the lead on the approach to the final fence and barely managed to clamber over the fence, jumping violently left into the bargain and interfering with 25/1-shot Arkwrisht, in second at the time, who, in turn, hampered the keeping-on Folsom Blue. Bellshill passed the post in fourth after a scramble for the line with three of the lightweights, General Principle, Isleofhopendreams and Forever Gold, and, rather surprisingly, the stewards saw fit to demote him from fourth to fifth. Folsom Blue may have been stopped in his tracks by the interference at the final fence, and he stayed on strongly again to finish a close fifth, but Bellshill's jockey was powerless to stop his mount's sudden change of direction. Bellshill's connections appealed against the decision of the Fairyhouse stewards (which had cost them €10,000 in prize money), trainer Willie Mullins

Andrea Wylie/Graham Wylie's "Bellshill"

saying 'I've never seen a horse disqualified for making a mistake in my life when a jockey wasn't to blame.' The appeal panel, however, didn't share connections' sense of injustice and the appeal was dismissed.

Consolation came for Bellshill and his connections at the Punchestown Festival where he was the shortest-priced of four runners for the Mullins stable in the Coral Punchestown Gold Cup. Bellshill was ridden by his Irish National jockey David Mullins who had also been narrowly denied in the Grand National at Aintree on Pleasant Company. Mullins rode Bellshill a little more patiently at Punchestown, although still having him close up as stablemate Djakadam made most of the running. Jumping well in the main, Bellshill was sent into the lead two out and, although idling on the run-in, was always holding the persistent, renewed challenge of Djakadam (second in the race for the fourth time) to score by three quarters of a length, with the favourite Road To Respect finishing eight lengths behind Djakadam after being left behind by the first two from the second last. Road To Respect, fourth in the Cheltenham Gold Cup, was the only one of the principals from that race to go on to Punchestown. For the record, he was beaten further at Cheltenham than at Punchestown, where he was followed home by Sub Lieutenant, the Mullins third string (judged on the betting) Killutagh Vic and the only British-trained challenger Sizing Granite. The twelve-runner Punchestown Gold Cup field made for a competitive renewal, despite the absence of the first three from Cheltenham, with the line-up including the winners of Ireland's three other Grade 1 open championship chases for the staying chasers. Outlander had won the Champion

Chase at Down Royal and Edwulf the Irish Gold Cup, with Road To Respect having won the Leopardstown Christmas Chase (formerly the Lexus) before finishing in the frame at Cheltenham. There is no doubt that it took a top-class performance to win at Punchestown and Bellshill, who is still relatively lightly raced over fences (he has won four of his seven starts), could well develop into a live contender for the 2019 Cheltenham Gold Cup, a race his trainer, for all his success, has yet to win.

Bellshill (IRE) (b.g. 2010)
- King's Theatre (IRE) (b 1991)
  - Sadler's Wells (b 1981)
    - Northern Dancer
    - Fairy Bridge
  - Regal Beauty (b 1981)
    - Princely Native
    - Dennis Belle
- Fairy Native (IRE) (b 1998)
  - Be My Native (br 1979)
    - Our Native
    - Witchy Woman
  - Amy Fairy (b 1981)
    - The Parson
    - Copp On

The workmanlike Bellshill has had his family background discussed in previous essays in this series but, to recap, he is by the now-deceased King's Theatre, who has been champion jumps sire in Britain and Ireland five times (King's Theatre's last crop are now six-year-olds and he should remain among the leading sires for a few more years yet, having finished a close second to Flemensfirth in the latest season). Bellshill is out of the lightly-raced Fairy Native who was well held in bumpers and a novice hurdle but has done well at stud, producing four winners so far. Bellshill's year-older brother Chieftain's Choice, a fairly useful performer at up to nineteen furlongs, was placed four times over hurdles and fences for Kevin Frost in the latest season, while another brother Foxbridge was a fairly useful handicap chaser who stayed three miles, as was Bellshill's half-brother In The Zone (by Bob Back). Much the most notable member of the family, however, is the top-class chaser One Man who won the King George VI Chase twice and the Queen Mother Champion Chase. One Man is out of a half-sister to Bellshill's grandam Amy Fairy who won a bumper before being successful over hurdles and fences. Bellshill usually travels strongly in his races but he stays extremely well (the Irish National is three miles five furlongs) and acts on heavy going. *W. P. Mullins, Ireland*

BELLS 'N' BANJOS (IRE) 8 b.g. Indian River (FR) – Beechill Dancer (IRE) (Darnay) [2017/18 c133, h–: c25g^5 c32.8s^{pu} c26s Mar 24] rangy gelding: winning hurdler: useful handicap chaser: fifth at Cheltenham in October: stays 23f: acts on heavy going: tried in cheekpieces: has suspect attitude. *Fergal O'Brien* c125 h–

BELLS OF AILSWORTH (IRE) 8 b.g. Kayf Tara – Volverta (FR) (Green Tune (USA)) [2017/18 c121, h112: c24.2s^3 c24.1s* c28.4v^3 c25s^{pu} Apr 14] good-bodied gelding: fair hurdler: useful handicap chaser: won at Bangor in December: third at Taunton (4¼ lengths behind Regal Flow) in March: stays 3½m: acts on good to firm and heavy going: wears tongue tie: held up. *Tim Vaughan* c130 h–

BELL WEIR 10 gr.g. Tobougg (IRE) – Belly Dancer (IRE) (Danehill Dancer (IRE)) [2017/18 c–, h98: h16.8g^4 h16.8g^2 h17.2d^3 h20.2g^2 Jul 5] lengthy gelding: modest handicap hurdler: fell first only chase start: stays 2½m: acts on soft and good to firm going: has worn headgear/tongue tie. *Kenneth Slack* c– h97

BELMONT JEWEL (IRE) 6 b.m. Westerner – Maddy's Supreme (IRE) (Supreme Leader) [2017/18 h19.9g^6 May 28] €6,500 3-y-o, £15,500 5-y-o: fifth foal: half-sister to useful hurdler/winning pointer Jessber's Dream (2¼m-2½m winner, by Milan): dam (h85) maiden hurdler (stayed 23f): off mark in points at fourth attempt: 11/2, sixth in mares maiden at Uttoxeter on hurdling debut: should do better. *Michael Scudamore* h– p

BELMONT PARK (FR) 7 br.g. Al Namix (FR) – Goldoulyssa (FR) (Cadoudal (FR)) [2017/18 h–: c16.1g^3 c23.6g^{pu} c25.7d^{ur} c21.7g^2 Nov 30] maiden hurdler: modest form over fences: stays 2¾m: in cheekpieces in 2017/18. *David Bridgwater* c96 h–

BELMOUNT (IRE) 9 b.g. Westerner – Artist's Jewel (Le Moss) [2017/18 c127, h–: c24d^3 c23.8g^4 c25.5g* c23.8m^6 c28.4v^F c24.2d^{pu} c27.3v^{pu} c23.8s Apr 25] well-made gelding: winning hurdler: fairly useful handicap chaser: won at Warwick in September: stays 3¼m: acts on good to firm and heavy going: usually wears cheekpieces: often let down by jumping over fences. *Nigel Twiston-Davies* c126 x h–

BEM

BE MY SEA (IRE) 7 b.g. Sea The Stars (IRE) – Bitooh (Diktat) [2017/18 h102: h21g² h23.1d* Jun 8] fair form over hurdles: won handicap at Bangor in June: stays 23f: acts on soft going: tried in cheekpieces/tongue tie. *Tony Carroll*   **h107**

BENABILITY (IRE) 8 b.g. Beneficial – Whataliability (IRE) (Leading Counsel (USA)) [2017/18 c85, h77: c21.6g^pu c23m^ur Nov 1] lengthy gelding: winning hurdler: modest chaser at best, no form in 2017/18: stays 2½m: acts on heavy going: usually wears headgear: has joined Zoe Davison. *Tim Vaughan*   **c– h–**

BEN ARTHUR (IRE) 8 b.g. Marienbard (IRE) – Oscartrainer (IRE) (Oscar (IRE)) [2017/18 h99: c17.4d⁶ c19.7d^ur c23.5s² c24v⁴ h24.1v² h21.7v⁶ Mar 10] point winner: fair handicap hurdler: modest form over fences: stays 3m: best form on soft/heavy going: in headgear last 4 starts: wears tongue tie. *Kim Bailey*   **c88 h100**

BENATAR (IRE) 6 b.g. Beneficial – Carrigeen Lily (IRE) (Supreme Leader) [2017/18 h138: c18.8g* c19.7s* c21d* c19.9s³ Mar 15] sturdy gelding: useful hurdler: smart form over fences: won novice handicap at Ascot (by 3¾ lengths from Space Oddity) and novice at Plumpton (by 9 lengths from Keeper Hill) in November, and Noel Novices' Chase again at Ascot (by short head from Finian's Oscar) in December: finished lame when third in JLT Novices' Chase (Golden Miller) at Cheltenham (12 lengths behind Shattered Love) in March: stays 21f: acts on heavy going: often races towards rear: remains open to improvement as a chaser. *Gary Moore*   **c150 p h–**

BENBECULA 9 b.g. Motivator – Isle of Flame (Shirley Heights) [2017/18 c–, h91§: h18.5d h16.8d⁴ h21.4s² h19v² h20.5v⁵ Apr 1] angular gelding: modest handicap hurdler: pulled up sole start over fences: stays 21f: acts on heavy going: wears blinkers: front runner: untrustworthy. *Richard Mitchell*   **c– h91 §**

BENBENS (IRE) 13 ch.g. Beneficial – Millicent Bridge (IRE) (Over The River (FR)) [2017/18 c139, h–: c25d c27.3s⁴ c28.8d* c24.2s c34v^pu c31.8g^pu c28.8d Apr 28] workmanlike gelding: winning hurdler: useful handicap chaser: won Betfair London National at Sandown (by neck from Sugar Baron) in December: stays 4m: acts on good to firm and heavy going. *Nigel Twiston-Davies*   **c133 h–**

BENDOMINGO (IRE) 7 b.g. Beneficial – Bobbies Storm (IRE) (Bob Back (USA)) [2017/18 h109: h21g* h20g⁵ h23g⁶ c20d² c25.6s^pu c19.9d⁶ Apr 24] fairly useful handicap hurdler: won at Warwick in May: poor form over fences: stays 25f: acts on good to soft going: has worn tongue tie. *Nigel Twiston-Davies*   **c72 h116**

BEN DUNDEE (IRE) 6 ch.g. Beneficial – Miss Dundee (IRE) (Bob Back (USA)) [2017/18 h20d* h16s⁶ h16s² h16s h16.8v h16.5d Apr 24] €50,000 3-y-o: sturdy gelding: second foal: dam, unraced, out of sister to very smart chaser Nick Dundee (stayed 3m): useful handicap hurdler: won at Punchestown in October: second at Leopardstown (3 lengths behind Trainwreck) in December: stays 21f: acts on heavy going: tried in tongue tie. *Gordon Elliott, Ireland*   **h136**

BENEAGLES (IRE) 6 b.g. Milan – Liss Rua (IRE) (Bob Back (USA)) [2017/18 h123p: h24.2d³ h24.2d⁵ h26s⁴ h25d Apr 26] useful-looking gelding: placed in Irish point: fairly useful handicap hurdler: stays 25f: acts on soft going: in headgear last 3 starts: often races towards rear. *Alan King*   **h119**

BENECHENKO (IRE) 6 br.g. Beneficial – Beann Ard (IRE) (Mandalus) [2017/18 h86p, b98: h21.4s² h23.1s³ h23.6v³ h20s² h23.1s h21.6v³ Apr 17] Irish point winner: bumper winner: fair maiden hurdler: will prove best at 3m+: acts on soft going: tried in cheekpieces. *Fergal O'Brien*   **h112**

BENEFICIAL JOE (IRE) 8 b.g. Beneficial – Joleen (IRE) (Bob's Return (IRE)) [2017/18 h118: c23.9g² c26.1d^F c23g^F h26.5m³ h26.4g⁵ h23.3g h23.3d* h27g² h24.2d Dec 1] sturdy gelding: fairly useful handicap hurdler: won at Uttoxeter in October: similar form over fences: best effort when second in novice handicap at Market Rasen in May: stays 27f: acts on good to firm and good to soft going: usually wears hood: often races towards rear. *Graeme McPherson*   **c119 h123**

BENEFIT NORTH (IRE) 7 ch.g. Beneficial – Hayley Cometh (IRE) (Supreme Leader) [2017/18 b18g h16s⁴ h16s³ h19.5v^F h16v⁴ Jan 15] €32,000 3-y-o: seventh foal: half-brother to fairly useful hurdler/chaser The Fresh Prince (2m-2½m winner, by Robin des Pres) and fairly useful hurdler/fair chaser Duke of Monmouth (2¾m-25f winner, by Presenting): dam (h101) 2½m hurdle winner: winning pointer: fair form in bumpers: better effort when third in maiden at Punchestown in November: similar form over hurdles: best effort when fourth in maiden at Down Royal in November: tried in hood: often in tongue tie: free-going sort, usually makes running. *Colin A. McBratney, Ireland*   **h104 b88**

BEN

BENEFIT OF LUCK (IRE) 6 ch.g. Beneficial – Shamrock Miss (IRE) (Bob's Return (IRE)) [2017/18 h95§, b84§: h25m³ c23.9gpu Jun 23] rather unfurnished gelding: multiple point winner: fair form over hurdles: pulled up in novice handicap on chasing debut: best effort at 25f: acts on good to firm going: one to treat with caution (has refused to race). *Harry Whittington*   c– § / h105 §

BENENDEN (IRE) 10 b.g. Moscow Society (USA) – Ashanti Dancer (IRE) (Dancing Dissident (USA)) [2017/18 c–x, h117: h23.9d^F h23.9gpu c23.9g⁶ h23.1g³ h23gpu c24dpu Oct 3] useful-looking gelding: fair handicap hurdler: fairly useful chaser at best, below form in 2017/18: stays 3¼m: acts on heavy going: has worn cheekpieces: tried in tongue tie: often races towards rear. *Michael Scudamore*   c98 / h109

BENIE DES DIEUX (FR) 7 b.m. Great Pretender (IRE) – Cana (FR) (Robin des Champs (FR)) [2017/18 c134P, h–: c20s* c16v* h19.9s* h20s* Apr 28]   c148 P / h151 p

    Willie Mullins could have taken his pick when comparing one of the current female stars of his stable with others of the same sex to have passed through his hands in recent seasons. But it wasn't Quevega, Annie Power or Vroum Vroum Mag whose names were mentioned when discussing Benie des Dieux, winner of the Grade 1 mares hurdles at the latest Cheltenham and Punchestown Festivals. Instead, Mullins referred to her as 'the female version of Douvan' judged on her work at home. Praise indeed, though no doubt Benie des Dieux's owners Rich and Susannah Ricci would settle for her enjoying a career as successful as those of Annie Power or Vroum Vroum Mag, who, like Douvan, both carried their colours. While Annie Power went on to prove herself in open company, winning the 2016 Champion Hurdle, her earlier wins included two editions of the Mares Champion Hurdle at Punchestown, a race which bore her name for the first time in 2018. A last-flight fall cost Annie Power certain victory at the 2015 Cheltenham Festival in the David Nicholson Mares' Hurdle, though Vroum Vroum Mag won that race a year later before winning the Punchestown Champion Hurdle (stable-companions Whiteout and Limini took the first two places in the Mares Champion at that meeting). The Mares Champion was only a Grade 3 race for much of the time that Quevega reigned as the top mare, and the six-times David Nicholson winner had the three-mile World Series Hurdle as her annual target at Punchestown, a race which she won every year from 2010 to 2013. Kept largely, but by no means exclusively, to races confined to their own sex, all three of these mares established prolific records for Mullins; Quevega won thirteen of her eighteen races for his yard, Annie Power thirteen out of fifteen and Vroum Vroum Mag twelve out of fifteen.

    Benie des Dieux has so far won five out of five since coming from France and, like Vroum Vroum Mag, she began her Irish career over fences. However, she managed only one appearance in the 2016/17 season, looking in a different league to her rivals in a beginners chase for mares at Limerick which she won by thirty lengths. It was almost a whole year later before Benie des Dieux was next seen out, confirming herself an exciting prospect by winning a five-runner listed mares chase at Carlisle in December, again making all and winning with any amount in hand by eight lengths. Back in Ireland in February, in a similar event at Naas, the Opera

OLBG Mares' Hurdle (David Nicholson), Cheltenham—a winning return to hurdles for Benie des Dieux (second right), who keeps on well to overhaul outsider Midnight Tour (checks) and below-par favourite Apple's Jade (left); the other mare in the picture La Bague Au Roi makes a mess of the flight and trails in last of the seven finishers

European Breeders' Fund Annie Power Mares Champion Hurdle, Punchestown—
Benie des Dieux confirms her Cheltenham superiority over Apple's Jade (No.1), who fades into third behind Augusta Kate (right)

Hat Mares' Chase, Benie des Dieux faced sterner opposition, with the useful pair Asthuria and Dinaria des Obeaux among her five rivals. Conceding weight to both (7 lb to stable-companion Asthuria), Benie des Dieux had less to spare, winning by two and a half lengths and three, but it was a comfortable success, Benie des Dieux impressing with her quick, accurate jumping.

Given the impression she had made over fences, Benie des Dieux had been at shorter odds for her other Cheltenham entry, the Ryanair Chase, but she took her chance in the David Nicholson instead, following the announcement of Vroum Vroum Mag's retirement in the week before the Festival. Vroum Vroum Mag failed to make it back to the track in the latest season after finishing lame when bidding to win the Punchestown Champion Hurdle again in 2017. Even assuming Benie des Dieux could translate her smart chasing form back to the smaller obstacles—her hurdles form in France much earlier in her career was no better than fairly useful— she faced no easy task dethroning the previous season's David Nicholson winner, the 2/1-on favourite Apple's Jade, who had herself begun her career with Mullins. Apple's Jade had won all four of her starts since the 2017 David Nicholson when she had beaten Vroum Vroum Mag by a length and a half with the other Mullins/ Ricci mare Limini just a nose back in third. On her latest outing, in the Christmas Hurdle at Leopardstown, Apple's Jade had beaten the subsequent Irish Champion Hurdle winner Supasundae. In a field of nine, the first single-figure field in the history of the David Nicholson, which was run again as the OLBG Mares' Hurdle, Benie des Dieux was a 9/2 chance with La Bague Au Roi, winner of all three of her starts in mares races during the season, the only other runner at single-figure odds on 5/1. As it turned out, the race took a lot less winning than had appeared likely, with both of Benie des Dieux's main rivals underperforming, particularly Apple's Jade who proved far too fresh for her own good after her break. Benefiting from a much more patient ride under Ruby Walsh, Benie des Dieux, who again travelled well, made good progress three out but didn't hit the front until the run-in, where she wandered but kept on well under a strong drive, with her jockey receiving a two-day ban for using his whip above the permitted level. Apple's Jade was beaten a length and a half by the winner into third behind the 33/1 runner-up Midnight Tour, while La Bague Au Roi, another who had done too much too soon, had only just been headed when making a mess of the final flight and trailed in last of the seven finishers. Benie des Dieux gave Mullins his ninth win in eleven runnings of the David Nicholson; in addition to Quevega's six-timer and Vroum Vroum Mag's victory, he also won the 2015 edition, in which Annie Power had crashed out, with second string Glens Melody.

It is only ten years since mares have had their own race at the Festival, while the addition of the Dawn Run Mares' Novices' Hurdle in 2016 (Mullins has won all three renewals to date) provides a second opportunity on the biggest stage for the producers of jump racing's future generations. Another development in the latest season was Cheltenham's staging of the very first card dedicated entirely to fillies and mares. Adapting the second day of the April meeting, which already had four such races, the 2018 card was scheduled to include three hurdles, three chases and a bumper (three of the races had listed status), though the day's headlines were dominated by the death of the Nickel Coin winner Dame Rose and the abandonment of the longest race on the card on welfare grounds due to the sudden change from weeks of unusually cold weather to an unseasonable heatwave.

The following week's Punchestown Festival featured a rematch between Benie des Dieux and Apple's Jade in the Irish Stallion Farms EBF Annie Power Mares Champion Hurdle though, despite her reverse at Cheltenham, Apple's Jade again started odds on to repeat her success of twelve months earlier when Mullins had supplied the next four home. Midnight Tour and Jer's Girl, who had been fifth at Cheltenham, took them on again, while Mullins also fielded the previous season's Dawn Run winner Let's Dance, she too carrying the 'Annie Power' colours of the Riccis. While Apple's Jade settled better than at Cheltenham, she again had no answer late on to Benie des Dieux who headed her approaching the last and kept on well for a three-length win over her stable's third string Augusta Kate, herself winner of the Grade 1 mares novices' hurdle at Fairyhouse twelve months earlier. Apple's Jade was only third again, with Let's Dance completing the frame. Augusta Kate had finished second at level weights behind Presenting Percy in the Galmoy Hurdle earlier in the season, and Benie des Dieux's beating of her represented better form than her Cheltenham success, matching the best of her efforts over fences.

Benie des Dieux won the last of her three starts on the Flat, over a mile and three quarters, before successfully switching to hurdles, winning twice at Auteuil and finishing third in a Group 3 for fillies and mares, the Prix Andre Michel, on what proved her final start there as a four-year-old for Isabelle Gallorini. She caught the eye of Pierre Boulard, Mullins' French agent, who was attracted by Benie des Dieux's 'masculine' physique—she's angular in appearance—her breeding, and, he also admitted, her name—'blessed by the gods'. Boulard apparently detected a lot of Robin des Champs (the sire of her dam) in her, and he was also the sire of Quevega

Mrs S. Ricci's "Benie des Dieux"

BEN

and Vautour. Benie des Dieux's own sire Great Pretender, who was fourth in the Prix du Jockey Club (over a mile and a half) and won both his starts over hurdles, is responsible for another of the Mullins stable's best horses Great Field. Although Great Field himself was missing from Punchestown, Benie des Dieux's sire had three winners at the meeting, with the useful Pravalaguna another successful mare for Mullins, while the Gordon Elliott-trained Dortmund Park won the two and a half mile Champion Novices' Hurdle. Benie des Dieux is the only runner to date out of her dam Cana who twice finished second from only four runs over hurdles in France. Cana's half-brother Choeur du Nord could become a more familiar name in future as he is standing as a stallion in France after his promising jumping career was cut short (he won two of his three starts over hurdles at three for Guillaume Macaire). Cana's half-sisters include some successful broodmares, one of them the dam of Ceasar's Palace who was the outstanding juvenile hurdler of his generation in France (rated 159p in *Chasers & Hurdlers 2010/11*) though he had a stop-start career thereafter, partnered on one occasion by Flat champion Christophe Soumillon. Grandam Cardoudalle gained all three of her wins at Auteuil, two over hurdles and one over fences. More distantly, Benie des Dieux's fourth dam had the less inspired name La Horse but she was the grandam of the very smart staying hurdler and Scottish Grand National runner-up Sweet Duke, and the family also includes the high-class two-mile hurdler Grandouet.

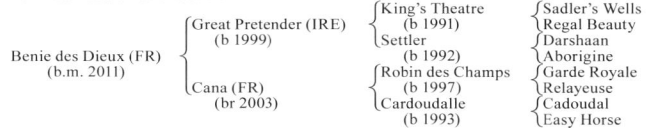

Benie des Dieux (FR) (b.m. 2011)	Great Pretender (IRE) (b 1999)	King's Theatre (b 1991)	Sadler's Wells
			Regal Beauty
		Settler (b 1992)	Darshaan
			Aborigine
	Cana (FR) (br 2003)	Robin des Champs (b 1997)	Garde Royale
			Relayeuse
		Cardoudalle (b 1993)	Cadoudal
			Easy Horse

Vroum Vroum Mag never went back over fences once being switched successfully to hurdles, and Mullins' question 'Are there the races to go for?' when discussing a possible return to the larger obstacles for Benie des Dieux may indicate that she too will remain over hurdles. There are, at present, no Grade 1 chases in either Britain or Ireland restricted to mares, which must make hurdling the more attractive proposition for a mare like Benie des Dieux who has proved herself equally adept in both disciplines. Rich Ricci, for one, says he'd love to see her back over fences, though he explained after Cheltenham that another reason for switching to hurdles was that, for all that she has an excellent jumping technique, she had been hard to keep sound in her hind quarters due to the greater effort required to jump fences. Benie des Dieux, who wore ear plugs at Cheltenham, is yet to race beyond two and a half miles, but will stay further, and she has raced only on soft or heavy ground. She was tried in cheekpieces earlier in her career in France. With further improvement to come, Benie des Dieux is on the way to adding her name to the mares who have provided the Mullins stable in recent seasons with jumping's greatest ever pool of female talent. *W. P. Mullins, Ireland*

BENI LIGHT (FR) 7 b.g. Crossharbour – Or Light (FR) (Sleeping Car (FR)) [2017/18 h62, b74: c20d^{pu} c18.2s^{pu} c17.5d^5 Apr 24] maiden hurdler: poor form over fences: best effort at 17f: acts on good to soft going: in hood last 2 starts. *Tom George* **c72 h–**

BENISSIMO (IRE) 8 b.g. Beneficial – Fennor Rose (IRE) (Kotashaan (FR)) [2017/18 c100, h112: h19.9v^6 h15.8v^5 h15.7v^{pu} Feb 25] fair hurdler at best, well below form in 2017/18: maiden chaser: tried in cheekpieces. *Tony Forbes* **c– h–**

BENNACHIE (IRE) 9 b.g. Milan – Stormy Lady (IRE) (Glacial Storm (USA)) [2017/18 c106§, h85§: h19.6g c20.3d^{ur} h20.5d^2 h19.2d^3 c19.9s^2 c19.7s* c21.7m* Apr 25] workmanlike gelding: poor handicap chaser nowadays: modest handicap chaser: won at Plumpton (conditional) and Taunton in April: stays 2¾m: acts on soft and good to firm going: usually wears cheekpieces: wears tongue tie: temperamental. *Tim Vaughan* **c94 § h83 §**

BENNY IN MILAN (IRE) 7 b.g. Milan – Chaparral Lady (IRE) (Broken Hearted) [2017/18 h107, b95: h19.1m* h17.2d h16.8g Sep 7] maiden pointer: bumper winner: fair handicap hurdler: won at Fontwell in June for Peter Fahey: stays 21f: acts on good to firm and good to soft going: has worn headgear: often races in rear: has joined F. Flood, Ireland. *Martin Todhunter* **h102**

BEN

BENNY'S BRIDGE (IRE) 5 b.g. Beneficial – Wattle Bridge (IRE) (King's Theatre (IRE)) [2017/18 b16.7d* b16.3s³ Mar 24] €34,000 3-y-o, £28,000 4-y-o: compact gelding: first foal: dam, lightly raced, closely related to useful 2m hurdle winner Snake Eyes out of useful hurdler/chaser up to 25f Be My Belle: fairly useful form in bumpers: won at Market Rasen in November: improved when third in Goffs UK Spring Sales Bumper at Newbury in March. *Fergal O'Brien* — **b99**

BENNYS GIRL (IRE) 10 b.m. Beneficial – Be My Flower (IRE) (Be My Native (USA)) [2017/18 c80, h–: c25.5g⁶ c16.1g⁴ c25.8m⁵ c25.8g⁴ c23g c23.9g⁵ c25.8m³ c25.8d⁴ c20.9s* c21.1v* c19.8v* Apr 27] maiden hurdler: modest handicap chaser: completed hat-trick in March/April, at Hereford, Sedgefield and Towcester (finished alone), last 2 mares events: stays 3¼m: acts on good to firm and heavy going. *Dai Williams* — **c86 h–**

BENNYS KING (IRE) 7 b.g. Beneficial – Hellofafaithful (IRE) (Oscar (IRE)) [2017/18 h124: c22.5s^pu Oct 19] good-topped gelding: fairly useful hurdler: pulled up in novice handicap on chasing debut: stays 2½m: acts on heavy going: usually races prominently: has joined Dan Skelton. *Venetia Williams* — **c– h–**

BENNY'S SECRET (IRE) 8 br.g. Beneficial – Greenhall Rambler (IRE) (Anshan) [2017/18 h92: h16.2m^pu h20.9d* h20.9g* h19.4d⁵ h24.3g Apr 20] fair handicap hurdler: won at Kelso in October and November: stays 21f: acts on soft going: has worn hood, including last 4 starts: has worn tongue tie: often races in rear. *N. W. Alexander* — **h103**

BENTELIMAR (IRE) 9 ch.g. Beneficial – Montel Girl (IRE) (Montelimar (USA)) [2017/18 c135, h140: c20s* c16g³ c22.5g^ur c22s² c24v⁶ c20.4s c16.3s³ c19.9s² c19.2v² c20.5s c15.8s* Apr 12] sturdy gelding: useful hurdler: smart chaser: won novice at Wexford (by 15 lengths from Dicosimo) in June and Red Rum Handicap Chase at Aintree (by 3¼ lengths from Theinval) in April: left J. R. Barry after fifth start: stays 25f, at least as effective at much shorter: acts on good to firm and heavy going: has worn headgear, including final start: usually races prominently. *Charlie Longsdon* — **c145 h–**

Zut Media Red Rum Handicap Chase, Aintree—the combination of first-time cheekpieces and a forcing ride from Jonathan Burke helps Bentelimar to his first win since joining present connections; the favourite Theinval is runner-up for the second year running

BEN

BENTONS LAD 7 br.g. Bollin Eric – Spirit of Ecstacy (Val Royal (FR)) [2017/18 c98, h88: c19.3s⁵ c25.2v^{pu} h20.6s⁴ h20.3g* Apr 20] point winner: modest handicap hurdler: won novice event at Southwell in April: modest form on chasing debut, little impact both starts over fences in 2017/18: stays 21f: acts on soft going: has worn headgear, including last 2 starts: has worn tongue tie: often races prominently. *Mark Walford* **c78 h92**

BEREA BORU (IRE) 10 b.g. Brian Boru – Wayward Venture (IRE) (Mister Mat (FR)) [2017/18 c103, h–: c24d c27.5g⁴ c26.1m^{pu} Jul 2] winning hurdler: useful chaser at best: stayed 3½m: acted on good to firm and heavy going: tried in headgear: wore tongue tie: dead. *Peter Bowen* **c123 x h–**

BERE HAVEN (IRE) 8 b.g. Papal Bull – Flower Drum (FR) (Celtic Swing) [2017/18 h20g³ h22.2d h16.7s h20g h27g⁴ Sep 7] won Irish point on debut: modest form over hurdles: left Jennie Candlish after second start: best effort at 27f: tried in tongue tie. *Ian O'Connor, Ireland* **h87**

BERGHOLT (IRE) 5 b.g. Sir Percy – Sularina (IRE) (Alhaarth (IRE)) [2017/18 h16.5s h15.6s⁶ Jan 3] modest maiden on Flat, stays 1½m: poor form over hurdles. *Tim Vaughan* **h77**

BERING UPSUN 7 b.g. And Beyond (IRE) – Bering Up (IRE) (Bering) [2017/18 h75, b80: h16.8d³ h16.4s h15.7v² Jan 24] modest form over hurdles: unproven beyond 17f: acts on heavy going: wears hood: front runner/races prominently. *James Ewart* **h95**

BERKELEY VALE 7 b.g. Three Valleys (USA) – Intriguing Glimpse (Piccolo) [2017/18 h16g^{pu} Aug 30] fair on Flat, stays 1¼m: in cheekpieces, pulled up in maiden on hurdling debut. *Roger Teal* **h–**

BERKSHIRE DOWNS 8 b.m. Tiger Hill (IRE) – Cut Corn (King's Theatre (IRE)) [2017/18 c87, h101: h20.5v⁵ h16v⁵ h23.8d Feb 14] poor maiden hurdler: maiden chaser: should stay 3m: acts on heavy going: wears cheekpieces: tried in tongue tie. *Sandy Thomson* **c– h69**

BERLIEF ARAMIS 8 b.g. Bertolini (USA) – Kaylifa Aramis (Kayf Tara) [2017/18 h19.7s^{pu} h21.7s⁶ Mar 27] no form over hurdles. *Alan Phillips* **h–**

BERMEO (IRE) 7 b.g. Definite Article – Miss Blueyes (IRE) (Dushyantor (USA)) [2017/18 c95, h94: h22d⁵ h23m h24.4s h19.2v⁶ h23.1d² Apr 24] modest handicap hurdler: maiden chaser: stays 3m: acts on good to firm and good to soft going: usually wears blinkers. *Johnny Farrelly* **c– h85**

BERNARDELLI (IRE) 10 b.g. Golan (IRE) – Beautiful Blue (IRE) (Xaar) [2017/18 c137x, h–: c20.5v⁴ c24.1v⁴ c23.4s⁴ c20.5v* Mar 9] winning hurdler: fairly useful handicap chaser: won at Ayr in March: stays 3m: acts on heavy going: wears headgear: often let down by jumping. *Nicky Richards* **c127 x h–**

BERRY DE CARJAC (FR) 7 ch.g. Epalo (GER) – Miria Galanda (FR) (Chef de Clan (FR)) [2017/18 c98, h92§: h16.3m* h16.8m² h16g⁴ h16d⁵ h16.8s h16.5g^F h16.5g Nov 30] workmanlike gelding: modest handicap hurdler: won at Stratford (amateur) in August: maiden chaser: stays 2½m: acts on good to firm going: has worn headgear/tongue tie: front runner/races prominently: temperamental. *Grace Harris* **c– h98 §**

BERTALUS (IRE) 9 b.g. City Honours (USA) – Deep Dalus (IRE) (Mandalus) [2017/18 c98§, h66§: h23.3g h24g^{pu} h24.3v⁵ h21.4v³ c23.4v* Apr 15] poor handicap hurdler: modest form over fences: won handicap at Newcastle in April: stays 3m: best form on soft/heavy going: has worn headgear, including in 2017/18: temperamental. *N. W. Alexander* **c95 § h79 §**

BERTIE BARNES (IRE) 7 b.g. Craigsteel – Mahon Rose (IRE) (Roselier (FR)) [2017/18 h90: h16s h21s h21s* h21v* Apr 27] fair handicap hurdler: won at Kempton and Towcester in April: stays 21f: best form on soft/heavy going. *Richard Phillips* **h106**

BERTIE BLAKE (IRE) 5 b.g. Beneficial – Diandrina (Mondrian (GER)) [2017/18 b–: h19.7s h19.7d⁶ h16.6d⁵ h19.6s Jan 26] modest form over hurdles: best effort at 2½m: acts on good to soft going. *Philip Kirby* **h86**

BERTIE BORU (IRE) 11 b.g. Brian Boru – Sleeven Lady (Crash Course) [2017/18 c127§, h–: c25g c30.2g Nov 17] strong, workmanlike gelding: maiden hurdler: fairly useful handicap chaser: stays 29f: acts on heavy going: wears cheekpieces: usually races nearer last than first: temperamental. *Philip Hobbs* **c119 § h–**

BERTIE LUGG 10 b.g. Beat All (USA) – Flakey Dove (Oats) [2017/18 c99, h98: c21.7m* c24.5g² c23m^{pu} Jul 5] winning chaser: fair form over fences: won handicap at Towcester (conditional) in May: stays 3m: acts on good to firm and heavy going: tried in tongue tie: has joined Tom Gretton. *Henry Oliver* **c108 h–**

BET

BERTIE MILAN (IRE) 13 b.g. Milan – Miss Bertaine (IRE) (Denel (FR)) [2017/18 c24.2g^F Jun 3] winning pointer: maiden hurdler: modest chaser, fell sole start in 2017/18: stays 31f: acts on soft going: wears headgear: temperamental. *N. W. Alexander*   c– § h–

BERTIE MY BOY (IRE) 9 b.g. Millenary – Slievemhuire (IRE) (Beneficial) [2017/18 h–: h23.9s^{pu} Dec 14] no form over hurdles. *Grant Cann*   h–

BERTIMONT (FR) 8 gr.g. Slickly (FR) – Bocanegra (FR) (Night Shift (USA)) [2017/18 c–, h135: h16.7s h15.8d h16.8g Apr 18] smallish gelding: useful handicap hurdler, below form in 2017/18: maiden chaser: unproven beyond 17f: acts on soft going: wears tongue tie. *Dan Skelton*   c– h111

BERWIN (IRE) 9 b.m. Lawman (FR) – Topiary (IRE) (Selkirk (USA)) [2017/18 h–: h20g May 26] no form over hurdles. *Sarah Robinson*   h–

BERYL N JEAN (IRE) 7 ch.m. Generous (IRE) – Scolboa House (IRE) (Bob's Return (IRE)) [2017/18 b16.2g^4 May 28] fifth foal: half-sister to fair hurdler All The Eights (2½m winner, by Loup Sauvage) and temperamental chaser Miss Dimples (21f winner, by Tikkanen): dam well held in 2 bumpers: in tongue tie, 18/1, fourth in mares bumper at Kelso. *Benjamin Arthey, Ireland*   b73

BESCOT SPRINGS (IRE) 13 b.g. Saddlers' Hall (IRE) – Silver Glen (IRE) (Roselier (FR)) [2017/18 c75, h101§: h23.3g^6 h23.3v h23.3s h22.7g^3 h24g^{pu} Nov 17] strong, good-bodied gelding: modest handicap hurdler: winning chaser: stays 3¼m: acts on good to firm and heavy going: wears headgear: usually races prominently: temperamental. *Lucinda Russell*   c– h97 §

BE SEEING YOU 7 ch.g. Medicean – Oshiponga (Barathea (IRE)) [2017/18 c65, h100: h21.6g^6 h23g^3 h20g^4 c20g Aug 23] fair handicap hurdler, below best in 2017/18: little show over fences: stays 23f: acts on good to firm going: wears headgear/tongue tie: has joined Matt Sheppard. *Trevor Wall*   c– h78

BEST BOY BARNEY (IRE) 12 b.g. Rashar (USA) – Graigue Lass (IRE) (Phardante (FR)) [2017/18 c105, h–: c23g^{pu} c25.8m^4 Jul 7] rangy gelding: maiden hurdler: fair chaser, no form in 2017/18: stays 3¼m: acts on any going: wears headgear/tongue tie: usually leads. *Jeremy Scott*   c– h–

BESTIARIUS (IRE) 6 b.g. Vinnie Roe (IRE) – Chione (IRE) (Mandalus) [2017/18 h107: h20.9d^3 Oct 8] fair form over hurdles: third in novice at Kelso on sole outing in 2017/18. *Nicky Richards*   h113

BEST PRACTICE (IRE) 7 br.g. Beneficial – Lemon Cello (IRE) (Accordion) [2017/18 h–: h15.7g^2 h16g^3 Jul 10] fair form over hurdles. *Jonjo O'Neill*   h101

BEST TO COME (IRE) 5 b.g. Stowaway – Nippy Nora (IRE) (King's Theatre (IRE)) [2017/18 b15.8d^6 Mar 22] €64,000 3-y-o: second foal: dam lightly-raced daughter of useful hurdler up to 3m Aine Dubh: 15/2, needed experience when sixth in bumper at Ludlow (20¼ lengths behind Rouge Vif): will improve. *Tom George*   b– p

BESTWORK (FR) 7 bl.g. Network (GER) – Harmony (FR) (Lute Antique (FR)) [2017/18 c86, h86: c16.1g* c15.6g^5 c20g* c19.4m^2 c21.6s^4 c20d^5 c19.9s* c15.9g^6 c20.2v^{pu} c20.5s^5 c20.5m* Apr 26] modest hurdler: fairly useful handicap chaser: won at Towcester in May, Uttoxeter and Stratford in July, Huntingdon in December and Kempton in April, 3 of them novice events: stays 2½m: acts on good to firm going: has worn hood: tried in tongue tie: can be moody. *Charlie Longsdon*   c124 h–

BETANCOURT (IRE) 8 ch.g. Refuse To Bend (IRE) – Orinoco (IRE) (Darshaan) [2017/18 h22.2d^5 h19.9g* h20.9d^6 c17.1g c19.2d^4 Dec 28] tall, useful-looking gelding: fell sole start in points: modest form over hurdles: won handicap at Sedgefield in October: similar form over fences: better effort when fourth in handicap at Catterick in December: stays 2½m: acts on good to soft going: has joined Stef Keniry. *James Ewart*   c87 h92

BE THAT AS IT MAY 5 b.m. Darbela (IRE) (Doyoun) [2017/18 b16s Feb 23] sister to useful bumper winner/top-class hurdler Darlan (2m/17f winner) and half-sister to fair hurdler Amie Magnifencent (2m-21f winner, by Mujahid): dam (h113), 2¼m/19f hurdle winner, also useful 1½m/2m winner on Flat: 2/1, tailed off in mares bumper at Warwick: clearly thought capable of much better. *Nicky Henderson*   b– p

BET ON BETTY 5 b.m. Flying Legend (USA) – Cadourova (FR) (Cadoudal (FR)) [2017/18 b16s^6 Mar 22] half-sister to fairly useful hurdler/useful chaser Minella Reception (2m-2½m winner, by King's Theatre): dam, French 2m chase winner, half-sister to useful hurdler/staying chaser Le Duc: well beaten in mares bumper. *Oliver Greenall*   b–

BET

BETTER DAYS (IRE) 7 gr.g. Daylami (IRE) – Miss Edgehill (IRE) (Idris (IRE)) [2017/18 c113, h84: c24.5g², c21.4g⁴ c24g* c25.6g Dec 6] workmanlike gelding: winning hurdler: fair handicap chaser: won at Kempton in October: stays 25f: best on good going or firmer: has worn tongue tie. *Nigel Twiston-Davies* **c113 h–**

BETTER GETALONG (IRE) 7 b.g. Gold Well – Arequipa (IRE) (Turtle Island (IRE)) [2017/18 b100: h16s* h16.4s³ h16v* h18.1v² h20sᵖᵘ Apr 14] good-topped gelding: bumper winner: useful form over hurdles: won novices at Ayr in October and January: third in Sharp Novices' Hurdle at Cheltenham (4½ lengths behind Slate House) in November: should stay 2½m: acts on heavy going. *Nicky Richards* **h131**

BETTERLATETHANNEVA (IRE) 7 b.m. Albano (IRE) – Acqua Pesante (IRE) (Distinctly North (USA)) [2017/18 h84, b79: h23.3d h19.9g⁵ h23m³ Jul 5] poor maiden hurdler: stays 23f: in cheekpieces last 2 starts: tried in tongue tie. *Robin Dickin* **h76**

BETTER NEWS 7 b.m. Fair Mix (IRE) – Welcome News (Bob Back (USA)) [2017/18 h21.6g h16gᵘʳ h15.8d⁴ h16.5m Apr 25] third foal: half-sister to fairly useful chaser Big News (3m winner, by Karinga Bay): dam winning pointer: well held completed start in points: poor form over hurdles: remains capable of better in handicaps. *Neil Mulholland* **h81 p**

BETWEEN THE WATERS (IRE) 7 ch.g. Indian River (FR) – Catch Ball (Prince Sabo) [2017/18 c86p, h96, b87: c23d³ c21.1m² c22.6m⁴ c17.8m⁴ c21d⁵ c19.3d² Oct 3] sturdy gelding: Irish point winner: modest form over hurdles: modest maiden chaser: stays 23f: acts on good to soft going: often in cheekpieces: tried in tongue tie. *Jamie Snowden* **c96 h–**

BEUVRON (FR) 8 ch.g. Martaline – Virginia River (FR) (Indian River (FR)) [2017/18 c25.8s³ c25.8m³ c25.8d² Jul 23] multiple point winner: winning hurdler: fair handicap chaser: stays 3¼m: acts on soft and good to firm going: in cheekpieces last 3 starts. *Martin Hill* **c107 h–**

BEWARE THE BEAR (IRE) 8 b.g. Shantou (USA) – Native Bid (IRE) (Be My Native (USA)) [2017/18 c145, h127+: c23.4v* c29.5vᵖᵘ c25s⁴ c31.8gᵖᵘ Apr 21] strong, workmanlike gelding: fairly useful hurdler: smart handicap chaser: won Rehearsal Chase at Newcastle (by 2¼ lengths from Bishops Road) in December: pulled up in both Welsh Grand National and Scottish Grand National: should stay 4m: acts on heavy going. *Nicky Henderson* **c147 h–**

BEYEH (IRE) 10 b.m. King's Best (USA) – Cradle Rock (IRE) (Desert Sun) [2017/18 c111, h–: c20g⁵ c17d⁵ h20.3g h15.7s⁵ h19.4s h20v⁴ h16s* h16s⁵ Mar 16] small mare: modest handicap hurdler: won at Fakenham (selling event) in February: fair form over fences: stays 2¾m: acts on heavy going: often races prominently. *Michael Appleby* **c106 h97**

BEYONDPERFECTION 7 b.m. And Beyond (IRE) – Pennepoint (Pennekamp (USA)) [2017/18 b16.2g b16.2d b16s Nov 29] fifth foal: dam unraced: no form in bumpers: left Jonathan Haynes after second start: tried in hood. *Philip Kirby* **b–**

BEYOND SUPREMACY (IRE) 6 ch.g. Beneficial – Slaney Athlete (IRE) (Warcraft (USA)) [2017/18 b–: h21.6vᵖᵘ h20.3s h23.1d⁴ Apr 24] useful-looking gelding: modest form over hurdles. *Jack R. Barber* **h88**

BEYONDTEMPTATION 10 ch.m. And Beyond (IRE) – Tempted (IRE) (Invited (USA)) [2017/18 h112: h16.2g³ h20.1g* h16.2gᶠ h20.1g h17.2g h22.1d h16.8g⁵ h20.1s³ h23.3vᵖᵘ h19.9g h16.2vᵖᵘ h20s⁶ h20.6s* h16vᵖᵘ h16.4v* h19.5v³ Feb 11] fair handicap hurdler: won at Hexham in May, and mares events at Newcastle in December and February (2 ran): stays 23f, at least as effective over shorter: acts on heavy going: wears hood/tongue tie: front runner. *Jonathan Haynes* **h110**

BEYOND THE CLOUDS 5 ch.g. Peintre Celebre (USA) – Evening (Mark of Esteem (IRE)) [2017/18 b100: b16g* h16.2d* h15.6m* h15.6s* h16g Apr 21] useful form in bumpers: won at Worcester (by 14 lengths from Mac Tottie) in September: similar form over hurdles: won novices at Kelso in October, and Musselburgh in November and February (by neck from Simply The Betts): usually travels strongly. *Kevin Ryan* **h137 b105**

BEYONDTHEFLAME 8 b.m. And Beyond (IRE) – Flame of Zara (Blushing Flame (USA)) [2017/18 h–: h16.8g h23.3g⁴ h20.1g⁴ h22.1d h23.3g⁴ h22.1gᵖᵘ h23.3d⁵ h23.3sᵖᵘ h25.3s⁵ h25.8sᵖᵘ h20.1d Apr 23] little form over hurdles: wears headgear: often wears tongue tie: usually leads. *Jonathan Haynes* **h70**

BEYOND THE GLEN 8 b.m. And Beyond (IRE) – Calabria (Neltino) [2017/18 h20.2gᵖᵘ h16.8v⁶ h19.9v⁶ h19.9g Apr 23] point winner: poor form over hurdles. *Chris Grant* **h75**

BEYOND THE LAW (IRE) 6 b.g. Westerner – Thegoodwans Sister (IRE) (Executive h123
Perk) [2017/18 h16v² h20s h19.6v⁴ h20v³ h19v* h18.8v* h22.3v⁴ h24vᵖᵘ h16.5d Apr 24]
€26,000 3-y-o: lengthy gelding: fourth foal: half-brother to bumper winner/fairly useful
hurdler Lookout Mountain (3¼m winner, by Flemensfirth): dam unraced half-sister to
fairly useful hurdler/smart chaser (winner up to 3m) Cailin Alainn: point winner: fairly
useful hurdler: won maiden at Limerick in December and minor event at Clonmel in
January: stays 2½m: acts on heavy going: wears tongue tie: front runner/races prominently.
M. F. Morris, Ireland

BEYOND THE STARS 7 b.m. And Beyond (IRE) – Treasured Memories (Cloudings h–
(IRE)) [2017/18 h19.9vᵖᵘ Apr 13] first foal: dam (h93) bumper/3m hurdle winner: failed to
complete in points/novice hurdle. *Maurice Barnes*

BHAKTI (IRE) 11 b.g. Rakti – Royal Bossi (IRE) (Spectrum (IRE)) [2017/18 h93§: h90
h23.9g⁶ h23.3d² h23g² Jun 14] strong, deep-girthed gelding: modest handicap hurdler:
stays 23f: acts on good to soft going: in cheekpieces last 2 starts. *Tom Lacey*

BIALCO (FR) 7 gr.g. Dom Alco (FR) – Lacanale (FR) (Kadalko (FR)) [2017/18 h19.4d c125
c19.4s c22.4s c18.4s² c17.4s c21.4v³ h22.8v⁵ h16v² h19.6s² Mar 24] second foal: dam h121
French 17f chase winner: fairly useful hurdler over hurdles: fairly useful chaser: second in
claimer at Auteuil in September: left P. Peltier after fifth start: stays 23f: best form on soft/
heavy going: has worn headgear: wears tongue tie. *Lucinda Russell*

BID ADIEU (IRE) 4 b.g. Pour Moi (IRE) – Thoughtless Moment (IRE) (Pivotal) h–
[2017/18 h16s h16gᵖᵘ Feb 24] fairly useful on Flat, stays 12.5f: 7/4, well held in juvenile
maiden at Wetherby on hurdling debut for Thomas Cooper: out of depth next time: wears
hood: has joined Richard Hughes. *Venetia Williams*

BIDDY BLACK 6 ch.m. Black Sam Bellamy (IRE) – Cosavita (FR) (Comte du Bourg h–
(FR)) [2017/18 b–: b16.2d⁵ h24gᵖᵘ Sep 6] failed to complete in points: poor form in b65
bumpers: pulled up in novice on hurdling debut. *Simon West*

BIENNIAL (IRE) 6 ch.g. Bienamado (USA) – Midnight Orchid (IRE) (Petardia) h97
[2017/18 h16.7g h16v⁵ h16vᵖᵘ h16v³ h17d h16g⁵ Apr 20] €10,000 3-y-o: brother to fair b61
hurdler/chaser Castletown Bridge (2m-27f winner): dam, 6f winner, half-sister to useful
hurdler/fairly useful chaser (stayed 21f) Buddy Marvel: unplaced in bumpers: modest form
over hurdles: left Andrew McNamara after first start. *Ian Duncan*

BIENTO MADAME 7 b.m. Robin des Champs (FR) – Histoire de Moeurs (FR) b83
(Kaldounevees (FR)) [2017/18 b15.7g² b16s⁵ b16g Sep 1] first foal: dam (c118/h107),
2m/17f hurdle/chase winner, also smart French 10.5f-1½m winner on Flat: modest bumper
performer: unplaced last 3 starts: has joined Dan Skelton. *Aaron Stronge, Ireland*

BIG BAD DOG (IRE) 4 b.g. Big Bad Bob (IRE) – Sunset Queen (IRE) (King's Theatre b–
(IRE)) [2017/18 b16v⁵ Mar 20] tailed off in bumper. *Micky Hammond*

BIG BAD DREAM (IRE) 6 b.g. Mountain High (IRE) – Stay At Home (IRE) (Blueprint b97
(IRE)) [2017/18 b86: b16v² b17d³ Mar 25] fairly useful form in bumpers: third at Carlisle
in March: will be suited by 2¼m+. *Donald Whillans*

BIGBADJOHN (IRE) 9 br.g. Vinnie Roe (IRE) – Celtic Serenade (IRE) (Yashgan) c139
[2017/18 c143, h–: c23.6dᵘʳ c24.1s c26g c23.8d c24s* c21.1sᵘʳ c28.8dᵖᵘ Apr 28] tall h–
gelding: winning chaser: useful handicap chaser: won at Kempton in February: left
Rebecca Curtis after fourth start: should stay extreme distances: acts on soft going: often
races towards rear. *Nigel Twiston-Davies*

BIG BANG DE LOIRE (FR) 7 b.g. Califet (FR) – Grischa (FR) (Septieme Ciel (USA)) c91
[2017/18 c19.7s⁴ c20.3s⁵ Dec 17] third foal: half-brother to winning French chasers Vertige h–
de Loire (17f winner, by Trempolino) and All In de Loire (19f winner, by Loup Solitaire):
dam French 11f-12.5f winner: off mark in points at third attempt: lightly-raced hurdler:
maiden chaser, fair form in 2014/15 when trained in France by G. Cherel: stays 2¼m: acts
on heavy going: has worn headgear. *Giles Smyly*

BIG BROTHER GEORGE (IRE) 6 b.g. Milan – Jade River (FR) (Indian River (FR)) c–
[2017/18 h108, b85: c24dᵖᵘ May 6] maiden hurdler: pulled up in novice handicap on h–
chasing debut: runner-up in points in 2018: in blinkers last 2 starts: in tongue tie last 3:
races prominently. *Oliver Greenall*

BIG CASINO 12 b.g. Court Cave (IRE) – Migsy Malone (Afzal) [2017/18 c123§, h–: c– §
c29.1mᵖᵘ c27.5g⁶ Jun 10] tall gelding: winning hurdler: fairly useful chaser at best, below h–
form in early-2017/18: in frame both starts in points later in season: stays 29f: acts on
heavy going: usually wears headgear: unreliable. *Nigel Twiston-Davies*

BIG

BIGCHEXTOCASH (IRE) 6 b.g. Stowaway – Monakeeba (IRE) (Snurge) [2017/18 b16d b16.8s^{pu} Feb 23] maiden Irish pointer: no form in bumpers. *Samuel Drinkwater*   b–

BIG CHUNKY (IRE) 5 b.g. Kalanisi (IRE) – Mystic Vic (IRE) (Old Vic) [2017/18 b16.2s Apr 27] tailed off in bumper. *Julia Brooke*   b–

BIGDEAL (FR) 5 gr.g. Montmartre (FR) – Rauxa (Singspiel (IRE)) [2017/18 b16.3d b17.7d h16.3s^{ur} h20.5v Jan 7] strong gelding: no form in bumpers/over hurdles: has joined Zoe Davison. *Gary Moore*   h– b–

BIG DIFFERENCE (IRE) 5 b.g. Presenting – Roque de Cyborg (IRE) (High Chaparral (IRE)) [2017/18 h21.2d^5 h15.3d Apr 22] €52,000 3-y-o: first foal: dam unraced half-sister to useful hurdler/high-class chaser (2½m-25f winner) Quito de La Roque and high-class hurdler (2½m-3m winner) Kazal: placed in Irish points: fair form over hurdles: better effort when fifth in novice at Ludlow in April: bred to stay 3m. *Ben Pauling*   h105

BIG EASY (GER) 11 b.g. Ransom O'War (USA) – Basilea Gold (GER) (Monsun (GER)) [2017/18 h–: h22.8m^3 h25g* h23g^6 h24.7s Nov 11] good-topped gelding: fairly useful handicap hurdler: won at Warwick in May: left Philip Hobbs after third start: stays 25f: acts on good to firm and heavy going: wears cheekpieces: often let down by jumping. *Ian Williams*   h129 x

BIG FELLA THANKS 16 b.g. Primitive Rising (USA) – Nunsdream (Derrylin) [2017/18 c128, h–: c20.8d^{pu} May 5] workmanlike gelding: winning hurdler: very smart chaser at best: stayed 3m: acted on good to firm and heavy going: tried in headgear: wore tongue tie: dead. *Tom George*   c– h–

BIG FRED (IRE) 7 gr.g. Tikkanen (USA) – Whadouno (IRE) (Abednego) [2017/18 b16v^5 h15.3v h16v^5 h15.8v^3 h19.5v h21.9v^2 Apr 1] sixth foal: half-brother to fairly useful hurdler/useful chaser Howwoulduno (2m winner, by Desert King), stays 2½m: dam winning pointer: fifth in bumper at Chepstow: fair form over hurdles: stays 2¾m: raced only on heavy going: usually races towards rear. *Bernard Llewellyn*   h100 b78

BIGIRONONHISHIP (IRE) 7 b.g. Beneficial – Portobello Lady (IRE) (Broken Hearted) [2017/18 c127, h–: c20.1s* c26.2v^5 Oct 26] tall gelding: winning hurdler: fairly useful chaser: won novice handicap at Hexham in October: likely to prove best up to 3m: raced only on soft/heavy going: often in tongue tie. *Rose Dobbin*   c125 h–

BIG JIM 9 b.g. Revoque (IRE) – Chilly Squaw (IRE) (Commanche Run) [2017/18 c104, h–: c16d^5 c16.2s* c15.5s^6 c15.5s^2 c16.4s^{pu} Mar 24] good-topped gelding: maiden hurdler: fairly useful handicap chaser: won at Warwick in January: stays 21f, as effective over shorter: acts on heavy going: front runner/races prominently. *Alex Hales*   c124 h–

BIGMARTRE (FR) 7 b.g. Montmartre (FR) – Oh La Miss (FR) (Le Balafre (FR)) [2017/18 c–, h130: c16m* c16.4g* c16.4s^2 c19.9s c20.5g* Apr 21] lengthy gelding: useful hurdler: smart chaser: won novice handicaps at Ludlow in October and Newbury (by 4½ lengths from Cyrname) in December, and Future Champions Novices' Chase at Ayr (by 1¾ lengths from Cobra de Mai) in April: second in handicap at Doncaster (short head behind Duke of Navan) in January: stays 2½m: acts on good to firm and heavy going: front runner/races prominently. *Harry Whittington*   c149 h–

BIG MEADOW (IRE) 7 b.g. Marienbard (IRE) – Lakyle Lady (IRE) (Bob Back (USA)) [2017/18 h118: h23.3d^4 h23.6v^6 c24.2s^2 c28.5v c24v* c23.8v^{pu} c24v^3 c24v^4 c23.6v^4 Apr 14] well-made gelding: maiden hurdler: fairly useful handicap chaser: won novice event at Uttoxeter in January: stays 3m: best form on soft/heavy going: has worn cheekpieces: front runner/races prominently. *Neil King*   c120 h98

BIG PENNY (IRE) 6 b.m. Oscar (IRE) – Lady Marnay (IRE) (Darnay) [2017/18 h97p: h20m^2 h19.6d* h20g^6 h24.4d^2 h24.4s Jan 26] off mark in Irish points at second attempt: fairly useful hurdler: won mares novice at Bangor in October: second in 2 handicaps (mares event second occasion) at Doncaster in December: stays 3m: acts on good to firm and good to soft going: tried in cheekpieces: in tongue tie last 3 starts. *Jonjo O'Neill*   h115

BIG PICTURE 6 b.g. Recharge (IRE) – Just Jenny (IRE) (King's Ride) [2017/18 h20.7m h20g h16.4d h15.8v^6 h17.7v h19.5v Apr 14] maiden pointer: poor maiden hurdler: left J. F. O'Shea after third start: stays 21f: tried in cheekpieces: often races in rear. *Johnny Farrelly*   h78

BIGPIPENOTOBACEE (IRE) 7 b.g. King's Theatre (IRE) – Another Dollar (IRE) (Supreme Leader) [2017/18 c–p, h109p: c19.9s^{pu} c19.2s* c20.9v Mar 10] fair form over hurdles: similar form over fences: won novice handicap at Market Rasen in February: stayed 19f: acted on soft going: often raced towards rear: dead. *Tom George*   c112 h–

BIG RIVER (IRE) 8 b.g. Milan – Call Kate (IRE) (Lord Americo) [2017/18 h136: c23.4g* c21.6v^{pu} c24s^3 c23.4v* c24v^2 Mar 17] workmanlike gelding: useful hurdler: similar form over fences: won novice at Kelso in October and minor event there (by 4½ lengths from Shantou Flyer) in February: stays 3¼m: acts on heavy going: wears tongue tie: often races towards rear. *Lucinda Russell* — c144 h–

BIG ROBIN (IRE) 6 b.m. Robin des Champs (FR) – Melodique (Kahyasi) [2017/18 h–, b–: h19s* h21.7v^3 h20.5g^4 Apr 21] has had breathing operation: off mark in Irish points at second attempt: fair form over hurdles: won mares novice at Taunton in February. *Nicky Henderson* — h113

BIG THUNDER 8 gr.g. Dalakhani (IRE) – Charlotte O Fraise (IRE) (Beat Hollow) [2017/18 h108: h15.7d^R h19.3s^3 ab16.3g^2 Mar 3] maiden hurdler, fair form at best: stays 2½m: acts on soft going: tried in cheekpieces. *Micky Hammond* — h84

BIG TIME DANCER (IRE) 5 b.g. Zoffany (IRE) – Final Opinion (IRE) (King's Theatre (IRE)) [2017/18 h16s^3 h16.8s^4 Nov 28] fair on Flat, stays 1¼m: fair form over hurdles: better effort when third in novice at Wetherby in November: will stay further than 2m: has joined Jennie Candlish. *Brian Ellison* — h109

BIG TIME FRANK (IRE) 7 b.g. Bienamado (USA) – Pure Spirit (IRE) (Hubbly Bubbly (USA)) [2017/18 h16v^{pu} h16.5g h20.5^{pu} h21.4v^3 c25.2s^{pu} c24.5v^3 c24.5s^3 c25.1v^4 Mar 8] poor form over hurdles/fences. *Polly Gundry* — c82 h82

BIG WATER (IRE) 10 ch.g. Saffron Walden (FR) – Magic Feeling (IRE) (Magical Wonder (USA)) [2017/18 c–, h113: c20.9v^{pu} Feb 18] tall gelding: winning hurdler: useful chaser at best: failed to complete in 2017/18, including in points: stays 3m: acts on heavy going. *G. M. Davies* — c– h–

BILL AND BARN (IRE) 7 br.g. Presenting – Forgotten Star (IRE) (Don't Forget Me) [2017/18 h83: h26d^6 h20.5d^5 h23.6v* c20.2v^2 h23.6v^4 Feb 2] sturdy gelding: won both starts in points: fair form over hurdles: won conditionals novice at Chepstow (dead-heated with Rhaegar) in December: 9/4, second in novice handicap at Wincanton (10 lengths behind Le Boizelo) on chasing debut: stays 3m: best form on heavy going: open to improvement over fences. *Paul Nicholls* — c121 p h111

BILLBUSHAY (IRE) 9 b.g. Westerner – Oscareen (IRE) (Oscar (IRE)) [2017/18 h121: h17.7d^{pu} Nov 19] fairly useful hurdler, pulled up sole start in 2017/18: stayed 2¼m: acted on good to firm and good to soft going: tried in cheekpieces/tongue tie: usually raced close up: dead. *Dr Richard Newland* — h–

BILL D'ARON (FR) 7 ch.g. Dom Alco (FR) – Nobless d'Aron (FR) (Ragmar (FR)) [2017/18 h94: h16.4v h17d c20.9s^{pu} Apr 8] no form over hurdles: pulled up in novice handicap on chasing debut: usually in headgear. *James Ewart* — c– h–

BILLING (IRE) 10 b.g. Milan – Melodic Tune (IRE) (Roselier (FR)) [2017/18 c24g^{ur} Jun 26] sturdy gelding: multiple point winner: maiden hurdler: no show on chasing debut: should be suited by further than 2½m: tried in blinkers: temperament under suspicion. *Jacqueline Coward* — c– h–

BILLINGSLEY (IRE) 6 b.g. Millenary – Retain That Magic (IRE) (Presenting) [2017/18 b88: h21.2v h16v* h16v* Apr 14] fair form over hurdles: won novices at Chepstow in February and April: front runner/races prominently: remains with potential. *Alastair Ralph* — h113 p

BILLY BRONCO 7 ch.g. Central Park (IRE) – Nan (Buckley) [2017/18 h118: c23.8v^3 c23.6v^4 c30s^2 c34v Mar 17] fairly useful hurdler: similar form over fences: placed in novice at Ffos Las in November and handicap at Catterick in January: stays 3¾m: raced only on soft/heavy going: still unexposed as a chaser. *Evan Williams* — c116 p h–

BILLY CONGO (IRE) 11 b.g. Zagreb (USA) – Delicate Child (IRE) (Son of Sharp Shot (IRE)) [2017/18 h–: h19.2v Feb 1] fair hurdler at best, very lightly raced and no form since 2015/16: wears tongue tie. *Richard Hawker* — h–

BILLY DUTTON 12 ch.g. Sir Harry Lewis (USA) – Tinoforty (FR) (Saint Estephe (FR)) [2017/18 h23.6s^4 h21.6v^4 h22.8v h23.9v^4 h23.1s^5 Feb 23] strong gelding: fairly useful handicap hurdler: fourth at Exeter in December: maiden chaser: stays 3m: acts on heavy going: tried in cheekpieces. *Chris Down* — c– h115

BILLY ELLIOTT 6 gr.g. Schiaparelli (GER) – Ladylliat (FR) (Simon du Desert (FR)) [2017/18 b–: h15.7m^F h20s^5 h16g^4 h16g h21.6d^{pu} h25g^{pu} Nov 5] modest form over hurdles: best effort at 2½m: tried in cheekpieces. *Kim Bailey* — h85

BIL

BILLY FLIGHT (FR) 6 b.g. Walk In The Park (IRE) – Moon Flight (FR) (Saint Preuil (FR)) [2017/18 h20.7m h24g h25m* h24.6g c23.5g^6 c25.1g c25.5d c25d^{pu} h19.7s^{pu} c25.2s^F h19.9v^{pu} Mar 13] €60,000 3-y-o: fourth foal: half-brother to fairly useful French chaser Speedy Flight (2¼m-2½m winner) and French 17f hurdle winner Soon Flight (both by Califet): dam, French 17f-2½m hurdle/chase winner, half-sister to smart hurdler/very smart French chaser (stayed 27f) Sunny Flight: fair handicap hurdler: won at Ballinrobe in May: modest form over fences: left Noel Meade after eighth start: stays 25f: acts on good to firm going: has worn blinkers: often races towards rear: temperamental. *Noel Wilson* — **c95 §** / **h101 §**

BILLYGWYN TOO 5 b.g. Dr Massini (IRE) – Lady Prunella (IRE) (Supreme Leader) [2017/18 b16.8d* Apr 24] £4,000 4-y-o: half-brother to several winners, including fair chaser Bollitree Bob (2m-2¼m winner, by Bob's Return) and fair/ungenuine hurdler/chaser Marsh Court (19f/2½m winner, by Overbury): dam (h73), second in 21f hurdle on only start, half-sister to useful staying chaser Latent Talent: off mark in points at second attempt: 9/1, won maiden bumper at Exeter (by ¾ length from Kootenay River) in April: will stay at least 2½m. *J. W. Tudor* — **b100**

BILLY HICKS 7 b.g. Kayf Tara – Michelle's Ella (IRE) (Ela-Mana-Mou) [2017/18 h110: h18.5v^2 h19.5v^6 h15.7v^4 h19.9v^5 Apr 7] runner-up in point on debut: fair handicap hurdler: stays 19f: raced only on soft/heavy going: often in hood. *Samuel Drinkwater* — **h107**

BILLY MERRIOTT (IRE) 12 b.g. Dr Massini (IRE) – Hurricane Bella (IRE) (Taipan (IRE)) [2017/18 c23.4s^2 c22.6d^2 Apr 22] sturdy gelding: easy winner on point debut: winning hurdler: fairly useful maiden chaser nowadays: second in hunter at Newbury in March: stays 21f: acts on soft going: has worn tongue tie. *Mrs C. Fry* — **c119** / **h–**

BILLY MY BOY 9 b.g. Volochine (IRE) – Key West (FR) (Highest Honor (FR)) [2017/18 h108: h16m^3 h15.8g^5 h16.8g^2 h16g h16.8d c16.3g^{pu} c16.5g Oct 25] fair handicap hurdler: no form over fences: stays 19f: acts on good to firm going: wears headgear: tried in tongue tie: usually races close up. *Chris Down* — **c–** / **h104**

BILLY TEAL 13 ch.g. Keen – Morcat (Morston (FR)) [2017/18 h16.7d^{pu} Nov 23] no form over hurdles/fences: tried in cheekpieces. *Lee James* — **c–** / **h–**

BILLY TWO TONGUES 10 b.g. Heron Island (IRE) – Ranahinch (IRE) (Persian Mews) [2017/18 c119, h–: c23m^4 c24s^3 c24g h23.1s^6 c25.5d^5 Nov 10] modest handicap hurdler: fairly useful handicap chaser: fourth at Worcester in July: stays 25f: acts on good to firm and heavy going: tried in tongue tie: has joined Johnny Farrelly. *Jeremy Scott* — **c116** / **h79**

BINDON MILL 9 b.g. Tamure (IRE) – Singing Cottage (Greensmith) [2017/18 c120, h106: c24.2s^4 c26.2d c30.7v^F c28.5v^{pu} Jan 7] maiden hurdler: fair handicap chaser: should stay long distances: best form on soft/heavy going. *Victor Dartnall* — **c114** / **h–**

BINGE DRINKER (IRE) 9 b.g. Spadoun (FR) – Our Honey (IRE) (Old Vic) [2017/18 c140p, h–: c23.6v Dec 9] winning hurdler: twice-raced over fences, useful form when winning novice in 2016/17 for Rebecca Curtis: well held next time: stays 3m: acts on heavy going. *Paul Nicholls* — **c–** / **h–**

BINGO D'OLIVATE (FR) 7 b.g. Laverock (IRE) – Ombrelle de L'Orme (FR) (Marchand de Sable (USA)) [2017/18 c–, h117: c16.2g^6 c20.5g^6 h16.2g^6 h16.7g^{pu} h17s h16.2s^3 h20.1v^3 h15.7v h16.4v^6 h16v^F c20.1v^F c15.6d^6 Apr 23] angular gelding: modest handicap hurdler: similar form over fences: left Noel Williams after second start: stays 2½m: acts on heavy going: wears headgear: often races in rear. *Gemma Anderson* — **c85** / **h90**

BIRCH BANK 5 b.g. Multiplex – Dolly Duff (Alflora (IRE)) [2017/18 b–: b16d h15.8v^6 h19.7v^6 h19.3v^3 h27v^5 Apr 13] no form in bumpers: poor form over hurdles: left William Kinsey after first start: bred to be suited by further than 2½m: tried in tongue tie. *Donald McCain* — **h80** / **b–**

BIRCH HILL (IRE) 8 b.g. Kalanisi (IRE) – Miss Compliance (IRE) (Broken Hearted) [2017/18 h122: h16.8v^{pu} h15.8s* h15.8d^6 h15.6s Apr 14] well-made gelding: won completed start in Irish points: fairly useful handicap hurdler: won at Huntingdon in February: stays 21f: acts on soft going: tried in cheekpieces: wears tongue tie: often races in rear. *Sophie Leech* — **h118**

BIRCH VALE (IRE) 6 br.m. Presenting – Oscar Rebel (IRE) (Oscar (IRE)) [2017/18 b76: b16s^2 b16.8s^2 h20.6v^4 h16.8v* h16.2s^2 Apr 27] fair form in bumpers: similar form over hurdles: won mares novice at Sedgefield in March: should be suited by 2½m: front runner/races prominently. *Donald McCain* — **h108** / **b88**

BISCUIT 7 ch.m. Black Sam Bellamy (IRE) – Falcon's Gunner (Gunner B) [2017/18 b86: h18.5s^{pu} h15.7g^6 h19.7s h20.3g^{pu} Apr 20] poor form over hurdles: should be suited by further than 2m: in tongue tie last 3 starts. *Kim Bailey* — **h71**

BIT

- **BISE D'ESTRUVAL (FR)** 7 b.m. Kingsalsa (USA) – Option d'Estruval (FR) (Epervier Bleu) [2017/18 c–, h–: h16g⁵ h15.7g² h16g⁵ Sep 12] modest maiden hurdler: little show over fences: stayed 2¼m: acted on good to soft going: often in tongue tie: often travelled strongly, found little: dead. *Dan Skelton*
  c–
  h87 §

- **BISHOP OF BLING (IRE)** 5 b.g. Big Bad Bob (IRE) – Convent Girl (IRE) (Bishop of Cashel) [2017/18 h96: h21.2d Apr 24] fair maiden on Flat, stays 1½m: modest form over hurdles for Dr Richard Newland, well held sole start in 2017/18: tried in cheekpieces. *Alastair Ralph*
  h–

- **BISHOPS COURT** 8 b.g. Helissio (FR) – Island of Memories (IRE) (Beneficial) [2017/18 c132, h103: c20.2s c20.5d³ c15.7v* c20.5dᵖᵘ c16vᵖᵘ c21.6g² Apr 20] tall gelding: maiden chaser: useful handicap hurdler: won at Wincanton (by 8 lengths from Coeur Tantre) in December: stays 2½m: acts on heavy going: wears headgear/tongue tie. *Neil Mulholland*
  c133
  h–

- **BISHOPS ROAD (IRE)** 10 b.g. Heron Island (IRE) – Nice Resemblance (IRE) (Shernazar) [2017/18 c146, h–: c23.4v² c29.5vᵖᵘ c24.2s c20s Feb 23] compact gelding: winning hurdler: useful handicap chaser: second in Rehearsal Chase at Newcastle (2¼ lengths behind Beware The Bear) in December: stays 3½m: acts on heavy going: has worn headgear, including final start. *Kerry Lee*
  c144
  h–

- **BISOUBISOU** 6 b.m. Champs Elysees – Marathea (FR) (Marathon (USA)) [2017/18 h–, b–: h16.3g h16s h15.7d⁶ h20.6s⁴ h20v* h23.9s h15.8s⁶ Mar 14] angular mare: poor handicap hurdler: won at Fakenham (conditional) in January: stays 21f: best form on soft/ heavy going: often wears headgear/tongue tie: often races towards rear. *Olly Murphy*
  h82

- **BISTOURI D'HONORE (FR)** 6 b.g. Ballingarry (IRE) – Elivette (FR) (Arvico (FR)) [2017/18 h109, b85: h16.8g* h18.5d³ Jul 23] well-made gelding: multiple point winner: fair handicap hurdler: won lady amateur event at Newton Abbot in June: stays 2¾m, effective at shorter: acts on good to firm going: in headgear last 2 starts. *Paul Nicholls*
  h112

- **BITE MY TONGUE (IRE)** 5 b.g. Vale of York (IRE) – Near Relation (Distant Relative) [2017/18 h15.7sᵖᵘ h15.8s h15.7vᵖᵘ h15.7vᵖᵘ Feb 25] no form on Flat/over hurdles: in cheekpieces last 2 starts. *John O'Neill*
  h–

- **BITE THE BISCUIT (IRE)** 6 b.g. Getaway (GER) – Kiltoome Scot (IRE) (Oscar (IRE)) [2017/18 h85, b82: h23mᵖᵘ May 11] placed in points: modest form over hurdles, pulled up sole start in 2017/18: tried in cheekpieces. *Philip Hobbs*
  h–

- **BIT OF A CHARLIE** 9 b.g. Emperor Fountain – Win A Hand (Nearly A Hand) [2017/18 h19s h19.5s Apr 27] lengthy, angular gelding: poor form over hurdles: tried in tongue tie. *Robert Walford*
  h62

- **BIT OF A GEORDIE** 5 br.m. Geordieland (FR) – Gaelic Gold (IRE) (Good Thyne (USA)) [2017/18 b16.8g b16.8v⁴ Mar 13] half-sister to 3 winners, including smart hurdler/ useful chaser Bitofapuzzle (19f-3m winner, by Tamure) and bumper winner/fairly useful hurdler Golden Gael (2m-2½m winner, by Generous): dam unraced: no form in bumpers. *Tom Gretton*
  b–

- **BIT OF A QUIRKE** 5 ch.g. Monsieur Bond (IRE) – Silk (IRE) (Machiavellian (USA)) [2017/18 h15.7d h20.1v³ h16.7g² h15.8d⁵ Nov 3] fair on Flat, stays 1¼m: modest form over hurdles. *Mark Walford*
  h96

- **BIT SPICY (IRE)** 7 gr.m. Tikkanen (USA) – Like A Bolt (IRE) (Lahib (USA)) [2017/18 h–, b62: h15.9g⁶ h19.2gᵖᵘ h15.9dʳʳ Oct 23] no form over hurdles, refused to race final start. *Rebecca Woodman*
  h–

- **BITTER VIRTUE** 7 b.m. Lucarno (USA) – Avoine (IRE) (Saddlers' Hall (IRE)) [2017/18 h94: h18.7g* h16d h20.3d⁴ h20m⁶ h20g⁵ h19g⁵ h20g Oct 17] rather leggy mare: fair handicap hurdler: won mares event at Stratford in May: stays 2½m: acts on good to firm going: tried in cheekpieces: wears tongue tie. *David Dennis*
  h100

- **BITUMEN BELLE** 6 b.m. Oscar (IRE) – Midnight Pond (IRE) (Long Pond) [2017/18 b–: b16.7v ab16.3g ab16.3g⁵ h22.8s³ Mar 21] poor form in bumpers: 33/1, third in mares novice at Haydock (16¾ lengths behind Skewiff) on hurdling debut: may prove best at shorter than 23f. *Philip Kirby*
  h89
  b71

- **BITVIEW COLIN (IRE)** 7 ch.g. Whitmore's Conn (USA) – Madame Stella (FR) (Snurge) [2017/18 h24g c19.9d⁴ c20m³ c16.8s³ c16g h19.5s h20.1s* c24.2sᶠ c20.5vᵖᵘ c20.4v³ Dec 17] compact gelding: fair handicap hurdler: won at Hexham in October: fair maiden chaser: stays 2½m: acts on good to firm and heavy going: wears blinkers/tongue tie: front runner/races prominently. *John Patrick Ryan, Ireland*
  c106
  h111

BIV

BIVOUAC (FR) 7 b.g. Califet (FR) – Pazadena (FR) (Ragmar (FR)) [2017/18 c127, h–: c24s^{pu} Jan 25] lengthy, good sort: placed in points: winning hurdler: fairly useful chaser at best, pulled up sole start under Rules in 2017/18: stayed 2½m: acted on heavy going: tried in cheekpieces: dead. *J. P. Owen*   c– h–

BIZET (IRE) 4 b.g. Helmet (AUS) – Morinda (Selkirk (USA)) [2017/18 h15.8g h16g^6 Oct 22] compact gelding: modest maiden on Flat, stays 1½m: no form over hurdles: in blinkers second start. *John Ryan*   h–

BLACKADDER 6 b.g. Myboycharlie (IRE) – Famcred (Inchinor) [2017/18 h76x: h16.5v Apr 12] poor maiden hurdles: will prove best at sharp 2m: acts on good to firm going: usually wears hood: often let down by jumping. *Mark Gillard*   h– x

BLACK ANTHEM (IRE) 6 b.g. Royal Anthem (USA) – Rockababy (IRE) (King's Ride) [2017/18 h105, b–: h16.8g h20g^2 h23g^3 h21.6d^2 h19.3d h19.5s h21.4v^{pu} h19.5v^{pu} h15.3v^6 Mar 28] in frame twice in Irish maiden points: modest maiden hurdler: stays 2¾m: acts on soft going: usually races close up. *Brian Barr*   h95

BLACK ART 6 ch.g. Black Sam Bellamy (IRE) – Art Series (Kalanisi (IRE)) [2017/18 b85: h16.2s^2 h19.3d^4 h16.8s^2 h16.8s* h16.8v* h19.9v^5 Mar 23] workmanlike gelding: fair form over hurdles: won handicaps at Sedgefield (twice) in January: may prove best at 2m: acts on heavy going: often races prominently. *Sue Smith*   h114

BLACK BANJO (IRE) 9 br.g. Hawkeye (IRE) – Corkscrew Hill (IRE) (Golan (IRE)) [2017/18 h20g h19.6g h20g h23.3d c15.7g^5 Apr 20] point winner: little form over hurdles: 66/1, fifth in novice at Southwell (24¾ lengths behind Peter The Mayo Man) on chasing debut, probably flattered: left Matt Sheppard after first start: has worn headgear: wears tongue tie. *Claire Dyson*   c93 ? h–

BLACKBIRD 5 b.m. Black Sam Bellamy (IRE) – Daurica (Dolpour) [2017/18 b15.8s ab16d Mar 5] second foal: dam (h117) 2½m/21f hurdle winner: no form in bumpers. *Stuart Edmunds*   b–

BLACKBOW (IRE) 5 b.g. Stowaway – Rinnce Moll (IRE) (Accordion) [2017/18 b16d* b16s* b16.4s^5 b16.3s^2 Apr 25] €32,000 3-y-o, £150,000 4-y-o: good-topped gelding: first foal: dam unraced: winning pointer: smart form in bumpers: won maiden at Leopardstown in December and Grade 2 there (by 1½ lengths from Rhinestone) in February: second in Champion INH Flat Race at Punchestown (1¼ lengths behind Tornado Flyer) in April. *W. P. Mullins, Ireland*   b123

BLACK BUBLE (FR) 5 b.g. Valanour (IRE) – Miss Bubble Rose (FR) (Sevres Rose (IRE)) [2017/18 h94: h16g^{ur} h16d^{pu} h16s^3 h19.6d* Apr 21] fair handicap hurdler: won at Bangor in April: stays 2½m: acts on good to soft going. *Tony Carroll*   h108

BLACK CORTON (FR) 7 br.g. Laverock (IRE) – Pour Le Meilleur (FR) (Video Rock (FR)) [2017/18 c–p, h135: c17.4d* c20g^2 c23g* c21.6m* c21g* c24.4g* c24.4s* c23.4g^2 c24d* c23.8s* c24.4s^5 c25s^4 Apr 13]   c151 h–

Pitchcroft, the small piece of arable land which acts as one of Worcester's main flood plains, has a long history with the horse. It is rumoured that horse racing has been staged on Pitchcroft since as early as 1700, though archive copies of long-standing local newspaper *Berrow's Worcester Journal* (which itself began life in 1690) reveal that the earliest recorded evidence of a race meeting held there came on June 27th 1718. To commemorate the 300th anniversary of this date, racing historian Chris Pitt has produced a book, published in conjunction with Worcester racecourse, detailing the significant moments during those three centuries of action at one of Britain's oldest National Hunt tracks. Among the high points, the Worcester Grand Annual Handicap was one of the most prestigious steeplechases in the country during the mid-1800s, whilst, at the other end of the scale, a flirtation with Flat racing came to an end in August 1966 because of its unpopularity with the local public—Flat fixtures repeatedly made a loss, whereas jumping was profitable because it was far more popular with racegoers. Worcester's chase course, in particular, proved a popular hunting ground for top stables during the 'seventies and 'eighties, when it was often used as an ideal testing ground for horses needing experience early in their chasing career. Dual Champion Hurdle winner Comedy of Errors (aged ten) had his only chase start at Worcester, finishing runner-up, and other legendary performers including Tingle Creek, Night Nurse, Silver Buck and Wayward Lad raced over fences (all with success) at Worcester during this era. There is a picture on page 814 of *Chasers & Hurdlers 1982/83* of Wayward Lad beating Night Nurse in the

Worcester racecourse—a common theme during Worcester's 300-year history has been the adjoining River Severn bursting its banks (top), which prompted the decision to switch to summer racing instead (bottom)

Worcester Evening News Chase. Record-breaking champion jockey John Francome was certainly an advocate of Worcester, having ridden the first and thousandth winner of his decorated career there—'two long straights, decent fences and nearly always good ground' is Francome's glowing verdict on the track.

In truth, however, arguably the most famous fact about Worcester racecourse is that it is close to the River Severn and has endured regular floods down the years. The course's susceptibility to waterlogging, combined with the unpredictable timing of the floods, prompted a radical rethink in the mid-'nineties, when the course's then-manager Jack Bennett approached fellow racecourses (plus then-governing body the BHB) about introducing a new summer jumping programme as part of the calendar. As a result, from 1995 Worcester scrapped all its winter fixtures in favour of summer ones, a situation which remains until today. Alas, the restructuring didn't mean the end of costly abandonments. Unprecedented rainfall in June 2007 resulted in most parts of the United Kingdom falling victim to serious flooding and, true to form, Worcester was one of the worst-hit areas. Further heavy rain the following month resulted in even more extensive flooding in the area and wiped out all of the track's remaining fixtures until late-April 2008, with the lost income (plus extensive repair work needed) even prompting rumours that the course might never stage racing again. The rumours proved to be wide of the mark, though things haven't always been plain sailing at Worcester since the resumption, with a meeting on July 1st 2009 having to be abandoned on horse welfare grounds due, ironically, to an insufficient supply of water at the course during sweltering temperatures (though the course has always disputed that headline-grabbing version of events). In addition, plenty of modern-day racing professionals would probably take issue with Francome's aforementioned testimonial, particularly as Worcester uses portable fences and fixed-brush hurdles nowadays, both of which are sometimes unpopular with trainers and jockeys. As for the 'nearly always good ground' bit, the course fell some way short of meeting that requirement for its October 12th fixture during the latest season, when a spate of going-related non-runners resulted in Worcester being

32Red Kauto Star Novices' Chase, Kempton—
Black Corton reverses Newbury placings with Elegant Escape

branded 'a joke' by racegoers and trainers alike. The official going description was changed from 'good' to 'good to firm' after the opening race, but trainers clearly felt conditions were even firmer than that—Timeform called the ground 'firm' throughout—and withdrew thirty-two horses from the final six races on the card, reducing two of those contests to a match. 'It's very disappointing,' remarked Alan King, one of the trainers in question, 'although that's not the biggest problem I have with Worcester. The facilities for owners and trainers are just awful, the worst of any course I go to. In this day and age, it's not acceptable and something needs to be done.' Similar complaints were made after a weekend meeting in June 2018, when owners and trainers were queuing up to brand the course's facilities as 'horrendous', with several vowing to boycott the course in future. Arena Racing Company, which now runs the course under lease from Worcester City Council, vowed to investigate the complaints.

Despite all of this, Worcester still has a habit of attracting above-average performers early in their chasing career. Paul Nicholls is clearly still an advocate and sent San Benedeto to contest a two and a half mile novice chase there in late-June 2016, after he had opened his account over fences several weeks earlier. A strong late rally by San Benedeto saw him claim a last-gasp win at Worcester that day, a feat he repeated when landing the Grade 1 Maghull Novices' Chase by a head at Aintree some nine and a half months later (with three further wins in between). The Nicholls-trained Black Corton contested the same Worcester novice chase in the latest season and was sent off at odds-on, having also recently opened his account over fences (at Fontwell earlier in June). Although he failed to emulate San Benedeto on the day, having to settle for a close second behind Forever Field after conceding first run to that rival in a muddling race, Black Corton went on to surpass his stable-companion's 2016/17 achievements. He won seven of his ten subsequent starts, notably the Grade 1 Kauto Star Novices' Chase (his penultimate win) at Kempton in December, and his total haul of eight successes gave him more wins than any other horse on British and Irish soil during 2017/18. A big feature of that winning spree was Black Corton's association with Bryony Frost, who rode him for those final ten starts, taking over from then-stable jockey Sam Twiston-Davies, who had ridden him on the two outings in June. Frost's first ride on Black Corton came back at Worcester in July, where a more forcing ride saw the sure-footed Black Corton make all to beat odds-on Knight of Noir by thirteen lengths. Another wide-margin win in a small field for another novice followed at Fontwell the following month, when Black Corton comprehensively reversed those Worcester placings with Forever Field (beating him by fourteen lengths on terms 1 lb worse), before he then lowered the colours of more experienced rivals (which included stable-companion Frodon back in a race-rusty third) in a quite valuable intermediate chase at Newton Abbot in October. Plans to put Black Corton away in order to freshen him up for another summer campaign were shelved after further wins in novice chases at Cheltenham in late-October (when Newton Abbot runner-up Sizing Tennessee might have won had he not fallen two out) and November, his four-length defeat of Ballyoptic in the latter a clear illustration of the improvement made in the course of this five-timer—Ballyoptic was rated 19 lb higher than Black Corton over hurdles by Timeform. Black Corton's next start came in the Grade 2 John Francome Novices' Chase at Newbury in December—ironically, a contest known as the Worcester Novices' Chase until the latest season (it was also staged at Worcester until 2000)—and his three quarters of a length defeat by Elegant Escape (who received 3 lb) was used as evidence by many that Black Corton had finally had his limitations exposed, particularly as the short-priced favourite Fountains Windfall would have gone close but for falling three out. Such thinking was soon shown to be hasty, however, as

Sodexo Reynoldstown Novices' Chase, Ascot—a canny front-running ride by Bryony Frost aboard Black Corton which brings him an eighth win of the season, more than any other horse, this one over Ms Parfois (white face) and Mount Mews (noseband)

The Brooks, Stewart Families & J. Kyle's "Black Corton"

Black Corton proved better than ever when picking up the winning thread on his next two starts. If anything, Fountains Windfall looked an even bigger danger than at Newbury when falling four out in the Kauto Star at Kempton on Boxing Day, though the fact that Black Corton (who was left in front after that incident) convincingly reversed Newbury form with eventual runner-up Elegant Escape suggests it would have been a closely-run thing either way. There were no such imponderables in the Sodexo Reynoldstown Novices' Chase at Ascot in February when Black Corton dictated matters under a canny ride before running out a comprehensive eight-length winner from Ms Parfois, a stable-companion of the ill-fated Fountains Windfall (who died in a schooling accident at home earlier in February).

Black Corton had undoubtedly been underestimated by punters and pundits alike for much of the winter—Ascot was the first time in five starts that he had been sent off favourite, which is a telling statistic given he'd been raced primarily in small fields. Of Black Corton's eight wins in 2017/18, three came in three-runner events, two apiece in four-runner (including the Reynoldstown) and five-runner ones, whilst his Kauto Star win came at the expense of just six rivals. The paucity of runners has been a recurring theme in leading novice chases on British soil in recent years, whilst the fact that Black Corton met just three runners from the powerhouse stable of British champion trainer Nicky Henderson during the whole of his twelve-race campaign is arguably a further illustration that there is something wrong with the novice chasing programme. By contrast, the Grade 1 Flogas Novices' Chase at Leopardstown, an equivalent RSA Chase trial to the Reynoldstown staged earlier in February, attracted an ultra-competitive field of eleven, which included five runners from record-breaking Irish champion trainer Willie Mullins and a further four from his great rival Gordon Elliott, though victory went to the Henry de Bromhead-trained Monalee in a tight finish. This greater strength in depth among the Irish novices showed itself at the following month's Cheltenham Festival, with Irish yards winning all four of the meeting's graded novice chases (they completed the same whitewash in 2015) thanks to Footpad in the Arkle, Rathvinden (who had unseated in the Flogas) in the National Hunt Chase, Presenting Percy in the RSA and Shattered Love in the Golden Miller (Flogas seventh The Storyteller also won one of the handicaps, the Plate). Monalee chased home Presenting Percy (albeit seven lengths adrift) to ensure an Irish one, two in the RSA, whilst the Flogas runner-up Al Boum Photo would also have been placed but for falling two out. As for the 5/1-shot Black Corton (shortest priced of the home-trained challengers), he was harried by Monalee from an early stage and didn't jump so well as usual, eventually fading to be last of five finishers (beaten a total of seventeen and a quarter lengths), just behind old rivals Elegant Escape and Ballyoptic. At first glance, Black Corton's remote fourth to the Henderson-trained Terrefort in the Mildmay Novices' Chase at Aintree on his final outing was even more disappointing, particularly as Ms Parfois and Elegant Escape filled the places, though Black Corton had been on the go for over twelve months by this stage and it might simply have been one race too many at the end of a busy campaign.

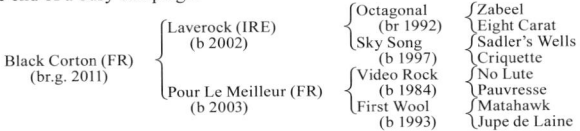

Black Corton (FR) (br.g. 2011)
- Laverock (IRE) (b 2002)
  - Octagonal (br 1992)
    - Zabeel
    - Eight Carat
  - Sky Song (b 1997)
    - Sadler's Wells
    - Criquette
- Pour Le Meilleur (FR) (b 2003)
  - Video Rock (b 1984)
    - No Lute
    - Pauvresse
  - First Wool (b 1993)
    - Matahawk
    - Jupe de Laine

The lengthy Black Corton is the second foal out of twice-raced maiden Pour Le Meilleur and her only winner to date, though his two-years-older half-sister Victoire de Corton (by Robin des Champs) was placed twice over two and a quarter miles on both starts over hurdles. Pour Le Meilleur has produced four foals (all as yet unraced) since Black Corton, namely the 2012 filly Comete de Corton (by Network) and 2013 gelding Diego de Corton (by Alberto Giacometti), plus two further half-brothers in Gala de Corton (by Secret Singer) and Hermes de Corton (by Coastal Path) in 2016 and 2017 respectively. Black Corton is undoubtedly the star name in this family, though several above-average performers can be found further back, including the useful hurdler Unika La Reconce (a half-sister to Pour Le Meilleur) and useful staying chaser Ciel de Brion (a half-sister to Black Corton's grandam First Wool). The Francois Doumen-trained Ciel de Brion contested several valuable handicap chases on British soil in the late-'nineties, including finishing fourth to Suny Bay in the 1997 Hennessy Cognac Gold Cup. That Newbury showpiece (now known as the Ladbrokes Trophy) could well be an autumn target for Black Corton too, though the chances are that he will start 2018/19 no better than averagely-handicapped and a campaign geared around a tilt at the Grand National (Ciel de Brion fell five out in the 1998 renewal when still in contention) may turn out to be a longer-term plan. Black Corton's prominent style of racing and sound jumping should stand him in good stead around Aintree, whilst Bryony Frost—who unfortunately faces time on the sidelines after a bad fall at Newton Abbot at the start of the 2018/19 season—got her eye in over the fences when finishing fifth on Milansbar on her National debut in April.

Stamina is still an unknown quantity so far as the Grand National is concerned for Black Corton who remains unproven beyond three miles. His reserves seemed to be stretched by rain-softened conditions in the Mildmay, though, as was stated earlier, there must be a chance he was over the top by then and he is certainly worth a try over longer distances. Black Corton is versatile with regards to underfoot conditions, having shown his form on going ranging from good to firm to soft. He has been tongue tied since his second start on British soil and was also fitted with a hood prior to teaming up with Frost. However, he has proved a model of consistency for most of this period and—even though wins are likely to be harder to come by from now on—he is a great credit to his connections. *Paul Nicholls*

BLA

BLACKDOWN HILLS 8 b.m. Presenting – Lady Prunella (IRE) (Supreme Leader) [2017/18 h57: h15.3v⁴ h16.5m² Apr 25] bumper winner: fair form over hurdles: should stay at least 2½m. *Seamus Mullins*   **h107**

BLACKFIRE (FR) 6 br.g. Kingsalsa (USA) – Sister Celestine (Bishop of Cashel) [2017/18 h94: h19d h16g⁵ h23g⁶ c20g c19.4g⁴ c16.5g⁴ Aug 1] rather leggy gelding: poor maiden hurdler: similar form over fences: unproven beyond 17f: acts on soft going: wears headgear: in tongue tie last 2 starts: often races towards rear. *Tom Symonds*   **c71** **h69**

BLACK FRANKS ANGEL 8 b.m. Black Sam Bellamy (IRE) – City of Angels (Woodman (USA)) [2017/18 h22s^pu c19.7s³ c25.7v^pu Mar 12] half-sister to numerous winners, including useful hurdler/smart chaser I'm So Lucky (2m-2½m winner, by Zilzal) and useful hurdler Dream Esteem (2m winner, by Mark of Esteem): won point on debut: modest form over hurdles: poor form over fences: left Henry de Bromhead after first start: stays 23f: acts on good to soft going: sometimes in cheekpieces. *Johnny Farrelly*   **c67** **h–**

BLACK IVORY 6 b.g. Revoque (IRE) – Annie's Gift (IRE) (Presenting) [2017/18 h113, b95: h24.7d² h20v⁴ h25s* h22.8v^bd Feb 17] fairly useful handicap hurdler: won at Aintree in December and Warwick (by 1¼ lengths from Sykes) in January: fatally injured when brought down fifth in race won by Tommy Rapper at Haydock: stayed 25f: acted on heavy going: often raced prominently, usually travelled strongly. *Ruth Jefferson*   **h125**

BLACK JACK JAXON 6 gr.g. Fair Mix (IRE) – No Virtue (Defacto (USA)) [2017/18 b–: b16f⁶ h20g^pu h19.7s^pu h23.8s^pu Feb 21] runner-up both starts in points: no form in bumpers/over hurdles: tried in cheekpieces: in tongue tie last 2 starts. *Steve Flook*   **h–** **b–**

BLACK JACK ROVER (IRE) 9 b.g. Vinnie Roe (IRE) – Kilgefin Tina (IRE) (City Honours (USA)) [2017/18 c21.2s c21.2d² Aug 26] won Irish maiden point on debut: winning hurdler: fair form over fences: better effort when second in novice at Cartmel in August: stays 25f: acts on good to firm going. *Donald McCain*   **c109** **h–**

BLACKJACKTENNESSEE 4 b.g. Fair Mix (IRE) – No Virtue (Defacto (USA)) [2017/18 b15.7g³ b13.7g h15.8v^ro h15.8s h16.2s h15.8d⁵ Apr 24] leggy gelding: poor form in bumpers: no form over hurdles: tried in hood. *Steve Flook*   **h–** **b72**

BLACK JEWEL (IRE) 8 br.g. Scorpion (IRE) – Sapphire Eile (Mujtahid (USA)) [2017/18 c25.2g⁵ c21d c23.5d c24d h19.6d^pu Apr 21] modest maiden hurdler/chaser: stays 25f: acts on good to soft going: often wears headgear: has worn tongue tie. *Paul W. Flynn, Ireland*   **c86** **h–**

BLACK KALANISI (IRE) 5 b.g. Kalanisi (IRE) – Blackthorne Winter (IRE) (Old Vic) [2017/18 b15.8g⁴ ab16g Feb 19] second foal: dam, runner-up sole start in point, half-sister to useful hurdler (2m-2½m winner) Amstecos: fair form in bumpers: better effort when fourth at Ludlow in November. *Ben Pauling*   **b90**

BLACK KETTLE (IRE) 8 b.g. Robin des Pres (FR) – Whistful Suzie (IRE) (Eurobus) [2017/18 h16m h20g c16.4g² c16d⁴ c15.7d⁴ c16.4v³ c16.3v* Apr 14] has had breathing operation: modest maiden hurdler: similar form over fences: won handicap at Newcastle in April: left Christian Delcros after second start: stays 19f: acts on heavy going: often wears cheekpieces: usually wears tongue tie: usually races close up. *Rebecca Menzies*   **c95** **h–**

BLACK LIGHTNING (IRE) 5 br.g. Whitmore's Conn (USA) – Annie May (IRE) (Anshan) [2017/18 b17.7s² b16.3s b17.7s³ Apr 15] £12,000 3-y-o: first foal: dam (c110/h104), 2m-2½m hurdle/chase winner (stayed 25f), half-sister to useful hurdler/chaser (stays 3m) Fagan and useful chaser (stays 25f) Creevytenant: fair form in bumpers: best effort when second at Plumpton on debut. *Nick Gifford*   **b94**

BLACKMILL (IRE) 7 b.g. Kalanisi (IRE) – Lady of The Mill (IRE) (Woods of Windsor (USA)) [2017/18 h23.1v⁵ h23.9s⁶ h23.8s⁵ c20.9v⁴ c25.1v^pu c24.2d⁵ Apr 24] €28,000 3-y-o, £25,000 4-y-o: third foal: brother to fair hurdler Mr Steadfast (17f winner), stayed 2½m: dam unraced half-sister to useful hurdler/smart chaser (stayed 3½m) Strath Royal and to dam of Irish Grand National winner Niche Market: multiple point winner: modest form over hurdles: fair form over fences: best effort when fourth in novice handicap at Hereford in March: stays 3m: best form on soft/heavy going: tried in cheekpieces: in tongue tie last 4 starts. *David Dennis*   **c103** **h98**

BLACK MISCHIEF 6 b.g. Black Sam Bellamy (IRE) – Miss Mitch (IRE) (King's Theatre (IRE)) [2017/18 h12¹p, b93: h16g⁴ h19.5d⁵ h21d⁵ h19.6s³ h16.5s³ h21m* Apr 26] fairly useful hurdler: won maiden at Warwick in May and handicap at Kempton in April: stays 21f: acts on good to firm going: often wears cheekpieces: in tongue tie last 2 starts. *Harry Fry*   **h128**

BLA

BLACK NARCISSUS (IRE) 9 b.m. Westerner – Arcanum (IRE) (Presenting) [2017/18 c105, h102: c23.6s^{pu} c23.8v^3 c25.2s^{pu} c24v^{pu} c24.5v^5 h23.9s c23.5v^2 c26.3v* c26.7v^{pu} Apr 9] has had breathing operation: fair hurdler at best: modest handicap chaser: won at Sedgefield in March: stays 3¼m: acts on heavy going: usually wears headgear: wears tongue tie: often races towards rear: untrustworthy. *Alexandra Dunn*   **c97 §** **h– §**

BLACK N BLUE 6 ch.g. Galileo (IRE) – Coyote (Indian Ridge) [2017/18 b16.2s Apr 27] tailed off in bumper. *R. Mike Smith*   **b–**

BLACK OP (IRE) 7 br.g. Sandmason – Afar Story (IRE) (Desert Story (IRE)) [2017/18 b111: h16.3d^4 h20.8s* h20.3v^2 h21.1s^2 h20s* Apr 14]   **h152**

In an era when some National Hunt stallions cover books of upwards of three hundred mares—the busiest sire in the British Isles in 2017 was Soldier of Fortune who had a book of 352— it's only to be expected that such well patronised sires will have more than one good horse in a given crop or season. On the other hand, the odds appear stacked against a stallion like Sandmason, who apparently covered a single mare in 2017—which was one more than the year before. The twenty-one-year-old Sandmason, who stands for just €1,000 at Lacken Stud in County Wexford, has had better patronage in the past (and will be even more popular now), but a grand total of twenty-four horses sired by him listed on Timeform's base attests to the lack of opportunities he has been given. Only five of his offspring have won any sort of race under Rules—two have won a maiden hurdle, and another an Irish bumper—but against all the odds the two others developed into a couple of the best British-trained novice hurdlers of the latest season, each winning a Grade 1 prize at one of the major spring festivals.

Black Op and the year-younger Summerville Boy were both bred by Lacken Stud's owner Paul Rothwell before initially going their separate ways, though not the least remarkable aspect of the pair's success is that they have ended up racing for the same trainer and owner, namely Tom George and Roger Brookhouse. Black Op failed to find a buyer when first put through the ring in Ireland as a three-year-old, but a twenty-five-length win on his only start in Irish points two years later made him a much more attractive proposition when he was offered again, shortly after that success, at the inaugural Aintree Sales held at the 2016 Grand National meeting. Purchased for £210,000 by Brookhouse, who has invested heavily in pointers over the years, Black Op was one of half a dozen six-figure lots at the sale, along with Samcro whom Black Op was to run into at Cheltenham in the latest season. Black

Betway Mersey Novices' Hurdle, Aintree—
Black Op overcomes a mistake at the last to edge out Lostintranslation (right) in a grandstand finish

Mr R. S. Brookhouse's "Black Op"

Op looked a good prospect for his new connections straight away when beating Claimantakinforgan in a bumper at Doncaster on his debut the following February, so impressive that he started favourite for the Grade 2 bumper at Aintree that spring, though managing only ninth in a modestly-run race that turned into too much of a test of speed for him. Black Op fared much better at the latest Grand National meeting, ending his first season over hurdles with victory in the Betway Mersey Novices' Hurdle a day after the winner of that bumper the year before, Lalor, had won the Grade 1 Top Novices' Hurdle over two miles.

Second favourite Black Op was a game half-length winner of the Mersey from Lostintranslation who had finished seventh to Summerville Boy in the Supreme Novices' at Cheltenham. Black Op would doubtless not have had to work quite so hard for his success had he jumped better in the closing stages. After travelling strongly through the race in a handy position, he went on turning into the home straight. But there were still plenty in touch, notably unbeaten favourite On The Blind Side, when Black Op put in a sloppy jump three out, though a worse mistake by the favourite at the next ended his chance. Black Op still had Lostintranslation and the mare Momella upsides him at the final flight which Black Op also hit, losing momentum and handing the lead to Lostintranslation on his inner. To his credit Black Op rallied, and with the leading pair neck and neck, Black Op proved just the stronger in the final fifty yards. Momella was beaten another three lengths into third, though the presence in fourth of the maiden Aye Aye Charlie, who had finished a lot further behind Black Op in two previous meetings at Cheltenham, holds down the level of the form. On The Blind Side was only sixth of the nine finishers.

Black Op certainly wasn't winning a good race out of turn. He had finished fourth behind Lostintranslation on his hurdling debut in a maiden at Newbury in December before easily landing the odds in a similar event at Doncaster the following month when stepping up to two and a half miles. At Doncaster too, his jumping left something to be desired, while a last-flight error proved costly when he took on Santini in the Classic Novices' Hurdle at Cheltenham later the same month, the pair finishing a long way clear of Aye Aye Charlie in third, with Santini eventually getting the better of the argument by three quarters of a length despite Black Op keeping on well. Back at Cheltenham for the Baring Bingham, Black Op was the leading British hope against the much-vaunted Samcro and ran his best race to date to be beaten two and three quarter lengths. That was the closest any of his opponents came to beating Samcro all season, though Black Op was really no match for the impressive winner, although he again stuck to his task after a mistake at the last. Black Op finished five lengths clear of the third Next Destination who was another to frank the form when he won at the Punchestown Festival.

```
                    ┌ Sandmason      ┌ Grand Lodge    ┌ Chief's Crown
                    │   (ch 1997)    │   (ch 1991)    │ La Papagena
                    │                │ Sandy Island   │ Mill Reef
Black Op (IRE)      ┤                │   (ch 1981)    │ Sayonara
   (br.g. 2011)     │                ┤                ┤
                    │                │ Desert Story   │ Green Desert
                    │                │   (b 1994)     │ Aliysa
                    └ Afar Story (IRE)│                │
                        (b 2001)     │ Afarka         │ Kahyasi
                                     │   (b 1993)     │ Afasara
```

Black Op's sire Sandmason was an entirely home-grown product of Lord Howard de Walden's Plantation Stud, by the Dewhurst winner Grand Lodge out of Lancashire Oaks winner Sandy Island, herself a close relative of Derby winner Slip Anchor. Injury at three put paid to any Derby hopes for Sandmason, but he won the following season's Hardwicke Stakes at Royal Ascot before leaving Henry Cecil to race in Australia where he failed to make much impact, his performances including finishing last of all in Media Puzzle's Melbourne Cup. Sandmason began his stud career with one season in New Zealand before being returned to Europe and settling in Ireland. The sales catalogue refers to Black Op's dam Afar Story as having 'run a few times in point-to-points' though the stark truth was that she was pulled up on all four of her starts in Ireland. Whilst lacking ability herself, Afar Story came from a good family. Her dam Afarka was fairly useful in Ireland, both on the Flat, successful at a mile and a half, and over hurdles, winning at up to three miles. Afarka bred three winners, the best of them being Younevercall who was useful at up to three miles over hurdles. Afarka was a half-sister to the useful hurdler Afarad, who was placed in the three big juvenile hurdles at Cheltenham, Aintree and Punchestown, and, incidentally, was by Sandmason's relative Slip Anchor. Afarka's half-sisters, meanwhile, produced the half-brothers Afsoun, third in a Champion Hurdle, and the latest season's Cleeve Hurdle winner Agrapart, as well as the popular cross-country chaser and Grand National runner-up Balthazar King. Black Op is a tall, good-topped gelding, every inch a chaser on looks and a really exciting prospect for novice events over two and a half miles or more, though he won't be able to treat the larger obstacles with quite so much disregard as he did his hurdles. He usually travels strongly, acts on heavy ground and was tongue tied for his last three starts. *Tom George*

BLACK PIRATE 6 b.g. Black Sam Bellamy (IRE) – Proper Posh (Rakaposhi King) **b107**
[2017/18 b16v* b16v* b16g² Apr 21] £12,000 3-y-o, £75,000 5-y-o: seventh foal: dam, little sign of ability, half-sister to useful hurdler/smart chaser (stayed 3m) Hobbs Hill: won point on debut: useful form in bumpers: won at Wetherby (by 8 lengths from Court Master) and Ayr (conditionals/amateur event, by 4 lengths from Big Bad Dream) in February: will be suited by 2½m+. *James Ewart*

BLACK PRINCE (FR) 4 b.g. Falco (USA) – Thamara (USA) (Street Cry (IRE)) **h104**
[2017/18 h15.3g² Oct 29] fair on Flat, stays 2m: in tongue tie, 5/1, second in juvenile at Wincanton (5 lengths behind Thounder) on hurdling debut. *Anthony Honeyball*

BLACK SAM BELLA 6 b.m. Black Sam Bellamy (IRE) – Newton Mo (Homo Sapien) **h107**
[2017/18 b98: h19.6d² h21.2g³ h18.6d² Dec 7] won point on debut: fair form over hurdles: best effort when second in mares novice at Bangor in October: will prove suited by 2½m+. *Dan Skelton*

Randox Health Becher Handicap Chase, Aintree—
an impressive win for the previous season's Grand National fourth Blaklion and Gavin Sheehan
ahead of Aintree regular The Last Samuri (noseband), who finishes one place closer than in 2016

BLACK TULIP 6 ch.m. Black Sam Bellamy (IRE) – Combe Florey (Alflora (IRE)) [2017/18 h88, b–: h22g* h20g² h19.9g⁶ h20s⁴ h21v* h19.4s h20.5s h24.3g³ Apr 20] compact mare: fairly useful hurdler: won handicap at Stratford in May and mares novice at Warwick in December: stays 3m: acts on heavy going. *Henry Daly*   **h117**

BLACKWELL SYNERGY (FR) 12 b.g. Antarctique (IRE) – Pyu (GER) (Surumu (GER)) [2017/18 c–x, h95: h23.3d⁶ h23.1g⁵ h23.3d h23.6s^pu h23.4s⁴ h23.4s h24.4s⁶ h25s^pu h21v⁵ Apr 27] angular gelding: poor handicap hurdler: winning chaser (sketchy jumper): stays 3m: acts on soft going: has worn headgear: usually races close up: often races lazily. *Tracey Leeson*   **c– x** **h67 §**

BLAIRS COVE 6 b.g. Presenting – Raitera (FR) (Astarabad (USA)) [2017/18 h129p, b93: h19g* h19g² h16g* h21.1g⁵ h19.3d³ h24.4d³ h19s⁶ h19.9v h16.5v⁴ Feb 4] well-made gelding: fairly useful hurdler: won novices at Warwick in May and September: stays 3m: acts on good to soft going: wears tongue tie. *Dan Skelton*   **h120**

BLAKE DEAN 10 b.g. Halling (USA) – Antediluvian (Air Express (IRE)) [2017/18 c91, h95: h21.6g h21.6d^pu h21.6m h23m^F Jul 5] rather sparely-made gelding: modest chaser: well below form in 2017/18: maiden chaser: usually wears headgear/tongue tie. *Chris Gordon*   **c–** **h–**

BLAKEMOUNT (IRE) 10 br.g. Presenting – Smashing Leader (IRE) (Supreme Leader) [2017/18 c133, h–: c24.2d⁶ c26.2v⁴ Apr 7] compact gelding: winning hurdler: useful handicap chaser, below best in 2017/18 after long absence: stays 33f: acts on heavy going: front runner/races prominently. *Sue Smith*   **c116** **h–**

BLAKERIGG (IRE) 7 b.g. Presenting – Azalea (IRE) (Marju (IRE)) [2017/18 h–: h20.9g c17.1g⁵ c19.1s² c24.5d^pu Mar 25] well-made gelding: little form over hurdles: modest form over fences: best effort when second in novice handicap at Doncaster in January: should stay 2½m+: acts on soft going. *Nicky Richards*   **c96** **h–**

BLAKLION 9 b.g. Kayf Tara – Franciscaine (FR) (Legend of France (USA)) [2017/18 c158, h–: c24.2s² c25.9v* c28.4v² c34.3s^bd c28.8d^pu Apr 28] angular gelding: winning hurdler: high-class handicap chaser: won Becher Chase at Aintree (by 9 lengths from The Last Samuri) in December: second in Charlie Hall Chase at Wetherby (½ length behind Bristol de Mai) in November: brought down first in Grand National at Aintree in April: stays 29f: acts on heavy going: tried in hood. *Nigel Twiston-Davies*   **c160** **h–**

BLE

BLAMEITALONMYROOTS (IRE) 8 b.m. Turtle Island (IRE) – Makingyourmindup (IRE) (Good Thyne (USA)) [2017/18 c123, h–: c26.2d⁶ c23.6v c26.7v² c24s⁵ c28.4vᵖᵘ Mar 31] angular mare: winning hurdler: fairly useful handicap chaser: second at Wincanton in January: stays 27f: acts on heavy going: tried in cheekpieces. *Oliver Sherwood*   **c119**   **h–**

BLANDFORDS GUNNER 9 b.g. Needle Gun (IRE) – Miss Millbrook (Meadowbrook) [2017/18 c117, h–: c16.4d² c18.2s³ Dec 14] rangy gelding: maiden hurdler: fairly useful handicap chaser: second at Doncaster in December: stays 19f: acts on soft and good to firm going: in cheekpieces last 2 starts. *Richard Price*   **c115**   **h–**

BLAST OF KOEMAN (IRE) 7 ch.g. Shantou (USA) – Erintante (IRE) (Denel (FR)) [2017/18 h122, b107: h20.5d⁵ c20d⁴ c16s* c17d³ c17s⁴ c21.3s² c20s² Apr 25] fairly useful hurdler: useful form over fences: won novice at Fairyhouse in November: second in Guinness Handicap Chase at Punchestown (neck behind Patricks Park) in April: stays 21f: acts on soft going: tried in cheekpieces: wears tongue tie. *Robert Tyner, Ireland*   **c136**   **h–**

BLAYDON (IRE) 5 b.g. Milan – Pretty Impressive (IRE) (Presenting) [2017/18 b16.2v³ b16.2d Apr 23] little form in bumpers. *Lucinda Russell*   **b71**

BLAZER (FR) 7 ch.g. Network (GER) – Juppelongue (FR) (Trebrook (FR)) [2017/18 c136p, h–: c16g* c16.7v⁴ Apr 1] sturdy gelding: winning hurdler: useful form over fences: won maiden at Punchestown in May: fourth in novice handicap at Fairyhouse (4¼ lengths behind Bel Ami de Sivola) in April: stays 3m: acts on heavy going: remains with potential as a chaser. *W. P. Mullins, Ireland*   **c137 p**   **h–**

BLAZING GLEN (IRE) 10 ch.g. Beneficial – Kofiyah's Rose (IRE) (Roselier (FR)) [2017/18 c–, h–: h19d⁶ c23d² c23.9gᴿ c20gᵖᵘ h20.7sᵖᵘ h15.8g Apr 24] maiden hurdler/chaser, little form in 2017/18: stays 23f: acts on soft going: temperamental. *Alan Jessop*   **c80 §**   **h–**

BLAZING GOLD 5 b.m. Fair Mix (IRE) – Playing With Fire (IRE) (Witness Box (USA)) [2017/18 b13.7d⁵ b16d Apr 26] unfurnished mare: first foal: dam (c108/h105), 2m/17f hurdle/chase winner, half-sister to fair hurdler/fairly useful chaser (stayed 3¼m) Merry Path: little impact in bumpers. *Robin Dickin*   **b58**

BLAZON 5 b.g. Dansili – Zante (Zafonic (USA)) [2017/18 b101: h16g⁵ h15.8s h16.3g² h20s⁴ h15.8d⁴ Mar 26] bumper winner: fair form over hurdles: stays 2½m: acts on soft going: tried in cheekpieces: front runner/races prominently. *Kim Bailey*   **h106**

BLENHEIM WARRIOR 6 gr.g. Galileo (IRE) – Crystal Swan (IRE) (Dalakhani (IRE)) [2017/18 h15.8s Mar 14] fair on Flat, stays 1¾m: well held in maiden on hurdling debut. *Paul Webber*   **h–**

BLESS THE WINGS (IRE) 13 b.g. Winged Love (IRE) – Silva Venture (IRE) (Mandalus) [2017/18 c145, h115+: c28sᵖᵘ c29sᵖᵘ c30.2d* c30.2sᶠ c29vᵖᵘ c34.3s³ c33.5d⁴ Apr 26] sturdy gelding: fairly useful hurdler: smart handicap chaser: won cross-country event at Cheltenham (by 2½ lengths from Cantlow) in December: stays 4¼m: acts on good to firm and heavy going: wears headgear: has worn tongue tie. *Gordon Elliott, Ireland*   **c145**   **h–**

BLETCHLEY CASTLE (IRE) 9 b.g. Dylan Thomas (IRE) – Zaafran (Singspiel (IRE)) [2017/18 h109: h21mᵖᵘ h15.8g c21m² Jul 7] point winner: fair hurdler: 10/1, second in novice handicap at Newton Abbot (6 lengths behind Braqueur d'Or) on chasing debut: stays 19f: acts on soft and good to firm going: wears tongue tie: front runner/often races freely. *Seamus Durack*   **c109**   **h–**

BLEU BERRY (FR) 7 b.g. Special Kaldoun (IRE) – Somosierra (FR) (Blushing Flame (USA)) [2017/18 h143: h16s h21.1s* h20v⁴ h16s³ Apr 27] smart hurdler: won Coral Cup   **h147**

Coral Cup Handicap Hurdle, Cheltenham—an eleventh hour spare ride for Mark Walsh provides him with a first Cheltenham Festival winner, as Bleu Berry (second right) pounces late to defeat Topofthegame (third right) and Barra (star on chest)

Luke McMahon's "Bleu Berry"

at Cheltenham (by neck from Topofthegame) in March: third in Punchestown Champion Hurdle (22¼ lengths behind Supasundae) in April: stays 21f: acts on heavy going: tried in cheekpieces: often races in rear. *W. P. Mullins, Ireland*

BLEU ET NOIR 7 b.g. Enrique – Gastina (FR) (Pistolet Bleu (IRE)) [2017/18 h125: h16.5g Jun 16] fairly useful hurdler, well held sole start in 2017/18: stays 19f: acts on heavy going: wears hood: front runner/races freely: fair on Flat, won maiden in 2017. *Tim Vaughan*   h–

BLEU ET ROUGE (FR) 7 gr.g. Charming Groom (FR) – Lady du Renom (FR) (Art Francais (USA)) [2017/18 c142, h–: h16s h15.7d⁴ h16.3v² h16.8v h16v⁴ h24d Apr 26] lengthy gelding: smart handicap hurdler: second in Betfair Hurdle at Newbury (4½ lengths behind Kalashnikov) in February: fourth in Racing Welfare Handicap Hurdle at Ascot in December: useful form over fences: stays 19f: acts on heavy going: often wears tongue tie: usually races towards rear. *W. P. Mullins, Ireland*   c–
h151

BLINDING LIGHTS (IRE) 13 b.g. Snurge – Tender Return (IRE) (Strong Gale) [2017/18 c98: c25.5g⁵ May 5] multiple point winner: modest chaser, well held sole start in 2017/18: stays 25f: acts on firm going: usually wears cheekpieces: wears tongue tie. *Mary Sanderson*   c–

BLOODY NOSE (IRE) 6 b.g. Kalanisi (IRE) – Renvyle Society (IRE) (Moscow Society (USA)) [2017/18 b–: h20g h21.2gᵖᵘ h23.6v⁶ h19.9vᵖᵘ Feb 10] little show over hurdles: tried in hood. *Mark Bradstock*   h62

BLOTTOS (IRE) 6 b.g. Westerner – Autumn Beauty (IRE) (Darnay) [2017/18 b84: h20dᶠ h16.8s* h19.3s² h19.9v* h19.3v* h20.5vᵖᵘ h19.9vᵖᵘ Mar 23] fairly useful hurdler: won maiden in December and novice in January both at Sedgefield, and handicap at Carlisle in February: will be suited by further than 2½m: acts on heavy going: usually races close up. *Sue Smith*   h123

Martin Pipe Conditional Jockeys' Handicap Hurdle, Cheltenham—
Blow By Blow ensures Gordon Elliott is top trainer at the Festival thanks to an excellent front-running ride from Donagh Meyler; he is also a record-breaking seventh winner at the meeting for owners Gigginstown House Stud

BLOW BY BLOW (IRE) 7 ch.g. Robin des Champs (FR) – Shean Rose (IRE) (Roselier (FR)) [2017/18 h16s³ h18s² h23v* h20v⁶ h20s* h20.3v* h20v⁴ h24s Apr 25] smart bumper winner: smart hurdler: won maiden at Navan (by 1½ lengths from As You Were) in December, Michael Purcell Memorial Novices' Hurdle at Thurles (by 14 lengths from Gun Digger) in February and Martin Pipe Conditional Jockeys' Handicap Hurdle at Cheltenham (by 5 lengths from Discorama) in March: should stay at least 3m: acts on heavy going: usually wears blinkers: wears tongue tie: usually races close up. *Gordon Elliott, Ireland* **h149**

BLU CAVALIER 8 b.g. Kayf Tara – Blue Ride (IRE) – (King's Ride) [2017/18 h18.5d² h18.5v⁴ h19.5s⁴ h15.3v* h19v* h19.8d* Apr 22] fairly useful form over hurdles: completed hat-trick in maiden at Wincanton in March, and novices at Taunton and Wincanton in April: stays 2½m: acts on heavy going: front runner/races prominently, usually travels strongly. *Paul Nicholls* **h129**

BLUE APRIL (FR) 7 b.g. Blue Bresil (FR) – Royale Little (FR) (Garde Royale) [2017/18 h84§: h19.6s⁶ h15.9s⁴ h17.7v* h15.9v h16v² h16s⁶ Mar 22] compact gelding: poor handicap hurdler: won at Fontwell in January: stays 2¼m: acts on heavy going: wears headgear: one to treat with caution (has refused to race). *Jeremy Scott* **h83 §**

BLUE BALLERINA (IRE) 4 bl.f. Fame And Glory – Peinture Rose (IRE) (Marathon (USA)) [2017/18 b15.v⁵ Apr 7] €20,000 3-y-o: third foal: closely related to fair hurdler All Is Good (2m winner, by Scorpion): dam unraced: well beaten in mares bumper. *Oliver Greenall* **b–**

BLUE BATON (IRE) 5 b.m. Presenting – Blu Louisiana (IRE) (Milan) [2017/18 b15.6s³ b15.6d⁵ b17d⁴ h16.2s Apr 27] third foal: sister to bumper winner Peculiar Places: dam once-raced half-sister to very smart hurdler (stayed 21f) Dunguib (by Presenting): modest form in bumpers: well held in mares novice on hurdling debut. *Lucinda Russell* **h– b77**

BLUE BULLET (FR) 7 b.g. Le Fou (IRE) – Jiletta (FR) (Passing Sale (FR)) [2017/18 h–, b89: h15.8d h16d⁶ h16d⁶ h15.3v² Dec 26] fair form over hurdles: will be suited by 2½m: acts on heavy going: tried in cheekpieces: often in tongue tie. *Jamie Snowden* **h103**

BLUE CANNON (IRE) 10 b.g. High Chaparral (IRE) – Blushing Barada (USA) (Blushing Groom (FR)) [2017/18 c–, h–§: c20.1g⁶ c24.2g Jun 25] winning hurdler: fairly useful chaser at best, retains little ability: stays 2½m: acts on soft and good to firm going: has worn headgear: temperamental. *Valerie Jackson* **c66 § h– §**

BLUE COMET 7 br.g. Blueprint (IRE) – Be My Valentine (IRE) (Be My Native (USA)) [2017/18 h106, b71: h20.6g³ h20.2g³ h20.6g* h23.1g* h23.1g* Oct 21] fairly useful hurdler: completed hat-trick at Market Rasen in novice in July, and handicaps in August and October: stays 23f: best form on good going: usually wears tongue tie: front runner/races prominently. *Fergal O'Brien* **h125**

BLU

BLUE COVE 13 ch.g. Karinga Bay – Meadow Blue (Northern State (USA)) [2017/18 h65: c24.2g^{pu} h25.3s^3 h27v^6 Mar 23] workmanlike gelding: maiden hurdler: pulled up in novice handicap on chasing debut: tried in cheekpieces: has worn tongue tie: often races towards rear. *Lynn Siddall* — c– h–

BLUE EMPYREAN (IRE) 8 b.g. Generous (IRE) – Maldagora (IRE) (Luso) [2017/18 h21.3g^4 h21.8g^6 h21.8g^3 h22s c16.2v^3 c16v^2 c16v* c20v* c24.1v^3 h24v^{pu} Apr 12] bumper winner: fair maiden hurdler: fairly useful form over fences: won handicaps at Naas and Down Royal in January: left Gordon Elliott after fourth start: stays 2¾m: acts on heavy going: wears cheekpieces. *R. K. Watson, Ireland* — c118 h104

BLUE FLIGHT (FR) 5 b.g. Blue Bresil (FR) – Lover Flight (FR) (Saint Cyrien (FR)) [2017/18 b16v^2 b16.2s^3 h23.8s^4 h21v^3 h20.2s* Apr 25] fourth foal: half-brother to fairly useful hurdlers Love Flight (French 15f winner, by Irish Wells) and Holly Flight (19f winner, by Walk In The Park): dam French 17f hurdle winner: off mark in Irish points at third attempt: fairly useful form in bumpers: better effort when second at Chepstow in December: fair form over hurdles: won maiden at Perth in April. *Nigel Twiston-Davies* — h113 b97

BLUEFORTYTWO 5 gr.g. Overbury (IRE) – Celine Message (Silver Patriarch (IRE)) [2017/18 b16v^2 b16.2s^4 Apr 27] £6,500 3-y-o: second foal: dam unraced: fair form in bumpers: better effort when second at Ayr in January for Donald Whillans: will stay further than 2m. *James Ewart* — b92

BLUE HUSSAR (IRE) 7 b.g. Montjeu (IRE) – Metaphor (USA) (Woodman (USA)) [2017/18 h118: h16d^6 h18.9v^4 h16.2s^{pu} Jan 14] fair handicap hurdler: stays 2¼m: acts on soft going: races prominently. *Micky Hammond* — h108

BLUE JACKET (USA) 7 ro.m. Mizzen Mast (USA) – Complex (USA) (Unbridled's Song (USA)) [2017/18 h16.2d^{pu} Oct 8] fair on Flat, stays 7f: no form in 2 starts over hurdles. *Dianne Sayer* — h–

BLUE KANGAROO (FR) 5 b.g. Blue Bresil (FR) – Mascotte du Maine (FR) (Maresca Sorrento (FR)) [2017/18 b–: b16.7d^3 b15.8s Oct 21] sturdy gelding: little impact in bumpers for various trainers: in hood both 2017/18 starts: tried in tongue tie. *Peter Bowen* — b69

BLUE KASCADE (IRE) 11 ch.g. Kaieteur (USA) – Lydia Blue (IRE) (Eve's Error) [2017/18 c116, h–: c26.2g^{pu} c23.8m^4 c24.3v^6 Nov 15] winning hurdler: fairly useful handicap chaser: won at Musselburgh in November: stays 3m: acts on good to firm and heavy going: has worn headgear, including in 2017/18: front runner/races prominently. *Sandy Thomson* — c117 h–

BLUE MERLIN 5 b.g. Fair Mix (IRE) – Mighty Merlin (Royal Applause) [2017/18 b15.7g Oct 26] 9/2, eighth in maiden bumper at Southwell. *Fergal O'Brien* — b–

BLUE MOUNTAIN BOY (IRE) 6 b.g. Blueprint (IRE) – Thegirlfromgalway (IRE) (Royal Dane (IRE)) [2017/18 b18g^8 c24.2d^{pu} Apr 24] multiple point winner: tailed off in maiden bumper: pulled up in novice hunter on chasing debut: left Terence O'Brien after first start. *T. Ellis* — c– b–

BLUE N YELLOW (IRE) 5 b.g. Jeremy (USA) – Bluemamba (USA) (Kingmambo (USA)) [2017/18 b16g* Jul 10] fourth foal: half-brother to 3 winners, including fairly useful hurdler Blue Atlantic (17f winner, by Stormy Atlantic): dam French 1m winner (including Poule d'Essai des Pouliches): 3/1, won bumper at Worcester (by 2¼ lengths from Mythical Prince) on debut. *Johnny Farrelly* — b96

BLUE RHYTHM (IRE) 6 b.g. Milan – Madame Jean (FR) (Cricket Ball (USA)) [2017/18 h63, b–: h23.3d^4 h24g^2 h25.6d^F Jun 6] modest form over hurdles: fell on point debut: stays 3m: acts on good to soft going: in cheekpieces last 3 starts: often races prominently. *Evan Williams* — h91

BLUE SIRE (FR) 7 b.g. Day Flight – Hirlish (FR) (Passing Sale (FR)) [2017/18 h103: h16v^{pu} h16.5s^{pu} Jan 20] compact gelding: maiden hurdler: tried in visor/tongue tie: dead. *Nigel Hawke* — h–

BLUE VALENTINE (FR) 7 b.m. Born King (JPN) – Pompom Girl (FR) (Lost World (IRE)) [2017/18 h19.4d^F h16v^5 Feb 3] has had breathing operation: second foal: dam French 1½m-15f winner: modest form over hurdles. *Harry Whittington* — h89

BLUNDER BUSS (IRE) 5 b.g. Court Cave (IRE) – Shantou Rose (IRE) (Shantou (USA)) [2017/18 b17g h20.4g^6 h21.2g^2 h20s^3 h20.5v^3 h19.4d* Mar 16] first foal: dam lightly-raced half-sister to useful hurdler/smart chaser (stayed 3½m) Cannington Brook: fair form in bumpers: fairly useful form over hurdles: won handicap at Musselburgh in March: left Miss Elizabeth Doyle after third start: likely to stay 3m: acts on soft going: front runner/races prominently. *Chris Grant* — h117 b85

BOB

BLUSHING RED (FR) 4 ch.g. Le Havre (IRE) – Boliche (Key of Luck (USA)) [2017/18 h16.5v h15.3d^6 Apr 22] fairly useful on Flat, stays 12.5f: well held both starts over hurdles. *Emma Lavelle* — **h67**

BOAGRIUS (IRE) 6 ch.g. Beneficial – Greenhall Rambler (IRE) (Anshan) [2017/18 h113, b104: c20.2g^{pu} c17.2s^2 c19.9s^3 Feb 4] point/bumper winner: fair form over hurdles: fairly useful form over fences: best effort when second in handicap at Market Rasen in December: stays 21f: acts on soft going: in tongue tie last 2 starts. *Tom George* — **c117 h–**

BOA ISLAND (IRE) 8 b.g. Trans Island – Eskimo Kiss (Distinctly North (USA)) [2017/18 c126, h106: c23.6d c26.7g c31.8g^{pu} Apr 21] strong gelding: maiden hurdler: fairly useful chaser at best, no form in 2017/18: left Paul Nicholls after second start: sometimes in headgear: usually wears tongue tie. *James Moffatt* — **c– h–**

BOALS CORNER (IRE) 6 b.m. Coroner (IRE) – Briefs Lady (Laveron) [2017/18 h16m h20.2v^{pu} Sep 27] second foal: dam unraced half-sister to fairly useful hurdler (stayed 2½m) Dr Flynn: no form in bumper/over hurdles: in hood last 2 starts. *Stephen Francis Magee, Ireland* — **h–**

BOARD OF TRADE 7 ch.g. Black Sam Bellamy (IRE) – Realms of Gold (USA) (Gulch (USA)) [2017/18 h122: h20.6s^3 h24.3g Apr 20] fairly useful handicap hurdler: third at Market Rasen in February: stays 3m: acts on soft going. *Alan King* — **h117**

BOARDWALK EMPIRE (IRE) 11 b.g. Overbury (IRE) – Mighty Mandy (IRE) (Mandalus) [2017/18 c–, h–: h21.6v^{pu} h21.4s^{pu} h23v^4 h23.6v^6 h25s^5 Apr 15] good-bodied gelding: fairly useful handicap hurdler at best, well below form in 2017/18: maiden chaser: stays 3m: acts on heavy going: has worn headgear/tongue tie: front runner/races prominently. *Kate Buckett* — **c– h73**

BOBBIE'S DIAMOND (IRE) 8 b.g. Vinnie Roe (IRE) – Betty's The Best (IRE) (Oscar (IRE)) [2017/18 c16g^F c19.5s^5 c16.5s c17d^{pu} c21s c16.5v* c20.5v^2 c21.5v^6 c17.1v^{ur} h20.5g Apr 21] winning hurdler: fair chaser: won novice at Ayr in February: left A. J. Martin after fifth start: stays 2½m: acts on heavy going: has worn tongue tie: usually races towards rear. *Andrew Hamilton* — **c113 h–**

BOBBLE BORU (IRE) 10 b.m. Brian Boru – Balreask Lady (IRE) (Shardari) [2017/18 c96x, h103: h16g^2 h15.8d^6 h16g^6 h15.3g^5 Oct 29] angular mare: modest handicap hurdler: winning chaser: stays 2½m: acts on heavy going: has worn headgear: tried in tongue tie: front runner/races prominently: often let down by jumping over fences. *Matt Sheppard* — **c– x h99**

BOBBLE EMERALD (IRE) 10 ch.g. Rudimentary (USA) – Aunt Emeralds (IRE) (Roselier (FR)) [2017/18 c–, h112: h19.2m^3 h16g h20.3d* h16.4g* Oct 27] lengthy gelding: fairly useful handicap hurdler: won at Southwell and Cheltenham (conditional) in October: pulled up only start over fences: has won over 3m, at least as effective at 2m: acts on good to firm and heavy going: wears headgear: has worn tongue tie, including 2017/18: front runner/races prominently. *Martin Keighley* — **c– h119**

BOBBY DOVE 11 b.g. Fraam – Flakey Dove (Oats) [2017/18 h21.6g^{pu} Sep 2] poor maiden handicap hurdler: winning chaser: unproven beyond 17f: acts on soft going: tried in cheekpieces/tongue tie. *Bernard Llewellyn* — **c– h–**

BOBCATBILLY (IRE) 12 b.g. Overbury (IRE) – Cush Jewel (IRE) (Executive Perk) [2017/18 c19.4g^{pu} c20g^3 Jun 25] tall, useful-looking gelding: maiden hurdler: fair handicap chaser nowadays: stays 3m: acts on good to firm and heavy going. *Ian Williams* — **c109 h–**

BOB FORD (IRE) 11 b.g. Vinnie Roe (IRE) – Polar Lamb (IRE) (Brush Aside (USA)) [2017/18 c121§, h124§: c23.6d* c26.1d^5 c23.6v^F c34v^{pu} c27.9v^{pu} Apr 1] tall gelding: winning hurdler: fairly useful handicap chaser: won veterans event at Chepstow in October: left Alastair Ralph after first start: stays 3½m: acts on heavy going: wears headgear: tried in tongue tie: unreliable. *Dr Richard Newland* — **c128 § h– §**

BOB MAHLER (IRE) 6 b.g. Mahler – Cooladurragh (IRE) (Topanoora) [2017/18 h112, b92: h21.6v^5 h21.6d^3 h19.9v^2 h22v^2 h24.1d* h24.3g^2 Apr 20] rangy, useful-looking gelding: useful hurdler: won novice at Wetherby in March: second in handicap at Ayr in April: will probably stay further than 3m: acts on heavy going: in cheekpieces last 2 starts: temperamental. *Warren Greatrex* — **h128 §**

BOBO MAC (IRE) 7 gr.g. Whitmore's Conn (USA) – Blazing Love (IRE) (Fruits of Love (USA)) [2017/18 h123, b94: h20d h19.6s^4 h24d^F c19.9s^5 c24.2s^F c23.4s^4 h25d* Apr 26] sturdy gelding: useful handicap hurdler: won at Warwick (by ¾ length from Frankly Speaking) in April: fairly useful form over fences, has been let down by jumping: stays 25f: acts on heavy going: tried in cheekpieces. *Tom Symonds* — **c122 h130**

145

BOB

BOBONYX 8 b.g. Phoenix Reach (IRE) – Twist The Facts (IRE) (Un Desperado (FR)) [2017/18 c73, h56: c20s⁵ c26v² c25.1v² c24.5v² c24.2v c24.5v³ c26.3v² Apr 13] maiden hurdler: poor maiden chaser: stays 3¼m: acts on heavy going: has worn headgear: tried in tongue tie. *Dai Williams* — **c78 h–**

BOB'S BOY 5 b.g. Showcasing – Tech Zinne (Zinaad) [2017/18 h101: h16m⁴ h16.3m^pu Aug 24] modest form over hurdles, below best both starts in 2017/18: left Warren Greatrex after first start: raced around 2m: acts on soft going: in cheekpieces last 2 starts: tried in tongue tie: usually races prominently. *Oliver Greenall* — **h62**

BOB TUCKER (IRE) 11 b.g. Brian Boru – Acumen (IRE) (Phardante (FR)) [2017/18 c127, h–: c24d⁴ c23.8m c25d² Oct 29] workmanlike gelding: winning hurdler: fairly useful handicap chaser: second in veterans event at Aintree in October: stays 29f: acts on good to firm and heavy going: often wears headgear: tried in tongue tie. *Charlie Longsdon* — **c125 h–**

BOCASIEN DESBOIS (FR) 7 gr.g. Smadoun (FR) – Quocasienne (FR) (Ungaro (GER)) [2017/18 h71: h16.2d h20.9d h24g² h19.3d⁶ c21.4s* Mar 26] modest maiden hurdler: 9/2, won novice handicap at Market Rasen (by 1¾ lengths from Kings Temptation) on chasing debut: stays 3m: acts on soft going. *Martin Todhunter* — **c91 h89**

BODACIOUS NAME (IRE) 4 b.g. Famous Name – Nice Wee Girl (IRE) (Clodovil (IRE)) [2017/18 h16.2v^pu Sep 27] fair on Flat, stays 21.5f: excuses when pulled up in juvenile handicap hurdling debut: sure to do better. *John Quinn* — **h– p**

BOETHIUS 5 b.g. Manduro (GER) – Perfect Note (Shamardal (USA)) [2017/18 h88: h15.9d^pu Oct 23] maiden hurdler, modest form on standout effort: tried in visor. *Tim Vaughan* — **h–**

BOGARDUS (IRE) 7 b.g. Dalakhani (IRE) – Sugar Mint (IRE) (High Chaparral (IRE)) [2017/18 h96: h16s h19.3d⁶ h15.6g Dec 18] fair on Flat, stays 12.5f: modest form on hurdling debut: little impact in 2017/18: has joined Lawrence Mullaney. *Patrick Holmes* — **h–**

BOGOSS DU PERRET (FR) 7 b.g. Malinas (GER) – Lady Paques (FR) (Lights Out (FR)) [2017/18 c–, h81: c21g² c25.8g* c24.2s^pu Nov 15] angular gelding: maiden hurdler: modest form over fences: won novice handicap at Newton Abbot in September: stays 3¼m: best form on good going: tried in blinkers: front runner/races prominently. *Jimmy Frost* — **c93 h–**

BOHEMIAN RHAPSODY (IRE) 9 b.g. Galileo (IRE) – Quiet Mouse (USA) (Quiet American (USA)) [2017/18 h97: h16.7g h18.5d² h20.3d h16.8s⁶ h19m h21.2g⁶ h24s³ h21.6v^ur h19.5v³ h26s c24.2v^pu Apr 17] sturdy gelding: modest handicap hurdler: pulled up in novice hunter on chasing debut: left Brendan Powell after first start, Brian Barr after tenth: stays 3m, effective at much shorter: acts on good to firm and heavy going: usually wears headgear. *Matthew Hampton* — **c– h94**

BOHERBUOY (IRE) 6 b.g. Galileo (IRE) – Potion (Pivotal) [2017/18 h16.4g* h16.5g⁵ h16v³ h16s Feb 3] brother to fair hurdler Mad For Road (17f winner): fairly useful on Flat, stays 1¼m: useful form over hurdles: won maiden at Sligo in July: third in handicap at Listowel (1¾ lengths behind Lagostovegas) in September. *N. Madden, Ireland* — **h131**

BOHER CALL (IRE) 11 b.g. Indian River (FR) – Cill Fhair (IRE) (Naheez (USA)) [2017/18 c20m³ c19d c20.5m⁴ Apr 26] point winner: fair handicap chaser: left Paul W. Flynn after second start: stays 21f: acts on good to firm and heavy going: has worn headgear: wears tongue tie: usually races close up. *Richard J. Bandey* — **c111**

BOHER LAD (IRE) 11 b.g. Gold Well – Shindeesharnick (IRE) (Roselier (FR)) [2017/18 c67, h101: h23g⁴ h26s⁵ h24v⁴ h24.2s h25s⁴ Apr 15] smallish gelding: point winner: fair handicap hurdler: well held only chase start: stays 3¼m: acts on good to firm and heavy going: has worn headgear/tongue tie. *Alan Phillips* — **c– h100**

BOHERNAGORE (IRE) 9 b.g. Tajraasi (USA) – Brownies Haven (IRE) (Bob Back (USA)) [2017/18 h91: h15.8d⁵ h18.6g^pu h16.8g² h15.8g² h18.1g h15.8g^f h15.7g h20.7g^F Nov 14] compact gelding: maiden pointer: modest handicap hurdler: stays 2¼m: acts on good to soft going: wears headgear: front runner. *Philip Kirby* — **h89**

BOIS D'EBENE (IRE) 4 b.f. Big Bad Bob (IRE) – Mpumalanga (Observatory (USA)) [2017/18 h15.8s^pu Jan 10] half-sister to useful hurdler Tea In Transvaal (winner around 2m, by Teofilo): fair maiden on Flat, stays 1m: pulled up in fillies juvenile on hurdling debut. *Evan Williams* — **h–**

BOITE (IRE) 8 b.g. Authorized (IRE) – Albiatra (USA) (Dixieland Band (USA)) [2017/18 h138: h21.4v² h19s* h22.8v^F h24s h21.5s⁵ Apr 28] rather leggy gelding: has had breathing operation: useful handicap hurdler: won at Taunton (by 11 lengths from Monbeg Legend) in January: stays 21f: acts on heavy going: has worn cheekpieces, including final 2017/18 start: tried in tongue tie: usually races close up. *Warren Greatrex* — **h139**

BON

BOLD DUKE 10 b.g. Sulamani (IRE) – Dominant Duchess (Old Vic) [2017/18 h87: c100
c16.5s³ c20.3d² c20g² c24.1g⁴ c22.6g^pu c17.4g^F Oct 31] winning hurdler: fair form over h–
fences: stayed 2½m: acted on heavy going: tried in headgear: dead. *Edward Bevan*

BOLD IMAGE (IRE) 7 b.m. Milan – Golden Bay (Karinga Bay) [2017/18 b81p: h20.5s h101
h19.2v⁶ h17.7v h21.7d⁶ h24.6s h21.6s³ Apr 23] bumper winner: fair form over hurdles:
stays 2¾m: acts on good going: has joined Dan Skelton. *Suzy Smith*

BOLDMERE 5 b.g. Multiplex – Pugnacious Lady (Hernando (FR)) [2017/18 b15.3d⁵ b95
Apr 22] third foal: dam maiden on Flat (stayed 1½m): 20/1, fifth in bumper at Wincanton
(6½ lengths behind Samarquand). *Graeme McPherson*

BOLD PLAN (IRE) 4 b.g. Jeremy (USA) – Kings Orchid (IRE) (King's Theatre (IRE)) b103 p
[2017/18 b15.3d² Apr 22] €28,000 3-y-o, £195,000 4-y-o: first foal: dam (h81) maiden
hurdler (best effort at 2m): won Irish point on debut: 6/1, shaped very well when second in
bumper at Wincanton (neck behind Samarquand): useful prospect. *Evan Williams*

BOLERO COLLONGES (FR) 7 gr.g. Fragrant Mix (IRE) – Katy Collonges (FR) c–
(Lute Antique (FR)) [2017/18 c–, h56; h16.8g⁶ May 16] maiden hurdler/chaser, little form h–
in Britain: has worn headgear: tried in tongue tie. *Simon Waugh*

BOLISTER (FR) 7 b.g. Le Balafre (FR) – Girlish (FR) (Passing Sale (FR)) [2017/18 h–
h100: h16m⁵ May 1] sturdy gelding: modest hurdler, well held sole start in 2017/18: bred
to stay beyond 2m. *Gary Moore*

BOLLIN ACE 7 b.g. Bollin Eric – Bollin Annabel (King's Theatre (IRE)) [2017/18 h129: c129
h19.7s^F c16.4v⁴ c16.3s² c15.9v* c20.6s⁵ c20d² c20.1s² Apr 26] fairly useful handicap h118
hurdler: similar form over fences: won maiden at Leicester in March: second in novice at
Carlisle later in month: stays 21f: acts on heavy going: usually wears headgear: tried in
tongue tie: front runner/races prominently. *Tim Easterby*

BOLLIN JULIE 11 b.m. Bollin Eric – Bollin Nellie (Rock Hopper) [2017/18 h78: h23.3g h–
May 23] poor hurdler: stays 25f: acts on heavy going: in blinkers sole 2017/18 start.
Donald Whillans

BOLLIN LINE 11 b.g. Bollin Eric – Leading Line (Leading Man) [2017/18 c87, h–: c97
c19.2g⁵ c17.4g⁶ h16.7g* h16.2d³ h19.6g^bd h15.8g* h16.8g* h15.8g* h21.2g* c16.4s⁴ h105
c20.2v^ur c15.7d⁷ Dec 19] sturdy gelding: fair hurdler: won conditional/amateur seller at
Market Rasen in August, and completed hat-trick in handicaps at Sedgefield and Ludlow
(2) in November: modest handicap chaser: won at Catterick in December: stays 21f: acts
on soft going: tried in hood: races well off pace. *Lucinda Egerton*

BOLVING (IRE) 7 b.g. Stowaway – Kiniohio (FR) (Script Ohio (USA)) [2017/18 h81: h98
h19.5d h16.3s h16.3s h21s² Apr 9] useful-looking gelding: modest form over hurdles: stays
21f: acts on soft going: sometimes in hood/tongue tie. *Victor Dartnall*

BOMBAY RASCAL 5 ch.m. Indian Haven – Kohiba (IRE) (Rock of Gibraltar (IRE)) h–
[2017/18 b16.8m⁶ h16v^vo h16.5s^pu Jan 20] fourth foal: half-sister to fair hurdler Kohuma b–
(2m winner, by Halling): dam German 7f winner on only start: no sign of ability, including
on Flat. *Robert Waiford*

BOMBER COMMAND (FR) 6 gr.g. Al Namix (FR) – Ballade Nordique (FR) (Royal h109
Charter (FR)) [2017/18 h98p, b79; h15.8d² h15.7d² h15.8g* Jun 21] fair form over hurdles:
won maiden at Uttoxeter in June: raced around 2m: acts on good to soft going: usually
races close up. *Tom George*

BOMBER'S MOON 7 b.g. Erhaab (USA) – Flaviola (IRE) (Moscow Society (USA)) h96
[2017/18 b95: b15.7d⁶ h15.7s⁶ h15.8d³ h23.1d Apr 21] sturdy gelding: fair form in b84
bumpers: modest form over hurdles: best effort when third in maiden at Huntingdon in
March: tried in tongue tie. *Nigel Twiston-Davies*

BONBON AU MIEL (FR) 7 b.g. Khalkevi (IRE) – Friandise Ii (FR) (Mistigri) [2017/18 c142
h139: c23.5v⁴ c20v* c24.4s^F Mar 14] good-topped gelding: useful form over hurdles: h–
similar form over fences: won maiden at Navan (by 11 lengths from Turcagua) in January:
behind when fell last in RSA Insurance Novices' Chase at Cheltenham: stays 2½m: acts on
heavy going: in tongue tie last 2 starts. *W. P. Mullins, Ireland*

BON CHIC (IRE) 9 b.m. Presenting – Homebird (IRE) (Be My Native (USA)) [2017/18 c118 §
c124, h113: h25.4d^ur c21.2g³ c23.8g⁶ c21.2g² c20g^pu h24.7d* h24.7s h24.3g^ro Apr 20] h119 §
useful-looking mare: fairly useful handicap hurdler: won at Aintree (conditional) in
October: fairly useful handicap chaser: third at Cartmel in July: stays 25f: acts on soft and
good to firm going: wears headgear: often heads: unreliable. *James Moffatt*

BON

BONDS CONQUEST 9 ch.g. Monsieur Bond (IRE) – Another Conquest (El Conquistador) [2017/18 c72, h–: c19.4v^pu c24.5s^4 c16s^4 c20.2v* Mar 9] maiden hurdler: poor handicap chaser: won at Leicester in March: stays 25f: acts on heavy going: wears headgear: front runner/races prominently. *Seamus Mullins* — **c78 h–**

BONNE QUESTION (FR) 9 gr.g. Tagula (IRE) – Amonita (GER) (Medaaly) [2017/18 h115: h15.7s h16v^5 Mar 20] sturdy gelding: fair hurdler, lightly raced: unproven beyond 17f: raced only on soft/heavy going. *Venetia Williams* — **h100**

BONNET'S VINO 10 b.m. Grape Tree Road – Bonnet's Pieces (Alderbrook) [2017/18 c110, h108: h20d^2 h20.6d^3 h21.2s^6 Feb 21] lengthy, medium-sized mare: fair handicap hurdler: fair chaser: stays 23f: acts on heavy going. *Pam Sly* — **c– h107**

BONNIE BLACK ROSE 8 b.m. Black Sam Bellamy (IRE) – Fragrant Rose (Alflora (IRE)) [2017/18 h16g h16.8v^5 h15.8s h21.2d^6 h21.2s h25.6v^pu Feb 5] poor form over hurdles: often wears hood. *Arthur Whiting* — **h75**

BONNY KATE (IRE) 8 ch.m. Beneficial – Peppardstown (IRE) (Old Vic) [2017/18 c142, h–: c24v^3 c24.5d^pu c23v^pu c26.2v^2 c21s^5 Apr 27] winning hurdler: useful handicap chaser: third in Troytown Handicap Chase at Navan (10¾ lengths behind Mala Beach) in November: stays 3½m: acts on heavy going: in cheekpieces last 2 starts. *Noel Meade, Ireland* — **c135 h–**

BONOBO (IRE) 11 b.g. Quws – Better Folly (IRE) (Rhoman Rule (USA)) [2017/18 c99, h116: c19.4g^3 c16.3m^ur h18.5d* c17.4d^2 c16v^pu Nov 12] modest hurdler: won seller at Newton Abbot in September: fair maiden chaser: stays 19f: acts on soft and good to firm going: often wears headgear: tried in tongue tie: often let down by jumping over fences. *Evan Williams* — **c106 x h98**

BON PAPA (FR) 7 br.g. Network (GER) – Gibelotte (FR) (Royal Charter (FR)) [2017/18 h116, b107: c16.1s* c24s^3 c21s c16.7v^2 c16d^3 Apr 26] fairly useful form over hurdles: smart form over fences: won maiden at Punchestown (by 11 lengths from Light That) in November: placed in handicaps at Fairyhouse (novice, 1½ lengths behind Bel Ami de Sivola) and Punchestown (10 lengths behind Cadmium) in April: will prove best at short of 3m: acts on heavy going: in tongue tie last 3 starts. *W. P. Mullins, Ireland* — **c145 h–**

BONZA GIRL 5 b.m. Midnight Legend – Purple Patch (Afzal) [2017/18 b16d h18.5s h21.4v h16.8s^6 h15.3v^4 Apr 9] second foal: half-sister to a winning pointer by Central Park: dam (h106) 2m hurdle winner (stayed 2¾m): tailed off in bumper: poor form over hurdles. *Jeremy Scott* — **h82 b–**

BOOBOROWIE (IRE) 5 b.g. Big Bad Bob (IRE) – Rejuvenation (IRE) (Singspiel (IRE)) [2017/18 h17.7v h15.5v h17.7s^5 h16.8v Apr 13] fair maiden on Flat, stays 1¼m: little show over hurdles. *Ali Stronge* — **h69**

BOOGIE LIFE 7 b.m. Tobougg (IRE) – Life Is Life (FR) (Mansonnien (FR)) [2017/18 h67p, b–: h16.2g h16.2g^3 h16v^pu h15.6g^5 ab16.3g^6 h19.4d^pu h24.3g^pu Apr 20] lengthy mare: poor maiden hurdler: best effort at 2m: usually races prominently: has joined Donald McCain. *Jim Goldie* — **h81**

BOOK DIRECT (IRE) 7 b.g. Kayf Tara – Sinnaja (Sinndar (IRE)) [2017/18 h117p: h19v^pu Apr 12] third in Irish point: fair form over hurdles, shaped as if amiss sole start in 2017/18. *Philip Hobbs* — **h–**

BOOK OF EXCUSES (IRE) 10 b.g. Brian Boru – Out of Danger (IRE) (Darnay) [2017/18 c19.8g^pu May 22] winning chaser: fair maiden chaser at best: stayed 3m: acted on firm going: wore tongue tie: dead. *Barry Brennan* — **c– h–**

BOOK OF GOLD (IRE) 6 b.g. Flemensfirth (USA) – Ballerina Queen (IRE) (Be My Native (USA)) [2017/18 b92: h20g^6 h20.5s^3 h20.5s^4 h20.8s^2 h24.2v^3 h23.6s h25.8v^pu Mar 17] sturdy gelding: fairly useful maiden hurdler: third in handicap at Newbury in February: stays 3m: acts on heavy going: in cheekpieces last 2 starts: front runner/races prominently. *Oliver Sherwood* — **h118**

BOOK OF LOVE (IRE) 9 b.g. Kutub (IRE) – Love's Always Game (IRE) (Camden Town) [2017/18 h19.3d c16.4v^4 h20.2s Apr 27] won sole start in Irish points: maiden hurdler: tailed off in novice handicap on chasing debut: tried in cheekpieces. *Martin Todhunter* — **c– h–**

BOOLA RIVER (IRE) 8 b.m. Craigsteel – Hy Kate (IRE) (Over The River (FR)) [2017/18 h21.7v^3 h19.5s h21.7v h23.1v^R h23.9m^pu Apr 25] fifth foal: half-sister to a winning pointer by Double Eclipse: dam placed in point: Irish point winner: little show over hurdles. *Seamus Mullins* — **h60**

BOR

BOOYAKASHA (IRE) 6 b.g. Presenting – Land of Honour (Supreme Leader) [2017/18 b79p: h19.3d³ h16.2s h16v⁶ Mar 9] modest form over hurdles: best effort when third in novice at Catterick in December: bred to be suited by 2½m+. *Nicky Richards* **h90**

BORAK (IRE) 6 b.g. Kodiac – Right After Moyne (IRE) (Imperial Ballet (IRE)) [2017/18 h101: h16.5m³ Apr 25] modest handicap hurdler: will stay 2½m: acts on good to firm and heavy going: tried in cheekpieces: has worn tongue tie. *Bernard Llewellyn* **h92**

BORDEAUX BILL (IRE) 7 b.g. Craigsteel – Laura Croft (IRE) (Mister Lord (USA)) [2017/18 h128p, b90: c16.4d^F c17.2g⁵ c21.4d² c24.2s* ab16g* c24.2s^pu Mar 16] lengthy gelding: won jumpers bumper at Southwell in March: fairly useful form over hurdles: similar form over fences: won 3-runner novice at Wetherby in December: stays 3m: acts on soft going: often races towards rear. *Brian Ellison* **c126 h–**

BORDER BREAKER (IRE) 9 br.g. Indian Danehill (IRE) – Flying Answer (IRE) (Anshan) [2017/18 c–, h–: h20.1g² h23.9m h20.1g² h23.9g⁵ h23.3g⁴ h20.2d¹ h20.1d^pu c24.2v^pu c19.9d⁵ Apr 24] angular gelding: fair handicap hurdler: fairly useful chaser at best, below form in 2017/18: left Simon Waugh after eighth start: stays 3m: acts on soft going: usually wears headgear/tongue tie. *Sam England* **c97 h104**

BORDERLINEDECISION (IRE) 6 b.g. King's Theatre (IRE) – Dani California (Beat All (USA)) [2017/18 h16g h15.8g h16g h18.6g⁶ h21.6g⁵ h15.8g* Sep 13] second foal: brother to bumper winner Dani Theatre: dam (h132), 2m hurdle winner, also 1½m-2m winner on Flat: fair handicap hurdler: won at Uttoxeter in September: left N. Madden after first start: stays 19f: best form on good going: has worn tongue tie, including last 3 starts. *Jonjo O'Neill* **h101**

BORDER VICTOR 6 b.g. Beat All (USA) – Sambara (IRE) (Shardari) [2017/18 h91, b–: h21.3s h23.8g^pu h24.1s h20.5v³ h24.1d² h19.3v² Apr 17] modest maiden hurdler: stays 3m: acts on heavy going: often wears headgear: irresolute. *Barry Murtagh* **h85 §**

BORED OR BAD (IRE) 6 b.g. Oscar (IRE) – Siberiansdaughter (IRE) (Strong Gale) [2017/18 h–: h23.3g⁴ May 28] poor maiden hurdler: wore cheekpieces sole 2017/18 start: tried in tongue tie: often races towards rear. *David Dennis* **h–**

BOREHAM BILL (IRE) 6 b.g. Tikkanen (USA) – Crimond (IRE) (Zaffaran (USA)) [2017/18 b105: h20.5d⁴ h19.6s⁴ h20.3v* h21.7s² h20.3g Apr 18] workmanlike gelding: useful bumper performer: fairly useful form over hurdles: won maiden at Southwell in February: second in novice at Fontwell in March: stays 2¾m: acts on heavy going: usually leads: temperament under suspicion. *Ben Pauling* **h121**

BORIC 10 b.g. Grape Tree Road – Petrea (St Ninian) [2017/18 c110, h–: c24.5s² c29.2g² c23.4v⁴ c27.6s⁶ c25.2s² c32.6s^pu c30.6s⁴ Apr 27] maiden hurdler: fairly useful handicap chaser: second at Sedgefield in November: stays 31f: acts on soft going: wears headgear. *Simon Waugh* **c125 h–**

BORIS GRISHENKO (IRE) 5 ch.g. Sixties Icon – Tetou (IRE) (Peintre Celebre (USA)) [2017/18 b16.6s⁵ b18.8g² b16.2d³ h16s h16v Sep 29] €36,000 3-y-o: fourth foal: half-brother to useful 2m hurdler/chaser Tetlami (by Daylami): dam 1¼m winner: fair form in bumpers: modest form over hurdles: tried in hood. *Gordon Elliott, Ireland* **h88 b86**

BORN A SAINT 5 ch.g. Phoenix Reach (IRE) – Kind Nell (Generous (IRE)) [2017/18 h19.3v^pu Jan 24] pulled up in novice hurdle. *Laura Morgan* **h–**

BORN FOR WAR (IRE) 6 ch.g. Wareed (IRE) – Oscar Bird (IRE) (Oscar (IRE)) [2017/18 b88: h16s⁵ h20.3s⁵ h15.8s Jan 10] runner-up in Irish maiden point: modest form over hurdles. *Tom George* **h90**

BORN IN THORNE 5 b.m. Haafhd – Royal Nashkova (Mujahid (USA)) [2017/18 ab16g² Mar 2] fourth foal: half-sister to 9f-1¼m winner Artful Prince (by Dutch Art): dam unraced: 5/2, second in maiden bumper at Southwell (4½ lengths behind Flash The Steel). *Ivan Furtado* **b85**

BORN LEGEND (IRE) 4 b.g. Born To Sea (IRE) – Hallowed Park (IRE) (Barathea (IRE)) [2017/18 h16.8g^pu h15.9m⁶ h15.8m^pu h15.8s³ h16.7s* h17.7v^pu h16.3v h16s⁵ h16v^pu h15.3v^pu Apr 26] sturdy gelding: has had breathing operation: fair modest form on Flat, stays 1¼m: modest hurdler: won juvenile maiden at Bangor in November: best effort at 17f: acts on soft going: wears headgear: front runner/races prominently. *Oliver Sherwood* **h98**

BORN SURVIVOR (IRE) 7 b.g. King's Theatre (IRE) – Bob's Flame (IRE) (Bob Back (USA)) [2017/18 h142: c15.2s* c21.6v³ c15.7v³ c16.3v c24.1g Apr 21] useful-looking gelding: useful hurdler: similar form over fences: won novice at Wetherby in November: third in graduation event at Haydock (11½ lengths behind Clan des Obeaux) later in month: stays 21f: acts on heavy going: tried in cheekpieces: often travels strongly. *Dan Skelton* **c139 h–**

BOR

BORN TO BOOGIE 4 b.f. Bahri (USA) – Turtle Dove (Tobougg (IRE)) [2017/18 h16.2g⁵ Jun 3] poor maiden on Flat, best effort at 5f: tailed off in juvenile on hurdling debut: has joined Bill Turner. *Chris Grant*   h–

BORN TO SIZE (GER) 6 b.g. Sholokhov (IRE) – Beyonce (GER) (Samum (GER)) [2017/18 h16d² h16s h16.5g c18g* c18.9sᵖᵘ c18.2.5sᶠ Feb 4] first foal: dam unraced: modest form over hurdles: fair form over fences: won maiden at Thurles (by 4 lengths from Youcantcallherthat) in October on final start for W. J. Burke: stays 2¼m: acts on good to soft going: has worn hood: tried in tongue tie. *Kayley Woollacott*   c111 h97

BORUMA (IRE) 8 b.g. Brian Boru – Itlallendintears (IRE) (Lil's Boy (USA)) [2017/18 c–, h109: h17.2m⁴ h22.1d* h22.1g* h22.1sᶠ h25.4d⁶ h19.7s⁶ h20.5gᵘʳ Apr 21] fairly useful handicap hurdler: won at Cartmel in May and June: maiden chaser (likely to have won both starts over fences in 2014/15 but for falling): stays 2¾m: acts on good to firm and heavy going: tried in hood. *James Moffatt*   c– h118

BORU'S BROOK (IRE) 10 b.g. Brian Boru – Collybrook Lady (IRE) (Mandalus) [2017/18 h15.9dᵖᵘ Feb 26] good-topped gelding: fairly useful hurdler at best, pulled up sole start in 2017/18: winning chaser: unproven beyond 2m: acts on heavy going: tried in blinkers. *Suzi Best*   c– h–

BOSS DES MALBERAUX (FR) 7 b.g. Antarctique (IRE) – Scavenger (FR) (Nashamaa) [2017/18 b17m⁴ May 11] 7/2, tailed off in bumper. *Simon West*   b–

BOSS DES MOTTES (FR) 7 b.g. Califet (FR) – Puszta des Mottes (FR) (Useful (FR)) [2017/18 c123, h–: c16.4g⁴ c20.3g⁴ c17.3d² c15.7g⁵ c17.3g³ c17.2g³ c20.3g⁴ c15.6d³ c19.3d⁶ Oct 3] rather slightly-built gelding: winning hurdler: modest handicap chaser nowadays: stays 19f: acts on soft and good to firm going: wears headgear: usually wears tongue tie. *Henry Hogarth*   c99 h–

BOSS IN BOOTS (IRE) 10 gr.g. King's Theatre (IRE) – Grey Mo (IRE) (Roselier (FR)) [2017/18 c95§, h85§: h20d May 27] angular gelding: one-time fair hurdler, tailed off sole start in 2017/18: modest chaser: stays 2¾m: acts on good to firm and heavy going: wears headgear: usually races towards rear: not one to rely on. *Tim Vaughan*   c– § h– §

BOSS MANS LADDER (IRE) 6 b.g. Mahler – Glen Supreme (IRE) (Supreme Leader) [2017/18 h26d⁵ h20.5d h20.5s h16s h25s h26.4d* Apr 22] £16,000 5-y-o: unfurnished gelding: seventh foal: half-brother to a winning pointer by Shantou: dam unraced half-sister to fairly useful hurdler/chaser (2½m-3m winner) Noisy Miner: third on debut in Irish point: fair form over hurdles: won handicap at Stratford in April: will stay long distances: acts on good to soft going: tried in cheekpieces. *Ben Pauling*   h107

BOSTIN (IRE) 10 ch.g. Busy Flight – Bustingoutallover (USA) (Trempolino (USA)) [2017/18 h86: h25g* h25.6d² h21.6m³ h24g Jul 16] modest handicap hurdler: won at Plumpton in May: stays 3¼m: acts on good to firm and good to soft going: usually races towards rear. *Daniel O'Brien*   h91

BOSTON BLUE 11 b.g. Halling (USA) – City of Gold (IRE) (Sadler's Wells (USA)) [2017/18 c102§, h89§: c16.1g² c15.9m⁴ Nov 20] quite good-topped gelding: winning hurdler: fair form over fences: stays 2½m: acts on good to firm and heavy going: often races lazily/looks reluctant. *Tony Carroll*   c92 § h– §

BOSTON DE LA ROCHE (FR) 7 b.g. Malinas (GER) – Quesland de La Roche (FR) (Arnaqueur (USA)) [2017/18 h97: h15.8g⁵ May 9] modest maiden hurdler: best efforts around 2m: best form on good going: dead. *Dan Skelton*   h92

BOUDRY (FR) 7 b.g. Crossharbour – Lavande (FR) (Iris Noir (FR)) [2017/18 h85: h16g⁵ h20g⁶ h22g h18.8d⁵ h16s h21.3d h18.1v Apr 16] workmanlike gelding: fair maiden hurdler: left Gordon Elliott after fifth start: stays 2½m: acts on good to soft going: sometimes in tongue tie: often races towards rear. *Rose Dobbin*   h101

BOUGGIETOPIECES 8 b.g. Tobougg (IRE) – Bonnet's Pieces (Alderbrook) [2017/18 c96§, h–: c21.1mᵖᵘ c20.9sᵖᵘ Jan 29] winning hurdler: fair chaser at best, pulled up both starts in 2017/18: left Tim Vaughan after first one: stays 3m: acts on soft and good to firm going: tried in cheekpieces/tongue tie: temperamental. *A. B. Leyshon*   c– § h–

BOUGHTBEFORELUNCH (IRE) 5 b.g. Dubai Destination (USA) – Anie (IRE) (Saffron Walden (FR)) [2017/18 h90: h19.9d h16.3s h15.8s Jan 26] lengthy, rather unfurnished gelding: little impact over hurdles. *Paul Webber*   h70

BOUND FOR GLORY (IRE) 12 b.g. Witness Box (USA) – Musical View (IRE) (Orchestra) [2017/18 c105, h–: c21.1s² c22.6d⁵ c21.1s⁶ Apr 12] lengthy gelding: multiple point winner: winning hurdler: fair chaser: stays 23f: acts on soft and good to firm going: tried in blinkers: wore tongue tie in 2017/18. *D. M. G. Fitch-Peyton*   c114 h–

BOY

BOUND HILL 9 b.g. Kayf Tara – Ardent Bride (Ardross) [2017/18 c93, h101§: h21m^pu h20s c19.5v³ Dec 11] strong gelding: fair hurdler, below form in 2017/18: modest form over fences: stays 19f: acts on heavy going: wears headgear: front runner, tends to find little: temperamental. *Fiona Shaw* — **c88 §**, **h– §**

BOURBON PRINCE 7 ch.g. Aqlaam – Good Enough (FR) (Mukaddamah (USA)) [2017/18 c82, h–: c16.4g May 16] maiden hurdler: poor form over fences: unproven beyond 17f: acts on good to soft going: tried in hood: has worn tongue tie. *Sam England* — **c–**, **h–**

BOURNE 12 gr.g. Linamix (FR) – L'Affaire Monique (Machiavellian (USA)) [2017/18 h111§: h23.3g⁵ h22.1d⁵ h27g⁶ h24.6s³ Dec 3] close-coupled gelding: fair handicap hurdler: stays 3¼m: acts on heavy going: usually wears headgear: temperamental. *Donald McCain* — **h105 §**

BOURNVILLE (IRE) 4 b.f. Casamento (IRE) – Passaggio (Pivotal) [2017/18 ab16.3g* ab16.3g* Mar 3] fourth foal: half-sister to winning sprinters by Intense Focus and Moss Vale: dam unraced half-sister to fair hurdler/fairly useful chaser (stayed 3½m) Noble Concorde: fairly useful form in bumpers: won at Newcastle in February (mares) and March. *K. R. Burke* — **b95**

BOUTAN 5 gr.m. Tobougg (IRE) – High Tan (High Chaparral (IRE)) [2017/18 h96: h18.5v h16.6⁶ h16v h15.8v² h16.5s⁶ Jan 9] poor maiden hurdler: left Bernard Llewellyn after first start: raced mainly around 2m: acts on heavy going: wears cheekpieces. *Grace Harris* — **h84**

BOUVREUIL (FR) 7 b.g. Saddler Maker (IRE) – Madame Lys (FR) (Sheyrann) [2017/18 c147, h–: c19.9d c22.4g⁶ c16.3v^bd c21.1s^pu Apr 13] useful-looking gelding: winning hurdler: smart handicap chaser: below best in 2017/18, though had excuses first 3 starts: stays 21f: acts on heavy going: has worn hood, including in 2017/18: wears tongue tie: often races towards rear: can look tricky (has high head carriage). *Paul Nicholls* — **c122**, **h–**

BOWBAN 4 b.c. Makfi – Serafina's Flight (Fantastic Light (USA)) [2017/18 h16.7g^ur Jun 23] fairly useful maiden on Flat, stays 1¼m: well held when stumbled and unseated last in juvenile at Market Rasen on hurdling debut: should do better. *Brian Ellison* — **h– p**

BOWIE (IRE) 11 br.g. Pelder (IRE) – La Fenice (IRE) (Krayyan) [2017/18 c–, h108: h18.6g³ h20.6g⁴ h20.5s h18.6s² h18.6v Jan 17] smallish gelding: fair handicap hurdler: pulled up sole start over fences: stays 21f: acts on good to firm and heavy going: tried in cheekpieces: often races prominently. *Nick Kent* — **c–**, **h105**

BOWLER BILL 5 gr.g. Great Palm (USA) – Overthrow (Overbury (IRE)) [2017/18 b16.8g⁵ b15.7g May 24] no form in bumpers: has joined David Thompson. *Chris Grant* — **b–**

BOXER BEAT (IRE) 11 b.g. Xaar – Pantoufle (Bering) [2017/18 c74, h–: h23.8s^pu h16.2s h16.7v c16d c17.4d⁵ Apr 21] fair maiden hurdler at best, no form in 2017/18: modest handicap chaser nowadays: stays 2½m: acts on soft and good to firm going: has worn headgear/tongue tie. *Lady Susan Brooke* — **c92**, **h–**

BOX OFFICE (FR) 7 b.g. Great Pretender (IRE) – Quelle Mome (FR) (Video Rock (FR)) [2017/18 c117, h–: c23.9g⁴ c25.5m³ c24g³ h19.2s⁴ h19v h21v^pu Mar 28] good-topped gelding: fair handicap hurdler/chaser: stays 19f: acts on soft going: has worn tongue tie, including in 2017/18: often races towards rear. *Jonjo O'Neill* — **c110**, **h105**

BOYFROMNOWHERE (IRE) 11 br.g. Old Vic – Eist Do Gale (IRE) (Strong Gale) [2017/18 c108§, h–: c25.2s⁴ c25.2d^bd c29.6v³ c29.2v⁵ c24.1s⁵ c27.5d² Apr 22] sturdy gelding: winning hurdler: modest handicap chaser: stays 3¾m: acts on heavy going: has worn headgear, including final start: wears tongue tie: temperamental. *Adrian Wintle* — **c97 §**, **h–**

BOYGOJUMPING 6 ch.g. Midnight Legend – Maisie Malone Vii (Damsire Unregistered) [2017/18 c–: c21.1s⁵ May 18] multiple point winner: little show in hunter chases. *Martin Peaty* — **c–**

BOYHOOD (IRE) 7 b.g. Oscar (IRE) – Glen Dubh (IRE) (Supreme Leader) [2017/18 h123p: h19.5d* h24.2d⁴ h24s* Jan 1] good-topped gelding: useful handicap hurdler: won at Lingfield in November and Cheltenham (by 7 lengths from Red Rising) in January: stays 3m: acts on soft going: open to further improvement. *Tom George* — **h135 p**

BOY IN A BENTLEY (IRE) 8 b.g. Kayf Tara – All Our Blessings (IRE) (Statoblest) [2017/18: h109, h15.7g² h18.7g² h22.1d* h19.9g* h19.9g^pu h21.2g h20.5s Apr 15] lengthy gelding: fair hurdler: won novices at Cartmel in August and Sedgefield (conditional) in September: well held on chasing debut: left Kim Bailey after first start: stays 23f: acts on soft going: wears headgear/tongue tie: often races prominently: temperamental. *Neil Mulholland* — **c–**, **h107 §**

BOY

BOY NAMED SIOUX 7 b.g. Indian Danehill (IRE) – Annie's Gift (IRE) (Presenting) [2017/18 b16v h16.7s³ h20.6v^{pu} Apr 14] second foal: half-brother to 1¾m-2m winner Anne's Valentino (by Primo Valentino): dam unraced half-sister to useful hurdler/smart chaser (stayed 3¾m) According To Pete: well beaten in bumper: modest form over hurdles: better effort when third in novice at Market Rasen in March: has joined Colin Tizzard. *Ruth Jefferson* h99 b–

BOY'S ON TOUR (IRE) 6 b.g. Beneficial – Galant Tour (IRE) (Riberetto) [2017/18 b16.2d⁴ h20.9d^{pu} h15.6m⁵ h19.4g⁵ h15.6g c19.9s⁴ c19.9s² c19.9s⁶ Feb 4] €11,000 3-y-o, €33,000 5-y-o: sixth foal: brother to bumper winner/fair 2½m hurdle winner Tour de Ville, and half-brother to useful hurdler/chaser On Tour (2m-2½m winner, by Croco Rouge) and fairly useful hurdler/chaser Galant Ferns (2¾m-25f winner, by Bob Back): dam (h102) 2½m/2¾m hurdle winner: Irish maiden point winner: fourth in bumper: poor form over hurdles: modest form over fences: best effort when second in handicap at Musselburgh in January: stays 2½m: acts on soft going: sometimes in hood. *Lucinda Russell* c95 h80 b78

BOYTONRATH (IRE) 8 b.m. Beneficial – Rossbrook (IRE) (Presenting) [2017/18 h18.8g h16d² h16g² h16.5s⁶ h16v⁴ h16.8g Nov 2] second foal: dam, poor maiden hurdler/chaser, half-sister to fairly useful hurdler/chaser (2½m-25f winner) Baily Storm: modest maiden hurdler: unproven beyond 2m: acts on heavy going. *Gordon Elliott, Ireland* h90

BRAAVOS 7 br.g. Presenting – Tatanka (IRE) (Lear Fan (USA)) [2017/18 h122: h23.3d² h24g³ h20.3g* c22.6s^{pu} c18g h21m⁵ Apr 26] well-made gelding: fairly useful handicap hurdler: won at Southwell in September: no form over fences: stays 3m: acts on heavy going. *Philip Hobbs* c– h128

BRACE YOURSELF (IRE) 5 ch.g. Mahler – Angelica Garnett (Desert Story (IRE)) [2017/18 b16v* b16s³ b16v² Apr 2] £165,000 4-y-o: fifth foal: half-brother to fairly useful hurdler Expedite (2½m-23f winner, by Brian Boru): dam, 1½m winner, half-sister to useful hurdler/fairly useful chaser (stayed 25f) De Soto: runner-up in point: useful form in bumpers: won maiden at Down Royal (by 24 lengths from Dorydalis) in December: second at Fairyhouse (2¾ lengths behind Getaway John) in April: will be suited by at least 2½m. *Noel Meade, Ireland* b113

BRACKA LILY (IRE) 6 b.m. Mahler – Hep To The Jive (FR) (Bahri (USA)) [2017/18 b16g⁶ b15.8m h16s h18s h16v h21v^{pu} h16.8g Apr 23] seventh foal: half-sister to 19f bumper winner King'sandqueen's (by King's Theatre): dam, French 13f winner, half-sister to high-class hurdler/very smart chaser (stayed 29f) Bounce Back: well held in bumpers/over hurdles. *Noel C. Kelly, Ireland* h82 b67

BRADDAN HEAD 5 br.g. Recharge (IRE) – Solid Land (FR) (Solid Illusion (USA)) [2017/18 h16.6s h20.6s⁵ h21d⁵ Apr 26] sturdy gelding: seventh foal: half-brother to useful hurdler/chaser Grandads Horse (19f-3m winner, by Bollin Eric): dam (h104) lightly raced over hurdles: green in bumper: modest form over hurdles: better effort when fifth in maiden at Warwick in April: open to further improvement. *Charlie Longsdon* h97 p b–

BRADFORD BRIDGE (IRE) 8 b.g. Milan – Isis du Berlais (FR) (Cadoudal (FR)) [2017/18 h112: c19.5g^{pu} c20.2g⁶ c19.4v² c23s^{pu} h23.9v^{pu} Feb 4] fair form over hurdles: similar form over fences: stays 2½m: acts on heavy going. *Philip Hobbs* c102 h–

BRAES OF LOCHALSH 7 b.g. Tiger Hill (IRE) – Gargoyle Girl (Be My Chief (USA)) [2017/18 h–: h20.5v⁶ h19v Dec 22] fair on Flat, stays 17.5f: poor form over hurdles: tried in cheekpieces. *Jim Goldie* h82

BRAHMA BULL (IRE) 7 ch.g. Presenting – Oligarch Society (IRE) (Moscow Society (USA)) [2017/18 b17.6d* b16v* b16v* h23.6d* h21.1s h24s⁶ Apr 25] €170,000 3-y-o: workmanlike gelding: first foal: dam (c101/h127), bumper/2m hurdle winner, half-sister to Irish Grand National winner Thunder And Roses (by Presenting): useful form when winning all 3 starts in bumpers, at Ballinrobe in July, Listowel in September and Tipperary in October: fairly useful form over hurdles: won maiden at Thurles in November: stiff tasks next 2 starts: should still do better over hurdles. *W. P. Mullins, Ireland* h126 p b111

BRAHMS DE CLERMONT (FR) 7 b.g. Califet (FR) – Colline de Clermon (FR) (Vertical Speed (FR)) [2017/18 h106, b109: h16.8m* h19g³ h20d² h16.5g* h16.5s* h15.6s⁴ ab16d⁴ h16g* Apr 20] useful hurdler: won maiden at Exeter in May, and novices at Taunton in November/December and Ayr (by 2 lengths from Deyrann de Carjac) in April: stays 2½m: acts on soft and good to firm going: front runner/races prominently. *Paul Nicholls* h131

BRAIN POWER (IRE) 7 b.g. Kalanisi (IRE) – Blonde Ambition (IRE) (Old Vic) [2017/18 h158: c18d* c15.5d^{ur} c16.8v^F c15.9s^2 c19.99^F Apr 12] rangy gelding: very smart hurdler: smart form over fences: won novice at Kempton (by 28 lengths from War Sound) in November: second in Arkle Chase at Cheltenham (14 lengths behind Footpad) in March: raced mainly around 2m: acts on soft going: has worn cheekpieces: tried in tongue tie: often travels strongly. *Nicky Henderson*   **c154 h–**

BRAMBLE BROOK 8 b.g. Kayf Tara – Briery Ann (Anshan) [2017/18 c115, h107: c20.9s^2 c25.8g^2 c20.9s^3 c19.7v* c19.5v^3 c17.8v* c20.9v^6 c20.2v^4 c20.2d^3 Apr 22] strong gelding: maiden hurdler: fairly useful handicap chaser: won at Plumpton in January and Fontwell in February: stays 3¼m, fully effective at much shorter: acts on heavy going: in cheekpieces last 2 starts: wears tongue tie: front runner/races prominently: temperamental. *Colin Tizzard*   **c117 § h–**

BRANDON HILL (IRE) 10 b.g. Beneficial – Annesbanker (IRE) (Anshan) [2017/18 c132, h–: c23.8d^2 c24s^3 c24s^2 c20.5s c23.8s^4 Apr 25] lengthy gelding: winning hurdler: useful handicap chaser: second at Kempton (length behind Bigbadjohn) in February: stays 3m: acts on heavy going: front runner. *Tom George*   **c136 h–**

BRANDY AND RED (IRE) 9 b.g. Presenting – Mildan Grace (Afzal) [2017/18 c24.2m^3 c24.2v^{pu} Apr 17] point winner: poor form in hunter chases: better effort when third at Exeter in May: left G. Chambers after first start. *P. D. Rogers*   **c83**

BRANDY BREEZE 7 b.m. Rob Roy (USA) – Ginger Brandy (Bollin Terry) [2017/18 b16.2s b16.2g Nov 11] sturdy mare: first foal: dam unraced: no form in bumpers. *Jean McGregor*   **b–**

BRANDY BURN 7 b.m. Indian Danehill (IRE) – Kingennie (Dunbeath (USA)) [2017/18 b–: b16.2d^4 h16.8g^2 h16.7g h19.7d Oct 18] little impact in bumpers/over hurdles. *Peter Niven*   **h– b67**

BRANSTON DOYEN 5 b.m. Doyen (IRE) – Julatten (IRE) (Alhaarth (IRE)) [2017/18 b16.8s^6 b16.6s Jan 27] third foal: dam, modest maiden on Flat (stayed 1¼m), failed to complete both starts over hurdles, sister to high-class hurdler (2m-19f winner) Iktitaf: well held in bumpers: in hood first start. *Malcolm Jefferson*   **b–**

BRAQUEUR D'OR (FR) 7 b.g. Epalo (GER) – Hot d'Or (FR) (Shafoun (FR)) [2017/18 h101, b69: h21g^3 c25.8m^2 c22.6g* c21m* c20s^3 c22.6m^2 h21.6d^2 c23.8m* c23.8g^3 c26g^4 c24d^2 c24.1g Apr 21] tall, angular gelding: fair form over hurdles: useful handicap chaser: won at Stratford and Newton Abbot in July, and Ludlow in October: third in Sodexo Gold Cup (Handicap Chase) at Ascot in November: stays 3¼m: acts on good to firm and good to soft going. *Paul Nicholls*   **c139 h112**

BRASCOE (IRE) 6 b.g. Craigsteel – Mandysue (IRE) (Mandalus) [2017/18 b15.7v^5 h24.1d^4 h22d Apr 22] third foal: half-brother to a winning pointer by Great Palm: dam unraced sister to fairly useful hurdler/top-class chaser (stayed 29f) Sir Rembrandt: runner-up both completed starts in Irish maiden points: well beaten in bumper: modest form over hurdles. *Jonjo O'Neill*   **h88 b–**

BRASS MONKEY (IRE) 11 b.g. Craigsteel – Saltee Great (IRE) (Fourstars Allstar (USA)) [2017/18 c–, h95: h21m^3 h22d^{pu} h19.9g h23.3d^6 Sep 24] poor handicap hurdler nowadays: maiden chaser: stays 3m: acts on good to firm and heavy going: often wears headgear: tried in tongue tie. *Martin Keighley*   **c– h84**

BRAVE DANCING 4 b.g. Mount Nelson – Purring (USA) (Mountain Cat (USA)) [2017/18 h17.4s^2 h17.4v^4 h17.4v* h16.4s^{pu} c18.4d^2 Apr 20] fair form on Flat: fairly useful form over hurdles: won 4-y-o event at Pau in February: always behind in Fred Winter Juvenile Handicap Hurdle at Cheltenham next time: in cheekpieces, fair form when second at Angers on chasing debut (should improve): has worn tongue tie. *David Cottin, France*   **c101 p h115**

BRAVE EAGLE (IRE) 6 b.g. Yeats (IRE) – Sinful Pleasure (IRE) (Sinndar (IRE)) [2017/18 h123p: h16.8s^2 h20.5v* h20.3v h20.3g^{ur} Apr 18] lengthy gelding: third both starts in Irish maiden points: useful form over hurdles: won handicap at Newbury (by ½ length from Theligny) in December: will be suited by 3m: acts on heavy going: usually races prominently. *Nicky Henderson*   **h130**

BRAVE HELIOS 8 b.g. High Chaparral (IRE) – Renowned (IRE) (Darshaan) [2017/18 c111, h–: h23g^2 c22.6g^2 c25.8d^6 h25g^5 h25g Nov 5] rather leggy gelding: modest handicap hurdler: modest maiden chaser: stays 25f: acts on good to firm and heavy going: wore headgear/tongue tie in 2017/18. *Richard Phillips*   **c93 h97**

BRA

BRAVE JAQ (FR) 7 ch.g. Network (GER) – Galaxie (FR) (Useful (FR)) [2017/18 h–: c22.6d^{pu} Apr 22] placed once from 2 starts in points: maiden hurdler: pulled up in hunter chasing debut: best effort at 2m: acts on soft going: usually wears hood: tried in tongue tie. *R. D. Potter*   c– h–

BRAVENTARA 7 b.m. Kayf Tara – L'Aventure (FR) (Cyborg (FR)) [2017/18 h112: h23.8v^3 h24v^2 h25.5s^F Mar 27] lengthy mare: fairly useful handicap hurdler: second in mares event at Towcester in February: stays 3¼m: acts on good to firm and heavy going. *Tom George*   h118

BRAVE SPARTACUS (IRE) 12 b.g. Spartacus (IRE) – Peaches Polly (Slip Anchor) [2017/18 c–, h116: h20.1g^4 c21.2d^3 c20.1m^2 c21.4g^2 c20.1d^5 c21.2g* c21.4g^{pu} h16v Mar 20] good-topped gelding: fair hurdler: fairly useful handicap chaser: won at Cartmel in August: stays 21f: acts on good to firm and heavy going: has worn hood: usually leads. *Gillian Boanas*   c128 h105

BRAW ANGUS 8 b.g. Alflora (IRE) – Suilven (Teenoso (USA)) [2017/18 h108: h23.1s^4 h23.1v^5 h23.8s^{pu} h25s^{pu} h19.5s^{pu} Apr 27] fair handicap hurdler: stays 21f: acts on heavy going: in cheekpieces last 2 starts: temperament under suspicion. *Kim Bailey*   h98

BREAKING BITS (IRE) 11 br.g. Oscar (IRE) – Lantern Lark (IRE) (Be My Native (USA)) [2017/18 h108: h19.3m* h20g Jun 3] workmanlike gelding: modest handicap hurdler: won at Carlisle in May: stays 2¾m: acts on firm and good to soft going: tried in cheekpieces: front runner/races prominently. *Jamie Snowden*   h98

BREAKING GROUND (IRE) 6 b.g. Echo of Light – Mayfair (Green Desert (USA)) [2017/18 b16.8m h16g^3 h16m^6 h16g h15.8g h19.8s h19.8s^5 h23.9s h20.5v h21.4s* h19.8v^{ur} h19.7s^5 h21s^5 h23.1d* Apr 24] £16,000 5-y-o: half-brother to several winners, including fair hurdler/useful chaser Sou'wester (2m-2½m winner, by Fleetwood), stayed 23f, and modest hurdler Drawn Free (2m winner, by Tagula): dam 6f winner: disqualified (positive sample) after first past post on last of 6 starts in Irish points: tailed off in bumper: modest handicap hurdler: won at Wincanton in February and Exeter in April: stays 23f: acts on soft going: tried in headgear: wears tongue tie: often travels strongly. *Richenda Ford*   h96 b–

BREAKING WAVES (IRE) 4 b.g. Yeats (IRE) – Acoola (IRE) (Flemensfirth (USA)) [2017/18 b15.8d* Mar 26] €30,000 3-y-o: fifth foal: half-brother to bumper winner/smart hurdler Ok Corral (2m-21f winner, by Mahler), stays 3m, and bumper winner/fairly useful hurdler Lithic (2m-21f winner, by Westerner): dam, winning pointer, sister to very smart hurdler/top-class chaser (stayed 29f) Tidal Bay: 12/1, won conditionals/amateur bumper at Huntingdon (impressively, by 2¾ lengths from Some Day Soon) on debut: likely to improve. *Noel Williams*   b102 p

BREAN GOLF BIRDIE 6 br.m. Striking Ambition – Straight As A Die (Pyramus (USA)) [2017/18 h81: h18.5m h16g^3 h16.8d h16.8s h15.3s^4 h15.3v^6 h16.5s h15.3v^{pu} Mar 28] stocky, plain mare: poor maiden hurdler: wears hood: often races towards rear. *Carroll Gray*   h76

BREATH OF BLIGHTY (FR) 7 b.g. Policy Maker (IRE) – Nosika d'Airy (FR) (Oblat (FR)) [2017/18 c120, h102: c20.3g^6 c19.9g^4 c18g^6 c20.5d^2 c20.5d^F Jan 13] maiden hurdler: fairly useful handicap chaser: second at Kempton in November: stayed 2½m: acted on soft and good to firm going: tried in cheekpieces: wore tongue tie: dead. *Paul Webber*   c117 h–

BRECON HILL (IRE) 5 b.g. Arcano (IRE) – Bryanstown Girl (IRE) (Kalanisi (IRE)) [2017/18 b92: b16.8g^2 b16.7g* h15.8s^5 Feb 22] fairly useful form in bumpers: won at Market Rasen in May: 20/1, shaped well when fifth in novice at Huntingdon (9 lengths behind Starcrossed) on hurdling debut: left Sally Haynes after second start: likely to improve. *Sarah Humphrey*   h107 p b102

BREDON HILL LAD 11 ch.g. Kirkwall – Persian Clover (Abutammam) [2017/18 c98, h–: c16v* c17.8v^4 c19.4v^{pu} c17.8v^3 c19.4v^3 Apr 1] lengthy gelding: winning hurdler: fair handicap chaser: won at Ffos Las in November and Fontwell in December: stays 3m: acts on heavy going: wears cheekpieces/tongue tie: front runner/races prominently. *Susan Gardner*   c106 h–

BREDON HILL LEO 6 b.g. Sulamani (IRE) – Persian Clover (Abutammam) [2017/18 b15.8d^4 b16d Oct 15] poor form in bumpers. *Susan Gardner*   b67

BREEZE ALONG 8 ch.g. Denounce – Briery Breeze (IRE) (Anshan) [2017/18 h–: c15.7d^3 h15.8d^6 h15.5v^5 Jan 31] lengthy gelding: little form over hurdles: 40/1, third in novice at Southwell (20 lengths behind Chirico Vallis) on chasing debut: in hood/tongue tie last 3 starts: has joined Dan Skelton. *Sam Thomas*   c82 h58

BRI

BRELADE 6 b.g. Presenting – Polivalente (FR) (Poliglote) [2017/18 h139, b108: c18v² c16.2d² c17v² c16.2s⁴ c16v³ h16.8v h16v² h16g⁵ Apr 21] sturdy gelding: useful handicap hurdler: fifth in Scottish Champion Hurdle at Ayr (4¾ lengths behind Midnight Shadow) in April: similar form over fences: second in maidens at Punchestown (7 lengths behind Petit Mouchoir) in October and Navan (11 lengths behind Footpad) in November: stays 2¼m: acts on heavy going: in tongue tie last 3 starts. *Gordon Elliott, Ireland* — **c134 h136**

BRELAN D'AS (FR) 7 b.g. Crillon (FR) – Las de La Croix (FR) (Grand Tresor (FR)) [2017/18 h139p: c20.9s³ c24.2v³ c19.2v⁵ h20.3v h20.3g Apr 18] fairly useful form over hurdles: similar form over fences: best effort when third in maiden at Ffos Las in October, though found less than looked likely: stays 2½m: acts on soft going: usually wears hood: wears tongue tie: usually races towards rear. *Paul Nicholls* — **c123 h125**

BRERETON (IRE) 7 b.g. Kalanisi (IRE) – Westgrove Berry (IRE) (Presenting) [2017/18 h81: h19d c23.6g c20g^F c19.4v⁶ Jan 19] useful-looking gelding: poor form over hurdles: little impact over fences: in cheekpieces last 2 starts: often wears tongue tie: has joined Richard Harper. *Richard Woollacott* — **c– h–**

BRESLIN 5 ch.g. Atlantic Sport (USA) – Aries (GER) (Big Shuffle (USA)) [2017/18 h15.7g⁶ h17.7v^pu Dec 26] fair on Flat, stayed 2m: no form over hurdles: dead. *Sheena West* — **h–**

BREWIN'UPASTORM (IRE) 5 b.g. Milan – Daraheen Diamond (IRE) (Husyan (USA)) [2017/18 b16.2s²* b16.3v⁴ Feb 10] €35,000 3-y-o, £250,000 4-y-o: brother to useful 19f hurdle winner Get Back In Line, closely related to fairly useful hurdler/useful chaser Glam Gerry (2½m/21f winner, by Dr Massini), and half-brother to 2 winners, including useful hurdler/chaser Kimberlite King (2m-21f winner, by Good Thyne): dam unraced: won point on debut: useful form in bumpers: won conditionals/amateur event at Hereford (impressively, by 9 lengths from Portrush Ted) in January: shaped well when fourth in listed event at Newbury (13½ lengths behind Acey Milan) in February: good prospect. *Olly Murphy* — **b112 p**

BRIAC (FR) 7 b.g. Kapgarde (FR) – Jarwin Do (FR) (Grand Tresor (FR)) [2017/18 h99: h15.9d⁴ h15.9v⁶ h15.9v⁵ h16v* h16s³ Mar 9] modest handicap hurdler: won at Sandown (conditional) in February: stays 2½m: acts on heavy going: tried in headgear: front runner/ races prominently. *Mark Pattinson* — **h96**

BRIAN BORANHA (IRE) 7 b.g. Brian Boru – Tapneiram (IRE) (Kahyasi) [2017/18 h108: h23.1g² h23.1g² c19.2g² c21.4g⁴ c24.2g² c24.2d* Sep 5] rather lightly-built gelding: fair handicap hurdler: fairly useful form over fences: won novice handicap at Hexham in September: will stay long distances: acts on soft going. *Peter Niven* — **c121 h107**

BRIANSTORM (IRE) 6 b.g. Brian Boru – Coco Moon (IRE) (Classic Cliche (IRE)) [2017/18 b16.8g⁴ h16.4g³ h15.5d² h16.3s³ h16.5s* h16s* h20s^pu Apr 14] €3,500 3-y-o, €40,000 4-y-o: well-made gelding: second foal: dam unraced half-sister to useful hurdler/ chaser (stays 25f) Warden Hill: winning Irish pointer: fair form in bumpers: better effort when third at Cheltenham: fairly useful form over hurdles: won novices at Taunton in January and Sandown in March: should stay beyond 2m: acts on soft going: wears hood: usually leads: has joined Venetia Williams. *Warren Greatrex* — **h121 b94**

BRICBRACSMATE 10 b.g. Revoque (IRE) – Blissphilly (Primo Dominie) [2017/18 h100: h16.7g³ May 21] modest form over hurdles: in cheekpieces last 2 starts. *Michael Mullineaux* — **h84**

BRIDANE REBEL (IRE) 7 b.m. Milan – Rebel Dream (IRE) (Dushyantor (USA)) [2017/18 b16.2g³ h22.1d⁵ h15.8m h15.8g* h19.9d⁴ h23.9s⁶ h15.8d² h16.8d h19.6s⁵ h25v³ h23.1v* h25.5s⁴ Mar 27] fair hurdler: won conditionals novice at Uttoxeter in July and mares handicap at Market Rasen (by 6 lengths from Milly Baloo) in March: stayed 25f: acted on heavy going: often wore headgear: usually wore tongue tie: dead. *Jennie Candlish* — **h105 b75**

BRIDEY'S LETTUCE (IRE) 6 b.g. Iffraaj – Its On The Air (IRE) (King's Theatre (IRE)) [2017/18 h16.7g h15.5d⁶ h15.5s³ h20.6s Dec 26] fair on Flat, stays 16.5f: modest form over hurdles: in hood last 2 starts. *Charles Pogson* — **h88**

BRIDGE OF CALLY (IRE) 5 b.g. September Storm (GER) – Cathy's Pal (IRE) (Exit To Nowhere (USA)) [2017/18 b69: b15.7g⁶ h15.8d⁵ h15.7s⁵ h15.7v³ h19s⁶ Mar 26] poor form in bumpers: fair form over hurdles: should stay beyond 2m: usually leads. *Harry Whittington* — **h104 b74**

BRIDLE LOANAN (IRE) 5 b.g. Getaway (GER) – Hanora O'Brien (IRE) (Bob Back (USA)) [2017/18 b17.7s⁴ Apr 15] €10,500 3-y-o: fourth foal: half-brother to fairly useful hurdler Mr Nicolls (17f winner, by Oscar): dam unraced half-sister to useful hurdler (17f winner) Milo Man: completed only once in 4 starts in Irish points, though clear when fell last on final one: 12/1, some encouragement when fourth in bumper at Plumpton (22¼ lengths behind Baddesley Knight): open to improvement. *Gary Moore* — **b77 p**

BRI

BRIERY BELLE 9 b.m. King's Theatre (IRE) – Briery Ann (Anshan) [2017/18 c139, h–: c23.9g⁴ Nov 9] strong mare: winning hurdler: useful chaser, below form sole start in 2017/18: stays 3m: acts on heavy going: often races prominently. *Henry Daly*   **c122** **h–**

BRIERY EXPRESS 5 b.m. Rail Link – Blackbriery Thyne (IRE) (Good Thyne (USA)) [2017/18 b16.5v² Apr 12] fourth foal: half-sister to bumper winner/fairly useful hurdler Meadowcroft Boy (2m/17f winner, by Kayf Tara): dam (h109), 2m hurdle winner, half-sister to useful hurdler/chaser (stays 21f) Briery Queen and useful staying chaser Briery Fox: in hood, 10/1, promise when second in mares maiden bumper at Taunton (8 lengths behind Miss Heritage): better to come. *Noel Williams*   **b86 p**

BRIERY QUEEN 9 b.m. King's Theatre (IRE) – Briery Gale (Strong Gale) [2017/18 h140: c19.2s* Nov 15] useful-looking mare: useful hurdler: 8/1, won novice at Exeter (comfortably by 3¼ lengths from Chameron) on chasing debut: stays 21f: acts on soft going: wears hood: often races towards rear/travels strongly: open to improvement over fences. *Noel Williams*   **c140 p** **h–**

BRIGADE OF GUARDS (IRE) 4 b.g. Presenting – Lasado (IRE) (Jurado (USA)) [2017/18 b16g⁵ b16.3s Mar 24] £50,000 3-y-o: sturdy gelding: brother to bumper winner Captain Woodie and half-brother to several winners, including fairly useful hurdler/useful chaser Coverholder (2m-23f winner) and useful hurdler Not Many Left (2½m winner) (both by Oscar): dam unraced half-sister to top-class chaser (stayed 3¼m) Harbour Pilot: fair form in bumpers: better effort when fifth at Kempton in February. *Alan King*   **b87**

BRIGADIER BOB (IRE) 5 b.g. Excellent Art – Plausabelle (Royal Applause) [2017/18 b16s² h15.8v⁴ h16.7s⁴ Mar 24] €20,000 3-y-o: good-topped gelding: third foal: dam 1m-9.5f winner: second in maiden bumper at Warwick (12 lengths behind Thebannerkingrebel): modest form over hurdles. *Kerry Lee*   **h88** **b86**

BRIGHT NEW DAWN (IRE) 11 br.g. Presenting – Shuil Dorcha (IRE) (Bob Back (USA)) [2017/18 c145§, h127§: c15.9d⁶ c20.2v^{tt} c16s^F c16.3v Mar 16] rangy, useful-looking gelding: fairly useful hurdler: smart handicap chaser, below best in 2017/18: stays 3m: acts on heavy going: has worn headgear/tongue tie: one to treat with caution (refused to race second start). *Venetia Williams*   **c131 §** **h– §**

BRIGHT PROSPECT (IRE) 9 b.g. Kutub (IRE) – Bright Future (IRE) (Satco (FR)) [2017/18 c116, h87: c23.8m² c23.4s* c20d⁵ Mar 31] winning hurdler: fair handicap chaser: won at Kelso in January: stays 3m: acts on soft going: often wears cheekpieces. *Jackie Stephen*   **c112** **h–**

BRIGHTS PARK (IRE) 6 b.g. Mahler – Ellesmere (IRE) (Turtle Island (IRE)) [2017/18 b16.7g b20.8d h16.7s⁶ h18.6v⁶ Jan 17] £4,500 3-y-o: second foal: dam, little form in points, half-sister to useful hurdler/fairly useful chaser (stayed 4¼m) Earth Planet: well beaten in bumper: modest form over hurdles: bred to stay 3m+. *Nick Kent*   **h95** **b–**

BRIGHT TOMORROW (IRE) 7 b.g. Robin des Pres (FR) – Gweedara (IRE) (Saddlers' Hall (IRE)) [2017/18 c22.5g⁵ h17.7g h16g h21.2d³ h21.3s² h23.1v h21.4d^{ur} Apr 22] €20,000 3-y-o: first foal: dam unraced half-sister to very smart chaser (stayed 31f) Hey Big Spender: fair handicap hurdler: fairly useful chaser, well held sole start over fences in 2017/18: left Mrs J. Harrington after first start: stays 21f: acts on soft and good to firm going: has worn cheekpieces, including last 3 starts: usually wears tongue tie: often races prominently: often let down by jumping. *Warren Greatrex*   **c– x** **h108**

BRIGID JO (IRE) 5 ch.m. Presenting – Tchouina (FR) (Broadway Flyer (USA)) [2017/18 h15.8d^{ro} h20.6g⁶ Aug 19] fifth foal: half-sister to Miss Chief (2¼m hurdle winner in France, by Shirocco): dam (h96), placed over hurdles in France (10.5f winner on Flat), half-sister to useful French hurdler (2¼m-19f winner) Magic Fabien: no form over hurdles, ran out on debut. *Nigel Hawke*   **h–**

BRILLARE MOMENTO (IRE) 7 b.m. Milan – Sunshine Leader (IRE) (Supreme Leader) [2017/18 h136p, b95: h21.6g² h21.1g* h20.3s h16s⁴ h19.2s* h20.3v h20.3g Apr 19] well-made mare: has had breathing operation: useful hurdler: won novice at Cheltenham in October and handicap at Towcester (by 1¼ lengths from Red Indian) in February: stays 2¾m: acts on heavy going: in cheekpieces last 2 starts: tried in tongue tie: front runner/races prominently. *Martin Keighley*   **h134**

BRINESTINE (USA) 9 b.g. Bernstein (USA) – Miss Zafonic (FR) (Zafonic (USA)) [2017/18 c89, h86: c18.2m³ Apr 25] angular gelding: modest hurdler: similar form over fences: unproven beyond 17f: best form on good going: often wears headgear: wears tongue tie. *Emma-Jane Bishop*   **c77** **h–**

BRI

BRING BACK CHARLIE 8 b.g. Green Card (USA) – Nafertiti (IRE) (Bob Back (USA)) [2017/18 h85: h15.8g³ h15.8g⁶ h18.7m² h20g⁴ h16.3m⁴ h16.3g² h15.8g³ Nov 9] modest handicap hurdler: should stay 2½m: acts on good to firm and good to soft going: wears cheekpieces. *Nigel Twiston-Davies*   **h89**

BRIO CONTI (FR) 7 gr.g. Dom Alco (FR) – Cadoulie Wood (FR) (Cadoudal (FR)) [2017/18 h140p, b97: c20d* Nov 13] good-topped gelding: useful hurdler: 2/5, won novice at Carlisle (by short head from Alzammaar) on chasing debut: stays 21f: acts on heavy going: strong traveller: remains open to significant improvement over fences despite absence. *Paul Nicholls*   **c129 P h–**

BRISTOL DE MAI (FR) 7 gr.g. Saddler Maker (IRE) – La Bole Night (FR) (April Night (FR)) [2017/18 c159, h–: c24.2s* c25.6v* c24d⁶ c25.3v³ c25s² Apr 12]   **c165 x h–**

There was a slightly different look to the programme on Betfair Chase day at Haydock in the latest season. The long-standing 'Fixed Brush' Handicap Hurdle was superseded by the more valuable Betfair Stayers Handicap Hurdle over conventional obstacles and, more significantly, the £100,000 Betfair Price Rush Hurdle, a relatively new conditions event which unfortunately coincided with a period when good two-mile hurdlers in Britain have been in particularly short supply, was discontinued after just three runnings (the race never attracted a field bigger than the five who lined up for the first edition and it suffered from being run just seven days before the Grade 1 'Fighting Fifth' at Newcastle). As for the big race itself, the thirteenth running of the Betfair Chase (registered as the Lancashire Chase) was contested over a new distance of three miles, one furlong and 125 yards, almost a furlong and a half longer than previously. Concerns had been expressed about the three-mile start on the chase course because it was so close to the first bend, with some jockeys apparently warning about the dangers of a hectic scramble in a big field (though the Betfair has never had a double-figure field). Moving back

bet365 Charlie Hall Chase, Wetherby—a record fifth win in the race for Nigel Twiston-Davies and a 1,2 for the stable too, with the grey Bristol de Mai holding off the rallying Blaklion

Betfair Chase, Haydock—yet another wide-margin win in bottomless ground at Haydock for Bristol de Mai; three-times winner Cue Card (noseband) plugs on for second

the start, closer to the stands so that the runners do not go straight into a bend, means that there are now nineteen fences instead of eighteen, with the last fence in the final straight being jumped three times.

Extending the distance of the Betfair Chase had not the slightest bearing on the result of the latest running which mud-loving Bristol de Mai would almost certainly have won at any distance from two miles to four miles on the day. If it's soft or heavy, and it's Haydock, Bristol de Mai is in his element, as he has demonstrated on his three appearances at the track. Racing with plenty of enthusiasm and making much or all of the running on each of the three occasions, he has run away with the Grade 2 Altcar Novices' Chase by thirty-two lengths (in the 2015/16 season), the Peter Marsh Handicap under 11-2, off a BHA mark of 154, by twenty-two (in the 2016/17 season) and now the Grade 1 Betfair Chase by fifty-seven lengths. That last performance gave Bristol de Mai the distinction of being the widest-margin winner of any Grade 1 race over jumps, succeeding Apple's Jade who won the Anniversary Hurdle at the 2016 Aintree Grand National meeting by fifty-one lengths. Judges are now able to record winning distances up to two hundred lengths, though, before 2009, a margin of more than thirty lengths was officially returned as 'a distance'. Official distances are calculated according to a length-per-second scale that varies with the prevailing going; the runner-up in the Betfair, Cue Card, finished fourteen and a quarter seconds behind Bristol de Mai which, using four lengths per second (for soft/heavy ground), converts to fifty-seven lengths (had the Betfair been run on good ground, the calculation would have been five lengths per second, converting to seventy-one lengths).

The withdrawal of Cheltenham Gold Cup winner Sizing John in the week leading up to the race, on account of the heavy ground, took some of the gloss off the latest Betfair Chase. However, the field of six still contained three Grade 1 winners from the current calendar year, the veteran Cue Card (trying to equal Kauto Star's four Betfair Chase victories), Outlander (winner of the Champion Chase at Down Royal last time) and Tea For Two (who had beaten Cue Card into second in the Aintree Bowl). It was Bristol de Mai who started a short-priced favourite, though, having won the bet365 Charlie Hall Chase with a 6-lb penalty at Wetherby in game fashion three weeks earlier from his stablemate Blaklion. Cue Card and the 2015 Cheltenham Gold Cup winner Coneygree both returned to action in the Charlie Hall, and Cue Card still held every chance when falling five out (Coneygree had been pulled up soon after making a bad mistake at the eighth when possibly unsighted by the low-lying sun, which Cue Card's jockey also blamed).

Bristol de Mai's rivals in the Betfair Chase were floundering a long way from home and his complete demolition of them—for the record, Outlander finished third, nine lengths behind Cue Card—begged the question of how much credit Bristol de Mai should be given. Taking the form at anything like face value would have sent Bristol de Mai's rating 'off the scale', even making adjustments for the fact that extreme conditions can often lead to fields finishing strung out and a winner's superiority being exaggerated. The conservative view eventually taken of Bristol de Mai's performance had all his rivals running way below form, though a time comparison with the following handicap over the same distance (in which only two finished) suggested Bristol de Mai had probably recorded a performance into the 170s (Bristol de Mai's time was ten seconds faster than the winner of the handicap and he ran to a timefigure of 174, one of the highest recorded in the first season of Timeform timefigures for jumps courses in Britain and Ireland, about which there is more in the essays on Footpad and Min).

Whatever he achieved in terms of form, Bristol de Mai deserves plenty of credit for maintaining a relentless gallop in bottomless conditions in the Betfair Chase, and for winning without coming off the bridle. However, it was obvious that none of his rivals could have given anything like their true running and the conservative assessment of his Haydock performance was borne out on the balance of the form he showed on his three subsequent appearances. He managed only sixth of seven finishers, well beaten behind Might Bite, in the King George VI Chase at Kempton, seemingly not the same horse away from the mud, although his jumping also let him down on this occasion when he finally lost his place with a bad mistake at the third last. Conditions were in his favour on his two other outings when he ran much better. His less than fluent jumping again counted against him when he was a creditable third to Definitly Red and American in the Cotswold Chase at Cheltenham at the end of January, one paced after holding every chance on the home turn. Bristol de Mai saved his best until last and got right back on track with a much better effort against odds-on Might Bite in the Betway Bowl at Aintree. Might Bite and Bristol de Mai dominated the race throughout, with Bristol de Mai making most, at times joined by Might Bite, until outclassed in the home straight. Bristol de Mai was eventually beaten seven lengths, as Might Bite asserted from the third last, but he

Mr Simon Munir & Mr Isaac Souede's "Bristol de Mai"

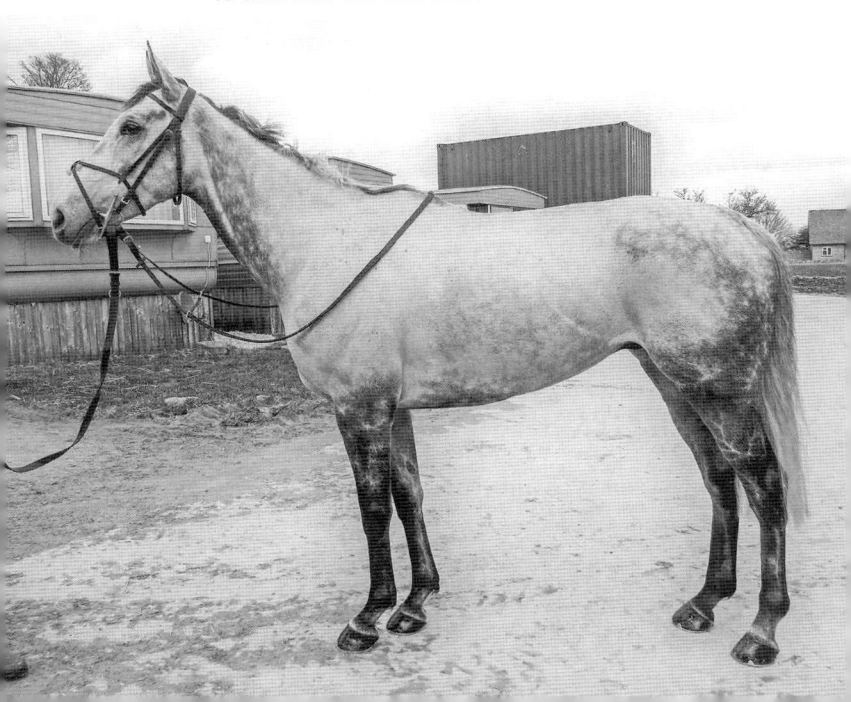

emerged with plenty of credit from a race that was a fine spectacle. Clan des Obeaux kept on for third, three and a quarter lengths behind Bristol de Mai, with Sizing Codelco and Sub Lieutenant probably flattered in fourth and fifth, ahead of the well-held Tea For Two who never promised to repeat his heroics of twelve months earlier (Definitly Red unseated his rider early on after a bad mistake).

Bristol de Mai (FR) (gr.g. 2011)
- Saddler Maker (IRE) (b 1998)
  - Sadler's Wells (b 1981)
    - Northern Dancer
    - Fairy Bridge
  - Animatrice (b 1985)
    - Alleged
    - Alexandrie
- La Bole Night (FR) (gr 1999)
  - April Night (gr 1986)
    - Kaldoun
    - My Destiny
  - Grageline (b 1994)
    - Hellios
    - Rousseliere

Bristol de Mai, a tall gelding, seems to have been featuring in good races for some time but this is the first occasion that he has had an essay in *Chasers & Hurdlers*. After starting his career in France, he made his mark in Britain as a juvenile hurdler by winning the Finale Juvenile Hurdle at Chepstow (in extremely testing conditions) and reaching a place in the Anniversary Hurdle at Aintree (on good ground). He looked the type to progress and made into a smart novice chaser in his second season when his four victories also included the Grade 1 Scilly Isles Novices' Chase, as well as the Altcar at Haydock, before putting up his best effort when runner-up to Black Hercules in the Golden Miller at the Cheltenham Festival. Bristol de Mai made up into a very smart chaser in 2016/17—when the Peter Marsh gave him his only victory—and progressed again in the latest season when the Betfair Chase provided him with a third Grade 1.

Bristol de Mai's sire the Sadler's Wells stallion Saddler Maker died in May 2016 and, typically, his reputation has soared since his demise as he has also enjoyed success with the fine mare Apple's Jade and such as the high-class Alpha des Obeaux, the useful juvenile hurdler Apple's Shakira (a sister to Apple's Jade) and the useful novice chaser Dinaria des Obeaux in the latest season. Like Bristol de Mai, most of Saddler Maker's progeny are AQPS (Autre Que Pur Sang, or other than thoroughbred). Saddler Maker never won a race and, when he took up stallion duties at the age of seven (he was a close relation to French champion jumps sire Poliglote), he received only very modest support at first (his first three crops reportedly comprising only fifteen foals). He had stronger backing in the period before his death, his last crop in 2017 numbering more than fifty. Bristol de Mai's dam La Bole Night, a selle francais (French saddlebred), was only lightly raced but Bristol de Mai is the third of her first four foals to have been successful, the others being the French mile and a half winner Riva (by Winning Smile) and the French fourteen and a half furlong winner Ula de Mai (by Passing Sale). Bristol de Mai stays three and a quarter miles and, although he has won on good to soft going, he revels in the mud. A sketchy jumper sometimes, he usually makes the running or races prominently. He was equipped with ear plugs in the Charlie Hall Chase and the Betfair Chase, both of which are likely to be on his agenda again in 2018/19. *Nigel Twiston-Davies*

BRITANIO BELLO (FR) 7 b.g. Irish Wells (FR) – Tchi Tchi Bang Bang (FR) (Perrault) [2017/18 c–, h–: c16.5g^5 c19.7s^{ur} c23.5s^{pu} Dec 5] tall, angular gelding: winning hurdler: little show over fences. *Gary Moore*   c–
h–

BROADWAY BELLE 8 b.m. Lucarno (USA) – Theatre Belle (King's Theatre (IRE)) [2017/18 h73: h23.9g^2 h23.3s^4 h22.7g^5 h23.4s^3 h24.1s h25.8s^3 h25.3s^2 h27v* h27v^6 Apr 13] modest handicap hurdler: won at Sedgefield in March: stays 27f: acts on good to firm and heavy going: races prominently. *Chris Grant*   h85

BROADWAY BUFFALO (IRE) 10 ch.g. Broadway Flyer (USA) – Benbradagh Vard (IRE) (Le Bavard (FR)) [2017/18 c22.9v^{ur} c23s^5 Jan 9] good-topped gelding: winning hurdler: smart handicap chaser, off nearly 2 years before return: stays 4m: acts on heavy going: wears headgear: usually wears tongue tie. *David Pipe*   c132
h–

BROADWAY DREAMS 4 b.g. Oasis Dream – Rosa Eglanteria (Nayef (USA)) [2017/18 h15.3g^6 h16d^5 h16s^6 Dec 4] fairly useful maiden on Flat, stays 1¼m: well held in juvenile hurdles. *Michael Blake*   h61

BROADWAY SYMPHONY (IRE) 11 ch.g. Broadway Flyer (USA) – Flying Hooves (IRE) (Orchestra) [2017/18 c23.8d[6] Mar 22] workmanlike gelding: has had breathing operation: point winner: maiden hurdler: fair chaser at one time, well held sole start under Rules in 2017/18: stays 3m: acts on heavy going: tried in hood. *Tracey L. Bailey*   c75 h–

BROCKTON GANDT 6 br.m. Erhaab (USA) – Oyster Bay (Mandalus) [2017/18 b–: h22g[pu] h16.7s h21.2d[pu] Dec 20] no form in bumper/over hurdles: in hood last 2 starts. *Mike Hammond*   h–

BRODY BLEU (FR) 11 b.g. Kotky Bleu (FR) – Brodie Blue (FR) (Agent Bleu (FR)) [2017/18 c118, h–: c23g[3] c19.2g h22g Aug 3] strong gelding: maiden hurdler: fairly useful chaser at best, below form in 2017/18: left Miss L. Wallace after first start: stays 3m: acts on good to firm and heavy going: tried in cheekpieces: in tongue tie last 2 starts. *Alexandra Dunn*   c87 h–

BROKE AWAY (IRE) 6 br.m. Stowaway – Not Broke Yet (IRE) (Broken Hearted) [2017/18 b16s[5] b16.7g[4] b16.8m b16.7g Oct 31] first foal: dam (h106) 2m hurdle winner: modest form in bumpers: left Ms Margaret Mullins after second start: tried in hood. *Alexandra Dunn*   b81

BROKEN EAGLE (USA) 10 b.g. Broken Vow (USA) – Tricky Bird (USA) (Storm Bird (CAN)) [2017/18 c106, h–: c16.3d[pu] c23.6m* c27.5d[pu] Jun 9] leggy, close-coupled gelding: prolific point winner: maiden hurdler: fairly useful hunter chaser: won novice at Huntingdon in May: stays 3m: acts on good to firm going: wears tongue tie. *Alan Hill*   c116 h–

BROKEN QUEST (IRE) 6 b.g. Ask – Broken Thought (IRE) (Broken Hearted) [2017/18 b20s[4] h21.6s h16.8v[pu] h19.6s* h21s* h19.8v* h20.5v[3] h21.4v[5] Apr 9] €10,500 3-y-o: second foal: closely related to fairly useful hurdler Never Equalled (2m-2½m winner, by Brian Boru): dam maiden pointer: off mark in Irish maiden points at second attempt: fairly useful handicap hurdler: completed hat-trick at Huntingdon in January, and Kempton and Sandown in February: stays 21f: raced only on soft/heavy going: usually wears tongue tie. *David Dennis*   h119

BRONCO BILLY (IRE) 8 b.g. Flemensfirth (USA) – La Fisarmonica (IRE) (Accordion) [2017/18 c110, h–: c24g[4] c26.1g[pu] c25.5d[6] c25.2g[pu] Nov 29] well-made gelding: winning hurdler: fair handicap chaser: won at Warwick in May: stays 25f: acts on good to soft going: usually wears cheekpieces: wears tongue tie: temperament under suspicion. *Jonjo O'Neill*   c110 h–

BRONZALLURE (IRE) 5 b.g. Dubai Destination (USA) – Satco Street (IRE) (Satco (FR)) [2017/18 b16.7g[5] h16.7s h16.7s h16.7v h21s Apr 9] some encouragement in bumper on debut: little show over hurdles: should be suited by further than 17f: tried in cheekpieces: wears tongue tie. *Oliver Greenall*   h72 b74

BROOM TIP (IRE) 6 b.g. Flemensfirth (USA) – Norabelle (FR) (Alamo Bay (USA)) [2017/18 h98b, b–: h16.3g[4] h19.5v[pu] h23.8s c20.3d[F] Apr 21] fair form over hurdles: fell 2 out in novice handicap won by Kapcorse at Bangor on chasing debut, might have been placed: should stay 2¾m+: acts on soft going: often races towards rear. *Tom George*   c110 h107

BROTHER BENNETT (FR) 8 gr.g. Martaline – La Gaminerie (FR) (Cadoudal (FR)) [2017/18 c88, h–: c16.3s[3] c16.3s[4] h15.8v[3] c17v[6] c16.5d[5] c17s* Apr 15] well-made gelding: poor maiden hurdler: poor handicap chaser: won at Plumpton in April: unproven beyond 17f: acts on heavy going: has worn headgear, including last 4 starts: wears tongue tie: temperamental. *Zoe Davison*   c80 § h79

BROTHER BRIAN (IRE) 10 b.g. Millenary – Miner Detail (IRE) (Presenting) [2017/18 c19.1d[3] Dec 15] lengthy gelding: useful hurdler: 7/1, third in novice at Doncaster (29 lengths behind Peter The Mayo Man) on chasing debut after 32-month absence: barely stays 3m: acts on soft going, probably on good for firm: should improve over fences. *Hughie Morrison*   c107 p h–

BROTHERLY COMPANY (IRE) 6 b.g. Fast Company (IRE) – Good Lady (IRE) (Barathea (IRE)) [2017/18 h119: h19.1g[F] h18.5m[3] h20m h16.6d[pu] h19.3s[3] ab16g[2] Mar 2] angular gelding: fairly useful handicap hurdler: third at Newton Abbot in May: left Harry Fry after third start: stays 19f: acts on soft and good to firm going: tried in cheekpieces: often races prominently. *Joanne Foster*   h116

BROTHER NORPHIN 6 b.g. Norse Dancer (IRE) – Orphina (IRE) (Orpen (USA)) [2017/18 h–, b–: h17.7v[3] h15.9v[6] h24s[3] h23v[2] h23.9s[2] h23.1v[pu] Apr 8] poor maiden hurdler: stayed 3m: acted on heavy going: tried in headgear/tongue tie: often raced towards rear: dead. *Seamus Mullins*   h77

BRO

BROTHER SCOTT 11 b.g. Kirkwall – Crimson Shower (Dowsing (USA)) [2017/18 c88, h–: c20.1g³ c15.6g² c21.2g* c21.2s* c21.2d⁶ c19.3g² c21.1g² c19.3d c21.1g⁶ c20d² c20s Dec 3] winning hurdler: modest handicap chaser: won at Cartmel in June and July: left Sue Smith after fourth start: best at shorter than 2¾m: acts on good to firm and heavy going: front runner/races prominently. *Barbara Butterworth* **c97 h–**

BROTHER TEDD 9 gr.g. Kayf Tara – Neltina (Neltino) [2017/18 c135, h145: c20g* c21m² Jun 16] well-made gelding: smart hurdler: useful chaser: won 3-runner maiden at Uttoxeter (by ½ length from Beat That) in May: will stay 3m: acts on good to firm and heavy going: often races prominently. *Philip Hobbs* **c136 h–**

BROUGHTONS ADMIRAL 4 b.g. Born To Sea (IRE) – Chanter (Lomitas) [2017/18 h16.2s⁵ h16.8v⁴ ab16d⁴ h16.2s* h16.5s⁵ Apr 14] neat gelding: fair maiden on Flat, stays 2m: fair form over hurdles: won juvenile maiden at Hereford in March: in cheekpieces last 3 starts. *Alastair Ralph* **h113**

BROUGHTONS RHYTHM 9 b.g. Araafa (IRE) – Broughton Singer (IRE) (Common Grounds) [2017/18 h114: h16d⁶ h17.7v³ c18.2s³ c15.7v² Apr 9] lengthy gelding: fair handicap hurdler: similar form over fences: better effort when second in novice handicap at Wincanton in April: stays 19f: acts on heavy going. *Oliver Sherwood* **c108 h107**

BROUGHTONS STAR (NZ) 11 ch.g. Starcraft (NZ) – Marrakech (IRE) (Barathea (IRE)) [2017/18 h103: h17.2m h20.4d^F h16g³ h16.2g² h16.2m⁴ h16.3g² h16s* h16.7g h16s⁴ c19.2v^pu Sep 22] workmanlike gelding: fair handicap hurdler: won at Sligo in August: pulled up in maiden on chasing debut: stayed 21f: acted on soft and good to firm going: wore hood: tried in tongue tie: dead. *Gordon Elliott, Ireland* **c– h103**

BROWN BEAR (IRE) 7 b.g. Yeats (IRE) – Moray Firth (UAE) (Halling (USA)) [2017/18 c96, h92: c21.7m⁶ h21.6d* c21.1m* h19.3g* h21g⁵ c17.8v^pu c21.6d⁶ Feb 25] useful-looking gelding: fair handicap hurdler: won at Fontwell in May and Ascot (novice) in November: fair handicap chaser: won at Fontwell in June: stays 2¾m: acts on good to firm and good to soft going: usually wears cheekpieces. *Nick Gifford* **c104 h111**

BROWN PADDY (IRE) 8 b.g. Morozov (USA) – River Breeze (IRE) (Sharifabad (IRE)) [2017/18 h–, b–: h25d^pu May 1] maiden pointer: little show in bumper/over hurdles. *Laura Hurley* **h–**

BROWN REVEL 9 b.m. Revoque (IRE) – Brown Seal (Arctic Lord) [2017/18 c23g⁵ c22.6m⁵ h23d⁵ h24d⁴ c24s^pu c25.5s^pu Nov 22] third foal: half-sister to a winning pointer by Sir Harry Lewis: dam winning pointer: point winner: no form over hurdles/fences: in tongue tie last 3 starts. *Steve Flook* **c– h–**

BROWN TRIX (IRE) 8 b.g. Flemensfirth (USA) – Five Trix (Minster Son) [2017/18 c–: c19.3g⁶ c21.6g^pu c23.8g⁵ c19.3d c24s¹ c24d^pu c26d c25.2v^F c20.1v* c23.9s⁴ c20.1v³ Mar 15] maiden pointer: poor handicap chaser: won at Newcastle in February: left Victor Thompson after third start: stays 2½m: best form on heavy going: wears cheekpieces/ tongue tie: often leads: has bled. *Sam England* **c80**

BROWNVILLE 9 b.g. Kayf Tara – Cool Spice (Karinga Bay) [2017/18 c116, h–: c26.1g* c24d⁵ c26.1d^pu c25.5s⁴ c27.9v^pu Apr 1] winning hurdler: fair handicap chaser: won at Uttoxeter in May: stays 3¾m: acts on heavy going: wears cheekpieces/tongue tie: usually races towards rear. *Nigel Twiston-Davies* **c113 h–**

BRUCE ALMIGHTY (IRE) 7 b.g. Yeats (IRE) – Lady Rolfe (IRE) (Alzao (USA)) [2017/18 h105: c20.3d^pu Jun 8] stocky gelding: fair hurdler: pulled up in novice handicap on chasing debut: stays 21f: acts on good to soft going: often in cheekpieces: temperamental. *Donald McCain* **c– § h– §**

BRUICHLADDICH 6 b.g. Westerner – Highland Cherry (Milan) [2017/18 h100, b60: h24.3v² h22.8v² h22.7v^F Feb 15] fairly useful form over hurdles: second in handicap at Ayr in January: stayed 3m: acted on heavy going: often raced prominently: dead. *Iain Jardine* **h119**

BRUNEL WOODS (IRE) 6 b.g. Oscar (IRE) – Golden Bay (Karinga Bay) [2017/18 b93: h16g² Oct 17] fair form in bumpers: 7/1, second in novice at Worcester (21 lengths behind Sword of Fate) on hurdling debut: will be suited by further than 2m: capable of better. *David Dennis* **h85 p**

BRUNSWICK GOLD (IRE) 13 ch.g. Moscow Society (USA) – Tranbu (IRE) (Buckskin (FR)) [2017/18 c21.1s³ May 18] tall, good-topped gelding: multiple point winner: winning hurdler: fair hunter chaser: stays 25f: acts on heavy going: has worn cheekpieces: tried in tongue tie. *S. C. Robinson* **c95 h–**

BRUSHED UP 5 b.m. Doyen (IRE) – Definite Artist (IRE) (Definite Article) [2017/18 b15.8g* b15.8v4 h15.7v4 Mar 29] second foal: dam (b91) second from 2 starts in bumpers: fair form in bumpers: won mares event at Ludlow in December: 12/1, fourth in mares maiden at Towcester (38 lengths behind Phoeniciana) on hurdling debut: should improve. *Tom Symonds* — **h62 p b88**

BRUTAL (IRE) 4 b.g. Pivotal – Loreto (IRE) (Holy Roman Emperor (IRE)) [2017/18 h16d* h17g6 h16.2v2 Sep 27] useful on Flat, stays 9.5f: fair form over hurdles: won juvenile maiden at Cork in August: tried in cheekpieces: wears tongue tie. *Gordon Elliott, Ireland* — **h101**

BRYDEN BOY (IRE) 8 b.g. Craigsteel – Cailin Vic Mo Cri (IRE) (Old Vic) [2017/18 h127: h24.3v5 h23.1v4 h21.4v4 h24.1v2 h22.8v h24g Apr 18] workmanlike gelding: fairly useful handicap hurdler: second at Wetherby in February: stays 3¼m: acts on heavy going: often wears cheekpieces: tried in tongue tie. *Jennie Candlish* — **h126**

BRYNMAWR 8 b.g. Double Trigger (IRE) – Little Feat (Terimon) [2017/18 h112: h23.9s5 h15.7v h20.3v* h19.5v2 h21.4v2 Apr 9] fairly useful handicap hurdler: won novice event at Southwell in March: stays 21f: raced only on soft/heavy going: tried in cheekpieces: usually races prominently. *Colin Tizzard* — **h120**

BUACHAILL ALAINN (IRE) 11 b.g. Oscar (IRE) – Bottle A Knock (IRE) (Le Moss) [2017/18 c128§, h–: c29.4d5 c25g2 c23g2 c25.5g5 c29.2g5 c28.4vpu Nov 25] good-topped gelding: has had breathing operation: winning hurdler: fairly useful handicap chaser: second at Worcester in August: stays 29f: acts on good to firm and heavy going: wears headgear/tongue tie: lazy/moody. *Peter Bowen* — **c123 § h–**

BUBBLE O'CLOCK (IRE) 5 ch.g. Robin des Champs (FR) – Flaithiuil (IRE) (Presenting) [2017/18 b16d Oct 15] first foal: dam unraced half-sister to useful hurdler (stays 21f) My Wigwam Or Yours: tailed off in bumper. *Paul Nicholls* — **b–**

BUBBLES ARCADE 6 b.m. Arkadian Hero (USA) – Alwariah (Xaar) [2017/18 b16.8m* b16.8m3 Jul 7] third foal: dam maiden (stayed 7f): maiden pointer: modest form in bumpers: won conditionals/amateur event at Newton Abbot in June: modest form on Flat. *Rod Millman* — **b77**

BUBLE (IRE) 9 b.g. Milan – Glorious Moments (IRE) (Moonax (IRE)) [2017/18 h108: h20.3g3 c24gpu h21.6m* h18.7g2 h20g* h18.5d5 Sep 11] runner-up 3 of 4 starts in Irish points: fair hurdler: won maiden at Newton Abbot in July and claimer at Worcester in August: pulled up in novice handicap on chasing debut: should stay 3m: acts on good to firm and good to soft going: usually in cheekpieces: often races prominently. *David Bridgwater* — **c– h109**

BUBSY BURBIDGE 7 b.g. Helissio (FR) – Twin Time (Syrtos) [2017/18 h95: c15.7g6 c19.2g4 h15.8v4 Dec 22] modest maiden hurdler: no form over fences: unproven beyond 2m: acts on heavy going: usually races close up. *Neil Mulholland* — **c– h87**

BUCHE DE NOEL (FR) 7 ch.m. Coastal Path – Kyrie (FR) (Lute Antique (FR)) [2017/18 h20d4 Sep 29] lengthy mare: fairly useful handicap hurdler, off 18 months before only outing in 2017/18: winning chaser: stays 2¼m: acts on soft and good to firm going. *Jamie Snowden* — **c– h117**

BUCK BRAVO (IRE) 6 b.g. Mahler – Damoiselle (Sir Harry Lewis (USA)) [2017/18 h70 h20vpu h20v6 h15.8v4 h15.8s Jan 10] placed in points: little form over hurdles: in tongue tie last 3 starts. *David Rees* — **h70**

BUCKBY BOY 5 br.g. Shirocco (GER) – Fair View (GER) (Dashing Blade) [2017/18 b85: b16.7g h19.5d h15.8d6 h18.6d4 h20.3gpu Apr 20] fair in bumpers: modest form over hurdles: usually raced towards rear: dead. *Dan Skelton* — **h90 b–**

BUCKHORN TIMOTHY 9 b.g. Tamure (IRE) – Waimea Bay (Karinga Bay) [2017/18 c134, h–: h25.8g4 h19.8s* c29.5vpu Jan 6] useful handicap hurdler: won at Fontwell in October and Wincanton (by ½ length from Winning Spark) in November: useful chaser, pulled up sole start over fences in 2017/18: stays 3¼m: acts on heavy going. *Colin Tizzard* — **c– h130**

BUCKING THE TREND 10 b.g. Kayf Tara – Macklette (IRE) (Buckskin (FR)) [2017/18 c130, h127: h23.9g Oct 28] good-topped gelding: fairly useful hurdler, below form only start in 2017/18: useful chaser: stays 25f: acts on heavy going: often in cheekpieces: in tongue tie last 2 starts. *Tim Vaughan* — **c– h–**

BUCKLED 8 b.g. Midnight Legend – Mulberry Wine (Benny The Dip (USA)) [2017/18 c–, h107: h20.2v3 h22.7g* h23.8m2 h19.4g* h19.4d5 Mar 16] fairly useful handicap hurdler: won at Kelso (conditional) in October and Musselburgh in December: maiden chaser: stays 3m: acts on firm and soft going: has worn hood: usually races close up. *Sandy Thomson* — **c– h119**

BUC

BUCKLE STREET 5 br.g. Cacique (IRE) – Rose Row (Act One) [2017/18 h114: h23g² h23.3d³ h21.1g⁶ h21.1s⁵ h25.3d* h24s³ h23.5s^ur h24.4s* h24g Apr 18] compact gelding: useful handicap hurdler: won at Catterick in December and Doncaster (by 1¼ lengths from Classic Ben) in February: stays 25f: acts on soft going: wears cheekpieces/tongue tie. *Martin Keighley* **h130**

BUCK MAGIC (IRE) 12 b.g. Albano (IRE) – Green Sea (Groom Dancer (USA)) [2017/18 c19.4g^pu c23g Jul 27] tall gelding: multiple point winner: winning hurdler: fairly useful maiden chaser at best, has deteriorated: stays 3m: acts on soft going: has worn headgear, including in 2017/18. *Alexandra Dunn* **c92 h–**

BUCKONTUPENCE (IRE) 10 b.g. Brian Boru – Miss Od (IRE) (Good Thyne (USA)) [2017/18 h99: h23.1g^pu c19.8g^pu h20g^ur h22g^pu h23g^ur Jul 27] Irish point winner: modest maiden hurdler: pulled up in novice handicap on chasing debut: stays 25f: acts on good to firm going: wore headgear in 2017/18: ungenuine. *James Evans* **c– h93 §**

BUCK'S LAD 8 b.g. Double Trigger (IRE) – April Attraction (FR) (Mark of Esteem (IRE)) [2017/18 h96, b–: h16.8m⁵ May 9] modest form on first of 2 starts over hurdles. *Victor Dartnall* **h–**

BUDARRI 5 b.g. Supreme Sound – Amtaar (Nayef (USA)) [2017/18 b–: h16.2v³ h16.2v⁶ h16v⁴ h17v⁵ h17d h16.8v² h16.8g⁴ Apr 23] modest maiden hurdler: raced around 2m: acts on heavy going: usually wears hood. *Stuart Coltherd* **h96**

BUDLE BAY (IRE) 6 b.g. Scorpion (IRE) – Argus Gal (IRE) (Alzao (USA)) [2017/18 b16.2g Jun 17] tailed off in bumper. *Simon Waugh* **b–**

BUFFALO BALLET 12 b.g. Kayf Tara – Minora (IRE) (Cataldi) [2017/18 c109, h99: c20.5s² c24.3v⁴ c24.5s⁵ c20.5v² c24.1v² c22.9s² c26.2v⁴ Apr 16] winning hurdler: fair maiden chaser: stays 3m: raced mainly on soft/heavy going: in cheekpieces last 2 starts: often races towards rear. *N. W. Alexander* **c108 h–**

BUFFALO SABRE (FR) 6 b.g. Turgeon (USA) – Kerry Rose (FR) (Tel Quel (FR)) [2017/18 c–, h99: c25.8d^pu Aug 22] modest form over hurdles: pulled up both starts in chases: won point soon after end of season: stays 2½m: acts on good to soft going: often in cheekpieces: sometimes in tongue tie. *Nigel Hawke* **c– h–**

BUGSIE MALONE (IRE) 8 b.g. Mahler – The Irish Whip (Presenting) [2017/18 c120, h118: h25m² c25g^F c27.7d⁴ c25.1v^pu c24s⁴ c24m* Apr 26] big gelding: fairly useful maiden hurdler: second in handicap at Plumpton: fairly useful handicap chaser: won at Kempton in April: stays 25f: acts on good to firm going: in cheekpieces last 2 starts: front runner/races prominently. *Chris Gordon* **c118 h116**

BUILDING FUTURES (IRE) 5 b.g. Kalanisi (IRE) – Lady of The Mill (IRE) (Woods of Windsor (USA)) [2017/18 b16s⁶ b15.3d Apr 22] lengthy gelding: no form in bumpers. *Jeremy Scott* **b–**

BUILDMEUPBUTTERCUP 4 ch.f. Sixties Icon – Eastern Paramour (IRE) (Kris Kin (USA)) [2017/18 b14s* ab16g² b15.7s* b17s⁵ Apr 12] workmanlike filly: second foal: dam (h94), 1½m bumper winner, also 1¼m-1½m winner on Flat: fairly useful form in bumpers: won fillies junior event at Warwick in November and mares event at Ascot in February: tried in blinkers. *Mick Channon* **b100**

BULFIN ISLAND (IRE) 9 b.g. Milan – Tournore Court (IRE) (Insan (USA)) [2017/18 h100: h25s^pu Feb 8] well-made gelding: won completed start in Irish maiden points: fair maiden hurdler, pulled up sole start in 2017/18: stays 3m: acts on soft going. *Alan King* **h–**

BULKOV (FR) 6 b.g. Zambezi Sun – Say Say (FR) (Garde Royale) [2017/18 c–, h123: h16.2d⁴ h16.2s² h16.8s* h16s⁵ h16.8s² h16v² h16.8v* Apr 13] tall gelding: fairly useful hurdler: won novices at Sedgefield in November, February and April: maiden chaser: stays 2¼m: acts on heavy going: usually leads, often travels strongly. *Micky Hammond* **c– h129**

BULLETPROOF (IRE) 12 b.g. Wareed (IRE) – Laura's Native (IRE) (Be My Native (USA)) [2017/18 c–, h106§: h16.8g⁴ h15.8g⁵ h18.5m³ h16.8g³ Aug 16] fair handicap hurdler: maiden chaser: stays 2¼m: acts on good to firm and good to soft going: wears headgear: has worn tongue tie: often races towards rear: unreliable. *Ken Cunningham-Brown* **c– h100 §**

BULLFROG (IRE) 5 b.m. Jeremy (USA) – Tramp Stamp (IRE) (King's Theatre (IRE)) [2017/18 ab16g* Nov 14] €44,000 3-y-o: first foal: dam (c123/h130) bumper/2m hurdle winner: 3/1, won mares bumper at Lingfield (by short head from Agathe Rosalie) on debut. *Gary Moore* **b82**

BULLIONAIRE (IRE) 5 b.g. Gold Well – Dontcallerthat (IRE) (Anshan) [2017/18 b105p: b15.7d² Dec 22] well-made gelding: useful bumper winner: second in listed event at Ascot (2¾ lengths behind Didtheyleaveuoutto) on sole start in 2017/18. *Harry Fry*   **b108**

BULLION (FR) 5 ch.g. Full of Gold (FR) – Ryde (FR) (Sillery (USA)) [2017/18 b16v³ b16v⁵ Jan 31] seventh foal: brother to French 19f hurdle/chase winner Innovate and half-brother to French 1¼m/11f winner Snap (by Bering): dam (c108/h110) French 15f-2¼m hurdle/chase winner: modest form in bumpers: better effort when third at Ayr in December: wears hood. *James Ewart*   **b83**

BULLS HEAD (IRE) 6 b.g. Darsi (FR) – Mrs Jenks (Gunner B) [2017/18 h16.4v* h20.5v* h16.4v² Apr 14] €8,000 3-y-o: half-brother to fair hurdler Ned's Island (21f winner, by Trans Island) and modest hurdler/fairly useful chaser Persian Gates (2½m-2¾m winner, by Anshan): dam unraced sister to high-class chaser (stayed 25f) Bobby Grant: third on completed start in points: fair handicap hurdler: won at Newcastle and Ayr in February: will stay 3m: acts on heavy going: often races towards rear. *Martin Todhunter*   **h108**

BUMBLE BAY 8 b.g. Trade Fair – Amica (Averti (IRE)) [2017/18 h100: h15.7d^pu h15.8g h15.8g^pu Jul 19] modest hurdler, no form in 2017/18: usually wears hood: wears tongue tie: often races towards rear. *Robert Stephens*   **h–**

BUMBLES BABE 5 b.m. Paco Boy (IRE) – Brooklyn's Sky (Septieme Ciel (USA)) [2017/18 b–: b16 2g⁶ May 10] no form in bumpers: dead. *Tim Reed*   **b–**

BUN DORAN (IRE) 7 b.g. Shantou (USA) – Village Queen (IRE) (King's Theatre (IRE)) [2017/18 c140, h–: c16.3s² c15.2s³ c20.5s³ c15.8s⁵ Apr 12] useful-looking gelding: winning hurdler: useful handicap chaser: third at Wetherby in January: stays 2½m, at least as effective around 2m: best form on soft/heavy going: tried in tongue tie: usually travels strongly. *Tom George*   **c140** / **h–**

BUNK OFF EARLY (IRE) 6 ro.g. Zebedee – Ctesiphon (USA) (Arch (USA)) [2017/18 h141: c17d² c16v^F h16.5d h20s⁴ Apr 28] compact gelding: smart form over hurdles: fourth in Ballymore Handicap Hurdle at Punchestown (2½ lengths behind Meri Devie) in April: useful form over fences: second in maiden at Leopardstown in December: yet to be asked for effort when fell 2 out in similar event won by Montalbano at Gowran in January: stays 2½m: acts on soft going: remains open to improvement as a chaser. *W. P. Mullins, Ireland*   **c138 p** / **h145**

BUONAROTTI BOY (IRE) 6 b.g. Galileo (IRE) – Funsie (FR) (Saumarez) [2017/18 h108: h16⁵ h16g⁶ h20g³ h16.2d Apr 26] fair handicap hurdler: left Gordon Elliott after third start: barely stays 2½m: acts on soft and good to firm going: wears headgear. *Sophie Leech*   **h107**

BUONARROTI (IRE) 7 b.g. Galileo (IRE) – Beauty Is Truth (IRE) (Pivotal) [2017/18 h15.8d Nov 25] fairly useful form on Flat, stays 15f: tongue tied, well beaten in maiden on hurdling debut. *Declan Carroll*   **h–**

BURBANK (IRE) 6 b.g. Yeats (IRE) – Spring Swoon (FR) (Highest Honor (FR)) [2017/18 h135p, b98: h20d c20d⁶ h19.3v³ h21.1s h21.4g Apr 21] tall gelding: useful handicap hurdler: third in Holloway's Handicap Hurdle at Ascot in January: 8/11, sixth in novice at Ludlow (32¼ lengths behind Hogan's Height) on chasing debut: stays 21f: acts on heavy going: in cheekpieces last 3 starts: should do better over fences. *Nicky Henderson*   **c– p** / **h139**

BURGESS DREAM (IRE) 9 b.g. Spadoun (FR) – Ennel Lady (IRE) (Erin's Hope) [2017/18 c67, h85: h25d⁶ h25.8g⁵ c23.5s^ur h24s c23.5v³ h23v³ h23v³ h24.2s c19.5s* Apr 6] tall, workmanlike gelding: modest handicap hurdler: poor handicap chaser: won at Fontwell in April: stays 3¼m: acts on heavy going: tried in cheekpieces. *Anna Newton-Smith*   **c80** / **h88**

BURGESS VIEW (IRE) 8 b.g. Kayf Tara – Dahara (FR) (Take Risks (FR)) [2017/18 c23g^pu h25.8m⁵ Aug 17] point winner: maiden hurdler: no form in chases: stays 3m: often in blinkers: sometimes wears tongue tie. *Mike Hammond*   **c–** / **h–**

BURLINGTON BERT (FR) 7 b.g. Califet (FR) – Melhi Sun (FR) (Mansonnien (FR)) [2017/18 h87, b101: h16.2d h20.9d⁵ h22.7g⁴ Nov 11] tall, angular gelding: bumper winner: modest form over hurdles: has worn tongue tie, including last 2 starts: usually finds little. *Jean McGregor*   **h90**

BUR

BURNING AMBITION (IRE) 7 b.g. Scorpion (IRE) – Wyndham Miss Sally (IRE) (Flemensfirth (USA)) [2017/18 c22.5v* c24.8v² c26.3v Mar 16] €20,000 4-y-o: tall gelding: fifth foal: half-brother to fairly useful hurdler/chaser Knockraha Pylon (2m-2¼m winner) and fair 2m hurdle winner Knockraha King (both by King's Theatre): dam unraced half-sister to fairly useful hurdler/fair chaser (stayed 25f) The Culdee: multiple point winner: useful form in chases: won maiden hunter at Limerick in December: best effort when second in hunter at Punchestown (2¾ lengths behind Gilgamboa) in February: remains open to improvement. *Pierce Michael Power, Ireland*   **c132 p**

BURNING BRIGHT 5 gr.g. Fair Mix (IRE) – Cee Cee Rider (Classic Cliche (IRE)) [2017/18 b16.7v Apr 11] in hood, tailed off in bumper. *Ben Case*   **b–**

BURNING DESIRE (IRE) 7 b.g. Galileo (IRE) – Flames (Blushing Flame (USA)) [2017/18 h–: h20m^pu Jul 5] lengthy gelding: placed in points: modest form at best over hurdles: tried in cheekpieces: sometimes in tongue tie. *Jimmy Frost*   **h–**

BURNING HEAT (IRE) 5 b.g. Rock of Gibraltar (IRE) – Burning Damask (USA) (Thunder Gulch (USA)) [2017/18 h109: h16g² h16.3g⁵ h16.3g^pu h19.6g^F h15.8g⁴ h19.6d Nov 25] angular gelding: fair maiden hurdler: left James Eustace after third start: unproven beyond 2m: acts on good to firm going: often in headgear. *Denis Quinn*   **h113**

BURNS CROSS (IRE) 6 b.g. Mahler – Strokestown Queen (IRE) (Presenting) [2017/18 b16.7v¹ b16.v⁶ b16.7d Apr 21] €27,000 3-y-o, €75,000 5-y-o: second foal: brother to modest hurdler Prince Mahler (2¾m-3m winner): dam unraced half-sister to fairly useful hurdler/chaser (2m-3m winner) Barton Nic: easy winner of Irish point on debut: fair form in bumpers: best effort when second at Bangor in January. *Neil Mulholland*   **b89**

BURN VALLEY 5 ch.m. With The Flow (USA) – Countess Point (Karinga Bay) [2017/18 b15.3v b16.8v⁶ h21.6s^pu Apr 23] fourth foal: sister to fairly useful hurdler/chaser Muffins For Tea (17f-23f winner), stays 3½m, and half-sister to modest hurdler Actlikeacountess (2½m winner, by Act One): dam (h101) bumper/17f hurdle winner: no form in bumpers/novice hurdle. *Colin Tizzard*   **h–** **b–**

BURRENBRIDGE HOTEL (IRE) 7 b.g. Ivan Denisovich (IRE) – Hearthstead Dancer (USA) (Royal Academy (USA)) [2017/18 h101, b–: h15.7g h20g^pu c16.4g⁵ c16g* c16.1s* c16.4v² c16v^pu c16.1v³ Mar 29] standout effort (fair form) over hurdles when won maiden in 2016/17: fairly useful form over fences: won handicaps at Hereford (novice) in November and Taunton in December: unproven beyond 2m: acts on good to firm and heavy going: has worn headgear: often races prominently. *Henry Oliver*   **c122** **h–**

BURREN LIFE (IRE) 6 br.g. Pelder (IRE) – Burren Valley (IRE) (Phardante (FR)) [2017/18 h20.2v* h21s³ h22.8v* h24v² h24v³ h20v⁵ h24v³ h22v^pu h24d Apr 26] £135,000 4-y-o: sixth foal: half-brother to 2 winners by Beneficial, including fair hurdler/fairly useful chaser Burren Ben (2½m-2¾m winner): dam (h66), lightly raced in bumpers/over hurdles, placed in points: fell in point on debut: placed in bumpers: useful hurdler: won maiden at Roscommon in September and novice at Thurles in November: third in Guinness Novices' Hurdle at Limerick in December: stays 3m: acts on heavy going: tried in blinkers. *Gordon Elliott, Ireland*   **h131**

BURROWS EDGE (FR) 5 b.g. Martaline – La Vie de Boitron (FR) (Lavirco (GER)) [2017/18 b16.3d² h16d⁴ h20.6s* h19.7v* h15.8v² h16s⁶ Apr 28] €36,000 3-y-o, €140,000 4-y-o: good-topped gelding: will make a chaser: second foal: half-brother to useful French 10.5f winner Burrows Park (by Astarabad): dam, French 1¾m winner, half-sister to fairly useful hurdler/smart chaser (stayed 25f) De Boitron: placed both starts in Irish points: second in bumper at Newbury (5 lengths behind Tidal Flow): fairly useful form over hurdles: won novices at Market Rasen in February and Hereford in March: will stay 3m: acts on heavy going. *Nicky Henderson*   **h126** **b98**

BURROWS LANE (FR) 7 b.g. Astarabad (USA) – Condoleezza (FR) (Mansonnien (FR)) [2017/18 h114, b93: h19g³ h20g² h19.9m* h20g³ h24g² h20g⁵ h20s³ Nov 14] bumper winner: fair hurdler: won handicap at Uttoxeter in July: stays 3m: acts on soft and good to firm going: usually wears cheekpieces/tongue tie. *Charlie Longsdon*   **h114**

BURROWS SAINT (FR) 5 b.g. Saint des Saints (FR) – La Bombonera (FR) (Mansonnien (FR)) [2017/18 h20s* h22.3v² h20.3v h20s³ Apr 27] second foal: dam (c126/h126), French 2¼m hurdle winner, sister to very smart French chaser (stayed 27f) Lagunak: useful hurdler: won maiden at Punchestown in November: third in Champion Novices' Hurdle at same course (12 lengths behind Dortmund Park) in April: fairly useful form over fences in 2016/17 for Guillaume Macaire: will stay 3m: acts on soft going: in tongue tie last 3 starts. *W. P. Mullins, Ireland*   **c–** **h134**

BUV

BURST YA BUBBLE (IRE) 6 b.g. Spadoun (FR) – Accordian Lady (IRE) (Accordion) [2017/18 h109, b67: h19.1g³ h15.8d* h15.8m² h19.3g h21.7d⁵ h19d* Apr 26] rangy gelding: fairly useful hurdler: won conditionals maiden at Uttoxeter in June and handicap at Warwick in April: stays 2¾m: acts on good to firm and good to soft going. *Seamus Mullins* **h115**

BURTONS WELL (IRE) 9 b.g. Well Chosen – Despute (IRE) (Be My Native (USA)) [2017/18 c134p, h–: c20.9g² c20.8s Jan 1] rangy gelding: winning hurdler: useful form over fences: second in handicap at Stratford (neck behind Romain de Senam) in October: went as if amiss next time: stays 21f: acts on heavy going. *Venetia Williams* **c136 h–**

BURY THE EVIDENCE 5 b.m. Phoenix Reach (IRE) – Madam Bijou (Atraf) [2017/18 b63: h20.3ro Nov 6] unplaced in bumpers/on Flat: ran out early on hurdling debut: in hood last 3 starts. *Derek Shaw* **h–**

BUSTER EDWARDS (IRE) 5 b.g. Kalanisi (IRE) – Hot Oscar (IRE) (Oscar (IRE)) [2017/18 h23d² Sep 3] €8,000 3-y-o, £17,000 4-y-o: first foal: dam (c101/h117), bumper/2½m-3m hurdle winner, half-sister to fairly useful hurdler (stayed 3m) Full Throttle: third in Irish point on debut: 11/4, second in maiden at Worcester (head behind Mister Mister) on hurdling debut: should progress. *David Pipe* **h104 p**

BUSTER MOON (IRE) 6 b.g. Darsi (FR) – Orinocco Blue (IRE) (Pistolet Bleu (IRE)) [2017/18 h19.5v⁴ h19.5v³ Mar 21] €5,000 3-y-o: third foal: dam (b78), ran once in bumper, half-sister to fair hurdlers/fairly useful chasers Avoca Promise (stayed 2½m) and Point Blank (stayed 3m): unplaced on completed start in Irish points: fair form over hurdles: better effort when third in maiden at Chepstow, dictating. *Jeremy Scott* **h106**

BUSTER THOMAS (IRE) 7 b.g. Westerner – Awesome Miracle (IRE) (Supreme Leader) [2017/18 h121: c24.2s³ c20.6vF c20v⁴ c24d⁵ c20.2d* Apr 22] runner-up in Irish point on debut: fairly useful form over hurdles: similar form over fences: won handicap at Wincanton in April: should be suited by 3m: acts on heavy going: tried in tongue tie: front runner/races prominently. *Emma Lavelle* **c121 h–**

BUSY BARO (IRE) 8 ch.g. Acambaro (GER) – Miss Busy Lizzy (IRE) (Supreme Leader) [2017/18 h120.3dpu h16v Jan 22] modest form at best over hurdles: usually wore hood: dead. *Paul Cowley* **h–**

BUTLERGROVE KING (IRE) 9 b.g. King's Theatre (IRE) – Sanadja (IRE) (Slip Anchor) [2017/18 c113, h–: c20m³ c20.9g* c21g² Jun 27] maiden hurdler: fair handicap chaser: won at Ffos Las in June: stays 3m: acts on good to firm and good to soft going: tried in cheekpieces: has worn tongue tie, including final start. *Dai Burchell* **c101 h–**

BUTNEY ISLAND (IRE) 8 b.g. Trans Island – Tash McGarry (IRE) (Publisher (USA)) [2017/18 c–, h105: h25dpu h21.6s Jun 5] sturdy gelding: fair hurdler, no form in 2017/18: tailed off only chase start: stays 2½m: acts on heavy going: tried in headgear. *Nick Mitchell* **c– h–**

BUVEUR D'AIR (FR) 7 b.g. Crillon (FR) – History (FR) (Alesso (USA)) [2017/18 c155p, h170: h16.4v* h16d* h16v* h16.4s* Mar 13] **c– h167**

Buveur d'Air kept his Champion Hurdle title in a season when he proved head and shoulders above the opposition in Britain but, on the day at Cheltenham, he was only a neck better than Ireland's top two-miler Melon. The style of Buveur d'Air's gritty second success in the Champion Hurdle contrasted with the ease of his three wins earlier in the season against a total of just nine rivals, only one of whom took him on again as one of his ten opponents at Cheltenham. In Britain at least, if not in Ireland, the two-mile hurdling division remains a weak one by historical standards, a situation which Buveur d'Air's connections exploited by abandoning a promising novice chase campaign to win his first Champion Hurdle. But that's taking nothing away from Buveur d'Air who is compiling the record of a true champion and is now the winner of twelve of his thirteen races over jumps, his only defeat coming when third in an exceptional Supreme Novices' Hurdle which threw up those other stars Altior and Min. When Min finished second to Altior again in the latest Queen Mother Champion Chase, it was the first time, in the interim, that any of the first three from that Supreme two years earlier had failed to pass the post first.

Having started out over fences the previous season, Buveur d'Air followed a much more traditional path to his second Champion Hurdle, beginning with the 'Fighting Fifth' Hurdle at Newcastle at the beginning of December. The likes of Comedy of Errors, Night Nurse and Sea Pigeon all won the 'Fighting Fifth' and Champion Hurdle in the same season, Comedy of Errors achieving that feat twice— all three were themselves dual winners of the Champion Hurdle. In what was a much more competitive era for two-mile hurdlers, that trio, along with Champion Hurdle regular Bird's Nest, won nine consecutive 'Fighting Fifths' between 1972 and 1980. Bird's Nest was demoted in the last of those editions from what would have been his fourth win in the race in favour of Sea Pigeon who thus gained his second success in the 'Fighting Fifth' before going on to win the Champion Hurdle for the second time that season. Kribensis became the next 'Fighting Fifth' winner to win the same season's Champion Hurdle in 1989/90, but the race's fortunes have tended to fluctuate since the 'golden age of hurdling', becoming a limited handicap for a time and being promoted to Grade 1 status in 2004.

Newcastle now finds itself a long way from the country's most powerful stables, but Nicky Henderson has long supported the 'Fighting Fifth' and Buveur d'Air was sent on the long journey from Lambourn in a bid to become his yard's fourth winner of the race after Landing Light in 2001, Punjabi in 2008 and My Tent Or Yours in 2013. Punjabi, who won a rearranged 'Fighting Fifth' staged at Wetherby, had been the last winner of the race to be successful at Cheltenham the following March. The last reigning Champion Hurdler to return in the 'Fighting Fifth' had been another from Seven Barrows, Binocular, though he was beaten at odds-on in 2010 (he was turned over at short odds on all three of his appearances in the race), despite its being run just down the road at Newbury that year after the weather had again claimed Newcastle. There were no similar worries for Buveur d'Air who looked in outstanding shape for his return to action, travelled strongly throughout and passed the post hard held to land odds of 6/1-on from the former dual winner Irving and the previous season's Fred Winter winner Flying Tiger. A steadily-run race in heavy ground, in which the two other runners in the field were outclassed, was never going to require Buveur d'Air to run to near his best form, but it promised plenty for the season ahead and came just weeks after the 2015 Champion Hurdle winner Faugheen had made an impressive return in the Morgiana Hurdle at Punchestown after the best part of two years off the track.

Henderson's previous 'Fighting Fifth' winners had gone on to the Christmas Hurdle at Kempton where both Landing Light and My Tent Or Yours had been successful. Punjabi would have gone close, too, but he fell two out, thereby missing out on the million pound bonus that existed at the time for any horse that won the 'Fighting Fifth', Christmas Hurdle and Champion Hurdle. Buveur d'Air faced only three opponents in the Christmas Hurdle, sponsored like the 'Fighting Fifth' by Unibet who also became the new backers of the Champion Hurdle. Handicappers Mohaayed and Chesterfield (the latter had run at Ascot three days earlier) had finished first and third in the previous season's Scottish Champion Hurdle which left The New One as Buveur d'Air's only credible opponent. The New One had been runner-up on his three previous appearances in the race and most recently had finished second to My Tent Or Yours, the rival who had beaten him in the first of those Christmas Hurdles four years earlier, in the International Hurdle at Cheltenham.

Unibet 'Fighting Fifth' Hurdle, Newcastle—
Buveur d'Air is far too strong for the 2014 and 2016 winner Irving

Unibet Christmas Hurdle, Kempton—another straightforward landing of the odds for Buveur d'Air, who easily sees off The New One (left), finishing runner-up in this race for a fourth time

The other valuable pre-Christmas weight-for-age two-mile hurdle in Britain, held at Haydock on Betfair Chase day just a week before the 'Fighting Fifth', failed to establish itself and was discontinued after just three runnings; The New One had won the first of them, a five-runner affair in 2014, while both subsequent editions had attracted fields of only four. At Kempton, another steadily-run race resulted in another easy win for the fluent-jumping Buveur d'Air who headed The New One at the final flight and readily outpaced him on the run-in to win by two and a quarter lengths, with Mohaayed and Chesterfield picking up the money for third and fourth. Straw Bear, Binocular (twice), Darlan, My Tent Or Yours and Yanworth had all won the Christmas Hurdle since 2007 for J. P. McManus, while Nicky Henderson was also winning it for the seventh time.

It was clear by now that Buveur d'Air didn't have much to fear from his British rivals in his quest to retain his Champion Hurdle crown, while Faugheen's capitulation at Leopardstown just three days after Buveur d'Air's win at Kempton suddenly left Ireland's main hope looking vulnerable. All that remained for Buveur d'Air to do before going to Cheltenham was to win the Contenders Hurdle at Sandown at the beginning of February for the second year running. John Constable, sixth of seven in the International, and the no-hoper Cap'n were his only rivals this time, and Buveur d'Air was untroubled to complete the task, even though he had to make his own running and his rider eased him a shade prematurely. The Swinton winner John Constable, along with the supplemented Kingwell Hurdle winner Elgin (another graduate from handicaps, having won the Greatwood earlier in the season), plus the Kingwell runner-up Ch'tibello and Buveur d'Air's 100/1 stablemate Charli Parcs, were all that could be mustered from Britain to take on the 6/4-on favourite at Cheltenham. Two more of Buveur d'Air's stable companions, Verdana Blue and three-times runner-up My Tent Or Yours, were both taken out due to the soft (officially 'heavy, soft in places') ground on which the Festival began.

While the Irish challenge was lacking the Irish Champion Hurdle winner Supasundae, who was waiting for the Stayers' Hurdle instead, the form of the Leopardstown contest, which had more strength in depth than any similar race that had taken place in Britain during the season up until then, was well represented at Cheltenham by Faugheen, Mick Jazz, Melon and Identity Thief. Faugheen's second place in the Irish Champion Hurdle signalled at least a partial recovery from his still unexplained flop in December in the Ryanair Hurdle which had been won by Mick Jazz. Faugheen started at 4/1 to win his second Champion Hurdle, while stable-companion Melon was a 7/1 chance despite finishing only fifth when fitted

Unibet Champion Hurdle Challenge Trophy, Cheltenham—much closer this time, with Buveur d'Air needing to pull out all the stops to beat Melon (right) and complete a clean sweep of Britain's three Grade 1 open two-mile hurdles; outsider Mick Jazz takes third

with a hood at Leopardstown last time. That represented a backwards step for the previous year's Supreme Novices' runner-up who had shaped well, taking a strong hold, when third behind My Tent Or Yours and The New One in the International. He had the headgear quickly dispensed with for the Champion Hurdle in which he wore ear plugs instead. Willie Mullins had four runners in all, his team completed by the previous season's Punchestown Champion Hurdle winner Wicklow Brave, having his first start since finishing in mid-division in the Melbourne Cup, and the former Baring Bingham winner Yorkhill who was returning to hurdles after losing his way over fences.

It might not have been a vintage line-up for a Champion Hurdle, but it produced an exciting finish and certainly a closer one than the betting predicted. It was well run, too, thanks to Charli Parcs taking up a pacemaking role on Buveur d'Air's behalf, something which also seemed to have the effect of unsettling customary front-runner Faugheen, wearing cheekpieces for the first time, who regained his early lead only briefly between three and two out. From then on, it chiefly concerned only Buveur d'Air and Melon, though Mick Jazz tried to go with them and was still only a couple of lengths down at the final flight which both leaders jumped well. Touching down together, Buveur d'Air and Melon continued their battle up the hill, Melon narrowly in front halfway up the run-in before Buveur d'Air pulled out a bit extra in the final fifty yards. The neck margin made it one of the closest finishes to a Champion Hurdle this century, along with the victories of Hardy Eustace, Punjabi and Jezki (the last-named pair ridden, like Buveur d'Air, by Barry Geraghty). Like the runner-up, 25/1 chance Mick Jazz showed improved form to finish third, beaten another three lengths, and he pulled nine lengths clear of Identity Thief in fourth. Elgin never landed a blow in fifth with Faugheen dropping out before completing the first six.

Geraghty's third Champion Hurdle was consolation for his missing the ride twelve months earlier on Buveur d'Air, which went to Noel Fehily when he was injured, while it was a seventh win in the race for both McManus and Henderson who had already become the most successful owner and trainer in the race's history with the first of Buveur d'Air's Champion Hurdles. Only Katchit ten years earlier had recorded a slower winning time in the Champion Hurdle this century and Geraghty stressed the unusually testing conditions when explaining his tactics afterwards. 'It is real winter conditions and very tacky down the back straight. Buveur d'Air won it the hard way. I was trying to save as much as I could off the turn in and then go for him as late as possible. He found what was needed.' Another of those neck winners, Hardy Eustace in 2005, had been the last Champion Hurdle winner to retain his title, though his second victory will be remembered as much for being the race that Harchibald lost. Harchibald, incidentally, had won the 'Fighting Fifth' and Christmas Hurdles that season leaving Buveur d'Air to become only the second horse after Kribensis to win those two races and the Champion Hurdle in the same campaign. Plenty of Champion Hurdle winners since Hardy Eustace have

BUY

made unsuccessful bids to win the race in successive seasons. Hardy Eustace went on to finish third in his hat-trick attempt, since when Brave Inca, Sublimity, Katchit, Punjabi, Hurricane Fly, Rock On Ruby and Jezki had all tried in vain. Hurricane Fly won his second Champion Hurdle, at the chief expense of Rock On Ruby, two years after his first win in 2011.

```
                          ┌ Crillon (FR)     ┌ Saumarez           ┌ Rainbow Quest
                          │  (br 1996)       │  (b or br 1987)    │ Fiesta Fun
                          │                  └ Shangrila          ┌ Riverman
Buveur d'Air (FR)        ┤                      (b 1978)          └ Garden Green
  (b.g. 2011)             │                  ┌ Alesso             ┌ Alleged
                          │ History (FR)     │  (b or br 1983)    └ Leandra
                          └  (b 1995)        └ Clair Deux Lune    ┌ Altayan
                                                (ch 1990)         └ Lili Dancer
```

Buveur d'Air had followed up his first Champion Hurdle win by beating My Tent Or Yours into second again in the Aintree Hurdle but an unsatisfactory scope ruled him out of a bid to complete the same double. Stable-companion L'Ami Serge won the Aintree Hurdle, while the Punchestown Champion Hurdle, in which Buveur d'Air would have met Melon again, was under consideration before his stable decided it would have no runners at all at that meeting, at which Ireland's powerhouse trainers Willie Mullins and Gordon Elliott were aiming nearly all their big guns. The main aim for Buveur d'Air in 2018/19 will no doubt be an attempt to become the sixth horse in the history of the Champion Hurdle to win the race three times. McManus owned the last to achieve that feat, Istabraq, who completed his hat-trick in 2000, while Henderson trained the previous triple winner before Istabraq, See You Then, who completed his treble in 1987 to join Hatton's Grace, Sir Ken and Persian War in the history books. See You Then helped Henderson secure his first two trainers' championships and Buveur d'Air has played an important part in putting Henderson back on top in the last couple of seasons some thirty years later (McManus also retained his title as champion owner). Fluent jumping and a turn of foot were Istabraq's chief assets. He was, after all, a blue-blooded son of Sadler's Wells. Buveur d'Air shares similar attributes, his notably slick jumping being another reason why he was returned to the smaller obstacles though, as previously detailed in his essays, his French AQPS pedigree makes him a very different animal to Istabraq in terms of breeding. His sire Crillon is also responsible for one of the best of the current crop of hurdlers in France, Alex de Larredya. Buveur d'Air, who has worn ear plugs in his two Champion Hurdles, stays two and a half miles and acts on heavy ground. His winning sequence over hurdles looks sure to extend into another season, though Samcro is potentially now among those who stand in the way of Buveur d'Air winning a third Champion Hurdle. *Nicky Henderson*

BUYER BEWARE (IRE) 6 br.g. Big Bad Bob (IRE) – Adoring (IRE) (One Cool Cat (USA)) [2017/18 c87p, h113: h15.6m⁶ h16.6d⁶ h19.4d⁶ Jan 1] fair handicap hurdler: failed to stay only chase start: stays 2¼m: acts on good to firm and good to soft going: has worn hood: has joined Lawrence Mullaney. *Patrick Holmes*   c–
h107

BUY MISTAKE (FR) 5 b.g. Soldier of Fortune (IRE) – Pyramid Painter (IRE) (Peintre Celebre (USA)) [2017/18 b16.2d² b16.2d² b16.8g³ Oct 25] £3,000 4-y-o: seventh foal: brother to French 10.5f winner Speed Run and half-brother to 2 winners in France, including useful 7.5f-12.5f winner Green Rock (by Green Tune): dam unraced: fairly useful form in bumpers: won conditionals/amateur event at Hexham in August: best effort when second at Perth in September. *Geoffrey Harker*   b104

BUYWISE (IRE) 11 b.g. Tikkanen (USA) – Greenogue Princess (IRE) (Rainbows For Life (CAN)) [2017/18 c146x, h132+: h19.6s c23.6v⁶ c24.2s* h23.4v c34.3sᵘʳ Apr 14]   c140
h–

Jumping enthusiasts love a gallant loser and it is no surprise that the enigmatic Buywise has built up a cult following over the years. He must have cost his legion of fans a small fortune with his series of near-misses in big handicaps, typically staying on strongly to be nearest at the finish after making mistakes and leaving himself poorly placed. His trademark efforts have included several at Cheltenham, headed by a very unlucky second, having to be switched, in the 2015 Paddy Power Gold Cup; a good third, arriving just too late, in the 2016 BetVictor Gold Cup; and,

171

32Red Veterans' Handicap Chase (Series Final), Sandown—
Buywise (at the height of his jump) is still only fifth two out, but a trademark strong late surge takes him to his first win over fences in almost four years

most recently, a creditable fourth, plotting his path from the back in familiar style, in the Ultima Handicap Chase at the 2017 Festival meeting. When Buywise lined up for the 32Red-sponsored Final of the 2017 Veterans' Chase Series at Sandown on his third start in the latest season, he hadn't won over fences for nearly four years— since the Silver Trophy Handicap at Cheltenham's 2014 April fixture—and hadn't won a race of any description for nearly three. The veterans series, in its third year, hasn't taken long to establish itself firmly in the calendar, with very well supported qualifiers (staged over the preceding year for ten-year-olds and upwards, who only have to run to qualify for the Final) and a very competitive Final.

A field of fourteen lined up for the latest Final, run at Sandown's early-January meeting, including the first five home from the previous year. Fourteen-year-old Pete The Feat made a valiant attempt to repeat his success and twelve-year-olds Gas Line Boy, Cloudy Too and Loose Chips finished in that order behind him to reach the first five again (the 2017 runner-up Theatrical Star came seventh). Buywise, who had qualified in a veterans chase at Exeter the previous February, seemingly contested the Final as something of an afterthought, following a seasonal pipe-opener down the field in a handicap hurdle at Bangor and a modest sixth in the Welsh Grand National Trial at Chepstow. Trainer Evan Williams revealed afterwards that Buywise had returned jarred up after his fourth at the Cheltenham Festival. 'We also had to do a bit of work on one of his hind legs, so he didn't have much of a summer holiday and I even thought it might be the end of the road for him, with hunter chases in the spring the only other likely option. But he's a tough old devil!' Buywise had never run before at Sandown, where connections thought the uphill finish would suit him, and, in another interesting move, he was ridden for the first time by Leighton Aspell. Buywise, a 12/1-shot, didn't quite follow the script on this occasion, his jumping holding together very well for Aspell, which enabled him to get into the race sooner than usual in a strongly-run race in which Loose Chips led them a merry dance for a long way. Making headway from four out after being dropped out, and with his jockey biding his time before a final effort, Buywise was coolly produced to lead on the run-in after Pete The Feat, who took over in front two out, jumped the last with a healthy lead. Buywise won by two lengths, with Gas Line Boy and Cloudy Too three lengths further behind Pete The Feat, in a heartwarming running of the race that served only to cement the popularity of the well-received veterans series which provides opportunities to extend the careers of old timers who might otherwise be lost to the game. So popular has the idea proven that there is lobbying for the Cheltenham Festival to have its own veterans chase. The most convincing suggestion is that the Kim Muir for amateurs, a race which caters for the same horses as the Ultima Handicap, might make way for a veterans chase, though there would be a danger that a Cheltenham Festival race for 'golden oldies' might steal some of the thunder from Sandown and affect the competitiveness of the Final there.

The Veterans' Chase Series Final was the clear highlight of the season for Buywise—who was badly hampered when unseating at the first Canal Turn in the Grand National (twelfth in 2016) on his only subsequent run over fences—and he will no doubt have Sandown in his sights again in the next season (though he will need to qualify). His trainer revealed, in an interesting feature after the Final in the *Racing Post*, a possible reason for Buywise's style of running. His movement is apparently a little restricted by his near-hind having been pinned before Williams bought him for 21,000 guineas as a six-year-old pointer. The pins were only found when the trainer had him scanned some time later. 'He takes an awful long time to warm up and that's why he tends to get behind and appears to take liberties with his fences.' Williams said he has had plenty of letters and emails over time with advice about how Buywise should be ridden—'usually telling us that we're doing it wrong'—but there seems to be no other way to ride him.

Buywise (IRE) (b.g. 2007)
- Tikkanen (USA) (gr 1991)
  - Cozzene (gr 1980)
    - Caro
    - Ride The Trails
  - Reiko (b 1979)
    - Targowice
    - Beronaire
- Greenogue Princess (IRE) (ch 1995)
  - Rainbows For Life (ch 1988)
    - Lyphard
    - Rainbow Connection
  - Trendy Princess (b 1982)
    - Prince Tenderfoot
    - Lendy

A lengthy gelding, Buywise is the best jumper sired by the Breeders' Cup Turf winner Tikkanen who was at stud in Japan before being imported to Ireland. Greenogue Princess, the dam of Buywise, was runner-up in a bumper and is a half-sister to the fairly useful staying chaser Fatherofthebride who was runner-up in a Kerry National and a Cork Grand National. Buywise is the only winner under Rules for Greenogue Princess, though a brother, Arnis Brack, was a winning pointer. Buywise's grandam Trendy Princess was an unraced sister to the Irish Cambridgeshire runner-up Tenderly, and his great grandam Lendy has featured in the extended pedigree of a number of notable jumpers. Lendy was the dam of the Grand National runner-up Zongalero and the grandam of Cheltenham Gold Cup winner and Grand National runner-up Garrison Savannah, and she is also the great grandam of the Punchestown Gold Cup winner China Rock. Buywise stays three miles (should get further) and acts on good to firm and heavy going. He has been tried in a visor. *Evan Williams*

BUZ BARTON (IRE) 10 b.g. Bach (IRE) – Cronin's Girl (IRE) (Oscar (IRE)) [2017/18 h80: h21.6g^{pu} h16.8s Jun 5] point winner: poor maiden hurdler: stays 2¾m: tried in cheekpieces. *Jimmy Frost* — h–

BYE BYE O BYE (IRE) 11 b.g. Kadeed (IRE) – Village Actress (IRE) (Actinium (FR)) [2017/18 h20v h19d^4 h20s^2 h21.1s c20v Apr 1] good-topped gelding: fair handicap hurdler: maiden chaser: stays 25f: acts on soft and good to firm going: has worn cheekpieces: wears tongue tie: usually races towards rear. *Michael C. Griffin, Ireland* — c– h108

BYGONES FOR COINS (IRE) 10 ch.m. Danroad (AUS) – Reservation (IRE) (Common Grounds) [2017/18 h82: h16.2g^2 h16.2g h16.7g^5 h18.6g^3 h15.7g^4 h21.2g^6 h18.1g h19.9g^{pu} h16.8g h20s h16d h16.8v^3 h15.7v^{pu} h19.7d^2 Mar 29] poor maiden hurdler: pulled up only chase start: stays 19f: acts on good to soft going: sometimes wears cheekpieces: wears tongue tie: front runner. *Kenny Johnson* — c– h75

BY RAIL 4 br.g. Rail Link – Soldata (USA) (Maria's Mon (USA)) [2017/18 h16s h15.8s h16d^6 Apr 7] fair on Flat in France for Y. Durepaire, stays 1¼m: little impact over hurdles: wears hood. *Nick Littmoden* — h–

BYRON BLUE (IRE) 9 br.g. Dylan Thomas (IRE) – High Society (IRE) (Key of Luck (USA)) [2017/18 h101: h20s^6 h22g^2 h24g* h21.6m^2 h25m^{pu} Sep 24] small gelding: fair handicap hurdler: won at Southwell in July: acts on good to firm and good to soft going: has worn hood: wears tongue tie: usually leads. *Brian Barr* — h107

BYRONEGETONEFREE 7 b.g. Byron – Lefty's Dollbaby (USA) (Brocco (USA)) [2017/18 h66: h20.2g h20.2g Jul 5] modest on Flat, stays 16.5f: little form over hurdles: raced mainly at 2m: tried in headgear. *Stuart Coltherd* — h–

BYT

BY THE BOARDWALK (IRE) 10 br.g. Presenting – Peripheral Vision (IRE) (Saddlers' Hall (IRE)) [2017/18 c125, h–: c23.9g³ c23.8m c25.6g⁴ c26.6s⁵ c20.5s Apr 9] strong gelding: has had breathing operation: maiden hurdler: fairly useful handicap chaser: third at Market Rasen in May: stays 3¼m: acts on good to firm and good to soft going: wears tongue tie: often races towards rear: signs of temperament. *Kim Bailey* — c121 h–

BY THE FIRESIDE 7 b.g. Dr Massini (IRE) – Dew Drop Inn (IRE) (Saddlers' Hall (IRE)) [2017/18 b66: b15.8g³ May 29] modest form in bumpers: in hood sole 2017/18 start. *Jo Davis* — b77

C

CABARET QUEEN 6 b.m. King's Theatre (IRE) – La Dame Brune (FR) (Mansonnien (FR)) [2017/18 h87: h20.6g⁴ h19.7d² h24s³ Dec 17] winning pointer: fair form over hurdles: won mares novice at Market Rasen in October: stays 2½m: in tongue tie last 3 starts. *Dan Skelton* — h108

CABERNET D'ALENE (FR) 6 b.g. Day Flight – Haifa du Noyer (FR) (Video Rock (FR)) [2017/18 h101: h16.7g⁴ h16g h18.5d* h19m⁶ h16.5g* h18.6v* h19.2s^pu Mar 7] good-topped gelding: fairly useful handicap hurdler: won at Newton Abbot (conditional) in September, Taunton in November and Market Rasen (conditional) in January: stays 19f: acts on good to firm and heavy going. *Nick Williams* — h117

CAB ON TIMES (IRE) 9 b.g. Indian Danehill (IRE) – Evening Fashion (IRE) (Strong Gale) [2017/18 c–, h–: c20.9d⁶ Jun 9] winning pointer: lightly-raced hurdler: no form in hunter chases: tried in cheekpieces. *S. Rea* — c– h–

CABRAGH (IRE) 9 b.g. Old Vic – Satco Street (IRE) (Satco (FR)) [2017/18 c114, h60: c26.3s³ c24.2v⁶ c24.2s Mar 9] maiden hurdler: fair chaser: left Sam England after first start: stays 3¼m: acts on soft going: has worn cheekpieces, including final start: usually races close up. *Charlie Mann* — c105 h–

CADEAU DU BRESIL (FR) 6 b.g. Blue Bresil (FR) – Melanie du Chenet (FR) (Nikos) [2017/18 c20m⁴ c19.5g⁶ c23.5v* c24v³ c24.2d⁴ Apr 24] €42,000 3-y-o colt: fifth foal: half-brother to fairly useful hurdler/useful chaser Antony (19f-3m winner, by Walk In The Park) and fair chaser Soleil d'Avril (25f winner, by Laveron): dam French 8.5f winner: fairly useful hurdler: won conditionals maiden at Limerick in 2016/17: fair form over fences: won 3-runner maiden at Towcester in March: left Gordon Elliott after second start: stays 3m: acts on heavy going: has worn tongue tie, including in 2017/18: often races towards rear. *Grant Cann* — c108 h–

CADEAU GEORGE 9 b.g. Relief Pitcher – Sovereign's Gift (Elegant Monarch) [2017/18 c–, h110: c26.2c24.2d^pu c24v^pu Dec 31] lengthy gelding: fair hurdler: useful chaser at best, no form in 2017/18: often wears headgear: front runner/races prominently: temperamental. *Ben Pauling* — c– § h–

CADEAUX'S FIRE 5 ch.m. Major Cadeaux – Confetti (Groom Dancer (USA)) [2017/18 b64: b16d h15.7g ab16d h20.7g Apr 24] angular mare: has had breathing operation: little form in bumpers: well held in maiden/novice hurdles: tried in tongue tie. *Charlie Longsdon* — h– b–

CADELLIN 7 b.g. Black Sam Bellamy (IRE) – Clotted Cream (USA) (Eagle Eyed (USA)) [2017/18 h88, b–: h19.3m² May 11] modest form over hurdles. *Donald McCain* — h98

CADEYRN (IRE) 6 b.g. Flemensfirth (USA) – Kapricia Speed (FR) (Vertical Speed (FR)) [2017/18 h95: h20d h19.5v⁴ h22v* h22s² h23.3v* Mar 17] strong, lengthy gelding: will make a chaser: winning pointer: bumper winner: fairly useful form over hurdles: won novices at Newcastle in January and Uttoxeter in March: stays 23f: acts on heavy going. *Michael Scudamore* — h121

CADIRA BEECHES 8 b.m. Lucarno (USA) – Gipsy Girl (Motivate) [2017/18 h–: h19.5v Mar 21] no form over hurdles. *Robert Stephens* — h–

CADMIUM (FR) 6 b.g. Early March – Mirquille (FR) (Passing Sale (FR)) [2017/18 c20v³ c17.5s* c18s⁴ c16d* Apr 26] second foal: half-brother to French 21f-27f chase winner Viva Libertad (by Robin des Pres): dam French 19f-21f chase winner: won only start over hurdles: smart form over fences: won maiden at Fairyhouse (by 5½ lengths from Veinard) in February and handicap at Punchestown (by 8 lengths from Coeur Joyeux) in April: should stay at least 2½m: acts on soft going: tried in cheekpieces: front runner/races prominently, often travels strongly: good prospect. *W. P. Mullins, Ireland* — c148 p h–

*Star Best For Racing Coverage Champion Hunters Chase, Punchestown—
Caid du Berlais routs his field under Mr Will Biddick to become the sole British-trained winner
at the 2018 Punchestown Festival*

CADORE (IRE) 10 b.g. Hurricane Run (IRE) – Mansiya (Vettori (IRE)) [2017/18 h72: h20.2g³ h20.2g⁵ h16.2s h23.8g h16.4v⁴ h20.2s Apr 27] leggy gelding: poor handicap hurdler nowadays: stays easy 3m: acts on heavy going: wears cheekpieces. *Lucy Normile*   **h71**

CADOUGARDE (FR) 5 br.g. Kapgarde (FR) – Sparkling Elisa (FR) (Cadoudal (FR)) [2017/18 b15.7d⁶ h16v⁶ Jan 31] €10,500 3-y-o: first foal: dam unraced: failed to complete both starts in points: unplaced in bumper: 50/1, sixth in maiden at Down Royal (16 lengths behind Celtic Rising) on hurdling debut. *Stuart Crawford, Ireland*   **h91 b71**

CAFE AU LAIT (GER) 8 b.g. Nicaron (GER) – Cariera (GER) (Macanal (USA)) [2017/18 h84: h15.9s³ h20.5v² h19.7v² h19.2v² h19.2v³ Feb 14] sturdy gelding: modest handicap hurdler: stays 21f: acts on good to firm and heavy going: usually in headgear: wears tongue tie. *Dan Skelton*   **h96**

CAGED LIGHTNING (IRE) 8 b.g. Haatef (USA) – Rainbow Melody (IRE) (Rainbows For Life (CAN)) [2017/18 h21.3s⁵ Nov 3] fairly useful on Flat, stays 2½m: modest maiden hurdler: should stay at least 2½m: acts on soft going: in cheekpieces last 3 starts. *Steve Gollings*   **h99**

CAGLIOSTRO (FR) 6 gr.g. Lord du Sud (FR) – Belle de Liziere (FR) (Bojador (FR)) [2017/18 h16g h20g⁵ Jun 14] placed in points: little form over hurdles: left Colin Bowe after first start. *David Dennis*   **h–**

CAID DES MALBERAUX (FR) 6 b.g. Antarctique (IRE) – Miss Nosybe (FR) (Millkom) [2017/18 h20g^pu Jun 3] won only start in points: pulled up in maiden on hurdling debut. *Paul Nicholls*   **h–**

CAID DU BERLAIS (FR) 9 b.g. Westerner – Kenza du Berlais (FR) (Kahyasi) [2017/18 c143, h143: c26.3v⁵ c24.5s* Apr 27] leggy gelding: useful hurdler: useful chaser: won Champion Hunters Chase at Punchestown (by 21 lengths from Timewaitsfornoone) in April: stays 3¼m: acts on heavy going: wears tongue tie. *Mrs Rose Loxton*   **c133 h–**

CAID DU LIN (FR) 6 gr.g. Della Francesca (FR) – Asia du Lin (FR) (Agent Bleu (FR)) [2017/18 h124: h16.3g² h16.7g³ h17.7g* h15.7g h15.8g² h16s² h15.7d h19.3v^pu h16.5s² Feb 20] sturdy gelding: useful handicap hurdler: won at Fontwell in October: second in listed event at Sandown (½ length behind A Hare Breath) in December: stays 19f: acts on soft going: wears headgear/tongue tie. *Dr Richard Newland*   **h130**

CAI

CAILLEACH ANNIE (IRE) 9 b.m. Blueprint (IRE) – Graineuaile (IRE) (Orchestra) [2017/18 c108§, h–: c23.6v³ c30.7v⁴ c24v* c27.9v Apr 1] winning hurdler: fair handicap chaser: won at Uttoxeter in December: stays 31f: acts on heavy going: has worn cheekpieces, including in 2017/18: has worn tongue tie, including last 4 starts. *Jackie du Plessis*   c111 h–

CAIRNSHILL (IRE) 7 gr.g. Tikkanen (USA) – Ilikeyou (IRE) (Lord Americo) [2017/18 h92: h21.8g⁴ h23.3g² h22.5g³ h24.8g⁴ h20v h20s Feb 24] fair handicap hurdler: won at Kilbeggan in June: stays 27f: acts on soft going: usually wears tongue tie: usually races in rear. *Mark McNiff, Ireland*   h101

CAIUS MARCIUS (IRE) 7 b.g. King's Theatre (IRE) – Ain't Misbehavin (IRE) (Trempolino (USA)) [2017/18 h122: h16.2g* h17.2g⁴ h16.2s² h16.7g h20d Oct 29] good-topped gelding: fairly useful handicap hurdler: won at Perth in May: should prove suited by 2¼m+: acts on soft going. *Nicky Richards*   h122

CAJUN FIDDLE (IRE) 7 b.m. Robin des Champs (FR) – Silk Style (Polish Precedent (USA)) [2017/18 h118: c19.9g⁴ c19.1d⁶ c20.5m^pu Apr 26] lengthy mare: fairly useful hurdler: fair form over fences: best effort when fourth in novice handicap at Huntingdon in October: stays 21f: acts on soft going. *Alan King*   c102 h–

CAKE DE L'ISLE (FR) 6 b.g. Fragrant Mix (IRE) – Taiga de L'Isle (FR) (Ragmar (FR)) [2017/18 h116, b–: h21.1g^ur h20.6d⁶ h19.4d² h24.4d Feb 8] rangy gelding: has had breathing operation: fairly useful handicap hurdler: second at Doncaster in December: stays 21f: acts on good to firm and good to soft going: in tongue tie last 2 starts: usually races close up. *Jonjo O'Neill*   h125

CALACH (FR) 6 gr.g. Fragrant Mix (IRE) – Nobless d'Aron (FR) (Ragmar (FR)) [2017/18 b72: b16v² Nov 4] fair form in bumpers: in hood, second in maiden event at Ayr on sole start in 2017/18. *James Ewart*   b85

CALARULES 5 gr.g. Aussie Rules (USA) – Ailincala (IRE) (Pursuit of Love) [2017/18 h92: h15.7s⁴ h19v³ Feb 4] modest maiden hurdler: should stay 19f+: acts on soft going: has worn headgear. *Tim Vaughan*   h93

CALCULATED RISK 9 ch.g. Motivator – Glen Rosie (IRE) (Mujtahid (USA)) [2017/18 c–, h95§: h19.8s Nov 23] rather leggy gelding: modest hurdler, well held sole outing in 2017/18: lightly-raced maiden chaser: stays 2½m: acts on heavy going: has worn cheekpieces: temperamental. *Alexandra Dunn*   c– h– §

CALETT MAD (FR) 6 b.g. Axxos (GER) – Omelia (FR) (April Night (FR)) [2017/18 c145+, h–: h23.9v* h23.9g* h21.1d⁵ h24.4s⁴ h26.1s* h24v^pu h23.9s* Apr 25] tall gelding: useful hurdler: won novices at Perth in September and Cheltenham in October, handicap at Musselburgh in February and 3-runner listed novice at Perth (by 31 lengths from Scorpion Sid) in April: smart chaser: stays 3¼m: acts on heavy going: wears tongue tie: usually travels strongly. *Nigel Twiston-Davies*   c– h140

CALIFORNIA SOUL (IRE) 7 b.g. Yeats (IRE) – Pointing North (USA) (Orientate (USA)) [2017/18 h20g h19.5m h16g* h16.2g² h20g⁵ h16g³ h16.2d h15.6m Nov 8] first foal: dam ran twice on Flat: once-raced on Flat: maiden pointer: fair hurdler: won maiden at Tramore in June: left Denis Hogan after seventh start: unproven beyond 2m: best form on good going: wears headgear: often races towards rear. *Rose Dobbin*   h106

CALIN DU BRIZAIS (FR) 7 b.g. Loup Solitaire (USA) – Caline du Brizais (FR) (Turgeon (USA)) [2017/18 c112, h100: c24d³ c25.8m* c25.8s* c26.1g² c25.8d⁴ h26.5d⁵ c25.8d⁴ Sep 22] fair handicap hurdler: fairly useful handicap chaser: won at Newton Abbot in May (novice) and June: stays 3¼m: acts on soft and good to firm going: usually wears headgear: has worn tongue tie. *Nigel Hawke*   c121 h98

CALINO D'AIRY (FR) 6 ch.g. Anzillero (GER) – Monita d'Airy (FR) (Oblat (FR)) [2017/18 c18.2v* c18.2s* c16.2s³ c17d c19.9s³ Apr 12] €20,000 3-y-o, £150,000 4-y-o: leggy gelding: fourth foal: brother to Unilo d'Airy (French 2m-21f hurdle/chase winner) and half-brother to 2 winners in France by Legolas, including Bolano d'Airy (2½m cross-country chase winner): dam unraced half-sister to fairly useful French hurdler/chaser (17f/2¼m winner) Inima d'Airy: won maiden point on debut: winning hurdler: smart form over fences: won maiden (by 3 lengths from Close Shave) and novice (by 2¾ lengths from Dont Tell No One) in October, both at Galway: third in Craddockstown Novices' Chase at Punchestown (15½ lengths behind Woodland Opera) in November and Manifesto Novices' Chase at Aintree (5¼ lengths behind Finian's Oscar) in April: stays 2½m: acts on heavy going: front runner/races prominently. *Henry de Bromhead, Ireland*   c145 h–

176

CALIPSO COLLONGES (FR) 6 b.g. Crossharbour – Ivresse Collonges (FR) (Video Rock (FR)) [2017/18 h17.2m h16.5s h20v h16v⁵ h20s h19.9v* h23.4s* h18.6v* h22.8s* h24g Apr 18] half-brother to several winners in France, including fair hurdler/fairly useful chaser Aramis Collonges (2¼m-2½m winner, by Dom Alco): dam French 1½m-13.5f winner: fairly useful handicap hurdler: won at Uttoxeter/Fakenham (novices) in February, and Market Rasen (conditional) and Haydock in March: unplaced in 2 starts over fences in France: left Thomas Cooper after fifth start: stays 23f: best form on soft/heavy going: in hood last 5 starts: tongue tied last 4: usually travels strongly. *Olly Murphy* — c—, h119

CALIPTO (FR) 8 b.g. Califet (FR) – Peutiot (FR) (Valanour (IRE)) [2017/18 c136, h–: c16.8g⁵ c19.2v⁵ c20s⁵ c20d* Mar 31] tall gelding: has had breathing operation: winning hurdler: useful handicap chaser: won at Carlisle (by 8 lengths from Pistol Park) in March: stays 2½m: acts on heavy going: has worn hood: has worn tongue tie, including in 2017/18. *Venetia Williams* — c140, h—

CALIVIGNY (IRE) 9 b.g. Gold Well – Summer Holiday (IRE) (Kambalda) [2017/18 c117, h–: c20v² c20d c20s² c24.1v⁵ c20.5v³ c20s⁶ c23.8s⁴ Apr 25] winning hurdler: fair maiden chaser nowadays: stays 3m: acts on heavy going: wears headgear: tried in tongue tie: temperament under suspicion. *N. W. Alexander* — c112, h—

CALIX DELAFAYETTE (FR) 6 b.g. Caballo Raptor (CAN) – Obepinedelafayette (FR) (Sleeping Car (FR)) [2017/18 b93: h16.2s⁵ h18.1v* Apr 16] sturdy gelding: bumper winner: fairly useful form over hurdles: won novice at Kelso (by 18 lengths from Sunny Destination) in April: likely to stay 2½m: wears hood. *James Ewart* — h117

CALLAGHAN (GER) 5 b.g. Cacique (IRE) – Cent Cheveux Blanc (GER) (Pentire) [2017/18 h–: h15.9m Sep 24] lengthy gelding: maiden on Flat: no form over hurdles: in headgear last 5 starts: wears tongue tie. *Tom Gretton* — h—

CALL CARLO 11 ch.g. Karinga Bay – Lady Widd (IRE) (Commanche Run) [2017/18 h19.7s c24.5v² c24v* c24.5vᵘʳ c26.2s⁴ Apr 27] maiden hurdler, tailed off after 47 months off on return in 2017/18: modest form over fences: won handicap at Southwell in March: stays 3m: acts on heavy going: tried in blinkers. *Venetia Williams* — c96, h—

CALL HIM ANYTHING 4 b.g. Mount Nelson – Focosa (ITY) (In The Wings) [2017/18 b16.2s Dec 16] 25/1, last in junior bumper. *Matthew Salaman* — b—

CALLING DES BLINS (FR) 6 b.m. Konig Turf (GER) – Quelye des Blins (FR) (Silver Rainbow) [2017/18 h73p: h15.8m² h17.7m⁴ c16.3d⁴ Jul 31] modest form over hurdles: 6/1, well-beaten last of 4 in novice handicap at Newton Abbot on chasing debut: unproven beyond 2m: acts on good to firm going: wears tongue tie: usually races nearer last than first: takes strong hold. *Dan Skelton* — c—, h94

CALL IT MAGIC (IRE) 8 ch.g. Indian River (FR) – Luas Luso (IRE) (Luso) [2017/18 h24d⁵ c23s² c22.5s* h23.2v⁴ c23.5v³ c29v Apr 2] winning pointer: fairly useful maiden hurdler at best: useful chaser: won minor event at Ballinrobe in September and handicap at Galway (by 5½ lengths from The Winkler) in October: stays 3m: acts on heavy going: in blinkers last 5 starts: usually leads. *Ross O'Sullivan, Ireland* — c138, h109

CALL ME (IRE) 7 b.g. Craigsteel – Wake Me Gently (IRE) (Be My Native (USA)) [2017/18 h22.7g⁵ h22.7s⁶ h22v⁵ h25vᵖᵘ Feb 19] £10,000 6-y-o: angular gelding: brother to fairly useful 21f chase winner Jack Steel and fair 21f hurdle winner Ample Appeal: dam unraced half-sister to fair hurdler/fairly useful chaser (stays 3¼m) Belmount: winning pointer: modest form over hurdles. *Lucy Normile* — h97

CALL ME LORD (FR) 5 b.g. Slickly (FR) – Sosa (GER) (Cape Cross (IRE)) [2017/18 h141p: h15.8g³ h16s* h15.3s³ h16v² h21.5s* Apr 28] tall gelding: has scope: will make a chaser: very smart hurdler: won handicap at Sandown (by 3¼ lengths from Our Merlin) in January and Select Hurdle there (by 16 lengths from Lil Rockerfeller, relishing step up in trip) in April: stays 21f: acts on heavy going: often travels strongly. *Nicky Henderson* — h154

CALL ME SID 6 b.g. Schiaparelli (GER) – Zolotaya (Kayf Tara) [2017/18 b–: h21.4s h21.2s* h19.2d⁴ h19.5s Apr 27] fairly useful form over hurdles: won maiden at Ludlow in January: will stay 3m: front runner/races prominently. *Jennifer Mason* — h115

CALL ME VIC (IRE) 11 b.g. Old Vic – Call Me Dara (IRE) (Arapahos (FR)) [2017/18 c136, h–: c25g⁶ c25d⁴ c19.1d⁴ c23.4sᵖᵘ c24s c19.4dᵖᵘ Apr 22] good-topped gelding: winning hurdler: useful handicap chaser: fourth at Doncaster (7¾ lengths behind Markov) in December: lost form after: stays 3¼m: acts on good to firm and heavy going: in blinkers last 2 starts: front runner/races prominently. *Tom George* — c132, h—

CAL

CALL SIGN CHARLIE (IRE) 4 gr.f. Arakan (USA) – Ardea Brave (IRE) (Chester House (USA)) [2017/18 b13.7g Apr 20] fourth foal: half-sister to 2 winners on Flat, including smart 7f/1m winner Captain Joy (by Dark Angel): dam 11.5f/1½m winner: tailed off in bumper. *Brian Barr*   **b–**

CALLTHEBARMAN (IRE) 4 b.g. Lord Shanakill (USA) – African Scene (IRE) (Scenic) [2017/18 h16s⁶ h16v h16v h16v h16vᵖᵘ h15.8s* Mar 14] half-brother to several winners, including useful hurdler Jer's Girl (2m-2½m winner, by Jeremy) and modest hurdler/chaser Scenic Star (2¾m/23f winner, by Erewhon): dam lightly raced on Flat: modest form over hurdles: won lady riders handicap at Huntingdon in March: raced only at 2m: acts on soft going: in tongue tie last 3 starts. *Gavin Patrick Cromwell, Ireland*   **h99**

CALL THE COPS (IRE) 9 b.g. Presenting – Ballygill Heights (IRE) (Symboli Heights (FR)) [2017/18 c–, h109: h16.2g⁴ h21.5d⁵ h20.6g h16.2v Sep 14] sturdy gelding: useful handicap hurdler at best, well below form since 2015/16: behind when refused last on chasing debut: stays 3m: acts on good to firm and heavy ground: wears headgear. *Ben Haslam*   **c–** **h108**

CALL THE TAXIE (IRE) 7 b.g. Scorpion (IRE) – Mystic Moonbeam (IRE) (Supreme Leader) [2017/18 c20s* c22.5v³ c22.6s⁵ c24.5dᶠ c25vᵖᵘ h20v² h24v² h23.1s³ Mar 12] €6,000 3-y-o, £25,000 5-y-o: fourth foal: dam once-raced half-sister to smart hurdle winner around 2m Farmer Brown: useful handicap hurdler: second at Gowran (1¾ lengths behind Laid Back Luke) and Punchestown in February: similar form over fences: won maiden at Navan in September: third in minor event at Galway (9 lengths behind A Genie In Abottle) in October: stays 3m: acts on heavy going: has worn cheekpieces, including last 3 starts: tried in tongue tie. *Ellmarie Holden, Ireland*   **c134** **h134**

CALL TO ORDER 8 b.g. Presenting – Theatre Girl (King's Theatre (IRE)) [2017/18 h123: c24g² c20d h23.8d² Apr 24] well-made gelding: fairly useful handicap hurdler: second at Ludlow in April: similar form over fences: better effort when second in novice at Uttoxeter in September: stays 3m: acts on soft going: has worn cheekpieces, including final start: remains capable of better as a chaser. *Jonjo O'Neill*   **c117 p** **h118**

CALL ZAC (IRE) 9 b.g. Zerpour (IRE) – Dolly of Dublin (IRE) (Be My Native (USA)) [2017/18 c–: c20.1g⁵ c23.8g⁴ c24.2g Jun 3] maiden pointer: modest form in chases: tried in visor: in tongue tie last 4 starts. *Iain Jardine*   **c85**

CALVA D'HONORE (FR) 7 b.g. Khalkevi (IRE) – Elivette (FR) (Arvico (FR)) [2017/18 h107, b94: h20.3g³ h16g⁵ Jul 18] bumper winner: fair maiden hurdler: should stay 2½m: acts on good to soft going: usually leads. *Ben Pauling*   **h105**

CALYPSO DELEGATOR (IRE) 5 b.g. Lilbourne Lad (IRE) – Amber Nectar (IRE) (Barathea (IRE)) [2017/18 h–: h16.2d h16s h15.7d h15.7d³ h15.7s Jan 11] modest form over hurdles: raced only at 2m: acts on good to soft going: in headgear last 2 starts. *Micky Hammond*   **h87**

CALYPSO STORM (IRE) 7 b.g. Trans Island – Valin Thyne (IRE) (Good Thyne (USA)) [2017/18 h19.7s⁶ Jan 13] modest form in bumpers: 66/1, sixth in novice at Wetherby (36¼ lengths behind Noble Robin) on hurdling debut: bred to be suited by 2½m+. *Rebecca Menzies*   **h77**

CAMAKASI (IRE) 7 b.g. Camacho – Innocence (Unfuwain (USA)) [2017/18 h–: h15.9m Sep 24] sturdy gelding: fairly useful on Flat, stays 1½m: maiden hurdler, well held sole start in 2017/18: has worn headgear/tongue tie. *Ali Stronge*   **h–**

CAMAPLU (FR) 6 gr.m. Turgeon (USA) – Line Tzigane (FR) (Bonnet Rouge (FR)) [2017/18 h–: h16.3g⁴ h18.7g³ h15.8d⁶ Jul 28] poor form over hurdles: should stay beyond 2m. *David Bridgwater*   **h78**

CAMILLAS WISH (IRE) 9 b.m. Presenting – Take Ine (FR) (Take Risks (FR)) [2017/18 c23m* c23.4g* h23.3g* c25.5g* h23.9g⁵ c25.5s* c25.5g⁵ c29.2g c26.3sᵖᵘ c26.3v⁴ Mar 23] fair handicap hurdler: won novice event at Fakenham and mares event at Uttoxeter in June: fair chaser: won hunter at Down Royal in May, and handicaps at Cartmel in June and July: left J. T. R. Dreaper after first start, Richard Ford after seventh: stays 3¼m: acts on good to firm and heavy going: has worn cheekpieces. *Micky Hammond*   **c112** **h100**

CAMINO LADY (IRE) 8 br.m. Robin des Pres (FR) – Andromeda (IRE) (Barathea (IRE)) [2017/18 h19.3dᵖᵘ Dec 19] €2,500 3-y-o: seventh foal: half-sister to a winning pointer by Bob Back: dam lightly raced: in tongue strap, pulled up in novice hurdle. *David Thompson*   **h–**

CAMPEADOR (FR) 6 gr.g. Gris de Gris (IRE) – Royale Video (FR) (Video Rock (FR)) [2017/18 h153p: h16s* h16.2sᶠ h16s³ Dec 29] useful-looking gelding: smart hurdler: won minor event at Punchestown (by 1¾ lengths from Wakea) in October: raced around 2m: acts on heavy going: often in hood: tried in tongue tie. *Gordon Elliott, Ireland*   **h151**

CAMRON DE CHAILLAC (FR) 6 br.g. Laverock (IRE) – Hadeel (Polish Precedent (USA)) [2017/18 h105: h20s⁶ h19.5v⁵ h15.3v³ h19s* h21.2v* h23.9v^pu h19.5v⁵ h21.7s³ Apr 6] close-coupled gelding: fairly useful handicap hurdler: won at Taunton (conditional) in December and Sedgefield in January: third at Fontwell in April: stays 2¾m: acts on good to firm and heavy going: usually wears headgear: usually leads. *Nigel Hawke*   **h116**

CANARDIER (FR) 6 b.g. Crillon (FR) – Idylle du Marais (FR) (Panoramic) [2017/18 b109p: h20s³ h16c⁵ Dec 26] bumper winner: useful form over hurdles: better effort when third in maiden at Fairyhouse (5 lengths behind Jetz) in November: tried in hood: remains capable of better. *Dermot Anthony McLoughlin, Ireland*   **h130 p**

CANDLELIGHT STORY 8 b.m. Kayf Tara – Foehn Gale (IRE) (Strong Gale) [2017/18 h19.9d h15.8d h16.7g Oct 31] sister to fair hurdler/fairly useful chaser Circus of Dreams (2m-3m winner) and a winning pointer, and half-sister to several winners, including bumper winner/fair chaser Super Road Train (3m-3½m winner, by Petoski): dam unraced: little impact in novice/maiden hurdles: should do better. *Jennie Candlish*   **h– p**

CANDYMAN CAN (IRE) 8 b.g. Holy Roman Emperor (IRE) – Palwina (FR) (Unfuwain (USA)) [2017/18 h15.7v^pu h15.8d⁴ Apr 24] lengthy, rather sparely-made gelding: fairly useful at one time on Flat: modest maiden hurdler: best effort at 2½m: acts on good to soft going: tried in hood. *Laura Hurley*   **h94**

CANDY MIX 5 gr.m. Fair Mix (IRE) – Escapado (USA) (Red Ransom (USA)) [2017/18 b15.8g b16m Jul 5] second foal: dam unraced half-sister to useful hurdler/fairly useful chaser (2m winner) Mutual Friend: no form in bumpers. *Roy Brotherton*   **b–**

CANELIE (FR) 6 b.m. Gentlewave (IRE) – Medjie (FR) (Cyborg (FR)) [2017/18 h16d⁴ h20v^pu h19s* h18s^pu h19v^pu Apr 12] half-sister to several winners, including useful hurdler Upsie (2m-2½m winner, by Le Balafre): dam unraced sister to useful/ungenuine chaser Nadover (stayed 31f): multiple bumper winner in France: fairly useful handicap hurdler: won at Taunton in January: left Gordon Elliott after second start: stays 19f: acts on heavy going: in tongue tie last 2 starts. *Harry Fry*   **h128**

CANELO (IRE) 5 ch.g. Mahler – Nobody's Darling (IRE) (Supreme Leader) [2017/18 h19.5d² h21.4s² h23.9s⁵ h19.4s* h19.8v⁴ h21.7g* Apr 20] €9,000 3-y-o, £26,000 4-y-o: sturdy gelding: sixth foal: half-brother to fair hurdler/chaser Debt To Society (19f-27f winner) and a winning pointer (both by Moscow Society): dam unraced: runner-up in point: fairly useful form over hurdles: won novices at Doncaster in February and Fontwell in April: should stay 3m: acts on soft going. *Alan King*   **h124**

CANFORD CHIMES (IRE) 5 b.g. Canford Cliffs (IRE) – Appleblossom Pearl (IRE) (Peintre Celebre (USA)) [2017/18 b90: b13.6g* b16.7g Jun 23] fair form in bumpers: won at Fontwell in May: left Alan King after first start. *Philip Kirby*   **b90**

CANFORD KILBEY (IRE) 5 b.m. Canford Cliffs (IRE) – Sweet Namibia (IRE) (Namid) [2017/18 h–: h16.8g⁶ May 4] modest on Flat: little form over hurdles. *Tony Coyle*   **h–**

CANGODEMAYO 6 b.m. Lucarno (USA) – Cadoutene (FR) (Cadoudal (FR)) [2017/18 b17d h21.2d⁵ h20.5s^pu Jan 17] sixth foal: half-sister to fairly useful hurdler/chaser Cecil Corbett (2¼m-23f winner, by Bollin Eric) and French hurdler Muhtatene (15f winner, by Muhtathir): dam unraced half-sister to fair hurdler/fairly useful chaser (stayed 3m) Blu Teen: Irish point winner: tailed off in mares bumper: poor form over hurdles. *Ben Pauling*   **h79 b–**

CANICALLYOUBACK 10 b.g. Auction House (USA) – Island Colony (USA) (Pleasant Colony (USA)) [2017/18 c126, h104: h16d⁴ c16.2g⁵ c19.4g⁵ c17g³ c16.5g c17g³ h16.5g c15.9d³ c18.2s^pu Feb 20] fair handicap hurdler/chaser nowadays: stays 19f: acts on good to firm and good to soft going: tried in visor. *Evan Williams*   **c112 h102**

CAN MESTRET (IRE) 11 b.g. Millenary – River Anita (IRE) (Riverhead (USA)) [2017/18 c17.4s² May 18] smallish gelding: multiple point winner: fair hunter chaser: stays 21f: acts on heavy going: has worn hood. *S. R. Andrews*   **c110**

CANNY STYLE 5 b.m. Canford Cliffs (IRE) – Stylish One (IRE) (Invincible Spirit (IRE)) [2017/18 h17d² h15.6g* h16.8s³ h15.6d³ Feb 14] fairly useful on Flat: fair form over hurdles: won mares maiden at Musselburgh in November: likely to prove best at sharp 2m. *Kevin Ryan*   **h108**

CANNY TOM (IRE) 8 b.g. Jimble (FR) – Tombazaan (IRE) (Good Thyne (USA)) [2017/18 h102: h18.8g^f h16.5m⁴ h18.8g² h16.5m³ h16.7g² h16.4g² h16g² h16.6s h16g² h16s* h16.5s h17.3v² c16d³ c19.2d* c18.2s⁶ h16.4d Nov 17] sturdy gelding: fair hurdler: won maiden at Tramore in August: fair form over fences: won maiden at Downpatrick in October: stays 2½m: acts on good to firm and heavy going: tried in hood: wears tongue tie: usually races towards rear. *Gordon Elliott, Ireland*   **c114 h106**

CAN

CANOODLE 6 b.m. Stimulation (IRE) – Flirtatious (Generous (IRE)) [2017/18 h109, b85: h16.3g⁶ h15.8g³ h19.4s⁵ h19.8d² Apr 22] leggy mare: bumper winner: fair handicap hurdler: barely stays 19f: acts on good to firm and good to soft going: wears headgear. *Hughie Morrison*   **h114**

CANTLOW (IRE) 13 b.g. Kayf Tara – Winnowing (IRE) (Strong Gale) [2017/18 c147, h122+: h23d c30.2g⁴ c30.2d² c30.2s^pu c33.5d⁵ Apr 26] well-made gelding: useful hurdler at best: useful chaser: second in cross-country event at Cheltenham (2½ lengths behind Bless The Wings) in December: stayed 33f: acted on good to firm and heavy going: refitted with headgear last 4 starts: tried in tongue tie: dead. *Enda Bolger, Ireland*   **c142 h–**

CANTON PRINCE (IRE) 7 b.g. Shantou (USA) – Hasainm (IRE) (Grand Lodge (USA)) [2017/18 h124, b96: h20d³ h19.7s⁴ Nov 4] bumper winner: fairly useful handicap hurdler: stays 2½m: acts on soft going. *Tim Vaughan*   **h123**

CANT PAY WONT PAY (IRE) 10 b.g. Flying Legend (USA) – Kadastrofs Prize (IRE) (Kadastrof (FR)) [2017/18 c23.5g* c22.1g² c24g c23.5v² c24.2d^ur c24.2s³ c26.3s^ur c25.2v c20.1v⁵ h24.1d Mar 29] point winner: well held in handicap on hurdling debut: modest chaser: won maiden hunter at Downpatrick in May: left Mark Fahey after fourth start: stays 23f: acts on heavy going: has worn headgear, including in 2017/18: tried in tongue tie. *Rose Dobbin*   **c97 h–**

CANYON CITY 5 b.g. Authorized (IRE) – Colorado Dawn (Fantastic Light (USA)) [2017/18 h16g³ h15.8g* h15.8g³ h15.5v⁵ h16s Mar 16] good-topped gelding: fairly useful maiden on Flat: fair form over hurdles: won novice at Huntingdon in October: raced only at 2m: best form on good going. *Neil King*   **h114**

CANYOUHEARMENOW (IRE) 7 b.g. Trans Island – First of April (IRE) (Presenting) [2017/18 h20.5d h15.9s h19.2v c17v c21.7v^pu c23.5v c26v* c26.2s⁵ Apr 27] no form over hurdles: poor form over fences: won handicap at Fontwell in March: stays 3¼m: acts on heavy going: in headgear last 5 starts, tongue tied last 2. *Diana Grissell*   **c72 h–**

CANYOURINGMEBACK (IRE) 6 b.g. Robin des Pres (FR) – Hunters Bar (IRE) (Treasure Hunter) [2017/18 h17.7v² h15.5v⁶ h21.7d c19.4d⁶ Apr 22] €7,000 3-y-o, £52,000 5-y-o: fourth foal: dam (c93/h107) bumper/19f hurdle winner: Irish point winner: fair form over hurdles: 9/1, sixth in novice handicap at Stratford (29 lengths behind Zamparelli) on chasing debut: best effort at 2¼m: acts on heavy going: tried in hood. *Nick Gifford*   **c82 h103**

CAPARD KING (IRE) 9 b.g. Beneficial – Capard Lady (IRE) (Supreme Leader) [2017/18 c127, h–: c25g c26.1d⁶ c26d³ c24s^ur c24d³ c25.5s² c29.2v³ c24g Apr 20] sturdy gelding: winning hurdler: fairly useful handicap chaser: placed 4 times in 2017/18: stays 29f: acts on heavy going: wears cheekpieces: usually leads: temperamental. *Jonjo O'Neill*   **c121 § h–**

CAP D'AUBOIS (FR) 6 br.g. Snow Cap (FR) – Caline Grace (FR) (Marmato) [2017/18 h136: h24d* h22.8s h24.4g⁴ c23s² c21s c21.5v³ Jan 27] fairly useful hurdler: won minor event at Tipperary in July: useful form over fences: best effort when second in maiden at same course (¾ length behind Death Duty) in October: stays 3m: acts on soft going: tried in tongue tie. *W. P. Mullins, Ireland*   **c136 h121**

CAP DU NORD (FR) 5 br.g. Voix du Nord (FR) – Qualite Controlee (FR) (Poliglote) [2017/18 h16g⁶ h16d h16s⁶ h16s* h15.7v³ h16.5s^pu h21.6s⁴ Apr 23] sturdy gelding: fourth foal: half-brother to 3 winners, including useful hurdler Qualando (2m-19f winner, by Lando) and bumper winner Au Quart de Tour (2m winner, by Robin des Champs): dam, French 17f-19f hurdle/chase winner, also 13f winner on Flat: second on completed start in Irish maiden points: fair hurdler: won novice handicap at Sandown in December: unproven beyond 2m: acts on soft going. *Christian Williams*   **h105**

CAPE CASTER (IRE) 7 br.g. Cape Cross (IRE) – Playboy Mansion (IRE) (Grand Lodge (USA)) [2017/18 c115, h117: c16.5m* c16.3s² c15.7g³ c17g² c16.5g⁵ Sep 18] rather leggy gelding: winning hurdler: fairly useful handicap chaser: won at Worcester in May: raced mainly around 2m: acts on good to firm and heavy going: often let down by jumping over fences. *Evan Williams*   **c117 x h–**

CAPE HIDEAWAY 6 b.g. Mount Nelson – Amiata (Pennekamp (USA)) [2017/18 h98: h20.6g² h20.1g* h20g⁴ h16.2v^pu h16.6d h21.3s h18.6v² h16.8v² h16.7v⁴ h20.1d⁴ Apr 23] fair handicap hurdler: won at Hexham in May: stays 21f: acts on heavy going: wears cheekpieces: usually races close up. *Mark Walford*   **h110**

CAPELAND (FR) 6 b.g. Poliglote – Neiland (FR) (Cyborg (FR)) [2017/18 h121: h18.7g² h19.8s⁴ h15.3v² Dec 7] good-topped gelding: fairly useful handicap hurdler: made frame all 3 starts in 2017/18: stays 2½m: acts on heavy going: in hood last 3 starts: tried in tongue tie: strong traveller. *Paul Nicholls*   **h127**

CAP

CAPE OF GLORY (IRE) 5 br.g. Cape Cross (IRE) – Stairway To Glory (IRE) (Kalanisi (IRE)) [2017/18 h110: h19.6g^6 h19.9g^2 h20.9g^2 h16.8s^3 Dec 8] close-coupled gelding: fairly useful on Flat: fair form over hurdles: stays 21f: acts on good to soft going: wears headgear: often races prominently/travels strongly. *Keith Dalgleish*   **h111**

CAP HORNER (FR) 6 gr.g. Apsis – Rapsodie Sea (FR) (April Night (FR)) [2017/18 h96, b63: h23s^3 h23.3d^3 h19.9m^5 c23.6v^{pu} c23.5s* c23s^{pu} c19.2v^4 c20.2v^4 c21.6d^2 c28.4s* c25.7s^3 Apr 15] fair form over hurdles: fair handicap chaser: won at Lingfield (novice) in December and Taunton in March: stays 3½m: acts on soft and good to firm going. *Seamus Mullins*   **c112 h108**

CAPITAINE (FR) 6 gr.g. Montmartre (FR) – Patte de Velour (FR) (Mansonnien (FR)) [2017/18 h139: c16.3g* c17.2g* c15.5d^F h16.2g^2 Apr 18] good-topped gelding: useful handicap hurdler: smart form over fences: won maiden at Newton Abbot (by 10 lengths from The Gipper) in May and novice at Market Rasen (by 22 lengths from Western Miller) in October: raced mainly around 2m: acts on any going: has worn hood, including final start: usually races close up, often travels strongly. *Paul Nicholls*   **c146 h131**

CAPITOUL (FR) 6 b.g. Enrique – Ranavalo (GER) (Ungaro (GER)) [2017/18 h119: h16.7d^6 h16d^F h15.6d^6 h15.8v^6 h15.5v h16d^{ur} c16.5g* Apr 24] neat gelding: fair handicap hurdler: 7/1, won novice handicap at Huntingdon (by 10 lengths from Nightfly) on chasing debut: raced mainly around 2m: acts on soft going: tried in hood: likely to progress further as a chaser. *Dr Richard Newland*   **c126 p h109**

CAP'N (IRE) 7 b.g. Gamut (IRE) – Dawn Princess (IRE) (Old Vic) [2017/18 h15.8s h16v^3 h15.3s^5 h24v^4 c16d* Mar 22] workmanlike gelding: first foal: dam, second in point, sister to fairly useful hurdler/useful chaser (stayed 3m) Toby Lerone: no form on Flat (highly tried): well held over hurdles: 20/1, won 3-runner novice at Ludlow (by 2½ lengths from Tree of Liberty) on chasing debut: raced mainly at 2m: acts on good to soft going: tried in tongue tie. *Claire Dyson*   **c95 ? h95 ?**

CAPOTE (IRE) 10 b.g. Oscar (IRE) – Kinsellas Rose (IRE) (Roselier (FR)) [2017/18 c26.2d^F c23.6v^{ur} c24.2s^F h23.8s h24.4s^4 Feb 21] strong gelding: fairly useful form over hurdles, showed retains some ability final start: failed to complete all 3 outings over fences (off 3½ years before return): stays 25f: acts on heavy going: tried in cheekpieces: in tongue tie last 2 starts. *Jonjo O'Neill*   **c– x h106**

CAPPAWAY (IRE) 5 b.g. Getaway (GER) – Cappa Or (IRE) (Oscar (IRE)) [2017/18 b16.2g h16.5v^F h17.7s h19.2s^6 h16.8v Apr 17] unplaced in bumper: no form in maiden/ novice hurdles. *Evan Williams*   **h– b–**

CAPPIELOW PARK 9 b.g. Exceed And Excel (AUS) – Barakat (Bustino) [2017/18 c–, h104: h16s Apr 27] sturdy gelding: fair hurdler, well held sole outing in 2017/18: fairly useful chaser: stays 2½m: acts on heavy going: has worn headgear/tongue tie. *Tim Vaughan*   **c– h–**

CAPRICE D'ANGLAIS (FR) 6 gr.g. Kapgarde (FR) – Odile de Neulliac (FR) (Turgeon (USA)) [2017/18 c105, h105: h16g^6 h15.8g c20.2s^3 c19.4v^3 Feb 2] leggy gelding: modest handicap hurdler: fair handicap chaser: left Sam Thomas after second start: stays 2½m: acts on firm and soft going: wears headgear: in tongue tie last 2 starts: front runner/races prominently. *Charlie Longsdon*   **c102 h85**

CAPSIS DESBOIS (FR) 6 b.g. Apsis – Gesse Parade (FR) (Dress Parade) [2017/18 h100, b64: h21.4g^{pu} c20d^{pu} Nov 14] maiden hurdler: pulled up in novice handicap on chasing debut. *Gary Moore*   **c– h–**

CAP SOLEIL (FR) 5 b.m. Kapgarde (FR) – Move Again (FR) (Noir Et Or) [2017/18 b109: h16.3d* h16.3d^2 h18.9v* h16.8s^2 Mar 15] good-topped mare: unbeaten in 3 bumpers: useful form over hurdles: won mares novice at Newbury (by 7 lengths from Countister) in November and listed mares novice at Haydock (by neck from Angels Antics) in December: second in Dawn Run Mares' Hurdle at Cheltenham (18 lengths behind Laurina) in March: likely to stay 2½m. *Fergal O'Brien*   **h132**

CAP ST VINCENT (FR) 5 b.g. Muhtathir – Criquetot (FR) (Epervier Bleu) [2017/18 b–: h19s h15.3v^4 h15.8v^3 Apr 1] point winner: modest form over hurdles: best effort when third in novice at Ffos Las in April: left Paul Nicholls after first start. *Tim Vaughan*   **h97**

CAPSY DE MEE (FR) 6 b.g. Apsis – Koeur de Mee (FR) (Video Rock (FR)) [2017/18 h102: c19.4g^2 c16.4g^3 c16s^6 h23.5d h19.6s^{pu} Jan 26] rather unfurnished gelding: bumper winner: maiden hurdler, no form in 2017/18: fair form over fences: best effort when second in novice handicap at Stratford in August: stays 19f: best form on good to soft: tried in cheekpieces/tongue tie. *Jamie Snowden*   **c113 h–**

CAP

CAPTAIN BLACK 6 b.g. Black Sam Bellamy (IRE) – Midlem Melody (Syrtos) [2017/18 h19.3v⁶ h17d h20s h24.1v h17v h17d h19.3v³ Apr 17] sixth foal: dam (c90/h60) 2m-2½m hurdle/chase winner: poor maiden hurdler: stays 19f: acts on heavy going: usually races towards rear. *Stuart Coltherd* — **h84**

CAPTAIN BROWN 10 b.g. Lomitas – Nicola Bella (IRE) (Sadler's Wells (USA)) [2017/18 c–x, h118: h16.2g² h17.2g² h17.2d h16.2g⁵ Sep 20] rather leggy, lengthy gelding: fairly useful handicap hurdler: second at Cartmel in June: maiden chaser: best around 2m: acts on soft going: tried in headgear/tongue tie: often races towards rear: often let down by jumping over fences. *James Moffatt* — **c– x / h121**

CAPTAIN BUCK'S (FR) 6 b.g. Buck's Boum (FR) – Ombre Jaune (FR) (Brier Creek (USA)) [2017/18 h23.1m² h24.2d c23p³ c25.1v³ c23s² c23.8d² c26s c24.2d³ Apr 7] fairly useful form over hurdles: similar form over fences: second in handicaps at Taunton (novice) in January and Ludlow (amateur) in February: stays 25f: acts on heavy going: in cheekpieces last 5 starts: wears tongue tie. *Paul Nicholls* — **c125 / h118**

CAPTAIN CAMELOT (IRE) 9 b.g. Urban Ocean (FR) – Harneyspet (IRE) (Sharifabad (IRE)) [2017/18 c73: c23.6s Apr 27] multiple point winner: poor form in novice hunter chases: wears hood/tongue tie. *Miss C. Packwood* — **c–**

CAPTAIN CATTISTOCK 5 b.g. Black Sam Bellamy (IRE) – Pearl Buttons (Alflora (IRE)) [2017/18 h19.5d⁴ h21.4s⁴ h19.8v⁴ h19.3s⁴ h21.4v⁴ h20.3g⁴ Apr 18] €20,000 3-y-o: third foal: closely related to fair/ungenuine hurdler Pearlita (2¾m-3m winner, by Milan): dam unraced sister to fairly useful hurdler/useful chaser (2m-3¼m winner) Pearlysteps and half-sister to useful hurdler/fairly useful chaser (2m winner) Oyster Shell: point winner: useful form over hurdles: won novice in November, handicap in February and novice in March, all at Wincanton: fourth in novice at Cheltenham (4¼ lengths behind Diese des Bieffes) in April: will prove suited by 3m: acts on heavy going: in tongue tie last 5 starts: front runner/races prominently, usually travels strongly. *Paul Nicholls* — **h132**

CAPTAIN CHAOS (IRE) 7 ch.g. Golan (IRE) – Times Have Changed (IRE) (Safety Catch (USA)) [2017/18 c133p, h–: c23.6d⁶ c25s* c24.2s* c24.2v⁴ c23.9s* c25s⁵ Apr 13] lengthy, raw-boned gelding: winning hurdler: useful chaser: won novices at Aintree (by 19 lengths from Coastal Tiep) and Wetherby (by 1¼ lengths from Three Ways) in November, and Market Rasen in February: likely to stay extreme distances: best form on soft/heavy going: in blinkers last 5 starts: usually leads. *Dan Skelton* — **c141 / h–**

CAPTAIN CLAYTON (IRE) 11 b.g. Subtle Power (IRE) – Dont Hurry (IRE) (Muroto) [2017/18 h107: h19.3m³ May 11] fair hurdler, well held sole outing in 2017/18: stays 2¾m, effective at much shorter granted good test: acts on soft going: has worn tongue tie: usually races nearer last than first. *Simon West* — **h–**

CAPTAIN COCKLE 5 b.g. Indian Haven – Demand (Red Ransom (USA)) [2017/18 h16s Nov 28] little impact on Flat: tailed off in novice on hurdling debut. *Roger Teal* — **h–**

CAPTAIN DRAKE (IRE) 5 b.g. Getaway (GER) – Julika (GER) (Nebos (GER)) [2017/18 b15.7v* Mar 29] €36,000 3-y-o, £115,000 4-y-o: half-brother to useful hurdler/chaser Tornado In Milan (2m-2½m winner, by Milan): dam German 10.5f/11.5f winner: runner-up in point: in hood, 5/2, won maiden bumper at Towcester (by 1¾ lengths from J'ai Froid). *Harry Fry* — **b98**

CAPTAIN FELIX 6 b.g. Captain Gerrard (IRE) – Sweet Applause (IRE) (Acclamation) [2017/18 h105: h18.6g³ h18.6g⁵ h15.8g* h15.8g Oct 26] leggy gelding: fair handicap hurdler: won at Huntingdon in October: may prove best at around 2m: best form on good going: races prominently. *James Eustace* — **h109**

CAPTAIN FLASH (IRE) 9 b.g. Indian River (FR) – Westgate Run (Emperor Jones (USA)) [2017/18 c79, h–: h23g^pu May 26] little impact in points: maiden hurdler, pulled up sole start in 2017/18: winning chaser: stays 3m: acts on heavy going: in headgear last 5 starts: has worn tongue tie. *Jo Davis* — **c– / h–**

CAPTAIN GEORGE (IRE) 7 b.g. Bushranger (IRE) – High Society Girl (IRE) (Key of Luck (USA)) [2017/18 h55: h15.7m³ h15.8d² h19.1m² h16d⁶ h20f⁴ h20.5d⁵ h18.5s⁵ Apr 25] fair on Flat: modest maiden hurdler: stays 19f: acts on good to firm and good to soft going. *Michael Blake* — **h97**

CAPTAIN HOX (IRE) 9 b.g. Danehill Dancer (IRE) – Shangri La (IRE) (Sadler's Wells (USA)) [2017/18 c112§, h–: c20.1g⁶ c25g Jun 4] winning hurdler: fairly useful chaser at best, no form in 2017/18: stays 2½m: acts on heavy going: has worn headgear: wears tongue tie: has hung right/looked half-hearted. *Patrick Griffin, Ireland* — **c– § / h–**

CAR

CAPTAIN JACK 5 b.g. Mount Nelson – Court Princess (Mtoto) [2017/18 b–: h16.3g[5] h16s[5] h19.7g[3] h15.8s[5] h15.8s[5] h16v[3] Mar 28] fair form over hurdles: stays 2½m: acts on soft going. *Richard Price* — **h103**

CAPTAIN MORLEY 7 b.g. Hernando (FR) – Oval Office (Pursuit of Love) [2017/18 h95P: h19g[4] h16g[3] h16g Sep 12] well-made gelding: useful on Flat: fair form over hurdles. *David Simcock* — **h103**

CAPTAIN MOWBRAY 7 ch.g. Shami – Some Like It Hot (Ashkalani (IRE)) [2017/18 h101: h21.2g[6] c20.1g[5] c20.1g[3] c19.3d[F] c21.1g[2] c20.3d[5] c24.2s[*] c25.2d[3] c24s[3] ab16.3g[3] c24g[ur] Apr 20] fair maiden hurdler, below form sole outing in 2017/18: fair handicap chaser: won novice at Wetherby in December: stays 25f: acts on soft going: wears cheekpieces: held up. *Rebecca Menzies* — **c108 h–**

CAPTAINOFINDUSTRY (IRE) 9 b.g. Definite Article – Talk of Rain (FR) (Turgeon (USA)) [2017/18 c–, h–: h19.2g[*] h20.7g[*] h24g[6] h25g Oct 5] rangy gelding: fair handicap hurdler: won at Towcester and Huntingdon in May: no form over fences: stays 3m: acts on heavy going: has worn headgear: front runner/races prominently. *Mark Pitman* — **c– h112**

CAPTAIN PEACOCK 5 b.g. Champs Elysees – Blast Furnace (IRE) (Sadler's Wells (USA)) [2017/18 h15.8d[5] h20.8d[6] h20s[pu] Dec 19] dam sister to useful hurdler/fairly useful chaser (stayed 2½m) Run With The Wind: fairly useful on Flat: fair form over hurdles: best effort when sixth in novice at Doncaster in December: in blinkers last 2 starts. *Oliver Sherwood* — **h101**

CAPTAIN REDBEARD (IRE) 9 ch.g. Bach (IRE) – Diesel Dancer (IRE) (Toulon) [2017/18 c139, h–: c20.5v[3] c21.1v[6] c22.9v[*] c25.6v[2] h20.5v[*] c34.3s[ur] Apr 14] sturdy gelding: useful handicap hurdler: won at Ayr (by ¾ length from Elusive Theatre) in March: useful handicap chaser: won at Haydock (by 6 lengths from Catamaran du Seuil) in December: stays 3¼m: acts on heavy going. *Stuart Coltherd* — **c144 h141**

CAPTAIN SHARPE 10 ch.g. Tobougg (IRE) – Helen Sharp (Pivotal) [2017/18 c75§, h67§: c23.4g[pu] c24.2g[*] h23.3s[pu] c20v[5] c16.4s[pu] c23.8s[6] h19.9v[3] c19.3v[6] c16.4v[2] c16.3v[5] c15.6d[ur] Apr 23] sturdy gelding: poor hurdler: poor handicap chaser: won at Hexham in May: stays 3¼m, as effective at much shorter: acts on good to firm and heavy going: wears headgear: wears tongue tie: unreliable. *Kenny Johnson* — **c76 § h78 §**

CAPTAIN SIMON (IRE) 6 b.g. Dubai Destination (USA) – Gayephar (Phardante (FR)) [2017/18 b95: h16d h16s h16d Nov 27] well-made gelding: won point on debut: bumper winner: well held in novice/maiden hurdles. *Dan Skelton* — **h–**

CAPTAIN ZEBO (IRE) 6 b.g. Brian Boru – Waydale Hill (Minster Son) [2017/18 b16.7d[*] h16v[pu] Dec 28] sixth foal: closely related to fair hurdler Theatre Evening (2¾m winner, by King's Theatre): dam (h73), maiden hurdler (stayed 23f), half-sister to fairly useful hurdler/useful chaser (2½m/21f winner) Buckby Lane: won bumper at Bangor (by 15 lengths from Holryale) on debut: pulled up in maiden hurdle: left Ms N. M. Hugo after first start. *M. F. Morris, Ireland* — **h– b92**

CAPTIVA ISLAND (IRE) 5 b.g. Scorpion (IRE) – Sapphire Eile (Mujtahid (USA)) [2017/18 b16m[6] b15.8d[3] b16g[2] h16s[4] h15.8d[2] h19.9s[2] h16v[5] Jan 22] €20,000 3-y-o: half-brother to useful cross-country chaser Another Jewel (3m-4½m winner, by Saddlers' Hall) and bumper winner Tahrir Square (by Catcher In The Rye): dam, unraced, out of half-sister to Istabraq: fair form in bumpers: similar form over hurdles: left Gordon Elliott after third start: will stay at least 2¾m: tried in cheekpieces: signs of temperament. *Olly Murphy* — **h110 b87**

CARALINE (FR) 7 b.m. Martaline – Vie Ta Vie (FR) (Villez (USA)) [2017/18 c116, h–: c20s[4] c19.4s[*] c19.4v[3] c15.2v[2] c20v[3] c15.2d[2] c17.1v[*] Apr 7] winning hurdler: fairly useful handicap chaser: won at Wetherby in December and Kelso in April: stays 2½m: acts on heavy going: has worn headgear, including last 4 starts: wears tongue tie: usually races close up. *Micky Hammond* — **c128 h–**

CARD GAME (IRE) 9 b.m. Scorpion (IRE) – Cardona (Dashing Blade) [2017/18 h121: h17.2m[3] h20.1g[2] h16.2v Apr 7] small, compact mare: fairly useful handicap hurdler: second at Hexham in June: stays 21f: acts on soft and good to firm going. *Ruth Jefferson* — **h120**

CAREFULLY SELECTED (IRE) 6 b.g. Well Chosen – Knockamullen Girl (IRE) (Alderbrook) [2017/18 b20s[*] b16s[*] b16.4s[2] b16.3s[3] Apr 25] €10,000 3-y-o, £100,000 5-y-o: well-made gelding: second foal: dam unraced half-sister to dam of smart hurdler/ — **b123**

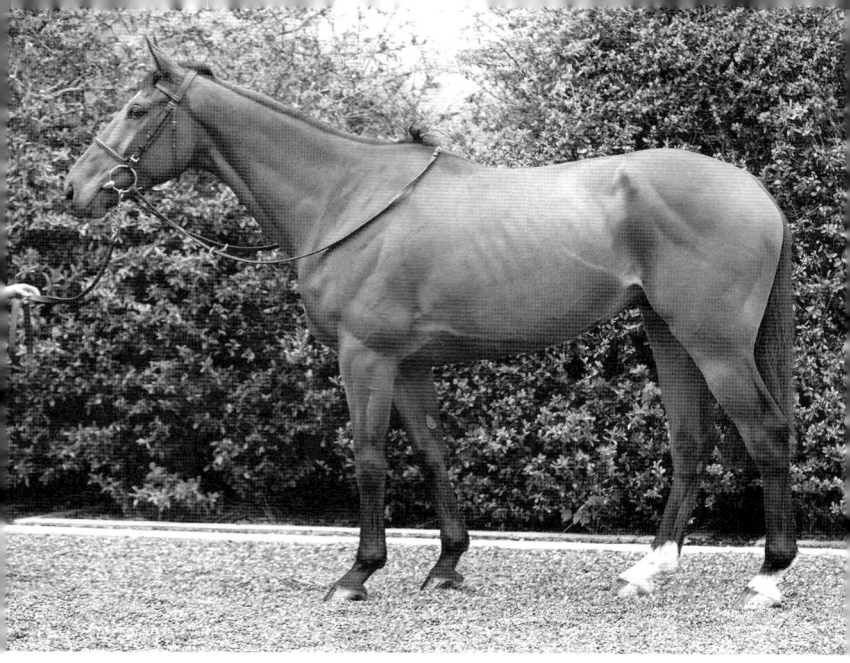

Miss M. A. Masterson's "Carefully Selected"

chaser (stayed 3m) Lord Sam: point winner: smart form in bumpers: won at Leopardstown (maiden) in December and Naas in February: placed in Champion Bumper (neck behind Relegate) at Cheltenham and Champion INH Flat Race (3 lengths behind Tornado Flyer) at Punchestown. *W. P. Mullins, Ireland*

CARIBERT (FR) 5 b.g. Ballingarry (IRE) – Cardamine (FR) (Garde Royale) [2017/18 b15.3s* b16.8v² b16.3s* Mar 24] £34,000 3-y-o: well-made gelding: half-brother to several winners in France, including useful hurdler/chaser Corscia (17f-21f winner, by Nickname): dam, French maiden hurdler, half-sister to fairly useful hurdler/useful chaser (stayed 3m) Caribou and to dam of smart hurdler/chaser (stays 2½m) Benie des Dieux: useful form in bumpers: won at Wincanton (by 4½ lengths from Hideaway Vic) in November and Goffs UK Spring Sales Bumper at Newbury (by 2¾ lengths from Hotter Than Hell) in March. *Harry Fry* **b112**

CARLI KING (IRE) 12 b.g. Witness Box (USA) – Abinitio Lady (IRE) (Be My Native (USA)) [2017/18 c119: c29.1m⁵ c26.1g³ May 28] fair handicap chaser: stays 29f: acts on heavy going: wears headgear: usually leads. *Caroline Bailey* **c108**

CARLINGFORD LOUGH (IRE) 12 b.g. King's Theatre (IRE) – Baden (IRE) (Furry Glen) [2017/18 c159, h121+: c25d c24sᵘʳ c20.2v⁵ c24dᵖᵘ c34.3sᵖᵘ Apr 14] lengthy gelding: winning hurdler: top-class chaser at best, no form in 2017/18: tried in tongue tie: held up. *John E. Kiely, Ireland* **c–** **h–**

CARLINGFORD PRINCE (IRE) 9 ch.g. Definite Article – Castle Hope (IRE) (Old Vic) [2017/18 h94: h22v⁶ Jan 30] placed in points: modest form over hurdles, very lightly raced: tried in hood. *Tim Reed* **h96**

CARLOS DU FRUITIER (FR) 6 b.g. Diableneyev (USA) – Odyssee Madrik (FR) (Antarctique (IRE)) [2017/18 b99: h19.6g² h19.7s* h19.4dᶠ h19.7sᵖᵘ h23.1v⁴ h20.3g Apr 18] useful-looking gelding: in frame both starts in Irish points: bumper winner: fairly useful form over hurdles: won novice at Wetherby in November: stays 2½m: acts on soft going. *Ben Pauling* **h126**

CARLTON RYAN (IRE) 10 b.g. Morozov (USA) – Dante's Arrow (IRE) (Phardante (FR)) [2017/18 c116: c24.1v^F c26.6s² h23.1s⁴ h25s⁵ h24.3g^F Apr 20] fair form over hurdles: fair handicap chaser: stays 27f: acts on heavy going: tried in cheekpieces. *Michael Easterby* c111 h108

CARNAROSS 9 b.g. Norse Dancer (IRE) – Miss Lewis (Sir Harry Lewis (USA)) [2017/18, h70: c16.4g⁵ c15.7d^F c15.6v^pu h16.2s h15.8d Nov 18] modest hurdler at best, no form in 2017/18: poor form over fences: raced around 2m: acts on heavy going: has worn tongue tie, including last 2 starts, when also in headgear. *Julia Brooke* c70 h–

CARNSPINDLE (IRE) 6 b.m. Ask – Whistling Gypse (IRE) (Good Thyne (USA)) [2017/18 h118, b94: h19.7s h21.6d⁶ h25d³ h19.5v³ h23.6s* h23.1s h24.3g⁵ Apr 20] tall mare: bumper winner: fairly useful handicap hurdler: won at Chepstow in February: stays 25f: acts on heavy going: in cheekpieces last 2 starts: often races prominently. *Warren Greatrex* h126

CARNTOP 5 b.g. Dansili – Milford Sound (Barathea (IRE)) [2017/18 h16g Feb 24] has had breathing operation: brother to fairly useful hurdler Quebec (17f winner): dam half-sister to useful hurdler (stayed 2½m) Silvertown: useful on Flat, stays 1½m: well beaten in Dovecote Novices' Hurdle on hurdling debut: capable of better with sights lowered. *Jamie Snowden* h– p

CAROBELLO (IRE) 11 b.g. Luso – Vic's Queen (IRE) (Old Vic) [2017/18 c72§, h–: c20g⁵ Jul 27] maiden hurdler: modest chaser at best, well held sole outing in 2017/18: stays 23f: acts on soft and good to firm going: has worn headgear, including last 4 starts: wears tongue tie, usually leads: temperamental. *Martin Bosley* c– § h–

CAROLE'S DESTRIER 10 b.g. Kayf Tara – Barton May (Midnight Legend) [2017/18 c152, h–: c26g c25.6v^pu c24s^pu c28.8d⁵ Apr 28] well-made gelding: winning hurdler: smart handicap chaser, well below form in 2017/18: stays 29f: acts on heavy going: tried in cheekpieces. *Neil Mulholland* c127 h–

CAROLE'S VIGILANTE (IRE) 7 ch.g. Flemensfirth (USA) – Gotta Goa (IRE) (Publisher (USA)) [2017/18 h20v³ h19.7s* h21.4v⁴ Mar 28] fair form over hurdles: won maiden at Hereford in January: will prove suited by 3m+: remains with potential. *Neil Mulholland* h110 p

CARQALIN (FR) 6 gr.g. Martaline – Mica Doree (FR) (Video Rock (FR)) [2017/18 c61, h–: c20d⁴ c26.7v⁴ c23.9v² c23.5v⁵ Jan 30] good-topped gelding: maiden hurdler: poor form over fences: unproved beyond 2½m: acts on good to soft going: wears headgear, tried in tongue tie. *Kim Bailey* c71 h–

CARRAIG MOR (IRE) 10 b.g. Old Vic – Lynrick Lady (IRE) (Un Desperado (FR)) [2017/18 c–, h–: c25.1v^pu Mar 28] lengthy, useful-looking gelding: point winner: winning hurdler: modest chaser at best, folded tamely in hunter sole outing under Rules in 2017/18: stays 25f: acts on soft going. *C. R. Barber* c– h–

CARRICKCROSS BOYE (IRE) 8 b.g. Trans Island – Ellie Forte (Alflora (IRE)) [2017/18 h20.5v⁶ c15.7v^F Jan 24] maiden pointer: no form under Rules: tried in hood. *Iain Jardine* c– h–

CARRICK ROADS (IRE) 4 ch.g. Robin des Champs (FR) – Jay Lo (IRE) (Glacial Storm (USA)) [2017/18 b15.3v b15.3d Apr 22] no form in bumpers. *Colin Tizzard* b–

CARRIED AWAY 6 b.m. Trans Island – Carry Me (IRE) (Lafontaine (USA)) [2017/18 h22d Apr 22] half-sister to useful chaser Present View (2½m-2¾m winner, by Presenting) and modest chaser Sturbury (2m winner, by Topanoora): dam unraced: well held in point: tailed off in novice hurdle. *Phil York* h–

CARRIED (IRE) 8 b.g. Footstepsinthesand – Tequise (IRE) (Victory Note (USA)) [2017/18 h16.8d h16g c17g⁵ c16d⁵ Aug 2] fairly useful on Flat: maiden hurdler: modest form over fences: better effort when fifth in maiden at Killarney in July: raced around 2m: best form on good going: has worn headgear, including last 3 starts: front runner/races prominently. *Mrs Prunella Dobbs, Ireland* c92 h–

CARRIG CATHAL 7 b.g. Fair Mix (IRE) – Blackwater Bay (IRE) (Supreme Leader) [2017/18 h140, b96: c22d^ur h20s h22v^pu h17.8v* h16.5d h20s Apr 28] winning pointer: useful handicap hurdler: won at Ballinrobe (by 2½ lengths from Prospectus) in April: unseated rider first on chasing debut: left Gordon Elliott after first start: stays 2½m: acts on good to firm and heavy going: tried in cheekpieces: in tongue tie last 4 starts: usually races nearer last than first. *S. J. Mahon, Ireland* c– h139

CAR

CARRIGDHOUN (IRE) 13 gr.g. Goldmark (USA) – Pet Tomjammar (IRE) (Accordion) [2017/18 c129, h–: c23.8v³ c24.5s⁴ c26.2v⁴ c29.2g⁴ Nov 2] lengthy gelding: winning hurdler: fairly useful handicap chaser: third at Perth in September: stays 4m: acts on good to firm and heavy going: usually in headgear: wears tongue tie: front runner/races prominently. *Maurice Barnes*   c122 h–

CARROLLS MILAN (IRE) 5 b.m. Milan – Native Crystal (IRE) (Be My Native (USA)) [2017/18 b15.7g⁶ Apr 20] £20,000 4-y-o: sister to modest hurdler/winning pointer Milan of Crystal (2m-21f winner), and closely related to fair hurdler Stronghaven (2m winner, by Oscar) and a winning pointer by Dr Massini: dam unraced half-sister to fairly useful hurdler/useful chaser (19f-3m winner) Saxophone: placed in Irish point: 14/1, sixth in conditional/amateur maiden bumper at Southwell. *Fergal O'Brien*   b80

CARRY ON ASIAN (IRE) 9 b.g. Asian Heights – Carry On Pierre (lRE) (Pierre) [2017/18 c26d^pu May 5] multiple point winner: in cheekpieces/tongue strap, pulled up in hunter on chasing debut. *Francesca Nimmo*   c–

CARRY ON SYDNEY 8 ch.g. Notnowcato – River Fantasy (USA) (Irish River (FR)) [2017/18 h105: h19.2g⁴ May 22] rather leggy gelding: fair handicap hurdler, below form sole outing in 2017/18: stays 3m: acts on soft going: wears headgear: front runner/races prominently. *Oliver Sherwood*   h88

CARTA BLANCA (IRE) 5 gr.m. Authorized (IRE) – Alicante (Pivotal) [2017/18 h15.6g^pu h19.3v Feb 19] modest maiden on Flat, stays 1½m: no form over hurdles: wears hood. *Gemma Anderson*   h–

CARTER MCKAY 7 gr.g. Martaline – Saxona (IRE) (Jade Robbery (USA)) [2017/18 b113: h16v* h16v³ h22s³ h20.3v Mar 16] workmanlike gelding: point winner: dual bumper winner: useful from chase maiden: won maiden at Gowran in November: third in Moscow Flyer Novices' Hurdle at Punchestown (13½ lengths behind Getabird) in January and Nathaniel Lacy & Partners Solicitors Novices' Hurdle at Leopardstown (2½ lengths behind Tower Bridge) in February: stays 2¾m. *W. P. Mullins, Ireland*   h136

CARTERS REST 15 gr.g. Rock City – Yemaail (IRE) (Shaadi (USA)) [2017/18 c80, h–: c17d^pu Jun 9] maiden pointer: winning hurdler: fair chaser at best, no form in 2017/18: stays 2½m: acts on heavy going: has worn headgear/tongue tie: often leads. *Mrs D. Walton*   c– h–

CARTWRIGHT 5 b.g. High Chaparral (IRE) – One So Marvellous (Nashwan (USA)) [2017/18 h16v² h16v* h16s⁴ h16v* h16.5d⁵ Apr 24] half-brother to useful hurdler Midnight Oil (2m winner, by Motivator), stayed 2½m: useful on Flat, stays 16.5f: similar form over hurdles: won maiden at Naas in February and listed novice at Navan (by ½ length from Articulum) in March: will be suited by further than 2m: acts on heavy going. *Gordon Elliott, Ireland*   h133

CARUMBA (IRE) 8 b.g. Gold Well – Sarah Marshall (IRE) (Flemensfirth (USA)) [2017/18 c–: h21.6m⁵ h21.6d^pu Jul 23] winning pointer: no form over hurdles: unseated rider first on chasing debut: wears cheekpieces. *Jackie du Plessis*   c– h–

CASABLANCA MIX (FR) 6 ch.m. Shirocco (GER) – Latitude (FR) (Kadalko (FR)) [2017/18 h123: c20f³ c19.9g² c19.9d* c17.5v^F Dec 21] bumper winner: fairly useful hurdler: useful form over fences: won mares novice at Huntingdon in November: in control when fell last in similar event at Exeter in December: stays 2½m: acts on heavy going: tried in cheekpieces: usually travels strongly: remains open to improvement as a chaser. *Nicky Henderson*   c141 p h–

CASACLARE (IRE) 4 b.g. Casamento (IRE) – Sarah Ann (IRE) (Orpen (USA)) [2017/18 h15.8g Oct 5] fair maiden on Flat, stays 1½m: in tongue tie, 22/1, too free when seventh in juvenile at Huntingdon on hurdling debut. *Jonjo O'Neill*   h–

CASA TALL (FR) 4 b.g. No Risk At All (FR) – Gribouille Parcs (FR) (Ungaro (GER)) [2017/18 h16.4d⁶ h17.4g³ h17.9g* h18.4s* h16.2s⁴ Apr 26] third foal: half-brother to Titi Loup (French 17f-21f hurdle/chase winner, by Loup Solitaire) and Creole Blue (French 17f hurdle winner, by Anabaa Blue): dam French 17f-19f chase winner: fairly useful form over hurdles: won juvenile events at Mont-de-Marsan and Bordeaux in November: left A. Chaille-Chaille after fourth start: stays 2¼m: acts on soft going: in hood first 4 starts. *Tom George*   h129

CASCAYE (FR) 6 br.m. Merlino Mago – Castyana (IRE) (Anabaa (USA)) [2017/18 h105, b81: h19.3s^pu h20.5v h19.8s Dec 9] fair hurdler at best, no form in 2017/18: usually wears cheekpieces: front runner/races prominently. *Kim Bailey*   h–

CASH AGAIN (FR) 6 br.g. Great Pretender (IRE) – Jeu de Lune (FR) (Useful (FR)) [2017/18 h110: h20.1v⁵ h16.8g c24.2s⁶ c20.3s^pu c19.3v* c21.1v³ c20s Apr 8] rather unfurnished gelding: maiden hurdler, no form in 2017/18: fair form over fences: won handicap at Sedgefield in January: stays 2½m: best form on soft/heavy going: often races in rear. *Ben Haslam*   c112 h–

CASHANOVA (IRE) 7 b.g. Arcadio (GER) – Starshade (IRE) (Oscar (IRE)) [2017/18 h105: h15.8g^bd h16g⁵ h16d⁶ h15.7s h19.6s c17v⁴ Apr 1] workmanlike gelding: fair maiden hurdler: well beaten in novice handicap on chasing debut: should stay beyond 2m: acts on soft going. *Nick Gifford*   c– h101

CASH IN MIND (IRE) 7 b.g. Creachadoir (IRE) – Dynamic Dream (USA) (Dynaformer (USA)) [2017/18 h16s² h16.4g⁶ h16.5v⁵ Nov 16] sturdy gelding: fairly useful on Flat: fair form over hurdles: best effort when second in maiden at Tipperary in October: likely to prove best at easy 2m. *Des Donovan, Ireland*   h110

CASH TO ASH (IRE) 5 b.g. Westerner – Knocklayde Rose (IRE) (Even Top (IRE)) [2017/18 h15.7v³ h16.7v⁴ h21.3d⁶ Mar 29] €25,000 3-y-o, resold €14,000 3-y-o: third foal: half-brother to fair hurdler Lagavara (2½m winner, by Exit To Nowhere), stays 3m: dam winning pointer: maiden Irish pointer: modest form over hurdles: best effort when fourth in novice at Market Rasen in March: should stay at least 2½m. *Mark Walford*   h95

CASIMIR DU CLOS (FR) 6 b.g. Blue Bresil (FR) – Cyrienne du Maine (FR) (Saint Cyrien (FR)) [2017/18 h15.7v⁵ Dec 6] down the field in maiden in France on sole outing on Flat: pulled up in Irish maiden point: well beaten in novice hurdle. *Stuart Coltherd*   h–

CASINO MARKETS (IRE) 10 br.g. Fruits of Love (USA) – Vals Dream (IRE) (Pierre) [2017/18 c138, h–: c21.4g h19f h20f⁴ h21g c20.8g Apr 18] tall gelding: fairly useful hurdler: useful chaser at best, no form over fences in 2017/18: stays 3m: acts on soft and good to firm going. *Emma Lavelle*   c– h126

CASK MATE (IRE) 5 b.g. Kalanisi (IRE) – Littleton Liberty (Royal Applause) [2017/18 b16.5s* b16s² h 16v² h16v² h16d² Dec 26] £18,000 3-y-o: sixth foal: brother to 2½m bumper winner/useful 19f hurdle winner Russian Bill (stayed 3m) and half-brother to modest hurdler/fair chaser Kyles Faith (2½m-3m winner, by Court Cave): dam little form on Flat: useful form in bumpers: won maiden event at Ballinrobe in September: fair form when second all 3 starts in maiden hurdles: in tongue tie last 5 starts: often races prominently, usually travels strongly. *Noel Meade, Ireland*   h113 b105

CASPER KING (IRE) 7 b.g. Scorpion (IRE) – Princess Supreme (IRE) (Supreme Leader) [2017/18 h123: h19.2g⁵ c20s^pu c20.2v^pu c19.2v^pu Apr 8] lengthy gelding: fairly useful hurdler: no form over fences: tried in blinkers: often races prominently. *Philip Hobbs*   c– h123

CASSE TETE (FR) 6 b.g. Poliglote – Ellapampa (FR) (Pampabird) [2017/18 c137, h115: c18.8d c20.8v c20s* c25s c25s Apr 14] lengthy gelding: maiden hurdler: useful handicap chaser: won at Warwick (by 5 lengths from Kylemore Lough) in February: should stay 3m: acts on soft going: often races towards rear. *Gary Moore*   c135 h–

CASSIS DE REINE 4 ch.f. Quatre Saisons – Reine de Violette (Olden Times) [2017/18 b13.2s³ b14d⁵ b14s² b12.6s Dec 20] lengthy, rather sparsely-made filly: fourth foal: dam maiden (stayed 1¼m): fair form in bumpers. *Bill Turner*   b85

CASSIVELLAUNUS (IRE) 6 b.g. Danehill Dancer (IRE) – Celtic Heroine (IRE) (Hernando (FR)) [2017/18 b–: h15.8d h17.7v h15.9v h15.9v h15.9v* h16m Apr 26] modest form over hurdles: won handicap at Plumpton (conditional) in February: raced mainly around 2m: acts on heavy going. *Daniel Steele*   h93

CASTAFIORE (USA) 5 b.m. Street Cry (IRE) – Showlady (USA) (Theatrical) [2017/18 h112: h16.3g⁵ h19.2g³ h16.6d* h19.7s² h15.8v* h16v h18.9v⁶ Mar 31] tall, angular mare: fairly useful handicap hurdler: won at Doncaster in December and Uttoxeter (mares) in February: stays 2½m: acts on heavy going: wears headgear: front runner/races prominently. *Charlie Longsdon*   h121

CASTARNIE 10 b.g. Alflora (IRE) – Just Jenny (IRE) (King's Ride) [2017/18 c115, h–: c24.2v² c24.2v⁴ c24.2v^pu c23s^pu Feb 4] strong gelding: maiden hurdler: fairly useful handicap chaser: second at Exeter in November: stays 25f: acts on heavy going: wears cheekpieces. *Robert Walford*   c117 h–

CASTERLY ROCK (IRE) 6 b.g. King's Theatre (IRE) – Alderbrook Girl (IRE) (Alderbrook) [2017/18 h106p, b–: h16d⁵ h15.8d² h17.7s³ Mar 7] tall gelding: fair form over hurdles: bred to be suited by 2½m+. *Philip Hobbs*   h111

CASTLEGRACE PADDY (IRE) 7 b.g. Flemensfirth (USA) – Thunder Road (IRE) (Mtoto) [2017/18 h133, b78: c16v* c18s* c16d⁵ Apr 26] useful hurdler: smart form over fences: won maiden at Fairyhouse (by 7½ lengths from Bravissimo) in December and   c145 p h–

listed novice at Thurles (by 3¾ lengths from Jett) in March: stays 2¼m: best form on soft/heavy going: front runner/races prominently, usually travels strongly: remains with potential as a chaser. *P. A. Fahy, Ireland*

CASTLE NORTH (IRE) 6 b.g. Stowaway – Fitanga (FR) (Fijar Tango (FR)) [2017/18 b16v² b16s² Apr 19] half-brother to several winners, including fair hurdler/winning pointer Once And Always (21f winner, by King's Theatre) and bumper winner/fair hurdler Tango Jim (2m winner, by Jimble): dam placed over hurdles/fences in France: fell in point on debut: useful form in bumpers: better effort when second in maiden at Fairyhouse (1½ lengths behind Dream Conti) in April. *W. P. Mullins, Ireland*   b105

CASTLE ON A CLOUD (IRE) 7 b.g. Flemensfirth (USA) – Ifyoucouldseemenow (IRE) (Saddlers' Hall (IRE)) [2017/18 h22.7s Jan 14] placed in Irish points: tailed off in novice on hurdling debut. *Chris Grant*   h–

CASTLETOWN (FR) 6 gr.g. Poliglote – Message Personnel (FR) (Mansonnien (FR)) [2017/18 c118, h105: h20.9d³ h16.8d² c15.7d⁶ h19.4d³ c19.3s² h20.5g² h20.2s* Apr 27] fair handicap hurdler: won at Perth in April: fair maiden chaser: stays 2¾m: acts on soft going: wears headgear: often races towards rear/travels strongly: no battler. *Pauline Robson*   c106 §
h105 §

CASTLEY LANE 12 b.g. Dapper – Holly (Skyliner) [2017/18 c–, h–: c19.4g^pu Aug 3] point winner: maiden hurdler/chaser, no form since 2015/16: stays 3m: best form on good going: usually wears headgear/tongue tie. *Sara Ender*   c–
h–

CASUAL CAVALIER (IRE) 10 br.g. Presenting – Asklynn (IRE) (Beau Sher) [2017/18 c115, h–: c15.2s³ c16.5v² c16.3v⁴ c15.2d Mar 29] maiden hurdler: fair handicap chaser: stays 2½m, effective at shorter: acts on heavy going. *George Bewley*   c105
h–

CATAMARAN DU SEUIL (FR) 6 b.g. Network (GER) – Fleur du Tennis (FR) (Video Rock (FR)) [2017/18 c121, h122: c21.4g c24.2d² c24.3v* c25.6v⁴ c22.9v² c19.4v⁴ Jan 23] winning chaser: useful handicap chaser: won at Ayr in November and Wetherby (by 2¾ lengths from Clan Legend) in January: stays 3m: acts on heavy going: wears headgear: usually travels strongly. *Dr Richard Newland*   c133
h–

CATCH A LUCKY STAR (IRE) 9 b.g. Luso – Badia Dream (IRE) (Old Vic) [2017/18 h–, b–: h19.5d h20.1g⁵ h20.5g^pu Jul 16] maiden pointer: poor maiden hurdler: stays 2½m: acts on soft going: has worn headgear, including final start. *Mark McNiff, Ireland*   h62

CATCHAMAT 9 b.m. Overbury (IRE) – More Flair (Alflora (IRE)) [2017/18 c–, h125: h23.1v⁵ h19.7s h25.8v⁶ h25s⁶ h20.2s⁶ Apr 25] multiple point winner: fairly useful hurdler, below form in 2017/18: pulled up in maiden hunter on chasing debut. *James Walton*   c–
h–

CATCHER ON THE GO (IRE) 8 b.g. Catcher In The Rye (IRE) – Suspicious Minds (Anabaa (USA)) [2017/18 h20g* h26.5d⁵ h19.5v⁴ h16.2s h15.8s Feb 22] well held in point: fair handicap hurdler: won at Ffos Las in June: stays 2½m: best form on good going: tried in tongue tie: lazy. *Evan Williams*   h107

CATCHING ON (IRE) 10 b.g. Milan – Miracle Lady (Bob's Return (IRE)) [2017/18 c–, h119: h23.3s h23.6s h19.9v⁴ h23.3v^pu c24.1v⁴ c23.6v² c23.6v^ur c29.6v⁴ h25.5v Mar 10] fair handicap hurdler: fairly useful handicap chaser nowadays: second at Chepstow in January: stays 3¾m: acts on heavy going: wears tongue tie: held up: often let down by jumping over fences. *Jonjo O'Neill*   c117 x
h113

CATCHIN TIME (IRE) 10 b.g. Chineur (FR) – Lady Dane (IRE) (Danetime (IRE)) [2017/18 h110: h15.5s⁵ h18.9v⁴ h15.5v h16s h15.3v⁴ h15.7v⁵ h15.8v³ Apr 7] lengthy gelding: modest handicap hurdler: raced mainly around 2m: acts on heavy going: has worn headgear, including last 4 starts: wears tongue tie: often races towards rear. *Laura Hurley*   h89

CATCH TAMMY (IRE) 12 br.g. Tamayaz (CAN) – Bramble Orchard (IRE) (Orchestra) [2017/18 c77, h–: c20.8d^pu May 5] lengthy gelding: maiden pointer: maiden hurdler: fairly useful chaser at best, retains little ability: stays 2½m: acts on soft going: has worn headgear: tried in tongue tie. *Mrs I. Barnett*   c–
h–

CATCHTHEMOONLIGHT 10 b.m. Generous (IRE) – Moon Catcher (Kahyasi) [2017/18 h95: h20g⁵ h16.2g⁵ h20.9d^pu h20s³ h16.4s h16.2v^pu h17d h20.2s² Apr 25] modest handicap hurdler: stays 2¾m: acts on soft and good to firm going: has worn hood: often races towards rear. *Lucinda Russell*   h90

CATHAL'S STAR 5 ch.g. Malinas (GER) – Hand Inn Glove (Alflora (IRE)) [2017/18 b16v⁵ Nov 4] 9/2, fifth in maiden bumper at Ayr (17¾ lengths behind Ask The Tycoon). *Malcolm Jefferson*   b66

CAULFIELDS VENTURE (IRE) 12 b.g. Catcher In The Rye (IRE) – Saddlers' Venture (IRE) (Saddlers' Hall (IRE)) [2017/18 c130§, h–: c25.5d⁵ c26.7g^pu c25.6g^F c25.6g^pu Dec 6] good-topped gelding: maiden hurdler: useful handicap chaser, below form in 2017/18: stays 3¼m: acts on firm and soft going: wears headgear: temperamental. *Emma Lavelle*   c117 §
h–

CEC

CAUSE OF CAUSES (USA) 10 b.g. Dynaformer (USA) – Angel In My Heart (FR) (Rainbow Quest (USA)) [2017/18 c154, h–: c21s c30.2spu Mar 14] good-topped gelding: winning hurdler: smart chaser at best, winning at 3 consecutive Cheltenham Festivals (2015-2017) and also runner-up in Grand National in last of those years: stayed 4¼m: acted on good to firm and heavy going: wore headgear/tongue tie: usually raced nearer last than first: has been retired. *Gordon Elliott, Ireland* — c–, h–

CAUSE TOUJOURS (FR) 6 b.g. Khalkevi (IRE) – Viana (FR) (Signe Divin (USA)) [2017/18 b109: h15.8s⁴ h15.8g² Nov 14] compact gelding: every chance when unseated last in Irish maiden point: useful bumper performer: fair form over hurdles: better effort when second in novice at Huntingdon in November: in tongue tie last 2 starts: should do better. *Dan Skelton* — h114 p

CAUTORILLO 6 ch.m. Black Sam Bellamy (IRE) – Cent Prime (Hernando (FR)) [2017/18 b–: b17.7s² h16.8v⁴ h21.2g Oct 26] modest form in bumpers: poor form over hurdles: tried in tongue tie. *Jamie Snowden* — h69, b80

CAVE HUNTER (IRE) 11 b.g. Court Cave (IRE) – Beasty Maxx (GER) (Keen) [2017/18 c113: c26.2gur May 28] multiple point winner: fair hunter chaser at best, unseated sole start under Rules in 2017/18: stays 3¼m: acts on good to firm and good to soft going: wears headgear/tongue tie. *Mrs Wendy Hamilton* — c–

CAVENTARA 6 b.g. Kayf Tara – L'Aventure (FR) (Cyborg (FR)) [2017/18 h–, b–: h16.2v³ h20.5v* Jan 2] fairly useful form over hurdles: won maiden at Ayr in January: will be suited by 2¾m+: open to further improvement. *Sandy Thomson* — h115 p

CAVERNOUS (IRE) 5 br.g. Court Cave (IRE) – Willoughby Sue (IRE) (Dabali (IRE)) [2017/18 ab16g⁶ Nov 28] €34,000 3-y-o: fourth foal: brother to smart hurdler/chaser Willoughby Court (2½m/21f winner) and closely related to bumper winner/useful chaser Markov (19f-2¾m winner, by Morozov): dam, well held on completed starts in bumpers, half-sister to very smart staying chaser Nil Desperandum: 6/4, sixth in bumper at Lingfield (21½ lengths behind Didtheyleaveuoutto): should do better. *Ben Pauling* — b– p

CAVE TOP (IRE) 6 b.g. Court Cave (IRE) – Cyrils Top Girl (IRE) (Top of The World) [2017/18 c109, b–: h16.8s⁸ h19.6g² h19.9v⁴ h19.9v¹ h21s¹ h19.9v⁵ h19.9v h19.3v² Apr 17] sturdy gelding: maiden Irish pointer: fairly useful handicap hurdler: won at Exeter (amateur) in October, and Uttoxeter in November and December: stays 2½m: acts on heavy going: front runner/races prominently. *Oliver Greenall* — h127

CAVIAR D'ALLEN (FR) 6 b.g. Laveron – Quadanse (FR) (Maille Pistol (FR)) [2017/18 h16m h16d⁴ h16.7d⁶ h16g⁴ h19s h19v² c18.2s⁵ Mar 26] third foal: dam unraced half-sister to smart French chaser (stayed 29f) Mikador: maiden pointer: modest form over hurdles: well beaten in novice handicap on chasing debut: stays 19f: acts on heavy going: tried in hood/tongue tie: front runner/races prominently. *Christian Williams* — c–, h99

CAVOK (IRE) 6 b.m. Kayf Tara – Timon's Present (Presenting) [2017/18 b16s³ Mar 22] first foal: dam (c72/h90), maiden jumper (stayed 2¾m), half-sister to useful hurdler/smart chaser (stays 2¾m) Rathlin (by Kayf Tara): won Irish point on debut: 7/2, third in mares bumper at Chepstow (4 lengths behind Meep Meep). *Ben Pauling* — b85

CAWDOR HOUSE BERT 11 b.g. Kayf Tara – Lady Shanan (IRE) (Anshan) [2017/18 c94, h–: c19.4v* c19.4v² c21spu Apr 23] winning hurdler: modest handicap chaser: won novice event at Ffos Las in February: stays 2½m: acts on heavy going: tried in cheekpieces: races well off pace, often travels strongly. *David Rees* — c98, h–

CAZZA CAZAM 4 b.f. Malinas (GER) – Flo The Machine (IRE) (Bach (IRE)) [2017/18 ab16g Mar 5] first foal: dam unraced half-sister to fairly useful hurdler/chaser (2½m-3m winner) Malapie: tailed off in bumper. *Clare Hobson* — b–

CEANN SIBHEAL (IRE) 9 b.g. Flemensfirth (USA) – Imperial Award (IRE) (Oscar (IRE)) [2017/18 c65, h–: h22.8v⁴ h23.3v⁴ c24v³ c24v¹ c24.5v³ c24v² Mar 28] lengthy gelding: fair handicap hurdler: similar form over fences: won handicap at Uttoxeter in February: stays 3¼m: acts on heavy going: wears headgear: in tongue tie last 4 starts: front runner/races prominently. *Warren Greatrex* — c111, h98

CEARA BE (IRE) 5 b.m. Oscar (IRE) – Pearl's A Singer (IRE) (Spectrum (IRE)) [2017/18 b70: h17d ab16g² ab16g* b17s Apr 12] rather unfurnished mare: fair bumper performer: won mares event at Lingfield in January. *Alex Hales* — b91

CECILATOR 4 b.f. Delegator – Cecily Parsley (Fantastic Light (USA)) [2017/18 h15.8d⁶ Jul 30] dam (c93/h67) 19f-2¾m chase winner (stayed 3m): modest maiden on Flat, stays 1½m: in cheekpieces, well beaten in juvenile on hurdling debut. *Noel Williams* — h–

CEC

CECILE DE VOLANGES 10 ch.m. Kheleyf (USA) – Fyvie (Grand Lodge (USA)) [2017/18 h20.3g Sep 6] multiple point winner: no form over hurdles: maiden chaser. *Mike Hawker* — c– h–

CEDAR VALLEY (IRE) 4 b.f. Flemensfirth (USA) – Lunar Path (IRE) (Night Shift (USA)) [2017/18 b16.5v* b17s Apr 12] €32,000 3-y-o: sturdy filly: fourth foal: half-sister to bumper winner Represented (by Presenting): dam (h108), French 2¼m hurdle winner, also 9f winner on Flat, half-sister to useful/unreliable staying chasers Celtic Son and Sonevafushi: fair form in bumpers: won mares event at Taunton in March: will be suited by 2½m. *Philip Hobbs* — b92

CEEGEM (IRE) 6 b.g. Kalanisi (IRE) – Aboo Who (IRE) (Aboo Hom) [2017/18 h93, b–: h20.2v⁴ h22.7g³ h19v⁶ h24.1v c24.2v^F Mar 15] modest maiden hurdler: beaten when fell 3 out in novice handicap at Hexham on chasing debut: should stay 3m: acts on heavy going: in headgear last 2 starts: often races prominently. *Lucinda Russell* — c– h85

CELER ET AUDAX 6 b.m. Kayf Tara – Wannaplantatree (Niniski (USA)) [2017/18 b16.3d^{su} b16.3g b15.8m⁶ b16.7g⁶ h19.5v^{ur} h15.8s h16v^{ur} h16s^{pu} h15.8d Apr 9] small, leggy mare: half-sister to several winners, including high-class hurdler/smart chaser Blazing Bailey (2m-3½m winner, by Mister Baileys): dam 1¾m-2m winner: poor form in bumpers: no form over hurdles. *John O'Shea* — h– b65

CELESTA (IRE) 10 b.g. Oscar (IRE) – Celestial Music (IRE) (Orchestra) [2017/18 h19.9m^{pu} Jul 2] maiden pointer: placed in bumpers: no form over hurdles: in headgear last 3 starts: tongue tied first 3 starts. *Sarah Hollinshead* — h–

CELESTIAL CHIMES (IRE) 7 ch.m. Mahler – Celestial Rose (IRE) (Roselier (FR)) [2017/18 h–, b–: h16d h19.2g^F h16g h21g^{pu} h15.7v⁵ h23.9m^{pu} Apr 25] poor maiden hurdler: bred to be suited by further than 2m: often races towards rear. *Robin Dickin* — h60

CELESTIAL DANCER (FR) 6 b.m. Dr Fong – Rabeera (Beat Hollow) [2017/18 h74: h16.3d⁴ May 21] modest maiden on Flat: poor form on hurdling debut in 2016/17: in visor, well held sole outing in 2017/18: wears tongue tie. *Nigel Twiston-Davies* — h–

CELESTIAL MAGIC 6 b.g. Black Sam Bellamy (IRE) – Mighty Merlin (Royal Applause) [2017/18 h116: h15.7d⁴ c15.7d¹ h15.8v⁴ h15.7v⁶ h21v⁴ Mar 28] fair handicap hurdler: fell first on chasing debut: unproven beyond 2m: acts on heavy going. *Richard Phillips* — c– h112

CELESTIAL PATH (IRE) 6 br.g. Footstepsinthesand – Miss Kittyhawk (IRE) (Hawk Wing (USA)) [2017/18 h88: h19d⁴ h16m³ h16.7g⁵ h16m Apr 26] useful on Flat: fair form over hurdles: will prove best at easy 2m: acts on good to firm going: in headgear last 5 starts: tried in tongue tie. *David Pipe* — h109

CELMA DES BOIS (FR) 6 b.g. Ballingarry (IRE) – Palafixe (FR) (Valanour (IRE)) [2017/18 h78, b86: h16m h20.7s⁵ h21.7g³ Apr 20] well-made gelding: third in Irish point: poor form over hurdles: stays 2¾m. *Richard Rowe* — h84

CELSIANA 4 ch.f. Sepoy (AUS) – Generous Lady (Generous (IRE)) [2017/18 b15.7g⁵ b13.2s⁶ Oct 24] half-sister to several winners, including fair hurdlers Highland Legacy (3¼m winner, by Selkirk) and Oasis Knight (19f/2½m winner, by Oasis Dream): dam useful 1½m-1¾m winner: behind in bumpers/Flat maiden: wears cheekpieces. *Marcus Tregoning* — b–

CELTIC ARTISAN (IRE) 7 ch.g. Dylan Thomas (IRE) – Perfectly Clear (USA) (Woodman (USA)) [2017/18 h93: h15.8g⁵ May 29] fair on Flat: modest handicap hurdler, below form sole outing in 2017/18: raced around 2m: acts on good to firm going: wears cheekpieces: in tongue tie last 2 starts. *Rebecca Menzies* — h81

CELTIC FLAMES (IRE) 8 gr.g. Celtic Swing – Don't Forget Shoka (IRE) (Don't Forget Me) [2017/18 h20.9g⁴ h17s⁶ h16.8d⁴ c15.6v* c16.3s⁴ c20.5v⁵ c19.9s^F c16.9d⁴ c19.2s⁴ Mar 26] fair form over hurdles: similar form over fences: won novice handicaps at Hexham in November and Musselburgh in March: stays 2½m: acts on heavy going: in cheekpieces last 4 starts: often let down by jumping over fences. *Lucinda Russell* — c110 x h101

CELTIC JOY (IRE) 5 b.g. Kayf Tara – No Time For Tears (IRE) (Celtic Swing) [2017/18 b15.3s⁵ b13.7s⁶ Jan 26] €70,000 3-y-o: first foal: dam, 1¾m winner, half-sister to fairly useful hurdler/fair chaser (stayed 3m) Snob Wells: modest form in bumpers: better effort when sixth at Huntingdon in January. *Emma Lavelle* — b83

CELTIC POWER 6 b.g. Rail Link – Biloxi (Caerleon (USA)) [2017/18 h16.2s⁵ Aug 19] modest on Flat, stays 2m: well beaten in novice on hurdling debut. *Jim Goldie* — h–

CELTIC SALLY (IRE) 6 b.m. Coroner (IRE) – Celtic Serenade (IRE) (Yashgan) [2017/18 b15.7g Jul 16] seventh foal: half-sister to fairly useful hurdler/useful chaser Bigbadjohn (2½m-3m winner, by Vinnie Roe): dam 2m-2½m hurdle/chase winner: maiden Irish pointer: 20/1, eighth in mares bumper at Southwell. *Fergal O'Brien*   b–

CELTIC SILVER 9 gr.g. Shirocco (GER) – As You Leave (IRE) (Kaldounevees (FR)) [2017/18 c22.6d[pu] Jun 9] multiple point winner: twice-raced hurdler in Ireland in 2014/15: in tongue tie, pulled on lady riders' hunter on chasing debut. *T. Ellis*   c– h–

CELTIC STYLE (IRE) 5 b.m. Craigsteel – Kissangel (IRE) (Namaqualand (USA)) [2017/18 b–: b16.8s b15.3v Apr 9] no form in bumpers. *Linda Blackford*   b–

CELTIC TUNE (FR) 7 b.g. Green Tune (USA) – Kerry Rose (FR) (Tel Quel (FR)) [2017/18 c103, h99: c25.5g[2] c25.5d[4] c24g[pu] c23g[pu] Jul 27] good-topped gelding: maiden hurdler: modest maiden chaser: stays 3¼m: acts on soft going: wears cheekpieces: usually in tongue tie: front runner/races prominently: temperamental. *Jonjo O'Neill*   c98 § h–

CENTRAL FLAME 10 ch.g. Central Park (IRE) – More Flair (Alflora (IRE)) [2017/18 c–, h–: c20d[pu] c23.4v[ur] c23.4s[3] c23.4v[3] c20.1s[3] Feb 24] big, strong gelding: winning hurdler: fairly useful maiden chaser: third in novice handicap at Newcastle in December: stays 23f: acts on heavy going: often races in rear. *James Walton*   c118 h–

CENTREOFEXCELLENCE (IRE) 7 b.g. Oscar (IRE) – Calm Approach (IRE) (Anshan) [2017/18 h68: h15.7m h20m[3] h18.7m[6] h16.3m h16d h19.9s h15.8d h19v[4] h15.7v[3] h19.6d* Apr 21] sturdy gelding: placed in Irish point: poor handicap hurdler: won at Bangor in April: left Gary Moore after third start: stays 2½m: acts on good to soft going: in hood last 3 starts: tongue tied 4 of last 5 starts: usually leads/races freely. *Steve Flook*   h77

CENTURIUS 8 ch.g. New Approach (IRE) – Questina (IRE) (Rainbow Quest (USA)) [2017/18 h116: c19.9s h16.2s[6] Apr 25] tall, good-topped gelding: fairly useful hurdler at best, well held second outing in 2017/18: tailed off in novice handicap on chasing debut: raced mainly at 2m: acts on heavy going. *Venetia Williams*   c– h–

CENTURO (USA) 5 ch.g. Cape Blanco (IRE) – Cats Copy (USA) (Cat's Career (USA)) [2017/18 h97: h16.7g h23g Jun 3] compact gelding: fair maiden on Flat, stays 1¾m: modest form at best over hurdles, below that level in 2017/18: wears headgear/tongue tie. *Jonjo O'Neill*   h77

CEPAGE (FR) 6 b.g. Saddler Maker (IRE) – Sience Fiction (FR) (Dom Alco (FR)) [2017/18 c135x, h–: c16.8d[2] c15.5s[3] c15.7s[4] c20.5s* c20.8g[4] Apr 18] stocky gelding: winning hurdler: useful handicap chaser: won at Kempton (by 1½ lengths from Cobra de Mai) in March: stays 21f: acts on soft going: often races towards rear: has won when sweating badly: prone to mistakes. *Venetia Williams*   c140 x h–

CEPORINE (FR) 6 gr.g. Cachet Noir (USA) – Cyclosporine (FR) (Mansonnien (FR)) [2017/18 h120§: h19.9v[2] h24.4s[pu] Feb 21] fairly useful form over hurdles: second in handicap at Uttoxeter in February: in hood last 2 starts: best treated with caution (very reluctant and unseated rider soon after start second run in 2016/17). *Richard Hobson*   h118 §

CERCA TROVA (IRE) 12 b.m. Brian Boru – Aran Dawn (IRE) (Phardante (FR)) [2017/18 h16s h16v c21v* h19v[5] c19.2s[6] Mar 25] modest hurdler at best, no form in 2017/18: modest handicap chaser: won at Tramore in January: stays 23f: acts on good to firm and heavy going: has worn hood: usually races in rear. *J. T. R. Dreaper, Ireland*   c88 h–

CEREAL KILLER (FR) 6 b.g. Buck's Boum (FR) – Dombrelle (FR) (Quart de Vin (FR)) [2017/18 b15.8s h23.8s[6] h21s h19s[3] Mar 26] €50,000 3-y-o: tall gelding: half-brother to 2 winners in France, including Batbayane Macalo (17f chase winner, by Crossharbour): dam French 11f/1½m winner: won both starts in points: unplaced in maiden bumper: fair form over hurdles: best effort when third in maiden at Taunton in March. *Paul Nicholls*   h104 b–

CERNUNNOS (FR) 8 b.g. Della Francesca (USA) – Jackette (USA) (Mr Greeley (USA)) [2017/18 c133§, h–: c25.5d[3] c22.6m[ur] c22.6m c24.1g[4] c24.2s[pu] c25.6g c19.4v Dec 9] useful-looking gelding: winning hurdler: fairly useful handicap chaser nowadays: won at Bangor in September: stays 3m: acts on soft going: usually in headgear: wears tongue tie: temperamental. *Tom George*   c119 § h–

CERVIN (FR) 6 b.g. Network (GER) – Outre Mer (FR) (Sleeping Car (FR)) [2017/18 h96: c19.4g[5] c16g[4] Nov 16] modest form over hurdles in France in 2016/17: no form over fences: tried in cheekpieces/tongue tie. *Tim Vaughan*   c– h–

CESAR COLLONGES (FR) 6 ch.g. Fragrant Mix (IRE) – Prouesse Collonges (FR) (Apple Tree (FR)) [2017/18 b–: h17s[4] h17d* h21.6v h17v[2] h16v[5] Apr 14] Irish point winner: fair form over hurdles: won novice at Carlisle in November: should stay at least 2½m: acts on heavy going: often travels strongly. *Evan Williams*   h112

CES

CESAR ET ROSALIE (FR) 6 ch.g. Network (GER) – Regle de L'Art (FR) (Video Rock (FR)) [2017/18 h117, b95: h20.2m* h19.6g² h19.8s⁶ h19s Dec 14] workmanlike gelding: bumper winner: fairly useful hurdler: won novice at Perth in July: second in handicap at Bangor in August: stays 2½m: acts on good to firm going: tried in hood: wears tongue tie. *Neil Mulholland*   **h115**

C'EST DEJA CA (FR) 6 ch.g. Dano-Mast – Ou Es Tu (FR) (Evening World (FR)) [2017/18 b16.8s⁴ Dec 8] £5,000 3-y-o: tall, leggy gelding: third foal: dam, third in 1½m French bumper, out of half-sister to King George VI Chase winner Algan: hinted at ability in bumper: should do better. *Tim Easterby*   **b– p**

C'EST DU GATEAU (FR) 6 b.g. Laveron – Programmee (FR) (Kahyasi) [2017/18 h19g⁵ h16.3g h16.8v⁵ h19.2v⁴ h15.8v h19.2v* h19.5v^F Apr 14] workmanlike gelding: third foal: half-brother to French chaser Belle Affaire (17f winner, by Coastal Path) and French hurdler Vie Sa Vie (2¼m winner, by Robin des Champs): dam, French 2¼m chase winner, half-sister to useful French 2¼m hurdle winner Sortie de Secours: modest handicap hurdler: won at Towcester (conditional) in March: stays 19f: acts on heavy going: wears tongue tie. *Tim Vaughan*   **h93**

C'EST JERSEY (FR) 6 b.g. Protektor (GER) – Myrtille Jersey (FR) (Murmure (FR)) [2017/18 h137: c21.5v² c24v^pu h21.1s h22v⁵ h20s² Apr 28] smallish gelding: useful handicap hurdler: second in Ballymore Handicap Hurdle at Punchestown (1¾ lengths behind Meri Devie) in April: useful form over fences: better effort when second in maiden at Fairyhouse (6 lengths behind Kemboy) in January: stays 21f: acts on heavy going: has worn headgear, including in 2017/18. *W. P. Mullins, Ireland*   **c136 h140**

CHAIN GANG 7 b.g. Midnight Legend – Gaspaisie (FR) (Beyssac (FR)) [2017/18 h125: h24v⁴ c20v⁴ c20s⁴ c21d^F h26.1s Feb 4] fairly useful handicap hurdler, below form in 2017/18: fair form over fences: best effort when fourth in maiden at Navan in December: stays 2½m: best form on soft/heavy going: held up. *Alan Fleming, Ireland*   **c113 h111**

CHAIN OF BEACONS 9 b.g. Midnight Legend – Millennium Girl (Skyliner) [2017/18 c108, h87: c21.1g³ c17.1g* c19.9d³ c16.4g² Apr 23] workmanlike gelding: maiden hurdler: fair handicap chaser: won at Kelso in November: stays 3m, at least as effective at much shorter: acts on good to soft going: wears tongue tie: usually races towards rear/travels strongly. *Katie Scott*   **c112 h–**

CHALLICO 6 ch.g. Presenting – Blue Ride (IRE) (King's Ride) [2017/18 b87: h18.5d⁴ h19m* h16.5g³ h16.5s³ Dec 30] tall gelding: bumper winner: fair form over hurdles: won novice at Taunton in November: stayed 19f: dead. *Paul Nicholls*   **h112**

CHALONNIAL (FR) 6 ch.g. Protektor (GER) – Kissmirial (FR) (Smadoun (FR)) [2017/18 h123: c20s⁶ Nov 12] tall, angular gelding: fairly useful form over hurdles: 6/1, shaped well when sixth in novice handicap at Sandown (16½ lengths behind Jameson) on chasing debut: tried in tongue tie: open to significant improvement over fences. *Harry Fry*   **c124 P h–**

CHAMBORD DU LYS (FR) 6 b.m. Great Pretender (FR) – Pot Jolie (FR) (Useful (FR)) [2017/18 h17g² h16.5m² May 29] second foal: dam French 9f-11.5f bumper winner: useful form over hurdles: second in mares handicap at Ballinrobe (6 lengths behind Is She Diesel) in May: unproven beyond 17f: acts on good to firm and heavy going: tried in hood. *W. P. Mullins, Ireland*   **h131**

CHAMERON (FR) 5 b.g. Laveron – Chamanka (FR) (Cadoudal (FR)) [2017/18 c19.2s² Nov 15] down the field in 2 Flat maidens in France: fairly useful form when winning both starts over hurdles at Auteuil for G. Cherel in 2016/17, including listed newcomers event: 6/1, second in novice at Exeter (3¼ lengths behind Briery Queen) on chasing debut: open to improvement as a chaser. *Paul Nicholls*   **c132 p h–**

CHAMPAGNE AT TARA 9 gr.g. Kayf Tara – Champagne Lil (Terimon) [2017/18 c134§, h–§: c21.3m³ c25g⁴ c23.8s^ur c24s^F c19.4d² Apr 22] rangy gelding: winning hurdler: useful handicap chaser: third at Haydock (4½ lengths behind Hammersly Lake) in May: stays 21f: acts on soft and good to firm going: has worn hood: tried in tongue tie: races towards rear, often travels strongly: faint-hearted, and best treated with caution. *Jonjo O'Neill*   **c131 § h– §**

CHAMPAGNE CHAMP 6 b.g. Champs Elysees – Maramba (Rainbow Quest (USA)) [2017/18 h15.3v³ h19.5s* h21s² Mar 17] rather leggy gelding: useful on Flat, stays 2¼m: fairly useful form over hurdles: won maiden at Chepstow in February. *Rod Millman*   **h122**

CHAMPAGNE CHASER 8 b.g. Tobougg (IRE) – Champagne Lil (Terimon) [2017/18 h103: h20.1d* c20.1s³ c20.9v^pu c19.9g^ur h19.5v⁴ h24.2s⁶ h19.5s³ Apr 27] lengthy gelding: fair handicap hurdler: won at Hexham in September: fairly useful form over fences: best effort when third in novice handicap at Hexham in October: stays 3m: acts on heavy going. *Tim Vaughan*   **c116 h107**

CHA

CHAMPAGNE CITY 5 ch.g. Tobougg (IRE) – City of Angels (Woodman (USA)) [2017/18 h16.8g⁴ h16.2g* h16.3g* h16.3g* h16d h16.4d³ h16.8s³ Dec 15] well-made gelding: half-brother to several winning jumpers, including useful hurdler/smart chaser I'm So Lucky (2m-2½m winner, by Zilzal) and useful hurdler Dream Esteem (2m winner, by Mark of Esteem): useful on Flat, stays 10.5f: fairly useful hurdler: won novices at Kelso in May and Stratford in June/July: third in handicaps at Cheltenham in November and December: raced around 2m: acts on soft going: usually races prominently. *Tom George* — **h123**

CHAMPAGNE EXPRESS 8 b.g. Kalanisi (IRE) – Marvellous Dream (FR) (Muhtathir) [2017/18 ab18d⁴ h20.3g* Apr 18] well-made gelding: placed in Irish points: fairly useful hurdler: fitter for comeback in jumpers bumper, won handicap at Cheltenham in April: stays 2½m: acts on soft going. *Nicky Henderson* — **h125**

CHAMPAGNE GEORGE (IRE) 8 gr.g. Acambaro (GER) – Charannah (IRE) (Red Sunset) [2017/18 h19.5dᵖᵘ h17.7v⁶ h20.3v² h22.8s³ h21.6s Apr 23] fair handicap hurdler: stays 23f: acts on heavy going: usually races close up. *Neil Mulholland* — **h104**

CHAMPAGNE JAMES (IRE) 10 b.g. Stowaway – Champagne Lady (IRE) (Turtle Island (IRE)) [2017/18 c17.4v² c16vᵖᵘ Feb 10] winning hurdler: useful maiden chaser at best: stayed 2½m: acted on heavy going: tried in blinkers: usually wore tongue tie: unreliable: dead. *Jamie Snowden* — **c118 §** **h–**

CHAMPAGNENDIAMONDS (IRE) 5 b.g. Milan – Shebeganit (IRE) (Alflora (IRE)) [2017/18 b16.2v² b15.8v² Mar 17] £21,000 3-y-o: medium-sized gelding: first foal: dam unraced half-sister to useful hurdler (stayed 2¾m) Couleur France: third in Irish point: fair form in bumpers: better effort when second at Kelso in January: will stay at least 2½m. *Lucinda Russell* — **b93**

CHAMPAGNE POPPY (IRE) 5 b.m. Scorpion (IRE) – Princess Supreme (IRE) – (Supreme Leader) [2017/18 b16d b16d Apr 26] £7,000 3-y-o: lengthy, rather unfurnished mare: sister to fairly useful hurdler Casper King (2m-2¼m winner) and half-sister to a winning pointer by Milan: dam unraced sister to useful hurdler/smart chaser (stayed 3m) Supreme Prince and useful hurdler/fairly useful chaser (17f-2¾m winner) Supreme Serenade: no form in bumpers. *Ben Pauling* — **b–**

CHAMPAGNE REEF 4 gr.f. Literato (FR) – Kritzia (Daylami (IRE)) [2017/18 b15.8s ab16d⁵ Mar 5] fifth foal: dam 1¾m winner: poor form in bumpers: last in Flat maiden. *Julia Feilden* — **b66**

CHAMPAGNE TO GO (IRE) 8 b.m. Beneficial – Terre d'Orient (FR) (Kabool) [2017/18 h100: h21.6g² h23.1vᵖᵘ c20.9vᵖᵘ h20.9vᵖᵘ h20.1d² Apr 23] Irish point winner: fair maiden hurdler: pulled up in novice handicap on chasing debut: left Kim Bailey after first start: stays 2¾m: acts on good to soft going: has worn cheekpieces, including in 2017/18. *Rebecca Menzies* — **c–** **h106**

CHAMPAGNE WEST (IRE) 10 b.g. Westerner – Wyndham Sweetmarie (IRE) (Mister Lord (USA)) [2017/18 c162x, h–: c20.6v⁵ c21v³ c25vᵖᵘ c20s Apr 25] well-made gelding: winning hurdler: high-class chaser, well below best in 2017/18: stays 25f, effective at shorter: acts on heavy going: tried in cheekpieces: front runner/races prominently. *Henry de Bromhead, Ireland* — **c135** **h–**

CHAMPAYNE GINGER (IRE) 7 ch.g. Stowaway – Katies Dancer (IRE) (Danehill Dancer (IRE)) [2017/18 c20g³ Jul 11] third in Irish point: modest maiden hurdler for Paul W. Flynn: 5/6, third in novice handicap at Uttoxeter (9½ lengths behind Bestwork) on chasing debut: stays 2½m: acts on heavy going: tried in cheekpieces: wears tongue tie. *Dan Skelton* — **c91** **h–**

CHAMPAYNE LADY (IRE) 6 ch.m. Robin des Champs (FR) – Magherareagh Lady (IRE) (Old Vic) [2017/18 b16d⁴ b16v h20s h16v² h16v* h16.8s³ Mar 15] €11,500 3-y-o: rather unfurnished mare: half-sister to fairly useful hurdler/chaser Falcarragh (2m-21f winner) and fairly useful 2m chase winner Shootin The Breeze (both by Alderbrook): dam unraced half-sister to useful chaser (stayed 3m) More Than A Stroll: fair form in bumpers: won maiden at Kilbeggan in May: similar form over hurdles: won mares maiden at Fairyhouse in February: should stay 2½m: best form on soft/heavy going: usually wears tongue tie. *Alan Fleming, Ireland* — **h114** **b92**

CHAMPERS ON ICE (IRE) 8 gr.g. Robin des Champs (FR) – Miss Nova (Ra Nova) [2017/18 c139, h–: h22.8v⁵ h24s Dec 15] tall, good-topped gelding: useful handicap hurdler: fifth in Betfair Stayers' Handicap Hurdle at Haydock in November: useful chaser: stays 3m: acts on heavy going: has worn headgear, including last 3 starts: tried in tongue tie. *David Pipe* — **c–** **h128**

CHA

CHAMPION CHASE (FR) 6 b.g. Voix du Nord (FR) – Darling Frisco (FR) (Trebrook (FR)) [2017/18 h100p: h15.7m⁴ c17.4d h20.5v⁶ h20.3v⁵ c20.3v² c19.7v² c19.7s² Apr 15] modest maiden hurdler: similar form over fences: left Kim Bailey after second start: stays 2½m: best form on soft/heavy going: in cheekpieces last 4 starts: tried in tongue tie. *Martin Bosley* — c93 h91

CHAMP (IRE) 6 b.g. King's Theatre (IRE) – China Sky (IRE) (Definite Article) [2017/18 b105: h21.6v² Jan 20] tall gelding: useful bumper winner: 2/1, plenty of promise when second in novice at Ascot (neck behind Vinndication) on hurdling debut: sure to improve. *Nicky Henderson* — h134 p

CHANCEANOTHERFIVE (IRE) 6 b.g. Dubai Destination (USA) – Ryhall (IRE) (Saddlers' Hall (IRE)) [2017/18 b16.2d* b16.4g* b15.6s² b17s Apr 13] €9,500 3-y-o: sturdy gelding: third foal: dam (h97) 23f hurdle winner out of fairly useful hurdler/useful chaser up to 3m Loshian: point winner: fairly useful form in bumpers: won at Perth in September and Newcastle in November: will stay 2¼m+. *Keith Dalgleish* — b104

CHANCEITON (IRE) 7 b.g. Vinnie Roe (IRE) – Lissnabrucka (IRE) (Lord Americo) [2017/18 h–: c26.2v² Apr 16] point winner: maiden hurdler: 7/1, second in maiden hunter at Kelso (21 lengths behind Diamond Brig) on chasing debut: seemingly stays 3¼m: acts on heavy going: in tongue tie last 4 starts. *Lucinda Russell* — c90 h–

CHANCEOFA LIFETIME (IRE) 11 ch.g. Beneficial – Bounty Queen (IRE) (King's Ride) [2017/18 c103, h–: c26.3s^pu c19.2s⁶ c16.4v⁶ c19.2s⁵ c23.4v⁵ c21.4d⁴ Apr 22] maiden hurdler: fair handicap chaser, well below best in 2017/18: stays 3¼m: acts on heavy going. *Victor Thompson* — c64 h–

CHANCE TAKEN 10 b.m. Overbury (IRE) – New Dawn (Rakaposhi King) [2017/18 c65p, h91: h16.7g⁶ Jun 23] sturdy mare: modest maiden hurdler, below form sole outing in 2017/18: well held only start over fences: stays 21f: acts on soft going: has worn headgear, including last 3 starts: tried in tongue tie. *Noel Williams* — c– h–

CHANDOS BELLE (GER) 5 b.m. Mamool (IRE) – Chandos Rose (IRE) (Mull of Kintyre (USA)) [2017/18 h97: h16g h19v⁴ h15.5v h18.6s³ h20.7s* h20.6v⁴ Apr 11] fair handicap hurdler: won mares event at Huntingdon in March: stays 21f: acts on heavy going: in tongue tie last 4 starts: usually travels strongly. *Stuart Edmunds* — h105

CHANGEOFLUCK (IRE) 10 b.g. Gold Well – Sotattie (Teenoso (USA)) [2017/18 c22.6d³ Jun 9] sturdy gelding: multiple point winner: maiden hurdler: modest form in chases: third in novice hunter at Stratford in June: stays 3m: acts on soft going: usually in cheekpieces: wears tongue tie. *Alan Hill* — c96 h–

CHANGE UR TUNE (IRE) 6 br.g. Milan – Sunny Native (IRE) (Be My Native (USA)) [2017/18 h19.7g h20v^pu h22d Apr 22] placed in Irish maiden point: no form over hurdles. *Sheila Lewis* — h–

CHANGING THE GUARD 12 b.g. King's Best (USA) – Our Queen of Kings (Arazi (USA)) [2017/18 c107x, h92§: h20.3g c17.4m³ h16.2g⁵ h18.7m c16.3d² c17.8d h16d⁵ c19.9d⁴ c16.3s⁵ h20v³ c16v⁴ c15.9v⁴ h16s⁴ c21s⁵ Apr 23] sturdy gelding: modest handicap hurdler/chaser nowadays: stays 21f: acts on good to firm and heavy going: wears headgear/tongue tie: often races prominently: temperamental. *Barry Brennan* — c96 h82 §

CHANKILLO 9 ch.g. Observatory (USA) – Seasonal Blossom (IRE) (Fairy King (USA)) [2017/18 c100§, h89§: c20.3s² h19.6d³ c19.4g⁴ c19.2g^pu Jul 9] compact gelding: modest maiden hurdler: fair handicap chaser: barely stays 23f: acts on heavy going: wears headgear: unreliable. *Sarah-Jayne Davies* — c100 § h92 §

CHANTARA ROSE 9 br.m. Kayf Tara – Fragrant Rose (Alflora (IRE)) [2017/18 c109, h101: c19.9s^pu Feb 8] fair hurdler: maiden chaser, pulled up sole start in 2017/18: stays 3m: acts on heavy going: wears cheekpieces: has worn tongue tie, including last 2 starts. *Neil Mulholland* — c– h–

CHANTECLER 7 b.g. Authorized (IRE) – Snow Goose (Polar Falcon (USA)) [2017/18 h97x: h16.8s h18.7g³ h20m⁴ h22g² h23g² h26.5d³ h21.6d⁶ Oct 12] lengthy gelding: fair maiden hurdler: stays 23f: acts on good to firm and good to soft going: has worn hood: wears tongue tie: often races freely: often let down by jumping. *Neil Mulholland* — h101 x

CHAPARRACHIK (IRE) 4 b.g. High Chaparral (IRE) – Chocolat Chaud (IRE) (Excellent Art) [2017/18 h17.7d^F Sep 10] fair maiden on Flats, form 1½m: weakening when fell 2 out in juvenile won by Lord E at Fontwell on hurdling debut. *Amanda Perrett* — h–

CHAPEL STILE (IRE) 6 b.g. Scorpion (IRE) – Peggy Cullen (IRE) (Presenting) [2017/18 h82p: h20.9d³ h22.7g² h24.4d* h23.1s* h24.3g* Apr 20] fairly useful handicap hurdler: won at Doncaster in December, Bangor in March and Ayr in April: will stay long distances: acts on soft going: responds generously to pressure. *Nicky Richards* — h126

CHARACTER ONESIE (IRE) 6 b.g. Dark Angel (IRE) – Flame Keeper (IRE) (Pivotal) **h99**
[2017/18 h16.7s⁵ h16.8s^su h15.6s² h16.4d³ Mar 16] fairly useful on Flat, stays 9f:
modest form over hurdles: raced around 2m: acts on soft going. *Donald McCain*

CHARBEL (IRE) 7 b.g. Iffraaj – Eoz (IRE) (Sadler's Wells (USA)) [2017/18 c155, h–: **c157**
h15.3s⁴ c15.5d⁴ c15.9s^F Mar 14] tall, useful-looking gelding: smart handicap hurdler at **h134**
best: very smart form over fences: 5½ lengths fourth of 6 to Politologue in Tingle Creek
Chase at Sandown in December: raced around 2m: acts on soft going: in cheekpieces last
2 starts: has worn tongue tie, including in 2017/18: races close up. *Kim Bailey*

CHARIN' CROSS 6 ch.g. Cockney Rebel (IRE) – Lush Lady (IRE) (Kris Kin (USA)) **h–**
[2017/18 h–, b–: h16.2g h19.3v h19.9s⁵ h19.9s Dec 26] no form in bumpers/over hurdles.
Micky Hammond

CHARLEMAR (FR) 6 b.g. Ballingarry (IRE) – Passemare (FR) (Useful (FR)) [2017/18 **h–**
h120: h23.1v Mar 11] useful-looking gelding: bumper winner: fairly useful hurdler at best,
dropped away tamely sole outing in 2017/18: unproven beyond 17f: acts on soft and good
to firm going. *Harry Whittington*

CHARLIE BREEKIE (IRE) 9 b.g. Alkaadhem – Highland Breeze (IRE) (Kotashaan **c–**
(FR)) [2017/18 h104: c23.6s^pu Apr 27] lengthy gelding: point winner: fair maiden hurdler: **h–**
pulled up in novice hunter on chasing debut: stays 2½m: acts on good to soft going: tried
in cheekpieces. *R. Llewellyn*

CHARLIE CHAPLIN (GER) 4 b.g. Lope de Vega (IRE) – Campina (Oasis Dream) **h98**
[2017/18 h15.8g⁶ h16g³ h15.8d h15.8s⁶ h15.8s h15.8d Apr 24] small, angular gelding:
modest maiden at best on Flat, stays 8.5f: similar form over hurdles: raced only at 2m: tried
in blinkers. *Robert Eddery*

CHARLIE COOK (IRE) 9 b.g. Royal Anthem (USA) – Supreme Baloo (IRE) (Supreme **h–**
Leader) [2017/18 h116: h23m⁶ May 11] well-made gelding: fairly useful hurdler, well
beaten sole outing in 2017/18: should stay further than 2½m: acts on good to firm and
heavy going. *Graeme McPherson*

CHARLIE MON (IRE) 9 ch.g. Presenting – Prowler (IRE) (Old Vic) [2017/18 c103§, **c95 §**
h–: c23d⁵ c23.6g* c25.5m³ c23g⁵ c23.9g³ c23.9g c25.8m* c26.3m² c22.7m⁶ Nov 20] **h–**
lengthy, workmanlike gelding: maiden hurdler: modest handicap chaser: won at
Huntingdon (novice) in May and Newton Abbot in August: stays 3¼m: acts on firm and
soft going: wears headgear: usually races close up: unreliable. *Mike Hammond*

CHARLIE PAPA LIMA (IRE) 7 b.g. Winged Love (IRE) – Fairylodge Scarlet (IRE) **c105**
(Mister Lord (USA)) [2017/18 h88: h15.7g² h20g⁴ h20.3g² h18.7g³ h18.6g⁴ h23.9d⁵ h21g⁵ **h105**
c18.2m² Apr 25] Irish point winner: fair maiden hurdler: 11/4, second in novice handicap
at Taunton (1¾ lengths behind Tikkinthebox) on chasing debut: stays 2½m: acts on good to
firm going: tried in hood/tongue tie: front runner/races prominently. *Harry Whittington*

CHARLIE PARKER (IRE) 5 b.g. Myboycharlie (IRE) – Solaria (IRE) (Desert Prince **h80**
(IRE)) [2017/18 h82: h21.6g⁴ h23g^pu h22g Aug 3] plain gelding: poor maiden hurdler:
stays 2¾m: acts on good to firm and heavy going: tried in cheekpieces: often races in rear.
Dominic Ffrench Davis

CHARLIE RASCAL (FR) 4 b.g. Myboycharlie (IRE) – Rascafria (USA) (Johannesburg **h110**
(USA)) [2017/18 h16.8d* h16.8g² h17.2d^pu Aug 28] modest maiden on Flat, unproven
beyond 1m: fair form over hurdles: won juvenile at Newton Abbot in July. *Neil Mulholland*

CHARLIE'S CHARM (IRE) 6 b.g. Golan (IRE) – Ben's Turn (IRE) (Saddlers' Hall **c110**
(IRE)) [2017/18 b79: h19.9g⁴ h16s⁵ h16d c19.2d⁶ h21.1s² c21v c21.3s^F Mar 9] rather leggy **h109**
gelding: fair form over hurdles: similar form over fences: every chance when fell last in
maiden won by Artic Pearl at Leopardstown in March: left Tim Fitzgerald after first start:
stays 21f: acts on soft going: tried in tongue tie. *Gavin Patrick Cromwell, Ireland*

CHARLIE SNOW ANGEL 9 b.g. Overbury (IRE) – Sister Seven (IRE) (Henbit (USA)) **c97**
[2017/18 c21.6g² c26.2g^pu c15.6v² c16.5v⁵ c16.3v* c16.4v^pu c17.1v³ c17.1v* Apr 16] **h–**
once-raced hurdler: modest handicap chaser: won at Newcastle in January and Kelso in
April: left C. Storey after first start: stays 2¾m: acts on heavy going: wears tongue tie.
Sandy Forster

CHARLIE STOUT (IRE) 7 br.g. Spadoun (FR) – Full of Elegance (FR) (Cadoudal **h130**
(FR)) [2017/18 h126, b78: h20v² h16s² h16s h16s h20v⁴ h16s h16s h16v⁶ h16s³ Apr 17] useful
handicap hurdler: placed 3 times in 2017/18: stays 2½m: acts on heavy going: tried in
cheekpieces: wears tongue tie: often travels strongly. *Shane Nolan, Ireland*

CHA

CHARLIE WINGNUT (IRE) 11 br.g. Westerner – Back To Stay (IRE) (Supreme Leader) [2017/18 c97, h96: c23.4g* c24g² c25.5g² c25.5s^pu c24.2g⁴ Aug 21] maiden hurdler: fair form over fences: won novice handicap at Kelso in May: stayed 25f: acted on soft going: front runner/raced prominently: dead. *Sue Smith* — c112 h–

CHARLI PARCS (FR) 5 b.g. Anabaa Blue – Ella Parcs (FR) (Nikos) [2017/18 h144: h16.3d² h15.7d h16.3v h16.4s^pu h16g⁴ Apr 21] tall, useful-looking gelding: useful handicap hurdler: fourth in Scottish Champion Hurdle at Ayr (3¾ lengths behind Midnight Shadow) in April: raced around 2m: acts on soft going. *Nicky Henderson* — h142

CHARMANT (FR) 6 b.g. Balko (FR) – Ravissante (FR) (Mad Tax (USA)) [2017/18 h101, b76: h16.8s* h16v⁴ h16.2s⁴ h15.6d² h16v⁴ Mar 9] fell in point: fairly useful handicap hurdler: won at Sedgefield (novice) and Ayr in December: raced around 2m: acts on heavy going: wears hood: tried in tongue tie: often races towards rear/travels strongly. *James Ewart* — h115

CHARMAYNE 6 b.m. Shirocco (GER) – Ancora (IRE) (Accordion) [2017/18 b16d b16s⁶ Nov 29] fifth foal: sister to bumper winner En Joule: dam unraced sister to very smart chaser (stayed 3¼m) The Tother One, closely related to top-class chaser (stays 3¼m) Carlingford Lough and half-sister to high-class chaser (stayed 21f) Thisthatandtother: no form in bumpers. *Stuart Edmunds* — b–

CHARMING LAD (IRE) 13 b.g. Dushyantor (USA) – Glens Lady (IRE) (Mister Lord (USA)) [2017/18 c–, h–: c29.2v^pu c23.8v^pu Apr 15] rangy gelding: fair maiden hurdler/chaser at best, no form since 2015/16: wears headgear/tongue tie. *Anthony Day* — c– h–

CHARMING ZEN (FR) 6 gr.g. Youmzain (IRE) – Niouumoun (FR) (Dadarissime (FR)) [2017/18 h136p: h16s h23.1v^F Feb 11] useful form at best over hurdles, no show in 2017/18: should stay further than 17f. *Nicky Henderson* — h–

CHARMIX (FR) 8 br.g. Laveron – Open Up (FR) (Fabulous Don (SPA)) [2017/18 c139, h–: h17.9s h23d c22v⁴ c19.5v^ur h24s c23.4v^F c23.8s⁶ Apr 25] well-made gelding: useful hurdler/chaser at best, below form in 2017/18: left Harry Fry after first start, Gordon Elliott after sixth: stays 3m: acts on heavy going: has worn headgear, including in 2017/18. *Sandy Thomson* — c126 h107

CHASE ME (IRE) 7 b.g. Mahler – Collatrim Choice (IRE) (Saddlers' Hall (IRE)) [2017/18 b61: h20.3g³ h19.9d h19.9d h19.7v⁵ c20.3v⁵ Feb 25] maiden pointer, runner-up 4 of 5 starts: poor form over hurdles: 7/1, fifth in novice handicap at Southwell (18½ lengths behind Normandy King) on chasing debut: often in hood: open to improvement as a chaser. *Sarah Hollinshead* — c74 p h81

CHASE THE SPUD 10 b.g. Alflora (IRE) – Trial Trip (Le Moss) [2017/18 c135, h–: c25.6v* c29.5v^pu c32.6s^pu c34.3s^pu Apr 14] workmanlike gelding: winning hurdler: smart handicap chaser: won at Haydock (by 6 lengths from Robinsfirth) in November: suited by extreme distances: acts on heavy going: tried in hood/tongue tie. *Fergal O'Brien* — c145 h–

CHASING HEADLIGHTS (IRE) 6 b.g. Getaway (GER) – Could Do (Cloudings (IRE)) [2017/18 b17s h22.2d h16.3g⁴ h18.7g h16.7g h16.8d⁵ h19.8v Mar 8] unplaced in point: tailed off in ladies maiden bumper: no form over hurdles: left Miss Elizabeth Anne Lalor after first start. *Alexandra Dunn* — h– b–

CHASMA 8 b.m. Kayf Tara – Luneray (FR) (Poplar Bluff) [2017/18 c97, h90: c20.3d* c20.2s c19.2s³ Feb 6] winning hurdler: fair form over fences: won handicap at Southwell in November: stays 2½m: acts on heavy going: tried in cheekpieces: wears tongue tie. *Michael Easterby* — c104 h–

CHASSEUR DE TETE (FR) 6 b.g. Coastal Path – Escomptee (FR) (Roi de Rome (USA)) [2017/18 b–: h16.2v h16s⁵ h16.7s⁵ h16v³ h17v h16v² h16.4v* Apr 15] fair hurdler: won novice handicap at Newcastle in April: will be suited by 2½m: raced only on soft/heavy going: in tongue tie last 3 starts. *Lucinda Russell* — h108

CHATEAU CHINON (FR) 6 b.g. Dream Well (FR) – Liesse de Marbeuf (FR) (Cyborg (FR)) [2017/18 h96, b83: c15.6v⁵ c17.2v⁴ Apr 11] modest form over hurdles: no form over fences: left Rebecca Menzies after first start: tried in hood: usually races nearer last than first. *Shaun Harris* — c– h–

CHATEAU CONTI (FR) 6 b.g. Vendangeur (IRE) – Regina Conti (FR) (Lavirco (GER)) [2017/18 h20s* h16s h24s Dec 28] second foal: half-brother to bumper winner Bingo Conti (by Coastal Path): dam, French 1½m bumper winner, half-sister to dam of Silviniaco Conti: bumper winner: useful hurdler: won minor event at Fairyhouse (by 2¼ lengths from The Storyteller) in November: stays 2½m: best form on soft/heavy going: usually races nearer last than first. *W. P. Mullins, Ireland* — h135

CHE

CHATEAU MARMONT (IRE) 5 b.g. Flemensfirth (USA) – Sliabh Geal Gcua (IRE) (Milan) [2017/18 b15.6s⁴ ab16.3g² Feb 24] €22,000 3-y-o, £100,000 4-y-o: first foal: dam won 2½m bumper on only start: second when fell last in Irish point: fairly useful form in bumpers: better effort when second at Newcastle in February. *Brian Ellison*   **b102**

CHATEAU ROBIN (IRE) 7 br.g. Robin des Pres (FR) – Bella With A Zee (IRE) (Persian Bold) [2017/18 h97p: c20.5v² c20.2v² c19.9d⁴ Apr 24] sturdy gelding: modest maiden hurdler: fair form over fences: best effort when second in novice handicap at Ayr in November: stays 2½m: acts on heavy going. *Kim Bailey*   **c106 h–**

CHATELIER (FR) 6 ch.g. Network (GER) – Elza III (FR) (Lazer (FR)) [2017/18 b15.8g⁵ h16g h16g h16g h15.8g h15.8v⁴ h16.6dᵘʳ Feb 8] last in bumper: poor form over hurdles: raced around 2m. *Samuel Drinkwater*   **h80 b–**

CHATEZ (IRE) 7 b.g. Dandy Man (IRE) – Glory Days (GER) (Tiger Hill (IRE)) [2017/18 h16v⁴ Dec 27] good-topped gelding: smart at one time on Flat: fairly useful form over hurdles: shaped as if retaining ability only 2 outings (one on Flat) since 2015. *Alan King*   **h99**

CHATO (FR) 6 ch.g. Malinas (GER) – Queen Bruere (FR) (Mansonnien (FR)) [2017/18 h88p, b99: h21.2v⁴ h21s h19d Apr 26] good-topped gelding: bumper winner: modest form over hurdles. *Alan King*   **h99**

CHEAT THE CHEATER (IRE) 11 b.g. Flemensfirth (USA) – Ballyclough Gale (Strong Gale) [2017/18 c92§, h–: c26.7vᶠ c24vᵖᵘ c24.5v Feb 1] compact gelding: winning hurdler: modest chaser at best, no form in 2017/18: wears headgear/tongue tie: lazy. *Claire Dyson*   **c– § h–**

CHEBSEY BEAU 8 b.g. Multiplex – Chebsey Belle (IRE) (Karinga Bay) [2017/18 h109: c21.4g* Jul 22] fair hurdler: 25/1, won novice handicap at Market Rasen (by 2¼ lengths from Lovely Job) on chasing debut: stays 21f: acts on good to firm and good to soft going. *John Quinn*   **c122 h–**

CHEEKY CHICA (IRE) 5 bl.m. Stowaway – Hats And Heels (IRE) (Flemensfirth (USA)) [2017/18 b13.7d² b15.8v⁶ Jan 3] first foal: dam (h115) bumper/19f hurdle winner: modest form in bumpers: better effort when second in maiden at Huntingdon in November. *Neil Mulhoiland*   **b82**

CHEENYS VENTURE 6 b.m. King's Theatre (IRE) – Daisies Adventure (IRE) (Flemensfirth (USA)) [2017/18 b–: h16.2g h20.6g⁴ h15.6g⁴ Dec 18] poor form over hurdles: in hood last 3 starts. *Sandy Thomson*   **h82**

CHEER'S DELBOY (IRE) 5 ch.g. Golan (IRE) – Lindy Lou (Hernando (FR)) [2017/18 h16.4g⁵ h16g⁵ h16s⁶ h21.2d⁶ Apr 24] workmanlike gelding: first foal: dam (h113), 17f hurdle winner, also 11.5f winner on Flat: runner-up on second of 2 starts in Irish maiden points: fair form over hurdles: should stay further than 2m: acts on soft going: often races towards rear. *Robin Dickin*   **h102**

CHEF D'EQUIPE (FR) 6 b.g. Presenting – Millesimee (FR) (Video Rock (FR)) [2017/18 c16.9s² c22.9s* h20.5d³ h20.5s⁶ c24.2d⁵ c20s* c18.8v Jan 20] useful-looking gelding: half-brother to several winners, including useful hurdler/fairly useful chaser Un Beau Matin (2¼m-2¾m winner, by Sagamix) and useful hurdler Vive La France (2m/17f winner, by Westerner): dam twice-raced half-sister to useful French 2¼m hurdle winner Sortie de Secours: fair maiden hurdler: fairly useful form over fences: won minor event at Auteuil in June and handicap at Sandown in January: left N. de Lageneste after second start: stays 3m: acts on soft going: in hood last 5 starts. *Philip Hobbs*   **c127 h110**

CHEF DES OBEAUX (FR) 6 b.g. Saddler Maker (IRE) – O Dame de Gene (FR) (Passing Sale (FR)) [2017/18 b105: h20.5d² h19.9v* h24.6s* h22.8v* h24vᵖᵘ h24.7sᵖᵘ Apr 13] tall gelding: useful bumper performer: similar form over hurdles: won conditional/amateur maiden at Uttoxeter in December, novice at Kempton in January and Prestige Novices' Hurdle at Haydock (by 15 lengths from Uppertown Prince) in February: stays 25f: acts on heavy going. *Nicky Henderson*   **h142**

CHEF D'OEUVRE (FR) 7 b.g. Martaline – Kostroma (FR) (Lost World (IRE)) [2017/18 c131x, h–: c26.2d c23.5sᵖᵘ h23.6v⁴ h24.3v² Jan 15] useful-looking gelding: winning pointer: fairly useful hurdler: second in handicap at Ayr in January: useful chaser at best, well below form both starts over fences in 2017/18: stays 25f: best form on soft/heavy going: usually in headgear: usually leads: temperament under suspicion: often let down by jumping over fences. *Warren Greatrex*   **c– x h118**

CHELSEA FLYER (IRE) 7 b.g. Westerner – Aktress (IRE) (Oscar (IRE)) [2017/18 h133: h20d⁵ h16d⁶ h16.6d⁵ ab16d Mar 5] well-made gelding: fairly useful hurdler, below best in 2017/18: stays 2½m: acts on good to soft going: tried in hood: tends to find little. *Emma Lavelle*   **h115**

CHE

CHELTENAM DE VAIGE (FR) 6 b.g. Forestier (FR) – Ratina de Vaige (FR) (April h102
Night (FR)) [2017/18 h93, b66: h15.9d² h20.7g² Nov 14] rather unfurnished gelding: fair
maiden hurdler: stays 21f: acts on heavy going. *Fergal O'Brien*

CHELTENHAM (FR) 6 b.m. Kap Rock (FR) – Sacree Mome (FR) (Dark Moondancer) c–
[2017/18 c20s^{pu} c24v^{pu} Dec 22] second foal: dam unraced: fair maiden hurdler for Francois h–
Nicolle in 2016/17: no form over fences: wore hood/tongue tie in 2017/18. *Oliver Greenall*

CHEQUE EN BLANC (FR) 6 b.g. Bernebeau (FR) – Necossaise (FR) (Michel h102
Georges) [2017/18 h97: h25d⁶ h24g⁶ h15.9d³ h21.7d³ h23.9s* h24.4s* h25v³ h24.2s²
h23.1v^{pu} Apr 17] lengthy gelding: fair handicap hurdler: won at Taunton in December and
Doncaster in January: left Tom Symonds after second start: will stay long distances: acts on
soft going: has worn headgear/tongue tie, including in 2017/18: usually races towards rear.
Gary Moore

CHEQUERED VIEW 5 b.m. Passing Glance – Blue Plaid (Clantime) [2017/18 b16d⁴ b85
b15.8g³ b15.8v⁴ b16.8g Apr 19] fourth foal: dam unraced: fair form in bumpers: in hood
last 3 starts. *Martin Keighley*

CHEROKEE PRINCE (IRE) 6 b.g. Westerner – Ara Blend (IRE) (Persian Mews) b93
[2017/18 b89p: b16.7g⁶ b15.6g⁶ Nov 30] fair form in bumpers. *Ronald O'Leary, Ireland*

CHERRY PRINCESS 8 gr.m. Act One – Francia (Legend of France (USA)) [2017/18 h74 §
h76: h17.2g h16.2d* h19.9g h16.8s^{pu} Nov 28] poor handicap hurdler: won at Hexham
in September: stays 2¾m, effective at shorter: acts on good to soft going: has worn
cheekpieces: in tongue tie last 3 starts: untrustworthy. *Barbara Butterworth*

CHESTERFIELD (IRE) 8 ch.g. Pivotal – Antique (IRE) (Dubai Millennium) [2017/18 h142
h148: h16.4s h15.7d h16d⁴ ab16d⁴ h16.8v⁴ h16g³ Apr 21] compact gelding: won jumpers
bumper at Kempton in March: useful handicap hurdler: third in Scottish Champion Hurdle
at Ayr (1¾ lengths behind Midnight Shadow) following month: best around 2m: acts on
heavy going: usually races nearer last than first, often travels strongly. *Seamus Mullins*

CHESTNUT BEN (IRE) 13 ch.g. Ridgewood Ben – Bensade (IRE) (Step Together (USA)) c103
[2017/18 c111, h–: c16.4g³ c19.3g² c19.2g⁴ c15.7g⁶ c20g⁶ c16.5f⁵ c15.8m³ c15.9m⁴ h–
c16.4d⁴ Dec 1] lengthy gelding: winning hurdler: fair handicap chaser: stays 2½m: acts
on good to firm and heavy going: tried in headgear: has worn tongue tie. *Peter Winks*

CHESTNUT STORM (IRE) 5 ch.m. Rip Van Winkle (IRE) – Always Attractive (IRE) h–
(King's Best (USA)) [2017/18 h–: h20.5d Dec 4] fair on Flat, stays 16.5f: no form over
hurdles. *Brian Barr*

CHEVALGRIS 8 gr.g. Verglas (IRE) – Danzelline (Danzero (AUS)) [2017/18 h97: h22d^{pu} h95
h22g³ h19.9d³ h20f² Oct 12] modest maiden hurdler: stays 2¾m: acts on any going: tried
in cheekpieces. *Dai Burchell*

CHEYONA (IRE) 6 b.m. Mr Dinos (IRE) – Ardilaun (IRE) (Darnay) [2017/18 b16s h–
b15.8d⁵ b21.6m⁴ h21.6d⁵ h18.5s Nov 15] first foal: dam, maiden hurdler/chaser (stayed b–
2½m), half-sister to fair hurdler/fairly useful chaser (stayed 3¼m) Black Anshan: no form
in bumpers/over hurdles. *Seamus Mullins*

CHEZ HANS (IRE) 4 b.g. Aizavoski (IRE) – Hidden Reserve (IRE) (Heron Island b–
(IRE)) [2017/18 b16.7d Apr 21] 15/8, seventh in conditionals/amateur bumper at Bangor.
Olly Murphy

CHICAGO LADY (IRE) 7 b.m. Stowaway – Gemmeus (IRE) (Bigstone (IRE)) h95
[2017/18 h20.6v⁶ h19.3v² h22.8s⁴ h19.3v⁶ Apr 17] €3,000 4-y-o, £12,000 5-y-o: second
foal: dam (h84) maiden hurdler (best at 2m): runner-up in Irish point: modest form over
hurdles: should stay beyond 2½m. *Donald McCain*

CHICAGO OUTFIT (IRE) 13 b.g. Old Vic – Lambourne Lace (IRE) (Un Desperado c100 §
(FR)) [2017/18 c117, h–: c23.8g⁵ c23.8m⁴ h23.8g^{pu} c24.1v^{ur} c24.2d* Apr 23] maiden h–
hurdler: fair handicap chaser nowadays: won at Hexham in April: stays 25f: acts on soft
and good to firm going: wears headgear: unreliable. *Leonard Kerr*

CHICA RAPIDA 6 ch.m. Paco Boy (IRE) – Tora Bora (Grand Lodge (USA)) [2017/18 h–
h16.8g^{pu} h16g^{pu} h16.8d³ h16.8v⁶ h16d^{pu} h16.8v^{ur} Nov 7] lengthy mare: fair maiden on Flat,
stays 7f: no form over hurdles. *Gail Haywood*

CHICKSGROVE SPRITE (IRE) 7 b.m. Scorpion (IRE) – Homebird (IRE) (Be My h82
Native (USA)) [2017/18 h72: h20.6g⁵ h23.3g³ h24g⁵ h19.2g⁵ h23d³ Sep 29] poor maiden
hurdler: stays 23f: acts on good to soft going: tried in cheekpieces: wears tongue tie: often
races towards rear: temperament under suspicion. *Neil Mulholland*

CHI

CHIC NAME (FR) 6 b.g. Nickname (FR) – Vuelta Al Ruedo (FR) (Ballingarry (IRE)) [2017/18 c128, h141: c24.2v³ c30.2s⁵ c26.2vᵖᵘ c30.6s* Apr 27] good-topped gelding: useful hurdler: useful chaser: won handicap at Perth in April: fifth in Glenfarclas Chase (Cross Country) at Cheltenham (17¾ lengths behind Tiger Roll) in March: stays 3½f: acts on heavy going: wears headgear. *Richard Hobson*   **c137 h–**

CHICORIA (IRE) 9 ch.g. Presenting – Coco Girl (Mystiko (USA)) [2017/18 h24.3v² h22.8v h24.3v⁵ h24v⁴ h20.5v* h22.7v* Apr 16] sturdy gelding: fair handicap hurdler: won at Ayr in March and Kelso in April: fairly useful chaser: stays 3m: acts on heavy going: tried in cheekpieces: temperamental. *Tristan Davidson*   **c– § h110 §**

CHIC THEATRE (IRE) 8 gr.g. King's Theatre (IRE) – La Reine Chic (FR) (Balleroy (USA)) [2017/18 h112: h16gᵖᵘ h16g⁵ h19.2m⁵ Aug 17] lengthy gelding: fair handicap hurdler, below form in 2017/18: stays 2½f: acts on heavy going: wears headgear/tongue tie: temperamental. *David Pipe*   **h93 §**

CHIDSWELL (IRE) 9 b.g. Gold Well – Manacured (IRE) (Mandalus) [2017/18 c126, h122: c20.1s² c23.4s² c24.5v³ c16.5v³ c20d³ c23.8sᵖᵘ Apr 25] rangy gelding: winning hurdler: useful handicap chaser: second at Newcastle (7 lengths behind Saints And Sinners) in December and Kelso (neck behind Bright Prospect) in January: stays 2⅜f: acts on heavy going: often races prominently. *Nicky Richards*   **c130 h–**

CHIEF BOTTLEWASHER (IRE) 7 b.g. Moss Vale (IRE) – Edwina (IRE) (Caerleon (USA)) [2017/18 c–, h79: c21.7mᵖᵘ May 4] poor hurdler: no form over fences: tried in hood. *Aytach Sadik*   **c– h–**

CHIEF BRODY 7 b.g. Phoenix Reach (IRE) – Cherry Plum (Medicean) [2017/18 h96: h16v* Mar 11] fair handicap hurdler: won at Warwick (conditional) on sole outing in 2017/18: unproven beyond 2m: acts on heavy going: tried in cheekpieces. *William Muir*   **h107**

CHIEF SITTINGBULL 5 ch.g. Indian Haven – Saharan Song (IRE) (Singspiel (IRE)) [2017/18 b73: b16s h19.5v Dec 9] poor form in bumpers: 100/1, seventh in novice at Chepstow (36¾ lengths behind Chooseyourweapon) on hurdling debut: likely to prove best at easy 2m. *Neil Mulholland*   **h76 b65**

CHIEFTAIN'S CHOICE (IRE) 9 b.g. King's Theatre (IRE) – Fairy Native (IRE) (Be My Native (USA)) [2017/18 h117: h16.2g² h15.8m³ c15.7g² c16g³ h15.5v h16v Feb 16] rather leggy gelding: fairly useful handicap hurdler: similar form over fences: better effort when second in novice at Southwell in July: stays 1⅞f: acts on heavy going: tried in cheekpieces. *Kevin Frost*   **c120 h114**

CHILDRENS LIST (IRE) 8 b.g. Presenting – Snipe Hunt (IRE) (Stalker) [2017/18 c138p, h123: c19.5s² c28.7vᵖᵘ c34.3sᵖᵘ Apr 14] good-topped gelding: useful hurdler: smart form over fences: second in minor event at Limerick (½ length behind Attribution) in October: stays 25f: acts on heavy going: remains open to improvement as a chaser. *W. P. Mullins, Ireland*   **c146 p h–**

CHILLI FILLI 5 ch.m. Presenting – Daprika (FR) (Epervier Bleu) [2017/18 b–p: b16.7s* h21.2g⁴ h15.8g³ h21.2d* h19s⁴ h20.3g⁵ Apr 19] fair form in bumpers: won mares event at Bangor in May: fairly useful form over hurdles: won novice at Ludlow in December: will stay 2¾m: acts on good to soft going: often races towards rear. *Henry Daly*   **h120 b90**

CHILL IN THE WOOD 9 br.m. Desert King (IRE) – Zaffaranni (IRE) (Zaffaran (USA)) [2017/18 c19.7dᵘʳ c23.6d* Apr 24] rather leggy mare: modest maiden hurdler: similar form over fences: won handicap at Huntingdon in April: stays 3m: acts on good to soft going: tried in cheekpieces. *Dominic Ffrench Davis*   **c88 h–**

CHILLI ROMANCE (IRE) 7 b.m. Flemensfirth (USA) – Blue Romance (IRE) (Bob Back (USA)) [2017/18 h95: h16.3g² h15.8g⁵ h16s² h16.5s³ h15.8s Mar 14] modest maiden hurdler: unproven beyond 2m: acts on soft going: has worn tongue tie, including last 5 starts: front runner/races prominently. *Fergal O'Brien*   **h91**

CHILLY MISS 9 b.m. Iceman – Fairlie (Halling (USA)) [2017/18 h104: h15.7g⁴ h20.3d³ h15.7g h20.3d² h19.9s Dec 26] fair handicap hurdler: stays 2½m: acts on good to firm and good to soft going: tried in cheekpieces. *Malcolm Jefferson*   **h101**

CHIMES OF DYLAN (IRE) 5 b.g. Court Cave (IRE) – What A Princess (IRE) (Alderbrook) [2017/18 b15.8s b16.5g h20.8s⁵ h21s h16d⁴ h21.7g² Apr 20] €16,000 3-y-o, £23,000 4-y-o: third foal: dam unraced half-sister to top-class chaser (2½m-3¼m winner) Celestial Gold and high-class hurdler (stayed 3m) Fivethreethree: fourth on second of 2 outings in Irish points: well held in bumpers: fair form over hurdles. *Neil King*   **h110 b–**

CHI

CHINATOWN BOY (IRE) 10 ch.g. Presenting – Asian Maze (IRE) (Anshan) [2017/18 c–, h–: c25.8m⁴ h23m Jul 5] well-made gelding: point winner: fairly useful maiden hurdler/chaser at best, lightly raced and below that level since 2015/16: stays 25f: acts on soft and good to firm going: sometimes in cheekpieces. *Charles Whittaker* c89 h–

CHIRICO VALLIS (FR) 6 b.g. Poliglote – Quora Vallis (FR) (Mansonnien (FR)) [2017/18 c15.7d* c16d^F c17.4v* c16.4v^F c15.9v² Feb 15] well-made gelding: third foal: half-brother to fair French 17f hurdle winner Athena Vallis (by Saint des Saints): dam, second in 2¾m hurdle in France on only start, half-sister to fairly useful French hurdler/smart chaser (17f-2¾m winner) Jerico Vallis: winning hurdler: useful form over fences: won novices at Southwell in November and Bangor (by 18 lengths from Champagne James) in December: raced around 2m: acts on heavy going: wears hood/tongue tie: temperament under suspicion (ran out once). *Neil Mulholland* c130 h–

CHITU (IRE) 8 b.g. Desert King (IRE) – Polly's Joy (IRE) (Oscar (IRE)) [2017/18 c132, h126: c16m² c16g* c20.1v³ c16.1g* c15.9g⁵ Oct 27] fairly useful hurdler: useful chaser: won novices at Perth in August and Towcester in October: stayed 2½m: acted on good to firm and heavy going: tried in hood: wore tongue tie: dead. *Patrick Griffin, Ireland* c132 h–

CHIVERS (IRE) 7 b.g. Duke of Marmalade (IRE) – Thara (USA) (Hennessy (USA)) [2017/18 h89: h20.5d h20.5s^pu Dec 3] maiden hurdler, no form in 2017/18: has worn headgear: temperament under suspicion. *Daniel Steele* h–

CHLOE'S COURT (IRE) 5 br.m. Court Cave (IRE) – Howaya Pet (IRE) (Montelimar (USA)) [2017/18 b15.3v⁴ h15.9v⁵ h21.7v⁴ h19.8v² Apr 9] fourth foal: sister to a winning pointer and half-sister to fairly useful hurdler/useful chaser Doing Fine (2¾m-3½m winner, by Presenting): dam (c130/h109) 3m-4m hurdle/chase winner: fourth in bumper at Wincanton: modest form over hurdles: best effort when second in maiden at same course in April: will prove suited by 3m+. *Robert Walford* h90 b66

CHOCOLATE DIAMOND (IRE) 7 ch.g. Intense Focus (USA) – Sagemacca (IRE) (Danehill Dancer (IRE)) [2017/18 h17.7v^pu h15.9d h15.9v h15.9s Apr 15] fair on Flat, stays 2m: no form over hurdles. *Daniel O'Brien* h–

CHOCOLAT NOIR (IRE) 5 b.m. Yeats (IRE) – Valrhona (IRE) (Spectrum (IRE)) [2017/18 h19.3d⁵ h19.3s⁴ h19.7s h17s h21.2g⁶ Apr 23] sister to fair hurdler/chaser Seven Kingdoms (2m-19f winner): fairly useful maiden hurdler on Flat, stays 13f: poor form over hurdles: tried in cheekpieces: often races towards rear. *Martin Todhunter* h80

CHOIX DE L'AMOUR (IRE) 6 br.g. Fruits of Love (USA) – Carlas Choice (IRE) (Exit To Nowhere (USA)) [2017/18 h19.7d^pu h20.6s^pu Dec 23] pulled up in 2 novice hurdles. *Tim Reed* h–

CHOIX DES ARMES (FR) 6 b.g. Saint des Saints (FR) – Kicka (Shirley Heights) [2017/18 b–: h19.3g h16.5s⁶ h15.3v³ h15.3v* h18.5v³ Apr 17] good-topped gelding: has had breathing operation: fair form over hurdles: won novice handicap at Wincanton in April: stays 19f: acts on heavy going: in hood last 5 starts: usually races towards rear, often travels strongly. *Paul Nicholls* h114

CHOOCHOOBUGALOO 6 b.m. Rail Link – Charmante Femme (Bin Ajwaad (IRE)) [2017/18 h–, b–: h18.7g^pu h20g May 26] lengthy mare: no form in bumpers/over hurdles: tried in hood. *Laura Young* h–

CHOOKIE ROYALE 10 ch.g. Monsieur Bond (IRE) – Lady of Windsor (IRE) (Woods of Windsor (USA)) [2017/18 h16.8s³ h15.6s h16.2s Apr 26] useful on Flat, best up to 7f: modest form over hurdles: best effort when third in novice at Sedgefield in November: will prove best at sharp 2m. *Keith Dalgleish* h99

CHOOSEYOURWEAPON (IRE) 5 br.g. Flemensfirth (USA) – Definite Love (IRE) (Definite Article) [2017/18 h19.5s* h19.5v* h21s⁴ h23.6s³ Mar 22] €30,000 3-y-o, £210,000 4-y-o: lengthy, well-made gelding: first foal: dam, maiden pointer, half-sister to fair hurdler/fairly useful chaser (21f-3m winner) He's The Guv'nor out of fair hurdler/useful chaser (stayed 25f) Love The Lord: won Irish point on debut: fairly useful form over hurdles: won maiden in November and novice in December, both at Chepstow: will stay 3m. *Evan Williams* h125

CHORAL BEE 9 b.m. Oratorio (IRE) – Chief Bee (Chief's Crown (USA)) [2017/18 h–: h15.8g⁶ h21.7d Nov 19] little form over hurdles: often in cheekpieces: has worn tongue tie, including in 2017/18. *Alan Jessop* h60

CHOSEN LUCKY (IRE) 7 b.g. Well Chosen – Melville Rose (IRE) (Phardante (FR)) [2017/18 c26d^pu May 5] prolific point winner: pulled up in hunter on chasing debut. *D. Summersby* c–

CH'

CHOSEN PATH (IRE) 5 b.g. Well Chosen – Karsulu (IRE) (Mukaddamah (USA)) [2017/18 h19.2g* h21.6sur h21s³ h21s* h20s Apr 14] €31,000 3-y-o, £60,000 4-y-o: rather unfurnished gelding: fourth foal: half-brother to fair chaser Stoleaway (3m winner, by Stowaway): dam (h65) maiden hurdler: third in Irish point: fairly useful form over hurdles: won novices at Fontwell in October and Kempton in March: stays 21f: acts on soft going. *Alan King* — **h128**

CHOSEN WELL (IRE) 9 b.g. Well Chosen – Killmaleary Cross (IRE) (Needle Gun (IRE)) [2017/18 c19.2v³ Dec 8] useful-looking gelding: has had breathing operation: point winner: fairly useful hurdler: similar form over fences: third in handicap at Exeter after 2-year absence: stays 23f: best form on heavy going: tried in tongue tie. *Alan King* — **c118 h–**

CHOUQUETTE 4 b.f. Fame And Glory – Mille Et Une (FR) (Trempolino (USA)) [2017/18 b12.4s⁵ b15.6d⁶ h16.2s³ Apr 27] fifth foal: half-sister to useful hurdler/smart chaser Hell's Kitchen (2½m winner, by Robin des Champs): dam (c113/h113), French 2m/17f hurdle/chase winner, sister to useful French hurdler/chaser up to 25f Madox: poor form in bumpers: 20/1, third in mares novice at Perth (11¼ lengths behind Floral Bouquet) on hurdling debut. *Lucinda Russell* — **h86 b70**

CHOZEN (IRE) 6 b.g. Well Chosen – Kneeland Lass (IRE) (Bob Back (USA)) [2017/18 h16g⁵ h16.7g⁴ h16.7d³ h16.8d* h15.8d⁶ h15.7v⁶ Jan 20] €21,000 3-y-o: third foal: half-brother to useful hurdler Mount Mews (2m-19f winner, by Presenting): dam, little form, sister to useful hurdler/high-class chaser (stayed 29f) Burton Port and half-sister to fairly useful hurdler/useful chaser (stays 21f) Burtons Well (by Well Chosen): runner-up on completed start in points: fair form over hurdles: won novice handicap at Carlisle in November: raced around 2m: acts on good to soft going: in hood last 5 starts: usually races in rear. *Tim Vaughan* — **h106**

CHRIS PEA GREEN 9 b.g. Proclamation (IRE) – Another Secret (Efisio) [2017/18 c16.8g c21dpu h19.2v⁴ h21.7v⁴ Jan 21] strong gelding: one-time useful hurdler/chaser, well below best in 2017/18 after long absence: stays 2½m: acts on heavy going: temperament under suspicion (has high head carriage): sketchy jumper of fences. *Gary Moore* — **c– x h102**

CHRIS'S DREAM (IRE) 6 b.g. Mahler – Janebailey (Silver Patriarch (IRE)) [2017/18 b16d⁶ h19.6v² h19v* h24v* h24v Mar 16] €17,000 3-y-o: rangy gelding: will make a chaser: second foal: half-brother to fairly useful 17f hurdle winner (later winner in USA, including Grade 1 3m event)/winning pointer Scorpiancer (by Scorpion): dam unraced: point winner: fair form in bumpers: useful form over hurdles: won maiden at Limerick in December and Surehaul Mercedes-Benz Novices' Hurdle at Clonmel (by 64 lengths from Carrigeen Acebo) in February: left Eugene M. O'Sullivan after third start: stays 3m: front runner/races prominently. *Henry de Bromhead, Ireland* — **h140 b85**

CHRISTMAS IN APRIL (FR) 6 b.g. Crillon (FR) – Similaresisoldofa (FR) (Kapgarde (FR)) [2017/18 h105p, b87: h20.6d³ h23.5d⁴ h24.2spu Mar 23] good-topped gelding: bumper winner: fair form over hurdles: stays 3m: acts on good to soft going: in hood last 4 starts. *Nicky Henderson* — **h111**

CHRISTMAS IN USA (FR) 6 b.g. Shaanmer (IRE) – Diamond of Diana (FR) (Kapgarde (FR)) [2017/18 c–, h94: h16.2g⁶ h23.3gpu h16.8d⁶ h16.8s⁴ h16.4s⁴ h16v² h19.7v⁶ h16.2sF Apr 26] poor maiden hurdler: twice-raced chaser: stays 2¼m: acts on heavy going: has worn headgear, including last 3 starts: wears tongue tie. *N. W. Alexander* — **c– h76**

CHRISTMAS TWENTY (IRE) 8 br.g. Zagreb (USA) – Celestial Gale (IRE) (Presenting) [2017/18 c–, h–: c19.3g³ c20.1v⁵ c19.2dpu c21.4vF h21.2v³ h25vpu h21.3d⁵ Mar 29] angular gelding: placed in Irish points: modest maiden hurdler/chaser: stays 21f: best form on soft/heavy going: wears headgear: often races in rear. *Micky Hammond* — **c95 h94**

CHRISTO 6 ch.g. Areion (GER) – Chantra (GER) (Lando (GER)) [2017/18 h15.5vpu h16.6sF Jan 26] fair on Flat (stayed 1¼m) for Frau C. Bersig: no form over hurdles: in tongue tie final start: dead. *Oliver Greenall* — **h–**

CHTI BALKO (FR) 6 br.g. Balko (FR) – Ina Scoop (FR) (Murmure (FR)) [2017/18 h120, b74: h16.3d³ h18.9v⁴ h15.7v* h16.2s⁵ h18.1v³ h16v h15.7s² Mar 31] angular gelding: placed in Irish point: useful handicap hurdler: won at Haydock in December: second there in March: raced around 2m: acts on good to soft going: usually leads. *Donald McCain* — **h138**

CH'TIBELLO (FR) 7 b.g. Sageburg (IRE) – Neicha (FR) (Neverneyev (USA)) [2017/18 h150: h16.8s⁴ h15.7v² h15.3s² h16.4s h16g Apr 21] useful-looking gelding: smart hurdler: second in Champion Hurdle Trial at Haydock (½ length behind The New One) in January and Kingwell Hurdle at Wincanton (2½ lengths behind Elgin) in February: raced around 2m: acts on good to firm and heavy going: tried in tongue tie. *Dan Skelton* — **h150**

201

CHU

CHU CHU PERCY 7 b.g. Tobougg (IRE) – First Katoune (FR) (Poliglote) [2017/18 h61, b66: h24.3s² h24g* h25.3s* h24.3v^{pu} Mar 9] winning pointer: fair handicap hurdler: won at Newcastle in November and Catterick (novice) in January: will stay long distances: acts on soft going: wears headgear: tried in tongue tie: races prominently. *Alistair Whillans* — **h107**

CHURCHFIELD CHAMP (IRE) 12 b.g. Norwich – Ash Dame (IRE) (Strong Gale) [2017/18 c17d Jun 9] tall gelding: multiple point winner: winning hurdler: fairly useful chaser at best, well held in hunter sole outing under Rules in 2017/18: stays 25f, effective at much shorter: acts on good to firm and heavy going: has worn headgear: wears tongue tie. *Kayley Woollacott* — **c–** **h–**

CHURCH HALL (IRE) 10 b.g. Craigsteel – Island Religion (IRE) (Religiously (USA)) [2017/18 h102: c20s* c20.6v^{ur} c22.4s⁶ h21.6s⁵ Apr 23] workmanlike gelding: fair handicap hurdler: fairly useful form over fences: won novice handicap at Lingfield in November: stays 3m: acts on soft going: in tongue tie last 5 starts. *Emma-Jane Bishop* — **c117** **h105**

CHURCH LEAP (IRE) 7 gr.g. High Chaparral (IRE) – Alambic (Cozzene (USA)) [2017/18 h–: h16s^{pu} h15.8d^{pu} Apr 24] tall, useful-looking gelding: has had breathing operation: bumper winner: maiden hurdler, no form in 2017/18: raced around 2m: in cheekpieces last 2 starts. *Patrick Chamings* — **h–**

CIARABELLA (IRE) 5 b.m. Gold Well – Fancy Fashion (IRE) (Broken Hearted) [2017/18 b16v b16v⁶ b16v³ Feb 26] second foal: dam, winning pointer, half-sister to fairly useful hurdler/fairly useful chaser (19f-2¾m winner) City Heights: no form in bumpers. *R. Mike Smith* — **b–**

CIBOIR (FR) 6 gr.g. Fragrant Mix (IRE) – Fleche Noir II (FR) (Quart de Vin (FR)) [2017/18 b–: h16.7g h16.7s Dec 26] no form in bumpers: tailed off in novice on hurdling debut: hooded first 2 starts. *Nick Kent* — **h–** **b–**

CILAOS EMERY (FR) 6 b.g. Califet (FR) – Queissa (FR) (Saint Preuil (FR)) [2017/18 h144, b102: h20s⁴ h16s² Dec 29] rather unfurnished gelding: bumper winner: very smart form over hurdles: second in Ryanair Hurdle at Leopardstown (1¾ lengths behind Mick Jazz) in December: stays 2½m: acts on soft going: in hood last 4 starts: front runner/races prominently. *W. P. Mullins, Ireland* — **h157**

CILAOS GLACE (FR) 5 br.g. Voix du Nord (FR) – Miss Glacee (FR) (Mister Mat (FR)) [2017/18 b16s Mar 17] well-made gelding: tailed off in maiden bumper. *Gary Moore* — **b–**

CILLIAN'S WELL (IRE) 8 b.g. Trans Island – Live A Lot (IRE) (Saddlers' Hall (IRE)) [2017/18 h98: h20g h19.2g² h18.7g* h16g² h18.5m* h16g⁴ h18.5g⁵ h16.8m³ h19.2d⁴ Sep 10] fair handicap hurdler: won at Stratford in June and Newton Abbot (conditional) in July: stays 19f: acts on good to firm going: wears headgear/tongue tie. *John Flint* — **h106**

CINDERFELLA 7 gr.g. Sagamix (FR) – Firecracker Lady (IRE) (Supreme Leader) [2017/18 h23.3v⁴ h25.5v³ Mar 10] fair form in bumpers: modest form over hurdles: better effort when fourth in novice at Uttoxeter: bred to stay 3m+. *Kerry Lee* — **h94**

CINEVATOR (IRE) 11 b.g. Dr Massini (IRE) – Hurricane Bella (IRE) (Taipan (IRE)) [2017/18 h17.2g h23g c25.1v^{pu} Mar 28] good-topped gelding: prolific point winner: fairly useful hurdler/chaser at best, no form in 2017/18: left Jeremy Scott after second start: usually wears headgear. *Miss E. M. G. Pickard* — **c–** **h–**

CINTEX (FR) 6 b.g. Assessor (IRE) – Precieuze (FR) (Video Rock (FR)) [2017/18 b17.7g³ b17.7d⁶ h22.2d² h20.5s h20.5v^{pu} h21.7d Feb 25] €32,000 3-y-o, £52,000 4-y-o: fourth foal: half-brother to French hurdler/chaser Voidirome (17f-19f winner, by Robin des Champs) and French chaser Be Work (2¼m-2½m winner, by Network): dam, unraced, closely related to smart hurdler/top-class chaser (stayed 3m) Impek: runner-up completed start in Irish maiden points: poor form in bumpers: fair form over hurdles. *Neil Mulholland* — **h102** **b68**

CIRCUIT COURT (IRE) 7 br.g. Court Cave (IRE) – Norwich Breeze (IRE) (Norwich) [2017/18 h21g^{pu} h25s⁶ h23.1d Apr 21] lengthy gelding: off mark in Irish points at fourth attempt: no form over hurdles. *Paul Webber* — **h–**

CITADEL (FR) 6 b.g. Al Namix (FR) – Oreli (FR) (Robin des Pres (FR)) [2017/18 c–, h–: c17.8s^F Mar 7] has had breathing operation: maiden hurdler: no form over fences, well backed when fell sole outing in 2017/18: tried in tongue tie: remains likely to do better as a chaser. *Dan Skelton* — **c– p** **h–**

CITRUS (FR) 6 b.g. Great Pretender (IRE) – Kelle Home (FR) (Useful (FR)) [2017/18 c– h96, b–: c22.6g^{pu} c20.9g^F Jun 1] lengthy gelding: modest hurdler: no form over fences: unproven beyond 2m: acts on good to soft going: usually in headgear/tongue tie. *David Pipe* — **h–**

CITY DREAMER (IRE) 4 ch.g. Casamento (IRE) – Cadescia (FR) (Cadeaux Genereux) [2017/18 h16.2g² h16.7g^{pu} h16.7g³ h15.9m* h16.7g* h16s² h16.6d³ h15.7s⁶ Mar 25] compact gelding: fair maiden on Flat, stays 2m: fairly useful hurdler: won juveniles at — **h127**

Plumpton and Market Rasen in September: second in Summit Juvenile Hurdle at Doncaster (10 lengths behind We Have A Dream) in December: raced around 2m: acts on soft and good to firm going: often races in rear/travels strongly. *Alan King*

CITY STAR 6 b.m. Black Sam Bellamy (IRE) – Danarama (Rock City) [2017/18 h21v[6] h15.3d Apr 22] second foal: dam winning pointer: poor form over hurdles. *Ben Pauling*   **h58**

CITY SUPREME (IRE) 8 b.g. Milan – Run Supreme (IRE) (Supreme Leader) [2017/18 c117, h115: c25.7s[4] c20.2v[pu] Mar 28] good-topped gelding: fairly useful hurdler: similar form at best over fences: stays 3¼m: acts on heavy going: has worn headgear: wears tongue tie: front runner/races prominently. *Anthony Honeyball*   **c95 h–**

CIVIL UNREST (IRE) 12 ch.g. Blueprint (IRE) – Yore (IRE) (Ore) [2017/18 c107x, h102: c15.6g[2] c19.2g[6] h16.2m h16.7g* h16.2g[2] c15.8g[4] h15.7s[pu] Jan 1] fair handicap hurdler: won at Bangor in August: fair form in chases: stays 2½m: acts on soft and good to firm going: wears headgear: front runner/races prominently: often let down by jumping/attitude. *James Ewart*   **c101 x h103 §**

CIVITESSES (FR) 6 b.m. Prince Kirk (FR) – Glenn Rose (FR) (Scooter Bleu (IRE)) [2017/18 h75, b–: h21.6m h16.8d Aug 22] maiden Irish pointer: maiden hurdler, no form in 2017/18: often in blinkers: usually races nearer last than first, often freely. *Brian Barr*   **h–**

CKALCO DES LOGES (FR) 6 b.g. Balko (FR) – Olla des Loges (FR) (Sleeping Car (FR)) [2017/18 h120: h19.6g* h22s[5] c19.9g[3] c18.9s[pu] c20v[pu] c18.2s[6] c24s[3] c21.2d[3] Apr 7] good-topped gelding: point winner: fairly useful hurdler: didn't need to be at best to win novice at Bangor in September: fair form in chases: stays 3m: acts on soft going: often wears tongue tie: often races prominently. *Dan Skelton*   **c109 h108**

CLAIMANTAKINFORGAN (FR) 6 b.g. Great Pretender (IRE) – Taquine d'Estrees (FR) (Take Risks (FR)) [2017/18 b115: h16.3d* h15.7d* h15.6s[3] h16.4s[5] h16g[2] Apr 21] good-topped gelding: smart bumper performer: similar form over hurdles: won novice at Newbury (by 2¼ lengths from Lostintranslation) in November and Kennel Gate Novices'   **h147**

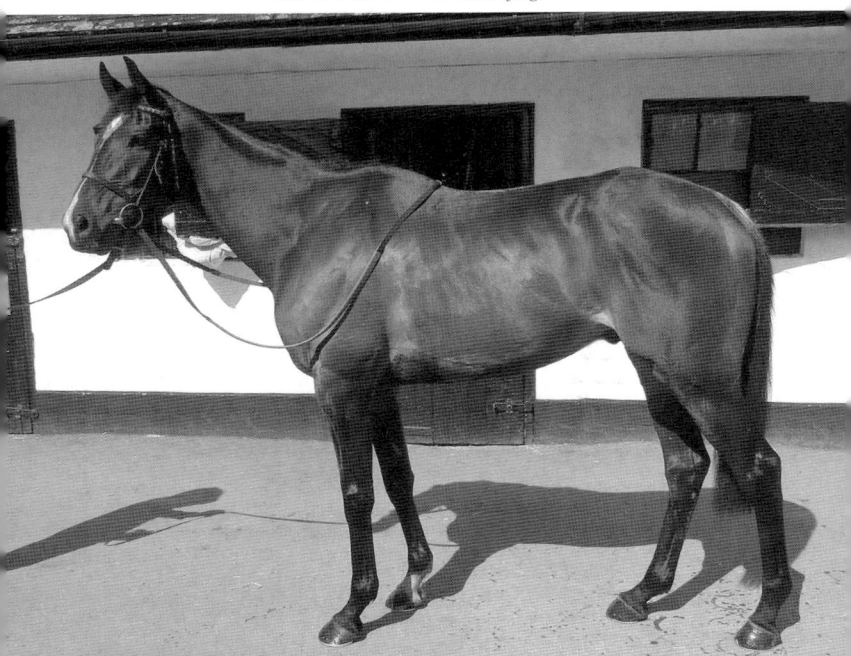

Grech & Parkin's "Claimantakinforgan"

CLA

Hurdle at Ascot (by 2¼ lengths from Dr Des) in December: second in Scottish Champion Hurdle at Ayr (1¼ lengths behind Midnight Shadow) in April: will prove suited by 2½m: acts on soft going: often travels strongly. *Nicky Henderson*

CLAN CHIEF 9 ch.g. Generous (IRE) – Harrietfield (Nicholas Bill) [2017/18 c77x, h–: c16g c20.1g^{pu} Jun 3] winning hurdler: maiden chaser, no form in 2017/18: has worn hood: has worn tongue tie, including in 2017/18. *N. W. Alexander* c–
h–

CLAN DES OBEAUX (FR) 6 b.g. Kapgarde (FR) – Nausicaa des Obeaux (FR) (April Night (FR)) [2017/18 c148, h–: c20.5d^2 c21.6v* c20.8s^2 c25s^3 Apr 12] well-made gelding: winning hurdler: high-class chaser: won graduation event at Haydock (by 7 lengths from Vintage Clouds) in November: third in Bowl Chase at Aintree (10¼ lengths behind Might Bite) in April: stays 25f: acts on heavy going: tried in tongue tie. *Paul Nicholls* c162
h–

CLAN LEGEND 8 ch.g. Midnight Legend – Harrietfield (Nicholas Bill) [2017/18 c122, h–: h16.2v* h18.9v^4 c20.6v* c19.4v^2 c20.1s^{ur} Feb 24] fairly useful handicap hurdler: won at Hexham in November: useful handicap chaser: won at Haydock in December: second at Wetherby in January: stays 21f: acts on heavy going: wears tongue tie: often travels strongly. *N. W. Alexander* c132
h124

CLARA SORRENTO (FR) 7 gr.g. Maresca Sorrento (FR) – Call Me Clara (FR) (Call Me Sam (FR)) [2017/18 h20.4d* h20.5d^2 h21g^2 h20d^2 Oct 19] €88,000 3-y-o: third foal: half-brother to French 2¼m hurdle winner Sweet Clara (by Assessor): dam ran twice over hurdles in France: useful hurdler: won novice at Punchestown in May: second in handicap there (2¼ lengths behind Ben Dundee) in October: stays 21f: acts on heavy going: wears hood: usually races close up. *Noel Meade, Ireland* h134

CLARCAM (FR) 8 b.g. Califet (FR) – Rose Beryl (FR) (Lost World (IRE)) [2017/18 c152, h129+: c16v^4 c16.7v^4 c21.1s^6 c20s Apr 25] good-topped gelding: winning hurdler: smart chaser: won Fortria Chase at Navan (by ½ length from Alisier d'Irlande) in November: stays 2¾m: acts on good to firm and heavy going: wears headgear/tongue tie. *Gordon Elliott, Ireland* c145
h–

CLASH OF D TITANS (IRE) 5 b.g. Gold Well – Give Us A Look (IRE) (Grand Plaisir (IRE)) [2017/18 b16.7s^5 h15.5v^3 h19.5v^2 h19.5v$^d6$ Mar 22] €12,000 3-y-o, £50,000 4-y-o: second foal: brother to a winning pointer: dam pulled up both starts in points: runner-up in Irish point: fifth in bumper at Bangor: fair form over hurdles: best effort when second in novice at Lingfield in February. *Warren Greatrex* h113
b95

CLASSICAL MILANO (IRE) 7 b.g. Milan – Miss Baden (IRE) (Supreme Leader) [2017/18 h104: h23.3v^{pu} h25.8g c21.1v^{pu} Feb 22] workmanlike gelding: in frame completed start in maiden points: fair hurdler at best, no form in 2017/18 (including on chasing debut). *George Bewley* c–
h–

CLASSICAL ROSE 6 b.m. Amadeus Wolf – Monaazalah (IRE) (Green Desert (USA)) [2017/18 h16v h16s h16.2s^6 Apr 26] fairly useful on Flat, stays 1m: poor form over hurdles: tried in tongue tie. *Gavin Patrick Cromwell, Ireland* h70

CLASSICAL SOUND (IRE) 6 b.g. Mahler – Sovienne (IRE) (Soviet Star (USA)) [2017/18 h71: h22.7g h20.1v^{pu} h19.9v^4 h27v^2 Apr 13] poor maiden hurdler: stays 27f: acts on heavy going. *Rose Dobbin* h78

CLASSIC BEN (IRE) 5 b.g. Beneficial – Dark Daisy (IRE) (Kotashaan (FR)) [2017/18 b16d^2 b16s^2 h20s* h19.6s* h24.4s h24.4s^2 h22.8v^6 Mar 31] lengthy gelding: second foal: dam winning pointer: fairly useful form when second in 2 bumpers: useful form over hurdles: won novices at Fakenham and Huntingdon in December: second in handicap at Doncaster (1¼ lengths behind Buckle Street) in February: will stay further than 3m: acts on soft going: tried in cheekpieces. *Stuart Edmunds* h132
b102

CLASSIC JEWEL (IRE) 11 b.g. Classic Cliche (IRE) – Be My Libby (IRE) (Be My Native (USA)) [2017/18 c24g* c25.8d^3 c24s^3 c21.7g^3 Nov 30] modest form over hurdles in Ireland for J. R. Barry: modest handicap chaser: won novice event at Uttoxeter in July: stays 3m: acts on soft going: usually wears headgear: has worn tongue tie, including last 4 starts: temperamental. *Evan Williams* c85 §
h–

CLASSICO DAIS (FR) 6 br.g. Al Namix (FR) – Fabema (FR) (Pure Hasard (FR)) [2017/18 h99: h26.4s^2 h23.6s^2 h24.1s h23.9v Mar 12] rangy, raw-boned gelding: modest maiden hurdler: stays 3¼m: acts on soft going: usually in cheekpieces. *Dan Skelton* h95

CLASSIC PALACE (IRE) 9 b.m. Classic Cliche (IRE) – Winconjon (IRE) (Oscar (IRE)) [2017/18 c–, h–: h22.1g^{pu} c20.1g^6 c21.2d^{pu} Aug 26] winning pointer: modest hurdler at best: little show in chases: tried in cheekpieces/tongue tie. *Dianne Sayer* c–
h–

Mr & Mrs P. K. Barber, G. Mason & Sir Alex Ferguson's "Clan des Obeaux"

CLASSIC TUNE 8 b.g. Scorpion (IRE) – Classic Fantasy (Classic Cliche (IRE)) [2017/18 **h–** h114: h20g h20.7s^{pu} Jan 26] fair hurdler, well below form both starts in 2017/18: stays 2½m: acts on soft going. *Claire Dyson*

CLASSULA 6 b.g. Sulamani (IRE) – Classic Fantasy (Classic Cliche (IRE)) [2017/18 b–: **h88** b13.7d^4 h15.8s h15.8s h15.8s h21s^3 Apr 9] poor form in bumpers: modest form over **b66** hurdles: in tongue tie last 3 starts. *Claire Dyson*

CLAUDE CARTER 14 b.g. Elmaamul (USA) – Cruz Santa (Lord Bud) [2017/18 c–, **c–** h96: h16.2g^5 h16.7g^4 h16.2d^5 h18.1g h19.9g^6 h15.7d h15.7d^6 Dec 28] neat gelding: fair **h72** handicap hurdler at best: fell sole outing over fences: stayed 2½m: acted on good to firm and good to soft going: wore headgear: dead. *Alistair Whillans*

CLAY ALLISON (IRE) 7 b.g. Primary (USA) – Cockpit Lady (IRE) (Commanche Run) **c–** [2017/18 h21.8g^6 h24g h19.6g^6 c26.3m^{ur} h25.8g^6 h20s^4 Dec 4] workmanlike gelding: poor **h81** maiden hurdler: unseated rider tenth in novice handicap at Taunton on chasing debut: left Noel Meade after second start: should stay further than 2m: tried in blinkers: wears tongue tie. *Olly Murphy*

CLAYTON 9 b.g. Peintre Celebre (USA) – Blossom (Warning) [2017/18 h116: h15.7g **h118** h17.7d^4 h16s* h16s h16v^2 Jan 30] lengthy gelding: fairly useful handicap hurdler: won at Lingfield in December: best at 2m: acts on heavy going: often wears tongue tie. *Gary Moore*

CLAYTON HALL (IRE) 5 b.g. Lilbourne Lad (IRE) – Hawk Dance (IRE) (Hawk Wing **h–** (USA)) [2017/18 h17.2d^F May 29] poor on Flat, stays 1¾m: in tongue tie, fell heavily second in novice on hurdling debut. *John Wainwright*

CLE

CLEARLY CAPABLE (IRE) 9 b.g. Bienamado (USA) – Spout Road (IRE) (Dr Massini (IRE)) [2017/18 h21.6g* h19.2g^pu h22g^pu h20g³ h18.5g* h20g³ h21s Apr 9] point winner: modest handicap hurdler: won at Newton Abbot in May and June (novice): maiden chaser in Ireland for Roy W. Tector: best from on good going: has worn headgear: in tongue tie last 3 starts: front runner. *Brian Barr* — c– h91

CLEMENCY 7 b.m. Halling (USA) – China Tea (USA) (High Chaparral (IRE)) [2017/18 h106: h15.7g³ h19.9d⁵ h16.3g h16s³ Nov 14] tall mare: fair handicap hurdler, below form in 2017/18: stays 21f: acts on heavy going. *Donald McCain* — h96

CLENAGH CASTLE (IRE) 8 b.g. King's Theatre (IRE) – Orwell's Marble (IRE) (Definite Article) [2017/18 c73, h–: c23.8d^pu c23.6s^pu Dec 26] point winner: maiden hurdler: maiden chaser, no form in 2017/18: often in cheekpieces: in tongue tie last 2 starts. *Jack R. Barber* — c– h–

CLENI WELLS (FR) 7 b.g. Poliglote – Kailasa (FR) (R B Chesne) [2017/18 c–, h112: h18.5m² h18.5s* h22.1s^pu h21.6g h18.5d³ h16.4g³ h16.8s⁶ c23g⁵ h20.5s Apr 15] workmanlike gelding: fair handicap hurdler: won at Newton Abbot in June: maiden chaser, well held sole outing over fences in 2017/18: stays 19f: acts on soft and good to firm going: wears headgear, usually races towards rear: inconsistent. *Martin Hill* — c– h113

CLIFF FACE (IRE) 5 b.m. Canford Cliffs (IRE) – Kotdiji (Mtoto) [2017/18 h16.5m⁴ Apr 25] half-sister to fairly useful hurdler Instant Karma (2m-2¼m winner, by Peintre Celebre) and fair hurdler Mister Carter (2m winner, by Antonius Pius): useful on Flat, stays 1½m: 7/2, fourth in mares novice at Taunton (8 lengths behind Cockney Wren) on hurdling debut. *Robert Stephens* — h100

CLIFFSIDE PARK (IRE) 9 b.g. Chevalier (IRE) – Lady Toulon (IRE) (Toulon) [2017/18 c17m h20s h16.5g⁴ h18.7g* c15.7g³ h20g⁵ h16d* h15.7d² h20.5d* h16.7s³ Dec 26] fairly useful hurdler: won seller at Stratford in July, conditionals selling handicap at Fakenham in October and conditionals seller at Leicester in December: fair maiden chaser: left Eoin Doyle after third start: stays 2¾m: acts on good to firm and heavy going: has worn headgear, including in 2017/18: tried in tongue tie. *Olly Murphy* — c104 h115

CLIFFS OF DOVER (IRE) 5 b.g. Canford Cliffs (IRE) – Basanti (USA) (Galileo (IRE)) [2017/18 h139p: h15.3s^pu Feb 17] useful hurdler: unsatisfactory display sole start in 2017/18 (won twice on Flat following month): raced around 2m: acts on good to firm going: often travels strongly. *Paul Nicholls* — h–

CLINTON HILL (IRE) 7 b.g. Flemensfirth (USA) – Smooching (IRE) (Saddlers' Hall (IRE)) [2017/18 b16v² b16v* b16v³ Mar 19] €60,000 3-y-o: third foal: dam unraced half-sister to smart hurdler up to 3m Moorish: useful form in bumpers: won maiden at Thurles (by 3 lengths from All For Joy) in February: bred to stay 3m. *W. P. Mullins, Ireland* — b107

CLOCK ON TOM 8 b.g. Trade Fair – Night Owl (Night Shift (USA)) [2017/18 h91: h18.7g⁵ h15.5s² h15.8v³ Dec 31] compact gelding: fair hurdler: unproven beyond 2m: acts on heavy going: often travels strongly. *Barry Leavy* — h99

CLONDAW ACE (IRE) 5 b.g. Flemensfirth (USA) – Peace Time Beauty (IRE) (Saddlers' Hall (IRE)) [2017/18 b16g Feb 24] off mark in Irish points at third attempt: tailed off in bumper. *Tim Vaughan* — b–

CLONDAW BANKER (IRE) 9 b.g. Court Cave (IRE) – Freya Alex (Makbul) [2017/18 c118, h–: c20.5g³ c20.1g c21.2s⁴ c24.2g^pu c21.6g⁶ c20.1v^pu h23.8m h16.8s^pu Nov 28] useful-looking gelding: fairly useful hurdler at best, no form in 2017/18: fairly useful maiden chaser: third in novice handicap at Kempton in May: left Nicky Henderson after first start: stays 2½m: acts on soft going: tried in cheekpieces. *Barry Murtagh* — c119 h–

CLONDAW BISTO (IRE) 7 b.g. September Storm (GER) – Solo Venture (IRE) (Abednego) [2017/18 h108: h17.7g h25d⁴ h23.1s³ h25v⁶ h23.5s⁴ h25v³ h21.6v^pu Apr 8] Irish point winner: fair maiden hurdler: stays 25f: acts on heavy going: in headgear last 5 starts: has worn tongue tie, including final start. *Suzy Smith* — h108

CLONDAW BUNNY (IRE) 5 b.g. Scorpion (IRE) – Super Sandie (IRE) (Dushyantor (USA)) [2017/18 b16.8d Apr 24] off mark in points at fourth attempt: tailed off in maiden bumper. *D. Summersby* — b–

CLONDAW CASTLE (IRE) 6 b.g. Oscar (IRE) – Lohort Castle (IRE) (Presenting) [2017/18 b105: h15.8d* h16.6d³ h16.2s* h16.8v Jan 27] useful-looking gelding: won completed start in Irish points: useful bumper performer: fairly useful form over hurdles: won maiden at Huntingdon in November and novice at Kelso in January: bred to stay further than 2m: strong traveller. *Tom George* — h129

CLO

CLONDAW CIAN (IRE) 8 br.g. Gold Well – Cocktail Bar (IRE) (Hubbly Bubbly (USA)) [2017/18 h133: c25s³ c23.8d² c23.9d² c23.8d^{pu} c28.5v c31.8s^{pu} c25s^{pu} Apr 14] lengthy gelding: useful hurdler: useful maiden chaser: second in novice handicap at Ascot (neck behind Toviere) in November: stays 3m: acts on heavy going: wears headgear: can take little interest, and isn't one to rely on. *Suzy Smith*   **c134 §**
h–

CLONDAW CRACKER (IRE) 7 b.g. Court Cave (IRE) – Twelve Pence (IRE) (Bob Back (USA)) [2017/18 h–: h20.3s h20.8d⁵ Feb 8] good-topped gelding: Irish point winner: won sole start in bumpers: little impact over hurdles. *Neil Mulholland*   **h–**

CLONDAW DRAFT (IRE) 10 b.g. Shantou (USA) – Glen Ten (IRE) (Mandalus) [2017/18 c122, h–: c19.4d* May 21] lengthy, useful-looking gelding: winning hurdler: fairly useful chaser: won novice handicap at Stratford sole start in 2017/18: stays 21f: acts on soft and good to firm going. *Donald McCain*   **c119**
h–

CLONDAW FIXER (IRE) 6 b.g. Court Cave (IRE) – The Millers Tale (IRE) (Rashar (USA)) [2017/18 b15.8v⁴ Mar 17] tall gelding: runner-up in Irish point: tailed off in bumper. *George Bewley*   **b–**

CLONDAW KAEMPFER (IRE) 10 b.g. Oscar (IRE) – Gra-Bri (IRE) (Rashar (USA)) [2017/18 c–, h132: h20d h19.6s² h19.4d^{pu} h21.4g Apr 21] rangy gelding: fairly useful handicap hurdler: second at Bangor in November: would have won but for unseating last on first of 2 starts over fences in 2014/15: stays 3m: acts on heavy going: usually in headgear: wears tongue tie: usually races prominently. *Donald McCain*   **c–**
h127

CLONDAW NATIVE (IRE) 6 b.g. Golan (IRE) – Great Outlook (IRE) (Simply Great (FR)) [2017/18 b16d⁴ h19.9d³ h19.6d² h21.6d* h24.4d³ h22.8v h24g Apr 18] €16,000 3-y-o: rather unfurnished gelding: half-brother to 3 winners, including smart hurdler/useful chaser Chasing Cars (2½m/21f winner, by Supreme Leader) and fairly useful hurdler Mackerye End (3m winner, by Milan): dam unraced: Irish point winner: fourth in bumper at Chepstow: fairly useful form over hurdles: won maiden at Ascot in December: third in handicap at Doncaster in February: stays 3m: acts on good to soft going: in cheekpieces last 2 starts: usually races prominently. *Stuart Edmunds*   **h128**
b91

CLONDAW RIGGER (IRE) 6 b.g. Stowaway – Daytona Lily (IRE) (Beneficial) [2017/18 h–, b63: h23.3d⁴ h23.1g c20g c24v² c25.2s* c25.7v⁵ c25.1v² c24v² c23.8v⁶ Apr 15] rather unfurnished gelding: Irish point winner: poor form over hurdles: modest handicap chaser: won novice event at Hereford in January: stays 25f: best form on soft/heavy going: wears tongue tie: front runner/races prominently. *Katy Price*   **c97**
h74

CLONDAW'S ANSWER (IRE) 6 b.g. Ask – Monabricka Lady (IRE) (Moscow Society (USA)) [2017/18 b15.3d Apr 22] Irish point winner: 12/1, eleventh in bumper at Wincanton (19 lengths behind Ebony Gale). *Kayley Woollacott*   **b–**

CLONDAW WARRIOR (IRE) 11 b.g. Overbury (IRE) – Thespian (IRE) (Tiraaz (USA)) [2017/18 h155: h16g⁶ h16d Aug 3] lengthy gelding: very smart hurdler, well below best in 2017/18: stays 3m: acts on soft going: usually wears headgear: often races in rear. *W. P. Mullins, Ireland*   **h–**

CLONDAW WESTIE (IRE) 7 b.g. Westerner – You're A Native (IRE) (Saddlers' Hall (IRE)) [2017/18 h–: h19.2v³ h20.5v c20.2v* c25.1v^{ur} c17.8v* c19.9d* c17.8s* Apr 6] smallish, angular gelding: modest form over hurdles: fairly useful form over fences: won handicaps at Leicester (novice) in February, Fontwell/Huntingdon (novice) in March and Fontwell in April: stays 2½m: acts on heavy going: wears cheekpieces/tongue tie: usually races prominently: open to further improvement as a chaser. *Lawney Hill*   **c122 p**
h88

CLOONACOOL (IRE) 9 b.g. Beneficial – Newhall (IRE) (Shernazar) [2017/18 c–, h128: h16.7g h16.5m² h15.8d⁶ Dec 20] sturdy gelding: useful hurdler/chaser at best: stayed 2½m: acted on good to firm and heavy going: wore headgear 4 of last 5 starts: usually travelled strongly: dead. *Stuart Edmunds*   **c–**
h115

CLOONE LADY (IRE) 6 b.m. Milan – Cloone Leader (IRE) (Supreme Leader) [2017/18 h19.6s⁴ h20.6s⁶ h20.7g² Apr 24] £40,000 6-y-o: well-made mare: fourth foal: dam (h99) 19f hurdle winner: Irish point winner: fair form over hurdles: easily best effort when second in mares novice at Huntingdon in April: open to further improvement. *Kim Bailey*   **h113 p**

CLO SACRE (FR) 6 b.g. Network (GER) – Legende Sacree (FR) (Hawker's News (IRE)) [2017/18 h66, b–: h23g⁴ h21.6d⁵ c16.3d³ c21.6g^{pu} Aug 24] runner-up completed start in points: poor form over hurdles/in chases: tried in blinkers/tongue tie. *Paul Nicholls*   **c67**
h81

CLO

CLOSE HOUSE 11 b.g. Generous (IRE) – Not Now Nellie (Saddlers' Hall (IRE)) [2017/18 c110, h–: c24.2m⁴ May 9] tall, sparely-made gelding: winning hurdler: fair chaser, below form sole outing in 2017/18: stays 3m: acts on heavy going: in headgear last 4 starts: has worn tongue tie. *Philip Kirby* — c68 h–

CLOSING CEREMONY (IRE) 9 b.g. Flemensfirth (USA) – Supreme Von Pres (IRE) (Presenting) [2017/18 h24.2d Nov 9] useful-looking gelding: useful handicap hurdler at best, showed retains some ability sole outing in 2017/18: well held only start over fences: stays 3¼m: best form on soft/heavy going. *Emma Lavelle* — c– h119

CLOTH CAP (IRE) 6 b.g. Beneficial – Cloth Fair (IRE) (Old Vic) [2017/18 b94: h20d⁵ h21.2g⁴ h19.9d h20.7s* h20.7s⁶ h24.3g^F Apr 20] fairly useful form over hurdles: won handicap at Huntingdon in December: stays 21f: acts on soft going. *Jonjo O'Neill* — h115

CLOUD HOPPER (IRE) 4 gr.g. Dubai Destination (USA) – Drain Hopper (Cloudings (IRE)) [2017/18 b13.7g h15.3g h17.7d h16.3s h19.2v⁶ Jan 8] compact gelding: tailed off in junior bumper: no form over hurdles. *Jamie Snowden* — h– b–

CLOUDY BEACH (IRE) 11 gr.g. Cloudings (IRE) – Niki Beach (IRE) (Needle Gun (IRE)) [2017/18 c23.6d^pu c20.3s⁶ c20s² c19.5v³ Jan 8] sturdy gelding: winning hurdler: fairly useful handicap chaser: second in veterans event at Lingfield in December: stays 2½m: acts on heavy going: tried in cheekpieces: inconsistent. *Venetia Williams* — c117 h–

CLOUDY BOB (IRE) 11 gr.g. Cloudings (IRE) – Keen Supreme (IRE) (Bob Back (USA)) [2017/18 c121§, h–: c24m⁴ c23.9g⁴ c24g² c23g⁴ c23s* c24.2v^R c20.9v³ Apr 10] lengthy gelding: winning hurdler: fairly useful handicap chaser: won at Taunton in February: left Pat Murphy after fourth start: stays 3m: acts on good to firm and heavy going: usually races nearer last than first. *Anthony Honeyball* — c125 h–

CLOUDY DREAM (IRE) 8 gr.g. Cloudings (IRE) – Run Away Dream (IRE) (Acceglio) [2017/18 c153, h–: c19.9d² c15.9s² c25v² c23.4s² c20.8s³ c19.9s⁵ Apr 13] good-topped gelding: winning hurdler: very smart chaser: placed in Old Roan Chase at Aintree in October, Shloer Chase at Cheltenham in November, Many Clouds Chase at Aintree in December, Betfair Denman Chase at Newbury in February and Ryanair Chase (Festival Trophy) at Cheltenham in March: barely stays testing 25f: acts on heavy going: often races towards rear/travels strongly: has joined Donald McCain. *Ruth Jefferson* — c157 h–

CLOUDY GLEN (IRE) 5 b.g. Cloudings (IRE) – Ribble (IRE) (Supreme Leader) [2017/18 b15.8v⁵ h21.7s h15.7v⁶ h16v² h15.3v³ h16s⁵ Apr 27] fourth foal: dam unraced half-sister to fairly useful hurdler (stayed 3m) Thames: well beaten in bumper: fair form over hurdles: tried in hood. *Venetia Williams* — h109 b–

CLOUDY TOO (IRE) 12 b.g. Cloudings (IRE) – Curra Citizen (IRE) (Phardante (FR)) [2017/18 c135, h121: h23.3s⁶ c25d c25.6v³ c24.2s⁴ c24.1v³ c28.4v^pu Mar 31] tall gelding: winning hurdler: fairly useful handicap chaser nowadays: fourth in Veterans' Handicap Chase Final at Sandown in January: stays 3¼m: acts on heavy going. *Sue Smith* — c127 h–

CLOVELLY 8 b.m. Midnight Legend – Chantilly Rose (Primitive Rising (USA)) [2017/18 h85, b–: h20.6g³ Nov 17] modest form over hurdles. *Rhona Brewis* — h85

CLUBS ARE TRUMPS (IRE) 9 b.g. Flemensfirth (USA) – Pairtree (Double Trigger (IRE)) [2017/18 c110§, h–: c24.5g^pu c23g² c23m⁶ c26m⁶ c24.1g³ c24d* c23.9g⁴ c29.2g⁴ Apr 26] maiden hurdler: fair handicap chaser: won at Southwell in October: stays 3¼m: acts on good to firm and good to soft going: wears headgear: tried in tongue tie: often races prominently: unreliable. *Jonjo O'Neill* — c111 § h–

CLUES AND ARROWS (IRE) 10 b.g. Clerkenwell (USA) – Ballela Girl (IRE) (Mandalus) [2017/18 c110, h–: c26.2g^pu c25.5g c20.3v^pu Feb 9] winning pointer/hurdler: maiden chaser, no form in 2017/18: left Rebecca Menzies after second start: has worn headgear, including in 2017/18. *Miss G. Walton* — c– h–

CLYNE 8 b.g. Hernando (FR) – Lauderdale (GER) (Nebos (GER)) [2017/18 h146: h15.8s² h18.9v³ c15.7v¹ h15.7v⁴ h19.2d⁴ h19.9v* h20s³ Apr 12] tall, angular gelding: smart hurdler: won handicap at Uttoxeter (by 2 lengths from Hitherjacques Lady) in March: third in Aintree Hurdle (6¾ lengths behind L'Ami Serge) in April: second in novice at Haydock (2 lengths behind Testify) on chasing debut: stays 2½m: acts on heavy going: not a fluent jumper, but should do better over fences. *Evan Williams* — c134 p h145 x

COASTAL DRIFT 4 b.g. Black Sam Bellamy (IRE) – Absalom's Girl (Saddlers' Hall (IRE)) [2017/18 b16.2s Jan 29] 10/1, well beaten in bumper. *Colin Tizzard* — b–

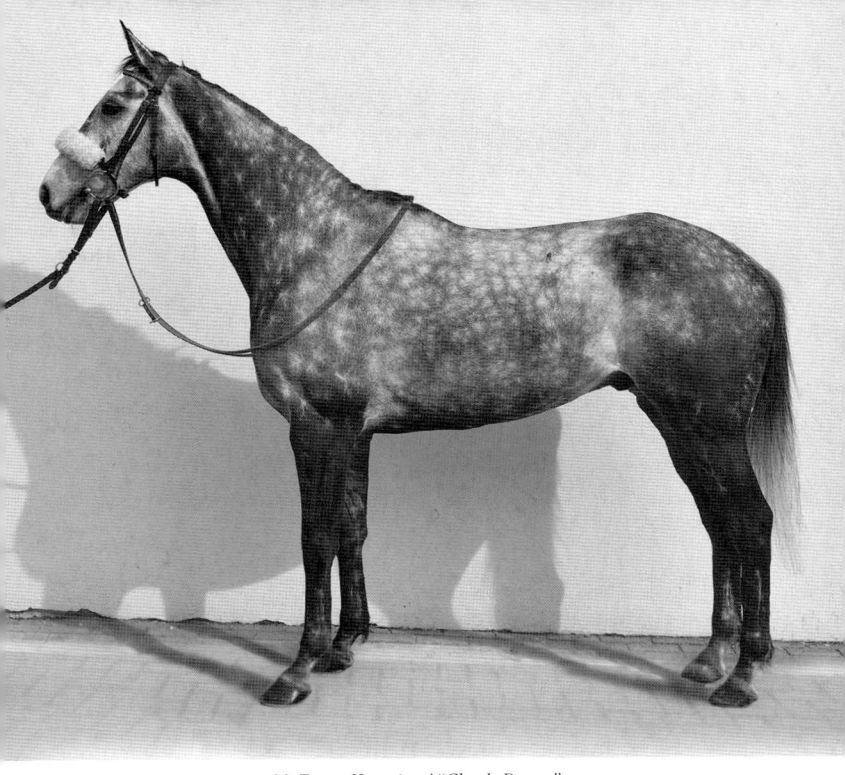

Mr Trevor Hemmings' "Cloudy Dream"

COASTAL TIEP (FR) 6 b.g. Coastal Path – Jaltiepy (FR) (Monjal (FR)) [2017/18 h133, b103: c24.2d* c25s² c25.3s^pu c20d² Feb 21] good-topped gelding: bumper winner: useful hurdler: similar form over fences: won maiden at Exeter in October: stays 3m: acts on good to soft going: sometimes in cheekpieces: ungenuine. *Paul Nicholls*   **c136 §**
h–

COBAJAYISLAND (IRE) 10 b.g. Heron Island (IRE) – Shinora (IRE) (Black Minstrel) [2017/18 c122, h–: c25.1v^pu c24s^pu c20.3g³ Apr 20] has had breathing operation: lightly-raced hurdler: fair handicap chaser: stays 3¼m: acts on heavy going: often travels strongly. *Michael Scudamore*   **c110**
h–

COBBLER'S SON 5 b.g. Black Sam Bellamy (IRE) – Cobbler's Queen (IRE) (Presenting) [2017/18 b15.8d h15.8d h16.7v^ur h15.8s h16v⁶ h20.6s h26.4d^pu Apr 22] well held in bumper: poor form over hurdles: in headgear last 2 starts. *Henry Daly*   **h68**
b–

COBOLOBO (FR) 6 br.g. Maresca Sorrento (FR) – Nanou des Brosses (FR) (Saint Cyrien (FR)) [2017/18 h116: h23.3d* h21.9v h25s^pu h20.5v^pu Jan 31] good-topped gelding: fairly useful handicap hurdler: won at Uttoxeter in November: should be suited by 3m: acts on soft going. *Jonjo O'Neill*   **h120**

COBRA DE MAI (FR) 6 b.g. Great Pretender (IRE) – Miria Galanda (FR) (Chef de Clan (FR)) [2017/18 h116: c16.2g* h16m* c16.5m* c17g^pu c16.4d* c15.9g⁵ c18.8g⁴ c20s* c20.5s² c20.5g² Apr 21] angular gelding: fairly useful handicap hurdler: won at Worcester in May: smart chaser: won novice handicap at Warwick and novice at Huntingdon in May,   **c145**
h120

209

COB

novice at Sedgefield in October and handicap at Warwick (by 2½ lengths from Drumlee Sunset) in February: second in Future Champions Novices' Chase at Ayr (1¾ lengths behind Bigmartre) in April: stays 2½m: acts on good to firm and heavy going: wears cheekpieces/tongue tie. *Dan Skelton*

COCKER 6 b.g. Shirocco (GER) – Treble Heights (IRE) (Unfuwain (USA)) [2017/18 h93: h16s⁴ h19.6s^pu h16s h21.7g Apr 20] poor maiden hurdler on balance: tried in cheekpieces. *Alan Blackmore*   **h73**

COCKLEY BECK (IRE) 6 b.m. Westerner – Bobnval (IRE) (Bob Back (USA)) [2017/18 b90: h16v² h19.7s³ h19v⁴ h17d⁴ Mar 31] bumper winner: fair form over hurdles: should be suited by further than 2m. *Nicky Richards*   **h100**

COCKNEY SEAGULL (IRE) 5 b.g. Watar (IRE) – Acountry Lane (IRE) (Norwich) [2017/18 b13.6g⁶ b17.7d h15.9v h21.7g^pu Apr 20] no form in bumpers/over hurdles: in headgear last 2 starts. *Linda Jewell*   **h–** **b–**

COCKNEY WREN 5 b.m. Cockney Rebel (IRE) – Compose (Anabaa (USA)) [2017/18 b94: h16g³ h15.8g⁴ h16.5m* Apr 25] rather sparely-made mare: bumper winner: fair form over hurdles: won maress novice at Taunton in April. *Harry Fry*   **h110**

COCO LIVE (FR) 6 b.g. Secret Singer (FR) – Iona Will (FR) (Kadalko (FR)) [2017/18 c–, h86: h20s May 17] Irish point winner: maiden hurdler, modest form at best: pulled up sole chase start: in cheekpieces/tongue tie last 2 starts. *Seamus Mullins*   **c–** **h–**

CODED MESSAGE 5 b.m. Oscar (IRE) – Ring Back (IRE) (Bob Back (USA)) [2017/18 b16s b15.7d⁶ b15.8v³ b16s⁴ Feb 23] third foal: half-sister to bumper winner/useful hurdler Midnight Jazz (2m-2½m winner) and fair hurdler Stepover (2m winner) (both by Midnight Legend): dam (h108) bumper/2m hurdle winner: fair form in bumpers. *Ben Case*   **b90**

CODE OF LAW 8 ch.g. Papal Bull – Fyvie (Grand Lodge (USA)) [2017/18 c92, h81: c22.6g³ c15.7d⁴ c20g^pu h20g c17.8m* c17.8d⁴ c19.7m³ Sep 24] maiden hurdler: modest handicap chaser: won at Fontwell in August: stays 21f: acts on soft and good to firm going: often wore cheekpieces in 2017/18: unreliable. *Neil Mulholland*   **c93 §** **h–**

CODY WYOMING 12 b.g. Passing Glance – Tenderfoot (Be My Chief (USA)) [2017/18 c122§, h–: c20.9s² c20.2s^pu c21.2s⁴ c21.2s⁵ c19.5v⁴ c19.5v⁴ c21.2s⁵ Feb 16] big, good-topped gelding: winning hurdler: fairly useful handicap chaser: won at Fakenham in December and Fontwell in January: stays 21f: acts on heavy going: wears cheekpieces/tongue tie: often races towards rear: temperamental. *Charlie Mann*   **c121 §** **h–**

COEUR BLIMEY (IRE) 7 b.g. Winged Love (IRE) – Eastender (Opening Verse (USA)) [2017/18 h114, b–: h16.4d⁵ h15.3v* h15.7d⁵ h21s⁶ h16.3v⁴ h23.6s Feb 24] workmanlike gelding: bumper winner: fairly useful handicap hurdler: won at Wincanton in December: sixth in Lanzarote Hurdle at Kempton in January: stays 19f: acts on heavy going: tried in cheekpieces: usually races prominently. *Susan Gardner*   **h126**

COEUR DE BRUME (FR) 6 b.g. Saint des Saints (FR) – Mabelle Lescribaa (FR) (Panoramic) [2017/18 h19.5s^pu Apr 27] in frame all starts over hurdles/fences in 2015/16 for A. Adeline de Boisbrunet: pulled up on belated return. *Johnny Farrelly*   **c–** **h–**

COEUR DE LION 5 b.g. Pour Moi (IRE) – Hora (Hernando (FR)) [2017/18 h137: h15.3s⁵ h20.5d h20.3v Mar 16] useful-looking gelding: useful on Flat, stays 2¼m: useful hurdler, below best in 2017/18: should be suited by further than 2m. *Alan King*   **h128**

COEUR PENSIF (FR) 6 br.g. Laveron – Lady Easter (FR) (Cadoudal (FR)) [2017/18 h24g⁴ h21.6d h21s³ h21s⁵ h19.8s h25d* Apr 24] £25,000 5-y-o: rather unfurnished gelding: second foal: dam pulled up in chase on only start in France: runner-up in Irish point: fairly useful form over hurdles: won handicap at Huntingdon in April: stays 25f: acts on soft going: tried in cheekpieces. *Ben Pauling*   **h117**

COEUR TANTRE (IRE) 7 ch.g. Fruits of Love (USA) – Ding Dong Belle (Minster Son) [2017/18 h109: h18.5g* h16.8d⁴ h21.6g^pu h17.7g³ c15.7s² c18.2s² c15.7v² Dec 26] fairly useful handicap hurdler: won at Newton Abbot (twice) in August: similar form over fences: stays 19f: acts on soft and good to firm going: has worn headgear, including final start: wears tongue tie: front runner/races prominently, often travels strongly. *Anthony Honeyball*   **c125** **h120**

COGBURN 6 ch.g. Black Sam Bellamy (IRE) – Realms of Gold (USA) (Gulch (USA)) [2017/18 b91: h19g² h19.6g⁴ Nov 5] useful-looking gelding: fair form in bumpers: similar form over hurdles: better effort when second in novice at Warwick in May: in eyeshields last 3 starts. *Alan King*   **h110**

COL

COGRY 9 b.g. King's Theatre (IRE) – Wyldello (Supreme Leader) [2017/18 c135x, h128: c25g* c26g^{pu} c29.2s^2 c24.2s^{ur} c20s^3 c25s c31.8g^{pu} Apr 21] sturdy gelding: winning hurdler: useful handicap chaser: won at Cheltenham (by 4 lengths from Singlefarmpayment) in October: second in Classic Chase at Warwick (11 lengths behind Milansbar) in January: stays 4m: acts on heavy going: usually wears headgear: often races prominently: often let down by jumping. *Nigel Twiston-Davies* — **c137 x h–**

COHESION 5 b.g. Champs Elysees – Winter Bloom (USA) (Aptitude (USA)) [2017/18 h15.9d^2 Oct 23] smart on Flat, winning 1¾m: 10/3, shaped with promise when second in maiden at Plumpton (8 lengths behind Highway One O One) on hurdling debut: sure to improve. *David Bridgwater* — **h99 p**

COILLTE LASS (IRE) 7 b.m. Beneficial – Black Mariah (IRE) (Bob's Return (IRE)) [2017/18 h133: c20f^5 c21.6d^5 c18.2s^4 h16.5s^6 h17.7v^2 h18.9v h21m^F Apr 26] useful-looking mare: Irish point winner: useful handicap hurdler, below form in 2017/18: modest form over fences: stays 2¾m: acts on good to soft going: in cheekpieces last 4 starts: tried in tongue tie: usually races close up. *Paul Nicholls* — **c95 h122**

COISA BLANCO (IRE) 5 b.g. Jeremy (USA) – Moon Legend (USA) (Gulch (USA)) [2017/18 h20.8s^6 h19.4s h20.6v^5 Mar 11] no form over hurdles. *Jonjo O'Neill* — **h–**

COJACK (IRE) 6 b.g. Presenting – In The Waves (IRE) (Winged Love (IRE)) [2017/18 h24g^5 h21g^{pu} Apr 26] good-topped gelding: no form over hurdles. *Mark Bradstock* — **h–**

COLBERT STATION (IRE) 14 b.g. Witness Box (USA) – Laurenca's Girl (IRE) (Commanche Run) [2017/18 c117, h110: c20d^4 May 16] strong gelding: point winner: winning hurdler: fair chaser, below form sole outing under Rules in 2017/18: stays 3¼m: acts on good to firm and heavy going: has worn headgear: wears tongue tie. *Jonjo O'Neill* — **c90 h–**

COLBY (IRE) 5 b.g. Witness Box (USA) – Wet And Dry (IRE) (Catcher In The Rye (IRE)) [2017/18 b15.6g^3 b16.8s^4 b16.4d^4 h19g^3 Apr 23] first foal: dam unraced: fair form in bumpers: 14/1, third in maiden at Sedgefield (8¾ lengths behind Hurricane Dylan) on hurdling debut: open to improvement. *Chris Grant* — **h101 p b90**

COLD AS ICE (FR) 6 gr.g. Montmartre (FR) – Turiama (FR) (Ashkalani (IRE)) [2017/18 h95p: h19.7s Jan 16] modest form on first of 2 starts over hurdles. *Venetia Williams* — **h–**

COLDITZ CASTLE (IRE) 4 ch.g. Getaway (GER) – Stowaway Sue (IRE) (Stowaway) [2017/18 b16d Apr 26] rather unfurnished gelding: 14/1, ninth in bumper at Warwick (19 lengths behind Umndeni). *Alan King* — **b73**

COLD KNIGHT 12 b.g. Sir Harry Lewis (USA) – Arctic Chick (Henbit (USA)) [2017/18 c98, h–: c21m^{pu} c19.4m^{pu} Jul 16] lengthy, useful-looking gelding: maiden hurdler: fair chaser at best, no form in 2017/18: stays 2½m: acts on soft and good to firm going: wears cheekpieces: tried in tongue tie: usually leads. *Tom Weston* — **c– h–**

COLD MARCH (FR) 8 b.g. Early March – Tumultueuse (FR) (Bering) [2017/18 c148, h–: h19s^3 c19.9s^{pu} c20s Apr 25] good-topped gelding: fairly useful maiden hurdler: smart handicap chaser at best, well below that level in 2017/18: stays 2½m: acts on good to firm and heavy going: has worn headgear, including in 2017/18. *Harry Whittington* — **c100 h115**

COLD SHOULDER 4 b.g. Passing Glance – Averami (Averti (IRE)) [2017/18 h16.7s^5 h17.7v^3 h17.7v^5 h15.5v^4 h15.8v^4 Feb 18] brother to fair hurdler Spectator (2m-19f winner) and half-brother to smart hurdler Taglietelle (2m-3m winner, by Tagula): fair form from 2 starts on Flat: modest form over hurdles: races freely. *Tom Symonds* — **h97**

COLD WESTON 5 ch.g. Malinas (GER) – Speed Bonnie Boat (Alflora (IRE)) [2017/18 b16g^6 b16g^5 Sep 3] poor form in bumpers. *Henry Daly* — **b59**

COLE HARDEN (IRE) 9 b.g. Westerner – Nosie Betty (IRE) (Alphabatim (USA)) [2017/18 c123p, h155: c23.8g^2 c23g^3 Aug 1] sturdy gelding: has reportedly had breathing operation: very smart hurdler: useful form over fences: best effort when second in maiden at Ffos Las (1¼ lengths behind Sir Ivan) in May: sustained knee injury after next start: stays 25f: acts on good to firm and heavy going: wears headgear: often in tongue tie: front runner. *Warren Greatrex* — **c133 h–**

COLIN'S BROTHER 8 b.g. Overbury (IRE) – Dd's Glenalla (IRE) (Be My Native (USA)) [2017/18 c125, h–: c19.9d^{ur} c16d* c20.2v* c16d^2 h20.3g Apr 18] angular gelding: fairly useful hurdler, well below final outing in 2017/18: useful handicap chaser: won at Ludlow in December and Leicester (by nose from Creep Desbois) in February: stays 21f: acts on heavy going: usually races towards rear. *Nigel Twiston-Davies* — **c132 h–**

bet365 Hurdle (West Yorkshire), Wetherby—
Colin's Sister gets the better of Wholestone in what was to become a season-long rivalry

COLIN'S SISTER 7 b.m. Central Park (IRE) – Dd's Glenalla (IRE) (Be My Native (USA)) [2017/18 h133p: h24.1s* h24.2d⁴ h20.3s³ h24v³ h24s⁴ Mar 15] long-backed mare: smart hurdler: won West Yorkshire Hurdle at Wetherby (by 2 lengths from Wholestone) in November: third in Relkeel Hurdle (6½ lengths behind Wholestone) and Cleeve Hurdle (11 lengths behind Agrapart), both at Cheltenham in January: stays 3m: acts on soft going: usually races towards rear. *Fergal O'Brien* **h150**

COLLA PIER (IRE) 9 b.m. Hawk Wing (USA) – Medalha Milagrosa (USA) (Miner's Mark (USA)) [2017/18 c125, h125: c16m³ c20m* h16.7gᵖᵘ Jul 8] angular mare: fairly useful hurdler at best, shaped as if amiss final outing in 2017/18: fairly useful chaser: won mares maiden at Down Royal in June: stays 21f: acts on soft and good to firm going: has worn hood/tongue tie: often races towards rear. *David Peter Dunne, Ireland* **c116 h–**

COLLODI (GER) 9 b.g. Konigstiger (GER) – Codera (GER) (Zilzal (USA)) [2017/18 c–, h110: h17.2g h16.8d⁵ h16.8gᵖᵘ h16.8vᵖᵘ Nov 26] compact gelding: fair handicap hurdler: fell only start over fences in 2015/16: raced around 2m: acts on good to firm and good to soft going: in cheekpieces last 2 starts: tried in tongue tie. *Neil Mulholland* **c– h102**

COLMERS HILL 8 b.g. Crosspeace (IRE) – My Dancing Kin (Baryshnikov (AUS)) [2017/18 c26v³ c26v² c26vᶠ c24.5vᵖᵘ c24.2v⁴ c26.2sᵖᵘ Apr 27] maiden hurdler: fair form over fences: stays 3¼m: acts on heavy going: in cheekpieces last 2 starts. *Jeremy Scott* **c101 h–**

COLONEL CUSTARD (IRE) 5 ch.g. Mahler – Criaire Princess (IRE) (Tidaro (USA)) [2017/18 b16.5m³ Apr 25] €25,000 3-y-o: fourth foal: half-brother to fairly useful hurdler/chaser The Gatechecker (19f/2½m winner, by Classic Cliche): dam (h114) 2m-3m hurdle winner: 6/1, third in bumper at Taunton (4¼ lengths behind Anytime Will Do). *Nicky Martin* **b97**

COLONEL FORSTER 6 b.g. Strategic Prince – Forsters Plantin (Muhtarram (USA)) [2017/18 b–: ab16.3g Apr 15] no form in bumpers. *Chris Grant* **b–**

COLONIAL DREAMS (IRE) 6 b.g. Westerner – Dochas Supreme (IRE) (Supreme Leader) [2017/18 b104: h21.2d³ h20.8s² h19.8vᶠ h19.3s* h20.6g* Apr 22] sturdy gelding: bumper winner: fairly useful form over hurdles: won maiden at Ascot in March and novice at Market Rasen in April: stays 21f: acts on heavy going: usually races prominently. *Nicky Henderson* **h123**

COLORADO GOLD 5 ch.m. Beat Hollow – Crevamoy (IRE) (Shardari) [2017/18 b15.7s[5] Mar 7] fourth foal: closely related to fairly useful hurdler/smart chaser Singlefarmpayment (3m/25f winner, by Milan): dam unraced half-sister to fairly useful hurdler/smart chaser (3m/25f winner) Aiteen Thirtythree and useful hurdler/smart chaser (stayed 3m) Sonofvic: fourth in point bumper: looked less than straightforward when well beaten in mares bumper at Catterick. *Tom Lacey* **b—**

COLORADO KID (IRE) 12 b.g. Presenting – Silent Orders (IRE) (Bob Back (USA)) [2017/18 c79, h–: c24.2g[4] c25.5g[3] Jun 30] twice-raced hurdler: poor handicap chaser: stays 25f: acts on good to firm going: in headgear last 4 starts. *Tim Easterby* **c73 h—**

COLREEVY (IRE) 5 b.m. Flemensfirth (USA) – Poetics Girl (IRE) (Saddlers' Hall (IRE)) [2017/18 b16v* b16s[3] b16.4s b16.3s* Apr 25] sturdy mare: fourth foal: half-sister to 3 winners, including bumper winner/useful hurdler Runfordave (2¼m winner, by Stowaway) and fairly useful hurdler/useful chaser Hurricane Darwin (2m-3m winner, by Westerner): dam once-raced half-sister to smart 2m hurdler Snap Tie: close up when fell in last point: useful form in bumpers: won mares maiden at Fairyhouse in December and EBF (Mares) INH Flat Race (Liss A Paoraigh) at Punchestown (by 5½ lengths from Black Tears) in April. *W. P. Mullins, Ireland* **b107**

COLROCKIN 7 b.g. Great Palm (USA) – Suetsu (IRE) (Toulon) [2017/18 h24v[pu] Apr 15] well held in bumper: pulled up in novice on hurdling debut. *Tracy Waggott* **h—**

COLT LIGHTNING (IRE) 5 b.g. Flemensfirth (USA) – Shannon Theatre (IRE) (King's Theatre (IRE)) [2017/18 h17s h17d[4] h16.7s[6] h19v[pu] h21.7s* h21.7v* h21.6v[pu] Apr 8] €48,000 3-y-o: first foal: dam unraced sister to useful hurdler/fairly useful chaser (stays 2½m) Blacklough: second in point: fair handicap hurdler: won at Hereford in January (novice) and March: stays 2¾m: acts on heavy going: front runner/races prominently. *Tom Lacey* **h108**

COLWINSTON (IRE) 8 b.g. Mustameet (USA) – Miss Jeanney (IRE) (Topanoora) [2017/18 h16s[5] h16s h16v[4] h19.5v[5] h16.5s Apr 14] fair maiden hurdler: stays 2½m: acts on heavy going: has worn tongue tie, including last 3 starts. *Miss Suzy Barkley, Ireland* **h102**

COMANCHE CHIEFTAIN (CAN) 6 b.g. Broken Vow (USA) – Platinum Preferred (CAN) (Vindication (USA)) [2017/18 h107: h15.8g* h16.3g* h15.8g[2] h16.3g* h16.3g[3] h15.9m[2] ab16d[5] h16.8g Apr 18] fairly useful hurdler: won handicap at Ffos Las in May, and novice in June and handicap in August, both at Stratford: raced around 2m: best form on good going: wears hood: front runner. *Neil King* **h124**

COMBER MILL (FR) 6 ch.g. Le Fou (IRE) – Kalistina (FR) (Sillery (USA)) [2017/18 h16m h16.5m h16.7g[6] h20d h15.8g[4] h15.8s* h19.7g h15.8v* h15.8v* h15.8s* h16.7s Mar 24] €20,000 3-y-o: half-brother to several winners, including fair/ungenuine hurdler Ouest Eclair (2m winner, by Sagacity) and French hurdler Salsavina (2¼m/19f winner, by Fly To The Stars): dam ran once on Flat: unplaced both starts in points: modest handicap hurdler: won at Uttoxeter in December and January, and Ludlow in February: left Colin A. McBratney after second start: likely to prove best at 2m: acts on heavy going: wears hood: has worn tongue tie, including last 4 starts: usually leads. *Alastair Ralph* **h99**

COMELY 6 b.m. Midnight Legend – Belle Magello (FR) (Exit To Nowhere (USA)) [2017/18 h94, b86: h21g[3] h23.9g* h23.5d[2] Dec 23] sturdy mare: fair in bumpers: similar form over hurdles: won novice handicap at Taunton in November: stays 3m: acts on soft going: often races prominently. *Nicky Henderson* **h104**

COME ON CHARLIE (FR) 6 b.g. Anzillero (GER) – End of Spring (FR) (Loup Solitaire (USA)) [2017/18 h15.3g h15.3v h15.8d[3] Mar 22] sixth foal: dam French 1¾m-17f hurdle/chase winner: modest form over hurdles: best effort when third in novice at Ludlow in March. *Philip Hobbs* **h96**

COME ON LOUIS 10 b.g. Grape Tree Road – Seamill (IRE) (Lafontaine (USA)) [2017/18 h–: h18.7m h20g h19.6g[4] h23.3d[3] h19.9s[pu] h16d Oct 31] point winner: poor maiden hurdler: stays 23f: acts on good to soft going: in blinkers last 5 starts: wears tongue tie. *Oliver Greenall* **h78**

COME ON LULU 7 ch.m. Calcutta – Flashing Floozie (Muhtarram (USA)) [2017/18 h69: h16.8g[5] h22.1d May 31] poor maiden hurdler: tried in cheekpieces/tongue tie. *David Thompson* **h65**

COME ON TEDDY (IRE) 4 b.g. Fame And Glory – Theatre View (IRE) (Old Vic) [2017/18 h16.8s[2] Feb 23] second foal: dam unraced sister to fairly useful staying chaser Theatre Knight: 20/1, second in bumper at Exeter (2¼ lengths behind Unwin Vc): will be suited by 2½m+. *Samuel Drinkwater* **b92**

Goffs Land Rover Bumper, Punchestown—clear-cut winner Commander of Fleet looks another exciting Gigginstown recruit from the pointing ranks

COMICAL RED 10 ch.g. Sulamani (IRE) – Sellette (IRE) (Selkirk (USA)) [2017/18 c93§, h68§: h23g^{pu} May 26] workmanlike gelding: modest hurdler at best, pulled up sole outing in 2017/18: maiden chaser: stays 27f: acts on good to firm and heavy going: wears headgear: has worn tongue tie: usually races prominently: ungenuine. *Mark Gillard*   c– § h– §

COMMANCHE RED (IRE) 5 ch.g. Mahler – Auntie Bob (Overbury (IRE)) [2017/18 b15.7d³ b16s* b17s⁶ Apr 13] €29,000 3-y-o: strong gelding: half-brother to 3 winners, including useful hurdlers Dani California (2m winner, by Beat All) and Oakly (2½m/21f winner, by Brian Boru): dam no form in bumpers: fairly useful form in bumpers: won maiden at Kempton in February: will prove suited by further than 2m. *Chris Gordon*   b102

COMMANDER OF FLEET (IRE) 4 b.g. Fame And Glory – Coonagh Cross (IRE) (Saddlers' Hall (IRE)) [2017/18 b16.5d* Apr 24] €47,000 3-y-o: second foal: half-brother to a winning pointer by Presenting: dam, bumper winner, half-sister to useful hurdler/chaser (2m-2½m winner) Sunset Lodge and fair hurdler/useful chaser (stayed 2½m) Atum Re: point winner: 5/1, won Goffs Land Rover Bumper at Punchestown (by 8½ lengths from Column of Fire) on debut under Rules: exciting prospect. *Gordon Elliott, Ireland*   b107 p

COMMERCIAL RUIN (IRE) 9 b.m. Zagreb (USA) – Sideways Sonia (Derrylin) [2017/18 h20.2m⁶ Jun 4] seventh foal: dam, placed in point, half-sister to useful hurdler/smart chaser (2m-21f winner) Hobbs Hill: Irish point winner: tailed off in novice hurdle. *Benjamin Arthey, Ireland*   h–

COMMODORE BARRY (IRE) 5 br.g. Presenting – Specifiedrisk (IRE) (Turtle Island (IRE)) [2017/18 b15.8s⁴ b15.8d Mar 26] €30,000 3-y-o, £85,000 4-y-o: brother to fair hurdler Lime Street (23f winner) and half-brother to several winners, including smart hurdler/very smart chaser Glencove Marina (2m-2¾m winner, by Spectrum) and fairly useful hurdler Theatre Territory (2m winner, by King's Theatre), stays 3m: dam unraced half-sister to Ascot Gold Cup winner Mr Dinos: runner-up in Irish point: fair form in bumpers: better effort when fourth at Huntingdon in December. *Kim Bailey*   b93

COMMODORE (FR) 6 gr.g. Fragrant Mix (IRE) – Morvandelle (FR) (Video Rock (FR)) [2017/18 h16.7s^{pu} h15.3v h16.7v⁴ h15.7v² h19.9v³ h19d Apr 26] compact gelding: sixth foal: half-brother to 2 French bumper winners, including 1¼m-15f winner Vougeot (by Special Kaldoun): dam maiden sister to high-class hurdler/smart chaser (stayed 2¾m) Osana and to dam of high-class staying chaser Notre Pere: fair maiden hurdler: won first of 2 starts over fences for A. Adeline de Boisbrunet in 2016/17: stays 21f: acts on heavy going. *Venetia Williams*   c– h106

COMPADRE (IRE) 7 b.g. Yeats (IRE) – Jolivia (FR) (Dernier Empereur (USA)) [2017/18 c113, h112: c24d² c24.1d c20.2g³ c19.9d* c21.4s^{pu} c20.5m² Apr 26] useful-looking gelding: lightly-raced hurdler: fairly useful handicap chaser: won at Huntingdon in November: stays 3m: acts on soft going: wears hood/tongue tie. *Jonjo O'Neill*   c120 h–

COMPETITION 6 b.g. Multiplex – Compolina (Compton Place) [2017/18 b–: h16.7g² Aug 6] fair maiden on Flat, stays 1½m: 28/1, second in maiden at Market Rasen (6 lengths behind Mcgroarty) on hurdling debut: in tongue tie last 3 starts: entitled to do better. *Brian Rothwell*   h103 p

COMPLEX KID 6 b.g. Multiplex – Life Is Life (FR) (Mansonnien (FR)) [2017/18 b17s Apr 8] tailed off in bumper. *Sandy Thomson*   b–

COMPLICE DU CHENET (FR) 6 b.g. Astarabad (USA) – Reine Irlandaise (FR) (Lost World (IRE)) [2017/18 b16.8d^{pu} Jul 31] pulled up in maiden bumper: dead. *Alan Jones*   b–

CON

COMRADE CONRAD (IRE) 4 br.g. Canford Cliffs (IRE) – View (IRE) (Galileo (IRE)) [2017/18 h17.7v⁴ h15.8s* h16.5v⁵ h15.7s³ h20.5g⁶ Apr 21] good-topped gelding: fairly useful on Flat, stays 13.5f: fair form over hurdles: won maiden at Ludlow in January: unproven beyond 2m: acts on soft going: in cheekpieces last 2 starts. *Dan Skelton* — h114

COMRAGH (IRE) 8 br.m. Desert King (IRE) – Akica (IRE) (Oscar (IRE)) [2017/18 h–: h21.2s^pu Jan 10] modest form over hurdles in 2015/16, pulled up both starts since: stays 2½m: acts on soft going. *Jeremy Scott* — h–

CONCEALED AMBITION (IRE) 6 br.g. Stowaway – Clairefontaine (Alflora (IRE)) [2017/18 h15.8s h15.7v⁶ Mar 21] no form over hurdles. *Tim Vaughan* — h–

CONEYGREE 11 b.g. Karinga Bay – Plaid Maid (IRE) (Executive Perk) [2017/18 c168, h–: c24.2s^pu c26g^pu Dec 2] strong gelding: winning hurdler: top-class chaser at best, won Cheltenham Gold Cup in 2014/15: very lightly raced since, shaped as if amiss both starts in 2017/18: stays 3¼m: acts on heavy going: front runner. *Mark Bradstock* — c–, h–

CONEY ISLAND (IRE) 7 b.g. Flemensfirth (USA) – Millys Gesture (IRE) (Milan) [2017/18 c159p, h–: c21d⁴ c21s^pu c20v^pu Apr 2] well-made gelding: winning hurdler: high-class form over fences: won graduation event at Ascot (by 9 lengths from Adrien du Pont) in December: pulled up other 2 starts in 2017/18: stays 3m: acts on heavy going. *Edward P. Harty, Ireland* — c160, h–

CONINGSBY 5 ch.g. Midnight Legend – Motcombe (IRE) (Carroll House) [2017/18 h18.5v² h21.3v² h23.3v⁴ Mar 17] fifth foal: half-brother to fair hurdler Rosa Imperialis (2¾m winner, by Imperial Dancer), bumper winner Fairey Delta (by Milan) and a winning pointer by King's Theatre: dam (c103) 21f-25f chase winner: point winner: fair form over hurdles. *Tom Lacey* — h113

CONNA CROSS (IRE) 7 b.g. Lecroix (GER) – Country Time (IRE) (Curtain Time (IRE)) [2017/18 h19.4g³ h16d⁶ h20v h20v⁴ c22d* h23d⁵ c20s⁶ h16v* h21v c20.5s* Apr 9] fair handicap hurdler: won at Cork (conditional) in November: fairly useful form over fences: won maiden at Tramore in October and handicap at Kempton in April: left James Joseph Mangan after ninth start: stays 23f: acts on heavy going: tried in hood. *Johnny Farrelly* — c125, h106

CONNETABLE (FR) 6 b.g. Saint des Saints (FR) – Montbresia (FR) (Video Rock (FR)) [2017/18 c125, h137: h26.5g h23.9g h25.3s⁵ h23.4s² h21d⁴ h26.1s³ h23.6s h24s³ h24.7s Apr 14] compact gelding: useful handicap hurdler: third in Pertemps Final at Cheltenham (2¾ lengths behind Delta Work) in March: winning chaser: stays 3¼m: acts on heavy going: wears headgear: usually races close up. *Paul Nicholls* — c–, h138

CONNIES CROSS (IRE) 11 b.g. Windsor Castle – Rockon-Beauty (IRE) (Mister Lord (USA)) [2017/18 c–: c32.5d^pu c23g⁵ c23v^pu Apr 12] multiple point winner: maiden hunter chaser, no form in 2017/18: left Mrs Sheila Crow after second start. *Mrs Sue Popham* — c–

CONQUER GOLD (IRE) 8 b.m. Gold Well – Ballinamona Wish (IRE) (Kotashaan (FR)) [2017/18 c124, h114: h20.5v h20.6s² h24.3v⁵ c24.1s⁶ Mar 24] fair handicap hurdler: fairly useful form over fences, well held sole outing in 2017/18: stays 3m well: acts on heavy going: often races prominently. *Nicky Richards* — c–, h114

CONRAD HASTINGS (IRE) 7 b.g. Flemensfirth (USA) – Berkeley House (IRE) (Beneficial) [2017/18 c19.9g* c22.7g* c20.5g² c20v⁵ c17s c20.4s^pu c21s^pu Apr 27] €60,000 3-y-o: lengthy gelding: third foal: half-brother to fair 2m hurdle winner Presenting Rose and a winning pointer (both by Presenting): dam (h95), bumper winner/maiden hurdler (stayed 3m), half-sister to Irish Grand National winner The Bunny Boiler: fairly useful hurdler: won maiden at Tipperary in 2016/17: useful chaser: won maiden at Kilbeggan in June and novice at Killarney in July: stays 23f: acts on heavy going. *Henry de Bromhead, Ireland* — c140, h–

CONTENTED (IRE) 5 gr.g. Dalakhani (IRE) – Leo's Spirit (IRE) (Fantastic Light (USA)) [2017/18 h15.3g³ h19g² h19.9s* h21.4v h20.5g Apr 21] €14,000 3-y-o: sixth foal: dam unraced half-sister to high-class 1m-11.5f winner Echo of Light: fair form over hurdles: won conditional/amateur novice at Sedgefield in December: stays 2½m: acts on soft going. *Philip Hobbs* — h114

CONTEUR D'HISTOIRE (FR) 6 b.g. Le Fou (IRE) – Page d'Histoire (FR) (Video Rock (FR)) [2017/18 h109, b–: c23d^pu h20g c17.4g⁵ c23g Sep 18] maiden hurdler, fair at best: modest form over fences: stays 21f: acts on soft going: tried in blinkers: wears tongue tie: usually races prominently. *Jonjo O'Neill* — c94, h–

CON

CONTRE TOUS (FR) 6 b.g. Forestier (FR) – Orphee de Vonnas (FR) (Jimble (FR)) [2017/18 c126, h87: c15.8s³ h15.7v* h17d³ c16.5g Apr 21] fairly useful hurdler: won novice at Southwell in February: fairly useful chaser: raced mainly around 2m: acts on good to firm and heavy going: usually in tongue tie. *Brian Ellison*   c119 h115

CONTROL ME (IRE) 4 b.f. Yeats (IRE) – Cullian (Missed Flight) [2017/18 b16.8d⁴ Apr 24] fifth foal: closely related to modest hurdler Fourina (21f winner, by Oscar): dam (c93/h95), 17f-21f hurdle/chase winner, half-sister to dam of very smart staying chaser Cane Brake: won point on debut: well beaten in maiden bumper. *Francesca Nimmo*   b–

COOKING FAT 7 ch.g. Tobougg (IRE) – Ostfanni (IRE) (Spectrum (IRE)) [2017/18 h131: h24.7g⁵ c19.4d² c20d^{ur} c21.6g² c19.1d⁵ c20.5v³ Mar 9] fairly useful handicap hurdler, below form on return in 2017/18: fairly useful form over fences: second in novice at Wetherby in October and handicap at Kelso in November: stays 25f: acts on soft going: in cheekpieces last 4 starts: often races towards rear. *Dianne Sayer*   c124 h100

COOLADERRY KING (IRE) 10 b.g. King Cheetah (USA) – Daly Lady (IRE) (Lord of Appeal) [2017/18 c106: c21.1s³ May 18] point winner: fair maiden chaser, below form sole outing under Rules in 2017/18: stays 3m: acts on good to soft going: has worn hood. *Miss Rose Grissell*   c86

COOLANLY (IRE) 6 b.g. Flemensfirth (USA) – La Fisarmonica (IRE) (Accordion) [2017/18 b16d* h20.5s² h21.1s h16.5s⁵ Apr 5³] €27,000 3-y-o: sturdy gelding: third foal: brother to fairly useful hurdler/fair chaser Bronco Billy (3m/25f winner) and fair hurdler/chaser Allez Cool (21f-25f winner): dam (h108), 2½m hurdle winner, half-sister to fairly useful hurdler/winning bumper (stayed 2½m) Joe Cullen: Irish point winner: won conditionals/amateur bumper at Chepstow (by ¾ length from Joyrider) in October: fairly useful form over hurdles: will prove best at 2½m+. *Fergal O'Brien*   h129 b99

COOLANURE (IRE) 9 b.m. Portrait Gallery (IRE) – Aiguille (IRE) (Lancastrian) [2017/18 c–x, h71: c23.4g² May 10] poor maiden hurdler/chaser: usually wears headgear: front runner/races prominently: often let down by jumping over fences. *Kenny Johnson*   c64 x h–

COOLE CHARMER (IRE) 9 ch.g. Flemensfirth (USA) – Ericas Charm (Alderbrook) [2017/18 c108, h96: h21.6d^{pu} h23.1g³ Oct 31] rangy, good sort: fell in point: modest maiden chaser, fair form at best: stays 23f: acts on good to soft going: tried in cheekpieces. *Neil Mulholland*   c– h94

COOLE CODY (IRE) 7 b.g. Dubai Destination (USA) – Run For Cover (IRE) (Lafontaine (USA)) [2017/18 c118: h18.5d* h21.6d* h21.1s* h24.7s^{pu} Apr 14] lengthy gelding: Irish point winner: useful hurdler: won novices at Newton Abbot (twice) in September and intermediate handicap at Cheltenham (by 3 lengths from Mischievious Max) in November: stays 2¾m: acts on heavy going: wears hood: tongue tied in 2017/18: front runner. *Michael Blake*   h139

COOLE HALL (IRE) 6 b.g. Flemensfirth (USA) – Coole Assembly (IRE) (Saddlers' Hall (IRE)) [2017/18 h115p: h20.9d* h22.7g² h22v* h22.7s* h22.8v⁶ Feb 17] sturdy gelding: Irish point winner: useful form over hurdles: won novices at Kelso in October, Newcastle (by 1¼ lengths from Senor Lombardy) in December and Kelso again (by 3¾ lengths from Knockrobin) in January: will be suited by 3m+: acts on heavy going: usually responds generously to pressure. *Rose Dobbin*   h131

COOLE WELL (IRE) 5 b.g. Gold Well – Bobs Lass (IRE) (Bob's Return (IRE)) [2017/18 b16.3s³ b16s⁵ Feb 9] £24,000 4-y-o: third foal: half-brother to fair hurdler/fairly useful chaser Benevolent (2m-3m winner, by Beneficial): dam unraced half-sister to fair hurdler/fairly useful chaser (2m-2½m winner) Bohemian Lass: runner-up in Irish point: fair form in bumpers: better effort when third at Newbury in January. *Ben Pauling*   b92

COOL GEORGE 10 b.g. Pastoral Pursuits – Magic Valentine (Magic Ring (IRE)) [2017/18 h20g⁵ Jun 14] compact gelding: fair maiden hurdler at best, lightly raced since 2013/14: pulled up sole start over fences: stays 2½m: acts on heavy going: tried in tongue tie. *Jackie du Plessis*   c– h92

COOLING 4 b.f. Firebreak – Esplanade (Danehill (USA)) [2017/18 b13.2s⁵ b13.7g² Nov 30] half-sister to 2 winners on Flat by Zamindar, including 1m-1¼m winner Embankment: dam (r), maiden on Flat, unraced in bumpers. *John Flint*   b82

COOLKING 11 b.g. King's Theatre (IRE) – Osocool (Teenoso (USA)) [2017/18 c119, h–: c27.7d^{pu} c24.2d^{pu} c28.5v c28.8v⁶ Feb 19] tall gelding: winning hurdler: fairly useful handicap chaser, well below form in 2017/18: stays 3¾m: acts on heavy going: usually wears headgear: tried in tongue tie: front runner/races prominently, tends to find little. *Gary Moore*   c76 h–

COO

COOL MACAVITY (IRE) 10 b.g. One Cool Cat (USA) – Cause Celebre (IRE) (Peintre **h125**
Celebre (USA)) [2017/18 h111: h15.7g* h16.4g[F] h16d[4] Nov 27] sturdy gelding: fairly
useful handicap hurdler: won at Towcester in October: raced mainly around 2m: acts on
good to firm going: has joined Alexandra Dunn. *Nicky Henderson*

COOLMEEN HILL (IRE) 7 b.g. Oscar (IRE) – Hazel's Tisrara (IRE) (Mandalus) **h108**
[2017/18 h17.2m* h16.2s[3] Aug 19] €38,000 3-y-o: fifth foal: closely related to fairly useful
hurdler/very smart chaser Sizing Granite (2m-2½m winner, by Milan), stays 3m, and half-
brother to fair 19f/2½m hurdle winner Doransfirth (by Flemensfirth) 2m
hurdle winner: maiden pointer: bumper winner: fair form over hurdles: won maiden at
Ballinrobe in May for Ellmarie Holden: wears tongue tie. *Susan Corbett*

COOL MIX 6 gr.g. Fair Mix (IRE) – Lucylou (IRE) (Bob Back (USA)) [2017/18 b99: **h124**
h16.2g[3] h16.4v[2] h16v[2] h16.2x* h16.4s[5] h20.5g* Apr 21] fairly useful form over hurdles:
won novice at Kelso in January and conditionals/amateur handicap at Ayr in April: stays
2½m: acts on heavy going: has worn hood: front runner/races prominently: free-going sort.
Iain Jardine

COOLOGUE (IRE) 9 b.g. Helissio (FR) – Scolboa (IRE) (Bob's Return (IRE)) [2017/18 **c–**
c141, h–: c25g[pu] c24s[pu] c26s[pu] c26g[pu] Apr 18] good-topped gelding: has had breathing **h–**
operation: winning chaser: useful chaser at best, no form in 2017/18: tried in tongue tie:
front runner/races prominently. *Charlie Longsdon*

COOL SKY 9 b.g. Millkom – Intersky High (USA) (Royal Anthem (USA)) [2017/18 **h117**
h118: h19.9g* h19.6s h20v[4] Dec 9] angular gelding: fairly useful handicap hurdler: won
at Uttoxeter in September: stays 2½m: acts on soft and good to firm going: tried in
cheekpieces. *Ian Williams*

COOPERESS 5 b.m. Sixties Icon – Vilnius (Imperial Dancer) [2017/18 h16.5m[5] h15.5d[5] **h79**
Nov 20] sturdy mare: modest on Flat, stays 1¼m: poor form over hurdles.

COOPER'S FRIEND (IRE) 9 b.g. Kayf Tara – Graphic Lady (IRE) (Phardante (FR)) **c107 §**
[2017/18 c119, h86: c24.2g[3] c20.1g[4] c20.1g c21.2s[pu] c20.1g[pu] c19.3g[4] c21.6g[3] c15.8m[4] **h–**
c20s[4] c19.3v[4] c19.9d[4] c15.6d[4] Apr 23] strong gelding: winning hurdler: fair handicap
chaser: stays 2¾m: acts on heavy going: usually wears headgear/tongue tie: temperamental.
R. Mike Smith

COOPERS SQUARE (IRE) 7 b.g. Mahler – Jessaway (IRE) (Dr Massini (IRE)) **c–**
[2017/18 h–: h19.9d c17.4d[pu] Oct 4] maiden Irish pointer: no form over hurdles: pulled up **h–**
in novice handicap on chasing debut. *Tom Weston*

COO STAR SIVOLA (FR) 6 b.g. Assessor (IRE) – Santorine (FR) (Della Francesca **c148**
(USA)) [2017/18 h139: c23.6d[5] c20.4d[3] c20.8s[2] c20.8v[4] c24.2s* c25s* c25s[pu] Apr 13] **h–**
rangy gelding: useful hurdler: smart chaser: won novice handicap at Exeter (by 14 lengths
from Ice Cool Champs) in February and Ultima Handicap Chase at Cheltenham (by neck
from Shantou Flyer) in March: stays 25f: acts on heavy going: often races prominently.
Nick Williams

COOTE STREET (IRE) 10 b.g. Winged Love (IRE) – Unknown Quality (Sabrehill **c–**
(USA)) [2017/18 c–, h–: c21.1g[pu] c23.4g[pu] Oct 28] point winner: no form under Rules: **h–**
tried in cheekpieces. *F. Jestin*

*Ultima Handicap Chase, Cheltenham—a first Festival win for jockey Lizzie Kelly as the novice
Coo Star Sivola (in front) holds off the persistent challenge of Shantou Flyer (visor)*

COP

COPAIN DE CLASSE (FR) 6 b.g. Enrique – Toque Rouge (FR) (Loup Solitaire (USA)) [2017/18 h130p: c18.8g³ c17.8d* c16s⁵ c16.5g⁴ Apr 20] well-made gelding: useful hurdler: similar form over fences: left almost second in novice at Fontwell in February: third in novice handicap at Ascot (6 lengths behind Benatar) in November: stays 19f: acts on good to soft going: tried in tongue tie: usually races close up. *Paul Nicholls* — **c130 h–**

COPERNICUS (IRE) 6 ch.g. Teofilo (IRE) – Nick's Nikita (IRE) (Pivotal) [2017/18 b90: h19d⁵ May 1] sturdy, lengthy gelding: bumper winner: well beaten in novice on hurdling debut: wore tongue tie: dead. *Charlie Longsdon* — **h70**

COPPER COIN 5 ch.g. Sulamani (IRE) – Silken Pearls (Leading Counsel (USA)) [2017/18 h16.7g⁸ b16.7v² b17s² Apr 8] fourth foal: half-brother to fairly useful hurdler Nordic Nymph (23f/3m winner, by Norse Dancer) and fair hurdler/chaser Brave Buck (2½m-25f winner, by Bollin Eric): dam (c103/h114) 2m-2¾m hurdle/chase winner: fairly useful form in bumpers: best effort when second at Carlisle in April. *Michael Scudamore* — **b98**

COPPERFACEJACK (IRE) 8 b.g. Robin des Pres (FR) – Leone des Pres (FR) (Tip Moss (FR)) [2017/18 c93§, h–: c24g⁴ c23.6g² c23.9g³ c24.5g* c26.3m* c23.9d³ c29.2g² Apr 26] workmanlike gelding: maiden hurdler: fair handicap chaser: won at Towcester in October and Taunton (novice) in November: stays 29f: acts on soft and good to firm going: has worn cheekpieces, including in 2017/18: wears tongue tie: usually leads. *Paul Webber* — **c109 h–**

COPPERHEAD 4 ch.g. Sulamani (IRE) – How's Business (Josr Algarhoud (IRE)) [2017/18 b15.3v b14s b16s Feb 9] sturdy gelding: poor form in bumpers. *Colin Tizzard* — **b69**

COPPER KAY 8 b.m. Kayf Tara – Presenting Copper (IRE) (Presenting) [2017/18 h130, b96: c20f⁴ h21.4s h20.3s⁶ c20s^F h20.3g Apr 19] useful-looking mare: fairly useful handicap hurdler: fair form over fences: fourth in mares novice at Worcester completed start: stays 21f: acts on heavy going. *Philip Hobbs* — **c102 h120**

COPPER PRINCE (IRE) 5 ch.g. Pelder (IRE) – Kora (IRE) (Mandalus) [2017/18 b13.7s Jan 26] tailed off in bumper. *Michael Appleby* — **b–**

COPPER WEST (IRE) 7 b.g. Westerner – Printing Copper (IRE) (Blueprint (IRE)) [2017/18 b17s⁴ h15.7d⁴ h21.2v³ h19.4s³ h17v⁵ Feb 19] medium-sized gelding: first foal: dam (h119), 2½m hurdle winner, half-sister to smart hurdler/chaser (stayed 21f) Copper Bleu: point winner: modest form in bumpers: fair form over hurdles: left Donal Coffey after first start: should be suited by 2½m+. *Tom George* — **h107 b84**

COPT HILL 10 b.g. Avonbridge – Lalique (IRE) (Lahib (USA)) [2017/18 h69: h17.2d⁶ h15.7g h16.2g h15.7d h15.7s h19.3d⁴ h16.8v⁶ h27v³ Mar 23] modest hurdler at best, no form in 2017/18: wears headgear: tried in tongue tie. *Julia Brooke* — **h–**

COQUIN MANS (FR) 6 b.g. Fragrant Mix (IRE) – Quissisia Mans (FR) (Video Rock (FR)) [2017/18 h24s* h24d* h16² h24v^su h20v* h16s⁴ Apr 27] first foal: dam, French 2m hurdle winner, also 1¼m winner on Flat: smart hurdler: won maiden at Limerick in 2016/17: also won minor events at Wexford in June and Cork in August, and Keelings Irish Strawberry Hurdle at Fairyhouse (by 5½ lengths from Diamond Cauchois) in April: second in Istabraq Hurdle at Tipperary and WKD Hurdle at Down Royal (4½ lengths behind Melon): stays 3m: acts on heavy going: usually wears hood: usually races close up. *W. P. Mullins, Ireland* — **h153**

CORAL POINT (IRE) 12 ch.g. Hawkeye (IRE) – Green Crystal (Green Dancer (USA)) [2017/18 c82, h–: c24.2m^pu May 9] multiple point winner: maiden hurdler: poor form in hunter chases. *B. Dowling* — **c– h–**

CORA SUNDROP 5 b.m. Kayf Tara – L'Ultima (FR) (Verglas (IRE)) [2017/18 b15.8m⁵ b16g Nov 1] fourth foal: dam, French 1¼m winner, half-sister to fairly useful French hurdler (2m-21f winner) Empereur du Monde: modest form in bumpers. *Tom Lacey* — **b75**

CORBETT COURT (IRE) 6 br.g. Court Cave (IRE) – Stefphonic (IRE) (Orchestra) [2017/18 h61: h16.8s h15.8v⁶ c20.9v^pu Dec 18] maiden hurdler: little form over hurdles: pulled up in novice handicap on chasing debut. *Debra Hamer* — **c– h–**

CORINDA 7 b.m. Midnight Legend – Conchita (St Ninian) [2017/18 b–: h20.1v⁵ Oct 14] no form in bumpers: well beaten in maiden on hurdling debut. *Simon Waugh* — **h–**

CORLAY (FR) 6 b.g. Saddler Maker (IRE) – Overn (FR) (Lesotho (USA)) [2017/18 h19.5s⁶ h23.1v h20.3v⁴ h24v² Mar 5] first foal: dam in frame both starts over hurdles in France at around 2m: fair form over hurdles: won 4-y-o event in France for N. Devilder in 2016/17: stays 3m: acts on heavy going: tried in cheekpieces. *Jonjo O'Neill* — **h109**

CORNBOROUGH 7 ch.g. Sir Percy – Emirates First (IRE) (In The Wings) [2017/18 h125: h16.5g⁴ h16d⁵ h16s² h16.8s⁴ h16.2s⁶ h20s Apr 13] compact gelding: fairly useful handicap hurdler: raced mainly around 2m: acts on soft going: tried in cheekpieces. *Mark Walford* — **h123**

CORNER CREEK (IRE) 8 b.g. Presenting – No Moore Bills (Nicholas Bill) [2017/18 c95 c–, h–: c22.5d[6] c22.5d[3] c24.2s[F] c24d* c25.6s[pu] c27.5d[ur] Apr 22] lightly-raced hurdler: h– modest handicap chaser: won at Southwell in December: stays 3m: acts on good to soft going: in cheekpieces last 3 starts. *Michael Scudamore*

CORNERSTONE LAD 4 b.g. Delegator – Chapel Corner (IRE) (Alhaarth (IRE)) h124 [2017/18 h16.2v* h16s[3] h15.7s* h15.7v[2] h16.2v[2] h17s[2] h16.2s[3] Apr 26] fair on Flat, stays 1¾m: fairly useful hurdler: won juveniles at Hexham in November and Catterick in January: second in Victor Ludorum Juvenile Hurdle at Haydock in February: will stay beyond 2m: raced only on soft/heavy going: in cheekpieces last 2 starts. *Micky Hammond*

CORNISH WARRIOR (IRE) 7 b.g. Oscar (IRE) – Ballylooby Moss (IRE) (Supreme h99 Leader) [2017/18 h104, b90: h19.8s[6] h21.1s h23.4v[4] h21s h21.6s[pu] Apr 23] fair handicap hurdler: stays 2½m: acts on heavy going: has worn cheekpieces, including final start: often races prominently. *Neil Mulholland*

COROBEREE (IRE) 5 b.g. Dansili – Cabaret (IRE) (Galileo (IRE)) [2017/18 h20g[6] h99 h16.3d[4] h16g[2] h15.7g[3] h16g h16s Jan 13] fairly useful on Flat, stays 1½m: modest form over hurdles: left Dan Skelton after fifth start: unproven beyond 2m: in headgear last 2 starts: tried in tongue tie. *Tony Coyle*

COROMANDEL 6 ch.g. King's Best (USA) – Novellara (Sadler's Wells (USA)) b– [2017/18 b16g Oct 25] 19,000 3-y-o: third foal: half-brother to 2 winners on Flat, including smart 9f-11f winner Disclaimer (by Dansili): dam useful 1¼m-1¾m winner: tailed off in bumper. *Dan Skelton*

CORRIE LOCH 6 b.m. King's Theatre (IRE) – Pennerose Bay (Karinga Bay) [2017/18 h– § h91, b75: h21g[rr] h20g[4] h15.7d h20g h15.8d Nov 3] angular mare: maiden hurdler, no form in 2017/18: left Alan King after first start: tried in hood/tongue tie: often races freely: has refused to race. *Tom Symonds*

CORRUPTION 4 b.f. Malinas (GER) – Blue Ride (IRE) (King's Ride) [2017/18 b15.7v b– Mar 29] sixth foal: half-sister to 3 winners, including fair hurdler/fairly useful chaser Sartorial Elegance (2¾m-3¼m winner) and bumper winner/fairly useful hurdler Blu Cavalier (15f-2½m winner) (both by Kayf Tara): dam (h129) bumper/2m-2¾m hurdle winner (stayed 25f): tailed off in maiden bumper. *Alexandra Dunn*

CORSECOMBE 6 ch.g. Norse Dancer (IRE) – Digyourheelsin (IRE) (Mister Lord b55 (USA)) [2017/18 b16.8s[6] b15.3v Apr 9] poor form in bumpers: in cheekpieces first start. *Mark Gillard*

CORSKEAGH EXPRESS (IRE) 7 gr.g. Daylami (IRE) – Zara's Victory (IRE) (Old c– Vic) [2017/18 h–: c21v[5] c22d[F] c21s c31.9v[pu] Nov 22] point winner: maiden hurdler: no h– form in chases. *Mark McNiff, Ireland*

COR WOT AN APPLE 7 b.g. Apple Tree (FR) – Chipewyas (FR) (Bering) [2017/18 c– c84, h93: h22g[5] h18.7m Jul 16] maiden chaser, no form in 2017/18: maiden chaser: stays h– 2½m: acts on good to firm and good to soft going: has worn cheekpieces, including in 2017/18: wears tongue tie: usually races close up. *Neil Mulholland*

CORZEAM (FR) 6 gr.g. Early March – Night Fever (FR) (Garde Royale) [2017/18 b82§: h103 § h15.7g[pu] h18.6d[pu] h15.7v[pu] h16v[3] Feb 19] good-bodied gelding: fair form when third in maiden at Lingfield, standout effort over hurdles: wears hood: has worn tongue tie, including in 2017/18: temperamental. *Nigel Twiston-Davies*

COSHESTON 5 ch.g. Black Sam Bellamy (IRE) – Rare Ruby (IRE) (Dilshaan) [2017/18 b90 p b17s[3] Apr 8] first foal: dam (h95), lightly raced over hurdles, 1¾m-2m winner on Flat: 25/1, third in bumper at Carlisle (7¾ lengths behind Largy Glory): should improve. *Jennie Candlish*

COSMEAPOLITAN 5 b.g. Mawatheeq (USA) – Cosmea (Compton Place) [2017/18 h119 p h105P: h16.3d Dec 2] good-topped gelding: useful on Flat, stays 1¾m: fairly useful form over hurdles: 4 lengths last of 7 in listed handicap at Newbury sole outing in 2017/18: remains open to improvement. *Alan King*

COSMIC BLUE (IRE) 6 b.m. Kalanisi (IRE) – Gift of Freedom (IRE) (Presenting) b– [2017/18 b15.7g b15.8d Jul 28] first foal: dam, no form in bumpers, out of half-sister to top-class 2m chaser Buck House: no form in bumpers. *Ian Mackie*

COSMIC DIAMOND 8 b.m. Multiplex – Lucy Glitters (Ardross) [2017/18 c–, h73: c– h18.7g[2] h19.6g* h19.5d h20.7g[3] h21g* h25s[4] Dec 26] angular mare: modest handicap h91 hurdler: won at Huntingdon in October and Towcester (mares event) in November: well held only start over fences in 2016/17: stays 21f: acts on soft going: tried in visor: wears tongue tie: often races towards rear. *Paul Webber*

COS

COSMIC KING (FR) 6 b.g. Kingsalsa (USA) – Kikinda (FR) (Daliapour (IRE)) [2017/18 h103, b83: h16g h20.3g⁴ Apr 20] lengthy gelding: fair form over hurdles: left Richard Phillips after first start: stays 2½m: best form on good going: usually wears hood: often races prominently. *Fergal O'Brien* — **h103**

COSMIC STATESMAN 6 ch.g. Halling (USA) – Cosmic Case (Casteddu) [2017/18 h89: h23.3g^{pu} h23.4g^R Jun 4] strong gelding: modest maiden hurdler at best: stayed 21f: acted on soft and good to firm going: wore headgear: dead. *Neil King* — **h–**

COSMIC TIGRESS 7 b.m. Tiger Hill (IRE) – Cosmic Case (Casteddu) [2017/18 h15.7g* h16g⁴ h15.8d Sep 24] modest form over hurdles: won handicap at Southwell in August: raced around 2m: acts on soft going. *John Quinn* — **h99**

COSMOS DES OBEAUX (FR) 6 b.g. Spanish Moon (USA) – Kore des Obeaux (FR) (Saint Cyrien (FR)) [2017/18 h119p: c23.4s^{pu} Dec 20] good-topped gelding: fairly useful hurdler: pulled up in novice handicap on chasing debut: stays 2¼m: acts on heavy going. *Nicky Henderson* — **c–** / **h–**

COSTA GALERA (IRE) 4 b.g. Rock of Gibraltar (IRE) – Albany Rose (IRE) (Noverre (USA)) [2017/18 ab16g⁵ Feb 19] 40/1, fifth in bumper at Lingfield (5¾ lengths behind Normal Norman). *Olly Murphy* — **b80**

COSTANTE VIA (IRE) 7 b.m. Milan – Spirit Rock (IRE) (Rock Hopper) [2017/18 b89: h20.7s h19.5s⁶ h19.9v⁴ h23.1v⁵ Apr 17] poor form over hurdles: should prove suited by 3m. *Nigel Twiston-Davies* — **h81**

COSTA PERCY 4 b.g. Sir Percy – Costa Brava (IRE) (Sadler's Wells (USA)) [2017/18 h16.2g* h16.7g* h16.7g² h16.2d³ Aug 21] fair on Flat, stays 1¾m: similar form over hurdles: won juveniles at Hexham and Market Rasen in June. *Jennie Candlish* — **h109**

COSTLY DREAM (IRE) 6 b.g. Yeats (IRE) – What Price Love (USA) (Repriced (USA)) [2017/18 b80: h20d h19.8d Apr 22] modest form sole start in bumpers: no form over hurdles. *Philip Hobbs* — **h–**

COSY CLUB (IRE) 4 br.g. So You Think (NZ) – Bali Breeze (IRE) (Common Grounds) [2017/18 h16s⁴ h16s³ h16.2s⁴ h16d* Mar 29] half-brother to modest hurdle winner around 2m Recognition (by Rip Van Winkle): dam (c72/h94), 2m hurdle winner, also 1¼m-1½m winner on Flat: modest on Flat, stays 7f: fair form over hurdles: won juvenile maiden at Wetherby in March: left A. P. Keatley after second start: will prove best at 2m: tried in tongue tie: likely to progress further. *Dan Skelton* — **h101 p**

COTSWOLD ROAD 8 b.g. Flemensfirth (USA) – Crystal Ballerina (IRE) (Sadler's Wells (USA)) [2017/18 h–§: h21.4g h19.8s^{pu} Nov 23] maiden hurdler, no form since 2015/16: in blinkers last 4 starts: has worn tongue tie, including in 2017/18. *Colin Tizzard* — **h–**

COTSWOLD WAY (IRE) 5 b.g. Stowaway – Rosies All The Way (Robellino (USA)) [2017/18 b14d⁵ h19s³ h19.5s h19.8d² Apr 22] £45,000 4-y-o: half-brother to 3 winners, including useful hurdler/chaser Immediate Response (2m-2¾m winner), stayed 3m, and fair hurdler/winning pointer King Maker (21f winner) (both by Strategic Choice): dam, maiden on Flat, half-sister to useful hurdler/smart chaser (stayed 25f) Eau de Cologne: fifth in bumper at Ludlow: fair form over hurdles: best effort when second in novice at Wincanton in April. *Philip Hobbs* — **h110** / **b80**

COTTERSROCK (IRE) 8 b.g. Robin des Pres (FR) – Toasted Oats (IRE) (Be My Native (USA)) [2017/18 c129, h–: h23g⁵ c16.5g^{pu} h20g^{pu} h21.1g h21.1s c25.2d^F Dec 28] strong gelding: fairly useful hurdler/chaser at best, well below form in 2017/18: should be suited by 3m: acts on good to soft going: often wears headgear: in tongue tie last 4 starts: often let down by jumping over fences. *Martin Keighley* — **c– x** / **h103**

COTTONWOOL BABY (IRE) 7 b.m. Gold Well – Golden Steppes (IRE) (Titus Livius (FR)) [2017/18 h–: h23.3d^{pu} h24g⁴ c21.4g^{pu} Aug 19] in frame in Irish points: poor maiden hurdler: pulled up in novice handicap on chasing debut: should stay 3m+: sometimes in headgear: usually races towards rear. *Michael Scudamore* — **c–** / **h74**

COTTSTOWN FOX (IRE) 9 ch.g. Bandari (IRE) – Cottstown Belle (IRE) (Flemensfirth (USA)) [2017/18 h21.6s Nov 15] workmanlike gelding: lightly-raced maiden hurdler, well held sole outing in 2017/18. *Neil Mulholland* — **h–**

COUDEFOUDRE (FR) 6 gr.g. Martaline – Chamoss World (FR) (Lost World (IRE)) [2017/18 h–: h23.6s^{pu} h15.8v⁵ h19.2v c20.3v^{ur} c18.2s⁴ c21s⁶ Apr 23] poor maiden hurdler: poor form over fences: tried in cheekpieces. *Venetia Williams* — **c66** / **h72**

COU

COUGAR KID (IRE) 7 b.g. Yeats (IRE) – Western Skylark (IRE) (Westerner) [2017/18 h96: h21.6d^{pu} h19.6g h19.6g h21.6m h15.8g³ h16.7d³ h16.8s⁵ h19.7g* h15.5d* h16.2s³ h23.1v⁵ h19.7s* h21.4s⁴ h16.2s⁵ Apr 25] lengthy gelding: fair handicap hurdler: won at Hereford in November, Leicester in December and Hereford again in January: stays 23f: acts on heavy going: has worn headgear, including last 3 starts: waited with. *John O'Shea* **h111**

COUGAR'S GOLD (IRE) 7 b.g. Oscar (IRE) – Top Her Up (IRE) (Beneficial) [2017/18 h–, b96: h21.9d⁴ h23.3d⁴ h22.1s* h22g⁵ c20.9v⁵ c21.4v⁵ h19.3s⁴ c24v⁷ Mar 5] fair form over hurdles: won handicap at Cartmel in July: modest form over fences: in cheekpieces, best effort when second in handicap at Southwell in March: stays 3m: acts on heavy going: wears tongue tie. *Peter Bowen* **c98 h100**

COULD YOU 6 b.m. Beat All (USA) – Wahiba Reason (IRE) (Robellino (USA)) [2017/18 b16.5v⁶ Apr 12] tailed off in bumper: dead. *Tim Pinfield* **b–**

COUNTER SHY (IRE) 5 b.g. Galileo (IRE) – Cross The Flags (IRE) (Flemensfirth (USA)) [2017/18 b94: h16g* h15.8s² h16.4d^{pu} Nov 17] fairly useful form over hurdles: won maiden at Worcester in September: would have been suited by 2½m: dead. *Jonjo O'Neill* **h115**

COUNTISTER (FR) 6 b.m. Smadoun (FR) – Tistairly (FR) (Fairly Ransom (USA)) [2017/18 h16.3d² h16.6d* h16v* h16.8s⁵ Mar 15] compact mare: first foal: dam unraced: multiple bumper winner in France for E. & G. Leenders, including of Group 2 events at Saint-Cloud and Maisons-Laffitte: fairly useful form over hurdles: won novices at Doncaster in December and Sandown in February: usually travels strongly. *Nicky Henderson* **h121**

COUNT MERIBEL 6 ch.g. Three Valleys (USA) – Bakhtawar (IRE) (Lomitas) [2017/18 h122, b95: h19.3s* h20d* h21.6d* h24s² h21s⁶ h19.3s⁵ h24.7s^{pu} Apr 13] good-bodied gelding: useful hurdler: won novices at Carlisle in October/November and Ascot by 8 lengths from Perfect Harmony) later in November: second in Albert Bartlett Novices' Hurdle (Bristol) at Cheltenham (2¾ lengths behind Kilbricken Storm) in December: stays 2¾m: acts on heavy going: usually leads. *Nigel Twiston-Davies* **h130**

COUNTRY DELIGHTS (IRE) 5 b.m. Mahler – Nadwell (IRE) (Gold Well) [2017/18 b16.2g⁶ b15.7d Nov 24] second foal: half-sister to fair hurdler Golden Jewel (2m winner, by Brian Boru): dam, unraced, closely related to fairly useful hurdler/chaser (stayed 3m) Vic Ville: no form in bumpers. *Hugh Burns* **b–**

COUNTRY'N'WESTERN (FR) 6 b.g. Samum (GER) – Cracking Melody (Shamardal (USA)) [2017/18 b95: b16g⁵ b16.8d⁴ Sep 22] fairly useful form at best in bumpers, disappointing both starts in 2017/18. *David Elsworth* **b69**

COUP DE PINCEAU (FR) 6 b.g. Buck's Boum (FR) – Castagnette III (FR) (Tin Soldier (FR)) [2017/18 h114p, b95: h21.4g² h21.1s⁶ h23.9s² h19.4s* h24g⁶ Apr 18] good-topped gelding: bumper winner: fairly useful form over hurdles: won maiden at Musselburgh in February: stays 3m: acts on soft going: in cheekpieces last 2 starts. *Paul Nicholls* **h127**

COUP DE VENT 7 b.m. Tobougg (IRE) – Pigment (Zamindar (USA)) [2017/18 h16.3g^{pu} Sep 9] workmanlike mare: modest on Flat, stays 1½m: modest form in bumpers in 2014/15: pulled up in novice on hurdling debut: held up. *John O'Shea* **h–**

COUR DES MALBERAUX (FR) 6 b.m. Le Malemortois (FR) – Domia (FR) (Highest Honor (FR)) [2017/18 b16.3g⁶ b16.8m⁶ Jul 7] first foal: dam French maiden (placed up to 11.5f): no form in bumpers: in hood second start. *Tony Newcombe* **b–**

COURT AFFAIRS 6 b.g. Court Cave (IRE) – Rock Money (IRE) (Deploy) [2017/18 b97: h21.4s h20.3s h15.8s⁵ h15.7s h21.6s⁶ Apr 23] won sole start in bumpers in 2016/17: modest form over hurdles: will be suited by further than 21f: acts on soft going. *Seamus Mullins* **h99**

COURT ARTIST (IRE) 7 b.m. Court Cave (IRE) – Native Artist (IRE) (Be My Native (USA)) [2017/18 b19.8g* h16g⁶ h20.2s* h20s* h18.9v³ h18s h22v³ h20s^{pu} Apr 28] closely related to bumper winner/fairly useful hurdler Araucaria (2½m winner, by Accordion) and half-sister to useful hurdler Private Malone (2½m-2¾m winner, by Darsi): dam (h104), placed all 3 starts in bumpers/over hurdles, out of half-sister to Grand National winner Corbiere: fair form in bumpers: won maiden at Kilbeggan in July: fairly useful hurdler: won mares maiden at Ballinrobe in September and mares event at Wexford in October: third in listed mares novice at Haydock (¾ length behind Cap Soleil) in December and Kerry Group EBF Shannon Spray Mares Novices' Hurdle at Limerick (7¼ lengths behind Lackaneen Leader) in March: stays 2¾m: acts on heavy going. *W. P. Mullins, Ireland* **h122 b88**

221

totepool Silver Trophy Handicap Hurdle, Chepstow—Court Minstrel (noseband) takes advantage of some late waywardness by Sam Spinner (second left) to repeat his 2015 win

COURT BALOO (IRE) 7 b.g. Court Cave (IRE) – Tremplin (IRE) (Tremblant) [2017/18 h85: h25.4g^{pu} h23.1g h23.3d^3 h23.3v^3 h23.3s h22.7g^4 h23.8g* h23.8s^2 c20.9s^{pu} Apr 8] poor handicap hurdler: won at Musselburgh in November: pulled up in novice handicap on chasing debut: stays 3m: acts on heavy going: usually wears headgear. *Alistair Whillans* c–
h82

COURT DISMISSED (IRE) 8 b.g. Court Cave (IRE) – Carramanagh Lady (IRE) (Anshan) [2017/18 c110§, h–: c24.1s^2 c24.2g* c23g* c24.1g^5 c21.1g^F c24g^5 Oct 22] compact gelding: winning hurdler: fair handicap chaser: won at Fakenham in June and Worcester in July: stays 25f: acts on soft going: wears headgear: front runner/races prominently: temperamental. *Donald McCain* c109 §
h–

COURT DREAMING (IRE) 5 b.g. Court Cave (IRE) – Louis's Teffia (IRE) (Presenting) [2017/18 b17d^5 Mar 25] €8,000 3-y-o: second foal: brother to bumper winner Judge Earle: dam, winning pointer, half-sister to fairly useful hurdler/useful chaser (stayed 3¾m) Night In Milan: 10/1, fifth in bumper at Carlisle (15 lengths behind Dr Sanderson): will be suited by 2½m+. *Nicky Richards* b81

COURT DUTY (IRE) 6 b.g. Court Cave (IRE) – Easter Duties (IRE) (Aristocracy) [2017/18 b–: b16s b16v h15.8v^4 h16v^4 h16v^3 h16v h16s^5 Apr 27] no form in bumpers: modest form over hurdles: raced only at 2m on soft/heavy going. *John Flint* h92
b–

COURT FRONTIER (IRE) 10 b.g. Court Cave (IRE) – Dame En Rouge (IRE) (Imperial Frontier (USA)) [2017/18 c128, h113: h24.2d^6 h23.6v c26.7v^4 c28.4s Mar 26] fair handicap hurdler: fairly useful handicap chaser: stays 31f: acts on good to firm and heavy going: has worn cheekpieces, including in 2017/18: tried in tongue tie: usually races nearer last than first. *Christian Williams* c123
h112

COURT IN FLIGHT (IRE) 6 b.m. Court Cave (IRE) – Flight Princess (IRE) (Swallow Flight (IRE)) [2017/18 h22.1d May 31] first foal: dam no form on Flat: maiden pointer: in cheekpieces, tailed off in mares maiden on hurdling debut. *Benjamin Arthey, Ireland* h–

COURT IN SESSION (IRE) 13 b.g. Court Cave (IRE) – Dangerous Dolly (IRE) (Jurado (USA)) [2017/18 c91§, h–§: h16m^2 c16.3m^6 h16.7g c16.5g^F Aug 1] useful-looking gelding: multiple point winner: poor handicap hurdler/chaser: unproven beyond 2m: acts on good to firm and good to soft going: has worn headgear, including last 2 starts: wears tongue tie: often races prominently: one to treat with caution (often reluctant/led in at start). *Matt Sheppard* c65 §
h75 §

COURTINTHEMIDDLE (IRE) 7 b.g. Court Cave (IRE) – Kilmessan (IRE) (Flemensfirth (USA)) [2017/18 h82: h23.6v h21v^pu Apr 27] runner-up in Irish point: poor hurdler, no show in 2017/18: stays 21f: acts on good to firm going. *Deborah Faulkner*   **h–**

COURT KING (IRE) 7 b.g. Indian River (FR) – Eliza Everett (IRE) (Meneval (USA)) [2017/18 h108: c24d^pu c20.3g* c24g* h23g² h25.4d² h26.5d⁴ c22.5s³ c26.3g³ c24.1s^pu Dec 2] fairly useful handicap hurdler: similar form over fences: won handicaps at Southwell (twice, novice second occasion) in June: stays 3¼m: acts on soft and good to firm going: wears headgear: has worn tongue tie, including in 2017/18: usually races prominently: one to treat with caution. *Peter Bowen*   **c123 §** / **h120 §**

COURTLANDS PRINCE 9 b.g. Presenting – Bathwick Annie (Sula Bula) [2017/18 h112: h16g^pu h20g³ h20.3d^pu Nov 21] fair handicap hurdler: should stay 2½m: acts on soft and good to firm going: wears tongue tie. *Neil Mulholland*   **h99**

COURT LIABILITY (IRE) 5 b.g. Court Cave (IRE) – Whataliability (IRE) (Leading Counsel (USA)) [2017/18 b17.7g* h21.2g* h19.7g* Nov 29] €14,000 3-y-o, £88,000 4-y-o: fifth foal: half-brother to modest hurdler/chaser Benability (2½m winner, by Beneficial): dam unraced half-sister to fair hurdler/smart chaser (stayed 3¼m) Treacle: runner-up in Irish point: won bumper at Fontwell (by neck from Solomon Grey) in October: fairly useful form over hurdles: won novices at Sedgefield and Hereford in November: will stay 2¾m+: open to further improvement. *Harry Whittington*   **h120 p** / **b102**

COURT MASTER (IRE) 5 b.g. Court Cave (IRE) – Lusos Wonder (IRE) (Luso) [2017/18 b16v² Feb 3] €20,000 3-y-o, €65,000 4-y-o: second foal: dam, runner-up in point, half-sister to useful hurdler/smart chaser (stayed 25f) Magnanimity: Irish point winner: 13/2, second in bumper at Wetherby (8 lengths behind Black Pirate): will be suited by 2½m+. *Michael Scudamore*   **b93**

COURT MINSTREL (IRE) 11 b.g. Court Cave (IRE) – Theatral (Orchestra) [2017/18 c–, h145: 15.7m⁴ h16.3g² h16d^f h16.3g⁴ h19.5h⁴ h20.5d h19.7s³ h19.3s h20s Apr 13] lengthy gelding: useful handicap hurdler: won Silver Trophy at Chepstow (by ½ length from Sam Spinner) in October: winning chaser: stays 19f: has form on soft going, but better under less testing conditions: races well off pace. *Evan Williams*   **c–** / **h144**

COURT OUT (IRE) 5 b.g. Court Cave (IRE) – Madame Martine (IRE) (Spadoun (FR)) [2017/18 b16.8d³ b16.5g Nov 16] modest form in bumpers: trained by Harry Whittington first start. *Jamie Snowden*   **b76**

COURTOWN OSCAR (IRE) 9 b.g. Oscar (IRE) – Courtown Bowe VII (Damsire Unregistered) [2017/18 c125, h125: c26.2v* c28.4v² Nov 25] fairly useful hurdler: useful handicap chaser: won at Carlisle in October: stays 3½m: acts on heavy going: tried in cheekpieces: front runner/races prominently. *Philip Kirby*   **c131** / **h–**

COURT PAINTER (IRE) 8 b.g. Court Cave (IRE) – Comings (IRE) (Grand Lodge (USA)) [2017/18 c–: c23.8s⁴ c25.2v^pu c19.9d⁴ c19.3v^pu c20.1v^pu c21.4s³ c20.9s^pu c21.4d⁶ Apr 22] point winner: poor maiden chaser: in cheekpieces last 3 starts. *Victor Thompson*   **c80**

COURT ROYALE (IRE) 5 b.g. Court Cave (IRE) – Windsor Dancer (IRE) (Woods of Windsor (USA)) [2017/18 b15.8g² Nov 9] €34,000 3-y-o: sixth foal: half-brother to bumper winner Kala Minstrel and bumper winner/fairly useful hurdler It's High Time (2m winner) (both by Kalanisi): dam, ran once over hurdles, 1¼m-1½m winner on Flat, half-sister to very smart hurdler/smart chaser (stays 19f) Court Minstrel (by Court Cave): 7/2, shaped well when second in bumper at Ludlow (¾ length behind Vinndication): open to improvement. *Evan Williams*   **b95 p**

COUSIN KHEE 11 b.g. Sakhee (USA) – Cugina (Distant Relative) [2017/18 c–, h115§: h21d² May 16] good-topped gelding: fairly useful on Flat: fairly useful handicap hurdler: second at Warwick sole outing in 2017/18: well held only chase start: stays 21f: acts on firm and soft going: tried in cheekpieces: temperamental. *Hughie Morrison*   **c–** / **h115 §**

COUSIN OSCAR (IRE) 6 b.g. Oscar (IRE) – On The Jetty (IRE) (Be My Native (USA)) [2017/18 h122, b81: h16.2g⁴ h17v⁶ c15.2d³ c19.9g² c19.9s⁵ Feb 4] sturdy gelding: second on completed start in Irish points: fairly useful handicap hurdler, below form in 2017/18: fair form over fences: stays 2½m: acts on soft going: tried in hood: front runner/races prominently. *Donald McCain*   **c110** / **h100**

COUSIN PETE 10 b.g. Kayf Tara – Leachbrook Lady (Alderbrook) [2017/18 c110: c23.9s² c26.3v³ Mar 16] multiple point winner: fairly useful form in hunter chases: best effort when third in Foxhunter Chase at Cheltenham in March: wears tongue tie. *Mrs Elizabeth Brown*   **c129**

COW

COWSLIP 9 b.m. Tobougg (IRE) – Forsythia (Most Welcome) [2017/18 c–, h106: h23.3d^{pu} h19.3s^3 h21.2g h23.1s* h18.9v^3 h19.7v^5 h19.6d^5 Apr 21] modest handicap hurdler nowadays: won at Bangor (conditional) in December: little impact in 2 chases in 2016/17: stays 25f: acts on soft going: wears cheekpieces. *Donald McCain* — c– h93

COYOACAN (FR) 6 b.g. Al Namix (FR) – Jetty Dancer (FR) (Smadoun (FR)) [2017/18 h110, b94: h16.3d^2 May 21] fair form over hurdles: second in novice at Stratford on sole outing in 2017/18: should prove suited by further than 2m: usually races prominently. *Warren Greatrex* — h110

CPM FLYER 4 b.g. Aqlaam – Zennor (Doyen (IRE)) [2017/18 b15.6s^5 Feb 4] 33/1, fifth in bumper at Musselburgh (12¼ lengths behind Seddon): will stay beyond 2m. *Brian Ellison* — b79

CRACKDELOUST (FR) 6 b.g. Daramsar (FR) – Magic Rose (FR) (Manninamix) [2017/18 h111: h16.2g^3 h16.2g^3 c16.4g^F h15.5s^4 h16.6d^4 h19.3s* h15.6s^5 h16g Apr 20] fairly useful handicap hurdler: won at Catterick in January: fell first on chasing debut: stays 19f: acts on good to firm and heavy going: in headgear last 3 starts. *Brian Ellison* — c– p h116

CRACK DU TAY (FR) 6 b.g. Ballingarry (IRE) – Bonjour Jandrer (FR) (Pennekamp (USA)) [2017/18 h98, b84: h21m^5 h20.3g h18.5d h19.9s Oct 19] modest maiden hurdler: tried in tongue tie. *Mark Wall* — h90

CRACKED REAR VIEW (IRE) 8 gr.g. Portrait Gallery (IRE) – Trip To Knock (Be My Chief (USA)) [2017/18 c24d^5 c25.3v^{pu} Dec 18] runner-up on completed start in points: fair hurdler: modest form over fences: better effort when fifth in novice handicap at Doncaster in December: should stay 2¾m+: acts on soft going: in headgear last 3 starts, tongue tied last 4. *Kim Bailey* — c88 h–

CRACKERDANCER (IRE) 8 b.m. Robin des Champs (FR) – Katie's Cracker (Rambo Dancer (CAN)) [2017/18 b109: h16v* h18v^F h22v^{pu} Mar 21] useful bumper performer: won listed mares event at Navan (by ¾ length from Cordovan Brown) in November: fair form over hurdles: won mares maiden at Limerick in December: should stay at least 2½m: wears tongue tie: front runner. *Ray Hackett, Ireland* — h114 b109

CRACKER JAK (IRE) 4 b.g. September Storm (GER) – Princess Jaffa (IRE) (Zaffaran (USA)) [2017/18 b17.7s^4 Mar 7] 9/2, last of 4 in bumper at Fontwell. *Suzy Smith* — b74

CRACKING DESTINY (IRE) 5 b.g. Dubai Destination (USA) – Cracking Gale (IRE) (Alderbrook) [2017/18 b16.4g b14d^4 h19.4s^6 Jan 26] £28,000 3-y-o, £100,000 4-y-o: good sort: first foal: dam, maiden pointer, half-sister to fairly useful hurdler/chaser (stays 2½m) Cracking Find: Irish point winner: fair form in bumpers: better effort when fourth at Ludlow in December: tailed off in maiden on hurdling debut: wears hood. *Nicky Henderson* — h– b86

CRACKING FIND (IRE) 7 b.g. Robin des Pres (FR) – Crack The Kicker (IRE) (Anshan) [2017/18 h117: c16d^3 c19.4d^3 c16.3g* c15.7d^5 c15.7s^3 c19.2s* c15.9s* c20.5g^6 Apr 20] point winner: winning hurdler: fairly useful chaser: won novice handicap at Newcastle in November, novice at Catterick in March and novice handicap at Carlisle in April: stays 2½m: acts on good to firm and heavy going: usually races close up. *Sue Smith* — c128 h–

CRACKING SMART (FR) 6 b.g. Great Pretender (IRE) – Maya du Frene (FR) (Le Pommier d'Or) [2017/18 h123p, b108: h20s* h24s* h20v^2 h20v^2 Jan 7] useful bumper performer: smart form over hurdles: won maiden at Punchestown (by 4 lengths from Shady Operator) in October and listed novice at Cork (by 8½ lengths from Robin des Foret) in November: second in Navan Novices' Hurdle (5½ lengths behind Next Destination) in December and Lawlor's of Naas Novices' Hurdle (length behind Next Destination) in January: stays 3m: acts on heavy going: tried in cheekpieces: usually in tongue tie: races prominently, responds generously to pressure: even better to come. *Gordon Elliott, Ireland* — h150 p

CRACK OF THUNDER (IRE) 9 b.g. September Storm (GER) – Keep Hunting (IRE) (Nestor) [2017/18 c25.5s^4 May 18] point winner: fair hurdler: fair maiden chaser, below form in hunter sole outing in 2017/18: probably stays 29f: acts on soft going: wears cheekpieces: temperamental. *Miss Rose Grissell* — c90 h– §

CRAFTY ROBERTO 10 ch.g. Intikhab (USA) – Mowazana (IRE) (Galileo (IRE)) [2017/18 c105, h110: c17d^2 c17.5v^6 h15.5v^3 c17v^2 c19.4d Apr 22] leggy gelding: fair handicap hurdler: fair maiden chaser: stays 2½m: acts on good to firm and heavy going: has worn headgear, including in 2017/18: wears tongue tie. *Alex Hales* — c101 h95

CRAGGAKNOCK 7 b.g. Authorized (IRE) – Goodie Twosues (Fraam) [2017/18 h121: h19g^4 h16g^5 h20.1g^5 h19.7s^2 h20.6s^5 h16d^4 Apr 22] good-topped gelding: fairly useful handicap hurdler: left Mark Walford after third start: stays 2½m: acts on soft going: usually wears cheekpieces: often races towards rear. *Richard Guest* — h114

CRE

CRAIGANBOY (IRE) 9 b.g. Zagreb (USA) – Barnish River (IRE) (Riverhead (USA)) [2017/18 c109, h77: c16.5s⁴ h19v⁵ c17.1v^pu h20.2s² Apr 26] fair maiden hurdler: fair chaser: stays 2½m: raced only on soft/heavy going: wears hood/tongue tie: held up. *N. W. Alexander*   **c100 h104**

CRAIGANEE (IRE) 11 b.g. Craigsteel – Hows She Going (IRE) (Strong Statement (USA)) [2017/18 c–, h99: h22.1s^pu Jul 24] tall gelding: fair hurdler, folded tamely sole outing in 2017/18: little impact in 2 starts over fences in 2016/17: stays 3m: acts on heavy going: has worn hood: wears tongue tie: usually leads. *Alexandra Dunn*   **c– h–**

CRAIGMOR (IRE) 6 b.g. Craigsteel – Twilight Princess (IRE) (Moscow Society (USA)) [2017/18 b15.8g h23.9v⁴ h20s³ h20s³ Dec 19] first foal: dam, winning pointer, half-sister to useful hurdler/fairly useful chaser (stayed 3m) Original Option: Irish point winner: considerate ride when eighth in bumper at Ludlow: best form over hurdles: best effort when third in novice at Fakenham in December. *Olly Murphy*   **h101 b–**

CRAIG STAR (IRE) 8 b.g. Craigsteel – Different Dee (IRE) (Beau Sher) [2017/18 h106: h21.2g² h17.2d³ h23.3g⁴ h16.7g³ h19.9g³ h20.9d* h16.2g^ur h16.8s² h19.4d² h18.1v* h16.8v⁶ h19.4d^ur Mar 16] fairly useful handicap hurdler: won at Kelso in October and January (amateur): stays 3m, effective at shorter: acts on heavy going: wears cheekpieces: often races prominently. *Donald McCain*   **h118**

CRANBROOK CAUSEWAY (IRE) 6 b.g. Mohaajir (USA) – Kingarriff Bell (IRE) (Mandalus) [2017/18 h19.9d h21.2d⁶ h19s^pu h18.6v h24v^pu Feb 25] second when hampered and fell last in Irish point: no form over hurdles: in headgear last 2 starts. *Graeme McPherson*   **h–**

CRANK EM UP (IRE) 7 b.g. Royal Anthem (USA) – Carrawaystick (IRE) (Old Vic) [2017/18 h110: c23.6v⁵ c24.2s³ c24v^pu c25.1v* c24v² c25.1v⁴ c26s^pu c29.2g^pu Apr 26] fair hurdler: fair handicap chaser: won novice event at Wincanton in January: will be suited by extreme distances: acts on heavy going: wears headgear: lazy, and one to treat with caution. *David Dennis*   **c110 § h–**

CRANSTAL (IRE) 5 b.g. Gold Well – Vincenta (IRE) (Bob Back (USA)) [2017/18 b15.8d h15.3d^pu Apr 22] down the field in bumper: pulled up in novice on hurdling debut. *Philip Hobbs*   **h– b67**

CRAWFORDS MILL (IRE) 6 br.m. Getaway (GER) – Lough Cuan (IRE) (Zaffaran (USA)) [2017/18 h16v⁶ h20s h21.4v⁴ h21.4v³ h17d c20v² Apr 17] €7,500 3-y-o: second foal: dam (c99/h117) 2m hurdle winner (stayed 3m): in frame all 4 starts in points: modest form over hurdles: 7/2, second in novice handicap at Carlisle (11 lengths behind Skipping On) on chasing debut: will be suited by 3m: best form on heavy going: likely to improve over fences. *Stuart Crawford, Ireland*   **c96 p h96**

CRAZY JACK (IRE) 10 b.g. Royal Anthem (USA) – Cindy's Fancy (IRE) (Shernazar) [2017/18 c109, h104: c20.3g³ c23.8d⁴ c20d³ Apr 9] tall gelding: winning hurdler: fair chaser nowadays: stays 3m: acts on heavy going: has worn cheekpieces. *Mrs A. R. Hewitt*   **c109 h–**

CREATIVE INERTA (IRE) 8 br.g. Balakheri (IRE) – Rambling Liss (IRE) (Presenting) [2017/18 b83: c21.1s² c24.2v^pu Apr 17] point winner: modest form in hunter chases: better effort when second in maiden event at Fontwell in May: tried in hood: wears tongue tie. *B. Clarke*   **c97**

CREEP DESBOIS (FR) 6 b.g. Great Pretender (IRE) – Brigade Mondaine (FR) (Arnaqueur (USA)) [2017/18 h119, b96: h21.1g c23.8d⁵ c21.2s* c20.2v² c19.9s⁶ Mar 31] good-topped gelding: fairly useful hurdler, below form on return in 2017/18: useful form over fences: won handicap at Fakenham in December: second in similar event at Leicester in February: stays 21f: acts on good to firm and heavy going: usually races prominently. *Ben Pauling*   **c132 h–**

CREEVYTENNANT (IRE) 14 b.g. Bob's Return (IRE) – Northwood May (Teenoso (USA)) [2017/18 c116: c23.8g* c21.4g³ c23.8g* h23.9v² h21.2g⁴ Nov 16] rangy gelding: fair form over hurdles: useful chaser: won hunter at Perth in May and handicap there (by ¾ length from Baileys Concerto) in August: stays 25f: acts on soft and good to firm going: has worn tongue tie, including in 2017/18: front runner. *Fergal O'Brien*   **c133 h113**

CRESSWELL BREEZE 8 b.m. Midnight Legend – Cresswell Willow (IRE) (Witness Box (USA)) [2017/18 c132, h–: c27.7d* c28.8d³ c29.2s⁵ c30.7s^pu Feb 23] tall, lengthy mare: winning hurdler: useful handicap chaser: won Southern National at Fontwell (by 3½ lengths from Cyclop) in November: third in Betfair London National at Sandown (3 lengths behind Benbens) in December: stays 29f: acts on heavy going: wears tongue tie: often races prominently. *Anthony Honeyball*   **c133 h–**

CRE

CRESSWELL LEGEND 7 b.g. Midnight Legend – Cresswell Willow (IRE) (Witness Box (USA)) [2017/18 b98: b16.7g h15.8g* h21.2g* h23.8d* h26.1s^2 h25d^{pu} Apr 26] sturdy gelding: Irish point winner: bumper winner: fairly useful form over hurdles: won novice at Ludlow in October, introductory event there in November and handicap at Musselburgh in January: stays 3¼m: acts on soft going: in tongue tie last 5 starts: front runner/races prominently. *Kim Bailey* **h127 b–**

CREST 7 b.g. Kayf Tara – Maiden Voyage (Slip Anchor) [2017/18 c23g^{pu} c23.4s c19.9s^5 c19.4s^6 Jan 13] winning hurdler: fairly useful maiden chaser, well below best in 2017/18: left Gordon Elliott after first start: tried in cheekpieces: has worn tongue tie, including in 2017/18: often races prominently: temperament under suspicion. *Micky Hammond* **c– h–**

CRIEVEHILL (IRE) 6 b.g. Arcadio (GER) – Ma Douce (IRE) (Mansonnien (FR)) [2017/18 h129: c15.9s c16d* c16.4g^3 c20.6v^2 c18.8v^4 c19.9v^2 c20v* c19.9s^2 Mar 31] lengthy gelding: fairly useful hurdler: useful handicap chaser: won at Lingfield in November and Sandown in March: stays 21f: acts on heavy going: has worn hood, including in 2017/18. *Nigel Twiston-Davies* **c139 h–**

CRIN AU VENT (FR) 6 b.g. Laveron – Tentative (FR) (Blushing Flame (USA)) [2017/18 h–: c17.4s^F May 20] winning hurdler: beaten when fell 3 out in novice won by Lofgren at Bangor on chasing debut: tried in hood/tongue tie. *Paul Nicholls* **c– h–**

CRINDLE CARR (IRE) 4 ch.g. Compton Place – Arley Hall (Excellent Art) [2017/18 h16d^6 h15.3g^5 Oct 29] modest maiden on Flat, stays 2m: poor form over hurdles. *John Flint* **h62**

CRINKLE CRAGS (IRE) 8 ch.g. Trans Island – Ashanti Dancer (IRE) (Dancing Dissident (USA)) [2017/18 c65§, h–§: c20.1g^3 c20.1g^{pu} Jun 17] modest hurdler at best: poor maiden chaser: stays 2½m: temperamental. *Nicky Richards* **c61 § h– §**

CRIQ ROCK (FR) 7 ch.g. Kap Rock (FR) – Criquetot (FR) (Epervier Bleu) [2017/18 h121: h24.5m^2 h21.4v^2 h21g^5 h24.6s^2 Apr 9] compact gelding: fairly useful maiden hurdler: stays 25f: acts on soft and good to firm going: held up. *Alan King* **h117**

CRISP STORY 7 b.m. Lucky Story (USA) – Rave On (ITY) (Barathea (IRE)) [2017/18 b15.7g b17s Oct 19] sister to useful 6f-1m winner Lucky Rave and half-sister to 7f winner Hit The Roof (by Auction House): dam maiden on Flat: no form in bumpers. *Peter Winks* **b–**

Dawn Homes Novices' Championship Handicap Chase, Ayr—the much improved Crosshue Boy (stars) overhauls long-time leader Dingo Dollar (white face) late on in this valuable new race for novices (a similar event was run at the Finale meeting at Sandown for hurdlers)

CRO

CRISTAL ICON (IRE) 4 b.f. Sixties Icon – Cristal Island (IRE) (Trans Island) [2017/18 h16v³ h16s⁵ h16v* h17s⁴ Apr 12] rather leggy filly: modest maiden on Flat, stays 11f: fairly useful form over hurdles: won maiden at Cork in March. *Thomas Mullins, Ireland* — **h116**

CRIXUS'S ESCAPE (IRE) 5 ch.g. Beneficial – Tierneys Choice (IRE) (Oscar (IRE)) [2017/18 b70: h16.2s* h16.2d* Apr 23] fairly useful form over hurdles: won maiden at Hexham in November and novice there in April: will be suited by 2½m: open to further improvement. *Gillian Boanas* — **h121 p**

CROCODILE DANCER 8 b.g. Croco Rouge (IRE) – She Likes To Boogy (IRE) (Luso) [2017/18 h68: h23.3d h20.3g⁶ May 16] poor maiden hurdler: should stay at least 23f. *Sam England* — **h57**

CROFTYS JOSH 4 b.g. Josr Algarhoud (IRE) – Little Missmoffatt (Karinga Bay) [2017/18 b13d Dec 2] well beaten in junior bumper. *Mark Weatherer* — **b–**

CROOKOFDEVON 9 b.g. Desideratum – Blue Morning (Balinbarbi) [2017/18 h–: h20.2g^pu May 17] no form: tried in cheekpieces: dead. *Jean McGregor* — **h–**

CROOKS PEAK 5 b.g. Arcadio (GER) – Ballcrina Girl (IRE) (Milan) [2017/18 b16.8g* b16.4s* b16.4s Mar 14] €16,000 3-y-o: useful-looking gelding: first foal: dam, unraced, closely related to fairly useful hurdler (2m-2½m winner) Diklers Oscar: useful form in bumpers: won at Newton Abbot (by 6 lengths from River Bray) in October and listed event at Cheltenham (by 1½ lengths from Air Navigator) in November. *Philip Hobbs* — **b107**

CROOKSTOWN (IRE) 11 b.g. Rudimentary (USA) – Millview Lass (IRE) (Jurado (USA)) [2017/18 c117x, h115: c19m* c20g^ur c21.4g⁶ h19.9d h18.6g⁵ c20s h20v^pu h20.5v^pu h20.6s Mar 26] rangy gelding: fairly useful handicap hurdler, below form in 2017/18: fairly useful handicap chaser: won at Haydock in May: stays 21f: acts on good to firm and heavy going: wears headgear. *Ben Case* — **c124 h102**

CROPLEY (IRE) 9 gr.g. Galileo (IRE) – Niyla (IRE) (Darshaan) [2017/18 h–: h26.4s³ h21.4g h16.5v h19.5s⁵ Apr 27] medium-sized gelding: modest handicap hurdler: stays 3¼m: acts on soft going: tried in blinkers: temperamental. *Dai Burchell* — **h84 §**

CROSSED MY MIND (IRE) 6 b.g. Beneficial – Coolvane (IRE) (Dr Massini (IRE)) [2017/18 h16s³ h16s³ h19.3v⁶ Jan 20] workmanlike gelding: second foal: dam unraced sister to smart hurdler/chaser (2m-3m winner) Massini's Magnet and closely related to fairly useful hurdler/useful chaser (stayed 25f) Twirling Magnet: fairly useful handicap hurdler: won maiden at Wexford in 2016/17: stays 21f: acts on soft going. *A. L. T. Moore, Ireland* — **h117**

CROSSHUE BOY (IRE) 8 b.g. Brian Boru – Gluais Linn (IRE) (Supreme Leader) [2017/18 c111, h125, b86: c17g c16g c20g c20d³ h20.5g⁴ h20v⁵ h20v c19.5v⁶ c17s* c16v* c19.6v* c16.7v³ c24.1g* Apr 21] useful-looking gelding: fairly useful handicap hurdler: useful chaser: won novice at Leopardstown, novice handicap at Wexford and novice at Down Royal, all in March, and valuable novice handicap at Ayr (by length from Dingo Dollar) in April: stays 3m, effective at shorter: acts on good to firm and heavy going: tried in cheekpieces: wears tongue tie: open to further improvement as a chaser. *Sean Thomas Doyle, Ireland* — **c141 p h122**

CROSS OF STEEL (IRE) 5 b.g. Craigsteel – Gaelic Million (IRE) (Strong Gale) [2017/18 b16.7d Apr 21] well beaten in bumper. *Jennie Candlish* — **b–**

CROSSPARK 8 b.g. Midnight Legend – Blue Shannon (IRE) (Be My Native (USA)) [2017/18 c136, h–: c19.9d⁴ c22.4g^pu c29.2s⁴ c20.2v⁴ c21.2d³ Apr 7] sturdy gelding: winning hurdler: useful handicap chaser: stays 3m: acts on heavy going: usually races prominently. *Caroline Bailey* — **c131 h–**

CROWDED ROOM (IRE) 12 b.g. Oscar (IRE) – Leadamurraydance (IRE) (Supreme Leader) [2017/18 c24.5v^R Mar 15] point winner: fair hurdler/chaser at best in Ireland for Michael Cunningham: tailed off when refused last in hunter chase sole outing under Rules in 2017/18: stays 25f: acts on heavy going: has worn headgear. *Callum Bickers-Price* — **c– h–**

CROWN HILL (IRE) 8 b.g. Definite Article – Silver Prayer (IRE) (Roselier (FR)) [2017/18 c124, h109: h26.4d² h23.1g⁴ h23.1v⁴ c19.4s² c24d² c28.4s⁴ Mar 26] fair handicap hurdler: fairly useful handicap chaser: stays 3½m: acts on heavy going: tried in hood: often races towards rear. *Johnny Farrelly* — **c120 h109**

CROWN THEATRE (IRE) 9 b.g. King's Theatre (IRE) – Palesa's Legacy (IRE) (Montelimar (USA)) [2017/18 c111, h111: c20g^pu Jun 25] winning hurdler: useful chaser at best, shaped as if amiss sole outing in 2017/18: stays 2¼m: acts on soft and good to firm going: wears tongue tie: held up: sometimes finishes weakly. *Jamie Snowden* — **c– h–**

CRU

CRUACHAN (IRE) 9 b.g. Authorized (IRE) – Calico Moon (USA) (Seeking The Gold (USA)) [2017/18 h86: c20.1g^{pu} h20.2v* h19v h23.8s^4 Jan 19] modest handicap hurdler: won at Perth in September: pulled up in novice on chasing debut: stays 2¾m, effective at shorter: acts on heavy going: wears headgear. *Lucy Normile*   c– h88

CRUCIAL MOMENT 4 b.g. Pivotal – Moonglow (Nayef (USA)) [2017/18 h15.8d* h16.7g^2 h16d^3 h16.7d* h16s* h15.6s^F Feb 4] good-topped gelding: modest on Flat, probably stayed 1¼m: fairly useful form over hurdles: won juveniles at Uttoxeter in July, Market Rasen in December and Sandown in January: raced around 2m: acted on soft going: dead. *Bill Turner*   h127

CRUCIAL ROLE 6 b.g. Westerner – The Lyme Volunteer (IRE) (Zaffaran (USA)) [2017/18 b86: h21.2m^{pu} h19.2g* h19.9d^4 h21.2d^2 h19.9v^2 h23.8s* h26s^2 h24v^{pu} Mar 16] well-made gelding: useful hurdler: won maiden at Towcester in May and handicap at Ludlow (by 13 lengths from Gamain) in January: will stay long distances: acts on heavy going. *Henry Daly*   h130

CRUISE IN STYLE (IRE) 12 b.m. Definite Article – Henrietta Street (IRE) (Royal Academy (USA)) [2017/18 c–§, h82§: h16d h16.8d Oct 12] workmanlike mare: modest hurdler at best, no form in 2017/18: winning chaser: stays 2½m: acts on any going: usually wins in headgear: wears tongue tie: untrustworthy. *Kevin Bishop*   c– § h– §

CRUISING BYE 12 b.g. Alflora – Althrey Flame (IRE) (Torus) [2017/18 c93x, h–: c24.1s* c24g^3 c25.5s h24v^3 c24.1s^2 c23.8v^2 Apr 15] poor handicap hurdler: modest handicap chaser: won at Bangor in May: left Gary Hanmer after third start: stays 29f: acts on good to firm and heavy going: wears headgear/tongue tie: often let down by jumping over fences. *Peter Bowen*   c97 x h81

CRUSHED (IRE) 4 b.g. Beat Hollow – Sel (Salse (USA)) [2017/18 h15.7s Jan 11] fairly useful on Flat, stays 1¼m: 15/8, tailed off in juvenile on hurdling debut: should do better. *Alan King*   h– p

CRY FURY 10 b.g. Beat Hollow – Cantanta (Top Ville) [2017/18 h87: h16d c16.5g^2 c16.5g^6 c20m^2 c16.5g c20g h23.3d^5 h19.5d^6 Oct 31] useful-looking gelding: poor maiden hurdler: poor form over fences: seems to stay 23f, effective at much shorter: acts on good to firm going: usually wears headgear/tongue tie: often races in rear: untrustworthy. *Matt Sheppard*   c83 § h71 §

CRYSTAL LAD (FR) 6 ch.g. Kapgarde (FR) – Qrystale Mag (FR) (Vertical Speed (FR)) [2017/18 h128, b90: c19.7d^5 c20s^5 c25.6g^3 c24s^3 c23.8s^4 h24g Apr 18] rather unfurnished gelding: fairly useful handicap hurdler, shaped better than result final outing in 2017/18: fairly useful form over fences: third in handicap at Ludlow in December: stays 3¼m: acts on soft going. *Gary Moore*   c122 h112 +

CRY WOLF 5 ch.g. Street Cry (IRE) – Love Charm (Singspiel (IRE)) [2017/18 h90: h23.3d h19.2g^6 h20.6g^3 h21.7d^4 h20.6s^{pu} h21.7s^4 h21s Feb 9] workmanlike gelding: modest maiden hurdler: stays 23f: acts on soft going: wears headgear: temperamental. *James Evans*   h92 §

CUBAN PETE (IRE) 6 b.g. Flemensfirth (USA) – Gee Whizz (FR) (Turgeon (USA)) [2017/18 b16.7s h19.5v^6 h19.2v h19.7v^3 h21.2d Apr 9] €45,000 3-y-o: sixth foal: half-brother to French chaser Brise du Large (17f-23f winner, by Phantom Breeze) and a winning pointer by Kaldounevees: dam, French 15f-21f hurdle/chase winner, half-sister to useful French hurdler/chaser (2¼m-3¼m winner) Vesube: shaped as if needed experience in bumper: modest form over hurdles. *Venetia Williams*   h87 b–

CUBOMANIA (IRE) 5 gr.g. Halling (USA) – Surrealism (Pivotal) [2017/18 h16d h16g h16v* h16v* h16v^2 Feb 11] fair form on Flat (best effort at 1¼m): fair hurdler: won handicaps at Down Royal (conditional) in December and Tramore in January: left Eugene M. O'Sullivan after second start: raced only at 2m: acts on heavy going: in tongue tie last 5 starts. *Gordon Elliott, Ireland*   h110

CUBSWIN (IRE) 4 b.f. Zamindar (USA) – Moonlight Rhapsody (IRE) (Danehill Dancer (IRE)) [2017/18 h16g* h15.8g^3 h16s^2 h19.4s h16.8g^2 h15.8d^{ur} Apr 24] small filly: fairly useful on Flat, stays 1½m: fair form over hurdles: won fillies juvenile at Fakenham in November: likely to prove best at around 2m: acts on soft going. *Neil King*   h105

CUCKLINGTON 7 b.g. Kayf Tara – Ardrom (Ardross) [2017/18 c93, h78: c25.1s^2 c25.7d* c25.1s* c25.1s^2 c23s^3 c25.1v^5 c23s^5 c25.1v* c23.6v^2 Apr 14] lengthy gelding: maiden hurdler: fair handicap chaser: won at Plumpton (novice) and Wincanton in November, and at latter course again (twice, novice on second occasion) in March: stays 3¼m: acts on heavy going: wears blinkers/tongue tie: front runner/races prominently, often travels strongly. *Colin Tizzard*   c114 h–

228

CUE

CUCKOO'S CALLING 4 b.f. So You Think (NZ) – Sinndarina (FR) (Sinndar (IRE)) b93
[2017/18 b13.7g* b14d* b14s³ Nov 22] first foal: dam useful French 9f-1½m winner: fair form in bumpers: won junior events at Huntingdon in October and Carlisle in November: fifth of 6 in Flat maiden. *James Bethell*

CUDDLES MCGRAW (IRE) 5 b.g. Court Cave (IRE) – Stefphonic (IRE) (Orchestra) h–
[2017/18 b16.3d h20.3g Apr 18] has had breathing operation: well beaten in bumper/ b–
novice hurdle (in tongue tie). *Fergal O'Brien*

CUE CARD 12 b.g. King's Theatre (IRE) – Wicked Crack (IRE) (King's Ride) c165
[2017/18 c174, h–: c24.2s^F c25.6v² c21s² c20.8s^{pu} Mar 15] h–

The self-appointed stewards of indignation who inhabit the Twittersphere were quick to demand Cue Card's retirement after he fell in the Charlie Hall Chase at Wetherby on his reappearance. It was his second fall in three starts—after he had crashed out at the third last in the previous season's Cheltenham Gold Cup—but there was absolutely no call for the heated response that followed, particularly the scurrilous accusation that Cue Card's connections were simply motivated by greed in keeping him in training. Cue Card had won two Grade 1 events the previous season, the Betfair Chase (for the third time) and the Ascot Chase (for the second), and had gone down by just a neck in the Aintree Bowl on his only other start after his fall in the Gold Cup. It clearly wasn't time, at the age of eleven, for him to say farewell to the big following that he had built up since he won the Champion Bumper at the Cheltenham Festival as a four-year-old (he won a Ryanair Chase too at 'jumping's biggest meeting' where he also finished in the frame in a Supreme Novices' Hurdle and an Arkle Trophy, as well as creating a big story when chasing a million-pound bonus—after winning the same season's Betfair and King George VI Chase—in the 2016 Gold Cup, a race in which he also fell at the third last). There was hardly any stage in Cue Card's career when he wasn't making headlines with some big-race success or other (he won nine Grade 1s) and his longevity undoubtedly contributed to his becoming one of the most popular racehorses of recent times. In one sense, at least, he had nothing more to prove. That, in itself, though, was no reason to retire him.

So long as a jumper is fit and well, and capable of winning races, owners will generally keep racing them, which they are fully entitled to do. Red Rum was still in training as a thirteen-year-old (retired through injury on the eve of the 1978 Grand National), Desert Orchid ran his last race when attempting a fifth win in the King George VI Chase at the age of twelve and Kauto Star's last appearance came at the age of twelve, after which he looked set for one final campaign, before plans were scrapped early in the 2012/13 season, following a remarkable comeback campaign in which he won a fourth Betfair Chase and a fifth King George VI Chase (there had been calls before that in some quarters for him to be retired after he had appeared to be losing his aura). Looking further back, Arkle's great contemporary Flyingbolt, struck down as a seven-year-old with the blood disease brucellosis, continued racing until he was twelve (third in the Cathcart at the Cheltenham Festival at that age) and there are plenty of other top chasers who have been kept going when no longer significant competitors in the top championship events. Age alone is no barrier. Sonny Somers—runner-up in that Cathcart in which Flyingbolt was third, incidentally—gained his last two victories at the age of eighteen and another popular favourite Peaty Sandy wasn't retired until the age of fourteen, showing the best form of his career at the age of thirteen when victory in the Eider Chase gave him his tenth course win at Newcastle. The first two in the latest Welsh Grand National, Raz de Maree and Alfie Spinner, were both thirteen-year-olds, while Pete The Feat, winner of the final of the previous year's Veterans' Chase series, gained another victory at Sandown in the latest season as a fourteen-year-old, and the exploits of that grand old stick Victory Gunner, retired at seventeen after winning his last race as a fifteen-year-old, are still fresh in the memory.

After his exit in the Charlie Hall, in which he was in the process of running well when coming down five out (his jockey blamed the low-lying sun), Cue Card went on three weeks later to finish second of five finishers in the Betfair Chase which was run in conditions that were little short of deplorable for a championship

Mrs Jean R. Bishop's "Cue Card"

event. Harry Cobden replaced regular partner Paddy Brennan at Haydock but Cue Card finished fifty-seven lengths behind the mud-loving winner Bristol de Mai. Paddy Brennan was back on board when Cue Card was next seen in the Betfair Ascot Chase in mid-February after defending champion Thistlecrack had been the stable's selected for the King George VI Chase and Cue Card's connections had also bypassed a listed chase at Kempton in January which had been earmarked before his training was temporarily interrupted by pus in a foot. The Ascot Chase produced one of the races of the season. Twelve-year-old Cue Card, a 9/1-shot on the day and conceding at least four years to each of his rivals, raced with zest and was in the firing line all the way before going down fighting in a fine battle with the favourite Waiting Patiently who retained his unbeaten record over fences by two and three quarter lengths, having to be ridden right out. Third-placed Frodon finished fifteen lengths behind Cue Card whose effort showed that he was still capable of top-class form. It was clear that Cue Card would be making another appearance at the Cheltenham Festival, either in the Gold Cup or the Ryanair Chase. He started second favourite to Un de Sceaux in the Ryanair—five years after his win in the race—but he was wisely pulled up by Paddy Brennan some way from home when it was clear he was not enjoying himself (the stewards inquired into his running and ordered him to be routine tested). That effort turned out to be Cue Card's swansong. He showed further signs at home of being something of a shadow of his former self and planned starts in the Bowl at Aintree, and then in the Oaksey Chase at Sandown's Finale meeting, were eventually shelved. He was paraded at the Sandown fixture and applauded into retirement.

CUL

```
                    ┌ King's Theatre (IRE)   ┌ Sadler's Wells    ┌ Northern Dancer
                    │     (b 1991)           │    (b 1981)       │ Fairy Bridge
Cue Card            │                        │ Regal Beauty      │ Princely Native
(b.g. 2006)         │                        │    (b 1981)       │ Dennis Belle
                    │                        ┌ King's Ride       ┌ Rarity
                    │ Wicked Crack (IRE)     │    (b 1976)       │ Ride
                    └     (b 1993)           │ Mighty Crack      │ Deep Run
                                             │    (b 1979)       │ Treize
```

The big, lengthy Cue Card has had his pedigree outlined in earlier editions of *Chasers & Hurdlers* (this is the eighth essay on him) and the only significant update is that his three-year-old half-brother by Gold Well was sold for £80,000 at the Cheltenham November Sales and is due to go into training with Paul Nicholls. Their dam Wicked Crack has produced just one other winner so far, the fair hurdler and fairly useful chaser Hidden Crack (by Lahib). The strong-travelling Cue Card often made the running and he stayed twenty-five furlongs and acted on heavy ground. He wore a tongue tie and, to counter a high head carriage, was equipped with a sheepskin noseband (although he did not wear one for the latest Ascot Chase). Racing's top performers do not resonate with the wider public as they once did—Arkle topped a *TV Times* popularity poll for 'most popular personality' back in 1966 with Bobby Moore, captain of England's World Cup winners, second and The Beatles third—but, to those close to the sport, Cue Card's contribution will be cherished for a long time. A most genuine racehorse, he deservedly became a real favourite and must have been a pleasure to own. *Colin Tizzard*

CUIL ROGUE (IRE) 10 b.g. Presenting – Coolshamrock (IRE) (Buckskin (FR)) [2017/18 h97: h23.9g⁴ h23g c20g⁵ Jul 11] point winner: modest maiden hurdler: 10/1, fifth in novice handicap at Uttoxeter (22½ lengths behind Bestwork) on chasing debut: left Nicky Richards after first start: stays 3m: acts on heavy going: has worn hood, including final start: has worn tongue tie, including last 2 starts. *Graeme McPherson* c79
h87

CUIRASSIER DEMPIRE (FR) 6 ch.g. Network (GER) – Juventhura (FR) (Video Rock (FR)) [2017/18 h100: c24g² c20.1g² c23g* c24.1d* Oct 4] won both completed starts in points: lightly-raced hurdler: useful form in chases: won novice handicaps at Worcester in August and Bangor in October: stays 3m: acts on good to soft going: often travels strongly: open to further improvement over fences. *Tom George* c134 p
h–

CUL DE POULE 6 b.g. Multiplex – Madam Blaze (Overbury (IRE)) [2017/18 b16g⁵ b16v⁶ h21.7s Jan 29] third foal: dam (h84), maiden hurdler (stayed 3m), sister to fairly useful hurdler/fair chaser (stayed 3¼m) Georgian King: modest form in bumpers: well beaten in maiden on hurdling debut: in tongue tie last 2 starts. *Martin Keighley* h–
b83

CULLY MAC (IRE) 7 b.g. Coroner (IRE) – Catch Those Kisses (Deploy) [2017/18 h–: h21.2g^pu h20.9d h16.4s h19.7v^F Feb 20] little form over hurdles: in cheekpieces last 2 starts. *Andrew Wilson* h–

CULM COUNSELLOR 9 ch.g. Erhaab (USA) – Miss Counsel (Leading Counsel (USA)) [2017/18 c–, h81: h21.6g⁵ h23g² h23g⁴ c20g^pu h20g⁴ c23g⁴ c25.8d* c25.8g² h26.4s* c25.1s^pu c26.3m⁴ Nov 1] workmanlike gelding: poor handicap hurdler: won at Stratford (amateur) in October: modest handicap chaser: won at Newton Abbot (conditional) in August: stays 3¼m: acts on soft and good to firm going: has worn headgear, including in 2017/18. *Chris Down* c85
h81

CULMINATION 6 b.g. Beat Hollow – Apogee (Shirley Heights) [2017/18 h105: h22.1m³ May 27] fair hurdler, better than result sole outing in 2017/18: unproven beyond 2m: acts on heavy going. *Donald McCain* h92 +

CULTIVATOR 7 b.g. Alflora (IRE) – Angie Marinie (Sabrehill (USA)) [2017/18 h136: c19.8g^pu c15.9m² c20.2s⁴ Jan 11] unfurnished gelding: useful hurdler: similar form over fences: best effort when second in maiden at Leicester (3½ lengths behind Tommy Silver) in November: stays 21f: acts on good to firm going: has worn hood. *Nicky Henderson* c132
h–

CULTRAM ABBEY 11 br.g. Fair Mix (IRE) – Kansas City (FR) (Lute Antique (FR)) [2017/18 c141, h119: c23.8m^pu c23.4s² c23.4v² c20.9v² c26.2v³ c23.8s* Apr 27] useful-looking gelding: winning hurdler: fairly useful chaser nowadays: won hunter at Perth in April: stays 27f: acts on heavy going: tried in cheekpieces. *Nicky Richards* c124
h–

231

CUL

CULTURE DE SIVOLA (FR) 6 b.m. Assessor (IRE) – Neva de Sivola (FR) (Blushing Flame (USA)) [2017/18 h115: h23.6d* h25d h26v³ h23.9v* h22.8v* Mar 31] unfurnished mare: fairly useful handicap hurdler: won at Chepstow in October, Taunton in February and Haydock in March: stays 3¼m: acts on heavy going. *Nick Williams* **h128**

CULVERWELL 7 b.g. Midnight Legend – Give Me Strength (IRE) (Flemensfirth (USA)) [2017/18 b17g May 19] point winner: in tongue tie, 25/1, seventh in conditionals/amateur bumper at Aintree. *Mrs Teresa Clark* **b–**

CUP FINAL (IRE) 9 ch.g. Presenting – Asian Maze (IRE) (Anshan) [2017/18 c120p, h122+: c19.3g² c20.1g² c21.4g c24.2g³ c21.6g⁵ c25.2d⁴ Nov 24] well-made gelding: useful hurdler at best: fairly useful chaser: second in novice at Hexham in June: stays 3¼m: acts on soft going: in tongue tie last 5 starts. *Ben Haslam* **c128 h–**

CUPID'S ICON 4 b.f. Sixties Icon – Flinders (Henbit (USA)) [2017/18 b16d Apr 26] lengthy filly: seventh foal: half-sister to modest hurdler Kayflin (2½m-2¾m winner, by Kayf Tara), stays 25f: dam (c84) 3m/3¼m winner: well beaten in bumper. *Emma Lavelle* **b–**

CUP OF AMBITION (IRE) 6 b.g. Vinnie Roe (IRE) – Sparkling Gem (IRE) (Revoque (IRE)) [2017/18 h99, b–: h16m^{ur} h21.2m^{pu} h21.6d^{pu} h20s⁵ c22.7d⁵ c19.2d^F h19.6s^{pu} h19.7s^{pu} Mar 27] point winner: modest maiden hurdler: let down by jumping in chases: in headgear last 5 starts: usually wears tongue tie. *Martin Keighley* **c– x h98**

CUP OF GOLD 6 b.m. Midnight Legend – Cee Cee Rider (Classic Cliche (IRE)) [2017/18 b15.7v Apr 27] second foal: dam (h103), 3m hurdle winner, half-sister to fairly useful hurdlers Smart Mover (stayed 25f) and Malindi Bay (winner up to 2¾m): little impact in points: well beaten in bumper. *Ben Case* **b–**

CURIOUS CARLOS 9 b.g. Overbury (IRE) – Classi Maureen (Among Men (USA)) [2017/18 h128: h17.2m* h16.5g² h16.7g^F h18.5g² h20.3g⁴ h16.3s⁶ h21.4g⁵ Apr 21] stocky gelding: useful handicap hurdler: won at Cartmel in May: second at Newton Abbot in August: stays 2½m: acts on good to firm and heavy going: has worn hood/tongue tie. *Peter Bowen* **h131**

CURRAGH HALL (IRE) 10 b.g. Saddlers' Hall (IRE) – Curragh Dane (IRE) (Danehill Dancer (IRE)) [2017/18 c19.3g c20.3v^{pu} c19.3g Apr 23] maiden pointer: modest hurdler: no form in chases: usually in headgear: wears tongue tie. *L. Humphrey* **c– h–**

CURRAIGFLEMENS (IRE) 10 b.g. Flemensfirth (USA) – Curraig Monashee (IRE) (Monashee Mountain (USA)) [2017/18 c26.3d⁶ c21.1s* c20.9d* c21.1s^{pu} Apr 12] fair hunter chaser: won at Fontwell in May and Stratford (handicap) in June: stays 25f: acts on soft going: tried in cheekpieces/tongue tie: usually races close up. *David Kemp* **c106**

CURRENT EXCHANGE (IRE) 13 ch.g. Beneficial – Musical Millie (IRE) (Orchestra) [2017/18 c98: c25.3d May 5] small gelding: fairly useful chaser at best, well held sole outing in 2017/18: stays 3¼m: acts on heavy going: wears headgear/tongue tie. *Francesca Nimmo* **c–**

CUSHEEN BRIDGE (IRE) 10 b.g. Oscar (IRE) – One Hell Ofa Woman (IRE) (Fourstars Allstar (USA)) [2017/18 c128, h108: c19.4d³ c19.1d³ c19.9s⁴ c21.2s⁶ c24g² Apr 20] sturdy gelding: winning hurdler: fairly useful handicap chaser: third at Wetherby in November and Doncaster in December: stays 3m: acts on soft going: tried in cheekpieces: wears tongue tie. *Charles Pogson* **c124 h–**

CUSHUISH 5 b.m. Yeats (IRE) – My Petra (Midnight Legend) [2017/18 b16.5v b16.5m Apr 25] £20,000 4-y-o: second foal: closely related to fairly useful hurdler/winning pointer My Dance (2¼m-2½m winner, by Kayf Tara): dam (c142/h134), 2m-19f hurdle/chase winner (also 11.6f winner on Flat), sister to fairly useful hurdler/useful chaser (stayed 25f) Midnight Appeal: no form in bumpers. *Bob Buckler* **b–**

CUT AND RUN 5 b.m. Getaway (GER) – Somethinaboutmolly (IRE) (Choisir (AUS)) [2017/18 b16.3g⁵ b16s h15.7v^{pu} Apr 27] second foal: half-sister to fairly useful chaser Somewhere To Be (19f/2½m winner, by Golan): dam unraced: no form in bumpers: in hood, pulled up in novice on hurdling debut. *Martin Keighley* **h– b–**

CUT THE CORNER (IRE) 10 br.g. Vinnie Roe (IRE) – Snipe Victory (IRE) (Old Vic) [2017/18 c121§, h100§: c23m³ c20g* c16d⁷ c19.4m² h21.6g⁵ c20d⁴ c23.8m⁵ c19.4g² c23.8g³ c16d¹ Apr 9] fairly useful handicap hurdler: useful handicap chaser: won at Uttoxeter (twice) in July: stays 3m, effective at much shorter: acts on good to firm and good to soft going: has worn headgear: often races prominently. *Alastair Ralph* **c133 h117**

232

CYR

CUT THE MUSTARD (FR) 6 br.m. Al Namix (FR) – Tadorna (FR) (Maresca Sorrento (FR)) [2017/18 h18v h16v⁵ h20.2v* h16.8s⁶ h20v h16.2d Apr 26] compact mare: second foal: half-sister to 13.5f bumper winner Burma (by Charming Groom): dam unraced: dual bumper winner in France: fair form over hurdles: won maiden at Punchestown in February: stays 2½m: acts on heavy going. *W. P. Mullins, Ireland* — **h112**

CYBALKO (FR) 5 b.g. Balko (FR) – Cybertina (FR) (Cyborg (FR)) [2017/18 b16.3d⁶ May 21] tailed off in bumper. *David Bridgwater* — **b–**

CYCLOP (IRE) 7 b.g. King's Theatre (IRE) – Tasmani (FR) (Turgeon (USA)) [2017/18 c118, h–: h24.7d c27.7d² c27.6s* c26.7v⁵ c28.8v⁴ c29.2v^pu c23.9v^ur Apr 11] good-topped gelding: fair handicap hurdler, below form on return in 2017/18: fairly useful handicap chaser: won at Market Rasen in December: stays 3½m: acts on heavy going: wears headgear/tongue tie: usually races prominently. *David Dennis* — **c121 h94**

CYDERCOURT (IRE) 5 b.g. Court Cave (IRE) – Lavender Track (IRE) (Pistolet Bleu (IRE)) [2017/18 b16v³ b16.2g⁴ b16.2v⁵ Apr 10] modest form in bumpers. *Nigel Twiston-Davies* — **b80**

CYPRUS AVENUE 6 b.m. Kayf Tara – Za Beau (IRE) (Beneficial) [2017/18 b16s⁵ b16.2g b16v b16.4s⁵ b16v⁴ h17d⁶ Mar 25] lengthy mare: second foal: dam (c97/h85) 2m-2½m chase winner: no form in bumpers: modest form over hurdles: best effort when fourth in maiden at Ayr in March: will stay further than 2m. *Ian Duncan* — **h90 b–**

CYRANO STAR (FR) 6 gr.g. Martaline – Quezac du Boulay (FR) (Useful (FR)) [2017/18 h84, b–: h17d h19.9s Dec 26] maiden hurdler, no form in 2017/18. *Andrew Crook* — **h–**

CYRIUS MORIVIERE (FR) 8 b.g. Vendangeur (IRE) – Sagesse Moriviere (FR) (Vaguely Pleasant (FR)) [2017/18 c135, h90: c19.4d⁴ h16.6d³ h15.8d² h20s Apr 13] lengthy gelding: point winner: fairly useful handicap hurdler nowadays: maiden chaser: best around 2m: acts on good to soft going: wears tongue tie: front runner/races prominently. *Ben Pauling* — **c– h124**

CYRNAME (FR) 6 b.g. Nickname (FR) – Narquille (FR) (Passing Sale (FR)) [2017/18 h115: h16d c16.5g* c16.4g² c16s* c20s² c20.5g* c19.9s⁴ Apr 12] good-topped gelding: fairly useful hurdler at best over hurdles: very smart form over fences: won novice handicap at Huntingdon in November, and Wayward Lad Novices' Chase (by 7 lengths from Shantou Rock) in December and Pendil Novices' Chase (by 11 lengths from The Unit) in February, both at Kempton: second in Scilly Isles Novices' Chase at Sandown (neck behind Terrefort) in February: stays 2½m: acts on soft going: wears hood/tongue tie: front runner. *Paul Nicholls* — **c156 h106**

32Red.com Wayward Lad Novices' Chase, Kempton—a bold front-running display by Cyrname

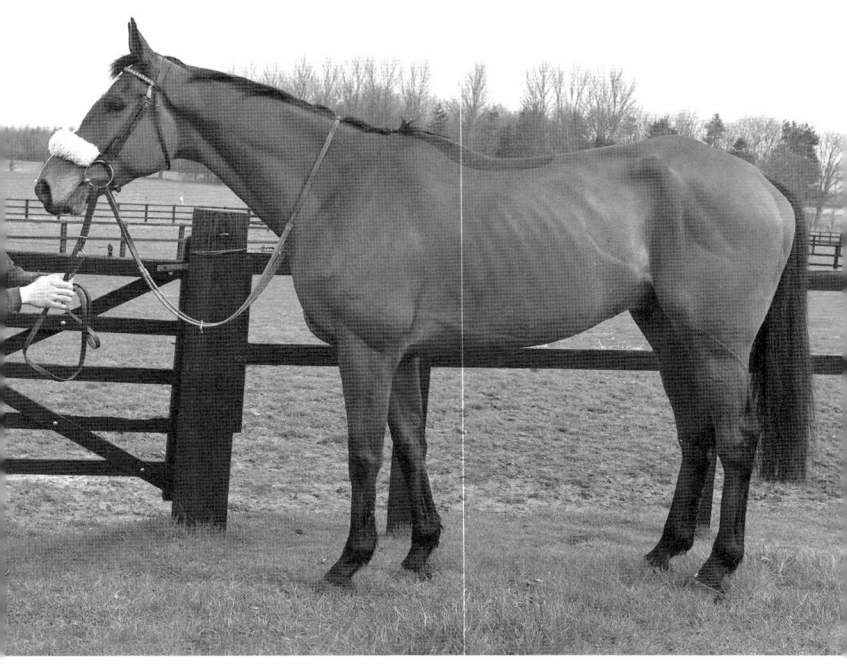

Mr & Mrs G. Calder & Mr P. M. Warren's "Cyrus Darius"

CYRUS DARIUS 9 b.g. Overbury (IRE) – Barton Belle (Barathea (IRE)) [2017/18 c–, h143: c20.5v* c21.6v⁴ c15.2s³ h18.1v* h20s⁵ Apr 12] good-topped gelding: smart hurdler: won Timeform Morebattle Hurdle at Kelso (by 12 lengths from Better Getalong) in February: useful form over fences: won handicap at Ayr in November: stays 2½m: acts on heavy going: often travels strongly: has joined Colin Tizzard. *Ruth Jefferson*

c143
h148

D

DA BABA ELEPHANT (IRE) 9 b.g. Subtle Power (IRE) – Queenofbenitstown (IRE) (Presenting) [2017/18 c–, h–: c20.1g c20.1g² c20.1g* c23.9g* c23g² Jul 10] lightly-raced hurdler: fair handicap chaser: won at Hexham and Market Rasen (novice) in June: stays 3m well: best form on good going: tried in cheekpieces: in tongue tie last 4 starts. *Ronan M. P. McNally, Ireland*

c102
h–

DABINETT MOON 10 b.m. Midnight Legend – Miss Crabapple (Sunyboy) [2017/18 c25.3d² c24.5g² c22.6d* c20.3vᵖᵘ Feb 9] prolific point winner: fair chaser: won lady riders' hunter at Stratford in June: stays 3m: acts on good to soft going (ran poorly on heavy final outing). *Mrs F. J. Marriott*

c104

DADSINTROUBLE (IRE) 8 b.g. Presenting – Gemini Lucy (IRE) (Glacial Storm (USA)) [2017/18 h135: c23dᶠ c23.4s⁴ c23sᵘʳ h23.1v⁵ h24s h24d Apr 26] sturdy gelding: useful handicap hurdler at best: fair form when fourth in novice handicap at Newbury, sole completed outing over fences: let down by jumping either side: stays 25f: acts on soft going. *Tim Vaughan*

c112
h124

DAHILLS HILL (IRE) 6 br.m. Mahler – Whites Cross (IRE) (Lord Americo) [2017/18 h22s⁶ h16.8d⁵ h24g⁶ h16g h20g h19d³ h21.7d h20.5dᵘʳ h21.2s* h18.6s² h25.5sᶠ Mar 27] sixth foal: half-sister to a winning pointer by Milan: dam, lightly raced in bumper/points,

h103

DAM

half-sister to fairly useful hurdler/smart chaser (stayed 3m) Mr Baxter Basics: point winner: fair handicap hurdler: won mares event at Ludlow in January: left David Kenneth Budds after sixth start: should stay beyond 21f: acts on soft going: tried in hood. *Graeme McPherson*

DAILY TRADER 4 ch.g. Medicean – Danehill Destiny (Danehill Dancer (IRE)) [2017/18 h15.8d^{pu} Apr 24] fair on Flat, stays 1½m: bled when pulled up on hurdling debut. *David Evans*   h–

DAISY DE SIVOLA (FR) 5 b.m. Assessor (IRE) – Kerrana (FR) (Cadoudal (FR)) [2017/18 c–, h118: c17.9s^{pu} h20.3s h23.8v^6 h19.5v* h21v^5 Mar 11] rather leggy mare: fair handicap hurdler: won at Chepstow in February: little show over fences: stays 19f: acts on heavy going. *Nick Williams*   c– h109

DAKKAR COLLONGES (FR) 5 br.g. Network (GER) – Karesse Collonges (FR) (Kadalko (FR)) [2017/18 h15.8s^5 h17.7g^3 h20s^F h20.3v h22d^4 Apr 22] fourth foal: dam, French 19f-25f chase winner, half-sister to useful hurdlers/smart staying chasers Vivaldi Collonges and Nenuphar Collonges: fair form over hurdles: trained in 2016/17 by Mlle A-S. Pacault: stays 2¾m: acts on soft going. *Ben Case*   h103

DAKLONDIKE (IRE) 6 b.g. Gold Well – Strong Irish (IRE) (Corrouge (USA)) [2017/18 h114, b77: c25.8g^4 c24.2s* c23.6s^4 c25.1v* c26v* c30s^{pu} Apr 28] tall gelding: useful hurdler: useful form over fences: won handicaps at Wetherby in November, and at Wincanton and Newbury (stayed on strongly when beating Grand Vision 3 lengths) in December: should stay long distances: best form on soft/heavy going: in cheekpieces last 5 starts: wears tongue tie: often races towards rear: no easy ride (can race lazily). *David Pipe*   c132 h–

DAKOTA GREY 7 gr.g. Fair Mix (IRE) – Miss Sassi (Terimon) [2017/18 c–, h–: h16.2v^6 h16.2v^4 h16.8s^3 h16.4s^F h20.5v^5 h17v h17s* h15.7g^5 Apr 20] fair handicap hurdler: won at Carlisle (conditionals) in April: pulled up both starts in novice chases: has form at 21f, but better at shorter when conditions are testing: best form on soft/heavy going: has worn headgear: tried in tongue tie: often races prominently, tends to find little. *Micky Hammond*   c– h102

DALAMAN (IRE) 7 b.g. Duke of Marmalade (IRE) – Crimphill (IRE) (Sadler's Wells (USA)) [2017/18 h68: h16d* h17.7s* h15.3s^2 h19.7s* Dec 26] lengthy gelding: fair handicap hurdler: won at Chepstow in October, Plumpton in November and Wetherby (novice) in December: stays 2½m: acts on soft going: tried in cheekpieces: has worn tongue tie. *Neil Mulholland*   h105

DALEELAK (IRE) 5 b.g. Arcano (IRE) – Alshamatry (USA) (Seeking The Gold (USA)) [2017/18 h17.7v^6 h15.9d h15.9s Apr 15] fair on Flat, stays 1m: no form over hurdles: tried in tongue tie. *Daniel O'Brien*   h–

DALIANCE (IRE) 9 ch.g. Dalakhani (IRE) – Everlasting Love (Pursuit of Love) [2017/18 c–, h102§: h20g^3 h21.6m^{pu} Aug 29] sturdy gelding: fair handicap hurdler: lightly-raced winning chaser: stays 23f: acts on heavy and good to firm going: wears headgear: temperamental. *Noel Williams*   c– § h102 §

DALI MAIL (FR) 5 gr.g. Satri (IRE) – Queenly Mail (FR) (Medaaly) [2017/18 b–p: b16.2v^3 b16.2v* b17s Apr 13] workmanlike gelding: fairly useful form in bumpers: won at Kelso in February: in tongue tie last 3 starts. *Donald Whillans*   b98

DALKADAM (FR) 7 gr.g. Martaline – Cadoudame (FR) (Cadoudal (FR)) [2017/18 c88, h94: h20.3g h15.8d c18.8d^3 c19.1d^4 c19.1s^5 Jan 26] strong, workmanlike gelding: modest handicap hurdler: modest maiden chaser: should stay 2½m: acts on heavy going: often in headgear: has worn tongue tie. *J. R. Jenkins*   c90 h–

DALMARELLA DANCER (IRE) 7 gr.m. Mastercraftsman (IRE) – Ting A Greeley (Mr Greeley (USA)) [2017/18 h90§: h16m h20g^5 h18g^{rr} h15.8g^{pu} Oct 26] temperamental maiden hurdler: refused to race third outing: one to leave alone. *David Peter Dunne, Ireland*   h– §

DAMBY'S STAR (IRE) 8 b.g. Kayf Tara – She Took A Tree (FR) (Sri Pekan (USA)) [2017/18 h79: h26.4s Oct 2] little form over hurdles: won point in 2018: tried in cheekpieces/tongue tie: front runner/races prominently. *Mark Bradstock*   h–

DAME DE COMPAGNIE (FR) 5 b.m. Lucarno (USA) – Programmee (FR) (Kahyasi) [2017/18 h15.8d* h16.4s^5 h19.3s^2 h20.3g* Apr 19] rather unfurnished mare: fourth foal: half-sister to 3 winners, including modest hurdler C'Est du Gateau (19f winner, by Laveron) and French chaser Belle Affaire (17f winner, by Coastal Path): dam, French   h131 p

235

*Huw Stevens, Jo Whiley Afterparty Onsale Mares' Novices' Hurdle, Cheltenham—
Dame de Compagnie (hoops) wins the opener on Cheltenham's first card exclusively for fillies and
mares; the headlines went to the others pictured, though, with fourth-placed Dame Rose (far side)
collapsing and dying after the race, whilst third-placed Banjo Girl (No.4) needed to be treated for
heat stress due to unseasonably hot weather, which resulted in a staying chase later in the afternoon
being abandoned on welfare grounds*

2¼m chase winner, half-sister to useful French 2¼m hurdle winner Sortie de Secours: bumper winner for A. Lacombe: useful form over hurdles: won mares maiden at Uttoxeter in November and listed mares novice at Cheltenham (by 1½ lengths from Just Janice) in April: also second in novice at Ascot (nose behind Point of Principle) in between: stays 2½m: acts on soft going: in hood last 3 starts: travels strongly: smart prospect. *Nicky Henderson*

DAME DU SOIR (FR) 5 br.m. Axxos (GER) – Kassing (FR) (Passing Sale (FR)) [2017/18 b12.9s² b11.9s* b11.9g³ b11.9s* h16.8s⁵ Feb 23] fourth foal: dam French 12.5f bumper winner: won bumpers at La Roche-Sur-Yon in October and Saint-Brieuc in November: left J. Provost and 7/4, threatened long way when fifth in mares novice at Exeter (7 lengths behind Love Lane) on hurdling debut: likely to improve. *David Bridgwater* **h98 p b?**

DAME ROSE (FR) 5 b.m. Network (GER) – Ile Rose (FR) (Le Riverain (FR)) [2017/18 b106: h16.2v* h16.3d³ h16.3d* h20.5vᵖᵘ h16.6s⁴ h16.4sᵖᵘ h20.3g⁴ Apr 19] useful bumper performer: useful hurdler: won novice at Hexham in October and listed mares novice at Newbury (by 9 lengths from Cap Soleil) in December: stayed 2½m: acted on heavy going: tried in tongue tie: front runner/raced prominently: dead. *Richard Hobson* **h130**

DAMIENS DILEMMA (IRE) 10 b.g. Wareed (IRE) – Olympos Belle (IRE) (Shahrastani (USA)) [2017/18 c99: c26.2g³ c22.6d c24.2g Jun 25] workmanlike gelding: multiple point winner: modest chaser: stays 3¼m: acts on good to firm and good to soft going. *Stuart Coltherd* **c90**

DAMMIT JANET (IRE) 5 b.m. Beneficial – Exitnell (Exit To Nowhere (USA)) [2017/18 b16s Nov 29] first foal: dam, winning pointer, half-sister to fairly useful hurdler/useful chaser (stays 3¼m) Potters Cross: tailed off in mares bumper: has joined Harry Whittington. *Thomas Cooper, Ireland* **b–**

DAMUT I'M OUT (IRE) 8 b.g. Gamut (IRE) – Five Cents More (IRE) (Flemensfirth (USA)) [2017/18 h24g h16.3g h16.7g h24.8g h20v Feb 14] point winner: poor form over hurdles: should stay beyond 2½m. *Gavin Patrick Cromwell, Ireland* **h78**

DANANDY (IRE) 11 b.g. Cloudings (IRE) – Tower Princess (IRE) (King's Ride) [2017/18 c22.6m⁶ c26m³ c24g⁶ Sep 26] sturdy gelding: winning pointer, including in 2018: winning hurdler: fairly useful handicap chaser: stays 3¼m: acts on good to firm and heavy going: wears headgear: often let down by jumping. *Philip Hobbs* **c120 x h–**

DAN

DANCECRAFT 4 b.f. Mastercraftsman (IRE) – Samba Chryss (IRE) (Galileo (IRE)) [2017/18 b15.7s⁵ b17.7d h21.7g^F h20.7g Apr 24] rather leggy filly: first foal: dam lightly raced on Flat in France: poor form in bumpers: in blinkers, laboured effort in mares event on completed start in novice hurdles. *Gary Moore*   h–
b72

DANCED EVERY DANCE (IRE) 5 b.m. Oscar (IRE) – Kinnegads Pride (IRE) (Be My Native (USA)) [2017/18 b15.6s Jan 19] €3,000 3-y-o: closely related to 2 winners by Old Vic, including fairly useful hurdler/chaser Cavite Beta (17f-21f winner), and half-sister to bumper winner/fairly useful hurdler Bangkok Pete (2½m-3m winner, by Alflora): dam (h75) lightly-raced half-sister to Hennessy Gold Cup winner Trabolgan: 22/1, behind in bumper at Musselburgh. *Donald Whillans*   b–

DANCE FLOOR KING (IRE) 11 b.g. Generous (IRE) – Strawberry Fool (FR) (Tel Quel (FR)) [2017/18 c121, h–: c20.2s c20.2s³ c20.5d⁵ c19.2v⁵ c25.1s^pu c20.5s Apr 9] lengthy gelding: maiden hurdler: useful handicap chaser at one time, largely out of sorts in 2017/18: stays 2½m: acts on good to firm and heavy going: tried in cheekpieces: often races prominently. *Nick Mitchell*   **c104**
h–

DANCE IN THE DUST (IRE) 7 b.g. Scorpion (IRE) – Samotracia (IRE) (Rock of Gibraltar (IRE)) [2017/18 h104: c21.4g^pu May 12] runner-up in Irish point on debut: maiden hurdler: in cheekpieces, pulled up in novice handicap on chasing debut: unproven beyond 2m: dead. *Jonjo O'Neill*   c–
h–

DANCEINTOTHELIGHT 11 gr.g. Dansili – Kali (Linamix (FR)) [2017/18 c–, h108: h19.2g^pu h19.9g* h16.2d² h20d⁶ h19s⁴ h19.3s⁶ h19.9v² h16.8v⁴ h21.2g⁵ Apr 23] sturdy gelding: fair handicap hurdler: won at Sedgefield in August: fell both starts over fences: stays 21f: acts on good to firm and heavy going: tried in cheekpieces: wears tongue tie: free-going front runner: amateur ridden. *Donald McCain*   c–
h107

DANCE OF FIRE 6 b.g. Norse Dancer (IRE) – Strictly Dancing (IRE) (Danehill Dancer (IRE)) [2017/18 h96: h16.2g⁴ h16.2d⁶ h15.6g Dec 18] modest maiden hurdler: stays 19f: acts on good to soft going: no headgear last 2 starts: often races towards rear. *N. W. Alexander*   **h86**

DANCE ROCK 5 b.g. Oasis Dream – Zee Zee Top (Zafonic (USA)) [2017/18 h17.2s² h16.7g² Aug 16] fair maiden on Flat, stayed 1¾m: runner-up both starts in maiden hurdles: dead. *Neil Mulholland*   **h103**

DANCING AMY (IRE) 5 ch.m. Doyen (IRE) – Dew Drop (Halling (USA)) [2017/18 b16.2g⁵ b16s⁵ h15.6s⁵ h16.4s³ h20.5v³ h17d⁵ Mar 31] first foal: dam unraced sister to fairly useful hurdler/fair chaser (2m winner) Stromstad: some promise in bumpers: modest form over hurdles: in tongue tie last 4 starts. *Lucinda Russell*   **h93**
b58

DANCING CONQUEST 8 b.m. Imperial Dancer – Another Conquest (El Conquistador) [2017/18 c–, h–: c17.5v⁴ c25.1v^pu c25.2s^pu c25.7v^F c19.7s^pu c24g⁵ Apr 26] strong mare: well held only start over hurdles: modest maiden chaser: probably stays 3¼m: acts on heavy going: prone to mistakes. *Seamus Mullins*   **c96 x**
h–

DANCING DOUG (IRE) 5 br.g. Kalanisi (IRE) – Drumcay Polly (IRE) (Le Bavard (FR)) [2017/18 b15.7d⁴ b16.8s^su b16.5s³ b17.7s² h15.9s² Apr 15] €8,000 3-y-o: useful-looking gelding: half-brother to several winners, including useful hurdler/high-class chaser Sound Investment (2m-2½m winner, by Dr Massini) and bumper winner/useful hurdler Gagewell Flyer (2m-2½m winner, by Deploy): dam unraced: fair form in bumpers: 5/2, length second to Six Gun Serenade in maiden at Plumpton on hurdling debut: open to improvement. *Sam Thomas*   **h103 p**
b87

DANCING HEARTS 5 b.m. Makfi – Danceabout (Shareef Dancer (USA)) [2017/18 b16d Nov 10] 8,000 3-y-o: sister to fair hurdler Making Shapes (2m winner) and half-sister to 3 winners on Flat: dam smart 7f/1m winner: tailed off in mares bumper. *Michael Scudamore*   b–

DANCING SHADOW (IRE) 9 br.g. Craigsteel – Be My Shadow (IRE) (Torus) [2017/18 c134, h83: h21.6v* c28.8d c32.8s^pu h23.1v⁴ h23.1d³ Apr 24] tall, angular gelding: fairly useful hurdler: won novice at Exeter in November: useful chaser at best: well below form both starts in 2017/18: stays 33f: acts on good to firm and heavy going: usually in headgear: temperamental. *Victor Dartnall*   c– §
h116 §

DANDOLO DU GITE (FR) 5 b.g. Khalkevi (IRE) – Lavande d'Epronière (FR) (Saint Cyrien (FR)) [2017/18 b15.3v³ b13.7s* Apr 6] third foal: dam unraced: runner-up in Irish point on debut: fairly useful form in bumpers: had breathing operation prior to winning at Fontwell (wore tongue tie) in April, staying on well. *Neil Mulholland*   **b102**

DAN

DANDRIDGE 9 ch.g. Doyen (IRE) – Arantxa (Sharpo) [2017/18 c143, h113: c17d c20s c16.8d⁶ c16.5g Apr 21] big, robust gelding: fair hurdler: useful chaser at best: disappointing in 2017/18 (had breathing operation prior to final start): tried in cheekpieces: wears tongue tie: usually races nearer last than first. *A. L. T. Moore, Ireland*   c– h–

DANDY DAN (IRE) 5 b.g. Midnight Legend – Playing Around (Act One) [2017/18 b15.8m* h21.2g* h20.8d² h19.6s⁵ h21.7g³ Apr 20] £34,000 3-y-o: first foal: dam unraced half-sister to fairly useful hurdlers Marcus (2¾m winner) and Tengo Ambro (stayed 2½m) out of National Hunt Chase winner Loving Around: won maiden bumper at Ludlow (by 4½ lengths from Inheritance Thief) in May: fairly useful form over hurdles: won novice at same course in November: disappointing last 2 starts: will stay 3m: in tongue tie last 4 outings: front runner/races prominently. *Kim Bailey*   h126 b99

DANDY DUKE (IRE) 7 b.g. Duke of Marmalade (IRE) – Quest For Eternity (IRE) (Sadler's Wells (USA)) [2017/18 h23.6v* h24s* h22.8v⁴ Dec 30] fairly useful handicap hurdler: won at Chepstow in November and Southwell (amateur event) in December: stayed 25f: best form on soft/heavy going: dead. *Tom George*   h119

DANDY MAG (FR) 5 br.g. Special Kaldoun (IRE) – Naiade Mag (FR) (Kadalko (FR)) [2017/18 h135: h16.5m² h19.4s³ Jun 11] neat gelding: useful form over hurdles: won minor event at Ballinrobe in May: third in Prix Alain du Breil at Auteuil (5 lengths behind Prince Ali) following month: stays 19f: acts on good to firm and heavy going: often leads. *W. P. Mullins, Ireland*   h141

DANDY WALK 4 b.f. Dandy Man (IRE) – Amatara (IRE) (Indian Haven) [2017/18 h16.8v⁵ h17.7v Dec 11] modest maiden on Flat (raced only at 6f): last both starts in juvenile hurdles. *Seamus Mullins*   h–

DANEHILLS WELL (IRE) 10 b.g. Indian Danehill (IRE) – Collatrim Choice (IRE) (Saddlers' Hall (IRE)) [2017/18 c91, h–: c20.1gᵖᵘ Jun 17] winning pointer: maiden hurdler: modest maiden chaser: pulled up only start in 2017/18: stays 2¾m: acts on soft going: wears headgear: tried in tongue tie: front runner/races prominently. *Alison Hamilton*   c– h–

DAN EMMETT (USA) 8 b.g. Flower Alley (USA) – Singing Dixie (USA) (Dixieland Band (USA)) [2017/18 c–, h–: c23.8v⁵ Nov 12] formerly fairly useful hurdler: not taken to chasing: stays 3¼m: acts on heavy going: tried in cheekpieces: often let down by jumping. *Michael Scudamore*   c– x h–

DAN GUN (IRE) 4 b.g. Intikhab (USA) – Lady Magdalena (IRE) (Invincible Spirit (IRE)) [2017/18 h16g h17.7g h16s Nov 7] poor form in juvenile hurdles. *John Joseph Hanlon, Ireland*   h79

DAN MCGRUE (IRE) 6 b.g. Dansant – Aahsaypasty (IRE) (Aahsaylad) [2017/18 h21.4s⁴ h23.9s⁴ h19s* h19s* Jan 20] sixth foal: dam unraced half-sister to useful hurdler/ fair chaser (2½m-3m winner) Rosin The Bow: bumper winner: fairly useful form over hurdles: won novices at Taunton in December and January: tongue tied 3 of last 4 starts: front runner/races prominently. *Paul Nicholls*   h118

DANNY KIRWAN (IRE) 5 b.g. Scorpion (IRE) – Sainte Baronne (FR) (Saint des Saints (FR)) [2017/18 b16g* b17s Apr 13] €19,000 3-y-o: tall gelding: third foal: half-brother to fairly useful hurdler Pilgrim Way (2½m-2¾m winner, by Kalanisi), stayed 3m: dam (b94), placed in bumpers, half-sister to fairly useful French hurdle/chase winner up to 21f Bingo Bell: easily won sole start in Irish maiden points: looked fine prospect when winning bumper at Kempton in February, quickening smartly out wide to lead 2f out: 11/4, possibly amiss in Grade 2 similar event won by Portrush Ted at Aintree 7 weeks later: remains open to plenty of improvement. *Paul Nicholls*   b103 P

DANNY O'RUAIRC (IRE) 6 b.g. Fast Company (IRE) – Tawoos (FR) (Rainbow Quest (USA)) [2017/18 h17.2d h17.2g h30 good-bodied gelding: little form over hurdles: tried in cheekpieces. *James Moffatt*   h–

DANNY THE DANCER 8 ch.g. Indian Haven – Invincible (Slip Anchor) [2017/18 c19.3g May 4] little sign of ability in varied company: tried in cheekpieces. *Mrs Lynne Ward*   c–

DANSEUR DU LARGE (FR) 5 gr.g. Martaline – Antagua (FR) (Cadoudal (FR)) [2017/18 h–, b–: h18.7g⁴ h16.7s⁶ May 20] well beaten in bumper: easily best effort over hurdles (modest form) when fourth in novice at Stratford. *Charlie Longsdon*   h95

DANS LE VENT (FR) 5 b.g. Skins Game – Boreade (FR) (Lost World (IRE)) [2017/18 b104: h15.8g³ h16.4g² h18.6d* h20.5v⁵ h20.6s³ h21.2d² h24.7s⁶ Apr 13] sturdy gelding: bumper winner: fairly useful hurdler: won novice at Market Rasen in November: improved last 3 starts, 21½ lengths sixth of 13 to Santini in Sefton Novices' Hurdle at Aintree final one: stays 25f: acts on heavy going: tried in cheekpieces: usually races close up. *Jamie Snowden*   h129

238

DAR

DANVINNIE 9 b.g. Midnight Legend – Top Gale (IRE) (Topanoora) [2017/18 c90, h–: c20.9g* c20g[pu] Jul 19] maiden hurdler: fair form over fences: won novice handicap at Ffos Las in June: possibly amiss next time: stays 21f: acts on heavy going: in headgear last 4 starts. *Oliver Sherwood* — **c102 h–**

D'ARCY'S SOUND (IRE) 8 b.g. Kalanisi (IRE) – Semillina (IRE) (Semillon) [2017/18 h18.5d[5] h16.7g h16.7v[3] h15.3v[5] h20.3v Feb 5] won Irish maiden point on debut: fair form over hurdles: well beaten in handicaps last 2 outings: unproven beyond 17f: acts on heavy going: usually races close up. *Venetia Williams* — **h103**

DARCY WARD (FR) 5 b.g. Doctor Dino (FR) – Alzasca (FR) (Grape Tree Road) [2017/18 h19s* h21.4v[6] h19m[2] Apr 25] £16,000 3-y-o: third foal: dam, French 13f winner, half-sister to fairly useful hurdler/smart chaser (stays 3½m) Pacha du Polder: winning pointer: fairly useful form in novice hurdles: won at Taunton in January: better effort after when second to Don't Ask at same track: should stay further than 19f. *Jack R. Barber* — **h124**

DAREBIN (GER) 6 ch.g. It's Gino (GER) – Delightful Sofie (GER) (Grand Lodge (USA)) [2017/18 h119: c16m[2] c16g* c16.5g[2] c20d[3] c16.8d[5] c19.5v[5] c15.5s* c16.8s[3] c16.5g[4] Apr 24] lengthy gelding: fairly useful hurdler: fairly useful chaser: won handicaps at Ludlow (novice event) in October and Sandown in March: stays 2¼m: acts on good to firm and heavy going: has worn headgear, including last 3 starts. *Gary Moore* — **c123 h–**

DARES TO DREAM (IRE) 4 br.f. Beneficial – Miss McGoldrick (IRE) (Kasakov) [2017/18 b12.4s Jan 13] third foal: dam, unraced, closely related to smart hurdler/high-class chaser (winner up to 2½m) Mister McGoldrick: well beaten in bumper. *Philip Kirby* — **b–**

DARE TO ACHIEVE 8 b.g. Galileo (IRE) – Mussoorie (FR) (Linamix (FR)) [2017/18 h16.8g[pu] May 10] fair form on hurdling debut: in hood, pulled up both starts since 22 months apart (saddle slipped second time): tried in tongue tie. *Robert Stephens* — **h–**

DARING KNIGHT 5 b.g. Dick Turpin (IRE) – Fairy Slipper (Singspiel (IRE)) [2017/18 h87: h16g[pu] h19.9g h16.3g Oct 21] poor maiden hurdler: left Clare Ellam after first start: best around 2m: acts on good to soft going: normally in headgear: in tongue tie last 2 starts. *Dan Skelton* — **h67**

DARIUS DES BOIS (FR) 5 b.g. Great Pretender (IRE) – Palafixe (FR) (Valanour (IRE)) [2017/18 h21.6d[5] h21.6d h21.2s h24.2s* h24.3g[2] Apr 20] tall gelding: chasing type: fourth foal: dam French maiden (second in 2¼m chase): unplaced on completed start in Irish points: fairly useful form over hurdles: won handicap at Newbury in March: further progress when second in novice handicap at Ayr: stays 3m: acts on soft going. *Nicky Henderson* — **h123**

DARK AND DANGEROUS (IRE) 10 b.g. Cacique (IRE) – Gilah (IRE) (Saddlers' Hall (IRE)) [2017/18 c–, h104: h16.2d[4] h16.2g h16.8s[2] h19.9s[5] h21.2v[5] h19.3s[6] h16.8v[2] h16v[4] h17s Apr 8] compact gelding: modest handicap hurdler: winning chaser: unproven beyond 17f: acts on heavy going: often wears headgear: tried in tongue tie: front runner/races prominently. *Simon Waugh* — **c– h97**

DARK ASTER 6 b.m. Alflora (IRE) – Westbourne (IRE) (King's Ride) [2017/18 h16.7v[4] h21s[3] h24v[5] Feb 14] placed in points: fair form over hurdles: best effort when third in mares novice at Warwick in January: wore hood: dead. *Richard Mitford-Slade* — **h103**

DARK ENEMY (IRE) 5 b.g. Dark Angel (IRE) – Headborough Lass (IRE) (Invincible Spirit (IRE)) [2017/18 h–: h16.8d[pu] Sep 11] sturdy gelding: little form over hurdles: tried in cheekpieces: in tongue tie last 4 starts. *Brendan Powell* — **h–**

DARK FLAME (IRE) 9 b.g. Gold Well – Glorys Flame (IRE) (Flemensfirth (USA)) [2017/18 c136, h–: c23.8g[4] Nov 4] strong gelding: winning hurdler: useful chaser: fourth in Sodexo Gold Cup (Handicap Chase) at Ascot, sole outing in 2017/18: stays 3m: has form on heavy going, possibly better suited by less testing conditions: usually races nearer last than first. *Richard Rowe* — **c129 h–**

DARK FORCE (FR) 5 gr.g. Gris de Gris (IRE) – Maciga (FR) (Gunboat Diplomacy (FR)) [2017/18 b64p: h16.8v[3] Apr 17] some promise in bumper/maiden hurdle. *Venetia Williams* — **h76 p**

DARK INVADER (FR) 6 b.g. Saint des Saints (FR) – Minirose (FR) (Mansonnien (FR)) [2017/18 h91: h20v[3] h20v[4] h15.5v[4] h19.5s[4] Mar 22] sturdy gelding: fair form over hurdles: stays 2½m. *Evan Williams* — **h100**

DARK MAHLER (IRE) 7 b.g. Mahler – Aries Rambler (IRE) (Shernazar) [2017/18 h94: c16g* c20s[6] Jan 10] third in Irish point on debut: modest form over hurdles: much better form when winning novice handicap at Ludlow on chasing debut: shaped like non-stayer in similar event there 8 weeks later: may prove best at around 2m: tried in tongue tie. *Emma Lavelle* — **c111 h–**

DAR

DARK SUNSET (IRE) 7 b.m. Scorpion (IRE) – Wilmott's Fancy (Buckley) [2017/18 h19.9d* h19.6g* h19.3v⁴ h20.5v⁵ h20.5d⁴ h24.4d* h25.3d⁴ h21.4v⁴ Mar 10] £8,000 6-y-o: sixth foal: half-sister to 3 winners, including bumper winner Alexander Seaview (by Bob Back) and fairly useful hurdler Lough Cuan (2m winner, by Zaffaran), stayed 3m: dam (h118), bumper/17f-19f hurdle winner, half-sister to winning hurdler/smart chaser (stayed 25f) Percy Smollett: runner-up in Irish maiden points: fair hurdler: won mares maiden at Uttoxeter in July, novice at Bangor (finished alone) in August and mares handicap at Doncaster in December: stays 25f: acts on heavy going: front runner/races prominently. *Donald McCain* — **h109**

DARK VALLEY (IRE) 8 b.g. Lend A Hand – Glorys Flame (IRE) (Flemensfirth (USA)) [2017/18 c24.2s³ Dec 27] placed twice from 3 starts in Irish maiden points in 2016: tailed-off last of 3 in novice on chasing debut. *Micky Hammond* — **c88 ?**

DARLAC (FR) 5 b.g. Lucarno (USA) – Pail Mel (FR) (Sleeping Car (FR)) [2017/18 b15.3d Apr 22] €42,000 3-y-o, £65,000 4-y-o: sixth foal: half-brother to fairly useful hurdler/smart chaser Alcala (2¼m-3¼m winner, by Turgeon) and French hurdler/chaser Bon Cheval (17f/2¼m winner, by Laverock): dam unraced half-sister to useful hurdler/winning chaser (2m-21f winner) Sang Bleu: runner-up on second start in Irish points: 10/1, seventh in bumper at Wincanton (10 lengths behind Ebony Gale). *Colin Tizzard* — **b83**

DARLING ALKO (FR) 5 b.g. Al Namix (FR) – Padalko Tatou (FR) (Kadalko (FR)) [2017/18 b14.9d* b16.8s Feb 23] first foal: dam French maiden: won bumper (maiden event) at Senonnes-Pouance on debut: left A. Lamotte d'Argy and 9/4, hung left when disappointing in similar race at Exeter 4 months later. *Colin Tizzard* — **b?**

DARLING DU LARGE (FR) 5 b.m. Kapgarde (FR) – Dissidente (FR) (Double Bed (FR)) [2017/18 b16.6s² b17s Apr 12] well-made mare: half-sister to French 6.5f winner Parisis (by Le Fou) and French 7.5f winner Bizertin (by Great Pretender): dam, French 1m-9.5f winner, half-sister to fairly useful hurdler/very smart chaser (stayed 2¾m) Mail de Bievre: better effort in mares bumpers (fair form) when second at Doncaster on debut: stiffer task in Grade 2 event at Aintree 11 weeks later. *Tom George* — **b92**

DARLING MALTAIX (FR) 5 b.g. Voix du Nord (FR) – Rosalie Malta (FR) (Lavirco (GER)) [2017/18 b16.8d⁵ h16.8g⁵ h16.5m³ h19gᶠ h16v h18.5d² Apr 24] tall gelding: second foal: dam placed in French bumpers at 12.5f: successful at Vichy on first of 2 starts in bumpers: fair form over hurdles: bred to be suited by further than 17f: acts on good to firm going: in hood last 5 starts: tried in tongue tie: usually races towards rear: headstrong. *Paul Nicholls* — **h111 b–**

DARLOA (IRE) 9 br.g. Darsi (FR) – Lady Lola (IRE) (Supreme Leader) [2017/18 h76: h16.8d h15.8d² h19g c18.2m⁶ Apr 25] poor maiden hurdler: well-held sixth in novice handicap at Taunton on chasing debut: unproven beyond 2m: acts on good to soft going: usually in headgear: wears tongue tie. *Victor Dartnall* — **c– h73**

DARLYN 5 b.m. Authorized (IRE) – Darariyna (IRE) (Shirley Heights) [2017/18 b16.2v⁴ Apr 10] closely related to bumper winner/fairly useful hurdler Jurby (15f/2m winner, by Motivator) and half-sister to several winners, including fairly useful hurdler/useful chaser Darenjan (2m-21f winner, by Alhaarth): dam 1½m-13.4f winner: 4/1, green when fourth of 6 in bumper at Hereford (20½ lengths behind Geordie B). *Henry Oliver* — **b58**

DARRY DESBOIS (FR) 5 ch.g. Ballingarry (IRE) – Tiwa (FR) (Dom Pasquini (FR)) [2017/18 b15.7s Feb 12] tailed off in bumper. *Martin Todhunter* — **b–**

DARSI IN THE PARK (IRE) 5 b.g. Darsi (FR) – Rock In The Park (IRE) (Rock Hopper) [2017/18 b16.6s Feb 21] won on completed start in Irish points: 14/1, well beaten in bumper. *Jonjo O'Neill* — **b–**

DARTAGNAN LE DUN (FR) 5 b.g. Kapgarde (FR) – Silvazeyra (FR) (Sheyrann) [2017/18 h17.9s⁴ h17.9s c17.4d⁵ c17.4s⁶ h16s h19.9vᵖᵘ h16.7s h15.8v Apr 7] fourth foal: half-brother to useful French hurdler/fairly useful chaser Alabama Le Dun (15f-2¼m winner, by Network): dam, French 2m/2¼m hurdle/chase winner, sister to useful French hurdler/chaser (15f-2½m winner) Silver Top: modest maiden hurdler: better effort in 4-y-o handicap chases at Auteuil when fifth: left J-P. Gallorini after fourth start: stays 2¼m: acts on soft going: in tongue tie last 2 starts. *Alex Hales* — **c105 h95**

DARTFORD WARBLER (IRE) 11 b.g. Overbury (IRE) – Stony View (IRE) (Tirol) [2017/18 c108, h103: c20v⁶ h23.3d² c20d⁵ c19.3s⁴ c21.4v⁴ c19.2s² c20.3g Apr 20] compact gelding: fair handicap hurdler/chaser: stays 23f: acts on heavy going: tried in cheekpieces: races prominently: best treated with caution. *Sue Smith* — **c96 § h100**

DAV

DARTMOOR GIRL (IRE) 4 b.f. So You Think (NZ) – Preveza (FR) (Dalakhani (IRE)) [2017/18 h15.3g h16.8v³ h16.5⁶ h16.8v⁵ Feb 11] poor maiden on Flat: no form over hurdles: in tongue tie last 2 starts. *Mark Gillard* h–

DARWINS FOX (FR) 12 b.g. Kahyasi – Parcelle de Sou (FR) (Ajdayt (USA)) [2017/18 c129, h–: c17.4s* c17d⁵ Jun 9] sturdy gelding: winning hurdler: fairly useful hunter chaser: won at Fontwell in May: best up to 2½m: acts on good to firm and heavy going: tried in cheekpieces: has worn tongue tie. *David Christie, Ireland* c126 h–

DARWINS THEORY (IRE) 10 b.g. Montjeu (IRE) – Thrift (IRE) (Green Desert (USA)) [2017/18 c–, h107: h16m³ h15.9d³ Feb 26] fair handicap hurdler: maiden chaser: stays 2¾m: acts on good to firm and heavy going: has worn headgear: wears tongue tie. *Fiona Shaw* c– h91

DASHEL DRASHER 5 b.g. Passing Glance – So Long (Nomadic Way (USA)) [2017/18 b15.3v* b16.4s b15.3d⁶ Apr 22] good-topped gelding: third foal: half-brother to fair hurdler Popping Along (19f/2½m winner, by Volochine): dam winning pointer: fairly useful form in bumpers: won at Wincanton in February. *Jeremy Scott* b98

DASHING OSCAR (IRE) 8 b.g. Oscar (IRE) – Be My Leader (IRE) (Supreme Leader) [2017/18 h126: h19.2g* h19.6s* h21d h19.8s⁴ Apr 28] lengthy gelding: useful handicap hurdler: won at Fontwell in October and Bangor (by 1¾ lengths from Clondaw Kaempfer) in November: stays 2½m: acts on heavy going: wears tongue tie: front runner/races prominently. *Harry Fry* h133

DASHING PERK 7 b.g. Kayf Tara – Dashing Executive (IRE) (Executive Perk) [2017/18 h113p, b94: h23.9g^F h21.4v* h23.4v h20s⁴ h19.8v^pu Mar 10] big, strong gelding: won Irish maiden point on debut: fairly useful form over hurdles: won novice at Wincanton in January: stays 3m: acts on heavy going: tried in cheekpieces: usually races prominently. *Dr Richard Newland* h118

DASSETT GOLD (FR) 5 b.g. Full of Gold (FR) – Marsavrile (FR) (April Night (FR)) [2017/18 b85: b16g⁶ h16.3d h23.3v^pu h21m^pu Apr 26] compact gelding: modest form in bumpers: no form over hurdles: tried in cheekpieces. *Paul Webber* h– b–

DAULYS ANTHEM (IRE) 10 br.g. Royal Anthem (USA) – Over Dubai (Overbury (IRE)) [2017/18 c94, h–: c19.4g* c17.4g* c16.3g⁵ Sep 2] maiden hurdler: fairly useful handicap chaser: left David Dennis, vastly improved when winning at Stratford and Bangor in August: lacklustre effort final start: barely stays 3m, and at least as effective around 2m: acts on soft going: tongue tied in 2017/18: usually races prominently. *Dan Skelton* c120 h–

DAUPHINE EREINE (FR) 6 b.m. Saint des Saints (FR) – Bellissima de Mai (FR) (Pistolet Bleu (IRE)) [2017/18 c109p, h–: c23.8d² c19.4s³ Apr 27] maiden hurdler: fairly useful form over fences: placed in handicaps at Ludlow and Chepstow in 2017/18: stays 3m: acts on soft going. *David Pipe* c126 h–

DAUPHINESS 6 b.m. Lucarno (USA) – Princess Angelique (FR) (Sagacity (FR)) [2017/18 b–: b16.7s h21.2g⁶ h19.6s h19.7s⁵ Jan 16] little form in bumpers/over hurdles. *Henry Daly* h56 b–

DAVERON (IRE) 10 b.g. Winged Love (IRE) – Double Doc (IRE) (Moonax (IRE)) [2017/18 c114, h94: h21g^pu h19s^pu h20.7s⁶ c16.1v c20.2v^pu c19.2v³ Apr 17] workmanlike gelding: fairly useful handicap hurdler/chaser in prime: regressed further in 2017/18: left Ben Pauling after fourth start: stays 21f: acts on heavy going: tried in headgear. *Richard Price* c71 h63

DAVE THE RAVE (IRE) 8 b.g. Craigsteel – Coolharbour Lady (IRE) (Lord Americo) [2017/18 h18.5d Oct 12] tailed off in bumper (for Ronald Thompson) and novice hurdle (hooded) 20 months apart. *Nicky Martin* h–

DAVID JOHN 7 b.g. Overbury (IRE) – Molly's Secret (Minshaanshu Amad (USA)) [2017/18 h96: c16.5g* c20.1g⁴ c20.3g³ c24g³ c24d² h23.1v^pu Nov 7] sturdy gelding: modest hurdler: fair form over fences: won novice handicap at Worcester in June: stays 3m: acts on good to soft going: has worn headgear, including last 3 starts: tried in tongue tie. *Tom Lacey* c108 h–

DAVIDS CHARM (IRE) 7 b.g. Milan – Have More (Haafhd) [2017/18 h20d* h21g* h16v² h16s* Dec 3] first foal: dam, lightly raced on Flat, half-sister to useful hurdler/very smart chaser (stayed 33f) Junior: well held only start on Flat: useful handicap hurdler: vast h137 p progress in 2017/18, winning at Listowel in June, Galway in August and Fairyhouse (by 2¾ lengths from Meri Devie) in December: stays 21f: acts on heavy going: in headgear last 4 starts: often travels strongly: likely to improve further. *John J. Walsh, Ireland*

DAVID'S PHOEBE (IRE) 5 br.m. Dubai Destination (USA) – Miss Compliance (IRE) (Broken Hearted) [2017/18 b16.8m^5 h16.7g^2 h16g^4 h16s* h19.4d Dec 15] £5,000 3-y-o: seventh foal: half-sister to fairly useful hurdler/useful chaser Bally Beaufort (2½m-25f winner, by Old Vic) and fairly useful hurdler Birch Hill (17f-21f winner, by Kalanisi): dam unraced half-sister to Grand National winner Comply Or Die: well beaten in mares bumper: fair form over hurdles: won mares handicap at Worcester in November: should stay beyond 2m: races prominently. *Tom Lacey*   h107 b–

DAWERANN (IRE) 9 b.g. Medicean – Dawera (IRE) (Spinning World (USA)) [2017/18 c16.3g^2 c16g^6 c16g^5 h16.2g^3 h23.9m^2 h23.9d^3 h23.9v^5 Sep 27] fair handicap hurdler: fair maiden chaser: effective from 2m to 3m: acts on good to firm and heavy going: has worn headgear, including last 5 starts: tried in tongue tie: often races towards rear. *Gordon Elliott, Ireland*   c111 h113

DAWNIERIVER (IRE) 8 br.m. Indian River (FR) – In Sin (IRE) (Insan (USA)) [2017/18 c111, h–: c21.1g^4 c23.9g c24g^2 c23g c25.2g^3 c24.2s^5 c24s^4 c23.9s^{pu} Feb 18] lengthy, rather sparely-made mare: maiden hurdler: fair handicap chaser: stays 3¼m: acts on soft and good to firm going: normally in cheekpieces: usually races towards rear. *Michael Scudamore*   c106 h–

DAWN MISSILE 6 b.g. Nayef (USA) – Ommadawn (IRE) (Montjeu (IRE)) [2017/18 h110: h23.3d^5 h25g Oct 17] good-topped gelding: fair form over hurdles: should stay beyond 2½m: acts on good to soft going: tried in cheekpieces: in tongue tie last 3 starts. *Nigel Twiston-Davies*   h93

DAWN SHADOW (IRE) 6 b.m. King's Theatre (IRE) – Corskeagh Shadow (IRE) (Beneficial) [2017/18 b16g^4 b16v^4 h18.9v^5 h19.8s* h18.2s^2 h16s* h16v^3 h20s^3 h18v^3 h16.8s^F h20v^4 h16.2d* Apr 26] sturdy mare: second foal: sister to a winning pointer: dam, bumper winner, sister to useful hurdler/fair chaser (stayed 2½m) Shadow Eile and fairly useful chaser (stays 29f) He Rock's: fairly useful bumper performer: fairly useful hurdler: won mares events at Clonmel (maiden) and Thurles in November, and Punchestown (listed novice, by length from Creation) in April: placed also in EBF Mares Hurdle at Leopardstown and Solerina Mares Novices' Hurdle at Fairyhouse (19 lengths behind Laurina): stays 2½m: acts on heavy going: usually races prominently. *Mrs D. A. Love, Ireland*   h127 b96

DAWN'S LITTLE LADY 6 b.m. Dr Massini (IRE) – Kopylova (Moscow Society (USA)) [2017/18 b16.8v^4 b16v^5 h21.6v^{pu} Apr 17] first foal: dam (h96), 19f-3m hurdle winner, half-sister to fairly useful chaser (stayed 3m) Merchant Royal: little show in bumpers/novice hurdle. *Sarah Robinson*   h– b–

DAWSON CITY 9 b.g. Midnight Legend – Running For Annie (Gunner B) [2017/18 c131, h–: c28.4v^4 c24.2v^{pu} c26.7v^3 c30.7s* c26s^2 c28.8d^6 Apr 28] sturdy gelding: winning hurdler: useful handicap chaser: won at Exeter (by 2 lengths from Shotgun Paddy) in February: good second at Newbury (8 lengths behind progressive Thomas Patrick) following month: out-and-out stayer: best form on soft/heavy going: has worn cheekpieces. *Polly Gundry*   c132 h–

DAYDREAM AULMES (FR) 5 b.g. Linda's Lad – My Wish Aulmes (FR) (Lyphard's Wish (FR)) [2017/18 b16g^4 b15.8d^2 b16.6s* Feb 21] €16,000 3-y-o, £15,000 4-y-o: half-brother to several winners, including fairly useful hurdler/useful chaser Ut Majeur Aulmes (2m winner, by Northern Park): dam French maiden: runner-up in point: fair form in bumpers: won at Doncaster in February: will stay at least 2½m. *Graeme McPherson*   b91

DAYDREAM ISLAND (IRE) 8 b.g. Trans Island – Ring Hill (Bering) [2017/18 c61, h–: c20.1g^6 c23.8g^3 c24.2g^{pu} h23.9g^6 c21.2s$^{p.t}$ h21.2g c23.8d^6 Mar 16] maiden hurdler: poor and error-prone maiden chaser: stays 3m: acts on heavy going: tried in hood. *Sheena Walton*   c70 x h–

DAY IN PARADISE 7 b.m. Tobougg (IRE) – Sunnyland (Sovereign Water (FR)) [2017/18 h–: h23.6v^5 h23.6v^{pu} Feb 2] poor form over hurdles. *Robert Stephens*   h67

DAYLAMI DAYS (IRE) 7 gr.g. Daylami (IRE) – Euro Gypsy (IRE) (Eurobus) [2017/18 h81p: h20g Jun 3] runner-up completed start in maiden points: better effort over hurdles when 11½ lengths behind 4 to Garo de Juilley in novice at Taunton in 2016/17: well beaten 2 months later. *Philip Hobbs*   h–

DEA

DAYLAMI KIRK (IRE) 7 b.g. Daylami (IRE) – Uptothefrontkirk (IRE) (Bob Back (USA)) [2017/18 b81: h19s h15.3v^{ro} h16.8v^4 Apr 17] tall, good-topped gelding: modest form in bumpers: some promise over hurdles: headstrong sort, makes running/races prominently: no easy ride (ran out second start). *Ron Hodges*   **h74**

DAY OF ROSES (IRE) 9 b.g. Acambaro (GER) – Dan's Choice (IRE) (Spanish Place (USA)) [2017/18 c–, h80: c25.5d* c25.5d* Jun 6] Irish point winner: poor form over hurdles: soon developed into much better chaser, winning handicaps at Fontwell in May and June (novice event, again easily): stays 25f: acts on heavy going. *Jeremy Scott*   **c100 h–**

DAYS OF HEAVEN (FR) 8 b.g. Saint des Saints (FR) – Daramour (FR) (Anabaa Blue) [2017/18 c143p, h122+: c19.4g^4 c20g^4 c21.4g c20.9g^4 c20.4s^{pu} c20.8g Apr 18] sturdy gelding: fairly useful hurdler: smart handicap chaser: won at Stratford and Uttoxeter (by 1½ lengths from Valseur du Granval) in May: stays 21f: acts on soft going: wears hood: free-going front runner: signs of temperament (edgy sort who has given trouble at start). *Nicky Henderson*   **c148 h–**

DAYTIME AHEAD (IRE) 7 gr.m. Daylami (IRE) – Bright Times Ahead (IRE) (Rainbows For Life (CAN)) [2017/18 h85: h21.6g^4 h19.8s* h20.5d^2 h21.4v^2 h19.5v^4 h23.9v^{pu} h20.5v^{ur} h21.4v^3 Apr 9] fair handicap hurdler: won at Wincanton in November and March: stays 2¾m: acts on heavy going: races towards rear. *Ron Hodges*   **h109**

DAZIBAO (FR) 5 ch.g. Muhaymin (USA) – Adjinne (FR) (Octagonal (NZ)) [2017/18 ab16g* b17s Apr 13] £58,000 3-y-o: smallish gelding: half-brother to 2 winners on Flat in France, including 6f-12.5f winner Riviera Paradise (by Tiger Hill): dam placed at 7f/1m in France: fair form when winning bumper at Lingfield in March: much stiffer task following month. *George Baker*   **b93**

DAZZLING OSCAR (IRE) 5 b.g. Oscar (IRE) – Zarinava (IRE) (Daylami (IRE)) [2017/18 b16d^6 Oct 15] well beaten in bumper: dead. *Jonjo O'Neill*   **b–**

DEADLY APPROACH 7 b.g. New Approach (IRE) – Speirbhean (IRE) (Danehill (USA)) [2017/18 c125, h86: c16m^3 c15.2d^{pu} Oct 18] maiden hurdler: fairly useful handicap chaser: raced around 2m: acts on good to soft going: has worn hood: wears tongue tie: front runner/races prominently. *Sarah-Jayne Davies*   **c111 h–**

DEADLY MOVE (IRE) 9 b.g. Scorpion (IRE) – Sounds Attractive (IRE) (Rudimentary (USA)) [2017/18 c111, h100: c23.8g^2 c24d^3 c24.1g^3 c20.3g* c24d Oct 3] strong gelding: multiple point winner: maiden hurdler: fair handicap chaser: won at Bangor in September: stays 3m: acts on heavy going: wears headgear/tongue tie: ungenuine. *Peter Bowen*   **c106 § h–**

DEADLY STING (IRE) 9 b.g. Scorpion (IRE) – Gaza Strip (IRE) (Hamas (IRE)) [2017/18 c–, h–: c20.9v^2 c21s^5 Mar 25] lengthy gelding: winning hurdler: fairly useful chaser at best: lightly raced and below form since 2015/16 stays 23f: acts on heavy going: wears cheekpieces: in tongue tie last 4 starts. *Paul H. Webb*   **c107 h–**

DEAL D'ESTRUVAL (FR) 5 b.g. Balko (FR) – Option d'Estruval (FR) (Epervier Bleu) [2017/18 h21v* h16s^2 h20.3v h16s^4 Apr 27] fifth foal: half-brother to useful hurdler Aurore d'Estruval (2m-2½m winner, by Nickname): dam, French 17f hurdle winner, half-sister to smart French chaser Garde d'Estruval: useful hurdler: won maiden at Tramore in January: best effort when second in Coral Hurdle (Handicap) at Leopardstown (1¼ lengths behind Off You Go) following month: stays 21f: acts on heavy going: often travels strongly: remains with potential. *W. P. Mullins, Ireland*   **h134 p**

DEALING RIVER 11 b.g. Avonbridge – Greensand (Green Desert (USA)) [2017/18 c111, h85: h16g h16.3m c17g^{pu} Sep 9] fair handicap hurdler/chaser: out of sorts in 2017/18: usually in cheekpieces: tried in tongue tie. *Caroline Bailey*   **c– h–**

DEANS ROAD (IRE) 9 ch.g. Golan (IRE) – Close To Home (IRE) (Be My Native (USA)) [2017/18 c136, h–: c19d* c22.5g c20.5g Aug 26] workmanlike gelding: point winner: successful only start over hurdles: useful handicap chaser: won at Listowel in June: below form both starts after: likely to stay 3m: acts on heavy going. *Henry de Bromhead, Ireland*   **c138 h–**

DEAR SIRE (FR) 6 gr.g. Al Namix (FR) – Polismith (FR) (Poliglote) [2017/18 h121, b95: h16.2g^5 h17.2d^4 h16.5g^5 h16.2g^2 h16.3m* h16.2d^2 h16.2s* h16.3g* h16.7g^5 h19.5d^4 h15.6d^F h15.6s* h16.5s^2 Apr 14] useful hurdler: won 5 times in 2017/18, including handicaps at Perth in August, Stratford in September and Musselburgh (by ¾ length from Forth Bridge) in February: stays 19f: acts on soft and good to firm going: wears hood: often races prominently. *Donald McCain*   **h137**

Bar One Racing Drinmore Novices' Chase, Fairyhouse—Death Duty maintains an unbeaten start to his chasing career with this clear-cut victory over Rathvinden (diamonds) and Snow Falcon

DEATH DUTY (IRE) 7 b.g. Shantou (USA) – Midnight Gift (IRE) (Presenting) [2017/18 h148: c23s* c18d* c20s* c17d^F Dec 26] well-made gelding: winning pointer: smart form over hurdles: quickly reached similar level over fences: won maiden at Tipperary and Buck House Novices' Chase at Punchestown in October and Drinmore Novices' Chase at Fairyhouse (by 3¼ lengths from Rathvinden) in December: 7/4, held in third when fell last in Racing Post Novices' Chase won by Footpad at Leopardstown final outing: missed remainder of season due to damaged ligaments: stays 23f, effective at shorter: acts on heavy going: usually races close up. *Gordon Elliott, Ireland*   **c154 +**   **h–**

DEAUVILLE CRYSTAL (FR) 5 b.m. Raven's Pass (USA) – Top Crystal (IRE) (Sadler's Wells (USA)) [2017/18 h123: c20d^6 c19.3g^3 c20s^3 c23.8d^4 h20.3s^{pu} h23.8s^{pu} Jan 18] good-topped mare: fairly useful hurdler at best: pulled up both starts in 2017/18: fair form over fences: stays 3m: acts on heavy going: tried in visor: wears tongue tie. *Nigel Hawke*   **c112**   **h–**

DEAUVILLE DANCER (IRE) 7 b.g. Tamayuz – Mathool (IRE) (Alhaarth (IRE)) [2017/18 h105: c16.5s^2 c16.5g* c16.3s* c16g^4 c16.5g^4 c17m^2 h20g^4 c19.9g* c16.3g* c19.1d* c20.8s c16s^4 c21.1s c20d^4 Apr 28] compact gelding: fair handicap hurdler: useful handicap chaser: won 5 times in 2017/18, beating Derintoher Yank 13 lengths in 3-runner novice event at Doncaster for final success: stays easy 21f: acts on heavy going: wears tongue tie. *David Dennis*   **c134**   **h100**

DEBACLE 5 b.g. Bach (IRE) – De Blanc (IRE) (Revoque (IRE)) [2017/18 h16.3d h18.6v Jan 17] sturdy gelding: well beaten both starts over hurdles. *James Eustace*   **h–**

DEBDEBDEB 8 b.m. Teofilo (IRE) – Windmill (Ezzoud (IRE)) [2017/18 h132: c20.1g* c24g* c23.9g^5 Nov 9] compact mare: useful hurdler: similar form over fences: won first 2 starts, namely novices at Hexham in May and Uttoxeter in September: last of 5 finishers behind Mia's Storm in listed mares novice at Market Rasen final outing: stays 3m: acts on soft going: has worn hood: front runner/races prominently. *Dan Skelton*   **c136**   **h–**

DEBECE 7 b.g. Kayf Tara – Dalamine (FR) (Sillery (USA)) [2017/18 h145: h24.7s^4 Apr 14] strong gelding: very much the type to make a chaser: useful handicap hurdler: lightly raced: off a year, fourth in Grade 3 at Aintree (11 lengths behind Mr Big Shot) only outing in 2017/18: stays 25f: acts on soft going: front runner/races prominently, usually travels strongly. *Tim Vaughan*   **h137**

DE BENE ESSE (IRE) 8 br.g. Scorpion (IRE) – Benedicta Rose (IRE) (Beneficial) [2017/18 c–, h–: c20.9s h23.9v^3 h21.9v* h23.1v^{pu} h19.5s Apr 27] workmanlike gelding: point winner: fair handicap hurdler: won at Ffos Las in April: no form in chases since winning novice at Exeter (match) on chasing debut in 2015/16: trained on 2017/18 reappearance only by Miss C. Packwood: stays 2¾m: best form on heavy going: often in headgear, including last 4 outings: often races in rear. *Adrian Wintle*   **c–**   **h100**

DEE

DE BLACKSMITH (IRE) 10 b.g. Brian Boru – Gift of The Gab (IRE) (Orchestra) [2017/18 c20.5g^{pu} c25.5d^3 Jun 6] good-topped gelding: point/hurdles winner: fairly useful maiden chaser at best: well below form both starts in 2017/18: stays 25f: acts on heavy going: usually in headgear: has had tongue tied: temperamental. *Gary Moore* — **c88 §**, **h–**

DE BOITRON (FR) 14 b.g. Sassanian (USA) – Pondiki (Sicyos (USA)) [2017/18 c32.5d May 5] compact gelding: has had breathing operation: point winner: winning hurdler: formerly smart handicap chaser: has deteriorated, though trip too far when well beaten in hunter only start in 2017/18: stays 25f, effective at much shorter: acts on good to firm and heavy going: tried in tongue tie. *Mrs Janet Ackner* — **c86**, **h–**

DEBROUILLARD (FR) 5 b.g. Irish Wells (FR) – Indecise (FR) (Cyborg (FR)) [2017/18 b16d Apr 26] rather unfurnished gelding: very green in bumper at Warwick. *Oliver Greenall* — **b56**

DEBUCHET (FR) 5 gr.g. Smadoun (FR) – Luzerne du Poitou (FR) (Royal Charter (FR)) [2017/18 b114: h16d^4 h16s^6 h16.4s h20s^F Apr 27] sturdy gelding: useful bumper performer: useful form over hurdles: highly tried last 3 starts, running creditably when falling 2 out in Grade 1 novice won by Dortmund Park final one: usually races close up. *Ms Margaret Mullins, Ireland* — **h135**

DECADE PLAYER (IRE) 10 b.g. Gamut – Ballindante (IRE) (Phardante (FR)) [2017/18 c113, h–: c17d^6 Jun 9] compact gelding: point/hurdles winner: fairly useful chaser at best: no form in hunters since early-2016/17: stays 19f: acts on soft and good to firm going: often in headgear: wears tongue tied: front runner/races prominently. *Miss Kelly Morgan* — **c64**, **h–**

DECIMUS (IRE) 11 b.g. Bienamado (USA) – Catch Me Dreaming (IRE) (Safety Catch (USA)) [2017/18 c–x, h111§: h25.6g^5 h26.5g^5 h26.5d Jul 23] lengthy, useful-looking gelding: fair handicap hurdler: winning chaser: stays 3¼m: acts on heavy and good to firm going: wears headgear: temperamental. *Jeremy Scott* — **c– x**, **h96 §**

DECKERS DELIGHT 7 b.m. Tobougg (IRE) – Oleana (IRE) (Alzao (USA)) [2017/18 h97: c20d^{pu} h20v^{pu} h23.9s h23.9v h23.9s^{ur} h23.1v Apr 8] poor handicap hurdler: pulled up in novice handicap on chasing debut: stays 3¼m: acts on heavy going: often in headgear: in tongue tie last 4 starts: usually races towards rear. *Nigel Hawke* — **c–**, **h69**

DECK OF CARDS (IRE) 6 br.g. Daylami (IRE) – Miss Edgehill (IRE) (Idris (IRE)) [2017/18 b16.5s Jan 9] tailed off in bumper. *Arthur Whiting* — **b–**

DE CLARE MAN 9 b.g. Kayf Tara – Douce Maison (IRE) (Fools Holme (USA)) [2017/18 h21d Nov 13] won twice in points: tailed off in novice on hurdling debut. *Diana Grissell* — **h–**

DE DANU'S BACH (IRE) 8 b.m. Bach (IRE) – The Dara Queen (Dara Monarch) [2017/18 h21.5v^{pu} h23.8s^5 c24v^4 h20v^6 c23v^{pu} Mar 29] half-sister to bumper winner/fairly useful chaser Pollardsfield (2m winner, by Arcane) and fair hurdler Rocky Ryan (23f winner, by Even Top): dam, 2m hurdle winner, also 1¼m winner on Flat: poor maiden on Flat: point winner: poor maiden hurdler: poor form over fences: best effort at 2½m: acts on soft going: tried in hood. *Nigel Slevin, Ireland* — **c61**, **h69**

DEDIGOUT (IRE) 12 b.g. Bob Back (USA) – Dainty Daisy (IRE) (Buckskin (FR)) [2017/18 c–, h143: c23.4v^{pu} c24.2s^{pu} h21.4v h19.7s h19.3v^6 h24.1v^4 h24.3v^2 h24.3v^2 h24.1v^5 h20.6v^4 Apr 15] big, deep-girthed gelding: fairly useful handicap hurdler nowadays: winning chaser: stays 3m: acts on heavy going: wears cheekpieces/tongue tie: usually races close up: signs of temperament. *Micky Hammond* — **c–**, **h121**

DE DOLLAR MAN (IRE) 7 ch.g. Vinnie Roe (IRE) – Dollar Bay (IRE) (Beau Sher) [2017/18 h138, b103: c24.2v^4 c19.2v* c19.4s^2 c19.2s^4 Mar 7] tall, lengthy gelding: bumper winner: useful hurdler: useful form over fences: won handicap at Exeter (by 5 lengths from Earthmoves) in December: should stay beyond 2½m: best form on soft/heavy going: usually races prominently. *Evan Williams* — **c133**, **h–**

DEDUCE (FR) 5 b.m. Iffraaj – Count The Cost (USA) (Cozzene (USA)) [2017/18 h–: h15.8d h15.6s Dec 5] poor form over hurdles: raced around 2m: acts on soft going. *James Eustace* — **h81**

DEEBAJ (IRE) 6 br.g. Authorized (IRE) – Athreyaa (Singspiel (IRE)) [2017/18 h103: h21.9g* h21.7s h19d Apr 26] lengthy gelding: fair handicap hurdler: won at Ffos Las in June: left Alexandra Dunn after second start: stays 2¾m: acts on heavy going: tried in visor/tongue tie: waited with. *Gary Moore* — **h109**

DEEP RESOLVE (IRE) 7 b.g. Intense Focus (USA) – I'll Be Waiting (Vettori (IRE)) [2017/18 h–: h18.6v Jan 17] fair on Flat (stays 1½m): fair hurdler at best: lightly raced and little form since 2014/15: stays 2¼m: best form on heavy going. *Sally Haynes* — **h–**

BetBright Trial Cotswold Chase, Cheltenham—a strong staying display by Definitly Red as he lowers the colours of market principals American and the grey Bristol de Mai

DEEPSAND (IRE) 9 br.g. Footstepsinthesand – Sinamay (USA) (Saint Ballado (CAN)) [2017/18 h114: h16.2g³ May 18] fair handicap hurdler: raced around 2m: acts on heavy going: has worn headgear: wears tongue tie: often races towards rear. *Lucinda Russell*   **h106**

DE FAOITHESDREAM (IRE) 12 br.g. Balakheri (IRE) – Cutteen Lass (IRE) (Tremblant) [2017/18 c132, h–: c19m⁵ c17g³ c16m⁶ c17.3s⁵ c16.3v³ c16d⁶ Nov 14] useful-looking gelding: winning hurdler: useful handicap chaser at best: nothing like so good in 2017/18: best around 2m: acts on good to firm and heavy going: best when ridden positively. *Evan Williams*   **c106 h–**

DEFI DU SEUIL (FR) 5 b.g. Voix du Nord (FR) – Quarvine du Seuil (FR) (Lavirco (GER)) [2017/18 h151p, b–: h19.3d⁴ h16s Feb 3] lengthy gelding: bumper winner: smart hurdler: unbeaten in 7 starts as a juvenile, most notable successes when landing Triumph Hurdle at Cheltenham and Anniversary Hurdle at Aintree (by 1¼ lengths from Divin Bere): seen out only twice (10 weeks apart) in 2017/18, again finding little when 26½ lengths seventh of 8 to Supasundae in Irish Champion Hurdle at Leopardstown: unproven beyond 17f: acts on soft going: often travels strongly. *Philip Hobbs*   **h126**

DEFINATELY VINNIE 8 ch.g. Vinnie Roe (IRE) – Sohapara (Arapahos (FR)) [2017/18 h78: h26.4s⁴ h25.8g³ h25.5g⁵ h26v² h26s⁴ h25.5v³ h26.4d Apr 22] modest hurdler: won maiden at Hereford in November: stays 3¼m: acts on heavy going: often races in rear. *Jane Mathias*   **h99**

DEFINING YEAR (IRE) 10 b.g. Hawk Wing (USA) – Tajaathub (USA) (Aljabr (USA)) [2017/18 h89: h22g⁵ h19.6m⁶ h22g^pu h15.8m* h15.8d* c16.5g³ Jul 18] modest handicap hurdler: won at Uttoxeter (twice) in July: 5/4, tame third in novice handicap at Worcester (18 lengths behind Adrrastos) on chasing debut, finding little: best at around 2m: acts on good to firm and good to soft going: wears tongue tie: often races towards rear/travels strongly. *Dan Skelton*   **c80 h95**

DEFINITE FUTURE (IRE) 9 b.g. Definite Article – Miss Marilyn (IRE) (Welsh Term) [2017/18 c124, h–: c19.9g* c20g* c20.3g^pu c16.5g⁶ c19.4d^pu Oct 18] winning hurdler: useful handicap chaser: won at Aintree in May and Worcester (by 3 lengths from Marquis of Carabas) in June: stayed 2½m: acted on soft and good to firm going: wore headgear: tried in tongue tie: dead. *Kerry Lee*   **c134 h–**

DEFINITELYANOSCAR (IRE) 5 b.m. Oscar (IRE) – Bobs Article (IRE) (Definite Article) [2017/18 b16.7s* b16.8g² Apr 19] €12,000 3-y-o, £8,000 4-y-o: fourth foal: half-sister to fairly useful/temperamental hurdler Towering (2m-23f winner, by Catcher In The Rye) and a winning pointer by Westerner: dam unraced sister to smart hurdler (2m winner) Staying Article and fairly useful hurdler/smart chaser (stayed 3m) Mossback: off mark in points at third attempt: fairly useful form in mares bumpers: won maiden event at Market Rasen in March: better form when second to Hawthorn Cottage in competitive race at Cheltenham month later, closing when running green (hung left) final 1f. *Harry Fry*   **b101**

DEL

DEFINITE OUTCOME (IRE) 9 b.g. Definite Article – Magical Theatre (IRE) (King's Theatre (IRE)) [2017/18 c126, h–: h24.7g^{pu} May 19] big, strong gelding: fairly useful hurdler at best: found nothing only appearance in 2017/18: fairly useful novice chaser previous season, though completed only once (when making successful chasing debut): stays 3m: acts on heavy going: in cheekpieces last 2 starts: in tongue tie last 4 starts: front runner/races prominently. *Richard Hobson*   c– h–

DEFINITE RUBY (IRE) 10 br.m. Definite Article – Sunset Queen (IRE) (King's Theatre (IRE)) [2017/18 c131, h124: c23m³ May 30] angular mare: fairly useful hurdler: useful handicap chaser: best up to 25f: acted on good to firm and heavy going: wore headgear: often raced prominently: dead. *Gordon Elliott, Ireland*   c133 h–

DEFINITE WINNER (IRE) 7 b.m. Definite Article – Sindabezi (IRE) (Magical Strike (USA)) [2017/18 h18.5v^{pu} h15.8s h15.3v h19.9v^{pu} Mar 17] has had breathing operation: sister to fairly useful hurdler/useful chaser Striking Article (2m-2½m winner) and bumper winner/fair hurdler Raichu (2m winner): dam (h112) bumper/2m-2¼m hurdle winner: no form over hurdles: in tongue tie last 2 starts. *Katy Price*   h–

DEFINITLY GREY (IRE) 7 gr.g. Daylami (IRE) – Caroline Fontenail (IRE) (Kaldounevees (FR)) [2017/18 h104: h21m^{pu} c23d^{pu} c23g² c23.6d* c24.2v^{pu} c23.8d⁶ c21.7s^{pu} c25.3g^{ur} Apr 18] good-topped gelding: winning hurdler: fair handicap chaser: won at Chepstow (conditionals event, by 18 lengths) in October: out of sorts since: stays 3m: acts on good to firm and good to soft going: wears tongue tie. *Charlie Longsdon*   c114 h–

DEFINITLY RED (IRE) 9 ch.g. Definite Article – The Red Wench (IRE) (Aahsaylad) [2017/18 c160, h141: c24.2s³ c25v* c25.3v* c26.3v⁶ c25s^{ur} Apr 12] sturdy gelding: winning hurdler: high-class chaser: won Many Clouds Chase at Aintree in December and Cotswold Chase at Cheltenham (by 8 lengths from American) in January: plugging-on sixth in Cheltenham Gold Cup, then unseated third in Bowl Chase won by Might Bite at Aintree final start: thorough stayer: acts on heavy going: front runner/races prominently: reliable. *Brian Ellison*   c164 h–

DEGOOCH (IRE) 9 ch.g. Gamut (IRE) – Blonde Ambition (IRE) (Old Vic) [2017/18 c122, h81: c19.9g⁵ h19.6d⁴ c19.4g* c19.4m^F c20d c15.2d³ h20s Nov 14] winning hurdler: fairly useful handicap chaser: won at Stratford in July: stays 21f: acts on soft and good to firm going: wears headgear: in tongue tie last 5 starts: races towards rear. *Johnny Farrelly*   c125 h92

DEISE DIAMOND (IRE) 7 b.g. Scorpion (IRE) – Lakeshore Lodge (IRE) (Taipan (IRE)) [2017/18 h94, b94: h22d^{pu} May 21] bumper winner: disappointing maiden hurdler: should be suited by 2½m: acts on good to soft going: tried in hood. *Neil King*   h–

DEISE VU (IRE) 10 b.g. Brian Boru – Deise Dreamer (IRE) (Beneficial) [2017/18 c103, h93: c16.5m^F c19.4m^{pu} c16.5g³ c16.5g³ c15.7d⁷ c17.4g³ c15.9d^{pu} Dec 7] winning pointer: maiden hurdler: fair handicap chaser: won at Southwell in October: best around 2m: acts on heavy going: has worn cheekpieces, including last 3 starts: tried in tongue tie: headstrong front runner. *Roy Brotherton*   c100 h–

DEJA BOUGG 7 b.m. Tobougg (IRE) – La Riveraine (USA) (Riverman (USA)) [2017/18 h102x: h23.3d* May 6] fair handicap hurdler: won mares event at Uttoxeter only start in 2017/18 stays 23f: acts on good to firm and heavy going: in tongue tie last 5 starts: often let down by jumping. *Neil Mulholland*   h105 x

DELANNOY 4 ch.g. Le Havre (IRE) – Raving Monsun (Monsun (GER)) [2017/18 h17.7g⁴ h17.7v⁵ h16m⁴ Apr 26] fair on Flat, stays 1¾m: easily best effort over hurdles (modest form) when fourth in juvenile at Fontwell in October: tried in cheekpieces. *Neil Mulholland*   h99

DELATITE 6 b.g. Schiaparelli (GER) – Desiree (IRE) (Desert Story (IRE)) [2017/18 b87: b15.7g⁴ b16.8g* Oct 3] fairly useful form in bumpers: won at Sedgefield in October: in cheekpieces first 3 outings. *John Berry*   b98

DELAYED REACTION 6 b.m. Black Sam Bellamy (IRE) – J'arrive (Generous (IRE)) [2017/18 b15.7v Mar 29] first foal: dam unraced daughter of fairly useful hurdler/fair chaser (2m winner) Delayed: tailed off in maiden bumper. *Peter Hedger*   b–

DELEGATE 8 ch.g. Robin des Champs (FR) – As You Leave (FR) (Kaldounevees (FR)) [2017/18 c17m⁶ c17.4d* c20.5g^{pu} c16.4s³ c19.9d* h16.8v⁴ c15.8s⁶ Apr 14] fair handicap hurdler: useful chaser: won maiden at Sligo in August and novice at Musselburgh (by 7 lengths from Divine Spear) in February: left Gordon Elliott after third start: stays 21f: acts on good to firm and heavy going: usually in tongue tie: usually races prominently. *Keith Dalgleish*   c135 h100

DEL

DELFACE (FR) 5 b.g. Della Francesca (USA) – Septieme Face (USA) (Lit de Justice (USA)) [2017/18 h15.8d* h15.5d h19.5s h18.5v[6] h19s[6] h15.5v[2] h19v[5] h16.5s[2] h16v h16s[3] Apr 27] half-brother to winners on Flat abroad by Verglas and Hurricane Cat: dam ran once in France: fair hurdler: won novice at Ffos Las in May: best around 2m: acts on heavy going: wears headgear: also in tongue tie last 5 starts. *David Pipe*   h108

DELGANY DEMON 10 b.g. Kayf Tara – Little Twig (IRE) (Good Thyne (USA)) [2017/18 c122, h112; c24.2s[pu] Nov 4] strong gelding: winning hurdler: useful maiden chaser at best: moody effort sole start in 2017/18: stays 3m: acts on heavy going: front runner/races prominently: temperamental. *Neil King*   c– § h–

DELIRE D'ESTRUVAL (FR) 5 b.g. Youmzain (IRE) – Question d'Estruval (FR) (Phantom Breeze) [2017/18 h20s[4] h15.7v* h20.5s[3] h15.7v[2] h20.3v h18.1v[4] Apr 16] third foal: half-brother to French hurdler/chaser Cadence d'Estruval (17f/2¼m winner, by Fragrant Mix): dam, French maiden (third in 2¼m hurdle), half-sister to fairly useful French hurdler/useful chaser (17f-21f winner) Vizir d'Estruval: bumper winner: fairly useful hurdler: won listed novice at Haydock (by neck from Midnight Shadow) in November and novice at Towcester (quickened clear before last when beating Harefield 9 lengths) in February: placed both starts in 4-y-o chases in France: stays 21f: acts on heavy going: front runner/races prominently. *Ben Pauling*   c– h129

DELIRIOUS LOVE (IRE) 6 b.g. Definite Article – Grangeclare Lark (IRE) (Old Vic) [2017/18 b16.6d b14s[6] Jan 18] poor form in bumpers. *Graeme McPherson*   b67

DELL' ARCA (IRE) 9 b.g. Sholokhov (IRE) – Daisy Belle (GER) (Acatenango (GER)) [2017/18 c–, h138: h20g[2] h20g[4] h23.9g[4] h24.2d* h25.3s[pu] h16.8s h19.6s[5] c20s[6] h24s c26g[3] Apr 18] leggy gelding: useful handicap hurdler: won at Newbury in November: useful handicap chaser: barely stays 3¼m: acts on good to firm and heavy going: wears headgear/tongue tie: often races in rear. *David Pipe*   c139 h140

DELL ORO (FR) 5 b.g. Walk In The Park (IRE) – Kallistea (FR) (Sicyos (USA)) [2017/18 b99: h15.7g* h16.3v[2] h19.6s[4] h20.3g[3] h21m[2] Apr 26] tall gelding: bumper winner: useful novice hurdler: won at Ascot in November: best effort when third at Cheltenham (3 lengths behind Diese des Bieffes) in April: will stay beyond 21f: best form on good going: sometimes idles (collared late when doing so at Kempton final start). *Gary Moore*   h133

DELTA BORGET (FR) 13 b.g. Kapgarde (FR) – L'Oceane (FR) (Epervier Bleu) [2017/18 c114, h–: c16.3d[bu] c19.2v[pu] Apr 8] maiden point winner: maiden hurdler: fairly useful chaser at best: pulled up both starts in 2017/18: stays 21f: acts on good to firm and heavy going: wears cheekpieces: tried in tongue tie: front runner/races prominently. *L. Jefford*   c– h–

DELTA WORK (FR) 5 br.g. Network (GER) – Robbe (FR) (Video Rock (FR)) [2017/18 h16d[2] h16.7g* h16v[3] h20v[3] h24v[2] h24s[4] h24v[3] h24s* h24s[2] Apr 25]   h150

'Ramsey, Xhaka, Ozil—you're *walking* on a football pitch at Wembley. Why are you walking? You're a disgrace. An absolute disgrace!' That was the verdict of former Manchester United and England stalwart Gary Neville whilst co-commentating on the League Cup Final in February in his new guise as Sky Sports' most-celebrated football pundit. As their team limped to a three-nil defeat against Manchester City, Neville went on to brand the aforementioned trio of Arsenal midfielders as 'spineless' for (in his view) giving up so soon, whilst he also singled out Shkodran Mustafi for 'pathetic defending' earlier in the game. Neville has been widely praised for his neutral analysis since hanging up his boots in favour of the microphone, with this pull-no-punches approach (even when passing judgement on former colleagues or rivals) proving particularly refreshing, and undoubtedly popular with viewers. This brave new world of outspoken sports broadcasting certainly isn't restricted to football either. Fans of England's most popular summer game will testify that strong opinions have long been a feature of cricket coverage, especially on the radio. Like Neville, former England cricket captain Michael Vaughan has made a successful switch to the commentary box, where he too hasn't been afraid to ruffle a few feathers. After England had been trounced by 340 runs in the second Test against South Africa during their 2017 series, which was just the second match as captain for Joe Root, Vaughan described the English batsmen as 'appalling' and accused them of 'lacking respect' for Test cricket. Root, who has known Vaughan since childhood, was clearly angered by his mentor's criticism and hit back by saying: 'I think that's very unfair—I can't believe he's actually said that to be honest.' Root and Vaughan patched things up before the next Test but, significantly, the latter stood by his comments and refused to apologise for them.

Pertemps Network Final Handicap Hurdle, Cheltenham—Delta Work (star on cap) takes advantage of a final-flight mistake by stable-companion Glenloe (hoops) to prevail by the narrowest of margins

Such outspokenness hasn't extended to the TV coverage of horse racing, however, where the name-calling still tends to be reserved for anyone who dares to criticise any of the participants. Paul Carberry's controversial ride on runner-up Harchibald in the 2005 Champion Hurdle, when he sat motionless until very late on, saw Channel 4's John McCririck warning viewers: 'Any of you criticising Paul Carberry, wash your mouth out with soap—you don't know what you're talking about.' McCririck's colleague Alastair Down labelled critics of Carberry's ride as 'imbeciles', having also lambasted owner John Hales earlier in the season for having the temerity to pass judgement on the rides given to one of his own horses—Hales, in a refreshingly honest answer to a journalist, had merely suggested Azertyuiop might have fared better against Moscow Flyer in the 2004 Tingle Creek if Ruby Walsh had pressurised that rival earlier, which were 'snivelling comments' made by a 'spoilt man' according to Down. Roll the clock forward thirteen years and, after a switch to ITV from Channel 4, it appears very little has changed if the immediate aftermath of the Pertemps Network Final at Cheltenham in March is anything to go by. A grandstand finish had just been fought out by Delta Work and 9/2 favourite Glenloe, with the latter going down by a rapidly-diminishing nose, losing momentum through a mistake at the last having arguably shaped like the best at the weights for most of the way.

Neither of the two ex-jockey pundits on duty that day, Luke Harvey and Sir Anthony McCoy, had discussed the possibility of there being an unlucky loser in the Pertemps Final until an interjection by Matt Chapman, McCririck's successor in the role of 'colourful' TV betting reporter, who suggested Glenloe's jockey Barry Geraghty would have won had he kicked for home earlier. 'What a terrific finish—but come on AP and Luke, every punter watching that race will have said "if Barry Geraghty didn't sit like he did, he would have won." It's all very well sitting like that if you don't make a mistake at the last, but the only thing that beat Glenloe there was the mistake at the final hurdle. Without that mistake he would—categorically, no doubt—have won!' Harvey dismissed this suggestion as 'absolute drivel', before adding 'I fail to see what he could have done any differently.' McCoy, Geraghty's predecessor in the role of retained jockey to Glenloe's owner JP McManus, was slightly more receptive to Chapman's criticism, acknowledging that a jockey would always love another go whenever he or she loses out in a tight finish, but even he rounded things off with a dig at the inquisitor: 'Barry Geraghty has had a lot more winners than the clown that just asked the question.' Chapman, of course, can be an acquired taste with his lively broadcasting style and such barbs from his colleagues might have been an attempt at banter to combat that, but surely it is the duty of an

Gigginstown House Stud's "Delta Work"

analyst to discuss these matters? Any experienced race-reader watching the latest Pertemps Final would have concluded Glenloe could be viewed as an unlucky loser and, although Chapman might have been guilty of over-egging the pudding a bit, his comments certainly weren't 'absolute drivel'. In truth, it is to be hoped horse-racing coverage never features the same extremes of criticism uttered by Messrs Neville and Vaughan earlier, particularly as (unlike in those sports) such comments could have direct consequences on people's livelihoods with, for example, jockeys losing out on rides and trainers losing out on horses. In addition, outspokenness for the sake of it also tends to encourage some of the keyboard warriors to be found on social media, with unfair abuse of jockeys through this medium already a problem. However, some middle ground can be found where constructive criticism or considered analysis of tactics can be made without great offence being taken on every occasion.

Ironically, one person who wasn't affected by the rights or wrongs of the debate surrounding the latter stages of the Pertemps Final was Glenloe's trainer Gordon Elliott, as he also saddled Delta Work. Not all punters felt aggrieved about the outcome either, as a late gamble on Delta Work saw him sent off second favourite at 6/1 (from 14/1 in the morning) in a field of twenty-three. Delta Work had been beaten on all five starts since running out a wide-margin winner when odds-on for a twenty-two-runner maiden hurdle at Punchestown back in May. That doesn't tell the whole story, however, as he had shown gradual improvement during much of that sequence. Indeed, he had been placed three times in graded novice company (including a third to his connections' outstanding prospect Samcro) prior to making the frame in two hot handicaps before Cheltenham, ridden by an inexperienced conditional when third to Kilfenora in a Pertemps qualifier at Punchestown on the final occasion. Davy Russell was back in the plate at Cheltenham, albeit only after being passed fit by the doctor following a fall from Bless The Wings over the cross-country course less than twenty-four hours earlier, which had seen him stood down from his final two intended rides on Wednesday's card. Happily there was no repeat of the jockey's experience in 2013, when Russell (on the back of another heavy fall

DEL

on the Wednesday) was forced to give up his remaining rides after finishing down the field in the Pertemps Final, a subsequent trip to hospital revealing a punctured lung—the fallout didn't end there, as a war of words broke out between medical officials on either side of the Irish Sea as to when the jockey could ride again (he was banned from riding on British soil until undergoing corrective surgery). Cheltenham nearly had to cancel fixtures the following autumn due to possible lack of medical cover caused by an official complaint to the General Medical Council investigating the decision by course doctors to allow Russell to ride on that Thursday card in the first place. All of which must have seemed a distant memory to Russell this time around, as Delta Work proved to be the first leg of a 377/1-treble on the card, those later wins on Balko des Flos and The Storyteller (the last-named also for Elliott) helping him to the title of leading jockey at the meeting for the first time—his final total of four wins being matched by compatriot Jack Kennedy, with Russell landing the prize thanks to more placed efforts.

'Davy is a master jockey and rides Cheltenham better than just about anyone; he has to be worth a couple of pounds at least around here in these handicaps and that can make such a big difference,' enthused winning owner Michael O'Leary, whose Gigginstown colours enjoyed their own treble on Thursday. Russell had Delta Work well positioned in mid-division from an early stage and tracked Glenloe for much of the way in a race that wasn't run at an end-to-end gallop. The decision to switch Delta Work when short of room on the long run to the last arguably proved crucial as Barry Geraghty might have been briefly unaware that Delta Work was challenging on the other side of Glenloe, who still looked to be travelling best at this stage. Delta Work took the lead when landing with more momentum at the last (despite a mistake of his own there) and, responding gamely to pressure, held off the rallying Glenloe to just get the better of the photo-finish, with outsiders Connetable (prominent throughout) and Taj Badalandabad faring best of the home-trained contingent in third and fourth respectively. Delta Work was the only novice in the Pertemps Final line-up and became the third successive novice winner of the race, following the Pat Kelly-trained pair Mall Dini and Presenting Percy in 2016 and 2017 respectively. By contrast, there had been just three novice winners in the previous twenty years, namely Kayf Aramis (2009), Oulart (2005) and Unsinkable Boxer (1998). As with Presenting Percy in 2017, Delta Work produced a performance which would also have seen him finish in the money in the Spa (the recognised staying championship for novice hurdlers) twenty-four hours later. It didn't take long for him to prove as much either, as he finished a neck in front of Spa winner Kilbricken Storm in the Grade 1 War of Attrition (branded as the Irish Daily Mirror) Novices' Hurdle at Punchestown on his final start. Delta Work had to give best in a tight finish this time, going down by a neck as he and Kilbricken Storm filled the minor placings behind hot favourite Next Destination. Delta Work again saw things out most gamely in the latter stages and the performance represented an excellent effort—the first three pulled twenty lengths clear of the remainder—whilst Delta Work's performance can be regardless all the more meritorious considering that much of the Elliott string was under a cloud during the Punchestown Festival (the yard closed down for several weeks shortly afterwards due to coughing).

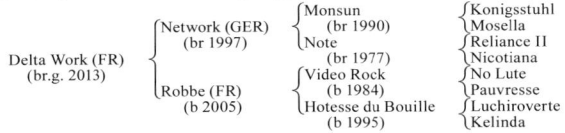

```
                          ┌ Network (GER)  ┌ Monsun         ┌ Konigsstuhl
                          │  (br 1997)     │  (br 1990)     ┤ Mosella
                          │                │                └ Reliance II
Delta Work (FR)           │                └ Note           ┌ Nicotiana
   (br.g. 2013)           ┤                   (br 1977)
                          │                                 ┌ No Lute
                          │ Robbe (FR)     ┌ Video Rock     ┤ Pauvresse
                          └  (b 2005)      │  (b 1984)
                                           │                ┌ Luchiroverte
                                           └ Hotesse du Bouille ┤
                                              (b 1995)          └ Kelinda
```

Delta Work's background isn't that of a typical Gigginstown recruit as he started life in French bumpers rather than Irish points, winning a mile and a half event at Lyon Parilly on the second of two outings for Emmanuel Clayeux in 2016/17. He is the second foal out of lightly-raced French mare Robbe, who made the frame twice at up to nineteen furlongs from just three starts over hurdles. Her first foal Cap York (by Ballingarry) was also snapped up by Gigginstown after tasting success in French bumpers, but so far has been restricted to just one outing in the famous maroon, white star, armlets and star on cap, finishing a promising sixth in a Leopardstown maiden hurdle for Noel Meade in mid-2016/17. Delta Work's year-younger half-brother Elwood (by Martaline) made it three winners from Robbe's first three runners when winning an eighteen-furlong hurdle in the French Provinces in late-April, while Robbe has since produced fillies in 2015 and 2016, named Foster's (by Cokoriko) and Gympie (by Lord du Sud) respectively. It's not the biggest surprise that Robbe was fast-tracked to stud as she hails from a fairly successful family. All six of her siblings to reach the track were successful over jumps, including the fairly useful chasers Sir Dream and Call of Duty (by Cap York's sire Ballingarry), who have both shown their form at up to twenty-one furlongs around Auteuil. Unraced grandam Hotesse du Bouille was also a half-sister to numerous winners, including the useful chaser at up to twenty-five furlongs Kenzo III. Fences are now likely to be on the agenda for the good-topped Delta Work too, particularly given his owners' usual policy of sending their chasing prospects over fences sooner rather than later. Delta Work has proved versatile with regards to trip, his two wins over hurdles coming at two miles and three miles, and he seems a very reliable sort (has made the frame on all eleven career starts), qualities which should continue to stand him in good stead. *Gordon Elliott, Ireland*

DELUSIONOFGRANDEUR (IRE) 8 b.g. Mahler – Olivia Rose (IRE) (Mujadil (USA)) [2017/18 c136, h–: c19.4d³ c29.2g³ c25.2d* c24.2s³ c32.8s⁵ c25.6v³ c34.3s^pu c26g Apr 18] lengthy gelding: winning pointer: winning hurdler: useful handicap chaser: won at Catterick in November: good third at Wetherby (Rowland Meyrick Chase, beaten neck by Get On The Yager) in December and Haydock (12 lengths behind Potters Legend) in March: stays 29f: acts on soft going: front runner/races prominently. *Sue Smith* c141 h–

DEMAND RESPECT 5 ch.g. Paco Boy (IRE) – Brilliance (Cadeaux Genereux) [2017/18 h16g h15.8g^pu h15.8g Nov 5] poor maiden on Flat: no form over hurdles: in tongue tie last 2 starts. *Laura Hurley* h–

DEMI SANG (FR) 5 b.g. Gris de Gris (IRE) – Morvandelle (FR) (Video Rock (FR)) [2017/18 h18.9g³ h17.4d² h18.9g* h16.9d³ c17.9s* c17.4s* c16v* c17s⁴ c20.4s^pu c20s^pu Apr 25] sturdy gelding: seventh foal: half-brother to 3 winners in France, including 21f chase winner Commodore (by Fragrant Mix): dam maiden sister to high-class hurdler/smart chaser (stayed 2¾m) Osana and to dam of high-class staying chaser Notre Pere: bumper winner: fairly useful form over hurdles: won 4-y-o event at Les Sables-d'Olonne in June: useful form over fences: won 4-y-o events at Auteuil (2, handicap on second occasion) in September and, having left Francois Nicolle, novice at Naas (by 1¼ lengths from Avenir d'Une Vie) in January: stays 19f: acts on heavy going. *W. P. Mullins, Ireland* c140 h116

DEMOGRAPHIC (USA) 9 b.g. Aptitude (USA) – Private Line (USA) (Private Account (USA)) [2017/18 h105: h24.4s Feb 21] fair handicap hurdler: below form sole start in 2017/18: stays easy 3m: acts on soft and good to firm going: wears visor: usually races close up. *Emma Lavelle* h69

DEMON D'AUNOU (FR) 5 b.g. Martaline – Jimagine II (FR) (Video Rock (FR)) [2017/18 h16.7g* h16.7s³ h19s⁴ h16.9g Apr 20] brother to fairly useful hurdler Coquine d'Aunou (2¼m winner) and half-brother to fairly useful French hurdler Quatre Vingt Treize (2¼m winner, by Michel Georges): dam, French maiden hurdler/chaser (placed up to 19f), half-sister to useful French hurdler/chaser (stayed 2¾m) Mysoko: placed both starts in French bumpers: fairly useful form over hurdles: won maiden at Market Rasen in October: in frame in novices next 2 starts: may prove best around 2m: often travels strongly. *Jonjo O'Neill* h125

DEMOOD (IRE) 9 b.m. Definite Article – Mood I'm In (GER) (Saddlers' Hall (IRE)) [2017/18 c22.6d^ur Jun 9] point winner: no promise either start over hurdles: unseated seventh in novice hunter on chasing debut. *Richard Pringuer* c– h–

DE NAME ESCAPES ME (IRE) 8 ch.g. Vinnie Roe (IRE) – Heartlight (IRE) (Accordion) [2017/18 h116: c18v c22d³ c20s⁴ c16.5s h16s^pu h24d³ Apr 26] sturdy gelding: useful handicap hurdler: good third at Punchestown (1¾ lengths behind A Great View) in April: only fair form over fences (remains capable of better): stays 3m: acts on heavy going: often in hood: in tongue tie last 3 starts. *Noel Meade, Ireland* c112 p h133

DE NAME EVADES ME (IRE) 6 b.g. Vinnie Roe (IRE) – Sound of The Crowd (IRE) (Accordion) [2017/18 h21s⁴ h24.6s³ Apr 9] €27,000 3-y-o: workmanlike gelding: fifth foal: half-brother to fairly useful hurdler Bull And Bush (19f-3m winner, by Presenting): dam h115 p unraced: Irish point winner: fairly useful form over hurdles: improved when 1¾ lengths third of 6 to Kilfilum Cross in novice at Kempton, despite appearing unsuited by steady gallop: will probably stay long distances: open to further progress. *Fergal O'Brien*

DENNY KERRELL 7 b.g. Midnight Legend – Tilla (Bin Ajwaad (IRE)) [2017/18 h77: c16.3g^{ur} c16.1g^2 h19.8v^4 c17.5d^{pu} Apr 24] poor maiden hurdler: poor form over fences: stays 2½m: acts on heavy going: has worn cheekpieces/tongue tie. *Seamus Mullins* **c81**
h71

DENSFIRTH (IRE) 5 b.g. Flemensfirth (USA) – Denwoman (IRE) (Witness Box (USA)) [2017/18 b16.8v^4 b16s^5 Feb 24] second foal: dam once-raced half-sister to Cheltenham Gold Cup winner Denman: fair form in bumpers: better effort when fourth to Supremely Lucky at Exeter: raced too freely 11 weeks later. *Paul Nicholls* **b88**

DENTLEY DE MEE (FR) 5 b.g. Lauro (GER) – Natty Twigy (FR) (Video Rock (FR)) [2017/18 b88: h16.8g^3 h16.5m* h21.2d^2 h21s h18.5s^3 h19.8v^2 h19v^2 Apr 12] useful-looking gelding: bumper winner: fairly useful hurdler: won maiden at Taunton in November: best effort when second to Sam's Gunner in EBF 'National Hunt' Novices' Handicap Hurdle Final at Sandown in March: stays 21f: acts on good to firm and heavy going: in cheekpieces last 2 starts. *Nick Williams* **h123**

DE PLOTTING SHED (IRE) 8 b.g. Beneficial – Lady Willmurt (IRE) (Mandalus) [2017/18 h147: c22.5s^2 c19v^5 c17s^2 c16v^2 c20.4s^{pu} c16.7s^2 c21s^{pu} Apr 27] useful-looking gelding: smart hurdler: useful maiden chaser: runner-up 4 times, including at Fairyhouse (went clear 2 out but faltered and headed late) in April: stays 3m: acts on heavy going: in tongue tie last 5 starts: has suspect attitude. *Gordon Elliott, Ireland* **c139**
h–

DE RASHER COUNTER 6 b.g. Yeats (IRE) – Dedrunknmunky (IRE) (Rashar (USA)) [2017/18 h21g^3 h21.6s^5 h16.6d^2 h19.2v* h20.3v^F h22.8v h20.5s^2 Mar 23] £10,500 3-y-o: lengthy gelding: third foal: half-brother to modest hurdler Lady Garvagh (2m winner, by Lucarno), stayed 2½m: dam (c94/h83) 2½m chase winner: point/bumper winner: fairly useful hurdler: won handicap at Fontwell in January: should stay beyond 2½m: acts on heavy going. *Emma Lavelle* **h126**

DERINTOHER YANK (IRE) 7 b.g. Dubai Destination (USA) – Anns Present (IRE) (Presenting) [2017/18 h120§, b94§: h16.7s^2 c17.3g^2 h20g^5 h23.9g h19.6g h16.7d* c15.9s* c15.9d^2 c16.4s^2 c19.1d^2 c19.9d^3 c15.9d^4 c15.9s^3 Apr 8] fairly useful handicap hurdler: won at Bangor in October: fairly useful handicap chaser: won novice event at Carlisle later in month: placed several times after: stays 2½m: acts on soft going: wears headgear: front runner: has flashed tail/carried head awkwardly. *Donald McCain* **c127 §**
h123 §

DERRIANA SPIRIT (IRE) 5 b.m. Flemensfirth (USA) – Distillery Lane (IRE) (Exit To Nowhere (USA)) [2017/18 b16.2g^2 b16v^2 b16.7v b17d* Mar 31] tall mare: fifth foal: half-sister to fairly useful hurdler/useful chaser Pure Vision (2m-2½f winner, by Milan): dam unraced half-sister to dam of useful hurdler/chaser (stays 25f) Peckhamecho: fairly useful form in bumpers: won mares event at Carlisle in March, making all and responding well once threatened. *Nicky Richards* **b97**

DERRINTOGHER BLISS (IRE) 9 b.g. Arcadio (GER) – His Fair Lady (IRE) (In The Wings) [2017/18 c126, h–: c24d^3 Oct 8] sturdy gelding: winning hurdler: maiden chaser, fairly useful at best: stayed 27f: acted on soft and good to firm going: wore cheekpieces: dead. *Kim Bailey* **c101**
h–

DERRYDOON 8 b.g. Multiplex – Wahiba Reason (IRE) (Robellino (USA)) [2017/18 h74, b–: h16.7s^3 h15.8g^6 h23.3g^5 Jun 21] poor maiden hurdler: unproven beyond 2m: acts on soft and good to firm going: has worn hood: usually in tongue tie. *Evan Williams* **h75**

DERRYFADDA (IRE) 9 b.g. Scorpion (IRE) – San Diego (IRE) (Leading Counsel (USA)) [2017/18 c23.6d Apr 24] good-bodied gelding: maiden hurdler: modest handicap chaser at one time: left Richard Ford/off 30 months before only start in 2017/18: stays 27f: acts on good to firm going: tried in tongue tie. *Sam England* **c–**
h–

DERRYNANE (IRE) 7 b.g. Oscar (IRE) – Tessano Queen (IRE) (Jurado (USA)) [2017/18 h70, b82: h16.3s^4 h15.7v* h19.3d^2 h16.8v^4 h16.8g Apr 23] fair handicap hurdler: won at Catterick in January: stays 19f: acts on heavy going: wears tongue tie: often travels strongly, but has found little. *Donald McCain* **h101**

DESERT CROSS 5 b.g. Arcano (IRE) – Secret Happiness (Cape Cross (IRE)) [2017/18 h93p: h16s h16.6d Dec 16] compact gelding: fairly useful on Flat, stays 1¾m: modest form at best over hurdles: may yet do better in handicaps. *Jonjo O'Neill* **h–**

DESERT CRY (IRE) 12 b.g. Desert Prince (IRE) – Hataana (USA) (Robellino (USA)) [2017/18 c–, h145: h20d* Nov 5] good-topped gelding: smart handicap hurdler: won at Carlisle (by ¾ length from Tomngerry) only outing in 2017/18: winning chaser: stays 23f: acts on heavy going: wears blinkers. *Donald McCain* **c–**
h147

DES

DESERT ISLAND DUSK 7 b.g. Superior Premium – Desert Island Disc (Turtle Island (IRE)) [2017/18 h105: h20.1g² h16.2g* h20.1g⁵ h16.2d⁵ h16.7g³ h19.9g h16.2d³ h16.2g h15.6m Nov 8] fair handicap hurdler: won at Hexham in June: stays 2½m: acts on good to firm and good to soft going: has worn hood: wears tongue tie. *Maurice Barnes*   **h104**

DESERTMORE HILL (IRE) 8 b.g. Beneficial – Youngborogal (IRE) (Anshan) [2017/18 h90: c16.5g* h16g⁶ c17.4g^pu c16.5g⁸ Sep 3] maiden hurdler: fair form over fences: won handicaps in June (novice) and September, both at Worcester: stays 19f: best form on good going: has worn hood: in tongue tie in 2017/18: often races in rear: has finished weakly. *Kerry Lee*   **c105 h68**

DESERTMORE VIEW (IRE) 10 b.g. Fruits of Love (USA) – The Iron Lady (IRE) (Polish Patriot (USA)) [2017/18 c–, h–; c16d³ Jul 28] prolific winning pointer: twice raced over hurdles: winning chaser: lightly raced and little form since 2014/15: stays 3m: best form on good going. *Ronald Harris*   **c59 h–**

DESERT QUEEN 10 b.m. Desert King (IRE) – Priscilla (Teenoso (USA)) [2017/18 c144, h126+: c23.9g² c19.9s³ Feb 22] good-topped mare: useful hurdler/chaser: third in listed mares event over fences at Market Rasen (14½ lengths behind Mia's Storm) in November: stays 3m: acts on soft going: wears tongue tie: free-going front runner: not straightforward (often plays up at start/slowly away). *Harry Fry*   **c133 h–**

DESERT RULER 5 b.g. Kheleyf (USA) – Desert Royalty (IRE) (Alhaarth (IRE)) [2017/18 h16.8s⁶ Dec 8] fairly useful on Flat, stays 12.5f: 16/1, sixth in maiden at Sedgefield (27 lengths behind Blottos) on hurdling debut. *Jedd O'Keeffe*   **h73**

DESERT SENSATION (IRE) 6 b.g. Authorized (IRE) – Awwal Malika (USA) (Kingmambo (USA)) [2017/18 h120: h23g h22s⁴ c26.2d Oct 31] sturdy gelding: fairly useful handicap hurdler at best: little enthusiasm for chasing when seventh in novice handicap at Chepstow: stays 3¼m: acts on soft and good to firm going: wears headgear/tongue tie: usually races close up. *Dr Richard Newland*   **c89 h108**

DESERT STING 9 b.g. Scorpion (IRE) – Skipcarl (IRE) (Carlingford Castle) [2017/18 h60: c22.6g* c24.1s^pu c22.5d³ c25.8m^R Aug 29] multiple winning pointer: maiden hurdler: modest form in chases: won novice handicap at Stratford in May: stays 23f: wears blinkers/tongue tie: front runner/races prominently: untrustworthy. *Oliver Greenall*   **c86 § h–**

DESHAN (GER) 7 b.g. Soldier Hollow – Desimona (GER) (Monsun (GER)) [2017/18 b80: b16.3d h16g⁴ h16.7g⁴ h16.7g⁶ h15.8d Oct 8] modest form in bumpers: standout effort over hurdles (modest form) when fourth in maiden at Bangor in August: in tongue tie last 4 starts: front runner/races prominently. *Tim Vaughan*   **h94 b–**

DESI DARU (IRE) 6 b.g. Indian Haven – Daiquiri (IRE) (Houmayoun (FR)) [2017/18 b15.8m⁶ h15.8g h15.8g⁶ Nov 5] no form, including on Flat: tried in blinkers. *Conrad Allen*   **h– b–**

DESILVANO 9 b.g. Desideratum – Cruz Santa (Lord Bud) [2017/18 h–: h25d^pu h24.4d h24.4s h26v⁵ h26.4d Apr 22] workmanlike gelding: point winner: useful novice hurdler in 2014/15: lightly raced and disappointing since: stays 25f: acts on heavy going: has worn cheekpieces: often races lazily. *James Evans*   **h90**

DESIREMOI D'AUTHIE (FR) 5 b.g. Cachet Noir (USA) – Toietmoi d'Authie (FR) (Al Namix (FR)) [2017/18 h15.8g² h16.5s h16.7g⁵ Feb 3] rather leggy gelding: first foal: dam, French bumper winner around 1¾m, half-sister to fairly useful French chaser (19f-21f winner) Curly d'Authie: bumper winner for F. Monnier: fair form over hurdles: tried in hood (usually races freely). *Alan King*   **h103**

DESPICABLE ME (IRE) 4 b.g. Gold Well – Bun Buns (IRE) (Bach (IRE)) [2017/18 b16d Apr 26] lengthy gelding: tailed off in bumper. *Henry Oliver*   **b–**

DESSINATEUR (FR) 5 b.g. Alberto Giacometti (IRE) – Castagnette III (FR) (Tin Soldier (FR)) [2017/18 b97: h16.8v⁴ h15.5v⁴ h21.2s⁵ h21.6s Apr 23] bumper winner: fair form over hurdles: should be suited by 21f+. *Venetia Williams*   **h101**

DESTIN D'AJONC (FR) 5 b.g. Martaline – Fleur d'Ajonc (FR) (April Night (FR)) [2017/18 h20v⁶ h16v³ h16s⁶ Apr 17] half-brother to fairly useful French hurdler/chaser Solotremp (17f-2½m winner, by Trempolino) and fairly useful French hurdler Polyfleur (2m winner, by Poliglote): dam, French 1¾m/15f winner, sister to fairly useful hurdler/chaser (17f-3m winner) Kerrigand: fair form only start on Flat: useful form over hurdles: won maiden at Auteuil in 2016/17 for Y. Fouin: third in Limestone Lad Hurdle at Naas (11¼ lengths behind Sandsend) in January and sixth in handicap at Leopardstown (7¾ lengths behind Grand Partner) in March: stays 2¼m: raced on soft/heavy going: tried in tongue tie. *Gordon Elliott, Ireland*   **h132**

DEY

DESTINED TO SHINE (IRE) 6 b.g. Dubai Destination (USA) – Good Shine (IRE) (Beneficial) [2017/18 b96: h17s⁶ h16s^{ur} h16s⁶ h16s h16.7s⁴ Mar 24] sturdy gelding: bumper winner: only modest form over hurdles: raced around 2m: acts on soft going: in tongue tie last 2 starts: often races freely. *Kerry Lee* — **h100**

DESTINEE ROYALE (FR) 5 b.m. Balko (FR) – Viana (FR) (Signe Divin (USA)) [2017/18 b15.7v* Apr 27] £56,000 3-y-o: sixth foal: half-sister to 3 winners, including useful hurdler Analifet (2m winner, by Califet), stayed 2½m, and bumper winner/fairly useful hurdler Cause Toujours (2m winner, by Khalkevi): dam French 17f hurdle/chase winner: 8/1, won mares bumper at Towcester (gamely by ½ length from Miss Heritage) on debut. *Venetia Williams* — **b89**

DESTINY'S GOLD (IRE) 8 b.g. Millenary – Knockhouse Rose (IRE) (Roselier (FR)) [2017/18 c116, h112: h16d^F h16.7g⁴ h19.9g* h20g³ h20.3g² h19.9d³ h24g⁴ h20g* h20.3g^{ur} h19.8s^{pu} Apr 28] tall gelding: fairly useful handicap hurdler: won at Uttoxeter in May and Worcester in September: twice-raced chaser: stays 2½m: acts on good to firm and good to soft going: wears headgear. *Dr Richard Newland* — **c–** **h124**

DESTINY'S STAR 6 br.g. Beneficial – Lady Cad (FR) (Cadoudal (FR)) [2017/18 h–: h21g^{pu} h20.8s^{pu} Jan 9] little form in maiden/novice hurdles. *Jonjo O'Neill* — **h–**

DESTRIER (FR) 5 b.g. Voix du Nord (FR) – Razia (FR) (Robin des Champs (FR)) [2017/18 b–: h15.5d⁴ h16v* h16g⁵ h16s² Apr 9] lengthy gelding: well held in bumper: fairly useful form over hurdles: won novices at Leicester in November and Wetherby in January: best effort when 2½ lengths second to Notre Ami in similar event at Kempton final outing. *Dan Skelton* — **h119**

DETONATE (FR) 5 gr.g. Al Namix (FR) – Tadorna (FR) (Maresca Sorrento (FR)) [2017/18 b15.6s⁶ Jan 3] poor form in bumpers: tried in hood/tongue tie. *James Ewart* — **b63**

DETOUR AHEAD 10 ch.m. Needwood Blade – My Tern (IRE) (Glacial Storm (USA)) [2017/18 c85, h–: c24.2g c23g^{pu} Jul 10] leggy, close-coupled mare: winning hurdler: poor handicap chaser: stays 2¾m: acts on good to firm and heavy going: wears headgear: tried in tongue tie: usually races prominently: often let down by jumping. *Clare Ellam* — **c55 x** **h–**

DETTE DE JEU (FR) 5 b.g. Desir d'Un Soir (FR) – Queltalent (FR) (Fado) [2017/18 b16v Feb 3] 15/2, shaped as if amiss in bumper at Wetherby. *Harry Whittington* — **b–**

DEVILS BRIDE (IRE) 11 b.g. Helissio (FR) – Rigorous (Generous (IRE)) [2017/18 c157, h–: c20.5s³ c20m³ c17g² c22.5g^F c20.5g⁵ c19.9d c21.1s c20s Apr 25] winning hurdler: smart handicap chaser: best effort in 2017/18 when third at Down Royal (½ length behind Sandymount Duke) in June: stays 23f: acts on soft and good to firm going: wears cheekpieces/tongue tie: often races prominently. *Henry de Bromhead, Ireland* — **c154 d** **h–**

DEVILS WATER 7 b.g. Overbury (IRE) – Reel Charmer (Dancing High) [2017/18 h100, b–: h23.9g^{pu} h19.3d^{pu} h15.6d h17d Mar 25] modest maiden hurdler: left George Charlton after first start: should stay beyond 19f: acts on good to soft going: in hood last 3 starts: has worn tongue tie. *Jane Walton* — **h78**

DEVITO'SGOLDENGIRL (IRE) 7 b.m. Gold Well – Caracool (FR) (Cadoudal (FR)) [2017/18 h20.2g⁶ h16.2m³ h16.2s² h23.9v^{pu} c19.9m Nov 8] third foal: dam, French maiden jumper, sister to useful French hurdler/chaser (17f-19f winner) Roc de Sivola and half-sister to useful French chaser (stayed 2¾m) Hercule Noir: Irish point winner: modest form over hurdles: last in novice handicap at Musselburgh on chasing debut: bred to stay beyond 2m: acts on soft going: in hood last 4 starts: wears tongue tie: usually races close up. *Lucinda Russell* — **c–** **h84**

DE VOUS A MOI (FR) 10 b.g. Sinndar (IRE) – Dzinigane (FR) (Exit To Nowhere (USA)) [2017/18 c125, h125: c20.5v h22.8v³ h22.8v⁵ c23.4v* Jan 30] fairly useful handicap hurdler: useful handicap chaser: won at Newcastle (by length from Newtown Lad) in January: stays 23f: acts on heavy going: has worn headgear: front runner/races prominently. *Sue Smith* — **c131** **h123**

DEXCITE (FR) 7 b.g. Authorized (IRE) – Belle Alicia (FR) (Smadoun (FR)) [2017/18 h117: h16.6d⁴ h16.2s Jan 14] well-made gelding: fair handicap hurdler: off 18 months prior to reappearance: stays 19f: acts on soft going: tried in hood: temperament under suspicion. *Tom George* — **h109**

DEYRANN DE CARJAC (FR) 5 b.g. Balko (FR) – Queyrann (FR) (Sheyrann) [2017/18 b78: b16d³ h16.6d³ h16g² Apr 20] rather unfurnished gelding: fairly useful form in bumpers: similar form when placed in novice hurdles at Doncaster and Ayr (2 lengths second of 5 to well-ridden Brahms de Clermont): will be suited by 2½m: remains open to improvement. *Alan King* — **h119 p** **b97**

DHA

DHAROOS (IRE) 5 ch.g. New Approach (IRE) – Cailiocht (USA) (Elusive Quality (USA)) [2017/18 h21.6d^{pu} h15.8g h19g Nov 16] fairly useful maiden on Flat (stays 1¾m) in 2016: little promise over hurdles. *Nigel Hawke*   h–

DIABLE DE SIVOLA (FR) 5 b.g. Noroit (GER) – Grande Route (IRE) (Lost World (IRE)) [2017/18 h128: h19.2g^2 h21.1s^4 h20.5v^F h16s^3 h20.3g Apr 18] rangy gelding: useful handicap hurdler: second at Fontwell in October and third at Chepstow (6 lengths behind Moabit) in February: should stay at least 21f: acts on heavy going. *Nick Williams*   h130

DIABLERETS (FR) 5 ch.g. Vendangeur (IRE) – Lavande (FR) (Iris Noir (FR)) [2017/18 h–: h16.5m h16.5g^F h15.3v^4 h16.5m Apr 25] lengthy gelding: no form over hurdles. *Kayley Woollacott*   h–

DIABLO DE ROUHET (FR) 5 b.g. Great Pretender (IRE) – Querelle d'Estruval (FR) (Panoramic) [2017/18 b16s b16.7d^6 h15.7s^5 h19.5v* h23.3v^2 ab16d^2 h21.1s Mar 14] plain gelding: third foal: dam maiden half-sister to fairly useful hurdler/chaser up to 3m Joueur d'Estruval: modest form in bumpers: fairly useful form over hurdles: won maiden at Chepstow in January: improved again when 3¾ lengths second to Game On in novice at Uttoxeter: often travels strongly. *Jo Hughes*   h121   b84

DIAKALI (FR) 9 gr.g. Sinndar (IRE) – Diasilixa (FR) (Linamix (FR)) [2017/18 h160: h20s^6 h21.5s^6 Apr 28] good-topped gelding: very smart hurdler at best: well held both starts in 2017/18: has form at 25f, but effective at much shorter: acts on heavy going: wears headgear: enthusiastic front runner. *Gary Moore*   h106

DIAMANT BLEU (FR) 5 b.g. Montmartre (FR) – Cate Bleue (FR) (Katowice (FR)) [2017/18 h115: h17.4d* h19.4d^6 h19.8s^6 c19.2v^4 c20v* c19.4v^5 Apr 3] sturdy gelding: fairly useful form over hurdles: won 4-y-o event at Auteuil in May: useful form over fences: won novice handicap at Sandown (beating Silverhow 8 lengths, overcoming mistakes) in March: stays 2½m: acts on heavy going: often races towards rear. *Nick Williams*   c130   h119

DIAMANT DE L'OUEST (FR) 5 b.g. Epalo (GER) – Ortezia (FR) (Evening World (FR)) [2017/18 b–: h19.9d^6 h16.7g h16.2s^4 h24.1s h21.2v h25v Feb 19] tall, rather unfurnished gelding: modest form over hurdles: unproven beyond 2m: acts on soft going: tried in cheekpieces. *Brian Ellison*   h86

DIAMOND BENNY (IRE) 6 b.g. Milan – Ben's Pride (Bollin Eric) [2017/18 h–, b–: h21g^5 h21.4g Oct 29] last in bumper: poor form over hurdles: tried in tongue tie. *Robert Stephens*   h66

DIAMOND BRIG 6 b.g. Black Sam Bellamy (IRE) – Lady Brig (Overbury (IRE)) [2017/18 c26.2v* Apr 16] second foal: brother to fairly useful hurdler/winning pointer Over To Sam (2¾m winner): dam, winning pointer, half-sister to fair hurdler/fairly useful chaser (2¾m-3¼m winner) Taramoss: won 3 of 4 starts in points: 5/4, won maiden hunter at Kelso (by 21 lengths from Chanceiton, easing clear from 2 out) on chasing debut: open to improvement. *Mrs Wendy Hamilton*   c107 p

DIAMOND CAUCHOIS (FR) 7 b.g. Crillon (FR) – Diamond Turtle (FR) (Limnos (JPN)) [2017/18 h20v^3 h20v* h24v^3 h21v* h20v^2 h24d^6 Apr 26] smart hurdler: won handicap in December and Boyne Hurdle in February (by 9 lengths from Lieutenant Colonel), both at Navan: good second in Keelings Irish Strawberry Hurdle at Fairyhouse (5½ lengths behind Coquin Mans) in April: stays 3m: acts on good to firm and heavy going: in tongue tie last 4 starts. *Gordon Elliott, Ireland*   h151

DIAMOND FORT (IRE) 6 ch.g. Gamut (IRE) – Ellie Forte (Alflora (IRE)) [2017/18 h116p, b88: h19.7s* h18.9v^{pu} h19.7s Jan 13] unplaced in Irish points: fairly useful form over hurdles: won handicap at Wetherby on return in November: disappointing both starts after: stays 2½m: acts on heavy going. *Fergal O'Brien*   h124

DIAMOND GAIT 5 b.m. Passing Glance – Milliegait (Tobougg (IRE)) [2017/18 b16d* b15.8s^2 b16v^5 b16.8g Apr 19] £8,500 3-y-o: sturdy mare: fourth foal: half-sister to bumper winner/fairly useful hurdler Gaitway (2m winner, by Medicean): dam, 7f winner (ran once over hurdles), half-sister to useful 2m hurdler Bold Gait out of half-sister to Champion Hurdle winner Royal Gait: fairly useful form in mares bumpers: won at Warwick in November: best effort when second in listed event at Huntingdon (2¼ lengths behind Duhallow Gesture) in December: in tongue tie last 3 starts. *Kim Bailey*   b98

DIAMOND GUY (FR) 5 b.g. Konig Turf (GER) – Unique Chance (FR) (Network (GER)) [2017/18 b100: h15.3g^4 ab18d^2 h15.3d* Apr 22] bumper winner: much better effort in novice hurdles at Wincanton (fairly useful form) when winning 14-runner event in April, beating Shoal Bay impressively by 2¼ lengths: in tongue tie last 3 starts: likely to progress further. *Paul Nicholls*   h115 p

DIE

DIAMOND JOEL 6 b.g. Youmzain (IRE) – Miss Lacroix (Picea) [2017/18 h16g Aug 1]   h–
formerly fairly useful staying handicapper on Flat, tailed off only start in 2018: little form
over hurdles, off 10½ months before return. *David Dennis*

DIAMOND KING (IRE) 10 b.g. King's Theatre (IRE) – Georgia On My Mind (FR)   c–
(Belmez (USA)) [2017/18 c144, h–: c21g⁵ h20v³ h21.1s^pu h23.1s* h20s^pu Apr 28] useful-   h135
looking gelding: useful hurdler nowadays: workmanlike winner of minor event at Thurles
in March: form in 2017/18 otherwise only when third in another minor event at
Punchestown (2¾ lengths behind Killultagh Vic) in December: useful novice chaser in
2016/17: stays 23f: acts on heavy going: wears tongue tie. *Gordon Elliott, Ireland*

DIAMOND REFLECTION (IRE) 6 b.g. Oasis Dream – Briolette (IRE) (Sadler's   h–
Wells (USA)) [2017/18 h63: h15.8g Sep 13] fair on Flat (stays 1¼m), successful in
January: poor maiden hurdler: will prove best around 2m: in headgear last 5 starts: wears
tongue tie. *Tom Weston*

DIAMOND REGGIE (IRE) 5 ch.g. Stowaway – Monilea Lady (IRE) (Accordion)   h–
[2017/18 b75: b16g h20v Nov 12] workmanlike gelding: poor form in bumpers: tailed off   b74
in maiden on hurdling debut. *Peter Bowen*

DIAMOND ROCK 7 b.g. Kayf Tara – Crystal Princess (IRE) (Definite Article) [2017/18   c110
h102: c17.4d c17.4g* c15.9d² c15.9s^pu Jan 11] winning hurdler: fair form over fences: won   h–
handicap at Bangor in October: stays 19f: acts on good to soft and good to firm going.
Henry Oliver

DIAMONDSARETRUMPS (IRE) 5 b.m. Dick Turpin (IRE) – Serial Sinner (IRE)   h–
(High Chaparral (IRE)) [2017/18 h15.8d^pu Jul 30] modest maiden on Flat, stays 7f: pulled
up in mares novice on hurdling debut. *Phil McEntee*

DICA (FR) 12 ch.g. Kapgarde (FR) – Easy World (FR) (Lost World (IRE)) [2017/18 c65,   c120
h–: c24.2g c20.1g* c20.1g² c21.2g² c17.3s³ c15.6g² c15.6v* c19.3d* c20.1g³ c19.3s*   h–
c15.7s* c15.9v⁵ Apr 17] winning hurdler: fairly useful handicap chaser: won at Hexham in
June and September, Sedgefield in October and December, and Catterick in March: stays
3¼m, but at least as effective at much shorter: acts on any going: has worn tongue tie: front
runner. *Paul Collins*

DICEY O'REILLY (IRE) 6 b.g. Stowaway – Moydrum Castle (IRE) (Arctic Lord)   h131
[2017/18 h16v⁴ h20s* h22s⁵ h24d^pu Apr 26] fourth foal: dam (h110) 2m-2½m hurdle
winner (stayed 3m): off mark in points on third attempt: useful form over hurdles: won
maiden at Leopardstown (by 3½ lengths from Mortal) in December: seemed amiss final
outing: tried in hood: in tongue tie last 3 starts. *Henry de Bromhead, Ireland*

DICK DARSIE (IRE) 8 br.g. Darsi (FR) – Hurricane Jane (IRE) (Strong Gale) [2017/18   c94 §
c100, h98: c24s^ur c26.3s² c24.2s* c24.2v^pu c24.1v⁵ c26.2d⁶ Mar 31] maiden hurdler: h–
modest handicap chaser: fortunate when winning novice at Wetherby in December: stays
3¼m: acts on heavy going: usually races nearer last than first: temperamental (usually soon
off bridle). *Sue Smith*

DICOSIMO (FR) 7 b.g. Laveron – Coralisse Royale (FR) (Tip Moss (FR)) [2017/18   c137 §
c22.5g² c20s² c19.9s c16g² c18.2s^pu c16g⁴ h19.3d⁵ h23.4s^pu h19.2s* h19v⁴ Apr 12] good-   h137 §
topped gelding: useful handicap chaser: won at Fontwell (by 5 lengths from Free Range)
in March: useful chaser: second in novice at Wexford (length behind Peregrine Run) in
July: left W. P. Mullins after sixth start: stays 2¾m: acts on heavy going: has worn hood,
including last 4 starts: often leads: temperamental. *Warren Greatrex*

DIDTHEYLEAVEUOUTTO (IRE) 5 ch.g. Presenting – Pretty Puttens (IRE) (Snurge)   b111 +
[2017/18 ab16g* b15.7d* b16.4s Mar 14] sturdy gelding: fourth foal: brother to bumper
winner Armaans Wish and half-brother to a winning pointer by Robin des Champs: dam
unraced half-sister to Cheltenham Gold Cup winner Denman: smart form in bumpers: won
at Lingfield (by 10 lengths from Ceara Be, displaying most impressive turn of foot) in
November and listed event at Ascot (readily by 2¾ lengths from Bullionaire) in December:
12/1, mid-field in Champion Bumper won by Relegate final start. *Nick Gifford*

DIEG MAN (FR) 5 ch.g. Kapgarde (FR) – Majestic Card (FR) (Ultimately Lucky (IRE))   h125
[2017/18 h17.9s² h17.9s* h19.9s* h19.3s h19.9v⁶ Mar 23] second foal: dam,
French maiden (placed up to 9.5f), sister to fairly useful French hurdler/chaser (2m/17f
winner) Like A Storm: fairly useful hurdler: won handicap at Auteuil (then left Y. Fouin) in
June, and novices at Sedgefield (conditionals event) in November and Catterick in January:
stays 2½m: acts on soft going: tried in cheekpieces/tongue tie. *Neil Mulholland*

DIE

DIEGO DU CHARMIL (FR) 6 b.g. Ballingarry (IRE) – Daramour (FR) (Anabaa   **c155 p**
Blue) [2017/18 h146: c16.3d* c16.3g³ c16.2s² c16.8s^F c15.8s* c15.5d⁵ Apr 28]   **h–**

    Diego du Charmil is getting closer to fulfilling the hopes expressed by his trainer when he was a juvenile that he will make 'a cracking two-mile chaser'. That prediction came after Diego du Charmil had won the Fred Winter Juvenile Handicap at the Cheltenham Festival on his British debut, after being allotted a handicap mark based solely on three placed efforts in juvenile hurdles in France for Arnaud Chaille-Chaille before the switch to Paul Nicholls. Diego du Charmil wasn't immediately sent chasing after winning the Fred Winter, improving into a useful two-mile handicap hurdler in his second season, but the long-term plan was put into effect in his latest campaign. Diego du Charmil beat his stablemate—and only opponent—Bagad Bihoue (who had already completed an early-season four-timer) on his chasing debut at Newton Abbot in September but then had the misfortune to strike into himself badly, managing only third to Shantou Rock, when seeking to follow up over the same course and distance the following month. 'He was only millimetres away from a fatal injury and he's lucky to be still with us,' says Paul Nicholls.

    That setback resulted in a four-month absence from the track, and the loss of valuable opportunities for Diego du Charmil to gain further experience. He made no impression on Arkle contender Saint Calvados in the Kingmaker Novices' Chase at Warwick on his return, finishing twenty-two lengths second, considerately ridden by Bryony Frost who was unable to claim her allowance on the day because of the status of the race. Diego du Charmil clearly wasn't ready for an Arkle challenge himself and plans to run him in the Grand Annual instead at the Cheltenham Festival were eventually shelved on account of the very soft going. Bryony Frost, able to claim her 3 lb this time, kept the mount on Diego du Charmil when he started a short-priced favourite in a valuable novice handicap at Ascot in late-March. He jumped boldly and accurately before coming down in unfortunate fashion at the third last, jumping the fence perfectly well but stumbling on landing. Diego du Charmil was still hard on the bridle when departing and looked like winning.

    Connections could have taken advantage of Diego du Charmil's handicap mark in Aintree's equivalent of the Grand Annual, the Red Rum, at the Grand National meeting, but instead he was thrown in at the deep end in Aintree's equivalent of the Arkle, the Doom Bar Maghull Novices' Chase. The Arkle third

Doom Bar Maghull Novices' Chase, Aintree—
Harry Cobden and Diego du Charmil lower the colours of odds-on Petit Mouchoir (grey)

Mrs Johnny de la Hey's "Diego du Charmil"

Petit Mouchoir started odds on, in a six-runner field lacking in depth for a Grade 1, but he became worked up beforehand and almost certainly didn't fully do himself justice on the day. Diego du Charmil was the one to take advantage, travelling well and jumping fluently in the main before leading on the bridle approaching the last and beating the keeping-on Petit Mouchoir by two and a half lengths, with front-running Shantou Rock six lengths further back in third. Diego du Charmil gave his stable a second Grade 1 at the meeting, following the success of Politologue in the Melling Chase the previous day. Politologue was ridden by the stable's number-one Sam Twiston-Davies but he didn't ride Diego du Charmil, with nineteen-year-old Harry Cobden, champion conditional in the 2016/17 season, taking over from Bryony Frost (who would not have been able to draw her allowance). Cobden and Frost—the latter became something of a 'media darling'—were both given more opportunities by Paul Nicholls in the latest season, riding a couple of dozen winners each for the yard. Twiston-Davies still received the lion's share of the rides at Manor Farm Stables and rode nearly fifty winners for the yard, but the emergence of Cobden and Frost eroded his position as the stable's top jockey. Twiston-Davies' seasonal total of one hundred and eight winners was his lowest since the days before he was appointed stable jockey in 2014 and he announced at the end of the season that he would be riding as a freelance in 2018/19. Harry Cobden, announced as Twiston-Davies' replacement as number-one, made an unlucky start to his new job when fracturing a bone in his neck in a fall riding at Market Rasen early in the new season for Colin Tizzard, who had been rumoured to be hoping to secure Cobden's services. Cobden seems likely to be back in time for the main part of the season, though the injury proved more serious than first reported. As for Diego du Charmil, he didn't fare so well in the Celebration Chase at Sandown's Finale meeting where, stepping into open company for the first time and again ridden by Cobden, he came last of

DIE

five finishers behind long odds-on Altior (with stablemate San Benedeto, ridden by Twiston-Davies, finishing runner-up at 33/1). Exactly what Diego du Charmil has achieved over fences so far is not completely straightforward to pin down on form, but there is no doubt that, considering his interrupted campaign, he remains a very interesting prospect for the top two-mile races. His trainer still retains plenty of faith in him, saying 'He's got a load of toe, he jumps well and there's a lot to come, he wants to mature a bit but he's a good horse.'

Diego du Charmil (FR) (b.g. 2012)
- Ballingarry (IRE) (b 1999)
  - Sadler's Wells (b 1981)
    - Northern Dancer
    - Fairy Bridge
  - Flamenco Wave (ch 1986)
    - Desert Wine
    - Armada Way
- Daramour (FR) (b 2005)
  - Anabaa Blue (b 1998)
    - Anabaa
    - Allez Les Trois
  - Negligente (b 1996)
    - Quest For Fame
    - Nobile Decretum

The tall, good-topped Diego du Charmil is by the French-based Sadler's Wells stallion Ballingarry who stands at a fee of €2,500 and has been represented by a number of above-average performers on this side of the Channel, including smart staying hurdler Aubusson. Diego du Charmil is the second foal out of the French Flat maiden Daramour whose first foal, Days of Heaven (by Saint des Saints), is a smart chaser for Nicky Henderson. The free-going Days of Heaven stays two and a half miles, but Diego du Charmil has been raced only at around two miles. He acts on soft going, wears a tongue tie and often travels strongly in his races. *Paul Nicholls*

DIESE DES BIEFFES (FR) 5 gr.g. Martaline – Chanel du Berlais (FR) (Saint Preuil (FR)) [2017/18 b76p: h17.7g* h16.5g* h16d² h21s⁵ h20.3v⁵ h20.3g* Apr 18] useful novice hurdler: successful at Fontwell (conditionals event) and Taunton in November, and at Cheltenham (by 2 lengths from Theclockisticking) in April: good fifth in competitive handicaps at Kempton and Cheltenham between last 2 wins: stays 21f: acts on heavy going: often races prominently: likeable type, still open to improvement. *Nicky Henderson* **h136 p**

DIFFERENT GRAVEY (IRE) 8 b.g. High Chaparral (IRE) – Newtown Dancer (IRE) (Danehill Dancer (IRE)) [2017/18 c144§, h–§: c19.4d⁶ c22.4gᵘʳ h21.4v Dec 26] tall gelding: high-class hurdler at best: no form since 2015/16, except when winning 4-runner maiden at Ascot following season on first of 2 starts over fences: stays 2½m: acts on heavy going: tried in cheekpieces: temperamental. *Polly Gundry* **c98 §** **h– §**

DIG A BIT DEEPER 5 b.g. Duke of Marmalade (IRE) – Dayia (IRE) (Act One) [2017/18 b61: h19.6dᵖᵘ h19.3s h16v⁵ h19.7v h24.1dᵖᵘ Mar 29] poor form in bumpers: no solid form over hurdles: often races freely close up. *Tim Easterby* **h–**

DIJON (IRE) 5 b.g. High Chaparral (IRE) – Royal Shyness (Royal Academy (USA)) [2017/18 b16.2g⁴ b16.2v Oct 14] £3,000 4-y-o: half-brother to several winners on Flat, including smart 7f/1m winner Commander Cave (by Tale of The Cat): dam useful 5.5f-6.5f winner: modest form when fourth to Fred The Foot on first of 2 starts in bumpers at Hexham. *John Quinn* **b82**

DIMINPETE 5 ch.g. Geordieland (FR) – Sonoma (IRE) (Dr Devious (IRE)) [2017/18 b16g b15.3s h16dᵖᵘ Nov 27] well beaten in bumpers: pulled up in novice on hurdling debut. *Jeremy Scott* **h–** **b–**

DIMPLE (FR) 7 gr.g. Montmartre (FR) – Dynella (FR) (Sillery (USA)) [2017/18 c116, h95: c23g³ c21.6gᵖᵘ c19.9d⁵ Mar 16] unbeaten in 3 points: maiden hurdler: fair chaser: left A. Slattery after first start: stays 21f: acts on good to soft going: has worn hood. *Iain Jardine* **c106** **h–**

DINARIA DES OBEAUX (FR) 5 b.m. Saddler Maker (IRE) – Indiana Jaune (FR) (Le Nain Jaune (FR)) [2017/18 h130: c16s* c20.6v* c20s⁴ c24s⁶ c20v* c16v³ c22.5v² c20s⁵ Apr 21] rather unfurnished mare: useful hurdler: similar form over fences: won maiden at Wexford in October, listed mares race at Clonmel (by 22 lengths) in November and Grade 2 mares novice at Thurles (by 8 lengths from Magic of Light) in January: stays 21f: best form on soft/heavy going: tried in cheekpieces: wears tongue tie: usually races prominently. *Gordon Elliott, Ireland* **c137** **h–**

DING DING 7 ch.m. Winker Watson – Five Bells (IRE) (Rock of Gibraltar (IRE)) [2017/18 h107: h21m⁶ h20.5g h20.5d* h25d⁶ h21.7v⁵ h20.7s h20.5v² h21.7d² h20.5v⁶ Mar 12] short-backed mare: fair handicap hurdler: won at Plumpton (good record there) in November: stays 2¾m: acts on good to firm and heavy going: often races towards rear. *Sheena West* **h107**

DIS

DINGO DOLLAR (IRE) 6 ch.g. Golden Lariat (USA) – Social Society (IRE) (Moscow Society (USA)) [2017/18 h126: c23.6g⁴ c24.2s^F c23.4s* c24d* c24.1g² Apr 21] useful-looking gelding: fairly useful hurdler: smart form over fences: won novice handicap at Newbury in December and novice at Doncaster in February: second in novice handicap at Ayr (length behind Crosshue Boy after forcing strong pace) final outing: stays 3¼m: acts on soft going: in cheekpieces last 2 starts: open to further improvement. *Alan King* — **c147 p**, **h–**

DINOS BENEFIT (IRE) 6 ch.m. Mr Dinos (IRE) – Beneficial Lady (IRE) (Beneficial) [2017/18 b15.7s⁴ h21.4v⁴ h16s* h16.6s³ h21.6s³ Apr 23] €1,200 3-y-o, £32,000 5-y-o: fifth foal: half-sister to a winning pointer by Royal Anthem: dam unraced half-sister to useful chaser (21f-29f winner) Trust Fund: won twice in Irish points: fourth in mares bumper at Towcester: modest form over hurdles: won mares novice at Chepstow in March: left Kayley Woollacott after second start: should stay at least 2½m: front runner/races prominently. *Colin Tizzard* — **h99**, **b83**

DINO VELVET (FR) 5 b.g. Naaqoos – Matgil (FR) (Grape Tree Road) [2017/18 h123: h16d⁵ h20.5d⁵ h21s h16.8v⁵ h16g* Apr 20] sturdy gelding: fairly useful handicap hurdler: won at Ayr in April: should stay beyond 2m: acts on soft going: often races towards rear. *Alan King* — **h124**

DINSDALE 5 b.g. Cape Cross (IRE) – Emmy Award (IRE) (Sadler's Wells (USA)) [2017/18 h116: h16d^pu h19.8s h16s⁴ h16d² h16m Apr 26] good-topped gelding: fair handicap hurdler: probably stays 19f: acts on soft going: has worn cheekpieces, including last 3 outings (also in tongue tie last 2). *Michael Scudamore* — **h111**

DIPLOMATE SIVOLA (FR) 5 ch.g. Noroit (GER) – None de Sivola (FR) (Cyborg (FR)) [2017/18 h16.9m* c17.9g² c18.4g c18.9d² c19.9g² c19.9g² h17.4s h17.4s⁶ h19.9s^F c20d⁴ c19.3g³ Apr 23] fourth foal: half-brother to fair French chaser Carnet d'Or Sivola (19f winner, by Assessor) and fair French hurdler Une Fois de Sivola (17f winner, by Kidder): dam French maiden hurdler/chaser: fair hurdler: won 4-y-o event at Nancy in May: fairly useful maiden chaser: runner-up 4 times in 4-y-o events in France: comfortably held in hunters last 2 outings: left A. Adeline de Boisbrunet after sixth start, Richard Chotard after ninth: stays 2½m: acts on soft and good to firm going. *Philip Hobbs* — **c115**, **h112**

DIPLOMATICO (USA) 5 b.g. Ambassador (GER) – Dulcet Tone (USA) (Empire Maker (USA)) [2017/18 h21g^pu h15.8s h15.8d Mar 26] fairly useful form on first of 2 starts on Flat in Germany: showed little in maiden/novice hurdles. *David Bridgwater* — **h–**

DIPPIN AND DIVING (IRE) 5 b.g. Kalanisi (IRE) – Supreme Dipper (IRE) (Supreme Leader) [2017/18 b16.4d Mar 16] tailed off in bumper. *George Bewley* — **b–**

DIRTY DEXTER 7 b.g. Beat All (USA) – Redlands Charm (Classic Cliche (IRE)) [2017/18 h–, b–: h22d^pu h24s⁴ h23.3v^pu h24s^pu h23.9v^pu h18.5v⁵ Apr 8] poor maiden hurdler: best effort at 3m on soft going: in headgear last 3 starts, also in tongue tie last 2. *Grace Harris* — **h64**

DISCKO DES PLAGES (FR) 5 b.g. Balko (FR) – Lady des Plages (FR) (Chamberlin (FR)) [2017/18 b15.7v⁶ b16.2s Apr 27] well held both starts in bumpers (sent off 11/4 for debut). *Richard Hobson* — **b–**

DISCORAMA (FR) 5 b.g. Saddler Maker (IRE) – Quentala (FR) (Lone Bid (FR)) [2017/18 h18s* h20v² h22.3v³ h16s h20.3v² h24s⁵ Apr 25] half-brother to French bumper winners Vitopoto (1½m winner, by Passing Sale) and Brichardier (15f winner, by Honolulu): dam unraced: useful form over hurdles: won maiden at Fairyhouse in December: did very well from poor position when 5 lengths second of 23 to Blow By Blow in Martin Pipe Conditional Jockeys' Handicap Hurdle at Cheltenham in March: stays 2½m: raced only on soft/heavy going: tried in hood: often races in rear. *Paul Nolan, Ireland* — **h136**

DISCOURS D'UN ROI (FR) 6 ch.g. Vision d'Etat (FR) – Reine de Lestrade (FR) (Sabrehill (USA)) [2017/18 h–: h16d^pu Oct 15] fairly useful winning juvenile hurdler in France in 2015/16: lightly raced and disappointing since: raced around 2m: acts on good to firm and good to soft going: tried in tongue tie. *Nicky Henderson* — **h–**

DISCOVERIE 10 b.g. Runyon (IRE) – Sri (IRE) (Sri Pekan (USA)) [2017/18 c112, h102: h16.2g⁵ h17d^ur h16.8s⁴ c15.7d⁶ c15.7s² c19.3v^pu h16.8v³ h15.7s* c16.4g⁵ Apr 23] lengthy gelding: modest handicap hurdler: won selling event at Catterick in March: fair handicap chaser: best around 2m nowadays: acts on good to firm and heavy going: wears headgear: signs of temperament. *Kenneth Slack* — **c110**, **h99**

DIS DONC (FR) 5 b.g. Kingsalsa (USA) – Skarina (FR) (Dark Moondancer) [2017/18 h16m h16g² h16s² h16s² h16v* h16v¹ h16.5d Apr 24] second foal: half-brother to French 1½m bumper winner/19f hurdle winner Chakina (by Fragrant Mix): dam lightly-raced half-sister to fairly useful hurdler (stayed 2½m) Ugolin de Beaumont: French bumper — **h130**

DIS

winner: useful hurdler: won maiden at Navan in February: further progress when second in handicap at same track (nose behind Monotype) following month: raced around 2m: acts on heavy going: has worn hood: often races prominently. *Noel Meade, Ireland*

DISKO (FR) 7 gr.g. Martaline – Nikos Royale (FR) (Nikos) [2017/18 c157, h–: c19.5s* Nov 4] useful-looking gelding: lightly-raced winning hurdler: high-class chaser: won Grade 2 event at Down Royal (by ½ length from Ballyoisin) on reappearance: not seen after (suffered hock problem, then stress fracture): stays 25f, effective at shorter: acts on soft going: wears hood: usually races close up. *Noel Meade, Ireland* — **c164 + h–**

DISSAVRIL (FR) 5 gr.m. Balko – Odile (FR) (Smadoun (FR)) [2017/18 b16.7v* b17s Apr 12] useful-looking mare: fifth foal: dam French 1¼m/11f bumper winner: fairly useful form in bumpers: left O. Sauvaget, won listed mares event at Market Rasen (impressively by 2½ lengths from Aimee de Sivola) in January: tailed off in Grade 2 mares event at Aintree subsequently: may prove best at around 2m. *Emma Lavelle* — **b104**

DISTANT HIGH 7 b.m. High Chaparral (IRE) – Distant Dreamer (USA) (Rahy (USA)) [2017/18 h77: h15.8d³ h16.8d⁴ h16g⁶ h19g Sep 26] poor maiden hurdler: unproven beyond 2m: acts on good to soft going: has worn headgear, including last 4 starts. *Richard Price* — **h77**

DISTANT SOUND (IRE) 11 b.g. Luso – Distant Dreams (IRE) (Saddlers' Hall (IRE)) [2017/18 h86: h20.3g⁴ h19.6g^pu h23.9g^pu h20.3d⁵ Dec 5] point winner: poor handicap hurdler: left Richard Hawker after reappearance: stays 21f: acts on heavy going: wears headgear: tried in tongue tie: often races towards rear. *Adrian Wintle* — **h76**

DISTIME (IRE) 12 b.g. Flemensfirth (USA) – Technohead (IRE) (Distinctly North (USA)) [2017/18 c96, h–: c21.1s Apr 12] workmanlike gelding: winning hurdler: useful chaser in prime: lightly raced and only fair form since 2015/16: stays 25f: acts on heavy going. *Mrs D. J. Ralph* — **c103 h–**

DISTINGO (IRE) 5 b.g. Smart Strike (CAN) – Distinctive Look (IRE) (Danehill (USA)) [2017/18 h17.9g³ h17.6s² h17.9s^ur h17.4s⁴ h15.9v* h17.7v² h16s* h16.5s^pu Apr 13] compact gelding: half-brother to high-class hurdler Supasundae (2m-21f winner, by Galileo), stays 3m: fair on Flat, stays 12.5f: fairly useful hurdler: won maiden at Plumpton in January and novice at Kempton in March: left Francois Nicolle after fourth start: stays 2¼m: acts on heavy going: often in headgear. *Gary Moore* — **h126**

DISTRACTED (IRE) 10 b.m. Publisher (USA) – Richmond Usa (IRE) (Insan (USA)) [2017/18 c105, h–: c25.3d^pu c25.5s³ c25.1v^pu Mar 28] point winner: maiden hurdler: modest chaser nowadays: left R. Thomas after second start: stays 27f: acts on heavy going: wears headgear: in tongue tie last 2 starts. *Alan Roberts* — **c86 h–**

DITES RIEN (IRE) 6 b.m. Kalanisi (IRE) – Our Soiree (IRE) (Milan) [2017/18 h91, b–: h21.6g³ May 10] modest maiden hurdler: stays 2¾m: best form on good going. *Neil Mulholland* — **h83**

DIVA DU MAQUIS (FR) 5 b.m. Buck's Boum (FR) – Qualine du Maquis (FR) (Video Rock (FR)) [2017/18 b16d² b15.7d⁴ b18.5v⁵ h20.7s⁴ h15.8s⁶ h21.2d Apr 9] third foal: dam unraced half-sister to fair hurdler/useful chaser (2m/17f winner) Lorient Express and fairly useful hurdler/useful chaser (stayed 3¼m) Nikola: in frame in bumpers at Warwick and Southwell: modest form over hurdles: will stay at least 2¾m. *Noel Williams* — **h93 b82**

DIVA RECONCE (FR) 5 b.m. Kap Rock (FR) – Kruscyna (FR) (Ultimately Lucky (IRE)) [2017/18 b94: h21.2d² Dec 20] won only start in bumpers: off 10 months, shaped well when 2½ lengths second of 12 to Chilli Filli in novice at Ludlow on hurdling debut: sure to progress. *Kim Bailey* — **h105 p**

DIVIN BERE (FR) 5 b.g. Della Francesca (USA) – Mofa Bere (FR) (Saumarez) [2017/18 h142: h15.7d h16.3v h16.8v^pu Mar 16] good-topped gelding: useful hurdler as a juvenile: left Nicky Henderson, little show in competitive handicaps in 2017/18: raced around 2m: acts on soft going: tried in tongue strap. *Paul Nicholls* — **h–**

DIVINE PORT (USA) 8 b.g. Arch (USA) – Out of Reach (Warning) [2017/18 h–: h18.1v³ Apr 16] fair handicap hurdler: off 2 years before sole outing in 2017/18: stays 2½m: acts on heavy going: tried in tongue tie. *Sally Haynes* — **h101**

DIVINE SPEAR (IRE) 7 b.g. Oscar (IRE) – Testaway (IRE) (Commanche Run) [2017/18 h127: c19.2d* c16.8d* c19.9d² Feb 14] strong gelding: fairly useful hurdler: useful form over fences: won maiden at Catterick (despite track not suiting) in November and novice handicap at Ascot (by 10 lengths from Exitas) in December: stays 21f: acts on heavy going: should do well in handicap chases in 2018/19. *Nicky Henderson* — **c143 p h–**

DIZOARD 8 b.m. Desideratum – Riviere (Meadowbrook) [2017/18 h20.2g h20.1d[6] h23.3v[pu] h19.9g[4] Oct 3] poor maiden hurdler: should stay beyond 2½m: acts on soft going: often in hood. *Iain Jardine* — h66

DIZZEY HEIGHTS (IRE) 6 b.m. Halling (USA) – Extreme Pleasure (IRE) (High Chaparral (IRE)) [2017/18 h86: h15.7g[6] h15.8d[5] h16g* h15.8g[6] h19g h23.4s[4] h16v[6] Jan 22] modest handicap hurdler: won at Fakenham in November: should stay beyond 2m: best form on good going: wears hood: in tongue tie last 2 starts: often races towards rear. *Neil King* — h86

DIZZY CHIEF 6 b.m. Erhaab (USA) – Dizzy Whizz (Kayf Tara) [2017/18 b16.7g[3] b17v[5] Apr 17] £2,600 4-y-o: first foal: dam (b88) bumper winner: modest form on first of 2 starts in bumpers. *Andrew Crook* — b76

DJAKADAM (FR) 9 b.g. Saint des Saints (FR) – Rainbow Crest (FR) (Baryshnikov (AUS)) [2017/18 c169, h–: c20.2v[2] c24d[pu] c24s[3] c26.3v[5] c24.5s[2] Apr 25] strong gelding: winning hurdler: top-class chaser at best, in frame in Cheltenham Gold Cup on 3 occasions: not quite the force of old in 2017/18, best efforts when second in John Durkan Memorial Punchestown Chase (beaten 7 lengths by Sizing John, had won 2 previous runnings) in December and Punchestown Gold Cup (¾ length behind Bellshill, runner-up in race for 4th time) in April: reportedly retired after sustaining hock injury in Grand Steeple-Chase de Paris at Auteuil shortly after end of season: stayed 3¼m: acted on heavy going: front runner/raced prominently. *W. P. Mullins, Ireland* — c165 h–

DJANGO DJANGO (FR) 5 gr.g. Voix du Nord (FR) – Lady Jannina (Sir Harry Lewis (USA)) [2017/18 b17.7g[4] h15.3s[5] h15.7s[6] h16.6s[2] h15.8s* h21g[4] h21s h16s Apr 28] €80,000 3-y-o: sturdy gelding: first foal: dam, in frame in bumpers, sister to fairly useful hurdler/chaser (stayed 3m) Top Totti out of half-sister to very smart staying chaser Antonin and to dam of top-class staying hurdler Mighty Man: fourth in bumper at Fontwell: fairly useful hurdler: won novice at Huntingdon in January: stays 21f: acts on soft going. *Jonjo O'Neill* — h118 b89

DJARKEVI (FR) 5 b.g. Khalkevi (IRE) – Onvavoir (FR) (Diableneyev (USA)) [2017/18 b16.8g[6] h16.6d h16.7g[3] Apr 22] €24,000 3-y-o, £68,000 4-y-o: third foal: dam unraced half-sister to dam of Grand National winner Pineau de Re: off mark at second attempt in Irish points: well beaten in bumper: better effort over hurdles (modest form) when third in maiden at Market Rasen: open to further improvement. *Charlie Longsdon* — h98 p b–

DJIN CONTI (FR) 5 b.g. Lucarno (USA) – Regina Conti (FR) (Lavirco (GER)) [2017/18 h17.4d[3] h16.5s[3] Jan 20] third foal: half-brother to useful hurdler Chateau Conti (2m-2½m winner, by Vendangeur) and bumper winner Bingo Conti (by Coastal Path): dam, French 1½m bumper winner, half-sister to dam of Silviniaco Conti: modest form on first of 2 starts over hurdles (left A. Adeline de Boisbrunet in between): remains capable of better. *Harry Whittington* — h99 p

DJINGLE (FR) 5 b.g. Voix du Nord (FR) – Jourie (FR) (Lute Antique (FR)) [2017/18 h16.9s[4] h17.9s* h17.9s[4] h16.8v[4] Feb 11] fifth foal: dam French 2½m chase winner: fairly useful form over hurdles: won 4-y-o event in September and listed race in November (by 6 lengths from Go For de Houelle), both at Auteuil: left A. Chaille-Chaille, possibly amiss in listed novice at Exeter: wears hood. *Paul Nicholls* — h129

D'NAILOR (IRE) 8 b.g. Stowaway – Lanesboro Lights (IRE) (Millfontaine) [2017/18 c97, h92: c21.2g[3] c21.2s[pu] Dec 4] maiden hurdler: modest handicap chaser: stays 21f: acts on heavy going: has worn cheekpieces, including last 5 starts. *Jennie Candlish* — c94 h–

DOCALI (IRE) 6 b.g. Dark Angel (IRE) – Housekeeping (Dansili) [2017/18 h–: h17.2d[pu] May 31] bad maiden hurdler: tried in blinkers/tongue tie. *Hugh Burns* — h–

DOC CARVER (IRE) 7 ch.g. Lakeshore Road (USA) – Tuney Tulip (IRE) (Taipan (IRE)) [2017/18 h16.7g[5] h15.5d[2] h16.7v[2] h15.7v[F] h15.9d[4] h16.8v[pu] Apr 8] £2,500 3-y-o: fourth foal: dam unraced half-sister to useful chaser (21f-29f winner) Trust Fund: winning pointer: tongue tied, well held in bumper (for R. Donohoe): fairly useful novice hurdler: second at Leicester in November and Bangor in January: lost form after falling next start: should stay further than 17f: acts on heavy going. *Henry Oliver* — h117

DOC PENFRO 6 b.g. Dr Massini (IRE) – Prescelli (IRE) (Snurge) [2017/18 b16v[4] b16v[4] b16.4s Mar 14] £65,000 4-y-o: rangy gelding: first foal: dam (c114/h114) ungenuine 21f/2¾m hurdle/chase winner: in front when fell last in Irish point: fair form in bumpers: best effort when fourth at Wetherby in February: will stay at least 2½m. *Kevin Frost* — b89

DOCTOR BARTOLO (IRE) 4 g.g. Sir Prancealot (IRE) – Operissimo (Singspiel (IRE)) [2017/18 h16s[2] h16.3s[2] h16s* Feb 23] sturdy gelding: fairly useful on Flat, stayed 12.5f: fairly useful form over hurdles: won juvenile at Warwick in February: dead. *Alan King* — h127

DOC

DOCTOR DEX (IRE) 5 b.g. Oscar (IRE) – Larnalee (IRE) (Presenting) [2017/18 b15.7d² b15.7d⁵ b16.2s² Apr 27] €41,000 3-y-o: first foal: dam (h95), 2¼m hurdle winner, half-sister to fairly useful hurdler/useful chaser (stayed 25f) Shuil Aris: fairly useful form in bumpers: second at Southwell (maiden) in November and Perth in April. *Tom George* **b98**

DOCTOR HAZE 7 b.g. Dr Massini (IRE) – Gypsy Haze (Romany Rye) [2017/18 h16v² h15.5d h23.1v³ h21.3d^pu Mar 29] half-brother to useful chaser Midnight Haze (2½m-25f winner, by Midnight Legend) and modest hurdler Sahara Haze (3¼m winner, by Rainbow High): dam winning pointer: winning pointer: fair form when second in novice at Chepstow on hurdling debut: went wrong way after: should be suited by 2½m+. *Kim Bailey* **h101**

DOCTOR LOOK HERE (IRE) 8 b.g. Dr Massini (IRE) – Eye Vision (IRE) (Taipan (IRE)) [2017/18 h110: h23.1m* h25g^pu May 25] good-topped gelding: fair handicap hurdler: won at Exeter in May: went wrong next time: stays 3¼m: acts on good to firm and heavy going: in cheekpieces last 2 starts: often travels strongly. *Susan Gardner* **h114**

DOCTOR PHOENIX (IRE) 10 br.g. Dr Massini (IRE) – Lowroad Cross (IRE) (Anshan) [2017/18 c138, h–: c17d² c16.7v* c16.5s c17s* c16s* c16v² c20v^F c16s⁵ Apr 24] winning hurdler: high-class chaser: left David Dennis, vast improvement in 2017/18, winning handicap at Cork in November, Dan Moore Memorial Handicap Chase at Fairyhouse in January and Grade 3 event at Naas (by 13 lengths from Alisier d'Irlande) in February: running even better when falling heavily 2 out (had taken off just in front) in Devenish Chase won by Un de Sceaux at Fairyhouse in April: stays 21f: acts on heavy going: wears cheekpieces/tongue tie: often races in rear: responds generously to pressure. *Gordon Elliott, Ireland* **c162 h–**

DOCTOR THEA 5 b.m. Multiplex – Kallithea (IRE) (Dr Fong (USA)) [2017/18 b73: b17s³ b16.2g⁵ h19.4d⁵ h19.4s h15.7s⁵ Mar 7] lengthy mare: modest form in bumpers: poor form in novice hurdles. *Jedd O'Keeffe* **h79 b82**

DOCTOR TIGER 7 b.g. Dr Massini (IRE) – Run Tiger (IRE) (Commanche Run) [2017/18 b16f³ h19.4s Jan 26] off mark in points at sixth attempt: tongue tied, tailed off in bumper/maiden hurdle. *Jack R. Barber* **h– b–**

Nick Bradley's "Doctor Phoenix"

DOL

DOCTOR WONG 6 b.g. Dr Massini (IRE) – Kitty Wong (IRE) (Supreme Leader) [2017/18 b16.8d⁶ Apr 24] placed in points: tailed off in maiden bumper. *Tom George*   b–

DODGYBINGO (IRE) 5 b.g. Roderic O'Connor (IRE) – Happy Flight (IRE) (Titus Livius (FR)) [2017/18 h108: h17.2m* h17g⁶ h17g h18.8g⁶ h16g Apr 20] rather leggy gelding: fairly useful hurdler: won minor event at Ballinrobe in May: left Noel Meade after fourth start: best around 2m: acts on soft and good to firm going: wears headgear: front runner/races prominently. *James Moffatt*   h120

DOES IT IN STYLE (FR) 5 b.g. Balko (FR) – Malta de Ronceray (FR) (Dress Parade) [2017/18 h–: h15.5d² h16.6s⁴ Jan 26] poor form over hurdles: will stay 2½m: acts on soft going: in cheekpieces last 2 starts. *Dan Skelton*   h74

DOESN'TBOTHERME (IRE) 7 b.m. Brian Boru – Nicky's Gun (IRE) (Needle Gun (IRE)) [2017/18 h–: h23.3g^pu May 13] maiden pointer: no promise in novice/maiden hurdle. *Victor Thompson*   h–

DOESYOURDOGBITE (IRE) 6 b.g. Notnowcato – Gilah (IRE) (Saddlers' Hall (IRE)) [2017/18 h133: h19.5d h20.5d h21d h23.4v⁵ h23.1v Mar 11] compact gelding: fairly useful handicap hurdler: standout effort in 2017/18 when fifth at Sandown: stays 23f: acts on heavy going: in cheekpieces last 3 starts: temperament under suspicion. *Jonjo O'Neill*   h116

DOING FINE (IRE) 10 b.g. Presenting – Howaya Pet (IRE) (Montelimar (USA)) [2017/18 c136, h123: h25.8g⁴ c25g³ c28.8d⁴ c31.8g⁴ Apr 21] deep-girthed gelding: lightly-raced hurdler: fairly useful form when fourth in handicap at Fontwell on reappearance: useful handicap chaser: creditable efforts in frame in 2017/18, 11 lengths fourth of 29 to Joe Farrell in Scottish Grand National at Ayr final outing: stays really well: acts on heavy going: wears headgear/tongue tie: held up: responds generously to pressure. *Neil Mulholland*   c136 h127

DOITFORJOE (IRE) 8 ch.g. Vinnie Roe (IRE) – Native Kin (USA) (Be My Native (USA)) [2017/18 h116: c23.8m³ c21m⁵ c20.3g³ c22.6g⁴ h23g c23g³ c25.7m* c25.8g^pu Oct 13] Irish point winner: fairly useful hurdler at best: fair handicap chaser: won at Plumpton in September: stays 3¼m: acts on good to firm going: wears tongue tie: usually races towards rear. *David Dennis*   c108 h–

DOITFORTHEVILLAGE (IRE) 9 b.g. Turtle Island (IRE) – Last Chance Lady (IRE) (Mister Lord (USA)) [2017/18 c133, h–: h16g c15.9g⁶ c15.9d* h16.3s⁴ h15.8s² c16.3v⁶ c15.8s⁴ Apr 12] angular gelding: fair maiden hurdler: useful handicap chaser: won at Cheltenham (by 2 lengths from Kapstadt) in November: has form at 3m, but races mostly around 2m: acts on heavy going: has worn hood: wears tongue tie: often races in rear. *Paul Henderson*   c138 h107

DOKTOR GLAZ (FR) 8 b.g. Mount Nelson – Deviolina (IRE) (Dr Devious (IRE)) [2017/18 c103p, h103: c23.4g^u c24.2d² c23.8g³ c24s⁵ c19.1s* c20s* Apr 8] fair hurdler: fair handicap chaser: won at Doncaster (novice) in January and Carlisle in April: stays 3m: acts on soft going: in visor last 5 starts: front runner/races prominently. *Rose Dobbin*   c110 h–

DOLATULO (FR) 11 ch.g. Le Fou (IRE) – La Perspective (FR) (Beyssac (FR)) [2017/18 c126, h–: c32.5d* May 5] close-coupled gelding: winning hurdler: fairly useful chaser: won hunter at Cheltenham only start in 2017/18: stayed 33f: acted on heavy going: wore headgear: often tongue tied: dead. *Ben Pauling*   c124 h–

DOLLAR AND A DREAM (IRE) 9 b.g. Fruits of Love (USA) – Gorgeous Georgina (IRE) (Tirol) [2017/18 h16d⁶ h16.3m⁵ h19.6g h16.7g h16.7g h15.8m⁶ h15.8g h18.6g Nov 9] angular gelding: fair hurdler, disappointing in 2017/18: left A. J. Martin after first start: let down by jumping over fences: unproven beyond 17f: acts on soft and good to firm going: has worn headgear, including last 3 starts: usually in tongue tie: not one to trust. *Michael Mullineaux*   c– x h87 §

DOLLY BORU 7 b.m. Brian Boru – Dolly Sparks (IRE) (Electric) [2017/18 b16s May 17] seventh foal: half-sister to fairly useful hurdler/useful chaser Falcon Island (2m winner, by Turtle Island): dam, ran once in point, half-sister to useful 2m hurdler/chaser Queen of Spades and to dam of smart hurdler/useful staying chaser Pettifour: tailed off in mares bumper. *Paul Davies*   b–

DOLLY DIAMOND 9 b.m. Erhaab (USA) – Solid Land (FR) (Solid Illusion (USA)) [2017/18 h22d⁴ May 21] modest maiden hurdler at best: stays 21f: acts on heavy going. *Graeme McPherson*   h–

DOLLYS DESTINATION (IRE) 5 b.m. Dubai Destination (USA) – Rehill Lass (IRE) (Shernazar) [2017/18 b16.3s⁶ b16s⁴ b16.8g² Apr 23] second foal: dam (h85) bumper winner: placed in Irish maiden point: fair form in bumpers. *Noel C. Kelly, Ireland*   b87

DOL

DOLLY'S DOT (IRE) 7 b.m. Vertical Speed (FR) – Our Dot (IRE) (Supreme Leader) [2017/18 h62, b–: h16.2s h19.9s[6] h16.8v[4] h23.8d h19.9v[4] h19.9v* h20.6v[2] h20.2s Apr 27] workmanlike mare: placed in points: poor handicap hurdler: won at Sedgefield in March: stays 21f: best form on heavy going: front runner/races prominently. *Victor Thompson* — **h80**

DOLOS (FR) 5 b.g. Kapgarde (FR) – Redowa (FR) (Trempolino (USA)) [2017/18 h134: h16d[2] h15.7g c18.8d* c21d[3] c15.5s[2] c16.3v c16.5g[2] Apr 21] good-topped gelding: useful handicap hurdler: second at Chepstow (4½ lengths behind Silver Streak) in October: smart form over fences: won maiden at Ascot (by 29 lengths) in November: best effort when second in listed handicap at Ayr (½ length behind Theinval) final outing: stays 19f: acts on soft going: wears tongue tie: travels strongly. *Paul Nicholls* — **c150 h132**

DOLPHIN VISTA (IRE) 5 b.g. Zoffany (IRE) – Fiordiligi (Mozart (IRE)) [2017/18 h16v[2] Jan 22] smart on Flat (stays 1¼m), won Cambridgeshire in 2017: 6/4, better than result when second in maiden at Fakenham (5 lengths behind Potters Midnight) on hurdling debut, finding test too much: sure to do better granted less testing conditions. *Martyn Meade* — **h102 p**

DOMESDAY BOOK (USA) 8 br.g. Street Cry (IRE) – Film Script (Unfuwain (USA)) [2017/18 c139, h–: c28.8d[pu] Apr 28] workmanlike gelding: winning hurdler: useful handicap chaser: won Fulke Walwyn Kim Muir Chase at Cheltenham (by ¾ length from Pendra) in 2016/17: pulled up in bet365 Gold Cup 14 months later: stays 3¼m: acts on heavy going: wears headgear: usually races close up. *Stuart Edmunds* — **c– h–**

DOMINATEUR (FR) 5 b.g. Desir d'Un Soir (FR) – Sourya d'Airy (FR) (Sheyrann) [2017/18 b15.7v[2] Feb 25] second foal: dam unraced half-sister to fairly useful French hurdler/chaser (2m-21f winner) Licara d'Airy: 9/1, shaped well when second in bumper at Southwell (5 lengths behind Katahdin): open to improvement. *Oliver Sherwood* — **b93 p**

DOMINGO (FR) 5 b.g. Special Kaldoun (FR) – Puligny Montrachet (FR) (Robin des Champs (FR)) [2017/18 c16.9v[3] c21.4s* c23.8v[6] c25.1v[pu] Mar 8] third foal: dam (h119) French 2¼m hurdle winner: lightly-raced maiden over hurdles: fair form over fences: won 4-y-o event at Lignieres in October, then left P. Peltier: stays 21f: acts on heavy going: in cheekpieces last 5 starts. *Jonjo O'Neill* — **c107 h–**

DOMTALINE (FR) 11 gr.g. Martaline – Domna Noune (FR) (Dom Pasquini (FR)) [2017/18 c119, h100: h17m* h16.2g[5] h18.6g[2] h20g c17.3g* h16.7g c19.2g[5] Aug 6] good-topped gelding: fair handicap hurdler: won at Carlisle in May: fairly useful handicap chaser: won at Cartmel in July: stays 3m: acts on good to firm and heavy going. *Peter Winks* — **c116 h103**

DONAPOLLO 10 b.g. Kayf Tara – Star of Wonder (FR) (The Wonder (FR)) [2017/18 c94§, h–: c23.4g h23.9g c24d[pu] Oct 3] workmanlike gelding: lightly-raced maiden hurdler: modest chaser at best: well below form in 2017/18: has worn cheekpieces: wears tongue tie: temperamental. *Rose Dobbin* — **c– § h– §**

DON BERSY (FR) 5 b.g. Califet (FR) – Tropulka God (FR) (Tropular) [2017/18 h133: h16v h15.7g h16s[2] h17d* h15.8d[4] Apr 9] good-topped gelding: useful handicap hurdler: won at Carlisle (by neck from Viserion) in March: probably stays 19f: acts on soft going: usually races prominently/travels strongly. *Tom Symonds* — **h132**

DON DES FOSSES (FR) 5 b.g. Denham Red (FR) – Sara des Fosses (FR) (Califet (FR)) [2017/18 b15.8v* h20.5v[4] Jan 23] £27,000 3-y-o, £35,000 4-y-o: second foal: dam unraced: won Irish point on debut: won at Uttoxeter (by length from Scorpion Haze) only outing in bumpers: 9/4, found nothing in novice at Leicester on hurdling debut (should do better). *Warren Greatrex* — **h71 p b94**

DONE A RUNNER (IRE) 12 b.g. Alderbrook – Last Wager (IRE) (Strong Gale) [2017/18 c77: c24.5g[3] May 15] multiple point winner: lightly-raced hunter chaser: in tongue tie last 3 starts. *D. Peters* — **c91**

DON FRANCO (IRE) 8 b.g. Oratorio (IRE) – Handora (IRE) (Hernando (FR)) [2017/18 c55, h–: c23.8g* c24.2g[5] c25.5g[2] h24g c25.5s* c24.1g[6] c25.5d[5] Aug 26] winning hurdler: modest handicap chaser: won at Perth in May and Cartmel in July: stays 25f: acts on heavy going: wears headgear: tried in tongue tie: races well off pace. *Stuart Crawford, Ireland* — **c98 h–**

DON HERBAGER (FR) 4 b.g. Saddler Maker (IRE) – Marie d'Altoria (FR) (Roi de Rome (USA)) [2017/18 h16.2s[5] h16.2v[4] Apr 10] €4,000 3-y-o: half-brother to several winners in France, including hurdlers Je Viens du Centre (17f winner, by Kotky Bleu) and Marie d'Altissima (17f-19f winner, by Voix du Nord): dam ran once on Flat: better effort in juvenile maiden hurdles at Hereford (modest form) when fourth of 5 to Royal Sunday in April. *Venetia Williams* — **h90**

DON

DON LAMI (FR) 5 ch.g. Honolulu (IRE) – Toutamie (FR) (Epalo (GER)) [2017/18 b17.7g* h24.4d² h20.3v³ h20.1d Apr 23] €55,000 4-y-o: first foal: dam unraced half-sister to staying chasers L'Ami (high class) and Kelami (useful): won Irish point on debut: won at Fontwell (by 6 lengths from It's Got Legs) only start in bumpers: fair form over hurdles: will stay beyond 3m. *Anthony Honeyball* — **h109 b99**

DONNA'S DELIGHT (IRE) 7 b.g. Portrait Gallery (IRE) – Hot Lips (IRE) (Good Thyne (USA)) [2017/18 b96: h19.3v* h22v⁴ h20.5v² h22v³ h19.3d² Mar 31] bumper winner: fairly useful form over hurdles: won novice at Carlisle in October: best effort when second to Uncle Alastair in novice at Ayr in December: will be suited by 3m: best form on heavy going. *Sandy Thomson* — **h120**

DONNA'S DIAMOND (IRE) 9 gr.g. Cloudings (IRE) – Inish Bofin (IRE) (Glacial Storm (USA)) [2017/18 c–, h126: h22.8v* h22.8v* h24s h25.8v² Apr 7] workmanlike gelding: smart hurdler: won handicap at Haydock (by 37 lengths) in January and Rendlesham Hurdle at same course (by 2¼ lengths from Agrapart) in February: unseated early only start over fences: stays 3¼m: acts on heavy going: races prominently. *Chris Grant* — **c– h144**

DONNAS DREAM (IRE) 5 b.m. Kalanisi (IRE) – Gerarda (IRE) (Toulon) [2017/18 ab16.3g⁶ b15.7s⁴ b17d⁵ Mar 31] €4,800 3-y-o: fourth foal: dam (h74), ran twice over hurdles, half-sister to useful hurdler/smart chaser (stayed 3¼m) Corket: poor form in bumpers. *Chris Grant* — **b71**

DONNYTWOBUCKETS (IRE) 4 b.g. Jeremy (USA) – Manorville (IRE) (Flemensfirth (USA)) [2017/18 b16.3s b13.7s⁵ Apr 6] £65,000 3-y-o: well-made gelding: third foal: half-brother to useful hurdler Us And Them (2m winner, by Stowaway): dam fair hurdler/chaser (2½m-2¾m winner): showed up long way in well-contested bumper at Newbury on debut: seemed to find next race coming too soon: remains capable of better. *Gary Moore* — **b– p**

DON SEBASTIAN (IRE) 7 b.g. High Chaparral (IRE) – Quick Thinking (IRE) – (Daylami (IRE)) [2017/18 h89: h24d h16.2g Aug 1] maiden Irish pointer: poor maiden hurdler: in headgear last 2 starts: tried in tongue tie: dead. *David Thompson* — **h–**

DON'T ACT UP 7 gr.g. Act One – Lucky Arrow (Indian Ridge) [2017/18 h–: h15.8s h16.3g⁴ Nov 2] off mark in Irish maiden points at fourth attempt: modest form over hurdles: best effort when fourth in novice at Stratford in November: will be suited by at least 2½m: better still to come. *Ian Williams* — **h89 p**

DON'T ASK (IRE) 5 b.g. Ask – Outback Ivy (USA) (Bob Back (USA)) [2017/18 b69p: b16.3d³ h16.7s* h19s³ h16v² h19m* Apr 25] fair form in bumpers: fairly useful form over hurdles: won novices at Bangor in December and Taunton (idling/flashing tail) in April: will prove suited by 2½m: usually leads. *Warren Greatrex* — **h125 b91**

DON'T BE FOOLED (IRE) 8 br.g. Misternando – Flemens Girl (IRE) (Flemensfirth (USA)) [2017/18 c15.7g⁴ c24gpu Sep 6] maiden point winner: no promise in novice chases. *Derek Shaw* — **c–**

DONT BE ROBIN (IRE) 6 b.g. Robin des Pres (FR) – Rainbow Times (IRE) (Jareer (USA)) [2017/18 b15.3v⁵ h16.5s³ h15.3v⁵ h15.3v⁴ h16v h16s⁴ Apr 27] fifth foal: half-brother to fair hurdler/modest chaser Shooting Times (2½m-3m winner, by Commanche Run) and modest chaser Willow Grange (3m winner, by Turtle Island): dam (c108) 25f chase winner: maiden Irish pointer: well beaten in bumper: modest form over hurdles: likely to be suited by 2½m+: acts on soft going. *Richenda Ford* — **h97 b61**

DONT CALL ME DORIS 8 b.m. Franklins Gardens – Grove Dancer (Reprimand) [2017/18 h15.8g Apr 24] rather leggy mare: lightly raced and little sign of ability. *Sarah Robinson* — **h–**

DONTCOUNTURCHIKENS (IRE) 4 b.g. Getaway (GER) – Stormy Breeze (IRE) (Glacial Storm (USA)) [2017/18 b15.8d³ Apr 24] seventh foal: half-brother to 2 winning pointers by Milan: dam unraced half-sister to fairly useful chaser (stayed 3¾m) Mac's Supreme and to dam of useful chaser (stayed 3m) Bennys Mist: 6/1 and tongue tied, third in bumper at Ludlow (8 lengths behind Imperial Aura) on debut. *David Dennis* — **b81**

DONTDILLYDALLY 5 b.m. Saint des Saints (FR) – Delayed (FR) (Fijar Tango (FR)) [2017/18 b17.7s⁴ h19.9dpu Sep 24] seventh foal: half-sister to 13f bumper winner Comte d'Anjou (by Desert King) and a winning pointer by Black Sam Bellamy: dam (c119/h121), 2m hurdle/chase winner, also 10.5f winner on Flat: favourite, fourth in mares bumper at Fontwell (13½ lengths behind Malindi Bay): pulled up in novice on hurdling debut: wears tongue tie. *Dan Skelton* — **h– b80**

Profile Systems Champion Novices' Hurdle, Punchestown—outsider Dortmund Park runs out a wide-margin winner of what ended up a substandard Grade 1 due to an incident two out which saw three significant runners depart

DON'T DOITTOME (IRE) 9 gr.g. Acambaro (GER) – Qui Plus Est (FR) (Dark Moondancer) [2017/18 c22.6d^F Jun 9] point winner: fell ninth in novice hunter on chasing debut: dead. *M. J. Felton*   c–

DONT DO MONDAYS (IRE) 11 b.g. Rashar (USA) – Bit of A Chance (Lord Ha Ha) [2017/18 c90, h–: c21.1s^{pu} May 18] winning hurdler: useful chaser at best: lightly raced and little form under Rules since 2015/16 (won points in March/April): stays 27f: acts on heavy going: wears headgear: tried in tongue tie. *N. A. Pearce*   c–
h–

DONT EVEN GO THERE (IRE) 7 b.g. Brian Boru – Foreal (IRE) (Bigstone (IRE)) [2017/18 h87, b–: h16.8m^4 h19g^6 h21.6m^3 Jun 16] poor form over hurdles: tried in cheekpieces: wears tongue tie. *Nicky Martin*   h60

DON'T HANG ABOUT 13 ch.g. Alflora (IRE) – Althrey Flame (IRE) (Torus) [2017/18 c92, h–: c22.5d^{pu} May 20] maiden hurdler: fair chaser at best: lightly raced and mostly well below form since early-2015/16: stays 3m: acts on good to firm and good to soft going: tried in cheekpieces: no easy ride. *Gary Hanmer*   c–
h–

DONTMINDDBOYS (IRE) 9 gr.g. Portrait Gallery (IRE) – Native Ocean (IRE) (Be My Native (USA)) [2017/18 c100, h85: c19.8g^2 c24.5g^2 c25.7d^3 c25.5s^2 c22.7d* c20v^3 c22.7s* c24.5s^2 c24.5v* c24.2d^{pu} Apr 24] tall gelding: maiden hurdler: fair handicap chaser: won at Leicester in December (novice event) and January, and at Towcester in March: stays 25f: acts on heavy going: tried in cheekpieces: has worn tongue tie. *Robin Dickin*   c102
h–

DON'T TELL GEORGE (FR) 5 b.g. Enrique – Anowa (FR) (Lost World (IRE)) [2017/18 b17.7d h20.5v^4 h17.7v^4 h20.5v^4 Apr 1] sixth foal: half-brother to 3 winners in France, including fairly useful hurdler/chaser Anowe de Jelois (17f-2½m winner) and hurdler Opale Jelois (17f/2¼m winner) (both by Red Guest): dam (h109) French 15f hurdle winner: very green in bumper: modest form over hurdles: best effort when fourth in novice at Plumpton in April: tried in hood. *Chris Gordon*   h87
b–

DON'T TELL MY MRS (IRE) 6 b.g. High-Rise (IRE) – Hazel Grove (IRE) (Definite Article) [2017/18 h23s^{pu} h20g^{pu} Jun 3] no show in novice/maiden hurdle at Worcester: tried in cheekpieces. *David Dennis*   h–

DONT TELL NO ONE (IRE) 10 b.g. Westerner – Kings Rose (IRE) (King's Ride) [2017/18 c22.5d^2 c22.7g* c18.2s^2 c24v^2 Nov 26] winning hurdler: useful form over fences: won maiden at Killarney in August: more improvement when second in Troytown Handicap Chase at Navan (2¾ lengths behind Mala Beach) in November: stays 3m: acts on heavy going: often travels strongly towards rear: usually responds generously to pressure: should progress further. *John E. Kiely, Ireland*   c134 p
h–

DONT TELL VAL 6 b.m. Midnight Legend – Tentsmuir (Arctic Lord) [2017/18 h73p, b92: h22.1d^2 h20.3g^3 h23.9g^{pu} Jul 6] bumper winner: modest form over hurdles: in tongue tie last 5 starts. *Fergal O'Brien*   h95

DON'T TOUCH IT (IRE) 8 b.g. Scorpion (IRE) – Shandora (IRE) (Supreme Leader) [2017/18 c152, h–: c18.2d^5 c17d^4 c17s^6 c17s^{ur} c16.3v^{pu} Mar 16] winning hurdler: very smart chaser as a novice, out of sorts in 2017/18: best around 2m: acts on heavy going: tried in cheekpieces. *Mrs J. Harrington, Ireland*   c122
h–

Gigginstown House Stud's "Dortmund Park"

DOODLE DANDY (IRE) 5 b.m. Starspangledbanner (AUS) – Grid Lock (IRE) (Van Nistelrooy (USA)) [2017/18 b–: h15.8d h15.8s h15.8s Jan 26] modest maiden on Flat (should stay 1¼m): well held in bumper/over hurdles: in hood last 2 starts. *Robin Mathew*   **h73**

DOOLIN 6 b.g. Rainbow High – Rabbit (Muhtarram (USA)) [2017/18 h–, b85: h19.2g h23.4g⁶ Nov 1] compact gelding: maiden pointer: poor form over hurdles: tried in cheekpieces: in tongue tie last 3 starts. *Charlie Mann*   **h–**

DORKING BOY 4 ch.g. Schiaparelli (GER) – Megasue (Kayf Tara) [2017/18 b16.7v* b16.3s Apr 25] third foal: dam (h108), bumper/2m hurdle winner, sister to Champion Bumper/Betfair Hurdle winner Ballyandy: fairly useful form in bumpers: won at Market Rasen on debut, forging clear: stiffer task at Punchestown just 2 weeks later: wears tongue tie. *Tom Lacey*   **b99**

DORKING COCK (IRE) 4 b.g. Winged Love (IRE) – Kiss Jolie (FR) (Cadoudal (FR)) [2017/18 b16.3s⁴ Mar 24] £44,000 3-y-o: good-topped gelding: fourth foal: dam, pulled up only start over hurdles in France, out of half-sister to dam of Cheltenham Gold Cup winner Long Run: 8/1, shaped as if needing experience when fourth in Goffs UK Spring Sales Bumper at Newbury (11 lengths behind Caribert). *Tom Lacey*   **b92**

DORTMUND PARK (FR) 5 b.g. Great Pretender (IRE) – Qena (FR) (Le Balafre (FR)) [2017/18 b11.9g* h16s⁶ h20v* h22.3v* h22s⁴ h24v h20s* Apr 27] good-bodied gelding: second foal: dam, French 11.5f bumper winner, half-sister to fairly useful French hurdler/ useful chaser (stayed 2¾m) United Park: won both starts in bumpers in France (for F. Foucher): smart form over hurdles: won maiden at Fairyhouse and novice at Thurles (by 16 lengths) in January, and Champion Novices' Hurdle at Punchestown (by 10 lengths from Whiskey Sour, aided by melee 2 out) in April: should stay 3m: acts on heavy going: in tongue tie last 5 starts. *Gordon Elliott, Ireland*   **h146 b?**

Crossed Fingers Partnership's "Double Shuffle"

DORTON GIRL 4 gr.f. Geordieland (FR) – Cash Crisis (IRE) (Ridgewood Ben) [2017/18 b14s Nov 22] first foal: dam winning pointer: tailed off in junior bumper. *Phil Middleton*   **b–**

DORY (IRE) 5 br.m. Westerner – Papal Princess (IRE) (Revoque (IRE)) [2017/18 b15.8g* b16.4s h16s² h20.7s⁵ Jan 12] £6,500 3-y-o: sturdy mare: fifth foal: half-sister to fairly useful hurdler/chaser Thanks For Tea (19f-3m winner) and fairly useful hurdler/fair chaser Teochew (2½m-3¼m winner) (both by Shantou): dam well held in bumpers/over hurdles: fair form in bumpers: won mares event at Uttoxeter in June, finding plenty: fair form when second in mares novice at Fakenham on hurdling debut: weakened over longer trip next time: bred to stay beyond 2m. *Warren Greatrex*   **h105 b92**

DOSTAL PHIL (FR) 5 b.g. Coastal Path – Quiphile (FR) (Panoramic) [2017/18 h16.7g⁴ Oct 31] first foal: dam French 11f-13f bumper winner: bumper winner in France in autumn 2016: 4/5, only fourth in novice at Bangor (6¾ lengths behind Whatmore) on hurdling debut a year later: clearly thought capable of better. *Philip Hobbs*   **h107 p**

DOTHRAKI RAIDER 7 b.g. Kayf Tara – French Spice (Cadeaux Genereux) [2017/18 h96: h15.7g⁴ Apr 20] workmanlike gelding: modest handicap hurdler: stays 2¾m: acts on good to firm going: tried in hood: wears tongue tie: usually races towards rear: has awkward head carriage. *Sophie Leech*   **h87**

DOTTIES DILEMA (IRE) 10 b.g. Pierre – Tellarue (IRE) (Rhoman Rule (USA)) [2017/18 h23g h19.6g⁴ c21.2d³ c22.1d* c23g* c20g⁵ h26.4s⁵ c24d* Nov 6] modest handicap hurdler: won at Cartmel in August: fair handicap chaser: won at Worcester in September and Southwell in November: stays 3m: acts on heavy and good to firm going: wears headgear/tongue tie: usually travels strongly, but has idled/found less than promised. *Peter Bowen*   **c103 h98**

DOU

DOUBLE ACCORD 8 ch.m. Double Trigger (IRE) – Got Tune (FR) (Green Tune (USA)) [2017/18 h98: c25.7d^ur c23g⁶ h25d^pu h23.9m Apr 25] modest hurdler at best: no form in 2017/18, including in 2 handicap chases: tried in blinkers: normally in tongue tie nowadays: usually leads. *Anthony Honeyball*   c–
h–

DOUBLE CHOCOLATE 15 b.g. Doubletour (USA) – Matching Green (Green Ruby (USA)) [2017/18 c98, h–: c22.6m⁶ Jul 16] maiden hurdler: fairly useful chaser at best: lightly raced and little form since winning reappearance in 2016/17: stays 3½m: acts on heavy and good to firm going: wears headgear: front runner/races prominently. *John O'Shea*   c–
h–

DOUBLE COURT (IRE) 7 b.g. Court Cave (IRE) – Miss Top (IRE) (Tremblant) [2017/18 h88: h20.6g h23.9v⁴ h21.2g⁴ h20v Dec 18] poor handicap hurdler: stays 23f: acts on good to firm and heavy going: usually in headgear. *Nigel Twiston-Davies*   h77

DOUBLEDISDOUBLEDAT (IRE) 11 ch.g. Vinnie Roe (IRE) – Castle Graigue (IRE) (Aylesfield) [2017/18 c99, h–: c23.8g⁶ May 18] workmanlike gelding: maiden hurdler: modest chaser nowadays: should be suited by 3m+: acts on good to soft going: front runner/races prominently. *Stuart Coltherd*   c–
h–

DOUBLE ROSS (IRE) 12 ch.g. Double Eclipse (IRE) – Kinross (Nearly A Hand) [2017/18 c148, h–: c23.6d⁴ c24.2s^ur c26g^pu c24.2s c26s⁴ c34.3s^pu Apr 14] strong gelding: winning hurdler: useful handicap chaser: fourth in veterans event at Chepstow (10¼ lengths behind Bob Ford) in October: inconsistent after: stays 3¼m: acts on heavy going: tried in cheekpieces/tongue tie. *Nigel Twiston-Davies*   c141
h–

DOUBLE SHUFFLE (IRE) 8 b.g. Milan – Fiddlers Bar (IRE) (Un Desperado (FR)) [2017/18 c152, h–: c19.4d² c21d² c24d² c25s c22.7d⁴ Apr 28] lengthy, useful-looking gelding: winning hurdler: high-class chaser: second in 1965 Chase at Ascot (8 lengths behind Top Notch) in November and King George VI Chase at Kempton (excelled himself when beaten length by Might Bite) in December: stays 3m: acts on soft going: wears hood: usually races prominently. *Tom George*   c162 ?
h–

DOUBLE TREASURE 7 b.g. King's Theatre (IRE) – Double Red (IRE) (Thatching) [2017/18 c121, h101: c21g* c20d* c19.8g* c20.4s c26g Apr 18] sturdy gelding: maiden hurdler: useful chaser: won handicaps at Newton Abbot and Worcester in September, and novice at Cheltenham (by 3¾ lengths from Two Taffs) in October: stays 21f: acts on good to firm and good to soft going: tried in hood: wears tongue tie: sound jumper. *Jamie Snowden*   c142
h–

DOUBLE U DOT EDE'S 9 b.g. Rock of Gibraltar (IRE) – Reveuse de Jour (IRE) (Sadler's Wells (USA)) [2017/18 c21.4g³ Jun 2] maiden hurdler: tailed off in maiden on chasing debut: probably stays 2¾m: acts on soft going: tried in hood: has worn tongue tie. *Lucinda Egerton*   c–
h–

DOUBLE WHAMMY 12 b.g. Systematic – Honor Rouge (IRE) (Highest Honor (FR)) [2017/18 c114, h–: c26.2g* May 28] leggy gelding: maiden hurdler: fairly useful handicap chaser: won at Kelso in May: stays 31f: acts on good to firm and heavy going: wears headgear: usually races in rear. *Iain Jardine*   c126
h–

DOUBLE W'S (IRE) 8 ch.g. Fruits of Love (USA) – Zaffre (IRE) (Mtoto) [2017/18 c145, h122: c17.1d⁵ c15.9g c16.4s⁵ c16.5g Apr 21] tall gelding: fairly useful hurdler: useful chaser at best, below that in 2017/18: enthusiastic sort, best around 2m: acts on soft going. *Ruth Jefferson*   c125
h–

DOUBLY CLEVER (IRE) 6 ch.g. Iffraaj – Smartest (IRE) (Exceed And Excel (AUS)) [2017/18 h119: h18.5m* h20m* h22.1s⁴ h20g² h20.3g³ Sep 6] workmanlike gelding: fairly useful handicap hurdler: won at Newton Abbot in May and Worcester in July: stays 2½m: acts on soft and good to firm going: has worn hood: tried in tongue tie. *Michael Blake*   h125

DOUGALSTAR (FR) 9 b.g. Layman (USA) – Concert House (IRE) (Entrepreneur) [2017/18 c25.6s^pu c21.2v^ur c19.2s^pu Feb 18] rather leggy gelding: maiden hurdler/chaser: failed to complete over fences in 2017/18: has worn headgear, including last 4 starts: tried in tongue tie: temperamental. *Jennie Candlish*   c– §
h–

DOUMBA (FR) 5 b.g. Royal Dragon (USA) – Roumba (FR) (Smadoun (FR)) [2017/18 b16.1v⁶ h16g Nov 1] well held in bumper/maiden hurdle: failed to complete in points subsequently. *Miss Katy Brown, Ireland*   h–
b–

271

DOU

DOUNIKOS (FR) 7 b.g. Smadoun (FR) – Baby Sitter (FR) (Nikos) [2017/18 c20v* c19.5v* c21s⁴ c24.4s^pu c29v^pu c24.5s^pu Apr 24] €52,000 3-y-o: rangy gelding: brother to French hurdler/chaser Nanette (17f-21f winner) and half-brother to 3 winners, including fairly useful hurdler Bonikos (19f/2½m winner, by Bonnet Rouge): dam French 1m winner: fairly useful form over hurdles: smart form over fences: won maiden at Gowran in November and Grade 2 novice at Limerick (by 4½ lengths from Tombstone) in December: best effort when 1½ lengths fourth of 11 to Monalee in Flogas Novices' Chase at Leopardstown next time: pulled up last 3 starts: should stay at least 3m: acts on heavy going. *Gordon Elliott, Ireland*   **c153 h–**

DOUVAN (FR) 8 b.g. Walk In The Park (IRE) – Star Face (FR) (Saint des Saints (FR)) [2017/18 c182, h–: c15.9s^F c16s² Apr 24] tall, good-topped gelding: winning hurdler: outstanding chaser at best: off a year (due to stress fracture of pelvis), going strongly when falling tenth in Queen Mother Champion Chase won by Altior at Cheltenham: 4/5, 2¾ lengths second of 9 to Un de Sceaux in Boylesports Champion Chase at Punchestown 6 weeks later: will stay 2½m+: acts on heavy going: front runner/races prominently: travels strongly: normally a fine jumper:. *W. P. Mullins, Ireland*   **c165+ h–**

DOUX PRETENDER (FR) 5 b.g. Great Pretender (IRE) – Lynnka (FR) (Passing Sale (FR)) [2017/18 b95p: h16.3s⁶ h16.6d² Feb 8] tall gelding: bumper winner: fairly useful form over hurdles: much better effort when second in novice at Doncaster in February: will stay beyond 2m. *Nicky Henderson*   **h122**

DOVE MOUNTAIN (IRE) 7 b.g. Danehill Dancer (IRE) – Virginia Waters (USA) (Kingmambo (USA)) [2017/18 h109: h16.3g² h16.7g³ h15.8m Oct 11] fair hurdler: raced around 2m: acts on soft going: wears headgear/tongue tie. *Olly Murphy*   **h101**

DOVILS DATE 9 gr.g. Clodovil (IRE) – Lucky Date (IRE) (Halling (USA)) [2017/18 h125: h23.1g⁵ h20.3g⁶ h20.6d h15.8d⁵ h24.4s h16.5s⁴ h19v Mar 12] sturdy gelding: fairly useful handicap hurdler at best: well below form in 2017/18: stays 2½m: acts on soft going: often races towards rear. *Tim Vaughan*   **h103**

DOWNLOADTHEAPP (IRE) 5 b.g. Definite Article – Chase A Dream (IRE) (Lord of Appeal) [2017/18 h15.9d^ur h19.9d h15.7s⁶ h15.8s⁶ h15.7v h16v Apr 14] fifth foal: dam (b86) second in bumper: form (modest) over hurdles only when mid-field in maiden at Huntingdon in March: should stay beyond 2m. *David Bridgwater*   **h91**

DOWN TIME (USA) 8 b.g. Harlan's Holiday (USA) – Frappay (USA) (Deputy Minister (CAN)) [2017/18 c–, h86: c24.2g^pu h19.3d^ur Dec 19] leggy gelding: fair hurdler/chaser at best: failed to complete both starts in 2017/18 (left Brian Ellison in between), though won on Flat subsequently: stays 3m: acts on good to soft going: normally in headgear: has worn tongue tie: usually races nearer last than first. *Paul Midgley*   **c– h–**

DOWNTOWN GETAWAY (IRE) 5 b.g. Getaway (GER) – Shang A Lang (IRE) (Commander Collins (IRE)) [2017/18 b16s* Dec 3] fourth foal: half-brother to fairly useful hurdler/chaser Timeforwest (2½m-3m winner, by Westerner): dam (b72), ran twice in bumpers, closely related to fairly useful hurdler/smart chaser (stayed 2½m) Down In Neworleans and half-sister to smart hurdler (stayed 21f) Chomba Womba: 14/1, looked good prospect when won maiden bumper at Fairyhouse (by 12 lengths from Remastered) on debut, storming clear: sold £350,000 later in month, joined Nicky Henderson. *Ms Margaret Mullins, Ireland*   **b114**

DOYEN DYNAMO 9 b.g. Doyen (IRE) – Fancy Shawl (Polish Precedent (USA)) [2017/18 h20g⁴ Jun 14] point winner: modest form in bumpers in 2014/15: in cheekpieces, tailed off in maiden on hurdling debut: in tongue tie last 3 starts. *Polly Gundry*   **h–**

D'PINESFLYER (IRE) 6 b.m. Westerner – Diskretion (GER) (Acatenango (GER)) [2017/18 h17g⁵ h19g⁴ h21g h20.1d^pu Sep 5] modest maiden hurdler: left Patrick Neville after third start: stays 2½m: acts on good to soft going. *Johnny Farrelly*   **h94**

DRACONIEN (FR) 5 br.g. Linda's Lad – Holding (FR) (Useful (FR)) [2017/18 h19.3v* h18.8v² h16v^ur h16v² h16.5d* Apr 24]   **h149**

Following a stable that had a record eighteen winners at the Punchestown Festival sounds like a profitable system, but it wasn't quite that simple. No fewer than half of Willie Mullins' winners were not the stable's first string in their races, judged by the betting, and at 25/1 Draconien caused the biggest upset of them all when the outsider of four from his yard in the Herald Champion Novices' Hurdle on the opening day, providing the first victory of a momentous week which clinched another Irish trainers' title for Mullins. The likes of Hurricane Fly, Faugheen and

Herald Champion Novices' Hurdle, Punchestown—25/1-shot Draconien gets the ball rolling in a record-breaking week for trainer Willie Mullins, showing much improved form to beat Vision des Flos (left) and Mengli Khan (right)

Douvan had all won the race for Mullins in the past, with names such as Dawn Run, Moscow Flyer, Brave Inca and Jezki also on the roll of honour, though the 2017 renewal had also seen a Mullins-trained favourite beaten by a lesser-fancied stable companion when Melon was beaten by Cilaos Emery. It was hard to see Draconien turning the tables on Getabird from their meeting earlier in the month in the Rathbarry & Glenview Studs Novices' Hurdle at Fairyhouse where Draconien was readily beaten twelve lengths into second, particularly as he was meeting the 11/10 favourite on terms 6 lb worse at Punchestown. But just as he had in the Supreme Novices' at Cheltenham, Getabird proved a let-down, at the same time as the much more patiently-ridden Draconien showed considerable improvement on anything he had achieved previously since joining the yard from France.

Less testing ground at Punchestown might have been one factor in Draconien's improvement as he had raced only on heavy ground until then. He was also suited by coming off a good pace in a contest where all the pace-setters finished well beaten; Getabird raced too freely early on and, along with outsiders Hardline and Beyond The Law who had pressed him for the lead, he was a spent force by the time Draconien arrived on the scene jumping the last. Ridden as he had been at Fairyhouse by Noel Fehily, Draconien crept closer from four out before looming up early in the straight, though he had to wait for a gap before jumping on at the final flight and being driven clear to win by two and a quarter lengths. Fehily was one of no fewer than ten different jockeys who partnered Mullins' Punchestown winners. Runner-up to Draconien was the only British-trained challenger Vision des Flos, beaten a similar distance when second in the Top Novices' Hurdle at Aintree, while another seven lengths back in third was the Royal Bond Novices' winner Mengli Khan who came out best of Gordon Elliott's three runners after being close up when making a bad mistake at the last. Getabird actually fared worst of the four from his stable, back in seventh behind Whiskey Sour (fourth) and Sharjah (sixth). Draconien's last two races belatedly confirmed the big impression he had made much earlier in the season on his hurdling debut when running away with an amateur riders maiden at Clonmel in December by twelve lengths. He was beaten a long way in second by Beyond The Law in a minor event there next time and then unseated his rider early on in a listed novice at Navan in March won by Cartwright who went on to finish fifth in the Herald Champion.

Clipper Logistics Group Ltd's "Draconien"

Draconien (FR) (br.g. 2013)
- Linda's Lad (b 2003)
  - Sadler's Wells (b 1981)
    - Northern Dancer
    - Fairy Bridge
  - Colza (b 1991)
    - Alleged
    - Dockage
- Holding (FR) (b 1995)
  - Useful (b 1986)
    - Vorias
    - Etoile du Berger III
  - Bentry (b 1985)
    - Ben Trovato
    - Trypha

Mullins likes to give his French imports plenty of time and Draconien's Irish debut came more than a year after his only start in France for Yohann Gourraud when he finished fourth in a bumper. Not just any bumper, though, because he made his debut in the Prix Jacques de Vienne at Saint-Cloud, the top race for AQPS three-year-olds. The winner of that race, incidentally, Delirant was subsequently bought by J. P. McManus to go into training with David Pipe. Draconien is a first Grade 1 winner for his sire Linda's Lad, winner of the Criterium de Saint-Cloud and Lingfield Derby Trial for Andre Fabre. Draconien's dam Holding ran only twice in AQPS races, finishing second on her debut and unseating her rider on her other start. Draconien is her sixth winner, the best of the others being the fairly useful chaser Nasthazya (by Rochesson), a winner at up to nearly three miles and twice successful at Auteuil. His other winning siblings include Vroum (by Passing Sale), a former winner of the Jacques de Vienne, and Bol d'Air (by Blue Bresil) who won a couple of two-mile hurdles for Chris Gordon in 2016/17. Draconien's year-older brother Cash Back has followed him to Ireland after finishing second on both his starts over hurdles at Auteuil in the autumn. Draconien's thoroughbred grandam

Bentry won an eleven-furlong claimer at Clairefontaine but has mostly produced jumpers at stud, including Le Khoumf, who was a fairly useful hurdler at around two miles in Britain, and the mare Benefique, a winner of seven races over hurdles and fences at Auteuil and second in the top chase of the autumn for four-year-olds, the Prix Maurice Gillois. A chasing career probably beckons now for Draconien who should stay two and a half miles. *W. P. Mullins, Ireland*

DRAFT PICK (IRE) 5 b.g. Court Cave (IRE) – Kilmington Breeze (IRE) (Roselier (FR)) [2017/18 b17g May 19] maiden pointer, runner-up both starts in 2018: tailed off in bumper. *Tom Weston* — b–

DRAGON DE LA TOUR (FR) 7 b.g. Royal Dragon (USA) – Turga de La Tour (FR) (Turgeon (USA)) [2017/18 h98: h20.3g c23.6g^3 c20g^6 Jun 25] modest maiden hurdler: better effort in handicap chases (modest form) when third in novice event at Huntingdon: may prove best short of 3m: acts on good to firm going: in cheekpieces last 4 starts. *Dan Skelton* — c97 h66

DRAGON DU CLOS (FR) 5 b.g. Policy Maker (IRE) – Fany des Planches (FR) (Shafoun (FR)) [2017/18 h16.7g Sep 1] tailed off in maiden hurdle. *Nigel Twiston-Davies* — h–

DRAGONFLI 6 b.g. Revoque (IRE) – Chiddingfold Chick (Zaffaran (USA)) [2017/18 h–, b–: h19.9s^4 h19.3d^3 Dec 19] well held in bumpers: modest form over hurdles: will stay further than 2½m. *Lucinda Egerton* — h87

DRAGON KHAN (IRE) 9 b.g. Dr Fong (USA) – Desert Magic (IRE) (Green Desert (USA)) [2017/18 h93: h17.7d^6 h15.8d h15.8v^5 h15.5v^3 h15.8v^2 h17.7s^4 Apr 6] poor handicap hurdler: left John O'Shea after first start: unproven beyond 2m: best form on soft/heavy going: has worn headgear: wears tongue tie: often travels strongly. *Rosemary Gasson* — h83

DRAGON'S DEN (IRE) 11 b.g. Antonius Pius (USA) – Tallassee (Indian Ridge) [2017/18 c–, h106: h23.1m^5 c23g^6 c19.4g^3 c22.6m^5 c19.2v^{pu} Jan 1] compact gelding: fairly useful hurdler at best: similar form when winning maiden at Exeter (match) on chasing debut in 2015/16: just fair form in handicaps in 2017/18: has form at 3m, probably better at shorter: acts on good to firm and heavy going: tried in hood: in tongue tie last 3 starts: usually races nearer last than first. *Jackie du Plessis* — c103 h–

DRAGOON GUARD (IRE) 7 b.g. Jeremy (USA) – Elouges (IRE) (Dalakhani (IRE)) [2017/18 h96: h21.6d^6 h18.5m h19.5d h18.5v^{pu} h16.5g Nov 16] neat gelding: modest maiden hurdler at best: no form in 2017/18 (left Anthony Honeyball after first start): tried in headgear: normally tongue tied. *Katie Stephens* — h–

DRAMA KING (IRE) 7 b.g. King's Theatre (IRE) – Miss Arteea (IRE) (Flemensfirth (USA)) [2017/18 h19s^6 h18.5v^{pu} Feb 11] sturdy gelding: little promise in bumper (in cheekpieces, looked wayward) and novice hurdles. *David Pipe* — h–

DRAMATIC PAUSE (IRE) 5 b.g. Oscar (IRE) – Night Heron (IRE) (St Jovite (USA)) [2017/18 b16v* Dec 9] €18,000 3-y-o: third foal: half-brother to modest hurdler Way of The World (2½m winner, by Flemensfirth): dam unraced half-sister to useful hurdler (2½m-2¾m winner) Flemenson: failed to complete both starts in points: 20/1, created good impression when winning bumper at Chepstow by 3 lengths from Blue Flight. *Tom Symonds* — b101

DR ANUBIS (IRE) 13 ch.g. Beneficial – Gaelic (IRE) (Strong Gale) [2017/18 c16.3d^{pu} c23g^{pu} c20g^{pu} Jun 25] plain gelding: of little account nowadays: left David Lewis after second start: has worn headgear/tongue tie: ungenuine. *Alan Phillips* — c– § h–

DR DES (IRE) 7 b.g. Double Eclipse (IRE) – Dans Belle (IRE) (Rising) [2017/18 h16.3g* h15.7g^2 h15.7d^2 h19.2v* h19.2d h19.2v* Mar 29] £11,000 6-y-o: sturdy gelding: fourth foal: half-brother to winning pointers by Dr Massini and Alderbrook: dam, winning pointer, half-sister to fair hurdler/fairly useful chaser (stayed 23f) Danaeve: in frame completed starts in Irish points: useful form over hurdles: won maiden at Stratford in October, and novices at Towcester in February and March (by 18 lengths from Piton Pete): also ran well when second in Kennel Gate Novices' Hurdle at Ascot (2¼ lengths behind Claimantakinforgan) in December: stays 19f: acts on heavy going: front runner/races prominently. *Henry Oliver* — h135

DR DUNRAVEN 7 b.g. Dr Massini (IRE) – Bajan Girl (FR) (Emperor Jones (USA)) [2017/18 c68, h101: h15.8d^2 h19s h16.6s^{pu} h15.7g^3 Apr 20] modest maiden hurdler: twice-raced chaser: stays 2½m: acts on good to soft going: often in headgear: tried in tongue tie. *Martin Keighley* — c– h97

DRE

DREAM BAIE (FR) 5 b.g. Crillon (FR) – Montaraza (FR) (Anabaa Blue) [2017/18 b18v⁴ h16.1s⁴ h15.9s^pu h15.9d h15.8s³ h15.8d Apr 24] €23,000 3-y-o: first foal: dam fairly useful French 2m hurdle winner: fourth in maiden bumper at Sligo: fair form in maiden at Galway on hurdling debut: left Joseph Patrick O'Brien, went wrong way subsequently: raced around 2m: tongue tied. *Michael Roberts*   **h102 b74**

DREAM BERRY (FR) 7 gr.g. Dream Well (FR) – Kalberry (FR) (Kaldounevees (FR)) [2017/18 c–p, h144: h20.3v h20s⁶ Apr 28] rather leggy gelding: useful handicap hurdler: shaped well in competitive events both outings in 2017/18, 6 lengths sixth of 24 to Meri Devie in Ballymore Handicap Hurdle at Punchestown final one: possibly amiss sole start over fences: will be suited by further than 21f: acts on heavy going: wears tongue tie: often travels strongly. *Jonjo O'Neill*   **c– h142**

DREAM BOLT (IRE) 10 ch.g. Urban Ocean (FR) – Riviera Dream (IRE) (Over The River (FR)) [2017/18 c120, h–: c21m* c17g⁴ c16m^pu c16.4g⁴ c18.2s* c18.8d³ c20.8v^pu c15.7s⁵ c21s² Apr 23] rather leggy gelding: winning hurdler: fairly useful handicap chaser: won at Newton Abbot in May, Stratford in June and Taunton in December: stays 21f: acts on firm and soft going: tried in tongue tie: usually races towards rear. *David Rees*   **c127 h–**

DREAM BROTHER (IRE) 6 b.g. Oscar (IRE) – Warmley's Gem (IRE) (Phardante (FR)) [2017/18 b16d Apr 26] well-made gelding: Irish point winner: 11/1, eighth in bumper at Warwick (15¾ lengths behind Umndeni), doing too much too soon. *Warren Greatrex*   **b79**

DREAMCATCHING (FR) 5 b.g. Al Namix (FR) – New Zealand (FR) (Smadoun (FR)) [2017/18 h117: h16.4g c16g⁵ c15.7s^pu Nov 23] good-topped gelding: bumper winner in France: fairly useful juvenile hurdler in 2016/17: disappointing on return, and in novice handicap chases subsequently: stays 2½m: acts on firm and good to soft going. *Paul Nicholls*   **c– h88**

DREAM CHOPE (FR) 9 ch.g. Muhaymin (USA) – Snow In Summer (FR) (Limnos (JPN)) [2017/18 c20.8d^pu May 5] maiden pointer: winning hurdler in France: lightly-raced maiden chaser: pulled up in hunter sole start under Rules in 2017/18: tried in headgear. *Miss L. Luxton*   **c– h–**

DREAM CONTI (FR) 5 br.g. Lauro (GER) – Posterite (FR) (Video Rock (FR)) [2017/18 b16s* Apr 19] €235,000 3-y-o: third foal: half-brother to useful hurdler Bello Conti (2m winner, by Coastal Path), stayed 2½m: dam once-raced half-sister to fairly useful hurdler/ smart chaser (stayed 25f) Oedipe and fairly useful hurdler/useful chaser (stayed 3½m) Tour des Champs: 2/1, looked useful prospect when won maiden bumper at Fairyhouse (readily by 1½ lengths from Castle North) on debut. *Noel Meade, Ireland*   **b107 p**

DREAM FLYER (IRE) 11 ch.g. Moscow Society (USA) – Bright Choice (IRE) (The Parson) [2017/18 c105, h–: c24.2g⁵ c29.4d⁴ May 29] winning hurdler: fair handicap chaser: below par both outings in 2017/18: stays 3¼m: acts on soft going: has worn headgear/tongue tie: front runner/races prominently. *Keith Dalgleish*   **c94 h–**

DREAM FREE 5 b.g. Oasis Dream – Freedonia (Selkirk (USA)) [2017/18 h16.8s^pu Dec 8] modest maiden on Flat, stays 1½m: in cheekpieces/tongue tie, pulled up in maiden on hurdling debut. *Mark Walford*   **h–**

DREAMLINER 5 b.g. Samraan (USA) – Oklahoma (Shareef Dancer (USA)) [2017/18 b15.6s b14s h15.8s h15.8s Mar 14] little form bumpers/maiden hurdles: in hood last 3 starts. *Christopher Kellett*   **h– b–**

DREAMSOFTHEATRE (IRE) 10 gr.g. King's Theatre (IRE) – Caroline Fontenail (IRE) (Kaldounevees (FR)) [2017/18 c123, h–: c29.1m⁴ c23.9g² h25g⁵ h23.1s⁵ h24.4s h25d^pu Apr 24] workmanlike gelding: fair handicap hurdler/chaser nowadays: won over hurdles at Huntingdon in October: stays 29f: acts on soft and good to firm going: wears cheekpieces/tongue tie: often races towards rear: temperamental. *Jonjo O'Neill*   **c103 § h106 §**

DREAM VOICE (IRE) 5 b.m. Approve (IRE) – Louve Sereine (FR) (Sadler's Wells (USA)) [2017/18 h15.8d^pu Oct 8] fair form on Flat: pulled up in maiden on hurdling debut. *John Holt*   **h–**

DRENEK (FR) 5 gr.g. Turgeon (USA) – Sireva (FR) (Simon du Desert (FR)) [2017/18 b16.2v⁵ Jan 25] hooded, tailed off in bumper. *James Ewart*   **b–**

DRESDEN (IRE) 10 b.g. Diamond Green (FR) – So Precious (IRE) (Batshoof) [2017/18 c141, h–: c20.9g⁶ c20s³ c21.1v c15.7s* c15.2v* c16.3v^F Mar 16] winning hurdler: smart handicap chaser: won at Catterick in January and Wetherby (by 1¼ lengths from Caraline) in February: stayed 2½m: acted on good to firm and heavy going: dead. *Henry Oliver*   **c145 h–**

DRO

DREWMAIN LEGEND 6 b.m. Midnight Legend – Ryders Hill (Zaffaran (USA)) **h97**
[2017/18 h79, b–: h21.6s h16.v³ h16.5s² h15.9v h19.5v* Apr 14] modest handicap hurdler: won novice event at Chepstow in April: should stay 21f+: acts on heavy going: tried in cheekpieces. *Ali Stronge*

DR HOOVES (IRE) 5 b.g. Yeats (IRE) – Sejour (IRE) (Bob Back (USA)) [2017/18 b72p: **b91**
b15.6s² b16.2v² b17s Apr 8] fair form in bumpers: in tongue tie last 3 starts. *Lucinda Russell*

DRIFT 5 b.m. With The Flow (USA) – Lady Exe (Karinga Bay) [2017/18 b15.7v Apr 27] **b–**
£2,500 4-y-o: second foal: dam, no form, sister to fairly useful chaser Earl's Kitchen (stayed 3¾m): tailed off in mares bumper. *Noel Williams*

DRIFTWOOD HAZE 10 b.g. Nomadic Way (USA) – Kristal Haze (Krisinsky (USA)) **c–**
[2017/18 c–, h125: h22.8m h23g h23.9v⁴ h21.9v⁵ h23.6v⁵ Jan 6] angular gelding: winning **h109**
pointer: fairly useful hunter chase at best: below form in 2017/18: well held in novice hunter only start in chase: stays 3m: acts on heavy going: tried in blinkers. *Phillip Dando*

DRIFTWOOD PRIDE (IRE) 10 b.g. Balmont (USA) – Olivia's Pride (IRE) (Digamist **c94**
(USA)) [2017/18 c94: c20.8pu c20.9d⁴ c20.5mpu Apr 26] point winner: modest form in hunter chases: stays 23f: acts on good to soft going: wears headgear: tried in tongue tie. *Miss Jane Western*

DRILL BABY DRILL 7 b.m. Black Sam Bellamy (IRE) – Tulipa (POL) (Jape (USA)) **h92 p**
[2017/18 h22.8s² h21.6s⁴ Apr 23] fifth foal: half-sister to modest chaser On The Case (2m winner, by Generous), stayed 2½m: dam (h119), 2m/17f hurdle winner, also winner up to 13f on Flat: modest form over hurdles: will be suited by 3m: remains open to improvement. *Tom George*

DRINKS INTERVAL 6 b.m. King's Theatre (IRE) – Dame Fonteyn (Suave Dancer **h120**
(USA)) [2017/18 b84: b16s⁴ h16.8v* h21.2g* h16.3d⁵ h21.4vF h15.3v³ h24.6s³ h24.3g⁴ **b63**
Apr 20] sturdy mare: poor form in bumpers: fairly useful hurdler: won mares novices at Newton Abbot and Ludlow, both in October: third in mares handicap at Kempton in April: stays 25f: acts on heavy going: wears tongue tie: often races towards rear. *Colin Tizzard*

DRIVE ON LOCKY (IRE) 11 b.g. Milan – Husyans Beauty (IRE) (Husyan (USA)) **h68**
[2017/18 h94: h24g h25.8mF h23.3d h23.9m h21.6vpu h15.9vur h21.4spu Feb 17] stocky gelding: modest handicap hurdler at best: little form in 2017/18: stays 25f: acts on soft going: wears headgear: normally in tongue tie. *Johnny Farrelly*

DRIVE THE BUS (IRE) 9 b.g. Helissio (FR) – Curraghs Annie (IRE) (Darazari (IRE)) **c–**
[2017/18 c23.8pu Mar 22] winning hurdler/chaser: pulled up in hunter chase only start **h–**
under Rules in 2017/18: stays 2½m: acts on soft going: usually in cheekpieces/tongue tie: held up. *Mrs B. Thomas*

DR MIKEY (IRE) 9 b.g. Dr Massini (IRE) – Nicola Marie (IRE) (Cardinal Flower) **h140**
[2017/18 h133, b101: h16v* Apr 1] dual bumper winner: useful form over hurdles: won minor event at Cork (by 4¼ lengths from Brelade), only start in 2017/18: raced around 2m: acts on heavy going: tried in hood: usually leads. *Ms M. Flynn, Ireland*

DR MOLONEY (IRE) 11 b.g. Dr Massini (IRE) – Solal Queen (Homo Sapien) [2017/18 **c107 §**
c110, h–: c20.1g³ c20.1m⁵ c20.1sF c25.5dF c20.1v² c21v⁴ c19.2d Oct 13] winning hurdler: **h–**
fair maiden chaser: barely stays 3m: acts on good to firm and heavy going: normally in headgear: has worn tongue tie: has joined Olly Murphy: irresolute. *Stuart Crawford, Ireland*

DROMNEA (IRE) 11 b.g. Presenting – Fifth Imp (IRE) (Commanche Run) [2017/18 **c133 d**
c133, h–: c20v* c24s⁶ c22.5s⁶ c24.5dF c21s Feb 4] big, strong gelding: winning hurdler: **h–**
useful chaser: won minor event at Listowel (by 2¾ lengths from Hidden Cyclone) in September: disappointing after: stays 3m: acts on heavy going: has worn tongue tie, including last 2 starts (when also in headgear). *M. F. Morris, Ireland*

DROPS OF JUPITOR (IRE) 6 gr.m. Dylan Thomas (IRE) – Fancy Intense (Peintre **h108**
Celebre (USA)) [2017/18 b89: h15.9d h18.5s² h18.5v* h16s⁶ h21.4v⁶ h16.8s⁴ h18.5vpu Apr 17] tall, good-topped mare: pulled up in point: bumper winner: fair hurdler: won mares novice at Exeter in December: best up to 19f: acts on heavy going: hooded over hurdles bar final outing: usually races freely in rear. *Anthony Honeyball*

DROPZONE (USA) 9 b.g. Smart Strike (CAN) – Dalisay (IRE) (Sadler's Wells (USA)) **c–**
[2017/18 c–, h78§: h21.6s⁴ h23m⁴ h23.1d⁴ Apr 24] sturdy gelding: poor handicap hurdler: **h72 §**
maiden chaser: stays 3m: acts on good to firm and good to soft going: usually in headgear: tried in tongue tie: temperamental (usually races lazily in rear). *Brian Forsey*

DRO

DROVERS LANE (IRE) 6 b.g. Oscar (IRE) – Minnie Turbo (IRE) (General View) [2017/18 b16.3s h21s⁵ Feb 10] off mark in Irish points at second attempt: eighth in bumper at Newbury: 16/1, fifth in novice at Warwick (18½ lengths behind Louse Talk) on hurdling debut. *Rebecca Curtis* — h99 b–

DR RHYTHM (IRE) 5 b.g. Kalanisi (IRE) – Muscova Rose (IRE) (Sevres Rose (IRE)) [2017/18 b15.7d Nov 25] €15,500 3-y-o: rather unfurnished gelding: first foal: dam unraced half-sister to useful hurdler/very smart chaser (2m-2¼m winner) Andreas: wide-margin winner only start in points: 4/1, well beaten in bumper at Ascot: clearly thought capable of better. *Paul Nicholls* — b– p

DR ROBIN (IRE) 8 b.g. Robin des Pres (FR) – Inter Alia (IRE) (Dr Massini (IRE)) [2017/18 c116, h–: c23g⁴ c23m⁴ c24.1g⁶ c24.8vᵖᵘ Apr 15] lengthy gelding: winning hurdler: fairly useful handicap chaser: won at Worcester in July: stays 3m: acts on soft and good to firm going: wears headgear: tried in tongue tie: often races lazily: temperamental. *Peter Bowen* — c119 § h–

DR SANDERSON (IRE) 4 b.g. Jeremy (USA) – Guydus (IRE) (Old Vic) [2017/18 b17d* Mar 25] €17,000 3-y-o: first foal: dam (c89/h98) ungenuine 2½m-3¼m hurdle/chase winner: 3/1, green when won bumper at Carlisle (by ½ length from Minella Mystics) on debut: will stay 2¼m+. *Stuart Crawford, Ireland* — b99

DRUID'S DIAMOND 5 b.g. Piccolo – Faithful Beauty (IRE) (Last Tycoon) [2017/18 h16.2v⁴ h16.7g⁴ h15.8d³ h16.7dᵖᵘ h16.7d⁴ Dec 7] half-brother to useful hurdler Ubi Ace (2m winner, by First Trump) and modest chaser Charlie George (2m winner, by Idris): modest maiden on Flat, stays 1½m: modest form over hurdles: will prove best at 2m: acts on heavy going: tried in headgear. *Mark Walford* — h98

DRUID'S FOLLY (IRE) 8 b.g. Beneficial – Sweet Vale (IRE) (Supreme Leader) [2017/18 h121: c16.5sᵖᵘ c19.4dᵖᵘ h19.8s⁴ h21.6v h18.5v h19.2v h21.7g² Apr 20] tall gelding: fair handicap hurdler nowadays: let down by jumping in 2 novice handicap chases (then left Fergal O'Brien): stays 2¾m: acts on good to soft going: in hood last 5 starts: wears tongue tie: often races in rear. *Robert Walford* — c– h98

DRUMACOO (IRE) 9 b.g. Oscar (IRE) – My Native (IRE) (Be My Native (USA)) [2017/18 c–, h–: h20v⁵ c23.5v² h20s⁴ h22vᵖᵘ c24.5sᵖᵘ Apr 28] tall gelding: formerly useful hurdler: lightly-raced chaser, smart as a novice: better run in 2017/18 when close second in minor event at Fairyhouse in February: stays 3m: acts on heavy going: has worn hood. *M. Hourigan, Ireland* — c138 h128

DRUMCLIFF (IRE) 7 b.g. Presenting – Dusty Too (Terimon) [2017/18 h124: h19.5d c15.7s⁴ c18.8v⁴ c16.2s⁴ c20.8sᵖᵘ Mar 15] well-made gelding: fairly useful maiden hurdler: immediately made into better chaser in 2017/18: won handicaps at Wincanton (novice) in November and Ascot (amateur) in January: stays 19f: acts on heavy going: wears tongue tie: usually races towards rear: sometimes found little over hurdles. *Harry Fry* — c143 h114

DRUMCONNOR LAD (IRE) 8 b.g. Winged Love (IRE) – Drumconnor Lady (IRE) (Shahrastani (USA)) [2017/18 c17d⁴ c20v² c17v* c21.3s Mar 9] winning hurdler: useful form over fences: won novice at Navan in February: best run when second in maiden at Cork (3 lengths behind Livelovelaugh) previous outing: stays 2½m: acts on heavy going: wears tongue tie. *A. P. Keatley, Ireland* — c131 h–

DRUMHART (IRE) 9 ch.g. Beneficial – Nancylu (IRE) (Luso) [2017/18 c112, h–: c20m c20m³ c19.2g⁶ c19.9s⁶ h23.9m⁵ c19.2g⁶ c20.9s Jan 29] winning pointer: maiden hurdler: fair handicap chaser: left Colin A. McBratney after sixth start: acts on good to firm and good to soft going: usually in tongue tie: often races in rear. *Mrs D. J. Ralph* — c100 h–

DRUMLANG (IRE) 12 b.g. Soviet Star (USA) – Sherekiya (IRE) (Lycius (USA)) [2017/18 c78, h–: c19.4g² c20g c20.3d² c19.7d⁵ Oct 23] rather leggy gelding: winning hurdler: fairly useful handicap chaser at best: only poor form since 2015/16: stays 21f: acts on good to firm and good to soft going: often in headgear: tried in tongue tie. *Kevin Frost* — c84 h–

DRUMLEE CITY (IRE) 6 b.g. City Honours (USA) – Alentio (IRE) (Luso) [2017/18 b84: h21.6vᵖᵘ h20.5d⁵ h19s h23.4s² h24v* Mar 15] compact gelding: third in Irish point on debut: fair form over hurdles: improved when won handicap at Towcester in March: will stay further than 3m: acts on heavy going: tried in cheekpieces. *Nick Mitchell* — h109

DRUMLEE SUNSET (IRE) 8 br.g. Royal Anthem (USA) – Be My Sunset (IRE) (Bob Back (USA)) [2017/18 c136, h116: c19.1d² c20.8v c20s² Feb 23] compact gelding: fairly useful hurdler: useful handicap chaser: second at Warwick (2½ lengths behind Cobra de Mai) in February: should stay beyond 2½m: acts on soft going: tried in tongue tie: possibly not straightforward. *Tom George* — c131 h–

DRUMLYNN (IRE) 7 b.g. Definite Article – Miss Florida (IRE) (Florida Son) [2017/18 b16g* b15.8d³ Jul 28] £12,500 5-y-o: half-brother to fair chaser Aboo Who (3m winner, by Aboo Hom) and winning pointers by Reprimand and Anshan: dam (b68), ran once in bumper, sister to useful chaser (stayed 2½m) Kurakka: placed in points: fair form in bumpers: won conditionals/amateur event at Worcester in June: will stay at least 2½m. *Nicky Henderson* — **b91**

DRUMNAGREAGH (IRE) 5 b.m. September Storm (GER) – Saffron Pride (IRE) (Be My Native (USA)) [2017/18 b16.2m⁴ b16.4d⁶ b16v h16s h16v h16.6v h18.8s⁶ h16s Apr 19] seventh foal: sister to fair hurdler/chaser Weyburn (2½m winner) and half-sister to fair hurdler Generous Helpings (25f winner, by Generous): dam unraced: pulled up in point: modest form in bumpers: poor form over hurdles: unproven beyond 2m: tried in tongue tie. *Stuart Crawford, Ireland* — **h72 b77**

DRUMS OF WAR (IRE) 6 b.g. Youmzain (IRE) – Min Asl Wafi (IRE) (Octagonal (NZ)) [2017/18 b87: b16.2g³ b16.8g h16.8s⁶ h19.4g² h16.2v⁴ h16.8v* h16.7g⁴ Apr 22] fair form in bumpers: fair form over hurdles: won novice handicap at Sedgefield in March: stays 19f: acts on heavy going: in cheekpieces last 2 starts. *Chris Grant* — **h106 b87**

DRUMVIREDY (IRE) 9 b.m. Flemensfirth (USA) – Leitrim Bridge (IRE) (Earl of Barking (IRE)) [2017/18 c108§, h105§: c23.8vᵘʳ c25.1sᵖᵘ h19.5v⁶ Jan 19] sturdy mare: fair hurdler/novice chaser at best: no form in 2017/18: stays 3m: acts on heavy going: unreliable. *Venetia Williams* — **c– § h– §**

DRUNKEN PIRATE 5 b.g. Black Sam Bellamy (IRE) – Peel Me A Grape (Gunner B) [2017/18 b15.3d⁶ Apr 22] sixth foal: half-brother to bumper winner/useful hurdler Letsby Avenue (2½m-2¾m winner, by Tikkanen) and bumper winner Coyaba (by Midnight Legend), stays 21f: dam unraced sister to useful chaser (2m-21f winner) Air Shot and useful staying hurdler Flying Gunner, and half-sister to useful chaser (stayed 25f) Windross: 10/1, plenty of promise when sixth in bumper at Wincanton (7¼ lengths behind Samarquand), looming up 2f out before running green: good deal better to come. *Noel Williams* — **b94 p**

DR WELLS 6 b.g. Dr Massini (IRE) – Aristi (IRE) (Dr Fong (USA)) [2017/18 b15.7d h19.5vᵖᵘ Jan 19] looked very green in maiden bumper: pulled up in novice on hurdling debut. *Peter Bowen* — **h– b–**

DUBAI ANGEL (IRE) 7 b.g. Dubai Destination (USA) – Just Another Penny (IRE) (Terimon) [2017/18 h129, b112: c15.9s³ c20.1s³ h20.2s² Apr 27] useful bumper performer: fairly useful hurdler: good second in handicap at Perth only outing: useful form over fences: third in handicaps at Carlisle (novice) and Newcastle (looked big threat long way when beaten 11½ lengths by Saints And Sinners): stays 2¾m: acts on heavy going. *Ruth Jefferson* — **c132 h128**

DUBAI CELEBRITY 6 b.g. Sakhee (USA) – Aljana (IRE) (Exceed And Excel (AUS)) [2017/18 h99: h16.8g² h17.2g Jun 30] modest maiden hurdler: unproven beyond 17f: acted on good to firm going: wore cheekpieces last 3 starts: dead. *Chris Grant* — **h98**

DUBAI DEVILS (IRE) 7 b.g. Dubai Destination (USA) – Saddlers Leader (IRE) (Saddlers' Hall (IRE)) [2017/18 h108: h23.9g³ h23.9m² h24.8dᵖᵘ c24.2s⁵ c20v⁵ Nov 25] workmanlike gelding: maiden pointer: fair maiden hurdler: similar form when fifth in novice handicap at Hexham on first of 2 outings over fences: stays 3m: acts on good to firm and heavy going: has worn cheekpieces. *Paul Stafford, Ireland* — **c100 h109**

DUBAI DIRHAM 5 ch.m. Dubai Destination (USA) – Rolline (IRE) (Revoque (IRE)) [2017/18 b65: b13.7d ab16g³ ab16g h15.9s Apr 15] rather unfurnished mare: modest form in bumpers: 11/1, seventh in maiden at Plumpton (12¼ lengths behind Six Gun Serenade) on hurdling debut. *Suzy Smith* — **h– b79**

DUBAI FLYER (IRE) 5 b.g. Dubai Destination (USA) – Kalyfa Royale (IRE) (Blueprint (IRE)) [2017/18 b17.3g h22.1g h16.7sᵖᵘ Aug 5] no promise in maiden bumper/hurdles. *Noel C. Kelly, Ireland* — **h– b–**

DUBAWI ISLAND (FR) 9 b.g. Dubawi (IRE) – Housa Dancer (FR) (Fabulous Dancer (USA)) [2017/18 c–, h–: h19.8s h19.7s Jan 16] round-barrelled gelding: useful hurdler at best: lightly raced and little form since 2015/16 (no aptitude for chasing sole try): stays 21f: acts on heavy going: tried in blinkers. *Venetia Williams* — **c– h–**

DUBH DES CHAMPS (IRE) 6 br.g. Robin des Champs (FR) – Aneda Dubh (IRE) (Presenting) [2017/18 h–: h22.1d⁴ Aug 28] well held both starts in novice hurdles. *Philip Kirby* — **h71**

DUBLIN INDEMNITY 6 b.g. Presenting – Tazzarine (FR) (Astarabad (USA)) [2017/18 h–: b16.2sᵖᵘ h15.3vᵖᵘ Mar 28] no promise in bumpers/maiden hurdle: tried in cheekpieces. *Kerry Lee* — **h– b–**

DUC

DUCA DE THAIX (FR) 5 b.g. Voix du Nord (FR) – Nouca de Thaix (FR) (Subotica (FR)) [2017/18 h16v⁴ h16v* h16v⁶ h16.8v h16s h16.5d Apr 24] lengthy gelding: fifth foal: half-brother to fairly useful hurdler/smart chaser Antartica de Thaix (19f/2½m winner) and French hurdler/chaser Vica de Thaix (17f/2¼m winner) (both by Dom Alco): dam French 1½m bumper winner: bumper winner for G. Cherel: useful hurdler: won Irish Independent Hurdle at Limerick (by 2½ lengths from Us And Them) in December: stays 2¼m: acts on heavy going: in tongue tie last 3 starts: patiently ridden. *Gordon Elliott, Ireland* — h133

DUC DE SEVILLE (IRE) 6 b.g. Duke of Marmalade (IRE) – Splendid (IRE) (Mujtahid (USA)) [2017/18 c–,x, h65: h22g^pu h22.1m⁴ h23.4g^pu Jun 4] of little account nowadays: has worn headgear. *Michael Chapman* — c– x, h–

DUC DES GENIEVRES (FR) 5 gr.g. Buck's Boum (FR) – Lobelie (FR) (Round Sovereign (FR)) [2017/18 h17.9s* h20v³ h16s² h21.1s⁵ h20v⁵ h20s⁶ Apr 27] sturdy gelding: fourth foal: dam, French 1½m bumper winner, half-sister to fairly useful hurdler/chaser (stayed 3¼m) Pacha d'Oudairies: smart form over hurdles: won 4-y-o event at Moulins (then left E. Vagne) in May: much better form subsequently, including when third in Lawlor's of Naas Novices' Hurdle (4 lengths behind Next Destination) in January and second in Deloitte Novices' Hurdle at Leopardstown (beaten 5½ lengths by Samcro) in February: stays 21f: raced on soft/heavy going: usually races towards rear. *W. P. Mullins, Ireland* — h145

DUC KAUTO (FR) 5 b.g. Ballingarry (IRE) – Kauto Lorette (FR) (Useful (FR)) [2017/18 b15.8s h16.5s Dec 14] well held in maiden bumper/novice hurdle. *Colin Tizzard* — h–, b–

DUCLOYNE LADY (IRE) 9 b.m. Oscar (IRE) – Lizes Birthday (IRE) (Torus) [2017/18 c–, h75: h19d⁵ h19.9s⁶ Oct 19] point winner: poor form over hurdles: runner-up in mares maiden hunter at Cork sole start in chase: should stay beyond 19f: acts on heavy going. *Henry Oliver* — c–, h79

DUDE ALERT (IRE) 8 b.g. Windsor Knot (IRE) – Policy (Nashwan (USA)) [2017/18 h20.7s h15.9v⁶ Mar 12] tall gelding: of little account: wears headgear: one to avoid. *Mark Hoad* — h– §

DU DESTIN (FR) 5 gr.g. Fuisse (FR) – Parenthese (FR) (Fragrant Mix (IRE)) [2017/18 b16.3d h20.8s h19.2v⁶ h19.4s h16s Apr 9] €70,000 3-y-o: fifth foal: dam, French 19f chase winner (also 1m winner on Flat), half-sister to dam of useful hurdler/smart chaser (stays 21f) Invitation Only: down field in bumper at Newbury: poor form in maiden/novice hurdles: will be suited by 2¾m+: should still do better. *Nicky Henderson* — h73 p, b–

DUDETTE 6 ch.m. Apple Tree (FR) – Whatagale (Strong Gale) [2017/18 b–: h22.1d h20.3g⁴ h22v^pu h25.3s⁴ h23.3v⁶ Mar 15] little form in bumper/over hurdles. *Andrew Crook* — h74

DUEL AT DAWN (IRE) 8 b.g. Presenting – Phillis Hill (Karinga Bay) [2017/18 h132: c23.6d² c24.2v* c25.3s² c24s² c31.8s^pu Mar 13] sturdy gelding: useful hurdler: useful novice chaser: won at Exeter in November: runner-up after at Cheltenham (6 lengths behind Sizing Tennessee) and Warwick (listed, beaten 5 lengths by Ms Parfois): should stay beyond 25f: acts on heavy going: in cheekpieces last 5 starts: races prominently. *Alex Hales* — c142, h–

DUELING BANJOS 8 gr.g. Proclamation (IRE) – Kayf Lady (Kayf Tara) [2017/18 c130, h–: c24.2s² c25d c25.6g^F h24.4d Feb 8] big, strong gelding: winning hurdler: useful handicap chaser: stays 3m: acts on heavy going: has worn cheekpieces, including on 3 of 4 appearances in 2017/18: in tongue tie last 4 starts. *Kim Bailey* — c129, h–

DUFFY ALLEN (FR) 5 b.g. Lucarno (USA) – Parade (FR) (Robin des Champs (FR)) [2017/18 b81: b16.7g⁶ h20.6g³ h19.9d h19.3d² Dec 19] poor form in bumpers: fair form over hurdles: best effort when second in novice at Catterick in December: will be suited by 2¾m+: remains with potential. *Nick Kent* — h96 p, b72

DUHALLOWCOUNTRY (IRE) 12 b.g. Beneficial – Milltown Lass (IRE) (Mister Lord (USA)) [2017/18 c80§, h–§: c16.4g c15.8m⁶ c16.4s c16.4s⁵ c16.3v⁶ c16.4v⁶ c16.3v^pu c15.6d Apr 23] winning pointer: maiden hurdler: poor handicap chaser: wears headgear: usually races close up: temperamental. *Victor Thompson* — c– §, h– §

DUHALLOW GESTURE (IRE) 6 b.m. King's Theatre (IRE) – Rare Gesture (IRE) (Shalford (IRE)) [2017/18 b18g⁴ b15.8s* b17s³ Apr 12] €40,000 3-y-o: good-topped mare: half-sister to several winners, including modest hurdler/fairly useful chaser Me And Ben (2½m-3m winner, by Revoque) and fairly useful hurdler/chaser Cogryhill (2¾m-25f winner, by Presenting): dam unraced half-sister to smart hurdler/chaser Wichita Lineman (by King's Theatre) and top-class hurdler Rhinestone Cowboy, both stayed 3m: winning pointer: fairly useful bumper performer: won mares maiden at Tipperary (left Damien — b103

Murphy after) in May and listed mares event at Huntingdon (by 2¼ lengths from Diamond Gait) in December: further improvement when third in Nickel Coin Mares' National Hunt Flat Race at Aintree (4 lengths behind Getaway Katie Mai) final outing. *Anthony Honeyball*

DUHALLOW LAD (IRE) 6 b.g. Papal Bull – Macca Luna (IRE) (Kahyasi) [2017/18 b19d h16v h16.8v^{pu} h16.7v h19.2v^3 h16.3s^2 c19.7v* c19.2v^2 Apr 8] half-brother to several winners, including fair hurdler Moonwalking (2½m winner, by Danehill Dancer) and fair chaser Celtic Intrigue (3m-3¼m winner, by Celtic Swing): dam 1m-1½m winner: maiden pointer: seventh in bumper at Cork (for L. J. Archdeacon): fair maiden hurdler: better form in novice handicap chases, winning at Plumpton in March and runner-up at Exeter following month: best up to 2½m: raced on going softer than good (acts on heavy): remains open to improvement over fences. *Alan Jones*   c114 p h100 b–

DUHALLOW TORNADO (IRE) 6 b.g. Golden Tornado (IRE) – Cappard Ridge (IRE) (Executive Perk) [2017/18 c25.2s* c26.2v* Apr 7] £25,000 5-y-o: half-brother to fairly useful hurdler/fair chaser Clashnabrook (2¼m-21f winner, by Alderbrook) and fair chaser Allmyown (21f winner, by Mr Combustible): dam unraced half-sister to useful hurdler/fair chaser Jet Rules (2½m-25f winner) and useful hurdler Jet Tabs (2¾m-3¼m winner): multiple point winner: fairly useful form in hunter chases, winning at Catterick (novice) in March and Kelso in April: likely to progress further. *C. C. Pimlott*   c125 p

DUKE ARCADIO (IRE) 9 b.g. Arcadio (GER) – Kildowney Duchess (IRE) (Jurado (USA)) [2017/18 c112, h–: c24d^{pu} May 6] won Irish maiden point on debut: lightly-raced maiden hurdler: disappointing over fences since promising chasing debut in 2016/17: stays 3m: acts on soft going: tried in blinkers. *Oliver Sherwood*   c– h–

DUKE DEBARRY (IRE) 7 b.g. Presenting – Blue Dante (IRE) (Phardante (FR)) [2017/18 b88: h21d^4 h18.9v^2 h24.6s^4 h24.4s^6 h19.3v* Apr 17] fairly useful form over hurdles: landed odds in novice at Carlisle in April: stays 21f: acts on heavy going: often races prominently. *Nicky Henderson*   h115

DUKE DES CHAMPS (IRE) 8 b.g. Robin des Champs (FR) – Ballycowan Lady (IRE) (Accordion) [2017/18 c22.4v^2 c23.4v^3 Feb 10] lengthy gelding: winning hurdler: much better effort in novice handicap chases at Newbury (useful form) when 3¼ lengths second to Rocklander: weakened badly from 2 out 6 weeks later: stays 2¾m: acts on heavy going. *Philip Hobbs*   c135 h–

DUKE OF KILCORRAL (IRE) 5 gr.g. Duke of Marmalade (IRE) – Miss Shaan (FR) (Darshaan) [2017/18 b16d^6 h19.5v h16.7v h16.7v^2 h21.7d^{ur} h19.2v^2 h19.2s^2 Apr 6] half-brother to several winners on Flat, including useful 5f-1m winner Bahceli (by Mujadil): dam ran twice on Flat in France: well held in bumpers (trained in 2016/17 by M. P. Sunderland): fairly useful form over hurdles: second in handicap at Fontwell in March and in novice there in April: stays 19f: acts on heavy going. *Neil Mulholland*   h116 b73

DUKE OF NAVAN (IRE) 10 b.g. Presenting – Greenfieldflyer (IRE) (Alphabatim (USA)) [2017/18 c139, h–: c15.8s^3 c16.4g^F c15.2s^2 c16.4s* c16.5g^3 Apr 21] well-made gelding: winning hurdler: smart handicap chaser: won at Doncaster (by short head from Bigmartre) in January: stays 2¼m: acts on good to firm and heavy going: enthusiastic sort. *Nicky Richards*   c145 h–

DUKE OF SONNING 6 ch.g. Duke of Marmalade (IRE) – Moonshadow (Diesis) [2017/18 h–: h16.2g^6 h19.9g h16g^6 h16d^5 Sep 29] modest handicap hurdler: unproven beyond 2m: acts on good to soft going: in blinkers last 4 starts: often races freely. *Shaun Harris*   h94

DUKE STREET (IRE) 6 b.g. Duke of Marmalade (IRE) – Act of The Pace (IRE) (King's Theatre (IRE)) [2017/18 h133: c20g^3 c18.8g Nov 4] compact gelding: useful hurdler: useful form over fences: better effort when third in maiden at Worcester (1½ lengths behind Wait For Me) on chasing debut: let down by jumping at Ascot after: stays 21f: acts on soft and good to firm going: has worn cheekpieces, including last 4 starts: often races prominently. *Dr Richard Newland*   c130 h–

DULCE PANEM (FR) 6 ch.g. Panis (USA) – Danissima (FR) (Fabulous Dancer (USA)) [2017/18 c17.4s^F h16.8d^5 h19.3d^4 h16v^3 h18.9v^2 h19.2v^6 h19.7v^{bd} Feb 20] half-brother to 3 winners in France, including smart hurdler/fairly useful chaser Dulce Leo (2¼m-21f winner, by Priolo): ran once on Flat: fair maiden hurdler: similar form on chasing debut, but not completed over fences since: left B. de Montzey after first start: stays 19f: acts on heavy going: has worn cheekpieces, including last 3 starts: usually races nearer last than first. *Rebecca Menzies*   c– h100

DUN BAY CREEK 7 b.g. Dubai Destination (USA) – Over It (Overbury (IRE)) [2017/18 h110: h21g^F May 13] lengthy gelding: lightly-raced hurdler, fair at best: should stay 3m: acts on good to soft going. *Alan King*   h–

DUN

DUNCOMPLAINING (IRE) 9 b.g. Milan – Notcomplainingbut (IRE) (Supreme Leader) [2017/18 c87p, h100p: c20.2s Jan 11] big, rangy gelding: bumper winner: lightly-raced maiden hurdler, fair form at best: some promise in novice event on first of 2 starts in handicap chases: will stay beyond 21f: acts on soft going: tongue tied in 2016/17. *Oliver Sherwood*   c– h–

DUN FAW GOOD 11 br.g. Grape Tree Road – Dun Rose (Roscoe Blake) [2017/18 c91: c19.3s⁴ c23.8d² c23.8d* Mar 16] multiple point winner: modest handicap chaser: won at Musselburgh in March: stays 25f: acts on good to soft going. *James Walton*   c89

DUNKEREEN (IRE) 5 b.g. Scorpion (IRE) – Malabar Rose (IRE) (Oscar Schindler (IRE)) [2017/18 b16s⁴ b16.8s³ h16v^pu Jan 1] poor form in bumpers: pulled up in maiden on hurdling debut: tried in hood: in tongue tie last 2 starts. *Olly Murphy*   h– b65

DUNLY (FR) 5 b.g. Gris de Gris (IRE) – Octavine du Meix (FR) (Le Tajer (FR)) [2017/18 b87: h20.5v Nov 15] placed in 4 bumpers in 2016/17: 14/1, seventh in maiden at Ayr (28¾ lengths behind Victoria Says) on hurdling debut: should do better. *James Ewart*   h– p

DUNN'S RIVER (FR) 7 gr.g. Mastercraftsman (IRE) – Prairie Moon (Halling (USA)) [2017/18 h21.2g h19g⁶ h21.7g⁵ Apr 20] multiple winning pointer: modest maiden hurdler, lightly raced: stays 2¾m: acts on good to soft going: in blinkers last 2 starts: tried in tongue tie. *Jack R. Barber*   h91

DUNRAVEN DOC 7 b.g. Dr Massini (IRE) – Aphrodisias (FR) (Double Bed (FR)) [2017/18 b17g⁶ May 19] seventh foal: half-brother to 3 winners, including modest hurdler Solitairy Girl (19f winner, by Loup Solitaire): dam unraced sister to smart French hurdler/high-class chaser (stayed 27f) Matinee Lover: won twice in points in 2017: in hood/tongue tie, found little in bumper at Aintree. *David Brace*   b–

DUNRAVEN STORM (IRE) 13 br.g. Presenting – Foxfire (Lord Americo) [2017/18 c143x, h–: c18m³ c19.4g⁶ Jun 10] sturdy gelding: winning hurdler: smart handicap chaser in prime: below form both starts in 2017/18, markedly so final one: stays 19f: acts on heavy going: usually leads: often let down by jumping. *Philip Hobbs*   c128 x h–

DUN SCAITH (IRE) 10 b.g. Vinnie Roe (IRE) – Scathach (IRE) (Nestor) [2017/18 c–, h106§: h20g⁶ h20.3g³ h25.4s⁵ h16.3s h15.8v² h16.7v^ur Feb 9] fair handicap hurdler: fell both starts in maiden chases: best up to 3m: acts on good to firm and heavy going: often hooded: wears tongue tie: usually races towards rear: temperamental. *Sophie Leech*   c– h101 §

DUNSTALL DOLLY 5 b.m. Midnight Legend – Toungara (FR) (Smadoun (FR)) [2017/18 b15.8v⁶ Apr 7] first foal: dam lightly-raced sister to fairly useful hurdler/top-class chaser (stayed 25f) Nacarat: 7/2, tailed off in mares bumper at Uttoxeter. *Tom George*   b–

DUNVEGAN (FR) 5 gr.g. Le Havre (IRE) – Or des Joncs (FR) (Turgeon (USA)) [2017/18 b16s² b16v² b16v* b16s⁶ b20s² b16.2d* Apr 26] second foal: dam unraced: useful bumper performer: won at Fairyhouse (maiden) in January and Punchestown (by 1¾ lengths from Voix des Tiep) in April: 4/1, shaped well when second in maiden at Leopardstown (7½ lengths behind Pallasator) on hurdling debut: should do better. *P. A. Fahy, Ireland*   h122 p b112

DURBANVILLE 6 b.g. Black Sam Bellamy (IRE) – Kealshore Lass (Alflora (IRE)) [2017/18 h96: h19.3v* h24.1s³ h25.3d³ h19.4s⁶ h24.3v⁵ Feb 26] fair handicap hurdler: won at Carlisle in October: stays 3m: acts on heavy going: tried in cheekpieces: often races prominently. *James Ewart*   h105

DURSEY SOUND (IRE) 10 b.g. Milan – Glendante (IRE) (Phardante (FR)) [2017/18 c119, h–: c24.2g³ c26.1d² c25.5g⁴ c24.1g Aug 16] well-made gelding: winning hurdler: fair handicap chaser: stays 3¼m: acts on heavy going: tried in headgear/tongue tie: usually races towards rear: not straightforward. *Ben Haslam*   c106 h–

DUSKY HERCULES (IRE) 4 b.g. Shantou (USA) – Annalecky (IRE) (Bob's Return (IRE)) [2017/18 b15.3v Apr 9] half-brother to several winners, including smart hurdler/very smart chaser Black Hercules (2m-3m winner, by Heron Island) and fairly useful hurdler Tourboy (3m winner, by Whitmore's Conn): dam unraced: 14/1, seventh in bumper at Wincanton. *David Pipe*   b–

DUSKY LARK 8 b.g. Nayef (USA) – Snow Goose (Polar Falcon (USA)) [2017/18 c140, h–: c24.1s^pu h18.5v³ h21.4s³ c19.9s⁴ c21s^ur Apr 23] good-topped gelding: fairly useful handicap hurdler/useful handicap chaser at best: below form in 2017/18: stays 2½m: acts on heavy going: in cheekpieces last 2 starts: often tongue tied: front runner/races prominently: often let down by jumping over fences. *Robert Walford*   c117 x h114

DUSKY LEGEND 8 b.m. Midnight Legend – Tinagoodnight (FR) (Sleeping Car (FR)) [2017/18 h138: c20f² c17.4s² c16.4g^F h16.6s³ h21.1s^F Mar 14] sturdy mare: useful hurdler: similar form over fences: running best race (keeping on and looking set to go close) when falling 2 out in novice handicap won by Bigmartre at Newbury in December: stays 2½m: acts on heavy going: remains with potential as a chaser. *Alan King*   c143 p
h123

DUSKY RAIDER (IRE) 5 gr.g. Clodovil (IRE) – Rahila (IRE) (Kalanisi (IRE)) [2017/18 h89: h16.8m³ h15.8g h16d⁶ h15.8d* h16.8v Nov 26] fair form over hurdles: won handicap at Uttoxeter in October: unproven beyond 2m: acts on good to soft going. *Tim Vaughan*   h102

DU SOLEIL (FR) 6 ch.g. Zambezi Sun – Cykapri (FR) (Cyborg (FR)) [2017/18 h111p: h15.8d* h18.9v^F h15.5v² h20.5v^{pu} h19.9v Mar 17] fairly useful form over hurdles: won novice at Uttoxeter in November: best around 2m (weakened badly at testing 2½m): acts on heavy going: tried in hood: front runner/races prominently. *Venetia Williams*   h118

DUSTY PEARL 5 b.g. Frozen Fire (GER) – Kahooting (Kahyasi) [2017/18 b17g³ h19.9d⁵ Oct 8] runner-up on second of 2 starts in maiden points: inadequate test when third in conditionals/amateur bumper at Aintree (for Francesca Nimmo): 6/1, well held in conditionals maiden at Uttoxeter on hurdling debut. *Kim Bailey*   h74
b80

DUTCH ARTIST (IRE) 6 ch.g. Dutch Art – Baltic Princess (FR) (Peintre Celebre (USA)) [2017/18 h15.7d⁶ h16.8s⁵ h15.7d Dec 28] fair on Flat, unproven beyond 1m: modest form when sixth in novice at Catterick on hurdling debut: didn't progress: tried in tongue tie. *Alan Brown*   h85

DUTCH CANYON (IRE) 8 b.g. Craigsteel – Chitabe (IRE) (Lord of Appeal) [2017/18 c72§, h76§: c23.8g⁶ c20.1g⁵ c23.8d³ c23.8s⁵ h23.8d² h23.9s Apr 25] poor maiden hurdler/chaser: stays 3m: acts on good and good to firm going: regularly in headgear: has worn tongue tie: ungenuine. *N. W. Alexander*   c60 §
h81 §

DUTCH COED 6 b.g. Dutch Art – Discoed (Distinctly North (USA)) [2017/18 b16.4g b15.7d Dec 19] tailed off in bumpers: modest form on Flat subsequently. *Tina Jackson*   b–

D'WATERSIDE 4 b.g. Sir Percy – Santorini Sunset (Haafhd) [2017/18 h15.8v h15.8s h15.8d⁴ h15.8d Apr 24] neat gelding: modest maiden on Flat, stays 11f: modest form over hurdles: tried in hood. *David Loughnane*   h93

DWYNANT 5 gr.m. Multiplex – Nant Y Mynydd (Piccolo) [2017/18 h20g⁵ h17.2g³ h16g h19.6g Aug 16] modest maiden on Flat, stays 8.5f: winning pointer: little promise over hurdles, making mistakes: hooded first 3 outings. *David Loughnane*   h–

DYLANSEOGHAN (IRE) 9 b.g. Pierre – Sabbatical (IRE) (Jurado (USA)) [2017/18 c85, h–: c22.7d² c23.6s^{pu} c22.7s^{ur} c20.2v³ c20.2v² c24s³ c27.5d* Apr 22] winning pointer: maiden hurdler: fair handicap chaser: won at Stratford in April: stays 3½m: acts on heavy going: in cheekpieces 4 of last 5 outings. *Zoe Davison*   c104
h–

DYLAN'S STORM (IRE) 6 b.g. Zebedee – Storm Lady (IRE) (Alhaarth (IRE)) [2017/18 h54: h16.8g⁶ h16.8g May 16] modest maiden pointer: poor maiden hurdler: best around 2m: acts on good to soft going: tried in cheekpieces: usually tongue tied. *Peter Niven*   h63

DYLIEV (FR) 5 ch.m. Dylan Thomas (IRE) – Coreliev (IRE) (Fasliyev (USA)) [2017/18 h16d⁶ h18.6d⁵ h15.8s⁵ h15.8s³ Feb 22] fairly useful on Flat, stays 10.5f: modest form over hurdles: in hood last 3 starts. *Caroline Bailey*   h98

DYLLAN (IRE) 5 b.g. Zebedee – Luvmedo (IRE) (One Cool Cat (USA)) [2017/18 h16.3g^{pu} Oct 21] fair on Flat, stays 7f: pulled up in seller on hurdling debut. *Ruth Carr*   h–

DYNAMIC ISLAND (IRE) 7 b.g. Island House (IRE) – Curragh Barn Lass (IRE) (Supreme Leader) [2017/18 c26.2v^{pu} Apr 16] dual point winner: tongue tied, pulled up in maiden hunter on chasing debut. *Mrs L. Bevin*   c–

DYNAMITE DOLLARS (FR) 5 b.g. Buck's Boum (FR) – Macadoun (FR) (Cardoun (FR)) [2017/18 b97: h16d* h16.8v* h15.7v³ h19.8s⁵ h20.5v⁵ h19.4s² Feb 21] good-topped gelding: fairly useful form over hurdles: won novices at Chepstow in October and Exeter in November: stays 19f: acts on heavy going: usually races prominently/travels strongly. *Paul Nicholls*   h127

DYNAMO FRANKIE (IRE) 11 b.g. Beneficial – River View (IRE) (Flemensfirth (USA)) [2017/18 c26d^{pu} May 5] winning pointer: pulled up in hunter on chasing debut. *W. M. Wanless*   c–

DYNAMO (IRE) 7 b.g. Galileo (IRE) – Trading Places (Dansili) [2017/18 c–x, h67x: h24g⁵ h21.6m Jun 15] disappointing maiden hurdler: also let down by jumping over fences: unproven beyond 17f: acts on soft going: in cheekpieces last 3 starts: wears tongue tie. *Jamie Snowden*   c– x
h71 x

DYS

DYSIOS (IRE) 10 b.g. Invincible Spirit (IRE) – Hataana (USA) (Robellino (USA)) [2017/18 c132, h–: h16v³ h20v* h20d c17d c17s³ c17s⁵ h22v^pu Apr 2] useful handicap hurdler: won at Gowran (by 10 lengths from Young Turk) in September: fairly useful handicap chaser: third in Dan Moore Memorial Handicap Chase at Fairyhouse in January: stays 2½m: acts on heavy going: tried in cheekpieces: wears tongue tie. *Denis W. Cullen, Ireland*   **c128 h130**

E

EAGER TO KNOW (IRE) 8 b.g. Sayarshan (FR) – Drew (IRE) (Double Schwartz) [2017/18 h79: h23.9g³ h23.3g³ c23.8d^F c19.3s^pu Jan 12] winning pointer: poor maiden hurdler: failed to complete both starts in chases: stays 27f: acts on good to firm going: often races towards rear. *Micky Hammond*   **c– h80**

EAGLE RIDGE (IRE) 7 b.g. Oscar (IRE) – Azaban (IRE) (Be My Native (USA)) [2017/18 b18g h16v⁶ h16.2v h16v³ h18.9s^pu Mar 21] €44,000 3-y-o: half-brother to 3 winners, including fairly useful hurdler/useful chaser King of The Wolds (2m-25f winner, by Presenting): dam unraced half-sister to winning hurdler/useful chaser (stays 29f) Pete The Feat out of Supreme Novices' Hurdle winner Tourist Attraction: runner-up in Irish point: modest form in bumpers/over hurdles: left J. R. Barry after first start: should be suited by further than 2m: often races towards rear. *N. W. Alexander*   **h97 b–**

EAMON AN CNOIC (IRE) 7 b.g. Westerner – Nutmeg Tune (IRE) (Accordion) [2017/18 h125: c15.2s^F c20.6v* c15.7v³ c19.7v* c25s h20s^pu Apr 13] tall gelding: fairly useful form over hurdles, won twice in 2016/17: useful form over fences: won novice at Haydock in December and 3-runner novice handicap at Plumpton in February: stays 21f: acts on heavy going: in cheekpieces last 2 starts: often races prominently/travels strongly. *David Pipe*   **c134 h–**

EARCOMESTOM 6 b.g. Passing Glance – Earcomesannie (IRE) (Anshan) [2017/18 b16.4g b15.8g b16.2g h21s h19s h21v⁶ h20.3g Apr 20] workmanlike gelding: twice-raced pointer: no form in bumpers: poor form over hurdles: in hood last 2 starts: tried in tongue tie. *Peter Pritchard*   **h77 b–**

EARLOFTHECOTSWOLDS (FR) 4 bl.g. Axxos (GER) – Sissi Land (FR) (Grey Risk (FR)) [2017/18 b16d Apr 7] £19,000 3-y-o: second foal: dam in frame in French bumpers at 1½m: 5/1, green when third in bumper at Fakenham (3½ lengths behind Before Midnight). *Nigel Twiston-Davies*   **b89**

EARLS FORT (IRE) 8 b.g. Kalanisi (IRE) – Lillando (IRE) (Lando (GER)) [2017/18 h115: h20.1g^F h19.9g⁶ c16g⁵ c19.4g c23g^pu Aug 30] fair hurdler: no form in 2017/18, including over fences: stayed 21f: wore cheekpieces/tongue tie: dead. *Neil Mulholland*   **c– h–**

EARLSHILL (IRE) 7 b.g. Milan – Mrs Marples (IRE) (Sexton Blake) [2017/18 h112: h19.9d³ h23.4v⁵ h21g h21d* Apr 26] sturdy gelding: Irish point winner: fairly useful hurdler: won maiden at Warwick in April: left Dan Skelton after third start: should stay beyond 21f: acts on heavy going: usually in tongue tie: often races prominently. *Stuart Edmunds*   **h116**

EARLY BOY (FR) 7 b.g. Early March – Eclat de Rose (FR) (Scribe (IRE)) [2017/18 h–: h15.7d^pu h15.7d h16v Feb 20] no form in bumpers/over hurdles: tried in eyeshields. *Andrew Crook*   **h–**

EARLY DOORS (FR) 5 b.g. Soldier of Fortune (IRE) – Ymlaen (IRE) (Desert Prince (IRE)) [2017/18 h16s* h16v* h16s² h16s h20.3v³ h20s Apr 28] €36,000 3-y-o: seventh foal: half-brother to 3 winners on Flat, including useful French 7f-11f winner Landym (by Lando): dam, 6f winner, half-sister to useful hurdler (15f-17f winner) Smaoineamh Alainn: bumper winner: useful form over hurdles: won maiden at Wexford in October and Fishery Lane Hurdle at Naas (by 2 lengths from Meri Devie) in November: second in Royal Bond Novices' Hurdle at Fairyhouse (5½ lengths behind Mengli Khan) in December and third in Martin Pipe Conditional Jockeys' Handicap Hurdle at Cheltenham (6¼ lengths behind Blow By Blow) in March: stays 2½m: acts on heavy going. *Joseph Patrick O'Brien, Ireland*   **h140**

EARLY DU LEMO (FR) 5 gr.g. Early March – Kiswa (FR) (Top Waltz (FR)) [2017/18 h119p: h16.3s² h15.9v⁵ Apr 1] good-topped gelding: fairly useful form over hurdles: second in handicap at Newbury in March: raced around 2m: acts on soft going. *Gary Moore*   **h122**

EARLY LEARNER 6 b.m. Sulamani (IRE) – Slow Starter (IRE) (Dr Massini (IRE)) [2017/18 b16.7v Jan 17] €17,000 3-y-o, £28,000 5-y-o: sixth foal: half-sister to winning pointers by Vinnie Roe and Loup Sauvage: dam unraced half-sister to useful hurdler/smart   **b–**

EAS

chaser (stayed 3m) Risk Accessor and to dam of smart hurdler/useful chaser (stayed 2½m) Raya Star: won Irish mares maiden point on debut: tailed off in listed mares bumper. *Kim Bailey*

EARLY RETIREMENT (IRE) 6 b.g. Daylami (IRE) – Deep Lilly (Glacial Storm (USA)) [2017/18 h105: h20.3g* h24.1d² h24.4s⁵ h22.8vᵖᵘ Mar 31] fairly useful handicap hurdler: won at Southwell in October: stays 3m: acts on heavy going: tried in cheekpieces. *Caroline Bailey*   **h116**

EARTH LADY 6 b.m. Presenting – Simply Divine (IRE) (Be My Native (USA)) [2017/18 h98p, b68: h19gᵖᵘ h15.7sᵖᵘ h17dᵖᵘ Mar 31] maiden hurdler, no form in 2017/18: left Philip Hobbs after first start: usually races towards rear. *Martin Todhunter*   **h–**

EARTH LEADER (IRE) 5 br.g. Presenting – Full of Spirit (IRE) (Exit To Nowhere (USA)) [2017/18 b15.3s⁶ Nov 11] well beaten in bumper. *Paul Nicholls*   **b–**

EARTH MOOR (IRE) 4 ch.g. Ask – Merrylas (IRE) (Mister Lord (USA)) [2017/18 b15.3v⁴ Apr 9] 16/1, fourth in bumper at Wincanton (12¼ lengths behind Unwin Vc). *Philip Hobbs*   **b78**

EARTHMOVES (FR) 8 b.g. Antarctique (IRE) – Red Rym (FR) (Denham Red (FR)) [2017/18 c106, h122: c23.8g⁴ c19.4d* c21.4g* c21.4g h24.7sᵖᵘ c19.2v² c23sᵖᵘ c25.2s⁵ Feb 12] lengthy gelding: winning hurdler: fairly useful handicap chaser: won at Ffos Las (novice) in May and Market Rasen in June: stays 21f: acts on heavy going: wears headgear/ tongue tie: often races prominently: signs of temperament. *Peter Bowen*   **c127 h–**

EARTH STORM (IRE) 6 b.g. Getaway (GER) – Aguida (FR) (Kahyasi) [2017/18 h21d h23.9s h21s Feb 9] €10,000 4-y-o: fourth foal: dam lightly-raced half-sister to very smart French hurdler/useful chaser (17f-25f winner) Astonville: winning pointer: mid-field at best in novice/maiden hurdles: should stay at least 3m. *Jack R. Barber*   **h85**

EASTER DAY (FR) 10 b.g. Malinas (GER) – Sainte Lea (FR) (Sirk) [2017/18 c–, h124: h25g³ h25s⁵ Jan 26] useful-looking gelding: fairly useful handicap hurdler: winning chaser: left Henry Spiller after first start: stays 3¼m: acts on heavy going: has worn headgear: usually races towards rear. *Oliver Sherwood*   **c– h123**

EASTER GOLD (FR) 4 b.f. Kapgarde (FR) – Une Dame d'Or (FR) (Astarabad (USA)) [2017/18 b15.8v² b16d⁵ Apr 26] £24,000 3-y-o: close-coupled filly: first foal: dam (b78), second in bumper on only start, half-sister to fairly useful/unreliable hurdler/chaser (stayed 3¼m) River d'Or: fair form in bumpers: better effort when second in mares event at Uttoxeter. *Lucy Wadham*   **b89**

EASTER IN PARIS (IRE) 9 b.m. Bienamado (USA) – Easter Saturday (IRE) (Grand Plaisir (IRE)) [2017/18 c94, h92: h21.7d c19.7s² h21.2sᵖᵘ c19.2s⁴ Feb 6] lengthy mare: maiden hurdler: modest handicap chaser, below form in 2017/18: stays 2¾m: acts on heavy going: tried in hood: front runner/races prominently. *Paul Henderson*   **c71 h–**

EASTER MYTTON 6 b.m. Overbury (IRE) – Ma Dame Mytton (Hunting Lion (IRE)) [2017/18 b–: h19.3dᵖᵘ Nov 24] no show in bumper/novice hurdle. *Hugh Burns*   **h–**

EASTERN LADY (IND) 5 ch.m. Dancing Forever (USA) – Oriental Lady (IRE) (King's Best (USA)) [2017/18 h16g h15.8g⁴ h15.8g⁴ h16.2g⁵ h16.2s⁵ h16.5s Jan 9] maiden on Flat: poor form over hurdles: raced only at 2m: usually in hood/tongue tie. *Richard Price*   **h84**

EAST INDIES 5 b.g. Authorized (IRE) – Elan (Dansili) [2017/18 h112: h15.9m* h15.3s h15.7g h15.8g⁶ Nov 14] rather leggy gelding: fairly useful handicap hurdler: won at Plumpton in September: stays 2¼m: acts on good to firm and good to soft going: has worn hood: often races freely. *Gary Moore*   **h116**

EASTLAKE (IRE) 12 b.g. Beneficial – Guigone (FR) (Esprit du Nord (USA)) [2017/18 c150§, h–§: c15.9g c16.3v c21.1s Apr 13] rangy gelding: has had breathing operation: winning hurdler: smart chaser at best, no form in 2017/18: stays 21f: has worn cheekpieces: wears tongue tie: unreliable. *Jonjo O'Neill*   **c– § h– §**

EASTVIEW BOY 7 ch.g. Iktibas – Eastview Princess (J B Quick) [2017/18 c114, h109: h16.8v* h20.6v* h16.2d Apr 26] workmanlike gelding: fairly useful handicap hurdler: won at Sedgefield in March and Newcastle in April: fair chaser: stays 21f: acts on heavy going: tried in cheekpieces. *Philip Kirby*   **c– h115**

EAST WING (IRE) 6 b.g. Winged Love (IRE) – Eastender (Opening Verse (USA)) [2017/18 b15.8d² b15.8d h16.5g h15.9s h15.3v h18.5s Feb 23] €18,000 3-y-o: sixth foal: brother to smart bumper winner/fairly useful hurdler Coeur Blimey (stays 19f) and fairly useful hurdler/chaser Just Get Cracking (2m-21f winner): dam lightly-raced half-sister to very smart/temperamental hurdler (stayed 3m) Westender: fair form when second in bumper on debut: disappointing after, mainly over hurdles: usually in tongue tie. *Anthony Honeyball*   **h– b89**

285

EAS

EASYONDEYE (IRE) 12 b.g. Beneficial – Lady of Appeal (IRE) (Lord of Appeal) [2017/18 c–, h–: c20.2s c19.4v[pu] Jan 19] point winner: once-raced hurdler: fair chaser at best: stays 21f: acts on heavy going: in tongue tie last 2 starts. *Debra Hamer*   **c73 h–**

EASY STREET (IRE) 8 b.g. High Chaparral (IRE) – Victorine (IRE) (Un Desperado (FR)) [2017/18 c127, h104: c19.9g[6] c20.1m Jun 4] maiden hurdler: fairly useful chaser, well below best both starts early in 2017/18: stays 25f: acts on soft and good to firm going: often races in rear: often let down by jumping. *Jonjo O'Neill*   **c– x h–**

EAT MY DIRT (IRE) 6 b.g. Mahler – Aos Dana (IRE) (Fourstars Allstar (USA)) [2017/18 b15.8d* b16.3g[5] Jul 4] €8,000 3-y-o: seventh foal: brother to a winning pointer and half-brother to fair hurdler Stanton Court (2m winner, by Hubbly Bubbly): dam placed in points: modest form in bumpers: won at Ffos Las in May. *Ian Williams*   **b83**

EATON HILL (IRE) 6 b.g. Yeats (IRE) – Guilt Less (FR) (Useful (FR)) [2017/18 h120, b89: h21.1g h21.6d[6] h19.9v[3] h20s[2] Apr 13] good-topped gelding: fairly useful handicap hurdler: second to Jester Jet in Grade 3 at Aintree (tongue tied) in April: likely to stay further than 2¾m: acts on soft going: often races towards rear. *Kerry Lee*   **h125**

EATON MILLER (IRE) 6 b.g. Milan – Four Fields (IRE) (Fourstars Allstar (USA)) [2017/18 b15.7d h15.8d h15.8d h15.8s h19.2v[5] h20v[4] h21.7v Mar 10] well held in bumper: poor form over hurdles: will be suited by 2¾m+: acts on heavy going. *Tom Symonds*   **h76 b–**

EATON ROCK (IRE) 9 b.g. Rocamadour – Duchess of Kinsale (IRE) (Montelimar (USA)) [2017/18 c96, h–: c20.3g[2] c20.9g[2] c23g Jul 27] winning hurdler: modest handicap chaser: stays 3m: acts on heavy going: in cheekpieces last 3 starts: wears tongue tie nowadays. *Tom Symonds*   **c93 h–**

EAU DE NILE (IRE) 5 b.g. Robin des Champs (FR) – Rivervail (IRE) (River Falls) [2017/18 b–: b16f[4] h16s h15.8d h15.8s h21.2d[F] Apr 24] useful-looking gelding: modest form in bumpers/over hurdles. *Henry Daly*   **h90 b79**

EBONY EXPRESS 9 bl.g. Superior Premium – Coffee Ice (Primo Dominie) [2017/18 h15.8m* h16.7g Jul 22] sturdy gelding: fairly useful handicap hurdler: won at Uttoxeter in July after 16-month absence: should stay 2½m: acts on good to firm and heavy going: tried in cheekpieces/tongue tie. *Dr Richard Newland*   **h120**

EBONY GALE 4 br.g. Shirocco (GER) – Glenora Gale (IRE) (Milan) [2017/18 b16s[6] b15.3d* Apr 22] €46,000 3-y-o: lengthy gelding: first foal: dam (h109), untrustworthy bumper/2½m hurdle winner, out of half-sister to useful staying chaser Frazer Island: fairly useful form in bumpers: won at Wincanton in April. *Philip Hobbs*   **b97**

EBONY ROSE 6 br.m. Kalanisi (IRE) – Cogolie (FR) (Cyborg (FR)) [2017/18 b73§: h20.6g[2] h20.2g* h23.3d[3] h23.9d* h20.1s[4] h23.8m[5] h24.6s* Dec 3] fair hurdler: won maiden at Perth in August, and handicaps at same course in September and Carlisle in December: stays 25f: acts on soft going: wears hood: in tongue tie last 5 starts: races well off pace. *Susan Corbett*   **h112**

EBONYS ENCORE (IRE) 6 b.m. Oscar (IRE) – Ebony Queen (Classic Cliche (IRE)) [2017/18 h20.6g[3] h18.5v h20.7d Mar 26] €4,000 3-y-o, £35,000 5-y-o: fourth foal: half-sister to a winning pointer by Presenting: dam (b76), lightly raced in bumpers/over hurdles, half-sister to fairly useful hurdler/chaser (21f/2¾m winner) Carlitos out of useful 2m hurdler/chaser Queen of Spades: won Irish point on debut: modest form over hurdles: remains open to improvement. *Jonjo O'Neill*   **h96 p**

ECHNATON (GER) 5 b.g. Lord of England (GER) – Easy Sunshine (IRE) (Sadler's Wells (USA)) [2017/18 b–: b16g h16s h15.8s h16.6d c21.4s[4] Mar 26] no form in bumpers/over hurdles: 16/1, showed more when fourth in novice handicap at Market Rasen (8¾ lengths behind Bocasien Desbois) on chasing debut, despite not jumping well: has worn hood: tried in tongue tie: often races prominently: open to improvement over fences. *Lucy Wadham*   **c90 p h– b–**

ECHO BEAT (IRE) 5 b.m. Beat Hollow – Calendula (Be My Guest (USA)) [2017/18 b–: ab16.3g ab16.3g Mar 3] no form in bumpers. *Tracy Waggott*   **b–**

ECHO EXPRESS (IRE) 6 b.g. Echo of Light – If Dubai (USA) (Stephen Got Even (USA)) [2017/18 b92: h16.2g[2] h16.2v[3] h16v[6] h20.2s Apr 27] bumper winner: modest form over hurdles. *Nicky Richards*   **h95**

ECHO LADY (IRE) 7 b.m. Kayf Tara – Echo Queen (IRE) (Luso) [2017/18 h16.5m h16g h24g[6] h17.6d[6] h16s[3] h20.1s[6] Oct 6] third foal: half-sister to useful hurdler/chaser Kilcarry Bridge (2m-3m winner, by Balakheri) and fair hurdler/fairly useful chaser New Kid In Town (2½m-3m winner, by Gamut): dam unraced sister to Irish Grand National winner Hear The Echo: poor maiden hurdler nowadays: unproven beyond 17f: acts on soft and good to firm going: wears tongue tie. *John Patrick Ryan, Ireland*   **h82**

286

ECHO WATT (FR) 4 gr.g. Fragrant Mix (IRE) – Roxane du Bois (FR) (Passing Sale (FR)) [2017/18 b15.8v* h16s⁴ h16sᵘʳ h20.3v⁶ h23v⁵ Feb 19] useful-looking gelding: third foal: dam placed in French bumpers around 1½m: won maiden bumper at Ffos Las (by 9 lengths from Potters Tale) in December: modest form over hurdles: should stay further than 2m: in hood last 2 starts: often leads. *Richard Hobson*   h97 b89

ECLAIR DE GUYE (FR) 4 gr.g. Lord du Sud (FR) – Jouvence de Guye (FR) (Hawker's News (IRE)) [2017/18 b11.4g⁴ b16d⁶ Apr 7] unplaced in bumpers: left G. Taupin after first start. *Lucy Wadham*   b?

ECOLE D'ART (IRE) 4 b.g. Nathaniel (IRE) – Danehill Dreamer (USA) (Danehill (USA)) [2017/18 h15.7sᵘʳ Jan 11] fair form on Flat for A. Fabre, stays 10.5f: behind when unseated last in juvenile hurdle. *Malcolm Jefferson*   h–

ECO WARRIOR 8 b.g. Echo of Light – Kryssa (Kris) [2017/18 c19.3g⁶ Apr 23] good-topped gelding: winning pointer: maiden hurdler: yet to complete in chases: unproven beyond 17f: acts on heavy going: tried in headgear. *N. Orpwood*   c– h–

EDDIEMAURICE (IRE) 7 ch.g. Captain Rio – Annals (Lujain (USA)) [2017/18 h120: c20.9sᵖᵘ c16s⁴ h15.7g⁴ h16v² h16.8v⁶ h16s⁵ h16v⁴ Apr 14] compact gelding: fairly useful handicap hurdler: second at Kempton in December: fair form over fences: better effort when fourth in novice handicap at Chepstow: unproven beyond 2m: acts on heavy going: tried in headgear: often races towards rear. *John Flint*   c109 h118

EDDIES MIRACLE (IRE) 10 b.g. Beat of Drums – Ballinamona Gold (IRE) (Pierre) [2017/18 c22.1g⁶ c24v⁶ c21.5s⁴ c19.6v* c21.1sᵘʳ Apr 12] multiple point winner: fair form in chases: won hunter at Down Royal in March: generally let down by jumping otherwise, notably on debut under Rules: should stay beyond 21f: acts on heavy going. *David Christie, Ireland*   c114 x

EDDIES PEARL (IRE) 8 b.m. Craigsteel – Florida Bay (IRE) (Florida Son) [2017/18 h18.5s h16v h19v⁶ Apr 12] €1,700 3-y-o: half-sister to fairly useful hurdler/chaser Majestic Mayhem (2½m winner, by Luso), stayed 25f: dam unraced sister to top-class chaser (stayed 3¼m) Florida Pearl: winning pointer: no form in bumper/novice hurdles. *Brian Forsey*   h–

EDDY 9 b.g. Exit To Nowhere (USA) – Sharway Lady (Shareef Dancer (USA)) [2017/18 h69: h19.9d* h23.3d* h22g⁶ h20g⁶ h23.3d⁵ h21.6d* h21.6s² h23.1vᵘʳ h23.1v² h23.5d Dec 23] strong gelding: fair handicap hurdler: won at Uttoxeter in May and June, and Exeter (novice) in October: stays 23f: acts on heavy going: tried in hood: has worn tongue tie, including last 5 starts: usually races towards rear, often travels strongly. *Susan Gardner*   h100

EDEIFF'S LAD 11 ch.g. Loup Sauvage (USA) – Ede'iff (Tragic Role (USA)) [2017/18 c75, h–: c24.2s³ c20.3gᵖᵘ Apr 20] point winner: maiden hurdler: poor chaser: stays 3m: acts on heavy going: wears hood. *L. Humphrey*   c78 h–

EDLOMOND (IRE) 12 gr.g. Great Palm (USA) – Samardana (IRE) (Hernando (FR)) [2017/18 c89§, h–: c16.1gᵖᵘ May 22] tall gelding: winning hurdler: fair chaser at best, has lost his way: wears headgear/tongue tie: temperamental. *Bill Turner*   c– § h–

EDVARDO (IRE) 8 b.g. Oscar (IRE) – Shedan (IRE) (Perpendicular) [2017/18 h16.8v² h21.4vᵇᵈ Jan 6] fair handicap hurdler: stayed 21f: best form on heavy going: tried in cheekpieces/tongue tie: dead. *Richard Woollacott*   h110

EDWARD ELGAR 7 ch.g. Avonbridge – Scooby Dooby Do (Atraf) [2017/18 h100§: c21.7m⁴ c19.8g³ c22.5d² c24gᵖᵘ c21.7g⁶ c19.8s³ c20.2s h19.2v⁴ h20.6s⁵ Mar 26] sturdy gelding: modest handicap hurdler/maiden chaser: stays 2¾m: acts on heavy going: wears headgear: temperamental. *Caroline Bailey*   c95 § h91 §

EDWULF 9 b.g. Kayf Tara – Valentines Lady (IRE) (Zaffaran (USA)) [2017/18 c150+, h–: c24dᵖᵘ c24s* c26.3v c24.5s Apr 25]   c161 h–

The centre-piece of the inaugural two-day Dublin Racing Festival at Leopardstown in February, the Unibet-sponsored Irish Gold Cup, produced a winner with a particularly heartwarming story. Rank outsider Edwulf may have been a fortunate winner on the day—Killultagh Vic fell at the last with victory in his grasp—but the media coverage afterwards read like a fairytale. The horse's tough constitution, and the efforts of the Cheltenham racecourse vets and the owner's own vets, had resulted in his being saved—after most feared the worst—when he fell in full view of the packed Cheltenham stands in the previous season's National Hunt Chase. Edwulf was in second behind Tiger Roll when he began to falter going to the

Unibet Irish Gold Cup, Leopardstown—Killultagh Vic and Paul Townend crash out at the last, leaving the way for 33/1-shot Edwulf (hoops) to overhaul Outlander

final fence, and he was still second when he went wrong on the run-in, becoming uncoordinated and staggering to a halt. He eventually collapsed and it looked as if he had suffered a seizure. The green screens were erected and the vets moved in.

Edwulf underwent treatment, reportedly having a fit and suffering temporary blindness as he lay on the ground behind the screens, and he was down for over forty minutes being treated for oxygen deprivation brought on by extreme exertion and possibly heat stress. With the help of members of the local fire service, Edwulf was put on a mat and pulled to the side of the track as the next race was delayed. When injured horses are down for as long as Edwulf, they rarely get up, but Edwulf managed to regain his feet, still quite uncoordinated, and was taken by horse ambulance to Three Counties Equine Hospital at nearby Tewkesbury. It seemed something of a miracle when it was discovered the next day that he was still alive, and it wasn't much longer before he was able to be returned to Ireland. Edwulf spent the summer at his owner's Martinstown Stud and, after many must have assumed his racing career was over, he went back into training in the autumn at Joseph O'Brien's burgeoning County Kilkenny stable which now houses a string of around one hundred and fifty, split evenly between Flat and jumping. O'Brien said there were 'no major plans' for Edwulf except to 'start him off and take it from there, the vets say we have no reason to fear a recurrence of what happened at Cheltenham.'

When Edwulf was pulled up in the Leopardstown Christmas Chase on his reappearance, after being tailed off some way from home, victory in the Irish Gold Cup on his next start must have seemed beyond the wildest dreams of all but those closest to him. Edwulf was available in places at 100/1 on the morning of the race (eventually sent off at 33/1) in which half the field had taken part in the Christmas Chase six weeks earlier. The Christmas Chase quintet supplied the first three in the Irish Gold Cup, the patiently-ridden Edwulf making smooth headway from the third last and staying on to lead in the final hundred yards to win by a neck from the Christmas Chase third Outlander (who had been left in front at the last when Killultagh Vic fell). Djakadam, pulled up in the Christmas Chase, bounced back from that rare poor effort to finish third, ten lengths behind Outlander, after making much of the running. Our Duke, who was sent off favourite, and the Christmas Chase fifth and sixth Valseur Lido and Alpha des Obeaux were the only other finishers. The two other runners representing Edwulf's owner, Anibale Fly and Minella Rocco, were making no impression when they fell at the second last and the last respectively.

EDW

J. P. McManus said at first that he was 'lost for words' when interviewed on At The Races afterwards, but then went on to provide a moving account of Edwulf's remarkable recovery that could have left no one in any doubt about his passion for the game, paying particular tribute to all who had helped at Cheltenham and during the horse's rehabilitation. He also revealed the reason—'a little each-way'—that Edwulf's odds had contracted from 100/1 to 33/1! Edwulf was among six of the Irish Gold Cup runners who went on to contest the Cheltenham Gold Cup, as did the Christmas Chase winner Road To Respect who, by design, hadn't run since that victory. There were nine Irish-trained challengers for steeplechasing's blue riband, with Anibale Fly and Road To Respect doing best of them to complete the frame behind Native River and Might Bite. Edwulf started at 20/1 and finished eighth of nine finishers, making some headway four out but weakening from the next (the vets reported that he was suffering from mild heat exhaustion afterwards). Edwulf again ran some way below his Irish Gold Cup form on his only other start, when seventh of ten finishers behind Bellshill, Djakadam and Road To Respect in the Punchestown Gold Cup at the end of April. Mr Derek O'Connor, who had been in the saddle in the National Hunt Chase, rode Edwulf in all his races in the latest season (he became the first amateur to win the Irish Gold Cup).

Edwulf (b.g. 2009)	Kayf Tara (b 1994)	Sadler's Wells (b 1981)	Northern Dancer
			Fairy Bridge
		Colorspin (1983)	High Top
			Reprocolor
	Valentines Lady (IRE) (b 2001)	Zaffaran (b 1985)	Assert
			Sweet Alliance
		Jessica One (b 1991)	Supreme Leader
			Lochadoo

Mr John P. McManus' "Edwulf"

EEZ

Edwulf, a tall gelding who has severe stringhalt, is the second successive Irish Gold Cup winner to have been bred, not in Ireland, but in Britain. Neither the 2017 winner Sizing John, nor Edwulf, were the product of sending British-based mares to Irish stallions either. Their dams were raced on the northern jumping circuit and Sizing John and Edwulf were both sired by British-based stallions and were bred in northern England, Sizing John near Whitby on the Yorkshire coast and Edwulf not far away at Guisborough in Cleveland. Edwulf's sire Kayf Tara, who has been the star name among British-based jumping sires for a number of years, twice won the Gold Cup at Royal Ascot and there is stamina on the distaff side of Edwulf's pedigree too. His dam Valentines Lady, a bumper winner (who gained 'black type' when third in the mares bumper at the Grand National meeting), won over hurdles at three miles for Saltburn trainer Keith Reveley. Unfortunately, she has had very few progeny (reportedly difficult to keep in foal), though her only other offspring to reach the racecourse, the progressive six-year-old Grand Morning (by Sizing John's sire Midnight Legend), has also carried the McManus colours to success, completing a hat-trick over hurdles (his final win at two and three quarter miles) in the latest season. Edwulf's grandam Jessica One won a bumper and five hurdle races (at up to two and three quarter miles) for Mary Reveley before being bought privately at the end of her racing career by Edwulf's breeder, Cleveland-based farrier Ivor Valentine and his wife, who sold Edwulf for £24,000 at Doncaster Sales as a foal (he went through the ring two years later for just €30,000 at the Derby Sale). Edwulf raced under Rules for Ben Pauling and Aidan O'Brien before joining Joseph O'Brien in the 2016/17 season. He stays twenty-five furlongs and has shown his best form on soft and heavy going. He wears a tongue tie. *Joseph Patrick O'Brien, Ireland*

EEZ EH (IRE) 5 b.g. Jeremy (USA) – Step With Style (USA) (Gulch (USA)) [2017/18 h16.8g^4 Aug 31] fair on Flat, stays 1½m: 20/1, fourth in novice at Sedgefield (29½ lengths behind Gibson Park) on hurdling debut. *Keith Dalgleish*   h77

EGGESFORD 4 b.g. Foxwedge (AUS) – Elegant Pride (Beat Hollow) [2017/18 h15.3g^{pu} h15.8g h16.8v^F h16.5v h16.5v Apr 12] once-raced on Flat: no form over hurdles: tried in hood. *Laura Young*   h–

EH GEORGES (FR) 4 b.g. Coastal Path – Lady de Vesvre (FR) (Sassanian (USA)) [2017/18 b12.2g^5 h16.4d^4 h15.4g^9* c17.9g* c17.4s^5 Apr 18] well-made gelding: sixth foal: half-brother to French 1½m/13f bumper winner Urfa (by Voix du Nord): dam, French 17f-21f chase winner, sister to useful chaser (stayed 4m) Kock de La Vesvre: fifth in maiden bumper at Cluny: fair form over hurdles: won juvenile at Vichy in September: 23 lengths fourth to Apple's Shakira in Prestbury Juvenile Hurdle at Cheltenham next time: fair form over fences: won 4-y-o event at Lignieres in March: stays 2¼m: has worn tongue tie: remains with potential. *Emmanuel Clayeux, France*   c109 p / h113 p / b–

EJAYTEEKAY 5 b.m. Big Bad Bob (IRE) – Lovely Dream (IRE) (Elnadim (USA)) [2017/18 h16d h18v h16s h16v^4 h15.8v^5 Feb 10] fairly useful on Flat, stays 11.5f: modest form over hurdles: usually races nearer last than first. *Gavin Patrick Cromwell, Ireland*   h91

EL BANDIT (IRE) 7 b.g. Milan – Bonnie Parker (IRE) (Un Desperado (FR)) [2017/18 h141: c25.5d* May 16] tall, useful-looking gelding: useful hurdler: 4/11, won 3-runner novice at Warwick (by 16 lengths from Shelford, with plenty in hand) on chasing debut early in season: stays 3¼m: acts on good to soft going: tried in hood: not seen out again but should still improve over fences. *Paul Nicholls*   c141 p / h–

EL DEGUELLO 5 b.m. Shirocco (GER) – Competa (Hernando (FR)) [2017/18 ab16g b16d Apr 26] unfurnished mare: seventh foal: half-sister to 3 winners, notably Champion Hurdle winner Punjabi (by Komaite) and fairly useful hurdler/useful chaser Attribution (2m-19f winner, by Alhaarth): dam unraced: little impact in bumpers. *Tony Carroll*   b–

ELECTORAL (IRE) 5 b.g. Rip Van Winkle (IRE) – Sumingasefa (Danehill (USA)) [2017/18 b69: b16.7g Oct 31] little show in bumpers. *Sarah-Jayne Davies*   b–

ELEGANT ESCAPE (IRE) 6 b.g. Dubai Destination (USA) – Graineuaile (IRE) (Orchestra) [2017/18 h133: c23.6d^2 c24.2v^2 c23.4g* c24d^2 c24.2v* c24.4s^3 c25s^3 Apr 13] well-made gelding: useful hurdler: smart chaser: won Ladbrokes John Francome Novices' Chase at Newbury (by ¾ length from Black Corton) in December and graduation event at Exeter (by 13 lengths from Ramses de Teillee) in February: second in Kauto Star Novices' Chase at Kempton (1½ lengths behind Black Corton) in between, and third in RSA Insurance   c151 / h–

Mr J. P. Romans' "Elegant Escape"

Novices' Chase at Cheltenham (14 lengths behind Presenting Percy) in March and Mildmay Novices' Chase at Aintree (in cheekpieces, 12¾ lengths behind Terrefort) in April: will be suited by 3½m+: acts on heavy going: usually races close up. *Colin Tizzard*

ELEGANT (IRE) 7 b.m. Oscar (IRE) – Good Thought (IRE) (Mukaddamah (USA))   **h–**
[2017/18 b77: h20.7g Apr 24] lengthy mare: modest form in bumpers: well beaten in mares novice on hurdling debut. *Michael Roberts*

ELGIN 6 b.g. Duke of Marmalade (IRE) – China Tea (USA) (High Chaparral (IRE))   **h157**
[2017/18 h143, b98: h16d4 h15.7g* h16.4s* h15.7d6 h15.3s* h16.4s5 Mar 13]

Racing's dalliances with borrowing titles for its big meetings from golf's 'majors' has finally been consigned to history. The North West Masters—billed as 'the most exciting weekend of jump racing in Britain'—was first introduced in November 2005 but proved short-lived because the terrestrial TV partner at the time Channel 4 changed its stance on showing racing on a Sunday afternoon. The Masters combined the Betfair Chase meeting at Haydock with the Becher Chase meeting the following day at Aintree, but the Aintree executive moved its valuable card to an early-December Saturday when free-to-air TV coverage was dropped. An even earlier marketing initiative involved Cheltenham rebranding the three-day meeting staged in November as The Open, which seemed an odd title for a race meeting when it was first introduced and took some years to be adopted in widely accepted parlance. The Open has developed into much the biggest meeting on Cheltenham's programme after the Festival and its rising popularity led to the Royal and Ancient Golf Club, organisers of golf's Open the oldest of that sport's four

Unibet Greatwood Handicap Hurdle, Cheltenham—the most valuable win of a profitable campaign for Elgin as he edges out the grey Misterton; 2015 winner Old Guard (noseband) rallies for third while the other horse pictured William H Bonney fades into fifth

'majors', claiming that it was creating confusion and hampering efforts to promote its own event. Cheltenham's executive agreed to drop the title in the latest season to 'help both parties promote their respective events and avoid a clash of words in the modern world of digital marketing.'

Considering that there is plenty of opportunity for confusion between racing's Cheltenham Festival and the same town's prestigious performing arts versions, Cheltenham's decision to drop The Open title was a curious one. How much scope is there for potential customers to confuse The Open at Cheltenham and golf's Open, events which are months apart anyway? Leaving that argument aside, Cheltenham's decision to rebrand its meeting urbanely as 'the November meeting' from 2017 onwards presumably leaves the way open for a sponsor in the future for a fixture still known to some of the older generation as the Mackeson meeting after the name of the long-term sponsor of the big handicap there. The first of Cheltenham's big pre-Christmas handicaps, now run as the BetVictor Gold Cup, has enjoyed much more continuity with its sponsors than the other major traditional big handicap run at Cheltenham in December, which went under the name of the Caspian Caviar Gold Cup in the latest season. Mackeson's sponsorship of the November race ended with the 1995 running and, after spells under the Murphy's and Thomas Pink banners, the big handicap was run from 2003 to 2015 as the Paddy Power Gold Cup, continuity of sponsorship undoubtedly helping to fix the meeting in the public consciousness.

The latest November meeting was one for the mudlarks with 25/1-shot Splash of Ginge taking the second running of the BetVictor Gold Cup on the Saturday as the rain kept on and on. However, it was the condition of the ground on Sunday, the last of the three days, that became a big talking point. After partnering Cloudy Dream to finish second in the Shloer Chase, a mud-spattered Brian Hughes told ITV that the track 'should be ashamed of themselves, watering so much—that's horrendous ground.' Another jockey described conditions as 'like galloping through PVA glue' as the going deteriorated after twelve millimetres of rain on Saturday, not helped by the fact that Sunday's card also opened with a nineteen-runner handicap hurdle which inevitably compounded the situation on that part of the track. Cheltenham's clerk of the course Simon Claisse defended the criticism by explaining that the priority was to preserve ground on the inner of both the chase and hurdles tracks (the November meeting is on the Old Course) for the Festival meeting. 'If we use the ground in November and December and trash it, and it doesn't recover, then we could run into an awful lot of trouble come March,' Claisse said, acknowledging that the track could not provide fresh ground each day in bad conditions at the November and December meetings. He justified the course's watering policy by pointing out that he had had to irrigate before the Showcase meeting in October so the going did not become good to firm—'for obvious welfare reasons.'

No doubt the question of whether Cheltenham perhaps stages one meeting too many will form part of the review ordered after the death of six horses at the Festival. The International meeting in December featured the highly-publicised death of the BetVictor runner-up Starchitect who was on his way to victory, in a clear lead, in the Caspian Caviar Gold Cup when he suffered a devastating hind leg

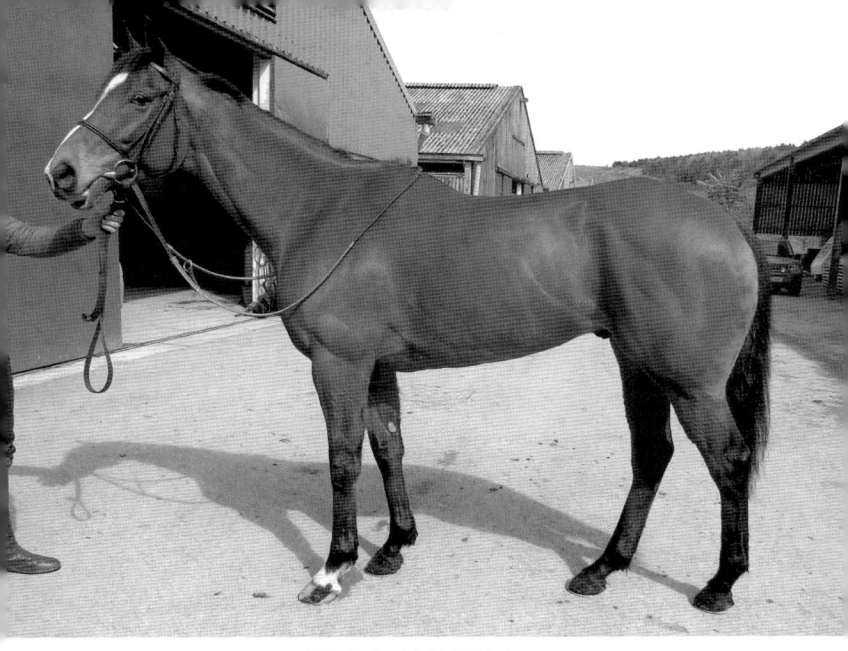

Elite Racing Club's "Elgin"

injury on the flat before the penultimate obstacle, at around the place where the Old Course crosses the New at the bottom of the hill, where the surface tends to become more worn. It should be said that an examination afterwards by BHA officials found no problem with the conditions, though the racing manager for Starchitect's owners described the ground as 'churned and softer there than the rest of the track.'

The narrowing of the track at the November meeting, because of the need to preserve the inner sections for March, resulted in Sunday's racing being rendered somewhat unsatisfactory by the conditions handing a significant advantage to the runners steering a wide route in search of fresher ground. The winner of Sunday's big race, the Unibet Greatwood Handicap Hurdle, 10/1-shot Elgin, went round the houses, as did all of the first four who also took the favoured route towards the outer rail. The gallop wasn't strong for a race of the Greatwood's usual competitiveness but the race still developed into a slog, with Elgin edging ahead of front-running Misterton soon after the last and holding on by a neck, with Old Guard and top weight The New One completing the frame. The Greatwood also featured a fatality when the favourite London Prize took a bad fall.

Elgin already had a big handicap under his belt going into the Greatwood, having won the William Hill Handicap Hurdle at Ascot earlier in the month, a race that featured plenty of progressive types. He continued to improve, following his Greatwood win with a creditable sixth under top weight in the valuable Racing Welfare Handicap at Ascot's Christmas meeting and then doing even better when successfully conceding weight to five opponents in the Betway Kingwell Hurdle at Wincanton in February. The performance in beating favourite Ch'tibello by two and a half lengths, after being patiently ridden and making up his ground in smooth fashion, encouraged owners Elite Racing Club to supplement Elgin for the Champion Hurdle at a cost of £20,000. He travelled well for a long way at Cheltenham but couldn't quicken in the straight, managing fifth behind Buveur d'Air, beaten around

ELI

fourteen lengths by the winner. His trainer's after-race quote that 'we can do no more over hurdles' prefaced a switch to the Flat for Elgin who, by June, had qualified himself for a mark in good handicaps—still looking relatively unexposed—with his three runs including smoothly landing the odds in a couple of novice events at Chelmsford and Catterick on his second and third starts.

Elgin (b.g. 2012)
- Duke of Marmalade (IRE) (b 2004)
  - Danehill (b 1986) — Danzig / Razyana
  - Love Me True (ch 1998) — Kingmambo / Lassie's Lady
- China Tea (USA) (b 2006)
  - High Chaparral (b 1999) — Sadler's Wells / Kasora
  - Molasses (ch 1998) — Machiavellian / Lingerie

The lengthy, useful-looking Elgin is a half-brother to the fair hurdler Clemency (by Halling) out of the unraced China Tea (for whom Elite paid 60,000 guineas as a yearling). China Tea is a sister to the smart French mile and a half performer Magadan who is now at stud in that country (fee €1,500). China Tea and Magadan are out of an unraced daughter of the Niarchos family's outstanding broodmare Lingerie who became the dam of Oaks winner Light Shift and the brother and sister Limnos and Shiva, both of whom also made their mark in pattern company. Light Shift is the dam of the 2017 Eclipse and Juddmonte International winner Ulysses, while a full sister to her bred another of the top performers in the 2017 European Flat season, Cloth of Stars, who won the Prix Ganay and finished second in the Prix de l'Arc (one place ahead of Ulysses). Elgin will never attain the heights achieved on the Flat by some of the more illustrious members of his family but he should more than pay his way. He showed very smart form over hurdles raced at around two miles, usually travelling strongly in his races. He acts on soft going. *Alan King*

ELITE GARDE (FR) 4 b.g. Kapgarde (FR) – Queyrann (FR) (Sheyrann) [2017/18 b16v⁴ b16v Apr 1] €40,000 3-y-o: fourth foal: dam unraced: fair form in bumpers: better effort when fourth at Warwick in March. *Paul Webber* **b85**

ELIXIR DE NUTZ (FR) 4 gr.g. Al Namix (FR) – Nutz (FR) (Turgeon (USA)) [2017/18 b13.9g* h16.8v⁶ Jun 27] tall gelding: half-brother to 3 winners in France, including hurdler/chaser Calnutz (17f-21f winner, by Balko): dam maiden half-sister to useful hurdler/chaser (stays 2½m) Bonbon Au Miel: won at Argentan in October, only start in bumpers for G. Cherel: 10/1, shaped as if amiss when tailed off in Finesse Juvenile Hurdle at Cheltenham on hurdling debut. *Philip Hobbs* **h–** **b?**

ELIZABETHS WISH 8 gr.m. Fair Mix (IRE) – Margarets Wish (Cloudings (IRE)) [2017/18 h20m⁵ h20g^pu Jun 14] second foal: dam (h79), 2m hurdle winner, also 1¼m winner on Flat: little show in maiden hurdles: won twice in points in 2018. *Trevor Wall* **h77**

ELKSTONE 7 b.g. Midnight Legend – Samandara (FR) (Kris) [2017/18 c97§, h–: c15.7d³ c15.7g⁵ c19.2g² c21.4d⁴ c15.7v⁴ Feb 5] maiden hurdler: modest maiden chaser: stays 19f: acts on soft going: wears hood: has worn tongue tie: irresolute. *Caroline Bailey* **c92 §** **h–**

ELLARY 7 b.m. Mahler – Reine des Reines (IRE) (Supreme Leader) [2017/18 b15.8d² Jun 7] €20,000 3-y-o, £1,200 5-y-o: fourth foal: dam (h110), bumper/2m hurdle winner (stayed 2½m), half-sister to useful hurdler (stayed 3m) Grand Theatre: 8/1, second in mares bumper at Uttoxeter (8 lengths behind Rose of Cimarron). *Stuart Edmunds* **b83**

ELLA'S DENE 7 ch.m. Millkom – Oh So Perky (IRE) (Executive Perk) [2017/18 b16.8s h19.3d^pu h17s Apr 8] first foal: dam winning pointer: no show in bumper/over hurdles. *Tim Reed* **h–** **b–**

ELLENS WAY 6 b.m. Black Sam Bellamy (IRE) – Function Dreamer (Overbury (IRE)) [2017/18 h114: h21.4s⁶ h19.8s h21.7v* h23.8v* Jan 3] placed both starts in Irish maiden points: fairly useful handicap hurdler: won at Fontwell (mares) in December and Ludlow in January: stays 3m: raced only on soft/heavy going: often races prominently. *Jeremy Scott* **h128**

ELLIE MAC (IRE) 5 b.m. Court Cave (IRE) – Dizzy's Whisper (IRE) (Supreme Leader) [2017/18 h16v^pu h16v h16d* h18s h16.8s h16.2d⁴ Apr 26] €8,500 3-y-o: rather unfurnished mare: fifth foal: half-sister to bumper winner Thisonetime (by Kalanisi) and a winning pointer by Kahyasi: dam unraced: fairly useful form over hurdles: won maiden at Leopardstown in December: best effort when fourth in listed mares novice won by Dawn Shadow at Punchestown final start: unproven beyond 2m: acts on good to soft going. *Henry de Bromhead, Ireland* **h120**

EME

EL MASSIVO (IRE) 8 b.g. Authorized (IRE) – Umthoulah (IRE) (Unfuwain (USA)) **h100**
[2017/18 h110: h19.9d h20.3g^{pu} Oct 26] fair handicap hurdler: unproven beyond 17f: acted on heavy and good to firm going: dead. *Harriet Bethell*

ELMONO (FR) 7 ch.g. Epalo (GER) – Monareva (FR) (Montjeu (IRE)) [2017/18 h16.2s^3 **h101**
Apr 25] fairly useful hurdler at best in France: showed retains some ability only start in 2017/18: stays 19f: acts on soft going: often races towards rear. *Lucinda Russell*

ELOCUTION 5 b.m. Paco Boy (IRE) – Speech (Red Ransom (USA)) [2017/18 h–: h16s **h–**
Nov 28] modest on Flat, stays 1¾m: no form over hurdles: tried in hood. *Sheena West*

EL PRESENTE 5 b.g. Presenting – Raitera (FR) (Astarabad (USA)) [2017/18 b16d^3 **h115**
h19.6g* h19.6g^3 h19.6s^3 h19.8d^5 Apr 22] €54,000 3-y-o: third foal: brother to fairly useful **b84**
hurdler (2m-19f winner) Blairs Cove: dam unraced half-sister to top-class chaser (best around 2m) Golden Silver: third in bumper at Warwick: fairly useful form over hurdles: won maiden at Huntingdon in October: will stay beyond 2½m: usually races prominently. *Kim Bailey*

EL SCORPIO (IRE) 6 b.g. Scorpion (IRE) – El Monica (IRE) (Kahyasi) [2017/18 **h79**
b16.2g b14s h19.6s^6 h16.2v^4 h15.8g Apr 24] workmanlike gelding: mid-field at best in **b75**
bumpers: poor form over hurdles. *John Groucott*

EL TERREMOTO (FR) 6 b.g. Spirit One (FR) – By Decree (USA) (With Approval **c–**
(CAN)) [2017/18 c–, h124: h18.7g* h18.9v^6 h21s Jan 13] lengthy gelding: useful handicap **h134**
hurdler: won at Stratford (by 7 lengths from Capeland) in October: runner-up only start over fences: stays 2¾m: acts on heavy going. *Nigel Twiston-Davies*

ELTON DES MOTTES (FR) 4 b.g. Maresca Sorrento (FR) – Ouheut des Mottes (FR) **b91 p**
(Ungaro (GER)) [2017/18 b16.7g^5 Apr 22] £65,000 3-y-o: second foal: dam 15f-19f hurdle winner: 8/1, promise when fifth in bumper at Market Rasen (4¼ lengths behind Northern Soul), left poorly placed: sure to progress. *Dan Skelton*

ELUSIVE COWBOY (USA) 5 ch.g. Elusive Quality (USA) – Sarmad (USA) **h94**
(Dynaformer (USA)) [2017/18 h59: h15.7m^2 h15.7g^6 h18.5m h20.5d h15.9v h21.7g^{pu} Apr 20] close-coupled gelding: maiden hurdler, standout effort when second in novice at Towcester: had various trainers in 2017/18: in cheekpieces last 2 starts. *Michelle Bryant*

ELUSIVE THEATRE (IRE) 7 b.m. King's Theatre (IRE) – Miss Best (FR) (Grand **c121**
Tresor (FR)) [2017/18 h119: c21.2d* c20.1g^F c15.9s^5 h22.6v h20.3s^5 h21.4v* c23.4v^2 **h126**
h20.5v^2 c20d^3 h24.3g^{pu} Apr 20] neat mare: fairly useful handicap hurdler: won at Ayr in January: similar form over fences: won maiden at Cartmel in May: possibly best at short of 3m when conditions are testing: acts on heavy going: has worn hood. *Stuart Crawford, Ireland*

ELVIS MAIL (FR) 4 gr.g. Great Pretender (IRE) – Queenly Mail (FR) (Medaaly) [2017/18 **b71**
b14.6s^4 b16.2v^4 b16v^3 Mar 10] poor form in bumpers: tried in hood. *N. W. Alexander*

ELVIZ 4 b.g. Medicean – Estrela (Authorized (IRE)) [2017/18 ab16g^6 b15.8d Mar 26] **b–**
limited impact in bumpers. *Tony Carroll*

ELYSIAN PRINCE 7 b.g. Champs Elysees – Trinkila (USA) (Cat Thief (USA)) [2017/18 **h95**
h103: h15.8g h15.8g^6 h18.7g^2 h16.5g h15.5s Dec 3] fair handicap hurdler, largely well below best in 2017/18: stays 19f: acts on good to firm going: tried in visor: often wears tongue tie: usually races prominently. *Neil King*

EMBOLE (FR) 4 b.g. Buck's Boum (FR) – Urielle Collonges (FR) (Dom Alco (FR)) **h122**
[2017/18 b12.2g^4 h16.4v^3 h15.8s^5 h15.3s* h16.4s h16g^3 Apr 20] close-coupled gelding: **b?**
first foal: dam, French 1½m bumper winner and second only start over hurdles, sister to useful hurdlers/chasers Robinson Collonges (stayed 21f) and Quentin Collonges (stayed 29f): last of 7 in a bumper for Emmanuel Clayeux: fairly useful form over hurdles: won novice at Wincanton in February: third in handicap at Ayr in April: raced around 2m: acts on heavy going: in hood last 4 starts: in tongue tie last 3. *Dan Skelton*

EMELL 8 ch.g. Medicean – Londonnetdotcom (IRE) (Night Shift (USA)) [2017/18 **h84**
h16.5s h16.5s^F h16.6s^4 Jan 26] useful at best on Flat, stays 8.5f: poor form over hurdles. *Tim Vaughan*

EMERALD CHIEFTAN (IRE) 8 b.g. Oscar (IRE) – Its Only Gossip (IRE) (Lear Fan **h107**
(USA)) [2017/18 h19.9v^2 h19.9v^6 h23.1d^6 Apr 21] £13,000 8-y-o: third foal: half-brother to fairly useful hurdler/useful chaser Westerner Point (2m-3m winner, by Westerner): dam, maiden on Flat/ran once over hurdles, closely related to smart hurdler/fairly useful chaser (stayed 21f) Montalcino: off mark in Irish points at fifth attempt: fair form in novice/ maiden hurdles. *Rebecca Menzies*

EMERALD ROSE 11 b.m. Sir Harry Lewis (USA) – Swiss Rose (Michelozzo (USA)) [2017/18 c116, h–: c23.9g* c27.5g³ c24.1s³ c27.6s³ c24.1s¹ Mar 24] angular mare: winning hurdler: fairly useful handicap chaser: won at Market Rasen in May: should stay beyond 3½m: acts on good to firm and heavy going: wears cheekpieces. *Julian Smith* **c117 h–**

EMERGING FORCE (IRE) 8 b.g. Milan – Danette (GER) (Exit To Nowhere (USA)) [2017/18 c140p, h–: c23.8g Nov 4] tall gelding: winning hurdler: useful chaser: should be suited by further than 3m: acts on soft and good to firm going: usually leads. *Harry Whittington* **c130 h–**

EMERGING TALENT (IRE) 9 b.g. Golan (IRE) – Elviria (IRE) (Insan (USA)) [2017/18 c21v² Oct 2] tall gelding: useful hurdler: 6/5, second in novice at Newton Abbot (3½ lengths behind Kayf Adventure) on chasing debut in autumn after 18-month absence: stays 21f: acts on heavy going: tried in hood: in tongue tie last 5 starts: seemed sure to progress over fences but not seen out again. *Paul Nicholls* **c126 p h–**

EMIGRATED (IRE) 5 b.g. Fastnet Rock (AUS) – Ecoutila (USA) (Rahy (USA)) [2017/18 h21.8g² h20.4d h21g h19.9g⁵ c20d h15.5v^pu h15.8s Feb 8] modest on Flat, stays 1¼m: modest maiden hurdler: tailed off in maiden on chasing debut: left Gavin Patrick Cromwell after fifth start: stays 2¾m: best form on good going: in headgear last 5 starts: has worn tongue tie. *Derek Shaw* **c– h92**

EMILYOGUE (IRE) 5 b.m. Scorpion (IRE) – Presenting Tara (IRE) (Presenting) [2017/18 h16d h17g h20d h17v⁶ Apr 17] first foal: dam unraced sister to fairly useful hurdler (stayed 3m) Ninth Legion: maiden hurdler, no form in 2017/18: tried in tongue tie. *John Patrick Ryan, Ireland* **h–**

EMINENT POET 7 b.g. Montjeu (IRE) – Contare (Shirley Heights) [2017/18 h129: h20d h23.3v⁵ h22.8v* h23.6v³ h26s h23.6s⁶ h24.1v* h25.8v^pu Apr 7] compact gelding: useful handicap hurdler: won at Haydock in December and Wetherby (by 2¾ lengths from Warthog) in March: stays 3¼m: best form on soft/heavy going. *Venetia Williams* **h130**

EMISSAIRE (FR) 4 b.g. Kap Rock (FR) – Jacee (FR) (Royal Charter (FR)) [2017/18 b13.6v* b14.6s b16.2s Apr 27] sixth foal: half-brother to fairly useful French hurdler/smart chaser Bon Augure (17f-2¾m winner, by My Risk): dam unraced: fair form in bumpers: won junior event at Ayr in November: tried in hood. *Lucinda Russell* **b92**

EMITOM (IRE) 4 b.g. Gold Well – Avenging Angel (IRE) (Heron Island (IRE)) [2017/18 b16d* Apr 26] £30,000 3-y-o: good-topped gelding: fourth foal: brother to a winning pointer: dam unraced half-sister to a winning hurdler (stayed 3¼m) Melody Maid: 11/2, won 18-runner bumper at Warwick (by 1¾ lengths from Moor Freedom) on debut. *Warren Greatrex* **b95**

EMMA BEAG (IRE) 7 b.m. Westerner – Emma Jane (IRE) (Lord Americo) [2017/18 h24d h17d h16.8s h25.3s² h19.9v⁶ h20.6s Mar 26] first foal: dam (c134/h118) 19f-25f hurdle/chase winner: fair hurdler, below best in 2017/18: left Miss Elizabeth Doyle after first start: stays 3m: acts on heavy going: has worn hood, including last 5 starts: usually races in rear. *Julia Brooke* **h89**

EMMPARA 4 ch.g. Black Sam Bellamy (IRE) – Maria Antonia (IRE) (King's Best (USA)) [2017/18 b13.7v⁶ b15.3d Apr 22] last in bumpers: wears hood. *Philip Hobbs* **b–**

EMPEROR COMMODOS 11 b.g. Midnight Legend – Theme Arena (Tragic Role (USA)) [2017/18 c100§, h–§: h16g^pu h16g⁶ c16g⁴ Nov 29] sturdy gelding: maiden hurdler/chaser, no form in 2017/18: usually wears headgear: has worn tongue tie, including last 4 starts: prone to mistakes over fences: untrustworthy. *Robin Mathew* **c– § h– §**

EMPEROR'S CHOICE (IRE) 11 b.g. Flemensfirth (USA) – House-Of-Hearts (IRE) (Broken Hearted) [2017/18 c127, h–: c28.4v³ c27.3v* c29.5v^F c30.7s^ur c28.4v^pu Mar 12] good-topped gelding: winning hurdler: fairly useful handicap chaser: won at Haydock in December: stays 33f: acts on heavy going: wears headgear: inconsistent. *Venetia Williams* **c126 h–**

EMPIRE DE MAULDE (FR) 4 b.g. Spanish Moon (USA) – Ondine de Brejoux (FR) (Murmure (FR)) [2017/18 b8.9g* b8.9d* b10.9m² b10.9m* b11.9g* h16v⁴ h16.4v⁴ Feb 5] won 4 bumpers in Corsica for D. Ferir: poor form when fifth in maiden in hurdles: has worn hood. *James Ewart* **h77 b?**

EMPREINTE RECONCE (FR) 4 b.f. Voix du Nord (FR) – Petite Fille (FR) (Robin des Champs (FR)) [2017/18 b12.6s⁵ Dec 20] third foal: half-sister to French 2½m chase winner Un Dom du Ciel (by Dom Alco): dam unraced half-sister to useful hurdler/fairly useful chaser (stayed 21f) Image de Marque II and to dam of high-class chaser (stayed 25f) Quel Esprit: won bumper at Lignieres in 2016/17 for A. Lacombe: didn't see race out on British debut. *Colin Tizzard* **b66**

EMPTY MARMALADES (FR) 7 b.g. Poliglote – Arvicaya (Kahyasi) [2017/18 h16d h16.5s Dec 14] maiden hurdler, no form in 2017/18. *Gary Moore* **h–**

ENN

ENA BAIE (FR) 4 b.f. Crillon (FR) – Trema Baie (FR) (Snow Cap (FR)) [2017/18 b10.9g² b11.9d* b14s⁴ Jan 1] good-topped filly: first foal: dam French 11f-14.5f bumper winner: won Group 3 bumper at Le Lion-d'Angers in July for Y. Fertillet: fourth in listed event at Cheltenham on British debut. *Harry Fry* — **b?**

ENCHANTED MOMENT 6 b.m. Lawman (FR) – Gentle Thoughts (Darshaan) [2017/18 h15.7g Aug 20] half-sister to 3 winning hurdlers, including Blue Bajan (very smart 2m winner, by Montjeu) and Aine's Delight (fairly useful 2m winner, by King's Best): modest/ungenuine maiden on Flat: well beaten in mares novice on hurdling debut. *Olly Murphy* — **h–**

ENDEAVOR 13 ch.g. Selkirk (USA) – Midnight Mambo (USA) (Kingmambo (USA)) [2017/18 c102§, h90§: c17.3d* c17.3g⁶ c17.3s^pu h17.2s h16.2d h18.1g* c15.8m⁵ c15.8g⁶ h15.6g c19.9s⁵ Jan 19] poor handicap hurdler: won at Kelso in September: modest handicap chaser: won at Cartmel in May: stays 2½m: acts on any going: has worn cheekpieces: unreliable. *Dianne Sayer* — **c91 §** / **h72 §**

ENDLESS CREDIT (IRE) 8 b.g. High Chaparral (IRE) – Pay The Bank (High Top) [2017/18 c123, h110: c17.1g⁴ May 28] winning hurdler: fairly useful form over fences: raced around 2m: acts on soft going: tried in tongue tie: front runner/races prominently. *Micky Hammond* — **c108** / **h–**

ENDLESS FLIGHT (IRE) 4 b.g. Winged Love (IRE) – Lady Oakwell (IRE) (King's Ride) [2017/18 b16s³ b16.3s⁵ Mar 24] £18,000 3-y-o: brother to fair hurdler/fairly useful chaser Posh Bird (2½m-3¾m winner) and a winning pointer, and half-brother to bumper winner/fair hurdler Ballykelly (19f winner, by Insan): dam failed to complete both starts in points: modest form in bumpers. *Susan Gardner* — **b84**

ENDLESS RIVER 5 b.m. Tobougg (IRE) – Blaeberry (Kirkwall) [2017/18 h16.8d^pu h16d h16.5m Apr 25] dam useful 19f-3m hurdle/chase winner: no form on Flat/over hurdles: left Mrs J. Harrington after second start. *Alan King* — **h–**

ENEKO (FR) 4 bl.g. Laverock (IRE) – Kaline Collonges (FR) (Video Rock (FR)) [2017/18 b11.4d⁶ b11.9g* h16.2v* h16s⁴ h16.2v² h19.4g⁵ Dec 18] second foal: dam maiden in bumpers/over jumps in France: won bumper at La Roche-sur-Yon in June: fair form over hurdles: won juvenile at Perth in September: left Alain Couetil after second start. *Keith Dalgleish* — **h111** / **b?**

ENGLAND EXPECTS 4 b.f. Mount Nelson – Fanny's Fancy (Groom Dancer (USA)) [2017/18 h15.7d h15.7s^pu Jan 1] fair maiden on Flat, stays 1¼m: no form over hurdles: wears hood. *K. R. Burke* — **h–**

ENGLISH PALE (IRE) 5 b.g. Elusive Pimpernel (USA) – Terme Cay (USA) (Langfuhr (CAN)) [2017/18 h17.6d^pu h16.5g³ h16v h15.8d⁴ Nov 27] fair maiden hurdler: left Mrs J. Harrington after third start: will prove best around 2m: acts on soft going: has worn headgear/tongue tie. *John Flint* — **h103**

EN JOULE 7 ch.m. Shirocco (GER) – Ancora (IRE) (Accordion) [2017/18 h89, b89: h20g h24g^pu h22g Aug 3] bumper winner: maiden hurdler, no form in 2017/18: in cheekpieces last 3 starts: usually races prominently. *Neil Mulholland* — **h–**

ENJOY RESPONSIBLY (IRE) 9 b.g. Flemensfirth (USA) – Spice Patrol (IRE) (Mandalus) [2017/18 c113, h–: c21.2g² c24.1s⁵ c21.2s⁴ c20.5g³ c21.2s* c20.8g Apr 18] workmanlike gelding: maiden hurdler: fairly useful handicap chaser: won at Fakenham in November and March: stays 21f: acts on soft and good to firm going: has worn headgear/tongue tie: often races towards rear. *Oliver Sherwood* — **c128** / **h–**

ENLIGHTEN 4 b.g. Kayf Tara – Rapturous (Zafonic (USA)) [2017/18 b15.6s³ b16g⁶ Apr 21] seventh foal: dam unraced: fair form in bumpers. *Michael Easterby* — **b88**

EN MEME TEMPS (FR) 4 b.g. Saddler Maker (IRE) – Lady Reine (FR) (Ragmar (FR)) [2017/18 b16s⁶ Feb 24] 3/1, sixth in conditional/amateur maiden bumper at Chepstow (22 lengths behind Supremely Lucky, carrying head high). *Tom Lacey* — **b66**

ENMESHING 5 ch.g. Mastercraftsman (IRE) – Yacht Club (USA) (Sea Hero (USA)) [2017/18 h78: h16.8g^pu h16g Aug 1] fair on Flat, stays 1½m: limited impact over hurdles: tried in cheekpieces. *Alexandra Dunn* — **h–**

ENNISCOFFEY OSCAR (IRE) 6 b.g. Oscar (IRE) – Enniscoffey (IRE) (Old Vic) [2017/18 h113: h18.5d⁴ h20d h21d³ h20.8d* h24.4s* h24v h19.8s Apr 28] tall gelding: second when fell last only start in Irish points: useful bumper performer: useful hurdler: won novice at Doncaster in December and River Don Novices' Hurdle there (by short head from Shannon Bridge) in January: stays 3m: acts on soft going. *Emma Lavelle* — **h134**

ENN

ENNISTOWN 8 b.g. Authorized (IRE) – Saoirse Abu (USA) (Mr Greeley (USA)) [2017/18 h136: h26.5d^{pu} h20d^6 Sep 29] good-topped gelding: useful hurdler at best, no form in 2017/18: stays 25f: acts on soft going: has worn headgear: wears tongue tie: usually races nearer last than first: has joined Anthony Honeyball: temperamental. *David Pipe* — h– §

ENOLA GAY (FR) 5 b.g. Fuisse (FR) – Enolaland (FR) (Daliapour (IRE)) [2017/18 h118: h15.8d^2 h19.3g h15.7d* c16.1s^2 c22.7v^2 h16s Apr 28] useful-looking gelding: fair hurdler: won maiden at Catterick in December: similar form over fences: better effort when second in novice handicap at Taunton in January: should stay beyond 2m: acts on soft going: usually races close up. *Venetia Williams* — c112 h112

EN PASSE (IRE) 9 b.m. Flemensfirth (USA) – Asklynn (IRE) (Beau Sher) [2017/18 c26d^5 May 5] multiple point winner: lightly-raced hurdler: 33/1, fifth in hunter at Cheltenham (13¾ lengths behind Woodfleet) on chasing debut: has worn tongue tie. *H. C. Pauling* — c94 h–

ENRICHISSANT (FR) 4 b.g. Speedmaster (GER) – Quibble (FR) (Jimble (FR)) [2017/18 b12.4g b11.9d^3 b12.9d^2 b16.3s^4 b16.3v Feb 10] fourth foal: half-brother to French bumper winners Bambouzle (1½m-15f winner, by Forestier) and Dont Hesitate (12.5f/13f winner, by Diamond Boy): dam placed in French bumpers up to 15f: fair bumper performer: placed twice in France and fourth at Newbury: left Francois Doumen after second start, D. Windrif after third. *David Bridgwater* — b88

ENZANI (IRE) 7 b.g. Cape Cross (IRE) – Eytarna (IRE) (Dubai Destination (USA)) [2017/18 h102: h16.2g* h16.2g* Jun 17] fair form over hurdles: won maiden at Perth in May and novice at Hexham in June: stays 19f: best form on good going: often in cheekpieces: wears tongue tie: has joined Gordon Elliott. *John McConnell, Ireland* — h113

EOLIAN 4 b.g. Poet's Voice – Charlecote (IRE) (Caerleon (USA)) [2017/18 h16s^5 Feb 23] half-brother to useful hurdler Ghimaar (2m-2½m winner, by Dubai Destination) and fairly useful hurdler Man Look (2m-2½m winner, by Nayef): fair/temperamental on Flat, stays 1½m: 14/1, fifth in juvenile at Warwick (32¾ lengths behind Doctor Bartolo) on hurdling debut, reportedly lame. *Olly Murphy* — h84

EPHRAIM 7 b.g. Rail Link – Enrica (Niniski (USA)) [2017/18 h23.3d^{pu} Nov 3] good-topped gelding: fairly useful hurdle winner, no show in handicap only start in 2017/18. *Charlie Mann* — h–

EQUITY SWAP (IRE) 9 ch.g. Strategic Prince – Medicean Star (IRE) (Galileo (IRE)) [2017/18 c–, h–: h16g^2 h19.6g^5 h21.6m^3 Aug 29] sturdy gelding: fair handicap hurdler: lightly-raced chaser: stays 2¾m: acts on good to firm and good to soft going: has worn cheekpieces: tried in tongue tie. *Debra Hamer* — c– h100

EQULEUS 6 b.g. Equiano (FR) – Merle (Selkirk (USA)) [2017/18 h90: h21.6g h18.5m h16g^6 h16.8g Jun 27] maiden hurdler, no form in 2017/18: tried in cheekpieces: in tongue tie last 5 starts. *Katie Stephens* — h–

EQUUS AMADEUS (IRE) 5 b.g. Beat Hollow – Charade (IRE) (Danehill (USA)) [2017/18 b89: b16.8m* h19.9g* h19.5d^{pu} h21s^5 h16s^3 Apr 28] lengthy gelding: fair form in bumpers: won at Exeter in May: fairly useful form over hurdles: won maiden at Uttoxeter in September: placed in novice at Kempton and novice handicap at Sandown last 2 starts: stays 2½m: acts on soft going. *Tom Lacey* — h125 b93

EQUUS FLIGHT (IRE) 5 b.g. Vinnie Roe (IRE) – Maiden Flight (IRE) (Jurado (USA)) [2017/18 b16v^4 h23.6v^{pu} Jan 19] placed twice from 3 starts in Irish points: showed a bit when fourth in bumper at Chepstow: pulled up in maiden on hurdling debut (tongue tied). *Peter Bowen* — h– b80

EQUUS LEADER (IRE) 4 b.g. Getaway (GER) – Good Looking Woman (IRE) (Oscar (IRE)) [2017/18 b16d Apr 26] workmanlike gelding: 14/1, twelfth in bumper at Warwick (16½ lengths behind Emitom, hampered home turn). *Peter Bowen* — b–

EQUUS MILLAR (IRE) 5 b.g. Masterofthehorse (IRE) – Lets Get Busy (IRE) (Presenting) [2017/18 h19.6g^F h20g^4 h16.7s^4 h16s Jan 13] rather unfurnished gelding: third foal: dam (h78) 2¾m hurdle winner: fair form over hurdles: in hood last 2 starts. *Nigel Twiston-Davies* — h104

EQUUS SECRETUS (IRE) 6 b.g. Brian Boru – Bodega Bay (IRE) (Presenting) [2017/18 h19.6g* h24d* h24s^3 h19.6s^6 Feb 8] £7,000 3-y-o, £600 4-y-o, £30,000 5-y-o: strong gelding: chasing type: second foal: dam (c91/h74) maiden jumper: won point on debut: useful form over hurdles: won novices at Huntingdon and Southwell (by 6 lengths from Another Stowaway) in November: disappointing last 2 starts: will stay beyond 3m. *Ben Pauling* — h130

ESP

ERAGON DE CHANAY (FR) 4 b.g. Racinger (FR) – Rose Celebre (FR) (Authorized (IRE)) [2017/18 h16.7g³ h15.8s* h16.4s³ h16.6d⁴ h16v* h16.4s h15.7s² Mar 25] close-coupled gelding: first foal: dam unraced: fairly useful hurdler: won juveniles at Hyeres before start of season (for A. Adeline de Boisbrunet) and Ffos Las in October, and juvenile handicap at Sandown in March: likely to stay 2½m: acts on heavy going. *Gary Moore* — **h124**

ERICAS LAD 7 b.g. Mutazayid (IRE) – Kingsmill Quay (Noble Imp) [2017/18 h25.5v⁵ h21.6v⁶ Apr 17] placed in points: well beaten in novice hurdles. *Jackie du Plessis* — **h–**

ERICK LE ROUGE (FR) 4 ch.g. Gentlewave (IRE) – Imperia II (FR) (Beyssac (FR)) [2017/18 h16.7s⁴ h16.3s⁴ h16.8v⁵ h16v² Mar 10] lengthy gelding: fifth foal: half-brother to fairly useful hurdler/smart chaser Ornais (19f-3m winner, by Michel Georges) and fairly useful French hurdler Capharnaum (2¼m winner, by Le Triton): dam French maiden half-sister to fairly useful hurdler/useful chaser (stayed 25f) Napolitain: fair form over hurdles. *Nick Williams* — **h100**

ERIC THE THIRD (IRE) 9 b.g. Mountain High (IRE) – Commanche Princess (IRE) (Commanche Run) [2017/18 h16g h16g h18g h18.8g³ h18.8g³ c19.2v c18gᵖᵘ h16.5mᶠ Apr 25] poor handicap hurdler: no form over fences: left P. J. Rothwell after seventh start: stays 19f: acts on good to soft going: tried in hood/tongue tie. *Tim Vaughan* — **c–** / **h78**

ERMYN'S EMERALD 6 b.g. Alflora (IRE) – Emerald Project (IRE) (Project Manager) [2017/18 h80: h16gᵖᵘ h19.6g h15.9d⁵ h19.2v Dec 26] modest maiden hurdler: unproven beyond 2m: acts on good to soft going. *Pat Phelan* — **h85**

ERNBRA 8 ch.m. Young Ern – Inbra (Infantry) [2017/18 h15.7gᵖᵘ May 24] second foal: dam unraced: pulled up in mares novice hurdle. *Laura Morgan* — **h–**

E SI SI MUOVE (IRE) 6 b.g. Galileo (IRE) – Queen of France (USA) (Danehill (USA)) [2017/18 b65: b16.7g Apr 22] mid-field at best in bumpers, racing freely. *Andrew Crook* — **b–**

ESKENDASH (USA) 5 ch.g. Eskendereya (USA) – Daffaash (USA) (Mr Greeley (USA)) [2017/18 b93: h16s⁴ h15.8d³ h16.6d³ h15.8d² h15.8g³ Apr 24] workmanlike gelding: fairly useful form over hurdles: placed in maidens/handicaps: will prove best at sharp 2m: acts on good to soft going: usually travels strongly. *Pam Sly* — **h122**

ESPALION (FR) 4 b.g. Khalkevi (IRE) – Somosierra (FR) (Blushing Flame (USA)) [2017/18 b16d⁵ Apr 7] 25/1, fifth in bumper at Fakenham (20½ lengths behind Before Midnight). *Tim Vaughan* — **b66**

ESPOIR D'ALLEN (FR) 4 b.g. Voix du Nord (FR) – Quadanse (FR) (Maille Pistol (FR)) [2017/18 h16s* h16s* h16s* h16d* h16s⁴ Feb 4] fourth foal: dam unraced half-sister to smart French chaser (17f-2½m winner) Mikador: bumper winner in France: useful form over hurdles: won juveniles at Punchestown in October and Down Royal in November, and — **h142**

Knight Frank Juvenile Hurdle, Leopardstown—
Espoir d'Allen (hoops) maintains his unbeaten start over hurdles by landing the odds from the Gigginstown-owned pair Farclas (big white face) and Mitchouka (white cap)

Mr John P. McManus' "Espoir d'Allen"

Bar One Racing Juvenile Hurdle at Fairyhouse (by 4½ lengths from Mitchouka) and Knight Frank Juvenile Hurdle at Leopardstown (by 1¼ lengths from Farclas) in December: well beaten in Spring Juvenile Hurdle at Leopardstown final start: raced around 2m: acts on soft going: usually travels strongly. *Gavin Patrick Cromwell, Ireland*

ESPOIR DE TEILLEE (FR) 6 b.g. Martaline – Belle de Lyphard (FR) (Lyphard's Wish (FR)) [2017/18 b97: h19.3d* Nov 24] in front when fell last in Irish maiden point: bumper winner: 4/6, also won novice at Catterick (in good style by 16 lengths from Jack Devine) on hurdling debut in November: not seen out again but should still progress. *Neil Mulholland* **h124 p**

ESPOIR MORIVIERE (FR) 4 ch.g. Saddex – Sagesse Moriviere (FR) (Vaguely Pleasant (FR)) [2017/18 h16.2d⁵ Apr 23] 12/1, fifth in novice hurdle at Hexham (31¾ lengths behind Crixus's Escape) on debut. *Rose Dobbin* **h73**

ESPRESSO FREDDO (IRE) 4 b.g. Fast Company (IRE) – Spring Bouquet (IRE) (King's Best (USA)) [2017/18 h16g⁴ Oct 22] close-coupled gelding: fairly useful on Flat, probably best at 7f: well beaten in juvenile on hurdling debut. *Robert Stephens* **h–**

ESPRIT DE SOMOZA (FR) 4 b.g. Irish Wells (FR) – Topaze de Somoza (FR) (Discover d'Auteuil (FR)) [2017/18 h16s⁵ h15.8s* h16.5s² h16.4s Mar 14] tall gelding: second foal: dam unraced sister to smart French hurdler/chaser (stayed 2¾m) Or Noir de Somoza: fairly useful form over hurdles: won juvenile at Huntingdon in January: will stay beyond 2m. *Nick Williams* **h125**

ESSTEEPEE 9 b.g. Double Trigger (IRE) – Lamper's Light (Idiot's Delight) [2017/18 c23.6s⁵ Apr 27] winning pointer: maiden hurdler: well beaten in novice hunter on chasing debut: best effort at 2½m: acts on soft going: tried in cheekpieces/tongue tie. *Mrs Sherree Lean* **c74 h–**

ESTHER DU CLOS (FR) 4 b.g. Blue Bresil (FR) – Mascotte du Maine (FR) (Maresca Sorrento (FR)) [2017/18 b15.7gᵖᵘ Oct 11] fatally injured in bumper. *Christian Williams* **b–**

EUX

ETAMINE DU COCHET (FR) 4 gr.f. Martaline – Nuance du Cochet (FR) (Siam (USA)) [2017/18 h16d² Nov 10] fifth foal: dam unraced half-sister to useful French hurdler/chaser (17f-3m winner) Leader du Cochet: 14/1, promise when second in juvenile hurdle at Warwick (10 lengths behind We Have A Dream) on debut in autumn: will stay further than 2m: not seen out again but should still progress. *Dan Skelton*   **h103 p**

ETERNALLY YOURS 5 b.m. Sulamani (IRE) – Well Disguised (IRE) (Beneficial) [2017/18 b15.6g⁴ b16.8s* b15.6d⁴ h20.6v* Apr 14] second foal: dam (h108), 2m hurdle winner, half-sister to fairly useful/unreliable staying chaser French Executive: fair form in bumpers: won mares event at Sedgefield in December 5/2, also won novice at Newcastle (easily by 3 lengths from Love At Dawn) on hurdling debut: better to come. *Donald Whillans*   **h93 p** / **b91**

ETHELWYN 8 ch.m. Alflora (IRE) – Our Ethel (Be My Chief (USA)) [2017/18 h105: c15.7g⁵ c20g³ c24d⁴ h20.1d⁵ Sep 5] fair hurdler at best: modest form over fences: best effort when third in novice handicap at Uttoxeter in June: stays 2¾m: acts on good to soft going: tried in cheekpieces: temperament under suspicion. *Malcolm Jefferson*   **c91** / **h–**

ETHERIDGE ANNIE 9 b.m. Leander – Lady Harriet (Sir Harry Lewis (USA)) [2017/18 h77: h23.3d^F May 6] maiden hurdler: tried in cheekpieces/tongue tie. *Hugo Froud*   **h–**

ET MOI ALORS (FR) 4 b.g. Kap Rock (FR) – Qui L'Eut Cru (FR) (Lavirco (GER)) [2017/18 h15.7v^F h16v² h17s⁶ Apr 12] useful-looking gelding: fifth foal: half-brother to 3 winners in France, including chaser Brio des Villerets (2¼m-2¾m winner, by Malinas): dam once-raced half-sister to useful 2m hurdle winner Unika La Reconce and to dam of useful hurdler/smart chaser (stays 3m) Black Corton: fairly useful form over hurdles: in control when fell last in juvenile at Ascot on debut. *Gary Moore*   **h117**

ETOO SPORT (FR) 4 b.g. Great Journey (JPN) – Theloune (FR) (Cardoun (FR)) [2017/18 h17.4d³ h17.4d⁶ h16.2d^{pu} h16.2s^{pu} c16.9v⁶ c16.9m⁵ Apr 22] fourth foal: half-brother to French chaser Bahia de Cerisy (19f winner, by Sleeping Car): dam, French 2¼m hurdle winner, half-sister to fair French hurdler/fairly useful chaser (17f-19f winner) Cathelie: fair form in juvenile hurdle on debut: showed nothing after, including over fences: trained third/fourth starts only by Richard Hobson: tried in cheekpieces. *F. Matzinger, France*   **c–** / **h100**

ETTILA DE SIVOLA (FR) 4 b.g. Noroit (GER) – Wild Rose Bloom (FR) (Kaldounevees (FR)) [2017/18 b13d* Dec 1] fifth foal: half-brother to useful French hurdler/chaser Attila de Sivola (17f-21f winner, by Kapgarde) and bumper winner/winning pointer Cirano de Sivola (by Vendangeur): dam unraced half-sister to useful hurdler (2m-2½m winner) Dance Floor King: 15/2, won junior bumper at Doncaster (by head from Skyline) on debut. *James Ewart*   **b85**

EURATO (FR) 8 ch.g. Medicean – Double Green (IRE) (Green Tune (USA)) [2017/18 h19.9d h24.4d⁶ h18.6v⁵ Jan 17] fairly useful at best on Flat, stays 2m: modest form over hurdles: wears cheekpieces. *Steve Gollings*   **h98**

EUREU DU BOULAY (FR) 4 b.g. Della Francesca (USA) – Idole du Boulay (FR) (Useful (FR)) [2017/18 b11.4g⁴ b11.9g² b14.4g³ h17.9s h17.6s⁵ h17.9g² h17.6s* h16.4s^{pu} h19v⁵ Apr 12] good-topped gelding: sixth foal: brother to French 13.5f bumper winner Ugoline du Boulay and half-brother to French chaser Violette du Boulay (17f-21f winner, by Until Sundown): dam, French 11.5f-13f bumper winner, sister to fair hurdler/useful chaser (stayed 2½m) Provocative: placed in bumpers: fairly useful form over hurdles: won juvenile at Fontainebleau in November: left B. Lefevre after seventh start: stays 2¼m: acts on soft going: has worn cheekpieces/tongue tie. *Richard Hobson*   **h120** / **b?**

EUR GONE WEST (IRE) 5 b.g. Westerner – Floating Euro (IRE) (Beneficial) [2017/18 b15.8d⁶ b16.8v Dec 8] third in Irish point on debut: mid-field in bumpers: tried in tongue tie. *David Pipe*   **b74**

EURKASH (FR) 4 b.g. Irish Wells (FR) – Meralda (FR) (Baby Turk) [2017/18 b16d Apr 26] useful-looking gelding: sixth foal: half-brother to fairly useful French hurdler/chaser Durkash (17f/2¼m winner, by Blue Bresil) and fair French hurdler/fairly useful chaser Urkashe (2¼m-2¾m winner, by Clety): dam, French maiden, sister to useful French hurdler/fairly useful chaser (19f winner) Hurkash: 66/1, seventh in bumper at Warwick (6¼ lengths behind Emitom). *Paul Webber*   **b86**

EUXTON LANE (IRE) 6 b.g. Getaway (GER) – Local Hall (IRE) (Saddlers' Hall (IRE)) [2017/18 b16.7g³ h18.6d⁵ h16.6s h15.7v² h17.7s* h20.5s* h20s Apr 14] €57,000 3-y-o: strong gelding: will make a chaser: third foal: dam, unraced, out of sister to fairly useful hurdler/useful chaser (stayed 21f) Certainly Strong: fourth in bumper at Bangor: useful form over hurdles: won maiden at Fontwell and novice at Newbury (by 3 lengths from De Rasher Counter) in March: stays 21f: acts on soft going: often travels strongly. *Oliver Sherwood*   **h134** / **b96**

EVA

EVA'S OSKAR (IRE) 4 gr.g. Shirocco (GER) – Sardagna (FR) (Medaaly) [2017/18 b16v Apr 14] 7/1, well held in bumper at Chepstow. *Tim Vaughan* — b–

EVENING HUSH (IRE) 5 b.m. Excellent Art – Applause (IRE) (Danehill Dancer (IRE)) [2017/18 h128: h16s h15.7^F Dec 23] angular mare: fairly useful hurdler at best: raced around 2m: acted on soft going: usually led: dead. *Evan Williams* — h–

EVERLANES 5 br.m. Shirocco (GER) – Good Thinking (Kayf Tara) [2017/18 b15.7d* b15.8s^5 b15.7v^4 Apr 27] first foal: dam unraced half-sister to useful hurdler/top-class chaser (stayed 21f) Wishfull Thinking: fair form in bumpers: won mares event at Southwell in November: in tongue tie last 2 starts. *Anthony Honeyball* — b89

EVER SO MUCH (IRE) 9 b.g. Westerner – Beautiful World (IRE) (Saddlers' Hall (IRE)) [2017/18 c104, h99: c20.1g^6 h21.2g^5 h19.9g^3 c21.1g^5 h21.2v h21.2g* Apr 23] modest handicap hurdler: won at Sedgefield in April: fair chaser at best: stays 21f: acts on good to firm and good to soft going: wears headgear. *Ben Haslam* — c86 h93

EVERYBODY'S TALKIN (IRE) 5 ch.g. Robin des Champs (FR) – Miss Otis Regrets (IRE) (Bob Back (USA)) [2017/18 h23.1s^6 h15.7s h20.8d^4 h22v^4 Apr 14] £65,000 4-y-o: fourth foal: half-brother to fairly useful hurdler/chaser Marquis of Carabas (19f winner, by Hurricane Run) and a winning pointer by Yeats: dam (b81), bumper winner on only start, half-sister to fairly useful hurdler/chaser (stayed 3m) Aneyeforaneye: off mark in Irish points at third attempt: fair form over hurdles: wears tongue tie. *Nigel Twiston-Davies* — h104

EVERY CHANCE (IRE) 5 b.g. Frozen Power (IRE) – Runway Dancer (Dansili) [2017/18 h19.9g^6 Apr 23] half-brother to German 17f chase winner Batya (by Whipper): fairly useful on Flat, stays 1¾m: 10/1, sixth in maiden at Sedgefield (20¼ lengths behind Hurricane Dylan) on hurdling debut. *Noel C. Kelly, Ireland* — h88

EVERYDAY EVERYHOUR 7 b.g. Presenting – Candello (Supreme Leader) [2017/18 c19.5g^2 c23.6s^4 c19.9g^6 c18.9s^{pu} Jan 16] €62,000 3-y-o: fourth foal: half-brother to bumper winner/modest hurdler Julia Too (2m winner, by King's Theatre): dam (b98) bumper winner: won 2-runner point on debut: winning hurdler: fair form in chases: left Gordon Elliott after third start: stays 25f: best form on good going: tried in cheekpieces: front runner/races prominently. *Kerry Lee* — c114 h–

EXCALIBUR (POL) 5 gr.h. Youmzain (IRE) – Electra Deelites (With Approval (CAN)) [2017/18 h16.2v^5 h19.9v h19.3v Apr 17] won over 1¼m on Flat for W. Olkowski in Poland in 2017: well beaten in novice hurdles. *Micky Hammond* — h–

EXCELLENT PUCK (IRE) 8 b.g. Excellent Art – Puck's Castle (Shirley Heights) [2017/18 h16g^{pu} Jul 27] fair on Flat, stays 16.5f: pulled up in novice on hurdling debut. *Shaun Lycett* — h–

EXCELLENT RESULT (IRE) 8 b.g. Shamardal (USA) – Line Ahead (IRE) (Sadler's Wells (USA)) [2017/18 h120: h20.6g^5 Jul 22] sturdy gelding: fairly useful hurdler: fit from Flat, ran poorly in cheekpieces only start in 2017/18: unproven beyond 2m: acts on good to firm going: usually races close up. *Richard Spencer* — h91

EXCELLENT TEAM (IRE) 6 b.g. Teofilo (IRE) – Seradim (Elnadim (USA)) [2017/18 h126: h16g^4 h16.3g^6 h16g h16.7g h16.8g^4 h16d^4 h15.8m* h15.8g^5 h15.8s h19v^{pu} h16d^6 h19d Apr 26] rather leggy gelding: fair handicap hurdler: won at Ludlow (conditional) in October: lost form after: stays 2½m: acts on good to firm and good to soft going: wears tongue tie. *Dan Skelton* — h106

EXCITABLE ISLAND (IRE) 11 b.g. Heron Island (IRE) – Miss Excitable (IRE) (Montelimar (USA)) [2017/18 c97: c26d^2 c25.5s^2 May 18] multiple winning pointer: fair form when placed in hunter chases: should be suited by further than 3¼m. *N. W. Padfield* — c107

EXCLUSIVE RIGHTS 10 b.m. Fair Mix (IRE) – Rosie Ring (IRE) (Phardante (FR)) [2017/18 c87, h–: c17d^2 c22.6d^{pu} Apr 22] winning pointer: lightly-raced hurdler: modest form in chases: better effort in 2017/18 when second in hunter at Stratford: left Mrs Pauline Harkin after: stays 23f, as effective at much shorter: acts on good to firm and good to soft going. *Mrs Claire Hardwick* — c91 h–

EXITAS (IRE) 10 b.g. Exit To Nowhere (USA) – Suntas (IRE) (Riberetto) [2017/18 c–, h113: c16.5g^{pu} c19.4g^5 c21d^5 c15.6d^2 c17g* c20d^7 c18g^4 c16.8g* c15.9d^3 h16s c16.8d^2 c19.9s^4 Jan 12] lengthy gelding: winning pointer: useful handicap chaser: won at Stratford in September, Kempton (novice) in October and Ascot (listed, by 7 lengths from Quite By Chance) in November: stays 19f: acts on heavy going: has worn tongue tie. *Phil Middleton* — c132 h–

EXIT TO FREEDOM 12 ch.g. Exit To Nowhere (USA) – Bobanvi (Timeless Times (USA)) [2017/18 c–, h74[8]: h20.6g[5] h20.6g h20.1d h22.1d[4] h27g[ur] h23.3d[2] h20.9d[5] h22.7g[pu] h24g h23.1d[pu] h16.7s[5] Dec 26] poor handicap hurdler: fell first only chase start: stays 23f: acts on firm and soft going: wears headgear: has worn tongue tie: front runner/races prominently: unreliable. *John Wainwright* c–
h69 §

EXMOOR MIST 10 gr.g. Kayf Tara – Chita's Flora (Alflora (IRE)) [2017/18 c–, h–: c16.5g c16.4s c18.2s[2] c16.4s[6] c18.2v* Apr 12] rangy handicap chaser: won at Taunton in April: stays 2¼m: acts on heavy going: in headgear last 4 starts: wears tongue tie: untrustworthy. *Victor Dartnall* c106 §
h–

EXOTIC FRIEND (IRE) 10 ch.g. Croco Rouge (IRE) – Prima Nox (Sabrehill (USA)) [2017/18 h100: h23m[pu] May 11] workmanlike gelding: fair hurdler: stays 2½m: acts on good to soft going. *Adrian Wintle* h–

EX PATRIOT (IRE) 5 b.g. Elusive Pimpernel (USA) – Carolobrian (IRE) (Mark of Esteem (IRE)) [2017/18 h137: h16v[3] h16v[3] h20v* h20v[2] h24v h18s[5] Mar 9] sparely-made gelding: useful hurdler: won minor event at Limerick in December: third in handicap at Listowel (2 lengths behind On The Go Again) and Istabraq Hurdle at Tipperary (4 lengths behind Jezki) earlier in season, and second in minor event at Punchestown (2¾ lengths behind Killultagh Vic) later in December: stays 2½m: best form on soft/heavy going: often races prominently. *Ellmarie Holden, Ireland* h140

EXPEDITE (IRE) 7 b.g. Brian Boru – Angelica Garnett (Desert Story (IRE)) [2017/18 c–, c–, h125: h20.6g h20g h24g Jun 3] compact gelding: fairly useful hurdler: below form both starts in 2017/18: unseated first only chase start: stays 3m: acts on soft and good to firm going: usually wears cheekpieces nowadays: front runner/races prominently: signs of temperament. *Ben Pauling* c–
h–

EXPRESSTIME (IRE) 5 b.m. Scorpion (IRE) – Glenair Dante (IRE) (Phardante (FR)) [2017/18 c23.4v[3] h19.9v[pu] c20d[F] Mar 31] £24,000 5-y-o: eighth foal: half-sister to a winning pointer by Heron Island: dam, winning pointer, half-sister to useful hurdler/smart chaser (2m winner) Blueberry Boy: runner-up both starts in Irish points: modest form when third of 4 in mares novice chase at Kelso, only completed start under Rules: tried in tongue tie. *Chris Grant* c90
h–

EXTRA BALD (FR) 4 b.g. Linda's Lad – Palatyne (FR) (Passing Sale (FR)) [2017/18 b16.7d[5] Apr 21] fourth foal: dam unraced half-sister to prolific French cross-country chaser (winner up to 3¾m) Archy Bald: 8/1, fifth in bumper at Bangor. *Richard Hobson* b68

EXXARO (IRE) 8 b.g. Presenting – Mandys Gold (IRE) (Mandalus) [2017/18 c20g[4] c21s[2] c23g[2] c23g[2] c21m[2] c24g[4] c23.8m c19.5d[pu] Nov 9] sturdy gelding: winning hurdler: fairly useful maiden chaser: left M. F. Morris after final 2016/17 start: stays 23f: acts on good to firm going: usually wears headgear: in tongue tie last 4 starts: often races prominently/lazily: one to treat with caution. *Colin Tizzard* c128 §
h–

EYES OF A TIGER (IRE) 7 ch.g. Golan (IRE) – Backtothekingsnest (IRE) (King's Theatre (IRE)) [2017/18 h115: c19.3g* c16.3g* c20.1m c16.4d[3] c17.2g[4] Oct 21] fair hurdler: fairly useful form over fences: won novice at Sedgefield in May and 2-runner novice handicap at Fakenham in June: stays 19f: acts on heavy going: usually wears hood: front runner/races prominently. *Brian Ellison* c127
h–

EYESOPENWIDEAWAKE (IRE) 7 b.g. Stowaway – Namesake (Nashwan (USA)) [2017/18 h15.7g* c18d* c15.7d[4] Dec 5] €38,000 3-y-o: fourth foal: half-brother to 5f/6f winner Kheley (by Kheleyf): dam unraced half-sister to useful hurdler/chaser (stayed 3m) Locksmith: fair form over hurdles: won maiden at Southwell in June: fairly useful form over fences: won novice handicap at Kempton in November: stays 2¼m: acts on good to soft going: tried in hood/tongue tie: front runner/races prominently. *Harry Whittington* c124
h107

EY UP ROCKY 5 b.g. Dylan Thomas (IRE) – Polo (Warning) [2017/18 b16.2g* h19.6s[F] h16.5s[pu] h16.7g[4] Apr 22] half-brother to several winners on Flat, including winner around 1¼m Stephano (by Efisio): dam 1m-1¼m winner: won bumper at Kelso (by head from Senor Lombardy) in September, only outing for Micky Hammond: modest form when fourth in maiden at Market Rasen on completed start over hurdles. *Jonjo O'Neill* h94
b101

F

FABULOUS SAGA (FR) 6 b.g. Saint des Saints (FR) – Fabalina (FR) (Dear Doctor (FR)) [2017/18 b18g* b20d[2] b16d[2] h21.5s* h20v* h21s[2] h24s[3] h24v* h24v* h22s h24v Mar 16] angular gelding: fourth foal: half-brother to French hurdler/chaser Fabulous Valley (17f-21f winner, by Vatori): dam French 1m-1¼m winner: won maiden point on debut: h141
b106

FAB

useful form in bumpers: won maiden at Tipperary in May: useful hurdler: won maiden at Ballinrobe in August, novice at Listowel in September, Kerry Group Stayers Novices' Hurdle at Cork in December and Guinness Novices' Hurdle at Limerick (by 3¾ lengths from Delta Work) in December: stays 3m: acts on heavy going: in tongue tie last 4 starts: front runner. *W. P. Mullins, Ireland*

FACT FLOW (IRE) 9 br.g. Whitmore's Conn (USA) – Beaver Run (IRE) (Be My Native (USA)) [2017/18 h15.8d h16.4g h15.8v⁵ c16s⁵ c18.2v⁴ Apr 12] sturdy gelding: maiden pointer: no form under Rules: tried in cheekpieces. *Dai Burchell*   c– h–

FACTION 5 b.g. Champs Elysees – Belladera (IRE) (Alzao (USA)) [2017/18 h98: h19.6s³ h19.9g² h23m Jul 5] modest maiden hurdler: should stay further than 2½m: in cheekpieces last 2 starts. *Nigel Hawke*   h92

FACT OF THE MATTER (IRE) 8 b.g. Brian Boru – Womanofthemountain (IRE) (Presenting) [2017/18 c122, h–: c25g³ c26.1m c25.5g* c25.5g³ c25.1s^pu c31.8g Apr 21] has had breathing operation: maiden hurdler: fairly useful handicap chaser: won at Cartmel in August: stays 25f: acts on good to firm going: usually in hood: wears tongue tie: often races prominently. *Jamie Snowden*   c128 h–

FADAS (FR) 5 gr.m. Davidoff (GER) – Winkle (FR) (Turgeon (USA)) [2017/18 h116: h15.7g^pu Jun 26] fairly useful hurdler, folded tamely sole outing in 2017/18: stays 2¼m: acts on soft going: in cheekpieces/tongue tie last 4 starts. *Dan Skelton*   h–

FAGAN 8 gr.g. Fair Mix (IRE) – Northwood May (Teenoso (USA)) [2017/18 c23.8g* c20.1v² c24.4g² c31.8g^pu Apr 21] good-topped gelding: useful hurdler: similar form over fences: won novice at Perth in July: stays 3m: acts on heavy going. *Gordon Elliott, Ireland*   c143 h–

FAGO (FR) 10 b.g. Balko (FR) – Merciki (FR) (Villez (USA)) [2017/18 c–§, h–: c23.8s² Apr 27] good-topped gelding: winning hurdler: one-time smart chaser: month on from point win, well beaten in hunter sole outing under Rules in 2017/18: stays 2¾m: acts on heavy going: has worn hood: wears tongue tie: temperamental. *Mrs L. A. Colthred*   c– § h–

FAHEEM 7 b.g. Halling (USA) – White Star (IRE) (Darshaan) [2017/18 h83, b88: h16.3d⁶ h16.5g Nov 30] fair form in bumpers: poor form over hurdles. *Lydia Richards*   h76

FAINT HOPE 6 ch.g. Midnight Legend – Rhinestone Ruby (Kayf Tara) [2017/18 h80: b16.8m⁶ b16d h19g³ h19.7s⁵ h19s⁵ h20v³ Apr 15] poor form in bumpers: fair form over hurdles: tried in tongue tie: usually races nearer last than first. *Grace Harris*   h108 b67

FAIR ASK 10 gr.m. Fair Mix (IRE) – Ask Me Not (IRE) (Shernazar) [2017/18 h62: h19.6s May 20] point winner: little form over hurdles: in cheekpieces last 2 starts. *Gary Hanmer*   h–

FAIR FRANK 7 gr.g. Fair Mix (IRE) – Firstflor (Alflora (IRE)) [2017/18 b–: b16g h15.7g⁵ h16.3g³ h18.7m⁴ c15.7g* c15.9m Nov 20] no form in bumpers: poor form over hurdles: modest form over fences: won novice handicap at Southwell in October. *David Bridgwater*   c97 h72 b–

FAIR LOCH 10 gr.g. Fair Mix (IRE) – Ardentinny (Ardross) [2017/18 c129§, h–§: c16m^pu c15.2d⁴ c17.1g c17.2s* c15.2v⁶ ab16.3g³ Mar 3] good-topped gelding: winning hurdler: fairly useful handicap chaser: won at Market Rasen in December: raced mainly around 2m: acts on heavy going: tried in headgear: has worn tongue tie: temperamental. *Brian Ellison*   c124 § h– §

FAIRMOUNT 7 gr.g. Fair Mix (IRE) – Miss Chinchilla (Perpendicular) [2017/18 b15.7g⁵ b16d³ h16s⁶ h15.8v* h20.3v^pu Apr 21] medium-sized gelding: has had breathing operation: fifth foal: brother to fair hurdler Grand Enterprise (3m winner), and half-brother to useful chaser Dare To Endeavour (2½m-3m winner) and fair hurdler/chaser Allchilledout (19f-3m winner, both by Alflora): dam (h114) 2m-21f hurdle winner: fair form in bumpers: fairly useful form over hurdles: won novice at Ffos Las in December: should stay 2½m: front runner/races prominently. *Martin Keighley*   h117 b92

FAIR OAKS 6 gr.m. Fair Mix (IRE) – School Days (Slip Anchor) [2017/18 b16s^pu b15.7d Dec 19] £600 3-y-o: sixth foal: dam 1m winner: no form in bumpers. *Kevin Hunter*   b–

FAIR TO MIDDLING 8 gr.g. Fair Mix (IRE) – Mtilly (Mtoto) [2017/18 h106: c22.5g³ c19.4g³ c25.5d² c24g^F c25.7m^ur h20.6d Dec 7] fair hurdler, well held final outing in 2017/18: fair form over fences: stays 25f: acts on good to soft going: wears headgear: has worn tongue tie, including last 5 starts. *Peter Bowen*   c100 h–

FAIRWAY FREDDY (IRE) 5 b.g. Elusive Pimpernel (USA) – Silent Supreme (IRE) (Supreme Leader) [2017/18 b16g³ h16s h15.8s Feb 22] £26,000 3-y-o: half-brother to fairly useful hurdler/useful chaser Have You Seen Me (2m-2½m winner, by Beneficial) and fair hurdler/chaser Millers Reef (2m-25f winner, by Bob Back): dam unraced sister to very smart chaser up to 3m Nick Dundee and high-class hurdler/smart chaser (2m-2½m winner) Ned Kelly: third in conditionals/amateur bumper at Fakenham (1½ lengths behind Kaloci): no form over hurdles. *Nick Gifford*   h– b90

FAR

FAIR WESTERNER (IRE) 6 b.g. Westerner – Fair Milan (IRE) (Milan) [2017/18 b16g b15.7g Oct 26] pulled up in 2 Irish points: in tongue tie, well held in 2 bumpers (hooded second occasion). *Ali Stronge*   b–

FAIRY POL (IRE) 5 b.m. Milan – Culmore Lady (IRE) (Insan (USA)) [2017/18 b16.7s⁶ h15.7g* h18.5s⁵ h21.2d³ h19.2s h21.2d⁶ Apr 9] £6,000 3-y-o: fifth foal: dam (h80) bumper winner/maiden hurdler (stayed 2½m): sixth in mares bumper at Bangor: fair form over hurdles: won mares maiden at Towcester in October: stays 21f: acts on good to soft going: usually races prominently. *Henry Oliver*   h110 b66

FAITH JICARO (IRE) 11 b.m. One Cool Cat (USA) – Wings To Soar (USA) (Woodman (USA)) [2017/18 c88, h83: h18.7g h18.7m h23g Jul 27] fair hurdler at best, no form in 2017/18: winning chaser: often wears cheekpieces: has worn tongue tie, including final start. *Mark Brisbourne*   c– h–

FALCARRAGH (IRE) 11 ch.g. Alderbrook – Magherareagh Lady (IRE) (Old Vic) [2017/18 c–§, h107§: c19.9g h23.3g h21.7gᵖᵘ Aug 24] lengthy gelding: fairly useful hurdler/chaser at best, no form in 2017/18: tried in cheekpieces: usually races towards rear. *Tim Vaughan*   c– h–

FALCONS FALL (IRE) 7 ch.g. Vertical Speed (FR) – Ellie Park (IRE) (Presenting) [2017/18 h118: h24.3vᵖᵘ h23.6v c24sᵖᵘ h26s Feb 10] fairly useful hurdler at best, no form in 2017/18: pulled up in novice handicap on chasing debut: tried in cheekpieces. *Tom Symonds*   c– h–

FALCON SUN (FR) 4 b.g. Falco (USA) – Pray For Sun (IRE) (Fantastic Light (USA)) [2017/18 h15.8s² h16s³ h16.8s⁶ Mar 24] £6,000 3-y-o: fifth foal: half-brother to 2 winners on Flat in France, including useful 1½m winner Fantastic Love (by Azamour): dam French 11f winner: fair form over hurdles: will stay 2½m: tried in tongue tie. *Dan Skelton*   h105

FALCOS (FR) 6 ch.g. Falco (USA) – Olvera (IRE) (Sadler's Wells (USA)) [2017/18 h108: h16.8g h15.7g h15.8d Jul 28] maiden hurdler, no form in 2017/18: in tongue tie last 2 starts. *Rebecca Menzies*   h–

FAMOUS MILLY (IRE) 4 b.f. Famous Name – Gilah (IRE) (Saddlers' Hall (IRE)) [2017/18 h16s² h17v* h16vᶠ Jan 6] half-sister to several winning jumpers, including useful hurdler/fairly useful chaser Ainama (2m-3m winner, by Desert Prince) and useful hurdler Doesyourdogbite (2½m/21f winner, by Notnowcato): fairly useful on Flat, stays 1m: similar form over hurdles: won listed fillies juvenile race at Aintree (by 17 lengths from Malaya) in December: wears tongue tie. *Gavin Patrick Cromwell, Ireland*   h120

FANTASY KING 12 b.g. Acclamation – Fantasy Ridge (Indian Ridge) [2017/18 c121, h102: c21.2d⁶ h17.2d⁵ h17.2g⁴ c17.3s⁶ c17.3g⁵ c17.1gᵖᵘ Sep 20] tall gelding: fair handicap hurdler: fairly useful chaser at best, no form over fences in 2017/18: stays 21f: acts on firm and good to soft going: tried in cheekpieces: has worn tongue tie, including final start: often races towards rear. *James Moffatt*   c– h96

FARCLAS (FR) 4 gr.g. Jukebox Jury (IRE) – Floriana (GER) (Seattle Dancer (USA)) [2017/18 h16d² h16s² h16.8v* h16s⁵ Apr 28]   h149

In contrast to the previous season, when Defi du Seuil had been much the most dominant juvenile hurdler, including both the Triumph and Anniversary Hurdles among his seven successes, the honours were spread more evenly among the latest crop of four-year-olds. In fact, for the Triumph Hurdle winner Farclas, his Cheltenham Festival success was the only win in four starts. The Triumph result confirmed that some of the strongest form in the division beforehand was to be found in Ireland. But that didn't stop the main British hope, the Nicky Henderson-trained filly Apple's Shakira, being sent off the 6/5 favourite in her bid to become a third consecutive winner of the Triumph for J. P. McManus after Ivanovich Gorbatov and Defi du Seuil. A sister to Apple's Jade, who had been runner-up to Ivanovich Gorbatov two years earlier, Apple's Shakira had won all three of her starts for Henderson, each of them races at Cheltenham which Defi du Seuil had won the previous season. Apple's Shakira had impressed with the style of her wins, though they were generally lacking in substance, her last couple of victories gained at odds of 10/1-on and 7/1-on against rivals who weren't considered worthy of taking her on again in the Triumph. McManus had another Triumph candidate compiling an unbeaten record in Ireland in Espoir d'Allen though, after winning all four of his starts before the turn of the year, his bubble burst in the Spring Juvenile Hurdle at the Dublin Racing Festival when he finished a well-beaten fourth of the five runners

JCB Triumph Hurdle, Cheltenham—
Irish juveniles dominate as Farclas reverses Leopardstown placings with Mr Adjudicator (right) and provides jockey Jack Kennedy with a fourth winner at the 2018 Festival

and wasn't seen out again. The Leopardstown race threw up the pair who went on to fight out the finish of the Triumph, Mr Adjudicator coming out on top by a length and a quarter from Farclas. Farclas didn't go down without a fight when he was headed at the last after taking the lead entering the straight. Both horses had made their hurdling debut in juvenile contests at Leopardstown's Christmas meeting, Mr Adjudicator smoothly winning a maiden event, while Farclas had been pitched straight into a meeting with odds-on Espoir d'Allen in the Grade 2 Knight Frank Juvenile Hurdle, showing useful form in staying on to be beaten a length and a quarter. Both Mr Adjudicator and Farclas had shown fairly useful form on the Flat, with Farclas winning a mile and a half maiden at Clairefontaine on the last of his four starts in France for Jean-Michel Lefebvre.

Though Mr Adjudicator and Farclas had pulled a long way clear in a good time at Leopardstown, the form of their race was generally somewhat underestimated and they were sent off at 8/1 and 9/1 respectively for the JCB-sponsored Triumph. As well as Apple's Shakira, Stormy Ireland (along with Mr Adjudicator one of four Mullins runners), and the Alan King-trained Redicean were also ahead of them in the betting. Stormy Ireland had routed her field on her only start for Mullins (by an official margin of fifty-eight lengths), while Redicean had completed a hat-trick of wins at Kempton in the Adonis Juvenile Hurdle. The days of thirty-runner fields for the Triumph Hurdle have long gone, particularly since the addition to the Festival programme in 2005 of the handicap for four-year-olds, the Fred Winter, and the latest field of nine was the first single-figure line-up since the Triumph was moved from Cheltenham's April meeting; only seven runners contested the race in 1965 (on officially firm ground) when fields in general were decimated by a coughing epidemic. The heavy going on the final day of the latest championship meeting was more reminiscent of bygone Festivals, however, and the emphasis that conditions placed on stamina looked to suit Farclas. He and Mr Adjudicator came through to jump the final flight in a share of the lead and it was Farclas who proved the stronger up the hill, keeping on gamely under a strong drive to win by a length and three quarters. Mr Adjudicator had no more to give in the last hundred yards but finished three and a half lengths clear of his stable's 33/1-shot Sayo in third, with Apple's Shakira staying on to complete the frame clear of the three other finishers. Stormy Ireland had just been headed by the first two when taking a tired fall at the final flight.

Farclas took his jockey Jack Kennedy's number of wins at the latest Festival to four and put him alongside Davy Russell, though Russell clinched the top jockey award at the meeting by virtue of having also ridden a runner-up. Kennedy's other wins came on Samcro and Shattered Love, both in the Gigginstown colours of Farclas, and on Veneer of Charm in the Fred Winter (trainer Gordon Elliott did the double in the two juvenile hurdles). Kennedy has some way to go to match Russell's Festival record of twenty-two successes which includes riding at least one winner at every Festival since 2006. Having broken his Festival duck on Labaik in the 2017 Supreme, Kennedy has time on his side, though, as he only turned nineteen

Gigginstown House Stud's "Farclas"

in April. Russell rode Gordon Elliott's previous Triumph Hurdle winner Tiger Roll in 2014, three months after he had been sacked as Gigginstown's retained rider, his partnership with Tiger Roll coming about when Bryan Cooper was badly injured in a fall in the Fred Winter two days earlier. Russell successfully resumed his partnership with Tiger Roll in the latest Grand National. Farclas was unable to confirm his superiority over Mr Adjudicator when the pair met for a third time in the Champion Four Year Old Hurdle at Punchestown. Farclas looked short of pace, finishing only fifth in a race which tested stamina much less than the Triumph, while Mullins-trained runners swept the first four places, though Mr Adjudicator was beaten three lengths into second behind Saldier who had finished a well-held fifth at Cheltenham on just his second start over hurdles.

Farclas (FR) (gr.g. 2014)	Jukebox Jury (IRE) (gr 2006)	Montjeu (b 1996) — Sadler's Wells / Floripedes
		Mare Aux Fees (gr 1988) — Kenmare / Feerie Boreale
	Floriana (GER) (b 2005)	Seattle Dancer (b 1984) — Nijinsky / My Charmer
		Florilla (ch 1997) — Big Shuffle / Furiella

The good-topped Farclas comes from the first crop of Jukebox Jury whose biggest win came when dead-heating with Duncan in the Irish St Leger. His other Group 1 success had come two years earlier at Cologne and it was in Germany that Jukebox Jury began his stud career at Gestut Etzean, the same stud which bred Elliott's Gold Cup winner Don Cossack. However, with his sire Montjeu building a reputation as a sire of jumps stallions (Tiger Roll is by one of Montjeu's Derby-winning sons Authorized), Jukebox Jury was acquired to stand his first season at Burgage Stud in County Carlow in the spring, with Farclas proving a timely advertisement for him. Farclas' dam Floriana won her first race in her native

FAR

Germany, where she was listed-placed, but was trained for most of her career in Switzerland where she won another six races at up to eleven furlongs. Farclas is Floriana's second foal and the only one to have raced to date. Floriana was one of five winners out of the once-raced Florilla, the others including Florishwells d'Ete who was a fairly useful winner over hurdles and fences at around two miles for Willie Mullins and owner J. P. McManus. Great grandam Furiella was just a fair sprint handicapper for Pat Haslam but she was from a famous family of classic performers, developed by the Moller brothers' White Lodge Stud, being out of a half-sister to Derby winner Teenoso. Another Derby winner descending from the same family is Sir Percy, sire of Presenting Percy. Furiella's half-sister Norpella became dam of the smart seven-furlong and mile performer Sugarfoot and hurdler Carlito Brigante, though *not* the Carlito Brigante who won the 2011 Coral Cup for Farclas' connections. This was his older namesake trained by Paul Webber who won the 1997 Imperial Cup.

Assessing what the future might hold for recent Triumph Hurdle winners has been a thankless task. The last three winners, Peace And Co, Ivanovich Gorbatov and Defi du Seuil have all been singularly disappointing since showing so much promise in their juvenile hurdle seasons. When the first of those won a novice chase at Hexham very early in the latest season, it was the only success any of the trio has registered since their four-year-old days. On the other hand, who could have foreseen their immediate predecessor going on to win a Grand National? Farclas doesn't look a Champion Hurdle contender, certainly not if it is contested under the conditions which normally prevail at the Cheltenham Festival. Proven on heavy going, Farclas will stay two and a half miles and should win more races when stepped up in trip. He was tongue tied for his last two starts at Cheltenham and Punchestown. *Gordon Elliott, Ireland*

FAR CRY 5 b.m. Sakhee's Secret – Yonder (And Beyond (IRE)) [2017/18 ab16g³ ab16d⁶ Mar 5] second foal: sister to 8.6f winner Kissy Suzuki: dam (h95), 13f bumper winner (placed up to 21f over hurdles), also 1½m-1¾m winner on Flat: modest form in bumpers: better effort when third in mares event at Lingfield in January. *Hughie Morrison* **b83**

FARE THEE WELL (IRE) 8 b.g. Duke of Marmalade (IRE) – Bowstring (IRE) – (Sadler's Wells (USA)) [2017/18 h19.5vᵖᵘ h19.2vᵖᵘ Mar 29] in frame both starts in Irish points in 2014: no form over hurdles. *Sarah Humphrey* **h–**

FARMER BOY (IRE) 5 b.g. Scorpion (IRE) – Absent Beauty (IRE) (Dancing Dissident (USA)) [2017/18 b16.8m⁴ h20v h19s⁴ h20.7s⁶ Feb 22] €7,000 3-y-o: half-brother to several winners, including fairly useful hurdler Riverboatman (2m winner, by Lahib) and fair hurdler Swinton Diamond (21f winner, by Dubai Destination): dam (h80), lightly raced over hurdles, 12.5f winner on Flat: well beaten in bumper: modest form over hurdles. *Nigel Hawke* **h88 b–**

FARMER LAD (IRE) 5 b.g. Scorpion (IRE) – Gortnagowna (IRE) (Moscow Society (USA)) [2017/18 b16.8m⁶ h16v h18.5vᵖᵘ Jan 1] tailed off in bumper: no form over hurdles. *Nigel Hawke* **h– b–**

FARMER MATT (IRE) 12 b.g. Zagreb (USA) – Ashville Native (IRE) (Be My Native (USA)) [2017/18 c23.9s⁴ Feb 6] lengthy, useful-looking gelding: point winner: winning hurdler: fair chaser nowadays: stays 3m: acts on heavy going: wore cheekpieces sole outing in 2017/18: wears tongue tie. *Thomas Murray* **c100 h–**

FARM THE ROCK (IRE) 7 b.g. Yeats (IRE) – Shades of Lavender (IRE) (Peintre Celebre (USA)) [2017/18 h109, b78: c16.2g⁵ c20.2g² c20.9sᶠ c20sᶠ c20.3d⁴ Apr 21] point winner: maiden hurdler: fair form over fences: should stay beyond 21f: acts on good to soft going: often in tongue tie. *Katy Price* **c108 h–**

FAROCCO (GER) 5 b.g. Shirocco (GER) – Fantasmatic (GER) (Lomitas) [2017/18 b16.2d b16.2d h16.2g h17d Nov 13] little impact in bumper/over hurdles: in tongue tie last 2 starts. *Maurice Barnes* **h– b–**

FARRAH'S CHOICE 6 b.m. Equiano (FR) – Esplanade (Danehill (USA)) [2017/18 h–: h15.8m⁶ h16.3g h15.7gᵖᵘ Jun 26] maiden on Flat: no form over hurdles: tried in tongue tie. *James Grassick* **h–**

FAST PLAY (IRE) 6 b.m. Fast Company (IRE) – Akariyda (IRE) (Salse (USA)) [2017/18 h16.7g h19.6g⁴ h18.7g Nov 2] half-sister to fairly useful hurdler Wise Move (21f winner, by Kalanisi): fair on Flat, stays 1½m: poor form over hurdles. *Conor Dore* **h62**

FATHER EDWARD (IRE) 9 b.g. Flemensfirth (USA) – Native Side (IRE) (Be My c–
Native (USA)) [2017/18 c132, h–: c22.6m^{pu} c26m^{ur} Aug 17] sturdy gelding: winning h–
hurdler: useful chaser at best, no form in 2017/18: stays 25f: acts on soft and good to firm
going: wears headgear: has worn tongue tie, including last 2 starts. *David Pipe*

FAUGHEEN (IRE) 10 b.g. Germany (USA) – Miss Pickering (IRE) (Accordion) h165
[2017/18 h16.2s* h16s^{pu} h16s^2 h16.4s^6 h24d* Apr 26]

History was abundant as the 2015 Champion Hurdle winner Faugheen winning the race again after a hiatus of three years. For one thing, only two horses older than nine, Hatton's Grace and Sea Pigeon, have ever won the two-mile hurdlers' championship. Hatton's Grace was ten when winning the race for the second time in 1950 before becoming the first triple winner a year later. Sea Pigeon was successful for the first time as a ten-year-old in 1980, also winning it again aged eleven. But it wasn't simply a matter of age where Faugheen was concerned. No Champion Hurdler has ever regained his crown three years later, and only two, Comedy of Errors and Hurricane Fly, have ever won it back after losing it. What's more, Faugheen had spent much of the intervening period convalescing from a series of setbacks which had ruled him out of both Champion Hurdles following his victory. A suspensory injury initially kept him off the track, causing him to miss the 2016 Champion Hurdle which went instead to the same connections' Annie Power who was supplemented to replace him. Willie Mullins had been expecting Faugheen to return 'as good as new' in the 2016/17 season, with the Morgiana Hurdle at Punchestown that autumn intended to mark his reappearance. But a bruised foot caused him to miss that race, delaying his planned comeback until the Irish Champion Hurdle the following January, the race in which he had put up a career-best effort, and one of the best by any hurdler this century, when slamming his high-class stable-companions Arctic Fire and Nichols Canyon twelve months earlier. What was first thought to be a pulled muscle ruled Faugheen out of the Irish Champion and, when the diagnosis turned out to be something more serious, a stress fracture, it put paid for the second year running to any hopes of his contesting the Champion Hurdle at Cheltenham and consigned him to a whole season on the sidelines.

Faugheen did at least make the line-up for the latest Champion Hurdle, though he couldn't make history, as he was beaten more than twenty lengths into sixth behind the winner for the second year Buveur d'Air. It was the only occasion during the season, incidentally, that Faugheen was able to team up with Ruby Walsh, successful on him in 2015. Walsh was himself in the wars for much of the season. But Faugheen's campaign was anything but a failure. He actually made two successful comebacks of sorts which bookended his campaign, in the first of them putting his various setbacks and lengthy absence behind him, and in the second bouncing back from that heavy defeat in the Champion Hurdle to win over three miles. He might not have been as brilliant as he once was, his invincibility a thing of the past, but his two wins, both of them at Punchestown, showed he retained a considerable amount of ability, and enthusiasm, and put him right up with the best hurdlers that raced in the latest season. A year later than scheduled, Faugheen finally returned to action after a twenty-two-month absence in the Unibet Morgiana Hurdle in November, with Paul Townend in the saddle after Walsh broke his leg in a fall at the track the day before. It was in the same race two years earlier that Faugheen had met with the first defeat of his career, having won a point, a bumper, and all nine of his starts over hurdles. Defeat by his own stable-companion Nichols Canyon was a shock result at the time, though perhaps less so now given that Nichols Canyon went on to win a Stayers' Hurdle. Faugheen's three rivals in the latest Morgiana included fellow nine-year-old Jezki, the 2014 Champion Hurdle winner who had himself successfully returned from a lengthy absence the previous January. Jezki and one of the two five-year-olds in the field, Campeador, had both won races the previous month, but Faugheen was the subject of strong support and, unlike in 2015, gave those who backed him at very short odds little cause for concern, except for some alarm when he had to reach for the fourth last. Faugheen could hardly have won more convincingly, in fact, making all, with Jezki under the whip to stay in touch and the two others already beaten off as he turned for home full of running.

Ladbrokes Champion Stayers' Hurdle, Punchestown—
David Mullins slips his field as Faugheen rolls back the years to thrash stable-companions Penhill (hooped cap) and Shaneshill (third, on rails)

In style at least, it was a performance reminiscent of the 'old' Faugheen, right down to the less than fluent leap he put in at the last, as he drew sixteen lengths clear of Jezki, with outsider Swamp Fox inheriting a remote third after Campeador fell heavily at the last. Perhaps the most noteworthy measure of Faugheen's win was his timefigure (equivalent to a timerating of 169) which wasn't bettered by another hurdler all season.

Historical precedents aside, Faugheen's sparkling return raised the prospect of Buveur d'Air having a fight on his hands to retain his Champion Hurdle title, with Faugheen as low as 7/4 after the Morgiana to win back his crown. Buveur d'Air's impressive return of his own in the 'Fighting Fifth' at Newcastle a fortnight later whetted the appetite still further for their possible clash at Cheltenham, but it wasn't long before Faugheen's participation in yet another Champion Hurdle was thrown into doubt. In an upset that rivalled his 2015 Morgiana defeat, Faugheen was beaten at odds of 11/2-on on his next start in the Ryanair Hurdle at Leopardstown. Even before the field reached the fourth hurdle, alarm bells began ringing when stable-companion Cilaos Emery took over in front from Faugheen, and as soon as the pace quickened after three out Faugheen dropped to last in a matter of strides before being pulled up and then dismounted at the next flight, leaving Mick Jazz and Cilaos Emery to fight out the finish. As a precaution, Faugheen was brought back in the horse ambulance, but he was reported to be sound afterwards and various tests failed to reveal anything to explain his dismal performance. Faugheen therefore lined up for the Irish Champion Hurdle in early-February when there was still enough confidence in him for him to start at a shade of odds on ahead of stable-companion Melon, with Mick Jazz also in the line-up. Faugheen showed more of his customary zest and put his puzzling defeat firmly behind him, although he was headed on the run-in by Supasundae who was dropping back from three miles and ran out the winner by two and a quarter lengths. Wearing cheekpieces for the first time, Faugheen was sent off the 4/1 second favourite behind Buveur d'Air in the Champion Hurdle, seemingly having the beating of Melon and Mick Jazz, as well as Identity Thief, on their form in the Irish Champion Hurdle. However, while that trio filled the frame behind Buveur d'Air, Faugheen finished a long way behind the principals after Buveur d'Air's pacemaker Charli Parcs had cut out much of the running, Faugheen taking over only briefly between three out and the second last before being left behind. 'Ruby got off him and said he just wants a longer trip nowadays,' commented trainer Willie Mullins afterwards.

A similar conclusion had been reached by connections of the former Champion Hurdle winners Hurricane Fly and Jezki when they were beaten into third and fourth behind Faugheen in the 2015 Champion Hurdle. Having won the Aintree Hurdle, Jezki went on to beat Hurricane Fly in what was then the World Series Hurdle at Punchestown. Whereas three miles was uncharted territory for both of them, Faugheen had been campaigned principally as a stayer in his formative runs over hurdles, gaining the first graded success of his career in his only previous race over three miles at Limerick. Even so, three consecutive defeats had raised doubts about Faugheen recapturing even his Morgiana form. With Mullins going all out to retain his trainers' title in Ireland, Faugheen was one of no fewer than seven from his stable in the Ladbrokes Champion Stayers' Hurdle at Punchestown. Faugheen was only third among them in the betting which was headed by 2/1 favourite Penhill, winner of the Stayers' Hurdle at Cheltenham and the mount of Paul Townend, while Bacardys, a last-flight faller when likely to have finished third behind Penhill, was next at 4/1. David Mullins took the ride on 11/2-chance Faugheen, while 6/1-shot Identity Thief was the shortest of those not trained by Mullins, having himself stepped up in trip from finishing fourth in the Champion Hurdle to win the Liverpool Hurdle at Aintree. Notwithstanding his shock defeat in the 2015 Morgiana, Faugheen has an excellent record at Punchestown. He won his bumper there, as well as his very first start over hurdles, while his two appearances at previous Festivals at the track had seen him land the Herald Champion Novices' Hurdle and Punchestown's Champion Hurdle. Jezki was a former winner of those two Festival races as well, and Faugheen emulated him by adding the Champion Stayers' to his Punchestown record, with Jezki among those he beat.

The three-mile hurdle start at Punchestown is at the very entrance to the back straight, and David Mullins got Faugheen off to a flier as soon as the tapes went back while some of his rivals were still walking round the paddock, establishing a lead that was never to be relinquished. Bacardys and sole British challenger La Bague Au Roi were the only two in touch with Faugheen for much of the way, with Penhill and another stable companion Shaneshill in turn clear of the main pack. Of Faugheen's closest pursuers, only Penhill proved a threat when ridden to challenge off the home turn, but Faugheen kept up the gallop to pull away again on the run to the final flight, drawing further clear on the run-in to beat Penhill by thirteen lengths. Shaneshill kept on to finish another four and three quarters back in third, completing a one, two, three for the stable, and was in turn well clear of Identity Thief who fared best of those who never looked like landing a blow. Faugheen's victory was a seventh in the race for Willie Mullins, four of those wins provided by the mare Quevega, while it took Faugheen's own Grade 1 score to eight. Willie Mullins conceded afterwards that Faugheen had things go his way right from the off, also saying that his work beforehand had apparently given little indication of what was to come. 'Myself and Ruby were standing at the gallops the other morning when he came up. I don't know how slow he came up but the two of us looked at one another and we just turned over the gallop and said "Well, we'll run him anyhow"'. Plenty of headlines claimed Faugheen was 'back to his best' at Punchestown but, with neither Penhill nor Identity Thief showing the form of their wins at Cheltenham and Aintree, Faugheen was still some way below that outstanding performance he put up to win the 2016 Irish Champion Hurdle, in which he scored by fifteen lengths to earn a rating of 176. He has, though, been rated the season's top staying hurdler, just ahead of Penhill and Sam Spinner.

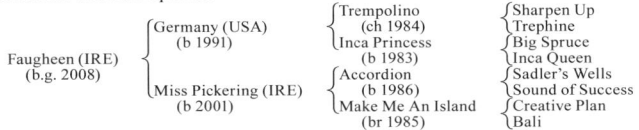

Faugheen (IRE) (b.g. 2008)
- Germany (USA) (b 1991)
  - Trempolino (ch 1984)
    - Sharpen Up
    - Trephine
  - Inca Princess (b 1983)
    - Big Spruce
    - Inca Queen
- Miss Pickering (IRE) (b 2001)
  - Accordion (b 1986)
    - Sadler's Wells
    - Sound of Success
  - Make Me An Island (br 1985)
    - Creative Plan
    - Bali

Plans to run Faugheen in the Grande Course de Haies d'Auteuil had to be shelved when he returned sore from Punchestown. Examination revealed a growth 'the size of a mandarin orange' in his groin area which was removed in a successful operation. There was speculation that it might have accounted for his loss of form earlier in the season, though if so it clearly didn't trouble him much on his final start. Retirement had been looming for Faugheen if he had finished down the field at Punchestown—his 'last chance saloon' in the words of his trainer—but instead a novice chasing campaign could be on the cards for him in 2018/19. It would be very late in the day to go chasing with Faugheen, though he is a good-topped gelding with the size for fences and is relatively lightly raced for his age, having still had only eighteen starts under Rules. If he does go chasing, Faugheen would be a year older than Limestone Lad, another top-class Irish hurdler who briefly switched to fences late in life. Limestone Lad won four of his six novice chases, showing smart form, but he was less adept over fences and soon reverted to hurdling. He went on to win another eleven races back over the smaller obstacles, including two more Morgiana Hurdles (a race he won three times in all) and the Champion Stayers' at Punchestown.

Since Faugheen's last essay in *Chasers & Hurdlers* his two-years younger half-brother Telmadela (by Definite Article), a winning pointer, has proven just a poor maiden over hurdles in Britain. A possible third runner in future for their unraced dam Miss Pickering is five-year-old Osmotic (by Fracas), bought by Gigginstown for €60,000 as a three-year-old. Meanwhile, Faugheen's sire Germany has come up with a jumper who might rank alongside Faugheen in terms of ability one day in Samcro, also a graduate of the pointing field and bumpers, and with the potential to win a Champion Hurdle. Faugheen stays three miles well and acts on heavy and good to firm ground. *W. P. Mullins, Ireland*

FAUVE (IRE) 7 b.g. Montjeu (IRE) – Simaat (USA) (Mr Prospector (USA)) [2017/18 h18.5m h18.5g⁶ h16.8d^tr Jul 23] sturdy gelding: maiden hurdler, modest form at best: tried in headgear/tongue tie: temperamental: dead. *Richard Hawker*   **h58 §**

FAVORITE GIRL (GER) 10 b.m. Shirocco (GER) – Favorite (GER) (Montjeu (IRE)) [2017/18 c–, h118: h16g⁶ May 25] compact mare: fairly useful hurdler, well held sole outing in 2017/18: little promise in 2 starts over fences: probably best around 2m: acts on heavy going: front runner/races prominently. *Michael Appleby*   **c– h–**

FAVORITO BUCK'S (FR) 6 b.g. Buck's Boum (FR) – Sangrilla (FR) (Sanglamore (USA)) [2017/18 c102, h–: c20.2g^F c18d³ c20.5d^pu c20.5g* c20.5s c26g* Apr 20] tall gelding: winning chaser: useful chaser: won handicap at Kempton in February and novice at Fontwell (by 2½ lengths from Toviere) in April: stays easy 3¼m: acts on soft going: tried in cheekpieces/tongue tie. *Paul Nicholls*   **c132 h–**

FAWSLEY SPIRIT (IRE) 5 b.g. Stowaway – Apple Trix (IRE) (Flemensfirth (USA)) [2017/18 h21.7s³ h20.7s³ h21v Mar 28] €40,000 3-y-o: first foal: dam unraced sister to useful hurdler/chaser (stayed 29f) Beg To Differ: fair form over hurdles: best effort when third in maiden at Huntingdon in February: should be suited by further than 2½m: wears blinkers. *Ben Pauling*   **h108**

FAYONAGH (IRE) 7 b.m. Kalanisi (IRE) – Fair Ina (IRE) (Taipan (IRE)) [2017/18 b118: h16d* Oct 7] lengthy mare: smart bumper performer: won Champion Bumper at Cheltenham in 2016/17: 2/13, won maiden at Fairyhouse (by 2½ lengths from Rock Road) sole outing over hurdles: broke leg on gallops later in October: usually led/responded generously to pressure: dead. *Gordon Elliott, Ireland*   **h107**

FEAR GLIC (IRE) 12 b.g. Dr Massini (IRE) – Graineuaile (IRE) (Orchestra) [2017/18 c126, h–: c20d c23.6d^pu c21.7g⁶ c20.9s³ c20.9pu Jan 1] winning hurdler: fairly useful handicap chaser, below form in 2017/18: stays 23f: acts on soft and good to firm going: often races prominently. *Jackie du Plessis*   **c103 h–**

FEARNIE LOU (IRE) 4 b.f. Mahler – Wet And Dry (IRE) (Catcher In The Rye (IRE)) [2017/18 b16d Apr 26] compact filly: second foal: dam unraced: well beaten in bumper. *Christian Williams*   **b–**

FEARSOME FRED 9 b.g. Emperor Fountain – Ryewater Dream (Touching Wood (USA)) [2017/18 h85: h19g h23.9s² h23.3v³ h24s² h23.9v h23.1d³ Apr 24] runner-up in point: modest maiden hurdler: stays 3m: acts on soft going. *Dr Jeremy Naylor*   **h91**

FEAST OF FIRE (IRE) 11 ch.g. St Jovite (USA) – Bellagrana (Belmez (USA)) [2017/18 c95, h84: c23.9g^pu c24.2d c26d Dec 2] tall gelding: winning hurdler: modest chaser at best, no form in 2017/18: wears headgear: tried in tongue tie. *Joanne Foster*   **c– h–**

FEDERICI 7 b.g. Overbury (IRE) – Vado Via (Ardross) [2017/18 c131, h111: c24.5s⁵ c21.6g* c25.9v⁴ c20.6v⁵ c24s⁵ c23.8d³ c30.2s^pu Mar 14] fair hurdler: fairly useful handicap chaser nowadays: won at Kelso in November: stays 3¾m: acts on heavy going: wears headgear: front runner/races prominently. *Donald McCain*   **c129 h–**

FEEL THE PINCH 4 b.g. Librettist (USA) – Liqueur Rose (Alflora (IRE)) [2017/18 b14s b16s Feb 24] good-topped gelding: no form in bumpers. *Fergal O'Brien*   **b–**

FELIX DESJY (FR) 5 ch.g. Maresca Sorrento (FR) – Lamadoun (FR) (Smadoun (FR)) [2017/18 b16d* b16s* b16.3s⁵ b16.3s⁵ Apr 25] €29,000 3-y-o: unfurnished gelding: third foal: half-brother to French 11.5f-13.5f winner Carladoun (by Roli Abi): dam, French 19f chase winner, closely related to fairly useful hurdler (stayed 2½m) L'Eau du Nil: won point on debut: useful form in bumpers: won at Punchestown (maiden) in October and Down Royal in November: tried in hood. *Gordon Elliott, Ireland*   **b112**

FID

FELIX MENDELSSOHN (IRE) 7 b.g. Galileo (IRE) – Ice Queen (IRE) (Danehill **h110**
Dancer (IRE)) [2017/18 b16.7g³ h19.5sur h16s⁶ h16v⁵ Dec 22] useful on Flat, stays 1½m:
fair form over hurdles: left Joseph Patrick O'Brien after third start: tongue tied first 4 starts.
Stuart Coltherd

FENCOTE BELLE (IRE) 5 b.m. Presenting – Hannigan's Lodger (IRE) (Be My Native **h–**
(USA) [2017/18 b16.2g b16.2g h19.7spu h19.9spu Jan 12] sister to fairly useful hurdler **b–**
Leave At Dawn (2m-2¾m winner) and fairly useful chaser Present Lodger (2½m winner),
and half-sister to 3 winners: dam (c129/h107) 17f-2½m hurdle/chase winner: no form in
bumpers/over hurdles. *Malcolm Jefferson*

FENLONS COURT (IRE) 6 b.g. Court Cave (IRE) – Classic Note (IRE) (Classic Secret **h97**
(USA)) [2017/18 b17.7g⁶ h15.3s³ h16s⁵ h17.7v⁶ h21.4v⁶ h19.8s⁴ h19.5s⁶ Apr 27] fourth **b82**
foal: half-brother to fair hurdler/fairly useful chaser Tangolan (2½m-3m winner, by Golan):
dam (h108) bumper winner/2m hurdle winner: placed in Irish points: sixth in bumper at
Fontwell: modest form over hurdles: stays 2½m: acts on soft going. *Seamus Mullins*

FENLON'S HILL (IRE) 7 b.g. Court Cave (IRE) – Eva's Lass (IRE) (Flemensfirth **c118**
(USA)) [2017/18 c21.7g⁵ c23.5g² h20g⁶ c20d³ c21drr c20.1s² c18.2s* c21d* c17s² c20.3d⁶ **h94**
Apr 21] modest maiden hurdler: fairly useful chaser: won handicaps at Galway in
September and Fairyhouse (conditional) in October: second in novice at Leopardstown in
March: stays 23f: acts on soft going: tried in cheekpieces: has worn tongue tie. *Paul
Stafford, Ireland*

FERGALL (IRE) 11 br.g. Norwich – Gaybrook Girl (IRE) (Alderbrook) [2017/18 c–, **c–**
h133: h15.7mF h16d h15.7d Dec 23] sturdy gelding: useful handicap hurdler: jumped **h135**
poorly only outing over fences: stayed 2½m: acted on soft and good to firm going: in
cheekpieces last 4 starts: deaf. *Seamus Mullins*

FERGAL MAEL DUIN 10 gr.g. Tikkanen (USA) – Fad Amach (IRE) (Flemensfirth **c110**
(USA)) [2017/18 c123, h–: c27.7d⁶ c26v⁵ c19.5vur c20v⁵ c21.6dF c20.3gpu Apr 20] rangy **h–**
gelding: maiden hurdler: fairly useful handicap chaser, below form in 2017/18: stays 3m:
acts on heavy going: has worn headgear, including last 4 starts: has worn tongue tie,
including last 3 starts. *Colin Tizzard*

FERNANDO (IRE) 14 b.g. Fruits of Love (USA) – Dancing Venus (Pursuit of Love) **c–**
[2017/18 h21.2mpu c20gpu Sep 18] point winner: little form under Rules: tried in hood/ **h–**
tongue tie. *Ken Wingrove*

FERNAN (IRE) 6 br.g. Robin des Champs (FR) – Rosa Rugosa (IRE) (In The Wings) **h99 p**
[2017/18 b96: h16.2g⁵ Oct 28] fairly useful form in bumpers: 11/1, fifth in maiden at Kelso
(9 lengths behind Some Reign) on hurdling debut: should improve. *Malcolm Jefferson*

FERNGROVE (USA) 7 gr.g. Rockport Harbor (USA) – Lucky Pipit (Key of Luck **h–**
(USA)) [2017/18 h16g h16spu Dec 27] maiden on Flat: little form over hurdles: in hood/
tongue tie last 3 starts. *Susan Corbett*

FERROBIN (IRE) 4 br.g. Robin des Champs (FR) – Fedaia (IRE) (Anabaa (USA)) **b87 p**
[2017/18 b15.8d² Apr 24] €45,000 3-y-o: first foal: dam unraced half-sister to Auronzo out
of Fedian, both group-winning jumpers up to 2¼m/19f in Italy: 4/1, shaped with promise
when second in bumper at Ludlow (4 lengths behind Imperial Aura): better to come.
Dan Skelton

FESTIVAL DAWN 6 b.m. Kayf Tara – Keel Road (IRE) (Luso) [2017/18 h19s² Feb 20] **h112 p**
first foal: dam (c101) 3m chase winner: maiden pointer: 12/1, promise when second in
mares novice at Taunton (length behind Big Robin) on hurdling debut: should improve.
Philip Hobbs

FESTIVE AFFAIR (IRE) 10 b.g. Presenting – Merry Batim (IRE) (Alphabatim (USA)) **c135**
[2017/18 c127: c16m* c16.2g⁴ c16m* c16.8g c15.9d c16.4g c16d² Dec 20] tall gelding:
useful handicap chaser: won at Ludlow in May and Uttoxeter (by 1½ lengths from
Hammersly Lake) in July: raced mainly around 2m: acts on good to firm and good to soft
going: usually in cheekpieces: wears tongue tie: front runner/races prominently. *Jonjo
O'Neill*

FFORBIDDEN LOVE 4 b.f. Fastnet Rock (AUS) – Trinkila (USA) (Cat Thief (USA)) **b80**
[2017/18 b12.4s³ b12.4s³ ab16g⁴ b16.8g Apr 19] fourth foal: closely related to fair hurdler
Elysian Prince (2m winner, by Champs Elysees), stays 19f: dam 8.6f winner: modest form
in bumpers: won mares event at Lingfield in January: tried in tongue tie. *Neil King*

FIDDLER'S FLIGHT (IRE) 12 b.g. Convinced – Carole's Dove (Manhal) [2017/18 **h67**
h73: h15.8d h15.8d h19.9s³ h19.9s h19.7v⁶ ab16g⁶ h19.9v h19.9vpu Mar 23] poor handicap
hurdler: stays 2½m: acts on heavy going: usually wears headgear: usually races in rear.
John Norton

FID

FIDELITY 6 b.g. Halling (USA) – Sir Kyffin's Folly (Dansili) [2017/18 h69: h16d² h15.8g² h16g² h19g Nov 30] poor maiden hurdler: unproven beyond 2m: acts on good to soft going: usually races towards rear. *Jonathan Geake* — **h79**

FIDUX (FR) 5 b.g. Fine Grain (JPN) – Folle Tempete (FR) (Fabulous Dancer (USA)) [2017/18 h128: h16d⁴ h16s^ur h16s⁴ h19s⁴ h16v h19.8s³ Apr 28] compact gelding: fairly useful handicap hurdler: probably stays 19f: acts on good to soft going. *Alan King* — **h128**

FIELD MASTER (IRE) 5 b.g. Doyen (IRE) – West Hill Rose (IRE) (Roselier (FR)) [2017/18 b16.3d b16.2s Jan 29] no form in bumpers. *Emma Lavelle* — **b–**

FIELDS OF FORTUNE 4 b.g. Champs Elysees – Widescreen (USA) (Distant View (USA)) [2017/18 h16d^ur h16s⁵ h16v⁴ Mar 28] fair maiden on Flat, stays 1¾m: fair form over hurdles: fourth when unseated rider last in juvenile won by We Have A Dream at Warwick in November, best effort. *Alan King* — **h107**

FIELDS OF GLORY (FR) 8 b.g. King's Best (USA) – Lavandou (Sadler's Wells (USA)) [2017/18 c105, h–: c22.6g⁴ c20.2s Jan 11] winning hurdler: fair handicap chaser: best up to 2½m: acts on heavy going: wears tongue tie. *Tim Vaughan* — **c102 h–**

FIFTY PEACH WAY 6 b.m. Black Sam Bellamy (IRE) – Aphrodisia (Sakhee (USA)) [2017/18 b15.8g b16.6s b15.8d⁵ Apr 24] £650 3-y-o: first foal: dam 1m-1¼m winner: poor form in bumpers. *Alex Swinswood* — **b72**

FIFTY SHADES (IRE) 5 gr.g. Tajraasi (USA) – Baylough Mist (IRE) (Cloudings (IRE)) [2017/18 h16g⁶ h16g h18.5d^pu h16.2v⁶ c24g⁴ Apr 26] €5,000 3-y-o: good-topped gelding: first foal: dam unraced: little impact in points: no form over hurdles: 33/1, fourth in novice handicap at Warwick (16¼ lengths behind Posh Totty) on chasing debut: left Sean Thomas Doyle after second start: best effort at 3m: usually races towards rear: capable of better as a chaser. *Christian Williams* — **c77 p h–**

FIGEAC (FR) 4 gr.g. Kendargent (FR) – Faviva (USA) (Storm Cat (USA)) [2017/18 h15.8s h15.8g⁶ h15.8d ab16d³ h16.5m⁶ Apr 25] fairly useful on Flat in France, stays 1½m: modest form over hurdles: in tongue tie last 4 starts. *Nick Littmoden* — **h91**

FIGHT AWAY BOYS (IRE) 10 ch.g. Vertical Speed (FR) – Say Ya Love Me (IRE) (Presenting) [2017/18 c–, h–: c24.2g h23.8g⁴ Nov 30] multiple point winner: poor maiden hurdler: little form in hunter chases: left Mrs Caroline Crow after first start: sometimes in headgear: tried in tongue tie. *N. W. Alexander* — **c57 h67**

FIGHT COMMANDER (IRE) 9 b.g. Oscar (IRE) – Creidim (IRE) (Erins Isle) [2017/18 c112, h–: c24g⁴ c25.7d³ c25.1v³ c29.2v² c21.7v² Apr 27] lengthy gelding: maiden hurdler: fair handicap chaser: stays 29f: acts on good to firm and heavy going: usually in headgear: temperamental. *Oliver Sherwood* — **c105 § h–**

FIGHT FOR LOVE (FR) 5 b.g. Fuisse (FR) – Love Affair (FR) (Arctic Tern (USA)) [2017/18 b–: ab16g⁵ h17.7v⁵ Jan 21] modest form in bumpers: well beaten in novice on hurdling debut. *Laura Mongan* — **h– b82**

FIGHTING BACK 7 b.g. Galileo (IRE) – Maroochydore (IRE) (Danehill (USA)) [2017/18 h16.6s^pu h16.2v⁴ h16.8v⁴ Apr 13] fair maiden on Flat in 2014: poor form over hurdles. *Henry Hogarth* — **h68**

FIG'S PRIDE (IRE) 5 br.m. Stowaway – Roseboreen (IRE) (Roselier (FR)) [2017/18 b16.2g b16.2v⁶ b17d Mar 31] sturdy mare: seventh foal: sister to modest chaser Spirit of Hale (3m winner) and half-sister to fairly useful hurdler/chaser Beauboreen (19f-3¼m winner, by Revoque): dam, winning pointer, half-sister to useful hurdler/smart chaser (2m-2½m winner) Fiendish Flame and fair hurdler/useful chaser (stayed 25f) Will Be Done: no form in bumpers: has worn hood. *N. W. Alexander* — **b–**

FILATORE (IRE) 9 ch.g. Teofilo (IRE) – Dragnet (IRE) (Rainbow Quest (USA)) [2017/18 h89§: h23.6d h25s³ h19.9v h20.5v⁴ h19.5v⁵ h20v h23v⁵ h23.6v⁵ h21.9v² Apr 1] sturdy gelding: poor handicap hurdler: stays 2¾m: acts on heavy going: wears headgear: has worn tongue tie: front runner/races prominently: moody. *Bernard Llewellyn* — **h74 §**

FILEMON 6 gr.g. Kayf Tara – L'Ultima (FR) (Verglas (IRE)) [2017/18 b13.6g⁴ h16.3d h16.3s h16.3v Feb 10] £35,000 4-y-o: lengthy gelding: third foal: dam, French 1¼m winner, half-sister to fairly useful French hurdler (2m-21f winner) Empereur du Monde: fourth in bumper at Fontwell (7 lengths behind Canford Chimes): no form over hurdles: tried in hood: wears tongue tie. *Jamie Snowden* — **h– b83**

FILLE DES CHAMPS (IRE) 7 b.m. Robin des Champs (FR) – South Queen Lady (IRE) (King's Ride) [2017/18 h94: h23.3d² h23.6v⁵ h23.8v⁴ h21.2s² h26s h23.1v³ h23.3v^pu Apr 7] fair handicap hurdler: stays 3m: acts on heavy going: usually wears tongue tie: often races towards rear. *Evan Williams* — **h101**

FIN

FILLYDELPHIA (IRE) 7 b.m. Strategic Prince – Lady Fonic (Zafonic (USA)) [2017/18 h16.7d^{pu} h15.7d^4 Dec 28] modest on Flat: poor maiden hurdler on balance: raced around 2m. *Patrick Holmes* — **h75**

FINAGHY AYR (IRE) 10 ch.g. Lahib (USA) – Ali Ankah (IRE) (Insan (USA)) [2017/18 c103x, h–: c24.3v^5 c24.5s* c24.1v^2 c24.1v^2 c31.9v^2 c26.2d Mar 31] winning hurdler: fair handicap chaser: won at Carlisle in December: stays 4m: acts on heavy going: wears cheekpieces: tried in tongue tie: makes mistakes. *Ian Duncan* — **c102 x / h–**

FINAL CHOICE 5 b.g. Makfi – Anasazi (IRE) (Sadler's Wells (USA)) [2017/18 h117: h16.3s^3 h19.9v^6 h16.5s Apr 14] good-topped gelding: fairly useful handicap hurdler: won at Wetherby in March: should stay beyond 2m: acts on heavy going: often in cheekpieces: tried in tongue tie: often races prominently. *Warren Greatrex* — **h117**

FINAL COUNTDOWN 7 ch.g. Selkirk (USA) – Culture Queen (King's Best (USA)) [2017/18 h91: h16.2g^{pu} h17m^2 h16.2g^5 May 23] modest maiden hurdler: raced around 2m: acts on good to firm going: has worn cheekpieces, including last 4 starts: often races towards rear: often let down by jumping. *Rebecca Menzies* — **h89 x**

FINAL FLING (IRE) 7 b.g. Milan – Supreme Singer (IRE) (Supreme Leader) [2017/18 h83: h23.9g h23.3g^2 h23.9d h23.3d* h23.3s^3 c19.9m^5 c26d^6 h24.1s* h24.1v* Jan 23] fair handicap hurdler: won at Hexham in August, and Wetherby in December and January: poor form over fences: stays 3¼m: acts on good to firm and heavy going: wears cheekpieces. *Rose Dobbin* — **c81 / h101**

FINAL NUDGE (IRE) 9 b.g. Kayf Tara – Another Shot (IRE) (Master Willie) [2017/18 c139, h–: c25.1s^2 c29.5v^3 c24.2s^5 c26s c34.3s^F Apr 14] strong gelding: winning hurdler: useful handicap chaser: second in Badger Ales Trophy Handicap Chase at Wincanton (head behind Present Man) in November: probably best up to 29f: acts on heavy going: has worn cheekpieces, including in 2017/18. *David Dennis* — **c139 / h–**

FINAL REMINDER (IRE) 6 b.m. Gold Well – Olde Kilcormac (IRE) (Supreme Leader) [2017/18 h69: h20.2m^5 h23.8g^5 Dec 18] Irish point winner: poor form over hurdles: best effort at 3m. *N. W. Alexander* — **h84**

FINALSHOT 5 b.g. Phoenix Reach (IRE) – Ryoshi (Rakaposhi King) [2017/18 b16.6s^2 b16d^6 Apr 26] useful-looking gelding: third foal: dam (b76), third only start in points, also ran once in bumper: fairly useful form in bumpers: better effort when second at Doncaster on debut. *Henry Daly* — **b96**

FINANCIAL CLIMATE (IRE) 11 b.g. Exit To Nowhere (USA) – Claudia's Pearl (Deploy) [2017/18 c106, h–: c24.5g^{pu} May 22] lengthy gelding: winning hurdler: fairly useful chaser at best, folded tamely sole outing in 2017/18: stays 3¼m: acts on heavy going: wears headgear. *Oliver Sherwood* — **c– / h–**

FIN AND GAME (IRE) 6 b.g. Oscar (IRE) – Miss Cilla (IRE) (Shernazar) [2017/18 b92: h16s* h16.7v* ab16g* h16g^4 Apr 20] fairly useful form over hurdles: won novices at Wetherby in November and Bangor in January: also won 3-runner jumpers bumper at Southwell in March: will stay beyond 2m: usually races prominently. *Donald McCain* — **h125**

FINCH FLYER (IRE) 11 ch.g. Indian Ridge – Imelda (USA) (Manila (USA)) [2017/18 c–§, h–: c20g^{pu} c22.6m^{pu} h18.7g Jul 23] stocky gelding: winning hurdler/maiden chaser, no longer of any account: usually wears headgear: has worn tongue tie, including in 2017/18: temperamental. *Aytach Sadik* — **c– § / h– §**

FINDUSATGORCOMBE 6 b.g. Tobougg (IRE) – Seemma (Romany Rye) [2017/18 h–: h16.8d^3 h25.8m* h21.6g h25s h21.4s^{pu} h23.1d^6 Apr 24] point winner: poor handicap hurdler: won at Fontwell in August: stays 3¼m: acts on good to firm going: often races freely. *Jimmy Frost* — **h79**

FINE ARK 5 b.m. Multiplex – Do It On Dani (Weld) [2017/18 b15.8m b20.6g^{pu} Nov 9] seventh foal: half-sister to modest chaser Dingo Bay (2½m-25f winner, by Karinga Bay): dam (h111), 3m-27f hurdle winner, half-sister to fairly useful hurdler/fair chaser (2m-2½m winner) Jessolle: no show in bumper/maiden hurdle. *Henry Daly* — **h– / b–**

FINE JEWELLERY 9 b.g. Epalo (GER) – Lola Lolita (FR) (Dom Alco (FR)) [2017/18 c73, h75: c19.8g* c21g^{pu} Aug 16] maiden hurdler: poor form over fences: won novice handicap at Towcester in May: stays 2½m: best form on good going: has worn hood/tongue tie. *Jamie Snowden* — **c81 / h–**

FIN

FINE RIGHTLY (IRE) 10 b.g. Alflora (IRE) – Bealtaine (IRE) (Zaffaran (USA)) **c139**
[2017/18 c142, h135: c16v³ c20s³ h20v² h20v c25.6v⁵ c20v⁴ c24.5s⁴ Apr 28] useful **h134**
handicap hurdler: second at Navan (8 lengths behind Diamond Cauchois) in December: useful handicap chaser: third in Fortria Chase at same course (2½ lengths behind Clarcam) in November: stays 3¼m: acts on heavy going: has worn hood, including last 3 starts: has worn tongue tie, including in 2017/18: usually races nearer last than first. *Stuart Crawford, Ireland*

FINGAREETA 5 b.m. Schiaparelli (GER) – Annie's Answer (IRE) (Flemensfirth (USA)) **b88**
[2017/18 b15.8g² b15.7g* Jul 16] fourth foal: sister to bumper winner/fair 2m hurdle winner Schiaparannie: dam (c110/h130) bumper and 2m/17f hurdle winner: fair form in bumpers: won mares event at Southwell in July: wears hood. *Malcolm Jefferson*

FINGERONTHESWITCH (IRE) 8 b.g. Beneficial – Houseoftherisinsun (IRE) **c–**
(Fourstars Allstar (USA)) [2017/18 c131, h–: c20.2s^pu h23.9v² h22.8v⁶ h22.8v² h26s⁵ **h120**
h24.4d⁴ h22.8v Mar 31] lengthy gelding: fairly useful handicap hurdler nowadays: second at Ffos Las in November: useful chaser at best, possibly amiss on return: stays 3m: acts on heavy going: wears cheekpieces/tongue tie: often races towards rear. *Neil Mulholland*

FINGERS CROSSED (IRE) 8 b.g. Bach (IRE) – Awesome Miracle (IRE) (Supreme **c82**
Leader) [2017/18 c97, h–: c20.5g⁴ c16g³ c20.2g⁵ Dec 3] good-topped gelding: winning **h–**
hurdler: modest maiden chaser, below form in 2017/18: should stay 2½m: acts on soft going: tried in hood: in tongue tie last 2 starts. *Paul Webber*

FINIAN'S OSCAR (IRE) 6 b.g. Oscar (IRE) – Trinity Alley (IRE) (Taipan (IRE)) **c156**
[2017/18 h155: c19.4d* c20.4d* c15.5d³ c21d² h24v^pu c19.9s⁵ c19.9s* c24.5s^co **h–**
Apr 24]

Substantial investment in both established and untried stock by the late Alan Potts (who died in November aged eighty) has seen the Potts's emerald green, yellow chevron and sleeves, red cap, become a regular sight in the big races over recent seasons. Of the exciting talent coming through the ranks, dual Grade 1-winning novice hurdler Finian's Oscar became perhaps one of only a handful of recent big-money Irish point-to-point buys to really live up to the hype. He won the first of his two Grade 1s just three months after winning his point at Portrush and, given his background and rangy physique, he was an eagerly-anticipated novice chasing prospect at the beginning of the most recent season. The ill-fated Finian's Oscar began his season over fences in the same two and a half mile novice at Chepstow that stablemate Cue Card had won six years earlier and, after justifying short odds in that race and another novice at Cheltenham over the same trip, he was dropped to two miles for the Henry VIII Novices' Chase at Sandown in early-December. Though he'd travelled well in a Tolworth Hurdle, Finian's Oscar had really looked a stayer when winning the Mersey Novices' Hurdle at Aintree in his first season, and he seemed to be unable to cope with the drop back to the minimum trip at Sandown. Sent off the 13/8 favourite, he got the first fence all wrong and was labouring badly by the sixth, eventually finishing tailed off.

Big Buck's Celebration Manifesto Novices' Chase, Aintree—a final win for the ill-fated Finian's Oscar (No.4), who comes home very strongly to overhaul the leader Rene's Girl

Ann & Alan Potts Limited's "Finian's Oscar"

    Trainer Colin Tizzard didn't seem sure that the drop in trip had been the issue in the Henry VIII, saying the following week: 'We don't really know why he didn't lie up. Was it all pace? I don't know. We will put a line through it, you can see he wasn't quite himself.' Despite those comments, Finian's Oscar was stepped back up in trip for his next run, just thirteen days after his Sandown flop, in the Noel Novices' Chase at Ascot. There was less emphasis on speed—he faced just two rivals over an extended two and a half miles at Ascot—but Finian's Oscar's jumping let him down again, so much so that even an adequate round would have seen him finish ahead of the winner Benatar. After Ascot, it was back to the drawing board with Finian's Oscar, who was brought back over the smaller obstacles for the Cleeve Hurdle: 'Bryan [Cooper] put up the idea after Ascot and it took a week to come round to that thinking. His jumping has been a bit of an issue but he is still a good horse and in really good form. He has always made a little noise so we have put a tongue-tie on and will see if we will be going for the Stayers' Hurdle.' The 'noise' Tizzard referred to may well have been behind Finian's Oscar's very tame finishing effort in the Cleeve, in which he had every chance turning for home before weakening and being pulled up by Bryan Cooper before the last.

    Finian's Oscar underwent a palate cauterisation before his return to chasing in the Golden Miller at the Cheltenham Festival where Robbie Power regained the ride from Bryan Cooper for the rest of the season. Finian's Oscar completed this time, but his jumping was still unconvincing (despite the application of first-time cheekpieces), as was his finishing effort. The latter certainly changed on his next start in the Manifesto Novices' Chase at Aintree after Finian's Oscar had put himself on the back foot down the back straight with some customary sloppy leaps. He was

FIN

matched at 229/1 on Betfair in running, before rallying strongly down the home straight and surging into the lead after the last. Finian's Oscar continued the good work and looked to have finally got the hang of chasing on his next start back at three miles in the Growise Champion Novices' Chase at Punchestown. He jumped better than he had done at Cheltenham and Aintree, despite being in a bigger field, and was in the process of running well (responding to pressure in second) when carried out at the last fence in a bizarre incident which is covered in the essay on Al Boum Photo.

Finian's Oscar (IRE) (b.g. 2012)
- Oscar (IRE) (b 1994)
  - Sadler's Wells (b 1981)
    - Northern Dancer
    - Fairy Bridge
  - Snow Day (b 1978)
    - Reliance II
    - Vindaria
- Trinity Alley (IRE) (b 2001)
  - Taipan (b 1992)
    - Last Tycoon
    - Alidiva
  - Trinity Gale (b 1988)
    - Strong Gale
    - Trinity Air

Finian's Oscar might well have scaled even greater heights given another season over fences, especially considering his improved round of jumping at Punchestown, but, sadly, he died of organ failure after undergoing an operation for colic over the summer. Finian's Oscar's pedigree was covered in detail in his essay in *Chasers & Hurdlers 2016/17*, since when his year-younger half-brother School Boy Hours (by Presenting)—the third foal out of Trinity Alley—finished an eye-catching third on his hurdling debut at Navan in March for trainer Noel Meade in the colours of J. P. McManus. *Colin Tizzard*

FINISH THE STORY (IRE) 12 b.g. Court Cave (IRE) – Lady of Grange (IRE) (Phardante (FR)) [2017/18 c105, h100: c25.5d² c26v⁴ c21.7v^pu c24.5v⁵ c26.7v^ur c26.2s^ur Apr 27] compact gelding: fair hurdler: modest handicap chaser nowadays: out-and-out stayer: acts on heavy going: wears headgear/tongue tie. *Johnny Farrelly*   c90 h–

FINLEY'S EYES (IRE) 5 b.g. Beneficial – Badia Dream (IRE) (Old Vic) [2017/18 b17s⁵ Apr 8] €75,000 3-y-o: fourth foal: half-brother to bumper winner/fairly useful hurdler Listen To The Man (15f-2½m winner, by Court Cave): dam unraced half-sister to useful chaser (stayed 27f) Scotmail Boy: 5/2, fifth in bumper at Carlisle (10½ lengths behind Largy Glory): should prove capable of better. *Dan Skelton*   b87 p

FINNEGAN'S GARDEN (IRE) 9 b.g. Definite Article – Tri Folene (FR) (Nebos (GER)) [2017/18 c76, h–: c22.5d⁵ c20.2g² c19.7s* c19.4v^ur c16v² c16v³ c16s³ c16v* c16v^ur c19.7v* Apr 1] maiden hurdler: modest handicap chaser: won at Plumpton in December, Lingfield (conditional) in March and Plumpton again in April: stays 2½m: acts on heavy going: has worn hood. *Zoe Davison*   c95 h–

FINULA (IRE) 6 b.g. Robin des Champs (FR) – Glens Ruby (IRE) (Presenting) [2017/18 h109, b75: h21g^ur h20s⁶ h20.7s^pu Dec 26] fair handicap hurdler, below form in 2017/18: should stay beyond 2m: acts on good to soft going: in tongue tie last 3 starts. *Brendan Powell*   h91

FIOSRACH (IRE) 8 b.g. Bachelor Duke (USA) – Saana (IRE) (Erins Isle) [2017/18 h102: h17.2d² h17.2g⁶ h17.2s⁴ h16.8g Sep 7] fair handicap hurdler: unproven beyond 17f: acts on soft going: has worn cheekpieces, including in 2017/18: in tongue tie last 2 starts. *James Moffatt*   h106

FIRE AHEAD (IRE) 5 b.g. Yeats (IRE) – Ring of Fire (USA) (Nureyev (USA)) [2017/18 h16.6s h16.6s h16v h16.5v^pu Apr 12] pulled up only start in Irish points: poor form over hurdles. *Ian Williams*   h58

FIREBIRD FLYER (IRE) 11 b.g. Winged Love (IRE) – Kiora Lady (IRE) (King's Ride) [2017/18 c134d, h–: h23.9v³ c29.5v^F c25.2s c23.8v c23.6s Mar 22] small, sturdy gelding: fair handicap hurdler nowadays: useful chaser at best, no form over fences in 2017/18: stays 33f: acts on heavy going: has worn cheekpieces, including final start: has worn tongue tie: held up. *Evan Williams*   c– h104

FIRE IN HIS EYES (IRE) 7 br.g. Stowaway – Carrigeen Kohleria (IRE) (Luso) [2017/18 c80, h129: h20s⁴ c18s³ c18v⁴ c25v c21.6v² c23v² c20v² c19.6v² c22.5s⁶ Apr 17] fairly useful hurdler, below form on return in 2017/18: fairly useful maiden chaser: stays 25f: acts on heavy going: in headgear last 5 starts: wears tongue tie: front runner/races prominently. *Gordon Elliott, Ireland*   c120 h86

FIRE PALACE 4 b.f. Royal Applause – Inflammable (Montjeu (IRE)) [2017/18 h16g⁶ Nov 1] fair on Flat, stays 1m: tailed off in fillies juvenile on hurdling debut. *Robert Eddery*   h–

FIRE ROCK (IRE) 7 b.g. Scorpion (IRE) – Cooline Jana (IRE) (Presenting) [2017/18 c– h–: c16g^F h23.9g⁴ h23.9d Aug 2] poor maiden hurdler: fell heavily second in novice h78 handicap on chasing debut. *Nicky Richards*

FIRMOUNT GENT (IRE) 12 b.g. Beneficial – Tinkers Lady (Sheer Grit) [2017/18 c97 c20g³ c17.8m⁵ c17.4d* c15.7g³ c19.7d^{ur} c23.6g⁴ c19.3g^{pu} Apr 23] lengthy, plain gelding: h– raced twice over hurdles for Miss Hilary McLoughlin: modest novice chaser: won novice event at Bangor in October: left Dan Skelton after sixth start: stays 23f: acts on good to soft going: usually wore cheekpieces/tongue tie in 2017/18. *Mrs B. Ewart*

FIRST ASSIGNMENT (IRE) 5 b.g. Vinnie Roe (IRE) – Rebel Dream (IRE) (Dushyantor h121 (USA)) [2017/18 h19.5d² h20.3s⁴ h20.7s* h19.8v³ Mar 10] £40,000 4-y-o: third foal: half-brother to fair hurdler/winning pointer Bridane Rebel (2m-23f winner, by Milan): dam (c95/h95) winning pointer: won Irish point on debut: fairly useful form over hurdles: won handicap at Huntingdon in January: will stay 3m. *Ian Williams*

FIRST DESTINATION 6 b.m. Rail Link – Hollow Quaill (IRE) (Entrepreneur) b80 [2017/18 b16.7g* Aug 6] sixth foal: half-sister to 5f/6f winner Gower Princess (by Footstepsinthesand): dam 1m winner: 10/1, won bumper at Market Rasen (by short head from Soleglad), outbattling runner-up. *Robert Stephens*

FIRST DRIFT 7 ch.g. Generous (IRE) – Supreme Cove (Supreme Leader) [2017/18 h–, h118 b96: h20.8s⁴ h16.6d⁵ h16.6s* h16.7v⁸ h16.7s² Mar 26] Irish point winner: unbeaten in 2 bumpers: fairly useful form over hurdles: won novices at Doncaster in February and Market Rasen in March: should stay 2½m: acts on heavy going: front runner/races prominently. *Ben Case*

FIRST DU CHARMIL (FR) 6 ch.g. Ballingarry (IRE) – Famous Member (FR) (Peintre h111 Celebre (USA)) [2017/18 h108p: h15.7d³ h15.8s⁴ Jan 12] fair form over hurdles. *Samuel Drinkwater*

FIRST FANDANGO 11 b.g. Hernando (FR) – First Fantasy (Be My Chief (USA)) c– [2017/18 c–, h104: h26.4d May 21] sturdy gelding: fair hurdler, well beaten sole outing in h– 2017/18: winning chaser: stays 25f: acts on heavy going: has worn headgear, including last 4 starts: usually wears tongue tie. *Tim Vaughan*

FIRST FIGARO (GER) 8 ch.g. Silvano (GER) – Felina (GER) (Acatenango (GER)) h110 [2017/18 b17g* h16d h16v³ h16.5v Feb 21] angular gelding: smart bumper performer: won b115 at Killarney (by 4¾ lengths from Santiago de Cuba) in August: fair form over hurdles: best effort when third in maiden at Down Royal in January: has joined Venetia Williams. *D. K. Weld, Ireland*

FIRST FLOW (IRE) 6 b.g. Primary (USA) – Clonroche Wells (IRE) (Pierre) [2017/18 h133 b91: b16d⁴ h16s* h16.3v* h15.7v* h16.4s^{pu} Mar 13] well-made gelding: fair form in b91 bumpers: useful form over hurdles: won novice at Lingfield in November, introductory event at Newbury (by 20 lengths from Dell Oro) in December and Rossington Main Novices' Hurdle at Haydock (by 10 lengths from Midnight Shadow) in January: will stay at least 2½m. *Kim Bailey*

FIRST MOHICAN 10 ch.g. Tobougg (IRE) – Mohican Girl (Dancing Brave (USA)) h– [2017/18 h19v Mar 12] strong gelding: useful on Flat: fairly useful hurdler at best, well held sole outing in 2017/18: should stay beyond 2m: acts on good going. *Alan King*

FIRST OF NEVER (IRE) 12 b.g. Systematic – Never Promise (FR) (Cadeaux h66 § Genereux) [2017/18 h64§: h16.8g³ h15.8d⁴ h16.2g h16.6d⁵ Feb 8] poor maiden hurdler: stays 21f: acts on soft going: often travels strongly/finishes weakly. *Lynn Siddall*

FIRST QUEST (USA) 4 b.g. First Defence (USA) – Dixie Quest (USA) (Coronado's h94 Quest (USA)) [2017/18 h16s⁶ h16v⁶ h16s⁵ h15.9v h15.8s⁶ Feb 22] good-bodied gelding: fairly useful on Flat, stays 1¾m: modest form over hurdles: raced only at 2m. *Jim Boyle*

FIRST SUMMER 6 b.g. Cockney Rebel (IRE) – Silken Dalliance (Rambo Dancer h78 (CAN)) [2017/18 h73: h16.3g h15.8m⁶ h15.8g Jul 19] modest on Flat: poor form over hurdles: in cheekpieces 3 of 4 starts. *Shaun Harris*

FIRST UP (IRE) 4 b.g. Rip Van Winkle (IRE) – Doregan (IRE) (Bahhare (USA)) h99 [2017/18 h15.8g⁵ h15.8s⁶ h16.7d² h16s¹ Jan 13] half-brother to a winning jumper in Italy by Dane Friendly: dam Italian 2m hurdle winner: fairly useful on Flat, stays 1¼m: modest form over hurdles: in tongue tie last 2 starts. *Oliver Greenall*

FIRSTYMINI (FR) 7 gr.g. Slickly (FR) – Jolie Lola (FR) (Villez (USA)) [2017/18 c–, c– h–: h16.2g h16.2m³ h16.2g* h16.8g c20.1v^{pu} Oct 14] poor handicap hurdler: won at Perth h77 in August: maiden chaser: stays 19f: acts on good to firm and good to soft going. *R. Mike Smith*

FIR

FIRTH OF BAVARD 11 b.g. Flemensfirth (USA) – Ice Bavard (Le Bavard (FR)) [2017/18 h–: c20.5v^{pu} Jan 15] of no account. *Robert Goldie* — c– h–

FIRTH OF THE CLYDE 13 b.g. Flemensfirth (USA) – Miss Nel (Denel (FR)) [2017/18 c140, h–: c26.2g^4 c23.4v^4 Feb 5] tall gelding: maiden hurdler: useful handicap chaser: stays 3m: acts on heavy going: wears blinkers. *Ruth Jefferson* — c130 h–

FISCAL SPACE (IRE) 6 b.g. Court Cave (IRE) – Honeyed (IRE) (Persian Mews) [2017/18 b15.8s^6 h20v^3 h20v^4 h24.1v^5 Feb 3] €18,000 3-y-o, £46,000 4-y-o: closely related to 2 winners by Old Vic, including fair hurdler/useful chaser Gurkha Brave (2m-2½m winner), and half-brother to bumper winner/fair hurdler (15f-19f winner) Rainy Day Dylan and fairly useful chaser (2m winner, stays 2½m) Icing On The Cake (both by Spadoun): dam unraced half-sister to smart 2m hurdler Carobee: runner-up in Irish point: sixth in maiden bumper at Ffos Las: fair form over hurdles: best effort when third in maiden at same course in November. *Tom Symonds* — h109 b77

FISHERMAN FRANK 7 b.g. Rail Link – Ribbons And Bows (IRE) (Dr Devious (IRE)) [2017/18 b98: h19.9g^{bd} h19.9d^4 h19.9d^4 h19.3g^6 Nov 4] big gelding: bumper winner: fair form over hurdles: stayed 2½m: sometimes wore tongue tie: dead. *Michael Blake* — h108

FISHERMAN'S BLUES (IRE) 5 b.g. Zebedee – Southern Barfly (USA) (Southern Halo (USA)) [2017/18 h16.7g Aug 6] fairly useful maiden on Flat, stays 1½m: well held in maiden on hurdling debut. *Peter Niven* — h–

FISHERMAN'S TALE (IRE) 4 b.f. Jeremy (USA) – So You Said (IRE) (Definite Article) [2017/18 b16.8g Apr 19] £10,000 3-y-o: first foal: dam unraced half-sister to fairly useful hurdler/chaser (stays 29f) Henllan Harri: tailed off in mares bumper. *Giles Smyly* — b–

FIT FOR FIFTY 6 ch.g. Lucarno (USA) – Just For Jean (IRE) (Presenting) [2017/18 h81, b–: h17m^3 h19.9g h16.8g^4 h16.6s c20.9s^4 Apr 8] third on completed start in Irish points: poor maiden hurdler: well beaten in novice handicap on chasing debut: stays 21f: acts on good to firm going: often races prominently: entitled to do better as a chaser. *Donald McCain* — c– p h82

FIT FOR THE JOB (IRE) 6 b.g. Lawman (FR) – Spesialta (Indian Ridge) [2017/18 h18.7m Aug 24] fairly useful on Flat, stays 8.5f: well beaten in novice on hurdling debut. *Jonjo O'Neill* — h–

FIT THE BRIEF 8 b.m. Kayf Tara – Tulipa (POL) (Jape (USA)) [2017/18 h106: h20.3d^3 h15.7g^2 h16g^3 h19.9d^3 h19.9d^4 h21.6g^6 Oct 13] fair maiden hurdler: stays 2½m: acts on soft going: wears hood/tongue tie: temperamental. *Tom George* — h104 §

FITZHENRY (IRE) 6 b.g. Flemensfirth (USA) – She Took A Tree (FR) (Sri Pekan (USA)) [2017/18 c20s^5 c20v^3 c22.6s^2 c20.4v* h24s^2 c20s* c24v^2 Mar 23] €42,000 3-y-o: second foal: dam, French 6f-1m winner, half-sister to very smart hurdler (stayed 2½m) Jazz Messenger: fairly useful form over hurdles: useful handicap chaser: won at Thurles (conditional) in December and Naas (novice) in February: stays 3m: acts on heavy going: in cheekpieces last 2 starts: likely to progress further as a chaser. *Paul Nolan, Ireland* — c131 p h121

FITZ VOLONTE 11 br.g. Passing Glance – Swordella (Broadsword (USA)) [2017/18 c92, h–: c27.5d^{pu} Jun 9] workmanlike gelding: maiden chaser: modest chaser, stiff task sole outing in 2017/18: stays 3m: acts on soft going: has worn headgear, including last 3 starts. *Andrew Martin* — c– h–

FIVE BAR BRIAN (IRE) 4 br.g. Elusive Pimpernel (USA) – Vayenga (FR) (Highest Honor (FR)) [2017/18 b14.6s^2 Dec 23] €20,000 3-y-o: sixth foal: half-brother to useful 7f/1m winner Tigers Tale (by Tiger Hill): dam unraced: 20/1, second in junior bumper at Newcastle (2¼ lengths behind Star of Lanka). *Tim Reed* — b84

FIVE PIERS (IRE) 10 ch.g. Presenting – Gales Return (IRE) (Bob's Return (IRE)) [2017/18 c72, h–: c21.6g* May 10] point winner: maiden hurdler: modest form in chases: won novice hunter at Kelso, sole outing under Rules in 2017/18. *D. Holmes* — c92 h–

FIXED ASSET 6 b.g. Dr Massini (IRE) – Sharayna (Generous (IRE)) [2017/18 b16.7g Apr 22] well beaten in bumper. *Lucinda Egerton* — b–

FIXED RATE 5 b.g. Oasis Dream – Pretty Face (Rainbow Quest (USA)) [2017/18 h109: h21.2m^3 h17.7g^5 h20d* h20.5d^{pu} h19.4d* h19.4d^6 h20v^2 h15.8s^4 h16.8v^{pu} Apr 8] close-coupled gelding: fairly useful handicap hurdler: won at Fakenham in October and Doncaster in December: stays 21f: acts on good to firm and good to soft going: wears headgear/tongue tie: front runner/races prominently. *Charlie Mann* — h119

320

FLE

FIXE LE KAP (FR) 6 gr.g. Kapgarde (FR) – Lady Fix (FR) (Turgeon (USA)) [2017/18 h144: h18.9s* c19.7s² h19.3s h21.1s h24.7s Apr 14] good sort: useful hurdler: won listed event at Compiegne (by 1¼ lengths from Fafintadenient) in May: 1/5, second in novice at Plumpton (2¼ lengths behind Not Another Muddle) on chasing debut: stays 2½m: acts on heavy going: tried in cheekpieces: should do better as a chaser. *Nicky Henderson* **c126 p h138**

FIZZLESTIX (FR) 6 b.g. Bonbon Rose (FR) – Skipnight (Ashkalani (IRE)) [2017/18 h25d² h25.8v* h23.3v³ h26.4d² Apr 22] lengthy, rather unfurnished gelding: point winner: fair handicap hurdler: won at Fontwell (conditional) in March: stays 3¼m: acts on heavy going. *Chris Gordon* **h105**

FLAMING CHARMER (IRE) 10 ch.g. Flemensfirth (USA) – Kates Charm (IRE) (Glacial Storm (USA)) [2017/18 c116§, h–§: c23.6s² c16.2² c19.4v* c19.2v⁴ c18.8v⁵ c21.2s⁴ c20v⁵ Mar 10] tall gelding: winning hurdler: fairly useful handicap chaser: won at Chepstow in November: stays 3m: acts on heavy going: tried in cheekpieces: wears tongue tie: front runner/races prominently: untrustworthy. *Colin Tizzard* **c122 § h– §**

FLANAGANS FIELD (IRE) 10 b.g. Araafa (IRE) – Zvezda (USA) (Nureyev (USA)) [2017/18 h94: h15.8v² h20.5s³ h20v⁴ h17.7v⁴ h19v⁴ h15.8v³ h15.8v Apr 7] modest handicap hurdler: stays 21f: acts on good to firm and heavy going: wears headgear: has worn tongue tie, including final start: often races prominently. *Bernard Llewellyn* **h92**

FLASHEEN (IRE) 8 br.g. Flemensfirth (USA) – Afasheen (IRE) (Presenting) [2017/18 h21.6g⁵ h21.6m⁽ᵖᵘ⁾ Jul 7] no form in bumpers/over hurdles: in headgear/tongue tie last 2 starts. *Nigel Hawke* **h–**

FLASH GARDEN (IRE) 10 b.g. Heron Island (IRE) – Latin Lady (IRE) (Dr Massini (IRE)) [2017/18 c115: c21.6g⁽ᵖᵘ⁾ May 10] compact gelding: unbeaten in 4 points: fair form at best in hunter chases. *J. M. B. Cookson* **c–**

FLASHING GLANCE 5 b.g. Passing Glance – Don And Gerry (IRE) (Vestris Abu) [2017/18 h89: h16.7g⁶ h16.3g⁸* h16.8d² h16d³ h15.8d* h16g⁽ᵖᵘ⁾ Apr 21] smallish gelding: fairly useful form over hurdles: won novice at Stratford in September and handicap at Ludlow in March: raced around 2m: acts on good to soft going: sometimes in hood: front runner. *Tom Lacey* **h127**

FLASHJACK (IRE) 8 br.g. Soapy Danger – Open Miss (Dracula (AUS)) [2017/18 c118, h–: c23.8g⁴ h26v* h23.8s* h26s* h25.5v* h25.5v⁵ Apr 10] well-made gelding: fairly useful handicap hurdler: won at Warwick (conditional) in December, Ludlow (amateur, dead-heated) in January, Warwick again in February and Hereford in March: little show in chases since debut in that sphere: stays 3¼m: acts on heavy going: has worn cheekpieces: usually races towards rear. *Henry Daly* **c– h123**

FLASHMAN 9 ch.g. Doyen (IRE) – Si Si Si (Lomitas) [2017/18 c107§, h82§: c20.5g c17.8g² c19.7m² c17d¹ c25.7d c19.5s⁵ c17.8g⁵ Apr 20] workmanlike gelding: winning hurdler: fair handicap chaser: stays 2¼m: acts on soft going: wears headgear: temperamental. *Gary Moore* **c104 § h– §**

FLASH THE STEEL (IRE) 6 b.g. Craigsteel – Anna's Melody (IRE) (Luso) [2017/18 b14d² b14s³ ab16g* Mar 2] €1,600 3-y-o: first foal: dam unraced half-sister to useful staying hurdler No Hassle Hoff (by Craigsteel) out of half-sister to Scottish Grand National winner Moorcroft Boy: Irish point winner: fairly useful form in bumpers: won maiden at Southwell in March. *Dan Skelton* **b99**

FLAWLESS ESCAPE 5 gr.g. Sagamix (FR) – Sainte Kadette (FR) (Kadalko (FR)) [2017/18 b16v* h20s² h20.2s* h24s³ h20.3v Mar 16] €23,000 3-y-o: first foal: dam fair 2m-2¼m hurdle/chase winner: runner-up in point: won maiden bumper at Roscommon (by 5½ lengths from Chesterfield King) in September: useful form over hurdles: won maiden at Leopardstown in December: third in handicap there (3¾ lengths behind Total Recall) in February: front runner/races prominently: remains capable of better. *Gordon Elliott, Ireland* **h131 p b99**

FLAXEN FLARE (IRE) 9 ch.g. Windsor Knot (IRE) – Golden Angel (USA) (Slew O' Gold (USA)) [2017/18 c133, h103+: h20s² h20v³ c20v² c24.5d c25v⁽ᵖᵘ⁾ h20.3v h16v³ Apr 1] sturdy gelding: useful hurdler: third in Lismullen Hurdle at Navan (11½ lengths behind Apple's Jade) in November: fairly useful chaser: stays 21f: acts on heavy going: wears headgear. *Gordon Elliott, Ireland* **c127 h138**

FLED OR PLED (IRE) 6 b.g. Shantou (USA) – Desert Gail (IRE) (Desert Style (IRE)) [2017/18 h88: h22g⁽ᵖᵘ⁾ h24g⁶ c24g¹ c22.6g⁵ c23g⁶ c24.5g⁴ h23.1d Apr 24] poor handicap hurdler: poor form over fences: left David Dennis after sixth start: stays 3m: acts on good to firm going: usually in headgear/tongue tie: temperamental. *Tim Vaughan* **c76 § h60 §**

FLE

FLEETWOOD JACK (IRE) 7 ch.g. Fleetwood (IRE) – Titian Flame (IRE) (Titus Livius (FR)) [2017/18 h20.4g h20g h16g⁴ h24d^F h24g h19.6g^pu c20s^pu Oct 29] first foal: dam (h96§), 19f/2½m hurdle winner (stayed 3m), also 1m winner on Flat: modest form over hurdles: pulled up in maiden on chasing debut: should be suited by 2½m: often in headgear. *Miss Katy Brown, Ireland*   c–
h94

FLEMCARA (IRE) 6 b.g. Flemensfirth (USA) – Cara Mara (IRE) (Saddlers' Hall (IRE)) [2017/18 h103, b65: h21.4g⁵ h20s* h21.6v* h23.6v* h23.4v h21.1s Mar 14] sturdy gelding: runner-up in Irish point: fairly useful handicap hurdler: won at Worcester (novice) in November, Exeter in December and Chepstow in January: stays 3m: best form on soft/heavy going: wears tongue tie. *Emma Lavelle*   h127

FLEMENSKILL (IRE) 6 b.g. Flemensfirth (USA) – Nivalf (Gildoran) [2017/18 b97: h20s h20.5v h20.5v³ ab18d⁴ Mar 5] fairly useful form in bumpers: modest form over hurdles: best effort when third in novice at Plumpton in January: in hood last 3 starts: front runner/races prominently: temperament under suspicion. *Warren Greatrex*   h96

FLEMENS STORY (IRE) 7 b.g. Flemensfirth (USA) – Amelia Earhart (IRE) (Be My Native (USA)) [2017/18 h16.2g⁴ h22.7g³ Nov 11] £22,000 6-y-o: sturdy gelding: sixth foal: half-brother to modest hurcler Lady Wright (2½m winner, by King's Theatre) and a winning pointer by Bob Back: dam, fair 2½m-3m hurdle/chase winner, sister to high-class hurdler (2m-2¼m winner) Colonel Yeager: off mark in Irish points at fourth attempt: fair form over hurdles: better effort when fourth in maiden at Kelso in October. *Donald McCain*   h100

FLEMENSTRIX (IRE) 5 b.g. Flemensfirth (USA) – Laurens Trix (IRE) (Presenting) [2017/18 b16v⁴ Feb 2] €24,000 3-y-o: second foal: dam unraced sister to useful chaser (stayed 3¼m) A Good Skin and half-sister to Champion Bumper winner/smart hurdler (stayed 3m) Cousin Vinny: tailed off in bumper. *Charlie Longsdon*   b–

FLEMERINA (IRE) 9 b.m. Flemensfirth (USA) – Ballerina Laura (IRE) (Riot Helmet) [2017/18 h94: h17s⁴ h19.9g⁴ h24g h24.1s³ c19.3s³ c19.2s² c21.3v² h23.1v c24.2d^F Apr 23] modest handicap hurdler: similar form over fences: stayed 3m: acted on heavy going: temperamental: dead. *Sue Smith*   c94 §
h92 §

FLEMINATOR 6 b.m. Flemensfirth (USA) – Misleain (IRE) (Un Desperado (FR)) [2017/18 b–: b17s h16.2s^pu Nov 10] lengthy mare: no form: dead. *Gillian Boanas*   h–
b–

FLEMINPORT (IRE) 5 b.g. Flemensfirth (USA) – Geek Chic (IRE) (Saffron Walden (FR)) [2017/18 h16d³ h19.9d h21.7s* h19.5v* h19.9v⁴ Mar 17] £140,000 4-y-o: first foal: dam, winning pointer, closely related to useful hurdler/smart chaser (stayed 3m) Tumbling Dice: runner-up on completed start in Irish points: fairly useful form over hurdles: won maiden at Hereford in January and novice at Lingfield in February: will be suited by 3m: best form on soft/heavy going: remains with potential. *Jonjo O'Neill*   h124 p

FLETCHERS FLYER (IRE) 10 b.g. Winged Love (IRE) – Crystal Chord (IRE) (Accordion) [2017/18 c144, h–: c25.1s^pu c28.8d c24.2v^pu c30s³ Apr 28] good-topped gelding: winning hurdler: fairly useful handicap chaser nowadays: third at Punchestown in April: stays 3¼m: acts on heavy going: in cheekpieces last 3 starts: wears tongue tie: front runner/races prominently, tends to find little. *Harry Fry*   c124
h–

FLEUR DU POMMIER 5 br.m. Apple Tree (FR) – Jersey Countess (IRE) (Supreme Leader) [2017/18 b–: b17d b15.7d⁵ h15.8s⁴ h16v^pu h15.8d h15.8d Apr 24] modest form in bumpers: poor form over hurdles: likely to stay 2½m. *G. C. Maundrell*   h70
b82

FLEUR DU WELD 10 ch.m. Weld – Midnight Walker (Exodal (USA)) [2017/18 h87: h21.6g² May 10] modest form over hurdles: stays 2¾m: acts on good to firm going: in tongue tie last 3 starts. *Gail Haywood*   h88

FLICHITY (IRE) 13 br.g. Turtle Island (IRE) – Chancy Gal (Al Sirat) [2017/18 c–§, h–§: c16d c22.5d⁴ c24s⁶ c19.2g⁵ Nov 9] leggy gelding: winning hurdler/chaser, of little account nowadays: has worn headgear, including last 5 starts: ungenuine. *John Cornwall*   c– §
h– §

FLIC OU VOYOU (FR) 4 b.g. Kapgarde (FR) – Hillflower (FR) (Sabrehill (USA)) [2017/18 b13.7g⁴ Apr 20] 13/8, fourth in bumper at Fontwell (16½ lengths behind Kalinihta). *Paul Nicholls*   b69

FLIGHT TO MILAN (IRE) 5 b.g. Milan – Kigali (IRE) (Torus) [2017/18 h19.7g⁶ h16.5s h16.5v³ h16.5v² h16.5s⁵ Mar 26] €40,000 3-y-o: brother to useful hurdler/chaser Barrakilla (19f/2½m winner) and half-brother to 3 winners, including smart hurdler/high-class chaser China Rock (2¼m-25f winner, by Presenting): dam (b68), ran twice in bumpers, out of half-sister to Grand National second Zongalero and to dam of Cheltenham Gold Cup winner Garrison Savannah: fair form over hurdles: raced around 2m since debut: best form on heavy going. *Evan Williams*   h107

FLU

FLIGHT TO NOWHERE 6 ch.m. Aeroplane – River Beauty (Exit To Nowhere (USA)) h94
[2017/18 h84, b–: h16d⁴ h15.8g h15.8v^F h16.5s⁴ h15.9v h16s* h16.2v⁴ h16.3d⁶ Apr 22]
modest handicap hurdler: won at Chepstow in March: raced only at 2m: acts on soft going:
has worn hood: wears tongue tie. *Richard Price*

FLIGHTY FILIA (IRE) 6 gr.m. Raven's Pass (USA) – Coventina (IRE) (Daylami h88
(IRE)) [2017/18 h88: h21.6g h21.6m⁴ h21.6g^pu h18.5s^pu Apr 23] workmanlike mare:
modest maiden hurdler: stays 2¾m: acts on good to firm going. *Jimmy Frost*

FLINTHAM 9 b.g. Kayf Tara – Plaid Maid (IRE) (Executive Perk) [2017/18 c139, h–: c128
c24.2v² c24s⁵ c23.6s² Feb 24] sturdy gelding, has had breathing operation: useful hurdler: h–
useful maiden chaser: second in novice at Exeter in November: stays 3¼m: acts on heavy
going: wears headgear: tried in tongue tie: front runner. *Mark Bradstock*

FLOBURY 10 b.m. Overbury (IRE) – Miss Flora (Alflora (IRE)) [2017/18 h90: h19.9d⁶ h54
h23.1s^pu Dec 2] smallish mare: modest handicap hurdler, well below form in 2017/18:
stays 23f: acts on soft going: held up. *Barry Leavy*

FLOKI 4 b.g. Kalanisi (IRE) – La Dame Brune (FR) (Mansonnien (FR)) [2017/18 b16d b86 p
Apr 26] rangy gelding: half-brother to fair 21f hurdle winners Cabaret Queen (by King's
Theatre) and Internal Transfer (by Kayf Tara), latter also winning pointer: dam (h113),
unreliable 2½m/21f hurdle winner, half-sister to fairly useful hurdler/useful chaser (2m-21f
winner) Nikos Eros: 16/1, better than result when eighth in bumper at Warwick (6¼
lengths behind Emitom), not clear run home turn: capable of better. *Dan Skelton*

FLORAL BOUQUET 5 bl.m. Fair Mix (IRE) – Florarossa (Alflora (IRE)) [2017/18 b83: h112
h15.7g³ h18.5v⁶ h15.8d* h16.2s* Apr 27] lengthy mare: has had breathing operation: fair
form over hurdles: in tongue tie, won mares novices at Ludlow and Perth in April: front
runner/races prominently. *Jamie Snowden*

FLORAL FANTASY (IRE) 8 b.m. Flemensfirth (USA) – Fantastic Fleur (GER) c84
(Winged Love (IRE)) [2017/18 c19.5g⁶ c25.3s^pu c20g^pu Sep 13] second foal: dam (h91), h–
2m hurdle winner, half-sister to very smart hurdler/chaser (stayed 21f) Foreman: point
winner: fairly useful hurdler: won mares handicap at Downpatrick in 2016/17: modest
maiden chaser: left Enda Bolger after second start: stays 2¼m: acts on heavy going: tried
in visor: often races in rear. *Jonjo O'Neill*

FLORAL QUEEN 5 b.m. Emperor Fountain – Florentino (Efisio) [2017/18 b–: b15.7d b–
b13.7v⁶ Jan 21] no form in bumpers. *Neil Mulholland*

FLORAMOSS 7 b.m. Alflora (IRE) – Brackenmoss (IRE) (Supreme Leader) [2017/18 h99
h101, b76: h19.9g h23.3v⁴ h19.7v⁴ h19v³ h25.3s³ h24.1d³ h17v⁴ Apr 17] fair maiden
hurdler: stays 25f: acts on heavy going. *Gillian Boanas*

FLORESCO (GER) 8 ch.g. Santiago (GER) – Fiori (GER) (Chief Singer) [2017/18 c98 p
h122: h18.5m⁵ c16g⁴ h19s Dec 14] compact gelding: fairly useful hurdler, below form in h109
2017/18: 12/1, fourth in novice handicap at Ludlow (19½ lengths behind Darebin) on
chasing debut: stays 2¼m: acts on heavy going: in headgear last 5 starts: usually wears
tongue tie: entitled to do better as a chaser. *Richard Woollacott*

FLORIDA CALLING (IRE) 9 ch.g. Presenting – Miami Nights (GER) (Tertullian c104
(USA)), c–, h–: c24g² c23.8m² c22.6m⁴ c23.6g⁶ Oct 17] lengthy gelding: Irish h–
point winner: lightly-raced hurdler: fair maiden chaser: stays 3m: acts on good to firm
going: tried in cheekpieces: front runner/races prominently. *Tom George*

FLORRIE FORBES 5 g.g. Gold Well – Miss Orphan (FR) (Round Sovereign (FR)) h126
[2017/18 h19.7s³ h20.5s⁴ h23.3v³ h24.1v³ h20.6v* h22v² Apr 14] £31,000 3-y-o, £28,000
4-y-o: half-brother to fair hurdler Forest Silver (2½m winner, by Silver Patriarch), stayed
3m: dam (h123), 2m/17f hurdle winner, also 10.5f winner on Flat: runner-up in Irish point:
fairly useful form over hurdles: won novice at Market Rasen in March: second in novice
handicap at Newcastle in April: stays 3m: raced only on soft/heavy going. *Alex Hales*

FLO'SBOY SAM 5 b.g. Tobougg (IRE) – Madam Flora (Alflora (IRE)) [2017/18 h–, b–: h92 §
h15.9d⁴ h15.9d h19s^pu h19v^vr h15.3v^pu Apr 9] modest form over hurdles: best effort at 2m:
tried in blinkers: one to leave alone (has refused to race). *Colin Tizzard*

FLOW WITH EVE 9 b.m. With The Flow (USA) – Vercheny (Petoski) [2017/18 h92: h94
h20v² h16.6d⁶ h20.7s Mar 14] sturdy mare: modest maiden hurdler: stays 2½m: acts on
heavy going: has worn headgear, including last 2 starts: in tongue tie last 3 starts: usually
races in rear. *Olly Murphy*

FLUGZEUG 10 gr.g. Silver Patriarch (IRE) – Telmar Flyer (Neltino) [2017/18 c79, h85: c79
c25.5g* c25.7g³ c25.5d^pu c25.8d^pu h25.8g h25.8g h25s^pu c26v^pu Mar 17] modest hurdler at h–
best, no form in 2017/18: poor handicap chaser: won at Fontwell in May: stays 3¼m: acts
on good to firm and heavy going: wears cheekpieces. *Seamus Mullins*

323

FLY

FLY CAMP (IRE) 8 gr.g. Westerner – Pearlsforthegirls (Cloudings (IRE)) [2017/18 h126: h24s h25s^F Jan 13] lengthy gelding: won completed start in Irish points: fairly useful hurdler at best, no form in 2017/18: stays 2½m: acts on soft going. *Nicky Henderson* — h–

FLYCORN (IRE) 12 b.g. Winged Love (IRE) – Scathach (IRE) (Nestor) [2017/18 c21.2g^5 c21.2s^5 c20.1v^{ro} c20s Sep 23] medium-sized gelding: useful hurdler at best: poor form over fences: stays 21f: acts on good to firm and heavy going: has worn tongue tie. *Stuart Crawford, Ireland* — c70 h–

FLY DU CHARMIL (FR) 7 b.g. Saint des Saints (FR) – Famous Member (FR) (Peintre Celebre (USA)) [2017/18 h16.3d^4 h21s^{pu} h15.8v* h19.5s^{pu} Mar 22] sturdy gelding: point winner: fair handicap hurdler: won at Ffos Las in February: should be suited by further than 2m: acts on heavy going: in cheekpieces last 2 starts. *Warren Greatrex* — h107

FLY HOME HARRY 9 b.g. Sir Harry Lewis (USA) – Fly Home (Skyliner) [2017/18 c100, h–: c21.6g^2 c23.8g* c22.7m^{pu} c23.6s* c25.5s c29.2g^{pu} Apr 26] maiden hurdler: fair handicap chaser: won at Ludlow in October and Huntingdon in January: stays 3m: acts on soft going: usually in cheekpieces: wears tongue tie: front runner/races prominently: temperament under suspicion. *Charlie Longsdon* — c112 h–

FLYING ANGEL (IRE) 7 gr.g. Arcadio (GER) – Gypsy Kelly (IRE) (Roselier (FR)) [2017/18 c154, h–: c21g^5 c21d^4 c25v^3 c24s c21.1s Apr 13] good-topped gelding: has had breathing operation: winning hurdler: smart chaser: third in Many Clouds Chase at Aintree (15 lengths behind Definitly Red) in December: best up to 25f: acts on heavy going: tried in tongue tie: inconsistent. *Nigel Twiston-Davies* — c152 h–

FLYING AWAY 4 b.g. Arvico (FR) – Tyre Hill Lilly (Jupiter Island) [2017/18 b16v Apr 14] well beaten in bumper. *Susan Gardner* — b–

FLYING EAGLE (IRE) 10 b.g. Oscar (IRE) – Fille d'Argent (IRE) (Desert Style (IRE)) [2017/18 c21.4g^4 c21.2s* c20.1s^{pu} c21.2d* c20d c19.4s^3 c21.1s^{ur} Apr 13] lengthy, good sort: winning hurdler: fairly useful chaser: won maiden at Cartmel in July and novice there in August: stays 3m: acts on good to firm and heavy going: usually wears headgear: has worn tongue tie, including final start: temperamental. *Peter Bowen* — c121 § h–

FLYING FEATHERS (IRE) 5 b.m. Westerner – Miss Molly Malone (IRE) (Accordion) [2017/18 b15.7g Apr 20] €4,200 3-y-o: second foal: dam (b84), third in bumper on only start, closely related to fairly useful hurdler/chaser Nicolas Chauvin (2m winner): last in bumper. *Louise Allan* — b–

FLYING JACK 8 b.g. Rob Roy (USA) – Milladella (FR) (Nureyev (USA)) [2017/18 h94: h16.2g^6 c19.3g^6 c24.2g^6 c20.1g^{ro} h23.3g^2 h20.1d* h20.1d^{ur} c19.3g^4 c24.2s^F Nov 10] long-backed gelding: modest hurdler: won handicap at Hexham in August: fair form over fences: stays 3m: acts on good to heavy going: tried in cheekpieces/tongue tie. *Maurice Barnes* — c105 h98

FLYING TIGER (IRE) 5 bl.g. Soldier of Fortune (IRE) – Ma Preference (FR) (American Post) [2017/18 h133: h15.3s^3 h16.4v^3 h16.6d^4 h15.3s^4 h16.8v h16g Apr 21] good-topped gelding: useful handicap hurdler: third in Elite Hurdle at Wincanton (4¾ lengths behind London Prize) in November and Fighting Fifth Hurdle at Newcastle (4½ lengths behind Buveur d'Air) in December: raced around 2m: acts on heavy going: held up. *Nick Williams* — h137

FLYING VERSE 6 b.g. Yeats (IRE) – Flight Sequence (Polar Falcon (USA)) [2017/18 b15.8m^5 b16g^4 h16.3m^3 h19.7g h16.5s h20.8s h19.3d^5 h19.7s^6 Mar 27] half-brother to several winners, including useful hurdler/chaser Roman Flight (2m-21f winner, by Antonius Pius): dam 1¼m winner: modest form in bumpers: poor form over hurdles: in cheekpieces last 2 starts: often races in rear. *David Dennis* — h83 b79

FLYNNVINCIBLE 7 b.g. Tobougg (IRE) – Shiny Thing (USA) (Lear Fan (USA)) [2017/18 h20s h16v^3 h15.7s^4 Feb 8] second foal: dam (h104), 2m hurdle winner (stayed 19f), also 1¼m winner on Flat: modest form over hurdles: left Edward Stanners after first start: best effort at 2m: acts on heavy going: usually races towards rear. *Olly Murphy* — h99

FLY RORY FLY (IRE) 6 b.g. Milan – Thousand Wings (GER) (Winged Love (IRE)) [2017/18 h21.8g* h24.8d^3 c23.6s^F c25.1g^2 c22.5d c20.1s^4 Apr 26] €115,000 3-y-o: fifth foal: closely related to bumper/modest 2m hurdle winner Oscar Wings (by Oscar), stayed 2½m: dam, German 1½m winner, sister to fairly useful hurdler (stayed 3m) True Lover: fair form over hurdles: won maiden at Downpatrick in May: fair useful form over fences: second in maiden at Wexford in July: left Noel Meade after fifth start: stays 25f: acts on heavy going: usually in blinkers: has worn tongue tie, including final start. *N. W. Alexander* — c121 h104

FOO

FLY VINNIE (IRE) 9 b.g. Vinnie Roe (IRE) – Great Days (IRE) (Magical Strike (USA)) [2017/18 h–: h23.3g^{pu} h23.8m* h24.6s h23.8d Jan 1] maiden Irish pointer: fairly useful handicap hurdler: won at Musselburgh in November: left Sandy Thomson after first start: stays 3m: acts on soft and good to firm going: front runner/races prominently. *Alistair Whillans* **h120**

FLY WEST (IRE) 10 b.g. Westerner – Flying Nora (IRE) (Topanoora) [2017/18 c26d^3 c23v^F Apr 12] multiple point winner: fair form in hunter chases: in hood last 2 starts. *E. Walker* **c106**

FOCACCIA (IRE) 7 b.g. Milan – Dantes Term (IRE) (Phardante (FR)) [2017/18 h108: h16g^3 h20g^2 h15.8d^2 h20g h16.7d* h18.6s Dec 26] fair handicap hurdler: won at Market Rasen (conditional) in December: stayed 2½m: acted on good to firm and good to soft going: in cheekpieces/tongue tie last 3 starts: dead. *Dan Skelton* **h112**

FOLLOWMYBUTTONS (IRE) 8 br.g. Kalanisi (IRE) – Clondalee (IRE) (Presenting) [2017/18 c–, h101: c21.7m^{pu} May 4] fairly useful hurdler: no form over fences: stays 19f: in tongue tie last 5 starts. *David Arbuthnot* **c–** **h–**

FOLLOW THE BEAR (IRE) 6 b.g. King's Theatre (IRE) – Mrs Dempsey (IRE) (Presenting) [2017/18 h115: h24.5m* h20.3g^2 h20g^3 h23.1v^4 Jan 4] good-topped gelding: point winner: fairly useful hurdler: won novice at Kempton in May: third in novice handicap at Worcester in October: stays 3m: acts on soft and good to firm going: often leads. *Nicky Henderson* **h124**

FOLLOW THE SWALLOW (IRE) 10 b.g. Dr Massini (IRE) – Old Chapel (IRE) (Royal Fountain) [2017/18 c116x, h54: c23g^{pu} c20.3s c18.9s^{pu} Jan 16] strong, close-coupled gelding: well held sole outing over hurdles: fairly useful chaser at best, no form in 2017/18: in visor/tongue tie last 2 starts: often races in rear: often let down by jumping. *Graeme McPherson* **c– x** **h–**

FOLLY BERGERE (IRE) 5 ch.m. Champs Elysees – Rainbow Queen (FR) (Spectrum (IRE)) [2017/18 h84p: h20.7d^6 Mar 26] fairly useful on Flat, stays 2m: fair form over hurdles: sixth in mares novice at Huntingdon on sole outing in 2017/18: will stay 2¾m+. *James Eustace* **h102**

FOLSOM BLUE (IRE) 11 b.g. Old Vic – Spirit Leader (IRE) (Supreme Leader) [2017/18 c139§, h95: h24v* h22.6v^4 h23.4v^4 c28.7v^4 c29v^4 h24d Apr 26] sturdy gelding: useful handicap hurdler: smart handicap chaser: won at Clonmel in September (Irish National Principle), promoted fourth in Irish Grand National Chase at Fairyhouse (1½ lengths behind General Principle) in April: stays 29f: acts on heavy going: has worn headgear, including last 4 starts: wears tongue tie: often races prominently. *Gordon Elliott, Ireland* **c148** **h129**

FONTSANTA (IRE) 5 b.g. Flemensfirth (USA) – Day's Over (Overbury (IRE)) [2017/18 b13.7v* b16.8s^4 Feb 23] €110,000 3-y-o: first foal: dam (h71) maiden half-sister to useful hurdler (2m-2¼m winner) Dusky Lord out of sister to high-class chaser up to 2½m Deep Sensation: fair form in bumpers: won at Fontwell in January: wears hood. *Emma Lavelle* **b94**

FOOL TO CRY (IRE) 5 ch.m. Fast Company (IRE) – Islandagore (IRE) (Indian Ridge) [2017/18 h107: h16g^5 h19g^2 h21.1g h15.8d^3 h15.7s^4 Dec 17] small mare: fair handicap hurdler: stays 19f: acts on good to firm and good to soft going. *Johnny Farrelly* **h114**

FOOTPAD (FR) 6 b.g. Creachadoir (IRE) – Willamina (IRE) (Sadler's Wells (USA)) [2017/18 h159: c17v* c17d* c17s* c15.9s* c16d* Apr 26] **c174 p** **h–**

'The four horses of the apocalypse' is becoming almost an annual bookmakers' promotion on the opening day of the Cheltenham Festival. It is three years since Annie Power's spectacular last-flight fall in the David Nicholson Mares' Hurdle saved 'the old enemy' from a payout of tens of millions of pounds after short-priced Willie Mullins-trained favourites had won the Supreme Novices' Hurdle, the Arkle and the Champion Hurdle. On that occasion, Ladbrokes claimed 'It would have been worse than Dettori Day in 1996 [the 'Magnificent Seven' at Ascot] if Annie Power hadn't come unstuck.' A similar story was played out the following year when Mullins again had the favourites for the same opening-day events (three of the four won, though the accumulator went down in the very first race when Min was beaten by Altior). Ladbrokes took things a step further by warning the London Stock Market, the week before the latest Festival, that it was bracing itself for 'a monstrous payout' as punters waded into a four-horse accumulator on favourites Getabird, Footpad, Buveur d'Air and Apple's Jade in the same four races.

325

*Racing Post Novices' Chase, Leopardstown—
an imperious display by Footpad as he saunters clear of Any Second Now*

'We've had our fair share of disastrous Tuesdays at the Festival and this year could be the biggest one yet,' said a spokesperson. In the face of the warning, incidentally, Ladbrokes shares went up!

Stock market investors proved better judges than the Cheltenham racegoers on this occasion, with those punters banking on the Mullins-trained Getabird in the opening Supreme Novices' Hurdle knowing their fate some way from home. The Gordon Elliott-trained 'banker' Apple's Jade was also beaten—at 2/1-on—in the Mares' Hurdle but, in the two other races, Footpad and reigning champion Buveur d'Air landed the odds in the Arkle and the Champion Hurdle respectively. Footpad's victory extended his unbeaten run over fences to four since being switched from hurdling and, although the Arkle attracted the smallest field in its history, he produced a top-class performance, on a par with those of Un de Sceaux, Douvan and Altior in winning the race in recent years. Footpad made it five in a row when romping home in the Ryanair Novices' Chase at the Punchestown Festival and, still only six, has time on his side (in more ways than one, as will be revealed).

The Arkle was Footpad's third appearance at the Cheltenham Festival, the first of them coming when he was third in the Triumph Hurdle in his first season with Willie Mullins, following his acquisition from France after finishing second in a useful conditions hurdle for three-year-olds at Auteuil for Robert Collet. Footpad won France's top juvenile event, the Prix Alain du Breil at Auteuil, for Mullins after the end of that first season (the second of two wins in France for him that summer) and he was also beaten in a photo for the Prix Renaud du Vivier over the same course and distance on his return from a short summer break. The Renaud du Vivier was the first of five successive Grade 1 races which Footpad contested as he developed into a very smart hurdler in his second season. He didn't manage to win one, but he finished in the frame in the Irish Champion Hurdle, the Champion Hurdle at Cheltenham and the Champion Stayers' Hurdle at Punchestown on his last three outings. Footpad ran as if barely getting the three miles at Punchestown and he has been kept at around two miles over fences so far (though connections are said to be considering stepping him up in trip again in the next season).

Six of the eleven runners in the 2017 Champion Hurdle—a much higher proportion than usual—went on to win over fences in the latest season and Footpad proved easily the best of them, turning the tables convincingly on the Irish Champion Hurdle winner and Champion Hurdle third Petit Mouchoir on each of the three occasions that they met over fences. The first of those meetings came in the Frank Ward Solicitors Arkle Novices' Chase which formed part of the newly-instituted two-day Dublin Racing Festival at Leopardstown in early-February (the Arkle was the principal supporting race for the Champion Hurdle on the first day, along with a third Grade 1 in the newly-promoted Golden Cygnet Novices' Hurdle, branded as the Nathaniel Lacy & Partners Solicitors Novices' Hurdle). Footpad was already a Grade 1 winner over fences, having followed a scintillating display in a maiden chase at Navan in November with an equally impressive win in the Racing Post Novices' Chase at Leopardstown's Christmas meeting. Footpad's jumping was superb in both those races, which he won by a double-figure margin, being in complete command before the final fence on each occasion. Footpad's success in the Racing Post Novices' Chase was the third in a row in the race for his trainer, following Douvan in 2015 and Min in 2016, and Footpad lined up for the Arkle at Leopardstown already a hot favourite in the ante-post market for the Arkle at Cheltenham. He was odds-on for Cheltenham with nearly all bookmakers after again jumping like an old hand and winning very smoothly by five lengths and nineteen lengths from Petit Mouchoir and the Racing Post Novices' Chase runner-up Any Second Now.

    The fields for the Arkle Trophy (sponsored for the seventh year by the Racing Post) have shrunk in recent times, coinciding with the inauguration of the Golden Miller Novices' Chase (over the intermediate distance of two and a half miles). The Golden Miller was introduced at the 2011 Festival and fast-tracked to Grade 1 after just three years. Its introduction has undoubtedly affected the strength in depth of the Arkle which has had only one double-figure field in its last seven runnings. The previous smallest field for the Arkle, the six which lined up in 2012, owed something to the reputation that odds-on Sprinter Sacre had already established by then. It could perhaps also be said that the latest field of just five was at least, in part, a measure of Footpad's reputation, but it must be a cause for worry that he beat the smallest field for a race at the Festival for more than thirty years (Half Free beat three opponents in 1987 in the Cathcart Challenge Cup, a race discontinued after 2004). Petit Mouchoir was again among Footpad's opponents at Cheltenham, the pair up against a home-trained trio headed by the very smart, bold-jumping front runner Saint Calvados who had won all three of his races over fences, the most recent of them the Kingmaker Novices' Chase at Warwick where he had won by twenty-two lengths from Diego du Charmil.

    The unusually testing going for the Festival seemed sure to suit the proven Saint Calvados who started 11/4 second favourite behind Footpad, who was sent off at 6/5-on. An overly-strong gallop, as Saint Calvados and Petit Mouchoir battled it out from an early stage, probably set up the race for Footpad. Petit Mouchoir and Saint Calvados (with whom something may have been amiss) cut each other's throats and the unflappable Ruby Walsh ('I thought they were going quick enough'), who had just returned from four months on the sidelines with a broken leg, eventually settled

Frank Ward Solicitors Arkle Novices' Chase, Leopardstown—a minor scare at the last for Footpad who has already taken the measure of the grey Petit Mouchoir

*Racing Post Arkle Challenge Trophy Novices' Chase, Cheltenham—
Petit Mouchoir again has to settle for minor honours, losing second to Brain Power (left) late on as
Footpad storms clear under Ruby Walsh from two out*

Footpad well back from the leading pair who had an advantage of fifteen to twenty lengths over him for much of the race. Footpad made a bad mistake at the sixth of the thirteen fences but, after a momentary scare for his supporters, he was soon back on the bridle and began to make inroads into the deficit before the fourth last. Close up three out and in front before the second last, Footpad stayed on strongly in the home straight to win by fourteen lengths from 14/1-shot Brain Power who picked up the pieces to finish second, three quarters of a length ahead of the tiring Petit Mouchoir who had been clear of the field four out. Saint Calvados had lost touch with Petit Mouchoir before that and trailed home thirty-eight lengths behind Petit Mouchoir, beating only 66/1 outsider Robinshill who was always behind.

Ruby Walsh was aboard Footpad in a race for the first time since the combination's fourth behind Buveur d'Air in the previous season's Champion Hurdle. Walsh excelled on Footpad in the Arkle and went on to complete a double on the day when partnering Benie des Dieux to win the Mares' Hurdle, a success that gave him his fifty-eighth Cheltenham Festival winner. Unfortunately, Walsh's return to action was short-lived as he aggravated his leg fracture in a fall in the following day's RSA Chase and didn't ride again for the rest of the season. Willie Mullins, the trainer of Benie des Dieux as well as Footpad, went on to land a first-day treble when Rathvinden (ridden by Mr Patrick Mullins) won the National Hunt Chase. There were seventeen Irish-trained winners at the latest Cheltenham Festival (two fewer than the record set the previous year) and, although Willie Mullins couldn't match the eight-winner haul of Gordon Elliott, his own total of seven took him to sixty-one winners at the Festival over the years and enabled him to supplant Nicky Henderson (who now has sixty) as the leading trainer in Festival history.

Footpad's spectacular performance in the Arkle was more than backed up by the clock. Thanks to changes by the British Horseracing Authority to the ways race distances are measured, and a wholesale remeasuring of courses—following an investigation by Timeform in the 2014/15 season which revealed some alarming inaccuracies—it has become possible for accurate timefigures to be returned from all jumps courses in Britain (and those courses in Ireland whose historical race times and distances have stood up to close scrutiny). Timeform timefigures for the jumpers were published for the first time in the latest season, although the project had been in the planning for some time, held back also because exact race distances

FOO

were not available either (the BHA now stipulates that additional or reduced yardage, from that which has been advertised, must be made public so that the exact race distance is known). As on the Flat, the use of Timeform standard times, for which the mathematics is much more complex than simply using record times or averaging the best ten times from the last five years, for example, enables the merit of times at the same distance, at vastly different tracks, to be compared. Footpad recorded a timefigure equivalent to a timerating of 179 in winning the Arkle, a time performance bettered over the season only by Altior when he won the Queen Mother Champion Chase. A timefigure is necessarily dictated to some degree by the pace of a race and, if the early gallop is not what it should have been, the resulting timefigure will be slow. The strength of 'time', as a guide to true merit, is that a very fast time performance establishes a horse without question as a good horse. A time performance can sometimes reveal exceptional merit before it can be recognised by other means and, with Footpad, his timefigure reveals that he is a better horse than he can be rated on the basis of comparative form—better, in all probability, than his Timeform rating, which makes him an extremely exciting prospect. Saint Calvados is another 'fast-timer' to watch out for, despite his eclipse in the Arkle; he recorded a timerating of 165 when winning the Kingmaker at Warwick, some way in advance of his form rating. There is more about the practical value and use of timefigures in the essay on Min.

Footpad's fifth victory over fences came in the Ryanair Novices' Chase at the Punchestown Festival, after he had been earmarked at first, at the behest of his owners, for the Maghull Novices' Chase at Aintree. An unsatisfactory scope kept him out of the Maghull, in which Diego du Charmil upset the odds laid on Petit Mouchoir. Petit Mouchoir went on to meet Footpad again at Punchestown but with Petit Mouchoir running below his best—possibly feeling the effects of his race in the Maghull—Footpad wasn't extended to maintain his unbeaten record over fences. He made all, again jumping superbly, and won with plenty in hand by twelve lengths from British-trained 25/1-shot Optimus Prime.

Ryanair Novices' Chase, Punchestown—Daryl Jacob does the steering this time as Footpad rounds off a superb novice campaign with another very fluent display

Mr Simon Munir & Mr Isaac Souede's "Footpad"

Footpad (FR) (b.g. 2012)	Creachadoir (IRE) (b 2004)	King's Best (b 1997)	Kingmambo
			Allegretta
		Sadima (b 1998)	Sadler's Wells
			Anima
	Willamina (IRE) (b 1999)	Sadler's Wells (b 1981)	Northern Dancer
			Fairy Bridge
		Animatrice (b 1985)	Alleged
			Alexandrie

Footpad, a good-topped gelding, is closely related to the fairly useful French seventeen-furlong hurdle/chase winner Wild Mania (by Footpad's grandsire King's Best) and a half-brother to three other winners, the best of whom was Organisateur (by Highest Honor), a very smart hurdler at up to twenty-one furlongs for Paul Nicholls before going on to perform with credit over hurdles and in races over timber in the United States. Footpad is by the good miler Creachadoir, who was also represented by the useful juvenile hurdler Mitchouka in the latest season. Creachadoir initially stood under the Darley banner at Haras du Logis in Normandy, nearby his half-brother Youmzain who finished second in three consecutive Prix de l'Arcs and was probably part of the cause of Creachadoir suffering a lack of patronage (Footpad is one of thirty-three foals in his second crop, while Mitchouka is one of only fourteen in his fourth). Creachadoir has been at Haras de Lonray in recent seasons and stood at €3,500 in 2018. He himself is out of a Sadler's Wells mare, and Footpad's dam Willamina, a winner in France at eleven and a half furlongs and also a sister to the late Saddler Maker (sire of such as Bristol de Mai and Apple's Jade), is herself a daughter of Sadler's Wells. Willamina hails from the Wertheimer studs and is from the same family as the now-deceased Poliglote (a champion sire in France both on the Flat and several times over jumps) who was by Sadler's Wells out of Alexandrine, Footpad's great grandam. Willamina was weeded out of the Wertheimer studs at the Deauville Sales in December 2007 when Robert Collet bought her for €145,000. Footpad is the last of seven foals produced by Willamina whose better performers on the racecourse have all been jumpers, who also include Wanaba (by Anabaa) whose six wins included the Prix General de Rougemont, a listed handicap over hurdles at Auteuil (where he was also third in the Group 2 Prix Amadou).

Footpad's achievements have thrust his sire and his distaff family into the limelight and he seems sure to enhance the reputation of both even further. A clash between him and Altior over two miles would be worth going a long way to see, but, with Altior looking increasingly as if a step up in trip might suit him and Footpad's connections reportedly mulling over stepping him up in trip (connections have even talked of him as a possible Gold Cup horse), that particular meeting seems to be in the lap of the gods. Footpad has shown that he stays at least nineteen furlongs and that he acts on heavy going (though he doesn't need the mud). Tried in a hood earlier in his career, he is a strong traveller in his races and usually races prominently or makes the running. It bears repeating that he is a splendid jumper of fences and will almost certainly go on to even better things in that sphere, whatever campaign is mapped out for him. *W. P. Mullins, Ireland*

FORBIDDING (USA) 5 ch.g. Kitten's Joy (USA) – La Coruna (USA) (Thunder Gulch (USA)) [2017/18 b81: h17g⁵ May 19] modest form in bumpers: tailed off in novice on hurdling debut. *George Charlton* h–

FOR CARMEL (IRE) 8 b.g. Mr Dinos (IRE) – Bobalena (IRE) (Bob Back (USA)) [2017/18 h19.5d h23.6v² c23.5s³ c26v² c23.5v² h23.1s^pu c23.6s c21s* Apr 23] point winner: modest maiden hurdler: fair form over fences: won handicap at Newton Abbot in April: stays 3¼m: acts on heavy going: wears tongue tie: usually races nearer last than first (disputed lead for win). *Paul Henderson* c104 h95

FOREST BIHAN (FR) 7 ch.g. Forestier (FR) – Katell Bihan (FR) (Funny Baby (FR)) [2017/18 c151, h124: c17.1d* c17.5v^pu c16s³ c16.4s⁴ ab16.3g* c16.5g⁶ Apr 21] good-topped gelding: won jumpers bumper at Newcastle in March: winning hurdler: smart handicap chaser: won at Kelso (by 1¾ lengths from Simply Ned) in October: third in Desert Orchid Chase at Kempton (27 lengths behind Politologue) in December: stays 19f: acts on heavy going: has worn headgear, including last 2 starts. *Brian Ellison* c154 h–

FOREST DES AIGLES (FR) 7 b.g. Balko (FR) – Rose des Aigles (FR) (Le Nain Jaune (FR)) [2017/18 c116, h–: c20.1s* c20s* c24.1v* c25.6v^pu Jan 20] winning hurdler: useful handicap chaser: won at Hexham in October, and Carlisle and Bangor in December: stays 3m: best form on soft/heavy going: wears tongue tie: usually travels strongly. *Lucinda Russell* c132 h–

FOREST FUSION (IRE) 4 b.g. Flemensfirth (USA) – Qui Plus Est (FR) (Dark Moondancer) [2017/18 b15.7s Feb 12] 13/2, well held in maiden bumper. *Tim Easterby* b–

FOREVER FIELD (IRE) 8 b.g. Beneficial – Sarahs Reprive (IRE) (Yashgan) [2017/18 h132: c20.5m² c21.7g² c20g* c21.6m² c23.8m c20.5d Nov 27] useful hurdler: useful form over fences: won novice at Worcester in June: stays 21f: acts on good to firm going. *Nicky Henderson* c131 h–

FOREVER GOLD (IRE) 11 b.g. Gold Well – Clonbrook Lass (IRE) (Lord Americo) [2017/18 c135, h126: h20d^F c29s² c24.5d^ur c28.7v^pu c29v³ c30s^ur Apr 28] fairly useful handicap hurdler, fell on return in 2017/18: useful handicap chaser: third in Irish Grand National Chase at Fairyhouse (baulked last when beaten only ¾ length by General Principle) in April: stays 3¾m: acts on heavy going: usually wears headgear: in tongue tie last 2 starts. *Edward Cawley, Ireland* c139 h–

FOREVER MY FRIEND (IRE) 11 b.g. King's Theatre (IRE) – Kazan Lady (IRE) (Petardia) [2017/18 c119§, h–: c19.9g³ c19.4g* c20g⁴ h15.8g³ c21.2g⁵ c20d⁶ Apr 9] smallish gelding: maiden hurdler: fairly useful handicap chaser: won at Stratford in June: stays 3m: acts on soft and good to firm going: wears headgear: tried in tongue tie: unreliable. *Mickey Bowen* c123 § h65 §

FOR

FOREWARNING 4 b.g. Cacique (IRE) – Buffering (Beat Hollow) [2017/18 b13.1g^2 b13.6v^3 b15.6s^5 Jan 19] 5,000 3-y-o: third foal: half-brother to useful 1m winner Roller (by Rail Link): dam useful French 9.5f winner: fair form in bumpers: best effort when second in junior event at Market Rasen in October: wears tongue tie. *Susan Corbett* — **b91**

FORGE MEADOW (IRE) 6 b.m. Beneficial – Ballys Baby (IRE) (Bob Back (USA)) [2017/18 h134: h16v^6 h16s^5 h16s^5 h18.2s* h20s^2 h16v^2 h16v* h20v^{pu} h20s^{pu} Apr 28] useful hurdler: won listed mares event at Punchestown (by 7½ lengths from Dawn Shadow) in November and Red Mills Trial Hurdle at Gowran (by 1½ lengths from Identity Thief) in February: second in EBF Mares Hurdle at Leopardstown in December and Limestone Lad Hurdle at Naas in January: stays 2½m: acts on heavy going: tried in hood: front runner. *Mrs J. Harrington, Ireland* — **h143**

FORGET ME KNOT (IRE) 5 b.m. Presenting – J'y Reste (FR) (Freedom Cry) [2017/18 b17d Oct 29] half-sister to several winners, including fairly useful hurdler/very smart chaser J'Y Vole (2m-21f winner, by Mansonnien): dam, French 15f-2¼m hurdle winner (also 11f-1¾m winner on Flat), out of half-sister to dam of Cheltenham Gold Cup winner Long Run: 20/1, thirteenth in mares bumper at Aintree (23½ lengths behind Grageelagh Girl): should do better. *Emma Lavelle* — **b– p**

FORGETTHESMALLTALK (IRE) 6 b.g. Flemensfirth (USA) – Mylane du Charmil (FR) (Saint Cyrien (FR)) [2017/18 h106, b76: h23.1s^3 h23.1s^2 h23.5d^2 h24.3g Apr 20] sturdy gelding: Irish point winner: fairly useful form over hurdles: stays 3m: acts on soft going: often travels strongly. *Alan King* — **h116**

FORGE VALLEY 14 b.g. Bollin William – Scalby Clipper (Sir Mago) [2017/18 c67: c24.2g c25.5d^2 May 31] lengthy gelding: multiple point winner: modest maiden hunter chaser: stays 3¼m: acts on soft going: wears cheekpieces: usually races close up. *Miss G. Walton* — **c94**

FOR GOOD MEASURE (IRE) 7 b.g. King's Theatre (IRE) – Afdala (IRE) (Hernando (FR)) [2017/18 h135: c16g^4 c20.5g^3 Feb 24] sturdy gelding: similar form over fences: better effort when third in Pendil Novices' Chase at Kempton (16 lengths behind Cyrname) in February, having hopeless task from position: stays 25f: acts on heavy going: races towards rear: better to come as a chaser. *Philip Hobbs* — **c132 p h–**

FORGOTTEN GOLD (IRE) 12 b.g. Dr Massini (IRE) – Ardnataggle (IRE) (Aristocracy) [2017/18 c139, h–: c23.6d^{pu} c26.7g^2 Oct 29] stocky gelding: winning hurdler: useful handicap chaser: second at Wincanton (2¼ lengths behind Mr Mix) in October: stays 27f: acts on any going: in headgear last 5 starts: usually races close up. *Tom George* — **c138 h–**

FORGOTTEN HERO (IRE) 9 b.g. High Chaparral (IRE) – Sundown (Polish Precedent (USA)) [2017/18 h15.7g^2 h15.8g^2 h16g^5 Aug 23] useful on Flat: fair form over hurdles: wears tongue tie. *Kim Bailey* — **h104**

FORGOT TO ASK (IRE) 6 b.g. Ask – Lady Transcend (IRE) (Aristocracy) [2017/18 b100p: b17.7g h19.5d^5 h15.5d^4 h16.3s^4 Jan 17] runner-up both completed starts in Irish points: bumper winner: fair form over hurdles: best effort when fourth in novice at Newbury in January: should be suited by at least 19f: remains with potential. *Tom George* — **h109 p b–**

FOR INSTANCE (IRE) 8 b.g. Milan – Justamemory (IRE) (Zaffaran (USA)) [2017/18 h120: h24.5m^3 c23g* h23g* Jul 18] Irish point winner: fairly useful hurdler: won novice at Worcester in July: 5/2, also won novice at same course (by ½ length from Masterofdeception) on chasing debut: stays 3m: acts on good to firm and good to soft going: tried in cheekpieces: open to improvement as a chaser. *Jonjo O'Neill* — **c125 p h119**

FOR JIM (IRE) 6 gr.g. Milan – Dromhale Lady (IRE) (Roselier (FR)) [2017/18 h16.7v^6 h15.7v^6 h16v^6 h15.8s^5 h19.6d^2 Apr 21] €18,000 3-y-o: sixth foal: closely related to fair hurdler For Gortnatona (2¼m winner, by Oscar) and half-brother to fairly useful hurdler Jean Fleming (19f-2¾m winner, by Flemensfirth), both winning pointers: dam (c119/h121) 2m-2¾m hurdle/chase winner: unplaced in Irish points: modest form over hurdles: will be suited by 2½m+: acts on good to soft going: open to further improvement. *Jennie Candlish* — **h96 p**

FORMIDABLEOPPONENT (IRE) 11 b.g. Arakan (USA) – Sliding (Formidable (USA)) [2017/18 c111, h–: c24.2g^{pu} c20.1m^6 c20.1g^5 c23.4g Oct 28] winning hurdler: fair handicap chaser, below form in 2017/18: stays 3m: acts on soft and good to firm going: wears blinkers: has worn tongue tie. *William Young Jnr* — **c89 h–**

FORRARDON XMOOR 9 gr.g. Fair Mix (IRE) – The Nuns Song (Sir Harry Lewis (USA)) [2017/18 c24.2m^2 c21.2d^{bd} May 29] multiple point winner: maiden hurdler: poor form when second in hunter at Exeter, completed start in chases: best effort at 3m: acts on good to firm going: tried in tongue tie. *D. M. G. Fitch-Peyton* — **c84 h–**

FOR

FORT CARSON (IRE) 12 b.g. Stowaway – The Red One (IRE) (Camden Town) [2017/18 h108: h16.7g May 12] fair hurdler: stayed 2½m: acted on heavy going: often wore headgear: tried in tongue tie: front runner/raced prominently: dead. *Neil King* h–

FORT GABRIEL (FR) 7 ch.g. Ange Gabriel (FR) – Forge Neuve (FR) (Tel Quel (FR)) [2017/18 c86, h–: c21.2m⁴ c25.5m* c23.8g* c25.8m* c24s⁴ c22.6m³ c25.7m² c26g⁵ Oct 6] maiden hurdler: fair handicap chaser: won at Fontwell and Ffos Las in June, and Newton Abbot in July: left Fiona Kehoe after first start: stays 3¼m: acts on good to firm going: wears headgear: front runner/races prominently. *David Bridgwater* c112 h–

FORTH BRIDGE 5 b.g. Bernardini (USA) – Sally Forth (Dubai Destination (USA)) [2017/18 h133: c16.2g⁴ c20.3d³ h19.4d^pu h15.6s² h16.8g² Apr 18] lengthy, useful-looking gelding: useful handicap hurdler: second at Musselburgh (¾ length behind Dear Sire) in February and Cheltenham (conditionals/amateur event, 6 lengths behind Magic Dancer) in April: fair form over fences: should stay beyond 2m: acts on soft going: tried in cheekpieces/tongue tie: front runner/races prominently. *Charlie Longsdon* c113 h134

FORTH CAVE (IRE) 6 b.g. Court Cave (IRE) – Supreme Departure (IRE) (Supreme Leader) [2017/18 h20.1v⁶ h19.7d⁶ h19.3v⁶ Apr 17] in frame in Irish points: no form over hurdles: left Joanne Foster after second start. *Dianne Sayer* h–

FORTHEFUNOFIT (IRE) 9 b.g. Flemensfirth (USA) – Sommer Sonnet (IRE) (Taipan (IRE)) [2017/18 c89, h131: h25d Apr 26] sturdy gelding: useful hurdler, tired sole outing in 2017/18: didn't take to chasing: stays 3m: acts on heavy going: usually in cheekpieces. *Jonjo O'Neill* c– h118

FORTIFIED BAY (IRE) 6 b.g. Makfi – Divergence (USA) (Red Ransom (USA)) [2017/18 h118, b103: h20m² h21.9d³ May 27] bumper winner: fair maiden hurdler: stays 21f: acts on good to firm and heavy going. *Alan King* h110

FORT JEFFERSON 5 br.g. Passing Glance – Florida Heart (First Trump) [2017/18 h15.8v² h15.8v⁵ h15.8s⁶ h18.6v³ h17s⁴ h16.8g² Apr 28] fair on Flat, stays 1¼m: fair form over hurdles: unproven beyond 17f: acts on heavy going: often in headgear: usually races nearer last than first. *Oliver Greenall* h102

FORT SMITH (IRE) 9 b.g. Presenting – Land of Honour (Supreme Leader) [2017/18 c98§, h96§: c19.9d^pu Nov 25] maiden hurdler: useful chaser at best, pulled up sole outing in 2017/18: stays 3f: acts on soft going: usually wears headgear/tongue tie: one to leave alone. *Oliver Sherwood* c– § h– §

FORTUNATE GEORGE (IRE) 8 b.g. Oscar (IRE) – Fine Fortune (IRE) (Bob Back (USA)) [2017/18 h130: c21.6g⁵ c23g² c19.9d⁵ c21d* c23.8d c21v³ h21.4s⁴ h24.7s Apr 14] good-topped gelding: useful handicap hurdler: won at Wincanton (by 5 lengths from Watcombe Heights) in February: fairly useful form over fences: won handicap at Ascot in November: stays 3m: acts on heavy going: usually wears visor. *Emma Lavelle* c129 h133

FORTUNES HIDING (IRE) 5 b.g. Beat Hollow – Sambre (FR) (Turgeon (USA)) [2017/18 b16d Oct 15] 7/1, eighth in bumper at Chepstow. *Peter Bowen* b–

FORT WORTH (IRE) 9 b.g. Presenting – Victorine (IRE) (Un Desperado (FR)) [2017/18 c130, h–: c24m³ c23.8g² c23g* c25.5g^F Sep 26] well-made gelding: winning hurdler: useful handicap chaser: won at Worcester in June: stayed 25f: acted on good to firm and good to soft going: tried in cheekpieces: in tongue tie last 3 starts: usually raced towards rear: dead. *Jonjo O'Neill* c136 h–

FORTY CROWN (IRE) 12 b.g. Court Cave (IRE) – Forty Quid (IRE) (Exhibitioner) [2017/18 c–, h115§: h19.9g⁴ h20.9g⁵ h24.6s c20.5v^pu h21.3d h22.7v³ Apr 16] good-topped gelding: fair handicap hurdler, maiden chaser: stays 25f: acts on heavy going: has worn headgear, including in 2017/18: usually races close up: temperamental. *George Bewley* c– § h105 §

FORTYSHADESOFBAY (IRE) 5 b.m. Lope de Vega (IRE) – Mureefa (USA) (Bahri (USA)) [2017/18 b16.2g Nov 11] €3,000 3-y-o: smallish mare: half-sister to several winners on Flat, including useful 1m-1¼m winner Habalwatan (by In The Wings): dam ran twice on Flat: well beaten in mares bumper. *S. Curling, Ireland* b–

FOR YES (IRE) 9 b.g. Kutub (IRE) – Oscartain (IRE) (Oscar (IRE)) [2017/18 h–: c24.2g^pu c20.1g³ c15.6g⁵ c26.6s⁵ c26.2v³ Apr 16] multiple point winner: maiden hurdler: fair form over fences: best effort at 2½m: in visor last 2 starts: sometimes in tongue tie. *Mrs L. A. Coltherd* c100 h–

FORZA MILAN (IRE) 6 b.g. Milan – Nonnetia (FR) (Trempolino (USA)) [2017/18 h124p, b87: h23g⁶ h24.7s² h24.2d² h24s^pu Mar 15] useful-looking gelding: useful handicap hurdler: second at Newbury (1½ lengths behind The Organist) in December: stays 25f: acts on heavy going: tried in tongue tie. *Jonjo O'Neill* h135

FOU

FOU ET SAGE (FR) 7 b.g. Sageburg (IRE) – Folie Lointaine (FR) (Poliglote) [2017/18 c135, h–: h16.7g h15.7g h19.8s³ c18.9s³ c20.1s² c19.1d⁴ Apr 17] sturdy, lengthy gelding: fairly useful handicap hurdler: third at Wincanton in November: useful chaser: left Harry Whittington, below best back in France last 3 starts: stays 21f: acts on heavy going: tried in tongue tie. *P. Peltier, France*   **c114 h120**

FOUNDATION MAN (IRE) 11 b.g. Presenting – Function Dream (IRE) (Strong Gale) [2017/18 c127, h–: c20g⁴ c20g⁵ c21.4g⁵ c24.1g⁵ c21g c19.9g⁵ c20.2s⁶ c20.2s⁵ c21.2s² Dec 4] very big gelding: has reportedly suffered breathing problems: maiden hurdler: fairly useful handicap chaser: stays 3m: acts on firm and soft going: has worn headgear/tongue tie: temperamental. *Jonjo O'Neill*   **c117 § h–**

FOUNTAINS WINDFALL 8 b.g. Passing Glance – Fountain Crumble (Dr Massini (IRE)) [2017/18 h144+: h24.1s⁵ c20.3d* c23.4gᶠ c24dᶠ c24d* Jan 13] well-made gelding: useful hurdler: smart form over fences: won novice at Southwell (by 11 lengths from Stowaway Magic) in November and handicap at Kempton (by 9 lengths from Ballykan) in January: stayed 25f: acted on heavy going: usually led, often travelled strongly: dead. *Anthony Honeyball*   **c153 h–**

FOUR MILE BEACH 5 gr.g. Dalakhani (IRE) – Rappel (Royal Applause) [2017/18 h89§: h16.8g⁵ h16.8g⁵ Nov 2] modest maiden hurdler: raced around 2m: acts on good to firm going: usually wears headgear: temperamental. *Malcolm Jefferson*   **h85 §**

FOUROVAKIND 13 b.g. Sir Harry Lewis (USA) – Four M's (Majestic Maharaj) [2017/18 c117, h–: c24s² c22.2vᶠ c23.6sᵖᵘ Mar 22] winning hurdler: fairly useful chaser: second in hunter at Warwick in January: stays 31f: acts on heavy going: wears blinkers: usually races nearer last than first. *Matt Hazell*   **c117 h–**

FOURTH ACT (IRE) 9 b.g. King's Theatre (IRE) – Erintante (IRE) (Denel (FR)) [2017/18 c135, h108: c23.8g h21.7v* h23.4v c20.5g⁴ c24.2v³ c23.8dᵖᵘ Apr 9] angular gelding: fairly useful handicap hurdler: won at Fontwell in January: fairly useful handicap chaser: third at Sandown in March: stays 3½m: acts on good to firm and heavy going: has worn headgear, including last 2 starts: wears tongue tie: front runner/races prominently. *Colin Tizzard*   **c125 h119**

FOX APPEAL (IRE) 11 b.g. Brian Boru – Lady Appeal (IRE) (Phardante (FR)) [2017/18 c144, h–: c21g² c20.3g c21.6g⁴ c23.6d² c25.1s⁵ c22.7g² c24.2sᶠ c24sᵖᵘ c23.8s⁴ Mar 25] smallish gelding: winning hurdler: useful handicap chaser: second 3 times in 2017/18: stays 3m: acts on good to firm and heavy going: wears headgear/tongue tie: often let down by jumping. *Emma Lavelle*   **c140 x h–**

FOXCUB (IRE) 10 b.g. Bahri (USA) – Foxglove (Hernando (FR)) [2017/18 c86, h–: c24.2s* c25.2s Mar 7] sturdy gelding: point winner: useful hurdler at best: fair form in chases: won hunter at Fakenham in February: stays 25f: acts on heavy going: has worn cheekpieces, including in 2017/18. *R. D. Potter*   **c100 h–**

FOX NORTON (FR) 8 b.g. Lando (GER) – Natt Musik (FR) (Kendor (FR)) [2017/18 c170, h–: c15.9s* c15.5d² c24dᵖᵘ Dec 26] well-made gelding: winning hurdler: top-class chaser: won Shloer Chase at Cheltenham (by 8 lengths from Cloudy Dream) in November: second in Tingle Creek Chase at Sandown (½ length behind Politologue) 3 weeks later: not himself in King George VI Chase at Kempton, and not seen out again (suffered suspensory injury): stays 2½m: acts on soft going: wears hood. *Colin Tizzard*   **c167 h–**

FOXROCK (IRE) 10 b.g. Flemensfirth (USA) – Midnight Light (IRE) (Roselier (FR)) [2017/18 c142, h–: c23.7v² c26.3vᵖᵘ Mar 16] lengthy, workmanlike gelding: winning hurdler: useful chaser nowadays: second in hunter at Thurles in January: stays 25f: acts on heavy going: wears headgear/tongue tie. *Alan Fleming, Ireland*   **c126 h–**

Shloer Chase, Cheltenham—a second successive win in the race for Fox Norton, which proves to be the highlight of Bryan Cooper's brief tenure as retained rider in Britain for the Potts horses

FRA

FOXTAIL HILL (IRE) 9 b.g. Dr Massini (IRE) – Flynn's Girl (IRE) (Mandalus) [2017/18 c141, h–: c15.9g* c20.4s c20.8s⁶ c16.4s c16.3v c16.5g Apr 21] workmanlike gelding: winning hurdler: useful handicap chaser: won at Cheltenham (by neck from Le Prezien) in October: stays 21f: acts on soft going: usually leads. *Nigel Twiston-Davies* **c141 h–**

FOXTROT JULIET 5 b.m. Shirocco (GER) – Miami Explorer (Pennekamp (USA)) [2017/18 ab16g ab16g⁴ b16.8g⁴ Apr 23] fourth foal: dam (h106), 2m hurdle winner, half-sister to Grand National winner Rule The World: modest form in bumpers. *Olly Murphy* **b78**

FOXY ACT 7 ch.m. Act One – Brown Fox (FR) (Polar Falcon (USA)) [2017/18 h74, b–: h18.5m* h21.6m² h16.8m* h21.6d* h20g h22s^pu h15.3v⁴ h24.6s Apr 9] fairly useful hurdler: won mares novices at Exeter and Newton Abbot in June, and novice at Newton Abbot in July: stays 2¾m: acts on good to firm and good to soft going: usually leads. *Chris Down* **h115**

FOXY LASS 4 b.f. Foxwedge (AUS) – Domitia (Pivotal) [2017/18 h16d h16v⁶ h16.5s* h16v² h16s h16v⁴ h16.8g⁶ Apr 19] little impact on Flat: fair hurdler: won juvenile maiden at Ballinrobe in September: raced around 2m: best form on soft/heavy going: tried in blinkers: usually leads. *Denis Hogan, Ireland* **h102**

FRAMPTON (IRE) 9 b.g. Presenting – Drumavish Lass (IRE) (Oscar (IRE)) [2017/18 c–, h–: h23m^pu May 11] sturdy gelding: fairly useful hurdler/chaser at best, has lost his form: wears headgear. *Charlie Longsdon* **c– h–**

FRANCE DU LUKKA (FR) 4 bl.f. Kap Rock (FR) – Orlamonde Queen (FR) (Royal Charter (FR)) [2017/18 b16.2s b16.8v⁶ h16.7v⁶ h16.8s Feb 23] half-sister to fair hurdler/chaser Dom Lukka (17f-3¼m winner, by Dom Alco): dam lightly raced in France: no form in bumpers/novice hurdle: tried in hood. *Jackie du Plessis* **h– b–**

FRANCKY DU BERLAIS (FR) 5 b.g. Saint des Saints (FR) – Legende du Luy (FR) (Bonnet Rouge (FR)) [2017/18 b16g³ b16.7g b16.7v⁶ h16s² Apr 27] €23,000 3-y-o: first foal: dam, French 17f-2½m hurdle/chase winner, half-sister to fairly useful French hurdler/high-class chaser (stays 27f) Saint Palois (by Saint des Saints): modest form in bumpers: 25/1, second in maiden at Chepstow (3½ lengths behind Arian) on hurdling debut: tried in hood/tongue tie. *Peter Bowen* **h110 b77**

FRANKIE BALLOU (IRE) 9 br.g. Norwich – One Up (IRE) (Bob Back (USA)) [2017/18 c87, h–: h19.3d c19.2d² c19.3s^pu c16.4v* c16.4v* c16.4v² c16.4v* Apr 13] quite good-topped gelding: maiden hurdler: fair handicap chaser: won at Sedgefield in February, March and April (novice): stays 2½m, most effective at shorter: best form on soft/heavy going: usually wears headgear: tried in tongue tie: front runner/races prominently. *Joanne Foster* **c103 h–**

FRANKIE RAPPER (IRE) 6 b.g. Milan – Parkdota (IRE) (Good Thyne (USA)) [2017/18 b85: h15.7d h20g³ h21d Nov 13] fair form in bumpers: modest form over hurdles: best effort when third in maiden at Worcester in October. *Dan Skelton* **h89**

FRANKLY SPEAKING 8 ch.g. Flemensfirth (USA) – No More Money (Alflora (IRE)) [2017/18 h19.5v⁵ h19.5v h23.6v³ h20.3v⁴ h23.3v² h25d² Apr 26] lengthy gelding: fair form over hurdles: stays 25f: acts on heavy going: usually races towards rear. *Tom Symonds* **h112**

FRANK N FAIR 10 br.m. Trade Fair – Frankfurt (GER) (Celtic Swing) [2017/18 c85?, h73: c25.7g^pu c19.7d² c24.2s^ur c25.7d* c25.7* c28.5v³ c25.7v⁴ h25.5s c25.7s² Apr 15] modest hurdler at best: fair handicap chaser: won at Plumpton (twice) in December: stays 3½m: acts on heavy going: tried in cheekpieces: usually races in rear. *Zoe Davison* **c104 h–**

FRANK THE SLINK 12 b.g. Central Park (IRE) – Kadari (Commanche Run) [2017/18 c86, h–: c24.2g³ c24.5g⁶ c24.2s* c26d Dec 2] strong gelding: maiden hurdler: poor handicap chaser nowadays: won at Hexham (conditional) in November: stays 3¼m: acts on heavy going: has worn cheekpieces, including in 2017/18: in tongue tie last 2 starts: front runner/races prominently. *Micky Hammond* **c78 h–**

FRANTICAL 6 b.g. Observatory (USA) – Quest For Freedom (Falbrav (IRE)) [2017/18 h16.3g Sep 9] fair on Flat, stays 1¼m: tailed off in novice on hurdling debut. *Tony Carroll* **h–**

FRANZ KLAMMER 6 b.g. Midnight Legend – Ski (Petoski) [2017/18 h–, b69: h16.3g⁶ h16.3g⁵ h15.7d^ur h16.5s h20.3g Apr 20] modest form over hurdles. *Charlie Longsdon* **h94**

FRASER CANYON 6 b.g. Halling (USA) – Valley of Gold (FR) (Shirley Heights) [2017/18 h99: h25.8g⁵ h23.1v^pu h23.8g* h23.8s² Jan 19] modest handicap hurdler: won at Musselburgh in December: stays 3m: acts on soft going: in headgear last 3 starts: wears tongue tie. *Tim Vaughan* **h96**

FRE

FREDDIES PORTRAIT (IRE) 9 gr.g. Portrait Gallery (IRE) – Phara (IRE) (Lord Americo) [2017/18 c113, h–: h18.9v[5] c20v[6] c25.6s[pu] c19.2s[5] c19.8v[pu] Mar 29] point winner: fair hurdler/chaser, below form in 2017/18: stays 2½m: acts on heavy going: in blinkers last 2 starts, tongue tied last 5: front runner: temperamental. *Donald McCain* — **c80 §**
h–

FREDDY WITH A Y (IRE) 8 b.g. Amadeus Wolf – Mataji (IRE) (Desert Prince (IRE)) [2017/18 h15.8g Nov 14] workmanlike gelding: fair on Flat, barely stays 1¼m: tailed off in novice on hurdling debut. *J. R. Jenkins* — **h–**

FREDERIC 7 b.g. Zamindar (USA) – Frangy (Sadler's Wells (USA)) [2017/18 h119: h16.8g[2] Oct 3] fairly useful on Flat: fairly useful handicap hurdler: second at Sedgefield sole outing in 2017/18: stays 19f: acts on good to soft going. *Keith Dalgleish* — **h119**

FRED LE MACON (FR) 9 b.g. Passing Sale (FR) – Princess Leyla (Teenoso (USA)) [2017/18 h99§: c16g c23.4g[2] c20.1g[pu] Jun 17] smallish gelding: modest hurdler: similar form over fences: stayed 2¾m: acted on heavy going: tried in cheekpieces: temperamental: dead. *Martin Todhunter* — **c85 §
h– §**

FRED'S FILLY 5 ch.m. Avonbridge – Regal Quest (IRE) (Marju (IRE)) [2017/18 h15.3d Apr 22] poor maiden on Flat, raced mainly at sprint trips: in hood, well beaten in novice on hurdling debut. *Nick Mitchell* — **h–**

FRED THE FOOT (IRE) 6 b.g. Scorpion (IRE) – Rainy Season (IRE) (Sulamani (IRE)) [2017/18 b16.2g* h16d h16.6v[5] h16v[5] Apr 1] €17,000 3-y-o: third foal: brother to modest 23f hurdle winner Motts Cross: dam, unraced, closely related to useful hurdler/fairly useful chaser (stayed 3m) Top Strategy: runner-up in point: fairly useful form in bumpers: won at Hexham in June: fair form over hurdles: best effort when fifth in maiden at Fairyhouse in April: will be suited by 2½m+: wears tongue tie: often races towards rear: better to come. *John McConnell, Ireland* — **h99 p
b98**

FREE BOUNTY 5 b.g. Dick Turpin (IRE) – Native Ring (FR) (Bering) [2017/18 h–: h20.3g[5] h16g[5] h15.7g h20.7g[4] h20.7s Dec 26] neat gelding: modest form over hurdles: stays 21f: wears tongue tie. *Neil Mulholland* — **h99**

FREEDOM RUN 5 ch.m. Presenting – Mathine (FR) (Malinas (GER)) [2017/18 b15.8s[6] Feb 8] first foal: dam, pulled up only start over hurdles in France, half-sister to Cheltenham Gold Cup winner Long Run: 9/1, shaped as if needed experience when sixth in mares bumper at Huntingdon (16¼ lengths behind Sparkling Dawn). *Emma Lavelle* — **b74**

FREE OF CHARGE (IRE) 9 ch.g. Stowaway – Sweetasanu (IRE) (Sri Pekan (USA)) [2017/18 c94§, h–: c20g c24g[2] c24.4d Aug 9] winning hurdler: modest maiden chaser nowadays: stays 3½m: acts on firm and soft going: usually in blinkers/tongue tie nowadays: jumps none too fluently: unreliable. *Gordon Elliott, Ireland* — **c90 §
h–**

FREE ONE (IRE) 6 b.g. Fast Company (IRE) – Tatamagouche (IRE) (Sadler's Wells (USA)) [2017/18 h–: h16g[5] h15.8g[2] h16.7g[3] h17.7g h15.9d[F] Dec 4] fair at best on Flat: fair form over hurdles: usually wore hood: dead. *Jo Davis* — **h100**

FREE RANGE (IRE) 8 b.g. Subtle Power (IRE) – Tullyspark Rose (IRE) (Beneficial) [2017/18 h16g* h19.9s[2] c21.4s[4] c20s[3] c23.6s[4] h19.2s[2] h21.3d[4] c20.3g[4] Apr 20] £10,000 7-y-o: first foal: dam unraced half-sister to fairly useful hurdler (2m-2½m winner) Destiny's Gold out of sister to top-class staying chaser The Grey Monk: Irish point winner: fair form over hurdles: won maiden at Fakenham in November: similar form over fences: left Dan Skelton after seventh start: stays 2½m: acts on soft going: in headgear last 5 starts. *Micky Hammond* — **c111
h112**

FREE RETURN (IRE) 7 b.g. Mr Combustible (IRE) – Marisha (IRE) (Gulland) [2017/18 c–, h67: c24.1s[pu] May 20] runner-up on second of 2 starts in Irish points: little form under Rules: in cheekpieces last 4 starts. *Tom Weston* — **c–
h–**

FREE SCORPION (IRE) 7 b.m. Scorpion (IRE) – Free Dreamer (IRE) (Turtle Island (IRE)) [2017/18 h20g Jul 27] third foal: dam unraced half-sister to smart hurdler/useful chaser (stayed 3m) Deputy Dan: maiden pointer: modest form at best over hurdles for M. Hourigan: well held sole outing in 2017/18: should stay beyond 2m: in tongue tie last 5 starts: often races towards rear. *Dan Skelton* — **h–**

FREE STONE HILL (IRE) 8 b.g. Beneficial – Claramanda (IRE) (Mandalus) [2017/18 h111: h16.3g* h20g[3] h16.3m[2] h16g[2] h16.8g[3] h15.9m[5] c19.5g[2] c18g[f] c16g[3] h15.8s c16s[3] Mar 17] workmanlike gelding: fair handicap hurdler: won at Stratford in May: similar form over fences: second in novice handicap at Fontwell in October: stays 19f: acts on good to firm going: wears tongue tie: usually races nearer last than first. *Dan Skelton* — **c115
h114**

FREE TRAVEL (IRE) 7 b.g. Stowaway – Janet Lindup (Sabrehill (USA)) [2017/18 h20.5s h21s[6] Dec 21] third in Irish point: little impact over hurdles. *Ben Case* — **h63**

336

FREEWHEEL (IRE) 8 br.g. Galileo (IRE) – La Chunga (USA) (More Than Ready (USA)) [2017/18 h88: h19.9g³ h20.6g⁵ h19.7s^pu h16.4s Dec 23] fairly useful on Flat: poor maiden hurdler: left Lucinda Egerton after second start: stays 2½m: acts on good to soft going: tried in tongue tie. *Tina Jackson* — h80

FREE WORLD (FR) 14 b.g. Lost World (IRE) – Fautine (FR) (Fast Topaze (USA)) [2017/18 c93, h–: c20.9d^pu c20.3v³ c20v^pu c17.8s³ Mar 7] well-made gelding: winning hurdler: modest handicap chaser, below form in 2017/18: stays 2½m: acts on heavy going: tried in hood: has worn tongue tie: usually leads. *Lady Susan Brooke* — c67 h–

FRELIA (IRE) 7 b.m. Oscar (IRE) – Hannabelle (IRE) (Rudimentary (USA)) [2017/18 c25.3d* c25.5s² May 18] £1,600 3-y-o: first foal: dam unraced: multiple point winner: fair form in chases: won mares hunter at Cheltenham in May. *D. C. Gibbs* — c109

FRENCH CRUSADER (FR) 5 b.g. Kapgarde (FR) – Largesse (FR) (Saumarez) [2017/18 b13.7d⁴ h16.6s⁵ h19.4s² Feb 21] €70,000 3-y-o: half-brother to several winners on Flat in France, including 1m winner Grandes Illusions (by Kendor): dam unraced: won maiden bumper at Huntingdon (by 2 lengths from Cheeky Chica) in November: fairly useful form over hurdles: better effort when second in novice at Doncaster in February: remains with potential. *Nicky Henderson* — h122 p b95

FRENCH SEVENTYFIVE 11 b.g. Pursuit of Love – Miss Tun (Komaite (USA)) [2017/18 c84, h82: c23.4g⁶ c22.5d⁴ h24g^pu c24.2g^pu h24g³ h24g⁵ c23.4g⁵ c24d⁴ c24d³ c25.6s⁴ Dec 17] poor handicap hurdler/chaser: stays 3m: acts on soft going: wears headgear. *Gillian Boanas* — c72 h66

FRENCH TICKET 7 b.g. Bollin Eric – Merry Tina (Tina's Pet) [2017/18 b91: b16.2g⁴ b16.2g h20.6s^pu Dec 23] modest form in bumpers: pulled up in novice on hurdling debut. *James Walton* — h– b83

FRESH BY NATURE (IRE) 11 b.m. Flemensfirth (USA) – Star Alert (IRE) (Darazari (IRE)) [2017/18 c–x, h99§: h23.3d³ h23.3d^pu May 20] sturdy mare: fair handicap hurdler: winning chaser: stayed 27f: acted on good to firm and heavy going: refitted with headgear last 3 starts: often let down by jumping/attitude: dead. *Harriet Bethell* — c– x h102 §

FRESH NEW DAWN (IRE) 6 ch.g. Flemensfirth (USA) – Star Shuil (IRE) (Soviet Star (USA)) [2017/18 b16.8g² h23.9v³ h16v² h18.6v⁴ h21s⁴ h21.2s⁴ h26v³ Mar 28] £20,000 5-y-o: first foal: dam, well beaten in bumpers, half-sister to fairly useful hurdler/fair chaser (stayed 3m) King Ar Aghaidh out of Stayers' Hurdle winner Shuil Ar Aghaidh: runner-up in Irish point: second in bumper at Sedgefield: fair form over hurdles: should stay 3m: raced mainly on soft/heavy going: tried in hood: often races towards rear. *Olly Murphy* — h109 b94

FRIARY GOLD (IRE) 6 b.g. Mountain High (IRE) – Platinium Ambition (IRE) (Good Thyne (USA)) [2017/18 b18g² b16g⁶ h16d⁵ h21.4g⁶ h16.7s Nov 15] second foal: dam unraced sister to fairly useful hurdler/useful chaser (stayed 2½m) Soltero: maiden pointer: fairly useful form in bumpers: modest form over hurdles: left Declan Queally after third start: tried in tongue tie. *Katy Price* — h89 b97

FRIDAY FEELING 4 b.f. Schiaparelli (GER) – Lac Marmot (FR) (Marju (IRE)) [2017/18 b14s b14s Jan 1] rather unfurnished filly: half-sister to several winners, including fairly useful hurdler/useful chaser Midnight Appeal (2½m-3m winner) and useful hurdler/chaser My Petra (2m-19f winner) (both by Midnight Legend): dam unraced: no form in bumpers. *John O'Shea* — b–

FRIDAY NIGHT LIGHT (FR) 5 b.g. Air Chief Marshal (IRE) – Peninsula (FR) (Dansili) [2017/18 h16.5s³ h16.8v² h16.3s* h16.5v² h19.3s² h16v^pu h16s Apr 28] good-topped gelding: useful on Flat in France, stays 1½m: fairly useful handicap hurdler: won at Newbury in January: stays 19f: raced only on soft/heavy going: in headgear last 4 starts: wears tongue tie. *David Pipe* — h122

FRIENDLY ROYAL (IRE) 9 b.g. Royal Anthem (USA) – Friendly Girl (IRE) (King's Ride) [2017/18 c19.3g c24.2v³ Sep 14] sturdy gelding: maiden hurdler: poor handicap chaser: stayed 2¾m: acted on heavy going: in tongue tie last 2 starts: dead. *Sam England* — c80 h–

FRIENDSHIP BAY 14 b.g. Midnight Legend – Friendly Fairy (Gunner B) [2017/18 h92: h19d⁶ h20.5s h16.7s⁴ Dec 26] workmanlike gelding: poor maiden hurdler nowadays: stays 21f: acts on good to soft going: often races towards rear. *James Evans* — h82

FRIENDS IN HEAVEN (IRE) 6 b.g. Asian Heights – Native Bev (IRE) (Be My Native (USA)) [2017/18 h16.2s Apr 26] runner-up on completed start in Irish points: well held in novice on hurdling debut. *Andrew Wilson* — h–

FRI

FRIGHTENED RABBIT (USA) 6 b.g. Hard Spun (USA) – Champagne Ending (USA) (Precise End (USA)) [2017/18 h95: h16.2g² h16.2g h17.2s h19.3v^{ur} h17d h17s⁵ h16.8g⁶ Apr 23] sparely-made gelding: modest handicap hurdler: left Susan Corbett after third start: raced mainly around 2m: acts on heavy going: often wears headgear/tongue tie: front runner/races prominently, often freely. *Dianne Sayer*   **h89**

FRIZZLE 5 b.m. Rocamadour – Dizzy Frizzy (Loup Sauvage (USA)) [2017/18 ab16g⁵ b15.7s Dec 21] third foal: half-sister to bumper winner/useful hurdler No Comment (19f/2½m winner, by Kayf Tara), stays 25f: dam unraced half-sister to useful hurdler/smart chaser (2m-2½m winner) Aran Concerto: poor form in bumpers. *Emma Lavelle*   **b68**

FRODON (FR) 6 b.g. Nickname (FR) – Miss Country (FR) (Country Reel (USA)) [2017/18 c148, h–: c21g³ c24.2s² c21d³ c23.8d² c20.8v* c21s³ c20.8s⁵ c20.8g Apr 18] rather unfurnished gelding: winning hurdler: high-class chaser: won Grade 3 handicap at Cheltenham (by 17 lengths from Shantou Flyer) in January: placed in listed event at Sandown (8 lengths behind Might Bite) and 1965 Chase at Ascot (10¼ lengths behind Top Notch), both in November, and Betfair Ascot Chase (17¾ lengths behind Waiting Patiently) in February: stays 3m: acts on good to firm and heavy going: wears tongue tie: usually races prominently. *Paul Nicholls*   **c160 h–**

FROM THE HEART (IRE) 4 b.g. Jeremy (USA) – Zephyr Lilly (IRE) (Alhaarth (IRE)) [2017/18 b16g b15.8d Mar 26] little impact in bumpers. *Philip Hobbs*   **b–**

FRONTLINE (IRE) 10 b.g. King's Theatre (IRE) – Thunder Road (IRE) (Mtoto) [2017/18 c–, h–: c18d c15.7v^{pu} Feb 5] robust gelding: fairly useful hurdler: maiden chaser, no form in 2017/18: stays 2¼m: acts on heavy going: tried in headgear/tongue tie. *Paul Cowley*   **c– h–**

FROSTY DAWN 10 b.m. Desideratum – Frosty Petal (Silver Patriarch (IRE)) [2017/18 h23.3g^{pu} h25.6v² h24v^F h23.3v^{pu} Mar 17] placed in points: form (poor) over hurdles only when second in mares handicap at Southwell in February: tried in blinkers. *Mike Sowersby*   **h71**

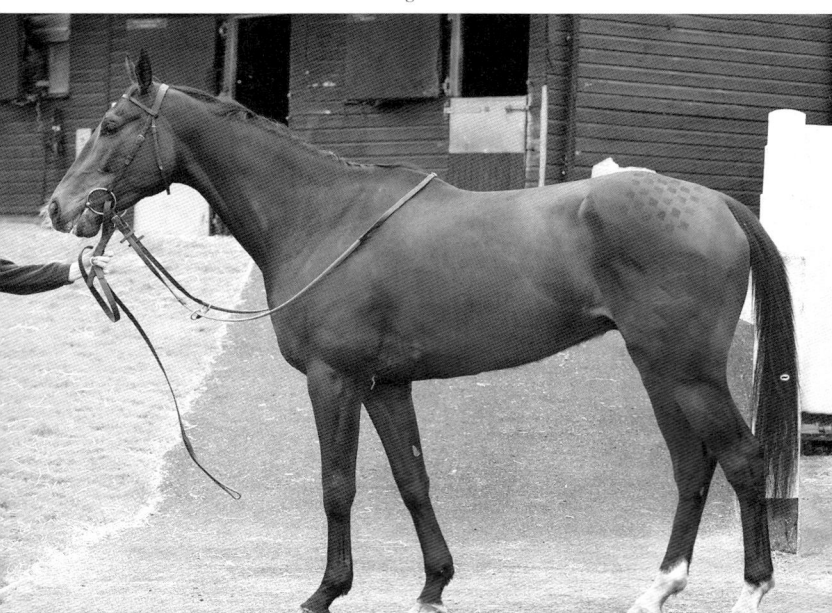

Mr P. J. Vogt's "Frodon"

FUL

FROZEN FLAME (IRE) 5 b.g. Frozen Fire (GER) – Flame Supreme (IRE) (Saddlers' Hall (IRE)) [2017/18 h19.6g⁶ h20.8s⁴ h19.4s⁵ h25d⁴ Apr 24] €1,800 3-y-o, £145,000 4-y-o: sturdy gelding: fourth foal: half-brother to fairly useful hurdler Reverant Cust (2m winner, by Daylami) and modest hurdler The Ballyboys (19f winner, by Westerner): dam, tailed off in bumper, closely related to fairly useful hurdler (stays 21f) Run To Milan: runner-up in Irish point: fair form over hurdles. *Jonjo O'Neill* — h109

FROZEN MOTION 6 b.m. Black Sam Bellamy (IRE) – Katys Jools (King's Theatre (IRE)) [2017/18 h20.7s h21.4v⁵ Feb 1] £8,500 4-y-o, £42,000 5-y-o: first foal: dam, well held in bumpers, sister to useful hurdler (stayed 3m) Palace Jester and half-sister to useful hurdler/chaser (stayed 3m) Bakbenscher: Irish point winner: poor form over hurdles: in hood second start. *Charlie Longsdon* — h80

FROZEN OUT (IRE) 5 b.g. Frozen Power (IRE) – Liscoa (IRE) (Foxhound (USA)) [2017/18 b16v ab16.3g⁴ h16.2d Apr 23] modest form in bumpers: well beaten in novice on hurdling debut. *Tim Easterby* — h– b77

FROZEN OVER 10 b.g. Iceman – Pearly River (Elegant Air) [2017/18 h91: h16d⁴ h18.7g^ur h16.8d h16.8g⁶ h16d² h16d⁴ h15.8m² Oct 11] compact gelding: modest handicap hurdler: raced mainly around 2m: acts on firm and good to soft going: has worn headgear: wears tongue tie. *Chris Down* — h87

FROZON 5 b.g. Kheleyf (USA) – Crozon (Peintre Celebre (USA)) [2017/18 h16.7s h15.7d h16.6d h15.7d^R Dec 28] modest on Flat, stays 1½m: no form over hurdles. *Harriet Bethell* — h–

FS LOLA 4 ch.f. Arvico (FR) – Semi Colon (FR) (Robin des Champs (FR)) [2017/18 b13.2s Oct 24] first foal: dam (c107/h123) bumper/19f hurdle winner (stayed 21f): tailed off in junior bumper. *Martin Hill* — b–

FUHGEDDABOUDIT 11 ch.g. Generous (IRE) – Serraval (FR) (Sanglamore (USA)) [2017/18 c91x, h96: h20.3g² h21.6s² h20g^pu Jul 10] modest maiden hurdler/chaser: stays 23f: acts on good going: wears cheekpieces: often let down by jumping over fences. *Seamus Mullins* — c– x h92

FULL CRY (IRE) 8 b.g. Milan – Gaye Melody (IRE) (Un Desperado (IRE)) [2017/18 c134, h–: c23m⁵ c22.5g c20s² c22.6s⁵ c24.5d Dec 27] winning hurdler: useful handicap chaser: second at Wexford (short head behind Tesseract) in October: stays 3m: acts on soft and good to firm going: often in cheekpieces: wears tongue tie. *Henry de Bromhead, Ireland* — c132 h–

FULL (FR) 6 b.g. Mr Sidney (USA) – Funny Feerie (FR) (Sillery (USA)) [2017/18 h127: h16g⁴ h16g⁶ h15.7g² c16.5g² c16.5d² c18d Nov 13] fair maiden hurdler: fairly useful form over fences: best effort when second in handicap at Worcester in September: unproven beyond 17f: acts on soft going: often races towards rear. *Neil Mulholland* — c118 h109

FULL GLASS (FR) 5 b.g. Diamond Green (FR) – Full Tune (FR) (Green Tune (USA)) [2017/18 c21.9s^m h18.9s* c21.9s³ c20.5g³ Apr 20] third foal: dam, French 19f hurdle winner, half-sister to fair hurdler/useful staying chaser Full Jack: fairly useful form over hurdles: won 4-y-o event at Cholet in October: useful chaser: third in Prix Morgex at Auteuil in November and listed handicap at Ayr (6 lengths behind Value At Risk) in April: left Guillaume Macaire after fourth start: stays 2¾m: acts on soft going: open to further improvement as a chaser. *Alan King* — c141 p h124

FULL IRISH (IRE) 7 b.g. Flemensfirth (USA) – Miss Kettlewell (IRE) (Saddlers' Hall (IRE)) [2017/18 h126: c16.2d⁴ c23.5s* c22.9v⁴ c20.8v⁵ c24.4s^pu Mar 14] well-made gelding: fairly useful hurdler: useful form over fences: won intermediate handicap at Lingfield (by 7 lengths from Two Smokin Barrels) in November: stays 23f: acts on heavy going: tried in cheekpieces: in tongue tie last 2 starts: usually races nearer last than first. *Emma Lavelle* — c134 h–

FULL JACK (FR) 11 b.g. Kahyasi – Full Contact (FR) (Cadoudal (FR)) [2017/18 c118, h106: c29.4d h23.8s³ c32.8s* Feb 3] fair handicap hurdler: fairly useful handicap chaser: won at Musselburgh in February: left Pauline Robson after first start: stays 33f, effective at much shorter: acts on good to firm and heavy going: often wears headgear. *Sandy Thomson* — c121 h106

FULL OF MISCHIEF (IRE) 10 ch.m. Classic Cliche (IRE) – Drama Chick (Riverwise (USA)) [2017/18 h–: h19.2d^pu Feb 25] fourth in bumper on debut: lightly raced and no form since. *Richard Rowe* — h–

FULL SHIFT (FR) 9 b.g. Ballingarry (IRE) – Dansia (GER) (Lavirco (GER)) [2017/18 c127, h–: c17.1g⁴ c17.1g^pu c20.1s^pu Dec 23] well-made gelding: winning hurdler: useful chaser at best, no form in 2017/18: stays 21f: acts on soft going: often in cheekpieces/tongue tie. *Ben Haslam* — c– h–

339

FUL

FULL TROTTLE (IRE) 9 ch.g. Vertical Speed (FR) – Keerou Lady (IRE) (Be My Native (USA)) [2017/18 c118: c20.8d* c20.9s² c20d* Apr 9] has had breathing operation: prolific point winner: fairly useful form in hunter chases: won at Cheltenham in May and Ludlow in April: stays 2¾m: acts on heavy going: tried in hood: wears tongue tie. *Miss L. Thomas*   **c127**

FUTURE BOY (IRE) 6 b.g. Beneficial – Money Clip (IRE) (Oscar (IRE)) [2017/18 h15.8g h21d Apr 26] workmanlike gelding: placed once from 4 runs in Irish points: no form over hurdles. *Robin Dickin*   **h–**

FUTURE SECURITY (IRE) 9 ch.g. Dalakhani (IRE) – Schust Madame (IRE) (Second Set (IRE)) [2017/18 h20.6s² Feb 6] fair hurdler: won minor event at Nancy in 2016/17 for C. von der Recke: stays 21f: acts on soft and good to firm going: tried in visor: wears tongue tie. *Dan Skelton*   **h108**

FUZZY LOGIC (IRE) 9 b.g. Dylan Thomas (IRE) – Gates of Eden (USA) (Kingmambo (USA)) [2017/18 c89, h93: h21.6m⁶ Jun 15] modest handicap hurdler: maiden chaser: stays 21f: acts on soft and good to firm going: wears headgear. *Bernard Llewellyn*   **c–** **h87**

G

GABRIAL THE GREAT (IRE) 9 b.g. Montjeu (IRE) – Bayourida (USA) (Slew O' Gold (USA)) [2017/18 c136, h118: c21g⁵ c16.2g³ c16.5g² c16.5g⁴ h20.3g² h19.5d⁶ Nov 14] lengthy gelding: fairly useful handicap hurdler: second at Southwell in September: useful handicap chaser: fourth at Worcester (2¾ lengths behind Abidjan) in August: won on point debut in April: stays 2½m: acts on soft and good to firm going: has worn headgear, including last 3 starts: usually wears tongue tie: races towards rear: often travels strongly, but no battler. *David Pipe*   **c136 §** **h121 §**

GABRIEL ARCHER (IRE) 6 b.g. Yeats (IRE) – Miss Bedlam (IRE) (Presenting) [2017/18 b17.2m h16d h16sᵖᵘ Nov 8] well held in bumper (for Joseph Patrick O'Brien): no show in 2 maiden hurdles (for Henry de Bromhead on first occasion): tried in tongue tie. *Alexandra Dunn*   **h–** **b–**

GAELIC FLOW 7 ch.g. With The Flow (USA) – Gaelic Lime (Lomitas) [2017/18 h66, b–: h19.8s h23.9s h23.1d Apr 24] poor maiden hurdler: signs of temperament. *Chris Down*   **h55**

GAELIC POET (IRE) 4 b.g. Yeats (IRE) – Hasainm (IRE) (Grand Lodge (USA)) [2017/18 b16s Mar 17] rather unfurnished gelding: 25/1, ninth in maiden bumper at Kempton. *Tim Vaughan*   **b–**

GAELIC PRINCE (FR) 6 b.g. Martaline – Gaelic Jane (FR) (Hero's Honor (USA)) [2017/18 h16.8vᵘʳ Nov 7] €160,000 3-y-o: strong gelding: half-brother to 3 winners, including fairly useful French hurdler Gaelic Joy (19f winner, by Turgeon) and fairly useful French hurdler/fair chaser Gaelic Ocean (17f/2½m winner, by Urban Ocean): dam French maiden on Flat: hampered and unseated first in novice hurdle at Exeter. *Philip Hobbs*   **h– p**

GAELIC SURPRISE 6 b.m. Arvico (FR) – Gaelic Lime (Lomitas) [2017/18 b74: b16.8m³ h21.6mᶠ h21.6gᵖᵘ Aug 16] angular mare: poor form in bumpers: little impact over hurdles: usually races towards rear. *Stuart Kittow*   **h–** **b73**

GALACTIC POWER (IRE) 8 ch.g. Gamut (IRE) – Celtic Peace (IRE) (Deploy) [2017/18 c–, h90: h19.2g³ h18.5v⁵ h21.2d* h20.7s² h23.8s⁴ h21.2s* h21v³ h23.8dᵖᵘ Apr 24] compact gelding: fair handicap hurdler: won at Ludlow in November and February: well beaten on chasing debut: stays 21f: acts on soft and good to firm going: usually races in rear. *Robin Dickin*   **c–** **h101**

GALE FORCE OSCAR (IRE) 13 br.g. Oscar (IRE) – Distant Gale (IRE) (Strong Gale) [2017/18 c84§, h–§: c24.1sᵖᵘ May 20] smallish, angular gelding: maiden hurdler: fair hunter chaser at best: stays 3¼m: acts on good to firm and heavy going: has worn headgear: wears tongue tie: often races towards rear: temperamental. *Tom Symonds*   **c– §** **h– §**

GALIZZI (USA) 7 b.g. Dansili – Dancing Abbie (USA) (Theatrical) [2017/18 h18.5g h19.2d Sep 10] sturdy gelding: fairly useful hurdler for John Ferguson, no form in 2017/18: unproven beyond 2m: acts on good to soft going: tried in cheekpieces: usually wears tongue tie: has joined J. Reynier, France, placed on Flat in 2018. *Tim Vaughan*   **h–**

GALLAHERS CROSS (IRE) 6 b.g. Getaway (GER) – Raheen Lady (IRE) (Oscar (IRE)) [2017/18 b16.1s* b15.7d⁴ Dec 22] sturdy gelding: second foal: half-brother to a winning pointer by Millenary: dam unraced half-sister to fair hurdler/fairly useful chaser (stayed 3m) Lord Strickland: point winner: useful form in bumpers: won maiden at Galway   **b107**

(by 6½ lengths from Monstrosity) in October: improved when fourth in listed event at Ascot (3 lengths behind Didtheyleaveuoutto) in December: left Peter Fahey after first start: will be suited by further than 2m. *Nicky Henderson*

GALLERY EXHIBITION (IRE) 11 b.g. Portrait Gallery (IRE) – Good Hearted (IRE) (Broken Hearted) [2017/18 c131, h–: c24m⁶ c26.6s³ c21.1s Apr 12] rangy gelding: winning hurdler: useful chaser, below best in 2017/18: stays 25f: acts on soft and good to firm going: wears tongue tie. *Kim Bailey*   c103 h–

GALLEY GREY (IRE) 7 gr.m. Great Palm (USA) – Sabi Sand (Minster Son) [2017/18 b16.8g Oct 3] fifth foal: half-sister to a winning pointer by Definite Article: dam (c88/h64), 3m/3¼m chase winner, half-sister to useful hurdler/chaser (2½m-33f winner) Tyneandthyneagain: tailed off in bumper. *Ray Craggs*   b–

GALROS LADY (IRE) 8 b.m. Alhaarth (IRE) – Alleged Touch (USA) (Alleged (USA)) [2017/18 c82, h71: c23g³ c24d Nov 6] maiden hurdler: poor handicap chaser: best effort at 2½m: acts on good to firm going: usually wears cheekpieces: tried in tongue tie. *Tim Vaughan*   c68 h–

GALUPPI 7 b.g. Galileo (IRE) – La Leuze (IRE) (Caerleon (USA)) [2017/18 h16d³ h20f⁵ Oct 12] modest handicap hurdler: unproven beyond 2m: acts on soft going: often wears visor. *J. R. Jenkins*   h92

GALVESTON (IRE) 9 ch.g. Presenting – Rare Gesture (IRE) (Shalford (IRE)) [2017/18 h99: h23.9s⁴ h23.3v⁵ h23.9v⁵ Sep 28] in frame both completed starts in maiden points: modest maiden hurdler: stays 23f: acts on soft going: has worn tongue tie, including in 2017/18: has joined Thomas Foley. *Gordon Elliott, Ireland*   h90

GALWAY JACK (IRE) 13 b.g. Witness Box (USA) – Cooldalus (IRE) (Mandalus) [2017/18 c128: c20.3g* c24.2v* c20v* c20.3g* Apr 20] rangy gelding: useful hunter chaser, unbeaten in 2017/18: won at Southwell in May, Wetherby in February, Warwick in March and Southwell again (by ¾ length from Shotavodka) in April: stays 3m: acts on heavy going: tried in tongue tie: bold-jumping front runner. *G. T. H. Bailey*   c130

GAMAIN (IRE) 9 b.g. Gamut (IRE) – Glass Curtain (IRE) (Old Vic) [2017/18 c91, h–: h21.6m⁶ h26.5d* h23.3v³ c23.8v³ c30.7v⁵ h23.8s³ h23.8s² c25.1s* Feb 17] fair handicap hurdler: won at Newton Abbot in September: fair handicap chaser: won at Wincanton in February: stays 3¼m: acts on heavy going: wears headgear: often travels strongly. *Nick Williams*   c109 h107

GAMBLING GAMUT (IRE) 6 ch.g. Gamut (IRE) – Red Promise (IRE) (Old Vic) [2017/18 h23.9sᵖᵘ Dec 14] unplaced completed start in Irish points: pulled up in novice on hurdling debut. *Alexandra Dunn*   h–

GAMBOL (FR) 8 ch.g. New Approach (IRE) – Guardia (GER) (Monsun (GER)) [2017/18 c97, h102: c16.4gᵖᵘ h18.7g³ Jul 23] smallish gelding: modest hurdler: similar form over fences: should stay beyond 19f: acts on good to firm and good to soft going: usually wears headgear/tongue tie: often races towards rear. *Ian Williams*   c– h81

GAMBOLING GIGI 6 ch.m. Black Sam Bellamy (IRE) – Gundreda (Gunner B) [2017/18 b16.7g Oct 31] fourth foal: dam unraced sister to useful chaser (21f-3¼m winner) Gunner Welburn: in tongue tie, well held in bumper at Bangor. *Gary Hanmer*   b–

GAME AS A PHEASANT 8 ch.g. Supreme Sound – Burnaby Belle (IRE) (Elnadim (USA)) [2017/18 c26dᵖᵘ May 5] point winner: tailed off in bumper: pulled up in hunter on chasing debut. *Mrs C. A. Coward*   c–

GAMEKEEPER BILL 4 b.g. Beat All (USA) – Granny McPhee (Bahri (USA)) [2017/18 b13.7g⁵ b13.1g b15.3v b15.8s⁶ h15.8d h16s Apr 9] rather unfurnished gelding: poor form in bumpers: no form over hurdles. *Alan Bailey*   h– b74

GAME ON (IRE) 6 b.g. Gamut (IRE) – Dar Dar Supreme (Overbury (IRE)) [2017/18 b92: h19.9d⁴ h21.3s² h20.5v* h23.3v* h19.8v h25.5v² Apr 10] well-made gelding: fairly useful form over hurdles: won novices at Plumpton in January and Uttoxeter in February: stays 3¼m: best form on soft/heavy going: front runner/races prominently. *Lucy Wadham*   h124

GANACHE (IRE) 5 b.g. Scorpion (IRE) – Spring Baloo (IRE) (Definite Article) [2017/18 b16s³ b16d³ Apr 26] €50,000 3-y-o: good-topped gelding: second foal: dam unraced half-sister to top-class hurdler/very smart chaser (2m-21f winner) Oscar Whisky: fair form in bumpers: better effort when third at Warwick in April. *Nicky Henderson*   b93

GANBEI 12 ch.g. Lomitas – Native Ring (FR) (Bering) [2017/18 c125, h119: h24d c24.2d⁵ Mar 29] sturdy gelding: fairly useful handicap hurdler/chaser, below best in 2017/18: stays 3¼m: acts on soft and good to firm going: tried in cheekpieces: sometimes in tongue tie: often races towards rear. *Michael Easterby*   c115 h102

GAN

GANG WARFARE 7 b.g. Medicean – Light Impact (IRE) (Fantastic Light (USA)) [2017/18 h15.8d[5] h19.1m[6] h15.8g h19g[5] h15.7d[4] Dec 28] useful on Flat, stays 2¼m: fair form over hurdles: best effort at 2m: acts on good to soft going: in cheekpieces last 2 starts: often races towards rear. *Alexandra Dunn*   **h104**

GANNICUS 7 b.g. Phoenix Reach (IRE) – Rasmani (Medicean) [2017/18 h104: h16g* h16g[6] h17.7g h20.6g[5] ab16d Mar 5] rather leggy gelding: modest hurdler: won maiden at Fakenham in June: unproven beyond 2m: best form on good going: usually wears cheekpieces: wears tongue tie. *Brendan Powell*   **h99**

GARDE FORESTIER (FR) 6 b.g. Forestier (FR) – Nette Rousse (FR) (Robin des Pres (FR)) [2017/18 h97: h15.3s* h15.8s[3] h21.4v[pu] Apr 9] fair handicap hurdler: won conditional/amateur novice at Wincanton in November: left Charles Whittaker after first start: best around 2m: acts on soft going: wears tongue tie. *Seamus Mullins*   **h108**

GARDEFORT (FR) 9 b.g. Agent Bleu (FR) – La Fresnaie (FR) (Exit To Nowhere (USA)) [2017/18 c145, h–: c19.9s[4] Nov 11] rangy gelding: winning hurdler: useful handicap chaser: fourth at Aintree (10½ lengths behind On Tour) on sole start in 2017/18: stays 21f: acts on good to firm and heavy going: tried in cheekpieces: often travels strongly. *Venetia Williams*   **c137 h–**

GARDE LA VICTOIRE (FR) 9 b.g. Kapgarde (FR) – Next Victory (FR) (Akarad (FR)) [2017/18 c159, h151: h19.4s[2] c17.5v[4] c16.3v Mar 16] tall gelding: smart hurdler at best: second in listed event at Auteuil (2 lengths behind Azucardel) in October: very smart chaser, below form in 2017/18: stays 2½m: acts on good to firm and heavy going: usually races close up. *Philip Hobbs*   **c129 h135**

GARDINERS HILL (IRE) 8 br.g. Stowaway – Mysterious Lass (IRE) (Satco (FR)) [2017/18 c110, h–: c23.8g[6] c23.6s c19.4v[bd] c25.1v[pu] c25.5s[3] c25.1s[pu] Feb 17] sturdy gelding: has had breathing operation: maiden hurdler: modest handicap chaser: stays 25f: acts on heavy going: often wears tongue tie: often races towards rear. *David Rees*   **c98 h–**

GARO DE JUILLEY (FR) 6 b.g. Ungaro (GER) – Lucy de Juilley (FR) (Goldneyev (USA)) [2017/18 h111: h15.3s[2] h16s[3] h19s[3] h21.4d[F] Apr 22] unfurnished gelding: fairly useful handicap hurdler: second at Wincanton in October: stays 19f: acts on soft going: tried in hood: wears tongue tie: often races freely: has bled. *Paul Nicholls*   **h120**

GARRAHALISH (IRE) 10 b.g. Presenting – Savu Sea (IRE) (Slip Anchor) [2017/18 c111, h–: c20g[2] c21m[4] c24.2g[F] Jun 25] winning hurdler: fair handicap chaser: stayed 21f: acted on good to firm and heavy going: tried in cheekpieces/tongue tie: usually raced close up: dead. *Robin Dickin*   **c111 h–**

GARRAN CITY (IRE) 7 ch.g. City Honours (USA) – Native Orchid (IRE) (Be My Native (USA)) [2017/18 h19.5s[3] h19.5v[2] h23.9v[6] Apr 15] £40,000 5-y-o: half-brother to fairly useful chaser Hunters Lodge (2¾m-3m winner, by Subtle Power), stays 29f, and fair hurdler Native Optimist (23f/3m winner, by Broadway Flyer): dam lightly-raced half-sister to useful hurdler/fair chaser (stayed 2½m) Camden Venture: won sole start in Irish maiden points: fairly useful form over hurdles: best effort when third in maiden at Chepstow in February. *David Pipe*   **h116**

GARRANE (IRE) 6 b.g. Tikkanen (USA) – Ballooley (IRE) (Winged Love (IRE)) [2017/18 h19.2g h21.4g h21.6s h21.2d[4] h26v[4] h21.4s[3] h23.9v* h23.6v[4] h23.1v[pu] Apr 17] €11,000 3-y-o: fourth foal: dam unraced half-sister to fairly useful chaser (best around 2½m) Jaffa: maiden Irish pointer: fair handicap hurdler: won at Taunton and Chepstow in March: stays 3¼m: acts on heavy going. *Jeremy Scott*   **h105**

GARRETTSTOWN (IRE) 5 b.g. Doyen (IRE) – Azur (IRE) (Brief Truce (USA)) [2017/18 b16v* Apr 14] seventh foal: half-brother to fairly useful hurdler Bandon Roc (19f-25f winner, by Shirocco): dam 7f-12.6f winner: 5/1, won bumper at Chepstow (by 8 lengths from Nikap) on debut. *Olly Murphy*   **b104**

GASK RIDGE (IRE) 8 b.g. High Chaparral (IRE) – Creative Approach (IRE) (Toulon) [2017/18 h91, b78: h21m[6] h16d[5] h20g[3] h23g[6] Jul 27] lengthy gelding: modest maiden hurdler: won point soon after end of season: stays 2½m: best form on good going: in hood last 3 starts: usually races nearer last than first. *Christian Williams*   **h88**

GAS LINE BOY (IRE) 12 b.g. Blueprint (IRE) – Jervia (Affirmed (USA)) [2017/18 c145, h–: c25d[F] c21.1v* c24.2s[3] c34.3s Apr 14] tall, useful-looking gelding: winning hurdler: smart handicap chaser: won Grand Sefton Chase at Aintree (by 4½ lengths from Ultragold) in December: third in veterans event at Sandown in January: stays 29f: acts on heavy going: wears headgear: often travels strongly. *Ian Williams*   **c148 h–**

GEN

GASOLINE (IRE) 6 b.g. Mahler – Judelle de Thou (FR) (Trebrook (FR)) [2017/18 h78, b74: h23.3g^{pu} h15.7g h21.2g^{pu} h23.3d^{pu} h19.9g^{pu} Oct 3] little form over hurdles: tried in blinkers: has worn tongue tie. *Mike Sowersby* — **h–**

GASSIN GOLF 9 b.g. Montjeu (IRE) – Miss Riviera Golf (Hernando (FR)) [2017/18 h127: h16v h16s^3 h19.7s^4 h16v^3 h16v h16.2v^4 Apr 7] useful-looking gelding: fairly useful handicap hurdler: third at Sandown in January and February: stays 19f: acts on heavy going: usually wears headgear/tongue tie: best treated with caution. *Kerry Lee* — **h119 §**

GAUCHO 5 b.g. Shirocco (GER) – Gulshan (Batshoof) [2017/18 b16.4g b13.7d^6 Nov 25] tall gelding: well held in bumpers. *Nigel Twiston-Davies* — **b–**

GAUCHO GIL (IRE) 5 b.g. Getaway (GER) – Ballys Baby (IRE) (Bob Back (USA)) [2017/18 b16.8s^5 b16.7d Apr 21] well held in bumpers: in hood first start. *Philip Hobbs* — **b–**

GAUVAIN (GER) 16 b.g. Sternkoenig (IRE) – Gamina (GER) (Dominion) [2017/18 c117§, h–: c21.1s^4 May 18] good-topped gelding: multiple point winner: winning hurdler: high-class chaser in prime: stays 3m: acts on soft and good to firm going: often wears headgear: wears tongue tie: unreliable. *Miss V. Collins* — **c89 §, h–**

GAYEBURY 8 b.g. Overbury (IRE) – Gaye Sophie (Environment Friend) [2017/18 h136: h24.1s^{pu} h22.8v c23.8g^F Dec 6] sturdy gelding: useful hurdler at best, below form in 2017/18: narrowly in front when fell fatally 2 out in novice won by Western Climate at Ludlow on chasing debut: stayed 3m: acted on heavy going: tried in cheekpieces. *Evan Williams* — **c132, h–**

GAYTON 4 ch.f. Haafhd – Wistow (Sir Harry Lewis (USA)) [2017/18 b15.7g Apr 20] second foal: dam (c125/h121) 23f-25f hurdle/chase winner: 12/1, eighth in conditional/amateur maiden bumper at Southwell (11¼ lengths behind dead-heaters Indefatigable and Sweet Adare). *Pam Sly* — **b73**

G'DAY AUSSIE 5 b.g. Aussie Rules (USA) – Moi Aussi (USA) (Mt Livermore (USA)) [2017/18 h109: h16.7g^5 h18.6g^{pu} Aug 19] fair handicap hurdler, below form in 2017/18: unproven beyond 17f: acts on good to soft going: wears cheekpieces: often races towards rear: has joined Dave Roberts. *Brian Ellison* — **h94**

GENERAL ALLENBY 4 b.g. Medicean – Cat Hunter (One Cool Cat (USA)) [2017/18 h16.8s^3 Apr 23] dam half-sister to smart hurdler/very smart chaser (2m winner) Charbel: modest on Flat, stays 2m: 16/1, third in novice at Newton Abbot (30¾ lengths behind Higgs) on hurdling debut: will stay further than 2m: open to improvement. *Henry Tett* — **h72 p**

GENERAL BUX 7 b.g. Lucarno (USA) – Cadoutene (FR) (Cadoudal (FR)) [2017/18 h–: c23.6d^6 h16s h16s^4 Dec 19] big gelding: modest form over hurdles: fourth in handicap at Fakenham in December: tailed off in novice on chasing debut: left Suzy Smith after first start: should be suited by at least 2½m: remains capable of better over hurdles. *Olly Murphy* — **c–, h94 p**

188Bet Grand Sefton Handicap Chase, Aintree—Gas Line Boy (No.2) and Robbie Dunne overcome a troubled passage to land this valuable prize from course specialist Ultragold (left)

GENERAL CONSENSUS 6 br.g. Black Sam Bellamy (IRE) – Charlottes Webb (IRE) (Luso) [2017/18 h19.5d h21v* h24s Apr 25] €35,000 3-y-o: first foal: dam (h90), winning pointer, half-sister to useful hurdler (stayed 3m) Kilcrea Kim: maiden pointer: fairly useful form when third at Punchestown only start in bumpers: fair form over hurdles: won maiden at Warwick in March. *Samuel Drinkwater* — h114

GENERAL CUSTARD 5 b.g. Shirocco (GER) – Diamant Noir (Sir Harry Lewis (USA)) [2017/18 b15.8v⁴ b17v² h21v^{pu} Mar 28] poor form in bumpers: pulled up in maiden on hurdling debut. *Olly Murphy* — h– b67

GENERAL GINGER 8 ch.g. Generous (IRE) – Nuzzle (Salse (USA)) [2017/18 h–: h15.3s h15.5d³ h19s⁴ ab18d* Mar 5] won jumpers bumper at Kempton in March: fairly useful handicap hurdler: third at Leicester in November: stays 19f: acts on good to firm and good to soft going: wears tongue tie. *Harry Fry* — h115

GENERAL GAMBUL 11 b.g. General Gambul – Gold Charm (Imperial Fling (USA)) [2017/18 c88, h–: c26.7v⁵ c25.1v^{pu} c19.4v^{pu} c23.5v* c25.1s² c25.7v^{pu} c25.1v³ c24.2v³ c21s² Apr 23] tall, angular gelding: winning hurdler: modest handicap chaser: won at Lingfield in January: stays 3¼m: acts on heavy going: wears headgear: front runner. *Ron Hodges* — c90 h–

GENERAL MAHLER (IRE) 8 b.g. Mahler – High Dough (IRE) (High Roller (IRE)) [2017/18 h112: h19.7s h19.4d⁵ c21.4s² c24s⁴ c26.6s³ h25d^F h24.3g Apr 20] has had breathing operation: modest handicap hurdler: fair form over fences: best effort when second in novice handicap at Market Rasen in December: barely stays 3¼m: acts on heavy going: usually wears tongue tie: often races in rear. *Brian Ellison* — c112 h95

GENERAL MALARKEY (IRE) 6 b.g. Scorpion (IRE) – Andreas Benefit (IRE) (Beneficial) [2017/18 b81: h21.2s^{pu} h20.3v Feb 5] little impact in bumpers/over hurdles. *Nigel Twiston-Davies* — h–

GENERAL PICTON (IRE) 6 b.g. Beneficial – Back To Cloghoge (IRE) (Bob Back (USA)) [2017/18 h19.5s Apr 27] tailed off in novice hurdle. *Kim Bailey* — h–

GENERAL PRINCIPLE (IRE) 9 b.g. Gold Well – How Provincial (IRE) (Be My Native (USA)) [2017/18 c140, h–: h24v² c24v c24.5d c21s⁴ c21.3s⁶ c29v* Apr 2] — c142 h134

Watching the two superpower jumping trainers in Ireland marshalling their vast forces can be fascinating. Fifteen-times British champion Martin Pipe ran ten horses in the 2001 Grand National and Flat trainer David 'Dandy' Nicholls once ran twelve in a Stewards' Cup consolation handicap, but it is by no means such a rarity nowadays to see a mob-handed approach adopted in Ireland's valuable handicaps. The stables of Willie Mullins and Gordon Elliott both threw the kitchen sink at particular races in the latest season, Mullins saddling thirteen of the twenty-four runners in a handicap hurdle on the last day of the Punchestown Festival (they filled four of the first five places) while Elliott, who frequently makes a multiple challenge for Ireland's most valuable handicap chases, had fielded thirteen runners himself in the Boylesports Irish Grand National at Fairyhouse on Easter Monday (the day he also passed two hundred winners for the season). Thirteen runners in the same race was a record, overkill even by the practice of Elliott who had run nine in the race the previous year, and, with Mullins saddling four, the pair accounted for over half the Irish National field (they had provided forty-eight of the ninety-seven original entries). British trainers seem to have virtually given up when it comes to the Irish National—there was one British challenger in 2017 and none at all for the latest running—while in Ireland there are plenty who think the crushing domination of the Mullins and Elliott stables is not healthy for the game. Furthermore, eight of the Elliott runners in the Irish National were owned by Gigginstown House Stud who were also represented by horses saddled by Mouse Morris and Joseph O'Brien which brought the Gigginstown team to ten, one third of the field (they had run thirteen in the race the year before). Gigginstown had won the Irish National on three occasions, with Hear The Echo (2008), Thunder And Roses (2015) and Rogue Angel (2016), but, rather surprisingly, both Willie Mullins and Gordon Elliott were still waiting for their first success in the Fairyhouse showpiece.

The ill-fated Our Duke, the previous year's impressive winner, originally headed the Irish Grand National weights but, on the day, four of the Gigginstown contingent—Outlander, the Thyestes Chase winner Monbeg Notorious, the smart novice Dounikos and Lord Scoundrel (all trained by Elliott)—filled four of the top

Boylesports Irish Grand National Chase (Extended Handicap), Fairyhouse—mayhem as leader Bellshill throws away his winning chance by barely clearing the last, hampering several in the process, notably Arkwrisht (second right) ...

five slots, with the Mullins-trained Bellshill (penalised 8 lb for a win in the Bobbyjo Chase) second top weight behind Outlander. The Mullins quartet also included the 13/2 favourite Pairofbrowneyes, who had won the Leinster National, and the 16/1-shot Isleofhopendreams who had finished second to another of the well-backed runners Folsom Blue (Elliott-trained) in the Punchestown Grand National Trial. Folsom Blue was among the Irish Grand National runners who had done well in the race before (fourth and fifth in previous years) and that group also included Thunder And Roses (who had added a fourth place in 2017 to his record), the veteran Bless The Wings (runner-up in the two previous years) and General Principle, another of the Gigginstown/Elliott battalion, who had finished fifth as a novice the previous year. General Principle had been a 16/1-shot on that occasion and the mount of Bryan Cooper who was then Gigginstown's first jockey; Cooper's once-burgeoning career has gone into decline since being displaced from that job in the summer, before being appointed by Alan Potts to ride his horses trained in Britain by

... allowing General Principle (second left) to just get the better of Isleofhopendreams (left) in a grandstand finish; Forever Gold (right) pipped Bellshill (later demoted) for third

Gigginstown House Stud's "General Principle"

Colin Tizzard, only to hold that post for just a short time after Potts's death before being replaced by Robbie Power (Cooper had been told initially that he would still ride for Gigginstown but would no longer have first call, but he didn't have the mount on any of the ten Gigginstown runners in the latest Irish National, in which he picked up a spare ride for Willie Mullins on the promising novice Kemboy who, alas, didn't get very far on his first foray into handicaps).

General Principle had been running in fiercely competitive valuable handicaps all season but the only time he had reached the frame had been in the Leopardstown Chase (branded as the Chanelle Pharma) in February when he shaped well enough to suggest he wasn't handicapped out of things, running on to finish fourth after still having plenty to do three out. Davy Russell, who rode him that day, was on Dounikos in the Irish National while Jack Kennedy, who had ridden General Principle in his other races over fences during the season, was on Monbeg Notorious. J. J. Slevin had the mount on 20/1-shot General Principle who was ridden closer to the pace than usual and travelled fluently before coming under pressure from the third last in a race that was run under conditions that were at the very limit of raceable after heavy rain turned the track into a quagmire (the remaining day of the Easter Festival was abandoned because of waterlogging). As General Principle moved into fourth approaching the final fence, he suddenly benefited from dramatic happenings just in front of him when the leader Bellshill slowed and veered left, barely clambering over the fence as he severely hampered second-placed Arkwrisht in an incident in which the staying-on lightweight Forever Gold was baulked, along with Folsom Blue who was coming with a strong challenge. Isleofhopendreams briefly grabbed the initiative in a five-horse, last-gasp scramble for the line, but the very strongly-ridden General Principle clawed him back in the dying strides to win by a head, with Forever Gold half a length away third, and Bellshill a further head back in fourth, three quarters of a length in front of the rallying Folsom Blue who stayed on strongly again from the last and was promoted to fourth afterwards by the stewards who were also kept busy issuing a seven-day ban to the winning jockey for using his whip with excessive force and a three-day ban for Danny Mullins who rode the runner-up and was deemed not to have given his mount enough time to respond to the whip. Only eight of the runners completed the course, the last of them Monbeg Notorious giving his trainer three finishers from an all-out assault that finally fulfilled his ambition to triumph in Ireland's richest jumps race (total prize money nowadays €500,000).

General Principle (IRE) (b.g. 2009)
— Gold Well (b 2001)
—— Sadler's Wells (b 1981) —— Northern Dancer / Fairy Bridge
—— Floripedes (b 1985) —— Top Ville / Toute Cy
— How Provincial (IRE) (b 1996)
—— Be My Native (br 1979) —— Our Native / Witchy Woman
—— Jazz Bavard (b 1984) —— Le Bavard / Jazz Music

The lengthy, well-made General Principle is typical of the slow-maturing, chasing types nurtured by the Gigginstown operation which makes a huge financial commitment to Irish racing. General Principle was bought by his trainer for £80,000 as a five-year-old at the Cheltenham December Sales, a fortnight after he had made a winning debut in an Irish maiden point, and he didn't make his first appearance under Rules until he was six. A useful bumper winner (contested the Champion Bumper at Cheltenham), he went on to show fairly useful form over hurdles before being sent chasing as a seven-year-old. By the now-deceased Gold Well (an unraced brother to Montjeu), General Principle is the seventh foal produced by How Provincial, an unraced half-sister to Sounds Strong who was a useful staying handicap chaser at his best. How Provincial's other winners include the useful handicap chaser Saints And Sinners (a brother to General Principle) and a couple of useful staying chasers in Bella Mana Mou (by Snurge) and Wicked Willy (by Arcadio). Their unraced grandam Jazz Bavard was out of the bumper winner Jazz Music, a sister and half-sister to the staying chasers Stephen's Society and Slaves Dream. The latter was runner-up in the Scottish Grand National (he also won the Great Yorkshire Chase), while Stephen's Society earned fame for winning the 1973 Velka Pardubicka under British amateur Chris Collins. General Principle, who has worn a tongue tie on his last four starts, stays twenty-nine furlongs and acts on heavy going. *Gordon Elliott, Ireland*

GENEROUS CHIEF (IRE) 10 br.g. Generous (IRE) – Yosna (FR) (Sicyos (USA)) [2017/18 c101§, h107§: h26.4d h26.5g h23g[5] h26.5d c23g[3] h25g[2] h25g[3] c23m[6] h25g[3] Nov 5] good-topped gelding: fair handicap hurdler: modest handicap chaser: stays 27f: acts on soft and good to firm going: wears headgear: front runner/races prominently: lazy sort who needs treating with caution. *Graeme McPherson* c98 § h102 §

GENEROUS DAY (IRE) 6 b.g. Daylami (IRE) – Our Pride (Generous (IRE)) [2017/18 h96, b–: h15.8d[2] h15.7d* h15.5s[3] h18.6s* h20.6s[4] h16.7g[3] Apr 22] fair handicap hurdler: won at Southwell in November and Market Rasen in December: stays 21f: acts on soft going: usually races prominently. *Henry Oliver* h111

GENEROUS HELPINGS (IRE) 9 ch.g. Generous (IRE) – Saffron Pride (IRE) (Be My Native (USA)) [2017/18 c–x, h101x: h23.9s[6] h21.7g Apr 20] fair hurdler, below form in 2017/18: maiden chaser: stays 25f: acts on good to firm and good to soft going: usually wears headgear: often let down by jumping. *Gary Moore* c– x h– x

GENI JOHNSON (IRE) 6 b.m. Mountain High (IRE) – Garrymorris (IRE) (Old Vic) [2017/18 b16g b18g[6] b16d h21d h19.8g h16.9s h20v[ur] h15.3v h18.5s[3] Apr 23] fifth foal: dam unraced daughter of fairly useful hurdler/useful chaser up to 3m Letterlee: no form in bumpers: poor form over hurdles: left J. R. Barry after sixth start: should stay 2½m: acts on soft going: tried in cheekpieces: often races towards rear. *Alexandra Dunn* h83 b–

GENRES 6 b.g. Champs Elysees – Musical Horizon (USA) (Distant View (USA)) [2017/18 h16.6d[pu] Dec 16] fair on Flat, stays 12.5f: pulled up in novice on hurdling debut. *Rebecca Menzies* h–

GEN

GENTLEMAN FARMER 6 ch.g. Tobougg (IRE) – Sweet Shooter (Double Trigger (IRE)) [2017/18 h–, b–: h16.8s h16.8v h19g Nov 16] tall, lengthy gelding: won on second of 2 starts in points: little impact over hurdles. *Richard Hawker*   h–

GENTLEMAN JAMES 6 b.g. Sixties Icon – Cashback Rose (IRE) (Alflora (IRE)) [2017/18 h–: h23.9g h19.9g h19.9s Dec 26] poor maiden hurdler: tried in tongue tie. *Dianne Sayer*   h61

GENTLEMAN JON 10 b.g. Beat All (USA) – Sudden Spirit (FR) (Esprit du Nord (USA)) [2017/18 c131, h–: c25.8g³ c21m⁴ c26.1m⁵ c20s² c23g³ c20.2s⁵ c26.7g³ c25d^F c22.4g³ c24.2v^{pu} Feb 11] tall, well-made, attractive gelding: winning hurdler: fairly useful handicap chaser: second at Uttoxeter in July and third at Newbury in December: stays 27f: acts on good to firm and heavy going: wears blinkers/tongue tie: usually races prominently: temperamental. *Colin Tizzard*   c125 §
h–

GEOPHONY (IRE) 4 b.g. Canford Cliffs (IRE) – Dawn Chorus (IRE) (Mukaddamah (USA)) [2017/18 h16.2v^{pu} h15.8g Oct 5] fair on Flat, stays 1m: no form over hurdles. *Mark Johnston*   h–

GEORDIE B 5 br.g. Geordieland (FR) – Sari Rose (FR) (Vertical Speed (FR)) [2017/18 b16.2v* Apr 10] £40,000 2-y-o: sixth foal: half-brother to modest hurdlers Amber Flush (23f-25f winner, by Sir Harry Lewis) and Silent Sun (2m winner, by Lucarno): dam, French 17f hurdle winner, half-sister to very smart French chaser (stayed 29f) Indien Bleu: 7/2, won bumper at Hereford (by ½ length from Little Rory Mac) on debut. *Venetia Williams*   b94

GEORDIE DES CHAMPS (IRE) 7 br.g. Robin des Champs (FR) – Kilcoleman Lady (IRE) (Presenting) [2017/18 h137: c25s⁴ c23s* c25.2s² c20d³ Apr 28] useful-looking gelding: useful hurdler: similar form over fences: won novice handicap at Taunton (by 3¾ lengths from Captain Buck's) in January and novice at Hereford in March: stays 25f: acts on soft going: tried in tongue tie: remains open to improvement over fences. *Rebecca Curtis*   c135 p
h–

GEORDIELAD 4 ch.g. Geordieland (FR) – Adees Dancer (Danehill Dancer (IRE)) [2017/18 h16sp^u Nov 29] no form on Flat: pulled up in juvenile maiden on hurdling debut. *Oliver Sherwood*   h–

GEORDIELANDGANGSTA 5 br.g. Geordieland (FR) – Dunsfold Duchess (IRE) (Bustino) [2017/18 b17v⁶ h16.2s Apr 26] second on completed start in points: little impact in bumper: 100/1, seventh in novice at Perth (23¼ lengths behind Asylo) on hurdling debut. *Rose Dobbin*   h74
b–

GEORGE GENTLY (FR) 5 b.g. Gentlewave (IRE) – Sindibad (USA) (Rock of Gibraltar (IRE)) [2017/18 h15.7v^{pu} h16s Mar 17] lengthy gelding: fairly useful form when second in juvenile hurdle at Enghien on debut, little show both starts in 2017/18. *Dan Skelton*   h–

GEORGE HERBERT 7 b.g. Yeats (IRE) – Colorado Dawn (Fantastic Light (USA)) [2017/18 h88: h19d h18.7g⁶ h18.6g^{pu} Aug 6] maiden pointer: little impact over hurdles: often wears cheekpieces: temperament under suspicion. *Fergal O'Brien*   h–

GEORGIAN FIREBIRD 8 b.m. Firebreak – Skovshoved (IRE) (Danetime (IRE)) [2017/18 h16s^F h15.8v⁶ h20.7s³ h21v^{pu} Mar 28] modest handicap hurdler: stays 21f: acts on heavy going. *Barry Leavy*   h93

GEORGIESHORE (IRE) 10 b.g. Turtle Island (IRE) – Pride of St Gallen (IRE) (Orchestra) [2017/18 h78: h15.5d⁴ h19.9v³ h15.5v* h15.5v⁵ h16v⁶ c16v² h15.7v Mar 15] well-made gelding: modest handicap hurdler: won at Leicester in January: well beaten in novice on chasing debut: stays 2½m: acts on heavy going: wears headgear. *Zoe Davison*   c61
h86

GEORGINA JOY 5 b.m. Midnight Legend – First Katoune (FR) (Poliglote) [2017/18 h16g h16.8d⁶ h16.8v h15.3g h21g⁶ h23.9s² h23.9v^{pu} h23.1d² Apr 24] third foal: half-sister to fair hurdlers Southport (17f winner, by Robin des Pres) and Chu Chu Percy (3m/25f winner, by Tobougg), latter also winning pointer: dam, unraced, out of useful French hurdler/winning chaser around 2¼m Katoune: poor maiden hurdler: stays 3m: acts on soft going: in tongue tie last 3 starts: usually leads. *Nigel Hawke*   h74

GERMANY CALLING (IRE) 9 b.g. Germany (USA) – Markir (IRE) (Flemensfirth (USA)) [2017/18 c141, h–: c21.4g^{pu} c19.4g⁶ Nov 2] lengthy gelding: winning hurdler: useful chaser, well below best in 2017/18: stays 2½m: acts on soft and good to firm going: wears cheekpieces/tongue tie: front runner/races prominently. *Charlie Longsdon*   c–
h–

GERONIMO 7 ch.g. Kadastrof (FR) – Triggers Ginger (Double Trigger (IRE)) [2017/18 h20.5v² h20.5v² h25d² h22.7v² Apr 16] first foal: dam (c83/h86), winning pointer/maiden under Rules (stayed 3m), half-sister to fairly useful chaser (3m winner) Silver Commander: fair form when runner-up all starts over hurdles: stays 25f. *Sandy Thomson*   h109

GET

GERTIE GETAWAY (IRE) 6 b.m. Getaway (GER) – Aroseforclare (Royal Vulcan) [2017/18 b16.8m⁴ h16m⁴ h19s^pu Dec 30] €2,500 3-y-o: eighth foal: half-sister to 2 winning pointers by Bienamado: dam, of little account, half-sister to dam of useful hurdler/smart chaser (best up to 21f) I'msingingtheblues: shaped as if needed experience in bumper: modest form over hurdles: better effort when fourth in novice at Worcester. *Philip Hobbs* **h85 b72**

GETABIRD (IRE) 6 b.g. Getaway (GER) – Fern Bird (IRE) (Revoque (IRE)) [2017/18 b116: h20v* h16v* h16.4s h16v* h16.5d h20s^pu Apr 27] **h144**

    For once, it wasn't a Willie Mullins-trained novice hurdler who was the main focus of hype going into Cheltenham. The achievements of Samcro saw to that, though Getabird had established no small reputation himself and, at 7/4, he started a shorter price than any of his predecessors from the same stable, Vautour, Douvan, Min and Melon, who had been sent off either favourite or joint favourite for the four preceding editions of the Supreme Novices' Hurdle. In fact, Getabird had a very similar profile to Samcro leading up to the Festival, maintaining an unbeaten record over hurdles after graduating from points and showing lots of ability in bumpers. The pair had actually begun their careers together as four-year-olds in the hands of Ireland's leading handler of pointers Colin Bowe. Unlike Samcro's record, however, that of Getabird wasn't entirely without blemish as he had run out in the early stages of his debut between the flags. Both horses had gone on to fetch six-figure sums to join Ireland's opposing superpowers, Samcro going to Gigginstown and Gordon Elliott, and Getabird to Rich and Susannah Ricci and Mullins. A clash between the two could have taken place in the Supreme but, with Samcro waiting instead for the Baring Bingham, Getabird had a favourite's chance of becoming his owners' fourth winner of the Festival opener in the last six runnings, following Champagne Fever, Vautour and Douvan. However, after making much of the running, Getabird was soon done with and eventually eased to finish a well-held eleventh of the fifteen finishers behind Summerville Boy. Getabird had two cracks at restoring his reputation at a major festival when turning out for both the two-mile and two-and-a-half-mile Champion Novices' Hurdles at Punchestown. His double shift was no doubt prompted by Samcro's absence from the longer contest in favour of the meeting's Champion Hurdle. Getabird raced too freely when well beaten in the two-mile contest, but was in the process of running a much better race three days later when he and stablemate Scarpeta were badly hampered and brought to a standstill by a faller two out who sent them into the rails.

Sky Bet Moscow Flyer Novices' Hurdle, Punchestown—Getabird rockets to the head of the ante-post betting for the Supreme Novices' with an impressive display

GET

Getabird hasn't had much luck at the big festivals to date, as he had failed to make Cheltenham at all the previous season after being ante-post favourite over the winter for the Champion Bumper. He had earned that position with wins at Fairyhouse (backed off the boards when winning impressively by twelve lengths) and Gowran, though he had to work harder to beat three rivals at odds of 10/1-on on the second occasion and was found to be lame afterwards. Getabird had only the ill-fated Cheltenham and Punchestown winner Fayonagh, and Paloma Blue who had chased her home at Punchestown, above him in the bumper ratings in *Chasers & Hurdlers 2016/17*, Getabird rated 116 and Samcro, winner of all three of his bumpers, on 115p. Getabird had only two races over hurdles prior to Cheltenham, both at Punchestown. Returning from almost eleven months off the course in December, he just needed keeping up to his work to land the odds in a maiden by seven lengths from the useful Impact Factor. That was over two and a half miles, and Getabird was dropped back to two miles for the following month's Sky Bet Moscow Flyer Novices' Hurdle, a Grade 2 contest which Vautour, Douvan and Min had all won before going for the Supreme. Mullins ran two others in a field of six, though it was essentially a two-horse race between even-money Getabird and the Gordon Elliott-trained Mengli Khan who had already shown smart form when winning the Royal Bond Novices' Hurdle at Fairyhouse. Mengli Khan had since blotted his copybook when running out in the Future Champions Novices' Hurdle at Leopardstown and had to concede 6 lb to Getabird because of a penalty for his Grade 1 win in the Royal Bond. Mengli Khan went on to finish in front of Getabird twice later in the season, when third in both the Supreme and over two miles at Punchestown, but there was no mistaking Getabird's superiority in the Moscow Flyer. Making all under Mr Patrick Mullins, who had ridden him in both his bumpers, Getabird travelled strongly before stretching clear of Mengli Khan in the straight for an impressive nine-length success. Getabird was similarly dominant in between Cheltenham and Punchestown when putting up a slightly better performance still to win another Grade 2 contest, the Rathbarry & Glenview Studs Novices' Hurdle at Fairyhouse in early-April. Back under Paul Townend this time, Getabird enjoyed an easier lead than he had in the Supreme and banished memories of that performance with a ready win, settling better than at Cheltenham and quickening entering the straight before pulling twelve lengths clear of stable-companion Draconien to whom he was conceding 6 lb. The runner-up turned that form on its head when having Getabird back in seventh at level weights at Punchestown, while the third and fourth at Fairyhouse, Hardline and Sharjah, also ran well below their best in the same race next time.

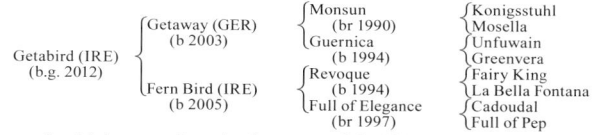

Getabird (IRE) (b.g. 2012)
- Getaway (GER) (b 2003)
  - Monsun (br 1990)
    - Konigsstuhl
    - Mosella
  - Guernica (b 1994)
    - Unfuwain
    - Greenvera
- Fern Bird (IRE) (b 2005)
  - Revoque (b 1994)
    - Fairy King
    - La Bella Fontana
  - Full of Elegance (br 1997)
    - Cadoudal
    - Full of Pep

Getabird comes from the first crop of the high-class Getaway who began his racing career in France with Andre Fabre before being returned to his native Germany. He started out as a stayer but raced mainly over a mile and a half later on, winning twice at Group 1 level, including the Grosser Preis von Baden. Standing at Grange Stud, Getaway has been second only to another Coolmore jumps stallion, Soldier of Fortune, in terms of the number of mares he has covered in recent seasons. Getabird and the smart Nicky Henderson-trained mare Verdana Blue are the pick of Getaway's early runners to date. Getabird quickly made amends for his misdemeanour on his pointing debut by winning his next start before he was sold days later at Goffs Punchestown Sale for €200,000. Getaway's offspring have proven especially popular at boutique sales, and Getabird is far from being the most expensive of them; Downtown Getaway, who won the same Fairyhouse bumper in which Getabird had himself made his Rules debut a year earlier, was bought to join Nicky Henderson from Mags Mullins for £350,000 at Cheltenham in December. Getabird is the first foal out of his dam Fern Bird who was pulled up in her only start in an Irish point, while grandam Full of Elegance was unraced but has produced

GET

the useful staying chaser Relentless Dreamer. This is a very successful family, as great grandam Full of Pep was a prolific broodmare in France and is notable now for being the grandam of Cheltenham Gold Cup and dual King George winner Long Run. Mullins trained another good winner descending from Full of Pep in great granddaughter J'Y Vole whose successes included the Dr P. J. Moriarty Novices' Chase, as well as finishing third in the Ryanair Chase. Full of Pep produced good winners of her own, too, including Full of Ambition who was second in the Grande Course de Haies d'Auteuil.

Not everything went smoothly for Getabird in his first season over jumps but the positives outweighed the negatives and he should make an exciting novice chaser. He is a strong, compact gelding and his style of racing should make him hard to peg back over fences. Having tended to race freely when taken on for the lead in the Supreme, and on his first start at the Punchestown Festival, he settled better when fitted with an Australian noseband on his final start. Getabird stays two and a half miles, but is fully effective over two. While his best performances came on heavy ground in the latest season, his bumper wins show that he does not require conditions that are testing. He wore ear plugs in the Supreme Novices' Hurdle. *W. P. Mullins, Ireland*

GETAREASON (IRE) 5 ch.g. Getaway (GER) – Simple Reason (IRE) (Snurge) [2017/18 b17.3s* b16.2d³ Apr 26] £8,000 3-y-o, £140,000 4-y-o: third foal: dam unraced half-sister to fairly useful hurdler/useful chaser (stays 3m) Jet Master: useful form in bumpers: won maiden at Downpatrick (by 4¼ lengths from Ruthless Article) in March: improved when third at Punchestown (6¼ lengths behind Dunvegan) month later. *W. P. Mullins, Ireland* **b105**

GETAWAY BAY (IRE) 6 b.g. Getaway (GER) – Wayward Star (IRE) (Old Vic) [2017/18 h16.2v^pu Oct 14] maiden Irish pointer: pulled up in novice on hurdling debut. *Sue Smith* **h–**

GETAWAY GERRY 4 b.g. Getaway (GER) – Loch Dhu (IRE) (Oscar (IRE)) [2017/18 b16.2d⁶ Apr 23] 50/1, sixth in bumper at Hexham (16 lengths behind Melekhov). *Katie Scott* **b69**

GETAWAY JOHN (IRE) 5 ch.g. Getaway (GER) – Present Your Own (IRE) (Presenting) [2017/18 b16s² b16v* b16v* b16.3s Apr 25] €30,000 3-y-o: third foal: dam placed in point: smart bumper performer: won at Punchestown in February and Fairyhouse (by 2¾ lengths from Brace Yourself) in April: should prove suited by further than 2m: usually responds generously to pressure. *Gordon Elliott, Ireland* **b115**

GETAWAY KATIE MAI (IRE) 5 br.m. Getaway (GER) – Carrigmoorna Style (IRE) (Dr Massini (IRE)) [2017/18 b16.2d* b16s² b17s* Apr 12] neat mare: sixth foal: half-sister to fair hurdler Koultas King (2½m-2¾m winner, by Exit To Nowhere): dam unraced half-sister to useful hurdler/chaser (winner up to 25f) Control Man: runner-up in point on debut: useful form in bumpers: won mares event at Ballinrobe (by ¾ length from Motown Girl) in August and Nickel Coin Mares' National Hunt Flat Race at Aintree (by 1¼ lengths from Midnightreferendum) in April: second in Grade 2 at Leopardstown (1½ lengths behind Relegate) in between: will be suited by further than 2m. *John Queally, Ireland* **b108**

Goffs Nickel Coin Mares' Standard Open NH Flat Race, Aintree—Irish-trained favourite Getaway Katie Mai (No.5) comes from a seemingly impossible position to score under some controversially hard driving from Mr Jamie Codd who picks up a 17-day whip ban and £400 fine

GET

GETAWAY TRUMP (IRE) 5 b.g. Getaway (GER) – Acinorev (IRE) (Cape Cross (IRE)) [2017/18 b16s⁴ b15.3v⁶ Apr 9] €11,500 3-y-o, £90,000 4-y-o: third foal: dam (b80), ran twice in bumpers, half-sister to useful hurdler/fairly useful chaser (stayed 3m) Paco Jack: off mark in Irish points at third attempt: best form in bumpers: better effort when fourth in maiden at Kempton in February. *Paul Nicholls* **b89**

GET BACK TO ME (IRE) 11 br.g. Presenting – My Name's Not Bin (IRE) (Good Thyne (USA)) [2017/18 c74, h79: c20.5g^pu c20.9g^pu Jun 20] maiden hurdler/chaser, no form in 2017/18: stays 2¾m: acts on good to soft going: sometimes in tongue tie: often races lazily. *Simon Earle* **c–** **h–**

GET HOME NOW 10 b.g. Diktat – Swiftly (Cadeaux Genereux) [2017/18 h100: h21.6g² h20d⁴ h23.3g³ h20m* h19.2m* h18.6g* h21.1p^pu Oct 27] sturdy gelding: fairly useful handicap hurdler: won at Worcester (conditional) in July, Fontwell in August and Market Rasen in September: stays 2½m: acts on firm and soft going: often wears headgear: wears tongue tie: front runner/races prominently. *Peter Bowen* **h122**

GET INVOLVED (IRE) 9 b.g. Milan – Strong Red (Strong Gale) [2017/18 c113x, h101: c23g* c24gf Sep 26] tall gelding: fair hurdler: fair handicap chaser: won at Worcester in June: fell fatally at Warwick: stayed 25f: acted on heavy going: often wore headgear/tongue tie. *Robin Dickin* **c106 x** **h–**

GETONSAM 6 ch.g. Black Sam Bellamy (IRE) – Pennepoint (Pennekamp (USA)) [2017/18 h86, b–: h16.2g h16.2g⁶ h16.4s^pu h15.7s^pu Jan 1] little sign of ability: sometimes in hood: wears tongue tie: front runner/races prominently, often freely. *Jonathan Haynes* **h–**

GET ON THE YAGER 8 b.g. Tamure (IRE) – Florentino (Efisio) [2017/18 h131: c22.5s⁶ c19.4d⁶ c26v* c24.2s* c20.3v² c34v c31.8g^pu Apr 21] good-topped gelding: useful hurdler: useful handicap chaser: won at Fontwell and Rowland Meyrick Chase at Wetherby in December: second in novice at Southwell (2½ lengths behind Two Swallows) in February: stays 3¼m: acts on heavy going: usually races towards rear. *Dan Skelton* **c138** **h–**

GET OUT THE GATE (IRE) 5 b.g. Mahler – Chartani (IRE) (King's Theatre (IRE)) [2017/18 h16s⁴ h21s⁴ h21.4v⁶ Apr 9] €26,000 3-y-o: tall gelding: will make a chaser: second foal: dam (c102/h89), 2m hurdle/chase winner (stayed 2½m), half-sister to fairly useful hurdler (2m winner) Dul Ar An Ol: won Irish point on debut: fairly useful form over hurdles: best effort when fourth in novice at Sandown in December: should stay beyond 2m. *Paul Nicholls* **h116**

GET READY FREDDY 8 b.g. Sixties Icon – Summer Shades (Green Desert (USA)) [2017/18 c80, h60: c16g⁴ c16.5g* h16.3m² c16d* c16.5f⁴ h16.8s Oct 24] sparsely-made gelding: poor maiden hurdler: fair handicap chaser: won at Worcester in August and Uttoxeter in September: left Nick Mitchell after first start: unproven beyond 2m: acts on good to firm and good to soft going: tried in cheekpieces: wears tongue tie: often races in rear. *Dan Skelton* **c102** **h77**

GET RHYTHM (IRE) 8 b.g. Kayf Tara – Ninna Nanna (FR) (Garde Royale) [2017/18 h112, b75: h16g² h16.7d* c16g* c16d² c15.7d³ c16.4s⁵ c17.4df Apr 21] good-topped gelding: fairly useful hurdler: won maiden at Bangor in June: similar form over fences: won novice handicap at Ffos Las in June: second in handicap at Lingfield in November: unproven beyond 17f: acts on heavy going: usually leads. *Tom George* **c120** **h117**

GETTYSBURG ADDRESS (IRE) 7 b.g. Milan – Cat Burglar (IRE) (Robellino (USA)) [2017/18 h24g³ h20g³ h19.9g² h21.6g* h20.1d* Sep 5] €55,000 3-y-o: third foal: half-brother to fairly useful hurdler/chaser Skylander (17f-23f winner, by Flemensfirth): dam maiden on Flat: fairly useful hurdler: won maiden at Newton Abbot in August and novice at Hexham in September: left Noel Meade after first start: stays 3m: acts on heavy going: wears headgear: tried in tongue tie: front runner/races prominently. *Dr Richard Newland* **h120**

GET WISHING (IRE) 6 b.g. Getaway (GER) – Third Wish (IRE) (Second Empire (IRE)) [2017/18 b–: h16s h16.5g h16.8v³ h19.9v⁴ h16v^pu h15.3v⁶ Apr 9] modest form over hurdles: best effort at 17f: acts on heavy going: sometimes in hood: often wears tongue tie. *Victor Dartnall* **h86**

G FOR GINGER 8 ch.m. Lucarno (USA) – Kaream (Karinga Bay) [2017/18 h57, b89: h16g² h16g* h21.6g⁵ h19g Nov 16] bumper winner: fair form over hurdles: won mares maiden at Worcester in September: should stay 2½m: best form on good going: tried in hood: usually wears tongue tie: usually races close up. *Anthony Honeyball* **h108**

GHINIA (IRE) 7 b.m. Mastercraftsman (IRE) – Jorghinia (FR) (Seattle Slew (USA)) [2017/18 h15.7d⁵ h16s⁵ Dec 19] fair on Flat, stays 1¼m: well held in 2 novice hurdles. *Pam Sly* **h–**

352

GIN

GIBBES BAY (FR) 6 gr.g. Al Namix (FR) – Nouvelle Donne (FR) (Sleeping Car (FR)) [2017/18 h106, b93: h19.8s² h21.4g c24d^{ur} c24d^F Feb 8] tall gelding: bumper winner: fairly useful form over hurdles: second in novice handicap at Wincanton in October: departed early both starts over fences: should stay 21f: acts on soft and good to firm going. *Paul Nicholls*   c– h115

GIBB HILL 4 ch.g. Frozen Fire (GER) – River Reine (IRE) (Lahib (USA)) [2017/18 b15.3v⁵ Dec 7] workmanlike gelding: well beaten in junior bumper. *Bob Buckler*   b–

GIBBSTOWN (IRE) 12 b.m. Bob Back (USA) – Kitty Maher (IRE) (Posen (USA)) [2017/18 c98§, h–: c23s c24.4v⁵ c23.5d c24.6v c21v⁴ c24.1v³ c24.1v⁶ c24.2d² Apr 23] maiden hurdler: modest handicap chaser: stays 25f: acts on heavy going: has worn headgear, including last 3 starts: has worn tongue tie: temperamental. *Paul Stafford, Ireland*   c89 § h–

GIBENO (IRE) 4 b.g. Fastnet Rock (AUS) – Dance To The Top (Sadler's Wells (USA)) [2017/18 b13.7g h15.7v^{pu} Feb 5] has had breathing operation: well beaten in junior bumper: pulled up in novice on hurdling debut: wears tongue tie: fair form on Flat for Michael Appleby, best effort at 7f. *Dan Skelton*   h– b–

GIBRALFARO (IRE) 6 b.g. Dalakhani (IRE) – Ronda (Bluebird (USA)) [2017/18 h141: c20.3g³ h17h* Apr 14] compact gelding: useful hurdler: won allowance race at Tryon in April: last of 3 in novice at Bangor (15 lengths behind Modus) on chasing debut (should do better): left Alan King after first start: stays 21f: acts on hard and soft going: has worn headgear. *Jack O. Fisher, USA*   c113 p h123

GIBSON PARK 5 b.g. Poet's Voice – Fifty (IRE) (Fasliyev (USA)) [2017/18 h115p: h18.7g² h16m² h16.8g* h16.8g³ h17.7m² c16.1g² Oct 11] fairly useful hurdler: won novice at Sedgefield in August: 8/11, second in novice at Towcester (7 lengths behind Chitu) on chasing debut: stayed 2¼m: acted on good to firm going: usually raced prominently/travelled strongly: dead. *Dan Skelton*   c99 h126

GIFT FROM GOD 5 b.g. Teofilo (IRE) – Piffling (Pivotal) [2017/18 h–: h15.8m h16.3d^{pu} h20g^{pu} Oct 25] modest at best on Flat, stays 6f: no form over hurdles: left Hugo Froud after second start: tried in hood: wears tongue tie. *Anthony Honeyball*   h–

GI JAYNE (IRE) 7 b.m. Millenary – Lady of Appeal (IRE) (Lord of Appeal) [2017/18 h16.8d^{bd} c16g h20g h15.8d h20g^{pu} h19.2v^{pu} h21.7d h21.7v^{pu} Mar 10] has had breathing operation: fifth foal: half-sister to 3 winners by Beneficial, including fairly useful hurdler/useful chaser Alamein (2m/17f winner) and fairly useful hurdler/winning pointer Quiet Candid (2m/17f winner): dam unraced half-sister to useful staying chaser Midnight Caller: maiden pointer: poor maiden hurdler: well held in maiden on chasing debut: left Jonathan Fogarty after third start: stays 2½m: acts on good to soft going: in hood last 3 starts: usually wears tongue tie: often races towards rear: has bled. *Dan Skelton*   c78 h61

GILGAMBOA (IRE) 10 b.g. Westerner – Hi Native (IRE) (Be My Native (USA)) [2017/18 c147+, h–: c22v* c23.7v* c24.8v* Feb 11] rangy gelding: winning hurdler: useful hunter chaser nowadays: won at Down Royal in December, Thurles in January and Punchestown (by 2¾ lengths from Burning Ambition) in February: stays 25f: acts on heavy going: tried in cheekpieces. *Enda Bolger, Ireland*   c134 + h–

GILLY GRACE 8 b.m. Morpeth – Miss Grace (Atticus (USA)) [2017/18 h77: h20g h19.9d h18.5v⁴ h16.5s h23.9s⁵ h19.7s⁴ c19.4d Apr 22] poor maiden hurdler: well beaten in novice handicap on chasing debut: stays 19f: acts on soft going: tried in cheekpieces. *Jimmy Frost*   c– h63

GILT SHADOW (IRE) 10 b.g. Beneficial – Baile An Droichid (IRE) (King's Ride) [2017/18 c–, h141: c19.5s^F Nov 3] rangy gelding: useful hurdler: similar form over fences: upsides when fell fatally last in maiden won by Tombstone at Down Royal: stayed 21f: acted on heavy and good to firm going: tried in hood. *Stuart Crawford, Ireland*   c141 h–

GIN AND TONIC 8 ch.g. Phoenix Reach (IRE) – Arctic Queen (Linamix (FR)) [2017/18 c–, h79: h15.8d⁴ h15.8d⁴ c17.2g³ c16.4g c15.7d^{pu} h16g c16.3s³ h16v* c16.3s⁴ h15.8s Mar 14] poor handicap hurdler: won at Fakenham in December: modest form over fences: unproven beyond 17f: acts on heavy going: wears headgear: front runner/races prominently. *Michael Wigham*   c93 h79

GIN COBBLER 12 b.g. Beneficial – Cassia (Be My Native (USA)) [2017/18 c90§, h–: c15.6g³ May 13] maiden hurdler: modest handicap chaser: stays 2½m: acts on good to firm and heavy going: often races freely: unreliable. *Victor Thompson*   c70 § h–

GINGE DE SOPHIA (IRE) 5 b.m. Presenting – Me Grannys Endoors (IRE) (Tremblant) [2017/18 b74: h16.8v³ h15.8d⁴ h21s⁴ Nov 22] compact mare: modest form over hurdles: best effort when fourth in mares maiden at Uttoxeter in November: should stay 2½m: in tongue tie last 3 starts. *Nigel Twiston-Davies*   h98

GIN

GINGER FIZZ 11 ch.m. Haafhd – Valagalore (Generous (IRE)) [2017/18 h101: h15.7g⁴ h17.7m* h15.7g⁵ h16g* h16g h15.8d⁴ h16g³ h16s⁴ Nov 14] lengthy, angular mare: fair handicap hurdler: won mares events at Fontwell in June and Worcester in August: stays 2¼m: acts on good to firm and good to soft going: wears headgear/tongue tie: usually leads. *Ben Case* — **h104**

GINGILI 8 b.g. Beat All (USA) – Gentian (Generous (IRE)) [2017/18 c–, h110§: h23m² h23.9g² c26m* c25.8dᵖᵘ c24.2s* Oct 24] fair handicap hurdler: won at Worcester in June: fairly useful form over fences: won handicaps at Fontwell in August and Exeter in October: stays 3¼m: acts on soft and good to firm going: wears headgear/tongue tie: often races prominently: moody and can't be relied on. *Johnny Farrelly* — **c127 §**, **h116 §**

GINNY BRIG 7 b.m. Great Palm (USA) – Royal Reference (Royal Fountain) [2017/18 b16.2m⁶ b16.2g⁵ b16.2m⁴ b20.2g h23.3dᵖᵘ Aug 21] fourth foal: dam winning pointer: poor form in bumpers: no form over hurdles. *Lisa Harrison* — **h–**, **b63**

GINO TRAIL (IRE) 11 br.g. Perugino (USA) – Borough Trail (IRE) (Woodborough (USA)) [2017/18 c146, h–: c17.5v³ c15.2s* c16.3s* c15.5s² c15.5s* c16.3v² c15.8s³ Apr 12] good-topped gelding: winning hurdler: smart handicap chaser: won at Wetherby (by 7 lengths from Pain Au Chocolat) in November, Cheltenham (by 1¼ lengths from Bun Doran) in December and Sandown (by ½ length from Dolos) in February: also ran well when second at Sandown (8 lengths behind Speredek) and in Grand Annual at Cheltenham (4½ lengths behind Le Prezien): best at 2m: acts on heavy going: wears headgear: front runner. *Kerry Lee* — **c153**, **h–**

GIVEAWAY GLANCE 5 br.m. Passing Glance – Giving (Generous (IRE)) [2017/18 h117: h16.3g² h16sᵖᵘ h15.8g⁵ h15.8d Mar 26] fairly useful handicap hurdler: second in mares event at Stratford in October: raced at 2m: acts on soft going: tried in hood: often races towards rear. *Alan King* — **h125**

GIVE BATTLE (IRE) 6 b.g. Intikhab (USA) – Hugs 'N Kisses (IRE) (Noverre (USA)) [2017/18 h20d Sep 29] fair maiden hurdler at best, well held sole start in 2017/18: unproven beyond 2m: acts on heavy going. *Pat Coffey, Ireland* — **h–**

GIVE HIM TIME 7 b.g. Kalanisi (IRE) – Delayed (FR) (Fijar Tango (FR)) [2017/18 c72, h103: c17.4g² c17.8g³ Nov 10] placed in Irish maiden point: maiden hurdler: modest form over fences: stays 2¼m: acts on soft going: often wears headgear: in tongue tie last 3 starts. *Nick Gifford* — **c97**, **h–**

GIVE ME A COPPER (IRE) 8 ch.g. Presenting – Copper Supreme (IRE) (Supreme Leader) [2017/18 h136p: c23.4gᵘʳ c24d* Nov 13] useful hurdler: similar form over fences: won 2-runner novice at Kempton in November: stays 3m: acts on heavy going: in tongue tie last 3 starts: usually races close up: open to improvement as a chaser. *Paul Nicholls* — **c140 p**, **h–**

GIVING BACK 4 br.f. Midnight Legend – Giving (Generous (IRE)) [2017/18 ab16d* b16.8g Apr 19] £32,000 3-y-o: fifth foal: half-sister to fairly useful 2m hurdle winners Giveaway Glance and Forgiving Glance (both by Passing Glance): dam useful 7f winner who stayed 1¼m: fair form in bumpers: won maiden at Kempton in March. *Alan King* — **b90**

GLANCE BACK 7 b.g. Passing Glance – Roberta Back (IRE) (Bob Back (USA)) [2017/18 h87, b–: h16.5g c15.9s³ c15.9v* c15.2dᶠ Mar 29] lengthy gelding: poor form over hurdles: modest form over fences: won handicap at Leicester in February: raced at around 2m: acts on heavy going: tried in hood: wears tongue tie: usually leads. *Emma-Jane Bishop* — **c97**, **h–**

GLANVILLES GUEST 6 ch.m. Sulamani (IRE) – Doubly Guest (Baratheà Guest) [2017/18 b88: h15.7g³ h18.5s⁴ h20g⁵ Jul 10] bumper winner: poor form over hurdles: should stay 2½m: often races towards rear. *Nick Mitchell* — **h84**

GLEANN NA NDOCHAIS (IRE) 12 b.g. Zagreb (USA) – Nissereen (USA) (Septieme Ciel (USA)) [2017/18 c113, h–: c20.1g c20.1gᵘʳ c15.6gᵖᵘ Aug 21] winning hurdler: fair chaser, no form in 2017/18: often races towards rear: not a fluent jumper over fences. *Alistair Whillans* — **c– x**, **h–**

GLENCAIRN VIEW (IRE) 8 ch.g. Flemensfirth (USA) – Ballerina Laura (IRE) (Riot Helmet) [2017/18 h24s⁴ c21v⁶ c18s⁴ c21v² c25v* c23v³ c24v* c31.8gᵖᵘ Apr 21] fair form over hurdles: fairly useful handicap chaser: won at Punchestown (amateur) in January and Navan (novice) in March: stays 25f: acts on heavy going. *Anthony Mullins, Ireland* — **c128**, **h99**

GLENFORDE (IRE) 7 ch.g. Flemensfirth (USA) – Feel The Pride (IRE) (Persian Bold) [2017/18 h108: c23.6v⁴ c20v² c19.9s⁴ c20.3dᵖᵘ Apr 21] has had breathing operation: runner-up on second of 2 starts in Irish maiden points: fair form over hurdles: fairly useful form over fences: second in handicap at Uttoxeter in December: stays 2½m: acts on heavy going: in cheekpieces last 2 starts: tried in tongue tie. *Kim Bailey* — **c115**, **h–**

GLI

GLENGRA (IRE) 9 gr.g. Beneficial – Zaraza (IRE) (Darshaan) [2017/18 c108, h93: c23.6g6 Nov 14] rather leggy gelding: placed in Irish points: modest form over hurdles: fair form on chasing debut, well held sole start in 2017/18: stays 21f: best form on good going: often races towards rear, tends to find little. *Ian Williams* — **c68 h—**

GLENLOE (IRE) 7 br.g. Kayf Tara – Mandys Native (IRE) (Be My Native (USA)) [2017/18 h20v2 h22.6v2 h24s3 h24s2 h24d5 Apr 26] tall gelding: brother to useful hurdler/chaser Alfie Sherrin (2m-3m winner), stayed 29f, and useful hurdler/chaser Hawkes Point (3m-29f winner): dam (h92) 21f hurdle winner/winning pointer (stayed 25f): smart handicap hurdler: second in Pertemps Final at Cheltenham (beaten nose by Delta Work) in March and fifth at Punchestown (3¾ lengths behind A Great View) in April: stays 3m: acts on heavy going: usually responds generously to pressure. *Gordon Elliott, Ireland* — **h144**

GLENLORA 5 ch.m. Supreme Sound – Rainha (Alflora (IRE)) [2017/18 b16v Dec 22] first foal: dam winning pointer: tailed off in bumper. *Sandy Thomson* — **b—**

GLENMA (IRE) 7 br.g. Scorpion (IRE) – Scoop Thirty Nine (Petoski) [2017/18 h75: h21.4v4 Mar 10] poor maiden hurdler: stays 2½m: acts on soft going. *R. Mike Smith* — **h—**

GLENMONA (IRE) 6 b.m. Dubai Destination (USA) – Sabbiosa (IRE) (Desert Prince (IRE)) [2017/18 b16.3s2 b16.4sur Nov 18] off mark in Irish points at second attempt: fair form in bumpers: second in mares event at Stratford in October: fatally injured in listed race won by Posh Trish at Cheltenham. *Harry Whittington* — **b89**

GLENO (IRE) 6 ch.g. Ask – Lwitikila (Denel (FR)) [2017/18 b93: b16v* Mar 10] fair form in bumpers: won 3-runner event at Ayr on sole start in 2017/18: has joined Gary Moore. *Stuart Crawford, Ireland* — **b91**

GLEN ROCCO 7 ch.g. Shirocco (GER) – Adees Dancer (Danehill Dancer (IRE)) [2017/18 h19.5d6 h15.5d5 h20.5v3 Jan 7] €48,000 3-y-o, £80,000 5-y-o: fourth foal: half-brother to 3 winners, including fair 2m hurdle winner Dubawi Dancer (by Dubawi): dam maiden on Flat: off mark in Irish maiden points at second attempt: modest form over hurdles: best effort when fifth in novice at Leicester in December: should be suited by 2½m+: remains open to improvement. *Nick Gifford* — **h97 p**

GLENS HARMONY (IRE) 6 b.m. King's Theatre (IRE) – Glens Music (IRE) (Orchestra) [2017/18 b16v2 h16d* h16.2d Apr 26] sister to bumper winner/smart hurdler Glens Melody (2¼m-2¾m winner), closely related to useful hurdler Lean Araig (2m-3m winner, by Old Vic) and half-sister to 2 winners, including bumper winner/useful hurdler Ceol Rua (2m-2¼m winner, by Bob Back): dam, (c127/h134) 2m-2½m hurdle/chase winner, also 2m winner on Flat: useful form in bumpers: second in listed mares event at Gowran (2 lengths behind Ainsi Va La Vie) in September: fairly useful form over hurdles: won mares maiden at Thurles in October: will be suited by further than 2m: often travels strongly. *W. P. Mullins, Ireland* — **h117 b108**

GLENS WOBBLY 10 ch.g. Kier Park (IRE) – Wobbly (Atraf) [2017/18 h19.5s h19g Nov 16] fairly useful on Flat, stays 13f: no form over hurdles: has joined Dominic Ffrench Davis. *Jonathan Geake* — **h—**

GLENTEENEASAIGH (IRE) 10 gr.g. Vinnie Roe (IRE) – Edward Street (IRE) (Rhoman Rule (USA)) [2017/18 c20m3 c24g4 c24d5 Dec 5] multiple point winner: maiden hurdler: poor form over fences: stayed 19f: acted on soft going: tried in visor: in tongue tie in 2017/18: dead. *Tim Vaughan* — **c73 h—**

GLENTROOL 5 b.g. Passing Glance – Killala Bay (IRE) (Executive Perk) [2017/18 b17.7s3 b16.2s3 b17v* b17s Apr 8] sixth foal: half-brother to a winning pointer by Midnight Legend: dam lightly raced in bumpers/over fences: fair form in bumpers: won at Carlisle in March: will be suited by 2½m+. *Sam Thomas* — **b92**

GLIMPSE OF GOLD 7 b.g. Passing Glance – Tizzy Blue (IRE) (Oscar (IRE)) [2017/18 h97: h16d c17d5 c16.1sur c19.1spu h15.8v4 Apr 7] modest handicap hurdler: no form over fences: stays 2½m: acts on soft going: wears tongue tie: often races in rear. *Tim Vaughan* — **c— h89**

GLINGER FLAME (IRE) 6 ro.g. Daylami (IRE) – Titian Flame (IRE) (Titus Livius (FR)) [2017/18 b16.4g3 Nov 17] €20,000 3-y-o: second foal: dam (h96), unreliable 19f/2½m hurdle winner (stayed 3m), also 2m winner on Flat: 7/1, shaped well when third in bumper at Newcastle (5 lengths behind Chanceanotherfive): should improve. *Nicky Richards* — **b87 p**

GLINGERSIDE (IRE) 7 b.g. Milan – Kettle 'N Cran (IRE) (Zaffaran (USA)) [2017/18 h115, b–: c20.5spu c20.5v5 h19.7spu h16v4 h19.4s4 h17v h20.2s5 Apr 27] modest handicap hurdler nowadays: no form over fences: stays 2½m: acts on heavy going. *R. Mike Smith* — **c— h99**

The Megsons' "Global Citizen"

GLITTERING LOVE (IRE) 6 b.g. Winged Love (IRE) – Glittering Image (IRE) (Sadler's Wells (USA)) [2017/18 h–, b–: h19.9v⁴ Apr 13] won last 4 of 5 starts in points: modest form over hurdles: tried in tongue tie: often races towards rear. *Nicky Richards* — h89

GLOBAL BONUS (IRE) 9 b.g. Heron Island (IRE) – That's The Bonus (IRE) (Executive Perk) [2017/18 h20s² h20.3d³ Jun 6] fair form over hurdles. *Caroline Bailey* — h113

GLOBAL CITIZEN (IRE) 6 b.g. Alkaadhem – Lady Willmurt (IRE) (Mandalus) [2017/18 b16f* h20d⁵ h15.8d² h15.7v* h16g* h16.5s⁶ Apr 13] £275,000 5-y-o: sturdy gelding: seventh foal: brother to useful hurdler/chaser A Hare Breath (2m-21f winner) and half-brother to bumper winner/smart hurdler De Plotting Shed (19f-2¾m winner, by Beneficial): dam, maiden hurdler/chaser, best effort at 2m: won Irish point on debut, and also landed 3-runner bumper at Worcester (by 7 lengths from Hattaab) in October: smart form over hurdles: won novice at Southwell (by 8 lengths from Euxton Lane) and Dovecote Novices' Hurdle at Kempton (by 9 lengths from Scarlet Dragon) in February: left Jonjo O'Neill after third start: unproven beyond 2m: acts on heavy going: front runner/races prominently, strong traveller. *Ben Pauling* — h142, b104

GLOBAL DOMINATION (IRE) 10 b.g. Alflora (IRE) – Lucia Forte (Neltino) [2017/18 c20.3d⁶ c25.6s³ c23.6s² c23.9s³ c19.9s² c21.2d* Apr 7] maiden hurdler: modest handicap chaser: won at Fakenham in April: stays 3m: acts on heavy going: usually wears cheekpieces: in tongue tie last 2 starts: often races in rear. *Caroline Bailey* — c85, h–

GLOBAL FERT (IRE) 8 b.g. Flemensfirth (USA) – Global Diamond (IRE) (Classic Music (USA)) [2017/18 h87: h19.9g h19.4d⁴ h15.8v* h16v h20v² Apr 1] second on completed start in points: fair handicap hurdler: won novice event at Uttoxeter in December: left Noel C. Kelly after fourth start: stays 2½m: acts on heavy going: often wears tongue tie: often travels strongly. *T. Gibney, Ireland* — h110

GOD

GLOBALISATION (IRE) 8 b.g. Tikkanen (USA) – On A Mission (IRE) (Dolphin Street (FR)) [2017/18 c116, h101: c23.8g^{pu} May 9] maiden hurdler: fairly useful chaser, pulled up sole start in 2017/18: stays 3m: acts on heavy going: usually wears headgear: wears tongue tie. *Rebecca Curtis*   c– h–

GLOBAL STAGE 7 b.g. Multiplex – Tintera (IRE) (King's Theatre (IRE)) [2017/18 h121, b107: h20.5s* h24s⁴ h22.8v^{pu} Feb 17] strong, good-topped gelding: Irish point winner: useful bumper performer: fair hurdler: won maiden at Ayr in October: should stay at least 2¾m: acts on good to soft going: tried in cheekpieces: usually races close up. *Fergal O'Brien*   **h113**

GLOBAL THRILL 9 b.g. Big Shuffle (USA) – Goonda (Darshaan) [2017/18 h94§: h18.5d h16.3s* h16.3g* h15.3g³ h16d* h15.3v³ h16v h16s Apr 27] good-topped gelding: fair handicap hurdler: won at Stratford (twice) in October and Kempton in November: best around 2m: acts on heavy going: has worn headgear: wears tongue tie: usually races towards rear. *Bernard Llewellyn*   **h104**

GLOBAL TOUR (IRE) 5 b.g. Arakan (USA) – Galant Tour (IRE) (Riberetto) [2017/18 b16.8g h17g h18.8s Mar 25] well held in bumper/over hurdles: left David Harry Kelly after second start: tried in hood/tongue tie. *Paul W. Flynn, Ireland*   h– b–

GLOI 7 b.m. Overbury (IRE) – Go Gwenni Go (Bold Fox) [2017/18 h15.7d b15.8g h15.8s h15.8s h19s Feb 20] first foal: dam no form in bumpers/over hurdles: poor form in bumpers/over hurdles: tried in hood. *Debra Hamer*   **h64 b60**

GLORVINA (IRE) 4 b.f. Dragon Pulse (IRE) – Hawk Dance (IRE) (Hawk Wing (USA)) [2017/18 h17.2d* h16.7g h15.8s² h15.5d³ h16s⁶ h16s³ h16.7v Feb 9] compact filly: fair on Flat, stays 8.5f: modest hurdler: won juvenile at Cartmel in August: raced around 2m: acts on soft going: front runner/races prominently. *Charlie Mann*   **h97**

GLORY HUNTER (IRE) 8 b.g. Brian Boru – Fae Taylor (IRE) (Desert Style (IRE)) [2017/18 c22.6d^{pu} Jun 9] point winner: pulled up in novice hunter on chasing debut. *Mrs Pauline Harkin*   c–

GNARLY 6 b.m. Midnight Legend – Diamant Noir (Sir Harry Lewis (USA)) [2017/18 h19.5s Feb 24] seventh foal: half-sister to fairly useful hurdler Wild Rhubarb (3m winner, by Hernando), bumper winner/modest hurdler Amber Cloud (2m winner, by Lomitas) and a winning pointer by Presenting: dam (h134) bumper/2m-3m hurdle winner: placed in point: 20/1, eighth in maiden at Chepstow on hurdling debut. *Jonjo O'Neill*   **h67**

GOAL (IRE) 10 b.g. Mujadil (USA) – Classic Lin (FR) (Linamix (FR)) [2017/18 c–, h101: h16d⁶ h15.8g^{ur} h16.5g h16.5g³ Nov 30] modest handicap hurdler: fell sole start over fences: stays 2¼m: acts on good to firm and good to soft going: wears headgear/tongue tie: often races towards rear. *Tracey Watkins*   c– **h96**

GO AS YOU PLEASE (IRE) 5 b.g. Jeremy (USA) – Aweebounce (IRE) (Dubawi (IRE)) [2017/18 b16.7d² Apr 21] £40,000 3-y-o: first foal: dam unraced half-sister to smart Scandinavian performer up to 1½m Hurricane Red: 14/1, caught eye when second in conditionals/amateur bumper at Bangor (4½ lengths behind Norman Stanley), closing all way to line: sure to improve. *Paul Webber*   **b92 p**

GO CONQUER (IRE) 9 b.g. Arcadio (GER) – Ballinamona Wish (IRE) (Kotashaan (FR)) [2017/18 c140, h–: c21.6g* c23.8g* c23.8d^F c24g⁵ c20.8g Apr 18] strong gelding: winning hurdler: smart handicap chaser: won at Fontwell (by 2 lengths from As de Mee) in October and Sodexo Gold Cup at Ascot (by 4½ lengths from Rock Gone) in November: stays 3m: acts on soft going: tried in tongue tie: strong-travelling front runner. *Jonjo O'Neill*   **c150 h–**

GODSMEJUDGE (IRE) 12 b.g. Witness Box (USA) – Eliza Everett (IRE) (Meneval (USA)) [2017/18 c116§, h81: c25.5d* May 16] winning hurdler: smart chaser at best for Alan King, won Scottish Grand National at Ayr in 2012/13: stayed 4m: acted on heavy going: wore headgear/tongue tie: dead. *David Dennis*   c– h–

GOD'S OWN (IRE) 10 b.g. Oscar (IRE) – Dantes Term (IRE) (Phardante (FR)) [2017/18 c165, h–: c19.9d⁶ c20.5d³ c15.9s³ c15.5d³ Apr 28] sturdy, good-topped gelding: winning hurdler: top-class chaser, not quite at best in 2017/18: third in Queen Mother Champion Chase at Cheltenham (18 lengths behind Altior) in March and Celebration Chase at Sandown (7 lengths behind same horse) in April: stays 21f: acts on soft going: tried in tongue tie. *Tom George*   **c154 + h–**

GOD WILLING 7 b.g. Arch (USA) – Bourbon Ball (USA) (Peintre Celebre (USA)) [2017/18 h16s Nov 4] fairly useful on Flat, stays 9f: tailed off in novice on hurdling debut. *Declan Carroll*   h–

GOF

GOFAST DE SAUNIERE (FR) 5 b.g. Ange Gabriel (FR) – Aiglette (FR) (Kingsalsa (USA)) [2017/18 b15.7v Mar 29] pulled up in Irish point: tailed off in maiden bumper. *Jo Hughes* — b–

GO FORRIT (IRE) 4 b.g. Jeremy (USA) – Ben Roseler (IRE) (Beneficial) [2017/18 b13.7s⁴ Apr 6] in hood, well beaten in bumper. *David Arbuthnot* — b–

GOFORTHECRAIC (IRE) 5 b.g. Arcadio (GER) – Valin Thyne (IRE) (Good Thyne (USA)) [2017/18 b16d Oct 15] fourth foal: dam, placed in points, half-sister to fairly useful chaser (stayed 3m) Listen Boy: won point on debut: 2/1, well beaten in bumper at Chepstow: has joined Harry Fry: should do better. *Dan Skelton* — b– p

GOG ELLES (IRE) 4 b.f. Helmet (AUS) – Hear My Cry (USA) (Giant's Causeway (USA)) [2017/18 h16.5v h16.8s^pu Feb 23] modest maiden on Flat, stays 1¼m: no form over hurdles. *Katie Stephens* — h–

GOGO BALOO 6 b.m. Schiaparelli (GER) – Tarabaloo (Kayf Tara) [2017/18 h87, b–: h19.7s⁶ h25.3s³ h19.7v³ h24v Apr 14] has had breathing operation: pulled up in point: modest form over hurdles: should stay 2½m+: acts on heavy going. *Tim Easterby* — h94

GO GO LUCAS (IRE) 5 ch.g. Golan (IRE) – Bob Girl (IRE) (Bob Back (USA)) [2017/18 b84: b16.7g h16.2s* h20s² Dec 3] modest form in bumpers: fairly useful form over hurdles: won maiden at Hexham in November: stayed 2½m: often raced towards rear: dead. *Simon West* — h122 b–

GOINGFORAMOOCH 7 b.m. Primo Valentino (IRE) – Emmasflora (Alflora (IRE)) [2017/18 h–, b–: h21.6g^pu May 10] no show in bumpers/over hurdles: tried in hood. *Katie Stephens* — h–

GOING FOR BROKE (IRE) 8 b.g. Gold Well – Kokopelli Star (Hernando (FR)) [2017/18 h117: h16g⁵ c16.3d³ c17m^ur c20g* c20d⁴ c16g⁵ Oct 26] fair handicap hurdler: fairly useful form over fences: won novice handicaps at Newton Abbot in July and Worcester in September: stays 2½m: acts on good to soft going: wears cheekpieces: usually wears tongue tie: has joined Stephanie Moore, USA. *Rebecca Curtis* — c124 h108

GOING GOLD (IRE) 6 b.g. Gold Well – Wednesday Girl (IRE) (Rudimentary (USA)) [2017/18 b90: b15.7d² h16s⁴ h19.4s⁴ h16s³ h19.3d* h16.8g⁶ h16s Apr 28] lengthy gelding: won Irish maiden point on debut: fairly useful form in bumpers: second at Catterick in November: similar form over hurdles: won novice at Carlisle in March: sixth in conditionals/amateur handicap at Cheltenham in April: stays 19f: acts on soft going: often races prominently: has joined Ian Williams. *Richard Hobson* — h119 b96

GOLAN DANCER (IRE) 10 b.g. Golan (IRE) – Seductive Dance (Groom Dancer (USA)) [2017/18 c98§, h99§: c16.3m^pu Jun 16] good-topped gelding: modest maiden hurdler/chaser: little impact in points: stays 19f: acts on heavy going: has worn headgear: quirky sort. *Jimmy Frost* — c– § h– §

GOLANDER (IRE) 8 b.g. Golan (IRE) – Bonnie And Bright (IRE) (Topanoora) [2017/18 c23g^pu c25.8d^pu c25.8g^pu h21.6d⁴ h18.5v⁶ h16.8d⁶ Oct 12] point winner: poor maiden hurdler: little show over fences: left T. J. Nagle Jnr after first start: best effort at 2m: acts on good to firm going: has worn cheekpieces, including last 3 starts: tried in tongue tie: races towards rear. *Carroll Gray* — c– h68

GOLAN FORTUNE (IRE) 6 b.g. Golan (IRE) – Ballyknock Alainn (IRE) (Witness Box (USA)) [2017/18 h20.3g³ h19.9d³ h21.1g h19.8s* h21g^f h21.6d* h21d* h23.4v² h22.8v³ h24.7s Apr 14] £42,000 5-y-o: lengthy gelding: third foal: half-brother to a winning pointer by Indian Danehill: dam (h71), winning pointer, half-sister to useful hurdler (stayed 2½m) Finns Cross: won completed start in Irish maiden points: useful handicap hurdler: won at Sandown (conditional) in November, and Ascot (conditional) and Kempton in December: second at Sandown (1½ lengths behind Topofthegame) in February: stays 23f: acts on heavy going: wears cheekpieces: usually travels strongly. *Phil Middleton* — h136

GOLANOVA 10 b.g. Golan (IRE) – Larkbarrow (Kahyasi) [2017/18 c109§, h95§: c21.1g³ h25m² c20.3d^f Jun 6] modest handicap hurdler: fair handicap chaser: stayed 3¼m: acted on good to firm and heavy going: often wore cheekpieces: dead. *Gary Moore* — c106 § h99 §

GOLCONDA PRINCE (IRE) 4 b.g. Arcano (IRE) – Mujarah (IRE) (Marju (IRE)) [2017/18 h15.8g⁵ h16s^F Dec 4] fair on Flat, stays 1¼m: modest form over hurdles: better effort when fifth in juvenile at Huntingdon in November: will prove best at easy 2m. *Richard Fahey* — h97

GOLD BLADE (IRE) 5 b.g. Gold Well – Supreme Evening (IRE) (Supreme Leader) [2017/18 b16s Feb 9] well beaten in maiden bumper. *Nicky Henderson* — b–

GOL

GOLD CHAIN (IRE) 8 b.m. Authorized (IRE) – Mountain Chain (USA) (Royal **h107 §**
Academy (USA)) [2017/18 h106§: h16.2g* h20.2g* h24.7g[5] h20.2g[3] h17.2s[4] h23.9g[3]
h22.1d[6] h20.2v[pu] Sep 28] neat mare: fair handicap hurdler: won mares event and
conditionals event at Perth in May: stays 2½m: acts on soft and good to firm going: wears
headgear/tongue tie: untrustworthy. *Dianne Sayer*

GOLD CLASS 7 ch.g. Firebreak – Silken Dalliance (Rambo Dancer (CAN)) [2017/18 **h101**
h94: h16.7g* h16.7g h16.3g[4] h18.7g[3] h15.5[4] Dec 3] fair hurdler: won lady amateur
handicap at Market Rasen in July: left Olly Murphy after fourth start: stays 21f: acts on
good to soft going: wears headgear/tongue tie. *Clare Hobson*

GOLDEN BIRTHDAY (FR) 7 b.g. Poliglote – Gold Or Silver (FR) (Glint of Gold) **h139**
[2017/18 h118, b98: h19g* h18.5s[3] h18.5d[7] h21.6g* Sep 2] bumper winner: useful
handicap hurdler: won at Warwick in May, and Newton Abbot in July and September (by
10 lengths from Wait For Me): stays 2¾m: acts on heavy going: in tongue tie last 3 starts:
often travels strongly. *Harry Fry*

GOLDEN CANNON 7 b.m. Winker Watson – Kalmina (USA) (Rahy (USA)) [2017/18 **h69**
b–: h15.8g Apr 24] poor maiden on Flat: 250/1, seventh in maiden at Huntingdon on
hurdling debut. *Sheena West*

GOLDEN DOYEN (GER) 7 b.g. Doyen (IRE) – Goldsamt (GER) (Rienzi (EG)) **c114 x**
[2017/18 c134x, h138: h25.4d[3] c23g[3] Jun 25] useful-looking gelding: useful handicap **h126**
hurdler: also useful over fences, below best final start in 2017/18: stays 3m: acts on soft
going: tried in cheekpieces: often let down by jumping over fences. *Philip Hobbs*

GOLDEN ESTHER (IRE) 5 b.m. Scorpion (IRE) – Mascareigne (FR) (Subotica (FR)) **b–**
[2017/18 b15.7d b16.2s Jan 16] half-sister to fairly useful hurdler/chaser Urtheoneiwant
(2m-3m winner, by Kayf Tara) and bumper winner Nurse Ratched (by Presenting): dam,
French 2m hurdle winner, also winner around 1½m on Flat: no form in bumpers.
Alan Phillips

GOLDEN FRIDAY (IRE) 5 b.g. Gold Well – Azulada (FR) (Pistolet Bleu (IRE)) **b84**
[2017/18 b16g[5] b16.7s Dec 2] €9,000 3-y-o: half-brother to fair hurdler Lady Olwyn
(2½m/21f winner, by Revoque) and fair hurdler/chaser Azulada Bay (21f-27f winner, by
Karinga Bay): dam, French 2m hurdle winner, also winner 1¼m-1½m on Flat: modest
form in bumpers: better effort when fifth in conditionals/amateur event at Fakenham: will
prove suited by further than 2m: has joined Donald McCain. *Sam Thomas*

GOLDEN INVESTMENT (IRE) 9 b.g. Gold Well – Mangan Pet (IRE) (Over The **c109**
River (FR)) [2017/18 c109, h109: c25.5m[2] c25.5d[2] c24.2d* c24.5s[4] c25.2d[4] c30s[ur] **h–**
c25.2s[F] c24.5d[4] Mar 25] angular gelding: fair hurdler: fair handicap chaser: won at
Wetherby in November: stays 25f: acts on good to soft and good to firm going: wears hood/tongue
tie. *Donald McCain*

GOLDEN JEFFREY (SWI) 5 b.g. Soldier Hollow – Ange Doree (FR) (Sinyar (IRE)) **h124**
[2017/18 b97: b16.2g* h20.2m[F] h17.2d* h16.2v* h16.4g[4] h15.6m[2] h21.1s ab16.3g[5] h16.4s **b95**
h17d[6] h16.2v h20.5g[5] Apr 21] sturdy gelding: fairly useful form in bumpers: won at Kelso
in May: fairly useful hurdler: won novices at Cartmel in August and Perth in September:
best around 2m: acts on good to firm and heavy going: tried in blinkers. *Iain Jardine*

GOLDEN JET (IRE) 5 b.g. Golan (IRE) – Could Do (Cloudings (IRE)) [2017/18 **h–**
h16.7g[6] h16g h21d h25d[pu] h20.3d[pu] Dec 5] of no account: tried in blinkers. *Clare Hobson*

GOLDEN MILAN (IRE) 10 b.g. Milan – Belle Provence (FR) (Phantom Breeze) **c–**
[2017/18 c–, h–: h24.4s c24.5s[pu] Feb 8] useful-looking gelding: point winner: fair hurdler/ **h–**
maiden chaser at best, no form since 2015/16: often wears headgear: usually wears tongue
tie. *Alan Phillips*

GOLDEN SANDSTORM (IRE) 9 ch.g. Golden Tornado (IRE) – Killoughey Fairy **h–**
(IRE) (Torus) [2017/18 h19.5v[F] h20.3v[pu] Feb 5] little show in bumpers/over hurdles: tried
in tongue tie. *Daniel Loughnane*

GOLDEN SOVEREIGN (IRE) 4 b.g. Gold Well – Fugal Maid (IRE) (Winged Love **b89**
(IRE)) [2017/18 b16v[3] Apr 14] €38,000 3-y-o: fifth foal: half-brother to useful hurdler/
winning bumper winner Red Rising (3m/25f winner) and bumper winner/fairly useful hurdler
Sizinguptheamazon (19f winner) (both by Flemensfirth): dam, unraced, half-sister to fair
hurdler/useful chaser (stayed 29f) Manus The Man: 9/2, third in bumper at Chepstow (9¾
lengths behind Garrettstown). *Philip Hobbs*

GOLDEN SPEAR 7 ch.g. Kyllachy – Penmayne (Inchinor) [2017/18 h128: h16s[2] h17g[6] **h130**
h16s h16s[4] h16.5d Apr 24] angular gelding: useful handicap hurdler: second at Galway
(2 lengths behind Top Othe Ra) in August: unproven beyond 2m: acts on soft going: has
worn cheekpieces: wears tongue tie: often races towards rear. *A. J. Martin, Ireland*

359

Lavazza Silver Cup Handicap Chase, Ascot—a first win in this race in 23 years for trainer Nicky Henderson as Gold Present (hooped cap) overhauls the leader Frodon

GOLDEN SUNRISE (IRE) 5 ch.g. Stowaway – Fairy Dawn (IRE) (Old Vic) [2017/18 b87: h18.5d h21.6v³ h19.5v² h23.9s⁴ h18.5v* h21.7s³ h23.1d² Apr 24] workmanlike gelding: fairly useful hurdler: won novice at Exeter in February: placed in similar events at Fontwell in March and Exeter in April: stays 23f: acts on heavy going: tried in tongue tie: often races prominently. *Colin Tizzard* — **h120**

GOLDEN TOWN (IRE) 7 b.g. Invincible Spirit (IRE) – Princesse Dansante (IRE) (King's Best (USA)) [2017/18 h102: h16.2g² h17.2d³ h17.2s³ h16.2g³ h17.2d³ h16.8g⁵ h16s h16.2s³ Apr 26] fair maiden hurdler: raced around 2m: acts on soft going: has worn headgear: often wears tongue tie. *James Moffatt* — **h104**

GOLDEN VISION (FR) 6 bl.m. Vision d'Etat (FR) – My Gold du Fanil (FR) (Goldneyev (USA)) [2017/18 h121: c20v^pu Mar 11] tall mare: fairly useful hurdler: pulled up in handicap on chasing debut on sole 2017/18 start: stays 2¼m: acts on soft going: tried in cheekpieces: in tongue tie last 3 starts: often leads. *Dan Skelton* — **c–** **h–**

GOLDEN WHISKY (IRE) 5 ch.g. Flemensfirth (USA) – Derry Vale (IRE) (Mister Lord (USA)) [2017/18 b17d⁵ b15.3v⁶ h15.7v⁴ h19s^F Mar 26] £34,000 3-y-o: seventh foal: brother to smart hurdler/winning pointer Topofthegame (2¾m/23f winner): dam unraced half-sister to smart hurdler (best up to 21f) Artadoin Lad: modest form in bumpers: fair form over hurdles: bred to be suited by 2½m+. *Evan Williams* — **h109** **b79**

GOLD FIELDS 4 b.g. Sakhee (USA) – Realms of Gold (USA) (Gulch (USA)) [2017/18 b14s Jan 1] rather unfurnished gelding: tailed off in listed bumper. *Laura Morgan* — **b–**

GOLD INGOT 11 ch.g. Best of The Bests (IRE) – Realms of Gold (USA) (Gulch (USA)) [2017/18 c113, h–: c19.9m⁴ c20.3d* c19.2g⁴ c23.9g^pu c20g³ c24d⁵ Oct 3] good-topped gelding: winning hurdler: fair handicap chaser: won at Southwell in June: stays 3m: acts on heavy going: usually wears cheekpieces: usually races close up. *Caroline Bailey* — **c107** **h–**

GOLD MOUNTAIN (IRE) 8 b.g. Gold Well – La Belle de Serk (IRE) (Shernazar) [2017/18 c120p, h98: c21m³ c20.2g⁵ h23.9g³ Nov 30] runner-up in Irish point: fair form over hurdles: fairly useful form over fences: third in handicap at Newton Abbot in May: stays 3m: acts on good to firm going: wears tongue tie: often races towards rear: has joined Martin Keighley. *Alexandra Dunn* — **c116** **h113**

GOLD OPERA (IRE) 9 b.g. Gold Well – Flute Opera (IRE) (Sharifabad (IRE)) [2017/18 c125, h–: c24.3v⁴ c27.3v^pu c23.4s⁵ c23.4v⁵ c26.9v^pu c20.1v* Apr 15] maiden hurdler: fairly useful handicap chaser: won at Newcastle in April: stays 3m: acts on heavy going: wears headgear: often races prominently: has joined Keith Dalgleish: temperamental. *N. W. Alexander* — **c121 §** **h–**

GOO

GOLD PRESENT (IRE) 8 br.g. Presenting – Ouro Preto (Definite Article) [2017/18 c143, h–: c22.4g* c23.8d* c25s^{pu} c31.8g^{pu} Apr 21] lengthy gelding: winning hurdler: very smart handicap chaser: won at Newbury (by neck from Warriors Tale) and Silver Cup at Ascot (by 3 lengths from Frodon) in December: pulled up in Ultima Handicap Chase at Cheltenham and Scottish Grand National at Ayr (probably failed to stay) last 2 starts: stays 3m: acts on good to soft going. *Nicky Henderson* — **c155 h–**

GOLDSLINGER (FR) 6 b.g. Gold Away (IRE) – Singaporette (FR) (Sagacity (FR)) [2017/18 h96: h19.2v^{pu} h15.9v^5 h17.7s^3 h18.5s* Apr 23] neat gelding: fair handicap hurdler: won novice event at Newton Abbot in April: stays 2¼m: acts on soft going: tried in hood. *Gary Moore* — **h100**

GOLIATH (IRE) 6 br.g. Golan (IRE) – Lady Shanakill (IRE) (Witness Box (USA)) [2017/18 b–: h19.0v^{pu} h19.3d^{pu} Mar 31] no show in bumper/novice hurdles: tried in cheekpieces. *Keith Dalgleish* — **h–**

GO LONG (IRE) 8 b.g. Hurricane Run (IRE) – Monumental Gesture (Head For Heights) [2017/18 h–: h18.5v^4 h16.5v^3 Feb 4] rangy gelding: will make a chaser: runner-up in Irish maiden point: fairly useful hurdler: third in handicap at Taunton in February: likely to stay 2½m: acts on heavy going. *Evan Williams* — **h125**

GONALSTON CLOUD (IRE) 11 gr.g. Cloudings (IRE) – Roseoengus (IRE) (Roselier (FR)) [2017/18 c132, h–: h21.3s c30s^5 c32.8s^{pu} c24.2d* c23.9d^2 Apr 22] maiden hurdler: useful handicap chaser: won at Wetherby (by 3¾ lengths from Goodtoknow) in March: second at Market Rasen (1¼ lengths behind Wolf Sword) in April: stays 33f: acts on heavy going: usually wears cheekpieces. *Nick Kent* — **c130 h–**

GONEINAGLANCE 9 b.m. Passing Glance – It's Missy Imp (Fearless Action (USA)) [2017/18 h19.5s^F Nov 28] modest form over hurdles in 2014/15, struggling when fell 2 out in maiden on sole start since. *Andrew Martin* — **h–**

GONE PLATINUM (IRE) 9 b.g. Mountain High (IRE) – Miss Platinum (IRE) (Oscar (IRE)) [2017/18 c19.4d^2 c22.6d^5 h18.5d c17.4g c16v^3 Apr 15] fair maiden hurdler, well held sole start in 2017/18: similar form over fences: stays 19f: acts on good to firm and heavy going: tried in cheekpieces: tongue tied in 2017/18. *David Rees* — **c107 h–**

GONE TOO FAR 10 b.g. Kayf Tara – Major Hoolihan (Soldier Rose) [2017/18 c133, h–: c19.2m^4 c23.8g^5 Jun 1] well-made gelding: winning hurdler: useful handicap chaser, below best in 2017/18: best up to easy 23f: acts on soft and good to firm going: wears headgear: unreliable. *David Pipe* — **c116 § h–**

GONNABEGOOD (IRE) 7 b.g. Kutub (IRE) – Angels Flame (IRE) (Un Desperado (FR)) [2017/18 h78: h21.6s^4 h21.6v* h21.6v^2 c25.2s^{pu} h24s* h23.1v^4 h23.1d^6 Apr 24] modest handicap hurdler: won at Exeter in November and Towcester in February: pulled up in novice handicap on chasing debut: stays 3m: acts on heavy going: wears cheekpieces: should do better over fences. *Jeremy Scott* — **c– p h87**

GOOD AND HARDY (IRE) 5 b.g. Westerner – Kilganey Maid (IRE) (Rudimentary (USA)) [2017/18 b16v^5 Apr 14] off mark in Irish points at third attempt: 2/1, fifth in bumper at Chepstow (18½ lengths behind Garrettstown). *Fergal O'Brien* — **b80**

GOOD BOY BOBBY (IRE) 5 b.g. Flemensfirth (USA) – Princess Gaia (IRE) (King's Theatre (IRE)) [2017/18 b16s* b16v* b16.3v^3 b16v* Mar 20] €80,000 3-y-o: good-topped gelding: chasing type: second foal: half-brother to bumper winner Monastery (by Presenting): dam (h94), in frame in bumpers/maiden hurdle, sister to very smart hurdler (stayed 3m) Voler La Vedette and half-sister to useful staying hurdler/chaser Hennessy: useful form in bumpers: won at Chepstow in November and January, and Wetherby (by 3¾ lengths from Manon) in March: will be suited by 2½m+: tried in hood. *Nigel Twiston-Davies* — **b113**

GOOD EGG (IRE) 15 b.g. Exit To Nowhere (USA) – Full of Surprises (IRE) (Be My Native (USA)) [2017/18 c20.8d^2 May 5] well-made gelding: multiple point winner: fair chaser: stays 25f: acts on heavy going: tried in cheekpieces. *Miss Sarah Rippon* — **c114**

GOOD EVENT 10 b.g. Goodricke – Eventuality (Petoski) [2017/18 h16.3g^{pu} h16.3m^4 h18.7m^6 Aug 24] poor form over hurdles: pulled up in points. *Peter Hiatt* — **h67**

GOODGIRLTERESA (IRE) 8 b.m. Stowaway – Decheekymonkey (IRE) (Presenting) [2017/18 h84, b92: h20s^2 h21.4s h20.7s^6 h21.2d^5 Apr 9] off mark in Irish points at fourth attempt: fair maiden hurdler: stays 21f: acts on heavy going: wore tongue tie in 2017/18. *Neil Mulholland* — **h100**

GOO

GOOD MAN HUGHIE (IRE) 9 ch.g. Flemensfirth (USA) – Good Dawn (IRE) (Good Thyne (USA)) [2017/18 h95: c19.7s³ c17v c16v² c20.3v^pu Mar 5] Irish point winner: modest hurdler: similar form in chases: stays 19f: acts on heavy going: has worn headgear, including in 2017/18: tried in tongue tie: has joined Barry Brennan. *Gary Moore*   c92 h–

GOOD MAN (IRE) 5 ch.g. New Approach (USA) – Garden City (FR) (Majorien) [2017/18 b16.2m Jun 4] modest maiden on Flat, stays 12.5f: well beaten in bumper. *Karen McLintock*   b–

GOOD MAN JIM (FR) 5 gr.g. Martaline – Precious Lucy (FR) (Kadrou (FR)) [2017/18 b16d Apr 26] good-topped gelding: off mark in Irish points at second attempt: tailed off in bumper. *Tom George*   b–

GOOD MAN PAT (IRE) 5 b.g. Gold Well – Basically Supreme (IRE) (Supreme Leader) [2017/18 h18.5d³ h22g² h24.5d² h21.6d⁴ h23.1v* h24v* h24.7s^pu Apr 13] €15,000 3-y-o, £70,000 4-y-o: good-topped gelding: seventh foal: closely related to a winning pointer by Oscar: dam unraced: off mark in Irish points on second attempt: fairly useful hurdler: won novices at Bangor in February and Southwell in March: stays 3m: acts on heavy going: usually travels strongly. *Alan King*   h128

GOOD MAN VINNIE (IRE) 7 ch.g. Vinnie Roe (IRE) – Pellerossa (IRE) (Good Thyne (USA)) [2017/18 h21.6v⁵ h16.8s c18d⁶ c23.8d² h21.6d⁴ c24d⁶ h21.4d Apr 22] workmanlike gelding: fourth foal: brother to fair hurdler Roving Lad (2¼m-21f winner): dam, winning pointer, half-sister to fair hurdler/fairly useful chaser (stayed 25f) Presentandcorrect: Irish point winner: modest form over hurdles: fair form over fences: best effort when second in novice handicap at Ludlow in November: stays 3m: acts on soft going. *Paul Henderson*   c107 h96

GOOD NEWS 6 b.g. Midnight Legend – Venetian Lass (First Trump) [2017/18 b84: h19.1g⁴ h21.6d⁴ h21g³ h25.8g⁴ h23.9g⁵ h21s^pu Apr 9] modest form over hurdles: should be suited by 3m: acts on good to soft going. *Lydia Richards*   h91

GOODNIGHT CHARLIE 8 gr.m. Midnight Legend – Over To Charlie (Overbury (IRE)) [2017/18 h82: h25d⁴ h19.2g* h19.2v h19.2v^pu h26s c21.4s^pu c24g² Apr 26] workmanlike mare: point winner: modest handicap hurdler: won at Warwick and Towcester (amateur) in May: similar form over fences: better effort when second in novice handicap at Warwick: stays 25f: acts on soft going: usually wears headgear: usually races close up. *Caroline Fryer*   c96 h96

GOODNIGHTIRENE (IRE) 8 ch.m. Indian River (FR) – Markskeepingfaith (IRE) (Ajraas (USA)) [2017/18 h23g^pu h20s^pu c20s c24v^pu c26v^F Jan 21] point winner: maiden hurdler, modest form on standout effort: no form over fences: wore hood: tried in tongue tie: dead. *Laura Young*   c– h–

GOODNIGHT VIENNA (IRE) 12 b.g. High Roller (IRE) – Curragh Bridge (Pitpan) [2017/18 c–: c32.5d^pu May 5] multiple point winner: little impact in hunter chases: tried in cheekpieces. *Mrs L. Redman*   c–

GOODTOKNOW 10 b.g. Presenting – Atlantic Jane (Tamure (IRE)) [2017/18 c142, h–: c26.7g^ur c25.9v^pu c29.2s^pu c25.2s c28.4v^pu c24.2d² c23.8d² Apr 24] useful-looking gelding: winning hurdler: fairly useful handicap chaser: first past post at Ludlow (demoted after bumping rival run-in) in April: stays 29f: acts on heavy going: wears headgear. *Kerry Lee*   c125 h–

GOOD TRADITION (IRE) 7 b.g. Pivotal – Token Gesture (IRE) (Alzao (USA)) [2017/18 h114: h19.6d⁵ h20.2g⁴ ab16g* h16.7s³ Mar 24] won jumpers bumper at Southwell in March: fair handicap hurdler: stays 19f: acts on soft going: tried in cheekpieces. *Donald McCain*   h110

GOOHAR (IRE) 9 b.g. Street Cry (IRE) – Reem Three (Mark of Esteem (IRE)) [2017/18 c119, h–: c26.2v c24.2v⁵ c25.6s² c23.8d* c23.8d³ Apr 9] rangy gelding: winning hurdler: fairly useful handicap chaser: won at Ludlow (amateur) in February: stays 3¼m: acts on heavy going: wears cheekpieces: shows signs of temperament. *Henry Daly*   c120 h–

GO ON HENRY (IRE) 10 b.g. Golan (IRE) – The Millers Tale (IRE) (Rashar (USA)) [2017/18 c93, h–: c19.4m³ c19.4g⁴ c20g* c16g^ur c23.8d^pu h15.8g⁴ h16.2s h20.5v Jan 11] poor form over hurdles: modest handicap chaser: won at Ludlow (amateur) in October: stays 3m: acts on good to firm going: wears headgear/tongue tie. *Matt Sheppard*   c89 h77

GOONJIM (IRE) 7 ch.g. Beneficial – Clogga Native (IRE) (Good Thyne (USA)) [2017/18 c80, h69: c17.4d² c16.3m⁵ Jun 16] maiden hurdler: poor chaser: stays 2½m: acts on soft going: usually wears hood, not in 2017/18: wears tongue tie: races towards rear, tends to find little. *Alexandra Dunn*   c77 h–

GOOSE MAN (IRE) 6 b.g. Gold Well – Young Amelie (FR) (Garde Royale) [2017/18 h20.4d² c20s² c20v* c16.2v* Jan 31] third foal: half-brother to bumper winners Young Palm (by Great Palm) and Young Ambition (at 2½m, by Heron Island): dam once-raced   c132 p h104 half-sister to useful 2m chaser Best Lover: fair form over hurdles: useful form over fences: won novices at Navan in December and Down Royal in January: stays 3m: acts on heavy going: capable of better still as a chaser. *Tom J. Taaffe, Ireland*

GOOSEN MAVERICK (IRE) 7 b.g. Morozov (USA) – Bonny River (IRE) (Exit To Nowhere (USA)) [2017/18 c–, h75, b–: c25.1s[4] c24d[3] c25.5s* c25.6s[pu] c25.1v[3] c26v[ur] c24g Apr 26] compact gelding: maiden hurdler: poor handicap chaser: won at Warwick in November: stays 25f: acts on heavy going: often let down by jumping. *Grant Cann* c81 x
h–

GORES ISLAND (IRE) 12 b.g. Beneficial – Just Leader (IRE) (Supreme Leader) [2017/18 c121, h109: c19.7g[2] c19.9d[pu] c20.5d c16.1s[2] c17.8v[3] c17.8v[3] c19.7s[6] Apr 15] tall, lengthy gelding: fair hurdler: fairly useful handicap chaser, generally below best in 2017/18: stays 21f: acts on heavy going: has worn headgear, including in 2017/18: temperamental. *Gary Moore* c112 §
h– §

GORING ONE (IRE) 13 b.g. Broadway Flyer (USA) – Brigette's Secret (Good Thyne (USA)) [2017/18 c94, h–: c22.6g[5] c21.6d[3] c26.7v* c26v* c26v[3] c25.1s[5] c25.1v[pu] c27.5d[3] Apr 22] compact gelding: maiden hurdler: modest handicap chaser: won at Wincanton and Fontwell in December: stays 27f: acts on good to firm and heavy going: often wears headgear: usually races close up. *Anna Newton-Smith* c94
h–

GORRAN HAVEN (IRE) 8 ch.g. Stowaway – Diminished (IRE) (Alphabatim (USA)) [2017/18 c93: c20.3g[6] c24d[4] c25.5s[4] Nov 22] maiden pointer: poor maiden chaser: stays 2½m: best form on good going: sometimes in headgear: has worn tongue tie: often races prominently. *Caroline Bailey* c78

GORSKY ISLAND (IRE) 10 b.g. Turtle Island (IRE) – Belle Magello (FR) (Exit To Nowhere (USA)) [2017/18 c–, h–: c23.8g c27.5g[2] c25.1v[pu] c25.6s[3] c26.6s[pu] c24s[pu] c24g[5] Apr 20] good-topped gelding: maiden hurdler: fairly useful handicap chaser: second at Stratford in June: stays 1½m: acts on soft going: tried in cheekpieces. *Tom George* c120
h–

GORTNAGIRL (IRE) 6 b.m. Mahler – Rebel Flyer (IRE) (Presenting) [2017/18 h20.7d h21d[6] Apr 26] £15,000 5-y-o: rather unfurnished mare: second foal: half-sister to fair hurdler Troublesombrothers (2m winner, by Heron Island): dam, winning pointer, half-sister to useful hurdler/fairly useful chaser (2m-2½m winner) Treaty Flyer: off mark in Irish points at fifth attempt: modest form over hurdles: wears tongue tie. *Paul Cowley* h86

GORTROE JOE (IRE) 6 b.g. Beneficial – Rowlands Star (IRE) (Old Vic) [2017/18 b85p: h16.4g[3] h15.7v[5] h15.8d[4] h21.2s[4] Jan 18] useful-looking gelding: has scope: placed on completed start in Irish maiden points: fair form over hurdles: often travels strongly. *Dan Skelton* h114

GOSHEVEN (IRE) 5 b.g. Presenting – Fair Choice (IRE) (Zaffaran (USA)) [2017/18 b15.3v[5] h21s[3] h20.3g[5] Apr 18] well-made gelding: fifth foal: half-brother to useful hurdler/chaser Vesper Bell (2½m-3m winner), stayed 3¾m, and fairly useful chaser Aurora Bell (2¾m-3m winner) (both by Beneficial): dam ran twice in bumpers: held back by inexperience in bumper: fairly useful form over hurdles: better effort when fifth in novice at Cheltenham in April: will be suited by 2¾m+: will go on improving. *Philip Hobbs* h125 p
b72

GOT AWAY (FR) 5 b.m. American Post – Hideaway Girl (Fasliyev (USA)) [2017/18 h17.9s[4] c18.4s* c21.4s[4] h17.9s c16.4v[F] c22.7s* c19.9s[pu] c21s[F] Apr 27] strong mare: third foal: half-sister to French 6f-7.5f winner Got Breizh (by Footstepsinthesand): dam maiden (stayed 1m): useful hurdler: fourth in listed race at Auteuil in May: similar form over fences: won minor event at Auteuil in June and listed mares event at Leicester (by 4½ lengths from Antartica de Thaix) in January: left P. Peltier after fourth start: stays 23f: acts on heavy going: often wears headgear. *Oliver Sherwood* c137
h137

GOTHIC EMPIRE (IRE) 6 b.g. Dark Angel (IRE) – Box of Frogs (IRE) (One Cool Cat (USA)) [2017/18 h16s h15.8g[4] Apr 24] leggy gelding: fairly useful on Flat, stays 7f: fair form over hurdles: better effort when fourth in maiden at Huntingdon: should improve again. *Richard Rowe* h102 p

GOT THE NAC (IRE) 9 br.g. Beneficial – Hey Jude (IRE) (Mandalus) [2017/18 c–, h–: c20.9s[ur] Jan 29] winning hurdler: useful form at best over fences, unseated rider in hunter sole start under Rules (won Irish point in October) in 2017/18: unproven beyond 2m: acts on heavy going: tried in hood. *Mrs Kim Smyly* c–
h–

GOULANE CHOSEN (IRE) 9 b.g. Well Chosen – Vixen's Cry (IRE) (Miner's Lamp) [2017/18 c20.3s* h20v c18s[2] c18v* h19v[6] c20s[F] Apr 25] winning pointer: fairly useful hurdler at best, below form in 2017/18: useful chaser: won minor event at Clonmel in November and handicap at Gowran (by 7 lengths from La Bella Vida) in March: left Paul Patrick Moloney after fourth start: stays 2¾m: acts on heavy going: has worn cheekpieces. *Seamus Spillane, Ireland* c136
h–

GOU

GOUTEZ MOI (FR) 5 b.g. Dragon Dancer – Titi Jolie (FR) (Blushing Flame (USA)) [2017/18 b16s⁵ b16s⁴ b15.8d Mar 26] €23,000 3-y-o: rather unfurnished gelding: second foal: half-brother to French hurdler La Pleine Lune (17f winner, by Early March): dam, French maiden hurdler (second at 15f), half-sister to fairly useful French hurdler/chaser (15f-19f winner) Mister Emily: fair form in bumpers: best effort when fourth in maiden at Kempton in February. *Laura Mongan* — **b87**

GOWANAUTHAT (IRE) 10 ch.g. Golan (IRE) – Coolrua (IRE) (Commanche Run) [2017/18 c131, h–: c19.2g^{pu} c21.6g^{ur} c24.2d^{pu} c26d⁴ c15.9v⁵ Mar 9] winning pointer: maiden hurdler: useful chaser, well below best in 2017/18: left Charlie Mann after third start: stays 3m: acts on good to firm and heavy going: usually wears cheekpieces: wears tongue tie: front runner/races prominently. *Francesca Nimmo* — **c85 h–**

GOWELL (IRE) 7 b.m. Gold Well – Glen Supreme (IRE) (Supreme Leader) [2017/18 c–, h90: h21g⁵ h21.6m c20d³ c20s c25.1v⁴ c26v^{pu} c23.5v Jan 30] modest form over hurdles: poor handicap chaser: stays 2½m: acts on soft going: in blinkers last 2 starts: in tongue tie last 3: ungenuine. *Seamus Mullins* — **c82 § h– §**

GO WEST YOUNG MAN (IRE) 10 b.g. Westerner – Last of Her Line (Silver Patriarch (IRE)) [2017/18 c119§, h119§: c25.5m⁴ c18g c19.9d^{ur} c22.9v^{pu} c20s c20.2v⁵ c20.3d² Apr 21] rangy gelding: fairly useful hurdler: fair maiden chaser nowadays: stays 3m: acts on good to firm and heavy going: temperamental. *Henry Daly* — **c113 § h– §**

GOWITHTHEFLOW (IRE) 5 b.g. Westerner – Maryiver (IRE) (Runyon (IRE)) [2017/18 h19.5s² h20.5s² h20.8d⁸ h21.1s Mar 14] €19,000 3-y-o, £75,000 4-y-o: sturdy gelding: second foal: half-brother to fairly useful hurdler/winning pointer Lough Derg Farmer (21f/2¾m winner, by Presenting): dam (c112/h114) 2m-21f hurdle/chase winner: won Irish maiden point on debut: useful form over hurdles: won novice at Doncaster (by 1¼ lengths from Paisley Park) in February. *Ben Pauling* — **h130**

GRAASTEN (GER) 6 ch.g. Sholokhov (IRE) – Golden Time (GER) (Surumu (GER)) [2017/18 h118: h20.5v* h21s⁶ Mar 17] good-topped gelding: fairly useful handicap hurdler: won at Plumpton in February: stays 21f: acts on heavy going. *Gary Moore* — **h125**

GRACE DONT WAIT (IRE) 7 b.m. Acambaro (GER) – So Musical (IRE) (Old Vic) [2017/18 b16d b16g Jun 3] first foal: dam (b79) second in bumper: no form in bumpers. *Rob Summers* — **b–**

GRACEFUL LEGEND 7 b.m. Midnight Legend – Clover Green (IRE) (Presenting) [2017/18 h120: h16.3g³ h16s⁶ h21.6d* h20.3s³ h21.1s Mar 14] compact mare: useful handicap hurdler: won mares event at Ascot in November: third in another mares event at Cheltenham (5½ lengths behind Momella) in December: stays 2¾m: acts on soft going: often wears cheekpieces. *Ben Case* — **h132**

GRACE TARA 9 b.m. Kayf Tara – Fenney Spring (Polish Precedent (USA)) [2017/18 h111: c20s¹ c24.2s⁴ c22.5v⁴ c25.2v² c24.1s⁵ h24.6s⁵ Apr 9] Irish point winner: fair handicap hurdler: similar form over fences: stays 25f: best form on soft/heavy going: often wears tongue tie: often travels strongly. *Michael Scudamore* — **c106 h105**

GRACIE STANSFIELD 4 ch.f. Peintre Celebre (USA) – Ex Gracia (Efisio) [2017/18 b13.7g⁴ b13.1g⁶ b13.6v⁶ Nov 15] second foal: half-sister to 6f winner Questo (by Monsieur Bond): dam ran twice on Flat: poor form in bumpers: has joined Tony Carroll. *Philip Kirby* — **b68**

GRAGEELAGH GIRL (IRE) 7 b.m. Craigsteel – Smiths Lady (IRE) (Anshan) [2017/18 b16.2g* b17d² b16.4s² b15.8s Dec 26] £20,000 6-y-o: useful-looking mare: sixth foal: half-sister to a winning pointer by Heron Island: dam unraced daughter of fairly useful staying hurdler Accountancy Lady: Irish point winner: fairly useful form in bumpers: won at Perth in July, and also first past post in mares event at Aintree (demoted for causing interference) in October: second in listed mares race at Cheltenham (3¼ lengths behind Posh Trish) in November. *Fergal O'Brien* — **b101**

GRAMS AND OUNCES 11 b.g. Royal Applause – Ashdown Princess (IRE) (King's Theatre (IRE)) [2017/18 c110, h99: h16.8d² h19.5d³ h15.8d h15.9s^F h15.7v² h16v⁶ Apr 14] sturdy gelding: modest handicap hurdler: maiden chaser: stays 2½m: acts on good to firm and heavy going: often wears cheekpieces: wears tongue tie. *Grace Harris* — **c– h96**

GRANARD (IRE) 6 br.g. Getaway (GER) – Yes Darling (IRE) (Oscar (IRE)) [2017/18 b16s³ h21.9v* h20.6v⁴ Apr 14] first foal: dam, unraced, out of half-sister to top-class chaser (winner up to 25f) Merry Gale: runner-up second of 2 starts in Irish maiden points: third in bumper at Warwick: fairly useful form over hurdles: easily won 3-runner novice at Ffos Las in April: likely to stay 3m. *Nigel Twiston-Davies* — **h118 b85**

GRANDADS HORSE 12 br.g. Bollin Eric – Solid Land (FR) (Solid Illusion (USA)) [2017/18 c129, h–: c24.3v³ c22.7g⁵ c24vᵖᵘ c24s⁶ c29.2g⁵ Apr 26] strong gelding: winning hurdler: fairly useful handicap chaser: third at Ayr in November: stays 25f: acts on soft and good to firm going: has worn headgear, including in 2017/18: has worn tongue tie. *Jennie Candlish*   **c121 h–**

GRAND COUREUR (FR) 6 b.g. Grand Couturier – Iris du Berlais (FR) (Bonnet Rouge (FR)) [2017/18 h102: h15.8d⁵ h20s⁴ c17.4d c20g² c20.2gᵖᵘ c17.4dᵖᵘ Apr 21] rather unfurnished gelding: maiden hurdler, fair at best: modest form over fences: left Nick Williams after fifth start: stays 2½m: acts on good to soft going: tried in cheekpieces. *Barry Leavy*   **c94 h89**

GRAND ENTERPRISE 8 b.g. Fair Mix (IRE) – Miss Chinchilla (Perpendicular) [2017/18 c–, h104: h23.3g³ h22.1dᶠ h23.3vᵖᵘ Oct 14] fair handicap hurdler: maiden chaser: stays 27f: acts on good to firm and good to soft going: often travels strongly. *Henry Hogarth*   **c– h104**

GRAND INQUISITOR 6 b.g. Dansili – Dusty Answer (Zafonic (USA)) [2017/18 h16.5m⁴ h15.8d Nov 25] good-topped gelding: useful on Flat, stays 1½m: modest form over hurdles: better effort when fourth in maiden at Taunton in November. *Ian Williams*   **h92**

GRAND INTRODUCTION (IRE) 8 b.g. Robin des Pres (FR) – What A Breeze (IRE) (Naheez (USA)) [2017/18 c23.6vᵖᵘ c24.2sᵖᵘ c24.5s* c24.5vᵖᵘ Feb 14] maiden hurdler: fair form over fences: won handicap at Towcester in February: stays 3m: acts on heavy going: often in tongue tie. *Fergal O'Brien*   **c101 h–**

GRANDIOSO (IRE) 11 b.g. Westerner – Champagne Warrior (IRE) (Waajib) [2017/18 c120, h–: c15.9vᵖᵘ c23.8d Mar 22] well-made gelding: winning hurdler: smart chaser at best, no form in hunters in 2017/18: stayed 23f: acted on good to firm and heavy going: tried in cheekpieces: wore tongue tie: usually raced towards rear: dead. *Steve Flook*   **c– h–**

GRAND MORNING 6 b.g. Midnight Legend – Valentines Lady (IRE) (Zaffaran (USA)) [2017/18 h16.2s³ h16v* h16v* h22v* Apr 14] £68,000 3-y-o: well-made gelding: second foal: half-brother to winning hurdler/high-class chaser Edwulf (19f-3m winner, by Kayf Tara): dam (h102) bumper and 2¾m-3m hurdle winner: fairly useful form over hurdles: won maiden at Ayr in January, novice there in February and novice handicap at Newcastle in April: in tongue tie last 2 starts: likely to progress further. *Lucinda Russell*   **h123 p**

GRAND PARTNER (IRE) 10 b.g. Millenary – Bens Partner (IRE) (Beneficial) [2017/18 h134: c16g c16g c17g h20vᵖᵘ h20v⁴ h20v³ h20v h16s³ h16v* h20s⁵ h16.5dᶠ Apr 24] tall, workmanlike gelding: useful handicap hurdler: won at Leopardstown (by 1¼ lengths from Chesterfield King) in March: fifth in Grade 3 at Aintree (2¼ lengths behind Jester Jet) in April: modest form over fences: stays 3m: acts on good to firm and heavy going: has worn headgear. *Thomas Mullins, Ireland*   **c96 h135**

GRAND RIGEL (IRE) 5 b.g. Grandera (IRE) – Nora D (IRE) (Revoque (IRE)) [2017/18 b16.8v h19sᵖᵘ Dec 30] no show in bumper/novice hurdle. *David Pipe*   **h– b–**

GRAND SANCY (FR) 4 b.g. Diamond Boy (FR) – La Courtille (FR) (Risk Seeker) [2017/18 b13.1g⁴ h15.3v² h15.3v² h16.5v² h16.4sᵖᵘ Mar 14] good-topped gelding: first foal: dam fair French 17f/2¼m hurdle/chase winner: fair form in bumpers: better effort when second in junior event at Wincanton in December: similar form over hurdles: usually wears hood. *Paul Nicholls*   **h112 b89**

GRANDTURGEON (FR) 11 gr.g. Turgeon (USA) – Grande Symphonie (FR) (Big John (FR)) [2017/18 c24s* c22.2v³ Feb 17] prolific point winner: fairly useful form in chases: won hunter at Warwick in January: wears tongue tie. *Philip Rowley*   **c122**

GRAND TURINA 7 b.m. Kayf Tara – Cesana (IRE) (Desert Prince (IRE)) [2017/18 h113: h19.6gᵖᵘ h19.4s h20.7s⁵ h18.6s⁴ h23.1v⁴ Mar 11] sturdy mare: fair handicap hurdler: stays 21f: acts on heavy going: has worn hood: usually races close up. *Venetia Williams*   **h110**

GRAND VISION (IRE) 12 gr.g. Old Vic – West Hill Rose (IRE) (Roselier (FR)) [2017/18 c127, h–: c20s* c26v² c20.2v* c26.3v⁶ c21.1s⁵ Apr 12] tall gelding: winning hurdler: useful handicap chaser: won at Lingfield (veterans) in December and Wincanton (by 7 lengths from Kayf Adventure) in February: stays 3¼m: acts on heavy going: has worn cheekpieces: usually races close up. *Colin Tizzard*   **c133 h–**

GRANIA O'MALLEY (IRE) 5 ch.m. Beat Hollow – Oh Susannah (FR) (Turgeon (USA)) [2017/18 b90: b16.7s² b15.8m² h15.8s⁴ h15.8g⁵ h19.7s h16s h16.7v⁵ h16.5v² Mar 12] rather unfurnished mare: fair form in bumpers: similar form over hurdles: unproven beyond 2m: acts on heavy going: often races towards rear. *Evan Williams*   **h101 b93**

GRA

GRAN MAESTRO (USA) 9 ch.g. Medicean – Red Slippers (USA) (Nureyev (USA)) [2017/18 c101, h120: h17m³ h15.7d⁴ h16.3g⁶ h19.9m² h23.3d³ h22.1s² h19.6g⁴ h24.1d⁴ h23.6d⁶ h21.1s h20.5s h16.6d² h16s* h15.7s⁶ Feb 12] plain gelding: fair handicap hurdler: won at Wetherby in January: maiden chaser: stays 2½m: acts on soft and good to firm going: wears headgear: has worn tongue tie. *Peter Winks* — c–, h109

GRANNY BIDDY (IRE) 7 b.m. Flemensfirth (USA) – Calomeria (Groom Dancer (USA)) [2017/18 h20.7m³ h21.5g h20d h16g⁴ h17g⁵ h21g* h20v* h20.2s² h19d* h20s* h20v* h24vᵖᵘ Dec 10] €30,000 4-y-o: fifth foal: sister to bumper winner/fairly useful chaser Bandit Country (2¾m winner) and half-sister to fair hurdler Res Ipsa Loquitur (2m/17f winner, by Beneficial): dam (h111), 2m hurdle winner, sister to smart hurdler (winner up 21f) Son of Flicka: useful handicap hurdler: won at Tramore in August, Listowel in September, and Cork in October and November (twice): stays 3m: acts on good to firm and heavy going: wears headgear: often races prominently, usually travels strongly. *Michael Winters, Ireland* — h130

GRAN PARADISO (IRE) 6 ch.g. Galileo (IRE) – Looking Lovely (IRE) (Storm Cat (USA)) [2017/18 h109: h21.2g⁴ May 4] fair handicap hurdler: stays 21f: acts on good to soft going: wears cheekpieces: in tongue tie last 2 starts: usually races towards rear, often lazily: has joined Dan Skelton. *Micky Hammond* — h96

GRANVILLE ISLAND (IRE) 11 b.g. Flemensfirth (USA) – Fox Glen (Furry Glen) [2017/18 c120, h118: c20dᶠ c22.9v⁴ c20.6v⁴ c19.4s³ c20v* c20v* c20.2v* Mar 9] workmanlike gelding: fairly useful hurdler: fairly useful handicap chaser: completed hat-trick at Uttoxeter in January, Carlisle in February and Leicester in March: stays 2½m: acts on heavy going: tried in cheekpieces: strong traveller, has found little. *Jennie Candlish* — c128, h–

GRAPE TREE FLAME 10 ch.m. Grape Tree Road – Althrey Flame (IRE) (Torus) [2017/18 h117: h23.3d³ May 20] sturdy mare: fairly useful handicap hurdler: stays 27f: acts on heavy going: wears headgear. *Peter Bowen* — h107

GRAPEVINE (IRE) 5 b.g. Lilbourne Lad (IRE) – High Vintage (IRE) (High Chaparral (IRE)) [2017/18 h16.5s⁵ h16.3v⁴ ab16d* h16s⁵ h16s Apr 28] good-topped gelding: fairly useful on Flat, stays 1¼m: won jumpers bumper at Kempton (by ½ length from Diablo de Rouhet) in March: fair form over hurdles: remains open to improvement. *Nicky Henderson* — h106 p

GRAY DAY (IRE) 7 gr.g. Daylami (IRE) – Carrigeen Diamond (IRE) (Old Vic) [2017/18 h116, b82: c20d⁵ Oct 8] fairly useful form over hurdles: 22/1, showed aptitude when 13 lengths fifth of 9 to Aqua Dude in maiden at Uttoxeter on chasing debut: stays 23f: acts on soft going: front runner/races prominently: should progress as a chaser. *Donald McCain* — c122 p, h–

GRAYHAWK (IRE) 8 gr.g. Kalanisi (IRE) – Saddler Regal (IRE) (Saddlers' Hall (IRE)) [2017/18 c73s, h–: c17.4d⁴ c21.6dᵖᵘ c19.7s⁴ Dec 18] sturdy gelding: twice-raced hurdler: little form in chases: won point in March: usually in cheekpieces: often races prominently. *Diana Grissell* — c59 x, h–

GRAYS CHOICE (IRE) 7 b.g. Well Chosen – Pennyworth (IRE) (Zaffaran (USA)) [2017/18 h86: c20.3vᵖᵘ c15.7d⁵ h19.5v h21v³ Apr 27] poor maiden hurdler: no form over fences: left George Bewley after second start: best effort at 2¾m: acts on soft going: has worn cheekpieces: tried in tongue tie. *Henry Oliver* — c–, h68

GRAYSTOWN (IRE) 6 b.g. Well Chosen – Temple Girl (IRE) (Luso) [2017/18 h16s³ h20.5v² h18.9v⁶ h16v⁵ h15.7v⁵ h15.6s h16v⁶ h20.9vᵖᵘ h17v³ Apr 17] second foal: dam unraced: placed twice in Irish points: fair maiden hurdler: stays 2½m: best form on heavy going. *Stuart Coltherd* — h106

GRAY WOLF RIVER 7 gr.m. Fair Mix (IRE) – Inkpen (Overbury (IRE)) [2017/18 h–: c16.1g⁵ c17.4dᵖᵘ May 28] plain mare: won completed start in points: maiden hurdler: no form over fences: tried in hood: often races freely. *Richard Harper* — c–, h–

GREAT COLACI 5 b.g. Sulamani (IRE) – Fairlie (Halling (USA)) [2017/18 h16.7g⁶ h15.6m h15.7d h16.7dᶠ h15.6s Jan 3] modest on Flat, stays 7f: poor form over hurdles: raced around 2m. *Gillian Boanas* — h78

GREAT EXPECTATIONS 10 b.g. Storming Home – Fresh Fruit Daily (Reprimand) [2017/18 h16g⁵ Jun 4] modest on Flat, stays 7f: no form over hurdles: wears tongue tie. *J. R. Jenkins* — h–

GREAT FIELD (FR) 7 b.g. Great Pretender (IRE) – Eaton Lass (IRE) (Definite Article) [2017/18 c170p, h–: c16v* Mar 23] — c170 p, h–

A scattergun approach to placing horses can often reap dividends if a trainer has an embarrassment of riches in his yard, as the record in recent years of leading Flat trainer Aidan O'Brien can testify. Three of O'Brien's last five British classic wins went to a horse which wasn't the Ballydoyle first string, with the 2017 Derby perhaps the best example. O'Brien saddled six of the eighteen runners, including the 40/1 winner Wings of Eagles, who swooped late to beat Ballydoyle first string Cliffs of Moher in a thrilling finish, a sixth Derby win for the combination of O'Brien and the Coolmore partners a triumph for weight of numbers from the outset, Coolmore having entered no fewer than fifty-nine yearlings at the initial entry stage back in December 2015. O'Brien's nearest equivalent in the Irish National Hunt ranks, record-breaking champion trainer Willie Mullins, has tended to keep his star performers apart as much as possible down the years (the O'Brien horses are mostly in the same or similar ownership which allows more latitude for multiple entries).

However, Mullins resorted to the kitchen sink treatment at the latest Punchestown Festival as his battle with great rival Gordon Elliott for the 2017/18 trainers' championship in Ireland reached fever pitch, both yards mob-handed in most of the races (prize money mostly went down to sixth). Mullins certainly benefited from his increased number of runners (the figures are in the essay on Kemboy), with exactly half of his yard's record-breaking eighteen winners over the five-day meeting being provided by horses which weren't the Closutton first string. The Boylesports Champion Chase on the Tuesday was a case in point, with Un de Sceaux lining up for battle alongside no fewer than three stable companions—the popular front runner had met just three other Closutton inmates during his seventeen previous starts over fences (and just five in total from twenty-seven career starts for Mullins). Indeed, Un de Sceaux had sidestepped the Queen Mother Champion Chase in favour of the Ryanair Chase (first in 2017, runner-up in 2018) at the last two Cheltenham Festivals to avoid a clash with stable companions who were presumably ranked higher in Mullins' pecking order. Un de Sceaux's connections could possibly have been forgiven for having 'what if' thoughts after Un de Sceaux lowered the colours of the Susannah Ricci-owned pair Douvan (second) and Min (fourth) at Punchestown—the fourth Mullins runner, outsider Ballycasey (one of that Mullins trio that Un de Sceaux had actually met before), claimed the €2,750 for sixth place!

Ironically, however, potentially the most exciting two-mile chaser within the Mullins ranks—judged on Timeform ratings—was actually missing from that Punchestown Champion Chase line-up. Great Field had spent the vast majority of the season on the sidelines, and another injury setback the weekend before the Punchestown Festival must have been especially frustrating for his connections. As a result, there is very little to add about Great Field in 2017/18 and, because of that, there is a danger that he will go under the radar for the second season running, particularly when it comes to British racegoers, his sole effort on British soil having come when he was pulled up after proving far too headstrong in the 2016 County Hurdle (for which he was sent off joint favourite). It should be stressed, however, that Great Field can still boast an unbeaten record over fences, with the form of those (largely very easy) wins continuing to stand up well to close inspection.

In truth, Great Field's latest win, in the Grade 2 toals.com Bookmakers Webster Cup Chase at Navan in late-March, might not have seemed quite so impressive as some of his previous performances at first glance, but subsequent events showed it in a better light. Having run out of time to take up any engagements at either the Dublin Racing Festival or the Cheltenham Festival, Great Field was probably entitled to benefit from his belated reappearance and he was an easy-to-back 11/8 favourite, conceding weight to all five of his rivals on heavy ground. As it was, Great Field picked up where he left off in his 2016/17 novice campaign, cutting a dash out in front under his now-regular jockey Jody McGarvey (who himself missed much of the latest season through injury). Great Field's fast and low jumping technique can provide the odd white-knuckle moment for his supporters, but he was notably accurate at Navan and seemed set for another wide-margin win for most of the way. His eleven-month absence began to tell in the latter stages, however, and his margin of victory was cut down late by the patiently-ridden Doctor Phoenix (receiving 4 lb), who was just a length and three quarters behind at the line, the pair pulling eighteen lengths clear of the remainder. McGarvey always had matters under control, though, and Great Field's superiority over Doctor Phoenix on the day was clearly a good deal greater than that final margin. The effort was made to look even

GRE

better by the performance of Doctor Phoenix next time. In receipt of 5 lb, he seemed set to beat Un de Sceaux before he came down two out in the Grade 2 Devenish Chase over two and a half miles on Fairyhouse's Irish Grand National card (Doctor Phoenix's stable was under a cloud when he subsequently managed only fifth in the Boylesports Champion Chase).

```
                    ┌ Great Pretender (IRE) ┌ King's Theatre    ┌ Sadler's Wells
                    │ (b 1999)              │ (b 1991)          │ Regal Beauty
                    │                       │ Settler           │ Darshaan
Great Field (FR)    │                       │ (b 1992)          │ Aborigine
  (b.g. 2011)       │                       
                    │ Eaton Lass (IRE)      ┌ Definite Article  ┌ Indian Ridge
                    │ (br 2001)             │ (b 1992)          │ Summer Fashion
                                            │ Cockney Lass      │ Camden Town
                                            │ (ch 1983)         │ Big Bugs Bomb
```

Great Field's pedigree was discussed in detail in *Chasers & Hurdlers 2016/17* and there isn't much to add other than to report two further wins for his half-brother Deadheat (by Buck's Boum), who developed into a fairly useful hurdler/chaser at up to two and three quarter miles in France during the latest season. Another half-brother Unexcepted (by Anzillero) is heading to Ireland, though, having been bought for £200,000 at the Cheltenham November Sales after finishing third in an Auteuil juvenile hurdle in October (for Emmanuel Clayeux) on his only start to date. The unraced dam Eaton Lass has produced one more foal since the aforementioned trio, her 2017 filly Perle Baie (by Kitkou). On breeding, Great Field should stay a fair bit further than two miles but, given his style of racing, it would be perfectly understandable if he was kept around the minimum. Top two-mile prizes will presumably be on the agenda in 2018/19, when hopefully he will be seen much more regularly. It is also to be hoped that he gets the opportunity to prove himself against tip-top opposition, even if the competition comes from within his own stable. There shouldn't be an issue over juggling jockeys within the yard, bearing in mind McGarvey's association with Great Field. J.P. McManus' other retained riders Barry Geraghty and Mark Walsh will presumably get the call should anything happen to McGarvey, which frees up the likes of Ruby Walsh and Paul Townend to ride for the yard's other powerful owners. Great Field remains a top-notch prospect, and there is very much the possibility of even better to come, and he should certainly not be underestimated. His ante-post odds of 25/1 at the time of writing for the 2019 Queen Mother Champion Chase are guilty of doing that, considering the form he has already shown. *W. P. Mullins, Ireland*

GREAT FIGHTER 8 b.g. Street Cry (IRE) – Evil Empire (GER) (Acatenango (GER)) [2017/18 h130: h15.7m³ h16g Apr 20] fairly useful hurdler: third in Swinton Handicap at Haydock in May: stays 19f: acts on good to firm and good to soft going: wears headgear: races towards rear, usually travels strongly. *Jim Goldie* — h116

GREAT LOVER (FR) 6 gr.g. Smadoun (FR) – Dominelle (FR) (Pinmix (FR)) [2017/18 h15.3g^{pu} h15.8d h16.5v⁴ h16v⁵ h16v Apr 14] second foal: dam, French maiden, half-sister to fairly useful French hurdler/fair chaser (17f/2¼m winner) Eliga: modest form over hurdles: best effort at 2m: acts on heavy going: usually races towards rear. *Philip Hobbs* — h97

GREAT TEMPO (FR) 5 b.g. Great Pretender (IRE) – Prima Note (FR) (Nononito (FR)) [2017/18 h115: h17.7d h24.1s h19.5v³ h21.7s Apr 6] rather leggy gelding: fair handicap hurdler: stays 19f: acts on heavy going: wears headgear. *David Pipe* — h103

GRECIAN KING 5 b.g. Kheleyf (USA) – Grecian Air (FR) (King's Best (USA)) [2017/18 h15.8g h15.7s h15.7d⁶ h15.7v h15.6d³ h15.7g Apr 20] half-brother to fair hurdler Magic Skyline (2m/17f winner, by Refuse To Bend): dam half-sister to useful hurdler/ fairly useful chaser (2m-19f winner) Desert Air: modest maiden on Flat, stays 1¼m: modest form over hurdles: raced only at 2m: acts on good to soft going: often in hood: often races towards rear/freely. *Laura Morgan* — h89

GREEN FLAG (IRE) 11 b.g. Milan – Erin Go Brea (IRE) (Un Desperado (FR)) [2017/18 c112, h–: c24.2v^{pu} Oct 14] winning hurdler: useful chaser at best, pulled up sole start in 2017/18: stayed 4m: acted on good to firm and heavy going: tried in tongue tie: dead. *Lucinda Russell* — c– h–

GREEN LIGHT 7 b.g. Authorized (IRE) – May Light (Midyan (USA)) [2017/18 h94p: ab16g³ h16.8v⁴ Apr 13] fairly useful at best on Flat, stays 1½m: twice raced over hurdles, well held in novice in April. *Brian Ellison* — h–

GRE

GREEN OR BLACK (IRE) 6 gr.m. Zebedee – Boucheron (Galileo (IRE)) [2017/18 h89p: h16g^3 h16.8v^2 h16s^2 Nov 14] fair form over hurdles: will prove best at sharp 2m. *Neil Mulholland*   **h104**

GREENSALT (IRE) 10 b.g. Milan – Garden City (IRE) (Shernazar) [2017/18 c25.2s^3 c21.1s^3 Apr 12] multiple point winner: maiden hurdler: fairly useful form over fences: better effort in 2017/18 when third in Foxhunters' Chase at Aintree (beaten 6½ lengths by Balnaslow) in April: stays easy 25f: acts on heavy going: tried in cheekpieces: wears tongue tie. *W. H. Easterby*   **c122 h–**

GREEN TIKKANA 5 gr.m. Tikkanen (USA) – Think Green (Montjeu (IRE)) [2017/18 b72: h16v^6 h15.7s^4 h16v^3 h24.3v^4 h27v^{pu} Mar 23] leggy mare: modest form over hurdles: stays 3m: acts on heavy going: usually races nearer last than first. *James Ewart*   **h91**

GREEN WINTER (IRE) 10 ch.g. Well Made (GER) – Assistine (IRE) (Oscar (IRE)) [2017/18 c–: c27.5d^{pu} Jun 9] multiple point winner: no form in novice hunter chases. *J. R. Bryan*   **c–**

GREENWORLDSOLUTION 6 b.g. Lucarno (USA) – Basford Lady (IRE) (Accordion) [2017/18 h63: h16.7g^2 h15.8g h15.8g^3 h18.6g^6 h19.6g^6 h19.6g^2 h19.9g^2 h19.3v h16.8g Nov 2] modest maiden hurdler: stays 2½m: best form on good going: tried in visor: usually wears tongue tie. *Jennie Candlish*   **h91**

GREEN ZONE (IRE) 7 b.g. Bushranger (IRE) – Incense (Unfuwain (USA)) [2017/18 h97: h16.2m^5 h20.2g* h16.2m* h19.9d* h16.2s^4 h23.9d h19.9d h24.7d^{pu} h20.9g^4 Nov 11] compact gelding: fair handicap hurdler: won at Perth (twice) and Uttoxeter in July: stays 21f: acts on soft and good to firm going: usually races towards rear. *Lisa Harrison*   **h105**

GREGARIOUS (IRE) 5 gr.g. Big Bad Bob (IRE) – Sense of Greeting (IRE) (Key of Luck (USA)) [2017/18 h111: c18d^{pu} c15.5d^4 c17v^2 c16v^F h15.7v* h16d^3 h19d^4 Apr 26] well-made gelding: fair handicap hurdler: won at Towcester in March: similar form over fences: stays 19f: acts on heavy going: usually wears hood: often wears tongue tie. *Lucy Wadham*   **c106 h114**

GRETTA ROSE 6 b.m. Proclamation (IRE) – Realms of Roses (Mister Baileys) [2017/18 h22.1d h23.9d^4 Aug 2] fifth foal: dam unraced half-sister to fair hurdler/fairly useful chaser (stayed 3m) Gold Ingot and fairly useful hurdler (19f/21f winner) Kenai Peninsula: off mark in points at fourth attempt: poor form over hurdles. *Susan Corbett*   **h73**

GREYBOUGG 9 gr.g. Tobougg (IRE) – Kildee Lass (Morpeth) [2017/18 c130, h–: c19.9d^{ur} c16.4g^6 c20.1s^5 c21.1s^{pu} Apr 13] lengthy gelding: winning hurdler: useful handicap chaser: below best in 2017/18, though had excuses: stays 3m, at least as effective at much shorter: acts on good to firm and heavy going: has worn hood: front runner. *Nigel Hawke*   **c115 h–**

GREY CHARLIE 4 gr.g. Hellvelyn – Phoenix Rising (Dr Fong (USA)) [2017/18 ab16g^4 Mar 2] well beaten in maiden bumper/on Flat debut. *Ivan Furtado*   **b–**

GREYED A (IRE) 7 gr.g. Daylami (IRE) – Broadcast (Broadsword (USA)) [2017/18 h105: h18.5d c20d^{pu} c26v* c26v* c23.6v^{pu} c24v^2 c25.7d^2 Feb 26] fair hurdler: similar form over fences: won handicaps at Fontwell in December and January, and Plumpton in February: stays 3¼m: acts on heavy going: tried in cheekpieces: usually leads. *Dr Richard Newland*   **c114 h–**

GREY GOLD (IRE) 13 gr.g. Strategic Choice (USA) – Grouse-N-Heather (Grey Desire) [2017/18 c146, h–: c19.4s* c19.4s^{ur} c19.4v^4 c19.4v^5 c16v^5 c15.9v^3 Apr 17] rather leggy gelding: winning hurdler: fairly useful chaser nowadays: won claimer at Ffos Las in October: third in handicap at Carlisle in April: stays 2½m: acts on heavy going. *Kerry Lee*   **c121 h–**

GREY MESSENGER (IRE) 9 gr.g. Heron Island (IRE) – Turlututu (FR) (Turgeon (USA)) [2017/18 c60, h69: c20.2s^{ur} c21.7m^{ur} Apr 25] sturdy gelding: maiden hurdler: poor form over fences: stays 23f: tried in cheekpieces: wears tongue tie. *Emma-Jane Bishop*   **c67 h–**

GREY MONK (IRE) 10 gr.g. Alderbrook – Thats The Bother (IRE) (Roselier (FR)) [2017/18 c–, h108§: h23.1g^5 h20.3d^5 h25g^5 h25g Nov 5] modest handicap hurdler: maiden chaser: stays 23f: acts on good to firm and heavy going: wears headgear/tongue tie: usually races close up: temperamental. *Sara Ender*   **c– h94 §**

GREY STORM (IRE) 7 gr.g. September Storm (GER) – Lady Blayney (IRE) (Mazaad) [2017/18 h–: h20.2g h20.2g^6 h19.6g Aug 16] won Irish point on debut: no form over hurdles: often wears tongue tie: often races towards rear. *Rose Dobbin*   **h–**

Caspian Caviar Gold Cup Handicap Chase, Cheltenham—the tragic demise of clear leader Starchitect leaves the grey Guitar Pete, Clan des Obeaux (centre) and King's Odyssey (noseband, right) to fight out the finish

GREY WATERS (IRE) 4 gr.f. Mastercraftsman (IRE) – Pelican Waters (IRE) (Key of Luck (USA)) [2017/18 h16d² h17g* h16v* h17v⁵ h16d⁴ h16s³ Feb 4] fairly useful form over hurdles: won juveniles at Killarney in August and Listowel in September: third in Spring Juvenile Hurdle at Leopardstown (17¼ lengths behind Mr Adjudicator) in February: raced around 2m: acts on heavy going. *Joseph Patrick O'Brien, Ireland* — **h118**

GRIFFINGTON 9 b.g. Fantastic Spain (USA) – Sound Check (Formidable (USA)) [2017/18 h–: h23s^pu May 17] pulled up both starts in novice hurdles: wears hood. *Grace Harris* — **h–**

GRIMTHORPE 7 ch.g. Alflora (IRE) – Sally Scally (Scallywag) [2017/18 b–: b15.7d h19.3s^pu h19.9s^pu h16.8v^pu Apr 13] no form in bumpers/over hurdles. *Tina Jackson* — **h–** **b–**

GRIS DE PRON (FR) 5 b.g. Gris de Gris (IRE) – Say Say (FR) (Garde Royale) [2017/18 h116: h17g⁴ c16.4g⁴ c16.3g^F Nov 17] fairly useful hurdler, below form on return in 2017/18: fair form over fences: yet to be asked for effort when fell 2 out in novice handicap won by Cracking Find at Newcastle: left Oliver Greenall after first start: unproven beyond 17f: acts on good to soft going: often in hood: sometimes in tongue tie: often races towards rear: should do better as a chaser. *Henry Hogarth* — **c112 p** **h79**

GRISSOM (FR) 10 ch.g. Sabrehill (USA) – Nuit de Chine (FR) (Valanour (IRE)) [2017/18 h18.5d^pu Sep 22] point winner: maiden hurdler/chaser: should stay beyond 19f: acts on soft going: often wears tongue tie. *Jimmy Frost* — **c–** **h–**

GROUNDUNDERREPAIR (IRE) 7 b.g. Milan – Discerning Air (Ezzoud (IRE)) [2017/18 h110, b81: h21.4g³ h19s² h24s² h23.9v³ h25.5v* Apr 10] fairly useful handicap hurdler: won at Hereford in April: thorough stayer: acts on heavy going: in cheekpieces last 2 starts. *Warren Greatrex* — **h120**

GROUSE LODGE (IRE) 12 b.g. Well Chosen – Arctic Jane (IRE) (Dayeem (USA)) – [2017/18 c20.3g Apr 20] workmanlike gelding: multiple point winner: winning hurdler: fairly useful chaser at best, well held in late-season hunter: stays 3¼m: acts on heavy going: has worn headgear. *Mrs Emma Clark* — **c–** **h–**

GROVE SILVER (IRE) 9 gr.g. Gamut (IRE) – Cobbler's Well (IRE) (Wood Chanter) [2017/18 c123, h–: c29.2g c20.1v c24v³ c25.6s^F c24v⁴ c20v* c20s⁵ Apr 8] rather leggy gelding: winning hurdler: fairly useful handicap chaser: won at Carlisle in March: stays 29f, effective at much shorter when conditions are testing: acts on heavy going: wears headgear: tried in tongue tie. *Jennie Candlish* — **c118** **h–**

GROW NASA GROW (IRE) 7 ch.g. Mahler – Dereenavurrig (IRE) (Lancastrian) [2017/18 h–: h19.9g³ h19.9g⁵ c16.4g c23.6g^pu c24.2s^pu c19.1s³ c20.2v⁴ c15.7v⁵ Mar 5] tall gelding: little show over hurdles: poor form over fences: should be suited by further than 2½m. *Peter Winks* — **c77** **h57**

GUANCIALE 11 b.g. Exit To Nowhere (USA) – Thenford Lass (IRE) (Anshan) [2017/18 c100§, h–§: c16.5m³ c16.3m^pu h16.8g^pu Jun 27] lengthy gelding: modest hurdler at best: modest handicap chaser: stays 3m: acts on good to firm and heavy going: wears cheekpieces: has worn tongue tie: often races towards rear: unreliable. *Dai Burchell* — **c98 §** **h– §**

GUARACHA 7 ch.g. Halling (USA) – Pachanga (Inchinor) [2017/18 c89, h77: c16.3d⁶ Jul 31] winning hurdler: fair chaser at best, well held sole start in 2017/18: stays 2½m: acts on heavy going: usually wears headgear. *Alexandra Dunn* — **c–** **h–**

GWE

GUARDS CHAPEL 10 b.g. Motivator – Intaaj (IRE) (Machiavellian (USA)) [2017/18 c–, h112§: h20.5s h19.5s² h19.2v⁵ Mar 17] rather leggy gelding: fair handicap hurdler: well held only outing over fences: stays 21f: acts on good to firm and good to soft going: usually wears headgear: usually races nearer last than first: moody. *Gary Moore* — **c–** **h107 §**

GUERRILLA TACTICS (IRE) 8 b.g. Presenting – Karens Flight (IRE) (Broadway Flyer (USA)) [2017/18 h21.6g³ h21.6m³ h22g⁴ c25.8g³ h26g* c25.1s* c26.7vF c25.1d⁴ Apr 22] modest form over hurdles: won handicap at Warwick in September: fair form over fences: won novice handicap at Wincanton in October: thorough stayer: acts on soft going: races prominently. *Jeremy Scott* — **c102** **h96**

GUIDING STARS (FR) 5 b.g. Bonbon Rose (FR) – Furika (FR) (Kadalko (FR)) [2017/18 b–: b16g² b15.8s b16.7v⁴ Apr 11] fair form in bumpers: tried in hood. *Harry Whittington* — **b89**

GUITAR PETE (IRE) 8 gr.g. Dark Angel (IRE) – Innishmore (IRE) (Lear Fan (USA)) [2017/18 c114+, h138+: h22.8m h20.6g² c20.1d² c21.4g² c19.4s* c20.4s c20.8s* c21vur c20.8s⁶ c20.5g Apr 20] rather leggy gelding: useful handicap hurdler: second at Market Rasen (4½ lengths behind Whatzdjazz) in July: useful handicap chaser: won listed event at Wetherby in November and Caspian Caviar Gold Cup at Cheltenham (by 2¾ lengths from Clan des Obeaux after clear leader broke down) in December: stays 21f: acts on good to firm and heavy going: has worn headgear/tongue tie. *Nicky Richards* — **c138** **h130**

GUMBALL 4 gr.g. No Risk At All (FR) – Good Time Girl (FR) (Slickly (FR)) [2017/18 h16.3s* h16d⁶ h16.4s² h15.8s² h16.8vpu h17s² h15.8d* Apr 24] sturdy gelding: first foal: dam, French 7f winner, sister to useful hurdler/fairly useful chaser (stayed 23f) Olofi: useful hurdler: won juveniles at Stratford and Chepstow in October, and novice at Ludlow in April: second in Anniversary Hurdle at Aintree (7 lengths behind We Have A Dream) earlier in April: will probably stay beyond 2m: acts on soft going: tried in tongue tie. *Philip Hobbs* — **h140**

GUNFLEET (IRE) 6 b.g. Oscar (IRE) – Lady Lincon (IRE) (Great Palm (USA)) [2017/18 b96: h19.2g² h19.9d⁵ h20.3s* h24.4d⁷ Feb 8] bumper winner: useful form over hurdles: won novice at Southwell in December and handicap at Doncaster (by ½ length from Nautical Nitwit) in February: will stay beyond 3m: tried in hood: often races freely: open to further improvement. *Emma Lavelle* — **h130 p**

GUNNER LINDLEY (IRE) 11 ch.g. Medicean – Lasso (Indian Ridge) [2017/18 h81: h16.2g⁴ h16.2g⁴ h16.2g Jun 25] poor maiden hurdler: unproven beyond 17f: acts on good to soft going: has worn headgear: front runner/races prominently. *Stuart Coltherd* — **h75**

GUN SHY (IRE) 10 b.g. Norwich – Debbies Scud (IRE) (Roselier (FR)) [2017/18 h20gpu h19.2m c19.4v⁵ c20.9v⁵ Apr 10] fairly useful hurdler/chaser at best for Gary Moore, no form in 2017/18. *Deborah Faulkner* — **c–** **h–**

GUSTAVE MAHLER (IRE) 8 ch.g. Mahler – Kloetta (IRE) (Grand Lodge (USA)) [2017/18 h106, b93: h16g* h15.7g* h16g² h18.5d* h19.9g³ h19.5dpu Oct 15] sturdy gelding: point winner: bumper winner: fairly useful hurdler: won novices at Worcester in May, Southwell in June and Newton Abbot in August: stays 2½m: acts on good to soft going: front runner. *Alastair Ralph* — **h126**

GUSTAV (IRE) 8 b.g. Mahler – Pakaradyssa (FR) (Roakarad) [2017/18 c91, h91: c20.2v³ c19.4v³ c17.5d* Apr 24] compact gelding: maiden hurdler: modest handicap chaser: won at Exeter in April: stays 21f: acts on soft going: wears cheekpieces: usually races close up. *Zoe Davison* — **c99** **h–**

GUYBOY 5 b.g. Like A Boy – Left Nostril (IRE) (Beckett (IRE)) [2017/18 b14d Dec 20] tailed off in bumper. *Sarah-Jayne Davies* — **b–**

GVS IRPORTENSA (IRE) 6 ch.m. Trans Island – Greenfield Noora (IRE) (Topanoora) [2017/18 b88: h18.7g* Aug 3] fair form in bumpers: 3/1, won 9-runner maiden at Stratford on hurdling debut by length from Boy In A Bentley: will stay 2½m: tried in cheekpieces. *Warren Greatrex* — **h94**

GWALIA (IRE) 5 b.g. Beat Hollow – Payphone (Anabaa (USA)) [2017/18 b16.5g² b16v² b13.7s² Apr 6] €16,000 3-y-o: seventh foal: brother to bumper winner/fairly useful hurdler Call Back (2m/17f winner) and half-brother to 2 winners on Flat: dam useful French 5.5f winner: fair form in bumpers: best effort when second at Fontwell in April. *Evan Williams* — **b92**

GWENCILY BERBAS (FR) 7 b.g. Nickname (FR) – Lesorial (FR) (Lesotho (USA)) [2017/18 c132, h–: c17g² c24.9s* c16.5s c16v³ c21sur Feb 4] winning hurdler: useful chaser: won maiden at Roscommon in June: third in novice at Naas (9¼ lengths behind Demi Sang) in January: stays 25f: acts on heavy going: tried in headgear: sometimes wears tongue tie: usually races prominently. *Alan Fleming, Ireland* — **c130** **h–**

GWI

GWILI SPAR 10 ch.g. Generosity – Lady of Mine (Cruise Missile) [2017/18 c71§, h69§: h23.3d h19.9g[4] c20g[F] h20g[pu] h15.8g[5] h19.6g[pu] h16d[4] h15.8g Sep 13] poor maiden hurdler: poor chaser: stays 2½m: acts on good to soft going: has worn hood: often wears tongue tie: ungenuine. *Laura Hurley*   c– §
h67 §

H

HAAFAPIECE 5 ch.g. Haafhd – Bonnet's Pieces (Alderbrook) [2017/18 b95: h16.3g[4] h18.6d[4] h15.7s[4] h16m[4] Apr 26] bumper winner: fair form over hurdles. *Pam Sly*   h110

HAAFAPRINCESS 5 b.m. Haafhd – Mystic Glen (Vettori (IRE)) [2017/18 b16.4d[5] Mar 16] first foal: dam (c81/h75), ungenuine 2m hurdle/chase winner, half-sister to useful hurdler (2m-2¼m winner) Clever Cookie: well held in bumper. *Peter Niven*   b–

HAASAB (IRE) 5 b.g. Sakhee (USA) – Badweia (USA) (Kingmambo (USA)) [2017/18 b15.7g[6] b16.7g[4] ab16g[3] b15.7d[2] h19.3v[5] h24v[3] h15.8d h20.6g[5] Apr 22] £3,500 3-y-o: fourth foal: half-brother to smart 7f/1m winner Mitraad (by Aqlaam): dam 6f/7f winner: placed in bumpers: modest form over hurdles: often in headgear: often races towards rear. *Laura Morgan*   h96
b88

HAB SAB (IRE) 6 b.g. Papal Bull – Tamburello (IRE) (Roi Danzig (USA)) [2017/18 h–, b–: h20.5s[5] h20.5d c17v c25.7v[pu] Apr 1] good-topped gelding: poor form over hurdles: no show over fences. *Linda Jewell*   c–
h79

HADFIELD (IRE) 6 b.g. Sea The Stars (IRE) – Rezyana (AUS) (Redoute's Choice (AUS)) [2017/18 h116: h20s[3] h19.5s[3] h23.3v[5] Dec 22] fairly useful handicap hurdler: third at Worcester in November: should stay beyond 2½m: acts on soft going: wears cheekpieces/tongue tie: unreliable. *Neil Mulholland*   h118 §

HAIGHALL (IRE) 6 b.g. Scorpion (IRE) – Longwhitejemmy (IRE) (Rashar (USA)) [2017/18 h75: h20d[F] h19.9s[5] Dec 8] twice-raced over hurdles, running to fair level when fell 2 out in novice won by Count Meribel at Carlisle: dead. *Chris Grant*   h101

HAINAN (FR) 7 gr.g. Laveron – Honor Smytzer (Highest Honor (FR)) [2017/18 c130, h–: h24.3v[pu] c28.4v* c25.6v[3] c32.6s[4] c34v[pu] Mar 17] winning hurdler: useful handicap chaser: won at Haydock by 12 lengths from Courtown Oscar) in November: third in Peter Marsh Chase there (13¾ lengths behind The Dutchman) next time: stays 3½m: acts on heavy going: front runner/races prominently: signs of temperament. *Sue Smith*   c138
h–

HALCYON DAYS 9 b.g. Generous (IRE) – Indian Empress (Emperor Jones (USA)) [2017/18 c113, h–: c16.5s[2] c15.7d[4] c16.3v[pu] c17.1v[pu] c17.1v[2] Apr 16] maiden hurdler: fair handicap chaser: stays 19f: acts on heavy going: wears headgear: usually races close up. *Rebecca Menzies*   c110
h–

HALDON HILL (IRE) 5 b.g. Mahler – Qui Plus Est (FR) (Dark Moondancer) [2017/18 b16v[4] Apr 14] fourth foal: half-brother to a winning pointer by Acambaro: dam unraced half-sister to fairly useful hurdler/useful chaser (stayed 2¾m) Requin: 7/1, fourth in bumper at Chepstow (15¾ lengths behind Garrettstown). *Victor Dartnall*   b84

HALLINGHAM 8 b.g. Halling (USA) – In Luck (In The Wings) [2017/18 h87: h16g[2] h15.7d[6] Nov 21] stocky, compact gelding: modest on Flat, stays 1½m: modest handicap hurdler: stays 19f: acts on good to firm going: wore headgear in 2016/17: usually races prominently. *Ken Cunningham-Brown*   h81

HALLINGS COMET 9 ch.g. Halling (USA) – Landinium (ITY) (Lando (GER)) [2017/18 c–, h–: h16g* h16g[2] h16g* h16g* h20d* h21.1g[4] h19.5d[2] Nov 14] sturdy gelding: fairly useful handicap hurdler: won at Worcester in June, July and September (twice): winning chaser: stays 2½m: acts on good to firm and good to soft going: front runner. *Shaun Lycett*   c–
h120

HALLING'S WISH 8 br.g. Halling (USA) – Fair View (GER) (Dashing Blade) [2017/18 c–, c17.4g[4] c21.1m[5] h18.7g[4] Sep 9] fair hurdler/maiden chaser at best, well held in 2017/18: stays 2¾m: acts on good to firm and good to soft going: wears blinkers: has worn tongue tie. *Gary Moore*   c–
h–

HALLY'S KITCHEN 6 b.m. Getaway (GER) – Crystal Ballerina (IRE) (Sadler's Wells (USA)) [2017/18 b–: b17.7d b16.3s h18.5v[6] h18.5s[6] h19.2s[5] h23.1d Apr 24] little show in bumpers/over hurdles: tried in tongue tie. *Fiona Shaw*   h75
b–

HALO MOON 10 br.g. Kayf Tara – Fragrant Rose (Alflora (IRE)) [2017/18 c20.3s c24.2v[3] c24s[2] c22.4s[3] Mar 23] well-made gelding: maiden hurdler: fairly useful handicap chaser: second in veterans event at Doncaster in February and third at Newbury in March: stays 3m: acts on heavy going: wears cheekpieces. *Neil Mulholland*   c122
h–

HAMELIN POOL 4 b.g. High Chaparral (IRE) – Presbyterian Nun (IRE) (Daylami (IRE)) [2017/18 h16.7s ab16g⁴ Mar 2] has had breathing operation: no form, including on Flat. *Michael Chapman*   **h–**

HAMMERSLY LAKE (FR) 10 b.g. Kapgarde (FR) – Loin de Moi (FR) (Loup Solitaire (USA)) [2017/18 c140, h139: c21.3m* c16m² c20.3g² c20.1d* h21g⁵ c25spu Apr 14] good-topped gelding: useful hurdler at best: smart handicap chaser: won at Haydock (by 2½ lengths from Kilcrea Vale) in May and Perth (by 4 lengths from Guitar Pete) in September: left Nicky Henderson after first start: stays 21f: acts on good to firm and heavy going: usually races towards rear. *Charlie Longsdon*   **c154** **h–**

HANDS OF STONE (IRE) 6 b.g. Shantou (USA) – Hayabusa (Sir Harry Lewis (USA)) [2017/18 b89: h19.9dF h21.2m⁵ h16.8s h16s h20v⁶ h17.7v h20v⁶ h21.9v⁴ Apr 1] lengthy, rather unfurnished gelding: poor maiden hurdler: tried in cheekpieces: usually in tongue tie. *Evan Williams*   **h85**

HANDSOME DAN (IRE) 12 b.g. Busy Flight – Beautiful City (IRE) (Jurado (USA)) [2017/18 c–, h115: h18.6g² h21.2g⁶ Nov 6] fairly useful handicap hurdler, winning chaser: stays 3m, effective at much shorter: acts on good to firm and good to soft going: tried in blinkers/tongue tie: races well off pace. *Sarah Hollinshead*   **c–** **h118**

HANDSOME SAM 7 ch.g. Black Sam Bellamy (IRE) – Rose Marine (Handsome Sailor) [2017/18 c106, h108: c19.4vpu c20g⁵ c25.2s³ c25.2spu h15.5v Jan 31] lengthy gelding: winning hurdler: maiden chaser, below best in 2017/18: stays 3m: acts on heavy going: has worn headgear, including in 2017/18: in tongue tie last 5 starts: temperamental. *Matt Sheppard*   **c93 §** **h– §**

HANDY HOLLOW (IRE) 5 ch.g. Beat Hollow – Hesperia (Slip Anchor) [2017/18 b16.2d² h16.2d² h16.2s³ h16.2s³ h16.8s h15.8s⁶ h16.8vpu Mar 13] smallish, angular gelding: brother to useful hurdler Hollow Tree (2m/17f winner), stays 3m, and half-brother to several winners, including fair hurdler Western Point (2m winner, by Pivotal): dam useful French 11f/1½m winner: fair form in bumpers: better effort when second in conditionals/amateur event at Stratford: modest form over hurdles: will be suited by further than 2m: usually wears hood. *Donald McCain*   **h91** **b88**

HANGARD 6 b.g. Black Sam Bellamy (IRE) – Empress of Light (Emperor Jones (USA)) [2017/18 b16s* b16v⁴ h21.4vpu ab16g³ h20.1v³ h19.9v h16.2d⁴ Apr 23] £13,000 3-y-o: brother to fair 21f hurdle winner/winning pointer Belle Empress, closely related to 2 winners, including useful hurdler/chaser Rons Dream (2m-25f winner, by Kayf Tara), and half-brother to 2 winners by Definite Article, including bumper winner/useful chaser Fistral Beach (2½m/21f winner, stayed 3m): dam, lightly raced on Flat, half-sister to high-class hurdler/very smart chaser (winner up to 2½m) Wahiba Sands: modest form in bumpers: won maiden at Ayr in October: fair form over hurdles: front runner/races prominently. *Philip Kirby*   **h109** **b75**

HANSUPFORDETROIT (IRE) 13 b.g. Zagreb (USA) – Golden Needle (IRE) (Prince of Birds (USA)) [2017/18 c105, h74: c22.5d² c26.1d c26.1v⁵ c24v⁷ c24.2v⁴ h20.5v² c23.6v⁴ c25.1s⁴ c25.7vpu c23.8v⁴ c26.2s³ Apr 27] strong gelding: fairly useful hurdler at one time: fair handicap chaser nowadays: won at Uttoxeter in December: stays 3¼m: acts on heavy going: often wears cheekpieces: wears tongue tie: often races towards rear. *Bernard Llewellyn*   **c100** **h90**

HAPPY DIVA (IRE) 7 b.m. King's Theatre (IRE) – Megans Joy (IRE) (Supreme Leader) [2017/18 h131: c15.9v³ c24d² c23.4s² c20s⁴ c20.3v* c19.9s² c21s⁴ Mar 25] good-bodied mare: useful hurdler: useful chaser: won small-field novices at Ludlow in January, Bangor (mares) in February and Ascot in March: has won over 3m, but at least as effective at shorter: acts on heavy going: wears tongue tie: strong traveller. *Kerry Lee*   **c140** **h–**

HAPPY RING HOUSE (IRE) 9 b.g. Muhtathir – Pink Topaz (USA) (Tiznow (USA)) [2017/18 c–: h19.6spu h23.1vF Jan 4] winning pointer: failed to complete all 3 starts under Rules: tried in cheekpieces: in tongue tie last 2 starts. *Mike Hammond*   **c–** **h–**

HARAMBE 5 b.g. Malinas (GER) – Crystal Princess (IRE) (Definite Article) [2017/18 b14d* b16.7v² b17s³ Apr 13] £18,000 3-y-o: rather unfurnished gelding: third foal: half-brother to fair hurdler/chaser Diamond Rock (17f-19f winner, by Kayf Tara) and modest hurdler Reivers Lodge (23f winner, by Black Sam Bellamy): dam unraced half-sister to useful hurdler (19f winner) Bags Groove: useful form in bumpers: won at Ludlow (by neck from Flash The Steel) in December: best effort when third in Grade 2 at Aintree (3¼ lengths behind Portrush Ted) in April. *Alan King*   **b108**

HAR

HARANGUE (IRE) 10 br.g. Street Cry (IRE) – Splendeur (FR) (Desert King (IRE)) [2017/18 c–, h–: h21.6m* Jun 15] fair handicap hurdler: landed gamble at Fontwell in June after 11-month absence/leaving Paul John Gilligan, finishing lame: winning chaser: stays 3¼m, effective at shorter: acts on good to firm and heavy going: usually wears headgear/tongue tie. *Peter Fahey, Ireland*   c– h110

HARBOUR FORCE (FR) 4 b.g. Harbour Watch (IRE) – Dam Beautiful (Sleeping Indian) [2017/18 h15.8m^{ro} h16d^4 h15.8s^3 h16d^{pu} h16.8v^{pu} Nov 26] maiden on Flat: modest form over hurdles: tried in headgear: usually races towards rear. *Neil Mulholland*   h93

HARDBACK (IRE) 7 b.g. Morozov (USA) – Alphablend (IRE) (Alphabatim (USA)) [2017/18 h16.3g* h19.8g^F h16.6v^3 h20.4s^4 h20s h16s* h16s Mar 9] €24,000 3-y-o: seventh foal: half-brother to fairly useful 2m hurdle winner/winning pointer Laser Hawk and another winning pointer (both by Rashar): dam unraced: unseated on sole point start: useful hurdler: won maiden at Sligo in August and novice handicap at Leopardstown (by head from Low Sun) in December: stays 2½m: acts on heavy going: in tongue tie last 2 starts: often races prominently. *Joseph Patrick O'Brien, Ireland*   h131

HARDLINE (IRE) 6 b.g. Arcadio (GER) – Hidden Reserve (IRE) (Heron Island (IRE)) [2017/18 h118p, b105: h18.8v^2 h16s* h16.5v* h16s^3 h16s^3 h16v* h16s* h16v^3 h16.5d Apr 24] won maiden point on debut: useful bumper performer: useful hurdler: won maiden at Wexford in October, minor event at Clonmel in November, listed event at Punchestown (by 2¼ lengths from Riders Onthe Storm) in February and Grade 2 novice at Naas (by ½ length from Impact Factor) in February: unproven beyond 2m: acts on heavy going: wears hood. *Gordon Elliott, Ireland*   h139

HARDNESS (IRE) 5 b.g. Makfi – Hideaway (FR) (Cape Cross (IRE)) [2017/18 h16v h15.3v h16.3v h15.3v h16.5m Apr 25] fair maiden on Flat in France, stays 11.5f: poor form over hurdles. *Philip Hobbs*   h75

HARDROCK DAVIS (FR) 7 b.g. Saint des Saints (FR) – Trumpet Davis (FR) (Rose Laurel) [2017/18 h66, b71: h21.4v^5 h16.8v^F h16.8g Apr 23] modest form over hurdles, best effort on return: tried in hood. *Keith Dalgleish*   h85

HARD STATION (IRE) 9 b.g. Bandari (IRE) – Vinecroft (IRE) (Executive Perk) [2017/18 c26s^{pu} Feb 21] point winner: once-raced hurdler: fair form at best in chases, won both starts in hunters in early-2016/17 for J. P. O'Keeffe: folded tamely on belated return: stays 3m: in hood last 4 starts. *Richard J. Bandey*   c– h–

HARDTOROCK (IRE) 9 b.g. Mountain High (IRE) – Permissal (IRE) (Dr Massini (IRE)) [2017/18 c–, h64: c23g^{ur} c24g^6 c21.6g* c23g c21.6g^3 c19.7d^{pu} c21.6d^{pu} Nov 19] sturdy gelding: maiden hurdler: poor handicap chaser: won novice event at Fontwell in August: stays 2¾m: best form on good going: has worn cheekpieces, including in 2017/18: often wears tongue tie: unreliable. *Seamus Mullins*   c72 § h–

HAREFIELD (IRE) 5 b.g. Doyen (IRE) – Bobbi's Venture (IRE) (Bob Back (USA)) [2017/18 b95: h16.8s^4 h16s* h20.5v^2 h15.7v^2 h16v^F Mar 28] rangy, rather unfurnished gelding: fairly useful form over hurdles: won novice at Warwick in November: should stay 2½m+: acts on heavy going. *Alan King*   h122

HARGAM (FR) 7 gr.g. Sinndar (IRE) – Horasana (FR) (Galileo (IRE)) [2017/18 h139: c16d^2 c17.4s^2 c20d c19.9v^{pu} c20v^{pu} Jan 27] rather leggy gelding: smart hurdler at one time: fairly useful form when second in maiden at Uttoxeter on chasing debut: went wrong way after: left Nicky Henderson after second start: unproven beyond 17f: acts on soft and good to firm going: tried in cheekpieces: races towards rear, often lazily. *John Quinn*   c119 h–

HARLEY REBEL 6 br.g. Cockney Rebel (IRE) – Al Kahina (Mark of Esteem (IRE)) [2017/18 h20m Jul 5] leggy gelding: fairly useful hurdler in 2015/16, no show only start since: stays 19f: best form on soft/heavy going: tried in cheekpieces. *Neil Mulholland*   h–

HARLEYS MAX 9 b.g. Winged Love (IRE) – Researcher (Cosmonaut) [2017/18 c96, h–: c17.1v^F Apr 16] maiden hurdler: modest handicap chaser: let down by jumping only start in 2017/18: stays 2¾m: acts on soft and good to firm going. *Susan Corbett*   c– h–

HARMONIC LADY 8 ch.m. Trade Fair – First Harmony (First Trump) [2017/18 h15.8v^{pu} h15.7s^{pu} Jan 1] 1¼m winner on Flat: failed to complete all 3 starts in points: lightly raced over hurdles, modest form at best: tried in tongue tie. *Mike Sowersby*   h–

HARMONISE 4 b.f. Sakhee's Secret – Composing (IRE) (Noverre (USA)) [2017/18 h15.7v^{bd} h15.9v* h16g^5 h17.7v^5 h16.8g^{ur} Apr 19] smallish, angular filly: closely related to fair maiden Abundantly (17f/2¼m winner, by Sakhee): fairly useful on Flat, stays 1¼m: fair form over hurdles: won mares novice at Plumpton in February: unproven beyond 2m: best form on heavy going: usually in hood: tried in tongue tie: usually leads. *Sheena West*   h108

HAT

HAROON (IRE) 4 ch.g. Lope de Vega (IRE) – Hazarista (IRE) (Barathea (IRE)) [2017/18 h16d[6] h16.8g[pu] Oct 25] fair maiden on Flat, stays 9f: poor form on first of 2 starts over hurdles: wears tongue tie. *Tony Coyle* — h69

HARRISONS PROMISE 6 b.m. Westerner – Hello My Lovely (Presenting) [2017/18 b86: b16.2g[3] b16s* b16.7v[5] Jan 17] close-coupled mare: fair form in bumpers: won mares event at Wetherby in November: will stay further than 2m: in tongue tie last 3 starts. *Susan Corbett* — b94

HARRY HUNT 11 b.g. Bertolini (USA) – Qasirah (IRE) (Machiavellian (USA)) [2017/18 c109§, h109§: c21.1g[2] c21.5v* c26.3s[4] c21.4v[6] Jan 17] lengthy gelding: fair hurdler: fair handicap chaser: won at Ayr in November: stays 3m: acts on heavy going: has worn headgear: unreliable. *Graeme McPherson* — c110 § / h– §

HARRY THE VIKING 13 ch.g. Sir Harry Lewis (USA) – Viking Flame (Viking (USA)) [2017/18 c124§, h–: c26.2d* c27.3v[3] c26.2v[pu] c30.6s Apr 27] useful-looking gelding: winning hurdler: fairly useful handicap chaser: won at Carlisle in November: stays 33f: acts on heavy going: wears headgear: front runner/races prominently: temperamental. *Sandy Thomson* — c122 § / h–

HARRY TOPPER 11 b.g. Sir Harry Lewis (USA) – Indeed To Goodness (IRE) (Welsh Term) [2017/18 c141x, h–: c24.2v[2] c24.1v[pu] c27.9v[pu] Apr 1] useful-looking gelding: winning hurdler: top-class chaser at best: won Charlie Hall Chase at Wetherby and Denman Chase at Newbury in 2013/14, lightly raced and not same force after: stayed 25f: acted on heavy going: wore cheekpieces: usually raced prominently: often let down by jumping: has been retired. *Kim Bailey* — c130 x / h–

HARTFORTH 10 ch.g. Haafhd – St Edith (IRE) (Desert King (IRE)) [2017/18 h115§: h24.6s h24.3v Jan 2] smallish gelding: fairly useful hurdler at best, no form in 2017/18: stays 27f: acts on heavy going: tried in cheekpieces: often races prominently: unreliable. *Donald Whillans* — h– §

HARTSHORNE ABBIE (IRE) 5 ch.m. Getaway (GER) – Lala Nova (IRE) (Zaffaran (USA)) [2017/18 b13.7s Jan 26] sixth foal: half-sister to winning pointers by Oscar and Robin des Champs: dam (c106/h93), 2m/17f hurdle/chase winner, half-sister to useful hurdler/chaser (stays 3m) Wadswick Court: well beaten in bumpers. *Martin Keighley* — b–

HARTSIDE (GER) 9 b.g. Montjeu (IRE) – Helvellyn (USA) (Gone West (USA)) [2017/18 h113: h16.8g h17s h16d h16.8s[6] h15.7d[F] h15.7s[3] h15.7s[4] h15.7v[4] h16.6d[4] h16v[5] h17d[3] h15.8v[5] Apr 7] sturdy gelding: modest handicap hurdler: won at Doncaster (conditional) in February: unproven beyond 17f: acts on heavy going: usually wears headgear: also wears tongue tie nowadays. *Peter Winks* — h90

HARVEY (IRE) 7 br.m. Presenting – One Swoop (IRE) (Be My Native (USA)) [2017/18 h74, b–: h18.7g h21.6d[5] Jun 6] sturdy mare: little form: dead. *Laura Mongan* — h–

HATCHER (IRE) 5 b.g. Doyen (IRE) – African Keys (IRE) (Quws) [2017/18 b99: b16g* h15.8g[2] h15.8g[5] h15.7g[5] h15.8g[2] Apr 24] lengthy gelding: fairly useful form in bumpers: won (for second time) at Worcester in September: fair form over hurdles: bred to stay further than 2m: wears hood: usually races towards rear, often freely: not straightforward. *Dan Skelton* — h114 / b97

HATCHET JACK (IRE) 6 b.g. Black Sam Bellamy (IRE) – Identity Parade (IRE) (Witness Box (USA)) [2017/18 h16.8s h26d[3] h20.5d[4] h23.5d[5] h21.4v[2] h23.5s[3] h22.8v[3] Mar 31] €9,000 3-y-o: workmanlike gelding: first foal: dam (c104/h104) 2½m-3m hurdle/chase winner, maiden pointer: fairly useful maiden hurdler: stays 3¼m: acts on heavy going: waited with. *Paul Henderson* — h118

HATEM (FR) 5 gr.g. Kendargent (FR) – Escolhida (IRE) (Montjeu (IRE)) [2017/18 h101: h15.8m[5] h16d[4] h18.6g[6] ab16d Mar 5] 1m winner on Flat in France: maiden hurdler, fair form at best: left Caroline Bailey after first start: tried in blinkers/tongue tie: often races towards rear. *Nick Littmoden* — h–

HATTAAB 5 b.g. Intikhab (USA) – Sundus (USA) (Sadler's Wells (USA)) [2017/18 b83: b16f[2] b16.5g[5] h15.8d[6] h15.8s h15.8s Jan 26] maiden in bumpers: fair form over hurdles: best effort when sixth in novice at Ludlow in December. *Tom George* — h101 / b89

HATTONS HILL (IRE) 9 b.g. Pierre – Cluain Chaoin (IRE) (Phardante (FR)) [2017/18 c85, h–: c24.2g* c24.2g* c24.2g* c31.9v[pu] c25.2d[pu] c24v[pu] Feb 10] maiden hurdler: fair handicap chaser: completed 5-timer at Hexham in spring 2017: disappointing after a break last 3 starts: stays 3m: acts on heavy going: wears cheekpieces nowadays. *Henry Hogarth* — c106 / h–

375

HAU

HAULANI (USA) 4 ch.g. Algorithms (USA) – License To Speed (USA) (Thunder Gulch (USA)) [2017/18 h15.7d³ h16v² c24.2s⁶ h24.1s⁶ ab16g³ h18.8s^pu h16.4v⁵ Apr 15] neat gelding: fairly useful on Flat, stays 1¼m: fair form over hurdles: best effort at 2m: acts on heavy going: tried in blinkers: in tongue tie last 2 starts. *Brian Ellison* — **h108**

HAUL AWAY (IRE) 5 b.g. Stowaway – Lisacul Queen (IRE) (Old Vic) [2017/18 b16.7g⁴ h21.2g² Nov 16] €40,000 3-y-o: second foal: dam unraced sister to fairly useful hurdler (2½m winner) Talbot Road: fourth in bumper at Bangor (4 lengths behind One For Rosie): 11/2, fairly useful form when second in introductory event at Ludlow (3¼ lengths behind Cresswell Legend) on hurdling debut: wears hood. *Nicky Henderson* — **h116 b95**

HAUL US IN (IRE) 6 br.m. Kalanisi (IRE) – Shuilan (IRE) (Good Thyne (USA)) [2017/18 h95, b59: c20.1v² c24.2s⁶ h24.1s⁶ h20.5v² h25v² h21.4v* h20.9v* h24.3g Apr 20] fair handicap hurdler: completed hat-trick at Ayr (mares), Hexham and Kelso in March/April: modest form over fences: better effort when second in novice handicap at Hexham: stays 25f: best form on soft/heavy going: has worn headgear: front runner/races prominently: has looked hard ride. *Lucinda Russell* — **c85 h110**

HAVANA BEAT (IRE) 8 b.g. Teofilo (IRE) – Sweet Home Alabama (IRE) (Desert Prince (IRE)) [2017/18 h16.7d² h20g² h19.9m³ h15.8d* h16.5s* Apr 14] fairly useful on Flat, stays 2½m: useful form over hurdles: won maiden at Huntingdon in March and conditionals/amateur handicap at Aintree (by 10 lengths from Dear Sire) in April: stays 2½m: acts on soft going. *Tony Carroll* — **h130**

HAVANA JACK (IRE) 8 b.g. Westerner – Hackler Poitin (IRE) (Little Bighorn) [2017/18 c96: c21.6g⁴ c26.2g^pu c23.4g* c21.5v⁶ c23.8g² c23.8s^ur c24.1v^pu c21.5v⁵ c21.6v³ Apr 16] modest handicap chaser: won at Kelso in October: stays 3¼m: acts on good to firm and heavy going: has worn headgear. *Leonard Kerr* — **c91**

HAVE A GO HERO (IRE) 10 b.g. Flemensfirth (USA) – Blue Bank (IRE) (Burslem) [2017/18 c110: c23.9d⁴ Nov 23] fair handicap chaser: stays 25f: acts on good to soft going: in visor last 3 starts. *Dai Williams* — **c109**

HAVE YOU HAD YOURS (IRE) 12 br.g. Whitmore's Conn (USA) – Mandys Moynavely (IRE) (Semillon) [2017/18 c97, h–: c20.1g^ur c20.1g⁵ Jun 17] lightly-raced hurdler: fair chaser at best, retains little ability: tried in cheekpieces. *Jane Walton* — **c– h–**

HAVISHAM 6 b.g. Mount Nelson – Ile Deserte (Green Desert (USA)) [2017/18 h15.9d⁵ h15.9s⁶ h15.8d h16.8v^pu Apr 17] fairly useful on Flat, stays 17f: poor form over hurdles: tried in hood: in tongue tie last 3 starts. *Jamie Snowden* — **h76**

HAWKHURST (IRE) 8 b.g. Flemensfirth (USA) – Silaoce (FR) (Nikos) [2017/18 c112§, h120§: h23.3g² h20.1g³ h20.1g³ c23.8m^pu h19.9g⁶ Aug 31] multiple point winner: fair maiden hurdler/chaser: stays 3m: acts on heavy going: wears headgear: has worn tongue tie: often races in rear: temperamental. *Ben Haslam* — **c– § h102 §**

HAWTHORN COTTAGE (IRE) 5 b.m. Gold Well – Miss Kilkeel (IRE) (Religiously (USA)) [2017/18 b15.8s³ b17.7d² b16.8g* Apr 19] £20,000 4-y-o, resold £30,000 4-y-o: fifth foal: dam (h101) 2¼m hurdle winner: off mark in Irish points at fifth attempt: fairly useful form in bumpers: won mares event at Cheltenham (in cheekpieces, by ½ length from Definitelyanoscar)) in April. *Amy Murphy* — **b98**

HAY JAMES 7 gr.g. Proclamation (IRE) – Rose Bien (Bien Bien (USA)) [2017/18 b16.6d h23.4v^pu h15.7v^pu Feb 25] no form in bumper/over hurdles. *Shaun Harris* — **h– h–**

HAYLEY BELLE (IRE) 7 b.m. Flemensfirth (USA) – Tart of Tipp (IRE) (Saddlers' Hall (IRE)) [2017/18 h24s^pu Dec 17] €9,500 3-y-o, £48,000 5-y-o: fifth foal: sister to bumper winner/fair hurdler Josephine Marcus (2¼m winner) and a winning pointer, and half-sister to modest chaser Troubled (3m winner, by Vinnie Roe): dam unraced half-sister to Supreme Novices' Hurdle winner Destriero and to dam of Cheltenham Gold Cup winner Coneygree: off mark in Irish points at second attempt: jumped badly right when pulled up in mares novice on hurdling debut. *Mark Bradstock* — **h–**

HAZAMAR (IRE) 5 gr.g. Manduro (GER) – Hazarafa (IRE) (Daylami (IRE)) [2017/18 h108: h17.2d⁶ h16.8g⁶ c15.7g^F Aug 20] good-topped gelding: fair hurdler at best: likely to finish no better than fourth when fell heavily 3 out in novice won by Azzuri at Southwell on chasing debut: will prove best at 2m: acts on good to firm going: usually in cheekpieces: wears tongue tie. *Sophie Leech* — **c88 h90**

HAZARIBAN (IRE) 9 b.g. Kahyasi – Hazarista (IRE) (Barathea (IRE)) [2017/18 h19.5s^pu h20v⁶ h19d h20.5d^pu Dec 7] useful hurdler at one time, has deteriorated: stays 2¾m: acts on heavy going: tried in cheekpieces: wears tongue tie: usually races towards rear. *Seamus Fahey, Ireland* — **h102**

HEA

HAZEL HILL (IRE) 10 b.g. Milan – Resenting (IRE) (Presenting) [2017/18 c22.7v* c24.5v* Mar 15] second foal: half-brother to a winning pointer by Westerner: dam maiden pointer: prolific winning pointer: fairly useful form in chases: easily won hunters at Leicester in February and Towcester in March: open to improvement. *Philip Rowley* — c116 p

HAZY MANOR (IRE) 4 b.f. Tagula (IRE) – Hazarama (IRE) (Kahyasi) [2017/18 h16g⁴ h15.7d² h19.7v⁴ h20.2s Apr 25] sister to fair hurdler Jesmond Lodge (2m winner) and fairly useful hurdler Domino Dancer (2m/17f winner), and half-sister to fair hurdler Whats The Plot (2m winner, by Alfred Nobel): maiden on Flat: modest form over hurdles: should stay further than 2m: in hood last 3 starts. *Julia Brooke* — h98

HAZY TOM (IRE) 12 b.g. Heron Island (IRE) – The Wounded Cook (IRE) (Muroto) [2017/18 c108, h–: c21.1s⁵ c20v⁵ c21s⁶ Mar 25] tall, lengthy gelding: winning hurdler: useful chaser at best, no form under Rules in 2017/18 (won point in April): tried in headgear: in tongue tie last 2 starts. *Miss K. Phillips-Hill* — c– h–

HEAD HIGH (IRE) 5 gr.g. Mastercraftsman (IRE) – Elisium (Proclamation (IRE)) [2017/18 h107: h16.7s h16.7g h15.8m Oct 11] fair hurdle winner, well below best in 2017/18: will prove best at sharp 2m: acts on good to soft going: usually races towards rear. *Sarah Hollinshead* — h87

HEAD HUNTER (IRE) 5 b.g. Rip Van Winkle (IRE) – Superfonic (FR) (Zafonic (USA)) [2017/18 b85: b15.8d b17.7d Dec 4] fair form on debut in bumpers, well held both starts in 2017/18. *Michael Scudamore* — b–

HEAD LAD (FR) 5 b.g. Linda's Lad – Orabelle (FR) (Freedom Cry) [2017/18 h16s h16.3s h16s h16.7g Apr 22] useful-looking gelding: no form over hurdles. *Jonjo O'Neill* — h–

HEAD TO THE STARS 7 br.g. Kayf Tara – Sail By The Stars (Celtic Cone) [2017/18 h118: h20d⁶ h23.4s⁵ h21.4v* h20.5v² h23.1v² h22.8v² h24g^pu Apr 18] rangy gelding: useful handicap hurdler: won at Wincanton in January: second at Haydock (1¼ lengths behind Culture de Sivola) in March: stays 23f: acts on heavy going. *Henry Daly* — h132

HEAR NO EVIL (IRE) 6 b.g. Getaway (GER) – Listening (IRE) (King's Theatre (IRE)) [2017/18 b96: h20s* h22v³ h19.3s* Jan 11] placed in bumpers: fairly useful form over hurdles: won novices at Aintree in November and Catterick (tongue tied, by length from Sam's Gunner) in January: often travels strongly. *Dan Skelton* — h128

HEARTASIA (IRE) 5 b.m. Danehill Dancer (IRE) – Big Heart (Mr Greeley (USA)) [2017/18 b90: b16.2g* h15.6g³ h15.6s³ h16.4v² Jan 30] fairly useful form in bumpers: won (for second time) mares event at Kelso in May: fair form over hurdles: best effort when second in handicap at Newcastle in January: in hood last 5 starts: wears tongue tie: often races towards rear/travels strongly. *Susan Corbett* — h101 b102

HEAR THE CHIMES 9 b.g. Midnight Legend – Severn Air (Alderbrook) [2017/18 h106: h16.7g² h15.8g⁴ h16.8s³ h15.5v h15.8s⁵ h16.7s³ h15.7g⁶ Apr 20] sturdy gelding: modest handicap hurdler: unproven beyond 17f: acts on heavy going: often races in rear. *Shaun Harris* — h97

HEART O ANNANDALE (IRE) 11 b.g. Winged Love (IRE) – She's All Heart (Broken Hearted) [2017/18 c89x, h83: c26.2g* h23.3g⁶ c24.2g⁶ c25.5g⁶ h23.9d Aug 2] poor handicap hurdler: modest handicap chaser: won at Kelso in May: stays 27f: acts on soft going: wears headgear/tongue tie: often let down by jumping over fences. *Iain Jardine* — c85 x h–

HEART OF KERNOW (IRE) 6 b.g. Fruits of Love (USA) – Rathturtin Brief (IRE) (Saddlers' Hall (IRE)) [2017/18 h83: h20.1v* h23.3s* Oct 6] fair form over hurdles: won maiden at Hexham in September and novice there (fortunate) in October. *Nigel Hawke* — h104

HEATHER BURNING (IRE) 7 b.g. Mountain High (IRE) – Go To Blazes (IRE) (Aahsaylad) [2017/18 b78: h17s h16s h15.7d h15.6g⁶ Dec 18] showed a bit in bumper on debut: no form over hurdles. *Rose Dobbin* — h–

HEATH KING (IRE) 8 b.g. Fruits of Love (USA) – Shamaiyla (FR) (Sendawar (IRE)) [2017/18 h–: h15.8v Nov 12] behind on completed start in points: poor form in bumpers: well held over hurdles. *Miss Imogen Pickard* — h–

HEAVEN DREAM (FR) 6 b.g. Linda's Lad – Maia Eria (FR) (Volochine (IRE)) [2017/18 b15.8s⁵ h21.6v^pu h18.9s⁴ h19.4s⁴ Apr 18] good-bodied gelding: sixth foal: closely related to useful French hurdler Password (2¼m/19f winner, by Poliglote) and half-brother to useful French hurdler Wonder Charm (17f/2¼m winner, by Shamardal): dam smart French 2¼m-2½m hurdle winner: some encouragement in maiden bumper: fairly useful form over hurdles: left Venetia Williams, fourth in minor events at Fontainebleau and Auteuil. *Mlle A-S. Pacault, France* — h116 b77

HEA

HEAVENLY GAIT 6 b.m. Revoque (IRE) – Still Runs Deep (Karinga Bay) [2017/18 b–: h16.8g^{pu} h16.2g Jun 3] no form: tried in hood. *Jason Ward*   h–

HEAVENLY PROMISE (IRE) 7 ch.m. Presenting – Ambrosia's Promise (IRE) (Minster Son) [2017/18 c67, h78, b–: c24.1s^F h23.8d^5 c20g^{ur} c20.3v^3 c25.2s^4 c20.2v^5 c20.9s^2 c24.1d* Apr 21] maiden hurdler: poor handicap chaser: won novice event at Bangor in April: stays 3m: acts on heavy going: has worn hood: often races towards rear. *John Groucott*   c80 h–

HEAVEN SCENT 5 ch.m. Phoenix Reach (IRE) – Hel's Angel (IRE) (Pyrus (USA)) [2017/18 h101: h19.3m^3 h20.3d^6 h24.7g h20.2g h22.1s h19.9g^5 Oct 3] modest handicap hurdler: stays 2½m: acts on good to firm and heavy going: wore headgear in 2017/18: often let down by jumping. *Donald McCain*   h93 x

HECLA (IRE) 5 b.m. Beat Hollow – Clairefontaine (Alflora (IRE)) [2017/18 b17s^6 Oct 19] fourth foal: closely related to modest hurdler/chaser Normandy King (2½m winner, by King's Theatre): dam unraced half-sister to useful hurdlers/chasers Value At Risk (stays 2½m) and Battlecry (stayed 3½m): kicked before start when tailed off in mares bumper. *Stuart Crawford, Ireland*   b–

HECTON BAY (IRE) 7 b.g. Trans Island – Reserve The Right (IRE) (Double Eclipse (IRE)) [2017/18 h19.2d^{pu} Feb 25] pulled up in novice hurdle. *Linda Jewell*   h–

HEDGEINATOR (IRE) 8 ch.g. Beneficial – Annalecky (IRE) (Bob's Return (IRE)) [2017/18 c21d* c20g^4 c23.6d^5 c23.8v^5 c24.2d^2 c23.8v* c26.3s* Jan 12] €20,000 3-y-o: workmanlike gelding: fourth foal: half-brother to smart hurdler/very smart chaser Black Hercules (2m-3m winner, by Heron Island): dam unraced: point winner: lightly-raced hurdler: fair handicap chaser: won at Newton Abbot in August, and Ludlow (conditional/amateur) and Sedgefield in January: stays 3¼m: acts on heavy going: in cheekpieces last 4 starts: tried in tongue tie: front runner/races prominently. *Christian Williams*   c111 h–

HEDLEY LAMARR (IRE) 8 b.g. Gold Well – Donna's Tarquin (IRE) (Husyan (USA)) [2017/18 c121, h–: c23.8m^2 h23.1g Jun 2] winning hurdler: maiden chaser, fairly useful at best: stays 3m: acts on soft going: in headgear last 3 starts. *Jonjo O'Neill*   c110 h–

HE IS ROSY (IRE) 6 b.g. Helissio (FR) – Sister Rose (IRE) (Roselier (FR)) [2017/18 h20s^6 h15.8d^6 h19.9d h15.3v Apr 9] off mark in Irish maiden points at third attempt: little form over hurdles. *Susan Gardner*   h–

HEIST (IRE) 8 b.g. Galileo (IRE) – Matikanehanafubuki (IRE) (Caerleon (USA)) [2017/18 c127, h120: h23.9d* h23.9g^3 c24.2g* c23.8g^4 h20.2g h24.4g^3 c23.8m c25s c30s Apr 28] compact gelding: fairly useful handicap hurdler: won at Ffos Las in May: useful handicap chaser: won at Hexham (by 5 lengths from Presenting Junior) in June: stays 3¼m: acts on good to firm and good to soft going: wears headgear/tongue tie. *Patrick Griffin, Ireland*   c131 h118

HELAMIS 8 b.m. Shirocco (GER) – Alnoor (USA) (Danzig (USA)) [2017/18 h15.8s^5 h15.8v Apr 7] modest hurdler at best, no form in 2017/18 after long absence: stays 2½m: acts on heavy going: has worn headgear. *Barry Leavy*   h–

HELF (IRE) 4 b.g. Helmet (AUS) – Causeway Song (USA) (Giant's Causeway (USA)) [2017/18 h16.6s h15.8d^5 h19.6d Apr 21] fair maiden on Flat, stays 1½m: no form over hurdles: wears tongue tie. *Oliver Greenall*   h–

HELIOBLU BARELIERE (FR) 5 b.g. Heliostatic (IRE) – Lonia Blue (FR) (Anabaa Blue) [2017/18 b15.8d b13.7s^3 Apr 6] poor form in bumpers. *Ivan Furtado*   b70

HELIUM (FR) 13 b.g. Dream Well (FR) – Sure Harbour (SWI) (Surumu (GER)) [2017/18 c118, h102: c17d^2 c19.4g^5 c19.9g^{pu} c20.9s^{ur} c16.5g^3 c19.7s^6 c16.1s^6 c16.1v^5 Mar 12] strong gelding: fair hurdler: fairly useful handicap chaser: largely out of sorts in 2017/18: stays 2½m: acts on any going: tried in cheekpieces: has worn tongue tie: unreliable. *Alexandra Dunn*   c107 § h–

HELLO BERTIE 6 b.g. Kayf Tara – I'm Delilah (Overbury (IRE)) [2017/18 b97: b15.7g^3 h16.2v^2 h19.7d^5 h15.7d Nov 24] third in bumpers: modest form over hurdles: best effort when second in novice at Perth in September. *Malcolm Jefferson*   h92 b87

HELLO FELLAS (IRE) 6 b.g. Gold Well – Archdale Ambush (IRE) (Heron Island (IRE)) [2017/18 b96: h17s^5 h16.4g^5 h16.8s Dec 8] runner-up in bumper: modest form over hurdles: best effort when fifth in novice at Carlisle in October: tried in hood. *Nicky Richards*   h96

HELLO GEORGE (IRE) 9 b.g. Westerner – Top Ar Aghaidh (IRE) (Topanoora) [2017/18 h131: h24.3v^2 h24.2d^3 Dec 1] lengthy gelding: useful handicap hurdler, lightly raced nowadays: placed at Ayr in November and Newbury (4 lengths behind The Organist) in December: stays 3m: acts on good to firm and heavy going: wears cheekpieces. *Philip Hobbs*   h131

HER

HELLORBOSTON (IRE) 10 b.g. Court Cave (IRE) – Helorhiwater (IRE) (Aristocracy) [2017/18 h23.3g Jun 3] lengthy gelding: winning hurdler: maiden chaser: won twice in points in 2018: stays 27f: acts on heavy going: wears headgear. *Donald McCain*   c– h–

HELLO SWEETIE 9 b.m. Westerner – Knock Down (IRE) (Oscar (IRE)) [2017/18 c17m* c17m* c20m6 h16g5 h17.6d* h16.5g6 h16.2d4 h16.7g2 h16s5 h18.2s Nov 18] fairly useful handicap hurdler: won at Ballinrobe in July: second in listed event at Market Rasen in September: fairly useful handicap chaser: won at Ballinrobe (twice) in May: stays 2¼m: acts on good to firm and heavy going: has worn hood: wears tongue tie. *P. E. Collins, Ireland*   c121 h116

HELL'S KITCHEN 7 b.g. Robin des Champs (FR) – Mille Et Une (FR) (Trempolino (USA)) [2017/18 c132F, h–: c16d2 c16.4gur c20.5d* c21spu Feb 4] big, well-made gelding: winning hurdler: smart form over fences: won novice handicap at Kempton (by 1½ lengths from Mister Whitaker) in December: stays 21f: acts on heavy going: in hood last 4 starts: in tongue tie last 3. *Harry Fry*   c146 h–

HELMSLEY LAD 7 gr.g. Fair Mix (IRE) – Wuchowsen (IRE) (King's Ride) [2017/18 h113, h97: h19.9g5 h20.9g6 h16.6d Dec 16] tall gelding: bumper winner: fair maiden hurdler: front runner/races prominently: temperamental. *Malcolm Jefferson*   h96 §

HELPSTON 14 b.g. Sir Harry Lewis (USA) – Chichell's Hurst (Oats) [2017/18 c101, h–: c27.2spu May 18] big, rangy gelding: placed in points, including in 2018: winning hurdler: smart chaser at one time: stays 25f: acts on soft going: tried in cheekpieces: in tongue tie last 2 starts. *S. R. Andrews*   c– h–

HELUVAGOOD 6 b.g. Helissio (FR) – Cape Siren (Warning) [2017/18 h95: h19.5vpu h21.6v4 h20.5v4 h21.4s6 h19.5s* h19.5v2 Apr 14] lengthy gelding: fair handicap hurdler: won novice event at Chepstow in March: stays 19f: raced mainly on soft/heavy going: wears tongue tie. *Victor Dartnall*   h100

HENLLAN HARRI (IRE) 10 br.g. King's Theatre (IRE) – Told You So (IRE) (Glacial Storm (USA)) [2017/18 c127, h112: c26.1m4 h23g3 c25.1spu c26v6 Dec 30] lengthy gelding: fairly useful handicap hurdler/chaser: stays 29f: acts on good to firm and heavy going: usually wears headgear: has worn tongue tie, including final start: front runner/races prominently. *Peter Bowen*   c124 h124

HENPECKED 8 b.m. Footstepsinthesand – Poule de Luxe (IRE) (Cadeaux Genereux) [2017/18 h81: h16.2g3 h16.2g5 Jul 6] fairly useful on Flat, stays 13f: modest form over hurdles: raced around 2m: wears cheekpieces. *Alistair Whillans*   h88

HENRI PARRY MORGAN 10 b.g. Brian Boru – Queen of Thedaises (Over The River (FR)) [2017/18 c134x, h–: c19.9d2 c25.6vur c28.5v5 c24.2vpu c27.9v* c31.8gpu Apr 21] sturdy gelding: winning hurdler: useful handicap chaser: won at Ffos Las (by 4½ lengths from Jennys Surprise) in April: stays 3½m: acts on good to firm and heavy going: usually wears headgear: wears tongue tie: often let down by jumping. *Peter Bowen*   c137 x h–

HENRY'S JOY (IRE) 6 b.g. Craigsteel – Shocona (Oscar Schindler (IRE)) [2017/18 b17s2 h16.7s4 h19.9s2 h19.3v5 h19.9v* h20.2s Apr 26] £25,000 4-y-o: first foal: dam winning pointer: placed both starts in Irish points: second in bumper at Aintree: fair form over hurdles: won handicap at Sedgefield in March: bred to stay further than 2½m: raced only on soft/heavy going: front runner/races prominently. *Donald McCain*   h114 b87

HENRYVILLE 10 b.g. Generous (IRE) – Aquavita (Kalaglow) [2017/18 c147, h–: c21g* c20g3 c21.4g c20s5 c20.3gur h21.6g c25gpu Oct 28] sturdy gelding: winning hurdler: smart handicap chaser: won at Newton Abbot (by 5 lengths from Fox Appeal) in May: stays 25f: acts on soft and good to firm going: wears hood/tongue tie: races well off pace. *Harry Fry*   c147 h–

HEPBURN 5 b.m. Sixties Icon – Mighty Splash (Cape Cross (IRE)) [2017/18 c91, h97: h20.5v2 c21.3v3 c20.9s4 c21.1vur Apr 13] modest form over hurdles/fences: stays 21f: acts on heavy going: tried in cheekpieces: wears tongue tie: front runner/races prominently. *Ali Stronge*   c91 h97

HEPIJEU (FR) 7 b.g. Palace Episode (USA) – Helenjeu (Montjeu (IRE)) [2017/18 c106§, h–: c20.9d3 h19.9m* c22.6g2 c20g2 c23g5 c20.3g4 c21.4g2 c23.6g2 c20.3s2 c23.6s5 Jan 12] good-topped gelding: winning hurdler: fair handicap chaser: won at Huntingdon in May: left Charlie Longsdon after eighth start: barely stays 23f: acts on soft and good to firm going: wears headgear: usually wears tongue tie: often leads. *Geoffrey Deacon*   c104 h–

HERBERT PARK (IRE) 8 b.g. Shantou (USA) – Traluide (FR) (Tropular) [2017/18 c125, h130: c23.8m4 c24.2d* Apr 24] tall gelding: useful hurdler at one time: fair chaser nowadays: won novice hunter at Exeter in April: had also won point 2 months earlier: left David Pipe after first start: stays 3m: acts on heavy going: usually wears headgear: temperamental. *R. J. Alford*   c110 § h–

HER

HER DREAM (IRE) 6 b.m. Yeats (IRE) – High Benefit (IRE) (Beneficial) [2017/18 b–: b16v^{ur} h20.7d^{pu} h16s h21d Apr 26] rather unfurnished mare: no form in bumpers/over hurdles: in tongue tie last 4 starts. *Claire Dyson* **h– b–**

HERDSWICK HOLLOA (IRE) 7 ch.g. Marienbard (IRE) – Cash A Lawn (IRE) (Executive Perk) [2017/18 h79, b75: h25.8g^2 h25g h25d Mar 26] modest maiden hurdler: best effort at 3¼m: tried in tongue tie. *Neil King* **h95**

HERE COMES LOVE (IRE) 8 b.g. Winged Love (IRE) – Heres McGoogan (IRE) (Shaamit (IRE)) [2017/18 c74, h81: c16g^6 c15.6g^4 c23.8g^{pu} c21.2s c16d^4 c23.8v^4 c23.4d^4 c20.5s^5 c17.1g c24.2v^{pu} Nov 22] maiden hurdler: poor maiden chaser: left Patrick Griffin after third start: stays 2½m: acts on heavy going: has worn cheekpieces: has worn tongue tie, including last 3 starts. *William Young Jnr* **c81 h–**

HERE COMES MOLLY (IRE) 7 ch.m. Stowaway – Grange Melody (IRE) (Presenting) [2017/18 h72: h22.1g^5 h26.4s Oct 2] maiden hurdler/pointer: tried in hood: has worn tongue tie. *Tracey Barfoot-Saunt* **h–**

HERECOMESNELSON (IRE) 9 b.g. Morozov (USA) – Undesperado View (IRE) (Un Desperado (FR)) [2017/18 h16.8d h25.8s h19.7v^{pu} h20.2s Apr 27] maiden hurdler, no form in 2017/18: tried in hood. *Katie Scott* **h–**

HERECOMESTHEBOOM (IRE) 6 b.g. Darsi (FR) – Dympnajane (Dushyantor (USA)) [2017/18 b16.4g* b15.7d b15.8d^3 Mar 22] £21,000 5-y-o: lengthy gelding: first foal: dam unraced: runner-up in Irish point on debut: useful form when won at Cheltenham (by 1¼ lengths from Ainchea) in October, easily best effort in bumpers. *Fergal O'Brien* **b106**

HERE I AM (IRE) 11 b.g. Presenting – The Last Bank (IRE) (Phardante (FR)) [2017/18 c–, h–: c15.5d c16.4s^{pu} c17.8g^2 Apr 20] workmanlike gelding: maiden hurdler: fair handicap chaser: stays 2½m: acts on soft and good to firm going: tried in cheekpieces. *Diana Grissell* **c103 h–**

HERE'S BINGO 5 b.g. With The Flow (USA) – Winter Scene (IRE) (Oscar (IRE)) [2017/18 b16.8v^3 b16.8s Feb 23] second foal: half-brother to a winning pointer by Rainbow High: dam, winning pointer, closely related to fair hurdler/fairly useful chaser (stayed 2½m) The Entomologist: fair form in bumpers: better effort when third at Exeter in February. *Susan Gardner* **b85**

HERE'S HERBIE 10 b.g. Classic Cliche (IRE) – Tyre Hill Lilly (Jupiter Island) [2017/18 c–, h121: h19s^4 h18.5v^F h19s^3 h19.8v^4 h19v^2 Apr 12] workmanlike gelding: fairly useful handicap hurdler: fell both starts over fences: stays 21f: acts on heavy going: wears tongue tie. *Susan Gardner* **c– h117**

HERESMYNUMBER (IRE) 8 b.g. Kalanisi (IRE) – Broken Rein (IRE) (Orchestra) [2017/18 h95: h24s h20v^3 c20.2v^3 c21.2s* c21.2d^2 c26.3v* c26.2s^F Apr 27] sturdy gelding: modest maiden hurdler: fair form over fences: won handicaps at Fakenham (novice) in March and Sedgefield in April: stays 3¼m: acts on heavy going: wears cheekpieces/tongue tie: often races prominently. *Ali Stronge* **c99 h87**

HEREWEGO HEREWEGO (IRE) 7 b.g. Kalanisi (IRE) – Downtown Train (IRE) (Glacial Storm (USA)) [2017/18 h16g* h20.6s^2 h19.8v^2 Feb 16] rangy, useful-looking gelding: fairly useful form over hurdles: won novice at Warwick in October: second after in novice at Market Rasen and novice handicap at Sandown: stays 21f: acts on heavy going. *Alan King* **h126**

HERITAGE WAY 9 b.g. Tamayaz (CAN) – Morning Caller (IRE) (Zaffaran (USA)) [2017/18 c21.4s^{pu} c20.9s^F c24.2d Apr 23] bumper winner: no form over hurdles/fences. *Henry Hogarth* **c– h–**

HERMANUS (IRE) 6 ch.m. Golan (IRE) – Almost Trumps (Nearly A Hand) [2017/18 b93: h16v^5 h21.3s h19.7s^4 h19.4s^{ur} h20.6v^5 h15.7v^3 Mar 5] bumper winner: modest form over hurdles: stays 2½m: acts on heavy going: tried in cheekpieces. *James Ewart* **h93**

HERMINATOR (FR) 8 br.g. Night Tango (GER) – Roannaise (FR) (Octagonal (NZ)) [2017/18 h19d Apr 26] good-topped gelding: maiden hurdler, well held only start since leaving W. P. Mullins: winning chaser in France: stays 2¼m: acts on heavy going: in tongue tie last 2 starts. *Tom Lacey* **c– h–**

HERMOSA VAQUERA (IRE) 8 ch.m. High Chaparral (IRE) – Sundown (Polish Precedent (USA)) [2017/18 h97: h17.7m^2 Aug 17] fair on Flat, stays 1½m: modest handicap hurdler: stays 21f: acts on good to firm and good to soft going: wears cheekpieces: has worn tongue tie. *Gary Moore* **h98**

HERNANDES (FR) 4 gr.g. Clodovil (IRE) – Gontcharova (IRE) (Zafonic (USA)) [2017/18 h15.8g^4 h16d h15.8g^5 Nov 16] fair maiden on Flat: modest form over hurdles: best effort when fourth in juvenile at Huntingdon in October. *Ian Williams* **h96**

HID

HEROES OR GHOSTS (IRE) 9 br.g. Indian River (FR) – Awomansdream (IRE) (Beneficial) [2017/18 c106, h–: c23d* c23g c24.1g[6] c24g[4] c24g[2] c24d[pu] c21.7s[4] c25.5s Feb 23] rangy gelding: maiden hurdler: fair handicap chaser: won novice event at Worcester in May: stays 3m: acts on heavy going: tried in cheekpieces. *Jo Davis*   c109 h–

HERON HEIGHTS (IRE) 9 b.g. Heron Island (IRE) – Inter Alia (IRE) (Dr Massini (IRE)) [2017/18 c140, h–: h21g c22.5g[bd] c22.5g c21s c24.5s* Apr 28] tall, close-coupled gelding: maiden hurdler: useful handicap chaser: won at Punchestown (by 7 lengths from Rogue Angel) in April: stays 25f: acts on heavy going: in cheekpieces last 2 starts: wears tongue tie. *Henry de Bromhead, Ireland*   c141 h–

HERO'S CREEK (IRE) 5 br.g. Kalanisi (IRE) – Iktitafs Sister (IRE) (Val Royal (FR)) [2017/18 b15.7v[6] Feb 25] tailed off in bumper. *Ben Pauling*   b–

HE'S A GOER (IRE) 4 b.g. Yeats (IRE) – Tessas Girl (IRE) (Catcher In The Rye (IRE)) [2017/18 b14.6s[3] b16.2s b15.8v[4] Apr 15] modest form in bumpers. *Tom Lacey*   b79

HE'S A TOFF (IRE) 4 br.g. Dandy Man (IRE) – Prevarication (IRE) (In The Wings) [2017/18 h16.3s[pu] h16.3v[6] h16.5m Apr 25] close-coupled gelding: modest maiden on Flat, stays 1m: no form over hurdles. *Jo Davis*   h–

HES OUR ROBIN (IRE) 8 b.g. Robin des Pres (FR) – Poly Sandstorm (IRE) (Presenting) [2017/18 c109, h104: h16.7g h16.7s h15.7s h16.6s h15.8s[4] h16.7s[6] h16.8g[3] Apr 23] modest maiden hurdler nowadays: lightly-raced chaser: stays 21f: acts on good to firm and heavy going: wears hood: has worn tongue tie. *Michael Mullineaux*   c– h86

HESTINA (FR) 5 b.m. Soldier of Fortune (IRE) – Diagora (FR) (Highest Honor (FR)) [2017/18 h116p: h15.8m[2] h16.7g* h16.0s[2] Oct 3] fairly useful hurdler: won novice at Market Rasen in July: raced around 2m: acts on good to firm going: wears hood/tongue tie. *Dan Skelton*   h119

HEURTEVENT (FR) 9 b.g. Hold That Tiger (USA) – Sybilia (GER) (Spectrum (IRE)) [2017/18 c95, h–: c16.5g c16.5g[5] c20g[6] c24.5g c21.7g[4] c19.8s[ur] c20.2s c16.1v[2] c19.7v[4] c23.6d[5] Apr 24] angular gelding: winning hurdler: poor handicap chaser nowadays: unproven beyond 17f: acts on soft going: has worn headgear/tongue tie, including in 2017/18. *Tony Carroll*   c69 h–

HEY BILL (IRE) 8 b.g. Indian Danehill (IRE) – Grange More (IRE) (Ridgewood Ben) [2017/18 h112: h23.1g[pu] h23.6s c24d[4] c20s* c23s[bd] c19.0d[2] c23.8d* Apr 24] winning hurdler: fairly useful form over fences: won handicaps at Ludlow in January (novice) and April (awarded race): stays 3m: acts on soft going: usually races prominently. *Graeme McPherson*   c124 h–

HEY BOB (IRE) 6 br.g. Big Bad Bob (IRE) – Bounty Star (IRE) (Fasliyev (USA)) [2017/18 h79§: h16.8g[2] h16.8g[4] h17.2d[5] h16.2g[4] h15.8d[4] h16.8g[3] h15.8g h15.7d* h15.6s[3] Jan 3] close-coupled gelding: poor handicap hurdler: won at Southwell (conditional) in November: unproven beyond 17f: acts on soft going: wears tongue tie: often races freely: temperamental. *Chris Grant*   h75 §

HEY BUD 5 b.g. Fair Mix (IRE) – Azione (Exit To Nowhere (USA)) [2017/18 b16.5s[2] b15.8d[4] Mar 22] first foal: dam (h96), unreliable 2m/17f hurdle winner, half-sister to fairly useful hurdler (stays 21f) Brynmawr. fair form in bumpers: better effort when second at Taunton in January. *Jeremy Scott*   b85

HEYDOUR (IRE) 5 br.g. Presenting – Our Lucky Venture (IRE) (Golan (IRE)) [2017/18 b16.3d h20.6s Feb 6] first foal: dam unraced half-sister to smart hurdlers Movewiththetimes (15f-2¼m winner) and Venture Capital (stayed 2¾m) (both by Presenting): well beaten in bumper/novice hurdle. *Mick Channon*   h– b–

HEY LISTEN (IRE) 6 b.g. Kutub (IRE) – Crescendor (FR) (Lavirco (GER)) [2017/18 c–: h23.3g[pu] h16.2d[3] h23.9v[pu] h16.2g[6] c19.9g[pu] h15.6g h15.6d[4] h16.2s[2] Apr 26] point winner: modest maiden hurdler: little show in chases: unproven beyond 2m: acts on soft going: sometimes in cheekpieces: usually races towards rear. *Lucinda Russell*   c– h96

HIDDEN CARGO (IRE) 6 b.g. Stowaway – All Heart (Alhaarth (IRE)) [2017/18 h115, b88: h18.5d[pu] h19s[6] h24.4s Jan 25] useful-looking gelding: fair maiden hurdler: stays 19f: acts on good to soft going. *Alan King*   h102

HIDDEN CYCLONE (IRE) 13 b.g. Stowaway – Hurricane Debbie (IRE) (Shahanndeh) [2017/18 c–x, h150x: c21g[2] h22.8s c20v[2] h16s Oct 18] workmanlike gelding: smart hurdler/very smart chaser: below best in 2017/18: stays 23f: acts on heavy going: wears headgear: often let down by jumping. *John Joseph Hanlon, Ireland*   c130 x h138 x

HID

HIDDEN DILEMMA (IRE) 5 b.m. Winged Love (IRE) – Kiss Jolie (FR) (Cadoudal (FR)) [2017/18 h16v h16s h16.2s⁴ Apr 27] third foal: dam, pulled up only start over hurdles in France, out of half-sister to dam of Cheltenham Gold Cup winner Long Run: third on completed start in points: poor form over hurdles: best effort when fourth in mares novice at Perth. *Stuart Crawford, Ireland*   h84

HIDDEN GLEN (IRE) 5 ch.g. Stowaway – Gleanntan (IRE) (Lil's Boy (USA)) [2017/18 b15.7g⁴ b15.7d b16.6s Feb 21] €47,000 3-y-o: well-made gelding: second foal: half-brother to fair hurdler Undisputed (2¼m winner, by King's Theatre): dam (b90) placed all 3 starts in bumpers: fairly useful form in bumpers: won maiden at Southwell in October. *Ben Pauling*   b95

HIDDEN IMPACT (IRE) 7 br.g. Oscar (IRE) – Maiden Flight (IRE) (Jurado (USA)) [2017/18 b87: b16d h20s h23.9s^pu Dec 14] runner-up in Irish maiden point/on first of 2 starts in bumpers: limited impact in novice hurdles: usually in tongue tie. *Rebecca Curtis*   h– b–

HIDDEN OASIS (IRE) 7 b.g. Lawman (FR) – Spesialta (Indian Ridge) [2017/18 h16g³ h16g⁵ h15.8g⁵ h15.7d⁵ h16.5s Dec 14] dam half-sister to useful hurdler (2½m winner) Jalingo: fair on Flat nowadays, stays 1¼m, won at Saint Moritz for C. von der Recke in February: modest form over hurdles: raced only at 2m: tried in tongue tie. *Jonjo O'Neill*   h94

HIDDEN REBEL 6 b.m. Cockney Rebel (IRE) – Medicea Sidera (Medicean) [2017/18 h16.4g^R Nov 17] fairly useful on Flat, stays 1¼m: in hood, 12/1, behind until refused fourth in novice at Newcastle on hurdling debut: one to leave alone. *Alistair Whillans*   h– §

HIDEAWAY VIC (IRE) 5 b.g. Stowaway – Cailin Vic Mo Cri (IRE) (Old Vic) [2017/18 b15.3s² b17.7s* b15.3v² Feb 1] £24,000 3-y-o: third foal: brother to a winning pointer and half-brother to fairly useful hurdler Bryden Boy (19f-3m winner, by Craigsteel): dam (h113), bumper/2½m hurdle winner, half-sister to useful hurdler (stayed 2½m) Prince of Steal: fairly useful form in bumpers: won at Plumpton in December: in tongue tie last 2 starts. *Anthony Honeyball*   b99

HIER ENCORE (FR) 6 ch.g. Kentucky Dynamite (USA) – Hierarchie (FR) (Sillery (USA)) [2017/18 h15.9v h19.2v³ h16v⁶ h20.5v⁶ h21.7g⁴ Apr 20] modest maiden on Flat, stays 16.5f: poor form over hurdles: tried in hood. *Nigel Dunger*   h61

HIGGS (IRE) 5 b.g. Scorpion (IRE) – Captain Supreme (IRE) (Captain Rio) [2017/18 b15.8m⁴ b14d h16v² h16.8s* Apr 23] €18,000 3-y-o: first foal: dam unraced sister to useful hurdler (2½m winner) Allure of Illusion and half-sister to smart hurdler/chaser (stayed 21f) Blackstairmountain: modest form in bumpers: fair form over hurdles: won novice at Newton Abbot in April: bred to stay further than 2m. *Sarah-Jayne Davies*   h110 b79

HIGH ASPIRATIONS (IRE) 10 b.g. Dr Massini (IRE) – Divining (IRE) (Dowsing (USA)) [2017/18 c94, h–: c21.7m⁴ c20.9d⁴ c19.4g⁵ c25.8d^pu Aug 22] dipped-backed gelding: maiden hurdler: fair handicap chaser at one time, little form in 2017/18: stays 3¼m: acts on good to firm and heavy going: has worn headgear: often races prominently. *Michael Blake*   c75 h–

HIGH BRIDGE 7 b.g. Monsun (GER) – Ameerat (Mark of Esteem (IRE)) [2017/18 h140: h15.7g³ h16.3d* h16.3v Feb 10] workmanlike gelding: useful handicap hurdler: won listed event at Newbury (by 1¼ lengths from Charli Parcs) in December: raced around 2m: acts on good to soft going. *Ben Pauling*   h142

HIGHBURY HIGH (IRE) 11 gr.g. Salford Express (IRE) – Betseale (IRE) (Step Together (USA)) [2017/18 c109x, h96: c21.1d⁴ c19.2g⁶ c20.3g² c19.3g* c21.4g⁶ c22.4s^pu Mar 23] angular gelding: winning hurdler: fair handicap chaser: won at Sedgefield in August: stays 2¾m: acts on good to firm and heavy going: wears headgear/tongue tie: often races towards rear: often let down by jumping. *Neil Mulholland*   c112 x h–

HIGH COUNSEL (IRE) 9 br.g. Presenting – The Bench (IRE) (Leading Counsel (USA)) [2017/18 c90, h–: c24g⁴ c22.7m² c25.2g* Nov 29] point winner: winning hurdler: modest handicap chaser: won at Hereford in November: stays 25f: acts on good to firm and good to soft going: has worn headgear, including last 4 starts: often races towards rear: signs of temperament (has been reluctant at start). *Gary Hanmer*   c93 h–

HIGH EXPECTATIONS (FR) 7 b.g. High Rock (IRE) – Tashifiya (FR) (Sendawar (IRE)) [2017/18 h16.4g^ur h15.5d⁴ h16.5s^pu Apr 14] compact gelding: fairly useful handicap hurdler: won at Leicester in November: unproven beyond 2m: acts on soft going. *Gordon Elliott, Ireland*   h117

HIGH HATTON 9 b.g. Silver Patriarch (IRE) – Leroy's Sister (FR) (Phantom Breeze) [2017/18 c108: c25.3d c23.6s⁶ Apr 27] multiple point winner: maiden chaser, well held in hunters in 2017/18: stays 27f: acts on good to firm going: tried in hood/tongue tie. *J. W. Tudor*   c73

HIG

HIGHLAND CASTLE 10 b.g. Halling (USA) – Reciprocal (IRE) (Night Shift (USA)) [2017/18 h–: h22.1g Jun 30] smart at one time on Flat, stays 2m, no form in 2017: well held in novice/maiden hurdles: wears tongue tie. *Lucinda Egerton* — **h–**

HIGHLAND FLING (IRE) 6 br.g. Country Reel (USA) – High Fun (FR) (Kahyasi) [2017/18 h118: h21g^4 h20v* h16s h20v h16s c17.5s^F c20v^6 c20.1s^{pu} Apr 26] fairly useful handicap hurdler: won at Listowel in September: running to similar level when falling last in maiden at Fairyhouse on first of 3 starts over fences: stayed 21f: acted on heavy going: often tongue tied: dead. *Gavin Patrick Cromwell, Ireland* — **c125 h128**

HIGHLAND HUNTER (IRE) 5 gr.g. Subtle Power (IRE) – Loughine Sparkle (IRE) (Beneficial) [2017/18 b16.2v* b17s Apr 13] €12,500 3-y-o: sturdy gelding: second foal: half-brother to bumper winner/winning pointer Scully's Dream (by Taylor Stone): dam unraced: won Irish point on debut: fairly useful form in bumpers: won at Kelso in January. *Lucinda Russell* — **b99**

HIGHLAND LODGE (IRE) 12 b.g. Flemensfirth (USA) – Supreme Von Pres (IRE) (Presenting) [2017/18 c143§, h–: c25.9v^3 c25.6v^{pu} Jan 20] strong gelding: winning hurdler: useful handicap chaser: third in Becher Chase at Aintree (14 lengths behind Blaklion) in December (also won/second in race previous 2 years): stays 27f: acts on heavy going: wears headgear: temperamental. *James Moffatt* — **c134 § h–**

HIGHLAND PEAK 6 b.g. Distant Peak (IRE) – Flower Appeal (Diktat) [2017/18 h–, b68: h20.2g h20.2g^5 h23.9s h20.9d^6 h20.2s^6 Apr 27] poor form over hurdles: tried in tongue tie. *Jackie Stephen* — **h83**

HIGHLAND RIVER 12 b.g. Indian Creek – Bee One (IRE) (Catrail (USA)) [2017/18 h20g c20g^{pu} Jul 27] modest hurdler/chaser at best, no form in 2017/18: has worn headgear: tried in tongue tie: ungenuine. *Edward Bevan* — **c– § h– §**

HIGH NOON (IRE) 6 b.g. Westerner – Seymourswift (Seymour Hicks (FR)) [2017/18 b99: h19.5d^6 h20.5s^5 h22d^6 Apr 22] third in bumper: fair form over hurdles: best effort when sixth in maiden at Chepstow in October. *Emma Lavelle* — **h100**

HIGH RAIL 6 b.g. High Chaparral (IRE) – Cool Catena (One Cool Cat (USA)) [2017/18 b15.7d Nov 25] compact gelding: pulled up in bumper (hooded). *Tony Newcombe* — **b–**

HIGHSALVIA COSMOS 7 b.g. High Chaparral (IRE) – Salvia (Pivotal) [2017/18 h16.3g^5 Jun 10] workmanlike gelding: maiden hurdler, fair form at best: tried in blinkers: in tongue tie last 4 starts. *Mark Hoad* — **h84**

HIGH SCHOOL DAYS (USA) 5 ch.m. Elusive Quality (USA) – Baroness Richter (IRE) (Montjeu (IRE)) [2017/18 h17g^2 h16d^2 h16.5d^3 h16g^3 h16v* h16s* h16v* h16v^4 h16.8s^{pu} h20v h16.5d Apr 24] compact mare: fairly useful on Flat in France, stays 1¼m: fairly useful hurdler: won handicap at Gowran in September, novice at Wexford in October and handicap at Thurles in December: unproven beyond 17f: acts on heavy going: often races towards rear. *Henry de Bromhead, Ireland* — **h128**

HIGH SECRET (IRE) 7 b.g. High Chaparral (IRE) – Secret Question (USA) (Rahy (USA)) [2017/18 h130: h15.7m h15.8g^5 h19.4d^5 Dec 15] good-topped gelding: useful hurdler, well below best in 2017/18: unproven beyond 2m: best form on good going: tried in cheekpieces: often races prominently: has joined Dan Skelton. *Paul Nicholls* — **h111**

HIGHWAY GIRL 5 b.m. Kayf Tara – Whichway Girl (Jupiter Island) [2017/18 b15.8s^3 b16.6s^3 Jan 27] fifth foal: half-sister to 3 winners, including fairly useful hurdler Nightline (2½m winner), stays 3m, and fair 2m chase winner Nightfly (both by Midnight Legend): dam, winning pointer, half-sister to useful hurdler/smart chaser (stayed 3¼m) Alderburn: fair form when third in bumpers at Huntingdon and Doncaster (mares): likely to be suited by further than 2m. *Charlie Longsdon* — **b87**

HIGHWAY ONE O ONE (IRE) 6 br.g. Stowaway – High Accord (IRE) (Accordion) [2017/18 b16.8d* h15.9d* h17.7g^2 h16d^2 h17.7v* h16v h16s* h16s^2 Apr 28] €42,000 3-y-o: rather unfurnished gelding: third foal: half-brother to bumper winner Pearl Diamond (by Arcadio): dam, unraced, closely related to fair hurdler/fairly useful chaser (stayed 2½m) Avoca Promise: placed twice in Irish maiden points: won at Newton Abbot (by 15 lengths from Point of Principle) in September, only start in bumpers: useful hurdler: won maiden at Plumpton in October, and novices at Fontwell in December and Kempton (by 5 lengths from Equus Amadeus) in April: stays 2¼m: acts on heavy going: front runner/races prominently. *Chris Gordon* — **h137 b101**

HIGHWAY STAR (FR) 6 b.g. Vision d'Etat (FR) – Lyli Rose (FR) (Lyphard's Wish (FR)) [2017/18 b95: b17.7g ab16g^6 Feb 19] fair form in bumpers, best effort when third in 2016/17: should stay further than 2m. *Sarah Humphrey* — **b82**

HIG

HIGHWAY STORM (IRE) 8 b.g. Stowaway – Snow In Summer (IRE) (Glacial Storm (USA)) [2017/18 c117, h–: c25g c26.1d³ c24.2s^{pu} Nov 4] winning hurdler: fairly useful chaser: stays 3¼m: acts on heavy going: usually wears cheekpieces: front runner/races prominently. *Richard Hobson*   **c116 h–**

HIGH WELLS 4 b.g. High Chaparral (IRE) – Valencha (Domedriver (IRE)) [2017/18 h15.9m³ h15.8m³ h17.7s Apr 6] fair on Flat, stays 12.5f: modest form over hurdles: wears blinkers. *Seamus Durack*   **h87**

HIGH WHEELER (IRE) 7 b.g. Kalanisi (IRE) – Penny Farthing (Mind Games) [2017/18 h–, b88: h21v^{pu} Apr 27] no form over hurdles. *Caroline Fryer*   **h–**

HIJA 7 b.m. Avonbridge – Pantita (Polish Precedent (USA)) [2017/18 h80: h23s³ h21.6s^{ur} h21.6m⁵ h23m⁵ h23.9m Apr 25] poor handicap hurdler: stays 3m: acts on good to firm and good to soft going: wears cheekpieces. *Gail Haywood*   **h74**

HIJRAN (IRE) 5 ch.m. Mastercraftsman (IRE) – Sunny Slope (Mujtahid (USA)) [2017/18 h15.7s⁶ h15.8s⁶ h16v³ h15.7v² h16.7s* Mar 24] fair on Flat, stays 8.5f: fair form over hurdles: won handicap at Bangor in March: raced around 2m: raced only on soft/heavy going. *Henry Oliver*   **h107**

HILAND OSCAR (IRE) 9 b.g. Oscar (IRE) – Be My Treasure (IRE) (Be My Native (USA)) [2017/18 h20.5v^{pu} h21.7g^{pu} Apr 20] little impact in Irish points: no form over hurdles: tried in hood/tongue tie. *Paddy Butler*   **h–**

HILLARY VIEW (IRE) 6 b.g. Court Cave (IRE) – Tearaway Lady (IRE) (Tidaro (USA)) [2017/18 h19.5v h19.5v⁴ h23.6v⁶ h20v* h21v⁶ Mar 11] €11,000 3-y-o, £20,000 5-y-o: strong gelding: will make a chaser: half-brother to fair/temperamental chaser Wait No More (19f-3¼m winner, by Strategic Choice) and closely related/half-brother to 3 winning pointers: dam unraced half-sister to fairly useful cross-country chaser (3m winner) Tearaway King: winning pointer: modest form over hurdles: won handicap at Ffos Las in February: best effort at 2½m: acts on heavy going: tried in cheekpieces. *Peter Bowen*   **h98**

HILLCREST FIRE (IRE) 4 b.f. Fast Company (IRE) – Firecrest (IRE) (Darshaan) [2017/18 h15.5d* h17v³ h15.8s⁴ ab16d³ h16.8g³ Apr 19] half-sister to several winning jumpers, including useful hurdler All Set To Go (winner around 2m, by Verglas) and fairly useful hurdler/useful chaser Tocororo (2m-2¾m winner, by Teofilo): useful on Flat, stays 10.5f: fair form over hurdles: won fillies juvenile at Leicester in November: in hood last 2 starts: usually races prominently/freely. *Stuart Edmunds*   **h104**

HILL FORT 8 b.g. Pivotal – Cairns (UAE) (Cadeaux Genereux) [2017/18 h104: h16d² h16.7s³ h18.5d h16.5g h16.2s h20.5v³ h16s h25d⁵ h19.2v² h20.5v³ c20.9v³ Apr 10] modest handicap hurdler: 14/1, third in novice handicap at Hereford (6½ lengths behind One Style) on chasing debut: left Matt Sheppard after sixth start: stays 21f: acts on good to firm and heavy going: wears headgear/tongue tie. *Alexandra Dunn*   **c89 h96**

HILL OF GOLD (IRE) 10 ch.g. Beneficial – Cap The Waves (IRE) (Roselier (FR)) [2017/18 c100: c24.2m⁵ May 9] winning pointer/hunter chaser, well beaten only start under Rules in 2017/18: stays 3m: wears headgear. *David Kemp*   **c–**

HILLS OF CONNEMARA (IRE) 6 gr.m. Tikkanen (USA) – Desirable Rhythm (IRE) (Hernando (FR)) [2017/18 h16.2v³ ab16.3g⁵ h19.3v⁶ h24.1d² Mar 29] €2,500 4-y-o, £17,000 5-y-o: fourth foal: dam (b86) bumper winner: won Irish point on debut: poor form in bumpers: fair form over hurdles: better effort when second in novice at Wetherby (tongue tied). *Susan Corbett*   **h109 b72**

HILLS OF DUBAI (IRE) 9 ch.g. Dubai Destination (USA) – Mowazana (IRE) (Galileo (IRE)) [2017/18 h109: c20.5v* c20.5v* c20.6s² c23.4v³ Apr 7] maiden hurdler: fairly useful form over fences: won handicaps at Ayr in January, first one novice event: stays 2½m: acts on heavy going: usually leads. *Donald McCain*   **c117 h–**

HINDON ROAD (IRE) 11 b.g. Antonius Pius (USA) – Filoli Gardens (Sanglamore (USA)) [2017/18 c115§, h–: c20.3v^{pu} Feb 9] rather leggy gelding: maiden pointer: winning hurdler: fairly useful chaser at best, pulled up in hunter only start under Rules in 2017/18: stays 3m: acts on soft going: often wears cheekpieces: travels strongly, but often flatters to deceive. *Mrs C. Drury*   **c– § h–**

HINT OF GREY (IRE) 5 gr.m. Mastercraftsman (IRE) – Anamarka (Mark of Esteem (IRE)) [2017/18 h114: h16.2g* h15.8g² h15.7g⁴ h17v⁴ h16s⁵ Nov 14] fair hurdler: won novice at Hexham in May: raced around 2m: acts on soft going: has worn hood: has joined Gary Moore. *Don Cantillon*   **h108**

HINT OF MINT 9 b.g. Passing Glance – Juno Mint (Sula Bula) [2017/18 h135: h16g^{pu} Oct 22] sturdy gelding: useful hurdler: went wrong only start in 2017/18: stays 2½m: acts on good to firm and heavy going: tried in cheekpieces. *Harry Fry*   **h–**

HOL

HIS DREAM (IRE) 5 b.g. Yeats (IRE) – Rosa Muscosa (USA) (Dixie Union (USA)) [2017/18 b16m* h16.8v[6] h16.7s[5] h18.6v Jan 17] sturdy gelding: first foal: dam maiden on Flat (best at 7f): fairly useful form in bumpers: won at Down Royal in May, then left Ellmarie Holden: well held in novice hurdles. *Jonjo O'Neill*   h72 b104

HIT AND RUN (IRE) 6 b.g. Getaway (GER) – Arrive In Style (IRE) (King's Theatre (IRE)) [2017/18 h94, b76: h16.2g[3] h15.8d[6] h16.8s[2] h19.9s* h15.7s[3] h15.7s[2] h16.7s h17s[2] Apr 8] fair handicap hurdler: awarded race at Sedgefield in December: stays 2½m: acts on soft going: has worn headgear, including last 4 starts. *Donald McCain*   h106

HITCHHIKER (IRE) 7 b.g. Milan – No Easy Way (IRE) (Mandalus) [2017/18 h21.6v[pu] Nov 7] lengthy gelding: pulled up in novice hurdle. *Laura Young*   h–

HI THERE SILVER (IRE) 4 gr.g. Clodovil (IRE) – Elaborate (Sadler's Wells (USA)) [2017/18 h17.7d[pu] h15.9m[5] h17.7g h15.3g Oct 29] modest maiden on Flat, stays 1½m: no form over hurdles. *Michael Madgwick*   h–

HITHERJACQUES LADY (IRE) 6 br.m. Robin des Champs (FR) – Crackin' Liss (IRE) (Bob Back (USA)) [2017/18 h120, b–: h21.6d[3] h19.8s[3] h23.5v[pu] h19.9v[2] h24.3g Apr 20] sturdy mare: has had breathing operation: bumper winner: fairly useful handicap hurdler: second at Uttoxeter in March: stays 2¾m: acts on heavy going: front runner/races prominently. *Oliver Sherwood*   h125

HI TIDE (IRE) 14 br.g. Idris (IRE) – High Glider (High Top) [2017/18 c–, h77: h15.7g[5] h16d h15.7d[pu] Nov 6] sturdy gelding: poor hurdler nowadays: winning chaser: stays 2½m: tried in cheekpieces/tongue tie. *J. R. Jenkins*   c– h–

HITMAN FRED (IRE) 5 b.g. Getaway (GER) – Garravagh Lass (IRE) (Oscar (IRE)) [2017/18 b16.2v[2] h16.2v[5] Feb 15] €20,000 3-y-o, £90,000 4-y-o: first foal: dam, little impact in points, closely related to fairly useful hurdler/useful chaser (stays 25f) According To Trev and half-sister to useful hurdler (stays 3m) Skipthecuddles: won Irish point on debut: fairly useful form in bumpers: better effort when second at Kelso in January. *Rose Dobbin*   b99

HIT THE HEADLINES (IRE) 12 b.g. Flemensfirth (USA) – Heather Breeze (IRE) (Lord Americo) [2017/18 c75, h–: h19.5v[pu] Jan 30] tall gelding: winning hurdler: maiden chaser: stays 21f: acts on soft going: tried in cheekpieces: often in tongue tie nowadays: weak finisher. *Nigel Dunger*   c– h–

HIT THE HIGHWAY (IRE) 9 b.g. Pierre – Highway Belle (IRE) (Germany (USA)) [2017/18 c119, h–: c24g[4] h19s[ur] h21.6v h19.2v[5] h20.5v[pu] h21.7d h24.2s[3] h21.7s[2] Apr 6] useful-looking gelding: point winner: fairly useful handicap hurdler: maiden chaser: left Giles Smyly after fifth start: stays 3m: best form on soft/heavy going: tried in cheekpieces: has worn tongue tie, including in 2017/18: front runner/races prominently. *Chris Gordon*   c– h121

HOGAN'S HEIGHT (IRE) 7 b.g. Indian River (FR) – Electre du Berlais (FR) (Royal Charter (FR)) [2017/18 h106, b66: h21.6v[2] c20d c19.8g[2] c20d* c19.4s* c20.6s* c25s[6] Apr 13] sturdy gelding: fair form over hurdles: useful form over fences: won novices at Ludlow in December and Wetherby in January, and novice handicap at Haydock in March: may prove best at around 2½m: acts on heavy going: tried in hood: wears tongue tie: front runner/races prominently. *Jamie Snowden*   c138 h114

HOKE COLBURN (IRE) 6 b.g. Beneficial – Ravaleen (IRE) (Executive Perk) [2017/18 h106, b95: h18.5d[pu] h20.3d* h25s[6] h25d[pu] Apr 24] compact gelding: has had breathing operation: bumper winner: fair handicap hurdler: won at Southwell in November: should stay beyond 2½m: acts on soft going. *Harry Whittington*   h106

HOLBROOK PARK 8 b.g. Midnight Legend – Viciana (Sir Harry Lewis (USA)) [2017/18 h119: c24.2s* c23.4s[pu] c20.2v[pu] c23.6s[pu] c19.7v[2] c19.7d* c19.5s[4] c25.7s* Apr 15] fairly useful hurdler: fairly useful chaser: won maiden at Fakenham in November, novice at Plumpton in February and handicap at Plumpton again in April: stays 3¼m: acts on heavy going: tried in cheekpieces: has worn tongue tie, including often in 2017/18. *Neil King*   c127 h–

HOLDBACKTHERIVER (IRE) 6 b.g. Presenting – Fairy Lane (IRE) (Old Vic) [2017/18 b85: h15.8v[ur] h16v[3] h19s[5] h19.8v[2] h15.8v[5] h21.6v* Apr 8] good-topped gelding: fairly useful handicap hurdler: won novice event at Exeter in April: stays 2¾m: acts on heavy going: usually races close up. *Evan Williams*   h116

HOLDING PATTERN (IRE) 6 b.m. Teofilo (IRE) – Meon Mix (Kayf Tara) [2017/18 b16g* b16s[3] b16.4s[6] b16.3s Apr 25] good-topped mare: fourth foal: half-sister to 1m-1¼m winner Sublimation (by Manduro): dam lightly-raced maiden (should have stayed 1½m): fairly useful form in bumpers: won maiden at Thurles in October: wears hood/tongue tie. *Mrs J. Harrington, Ireland*   b97

HOL

HOLD ME TIGHT (IRE) 4 b.g. Zoffany (IRE) – All Embracing (IRE) (Night Shift (USA)) [2017/18 h17.7g⁶ h16.8v² h16.3v⁵ Dec 30] workmanlike gelding: modest maiden on Flat, stays 12.5f: modest form over hurdles: best effort when second in juvenile at Exeter in November: wears tongue tie. *Polly Gundry*   **h94**

HOLD THE BUCKS (USA) 12 b.g. Hold That Tiger (USA) – Buck's Lady (USA) (Alleged (USA)) [2017/18 h15.9vᵖᵘ Jan 7] fair hurdler at best: very lightly raced and no form since 2014/15, including over fences: unproven beyond 17f: acts on heavy going: has worn headgear. *Daniel Steele*   **c– h–**

HOLEINTHEWALL BAR (IRE) 10 b.g. Westerner – Cockpit Lady (IRE) (Commanche Run) [2017/18 c125, h115: c25.2g⁴ h20m c19.9s⁵ c16.3g⁶ c20.9sᵖᵘ c20.2s c17.5d⁶ Apr 24] fairly useful handicapper at best, well below that in 2017/18: left Gordon Elliott after third start: stays 21f: acts on good to firm and heavy going: usually wears headgear: tried in tongue tie. *Tracey Barfoot-Saunt*   **c99 h–**

HOLLIES PEARL 8 b.m. Black Sam Bellamy (IRE) – Posh Pearl (Rakaposhi King) [2017/18 h–: h23.9d³ May 27] fairly useful handicap hurdler: lame only start in 2017/18: stays 3m: acts on soft going: in headgear last 5 starts: also often in tongue tie. *Peter Bowen*   **h119**

HOLLOW CREST (IRE) 5 b.m. Beat Hollow – Johnston's Crest (IRE) (Be My Native (USA)) [2017/18 b17d b16v³ b16s⁴ Dec 29] closely related to 3 winners by King's Theatre, including bumper winner/fairly useful hurdler Little Hercules (2m winner, stayed 2¾m), and half-sister to winning pointers by Presenting and Moscow Society: dam (h88), maiden hurdler (stayed 3m), half-sister to fairly useful hurdler (stayed 3m) Arctic Court: modest form in bumpers: should be suited by further than 2m: wears hood. *James A. Nash, Ireland*   **b84**

HOLLOWGRAPHIC (IRE) 5 ch.g. Beat Hollow – Corskeagh Shadow (IRE) (Beneficial) [2017/18 b16v* Dec 10] €80,000 3-y-o: third foal: closely related to bumper winner/fairly useful hurdler Dawn Shadow (2m-2½m winner, by King's Theatre): dam (h89), bumper winner, sister to useful hurdler/fair chaser (stayed 2½m) Shadow Eile: smart form in bumpers: improved from debut when won maiden at Punchestown (by 13 lengths from Dunvegan) in December. *W. P. Mullins, Ireland*   **b115**

HOLLOW PARK (IRE) 6 b.m. Flemensfirth (USA) – Love And Beauty (IRE) (Presenting) [2017/18 h90, b–: h21.6g h19.6d⁴ h15.8s h23.6s⁵ h21g h23.3v³ h23.9m* Apr 25] runner-up in 8 runs in point: poor handicap hurdler: won mares event at Taunton in April: stays 3m: acts on good to firm going: in tongue tie last 2 starts: front runner/races prominently. *Katy Price*   **h77**

HOLLY BUSH HENRY (IRE) 7 b.g. Yeats (IRE) – Maslam (IRE) (Robellino (USA)) [2017/18 c133, h–: h15.7m h15.8m⁶ h16.8d⁶ h20.3g⁵ h23g* h25m* h23.9g⁶ h24.7s⁴ h23.4s* c24s⁴ c24.2v* c24.2s² c23.8s⁵ c25s⁶ Apr 14] lengthy gelding: useful handicap hurdler: won at Worcester and Plumpton in September, and Sandown (by neck from Connetable) in December: useful handicap chaser: won at Fakenham in January: second in Masters Handicap Chase at Sandown (¾ length behind Ballydine) in February: left Graeme McPherson after first start: stays 25f: acts on good to firm and heavy going: has worn headgear, including last 3 starts: has worn tongue tie: often travels strongly. *Phil Middleton*   **c131 h132**

HOLLY FLIGHT (FR) 6 b.m. Walk In The Park (IRE) – Lover Flight (FR) (Saint Cyrien (FR)) [2017/18 h16.5g⁴ h20.2g h20.3g Apr 19] third foal: half-sister to fairly useful French 15f hurdle winner Love Flight (by Irish Wells): dam, French 17f hurdle winner, out of half-sister to smart French hurdler/chaser (stayed 27f) Sunny Flight: fairly useful form over hurdles: fourth in mares handicap at Galway in August: left Alan Fleming after second start: stays 19f: acts on good to soft going: tried in hood: in tongue tie last 5 starts: often races towards rear. *Dan Skelton*   **h116**

HOLLYWOOD ALL STAR (IRE) 9 b.g. Kheleyf (USA) – Camassina (IRE) (Taufan (USA)) [2017/18 h96: h15.9s⁶ h15.5v h16s² h15.7vᵖᵘ h16v² Apr 14] compact gelding: modest handicap hurdler: stays 2½m: acts on heavy going: in tongue tie last 3 starts. *Graeme McPherson*   **h95**

HOLLYWOOD KEN (IRE) 5 b.g. Arcano (IRE) – Third Dimension (FR) (Suave Dancer (USA)) [2017/18 h100: h16gᵖᵘ h21.6d h19m h17.7s* h16s* Apr 27] workmanlike gelding: well held in point: fair handicap hurdler: won at Fontwell and Chepstow in April: left Richard Woollacott after third start: stays 2¼m: acts on soft going: has worn headgear: wears tongue tie. *Fiona Shaw*   **h114**

HOLLYWOOD ROAD (IRE) 5 b.g. Kodiac – Rinneen (IRE) (Bien Bien (USA)) [2017/18 h118: h15.7g⁵ Oct 11] fairly useful hurdler: well held only start in 2017/18: raced only at 2m: acts on good to firm going: sometimes in blinkers: has joined Gary Moore. *Don Cantillon*   **h–**

HON

HOLRYALE (IRE) 6 b.g. Trans Island – Lady Ramona (IRE) (Lord Americo) [2017/18 b15.8d* b16.7d² b18.5d² h16d² h15.8d⁴ Nov 25] €5,800 3-y-o: third foal: half-brother to a winning pointer by Arcadio: dam (c102) 19f chase winner (stayed 2¾m): in frame both starts in Irish maiden points: fair form in bumpers: won at Uttoxeter in May: fair form over hurdles: best effort when second in novice at Newton Abbot in September: tried in tongue tie: front runner/races prominently. *Dan Skelton* **h109 b90**

HOLY CROSS (IRE) 7 b.g. Yeats (IRE) – Bleu Ciel Et Blanc (FR) (Pistolet Bleu (IRE)) [2017/18 c–, h100: h23.3gᵖᵘ h20g h18.7gᵖᵘ Jul 23] maiden hurdler, no form in 2017/18: unseated only chase start: has worn headgear, including final start: wears tongue tie: often races towards rear. *Claire Dyson* **c– h–**

HOLY STREET (IRE) 6 b.g. Presenting – Vigna Maggio (FR) (Starborough) [2017/18 b64p: h15.8d h19.9d² h21.6d³ h23.3g⁵ Jul 19] modest form over hurdles: placed in points in 2018. *Alan King* **h91**

HOLY TIGER 7 b.g. Tiger Hill (IRE) – Divina Mia (Dowsing (USA)) [2017/18 b16vᵖᵘ Dec 31] pulled up in bumper. *Henry Tett* **b–**

HOMERS ODYSSEY 8 b.g. Overbury (IRE) – Aikaterine (Kris) [2017/18 h92, b83: h20.5d³ Oct 23] workmanlike gelding: modest maiden hurdler: below form only start in 2017/18: stays 25f: acts on soft going: often races prominently. *Chris Gordon* **h67**

HONEST INTENT 7 b.g. Fair Mix (IRE) – Just Jenny (IRE) (King's Ride) [2017/18 h100, b–: h18.6gᵖᵘ h21.2gᵖᵘ h23d² c24.2ᶠ Dec 26] modest maiden hurdler: in command when fell fatally 2 out in novice handicap at Wetherby on chasing debut: left Ronald Thompson after third start: stayed 3m: acted on soft going: tried in hood: usually raced close up/freely. *Mark Walford* **c103 h98**

HONEST VIC (IRE) 5 b.g. Kalanisi (IRE) – Miss Vic Lovin (IRE) (Old Vic) [2017/18 b79: b15.7g* h16g⁶ h16.3g* h15.8d⁵ h20.5g⁵ Apr 18] fair form in bumpers: won maiden at Towcester in May: fairly useful form over hurdles: won novice at Stratford in November: fifth in handicap at Cheltenham in April: stays 2½m: open to further improvement. *Henry Daly* **h122 p b90**

HONEYCHILE RYDER 7 ch.m. Black Sam Bellamy (IRE) – Dusky Dante (IRE) (Phardante (FR)) [2017/18 h61: h24.1s⁵ c21.3vᴿ h19.7v h24v³ Apr 14] poor maiden hurdler: no show on chasing debut: stays 3m: acts on heavy going: tried in hood: races towards rear. *Dianne Sayer* **c– h65**

HONEY P (IRE) 7 b.m. Winged Love (IRE) – Luck's A Lady (IRE) (Insan (USA)) [2017/18 b17.7g May 14] second foal: dam (h88), bumper winner/maiden hurdler (stayed 3m), half-sister to fair hurdler/useful French chaser (winner up to 21f) Fire Ball: tailed off in bumper. *Steve Woodman* **b–**

HONEY POUND (IRE) 10 b.g. Big Bad Bob (IRE) – Moon Review (USA) (Irish River (FR)) [2017/18 c–x, h114: h15.7g⁴ h16g⁵ h16.8dᵖᵘ Jul 31] workmanlike gelding: fair handicap hurdler, below form in 2017/18: lightly-raced chaser (sketchy jumper): stays 2¼m: acts on soft and good to firm going: wears hood: often races towards rear: temperamental. *Tim Vaughan* **c– x h90 §**

HONGKONG ADVENTURE 5 b.g. Roderic O'Connor (IRE) – Queen Margrethe (Grand Lodge (USA)) [2017/18 h–: h18.7g⁵ h18.6g⁵ h20.3g⁵ h16.8d⁴ h18.5v h16d³ h18.7g Nov 2] leggy gelding: modest maiden hurdler: may prove best at around 2m: best form on good going: in headgear last 3 starts: usually in tongue tie. *Olly Murphy* **h89**

HONKYTONKTENNESSEE (IRE) 9 b.g. Scorpion (IRE) – Polly Platinum (IRE) (Phardante (FR)) [2017/18 c106p, h109: h25d⁴ c20.3d² c22.6g³ c22.6m* c21dᶠ h19.9g⁵ c20g² c19.9g⁶ h16d² c25g c20dᶠ Apr 9] rangy gelding: fair handicap hurdler: fairly useful chaser: won handicap at Stratford in July: left Dan Skelton after third outing, failed to complete most subsequent starts (mainly in points): stays 3¼m: acts on good to firm and good to soft going: usually wears headgear: irresolute. *R. W. J. Willcox* **c118 § h105 §**

HONOURABLE EXIT (IRE) 11 b.g. Exit To Nowhere (USA) – Honor Love (FR) (Pursuit of Love) [2017/18 c–, h84: c24.2m⁴ May 9] multiple point winner: maiden hurdler: poor form in chases: has worn hood. *J. Tickle* **c78 h–**

HONOURABLE HENRY 8 b.g. Kayf Tara (IRE) – Kingara (Karinga Bay) [2017/18 h–: c23gᵖᵘ c23g⁴ c23sᵖᵘ Dec 30] winning pointer: no form under Rules: tried in cheekpieces. *Sarah-Jayne Davies* **c– h–**

HONOUR A PROMISE 10 b.m. Norse Dancer (IRE) – Motcombe (IRE) (Carroll House) [2017/18 h15.7d Nov 21] maiden hurdler: no form over fences: wears headgear: signs of temperament. *Paul Webber* **c– h–**

HON

HONOUR PROMISE (IRE) 6 b.m. Jeremy (USA) – Karenaragon (Aragon) [2017/18 h91: h20g[pu] Jul 18] modest hurdler at best: unproven beyond 17f: acts on good to soft going: usually wears cheekpieces. *Bernard Llewellyn* — h–

HOO BALLY DIVA (IRE) 7 b.m. Scorpion (IRE) – Dr Sandra (IRE) (Dr Massini (IRE)) [2017/18 h98: h23.9s* Feb 20] sturdy mare: modest hurdler: won mares handicap at Taunton, only start in 2017/18: stays 3¼m: acts on soft going: often races prominently. *Bob Buckler* — h96

HOOK LANE ROOBEE 5 b.g. Spendent – Sharp Action (Overbury (IRE)) [2017/18 b17.7d* Dec 4] first foal: dam placed in point: 28/1, won bumper at Plumpton (by ½ length from Seaston Spirit) on debut: will stay at least 2½m. *Suzy Smith* — b94

HOOLA HULA 5 br.m. Yeats (IRE) – Dancing Dasi (IRE) (Supreme Leader) [2017/18 h90p, b81: h18.5m[3] h16s h19.7g h21.7s[pu] h23.9s[pu] h16.5v h23.9m Apr 25] rather unfurnished mare: poor maiden hurdler: tried in cheekpieces. *Susan Gardner* — h83

HOOLIGAN JACK 5 ch.g. Daylami (IRE) – Stravaigin (Primitive Rising (USA)) [2017/18 h16.4v[pu] h16v h19.3d[6] Mar 31] little show in maiden/novice hurdles. *Iain Jardine* — h–

HOOVES THE DADDY (IRE) 5 b.g. Robin des Pres (FR) – Countessdee (IRE) (Arctic Lord) [2017/18 b–: h15.8d h16s[pu] h16.2v h19.3d h19.3v[pu] Mar 8] has had breathing operation: no form in bumpers/over hurdles: left Seamus Mullins after first start. *Sue Smith* — h– b–

HOPE FOR GLORY 9 b.g. Proclamation (IRE) – Aissa (Dr Devious (IRE)) [2017/18 c–, h63: c16.4g* May 16] little form over hurdles: poor form over fences: won handicap at Sedgefield in May: unproven beyond 2m: has worn headgear: wears tongue tie: usually leads. *Maurice Barnes* — c83 h–

HOPE'S WISHES 8 b.m. Kayf Tara – Otarie (FR) (Lute Antique (FR)) [2017/18 h112: h20m[5] h19.9d[2] h15.8v[4] h15.9d[6] c15.9v[2] h15.3v[6] Mar 28] fair handicap hurdler: 13/2, second in maiden at Leicester (16 lengths behind Bollin Ace) on chasing debut: stays 2½m: acts on good to firm and heavy going: tried in cheekpieces. *Barry Brennan* — c92 h102

HORACE HAZEL 9 b.g. Sir Harry Lewis (USA) – Kaream (Karinga Bay) [2017/18 c112, h110: h24m[3] h26.4d[3] h21.5d[2] h23.3g[3] h23.3d[4] h26.5d[3] Aug 22] good-topped gelding: fair handicap hurdler: winning chaser: stays 3¼m: acts on soft going: has worn headgear/tongue tie, including in 2017/18: usually leads. *Anthony Honeyball* — c– h110

HORATIO HORNBLOWER (IRE) 10 b.g. Presenting – Countess Camilla (Bob's Return (IRE)) [2017/18 c120, h–: c23g[3] c24v[4] c23.4s* c23.8d[5] c24.2v[2] c25.6v[2] c23.8v[3] Apr 15] rangy gelding: winning hurdler: fairly useful handicap chaser: won at Newbury in January: second at Sandown and Haydock in March: barely stays 3¼m: acts on good to firm and heavy going: often in cheekpieces in 2017/18: usually races towards rear. *Nick Williams* — c121 h–

HORSE FORCE ONE (IRE) 7 b.g. Kalanisi (IRE) – Oilpainting (IRE) (Welsh Term) [2017/18 b16.8m* b16.8m* h21.6d[3] Jul 23] point winner: fairly useful form in bumpers: won at Newton Abbot in May and July: 4/7, third in maiden at same course (23 lengths behind Whoshotwho) on hurdling debut: should do better. *Philip Hobbs* — h91 p b96

HORSEGUARDSPARADE 7 b.g. Montjeu (IRE) – Honorlina (FR) (Linamix (FR)) [2017/18 c98, h109: c20m[pu] May 11] sturdy gelding: fair maiden hurdler: little enthusiasm for chasing: stays 3m: acts on good to soft going: wears cheekpieces: often races towards rear. *Nigel Twiston-Davies* — c– h–

HORSESHOE BAY (IRE) 6 b.g. Arch (USA) – Sweepstake (IRE) (Acclamation) [2017/18 h16g* h20d[6] Sep 29] useful on Flat, stays 13f: fair form over hurdles: won maiden at Worcester in August: disappointing next time. *Dan Skelton* — h109

HOT GOSSIP (IRE) 4 b.f. Fast Company (IRE) – On The Make (IRE) (Entrepreneur) [2017/18 h16.2v[3] h15.6s[6] h15.7s Mar 7] poor maiden on Flat: poor form over hurdles. *Dianne Sayer* — h78

HOT LICK 4 b.g. Phoenix Reach (IRE) – Sweet Mandolin (Soviet Star (USA)) [2017/18 h16.2g[4] h16.7g[3] Jun 23] modest maiden on Flat, stays 1½m: well held in juvenile hurdles: in hood/tongue tie first start. *Dan Skelton* — h–

HOT N SASSY (IRE) 4 ch.f. Arcano (IRE) – Cheeky Weeky (Cadeaux Genereux) [2017/18 h16.8d[pu] Jul 23] half-sister to fair hurdler Cellarmaster (2m winner, by Alhaarth): poor maiden on Flat: pulled up in juvenile on hurdling debut. *Polly Gundry* — h–

HUG

HOT RYAN 5 b.m. Midnight Legend – Darn Hot (Sir Harry Lewis (USA)) [2017/18 b16.8d Apr 24] first foal: dam (c107) 23f chase winner: off mark in points at second attempt: tailed off in maiden bumper. *Chris Honour* — b–

HOT SMOKED 5 br.m. Eastern Anthem (IRE) – Waheeba (Pivotal) [2017/18 b16.5m⁶ Apr 25] second foal: dam lightly raced on Flat: well beaten in bumper. *Robert Walford* — b–

HOTTER THAN HELL (FR) 4 ch.f. No Risk At All (FR) – Ombrelle (FR) (Octagonal (NZ)) [2017/18 b16.3s² Mar 24] £16,000 3-y-o: rather unfurnished filly: sixth foal: half-sister to bumper winner/fairly useful hurdler Aurillac (19f winner, by Martaline): dam lightly-raced half-sister to fairly useful hurdler/smart chaser (2m-21f winner) Jim and useful French hurdler/fairly useful chaser (17f-19f winner) Mesange Royale: 25/1, second in Goffs UK Spring Sales Bumper at Newbury (2¾ lengths behind Caribert) on debut. *Alan King* — b95

HOUBLON DES OBEAUX (FR) 11 b.g. Panoramic – Harkosa (FR) (Nikos) [2017/18 c142, h–: c24.2s* c28.8d⁶ c24.2s⁵ c25.2s³ c32.6s^pu c23.8s³ c34.3s^F c28.8d Apr 28] good-topped gelding: winning hurdler: useful handicap chaser: won veterans event at Sandown in November: stays 33f: acts on heavy going: wears headgear. *Venetia Williams* — c142 h–

HOUNDSCOURT (IRE) 11 b.g. Court Cave (IRE) – Broken Rein (IRE) (Orchestra) [2017/18 c86§, h81§: c26.3s^pu h24.1s⁴ c25.2v^pu h24v* h27v⁴ Mar 23] modest handicap hurdler: won at Southwell in February: winning chaser: stays 27f: acts on heavy going: usually wears headgear: wears tongue tie: unreliable. *Joanne Foster* — c– § h88 §

HOUSE OF FRAUDS (IRE) 10 b.g. Storming Home – Bogus Penny (IRE) (Pennekamp (USA)) [2017/18 h16.5s^pu Feb 20] little form on Flat: pulled up in novice on hurdling debut. *Tony Newcombe* — h–

HOUSEPARTY 10 b.g. Invincible Spirit (IRE) – Amusing Time (IRE) (Sadler's Wells (USA)) [2017/18 c–§, h–: c17.8m² c17.8d⁵ Sep 10] compact gelding: maiden pointer/hurdler: poor handicap chaser: stays 2¼m: has worn headgear, including last 2 starts when also tongue tied: unreliable. *Nick Gifford* — c66 § h–

HOW ABOUT IT (IRE) 9 b.g. Kayf Tara – Midnight Gift (IRE) (Presenting) [2017/18 c108§, h–: h25g⁵ h25d⁴ h21.6v c24v⁴ h25d⁵ Mar 26] lengthy gelding: modest maiden hurdler/handicap chaser nowadays: stays 25f: acts on heavy going: wears headgear: tried in tongue tie: temperamental. *Alexandra Dunn* — c86 § h96 §

HOWABOUTNEVER (IRE) 10 b.g. Shantou (USA) – Sarah's Cottage (IRE) (Topanoora) [2017/18 h–: h20g h24g⁵ h20g* h21.4s h19.7s^pu Mar 27] smallish gelding: modest handicap hurdler: won selling event at Worcester in July: stays 3¼m: acts on heavy going: wears headgear: temperamental. *Roger Teal* — h92 §

HOWLONGISAFOOT (IRE) 9 b.g. Beneficial – Miss Vic (IRE) (Old Vic) [2017/18 c121, h–: c21.6g⁶ c20.2s^pu c19.7s⁵ c26v⁶ c19.5v⁵ c25.7v^pu c21.6v^pu h25s⁶ Apr 15] strong gelding: winning hurdler: fairly useful chaser: out of sorts in 2017/18: best at short of 3m: acts on heavy going: has worn headgear, including final start: often races lazily. *Chris Gordon* — c– h–

HOWS JOHNNY 5 b.g. Multiplex – Compton Chick (IRE) (Dolphin Street (FR)) [2017/18 b16.7d⁴ Jun 8] well beaten in bumper: fell last when holding place claims all 3 starts in points. *John Wainwright* — b–

HOW'S MY FRIEND 13 b.g. Karinga Bay – Friendly Lady (New Member) [2017/18 c91, h–: h25.8g^pu c24d⁶ c25.1s² c26.7v² c24.5v* c21.7v* c24.5v* Mar 15] workmanlike gelding: maiden hurdler: modest handicap chaser: completed hat-trick at Towcester in February/March: stays 27f: acts on good to firm and heavy going: has worn tongue tie: responds generously to pressure. *Grant Cann* — c97 h–

HUFF AND PUFF 11 b.g. Azamour (IRE) – Coyote (Indian Ridge) [2017/18 c121, h–: c20.9v* c23.9d³ Apr 22] tall, workmanlike gelding: winning hurdler: fairly useful form over fences: won handicap at Hereford in April after 13-month absence: stays 3m: acts on good to firm and heavy going: often races prominently. *Venetia Williams* — c123 h–

HUGHESIE (IRE) 9 b.g. Indian Danehill (IRE) – Collatrim Choice (IRE) (Saddlers' Hall (IRE)) [2017/18 c–, h96: h22g⁵ c21m² c21g^F h20g⁶ Aug 1] lengthy gelding: maiden hurdler: fair handicap chaser nowadays: stays 21f: acts on good to firm and heavy going: has worn headgear, including in 2017/18: wears tongue tie. *Evan Williams* — c109 h92

389

HUG

HUGOS HORSE (FR) 5 gr.g. Turgeon (USA) – Bella Eria (FR) (Nikos) [2017/18 h21.6s^{pu} Nov 15] off mark in points at fifth attempt in April: pulled up in novice on hurdling debut. *Paul Nicholls*   h–

HUGO'S REFLECTION (IRE) 6 b.g. Robin des Champs (FR) – Dawn Court (Rakaposhi King) [2017/18 b–: b15.8v^4 h19.5v Jan 6] rangy gelding: little show in bumpers/maiden hurdle. *Ben Case*   h– b–

HUMBEL BEN (IRE) 15 br.g. Humbel (USA) – Donegans Daughter (Auction Ring (USA)) [2017/18 c90x, h76: c16.3d^3 c17.8d Sep 10] tall gelding: winning hurdler: modest handicap chaser: stays 2¾m: acts on heavy going: usually wears cheekpieces: has worn tongue tie: sketchy jumper. *Alan Jones*   c88 x h–

HUMPHREY BOGART (IRE) 5 b.g. Tagula (IRE) – Hazarama (IRE) (Kahyasi) [2017/18 h16g Feb 24] brother to fair hurdler Jesmond Lodge (2m winner) and fairly useful hurdler Domino Dancer (2m/17f winner), and half-brother to fair hurdler Whats The Plot (2m winner, by Alfred Nobel): smart on Flat, stays 1½m: needed experience when well beaten in Dovecote Novices' Hurdle at Kempton (hooded) after 19-month absence: should prove capable of much better. *Nicky Henderson*   h– p

HUNTERS CALL (IRE) 8 b.g. Medaaly – Accordiontogelica (IRE) (Accordion) [2017/18 h16.4d^4 h24.7d^5 h20.5g^3 h15.7d* Dec 23]   **h130**

Few jumps trainers have made as big an impact in their first season as Olly Murphy in 2017/18. A return of forty-seven winners compares very favourably with other trainers who have taken out a licence since the turn of the century. Multiple Grade 1-winning trainer Harry Fry sent out just twenty winners when starting out in 2012/13, while Dan Skelton, who saddled more winners (one hundred and fifty-six) than anyone else in Britain in the latest season, was responsible for just twenty-seven winners in his first season in 2014/15. Murphy certainly made a better fist of his first domestic campaign than long-time mentor Gordon Elliott managed in his native Ireland—Elliott recorded his first winner under Rules courtesy of Arresting at Perth in June 2006, but had still to record a winner in Ireland when Silver Birch won the Grand National the following year! Elliott, of course, is now firmly established as one of the pre-eminent trainers, and his tally of two hundred and ten wins in Ireland in 2017/18 eclipsed Willie Mullins' previous record for number of wins in a season by seventeen (a Mullins four-timer on the final day of the season at Punchestown took him to two hundred and twelve winners to regain the record!)

Gordon Elliott owes much of his success to his mastery of placing horses, something which Murphy learned during his time as assistant trainer at Cullentra House. Appearing alongside Elliott on the panel at a Cheltenham preview hosted by Betfair, Murphy revealed 'The one thing he (Elliott) told me was to go home and train winners. Don't worry about going to Newbury, putting on a tweed suit and going for a nice lunch. Go to your smaller tracks and try to run your horses in the right races. You look at Gordon's horses now and, in the summer, he gets as big a buzz winning with a horse which no one else can win with. I've tried to emulate him on a very, very small scale, trying to get going by training bad horses and just trying to catch people's attentions that way.' Murphy later added that he wasn't going to run horses at Cheltenham 'just to go there on the beer' and he would likely be watching a 0-100 handicap hurdle at Fakenham around the time of the Gold Cup. True to his word, Murphy saddled just one runner at the Cheltenham Festival—Oxford Blu who was pulled up in the Fred Winter—and he saddled a winner, three seconds and a third from five runners at Fakenham on Gold Cup afternoon!

Murphy moved back from Ireland at the beginning of May and started training at Warren Chase Stables in Stratford-upon-Avon, on the same three-hundred-and-fifty-acre estate as his mother Anabel Murphy, who has been training on a small scale herself for over thirty years (his father Aiden Murphy is a well-known bloodstock agent). Murphy's admiration for what Elliott has achieved is evident from the facilities at Warren Chase. In addition to sixty-five boxes, two horse walkers and a seven-furlong fibresand gallop, Murphy also has a half-mile circuit and a quarter-mile cantering ring modelled on those at Cullentra House. Murphy made the perfect start to his training career with his first runner Dove Mountain, previously trained by both Gordon Elliott and Anabel Murphy, winning a

Racing Welfare Handicap Hurdle, Ascot—the highlight of a very successful first campaign for rookie trainer Olly Murphy as Hunters Call gets the better of the grey Silver Streak

class six handicap on the Flat at Brighton in early-July, and he had to wait only five days before his first success over obstacles, Gold Class leading home a one, two for the stable in a lady amateur riders handicap hurdle at Market Rasen. Overall Murphy saddled eleven winners from twenty-four runners in July, operating at a forty-six per cent strike rate.

By far the biggest success of Murphy's short training career to date, however, came courtesy of Hunters Call in the seventeen-runner Racing Welfare Handicap Hurdle at Ascot in December, a race worth £85,425 to the winner. Hunters Call joined Murphy from John Neilan, for whom he had won just one of his nine starts over hurdles in Ireland, and he started out for his new yard at Ascot from a mark 8 lb higher than when last seen finishing third in a two and a half mile handicap at Sligo in August. Though not obviously well handicapped, there were signs that a big run was expected from Hunters Call at Ascot, with Jack Kennedy coming over from Ireland to take the ride, a gamble on the day seeing Hunters Call's odds contract from 16/1 in the morning to an SP of 9/1. Unusually for such a big field, the pace was only steady and Hunters Call perhaps benefited from making his move before most of the others, though it is unlikely to have made any difference to the result, such was the ease of his success. He was still virtually on the bridle when leading two out and never looked in any danger of defeat, finishing three lengths clear at the line with Silver Streak taking second ahead of Verdana Blue and Bleu Et Rouge. That there was just eight lengths between the second and the ninth reflected the nature of the race, a competitive field in a blanket finish for which the gallop was largely responsible. It was to Hunters Call's credit that he was able to put distance between himself and the remainder, his commanding victory suggesting that he had yet to reach his full potential. However, after missing the Betfair Hurdle to protect his handicap mark for Cheltenham, the rest of his season was eventually curtailed because of an injury. He was found to have some heat in his foot in the week before an intended run in the County Hurdle and was swiftly ruled out, a blow Murphy described as 'a kick in the balls' during the aforementioned Betfair preview night. At first, the setback was deemed only minor and it was thought that it would allow him to return for another of the major end-of-season festivals, with the Scottish Champion Hurdle at Ayr mentioned as a possible target. That optimism turned out to be misplaced, though, and Hunters Call was not seen out again.

391

HUN

```
Hunters Call (IRE)   ┌ Medaaly         ┌ Highest Honor    ┌ Kenmare
(b.g. 2010)          │  (gr 1994)      │  (gr 1983)       │ High River
                     │                 │ Dance of Leaves  │ Sadler's Wells
                     │                 │  (b 1987)        │ Fall Aspen
                     │ Accordiontogelica(IRE) ┌ Accordion  │ Sadler's Wells
                     │  (b 2004)       │  (b 1986)        │ Sound of Success
                     │                 │ Evangelica       │ Dahar
                     └                 └  (b 1990)        └ Rebut
```

Hunters Call's sire Medaaly, winner of the 1996 Racing Post Trophy, died in 2010. He was at stud in France and South Africa before being sent to stand in Ireland as a National Hunt stallion in 2008, with the top-class chaser Medermit and the very smart hurdler/useful chaser Sky's The Limit standing out among his best progeny. Hunters Call is the second foal out of the unraced Accordiontogelica, a sister to the useful hurdler/smart chaser (stayed three miles) Call The Police, and he is a half-brother to the modest bumper performer Angelica Yeats (by Yeats), who is yet to win in nine starts (well held on sole hurdling start) for John Neilan. Grandam Evangelica went from winning a selling hurdle to contesting the Grand National during her time with Martin Pipe for whom she proved a fairly useful, but not always reliable, staying chaser. Hunters Call, who failed to complete on either of his starts in points, was sent to the Cheltenham November Sales six days after making a winning hurdling debut at Naas in 2015, but was led out unsold at £85,000. He was owned by his breeder Michael Ward, who eventually sold him privately in the weeks leading up to that Ascot success for his first-season trainer. A lengthy gelding, Hunters Call has the option of going novice chasing in the next season, though he could yet have more to offer if kept over hurdles, with a BHA mark of 137 unlikely to anchor him given the manner of his Ascot victory. Hunters Call is a strong traveller who has been tried at twenty-five furlongs, but is probably best at two miles. He acts on heavy going and it is worth reiterating that he remains open to further progress for a young trainer who has quickly shown himself to be a dab hand at improving recruits from other yards. *Olly Murphy*

HUNTERS LODGE (IRE) 12 ch.g. Subtle Power (IRE) – Native Orchid (IRE) (Be My Native (USA)) [2017/18 c–§, h–: c24.5g[5] May 15] strong gelding: 3-time winning pointer: maiden hurdler: fairly useful chaser at best, no form in 2017/18: stays 29f: acts on heavy going: has worn headgear, including in 2017/18: in tongue tie last 2 starts: hard ride, not one to trust. *Alan Hill* **c– § h–**

HUNT POLITICS 6 b.g. Black Sam Bellamy (IRE) – Jaunty Flight (Busy Flight) [2017/18 b16.3s b15.7v[4] b17.7s[3] h20.5s[5] h21.6v[4] Apr 17] compact gelding: off mark in points at second attempt: modest form in bumpers: poor form over hurdles: better effort when fifth in novice at Newbury. *Warren Greatrex* **h80 b79**

HUNTRESS (IRE) 6 b.m. Flemensfirth (USA) – Madgehil (IRE) (Anshan) [2017/18 b91: h19.2g h19.4s ab18d h20.7g Apr 24] compact mare: bumper winner: poor form over hurdles. *Suzy Smith* **h60**

HUNTSMAN SON (IRE) 8 b.g. Millenary – Daly Lady (IRE) (Lord of Appeal) [2017/18 h103p: h19.9d[2] h20.6d* h19.4d* h20.5v[4] h16.8v[2] h16v[4] Mar 10] well-made gelding: won both completed starts in Irish points: fairly useful handicap hurdler: won at Market Rasen and Doncaster (novice) in December: second at Cheltenham in January: stays 21f: acts on heavy going. *Alex Hales* **h129**

HURLSTONE POINT 5 br.m. Scorpion (IRE) – Dudeen (IRE) (Anshan) [2017/18 b16g b15.7d h21.6s[pu] Apr 23] fourth foal: half-sister to 3 winners, including fairly useful hurdler Catherines Well (19f winner, by Kayf Tara): dam (h89), 2½m hurdle winner, half-sister to fairly useful staying hurdler Helm: no form in bumpers: pulled up in mares novice on hurdling debut. *Philip Hobbs* **h– b–**

HURRICANE DARWIN (IRE) 8 b.g. Westerner – Poetics Girl (IRE) (Saddlers' Hall (IRE)) [2017/18 h22s[4] h20m c20s* h24s* c24v c24v[4] c30.2s[pu] c24s[2] Apr 28] sturdy gelding: fairly useful handicap hurdler: won at Clonmel in November: useful chaser: won handicap at Navan (by 1¾ lengths from Whatareudoingtome) in September: stays 3m: acts on heavy going: usually in tongue tie: often races towards rear. *Alan Fleming, Ireland* **c130 h124**

HURRICANE DYLAN (IRE) 7 b.g. Brian Boru – Definetly Sarah (IRE) (Definite Article) [2017/18 h20.3v[5] h20.6v[3] h19.9v[2] h19.9g* Apr 23] placed both starts in Irish maiden points: fairly useful form over hurdles: won maiden at Sedgefield in April: stays 21f. *Kevin Frost*   **h116**

HURRICANE HOLLOW 8 b.g. Beat Hollow – Veenwouden (Desert Prince (IRE)) [2017/18 h16s h16s[3] h19.8v[2] h16.5s h15.7s[pu] Mar 7] smallish, leggy gelding: fairly useful handicap hurdler: second at Wincanton in February: stays 2½m: acts on good to firm and heavy going: tried in cheekpieces: usually races towards rear: has joined Keith Dalgleish. *Dan Skelton*   **h124**

HURRICANE MINNIE 5 b.m. Authorized (IRE) – Hurricane Milly (IRE) (Milan) [2017/18 b16d b15.8g[5] b16.6s Jan 27] first foal: dam (b96), bumper winner, closely related to smart staying chasers Darkness and Cantlow: modest form in bumpers: bred to be suited by further than 2m: wears hood. *Alan King*   **b77**

HURRICANE RIDGE (IRE) 9 b.g. Hurricane Run (IRE) – Warrior Wings (Indian Ridge) [2017/18 h16.8g h18.5d[3] h18.5v[3] h21.6s Oct 24] maiden pointer: modest handicap hurdler: winning chaser: stays 21f: acts on heavy and good to firm going: has worn headgear. *Jimmy Frost*   **c–** **h92**

HURRICANE RITA (FR) 8 gr.m. Sagamix (FR) – Madonna da Rossi (Mtoto) [2017/18 h92: h21g[2] h20v[pu] h16v* h16s[5] h15.7v[2] h15.7v[6] h16s[3] h15.7g Apr 20] has had breathing operation: modest handicap hurdler: won at Fakenham in January: left Olly Murphy after fifth start: stays 2¾m: acts on heavy going: wears headgear: has worn tongue tie, including in 2017/18. *Conor Dore*   **h95**

HURRICANE VOLTA (IRE) 7 ch.g. Hurricane Run (IRE) – Haute Volta (FR) (Grape Tree Road) [2017/18 h–: h20.5v[3] h16v[2] Apr 16] fair form over hurdles: best effort at 2m: acts on heavy going: usually in cheekpieces: in tongue tie last 2 starts. *Gordon Elliott, Ireland*   **h107**

HURRY HENRY (IRE) 9 b.g. Blueprint (IRE) – Tower Princess (IRE) (King's Ride) [2017/18 c103, h–: c15.7s[pu] c19.4v[pu] c19.2v[pu] Dec 21] tall gelding: winning hurdler: maiden chaser, no form in 2017/18: tried in cheekpieces: in tongue tie last 5 starts. *Richenda Ford*   **c–** **h–**

HYMN AND A PRAYER 5 br.g. Eastern Anthem (IRE) – Kryssa (Kris) [2017/18 b16.2g[3] b16s Feb 6] sixth foal: closely related to a Flat winner abroad by Singspiel and half-brother to 1¼m-1½m winner/winning pointer Eco Warrior (by Echo of Light): dam, 5f-1m winner, half-sister to smart hurdler/chaser (stays 21f) Modus: modest form in bumpers: easily better effort when third at Hereford in November. *Fiona Shaw*   **b81**

I

I AM COLIN 9 b.g. Zafeen (FR) – Dd's Glenalla (IRE) (Be My Native (USA)) [2017/18 c123, h–: c24.2v[pu] Nov 7] strong gelding: winning hurdler: fairly useful chaser, pulled up sole outing in 2017/18: stayed 3m: acted on heavy going: usually wore cheekpieces: dead. *Nigel Twiston-Davies*   **c78** **h–**

I AM SAM 7 b.g. Black Sam Bellamy (IRE) – Flinders (Henbit (USA)) [2017/18 h19.5d h23.6v h20.5v[5] c24g[6] Apr 26] tall gelding: fifth foal: closely related to modest hurdler Kayflin (2½m-2¾m winner, by Kayf Tara): dam (c84/h76) 3m-3¼m chase winner: last of 3 finishers on completed start in points: poor form over hurdles: 11/1, sixth in novice handicap at Warwick (33¾ lengths behind Posh Totty) on chasing debut: wears hood. *Emma Lavelle*   **c–** **h82**

IBALLISTICVIN 5 b.g. Rail Link – Guntakal (IRE) (Night Shift (USA)) [2017/18 h17.7m[4] Aug 17] half-brother to a winning hurdler in Italy by Spectrum: fair on Flat, stays 13.5f: 9/2, fourth in novice at Fontwell (15 lengths behind Balancing Time) on hurdling debut: should improve. *Gary Moore*   **h91 p**

IBIS DU RHEU (FR) 7 b.g. Blue Bresil (FR) – Dona du Rheu (FR) (Dom Pasquini (FR)) [2017/18 c145, h–: c23.4v[4] c20.4s[5] c25s[5] Apr 14] well-made gelding: winning hurdler: useful maiden chaser: stays 3m: acts on heavy going: has worn hood: wears tongue tie. *Paul Nicholls*   **c134** **h–**

IBLEO (FR) 5 b.g. Dick Turpin (IRE) – Mahendra (GER) (Next Desert (IRE)) [2017/18 h114: h16d Oct 14] fair form over hurdles for P. Leblanc in 2016/17: little show both starts in Britain: has worn: tried in cheekpieces. *Venetia Williams*   **h–**

IBS

IBSEN (IRE) 9 b.g. Dubawi (IRE) – Really (IRE) (Entrepreneur) [2017/18 h22.8v Nov 25] small, close-coupled gelding: fairly useful on Flat, stays 2m: fairly useful hurdler, won twice in 2015/16: lightly raced since, stiff task sole outing in 2017/18: stays 2¾m: acts on heavy going: often wears headgear: in tongue tie last 3 starts. *Gordon Elliott, Ireland*   h–

ICANMOTOR 11 b.m. Midnight Legend – Lochnagold (Lochnager) [2017/18 h82: h24g* h23.3g⁶ h22g³ c19.4gᵖᵘ Jul 23] modest handicap hurdler: won at Southwell in May: pulled up in novice handicap on chasing debut: stays 3m: acts on good to firm and good to soft going: has worn cheekpieces, including last 4 starts: wears tongue tie: often travels strongly. *Fergal O'Brien*   c– h92

I CARE DES SOURCES (FR) 4 gr.f. Turgeon (USA) – Baraka du Berlais (FR) (Bonnet Rouge (FR)) [2017/18 b13.7g b14s h20.7s Jan 12] fourth foal: half-sister to useful hurdler Let's Dance (2m-2½m winner, by Poliglote) and bumper winner Lad of Luck (by Soldier of Fortune): dam useful French hurdler/fairly useful chaser (17f/2¼m winner): poor form in bumpers: well held on hurdling debut: tried in tongue tie. *Jonjo O'Neill*   h– b62

ICE COOL CHAMPS (IRE) 7 ch.g. Robin des Champs (FR) – Last of Many (IRE) (Lahib (USA)) [2017/18 h116p, b99: h19.7s³ h23.3v* c23.6v⁵ c24.2s² c23.4s³ Mar 23] well-made gelding: fairly useful form over hurdles: won handicap at Uttoxeter in November: similar form over fences: best effort when second in novice handicap at Exeter in February: stays 3m: acts on heavy going. *Philip Hobbs*   c122 h128

ICE KONIG (FR) 9 gr.g. Epalo (GER) – Isarwelle (GER) (Sternkoenig (IRE)) [2017/18 h94: h21.6s h21.6m⁴ h19g h19s h15.5v Jan 31] rather leggy gelding: modest handicap hurdler: stays 2¾m: acts on good to firm and good to soft going: has worn tongue tie, including in 2017/18. *Jimmy Frost*   h85

ICE TRES 9 br.m. Iceman – Tup Tim (Emperor Jones (USA)) [2017/18 h16.5s⁵ h19v⁶ h16.5m* Apr 25] modest handicap hurdler: won at Taunton in April: unproven beyond 17f: acts on good to firm and good to soft going: usually wears headgear: has worn tongue tie. *Chris Down*   h85

ICING ON THE CAKE (IRE) 8 b.g. Spadoun (FR) – Honeyed (IRE) (Persian Mews) [2017/18 c128, h113p: c19.9g⁵ c23.8d c20.2v⁵ c21s⁴ Apr 23] good-topped gelding: lightly-raced hurdler: fairly useful handicap chaser: stays 2½m: acts on soft going: often races towards rear. *Oliver Sherwood*   c118 h–

ICONIC SKY 5 gr.m. Sixties Icon – Kentucky Sky (Cloudings (IRE)) [2017/18 h106: h21.6d h15.7s³ h15.5v⁵ h18.6s* h20.5v² h20d³ h20.6g* Apr 22] compact mare: fairly useful handicap hurdler: won maiden events at Market Rasen in February and April: stays 21f: acts on heavy going: wears cheekpieces. *Lucy Wadham*   h122

I'D BETTER GO NOW (IRE) 5 b.g. Alkaadhem – Pohutakawa (FR) (Affirmed (USA)) [2017/18 b16.7g⁵ Oct 31] €55,000 3-y-o: closely related to 7f-1½m winner Speagle (by Desert Sun) and half-brother to useful hurdler/smart chaser Carthalawn (2m/17f winner, by Foxhound): dam unraced: 10/1, fifth in bumper at Bangor (4¼ lengths behind Ballygomartin). *Charlie Longsdon*   b96

IDDER (IRE) 7 br.g. Authorized (IRE) – Epiphany (Zafonic (USA)) [2017/18 h110: h17m* h22.15 h16d h17v³ h17d Nov 13] fair handicap hurdler: won at Carlisle in May: should stay further than 17f: acts on good to firm and heavy going: wears cheekpieces. *James Moffatt*   h109

IDEE DE GARDE (FR) 5 b.g. Kapgarde (FR) – Idee Recue (FR) (Sicyos (USA)) [2017/18 b16v* Jan 2] €52,000 3-y-o: fifth foal: dam French 2m/17f hurdle/chase winner: 2/1, won bumper at Ayr (by length from Bluefortytwo) on debut, keeping on gamely: useful prospect: has joined Dan Skelton. *Nicky Richards*   b93 p

IDENTITY THIEF (IRE) 8 b.g. Kayf Tara – Miss Arteea (IRE) (Flemensfirth (USA)) [2017/18 c147, h–: h16s⁶ h16v² h16.4s¹ h24.7s* h24d⁴ Apr 26]   c– h161

'It's the first time in fifteen years my brother has bought me a two-mile hurdler and he'll probably never jump a fence!' joked Michael O'Leary after his Mengli Khan had won the Bar One Racing Royal Bond Novices' Hurdle at Fairyhouse in December, his remark reinforcing the point that hurdling is normally only a means to an end so far as Gigginstown House Stud is concerned. Most of the horses that Gigginstown buys are graduates from the Irish point-to-point field, embryonic chasers whose careers over hurdles very rarely last more than one season. Many of the operation's eighty Grade 1 wins under Rules have come in staying chases, the milestone achieved when Dortmund Park won the Profile Systems Champion Novices' Hurdle on the penultimate day of the Punchestown Festival, thirteen years

394

Ryanair Stayers' Hurdle (Liverpool), Aintree—Identity Thief reinvents himself as a stayer with a clear-cut victory over the consistent Wholestone

after subsequent Gold Cup winner War of Attrition gave Gigginstown its first in the Swordlestown Cup Novices' Chase at the same meeting. Forty-seven of the eighty have come over fences, including a second Gold Cup with Don Cossack in 2016 and multiple wins in the Leopardstown Christmas Chase, the Irish Gold Cup and the Punchestown Gold Cup, the three most valuable Grade 1 staying chases in Ireland. Thirty-one of the total have come in Grade 1 hurdle races, and horses who were not in their novice/juvenile seasons have been responsible for just twelve of those. Lieutenant Colonel won both the Hatton's Grace Hurdle at Fairyhouse and the Christmas Hurdle at Leopardstown for Sandra Hughes in 2014/15, having failed to meet expectations on his chasing debut at Naas earlier that season; Identity Thief produced a very smart effort on just his sixth hurdling start to win the 'Fighting Fifth' Hurdle at Newcastle in 2015/16, the same season in which Prince of Scars graduated from handicaps to give Gigginstown a second consecutive win in the Christmas Hurdle; Apple's Jade recorded a hat-trick of Grade 1 successes in 2016/17, adding to Petit Mouchoir's wins in the Ryanair Hurdle and the Irish Champion Hurdle at Leopardstown; and, in the latest season, Apple's Jade won the Hatton's Grace for the second year in succession before taking the step up to three miles in her stride in the Christmas Hurdle, while Identity Thief proved a revelation, stepped up markedly in trip, when winning the Ryanair Stayers' Hurdle at Aintree.

Identity Thief's career had not gone to plan in the intervening period since the highs of his 2015/16 campaign, with his debut season over fences the following year going awry after an encouraging start, resulting in him eventually ending up back over hurdles, bringing up the rear in both the Aintree Hurdle and the Punchestown Champion Hurdle. Chasing was put on the back-burner in the latest season and when Identity Thief finally made his reappearance in February, it was in the Irish Champion Hurdle at Leopardstown, where he shaped as if needing the run in sixth (beaten over twenty-five lengths behind Supasundae). Identity Thief duly stepped up on that form when a length and a half second to Forge Meadow in the Red Mills Trial Hurdle at Gowran two weeks later, and took another step forward when twelve lengths fourth behind Buveur d'Air in the Champion Hurdle at Cheltenham, producing his best effort since his second behind Vroum Vroum Mag in the Punchestown Champion Hurdle in April 2016.

There was little in those three performances over two miles to draw encouragement for what was to come on his next start in the Ryanair Stayers' Hurdle (registered as the Liverpool Hurdle) at Aintree. With quite a few in the line-up seemingly making up the numbers, the race lacked the depth of the Stayers' Hurdle at Cheltenham, the form of which was represented by Wholestone (third), Sam Spinner (fifth), The Worlds End (seventh) and Lil Rockerfeller (thirteenth). Sam Spinner was sent off the 6/5 favourite at Aintree, having been unsuited by the run of the race at Cheltenham, with the other Stayers' Hurdle runners also going off shorter in the betting than 14/1-shot Identity Thief, as did the National Spirit Hurdle winner Old Guard (12/1). The race appeared to be developing as many would have expected when Sam Spinner moved to the head of affairs in the back straight, but Wholestone and Identity Thief were both travelling sweetly in his slipstream and that pair went on after two out, with Identity Thief finding most in his first race at three miles to assert in the closing stages, pulling five lengths clear of Wholestone with Sam Spinner another ten lengths back in third. Sam Spinner was well below the form of his Long Walk Hurdle victory at Ascot earlier in the season, but there was no reason to think that Wholestone had not run to his best and Identity Thief's performance was well up to standard for the race, producing a clear career best to record the second Grade 1 win of his career, some twenty-nine months after his first. Following the Ryanair Chase success of stablemate Balko des Flos, incidentally, Identity Thief's win was also the second in major races sponsored by Ryanair in the latest season to be won by Michael O'Leary, CEO of the company, who had endured no luck in his company's sponsored events in previous years. Identity Thief's win was a first Grade 1 success in Britain for Sean Flanagan, who rode him in each of his five starts in the latest season and was credited with the suggestion to step him up to three miles at Aintree, feeling that his mount 'had just hit a flat spot mid-race [at Cheltenham] before staying on well at the end.'

Identity Thief (IRE) (b.g. 2010)
- Kayf Tara (b 1994)
  - Sadler's Wells (b 1981)
    - Northern Dancer
    - Fairy Bridge
  - Colorspin (b 1983)
    - High Top
    - Reprocolor
- Miss Arteea (IRE) (b 2002)
  - Flemensfirth (b 1992)
    - Alleged
    - Etheldreda
  - Merric (ch 1991)
    - Electric
    - Merry Proverb

There was certainly the requisite stamina in Identity Thief's pedigree to suggest that the step up to three miles would not be an issue for him. He is by the dual Ascot Gold Cup winner Kayf Tara, the sire of plenty of good stayers, and out of the unraced mare Miss Arteea, a daughter of stamina influence Flemensfirth. Identity Thief is the third foal out of Miss Arteea, a half-sister to the useful chaser (best at up to two and a half miles) Arteea, and he is a half-brother to the useful but unreliable hurdler Oscarteea (stayed three miles, by Oscar), who is reported to have died since last seen finishing well held in a handicap hurdle at Newbury in December. The only other progeny of Miss Arteea to have made it to the racecourse so far are Queen Deirdre (by King's Theatre), who won one of her two starts in bumpers for Willie Mullins, and the David Pipe-trained Drama King (also by King's Theatre), who has failed to make an impression in three starts. Henry de Bromhead paid €135,000 for a three-year-old close relative (by Milan) to Identity Thief at the Derby Sale in June 2018. Identity Thief was sold as a foal to Ian Ferguson for €15,000 and three years later he was returned to the ring at the Derby Sale where trainer Gordon Elliott went to €40,000 to secure him on behalf of Gigginstown. Identity Thief has certainly proved a good buy, with his career earnings standing at over £325,000, with more to come from him over three miles in all probability. He can have his run excused when well held behind Faugheen in the Champion Stayers' Hurdle at Punchestown on his final start, when he possibly found the race coming too soon after just twelve days off. He is better judged on his Aintree form for now. Identity Thief still has the option of going back over fences, but it is more likely that he will have a campaign geared around a crack at the Stayers' Hurdle at Cheltenham in the next season. A rather leggy gelding, Identity Thief stays three miles and acts on heavy going. *Henry de Bromhead, Ireland*

I'DLIKETHEOPTION (IRE) 7 b.g. Presenting – Supreme Dreamer (IRE) (Supreme Leader) [2017/18 c127, h112: c19.2g* c21.4g c20.5g6 Feb 24] winning hurdler: fairly useful handicap chaser: won at Market Rasen in May: stays 21f: acts on good to firm and good to soft going: wears tongue tie: often races towards rear. *Jonjo O'Neill*

IFANDABUT (IRE) 6 b.g. Scorpion (IRE) – Native Wonder (IRE) (Good Thyne (USA)) [2017/18 b16d⁵ h19.5d h21.4s h16.7v Jan 4] £22,000 3-y-o: third foal: dam, winning pointer, half-sister to fairly useful hurdler/useful chaser (stayed 3m) Hangover: fifth in bumper at Warwick (10¼ lengths behind Rhaegar): no form over hurdles. *Venetia Williams* — h– b81

IFANDBUTWHYNOT (IRE) 12 b.g. Raise A Grand (IRE) – Cockney Ground (IRE) (Common Grounds) [2017/18 c130, h117: c17.1g^{ur} c15.2s³ c16d⁴ c15.9d² c16d⁴ Apr 9] workmanlike gelding: winning hurdler: fairly useful handicap chaser: unproven beyond 2m: acts on good to firm and heavy going: has worn hood: usually tongue tied: front runner. *Tim Easterby* — c127 h–

IF THE CAP FITS (IRE) 6 b.g. Milan – Derravaragh Sayra (IRE) (Sayarshan (FR)) [2017/18 b115: h18.5d⁴ h16.7s* h16d* Dec 26] good-topped gelding: smart bumper performer: similar form over hurdles: unbeaten in 3 novices, at Exeter in October, Bangor in November and Kempton (beating Diese des Bieffes by 5 lengths) in December: will be suited by 2½m+: front runner/races prominently: exciting prospect. *Harry Fry* — h149 p

IF YOU SAY RUN (IRE) 6 b.m. Mahler – De Lissa (IRE) (Zaffaran (USA)) [2017/18 b104p: h19.5d* h21.2g² h15.3v* h16.5s² h19.8v² h20.5s^{pu} Mar 24] good-topped mare: Irish point winner: bumper winner: fairly useful form over hurdles: won mares novices at Chepstow in October and Wincanton in December: second in Jane Seymour Mares' Novices' Hurdle at Sandown in February: stays 21f: acts on heavy going: wears tongue tie. *Paul Nicholls* — h128

IGOUGO (IRE) 5 ch.g. Where Or When (IRE) – Giolldante (IRE) (Phardante (FR)) [2017/18 b15.8v⁶ h18.5v^{pu} h18.5v⁴ Apr 8] no show in bumper/over hurdles: tried in hood/tongue tie. *Jeremy Scott* — h– b–

I JUST KNOW (IRE) 8 b.g. Robin des Pres (FR) – Desperado Queen (IRE) (Un Desperado (FR)) [2017/18 c133, h–: c24.5s³ c20d⁴ c30s* h23.3v² c34.3s^{F} Apr 14] good-topped gelding: maiden hurdler: useful handicap chaser: won at Catterick (by 15 lengths from Billy Bronco) in January: thorough stayer: acts on heavy going: bold-jumping front runner. *Sue Smith* — c136 h112

I KNOW THE CODE (IRE) 13 b.g. Viking Ruler (AUS) – Gentle Papoose (Commanche Run) [2017/18 c71, h–: c22.5d^{pu} May 20] angular gelding: modest hurdler at best: poor chaser: little form since 2014/15: stays 2½m: acts on heavy going: often races towards rear. *Lynn Siddall* — c– h–

ILEWINDELILAH 10 b.m. Grape Tree Road – Bridepark Rose (IRE) (Kemal (FR)) [2017/18 h–: h16.8g h25.8g* h25g² h25g⁶ Nov 5] modest handicap hurdler: won at Fontwell in October: stays 3¼m: best form on good going: often wears headgear. *Charlie Mann* — h84

ILEWIN GEEZ 8 ch.g. Generous (IRE) – Ilewin Janine (IRE) (Soughaan (USA)) [2017/18 h16.6s² h16s⁵ Apr 9] bumper winner: fair form over hurdles: better effort when second in novice at Doncaster in February: likely to stay 2½m. *Charlie Mann* — h112

I'LL BE YOUR CLOWN (IRE) 7 b.g. Aqlaam – Lady Avenger (IRE) (Namid) [2017/18 h113: h16.7g* h15.7d³ h15.7g⁵ h15.3s h16d^{pu} h16.5g h16.5s Dec 14] fair hurdler: won novice at Market Rasen in May: left Dan Skelton after third start: raced around 2m: acts on heavy going: tried in tongue tie. *Steven Dixon* — h109

I'LLHAVEALOOK (IRE) 13 b.g. Milan – Kelly's Native (IRE) (Be My Native (USA)) [2017/18 h95§: h22d³ May 21] point winner: modest handicap hurdler: stays 3m: acts on heavy going: wears headgear: front runner/races prominently: temperamental. *Katie Stephens* — h94 §

I'LL RUN WITH YOU (IRE) 5 b.m. Darsi (FR) – Suzy Q (IRE) (King's Ride) [2017/18 h22.1d⁵ h20.2v h16.8v Mar 23] €5,000 3-y-o: eighth foal: dam, showed a little ability in bumpers, half-sister to useful hurdler/chaser (stayed 21f) The Railway Man: little show in Irish points/novice hurdles. *Dianne Sayer* — h–

ILLTELLMEMA (IRE) 6 gr.m. Milan – Cullenstown Lady (IRE) (Wood Chanter) [2017/18 h21.7v² h19.2s³ h18.5d^{F} Apr 24] £27,000 6-y-o: sister to modest hurdler Queeny (2½m-25f winner) and half-sister to 2 winners, including fair hurdler Ikansea (2¼m winner, by Scribano): dam (c106/h119) 2m-3m hurdle/chase winner: point winner: modest form over hurdles: best effort when second in mares novice at Fontwell in March: tried in hood. *Suzy Smith* — h94

ILOVEMINTS 6 b.m. Kayf Tara – La Harde (FR) (Valanour (IRE)) [2017/18 b88: h15.8v^{F} h15.8v⁵ h16v³ Apr 14] bumper winner: modest form over hurdles: best effort when third in novice at Chepstow in April: tried in hood/tongue tie. *David Pipe* — h91

ILS

IL SASSICAIA 5 b.g. Dick Turpin (IRE) – Step Fast (USA) (Giant's Causeway (USA)) [2017/18 h–: h20.2g^{pu} May 17] modest maiden on Flat, stays 1¼m: no form over hurdles: tried in cheekpieces/tongue tie. *Jackie Stephen* — h–

IL SICARIO (IRE) 4 b.g. Zebedee – Starring (FR) (Ashkalani (IRE)) [2017/18 h16.8g^5 h17.7d h16.3s^2 h15.3g Oct 29] half-brother to fair hurdler Goodwood Starlight (2m/17f winner, by Mtoto): fair on Flat, stays 1¼m: modest form over hurdles: tried in headgear. *Bill Turner* — h92

IMADA (IRE) 8 br.g. Arcadio (GER) – Anck Su Namun (IRE) (Supreme Leader) [2017/18 h16.2s h16v^2 Mar 9] bumper winner: fair form over hurdles, lightly raced: should stay beyond 2m: acts on heavy going. *Nicky Richards* — h113

I'M A GAME CHANGER (IRE) 6 b.g. Arcadio (GER) – Drinadaly (IRE) (Oscar (IRE)) [2017/18 h132: h16.7g^6 h16d^5 h15.8d* h16g Apr 21] useful-looking gelding: useful handicap hurdler: won at Ludlow (by 2 lengths from Mister Universum) in April: raced around 2m: acts on soft going: often races towards rear. *Philip Hobbs* — h136

I'M ALWAYS TRYING (IRE) 5 b.g. Westerner – Pepsi Starlet (IRE) (Heavenly Manna) [2017/18 b15.8v^5 h15.8v^3 h20.5v^2 h23.3v^{pu} Apr 7] €57,000 3-y-o: brother to fairly useful hurdler/chaser Queens Wild (17f-2¾m winner), closely related to a winning pointer by Catcher In The Rye and half-brother to 3 winners, including fairly useful chaser The Phantom Piper (2½m winner, by Snurge); dam unraced: fifth in bumper at Ffos Las: modest form over hurdles: should stay 3m: tried in cheekpieces. *David Pipe* — h94 b73

I'M AN IZZ WIZZ (IRE) 10 ch.g. Desert King (IRE) – Lovely Native (IRE) (Be My Native (USA)) [2017/18 c23.5g^6 c19.2g* c20m^5 c20d* c20.1s^3 h24.4g^5 c21.4g* Sep 30] twice-raced hurdler: fairly useful handicap chaser: won at Downpatrick in June, Wexford in July and Market Rasen in September: stays 3m: acts on good to firm and heavy going. *Liam Lennon, Ireland* — c119 h–

I'M BRITISH 5 b.g. Aqlaam – Libritish (Librettist (USA)) [2017/18 b–: b15.8g^4 Jul 19] poor form in bumpers. *Sarah Humphrey* — b68

I'M IN CHARGE 12 b.g. Rakaposhi King – Cloudy Pearl (Cloudings (IRE)) [2017/18 c118, h103: h24v^3 Apr 27] workmanlike gelding: fair handicap hurdler: fairly useful chaser: stays 27f: acts on good to firm going: usually wears tongue tie, not sole outing in 2017/18: usually races nearer last than first. *Grant Cann* — c– h94

IMJOEKING (IRE) 11 b.g. Amilynx (FR) – Go Franky (IRE) (Hollow Hand) [2017/18 c130, h–: c15.8s^6 c21.1v^5 c16.2s^2 c16.5v* Mar 10] big gelding: winning hurdler: useful handicap chaser: won at Ayr (by neck from Monbeg River) in March: stays 2½m: acts on good to firm and heavy going: wears tongue tie: usually races close up. *Lucinda Russell* — c131 h–

IMPACT FACTOR (IRE) 6 b.g. Flemensfirth (USA) – Hello Kitty (IRE) (Houmayoun (FR)) [2017/18 h20v^2 h16d^2 h16v* h16s^2 h16.5s Apr 13] €41,000 4-y-o: sturdy gelding: first foal: dam (c116/h119) 2½m-23f hurdle/chase winner: useful form over hurdles: won maiden at Punchestown in January: stays 2½m: acts on heavy going. *Mrs J. Harrington, Ireland* — h132

IMPERIAL ACOLYTE 4 b.g. Kalanisi (IRE) – Isabello (IRE) (Presenting) [2017/18 b16.2s^5 Apr 27] €22,500 3-y-o: fourth foal: half-brother to bumper winner Odello (by King's Theatre): dam unraced half-sister to useful hurdler/chaser (stayed 3m) Banjaxed Girl: mid-field in bumper at Perth: should do better. *Nigel Twiston-Davies* — b64 p

IMPERIAL AURA (IRE) 5 b.g. Kalanisi (IRE) – Missindependence (IRE) (Executive Perk) [2017/18 b16s^3 b15.8d* Apr 24] €26,000 3-y-o: third foal: half-brother to fair hurdler/fairly useful chaser Pawn Star (2¾m-3m winner, by Beneficial): dam (h95) bumper winner: fair form in bumpers: won at Ludlow in April: will stay beyond 2m. *Kim Bailey* — b94

IMPERIAL CIRCUS (IRE) 12 b.g. Beneficial – Aunty Dawn (IRE) (Strong Gale) [2017/18 c23s^{pu} Jan 9] lengthy gelding: multiple point winner: winning hurdler: fairly useful chaser at best, pulled up in hunter sole outing under Rules in 2017/18: stays 31f: acts on good to firm and heavy going: has worn headgear: tried in tongue tie. *Richard Mitford-Slade* — c– h–

IMPERIAL ELIXIR (IRE) 5 b.g. Doyen (IRE) – Blond's Addition (IRE) (Lord Americo) [2017/18 b16.8g^6 b16.6d^5 Dec 1] €22,000 3-y-o: fifth foal: half-brother to fairly useful hurdler/winning pointer Steely Addition (21f-3m winner, by Craigsteel): dam unraced: modest form in bumpers: will stay further than 2m. *Fergal O'Brien* — b83

IMPERIAL ELOQUENCE (IRE) 6 b.g. Kalanisi (IRE) – Babble On (IRE) (Anita's Prince) [2017/18 b106: h19d^F h16.8g^4 h20s^2 h22v^5 h19.4s^4 Feb 3] rangy gelding: useful bumper performer: fair form over hurdles: best effort at 2½m: acts on soft going. *Fergal O'Brien* — h109

IND

IMPERIAL KNIGHT (IRE) 6 b.g. Mahler – And Whatever Else (IRE) (Bob Back (USA)) [2017/18 b15.8g b15.7d² Apr 21] first foal: dam (h104), 3m hurdle winner/winning pointer, half-sister to useful hurdler (stays 21f) Bags Groove: fair form when placed in bumpers. *Olly Murphy* **b92**

IMPERIAL NEMESIS (IRE) 5 b.g. Stowaway – Liss Alainn (IRE) (Flemensfirth (USA)) [2017/18 b15.8g b15.7v³ b16s h16.2s² Apr 26] €26,000 3-y-o: third foal: half-brother to smart hurdler/winning pointer Next Destination (19f-3m winner, by Dubai Destination): dam unraced half-sister to useful hurdler (stays 3m) Kilfenora: fair form in bumpers: 10/1, second in novice at Perth (2¾ lengths behind Asylo) on hurdling debut: will be suited by 2½m: likely to improve. *Nigel Twiston-Davies* **h104 p b86**

IMPERIAL PRESENCE (IRE) 7 ch.g. Presenting – Penneyrose Bay (Karinga Bay) [2017/18 c131, h–: c20g⁵ c16.4s² Mar 24] strong gelding: winning hurdler: useful handicap chaser: should stay beyond 2m: acts on good to soft going: tried in hood: front runner/races prominently. *Philip Hobbs* **c123 h–**

IMPERIAL PRINCE (IRE) 9 b.g. Subtle Power (IRE) – Satco Rose (IRE) (Satco (FR)) [2017/18 h24.3v^pu h24.3v c20.5v^pu c19.9s c20.1s³ Apr 26] hurdle winner at best, no form first 2 starts in 2017/18: modest form over fences: best effort when third in novice handicap at Perth in April: stays 23f: acts on heavy going. *Ian Duncan* **c94 h–**

IMPORTANT MOMENT (IRE) 9 b.g. Milan – Cuiloge Lady (IRE) (Beneficial) [2017/18 h112: h20.2g h20m⁴ Jun 23] point winner: fair form over hurdles, little impact in 2017/18: stays 3m: acts on soft going: in tongue tie last 4 starts. *Stuart Crawford, Ireland* **h85**

IMPULSIVE STAR (IRE) 8 b.g. Busy Flight – Impulsive Ita (IRE) (Supreme Leader) [2017/18 h132p: c25.2d^F c25.2s² c23.6v³ c31.8s⁴ Mar 13] well-made gelding: useful hurdler: similar form over fences: fourth to Rathvinden in National Hunt Chase at Cheltenham in March: stays 25f: acts on heavy going: in cheekpieces last 2 starts: front runner/races prominently. *Neil Mulholland* **c134 h–**

I'M STILL WAITING (IRE) 6 ch.g. Stowaway – Prima Dona Sivola (FR) (Apple Tree (FR)) [2017/18 h96, b–: h21d May 16] placed in point: maiden hurdler, modest form on standout effort: tried in hood: often races prominently. *Fergal O'Brien* **h–**

I'M TO BLAME (IRE) 5 b.g. Winged Love (IRE) – Swap Shop (IRE) (Lord Americo) [2017/18 b15.8d⁴ b15.6s* Jan 19] £30,000 3-y-o: brother to 2½m bumper winner/fairly useful 2¾m hurdle winner Showem Silver: dam unraced half-sister to useful hurdler/smart chaser (2m-2½m winner) Aran Concerto: fairly useful form in bumpers: won both starts, at Catterick in November and Musselburgh in January. *Keith Dalgleish* **b101**

INAJIFFY (IRE) 5 b.m. Mahler – Spirit of Clanagh (IRE) (Zagreb (USA)) [2017/18 b16.2g b16.8s Dec 26] €3,500 3-y-o: sturdy mare: second foal: dam unraced half-sister to useful hurdler/smart chaser (stayed 35f) Double Seven: no form in bumpers: in tongue tie second start. *George Bewley* **b–**

INAMINNA (IRE) 7 b.g. Oscar (IRE) – Amber Trix (IRE) (Scribano) [2017/18 b17.7g³ h19s⁴ h15.3v³ h15.6s* Apr 27] €22,000 6-y-o: first foal: dam (h100) bumper winner/maiden hurdler (stayed 2½m): Irish point winner: placed in bumper: fairly useful form over hurdles: won handicap at Chepstow in April: will go on improving. *Neil Mulholland* **h116 p b68**

INCHCOLM (IRE) 8 br.g. Presenting – Rose of Inchiquin (IRE) (Roselier (FR)) [2017/18 c83, h–: c26.2g² c24.2g² c24d^pu c24.2d⁶ c26.3s^pu c24.2s² c23.9v³ c25.2d^pu Feb 2] placed in Irish points: maiden hurdler: poor maiden chaser: stays 3¼m: acts on soft going: has worn headgear, including final start: tried in tongue tie: often races in rear: temperamental. *Micky Hammond* **c82 § h–**

INCH LALA (IRE) 6 ch.m. Mahler – Aboo Lala (IRE) (Aboo Hom) [2017/18 b78: h21s³ h20.5s h21.4v³ h19s⁵ h23.1v^pu Apr 17] placed in Irish point: fair form over hurdles: left Neil Mulholland after third start: should stay 3m: acts on heavy going: often leads. *Johnny Farrelly* **h100**

INCLUDED 6 b.m. Champs Elysees – Cordoba (Oasis Dream) [2017/18 h15.8g³ h16g* h17.2s³ Jul 22] fair on Flat, stays 1½m: modest form over hurdles: won maiden at Worcester in June: wears tongue tie. *David Dennis* **h97**

INCUS 5 b.g. Bertolini – Cloudchaser (IRE) (Red Ransom (USA)) [2017/18 h15.8v⁴ h16.7v Dec 15] fair on Flat, stays 2m: poor form over hurdles. *Ed de Giles* **h71**

INDEFATIGABLE (IRE) 5 b.m. Schiaparelli (GER) – Spin The Wheel (IRE) (Kalanisi (IRE)) [2017/18 b16v³ b15.7g* Apr 20] first foal: dam unraced: fair form in bumpers: won conditional/amateur maiden at Southwell (dead-heated) in April: left S. Curling after first start. *Paul Webber* **b89**

IND

INDIAN CASTLE (IRE) 10 b.g. Dr Massini (IRE) – Indian Legend (IRE) (Phardante (FR)) [2017/18 c132, h–: c25g² c25d⁶ c29.2s c24s^pu c25.7s⁴ Apr 15] tall gelding: winning hurdler: fairly useful handicap chaser: stays 3¼m: acts on heavy going: often wears headgear. *Ian Williams* — c125 h–

INDIAN HARBOUR 5 b.g. Indian Haven – Hawait Al Barr (Green Desert (USA)) [2017/18 b82: b15.7d⁴ h19.3s^ur h16.2d³ Apr 23] poor form in bumpers: fair form when third in novice at Hexham, completed start over hurdles. *Sally Haynes* — h109 b62

INDIAN HAWK (IRE) 6 b.g. Westerner – Yorkshire Girl (IRE) (Anshan) [2017/18 h21.2v* h24.4s h19s* h19.8v^pu h20d⁵ c21.7v² Apr 27] €36,000 3-y-o, £110,000 5-y-o: useful-looking gelding: first foal: dam, no form, half-sister to fairly useful hurdler/useful chaser (stayed 3m) Banasan: point winner: fairly useful form over hurdles: won maiden at Ludlow in January and novice at Warwick in February: 1/2, second in maiden at Towcester (7 lengths behind Malapie) on chasing debut: stays 2¾m: acts on heavy going: capable of better as a chaser. *Nicky Henderson* — c116 p h123

INDIAN HERCULES (IRE) 6 b.g. Whitmore's Conn (USA) – Carrawaystick (IRE) (Old Vic) [2017/18 b–p: h19.9d* h21.3s⁶ h21.7s⁵ h20.5v³ h19.5s³ Apr 27] Irish point winner: fairly useful form over hurdles: won maiden at Uttoxeter in November: third in novice at Chepstow in April: should stay 2¾m: acts on heavy going: often races prominently. *Warren Greatrex* — h119

INDIAN MONSOON (IRE) 6 b.g. Monsun (GER) – Madhya (USA) (Gone West (USA)) [2017/18 h20v h20v⁴ h20v² h16s Feb 3] fair maiden on Flat (stays 1¼m) for Sir Michael Stoute in 2015: useful hurdler: won novice at Cork in 2016/17: second in handicap there in January: stays 2½m: acts on heavy going: often wears headgear. *Charles Byrnes, Ireland* — h133

INDIAN NATIVE (IRE) 8 b.m. Oscar (IRE) – Roman Native (IRE) (Be My Native (USA)) [2017/18 h109, b80: c20d⁴ c20s⁴ c21.7s³ c20.2v^pu c19.8v² Mar 29] point winner: fair hurdler: similar form over fences: stays 3m: acts on heavy going: in tongue tie last 3 starts: often races prominently. *Alex Hales* — c109 h–

INDIAN OPERA 6 b.m. Indian Danehill (IRE) – Minouchka (FR) (Bulington (FR)) [2017/18 b15.6d² b15.7s² b17d⁴ Mar 25] first foal: dam (c110/h95) 2½m-3½m chase winner: refused on sole point outing: fair form in bumpers. *Iain Jardine* — b89

INDIAN REEL (IRE) 8 br.g. Indian River (FR) – Ceilidh Dancer (Scottish Reel) [2017/18 h93: h16g⁶ h19.9s h21.2g h16.8s⁴ h19v³ h19.7v⁶ h15.5v* h15.7v⁴ h25d² h25s³ Apr 15] point winner: modest hurdler: won novice claimer at Leicester in January: stays 25f: acts on heavy going: usually wears cheekpieces: in tongue tie last 4 starts. *Fergal O'Brien* — h95

INDIAN RUPEE (IRE) 9 b.g. Indian Danehill (IRE) – Get A Few Bob Back (IRE) (Bob Back (USA)) [2017/18 c104x, h104: c16.5m^pu c16.5g^F Jun 3] sturdy gelding: fair hurdler: maiden chaser, fair form at best: stays 2½m: acts on soft going: wears hood. *Dai Williams* — c80 h–

INDIAN STREAM 9 ch.m. Generous (IRE) – Zaffarimbi (IRE) (Zaffaran (USA)) [2017/18 c143, h141: c23.6d h24.2v^pu h19.9s⁴ h20.3g Apr 19] lengthy, workmanlike mare: useful handicap hurdler: useful chaser, well held on return in 2017/18: stays 3m: acts on soft going: wears tongue tie: often races prominently. *Neil Mulholland* — c– h133

INDIAN TEMPLE (IRE) 9 b.g. Indian River (FR) – Ballycraggan (IRE) (Beneficial) [2017/18 c131, h–: c25g⁵ c20.1m* c20.1d³ c19.4d⁵ c19.9d³ c21.1s Apr 13] workmanlike gelding: maiden hurdler: useful handicap chaser: won at Perth (by 3½ lengths from Brave Spartacus) in June: stays 2¾m: acts on good to firm and heavy going: tried in cheekpieces: usually leads. *Tim Reed* — c132 h–

INDIAN VISION (IRE) 4 ch.g. Iffraaj – Sweet Fairnando (Hernando (FR)) [2017/18 h16.8g³ h15.7d⁵ h15.6d⁵ Jan 1] modest maiden on Flat, stays 1¼m: similar form over hurdles. *Micky Hammond* — h94

INDIAN VOYAGE (IRE) 10 b.g. Indian Haven – Voyage of Dreams (USA) (Riverman (USA)) [2017/18 c123, h–: c17.3d⁴ c20.1g⁴ c20.1m⁶ c17.2g⁵ c17.1g³ c16.5d⁵ c24.2v^pu c21.1g* c20.1v⁴ c19.3g^pu c15.9d⁵ c20d c16.4g⁴ Apr 23] strong gelding: maiden hurdler: fair handicap chaser nowadays: won at Sedgefield in October: stays 21f: acts on good to firm and heavy going: wears tongue tie: often races prominently: unreliable. *Maurice Barnes* — c111 § h–

INDIGO ISLAND (IRE) 9 b.g. Trans Island – Go Indigo (IRE) (Cyrano de Bergerac) [2017/18 c20.3v^pu Feb 9] point winner: modest maiden hurdler: maiden chaser, pulled up sole outing under Rules in 2017/18: stays 2½m: acts on heavy going: has worn cheekpieces/tongue tie. *R. A. Owen* — c– h–

400

INDIGO STAMP 7 b.g. Rainbow High – Philatelic Lady (IRE) (Pips Pride) [2017/18 b15.3s b16v h18.5v^{pu} h15.3s^6 h19s^6 h15.3d Apr 22] has had breathing operation: well beaten in bumpers: little form over hurdles. *Mark Gillard* — h75, b–

INDIROCCO (GER) 5 ch.g. Shirocco (GER) – Indigo Girl (GER) (Sternkoenig (IRE)) [2017/18 h105P: h19.3s^6 h21d^4 Apr 26] good-topped gelding: fair form over hurdles. *Dan Skelton* — h108

INDY FIVE (IRE) 8 b.g. Vertical Speed (FR) – Beesplease (IRE) (Snurge) [2017/18 h115: h21.6v c23s* c23.4s^F c23.4v* c24.1v^2 c31.8g^F Apr 21] winning hurdler: useful form over fences: won novice handicaps at Taunton in December and Newbury in February: second in handicap at Ayr in March: should stay long distances: acts on heavy going: front runner/races prominently. *David Dennis* — c137, h–

INDY ISLAND (IRE) 9 gr.m. Indian Danehill (IRE) – Another Sparkle (Bustino) [2017/18 c–, h97: c24d^4 c20g^{pu} c21.6d^{pu} Nov 19] point winner: modest hurdler: similar form over fences: stays 3m: acts on soft going: tried in cheekpieces. *Charlie Longsdon* — c95, h–

IN FAIRNESS (IRE) 9 b.g. Oscar (IRE) – Dix Huit Brumaire (FR) (General Assembly (USA)) [2017/18 c96, h–: c24.2m^2 May 9] tall, useful-looking gelding: placed in point: winning hurdler: maiden chaser nowadays: stays 3m: acts on soft going. *E. Turner* — c94, h–

INFINITE SUN 7 b.g. And Beyond (IRE) – Kingussie Flower (Scottish Reel) [2017/18 b94: h18.6d^6 h20.6g^3 Apr 22] good-topped gelding: chasing type: bumper winner: fair form over hurdles: better effort when third in novice at Market Rasen in April: in tongue tie last 3 starts: held up. *Fergal O'Brien* — h101

IN FOCUS (IRE) 7 ch.g. Intense Focus (USA) – Reine de Neige (Kris) [2017/18 h16.4g Nov 17] modest on Flat, stays 2m: in hood, 40/1, dropped away quickly in novice on hurdling debut. *Dianne Sayer* — h–

INFORMATEUR (FR) 5 b.g. Maresca Sorrento (FR) – Isarella (GER) (Second Set (IRE)) [2017/18 h15.7v^2 b16v h19.3v^3 Apr 17] fifth foal: dam, 2m/2¼m hurdle winner in Italy, also 7f/1m winner on Flat in Germany: fair form in bumpers: 14/1, third in novice at Carlisle (9½ lengths behind Duke Debarry) on hurdling debut: open to improvement. *Sue Smith* — h100 p, b87

INGLEBY HOLLOW 6 ch.g. Beat Hollow – Mistress Twister (Pivotal) [2017/18 h16.6s^5 h16.8v^3 Feb 22] fair on Flat, stays 2m: modest form over hurdles: better effort when third in novice at Sedgefield in February: wears tongue tie: open to further improvement. *David O'Meara* — h93 p

INHERITANCE THIEF 6 b.g. Black Sam Bellamy (IRE) – Red And White (IRE) (Red Ransom (USA)) [2017/18 b15.8m^2 b16.7d^2 b16.7s^2 Apr 22] second foal: closely related to modest hurdler Pink Tara (2½m winner, by Kayf Tara): dam (h96), maiden hurdler (best around 2m), 6f winner on Flat: fair form in bumpers. *Venetia Williams* — b93

INIESTA (IRE) 7 b.g. Galileo (IRE) – Red Evie (IRE) (Intikhab (USA)) [2017/18 h16.8d^2 h23.3g^6 h18.5d h16.3g* h15.8g^3 h15.8g^2 h15.5v^2 h19.5s^3 h18.5s^2 Apr 23] sturdy gelding: fair hurdler: won seller at Stratford in October: left Fergal O'Brien after sixth start: stays 2¼m: acts on soft going: wears headgear: front runner/races prominently. *Michael Blake* — h103

INIS MEAIN (USA) 11 b.g. Bernstein (USA) – Runaway Fields (USA) (Runaway Groom (CAN)) [2017/18 c16.3v^3 c23s^3 c20d c30.2g^6 c17s^3 c19.5v^4 c20s^3 c16.2v^4 c22v c16.7s^3 Apr 17] well-made gelding: winning hurdler: useful maiden chaser: third in Grade 3 novices at Roscommon (length behind Landofhopeandglory) in September and Navan (7¼ lengths behind Tombstone) in December: stays 3m: acts on heavy going: tried in cheekpieces: has worn tongue tie: often leads. *Denis Hogan, Ireland* — c131, h–

INK MASTER (IRE) 8 b.g. Whitmore's Conn (USA) – Welsh Connection (IRE) (Welsh Term) [2017/18 c129, h–: c19.2m^2 c16.5g* c16.5g^6 c16.5g^{pu} h16.8g^3 h19.9g^6 c15.8s h16.6d c15.7s^5 c15.8s^5 Feb 3] workmanlike gelding: fair handicap hurdler: fairly useful handicap chaser: won at Worcester in June: left Philip Hobbs after fourth start: unproven beyond 2m: acts on good to firm and good to soft going: wears hood: in tongue tie last 2 starts: front runner. *Donald McCain* — c128, h112

INNER DRIVE (IRE) 10 b.g. Heron Island (IRE) – Hingis (IRE) (Shernazar) [2017/18 c–, h131: h20d^4 Oct 29] point winner: useful form over hurdles, very lightly raced: once-raced chaser: stays 21f: acts on soft going. *Alan King* — c–, h132

INNISCASTLE LAD 6 b.g. Kyllachy – Glencal (Compton Place) [2017/18 h16.7d^5 h16.8g^2 h16.4g^3 h16.8s^4 h15.7s h16.2s^4 ab16.3g^3 h17s^3 Apr 8] fairly useful on Flat, stays 10.5f: fair maiden hurdler: raced mainly around 2m: best form on good going: tried in blinkers. *Donald McCain* — h102

INN

INNISFREE LAD (IRE) 6 b.g. Yeats (IRE) – Tasmani (FR) (Turgeon (USA)) [2017/18 h–, b83: h15.8s h19.9d h23.9s[5] h23.3v[*] h24.4s[3] h25s[2] h21.4v[3] h25d Apr 24] rather unfurnished gelding: fair handicap hurdler: won at Uttoxeter in December: stays 25f: acts on heavy going. *David Dennis* — **h113**

INNIS SHANNON (IRE) 8 br.m. Stowaway – Put On Hold (IRE) (Lord Americo) [2017/18 c–x, h69x: h24.1d[pu] Mar 29] modest hurdler at best, little form since 2015/16: no form in chases: stays 2½m: acts on heavy going: tried in cheekpieces: usually races in rear: often let down by jumping. *George Bewley* — **c–**, **h– x**

INNOCENT GIRL (IRE) 9 b.m. King's Theatre (IRE) – Belle Innocence (FR) (Turgeon (USA)) [2017/18 c113, h88: h18.7m[3] c19.2g[2] h16.8d[2] c21g[2] Sep 2] sturdy mare: modest handicap hurdler: fairly useful handicap chaser: second at Newton Abbot in September: stays 21f: acts on firm and good to soft going: wears hood/tongue tie: usually races nearer last than first, often travels strongly. *Harry Fry* — **c117**, **h96**

INNOCENT TOUCH (IRE) 7 bl.g. Intense Focus (USA) – Guajira (FR) (Mtoto) [2017/18 h16.8g Apr 18] useful on Flat around 1½m: lightly-raced hurdler, fair form at best. *Henry Daly* — **h–**

INNOX PARK 8 b.g. Helissio (FR) – Redgrave Bay (Karinga Bay) [2017/18 h20m[pu] Jul 5] little form: often in cheekpieces. *Kevin Bishop* — **h–**

INN THE BULL (GER) 5 ch.g. Lope de Vega (IRE) – Ile Rousse (Danehill (USA)) [2017/18 h100p: h16d[4] h15.8g[3] h16d[3] h19s[pu] h15.8d[4] Dec 20] fairly useful on Flat, stays 1¾m: fair form over hurdles: won handicap at Worcester in September: should stay beyond 2m: acts on good to firm and good to soft going. *Alan King* — **h112**

IN ON THE ACT 8 b.g. Act One – Pequenita (Rudimentary (USA)) [2017/18 c82, h117: c16g[3] c19.4m[6] c17.8m[F] h16.8m[6] h15.8g[6] Sep 13] fair handicap hurdler at best: modest maiden chaser: stayed 21f: acted on good to soft going: tried in headgear: in tongue tie last 4 starts: often let down by jumping over fences: dead. *Evan Williams* — **c88 x**, **h66**

IN OUR BLOOD (IRE) 8 b.g. Oratorio (IRE) – Ruff Shod (USA) (Storm Boot (USA)) [2017/18 h16s h16d h16s h19.3v[3] h16v h20.5v[ur] Jan 2] fair maiden on Flat, stays 13f: poor form over hurdles: tried in cheekpieces. *Neil McKnight, Ireland* — **h83**

INSIGHT (IRE) 7 b.m. Bushranger (IRE) – Ribbon Glade (UAE) (Zafonic (USA)) [2017/18 h82: h22.1m[2] h20.3g[F] Jun 13] poor maiden hurdler: dead. *Lucinda Egerton* — **h84**

INSPIREUS (IRE) 5 b.g. Scorpion (IRE) – Miniconjou (IRE) (Be My Native (USA)) [2017/18 h15.9v[4] h18.5s[4] h21.4v[*] Mar 28] €7,500 3-y-o: seventh foal: half-brother to useful hurdler Thehillofuisneach (21f-25f winner, by Flemensfirth) and fairly useful/temperamental hurdler/chaser An Poc Ar Buile (19f-3m winner, by Mountain High): dam (h65) maiden hurdler: modest form over hurdles: should stay 21f. *Seamus Mullins* — **h90**

INSTANT ATTRACTION (IRE) 7 b.g. Tagula (IRE) – Coup de Coeur (IRE) (Kahyasi) [2017/18 h15.8d[5] Mar 26] half-brother to modest hurdler Wee Sonny (2m winner, by Refuse To Bend): useful at best on Flat, stays 8.5f: 8/1, shaped like non-stayer when fifth in maiden at Huntingdon on hurdling debut. *Jedd O'Keeffe* — **h94**

INSTANT KARMA (IRE) 7 b.g. Peintre Celebre (USA) – Kotdiji (Mtoto) [2017/18 h129: h16.3g[6] h16.4g Oct 27] rather leggy gelding: fairly useful hurdler at best, no form in 2017/18: left Michael Bell after first start: stays 2¼m: acts on soft and good to firm going: tried in tongue tie. *Jamie Snowden* — **h–**

INSTANT REPLAY (IRE) 6 ch.g. Fruits of Love (USA) – Ding Dong Belle (Minster Son) [2017/18 h–, b89: h20.9d h16s[6] h19.9s[4] c19.3s[*] c21.1v[*] c19.3v[2] c24.5d[F] Mar 25] modest form over hurdles: fairly useful form over fences: won novice handicaps at Sedgefield in January and February: will stay long distances: best form on soft/heavy going: often travels strongly. *Brian Ellison* — **c122**, **h93**

INSTINGTIVE (IRE) 7 b.g. Scorpion (IRE) – Fully Focused (IRE) (Rudimentary (USA)) [2017/18 c97, h65: h23.9d[5] h23.9s c20.1v[ur] h19.3v h16.8d h19v h16.4v[4] h16v[3] h16v[*] h17v[*] h19.7v[5] h17s[4] Apr 8] tall gelding: modest handicap hurdler: won at Ayr in February and Carlisle (novice) in March: winning chaser: unproven beyond 17f: best form on heavy going: tried in blinkers: has worn tongue tie: usually leads. *Lisa Harrison* — **c–**, **h87**

INTENSE TANGO 7 b.m. Mastercraftsman (IRE) – Cover Look (SAF) (Fort Wood (USA)) [2017/18 h123: h16d h16s[4] h18.9v[pu] Nov 25] useful hurdler at best, little impact in 2017/18: raced mainly around 2m: acts on good to soft going: in cheekpieces last 2 starts, tongue tied last 5: races prominently. *K. R. Burke* — **h98**

IOL

IN THE BUFF (IRE) 5 b.g. Fastnet Rock (AUS) – Sliabh Na Mban (IRE) (Sadler's Wells (USA)) [2017/18 b16.7g Jun 23] tailed off in bumper. *Tony Coyle* — b–

INTHEDEAL 4 b.g. Multiplex – Chebsey Belle (IRE) (Karinga Bay) [2017/18 b16.2v ab16.3g^{pu} ab16.3g^6 Mar 3] no form in bumpers. *Tim Easterby* — b–

IN THE HOLD (IRE) 8 b.g. Stowaway – Carrigeen Kerria (IRE) (Kemal (FR)) [2017/18 c25.2d* h23.9v^6 Mar 12] point winner: modest maiden hurdler: fair form over fences: won handicap at Catterick in February: stays 25f: acts on good to soft going. *Evan Williams* — c104 h83

IN THE PIPELINE (IRE) 5 b.g. Oscar (IRE) – Kerriemuir Lass (IRE) (Celtic Swing) [2017/18 b17.7s^5 Dec 18] well held in bumper. *Brendan Powell* — b–

IN THE ROUGH (IRE) 9 b.g. Scorpion (IRE) – Sounds Charming (IRE) (Presenting) [2017/18 c132, h–: c24d* c26.1m^3 Jul 2] workmanlike gelding: winning handicap chaser: won at Uttoxeter in May: third in Summer Cup there in July: stays 3¼m: acts on good to firm and heavy going: in cheekpieces last 2 starts. *Jonjo O'Neill* — c128 h–

IN THE TUB (IRE) 9 b.g. Kutub (IRE) – County Classic (Noble Patriarch) [2017/18 c–: h23.6v h21.6v^{pu} c19.4v^{pu} Jan 19] point winner: no form under Rules: tried in blinkers/tongue tie. *Carroll Gray* — c– h–

INTIFADAH (IRE) 6 b.g. Intikhab (USA) – Cuilaphuca (IRE) (Danetime (IRE)) [2017/18 h100: h20.3g h16.8s^{pu} h15.8g^4 h20g c17.4g c16.5g^6 Sep 3] compact gelding: fair handicap hurdler, below form in 2017/18: no form over fences: stays 2¼m: best form on good going: wears headgear/tongue tie: usually races nearer last than first: has joined Dan Skelton. *Tom Symonds* — c– h80

INTO THE BREACH (FR) 5 b.g. Al Namix (FR) – Arvicaya (Kahyasi) [2017/18 b16.6d b16.2v Jan 25] no form in bumpers. *James Ewart* — b–

INVESTIGATION 4 gr.g. Rip Van Winkle (IRE) – Syann (IRE) (Daylami (IRE)) [2017/18 h15.7s^6 h16v^{pu} ab16g^{rr} Mar 2] regressive on Flat: no form over hurdles: temperamental (refused to race in jumpers bumper). *Shaun Harris* — h– §

INVICTA LAKE (IRE) 11 b.g. Dr Massini (IRE) – Classic Material (Classic Cliche (IRE)) [2017/18 h25d h20.5s^4 h21.6d^5 c25.7v^3 c23s^F c25.7d^{ur} c24s^2 c25.1v^{pu} c25.7s^{ur} Apr 15] sturdy gelding: fair handicap hurdler: fair maiden chaser: stays 3¼m: acts on heavy going: wears cheekpieces. *Suzy Smith* — c108 h105

INVICTUS (GER) 6 b.g. Exceed And Excel (AUS) – Ivowen (USA) (Theatrical) [2017/18 h72: h15.8d^{pu} Oct 8] fair on Flat: maiden hurdler, little impact since 2015/16: raced around 2m: in headgear last 2 starts: often races freely. *David Loughnane* — h–

INVISIBLE CLOUDS (IRE) 5 gr.g. Cloudings (IRE) – Go My Dream (Tirol) [2017/18 b16.6d Dec 1] 13/2, held back by inexperience in bumper at Doncaster. *Warren Greatrex* — b–

INVISIBLE MAN (FR) 13 ch.g. Mansonnien (FR) – J'y Reste (FR) (Freedom Cry) [2017/18 c85, h–: c23g^4 c22.6d^3 Jun 9] gelding: multiple point winner: lightly-raced chaser nowadays: modest chaser nowadays: stays 3m: acts on soft and good to firm going: tried in cheekpieces: wears tongue tie. *Alastair Ralph* — c96 h–

INVITATION ONLY (IRE) 7 b.g. Flemensfirth (USA) – Norabelle (FR) (Alamo Bay (USA)) [2017/18 h15, b–: c20s* c20s^F c20v* c21s^3 c19.9s^{pu} c20v^3 c24.5s^{ur} Apr 24] sturdy gelding: winning hurdler: smart chaser: won maiden at Navan (by 4¼ lengths from Any Second Now) in December and Grade 3 novice at Punchestown (by 2½ lengths from Koshari) in January: third in Flogas Novices' Chase at Leopardstown (¾ length behind Monalee) in February and Ryanair Gold Cup Novices' Chase at Fairyhouse (8 lengths behind Al Boum Photo) in April: should stay beyond 21f: acts on heavy going: usually races close up. *W. P. Mullins, Ireland* — c154 h–

INVOLVE 4 b.g. Dansili – Popular (Oasis Dream) [2017/18 b13.7g b16.2s^6 h16s h15.8d Apr 24] poor form in bumpers: no form over hurdles. *Kim Bailey* — h– b67

IOLANI (GER) 6 b.g. Sholokhov (IRE) – Imogen (GER) (Tiger Hill (IRE)) [2017/18 b17.3g* h20d^3 h18.8g^2 h20.2g^F h16v^6 h18.9v h19.9s h19.3s h19.9v^4 h22v^{pu} Apr 14] first foal: dam German 1m winner: fairly useful form on Flat, winner at 1¾m: fairly useful form in bumpers: won maiden at Downpatrick in May: fair maiden hurdler: left W. P. Mullins after sixth start: barely stays 2½m: acts on heavy going: has worn tongue tie, including last 2 starts (when also in headgear). *Dianne Sayer* — h110 b103

ION

IONA DAYS (IRE) 13 br.g. Epistolaire (IRE) – Miss Best (FR) (Grand Tresor (FR)) [2017/18 c99, h–: c20.5g* c20.3d³ c21.4d² c19.7v³ Apr 1] tall gelding: lightly-raced hurdler: modest handicap chaser: won at Kempton in May: stays 3m: acts on good to firm and heavy going: usually wears headgear. *Julian Smith*   **c95 h–**

IORA GLAS (IRE) 9 gr.g. Court Cave (IRE) – Crossdrumrosie (IRE) (Roselier (FR)) [2017/18 c111, h118: h24.7g³ c24.1d* c23.8mᵖᵘ Jul 21] fairly useful handicap hurdler, below form on return in 2017/18: fairly useful handicap chaser: won at Bangor in June: stays 27f: acts on good to firm and heavy going: tried in cheekpieces: wears tongue tie. *Fergal O'Brien*   **c115 h95**

IOWEU 5 b.m. Cockney Rebel (IRE) – Doliouchka (Saumarez) [2017/18 ab16g Dec 5] half-sister to several winners on Flat, including useful French 1¼m-1f5f winner Hockney (by Zafonic): dam French 9f winner: 50/1, last of 7 in bumper at Lingfield. *Brian Barr*   **b–**

IPFLIBBYDIBBY (IRE) 6 b.g. Morozov (USA) – Sahara Storm (IRE) (Desert Prince (IRE)) [2017/18 b15.8g³ b16.8d b17.7g⁵ Aug 24] poor form in bumpers: in hood last 2 starts. *Sam Thomas*   **b71**

IRISH CAVALIER (IRE) 9 gr.g. Aussie Rules (USA) – Tracker (Bustino) [2017/18 c159, h–: c21mᵖᵘ Jun 16] good-topped gelding: winning hurdler: top-class chaser at best, won Charlie Hall Chase at Wetherby in 2016/17: stayed 3¼m: acted on heavy going: usually wore headgear: in tongue tie last 2 starts: usually raced towards rear: dead. *Rebecca Curtis*   **c– h–**

IRISH HAWKE (IRE) 6 b.g. Montjeu (IRE) – Ahdaab (USA) (Rahy (USA)) [2017/18 h94: h15.8m h20g⁶ h21.2g* h19.6g⁴ h22.7g h19.3d² Dec 19] modest handicap hurdler: won at Sedgefield in August: stays 21f: acts on good to soft going: tried in blinkers: wears tongue tie: often races towards rear. *Donald McCain*   **h89**

IRISH LEGIONNAIRE (IRE) 7 b.g. Kalanisi (IRE) – Harifana (FR) (Kahyasi) [2017/18 b16.3d³ Jun 9] placed on completed starts in points: modest form in bumpers. *Richard J. Bandey*   **b79**

IRISH OCTAVE (IRE) 8 b.g. Gamut (IRE) – Fairytaleofnewyork (IRE) (Zaffaran (USA)) [2017/18 c–, h64§: c23g* c22.5d* c24s* c24d⁴ c23.5vᵖ Jan 30] maiden hurdler: modest handicap chaser: won at Worcester in September and Uttoxeter (twice) in October: stays 3m: acts on heavy going: wears headgear: often races towards rear. *Rosemary Gasson*   **c93 h–**

IRISH ODYSSEY (IRE) 5 gr.g. Yeats (IRE) – Ma Furie (FR) (Balleroy (USA)) [2017/18 b17.7s* b17.7s Apr 15] fifth foal: closely related to useful hurdler/smart chaser King's Odyssey (2½m/21f winner) and bumper winner Queen Odessa (both by King's Theatre): dam (c122/h110) 2m-2½m hurdle/chase winner: fairly useful form in bumpers: won at Fontwell in March. *Neil Mulholland*   **b96**

IRISH PRINCE (IRE) 5 b.g. Presenting – Court Leader (IRE) (Supreme Leader) [2017/18 b16.3d b16.2g⁵ b16.3v⁵ h16.5s⁵ h16.5s Feb 20] €70,000 3-y-o: compact gelding: sixth foal: half-brother to smart bumper winner/hurdler Paloma Blue (2m winner, by Stowaway): dam (c123/h110), 2m-2½m hurdle/chase winner, sister to fairly useful hurdler/useful chaser (stayed 2¾m) Mount Sandel: modest form in bumpers: well held over hurdles: type to do better in handicaps. *David Pipe*   **h– p b75**

IRISH PROPHECY (IRE) 5 b.g. Azamour (IRE) – Prophets Honor (FR) (Highest Honor (FR)) [2017/18 b101: h16s* h16.6d² h16d⁶ h15.3d⁴ Apr 22] tall, good sort: unbeaten in 2 bumpers: fairly useful form over hurdles: won maiden at Sandown in November. *Emma Lavelle*   **h121**

IRISH ROE (IRE) 7 b.m. Vinnie Roe (IRE) – Betty's The Best (IRE) (Oscar (IRE)) [2017/18 b102: h15.7g* h17.2g* h16d² h16.6d* h16.6d⁴ h16.6s² h16.3vᵖᵘ h16g⁶ Apr 21] small, sparely-made mare: bumper winner: useful hurdler: won mares novices at Southwell in May and Cartmel in July, and handicaps at Doncaster (twice, intermediate event second occasion) in December: second in Doncaster Mares' Hurdle (¾ length behind Maria's Benefit) in January: raced around 2m: acts on soft going: usually travels strongly. *Peter Atkinson*   **h136**

IRISH THISTLE (IRE) 11 b.g. Luso – Which Thistle (IRE) (Saddlers' Hall (IRE)) [2017/18 c101x, h–: c20g⁴ c26.1g⁶ c21g³ c20g⁴ c17g⁴ c19.4g⁶ c16v⁴ c19.2vᵖᵘ c17.8g⁶ Apr 20] workmanlike gelding: winning hurdler: fair handicap chaser, largely below form in 2017/18: stays 23f: acts on good to firm and heavy going: has worn headgear, including in 2017/18: has worn tongue tie. *Dai Williams*   **c93 h–**

IRIS'S PROMISE 6 gr.m. Black Sam Bellamy (IRE) – Cheeky Mare (Derrylin) [2017/18 b–: h19.3m⁴ h22.1dᵖᵘ h15.8g h19.7vᵖᵘ Feb 20] no form over hurdles. *Jennie Candlish*   **h–**

IRON CHANCELLOR (IRE) 13 b.g. Alderbrook – Masriyna (IRE) (Shahrastani (USA)) [2017/18 c109, h–: c26.3d^{pu} May 5] lengthy gelding: multiple point winner: maiden hurdler: fair hunter chaser, pulled up sole outing under Rules in 2017/18: stays 3¼m: acts on heavy going: has worn headgear: temperamental. *Mrs Sue Popham* c– §
h–

IRONDALE EXPRESS 7 b.m. Myboycharlie (IRE) – Olindera (GER) (Lomitas) [2017/18 h89: h16v^6 h15.3v^2 h16v^5 Jan 30] modest maiden hurdler: raced around 2m: acts on heavy going: has worn cheekpieces: temperamental. *Barry Brennan* h84 §

IRON HORSE 7 b.g. Kayf Tara – What A Vintage (IRE) (Un Desperado (FR)) [2017/18 b65: h19.9v^3 Mar 17] well held in bumper: 25/1, third in novice at Uttoxeter (13¾ lengths behind Just Don't Ask) on hurdling debut. *Richard Phillips* h105

IRON IN THE SOUL 6 ch.g. Sulamani (IRE) – Go Classic (Classic Cliche (IRE)) [2017/18 b15.8g^4 b16.7g^5 h20g Jul 10] modest form in bumpers: tailed off in novice on hurdling debut. *Lucy Wadham* h–
b77

IRVING 10 b.g. Singspiel (IRE) – Indigo Girl (GER) (Sternkoenig (IRE)) [2017/18 h153: h16.4v^2 h19s^6 Jan 20] sturdy gelding: smart hurdler, below best both starts in 2017/18: raced around 2m: acts on heavy going: tried in cheekpieces/tongue tie. *Paul Nicholls* h138

ISAACSTOWN LAD (IRE) 11 b.g. Milan – Friends of Friends (IRE) (Phardante (FR)) [2017/18 c–, h125: h24.3v^3 h22.8v^F h22.8v^3 h22.8v^3 h24.1v^4 Mar 20] sturdy gelding: Irish point winner: fairly useful handicap hurdler: placed sole chase outing: stays 3¼m: acts on heavy going: tried in cheekpieces. *Nicky Richards* c–
h127

I SEE YOU WELL (FR) 5 b.g. Air Chief Marshal (IRE) – Bonne Mere (FR) (Stepneyev (IRE)) [2017/18 h114, b84: h20.5g* c16.3g^5 c18.8g^5 c15.7s^3 c16.8d^3 h21.7v^3 h19.2s^6 h21.7d h16.8v^5 Apr 8] compact gelding: fairly useful handicap hurdler: won at Plumpton (conditional) in May: fair form over fences: stays 2½m: acts on soft going. *Seamus Mullins* c113
h118

ISHARAH (USA) 5 b.g. Kitten's Joy (USA) – Menekineko (USA) (Kingmambo (USA)) [2017/18 h18s h19.9g Apr 23] useful on Flat, stays 16.5f: poor form over hurdles. *Noel C. Kelly, Ireland* h72

I SHOT THE SHERIFF (IRE) 11 b.g. Westerner – Sherin (GER) (Surumu (GER)) [2017/18 h128: h24.2d^{pu} h21s^{pu} Jan 13] useful-looking gelding: useful hurdler at best, no form in 2017/18: stays 2¾m: acts on heavy going: usually wears tongue tie. *Fergal O'Brien* h–

I SHOULD COCO 5 b.m. With The Flow (USA) – Follow The Dream (Double Trigger (IRE)) [2017/18 b16.8m^5 b16.8g^4 b16.3d^6 Sep 9] first foal: dam (b61), unplaced in bumpers, 1¾m-2¼m winner on Flat, half-sister to smart hurdler/chaser (stays 25f) Henryville: modest form in bumpers: little impact on Flat. *Karen George* b78

ISIS BLUE 8 b.g. Cockney Rebel (IRE) – Bramaputra (IRE) (Choisir (AUS)) [2017/18 h15.9d^4 h16v^3 h16.8v Apr 17] fair on Flat, stays 11f: modest form on standout effort over hurdles: left Neil Mulholland after second start: tried in tongue tie. *Keiran Burke* h96

ISKABEG LANE (IRE) 7 b.g. Westerner – Nosey Oscar (IRE) (Oscar (IRE)) [2017/18 h88: h15.8d^3 h16.2g c24.2s^{pu} c21.4d* c21.4s^3 c21.4v^3 c25.2d^2 c21.4v^F c20v^5 Mar 17] workmanlike gelding: fair form over hurdles: fair handicap chaser: won at Market Rasen in December: stays 25f: acts on heavy going: usually leads. *Sue Smith* c107
h100

ISKRABOB 8 ch.g. Tobougg (IRE) – Honour Bolton (Past Glories) [2017/18 h21.4s^{pu} c24.2d^{ur} c26g^5 Apr 20] workmanlike gelding: point winner: pulled up in novice on hurdling debut: little show in novice chases: left Neil Mulholland after first start. *Diana Grissell* c–
h–

ISLAND HEIGHTS (IRE) 9 b.g. Heron Island (IRE) – La Reina (IRE) (Executive Perk) [2017/18 c94, h121: h23.3v^4 Oct 14] compact gelding: fairly useful handicap hurdler, well below form sole outing in 2017/18: winning chaser: stays 25f: acts on heavy going: tried in visor. *Lucinda Russell* c–
h80

ISLAND RENDEZVOUS (IRE) 8 b.g. Trans Island – Verlaya (FR) (Vertical Speed (FR)) [2017/18 h89, b–: h22g^5 c24g^{ur} Jul 19] poor maiden hurdler: unseated ninth on chasing debut: in hood/tongue tie last 4 starts. *Jeremy Scott* c–
h63

ISLE OF EWE 7 b.m. Kayf Tara – Apple Town (Warning) [2017/18 h117p, b85: h18.6s^6 h21.3d^F Mar 29] fairly useful form over hurdles: in control when fell fatally last in handicap at Wetherby. *Tom Lacey* h120

ISLEOFHOPENDREAMS 11 b.g. Flemensfirth (USA) – Cool Island (IRE) (Turtle Island (IRE)) [2017/18 c136p, h126: h24s^{pu} c25v^{pu} c28.7v^2 c29v^2 c30s^2 Apr 28] winning hurdler: useful form over fences: second in handicap at Punchestown (1½ lengths behind Folsom Blue) in February and Irish Grand National Chase at Fairyhouse (head behind General Principle) in April: stays 3¾m: acts on heavy going. *W. P. Mullins, Ireland* c143
h–

ISL

ISLE ROAD (IRE) 9 b.g. Heron Island (IRE) – Corries Rein (IRE) (Anshan) [2017/18 c22.1g³ c23.6s^pu c16.5d Mar 26] point winner: maiden hurdler: modest form in chases: best effort when third in hunter at Downpatrick in May: left Jason Cairns after first start: stays 2¾m. *John David Riches* — c87 h–

IS LOVE ALIVE 9 ch.g. Presenting – Lovely Origny (FR) (Robin des Champs (FR)) [2017/18 c102, h–: c25.2s^pu c24.1d⁵ Apr 21] point winner: winning hurdler: fair maiden chaser, well below form in 2017/18: stays 3m: acts on soft going: has worn headgear: wears tongue tie. *Adrian Wintle* — c66 h–

ISTIMRAAR (IRE) 7 b.g. Dansili – Manayer (IRE) (Sadler's Wells (USA)) [2017/18 c–, h101: h21.6g h17.7d h18.7g⁵ h16.7g h20g Jul 18] fair handicap hurdler, well below best in 2017/18: twice-raced chaser: stays 2½m: acts on heavy going: has worn headgear, including last 4 starts: has worn tongue tie: has joined Dan Skelton. *Alexandra Dunn* — c– h56

ITCHY FEET (FR) 4 b.g. Cima de Triomphe (IRE) – Maeva Candas (FR) (Brier Creek (USA)) [2017/18 b13.7g² Apr 20] sixth foal: half-brother to French 19f chase winners Bandit d'Agrostis (by Discover d'Auteuil) and Dakota d'Agrostis (by Libourne): dam unraced: 10/3, second in bumper at Fontwell (3¼ lengths behind Kalinihta). *Olly Murphy* — b91

IT'LL DO RIGHTLY (IRE) 10 b.g. Westerner – Daring Hen (IRE) (Henbit (USA)) [2017/18 h19.3d* h19.9s³ Jan 12] half-brother to fairly useful hurdler/useful chaser Daring Article (2½m-3m winner, by Definite Article): dam, bumper winner, half-sister to high-class hurdler (2m-2¼m winner) Colonel Yeager: Irish point winner: fair form over hurdles: won novice at Catterick in December: will stay beyond 2½m. *Mrs Caroline McCaldin, Ireland* — h109

ITOLDYOU (IRE) 12 ch.g. Salford Express (IRE) – Adisadel (IRE) (Petardia) [2017/18 c103§, h–§: c29.1m² c25.7d⁵ c26v⁵ c23.5v c21.6v² c26v^ur Mar 17] sturdy gelding: lightly-raced hurdler: fair handicap chaser: stays 29f: acts on good to firm and heavy going: wears headgear: has worn tongue tie: usually races prominently: temperamental. *Linda Jewell* — c99 § h– §

ITSABOUTIME (IRE) 8 gr.g. Whitmore's Conn (USA) – Blazing Love (IRE) (Fruits of Love (USA)) [2017/18 h91: h18.5s Apr 23] angular gelding: modest maiden hurdler at best, offered little sole outing in 2017/18: should stay beyond 2½m: acts on heavy going. *Helen Nelmes* — h56

ITS'AFREEBEE (IRE) 8 br.g. Danroad (AUS) – Aphra Benn (IRE) (In The Wings) [2017/18 c139, h–: c21.4g^pu h23.9g h17.7d⁵ h18.9v⁵ h17.7v Dec 26] workmanlike gelding: useful hurdler/chaser at best, well below that level in 2017/18: stays 21f: acts on heavy going: has worn headgear, including final start: has worn tongue tie: increasingly lazy. *Dan Skelton* — c– h96

IT'S A GIMME (IRE) 11 b.g. Beneficial – Sorcera (GER) (Zilzal (USA)) [2017/18 c–, h–: c19.4g⁵ c19.4g² c21.4g c20d⁵ c23.6d³ c23.8d⁵ Dec 20] winning hurdler: useful handicap chaser: second at Stratford in June: stays 3m, effective at shorter: acts on soft and good to firm going: has worn tongue tie, including last 3 starts. *Jonjo O'Neill* — c128 h–

ITS A LITTLE RISKY 5 b.m. Windsor Castle – Risky Witness (IRE) (Witness Box (USA)) [2017/18 b15.7g⁶ Sep 6] first foal: dam unraced daughter of fairly useful 2m/17f hurdle winner Petite Risk: 12/1, sixth in maiden bumper at Southwell. *Tim Vaughan* — b–

IT'S ALL ABOUT ME (IRE) 6 b.m. King's Theatre (IRE) – Annie Spectrim (IRE) (Spectrum (IRE)) [2017/18 b81: ab16.3g⁴ ab16.3g⁴ h19.9g Apr 23] rather lightly-built mare: poor form in bumpers: well beaten in maiden on hurdling debut: should stay 2½m. *Micky Hammond* — h– b73

IT'S ALL AN ACT (IRE) 10 br.g. Presenting – Royal Lucy (IRE) (King's Ride) [2017/18 c–, c–x, h–: h15.9g⁴ h17.7d^pu h19g h19v⁵ c16.1v⁴ Mar 12] has had breathing operation: fair hurdler/fairly useful chaser at best, little form since 2015/16: left Daniel O'Brien after second start: has worn headgear/tongue tie, including in 2017/18: often races freely. *Tim Vaughan* — c– h65

ITS ALL GUESSWORK (IRE) 6 b.g. Mahler – La Lambertine (FR) (Glaieul (USA)) [2017/18 h110p, h108: b18.8g² h24g* h20.7d³ h22g³ h21.1g⁴ Oct 27] tall gelding: fair form in bumpers: fairly useful form over hurdles: won maiden at Bellewstown in July: stays 3m: acts on good to soft going: wears tongue tie: usually races nearer last than first. *Gordon Elliott, Ireland* — h123 b91

ITS ALL OR NOTHING 9 gr.g. Terimon – Little Vera (Carlingford Castle) [2017/18 c100: c24.2d^F Apr 24] multiple point winner: fair form in hunter chases. *Miss C. Rowe* — c104

IT'

IT'S A LONG STORY (IRE) 7 b.g. Court Cave (IRE) – Rockholm Girl (IRE) (Eve's Error) [2017/18 h–, h23.3g^{pu} h24g⁶ h27g c19.9m h24g⁶ Nov 17] poor maiden hurdler: well held in novice handicap on chasing debut: stays 3m: acts on soft going: tried in cheekpieces. *Barbara Butterworth*   c–
h70

ITSAMANSLIFE (IRE) 5 b.g. Mahler – Medieval Banquet (IRE) (Mister Lord (USA)) [2017/18 b16s h16v⁵ h19.7s⁶ h19.7s⁴ h21.2d Apr 24] €36,000 3-y-o: fourth foal: half-brother to fair chaser Sterling Stuff (3m winner, by Brian Boru): dam, winning pointer, out of half-sister to high-class hurdler (stayed 2½m) Vicario di Bray: placed both starts in Irish points: tailed off in bumper: modest form over hurdles: front runner/races prominently. *Katy Price*   h94
b–

IT'S A STEAL (IRE) 11 b.g. Craigsteel – Mimosa Rose (IRE) (Be My Native (USA)) [2017/18 c82, h100: h20g³ h23g⁵ h26.5d c19.2d^{pu} c23m³ c23g² c23.8v² c26v^{ur} c25.1d Apr 22] useful-looking gelding: fair maiden hurdler at best: poor handicap chaser nowadays: stays 3m: acts on heavy going: has worn cheekpieces, including final start: has worn tongue tie, including in 2017/18: temperamental. *Katie Stephens*   c80 §
h80 §

ITS A STING (IRE) 9 b.g. Scorpion (IRE) – Wyndham Sweetmarie (IRE) (Mister Lord (USA)) [2017/18 c17.4d³ c16.5g^F c16g^{ur} h16s^F ab18d³ c16.5g^{pu} Apr 24] good-bodied gelding: fairly useful maiden hurdler at best, behind when fell last fourth outing in 2017/18: modest maiden chaser: stays 19f: acts on soft going: has worn hood, including in 2017/18: often races in rear. *Oliver Sherwood*   c97
h–

IT'S BUSTER (IRE) 7 b.g. Stowaway – Late Guest (IRE) (Gothland (FR)) [2017/18 b15.7d⁴ b15.7d h17s h16.7g Apr 22] £9,500 5-y-o: third foal: dam unraced half-sister to fairly useful chaser (2m-2¾m winner) Mr Bossman: fair form in bumpers: no form over hurdles. *Sue Smith*   h–
b89

IT'S FINE WINE 5 b.g. Multiplex – Reem Two (Mtoto) [2017/18 b17.7d⁴ h21.2s Jan 18] third foal: brother to fairly useful hurdler Raise A Spark (2m-2½m winner): dam (h106) 17f-2½m hurdle winner (stayed 3m): fourth in bumper at Plumpton (11½ lengths behind Hook Lane Roobee): well beaten in maiden on hurdling debut. *Graeme McPherson*   h–
b80

IT'S GOT LEGS (IRE) 5 b.g. Getaway (GER) – Lady Cadia (FR) (Cadoudal (FR)) [2017/18 h17.7g² ab16g⁴ h16.8s h16v^{ur} h19.5v³ h15.9v³ Apr 1] £28,000 3-y-o: sturdy gelding: seventh foal: dam, lightly raced over hurdles in France, sister to dam of very smart hurdler/smart chaser (stayed 2½m) Geos: fair form in bumpers/over hurdles. *Gary Moore*   h107
b92

IT'S GRAND (IRE) 5 b.g. Westerner – Calomeria (Groom Dancer (USA)) [2017/18 b16g⁵ Jul 10] failed to complete 3 starts in Irish points: tailed off in bumper. *Donald McCain*   b–

ITSHARD TO NO (IRE) 9 b.g. Helissio (FR) – Miniballist (IRE) (Tragic Role (USA)) [2017/18 h104: h17.2d³ h18.7g⁵ c16s* Nov 8] fairly useful handicap hurdler at best: 6/1, won novice handicap at Chepstow (by neck from Swift Crusader) on chasing debut: stayed 2¼m: acted on heavy going: wore hood until last 6 starts: wore tongue tie: dead. *Kerry Lee*   c121
h106

IT'S NEVER ENOUGH 4 b.g. Equiano (FR) – Swynford Pleasure (Reprimand) [2017/18 b13.6v⁴ Nov 15] 5/2, fourth in junior bumper at Ayr (14¼ lengths behind Emissaire). *James Ewart*   b69

ITSNONOFURBUSINESS (IRE) 6 b.g. Flemensfirth (USA) – Moon Storm (IRE) (Strong Gale) [2017/18 b69p: h16.3g h21d h16d h23.1v* h26s³ h19.2s³ h23.1s⁶ Mar 26] point winner: fair handicap hurdler: won at Market Rasen in January: stays 3¼m: best form on soft/heavy going: in cheekpieces last 4 starts: races towards rear. *Dan Skelton*   h110

IT'S OBVIOUS (IRE) 6 gr.g. Tobougg (IRE) – Hiho Silver Lining (Silver Patriarch (IRE)) [2017/18 h15.3s⁴ h16.3s h18.5v⁴ h23.1v⁴ h23.9v c23s³ c28.4s⁶ Mar 26] £24,000 3-y-o, £85,000 4-y-o: workmanlike gelding: first foal: dam, winning pointer, half-sister to smart bumper winner/useful hurdler (stayed 3m) Secret Ploy: runner-up in Irish point: fair form over hurdles/fences: stays 23f: raced only on soft/heavy going: in headgear last 3 starts: in tongue tie 3 of last 4 starts. *David Pipe*   c110
h108

IT'S O KAY 5 b.m. Shirocco (GER) – Presenting Copper (IRE) (Presenting) [2017/18 b16.6s⁴ b16v² b16.8g* Apr 23] third foal: half-sister to bumper winner/useful hurdler Copper Kay (2m-19f winner, by Kayf Tara) and bumper winner Which One Is Which (by King's Theatre): dam (c139/h134), 2m-19f hurdle/chase winner, sister to useful hurdler/chaser (stays 3m) Give Me A Copper and half-sister to smart hurdler/chaser (stayed 21f) Copper Bleu: fair form in bumpers: won mares event at Sedgefield in April. *Olly Murphy*   b91

407

IT'

IT'S OSCAR (IRE) 11 b.g. Oscar (IRE) – Lady Bramble (IRE) (Be My Native (USA)) [2017/18 c–§, h87§: h22g³ h23g* h23g⁶ c20g³ c23g^{pu} Jul 10] tall gelding: modest handicap hurdler: won at Worcester in May: poor maiden chaser: best up to 3m: acts on good to firm and heavy going: wears headgear/tongue tie: ungenuine. *Alastair Ralph* — **c72 § h88 §**

ITS PANDORAMA (IRE) 8 b.g. Misternando – Gretchen's Castle (IRE) (Carlingford Castle) [2017/18 h16.2g⁴ h17.2d² h22.1g* h23.9m³ h19.9g h20.9d⁴ ab16g⁵ h19.9v² h23.1s Mar 26] pulled up in point: fair hurdler: won maiden at Cartmel in June: stays 2¾m: acts on heavy going: in headgear last 4 starts. *Brian Ellison* — **h110**

ITSTIMEFORAPINT (IRE) 10 b.g. Portrait Gallery (IRE) – Executive Pearl (IRE) (Executive Perk) [2017/18 c120, h–: c26.2v⁶ c30s^{pu} c29.6v* c31.9v⁴ c30.6s^{pu} Apr 27] maiden hurdler: fairly useful handicap chaser: won at Bangor in February: stays 4m: acts on heavy going: in blinkers last 3 starts: wears tongue tie. *Lucinda Russell* — **c117 h–**

IT'S YOUR MOVE (IRE) 6 b.g. Flemensfirth (USA) – Jeruflo (IRE) (Glacial Storm (USA)) [2017/18 h16.2g⁴ h19.9g³ h23.1g⁴ h19.9s³ h19.9v^F h19.9v² h24.3g Apr 20] placed in point: fair maiden hurdler: stays 2½m: acts on heavy going: in cheekpieces last 2 starts. *Brian Ellison* — **h112**

IVAN GROZNY (FR) 8 b.g. Turtle Bowl (IRE) – Behnesa (IRE) (Suave Dancer (USA)) [2017/18 h154: h16g³ h16d^{bd} h16v⁵ Oct 1] angular gelding: smart hurdler at best: third in Grimes Hurdle at Tipperary (5¼ lengths behind Plinth) in July: raced around 2m: acts on heavy going: wears hood: tried in tongue tie. *W. P. Mullins, Ireland* — **h141**

IVANHOE 8 b.g. Haafhd – Marysienka (Primo Dominie) [2017/18 h–: h20.5s^F h20.3v h15.8v⁵ h16s Mar 22] angular gelding: fair on Flat: fair hurdler at best, little form since 2015/16. *Michael Blanshard* — **h80**

IVANOVICH GORBATOV (IRE) 6 b.g. Montjeu (IRE) – Northern Gulch (USA) (Gulch (USA)) [2017/18 h152: h16.4s h16s h16.0s h16.8v h20s^{pu} h16.5d Apr 24] round-barrelled gelding: very smart hurdler at best, little impact in 2017/18: has worn headgear, including in 2017/18: wears tongue tie. *Joseph Patrick O'Brien, Ireland* — **h–**

IVORS INVOLVEMENT (IRE) 6 b.g. Amadeus Wolf – Summer Spice (IRE) (Key of Luck (USA)) [2017/18 h16.2v h16.8v h19.9v h16.8v⁵ Apr 13] modest on Flat, stays 1½m: poor form over hurdles. *Tina Jackson* — **h64**

IVOR'S QUEEN (IRE) 9 b.m. King's Theatre (IRE) – Sonnerschien (IRE) (Be My Native (USA)) [2017/18 c–p, h113: h16.3g⁴ c16.3d³ c17.8g⁴ h16.8g² h17.7g⁴ h15.3s⁴ h15.3g* h19.2g⁴ h15.3v⁴ c16.3s³ Feb 16] sturdy mare: fairly useful handicap hurdler: won at Wincanton in October: fair form over fences: stays 21f: acts on good to soft going: tried in hood: wears tongue tie. *Colin Tizzard* — **c112 h124**

IVOR THE FOX 6 b.g. Sakhee (USA) – Florie (Alflora (IRE)) [2017/18 b16.8s⁵ b15.7v Feb 25] soundly beaten in bumpers: in tongue tie second start. *Sara Ender* — **b–**

IWILLDOIT 5 b.g. Flying Legend (USA) – Lyricist's Dream (Dreams End) [2017/18 b13.7v⁵ b16.7d⁵ Apr 21] second foal: dam (h93) 2m hurdle winner (stayed 2½m): fair form in bumpers. *Sam Thomas* — **b90**

IZZO (GER) 5 b.g. Tertullian (USA) – Ioannina (Rainbow Quest (USA)) [2017/18 h17.9s* h19.4s³ h17.9s* h19.4s² h19.4s^F h19.4s⁵ h20s Apr 12] narrow, angular gelding: useful 9f winner on Flat in Germany: useful hurdler: won listed event at Compiegne in May and Prix de Maisons-Laffitte at Auteuil in September: 7 lengths second to De Bon Coeur in Prix Pierre de Lassus at Auteuil in October: well beaten in Aintree Hurdle final start: stays 19f: acts on soft going: wears hood: free-going type. *Mlle C. Fey, France* — **h144**

IZZY PICCOLINA (IRE) 10 b.m. Morozov – Chloara (IRE) (Flemensfirth (USA)) [2017/18 h–: h16.3d³ h23.3g Jun 15] maiden hurdler, lightly raced and no form since 2015/16: tried in cheekpieces. *Geoffrey Deacon* — **h–**

J

JABBEA (IRE) 6 b.g. Robin des Pres (FR) – Welsh Bea (IRE) (Welsh Term) [2017/18 b–: b16.6g⁶ h19.5v h18.5v Jan 1] rather unfurnished gelding: point winner: modest form in bumpers: no form over hurdles. *Mary Sanderson* — **h– b79**

JABOLTISKI (SPA) 6 b.g. Delfos (IRE) – Sonic Sea (IRE) (Zafonic (USA)) [2017/18 c112, h112: h21g⁵ May 13] good-topped gelding: fair handicap hurdler, well below form sole outing in 2017/18: fair form completed start over fences: stays 2¾m: acts on good to firm and heavy going: in cheekpieces last 2 starts. *Philip Hobbs* — **c– h89**

JABOTICABA (FR) 4 ch.g. Muhtathir – Janiceinwonderland (FR) (Ekraar (USA)) [2017/18 h16.4s* h16s² h16s⁶ Apr 9] fairly useful on Flat (stays 1¼m) for S. Wattel: similar form over hurdles: won newcomers race at Cagnes-sur-Mer in December, sole start for Mme P. Butel & J-L. Beaunez. *Alan King*   **h121**

JABULANI (FR) 5 gr.g. Martaline – Incorrigible (FR) (Septieme Ciel (USA)) [2017/18 b96: h21g² h21.1g³ h19.5d* h20.5d h19.3v h19.8v^pu Mar 10] good-bodied gelding: bumper winner: fairly useful form over hurdles: won novice at Lingfield in November: stays 21f: acts on good to soft going (won bumper on heavy). *Nigel Twiston-Davies*   **h119**

JACARNO 6 ch.g. Lucarno – Sparkling Jewel (Bijou d'Inde) [2017/18 b71: h15.7g⁴ h16.2v⁵ h16.4v⁶ h16s^bd h16s⁶ h19.7v h16.4v⁵ h15.7v⁶ h15.7s³ Mar 7] poor maiden hurdler: in headgear last 3 starts. *Andrew Crook*   **h74**

JACBEQUICK 7 b.g. Calcutta – Toking N' Joken (IRE) (Mukaddamah (USA)) [2017/18 h16s^pu h15.7d⁵ h16.7s⁴ Dec 26] fairly useful on Flat, stays 1½m: modest form in novice hurdles. *David O'Meara*   **h86**

JACK BEAR 7 b.g. Joe Bear (IRE) – Colins Lady (FR) (Colonel Collins (USA)) [2017/18 h90p: h16.8g h16.8s⁵ h15.7g Apr 20] fairly useful on Flat: modest maiden hurdler: left Harry Whittington after second start: front runner/races prominently. *Roger Teal*   **h82**

JACKBLACK 6 b.g. Crosspeace (IRE) – Saharan Royal (Val Royal (FR)) [2017/18 h111: h15.9g⁵ h16.3g³ h16g³ h17.7g⁴ h17.7d* Sep 10] fairly useful hurdler: won novices at Fontwell in August and September: stays 2¼m: acts on soft going: wears hood. *Brett Johnson*   **h115**

JACK DEVINE (IRE) 6 b.g. Kalanisi (IRE) – Sybil Says (IRE) (Flemensfirth (USA)) [2017/18 h21.2g⁵ h19.3d² h25.3s² h24.3g⁴ Apr 20] €18,000 3-y-o, £50,000 5-y-o: first foal: dam, unraced, out of sister to smart hurdler/very smart chaser (stayed 25f) Sackville: multiple Irish point winner: fair form over hurdles: tried in visor/tongue tie. *Rose Dobbin*   **h105**

JACKHAMMER (IRE) 4 b.g. Thewayyouare (USA) – Ask Annie (IRE) (Danehill (USA)) [2017/18 h16v Mar 9] fairly useful on Flat, stays 11f: tailed off in maiden on hurdling debut. *Dianne Sayer*   **h–**

JACK IN A BOX 8 b.g. Kayf Tara – La Dame Brune (FR) (Mansonnien (FR)) [2017/18 c97: c26.2d^pu c24.1d³ Apr 21] point winner: modest form in chases: stays 3m: acts on heavy going: in headgear last 2 starts. *Nigel Hawke*   **c98**

JACK LAMB 6 gr.g. Sulamani (IRE) – Charlotte Lamb (Pharly (FR)) [2017/18 h85: h16.8g⁴ h18.6g^pu h19.4d³ h19.4d^F Dec 15] modest form over hurdles: will be suited by 2½m+: acts on good to soft going. *Jedd O'Keeffe*   **h97**

JACKOFHEARTS 10 b.g. Beat Hollow – Boutique (Selkirk (USA)) [2017/18 c84, h–: c20.1g³ c16m⁵ c23.8m⁶ c23.8d⁵ c21.6v⁴ Apr 16] maiden hurdler: poor maiden chaser: tried in cheekpieces. *Jean McGregor*   **c68** / **h–**

JACKS LAST HOPE 9 b.g. King's Theatre (IRE) – Ninna Nanna (FR) (Garde Royale) [2017/18 h133: h20g* h20g⁵ h24g* h16.4d² h21.4g Apr 21] useful handicap hurdler: won at Aintree in May and Southwell (by 3¾ lengths from Kalifourchon) in August: 7/2, second in novice at Sedgefield (¾ length behind Cobra de Mai) on chasing debut: stays 3m: acts on heavy going: wears visor: sure to progress as a chaser. *Chris Grant*   **c115 p** / **h139**

JACK SNIPE 9 b.g. Kirkwall – Sea Snipe (King Luthier) [2017/18 c85, h87: c25.5m² c23.g* c25.8d* c24.1g c26g⁴ c25.1s^pu c25.7d^ur c23.8v⁴ Jan 3] maiden hurdler: fair handicap chaser: won at Worcester and Newton Abbot in July: will stay long distances: acts on good to firm and good to soft going: wears headgear: usually races prominently. *Jeremy Scott*   **c106** / **h–**

JACK THE HAT (IRE) 13 b.g. Dr Massini (IRE) – Aunt Rose (IRE) (Caribo) [2017/18 c20g c20.1g* h20.2d³ c20.5g^pu h19.8g² c18.4s^F h20d⁵ c25d⁴ Oct 19] modest handicap hurdler: fair handicap chaser: won at Perth in August: stays 2¾m: acts on good to firm and good to soft going: wears headgear/tongue tie. *Madeleine Tylicki, Ireland*   **c108** / **h93**

JACKTHEJOURNEYMAN (IRE) 9 b.g. Beneficial – Maslam (IRE) (Robellino (USA)) [2017/18 c100§, h88: h15.8m³ c16.5g² h16.7g c17.2g⁵ c16.5g⁴ h16.7d⁵ c16.1s⁵ c16.5d* h16.5m⁴ Apr 25] modest maiden hurdler: modest handicap chaser nowadays: won at Huntingdon in March: raced mainly around 2m: acts on good to firm and good to soft going: wears headgear/tongue tie: usually races close up. *Tom Gretton*   **c92** / **h88**

JAC

JACOBITE RISING (FR) 5 b.g. Rob Roy (USA) – Petillante Royale (FR) (Vertical Speed (FR)) [2017/18 b16.5g⁶ b16.4d h16g⁴ h16g* h16g⁴ Aug 23] fourth foal: dam unraced half-sister to useful French hurdler (2¼m/19f winner) Royal Surabaya: maiden pointer: poor form in bumpers: fair form over hurdles: won maiden at Worcester in August: left L. Byrne after second start: tried in tongue tie: usually races close up. *Charlie Longsdon* h110 b70

JAC THE LEGEND 9 b.g. Midnight Legend – Sky Burst (Gunner B) [2017/18 c116§, h106: h23.3g⁴ May 13] strong, compact gelding: winning pointer, placed once in 2018: fair handicap hurdler: fairly useful chaser: stays 29f: acts on soft going: wears headgear: temperamental. *Brian Ellison* c– § h105

J'AI FROID (IRE) 5 b.g. Flemensfirth (USA) – Park Wave (IRE) (Supreme Leader) [2017/18 b15.7v² Mar 29] half-brother to fairly useful hurdler/smart chaser Gallant Oscar (2½m-25f winner, by Oscar) and bumper winner/useful hurdler Enterprise Park (2m-2¾m winner, by Goldmark): dam unraced half-sister to useful cross-country chaser Risk of Thunder and to dam of top-class chaser up to 3m The Listener: fair form in bumpers. *Ben Case* b90

JAISALMER (IRE) 6 b.g. Jeremy (USA) – Shara (IRE) (Kahyasi) [2017/18 h119p: h21g⁴ h16.8v⁴ h15.9v* h17.7v* h15.9v^pu h16s Apr 28] stocky gelding: fairly useful hurdler: won novices at Plumpton in January and Fontwell in February: stays 21f: best form on heavy going: usually races close up. *Mark Bradstock* h127

JALEO (GER) 6 ch.g. New Approach (GER) – Jambalaya (GER) (Samum (GER)) [2017/18 h131: h20.5d h21d³ h19.7s⁶ h23.1s² h24.7s Apr 14] tall gelding: useful handicap hurdler: second at Bangor (2¾ lengths behind Chapel Stile) in March: stays 23f: acts on heavy going: tried in hood: usually races towards rear. *Ben Pauling* h135

JAMACHO 4 ch.g. Camacho – Obsessive Secret (IRE) (Grand Lodge (USA)) [2017/18 h17.2d³ h16.8g⁴ h15.6d³ ab16.3g* Mar 3] fairly useful maiden on Flat, stays 1¼m: won jumpers bumper at Newcastle in March: fair form over hurdles. *Brian Ellison* h106

JAMESGIFTKEYSANDAL (IRE) 7 b.g. Raintrap – Teanarco Lady (Averti (IRE)) [2017/18 h–: h20d h23.3g^pu h17.7m⁶ h18.5v^pu Oct 2] no form over hurdles: has worn hood, including in 2017/18: in tongue tie last 3 starts. *Robert Stephens* h–

JAMESON 6 br.g. Midnight Legend – Shatabdi (IRE) (Mtoto) [2017/18 h131, b103: c20.9s² c20s* c19.9g² c20.8s⁴ c16.4s⁴ c20.4s⁶ c20.8g⁵ Apr 18] good-topped gelding: winning hurdler: useful handicap chaser: won novice event at Sandown in November: second at Newbury in December: stays 21f: acts on soft going: has worn hood. *Nigel Twiston-Davies* c138 h–

JAMHOORI 10 b.h. Tiger Hill (IRE) – Tanasie (Cadeaux Genereux) [2017/18 h90: h16v Jan 22] fairly useful on Flat: lightly-raced maiden hurdler, well beaten sole outing in 2017/18: in visor last 2 starts. *Suzi Best* h–

JAMMIN MASTERS (IRE) 7 b.g. Sinndar (IRE) – Zara Million (ITY) (Zafonic (USA)) [2017/18 h19.7s² h19.5v⁵ h23.6v* h21.4v* h24d Apr 26] €18,000 3-y-o: sturdy gelding: fourth foal: dam ran twice in Italy: point winner: fairly useful form over hurdles: won maiden at Chepstow in January and handicap at Wincanton in April: runner-up both starts in hunter chases for T. M. Walsh in 2016/17: stays 3m: acts on heavy going: usually races close up. *Warren Greatrex* c– h127

JAMRHAM (IRE) 11 b.g. Great Palm (USA) – Appleway (IRE) (Lord Americo) [2017/18 c78, h–: c21.2m² May 9] point winner: pulled up sole outing over hurdles: poor handicap chaser: stays 21f: acts on good to firm and heavy going: in cheekpieces last 2 starts: wears tongue tie. *Sam Thomas* c82 h–

JAM SESSION (IRE) 6 ch.g. Duke of Marmalade (IRE) – Night Dhu (Montjeu (IRE)) [2017/18 h111: h16d May 1] bumper winner: fair form over hurdles: in cheekpieces, well held sole outing in 2017/18: tried in tongue tie. *Ian Williams* h–

J AND M GREENGAIRS 10 b.g. Flemensfirth (USA) – Smooth Technology (IRE) (Astronef) [2017/18 h20.5v^pu h19.4d⁵ h16.2s Apr 26] poor form over hurdles. *R. Mike Smith* h73

JANE LAMB 5 b.m. Haafhd – Lucinda Lamb (Kayf Tara) [2017/18 b83: b15.7d² b16.8s⁵ Dec 26] fair form in bumpers: tried in tongue tie. *Dan Skelton* b88

JANES BOUTIQUE (IRE) 7 b.m. Presenting – Supreme Touch (IRE) (Supreme Leader) [2017/18 b–: h21.2g⁵ h23.1s h24d⁴ c24.2s^pu c23s⁶ c25.2s^pu h24v^pu Feb 25] placed both starts in Irish points: poor form over hurdles: no form in chases. *Tom Symonds* c– h82

JARDIN DES PLANTES (FR) 8 ch.g. High Rock (IRE) – Dear Marianne (FR) (Akarad (FR)) [2017/18 h99: h16.7s² May 20] runner-up completed start in Irish maiden points: fair form over hurdles: wears tongue tie. *Donald McCain* h106

JAY

- **JARLATH** 7 b.g. Norse Dancer (IRE) – Blue Lullaby (IRE) (Fasliyev (USA)) [2017/18 c113, h–: h18.5d⁶ c20d* c19.5v² c19.5v² c21.2s³ Feb 16] good-topped gelding: fair handicap hurdler, shaped as if needing run on return: fair handicap chaser: won at Warwick in November: stays 21f: acts on good to firm and heavy going. *Seamus Mullins* — **c111 h75**

- **JAROB** 11 br.g. Beat All (USA) – Wishy (IRE) (Leading Counsel (USA)) [2017/18 c130, h131: h16.7g⁴ h20.2g c20s³ h24s Dec 28] useful handicap hurdler/chaser: stays 3m: acts on soft and good to firm going. *Andrew Lynch, Ireland* — **c136 h124**

- **JARVEYS PLATE (IRE)** 5 ch.g. Getaway (GER) – She's Got To Go (IRE) (Glacial Storm (USA)) [2017/18 b16.2s* Apr 27] €10,000 3-y-o: seventh foal: half-brother to fairly useful hurdler/chaser Behind Time (21f-3m winner, by Stowaway): dam (b77) in frame in bumpers: placed both starts in Irish points: 9/4, looked good prospect when won bumper at Perth by 3¾ lengths from Doctor Dex. *Fergal O'Brien* — **b104 p**

- **JASANI** 10 b.g. Gentleman's Deal (IRE) – Bred For Pleasure (Niniski (USA)) [2017/18 h19.2vᵖᵘ Mar 15] form (modest) only when winning novice handicap at Wetherby in 2015/16: tried in cheekpieces. *Roger Teal* — **h–**

- **JASSAS (FR)** 6 ch.g. Fuisse (FR) – Sylverina (FR) (Numerous (USA)) [2017/18 h16.4g* h19.4d⁶ h16.2s Jan 14] 2m winner on Flat in France: fair form over hurdles: won novice at Newcastle in November: should stay at least 2¼m: acts on soft going: tried in hood. *James Ewart* — **h103**

- **JAUNE ET BLEUE (FR)** 6 gr.m. Al Namix (FR) – Jaune de Beaufai (FR) (Ultimately Lucky (IRE)) [2017/18 h15.3v⁶ h16.2s³ h18.6s c20v* Mar 17] leggy mare: modest maiden hurdler: fair chaser: won newcomers event at Pau in 2015/16 for G. Cherel: also won handicap at Uttoxeter on sole outing over fences in 2017/18: stays 2½m: acts on heavy going. *David Dennis* — **c112 h95**

- **JAUNTY CLEMENTINE** 6 b.m. Lucarno (USA) – Jaunty Spirit (Loup Sauvage (USA)) [2017/18 h64, b–: h21g h21.2sᵖᵘ Jan 10] little form. *Brian Eckley* — **h–**

- **JAUNTY FLYER** 6 b.g. Sulamani (IRE) – Jaunty June (Primitive Rising (USA)) [2017/18 b87: h16d⁵ h20d⁴ h23.9v² h19.5v³ h19.3v* h24v⁴ h22d³ Apr 22] bumper winner: fairly useful hurdler: won novice at Catterick (dead-heated) in January: stays 3m: acts on heavy going: tried in tongue tie: front runner/races prominently. *Tim Vaughan* — **h115**

- **JAUNTY INFLIGHT** 9 b.g. Busy Flight – Jaunty Walk (Overbury (IRE)) [2017/18 c106, h97: c17.4gᵖᵘ h16.8sᵖᵘ h16.5sᵖᵘ Dec 14] sturdy gelding: modest hurdler/fair chaser at best, no form in 2017/18: left Dr Richard Newland after first start. *Chris Down* — **c– h–**

- **JAUNTY SORIA** 5 ch.m. Malinas (GER) – Jaunty Spirit (Loup Sauvage (USA)) [2017/18 b82: b15.8v⁵ Dec 31] modest form in bumpers. *Brian Eckley* — **b74**

- **JAUNTY THOR** 8 b.g. Norse Dancer (IRE) – Jaunty Walk (Overbury (IRE)) [2017/18 c97, h105: c20.3s³ c21.2g⁶ c16.3v² c16v⁴ c16sᵖᵘ h15.8v² h15.7g Apr 20] fair handicap hurdler: modest maiden chaser: stays 21f: acts on heavy going: often in headgear/tongue tie: often let down by jumping over fences. *Oliver Greenall* — **c95 x h100**

- **JAUNTY VELOCITY** 5 b.m. Sulamani (IRE) – Jaunty Walk (Overbury (IRE)) [2017/18 b16.2v³ Apr 10] fifth foal: half-sister to 3 winners, including modest hurdler/fair chaser Jaunty Inflight (2m-2¼m winner, by Busy Flight) and fair hurdler Jaunty Thor (2m winner, by Norse Dancer): dam, ran once in bumper, half-sister to useful hurdler/chaser (stayed 3m) Jaunty Flight: 9/1, third in bumper at Hereford (6½ lengths behind Geordie B). *Brian Eckley* — **b81**

- **JAXLIGHT** 6 b.m. Lucarno (USA) – Jaxelle (FR) (Lights Out (FR)) [2017/18 b15.7d⁴ b16.8v* b17s Apr 12] sturdy mare: fourth foal: dam, French maiden, half-sister to very smart staying chaser L'Ami and useful staying chaser Kelami: in front when fell in point: modest form in bumpers: won mares event at Sedgefield in March, only start for Patrick Holmes: trained by Dan Skelton on debut. *Andrew Crook* — **b83**

- **JAY ARE (IRE)** 9 b.g. Heron Island (IRE) – Vulpalm (IRE) (Great Palm (USA)) [2017/18 c19.7g⁴ c21.1d² Jun 6] twice-raced hurdler: fair handicap chaser: stays 21f: acts on soft going. *Gary Moore* — **c113 h–**

- **JAYO TIME (IRE)** 9 b.g. Morozov (USA) – Billythefilly (IRE) (Exit To Nowhere (USA)) [2017/18 c128, h–: h16.3g⁵ h23g c20d c24.2sᵖᵘ c20.3s³ c19.4vᵖᵘ c20.9s⁴ c18.9sᶠ c18.2s⁵ Feb 20] smallish, angular gelding: fair hurdler/useful chaser at best, well below that in 2017/18: stays 2¾m: effective at shorter: acts on soft and good to firm going: usually wears headgear: races towards rear. *Kerry Lee* — **c104 h–**

JAY

JAYTRACK PARKHOMES 4 b.g. Multiplex – Sudden Beat (Beat All (USA)) [2017/18 b13.7v* b16.4s Mar 14] £10,000 3-y-o: good-topped gelding: third foal: dam (b89), placed in bumpers, sister to fair hurdler/useful chaser (stays 27f) Gentleman Jon: fair form in bumpers: won conditionals/amateur event at Fontwell in February. *Colin Tizzard* **b86**

JAZZ THYME (IRE) 9 b.m. Helissio (FR) – Thyne Square (IRE) (Good Thyne (USA)) [2017/18 h88: h18.7m^2 h19.6g^2 h18.7m^2 h19g h20g Oct 17] modest maiden hurdler: stays 2½m: acts on good to firm going: has worn tongue tie, including in 2017/18. *Robert Stephens* **h93**

JAZZY (IRE) 5 b.g. Roderic O'Connor (IRE) – Lucayan Beauty (IRE) (Marju (IRE)) [2017/18 h105: h15.7g^5 May 15] leggy gelding: fair handicap hurdler, well below form sole outing in 2017/18: raced only at 2m: acts on good to firm going: wears headgear/tongue tie: usually leads. *Martin Keighley* **h66**

JEANNOT DE NONANT (FR) 6 ch.g. Full of Gold (FR) – Jolie Puce (FR) (General Assembly (USA)) [2017/18 c106+, h140: c19.9g^4 h20g^3 c22.5d^5 h19.9v^4 h24v* h21.1s h24.7s Apr 14] angular gelding: useful handicap hurdler: won at Southwell (by 3 lengths from Kansas City Chief) in February: fair form over fences: left Gordon Elliott after third start: stays 3m: acts on heavy going: wears headgear: tried in tongue tie. *Peter Bowen* **c106 h133**

JEBS GAMBLE (IRE) 7 b.g. Dubai Destination (USA) – Gentle Caribou (IRE) (Dushyantor (USA)) [2017/18 h87: h21.6g^5 h17.7d^2 h15.9d^4 h17.7v^2 h19.2v^3 Dec 26] modest maiden hurdler: stays 25f: acts on heavy going: in cheekpieces last 5 starts: often races towards rear. *Nick Gifford* **h99**

JEFFREY 5 ch.g. Apple Tree (FR) – Jambles (Muhtarram (USA)) [2017/18 b16.3s b15.3d Apr 22] no form in bumpers. *Robert Walford* **b–**

JENKINS (IRE) 6 b.g. Azamour (IRE) – Aladiyna (IRE) (Indian Danehill (IRE)) [2017/18 h142p, b–: h16.4s h16s h16s* h19.3v* h16.3v h16.8v^{pu} h20s Apr 13] good-topped gelding: bumper winner: useful handicap hurdler: won at Kempton and Ascot (Holloway's Handicap Hurdle, by 2¼ lengths from Air Horse One) in January: stays 19f: acts on heavy going: in headgear last 5 starts: usually races close up. *Nicky Henderson* **h144**

JENNIFER JUNIPER (IRE) 5 b.m. Kalanisi (IRE) – Assidua (IRE) (Anshan) [2017/18 b16s b15.7s^5 h21s^4 h23.8s h21.6s^{pu} Apr 23] €2,800 3-y-o, £30,000 4-y-o: seventh foal: half-sister to 3 winners, including fairly useful hurdler/winning pointerThe Kings Baby (2½m/21f winner) and modest hurdler The Kings Assassin (2¾m-3¼m winner) (both by King's Theatre): dam unraced: runner-up in Irish point: poor form in bumpers/over hurdles. *Fergal O'Brien* **h70 b70**

Ascot Spring Garden Show Holloway's Handicap Hurdle, Ascot—
champion conditional jockey James Bowen makes full use of his 5-lb claim as the blinkered Jenkins
proves too strong for the grey Air Horse One

JENNYS DAY (IRE) 7 b.g. Daylami (IRE) – Jennys Oscar (IRE) (Oscar (IRE)) [2017/18 h114, b87: h21.4g² h21.9v h21g h18.5v h23.8s⁶ h21s^{pu} h26.4d⁵ Apr 22] runner-up in point: fair handicap hurdler: stays 21f: acts on heavy going: tried in hood. *Katy Price* **h104**

JENNYS MELODY (IRE) 9 b.m. Gamut (IRE) – Pharaway Stream (IRE) (Phardante (FR)) [2017/18 h129: h24.7g⁶ h20v⁴ c21v² c24.1s^F Feb 22] useful hurdler: fairly useful form when second in mares maiden at Fairyhouse on completed start over fences: left Benjamin Arthey after first start: stayed 3m: acted on heavy going: tried in hood/tongue tie: dead. *Stuart Crawford, Ireland* **c123 h126**

JENNYS SURPRISE (IRE) 10 b.m. Hawk Wing (USA) – Winning Jenny (IRE) (Leading Counsel (USA)) [2017/18 c111, h–: c26.1d⁴ c25.1v⁴ c27.3v^{pu} c23.8v* c27.9v² c23.8s² Apr 27] workmanlike mare: winning hurdler: useful handicap chaser: won at Uttoxeter in November and Ffos Las in February: second in listed mares event at Perth (1¼ lengths behind Rons Dream) in April: stays 3½m: acts on heavy going: tried in cheekpieces: often races prominently. *Fergal O'Brien* **c133 h–**

JEN'S BOY 4 b.g. Malinas (GER) – Friendly Craic (IRE) (Mister Lord (USA)) [2017/18 b16.3s Mar 24] £65,000 3-y-o: rather unfurnished gelding: half-brother to 3 winners, including useful hurdler/very smart chaser Royal Regatta (2m-21f winner, by King's Theatre) and useful hurdler/smart chaser Three Musketeers (2½m-2¾m winner, by Flemensfirth): dam unraced: much better than result when down the field in Goffs UK Spring Sales Bumper at Newbury: sure to improve. *Nicky Henderson* **b– p**

JEPECK (IRE) 9 b.g. Westerner – Jenny's Jewel (IRE) (Be My Native (USA)) [2017/18 c118: c32.5d³ c27.5d⁴ c24.2s^{pu} c30.7v³ c27.6s⁴ c30.7s³ c28.4s³ c24.2d³ Apr 24] prolific point winner: fairly useful maiden chaser: third in hunter at Cheltenham in May: stays 33f: acts on heavy going: consistent. *Kayley Woollacott* **c117**

JEREMY'S JET (IRE) 7 b.g. Jeremy (USA) – Double Vie (IRE) (Tagula (IRE)) [2017/18 h15.8d⁵ h15.8g Nov 9] modest on Flat, stays 13f: poor maiden hurdler: raced mainly around 2m: acts on good to soft going: wears tongue tie. *Tony Carroll* **h81**

JERSEY BEAN (IRE) 5 b.g. Court Cave (IRE) – Jennifers Diary (IRE) (Supreme Leader) [2017/18 b16g² b15.7g* h16s³ h17.7v^{ur} h21.2s⁶ h19.2d* Feb 25] €44,000 3-y-o: good-topped gelding: fifth foal: closely related to smart hurdler Mischievous Milly (2m/17f winner, by Old Vic), stayed 21f, and half-brother to bumper winner Robinesse (by Robin des Champs): dam, placed in bumpers/over hurdles (stayed 3m), half-sister to useful chaser (stayed 25f) Alright Now M'lad: fairly useful form in bumpers: won at Ascot in November: fairly useful form over hurdles: won novice at Fontwell in February: should stay at least 2½m. *Oliver Sherwood* **h127 b96**

JERSEY BULL (IRE) 6 b.g. Clodovil (IRE) – Chaguaramas (IRE) (Mujadil (USA)) [2017/18 h15.9d Oct 23] fair on Flat: lightly-raced maiden hurdler, modest form at best: tried in hood. *Michael Madgwick* **h–**

JERSEY JEWEL (FR) 6 b.m. Naaqoos – Nikolenka (IRE) (Indian Ridge) [2017/18 h19.6d h15.7v^{pu} Feb 25] fair on Flat, stays 1½m: no form over hurdles: in cheekpieces second start: wears tongue tie. *Peter Bowen* **h–**

JER'S GIRL (IRE) 6 b.m. Jeremy (USA) – African Scene (IRE) (Scenic) [2017/18 h140: h16v⁴ h20v² h24.5d² h19.9s⁵ h20s Apr 28] angular mare: useful hurdler: second in Lismullen Hurdle at Navan (2 lengths behind Apple's Jade) and listed mares event at Kempton (½ length behind La Bague Au Roi) in November: stays 3m: acts on heavy going. *Gavin Patrick Cromwell, Ireland* **h140**

JERUSALEM BELLS (IRE) 9 b.g. Kalanisi (IRE) – Quit The Noise (IRE) (Un Desperado (FR)) [2017/18 c–, h–: c20g^{pu} c22.5d^{pu} Oct 8] point winner: maiden hurdler: no form in chases: wears tongue tie. *Alexandra Dunn* **c– h–**

JESSBER'S DREAM (IRE) 8 b.m. Milan – Maddy's Supreme (IRE) (Supreme Leader) [2017/18 h132: h21.4s³ c20.2v² Dec 26] Irish point winner: useful handicap hurdler: 6/4, second in mares novice at Wincanton (11 lengths behind Pearl Royale) on chasing debut: stays 21f: acts on heavy going: tried in blinkers: wears tongue tie: open to improvement as a chaser. *Paul Nicholls* **c125 p h135**

JESSE JUDE (IRE) 5 ch.g. Doyen (IRE) – La Belle Bleu (IRE) (Lahib (USA)) [2017/18 b16.8s⁶ ab16.3g h19.4d² Mar 16] €1,800 3-y-o: fifth foal: half-brother to a winning pointer by Heron Island: dam ran twice on Flat: poor form in bumpers: 100/1, showed bit more when second in novice at Musselburgh (8 lengths behind Bedrock) on hurdling debut. *Simon West* **h105 b71**

Alder Hey Children's Charity Handicap Hurdle, Aintree—Jester Jet (noseband) provides one of the highlights in a breakthrough season for trainer Tom Lacey as she holds off fellow outsider Eaton Hill (No.20)

JESTER JET 8 br.m. Overbury (IRE) – Hendre Hotshot (Exit To Nowhere (USA)) h135
[2017/18 h106: h23.9g² h24.7g³ h21.6d² h25d* h24s³ h24.6v^{pu} h21s² h20s* h19.8s Apr 28] leggy mare: useful handicap hurdler: won at Perth in May, Plumpton (mares) in December and Aintree (Grade 3, by ¾ length from Eaton Hill) in April: stays 25f: acts on good to firm and heavy going. *Tom Lacey*

JE SUIS CHARLIE 4 b.g. High Chaparral (IRE) – Fin (Groom Dancer (USA)) [2017/18 h117
h16.6d³ h15.6d² h15.6s³ Jan 19] half-brother to useful hurdler Fatcatinthehat (2m winner, by Authorized): fairly useful on Flat, stays 1¾m: similar form over hurdles: tried in cheekpieces. *John Quinn*

JET MASTER (IRE) 12 b.g. Brian Boru – Whats The Reason (IRE) (Strong Gale) c121 x
[2017/18 c127x, h114: h23.9g⁵ h16.2v* h16.2g⁶ c20.1g⁴ h16.8s⁶ c21.6s³ c23.8s^F Apr 25] h110
neat gelding: fair handicap hurdler: won at Perth in September: fairly useful handicap chaser: stays 3m: acts on good to firm and heavy going: wears hood/tongue tie: held up: often let down by jumping over fences. *N. W. Alexander*

JET SET (IRE) 6 b.m. Getaway (GER) – Lavender Track (IRE) (Pistolet Bleu (IRE)) h122
[2017/18 b17d³ h19.4d² h21.2v² h19.8s^F h20.5s h20.7g* Apr 24] €26,000 3-y-o, €80,000 b91
5-y-o: third foal: dam (h103), bumper/19f hurdle winner, half-sister to useful hurdler/high-class chaser (stayed 3¼m) Irish Cavalier and useful hurdler/smart chaser (stays 3m) Shattered Love: Irish point winner: third in mares bumper at Aintree (5 lengths behind Grageelagh Girl): fairly useful form over hurdles: won mares novice at Huntingdon in April: stays 21f: acts on heavy going: tried in tongue tie: front runner/races prominently. *Charlie Longsdon*

JETT (IRE) 7 b.g. Flemensfirth (USA) – La Noire (IRE) (Phardante (FR)) [2017/18 c137, c144
h132: c19v⁴ c18s* c17s² c17d³ c21s c18s* c18s² Mar 24] winning hurdler: useful chaser: h–
won maiden at Thurles in November and minor event there (by 4¼ lengths from Goulane Chosen) in February: second in listed novice at Thurles (3¾ lengths behind Castlegrace Paddy) in March: stays 23f, effective at shorter: acts on heavy going. *Mrs J. Harrington, Ireland*

JETZ (IRE) 6 b.g. Flemensfirth (USA) – Miss Squiff (IRE) (Saddlers' Hall (IRE)) h142
[2017/18 h20s³ h20s* h20v² h20v³ h20v⁴ h22s² h20v² h24s Apr 25] first foal: dam twice-raced close relative of Champion Hurdle winner Jezki and smart hurdler (stays 3m) Jetson, and half-sister to smart hurdler/useful chaser (stayed 2½m) Jered: useful hurdler: won maiden at Fairyhouse in November: second in Monksfield Novices' Hurdle at Navan (12 lengths behind Samcro) in November, Nathaniel Lacy & Partners Solicitors Novices' Hurdle at Leopardstown (head behind Tower Bridge) in February and Grade 2 novice at Fairyhouse (2¼ lengths behind Pallasator) in April: stays 2¾m: best form on soft/heavy going: in hood last 2 starts. *Mrs J. Harrington, Ireland*

JEU DE MOTS (FR) 5 b.g. Saint des Saints (FR) – Nanouska (GER) (Dashing Blade) c92
[2017/18 h20.1v⁴ c25.2s⁴ c20.2v³ c26g⁶ Apr 20] half-brother to several winners, including h66 p
useful hurdler/chaser Nambour (2¼m-2¾m winner, by Sholokhov): dam useful German 7.5f winner: runner-up both starts in points: better than result when well beaten in maiden on hurdling debut (open to improvement): modest form over fences. *Nick Williams*

JOE

JEWELLED PRINCE 6 ch.g. Zamindar (USA) – Diamond Lass (IRE) (Rock of Gibraltar (IRE)) [2017/18 h85: h16.8g⁶ h17.2d May 31] maiden hurdler, no form in 2017/18: in headgear last 4 starts: tried in tongue tie. *Joanne Foster*   **h–**

JEWELLERY (IRE) 11 b.m. King's Best (USA) – Eilean Shona (Suave Dancer (USA)) [2017/18 c84, h–: c20.1g⁴ h20.9d Oct 8] winning hurdler: poor handicap chaser nowadays: stays 3m: acts on good to firm and good to soft going: has worn headgear: wears tongue tie. *Katie Scott*   **c67** **h–**

JEZKI (IRE) 10 b.g. Milan – La Noire (IRE) (Phardante (FR)) [2017/18 h147: h16v* h16.2s² h24s⁵ h16s⁴ h18s* h20v^pu h24d Apr 26] smallish, strong gelding: smart hurdler nowadays: won Istabraq Hurdle at Tipperary (by 4 lengths from Coquin Mans) in October and minor event at Leopardstown (by 2 lengths from Lieutenant Colonel) in March: second in Morgiana Hurdle at Punchestown (16 lengths behind Faugheen) in November: effective at 2m to 3m: acts on good to firm and heavy going: has worn headgear, including last 4 starts. *Mrs J. Harrington, Ireland*   **h148 d**

JIGSAW FINANCIAL (IRE) 12 b.g. Brian Boru – Ardcolm Cailin (IRE) (Beneficial) [2017/18 h93: h20.3g^pu h23g² h20g* h16g⁵ h20.3g Jul 16] leggy gelding: modest handicap hurdler: won at Worcester in June: stays 3m: acts on good to firm and heavy going: tried in cheekpieces. *Laura Young*   **h93**

JIMINY CRICKET (IRE) 7 ch.g. Golden Lariat (USA) – Lady Smurfette (IRE) (Naheez (USA)) [2017/18 b15.7g⁴ h20.9d^pu h20.6v^pu h16.2d^pu Apr 23] fourth in maiden bumper at Southwell (9½ lengths behind Rococo Style): no form over hurdles. *Simon West*   **h–** **b75**

JIMMY 5 ch.g. Norse Dancer (IRE) – Isintshelovely (IRE) (Broken Hearted) [2017/18 b–: h19.2g h17.7v h19.2d Feb 25] modest form over hurdles. *Chris Gordon*   **h91**

JIMMY BELL 7 b.g. Tiger Hill (IRE) – Armada Grove (Fleetwood (IRE)) [2017/18 b83: b16.3d⁵ b16.8d h19.5v h19.7s² h21.7s⁵ h21.7v⁵ h19.7s² h23.9s⁴ Apr 25] modest at best in bumpers: modest form over hurdles: stays 2½m: acts on soft going: in cheekpieces last 2 starts. *John O'Shea*   **h98** **b–**

JIMMY BREEKIE (IRE) 8 b.g. Alkaadhem – Highland Breeze (IRE) (Kotashaan (FR)) [2017/18 h115, b96: h20s⁵ h20.2m* h20g² h16s⁶ h16v⁴ h20s³ h20v⁶ h19.3v⁵ Jan 24] failed to complete both starts in points: bumper winner: fairly useful hurdler: won novice at Perth in June: third in handicap at Fairyhouse in December: stays 2½m: acts on good to firm and heavy going: has worn hood. *Stuart Crawford, Ireland*   **h126**

JIMMY HIGH (IRE) 7 br.g. Mountain High (IRE) – Ballyknock Blaze (IRE) (Dr Massini (IRE)) [2017/18 b16.3d Jun 9] walked over in point: tailed off in bumper. *Andrew Nicholls*   **b–**

JIMMY THE JETPLANE (IRE) 10 b.g. Jimble (FR) – C'est Cool (IRE) (Roi Guillaume (FR)) [2017/18 c137, h–: c20.9v* c23.4s⁴ c24.5s⁵ Apr 27] well-made gelding: point winner: winning hurdler: fairly useful hunter chaser nowadays: won at Carlisle in March: stays 3¼m: acts on good to firm and heavy going: wears headgear: tried in tongue tie: usually races close up. *Francesca Nimmo*   **c121** **h–**

JIM THE DANGER 8 b.g. Lucarno (USA) – Kompete (Komaite (USA)) [2017/18 h19.1m^pu Jun 15] big gelding: no show in bumper/novice hurdle 27 months apart, tongue tied in former. *Gary Moore*   **h–**

JINSHA LAKE (IRE) 6 b.g. Galileo (IRE) – Al Ihsas (IRE) (Danehill (USA)) [2017/18 h89: h15.8g h15.8d Jul 30] sturdy gelding: modest hurdler at best, no form in 2017/18: tried in cheekpieces: wears tongue tie. *Evan Williams*   **h–**

JODIES JEM 8 br.g. Kheleyf (USA) – First Approval (Royal Applause) [2017/18 h103: h16.7g² h15.8g² h16.3g² h16g^F Jul 18] compact gelding: fair maiden hurdler: raced around 2m: best form on good going. *Michael Banks*   **h112**

JOE FARRELL (IRE) 9 b.g. Presenting – Luck of The Deise (IRE) (Old Vic) [2017/18 h129: c23.6d⁴ c23.8v² c23g⁴ c23.4s³ c23.4s* c31.8g⁴ Apr 21]   **c140** **h–**

Drainage problems contributed to Scotland's premier racecourse losing its big three-day Ayr Gold Cup meeting on the Flat in September, but there was no danger to its jumping showpiece, the Coral Scottish Grand National, which once again showed why it is one of jumping's great races. The Scottish National is Britain's most valuable handicap chase after the Aintree version and the Ladbrokes Trophy at Newbury, and, with a first prize of £122,442 and conditions just about perfect, the race was one of the highlights of the season. The prevailing good going—the Scottish National runners raced on fresh ground—came as a welcome change after a dismally wet winter which resulted in the spring festivals at Cheltenham and Aintree

Coral Scottish Grand National Handicap Chase, Ayr—Joe Farrell looks to have matters under control at the last ahead of fellow novices Ballyoptic (right) and the grey Vintage Clouds ...

being run in the mud and the entire Easter Monday programme being lost (Ayr itself had had fifteen jumps fixtures since November, all of those that were not cancelled being run on soft or heavy).

The Scottish National field was reduced to twenty-nine when the previous year's Eider Chase winner Mysteree was withdrawn after the deadline for reserves, but the betting was wide-open as usual with plenty of pre-race publicity about two so-called potential 'hat-trick horses'. There hasn't been an Irish-trained winner of the Scottish National in living memory but the 7/1 favourite Fagan, a novice, running in handicap company for the first time, was aiming to give his trainer Gordon Elliott a third major Grand National in as many weeks, following the success of General Principle in the Irish version and Tiger Roll at Aintree (the same unique treble had been attempted two years earlier by the Mouse Morris-trained Folsom Blue after the successes of Rogue Angel and Rule The World at Fairyhouse and Aintree). No horse had won the Scottish National in three successive years since before World War I (the race has been run at Ayr only since 1966), but second favourite Vicente, an 8/1-shot who might have run in the Grand National seven days earlier had the ground not been so testing, looked to have a fair chance of following up his successes in 2016 and 2017 (his BHA mark of 150 was 4 lb higher than for his two earlier wins, the first of them achieved while he was still a novice). Novices have a good record in the Scottish National and the Towton Novices' Chase winner and RSA Chase fourth Ballyoptic was the third runner at single-figure odds, his stable having had two previous novice winners, Captain Dibble and Earth Summit, who had finished fifth and seventh in the RSA Chase (the same yard had also been responsible for Sweet Duke, runner-up in the 1995 Scottish National after finishing fourth in the so-called 'novices' Gold Cup' at the Cheltenham Festival). Among the leading fancies at double-figure odds were other novices Vintage Clouds (second to Ballyoptic in the Towton), who had just missed the cut in the Grand National; the National Hunt Chase third Sizing Tennessee, seeking to follow three winners of the last seven runnings (Beshabar, Godsmejudge and Vicente) by winning the Scottish National after contesting the National Hunt Chase; and a second strong Irish-trained fancy in the progressive Glencairn View.

Those punters who banked on the novices proving the key again to the Scottish National were on the right lines. Novices finished first, second and third but the winner, the lightly-raced nine-year-old Joe Farrell having just his sixth outing over fences, was among the 33/1-shots and had hardly rated a mention in the race previews. He was from a stable that hadn't been firing on all cylinders over the winter and he had taken until the end of March to get off the mark over fences, in a six-runner novices' handicap at Newbury on his return from three months off. Joe Farrell won by seventeen lengths at Newbury after being left clear at the third last by the departure of Le Boizelo, his closest pursuer by that stage. The form wasn't easy to assess and an 11-lb rise in his BHA mark hardly made him look well-treated at Ayr. However, Joe Farrell was having his first crack at a marathon trip and he relished the stamina test, putting up an improved showing after being in touch all the way. There was no let-up in the gallop, with top weight Gold Present (who seemed not to stay in the end) among those forcing it, along with Vintage Clouds. Joe Farrell, whose jumping wasn't always fluent, was produced to take over at the fourth last and, as in the previous week's Grand National, the leader looked sure to win for long enough in the home straight. However, as with Tiger Roll (who held on in the end by a head from Pleasant Company), Joe Farrell was nearly caught as the strong-finishing Ballyoptic only just failed to peg him back. Joe Farrell clung on by a nose, the shortest possible margin, with the keeping-on Vintage Clouds (who had finished fourth in the Welsh National) four lengths further back in third, and Doing Fine a creditable fourth after coming from a long way back. Vicente finished a one-paced fifth after travelling well for much of the race and returned without his hind shoes, one of half a dozen runners who lost a shoe in the race, among them Joe Farrell. There were thirteen finishers, Fagan being among those pulled up after being beaten a long way out, while things were even worse for his compatriot Glencairn View who appeared to break down badly.

Joe Farrell's victory went some way to rescuing a poor season for his trainer Rebecca Curtis who had seen her string struggle to find its form and her stable strength fall from around fifty to just twenty (she had also endured turmoil in her private life). Pembrokeshire-based Curtis, who had only nine winners all season, enjoyed her biggest career success in the Scottish National on her first visit to Ayr, but she has been training for ten years and was in the winner's enclosure at the Cheltenham Festival four years in a row from 2012, with Teaforthree, At Fishers Cross, O'Faolains Boy and Irish Cavalier. Joe Farrell's success was also the biggest so far for his jockey Adam Wedge who had also had something of a mixed season, including being banned for twenty-one days for taking the wrong course on odds-on Report To Base at Exeter in January.

... but he's all out under Adam Wedge at the line to hold off the rallying Ballyoptic

JOE

Joe Farrell (IRE) (b.g. 2009)
- Presenting (br 1992)
  - Mtoto (b 1983)
    - Busted
    - Amazer
  - D'Azy (b 1984)
    - Persian Bold
    - Belle Viking
- Luck of The Deise (IRE) (b 2001)
  - Old Vic (b 1986)
    - Sadler's Wells
    - Cockade
  - Hope You're Lucky (ch 1982)
    - Quayside
    - Run of Luck

The good-topped Joe Farrell has something else in common with the Aintree winner Tiger Roll, in addition to just lasting home in a very valuable National after looking home and hosed. Like Tiger Roll, originally purchased to race for Godolphin on the Flat, Joe Farrell went through the hands of John Ferguson, long-time adviser to Sheikh Mohammed until he resigned in the summer of 2017. Ferguson trained in his own right over jumps for a while from Bloomfields in Newmarket, sending out a high ratio of winners to runners. He benefited from his long association with Sheikh Mohammed in acquiring a flow of useful Darley/Godolphin performers off the Flat which might otherwise have gone to the sales. In that respect, Joe Farrell, a jumping bred whom Ferguson bought for €26,000 as an unraced three-year-old, was far from typical of the usual Bloomfields recruits. Ferguson named him after a platoon sergeant in the Scots Guards that he had known in his army days, and Joe Farrell won two of his four bumpers, looking a useful hurdling prospect. By the time he made a winning start over timber as a seven-year-old, he was with Rebecca Curtis who bought him for only £10,000 at the Bloomfields dispersal at Cheltenham in April 2016, after John Ferguson gave up training. According to Curtis, he had 'broken down on both forelegs', which largely accounts for his having been sparingly raced. Joe Farrell's dam Luck of The Deise, an unraced half-sister to fairly useful staying hurdler Bondi Storm and fair staying hurdler/chaser Kilmington, has yet to breed another winner. The immediate family's main claim to fame is that Joe Farrell's great grandam Run of Luck was a sister to the top-class hunter chaser Eliogarty. Joe Farrell stays four miles and acts on heavy going, though he doesn't need the mud, as he showed in the Scottish National. *Rebecca Curtis*

JOEY SASA (IRE) 9 b.g. Winged Love (IRE) – Brescia (FR) (Monsun (GER)) [2017/18 h133, b110: h16d⁴ h18.8d⁸ h16.5d² h20s Apr 28] bumper winner: useful hurdler: won minor event at Downpatrick in October: second in handicap at Punchestown (2½ lengths behind True Self) in April: stays 2½m: acts on good to soft going. *Noel Meade, Ireland*   **h143**

JOG ON (IRE) 5 b.g. Definite Article – Azabu Juban (IRE) (Catcher In The Rye (IRE)) [2017/18 b15.3v⁶ Feb 1] well beaten in bumper. *Colin Tizzard*   **b–**

JOHN BISCUIT (IRE) 10 ch.g. Hawk Wing (USA) – Princess Magdalena (Pennekamp (USA)) [2017/18 c–, h80: h19.9g h19.6g⁶ h19.7g⁶ Nov 29] poor handicap hurdler: fell on sole start over fences: stays 21f: acts on good to soft going: tried in hood/tongue tie: usually races towards rear. *Jo Davis*   **c–** **h70**

JOHN CONSTABLE (IRE) 7 b.g. Montjeu (IRE) – Dance Parade (USA) (Gone West (USA)) [2017/18 h132: h15.7m* h16.7g* h16.8s⁶ h16v² h16.4s Mar 13] lengthy gelding: smart hurdler: won Swinton Handicap at Haydock (by 14 lengths from Optimus Prime) in May and Summer Hurdle (Handicap) at Market Rasen (by 2½ lengths from Red Tornado) in July: second in listed event at Sandown (1¾ lengths behind Buveur d'Air) in February: raced around 2m: acts on good to firm and heavy going: wears tongue tie: usually races towards rear/travels strongly. *Evan Williams*   **h150**

JOHNNY GO 8 b.g. Bollin Eric – Waverbeck (IRE) (Accordion) [2017/18 h97: h23.9g² c24.2g³ h23.9m⁵ c24.2g² c23.8m⁴ h23.9g* c23.8s³ Aug 19] modest handicap hurdler: won at Perth (amateur) in August: fair form over fences: stayed 3m: acted on soft going: often wore cheekpieces: dead. *Lisa Harrison*   **c100** **h98**

JOHNNY OCEAN (IRE) 6 b.g. Whitmore's Conn (USA) – Soda Bread (IRE) (Beneficial) [2017/18 h21.6d h23.3v^pu Dec 31] well-made gelding: Irish point winner: no form over hurdles. *Kim Bailey*   **h–**

JOHNNY OG 9 b.g. Flemensfirth (USA) – Mrs Roberts (Bob Back (USA)) [2017/18 c131, h–: c19.4g^pu May 8] workmanlike gelding: maiden hurdler: useful chaser at best, pulled up sole outing in 2017/18: stays 2½m: acts on heavy going: wears headgear: front runner/races prominently. *Martin Keighley*   **c–** **h–**

Betfred TV Summer Handicap Hurdle, Market Rasen—a profitable start to 2017/18 for John Constable (noseband) as he follows up his Swinton Hurdle win under leading Irish jockey Davy Russell

JOHNNY PEDLAR 7 b.g. Revoque (IRE) – Festival Fancy (Le Coq d'Or) [2017/18 b–: h16.2v⁵ h16v⁵ h18.1v³ Apr 16] modest form over hurdles: tried in hood. *Sandy Thomson*   **h86**

JOHNNYS LEGACY (IRE) 11 b.g. Ecton Park (USA) – Lexy May (USA) (Lear Fan (USA)) [2017/18 c–, h–: c20dᵘʳ Apr 9] sturdy gelding: maiden hurdler: modest chaser at best, lightly raced and no form since 2014/15: stays 3m: acts on heavy going: wears headgear: tried in tongue tie. *Miss Hannah Taylor*   **c–** **h–**

JOHNNY YUMA (IRE) 5 b.g. Alfred Nobel (IRE) – Rossbridge Lass (IRE) (Clerkenwell (USA)) [2017/18 b16.7g h16v h15.5d h16.7v⁵ h15.5v c24.1d⁴ Apr 21] €12,500 3-y-o: fourth foal: dam, ran twice in points, half-sister to high-class 2m hurdler Go Native: point winner: tailed off in bumper: poor form over hurdles: 12/1, fourth in novice handicap at Bangor (20 lengths behind Heavenly Promise) on chasing debut: capable of better as a chaser. *Katy Price*   **c82 p** **h83** **b–**

JOHN REEL (FR) 9 b.g. Country Reel (USA) – John Quatz (FR) (Johann Quatz (FR)) [2017/18 h90: h20g c15.7g* May 24] fairly useful hurdler at best, excuses on return in 2017/18: 7/2, won novice handicap at Southwell (by 6 lengths from Tiger Trek) on chasing debut: should stay beyond 2m: acts on heavy going. *David Evans*   **c124 p** **h–**

JOHNS LUCK (IRE) 9 b.g. Turtle Island (IRE) – Jemima Yorke (Be My Guest (USA)) [2017/18 c111, h–: c23.8vᵖᵘ c20.2v³ h23.8s h19.8v Mar 8] sturdy gelding: fair hurdler/chaser at best, no form in 2017/18: stays 3¼m, effective at much shorter: acts on heavy going: usually wears headgear. *Neil Mulholland*   **c–** **h–**

JOHN WILLIAMS (IRE) 9 b.g. Presenting – Duhallow Park (IRE) (Flemensfirth (USA)) [2017/18 c99, h–: c20.1gᵖᵘ c15.6v* c15.8m** c23.8g⁴ c19.9d² c17.1v⁴ Apr 16] maiden hurdler: fair handicap chaser: won at Hexham in October and Musselburgh in November: stays 2¾m, effective at shorter: acts on good to firm and heavy going: wears cheekpieces: usually leads. *Sandy Thomson*   **c102** **h–**

JOIN THE CLAN (IRE) 9 b.g. Milan – Millicent Bridge (IRE) (Over The River (FR)) [2017/18 c134, h–: c24d⁴ h25.4d⁴ c26.1m h25sᵖᵘ h24.4d⁵ Feb 8] workmanlike gelding: useful hurdler/chaser at best, below that in 2017/18: stays 3¼m: acts on heavy going: has worn headgear, including in 2017/18: often races towards rear. *Jonjo O'Neill*   **c123** **h113**

JOIN THE NAVY 13 b.g. Sea Freedom – Join The Parade (Elmaamul (USA)) [2017/18 h21.7d h19.5v h21s⁴ Apr 9] workmanlike gelding: fair handicap hurdler, below best in 2017/18: winning chaser: stays 21f: acts on heavy going: usually wears headgear: has worn tongue tie: races well off the pace: not straightforward (can look disinterested). *Kate Buckett*   **c–** **h91**

JOIN TOGETHER (IRE) 13 b.g. Old Vic – Open Cry (IRE) (Montelimar (USA)) [2017/18 c110§, h–: c32.5d⁴ May 5] multiple point winner: winning hurdler: fairly useful hunter chaser: stays 33f: acts on good to firm and heavy going: has worn headgear, including sole outing in 2017/18: temperamental. *Mrs Rose Loxton*   **c116 §** **h–**

JOK

JOKE DANCER 5 ch.g. Authorized (IRE) – Missy Dancer (Shareef Dancer (USA)) [2017/18 b65: h16.8g⁶ h16.4g² h15.7v* h15.7v⁵ h15.7v* h15.7s⁵ Mar 31] fairly useful hurdler: won novice at Haydock in December, and handicaps at same course in January and Newcastle in February: raced around 2m: acts on heavy going. *Sue Smith* — h124

JOKERS AND ROGUES (IRE) 10 b.g. Beneficial – Ashfield Girl (IRE) (Beau Sher) [2017/18 c–, h105: h17s^pu h19.3d⁵ c16.4s⁴ Dec 26] fair handicap hurdler, well below best in 2017/18: poor form over fences: stays 2½m: acts on heavy going: has worn tongue tie, including final start: front runner. *Kenneth Slack* — c76 h70

JOLIE CRICKETTE (FR) 6 b.m. Laverock (IRE) – Crickette River (FR) (Cricket Ball (USA)) [2017/18 c114, h97: h16v h20.2s⁵ Apr 25] modest handicap hurdler: fair chaser: stays 2½m: acts on soft going: usually wears blinkers. *N. W. Alexander* — c– h88

JOLIE FRANCINE (IRE) 6 gr.m. King's Theatre (IRE) – Belle Innocence (FR) (Turgeon (USA)) [2017/18 h20.6g⁴ h20.5s h15.7v³ Feb 1] fifth foal: sister to 2 winners, including modest hurdler/fair chaser Innocent Girl (2m-19f winner): dam won 2¼m listed hurdle in France: runner-up in Irish point: poor form over hurdles. *Charlie Longsdon* — h84

JOLLY JET (IRE) 6 b.m. Arcadio (GER) – Boarding Pass (IRE) (Accordion) [2017/18 h20.5s^pu h19.2d h21.7v^pu h24.6s⁶ Apr 9] €5,000 4-y-o: third foal: half-sister to fair/untrustworthy hurdler Transient Bay (2½m winner, by Trans Island), stays 23f: dam unraced: no form over hurdles. *Linda Jewell* — h–

JOLLY ROGER (IRE) 11 b.g. Oratorio (IRE) – Chalice Wells (Sadler's Wells (USA)) [2017/18 c–, h97: h15.8g^F May 9] close-coupled gelding: fairly useful hurdler at best, fell fatally sole outing in 2017/18: winning chaser: stayed 2½m: acted on any going: tried in cheekpieces. *Dai Burchell* — c– h80

JONAGOLD 7 b.g. Apple Tree (FR) – Single Handed (Cloudings (IRE)) [2017/18 c100, h108: c20.9d² c20.9g² c25.8d⁴ c20.9g² c21d³ c20.3d* c20.9s⁵ c23.8v^F Nov 12] point winner: maiden hurdler: fair handicap chaser: won at Bangor in October: stays 21f: acts on good to soft going: often in headgear: wears tongue tie: temperamental. *Evan Williams* — c102 § h–

JONJOELA (IRE) 7 b.m. Great Exhibition (USA) – Yorkshire Blade (IRE) (Sadler's Wells (USA)) [2017/18 h19.6g⁴ h20.6g⁴ h19.7g^F h21g^pu h23.4s⁵ h25d^ur Mar 26] fifth foal: dam unraced: point winner: well held in 2 bumpers in Ireland in 2015/16: poor form over hurdles: tried in hood. *Tracey Leeson* — h71

JONNIE SKULL (IRE) 12 b.g. Pyrus (USA) – Sovereign Touch (IRE) (Pennine Walk) [2017/18 c–, h68: h16m⁴ May 9] poor hurdler nowadays: once-raced chaser: tried in visor: wears tongue tie. *Phil McEntee* — c– h76

JONNIESOFA (IRE) 8 b.g. Well Made (GER) – Lucky Sarah (IRE) (Aahsaylad) [2017/18 c15.9v* c19v² Dec 30] workmanlike gelding: useful hurdler: similar form over fences: won maiden at Carlisle in October: stays 25f: acts on heavy going. *Rose Dobbin* — c137 h–

JONNY DELTA 11 ch.g. Sulamani (IRE) – Send Me An Angel (IRE) (Lycius (USA)) [2017/18 h112: h15.6m⁴ h19.4g^F Dec 18] fair handicap hurdler: stayed 19f: acted on good to firm and heavy going: dead. *Jim Goldie* — h101

JOSEPHINE K 5 b.m. Bahri (USA) – Montrachet Belle (Kadeed (IRE)) [2017/18 h66: h22.1g^pu h23.8g^pu h19.7s^pu Dec 26] little form: in tongue tie last 3 starts. *Susan Corbett* — h–

JOSEPH MERCER (IRE) 11 b.g. Court Cave (IRE) – Vikki's Dream (IRE) (Kahyasi) [2017/18 c94, h101: h24.1s h25.3d⁵ c26.3s^pu Jan 12] fair hurdler/modest chaser at best, no form in 2017/18: wore headgear: front runner/raced prominently: dead. *Tina Jackson* — c– h–

JOSIES ORDERS (IRE) 10 b.g. Milan – Silent Orders (IRE) (Bob Back (USA)) [2017/18 h21.6s⁶ c24s² c24s² c30.2d³ h20v c24v² c30.2s⁶ h20v^pu c33.5d² c24s* Apr 28] good-topped gelding: fairly useful handicap hurdler: useful chaser: won cross country event at Punchestown in April: stays 33f: acts on heavy going: has worn headgear, including in 2017/18: often races prominently. *Enda Bolger, Ireland* — c143 h119

JOSSES HILL (IRE) 10 b.g. Winged Love (IRE) – Credora Storm (IRE) (Glacial Storm (USA)) [2017/18 c156, h–: c21d⁶ c21.7s² c20.5d⁵ c24g^pu ab16d⁴ h24g^pu Apr 18] strong, useful-looking gelding: winning hurdler: smart chaser: second in Peterborough Chase at Taunton (3¼ lengths behind Top Notch) in December: disappointing after: stays 2½m: acts on good to firm and heavy going: wears headgear: front runner/races prominently. *Nicky Henderson* — c149 h–

JOUEUR BRESILIEN (FR) 6 b.g. Fuisse (FR) – Fille du Bresil (FR) (Smadoun (FR)) [2017/18 h116: c15.9s⁶ c16g² c16v³ Jan 3] lengthy, useful-looking gelding: fairly useful maiden hurdler: similar form over fences: should stay beyond 2m: acts on heavy going: tried in cheekpieces: usually races prominently. *Rebecca Curtis* — c120 h–

JUM

JOUR DE KLASS (FR) 6 ch.g. Prince Kirk (FR) – Meliades (FR) (Octagonal (NZ)) [2017/18 b16.8m⁴ b17.7g Aug 24] no form in bumpers. *Mark Usher* b–

JOVIAL JOEY (IRE) 7 b.g. St Jovite (USA) – Like A Bird (IRE) (Topanoora) [2017/18 c130, h101: c21.4g^pu c23.8g^ur c15.9d^pu c25.2d^pu Nov 24] maiden hurdler: useful chaser at best, no form in 2017/18: wears tongue tie: front runner/races prominently. *Maurice Barnes* c– h–

JOY AT MIDNIGHT 6 b.m. Midnight Legend – Flora Joy (Alflora (IRE)) [2017/18 b16m b16g Jul 18] second foal: dam unraced sister to fairly useful hurdler/chaser (stays 3m) Al Alfa: failed to complete all 3 starts in points: little show in bumper/maiden hurdle. *Richard Woollacott* h– b–

JOYCETICK (FR) 4 b.g. Myboycharlie (IRE) – Joyce (GER) (Chato (USA)) [2017/18 h16.9v³ h14.9d² h17.4g² h16.9g* h16s^pu h16m^F Apr 26] has had breathing operation: half-brother to fairly useful French hurdler/winning chaser Lilou Tag (2m-19f winner, by Hurricane Run): fairly useful on Flat in France, stays 1m: fairly useful form over hurdles: won claimer at Angouleme in September: left Francois Nicolle after fourth start: raced around 2m: in tongue tie last 2 starts. *Nick Littmoden* h118

JOYRIDER (IRE) 6 b.g. Stowaway – Aileen Supreme (IRE) (Presenting) [2017/18 b83: b16d² Oct 31] fairly useful form in bumpers: in hood first start. *Emma Lavelle* b98

JUBILEE LASS 6 b.m. Bach (IRE) – Kingaroy Lass (IRE) (Eurobus) [2017/18 b16.8g b16d h16v h19.5v^pu Dec 9] pulled up in point: no form in bumpers/over hurdles: dead. *Phillip Dando* h– b–

JUBILYMPICS 6 b.m. Kapgarde (FR) – Pepite de Soleil (FR) (Fly To The Stars) [2017/18 b87: b15.7m* h19.2v h17.7v³ h21.4v* h20.5v⁵ h20.5s³ h20.3g⁴ Apr 19] lengthy, rather unfurnished mare: fair form in bumpers: won mares event at Towcester in May: fairly useful form over hurdles: won novice at Wincanton in February: fourth in listed mares handicap at Cheltenham in April: will stay beyond 21f: acts on heavy going. *Seamus Mullins* h119 b88

JUDGE EARLE (IRE) 6 b.g. Court Cave (IRE) – Louis's Teffia (IRE) (Presenting) [2017/18 b83: b16.8g⁴ h19.7d² h21.2g⁶ h19.4g⁶ h18.1v³ h19.9v^pu h24.3g Apr 20] fair form in bumpers: won at Sedgefield in May: fair form over hurdles: should stay 2½m+: acts on heavy going. *Richard Fahey* h105 b86

JUDGE JOHN DEED (IRE) 7 ch.g. Robin des Champs (FR) – Milogan (IRE) (Milan) [2017/18 h21.6v^pu h21d Apr 26] €57,000 3-y-o: big gelding: second foal: dam unraced half-sister to useful hurdler/chaser (stayed 3½m) Tullymurry Toff: point winner: modest form over hurdles. *Paul Nicholls* h92

JUDGE JUDY (IRE) 5 b.m. Oscar (IRE) – The Bar Maid (Alderbrook) [2017/18 h19.2v^pu h19.2s Apr 6] fifth foal: dam (h110), 21f hurdle winner (stayed 3m), half-sister to fairly useful/moody hurdler/chaser (stayed 3m) Cornet: little form over hurdles: temperament under suspicion. *Lawney Hill* h74

JUGE ET PARTI (FR) 5 gr.g. Martaline – Nakota Rag (FR) (Nikos) [2017/18 b103p: h20v² h20v² h23.3v² h25.5v⁶ Mar 10] bumper winner: fairly useful form over hurdles: left Christian Williams after third start. *Nigel Twiston-Davies* h116

JUKEBOX JIVE (FR) 4 b.g. Jukebox Jury (IRE) – Sweetheart (Sinndar (IRE)) [2017/18 h17.7d* h16s⁴ Dec 8] smallish gelding: dam useful hurdler (2m-3m winner): useful on Flat, stays 2¼m: fairly useful form over hurdles: won juvenile at Fontwell in November: will stay 2½m: wears tongue tie. *Anthony Honeyball* h125

JULLY LES BUXY (FR) 8 b.m. Black Sam Bellamy (IRE) – Jadidh (Touching Wood (USA)) [2017/18 h–: h20.5v* h25v⁴ h21.4s⁵ h24v³ h23.1v* Apr 17] sturdy mare: fair handicap hurdler: won at Plumpton in January and Exeter in April: left Nick Mitchell after fourth start: stays 25f: acts on heavy going: tried in cheekpieces: in tongue tie last 2 starts. *Keiran Burke* h107

JUMBO DAVIS (IRE) 5 b.m. Doyen (IRE) – Banjo Davis (IRE) (Definite Article) [2017/18 b15.7v⁵ Apr 27] second foal: dam, bumper winner, half-sister to fairly useful hurdler (stays 3m) Small World: runner-up on completed start in Irish points: 7/2, fifth in mares bumper at Towcester (19¾ lengths behind Destinee Royale): open to improvement. *Harry Whittington* b63 p

JUMP AND JUMP (IRE) 8 br.m. Oscar (IRE) – My Twist (IRE) (Flemensfirth (USA)) [2017/18 c87, h92: c20g^pu c20g c17.8m⁶ c23m⁵ c23g³ Nov 30] sturdy mare: maiden hurdler/chaser: tried in cheekpieces/tongue tie: dead. *Johnny Farrelly* c71 h–

Liam & Valerie Brennan Memorial Florida Pearl Novices' Chase, Punchestown—
Jury Duty lowers the colours of his better-fancied stable-companion Shattered Love (mostly hidden)

JUMP FOR DOUGH (IRE) 7 b.g. Milan – Collopy's Girl (IRE) (Be My Native (USA)) [2017/18 h24d* h24.6g³ c24.2s⁴ c19.9g⁴ h23.8s* h23.8s* h26.1s⁵ Feb 4] good-topped gelding: fifth foal: dam twice-raced sister to fair hurdler/useful chaser Atum Re and half-sister to useful hurdler/chaser Sunset Lodge, both stayed 2½m: fairly useful handicap hurdler: won at Cork in May and Musselburgh (twice) in January: modest form over fences: left William O'Doherty after second start: stays 3¼m: acts on soft going. *Lucinda Russell* — **c92** **h115**

JUMPING JACK (IRE) 4 b.g. Sir Prancealot (IRE) – She's A Character (Invincible Spirit (IRE)) [2017/18 h15.9m⁴ h15.8g³ h16g² h15.8g² h16d² h15.9d² h15.7s⁴ h15.9v² Apr 1] good-quartered gelding: fairly useful on Flat, stays 1¼m: fair maiden hurdler: raced only at 2m: acts on heavy going. *Chris Gordon* — **h108**

JUNCTION FOURTEEN (IRE) 9 b.g. King's Theatre (IRE) – Chevet Girl (IRE) (Roselier (FR)) [2017/18 c144, h–: c21.4g^pu c23.6d⁴ c23.8g c22.4g⁴ ab16d⁶ c21.6g^F Apr 20] sturdy gelding: winning hurdler: useful handicap chaser: stays 3m: acts on soft and good to firm going: in visor last 5 starts: wears tongue tie: front runner/races prominently: temperamental. *Emma Lavelle* — **c137 §** **h–**

JUNE CARTER (IRE) 6 b.m. Scorpion (IRE) – Evidence (Machiavellian (USA)) [2017/18 h71: h19g h20.4s^pu h18.8g⁵ h21.8g⁵ h25d⁵ h21.5v⁶ h22.7g Oct 28] poor maiden hurdler: in blinkers last 4 starts: often races towards rear. *Mark McNiff, Ireland* — **h81**

JUNGLE GIRL 8 ch.m. Desideratum – Red Snow (Unfuwain (USA)) [2017/18 h19.9g Aug 31] second foal: dam lightly raced on Flat in France (second at 1½m)/in points: tailed off in novice hurdle. *John Wainwright* — **h–**

JUPITER CUSTOS (FR) 6 b.g. Le Havre (IRE) – Angel Rose (IRE) (Definite Article) [2017/18 h105: h16.7g³ May 21] fairly useful on Flat: fair form over hurdles. *Michael Scudamore* — **h104**

JUPITER'S GIFT (IRE) 6 b.m. Scorpion (IRE) – Presenting Ally (IRE) (Presenting) [2017/18 h–, h74: h21.6d³ h23m Jul 5] poor form over hurdles: in cheekpieces last 2 starts. *Kim Bailey* — **h77**

JURBY 8 b.g. Motivator – Darariyna (IRE) (Shirley Heights) [2017/18 h16.3g² h15.3v* h16.6d^pu h15.3v² h21.7s^F h15.7v* Apr 27] fairly useful form over hurdles: won novices at Wincanton in January and Towcester in April: will stay further than 2m: acts on heavy going. *Oliver Sherwood* — **h127**

422

JURY DUTY (IRE) 7 b.g. Well Chosen – Swan Heart (IRE) (Broken Hearted) [2017/18 h147: c22s* c20s² c22.6s⁴ c24s² c24v² c31.8s^ur c24.5s³ Apr 24] well-made gelding: smart hurdler: smart chaser: won maiden at Limerick (by 2½ lengths from Twiss's Hill) in October and Florida Pearl Novices' Chase at Punchestown (by ¾ length from Shattered Love) in November: also placed in Grade 3 novice at Cork, Neville Hotels Novices' Chase at Leopardstown, Grade 3 novice at Naas and Champion Novices' Chase at Punchestown: stays 25f: acts on heavy going: in tongue tie last 2 starts: often races towards rear. *Gordon Elliott, Ireland* **c150 +** **h–**

JURYS OUT (IRE) 5 b.g. Witness Box (USA) – No Complaints But (IRE) (Supreme Leader) [2017/18 h19.7s h19.5v Mar 21] no form over hurdles. *Venetia Williams* **h–**

JUSTADREAMYEKEN 6 b.g. Scorpion (IRE) – Loxhill Lady (Supreme Leader) [2017/18 b15.7s⁴ Feb 12] fourth foal: half-brother to bumper winner/useful hurdler Zulu Oscar (2m-21f winner, by Oscar) and fair hurdler/fairly useful chaser Royal Salute (2¼m-3¼m winner, by Flemensfirth): dam unraced half-sister to fair hurdler/fairly useful chaser (stayed 3m) Dorans Gold: 7/2, fourth in conditional/amateur maiden bumper at Catterick (7½ lengths behind The Some Dance Kid). *Harriet Graham* **b84**

JUST A FEELING 8 ch.m. Flemensfirth (USA) – Precious Lady (Exit To Nowhere (USA)) [2017/18 h–: h18.7g⁶ h15.8g h15.8d c23g^pu Oct 17] maiden hurdler, modest form at best: pulled up in maiden on chasing debut: left Paul Webber after first start: tried in visor/tongue tie. *Dan Skelton* **c–** **h68**

JUSTANOTHER MUDDLE 9 gr.g. Kayf Tara – Spatham Rose (Environment Friend) [2017/18 c16v^F Mar 5] tall gelding: has had breathing operation: fairly useful hurdler: off 2 years, fell heavily 4 out in novice won by Maestro Royal at Lingfield on chasing debut: should stay 3m. *Gary Moore* **c–** **h–**

JUST ANOTHER VODKA 6 gr.g. Double Trigger (IRE) – Par Excellence (Wizard King) [2017/18 b16d⁴ b16g b15.8d h19.7s h19s Jan 9] first foal: dam, showed nothing over hurdles/in points, 5f winner on Flat: modest form in bumpers: little form over hurdles: in hood last 3 starts. *Nicky Martin* **h60** **b83**

JUST A STING (IRE) 6 b.g. Scorpion (IRE) – Shanann Lady (IRE) (Anshan) [2017/18 b99: h21.6v² h16s³ h21.6v³ h21s Mar 17] lengthy gelding: will make a chaser: bumper winner: fairly useful form over hurdles. *Harry Fry* **h121**

JUSTATENNER 7 b.g. Northern Legend – Shelayly (IRE) (Zaffaran (USA)) [2017/18 c–p, h106: h23.9g h17.2d h20.2g⁵ h23.9d^pu h20.9d^F h19.3v⁶ h19.3d^F h23.8g³ h23.8s h17d⁶ h17s Apr 8] modest handicap hurdler: pulled up sole outing over fences: stays 3m: acts on heavy going: tried in headgear/tongue tie: races towards rear. *Barry Murtagh* **c–** **h85**

JUST A THOUGHT (IRE) 9 b.m. Stowaway – Carrig Lucy (IRE) (Phardante (FR)) [2017/18 b99: h19.5d² h26d² h21.4v² h20.5s³ h26s² h20.5s⁴ h20.3g Apr 19] smallish, angular mare: runner-up in Irish point: bumper winner: fairly useful maiden hurdler: stays 3¼m: acts on heavy going: often races prominently. *Rebecca Curtis* **h118**

JUST BEFORE DAWN (IRE) 9 b.g. Millenary – Knocka Beauty (IRE) (Allegoric (USA)) [2017/18 h123p: h20.2g* May 17] sturdy gelding: point/bumper winner: fairly useful form over hurdles: didn't need to repeat debut effort to win maiden at Perth on sole outing in 2017/18. *Tom George* **h106**

JUST BOBBY (IRE) 5 b.g. Black Sam Bellamy (IRE) – Blackwater Bay (IRE) (Supreme Leader) [2017/18 b90: b16.8g² b17d⁴ h16s⁶ h19.9v³ h19.9v* Apr 13] fair form in bumpers: similar form over hurdles: won novice at Sedgefield in April: usually races towards rear. *Micky Hammond* **h112** **b86**

JUST BROOKE 8 ch.m. Black Sam Bellamy (IRE) – Sports Express (Then Again) [2017/18 h–: h20.2g⁴ May 17] poor form over hurdles: tried in tongue tie. *N. W. Alexander* **h67**

JUST BRYAN 8 b.g. With The Flow (USA) – Straight Courage (Straight Knight) [2017/18 b–: h21.6d^pu Jul 31] no form in bumpers/novice hurdle: temperamental. *Colin Tizzard* **h– §**

JUST CALL ME AL (IRE) 5 br.g. Presenting – Tonaphuca Girl (IRE) (Saddlers' Hall (IRE)) [2017/18 b17s⁴ Apr 8] fifth foal: dam unraced half-sister to fairly useful hurdler/useful chaser (2m-21f winner) Donadino and fairly useful hurdler (stayed 3m) Raven Rock: 8/1, shaped well when fourth in bumper at Carlisle (8¾ lengths behind Largy Glory): open to improvement. *Gillian Boanas* **b90 p**

JUS

JUST CALL ME BLUE (IRE) 6 b.g. Blueprint (IRE) – Island-Bay (IRE) (Executive Perk) [2017/18 ab16g b16v[5] b16.2s Jan 16] no form in bumpers: wears cheekpieces. *Roger Teal* — b–

JUST CALL ME JENNI 7 b.m. Alflora (IRE) – Fairlie (Halling (USA)) [2017/18 b16.8s[pu] Dec 26] fifth foal: half-sister to 3 winners, including bumper winner/fair hurdler Chilly Miss (17f winner, by Iceman), stays 2½m, and fair hurdler Broctune Papa Gio (2m winner, by Tobougg): dam 6f-1¼m winner: pulled up in mares bumper. *Andrew Crook* — b–

JUST CAMERON 11 b.g. Kayf Tara – Miss Fencote (Phardante (FR)) [2017/18 c150, h–: c17.1d[6] c16.4g c15.2s* c15.2s[4] c16d[2] c20.5g[ur] Apr 20] tall gelding: winning hurdler: smart handicap chaser: won at Wetherby (by 1¾ lengths from Duke of Navan) in December: stays 2½m, usually races over shorter: acts on heavy going: has worn cheekpieces, including last 4 starts: wears tongue tie: often races prominently. *Micky Hammond* — c147 / h–

JUST CAUSE (IRE) 8 b.g. Court Cave (IRE) – Secret Can't Say (IRE) (Jurado (USA)) [2017/18 h24g c19.5g[2] c22.5d[6] c19.9g[F] c22d[5] c25.2s[5] Mar 7] multiple point winner: winning hurdler: fairly useful maiden chaser: left M. F. Morris after fifth start: stays 25f: acts on heavy going: often wears cheekpieces: tried in tongue tie: temperamental. *J. P. Owen* — c120 § / h–

JUST CHILLY 9 b.m. Kayf Tara – Your Punishment (IRE) (Montelimar (USA)) [2017/18 h16.8g h18.1g[5] h20.9d[2] h22.7g Oct 28] poor maiden hurdler: stays 21f: acts on heavy going: in hood last 4 starts. *Rose Dobbin* — h79

JUST DON'T ASK (IRE) 6 ch.g. Ask – Lucys Mate (IRE) (Supreme Leader) [2017/18 h19.7d[3] h19.5v[2] h20.5v* h19.9v* Mar 17] €8,500 3-y-o, £50,000 4-y-o: rangy gelding: will make a chaser: third foal: dam, bumper winner, half-sister to useful chaser (3m/25f winner) Meanus Dandy: winning pointer: fairly useful form over hurdles: won maiden at Ayr in February and novice at Uttoxeter in March: stays 2½m. *Charlie Longsdon* — h124

JUSTE POUR NOUS 5 b.g. Pour Moi (IRE) – Steam Cuisine (Mark of Esteem (IRE)) [2017/18 h101p: h17g[3] h16.3g[5] h15.7g[3] h20g h20g[pu] Aug 23] modest maiden hurdler: best effort at 2m: acts on good to firm going: wears headgear/tongue tie. *David Pipe* — h95

JUSTFORJAMES (IRE) 9 b.g. Dr Massini (IRE) – Over The Road (IRE) (Executive Perk) [2017/18 h117: c19.3g[5] c21.4s[5] c19.2v[3] c25.2s[4] c19.3v* c20s[3] c19.3g* Apr 23] winning hurdler: fairly useful handicap chaser: won at Sedgefield in March (novice) and April: stays 3m: acts on heavy going: has worn headgear, including last 3 starts. *Micky Hammond* — c117 / h–

JUST GEORGIE 8 b.g. Kayf Tara – Just Kate (Bob's Return (IRE)) [2017/18 c111, h–: h19.7s[6] c20.3s[2] c22.9v[ur] c23.4s[6] c24.2v* c20.6s[3] c23.4v[2] Apr 7] maiden hurdler: fairly useful handicap chaser: won at Wetherby in February: stays 3m: acts on heavy going: usually races prominently. *Sue Smith* — c117 / h92

JUSTICE KNIGHT (IRE) 6 b.g. Raven's Pass (USA) – New Story (USA) (Dynaformer (USA)) [2017/18 b–: h16.3m[5] h16.3g[su] h16.7g[5] h16g[6] h18.5v[2] h19g h21.7s[pu] h19.2v[pu] Feb 14] modest maiden hurdler: stays 19f: acts on heavy going: has worn hood: free-going front runner. *Michael Scudamore* — h91

JUSTIFICATION 10 b.g. Montjeu (IRE) – Colorspin (FR) (High Top) [2017/18 h115: h16d[5] h19s h19.8v[3] h20.5v[6] Feb 12] rather leggy gelding: fair handicap hurdler: stays 2½m: acts on soft going: often races in rear. *Gary Moore* — h101

JUST JANICE (IRE) 6 b.m. King's Theatre (IRE) – Liss Na Tintri (IRE) (Presenting) [2017/18 h120.5g[6] h19.8s* h20.6g[5] h16.5g[5] h19.5g[2] h22g[6] h20.2s[3] h16s[2] h20.4s* h16s* h18v h18s h22v h20.3g[2] Apr 19] first foal: dam, (h111) bumper winner/maiden hurdler (stayed 3m), out of very smart 2m-2½m hurdle winner Liss A Paoraigh: useful hurdler: won handicap at Clonmel in June, novice at Galway in October and EBF Lough Construction Ltd Mares Novices' Hurdle at Down Royal (by 4¼ lengths from Creation) in November: second in listed mares novice at Cheltenham (1½ lengths behind Dame de Compagnie) in April: stays 2¾m: acts on heavy going: has worn tongue tie: races well off pace. *John E. Kiely, Ireland* — h130

JUST JEREMY (IRE) 4 b.g. Jeremy (USA) – Taipers (IRE) (Taipan (IRE)) [2017/18 b13.7g[5] Apr 20] 10/1, fifth in bumper at Fontwell (18¾ lengths behind Kalinihta). *Gary Moore* — b66

JUST JOELLIOTT (IRE) 8 b.g. Great Exhibition (USA) – Solara (GER) (Danehill (USA)) [2017/18 h104: c25.8g[F] c26.2d[3] c23.6v[F] Nov 22] angular gelding: fair hurdler: similar front form over fences: third in novice handicap at Chepstow on completed start: stayed 3¼m: acted on good to soft going: tried in hood: wore tongue tie: often raced towards rear: dead. *Seamus Durack* — c104 / h–

JUST MIDAS (IRE) 5 b.g. Shantou (USA) – Desert Gail (IRE) (Desert Style (IRE)) **b84**
[2017/18 b16.8v⁴ b15.7v Mar 29] €32,000 3-y-o: fifth foal: brother to unreliable winning hurdler Fled Or Pled (21f-3m winner), closely related to fairly useful hurdler/chaser Court Red Handed (21f-25f winner, by Flemensfirth) and half-brother to fair hurdler/fairly useful chaser Clontarf (21f-3m winner, by Brian Boru): dam unraced: modest form in bumpers: better effort when fourth at Exeter on debut. *David Pipe*

JUST MILLY (IRE) 7 b.m. Milan – Out Performer (IRE) (Persian Bold) [2017/18 h115, **h125** b76: h23.3d⁶ h19.9g² h24.1d² h24.2d⁵ h20.6d³ h19.4d^F h20.6g² Apr 22] fairly useful handicap hurdler: stays 3m: acts on good to soft going: wears hood. *John Mackie*

JUST MINDED (IRE) 7 b.g. Kayf Tara – Georgia On My Mind (FR) (Belmez (USA)) **c116** [2017/18 h120, b93: c20d^F c15.6v^{pu} c25.2s³ c19.2s⁴ c19.3g² Apr 23] bumper winner: fairly **h–** useful hurdler: similar form over fences: stays 2½m: acts on soft going: tried in cheekpieces: temperament under suspicion. *Sue Smith*

JUST SO COOL (IRE) 7 gr.g. Acambaro (GER) – Lauras Dote (IRE) (Muroto) [2017/18 **h110** h19.6s* h19.8v⁴ h20.3v⁵ Mar 5] lengthy gelding: placed in point: fair handicap hurdler: won at Huntingdon (conditional) in January: stays 23f: acts on heavy going. *David Dennis*

JUST SPOT 11 ch.m. Baryshnikov (AUS) – Just Jasmine (Nicholas Bill) [2017/18 c–, h–: **c–** h18.5v² h15.3v* h19.2v h23.9s h19.7s³ h21.6v⁶ Apr 8] workmanlike mare: modest **h84** handicap hurdler: won novice event at Wincanton in December: winning chaser: stays 19f: acts on heavy going: has worn tongue tie. *Kevin Bishop*

JUSTTHEGREY (IRE) 6 gr.g. Getaway (GER) – Line White (FR) (Pitchounet (FR)) **b73** [2017/18 b15.7g⁵ Sep 6] 28/1, fifth in maiden bumper at Southwell (11½ lengths behind Rococo Style). *Rosemary Gasson*

JUST YOUR TYPE (IRE) 6 br.g. Morozov (USA) – Enistar (IRE) (Synefos (USA)) **h123** [2017/18 h20v² h22.8v⁴ h25.5v* Mar 10] €5,500 4-y-o, £40,000 5-y-o: third foal: brother to fairly useful hurdler/chaser Zanstra (19f-21f winner), stays 3m: dam unraced half-sister to useful hurdler/staying chaser Golden Chieftain: Irish point winner: fairly useful form over hurdles: won novice at Hereford in March: thorough stayer. *Charlie Longsdon*

K

KABANGA BAY 7 b.g. Overbury (IRE) – Cresswell Zoey (IRE) (Zaffaran (USA)) **h–** [2017/18 h104, b–: h19.2d⁶ Sep 10] winning pointer: maiden hurdler, well held only start under Rules in 2017/18: stays 21f: acts on soft and good to firm going. *Phil York*

KADDYS DREAM 7 b.m. Kadastrof (IRE) – Symbiosis (Bien Bien (USA)) [2017/18 **h94** h100p: h15.7s⁶ h19.6s⁴ h15.8s³ h20.7s Mar 14] modest maiden hurdler: stays 2½m: acts on soft going: sometimes in tongue tie. *Robin Dickin*

KAHALEESI 6 b.m. Shirocco (GER) – Maiden Voyage (Slip Anchor) [2017/18 h–, b72: **h–** h16.3s^{pu} Oct 2] useful-looking mare: no form over hurdles. *Olly Murphy*

KAHDIAN (IRE) 8 br.g. Rock of Gibraltar (IRE) – Katiykha (IRE) (Darshaan) [2017/18 **c75** h–: c18.2s³ c18.2m⁴ Apr 25] compact gelding: maiden hurdler: poor form over fences: **h–** stays 19f: acts on heavy and good to firm going: tried in cheekpieces/tongue tie. *Helen Rees*

KAKI DE LA PREE (FR) 11 b.g. Kapgarde (FR) – Kica (FR) (Noir Et Or) [2017/18 **c–** c138, h–: c23.8d^{pu} h25d⁵ Apr 26] good-bodied gelding: useful hurdler/chaser: should stay **h130** further than 25f: acts on heavy going. *Tom Symonds*

KALA CASTLE 6 b.g. Kalanisi (IRE) – Dancing Hill (Piccolo) [2017/18 b–: b15.7g⁶ **b–** May 15] last in bumpers: dead. *David Loder*

KALAHARI QUEEN 5 br.m. Kalanisi (IRE) – Queen's Leader (Supreme Leader) **h125 p** [2017/18 h19.5d h16s* h15.7s² h18.5s* h20.5s² Mar 24] lengthy mare: half-sister to fair hurdler/chaser Queen Olivia (2m-25f winner, by King's Theatre) and fair hurdler Mobile Sizer (2m winner, by Presenting): dam unraced: won point on debut: fairly useful form over hurdles: won mares novice at Lingfield in December and handicap at Exeter in February: second to Roksana in Mares 'National Hunt' Novices' Hurdle Finale at Newbury in March: stays 21f: acts on soft going: usually races close up: open to further improvement. *Jamie Snowden*

KAL

KALAHARRY (IRE) 6 b.g. Kalanisi (IRE) – Full Imperatrice (FR) (Dernier Empereur (USA)) [2017/18 h97: h20.1g³ h23.3g* Jun 3] modest handicap hurdler: won at Hexham (amateur) in June: stays 23f: best form on good going: often races towards rear. *Alistair Whillans* — **h98**

KALANISI GLEN (IRE) 8 br.g. Kalanisi (IRE) – Glen Ten (IRE) (Mandalus) [2017/18 h15.8g^F h16.3g² h16.2d³ Sep 5] sturdy gelding: runner-up on second of 2 starts in Irish maiden points: modest form over hurdles. *Jennie Candlish* — **h98**

KALANITI (IRE) 7 b.m. Kalanisi (IRE) – Miss Twinkletoes (IRE) (Zafonic (USA)) [2017/18 h109: c16.4g⁶ h15.7s² h15.6s⁴ h18.6s Feb 18] workmanlike mare: fair handicap hurdler: never a threat in novice handicap on chasing debut: unproven beyond 17f: acts on soft going: in cheekpieces last 2 starts. *Chris Grant* — **c– h109**

KALA NOIRE (IRE) 4 b.g. Kalanisi (IRE) – Lady Taipan (IRE) (Taipan (IRE)) [2017/18 b15.8s⁴ Mar 14] €15,000 3-y-o: sixth foal: dam, placed in points, out of sister to Grand National winner Royal Athlete: 14/1, fourth in bumper at Huntingdon (5¼ lengths behind That's A Given). *Sam Thomas* — **b89**

KALARIKA (IRE) 5 br.m. Kalanisi (IRE) – Katariya (IRE) (Barathea (IRE)) [2017/18 b79: h20.5d h16d h21.4v⁴ h16.5s h15.9v⁶ h15.3v² Apr 9] sturdy mare: modest handicap hurdler: won mares event at Taunton in March: best form at 2m: acts on heavy going: in cheekpieces/tongue tie last 4 starts. *Colin Tizzard* — **h86**

KALASHNIKOV (IRE) 5 br.g. Kalanisi (IRE) – Fairy Lane (IRE) (Old Vic) [2017/18 b101: h16s* h16.6d* h16s² h16.3v* h16.4s² Mar 13] — **h152 p**

The very first running of the race nowadays known as the Betfair Hurdle at Newbury fell to a five-year-old novice. The season's richest handicap hurdle started life in 1963 as the Schweppes Gold Trophy at Aintree when the sponsors, who had contributed a slice of the prize money for the two previous Grand Nationals, decided to put their name instead to a valuable new race on the opening day of the Grand National meeting. With a first prize of £7,825 2s 6d, the Schweppes Gold Trophy was worth more than that season's Champion Hurdle and only the Grand National itself and the Whitbread Gold Cup exceeded it in value. A field of forty-one—no 'maximum' fields back then—went to post with the weights headed by the previous season's Champion Hurdle winner Anzio on 12-7 (a future Champion Hurdle winner, Salmon Spray, was also in the field and finished fifth). Anzio ran well to be beaten only around a length and a half in fourth, but the winner was 20/1-shot Rosyth, carrying just 10-0, whose only win in four previous outings over hurdles had come in a novice at Windsor two starts earlier. The inaugural Schweppes Gold Trophy was marred by the serious injury sustained by reigning champion jockey Stan Mellor in a fall at the second flight, one which almost detached his lower jaw. Mellor had been set to win his fourth championship but, with his season ended, ironically it was Rosyth's jockey Josh Gifford who took the title. Rosyth himself has become rather an infamous name in the history of jump racing. He won the Schweppes again a year later when it moved to its permanent home of Newbury, though the improvement he showed on some much lesser performances in the meantime attracted the attention of the stewards and resulted in his trainer Ryan Price being warned off for a time and Gifford being suspended (Price won the Schweppes in four of its first five years, the last of those victories achieved with the controversial Hill House which brought the race further notoriety).

Five decades later, sponsorships by Schweppes and then by the Tote have run their course, and the Betfair Hurdle may not be the season's most valuable hurdle any more, but it is still the richest handicap hurdle and the latest running also went to a five-year-old novice. In fact, Kalashnikov became the seventh novice to win in the last nine renewals but there was no prospect of him sneaking into the race at the bottom of the handicap as Rosyth had done. Kalashnikov's smart novice form earned him a BHA mark of 141 and a weight of 11-5, though in a high-quality renewal he was receiving weight from no fewer than nine of his rivals in a present-day maximum field of twenty-four. After winning his only bumper at Wetherby the previous season, Kalashnikov had made a fine start to his hurdling career by winning novices at the same course in November and at Doncaster in December, both by ten lengths. He was beaten on his next start in the Tolworth Novices' Hurdle at Sandown but emerged with plenty of credit from a four-length

Betfair Hurdle (Handicap), Newbury—
Kalashnikov has only the riderless Silver Streak to contend with at the last

defeat at the hands of Summerville Boy, coming off the bridle a good way out but sticking to his task determinedly. Agrapart had finished third in the Tolworth before his win in the 2016 Betfair Hurdle, and Kalashnikov was sent off one of three 8/1 co-favourites at Newbury. The two other market leaders, Jenkins and Kayf Grace, were among a total of five fielded by Nicky Henderson, already successful in the race a record five times. Both had won on heavy ground last time out, conditions which prevailed again, and with little let-up in the gallop (which Jenkins helped to set), they finished well strung out in a race which put a premium on stamina. From mid-division, Kalashnikov improved into the first half dozen turning into the straight, coming off the bridle soon afterwards but running on strongly to lead between the final two hurdles as others faded. Willie Mullins' runner Bleu Et Rouge looked a big danger when cruising into contention from further back but Kalashnikov kept up the gallop to draw four and a half lengths clear at the line, with margins of eight lengths and nine back to the third and fourth Spiritofthegames and Coeur Blimey, and the two other co-favourites among those well beaten.

Jockey Jack Quinlan celebrated his biggest success crossing the line on Kalashnikov who also provided the highlight so far in the still early stages of the training career of Amy Murphy who was in just her second season with a licence. Before becoming the country's youngest licence-holder, Murphy spent some of her formative years as assistant trainer to Luca Cumani and she has remained in Newmarket where she trains Flat horses as well as jumpers. Kalashnikov very nearly provided his jockey and trainer with a Cheltenham Festival success to go with the Betfair Hurdle when he was beaten a neck in another meeting with Summerville Boy in the Supreme Novices' Hurdle. Running at least as well as he had at Newbury, Kalashnikov travelled better than in his two previous starts ridden closer to the pace and led two out, where Summerville Boy looked to have blundered his chance away, but was overhauled by the rallying winner in the final strides.

Kalashnikov (IRE) (br.g. 2013)
- Kalanisi (IRE) (b 1996)
  - Doyoun (b 1985)
    - Mill Reef
    - Dumka
  - Kalamba (b 1991)
    - Green Dancer
    - Kareena
- Fairy Lane (IRE) (b 2004)
  - Old Vic (b 1986)
    - Sadler's Wells
    - Cockade
  - Fairy Blaze (b 1991)
    - Good Thyne
    - Fairy Tree

Kalashnikov carries the yellow, purple diabolo colours of his trainer's father Paul Murphy, owner of Wychnor Park Stud. The stud's most successful broodmare to date is Carol's Crusader whose winners included the smart pair Mad Max, whose

Mr Paul Murphy's "Kalashnikov"

wins included the Manifesto Novices' Chase at Aintree, and Carole's Legacy who was runner-up at two Cheltenham Festivals, in the David Nicholson Mares' Hurdle and the three-mile handicap chase, as well as in the Bowl at Aintree. Kalashnikov isn't a home bred and he was bought for €35,000 as a foal and is the second good horse out of Fairy Lane to carry Murphy's colours after Kalashnikov's useful elder sister Kalane. She won the Mares' National Hunt Novices' Hurdle Finale at Newbury when with Charlie Longsdon and won the last two races of her career over fences at Doncaster, including a mares listed chase, by which time she had joined Murphy. A couple of Fairy Lane's other foals got off the mark during the latest season, with Pixie Lane (a mare by Gamut) winning over hurdles at Cork in July and Holdbacktheriver (by Presenting) landing a novice handicap hurdle at Exeter in April. All three of Kalashnikov's winning siblings have been successful over at least two and a half miles which isn't surprising as the unraced Fairy Lane is stoutly bred as well as being exceptionally well related, being a sister to Cheltenham Gold Cup and dual King George winner Kicking King. While Kicking King stayed beyond three miles in due course, he was campaigned mainly at around two miles earlier in his career, when, like Kalashnikov, he was second in the Supreme, before finishing runner-up in the Arkle at the following year's Festival. Another of Fairy Lane's brothers, the useful Four Commanders, was an even stouter stayer, finishing third in the National Hunt Chase. Kicking King and Four Commanders are the pick of nine winners out of Kalashnikov's unraced grandam Fairy Blaze, a daughter of the nine-furlong winner Fairy Tree. Everything points to the good-topped Kalashnikov being an exciting novice chasing prospect, with his strong finishes in testing conditions at two miles backing up the indications from his pedigree that he will be well suited by further. He wore ear plugs in the preliminaries for the Supreme but they were removed at the start. *Amy Murphy*

KALASKADESEMILLEY 7 b.g. Myboycharlie (IRE) – Congressional (IRE) (Grand Lodge (USA)) [2017/18 h101: h15.8g⁶ h16.3g³ h16g c19.4g⁵ c17g h16d⁵ h15.5d³ Dec 7] fair handicap hurdler: modest form over fences: left Martin Smith after fifth start: unproven beyond 17f: acts on good to firm going: in tongue tie last 2 starts. *Johnny Farrelly*   **c86 h101**

KALASTAR (IRE) 9 b.g. Kalanisi (IRE) – Katsura (Alflora (IRE)) [2017/18 c75§: c23.4g c24.2s³ c24.2dᵖᵘ c26.2dᵖᵘ c24.2d⁵ Apr 23] lengthy gelding: multiple winning pointer: poor maiden chaser: stays 3m: acts on soft going: has worn blinkers: temperamental. *Katie Scott*   **c71 §**

KALIFORNIA (IRE) 4 br.f. Kalanisi (IRE) – Carrigeen Kalmia (IRE) (Norwich) [2017/18 b15.7g Apr 20] €31,000 3-y-o: second foal: dam (c141), 2¼m-2½m chase winner, half-sister to dam of Irish Grand National winner Rogue Angel: 20/1, seventh in conditional/amateur maiden bumper at Southwell. *Henry Daly*   **b77**

KALIFOURCHON (FR) 7 gr.g. Martaline – Kaly Flight (FR) (Great Palm (USA)) [2017/18 h113: h20.6g² h23g h24g² c20g⁵ h23g⁵ c22.6gᶠ Nov 2] rather leggy gelding: fairly useful handicap hurdler: some promise over fences: stays 3m: best form on good going: has worn headgear, including last 4 starts: wears tongue tie: sometimes leads: remains open to improvement as a chaser. *David Pipe*   **c– p h115**

KALIMANTAN (IRE) 8 b.g. Azamour (IRE) – Kalamba (IRE) (Green Dancer (USA)) [2017/18 h23d* Sep 29] sturdy gelding: fair hurdler: fit from Flat, won seller at Worcester (visored) in September: stays easy 23f: acts on firm and soft going. *Tim Vaughan*   **h102**

KALINIHTA (IRE) 4 b.g. Kalanisi (IRE) – Valamareha (IRE) (Val Royal (FR)) [2017/18 b13.7g* Apr 20] €3,000 3-y-o: third foal: dam (h80), maiden hurdler, 7.5f/8.5f winner on Flat, half-sister to useful chaser (stays 2½m) All Together: 12/1, won bumper at Fontwell (readily by 3¼ lengths from Itchy Feet) on debut. *Noel Williams*   **b96**

KALMBEFORETHESTORM 10 ch.g. Storming Home – Miss Honeypenny (IRE) (Old Vic) [2017/18 h26.5d² h21.6s* Apr 23] close-coupled gelding: fair handicap hurdler: won at Newton Abbot in April: stays 3¼m: acts on soft and good to firm going: tried in tongue tie. *Helen Nelmes*   **h106**

KALOCI (IRE) 6 b.m. Stowaway – Eye And Ear (IRE) (Old Vic) [2017/18 b71: b15.8g³ b16g* b15.8s³ h15.5v* h15.9v² h15.7s² h20.5s Mar 24] unfurnished mare: fair form in bumpers: won conditionals/amateur event at Fakenham in November: fair form over hurdles: won novice at Leicester in January: left Kevin Bishop after first start: should stay 2½m: front runner/races prominently. *Stuart Edmunds*   **h110 b92**

KALONDRA (IRE) 7 b.g. Spadoun (FR) – Mystic Vic (IRE) (Old Vic) [2017/18 h143: c19.3g* c20.2s² c20.8s* c20s⁴ c20.8g³ Apr 18] workmanlike gelding: useful hurdler: smart form over fences: won maiden at Sedgefield in October and novice at Cheltenham (by 3¾ lengths from Coo Star Sivola) in December: third in Silver Trophy Chase (Limited Handicap) at Cheltenham (2¾ lengths behind Traffic Fluide) in April: stays 2¾m: acts on good to firm and heavy going: wears tongue tie: usually races towards rear, often travels strongly: open to more improvement over fences. *Neil Mulholland*   **c147 p h–**

KALUM RIVER (IRE) 4 b.g. Fame And Glory – King's Vintage (IRE) (King's Best (USA)) [2017/18 b16.5d* Apr 24] €3,000 3-y-o: third foal: dam 11f winner who stayed 2m: 16/1, won maiden bumper at Punchestown (by 1½ lengths from Barrington Court) on debut. *P. A. Fahy, Ireland*   **b108**

KANSAS CITY CHIEF (IRE) 9 b.g. Westerner – Badawi Street (Thowra (FR)) [2017/18 c26s² c24.9s h19.5s⁵ h21.4v⁵ h24.4s* h25.3d² h24v² h24s Mar 15] sturdy gelding: useful handicap hurdler: won at Doncaster (by 8 lengths from Amberjam) in January: useful handicap chaser: second at Killarney (3½ lengths behind Auvergnat) in May: left Miss M. L. Hallahan after second start: stays 3¼m: acts on heavy going: has worn cheekpieces, including last 4 starts. *Neil Mulholland*   **c133 h131**

KAPCORSE (FR) 5 br.g. Kapgarde (FR) – Angesse (FR) (Indian River (FR)) [2017/18 h16.8s⁶ h16.3d h19.8v⁶ c20.3d* Apr 21] well-made gelding: third foal: half-brother to useful hurdler Ria d'Etel (French 2¼m winner, by Martaline): dam French 2m/17f hurdle/chase winner: fair form over hurdles: 6/1, left that well behind when won novice handicap at Bangor (by 8 lengths from Go West Young Man, with plenty in hand) on chasing debut: stays 2½m: often races towards rear: possibly has his quirks, but useful chasing prospect. *Paul Nicholls*   **c125 p h103**

KAPDAD (FR) 4 ch.g. Kapgarde (FR) – Reveries (FR) (Montjeu (IRE)) [2017/18 b15.3v³ h16.3v² h16s³ h17.7v² Feb 15] compact gelding: fourth foal: dam unraced: third in junior bumper at Wincanton: fairly useful form over hurdles: best effort when second in juvenile at Fontwell in February: will stay 2½m. *Gary Moore*   **h118 b71**

KAP

KAPGA DE LILY (FR) 5 ch.m. Kapgarde (FR) – Louvisy (FR) (Loup Solitaire (USA)) [2017/18 b17s⁵ h15.7s* Mar 21] first foal: dam, French 17f/2¼m hurdle/chase winner, half-sister to fairly useful hurdler/smart chaser (stayed 2½m) Kapga de Cerisy (by Kapgarde): tailed off in mares bumper: 66/1, won 4-runner novice at Haydock (by 3¼ lengths from Think Ahead) on hurdling debut: likely to stay further than 2m. *Venetia Williams* — h106 b–

KAPGARDE KING (FR) 7 ch.g. Kapgarde (FR) – Cybertina (FR) (Cyborg (FR)) [2017/18 c99, h72: c25.8d³ c23.9g Aug 19] maiden hurdler: modest handicap chaser: stays 25f: acts on good to firm and good to soft going: usually wears hood. *Jamie Snowden* — c93 h–

KAPGARRY (FR) 5 b.g. Ballingarry (IRE) – Kaprissima (FR) (Epervier Bleu) [2017/18 b16s² Feb 24] fifth foal: half-brother to French hurdler Sikar (19f winner, by Kotky Bleu) and fair hurdler Western Wave (17f winner, by Westerner): dam (h112), French 17f/2¼m hurdle winner, half-sister to very smart hurdler/smart chaser (stayed 2½m) Geos: off mark in Irish points at fourth attempt: 8/1, second in conditional/amateur maiden bumper at Chepstow (2 lengths behind Supremely Lucky). *Nigel Twiston-Davies* — b96

KAP JAZZ (FR) 8 b.g. Kapgarde (FR) – Jazz And Liquer (FR) (Kahyasi) [2017/18 c123, h–: c26.2v c23.9g² c25.1v c22.4s Mar 23] sturdy gelding: winning hurdler: fairly useful handicap chaser: stays 3m: acts on soft going: tried in blinkers: often races prominently. *Venetia Williams* — c119 h–

KAPRICORNE (FR) 11 b.g. Kapgarde (FR) – Colombe Royale (FR) (Passing Sale (FR)) [2017/18 c75, h83: c25.8d² c25.8d³ c22.6g⁴ Oct 21] winning hurdler: poor maiden chaser: off mark in points soon after end of season: stays 3¼m: acts on heavy going: has worn headgear, including in 2017/18: wears tongue tie. *Dan Skelton* — c75 h–

KAPSTADT (FR) 8 b.g. Country Reel (USA) – King's Parody (IRE) (King's Best (USA)) [2017/18 h129: h16.7g³ c19.4g³ c16g² c15.9d² Nov 17] rather leggy gelding: fairly useful handicap hurdler: third in Summer Hurdle at Market Rasen: similar form over fences: second in handicaps at Ludlow (novice) and Cheltenham: unproven beyond 17f: acts on soft and good to firm going: has worn tongue tie. *Ian Williams* — c127 h126

KAPVILLE (FR) 11 ch.g. Kapgarde (FR) – Ville Eagle (FR) (Villez (USA)) [2017/18 c25.8gF c22.9d⁴ c22.4d* c29.8gF c22.9s² c22.4g² c25.8s* c30.2d c29.8s Apr 4] lengthy gelding: fair cross-country chaser: won at Le Lion-d'Angers in August and Lyon Parilly in November: well beaten at Cheltenham in December: stays 4½m: acts on heavy going: wears blinkers. *E. & G. Leenders, France* — c113 h–

KARALEE (FR) 7 gr.m. Martaline – Change Partner (FR) (Turtle Island (IRE)) [2017/18 h138: h16s³ h20s h16spu h18s³ h16v² h16s⁵ h20s Apr 28] useful hurdler: stays 2½m: acts on heavy going: in tongue tie last 5 starts: usually races towards rear. *W. P. Mullins, Ireland* — h134

KARAMOKO (IRE) 6 b.g. Manduro (GER) – Virevolle (FR) (Kahyasi) [2017/18 b16s² b15.6g h16.6s⁶ h17d Mar 25] poor form in bumpers/novice hurdles. *Nicky Richards* — h62 b68

KARA TARA 8 b.m. Kayf Tara – Matilda Too (IRE) (Definite Article) [2017/18 h79: h20.3g May 24] bumper winner: maiden hurdler, well held only start in 2017/18: stays 2½m: acts on soft going: tried in cheekpieces. *Malcolm Jefferson* — h–

KARINGO 11 ch.g. Karinga Bay – Wild Happening (GER) (Mondrian (GER)) [2017/18 c–x, h93: h20.2g⁶ h23.9m h23.9g² h23.9d h23.9s* h23.9vpu h22.7g Oct 28] poor handicap hurdler: won novice event at Perth in August: failed to complete both starts over fences: stays 3m: acts on soft and good to firm going: wears cheekpieces: often let down by attitude/jumping. *Lucy Normile* — c– x h81 §

KARL MARX (IRE) 8 b.g. Red Clubs (IRE) – Brillano (FR) (Desert King (IRE)) [2017/18 c–§, h82§: h16.8s³ h16.8g³ h16.8dpu h16.8g h19.8s⁴ h16v² h19.8v² h16.5v* Apr 12] leggy gelding: poor handicap hurdler: won at Taunton in April: no aptitude for fences: stays 3¼m, effective at much shorter: acts on any going: wears headgear: tried in tongue tie: temperamental. *Mark Gillard* — c– § h84 §

KASPERENKO 4 b.g. Archipenko (USA) – Jardin (Sinndar (IRE)) [2017/18 h16g⁶ Feb 24] useful on Flat, stays 1½m: well beaten in Adonis Juvenile Hurdle at Kempton (tongue tied). *Brendan Powell* — h–

KASTANI BEACH (IRE) 12 br.g. Alderbrook – Atomic View (IRE) (Old Vic) [2017/18 c–, h97: h16d³ h16.8s⁶ h15.9m h16.8s⁴ h17.7s² h15.9s⁵ h15.9v⁴ h16s⁵ h17.7s⁵ h19.8d³ Apr 22] angular gelding: modest handicap hurdler: winning chaser: effective at 2m when conditions are testing, and stays 3m: acts on heavy going: usually wears headgear. *Seamus Mullins* — c– h85

KATACHENKO (IRE) 9 b.g. Kutub (IRE) – Karalee (IRE) (Arokar (FR)) [2017/18 c132, h–: c19.9v² c21.6s⁶ c20.5g^F Apr 20] lengthy gelding: winning hurdler: useful handicap chaser: second at Aintree (nose behind Play The Ace) in December: stays 25f: acts on heavy going: has worn hood: usually leads: not one to trust. *Donald McCain*   **c133 §**
h–

KATAHDIN (IRE) 5 b.g. Kayf Tara – Keyaza (IRE) (Azamour (IRE)) [2017/18 b15.8s⁶ b15.7v* b16d⁴ Apr 26] tall gelding: first foal: dam (b93), bumper winner, half-sister to smart hurdler (stayed 19f) Pittoni: fairly useful form in bumpers: won at Southwell in February. *Lydia Pearce*   **b99**

KATALYSTIC (IRE) 7 br.g. Kalanisi (IRE) – Beltane Queen (IRE) (Strong Gale) [2017/18 h90, b85: h20.2g⁴ May 18] modest form over hurdles: stays 2½m: acts on soft going: often races towards rear. *Lucinda Russell*   **h91**

KATARA BAY 7 b.g. Kayf Tara – De Blanc (IRE) (Revoque (IRE)) [2017/18 h19.9d h19.9v⁵ h20.8s⁵ h24.1v⁶ h25d^F Mar 26] poor form over hurdles: tried in hood/tongue tie: often races in rear. *Barry Leavy*   **h69**

KATARRHINI 9 b.m. Kayf Tara – Dedrunknmunky (IRE) (Rashar (USA)) [2017/18 c–, h61: c22.6g May 8] maiden hurdler: no form over fences: has worn tongue tie. *Jo Davis*   **c–**
h–

KATEBIRD (IRE) 4 gr.f. Dark Angel (IRE) – She Basic (IRE) (Desert Prince (IRE)) [2017/18 h15.8d⁶ Apr 24] fairly useful on Flat, stays 10.5f: tailed off in novice on hurdling debut. *Oliver Greenall*   **h–**

KATENKO (FR) 12 b.g. Laveron – Katiana (FR) (Villez (USA)) [2017/18 c–, h–: c22.9s^pu c24v⁵ Apr 7] big, well-made gelding: winning hurdler: very smart chaser at best, lightly raced and little form since 2013/14: stays 25f: acts on heavy going. *Venetia Williams*   **c–**
h–

KATESON 5 gr.g. Black Sam Bellamy (IRE) – Silver Kate (IRE) (Insan (USA)) [2017/18 b16d* b17d² b15.7d b16v² b17s² Apr 13] lengthy, rather unfurnished gelding: first foal: dam (c136/h136) 2½m-3¼m hurdle/chase winner: useful bumper performer: won at Chepstow in October: second in Grade 2 at Aintree (3¼ lengths behind Portrush Ted) in April: will stay at least 2½m. *Tom Lacey*   **b108**

KATGARY (FR) 8 b.g. Ballingarry (IRE) – Kotkira (FR) (Subotica (FR)) [2017/18 c138, h–: c17.3d² c17g⁴ h16.2d³ c17.3g⁴ c19.4d⁴ h16.4v⁴ h16.2s² h18.1v⁴ h16.4v⁴ Apr 14] good-topped gelding: useful handicap hurdler: second at Kelso (neck behind Mirsaale) in January: useful handicap chaser: second at Cartmel (2½ lengths behind Oliver's Gold) in May: stays 21f: acts on any going: wears headgear: tried in tongue tie: front runner/races prominently. *Pauline Robson*   **c134**
h130

KATKEAU (FR) 11 b.g. Kotky Bleu (FR) – Levine (FR) (Luynes (USA)) [2017/18 c148, h–: c25d⁶ Oct 29] small, angular gelding: winning hurdler: smart handicap chaser: below form since winning very early in 2016/17: stays 25f: best form on soft/heavy going: wears hood/tongue tie. *David Pipe*   **c126**
h–

KATY MAY 7 b.m. Thethingaboutitis (USA) – Perry of Troy (Paris of Troy) [2017/18 b15.7m b16s May 17] second foal: dam failed to complete in points: fell in point on debut: well beaten in bumpers: tried in hood. *Mike Hammond*   **b–**

KATY P 6 b.m. Ask – Kingara (Karinga Bay) [2017/18 h108, b87: h23.3d² h21.6m* h26.5m⁴ h23g* Aug 30] leggy, unfurnished mare: fairly useful hurdler: won mares novice at Newton Abbot in May and handicap at Worcester in August: stays 23f: acts on soft and good to firm going: races towards rear, often travels strongly. *Philip Hobbs*   **h121**

KATY ROYAL 6 b.m. King's Theatre (IRE) – Water Stratford (IRE) (Jurado (USA)) [2017/18 h–, b–: h20.1d³ h19.9g⁴ h21.2g³ h20.6g² h25.3d⁴ h20.6v³ Jan 30] quite good-topped mare: fair maiden hurdler: should stay at least 3m: acts on heavy going: often races towards rear. *Chris Fairhurst*   **h104**

KAUTO LINGARRY (FR) 6 ch.g. Ballingarry (IRE) – Kauto Luisa (FR) (Jeune Homme (USA)) [2017/18 b–: b16.8m May 9] no form in bumpers. *Samuel Drinkwater*   **b–**

KAUTO RIKO (FR) 7 b.g. Ballingarry (IRE) – Kauto Relstar (FR) (Art Bleu) [2017/18 h112: c16.3s* c16.1s* c16v² c15.8s⁵ Apr 14] leggy gelding: fair hurdler: useful form over fences: won handicaps at Newcastle (novice) in December and Taunton in January: also first past post in another handicap at Hereford in March, but demoted after bumping rival: stays 21f: acts on good to firm and heavy going: often travels strongly. *Tom Gretton*   **c136**
h–

KAUTO THE KING (FR) 4 b.g. Ballingarry (IRE) – Kauto Luisa (FR) (Jeune Homme (USA)) [2017/18 b16v³ b16s⁴ b15.3v³ Apr 9] €42,000 3-y-o: sixth foal: dam unraced half-sister to dam of Kauto Star: fair form in bumpers: best effort when third at Wincanton in April: wears tongue tie. *Colin Tizzard*   **b90**

KAV

KAVANAGHS CORNER (IRE) 9 b.g. Coroner (IRE) – Annacarney (IRE) (Moscow Society (USA)) [2017/18 c81, h–: c20d^{pu} c20s c20.2s^4 c19.8s^2 c20.2v^2 c19.2v* Apr 17] maiden hurdler: poor handicap chaser: won at Exeter in April: stays 2½m: acts on heavy going: tried in hood: in tongue tie last 4 starts: often races towards rear. *Simon Earle* — **c83 h–**

KAVEMAN 6 b.g. Kayf Tara – Megalex (Karinga Bay) [2017/18 b59p: b13.6g^3 b15.7g^3 May 15] fair form in bumpers: best effort when third at Fontwell in May. *Gary Moore* — **b90**

KAYF ADVENTURE 7 b.g. Kayf Tara – My Adventure (IRE) (Strong Gale) [2017/18 h124: c21v* c20.5v^6 c19.8g^3 c20.2v* c20.2v^2 c20s^3 c20.4s c19.9s^2 Mar 24] tall gelding: fairly useful hurdler: useful chaser: won novice at Newton Abbot in October and handicap at Wincanton in January: stays 2¾m: acts on heavy going: often races towards rear/travels strongly. *Philip Hobbs* — **c137 h–**

KAYF BLANCO 9 b.g. Kayf Tara – Land of Glory (Supreme Leader) [2017/18 c129p, h130: h16.3g^2 c16.5m^F c16.3m^2 c16.1s^3 c15.2s^2 c19.4v^3 c20.5g^2 c16s^2 c19.4d^6 Apr 22] tall gelding: useful handicap hurdler: useful maiden chaser: second in handicaps at Kempton in February (neck behind Favorito Buck's) and March (novice, 2¼ lengths behind Vocaliser): stays 2½m: acts on heavy going: tried in hood/tongue tie. *Graeme McPherson* — **c130 h129**

KAYF CHARMER 8 b.m. Kayf Tara – Silver Charmer (Charmer) [2017/18 h92: h21.6g^4 h18.5v^{pu} h16v h21.6v^{ur} h15.5v h16s^3 h18.5v^{pu} Apr 17] has had breathing operation: poor handicap hurdler: stays 2½m: acts on heavy going: tried in blinkers. *Linda Blackford* — **h81**

KAYF GRACE 8 b.m. Kayf Tara – Potter's Gale (IRE) (Strong Gale) [2017/18 h119P: h15.7g^5 h16v* h16.3v h19.9s^F Mar 13] useful-looking mare: useful form over hurdles: won handicap at Kempton (by 1½ lengths from Eddiemaurice) in December: raced mainly around 2m: acts on heavy going. *Nicky Henderson* — **h131**

KAYFLEUR 9 b.m. Kayf Tara – Combe Florey (Alflora (IRE)) [2017/18 c110, h–: c24.2s* c21.7s^2 c22.5v^2 Jan 27] smallish, sturdy mare: winning hurdler: fairly useful handicap chaser: won mares event at Fakenham in November: second in mares novice event at Uttoxeter in January: stays 3m: acts on heavy going: often races towards rear. *Henry Daly* — **c115 h–**

KAYFLIN (FR) 10 b.m. Kayf Tara – Flinders (Henbit (USA)) [2017/18 c72, h83§: h25g^2 h21.6d* h23g^5 Jun 14] lengthy mare: modest handicap hurdler: won conditionals mares event at Fontwell in June: maiden chaser: stays 25f: acts on heavy going: wears headgear. *Linda Jewell* — **c– h86**

KAYF MOSS 10 b.g. Kayf Tara – Madam Mosso (Le Moss) [2017/18 c–, h97: h23.9v^{pu} h23.5s h24v^{pu} h23.3v* Apr 7] sturdy gelding: fair handicap hurdler nowadays: won at Uttoxeter in April: maiden chaser: stays 3m: best form on heavy going: wears headgear/tongue tie. *John Flint* — **c– h110**

KAYF STORM 5 gr.m. Kayf Tara – Royal Keel (Long Leave) [2017/18 b15.7s^4 b16.7s Mar 26] sister to 3 winners, including fairly useful hurdler/useful chaser Mystifiable (2¼m-2¾m winner) and fairly useful hurdler/chaser Long Lunch (2m-2½m winner), and half-sister to 2 winners, including useful hurdler/chaser Hidden Keel (2m-2½m winner, by Kirkwall): dam unraced half-sister to high-class 2m hurdler Relkeel: modest form in bumpers. *Kim Bailey* — **b79**

KAYF TIGER 9 b.g. Kayf Tara – La Marette (Karinga Bay) [2017/18 h19.8v^3 h16s^1 h23.1v^6 h19.6d^3 Apr 21] sturdy gelding: poor maiden hurdler: likely to prove best at 2½m+: acts on heavy going: tried in cheekpieces: in tongue tie last 4 starts. *Matt Sheppard* — **h65**

KAYLA 8 b.m. Kayf Tara – Palila (Petoski) [2017/18 h110: h24m^2 h25.6g^4 h23.1g^6 c24g^3 c24.1d^5 c23g^5 Oct 25] fair handicap hurdler: similar form over fences: best effort when third at Uttoxeter in September: stays 3m: acts on good to firm going: wears tongue tie. *Stuart Edmunds* — **c106 h112**

KEATING (IRE) 6 b.g. King's Theatre (IRE) – Tus Nua (IRE) (Galileo (IRE)) [2017/18 h102: h16.8g^4 h20g^{ur} Aug 30] sturdy gelding: fell in Irish maiden point: fair maiden hurdler: stays 2¾m: acts on soft going: tried in hood: in tongue tie last 2 starts. *David Pipe* — **h103**

KEBIR DE LA VIS (FR) 5 b.g. Sagacity (FR) – La Navarre (FR) (Baryshnikov (AUS)) [2017/18 b16.8d^5 b17.7g^6 Aug 24] no form in bumpers: tried in tongue tie. *Warren Greatrex* — **b–**

KEEL HAUL (IRE) 10 br.g. Classic Cliche (IRE) – Tara Hall (Saddlers' Hall (IRE)) [2017/18 c125, h102: c16.5g^6 c16d^4 c17.2s^F c17.8v^2 c15.7v^5 Feb 5] leggy gelding: winning hurdler: fair handicap chaser nowadays: stays 2¼m: acts on heavy going: wears headgear. *Henry Oliver* — **c111 h–**

KEEM BAY 4 b.f. Multiplex – Copsehill Girl (IRE) (Carroll House) [2017/18 h15.8s^{pu} Oct 19] dam (h108) 2½m/2¾m hurdle winner/winning pointer: no show in Flat maiden/juvenile hurdle. *Michael Mullineaux* — **h–**

KEM

KEEN'S TOKEN 12 b.g. Keen – Bella Mary (Derrylin) [2017/18 h22.2d Jul 11] no form. **h–**
Gary Sanderson

KEEPER HILL (IRE) 7 b.g. Westerner – You Take Care (IRE) (Definite Article) **c136**
[2017/18 h139: c22.6g* c19.7s² c24d* c19.9s^F c31.8s^F c24.1g^pu Apr 21] tall gelding: useful **h–**
hurdler: useful form over fences: won 2-runner novice at Stratford in November and
December Novices' Chase at Doncaster (by 8 lengths from Braqueur d'Or): let down by
jumping after: stays 3m: acts on soft going: usually races prominently. *Warren Greatrex*

KEEP IN LINE (GER) 6 b.g. Soldier Hollow – Kastila (GER) (Sternkoenig (IRE)) **h132**
[2017/18 h129: h16d² h16d³ h19.4d⁴ Dec 15] good-topped gelding: useful handicap
hurdler: third at Wetherby (4 lengths behind William of Orange) in November: should stay
2½m: acts on soft and good to firm going: often races towards rear. *Alan King*

KEEPIN TIME 6 b.m. Fair Mix (IRE) – Pipsacre (Kayf Tara) [2017/18 h–, b–: h19.6g **h–**
h20g⁶ h19g Sep 26] well held over hurdles: tried in tongue tie. *Dan Skelton*

KEEPINUPWITDJONES 6 b.g. Multiplex – Ceoperk (IRE) (Executive Perk) [2017/18 **h–**
b16.7g⁵ b16d⁵ b16g b15.6s⁴ h19.3v h16.2v h16.8v Feb 22] £9,000 3-y-o: third foal: dam **b82**
(c109/h100) 2m-2½m hurdle/chase winner: modest form in bumpers: well beaten in novice
hurdles: left A. L. T. Moore after third start: usually wears tongue tie. *Sharon Watt*

KEEP MOVING (FR) 6 b.g. Linda's Lad – Keeping Gold (FR) (Goldneyev (USA)) **c108**
[2017/18 c103, h–: c16.5g³ c17.5v² Nov 26] good-topped gelding: lightly raced over **h–**
hurdles: fair maiden chaser: unproven beyond 2¼m: acts on heavy going: usually races
towards rear. *Philip Hobbs*

KEEP ON TRACK (IRE) 11 ch.g. Rudimentary (USA) – Corries Rein (IRE) (Anshan) **c–**
[2017/18 c–, h–: c20.3g⁴ May 16] winning pointer: maiden hurdler: useful cross-country **h–**
chaser at one time, no longer of much account: tried in visor: in tongue tie last 3 starts.
Richard Walker

KEEP TO THE BEAT 7 b.m. Beat Hollow – Cadeau Speciale (Cadeaux Genereux) **h85**
[2017/18 h16d^ur h20.5d³ h20.7s h21.7g Apr 20] fair handicap hurdler, below best in
2017/18 after 2-year absence: stays 2½m: acts on good to firm going: has worn cheekpieces.
Pat Phelan

KEEPUP KEVIN 4 b.g. Haafhd – Black Salix (USA) (More Than Ready (USA)) **h–**
[2017/18 h15.8g Nov 5] fair on Flat, stays 1m: tailed off in juvenile on hurdling debut.
Pam Sly

KEEPYOURHEADUP 7 b.g. Sir Percy – Sweet Lemon (IRE) (Oratorio (IRE)) [2017/18 **h–**
h–: h17.7d^pu h19.5v^pu Jan 19] no form: in tongue tie last 2 starts. *Helen Nelmes*

KELKA 6 b.m. Exit To Nowhere (USA) – Scarvagh Diamond (IRE) (Zaffaran (USA)) **c120**
[2017/18 h125: c15.7v² c16.3s³ h16g Apr 20] fairly useful hurdler: similar form on first of **h–**
2 starts over fences: stays 21f: best form on soft/heavy going: usually leads. *Ruth Jefferson*

KELPIES MYTH 5 b.g. Dutch Art – Miss Respect (Mark of Esteem (IRE)) [2017/18 **h119**
b89: h16.2d⁶ h15.6m³ h15.6s⁴ h15.6s* h17s* h16s Apr 28] well-made gelding: bumper
winner: fairly useful form over hurdles: won handicap at Musselburgh in February and
novice at Carlisle in April: raced around 2m: acts on soft going: usually races close up.
Lucinda Russell

KELTUS (FR) 8 gr.g. Keltos (FR) – Regina d'Orthe (FR) (R B Chesne) [2017/18 c139, **c131**
h–: c25.5d² c26.1m Jul 2] rather leggy gelding: winning pointer: useful handicap chaser: **h–**
runner-up on second of 2 starts in points in late-2017: stays 25f: acts on good to firm and
heavy going: wears tongue tie. *Paul Nicholls*

KELVINGROVE (IRE) 8 b.g. Hurricane Run (IRE) – Silversword (FR) (Highest Honor **c121 §**
(FR)) [2017/18 h134: h22.8m c23g² c23g⁴ c23d⁶ c23.9g⁶ c25.6g^pu c23s* c25.3g⁶ Apr 18] **h123**
useful handicap hurdler: fairly useful handicap chaser: won novice event at Taunton in
December: stays 3m: acts on soft going: usually wears cheekpieces: temperamental. *Jonjo O'Neill*

KEMBOY (FR) 6 b.g. Voix du Nord (FR) – Vitora (FR) (Victory Note (USA)) **c157 p**
[2017/18 h140: c21.2v² c21.5v* c19.9s⁴ c29v^F c24v* c21s* Apr 27] **h–**
  Perennial Irish champion trainer Willie Mullins was an 11/4 chance at the
beginning of April to successfully make up a deficit of more than half a million
euros on rival Gordon Elliott by the end of the season. In an attempt to catch Elliott,
Mullins made more Punchestown Festival entries than he had ever done previously.
In the end, he saddled one hundred and seventeen runners, compared to sixty-three
the previous year, including an unusually high number in the handicaps at the

EMS Copiers Novices' Handicap Chase, Punchestown—a fine weight-carrying performance by Kemboy (stars on sleeves) in a typically competitive renewal of this valuable prize

meeting, up from eighteen to forty-five, including a record-equalling thirteen in the Ballymore Handicap Hurdle on the Saturday. Though Mullins started the week as the underdog, a six-timer on Wednesday—sandwiched by trebles on Tuesday and Thursday—saw him head into the penultimate day with a lead of over €400,000 which was significantly increased after the Supreme Horse Racing Club-owned Kemboy fared best of six runners from the yard when justifying favouritism in the EMS Copiers Novices' Handicap Chase, giving his trainer what turned out to be an unassailable lead in the title race after the Elliott-trained Samcro failed to land the Punchestown Champion Hurdle two races later.

The Supreme Horse Racing Club, with over six hundred members worldwide, has all its thirty horses with Willie Mullins. Supreme Carolina was the syndicate's first winner, in September 2011, and the outfit has enjoyed plenty of success since, including with the mare Airlie Beach who became its first Grade 1 winner when landing the Royal Bond Novices' Hurdle at Fairyhouse in 2016. Like Mullins himself, the Supreme Horse Racing Club has also had good winners on the Flat, with Pique Sous successful several times, most notably in the 2014 Queen Alexandra Stakes at Royal Ascot. A second Grade 1 success over jumps has so far proved elusive, as has a Cheltenham Festival winner (Pique Sous' third in the 2012 Champion Bumper the best so far), but the syndicate had plenty of reason to celebrate in the most recent season, as Kemboy's Punchestown win was his third of the campaign, having previously secured a landmark hundredth victory for the Supreme Horse Racing Club when surviving a late scare in a maiden chase at Fairyhouse in late-January. Well backed after a very promising second to Sutton Place on his chasing debut at the same venue on New Year's Day, Kemboy was in total control when hitting the last, with jockey Paul Townend doing extremely well to maintain the partnership after briefly losing his reins. Despite facing a steep rise in grade, Kemboy was again well backed in the Golden Miller Novices' Chase (branded as the JLT) at the Cheltenham Festival six weeks later and he ran creditably to finish fourth to Shattered Love—as he had done when fifth in the Baring Bingham (Neptune) Novices' Hurdle a year earlier. Ridden more patiently on this occasion by David Mullins, Kemboy would have done even better had he not made a bad mistake at the first ditch. Kemboy's jumping frailties again came to the fore on his first foray into handicap company when he fell at the first—under Bryan Cooper this time—in the Irish Grand National.

That was the first fall of Kemboy's ten-race career over jumps (he had one run on the Flat for Francis Matzinger in France back in 2015) and he was clearly none the worse for the experience when turned out just twelve days later in a five-runner Grade 3 novice chase at Limerick. Returned to calmer waters, Kemboy also proved himself over the longer trip, his jumping holding up much better this time as he provided another boost to the Golden Miller form, on the same day as Finian Oscar's win in the Manifesto at Aintree. Reunited with Paul Townend and ridden more positively, Kemboy was soon in front and jumped soundly in the main. He was well in command at the last, where the mistake on this occasion came from the eventual second Tombstone, who was held at the time, with Kemboy only having to be pushed out with hands and heels for an eight-length success. With a confidence-boosting win under his belt, Kemboy was back in action at the Punchestown Festival and was sent off at 11/4 in a big field, carrying joint top weight, for the EMS Copiers Novices' Handicap Chase, a valuable handicap dominated by Mullins since the race distance was shortened in 2007, and a contest won by the Supreme Horse Racing Club's own Avant Tout in 2016. Providing the syndicate with a second big handicap chase win in the space of two days, following Cadmium's win the previous afternoon, Kemboy led two out after a mainly sound round of jumping, and was driven out to score by five lengths, with runner-up A Rated eight lengths clear of the third Bel Ami de Sivola. With the race run at a true gallop on soft ground, the field was well strung out and eight of the eighteen starters failed to complete.

Kemboy (FR) (b.g. 2012)	Voix du Nord (FR) (b 2001)	Valanour (b 1992)	Lomond, Vearia
		Dame Edith (b 1995)	Top Ville, Girl of France
	Vitora (FR) (b 2004)	Victory Note (b 1995)	Fairy King, Three Piece
		Mosstraye (b 1993)	Tip Moss, Chevestraye

Supreme Racing Club, Brett T Graham & Kenneth Sharp's "Kemboy"

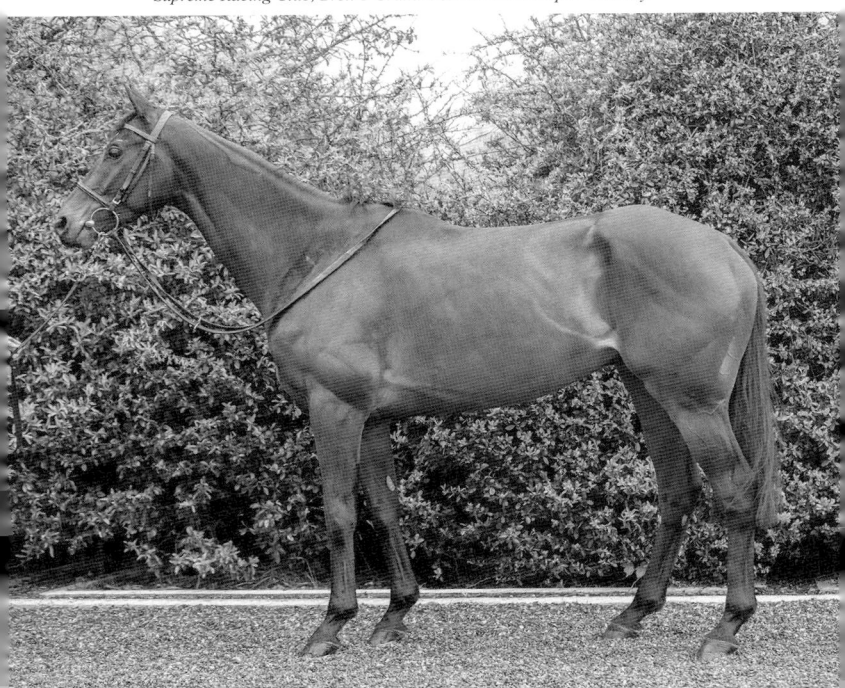

KEN

The sturdy Kemboy is by Voix du Nord, the sire of the Mullins-trained Vroum Vroum Mag, as well as graded winners Bachasson and Val de Ferbert. Kemboy is the second foal out of Vitora, a mile and a half winner in France and a half-sister to Relkeel Hurdle winner Karabak, a high-class staying hurdler in his prime, and Mossville, a fairly useful staying hurdler. Versatile with regards to trip, Kemboy looks the sort to win races at an even higher level in the next season. He stays three miles and acts very well on testing ground, with two of his four wins coming on heavy and another on soft. Kemboy wore ear plugs in the Golden Miller. He is open to further improvement as a chaser. *W. P. Mullins, Ireland*

KENNEDYS FIELD 5 b.g. Multiplex – Supreme Lady (IRE) (Supreme Leader) [2017/18 b16.2d⁵ b16.2v⁵ b15.6g h16.2s h16.4v³ h16v Feb 26] well held only completed start in Irish maiden points: poor form in bumpers/over hurdles: has worn hood. *Gemma Anderson* — **h80 b72**

KEN'S WELL (IRE) 7 b.g. Trans Island – Tiergarten (IRE) (Brief Truce (USA)) [2017/18 b16g² h16g² h20g* c20.2g⁴ Oct 29] €6,500 3-y-o: sixth foal: half-brother to fair hurdler/chaser Sum Laff (2½m-2¾m winner, by Publisher): dam, lightly raced over hurdles, maiden on Flat (stayed 1m): placed in bumpers: fair form over hurdles: won maiden at Wexford (hooded) in July: 20/1, fourth in novice handicap at Wincanton (21 lengths behind Wilberdragon) on chasing debut: left E. D. Linehan after third start: likely to stay at least 2¾m: front runner/races prominently: open to improvement. *Jo Davis* — **c100 p h108 p b95**

KENTFORD HEIRESS 8 b.m. Midnight Legend – Kentford Duchess (Jupiter Island) [2017/18 h110: h21d⁵ h26.5d² h21.7d² h25m³ h21.6g* h19.2g² h24.6s⁴ Apr 9] fair handicap hurdler: won mares event at Newton Abbot in October: stays 3¼m: acts on soft and good to firm going: held up. *Seamus Mullins* — **h112**

KENTFORD MALLARD 5 b.m. Sulamani (IRE) – Kentford Grebe (Teenoso (USA)) [2017/18 b15.3v ab16g Jan 30] sixth foal: closely related to fairly useful hurdler Swallowshide (2¾m winner, by Hernando) and half-sister to 2 winners, including bumper winner/useful hurdler Kentford Grey Lady (2½m-3m winner, by Silver Patriarch): dam (c105/h107) 2½m/21f hurdle/chase winner (stayed 3m): behind in bumpers. *Seamus Mullins* — **b–**

KENTFORD MYTH 8 b.m. Midnight Legend – Quistaquay (El Conquistador) [2017/18 c99, h103: h23s⁴ h20g⁶ h19.8s Nov 23] fair handicap hurdler, below best in 2017/18: winning chaser: barely stays 3¼m: acts on good to firm and heavy going: tried in tongue tie: often races towards rear. *Seamus Mullins* — **c– h78**

KENYAN (FR) 4 b.g. Kendargent (FR) – Landora (FR) (Lando (GER)) [2017/18 h16.3m⁵ h15.8d⁴ h16.8g³ h15.9m² h15.9d* h15.8d⁴ h19.5v^pu Nov 22] modest form on Flat: fair hurdler: won novice handicap at Plumpton in October: raced mainly around 2m: acted on good to firm and good to soft going: wore tongue tie: in cheekpieces last 5 starts: front runner/raced prominently, usually freely: dead. *Seamus Durack* — **h101**

KEPPEL ISLE (IRE) 9 b.g. Heron Island (IRE) – Wadi Khaled (FR) (Bering) [2017/18 c95, h–: c17.8m⁶ c17.8d^pu h17.7s³ Nov 20] good-topped gelding: modest hurdler/chaser at best, no form in 2017/18: tried in cheekpieces: usually leads. *Laura Mongan* — **c– h–**

KEREMAN (IRE) 4 b.g. Azamour (IRE) – Kerania (IRE) (Daylami (IRE)) [2017/18 h16.7g⁴ h16.8g⁴ h17.7d⁵ h15.9m⁵ Sep 24] brother to useful 1¼m-1½m winner Kerisa and half-brother to 3 winners on Flat, including useful 7f-1½m winner Karasiyra (by Alhaarth): dam ran once on Flat: modest form over hurdles: remains capable of better. *Dan Skelton* — **h94 p**

KERISPER (FR) 9 b.g. Robin des Champs (FR) – Tina Rederie (FR) (Cadoudal (FR)) [2017/18 c89p, h–: h23.9v Apr 15] Irish maiden point winner: fairly useful hurdler at best, well held sole start in 2017/18: some promise only chase start: stays 3m: acts on heavy going. *Nigel Twiston-Davies* — **c– h–**

KERRY'S BOY (IRE) 5 b.g. Oscar (IRE) – Kerry's Girl (IRE) (Flemensfirth (USA)) [2017/18 b16.4g^pu h19s⁶ h21.2d⁶ h21.7g⁴ Apr 20] £27,000 3-y-o: good sort: fourth foal: dam (h116), 19f hurdle winner, half-sister to useful hurdler/chaser (stayed 2¼m) St Pirran and fairly useful hurdler/useful chaser (stayed 29f) Guess Again: pulled up in bumper: modest form over hurdles: best effort when fourth in novice at Fontwell in April: in tongue tie last 3 starts. *Ben Pauling* — **h93 b–**

KESTREL VALLEY 4 b.f. Dr Massini (IRE) – Lady Karinga (Karinga Bay) [2017/18 b16.2s⁵ b15.8v h16.8s³ h16s⁴ Mar 22] first foal: dam (c106/h103), 2¾m hurdle winner, half-sister to useful hurdler/chaser (winner around 2m) Rock On Rocky: poor form in bumpers: fair form over hurdles: better effort when third in mares novice at Exeter in February: bred to be suited by 2½m+: in hood last 2 starts. *Matt Sheppard* — **h100 b74**

KIL

KEYBOARD GANGSTER (IRE) 7 b.g. Gamut (IRE) – Vic O'Tully (IRE) (Old Vic) [2017/18 b83§: h16v⁴ h16v* h15.7s³ h16.2v* Apr 7] useful form over hurdles: won novice at Ayr in February and handicap at Kelso (in hood, by ¾ length from Reverant Cust) in April: in tongue tie last 4 starts: races freely: quirky sort. *Donald Whillans*   **h130**

KEYBOARD WARRIOR (IRE) 6 b.g. Scorpion (IRE) – Our Shelly (IRE) (Rakaposhi King) [2017/18 b16.8m⁶ b16.8m² b16.8d⁴ Jul 31] maiden pointer: poor form in bumpers. *Paul Henderson*   **b74**

KEY TO THE WEST (IRE) 11 b.g. Westerner – Monte Solaro (IRE) (Key of Luck (USA)) [2017/18 c–, h105§: c20v c18.9sᵖᵘ c17.8g⁴ Apr 20] good sort: winning hurdler: modest handicap chaser nowadays: stays 2½m: acts on heavy going: has worn headgear/tongue tie, including in 2017/18: temperamental. *John Spearing*   **c92 §** / **h– §**

KHAGE (IRE) 5 b.g. Stowaway – Made Easy (IRE) (Rudimentary (USA)) [2017/18 b16d³ b16s⁵ Nov 12] well-made gelding: fourth foal: half-brother to useful hurdler/smart chaser Max Ward (2m-2½m winner, by Milan): dam unraced half-sister to smart hurdler/chaser (stayed 2½m) Made In Taipan: fair form in bumpers: better effort when third at Chepstow in October: wears hood. *Jonjo O'Neill*   **b92**

KHISMET 5 b.m. Kheleyf (USA) – Bisaat (USA) (Bahri (USA)) [2017/18 h97: h15.8g h16g³ h16.8g⁵ h16.7g² h15.8d³ h18.5d⁴ Oct 12] fair handicap hurdler: stays 19f: acts on good to firm and good to soft going: has worn cheekpieces, including final start. *John Flint*   **h102**

KHUDHA (IRE) 4 b.g. Helmet (AUS) – Seeking Dubai (Dubawi (IRE)) [2017/18 h16s⁵ h16s⁵ h16v⁴ h16.4s Mar 13] close-coupled gelding: fairly useful on Flat, stays 1½m: fair form over hurdles: wears cheekpieces. *Alan Fleming, Ireland*   **h107**

KICK ON DOTTIE (IRE) 5 ch.m. Getaway (GER) – Oddly Presented (IRE) (Presenting) [2017/18 b62p: b16.8g⁵ b16.2g⁴ h20.6g h16.8s h19.3dᵖᵘ Dec 19] poor form in bumpers: little show in novice hurdles. *Malcolm Jefferson*   **h–** / **b69**

KIKIMORA 5 gr.m. Malinas (GER) – Tikk Tokk (IRE) (Tikkanen (USA)) [2017/18 b–: h15.8d h15.8s h15.8d h21gᵖᵘ h19.6dᵖᵘ Apr 21] no form in bumper/over hurdles: in headgear/tongue tie last 2 starts. *Oliver Greenall*   **h–**

KILBREE KID (IRE) 11 b.g. Cloudings (IRE) – Bustingoutallover (USA) (Trempolino (USA)) [2017/18 c125, h–: c24d⁶ c27.5g⁵ c23.8g* c23.8g⁵ c24.2sᵖᵘ Oct 24] sturdy gelding: winning hurdler: fairly useful handicap chaser: won at Perth in July: stays 3¼m: acts on soft and good to firm going: wears headgear/tongue tie: often races prominently. *Tom George*   **c126** / **h–**

KILBREW BOY (IRE) 5 b.g. Stowaway – Bean Ki Moon (IRE) (King's Theatre (IRE)) [2017/18 b16d Apr 26] €4,000 3-y-o, £75,000 4-y-o: rather unfurnished gelding: third foal: dam unraced out of useful 2m hurdle winner Titled Dancer: second in Irish point on debut: in hood, 28/1, tenth in bumper at Warwick (7¾ lengths behind Emitom). *Ben Case*   **b85**

KILBRICKEN STORM (IRE) 7 b.g. Oscar (IRE) – Kilbricken Leader (IRE) (Supreme Leader) [2017/18 h16.8s³ h15.3s* h24s* h20.5v³ h24v* h24s³ Apr 25]   **h151**

The Spa Novices' Hurdle hasn't always met with universal approval in these pages since it was introduced into the Cheltenham Festival programme in 2005, when the meeting was expanded to four days. Timeform has argued that the new race (together with competing attractions for mares now available at the meeting too) has diluted the quality of the Festival's two established novice hurdles, the Supreme and the Baring Bingham, with leading performers often sidestepping the shorter races in favour of a supposedly easier opportunity. That certainly happened with the Jonjo O'Neill-trained pair Black Jack Ketchum and Wichita Lineman, who justified short-priced favouritism by wide margins in the Spa in 2006 and 2007 respectively, when they would also have been the market leaders in the corresponding years' Baring Bingham, their absences from the latter race robbing racegoers of some mouth-watering clashes in the process. Timeform was firmly against the decision to upgrade the Spa from Grade 2 to Grade 1 in 2008—also the year when current sponsors Albert Bartlett began their association with the race. Timeform has also argued that the Spa trip should be extended to make the contrast with the Baring Bingham more pronounced (there is just two furlongs, one hundred and eighty-seven yards between the two race distances). However, two miles seven furlongs and two hundred and thirteen yards on Cheltenham's New Course appears, in hindsight, to be more than

Albert Bartlett Novices' Hurdle (Spa), Cheltenham—33/1-shot Kilbricken Storm defeats the Nicky Henderson-trained pair Ok Corral (hoops & white cap) and Santini (second right)

enough of a test for young horses at such an early stage of their career and possibly explains why there have been six winners of the Spa aged seven or older in its fourteen renewals so far. By contrast, there has been just one winner aged over six of the Supreme or Baring Bingham during the same period, that being seven-year-old Captain Cee Bee who won the 2008 Supreme. The inaugural Spa winner Moulin Riche might have been just five but, in many other ways, he set the tone for what was to follow, having had plenty of racing (including a spell of chasing) and proving too strong on the day for largely less-experienced rivals. Moulin Riche is one of six Spa winners who were a second- or third-season novice and, on average, Spa winners are having their eleventh career start when they line up at Cheltenham.

The latest winner Kilbricken Storm falls below that average, having had seven career starts before tackling the Spa, including three runs in Irish points before joining present connections. Kilbricken Storm was one of just three runners in the field of twenty that were aged seven or older. He already had a course and distance win to his name too, having defeated the favourite Count Meribel by two and three quarter lengths in a disappointing four-runner renewal of the Grade 2 Bristol Novices' Hurdle (also sponsored by Albert Bartlett) at the International meeting in December. That was Kilbricken Storm's second win over hurdles. After catching the eye when third in a hot Exeter novice on his hurdling debut, he had run out a wide-margin winner of a Wincanton novice over just fifteen furlongs in November after being left clear by the final-flight fall of leader Mont des Avaloirs. Cheltenham punters clearly felt Kilbricken Storm had had his limitations exposed after a remote third to Poetic Rhythm in the Challow Hurdle at Newbury in late-December and he lined up for the Spa as a 33/1-shot. It was clear he hadn't given his true running at Newbury, however, and equally clear from an early stage in the Spa that he looked like putting up a much bolder showing. Always handy, the notably fluent Kilbricken Storm kept closer tabs on long-time leader Fabulous Saga than most of the market principals and, as a result, was better placed to pick up the pieces when that one faltered approaching the last. Despite tending to hang left off the bridle (something he also did in the Bristol), Kilbricken Storm kept going strongly and was always holding on from the last, beating the more patiently-ridden Nicky Henderson-trained pair Ok Corral (an eight-year-old, albeit a lightly-raced one) and the favourite Santini (having just his third start under Rules) by three lengths and a length and a half. Fabulous Saga faded into seventh in the end, while Poetic Rhythm (the other seven-year-old) came only tenth.

The victory of Kilbricken Storm proved a welcome fillip, after a trying first three days, for trainer Colin Tizzard who went on to complete a memorable double with Native River in the Cheltenham Gold Cup some forty minutes later. Heavy ground and a strong gallop meant the latest Spa was an even more gruelling test than usual (the time was over twenty-four seconds slower than Penhill clocked when winning twelve months earlier). The time and the conditions could cast some doubt as to the reliability of the form, particularly as Kilbricken Storm was the fifth successive Spa winner at double-figure odds and he is also the joint longest-priced winner, with Very Wood (2014) and Berties Dream (2010). Kilbricken Storm went a long way to dispelling such fears about the value of his Cheltenham victory with a solid effort on his only subsequent outing, when a very close third (beaten necks) to Next Destination and Delta Work in the War of Attrition (branded as the Irish Daily Mirror) Novices' Hurdle at the Punchestown Festival in April, again sticking to his task well in the latter stages as the first three pulled well clear of the remainder.

Kilbricken Storm (IRE) (b.g. 2011)	Oscar (IRE) (b 1994)	Sadler's Wells (b 1981)	Northern Dancer / Fairy Bridge
		Snow Day (b 1978)	Reliance II / Vindaria
	Kilbricken Leader (IRE) (b 1995)	Supreme Leader (b 1982)	Bustino / Princess Zena
		Kilbricken Star (b 1987)	Mandalus / Kilbricken Bay

Kilbricken Storm followed in the footsteps of previous Spa winners At Fishers Cross and Black Jack Ketchum (another seven-year-old winner) in being by Oscar out of a Supreme Leader mare. He might have won only once from those three starts in Irish maiden points, that victory coming with the aid of a wayward runner-up to boot, but the £22,000 Tizzard shelled out to secure him at the 2017 Doncaster Spring Sales still looked cheap at the time considering his pedigree. His year-younger half-brother I Know U Too Well (by Stowaway) had fetched €55,500 as an unraced store two years earlier and duly looked an exciting prospect when

A Selway & P Wavish's "Kilbricken Storm"

KIL

winning both of his starts in bumpers for Jonjo O'Neill in 2016/17 (unfortunately, though, he hasn't raced since then). Kilbricken Storm is also a half-brother to the winning Irish pointers Great Leader (by Great Palm) and Rainbow Sally (by Needle Gun), the latter now a broodmare, while his dam Kilbricken Leader (whose fourth foal he is) was a bumper winner who was also runner-up in a mares maiden hurdle over two and a half miles. Grandam Kilbricken Star was a winning Irish pointer who also won a two and three quarter mile maiden hurdle at Fairyhouse. Her main claim to fame, however, was that she was a sister to St Mellion Fairway, a remote fourth of five finishers in Earth Summit's gruelling Grand National and a useful staying hurdler earlier in his career, who would almost certainly have contested the Spa Hurdle in 1995 had the race existed then.

A strong gelding, Kilbricken Storm clearly handles the mud very well, having raced only on soft and heavy ground to date. His future almost certainly lies over fences and long distances should bring out the very best in him too, so it would be no surprise to see races such as the National Hunt Chase or the Scottish Grand National on the agenda for him in the next season should everything go to plan. Whether regular partner Harry Cobden will be in the saddle is another matter, though. Cobden has enjoyed plenty of success for the Tizzard stable in recent years, with six of the jockey's nine graded wins in 2017/18 provided by the Dorset yard, with Kilbricken Storm his first Cheltenham Festival winner. However, following the news in May that Cobden was to replace Sam Twiston-Davies as number one for Paul Nicholls (who supplied Cobden's three other graded wins in 2017/18), the latter will have first call when it comes to the big races. There is, however, unlikely to be a shortage of volunteers to ride Kilbricken Storm should a replacement be needed. *Colin Tizzard*

KILCARRY BRIDGE (IRE) 11 b.g. Balakheri (IRE) – Echo Queen (IRE) (Luso) [2017/18 c132x, h114: c23m* h20.5g⁵ c18.2s⁴ h16.3g² c20.5g* c24vᵖᵘ h20v³ h24v* c25d² h20v⁶ c16.5s c17s² c17s c18sᶠ c16v⁴ c29vᶠ h17.8v⁶ Apr 13] fairly useful handicap hurdler: won at Gowran in September: smart handicap chaser: won at Ballinrobe in May and Killarney (by length from The Winkler) in August: second in Grade 3 event at Punchestown (1½ lengths behind Road To Respect) in October: stays 25f, effective at much shorter: acts on good to firm and heavy going: wears tongue tie: usually leads: often let down by jumping over fences. *John Patrick Ryan, Ireland* **c146 x h125**

KILCASCAN 14 b.g. Alflora (IRE) – Peasedown Tofana (Teenoso (USA)) [2017/18 c92: c22.6g⁶ c22.6m⁶ c24vᵖᵘ c24.1s⁴ Mar 24] poor handicap chaser nowadays: stays 3¼m: acts on good to firm and heavy going: wears cheekpieces: usually leads. *Rosemary Gasson* **c73**

KILCREA BRIDGE 7 b.g. Kayf Tara – Ballyhoo (IRE) (Supreme Leader) [2017/18 c23.6s² Apr 27] €31,000 3-y-o: third foal: dam (h102) 21f-27f hurdle winner: point winner: fair maiden hurdler: left P. M. J. Doyle after final 2016/17 start: 6/1, second in novice hunter at Chepstow (19 lengths behind Tinkers Hill Tommy) on chasing debut: stays 3m: acts on soft going: tried in cheekpieces. *N. R. P. Williams* **c102 h–**

KILCREA VALE (IRE) 8 b.g. Beneficial – Inflation (FR) (Port Etienne (FR)) [2017/18 c143, h–: c21.3m² c21d³ c24d⁶ c21v² c20.5s⁵ c21.1s⁴ Apr 13] well-made gelding: winning hurdler: useful handicap chaser: second at Haydock (2½ lengths behind Hammersly Lake) in May and in bet365 Handicap Chase at Ascot (2¼ lengths behind Acting Lass) in January: stays 21f: acts on heavy and good to firm going: front runner/races prominently. *Nicky Henderson* **c138 h–**

KILCULLEN BELLAMY 6 b.m. Black Sam Bellamy (IRE) – Fenney Spring (Polish Precedent (USA)) [2017/18 b16.5v⁴ h16s³ Mar 22] £7,000 3-y-o, £10,000 6-y-o: fifth foal: closely related to 2 winners by Kayf Tara, including fair hurdler/winning pointer Grace Tara (19f-23f winner), and half-sister to bumper winner/useful hurdler Knight Bachelor (2½m-2¾m winner, by Midnight Legend), stayed 25f: dam (h69) bumper/2m hurdle winner (stayed 2½m): won completed start in Irish points: well beaten in mares bumper: 20/1, third in mares novice at Chepstow (7¼ lengths behind Dinos Benefit) on hurdling debut. *Evan Williams* **h86 b62**

KILCULLEN FLEM (IRE) 8 ch.g. Flemensfirth (USA) – Cansalrun (IRE) (Anshan) [2017/18 c105, h–: c24.2v* c24vᵖᵘ v9v* c28.4v³ c30s⁴ Apr 28] winning hurdler: fair handicap chaser: won at Hexham in October and March: stays 4m: acts on heavy going: wears headgear: front runner/races prominently. *Philip Kirby* **c114 h–**

KILCULLEN LADY (IRE) 8 b.m. Scorpion (IRE) – Glittering Star (IRE) (Good Thyne (USA)) [2017/18 h20.6g^{pu} h16.8s h19.3d^6 h20.8s^6 c21.3v^4 c24.2v^{pu} Mar 15] won Irish point on debut: no form under Rules: in headgear last 4 starts. *Henry Hogarth* c– h–

KILDISART (IRE) 6 br.g. Dubai Destination (USA) – Princess Mairead (IRE) (Blueprint (IRE)) [2017/18 b101p: h20d^2 h19.3g* h21d^2 h19.3s^5 h21s* h20s Apr 14] strong, compact gelding: runner-up in Irish maiden point: useful form over hurdles: won maiden at Ascot in November and handicap at Kempton (by 2¼ lengths from Zubayr) in March: stays 21f: acts on soft going: front runner/races prominently. *Ben Pauling* h140

KILFENORA (IRE) 6 b.g. Yeats (IRE) – Blazing Liss (IRE) (Supreme Leader) [2017/18 h131: c18.2v^F c16.2d^5 c19.5s^6 c17v c17v^3 c17s^{pu} h24v* h22v^{pu} Apr 2] useful handicap hurdler: won at Punchestown (by ½ length from Call The Taxie) in February: fairly useful form over fences: best effort when third in handicap at Navan in December: stays 3m: acts on heavy going. *Edward P. Harty, Ireland* c120 h131

KILFILUM CROSS (IRE) 7 gr.g. Beneficial – Singh Street (IRE) (Dolphin Street (FR)) [2017/18 h21.2v h23.8s^2 h23.6s* h24.6s* Apr 9] £50,000 5-y-o: second foal: dam (c81/h91), 2m-2½m hurdle winner, half-sister to fairly useful hurdler (2m-19f winner) Lucaindubai: winning Irish pointer: fairly useful form over hurdles: made all in novices at Chepstow in March and Kempton in April. *Kim Bailey* h123

KILFINICHEN BAY (IRE) 10 b.g. Westerner – Cailin Deas (IRE) (Pistolet Bleu (IRE)) [2017/18 c133, h–: c24d^5 c25.5d* c26.1m h23.3d^6 c23g^4 c25.5g^4 c26s^4 c21s^4 Mar 25] sturdy gelding: winning hurdler: useful chaser: won handicap at Fontwell in May: largely below form after: left Charlie Longsdon after sixth start: stays 3¼m: acts on good to firm and heavy going: tried in cheekpieces: has worn tongue tie, including usually in 2017/18: often races towards rear. *F. A. Hutsby* c129 h–

KILINAKIN (IRE) 8 ch.g. Definite Article – Topanberry (IRE) (Topanoora) [2017/18 h86: c20d^5 c15.9v* c19.9d c20.5s Apr 9] maiden hurdler: modest form over fences: won handicap at Leicester in March: bred to be suited by 3m+: acts on good to firm and heavy going. *Zoe Davison* c96 h–

KILLABRAHER CROSS (IRE) 11 gr.g. Kasmayo – Enoughrose (IRE) (Roselier (FR)) [2017/18 c84, h–: c25.7g^F c19.7d^{pu} Oct 23] maiden chaser: modest chaser at best: failed to complete in 2017/18, including in points: stays 2½m: acts on good to soft going: in cheekpieces last 4 starts: front runner/races prominently. *Paddy Butler* c– h–

KILLALA QUAY 11 b.g. Karinga Bay – Madam Bijou (Atraf) [2017/18 c128, h–: c23.6d c26.1d c24d^4 c23.4s^6 c24s^4 c25.6v^{pu} c24g^4 Apr 20] sturdy gelding: winning hurdler: fairly useful handicap chaser: stays 3m: acts on soft and good to firm going: wears headgear: front runner/races prominently: unreliable. *Charlie Longsdon* c125 § h–

KILLARE CASTLE (IRE) 8 b.g. Antonius Pius (USA) – Forloveofthestars (IRE) (Galileo (IRE)) [2017/18 c17g c19.5g^{pu} c20.6s c25.3g^{pu} c24d^F c18s^5 c21v^4 c21v^F c20v^{pu} c19.2s c24.1d^{ur} Apr 21] maiden hurdler: poor maiden chaser: in front when fell last in handicap at Tramore in January: left Gordon Michael Doyle after second start: stays 21f: acts on heavy going: usually in headgear in 2017/18: has worn tongue tie, including last 4 starts: front runner/races prominently. *Paul W. Flynn, Ireland* c74 h–

KILLARO BOY (IRE) 9 ch.g. Mr Dinos (IRE) – Auburn Roilelet (IRE) (Good Thyne (USA)) [2017/18 c131p, h–: h20v c21.3s^4 c29v^{bd} h21s^3 Apr 25] fair form over hurdles: useful form over fences: fourth in handicap at Leopardstown (8¾ lengths behind Spider Web) in March: stays 21f: acts on heavy going: wears hood. *Adrian Murray, Ireland* c131 h114

KILLER CROW (IRE) 9 ch.g. Presenting – Rivervail (IRE) (River Falls) [2017/18 c17m^6 c17m c23.4v^3 c20.9v^3 Mar 8] workmanlike gelding: winning hurdler: fair chaser nowadays: left Gordon Elliott after second start: stays 29f: acts on heavy going: usually wears headgear/tongue tie. *N. W. Alexander* c107 h–

KILLONE (IRE) 9 gr.g. Flemensfirth (USA) – Ceol Tire (IRE) (Roselier (FR)) [2017/18 c–, h98: h20.2g^5 May 17] maiden hurdler: pulled up sole chase start: best effort at 2m: in tongue tie last 3 starts. *Alison Hamilton* c– h68

KILLULTAGH VIC (IRE) 9 b.g. Old Vic – Killultagh Dawn (IRE) (Phardante (FR)) [2017/18 h20v* c24s^F c26.3v^{pu} c24.5s^5 Apr 25] sturdy gelding: smart hurdler: didn't have to be at best to win minor event at Punchestown (by 2¾ lengths from Ex Patriot) in c163 x h138

Mrs R Boyd, Mrs MJ Armstrong & JB Anderson's "Killultagh Vic"

December after 2-year absence: high-class form over fences: in narrow lead when falling last in Irish Gold Cup at Leopardstown in February: mistakes when pulled up in Cheltenham Gold Cup: stays 3m: acts on heavy going. *W. P. Mullins, Ireland*

KILMOGANNY (IRE) 6 b.g. Stowaway – Gowayourdat (IRE) (Saddlers' Hall (IRE)) [2017/18 h68: h21.6g h19.6s May 20] workmanlike gelding: twice-raced in Irish points: well held over hurdles. *Katy Price*   h–

KILMURVY (IRE) 10 b.g. Shantou (USA) – Spagna (IRE) (Definite Article) [2017/18 c120, h–: h23.1s c24v⁴ c25.6s⁴ c24.2vᵖᵘ c29.2g³ Apr 26] workmanlike gelding: winning hurdler: modest handicap chaser nowadays: stays 29f: acts on good to firm and heavy going: wears headgear/tongue tie: enthusiam on the wane. *Jeremy Scott*   c94 h–

KILRONAN CASTLE 7 ch.g. Indian River (FR) – Greatest Friend (IRE) (Mandalus) [2017/18 c108, h101: c24.1d⁶ c23.4g c20.2g* c19.1d⁵ c21.1v⁴ Feb 22] winning hurdler: fair handicap chaser: won at Leicester in December: stays 2¾m: acts on good to firm and heavy going: in cheekpieces last 3 starts: often leads. *Donald McCain*   c106 h–

KILTORMER (IRE) 6 b.m. Presenting – Lady Hillingdon (Overbury (IRE)) [2017/18 b16.2g⁶ b15.8g Jun 15] first foal: dam (c118/h130), 2m-2½m hurdle/chase winner, half-sister to useful hurdler (stayed 2¾m) Dangerously Good: no form in bumpers. *Donald McCain*   b–

KIMBERLEY POINT 5 b.m. Sixties Icon – Kingara (Karinga Bay) [2017/18 b16d² b16.7v b16.8g Apr 19] fifth foal: half-sister to fairly useful hurdler Katy P (21f-23f winner, by Ask) and a winning pointer by Kayf Tara: dam unraced half-sister to useful chaser (21f-3¼m winner) Gunner Welburn: fair form in bumpers: best effort when second in mares event at Warwick in November: tried in hood. *Alan King*   b88

KIMBERLITE CANDY (IRE) 6 b.g. Flemensfirth (USA) – Mandys Native (IRE) (Be My Native (USA)) [2017/18 h130: c20.9s⁵ c16d⁵ c17.4s³ c21.4s* c23.4sᵖᵘ c23.4v⁴ c24.2s³ c23.6v* Apr 14] rather unfurnished gelding: useful hurdle winner: useful handicap chaser: won novice events at Market Rasen in December and Chepstow (by 10 lengths from Cucklington) in April: will stay beyond 3m: acts on heavy going. *Tom Lacey*   c136 h–

KIN

KINARI (IRE) 8 b.g. Captain Rio – Baraza (IRE) (Kalanisi (IRE)) [2017/18 c110, h–: c24s* c26m⁴ c24g Sep 26] maiden hurdler: fairly useful handicap chaser: won at Uttoxeter in July: placed in points in 2018: stays 3¼m: acts on soft and good to firm going: wears headgear/tongue tie: usually races close up. *Peter Bowen* — **c115 h–**

KINCORA FORT (IRE) 9 b.g. Brian Boru – Glenview Rose (IRE) (Roselier (FR)) [2017/18 h20.5d⁴ h20.5s⁶ c19.9s² c20.2v* c19.9s* c22.4s⁵ Mar 23] useful-looking gelding: winning hurdler: fairly useful form over fences: won handicaps at Leicester in January and Huntingdon in February: stays 21f: acts on good to firm and heavy going: in tongue tie last 4 starts: often races prominently. *Noel Williams* — **c128 h93**

KINDLER 4 b.g. Firebreak – Neardown Beauty (IRE) (Bahhare (USA)) [2017/18 b14.6s⁶ Dec 23] 4/1, sixth in junior bumper at Newcastle: well held on Flat. *James Ewart* — **b61**

KING ALFONSO 9 br.g. Desert King (IRE) – Satire (Terimon) [2017/18 c81, h96: h16g³ h16.3g⁴ h16.8m⁴ c16.5g* c16.5d³ c16.5f³ h15.8g⁶ Oct 26] compact gelding: modest handicap hurdler nowadays: fair chaser: won novice at Worcester in September: unproven beyond 2m: acts on firm and soft going: tried in tongue tie. *Dai Burchell* — **c107 h92**

KING CALVIN (IRE) 6 b.g. King's Theatre – Lerichi (IRE) (Shardari) [2017/18 h22g⁴ h19.8v* h21.6v² Apr 17] £4,200 4-y-o: sixth foal: closely related to fairly useful hurdler/fair chaser Prince of Denial (19f2½m bumper, by Old Vic): dam maiden half-sister to very smart staying chaser Hey Big Spender: won twice in points: fairly useful form over hurdles: won maiden at Wincanton in March: will prove best at 2¾m+: wears tongue tie. *Jack R. Barber* — **h123**

KING CHARLIE (IRE) 8 b.g. Chevalier (IRE) – Desert Treat (IRE) (Desert Prince (IRE)) [2017/18 c78, h–: h25sᵖᵘ Apr 15] no form over hurdles: maiden chaser: stays 25f: acts on good to soft going: wears cheekpieces/tongue tie: usually races close up. *Suzy Smith* — **c– h–**

KING CNUT (FR) 4 ch.g. Kentucky Dynamite (USA) – Makadane (Danehill Dancer (IRE)) [2017/18 b13.7g b13.7g h17.7v⁶ h16v³ h16s⁴ h16s Feb 9] sturdy gelding: second foal: half-brother to French 10.5f winner First Conde (by Turtle Bowl): dam, French 9.5f-10.5f winner, half-sister to fairly useful French hurdler/chaser (15f-19f winner) Sparkie: no form in bumpers: modest form over hurdles. *Chris Gordon* — **h96 b–**

KING COOL 7 b.g. King's Theatre (IRE) – Cool Spice (Karinga Bay) [2017/18 h114: h20.5g⁵ c18d c19.9s c17vᵘʳ c17v⁵ c23.6s³ c25.7v² Apr 1] winning Irish pointer: fair handicap hurdler: modest form over fences: stays 3¼m: acts on heavy going: tried in cheekpieces/tongue tie. *Gary Moore* — **c90 h97**

KING GOLAN (IRE) 7 b.g. Golan (IRE) – Crimson Bow (GER) (Night Shift (USA)) [2017/18 h–, b–: h16.8g⁵ c19.3g⁵ c20g⁴ h24gᵖᵘ c16dᵘʳ c20dᵖᵘ c19.9m³ c19.2d³ Nov 24] maiden hurdler: poor form over fences: stays 2½m: acts on good to firm going: wears headgear/tongue tie: front runner/races prominently. *Kenny Johnson* — **c69 h–**

KING JULIEN (IRE) 5 b.g. Canford Cliffs (IRE) – Western Sky (Barathea (IRE)) [2017/18 h100: h20mᵖᵘ May 9] maiden hurdler: tried in tongue tie. *John Ryan* — **h–**

KING KAYF 9 b.g. Kayf Tara – Firecracker Lady (IRE) (Supreme Leader) [2017/18 c20.9vᵖᵘ Mar 10] strong gelding: bumper winner: maiden hurdler: pulled up in novice handicap on chasing debut after 2-year absence: bred to stay beyond 21f: acts on good to soft going: usually wears tongue tie. *Kerry Lee* — **c– h–**

KING MASSINI (IRE) 12 b.g. Dr Massini (IRE) – King's Linnet (IRE) (King's Ride) [2017/18 c–, h–: h23.9g⁵ Jun 22] workmanlike gelding: maiden hurdler, found little only start in 2017/18: winning pointer/chaser: stays 3¼m: acts on heavy going: has worn headgear, including last 2 starts. *Evan Williams* — **c– h–**

KING MURO 8 b.g. Halling (USA) – Ushindi (IRE) (Montjeu (IRE)) [2017/18 c122, h114: c17gᵖᵘ h17.2m⁵ h15.8g* c16g³ Jul 5] rather leggy gelding: fair hurdler: won conditionals seller at Uttoxeter in June: maiden chaser: better effort (fair form) in 2017/18 when last of 3 finishers in novice handicap at Perth: stays 19f: acts on good to firm and heavy going: usually in hood: wears tongue tie: usually races nearer last than first. *Fergal O'Brien* — **c111 h102**

KING OF ARAGON (IRE) 6 b.g. Montjeu (IRE) – Crazy Volume (IRE) (Machiavellian (USA)) [2017/18 h99: h15.6sᵖᵘ Jan 3] maiden hurdler, breathing problem only start in 2017/18: has worn headgear, including last 3 starts: usually tongue tied. *Iain Jardine* — **h–**

KING OF FASHION (IRE) 8 ch.g. Desert King (IRE) – French Fashion (IRE) (Jamesmead) [2017/18 h126: h24.3v⁴ h23.4vᵖᵘ h23.1s⁶ h24.3g⁶ Apr 20] rather leggy gelding: fairly useful handicap hurdler: left Ian Duncan after first start: stays 3m: acts on heavy going: wears tongue tie: often races towards rear. *Kerry Lee* — **h120**

KIN

KING OF GLORY 10 b.g. Kayf Tara – Glory Be (Gunner B) [2017/18 c118§, h–: c24.2s Oct 24] stocky gelding: maiden hurdler: fairly useful chaser, well held only start in 2017/18: stays 3m: best form on soft/heavy going: one to treat with caution (regularly flatters to deceive). *Venetia Williams*   **c74 §**
h–

KING OF MILAN (IRE) 8 b.g. Milan – Opera Mask (IRE) (Moscow Society (USA)) [2017/18 c95§, h–: c20.9d^{pu} c20g^4 c21.6g^{pu} Aug 24] winning pointer: no form over hurdles: maiden chaser: tried in headgear/tongue tie: temperamental: dead. *Des Donovan, Ireland*   **c57 §**
h–

KING OF REALMS (IRE) 6 b.g. King's Theatre (IRE) – Sunny South East (IRE) (Gothland (FR)) [2017/18 h101: h19.3g^2 h19s^2 h19.4s* h24g Apr 18] tall, good-topped gelding: bumper winner: fairly useful form over hurdles: won maiden at Doncaster in January: bred to stay 2½m+: remains open to improvement. *Ian Williams*   **h126 p**

KINGOFTHECOTSWOLDS (IRE) 4 b.g. Arcadio (GER) – Damoiselle (Sir Harry Lewis (USA)) [2017/18 b15.3v^4 b14s Jan 1] lengthy gelding: poor form in bumpers. *Nigel Twiston-Davies*   **b62**

KING OF THE DARK (IRE) 11 b.g. Zagreb (USA) – Dark Bird (IRE) (Lashkari) [2017/18 c88, h74: c25.8d^4 Aug 22] maiden hurdler: winning chaser, let down by jumping only outing (tongue tied) in 2017/18: stays 2¾m: acts on heavy going: tried in cheekpieces: often races prominently. *Katie Stephens*   **c63**
h–

KING'S CHORISTER 12 ch.g. King's Best (USA) – Chorist (Pivotal) [2017/18 c–, h55: h20.2g^{pu} May 18] compact gelding: modest hurdler at best, no show only outing in 2017/18: maiden chaser, often let down by jumping: tried in headgear: wears tongue tie. *Barry Murtagh*   **c– x**
h–

KINGS CROSS (FR) 8 b.g. King's Theatre (IRE) – Ladies Choice (FR) – Turgeon (USA) [2017/18 c97, h–: c24g^2 c26.1d^{pu} c23.9g^6 c21.6s^2 c23.6d^4 c26d^5 c19.4v^2 c23.5v^4 Jan 30] strong, compact gelding: maiden hurdler: modest handicap chaser: stays 3m: acts on heavy going: often wears headgear: usually tongue tied nowadays: unreliable. *Tony Carroll*   **c98 §**
h–

KINGS ECLIPSE (IRE) 8 b.g. Double Eclipse (IRE) – Good Times Ahead (IRE) (King's Ride) [2017/18 h76: h23.9g^5 h23.3d h23.3s^2 h24g^4 c26.3s* c26.3s^2 c26.3v^2 c30.6s^F Apr 27] modest maiden hurdler: fair form over fences: won novice handicap at Sedgefield in December: stays 31f: acts on heavy going: tried in hood: often races prominently. *Andrew Wilson*   **c99**
h85

KINGS INN (IRE) 4 b.g. Mawatheeq (USA) – Afnoon (USA) (Street Cry (IRE)) [2017/18 h16.5s^3 Dec 30] fair form up to 1½m on Flat: 2/1, not fluent when third in juvenile at Taunton (22 lengths behind Vaziani) on hurdling debut. *Paul Nicholls*   **h76**

KINGS LAD (IRE) 11 b.g. King's Theatre (IRE) – Festival Leader (IRE) (Supreme Leader) [2017/18 h19s^5 h21.7s^6 Apr 6] sturdy gelding: fairly useful handicap hurdler: winning chaser: stays 2½m: acts on heavy going: tried in cheekpieces: in tongue tie last 5 starts. *Colin Tizzard*   **c–**
h117

KINGSLEY (IRE) 5 b.g. Kalanisi (IRE) – Diva Antonia (IRE) (King's Theatre (IRE)) [2017/18 b–: b15.7d Nov 25] sturdy gelding: no form in bumpers/point. *Stuart Edmunds*   **b–**

KINGS LODGE 12 b.g. King's Theatre (IRE) – Mardello (Supreme Leader) [2017/18 c–§, h–: c24.2d^3 Apr 23] good-topped gelding: multiple winning pointer: winning hurdler: fairly useful chaser at best, no show either start in hunters: stays 2¾m: acts on soft going: in cheekpieces last 2 starts: tried in tongue tie: temperamental. *W. H. Easterby*   **c– §**
h– §

KINGS MONARCH 5 b.g. Schiaparelli (GER) – Monarch's View (King's Ride) [2017/18 h15.7s h16.3s^{ur} h19.5s^5 h16v^4 h16s^4 Apr 27] £15,000 3-y-o, resold £16,000 3-y-o, £60,000 4-y-o: seventh foal: half-brother to winning pointers by Midnight Legend (2) and Anshan: dam second in point: Irish point winner: fair form over hurdles. *Kerry Lee*   **h100**

KING'S ODYSSEY (IRE) 9 b.g. King's Theatre (IRE) – Ma Furie (FR) (Balleroy (USA)) [2017/18 c126, h–: c15.9d^3 c20.8s^3 c20.8v^3 c20.8s^3 Mar 15] well-made gelding: winning hurdler: useful handicap chaser: third in Brown Advisory & Merriebelle Stable Plate at Cheltenham (6¾ lengths behind The Storyteller) in March: stays 21f: acts on heavy going: often races prominently. *Evan Williams*   **c137**
h–

KING SPIRIT (IRE) 10 b.g. Fruits of Love (USA) – Tariana (IRE) (Revoque (IRE)) [2017/18 c19.9s^6 Feb 12] useful-looking gelding: maiden hurdler: fair chase winner, well held only start in 2017/18 after 4-year absence: stays 21f: acts on heavy going. *Tom Lacey*   **c–**
h–

KINGSPLACE (IRE) 6 b.g. Ask – Winsome Breeze (IRE) (Glacial Storm (USA)) [2017/18 b16.6d^2 b16v* Dec 31] fourth foal: closely related to useful/smart maiden chaser Mall Dini (2¾m-3m winner, by Milan) and half-brother to 2 winners, including fairly useful hurdler Landecker (2m-3¼m winner, by Craigsteel): dam unraced half-sister   **b95**

to fairly useful hurdler/chaser (winner up to 3m) Mr Babbage: runner-up in Irish point on debut: fairly useful form in bumpers: won at Warwick in December: will be suited by further than 2m. *Nigel Twiston-Davies*

KING'S REALM (IRE) 11 ch.g. King's Best (USA) – Sweet Home Alabama (IRE) (Desert Prince (IRE)) [2017/18 h16.8g Nov 2] good-topped gelding: fairly useful hurdler at best, no show only outing in 2017/18 after 28-month absence: well beaten only chase start: stays 19f: acts on soft and good to firm going: has worn tongue tie. *Tina Jackson*   c– h–

KING'S RESTE (IRE) 6 b.m. King's Theatre (IRE) – J'y Reste (FR) (Freedom Cry) [2017/18 b16d6 h19.9v4 h16.7s4 h15.8d4 h19.5spu Apr 27] half-sister to several winners, including fairly useful hurdler/very smart chaser J'Y Vole (2m-21f winner, by Mansonnien): dam, French 15f-2¼m hurdle winner (also 11f-1¾m winner on Flat), out of half-sister to dam of Cheltenham Gold Cup winner Long Run: well beaten in bumper: fair form over hurdles: in headgear last 4 starts: wears tongue tie. *Amy Murphy*   h103 b–

KINGS RYDE 6 b.g. King's Theatre (IRE) – Ryde Back (Bob Back (USA)) [2017/18 b16g3 h20.3g* h20g2 h23.9s3 Dec 14] first foal: dam (h131) bumper and 2½m/21f hurdle winner: third in conditionals/amateur bumper at Worcester: fairly useful form over hurdles: won novice at Southwell in September. *Nicky Henderson*   h123 b85

KING'S SOCKS (FR) 6 b.g. King's Best (USA) – Alexandrina (GER) (Monsun (GER)) [2017/18 c20.5s3 c20.8s5 c15.8spu Apr 12] good-topped gelding: has had breathing operation: useful hurdler: threatened on only start when listed event at Enghien and 2½ lengths second to Footpad in Prix Alain du Breil at Auteuil in 2016/17 for N. Bertran de Balanda: useful form over fences: won maiden at same course in 2015/16: third of 4 in graduation event at Kempton (8 lengths behind Modus) in February after 20-month absence: folded tamely final start: stays 2½m: acts on heavy going. *David Pipe*   c140 h–

KING'S SONG (FR) 8 b.g. King's Theatre (IRE) – Chanson Indienne (FR) (Indian River (FR)) [2017/18 c96, h83: h24g3 h21.5d3 c24g* c25.8dpu c25d* c28s Nov 5] poor handicap hurdler: fairly useful handicap chaser: won at Southwell in June and Punchestown in October: left David Dennis after fourth start: stays 25f: acts on soft going: usually wears headgear: wears tongue tie. *Gordon Elliott, Ireland*   c123 h70

KING'S TEMPEST 9 b.g. Act One – Queen of Spades (IRE) (Strong Gale) [2017/18 h113: h18.7g3 h16d c16gpu Nov 29] big, well-made gelding: bumper winner: maiden hurdler: pulled up in novice handicap on chasing debut: should be suited by further than 2m: acts on soft going: tried in cheekpieces/tongue tie: front runner/races prominently. *Warren Greatrex*   c– h97

KING'S TEMPLE (IRE) 5 b.g. Kalanisi (IRE) – I Don't Know (IRE) (Grand Plaisir (IRE)) [2017/18 b16d h19spu Dec 30] no show in bumper/novice hurdle. *Tim Vaughan*   h– b–

KINGS TEMPTATION 7 b.g. King's Theatre (IRE) – Temptation (FR) (Lando (GER)) [2017/18 h–, b78: h16g h16g5 h23.3g2 h21.6d4 h25g2 h24.5dF h23.5d c21.4s2 Mar 26] well-made gelding: fair maiden hurdler: 9/2, second in novice handicap at Market Rasen (1¾ lengths behind Bocasien Desbois) on chasing debut: stays 25f: acts on soft going: in tongue tie last 4 starts: should improve over fences. *Ben Case*   c103 p h104

KINGSTON (GER) 9 br.g. Dylan Thomas (IRE) – Katy Carr (Machiavellian (USA)) [2017/18 c108, h86: c19.9g c23.6v6 c21.6vpu c24s c21.4d5 Apr 22] sturdy gelding: winning hurdler/chaser, little form over fences in 2017/18: often wears headgear. *Tony Carroll*   c– h–

KINGSTON MIMOSA 6 b.g. Kheleyf (USA) – Derartu (AUS) (Last Tycoon) [2017/18 h93: h18.5m h19.2g6 h23.3d Sep 24] angular gelding: modest handicap hurdler, below form in 2017/18: stays 19f: acts on good to soft going: wears headgear: tried in tongue tie. *Mark Gillard*   h71

KING'S WALDEN 7 b.g. Fair Mix (IRE) – Clever Liz (Glacial Storm (USA)) [2017/18 b17g May 19] winning pointer: well beaten in bumper (tongue tied). *T. Ellis*   b–

KINGS WALK (IRE) 7 b.g. King's Theatre (IRE) – Shuil Sionnach (IRE) (Mandalus) [2017/18 h114: c15.2s3 h21g* h15.9v4 Apr 1] well-made gelding: fairly useful handicap hurdler: won at Kempton in February: 11/2, second of 3 finishers in novice at Wetherby (23 lengths behind Born Survivor) on chasing debut: stays 21f: acts on heavy going: usually races prominently: should do better over fences. *Colin Tizzard*   c106 p h120

KINGS WATCH (IRE) 7 b.g. Rainwatch – Leavemealoneawhile (IRE) (Be My Native (USA)) [2017/18 h16v h19.5v6 h16.7v4 h21vpu Mar 28] €2,500 3-y-o, £2,500 4-y-o: fourth foal: dam, winning pointer, half-sister to Grand National runner-up King Johns Castle: point winner: modest form over hurdles: tried in cheekpieces: wears tongue tie. *Richard Price*   h96

KIN

KINGSWELL THEATRE 9 b.g. King's Theatre (IRE) – Cresswell Native (IRE) (Be My Native (USA)) [2017/18 c133, h–: c30.2g* c30.2d⁴ Dec 15] lengthy gelding: winning hurdler: useful handicap chaser: won cross-country event at Cheltenham (by ¾ length from Vicomte du Seuil) in November: stays 31f: acts on heavy going: has worn cheekpieces, including last 5 starts: front runner/races prominently. *Michael Scudamore* — c136 h–

KING'S WHARF (IRE) 9 gr.g. Clodovil (IRE) – Global Tour (USA) (Tour d'Or (USA)) [2017/18 c134, h110: c17.1g* c19d h16.7g⁵ h19.9d h15.6m⁵ h15.6g c19.9d⁴ c15.8s⁶ Feb 3] fair handicap hurdler: useful handicap chaser: won at Kelso (by 23 lengths from Avidity) in May: left Gavin Patrick Cromwell after fourth start: stays 3m: acts on soft and good to firm going: has worn hood/tongue tie: often races prominently. *Sandy Thomson* — c131 h104

KING UTHER 8 b.g. Master Blade – Cadbury Castle (Midyan (USA)) [2017/18 c108: h23.1v⁴ h23.3v³ h26s* h24.2v² h25.8v³ Mar 17] good-topped gelding: fairly useful handicap hurdler: won at Warwick in January: stays 3¼m: acts on heavy going: in visor last 4 starts: front runner/races prominently: temperamental. *Chris Gordon* — h119 §

KING VINCE 5 gr.g. Mawatheeq (USA) – Tussah (Daylami (IRE)) [2017/18 b–: b16.8d* b17.7g* h15.9d³ h16s Nov 29] fair form in bumpers: won at Newton Abbot (maiden) in July and Fontwell in August: fair form over hurdles: better effort when third in maiden at Plumpton in November: left Stuart Kittow after second start: usually races prominently. *Jamie Snowden* — h103 b93

KIRUNA PEAK (IRE) 4 ch.f. Arcano (IRE) – Kirunavaara (IRE) (Galileo (IRE)) [2017/18 h17.7d² h16.3s³ h17v⁴ Dec 9] fair on Flat, stays 1¾m: modest form over hurdles: best effort when second in juvenile at Fontwell in September: wears tongue tie. *Fergal O'Brien* — h92

KISUMU 6 b.g. High Chaparral (IRE) – Arum Lily (USA) (Woodman (USA)) [2017/18 h89§: h16.2g³ h16.8g h16.8gᵖᵘ Nov 2] poor maiden hurdler nowadays: should stay beyond 2m: acts on soft going: has worn cheekpieces: temperamental. *Micky Hammond* — h83 §

KIT CASEY (IRE) 8 b.g. Robin des Pres (FR) – An Culainn Beag (IRE) (Supreme Leader) [2017/18 h70: c25d⁶ c23.6vᵖᵘ c20.9v⁶ Dec 18] winning pointer/hurdler: no form in chases: stays 3m: acts on heavy going: sometimes in hood/headgear. *Rebecca Curtis* — c– h–

KITCHAPOLY (FR) 8 b.g. Poliglote – Kotkicha (FR) (Mansonnien (FR)) [2017/18 c117, h–: c16.5g⁴ May 29] sturdy gelding: winning hurdler: fair handicap chaser, below form only start under Rules in 2017/18: stays 2½m: acts on good to firm and good to soft going: in tongue tie last 2 starts. *Dan Skelton* — c80 h–

KITEGEN (IRE) 12 b.g. Milan – Keen Gale (IRE) (Strong Gale) [2017/18 c–§, h–: h21.2mᵖᵘ c20.9gᶠ c21.1m Jun 15] tall, lengthy gelding: winning hurdler: fairly useful chaser at one time, well held only completed start in 2017/18: in cheekpieces/tongue tie last 2 starts: unreliable. *Robin Dickin* — c86 § h–

KITTEN ROCK (FR) 8 b.g. Laverock (IRE) – The Cat Eater (FR) (Tagel (USA)) [2017/18 c152+, h–: h16g² Jul 6] useful-looking gelding: very smart hurdler at one time: second in Grimes Hurdle at Tipperary (3½ lengths behind Plinth) only start in 2017/18: smart form over fences: stays 2½m: acts on heavy going: has worn hood. *E. J. O'Grady, Ireland* — c– h134

KITTY FISHER (IRE) 8 b.m. Scorpion (IRE) – Luck of The Deise (IRE) (Old Vic) [2017/18 h–, b–: h20.1d⁶ Apr 23] winning pointer: little show over hurdles. *Sandy Forster* — h–

KITTY POWER (IRE) 9 b.m. Presenting – Hannigan's Lodger (IRE) (Be My Native (USA)) [2017/18 h73: h16.8s⁵ Dec 8] poor form over hurdles: in hood last 5 starts: tried in tongue tie. *R. A. Curran, Ireland* — h–

KIWAYU 9 b.g. Medicean – Kibara (Sadler's Wells (USA)) [2017/18 h114: h20.6dᵖᵘ h24.4s Jan 26] has had breathing operation: fair hurdler at best, no form in 2017/18: stays 2½m: best form on good going: tried in cheekpieces/tongue tie: often travels strongly. *Mike Sowersby* — h–

KIWI MYTH 6 b.m. Midnight Legend – Kiwi Katie (Kayf Tara) [2017/18 b16s b16s h19.7g h18.5v³ h20.5s h20.5d⁶ h23.9mᵖᵘ Apr 25] second foal: half-sister to a winning pointer by Tobougg: dam unraced: well held in bumpers: modest form over hurdles: stays 21f: acts on heavy going: in tongue tie last 2 starts. *Fiona Shaw* — h89 b–

KK LEXION (IRE) 7 b.g. Flemensfirth (USA) – Kiloradante (IRE) (Phardante (FR)) [2017/18 h131: h21.1g³ h25.3s h18.9v³ h20.3g Apr 18] small gelding: fairly useful handicap hurdler: third at Cheltenham in October: best up to 21f: acts on soft going: usually races nearer last than first. *Tom George* — h127

KNO

KLARE CASTLE 6 b.g. Black Sam Bellamy (IRE) – Always Forgiving (Commanche **h99 p**
Run) [2017/18 b16.2d² b16.2v² h16v^ur Jan 23] £18,000 4-y-o: fourth foal: half-brother to **b100**
fair hurdlers Scooter Boy (2m winner, by Revoque) and Forgivienne (3m winner, by
Alflora), latter also winning pointer: dam unraced: fairly useful form when second in
bumpers at Hexham: third when unseated rider 2 out in novice won by Destrier at Wetherby
on hurdling debut: will be suited by further than 2m: open to improvement. *Sue Smith*

KLEPHT (IRE) 13 b.g. Great Palm (USA) – What A Mewsment (IRE) (Persian Mews) **c106**
[2017/18 c116, h–: c20.8d⁴ May 5] strong gelding: winning pointer/hurdler: fair chaser: **h–**
stays 2¾m: acts on good to firm and heavy going: wears tongue tie. *D. Holmes*

KLOUD GATE (FR) 6 ch.g. Astronomer Royal (USA) – Talkata (IRE) (Suave Dancer **h99**
(USA)) [2017/18 h16.3s⁶ h16s⁶ h16m³ Apr 26] rather leggy gelding: useful on Flat, stays
15.5f, left Gianluca Bietolini, France, after final start in 2017: modest form over hurdles:
best effort when third in novice at Kempton in April. *Gary Moore*

KNIGHT COMMANDER 5 br.g. Sir Percy – Jardin (Sinndar (IRE)) [2017/18 h74: **h109**
h16.8d* h15.8d³ h17.7g² h15.8d⁴ h21.3s⁴ Nov 3] rather sparely-made gelding: fair
handicap hurdler: won novice events at Newton Abbot and Uttoxeter in July: barely stays
21f: acts on good going: often races towards rear. *Olly Murphy*

KNIGHT DESTROYER (IRE) 4 b.g. Dark Angel (IRE) – Do The Deal (IRE) (Halling **h120**
(USA)) [2017/18 h17.2d² h15.8s* h16.7g² h16.8s³ h16.4s^F h15.7s⁵ Mar 25] strong gelding:
fairly useful on Flat, stays 1½m: fairly useful form over hurdles: won juvenile at Uttoxeter
in October: raced around 2m: acts on soft going: usually leads. *Jonjo O'Neill*

KNIGHTHOOD 4 b.g. Delegator – Love Roi (ITY) (Roi Danzig (USA)) [2017/18 **b83**
b16.3s⁶ Jan 17] half-brother to several winners, including a winning hurdler in Italy by
Hawk Wing: dam unraced Italian 6f-1m winner: 7/1, sixth in bumper at Newbury (5¾
lengths behind Morning Vicar). *Nicky Henderson*

KNIGHT IN DUBAI (IRE) 5 b.g. Dubai Destination (USA) – Bobbies Storm (IRE) **h131**
(Bob Back (USA)) [2017/18 b16.8g⁵ h21.3s* h21s³ h20.6s⁴ h21.1s Mar 14] €10,500 3-y-o, **b76**
£40,000 4-y-o: lengthy gelding: will make a chaser: sixth foal: half-brother to fair hurdler/
fairly useful chaser Abbey Storm (2½m/21f winner, by Presenting) and fair hurdler
Bendomingo (1¾m winner, by Beneficial), stays 25f: dam (b88), lightly raced in bumpers,
sister to high-class hurdler/smart chaser (stayed 3m) Back In Front and half-sister to fairly
useful hurdler/useful chaser (stays 3¼m) Another Hero: off mark in Irish points at second
attempt: promise when fifth in bumper at Sedgefield: useful form over hurdles: won novice
at Wetherby in December: third in Leamington Novices' Hurdle at Warwick (7 lengths
behind Mr Whipped) next time: may prove best short of 21f: in tongue tie last 2 starts.
Dan Skelton

KNIGHTLY PLEASURE 7 b.m. Kayf Tara – Kim Fontenail (FR) (Kaldounevees (FR)) **h76**
[2017/18 h100, b83: h19.2d⁶ h19.2v^pu Dec 11] well-made mare: bumper winner:
disappointing maiden hurdler: stays 19f: acts on heavy going: in cheekpieces last 4 starts:
temperament under suspicion. *Gary Moore*

KNIGHT OF NOIR (IRE) 9 b.g. Winged Love (IRE) – At Dawn (IRE) (Lashkari) **c136**
[2017/18 c117, h127: h24.7g* h23g* c23g² h25.4d⁵ c23d² c23.6d* c25s^pu h24.7s Apr 14] **h142**
workmanlike gelding: useful handicap hurdler: won at Aintree in May and Worcester (by 8
lengths from A Boy Named Suzi) in June: useful chaser: won novice at Chepstow (by 3½
lengths from Duel At Dawn) in October: left Neil Mulholland after sixth start: stays 25f:
acts on heavy going: has worn headgear: usually wears tongue tie: usually races close up.
Michael Blake

KNIGHT'S PARADE (IRE) 8 b.g. Dark Angel (IRE) – Toy Show (IRE) (Danehill **c–**
(USA)) [2017/18 c–, h105: h21.2g³ h19.6m² h20.7g² h19.1m⁴ h20.3g⁶ h20.3d⁴ h20d^pu **h99**
h19.7g Nov 29] fair handicap hurdler: little aptitude for chasing: stays 21f: acts on soft and
good to firm going: wears headgear/tongue tie: often races prominently. *Sarah Humphrey*

KNOCKADERRY FLYER (IRE) 9 b.g. Aolus (GER) – Tastao (IRE) (Camden Town) **c116**
[2017/18 c25.3d* May 5] fourth foal: half-brother to a winning pointer by Moonax: dam
pulled up both starts in points: winning pointer: 25/1, won hunter at Cheltenham (by 11
lengths from Always Archie) on chasing debut. *Paul King*

KNOCKANRAWLEY (IRE) 10 gr.g. Portrait Gallery (IRE) – Hot Lips (IRE) (Good **c131**
Thyne (USA)) [2017/18 c133, h–: c24.3v² c26v³ c25.6v^pu c30.7s⁵ c24.2s⁵ c30.7v³ Apr 17] **h–**
workmanlike gelding: winning hurdler: useful handicap chaser: second at Ayr in November:
stays 33f: acts on heavy going: wears headgear. *Kim Bailey*

KNO

KNOCKAN RUN (IRE) 7 b.g. Winged Love (IRE) – Knockans Flight (IRE) (Zaffaran (USA)) [2017/18 c24.2d^F Apr 24] off mark in Irish points at fourth attempt: fell seventh in novice hunter at Exeter on chasing debut. *Mrs Janet Ackner* — c–

KNOCKGRAFFON (IRE) 8 b.g. Flemensfirth (USA) – Gleaming Spire (Overbury (IRE)) [2017/18 c147, h–: c21g⁴ c16.3s⁵ c19.9d* c19.4v^F c20s⁴ c20.8g⁶ Apr 18] tall gelding: winning hurdler: useful handicap chaser: won at Musselburgh in January: left Dan Skelton after first start: stays 2½m: acts on soft going: in cheekpieces/tongue tie last 5 starts. *Olly Murphy* — c142 h–

KNOCK HOUSE (IRE) 9 ch.g. Old Vic – Lady's Gesture (IRE) (Anshan) [2017/18 c–, h115: h26.1s⁶ h25s² Apr 8] sturdy gelding: fairly useful handicap hurdler: second at Carlisle in April: winning chaser: stays 3¼m: acts on heavy going: has worn cheekpieces, including in 2017/18: tried in tongue tie. *Donald McCain* — c– h126

KNOCKLAYDE (IRE) 6 b.g. Mountain High (IRE) – Foret Noire (IRE) (Barathea (IRE)) [2017/18 h71: h24.3s^pu h20.5v^pu h23.3v^pu h20.6v⁶ Apr 14] poor maiden hurdler: in blinkers last 2 starts: often races towards rear. *Katie Scott* — h62

KNOCKLAYDE SNO CAT (IRE) 9 b.m. King's Theatre (IRE) – Sno-Cat Lady (IRE) (Executive Perk) [2017/18 h93: h23.9g h22.1d³ May 11] placed in Irish points: poor maiden hurdler: stays 3m: acts on heavy going: has worn hood: wears tongue tie: usually races towards rear. *Stuart Crawford, Ireland* — h76

KNOCKMAOLE BOY (IRE) 6 b.g. Echo of Light – Kashmir Lady (FR) (Rock of Gibraltar (IRE)) [2017/18 h16g² h16g^F h16.5m² h16.5m* h16g* h16.2s* h17.2d² Aug 26] dam half-sister to smart hurdler/useful chaser (2m-19f winner) Royal Shakespeare: fairly useful on Flat, stays 9.5f: fairly useful hurdler: won maiden at Down Royal in June, minor event at Limerick in July and novice at Perth in August: will prove best at 2m: acts on good to firm and heavy going: wears hood: in tongue tie last 5 starts: usually races prominently, strong traveller. *Gordon Elliott, Ireland* — h126

KNOCKNAMONA (IRE) 7 b.g. Trans Island – Faraday Lady (IRE) (Lord Americo) [2017/18 h86: h16.8g h16.2v c20.1v^F c21.1g c20v* h20.5s* c20.3v* c24.1v* c21.4v⁴ c21.4s⁶ Mar 26] modest handicap hurdler: won at Leicester in December: modest handicap chaser: won at Uttoxeter in November, Bangor in December and Ayr (novice) in January: stays 3m: acts on soft/heavy going. *Micky Hammond* — c98 h89

KNOCKNANUSS (IRE) 8 b.g. Beneficial – Dato Vic (IRE) (Old Vic) [2017/18 h15.9g* h15.9d² h15.9s² h17.7v* h16.3v^pu h19.5v⁴ Mar 5] first foal: dam unraced close relative of top-class 2m hurdler Dato Star: won Irish maiden point on debut: bumper winner for Michael Winters: fairly useful form over hurdles: won maiden at Plumpton in May and handicap at Fontwell in December: stays 2¼m: acts on heavy going: often races freely. *Gary Moore* — h128

KNOCKREA (IRE) 11 b.g. Pierre – Glynn Cross (IRE) (Mister Lord (USA)) [2017/18 h–: h16.2g³ h16.2g⁶ h20.2g^ur h17.2s^pu h19.9g^pu Oct 3] runner-up on completed start in Irish points: modest handicap hurdler nowadays: stays 2½m: acts on heavy and good to firm going: tried in tongue tie. *Gemma Anderson* — h87

KNOCKROBIN (IRE) 7 b.g. Robin des Pres (FR) – Tudor Style (IRE) (Montelimar (USA)) [2017/18 h20s⁴ h22.7s² h23.1v³ h19.6s* h19.9v² h23.9s^pu Apr 25] £22,000 6-y-o: half-brother to fair hurdler/chaser Tudor Fashion (2½m winner, by Presenting) and modest chaser Amber Knight (3m winner, by Rudimentary): dam (h91), 2½m hurdle winner, half-sister to useful hurdler/chaser (2m-2½m winner) Dawn Leader: won Irish point on debut: fairly useful form over hurdles: won novice at Bangor in March: stays 23f: raced only on soft/heavy going: in tongue tie last 4 starts: front runner/races prominently. *Donald McCain* — h128

KNOW THE SCORE (IRE) 5 b.g. Flemensfirth (USA) – Prairie Bell (IRE) (Sadler's Wells (USA)) [2017/18 b15.7v* b16.4s Mar 14] €55,000 3-y-o, £380,000 4-y-o: sturdy gelding: half-brother to useful hurdler/chaser Cailin Annamh (2¼m-2¾m winner, by Definite Article) and fairly useful hurdler Steel King (17f-3m winner, by Kalanisi): dam, lightly raced on Flat, sister to smart hurdler (stayed 3m) Mughas, and half-sister to fairly useful hurdler/smart chaser (stays 2½m) Sizing Platinum and smart hurdler (2m/17f winner) Pingshou: won Irish maiden point on debut: useful form in bumpers: won at Towcester (by 13 lengths from Milanstorm) in February: well held in Champion Bumper at Cheltenham. *David Pipe* — b105

KOALA KEEL (IRE) 6 gr.m. Kirkwall – Kayf Keel (Kayf Tara) [2017/18 b79: h19.3d⁵ h18.1v⁵ h16.2s^F Apr 27] placed in points: modest form over hurdles: closing when fell heavily last in mares novice won by Floral Bouquet at Perth in April, looking sure to be placed: in tongue tie last 3 starts. *N. W. Alexander* — h99

KUP

KOHUMA 8 ch.m. Halling (USA) – Kohiba (IRE) (Rock of Gibraltar (IRE)) [2017/18 h97: h16g^{pu} h16.2s^6 h16.5s* Jan 9] fair form over hurdles: won mares handicap at Taunton in January: raced around 2m: acts on soft going: front runner/races prominently. *Robert Walford* — **h101**

K O KENNY 7 b.g. Apple Tree (FR) – Cool Island (IRE) (Turtle Island (IRE)) [2017/18 h73: h19.9s h21.2v h24v^2 h24.1d^{pu} Mar 29] poor maiden hurdler: stays 3m: acts on heavy going: in cheekpieces last 2 starts. *Andrew Crook* — **h83**

KOOTENAY RIVER (IRE) 4 ch.g. Dubai Destination (USA) – Siwaara (IRE) (Peintre Celebre (USA)) [2017/18 b16.8d^2 Apr 24] £80,000 4-y-o: third foal: dam, lightly raced on Flat, half-sister to useful hurdler/fairly useful chaser (stayed 3m) Simarian: easy winner of point on debut: 11/10, second in maiden bumper at Exeter (¾ length behind Billygwyn Too). *Alan King* — **b98**

KOSHARI (FR) 6 br.g. Walk In The Park (IRE) – Honor May (FR) (Balleroy (USA)) [2017/18 h130+: c18v* c20v^2 c21sp^{pu} c20v* c21s^F Apr 27] useful hurdler: similar form over fences: won maiden at Thurles in December and minor event at Clonmel in March: second in Grade 3 novice at Punchestown (2½ lengths behind Invitation Only) in between: stays 2½m: acts on heavy going. *W. P. Mullins, Ireland* — **c143 h–**

KOSTAQUARTA (IRE) 11 ch.g. Beneficial – Aclare Thyne (IRE) (Good Thyne (USA)) [2017/18 c–, h–: c16s^{pu} c26v^{pu} c25.1v^{pu} c19.7v^5 Apr 1] strong gelding: multiple point winner: once-raced hurdler: maiden chaser, no form in 2017/18: wears cheekpieces/tongue tie: poor jumper. *Mark Gillard* — **c– x h–**

KOVERA (FR) 6 b.g. Antarctique (IRE) – Kesakao (FR) (Saint Estephe (FR)) [2017/18 h67: h15.8g h20g h21.6g^4 h23.3d Sep 24] poor maiden hurdler: best effort at 2¾m. *Tim Vaughan* — **h73**

KOZIER (GER) 4 ch.g. Muhtathir – Kasumi (GER) (Poliglote) [2017/18 h17.7g^2 Oct 6] fair on Flat, stays 2m: 11/8, second in juvenile at Fontwell (8 lengths behind Sussex Ranger) on hurdling debut: will stay further than 2¼m: should improve. *Alan King* — **h111 p**

KRACKATOA KING 10 b.g. Kayf Tara – Firecracker Lady (IRE) (Supreme Leader) [2017/18 c125§, h–: c24.2s^2 c26.1v* c25.1v^2 c29.2s c23.8v^4 c34v^6 Mar 17] well-made gelding: winning hurdler: fairly useful handicap chaser: won at Uttoxeter in November: second at Wincanton month later: stays 29f: raced only on soft/heavy going: wears headgear: often races prominently. *Kerry Lee* — **c124 h–**

KRIS SPIN (IRE) 10 br.g. Kris Kin (USA) – Auditing Empress (IRE) (Accordion) [2017/18 c86, h–: h25d^5 h24.3v* h23.3v^2 h25s^6 h23.4v h25.8v* h25.8v* Apr 7] workmanlike gelding: useful handicap hurdler: won at Ayr in November, Fontwell in March and Kelso (by 2¼ lengths from Donna's Diamond) in April: maiden chaser: stays 3¼m: acts on heavy going. *Kerry Lee* — **c– h142**

KRISTAL HART 9 b.m. Lucky Story (USA) – Moly (FR) (Anabaa (USA)) [2017/18 h95: h17.7d^4 h16.7g^4 h15.9d^2 h15.3v h16.5s Jan 9] modest maiden hurdler: unproven beyond 2m: acts on soft going: wears cheekpieces: often races towards rear. *Neil Mulholland* — **h90**

KRISTAL STAR 6 b.m. Midnight Legend – Royal Musical (Royal Abjar (USA)) [2017/18 h81, b76: h18.7g^5 h15.8m^6 h19.9g^6 h16.7g^{pu} h24g Jul 16] poor maiden hurdler: tried in blinkers: wears tongue tie. *Alex Hales* — **h69**

KRISTIAN GRAY (IRE) 9 b.g. Heliostatic (IRE) – Missfortuna (Priolo (USA)) [2017/18 c100: c25.3d^4 c27.5d^5 c24s^6 Jan 25] multiple point winner: modest chaser: stays 21f: acts on soft going: usually races prominently. *F. A. Hutsby* — **c92**

KRISTJANO (GER) 6 b.g. Nayef (USA) – Kalahari Dancer (Dalakhani (IRE)) [2017/18 h89: h18.5m^5 h16.8v^6 Nov 26] poor maiden hurdler. *Jimmy Frost* — **h–**

KRUGERMAC (IRE) 7 b.g. Kalanisi (IRE) – Vindonissa (IRE) (Definite Article) [2017/18 h99: h19.2s^6 h20.6v^3 Apr 11] tall, useful-looking gelding: fair hurdler, lightly raced: stays 21f: acts on heavy going: tried in visor. *Gary Moore* — **h108**

KUBLAI (IRE) 8 b.g. Laveron – Java Dawn (IRE) (Fleetwood (IRE)) [2017/18 c–, h116: h19.9d^5 h18.5m^6 h21.6m^2 h20m^3 h16.8g^2 h16.3m^2 h20.5v^4 h25s Apr 15] well-made gelding: modest handicap hurdler nowadays: pulled up both starts over fences: stays 2¾m: acts on soft and good to firm going: usually wears headgear/tongue tie nowadays: often travels strongly. *Alexandra Dunn* — **c– h91**

KUPATANA (IRE) 5 b.m. Westerner – Kildea Cailin (IRE) (Anshan) [2017/18 h20.5s^4 h19.5v* h16s^2 Mar 22] €1,700 3-y-o, £120,000 4-y-o: second foal: dam unraced: easy winner of Irish point on debut: fair form over hurdles: won maiden at Lingfield in March: tried in hood. *Nicky Henderson* — **h108**

KUR

KURAGINA (IRE) 4 b.f. Raven's Pass (USA) – Russian Society (Darshaan) [2017/18 b12.4s* b17s Apr 12] 5,000 3-y-o: useful-looking filly: half-sister to several winners, including fairly useful hurdler Skywards Reward (2m/17f winner, by Dubawi): dam, useful 1¼m winner, half-sister to useful 2m hurdler Buckwheat: modest form in bumpers: won junior event at Wetherby in December: well held in Grade 2 at Aintree. *Kenneth Slack* **b82**

KYLECRUE (IRE) 11 b.g. Gold Well – Sher's Adamant (IRE) (Shernazar) [2017/18 c134, h130: h20.5g⁵ c20v* c24vᵖᵘ c20v³ c20v⁵ h16.1s* h20v c16.7v⁵ c20sᵘʳ c21sᵖᵘ c18s⁵ c21.3s⁵ c24.5s³ Apr 28] useful handicap hurdler: won at Galway (by 1½ lengths from Prospectus) in October: useful handicap chaser: won at Listowel (by ½ length from The Gatechecker) in September: stays 25f: acts on good to firm and heavy going: wears headgear: has worn tongue tie: often races prominently. *John Patrick Ryan, Ireland* **c136 h134**

KYLEMORE LOUGH 9 b.g. Revoque (IRE) – One of The Last (Supreme Leader) [2017/18 c159, h–: c20.4sᵖᵘ c16.8v³ c20s² c20vᵖᵘ Apr 2] tall gelding: winning hurdler: very smart chaser: second in handicap at Warwick (5 lengths behind Casse Tete, tiring only run-in) in February: has won over 2¾m, probably better at shorter nowadays: acts on heavy going: tried in tongue tie: usually races prominently. *Harry Fry* **c159 h–**

L

LA BAGUE AU ROI (FR) 7 b.m. Doctor Dino (FR) – Alliance Royale (FR) (Turgeon (USA)) [2017/18 h132: h16s* h24.5d* h23.5v* h19.9s h24d Apr 26] tall, useful-looking mare: smart hurdler: won listed mares events at Wetherby and Kempton (by ½ length from Jer's Girl) in November and OLBG.com Mares' Hurdle (Warfield) at Ascot (by 16 lengths from Sainte Ladylime) in January: stays 3m well: acts on heavy going: races prominently/force pace: tough sort. *Warren Greatrex* **h145**

LABEL DES OBEAUX (FR) 7 b.g. Saddler Maker (IRE) – La Bessiere (FR) (Loup Solitaire (USA)) [2017/18 c151, h–: c23.6d c24.2s³ c26gᵖᵘ c24s⁶ c24g c31.8g⁶ Apr 21] compact gelding: winning hurdler: smart chaser: inconsistent in 2017/18, best effort when third in listed event at Sandown (8½ lengths behind Might Bite) in November: probably stays 4m: acts on heavy going: has worn cheekpieces, including last 4 starts: usually held up (but made all for 2 of 3 wins as a novice). *Alan King* **c149 h–**

LACKANEEN LEADER (IRE) 6 b.m. Oscar (IRE) – Shandora (IRE) (Supreme Leader) [2017/18 b16s³ h20s h18v² h16v* h20v* h22v* h20v² h24sᵖᵘ Apr 25] £40,000 5-y-o: seventh foal: half-sister to smart hurdler/chaser Don't Touch It (2m winner, by Scorpion) and fair hurdler I Never Knew That (2½m winner, by Anshan), stayed 3m: dam, ran twice in bumpers, half-sister to useful hurdler/very smart chaser (stayed 23f) Rubissimo: winning pointer: fair bumper winner: useful hurdler: won mares events at Fairyhouse (maiden) and Navan (handicap) in February, and Kerry Group EBF Shannon Spray Mares Novices' Hurdle (by 1¼ lengths from Moyhenna) at Limerick in March: also good second in Irish Stallion Farms EBF Mares Novices' Hurdle Championship Final at Fairyhouse (8½ lengths behind Laurina) in April: stays 2¾m: best form on heavy going: often travels strongly. *Gordon Elliott, Ireland* **h131 b86**

LAC SACRE (FR) 9 b.g. Bering – Lady Glorieuse (FR) (Le Glorieux) [2017/18 c108, h101: c24.2sᵖᵘ c23.8v⁶ c25.2g⁶ c25.3v³ c26v² c23.8v² c23.6s² c27.9v⁴ c30.6s² Apr 27] neat gelding: fair hurdler: fair handicap chaser: stays 31f: acts on heavy going: wears headgear/tongue tie. *John Flint* **c108 h–**

LA DAMA DE HIERRO 8 gr.m. Proclamation (IRE) – Altogether Now (IRE) (Step Together (USA)) [2017/18 c94, h–: c24.2gᵖᵘ May 13] winning hurdler: disappointing maiden chaser: stays 3¼m: acts on heavy going: in headgear last 2 starts. *Malcolm Jefferson* **c– h–**

LADIES DANCING 12 b.g. Royal Applause – Queen of Dance (IRE) (Sadler's Wells (USA)) [2017/18 c95, h75: c16.5mᵖᵘ h18.5m* c16.3mᵘʳ h18.5m⁶ h20g³ h16.8d³ h19m h18.5v Nov 7] angular gelding: modest handicap hurdler: won at Newton Abbot in May: lightly-raced maiden chaser, failed to complete both starts in 2017/18: stays 2¼m: acts on soft and good to firm going: has worn headgear: tried in tongue tie: front runner/races prominently. *Chris Down* **c– h89**

LADOFASH 4 b.g. Canford Cliffs (IRE) – Curras Spirit (Invincible Spirit (IRE)) [2017/18 h17.7g³ h17.7d⁵ h17.7v h20.5v⁵ h15.7s Mar 25] compact gelding: dam half-sister to useful hurdler (2m winner) Intense Tango: fair on Flat, stays 1½m: modest form over hurdles: stays 2¼m: acts on good to soft going: in cheekpieces last 4 starts. *Chris Gordon* **h99**

LAD

LAD OF LUCK (FR) 5 b.g. Soldier of Fortune (IRE) – Baraka du Berlais (FR) (Bonnet Rouge (FR)) [2017/18 b104p: h15.8s³ h19.6s³ h16s⁶ Apr 27] bumper winner: fair form over hurdles: shaped well when third in maiden at Huntingdon and novice at Bangor first 2 outings. *Jonjo O'Neill* **h107**

LADY ASH (IRE) 8 gr.m. Scorpion (IRE) – La Fiamma (FR) (General Assembly (USA)) [2017/18 h–: h21.6g^F May 10] poor form in bumpers/over hurdles: in headgear last 2 starts. *Robert Walford* **h71**

LADY AVERY (IRE) 6 b.m. Westerner – Bobs Article (IRE) (Definite Article) [2017/18 b–: h19.9d⁴ h22.1d May 31] £25,000 5-y-o: third foal: closely related to fairly useful/temperamental hurdler Towering (2m-23f winner, by Catcher In The Rye): dam unraced sister to smart hurdler (2m winner) Staying Article and fairly useful hurdler/smart chaser (stayed 3m) Mossback: Irish point winner: well held in bumper/over hurdles. *Alan Jones* **h63**

LADY BUTTONS 8 b.m. Beneficial – Lady Chapp (IRE) (High Chaparral (IRE)) [2017/18 h129: h16s² c17.4s* h20s⁴ h18s⁴ c16.3s* c15.8s⁴ Apr 14] lengthy mare: useful hurdler: second in listed mares event at Wetherby (2 lengths behind La Bague Au Roi) in November: took well to chasing: won novices at Bangor (listed mares) in November and Newcastle in February: stiffer task at Aintree final outing: best around 2m: acts on soft going: travels strongly. *Philip Kirby* **c140 h131**

LADY CHARTREUSE (IRE) 5 ch.m. Flemensfirth (USA) – Verde Goodwood (Lomitas) [2017/18 b16.7d⁶ Apr 21] €7,500 3-y-o: first foal: dam (h94), 2m hurdle winner (stayed 2½m), half-sister to useful hurdler (2m-21f winner) Argento Luna and useful hurdler/fairly useful chaser (19f-25f winner) Lyes Green: 10/1, sixth in conditionals/amateur bumper at Bangor (20 lengths behind Stoney Mountain). *Venetia Williams* **b59**

LADY CLITICO (IRE) 7 b.m. Bushranger (IRE) – Villa Nova (IRE) (Petardia) [2017/18 h–: h91: h15.6s h15.6d^F Feb 14] fair handicapper on Flat (stays 2m): fair maiden hurdler at best: ran poorly on completed start in 2017/18: raced around 2m: acts on heavy going: has worn headgear, including last 2 starts. *Rebecca Menzies* **h–**

LADY JAMESON (IRE) 7 b.m. Whitmore's Conn (USA) – Corbetstown Queen (IRE) (Oscar (IRE)) [2017/18 h21.6m^pu h16.8m³ h16g h16g^pu c17d^pu c23g^pu c24d^pu Dec 5] £5,000 6-y-o: second foal: half-sister to bumper winner/fairly useful hurdler Suit Yourself (17f winner, by Flemensfirth), stayed 2¾m: dam, ran twice in bumpers, half-sister to smart hurdler/very smart chaser (stayed 2½m) Fota Island: dual winner in points in 2016: no form otherwise: wears tongue tie. *Alexandra Dunn* **c– h–**

LADY KARINA 7 b.m. Kayf Tara – Lady Rebecca (Rolfe (USA)) [2017/18 h109p: h19s* h20.3s^F h19.5v Mar 21] lengthy mare: fairly useful form over hurdles: won handicap at Warwick in November: will stay 3m: raced on soft/heavy going. *Venetia Williams* **h115**

OLBG.com Mares' Hurdle, Wetherby—the prolific La Bague Au Roi (right) survives a blunder at the last to land the odds from Lady Buttons

LAD

LADY KNIGHT (IRE) 7 b.m. Champs Elysees – Knight's Place (IRE) (Hamas (IRE)) [2017/18 h16.3g⁶ Oct 21] rather leggy mare: poor stayer on Flat: little form over hurdles for various trainers: should stay beyond 2m: in headgear last 2 starts. *Sam Thomas*   h–

LADY LONDON (IRE) 7 b.m. Beneficial – Torduff Storm (IRE) (Glacial Storm (USA)) [2017/18 h–, b65; h20.9d^{pu} h22.7g⁵ h23.8g* h23.8g² h23.8s⁴ h20.2s³ Apr 25] quite good-topped mare: winning pointer: modest handicap hurdler: won at Musselburgh in November: stays 3m: acts on soft going: has worn headgear/tongue tie, including last 4 starts. *Rose Dobbin*   h89

LADY LONGSHOT 7 b.m. Needle Gun (IRE) – So Long (Nomadic Way (USA)) [2017/18 h91, b65: h18.7g³ h16.8s h15.3s³ h18.5v^{pu} Dec 8] modest maiden hurdler: stays 19f: acts on soft going: normally hooded: wears tongue tie. *Jeremy Scott*   h81

LADY LUNCHALOT (USA) 8 b.m. More Than Ready (USA) – Betty Johanne (USA) (Johannesburg (USA)) [2017/18 h18.7g⁴ h16g^F Jul 18] fair on Flat, stayed easy 1½m: poor form over hurdles: dead. *Polly Gundry*   h75

LADY MALEFICENT 4 b.f. Malinas (GER) – Lush Lady (IRE) (Kris Kin (USA)) [2017/18 b13.1g b16.7s⁵ Mar 26] second foal: dam, unraced, out of sister to high-class chaser (best up to 2½m) Function Dream: better effort in bumpers at Market Rasen (fair form) when fifth in mares maiden event in March. *Dan Skelton*   b87

LADY MARGORIE (IRE) 6 b.m. Winged Love (IRE) – Sure Quest (Sure Blade (USA)) [2017/18 b16.2g b16v b16v⁶ h18.8s⁶ h16s⁵ Apr 19] third foal: half-sister to a winning pointer by Flemensfirth: dam 9.7f-1½m winner: maiden in points: no form in bumpers (trained on first start by S. McConville): better effort over hurdles (modest form) when fifth in mares maiden at Fairyhouse in April: wears cheekpieces. *Alan A. H. Wells, Ireland*   h86 b–

LADY MARWAH (IRE) 5 b.m. Iffraaj – Eyrecourt (IRE) (Efisio) [2017/18 b17d b15.8s⁴ b16.8g Apr 19] 1,500 3-y-o: sixth foal: half-sister to useful/ungenuine 1½m-1¾m winner Saved By The Bell (by Teofilo): dam, ran twice on Flat, half-sister to fairly useful hurdler (stayed 2½m) Sayeh: fair form in bumpers. *Michael Scudamore*   b90

LADY MASTER 5 b.m. Native Ruler – Elmside Katie (Lord David S (USA)) [2017/18 b65: h15.7d h15.7s h15.7v⁶ h15.7v⁴ Feb 25] poor form in bumpers/over hurdles. *Caroline Bailey*   h73

LADY MIX 5 gr.m. Fair Mix (IRE) – Et Voila (Alflora (IRE)) [2017/18 b95: h19.6d⁶ h15.8d⁶ h16v⁵ h24.4d³ h23.1v⁶ h24.4s⁶ h19.9v³ Mar 13] fair maiden hurdler: stays 3m: acts on good to soft going (bumper winner on soft): in cheekpieces last 2 starts: front runner/races prominently. *Nigel Hawke*   h106

LADY OATCAKE (IRE) 5 b.m. Kalanisi (IRE) – Westgrove Berry (IRE) (Presenting) [2017/18 b16.2g May 28] fourth foal: half-sister to useful hurdler/chaser Jetstream Jack (19f-23f winner, by Beneficial) and fair hurdler Nendrum (2m winner, by Westerner): dam (h113), bumper/2m hurdle winner, half-sister to useful hurdler/smart chaser (stays 3¼m) Mendip Express: took little interest when tailed off in mares bumper. *N. W. Alexander*   b–

LADY OF LAMANVER 8 b.m. Lucarno (USA) – Lamanver Homerun (Relief Pitcher) [2017/18 h19.2g* h20.5s² h20.5s^{pu} Mar 24] tall mare: fairly useful handicap hurdler: won mares event at Fontwell in November: stays 2¾m: acts on heavy going: wears tongue tie: has raced freely. *Harry Fry*   h119

LADY OF LONGSTONE (IRE) 8 ch.m. Beneficial – Christdalo (IRE) (Glacial Storm (USA)) [2017/18 c112, h113: h23g⁵ h19.9d³ h23.3g⁶ h23g h26.5d⁴ h26.5d^{pu} h21.6v⁵ h20g⁵ h23.9m² h25.8g² h19g⁶ h19.7g⁵ Nov 29] workmanlike mare: fair handicap hurdler: lightly-raced maiden chaser: stays 3¼m: acts on soft and good to firm going: regularly wears headgear: tried in tongue tie. *David Pipe*   c– h104

LADY OF THE NIGHT 5 b.m. Midnight Legend – Even Flo (River Falls) [2017/18 b15.8v³ b16s² b16.8g Apr 19] first foal: dam (c104/h88) ungenuine 21f chase winner (stayed 3m): fair form in bumpers: best effort when second in mares event at Warwick in February: in tongue tie last 2 starts. *Kim Bailey*   b92

LADY OF THE REA (IRE) 7 b.m. Scorpion (IRE) – Sonnys Girl (IRE) (Broken Hearted) [2017/18 h20.6v⁴ h21.3v⁵ h19.7d⁴ Mar 29] £3,400 6-y-o: fifth foal: half-sister to fairly useful hurdler Dunroe Lady (2m-2½m winner, by Old Vic): dam, of little account, half-sister to fairly useful hurdler/chaser (stayed 2½m) Laureldean: maiden pointer: poor form over hurdles: tried in tongue tie. *Micky Hammond*   h62

LADY ROBYN (IRE) 8 b.m. Robin des Champs (FR) – Iseefaith (IRE) (Perugino (USA)) [2017/18 c–, h92, b86: c20.9s Mar 27] runner-up all 4 completed starts in Irish points: lightly-raced maiden hurdler/chaser: usually in cheekpieces: in tongue tie last 4 appearances: signs of temperament. *Peter Bowen*   c–
h–

LADY SAMBACK 6 ch.m. Black Sam Bellamy (IRE) – Bob Back's Lady (IRE) (Bob Back (USA)) [2017/18 b–: b15.8g^5 b16.2m^3 b17d^6 Mar 31] poor form in bumpers: wears tongue tie. *Maurice Barnes*   b61

LADY VESTA 5 b.m. Sir Percy – Lady Hestia (USA) (Belong To Me (USA)) [2017/18 b16.8g^2 b16.3d^2 b15.8m^3 Oct 11] second foal: sister to fair hurdler Perceus (2½m winner): dam 1½m-17f winner: fair form in bumpers: placed all 3 outings: wears headgear: has joined Cyril Murphy, USA. *Marcus Tregoning*   b86

LADY VITESSE 5 b.m. Rail Link – Sainte Gig (FR) (Saint Cyrien (FR)) [2017/18 b70: b15.8s h15.8s^5 h15.8v^6 h15.7v^6 Mar 29] unplaced in bumpers: best effort over hurdles (poor form) when sixth in maiden at Uttoxeter in February: in hood last 4 starts: tried in tongue tie. *Martin Keighley*   h80
b–

LADY VIVONA 10 gr.m. Overbury (IRE) – Ladylliat (FR) (Simon du Desert (FR)) [2017/18 h70: h20.2g^5 h21.2g^{ur} h23.3d^2 h19.9g^{pu} Oct 3] poor maiden hurdler: stays 23f: acts on good to soft going: tried in cheekpieces: has worn tongue tie: usually races prominently. *Lisa Harrison*   h76

LADY WETHERED (IRE) 6 br.m. Westerner – Vics Miller (IRE) (Old Vic) [2017/18 h73, b–: h19.8v^3 Apr 9] standout effort when 10 lengths third of 7 to Snuff Box in 2½m maiden hurdle at Wincanton, sole outing in 2017/18. *Linda Blackford*   h88

LA FILLE FRANCAISE (FR) 5 b.m. Kapgarde (FR) – Pondimari (FR) (Marignan (USA)) [2017/18 b80: h19.5d h16s^4 h15.7s^4 h19.6s^3 h19d^3 Apr 26] close-coupled mare: fair form over hurdles: in frame all 4 starts after reappearance: will stay beyond 2½m: acts on soft going: waited mth. *Robin Dickin*   h108

LAFTERLANDS (IRE) 7 b.g. Azamour (IRE) – Madam Gaffer (Tobougg (IRE)) [2017/18 b16.2d Aug 2] tailed off in bumper: dead. *Nicky Richards*   b–

LAGAVARA (IRE) 6 b.m. Exit To Nowhere (USA) – Knocklayde Rose (IRE) (Even Top (IRE)) [2017/18 h100, b77: h21.6g^3 h20.5d^4 h21.4v^{pu} h24v^3 h23.1v^6 h21.2d Apr 9] fair handicap hurdler: won mares event at Leicester in December: stays 3m: acts on heavy going. *Nigel Twiston-Davies*   h105

LAGOSTOVEGAS (IRE) 6 b.m. Footstepsinthesand – Reine de Coeur (IRE) (Montjeu (IRE)) [2017/18 h17g^{pu} h22.8s^3 h17g* h16v* h16v^3 h16.8v^5 h16.5d Apr 24] sturdy mare: smart handicap hurdler: won at Killarney in August and Listowel in September: also 5½ lengths fifth of 24 to Mohaayed in County Hurdle at Cheltenham: has form at 23f, but races almost exclusively around 2m: acts on heavy going. *W. P. Mullins, Ireland*   h144

LAHLOO 4 b.f. Native Ruler – Clipper Line (USA) (Mizzen Mast (USA)) [2017/18 b13.1g Oct 21] third foal: dam unraced: well beaten in junior bumper. *Nick Kent*   b–

LAKE CHAPALA (IRE) 9 b.g. Shantou (USA) – Rathcolman Queen (IRE) (Radical) [2017/18 c105§, h86§: c17.4g* h15.8m* h16.8s* h20g^4 h17.7g^4 h17.7g Oct 6] sturdy gelding: fair handicap hurdler: won at Huntingdon in May and Newton Abbot (conditionals) in June: fair handicap chaser: won at Fontwell earlier in May: stays 19f: acts on soft and good to firm going: wears headgear: tried in tongue tie: often travels strongly. *Chris Gordon*   c108
h104

LAKE FIELD (IRE) 9 b.g. Golan (IRE) – Rumson Way (IRE) (Petorius) [2017/18 c20d^2 c16.4s* c15.7d* c16.3v^3 c16d^5 c15.2d^6 Mar 29] sturdy gelding: winning hurdler: fairly useful form over fences: won handicaps at Newbury (conditionals) and Catterick (novice), both in December: probably stays 2½m: acts on heavy going: tried in tongue tie: often races prominently/travels strongly. *Kim Bailey*   c118
h–

LAKEFIELD REBEL (IRE) 12 b.g. Presenting – River Mousa (IRE) (Over The River (FR)) [2017/18 c90, h–: c24.2g^2 c26d^{pu} Dec 2] Irish point winner: maiden hurdler: modest maiden chaser: stays 4m: acts on soft going: tried in cheekpieces: often races towards rear. *Henry Hogarth*   c90
h–

LAKE MALAWI (IRE) 7 b.g. Westerner – Ariesanne (IRE) (Primo Dominie) [2017/18 h109: h23.9g^6 Aug 1] fair hurdler: disappointing only outing in 2017/18: stays 21f: acts on soft going. *Gordon Elliott, Ireland*   h–

LAKE PLACID 5 b.g. Champs Elysees – Phantom Wind (USA) (Storm Cat (USA)) [2017/18 h–: h16.8g h16.3d^5 h18.5d^6 Oct 12] poor form over hurdles: sometimes wore tongue tie: dead. *Nigel Hawke*   h61

LAK

LAKE SHORE DRIVE (IRE) 6 b.g. Thewayyouare (USA) – Labrusca (Grand Lodge (USA)) [2017/18 h94: h23.3g* h26.5g² Jun 27] fair handicap hurdler: won at Hexham in May: also successful on Flat in November: stays 3¼m: acts on good to firm and good to soft going: usually races in rear. *Johnny Farrelly*   h103

LAKESHORE LADY (IRE) 8 b.m. Lakeshore Road (USA) – Chiminee Chime (IRE) (Lord Americo) [2017/18 c101, h–: h20m* May 11] won Irish point on debut: fair hurdler: won conditionals seller at Worcester only appearance in 2017/18: winning chaser: stays 21f: acts on good to firm and heavy going: regularly wears headgear: tried in tongue tie: often races prominently. *David Bridgwater*   c– h101

LAKE TAKAPUNA (IRE) 7 b.g. Shantou (USA) – Close To Shore (IRE) (Bob Back (USA)) [2017/18 c22.5s c20.4s^pu c17d⁴ c21s^pu c16d Apr 26] €52,000 3-y-o: lengthy gelding: third foal: brother to fairly useful hurdler/chaser (19f-3¼m winner) Mr Shantu: dam unraced half-sister to useful hurdler/fairly useful chaser (stayed 3½m) Back To Bid: winning hurdler: fairly useful handicap chaser: best effort in 2017/18 when fourth at Leopardstown in December: stays 23f, effective at shorter: acts on heavy going. *J. Culloty, Ireland*   c123 h–

LAKETOUR LEADER (IRE) 6 b.g. Publisher (USA) – Gay da Cheen (IRE) (Tenby) [2017/18 b17.7g⁶ h20.5s h20.5d h17.7v⁵ h15.8s h15.8d Apr 24] Irish point winner: tailed off in bumper: poor form over hurdles: probably stays 21f: acts on soft going. *Richard Rowe*   h70 b–

LAKE VIEW LAD (IRE) 8 gr.g. Oscar (IRE) – Missy O'Brien (IRE) (Supreme Leader) [2017/18 c135, h–: c16.5v³ c23.4v* c22.9v³ c19.9v² c19.9v* c20.5v² c26.2v³ Apr 7] winning hurdler: useful novice chaser: won handicap events at Newcastle in December and Haydock in February: also second in Grade 2 race at Haydock (7 lengths behind Testify) in January and handicap at Ayr (beaten 1¼ lengths by Bernardelli) in March: stays 3¼m, at least as effective around 2½m: acts on heavy going: usually races close up: tough and genuine. *N. W. Alexander*   c137 h–

LAKE WASHINGTON (FR) 5 ch.g. Muhtathir – La Curamalal (IRE) (Rainbow Quest (USA)) [2017/18 b14d h19.7s^pu h16.5s h19.9v^pu h16.2v Apr 10] well beaten in bumper: no form over hurdles. *Venetia Williams*   h– b–

LALOR (GER) 6 b.g. It's Gino (GER) – Laviola (GER) (Waky Nao) [2017/18 b116: h16.8s² h15.7g³ h16.8s² h16.3v h16.5s* Apr 13]   h147

Bumper form doesn't work out much better than that of the 2017 running of Aintree's Grade 2 contest on the eve of the Grand National. It had looked a strong field at the time, with the third and fifth from the Champion Bumper at Cheltenham finishing close up again, and it certainly didn't disappoint as a source of future winners. Of the nineteen runners, fourteen had won at least once over hurdles before the Grand National meeting came round again, including nine of the first ten home, all showing at least fairly useful form. Several proved a fair bit better than that, with runner-up Enniscoffey Oscar and fifth-placed Claimantakinforgan winning Grade 2 novices during the season. The third and fourth, Western Ryder and If The Cap Fits, showed smart form, the latter unbeaten in three starts and looking an exciting prospect for Cheltenham before getting injured. Favourite Black Op finished only ninth at Aintree, but that support proved well justified in the long run as he turned out to be just about the pick of the field on form in the latest season, finding only Samcro too good in the Baring Bingham at Cheltenham before winning the Grade 1 Mersey Novices' Hurdle back at Aintree. Even the tailed-off last Larry had won twice in the interim, by the way.

Oddly, in view of the success of so many of those who had finished behind him at Aintree, one of the few horses still seeking to break his duck over hurdles twelve months later was the winner Lalor. He had sprung a surprise at 33/1, though he had been an impressive winner of the last of his three bumpers beforehand, all of them at Wincanton (he was later awarded his debut race too); the combination of less testing ground and a modest pace placed the emphasis on speed at Aintree and the conditions suited Lalor much better than the likes of Black Op. Although Lalor hadn't won over hurdles, he had gone close on his first three starts. He shaped well when beaten a short head by Onefortheroadtom on his reappearance at Exeter but didn't see his race out next time, under conditions which should have suited, when third to Mr One More at Ascot after going clear in the straight. On his third start, before Christmas at Cheltenham, Lalor matched his debut form but again didn't

Betway Top Novices' Hurdle, Aintree—
a poignant success for the connections of 14/1-shot Lalor (centre), who sheds his maiden tag over hurdles by defeating Vision des Flos (second right) and Bedrock (second left)

finish quite so well as might have been hoped, having the future Supreme Novices' winner Summerville Boy behind him in third but going down by two lengths in receipt of weight from Western Ryder.

A well-run handicap looked the sort of race which would see Lalor in the best light and he was made ante-post favourite for the Betfair Hurdle at Newbury in February, by which time he had undergone a breathing operation. Sent off at 14/1 on the day, a mistake four out effectively put paid to his chances and he finished down the field, with the heavy ground turning the race into much more of a test of stamina than speed. After missing Cheltenham, Lalor finally came good at Aintree, showing smart form—in keeping with the subsequent performances of those he had beaten there the year before—to win the Betway Top Novices' Hurdle. He clearly needed to improve on his previous efforts over hurdles and, as twelve months earlier, he upset some much better fancied rivals. The pair to beat looked to be the impressive Dovecote Novices' Hurdle winner Global Citizen and Vision des Flos who had finished sixth behind Samcro and Black Op at Cheltenham. Global Citizen disappointed under softer conditions than he had encountered at Kempton, but Vision des Flos ran right up to form in finishing two and a half lengths behind Lalor in second. On softer ground than twelve months earlier, Lalor saw his race out well, perhaps belatedly showing the benefit of his breathing operation. Leading after three out, he was joined by the outsider Bedrock at the second last but asserted again at the final flight and stayed on well, with Vision des Flos also keeping on well on the run-in to deprive Bedrock of second by three quarters of a length. The first three finished clear, with Global Citizen only sixth.

Lalor was reunited at Aintree with Richard Johnson for the first time since they had teamed up successfully a year earlier. Tragically, though, Richard Woollacott, who had celebrated the biggest success of his training career with Lalor in 2017, didn't live to see that promise fulfilled at the latest Grand National meeting. Johnson partnered another big winner for Woollacott in December when Beer Goggles pulled off a 40/1 shock in the Long Distance Hurdle at Newbury but, only the following month, found himself leading the tributes to the former champion point-to-point rider who was found dead at his Devon stable at the age of just forty.

LAM

Woollacott's wife Kayley, whose first winner since taking over the licence came at Exeter five days before Lalor's win at Aintree, described Lalor as the horse that had 'kept everything going'. Richard Woollacott had 'fallen in love' with the good-topped Lalor and bought him for €16,000 as a three-year-old at the Derby Sale, his looks making more appeal than his German Flat pedigree.

```
                         ┌ It's Gino (GER)  ┌ Perugino      ┌ Danzig
                         │   (b 2003)       │  (b 1991)     └ Fairy Bridge
                         │                  └ Imelda        ┌ Lomitas
Lalor (GER)              │                     (b 1998)     └ Ibidem
  (b.g. 2012)            │
                         │ Laviola (GER)    ┌ Waky Nao      ┌ Alzao
                         └   (b 2004)       │  (b 1993)     └ Waky Na
                                            └ Limaga        ┌ Lagunas
                                               (b 1993)     └ Lima
```

Lalor's sire It's Gino had not had any runners in Britain at the time and Lalor was one of just three for him in the latest season, though the two others were also successful, including Darebin who showed fairly useful form over fences. It's Gino went into the 2008 Arc as a smart Group 2 winner in Germany, starting at odds of more than 100/1 but excelling himself on what proved the final start of his career in dead-heating for third behind Zarkava (connections were aggrieved at not being given the position outright in a contentious photo-finish). Lalor's dam Laviola gained her only win over a mile at Bremen and Lalor is the second of her five reported foals to date, all of them by It's Gino. His older sister Lilydale was also a mile winner in Germany, while one of his younger sisters, Leyan, won over six furlongs as a two-year-old in Sweden. Grandam Limaga failed to win but was out of a listed-placed winner of four races, Lima, and bred some smart winners over longer trips. Limatus won a pair of listed staying contests in Germany and France, while a couple of his half-brothers did well further afield; Limario won Germany's top two-year-old race, the Preis des Winterfavoriten, before ending up in Dubai where he won a handicap at the Carnival, while Le Roi was exported to Australia where he was successful in Group 3 contests over a mile and a half and thirteen furlongs. Lalor has been raced only at around two miles and, although he won one of his bumpers on heavy ground, it may be that less testing conditions, which he hasn't managed to avoid for the most part so far, will prove to suit him ideally. Recent winners of the Top Novices' Hurdle have included My Tent Or Yours and Buveur d'Air, but Lalor makes more appeal as a future chaser than a top-notch hurdler, while his track record at Aintree would clearly make him one to note if sent back there in the next season.
Kayley Woollacott

LA MADRINA (IRE) 6 b.m. Milan – Edermine Blossom (IRE) (Bach (IRE)) [2017/18 **h–** h–, b–: h19g^{pu} h21.2g^5 h21.6v^{pu} h21.4v h16.5v^5 h18.5s Apr 23] has had breathing operation: little sign of ability: in cheekpieces 3 of last 4 outings: tried in tongue tie. *Katie Stephens*

LAMANVER ODYSSEY 6 b.m. Lucarno (USA) – Lamanver Homerun (Relief Pitcher) **h126** [2017/18 h116: h21.4s* h20.3s^F h21s^{pu} h18.5s^2 h18.9v^2 h24.3g^{pu} Apr 20] good-topped mare: fairly useful handicap hurdler: won mares event at Wincanton in November: also first past post at Haydock in March (beat The Delray Munky a neck), but demoted having hampered rival run-in): stays 2¾m: acts on heavy going: wears tongue tie: usually races close up. *Harry Fry*

LAMANVER PIPPIN 5 b.g. Apple Tree (FR) – Lamanver Homerun (Relief Pitcher) **b94** [2017/18 b15.3v^2 Apr 9] fourth foal: half-brother to 3 winners by Lucarno, including bumper winner/fairly useful hurdler Lamanver Odyssey (2¼m-21f winner) and fairly useful hurdler Lady of Lamanver (19f winner): dam (c136/h123) 19f-3m hurdle/chase winner: 7/1, shaped well when second in bumper at Wincanton (1¼ lengths behind promising Unwin Vc). *Harry Fry*

LAMBEAU FIELD (USA) 5 b.g. Cape Blanco (IRE) – Xinji (IRE) (Xaar) [2017/18 **c–** h107: c16.5g^4 c16.5f^{pu} h16g^{pu} Nov 1] compact gelding: fair maiden hurdler at best: no form **h–** in 2017/18, including over fences: raced only at 2m: acts on good to firm going: tried in cheekpieces/tongue tie: front runner/races prominently: has joined Leslie F. Young, USA. *Charlie Longsdon*

456

L'A

LAMB OR COD (IRE) 11 ch.g. Old Vic – Princess Lizzie (IRE) (Homo Sapien) [2017/18 c135, h–: c23.6d^{pu} c25g^F c25d c26.3s^2 Jan 1] lengthy gelding: has reportedly had breathing operation: winning hurdler: useful handicap chaser, well below best in 2017/18: stays 3¼m: has won on heavy going, but seems better under less testing conditions: has worn blinkers: wears tongue tie: often races towards rear. *Philip Hobbs*   **c114 h—**

LAMBS LANE (IRE) 6 b.g. Mahler – Ilikeyou (IRE) (Lord Americo) [2017/18 h24.8d^4 h16d h22d^3 h24v^{pu} h21d h21.1s h18.8s Mar 25] angular gelding: bumper winner: modest maiden hurdler: stays 2¾m: acts on good to soft going: tried in tongue tie: usually races nearer last than first. *P. J. Rothwell, Ireland*   **h96**

L'AMI SERGE (IRE) 8 b.g. King's Theatre (IRE) – La Zingarella (IRE) (Phardante (FR)) [2017/18 c143+, h161: h21.4s^2 h25.4s* h19.3d^2 h24.4d^2 c24s^3 h24s h20s* Apr 12]   **c153 + h163**

    Things must have seemed pretty bleak for Daryl Jacob in the spring of 2014, when the jockey was sidelined with a broken leg, knee and elbow as a result of a freak fall from the fractious Port Melon during the preliminaries for the Spa Novices' Hurdle at that year's Cheltenham Festival (Jacob had partnered Lac Fontana to win the County Hurdle less than half an hour earlier). To compound matters, the injured Jacob was sacked as stable jockey to then-champion trainer Paul Nicholls just over a month later. Although Nicholls offered Jacob the opportunity to stay on as number two to his replacement Sam Twiston-Davies, it was perfectly understandable that the jockey turned him down in favour of going freelance, arguing: 'I want to ride in the big races on the good horses as much as possible.' That ambition has been increasingly realised in recent seasons and, as a result, Jacob can have little cause to regret his decision to sever ties with Manor Farm Stables (the jockey didn't ride again for Nicholls until May 10th 2018). Jacob could have been forgiven for affording himself a wry smile at the end of the latest season when, exactly four years on from that low point, he achieved more than double the number of Grade 1 wins his former employer managed over the season (nine compared to Nicholls' four). Jacob's successor Twiston-Davies, meanwhile, ended the season by going freelance himself as Harry Cobden was appointed as stable jockey to Nicholls. All nine of Jacob's big-race wins came in the emerald green, dark green sleeves, and quartered cap of his current bosses, the big-spending owners Simon Munir and Isaac Souede, who have a high-quality string of around thirty horses in Britain on which Jacob now has first call. The link-up has proved beneficial to both parties, with continuity in the saddle a key factor given that the owners have their horses in Britain spread around six yards. The arrangement flourished at the Aintree Grand National meeting in April, when there were three lucrative wins at Grade 1 level (all provided by reigning champion trainer Nicky Henderson). The prolific winning juvenile We Have A Dream and promising novice chaser Terrefort both underlined their long-term prospects with their wins, but it was the success of L'Ami Serge in the Betway Aintree Hurdle which probably gave connections the most satisfaction.

    As discussed in these pages before, L'Ami Serge hasn't always proved the easiest horse to win with in recent years and even had a Timeform squiggle for a while. He had been runner-up eight times from his sixteen previous starts going into the Aintree Hurdle, and punters had also had their fingers burned when, starting a heavily-backed favourite, he was a fast-closing third (beaten less than a length) to Wakanda in the Sky Bet Handicap Chase at Doncaster in late-January. The reverses weren't always purely L'Ami Serge's fault, though. He showed some signs of a suspect attitude when first asked to quicken (hung left) in the Sky Bet Chase but he had a repeatedly troubled passage under stand-in jockey Davy Russell (Jacob was claimed to ride the Munir and Souede runners at Cheltenham's Trials meeting on the same afternoon) and he would have been widely viewed as a most unlucky loser but for his chequered reputation. In fairness, though, he stayed on very well inside the final hundred yards and would have been in front in another few strides. L'Ami Serge didn't do that much wrong either when runner-up in the Ascot Hurdle (left with too much to do behind Lil Rockerfeller) or the Long Walk Hurdle (beaten two and three quarter lengths by Sam Spinner) before the turn of the year, his weak-finishing tendencies exaggerated on those occasions up against notably tough front runners both times. Admittedly, his eighth in the Stayers' Hurdle at Cheltenham was harder

Betway Aintree Hurdle, Aintree—
L'Ami Serge (left) overhauls favourite Supasundae and outsider Clyne (noseband)

to defend, as he rather curled up on the stiff uphill climb to the finish after being produced to hold every chance at the last; that performance came in an unusually steadily-run affair which didn't play to his strengths and led to his obviously frustrated jockey labelling it 'the biggest balls of a race I've ever ridden in'. By contrast, the latest renewal of the Aintree Hurdle provided optimum conditions for the usually patiently-ridden L'Ami Serge—turning into a strongly-run affair over two and a half miles on testing ground. The outsider Diakali tore off into a clear early lead and plenty of the nine-strong field (among them 2014 winner The New One) failed to give their running in the face of the unrelenting gallop. It was manna from heaven for Jacob and L'Ami Serge, however, as the jockey was able to make full use of L'Ami Serge's ability to travel strongly though his races, particularly as he was given a good lead into the race when market principals Supasundae (runner-up in the Stayers') and My Tent Or Yours (also trained by Henderson) were sent—earlier than ideal—in pursuit of Diakali and another outsider Clyne. Still only fifth jumping two out, L'Ami Serge was produced with a strong run to sweep past Supasundae early on the run-in and was always holding on thereafter. L'Ami Serge had three lengths to spare over Supasundae at the line, with a further three and three quarter lengths back to the enterprisingly-ridden Clyne in third (possibly flattered after slipping the field early in the straight), while My Tent Or Yours (runner-up in 2016 and 2017) faded into fourth a further six lengths adrift.

L'Ami Serge (IRE) (b.g. 2010)	King's Theatre (IRE) (b 1991)	Sadler's Wells (b 1981)	Northern Dancer Fairy Bridge
		Regal Beauty (b 1981)	Princely Native Dennis Belle
	La Zingarella (IRE) (b 1998)	Phardante (b 1982)	Pharly Pallante
		In Memoriam (b 1988)	Buckskin Superdora

The Aintree Hurdle was the biggest success on British soil to date for L'Ami Serge, though his victory in the 2017 Grande Course de Haies d'Auteuil won him marginally more in prize money—his first two form figures for 2017/18 relate to runs at Auteuil (including the Grande Course) which were discussed in *Chasers & Hurdlers 2016/17*. A return trip to Auteuil in May for another tilt at the Grande

Course de Haies (which was brought forward a month this year to coincide with the Grand Steeple-Chase de Paris) proved unsuccessful, with a below-par L'Ami Serge managing only seventh behind the home-trained favourite De Bon Coeur. That was a rare blip from L'Ami Serge who has proved far more consistent than two of his siblings who were also seen out in 2017/18. Half-brother Sizing Codelco (by Flemensfirth) showed himself to be a high-class chaser when fourth to Might Bite in the Betway Bowl thirty-five minutes before the Aintree Hurdle, but that was very much his best effort in an otherwise frustrating campaign in which he often shaped like a horse with problems. L'Ami Serge's close relative Viens Chercher (by Milan) also lost his way in 2017/18, hinting at temperament when fitted with cheekpieces on his later starts, and he was sold cheaply (to join Peter Bowen) at the end of the campaign. The family has been discussed thoroughly in previous editions of *Chasers & Hurdlers* and there is little more to add, other than the fact that the dam La Zingarella has since produced the 2014 filly La Mistinguett (by Fame And Glory) and an as-yet-unnamed trio of colts by Oscar (2015), Yeats (2016) and Kayf Tara (2017).

A tall gelding who wears a hood nowadays, L'Ami Serge is a high-class performer over hurdles and has shown his form at two miles up to twenty-five furlongs. He is similarly versatile with regards to ground—although unraced on firmer than good, he has winning form on good, good to soft, soft and heavy. Such adaptability is likely to continue to stand him in good stead in the next season, when connections will surely be tempted to give him another try over fences. Although he has yet to reach quite the same heights in that sphere as over hurdles, his BHA chase mark reflects that and his luckless display in the Sky Bet Chase suggests he is more than capable of winning good races over fences off a mark of 154. Given that it usually turns into one of the season's most strongly-run races at around two and a half miles, the BetVictor Gold Cup at Cheltenham in November appeals as a possible autumn target. *Nicky Henderson*

LAMMTURNER (IRE) 6 b.m. Brian Boru – Deploy Or Die (IRE) (Deploy) [2017/18 h15.7s^F h19.9v^5 h19.9g Apr 23] second foal: dam unraced sister to smart hurdler (stayed 23f) Shinrock Paddy: little form over hurdles. *Joanne Foster*   **h–**

LANCASTER ROSE (IRE) 4 ch.f. Windsor Knot (IRE) – Tara Tara (IRE) (Fayruz) [2017/18 b15.7s^3 Mar 7] sixth foal: half-sister to fair hurdler/chaser To The Sky (2m/17f winner, by Saffron Walden) and a winning pointer by King's Theatre: dam, 5f winner, half-sister to dam of very smart hurdler (stayed 3m) Voler La Vedette: 8/1, third in conditionals/amateur mares bumper at Catterick (9¼ lengths behind Sea Story). *Sam Thomas*   **b73**

LANDECKER (IRE) 10 br.g. Craigsteel – Winsome Breeze (IRE) (Glacial Storm (USA)) [2017/18 c–, h118^5: h23.3g^2 h23.9v^4 h24.7d h25.8g^2 h24.6s^6 h25.8v* h22.7v^5 h25.8v^{pu} h26.6s Apr 26] rather leggy gelding: fairly useful handicap hurdler: won at Kelso in January: no aptitude sole start over fences: stays 3¼m: acts on heavy going: tried in headgear/tongue tie: races lazily towards rear. *N. W. Alexander*   **c–** **h116 §**

LANDIN (GER) 5 b.g. Sir Percy – Lupita (GER) (Niniski (USA)) [2017/18 h128: h20g* h20.5s^2 h20.5s^5 h19.8v* h19.5v* h20s^{pu} h19.8s^{pu} Apr 28] smallish gelding: fairly useful hurdler: won maiden at Worcester in October, novice handicap at Sandown in February and handicap at Lingfield in March: stays 2½m: acts on heavy going: tried in cheekpieces. *Seamus Mullins*   **h128**

LAND LEAGUE (IRE) 7 b.g. Touch of Land (FR) – Be My Sunset (IRE) (Bob Back (USA)) [2017/18 h113: h16.7g* h16.7g c18g^6 c16.3s^4 c19.9s^4 ab16d^3 Mar 5] tall gelding: Irish point winner: fair hurdler: won maiden at Bangor in September: below that level over fences: stays 2¼m: acts on heavy going: tried in tongue tie. *Stuart Edmunds*   **c102** **h114**

LANDMEAFORTUNE (IRE) 9 gr.g. Touch of Land (FR) – Mayrich (IRE) (Roselier (FR)) [2017/18 c99, h–: c23.8v* c26.2v Oct 26] maiden hurdler: fair handicap chaser: won at Perth in September: stayed 31f: acted on heavy going: sometimes wore headgear: dead. *Martin Todhunter*   **c107** **h–**

LANDOFSMILES (IRE) 5 b.g. Beneficial – Sadie Supreme (IRE) (Supreme Leader) [2017/18 b16.7s^2 b15.8v^3 Apr 15] €23,000 3-y-o, £16,000 5-y-o: first foal: dam unraced half-sister to fairly useful chaser (stayed 3m) Sound Witness: placed on second of 2 starts in Irish points: fair form when close second to Mick Manhattan in maiden at Bangor on first of 2 outings in bumpers. *Peter Bowen*   **b92**

LAND OF VIC 10 b.m. Old Vic – Land of Glory (Supreme Leader) [2017/18 c103, h116: h23.3d⁵ h24.7g* h23g⁴ h26.4g³ Jul 23] sturdy mare: fairly useful handicap hurdler: won mares event at Aintree in June: unconvincing over fences despite winning once from 4 starts: stays 25f: acts on heavy going: has worn headgear, including last 4 starts: tried in tongue tie: front runner/races prominently. *Peter Bowen*   c– h122

LANDSCAPE (FR) 10 b.g. Lando (GER) – Universelle (USA) (Miswaki (USA)) [2017/18 h88§: h25d^pu h15.9s² h15.9v⁴ h19.5v h25v^pu h15.9v³ Mar 12] rather leggy gelding: modest handicap hurdler nowadays: stays 25f: acts on heavy going: regularly wears headgear/tongue tie: usually races close up: unreliable. *Daniel Steele*   h86 §

LANGNESS (IRE) 5 b.g. Milan – Bally Robin (IRE) (Fourstars Allstar (USA)) [2017/18 h21.2d h20.6g⁴ Apr 22] €35,000 3-y-o: fifth foal: half-brother to a winning pointer by Beneficial: dam unraced half-sister to fairly useful hurdler/very smart chaser (stayed 25f) Billyvoddan: better effort in novice hurdles (modest form) when fourth at Market Rasen: will stay 3m. *Charlie Longsdon*   h99

LANSDOWNE ROAD (IRE) 10 b.g. Bienamado (USA) – Ballinamona Wish (IRE) (Kotashaan (FR)) [2017/18 h89: c24.2s^pu h19.7s c25.2v^F Jan 24] winning pointer: modest form on hurdling debut: none since, including over fences: tried in cheekpieces. *Joanne Foster*   c– h–

LANTA'S LEGACY 8 ch.m. Central Park (IRE) – Purple Patch (Afzal) [2017/18 c22.6g^pu c24g⁵ Jul 19] little form outside points: in tongue tie last 5 starts. *Jeremy Scott*   c56 h–

LAPALALA (IRE) 7 b.m. Oscar (IRE) – Lala Nova (IRE) (Zaffaran (USA)) [2017/18 h106: h19.9d⁶ Jul 11] fair maiden hurdler at best: no show sole start in 2017/18: should stay further than 2½m: acts on soft going: often races towards rear. *Philip Hobbs*   h–

LAPFORD LAD 6 ch.g. Arvico (FR) – State of Grace (Generous (IRE)) [2017/18 b16.8m⁴ b16.8v h19s^pu h18.5v h18.5s h15.3v h21.7g⁵ Apr 20] third foal: dam unraced daughter of fairly useful hurdler/chaser (stayed 21f) Vent d'Aout: modest form on first of 2 outings in bumpers: little form over hurdles. *Susan Gardner*   h64 b82

LARA TROT (IRE) 6 b.m. Scorpion (IRE) – Honour Own (IRE) (City Honours (USA)) [2017/18 h21s^pu h23.8s h21.2d h16s Apr 27] first foal: dam unraced half-sister to fairly useful hurdler/useful chaser (stayed 2¾m) Ballyholland: placed in Irish points: modest form over hurdles. *Robin Dickin*   h93

LARCH HILL (IRE) 5 ch.g. Presenting – Misty Move (IRE) (Saddlers' Hall (IRE)) [2017/18 h16.6s h19.9v^F Apr 7] no show in bumper/maiden hurdle. *Nigel Twiston-Davies*   h– b–

LARGY GLORY (IRE) 4 b.f. Fame And Glory – Esbeggi (Sabrehill (USA)) [2017/18 b17s* b16.3s Apr 25] sixth foal: half-sister to fairly useful hurdler/useful chaser Dunowen Point (2m-2½m winner) and fairly useful hurdler/chaser Mr Hudson (21f-3¼m winner) (both by Old Vic): dam unraced half-sister to useful hurdler (2¾m winner) Mischievious Max: won bumper at Carlisle on debut in April: left Stuart Crawford, stiffer task in Grade 3 mares event at Punchestown just 17 days later. *Mrs J. Harrington, Ireland*   b92

LARGY LEGS (IRE) 6 b.g. Getaway (GER) – Magneeto (IRE) (Brush Aside (USA)) [2017/18 h20.2m^pu Jun 4] Irish maiden pointer: in tongue tie, pulled up in novice on hurdling debut. *Stuart Crawford, Ireland*   h–

LARKBARROW LAD 5 b.g. Kayf Tara – Follow My Leader (IRE) (Supreme Leader) [2017/18 b15.7d³ b16g³ b15.3d² Apr 22] fourth foal: dam lightly-raced half-sister to very smart chaser (stayed 25f) Master of The Hall and smart chaser (stays 23f) Pairofbrowneyes and to dam of high-class hurdler (stays 21f) Samcro: fairly useful form in bumpers: placed all 3 starts, runner-up to Ebony Gale at Wincanton final one: wears tongue tie. *Philip Hobbs*   b97

LARKHALL 11 b.g. Saddlers' Hall (IRE) – Larkbarrow (Kahyasi) [2017/18 c77§, h–§: c20.3g⁵ c24.2g³ c24g² c15.7g⁴ c19.3d c23.6g³ c24d³ c15.9m⁵ c20.2g⁶ Dec 3] good-topped gelding: maiden hurdler: poor handicap chaser: stays 3m: acts on firm and good to soft going: tried in headgear/tongue tie: usually races towards rear: weak finisher (has bled). *Mike Sowersby*   c77 § h– §

LARRY 5 b.g. Midnight Legend – Gaspaisie (FR) (Beyssac (FR)) [2017/18 b96: h15.9d⁶ h17.7g^ur h16s⁴ h20.5v² h20.7s³ h20.5v* h19.2s* Apr 6] bumper winner: fairly useful hurdler: won novices at Plumpton in March and Fontwell in April: stays 21f: acts on heavy going: in tongue tie last 2 starts. *Gary Moore*   h126

LASTBUTNOTLEAST (IRE) 8 ch.m. Flemensfirth (USA) – Lakil Princess (IRE) (Bering) [2017/18 h127p: c20s^pu c19v* c22.7s³ h25.8v⁵ Apr 7] sturdy mare: unbeaten in mares novice hurdles in 2016/17: well held in handicap in 2017/18: useful form when   c130 h–

winning novice chase at Haydock (by 36 lengths from Jonniesofa) in December: disappointing over fences both starts either side (bled on chasing debut): stays 3m: raced on soft/heavy going: front runner/races prominently. *Donald McCain*

LAST GOODBYE (IRE) 7 b.g. Millenary – Welsh Ana (IRE) (Welsh Term) [2017/18 c140, h–: c24v c21s* c20.8s h24d Apr 26] good-topped gelding: useful hurdler: smart handicap chaser: won Leopardstown Handicap Chase (much improved when beating Vieux Morvan 9 lengths, finding plenty) in February: should be suited by further than 21f: acts on heavy going: in blinkers/tongue tie last 3 starts. *Miss Elizabeth Doyle, Ireland*   **c150 h124**

LASTIN' MEMORIES 6 b.g. Overbury (IRE) – Dusky Dante (IRE) (Phardante (FR)) [2017/18 h95, b78: h16.2g h20.1v h24.3v h24v^5 h16v^5 h19.7v^2 h20.9v^6 h18.1v^2 Apr 16] modest maiden hurdler: close second in conditionals handicap at Kelso final outing: stays 2½m: raced almost exclusively on heavy going: wears cheekpieces: usually races prominently. *Sandy Forster*   **h88**

LAS TUNAS (FR) 6 b.g. Country Reel (USA) – Grey Winner (FR) (Take Risks (FR)) [2017/18 c105, h114: c15.7d c16.5v^{pu} c17.1v^4 c19.2s^3 c17.2v^2 c19.2s^3 c17.1v^5 Apr 16] winning hurdler: modest handicap chaser nowadays: stays 19f: acts on heavy going: tends to find little. *R. Mike Smith*   **c86 h–**

LAST WATCH 5 br.m. Sagamix (FR) – Watcha (USA) (Blushing Stage (USA)) [2017/18 b16.2s^4 b17.7d Feb 26] sixth foal: half-sister to fair hurdler Arctic Watch (19f-2¾m winner, by Accondy): dam, ran once over hurdles, 8.5f winner in USA: modest form on first of 2 outings in bumpers. *David Bridgwater*   **b80**

LATE DATE (IRE) 7 b.g. Oscar (IRE) – Regents Ballerina (IRE) (Commanche Run) [2017/18 h102: h23.9g^6 h23.9m^6 h23.9s^5 Apr 25] Irish point winner: modest handicap hurdler: will stay beyond 3m: acts on heavy going. *Micky Hammond*   **h98**

LATE NIGHT LILY 7 b.m. Midnight Legend – Ready To Crown (USA) (More Than Ready (USA)) [2017/18 h122: h16.7g^F h16s^3 h15.8g^2 Dec 6] workmanlike mare: fairly useful handicap hurdler: placed both completed starts in 2017/18: stays 2½m: acts on good to firm and heavy going. *Dan Skelton*   **h124**

LATE ROMANTIC (IRE) 8 b.g. Mahler – Mere Gaye (IRE) (Gildoran) [2017/18 h100: h23.3v^{ur} Apr 7] multiple winner in points (successful both completed outings in 2018): fair form over hurdles: every chance when wandered and unseated approaching last in handicap won by Kayf Moss at Uttoxeter in April: will stay 3m: wears tongue tie. *Oliver Greenall*   **h113**

LATE SHIPMENT 7 b.g. Authorized (IRE) – Time Over (Mark of Esteem (IRE)) [2017/18 h119: h23.3v h23.6v^4 h26s^F h25.5v^5 h24.2s h23.9v^3 Apr 12] sturdy gelding: fair handicap hurdler: stays 3¼m: acts on heavy going: wears cheekpieces. *Nikki Evans*   **h111**

L'ATTENDUE (IRE) 4 br.f. Oscar (IRE) – Triptoshan (IRE) (Anshan) [2017/18 h19.9v^{pu} h16.8v h16d^4 h18.1v^{pu} Apr 16] fourth foal: sister to bumper winner Cruiseaweigh: dam unraced daughter of fairly useful hurdler/chaser (winner up to 25f) Triptodicks: poor juvenile hurdler. *Philip Kirby*   **h62**

L'AUBERGE DU BOIS (IRE) 6 br.g. Olden Times – Midway (IRE) (Warcraft (USA)) [2017/18 b16.2g^6 b16s h15.3v^2 h18.5d^5 Apr 24] half-brother to bumper winner/fair hurdler Josh's Dreamway (19f winner, by Deploy) and modest hurdler Hot Tottie (19f winner, by Lahib): dam unraced half-sister to useful chaser (stayed 3¼m) River Mandate: modest form in bumpers: similar form when second at Wincanton on first of 2 outings in maiden hurdles: likely to stay at least 19f. *Jeremy Scott*   **h98 b75**

LAUBERHORN 11 b.g. Dubai Destination (USA) – Ski Run (Petoski) [2017/18 c25.3d^6 May 5] prolific point winner in prime: formerly fair hurdler/maiden chaser: seen only twice under Rules since 2013/14: stays 2¾m: acts on soft and good to firm going: used to wear headgear. *Mrs Jo Paynter*   **c80 h–**

LAUGHARNE 7 b.g. Authorized (IRE) – Corsican Sunset (USA) (Thunder Gulch (USA)) [2017/18 h107: h21.4g^4 h23.5s^5 h23.9v^2 Apr 15] rather leggy gelding: fair handicap hurdler: left Luke Dace after first start: stays 3m: acts on good to firm and heavy going. *Tim Vaughan*   **h113**

LAUGHING LUIS 4 b.g. Authorized (IRE) – Leitzu (IRE) (Barathea (IRE)) [2017/18 b13.7g b14s^4 Jan 18] second foal: half-brother to 1¾m-2m winner Graceful Lady (by Sixties Icon): dam (h91), placed 2 of 3 starts over hurdles, 1m winner on Flat, closely related to fairly useful hurdler (stayed 2½m) Galianna: late headway in bumpers at Towcester and Ludlow (fourth of 12 to Rebound): will be suited by 2m+. *Nicky Henderson*   **b82**

LAUGHING MUSKETEER (IRE) 7 b.g. Azamour (IRE) – Sweet Clover (Rainbow Quest (USA)) [2017/18 h19d May 1] little form on Flat: tailed off in novice on hurdling debut. *Tracey Barfoot-Saunt*   **h–**

LAURINA (FR) 5 b.m. Spanish Moon (USA) – Lamboghina (GER) (Alkalde (GER)) [2017/18 h16v* h18v* h16.8s* h20v* Apr 1] **h150 p**

A race between Samcro and Laurina, with Laurina receiving the 7-lb mares allowance, would—arguably at least—have been anything but a walkover for Samcro. Comparing Laurina with the rivals of her own sex whom she actually beat, none of whom came close to testing her, is one way of putting her achievements into context, but perhaps the biggest compliment that can be paid to her is that she might have given the season's outstanding novice something to think about if their paths had crossed. The strength of opposition that Samcro and Laurina faced at Cheltenham was very different; a day after Samcro's impressive win over a good field in the Baring Bingham, Laurina maintained her unbeaten record for Willie Mullins with a runaway, eighteen-length victory in the Dawn Run Mares' Novices' Hurdle in which she was the easiest winner at the whole Festival.

The Grade 2 novice, which has been run as the Trull House Stud Mares' Novices' Hurdle since its inception in 2016, had previously been won by Laurina's stable-companions Limini and Let's Dance. The field of fourteen for the latest renewal, if anything, had even less strength in depth than those two editions, and the only one of Laurina's rivals who had shown a similar level of form beforehand was the confirmed front runner Maria's Benefit who had won her last five starts. Her wins had included a thirty-length success in a listed mares novice event at Taunton and a victory outside novice company in a Grade 2 mares hurdle at Doncaster on her most recent start when the opposition included Dusky Legend who had been placed in the first two editions of the Dawn Run. Maria's Benefit had company up front at Cheltenham as she was taken on by Cut The Mustard, one of Laurina's three stable-companions. Taking on Maria's Benefit for the lead resulted in her forcing too strong a pace and she was a spent force once they turned into the straight where the patiently-ridden Laurina cruised into the lead. She was already clear when not fluent at the last and pulled right away up the hill. Maria's Benefit finished only fourth in the end, with a short head separating the placed pair Cap Soleil and Champayne Lady, both of whom were ridden to pick up the pieces, coming from the rear.

*Trull House Stud Mares' Novices' Hurdle (Dawn Run), Cheltenham—
a bloodless success for odds-on Laurina*

*Irish Stallion Farms European Breeders Fund Mares Novices' Hurdle Championship, Punchestown—
Laurina maintains her 100% record for current connections with another effortless display*

      Laurina's win was the last of seven at the latest Cheltenham Festival for Willie Mullins, which wasn't quite enough to make him the Festival's leading trainer for a sixth time, though it did enable him to become the most successful trainer in Festival history. It was fitting that it should be a mare that gave him that record. Laurina was Mullins' sixty-first winner at the meeting, and it was another mare, Tourist Attraction, who gave him his very first Festival winner as a trainer (he rode three winners there as an amateur) in the 1995 Supreme Novices' Hurdle. Since then, Mullins has won three Champion Hurdles (including with a mare, Annie Power) and nine Champion Bumpers, including the latest edition with another mare, Relegate. The mare who has contributed most to Mullins' success at the Festival, though, is Quevega who set a record of her own when winning the David Nicholson Mares' Hurdle six times. Remarkably, Mullins has amassed more than half of his sixty-one wins over just the last five Festivals, setting a record of eight (which Gordon Elliott matched with a last-day double in the latest season) in 2015 alone. Nicky Henderson had been the Festival's most successful trainer since passing Fulke Walwyn's total of forty at the 2012 Festival. Buveur d'Air and Altior took Henderson's total to sixty at the end of the latest Festival. Paul Nicholls is the only other trainer to have saddled more than forty winners there, his two wins in March taking him to forty-three. The significance of setting a record previously held by a couple of Lambourn trainers was not lost on Mullins who said: 'When you start training, you hope for one winner here, that is the aspiration most Irish trainers have. This isn't something we ever dreamt of because we thought we couldn't do that with a base in Ireland.' Vincent O'Brien and Arkle's trainer Tom Dreaper had set the standard for Irish trainers at Cheltenham with totals of twenty-three and twenty-six respectively, mainly compiled in the 'fifties and 'sixties, though both men had their first taste of success at the Festival with Gold Cup winners shortly after the end of World War II, Dreaper training the 1946 winner Prince Regent and O'Brien saddling Cottage Rake who won the first of his three Gold Cups in 1948. Gordon Elliott, who didn't have his first Festival winners until 2011, is poised to become Ireland's second most successful trainer at Cheltenham with his total now standing at twenty-two.

LAU

Laurina had been impressive on both her starts for Mullins before Cheltenham, winning a maiden hurdle for mares at Tramore in December by fifteen lengths and then the Grade 3 Solerina Mares Novices' Hurdle at Fairyhouse in January, a race which Limini had also won, by eleven lengths with jockey Paul Townend barely having to move a muscle. After winning at Cheltenham the year before, Let's Dance had attempted to follow up in the Irish Stallion Farms EBF Mares Novices' Hurdle Championship Final at Fairyhouse (a race which Annie Power had won for the same connections in 2013 when it had become a Grade 1 for the first time). Let's Dance was beaten half a length by her stable-companion Augusta Kate but Laurina had no such problems and took the step up to two and a half miles in her stride. The pace was nothing like so strong as it had been at Cheltenham, which accounts for Laurina winning by a smaller margin as she was just asked to coast home to land the odds once she had cruised upsides two out. For the record, second favourite Lackaneen Leader, who had completed a hat-trick in a Grade 3 mares novice at Limerick, was eight and a half lengths back in second, with Alletrix and Dawn Shadow, the pair who had been placed in the Solerina, completing the frame. Dawn Shadow, who had fallen in the Dawn Run, went on to win a listed novice hurdle for mares at Punchestown but Laurina herself was one of the few exceptions among her stable's better horses in being absent during the final week of the Irish season.

Mullins' first two winners of the Dawn Run carried the colours of Rich and Susannah Ricci, but Laurina was the pick of a number of at least useful young hurdlers carrying the red, pink hoop and armlets of Sullivan Bloodstock Limited whose horses were out in force at the latest Cheltenham Festival. Owner Jered Sullivan had previously campaigned his horses under the banner of Potensis Bloodstock, with his company of the same name sponsoring Paul Nicholls' yard. Silviniaco Conti

Sullivan Bloodstock Limited's "Laurina"

had carried the red and pink silks to victory in the first of his two King Georges (his second came in the colours of his other part-owner Chris Giles) and Buveur d'Air had begun his career with Nicky Henderson in the same colours. Sullivan dispersed much of his bloodstock interests in the summer of 2016, but returned to ownership in a major way in the latest season, adding Mullins to a roster of trainers that still includes both Nicholls and Henderson. Baoulet Delaroque and Diese des Bieffes finished fifth in the Coral Cup and Martin Pipe respectively for those yards, as did Duc des Genievres for Mullins in the Baring Bingham. Chef des Obeaux was another to carry the Sullivan colours, though he disappointed for Henderson in the Spa. Adding to the owner's mixed fortunes at the Festival were Stormy Ireland, who ended up falling in the Triumph for which she was well fancied, and Sandsend who sustained a fatal injury in the County Hurdle, both of those trained by Mullins.

Laurina (FR)
(b.m. 2013)
- Spanish Moon (USA) (b 2004)
  - El Prado (gr 1989)
    - Sadler's Wells
    - Lady Capulet
  - Shining Bright (b 1989)
    - Rainbow Quest
    - Bourbon Girl
- Lamboghina (GER) (ro 1997)
  - Alkalde (br 1985)
    - Konigsstuhl
    - Astra
  - Landina (gr 1983)
    - Pentathlon
    - Landfrau

Laurina began her career, like Let's Dance, with Guillaume Macaire. She had two starts over hurdles at Fontainebleau in the spring of 2017, finishing second after a fall on her debut twelve days earlier. She is a tall, unfurnished mare by the high-class mile and a half performer Spanish Moon whose six wins for Khalid Abdullah and Sir Michael Stoute included the Grand Prix de Saint-Cloud which he won while serving a six-month ban from racing in Britain for giving trouble at the stalls. From the same Juddmonte family which has since produced Flintshire and Enable, Spanish Moon was given to the French National Studs by his owner. His first crop included Crack Mome who showed useful form over hurdles for Mullins as a novice, contesting the 2017 Supreme, something which no doubt played a part in the acquisition of Laurina who comes from a German family which has produced plenty of winners but no others of real note. Laurina cost her original owner only €8,000 as an unraced three-year-old. Her dam Lamboghina won twice in Germany at up to a mile and a quarter and Laurina is her seventh winner. Her six previous winners were all successful in France, with the three jumpers among them headed by the fairly useful winner at up to two and three quarter miles Lamigo (by American Post) who was successful in the latest season in a claiming chase at Auteuil and a handicap hurdle at Cagnes-sur-Mer. Lamboghina has also produced two other fillies by Spanish Moon. Laurina's older sister For Your Love won a claiming chase over nineteen furlongs, and her year-younger sister Immortality was sold for €25,000 at the Derby Sale in 2017 and has yet to race. Lamboghina was one of eight winners out of the German eleven-furlong winner Landina. The strong-travelling Laurina, who has raced only on soft or heavy ground to date, looks the most exciting prospect— male or female— among her stable's latest crop of novice hurdlers. How she goes about fulfilling that promise from now on depends largely on how ambitiously her connections decide to campaign her. Laurina could doubtless continue to clean up in mares races, but hopefully she will be given the chance at some stage to prove herself in open company as she has the potential to rank alongside some of the best mares to have passed through her trainer's hands. She wore ear plugs at Cheltenham.
W. P. Mullins, Ireland

LAURIUM 8 ch.g. Gold Away (IRE) – Silver Peak (FR) (Sillery (USA)) [2017/18 c141, h–: h24.2d^pu Nov 9] sturdy gelding: useful hurdler/novice chaser at best: pulled up over hurdles only start in 2017/18: stays 3m: acts on soft and good to firm going. *Nicky Henderson* c–
h–

LAVAL NOIR (FR) 7 b.g. Laveron – Vale of Honor (FR) (Singspiel (IRE)) [2017/18 h105p: h21d⁶ h20.5s h25s* h26s Feb 10] lengthy gelding: fair form over hurdles: won handicap at Huntingdon (conditionals) in December: should stay beyond 25f: acts on soft going: tried in cheekpieces: has had tongue tied, including for win. *Kim Bailey* h109

LAV

LA VATICANE (FR) 9 gr.m. Turgeon (USA) – Taking Off (FR) (Kahyasi) [2017/18 c137, h–: c25.8g^{pu} May 10] rather leggy mare: winning hurdler: useful chaser: stayed 3m: acted on heavy going: wore blinkers/tongue tie: often raced towards rear: dead. *David Pipe* c– h–

LAVELLA WELLS 10 b.m. Alflora (IRE) – Jazzy Refrain (IRE) (Jareer (USA)) [2017/18 h–: h16.2g^3 h23.3g^4 h22.1g^4 c16.4g h20.1s^4 h23.3s^6 h19.9d Nov 18] workmanlike mare: poor maiden hurdler: never going when well beaten in novice handicap on chasing debut: stays 23f: acts on soft going: often races prominently. *Sue Smith* c– h76

LA VOIX (FR) 6 b.m. Voix du Nord (FR) – Loupaline (FR) (Loup Solitaire (USA)) [2017/18 h54: h15.8d^{pu} Nov 18] little form over hurdles: tried in tongue tie. *Jimmy Frost* h–

LAWTOP LEGEND (IRE) 6 b.g. Milan – Nolagh Supreme (IRE) (Supreme Leader) [2017/18 b–: b16.8g h16.2s h16.4v^{pu} h16.7v Jan 4] sturdy gelding: little form in bumpers/over hurdles. *George Bewley* h– b–

LAZARUS (IRE) 4 b.g. Zoffany (IRE) – Knysna (IRE) (Rock of Gibraltar (IRE)) [2017/18 h16s^4 h15.8d^5 Mar 26] fair on Flat (stays 11.5f): better effort over hurdles when laboured fourth in juvenile at Fakenham. *Amy Murphy* h94

L'CHAMISE 5 b.m. Apple Tree (FR) – Colline de Fleurs (Alflora (IRE)) [2017/18 b17d^5 b15.8s^6 b17.7d^4 Feb 25] second foal: half-sister to bumper winner Summit Like Herbie (by Sulamani): dam (c92/h119), bumper/21f hurdle winner (stayed 25f), half-sister to fairly useful hurdlers/useful chasers Steel Summit (stays 25f) and On The Road (stays 2¾m): won point on debut: fair form in bumpers: best effort when fifth in mares event at Aintree in October. *Jack R. Barber* b88

LEADING SCORE (IRE) 8 b.g. Scorpion (IRE) – Leading Rank (IRE) (Supreme Leader) [2017/18 c96, h102: c20.1g^2 c20.1g^3 c23.8m^3 c21.4g^3 h27g^6 c17.1g^2 Nov 11] good-topped gelding: fair maiden hurdler at best: modest form over fences: stays 21f: acts on good to firm going: usually in headgear: temperament under suspicion. *James Ewart* c97 h83

LEANNA BAN 11 b.g. Alflora (IRE) – Gurleigh (IRE) (Pivotal) [2017/18 c111, h–: c25.5g c21.6g^2 c20.9s^{pu} c20.1s^R c19.4s^4 Jan 13] strong gelding: maiden handicap chaser nowadays: stays 25f: acts on heavy going: wears tongue tie: front runner: has finished weakly. *Tristan Davidson* c106 h–

LEAPAWAY (IRE) 6 b.g. Stowaway – Gisela (IRE) (King Charlemagne (USA)) [2017/18 h16s^5 h16.3s^4 h15.8s h15.8d Mar 26] lengthy gelding: third foal: half-brother to 5f winner Kylesku (by Moss Vale): dam ran twice on Flat: modest form over hurdles. *Philip Hobbs* h98

LEAP DEARG (IRE) 10 b.g. Beneficial – Wee Red Roo (IRE) (Supreme Leader) [2017/18 c16v^5 c15.7s^3 Mar 7] remote fourth in novice only outing over hurdles: useful chaser at best: largely disappointing since 2015/16: unproven beyond 17f: acts on heavy going: has worn headgear/tongue tie: usually races nearer last than first. *James A. Nash, Ireland* c106 h–

LEAVETHELIGHTON (IRE) 11 b.g. Oscar (IRE) – Royale Boja (FR) (Kadalko (FR)) [2017/18 c26.2v^2 Apr 7] point winner: maiden hurdler: fairly useful chaser: second in hunter at Kelso, sole start under Rules in 2017/18: stays 23f: acts on heavy going: regularly in cheekpieces. *John Dawson* c115 h–

LE BACARDY (IRE) 12 b.g. Bahhare (USA) – La Balagna (Kris) [2017/18 c116§, h–§: c20.8d^5 c20.9v^{pu} Feb 18] rangy gelding: winning hurdler: useful chaser at best: folded tamely in hunters in 2017/18: stays 2½m: acts on heavy going: usually in headgear: tried in tongue tie: usually races nearer last than first: temperamental. *A. Gardner* c– § h– §

LE BOIZELO (FR) 7 b.g. Irish Wells (FR) – Bois Tendre (FR) (Murmure (FR)) [2017/18 c19.2v^3 c19.2v^2 c20.2v* c20.2v^4 c23.4s^{ur} Mar 23] winning hurdler: fairly useful form over fences: won novice handicap at Wincanton in January: should stay beyond 2½m: acts on heavy going. *Robert Walford* c125 h–

LE BRAYE (IRE) 6 b.g. Court Cave (IRE) – Salsaparilla (FR) (Lost World (IRE)) [2017/18 h97: h24g^4 c21.5s^6 c25v^{pu} h23.9s* h20.2s^4 Apr 27] workmanlike gelding: winning pointer, but little show in 2 hunter chases: fair handicap hurdler: won at Perth (amateur) in April: left Dan Skelton after first start: stays 3m: acts on soft going: in tongue tie last 5 starts. *Gavin Patrick Cromwell, Ireland* c– h104

LE BREUIL (FR) 6 ch.g. Anzillero (GER) – Slew Dancer (Fabulous Dancer (USA)) [2017/18 h136, b101: h21d^5 h20v^2 h21.1s h20d* h19.8s^5 Apr 28] useful-looking gelding: bumper winner: useful handicap hurdler: won at Fakenham (by length from Sir Mangan) in April: stays 21f: acts on heavy going: in cheekpieces (ran respectably) final outing: often leads. *Ben Pauling* h140

466

LEG

LE CAPRICIEUX (FR) 7 b.g. Alberto Giacometti (IRE) – Eria Flore (FR) (Hero's **h104**
Honor (USA)) [2017/18 h107: h16s h15.9s* h19.6s^F h16s^3 h19.2v^F h16m^5 Apr 26] close-
coupled gelding: fair handicap hurdler: won at Plumpton in December: unproven beyond
2m: acts on soft going. *Gary Moore*

LECHLADE MAGICIAN (IRE) 5 b.g. Getaway (GER) – Run Supreme (IRE) **b101**
(Supreme Leader) [2017/18 b15.3v* b16.3v b15.8v^3 Mar 17] £16,000 3-y-o: good-topped
gelding: has scope: poor mover in slower paces: half-brother to 3 winners, including fairly
useful hurdler/chaser City Supreme (2½m-3m winner) and fairly useful hurdler Run To
Milan (2¼m winner, stays 21f) (both by Milan): dam unraced half-sister to useful hurdler/
fair chaser (stayed 25f) No Discount and fairly useful hurdler/useful chaser (stayed 2½m)
Old Flame: looked good prospect when winning bumper at Wincanton (by 12 lengths) in
December, but shaped as if amiss both starts after: will stay at least 2½m. *Anthony Honeyball*

LE COEUR NET (FR) 6 ch.g. Network (GER) – Silverwood (FR) (Garde Royale) **c105**
[2017/18 h99: h23.3d^5 h19.9d^6 c20d^4 c19.5v^{ur} c19.9s c17v* c17v^2 c19.7v^2 c17.8s^F c18.2v^2 **h91**
Apr 12] modest maiden hurdler: fair handicap chaser: won novice event at Plumpton in
January: has form over 3m, likely to prove best at much shorter: acts on heavy going: tried
in hood: normally in tongue tie: often travels strongly. *Anthony Honeyball*

LE CURIEUX (FR) 6 br.g. Lauro (GER) – La Curieuse (FR) (Robin des Champs (FR)) **c109**
[2017/18 h17g c18.2s^5 c18.2v c20s^{pu} c19.5v^6 c18.2s^5 c17.8v^4 Mar 17] compact gelding: **h–**
winning hurdler: disappointing maiden over fences: left John E. Kiely after third start:
stays 2¼m: acts on soft going: tried in tongue tie: has made mistakes. *Brendan Powell*

LE DAUPHIN (IRE) 7 b.g. Robin des Champs (FR) – Miss Denman (IRE) (Presenting) **h104**
[2017/18 h119: h20g h20.3g^5 h24.5d^6 Nov 27] good-topped gelding: fairly useful hurdler:
lightly raced and disappointing in handicaps in 2017/18: should stay beyond 21f: acts on
good to firm going. *Nicky Henderson*

LE DELUGE (FR) 8 b.g. Oratorio (IRE) – Princess Sofia (UAE) (Pennekamp (USA)) **h– §**
[2017/18 h–: h17.2s^{ro} Jul 24] regressive on Flat: clear when ran out early both starts in
maiden hurdles: wears tongue tie: one to avoid. *Micky Hammond*

LE DRAPEAU (FR) 6 ch.g. Satri (IRE) – La Bandera (Bahhare (USA)) [2017/18 b76: **h105**
h17d^3 h19.9s^4 h21.2v^2 h19.3v^4 h24.3g Apr 20] fair form over hurdles: probably stays 3m:
acts on heavy going: often races prominently. *Sue Smith*

LEE SIDE LADY (IRE) 8 ch.m. Mountain High (IRE) – Vicante (IRE) (Old Vic) [2017/18 **c65**
h104: h17.7m^3 c23g^3 h25.8m^2 c21.6s^{pu} h26g^4 Sep 26] winning pointer: fair handicap **h106**
hurdler: well below flat level both starts over fences: stays 3¼m: acts on good to firm and
heavy going: usually races towards rear: temperament under suspicion. *Neil Mulholland*

LEESWOOD LILY 5 b.m. Alflora (IRE) – Showtime Annie (Wizard King) [2017/18 **b–**
b75: b16.7s May 20] sparely-made mare: modest form in bumpers: well held sole outing in
2017/18. *Jennie Candlish*

LE FRANK (IRE) 6 b.g. King's Theatre (IRE) – Dream Lass (IRE) (Bob Back (USA)) **h91**
[2017/18 b84: h16.2v^4 h16v^3 h15.7v h20.2s^4 Apr 27] modest form over hurdles: should
stay at least 2½m: wears tongue tie: remains with some potential (well-bred sort). *Lucinda Russell*

LEFT BACK (IRE) 6 b.g. Oscar (IRE) – Baldrica (FR) (Lost World (IRE)) [2017/18 h–: **h–**
h23.3g^{pu} May 13] little form in maiden hurdles: returned to points subsequently, winning
in February: tried in hood: in tongue tie last 2 starts. *N. W. Alexander*

LEGAL EYES (IRE) 5 b.g. Court Cave (IRE) – Grass Tips (IRE) (Bob Back (USA)) **b98**
[2017/18 b16.7s^2 b16.7g^2 Apr 22] first foal: dam unraced half-sister to useful hurdler
(2½m-2¾m winner) Flemenson: fairly useful form in bumpers: runner-up at Bangor and
Market Rasen (beaten neck by Northern Soul). *Ben Pauling*

LEGAL LEGEND 11 b.g. Midnight Legend – Calamintha (Mtoto) [2017/18 c32.5d^5 May **c111**
5] multiple point winner: fair form in hunter chases: stays 33f. *C. Henn*

LEGAL OK (IRE) 6 b.g. Echo of Light – Desert Trail (IRE) (Desert Style (IRE)) **c94**
[2017/18 h94p, b–: h17.7d c17.4d^{pu} h21g^{po} c16g^2 c20g^{pu} Dec 6] tall gelding: Irish point **h–**
winner: lightly-raced maiden hurdler: modest form when second (beaten 14 lengths by
Dark Mahler) at Ludlow in November, sole completion in novice handicap chases:
unproven beyond 2m: acts on soft going: in headgear 4 of last 5 outings: tried in tongue tie:
usually leads/races freely. *Stuart Edmunds*

LE GAVROCHE (IRE) 5 b.g. Flemensfirth (USA) – Knockieran (IRE) (Oscar (IRE)) **h–**
[2017/18 b16s^6 h16v^6 h16.2v h16.4v^5 Feb 5] little show in bumper/novice hurdles. **b–**
Rose Dobbin

LEG

LEGENDE VOLANTE (FR) 5 ch.m. Flying Legend (USA) – J'y Vole (FR) (Mansonnien (FR)) [2017/18 b15.8g⁵ b15.8g h20.6g h20.3d⁴ Nov 6] first foal: dam (c156/h123) 2m-21f hurdle/chase winner: well held in bumpers and novice hurdles (hooded). *Amy Murphy* — h– b–

LEGEND LADY 7 b.m. Midnight Legend – Aoninch (Inchinor) [2017/18 h114: h19.2g⁵ h15.3v⁵ Jan 18] lightly-raced hurdler, fair at best: should stay further than 2m: acts on soft going. *Oliver Sherwood* — h–

LEGEND OF FRANCE 5 ch.m. Flying Legend (USA) – Bonne Anniversaire (Alflora (IRE)) [2017/18 b16s⁶ ab16g⁶ h15.9v⁴ h15.9d⁶ h15.8s h16s Apr 9] £2,500 3-y-o: rather unfurnished mare: half-sister to 3 winners, including fairly useful hurdler Grey Missile (21f winner, by Terimon) and fair hurdler Samedi Soir (2½m winner, by Black Sam Bellamy): dam unraced sister to useful hurdler (stayed 19f) Alph and half-sister to top-class hurdler (2m winner) Royal Derbi: modest form in bumpers: poor form over hurdles: will be suited by 2½m: often in hood: races in rear. *Pat Phelan* — h84 b77

LEGENDOFTHEKNIGHT 6 b.g. Midnight Legend – Pentasilea (Nashwan (USA)) [2017/18 b16s Jan 13] workmanlike gelding: tailed-off last in maiden bumper at Warwick. *Sarah Humphrey* — b–

LEGEND TO BE 8 b.g. Midnight Legend – Pentasilea (Nashwan (USA)) [2017/18 c24.2mᵖᵘ c19.2g⁴ c22.6g Aug 3] last in selling hurdle: little form in chases: returned to points subsequently, winning in April: in cheekpieces last 2 starts. *Sarah Humphrey* — c– h–

LEG LOCK LUKE (IRE) 8 b.g. Indian River (FR) – Delirious Tantrum (IRE) (Taufan (USA)) [2017/18 c98§, h–: h16.8d c23m* c23.8d³ c19.9d³ c24s⁴ Apr 9] lengthy gelding: maiden hurdler: fair handicap chaser: won at Taunton in November: stays 3m: acts on soft and good to firm going: usually in headgear/tongue tie: front runner/races prominently: temperamental. *Colin Tizzard* — c105 § h– §

LEITH HILL LAD 8 b.g. Kayf Tara – Leith Hill Star (Comme L'Etoile) [2017/18 h115: c21.6g⁶ c22.6g³ c25.7sᵖᵘ c23.6s⁵ c24s* c24.2d* Apr 24] good-topped gelding: fairly useful hurdler: fairly useful form over fences: won novice handicaps at Kempton and Exeter in April: stays 3m: acts on good to firm and heavy going: has been let down by jumping. *Charlie Longsdon* — c123 x h–

LEITH HILL LEGASI 9 b.m. Kahyasi – Leith Hill Star (Comme L'Etoile) [2017/18 c91, h–: c23.6s⁵ c26.7vᵖᵘ c24v³ c26v⁴ c24.5s⁵ c23.5v⁵ c26.2s² Apr 27] maiden hurdler: poor handicap chaser: stays 3¼m: acts on good to firm and heavy going: wears headgear/tongue tie: front runner. *Charlie Longsdon* — c83 h–

LE MARTALIN (FR) 7 ch.g. Martaline – Hembra (FR) (Croco Rouge (IRE)) [2017/18 h139, b107: c16s² c17vᵘʳ c17d³ c16v³ h20s Apr 25] useful novice hurdler in 2016/17: similar form when promising second in maiden at Wexford (neck behind Dinaria des Obeaux) on chasing debut: didn't progress: unproven beyond 2m: acts on soft going: wears headgear: regularly tongue tied: usually leads. *Noel Meade, Ireland* — c140 h–

LEMONADE DRINKER 5 gr.g. Fair Mix (IRE) – Sheknowsyouknow (Petrizzo) [2017/18 b15.3v Dec 26] tailed off in bumper. *Mike Hawker* — b–

LEMON'S GENT 11 br.g. Generous (IRE) – Lemon's Mill (USA) (Roberto (USA)) [2017/18 c109, h–: c19.2m³ May 9] big gelding: maiden hurdler: fair handicap chaser: stayed 3m: acted on good to firm and heavy going: wore headgear/tongue tie: made running/raced prominently: dead. *Paul Webber* — c84 h–

LE MUSEE (FR) 5 b.g. Galileo (IRE) – Delicieuse Lady (Trempolino (USA)) [2017/18 h15.3v² h16v² h19s* h20.3g Apr 18] has had breathing operation: once-raced on Flat: fairly useful form over hurdles: won maiden at Taunton in March: should stay further than 19f: wears tongue tie. *Nigel Hawke* — h118

LEODIS (IRE) 6 ch.g. Shirocco (GER) – Leonica (Lion Cavern (USA)) [2017/18 b88: b15.7g⁴ May 24] fair form both starts in bumpers: modest form on Flat subsequently. *Tom Tate* — b86

LEO LUNA 9 b.g. Galileo (IRE) – Eva Luna (USA) (Alleged (USA)) [2017/18 c126§, h–: c26v³ c28.5v⁴ c25.7v* c24.2vᵘʳ c26s² c25.7s⁶ Apr 15] tall gelding: winning hurdler: fairly useful handicap chaser: won at Plumpton (needed strong ride by Joshua Moore) in January: stays 3¼m: acts on heavy going: wears headgear: has worn tongue tie, including last 2 starts: front runner/races prominently: lazy/untrustworthy. *Gary Moore* — c121 § h–

LEOMAR (GER) 5 ch.g. Adlerflug (GER) – Lovana (IRE) (Darshaan) [2017/18 h16d⁴ h16.8d³ h16g³ h17.3g⁴ h18.8gᶠ h15.8s Mar 14] useful on Flat (stays 1¾m) in 2016: fair maiden hurdler: left Gordon Elliott after fifth start: should stay beyond 2m: acts on heavy going: tried in blinkers*: front runner/races prominently. *Dan Skelton* — h108

LEONASISLAND (IRE) 6 b.g. Trans Island – Ashanti Dancer (IRE) (Dancing Dissident (USA)) [2017/18 h16.2v Feb 15] pulled up in points: hooded, tailed off in novice on hurdling debut. *Stuart Coltherd* — **h—**

LEONCAVALLO (IRE) 6 br.g. Cape Cross (IRE) – Nafura (Dubawi (IRE)) [2017/18 h134: h19.6s6 Nov 15] neat gelding: useful handicap hurdler: faded only outing in 2017/18: unproven beyond 17f: acts on good to soft going: sometimes in cheekpieces. *Ben Pauling* — **h121**

LEORO (IRE) 4 ch.g. Campanologist (USA) – Ledicea (Medicean) [2017/18 h16.3s h15.7vpu Jan 20] workmanlike gelding: fairly useful on Flat (stays 2m), won in March/April: little impression in 2 juvenile hurdles (in tongue tie second one). *Charlie Mann* — **h—**

LEOSTAR 4 ch.g. Nathaniel (IRE) – Gaditana (Rainbow Quest (USA)) [2017/18 b15.6s5 b15.7s3 b16.4d2 b16g Apr 21] £11,000 3-y-o: second foal: dam, ran once on Flat, sister to fairly useful hurdler (stayed 19f) Migration: fair form in bumpers: will stay 2½m. *Alistair Whillans* — **b89**

LE PATRIOTE (FR) 6 b.g. Poliglote – Sentosa (FR) (Kaldounevees (FR)) [2017/18 h18.9s5 h17.9s h17.9s h21s h16.8v4 h19.3s* h16vpu Mar 10] €65,000 3-y-o: well-made gelding: fifth foal: half-brother to smart French hurdler/useful chaser La Segnora (17f-3m winner, by Turgeon): dam unraced: fairly useful handicap hurdler: won at Ascot in February: left M. Rolland after third start: stays 19f: acts on heavy going: in cheekpieces last 2 starts: strong-travelling sort: tracks pace. *Dr Richard Newland* — **h127**

LE PRECIEUX (FR) 5 b.g. Diamond Boy (FR) – Bab Khaldoun (FR) (Kaldoun (FR)) [2017/18 h15.7g h17.7v5 h16sF h17.7g6 Apr 20] good-topped gelding: closely related to fairly useful French hurdler La Bombonera (2¼m winner) and fairly useful French hurdler/very smart chaser Lagunak (17f-27f winner) (both by Mansonnien), and half-brother to fairly useful hurdler Gamede (2m winner, by Astarabad): dam French 10.5f winner: fair handicap hurdler: well held on chasing debut (in France): stays 2¼m: acts on heavy going. *Gary Moore* — **c— h109**

LE PREZIEN (FR) 7 br.g. Blue Bresil (FR) – Abu Dhabi (FR) (Saint Cyrien (FR)) [2017/18 c145, h—: c15.9g2 c20.4s3 c20.8s c16.3v* c19.9spu Apr 13] useful-looking gelding: winning hurdler: very smart chaser: won Grand Annual at Cheltenham (career-best effort, beating Gino Trail 4½ lengths) in March: pulled up quickly after bad mistake ninth in Melling Chase at Aintree final start: stays 2½m: acts on heavy going: wears tongue tie: waited with: has been held back by mistakes over fences. *Paul Nicholls* — **c156 x h—**

Johnny Henderson Grand Annual Challenge Cup Handicap Chase, Cheltenham—
Le Prezien (hoops) stays on to beat long-time leader Gino Trail (cheekpieces) in a race marred by three fatalities

LER

LE RICHEBOURG (FR) 5 br.g. Network (GER) – Fee Magic (FR) (Phantom Breeze) [2017/18 h17g* h17g* h16.6s* h16s⁶ h16s² h16s h16.8v Mar 16] angular gelding: fifth foal: half-brother to 3 winners, including top-class hurdler/very smart chaser Grands Crus (2½m-3m winner) and smart hurdler/useful chaser Gevrey Chambertin (2m-25f winner) (both by Dom Alco): dam unraced half-sister to Scottish Grand National winner Al Co: useful hurdler: won maiden at Killarney in May and novices at Killarney and Galway (by 5 lengths from Twobeelucky) in July: disappointing subsequently: bred to stay beyond 2m: acts on soft going. *Joseph Patrick O'Brien, Ireland* — h137

LERICHI BELLE (IRE) 7 b.m. King's Theatre (IRE) – Lerichi (IRE) (Shardari) [2017/18 h106, b84: h15.8d² h20.3g⁴ h21.2g⁴ h25s² h19.5v² h19.9v² h23.1vᵖᵘ Apr 17] fair maiden hurdler: stays 3m, effective at shorter: acts on heavy going: wears headgear: normally dropped out (has raced freely/made mistakes). *Martin Keighley* — h106

LE ROCHER (FR) 8 b.g. Saint des Saints (FR) – Belle du Roi (FR) (Adieu Au Roi (IRE)) [2017/18 h145: h19.5d h22.8v c17.5v* c16.2v* c21.4v* c19.2v³ c20.4sᵇᵈ Mar 13] tall gelding: fairly useful handicap hurdler: smart form over fences: won in small fields at Exeter (graduation, left alone 4 out) and Warwick (novice) in December, and at Market Rasen (graduation, by 1¼ lengths from Three Musketeers) in January: let down by jumping both starts after: stays 21f: acts on heavy going: front runner/races prominently. *Nick Williams* — c146 h123

LES ARCEAUX (IRE) 4 b.g. Arcano (IRE) – Amoureux (USA) (Deputy Minister (CAN)) [2017/18 h16v² h16v² h16v⁴ h17sᵖᵘ Apr 12] close-coupled gelding: progressive on Flat (stays 1½m) in 2017: fairly useful form over hurdles: runner-up in maidens at Punchestown and Naas first 2 starts. *Henry de Bromhead, Ireland* — h116

L'ES FREMANTLE (FR) 7 b.g. Orpen (USA) – Grand Design (Danzero (AUS)) [2017/18 c–, h–: h20.6g⁶ h15.7g h16.7g⁵ h16.2d h15.7d⁵ h20.7g h16.7d⁶ c16.3s⁵ c15.7v⁵ h16s⁵ Mar 16] plain gelding: of little account: has worn cheekpieces. *Michael Chapman* — c– h–

LESKINFERE (IRE) 5 b.g. Darsi (FR) – Taipans Girl (IRE) (Taipan (IRE)) [2017/18 h20d⁶ h19.6s⁴ h19.7s³ h23.1v Mar 11] £21,000 4-y-o: fourth foal: brother to fair chaser Tiny Dancer (2½m/21f winner), stays 25f, and half-brother to a winning pointer by Well Chosen: dam unraced half-sister to fair hurdler/fairly useful chaser (stayed 25f) Night Safe: third in Irish point on debut: fair form over hurdles: should stay 23f. *Oliver Greenall* — h106

LESSONS IN MILAN (IRE) 10 b.g. Milan – Lessons Lass (IRE) (Doyoun) [2017/18 c136, h–: c25.6vᵖᵘ c27.3vᶠ Dec 30] big, rangy gelding: winning hurdler: useful maiden chaser: stayed 4m: acted on heavy going: wore cheekpieces last 5 starts: usually raced close up but had lazy streak: dead. *Nicky Henderson* — c– h–

LETBESO (IRE) 10 ch.g. Vinnie Roe (IRE) – Go Hunting (IRE) (Abednego) [2017/18 c123§, h113§: c26d³ Feb 25] winning hurdler: fairly useful chaser at best: well beaten in hunter only outing under Rules in 2017/18: stays 3¼m: acts on good to firm and heavy going: wears headgear: often in tongue tie: temperamental. *Mrs K. Lawther* — c90 § h– §

LETEMGO (IRE) 10 b.g. Brian Boru – Leteminletemout (IRE) (Be My Native (USA)) [2017/18 c–, h102: h23.9m⁶ h20.2s⁵ h23.9d⁶ h23.3s h24.3s³ h23.3s⁵ h22.8v³ h24.3v⁶ h25.8s* h24.3v* h25v* h25dᵘʳ h25.8vᵖᵘ h24.3g³ h26.6s⁴ Apr 26] compact gelding: fair handicap hurdler: won at Kelso in January, and Ayr (conditionals) and Carlisle in February: lightly-raced maiden chaser: stays 27f: acts on good to firm and heavy going: used to wear headgear: tried in tongue tie: usually races in rear. *Andrew Hamilton* — c– h112

LETHIRATIT (IRE) 8 b.m. Zagreb (USA) – Clogga Native (IRE) (Good Thyne (USA)) [2017/18 c19.3g May 4] first foal: dam, winning pointer, out of half-sister to high-class staying chaser Scotton Banks: little form in points: also well held in varied company under Rules: tried in tongue tie. *M. V. Coglan* — c– h–

L'ETOILE (IRE) 5 ch.g. Champs Elysees – Cross Your Fingers (USA) (Woodman (USA)) [2017/18 b15.6g h19.3d⁵ h16.8v Feb 22] 15,000 3-y-o: fourth foal: brother to fairly useful hurdler Gallic Destiny (19f winner) and half-brother to a winner on Flat by Arch: dam unraced: seventh in maiden bumper at Musselburgh: no show in novice hurdles. *Micky Hammond* — h– b76

LET'S BE HAPPY (IRE) 4 gr.f. Mastercraftsman (IRE) – Corrozal (GER) (Cape Cross (IRE)) [2017/18 h15.8s⁵ h16s⁶ h15.3v⁶ Mar 8] half-sister to French hurdler Rockozal (2½m/19f winner, by Rock of Gibraltar): dam half-sister to fairly useful French hurdler (2m/17f winner) Cascavel: fair on Flat (stays 1½m): only poor form over hurdles. *Ali Stronge* — h78

LIC

LET'S DANCE (FR) 6 b.m. Poliglote – Baraka du Berlais (FR) (Bonnet Rouge (FR)) [2017/18 h141: h18.2s^F h20s* h24v^5 h24sf h20v^3 h20s^4 Apr 28] well-made mare: useful hurdler: won EBF Mares Hurdle at Leopardstown (by 8 lengths from Forge Meadow) in December: stays 2½m: acts on heavy going: in cheekpieces last 3 starts. *W. P. Mullins, Ireland* **h143**

LET'S GET AT IT (IRE) 5 b.g. Mustameet (USA) – Last Hope (IRE) (Jurado (USA)) [2017/18 b14d b17v^4 Apr 17] modest form in bumpers 4 months apart. *Harry Whittington* **b80**

LETS GET SERIOUS (IRE) 12 b.g. Overbury (IRE) – Vendimia (Dominion) [2017/18 c–§, h–: c32.5d c27.2s^2 May 18] good-topped gelding: winning hurdler: fair hunter chaser nowadays: stays 3½m: acts on heavy going: has worn headgear: not one to trust. *C. J. Miller* **c107 §** **h–**

LETS GO DUTCHESS 8 b.m. Helissio (FR) – Lets Go Dutch (Nicholas Bill) [2017/18 h98, b82: h16.8g^2 h20g* h24.7g^{pu} h21.4d^5 Apr 22] sturdy mare: fair handicap hurdler: won mares event at Aintree in May: stays 2¾m: acts on good to firm and good to soft going: usually races nearer last than first/travels strongly. *Kevin Bishop* **h107**

LETSKEEPIT SIMPLE (IRE) 8 b.g. Saffron Walden (FR) – Diaconate (IRE) (Cape Cross (IRE)) [2017/18 c21.1s^{pu} May 18] multiple point winner: pulled up in maiden hunter chase. *Ian Cobb* **c–**

LET'S SWAY 4 b.f. Authorized (IRE) – Let's Dance (IRE) (Danehill Dancer (IRE)) [2017/18 h16.5m^3 Apr 25] modest maiden on Flat: 200/1, better form when third in mares novice at Taunton (4 lengths behind Cockney Wren) on hurdling debut. *Tracey Barfoot-Saunt* **h105**

LET'S TANGO (IRE) 7 ch.g. Mahler – Miss Ogan (IRE) (Supreme Leader) [2017/18 h96: h19.5d h25d^{pu} Nov 25] good-topped gelding: modest maiden hurdler: poor efforts in 2017/18: should stay further than 2½m: acts on good to soft going: tried in cheekpieces. *Ben Case* **h–**

LETTHERIVERRUNDRY (IRE) 8 br.g. Diamond Green (FR) – Dissitation (IRE) (Spectrum (IRE)) [2017/18 c91, h116: h20g c20g^2 c20g^{pu} h17.7d^2 h20.6d^4 h15.7v^3 h19d^6 Apr 26] big, strong, workmanlike gelding: fair handicap hurdler: similar form over fences: stays 2½m: acts on good to soft going: wears cheekpieces: in tongue tie last 4 starts. *Brendan Powell* **c112** **h111**

LEVEL OF INTENSITY (IRE) 4 b.g. Intense Focus (USA) – Teofolina (IRE) (Teofilo (IRE)) [2017/18 h16.8g* h16.2v^3 h16s^5 h15.8s Feb 22] sturdy gelding: fair on Flat, stays 1½m: fair juvenile hurdler: won at Sedgefield in October: tried in cheekpieces: wears tongue tie. *Nigel Hawke* **h106**

LEXINGTON LAW (IRE) 5 b.g. Lawman (FR) – Tus Nua (IRE) (Galileo (IRE)) [2017/18 h92p: h16g^1 h15.9d h16.5g^4 Nov 16] fairly useful on Flat (stays 12.5f): fair form over hurdles: tried in cheekpieces. *Alan King* **h103**

LEX TALIONIS (IRE) 5 b.g. Thewayyouare (USA) – Dawn Air (USA) (Diesis) [2017/18 h16.7g h19.5s^4 h18.8v^F h16d^4 h16d* h16v^2 h16v^3 h16.3s h20.3v^3 h19.8s^2 h21.4v^4 h19.8d* Apr 22] fair maiden on Flat, stays 1¼m: fairly useful handicap hurdler: won at Punchestown in October and Wincanton (amateur) in April: left Noel Meade after seventh start: stays 2½m: acts on heavy going: in cheekpieces last 3 starts: wears tongue tie. *Charlie Mann* **h116**

LIBBY T VALANCE 7 b.m. Scorpion (IRE) – Dipp In The Dark (IRE) (Presenting) [2017/18 h95p, b83: h19.6d^3 h23.9g^6 Nov 30] bumper winner: modest form over hurdles: bred to stay 3m. *Rebecca Curtis* **h98**

LIBERTY BELLA 4 b.f. Librettist (USA) – Classy Crewella (Lahib (USA)) [2017/18 b16.7v^5 b16s^4 b15.8v^5 b15.7v Apr 27] second foal: dam tailed off in bumper only start: modest form in bumpers. *Brian Eckley* **b75**

LICKETY SPLIT (FR) 5 b.m. Buck's Boum (FR) – Sninfia (IRE) (Hector Protector (USA)) [2017/18 b15.7s b16.6s Jan 27] third foal: dam (c115/h100) 2m-2½m hurdle/chase winner: little show in bumpers. *Michael Scudamore* **b66**

LICKPENNY LARRY 7 gr.g. Sagamix (FR) – Myriah (IRE) (Strong Gale) [2017/18 h68: h15.8d^6 c16.5s^4 c21.4d^{ro} c19.9s^5 c19.1s^4 c21.7v^3 c20.2v^5 c17v* c16v* Apr 15] lengthy, angular gelding: poor form over hurdles: modest handicap chaser: won at Plumpton (novice) and Ffos Las in April: probably best at shorter than 2¾m: acts on heavy going: tried in hood: wears tongue tie: often travels strongly. *Tom Gretton* **c94** **h72**

471

LIE

LIEUTENANT COLONEL 9 br.g. Kayf Tara – Agnese (Abou Zouz (USA)) [2017/18 c126, h148: c19.5s³ h23d⁴ h24vᵖᵘ h21v² h18s² h16v* h20vᵖᵘ c21.2v⁴ h24dᵖᵘ Apr 26] tall gelding: useful hurdler nowadays: won minor event at Cork (by 1¼ lengths from Karalee) in March: lightly raced and disappointing over fences since successful chasing debut in 2016/17: stays 3m, effective at shorter: acts on good to firm and heavy going: wears headgear/tongue tie: untrustworthy. *Gordon Elliott, Ireland* — **c109 §** **h137 §**

LIEUTENANT GRUBER (IRE) 7 b.g. Scorpion (IRE) – Tanit Lady (IRE) (Presenting) [2017/18 h119, b91: h16.7s* h16.3g² h15.8g* h19.6gᵖᵘ Aug 16] strong, workmanlike gelding: bumper winner: fairly useful novice hurdler: won at Bangor (maiden) in May and Uttoxeter in July: should have stayed 2½m: acted on soft going: wore hood/tongue tie last 2 starts: dead. *Dan Skelton* — **h118**

LIFE KNOWLEDGE (IRE) 6 ch.g. Thewayyouare (USA) – Rosa Bellini (IRE) (Rossini (USA)) [2017/18 h95: h15.7s⁶ h16.6s⁶ h16.4d⁶ Mar 16] modest maiden hurdler: raced around 2m: acts on soft going. *Patrick Holmes* — **h83**

LIGHT BREAKS (IRE) 6 b.g. Dylan Thomas (IRE) – Anywaysmile (IRE) (Indian Ridge) [2017/18 h72: h23g Jun 14] poor maiden hurdler: will prove best short of 3m: in cheekpieces last 3 starts. *Nigel Twiston-Davies* — **h–**

LIGHTENTERTAINMENT (IRE) 10 b.g. King's Theatre (IRE) – Dochas Supreme (IRE) (Supreme Leader) [2017/18 c–, h112d: h16m² c16.5gᵖᵘ h18.7g⁴ h18.5d⁴ h18.5v² h19.9v³ h20s⁵ c20.3v⁵ c16v* c16v³ c16v⁵ Apr 15] workmanlike gelding: modest hurdler: modest form over fences: won handicap at Lingfield in February: stays 21f, effective at shorter: acts on heavy going: has worn cheekpieces, including last 3 starts: usually leads. *Barry Brennan* — **c91** **h92**

LIGHTHOUSE WARRIER (IRE) 8 b.g. Milan – Glannagaul (IRE) (Germany (USA)) [2017/18 b16.7g² b16.5g* h16v² Dec 10] second foal: dam unraced: won bumper point on debut in May 2016: useful form in bumpers: won maiden at Punchestown (impressive, by 9 lengths from Pershing Missile) in May: 3/1, second in maiden at Cork (5 lengths behind Athenean) on hurdling debut: wears tongue tie: promising. *Jonathan Sweeney, Ireland* — **h114 p** **b105**

LIGHTLY SQUEEZE 4 b.g. Poet's Voice – Zuleika Dobson (Cadeaux Genereux) [2017/18 h16v⁴ h17.7v⁴ h19.2s⁴ Apr 6] sturdy gelding: fairly useful on Flat, stays 1¼m: only poor form over hurdles: has worn headgear. *Philip Hide* — **h84**

LIGHT OF AIR (FR) 5 b.g. Youmzain (IRE) – Height of Vanity (IRE) (Erhaab (USA)) [2017/18 h93: h17.7d Sep 10] good-topped gelding: fair on Flat (stays 13f): form over hurdles only when fifth in juvenile on hurdling debut: in headgear last 2 starts. *Gary Moore* — **h–**

LIGHT THAT (IRE) 6 b.g. Echo of Light – Tucum (IRE) (Diktat) [2017/18 h131: h17gᵖᵘ h16.7g h16s h16.2s⁶ c16.1s² c16v¹ c17s³ h16.5d³ Apr 24] useful handicap hurdler: good third at Punchestown (3 lengths behind True Self) final outing: in frame all 3 starts over fences, best effort (fairly useful form) when 11 lengths second of 7 to Bon Papa in maiden at Punchestown: raced around 2m: acts on heavy going: tried in tongue tie: front runner/races prominently. *Mrs J. Harrington, Ireland* — **c115** **h130**

LIGNY (FR) 5 ch.g. Fuisse (FR) – Light Wave (FR) (Marignan (USA)) [2017/18 b–p: b14s Jan 18] good-topped gelding: down field in bumpers at Newbury and Ludlow (again 9/2) 10 months apart. *Nicky Henderson* — **b–**

LIKE SULLY (IRE) 10 b.g. Presenting – Swing Into Action (IRE) (Be My Native (USA)) [2017/18 c108, h–: c24m c23.6s⁶ c25.7d⁴ c26v⁶ c23.6d² Apr 24] good-topped gelding: winning hurdler: modest handicap chaser nowadays: stays 3¼m: acts on heavy going: tried in cheekpieces. *Richard Rowe* — **c91** **h–**

LILBITLUSO (IRE) 10 b.g. Luso – Izntitgreat (IRE) (Montelimar (USA)) [2017/18 c112, h–: c23.8sF c21.1sF Apr 12] multiple point winner: maiden hurdler: fair hunter chaser: stayed 3½m: acted on soft and good to firm going: tried in hood: usually raced prominently: dead. *J. J. O'Shea* — **c–** **h–**

LILLIAN (IRE) 7 b.m. Milan – Kay Tully (Kahyasi) [2017/18 h99: h25.6g* h24g² h26.5m* h26.4g* h26.5d³ h25.8g⁶ Oct 6] small mare: fairly useful handicap hurdler: won at Fontwell in May, and at Newton Abbot and Stratford in July: stays 3¼m: acts on good to firm and good to soft going: front runner/races prominently. *Seamus Mullins* — **h119**

LILLINGTON (IRE) 6 br.g. Westerner – Kind Word (IRE) (Yashgan) [2017/18 h111: c19.5g⁶ h21.4g h15.3v⁶ c18.2s³ c19.7vᵘʳ c18.2s² Mar 26] maiden hurdler: well held in handicaps in 2017/18: fair form over fences: stays 2¼m: acts on soft and good to firm going: tried in cheekpieces: wears tongue tie: temperament under suspicion. *Colin Tizzard* — **c102** **h–**

472

Coral Hurdle, Ascot—Lil Rockerfeller (cheekpieces) goes one better than in 2016

LILLIPUT LANE (IRE) 6 b.m. Yeats (IRE) – Charade (IRE) (Danehill (USA)) [2017/18 b16.8m³ b15.8g² b15.8s Dec 26] €10,000 3-y-o: second foal: dam, ran twice on Flat, half-sister to Champion Bumper runner-up Sophocles: fair form in bumpers. *Johnny Farrelly* **b87**

LILLY'S LEGEND 8 ch.m. Midnight Legend – Dalticia (FR) (Cadoudal (FR)) [2017/18 c54, h78: c23.4g* h24g^{ur} c24.2g² Jun 3] poor hurdler: similar form over fences: won selling handicap at Kelso in May: stays 25f: acts on good to firm and heavy going: wears cheekpieces. *Mark Walford* **c81 h–**

LIL ROCKERFELLER (USA) 7 ch.g. Hard Spun (USA) – Layounne (USA) (Mt Livermore (USA)) [2017/18 h162: h24.1s³ h19.3d* h24.4d⁶ h19.2d² h24s h24.7s^{pu} h21.5s² Apr 28] well-made gelding: smart hurdler: won Coral Hurdle at Ascot (by 1½ lengths from L'Ami Serge) in November: also placed in 2017/18 in West Yorkshire Hurdle at Wetherby, National Spirit Hurdle at Fontwell and Select Hurdle at Sandown (16 lengths behind Call Me Lord): stays 3m: acts on heavy going: normally in headgear: usually races prominently: tough. *Neil King* **h152**

LILY'S GEM (IRE) 5 b.m. Scorpion (IRE) – Kegster (IRE) (Bach (IRE)) [2017/18 b16v³ b17d² b17v* Apr 17] second foal: dam unraced half-sister to useful hurdler/chaser (stayed 2¼m) St Pirran and fairly useful hurdler/useful chaser (stayed 29f) Guess Again: fairly useful form in bumpers: won at Carlisle in April. *Stuart Crawford, Ireland* **b96**

LILYWHITE GESTURE (IRE) 9 b.m. Presenting – Loyal Gesture (IRE) (Darazari (IRE)) [2017/18 h99: h23.3d* h24.7g⁴ h20g⁴ h21.8g³ c22d³ c23d³ c20.1v* c20v^{pu} c20.6v^{pu} h23v Dec 16] rather leggy mare: fair handicap hurdler: won mares event at Uttoxeter in May: fair form over fences: won novice handicap at Hexham in September: stays 27f: acts on heavy going: wears tongue tie: usually races nearer last than first. *Gordon Elliott, Ireland* **c111 h104**

LIME STREET (IRE) 7 b.g. Presenting – Specifiedrisk (IRE) (Turtle Island (IRE)) [2017/18 c90, h94: h23.3g² h23.3g* h23.3d² h20g² h23g c20.9s⁴ h20v² h24.3g⁵ Apr 20] sturdy gelding: fair handicap hurdler: won novice event at Uttoxeter in June: well held in handicap chases: left Tom Symonds after first start: stays 3m: acts on heavy going: regularly in headgear/tongue tie nowadays. *Peter Bowen* **c83 h111**

LIMITED RESERVE (IRE) 6 b.g. Court Cave (IRE) – Lady Blackie (IRE) (Definite Article) [2017/18 h118, b86: h18.5s² h16.7g⁴ h15.7g² h18.9v* h18.9v* Dec 23] compact gelding: useful handicap hurdler: won at Haydock in November and December (landed odds by neck from Zalvados): stays 21f: acts on good to firm and heavy going. *Christian Williams* **h132**

LIMONCELLO (FR) 6 b.g. Maresca Sorrento (FR) – Isarella (GER) (Second Set (IRE)) [2017/18 h98: h21.6d⁵ c26.3m³ c22.7d h23.9s Dec 14] lengthy gelding: runner-up on last of 3 starts in points: modest maiden hurdler: poor form in chases: stays 23f: acts on heavy going: tried in headgear. *Nick Williams* **c80 h–**

473

LIN

LINCOLN COUNTY 7 b.g. Authorized (IRE) – Lane County (USA) (Rahy (USA)) [2017/18 h15.8d h19v^{pu} h18.6v^5 h21.2d^5 Apr 24] fair maiden hurdler at best: only poor form in handicaps in 2017/18: stays 2½m: acts on good to firm and good to soft going: has worn headgear: in tongue tie last 2 starts. *Oliver Greenall* — h78

LINED WITH SILVER (IRE) 9 gr.g. Cloudings (IRE) – Tinkers Lady (Sheer Grit) [2017/18 c89, h–: c16.5m* c16.1g^{pu} c16.1g^3 c20g^{pu} c22.6g^2 c17.8g^5 Nov 10] winning Irish pointer: maiden hurdler: modest handicap chaser: won at Worcester in May: probably stays 23f, though effective at much shorter: acts on good to firm going. *Alan Phillips* — c97 h–

LINENHALL (IRE) 6 ch.g. Stowaway – Option (IRE) (Red Ransom (USA)) [2017/18 b97: h22g* h21g^2 h24.4s^5 h24g Apr 18] fairly useful form over hurdles: won maiden at Stratford in November on hurdling debut: second in novice at Towcester next time: stiffer tasks both starts after: should be suited by 3m: tried in cheekpieces: front runner/races prominently. *Ben Pauling* — h124

L'INGANNO FELICE (FR) 8 br.g. Librettist (USA) – Final Overture (FR) (Rossini (USA)) [2017/18 h17s^3 h16.7g* Apr 22] fairly useful on Flat, stays 12.5f: fair form over hurdles: progressed further after winning maiden at Market Rasen in April: wears hood: open to more improvement. *Iain Jardine* — h109 p

LINGUINE (FR) 8 ch.g. Linngari (IRE) – Amerissage (USA) (Rahy (USA)) [2017/18 h115: h23.1m^3 h25.6g^6 h25m^4 h25d^2 h23.3d^5 h24d Dec 5] small gelding: fair handicap hurdler: stays 25f: acts on soft and good to firm going: normally in headgear: front runner. *Seamus Durack* — h109

LINKENHOLT (IRE) 6 ch.g. Robin des Champs (FR) – Honest Chance (FR) (Trempolino (USA)) [2017/18 b–: h18.5d h16g h15.5s^6 Dec 3] sturdy gelding: little form in bumpers/varied company over hurdles: went pointing after: tried in hood. *Oliver Sherwood* — h–

LION IN HIS HEART (IRE) 7 b.g. Westerner – Coolnasneachta (IRE) (Old Vic) [2017/18 h134, b97: c17g^{ro} c20s^{ur} h20g^3 h17g^3 h16v^{ro} h16.4g h20d^{pu} h16s^3 h20v^{pu} Jan 20] well-made gelding: useful handicap hurdler: failed to complete both starts over fences (still in front when ran out after 2 out in maiden won by Ask Nile at Killarney on chasing debut): should stay beyond 17f: acts on soft going: tried in blinkers: one to treat with plenty of caution. *Henry de Bromhead, Ireland* — c127 § h130 §

LION OF LACKABANE (IRE) 7 b.g. Welsh Lion (IRE) – Lackabane Julie (IRE) (Broken Hearted) [2017/18 h16g h16g h16g^5 h20g^{pu} Sep 12] maiden pointer: poor form over hurdles: tried in visor. *Mike Hammond* — h65

LIP SERVICE (IRE) 9 ch.g. Presenting – Top Her Up (IRE) (Beneficial) [2017/18 h21.1s^4 h19.8s^5 c23.9v^{pu} Apr 11] well-made gelding: fair form over hurdles: better form over fences as a novice: pulled up in handicap chase start in 2017/18: stays 2¾m: acts on heavy going: normally hooded: in tongue tie last 3 starts. *Fergal O'Brien* — c– h110

LISDOONVARNA LAD (IRE) 6 br.g. Westerner – Socialite Girl (Glacial Storm (USA)) [2017/18 b16g^2 b16.4s h16s* h15.7v^3 h19s^5 Feb 23] tall gelding: third foal: dam, little form, half-sister to fairly useful hurdler/useful chaser (stays 3¼m) Wizards Bridge: fairly useful form in bumpers: similar form over hurdles: won novice at Wetherby in December with ease on hurdling debut: better effort subsequently when third in Rossington Main Novices' Hurdle at Haydock (11½ lengths behind First Flow): bred to stay at least 19f. *Charlie Longsdon* — h118 b95

LISHEEN PRINCE (IRE) 7 b.g. Oscar (IRE) – Dino's Monkey (IRE) (Mr Dinos (IRE)) [2017/18 h119: h20.3g Apr 18] lengthy gelding: won Irish point on debut: fairly useful novice hurdler in 2016/17: off 16 months, shaped as if needing run in handicap at Cheltenham only outing since: stays 21f. *Olly Murphy* — h–

LISKEARD 6 b.g. Dansili – Quest To Peak (USA) (Distant View (USA)) [2017/18 b16.2d Aug 21] tailed off in bumper/Flat maiden: dead. *Andrew Crook* — b–

LISP (IRE) 4 ch.g. Poet's Voice – Hora (Hernando (FR) [2017/18 h17.7d^2 h15.9s* h17.7v* h15.7v^3 h16.4s^F Mar 14] sturdy gelding: half-brother to 3 winning hurdlers, including Thomas Campbell (smart 2m-25f winner, by Yeats) and Coeur de Lion (useful 2m winner, by Pour Moi): dam (h148) 19f-3m hurdle winner: fair maiden on Flat (should stay well beyond 1m): fairly useful form over hurdles: won novices at Plumpton in December and Fontwell in January: stays 2¼m: acts on heavy going. *Alan King* — h122

LISSYCASEY (IRE) 5 b.g. Rule of Law (USA) – Forever Mates (IRE) (Un Desperado (FR)) [2017/18 b16.7g h15.8d h15.8s⁴ h15.8s⁵ h15.7v^pu h19d² Apr 26] £16,000 4-y-o: rather unfurnished gelding: first foal: dam placed in points: runner-up on completed start in Irish points: well beaten in bumper: fairly useful form over hurdles: best run when second in handicap at Warwick in April: will be suited by 2½m: acts on soft going. *Sheila Lewis*   **h115 b–**

LISTEN DEAR (IRE) 8 b.m. Robin des Champs (FR) – Crescendor (FR) (Lavirco (GER)) [2017/18 c136p, h130p: c19.5g* May 21] lightly-raced winner over hurdles: useful form over fences: won mares event at Limerick sole outing in 2017/18: stays 19f: acts on soft going: usually leads: strong traveller. *W. P. Mullins, Ireland*   **c141 h–**

LISTEN FOR ME 8 b.m. Rainbow High – Teeton Bubbley (Neltino) [2017/18 h–p: h20m³ h19.9g² May 28] runner-up completed start in mares maiden points: fair form over hurdles: placed in mares maidens at Worcester and Uttoxeter. *Paul Webber*   **h101**

LISTEN TO THE MAN (IRE) 8 b.m. Court Cave (IRE) – Badia Dream (IRE) (Old Vic) [2017/18 h117: h16g* h15.8d* h16.7g* h16g² Oct 22] won Irish mares maiden point on debut: fairly useful hurdler: won novice at Worcester in June, mares novice at Uttoxeter in July and listed handicap at Market Rasen in September: effective at 2m to 2½m: acts on soft and good to firm going: front runner/races prominently. *Dan Skelton*   **h125**

LITE DUTIES (IRE) 9 b.g. Mountain High (IRE) – Kill Bill (IRE) (Warcraft (USA)) [2017/18 h20v* h24s Feb 4] useful handicap hurdler: won at Cork (by 1¾ lengths from Indian Monsoon) in January: not seen after poor effort next start: stays 3m: acts on heavy going. *Charles Byrnes, Ireland*   **h131**

LITHIC (IRE) 7 b.g. Westerner – Acoola (IRE) (Flemensfirth (USA)) [2017/18 h122p: h20g^F h20.6g* c17.2g³ c21.6d³ c20d² c24.2v^F h24g Apr 18] good-topped gelding: fairly useful hurdler: won novice at Market Rasen in June: fairly useful form over fences: best effort when second in novice handicap at Sandown in December: stays 2¾m: acts on soft and good to firm going: in cheekpieces last 3 starts: usually races towards rear. *Jonjo O'Neill*   **c124 h117**

LITTERALE CI (FR) 5 b.m. Soldier of Fortune (IRE) – Cigalia (Red Ransom (USA)) [2017/18 h113: h16.3g⁴ h15.8d* h15.3v³ h15.8d* Apr 22] fairly useful handicap hurdler: won lady amateur event at Ludlow in December and mares race at Stratford in April: raced around 2m: acts on soft going: usually travels strongly: all 3 wins for Miss A. B. O'Connor (7). *Harry Fry*   **h122**

LITTLE ACORN 7 b.m. Presenting – Whiteoak (IRE) (Oscar (IRE)) [2017/18 h100, b–: h21g* May 15] fair form over hurdles: in cheekpieces, won mares maiden at Kempton only outing in 2017/18: stays 21f. *Harry Fry*   **h107**

LITTLE ALLSTAR (IRE) 5 b.g. Morozov (USA) – Little Twinkle (IRE) (Fourstars Allstar (USA)) [2017/18 b15.8s h21.7s h20.7s h15.8d⁴ Mar 26] first foal: dam (h88) placed in bumpers/maiden hurdler: placed on sole start in Irish maiden points: seventh in bumper at Huntingdon: modest form over hurdles: wears tongue tie. *Sam Thomas*   **h94 b68**

LITTLE BAVINGTON 5 b.g. Strategic Prince – Vanilla Delight (IRE) (Orpen (USA)) [2017/18 b16.7g b15.8g⁶ Jul 19] little show in bumpers. *Philip Kirby*   **b–**

LITTLE BRUCE (IRE) 6 b.g. Yeats (IRE) – Lady Rolfe (IRE) (Alzao (USA)) [2017/18 h110: h20.1s⁵ h24.3v^pu h24.1d³ h21.3s³ h24.4s h25.5v h21.3v* Mar 20] fair hurdler: won seller at Wetherby in March: stays 3m: acts on heavy going: in headgear last 4 starts: tried in tongue tie: unreliable. *Philip Kirby*   **h108 §**

LITTLE CHUNK (IRE) 6 ch.g. Mr Dinos (IRE) – Daly Lady (IRE) (Lord of Appeal) [2017/18 h118, b81: h16.3g^pu h21.2g² h16d² c16v⁴ Jan 3] sturdy gelding: fairly useful handicap hurdler: left Warren Greatrex, runner-up at Ludlow and Kempton (conditionals) in November: well beaten in novice handicap on chasing debut: stays 21f: acts on good to soft going: in tongue tie last 3 starts: front runner/races prominently. *Kim Bailey*   **c– h120**

LITTLE DOTTY 9 br.m. Erhaab (USA) – Marsh Marigold (Tina's Pet) [2017/18 h93: h16.7g⁶ h16.7g⁵ Sep 1] lightly-raced maiden hurdler, modest at best: raced around 2m. *Giuseppe Fierro*   **h76**

LITTLE FRITZ (FR) 11 gr.g. Turgeon (USA) – Hunorisk (FR) (Mansonnien (FR)) [2017/18 c75x, h–: c24.2g^pu c21.2d⁵ h24.3s^pu Oct 30] maiden hurdler/chaser: little form since 2014/15: has worn tongue tie: often let down by jumping. *Leonard Kerr*   **c81 x h–**

LIT

LITTLE JIMMY 11 br.g. Passing Glance – Sementina (USA) (Silver Charm (USA)) [2017/18 c101, h94: h19.5d c16v[4] c17.8v[4] c15.7v[2] c16s[2] c16.4v[3] c16.3v[3] Apr 14] close-coupled gelding: maiden hurdler: modest handicap chaser: stays 21f: acts on heavy going: normally wears headgear: tongue tied: usually races towards rear. *Tom Gretton*   c92 h–

LITTLE JON 10 b.g. Pasternak – Jowoody (Gunner B) [2017/18 c130, h–: c20s[5] c22.4g[5] c20s[5] c23.8v[pu] c20.2v[2] c16d[F] Apr 24] tall gelding: maiden hurdler: fairly useful handicap chaser nowadays: stays 23f, at least as effective around 2½m: acts on heavy going: wears cheekpieces: front runner/races prominently: often let down by jumping. *Nigel Twiston-Davies*   c124 x h–

LITTLE LOTTE (IRE) 5 b.m. Kodiac – Dancing Steps (Zafonic (USA)) [2017/18 h90: h17g[8] h15.8g[6] h16.7g h16.8d[6] h18f[2] h16d Apr 22] modest handicap hurdler: won at Les Landes in May: trained second to fifth starts by Tom Gretton: unproven beyond 17f: acts on firm going: wears headgear: tried in tongue tie. *Mrs A. Corson, Jersey*   h89

LITTLE MILLIE (IRE) 6 b.m. Milan – Sweetbitter (FR) (Turgeon (USA)) [2017/18 h21s[2] h24s[2] h20.7s[6] h25.5s[5] h24.6s Apr 9] €9,000 3-y-o, £26,000 5-y-o: third foal: dam unraced half-sister to useful hurdler (2m-2¼m winner) Blue Shark: Irish point winner: fair form over hurdles: stays 25f: acts on soft going: tried in cheekpieces/tongue tie. *Neil King*   h106

LITTLE MISS POET 6 b.m. Yeats (IRE) – R de Rien Sivola (FR) (Robin des Champs (FR)) [2017/18 h120: h15.7g[5] h19v[4] h21.4d[3] Apr 22] lengthy mare: fairly useful handicap hurdler: should stay beyond 21f: acts on good to firm and heavy going. *Philip Hobbs*   h116

LITTLE PIPPIN 5 b.m. Sir Percy – Lady Le Quesne (IRE) (Alhaarth (IRE)) [2017/18 h16d[5] h18.9v[5] h18.6v Jan 17] dam half-sister to useful hurdler (2m winner) Diego Cao: modest on Flat, stays 8.5f: similar form over hurdles only when fifth in mares novice at Wetherby. *Tony Coyle*   h87

LITTLE POP 10 b.g. Pasternak – Flagship Daisy May (IRE) (Kahyasi) [2017/18 c110, h112: c15.7g[4] h15.8g[3] h16g[3] c17.2g[4] c16.5d[*] c15.2d[2] c16.8g[pu] c16.4d[pu] Dec 1] angular gelding: fair handicap hurdler: fairly useful handicap chaser: won at Southwell in June, Market Rasen in August and Worcester in September: unproven beyond 17f: acts on good to firm and good to soft going: wears hood: has worn tongue tie, including 4 of last 5 starts: front runner. *Nigel Twiston-Davies*   c120 h102

LITTLE RORY MAC (IRE) 4 b.g. Yeats (IRE) – Solar Quest (IRE) (King's Ride) [2017/18 b16.2v[2] Apr 10] closely related to fair hurdler Mill Quest (19f/2½m winner, by Milan) and half-brother to several winners, including fairly useful hurdlers/useful chasers Mister Hyde (2½m-3m winner, by Beneficial) and Glenquest (2m-3m winner, by Turtle Island), latter stayed 29f: dam 3m hurdle/chase winner: 2/1, signs of inexperience when second in bumper at Hereford (½ length behind Geordie B): should do better. *Philip Hobbs*   b91 p

LITTLE STAMPY (IRE) 7 ch.m. Artan (IRE) – Gold Stamp (Golden Act (USA)) [2017/18 h18.8g[4] h20g h22.1d Aug 26] half-sister to fairly useful hurdler Brads House (2¼m winner, by Rossini) and fair hurdler Littledean Jimmy (2¾m winner, by Indian Danehill): fair on Flat, stays 16.5f: fair maiden hurdler: stays 21f: acts on good to firm and good to soft going: has worn headgear, including last 4 starts. *D. Broad, Ireland*   h100

LITTLE VERN (IRE) 4 b.g. Oscar (IRE) – Silver Valley (IRE) (Henbit (USA)) [2017/18 b15.8d Mar 26] well beaten in bumper. *Colin Tizzard*   b–

LITTLE WINDMILL (IRE) 8 ch.g. Mahler – Ennismore Queen (IRE) (Glacial Storm (USA)) [2017/18 c107, h–: c19.7g[3] h25.8m[4] c25.7m[3] c24d c21.2g[2] c19.7s[3] c21.2s[pu] c21.2v[*] h20v[pu] c25.7d[2] c21.2d[pu] c20.3g[5] Apr 20] poor maiden hurdler: fair handicap chaser: won at Fakenham (amateur) in January: stays 3¼m: acts on good to firm and heavy going: wears headgear: has worn tongue tie, including last 5 starts: front runner: temperamental. *Neil King*   c100 § h65

LIVE FOR TODAY (IRE) 7 b.g. Alflora (IRE) – Uppermost (Montjeu (IRE)) [2017/18 c–: h16.5v h18.5s h16.5v Mar 12] winning pointer: no form in varied company under Rules: tried in tongue tie. *Kevin Bishop*   c– h–

LIVELOVELAUGH (IRE) 8 b.g. Beneficial – Another Evening (IRE) (Saddlers' Hall (IRE)) [2017/18 h135: c21.2s[3] c20v[*] c24v[3] c20.4s[F] Mar 13] good-topped gelding: won Irish maiden point on debut: useful hurdler: useful form over fences: won maiden at Cork (by 3 lengths from Drumconnor Lad) in January: failed to stay when third in Grade 3 novice at Naas (18½ lengths behind Moulin A Vent) later that month: best up to 21f: acts on heavy going: usually races prominently. *W. P. Mullins, Ireland*   c134 h–

LON

LIZ'S DREAM 5 b.m. Dick Turpin (IRE) – Whatcameoverme (USA) (Aldebaran (USA)) [2017/18 b17.7d* b16d Nov 10] sixth foal: half-sister to 3 winners on Flat, including 1m winner (stayed 11.6f) Dream Ruler (by Holy Roman Emperor): dam unraced: better effort in bumpers (modest form) when winning weak race at Fontwell in June: wears hood. *Laura Mongan*   **b81**

LIZZIE LANGTON 7 b.m. Kayf Tara – Madam Flora (Alflora (IRE)) [2017/18 h70: h16.5v⁴ h20.5v² h19.5vᶠ Apr 14] modest maiden hurdler: stays 21f: acts on heavy going: in tongue tie last 5 starts: usually races close up. *Colin Tizzard*   **h85**

LLANCILLO LORD (IRE) 8 b.g. Beneficial – Llancillo Lady (IRE) (Be My Native (USA)) [2017/18 c19.2s³ c19.2vᵖᵘ Dec 21] fairly useful novice hurdler in 2016/17: off a year, little promise both starts over fences: stays 2½m: acts on soft going: usually hooded: often in tongue tie. *Robert Walford*   **c–** **h–**

LLANTARA 7 b.m. Kayf Tara – Lady Llancillo (IRE) (Alflora (IRE)) [2017/18 h87: h16v² h19.2v h16.5s h15.8v² h15.7v⁵ h15.7v* h16.2v* Apr 10] fair handicap hurdler: won at Towcester in March and Hereford (mares) in April: unproven beyond 17f: acts on heavy going: wears tongue tie: often races towards rear. *Tom Symonds*   **h109**

LOCAL SHOW (IRE) 10 br.g. Oscar (IRE) – Loughaderra Rose (IRE) (Roselier (FR)) [2017/18 c–, h129: c24s⁶ c23.8s⁴ c23sᵖᵘ c19.3s² h21.2g Apr 23] lengthy gelding: winning hurdler: smart novice chaser in 2015/16: lightly raced and disappointing since: stays 3m: acts on heavy going: in blinkers last 2 starts. *Sarah Humphrey*   **c126** **h–**

LOCH GARMAN ARIS (IRE) 8 b.g. Jammaal – See Em Aime (IRE) (Little Bighorn) [2017/18 h–: h21.3vᵖᵘ h19.9v⁵ h16.7g Apr 22] bumper winner: no form in maiden/novice hurdles. *Gary Hanmer*   **h–**

LOCH LINNHE 6 b.g. Tobougg (IRE) – Quistaquay (El Conquistador) [2017/18 h107: h23.1v⁶ h23.1s² h23.3vᵖᵘ Apr 7] fair handicap hurdler: stays 23f: acts on soft going: in cheekpieces last 5 starts: tried in tongue tie: front runner/races prominently. *Mark Walford*   **h109**

LOCHNELL (IRE) 9 br.m. Winged Love (IRE) – Nothing For Ever (IRE) (Tikkanen (USA)) [2017/18 c82, h109: c20.5s⁴ c20.5v⁴ c19.3s² c24.1v* c24.1v² c32.6sᵖᵘ h24.3v⁴ Mar 9] rather leggy mare: modest handicap hurdler: fair handicap chaser: won at Ayr in December and January (sixth course success): stays 3¼m: acts on heavy going: often races in rear. *Ian Duncan*   **c110** **h86**

LOCKER ROOM TALK (IRE) 5 b.g. Beneficial – Whistling Gypse (IRE) (Good Thyne (USA)) [2017/18 b16.2s⁶ Jan 16] €50,000 3-y-o, £135,000 4-y-o: third foal: half-brother to bumper winner/fairly useful hurdler Carnspindle (17f-3m winner, by Ask): dam (c88/h74) maiden hurdler/chaser (stayed 25f): runner-up in Irish point: showed up long way in conditionals/amateur bumper at Hereford: capable of better. *Rebecca Curtis*   **b– p**

LOFGREN 7 b.g. Multiplex – Sherry Darling (IRE) (Alflora (IRE)) [2017/18 c105, h125: c21.7m² c17.4s* c17.1g* c15.8g² c21.2g⁴ c21.4g⁵ c20.5g⁵ c24g⁵ c31.8sᵖᵘ c16.5g² Apr 20] sturdy gelding: fairly useful hurdler: fairly useful chaser: won novice at Bangor and novice handicap at Kelso, both in May: should stay further than 2¾m: acts on soft and good to firm going: wears tongue tie. *Donald McCain*   **c127** **h–**

LOGICAL SONG (IRE) 7 b.g. King's Theatre (IRE) – Jaldemosa (FR) (Cadoudal (FR)) [2017/18 h16g h21g c23d² c17.4v* c20d³ c28s* Nov 5] fair handicap hurdler: useful chaser: won maiden at Sligo in September and Cork National (by 12 lengths from Raz de Maree) in November: effective at 17f to 3½m: acts on heavy going: usually travels strongly held up. *Ms Margaret Mullins, Ireland*   **c134** **h101**

LOG ON (IRE) 7 b.g. Scorpion (IRE) – Go Girl (IRE) (Saddlers' Hall (IRE)) [2017/18 h82: c20.1vᵖᵘ c24dᵖᵘ h19.3d h24.4s⁴ h19.7v c20.1vᶠ h25.3s⁶ h19.7v⁴ c21.6v⁵ Apr 16] poor maiden hurdler: poor form over fences: best short of 3m: acts on heavy going: in cheekpieces third to seventh starts: temperamental. *Rose Dobbin*   **c64 §** **h80 §**

LOMHARA 4 b.f. Bahri (USA) – Moonshine Malt (Superlative) [2017/18 b14d Nov 5] half-sister to 2 winners, including fairly useful/temperamental hurdler/chaser The Snail (19f-3m winner, by Namaqualand): dam unraced: hooded, tailed off in junior bumper at Carlisle. *Susan Corbett*   **b–**

LONDON GLORY 5 b.g. Archipenko (USA) – Reflected Image (IRE) (Refuse To Bend (IRE)) [2017/18 h16sᵖᵘ Dec 27] modest on Flat, stays 1¾m: in cheekpieces, pulled up in novice on hurdling debut. *David Thompson*   **h–**

Unibet Elite Hurdle (Limited Handicap), Wincanton—a final win for the ill-fated London Prize;
Lough Derg Spirit (left) chases him home

LONDONIA 6 gr.g. Paco Boy (IRE) – Snowdrops (Gulch (USA)) [2017/18 h90: h15.7m* **h104**
h17.7d* h15.8g² h16.3g h16.8g⁶ h15.8d³ Apr 24] fair handicap hurdler: won at Towcester
and Fontwell in May: stays 19f: acts on good to firm and good to soft going: wears hood/
tongue tie: races towards rear. *Graeme McPherson*

LONDON PRIZE 7 b.g. Teofilo (IRE) – Zibet (Kris) [2017/18 h133: h15.7m h15.3s* **h136**
h16.4s^F Nov 19] compact gelding: useful handicap hurdler: won Elite Hurdle at Wincanton
(by 3 lengths from Lough Derg Spirit) in November: raced around 2m (would have stayed
2½m): acted on soft going: wore cheekpieces last 2 starts: often raced prominently: fatally
injured at Cheltenham. *Ian Williams*

LONELY SOLDIER (IRE) 9 ch.g. Golan (IRE) – Crazy Bear (IRE) (King Charlemagne **h–**
(USA)) [2017/18 h–: h15.8g² Jun 21] maiden pointer: little promise in novice/maiden
hurdles: tried in in cheekpieces: wears tongue tie. *Dave Roberts*

LONE WOLF (IRE) 5 b.g. Gold Well – Luna Lovegood (IRE) (City Honours (USA)) **h126 p**
[2017/18 b16s³ b20s⁵ h16v³ b18s* Apr 27] €33,000 3-y-o: second foal: dam winning **b106**
pointer: useful form in bumpers: much improved when winning maiden at Punchestown
(by head from All For Joy) in April: 16/1, some encouragement when 4¾ lengths third to
Hardline in listed novice at Punchestown on hurdling debut (should do better): in tongue
tie after debut. *Joseph Patrick O'Brien, Ireland*

LONG HOUSE HALL (IRE) 10 b.g. Saddlers' Hall (IRE) – Brackenvale (IRE) (Strong **c145**
Gale) [2017/18 c149, h–: c24s⁴ Jan 27] useful-looking gelding: winning hurdler: smart **h–**
chaser: fourth in Sky Bet Chase (Handicap) at Doncaster (¾ length behind Wakanda) sole
outing in 2017/18: stayed 3m: acted on soft and good to firm going: wore hood/tongue tie:
dead. *Dan Skelton*

LONGHOUSE MUSIC 9 b.m. Gamut (IRE) – Soft Skin (IRE) (Rudimentary (USA)) **c89**
[2017/18 c21g^ur c16g⁵ c16g c17d⁵ c24.4d c21.2d^pu c22.5v^pu c24v⁵ Apr 2] second foal: dam
unraced: point winner: modest maiden chaser: should stay further than 17f: acts on good to
soft going: tongue tied except on third outing: temperament under suspicion. *S. Curling,
Ireland*

LOR

LONGHOUSESIGNORA (IRE) 6 b.m. Milan – Moscow Madame (IRE) (Moscow Society (USA)) [2017/18 h19.9d⁴ h19s⁵ h21v⁴ h21.2d² h20.2s Apr 25] £30,000 5-y-o: fourth foal: half-sister to fairly useful hurdler Moscow Presents (2m-3m winner, by Presenting): dam, of little account, half-sister to fairly useful hurdler/useful chaser (2½m-2¾m winner) Well Presented: winning Irish pointer: fair form over hurdles: will stay 3m: acts on heavy going. *Venetia Williams* — h106

LONG LUNCH 9 b.g. Kayf Tara – Royal Keel (Long Leave) [2017/18 c128, h–: c24m⁵ c24g⁴ Oct 5] good-bodied gelding: winning hurdler: fairly useful handicap chaser: stays 3m, effective at shorter: acts on good to firm and heavy going: wears cheekpieces/tongue tie: usually races in rear. *Charlie Longsdon* — c119 h–

LONGMORE (GER) 7 br.g. Mamool (IRE) – Linara (GER) (Windwurf (GER)) [2017/18 b–: c19.1d⁵ Dec 15] maiden Irish pointer: tailed off in bumper/novice chase. *Simon Waugh* — c–

LONGTOWN (IRE) 7 b.g. Scorpion (IRE) – Desirable Asset (IRE) (Zagreb (USA)) [2017/18 h118p: c24.2sᵖᵘ c19.4v⁶ c20.5s² Apr 9] lightly-raced winning hurdler: fairly useful form over fences: easily best effort when close second to Conna Cross in handicap at Kempton final start: stays 21f: raced on soft/heavy going: tried in tongue tie: travels strongly: open to further improvement as chaser. *Philip Hobbs* — c122 p h–

LONGUEVILLE FLIER (IRE) 9 b.g. Definite Article – Talk The Talk (Terimon) [2017/18 c–, h–: c23.4g³ c24.2g Jun 3] maiden hurdler: poor handicap chaser nowadays: stays 3¼m: acts on soft going: usually in headgear: has worn tongue tie, including last 2 outings. *Micky Hammond* — c70 h–

LOOE BAY 6 b.m. Kirkwall – Dragon Blue (Puget (USA)) [2017/18 b80: b16s⁵ Nov 29] little form in bumpers: tried in hood. *Dominic Ffrench Davis* — b–

LOOKFORARAINBOW 5 b.g. Rainbow High – Look Here's May (Revoque (IRE)) [2017/18 b79: b16.3g³ b16.7g⁵ b15.8d h19.9v⁵ Apr 7] modest form in bumpers: 50/1, fifth in maiden at Uttoxeter (18 lengths behind Secret Legacy) on hurdling debut: tried in hood: capable of better. *Sarah Hollinshead* — h95 p b83

LOOKING WELL (IRE) 9 b.g. Gold Well – Different Level (IRE) (Topanoora) [2017/18 c134, h–: c23.8m c32.8sᵘʳ c31.8gᵖᵘ Apr 21] winning hurdler: useful handicap chaser: in control when swerved and unseated approaching last at Musselburgh second start: out-and-out stayer: acts on soft and good to firm going. *Nicky Richards* — c137 h–

LOOK MY WAY 4 b.g. Pour Moi (IRE) – Casual Glance (Sinndar (IRE)) [2017/18 h16.4v² h15.8v⁴ h16.8v² h16.4s Mar 14] close-coupled gelding: dam half-sister to Imperial Cup winner Scorned: useful on Flat (stays 2¼m), better than ever in 2018: fairly useful juvenile hurdler: won at Ludlow in January: second either side at Newcastle and in Triumph Hurdle Trial (Finesse) at Cheltenham (8 lengths behind Apple's Shakira): will be well suited by at least 2½m. *John Quinn* — h127

LOOKS FROZEN (IRE) 4 ch.g. Frozen Fire (GER) – Miss Beverley (Beveled (USA)) [2017/18 b13.7g³ b13.7v² b15.8d Mar 22] lengthy, rather unfurnished gelding: half-brother to several winners, including fair chaser Owner Occupier (2m-2½m winner, by Foxhound) dam unraced: fair form in bumpers: placed first 2 outings. *Neil Mulholland* — b86

LOOKS LIKE POWER (IRE) 8 b.g. Spadoun (FR) – Martovic (IRE) (Old Vic) [2017/18 c107, h99: h15.8g² c19.4d⁴ c19.4v² c18.9s³ c23.6s* c19.8v⁴ c23.6v* Apr 14] fair handicap hurdler: fairly useful handicap chaser: won at Chepstow in March and April: stays 3m: acts on heavy going: wears headgear/tongue tie: often travels strongly. *Debra Hamer* — c123 h104

LOOKSNOWTLIKEBRIAN (IRE) 7 b.g. Brian Boru – Sheebadiva (IRE) (Norwich) [2017/18 h111: c26.2d² c20.9v* c20.5v* c26.2v⁶ Apr 16] fair hurdler: fairly useful form over fences: won novice handicap at Ffos Las in December and novice at Ay (landed odds despite jumping poorly) in February: again made mistakes final outing: stays 3¼m: acts on heavy going: often races towards rear. *Tim Vaughan* — c125 h–

LOOSE CHIPS 12 b.g. Sir Harry Lewis (USA) – Worlaby Rose (Afif) [2017/18 c140, h–: c23.6dᵖᵘ c24.2s³ c22.7g⁴ c24.2s⁵ c24.2s³ c24g c23.8s⁵ c24m⁶ Apr 26] good-topped gelding: winning hurdler: useful handicap chaser: stays 3½m: acts on good to firm and heavy going: wears headgear: front runner/races prominently: tough. *Charlie Longsdon* — c136 h–

LORD ALDERVALE (IRE) 11 br.g. Alderbrook – Monavale (IRE) (Strong Gale) [2017/18 c76, h–: c25.5g⁴ c25.5dᵖᵘ c21.1m³ c19.7d⁵ c21.6d² Nov 19] well-made gelding: point winner: maiden hurdler: poor maiden chaser: stays 3¼m: acts on soft and good to firm going: has worn headgear/tongue tie: usually leads. *Steve Woodman* — c77 h–

LOR

LORD BALLIM (FR) 8 ch.g. Balko (FR) – Lady Pauline (FR) (Hamas (IRE)) [2017/18 c129, h117: c23.8m⁶ c15.9g c24.2v^pu c20s^pu h19.3v³ h19v Mar 12] fairly useful handicap hurdler/chaser, below form over fences first 4 starts in 2017/18: should stay beyond 2½m: acts on heavy going: usually in headgear/tongue tie: usually races nearer last than first. *Nigel Hawke* — c106 h117

LORD BEN (IRE) 13 b.g. Beneficial – Lady Bluebell (IRE) (Mister Lord (USA)) [2017/18 c120, h114: c17.4g³ c17.2g⁴ c16.3g³ c16.5g² c15.9g c16.5g² c19.9d⁵ Nov 25] well-made gelding: fair hurdler: fair handicap chaser, on long losing run: stays 3m: acts on good to firm and heavy going: in headgear last 5 starts: front runner/races prominently. *Dai Williams* — c114 h–

LORD BRYAN (IRE) 7 b.g. Brian Boru – Run Cat (IRE) (Lord Americo) [2017/18 h108, b87: h21g^pu h21.4g⁶ c20.9v³ c19.4v* c19.2v^pu c20.2v c19.4v³ c20.9v* c19.4s* Apr 27] poor maiden hurdler: fairly useful handicap chaser: won at Chepstow in December, Hereford (novice) in March and Chepstow again in April: stays 3¼m, effective at shorter: acts on heavy going: wears tongue tie: front runner. *Peter Bowen* — c123 h84

LORD BUNNACURRY 7 ch.g. Black Sam Bellamy (IRE) – Lunareva (USA) (Nureyev (USA)) [2017/18 b–: h20.6g^pu h19.9m h23.1s^pu h24s^pu Dec 21] no sign of ability: tried in blinkers: in tongue tie last 2 starts: front runner. *Michael Mullineaux* — h–

LORD CONDI (IRE) 5 ch.g. Papal Bull – Wings To Soar (USA) (Woodman (USA)) [2017/18 b16.7g ab16g Feb 19] modest form in bumpers. *Martin Keighley* — b77

LORD COUNTY (FR) 4 gr.g. Lord du Sud (FR) – County County (FR) (Medaaly) [2017/18 h16.9g⁵ c16.9g⁵ h16.3s⁶ h15.8v³ h16.6s* h16.4v* h16.7v³ h18.9s⁵ h19.9v* Apr 7] good-topped gelding: third foal: dam, French 17f hurdle/chase winner, half-sister to useful hurdler (2m-2½m winner) County Zen: fairly useful handicap hurdler: won at Doncaster (novice) and Newcastle in January, and at Uttoxeter (found plenty) in April: fifth of 6 in maiden at Lyon Parilly on chasing debut, when left Emmanuel Clayeux: will prove suited by 21f+:acts on heavy going: has worn cheekpieces, including last 5 starts. *Oliver Greenall* — c– h117

LORD DUVEEN (IRE) 5 br.g. Doyen (IRE) – Afdala (IRE) (Hernando (FR)) [2017/18 h16.8s⁵ h16s² Mar 17] €62,000 3-y-o: tall gelding: closely related to 3 winners, including useful hurdler/smart chaser Balthazar King (2½m-31f winner), stayed 35f, and useful hurdler For Good Measure (2m/17f winner) (both by King's Theatre), stays 25f: dam unraced: fairly useful form in novice hurdles, shaping well when fifth to Onefortheroadtom in strong race at Exeter on debut: should still improve. *Philip Hobbs* — h116 p

LORD E (IRE) 4 b.g. Lord Shanakill (USA) – Elouges (IRE) (Dalakhani (IRE)) [2017/18 h17.7d⁴ h15.9m Sep 24] dam closely related to useful hurdler/chaser (stayed 3¼m) Pigeon Island: modest maiden on Flat (likely to stay at least 1½m): better form when winning juvenile at Fontwell in September on hurdling debut: bad mistake when well beaten in similar race at Plumpton next time. *Gary Moore* — h105

LORD FENDALE (IRE) 9 ch.g. Erewhon (USA) – Upton Lady (IRE) (Lord Upton (IRE)) [2017/18 h16.7d h15.8g h16.5s⁴ h16.5s⁴ h15.6s⁶ h15.7v h19.5v h20v Feb 18] modest handicap hurdler nowadays: should stay beyond 17f: acts on soft going: wears headgear: tried in tongue tie. *Tim Vaughan* — h94

LORD FRANKLIN 9 ch.g. Iceman – Zell (IRE) (Lend A Hand) [2017/18 h15.7d Dec 28] regressive on Flat: mistakes when well beaten in maiden on hurdling debut. *Andrew Crook* — h–

LORD GETAWAY (IRE) 6 b.g. Getaway (GER) – Terre d'Orient (FR) (Kabool) [2017/18 b15.7d h21.2v h21.6v⁶ h16.6d h20.3g² Apr 20] £9,500 5-y-o: good-topped gelding: fifth foal: half-brother to bumper winner Champagne To Go (by Beneficial), stays 2¾m: dam, 1m-1¼m winner, half-sister to useful chaser (2m/17f winner) Great Travel: winning Irish pointer: modest form only start in bumper: off 10 weeks, much improved form (fair) over hurdles when close second in novice handicap at Southwell: should be suited by further than 2½m. *James Evans* — h108 b80

LORD HEATHFIELD (IRE) 12 br.g. Classic Cliche (IRE) – Garryduff Bridge (IRE) (Taipan (IRE)) [2017/18 c115, h–: c27.6s^pu c24s⁴ c22.2v⁴ c23.6s^pu Mar 22] lengthy gelding: multiple winning pointer: maiden hurdler: formerly fairly useful chaser: below best (mainly in hunters) in 2017/18 (left Graeme McPherson after first start): stays 3¾m: acts on heavy going: wears headgear: front runner/races prominently. *Miss C. L. Mews* — c102 h–

LORD HUNTINGDON 5 b.g. Lord of England (GER) – Marajuana (Robellino (USA)) [2017/18 h110: h16.7s⁴ h16.7g* h15.9m³ h15.3s⁶ h16.6d⁶ Dec 2] fair handicap hurdler: won at Bangor in August: raced around 2m: acts on good to firm going: often travels strongly. *Alan King* — h114

LOS

LORD LANDEN (IRE) 13 br.g. Beneficial – Agua Caliente (IRE) (Old Vic) [2017/18 c98§, h–§: c20.9d* May 6] good-bodied gelding: maiden hurdler: modest handicap chaser: won at Uttoxeter sole start in 2017/18: best up to 2¾m: acts on good to firm and heavy going: used to wear headgear: wears tongue tie: often races freely/finishes weakly. *Fergal O'Brien* — c94 § / h– §

LORD MARMADUKE 5 ch.g. Duke of Marmalade (IRE) – Maid To Treasure (IRE) (Rainbow Quest (USA)) [2017/18 h16s⁶ h15.5d³ h15.8s⁴ h16s Mar 9] sturdy gelding: fair form only outing on Flat: similar form over hurdles: temperamental. *Paul Webber* — h107 §

LORD NAPIER (IRE) 5 b.g. Galileo (IRE) – Jacqueline (IND) (King Charlemagne (USA)) [2017/18 h16.2s⁵ h15.8s* h19.9v* h16.8v⁶ h20.2s* Apr 26] fairly useful maiden on Flat, stays 2m: fairly useful form over hurdles: won maiden at Ludlow in February, novice at Sedgefield in March and novice handicap at Perth in April: stays 2½m: raced only on soft/heavy going: usually races prominently/travels strongly. *Peter Bowen* — h126

LORDOFTHENIGHT (IRE) 6 b.g. Lord Shanakill (USA) – Begine (IRE) (Germany (USA)) [2017/18 b17.7s Apr 15] tailed off in bumper. *Neil Mulholland* — b–

LORD SCOUNDREL (IRE) 9 b.g. Presenting – Noble Choice (Dahar (USA)) [2017/18 c154, h–: c22.5g c24v^pu c21v^pu c25s^ur c29v^pu c20s Apr 25] winning hurdler: useful chaser nowadays: stays 25f: acts on good to firm and heavy going: has worn headgear, including last 4 starts: wears tongue tie. *Gordon Elliott, Ireland* — c141 / h–

LORD TOPPER 5 b.g. Sir Percy – Fugnina (Hurricane Run (IRE)) [2017/18 h110: h16m⁴ h19.1m⁶ h23.3g² c23g⁵ h26g² Sep 26] fair form over hurdles: only fifth to Cuirassier Dempire in novice handicap at Worcester on chasing debut (should do better): stays 3¼m: acts on good to firm going: tried in cheekpieces. *Jamie Snowden* — c– p / h114

LORD WALSINGHAM 4 b.g. Shirocco (GER) – Glorious Twelfth (IRE) (Old Vic) [2017/18 b16s Feb 9] £46,000 3-y-o: first foal: dam (h112), bumper/21f hurdle winner, closely related to fairly useful hurdler/useful chaser (stays 2½m) The West's Awake out of smart French hurdler/fairly useful chaser (2m-19f winner) Bilboa: 9/2, green/not knocked about in maiden bumper: should do better. *Alan King* — b– p

LORD WESSEX 7 b.g. Deltic (USA) – Society Night (IRE) (Moscow Society (USA)) [2017/18 b16.8d Jul 31] tailed off in maiden bumper. *Richard Mitchell* — b–

LORD WINDERMERE (IRE) 12 b.g. Oscar (IRE) – Satellite Dancer (IRE) (Satco (FR)) [2017/18 c146d, h–: c25.9v^F c34.3s^ur c30s Apr 28] workmanlike gelding: winning hurdler: formerly high-class chaser: won Cheltenham Gold Cup in 2014: well beaten sole completed start in 2017/18: stays 3¼m: acts on heavy going: tried in headgear/tongue tie: often races towards rear. *J. Culloty, Ireland* — c111 / h–

LORD WISHES (IRE) 11 b.g. Milan – Strong Wishes (IRE) (Strong Gale) [2017/18 c134, h124: h20.1g⁶ Jun 17] tall, good-bodied gelding: fairly useful handicap hurdler/useful chaser at best: stays 3m: acts on good to firm and heavy going: wears headgear: tried in tongue tie. *James Ewart* — c– / h102

LORENZO (IRE) 8 br.g. Flemensfirth (USA) – La Speziana (IRE) (Perugino (USA)) [2017/18 h20.2g⁶ May 17] winning pointer: no promise in bumpers and maiden hurdle (tongue tied). *Stuart Crawford, Ireland* — h–

LOS ALAMOS (IRE) 5 b.g. Galileo (IRE) – Artistique (IRE) (Linamix (FR)) [2017/18 b16m³ b16.8d* b16.5m⁴ h16d h16v⁵ Feb 8] closely related to high-class French 11f/1½m winner Montmartre (by Montjeu) and half-brother to several other winners on Flat: dam, useful French 15f winner, half-sister to useful French hurdler (2m-2¼m winner) Tertre: fair maiden on Flat (will prove suited by 1½m): useful form in bumpers: won at Punchestown (impressively by 11 lengths from Vocarium) in May: better effort in maiden hurdles when fifth at Thurles: wears tongue tie: front runner/races prominently: should do better again. *Joseph Patrick O'Brien, Ireland* — h103 p / b111

LOS CERRITOS (SWI) 6 ch.g. Dr Fong (USA) – La Coruna (SWI) (Arazi (USA)) [2017/18 h18.9s h17.9s h20g⁶ Jul 10] modest on Flat (stays 9f): well held over hurdles. *C. von der Recke, Germany* — h–

LOST HISTORY (IRE) 5 b.g. Strategic Prince – Prelude (Danzero (AUS)) [2017/18 h16s³ h16.3s h15.9v⁴ h16v⁵ Feb 19] workmanlike gelding: fair on Flat, stays 1½m: shaped well when third in big-field novice at Lingfield on hurdling debut: disappointing subsequently: will prove best at sharp 2m. *John Spearing* — h97

LOST IN NEWYORK (IRE) 11 b.g. Arakan (USA) – Lace Flower (Old Vic) [2017/18 c–, h70: h15.5d c19.2d⁶ h19.6d⁶ Apr 21] workmanlike gelding: poor hurdler/maiden chaser: best short of 3m: acts on soft and good to firm going: has worn headgear: tried in tongue tie: usually races nearer last than first. *Nick Kent* — c55 / h–

Taylor O'Dwyer's "Lostintranslation"

LOSTINTRANSLATION (IRE) 6 b.g. Flemensfirth (USA) – Falika (FR) (Hero's Honor (USA)) [2017/18 h16d² h16.3d² h16.3d* h15.7v⁶ h16.4s h20s² Apr 14] €38,000 3-y-o: strong gelding, will make a chaser: seventh foal: half-brother to a winning pointer by Overbury: dam, placed over hurdles, French 1m-1½m winner on Flat, half-sister to useful French hurdler/fairly useful chaser (17f/2¼m winner) Dark Steel: fourth in Irish maiden point: smart form over hurdles: won maiden at Newbury (by 3½ lengths from Admiral Barratry) in December: much improved last 2 outings, ½-length second to Black Op in Mersey Novices' Hurdle at Aintree final one: stays 2½m: acts on soft going: fine prospect for novice chases in 2018/19. *Colin Tizzard* **h147**

LOST LEGEND (IRE) 11 b.g. Winged Love (IRE) – Well Orchestrated (IRE) (King's Ride) [2017/18 c89§, h–: c23.8g³ c23.9g⁵ c26.1g* c24s² c24g³ Sep 26] lengthy gelding: winning hurdler: fairly useful handicap chaser nowadays: won at Uttoxeter in June: stays 3¼m: acts on good to firm and heavy going: has worn headgear: front runner/races prominently: moody. *Jonjo O'Neill* **c119 § h–**

LOSTNFOUND 5 b.m. Midnight Legend – La Cerisaie (Old Vic) [2017/18 b77p: h20.6g⁵ h15.8v* h16v² h19.9v² h20.5s^pu Mar 24] sturdy mare: fair form over hurdles: won mares novice at Uttoxeter in November: stays 2½m: acts on heavy going: tried in tongue tie: often races freely. *Jamie Snowden* **h107**

LOTS OV (IRE) 4 b.f. Rock of Gibraltar (IRE) – Bright Enough (Fantastic Light (USA)) [2017/18 b13.7g b13.1g b14d⁴ b12.4s⁴ Dec 9] fourth foal: half-sister to 2 winners on Flat, including useful 1¼m winner (stayed 1½m) Pack Leader (by Hurricane Run): dam 1m winner: first form in junior bumpers with 5¾ lengths fourth to Kuragina at Wetherby: poor form on Flat subsequently: tried in blinkers. *John Wainwright* **b72**

LOTUS POND (IRE) 10 b.g. Beneficial – Capard Lady (IRE) (Supreme Leader) [2017/18 c–, h–: c21.6g³ c21.2d^F c27.5d^pu Jun 9] multiple winning pointer: maiden hurdler: modest form over fences: should stay beyond 2¾m: acts on heavy going: tried in hood: in tongue tie last 4 starts. *W. Bryan* **c90 h–**

LOU

LOUD AND CLEAR 7 b.g. Dalakhani (IRE) – Whispering Blues (IRE) (Sadler's Wells (USA)) [2017/18 b101: h16.7d^3 h20.2g^2 h20.2s^5 Apr 26] dual bumper winner: only fair form over hurdles: tried in hood/tongue tie. *Iain Jardine* — h111

LOUD AS LIONS (IRE) 5 b.g. Flemensfirth (USA) – Misspublican (IRE) (Overbury (IRE)) [2017/18 b15.7d b16.2s^4 b16.8s Feb 23] useful-looking gelding: green, shaped like a stayer in bumpers. *Tom Symonds* — b62

LOUGHADERRA PRINCE (IRE) 9 b.g. Oscar (IRE) – Loughaderra Rose (IRE) (Roselier (FR)) [2017/18 c20.9s^5 Jan 29] fell on point debut: fair maiden hurdler: off 10 months/left Alan Fleming, shaped as if needing run in hunter on chasing debut: stays 2¾m: acts on soft going: front runner/races prominently. *Tom George* — c100 h–

LOUGH DERG FARMER (IRE) 6 b.g. Presenting – Maryiver (IRE) (Runyon (IRE)) [2017/18 h122p: c23.8d h24.2v^4 h23.5s Mar 25] sturdy gelding: Irish maiden point winner: fairly useful hurdler: 5/2, unsuited by track when pulled up in novice handicap at Ascot on chasing debut, jumping markedly left: should stay 3m: acts on soft going: in cheekpieces last 2 starts: temperament under suspicion. *Nicky Henderson* — c– h119

LOUGH DERG ISLAND (IRE) 10 b.g. Court Cave (IRE) – Clondalee Fred (IRE) (Jurado (USA)) [2017/18 c–, h98: c26.2v^{pu} Apr 16] point winner: modest maiden hurdler: pulled up both starts in chases: stays 2¾m: acts on heavy going: tried in tongue tie: weak finisher. *Mrs J. M. Hollands* — c– h–

LOUGH DERG JEWEL (IRE) 7 b.g. Oscar (IRE) – River Valley Lady (IRE) (Salt Dome (USA)) [2017/18 h118: c20.5v* c20.5v* c23.4s Jan 14] fairly useful hurdler: similar form in handicap chases: won novice events at Ayr in November and December (unchallenged): stays 25f, effective at shorter: acts on heavy going: usually leads. *Donald McCain* — c126 h–

LOUGH DERG SPIRIT (IRE) 6 b.g. Westerner – Sno-Cat Lady (IRE) (Executive Perk) [2017/18 h130: h15.3s^2 h16.3v^6 h20.3v^6 h19.8s Apr 28] well-made gelding: off mark in Irish maiden points at second attempt: useful handicap hurdler: good second in Elite Hurdle at Wincanton (3 lengths behind London Prize) on return: lightly raced after, twice shaping well: should prove best at further than 2m: acts on soft going. *Nicky Henderson* — h134

LOUGH DERG VOICES (IRE) 5 ch.g. Doyen (IRE) – Clemintine (IRE) (Common Grounds) [2017/18 h16g h23d^{pu} Sep 29] no sign of ability in points/over hurdles. *Pat Coffey, Ireland* — h–

LOUGH KENT 9 b.g. Barathea (IRE) – King's Doll (IRE) (King's Best (USA)) [2017/18 c–, h109: h17.2d* h17.2g* h17.2s^2 h17.2d^4 h16.8s^5 ab16.3g* h16g Apr 20] good-topped gelding: fairly useful handicap hurdler: won at Cartmel in May (conditionals) and June: also won jumpers bumper at Newcastle in March: winning chaser: stays 19f: acts on soft going: has worn cheekpieces. *James Moffatt* — c– h115

LOUGH LEGEND (IRE) 4 b.g. Watar (IRE) – Gibboghstown (IRE) (Second Empire (IRE)) [2017/18 b16v^3 b16.2d^3 Apr 23] modest form in bumpers: will stay beyond 2m. *Sue Smith* — b79

LOUGH RYN (IRE) 6 br.g. Court Cave (IRE) – Media View (IRE) (Presenting) [2017/18 b15.7d b20.7s^4 h16.8v^5 Apr 17] first foal: dam, winning pointer, third in 2½m bumper: fair form on first of 2 outings in bumpers: similar form in maiden on hurdling debut, though again found less than looked likely: disappointing next time. *Neil Mulholland* — h105 b–

LOUGH SALT (IRE) 7 b.g. Brian Boru – Castlehill Lady (IRE) (Supreme Leader) [2017/18 h110: h24.1d* h25.3d^6 ab16.3g^5 h21.3d^2 h25d Apr 24] close-coupled gelding: fairly useful handicap hurdler: won at Wetherby in October: stays 3m: acts on soft going: tried in cheekpieces: usually races towards rear. *Richard Guest* — h115

LOUGHVIEW LADDIE (IRE) 9 b.g. Shantou (USA) – Par Street (IRE) (Dolphin Street (FR)) [2017/18 h62, b–: h20.1g^F h16.2g h17.2g^3 h22g^{pu} h22.1d Aug 28] poor maiden hurdler: should prove suited by at least 2½m: has worn cheekpieces: wears tongue tie: often races towards rear: temperamental. *Noel C. Kelly, Ireland* — h67 §

LOUIS PHILLIPE (IRE) 11 ch.g. Croco Rouge (IRE) – Presenting's Wager (IRE) (Presenting) [2017/18 c89, h–: c25.8d^{pu} Jul 31] maiden hurdler: modest handicap chaser: went wrong only outing in 2017/18: stays 3¼m: acts on good to firm and good to soft going: in cheekpieces last 5 starts: has worn tongue tie. *Linda Blackford* — c– h–

LOU

LOUIS' VAC POUCH (IRE) 6 b.g. Oscar (IRE) – Coming Home (FR) (Exit To Nowhere (USA)) [2017/18 h124, b87: h19.5d⁶ h24.7s* h24s h24.7s Apr 14] useful-looking gelding: useful handicap hurdler: improved further when winning at Aintree (by 2¼ lengths from Forza Milan) in November: down field last 2 starts: stays 25f: acts on soft and good to firm going: wears hood: races freely, and tends to be ridden from well off pace. *Philip Hobbs*   **h138**

LOULOUMILLS 8 b.m. Rob Roy (USA) – Etching (USA) (Groom Dancer (USA)) [2017/18 h91: h22.7g² h22.1d⁵ h16.7g³ h20.2d h16.8g⁶ h20.9g⁵ Sep 20] modest handicap hurdler: stays 23f: acts on heavy going: tried in cheekpieces: wears tongue tie: front runner/ races prominently. *Maurice Barnes*   **h87**

LOUSE TALK (IRE) 6 b.g. Mahler – Foxy-Lady (IRE) (Yashgan) [2017/18 h21s* h19.3v* h24.7spu Apr 13] €21,000 3-y-o, £45,000 5-y-o: tall gelding: half-brother to fair hurdler/winning pointer Knockbrack Vic (2½m winner, by Old Vic): dam failed to complete both starts in points: off mark in Irish maiden points at second attempt: fairly useful form over hurdles: won novices at Warwick in February and Carlisle in March: stiff task final outing: should be suited by 3m. *Charlie Longsdon*   **h120**

LOU VERT (FR) 6 b.g. Vertigineux (FR) – Lourinha (FR) (Loup Solitaire (USA)) [2017/18 c116, h104: c20.1g* May 18] compact gelding: maiden hurdler: fairly useful form over fences: won handicap at Perth sole outing in 2017/18: stays 2½m: acts on good to firm going: tried in hood: wears tongue tie. *Paul Nicholls*   **c117 h–**

LOVATO (GER) 6 br.g. Lauro (GER) – Larella (GER) (Anabaa (USA)) [2017/18 h19.1g² h16.8g² h15.8m* h16g* h16.2sF Aug 19] half-brother to a winning hurdler/chaser in Italy by Sinndar: dam half-sister to fairly useful hurdler (stayed 3m) Landero: useful on Flat (stays 2m): fairly useful form over hurdles: won novices at Uttoxeter and Worcester in July: let down by jumping in handicap final start: unproven beyond 2m: acts on good to firm going: in cheekpieces last 3 starts. *Dr Richard Newland*   **h120**

LOVE AT DAWN (IRE) 5 br.m. Winged Love (IRE) – Presentingatdawn (IRE) (Presenting) [2017/18 b16.7g b16.2g h16.4s⁶ h16.8v⁵ h20.6v² Apr 14] angular mare: fourth foal: sister to fairly useful hurdler/chaser (2½m winner) Wishmoor: dam, ran twice in points, half-sister to useful hurdler/chaser (stays 25f) Knight of Noir (by Winged Love): poor form in bumpers: easily best effort in novice hurdles when second at Newcastle final outing, suited by increase in trip: will stay 3m. *Peter Niven*   **h90 b69**

LOVEHERANDLEAVEHER (IRE) 6 b.m. Winged Love (IRE) – Rowdy Exit (IRE) (Exit To Nowhere (USA)) [2017/18 h20.5sur Jan 17] £62,000 5-y-o: first foal: dam, winning pointer, half-sister to fairly useful chaser (stayed 23f) Rowdy Rampage: off mark in Irish points at second attempt: 8/1, unseated end of back straight in mares novice won by All Currencies at Newbury on hurdling debut. *Nicky Henderson*   **h– p**

LOVE LANE (IRE) 5 b.m. Stowaway – Inquisitive Look (Montjeu (IRE)) [2017/18 h15.7v⁴ h16.8s* h20.6g⁵ Apr 22] £10,000 4-y-o: first foal: dam (h99), maiden hurdler, 1¼m winner on Flat: placed in Irish points: fair form over hurdles: won mares novice at Exeter in February: should stay at least 2½m. *Henry Oliver*   **h106**

LOVELY BUBBLY 7 gr.g. Kayf Tara – Champagne Lil (Terimon) [2017/18 c94, h93: c20.3g c17.4d⁴ c16.3spu Dec 4] modest maiden hurdler: similar form on chasing debut: failed to progress: unproven beyond 17f: acted on good to firm and good to soft going: tried in visor: wore tongue tie: dead. *Tim Vaughan*   **c74 h–**

LOVELY JOB (IRE) 8 ch.g. Touch of Land (FR) – Wyckoff Queen (IRE) (Carefree Dancer (USA)) [2017/18 c24g* c21.4g² c24.2g* c25d² c23g* c26g⁴ Apr 18] workmanlike gelding: winning hurdler: useful handicap chaser: won novice events at Uttoxeter in June, Hexham in August and Taunton in November: stays 3¼m: acts on heavy going: front runner/races prominently: sound jumper. *Fergal O'Brien*   **c136 h–**

LOVELY SCHTUFF (IRE) 6 b.g. Court Cave (IRE) – The Long Bill (IRE) (Phardante (FR)) [2017/18 b15.6g⁵ h19.3d³ h20.2s³ Apr 25] £38,000 5-y-o: half-brother to bumper winner/fairly useful hurdler G'day Mate (2m winner, by Taipan) and fair hurdler/winning pointer Mister Mister (23f winner, by September Storm): dam unraced half-sister to fair hurdler/fairly useful chaser (2m-2¾m winner) King of The Arctic: off mark in Irish points at sixth attempt: fifth in maiden bumper at Musselburgh: better effort over hurdles (fair form) when third to Going Gold in novice at Carlisle on hurdling debut. *Jackie Stephen*   **h106 b84**

LOVELY TOUCH (IRE) 9 b.g. Humbel (USA) – My Touch (IRE) (Supreme Leader) [2017/18 h62: h21.6g* h20.3g* h20.3g² May 24] Irish maiden pointer: fair handicap hurdler: won at Fontwell and Southwell in May: much improved again when runner-up final start (finished lame): stays 2¾m: best form on good going. *Sam Thomas*   **h110**

484

LOVENORMONEY (IRE) 7 br.g. Winged Love (IRE) – Dixies Gem (IRE) (Anzillero (GER)) [2017/18 h119: h23.9v[6] h23.6v* h24s h23.1v* h24s Mar 15] good-topped gelding: won completed start in Irish maiden points: useful handicap hurdler: won at Chepstow in December and Exeter (by 6 lengths from Solomn Grundy) in February: stays 3m: acts well on heavy going: in headgear last 4 starts: front runner/races prominently: can look hard work. *Warren Greatrex* — h136

LOVERBOY (FR) 7 b.g. Winged Love (IRE) – Tartan Belle (Classic Cliche (IRE)) [2017/18 h19.2g[3] h19.6s Nov 15] ran once on Flat: fairly useful form over hurdles: left C. Gourdain and off 2½ years, much better effort in 2017/18 when third in handicap at Fontwell: stays 19f: acts on soft going. *Dan Skelton* — h115

LOVES DESTINATION 7 b.m. Dubai Destination (USA) – Bijou Love (IRE) (Winged Love (IRE)) [2017/18 h111: h17.7d[6] h19.8s[2] h24.6v[3] h21s[6] h20.5v[3] h24.6s[pu] Apr 9] lengthy mare: fair handicap hurdler: barely stays 3m: acts on heavy going. *Chris Gordon* — h114

LOVE THE LEADER (IRE) 10 b.g. Fruits of Love (USA) – Suelena (IRE) (Supreme Leader) [2017/18 c102, h109: h23.3d h19.9d h18.6g h18.5d[3] h20.3d h20.6g[pu] h21.4g h23.9g h19g Nov 30] modest handicap hurdler nowadays: lightly-raced winning chaser: thorough stayer: acts on heavy going: has worn headgear: usually races nearer last than first: sometimes races lazily. *Johnny Farrelly* — c–, h95

LOWANBEHOLD (IRE) 11 gr.g. Cloudings (IRE) – Marble Quest (IRE) (Roselier (FR)) [2017/18 c96, h–: c26.2g[3] c31.9v* c24.1v[3] c26.6s[4] c26.9v[4] c26.2d[3] c26.2v* c30.6s[6] Apr 27] maiden hurdler: fair handicap chaser: won at Hexham in November and Kelso in April: out-and-out stayer: acts on heavy going: tried in cheekpieces. *Sandy Forster* — c104, h–

LOWCARR MOTION 8 b.g. Rainbow High – Royalty (IRE) (Fairy King (USA)) [2017/18 h103§: h19.3m[2] c23.4g[pu] c24.2g[pu] c24g[pu] h21.2g h20.9d h24g Nov 17] modest handicap hurdler: no promise over fences: stays 25f: acts on soft going: usually in headgear nowadays: tried in tongue tie: temperamental. *Micky Hammond* — c– §, h86 §

LOWER HOPE DANDY 11 gr.g. Karinga Bay – Cheeky Mare (Derrylin) [2017/18 c135, h113: c24.2v[3] c26s[3] Mar 12] big, workmanlike gelding: fair hurdler: much better chaser after only 4 starts, shaping well when third in handicap at Newbury final outing in 2017/18: stays 3¼m: acts on heavy going: usually races close up. *Venetia Williams* — c129, h–

LOW SUN 5 b.g. Champs Elysees – Winter Solstice (Unfuwain (USA)) [2017/18 h16.7g* h16v[4] h16s[2] h16s h16s* h16.5d[4] h20s[5] Apr 28] fairly useful on Flat, stays 10.5f: useful hurdler: won maiden at Bellewstown in August and handicap at Fairyhouse in April: stays 2½m: acts on soft going: races prominently: ridden by Katie O'Farrell (7) last 3 outings. *W. P. Mullins, Ireland* — h135

LUBATIC (FR) 5 b.g. Sleeping Car (FR) – Luba (FR) (Mansonnien (FR)) [2017/18 b92: h17.7d[pu] h16d h16.3g h16v h20.7s[2] h15.9v[2] h16.5m Apr 25] rather unfurnished gelding: bumper winner: modest maiden hurdler: stays 21f: acts on heavy going: in hood last 3 starts (has raced freely). *Neil Mulholland* — h99

LUCA BRAZI (IRE) 6 b.g. Mahler – Carriacou (Mark of Esteem (IRE)) [2017/18 h–: h15.8m[5] h22g[4] h16g[pu] h23d[pu] h19.9d h15.5d[6] h15.5v[pu] c15.9v[ur] Mar 9] of no account: has worn hood: temperamental. *Aytach Sadik* — c– §, h– §

LUCARNO DANCER 8 b.m. Lucarno (USA) – Sing And Dance (Rambo Dancer (CAN)) [2017/18 h–: h16.2g[4] h18.1g h19.3v h16.2s* h16.8s[5] Nov 28] modest handicap hurdler: won at Hexham in November: should stay beyond 2m: acts on soft going: has worn hood/tongue tie, including throughout 2017/18. *Raymond Shiels* — h79

LUCCA LADY (IRE) 7 b.m. Milan – Trail Storm (IRE) (Supreme Leader) [2017/18 b18g[2] b16d[2] b16d[4] b16.3s* h20.6g[2] h20.6g[2] h16.3d[2] Apr 22] €15,500 3-y-o: fourth foal: dam (h104), 2½m hurdle winner, half-sister to fairly useful hurdler (2m-21f winner) Lady Zephyr: placed in points: fairly useful form in bumpers: won mares event at Stratford in October: fairly useful form over hurdles: best effort when close second in mares handicap at Stratford final outing: left R. P. Rath after third start: likely to stay beyond 2½m: front runner/races prominently. *Katy Price* — h116, b95

LUCCOMBE DOWN 8 b.g. Primo Valentino (IRE) – Flaming Rose (IRE) (Roselier (FR)) [2017/18 c–, h123: h22.8m[4] h23.1g[5] h23g[3] h23.3d h23g[2] h23.9g[3] h24s Dec 15] sturdy gelding: fairly useful handicap hurdler: little aptitude for chasing only attempt: stays 3m: acts on good to firm and good to soft going: has worn blinkers: front runner/races prominently. *Fergal O'Brien* — c–, h122

LUC

LUCKIME (IRE) 6 gr.g. Oscar (IRE) – Blossom Rose (IRE) (Roselier (FR)) [2017/18 b90p: b16d^5 h19.5s h19.6s^5 h21.2s^3 h25.3s* h25d^F h23.9v* Apr 12] fair form in bumpers: fairly useful form over hurdles: won novice at Catterick in February and handicap at Taunton in April: looks a thorough stayer: acts on heavy going. *Venetia Williams*   h124 b87

LUCKOFTHEDRAW (FR) 5 gr.g. Martaline – La Perspective (FR) (Beyssac (FR)) [2017/18 b80: b15.8g^4 b15.8v* b15.8v^3 h16v^4 h15.8v* h20v^2 Apr 15] fairly useful form in bumpers: left Christian Williams, won conditionals/amateur event at Ffos Las in November: fairly useful form over hurdles: won novice at same course in April: stays 2½m: in hood last 5 starts: remains with potential. *Nigel Twiston-Davies*   h118 p b95

LUCK OF THE LEGION (IRE) 5 b.m. Getaway (GER) – Grangeclare Flight (IRE) (Old Vic) [2017/18 b15.7d h15.7g Nov 30] €16,000 3-y-o: third foal: half-sister to fairly useful chaser Present Flight (23f-27f winner, by Presenting): dam (b94), bumper winner, sister to useful hurdler (stayed 2½m) Grangeclare Lark: well beaten in maiden bumper and maiden hurdle (needed experience). *Tom Lacey*   h– b–

LUCK'S BOY 5 b.g. Malinas (GER) – Mons Meg (Terimon) [2017/18 b13.7g Apr 20] down field in bumper at Fontwell. *Gary Moore*   b–

LUCKY ACCORD 6 ch.g. Schiaparelli (GER) – Prissie Lucinda (IRE) (Accordion) [2017/18 b16s h15.7v^5 Apr 27] lengthy, workmanlike gelding: green when well beaten in maiden bumper/novice hurdle. *Philip Hide*   h58 h–

LUCKY BOO (IRE) 9 b.m. Kodiac – Lucky April (Whittingham (IRE)) [2017/18 h16.2g h16.2g^{pu} May 28] poor maiden on Flat, stays 7f: no future over jumps: wears hood. *Hugh Burns*   h–

LUCKY ESTEEM 4 b.f. Yorgunnabelucky (USA) – Dream Esteem (Mark of Esteem (IRE)) [2017/18 h16.3m^{pu} Jul 16] dam (h143), 2m hurdle winner, half-sister to useful hurdler/smart chaser (stayed 21f) I'm So Lucky: modest maiden on Flat (stays 1m): off 11 months, pulled up in juvenile on hurdling debut. *Neil Mulholland*   h–

LUCKY LUCARNO 6 b.g. Lucarno (USA) – Sari Rose (FR) (Vertical Speed (FR)) [2017/18 b16.8s^{bd} b15.6s^4 h16.8v^6 Feb 22] lengthy gelding: has scope: shaped like a stayer in bumpers: needed experience in novice on hurdling debut. *Sue Smith*   h– b63

LUCKY PAT (IRE) 10 br.g. Spadoun (FR) – Little Well Lady (IRE) (Alderbrook) [2017/18 c20m^6 c17m^3 c19d^2 c17g^{bd} c18.2s^2 c20.5g^4 h19.5s^6 Sep 8] lightly-raced maiden on Flat: winning hurdler: useful handicap chaser: runner-up at Listowel and Galway (4 lengths behind Neverushacon) in 2017/18: best up to 2½m: acts on soft and good to firm going: has worn hood/tongue tie. *Mrs D. A. Love, Ireland*   c134 h98

LUCY MC (IRE) 7 gr.m. Tikkanen (USA) – Careless Abandon (IRE) (Mull of Kintyre (USA)) [2017/18 h95: h19d h15.8d May 20] maiden pointer: modest hurdler at best: regressed further in 2017/18: stays 2½m: acts on good to soft going. *Barry Leavy*   h–

LUMA'S GIFT 6 b.m. Apple Tree (FR) – Pems Gift (Environment Friend) [2017/18 b16.3g^6 b16s^6 h15.8s h21.2d Mar 22] seventh foal: sister to fair hurdler/fairly useful chaser Mick The Jiver (2¾m-3m winner) and half-sister to bumper winner Maggie Aron (by Generous): dam unraced: well beaten in bumpers (left Richard Hawker after debut) and over hurdles. *Claire Dyson*   h– b–

LUNA JUNE (IRE) 5 gr.m. Mahler – Halfway Home (Presenting) [2017/18 b16.5v^4 Apr 12] sixth foal: half-sister to fairly useful hurdler/useful chaser Balbriggan (2½m-3¼m winner) and modest hurdler/chaser Lily of Killarney (23f winner) (both by King's Theatre): dam unraced half-sister to bumper winner/very smart hurdler (stays 3m) Sam Spinner: 3/1, fourth in mares maiden bumper at Taunton (22½ lengths behind Miss Heritage). *Fergal O'Brien*   b66

LUNAR FLOW 7 b.g. With The Flow (USA) – Misty Move (IRE) (Saddlers' Hall (IRE)) [2017/18 c99, h79: c24d* c25.5d^3 c30.7v c24.2v^2 c24.2v^5 c24v* Apr 7] winning hurdler: fair handicap chaser: won at Uttoxeter in October and April (galloped clear strongly to take course record to 3-3): thorough stayer: acts on heavy going: usually in headgear nowadays: in tongue tie last 2 starts: usually races close up. *Jamie Snowden*   c114 h–

LUNAR LOGIC 6 b.g. Motivator – Moonmaiden (Selkirk (USA)) [2017/18 h93: h15.8g h16.7g^6 Aug 19] maiden hurdler: no promise in 2017/18: raced around 2m: has worn headgear: tried in tongue tie. *Sarah-Jayne Davies*   h–

LUNGARNO PALACE (USA) 7 b.g. Henrythenavigator (USA) – Good Time Sally (USA) (Forestry (USA)) [2017/18 h15.8s* h16s^3 Apr 9] fair on Flat (stays 2m, has shown quirks): fairly useful form over hurdles: won maiden at Huntingdon in March. *Fergal O'Brien*   h121

LUSO BENNY (IRE) 6 ch.g. Beneficial – Luas Luso (IRE) (Luso) [2017/18 b16.7g h21g³ h16.7g⁴ h23.3d² h20.9g⁶ h23.3s h19.4d h20.6s⁵ Dec 26] fourth foal: brother to fairly useful 2m hurdle winner Wes Hardin, and half-brother to bumper winner/useful chaser Call It Magic (2½m-23f winner, by Indian River) and a winning pointer by Marienbard: dam (b92) won bumper on only start: mid-field in bumpers: modest maiden hurdler: left Ms Margaret Mullins after hurdling debut: stays 23f: acts on good to soft going: tried in tongue tie: usually races nearer last than first: room for improvement in jumping. *Patrick Holmes* **h92 b81**

LUST FOR GLORY (IRE) 5 b.m. Getaway (GER) – Maisie Presenting (IRE) (Presenting) [2017/18 b15.7s³ Feb 17] €18,500 3-y-o, £240,000 4-y-o: first foal: dam unraced half-sister to useful hurdler (2½m winner) Theatre Bird: won Irish point on debut: 6/4, shaped well when third in mares bumper at Ascot (5 lengths behind Buildmeup-buttercup): should do better. *Nicky Henderson* **b86 p**

LUVLY BOY BLUE 7 b.g. Blueprint (IRE) – Mellouise (Handsome Sailor) [2017/18 h20.6v³ Apr 14] seventh foal: half-brother to bumper winner/fair hurdler Abzuson (3m winner) and a winning pointer (both by Abzu): dam showed little in bumpers/on Flat: 100/1 and tongue tied, third in novice hurdle at Newcastle (5 lengths behind Eternally Yours) on debut: entitled to do better. *Susan Corbett* **h96 p**

LYCIDAS (GER) 9 b.g. Zamindar (USA) – La Felicita (Shareef Dancer (USA)) [2017/18 h117: h16.2g* h16.5g³ Jun 16] fairly useful handicap hurdler: won at Kelso in May: stays 19f: acts on good to firm and heavy going: hooded prior to last 3 outings. *James Ewart* **h120**

LYGON ROCK (IRE) 5 b.g. Robin des Champs (FR) – Cute Lass (IRE) (Flemensfirth (USA)) [2017/18 b–: b16.7d⁴ h19.6s² h21.2s² h19s³ h21.7s³ Mar 27] much better effort in bumpers when fourth at Market Rasen on return: fairly useful form over hurdles: runner-up first 2 outings: will stay 3m: front runner/races prominently. *Henry Daly* **h115 b85**

LYNDSAYS LAD 5 b.g. Kayf Tara – Ceilidh Royal (Erhaab (USA)) [2017/18 b16s Feb 9] second foal: dam (b71), ran twice in bumpers, half-sister to useful hurdler/very smart chaser (stayed 3¼m) Barbers Shop: 7/1, seventh in maiden bumper at Kempton. *Nicky Henderson* **b76**

M

MAB DAB (IRE) 7 b.g. Papal Bull – Pret A Porter (UAE) (Jade Robbery (USA)) [2017/18 h106, b65: h21g⁶ h25.6g² h20.5d³ h25s² h21.7g* Apr 20] good-topped gelding: fair handicap hurdler: won at Fontwell in April: stays 25f: acts on good to firm going. *Linda Jewell* **h106**

MABELA 4 b.f. Oscar (IRE) – Histoire de Moeurs (FR) (Kaldounevees (FR)) [2017/18 b13.7g* b16.8g Apr 19] has scope: fourth foal: dam (c118/h107), unreliable 2m/17f hurdle/chase winner, also smart 10.5f-1½m winner on Flat: modest form in bumpers: won junior event at Huntingdon in November. *Dan Skelton* **b82**

MACARDLE (IRE) 5 b.g. Beneficial – Monavale (IRE) (Strong Gale) [2017/18 h16.1d⁴ b16v⁴ b16.4d³ h17s h16.2s⁵ Apr 26] €11,000 3-y-o, resold £26,000 3-y-o: brother to fair hurdler/fairly useful chaser Any Bets (2m-2½m winner) and half-brother to 2 winners, including fair hurdler Ballycrystal Court (19f winner, by Court Cave): dam, maiden hurdler, out of half-sister to Champion Hurdle winners Granville Again and Morley Street: fair form in bumpers: 16/1, fifth in novice at Perth (6¾ lengths behind Asylo) on hurdling debut: left Miss Elizabeth Doyle after second start. *Philip Kirby* **h98 b87**

MAC BELLA 6 ch.m. Black Sam Bellamy (IRE) – Macnance (IRE) (Mandalus) [2017/18 h–, b–: h15.7g^F h20.3g³ h16g⁴ h16g⁴ h19g⁴ Nov 16] modest form over hurdles: stays 19f. *Evan Williams* **h95**

MAC CENNETIG (IRE) 6 b.g. Brian Boru – Buslane (IRE) (Tidaro (USA)) [2017/18 h19.5d⁶ h16d⁴ h16d² h16.8s⁶ h16s^pu Dec 26] €3,500 3-y-o: second foal: dam unraced sister to smart hurdler/chaser (stayed 3¼m) Spendid: modest form in bumpers: modest maiden hurdler: left Joseph Patrick O'Brien after fourth start: best effort at 2m: acts on good to soft going: sometimes in tongue tie. *Micky Hammond* **h99**

MACKIE DEE (IRE) 6 b.g. Westerner – Whatdoyouthinkmac (IRE) (Supreme Leader) [2017/18 h94, b–: h19.3m³ h19.9g⁵ h20.3d³ h19.4d Dec 15] modest form over hurdles: stays 23f: best form on good going: usually in hood. *John Mackie* **h97**

MAC

MACKSVILLE (IRE) 5 gr.g. Mastercraftsman (IRE) – Fairest of All (IRE) (Sadler's Wells (USA)) [2017/18 h15.8s h15.7v[4] h15.8s[4] Mar 14] fair on Flat, stays 2m: modest form over hurdles: will stay 2½m. *James Eustace* — h94

MACK THE MAN (IRE) 4 b.g. Flemensfirth (USA) – Nifty Nuala (IRE) (Saddlers' Hall (IRE)) [2017/18 b15.3d Apr 22] 16/1, eighth in bumper at Wincanton (10¾ lengths behind Ebony Gale). *Evan Williams* — b80

MAC N CHEESE (IRE) 8 b.g. Milan – Fox Burrow (IRE) (Supreme Leader) [2017/18 h23.9v* c20.5v[3] c23.4v[F] h24.3v[6] h22.7v* Feb 15] fairly useful handicap hurdler: won at Perth in September and Kelso in February: similar form when third in novice handicap at Ayr completed start over fences: will stay long distances: best form on soft/heavy going: tried in hood. *Keith Dalgleish* — c118 h118

MAC TOTTIE 5 b.g. Midnight Legend – Tot of The Knar (Kayf Tara) [2017/18 b16g[4] b16g[2] b16.8d[2] b16g[2] Sep 3] first foal: dam (c120/h132) 2m-23f hurdle/chase winner: fair form in bumpers. *Neil Mulholland* — b88

MADAM ANNA (IRE) 5 b.m. Papal Bull – Melaaya (USA) (Aljabr (USA)) [2017/18 b17.7g* b16g[5] ab16g Jan 30] sixth foal: sister to Italian 7.5f/1m winner Papal Dream and half-sister to 6f winner Reve du Jour (by Iffraaj): dam 6f winner: modest form in bumpers: won at Plumpton in May: tried in hood. *Linda Jewell* — b81

MADAME CLAUD 5 ch.m. Champs Elysees – Change Partners (IRE) (Hernando (FR)) [2017/18 h16.8v[bd] h16s h19.2v[pu] h15.3v[pu] h16.8s h15.3v[pu] h23.9m[pu] Apr 25] half-sister to modest hurdler/chaser Lady Willa (2m/17f winner, by Footstepsinthesand) and 2m hurdle winner Lady Bridget (by Hawk Wing): dam half-sister to fairly useful hurdler/winning pointer (2m-2½m winner) Texas Ranger: fair on Flat, stays 2m: no form over hurdles: in headgear last 4 starts. *Mark Gillard* — h–

MADAME EMBER 5 br.m. Multiplex – Madam Blaze (Overbury (IRE)) [2017/18 b16g h16g h19.5d h18.7g Nov 2] fourth foal: dam (h84), maiden hurdler (stayed 3m), sister to fairly useful hurdler/fair chaser (stayed 3¼m) Georgian King: tailed off in bumper: no form over hurdles. *Matt Sheppard* — h– b–

MADAME FIONA 6 gr.m. Overbury (IRE) – Roslin (Roscoe Blake) [2017/18 b70: b15.7g[2] b15.8d[tr] h19.5s[5] h21.7s h21.7s[4] Mar 27] modest form in bumpers: poor form over hurdles: usually in headgear: temperamental. *Martin Keighley* — h81 § b79 §

MADAM SCULLY 5 ch.m. Flying Legend (USA) – Sally Scally (Scallywag) [2017/18 b16.8g Apr 23] third foal: dam winning pointer: 40/1, seventh of 8 in mares bumper at Sedgefield. *Tina Jackson* — b–

MAD FOR ACTION (IRE) 5 b.g. Beneficial – Subtle Hint (IRE) (Subtle Power (IRE)) [2017/18 h16.7g h15.8d[6] h15.7d h24.1v Jan 23] poor form over hurdles. *Jonjo O'Neill* — h75

MADINAT 4 ch.g. Haafhd – Let It Be (Entrepreneur) [2017/18 b15.7s b16.2d Apr 23] no form in bumpers. *Gillian Boanas* — b–

MAD JACK MYTTON (IRE) 8 b.g. Arcadio (GER) – Gilt Ridden (IRE) (Heron Island (IRE)) [2017/18 c133, h–: h16.5g* h16.7g[6] c16.5g* c16.5g[4] c16m[3] Oct 11] lengthy gelding: useful handicap hurdler: won at Aintree (by 2¾ lengths from Curious Carlos) in June: useful chaser: won novice at Worcester in September: stays 2½m, effective at shorter: acts on soft and good to firm going: in tongue tie last 3 starts. *Jonjo O'Neill* — c131 h133

MAEBH (IRE) 4 b.f. Doyen (IRE) – South Queen Lady (IRE) (King's Ride) [2017/18 b12.6s[3] b12.4s* b16v[3] b17s Apr 12] €8,500 3-y-o: lengthy filly: half-sister to 3 winners, including fairly useful hurdler/chaser Humbie (2m-3m winner, by Karinga Bay) and fair chaser Behemoth (23f winner, by Presenting): dam, maiden pointer, out of half-sister to dam of Cheltenham Gold Cup winner Denman: fair form in bumpers: won at Wetherby in January. *Seamus Mullins* — b86

MAESTRO ROYAL 9 b.g. Doyen (IRE) – Close Harmony (Bustino) [2017/18 h130: h21d[4] h20.5d c19.9s* c16v* c16.8s[4] Mar 25] tall gelding: useful handicap hurdler: similar form over fences: won maiden at Huntingdon in January and novice at Lingfield in March: stays 21f: acts on heavy going: tried in cheekpieces. *Nicky Henderson* — c131 h131

MAGGIE BLUE (IRE) 10 b.m. Beneficial – Top Ar Aghaidh (IRE) (Topanoora) [2017/18 c–, h105: h22.7g h23.3g[pu] Jun 3] fair hurdler, well beaten both starts in 2017/18: maiden chaser: stays 3¼m: acts on good to firm and heavy going: front runner/races prominently. *Harriet Graham* — c– h–

MAGGIE'S DAWN 6 b.m. Bach (IRE) – Maggie's Opera (Dr Massini (IRE)) [2017/18 h69: h23s[pu] May 17] little form over hurdles. *David Brace* — h–

MAG

MAGGIES LEGEND 5 b.m. Midnight Legend – Very Special One (IRE) (Supreme Leader) [2017/18 b16d b15.7s b20.7g^5 Apr 24] workmanlike mare: second foal: dam (c98/h122), 3¼m hurdle winner, half-sister to useful hurdler/chaser (stayed 3¾m) The Bishop Looney: no form in bumpers: 150/1, fifth in mares novice at Huntingdon (21 lengths behind Jet Set) on hurdling debut: in tongue tie last 2 starts. *Alex Hales*   h101 b–

MAGGIO (FR) 13 b.g. Trempolino (USA) – La Musardiere (FR) (Cadoudal (FR)) [2017/18 c132, h118: h21.4v^4 h21v^4 c26.2v^3 c34.3s^{pu} Apr 14] rather leggy gelding: fairly useful hurdler: useful chaser: third in minor event at Down Royal (19 lengths behind Mala Beach) in March: stays 25f: acts on good to firm and heavy going: has worn headgear, including in 2017/18: wears tongue tie. *Patrick Griffin, Ireland*   c132 h126

MAGICAL MAN 11 b.g. Lahib (USA) – Majestic Di (IRE) (Zaffaran (USA)) [2017/18 c89§, h–: c19.4s^4 c23.8v* c25.3v^4 c24.5v^6 c24.5v^6 Mar 29] maiden hurdler: modest handicap chaser: won at Ffos Las in November: stays 25f: acts on heavy going: usually wears headgear: often races towards rear: temperamental (has run out). *Debra Hamer*   c90 § h–

MAGICAL THOMAS 6 ch.g. Dylan Thomas (IRE) – Magical Cliche (USA) (Affirmed (USA)) [2017/18 h91: h19.9d h16g^5 h20g^3 h20g h17.7m* h15.9m^3 h16.8d Oct 12] modest handicap hurdler: won at Fontwell in August: stays 2¼m: acts on good to firm and heavy going: wears cheekpieces/tongue tie. *Neil Mulholland*   h91

MAGIC BULLET (IRE) 7 b.g. Flemensfirth (USA) – Some Bob Back (IRE) (Bob Back (USA)) [2017/18 h69, b79: h21g^5 May 15] modest form in bumpers: fair form over hurdles: in hood last 5 starts: usually races towards rear. *Nicky Henderson*   h102

MAGIC DANCER 6 b.g. Norse Dancer (IRE) – King's Siren (IRE) (King's Best (USA)) [2017/18 h109: h21d h15.8g^2 h16d* h16.4d* h15.7d ab16d h16.8g* Apr 18] sturdy gelding: fairly useful handicap hurdler: won at Kempton (conditional) and Cheltenham (novice) in November, and conditionals/amateur event at Cheltenham in April: left Charlie Longsdon after first start: has form at 21f, raced mainly around 2m: acts on soft going: wears cheekpieces/tongue tie: usually races towards rear. *Kerry Lee*   h128

MAGIC MONEY 10 b.m. Midnight Legend – Sticky Money (Relkino) [2017/18 c121, h111: c20.1m^4 c26.1m Jul 2] angular mare: fair hurdler: fairly useful handicap chaser, below form both starts in 2017/18: stays 25f: acts on good to firm and good to soft going: wears cheekpieces: often races towards rear. *Warren Greatrex*   c112 h–

MAGIC OF LIGHT (IRE) 7 b.m. Flemensfirth (USA) – Quest of Passion (FR) (Saumarez) [2017/18 h24v^3 c18d^2 c21s* c20.6v^F c20s^2 c20v^2 c21s c24.1s^2 c20s^1 c21s* Apr 27] €20,000 4-y-o: half-sister to smart hurdlers Mughais (2m-2¾m winner, by Sadler's Wells) and Pythagora (2m/17f winner) and fairly useful hurdler/smart chaser Sizing Platinum (2m-2¼m winner), latter pair by Definite Article: dam placed up to 15f on Flat in France: bumper winner: fair handicap hurdler: won at Punchestown in 2016/17: useful chaser: won maiden at Fairyhouse in November and mares handicap at Punchestown (by 1½ lengths from Goodthynemilan) in April: second in Grade 2 mares novice at Thurles (8 lengths behind Dinaria des Obeaux) in January: stays 3m: acts on heavy going: has worn headgear, including final start: usually races close up. *Mrs J. Harrington, Ireland*   c134 h105

MAGIC OF MILAN (IRE) 5 b.m. Milan – Laughing Lesa (IRE) (Bob Back (USA)) [2017/18 h16.7s h15.7s h17s^6 h15.8d^6 Apr 24] h106 4-y-o: medium-sized mare: closely related to 2 winners, including fair hurdler Knocklayde Vic (2m-2½m winner, by Old Vic), and half-sister to 2 winners, including fair chaser Basil Fawlty (23f winner, by Balakheri): dam, 2m hurdle winner, half-sister to top-class chaser (2m-25f winner) Merry Gale: unplaced in Irish point: poor form over hurdles. *Sam England*   h74

MAGIC RIVER (IRE) 7 ch.g. Indian River (FR) – All Magic (IRE) (Ashkalani (IRE)) [2017/18 h105: h20g^3 Jun 3] point winner: fair form over hurdles: should be suited by at least 2¼m. *Charles Whittaker*   h101

MAGIE DU MA (FR) 5 b.m. Sageburg (IRE) – To Much Fun (Act One) [2017/18 h130: h18.5s^4 c19.2g^2 c23g^4 Aug 1] good-topped mare: useful hurdler at best, below form since leaving P. Chevillard in 2016/17: fair form over fences: unproven beyond 17f: acts on soft going: in hood last 5 starts, tongue tied last 4. *David Pipe*   c102 h112

MAGISTRAL 8 b.g. Manduro (GER) – Tamalain (USA) (Royal Academy (USA)) [2017/18 h88: h16v h15.6s^{pu} Jan 3] fairly raced on Flat: lightly-raced maiden hurdler: in cheekpieces last 2 starts. *Linda Perratt*   h–

MAGNA CARTOR 8 b.g. Motivator – Hora (Hernando (FR)) [2017/18 h118: h16g^F h19.2g^6 h24s^{pu} Dec 28] lengthy gelding: fairly useful handicap hurdler: best at around 2m: acts on good to soft going: has worn hood. *John Joseph Hanlon, Ireland*   h122

MAG

MAGNA SAM 4 b.g. Black Sam Bellamy (IRE) – Angie Marinie (Sabrehill (USA)) [2017/18 b16s b16g Apr 21] unplaced in point: no form in bumpers. *Steve Flook* — h–

MAGNOLIA RIDGE (IRE) 8 b.g. Galileo (IRE) – Treasure The Lady (IRE) (Indian Ridge) [2017/18 h90: h16.8g[5] h16.2g[3] h16.7g[5] h18.6g[pu] h16.2d h19.9g[3] Oct 3] poor handicap hurdler nowadays: stays 2½m: best form on good going: wears headgear. *Mark Walford* — h82

MAGNUM (IRE) 5 gr.g. Lawman (FR) – Coventina (IRE) (Daylami (IRE)) [2017/18 h16.2g h16.2g[2] h15.8g[4] h16.2v h16.7g[5] h15.6m Nov 8] fairly useful maiden on Flat, stays 1½m: modest form over hurdles: best effort at 2m: tried in cheekpieces: in tongue tie last 5 starts. *Susan Corbett* — h87

MAGNUS ROMEO 7 b.g. Manduro (GER) – Chili Dip (Alhaarth (IRE)) [2017/18 h93: h15.8m h16.8d[4] h21.6s[pu] Oct 24] stocky gelding: modest maiden hurdler, no form in 2017/18: unproven beyond 17f: acts on soft and good to firm going: tried in blinkers: wears tongue tie. *Johnny Farrelly* — h–

MAGOO (IRE) 6 gr.g. Martaline – Noche (IRE) (Night Shift (USA)) [2017/18 h19.2v* Mar 17] half-brother to smart hurdler/very smart chaser Sam Winner (2m-27f winner, by Okawango): fair brother on Flat for Y. Durepaire, winner at 1¼m: fairly useful form over hurdles: won juvenile for Y. Fouin in 2016/17: in tongue tie, also won handicap at Fontwell on sole outing in 2017/18: open to further improvement. *Paul Nicholls* — h121 p

MAGUIRE'S GLEN (IRE) 10 b.g. Craigsteel – Next Venture (IRE) (Zaffaran (USA)) [2017/18 c111, h–: h20g[4] h18.5d[2] h21.6v* h23.1s[pu] h21.1s h21g[3] h23.3v[2] h21.4v[pu] c19.4v* c19.4v[4] c19.4s[4] Apr 27] fairly useful handicap hurdler: won at Newton Abbot in October: fair handicap chaser: won at Ffos Las in April: stays 23f: acts on heavy going: tried in cheekpieces. *Grace Harris* — c113 h115

MAHARI (IRE) 5 b.g. Duke of Marmalade (IRE) – Mission Secrete (IRE) (Galileo (IRE)) [2017/18 h17g[pu] h16v[3] h15.8d[pu] Mar 26] closely related to fair hurdler Miro (2¼m winner, by Rock of Gibraltar): useful on Flat for A. Fabre, stays 1½m: fair form when third in novice at Chepstow, standout effort over hurdles. *Kerry Lee* — h114

MAHLER BAY (IRE) 8 b.g. Mahler – Belalzao (IRE) (Alzao (USA)) [2017/18 h81: c19.3g[4] h20.6g c19.3g[5] c16d[pu] c19.3d c23.4g[4] c19.9m[6] h18.6d h16.8s Nov 28] maiden pointer: maiden hurdler, no form in 2017/18: poor form over fences: tried in headgear/tongue tie: temperamental. *Kenny Johnson* — c80 § h–

MAHLERDRAMATIC (IRE) 8 br.g. Mahler – Image of Vermont (IRE) (Accordion) [2017/18 h116: h18.6g[6] h16s[5] h20.5s c24.2s[pu] c19.9s[4] c20v[4] c19.2s[2] Mar 26] fair form over hurdles in 2016/17, well below that level in 2017/18: modest form over fences: should be suited by further than 2½m: acts on soft going: in cheekpieces last 4 starts: usually in tongue tie: usually races close up. *Brian Ellison* — c96 h79

MAHLER LAD (IRE) 8 b.g. Mahler – Sister Merenda (IRE) (Dr Massini (IRE)) [2017/18 c102, h–: c23.9g[pu] c26.3s[4] c23.8d* c26.2v[2] Apr 17] lightly-raced hurdler: fair handicap chaser: won at Musselburgh in February: stays 3¼m: acts on heavy going: wears headgear: front runner/races prominently. *Donald McCain* — c112 h–

MAHLERMADE (IRE) 5 ch.g. Mahler – Double Concerto (IRE) (Brahms (USA)) [2017/18 b83: b16b[6] h16s[2] h19.6d[5] Nov 25] modest form in bumpers: fair form over hurdles: better effort when second in maiden at Chepstow in November: should stay beyond 2m. *Alan King* — h108 b81

MAHLER'S FIRST (IRE) 6 b.g. Mahler – Fridays Folly (IRE) (Flemensfirth (USA)) [2017/18 b–: h23.1v[4] h23.6v[pu] h15.3v[5] h18.5v[pu] Apr 17] poor form over hurdles: tried in cheekpieces: usually races towards rear. *Victor Dartnall* — h84

MAHLERS STAR (IRE) 8 ch.g. Mahler – Celestial Rose (IRE) (Roselier (FR)) [2017/18 c112, h105: c20.5g[2] c23g[5] c21m[3] Jul 7] fair maiden hurdler: similar form over fences: stays 21f: acts on good to soft going: tried in visor/tongue tie. *David Bridgwater* — c105 h–

MAHLERVOUS (IRE) 5 b.g. Mahler – Brook Style (IRE) (Alderbrook) [2017/18 b78: b16.4s h15.7d* h15.7v[2] h16.5v[ur] h21v[2] h20.3g Apr 18] good-topped gelding: modest form in bumpers: fairly useful form over hurdles: won maiden at Southwell in December: will be suited by 3m: acts on good to soft going. *Warren Greatrex* — h117 b–

MAH MATE BOB (IRE) 6 b.g. Mahler – Bobset Leader (IRE) (Bob Back (USA)) [2017/18 h20.1v h20.1s[6] h16s Nov 29] workmanlike gelding: no form over hurdles. *George Bewley* — h–

MAID OF MILAN (IRE) 7 br.m. Milan – Joes Lady (IRE) (Win Quick (IRE)) [2017/18 h108: c25.8g* c22.5d³ c24.2s^F Nov 21] winning hurdler: fairly useful form over fences: won novice handicap at Newton Abbot in October: stays 3¼m: acts on soft and good to firm going: front runner. *Charlie Mann*   c116 h–

MAID OF TUSCANY (IRE) 7 b.m. Manduro (GER) – Tuscania (USA) (Woodman (USA)) [2017/18 h101: h16d^ur h15.9m⁶ h16.3g³ h15.8d^pu h15.7d³ Nov 21] modest handicap hurdler nowadays: stays 2¼m: acts on good to soft going: usually wears headgear. *Neil Mulholland*   h90

MAIN FACT (USA) 5 b.g. Blame (USA) – Reflections (Sadler's Wells (USA)) [2017/18 h20g⁴ h20.2g h19.9g h16.8s* h19.9s^pu h19.7v* h16.4v⁴ Apr 15] fairly useful on Flat in France, stays 11f: modest handicap hurdler: won at Sedgefield in November and Wetherby (novice) in March: stays 2½m: best form on soft/heavy going: in hood last 5 starts: usually races nearer last than first. *Dianne Sayer*   h98

MAIRE BANRIGH 6 b.m. King's Theatre (IRE) – La Marianne (Supreme Leader) [2017/18 h21.2d h15.8s Jan 12] £40,000 4-y-o, £320,000 5-y-o: third foal: half-sister to fairly useful hurdler/useful chaser Ballykan (2½m-3¼m winner, by Presenting): dam (c103/h108), 21f hurdle winner (stayed 3m), half-sister to useful hurdler/chaser (stayed 3m) Banjaxed Girl (by King's Theatre): Irish point winner: poor form over hurdles: tried tongue tied. *Dan Skelton*   h67

MAJESTIC GIRL (IRE) 5 b.m. Royal Applause – Pretty Majestic (IRE) (Invincible Spirit (IRE)) [2017/18 h15.7g Oct 11] modest maiden on Flat, stays 1m: tailed off in mares maiden on hurdling debut. *Steve Flook*   h–

MAJESTIC MAN (IRE) 5 b.g. Majestic Missile (IRE) – Windomen (IRE) (Forest Wind (USA)) [2017/18 b15.7g Oct 26] tailed off in maiden bumper: little impact on Flat. *Ronald Thompson*   b–

MAJESTIC MOLL (IRE) 6 b.m. King's Theatre (IRE) – Artist's Muse (IRE) (Cape Cross (IRE)) [2017/18 b89: h19.5d⁶ h21.2g² h19.4d* h20.3g Apr 19] bumper winner: fair form over hurdles: won mares novice at Doncaster in December: usually leads: remains open to improvement. *Emma Lavelle*   h112 p

MAJESTIC TOUCH (IRE) 7 br.g. Kalanisi (IRE) – Alexander Divine (Halling (USA)) [2017/18 h107p: h15.8d* May 6] fairly useful form over hurdles: won maiden at Uttoxeter on sole outing in 2017/18. *Philip Hobbs*   h115

MAJINGILANE (IRE) 6 b.g. Winged Love (IRE) – Kiora Lady (IRE) (King's Ride) [2017/18 h–: h19.9v h20.5v Jan 7] rather unfurnished gelding: no form over hurdles: tried in cheekpieces. *Warren Greatrex*   h–

MAJOR DAVIS (FR) 6 b.g. Vision d'Etat (FR) – Majorica Sancta (FR) (Saint des Saints (FR)) [2017/18 h100p, b86: h15.8m² h15.8g^ur h21.6m² Jul 7] angular gelding: fair form in bumpers: similar form over hurdles. *Warren Greatrex*   h101

MAJOR HINDRANCE (IRE) 8 ch.g. Kris Kin (USA) – Ten Dollar Bill (IRE) (Accordion) [2017/18 h108p: c22.5s c19.4v^bd c19.6v³ c19.2v* c20v³ c20v² c19.2v⁵ Apr 8] winning hurdler: fairly useful handicap chaser: won at Exeter in January: will be suited by 3m+: acts on heavy going: often races prominently: temperamental. *Henry Oliver*   c121 § h–

MAJOR RIDGE (IRE) 9 b.g. Indian Danehill (IRE) – Native Novel (IRE) (Be My Native (USA)) [2017/18 c82, h–: c24.2d c25.2v⁶ c26.3v³ c24.2d⁶ Apr 23] lightly-raced hurdler: poor handicap chaser: stays 3¼m: acts on heavy going: has worn tongue tie, including final start: usually races close home. *Micky Hammond*   c67 h–

MAKE IT HAPPEN (IRE) 9 b.g. Saffron Walden (FR) – Kelpie (IRE) (Kahyasi) [2017/18 c88, h–: h18.1g² h18.1v^ur h16v h18.1v* Apr 16] fair handicap hurdler: won at Kelso (conditional) in April: twice-raced chaser: stays 2½m: acts on heavy going: tried in cheekpieces: in tongue tie last 4 starts: front runner/races prominently. *Lucinda Russell*   c– h98

MAKE ME A FORTUNE (IRE) 10 b.g. Heron Island (IRE) – Biora Queen (IRE) (Old Vic) [2017/18 c105, h–: h24.1d h24s^pu h23.1v^pu Jan 17] medium-sized gelding: useful hurdler at best, no form in 2017/18: maiden chaser: wears cheekpieces: tried in tongue tie. *Steve Gollings*   c– h–

MAKES YOU STRONGER 6 ch.g. Major Cadeaux – Verus Decorus (IRE) (Titus Livius (FR)) [2017/18 b15.8d Nov 18] in tongue strap, tailed off in bumper. *Lisa Williamson*   b–

MAKITORIX (FR) 5 gr.g. Makfi – Goldamix (IRE) (Linamix (FR)) [2017/18 h16v* h16s^pu h16s⁴ h16v⁶ h16s⁴ h16s⁵ Feb 25] fairly useful on Flat for Y. Durepaire, stays 11.5f: h130

MAK

useful form over hurdles: won maiden at Listowel in September: fourth in Coral Hurdle (Handicap) at Leopardstown (5 lengths behind Off You Go) in February: raced only at 2m on soft/heavy going: in hood/tongue tie last 2 starts. *W. P. Mullins, Ireland*

MALA BEACH (IRE) 10 b.g. Beneficial – Peppardstown (IRE) (Old Vic) [2017/18 c22.5v² c24v* c24s^{pu} c26.2v* c24v² Apr 1] strong gelding: winning hurdler: very smart chaser: won Troytown Handicap Chase at Navan (by 2¾ lengths from Dont Tell No One) in November and minor event at Down Royal (by 9½ lengths from Bonny Kate) in March: second in Imperial Call Chase at Cork (2¼ lengths behind Sumos Novios) in April: likely to stay long distances: acts on heavy going. *Gordon Elliott, Ireland* **c155 h–**

MALACHITE 5 gr.g. Malinas (GER) – Kali (Linamix (FR)) [2017/18 b16g b15.7d³ b15.8s⁵ h20.7s* h19.8d⁶ Apr 22] tall, good-topped gelding: half-brother to several winners, including fairly useful hurdler/useful chaser Midnight Cowboy (19f2/2½m winner, by Midnight Legend), stays 3m, and fair hurdler Danceintothelight (2m-21f winner, by Dansili): dam 7f winner: fair form in bumpers: similar form over hurdles: won maiden at Huntingdon in February. *Nicky Henderson* **h111 b93**

MALACHYS GIRL (IRE) 5 b.m. Darsi (FR) – Borleagh Princess (IRE) (Presenting) [2017/18 b16.8g⁵ Apr 19] £28,000 4-y-o: fifth foal: half-sister to useful hurdler/smart chaser Monbeg Notorious (2¾m-25f winner, by Milan) and modest hurdler Katie's Hen (19f winner, by Shantou): dam (h84) lightly raced in bumpers/over hurdles: Irish point winner: in hood, 25/1, fifth in mares bumper at Cheltenham (4¼ lengths behind Hawthorn Cottage). *Ben Pauling* **b92**

MALAPIE (IRE) 10 b.g. Westerner – Victorian Lady (Old Vic) [2017/18 h113: h23.6s⁴ h23.3v⁴ h23.3v* h25s h20.5v* h23.5s h23.1v³ h22.8v h25.5v³ c21.7v* Apr 27] workmanlike gelding: fairly useful handicap hurdler: won at Uttoxeter in December and Leicester in January: 13/8, also won maiden at Towcester (by 7 lengths from Indian Hawk) on chasing debut: stays 3¼m: acts on heavy going. *Caroline Bailey* **c122 h122**

MALAYA (FR) 4 b.f. Martaline – Clarte d'Or (FR) (Kendor (FR)) [2017/18 h17.4s* h16d² h16s* h17v³ h16g² h15.7s* h17s Apr 12] useful-looking filly: fairly useful on Flat in France, stays 1m: useful hurdler: won listed event at Auteuil in May, Wensleydale Juvenile Hurdle at Wetherby (by 4 lengths from City Dreamer) in November and juvenile handicap at Ascot (by 3¾ lengths from Eragon de Chanay) in March: second in Adonis Juvenile Hurdle at Kempton (7 lengths behind Redicean) in February: left S. Culin after first start: raced around 2m: acts on soft going. *Paul Nicholls* **h133**

MALINAS JACK 4 b.g. Malinas (GER) – Sphere (IRE) (Daylami (IRE)) [2017/18 b13d³ b14s² b16.5d Apr 24] compact gelding: third foal: half-brother to 1¼m winner Inflexiball (by Refuse To Bend): dam (h83), lightly raced over hurdles, 1½m winner on Flat, half-sister to fairly useful hurdler (2½m winner) Isle of Ewe: fairly useful form in bumpers: best effort when second in listed event at Cheltenham (3¾ lengths behind Acey Milan) in January: left John Mackie after second start. *Henry de Bromhead, Ireland* **b102**

MALINDI BAY (FR) 5 b.m. Malinas (GER) – La Grande Villez (FR) (Villez (USA)) [2017/18 b17.7s* b16.3s h20.6g⁴ Oct 21] €4,500 3-y-o, £25,000 4-y-o: third foal: dam (c117/h121), 2m-2½m hurdle/chase winner, half-sister to fairly useful hurdler/very smart chaser American (by Malinas): Irish point winner: fair form in bumpers: won mares event at Fontwell in September: 14/1, fourth in mares novice at Market Rasen (12¼ lengths behind Cabaret Queen) on hurdling debut: should improve. *James Evans* **h91 p b92**

MALL DINI (IRE) 8 b.g. Milan – Winsome Breeze (IRE) (Glacial Storm (USA)) [2017/18 c145, h–: c22.5s⁵ c29s⁴ c20v⁵ c26s² c29v^{pu} Apr 2] good-topped gelding: winning hurdler: smart maiden chaser: second in Fulke Walwyn Kim Muir Chase at Cheltenham (½ length behind Missed Approach) in March: stays 3¼m: acts on heavy going: in blinkers last 2 starts: wears tongue tie: often races towards rear/travels strongly. *Patrick G. Kelly, Ireland* **c148 h–**

MALPREEDY (IRE) 6 b.m. Mahler – Miles Apart (IRE) (Roselier (FR)) [2017/18 h68, b–: h20g⁵ h20.6g h22.1g^{pu} h19.9v^{pu} h15.7v² h19.9v^{pu} Mar 23] poor maiden hurdler: in cheekpieces last 2 starts: tongue tied final start: usually races prominently. *David Loughnane* **h74**

MALTON ROSE (IRE) 7 b.m. Milan – Pharney Fox (IRE) (Phardante (FR)) [2017/18 b16g* h19.9g* Jul 19] £20,000 3-y-o: half-brother to 3 winners, including fairly useful hurdler/fair chaser Bale O'Shea (2m-2¾m winner, by Bob Back) and bumper winner Pharney Lady (by Flemensfirth): dam (b78), maiden in bumpers (ran once over hurdles), half-sister to fairly useful hurdler (stayed 2½m) Back To Ben Alder: won conditionals/ **h118 b98**

MAN

amateur bumper at Worcester (by 7 lengths from Mac Tottie) on debut: 8/13, also won conditionals maiden at Uttoxeter (by 25 lengths from Gettysburg Address) on hurdling debut 3 weeks later, but not seen out again. *Nicky Henderson*

MAMOO 5 ch.g. Sir Percy – Meredith (Medicean) [2017/18 h15.9g^2 h17.7m^3 h15.8d^5 h20d^4 h20s* h23.4s h20v^3 h20.3g^6 Apr 20] modest maiden on Flat, stays 1½m: modest handicap hurdler: won at Fakenham in December: stays 2½m: acts on soft and good to firm going: in headgear last 4 starts. *Neil King* **h99**

MANCE RAYDER (IRE) 5 b.g. Flemensfirth (USA) – J'y Viens (FR) (Smadoun (FR)) [2017/18 b93p: h21.6v^{pu} h19.5v^{pu} h23.1d^4 Apr 21] sturdy gelding: bumper winner: fair form when fourth in maiden at Bangor, standout effort over hurdles. *Philip Hobbs* **h111**

MAN FROM MARS 6 b.g. Schiaparelli (GER) – Diletia (Dilum (USA)) [2017/18 h119: h21s Jan 13] well-made gelding: fairly useful hurdler, excuses sole outing in 2017/18: unproven beyond 2m: acted on soft and good to firm going: dead. *Nick Williams* **h106**

MANGATA (FR) 4 b.g. Cape Cross (IRE) – Kong Moon (FR) (Hernando (FR)) [2017/18 h16d^{pu} h16.7s^{pu} h16s^{pu} Nov 29] fair maiden on Flat for H-A. Pantall, stays 11.5f: no form over hurdles. *Philip Kirby* **h–**

MANGO CAP (FR) 7 gr.g. Zambezi Sun – Medjai (FR) (Kendor (FR)) [2017/18 c113, h114: c16.2g^5 c19.4d^F May 21] sturdy gelding: fair hurdler/maiden chaser: stayed 3m: acted on heavy going: wore headgear/tongue tie: dead. *Matt Sheppard* **c109 h–**

MANHATTAN MEAD 8 ch.g. Central Park (IRE) – Honey Nut (Entrepreneur) [2017/18 c102, h–§: c23v^{pu} Apr 12] workmanlike gelding: point winner: fair maiden hurdler: similar form from 2 starts in chases: stays 3m: acts on soft and good to firm going: often in headgear: temperamental. *Paul Hamer* **c– § h– §**

MANHATTAN SPRING 7 b.g. Central Park (IRE) – Risky May (Petoski) [2017/18 h16v^6 h16.3s h16.3s^{pu} Jan 17] lengthy gelding: bumper winner: modest form over hurdles: will stay 2½m. *Seamus Mullins* **h94**

MAN IN BLACK (FR) 9 gr.g. Turgeon (USA) – Mimosa de Wasa (FR) (Roakarad) [2017/18 c84, h78: c19.8g^4 May 22] Irish point winner: modest maiden hurdler: poor form in chases: stays 21f: acts on heavy going: has worn cheekpieces, including sole outing in 2017/18: often races prominently. *Philip Kirby* **c68 h–**

MANITOWOC COUNTY (IRE) 6 b.g. Darsi (FR) – Murphys Appeal (IRE) (Lord of Appeal) [2017/18 h16.8g^4 h19.3v^3 h22.7g^6 h20.6s Dec 23] £30,000 4-y-o: close-coupled gelding: first foal: dam, poor maiden hurdler (stayed 21f), half-sister to fairly useful hurdler/useful staying chaser Willie John Daly: Irish point winner: fourth in bumper at Sedgefield: modest form over hurdles: should be suited by further than 19f. *Brian Ellison* **h97 b77**

MANKALA (IRE) 8 b.g. Flemensfirth (USA) – Maracana (IRE) (Glacial Storm (USA)) [2017/18 h20.6s^5 h21.4v^6 h21v^5 c20.3d^5 Apr 21] rangy gelding: fair form over hurdles: in tongue tie, 10/1, fifth in novice handicap at Bangor (18¼ lengths behind Kapcorse) on chasing debut. *Jennie Candlish* **c102 h104**

MANLEY COMMON (IRE) 6 b.g. Kayf Tara – Royalrova (FR) (Garde Royale) [2017/18 b16s Nov 8] well beaten in bumper: dead. *Venetia Williams* **b–**

MAN LOOK 6 b.g. Nayef (USA) – Charlecote (IRE) (Caerleon (USA)) [2017/18 h–: h16.8g* h16.2g* h16.7g^2 h16.8g^2 h20.9g^2 h21.2m^3 h19.6g* h16.4d h19.4g^3 ab16g^3 Mar 2] useful-looking gelding: fairly useful hurdler: won conditionals maiden at Sedgefield in May, novice at Perth in August and handicap at Bangor in October: stays 21f: acts on good to firm going: won in hood in 2017/18: usually leads. *Donald McCain* **h118**

MANNY OWENS (IRE) 6 b.g. Manduro (GER) – Arabian Coral (IRE) (Intikhab (USA)) [2017/18 h86p: h20f^5 h15.7g^3 h19.3d^2 h19.4d* h19.4d^6 Dec 15] fair handicap hurdler: won novice event at Doncaster in December: stayed 19f: acted on good to soft going: in cheekpieces last 4 starts: wore tongue tie: dead. *Jonjo O'Neill* **h107**

MAN OF LA MANCHA (IRE) 5 b.g. Zoffany (IRE) – Sarella Loren (USA) (Theatrical) [2017/18 h–: h16.2g^5 May 13] modest on Flat: well held completed start over hurdles: dead. *Ben Haslam* **h–**

MAN OF PLENTY 9 ch.g. Manduro (GER) – Credit-A-Plenty (Generous (IRE)) [2017/18 h118: h17.2d^5 h19.9d^4 h16d^2 h16.4g^2 h16.5m^3 h18.9v^2 h16s^5 h15.7d^5 h19.3v^4 h23.4v h16v^5 h21s^2 Apr 25] good-topped gelding: fairly useful handicap hurdler: stays 3m: acts on heavy going: has worn headgear, including in 2017/18: wears tongue tie: races well off pace. *Sophie Leech* **h125**

MAN

MAN OF STEEL (IRE) 9 b.g. Craigsteel – Knappogue Honey (IRE) (Anshan) [2017/18 c114, h–§; c27.2s* c25.5d* c27.5d^{pu} c20v^3 Feb 19] multiple point winner: maiden hurdler: fairly useful hunter chaser: won at Fontwell and Cartmel in May: stays 27f: acts on good to firm and heavy going: has worn headgear, including last 4 starts: wears tongue tie. *Alan Hill*   **c117 h–**

MAN OF THE NORTH 5 b.g. And Beyond (IRE) – Latin Beauty (IRE) (Sadler's Wells (USA)) [2017/18 b16.7v Feb 9] tailed off in bumper. *Tony Carroll*   **b–**

MANON 4 b.f. Malinas (GER) – La Creole (FR) (Astarabad (USA)) [2017/18 b16v^2 b15.7g Apr 20] second foal: dam, French 17f-19f hurdle/chase winner, half-sister to dual Scottish Grand National winner Merigo: fair form in bumpers: better effort when second at Wetherby in March. *Michael Easterby*   **b87**

MANTOU (IRE) 7 ch.g. Teofilo (IRE) – Shadow Roll (IRE) (Mark of Esteem (IRE)) [2017/18 c15.9v^6 c19.3g* Apr 23] little show in points: fairly useful hurdler: fair form in hunter chases: won novice event at Sedgefield in April: best up to 2½m: acts on good to soft going: in cheekpieces last 2 starts: usually wears tongue tie. *S. Allwood*   **c100 h–**

MANVERS HOUSE 5 b.g. Schiaparelli (GER) – Freydis (IRE) (Supreme Leader) [2017/18 b16s^2 Mar 17] lengthy gelding: sixth foal: half-brother to fairly useful hurdler/ winning pointer Kingscourt Native (3m winner, by King's Theatre) and a winning pointer by Revoque: dam (h86) 25f hurdle winner: 25/1, second in maiden bumper at Kempton (1¼ lengths behind Mister Fisher). *Robert Walford*   **b97**

MANWELL (IRE) 8 b.g. Gold Well – Roborette (FR) (Robore (FR)) [2017/18 h96: c15.7d^2 c20.3d^2 c20.3v^2 c15.7d^2 Dec 28] lengthy, workmanlike gelding: winning hurdler: fair form over fences: stays 2½m: acts on heavy going: tried in hood: wears tongue tie: usually races in rear. *Sam England*   **c105 h–**

MAN WITH VAN (IRE) 12 b.g. Milan – Delibonne (IRE) (Erdelistan (FR)) [2017/18 c–, h91: c25g h23.9g^4 h23.9g^3 c24.1g c24.2v^4 h20v h16v^5 h16v^5 Mar 9] point winner: fair handicap hurdler: useful handicap chaser at best, well below form in 2017/18: stays 3½m: acts on heavy going: often wears headgear: has worn tongue tie, including in 2017/18: usually races towards rear. *Patrick Griffin, Ireland*   **c89 h114**

MANY TALES 6 b.g. Multiplex – All Three Fables (Beat All (USA)) [2017/18 b15.8d^5 b16.6d^6 Dec 1] first foal: dam (h102) bumper/2m hurdle winner (stayed 2½m): modest form in bumpers. *John Mackie*   **b81**

MAOI CHINN TIRE (IRE) 11 b.g. Mull of Kintyre (USA) – Primrose And Rose (Primo Dominie) [2017/18 c–, h100: h15.8d^5 h16.2g^3 h20.9d h16d Nov 10] sturdy gelding: modest handicap hurdler: winning chaser: unproven beyond 17f: acts on good to firm going: has worn cheekpieces, including in 2017/18: tried in tongue tie. *Jennie Candlish*   **c– h97**

MAQUISARD (FR) 6 ch.g. Creachadoir (IRE) – Gioiosa Marea (IRE) (Highest Honor (FR)) [2017/18 h16v h16s h15.8d* h16.5s^F Apr 14] sturdy gelding: useful on Flat in France, stays 13f: fairly useful hurdler: won maiden at Pau for G. Cherel in 2015/16: also won handicap at Huntingdon in March: raced around 2m: acts on heavy going. *Gary Moore*   **h122**

MARANGU PASS 5 b.m. Kutub (IRE) – Shali San (FR) (Saint des Saints (FR)) [2017/18 b16.3s Oct 2] second foal: dam (c75/h106) bumper winner/maiden jumper (stayed 2¼m): tailed off in mares bumper. *David Pipe*   **b–**

MARATT (FR) 5 gr.g. Martaline – Lavi (FR) (Evening World (FR)) [2017/18 b16g b16.8v h17.7v^4 h17.7s^F Mar 7] little form in bumpers/over hurdles. *Seamus Mullins*   **h68 b–**

MARAWEH (IRE) 8 b.g. Muhtathir – Itqaan (USA) (Danzig (USA)) [2017/18 h105: h23.9g^{pu} h23.8m h23.8g^5 h23.8g^{pu} h20.9v^4 h23.9s^2 Apr 25] modest handicap hurdler nowadays: stays 3m: acts on soft and good to firm going: wears headgear: usually races close up: temperamental. *Lucinda Russell*   **h94 §**

MARBETH (IRE) 5 b.m. Frozen Power (IRE) – Suddenly (Puissance) [2017/18 h80: h17.2d h15.6d Feb 14] maiden hurdler, no form in 2017/18. *Hugh Burns*   **h–**

MARBLE MIST 6 gr.g. Martaline – Karolina (FR) (Pistolet Bleu (IRE)) [2017/18 h–, b–: h17.2s^{pu} Jul 24] angular gelding: little form over hurdles: tried in blinkers: in tongue tie last 2 starts: dead. *Evan Williams*   **h–**

MARBLE MOON (IRE) 6 b.g. Millenary – Royal Marble (IRE) (Anshan) [2017/18 b16g^3 b17d^2 b15.8v^4 h19s h16v h16.5v h19v^5 Apr 12] €15,000 3-y-o: second foal: dam unraced half-sister to fair hurdler/fairly useful chaser (winner up to 3m) Mercato: fair form when placed in bumpers: poor form over hurdles: left James Daniel Dullea after second start: should be suited by further than 17f. *Evan Williams*   **h66 b85**

494

MARCH IS ON (IRE) 5 b.g. Gold Well – Shannon Tiara (IRE) (Erins Isle) [2017/18 h21m[5] Apr 26] €10,000 3-y-o, £36,000 4-y-o: fifth foal: half-brother to fair hurdler Ceol Agus Ol (2½m winner, by Chevalier): dam unraced: Irish point winner: 12/1, fifth in novice at Kempton (38½ lengths behind Who's My Jockey) on hurdling debut. *Jonjo O'Neill*   **h83**

MARCH TO MILAN 7 b.m. Milan – Kay For Karbia (Kayf Tara) [2017/18 h19.3s[6] Oct 19] first foal: dam (b83), ran twice in bumpers, half-sister to fairly useful chasers Launde (stayed 21f) and Rosie Redman (stayed 3½m): tailed off in novice hurdle. *Julia Brooke*   **h–**

MARCILHAC (FR) 9 b.g. Smadoun (FR) – One Way (FR) (Exit To Nowhere (USA)) [2017/18 c132, h–: c23.6d[pu] c23.8g[2] c23.8d[5] c23.8d[2] Dec 20] well-made gelding: winning hurdler: useful handicap chaser: second at Ludlow in November and December: stays 3m: acts on heavy going: often races prominently. *Venetia Williams*   **c139 h–**

MARETTIMO (IRE) 4 b.g. Harbour Watch (IRE) – Renowned (IRE) (Darshaan) [2017/18 h16d[5] h15.3g[4] h15.8g[2] h17.7v[ur] h16.3s[5] h16.5s[2] h16s[6] Jan 25] tall gelding: half-brother to fairly useful hurdler Brave Helios (2m-25f winner, by High Chaparral) and fairly useful hurdler/winning chaser Legion d'Honneur (19f-21f winner, by Halling): little impact on Flat: modest maiden hurdler: raced mainly around 2m: acts on soft going. *Bill Turner*   **h93**

MARGUERITE ST JUST 8 b.m. Sir Percy – Ships Watch (IRE) (Night Shift (USA)) [2017/18 h78: h20g[pu] Jul 18] maiden pointer: maiden hurdler, pulled up sole outing in 2017/18: wears tongue tie. *Anthony Honeyball*   **h–**

MARIAH'S LEGEND 6 b.m. Flying Legend (USA) – Mariah Rollins (IRE) (Over The River (FR)) [2017/18 h114, b87: c17.4s[5] c18d[pu] h20v[ur] h19.4s[6] h21s[5] c19.9s[4] c16.3g[3] Apr 19] fairly useful handicap hurdler: fair form over fences: stays 21f: acts on soft going: has worn headgear, including final start. *Amy Murphy*   **c107 h118**

MARIA'S BENEFIT (IRE) 6 b.m. Beneficial – Youngborogal (IRE) (Anshan) [2017/18 b96: h16g[2] h16.8g* h16s* h15.8g* h16.5s* h16.6s* h16.8s[4] Mar 15] rather unfurnished mare: Irish point/bumper winner: useful hurdler: won 5 races on trot, novice at Newton Abbot in October, handicap at Sandown in November, mares handicap at Ludlow and listed mares novice at Taunton (by 30 lengths from If You Say Run) in December, and Yorkshire Rose Mares' Hurdle (by ¾ length from Irish Roe) at Doncaster in January: did too much too soon final start: raced around 2m: acts on soft going: enthusiastic front runner. *Stuart Edmunds*   **h137**

OLBG.com Yorkshire Rose Mares' Hurdle, Doncaster—
free-wheeling front runner Maria's Benefit has to dig very deep to hold off Irish Roe (right)

MAR

MARIENSTAR (IRE) 7 b.m. Marienbard (IRE) – Starofdonickmore (IRE) (Fourstars Allstar (USA)) [2017/18 h24d h16.3d* h20.7g^3 h21.7d^6 h19g^3 h24d^2 h23.3v^2 h25d^{pu} h21.7v^4 c22.5v^3 c24s^2 c25.2v^4 c22.2v^6 Mar 31] first foal: dam second from 3 starts in points: point winner: fair hurdler: won mares novice seller at Stratford in May, only start for Alexandra Dunn: fair form over fences: left Gerard J. O'Keeffe after first start: stays 3m: acts on heavy going: has worn tongue tie, including last 5 starts: front runner/races prominently. *Neil King* — c110 h110

MARI ME OSCAR (IRE) 8 b.m. Oscar (IRE) – Nostra (FR) (Limnos (JPN)) [2017/18 h–: c20g^2 c20g^3 May 28] maiden hurdler: poor form over fences: tried in cheekpieces/tongue tie. *Nikki Evans* — c77 h–

MARINERO (IRE) 9 b.g. Presenting – Peggy Maddock (IRE) (Oscar (IRE)) [2017/18 c142, h140: h20m^2 h20g^4 c25g c22.5g^{ur} h24d^3 c22s^4 h19.5d^5 c26s^{pu} c21s* Mar 25] rangy gelding: useful hurdler, below best in 2017/18: useful chaser: won hunter at Ascot (by 24 lengths from Numbercruncher) in March: left Henry de Bromhead after seventh start: stays 3m: acts on heavy going: has worn headgear/tongue tie, including in 2017/18. *David Christie, Ireland* — c131 h117

MARINERS MOON (IRE) 7 ch.g. Mount Nelson – Dusty Moon (Dr Fong (USA)) [2017/18 h79: h15.8d^6 h15.8d^2 h16d^5 h15.8g^4 h15.7g^5 h20.7g Nov 14] compact gelding: poor maiden hurdler: best effort at 2m: acts on good to soft going: in headgear last 5 starts: tried in tongue tie. *Caroline Bailey* — h82

MARJU'S QUEST (IRE) 8 b.g. Marju (IRE) – Queen's Quest (Rainbow Quest (USA)) [2017/18 c–, h115§: h16.7g h15.8g h20m^{pu} h18.6g^3 h18.6g^2 h18.6g^4 h16.7d^3 Nov 23] compact gelding: fair handicap hurdler: maiden chaser: stays 2½m: acts on good to soft going: tried in hood/tongue tie: front runner: temperamental. *Adrian Wintle* — c– h100 §

MARKET COURT (IRE) 7 b.g. Court Cave (IRE) – Piepowder (In The Wings) [2017/18 b62: h15.9v h19.5v^{pu} h16s^{pu} Apr 9] unplaced in bumper: no form over hurdles: tried in tongue tie. *Nick Gifford* — h–

MARKET ROAD (IRE) 8 gr.g. Tikkanen (USA) – Clydeside (IRE) (General Ironside) [2017/18 c–, h71: h19d* h23.3d^2 c20.9d* h21.6s* h23.6s^F h21.2g^3 h21.6v* c19.4v* c19.4v^4 c19.4v^{ur} Apr 1] fair handicap hurdler: won at Warwick (conditional) in May, and Exeter in October and December (amateur): fair form over fences: won handicaps at Ffos Las in May and Chepstow in February: stays 23f: acts on heavy going: has worn headgear: wears tongue tie: usually races towards rear, often travels strongly. *Evan Williams* — c109 h104

MARKOV (IRE) 8 b.g. Morozov (USA) – Willoughby Sue (IRE) (Dabali (IRE)) [2017/18 h120, b88: c21.6d* c19.1d* c19.9v^F c20.4s^{pu} c20d Apr 28] close-coupled gelding: bumper winner: fairly useful maiden hurdler: useful form over fences: won novice handicap at Fontwell in November and handicap at Doncaster in December: stays 3m: acts on good to firm and good to soft going: held up. *Ben Pauling* — c133 h–

MARK'S FOLLY (IRE) 5 ch.m. Stowaway – Accordeon Royale (IRE) (Accordion) [2017/18 b–p: b16.5v^5 h19m^4 Apr 25] unplaced in bumpers: tailed off in novice on hurdling debut. *Philip Hobbs* — h– b–

MARLAIS 6 b.g. Dylan Thomas (IRE) – Super Motiva (Motivator) [2017/18 h101: h15.8d^6 h17v h19.6g^{pu} h19.7g h21.2s^{pu} Jan 18] maiden hurdler, no form in 2017/18: tried in cheekpieces/tongue tie. *Arthur Whitehead* — h–

MARLEY FIRTH (IRE) 6 b.g. Flemensfirth (USA) – Merrill Gaye (IRE) (Roselier (FR)) [2017/18 h16v* h19.8s^4 h15.9v^6 h16v^3 h19.5v^5 h22d^5 Apr 22] £43,000 4-y-o: rather unfurnished gelding: half-brother to 3 fairly useful winners, including hurdler Strategic Approach (3m winner, by Bob Back) and chaser Divine Intavention (2m-25f winner, by Exit To Nowhere): dam unraced: Irish point winner: fairly useful form over hurdles: won novice at Chepstow in November: stays 2½m: best form on soft/heavy going: tried in tongue tie: tends to find little. *Dan Skelton* — h117

MARMAS 9 ch.g. Sir Percy – Kitabaat (IRE) (Halling (USA)) [2017/18 h19.6d Jun 8] fair hurdler at best, well held after very long absence sole outing in 2017/18. *John Mackie* — h–

MARMONT 5 ch.g. Winker Watson – Five Bells (IRE) (Rock of Gibraltar (IRE)) [2017/18 h94: h16m^6 h15.8m h16.8s^2 h15.8g h16.8d^3 h17.7v^3 h15.5v^5 h15.8s* h15.8s^2 h16s^2 Apr 27] rather leggy gelding: fair handicap hurdler: won novice event at Huntingdon in February: stays 2¼m: acts on soft going: in hood last 3 starts: has worn tongue tie, including in 2017/18: usually races prominently. *Jo Davis* — h108

MAROC 5 b.g. Rock of Gibraltar (IRE) – Zietory (Zieten (USA)) [2017/18 h98: h20.5s^{pu} h19.9v h16s^{pu} Jan 13] maiden hurdler, no form in 2017/18 (wore cheekpieces/tongue tie). *Nikki Evans* — h–

MAROCCHINO 5 gr.g. Tikkanen (USA) – Mocha (FR) (Mansonnien (FR)) [2017/18 b–: b15.6s Jan 3] no form in bumpers: in hood sole outing in 2017/18. *James Ewart* — b–

MARONETTE 5 b.m. Milan – Wyldello (Supreme Leader) [2017/18 h15.8g^5 h19.5v h16v^5 Apr 14] €50,000 3-y-o: rather unfurnished mare: fifth foal: closely related to fairly useful hurdler/useful chaser Cogry (19f-3¼m winner, by King's Theatre), stays 33f, and bumper winner/fairly useful hurdler The Caller (2m-3m winner, by Yeats): dam (h122), bumper/17f hurdle winner, sister to high-class hurdler (2m-25f winner) Marello: poor form over hurdles. *Tim Vaughan* — h66

MARQUIS OF CARABAS (IRE) 8 b.g. Hurricane Run (IRE) – Miss Otis Regrets (IRE) (Bob Back (USA)) [2017/18 h119: c20.3g^4 c16.5g^5 c19.4g* c20g^2 c21.4g^5 c19.4m^3 c20d^2 c19.4s^6 c21.4v^4 Apr 11] fairly useful hurdler: fairly useful handicap chaser: won at Ffos Las in June: stays 21f: acts on good to firm and heavy going. *David Dennis* — c126 h–

MARRACUDJA (FR) 7 b.g. Martaline – Memorial (FR) (Homme de Loi (IRE)) [2017/18 c140, h–: c18g^2 c16.8g^3 c16.4g^5 c15.8s* c21s^{ur} Apr 23] useful-looking gelding: winning hurdler: useful handicap chaser: won at Musselburgh (by 1¼ lengths from Baby King) in February: stays 2¼m: acts on soft going: has worn hood, including in 2017/18: wears tongue tie: often races prominently. *Paul Nicholls* — c142 h–

MARTABOT (FR) 7 gr.g. Martaline – Reine de Sabot (FR) (Homme de Loi (IRE)) [2017/18 h109: h21.4v^{pu} h19.5v h19v^3 h16.5s^6 h21.6v^5 Apr 8] fair maiden hurdler, below form in 2017/18: best around 2m: acts on soft going: in headgear last 4 starts: tried in tongue tie. *David Pipe* — h94

MARTEN (FR) 6 b.g. Martaline – Commande Blue (FR) (Commands (AUS)) [2017/18 b102: h20.3d^4 h19.6s^6 h21s^{pu} Feb 9] sturdy gelding: bumper winner: fair form over hurdles: won novice at Southwell in November: stays 2½m: front runner/races prominently. *Ben Pauling* — h114

MARTHA'S BENEFIT (IRE) 9 b.g. Beneficial – Trajectus (Homo Sapien) [2017/18 h70: c25.3d^{pu} c21.2d* c20.3v^{pu} Feb 9] point winner: maiden hurdler: modest form in chases: won maiden hunter at Cartmel in May: stays 21f: acts on good to soft going. *Andrew Nicholls* — c96 h–

MARTHA'S DREAM 4 ch.f. Captain Gerrard (IRE) – Rose Bounty (Polar Falcon (USA)) [2017/18 h16.5s^5 Dec 30] half-sister to 6f winner Mark of Meydan (by Mark of Esteem) and a winner in Japan by Fantastic Light: dam unraced half-sister to Poule d'Essai des Pouliches winner Rose Gypsy: well beaten in juvenile hurdle. *Sarah Robinson* — h–

MARTILA (FR) 6 b.m. Martaline – Paola Pierji (FR) (Cadoudal (FR)) [2017/18 h117: h16.2d^2 h16v* h16g^5 Apr 20] fairly useful handicap hurdler: won at Ayr in November: will stay 2½m: acts on heavy going: wears hood. *Pauline Robson* — h117

MARTILOO (FR) 8 b.m. Martaline – Paola Pierji (FR) (Cadoudal (FR)) [2017/18 c–, h–: c17.1g^2 c15.6g^3 c16g^2 c16d* c17.1g^2 c20.5v^{ur} c19.9s^2 c19.9s^3 c17.1v^4 Apr 7] maiden hurdler: fair handicap chaser: won at Perth in August: barely stays 21f: acts on soft going: has worn hood, including in 2017/18: usually wears tongue tie: often travels strongly. *Pauline Robson* — c109 h–

MARTIN CASH (IRE) 12 b.g. Oscar (IRE) – Native Singer (IRE) (Be My Native (USA)) [2017/18 c84, h–: c20.8d^{pu} May 5] lengthy, workmanlike gelding: maiden hurdler: fair chaser at best, out of depth sole outing under Rules in 2017/18: stays 21f: acts on heavy going: has worn headgear/tongue tie. *Mrs Jo Messenger* — c– h–

MARVELLOUS MONTY (IRE) 8 br.m. Oscar (IRE) – Montys Miss (IRE) (Presenting) [2017/18 h105: h20s^2 h20.3g h20.7s^4 h21.2s h25.5s^3 Mar 27] fair maiden hurdler: likely to prove best up to 3m: acts on heavy going: tried in tongue tie. *Johnny Farrelly* — h105

MARY ELEANOR 6 b.m. Midnight Legend – Lady Rebecca (Rolfe (USA)) [2017/18 b82: b17s^2 h20.6g* Nov 17] fair form in bumpers: 13/8, won mares maiden at Newcastle (by head from Katy Royal) on hurdling debut: entitled to progress. *Tom Lacey* — h101 p b86

MASH POTATO (IRE) 8 b.g. Whipper (USA) – Salva (Grand Lodge (USA)) [2017/18 h91: h15.8g^3 h17.2g^2 h15.8d^5 h17.2d^5 h16.2v^2 h15.8d^3 Oct 8] modest handicap hurdler: raced mainly around 2m: acts on soft going: wears cheekpieces/tongue tie. *Noel C. Kelly, Ireland* — h84

MAS

MASSEY'S WOOD 6 b.g. Black Sam Bellamy (IRE) – Reivers Moon (Midnight Legend) [2017/18 b16v* h20.2v² h20s⁵ h20v⁵ h24s* h24s Apr 17] €30,000 3-y-o: fourth foal: half-brother to bumper winner/fairly useful hurdler Reivers Lad (2m winner, by Alflora): dam (c109/h110) 21f-3m hurdle/chase winner: won maiden bumper at Listowel (by 31 lengths from Crumpledandcreased) in September: fairly useful form over hurdles: won maiden at Thurles in February: stays 3m: acts on soft going: tried in blinkers: usually leads/races freely. *Alan Fleming, Ireland* **h129 b105**

MASSINI MAN 5 b.g. Dr Massini (IRE) – Alleged To Rhyme (IRE) (Leading Counsel (USA)) [2017/18 b15.8d⁶ Mar 26] 10/1, sixth in conditionals/amateur bumper at Huntingdon (17¼ lengths behind Breaking Waves). *Tom George* **b80**

MASSINI'S LADY 7 b.m. Dr Massini (IRE) – Lady du Bost (FR) (Royal Charter (FR)) [2017/18 c–, h77§; h25.8s² h19v² c21.3v* c24.1v⁴ c23.4v⁶ Apr 15] poor maiden hurdler: similar form over fences: won handicap at Wetherby in February: stays 3¼m: best form on soft/heavy going: has worn headgear: front runner/races prominently: unreliable. *N. W. Alexander* **c80 § h77 §**

MASSINI'S TRAP (IRE) 9 b.g. Dr Massini (IRE) – Sparrow's Trap (IRE) (Magical Wonder (USA)) [2017/18 h131: h20d³ h20v⁵ h24s h20s Apr 13] smallish gelding: useful handicap hurdler: third at Aintree (4½ lengths behind Bags Groove) in October: stays 3m: acts on good to firm and heavy going: wears headgear: tried in tongue tie: held up. *James A. Nash, Ireland* **h133**

MASSINI'S VISION 6 b.m. Dr Massini (IRE) – Cathy's Dream (IRE) (Husyan (USA)) [2017/18 b16v⁵ b15.8v Dec 31] sixth foal: sister to a winning pointer and closely related to another by Kayf Tara: dam, winning pointer, half-sister to fair hurdler/useful staying chaser American Jennie: no form in bumpers. *Robert Stephens* **b–**

MASTEEN (FR) 6 b.g. Astarabad (USA) – Manson Teene (FR) (Mansonnien (FR)) [2017/18 b16.8s² Dec 8] 11/4, second in bumper at Sedgefield (21 lengths behind Theatre Legend): will stay 2½m. *Tony Coyle* **b61**

MASTER ARCHER (IRE) 4 gr.g. Mastercraftsman (IRE) – Kinigi (IRE) (Verglas (IRE)) [2017/18 h15.7s Dec 21] fairly useful maiden on Flat, stays 2m: 10/1, seventh in maiden at Towcester (30¼ lengths behind Al Shahir) on hurdling debut. *James Fanshawe* **h78**

MASTER BAKER 9 b.g. Kayf Tara – Fashion House (Homo Sapien) [2017/18 c23v* c24.2d² Apr 24] prolific point winner: fair form in hunter chases: in command before left alone last in maiden event at Taunton in April. *Mrs L. J. Jefford* **c114**

MASTER BILLIE (IRE) 4 ro.g. Mastercraftsman (IRE) – Billie Jean (Bertolini (USA)) [2017/18 h16gᵖᵘ h16g⁵ h17.7d Nov 19] sturdy gelding: poor maiden on Flat: no form over hurdles: tried in hood. *Roger Teal* **h–**

MASTER BONES (IRE) 9 b.g. Trans Island – Leaghillaun (IRE) (Turtle Island (IRE)) [2017/18 h20g h15.8d⁶ c20.3g⁶ c19.7mᵖᵘ Sep 24] maiden hurdler/chaser, no form in 2017/18: tried in visor when trained by J. G. Coogan in 2014/15. *Adrian Wintle* **c– h–**

MASTER BURBIDGE 7 b.g. Pasternak – Silver Sequel (Silver Patriarch (IRE)) [2017/18 c115p, h111: c20.2sF c19.7s* c19.1d³ c17.2sF c19.5s* Mar 7] strong gelding: fair hurdler: fairly useful form over fences: won handicaps at Plumpton in November and Fontwell in March: stays 21f: acts on soft going: wears cheekpieces: often travels strongly, usually waited with. *Neil Mulholland* **c124 h–**

MASTER CARD 5 ch.g. Presenting – Subtilty (With Approval (CAN)) [2017/18 b16s Feb 9] well beaten in maiden bumper. *Warren Greatrex* **b65**

MASTER DANCER 7 gr.g. Mastercraftsman (IRE) – Isabella Glyn (IRE) (Sadler's Wells (USA)) [2017/18 h113: h21.1g* h20.5d⁴ h21g Feb 24] good-topped gelding: fairly useful handicap hurdler: won at Cheltenham in October: stays 21f: acts on heavy going: wears cheekpieces. *Tim Vaughan* **h125**

MASTER DEE (IRE) 9 b.g. King's Theatre (IRE) – Miss Lauren Dee (IRE) (Montelimar (USA)) [2017/18 c142, h–: c20.1d³ c21.4g³ c19.9s² c24g* Feb 24] workmanlike gelding: winning hurdler: smart handicap chaser: won Betdaq Chase at Kempton (by 3¾ lengths from Ballykan) in February: stays 25f: acts on soft and good to firm going: has worn cheekpieces, including in 2017/18: wears tongue tie: consistent. *Fergal O'Brien* **c151 h–**

MASTER JAKE (IRE) 10 b.g. Pyrus (USA) – Whitegate Way (Greensmith) [2017/18 c135, h–: c25.8gᵖᵘ May 10] winning hurdler: useful chaser, pulled up sole outing in 2017/18: stayed 3m: acted on good to firm and heavy going: tried in cheekpieces: wore tongue tie: often travelled strongly: retired. *Dan Skelton* **c– h–**

MASTERMIND (IRE) 4 b.g. Nathaniel (IRE) – Snow Gretel (IRE) (Green Desert (USA)) [2017/18 h16s6 c23g2 Jun 3] rather leggy gelding: little impact on Flat: fairly useful hurdler: won juvenile maiden at Gowran in November and novice at Naas in February: second in Winning Fair Juvenile Hurdle at Fairyhouse (2¼ lengths behind Mitchouka) in February: raced only at 2m: acts on heavy going: tried in hood. *Charles O'Brien, Ireland* — **h120**

MASTEROFDECEPTION (IRE) 10 b.g. Darsi (FR) – Sherberry (IRE) (Shernazar) [2017/18 h112: c23g2 Jun 3] good-topped gelding: fairly useful hurdler: 10/1, second in novice at Worcester (½ length behind For Instance) on chasing debut: stays 3m: acts on soft and good to firm going: has worn headgear, including last 4 starts: in tongue tie last 3 starts. *Dr Richard Newland* — **c124 h–**

MASTER OF FINANCE (IRE) 7 ch.g. Mastercraftsman (IRE) – Cheal Rose (IRE) (Dr Devious (IRE)) [2017/18 h120§: h16.2g4 h16.8g2 h16.2g4 h16d h15.7d3 h16.8s h20.6s6 c16d5 c17.2v3 h17.7g3 Apr 20] sturdy gelding: has had breathing operation: fairly useful handicap hurdler: fair form over fences: left Malcolm Jefferson after fifth start: stays 2¼m: acts on soft going: wears headgear: temperamental. *Lucy Wadham* — **c106 § h114 §**

MASTER OF IRONY (IRE) 6 b.g. Makfi – Mother of Pearl (IRE) (Sadler's Wells (USA)) [2017/18 h131: h20.1g3 h16d* h16.3d4 h16vpu h16gur Apr 20] workmanlike gelding: useful handicap hurdler: won at Wetherby in October: stays 2½m: acts on soft going: in cheekpieces last 4 starts. *John Quinn* — **h130**

MASTER OF TARA (FR) 5 b.g. Kayf Tara – Ryme Bere (FR) (Until Sundown (USA)) [2017/18 b20s6 b16v* Feb 18] €75,000 3-y-o: second foal: dam, placed in French hurdles/chases up to 21f, half-sister to smart French hurdler/high-class chaser (stayed 27f) Matinee Lover: point winner: useful form in bumpers: won maiden at Navan (by 2¼ lengths from All For Joy) in February: likely to progress further. *Gordon Elliott, Ireland* — **b106 p**

MASTER OF VERSE (IRE) 9 b.g. Milan – Bacchonthebottle (IRE) (Bob Back (USA)) [2017/18 h130: c19.9g R c16g4 c17g6 c19.2g5 c16v5 c16.1spu h26spu c16dur Feb 21] winning pointer: winning hurdler: fair maiden chaser: left Noel Meade after fourth start: stays 21f: acts on good to firm and good to soft going: often in hood: has worn tongue tie, including in 2017/18. *Venetia Williams* — **c107 h–**

MASTERPLAN (IRE) 8 b.g. Spadoun (FR) – Eurolucy (IRE) (Shardari) [2017/18 c116, h–: c19.1d2 c20s2 c19.9s5 c20v3 c19.9s3 Mar 31] useful-looking gelding: winning hurdler: fairly useful handicap chaser: stays 2¾m: acts on soft and good to firm going: has worn headgear, including in 2017/18: has worn tongue tie: front runner/races prominently. *Charlie Longsdon* — **c117 h–**

*Betdaq Handicap Chase, Kempton—
the ultra-consistent Master Dee (right) swoops late to beat the 2016 fourth Ballykan (second right);
the nosebanded pair Theatre Territory and Art Mauresque (hoops) complete the frame*

MAS

MASTER RAJEEM (USA) 9 b.g. Street Cry (IRE) – Rajeem (Diktat) [2017/18 c103§, h100§: h20.1v^{pu} c26.3s^{pu} Nov 28] well-made gelding: fair hurdler/fairly useful chaser at best, no form in 2017/18: stays 27f: acts on heavy going: wears headgear: usually races prominently: temperamental. *Alison Hamilton* — c– §, h– §

MASTER RUFFIT (IRE) 10 ch.g. Blueprint (IRE) – Miss Ruffit (IRE) (Phardante (FR)) [2017/18 c124, h–: h16v h16v h22s h21.4v^{pu} c20.5v^F Mar 9] fairly useful hurdler/chaser at best, no form in 2017/18: tried in cheekpieces: dead. *Neil McKnight, Ireland* — c–, h–

MASTERS HILL (IRE) 12 gr.g. Tikkanen (USA) – Leitrim Bridge (IRE) (Earl of Barking (IRE)) [2017/18 c137, h113: c25d c22.7g^6 Dec 3] strong gelding: winning hurdler: useful chaser at best, no form in 2017/18: stays 3½m: acts on heavy going: wears headgear: has worn tongue tie, including final start. *Colin Tizzard* — c–, h–

MASTER SUNRISE (IRE) 9 ch.g. Blueprint (IRE) – Aunty Dawn (IRE) (Strong Gale) [2017/18 c87: c25.3d^3 c23g^2 May 26] point winner: modest form in hunter chases: in cheekpieces last 2 starts. *Mrs D. J. Ralph* — c93

MASTER THINKER (IRE) 4 b.g. Masterofthehorse (IRE) – Think Fast (IRE) (Songandaprayer (USA)) [2017/18 b13.7g^6 Apr 20] 6/1, sixth in bumper at Fontwell. *G. Hourigan, Ireland* — b61

MASTER TOMMYTUCKER 7 b.g. Kayf Tara – No Need For Alarm (Romany Rye) [2017/18 h18.5s* h21.6v* Apr 17] third foal: half-brother to fair hurdler Rouquine Sauvage (2m winner, by Loup Sauvage), stayed 21f: dam (c126/h120) 2m/17f hurdle/chase winner: fairly useful form over hurdles: won novices at Exeter in February and April: will go on improving. *Paul Nicholls* — h129 p

MASTER TRADESMAN (IRE) 7 ch.g. Marienbard (IRE) – Tobeornotobe (IRE) (Mister Lord (USA)) [2017/18 c26d^{pu} h21.2s^5 h21.7s^2 h23.1d^2 Apr 21] €16,000 3-y-o: third foal: dam (c101), 2½m-2¾m hurdle/chase winner (stayed 3m), half-sister to fairly useful hurdler (2m-23f winner) Nick The Beak: point winner: fair form over hurdles: best effort when second in maiden at Bangor in April: pulled up in hunter on chasing debut: should stay 3m+. *Richard Mitford-Slade* — c–, h113

MASTER VINTAGE 10 b.g. Kayf Tara – What A Vintage (IRE) (Un Desperado (FR)) [2017/18 h107: h16d^4 h16.5s^5 h19.4s^2 h21v^{pu} Mar 11] fair handicap hurdler: stays 19f: acts on heavy going: wears hood. *Richard Phillips* — h107

MASTER WORK (FR) 5 b.g. Network (GER) – Mascarpone (FR) (Mansonnien (FR)) [2017/18 h18.5d* h21.2g^4 h16s^5 h15.8d Mar 26] €40,000 3-y-o: second foal: dam (c111/h103) French 2½m/21f chase winner: fair form over hurdles: won novice at Exeter in October. *Philip Hobbs* — h112

MASTER WORKMAN (IRE) 12 b.g. Posidonas – Bobbie Magee (IRE) (Buckskin (FR)) [2017/18 c117: c24.2m* c27.5d Jun 9] multiple point winner: fairly useful hunter chaser: won at Fakenham in May: stays 3m: acts on good to firm and heavy going: wears cheekpieces. *David Kemp* — c120

MATCHAWAY (IRE) 9 b.g. Milan – Hatch Away (IRE) (Lord Americo) [2017/18 h121: h20g h15.7d^3 h20g^5 c16.5g^4 Oct 5] fairly useful handicap hurdler: 9/2, fourth in novice handicap at Huntingdon (18¾ lengths behind Mccabe Creek) on chasing debut: unproven beyond 17f: acts on soft going: usually in headgear: tried in tongue tie: should do better as a chaser. *Kerry Lee* — c103 p, h117

MATHAYUS (IRE) 5 b.g. Scorpion (IRE) – Prunelle (GER) (Waky Nao) [2017/18 b–: h20.6g^4 h22.1s^3 h21.2g^2 h19.9g* Oct 3] modest form over hurdles: won handicap at Sedgefield in October: often races prominently: will go on improving. *Sue Smith* — h99 p

MATORICO (IRE) 7 gr.g. Mastercraftsman (IRE) – Hashbrown (GER) (Big Shuffle (USA)) [2017/18 h–: h20.6g^4 c20g^4 c16.3v^4 c25d^5 c19.9s^{pu} c23s^3 c19.2s^6 Mar 26] rather leggy gelding: useful handicap hurdler: fairly useful form over fences: stays easy 25f: acts on heavy going: has worn headgear: usually wears tongue tie. *Jonjo O'Neill* — c120, h133

MATROW'S LADY (IRE) 11 b.m. Cloudings (IRE) – I'm Maggy (NZ) (Danseur Etoile (FR)) [2017/18 c95, h–: c21.6v^4 c26v^{pu} c21s^{pu} Apr 23] good-bodied mare: winning hurdler: modest handicap chaser, below form in 2017/18: stays 3m: acts on heavy going: wears headgear/tongue tie. *Neil Mulholland* — c83, h–

MATTHEW MAN 7 b.g. Bollin Eric – Garden Feature (Minster Son) [2017/18 h23.3g^{pu} c24.2d^{pu} Apr 23] maiden pointer: pulled up in maiden hurdle/hunter chase. *James Walton* — c–, h–

MATTS LEGACY (IRE) 6 b.g. Arcadio (GER) – How Provincial (IRE) (Be My Native (USA)) [2017/18 h–: b67: h15.8g^6 h18.5d h16d^3 h15.8v^{rr} h15.3v^{rr} h18.5s Apr 23] modest maiden hurdler: tried in hood: one to avoid (twice refused to race). *Tim Vaughan* — h §§

MAY

MAUNA KEA (IRE) 6 b.g. Mountain High (IRE) – The Bench (IRE) (Leading Counsel (USA)) [2017/18 h20.7m h21.8g h19.5v h23.1d⁴ Apr 24] €9,500 3-y-o: sixth foal: half-brother to fair hurdler/modest chaser High Counsel (23f-25f winner, by Presenting): dam unraced half-sister to smart hurdler (stayed 21f) Xenophon: modest maiden hurdler: once-raced chaser: left Ms Margaret Mullins after second start: should stay beyond 19f: acts on soft going: tried in headgear. *Polly Gundry*   c– h87

MAUREEN'S STAR (IRE) 5 b.m. Gold Well – Serpentine Mine (IRE) (Rashar (USA)) [2017/18 b16m h18.8g⁶ h21g h21.3g h20g⁵ h21.8g⁵ h18.8g⁵ h20.5v h16v h24v h24v Feb 11] €3,200 3-y-o: first foal: dam unraced half-sister to dams of useful hurdler Spiritofthegames (stays 21f) and useful hurdler/smart chaser Breedsbreeze (stayed 3m): unplaced both starts in Irish points: no form in bumpers: modest maiden hurdler: stays 2¾m: best form on good going: tried in blinkers. *Liam Lennon, Ireland*   h89 b–

MAURICIO (IRE) 4 ch.g. Helmet (AUS) – Essexford (IRE) (Spinning World (USA)) [2017/18 h16.3m⁶ h15.8d⁵ Jul 30] fair on Flat, stays 1¼m: poor form over hurdles. *Dr Richard Newland*   h59

MAX DO BRAZIL (FR) 6 b.g. Blue Bresil (FR) – Lili Valley (FR) (Cadoudal (FR)) [2017/18 h126: h24.7g^pu h21.6v h18.5v^pu h19.9v³ h23v⁶ Feb 19] sturdy gelding: fair handicap hurdler: stays 2½m: acts on heavy going: has worn headgear, including last 3 starts: wears tongue tie. *David Pipe*   h108

MAX DYNAMITE (FR) 8 b.g. Great Journey (JPN) – Mascara (GER) (Monsun (GER)) [2017/18 h16d h21.1s h20s^pu Apr 28] smart on Flat: useful handicap hurdler, below form in 2017/18: unproven beyond 17f: acts on heavy going. *W. P. Mullins, Ireland*   h123

MAX DYNAMO (FR) 8 b.g. Midnight Legend – Vivante (IRE) (Toulon) [2017/18 h58, b–: h19.5s h23.8d³ h24s² h24.4s⁵ h26s³ h25d³ Mar 26] poor maiden hurdler: stays 3¼m: acts on soft going: wears hood: usually races towards rear. *Jim Wilson*   h83

MAXED OUT KING (IRE) 10 ch.g. Desert King – Lady Max (IRE) (Mandalus) [2017/18 c111, h62: c19.3g* c15.7g³ c21.4g⁶ c20.1v⁵ c15.7d Dec 19] maiden hurdler: fair handicap chaser: won at Sedgefield in May: stays 2½m: acts on soft going: usually races close up. *Sue Smith*   c111 h–

MAX FORTE (IRE) 8 br.g. Indian River (FR) – Brook Forte (Alderbrook) [2017/18 h120: c24.2s^pu c20d^pu h21.4v h23.5s⁴ h23.8d Apr 24] rather leggy gelding: fair handicap hurdler: no form over fences: stays 3m: acts on good to soft going: in cheekpieces last 3 starts: front runner/races prominently. *Chris Down*   c– h113

MAXI MAC (IRE) 8 ch.g. Thousand Words – Crimada (IRE) (Mukaddamah (USA)) [2017/18 h15.8d^pu Jul 11] maiden hurdler, pulled up after long absence sole outing in 2017/18. *Trevor Wall*   h–

MAXIMUS MARIDIUS 7 br.g. Fair Mix (IRE) – Dutch Czarina (Prince Sabo) [2017/18 h99: h20.3g⁶ h16.8d⁶ c17.4g^F h20g² h16g² h15.8d³ c16.5f⁶ c16.4s³ Dec 26] angular gelding: point winner: fair maiden hurdler: modest form over fences: stays 2½m: acts on soft going: has worn headgear, including in 2017/18: tried in tongue tie: held up, travels well: open to further improvement as a chaser. *Samuel Drinkwater*   c96 p h105

MAX LIEBERMANN (IRE) 4 b.g. Galileo (IRE) – Anna Karenina (IRE) (Green Desert (USA)) [2017/18 h16s^pu ab16g* h15.8d³ Mar 26] little impact in maidens on Flat: won jumpers bumper at Southwell in March: fair form over hurdles: much better effort when third in maiden at Huntingdon: tried in tongue tie. *John Ryan*   h106

MAX MILAN (IRE) 9 b.g. Milan – Sunset Leader (IRE) (Supreme Leader) [2017/18 h23.9s^pu Jan 9] tall, useful-looking gelding: twice-raced hurdler, better effort (modest form) when sixth in maiden at Ascot in 2014/15. *David Arbuthnot*   h–

MAX MILANO (IRE) 13 b.g. Milan – Stellissima (IRE) (Persian Bold) [2017/18 h81: h20s^pu h19.2d h19.6s^pu Jan 12] sturdy gelding: fair hurdler at best, no form in 2017/18: has worn hood, including in 2017/18. *Alan Jessop*   h–

MAX WARD (IRE) 9 b.g. Milan – Made Easy (IRE) (Rudimentary (USA)) [2017/18 c145, h–: c16.8g⁶ c19.9d^pu c20.5s² Feb 9] good-topped gelding: winning hurdler: smart handicap chaser: second in graduation event at Kempton (3 lengths behind Modus) in February: stays 2½m: acts on soft going. *Tom George*   c145 h–

MAYDEN MASSINI 7 gr.g. Dr Massini (IRE) – Miss Tehente (FR) (Tehente (FR)) [2017/18 b–: b13.7d Nov 25] no form in bumpers. *Philip Hide*   b–

MAY MIST 6 b.m. Nayef (USA) – Midnight Mist (IRE) (Green Desert (USA)) [2017/18 b–: h15.8d^co h15.8s Jan 18] modest maiden on Flat: no form over hurdles. *Trevor Wall*   h–

MAY

MAYO STAR (IRE) 6 b.g. Stowaway – Western Whisper (IRE) (Supreme Leader) [2017/18 h106p, b91: h20.9d² Oct 8] bumper winner: fairly useful form over hurdles: second in novice at Kelso on sole outing in 2017/18: tried in hood: front runner/races prominently. *Malcolm Jefferson* — h118

MAY'S MILAN (IRE) 7 b.g. Milan – Opera Mask (IRE) (Moscow Society (USA)) [2017/18 b15.8v h20v^{pu} Dec 18] in frame both starts in Irish points: no show in bumper/maiden hurdle. *David Rees* — h– b–

MAYZE BELL 9 br.m. And Beyond (IRE) – Eleanor May (Crofthall) [2017/18 h67: h16.2v⁴ h24v² Apr 14] poor form over hurdles: often races towards rear. *Alistair Whillans* — h76

MAZALTO (IRE) 5 b.m. Teofilo (IRE) – Mazaaya (USA) (Cozzene (USA)) [2017/18 h15.8s^{ur} h17.7s^F h19.3s⁵ h16s^{pu} h16m⁵ Apr 26] lengthy mare: fair maiden on Flat, stays 16.5f: modest form over hurdles: stays 19f: acts on soft going: often races towards rear. *Pat Phelan* — h90

MAZURATI (IRE) 9 b.g. Definite Article – Mazuma (IRE) (Mazaad) [2017/18 c23.6g^{pu} c26d³ c25.6s^{pu} c24.5v c27.5d^{ur} Apr 22] compact gelding: point winner: maiden hurdler: poor form over fences: has worn headgear/tongue tie: ungenuine. *Ben Case* — c73 § h– §

MCCABE CREEK (IRE) 8 b.g. Robin des Pres (FR) – Kick And Run (IRE) (Presenting) [2017/18 c124, h123: c20.3g² c19.4g² c20g⁴ c19.2g⁴ c16.5g² c16.5g* c16.3g^{pu} Nov 1] sturdy gelding: winning hurdler: fairly useful handicap chaser: won novice event at Huntingdon in October: stays 21f: acts on soft and good to firm going: has worn headgear, including last 3 starts: usually races close up. *Caroline Bailey* — c122 h–

MCCOOLS GOLD 5 b.g. Yeats (IRE) – Gold Reef (Double Trigger (IRE)) [2017/18 h18.7g⁵ h16g Aug 23] dam (h126) 2m-2½m hurdle winner (stayed 3m): fair on Flat, stays 17f: modest form over hurdles: wears headgear. *Alan King* — h97

MCELLIGOTT (IRE) 5 b.g. Dark Angel (IRE) – Nina Blini (Bertolini (USA)) [2017/18 h15.8g^{pu} Jun 15] no form on Flat: pulled up in novice on hurdling debut. *Tom Lacey* — h–

MCGINTY'S DREAM (IRE) 7 b.g. Flemensfirth (USA) – Laboc (Rymer) [2017/18 h86: h24.3s c24.2v² c16.5v⁵ c20.1v c20.9v³ c24.2v² c20.1v² c24.2d^{ur} Apr 23] winning hurdler: poor maiden chaser: stays 3m: best form on soft/heavy going: wears headgear: often in tongue tie in 2017/18: usually races towards rear. *N. W. Alexander* — c81 h–

MCGOWAN'S PASS 7 b.g. Central Park (IRE) – Function Dreamer (Overbury (IRE)) [2017/18 b97: h16.4v⁵ h16v* h15.7v⁵ h16.2v³ h17s⁴ Apr 8] bumper winner: fairly useful form over hurdles: won maiden at Ayr in December: raced around 2m: best form on heavy going: often races prominently/freely. *Sandy Thomson* — h117

MCGROARTY (IRE) 7 b.g. Brian Boru – Uffizi (IRE) (Royal Academy (USA)) [2017/18 b20g* h16.7g² h16.7g* h16g* h21.6 ab18d⁶ h16.3s⁵ Mar 23] good-topped gelding: has had breathing operation: half-brother to several winners on Flat, including smart 6f-9f winner Momtic (by Shinko Forest): dam unraced: Irish point winner: fairly useful form in bumpers: won maiden at Ayr in June: similar form over hurdles: won maiden at Market Rasen and novice at Worcester in August: left David A. Kiely after first start: likely to prove best up to 2½m: best form on good going: in tongue tie last 5 starts: usually races prominently. *Dr Richard Newland* — h118 b98

MCKENZIE'S FRIEND (IRE) 7 b.g. Flemensfirth (USA) – Escrea (IRE) (Oscar (IRE)) [2017/18 h99: h21.2m^{pu} h16.2d h20.6g⁶ Oct 21] well-made gelding: fairly useful hurdler at best, no form in 2017/18: left Oliver Sherwood after first start: tried in blinkers. *Philip Kirby* — h–

MCLAREN VALE (IRE) 10 b.g. Darsi (FR) – Lunar Approach (IRE) (Mandalus) [2017/18 c81, h–: c25.3g⁴ h24g² c25.5s³ h24s^{pu} Oct 29] point winner: poor maiden hurdler/chaser: stays 25f: acts on soft going: tried in cheekpieces, including in 2017/18. *Thomas Coyle, Ireland* — c79 h80

MCNAMARAS BAND (IRE) 5 b.g. Getaway (GER) – Katies Pet (IRE) (Glacial Storm (USA)) [2017/18 b16g* Jun 3] fifth foal: half-brother to a winning pointer by King's Theatre: dam, lightly raced in points, half-sister to useful hurdler/top-class chaser (stayed 25f) Rince Ri: 5/2, won bumper at Worcester (by head from The Groovy Hoovy) on debut. *Philip Hobbs* — b89

MCVICAR 9 b.g. Tobougg (IRE) – Aries (GER) (Big Shuffle (USA)) [2017/18 c–, h109: h19.7s^{pu} h16.8s⁵ h25.3d⁴ Dec 28] small gelding: fair handicap hurdler, well below best in 2017/18: maiden chaser: stays 2½m: acts on heavy going: often wears cheekpieces. *John Davies* — c– h76

MEL

MEADOWCROFT BOY 9 b.g. Kayf Tara – Blackbriery Thyne (IRE) (Good Thyne (USA)) [2017/18 h–: h20.2d h16.2g* h17d² h16.8s h15.6d³ h15.6s⁵ Jan 19] angular gelding: has had breathing operation: fair handicap hurdler: won at Kelso in October: stays 2¼m: acts on soft going: has worn hood/tongue tie. *Alistair Whillans*   **h111**

MEAD VALE 5 ch.g. Schiaparelli (GER) – Devon Peasant (Deploy) [2017/18 h19.9d h19v³ Apr 12] half-brother to fairly useful hurdler Kolaphos (2¾m winner, by Kayf Tara) and a winning pointer by Generous: dam (h107) 17f hurdle winner: poor form over hurdles. *Nigel Hawke*   **h81**

MECHELEN 4 br.f. Malinas (GER) – Helen Wood (Lahib (USA)) [2017/18 b16.5v² b16.8g Apr 19] second foal: dam (c120/h110), 2m-19f hurdle/chase winner (also 1¼m winner on Flat), sister to fair hurdler/fairly useful chaser (stays 2¾m) Ashcott Boy: modest form in bumpers: better effort when second in mares event at Taunton in March: wears hood. *David Pipe*   **b84**

MEDAL OF FREEDOM (IRE) 8 b.g. Mahler – Clashwilliam Girl (IRE) (Seymour Hicks (FR)) [2017/18 b20, h77: c20.1g⁵ c24.2g⁵ May 23] placed all 3 completed starts in Irish points: maiden hurdler: poor maiden chaser: usually races towards rear. *Stuart Coltherd*   **c63** **h–**

MEDIEVAL BISHOP (IRE) 9 b.g. Bachelor Duke (USA) – On The Backfoot (IRE) (Bob Back (USA)) [2017/18 h24vᵖᵘ h19.6dᵖᵘ Apr 21] maiden hurdler, no form in 2017/18: has worn cheekpieces. *Tony Forbes*   **h–**

MEEP MEEP (IRE) 5 ch.m. Flemensfirth (USA) – Charming Leader (IRE) (Supreme Leader) [2017/18 b16s* b17s⁴ Apr 12] lengthy mare: half-sister to useful hurdler/winning pointer Westren Warrior (19f-3m winner, by Westerner); dam, unraced, sister to useful hurdler/chaser (stayed 29f) Feathered Leader: fairly useful form in bumpers: won mares event at Chepstow in March: improved when fourth in Nickel Coin Mares' National Hunt Flat Race at Aintree (4¼ lengths behind Getaway Katie Mai) in April: will be suited by 2½m. *Tom Lacey*   **b102**

MEGABOOST (IRE) 5 b.m. Court Cave (IRE) – Sweetasanu (IRE) (Sri Pekan (USA)) [2017/18 b16s⁶ h21v³ h15.7vᵖᵘ h20.7g Apr 24] £40,000 5-y-o: angular mare: sister to a winning pointer, and half-sister to fair hurdler Free of Charge (23f winner) and fair chaser Smuggler's Stash (3m-3¼m winner, both by Stowaway): dam unraced: runner-up in Irish point: sixth in mares bumper at Warwick: modest form over hurdles: best effort when third in mares novice at Towcester in March: tried in cheekpieces. *Ben Case*   **h96** **b66**

MEGABUCKS (IRE) 7 b.g. Well Chosen – Clonmayo (IRE) (Kasmayo) [2017/18 h87p, b81: h16g² h16d⁵ h20.5s³ c20s² Jan 10] point winner: fair form over hurdles: 3/1, second in novice handicap at Ludlow (length behind Hey Bill) on chasing debut: will stay further than 2½m: acts on soft going: often races prominently: sure to progress as a chaser. *Henry Oliver*   **c115 p** **h108**

MEGA FORTUNE (FR) 5 b.g. Soldier of Fortune (IRE) – Far Across (Common Grounds) [2017/18 h145: h18sᶠ Oct 8] well-made gelding: smart hurdler: pulling clear in 3-runner minor event at Limerick when falling fatally 2 out sole outing in 2017/18: unproven beyond 2m: acts on soft going: sometimes wore cheekpieces: front runner/raced prominently. *Gordon Elliott, Ireland*   **h135**

MEGA MIND (IRE) 5 ch.g. Captain Rio – Final Leave (IRE) (Glacial Storm (USA)) [2017/18 h15.8d h19.6sᵖᵘ h15.8s h19.2vᵖᵘ Feb 1] unplaced completed start in Irish points: no form over hurdles. *Sam Thomas*   **h–**

MELANGERIE 6 b.m. Fair Mix (IRE) – Angie Marinie (Sabrehill (USA)) [2017/18 b98: h16g⁵ h15.5d³ h15.8d* h15.8s* h19.2vᵖᵘ h20.3g Apr 19] bumper winner: fairly useful form over hurdles: won novice at Ludlow in December and mares novice there in January: barely stays 2½m: acts on soft going: has worn hood: often races prominently/travels strongly. *Nicky Henderson*   **h119**

MELCHIOR KING (IRE) 4 br.g. Stowaway – Miss Ira Zarad (IRE) (Darazari (IRE)) [2017/18 b16v⁶ Mar 11] well beaten in bumper. *Philip Hobbs*   **b–**

MELDRUM LAD (IRE) 9 b.g. Fruits of Love (USA) – Meldrum Hall (IRE) (Saddlers' Hall (IRE)) [2017/18 c131, h–: c18m⁴ c23.6g² c23.8g Nov 4] sturdy gelding: winning hurdler: fairly useful handicap chaser: second in novice event at Huntingdon in October: stays 3m: acts on firm and soft going: has worn headgear: wears tongue tie: usually races towards rear. *Seamus Durack*   **c125** **h–**

MEL

MELEKHOV (IRE) 4 b.g. Sholokhov (IRE) – Yorkshire Girl (IRE) (Anshan) [2017/18 b14s² b16s* b16.2d* Apr 23] second foal: half-brother to fairly useful hurdler/winning pointer Indian Hawk (19f-21f winner, by Westerner): dam, no form, half-sister to fairly useful hurdler/useful chaser (stayed 3m) Banasan: fairly useful form in bumpers: won at Fakenham (maiden) in February and Hexham in April. *Philip Hobbs* **b97**

MELLOW BEN (IRE) 5 b.g. Beneficial – Mellowthemoonlight (IRE) (Un Desperado (FR)) [2017/18 b17.7g⁵ h19.3g h16.3s⁵ h19.2v⁵ h16s⁶ h16s³ h17.7g* Apr 20] €32,000 3-y-o, £30,000 4-y-o: useful-looking gelding: seventh foal: brother to fair hurdler/chaser (2m-21f winner) Mullaghboy and half-brother to modest hurdler Hello Louie (2¾m winner, by Luso): dam (h85) 2m hurdle winner: runner-up sole start in Irish points: tailed off in bumper: fair form over hurdles: won handicap at Fontwell in April: stays 2¼m: acts on soft going: tried in hood. *Chris Gordon* **h110 b–**

MELODIC RENDEZVOUS 12 ch.g. Where Or When (IRE) – Vic Melody (FR) (Old Vic) [2017/18 c–, h138d: h15.3s Nov 11] lengthy, useful-looking gelding: high-class hurdler at best, well beaten sole outing in 2017/18: winning chaser: raced mainly around 2m: acted on heavy going: wore headgear: front runner/raced prominently: retired. *Jeremy Scott* **c– h–**

MELON 6 ch.g. Medicean – Night Teeny (Platini (GER)) [2017/18 h150: h16s* h16.8s³ h16s⁵ h16.4s² h16sF Apr 27] **h166**

The close finish to the Champion Hurdle, in which Melon went down by just a neck to odds-on Buveur d'Air, apparently wasn't the first time that their respective owners had found themselves wishing for opposing outcomes to a race. Buveur d'Air's owner J. P. McManus recalled afterwards how he and Melon's owner had become acquainted. 'I have had many a battle on the racecourse with Joe Donnelly. He was a bookmaker, I was a punter and half a bookmaker, and at the time they felt more important than this winner today.' Donnelly, who sold his bookmaking business to move into property investment, is also the owner [the horses run in the name of Mrs J. Donnelly, his wife] of the luckless Al Boum Photo who would have been placed but for a late fall in the RSA Chase at the latest Festival and was then denied victory in bizarre circumstances at Punchestown. Melon's second in the Champion Hurdle came twelve months after he had started a hot favourite for the Supreme Novices' on just his second start over hurdles. He was unfortunate to find the temperamental Labaik on a 'going day' on that occasion and also had to settle for second at Punchestown on his only other start in his novice season.

The well-regarded Melon had improvement to make to be a Champion Hurdle contender but, with only three starts over hurdles, that wasn't out of the question as he began the latest season, particularly if he proved more tractable. His season began well with victory in the Grade 2 WKD Hurdle at Down Royal at the beginning of November, when he landed the odds by four and a half lengths from stable-

WKD Hurdle, Down Royal—Melon lands the odds from stable-companion Coquin Mans

MEN

companion Coquin Mans, with Mick Jazz back in third. Returned to Cheltenham for the following month's International Hurdle, Melon couldn't justify favouritism but shaped encouragingly in finishing third behind the Champion Hurdle regulars My Tent Or Yours and The New One, holding every chance at the last and beaten only two and a quarter lengths behind the winner to whom he was conceding 6 lb. Melon took a strong hold behind the modest pace set by The New One and, for his next start in the Irish Champion Hurdle at Leopardstown, he wore a hood in the expectation that it would encourage him to settle better. Instead, the application of the headgear may have had an adverse effect as Melon produced his only disappointing performance to date in managing just fifth behind Supasundae. Melon wore ear plugs, with the hood left off, for the Champion Hurdle at Cheltenham where, as expected, a truly-run race showed him in a much better light. Well supported at 7/1, Melon travelled strongly in touch, jumped upsides Buveur d'Air two out, was still with him at the last and pushed him all the way to the line, giving best only in the last fifty yards. A rematch between the principals would have made for an interesting race at Punchestown, but still more fascinating, in Buveur d'Air's absence, was Melon's clash instead with top novice Samcro in the Punchestown Champion Hurdle. But just as that race was coming to the boil both protagonists fell independently three from home, with Melon looking sure to take a hand in the finish, though the same could just as well have been said of Samcro.

Melon (ch.g. 2012)
- Medicean (ch 1997)
  - Machiavellian (b 1987)
    - Mr Prospector
    - Coup de Folie
  - Mystic Goddess (ch 1990)
    - Storm Bird
    - Rose Goddess
- Night Teeny (ch 1997)
  - Platini (ch 1989)
    - Surumu
    - Prairie Darling
  - Nightrockette (b 1983)
    - Rocket
    - Nightlife

The well-made Melon is Flat-bred, from a family of German classic winners, and his pedigree was reviewed fully in *Chasers & Hurdlers 2016/17*. To recap his classic connections, his dam Night Teeny, a mile and a quarter winner in Germany, bred the German-trained Oaks d'Italia winner Night of Magic (by Peintre Celebre), while another of Melon's half-sisters by the same sire is the dam of the Deutsches Derby winner Nutan. Night Teeny's half-sister Night Petticoat won Germany's Oaks, the Preis der Diana, and produced a winner of the same race, Next Gina, as well as Next Desert, another winner of the Deutsches Derby. Nuit Polaire (by Kheleyf), another of Melon's half-sisters, is now dam of the smart French three-year-old Intellogent who won the Prix Jean Prat in July. Effective on soft ground, Melon is ideally suited by a well-run race at two miles. All being well, there will be other chances to see how he and Samcro measure up, a meeting that would be spiced up even more if Buveur d'Air was also in the line-up. Melon is overdue a Grade 1 success and, still with only seven completed starts over hurdles to his name, his trainer believes there is yet more improvement to come from him. *W. P. Mullins, Ireland*

MELROSE BOY (FR) 6 b.g. Saint des Saints (FR) – Pollypink (FR) (Poliglote) [2017/18 h117: h21.1s* h20.5s³ h21.7v* h23.4v³ h20.3v Mar 16] well-made gelding: useful hurdler: won handicap at Cheltenham (conditional) in November and novice at Fontwell in January: third in handicap at Sandown (3½ lengths behind Topofthegame) in February: stays 23f: acts on heavy going. *Harry Fry*   **h132**

MEMORYS 5 b.g. Oscar (IRE) – Kind Heart (Red Ransom (USA)) [2017/18 h16.2v h16.2d Apr 23] well-held third completed start in Irish points: no form over hurdles: wears tongue tie. *Donald McCain*   **h–**

MENAPIAN (IRE) 7 b.g. Touch of Land (FR) – Mannequin (IRE) (In The Wings) [2017/18 b63: h18.5d^F h18.5v Feb 11] little impact in bumpers/over hurdles. *Helen Nelmes*   **h63**

MENDIP EXPRESS (IRE) 12 br.g. King's Theatre (IRE) – Mulberry (IRE) (Denel (FR)) [2017/18 c133, h–: c26v⁴ c23.8s⁴ c24.2d* Apr 23] tall, good-topped gelding: prolific point winner: winning hurdler: useful hunter chaser: won at Hexham in April: stays 3¼m: acts on heavy going: wears tongue tie: front runner/races prominently. *Philip Hobbs*   **c129 h–**

MEN

MENGLI KHAN (IRE) 5 b.g. Lope de Vega (IRE) – Danielli (IRE) (Danehill (USA)) [2017/18 h136p: h16s* h16v* h16s* h16sro h16v² h16.4s³ h16.5d³ Apr 24]   **h149**

    Of the seven horses that ran in the 2015 Racing Post Trophy, runner-up Johannes Vermeer and fifth-placed Deauville went on to achieve the most on the Flat. Johannes Vermeer won the Group 1 Criterium International at Saint-Cloud on his next start, and, two years later, almost provided his trainer Aidan O'Brien with a first win in the Melbourne Cup, going down by just half a length to Rekindling, trained by Aidan's son Joseph. Ballydoyle stablemate Deauville has established himself as a smart performer, his wins including the very valuable Belmont Derby in the States. In terms of prize money, both Johannes Vermeer and Deauville have earned the sort of money which would make connections of National Hunt horses green with envy. Gigginstown House Stud bought Mengli Khan, a tailed-off last in the Racing Post Trophy, for 155,000 guineas at the Newmarket Autumn Sales a year later and he is yet to recoup his purchase price despite winning three races over hurdles, including a Grade 1 at Fairyhouse, and being placed in two other major Festival contests. While connections may never make a profit on Mengli Khan, the former Hugo Palmer-trained gelding who proved a useful middle-distance handicapper at three, is yet another fine advert for the training skills of Gordon Elliott who, in a slight rejig to his role for Gigginstown, will no longer train any of the point-to-point runners, instead focusing fully on the Gigginstown 'first team'. Mouse Morris will concentrate on the operation's younger horses, while Colin Bowe and Brian Hamilton—overseen by Pat Doyle—will take over the pointers from Eddie Hales, who retired from training in May to launch a new venture in the food business.

    Of the four other Racing Post Trophy runners, incidentally, the winner Marcel had one more run, finishing last in the Two Thousand Guineas, while Tony Curtis is still plying his trade in competitive handicaps over a mile. The third and fourth, Foundation and Port Douglas, failed to win another race in Britain or Ireland, and both were sent overseas, Foundation continuing to race under the Highclere Thoroughbred Racing Club banner in Australia, while Port Douglas changed hands privately in the winter of 2016 to race in Singapore after finishing fifth in the Irish Derby on his final start for Aidan O'Brien. Among the pick of those sent to the horses in training sales, many are sold to race abroad, or for winter campaigns on the all-weather, but Mengli Khan's sale to go jumping is one of several high profile exceptions which also include Adonis Hurdle winner Redicean (an 85,000-guinea purchase at the 2017 Newmarket Autumn Sales) and Stratum (a 160,000-guinea purchase at the 2016 Newmarket Autumn Sales), who chased home Mengli Khan in a Grade 3 hurdle at Navan in November and has since reverted to the Flat, winning a valuable handicap at Newbury in July 2018.

    Having shaped well in two starts in juvenile hurdles the previous season, Mengli Khan began his campaign with a clear-cut success in a thirty-runner maiden hurdle at Navan in September. He was stepped up in class for his next start, in a Grade 3 contest over the same course and distance in which he confirmed his improvement with a four-length win over Stratum. Mengli Khan was duly sent off even-money favourite to give his trainer a first win in the Bar One Racing Royal Bond Novices' Hurdle at Fairyhouse at the beginning of December. Showing form that at the time had been bettered, among the season's novices, only by his stable-companion Samcro, Mengli Khan travelled in mid-division before being produced to lead between the last two, staying on well for a five and a half length success over Early Doors, with a further fifteen lengths back to another Elliott-trained runner Hardline in third. On the back of his performance in a race won by the likes of Istabraq, Moscow Flyer, Hardy Eustace, Hurricane Fly and Jezki, Mengli Khan was made 8/1 favourite with the sponsors for the Sky Bet Supreme Novices' Hurdle.

    Mengli Khan's next start came in the Paddy Power Future Champions Novices' Hurdle at Leopardstown, a contender for the most dramatic race of the season. Having taken a lead from Hardline until halfway down the back straight, Mengli Khan was in front and travelling as well as anything when ducking out at the second last, crashing through the rail on the inside. Real Steel was left in front but—under strong pressure—was about to be headed by his stablemate Sharjah when both fell independently at the last. The Willie Mullins fourth string Whiskey Sour, who

MEN

had struggled to go the early gallop, came through for the unlikeliest of victories. After blotting his copybook at Leopardstown, Mengli Khan took on Getabird in the Moscow Flyer Novices' Hurdle at Punchestown just seventeen days later and got back on track to some extent, though he was beaten nine lengths and never threatened the winner, in the end running below the form he showed when winning the Royal Bond. The pace in the Moscow Flyer was nothing out of the ordinary, with Getabird enjoying the run of things from the front, and Mengli Khan's chance wasn't helped by the late withdrawal of his usual pacemaker Hardline due to a high temperature.

Mengli Khan made his first start over hurdles outside Ireland in the Supreme Novices' at the Cheltenham Festival, where, following a two-month break and fitted with a tongue-strap for the first time, he was sent off at 14/1, joint fifth favourite behind Getabird. Mengli Khan ran his best race of the season, beaten less than two lengths into third behind Summerville Boy, suited by the stronger gallop set by Getabird on this occasion. Mengli Khan was eventually beaten a neck and a length and three quarters by Summerville Boy and Kalashnikov. Mengli Khan signed off for the season by filling the same position in the Herald Champion Novices' Hurdle at the Punchestown Festival in late-April, shaping better than the bare result but unable to quite match his Cheltenham effort behind two less exposed runners in Draconien and Vision des Flos, a couple of late jumping errors ultimately contributing to Mengli Khan's undoing.

Mengli Khan (IRE) (b.g. 2013)	Lope de Vega (IRE) (ch 2007)	Shamardal (b 2002)	Giant's Causeway / Helsinki
		Lady Vettori (b 1997)	Vettori / Lady Golconda
	Danielli (IRE) (b 2002)	Danehill (b 1986)	Danzig / Razyana
		Ingabelle (b 1984)	Taufan / Bodelle

Gigginstown House Stud's "Mengli Khan"

MER

As with Identity Thief, the Flat-bred Mengli Khan does not have the typical profile of a Gigginstown House Stud recruit. By the Prix du Jockey Club winner Lope de Vega Mengli Khan is a brother to Very Special, a smart mare for Godolphin who won successive renewals of the Cape Verdi at Meydan in 2016 and 2017. Mengli Khan is also a half-brother to the useful miler Janicellaine (by Beat Hollow) and the ill-fated Fillies' Mile and Breeders' Cup Juvenile Fillies Turf winner Chriselliam (by Iffraaj), as well as the two-mile hurdler Akula (by Soviet Star) who was fairly useful in his prime. Mengli Khan's dam Danielli, a maiden who stayed thirteen furlongs, is out of the useful Irish sprinter Ingabelle making her a half-sister to the Premio Lydia Tesio and Princess Elizabeth Stakes winner Eva's Request and Moyglare Stud Stakes winner Priory Belle among others. A strong gelding, Mengli Khan has shown his best form on soft/heavy going and raced in a tongue strap on his last two starts. He wore ear plugs in the Supreme and has also worn ear plugs in the preliminaries of some of his other races. *Gordon Elliott, Ireland*

MERCENAIRE (FR) 4 gr.g. Soldier of Fortune (IRE) – Southwold (FR) (Take Risks (FR)) [2017/18 h16.8v* h16v³ h16.8v² h16.4s^pu Mar 14] good-topped gelding: fourth foal: brother to French 11.5f winner Aventuriere du Sud and half-brother to 2 other winners on Flat in France: dam French 1m/9.5f winner: fairly useful form over hurdles: won juvenile at Exeter in November: raced around 2m: acts on heavy going. *Nick Williams*   **h126**

MERCERS COURT (IRE) 10 b.g. Court Cave (IRE) – Vikki's Dream (IRE) (Kahyasi) [2017/18 c135, h117: c19.4g⁴ c22.6g^pu h25m⁵ c24.2d^F h20.5s c26d^pu c21.2s c19.4d Apr 22] angular gelding: fairly useful hurdler/useful chaser, well below best in 2017/18: stays 25f: acts on soft and good to firm going: tried in headgear/tongue tie: often races prominently. *Neil King*   **c116 h–**

MERCIAN KING (IRE) 7 b.g. Robin des Pres (FR) – Mariah Rollins (IRE) (Over The River (FR)) [2017/18 c110, h–: c17.4g² c17.8g* c16.5f* c16.3g³ c16.3s^F ab18d³ Mar 5] lengthy gelding: maiden hurdler: fairly useful handicap chaser: won at Fontwell in August and Worcester in October: stays 2½m, effective at shorter: acts on firm and soft going: has worn cheekpieces: usually races prominently. *Amy Murphy*   **c116 h–**

MERCIAN PRINCE (IRE) 7 b.g. Midnight Legend – Bongo Fury (FR) (Sillery (USA)) [2017/18 c136, h–: c19.4g³ c21.1v c20.5d* c19.4v* c20.8s c20.5g⁵ Apr 20] sturdy gelding: maiden hurdler: useful handicap chaser: won at Kempton in January and Wetherby in February: stays 21f: acts on heavy going: tried in tongue tie: usually races prominently. *Amy Murphy*   **c142 h–**

MERCIAN PRINCESS (IRE) 5 b.m. Saint des Saints (FR) – Bongo Fury (FR) (Sillery (USA)) [2017/18 b–: h16g Sep 12] lightly-made mare: no form in bumpers: in cheekpieces, well beaten in mares maiden on hurdling debut. *Amy Murphy*   **h–**

MERCY MERCY ME 6 b.g. Shirocco (GER) – Monsignorita (IRE) (Classic Cliche (IRE)) [2017/18 b16s* b16.4s b17s Apr 13] tall gelding: second foal: half-brother to a winning pointer by Kayf Tara: dam (h77), ungenuine maiden hurdler (stayed 2½m), out of sister to Champion Bumper winner/very smart hurdler (stayed 21f) Monsignor: useful form in bumpers: won at Sandown (by 3½ lengths from Classic Ben) in November. *Fergal O'Brien*   **b109**

MERE ANARCHY (IRE) 7 b.g. Yeats (IRE) – Maracana (IRE) (Glacial Storm (USA)) [2017/18 h99: h23m⁴ h23.3g Jul 19] fair handicap hurdler, below best in 2017/18: unproven beyond 2m: acts on soft going: tried in cheekpieces/tongue tie: usually races nearer last than first: signs of temperament. *Robert Stephens*   **h96**

MERIBEL MILLIE 7 b.m. Kayf Tara – Ede'iff (Tragic Role (USA)) [2017/18 h108, b79: c19.9g⁶ c20s⁶ h19.4s Jan 9] bumper winner: fair hurdler at best: poor form over fences: stays 2½m: acts on heavy going: tried in hood: wears tongue tie: usually races nearer last than first/freely: should do better as a chaser. *Neil Mulholland*   **c83 p h–**

MERI DEVIE (IRE) 5 ch.m. Spirit One (FR) – Folle Biche (FR) (Take Risks (FR)) [2017/18 h135+: h19.4s h16v² h16s² h16v⁴ h18s⁵ h20.2v* h16.8v h16s⁶ h20s* Apr 28] sturdy mare: smart hurdler: won listed mares event at Punchestown (by 5 lengths from Alletrix) in February and Ballymore Handicap Hurdle there (by 1¾ lengths from C'est Jersey) in April: second in Fishery Lane Hurdle at Naas (2 lengths behind Early Doors) in November: stays 2½m: acts on heavy going: has worn hood. *W. P. Mullins, Ireland*   **h145**

508

MIA

MERRION ROW (IRE) 10 b.g. Milan – Diklers Dante (IRE) (Phardante (FR)) [2017/18 c17g⁶ c24dpu Nov 6] no show in point: bumper winner: maiden hurdler: modest handicap chaser at best, won at Downpatrick in 2016/17:, below that level in 2017/18 left P. J. Rothwell after first start: stays 19f: acts on soft going: has worn hood/tongue tie, including in 2017/18: usually leads. *Martin Bosley* — c69 h—

MERRY MILAN (IRE) 6 b.g. Milan – Timerry (IRE) (Alphabatim (USA)) [2017/18 h21.2d⁶ h23.1d* Apr 21] closely related to several winning pointers by Oscar, including Oscar Delta (also useful 25f chase winner), and half-brother to a winning pointer by Kasmayo: dam unraced: Irish point winner: fair form over hurdles: won maiden at Bangor in April. *Nicky Martin* — h113

METHAG (FR) 5 b.m. Pour Moi (IRE) – Kyria (Grand Lodge (USA)) [2017/18 h77: h20.6d⁵ h15.5d⁶ Dec 7] close-coupled mare: fairly useful on Flat: poor maiden hurdler. *Alex Hales* — h76

MEXICAN BORDER (GER) 9 b.g. Sholokhov (IRE) – Moricana (GER) (Konigsstuhl (GER)) [2017/18 h90: h18.5m h18.7gpu Jun 20] modest hurdler at best, no form in 2017/18: unproven beyond 17f: acts on good to firm going: has worn hood: has worn tongue tie, including last 5 starts. *Martin Hill* — h—

MIAMI PRESENT (IRE) 8 b.g. Presenting – Miami Nights (GER) (Tertullian (USA)) [2017/18 c103, h107: c19.9m³ c19.4g² c21.4g* c24g* c24d⁴ c24g* c25.6g² Nov 16] good-topped gelding: winning hurdler: fairly useful handicap chaser: won at Market Rasen (novice) in August, and Southwell in September and October (novice): stays 3¼m: acts on soft going: wears headgear: front runner/races prominently. *Harriet Bethell* — c124 h—

MIA'S ANTHEM (IRE) 10 ch.g. Royal Anthem (USA) – Windmill View (IRE) (Glacial Storm (USA)) [2017/18 c127, h91: c20m⁶ c25g³ c23.8gpu Jul 5] angular gelding: winning hurdler: fairly useful handicap chaser, below form in 2017/18: stays 3¼m: acts on soft and good to firm going: has worn cheekpieces, including final start: wears tongue tie. *Noel C. Kelly, Ireland* — c100 h—

MIA'S STORM (IRE) 8 b.m. September Storm (GER) – Letitia's Gain (IRE) (Zaffaran (USA)) [2017/18 h121: h22.8m* c23.6d* c23.9g* c24dF c20.5gF Apr 21] sturdy mare: useful handicap hurdler: won at Haydock (by 8 lengths from Prime Venture) in May: smart form over fences: won novice at Chepstow (by 3¼ lengths from Elegant Escape) in October and listed mares event at Market Rasen (by 13 lengths from Antartica de Thaix) in November: stays 3m: acts on good to firm and heavy going: strong traveller. *Alan King* — c145 h132

Ballymore Handicap Hurdle, Punchestown—
the biggest win in a fine campaign for Rachael Blackmore as she steers Meri Devie (second right) to victory in a race dominated by Willie Mullins-trained runners, which also included runner-up C'est Jersey (blinkers) and the grey Bunk Off Early who came fourth

MIC

MICHAEL JAMES (IRE) 7 b.g. Baltic King – Flying Cockatoo (IRE) (Flying Spur (AUS)) [2017/18 h18.8d h16s h16.2s⁴ Nov 10] compact gelding: down the field in 4 starts on Flat: modest form over hurdles: wears tongue tie. *Paul Stafford, Ireland*   **h97**

MICHAEL'S MOUNT 5 ch.g. Mount Nelson – Dumnoni (Titus Livius (FR)) [2017/18 h16.6d* h16g³ h15.8d* h16.5s Apr 14] fairly useful on Flat, stays 1½m: fairly useful form over hurdles: won novices at Doncaster in February and Ludlow in March: third in Dovecote Novices' Hurdle at Kempton in between. *Ian Williams*   **h126**

MICHELE STROGOFF 5 b.g. Aqlaam – Maschera d'Oro (Mtoto) [2017/18 h16.8g Oct 25] fairly useful on Flat, stays 1¼m: tailed off in maiden on hurdling debut. *Tony Coyle*   **h–**

MICKEY BUCKMAN 5 b.g. Gleaming (IRE) – Mysaynoway (Overbury (IRE)) [2017/18 h19.1m⁵ Jun 15] well beaten in novice hurdle. *Gary Moore*   **h–**

MICKEY MILLER (IRE) 9 b.g. Millenary – Rare Harvest (IRE) (Phardante (FR)) [2017/18 c24.2g³ c21.2d³ May 29] multiple point winner: modest form in hunter chases. *John Dawson*   **c93**

MICKEYSMATEDUSTY 6 b.g. Revoque (IRE) – Dusty Anne (IRE) (Dushyantor (USA)) [2017/18 b16.8v Jan 1] tailed off in maiden bumper. *Mark Shears*   **b–**

MICKIEBLUEEYES (IRE) 6 b.g. Dilshaan – Killerig Park (I'm Supposin (IRE)) [2017/18 h–p: h20.5s⁶ h20.5s h19.6s⁴ h25d² Feb 26] modest form over hurdles: won handicap at Plumpton in February: stays 25f: acts on soft going: in tongue tie last 2 starts. *Diana Grissell*   **h99**

MICK JAZZ (FR) 7 b.g. Blue Bresil (FR) – Mick Maya (FR) (Siam (USA)) [2017/18 h148+: h16s³ h20s⁵ h16s* h16s³ h16.4s³ Mar 13]   **h161**

Death and taxes, yes, but not 20/1-on favourites in three-runner novice chases. The winner of two of his three starts over fences, showing useful form, Tree of Liberty looked the nearest thing to a racing certainty at Ludlow in March. One of his rivals, Over To Midnight, was a poor maiden hurdler who had finished tailed-off last on her only previous start over fences, while his other opponent, Cap'n, making his chasing debut, had finished in front of only one rival in four starts over hurdles and had been beaten eighty-nine lengths when last of four on his most recent start. To general consternation, in a slowly-run race in which he made several jumping errors, Tree of Liberty was headed by Cap'n at the final fence and was beaten two and a half lengths to become the shortest-priced loser over jumps in Britain (he was afterwards found to have bled).

Following the philosophy of 'never be afraid of one horse' had also paid off handsomely earlier in the season for the connections of Mick Jazz. Given the Grade 1 status of the race he won, and the fact that the long odds-on favourite who bit the dust was a former Champion Hurdle winner, the result of the Ryanair Hurdle at Leopardstown in December made a lot more headlines than the Ludlow race, though, inevitably, they were more about the shock defeat of Faugheen, who was sent off at 11/2-on, than Mick Jazz's victory. Faugheen had returned from a lengthy absence to win the Morgiana Hurdle at Punchestown the previous month by sixteen lengths and the top-class winner of the 2015 Champion Hurdle faced four rivals who had each shown just smart form at best. Willie Mullins also saddled the 6/1 second favourite Cilaos Emery, winner of the Herald Champion Novices' Hurdle at Punchestown at the end of the previous season, while Gordon Elliott supplied the three other runners, with 14/1-chance Mick Jazz joined by stable-companions Campeador (12/1) and The Game Changer (33/1). Campeador had been a long way behind Faugheen when falling at the last in the Morgiana, while Mick Jazz, who had finished third to Faugheen's stable-companion Melon in the WKD Hurdle at Down Royal on his reappearance, had since finished only fifth (one place behind Cilaos Emery) behind his own stablemate Apple's Jade when sent off at 25/1 for the Hatton's Grace Hurdle at Fairyhouse. It was clear some way out in the Ryanair that the favourite was in trouble, Faugheen relinquishing his lead to Cilaos Emery as early as before the fourth hurdle, and he was soon beaten once the pace quickened after the third last before being pulled up and dismounted. Less certain was which of the four remaining runners would be the one to take advantage. Cilaos Emery and Mick Jazz were the pair who pulled clear from the home turn and it was the latter who jumped into a narrow lead at the last before being driven a length and

MIC

three quarters ahead at the line. Campeador and The Game Changer took a remote third and fourth. Faugheen's stable-companion Nichols Canyon had been beaten in the same race twelve months earlier at 5/2-on, while Istabraq already looked beaten when falling at the last at odds of 4/1-on in 2000 in a race won by Moscow Flyer. Istabraq had won the three previous editions and was successful again a year later.

Quite what the first two in the latest Ryanair Hurdle had achieved in terms of form was obviously open to doubt, though another beating of Cilaos Emery entitled Mick Jazz to be credited with some improvement. There had been a neck between them in a listed novice hurdle at Punchestown the previous February and, while Cilaos Emery had gone on to better things afterwards, that had been Mick Jazz's final start of the season as he had to miss the County Hurdle when lame. Faugheen started odds on again when Mick Jazz faced him for a second time back at Leopardstown in the Irish Champion Hurdle in February, nothing having come to light to explain Faugheen's poor performance in the Ryanair. Faugheen duly got the better of the argument this time, with Mick Jazz finishing nearly five lengths behind him, but neither proved a match for Supasundae in the closing stages. The result seemed to confirm that Mick Jazz had been an opportunistic Grade 1 winner, but a career-best effort in the Champion Hurdle at Cheltenham showed him to be not far behind the best two-miler hurdlers around. He missed a run in the Red Mills Trial Hurdle at Gowran in between due to a temperature. Sent off at 25/1 at Cheltenham, Mick Jazz travelled well under a patient ride before moving on to the heels of the leading pair Buveur d'Air and Melon rounding the home turn. Though unable to land a blow, Mick Jazz kept on to be beaten a neck and three lengths into third and he pulled nine lengths clear of the fourth Identity Thief, putting up a high-class performance.

Although Mick Jazz ran only five times in the latest season—he wasn't in his stable's large team at the Punchestown Festival—that is more racing than he had had in any of his previous campaigns. After two runs over hurdles in France he joined Harry Fry and showed fairly useful form to be placed in a couple of juvenile hurdles at Newbury won by Old Guard and Top Notch. It was the best part of a year before Mick Jazz made the track again, starting joint favourite for the Greatwood Hurdle at Cheltenham for which he looked very well handicapped. However, he was pulled up on that occasion, found to be suffering from an irregular heartbeat, and it was almost

Ryanair Hurdle (December), Leopardstown—Mick Jazz takes full advantage of Faugheen's flop to claim his first Grade 1 win, chased home by Cilaos Emery (virtually hidden)

MIC

another twelve months before he was seen again. In the meantime, he had been bought at Doncaster Sales for just £27,000 by Elliott when owner Jared Sullivan dispersed most of his horses which had run under the Potensis Bloodstock banner. Buveur d'Air, incidentally, had also begun his career in the same colours, though, as recounted in the essay on Laurina, Sullivan returned to ownership on a large scale in the latest season. Mick Jazz finally got off the mark in a maiden hurdle at Clonmel and, before that listed win over Cilaos Emery, he came second to his stable's future Supreme Novices' winner Labaik in a Grade 3 novice at Navan and then finished third in a valuable handicap at Fairyhouse.

Mick Jazz is the best horse by his sire Blue Bresil to have raced in Britain or Ireland, though the latest Grand Annual winner Le Prezien isn't far behind him. Le Prezien was a second Cheltenham Festival winner for Paul Nicholls by the sire in three years after Ibis du Rheu who won the Martin Pipe in 2016. Le Prezien's brother Mont des Avaloirs showed useful form in novice hurdles for Nicholls in the latest season. Blue Bresil is a son of the smart French middle-distance horse Smadoun, best known in Britain as the sire of high-class chasers Nacarat and Smad Place. Blue Bresil had a much more interesting career (for three different trainers) than his three wins in minor company on the Flat might suggest. Along the way, he was also placed in a couple of trials for the Prix du Jockey Club, before finishing down the field in that race, and even more ambitiously fared no better when the rank outsider in that year's Arc won by Zarkava. Few Arc runners go jumping, but the following year Blue Bresil had five races over hurdles at Auteuil. He was again highly tried and failed to win, but showed smart form. In fact, thrown straight into Group 3 company, he went close to causing an upset on his hurdling debut when beaten only three quarters of a length in the Prix Jacques d'Indy by Long Run, then France's leading four-year-old hurdler. Having finished second in two more pattern races over hurdles, Blue Bresil ended his career with a win back on the Flat over fifteen furlongs. He was initially retired to stud in France but was moved to Yorton Farm in Britain for the 2016 covering season.

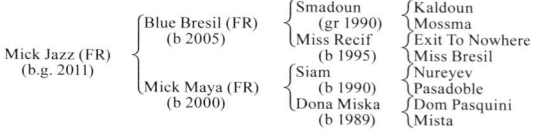

Mick Jazz (FR) (b.g. 2011)	Blue Bresil (FR) (b 2005)	Smadoun (gr 1990)	Kaldoun / Mossma
		Miss Recif (b 1995)	Exit To Nowhere / Miss Bresil
	Mick Maya (FR) (b 2000)	Siam (b 1990)	Nureyev / Pasadoble
		Dona Miska (b 1989)	Dom Pasquini / Mista

Mick Jazz's immediate relatives are from a more modest branch of one of the most famous French jumping families. His dam Mick Maya won a hurdle and two chases at up to nineteen furlongs in the French Provinces and she is also the dam of the bumper winner Mick Maestro (by Air Chief Marshal) who made a winning debut over hurdles at Uttoxeter for Tom George shortly after the end of the latest season. The other winner worth a mention is the useful Mick Thonic, another grandson of Mick Jazz's unraced grandam Dona Miska. He won a two-mile novice chase at Cheltenham for Colin Tizzard in 2016/17. Great grandam Mista, a winner over hurdles and fences at Auteuil, was a half-sister to Kotkie, the dam of Katko and Kotkijet who won five editions of the Grand Steeple-Chase de Paris between them. The well-made Mick Jazz didn't run badly in the Hatton's Grace over two and a half miles but a well-run two miles—he tends to travel strongly held up—suits him ideally and he acts on soft ground. He wears a hood and has had his tongue tied. He'll presumably be campaigned with the Champion Hurdle in mind again, though stable-companion Samcro may well be his stable's number-one Champion Hurdle contender by the time Cheltenham comes round again. It is also possible that Mick Jazz could be campaigned in the States where his owner is based. *Gordon Elliott, Ireland*

MICK MAESTRO (FR) 5 b.g. Air Chief Marshal (IRE) – Mick Maya (FR) (Siam (USA)) [2017/18 b86: b16.5s⁴ b13.7s Jan 26] fair form in bumpers. *Tom George* **b90**

MICK MANHATTAN (FR) 4 b.g. Blue Bresil (FR) – Normanville (IRE) (Anabaa Blue) [2017/18 b15.8v* Apr 15] first foal: dam, ran once on Flat in France, half-sister to useful 2m hurdle winner Wingtips: 8/1, won bumper at Ffos Las (by ½ length from Smiths Cross) on debut. *Evan Williams* — **b93**

MICK'S WISH (IRE) 6 b.g. Westerner – Bells Chance (IRE) (Needle Gun (IRE)) [2017/18 b16.2d⁶ b16.2d⁵ h22.7g h22.7s Jan 14] smallish gelding: poor form in bumpers: no form over hurdles. *Jackie Stephen* — **h–** **b69**

MICK THE POSER (IRE) 4 b.g. Art Connoisseur (IRE) – Naked Poser (IRE) (Night Shift (USA)) [2017/18 h15.8d² h16.8g² h17d⁴ h16s⁴ h16.2v³ h16.2s⁵ Apr 26] half-brother to fairly useful hurdler Artist's Muse (2m winner, by Cape Cross): modest on Flat, stays 1½m: fair form over hurdles: raced around 2m: acts on good to soft going: in cheekpieces last 5 starts: usually races prominently. *Jennie Candlish* — **h101**

MICK THONIC (FR) 8 gr.g. Maresca Sorrento (FR) – Mick Madona (FR) (Dadarissime (FR)) [2017/18 c135, h–: c21v³ c16mᵘʳ c15.9gᵖᵘ c15.9d c16dᵖᵘ c16v⁴ c16d⁶ h16g Apr 20] lengthy gelding: winning hurdler: useful handicap chaser, below form in 2017/18: stays 2½m: acts on heavy going: tried in blinkers: wears tongue tie. *Colin Tizzard* — **c121** **h110**

MICQUUS (IRE) 9 b.g. High Chaparral (IRE) – My Potters (USA) (Irish River (FR)) [2017/18 c75, h–: c19.7s⁴ c21.7m⁴ Apr 25] maiden hurdler: poor maiden chaser: has worn headgear, including in 2017/18. *Emma Lavelle* — **c59** **h–**

MIDAS GOLD (IRE) 6 b.g. Rip Van Winkle (IRE) – Hespera (Danehill (USA)) [2017/18 b89: b17d b16g Apr 21] bumper winner, well held in 2017/18. *Brian Ellison* — **b–**

MIDDLEBROW (IRE) 7 b.g. Oscar (IRE) – O What A Girl (IRE) (Anshan) [2017/18 h105, b90: h17.4g h16.2d⁴ c19.2d* c15.7bᵈ c19.9s* c16.9d² c20.3d Apr 21] bumper winner: poor maiden hurdler: fairly useful form over fences: won handicap at Catterick in November and novice handicap at Musselburgh in January: stays 2½m: acts on soft going: wears tongue tie: often races prominently. *Donald McCain* — **c116** **h68**

MIDNIGHT APPEAL 13 b.g. Midnight Legend – Lac Marmot (FR) (Marju (IRE)) [2017/18 c94x, h–: c22.6d⁶ Jun 9] good-topped gelding: multiple point winner: winning hurdler: useful chaser at best, typically let down by jumping sole outing under Rules in 2017/18: stays 25f: acts on good to firm and heavy going: often wears headgear/tongue tie. *Miss C. R. Hawker* — **c89 x** **h–**

MIDNIGHT CHEERS 7 b.m. Midnight Legend – Marrasit (IRE) (Zaffaran (USA)) [2017/18 h20.3vᵖᵘ Feb 5] fourth foal: dam winning pointer: pulled up in maiden hurdle. *Caroline Bailey* — **h–**

MIDNIGHT CHILL 6 b.g. Midnight Legend – Chilla Cilla (Glacial Storm (USA)) [2017/18 b90: h15.8d⁴ h15.7s h15.8s² h19.8vᵖᵘ h20.6s³ Apr 11] good-topped gelding: fair form over hurdles: should stay beyond 2m: acts on soft going: tried in tongue tie: front runner/races prominently. *Jamie Snowden* — **h114**

MIDNIGHT COWBOY 7 gr.g. Midnight Legend – Kali (Linamix (FR)) [2017/18 h118: c20.5m³ c20.5g* c20g* c21m³ c19.4m² c20d⁶ c21s³ Mar 25] lengthy gelding: point winner: winning hurdler: useful handicap chaser: won at Kempton and Warwick in May (novice events) and Stratford in August: left Alan King after sixth start: stays 3m: acts on good to firm and heavy going. *J. P. Owen* — **c133** **h–**

MIDNIGHT FRENSI 9 b.g. Midnight Legend – Flame O'Frensi (Tudor Flame) [2017/18 h21.7ᵖᵘ Jan 29] failed to complete all 3 starts in points: pulled up in maiden on hurdling debut. *Martin Wilesmith* — **h–**

MIDNIGHT FROLIC 6 b.m. Midnight Legend – Annie Greenlaw (Petoski) [2017/18 b17.7gᵖᵘ Nov 10] pulled up in bumper: dead. *Luke Dace* — **b–**

MIDNIGHT GEM 8 b.m. Midnight Legend – Barton Flower (Danzero (AUS)) [2017/18 h108: c21.4gᶠ h21.7d c19.9g c23.6g² c22.7d c20.3sᵖᵘ Dec 17] smallish mare: winning hurdler: fair form over fences: stays 3m: acts on good to firm and good to soft going: front runner/races prominently. *Charlie Longsdon* — **c103** **h–**

MIDNIGHT GLORY 6 b.m. Midnight Legend – Land of Glory (Supreme Leader) [2017/18 h109, b74: h23.1sᵖᵘ h21.6d⁴ h24.4d⁴ h24v⁴ h24.6s Apr 9] compact mare: fair handicap hurdler: stays 2¾m: acts on soft going. *Philip Hobbs* — **h104**

MIDNIGHT GYPSY 8 b.m. Midnight Legend – Romany Dream (Nomadic Way (USA)) [2017/18 h84: h18.7g⁴ h19.9g³ c21.6gᵖᵘ c20gᵖᵘ h19.6g³ h20g h19m* h19g* h19.7g Nov 29] sturdy mare: modest handicap hurdler: won conditionals/amateur event and mares event, both at Taunton in November: pulled up both starts over fences: stays 2½m: acts on good to firm going: wears hood: has worn tongue tie. *Stuart Kittow* — **c–** **h92**

MID

MIDNIGHT JAZZ 8 b.m. Midnight Legend – Ring Back (IRE) (Bob Back (USA)) [2017/18 h136: h15.8g[6] h19.8s[2] h21s[4] h19.9s[6] h20.3g[6] Apr 19] small mare: useful hurdler: second in listed mares event at Sandown (½ length behind Poppy Kay) in January: stays 2½m: acts on good to firm and heavy going: in cheekpieces last 4 starts: often travels strongly. *Ben Case* — **h133**

MIDNIGHT JITTERBUG 6 b.g. Midnight Legend – Heebie Jeebie (Overbury (IRE)) [2017/18 h89, b70: h16g[3] h17.7d[3] May 28] lengthy, rather unfurnished gelding: modest form over hurdles: stays 2m: acts on good to soft going. *Noel Williams* — **h96**

MIDNIGHT KATE (IRE) 4 gr.f. Midnight Legend – Primrose Time (Alflora (IRE)) [2017/18 b14.6s h15.7s h17s[5] h16.2s[5] Apr 27] first foal: dam (c112) bumper and 2m/17f chase winner: no form in bumpers: poor form over hurdles. *Jackie Stephen* — **h82 b–**

MIDNIGHT MAESTRO 6 b.g. Midnight Legend – Calamintha (Mtoto) [2017/18 h120: h15.7g[6] h15.7g h21d[5] h20.5s[2] Apr 15] useful-looking gelding: fairly useful handicap hurdler: stays 2½m: acts on heavy going. *Alan King* — **h124**

MIDNIGHT MAGIC 6 b.g. Midnight Legend – Arctic Magic (IRE) (Saddlers' Hall (IRE)) [2017/18 b–: h19g[4] h18.5m[6] h16.8s h16.3g h23.9g[3] h23.9s[bd] h24s[5] Dec 21] modest maiden hurdler: stays 3m: best form on good going: wears headgear/tongue tie. *David Pipe* — **h92**

MIDNIGHT MAN (FR) 4 ch.g. Evasive – Moon Tree (FR) (Groom Dancer (USA)) [2017/18 h16d h16.8g[5] Oct 25] fair maiden on Flat, stays 1m: modest form over hurdles: in tongue tie final start. *K. R. Burke* — **h91**

MIDNIGHT MERLOT 6 b.g. Midnight Legend – Peel Me A Grape (Gunner B) [2017/18 h94, b68: h20.3d[pu] c19.4s[4] c19.2s[pu] Feb 18] maiden hurdler: fair form over fences: better effort when fourth in novice at Wetherby in January: stays 21f: acts on soft going. *Noel Williams* — **c100 h–**

MIDNIGHT MIDGE 4 b.g. Midnight Legend – Posh Emily (Rakaposhi King) [2017/18 b13.7g b15.3v h16.5v[6] h15.3s Feb 17] neat gelding: poor form in bumpers/over hurdles. *Ron Hodges* — **h77 b70**

MIDNIGHT MONSOON 5 gr.m. Midnight Legend – Another Storm (Shambo) [2017/18 b16s[6] b16d[pu] Apr 7] first foal: dam (h106) 2½m-2¾m hurdle winner: poor form in bumpers. *Ben Case* — **b61**

MIDNIGHT MONTY 8 ch.g. Midnight Legend – Marello (Supreme Leader) [2017/18 c–, h110: h25m[4] c23m[2] c21.4v[2] c24.2v[2] c24.2s[3] c23.6v[pu] Apr 14] fair hurdler: fairly useful handicap chaser: left Tom Lacey after second start: stays 25f: acts on good to firm and heavy going: has worn blinkers, including in 2016/17: has worn tongue tie, including last 4 starts: front runner/races prominently. *Jamie Snowden* — **c117 h111**

MIDNIGHT MOOD 5 b.m. Aqlaam – Inflammable (Montjeu (IRE)) [2017/18 h16.3s Jan 17] modest on Flat, stays 11f: tailed off in novice on hurdling debut. *Dominic Ffrench Davis* — **h–**

MIDNIGHT MUSTANG 11 b.g. Midnight Legend – Mustang Molly (Soldier Rose) [2017/18 c82, h–: c23.6s[4] c24.5v[3] c23.6d[3] Apr 24] stocky gelding: maiden hurdler: poor handicap chaser: stays 3¼m: acts on heavy going: has worn cheekpieces, including in 2017/18. *Andrew Martin* — **c73 h–**

MIDNIGHT OWLE 8 ch.g. Midnight Legend – Owlesbury Dream (IRE) (Luso) [2017/18 h–: h23.3d h19.6s h19.6s[pu] h19.2v[4] h25d c15.7g Apr 20] workmanlike gelding: maiden hurdler, no form in 2017/18: well beaten in novice on chasing debut: wears tongue tie. *Claire Dyson* — **c– h–**

MIDNIGHT QUEEN 8 b.m. Rainbow High – Questionit (Sovereign Water (FR)) [2017/18 h–, b66: h19.6s[4] h20d[3] h21.6m h21.6m c21.6g[pu] Aug 24] point winner: poor maiden hurdler: pulled up in novice handicap on chasing debut: should stay 2¾m: acts on good to soft going: in headgear last 5 starts: often races lazily: temperament under suspicion. *John Flint* — **c– h71**

MIDNIGHTREFERENDUM 5 b.m. Midnight Legend – Forget The Ref (IRE) (Dr Massini (IRE)) [2017/18 b15.7s[3] b16s* b17s[2] Apr 12] rather unfurnished mare: second foal: dam, winning pointer, sister to fairly useful hurdler/chaser (19f-21f winner) Pocket Aces: useful form in bumpers: won mares event at Warwick in March (by length from Lady of The Night) in February: improved when second in Nickel Coin Mares' National Hunt Flat Race at Aintree (1¼ lengths behind Getaway Katie Mai) in April. *Alan King* — **b106**

MIDNIGHT REQUEST 9 b.g. Midnight Legend – Friendly Request (Environment Friend) [2017/18 c105x, h110: h23.1s* h23.1s[5] c19.2v[pu] h23.1s h21.4v[5] h23.9v[4] h19.5s Apr 27] fairly useful handicap hurdler: won at Exeter in October: winning chaser, often let down by jumping: stays 25f: acts on heavy going: has worn headgear, including last 2 starts: front runner/races prominently. *Nigel Hawke* — **c– x h115**

QTS Scottish Champion Hurdle (Limited Handicap), Ayr—
25/1-shot Midnight Shadow springs a surprise from Claimantakinforgan (hooped sleeves & cap) and 2017 winner Chesterfield (noseband)

MIDNIGHT SHADOW 5 b.g. Midnight Legend – Holy Smoke (Statoblest) [2017/18 b95: h15.8s* h15.7v² h17v² h15.7v² h15.7s^{ur} h16.5s h16g* Apr 21] workmanlike gelding: bumper winner: useful hurdler: won novice at Uttoxeter in October and Scottish Champion Hurdle (Limited Handicap) at Ayr (by 1¼ lengths from Claimantakinforgan) in April: second in Rossington Main Novices' Hurdle at Haydock (10 lengths behind First Flow) in January: will stay beyond 2m: acts on heavy going. *Sue Smith* **h137**

MIDNIGHT SHOT 8 b.g. Midnight Legend – Suave Shot (Suave Dancer (USA)) [2017/18 h129: c21.7m* c21.7g* c20.1g* c21.4g c20.3g⁵ c20d* c19.8g³ c20.8s c21.1s^{pu} c20d⁶ Apr 28] sturdy gelding: winning hurdler: useful chaser: won maiden and novice at Towcester in May, novice at Hexham in June and handicap at Uttoxeter (by 2¼ lengths from Petrou) in September: stays 23f: acts on soft and good to firm going: usually races close up. *Charlie Longsdon* **c135 h–**

MIDNIGHT SILVER 8 gr.m. Midnight Legend – Ruggtah (Daylami (IRE)) [2017/18 c108, h116: h21.9v⁴ h15.7s* Dec 17] fairly useful handicap hurdler: won mares event at Southwell in December: tried to refuse/unseated rider sole outing over fences in 2016/17: stays 3m: best form on soft/heavy going: wears tongue tie: usually races close up. *Jamie Snowden* **c– h119**

MIDNIGHT SONATA (IRE) 4 b.g. Big Bad Bob (IRE) – Symphonique (FR) (Epervier Bleu) [2017/18 b16.7g⁶ Apr 22] €45,000 3-y-o: sixth foal: dam, fairly useful French hurdler/chaser (15f-2¼m winner), also 7.5f winner on Flat: 8/1, green when sixth in bumper at Market Rasen (4¾ lengths behind Northern Soul): will improve. *Charlie Longsdon* **b90 p**

MIDNIGHT STROLL 6 b.g. Midnight Legend – Late For Class (IRE) (Bob's Return (IRE)) [2017/18 b108: h20v⁶ h16.1s* h20s* h20s⁴ h16s h19v^{pu} Apr 1] good-topped gelding: useful bumper performer: similar form over hurdles: won maiden at Galway in October and novice at Fairyhouse in December: stays 2½m: acts on soft going: tried in hood: often travels strongly. *Robert Tyner, Ireland* **h132**

MIDNIGHT TARGET 8 b.m. Midnight Legend – Right On Target (IRE) (Presenting) [2017/18 h107: c20.3g² c20d^F c20d² c20s² c23.6s* c24.1s⁴ c20.8g* Apr 19] fair hurdler: fairly useful chaser: won novice handicap at Huntingdon in February and listed mares novice handicap at Cheltenham in April: stays 3m: acts on soft going: wears hood/tongue tie: usually races close up. *John Groucott* **c117 h–**

MIDNIGHT TOUR 8 b.m. Midnight Legend – Uppermost (Montjeu (IRE)) [2017/18 h138: h19.6s³ h24.5d³ h24.6v⁴ h21s³ h19.9s² h20s⁶ Apr 28] smallish mare: useful hurdler: placed in handicap at Bangor (2¾ lengths behind Dashing Oscar) in November and David Nicholson Mares' Hurdle at Cheltenham (½ length behind Benie des Dieux) in March: stays 21f: acts on soft and good to firm going: often races towards rear. *Alan King* **h142**

MIDNIGHT TROUBLE 6 b.g. Midnight Legend – Friendly Request (Environment Friend) [2017/18 b16s⁴ h15.8v⁵ h21.2d Apr 9] sturdy gelding: fourth in maiden bumper at Warwick (16½ lengths behind Thebannerkingrebel): modest form over hurdles: will be suited by 3m. *Nigel Twiston-Davies* **h92 b79**

MIDNIGHT TUNE 7 b.m. Midnight Legend – Harmonic Motion (IRE) (Bob Back (USA)) [2017/18 h107: h21.4s² h21.4v* h24.6v⁴ h23.5v⁴ h19.8v* h20.5s Mar 24] compact mare: useful hurdler: won mares maiden at Wincanton and mares handicap at Kempton in **h131**

MID

December, and Jane Seymour Mares' Novices' Hurdle at Sandown (by 2¾ lengths from If You Say Run) in February: stays 25f: acts on heavy going: wears tongue tie: front runner, often travels strongly. *Anthony Honeyball*

MIDNIGHT WALK (IRE) 8 b.m. Oscar (IRE) – Lady Belvedere (IRE) (Lord Americo) [2017/18 h95, b–: h19.6s² h24.7g⁶ h17.2s⁵ h16.8g* h16g⁵ c15.7g² c19.3s* c15.9s⁴ c16.4g³ Apr 23] Irish point winner: fair hurdler: won mares novice at Sedgefield in September: similar form over fences: won mares handicap at same course in December: stays 2½m: acts on soft going: tried in hood: wears tongue tie. *Donald McCain* c108 h102

MIDTECH VALENTINE 7 b.m. Act One – Eveon (IRE) (Synefos (USA)) [2017/18 c88, h112: c20g³ h16.3g h19g³ h15.8g⁴ h19.4s h18.9v³ h20.6g³ Apr 22] lengthy mare: fair handicap hurdler: similar form over fences: stays 2½m: acts on heavy going: tried in cheekpieces/tongue tie: often races prominently. *Ian Williams* c104 h108

MIGHT BITE (IRE) 9 b.g. Scorpion (IRE) – Knotted Midge (IRE) (Presenting) [2017/18 c166, h–: c24.2s* c24d* c26.3v² c25s* Apr 12] c171 h–

For the first time in forty-five years, a single stable housed the favourites for Cheltenham's three greatest races, the Gold Cup, the Champion Hurdle and the Queen Mother Champion Chase, the last-named a relative late-comer to the triumvirate, inaugurated only in 1959 and taking time to attain its present supreme status. Amateur jockey Mr N. Henderson, claiming 7 lb, was in his very early days at Uplands in 1973 when the pre-eminent Fred Winter sent out Crisp on the opening day to try to regain the National Hunt Two-Mile Champion Chase (as it was known then), followed by reigning champion Bula on the second day when he attempted to win a third Champion Hurdle, and then Pendil, the best chaser in Britain, in the blue riband, the Gold Cup on Thursday, the final day of the three-day meeting. Ex-Australian Crisp, successful in the race two years earlier, started at 15/8-on but was beaten into third behind ex-American, Irish-trained Inkslinger (who went on to win the Cathcart on the final day as well). Bula was 6/5-on but couldn't produce his customary powerful finish from the last and managed only fifth behind Comedy of Errors. Pendil, a 6/4-on shot, came closest of the Winter triumvirate to victory as he narrowly failed to extend an unbeaten run of eleven over fences, stretching back to the November of the previous season; Pendil looked to have the Gold Cup in safe keeping when ridden clear from the second last but he faltered on the uphill climb to the finish and was caught and beaten a short head by The Dikler.

The Winter stable didn't go home empty-handed from that year's National Hunt meeting because Killiney won the Totalisator Champion Chase—the 'novices' Gold Cup'—on the opening day (the race had a bigger first prize than the Two-Mile Champion Chase and was run as the day's feature event, the third race on the card, just after the Champion Chase). Killiney was also an odds-on shot and he was never in much danger, extending his own unbeaten record over fences to eight. There was no more exciting prospect among that season's novices but he suffered a fatal injury in the Heinz Chase at Ascot on his next start, undoubtedly the biggest of the setbacks his stable had to suffer that season, which also included the heroic failure of Crisp in the Grand National, in which, under top weight of 12-0, he set up a commanding lead after jumping to the front at first Becher's and still held a fifteen-length advantage at the last. But Crisp tired badly and wandered approaching the elbow, allowing Red Rum, receiving 23 lb, to get up to win by three quarters of a length, the first two finishing twenty-five lengths clear in a time that smashed the race record by nearly twenty seconds. Fred Winter, incidentally, still ended the season, for the third year running, as leading trainer, something he went on to achieve eight times. As for Crisp, Bula and Pendil, all three resumed winning ways in the early part of the following season, Crisp breaking the course record when winning the Hermitage Chase at Newbury before turning the tables on Red Rum in a level weights meeting in the Doncaster Pattern Chase; Bula won the Black and White Whisky Gold Cup at Ascot after being sent chasing; and Pendil put up a magnificent performance under 12-7 to take the Massey-Ferguson Gold Cup at Cheltenham (Crisp and Bula were both sidelined by injury when the National Hunt meeting at Cheltenham came round once more, while Pendil, odds-on again, was brought down three out in the Gold Cup when travelling well).

516

Fred Winter won the last of his eight trainers' championships in the 1984/5 season, by which time Nicky Henderson, who had gone on to become Winter's assistant and a competent amateur rider, was training in his own right. Henderson succeeded Winter as champion trainer, winning the title in 1985/6 and 1986/7, but Martin Pipe was about to become the dominant force over jumps, revolutionising the training of jumpers as he won the trainers' championship fifteen times, his main rivals during that period being David Nicholson and then Paul Nicholls who was runner-up to Pipe for seven successive seasons before finally toppling him in 2005/6, after which Pipe retired at the age of just sixty. The keen battles between Pipe and Nicholls reflected one of the closest rivalries in the sport and Nicholls went on to enjoy a seven-year dominance of the trainers' championship after Pipe's retirement. No trainer has ever won the Gold Cup, the Champion Hurdle and the Queen Mother Champion Chase in the same season but Nicholls went very close in 2009 when only the neck of the Henderson-trained 22/1-shot Punjabi prevented Celestial Halo from taking the Champion Hurdle in the same year that Master Minded landed the odds for a second victory in the Queen Mother Champion Chase, and Kauto Star regained the Gold Cup after losing it to stablemate Denman the year before (Nicholls had a 1,2,4,5 in the Gold Cup in 2009 after a 1,2,3 in 2008 when Master Minded won his first Champion Chase and the stable had no runner in the Champion Hurdle). The 2008 and 2009 Cheltenham Festivals proved the high water mark for Manor Farm Stables—Big Buck's also won the first of his four World [Stayers'] Hurdles in 2009 to give the stable three of the four biggest championship events—and Paul Nicholls, who has been champion trainer ten times, is now finding his position being usurped by Nicky Henderson's Seven Barrows yard at Lambourn (Henderson's two trainers' championships in the 'eighties came when he was at Windsor House).

The major yards operate on a considerably larger scale nowadays than those of past champions such as Fred Winter and his contemporaries Peter Easterby and Michael Dickinson, but even Nicholls and Henderson, with strings of around a hundred and fifty, find it difficult to compete with the Irish stables run by perennial champion Willie Mullins and his close rival Gordon Elliott, who preside over two of the most powerful yards that jumping has even seen. The Mullins and Elliott raiding parties on the latest Cheltenham Festival yielded fifteen winners between

32Red King George VI Chase, Kempton—a third win in the race for trainer Nicky Henderson as Might Bite justifies favouritism from outsiders Double Shuffle (checked cap) and Tea For Two (right); 2016 winner Thistlecrack (left) is only fourth

MIG

them, Elliott clinching the trainers' trophy, after a fluctuating battle over the four days, with the victory of the appropriately-named Blow By Blow in the Martin Pipe Conditional Jockeys' Handicap Hurdle, the penultimate race of the meeting. That race provided a victory that was 'very special' for Gordon Elliott who worked for Martin Pipe at Pond House. The pair have become very good friends as Elliott has followed Pipe in building up, virtually from scratch, a big and very influential stable that has taken him right to the top of his profession. Just before Elliott began to seriously threaten his monopoly in Ireland, the master of Closutton Willie Mullins recorded a notable show of strength in Cheltenham's three big championships, Annie Power winning the 2016 Champion Hurdle (with stablemate Nichols Canyon third), Un de Sceaux coming second in the Champion Chase and Djakadam and Don Poli filling the places behind the Elliott-trained Don Cossack in the Gold Cup. Mullins nearly took the British trainers' championship that season, as well as the Irish, the issues not decided until the final day at Sandown after a thrilling scrap with Paul Nicholls.

In winning that tenth championship, Paul Nicholls won only two Grade 1 races in Britain and he has been finding it difficult to source the Grade 1 horses which not so long ago were much more plentiful at Manor Farm Stables. The latest trainers' championship in Britain went to Nicky Henderson for the second successive year, and the fifth time in all, helped considerably by the fact that his 'A-team', as he calls his best horses, was much stronger than that of Nicholls. Henderson-trained horses won thirteen of Britain's forty Grade 1s, while the Nicholls yard won four. Buveur d'Air, Altior and Might Bite were stars of the Henderson 'A-team' and they were the three who started favourite for the Champion Hurdle, the Queen Mother Champion Chase and the Gold Cup respectively. Henderson had won the two last-named in 2013 with Sprinter Sacre and Bobs Worth, but the trio he saddled in the Champion Hurdle that year finished out of the frame behind the Mullins-trained favourite Hurricane Fly. In the latest season, Buveur d'Air, who started at 6/4-on when retaining his Champion Hurdle crown, and Altior, who won the Queen Mother Champion Chase at evens (both beating Mullins-trained runners into second), set up the prospect of the big treble if 4/1-favourite Might Bite could land the Gold Cup. Might Bite had won the RSA Chase (as the 'novices' Gold Cup' is now known) twelve months earlier in the Cheltenham Festival's most dramatic finish, and had followed up at Aintree in the Mildmay Novices' in which he confirmed Cheltenham placings with his stablemate Whisper. Might Bite was clearly an exciting prospect, though his zestful racing character made him look more suited to a flat track like Kempton than to Cheltenham which places more emphasis on stamina and where, in any case, he hadn't shown his best side, nearly throwing the RSA Chase away on the run-in after being ten lengths clear at the last before unexpectedly veering sharply right and seemingly trying to pull himself up, his jockey getting him going again just in time. Might Bite would have won the Kauto Star Novices' Chase at Kempton on Boxing Day had he not fallen heavily at the final fence when eighteen lengths clear of his field, a mishap that cost him the distinction of becoming the first horse to win Britain's three most important races for staying novice chasers, the Kauto Star (formerly the Feltham), the RSA and the Mildmay. The King George VI Chase looked the obvious race for Might Bite in his second season over fences, with his trainer warning that 'the Gold Cup will be a different ball game ... although you never know!'

The Betfair Chase, the first leg of the 'Classic Triple Crown' which carries a million-pound bonus if the winner can add the King George and then the Gold Cup, was never on the agenda for Might Bite. 'The others can go and knock merry hell out of each other at Haydock, but the big test for Might Bite is Boxing Day,' said Nicky Henderson who warmed up Might Bite for Kempton in the Future Stars Intermediate Chase at Sandown in mid-November. Jumping boldly, 9/4-on shot Might Bite beat his three rivals in clear-cut fashion, extending his unbeaten run over fences to four since his fall in the Kauto Star. Starting 6/4 favourite for the 32Red King George VI Chase, Might Bite faced seven rivals, including the runaway winner of the Betfair, Bristol de Mai, and the previous year's King George winner Thistlecrack who had spent most of the intervening year on the injury list. Thistlecrack's stablemate Fox

Betway Bowl Chase, Aintree—Might Bite gains compensation for his Gold Cup reverse with a convincing beating of the grey Bristol de Mai

Norton, second in the Tingle Creek at Sandown and stepping up to three miles for the first time, was also in the line-up after the Tizzard stable took advantage of the decision to keep the same owners' Cheltenham Gold Cup winner Sizing John at home. Might Bite's own stablemate Whisper took him on for a third time after a very good second in the Ladbrokes Trophy (formerly the Hennessy) at Newbury. Might Bite's antics in the RSA Chase still featured strongly in King George previews, but he had been a straightforward ride in his races since and showed no sign of eccentricity at Kempton. He didn't have to improve on his previous form to win an average King George in which he never really looked in danger of defeat once he had taken the measure of front-running Bristol de Mai (who didn't jump so well as he can) and been sent into the lead four fences from the finish.

Might Bite had to be ridden two out and, after a prodigious leap at the last, he idled on the run-in, but he was always holding his closest pursuers, 50/1-shot Double Shuffle and 20/1-shot Tea For Two (in the frame for the second year) whom he beat by a length and two lengths. Thistlecrack's effort petered out after he had looked the main threat to Might Bite early in the home straight but he managed a respectable fourth, well ahead of Whisper (presumably not over his exertions at Newbury) and Bristol de Mai (not in the same form away from the mud) in fifth and sixth. Fox Norton ran poorly and was pulled up. Might Bite's regular jockey Nico de Boinville, who had had to sit out the Kauto Star twelve months earlier as he recuperated with a broken arm, said after the King George: 'He was always doing it very easily, travelling and jumping, and he always slightly idles; he jumped the last like he could have gone round again.' For trainer Nicky Henderson, who won the Christmas Hurdle on the same card with Buveur d'Air, Might Bite was a horse you could 'enjoy watching all day and night.'

Nicky Henderson also took the opportunity to reinforce his opposition—shared by many in the sport—to the Jockey Club's ambitions to redevelop Kempton for housing. Although the story had gone rather quiet since the announcement the previous January, the Jockey Club had reiterated that it still intends to go ahead. The loss of Kempton's historic jumps course would be a blow to the history and traditions of the sport, as outlined in last year's Annual in the essay on Thistlecrack. It came as a surprise that the course's importance is not recognised by the Jockey Club, an institution that everyone believed could be entrusted with protecting racing's heritage (it owns Cheltenham and Aintree, among other courses, both of which once had to be saved from developers in similar circumstances to those which

MIG

now face Kempton). There is, as yet, no 'Save Kempton' campaign on the scale of the massive public appeal to secure Aintree's future back in the 'eighties, but Nicky Henderson made another impassioned plea for a rethink. 'It's ridiculous, this is a proper racecourse with its own unique characteristics and I'll go down with it, they will be taking me in the bulldozer because I'll be handcuffed to the final ditch!' Might Bite's King George attracted its usual bumper crowd for the course of over 20,000 and provided Jockey Club Racecourses with an opportunity to take stock of what jumping would lose if Kempton was closed. Moving the main event to Sandown was suggested in the early part of the century when there were plans to sacrifice the National Hunt course at Kempton, to make way for an all-weather track for Flat racing. On that occasion jumping's supporters gained a reprieve when turf Flat racing eventually made way for an all-weather surface instead. The National Hunt track was actually repositioned closer to the grandstand, improving the atmosphere at Kempton's jumping fixtures. A King George at Sandown would be a different race, with an uphill finish and habitually more testing going than usually obtains at Kempton where the fast-draining three-mile course is among the fairest in the country. Kempton's King George has complemented the Cheltenham Gold Cup over the years, providing a very different test for the top staying chasers. A King George at Sandown would be in danger of looking much more like a rehearsal for Cheltenham, rather than the true mid-season stayers' championship that it is now—on a flat track and often under different conditions.

Might Bite wasn't seen out between the King George VI Chase and the Cheltenham Gold Cup, completing his preparation for the latter in a gallop after racing with Buveur d'Air (the pair led by Theinval) on Adonis Hurdle day at Kempton in February. With Sizing John under a cloud after a poor run in the Leopardstown Christmas Chase, Might Bite's position as ante-post favourite for the Gold Cup was threatened only by the prospect of the arduous ground conditions being created by heavy rain in the two months after Christmas. Cheltenham's clerk of the course described the forecast in the run up to the latest Festival as the most unsettled he had encountered in eighteen years in the job. It seemed at one time that the previous year's third Native River, a Welsh National winner with stamina to spare and proven on heavy going, would displace Might Bite at the head of the betting. However, on the day, in the absence of the previous year's winner Sizing John, they bet 4/1 Might Bite, 9/2 Our Duke (the previous year's Irish National winner) and 5/1 Native River, with 8/1 bar. Might Bite and the remorseless Native River went head-to-head from flagfall, neither putting a foot wrong as they raced ahead of the rest. The stamina-sapping conditions turned out to favour Native River, with Might Bite eventually outstayed after jumping superbly again and leading two out before being headed at the last and finding no extra in the last hundred yards. Might Bite went down by four and a half lengths on heavy going over the longest trip he has tackled so far in his career and emerged from the race with plenty of credit. For most of the contest, he travelled like the best horse and there was never any question of his shirking things in the closing stages where he had every opportunity to veer off course but instead fought all the way to the line. The winning time was an indication of just how testing the conditions were. Native River was only the third Gold Cup winner in thirty years to exceed seven minutes for the course.

Native River wasn't seen out again after Cheltenham but Might Bite went on to Aintree for the Betway Bowl in which he met the second and third from the King George again, Double Shuffle and Tea For Two (who had won the Bowl twelve months earlier), as well as coming up against Bristol de Mai and the Cotswold Chase winner Definitly Red who hadn't given his running in the Gold Cup. Reporting that Might Bite had been 'fresh and well at home since Cheltenham', Nicky Henderson nevertheless said he had his doubts about running him in the Bowl after such a gruelling encounter against Native River. The trainer need not have worried. Might Bite never put a foot wrong and gave a sparkling display, as good as any he has produced over fences, to beat Bristol de Mai, who made a much better fist of things than he had at Kempton, by seven lengths, with the youngest in the field six-year-old Clan des Obeaux a further three and a quarter lengths away in third (Tea For Two and Double Shuffle couldn't repeat their King George form, trailing in sixth and seventh, while Definitely Red unseated his rider at the third). With Willie Mullins and Gordon Elliott keeping most of their big guns in reserve for Punchestown, Nicky Henderson focussed on Aintree (he didn't have a single runner over the five days of Punchestown, saying he hadn't been 'keen on coming over for a drubbing'). The move paid off, with Seven Barrows having five Grade 1 winners at the Grand National meeting to Manor Farm Stables' two, which effectively secured the trainers' championship.

Might Bite certainly played his part in winning the seasonal championship for his trainer, along with Buveur d'Air and Altior, but he was seen out just four times in the campaign ('effectively three as he just had a canter round at Sandown,' according to his trainer). Might Bite is likely to be busier in the next season, all things being equal, with connections announcing the 'Classic Triple Crown', with its million-pound bonus, as the target (though that had been the plan initially for the luckless Sizing John in the latest season). 'He's here to race and I'd really love to have another crack at the Gold Cup on good ground,' said Henderson after Might Bite's win at Aintree. Provided he steers clear of injury and illness, Might Bite should make a bold bid to land the Betfair/King George/Gold Cup treble, something only Kauto Star has so far achieved in the same season. He is probably the best staying chaser in training under anything less extreme than the conditions he encountered in the Gold Cup, though he can certainly handle give in the ground (it was soft at Aintree and good to soft in the King George).

Might Bite (IRE) (b.g. 2009)
- Scorpion (IRE) (b 2002)
  - Montjeu (b 1996)
    - Sadler's Wells
    - Floripedes
  - Ardmelody (b 1987)
    - Law Society
    - Thistlewood
- Knotted Midge (IRE) (b 2000)
  - Presenting (br 1992)
    - Mtoto
    - D'azy
  - Bula Beag (b 1993)
    - Brush Aside
    - Bulabos

The Knot Again Partnership's "Might Bite"

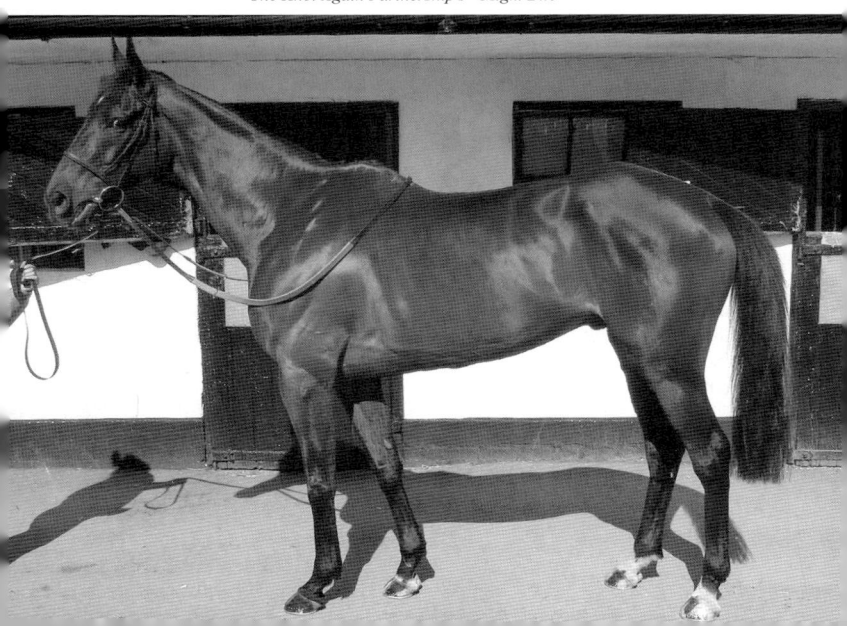

MIG

Might Bite is a tall gelding who was big and backward in his younger days and, having been sent to Seven Barrows to see if a buyer could be found, he was eventually purchased by the Knot Again Partnership, a syndicate which includes, among others, a few former members of the Not Afraid Partnership who had the 2013 Cheltenham Gold Cup winner Bobs Worth. Might Bite didn't see a racecourse until he was six and was fairly lightly raced in his first two seasons before making his mark in no uncertain terms in the 2016/17 season. His jumping of fences left something to be desired at first but he is now a superb jumper, a joy to watch when really on song. Might Bite's sire the St Leger winner Scorpion (Might Bite is from his first crop) was all the rage at first after being retired to Coolmore's jumping arm. Scorpion's sire Montjeu was making an impact as a sire of jumps sires and Scorpion covered huge books during much of his time at Coolmore (he received 348 mares in 2012, for example, making him the busiest sire in Britain and Ireland). However, some of Scorpion's earlier progeny showed signs of temperament and they earned something of an unfair reputation for being reluctant to battle. After patronage dried up—he had just twenty-one mares in the 2016 breeding season—Scorpion was moved to Shade Oak Stud in Shropshire (fee £3,000 in 2018) just in time for Might Bite's emergence as a tip-top novice chaser (his quirky performance in the RSA Chase was blamed in some quarters on his sire!). Don't Touch It, a Grade 1-winning novice hurdler, was another to show smart form over fences in 2016/17 and Scorpion has also been represented by a smart hurdler in the Henderson-trained Blue Fashion and by several useful chasers. Might Bite's dam, the Presenting mare Knotted Midge, was a winning pointer. Might Bite is her second foal, the first being the Grade 1-winning hurdler Beat That (by Milan) who won the Sefton Novices' Hurdle at Aintree and the War of Attrition Novices' Hurdle at Punchestown in the 2013/14 season for Seven Barrows. Might Bite has plenty of stamina on both sides of his pedigree—his dam is a sister to the useful Drombeag who stayed four miles—and he himself stays three and a quarter miles, although he can be keen and, as a strong traveller, is probably fully effective at distances short of three miles. He races prominently and is often a front runner, and it bears repeating that he is a splendid jumper. *Nicky Henderson*

MIGHTY ELSA 5 b.m. Schiaparelli (GER) – Tiger Moss (Classic Cliche (IRE)) [2017/18 b15.7d Nov 21] fourth foal: dam (h86) ungenuine 2½m hurdle winner (stayed 23f): 66/1, very green when tenth in mares bumper at Southwell. *Richard Phillips* b–

MIGHTY LEADER (IRE) 10 b.g. Milan – Madam Leader (IRE) (Supreme Leader) [2017/18 c–, h112: h26.4d* h23.9g⁶ h26.4g⁶ h23.1g* h24g⁵ h26.5d* h26.5g Oct 13] angular gelding: Irish point winner: fairly useful handicap hurdler: won at Stratford in May, Market Rasen in August and Newton Abbot in September: fell both starts in chases: stays 3¼m: acts on soft and good to firm going: wears headgear/tongue tie. *Fergal O'Brien* c– h123

MIGHTY MISSILE (IRE) 7 ch.g. Majestic Missile (IRE) – Magdalene (FR) (College Chapel) [2017/18 h114: h15.7g³ h19.1m h23g h16.5g h16.5g h24s^pu h21.4s Feb 17] sturdy gelding: fair handicap hurdler, below form in 2017/18: stays 2½m: acts on firm and soft going: often in headgear/tongue tie: temperament under suspicion. *Brian Barr* h91

MIGHTY THUNDER 5 b.g. Malinas (GER) – Cool Island (IRE) (Turtle Island (IRE)) [2017/18 b16.2m* b16.4g⁶ h19.4g h16.2v³ h16.2v⁵ h18.9s h20.2s³ Apr 26] €15,000 3-y-o: lengthy gelding: fifth foal: half-brother to fairly useful hurdler/useful chaser Isleofhopendreams (21f-3m winner, by Flemensfirth), stays 3¾m: dam unraced half-sister to useful chaser (stayed 3m) Stewarts House: fair form in bumpers: won at Perth in June: similar form over hurdles: will be suited by 2¾m: best form on heavy going: wears tongue tie. *Lucinda Russell* h107 b91

MIGHTY VIC (IRE) 10 b.g. Old Vic – Mighty Marble (IRE) (Satco (FR)) [2017/18 h17.7v³ h19.2d⁶ h21s⁶ h21.7s Apr 6] compact gelding: Irish point winner: modest form over hurdles: wears tongue tie. *Suzy Smith* h95

MIGHTY WHITEY (IRE) 12 b.g. Sesaro (USA) – Deeco Valley (IRE) (Satco (FR)) [2017/18 c–, h98: h16m h16.2g⁵ h17.2g* h16.3g⁵ h17.2d⁶ h16.2v³ h15.8m h18.8s h16.8g⁵ Apr 23] modest handicap hurdler: won at Cartmel (amateur) in July: winning chaser: stays 21f: acts on good to firm and heavy going: has worn headgear, including in 2017/18: wears tongue tie: front runner. *Noel C. Kelly, Ireland* c– h95

MIL

MILAN DIVA (IRE) 7 b.m. Milan – Shannon River (FR) (Nashamaa) [2017/18 h22.1d³ᵈ h18.8g⁴ h20g h16g Jul 22] €3,500 3-y-o: fourth foal: half-sister to French hurdler/chaser Shannon Falls (2m/17f winner, by Turgeon): dam unraced sister to dam of very smart French chaser Shannon Rock (stays 3¾m): runner-up on completed start in Irish points: poor form over hurdles: tried in cheekpieces. *Mrs Sarah Dawson, Ireland*   **h73**

MILANESQUE (IRE) 9 b.g. Milan – Longueville Quest (IRE) (Witness Box (USA)) [2017/18 c24.6vᵖᵘ c25v⁵ c23.6v c24v² c26.2vᵖᵘ Apr 17] once-raced hurdler: fair handicap chaser: won at Thurles in 2016/17: stays 3m: acts on heavy going: in blinkers last 2 starts: wears tongue tie. *Paul W. Flynn, Ireland*   **c99** **h–**

MILAN HART (IRE) 8 b.m. Milan – Queen of Harts (IRE) (Phardante (FR)) [2017/18 h–, b–: h18.5s⁶ h18.5gᵖᵘ Jun 27] maiden hurdler, no form in 2017/18. *Martin Hill*   **h–**

MILAN OF CRYSTAL (IRE) 9 b.m. Milan – Native Crystal (IRE) (Be My Native (USA)) [2017/18 c66, h82: h20g² h20g³ h19gᶠ h16g* h20g* h19.6g³ Oct 31] angular mare: point winner: modest handicap hurdler: won mares events at Warwick and Worcester in October: twice-raced chaser: stays 21f: acts on good to firm going: wears tongue tie: often races towards rear/travels strongly. *Dave Roberts*   **c–** **h96**

MILANSBAR (IRE) 11 b.g. Milan – Ardenbar (Ardross) [2017/18 c133, h–: c25.2d⁶ c23.6v³ c29.5vᵘʳ c29.2s* c32.6s⁵ c34v² c34.3s⁵ Apr 14] big gelding: winning hurdler: useful handicap chaser: won Classic Chase at Warwick (by 11 lengths from Cogry) in January: stays 4¼m (fifth in Grand National): acts on heavy going: in headgear last 5 starts: front runner/races prominently: unreliable (often sulks if unable to lead). *Neil King*   **c143 §** **h–**

MILANSTORM (IRE) 5 b.g. Milan – Deise Rose (IRE) (Glacial Storm (USA)) [2017/18 b15.7v² b16v* Mar 11] fifth foal: closely related to winning hurdler/pointer Roseini (2m winner, by Dr Massini), stayed 21f: dam winning pointer: fair form in bumpers: won at Warwick in March. *Nigel Twiston-Davies*   **b93**

Betfred Classic Handicap Chase, Warwick—Milansbar returns to form from out of the blue, teaming up with Bryony Frost for the first time; Cogry is a distant second

MIL

MILBOROUGH (IRE) 12 b.g. Milan – Fox Burrow (IRE) (Supreme Leader) [2017/18 c124, h124: c30s⁴ c32.6s^pu c24.1v^pu c28.4v^F c30.6s^pu Apr 27] good-topped gelding: winning hurdler: fairly useful handicap chaser nowadays: stays 33f: acts on good to firm and heavy going: in headgear last 2 starts: usually races nearer last than first. *Ian Duncan* — **c115 h–**

MILE HOUSE (IRE) 10 b.g. Close Conflict (USA) – Clogheen Lass (IRE) (Capricorn Line) [2017/18 h20g* c20g² Sep 18] lengthy gelding: winning pointer: useful handicap hurdler: won at Worcester in August after long absence: useful form over fences: second in maiden at same course (½ length behind Wait For Me) in September: stays 2¾m: acts on soft and good to firm going. *Robert Stephens* — **c131 h130**

MILES TO MILAN (IRE) 8 b.g. Milan – Princesse Rooney (FR) (Baby Turk) [2017/18 h–: h19.4s⁴ Jan 27] fair handicap hurdler, lightly raced: should stay beyond 19f: acts on heavy going. *Olly Murphy* — **h106**

MILEVA ROLLER 6 b.m. Multiplex – Alikat (IRE) (Alhaarth (IRE)) [2017/18 h–, b86: h15.7g⁴ h15.8m h22.1s⁶ h19.6g⁵ h23.3d h19.9g⁶ h24.3s Oct 30] poor maiden hurdler: left Jonjo O'Neill after fifth start: unproven beyond 2m: best form on good going: tried in headgear. *Lisa Harrison* — **h75**

MILGEN BAY 12 br.g. Generous (IRE) – Lemon's Mill (USA) (Roberto (USA)) [2017/18 c113, h–: c21.1d^pu Jun 6] good-topped gelding: maiden hurdler: fairly useful chaser at best, seemed amiss sole outing in 2017/18: stays 21f: acts on firm and soft going: has worn headgear: front runner/races prominently. *Oliver Sherwood* — **c– h–**

MILITARIAN 8 b.g. Kayf Tara – Mille Et Une (FR) (Trempolino (USA)) [2017/18 h94p, b–: c23.9s² c24v^pu c20.3g² Apr 20] strong gelding: point winner: lightly-raced hurdler: fairly useful form over fences: stays 3m: acts on soft going: tried in tongue tie: often races prominently. *Andrew Martin* — **c118 h–**

MILK KING (IRE) 5 gr.g. Cloudings (IRE) – Snow Keeper (Rocamadour) [2017/18 b16.3d b15.8d b15.7v b16.5m Apr 25] soundly beaten in bumpers: tried in tongue tie. *Dai Williams* — **b–**

MILKWOOD (IRE) 4 b.g. Dylan Thomas (IRE) – Tropical Lake (IRE) (Lomond (USA)) [2017/18 b15.3d Apr 22] half-brother to several winners, including fairly useful hurdler Seeability (3m winner, by Bob Back): dam, useful 2m hurdler, also 1m-1¾m winner on Flat: 25/1, seventh in bumper at Wincanton (11¼ lengths behind Samarquand): likely to improve. *Neil Mulholland* — **b86 p**

MILLANISI BOY 9 b.g. Kalanisi (IRE) – Millennium Rose (IRE) (Roselier (FR)) [2017/18 c125, h120: c23.6v^pu c23.6v* c23.4s² c26s^pu c23.6v⁵ Apr 14] workmanlike gelding: winning hurdler: fairly useful handicap chaser: won novice event at Chepstow in December: stays 3m: acts on heavy going: tried in cheekpieces last 4 starts: tried in tongue tie: front runner/races prominently. *Kayley Woollacott* — **c125 h–**

MILLE NAUTIQUE (FR) 7 b.g. Panis (USA) – Anoush (USA) (Giant's Causeway (USA)) [2017/18 c111, h–: c20.3g⁵ c19.2g² c19.2g* c19.2g³ Oct 5] lengthy gelding: maiden hurdler: fair handicap chaser: won at Market Rasen in August: stays 2½m: best form on good going: usually leads: inconsistent. *Alan King* — **c112 h–**

MILLEN DOLLAR MAN (IRE) 9 b.g. Millenary – Rare Dollar (IRE) (Bob's Return (IRE)) [2017/18 h16g h19.4g* h20d² h16.5s⁵ h24g^pu h19.8g h18.8v h19.2d h15.7d h16s⁴ h15.7v⁵ c16.5d⁶ c17s² c17.5d² Apr 24] poor handicap hurdler: won at Clonmel in May: poor form over fences: left W. Harney after seventh start: stays 21f: acts on soft going: has worn headgear, including in 2017/18: tried in tongue tie. *Alexandra Dunn* — **c73 h83**

MILL FORGE 11 b.g. Grape Tree Road – Agara (Young Ern) [2017/18 c19.2g h19.5v³ h20.2s* Apr 27] fair hurdler: in cheekpieces, won handicap at Perth in April: little form in chases: left Mark McCausland after first start: stays 2½m: acts on heavy going: tried in tongue tie. *Stuart Crawford, Ireland* — **c– h100**

MILL GREEN 6 b.g. Black Sam Bellamy (IRE) – Ceilidh Royal (Erhaab (USA)) [2017/18 b13.7s⁵ b15.8d⁴ Mar 26] first foal: dam (b71), ran twice in bumpers, half-sister to useful hurdler/very smart chaser (stayed 3¼m) Barbers Shop: fair form in bumpers: will be suited by 2½m+. *Nicky Henderson* — **b88**

MILLICENT SILVER 9 gr.m. Overbury (IRE) – Common Girl (IRE) (Roselier (FR)) [2017/18 c121§, h103§: h26v⁵ c25.5s⁴ c29.6v^pu c32.6s^ur c31.9v⁵ Mar 15] smallish, rather sparely-made mare: fair hurdler/fairly useful handicap chaser, below form in 2017/18: stays 31f: acts on heavy going: wears headgear: usually races towards rear: moody (usually races very lazily). *Nigel Twiston-Davies* — **c108 h82 §**

MIN

MILLIE THE MINX (IRE) 4 b.f. Medicean – Popocatepetl (FR) (Nashwan (USA)) [2017/18 b14d⁶ h15.7d h15.7s h16.6s Jan 26] closely related/half-sister to several winners on Flat; dam, maiden on Flat (stayed 1¾m), half-sister to fairly useful hurdler/chaser (2m/17f winner) Red Seventy: little impact in varied events, including on Flat. *Dianne Sayer* **h– b–**

MILLROSE BELL (IRE) 6 b.m. Flemensfirth (USA) – Laboc (Rymer) [2017/18 h20.1s³ h20.6g h19.9s⁶ h24v⁶ h24.3v h20.5v⁶ h23.3v⁵ h27v Apr 13] €12,000 3-y-o, £7,000 5-y-o: sturdy mare: sister to 2¾m hurdle winner McGinty's Dream and half-sister to fairly useful hurdler/winning pointer Abnaki (2¾m-27f winner, by Milan): dam, third in bumper, half-sister to Cheltenham Gold Cup winner See More Business: well-beaten third in Irish point: poor maiden hurdler. *Victor Thompson* **h77**

MILLY BALOO 7 b.m. Desideratum – Tarabaloo (Kayf Tara) [2017/18 c105, h99: c24.2s² c25.2d^ro h23.1v² c22.2v⁴ c23.9v³ Apr 11] fair handicap hurdler/chaser: stays 25f: acts on heavy going: often races prominently. *Tim Easterby* **c110 h105**

MILORD (GER) 9 br.g. Monsun (GER) – Montserrat (GER) (Zilzal (USA)) [2017/18 c101, h118: h21g h21g⁴ c22.6g⁵ h21g⁶ h21.2s h15.8d h25d Apr 24] compact gelding: fair handicap hurdler: similar form over fences: stays 3m: acts on good to firm and heavy going: wears headgear: front runner/races prominently: temperament under suspicion. *Kim Bailey* **c110 h107**

MILOSAM (IRE) 11 b.g. Milan – Lady Sam (IRE) (Topanoora) [2017/18 c23s^pu Jan 9] point winner: maiden hurdler: fair chaser at best, pulled up sole outing under Rules in 2017/18: stays 4m: acts on heavy going: wears headgear: temperamental. *G. Chambers* **c– § h–**

MILROW (IRE) 5 b.g. Tamayuz – Cannikin (IRE) (Lahib (USA)) [2017/18 h116: h16.3g³ h17.2g h16.3g⁶ h16.8d⁴ h21.6g³ h19.5d h23.9g² Oct 28] fairly useful hurdler: won seller at Stratford in August: left Dr Richard Newland after third start: stays 3m: acts on good to soft going: has worn cheekpieces, including in 2017/18: wears tongue tie. *Sophie Leech* **h123**

MILTON 6 br.g. Nomadic Way (USA) – Jesmund (Bishop of Cashel) [2017/18 b–: b17.7g⁶ May 14] no form in bumpers. *Diana Grissell* **b–**

MILZIPA (IRE) 6 b.g. Milan – Money For Buttons (IRE) (Alphabatim (USA)) [2017/18 h100, b83: h16d h20.7s Dec 26] useful-looking gelding: maiden hurdler, fair form at best. *Nicky Henderson* **h–**

MIND'S EYE (IRE) 6 b.g. Stowaway – Joleen (IRE) (Bob's Return (IRE)) [2017/18 h16d² h16s* h20s* h16s h21.1s h16.5s⁴ Apr 13] €43,000 3-y-o: well-made gelding: chasing type: third foal: half-brother to fairly useful hurdler Beneficial Joe (23f winner, by Beneficial), stays 27f: dam unraced half-sister to smart hurdler/top-class chaser (stayed 3m) Racing Demon: runner-up in point/bumpers: useful form over hurdles: won maiden at Fairyhouse in November and novice handicap at Leopardstown (by ¾ length from Darkest Flyer) in December: stays 2½m: acts on soft going. *Henry de Bromhead, Ireland* **h133**

MIND YOUR BACK (IRE) 5 b.g. Getaway (GER) – Local Hall (IRE) (Saddlers' Hall (IRE)) [2017/18 b15.7d⁵ Nov 6] €45,000 3-y-o: fourth foal: brother to fairly useful hurdler Euxton Lane (2¼m-2½m winner): dam, unraced, out of sister to fairly useful hurdler/useful chaser (stayed 21f) Certainly Strong: 8/1, fifth in maiden bumper at Southwell (13½ lengths behind Strong Glance): open to improvement. *Neil Mulholland* **b84 p**

MINELLA ARIS (IRE) 7 b.g. King's Theatre (IRE) – Liss Rua (IRE) (Bob Back (USA)) [2017/18 h121: c20.3g* c19.4d^F c23.4v^pu Feb 10] point winner: fairly useful hurdler: useful form over fences: won novice handicap at Southwell (by 6 lengths from Such A Legend) in May: stays 3m: acts on heavy going: wears tongue tie: often travels strongly. *Tom George* **c134 h–**

MINELLA ARTS (IRE) 9 br.g. Presenting – Norabelle (FR) (Alamo Bay (USA)) [2017/18 c22.6d⁶ Jun 9] multiple point winner: well beaten in bumper for John J. Nallen in 2014/15: in cheekpieces/tongue tie, well held in novice hunter at Stratford on chasing debut. *Miss C. Packwood* **c76**

MINELLA AWARDS (IRE) 7 b.g. Oscar (IRE) – Montys Miss (IRE) (Presenting) [2017/18 h142: h22.8v^pu h24d Apr 26] good sort: second in Irish point: smart handicap hurdler: stays 3m: acts on soft going: in tongue tie last 5 starts: often races towards rear. *Harry Fry* **h144**

MINELLACELEBRATION (IRE) 8 b.g. King's Theatre (IRE) – Knocktartan (IRE) (King's Ride) [2017/18 c131, h95: c24d* c25g² c25.5g^bd c23.6d⁵ c25g c24.1s⁶ Nov 15] sturdy gelding: winning handicap chaser: won at Uttoxeter in May: stays 25f: acts on heavy going. *Katy Price* **c136 h–**

MIN

MINELLA CHARMER (IRE) 7 b.g. King's Theatre (IRE) – Kim Hong (IRE) (Charnwood Forest (IRE)) [2017/18 c129p, h–: h16d^F h21d^6 h21.4g^F Apr 21] useful-looking gelding: useful handicap hurdler, let down by jumping in 2017/18: fairly useful form over fences: left Alan King after second start: stays 21f: acts on heavy going: usually wears tongue tie. *James Moffatt* c–
h118 x

MINELLA DADDY (IRE) 8 b.g. Flemensfirth (USA) – Old Moon (IRE) (Old Vic) [2017/18 c143, h127: c21v^4 c23.8s^2 c25s c28.8d^{pu} Apr 28] strong gelding: winning hurdler: useful handicap chaser: second in listed event at Ascot in February, standout effort in 2017/18: stays 25f: acts on good to firm and heavy going: wears headgear. *Peter Bowen* c138
h–

MINELLA ENCORE (IRE) 6 b.g. King's Theatre (IRE) – Stashedaway (IRE) (Treasure Hunter) [2017/18 b16s* b16s* b16s^4 Feb 3] £100,000 5-y-o: sixth foal: closely related/half-brother to 3 winning pointers: dam (c124/h124), 2m-2½m hurdle/chase winner, half-sister to Irish Grand National winner Glebe Lad: point winner: useful form in bumpers: won at Fairyhouse (maiden) and Leopardstown (by 1¾ lengths from The Gunner Murphy) in December. *W. P. Mullins, Ireland* b112

MINELLA FAIR (IRE) 7 b.g. Flemensfirth (USA) – Bell Walks Run (IRE) (Commanche Run) [2017/18 b105: h22s* h24v^5 h19s^3 h22v* Mar 20] runner-up in point: useful bumper performer: fairly useful form over hurdles: won maiden at Punchestown in November and novice at Clonmel (by 62 lengths) in March: should stay 3m: wears tongue tie: front runner/races prominently, often travels strongly. *Noel Meade, Ireland* h129

MINELLA FIVEO (IRE) 10 b.g. Westerner – Autumn Sky (IRE) (Roselier (FR)) [2017/18 c–, h111: h16d h16s^6 h16.2v^4 h16.7d^{su} h18.6v^4 h15.7g^2 Apr 20] well-made gelding: has had breathing operation: maiden pointer: modest handicap hurdler: fell only chase start: seems best around 2m: acts on heavy going: has worn cheekpieces. *Sue Smith* c–
h98

MINELLAFORDOLLARS (IRE) 6 b.g. King's Theatre (IRE) – Another Dollar (IRE) (Supreme Leader) [2017/18 b105: h16v^1 h19.5v* Dec 26] point/bumper winner: fairly useful form over hurdles: won maiden at Down Royal in December: will stay 2¾m+: likely to progress further. *Gordon Elliott, Ireland* h129 p

MINELLA FORFITNESS (IRE) 11 b.g. Westerner – Ring of Water (USA) (Northern Baby (CAN)) [2017/18 c121, h–: c20.5g^3 c19.2g* c15.7g^2 c19.2g^3 c20.3g^5 Sep 1] winning hurdler: fair handicap chaser nowadays: won at Market Rasen in June: stays 2¾m: acts on soft going: has worn headgear: usually races prominently/freely. *Charles Pogson* c102
h–

MINELLAFORLEISURE (IRE) 10 br.g. King's Theatre (IRE) – Dame Foraine (FR) (Raintrap) [2017/18 c–, h128: h16.6d h16s^5 Jan 13] lengthy gelding: fairly useful handicap hurdler, off 13 months before reappearance: well held completed start over fences: raced mainly around 2m: acts on good to soft going. *Alex Hales* c–
h113

MINELLA FOR ME (IRE) 8 b.g. King's Theatre (IRE) – Irish Mystics (IRE) (Ali-Royal (IRE)) [2017/18 h87: c16d^4 c15.9d^4 c20.2s^2 c19.9s^F c19.9d^6 Mar 26] good-topped gelding: lightly-raced gelding: fair form over fences: stays 2½m: acts on soft going: tried in hood: wears tongue tie: front runner/races prominently. *Tom George* c107
h–

MINELLA FOR VALUE (IRE) 12 br.g. Old Vic – Nightingale Express (IRE) (Strong Gale) [2017/18 c128, h–: c22.5s^2 c24d^2 c26.3v^{pu} Mar 16] raw-boned gelding: multiple point winner: winning hurdler: fairly useful chaser nowadays: second in hunter at Listowel in June: stays 3¼m: acts on any going: tried in visor. *Declan Queally, Ireland* c119
h–

MINELLA GATHERING (IRE) 9 b.g. Old Vic – A Plus Ma Puce (FR) (Turgeon (USA)) [2017/18 h87x: h25d^3 h21.4g h21.6v^2 h23.4s* h23.4v^2 h26s^6 h23.9v^5 h23.1v^{pu} Apr 17] compact gelding: modest handicap hurdler: won at Fakenham in December: stays 25f: best form on soft/heavy going: often let down by jumping. *Paul Henderson* h91 x

MINELLAHALFCENTURY (IRE) 10 b.g. Westerner – Shanakill River (IRE) (Anshan) [2017/18 c73§, h–: c24.2s^{pu} Mar 9] strong gelding: has had breathing operation: winning hurdler: useful chaser at best, let down by attitude both starts since 2015/16: stays 3m: acts on heavy going: has worn headgear: wears tongue tie. *Miss Claire Harris* c– §
h–

MINELLA MYSTICS (IRE) 5 b.g. Gold Well – Irish Mystics (IRE) (Ali-Royal (IRE)) [2017/18 b17d^2 Mar 25] £100,000 4-y-o: fifth foal: closely related to a winning pointer by King's Theatre and half-brother to useful hurdler/winning pointer Stowaway Magic (2m-21f winner, by Stowaway): dam, poor maiden hurdler, sister to dam of useful hurdler (stays 3m) Mr Whipped: runner-up in maiden point: 11/10, second in bumper at Carlisle (½ length behind Dr Sanderson). *John McConnell, Ireland* b99

MIN

MINELLA ON LINE (IRE) 9 b.g. King's Theatre (IRE) – Bally Bolshoi (IRE) (Bob Back (USA)) [2017/18 c133x, h–: h24.2d h19.2v³ c24s h24v³ c24.2s^F c21.1s^{ur} Apr 13] well-made gelding: fairly useful handicap hurdler: useful handicap chaser: stays 3¼m: acts on heavy going: has worn headgear, including last 2 starts: tried in tongue tie: front runner/races prominently: often let down by jumping of fences. *Oliver Sherwood*   **c133 x h116**

MINELLA PRESENT (IRE) 9 b.g. Presenting – Dabaya (IRE) (In The Wings) [2017/18 c139, h–: c20.5s⁶ Mar 17] strong gelding: winning hurdler: useful handicap chaser, not disgraced after long absence sole outing in 2017/18: stays 2½m: acts on good to firm and good to soft going: wears hood: has worn tongue tie. *Neil Mulholland*   **c120 h–**

MINELLA REBELLION (IRE) 6 b.g. King's Theatre (IRE) – Afdala (IRE) (Hernando (FR)) [2017/18 h102: h21m⁵ h20.1d^{pu} Sep 5] second in Irish point: maiden hurdler, fair form at best: tried in tongue tie. *Nicky Henderson*   **h83**

MINELLA ROCCO (IRE) 8 b.g. Shirocco (GER) – Petralona (USA) (Alleged (USA)) [2017/18 c167, h–: c25d⁴ c27.3s^{pu} c24d⁴ c24s^F Feb 4] big gelding: winning hurdler: top-class chaser, largely well below best in 2017/18 (late absentee from both Gold Cup and Grand National on account of very testing going): stays 4m: acts on soft going: has worn cheekpieces, including last 2 starts: usually wears tongue tie: often let down by jumping. *Jonjo O'Neill*   **c159 x h–**

MINELLA SCAMP (IRE) 9 b.g. King's Theatre (IRE) – Forgotten Star (IRE) (Don't Forget Me) [2017/18 c20.9v² c20.9v² c24v⁴ c21.4v³ Apr 11] maiden hurdler for A. J. Martin: fair maiden chaser: stays 21f: acts on heavy going: wears tongue tie. *Fergal O'Brien*   **c114 h–**

MINELLA STYLE (IRE) 8 b.g. King's Theatre (IRE) – Rose of The Erne (IRE) (Presenting) [2017/18 h110, b80: h16d⁵ h21d⁶ h19.3g h21.2g⁴ c20d c25.2s^{ur} Jan 16] Irish point winner: modest maiden hurdler: well held completed start in chases: left Neil King after second start: stays 19f. *Dai Williams*   **c– h94**

MINELLA SUITE (IRE) 7 br.g. Oscar (IRE) – Ballymaguirelass (IRE) (Phardante (FR)) [2017/18 c100p, h97, b–: c15.6v^F c16.5s⁵ c19.2d⁴ h25.8s Jan 14] big, lengthy gelding: Irish point winner: maiden hurdler/chaser, no form in 2017/18. *Rose Dobbin*   **c– h–**

MINELLATILLMORNING (IRE) 6 gr.g. King's Theatre (IRE) – Line Kendie (FR) (Bonnet Rouge (FR)) [2017/18 h80: h20g⁴ h15.3s h16s h19.0v* h19.2v* h19.5s² Mar 22] placed in Irish points: fair form over hurdles: won handicaps at Taunton (conditional) and Fontwell in February: stays 19f: best form on soft/heavy going: often travels strongly. *Neil Mulholland*   **h109**

MINELLA TREASURE (IRE) 8 b.g. King's Theatre (IRE) – Ringzar (IRE) (Shernazar) [2017/18 h99p: h23g³ h21.6d^{pu} Oct 12] runner-up both starts in Irish points: modest maiden hurdler. *Noel Williams*   **h93**

MINELLA TWEET (IRE) 10 b.g. King's Theatre (IRE) – Cara Mhaith (IRE) (Anshan) [2017/18 c21.1g* c20.3g* c17.4m⁴ c19.5g h21.6d c20.5d³ c19.2s³ c24s⁵ c20.5m³ Apr 26] lengthy gelding: fair hurdler for John J. Nallen: fair handicap chaser: won at Fontwell and Southwell in May: stays 21f: best form on good going: has worn hood, including final start: wears tongue tie: races well off pace. *Paul Henderson*   **c111 h–**

MINELLA VOUCHER (IRE) 7 b.g. King's Theatre (IRE) – All Rise (GER) (Goofalik (USA)) [2017/18 h16.7d h20g⁴ h16g h17.2d⁵ h20.3d⁶ h19.5d h19.2v⁶ h19.2v* c15.7v* c16.4v³ Mar 23] second foal: brother to French 17f hurdle winner King Dancer: dam lightly-raced half-sister to very smart hurdler/winning chaser (2m-2¾m winner) Auetaler: poor hurdler: won handicap at Towcester in February: modest form over fences: won novice handicap at Southwell in March: stays 19f: best form on heavy going: in tongue tie last 4 starts: usually races towards rear. *Alexandra Dunn*   **c89 h81**

MINELLA WEB (IRE) 9 b.g. King's Theatre (IRE) – Azalea (IRE) (Marju (IRE)) [2017/18 c98, h–: c19.7d³ c21.6d^{pu} Nov 19] lightly-raced hurdler: modest handicap chaser: stayed 23f: acted on good to firm going: tried in cheekpieces: wore tongue tie: temperamental: dead. *Colin Tizzard*   **c89 § h–**

MINELLA WHISPER 7 b.g. Kayf Tara – Celtic Native (IRE) (Be My Native (USA)) [2017/18 h23.3d⁵ h20.8d h19.6s⁶ h25s³ h25d* h26.4d³ Apr 22] €56,000 3-y-o: brother to useful chaser Ace High (3m winner, stayed 29f) and useful hurdler/chaser Premier Bond (2m-25f winner), and half-brother to 3 winners: dam (c116/h145) 2m-2¾m hurdle/chase winner: Irish point winner: fair form over hurdles: won handicap at Huntingdon in March: stays 3¼m: acts on good to soft going: often races prominently. *Richard Phillips*   **h102**

527

MIN

MINE NOW (IRE) 10 b.g. Heron Island (IRE) – Aisjem (IRE) (Anshan) [2017/18 h132: **h142**
h20m⁴ h22.8s² h22g² h24v h24s* h24s Mar 15] rather leggy gelding: point winner: useful
handicap hurdler: won at Leopardstown (by short head from A Great View) in December:
stays 3m: acts on good to firm and heavy going. *Peter Fahey, Ireland*

MINER DISTRACTION 10 b.m. Desert King (IRE) – Miner Yours (Miner's Lamp) **h–**
[2017/18 h16s h21.9v⁶ Apr 1] sturdy mare: maiden hurdler, no form in 2017/18 after long
absence: tried in tongue tie. *Debra Hamer*

MIN (FR) 7 b.g. Walk In The Park (IRE) – Phemyka (FR) (Saint Estephe (FR)) **c169**
[2017/18 c160P, h–: c20v* c17d² c17s* c15.9s² c19.9s² c16s⁴ Apr 24] **h–**

'The Race of Truth' is what the individual time trial is famously referred
to in cycling, the pitting of man or woman against just the stopwatch (with no
outside help from team mates) designed to reveal the strongest competitor. Time
trials traditionally have a big say in the outcome of cycling's flagship event, the
Tour de France. Five-times Tour winners Jacques Anquetil and Miguel Indurain both
largely owed their wins to dominating the time trial stages, whilst the 1989 Tour was
decided by a final stage time trial, when the American Greg LeMond overcame a
fifty-second deficit to defeat his great French rival Laurent Fignon on the Champs
Elysees by eight seconds, which remains the narrowest winning margin in Tour
history. Analysing the merits of time performances can vary from sport to sport, of
course, and it is sometimes not so simple as just focussing on the quickest time. For
example, the fastest lap in qualifying for motorcycling's premier class, MotoGP, can
sometimes be misleading as a measure of a rider's true pace and as a guide to what
might happen in the race itself, particularly as motorcycling is a sport where grid
position isn't quite so crucial as for the counterparts in Formula One. A prominent
grid position may be the result of one stellar lap posted under optimum conditions,
possibly significantly faster than any others the rider achieved during the practice
session. After a closer inspection of the lap charts, it usually pays to side with riders
who posted a series of consistently fast laps—nine-times world champion Valentino
Rossi is a master at concentrating on consistent race pace and regularly outperforms
his grid position (Rossi's wins are nearly double the number of pole positions he
has achieved).

In horse racing, a course record time can be similarly misleading, as it is
often just a reflection of a combination of the prevailing firm underfoot conditions
and the wind direction (in Flat races), coupled with the pace of the race, rather
than evidence of an outstanding performance by the winning horse. More detailed
and sophisticated analysis is required to assess the true merit of the time clocked.
Timeform, as the name implies, was a marriage between 'time' and 'form', and
its founder Phil Bull originally made his reputation by accurately assessing time
performances through 'racefigures' expressed in the decimal notation in seconds
(per five furlongs) faster or slower than a certain standard. When Timeform was
started, a rating and a racefigure appeared for each horse, the one a measure of its
form and the other a measure of its merit on time. The current incarnation, computer
timefigures, has been confined to Flat racing for most of its history, but Timeform
was able to extend the service to National Hunt racing in the latest season after a
prolonged period of research and development. The project was only able to get
off the ground properly once the BHA (under pressure from several parties after a
Timeform investigation in the 2014/15 season) instigated changes in 2015 to the
ways that race distances are accurately measured and recorded, a key factor being
that any alterations to the advertised trip must always be made public. Dolling out to
preserve ground has greater ramifications over jumps than on the Flat (courses such
as Market Rasen can regularly add nearly a furlong to the official distance as a result
of the practice). Increased confidence in the information provided by courses has
been vital in compiling a timefigure database.

No similar directive is currently in force in Ireland, so jumps timefigures
can only be returned for a handful of Irish courses where historical race times and
distances have stood up to close scrutiny. One of these is Gowran, the venue for
the comeback of the highly-regarded Min in November after injury had restricted
his novice chasing campaign in 2016/17 to just two starts (both yielding wins). At

Coral Dublin Chase, Leopardstown—
Min runs out a wide-margin winner of this new race; Simply Ned (left) and Special Tiara (stars) fill the minor placings after Ordinary World (stripes) blunders at the last

first glance, Min's winning margin at Gowran of thirty-six lengths (with a further sixty-nine lengths back to the third), starting at 9/1-on in a three-runner minor event, might have been dismissed as meaningless form against two vastly inferior rivals. A winning timefigure, equivalent to a timerating (on the Timeform scale) of 167, however, suggested there was substance to the performance and the figure illustrates how jumps timefigures can be a useful tool when assessing problematic form. Native River's reappearance win in the three-runner Denman Chase at Newbury (where he posted a timerating of 165) was another good example in the latest season of a top-class effort which represented stronger form on the clock than initial post-race impressions might have suggested. Both races took place under testing conditions and the state of the ground is one of the major factors to be taken into account when calculating timefigures, with other key components including the trip, standard times and closing sectionals. The last-named can be a good indicator as to whether a horse has done too much too soon in a race, and that was definitely a factor on Min's next start in the Grade 1 Paddy's Rewards Club Chase at Leopardstown's Christmas meeting. After racing freely at the head of affairs, 7/2-on Min was hard pressed to hold off the veteran British raider Simply Ned (who'd been placed in the last three renewals) by just half a length in a desperate finish. Min lost the race in the stewards' room after edging left under pressure and squeezing Simply Ned up against the rail on the run-in.

Reversing the placings in that race set the tone for a chastening few days for big-spending owner Rich Ricci, who would have won the Future Champions Novices' Hurdle some thirty-five minutes later but for Sharjah's final-flight fall; he then had to endure rare flops by his stalwart performers Djakadam and Faugheen (both pulled up) later on during the meeting. Paul Townend rode Min on his first two starts but he switched to the enigmatic Yorkhill instead in the inaugural edition of the Grade 2 Coral Dublin Chase back at Leopardstown in February, when Min (the mount of David Mullins) and Yorkhill faced four rivals. Punters certainly had not lost faith in Min, however, and he was heavily supported in to 11/8 favouritism, ahead of easy-to-back 7/4-shot Yorkhill. The money spoke in the race itself, with Yorkhill running a listless race to finish a well-beaten sixth behind an imperious Min, who gained ample consolation for that frustrating Christmas reverse by thrashing Simply Ned by twelve lengths this time, with the 2017 Queen Mother Champion Chase winner Special Tiara a further neck away in third.

As at Gowran, Min's impressive Dublin Chase performance was backed up by a similarly strong showing on the clock as he posted another timerating of 167. As a result, Min was the only runner going into the latest renewal of the Queen Mother Champion Chase who could boast two timefigures over fences above 165. Min was

MIN

reunited with Townend at Cheltenham, though it is worth noting that before stable jockey Ruby Walsh (back from injury for the Festival) had to sit things out, he sided with the other Ricci runner Douvan, who could boast the highest timefigure (172) in the Champion Chase line-up. Mr Patrick Mullins took over on Douvan, who was sent off 9/2 third choice behind Min at 5/2 and the even-money favourite Altior. Altior had never posted a timefigure over fences higher than 150 going into the Champion Chase, but that had been down to circumstances rather than anything else and, in a fiercely-run event, he duly confirmed himself the best around, recording a timefigure that was equivalent to a rating of 180, the best recorded by any horse over any distance all season. Altior defeated Min by seven lengths, coincidentally the same margin as when the pair were also first and second home in the 2016 Supreme Novices' Hurdle. The performance still represented a career-best effort by Min, who pulled eleven lengths clear of third-placed God's Own (Douvan fell four out when still travelling strongly at the head of affairs); the fact that Min traded at as low as 1.26 in-running on Betfair is an illustration of how easy Min seems to find things, even when racing at such a searching gallop.

Despite his obvious ability, Min is still waiting for his first Grade 1 win and he didn't have the stewards to blame for extending that drought, when going down by a neck to Politologue (only fourth at Cheltenham) in the Melling Chase at Aintree in April. The return to further probably stretched Min's stamina under the prevailing testing conditions. He gave his usual exuberant display and it was frustrating that he couldn't hold on after being produced to lead before the last, particularly as he clearly travelled and jumped like the best horse in the race for most of the way. Another defeat for Min on his final outing, just eleven days later, was much easier to excuse, though, as he was the only runner in the nine-strong Boylesports Champion Chase line-up who had contested races at both the Cheltenham and Aintree Festivals and it rather showed in his performance as he managed only a below-form fourth as his stable-companions Un de Sceaux and Douvan (the mount of Townend) fought out the finish.

```
                    ┌ Walk In The Park (IRE) ┌ Montjeu         ┌ Sadler's Wells
                    │ (b 2002)               │ (b 1996)        │ Floripedes
Min (FR)            │                        │ Classic Park    │ Robellino
(b.g. 2011)         │                        │ (b 1994)        │ Wanton
                    │                        ┌ Saint Estephe   ┌ Top Ville
                    │ Phemyka (FR)           │ (b 1982)        │ Une Tornade
                    └ (b 1996)               │ Stormyka        │ Akarad
                                             └ (b 1990)        └ Stormy Scene
```

The well-made Min has had his pedigree discussed in previous editions of *Chasers & Hurdlers* and there is nothing new to add, though it is worth repeating that he is out of a French mile and a quarter winner, and the longest distance over which any of his siblings have won is nineteen furlongs (over hurdles in the French Provinces). As a result, it's no surprise that two and a half miles looks the likely limit of Min's stamina range, at least for now, particularly given that he has a tendency to race freely. Min has raced only on good going or softer to date (acts on heavy), but is unlikely to be inconvenienced should he encounter firmer conditions. Despite his Punchestown defeat, Min boasts the strongest two-mile form, apart from star novice Footpad (who has posted a timefigure of 179), among the season's Irish chasers and it should not be long before he claims that elusive first Grade 1. He wore ear plugs in the Queen Mother Champion Chase. *W. P. Mullins, Ireland*

MINI DREAMS 6 b.m. Josr Algarhoud (IRE) – Mini Minster (Minster Son) [2017/18 b16.8s h16.8v^{pu} Mar 23] first foal: dam (h105) 2m-2½m hurdle winner: no show in mares bumper/novice hurdle. *Peter Atkinson* h–
b–

MINISTERFORSPORT (IRE) 7 b.g. Dubai Destination (USA) – Lady Alacoque (IRE) (Anshan) [2017/18 h16v* h18.8v⁴ h19v* Apr 1] first foal: dam unraced: multiple point winner: won only start in bumpers for Terence O'Brien: useful form over hurdles: won maiden at Limerick in December and handicap at Cork (by 1¼ lengths from Hareth) in April: will stay beyond 19f: tried in tongue tie. *Noel O'Neill, Ireland* h137

MINMORE GREY (IRE) 9 gr.g. Primary (USA) – Hopeful Memory (IRE) (Roselier (FR)) [2017/18 c–§, h–: c26d⁵ c25.1v^{pu} Mar 28] maiden pointer/hurdler: maiden chaser, no form in 2017/18: has worn headgear: temperamental. *Nick Lampard* c–§
h–

MINMORE PRESENT (IRE) 7 ch.g. Presenting – Ballagh Dawn (IRE) (Buckskin (FR)) [2017/18 c24s² c19.7d³ c26g⁴ Apr 20] €8,000 3-y-o: seventh foal: brother to fair hurdler Vodka 'N Tonic (17f winner) and half-brother to a winning pointer by Old Vic: dam, pulled up sole start in points, out of sister to top-class 2m-2½m chaser Waterloo Boy: point winner: fair form in novice chases. *Gary Moore* — c107

MINNIE ESCAPE 6 b.m. Getaway (GER) – Minnie Hill (IRE) (Oscar (IRE)) [2017/18 b15.3v Feb 1] first foal: dam (h121) 2m-2½m hurdle winner: tailed off in bumper. *Victor Dartnall* — b–

MINNIE MILAN (IRE) 9 b.m. Milan – Shiminnie (IRE) (Bob Back (USA)) [2017/18 h116: h25.4d⁶ h22.1g⁵ h25.4s h22.1d⁴ h19.9g h23.8m⁶ h23.8g⁴ h20s Dec 3] sturdy mare: fairly useful handicap hurdler, well below best in 2017/18: stays 3¼m: acts on good to soft going: in cheekpieces last 5 starts, tongue tied last 4: usually races prominently. *Barbara Butterworth* — h97

MINOTAUR (IRE) 6 b.g. Azamour (IRE) – Mycenae (Inchinor) [2017/18 h109: h20g³ h22.1m* h20g* Jun 16] fairly useful form over hurdles: won novices at Cartmel in May and Aintree in June: stays 2¾m: acts on good to firm going: usually travels strongly: open to further improvement. *Jonjo O'Neill* — h121 p

MINSTREL ROYAL 8 b.g. Kayf Tara – Close Harmony (Bustino) [2017/18 h118: h20.6g h18.7g³ h24.1d h19.7s h20s³ h20.5d² h19.3s⁵ Jan 11] strong gelding: will make a chaser: fair handicap hurdler: left Nicky Henderson after first start: stays 2¾m: acts on good to firm and good to soft going: wears tongue tie. *Philip Kirby* — h109

MIN TIKY (IRE) 6 b.m. King's Theatre (IRE) – Kon Tiky (FR) (Perrault) [2017/18 b–: h15.8d h17.7v h15.8g Apr 24] no form: tried in cheekpieces. *Mark Bradstock* — h–

MIRACLE CURE (IRE) 9 b.g. Whipper (USA) – Bring Back Matron (IRE) (Rock of Gibraltar (IRE)) [2017/18 c–, h105: h16m⁶ h15.7g⁶ h20g h20d h19d³ h16d³ h16d h16v h18.8v h16v Jan 25] close-coupled gelding: modest handicap hurdler: pulled up only start in chases: left Venetia Williams after second start: stays 2½m: acts on soft going: has worn headgear, including in 2017/18. *P. T. Flavin, Ireland* — c–, h96

MIRSAALE 8 ch.g. Sir Percy – String Quartet (IRE) (Sadler's Wells (USA)) [2017/18 h130: h16.2d⁴ h16.2s³ h16.2g* h16v⁴ h16.4v⁵ h23.8d h16.2s* h16.4s⁶ h17d³ h16.2v⁶ Apr 7] smallish, angular gelding: useful handicap hurdler: won at Perth in August, and Kelso in September and January: stays 19f: acts on soft going: tried in cheekpieces. *Keith Dalgleish* — h136

MIRS CHOICE (IRE) 8 b.m. Coroner (IRE) – Dummy Run (IRE) (Glacial Storm (USA)) [2017/18 h20.6g⁶ c24d⁴ c19.8gᵖᵘ Nov 30] sixth foal: half-sister to fairly useful hurdler/useful chaser Wuff (2½m-3m winner) and fair hurdler Markem (2½m winner) (both by Beneficial): dam unraced: point winner: well beaten in mares maiden hurdle: poor form in chases: tried in hood. *Tony Carroll* — c74, h–

MIRZAM (IRE) 4 gr.f. Mastercraftsman (IRE) – Luxie (IRE) (Acclamation) [2017/18 h16g⁵ h15.8v⁵ h15.8s⁶ h15.8d Apr 9] fairly useful on Flat, stays 1½m: poor form over hurdles. *Tom Symonds* — h74

MISCHIEVIOUS MAX (IRE) 5 ch.g. Dubai Destination (USA) – Saabga (USA) (Woodman (USA)) [2017/18 b16m⁵ b17g³ b16m* b20d³ h16.4g⁴ h20d² h21.8g* h16v² h16.6v² h20.4s² h21.1s² h20s h21.1s h24s Apr 17] neat gelding: half-brother to several winners, including 19f bumper winner Kolumbus (by Robin des Champs) and fairly useful hurdler Luggers Hall (2m winner, by Cape Cross): dam ran once on Flat: fairly useful form in bumpers: won maiden at Down Royal in May: useful hurdler: won maiden at Downpatrick in August: second in intermediate handicap at Cheltenham (3 lengths behind Coole Cody) in November: stays 2¾m: acts on heavy going. *Joseph Patrick O'Brien, Ireland* — h132, b95

MISFITS (IRE) 7 b.g. Beneficial – Park Rose (IRE) (Roselier (FR)) [2017/18 c102, h100: c17.1g⁴ c23.8d² c23.8s* c23.8d³ c23.8d⁴ c26.2d² c26.2v⁵ Apr 17] sturdy gelding: maiden hurdler: fair handicap chaser: won at Musselburgh in January: stays 3¼m: acts on soft going: tried in hood: wears tongue tie: front runner/races prominently. *Lucinda Russell* — c100, h–

MISS ADVENTURE (IRE) 6 b.m. Brian Boru – Blue Fire Lady (IRE) (Blueprint (IRE)) [2017/18 h19.5s² h21s⁵ h15.9v² h19.8v⁵ h15.9d³ h19.2v³ Mar 17] lengthy, angular mare: first foal: dam winning pointer: placed both starts in Irish points: fair form over hurdles: stays 2½m: acts on heavy going: in headgear last 5 starts. *Phil Middleton* — h105

MISS ALFIE ROSE 4 b.f. Nayef – Ariyfa (IRE) (Cape Cross (IRE)) [2017/18 b16.7s⁶ Mar 26] first foal: dam 8.6f winner: 66/1, sixth in mares maiden bumper at Market Rasen (13 lengths behind Definitelyanoscar). *Peter Niven* — b80

MIS

MISS AMELIA 5 b.m. Midnight Legend – Miss Pross (Bob's Return (IRE)) [2017/18 b16.2v h16s h20.6g[5] h16d[4] h16s[5] c19.4s[6] c19.2s c16.4v[5] Mar 23] second foal: sister to fair chaser Miss Conway (2m-19f winner): dam (c117/h106) 2m/17f hurdle/chase winner: tailed off in bumper: modest form over hurdles: no form over fences. *Mark Walford* — **c–** **h88** **b–**

MISS BENEFITZ (IRE) 7 ch.m. Beneficial – African Keys (IRE) (Quws) [2017/18 h92: h18.7g h20g h20.6g[6] h19.9g[pu] h16.3g[4] Aug 3] small mare: poor maiden hurdler: wears hood: temperamental. *Mike Hammond* — **h69 §**

MISS BISCOTTI 10 ch.m. Emperor Fountain – Bellacaccia (IRE) (Beau Sher) [2017/18 c96, h–: c25.3d[pu] c26.2g[2] May 28] winning hurdler: modest hunter chaser: stays 3¼m: acts on soft going: has worn cheekpieces: usually races close up. *Gary Rutherford* — **c90** **h–**

MISS CLYRO 8 b.m. Needle Gun (IRE) – Miss Millbrook (Meadowbrook) [2017/18 h16g h19.5d h16g h20.7g[pu] Nov 14] compact mare: sixth foal: sister to fairly useful chaser Blandfords Gunner (2m winner) and half-sister to 2 winners by Midnight Legend, including fairly useful hurdler/useful chaser Wychwoods Brook (2½m-25f winner): dam (c102) 3m/25f chase winner: maiden pointer: poor form over hurdles: in visor last 2 starts: wears tongue tie. *Richard Price* — **h73**

MISS CONWAY 7 br.m. Midnight Legend – Miss Pross (Bob's Return (IRE)) [2017/18 c83, h–: c16.4g[3] c20.1g[2] c15.6g* c19.2g* c15.6g* c15.6d[4] c20.1s[4] c17.2v[F] c15.6d Apr 23] neat mare: maiden hurdler: fair handicap chaser: won at Hexham in June, Market Rasen in July and Hexham again in August: stays 2½m: acts on good to soft going: usually leads. *Mark Walford* — **c103** **h–**

MISS CRICK 7 b.m. Midnight Legend – Kwaheri (Efisio) [2017/18 h127: h20.5g[3] h20g[3] h20g[3] h21.6g[6] c21.6g[3] c19.9d[3] Nov 25] lengthy mare: fairly useful handicap hurdler: similar form over fences: stays 2¾m: acts on soft going. *Alan King* — **c117** **h129**

MISSED APPROACH (IRE) 8 b.g. Golan (IRE) – Polly's Dream (IRE) (Beau Sher) [2017/18 c146, h–: h24.1s[pu] c26g[6] c29.2s[3] c32.8s[2] c26s* c28.8d[pu] Apr 28] lengthy gelding: has had breathing operation: winning hurdler: smart handicap chaser: won Fulke Walwyn Kim Muir Chase at Cheltenham (by ½ length from Mall Dini) in March: stays 4m: acts on heavy going: usually wears headgear: front runner/races prominently. *Warren Greatrex* — **c143** **h–**

MISS FEISTYPANTS 6 ch.m. Virtual – Fu Wa (USA) (Distant View (USA)) [2017/18 h71, b–: h20g c16.5g[4] c17.4d Oct 4] maiden hurdler: little form over fences: has worn hood: often races towards rear. *Seamus Mullins* — **c78** **h–**

Fulke Walwyn Kim Muir Challenge Cup Amateur Riders' Handicap Chase, Cheltenham—
Missed Approach (centre) repels the well-backed pair Mall Dini (left) and the grey Squouateur

MISS FLEMING 6 b.m. Flemensfirth (USA) – Uppermost (Montjeu (IRE)) [2017/18 **h96** h88: h15.7g⁴ h18.5s⁵ h19.9g² h20.5d³ h20.6s² h25.6vᵖᵘ Feb 5] modest maiden hurdler: stays 21f: acts on soft going: tried in visor: in tongue tie last 5 starts. *Tom George*

MISS GOTAWAY 9 b.m. Midnight Legend – Strollaway (IRE) (Jurado (USA)) [2017/18 **c–** c27.5dᵖᵘ Jun 9] multiple point winner: modest form over hurdles: pulled up both starts in **h–** chases: in tongue tie last 2 starts. *E. Walker*

MISS HAMDA (IRE) 4 gr.f. Mastercraftsman (IRE) – Erstwhile (FR) (Desert Prince **b72** (IRE)) [2017/18 b16v⁶ b16.8g⁶ Apr 23] seventh foal: half-sister to 3 winners on Flat, including useful 6f-9f winner Sikeeb (by Alhaarth): dam French 1½m winner: poor form in bumpers: left John Weymes after first start. *Brian Ellison*

MISS HERITAGE (IRE) 4 b.f. Pour Moi (IRE) – Haretha (IRE) (Alhaarth (IRE)) **b95 p** [2017/18 b16.5v* b15.7v² Apr 27] fourth foal: half-sister to 7f/1m winner Malekat Jamal (by Dutch Art): dam unraced: fairly useful form in bumpers: won mares maiden at Taunton in April: remains with potential. *David Elsworth*

MISS HONEY RYDER (IRE) 5 b.m. Stowaway – Seesea (IRE) (Dr Massini (IRE)) **b– p** [2017/18 b15.8s Feb 8] €50,000 4-y-o: second foal: half-sister to useful bumper winner/ smart hurdler Western Ryder (2m/17f winner, by Westerner), stays 2½m: dam (b81), lightly raced in bumpers, sister to fairly useful hurdler/useful chaser Glam Gerry and half-sister to useful hurdler/fairly useful chaser Kimberlite King (both stayed 21f): 3/1, very green when seventh in mares bumper at Huntingdon: should do better. *Warren Greatrex*

MISSION MARS 5 b.g. Kyllachy – Ashraakat (USA) (Danzig (USA)) [2017/18 h16.2gᵖᵘ **h–** h15.7gᵖᵘ Jun 26] little sign of ability. *Patrick Holmes*

MISSION TRIO (IRE) 6 b.g. Presenting – Miss Brandywell (IRE) (Sadler's Wells **h–** (USA)) [2017/18 b63: h19.7s h20.8d h19.3s⁵ Jan 1] little show in bumpers/over hurdles: tried in cheekpieces. *Patrick Holmes*

MISS JOEKING (IRE) 7 b.m. Alkaadhem – Go Franky (IRE) (Hollow Hand) [2017/18 **c75** h74: c16g⁵ c20.1g⁵ c24.2g* c25.5s⁶ Jul 22] winning hurdler: poor form over fences: won **h–** handicap at Hexham in June: stays 3m: acts on soft and good to firm going: in cheekpieces last 2 starts, tongue tied last 3. *Lucinda Russell*

MISS MACKIE (IRE) 7 b.m. Mr Combustible (IRE) – Grannys Kitchen (IRE) **c83** (Flemensfirth (USA)) [2017/18 h73: h19.3m⁵ h19.4m² c17.3s* c15.6g³ c15.6v⁵ c15.6d* Apr **h–** 23] maiden hurdler: poor form over fences: won handicaps at Cartmel in July and Hexham in April: raced mainly around 2m: acts on soft going: has worn cheekpieces, including in 2017/18. *R. Mike Smith*

MISS MAIDEN OVER (IRE) 6 br.m. Carlo Bank (IRE) – Rock Garden (IRE) **h–** (Bigstone (IRE)) [2017/18 h115, b–: h22sᵖᵘ h20.3d⁵ h21.7g⁶ h21.7d Sep 10] useful-looking mare: fairly useful hurdler at best, no form in 2017/18: left Fergal O'Brien after second start: tried in headgear. *Chris Gordon*

MISS MALARKY (IRE) 5 b.m. Presenting – The Shan Gang (IRE) (Anshan) [2017/18 **h–** b–: b15.7m⁶ b16s h16s Apr 9] rather unfurnished mare: no form in bumpers/novice hurdle: **b–** left Diana Grissell after first start. *Linda Jewell*

MISS MASH 7 b.m. Multiplex – Shanxi Girl (Overbury (IRE)) [2017/18 h100: h22d⁶ **c–** h17.2s² h20g² h19g⁴ h19.3s² c20sᵖᵘ h25sᵖᵘ Dec 26] compact mare: fair handicap hurdler: **h103 x** pulled up in handicap on chasing debut: stays 23f: acts on soft going: often races towards rear: often let down by jumping. *Henry Daly*

MISS MAYFAIR (IRE) 11 b.m. Indian Danehill (IRE) – Cocktail Party (USA) (Arctic **h96** Tern (USA)) [2017/18 h27g² h23.4g⁴ h25s* h25d² h25sᵖᵘ Dec 26] modest handicap hurdler: won at Plumpton in November: stays 27f: acts on heavy going: wears cheekpieces: usually leads. *Lawney Hill*

MISS MOBOT 8 b.m. Midnight Legend – Fleur de Nikos (FR) (Nikos) [2017/18 h120: **h123** h26.5m² h26.4g² h27g³ h21.2m² Oct 11] lengthy mare: fairly useful handicap hurdler: stays 3¼m: acts on good to firm going: often races prominently/travels strongly. *Philip Hobbs*

MISS MOLLY MAE (IRE) 6 b.m. Getaway (GER) – Miss Mary Mac (IRE) (Dushyantor **h–** (USA)) [2017/18 b17d h17.7v⁶ Jan 8] first foal: dam (c117/h116) 2½m hurdle/chase **b–** winner (stayed 3m): hinted at ability in mares bumper: well beaten in mares maiden on hurdling debut. *Neil Mulholland*

MISS NIGHT OWL 8 ch.m. Midnight Legend – Moyliscar (Terimon) [2017/18 h117, **h124** b93: h16.3g² h16s h16.2g⁴ Nov 29] compact mare: placed 3 times in Irish points: bumper winner: fairly useful handicap hurdler: won mares event at Stratford in October: raced around 2m: best form on good going: front runner. *Tom George*

MIS

MISS QUEST 6 b.m. Urgent Request (IRE) – Flighty Mist (Missed Flight) [2017/18 b16.2g h16.2g^{pu} Aug 1] first foal: dam (c90) 2m-2½m chase winner: no show in bumper/novice hurdle. *Sandy Forster* — h– b–

MISS QUOTED 6 b.m. Proclamation (IRE) – Ambience Lady (Batshoof) [2017/18 b16.8m b17.7s Sep 10] fourth foal: half-sister to 7f/1m winner Zebrano (by Storming Home): dam (c98/h76) bumper/2½m chase winner: no form, including on Flat. *Seamus Mullins* — b–

MISS ROCHER (IRE) 4 b.f. Arcadio (GER) – Madam Rocher (IRE) (Roselier (FR)) [2017/18 b16.5v^{pu} Apr 12] €1,000 3-y-o: seventh foal: half-sister to fair hurdler/fairly useful chaser Rowdy Rocher (2½m-3m winner, by Winged Love): dam unraced half-sister to fairly useful hurdler (stayed 2½m) Dr Flynn: pulled up in mares maiden bumper. *Nigel Hawke* — b–

MISS SERIOUS (IRE) 8 br.m. Kalanisi (IRE) – Burnt Out (IRE) (Anshan) [2017/18 c123, h–: h26.5m^6 h23.3d^5 h26.5d^F Aug 22] lengthy mare: fairly useful handicap hurdler, below form in 2017/18: fairly useful chaser: stays 3¼m: acts on good to firm and good to soft going: wears tongue tie. *Jeremy Scott* — c– h104

MISS SPENT (IRE) 8 b.m. Presenting – Cash And New (IRE) (Supreme Leader) [2017/18 h107: h19.9d* h18.5d^2 h21.7d^4 c16.5g^{pu} h16g^3 h19.9g^5 Nov 2] good-topped mare: fairly useful handicap hurdler: won mares event at Uttoxeter in July: third in listed event at Kempton (6 lengths behind Old Guard) in October: let down by jumping on chasing debut: stays 2½m: acts on good to soft going: has worn cheekpieces, including in 2017/18: wears tongue tie. *Dan Skelton* — c– h119

MISS TIGGY (IRE) 8 b.m. Milan – Rockwell College (IRE) (Supreme Leader) [2017/18 h–: h16v* h20.6s^3 h16v^4 Jan 15] fair hurdler: won mares maiden at Ayr in November: stays 21f: best form on heavy going. *Lucinda Russell* — h100

MISS TONGABEZI 9 b.m. Overbury (IRE) – Shiwa (Bustino) [2017/18 h116: h23.3d c20s c21.7s* c20.5s^3 c22.7v^3 c24.1s^{pu} Mar 24] compact mare: fairly useful hurdler: fair form over fences: won novice handicap at Towcester in December: third in listed mares event at Doncaster in January: stays 3m: acts on heavy going: wears hood/tongue tie: usually races close up. *Paul Webber* — c119 h108

MISS TYNTE (IRE) 6 b.m. Mahler – Top Quality (Simply Great (FR)) [2017/18 b86: b16d h16.5s^4 h15.9v^{ur} h16v^2 h16.5v^3 h21.2d* h24.3g Apr 20] modest form in bumpers: fair form over hurdles: won mares handicap at Ludlow in April: will prove best up to 21f: acts on heavy going: in headgear last 3 starts: often in tongue tie: often races towards rear/travels strongly. *David Pipe* — h111 b78

MISS YEATS (IRE) 7 b.m. Yeats (IRE) – Mrs Wallensky (IRE) (Roselier (FR)) [2017/18 h102: h21m^3 h19.5s^3 h23.5d h21s^5 h25d^4 Mar 26] good-topped mare: modest maiden hurdler: stays 25f: acts on soft going: front runner/races prominently. *Laura Mongan* — h97

MISTER BIG (IRE) 7 b.g. Scorpion (IRE) – Back To Roost (IRE) (Presenting) [2017/18 h107: h21.6m^{pu} h21.3s h15.5s^5 Dec 3] rangy gelding: maiden hurdler, no form in 2017/18: tried in blinkers. *Neil King* — h–

MISTER CHOW 4 ch.g. Nathaniel (IRE) – Skimmia (Mark of Esteem (IRE)) [2017/18 h16s^2 h16s* h15.7v^6 h18.8s* Mar 24] tall, good-topped gelding: fair on Flat, stays 13.5f: useful form over hurdles: won juvenile at Warwick in January and juvenile handicap at Newbury (by ½ length from Oistrakh Le Noir) in March. *Gary Moore* — h121

MISTER DICK (FR) 6 b.g. Great Journey (JPN) – Lyric Melody (FR) (Lyphard's Wish (FR)) [2017/18 c91, h94: c24g^5 h23.3g^{pu} h23g^6 h23g h23g^6 Aug 23] maiden pointer: modest hurdler/chaser at best, little show in 2017/18: stays 3m: acts on good to firm and heavy going: has worn headgear/tongue tie, including in 2017/18: front runner/races prominently: temperamental. *Jonjo O'Neill* — c– § h61 §

MISTER DON (IRE) 8 br.g. Presenting – Spring Flower (IRE) (Beneficial) [2017/18 c107, h82: c26.2g^5 c24.2g^3 c23.9g^2 c24.1g^2 c23.9g^2 c29.2g c26d* c32.8s^4 Feb 3] medium-sized, good-topped gelding: maiden hurdler: fairly useful handicap chaser: won at Doncaster in December: stays 31f: acts on good to firm and heavy going: wears cheekpieces: tried in tongue tie: often races prominently. *Rose Dobbin* — c118 h–

MISTER DRIFTER (IRE) 6 b.g. Stowaway – Graces Choice (IRE) (Luso) [2017/18 b82: h20g^5 h21.6v^6 h18.5d^6 h25g^4 h23.1v^6 h19v^6 h23.1v^{pu} Apr 8] fair maiden hurdler: stays 25f: has worn headgear, including last 4 starts: signs of temperament. *David Pipe* — h101

MIS

MISTER FIRST (FR) 12 b.g. Trempolino (USA) – Queen Running (FR) (Cadoudal (FR)) [2017/18 c128, h110: h24g^3 h24g^3 h21g 22.5g c22.6s c25d^{pu} h19.6v c20.5v^4 h21v^5 c22.5v^2 c17v^5 c20v^4 c21v^6 Feb 14] fair handicap hurdler/chaser: stays 25f: acts on good to firm and heavy going: has worn headgear, including last 2 starts: has worn tongue tie, including in 2017/18: often races towards rear: weak finisher and can't be relied on. *Robert Hennessy, Ireland* — **c108 §** / **h106 §**

MISTER FISHER (IRE) 4 b.g. Jeremy (USA) – That's Amazing (IRE) (Marignan (USA)) [2017/18 b16s* b17s Apr 13] €65,000 3-y-o: sturdy gelding: second foal: dam unraced half-sister to smart chaser (2m-2¼m winner) Fix The Rib and useful hurdler/chaser (stayed 3m) Frascati Park: fairly useful form in bumpers: won maiden at Kempton in March. *Nicky Henderson* — **b98**

MISTER FIZZ 10 b.g. Sulamani (IRE) – Court Champagne (Batshoof) [2017/18 h–: h23g h18.7g^3 h20.6d h16.8g^3 Apr 18] leggy gelding: fairly useful handicap hurdler: stays 2¾m: acts on good to firm and good to soft going: often in cheekpieces: front runner/races prominently. *Miss Imogen Pickard* — **h119**

MISTER MALARKY 5 ch.g. Malinas (GER) – Priscilla (Teenoso (USA)) [2017/18 b78: h21.4s^3 h19.5s^5 h16d* h16v h16v^3 h20.5v^2 h20.3g Apr 18] lengthy gelding: fairly useful hurdler: won novice at Kempton in November: will stay 3m: acts on heavy going: front runner/races prominently. *Colin Tizzard* — **h115**

MISTER MCCOY 5 b.g. Sea Freedom – Another Tino (Neltino) [2017/18 b15.8d Mar 26] tailed off in bumper. *Caroline Bailey* — **b–**

MISTER MISTER (IRE) 7 b.g. September Storm (GER) – The Long Bill (IRE) (Phardante (FR)) [2017/18 h21.6g^4 h16g h18.7g^3 h23d* h23.9g^{pu} h19.6g^5 Nov 5] useful-looking gelding: seventh foal: half-brother to bumper winner/fairly useful hurdler G'day Mate (2m winner, by Taipan): dam unraced half-sister to fair hurdler/fairly useful chaser (2m-2¾m winner) King of The Arctic: Irish point winner: fair form over hurdles: won maiden at Worcester in September: stays 23f: acts on good to soft going: usually in tongue tie. *Dai Williams* — **h102**

MISTER MIYAGI (IRE) 9 b.g. Zagreb (USA) – Muckle Flugga (IRE) (Karinga Bay) [2017/18 h147: h20.3g Apr 18] lengthy gelding: placed completed start in points: smart hurdler at best, found less than looked likely after long absence sole outing in 2017/18: stays 2½m: acts on good to soft going: usually races towards rear/travels strongly. *Stuart Edmunds* — **h–**

MISTER MOOSAH (IRE) 4 gr.g. Clodovil (IRE) – Hendrina (IRE) (Daylami (IRE)) [2017/18 h16d h16.8g^{pu} Oct 25] fair maiden on Flat, stays 1m: no form over hurdles: wears tongue tie. *Micky Hammond* — **h–**

MISTER RAINMAN (IRE) 6 b.g. Westerner – Khimki (IRE) (Moscow Society (USA)) [2017/18 b–: b16v h15.8v^{pu} h16.7v^6 Feb 9] no form in bumpers/over hurdles: tried in hood/tongue tie. *Adrian Wintle* — **h–** / **b–**

MISTER SERIOUS (IRE) 9 b.g. Kalanisi (IRE) – Mack Tack (IRE) (Shardari) [2017/18 h107: h21m Apr 26] point winner: fair form on hurdling debut in 2016/17, well beaten only start since. *Robert Walford* — **h–**

MISTER SHOWMAN 5 b.g. Showcasing – Theatre Royal (Royal Applause) [2017/18 h15.7m* h16d^2 h16.3g^3 h20.6g^3 h19.4d^4 Jan 1] fair on Flat, stays 13f: fair form over hurdles: won novice at Towcester in May: left Dan Skelton after fourth start: stays 19f: acts on good to firm and good to soft going: tried in cheekpieces/tongue tie. *Keith Dalgleish* — **h108**

MISTERTON 7 gr.g. Sagamix (FR) – Mighty Splash (Cape Cross (IRE)) [2017/18 h126, b99: h16.4s^2 h16.3v Feb 10] lengthy gelding: bumper winner: fairly useful handicap hurdler: won at Chepstow in October: second in Greatwood Hurdle at Cheltenham (neck behind Elgin) in November: stays 2½m: acts on soft going: usually races close up. *Harry Fry* — **h140**

MISTER UNIVERSUM (GER) 6 b.g. Cape Cross (IRE) – Miss Europa (IRE) (Monsun (GER)) [2017/18 h99: h16.8g^5 h16.7d^4 h16.3g* h16.7g* h18.7m^2 h16.3g^3 h15.8d^2 Apr 9] rather leggy gelding: fairly useful hurdler: won maiden at Stratford in July and novice at Bangor in August: second in handicap at Ludlow in April: stays 19f: acts on good to firm and good to soft going: in tongue tie last 5 starts: often races prominently/freely. *Dan Skelton* — **h123**

MISTER VALENTINE 5 b.g. Alflora (IRE) – Aberdeen Park (Environment Friend) [2017/18 b15.8v^5 b16s Feb 24] no form in bumpers. *Martin Keighley* — **b–**

Timeform Novices' Handicap Chase, Cheltenham—Mister Whitaker (left) and Theatre Territory (noseband) are about to pull clear of long-time leader Sizing Tennessee

MISTER WHITAKER (IRE) 6 b.g. Court Cave (IRE) – Benbradagh Vard (IRE) (Le Bavard (FR)) [2017/18 h111, b85: c21.6g³ c20d* c20.5d² c20.8v* c20.4s* Mar 13] lengthy, rather unfurnished gelding: lightly-raced hurdler: smart form over fences: won novice handicap at Carlisle (by 2 lengths from Solstice Star) in November, Timeform Novices' Handicap at Cheltenham (by 1¾ lengths from Theatre Territory) in January and Close Brothers Novices' Handicap Chase at Cheltenham (by head from Rather Be) in March: stays 21f: acts on good to firm and heavy going: open to further progress over fences. *Mick Channon*   **c146 p h–**

MISTRESS MASSINI 7 b.m. Dr Massini (IRE) – Mistress Willie (Master Willie) [2017/18 b86: b15.7m⁴ h20m⁴ May 11] sturdy mare: pulled up in point: fair form in bumpers: 7/1, fourth in mares maiden at Worcester (36½ lengths behind Whatzdjazz) on hurdling debut. *Anthony Honeyball*   **h78 b86**

MISTY BLOOM (IRE) 5 b.m. Yeats (IRE) – Misty Mountain (IRE) (Namaqualand (USA)) [2017/18 b16.3s ab16g⁵ ab16g² Jan 30] fifth foal: half-sister to 2 winners on Flat, including useful 6f-1m winner Corcovada (by Captain Rio): dam, 1m winner, half-sister to useful hurdler (2m/17f winner) Princeton Plains: modest form in bumpers. *Emma Lavelle*   **b79**

MISTY MAI (IRE) 8 b.m. Westerner – Arcanum (IRE) (Presenting) [2017/18 c–, h102: c22.5d⁵ c23.8v² c25.3v* h21.2s⁶ c23.8v⁵ c25.2v* c27.9v⁵ c23.8vᵖᵘ Apr 15] winning hurdler: fair handicap chaser: won at Ffos Las in December and Hereford (mares) in March: stays 25f: acts on heavy going. *David Rees*   **c113 h80**

MITCD (IRE) 7 gr.m. Mastercraftsman (IRE) – Halicardia (Halling (USA)) [2017/18 h86: h16.8g h16.8g³ h15.6s² Jan 3] modest handicap hurdler: stays 2½m: acts on good to soft going. *George Bewley*   **h88**

MITCHOUKA (FR) 4 b.g. Creachadoir (IRE) – Minnaloushe (FR) (Black Minnaloushe (USA)) [2017/18 h16g² h16s* h16s² h16d³ h16s* h16s* h16.4sᵖᵘ h16s² h16s⁶ Apr 28] half-brother to fair French hurdler Mitch (2¼m winner, by Zafeen): fairly useful on Flat in France, stays 1m: useful hurdler: won juveniles at Fairyhouse (maiden) and Punchestown in November, and at former course in January, and Winning Fair Juvenile Hurdle there (by 2¼ lengths from Mastermind) in February: raced only at 2m: acts on soft going: often travels strongly. *Gordon Elliott, Ireland*   **h138**

MIXBOY (FR) 8 gr.g. Fragrant Mix (IRE) – Leston Girl (FR) (Lesotho (USA)) [2017/18 c138, h–: c15.8s* c16s² Apr 26] angular gelding: winning hurdler: useful handicap chaser: won at Musselburgh in January: second at Perth in April: stays 21f, effective at shorter: acts on heavy going: has worn hood: front runner/races prominently. *Keith Dalgleish*   **c142 h–**

MOD

MIXCHIEVOUS 7 gr.g. Fair Mix (IRE) – Cheeky Mare (Derrylin) [2017/18 h105: h19.5v* h18.5v⁵ h25.5v Mar 10] good-topped gelding: fair handicap hurdler: won conditionals novice event at Chepstow in November: stays 2½m: acts on heavy going: usually races prominently: not straightforward. *Venetia Williams* — **h106**

MIZEN MASTER (IRE) 5 b.g. Captain Rio – Nilassiba (Daylami (IRE)) [2017/18 h97: h18.7g* h16.7g² h20.6g* h22.1d² h20.9g³ h21.1g h19.6s⁵ Nov 15] angular gelding: fairly useful hurdler: won novice handicap at Stratford in July and novice at Market Rasen in August: stays 2¾m: acts on good to soft going: tried in cheekpieces: wears tongue tie. *Olly Murphy* — **h121**

MOABIT (GER) 6 b.g. Azamour (IRE) – Moonlight Danceuse (IRE) (Bering) [2017/18 h132: c16.5m² c19.2g³ h16.5s⁴ h16s* h15.3v* h16.3s³ Mar 23] good-topped gelding: useful handicap hurdler: won at Chepstow in February and Wincanton (by 2½ lengths from Sea Wall) in March: underwhelming efforts over fences: strong-travelling sort, will prove best at 2m: acts on good to firm and heavy going: wears tongue tie. *Paul Nicholls* — **c99 h132**

MO CHAILIN (IRE) 7 b.m. Milan – Consultation (IRE) (Camden Town) [2017/18 h106: h19.9g³ Nov 2] fair handicap hurdler: stays 2½m: acts on heavy going: tried in blinkers. *Donald McCain* — **h107**

MODELIGO (IRE) 9 b.g. Indian Danehill (IRE) – Glens Lady (IRE) (Mister Lord (USA)) [2017/18 c112, h–: c17d³ c23g^pu c23.6s^F c19.4v c18.9s⁶ c19.4v^pu c16s⁵ c16v² c19.4v* Apr 14] angular gelding: winning hurdler: fair handicap chaser: won at Chepstow in April: stays 2½m: acts on heavy going: wears cheekpieces/tongue tie. *Matt Sheppard* — **c105 h–**

MODEM 8 b.g. Motivator – Alashaan (Darshaan) [2017/18 h139: c17g c19.5m* h16.5g² h19f² h20f² h21g² Oct 21] useful hurdler: second in A. P. Smithwick Memorial Handicap at Saratoga, New York Turf Writers Cup Handicap on same course, Lonesome Glory Handicap at Belmont (beaten 1¼ lengths by All The Way Jose) and Grand National Hurdle at Far Hills (beaten a nose by Mr. Hot Stuff): useful form over fences: won maiden at Ballinrobe (by 2¼ lengths from Rathvinden) in May: left Mrs J. Harrington after second outing: stays 2½m: acts on any going: often wears headgear: open to further improvement as a chaser. *Elizabeth Voss Murray, USA* — **c137 p h139**

*Close Brothers Novices' Handicap Chase, Cheltenham—
a second win in this race for top northern jockey Brian Hughes who drives Mister Whitaker
(white face) ahead of Rather Be (centre); outsider Rocklander is third*

Randox Health County Handicap Hurdle, Cheltenham—a first Festival winner for conditional Bridget Andrews as Mohaayed (second right) defeats fellow outsider Remiluc (right); Whiskey Sour (chevron) and Chesterfield (noseband, star on cap) complete the frame

MODERATOR (CZE) 8 b.g. Security Risk (USA) – Modrenka (CZE) (Laban (CZE)) [2017/18 h90: h19d³ h19g^pu May 25] modest form over hurdles: winning cross-country chaser in Czech Republic: often races towards rear. *Arthur Whitehead*   c– h95

MODULE (FR) 11 b.g. Panoramic – Before Royale (FR) (Dauphin du Bourg (FR)) [2017/18 c131, h–: c20.3v^pu Feb 9] useful-looking gelding: winning hurdler: very smart chaser in 2013/14, lightly raced and largely disappointing since: stays 2½m: acts on good to firm and heavy going: tried in cheekpieces/tongue tie. *Tom George*   c– h–

MODULUS 9 b.g. Motivator – Wild Academy (IRE) (Royal Academy (USA)) [2017/18 c–, h108: h16d h21.3s h16.4v⁵ h19.3s h19.9v⁵ h19.3d Mar 25] point winner: fair handicap hurdler, below form in 2017/18: pulled up only chase start: stays 2½m: acts on heavy going: wears headgear. *Peter Winks*   c– h98

MODUS 8 ch.g. Motivator – Alessandra (Generous (IRE)) [2017/18 h155: c20.3g* c20.2s* c19.2v^F c20.5s* c19.9s c19.9s⁵ Apr 12] lengthy gelding: very smart hurdler: smart form over fences: won novice at Bangor (by 5 lengths from Midnight Target) in October, Rising Star Novices' Chase at Wincanton (by 9 lengths from Kalondra) in November and graduation event at Kempton (by 3 lengths from Max Ward) in February: stays 21f: acts on soft going: has worn hood, including in 2017/18. *Paul Nicholls*   c147 h–

MOGESTIC (IRE) 9 b.g. Morozov (USA) – Crosschild (IRE) (Buckskin (FR)) [2017/18 h102: h21.6d² May 28] fair handicap hurdler: stays 3¼m: acts on heavy going: often races towards rear. *Seamus Mullins*   h96

MOHAAYED 6 b.g. Intikhab (USA) – Reyaada (Daylami (IRE)) [2017/18 h135p: h16.7g⁴ h16.4s h16.6d² h16d³ h16.8v* Mar 16] sturdy gelding: smart hurdler: won 2-runner intermediate hurdle at Market Rasen in May and County Handicap Hurdle at Cheltenham (33/1, by 2¾ lengths from Remiluc) in March: third of 4 in Christmas Hurdle at Kempton (6 lengths behind Buveur d'Air) in December: raced around 2m: acts on heavy going: wears tongue tie: often races towards rear. *Dan Skelton*   h146

MOIDORE 9 b.g. Galileo (IRE) – Flash of Gold (Darshaan) [2017/18 h114: h23.1g⁴ h23.1g³ h24g⁴ h23.3d⁶ h23.1g^pu h23.4g² h23.1v^ur h21.2v⁴ Jan 28] good-topped gelding: fair handicap hurdler: stays 23f: acts on heavy going: has worn headgear, including last 4 starts: tried in tongue tie. *Charles Pogson*   h104

MOLE TRAP 7 b.m. Kayf Tara – Fairly High (IRE) (Sri Pekan (USA)) [2017/18 h–, b63: h21.2m⁴ h21.6m^F h23.3d⁴ h23g⁴ h19.9d^pu Nov 18] poor form in bumpers/over hurdles. *Nicky Martin*   h73

MOLINEAUX (IRE) 7 b.g. King's Theatre (IRE) – Steel Grey Lady (IRE) (Roselier (FR)) [2017/18 h105: h21g⁴ h19.8s⁴ h19.7g³ h19s² h15.3v* h18.5s² h20.5s³ h19.5s* Apr 27] workmanlike gelding: fairly useful hurdler: won novices at Wincanton in February and Chepstow in April: stays 2½m: acts on heavy going: front runner/races prominently. *Colin Tizzard*   h123

MOLLIES GENT (IRE) 10 b.g. Court Cave (IRE) – Zaffalong (IRE) (Zaffaran (USA)) [2017/18 c101, h–: h22.1g c20.1g⁶ c24.2g h20g c24.4d⁶ h23.9s⁵ c25.2g c24.5g Oct 11] modest maiden hurdler: fair handicap chaser, below form in 2017/18: stays 3m: acts on soft going: has worn visor: usually wears tongue tie: front runner/races prominently. *Paul Stafford, Ireland*   c81 h88

MON

MOLLY CAREW 6 b.m. Midnight Legend – Moyliscar (Terimon) [2017/18 h108, b–: h19.5d³ h19.5s² h21.7v³ h19.5v h20.5v⁴ h21.2d⁵ Apr 9] fair handicap hurdler: stays 2½m: acts on heavy going: often races freely. *Neil Mulholland* — **h108**

MOLLY CHILDERS (IRE) 6 b.m. Stowaway – Hushaby (IRE) (Eurobus) [2017/18 b96: h16.7g³ h16g³ h20.6d* h20.3s⁴ h23.1v⁶ h24.6s² Apr 9] sturdy mare: runner-up completed start in points: fairly useful form over hurdles: won mares handicap at Market Rasen in November: stays 25f: acts on soft going: tried in cheekpieces: often races prominently. *Stuart Edmunds* — **h121**

MOLLY THE DOLLY (IRE) 7 b.m. Flemensfirth (USA) – Pistol Flash (IRE) (Pistolet Bleu (IRE)) [2017/18 b89: h21s* h18.9v⁴ h21s² h24v² Mar 5] point winner: fairly useful form over hurdles: won mares novice at Warwick in November: front runner/races prominently. *Dan Skelton* — **h119**

MOLTEN BROWN 13 b.g. Needle Gun (IRE) – Molten (Ore) [2017/18 c98: c23.8g⁴ c26.2g⁵ c22.6d^pu c23.8s^2d Apr 27] multiple point winner: modest hunter chaser: stays 3m: acts on soft and good to firm going: wears cheekpieces. *Tony Hogarth* — **c90**

MOMELLA (IRE) 6 ch.m. Sholokhov (IRE) – Missing Link (IRE) (Elusive Quality (USA)) [2017/18 h21.6g* h20d* h21.1d² h20.3s* h20s³ Apr 14] sturdy mare: third foal: half-sister to German/French 1m-12.5f winner Macao (by Motivator): dam unraced: Irish point winner: useful form over hurdles: won mares novice at Newton Abbot in May, novice at Fakenham in October and mares handicap at Cheltenham in December: placed in Hyde Novices' Hurdle at last-named course in November and Mersey Novices' Hurdle at Aintree (3½ lengths behind Black Op) in April: stays 2¾m: acts on soft going: often travels strongly. *Dan Skelton* — **h137**

MOMKINZAIN (USA) 11 b.g. Rahy (USA) – Fait Accompli (USA) (Louis Quatorze (USA)) [2017/18 c70, h79§: h20.2g h20.2d^pu Apr 20] maiden pointer: modest hurdler at best, no form in 2017/18: once-raced chaser: stays 21f: acts on soft and good to firm going: wears headgear/tongue tie: unreliable. *Lucinda Russell* — **c– h– §**

MONALEE (IRE) 7 b.g. Milan – Tempest Belle (IRE) (Glacial Storm (USA)) [2017/18 h149, b109: c20s* c24s^F c21s* c24.4s² c24.5s^F Apr 24] — **c157 p h–**

Jump racing in Ireland is riding the crest of a wave and has probably never been stronger. Cheltenham Festival success is one obvious measure of Irish dominance—nineteen Irish-trained winners in 2017 and seventeen in 2018—but the enhancing of domestic prize money and the generous opportunities for better-class horses in Ireland's racing programme have been crucial in attracting rich owners, including several who live outside Ireland. The inaugural two-day Dublin Racing Festival, in which existing races and new ones were brought together to create a magnificent weekend of racing in early-February, was another sign of Irish racing seizing the initiative from its British counterpart. The 'highlights' in Britain on the same weekend included the sight of Champion Hurdle favourite Buveur d'Air cantering over two opponents to land odds of 16/1-on in the Contenders Hurdle at Sandown (on the same card as the only Grade 1 on the day, the five-runner Scilly Isles Novices' Chase in which the favourite and second favourite finished thirty lengths clear). The previous weekend had featured Cheltenham's Trials day, supported by one of northern jumping's best days, Doncaster's late-January Saturday meeting, and the weekend after Sandown was Betfair Hurdle day at Newbury which also featured—for the second year running—straightforward victories in supporting events for Native River and Altior, having warm-up races for the Cheltenham Festival (the pair have faced just nine opponents between them in the Denman Chase and the Game Spirit in the past two years).

The Cheltenham Festival has become almost the be-all and end-all of the jumps season in Britain, with some of the top trainers reluctant to run good horses in competitive events between Christmas and the Festival, believing a hard race would be detrimental to their Cheltenham prospects. As a result, the quality and entertainment value of British jumping in the period leading up to Cheltenham has suffered. Predictably, most British trainers shunned the new Dublin Racing Festival because there was only five weeks to Cheltenham (combined with the possible effects of travel). The importance of the new fixture was not lost on Ireland's top stables who supported it with many of their biggest names. One of the main patrons of Willie Mullins, British-based American Rich Ricci, who has enjoyed plenty of

Cheltenham Festival success over the years, described the Dublin Racing Festival as 'hugely important for us with some of our top horses having questions to answer … We will know where we stand for the Cheltenham Festival after the weekend.' The meeting's seven Grade 1s all featured horses prominent in the ante-post market for Cheltenham and there were Cheltenham prospects on view in the other races too, while the meeting's handicaps were very well contested. There were more Grade 1s at the Dublin Racing Festival, incidentally, than are scheduled for the whole of the period between Christmas and the Cheltenham Festival in Britain, which, in itself, is a reflection of the fact that, if British jumping were to stage, as part of the preamble to Cheltenham, its own version of the Dublin Racing Festival (fraught with difficulties anyway), there would be no guarantee that the best horses would actually show up!

No fewer than eight Cheltenham Festival winners came from races run at the Dublin Racing Festival and others distinguished themselves too, with an overall total of twenty horses who ran on Leopardstown's big weekend making the frame at Cheltenham. Those performances should provide food for thought for trainers who propound the theory that running horses in competitive events close to Cheltenham damages their chances. It clearly did no harm to the likes of Footpad, Samcro, Farclas, Relegate and Rathvinden (all of whom won graded races at Cheltenham), or to The Storyteller, Bleu Berry and Delta Work who triumphed in valuable handicaps. Min, Supasundee, Mr Adjudicator and Monalee, the winners of the Coral Dublin Chase, a new Grade 2 on the first day, the Irish Champion Hurdle, the Spring Juvenile Hurdle and the Flogas (formerly Dr P. J. Moriarty) Novices' Chase, the last three Grade 1s, were second in the Queen Mother Champion Chase, the Stayers' Hurdle, the Triumph and the RSA Chase respectively at Cheltenham. Interestingly, both the Dublin Racing Festival and the Cheltenham Festival were run in very testing conditions, circumstances which, in the ordinary way, might have been expected to produce more in the way of a rash of beaten horses among those coming on to Cheltenham, rather than a spate of performances that seemed to repudiate the 'too close to Cheltenham' theory. Of course, had they not run so well at Cheltenham, connections of those who performed well at Leopardstown— particularly the winners—would have had the consolation of already picking up some good prize money, while, in the process, also helping to provide jump racing fans in Ireland with a terrific two days' racing.

The Flogas Novices' Chase (which is registered nowadays as the Scalp) has long been run on the Irish Gold Cup card, along with the Deloitte Novices' Hurdle and the Spring Juvenile, and all four of them were joined up, still on the same card but on a new, earlier date in February, to the Irish Champion Hurdle card (which includes the Arkle Novices' Chase and the important novice hurdle, registered as the Golden Cygnet, which became a Grade 1 in the latest season). The Coral Dublin Chase and two Grade 2 bumpers were added, with the coral.ie Handicap Hurdle, which has had various titles in its history (including The Ladbroke and the Pierse), and the newly-sponsored Chanelle Pharma Handicap Chase both transferred from a Leopardstown fixture traditionally held earlier in January (the Chanelle Pharma is the Leopardstown Chase whose proud history is littered with big names—Arkle won it three times, twice under 12-7—and it was a shame that the name seemed to disappear, particularly at a fixture claimed to be building on the tradition and prestige of Irish jumps racing). One other notable casualty, by the way, was the often significant hunter chase (the Raymond Smith Memorial) that has traditionally been run on Irish Gold Cup day. That no place could be found for it at the Dublin Racing Festival provoked criticism in some quarters on the grounds that it was a snub to those at the grassroots. The critics probably had a point, especially as space was found for *two* bumpers, including one restricted to mares (though that was won by Relegate from Getaway Katie May who went on to win the Nickel Coin at Aintree after Relegate had already beaten the geldings in Cheltenham's Champion Bumper).

The Flogas Novices' Chase attracted a representative field of eleven, in which Monalee and Sutton Place, both of whom had shown smart form over hurdles and made impressive chasing debuts, started 11/4 joint favourites, just ahead of Invitation Only who had already posted two smart efforts over fences, the last

Flogas Novices' Chase (Scalp), Leopardstown—Monalee (stars) comes out on top for the Henry de Bromhead stable in a race otherwise dominated by Mullins- and Elliott-trained runners; also pictured are the third Invitation Only (No.4), fourth Dounikos (No.3) and fifth Snow Falcon

when winning a Grade 3 novice at Punchestown. Monalee's impressive chasing debut had come in a strongly-contested maiden chase at Punchestown in November (when strongly-fancied Invitation Only had been an early faller). Monalee had long been regarded as the type to make an even better chaser (he had been runner-up to Penhill in the Spa Novices' Hurdle at Cheltenham the previous season) and he won easily from useful opposition at Punchestown, making all and jumping accurately. Unfortunately, his first mistake as a chaser ended his participation at the tenth fence in the Fort Leney Chase at Leopardstown (in which he started favourite) at the end of December. Monalee brought down Rathvinden on that occasion before the pair renewed rivalry in the Flogas Novices' Chase. Rathvinden failed to complete for the second successive outing, unseating his rider at the second last when out of contention, but Monalee resumed winning ways with a flawless display, making all and jumping superbly before finding plenty on the run-in to fend off Al Boum Photo, Invitation Only and Dounikos in a thrilling finish (Sutton Place's jumping let him down and he was eventually pulled up).

The first four from Leopardstown all went on to the Cheltenham Festival, with Monalee, Al Boum Photo and Dounikos contesting the 'novices' Gold Cup', the RSA Insurance Chase, and Invitation Only running in the Golden Miller. Irish-trained horses won all four graded novice events at the Festival and they looked set to complete a one, two, three in the RSA Chase when Al Boum Photo came down two out, looking set to finish third behind Presenting Percy and Monalee. Presenting Percy was a very good RSA winner, staying on well to win by seven lengths after being produced to lead at the second last, but Monalee's own performance—earning his second successive runner-up spot at the Festival—was on a par with some recent winners of the race and he barely put a foot wrong as he travelled strongly for much of the way, before proving no match for the winner at the business end. Elegant Escape fared best of the home contingent, filling third, seven lengths behind Monalee, after the departure of Al Boum Photo, while Ballyoptic came fourth, ahead of Black Corton who had enjoyed a fine season in a fairly weak staying novice division in Britain. Dounikos lost his place soon after four out and was pulled up.

Monalee, Al Boum Photo and Dounikos then took part in what had the makings of a cracking renewal of the Growise Champion Novices' Chase at the Punchestown Festival, a race that attracted Cheltenham Festival winners Shattered Love (Golden Miller), Rathvinden (National Hunt Chase) and The Storyteller (who had landed the Plate Handicap). The bizarre tale of The Storyteller's victory at Punchestown is recounted fully in the essay on Al Boum Photo (who should have won). Monalee, upsides and holding every chance when falling two out, wasn't involved in the late drama, though he would almost certainly have run creditably had he not come down (after jumping fluently until then). Monalee wouldn't have

MON

beaten Al Boum Photo, who was clearly going best when Monalee fell, but he looks a good prospect whose usually accurate and measured jumping should prove an asset in open company.

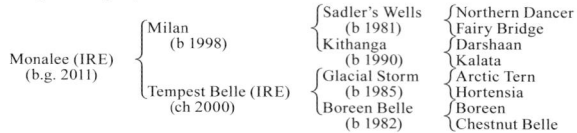

Monalee (IRE) (b.g. 2011)	Milan (b 1998)	Sadler's Wells (b 1981)	Northern Dancer Fairy Bridge
		Kithanga (b 1990)	Darshaan Kalata
	Tempest Belle (IRE) (ch 2000)	Glacial Storm (b 1985)	Arctic Tern Hortensia
		Boreen Belle (b 1982)	Boreen Chestnut Belle

Monalee, a tall gelding who always had the physical scope to make a chaser, is bred to stay well, being by the 2001 St Leger winner Milan, one of the stalwarts of Coolmore's National Hunt operation. Monalee's dam Tempest Belle never raced but is a half-sister to a couple of staying hurdler/chasers in the Thyestes Chase winner Be My Belle (dam of the fairly useful hurdler Snake Eyes) and Rose of Inchiquin (dam of the Irish Gold Cup runner-up Empire of Dirt who had an essay in *Chasers & Hurdlers 2016/17*). Both Be My Belle and Rose of Inchiquin went well in the mud, as did Monalee's grandam Boreen Belle, a useful staying hurdler who won the second running of what is now the Sefton Novices' Hurdle at Aintree. Monalee is his dam's third winner, all of them closely related, following the fair hurdler/fairly useful chaser Many Stars (by Oscar, a Sadler's Wells stallion like Monalee's sire) and the bumper winner/fair hurdler Brijomi Queen (by King's Theatre, also by Sadler's Wells). Many Stars won at up to three and a quarter miles and Monalee will stay further than three miles if tried. He acts on heavy going and usually makes the running or races prominently. Already very smart, he is open to further improvement over fences. *Henry de Bromhead, Ireland*

MON AMI BOB 5 ch.g. Schiaparelli (GER) – Maid of Perth (Mark of Esteem (IRE)) [2017/18 b–: ab16.3g ab16.3g⁴ b16.2s Apr 27] modest form in bumpers: in tongue tie last 3 starts. *James Bethell* — **b79**

MONANGO HIGH (IRE) 8 b.g. Mountain High (IRE) – Monanig Lady (IRE) (Alphabatim (USA)) [2017/18 h20.5vᵖᵘ Dec 22] little impact in points: pulled up in novice hurdle. *Stuart Coltherd* — **h–**

MONARCH'S GLORY (IRE) 8 b.g. Royal Anthem (USA) – Hazel's Glory (IRE) (Mister Lord (USA)) [2017/18 h22.1sᵖᵘ Jul 22] point winner: pulled up in novice hurdle. *Mike Sowersby* — **h–**

MONAR LAD (IRE) 6 b.g. Mountain High (IRE) – Cottage Lady (IRE) (Moscow Society (USA)) [2017/18 b–: h15.8d⁶ h17.2d⁵ h17.2g⁵ h15.8m⁵ h16.3s⁶ Oct 2] good-topped gelding: poor form over hurdles: raced around 2m: in tongue tie last 3 starts. *Dai Burchell* — **h78**

MONAR ROSE 6 b.m. Yeats (IRE) – Rhapsody Rose (Unfuwain (USA)) [2017/18 b92: h16d⁶ h15.7g⁴ h16.3d⁴ h16.3d⁶ h18.5s⁴ h18.9v c19.8vᵖᵘ Apr 27] lengthy, rather unfurnished mare: fair form over hurdles: won mares maiden at Towcester in May: shaped better than being pulled up suggests in handicap there on chasing debut: stays 19f: acts on heavy going: wears hood/tongue tie. *Ben Case* — **c– p / h110**

MONBEG CAVE (IRE) 6 b.g. Court Cave (IRE) – Reynella Cross (IRE) (Torus) [2017/18 h–: c16v⁴ c16.4vᶠ Apr 13] maiden hurdler: poor form over fences: tried in cheekpieces. *Martin Todhunter* — **c66 / h–**

MONBEG CHARMER (IRE) 7 br.g. Daylami (IRE) – Charming Present (IRE) (Presenting) [2017/18 h127: c23d⁴ c23.8g* c23.8d³ c24gᵖᵘ c20dᵖᵘ Apr 28] lengthy, angular gelding: fairly useful hurdler: useful form over fences: won handicap at Ludlow (by 1¾ lengths from Marcilhac) in November: stays 3m: acts on good to soft going: in hood last 5 starts, tongue tied last 4: front runner/races prominently. *Charlie Longsdon* — **c130 / h–**

MONBEG GOLD (IRE) 8 b.g. Gold Well – Little Hand (IRE) (Carroll House) [2017/18 c126, h–: h24.7g May 19] rangy gelding: fairly useful hurdler/chaser, well held sole outing (over hurdles) in 2017/18: stays 23f: acts on heavy going: has worn headgear. *Jonjo O'Neill* — **c– / h–**

MONBEG LEGEND 8 b.g. Midnight Legend – Reverse Swing (Charmer) [2017/18 h20.3d* h20g* h20g* h19s² h21g Feb 24] €14,000 3-y-o, £120,000 5-y-o: third foal: half-brother to modest hurdler/poor chaser Cleve Cottage (23f-3¼m winner, by Presenting): — **h126**

dam (c92/h77) 2m-3m hurdle/chase winner: Irish point winner: fairly useful form over hurdles: won maiden at Southwell and novice at Worcester in June, and another novice at Worcester in July: stays 2½m: acts on good to soft going. *Nicky Henderson*

MONBEG NOTORIOUS (IRE) 7 b.g. Milan – Borleagh Princess (IRE) (Presenting) [2017/18 h131, b108: c20v² c23.5v² c25.5v* c25v* c24v* c29v c24.5s² Apr 24] winning hurdler: smart chaser: won maiden at Punchestown (by 7½ lengths from Augustin) in December, Thyestes Handicap Chase at Gowran (by 11 lengths from Wounded Warrior) in January and Ten Up Novices' Chase at Navan (by ½ length from Mossback) in February: possibly flattered when second in eventful Champion Novices' Chase at Punchestown (6 lengths behind The Storyteller) in April: should stay long distances: acts on heavy going: wears headgear. *Gordon Elliott, Ireland*   **c149 h–**

MONBEG OSCAR (IRE) 6 b.g. Oscar (IRE) – Simply Joyful (Idiot's Delight) [2017/18 h111p, b89: h16s² h23.4s⁶ h15.8s² h20.3v² Feb 5] rather unfurnished gelding: Irish point winner: fairly useful form over hurdles: stays 2½m: acts on heavy going: front runner/races prominently. *Evan Williams*   **h117**

MONBEG RIVER (IRE) 9 br.g. Indian River (FR) – So Pretty (IRE) (Presenting) [2017/18 c129, h–: c19.4d² c19.1d* c18.8d c16.5v² c20.5g^F Apr 20] workmanlike gelding: maiden hurdler: useful handicap chaser: won at Doncaster (by 16 lengths from Drumlee Sunset) in December: stays 19f: acts on heavy going: tried in tongue tie: often travels strongly. *Martin Todhunter*   **c134 h–**

MONBEG THEATRE (IRE) 9 b.g. King's Theatre (IRE) – Amberina (IRE) (Bob Back (USA)) [2017/18 c19.4v* h23.1v² h21.4v^pu h21.2s² h21s³ h24g* Apr 18] sturdy gelding: fairly useful handicap hurdler: won at Cheltenham in April: fair form on completed chase start (off nearly 2 years before falling early on return): stays 3m: acts on heavy going: in cheekpieces last 4 starts: wears tongue tie: front runner/races prominently. *Jamie Snowden*   **c– h128**

MONBEG WORLDWIDE (IRE) 6 b.g. Lucarno (USA) – Molly Duffy (IRE) (Oscar (IRE)) [2017/18 b113: h20s² h16.3v³ Dec 7] point winner: unbeaten in 3 bumpers: useful form over hurdles: better effort when second in maiden at Fairyhouse (5 lengths behind Jetz) in November: stays 2½m+: usually races close up: remains open to improvement. *Gordon Elliott, Ireland*   **h130 p**

MONDAY CLUB 5 ch.g. Strategic Prince – Support Fund (IRE) (Intikhab (USA)) [2017/18 h97: h16.5g⁴ h16.2s^ur h16m³ Apr 26] neat gelding: fair maiden hurdler: raced only at 2m: acts on good to firm going: in headgear last 4 starts: usually races towards rear. *Dominic Ffrench Davis*   **h105**

Ten Up Novices' Chase, Navan—stamina is very much the order of the day as the favourite Monbeg Notorious holds off fellow Gigginstown runner Mossback

MON

MONDELLO (GER) 7 b.g. Soldier Hollow – Mandrella (GER) (Surumu (GER)) [2017/18 h97: h19.9d² h19.9d⁵ h23.6d⁵ h19.5v³ h23.9s^F Dec 14] modest maiden hurdler: stays 3m: acts on soft going: usually wears headgear/tongue tie: usually races nearer last than first. *Richard Woollacott* — **h98**

MONDERON (FR) 11 b.g. Laveron – Lomonde (FR) (Great Lakes) [2017/18 c94, h94: h20.7g⁴ c21.1m⁶ c20g^ur Oct 26] close-coupled gelding: winning hurdler: modest maiden chaser: stays 23f: acts on heavy going: has worn headgear, including last 5 starts: often in tongue tie: temperamental. *Fergal O'Brien* — **c92 §**, **h–**

MONDLICHT (USA) 8 b.g. Malibu Moon (USA) – Moonlight Cruise (USA) (Silver Deputy (CAN)) [2017/18 h104§: h16.2g³ h22.1d^tr h22.1g^rr h25.4s⁴ Jul 24] fair handicap hurdler: stays 25f: acts on heavy going: wears headgear: temperamental (twice refused to race in 2017/18). *James Moffatt* — **h99 §**

MONDO CANE (IRE) 11 b.g. Beneficial – La Vita E Bella (FR) (Le Nain Jaune (FR)) [2017/18 c–, h–: c24d⁴ c21.4d⁶ c20.3s³ c21.2v^ur c15.9v² c20.3v³ c15.9v² c23.6d Apr 24] winning hurdler: fair handicap chaser: stays 27f: acts on heavy going: wears headgear: often races towards rear. *Charles Pogson* — **c99**, **h–**

MON ELDORADO (FR) 6 b.g. Gentlewave (IRE) – Miryea (FR) (Shining Steel) [2017/18 b90p: b16.7g⁶ h16s³ h21.2v h16.7s^F Apr 1] fair form in bumpers: fairly useful form over hurdles: left Christian Williams, close up when fell heavily 2 out in novice at Market Rasen (tongue tied) in April: often in hood: tried in tongue tie: often races freely. *Peter Bowen* — **h119**, **b86**

MONETAIRE (FR) 12 b.g. Anabaa (USA) – Monitrice (FR) (Groom Dancer (USA)) [2017/18 c126, h–: c24d c23.4s^pu Mar 23] compact gelding: winning hurdler: modest chaser at best, no form under Rules in 2017/18 (won twice in points soon after end of season): left David Pipe after first start: best form up to 21f: acts on good to firm and heavy going: has worn headgear/tongue tie. *W. M. Wanless* — **c–**, **h–**

MONET MOOR 9 b.m. Morpeth – Miracle Monarch (Elegant Monarch) [2017/18 c–, h–: c20.9s⁶ c21s³ Apr 23] sturdy mare: maiden hurdler: poor form over fences: should prove suited by 3m: acts on soft going. *Jimmy Frost* — **c56**, **h–**

MONEY FOR NOTHING 9 b.g. Kayf Tara – Top of The Dee (Rakaposhi King) [2017/18 c94§, h88§: h15.7g h20g c16.3m⁴ c15.7d³ c19.7d^F h15.9d³ c21.2v³ c17v² c16.4v⁵ Feb 22] lengthy gelding: modest maiden hurdler/chaser nowadays: stays 2½m: acts on heavy going: wears headgear/tongue tie: usually races close up/freely: reluctant, and isn't one to trust. *Johnny Farrelly* — **c91 §**, **h81 §**

MONEYSTOWN (IRE) 8 b.m. Touch of Land (FR) – Karinga Duff (Karinga Bay) [2017/18 c55, h61: c17v⁴ c21.6d⁵ Feb 25] Irish point winner: little impact over hurdles: poor form over fences. *Linda Jewell* — **c81**, **h–**

MONEY TALKS 8 br.g. Motivator – Movie Mogul (Sakhee (USA)) [2017/18 c91, h103: h21m^pu May 1] workmanlike gelding: fair hurdler, pulled up sole start in 2017/18: maiden chaser: stays 21f: acts on soft and good to firm going: sometimes in headgear: has worn tongue tie: unreliable. *Michael Madgwick* — **c–**, **h– §**

MONFASS (IRE) 7 b.g. Trans Island – Ajo Green (IRE) (Moscow Society (USA)) [2017/18 h107: h17s h16.8s* h16.2s³ h15.7s³ h16v³ h16.2v⁵ h16.2s² Apr 25] fairly useful handicap hurdler: won at Carlisle in December: raced around 2m: best form on soft/heavy going: wears hood: held up. *Rose Dobbin* — **h115**

MONKEY PUZZLE 6 ch.g. Sulamani (IRE) – Hunca Munca (IRE) (Presenting) [2017/18 h115: h21.2m^pu May 14] runner-up in Irish point: fairly useful form when second on hurdling debut, shaped as if amiss only start since. *Oliver Sherwood* — **h–**

MONKSHOOD (IRE) 6 br.g. Stowaway – Flirthing Around (IRE) (Flemensfirth (USA)) [2017/18 h115p, b106: h22.5d* h20s* h24v⁴ h24v⁵ h24s^ur Apr 17] bumper winner: fairly useful hurdler: won maiden at Downpatrick in October and novice at Fairyhouse in November: stays 2¾m: acts on soft going: front runner/races prominently. *Gordon Elliott, Ireland* — **h129**

MONKSLAND (IRE) 11 b.g. Beneficial – Cush Jewel (IRE) (Executive Perk) [2017/18 c143, h147: h23d* h20v⁴ Nov 12] useful-looking gelding: useful hurdler nowadays: won minor event at Thurles in October: smart chaser: stays 3m: acts on heavy going: has worn hood, including in 2017/18: often races prominently. *Noel Meade, Ireland* — **c–**, **h136**

MONK'S VIEW 5 bl.g. Multiplex – Evelith Abbey (IRE) (Presenting) [2017/18 b16s b14d b15.3d Apr 22] poor form in bumpers. *Ben Pauling* — **b69**

MON

MON LINO (FR) 6 b.g. Martaline – Dalina (FR) (Trempolino (USA)) [2017/18 h22s* h21.6s* h22.6v³ h24s^pu h20v^pu c16.7s Apr 17] first foal: dam (h122), French 2¼m/19f hurdle winner, 10.5f-15f winner on Flat: pulled up in point: useful handicap hurdler: won maiden at Limerick in 2016/17: also won at Killarney in May and Galway in October: well beaten on chasing debut: stays 3m: best form on soft/heavy going: tried in cheekpieces. *Paul Nolan, Ireland*   c– h133

MON PALOIS (FR) 6 b.g. Muhaymin (USA) – Gastinaise (FR) (Cadoudal (FR)) [2017/18 b98: h20g* h23f* h23.9g⁴ h24d⁴ h21.4v⁵ h23.5s Feb 17] good-topped gelding: Irish point winner: bumper winner: fairly useful form over hurdles: won maiden at Ffos Las in May and novice at Worcester in October: stays 3m: acts on firm and good to soft going. *Kim Bailey*   h119

MON PARRAIN (FR) 12 b.g. Trempolino (USA) – Kadaina (FR) (Kadalko (FR)) [2017/18 c122§, h–: c27.2s³ c24s³ c21.1s^pu Apr 12] lengthy, useful-looking gelding: has had breathing operation: placed in points: lightly-raced hurdler: fair chaser nowadays: left Paul Nicholls after first start: stays 3¼m: acts on heavy going: wears headgear/tongue tie: unreliable. *Mrs Kim Smyly*   c108 § h–

MON PORT (IRE) 6 b.g. Scorpion (IRE) – Sounds Charming (IRE) (Presenting) [2017/18 b86: b16g* May 25] fair form in bumpers: won conditionals/amateur event at Warwick in May. *Ben De Haan*   b92

MONROCCO 5 b.m. Shirocco (GER) – Molly Flight (FR) (Saint Cyrien (FR)) [2017/18 b–: b15.7m h19.6d^F h15.7g⁶ h16g Oct 25] little impact in bumpers/over hurdles. *Kim Bailey*   h68 b–

MONSIEUR ARKADIN (FR) 7 b.g. Dream Well (FR) – Quenta des Bordes (FR) (Bateau Rouge) [2017/18 h104, b92: h25m* h23.3s^F h24.7d c24.2s⁵ c20.3d Apr 21] angular, rather lightly-made gelding: point/bumper winner: fair hurdler: won novice at Carlisle in May: no form in chases: stays 3¼m: acts on soft and good to firm going: tried in tongue tie. *Tim Vaughan*   c– h108

MONSIEUR BAGOT (IRE) 6 b.g. Robin des Pres (FR) – Hardabout (IRE) (Alderbrook) [2017/18 b16.2d Sep 11] tailed off in bumper. *Rebecca Menzies*   b–

MONSIEUR CO (FR) 5 b.g. Turgeon (USA) – Cayras Style (FR) (Trempolino (USA)) [2017/18 c121p, h128: c21.7g⁵ c19.1d^F c15.7v³ c21.2d⁴ c19.4d⁵ Apr 22] fairly useful hurdler: fairly useful handicap chaser: probably stays 19f: acts on heavy going: tried in blinkers: has worn tongue tie: usually races close up. *Paul Nicholls*   c121 h–

MONSIEUR GIBRALTAR (FR) 7 ch.g. Spirit One (FR) – Palabras de Amor (FR) (Rock of Gibraltar (IRE)) [2017/18, h–: c24.2m^pu c21s^ur Mar 25] good-topped gelding: won 5 of 6 starts in points: winning hurdler: useful chaser at best: looked set to finish no worse than second when unseated 4 out in hunter at Ascot in March: stays 21f: acts on good to firm and heavy going: has worn blinkers: has worn tongue tie, including final start: often travels strongly. *Mrs Rose Loxton*   c– ? h–

MONSIEUR JOURDAIN (IRE) 12 b.g. Royal Applause – Palwina (FR) (Unfuwain (USA)) [2017/18 c106, h–: c23.8g² c26.2g⁴ May 28] sturdy gelding: multiple point winner: winning hurdler: fair hunter chaser: stays 27f: acts on good to firm and heavy going: wears cheekpieces. *W. H. Easterby*   c101 h–

MONSIEUR LECOQ (FR) 4 b.g. Diamond Boy (FR) – Draga (FR) (Smadoun (FR)) [2017/18 h16.9s h17.7v³ Feb 15] seventh foal: half-brother to 3 winners in France, including chaser Alderic (19f-21f winner, by Take Risks): dam French 1¼m winner: fair form over hurdles: better effort when third in juvenile at Fontwell. *Nick Williams*   h114

MONSIEUR MURPHY (IRE) 8 b.g. Presenting – Mistress Cara (Terimon) [2017/18 h15.3g h16v⁴ h16.8s Dec 8] useful-looking gelding: maiden pointer: poor form over hurdles. *Neil Mulholland*   h77

MONTALBANO 6 ch.g. Monsieur Bond (IRE) – Alpen Glen (Halling (USA)) [2017/18 h138: c18s^F c17d^ur c16v* c18s^ur c20v c21s Apr 27] useful hurdler: similar form over fences: won maiden at Gowran in January: stays 2½m: acts on heavy going: wears hood. *W. P. Mullins, Ireland*   c139 h–

MONT CHOISY (FR) 8 b.g. Vic Toto (FR) – Rhapsodie St Eloi (FR) (Ragmar (FR)) [2017/18 h116x: h26.4d⁶ h23.3g³ h25.4s³ h26.5d* h27g^ur h25.8g h23g Oct 17] sturdy gelding: point winner: fairly useful handicap hurdler: won at Newton Abbot in August: stays 3¼m: acts on good to soft going: wears headgear: tried in tongue tie: often let down by jumping. *Peter Bowen*   h120 x

MONT DES AVALOIRS (FR) 5 b.g. Blue Bresil (FR) – Abu Dhabi (FR) (Saint Cyrien (FR)) [2017/18 b90p: b16d* h15.3s^F h17v* h16s³ h16g⁴ h16.7s* h16s⁴ Apr 28] tall gelding: fairly useful form in bumpers: won at Chepstow in October: useful form over   h136 b98

MON

hurdles: won novices at Aintree in December and Market Rasen in April: third in Tolworth Novices' Hurdle at Sandown (13 lengths behind Summerville Boy) in January: raced around 2m: best form on soft/heavy going: in hood last 3 starts: usually leads. *Paul Nicholls*

MONTE WILDHORN (IRE) 10 b.g. Old Vic – Miss Lloyds (IRE) (Take Risks (FR)) [2017/18 c88, h83: h22g³ h25g^{ur} May 29] poor handicap hurdler nowadays: lightly-raced maiden chaser: stays 2¾m: acts on heavy going: has worn cheekpieces/tongue tie. *David Bridgwater* — c– h78

MONTHYNE 7 ch.g. Nomadic Way (USA) – Captivating Tyna (IRE) (Presenting) [2017/18 h20.6s⁶ h19.5s h16.7s⁵ Mar 24] poor form in bumpers: no form over hurdles. *Warren Greatrex* — h–

MONTRACHET MIX (FR) 5 gr.g. Al Namix (FR) – La Collancelle (FR) (Sassanian (USA)) [2017/18 h–: h16.2v^{pu} h15.6m h17.4s^{pu} c19.9f⁶ Apr 22] good-topped gelding: poor form over hurdles: well held only outing over fences: left Patrick Holmes after second start. *L. Baudron, France* — c– h79

MONT ROYALE 10 b.g. Hurricane Run (IRE) – Wild Academy (IRE) (Royal Academy (USA)) [2017/18 c125, h–: c19m⁶ c21.2d* c21.4g⁵ c20s⁶ c20.3g⁶ c22.6g² c23.8m⁴ c25d^{pu} c25.6g^F c24m⁵ Apr 26] good-topped gelding: winning hurdler: fairly useful handicap chaser: won at Cartmel in May: stays 23f: acts on soft and good to firm going: has worn headgear, including in 2017/18: often races towards rear. *Jonjo O'Neill* — c128 h–

MONTYCRISTO 5 br.g. Motivator – Water Gipsy (Piccolo) [2017/18 h15.9s⁴ h17.7s^{ur} h15.9v Apr 1] modest maiden on Flat, stays 1¼m: similar form over hurdles. *Paul Henderson* — h85

MONTYDARKDESTROYER 7 b.g. Lucarno (USA) – Markila (FR) (Mark of Esteem (IRE)) [2017/18 h20.6v^{pu} Apr 14] little impact in bumpers: pulled up in novice on hurdling debut. *John Davies* — h–

MONTY MASSINI 7 b.g. Dr Massini (IRE) – Miss Montgomery (IRE) (Montekin) [2017/18 b15.8d⁶ h17.7m h18.5m⁵ h16.3g⁵ h25.8g Oct 7] little show in bumper/over hurdles. *Evan Williams* — h– b–

MONTY'S AWARD (IRE) 6 b.g. Oscar (IRE) – Montys Miss (IRE) (Presenting) [2017/18 b103: h15.8s³ h15.8d³ h16v h16.5m³ h19.3v^{pu} Jan 20] sturdy gelding: bumper winner: fair form over hurdles: should be suited by 2½m: acts on soft going: in hood last 2 starts. *Charlie Longsdon* — h104

MONZINO (USA) 10 b.g. More Than Ready (USA) – Tasso's Magic Roo (USA) (Tasso (USA)) [2017/18 c64x, h–§: h22.1g⁶ h23.4s³ Feb 16] workmanlike gelding: little form over hurdles/fences (sketchy jumper): ungenuine. *Michael Chapman* — c– x h– §

MOODY MAGGIE (IRE) 5 b.m. Milan – Golden Bay (Karinga Bay) [2017/18 b15.8s² ab16d² b16.8g⁴ Apr 19] sixth foal: sister to bumper winner Bold Image, and half-sister to bumper winner/fairly useful hurdler Watcombe Heights (2¼m winner, by Scorpion), stays 2¾m, and fairly useful chaser Old Pals Act (2½-2¾m winner, by Presenting): dam (h131) bumper and 21f/2¾m hurdle winner: fairly useful form in bumpers: will prove best at further than 2m. *Suzy Smith* — b95

MOONDAY SUN (USA) 9 gr.g. Mizzen Mast (USA) – Storm Dove (USA) (Storm Bird (CAN)) [2017/18 h126: h17g h16.5g* h16g⁵ h17g^F Jul 20] useful handicap hurdler: won at Punchestown (by 5 lengths from Bobabout) in May: raced around 2m: acts on good to firm and good to soft going: has worn hood: has worn tongue tie, including last 3 starts: races towards rear. *Gordon Elliott, Ireland* — h136

MOONLIGHT DANCER 5 gr.m. Kayf Tara – Dissolve (Sharrood (USA)) [2017/18 b15.8s⁵ h16v³ Mar 11] sister to fairly useful 2½m hurdle winner Bianco Fuji and closely related/half-sister to several winners, including bumper winner/useful hurdler Argento Luna (2m-21f winner, by Mtoto) and useful hurdler/fairly useful chaser Lyes Green (19f-25f winner, by Bien Bien), stayed 4m: dam (h78) 2m/17f hurdle winner (stayed 2¾m): fifth in mares bumper at Huntingdon: 25/1, third in novice at Warwick (20¾ lengths behind Piton Pete) on hurdling debut. *Dan Skelton* — h79 b75

MOONLIGHTER 5 b.g. Midnight Legend – Countess Camilla (Bob's Return (IRE)) [2017/18 b16.7s* b16.3v⁶ Feb 10] fifth foal: half-brother to 3 winners, including useful hurdler/chaser Horatio Hornblower (2m-3m winner, by Presenting) and fairly useful/untrustworthy chaser George Nympton (2m winner, by Alderbrook), stays 2½m: dam (h116), bumper/2m-2¾m hurdle winner, half-sister to very smart chaser (stayed 3m) Our Ben: useful form in bumpers: won at Bangor (by 6 lengths from Legal Eyes) in December. *Nick Williams* — b106

MOR

MOONLIGHT FLYER (IRE) 6 b.g. Broadway Flyer (USA) – Monteleena (IRE) (Montelimar (USA)) [2017/18 h65, b–: h19d h21.6d[4] h25.8g h18.5v[4] h21.6v[pu] h21.6v[pu] Dec 21] sturdy gelding: poor maiden hurdler: tried in cheekpieces. *Jeremy Scott* **h75**

MOONLIGHT HAZE 7 b.g. Helissio (FR) – Bella Haze (Midnight Legend) [2017/18 b–: b16g[3] b15.8v[ur] Nov 24] modest form in bumpers: tried in hood: dead. *Phillip Dando* **b83**

MOON RACER (IRE) 9 b.g. Saffron Walden (FR) – Angel's Folly (Wesaam (USA)) [2017/18 h133, b–: h16.3v h16.8v h21.4g* Apr 21] good-topped gelding: has had breathing operation: smart bumper performer: useful handicap hurdler: won at Ayr (by 1¼ lengths from Sky Khan) in April: stays 21f: acts on soft going: in tongue tie last 3 starts: often races prominently. *David Pipe* **h141**

MOON TRIP 9 b.g. Cape Cross (IRE) – Fading Light (King's Best (USA)) [2017/18 h64: h25.6d* h25.8g Nov 10] modest handicap hurdler: won at Fontwell in June: stays 3¼m: acts on soft going: tried in cheekpieces/tongue tie. *Geoffrey Deacon* **h90**

MOONTRIPPER 9 b.m. Doyen (IRE) – Moon Spinner (Elmaamul (USA)) [2017/18 h–: h20d[pu] h18.5s[2] h16g[5] h20g[5] h16.8d[5] h20g h15.8s[6] h19.5d h16v h20v[pu] h16.5s c16s[pu] c20.9s[5] c17.5d[4] Apr 24] point winner: poor maiden hurdler: poor form over fences: stays 2¼m: acts on soft going. *Phillip Dando* **c60 h76**

MOORES NOVELTY (IRE) 6 b.g. Sholokhov (IRE) – Moricana (GER) (Konigsstuhl (GER)) [2017/18 h16.2g h16v h16.2s h16.2s[pu] Apr 26] in frame completed starts in Irish points: limited impact over hurdles. *N. W. Alexander* **h–**

MOOR FREEDOM 5 b.m. Beat Hollow – Line Freedom (FR) (Freedom Cry) [2017/18 b16d[2] Apr 26] smallish, leggy mare: second foal: closely related to bumper winner Kayf Mariner (by Kayf Tara): dam (h137) bumper/2m-21f hurdle winner: 50/1, second in bumper at Warwick (1¾ lengths behind Emitom). *Polly Gundry* **b86**

MOORLANDS GEORGE 10 b.g. Grape Tree Road – Sandford Springs (USA) (Robellino (USA)) [2017/18 c106, h–: c25.1d[2] Apr 22] maiden hurdler: fair handicap chaser: stays 3¼m: acts on soft and good to firm going: wears tongue tie. *Jeremy Scott* **c108 h–**

MOORLANDS JACK 13 b.g. Cloudings (IRE) – Sandford Springs (USA) (Robellino (USA)) [2017/18 c108§, h–§: c20.5g[5] c20g[5] c22.6g[4] c21d* c19.2d[4] c20.5d[6] Nov 27] strong gelding: winning hurdler: fair handicap chaser: won at Newton Abbot in 2015: stays 23f: acts on soft and good to firm going: usually wears headgear: tried in tongue tie: unreliable. *Jeremy Scott* **c107 § h– §**

MOORLANDS MIST 11 gr.g. Fair Mix (IRE) – Sandford Springs (USA) (Robellino (USA)) [2017/18 c106§, h–: c22.6g[3] c23.9g[4] h20.1d[3] c24d[ur] h23.1g[3] h27g[5] c31.9v[2] c24.2s[pu] h24v[pu] h24v[pu] Feb 25] good-topped gelding: fair handicap hurdler: modest maiden chaser: stays extreme distances: acts on heavy going: has worn headgear, including in 2017/18: tried in tongue tie: temperamental. *Sara Ender* **c97 § h100 §**

MOORSTOWN (IRE) 8 b.g. Oscar (IRE) – Glacial Princess (IRE) (Glacial Storm (USA)) [2017/18 c88, h–: c23.8v[pu] c23.9v[4] c24.1v[pu] c24.1s c23.4v[4] Apr 15] maiden hurdler: poor handicap chaser: stays 3m: acts on heavy going: tried in blinkers: often in tongue tie: temperamental. *Lucinda Russell* **c81 § h–**

MORAL HAZARD (IRE) 9 br.g. Milan – Maria Thai (FR) (Siam (USA)) [2017/18 c107, h–: c23v[pu] Apr 12] multiple point winner: once-raced hurdler: fair form when second on chasing debut, pulled up both starts under Rules since: tried in tongue tie. *Miss Beverley Thomas* **c– h–**

MORE BUCK'S (IRE) 8 ch.g. Presenting – Buck's Blue (FR) (Epervier Bleu) [2017/18 c131, h–: c24.2s c26g Apr 18] well-made gelding: winning hurdler: useful chaser, below form both starts in 2017/18: stays 3m: acts on heavy going: has worn hood: wears tongue tie: usually races close up. *Paul Nicholls* **c110 h–**

MOREECE (IRE) 9 b.g. Chevalier (IRE) – Jumbo Romance (IRE) (Tagula (IRE)) [2017/18 c101, h85: c22.6d[ur] Jun 9] multiple point winner: fair maiden hurdler at best: similar form on chasing debut, unseated rider one start under Rules since: stays 3m: acts on soft and good to firm going: in headgear last 4 starts. *J. Lean* **c– h–**

MORELLO ROYALE (IRE) 8 b.m. King's Theatre (IRE) – Mystic Cherry (IRE) (Alderbrook) [2017/18 c–, h136: c20f c23.6d[4] c22.4d[2] h24.5d[4] c23.4s[6] Dec 20] compact mare: useful hurdler: fairly useful form over fences: stays 3m: acts on good to firm and heavy going: wears tongue tie: often races towards rear. *Colin Tizzard* **c127 h130**

MOR

MORE MADNESS (IRE) 11 b.g. Dr Massini (IRE) – Angelic Angel (IRE) (Phardante (FR)) [2017/18 c85, h81: h24g⁴ c24.2g⁴ c21.2g⁴ c25.5s⁴ h23.3v⁶ c24.2v² c24.2s c19.8s⁴ c25.2d² c23.8s³ c24.2v³ c26.3v⁵ Mar 23] poor maiden hurdler: modest handicap chaser: stays 25f: acts on heavy going: wears headgear: has worn tongue tie: temperamental. *Julia Brooke* **c85 §** **h79 §**

MORE OF THAT (IRE) 10 b.g. Beneficial – Guigone (FR) (Esprit du Nord (USA)) [2017/18 c159, h–: c24s⁶ c30.2d⁶ᵖᵘ c21d³ Dec 23] strong, lengthy gelding: winning hurdler: very smart chaser at best, no form in 2017/18: stayed 3¼m: acts on heavy going: has worn cheekpieces, including in 2017/18: tried in tongue tie: retired. *Jonjo O'Neill* **c–** **h–**

MORE THAN LUCK (IRE) 7 br.g. Gothland (FR) – Pretty Impressive (IRE) (Presenting) [2017/18 h97: c24d⁶ c20.9d² c25.8g³ c20.9g c23g* c22.7d³ h23.4v* c24.2v⁴ c25.5s⁶ h24vᵖᵘ h21v⁵ Mar 28] fair handicap hurdler: won at Fakenham in January: fair handicap chaser: won at Taunton in November: left Sam Thomas after fourth start: should stay beyond 3m: acts on heavy going: usually in headgear: wears tongue tie: often races in rear. *Olly Murphy* **c109** **h102**

MORE THAN TWO 8 b.m. Kayf Tara – Sweet Stormy (IRE) (Bluebird (USA)) [2017/18 h15.5sᵖᵘ h16.6sᵖᵘ Jan 9] third in bumper: no form over hurdles. *Barry Leavy* **h–**

MORGAN (IRE) 6 br.g. Big Bad Bob (IRE) – Gilt Ridden (IRE) (Heron Island (IRE)) [2017/18 h131, b104: h16.5g² h16g* h16.5g² h16h* h16v² h16v³ h16s⁴ h16s h16.5d⁵ Apr 24] bumper winner: useful hurdler: won novices at Wexford in June and Listowel in September: placed in Joe Mac Novices' Hurdle at Tipperary and For Auction Novices' Hurdle at Navan: raced around 2m: acts on heavy going: usually wears hood. *Gordon Elliott, Ireland* **h139**

MORGAN'S BAY 13 b.g. Karinga Bay – Dubai Dolly (IRE) (Law Society (USA)) [2017/18 c57x, h54: c20.5g⁴ c21.1dᵖᵘ Jun 6] strong gelding: maiden hurdler: fairly useful chaser at best, little encouragement since 2014/15: stays 2½m: acts on soft going: often let down by jumping. *Laura Mongan* **c90 x** **h–**

MORIANOUR (FR) 7 b.g. Valanour (IRE) – Moriane (FR) (Manninamix) [2017/18 h113p, b82: h19.8s⁶ h19.2v² h18.6v⁵ h16.8v⁴ Apr 8] fell in maiden point: fair hurdler: stays 2½m: acts on heavy going. *Evan Williams* **h112**

MORNEY WING (IRE) 9 b.g. Antonius Pius (USA) – Tillan Fuwain (FR) (Unfuwain (USA)) [2017/18 c124§, h–: c25gᵘʳ c27.7d c22.9v³ c24vᴿ c24.2v² c28.8vᵖᵘ c24.2s* c26s³ c29.2g⁶ Apr 26] workmanlike gelding: maiden hurdler: fair handicap chaser: won at Fakenham in March: stays 29f: acts on heavy going: wears headgear/tongue tie: unreliable. *Charlie Mann* **c111 §** **h–**

MORNING HERALD 7 br.m. Lucky Story (USA) – Wakeful (Kayf Tara) [2017/18 h121: h21g Feb 24] angular mare: fairly useful hurdler, little impression sole start in 2017/18: stays 3m: acts on good to firm going. *Martin Keighley* **h–**

MORNING REGGIE 9 gr.g. Turgeon (USA) – Nile Cristale (FR) (Northern Crystal) [2017/18 c120, h–: c21d⁶ c24pᵖᵘ c20v⁴ c22.4sᵖᵘ c20.3g⁶ Apr 20] well-made gelding: has had breathing operation: winning hurdler: fairly useful handicap chaser, below form in 2017/18: stays 3m: acts on heavy going: usually in headgear. *Oliver Sherwood* **c97** **h–**

MORNING ROYALTY (IRE) 11 b.g. King's Theatre (IRE) – Portryan Native (IRE) (Be My Native (USA)) [2017/18 c136, h114: h25.4d* c21.2g² c25.5g³ h19.7s⁴ c25.2s⁴ c20.1s³ Apr 26] small, sturdy gelding: fairly useful handicap hurdler: won at Cartmel in May: useful handicap chaser: stays 25f: acts on good to firm and heavy going: often races in rear. *James Moffatt* **c135** **h125**

MORNING SEQUEL 5 b.m. Revoque (IRE) – Silver Sequel (Silver Patriarch (IRE)) [2017/18 h16g h17.2g⁴ h15.8g⁵ Jul 11] half-sister to fair hurdler/fairly useful chaser Master Burbidge (19f-21f winner, by Pasternak) and fair hurdler Midnight Sequel (23f winner, by Midnight Legend): dam unraced half-sister to useful hurdler/chaser (stayed 2½m) Pass The Time: no form, including on Flat. *Neil Mulholland* **h–**

MORNING TIME (IRE) 12 b.g. Hawk Wing (USA) – Desert Trail (IRE) (Desert Style (IRE)) [2017/18 c65§, h64§: h17m⁴ h16.2g* h16.2g⁴ h16.2m⁶ c15.6gᶠ Aug 21] tall, good-topped gelding: poor handicap hurdler: won at Hexham (conditional) in June: poor chaser: raced mainly around 2m: acted on good to firm and heavy going: wore headgear/tongue tie: unreliable: dead. *Lucinda Russell* **c– §** **h71 §**

MORNING VICAR (IRE) 5 b.g. Beneficial – Mary's Little Vic (IRE) (Old Vic) [2017/18 b16.3s* b16.3v b16d² Apr 26] €50,000 3-y-o: useful-looking gelding: second foal: dam (h106), maiden hurdler (stayed 2¼m), out of half-sister to Triumph Hurdle **b105**

MOT

winner Baron Blakeney: useful form in bumpers: won at Newbury (by 2 lengths from Baddesley Knight) in January: best effort when second at Warwick (2¾ lengths behind Umndeni) in April. *Nicky Henderson*

MORNING WITH IVAN (IRE) 8 b.m. Ivan Denisovich (IRE) – Grinneas (IRE) (Barathea (IRE)) [2017/18 c–, h77: h16.7d* h16.4s* h19.4s² h15.6s³ h16.4d* h16.2s* Apr 25] fair handicap hurdler: won at Market Rasen in November, Newcastle in December, Musselburgh in March and Perth in April: maiden chaser: stays 2½m: acts on soft going: has worn headgear: wears tongue tie: often travels strongly. *Susan Corbett*   c– h110

MO ROUGE (IRE) 10 b.g. Croco Rouge (IRE) – Just A Mo (IRE) (Supreme Leader) [2017/18 c95§, h–: c26.2g⁴ c24.2g^pu h23.3d c23.4g Oct 28] fair maiden chaser/chaser at best, little show in 2017/18: stayed 3¼m: acted on good to firm and good to soft going: wore headgear: temperamental: dead. *Jackie Stephen*   c68 § h– §

MORTENS LEAM 6 b.g. Sulamani (IRE) – Bonnet's Pieces (Alderbrook) [2017/18 h105, b72: h16.7g³ h15.7g⁴ c15.2d² c21.2s* c19.4s⁵ c21.2s² h19.8d^ur Apr 22] fair maiden hurdler: fairly useful form over fences: won novice handicap at Fakenham in December: left Pam Sly after sixth start: stays 21f: acts on soft going: usually races nearer last than first. *Mike Hawker*   c122 h97

MORTHANALEGEND 9 b.g. Midnight Legend – Morwenna (IRE) (Zaffaran (USA)) [2017/18 c–, h–: h19.1g^rr h16g h23g^pu Jun 3] lengthy gelding: maiden hurdler, no form in 2017/18: pulled up only start over fences: wears tongue tie: temperamental. *Brendan Powell*   c– h– §

MOSCOW CALLING (IRE) 7 b.g. Morozov (USA) – Bubble Bann (IRE) (Hubbly Bubbly (USA)) [2017/18 h76: h23.9g^pu h20.6g h23.1g Aug 4] maiden hurdler, no form in 2017/18: often in headgear. *Nicky Richards*   h–

MOSCOW ME (IRE) 11 b.g. Moscow Society (USA) – Just Trust Me (IRE) (Warcraft (USA)) [2017/18 c87, h97: h15.7m⁵ May 4] modest handicap hurdler/chaser: raced around 2m: acts on soft and good to firm going: in cheekpieces last 2 starts. *Henry Oliver*   c– h89

MOSCOW MENACE (IRE) 11 b.g. Moscow Society (USA) – Sky Flagship (FR) (Sky Lawyer (FR)) [2017/18 c74, h–: c20.1g c23.4g May 10] multiple point winner: once-raced hurdler: poor handicap chaser: stayed 3¼m: acted on good to soft going: in blinkers last 5 starts: wore tongue tie: dead. *Katie Scott*   c61 h–

MOSSBACK (IRE) 8 b.g. Yeats (IRE) – Sejour (IRE) (Bob Back (USA)) [2017/18 c19v* c20v⁴ c24v^F c24v² c31.8s^F Mar 13] €62,000 3-y-o: strong, lengthy gelding: sixth foal: half-brother to smart 2m hurdle winner Staying Article (by Definite Article): dam unraced: winning hurdler: smart form over fences: won maiden at Naas (by 3 lengths from Snow Falcon) in November: second in Ten Up Novices' Chase at Navan (½ length behind Monbeg Notorious) in February: stayed 3m: best form on heavy going: raced prominently: dead. *Gordon Elliott, Ireland*   c146 h–

MOSS ON THE MILL 10 br.g. Overbury (IRE) – Mimis Bonnet (FR) (Bonnet Rouge (FR)) [2017/18 c127, h117: c25.6g⁶ c23.8d Apr 24] winning hurdler: useful handicap chaser, below form in 2017/18: stays 3¼m: acts on good to firm and heavy going: wears headgear. *Tom George*   c105 h–

MOSSPARK (IRE) 10 b.g. Flemensfirth (USA) – Patio Rose (Petoski) [2017/18 c119, h–: c26.7g⁵ c27.7d^pu c24.2v^pu Feb 16] tall gelding: winning hurdler: useful handicap chaser: stays 27f: acts on heavy going: has worn headgear: often races lazily. *Emma Lavelle*   c131 h–

MOSS STREET 8 b.g. Moss Vale (IRE) – Street Style (IRE) (Rock of Gibraltar (IRE)) [2017/18 c–, h106: h16m⁵ h15.8d May 20] small gelding: fair hurdler at best, no form since early-2016/17: winning chaser: stays 2½m: acts on soft and good to firm going: wears blinkers: has worn tongue tie: often races towards rear. *Conor Dore*   c– h–

MOST CELEBRATED (IRE) 5 b.g. New Approach (IRE) – Pietra Santa (FR) (Acclamation) [2017/18 h121: h16s^F h16.6d Dec 2] good-topped gelding: fairly useful hurdler at best, no form in 2017/18: raced around 2m: acts on good and good to firm going: in hood last 5 starts. *Neil Mulholland*   h–

MOSTLY BOB (IRE) 15 b.g. Bob Back (USA) – Town Gossip (IRE) (Indian Ridge) [2017/18 c24.2g⁵ c23.8g⁵ Jun 22] sturdy gelding: winning hurdler: poor handicap chaser nowadays: stays 3¼m: acts on soft and good to firm going: usually in blinkers: wears tongue tie: often let down by jumping/attitude. *Sophie Leech*   c56 § h–

MOTION TO STRIKE (IRE) 8 b.g. Beneficial – Comeragh Girl (IRE) (Imperial Ballet (IRE)) [2017/18 h86: h20.2g² h16.2g h16.2g h16.2g² h15.7s c20.9s⁵ Apr 8] Irish point winner: modest maiden hurdler: tailed off in novice handicap on chasing debut: stays 2½m: acts on soft going: has worn headgear, including in 2017/18: often races towards rear: irresolute. *Jackie Stephen*   c– h87 §

MOT

MOTLEY CREW 5 b.g. Mount Nelson – Greensand (Green Desert (USA)) [2017/18 b72: b15.8g[6] h16.8s[pu] Dec 8] poor form in bumpers: pulled up in maiden on hurdling debut. *Michael Easterby*   h– b–

MOTUEKA (IRE) 6 b.g. King's Theatre (IRE) – Tchouina (FR) (Broadway Flyer (USA)) [2017/18 b84: h20g[2] h23.1s[5] h23.3v[4] h23.1s[pu] Feb 23] fair form over hurdles: usually races nearer last than first: temperamental. *Philip Hobbs*   h111 §

MOULIN A VENT 6 gr.g. Sagamix (FR) – Bahia Blanca (FR) (Astarabad (USA)) [2017/18 h131, b109: h22s* c19.5s c20s[3] c23.5v* c24s[5] c24v* c24v[3] c29v[ur] c24v[5] Apr 12] fairly useful hurdler: won minor event at Navan in September: useful chaser: won maiden at Fairyhouse (by 18 lengths from Monbeg Notorious) in December and Grade 3 novice at Naas (by 4½ lengths from Jury Duty) in January: third in Ten Up Novices' Chase at Navan (19½ lengths behind Monbeg Notorious) in February: stays 3m: acts on heavy going: tried in blinkers. *Noel Meade, Ireland*   c139 h121

MOUNTAIN CLICHE (IRE) 11 b.g. Classic Cliche (IRE) – Quarry Girl (IRE) (Lord Americo) [2017/18 c24.2m* c21.1s[4] c25.8m[3] May 30] multiple point winner: once-raced hurdler: modest form in chases: won hunter at Exeter in May. *N. J. Dawe*   c98 h–

MOUNTAIN KING 9 b.g. Definite Article – Belle Magello (FR) (Exit To Nowhere (USA)) [2017/18 c134, h–: c24.9s c22.5g c20.1d* c23.8d[5] Sep 11] rangy gelding: winning hurdler: useful handicap chaser: won at Perth (by 18 lengths from Red Spinner) in August: stays 2½m: acts on heavy going: has worn cheekpieces, including last 2 starts: has worn tongue tie, including in 2017/18: usually races towards rear: hard to catch right, and is one to be wary of. *Gordon Elliott, Ireland*   c139 § h–

MOUNTAIN OF ANGELS 9 b.m. Midnight Legend – Landsker Missile (Cruise Missile) [2017/18 c20.9g[3] c19.4v[pu] Jan 19] point winner: no form under Rules: in hood last 2 starts. *Mary Evans*   c– h–

MOUNTAIN OF MOURNE (IRE) 9 ch.g. Mountain High (IRE) – Katies Native (IRE) (Be My Native (USA)) [2017/18 c–§, h104§: c24.2s[pu] h21.4v[5] h19.5v[2] h23.1s[4] h23.6v h23.1v[4] Apr 17] compact gelding: modest handicap hurdler: maiden chaser: stays 3m: acts on heavy going: has worn headgear, including last 4 starts: front runner/races prominently: temperamental. *Linda Blackford*   c– § h95 §

MOUNTAIN PATH 5 b.m. Mount Nelson – Vino (Efisio) [2017/18 b89: h16g[2] h16.7g[5] h15.7d[3] Nov 21] leggy mare: bumper winner: fair form over hurdles: best effort when second in maiden at Worcester in August. *Jonjo O'Neill*   h101

MOUNT BATUR (IRE) 5 ch.g. Mahler – Massini's Daughter (IRE) (Dr Massini (IRE)) [2017/18 b15.8d[4] Nov 18] fifth foal: half-brother to a winning pointer by Bach: dam, pulled up only start in points, half-sister to fairly useful hurdler (2¾m-25f winner) Chief Witness: 15/2, looked green when fourth in bumper at Uttoxeter (6¼ lengths behind Article Fifty). *Fergal O'Brien*   b87

MOUNT BECKHAM (IRE) 9 b.g. Desert King (IRE) – Nowhere Like Home (IRE) (Exit To Nowhere (USA)) [2017/18 c16g[4] c15.6g[2] c16d[3] c16.5s Nov 3] winning hurdler: fairly useful form over fences: stays 2½m: acts on soft going: tried in tongue tie. *Miss Clare Louise Cannon, Ireland*   c123 h–

MOUNTMELLICK GIRL (IRE) 6 b.m. Beneficial – Dream Witness (FR) (Sagamix (FR)) [2017/18 h25m[3] h24s[6] h23.9g[pu] Nov 16] third foal: dam (h96) 2¼m hurdle winner: poor maiden hurdler: stays 25f: acts on soft and good to firm going: has worn headgear, including last 4 starts: tried in tongue tie. *Brendan Duke, Ireland*   h82

MOUNT MEWS (IRE) 7 b.g. Presenting – Kneeland Lass (IRE) (Bob Back (USA)) [2017/18 h140p, b115: h16v[3] h16.3d[6] c19.1s* c24s[2] c23.8s[3] h21.1s Mar 14] well-made gelding: useful handicap hurdler: similar form over fences: won novice at Doncaster in January: third in Reynoldstown Novices' Chase at Ascot (12 lengths behind Black Corton) in February: stays 3m: acts on heavy going: remains capable of better as a chaser: has joined Donald McCain. *Ruth Jefferson*   c138 p h138

MOUNT OLIVER (IRE) 8 b.g. Mountain High (IRE) – Little Nancy (IRE) (Alphabatim (USA)) [2017/18 c16g c20.6s c24.5g[3] c23.8g[ur] c26v* c25.2d[3] Feb 2] modest handicap chaser: won at Fontwell in January: left Miss M. L. Hallahan after second start: stays 3¼m: acts on heavy going: in cheekpieces last 5 starts: often races prominently: often let down by jumping. *Neil Mulholland*   c85 x

MOUNT RUSHMOORE (IRE) 6 b.g. Shantou (USA) – Knock On The Door (IRE) (Saddlers' Hall (IRE)) [2017/18 b16v[3] h18.5v[2] h19.5s[2] h19s[4] Mar 26] €34,000 4-y-o, £28,000 5-y-o: fifth foal: half-brother to fair hurdler/fairly useful chaser Who's That   h116 b84

MRA

(2¼m/19f winner, by Kalanisi): dam no form: Irish point winner: third in bumper at Chepstow (15 lengths behind Good Boy Bobby): fairly useful form over hurdles: will stay 2½m: temperament under suspicion. *Colin Tizzard*

MOUNT VESUVIUS (IRE) 10 b.g. Spartacus (IRE) – Parker's Cove (USA) (Woodman (USA)) [2017/18 c71, h86: h15.7m[6] h21.6d[3] h21.6m[5] h21.6m[3] h25.8m[3] c25.8m[4] h20.3d[2] h25.8g[3] h21.4s[4] h23.9m[pu] Nov 1] compact gelding: poor handicap hurdler/chaser: barely stays 3¼m: acts on good to firm and heavy going: has worn cheekpieces: wears tongue tie: usually races in rear: no battler. *Paul Henderson*   **c68 h82 §**

MOVEWITHTHETIMES (IRE) 7 ch.g. Presenting – Dare To Venture (IRE) (Darazari (IRE)) [2017/18 h145: c15.9g[4] c20.4d[2] c20.8s[3] c20.8s[pu] Mar 15] well-made gelding: smart hurdler: useful form over fences: second in novice at Cheltenham (2¼ lengths behind Finian's Oscar) in November: stays 2½m: acts on soft going: often races towards rear. *Paul Nicholls*   **c140 h–**

MOVIE LEGEND 8 b.g. Midnight Legend – Cyd Charisse (Kayf Tara) [2017/18 c120, h109: c18g[3] c16.3s* c15.2s* c15.2s[4] c16.4s[6] c15.5v[2] c20v[pu] c21.2d[pu] Apr 7] workmanlike gelding: maiden hurdler: fairly useful handicap chaser: won at Fakenham in November and Wetherby in December: stays 23f: acts on good to firm and heavy going: wears cheekpieces: has worn tongue tie. *Lucy Wadham*   **c125 h–**

MOVIE SET (USA) 6 b.g. Dubawi (IRE) – Short Skirt (Diktat) [2017/18 h16s[F] h15.8g* Apr 24] good-topped gelding: fairly useful form on Flat up to 1½m: similar form over hurdles: won maiden at Huntingdon in April: open to improvement. *Richard Spencer*   **h115 p**

MOVING IN STYLE (IRE) 7 ch.g. Mountain High (IRE) – Good To Travel (IRE) (Night Shift (USA)) [2017/18 h16v h21.6d[pu] h15.3v h23.9s* h25s* Apr 15] €16,000 3-y-o: compact gelding: second foal: brother to bumper winner Le Legro: dam, 7f winner (no form over hurdles), half-sister to useful 2m hurdle winner In The Forge: Irish point winner: fair form over hurdles: won handicaps at Taunton (conditional) in March and Plumpton in April: stays 25f: acts on soft going. *Neil Mulholland*   **h104**

MOYNIHANS GIRL (IRE) 4 ch.f. Frammassone (IRE) – Catch Ball (Prince Sabo) [2017/18 h16.5s[pu] h16v h15.3s h16v Mar 21] half-sister to fair hurdler Keltic Crisis (3m winner, by Needle Gun) and modest hurdler/fair chaser TB Broke Her (2m-25f winner, by Indian River): dam (h134), 2½m-3m hurdle winner (1½m/13f winner on Flat), half-sister to smart hurdler (2m/17f winner) Satin Lover: no form over hurdles. *Laura Young*   **h–**

MOYROSS 7 b.g. Kayf Tara – Dancing Dasi (IRE) (Supreme Leader) [2017/18 h21.2s* h24d* h20v h22s[6] h24v[6] Feb 21] €22,000 3-y-o: second foal: dam (h112) 2m-2½m hurdle winner: point winner: in frame in 3 bumpers in 2016/17: useful form over hurdles: won maiden at Galway in September and novice at Cork in October: stays 3m: acts on heavy going. *Noel Meade, Ireland*   **h131**

MOZO 7 b.m. Milan – Haudello (FR) (Marignan (USA)) [2017/18 h90: h19.9d[5] h23.3v[3] h23.3v[2] h23.3v[pu] Mar 17] poor maiden hurdler: stays 23f: best form on heavy going: has worn hood, including in 2017/18: in tongue tie last 4 starts. *Anthony Honeyball*   **h77**

MR ADJUDICATOR 4 b.g. Camacho – Attlongglast (Groom Dancer (USA)) [2017/18 h16s* h16s* h16.8v[2] h16s[2] Apr 28]   **h147**

    When assessing the Irish challenge for the Triumph Hurdle—the pre-eminent race for four-year-old hurdlers—the form of the Spring Juvenile Hurdle is inevitably the place to start. There have been six Irish-trained winners of the Triumph in the last twenty-one runnings and all of them contested the Leopardstown race, now one of four Grade 1s on the second day of the newly-instituted Dublin Racing Festival. Commanche Court justified odds-on favouritism in the Leopardstown race when it was still a Grade 3 in 1997, before winning the twenty-eight-runner Triumph that season; Scolardy lost the Leopardstown race in the stewards' room in 2002, but went on to establish his superiority over Newhall, the beneficiary of his demotion, in no uncertain terms when winning by eleven lengths at Cheltenham; Our Conor ran out a clear-cut winner of the 2013 Spring Juvenile Hurdle, and went on to produce one of the best performances by a four-year-old in the *Chasers & Hurdlers* era when winning the Triumph by fifteen lengths; Tiger Roll finished runner-up in the Spring Juvenile on his debut for Gordon Elliott in 2014 before showing much improved form to go one better at Cheltenham; Ivanovich Gorbatov managed only fourth when sent off at odds-on heavy ground at Leopardstown in 2016, but bounced back on a sounder surface to beat Apple's Jade by a length and a quarter in the Triumph; and, in the latest season, Farclas was second in the Spring Juvenile Hurdle behind Mr Adjudicator, the pair pulling clear in a very good time, before going on to turn the tables in a protracted duel with the same rival at Cheltenham, where he won by a length and three quarters. Although only Commanche Court and Our Conor have completed the double in that period, the strength of the form of the Spring Juvenile has been proven time and again, particularly since it was promoted to Grade 1 in 2010 (the race was run as a Grade 2 between 2003 and 2009). Seven of the last eight winners of the Spring Juvenile have gone on to win or finish placed in the Triumph, and the exception, the 2015 winner Petite Parisienne, one of six mares to have won the Spring Juvenile since its inception in 1994, was hardly disgraced when fifth at Cheltenham.

Mr Adjudicator's win in the latest renewal of the Tattersalls Ireland-sponsored Spring Juvenile Hurdle was a fourth in the race for Willie Mullins, making him the leading trainer in its history, though he could easily have had five wins if the stewards had not intervened after Scolardy was first past the post in 2002. That demotion, which was upheld by the Turf Club on appeal, robbed connections of the €100,000 bonus on offer for any horse which won what was then known as the Cashmans Bookmakers Juvenile Hurdle and the Triumph in the same season (the bonus to be split between the trainer and the owner). The verdict clearly still rankled with Mullins when he was interviewed after Scolardy's Cheltenham success. 'It's still hard to see how we lost that race,' he said. 'But we're still happy enough. We got our bonus today.' The essay on Newhall in *Chasers & Hurdlers 2001/02* explained that there was 'a clear case for awarding her the race', with Scolardy having nudged her when squeezing through to lead two out, before just half a length separated them at the line. Coming into the latest renewal, Mr Adjudicator boasted a profile closer to that of Scolardy and Mister Hight, Mullins' first winner of the Spring Juvenile in 2006, than French recruits Petite Parisienne and Footpad, who recorded successive wins in the race for their trainer in 2015 and 2016. Scolardy had already run fourteen times on the Flat for Mullins when making his hurdling bow in the October of his three-year-old season, whilst Mister Hight had ten Flat starts under his belt when lining up for the first time over hurdles at Leopardstown's Christmas meeting, the same starting point for Mr Adjudicator's hurdling career in the latest season. Mr Adjudicator arrived at Mullins' yard having won two out of twelve starts on the Flat for Joseph Murphy, showing fairly useful form when winning an eleven-furlong apprentice handicap on his final outing at Killarney in August. He looked a potentially useful recruit to hurdling right from the start, when making a smooth winning debut at Leopardstown four months later, always travelling strongly in a steadily-run affair and going on early in the straight, driven clear to win by seven and a half lengths.

Only five runners went to post for the Spring Juvenile Hurdle, with the betting headed by 5/4-on Espoir d'Allen, who was unbeaten in four starts over hurdles, including the Grade 2 Knight Frank Juvenile Hurdle over course and distance the time before, at the same meeting at which Mr Adjudicator made his debut. Farclas was a length and a quarter behind Espoir d'Allen on that occasion, shaping promisingly for one making his first appearance over obstacles, and he was sent off the joint second favourite with Mr Adjudicator at 3/1, with rank outsiders Grey Waters (33/1) and Tenth Amendment (66/1) having finished only fourth and fifth respectively behind Espoir d'Allen on their previous starts. Tenth Amendment took them along in the early stages before being headed by the strong-travelling Espoir d'Allen three out. The alarm bells also began to ring for the favourite soon afterwards, however, and he weakened so quickly in the straight that he was most likely amiss on the day (not seen out again). That left Mr Adjudicator and Farclas to battle out the finish, with the former coming through from behind and having to pull out all the stops to get the verdict by a length and a quarter. The first two finished well clear of the third in a time over a second faster than Samcro recorded when winning the Deloitte Novices' Hurdle later on the same card. Mr Adjudicator couldn't confirm the placings with Farclas on stamina-sapping heavy ground in the Triumph Hurdle at Cheltenham, but he improved further himself at the Festival, and he looked unlucky not to finish closer when second (three lengths behind stablemate

Saldier) on his final start in the Champion Four Year Old Hurdle at the Punchestown Festival, running on after being forced to switch after having anything but a smooth passage between the final two flights.

Mr Adjudicator (b.g. 2014)
- Camacho (b 2002)
  - Danehill (b 1986)
    - Danzig
    - Razyana
  - Arabesque (b 1997)
    - Zafonic
    - Prophecy
- Attlongglast (b 2001)
  - Groom Dancer (b 1984)
    - Blushing Groom
    - Featherhill
  - My Way (b 1995)
    - Marju
    - Ausherra

A rather leggy gelding, Mr Adjudicator is a rare National Hunt performer for his sire Camacho, a son of Danehill who produced his best effort when runner-up in the Jersey Stakes in 2005, when Royal Ascot was run at York. Camacho stands at Yeomanstown Stud in Ireland at a fee of €7,500 and has been a good source of two-year-old winners; Teppal provided him with a first Group 1 winner when winning the Poule d'Essai des Pouliches at Longchamp in May. Camacho has had just five individual winners over jumps at the time of writing, with Mr Adjudicator by far the best, ahead of El Beau, who was a fairly useful juvenile hurdler himself in 2014/15. Mr Adjudicator is the fifth foal out of the unraced Attlongglast, a half-sister to the fairly useful hurdler Devil To Pay, and he is a half-brother to three winners on the Flat by Multiplex including useful winner at up to a mile Multi Bene. The only other progeny of Attlongglast to have raced over jumps so far is Multigifted (winner at up to two miles on the Flat) who has shown just modest form over hurdles so far.

Mr David Bobbett's "Mr Adjudicator"

MRA

Mr Adjudicator was sold as a yearling at the Doncaster Sales for £21,000 and raced on the Flat in his trainer's own colours, before being sold privately to go hurdling. The top four-year-olds find it notoriously difficult to make an impact in their second season over hurdles, but Mr Adjudicator has made such a promising start that it would be no surprise if he made his mark, especially on a sounder surface than he has encountered so far in this sphere, which might suit him better (testing for all four of his starts). He showed form on a firmer surface on the Flat. Mr Adjudicator was tried in cheekpieces/blinkers on the Flat and wore a hood for his hurdling debut, but was not fitted with headgear again in the latest season (though he wore ear plugs in the Triumph). He was declared to run in the Prix Alain du Breil at Auteuil after the end of the British jumps season, but was withdrawn by the stewards after falling foul of the new regulations introduced in January which require that any horse racing in France has to be vaccinated against equine herpes, the virus which ravaged Jean-Claude Rouget's stable in 2017. *W. P. Mullins, Ireland*

MR ANTOLINI (IRE) 8 b.g. Catcher In The Rye (IRE) – Victory Run (IRE) (Old Vic) [2017/18 h16.5g[6] h16g[4] h16.7g h20g[4] h21g h16.6v[6] h16d[3] h15.5v* h19.6s[2] h16v* h15.9v[2] Apr 1] rather leggy gelding: maiden pointer: bumper winner: useful handicap hurdler: won maiden at Gowran in 2016/17: also won at Leicester in January and Imperial Cup at Sandown (by neck from Call Me Lord) in March: left Garrett James Power after seventh start: stays 2½m: acts on heavy going: has worn hood. *Nigel Twiston-Davies* — **h136**

MR BACHSTER (IRE) 13 b.g. Bach (IRE) – Warrior Princess (IRE) (Mister Lord (USA)) [2017/18 c95, h–: c20.3d[pu] h21.2g[5] c20.3v[4] c16.1v[4] Feb 1] compact gelding: maiden hurdler: modest handicap chaser, below form in 2017/18: stays 2½m: acts on heavy going: wears cheekpieces: often races prominently. *Kerry Lee* — **c74 h74**

MR BANKS (IRE) 7 br.g. Kalanisi (IRE) – She's Supersonic (IRE) (Accordion) [2017/18 h20.3d[pu] Dec 5] maiden hurdler, shaped as if amiss after long absence only outing in 2017/18: in headgear last 3 starts. *Paul Webber* — **h–**

MR BIG SHOT (IRE) 7 br.g. Flemensfirth (USA) – Une Etoile (IRE) (Un Desperado (FR)) [2017/18 h125p: h20.3v h24.7s* Apr 14] big gelding: bumper winner: smart form over hurdles: won Grade 3 handicap at Aintree (by ¾ length from Now McGinty) in April: stays 25f: open to further improvement. *David Pipe* — **h142 p**

MR BOSS MAN (IRE) 10 b.g. Beneficial – Sarah Massini (IRE) (Dr Massini (IRE)) [2017/18 c24.5g[F] c25g* h20g c25g[2] c22.5s h22.5s[F] c18d[4] h24s c19.9d[5] c19.6v[3] c24.5s[F] Apr 28] fairly useful handicap hurdler/chaser: won at Kilbeggan in June: second in Midlands National Handicap Chase there in July: stays 25f: acts on good to firm and heavy going: has worn headgear. *Nigel Slevin, Ireland* — **c118 h114**

MR BROWNSTONE (IRE) 4 b.g. Sakhee (USA) – Sweet Child O'Mine (Singspiel (IRE)) [2017/18 b13.2s b13.7g Nov 30] no form in bumpers/sole outing on Flat: wears tongue tie. *Brendan Powell* — **b–**

*Matchbook Imperial Cup Handicap Hurdle, Sandown—
a second Imperial Cup in three years for trainer Nigel Twiston-Davies as 20/1-shot Mr Antolini
(checks) narrowly gets the better of top-weight Call Me Lord (second left)*

Gaskells Handicap Hurdle, Aintree—the imposing Mr Big Shot (centre) holds off Now McGinty (left) to land this valuable prize; long-time leader Debece (partly hidden) fades into fourth

MR CAFFREY 6 b.g. Duke of Marmalade (IRE) – Quest For Eternity (IRE) (Sadler's Wells (USA)) [2017/18 h92: h20g⁶ h18.7m* h20g* Jul 27] fair handicap hurdler: won at Stratford (conditional) and Worcester in July: left John Flint after first start: stays 2¾m: acts on good to firm and good to soft going: wears headgear: temperamental. *Dr Richard Newland*   **h100 §**

MR CARDLE (IRE) 9 b.g. Golan (IRE) – Leave Me Be (IRE) (Be My Native (USA)) [2017/18 c95§, h–§: c16.5m^F May 11] modest maiden hurdler/chaser, fell fatally sole outing in 2017/18: stayed 23f: acted on firm and soft going: wore headgear: often raced towards rear: temperamental. *Steve Flook*   **c– §** / **h– §**

MR DORRELL SAGE (FR) 5 b.g. Sageburg (IRE) – Miss Breezy (FR) (Sicyos (USA)) [2017/18 b–: b16s Feb 9] well held in bumpers. *Oliver Sherwood*   **b–**

MR FENTON (IRE) 7 b.g. Trans Island – Carnagh Girl (IRE) (Saddlers' Hall (IRE)) [2017/18 h112: h23g² h20.3g h25g Oct 5] chunky gelding: fair maiden hurdler: stays 23f: acts on good to firm and soft going: tried in headgear: temperamental. *Emma Lavelle*   **h109 §**

MR FICKLE (IRE) 9 b.g. Jeremy (USA) – Mamara Reef (Salse (USA)) [2017/18 h114§: h19.8s h19.5s h21d h16v h18.5v^pu Apr 17] smallish gelding: fairly useful hurdler at best, no form in 2017/18: has worn headgear: usually races nearer last than first: temperamental. *Gary Moore*   **h– §**

MR FIFTYONE (IRE) 9 b.g. Jeremy (USA) – Maka (USA) (Diesis) [2017/18 c140, h–: c16g³ c17g³ c17d c15.9g c16d⁴ Apr 26] sturdy gelding: winning hurdler: useful handicap chaser: stays 2½m: acts on good to firm and heavy going: has worn cheekpieces, including last 2 starts. *Mrs J. Harrington, Ireland*   **c138** / **h–**

MR FITZROY (IRE) 8 ch.g. Kyllachy – Reputable (Medicean) [2017/18 c120, h118: h17.9s h15.8v⁴ c16.1s^F c18.2s^ur h19.5v h19.9v⁴ Apr 7] small gelding: has had breathing operation: fairly useful handicap hurdler, below form in 217/18: maiden chaser, failed to complete both starts over fences in 2017/18: stays 2¼m: best form on soft/heavy going: tried in cheekpieces: has worn tongue tie, including last 5 starts. *Jo Davis*   **c–** / **h95**

MR GLOBETROTTER (USA) 5 b.g. Henrythenavigator (USA) – Sunshine For Life (USA) (Giant's Causeway (USA)) [2017/18 h97: h16.2g h19.9g Oct 3] poor maiden hurdler. *Iain Jardine*   **h81**

MRG

MR GREY (IRE) 10 gr.g. Great Palm (USA) – Presenting Shares (IRE) (Presenting) [2017/18 c122, h–: h20.5d⁶ Nov 6] strong, lengthy gelding: point winner: fairly useful hurdler at best, well held sole start in 2017/18: fairly useful form in chases: stays 2½m: acts on soft going: wears tongue tie. *Ben Case*   **c–** **h–**

MR GRUMPY 5 b.g. Sir Percy – Panna (Polish Precedent (USA)) [2017/18 h81p: h16.2g² h16.2m³ Jun 4] fair form over hurdles: tried in hood. *Lucinda Russell*   **h105**

MR JACK (IRE) 6 ch.g. Papal Bull – Miss Barbados (IRE) (Hawk Wing (USA)) [2017/18 h21s^pu h17.7v^pu h15.9v⁴ h15.9s³ Apr 15] second foal: dam unraced: fair form over hurdles. *Linda Jewell*   **h101**

MR JIM 9 b.g. Fraam – Coddington Susie (Green Adventure (USA)) [2017/18 c94: c21.7m² c15.9m³ c21.4d⁵ c20.2s⁵ c19.7s^ur Apr 15] modest handicap chaser: stays 2¾m: acts on good to firm going. *Tony Carroll*   **c92**

MR KIT CAT 8 ch.g. Lucarno (USA) – Makeabreak (IRE) (Anshan) [2017/18 h117: h16m² h18.5m⁶ c16.5g⁴ c16.3g² c16.5d⁴ c16.5f^pu Oct 12] good-topped gelding: fairly useful handicap hurdler: fair form over fences: will stay 2½m: acts on good to firm and good to soft going: has worn hood, including in 2017/18. *Evan Williams*   **c102** **h116**

MR KITE 7 b.g. Sixties Icon – Mar Blue (FR) (Marju (IRE)) [2017/18 h107: h15.6s⁶ h16.7s³ Feb 18] well-made gelding: fair handicap hurdler: raced mainly around 2m: acts on soft going: wears tongue tie: often races towards rear. *Susan Corbett*   **h105**

MR LANDO 9 b.g. Shirocco (GER) – Capitana (GER) (Lando (GER)) [2017/18 c–, h102: h16.7g⁵ h18.5v h16.5s² h19v² h15.9v* h16s⁴ Mar 22] close-coupled gelding: fair handicap hurdler: won at Plumpton in March: once-raced chaser: stays 19f: acts on good to firm and heavy going: has worn headgear, including in 2017/18: has worn tongue tie, including last 4 starts: usually leads. *Johnny Farrelly*   **c–** **h102**

MR LOVE (IRE) 6 b.g. Winged Love (IRE) – Bonny Rathlin (IRE) (Beauchamp King) [2017/18 h104: c24.2s⁴ c22.7s³ c24v^pu c21.4v² c24v⁵ Mar 28] sturdy gelding: runner-up in Irish point: lightly-raced hurdler: fair form in chases: stays 3m: acts on heavy going: in headgear last 2 starts: usually races towards rear: temperamental. *Lucy Wadham*   **c105 §** **h–**

MR MACHO (IRE) 6 b.g. Flemensfirth (USA) – Accordian Rules (IRE) (Accordion) [2017/18 b16.7d⁶ Apr 21] €44,000 3-y-o: fifth foal: dam, unraced, from family of top-class hurdler/very smart chaser (stayed 3¼m) Time For Rupert (by Flemensfirth): 12/1, very green when sixth in conditionals/amateur bumper at Bangor (15¼ lengths behind Norman Stanley): should improve. *Kim Bailey*   **b– p**

MR MAFIA (IRE) 9 b.g. Zerpour (IRE) – Wizzy (IRE) (Presenting) [2017/18 c102, h93: h22g² c22.6g⁵ h20g h18.7m* h20g² c20.3d⁴ c23.6d^ur h21.2g h19.7g h19.4d⁴ h15.7d⁵ Dec 28] modest handicap hurdler: won novice event at Stratford in August: fair handicap chaser, below form in 2017/18: stays 3m: acts on good to firm and good to soft going: has worn tongue tie: held up. *Tony Carroll*   **c73** **h92**

MR MAGILL (FR) 6 b.g. Hamairi (IRE) – Marie Cuddy (IRE) (Galileo (IRE)) [2017/18 h15.9v h19s h15.3v^pu h16.5s Feb 20] poor maiden on Flat: no form over hurdles: wears hood: tried in tongue tie. *Nick Mitchell*   **h–**

MR MCGUINESS (IRE) 8 b.g. Kalanisi (IRE) – Maig Mandy (IRE) (Mandalus) [2017/18 h108: h21g² h20g* h20g* h20m⁴ h20g⁵ h23g⁵ h21.1g c20d^pu Nov 27] lengthy gelding: fairly useful handicap hurdler: won at Worcester (twice) in June: pulled up in maiden on chasing debut: stays 23f: acts on good to firm and good to soft going: usually races towards rear. *Rosemary Gasson*   **c–** **h120**

MR MEDIC 7 b.g. Dr Massini (IRE) – Danse Slave (FR) (Broadway Flyer (USA)) [2017/18 c117p, h–: c20d⁶ c19.2d* c19.9d³ c18.8d* Dec 23] sturdy gelding: maiden hurdler: useful handicap chaser: won at Exeter in October and Ascot (by short head from Rock On Rocky) in December: stays 2½m: acts on good to firm and good to soft going. *Robert Walford*   **c132** **h–**

MR MERCURIAL (IRE) 10 b.g. Westerner – Arcanum (IRE) (Presenting) [2017/18 c125: c27.5d^pu c23.8d* c23.8d* Apr 24] good-topped gelding: multiple point winner: fairly useful chaser: won hunters at Ludlow in March and April: stays 3½m: acts on soft and good to firm going: often in headgear: wears tongue tie: often travels strongly. *Mrs Sheila Crow*   **c123**

MR MIX (FR) 7 gr.g. Al Namix (FR) – Royale Surabaya (FR) (Turgeon (USA)) [2017/18 c120p, h138: c23g² c23.6d³ c26.7g* c25.1s^pu c24d³ c24.1g Apr 21] angular gelding: useful hurdler: useful chaser: won novice at Worcester in May and handicap at Wincanton in October: stays 27f: acts on heavy going: has worn cheekpieces, including final start. *Paul Nicholls*   **c141** **h–**

MR MONOCHROME 7 br.g. Indian Danehill (IRE) – Our Ethel (Be My Chief (USA)) [2017/18 h127, b96: c20.1v⁴ Sep 28] leggy, useful-looking gelding: bumper winner: fairly useful hurdler: 16/1, fourth in novice at Perth (27 lengths behind Ballyandy) on chasing debut: front runner/races prominently. *Malcolm Jefferson*   c110 h–

MR MOSS (IRE) 13 b.g. Moscow Society (USA) – Yesterdays Gorby (IRE) (Strong Gale) [2017/18 c105, h80: c20.8d^pu May 5] good-topped gelding: point winner: maiden hurdler: fair hunter chaser, pulled up sole outing under Rules in 2017/18: stays 3¼m: acts on good to firm and heavy going: has worn headgear, including final start: has worn tongue tie. *S. Rea*   c– h–

MR MOUNTAIN (IRE) 8 b.g. Mountain High (IRE) – Not Mine (IRE) (Oscar (IRE)) [2017/18 c–, h113: c21m⁶ c21g^pu Jun 27] lengthy gelding: fair hurdler: no form over fences: stays 2¾m: has worn hood: tried in tongue tie. *Emma Lavelle*   c– h–

MR MUDDLE 11 gr.g. Imperial Dancer – Spatham Rose (Environment Friend) [2017/18 c112, h–: c19.7s² c18.2s⁵ c16v⁵ c17.8v⁵ c17.8v⁵ Apr 15] compact gelding: winning hurdler: fair handicap chaser nowadays: stays 2¾m: acts on heavy going: wears headgear. *Gary Moore*   c108 h–

MR MULLINER (IRE) 9 br.g. Millenary – Mrs Battle (IRE) (Be My Native (USA)) [2017/18 c–, h108: c23.5g^pu h20.5g⁶ h24g^pu h21.2d^pu h23.8s^pu h26s c25.1d^pu Apr 22] fair hurdler at best, no form in 2017/18: maiden chaser: left Mark McNiff after third start: has worn headgear, including in 2017/18: wears tongue tie. *Paul Henderson*   c– h–

MR ONE MORE (IRE) 6 b.g. Asian Heights – Norah's Quay (IRE) (Witness Box (USA)) [2017/18 b102: h16.3g* h15.7g* h15.7d⁶ h19.6s⁵ Feb 8] sturdy gelding: bumper winner: fairly useful form over hurdles: won maiden at Stratford in October and introductory event at Ascot in November: often races towards rear. *Harry Fry*   h119

MR PUMBLECHOOK 4 b.g. Midnight Legend – Definitely Pip (IRE) (Definite Article) [2017/18 b16s⁶ b16.3s⁶ Mar 24] sturdy gelding: modest form in bumpers. *Alan King*   b76

MR RAJ (IRE) 10 b.g. Oscar (IRE) – Chapel Wood Lady (IRE) (Zaffaran (USA)) [2017/18 c110: c19.3g* May 4] multiple point winner: fair chaser: won novice hunter at Sedgefield on sole outing in 2017/18: in tongue tie last 2 starts. *T. Gallagher*   c109

MR ROBINSON (FR) 11 b.g. Robin des Pres (FR) – Alberade (FR) (Un Desperado (FR)) [2017/18 c62, h–: c15.6g⁵ c29.4d c19.3g⁶ Aug 31] maiden hurdler: poor chaser, no form in 2017/18: has worn headgear, including in 2017/18: not straightforward. *Lucinda Egerton*   c– h–

MR SANDGATE (IRE) 5 b.g. Sandmason – Ballybeg Princess (IRE) (The Bart (USA)) [2017/18 b–: b16v h20.5v^pu h16.2s Apr 26] no form in bumpers/over hurdles. *R. Mike Smith*   h– b–

MR SATCO (IRE) 10 b.g. Mr Combustible (IRE) – Satlin (IRE) (Satco (FR)) [2017/18 c116§, h–: c20d² c20.9d Jun 9] workmanlike gelding: point winner: winning hurdler: fairly useful chaser: stays 3m: acts on good to firm and good to soft going: wears headgear: usually races: moody, and not one to trust. *Mrs Emma Oliver*   c119 § h–

MR SAWYER 9 b.g. Striking Ambition – Willows World (Agnes World (USA)) [2017/18 c94: c16.3d^pu c20.9d⁵ c21g⁵ c16.5g^pu Sep 3] multiple point winner: modest maiden chaser: left K. Jacka after second start. *Tim Vaughan*   c85

MRS BELLAMY 5 b.m. Black Sam Bellamy (IRE) – Jaxelle (FR) (Lights Out (FR)) [2017/18 b16s⁵ Feb 16] fifth foal: half-sister to bumper winner Jaxlight (by Lucarno); dam, French maiden, half-sister to very smart staying chaser L'Ami and useful staying chaser Kelami: 12/1, fifth in maiden bumper at Fakenham (12¼ lengths behind Melekhov). *Michael Appleby*   b73

MRS BURBIDGE 8 b.m. Pasternak – Twin Time (Syrtos) [2017/18 c–, h96: h16g* c19.7d² c20.9s³ Mar 27] modest handicap hurdler: won mares event at Worcester in September: similar form in chases: stays 2½m: acts on heavy going: wears cheekpieces/tongue tie: often travels strongly. *Neil Mulholland*   c91 h97

MR SCAFF (IRE) 4 br.g. Vocalised (USA) – Nancy Rock (IRE) (Rock of Gibraltar (IRE)) [2017/18 h17.7g Oct 6] modest maiden on Flat, stays 1½m: tailed off in juvenile hurdle. *Paul Henderson*   h–

MR SCRUMPY 4 b.g. Passing Glance – Apple Days (Sovereign Water (FR)) [2017/18 b16.7g³ Apr 22] third foal: half-brother to bumper winner Rosemary Russet (by Midnight Legend); dam, winning pointer, half-sister to useful chaser (stayed 29f) Strongbows Legend: 16/1, third in bumper at Market Rasen (3 lengths behind Northern Soul): sure to progress. *Jedd O'Keeffe*   b94 p

MRS

MR SELBY 9 b.g. Terimon – Bee-A-Scally (Scallywag) [2017/18 h–: h22.1d^{pu} May 29] maiden pointer: fair form when won novice in 2015/16, standout effort over hurdles: tried in hood: dead. *James Moffatt*   **h–**

MRS GRASS 11 ch.m. And Beyond (IRE) – Tempted (IRE) (Invited (USA)) [2017/18 h77§: h17m h17.2d h16.2d⁶ h16.2v⁵ h20.1s* h17s⁵ h16.2s² Nov 10] small mare: poor handicap hurdler: won mares event at Hexham in October: stays 2½m: acts on heavy going: wears headgear: has worn tongue tie, including up 2017/18: front runner/races prominently. *Jonathan Haynes*   **h78**

MR SHAHADY (IRE) 13 b.g. Xaar – Shunaire (USA) (Woodman (USA)) [2017/18 c–, h–: c19.3g^{pu} c21.6g^{pu} May 10] point winner: maiden hurdler: no form in chases (often let down by jumping): has worn headgear. *Victor Thompson*   **c– x h–**

MR SHANTU (IRE) 9 b.g. Shantou (USA) – Close To Shore (IRE) (Bob Back (USA)) [2017/18 c128, h126x: h23g⁶ h20g⁶ h23g c23.8g⁴ c23.9d^{pu} Apr 22] good-topped gelding: fairly useful handicap hurdler/chaser: stays 3¼m: acts on good to firm going: usually wears headgear/tongue tie: often let down by jumping over hurdles. *Jonjo O'Neill*   **c114 h118 x**

MRS HYDE (IRE) 5 b.m. Flemensfirth (USA) – Funny Times (Silver Patriarch (IRE)) [2017/18 b17.7d⁵ Feb 26] £17,000 4-y-o: fourth foal: sister to bumper winner/fairly useful hurdler Flementime (2½m winner): dam bumper winner out of sister to smart staying jumper Better Times Ahead: 11/4, fifth in mares bumper at Plumpton (22¾ lengths behind Queen's Magic): should do better. *Shaun Lycett*   **b78 p**

MRS MIGGINS (IRE) 5 b.m. Presenting – Carrigeen Lunaria (IRE) (Saddlers' Hall (IRE)) [2017/18 b16.8v³ b16.5v Mar 12] £8,000 3-y-o, resold £48,000 3-y-o: third foal: dam, winning pointer, half-sister to useful hurdler/smart chaser (stays 21f) Benatar: poor form in bumpers. *David Pipe*   **b72**

MR SNIPS 5 b.g. Indian Haven – Madam'x (Xaar) [2017/18 b16s b16s b16.7g Apr 22] smallish gelding: no form in bumpers. *Clive Drew*   **b–**

MR SNOOZY 9 b.g. Pursuit of Love – Hard To Follow (Dilum (USA)) [2017/18 c–, h108: h18.6g* h19.7s⁴ h18.6s⁶ h20.6v Apr 11] sturdy gelding: fair handicap hurdler: won at Market Rasen in November: pulled up only start over fences: stays 2¾m: acts on soft and good to firm going: wears headgear: usually races close up. *Mark Walford*   **c– h114**

MRSROBIN (IRE) 8 b.m. Robin des Pres (FR) – Regents Dancer (IRE) (Flemensfirth (USA)) [2017/18 c101, h–: h23.3g* h23.9g^{pu} c25.8m^{pu} c23m² Nov 1] lengthy mare: modest hurdler: won novice handicap at Uttoxeter in May: modest handicap chaser: stays 3¼m: acts on good to firm and good to soft going: has worn headgear, including in 2017/18: usually races close up: ungenuine. *Barry Brennan*   **c85 § h87 §**

MR SYNTAX (IRE) 14 b.g. King's Theatre (IRE) – Smile Awhile (USA) (Woodman (USA)) [2017/18 c107§, h–: c22.6d³ Apr 22] tall, lengthy gelding: point winner: maiden hurdler: fair chaser nowadays: stays 3m: acts on good to firm and heavy going: tried in cheekpieces: has worn tongue tie: often races towards rear: no battler. *Miss Michelle Bentham*   **c93 § h–**

MR WASHINGTON (IRE) 5 b.g. Vinnie Roe (IRE) – Anna Bird (IRE) (Be My Native (USA)) [2017/18 b16v³ b16.2s⁶ h19.7v² h16.2v³ Apr 10] €2,500 3-y-o, £40,000 4-y-o: seventh foal: dam unraced: point winner: modest form in bumpers: similar form over hurdles: better effort when second in novice at Hereford in March: in tongue tie last 2 starts. *David Dennis*   **h90 b82**

MR WEST COAST (IRE) 5 b.g. Dubai Destination (USA) – Camas North (IRE) (Muharib (USA)) [2017/18 b15.3d Apr 22] in tongue strap, 7/2, twelfth in bumper at Wincanton (19½ lengths behind Ebony Gale). *Harry Fry*   **b–**

MR WHIPPED (IRE) 5 br.g. Beneficial – Dyrick Daybreak (IRE) (Ali-Royal (IRE)) [2017/18 h16d* h20.5s* h21s* h23.8s² h24v^{pu} Mar 16] €26,000 3-y-o, £160,000 4-y-o: well-made gelding: sixth foal: dam (h118), 2m-2½m hurdle winner, also 1¾m-2m winner on Flat: Irish point winner: useful form over hurdles: won novices at Kempton and Newbury in December, and Leamington Novices' Hurdle at Warwick (by length from Paisley Park) in January: stays 3m: acts on soft going. *Nicky Henderson*   **h140**

MR WITMORE (IRE) 8 b.g. Whitmore's Conn (USA) – Bright Future (IRE) (Satco (FR)) [2017/18 c–, h87: c20.1g³ c20.1g⁶ c23.9g^F h20g c15.6g h16.2g c17.1g³ c15.6v³ c19.2d⁵ c19.9d^{ur} c16.4v⁴ c20.9v² c20.1v* c20.9s³ Apr 8] workmanlike gelding: maiden hurdler: modest handicap chaser: won at Hexham in March: stays 21f: acts on heavy going: wears headgear: tried in tongue tie: not one to trust. *Kenny Johnson*   **c86 § h–**

Mr M. R. Chapman's "Ms Parfois"

MSASSA (FR) 4 b.g. Sholokhov (IRE) – Ramina (GER) (Shirocco (GER)) [2017/18 h16v* h16s⁵ h16s⁴ Apr 28] first foal: dam, German 1m-1¼m winner, half-sister to fairly useful hurdler (stayed 19f) Mountain Fighter: useful form over hurdles: won maiden at Wexford in March: fourth in Champion Four Year Old Hurdle at Punchestown: will be suited by at least 2¼m: likely to progress further. *W. P. Mullins, Ireland*   **h136**

MS PARFOIS (IRE) 7 ch.m. Mahler – Dolly Lewis (Sir Harry Lewis (USA)) [2017/18 h118, b87: c24d³ c20.8s* c23.4s* c24s* c23.8s² c31.8s² c25s² Apr 13] lengthy mare: winning hurdler: smart chaser: won mares handicap at Cheltenham and listed mares novice at Newbury in December, and listed novice at Warwick (by 5 lengths from Duel At Dawn) in January: second after in Reynoldstown Novices' Chase at Ascot (8 lengths behind Black Corton), National Hunt Chase at Cheltenham (½ length behind Rathvinden) and Mildmay Novices' Chase at Aintree (3¾ lengths behind Terrefort): thorough stayer: acts on heavy going: has worn hood, including in 2017/18: wears tongue tie: front runner/races prominently, usually travels strongly: good jumper. *Anthony Honeyball*   **c146 h–**

MTADA SUPREME (IRE) 13 b.g. Bishop of Cashel – Tullabards Leader (IRE) (Supreme Leader) [2017/18 c24.5g³ c25g c24s* c30.2d^pu c24v c22.5s^pu Apr 17] angular gelding: multiple point winner: fairly useful chaser: won cross-country event at Punchestown in November: stays 25f: acts on heavy going. *Peter Maher, Ireland*   **c129**

MUCH TOO MUCH 5 b.m. Stimulation (IRE) – Complication (Compton Place) [2017/18 b17d ab16g⁴ ab16g⁵ Jan 30] fifth foal: half-sister to 2 winners on Flat, including 8.5f winner Maunsells Duke (by Bachelor Duke): dam 6f winner: poor form in bumpers. *Hughie Morrison*   **b74**

MUCKLE ROE (IRE) 9 b.g. Westerner – Island Crest (Jupiter Island) [2017/18 c117, h–: c25.5d* c24.2v⁶ c29.2v² c28.4v⁴ c23.8d Apr 24] tall gelding: maiden hurdler: fairly useful handicap chaser: won at Warwick in May: stays 29f: acts on heavy going: often races towards rear: often let down by jumping. *Nigel Twiston-Davies*   **c123 x h–**

MUF

MUFFINS FOR TEA 8 ch.g. With The Flow (USA) – Countess Point (Karinga Bay) [2017/18 h110: h16.8g* h20s³ c17.5s³ c16s^F c16s³ c23s* c25.1v² c28.4s² Mar 26] fair handicap hurdler: won at Newton Abbot (conditional) in May: fairly useful form over fences: won novice handicap at Taunton in February: stays 3½m: acts on heavy going: wears tongue tie: often races prominently. *Colin Tizzard* **c129 h114**

MUFTAKKER 4 gr.g. Tamayuz – Qertaas (IRE) (Linamix (FR)) [2017/18 ab16.3g Apr 15] 20/1, shaped as if needed experience when ninth in bumper at Newcastle (5¼ lengths behind Summer Lightening). *John Norton* **b77**

MUHTARIS (IRE) 8 b.g. Teofilo (IRE) – Fann (USA) (Diesis) [2017/18 h–: h18.5v⁵ Apr 17] sturdy gelding: fairly useful handicap hurdler, below form only 2 starts since 2015/16: stays 21f: acts on heavy going: has worn cheekpieces, including in 2017/18. *Ian Williams* **h72**

MUIRSHEEN DURKIN 4 b.g. Fastnet Rock (AUS) – Be My Queen (IRE) (Sadler's Wells (USA)) [2017/18 h15.7d⁶ Dec 19] fairly useful on Flat, stays 8.5f: well beaten in juvenile hurdle. *Neville Bycroft* **h–**

MULCAHYS HILL (IRE) 6 b.g. Brian Boru – Belsalsa (FR) (Kingsalsa (USA)) [2017/18 b93: b16.3d* h20v* h20.5v² h20.3v⁴ h24v^{pu} Mar 16] rather unfurnished gelding: point winner: fairly useful form in bumpers: won at Stratford in May: smart form over hurdles: won maiden at Ffos Las (by 1¼ lengths from Juge Et Parti) in November: second in Challow Novices' Hurdle at Newbury (short head behind Poetic Rhythm) in December: should be suited by 3m: front runner/races prominently: has flashed tail. *Warren Greatrex* **h138 b103**

MULLAGHBOY (IRE) 7 b.g. Beneficial – Mellowthemoonlight (IRE) (Un Desperado (FR)) [2017/18 h102, b–: h20d³ h16s* h20s³ c21.2s^F c21.2v* c17.8v⁴ Jan 21] modest hurdler: won amateur novice handicap at Fakenham in May: fair form over fences: won novice handicap at same course in January: stays 21f: best form on soft/heavy going: wears hood: usually tongue tied: often races towards rear. *Olly Murphy* **c103 h99**

MULLAGHMURPHY BLUE (IRE) 7 br.g. Beneficial – Blue Phase (IRE) (Bob Back (USA)) [2017/18 c23.5g² c22.1g^{su} c20d⁴ c16d³ c23.5d³ c19.9m* h21.2g² c19.9g* c19.9s³ Jan 3] first foal: dam (h93), maiden hurdler (best form at 2m), half-sister to fairly useful hurdler (2½m-2¾m winner) Mrs Wallensky: 5/4, second in handicap at Ludlow only start over hurdles (open to improvement): fair handicap chaser: won novice events at Musselburgh in November and December: stays 23f: acts on good to firm and good to soft going: in tongue tie last 5 starts: strong traveller. *J. T. R. Dreaper, Ireland* **c110 h95 p**

MULTELLIE 6 b.g. Multiplex – Bollin Nellie (Rock Hopper) [2017/18 h16s Dec 27] fairly useful on Flat, stays 1¾m: tailed off in novice hurdle. *Tim Easterby* **h–**

MULTICULTURE (IRE) 6 b.g. Mount Nelson – Gracious Melange (Medicean) [2017/18 h129: h15.7m May 13] good-topped gelding: fairly useful hurdler, well held sole outing in 2017/18: raced around 2m: best form on heavy going: front runner/races prominently, usually travels strongly. *Philip Hobbs* **h–**

MULTIGIFTED 5 b.m. Multiplex – Attlongglast (Groom Dancer (USA)) [2017/18 h98: h20.5d⁴ h16s³ h15.3v⁴ Jan 6] modest maiden hurdler: unproven beyond 2m: raced only on ground softer than good: in tongue tie last 4 starts. *Michael Madgwick* **h97**

MULTITALENTED 5 b.g. Multiplex – Star Welcome (More Welcome) [2017/18 b15.7d⁶ b15.7v⁴ h16v ab16g³ Mar 2] third foal: half-brother to smart 8.6f-1½m winner Myplacelater (by Where Or When): dam 1¼m winner: modest form in bumpers. *Tom Tate* **b82**

MUMGOS DEBUT (IRE) 10 b.g. Royal Anthem (USA) – Black Queen (IRE) (Bob Back (USA)) [2017/18 c115, h–: c20.1v* c20v c16.5v c16.5v⁶ c21.5v⁴ c17.1v³ Apr 16] has had breathing operation: maiden hurdler: fair handicap chaser: left alone after sole rival unseated first at Perth in September: stays 2½m: acts on heavy going: wears tongue tie. *Lucinda Russell* **c105 h–**

MUNSAAB (IRE) 12 b.g. Alhaarth (IRE) – Claustra (FR) (Green Desert (USA)) [2017/18 c119, h–: c25.5m* c21.2g⁶ c25.1g² c21.2g⁴ c20.5v³ c26.2v Oct 26] winning hurdler: fairly useful handicap chaser: won at Cartmel in May: stays 25f: acts on good to firm and heavy going: wears headgear: has worn tongue tie. *James Moffatt* **c119 h–**

MUNSTEAD PRIDE 6 ch.g. Sir Percy – Memsahib (Alzao (USA)) [2017/18 h16.3g h20.6v h20.2v^{pu} Sep 28] fairly useful on Flat, stays 1¾m: maiden hurdler, no form in 2017/18: often races towards rear. *Gordon Elliott, Ireland* **h–**

MURPHY'S NAILS 6 b.g. Milan – Definite Artist (IRE) (Definite Article) [2017/18 h62, b–: h19.7s³ h23.8s h19.5v^{pu} Apr 14] poor form over hurdles: tried in cheekpieces: often races prominently. *Kerry Lee* **h83**

MURRAYANA (IRE) 8 b.g. King's Theatre (IRE) – Royalrova (FR) (Garde Royale) [2017/18 c–, h–: c26.3d^{pu} May 5] point winner: fairly useful hurdler: maiden chaser, pulled up in hunters only 2 starts under Rules since 2015/16: stays 25f: acts on heavy going: tried in cheekpieces: wears tongue tie. *N. A. Pearce*   **c–**
h–

MURRAY MOUNT (IRE) 8 b.g. Trans Island – Ash (Salse (USA)) [2017/18 c83, h97: c20.9d^{ur} c20.3g* c20.3d^4 c20g* c20m^4 c20g^2 c25g^{pu} Oct 27] good-topped gelding: winning hurdler: fair handicap chaser: won at Southwell in May and Worcester in June: stays 2½m: best form on good going: tried in blinkers. *Henry Oliver*   **c109**
h–

MUSICAL MOON 8 b.g. Piccolo – Lunasa (IRE) (Don't Forget Me) [2017/18 h–: h20m^{pu} May 11] failed to complete in points: no form over hurdles: in headgear last 5 starts: dead. *Steve Flook*   **h–**

MUSICAL SLAVE (IRE) 5 b.g. Getaway (GER) – Inghwung (Kayf Tara) [2017/18 h18.6d^6 Nov 23] second foal: dam (h121), 2½m-2¾m hurdle winner (stayed 3¼m), half-sister to fairly useful hurdler (19f/2½m winner) Florafern out of useful chaser up to 3¼m Mossy Fern: shaped well when sixth in bumper at Punchestown in 2016/17: well beaten in novice hurdle. *Philip Hobbs*   **h–**

MUSICAL STARDUST 5 b.m. Passing Glance – Royal Musical (Royal Abjar (USA)) [2017/18 ab16g^6 b13.7g Apr 20] half-sister to fair chaser Midnight Chorister (2m/17f winner, by Midnight Legend): dam little form on Flat: poor form in bumpers. *Sam Thomas*   **b56**

MUSKETEER 6 ch.g. Schiaparelli (GER) – Suave Shot (Suave Dancer (USA)) [2017/18 b60: h19.9m h21.6d^5 Jul 31] poor form in bumpers: no form over hurdles: tried in hood. *Robert Stephens*   **h–**

MUSTANG ON 8 b.g. Croco Rouge (IRE) – More To Life (Northern Tempest (USA)) [2017/18 h102: c21.4g^2 May 12] workmanlike gelding: fair maiden hurdler: 12/1, second in novice handicap at Market Rasen (11 lengths behind Running Wolf) on chasing debut: stays 21f: acts on soft going: has worn hood. *Nick Kent*   **c98**
h–

MUST HAVEA FLUTTER (IRE) 6 b.g. Mustameet (USA) – Secret Flutter (IRE) (Entrepreneur) [2017/18 h20.5d^6 h15.9s h19s c15.9s^4 c19.2s* c19.9s^2 c19.2s* Mar 26] third foal: half-brother to a winning pointer in Catcher In The Rye: dam (h89) 2m hurdle winner: in frame in Irish points: modest form over hurdles: fairly useful form over fences: won handicaps at Market Rasen in February and March: stays 21f: acts on soft going: has worn hood: often travels strongly: open to further improvement. *Dan Skelton*   **c124 p**
h93

MUSTMEETALADY (IRE) 8 b.g. Mustameet (USA) – Ladymcgrath (IRE) (Jamesmead) [2017/18 c129, h–: c25g c22.5s c24.2d^{ur} c24d* c24s Jan 27] good-topped gelding: winning hurdler: fairly useful handicap chaser: won at Doncaster in December: stays 3½m: acts on soft going: wears cheekpieces: usually races towards rear. *Jonjo O'Neill*   **c129**
h–

MUTAMAYEL (IRE) 4 b.g. Mawatheeq (USA) – Musharakaat (IRE) (Iffraaj) [2017/18 ab16.3g Apr 15] no show in bumper. *John Norton*   **b–**

MUTAWAASEL 6 b.g. Teofilo (IRE) – Muwakleh (Machiavellian (USA)) [2017/18 b16.8g^3 h16.8g h16s^5 h16s Dec 27] sturdy gelding: modest form in bumpers: similar form over hurdles: best effort when fifth in novice at Wetherby in November. *Sue Smith*   **h86**
b80

MUTHABIR (IRE) 8 b.g. Nayef (USA) – Northern Melody (IRE) (Singspiel (IRE)) [2017/18 h112: h23.3g^4 h23.3d^4 h21.2g^3 h24.5d* h24.4s h19.8s^5 h23.8d^4 Apr 24] sturdy gelding: fairly useful handicap hurdler: won at Kempton in November: stays 3m: acts on heavy going: tried in cheekpieces. *Richard Phillips*   **h116**

MUTOONDRESDASHORSE 4 ch.g. Harbour Watch (IRE) – Mutoon (IRE) (Erhaab (USA)) [2017/18 h15.8g^6 h15.3d Apr 22] fairly useful on Flat, stays 7f: no form over hurdles. *Nigel Hawke*   **h–**

MUWALLA 11 b.g. Bahri (USA) – Easy Sunshine (IRE) (Sadler's Wells (USA)) [2017/18 c95§, h–: c16.4g* c17.3d^5 h16.2m^6 c15.7g^{ur} c16g^2 c20.1m^2 c17.2g^2 c16d^2 c16d^3 c17.2g^2 c19.3g^3 c17.1g^5 c19.3d^5 c15.2d^5 h22.7g c15.8m^2 c20.1g^2 c15.8g^3 Nov 30] sturdy, good-bodied gelding: modest hurdler at best, shows no form in 2017/18: fair handicap chaser: won at Sedgefield in May and Market Rasen in July: stays 2½m: acts on soft and good to firm going: has worn cheekpieces: wears tongue tie: temperamental. *Lisa Harrison*   **c106 §**
h– §

MY ANCHOR 7 b.g. Mount Nelson – War Shanty (Warrshan (USA)) [2017/18 c–, h83: h19.6d Apr 21] sturdy gelding: maiden hurdler: pulled up only start over fences: stays 21f: acts on good to soft going: has worn tongue tie: usually races towards rear. *Anthony Day*   **c–**
h–

MYB

MY BETTY (IRE) 10 b.m. Definite Article – Banusal (IRE) (Lord Americo) [2017/18 h17.5g³ h16gF h16.4g³ h24.8g⁶ h16s h16s⁶ h16d⁵ h19.9g Nov 2] fair handicap hurdler: winning chaser: stays 2½m: acts on good to firm and good to soft going: tried in tongue tie: usually races close up. *Peter Croke, Ireland*   c–
h104

MY BOY JAMES (IRE) 6 br.g. Getaway (GER) – Parkality (IRE) (Good Thyne (USA)) [2017/18 h111, b84: h16s⁴ h16s⁶ Jan 13] lengthy gelding: fair maiden hurdler: raced around 2m: acts on soft going. *Laura Mongan*   h103

MYBOYSAM 4 b.g. Delegator – Fantastisch (lRE) (Fantastic Light (USA)) [2017/18 b13.7g² b13.7s Jan 26] smallish gelding: third foal: dam (h102), 17f hurdle winner (1m winner on Flat), half-sister to useful hurdler/chaser (stayed 2½m) Manyriverstocross: fair form in bumpers. *Alan King*   b87

MY BROTHER SYLVEST 12 b.g. Bach (IRE) – Senna da Silva (Prince of Birds (USA)) [2017/18 c–§, h109§: h15.7gᵖᵘ h20gᵖᵘ Jun 14] sturdy gelding: useful hurdler at best, no form in 2017/18: winning chaser: stays 2¾m: acts on firm and soft going: often in headgear: has worn tongue tie: usually leads: unreliable. *Brian Barr*   c– §
h– §

MY BROWN EYED GIRL 5 b.m. Ferrule (IRE) – Chalosse (Doyoun) [2017/18 h–: h23.3sᵖᵘ h23.8gᵖᵘ h24.1sᵖᵘ h19.9v⁵ h19.7v³ h21.3v³ Mar 20] small, leggy mare: poor maiden hurdler: has worn headgear, including in 2017/18: wears tongue tie. *Susan Corbett*   h68

MY CHARITY (IRE) 7 b.g. King's Theatre (IRE) – Benefit Ball (IRE) (Beneficial) [2017/18 b–: b16.7g⁵ h20g² h20.8d³ h20.3s h21g h22d² Apr 22] tall gelding: fair form in bumpers: fairly useful form over hurdles: second in maiden at Worcester in October: stays 2¾m. *Graeme McPherson*   h116
b86

MY COUSIN RACHEL (IRE) 7 br.m. Presenting – Countess Camilla (Bob's Return (IRE)) [2017/18 h96, b–: h20gᵖᵘ May 26] well-made mare: modest hurdler, excuses sole outing in 2017/18: unproven beyond 2m: acts on good to soft going: in cheekpieces last 2 starts: wears tongue tie: signs of temperament. *Kim Bailey*   h–

MY DANCE 6 b.m. Kayf Tara – My Petra (Midnight Legend) [2017/18 b16.3d⁴ b16d h19.2v⁴ h17.7v* h20.5v* Jan 29] first foal: dam (c142/h134), 2m-19f hurdle/chase winner (also 11.6f winner on Flat), sister to fairly useful hurdler/useful chaser (2½m-3m winner) Midnight Appeal: point winner: modest form in bumpers: fair form over hurdles: won mares maiden at Fontwell and novice at Plumpton in January: likely to stay beyond 2½m: sometimes in tongue tie: front runner: open to further improvement. *Anthony Honeyball*   h114 p
b78

MY DIAMOND (IRE) 7 b.g. Brian Boru – Our Idol (IRE) (Mandalus) [2017/18 h–: h23.9gᵖᵘ h19v³ c20.3vᵖᵘ c21.7mᵘʳ Apr 25] poor maiden hurdler: no form over fences: has worn headgear, including in 2017/18: often races prominently. *Laura Young*   c–
h66

MYDOR (FR) 8 ch.g. Stormy River (FR) – Fabulousday (USA) (Diesis) [2017/18 c108, h129: h24.1v Feb 3] lengthy gelding: useful hurdler at best, well beaten sole outing in 2017/18: maiden chaser: stays 3m: acts on heavy going: wears headgear: has worn tongue tie: usually races towards rear. *Kenneth Slack*   c–
h–

MY ESCAPADE (IRE) 7 ch.m. Tamayuz – Highly Respected (IRE) (High Estate) [2017/18 c–, h90: h20.2s³ Apr 27] modest maiden hurdler: once-raced chaser: stays 2½m: acts on soft and good to firm going. *Simon Waugh*   c–
h85

MY HOMETOWN (IRE) 8 b.g. Presenting – Amathea (FR) (Exit To Nowhere (USA)) [2017/18 c19dF c22.7g⁵ c24vᵖᵘ c20s⁵ c20s c24s⁴ c30.2d⁶ c24v c33.5dF c24sᵘʳ Apr 28] rangy gelding: brother to fair 21f chase winner Painted Lady and half-brother to 3 winners, including fair/ungenuine hurdler/chaser Insignia (19f-2¾m winner, by Royal Applause): dam French 1m winner: point winner: won only start over hurdles in 2014/15: fairly useful maiden chaser: stays 3m: best form on soft/heavy going: tried in tongue tie: front runner. *Enda Bolger, Ireland*   c120
h–

MY IDEA 12 b.g. Golan (IRE) – Ghana (GER) (Bigstone (IRE)) [2017/18 c100, h–: c20.1g⁶ c20.1g⁴ c20.1g⁵ c15.6g⁵ c15.6d* c15.6v³ c19.3d⁴ c15.6v⁶ c15.8m c19.2dᵖᵘ Nov 24] rather leggy gelding: winning chaser: poor handicap chaser: won at Hexham in September: stays 25f: acts on heavy going: usually in cheekpieces: wears tongue tie. *Maurice Barnes*   c84
h–

MY JAMAICAN GUY (IRE) 5 b.g. Duke of Marmalade (IRE) – Mustique Dream (Don't Forget Me) [2017/18 h15.6m h20.6s Dec 23] no form in Flat maiden/novice hurdles. *Iain Jardine*   h–

MY LAD PERCY 10 b.g. Central Park (IRE) – Only Millie (Prince Daniel (USA)) [2017/18 h20s⁵ Nov 14] lengthy gelding: fair handicap hurdler, shaped as if retaining ability after long absence sole outing in 2017/18: maiden chaser (often let down by jumping): stays 25f: acts on good to firm and good to soft going: often wears cheekpieces. *Martin Keighley* — c– x h96

MY LADY GREY 4 gr.f. Presenting – Wassailing Queen (Generous (IRE)) [2017/18 b15.7s⁶ b16.7s⁴ b15.7g³ Apr 20] £38,000 3-y-o: first foal: dam (h101), bumper winner, half-sister to useful hurdler/smart chaser (stayed 3¼m) Bob Bob Bobbin out of very smart hurdler/smart chaser (stayed 3m) Absalom's Lady: fair form in bumpers. *Colin Tizzard* — b85

MY LIEGE (IRE) 7 b.g. Marienbard (IRE) – Smashing Leader (IRE) (Supreme Leader) [2017/18 h16.7v⁵ h25s⁵ h19.9v³ Apr 7] bumper winner: fair form over hurdles: best effort when third in maiden at Uttoxeter in April. *Evan Williams* — h99

MY LITTLE CRACKER (IRE) 8 b.m. Scorpion (IRE) – Cailin Gruaig Dubh (IRE) (Danehill Dancer (IRE)) [2017/18 c80, h115: c16gpu h19.3s⁴ Oct 19] fairly useful handicap hurdler, below form final outing in 2017/18: little form in chases: stays 19f: acts on heavy going: wears cheekpieces: front runner/races prominently. *Iain Jardine* — c– h83

MY LORD 10 br.g. Ishiguru (USA) – Lady Smith (Greensmith) [2017/18 h15.9m h20.5d⁶ h17.7s⁴ Nov 20] fair hurdler at best, no form in 2017/18: has worn headgear. *Michelle Bryant* — h–

MY MO (FR) 6 b.g. Silver Frost (IRE) – Anna Ivanovna (FR) (Fasliyev (USA)) [2017/18 h112: h20.2g⁶ c19.4g Aug 3] fair hurdler, well held on return: well beaten in novice handicap on chasing debut: stays 2½m: acts on good to firm going: wears cheekpieces: usually races close up. *David Dennis* — c– h–

MY NOBLE FRIEND 7 b.g. Overbury (IRE) – Karinga Princess (Karinga Bay) [2017/18 b15.8mF May 14] in hood, tailed off when fatally injured in bumper. *Ken Wingrove* — b–

MY NOSY ROSY 10 b.m. Aflfora (IRE) – Quiz Night (Kayf Tara) [2017/18 c19.9m⁵ May 23] point winner: winning hurdler: modest chaser at best, well held after long absence sole outing in 2017/18: stayed 21f: acted on good to firm and heavy going: wore headgear/tongue tie: dead. *Ben Case* — c– h–

MY OLD GOLD (IRE) 8 b.m. Gold Well – Tenbo (IRE) (Sexton Blake) [2017/18 h16v³ h20.6v² h21.4v² h25s⁴ h26.6s² Apr 26] seventh foal: closely related to fair chaser My Old Piano (23f winner, by Dr Massini): dam, well beaten in bumpers, half-sister to useful hurdler (winner up to 3m) Treasure Again: point winner: fairly useful form over hurdles: won handicap at Carlisle in April: stays 27f: raced only on soft/heavy going: usually travels strongly. *Nicky Richards* — h118

MYPLACEATMIDNIGHT 6 b.g. Midnight Legend – Zahra's Place (Zaha (CAN)) [2017/18 b99: b16g⁴ b16.7v³ Apr 11] fairly useful form in bumpers. *Neil King* — b96

MY RENAISSANCE 8 b.g. Medicean – Lebenstanz (Singspiel (IRE)) [2017/18 h68p: h17.2d* h17.2g⁴ h16.7g⁶ h17.2s² c17.4g⁴ c16.4g* ab16.3g Mar 3] poor handicap hurdler: won at Cartmel in May: similar form over fences: won novice handicap at Sedgefield in September: unproven beyond 17f: acts on good to soft going: has worn headgear, including in 2017/18: has worn tongue tie: front runner/races prominently. *Sam England* — c82 h76

MYROUNDORURS (IRE) 8 b.g. Arakan (USA) – Six Bob (IRE) (Anshan) [2017/18 c109, h–: c15.7v³ Feb 5] maiden chaser: unproven beyond 2m: acts on good to firm going: wears hood: front runner. *Robin Dickin* — c103 h–

MYSTEREE (IRE) 10 b.g. Gold Well – Hillside Native (IRE) (Be My Native (USA)) [2017/18 c136, h–: c29.5vpu c28.4v³ Feb 17] angular gelding: winning hurdler: useful chaser at best, no form in 2017/18: stays 33f: acts on heavy going: usually races towards rear. *Michael Scudamore* — c– h–

MYSTICAL CLOUDS (IRE) 5 gr.g. Cloudings (IRE) – Silent Valley (Forzando) [2017/18 b16g ab16g⁴ h19.4s³ h21d³ Apr 26] €26,000 3-y-o: useful-looking gelding: closely related to useful hurdler/chaser Rum And Butter (19f/2½m winner, by Milan) and half-brother to useful hurdler/fairly useful chaser Red Not Blue (2½m-3m winner, by Blueprint): dam (h86), unreliable 2m hurdle winner, also 1¼m winner on Flat: fair form in bumpers: fairly useful form over hurdles: third in novice at Doncaster and maiden at Warwick. *Alan King* — h119 b88

MYSTICAL KNIGHT 9 b.g. Kayf Tara – Dark Diva (Royal Fountain) [2017/18 c135, h–: c24.1v³ c23.8spu c23.8vpu c22.4s⁴ Mar 23] well-made gelding: winning hurdler: fairly useful handicap chaser nowadays: stays 25f: acts on heavy going: wears tongue tie: often races towards rear. *Rebecca Curtis* — c123 h–

MYS

MYSTIC SKY 7 b.m. Midnight Legend – Kentucky Sky (Cloudings (IRE)) [2017/18 h117: h20m[4] h20.3d[2] h15.7g* h16.7g[4] h19.8s Apr 28] lengthy mare: has had breathing operation: fairly useful handicap hurdler: won mares event at Southwell in June: stays 2½m: acts on good to soft going: wears blinkers: often races towards rear. *Lucy Wadham* — **h121**

MYSTIC THEATRE (IRE) 7 b.m. King's Theatre (IRE) – Mystic Cherry (IRE) (Alderbrook) [2017/18 b16m* h19.8g* h19.5g* h16.7g* h20v* h16s[F] Nov 3] €31,000 3-y-o: fifth foal: sister to useful hurdler Morello Royale (21f-3m winner) and closely related to a winning pointer by Brian Boru: dam unraced: point winner: fairly useful form in bumpers: won at Tipperary in May: useful form over hurdles: won mares maiden at Kilbeggan in July, mares novice at same course and mares event at Bellewstown (by 16 lengths from Jaime Sommers) in August, and listed mares event at Gowran (by 10 lengths from Polar Present) in September: stays 2½m: acts on heavy going: front runner, usually travels strongly: remains with potential. *W. P. Mullins, Ireland* — **h135 p / b103**

MYSTIFIABLE 10 gr.g. Kayf Tara – Royal Keel (Long Leave) [2017/18 c132, h–: c19.4d[4] c21.1v[4] c16.4s[3] c21.1s Apr 13] sturdy gelding: winning hurdler: fairly useful handicap chaser: stays 2¾m: acts on soft going: tried in hood: wears tongue tie: usually races prominently. *Fergal O'Brien* — **c121 / h–**

MY STORY (IRE) 6 b.g. Court Cave (IRE) – Holloden (IRE) (Shantou (USA)) [2017/18 b77p: b16.8m[5] May 9] Irish point winner: modest form in bumpers. *Neil Mulholland* — **b80**

MY STROPPY POPPY 9 b.m. Multiplex – Aspen Ridge (IRE) (Namid) [2017/18 h–: h15.7g[pu] Jun 13] little form, including on Flat: wears hood: in tongue tie last 2 starts. *David Dennis* — **h–**

MY TENT OR YOURS (IRE) 11 b.g. Desert Prince (IRE) – Spartan Girl (IRE) (Ela-Mana-Mou) [2017/18 h163: h16.8s* h20s[4] Apr 12] strong, rangy gelding: top-class hurdler at best: won International Hurdle at Cheltenham (by 1¼ lengths from The New One) in December: keen sort, best around 2m: acts on soft and good to firm going: wears hood. *Nicky Henderson* — **h159**

MYTHICAL LEGEND 7 ch.m. Midnight Legend – Materiality (Karinga Bay) [2017/18 h91: h19.2v[3] h20.7s h20.7g[6] Apr 24] workmanlike mare: modest form over hurdles: should stay 2½m+. *Emma Lavelle* — **h97**

MYTHICAL PRINCE (IRE) 6 b.g. Beneficial – Conker Nails (IRE) (Carroll House) [2017/18 b16.2g[2] b16g[2] Jul 10] €30,000 3-y-o: second foal: dam (c95/h97), 2m/2¼m hurdle/chase winner, half-sister to fairly useful hurdler (2m winner) Woodpole Academy (by Beneficial): failed to complete in points: fairly useful form when second in bumpers. *Ronald O'Leary, Ireland* — **b95**

Unibet International Hurdle, Cheltenham—
a first win in nearly four years for My Tent Or Yours (hoops), in receipt of weight from three-times International winner The New One (centre) and Melon (right)

NAN

MY TURGEON (FR) 5 gr.g. Turgeon (USA) – My Belle (FR) (Smadoun (FR)) [2017/18 b17v⁴ Mar 8] third foal: dam, French 17f/2¼m chase winner, half-sister to smart hurdler/useful chaser (stays 21f) Le Rocher: 2/1, fourth in bumper at Carlisle (22 lengths behind Glentrool): clearly thought capable of better. *Ben Pauling* **b66 p**

MY VALENTINO (IRE) 5 ch.g. Duke of Marmalade (IRE) – Nadwah (USA) (Shadeed (USA)) [2017/18 h–: h20.2g h17.2s Jul 24] modest maiden on Flat: no form over hurdles: has worn cheekpieces, including in 2017/18. *Dianne Sayer* **h–**

MZUZU (IRE) 6 b.g. Oscar (IRE) – Tempest Hill (IRE) (Presenting) [2017/18 b16v³ h20.3g Apr 18] £62,000 5-y-o: first foal: dam unraced: winning pointer: well-held third in bumper: 100/1, shaped well when eighth in novice at Cheltenham (14¼ lengths behind Diese des Bieffes) on hurdling debut: should improve. *Tom George* **h117 p** **b66**

N

NAASIK 5 b.g. Poet's Voice – Shemriyna (IRE) (King of Kings (IRE)) [2017/18 b66: b16.8g³ b16.7g³ h16.8s h16.6s h15.7v⁵ h21.2g Apr 23] modest form in bumpers: poor form over hurdles. *John Norton* **h70** **b81**

NABATEAN (IRE) 7 b.g. Rock of Gibraltar (IRE) – Landinium (ITY) (Lando (GER)) [2017/18 h20.5dᵖᵘ Dec 1] lengthy gelding: smart on Flat, stays 1¾m: pulled up in novice hurdle after 2½-year absence. *Shaun Lycett* **h–**

NABHAN 6 b.g. Youmzain (IRE) – Danidh Dubai (IRE) (Noverre (USA)) [2017/18 h–: h15.8m³ h18.5g³ h16.7d h15.3s⁵ h19.6g⁶ h16s Apr 27] angular gelding: fair handicap hurdler: should stay 2½m: acts on heavy going: often in cheekpieces/tongue tie. *Bernard Llewellyn* **h111**

NACHI FALLS 5 ch.g. New Approach (IRE) – Lakuta (IRE) (Pivotal) [2017/18 h117: c19.2g³ c23g* c22.6m⁴ c24g² h23.9gᵖᵘ Oct 28] compact gelding: fairly useful hurdler: similar form over fences: won maiden at Worcester in August: stays 3m: acts on good to soft going: wears tongue tie. *Nigel Hawke* **c119** **h–**

NAGAMAAT (IRE) 4 b.f. Raven's Pass (USA) – Shawka (Oasis Dream) [2017/18 h15.8gᵖᵘ Nov 16] last all 4 starts on Flat: pulled up in juvenile on hurdling debut. *Nikki Evans* **h–**

NAILER (IRE) 8 b.g. Coroner (IRE) – Celtic Serenade (IRE) (Yashgan) [2017/18 h–, b–: h17.2d⁴ h17.2d⁴ h19.9g³ h16.4s Dec 23] fair form over hurdles: best effort at 17f: acts on good to soft going: tried in hood: usually tongue tied. *Tristan Davidson* **h101**

NAKADAM (FR) 8 b.g. Nickname (FR) – Cadoudame (FR) (Cadoudal (FR)) [2017/18 c108, h–: c21.5v² c24.3v² c24.1v³ Dec 22] maiden hurdler: fair handicap chaser: stays 31f, at least as effective over much shorter: acts on heavy going: wears cheekpieces/tongue tie: usually races towards rear, often travels strongly: consistent. *R. Mike Smith* **c108** **h–**

NALIM (IRE) 12 b.g. Milan – Hati Roy (IRE) (Lafontaine (USA)) [2017/18 c24.2g Jun 3] maiden hurdler: modest chaser at best, well held only start in 2017/18: should stay beyond 3¼m: acts on heavy going: wears headgear: temperamental. *Harriet Bethell* **c– §** **h– §**

NALINKA DE LA MARE (FR) 5 gr.m. Martaline – Fidji de La Mare (FR) (Tel Quel (FR)) [2017/18 b15.8m⁴ b17d Oct 29] €35,000 3-y-o, resold £50,000 3-y-o: half-sister to several winners in France, including chaser Springa de La Mare (17f-25f winner, by Kaldounevees): dam unraced: modest form in bumpers. *Gary Moore* **b78**

NAMPARAROO 9 b.m. Kayf Tara – Silk Stockings (FR) (Trempolino (USA)) [2017/18 h16d⁵ h15.7g² h15.7g² h19.9d² Jul 28] modest form over hurdles. *David Bridgwater* **h98**

NANACAULSITESKER (IRE) 6 b.m. Echo of Light – Annieirwin (IRE) (Perugino (USA)) [2017/18 h16.4d h16.5d h17d Mar 31] no form on Flat: poor maiden hurdler: left John G. Carr after second start: raced around 2m: often in hood: often races towards rear. *Alan Berry* **h65**

NANDO (GER) 6 b.g. Dai Jin – Natalis (GER) (Law Society (USA)) [2017/18 b79p: b16.2m⁵ h16v² h16v⁵ h20.2s⁵ Apr 25] modest form in bumpers: fair form over hurdles: best effort when second in maiden at Ayr in January: tried in hood. *Nicky Richards* **h112** **b81**

NANNY MAKFI (IRE) 5 b.m. Makfi – Pan Galactic (USA) (Lear Fan (USA)) [2017/18 h15.3v h18.5v² Apr 8] half-sister to 3 winners, including fairly useful hurdler/chaser Megaton (17f-3m winner, by Nashwan) and fairly useful hurdler Engrossing (2m winner, by Tiger Hill): modest maiden on Flat, stays 1½m: poor form over hurdles: wears tongue tie. *Brian Barr* **h68**

565

NAN

NANSAROY 8 br.g. Indian River (FR) – Jurado Park (IRE) (Jurado (USA)) [2017/18 c123, h–: c21.3m⁴ c23.6vᵘʳ c19.4v c25.6s⁶ c20.9s³ c19.4v⁴ c18.2sᶠ Mar 26] angular gelding: winning hurdler: fairly useful maiden chaser, largely below form in 2017/18: stays 3m: best form on soft/heavy going: has worn headgear, including in 2017/18: often races towards rear. *Evan Williams*   **c118 d** / **h–**

NARANJA 6 ch.m. Black Sam Bellamy (IRE) – Full of Fruit (FR) (Apple Tree (FR)) [2017/18 h102, b95: h20.5d³ h19.5s* h19.8v⁶ h17.7v³ h24.3g* Apr 20] lengthy mare: bumper winner: fairly useful hurdler: won mares maiden at Lingfield in November, and mares handicaps at Chepstow in January and Ayr in April: stays 3m: acts on heavy going: tried in tongue tie: usually races close up. *Jamie Snowden*   **h119**

NATHANS PRIDE (IRE) 10 ch.g. Definite Article – Tricias Pride (IRE) (Broken Hearted) [2017/18 c–, h125: h20g⁴ h20g h21.1g c19.9g* h19.4g² Dec 18] workmanlike gelding: fairly useful handicap hurdler: similar form over fences: won novice handicap at Musselburgh in November: stays 2½m: acts on good to firm going: in tongue tie last 5 starts. *Tim Vaughan*   **c123** / **h119**

NATIVE GAMUT (IRE) 8 b.g. Gamut (IRE) – Gonearethedays (IRE) (Be My Native (USA)) [2017/18 c24s³ c15.9v³ c24.2dᵖᵘ Apr 7] off mark in points at seventh attempt: modest form in chases. *Alastair Ralph*   **c88**

NATIVE OPTIMIST (IRE) 11 b.g. Broadway Flyer (USA) – Native Orchid (IRE) (Be My Native (USA)) [2017/18 h–: h23.3g h20.1g⁴ h23.9g* h25.4s h23.3d h23.9d² h23.3v* h24.3v h24.6s² h25.8v h25dᵖᵘ h26.6s Apr 26] angular gelding: fair handicap hurdler: won at Perth in July and Hexham in October: stays 25f: acts on heavy going: tried in tongue tie: usually races towards rear: temperamental. *Sheena Walton*   **h108 §**

NATIVE RIVER (IRE) 8 ch.g. Indian River (FR) – Native Mo (IRE) (Be My Native (USA)) [2017/18 c166, h153: c23.4s* c26.3v* Mar 16]   **c172** / **h–**

Which was the greatest Cheltenham Gold Cup? The biography of five-times winner Golden Miller by Gregory Blaxland, first published in 1972, has a chapter entitled *The greatest Gold Cup* which recounts the legendary battle between Golden Miller and Thomond II in 1935, the year after Golden Miller had completed the Gold Cup/Grand National double (he had won all his races since). The 1935 Gold Cup was moved to the last day of the National Hunt meeting as the grand climax and was widely expected to provide a comfortable fourth win in the race for Golden Miller until the very late decision to run Thomond (after his American owner's intended runner was reportedly injured). Thomond had beaten Golden Miller over two and a half miles at Kempton's Christmas meeting fifteen months before their meeting in the 1935 Gold Cup and had lost just once since (when third to Golden Miller in the Grand National under 12-4). The prospect of the 'clash of the giants' drew a crowd of 16,367, far exceeding the expectations of the Cheltenham management (the situation on the roads around Cheltenham was chaotic and there was 'a fearsome scrimmage' at Paddington station for places on the special trains from London, while race cards were sold out long before the first race, despite twice the normal number being printed). The Gold Cup programme opened with a selling chase and a selling hurdle before the Gold Cup, and motorists were still trying to park and the last of the pedestrians making their way from the station when the second race was run. The Gold Cup had a field of five in which Golden Miller was sent off at 2/1-on and Thomond at 5/2, with 100/7 bar. Southern Hero led the field out on to the second circuit 'as if they were heading for home in a two-mile chase' and Golden Miller and Thomond moved through at the third from home and had the race between them from that point, two 'incredible battlers hurling themselves [over the last two fences], still in perfect unison.' For thirty yards or so after the final fence, Thomond's head was in front but Golden Miller got up to win by three quarters of a length (beating Easter Hero's course record by 27 seconds). Pandemonium broke out as racegoers jockeyed for positions to obtain a close-up view of the pair as they returned.

Among those at Cheltenham on hand to congratulate Golden Miller's connections was The Honourable George Lambton, one of the greatest trainers in the era that bridged the nineteenth and twentieth centuries (his long partnership with the 16th and 17th Earls of Derby was one of the most significant in the history of Flat racing, and he also purchased the yearlings on which the then-Aga Khan's successful racing empire was founded). Lambton spoke to the trainers of both Golden Miller and Thomond after the Gold Cup and told them that he had witnessed no finer race. Lambton wrote racing's most famous memoir *Men and Horses I Have Known* which is quoted in the biography of Golden Miller in the context of a comment made to Lambton by Fred Archer after Ormonde had beaten Minting by two lengths in the 1886 Two Thousand Guineas, the pair having drawn right away from their rivals until Minting gave best halfway up the final hill. It had been Archer's contention that 'when you get two smashing good horses trying to cut each other down over the Rowley Mile the pressure is so great that one or the other is sure to crack; it may be just a toss up which gives way first, but the one who does will have no struggle left.' In *Men and Horses I Have Known*, George Lambton also recalled the 'race of the century' between Ard Patrick and Sceptre in the 1903 Eclipse, which represented his perfect race—'About the best thing in racing is when two good horses single themselves out from the rest of the field and have a long drawn-out struggle.'

The Cheltenham Gold Cup has produced such occasions in its long history, including, for example, Arkle's victory over an outstanding reigning champion in Mill House in the 1964 edition. There were only four runners but the race didn't disappoint with Mill House, as expected, attempting to nullify Arkle's turn of foot by forcing the pace. Mill House stretched into a three-length lead from the start and, with half a mile to go, showed no sign of stopping. By the second last, however, Arkle was upsides, with both horses still full of running. Arkle was just in front over the last and went on to win by five lengths, Mill House's effort to renew his challenge proving to no avail. Arkle's amazing career did much to put National Hunt racing on a par with the Flat in popularity, something which could also be said over two decades later of Desert Orchid whose gritty victory in the 1989 Gold Cup was voted the greatest race of all time in a *Racing Post* poll in 2005. Hours of rain turned the going heavy—conditions were atrocious—and, with snow falling in the morning, the Gold Cup-day programme was given the go-ahead only after the course passed a midday inspection. The race was marred by the fatal fall of Ten Plus who

1935 Cheltenham Gold Cup—
Golden Miller and Thomond II (right) battle it out in front of a then-record crowd

was in the lead, still travelling strongly, when he came down three out. The 25/1-shot Yahoo looked all over the winner after taking over approaching the second last where Desert Orchid gave the impression of having little left; but Desert Orchid refused to give up and he was back almost upsides Yahoo crossing the last before forging ahead halfway up the run-in to win by a length and a half.

The four Gold Cups between 2008 and 2011 provided another glorious spell in the history of steeplechasing's most important championship. Those races featured four meetings between stablemates Kauto Star and Denman, neither any longer with us because Denman had to be put down in June 2018 after his health worsened. The popularity of the pair was amplified by their rivalry and by their different racing styles, Denman's relentless galloping instrumental in a never-to-be-forgotten triumph in the 2008 Gold Cup over Kauto Star, the versatile chaser with speed who was the reigning champion. Denman was an exhilarating sight that day, out in front jumping superbly, and the game was up for Kauto Star some way out. The much-hyped pulsating head-to-head encounter between Kauto Star and Denman never really came to fruition, the biggest disappointment in that regard being the 2010 Gold Cup, billed as 'The Decider' between the two Gold Cup winners, after Kauto Star had won his second Gold Cup by thirteen lengths from Denman in 2009. The 2010 Gold Cup was supported by a huge public relations campaign, but the race saw Imperial Commander win from Denman after Kauto Star had fallen. The final meeting of Denman and Kauto Star in the 2011 Gold Cup did look for two hundred yards, as the pair threatened to pull away rounding the home bend, as if it might deliver the head-to-head encounter that had been hoped for in previous years (Long Run ran them down in the home straight, Denman finishing second in the race for the third time and taking his match score with third-placed Kauto Star to three-one).

The Kauto Star/Denman era provided ample evidence of the truism that great occasions don't always generate the races that might be anticipated. Close, compelling encounters can't be produced to order. That said, there were those who firmly predicted a nip-and-tuck Gold Cup duel in the latest season between two of the market leaders, the King George VI Chase winner Might Bite and the previous year's Gold Cup third Native River, for whom the very testing conditions provided the sort of stamina test he relishes. Back in 2010, Racing for Change (now renamed Great British Racing) hired a 'battle bus' to tour the country, and arranged a photo-shoot with heavy weight boxing champion David Haye, as part of the promotion for *Kauto Star v Denman: The Decider* which also involved the distribution of rosettes and scarves in the racing colours carried by the pair. It was rare to see so many racing fans adopting such obvious partisanship and, perhaps because the clash was hyped so much beforehand, it produced feelings of let-down and disappointment when neither group of supporters had a winner to cheer. 'Two-horse races' have a habit of failing to live up to their billing anyway, though it is perhaps stretching things to say that the latest Gold Cup was viewed beforehand by everyone as a head-to-head between Might Bite and Native River. The pair started at 4/1 and 5/1 respectively, separated in the betting market by the main Irish-trained challenger Our Duke, a stablemate of the previous year's winner Sizing John who couldn't defend his title because of injury. Native River had made a smooth winning comeback in the Denman Chase at Newbury in February after coming back late into training because of jarring in the previous year's Gold Cup which caused Native River some ligament trouble.

Native River shaped as if he was as good as ever at Newbury and, when Sizing John defected from the Gold Cup, Native River was left as the main challenger on form to Might Bite. Our Duke, winner of the Irish Grand National by fourteen lengths as a novice, looked on the up again, after suffering a back problem, when winning the Red Mills Chase at Gowran (the runner-up Presenting Percy had made that form look all the better when winning the RSA Chase earlier in the meeting). Ireland supplied nine of the fifteen who went to post for the third and last Timico-sponsored Cheltenham Gold Cup (there were three late withdrawals on account of the worsening going), the challenge from across the water also including Killultagh Vic who had looked set to win the Irish Gold Cup when departing at the final fence at Leopardstown. Edwulf, the beneficiary of Killultagh Vic's misfortune,

Betfair Denman Chase, Newbury—a winning reappearance for Native River, who looks every bit as good as ever in beating the grey Cloudy Dream easily

was also in the Cheltenham Gold Cup line-up, as was Road To Respect, winner of the Leopardstown Christmas Chase (from Balko des Flos who had gone on to win the Ryanair Chase twenty-four hours before the Gold Cup). Djakadam was back for a fourth crack at the race while Total Recall was out to emulate Mandarin, Arkle, Bregawn, Denman and Bobs Worth by winning the Hennessy (now the Ladbrokes Trophy) and the Gold Cup in the same season. Of the British-trained Gold Cup runners backing up Might Bite and Native River, only the Cotswold Chase winner Definitly Red—a rare northern challenger for the blue riband nowadays—started at shorter than 25/1.

With the prevailing heavy going ensuring that the emphasis was going to be on stamina, Native River's jockey Richard Johnson set out to force the pace, and make full use of his mount's fast and accurate jumping. Might Bite kept tabs on Native River from early on, also jumping splendidly in the main, and the pair gradually piled the pressure on their rivals from the water jump on the final circuit. They made the race almost entirely their own from a long way out, holding an advantage of five or six lengths at the final open ditch, six from home. Native River's bold jumping had continually taken the eye, but Might Bite was always poised just behind him and, as they swung into the home straight with two to jump, there was very little between them. Might Bite had his nose in front at the second last, looking to be travelling just the better, but Native River fought back under strong pressure and was back in front again jumping the final fence, although Might Bite's jockey still hadn't asked for everything from his mount. When push came to shove, however, Native River proved too strong, finding plenty up the steep climb to the finish and outstaying Might Bite who cracked with a hundred yards to go and was beaten four and a half lengths in the end (having 'no struggle left', to use Fred Archer's words quoted earlier).

The winning margin flattered Native River and was hardly fair to Might Bite who had looked the better horse for so much of the race (Might Bite's trainer pointed out that the worst of the ground was after the last, where the surface was

Timico Cheltenham Gold Cup Chase, Cheltenham—
Native River and Might Bite lead the way over the second in front of packed stands ...

chewed up and the fresh ground reserved for the Gold Cup ran out). Take nothing away, however, from Native River who took his golden chance under conditions that played very much to his four greatest strengths, stamina, tenacity, fine jumping and the ability to produce his best in very testing ground. What would have happened on good ground can only be guessed at, though Might Bite's trainer wasn't alone in thinking Might Bite would have won. Native River's winning time of 7m 2.6sec was testament to the gruelling underfoot conditions, which were reminiscent of some of the Gold Cups in the 'seventies and early-'eighties. Native River and Bobs Worth (7m 1.70sec in 2013) are the only Gold Cup winners to exceed seven minutes since Desert Orchard won in that notorious mud bath in 1989. Desert Orchid's winning time was 7m 17.84sec, and was the slowest since Ten Up's 7m 51.4sec in 1975.

L'Escargot's 8m 0.7sec in 1971 is the slowest time since the Gold Cup was switched from the Old Course to the New Course in 1967, after which the Gold Cup course remained more or less unaltered until the introduction of the four-day Festival in 2005. The line of the chase course on the New Course is now moved in seven yards on the Friday to provide fresh ground, in effect reducing the distance of Gold Cups run since 2004 by about eighty-four yards, equating to around six seconds. The drawn-out duel between Native River and Might Bite deserves to go down in history as an enthralling encounter that produced one of the finest sights in modern racing, as the pair stretched further clear of their field racing down the hill and turned for home together before fighting out a thrilling climax in the home straight. For the record, Irish-trained 33/1-shot Anibale Fly ran the race of his life to take third, staying on well from mid-division to finish only four lengths behind Might Bite, with Road To Respect, one of the few in the main bunch to look at any stage as if he might get involved in the battle up ahead, completing the frame a further four lengths adrift. Djakadam came fifth and Definitely Red, in trouble a long way out, sixth.

... still nothing between them two circuits later, though Native River (noseband) proves the stronger up the run-in

There were nine finishers, with Tea For Two, Edwulf and American bringing up the rear. Total Recall was running well when he departed at the third last, in sixth place and only just behind Anibale Fly at the time. Killultagh Vic and Our Duke were both let down by their jumping on the day.

Native River's triumph was the first in the Gold Cup for trainer Colin Tizzard whose stable did not enjoy the smoothest of runs with its potential Gold Cup horses in the latest season, Thistlecrack having to miss the race for the second successive year because of injury, while the veteran Cue Card, who like Thistlecrack is a King George VI Chase winner, eventually missed the Gold Cup in favour of the Ryanair Chase, in which he was pulled up. Native River provided Richard Johnson with his second Gold Cup, eighteen years after the success of Looks Like Trouble. Johnson broke the rules on Native River, using his whip above the permitted level, which resulted in his being suspended for seven days and being fined £6,550 (around a fifth of his prize money). 'He answered every call,' said Johnson of Native River. 'It is disappointing but I broke the rules. Hopefully it will take nothing away from him and his performance.' Johnson's excessive use of the whip on this occasion—one of six whip suspensions imposed at the Festival (five of them winning rides)—exposed the reality that the whip rules will continue to be broken because they put jockeys in a dilemma, one which is even greater in a big race like the Gold Cup, of having to choose between incurring a suspension (and sometimes a fine) or possibly losing a race.

Racing is about finding the best horses and the whip has always been very much part of the game. Used correctly and skilfully, the whip is not a welfare issue in racing but, when a jockey is found guilty of a whip offence in a big race, it is nearly always overplayed in media reports. Today's society is ultra-sensitive and such reports tend to give racing a bad name (until the last decade, racecourses did not routinely relay to the crowd the results of stewards inquiries into whip offences, but it would be impossible to keep such basic information from the race-going public nowadays). In truth, the current whip rules are not fair to jockeys, who are put in the cauldron of a big occasion, with so much at stake, but then expected, in the heat of battle at the end of the race, to behave as if they were at a vicarage tea party! The debate about the whip remains as heated as ever and, perhaps if the authorities were really serious about moving the subject down the agenda, they might consider the admittedly draconian solution of applying suspensions at big meetings, in extreme cases, to the *next* big meeting. If a jockey is banned for three days at the Cheltenham Festival, he misses the Grand National meeting. That would be a greater deterrent even than banning jockeys, in extreme cases, from riding the horse on whom the suspension has been occurred in its next race, an earlier solution suggested in these pages. The rules are the rules and racecourse stewards have shown time and again that they do not exercise discretion, even on the major occasions when racing is in the spotlight. In that situation, increasing the penalties for riding indiscretions and whip offences in big races is the only practical way to stop such offences and to counter the negative publicity that is often created by them.

Native River (IRE) (ch.g. 2010)
- Indian River (FR) (b 1994)
  - Cadoudal (br 1979)
    - Green Dancer
    - Come To Sea
  - The Fun (b 1979)
    - Funny Hobby
    - The Lark
- Native Mo (IRE) (b 1996)
  - Be My Native (br 1979)
    - Our Native
    - Witchy Woman
  - Milford Run (b 1985)
    - Deep Run
    - Belle of The West

The well-made Native River has had his pedigree examined in the last two editions of *Chasers & Hurdlers* and there is very little to add. He is by Indian River, a stallion bred and raced in France, and his dam has a traditional Irish jumping background. Native Mo never ran but has bred three winners, the others being the winning hurdler/useful chaser Orpheus Valley (by Beneficial) and the useful hurdler Mahler Ten (by Mahler). She was also represented on the racecourse in the latest season by One Night In Milan (by Milan) who ran three times without success in bumpers and a novice hurdle for Paul Nicholls and should do better in time. Native River's grandam Milford Run was a bumper winner (half-sister to the

Brocade Racing's "Native River"

very smart Minella Lad, third in the 1994 Stayers' Hurdle) and his great grandam Belle of The West was a useful chaser. Native River went through the sale-ring cheaply at Fairyhouse as a foal and found his way to the Tizzard stable and owners Brocade Racing after unseating his rider at the last in an Irish maiden point for Cork trainer Denis Ahern in March 2014 as a four-year-old. He reportedly changed hands privately for less than six figures, slipping under the radar of Ireland's biggest owners. It was a similar story with the Queen Mother Champion Chase winner Altior who was bought as a store for €60,000 from the Land Rover Sale. Along with French-bred Buveur d'Air, the Irish-breds Native River and Altior kept the Cheltenham Festival's three most valuable and prestigious races in Britain, some consolation for the 17-11 thrashing that Irish trainers gave their British counterparts at the meeting. Native River should be back to defend his crown in the next season when further clashes between him and Might Bite will be worth going a long way to see. A thorough stayer who is in his element forcing the pace—he goes really well for Richard Johnson—Native River will get the Grand National trip, though his owners are said to be reluctant to run him in that race, despite his looking a natural for it. The ground was good when he won the Hennessy (now the Ladbrokes Trophy) as a six-year-old, and when he was third in the 2017 Gold Cup, so he doesn't need the mud, although he handles testing conditions extremely well. He wears cheekpieces (he had a lazy streak when younger) but is thoroughly game and genuine. *Colin Tizzard*

NATIVE ROBIN (IRE) 8 br.g. Robin des Pres (FR) – Homebird (IRE) (Be My Native (USA)) [2017/18 c–, h–: c20d c17.5v⁴ c20v* c19.5v* c20.2s⁴ c19.9s⁵ h21.6s Apr 23] maiden hurdler: fair handicap chaser: won at Warwick in December and Fontwell in January: stays 2½m: acts on heavy going. *Jeremy Scott*   c114 h–

NATIVE SOLDIER (IRE) 4 b.g. Sepoy (AUS) – Electra Star (Shamardal (USA)) [2017/18 h16d Nov 10] fairly useful at best on Flat, stays 1¼m: tailed off in juvenile on hurdling debut. *John Flint*   h–

NATTER JACK CROAK (IRE) 6 b.g. Gold Well – Native Euro (IRE) (Be My Native (USA)) [2017/18 b75: h16d h23.1s² h23.6v⁴ h23.5d h20.7s⁴ Jan 26] workmanlike gelding: won Irish maiden point on debut: fair form over hurdles: left Rebecca Curtis after fourth start: stays 23f: acts on soft going. *Nigel Twiston-Davies* h105

NAUTICAL NITWIT (IRE) 9 b.g. Let The Lion Roar – Mrs Pugwash (IRE) (Un Desperado (FR)) [2017/18 h129: h22.1s³ h25.4d⁴ h23g³ h24.1d³ h24.7s⁶ h24d h24.4d² ab16g³ ab16.3g* h22.8v⁵ Mar 31] compact gelding: won jumpers bumper at Newcastle in March: useful handicap hurdler: second at Doncaster (½ length behind Gunfleet) in February: stays 25f: acts on good and good to firm going. *Philip Kirby* h130

NAUTICAL TWILIGHT 8 gr.m. Proclamation (IRE) – Anabranch (Kind of Hush) [2017/18 c104, h107: h16.7d⁶ h15.7s² h16.8v h16.8v⁵ Feb 22] lengthy mare: modest handicap hurdler: winning chaser: unproven beyond 17f: acts on heavy going: wears headgear: front runner/races prominently: untrustworthy. *Ruth Jefferson* c– §
h99 §

NAVAJO WAR DANCE 5 b.g. Makfi – Navajo Rainbow (Rainbow Quest (USA)) [2017/18 h15.8d h17.7v³ h16.3s h19.2v⁴ Feb 15] fairly useful on Flat, stays 10.5f: fair form over hurdles. *Ali Stronge* h106

NAYATI (FR) 4 b.g. Spirit One (FR) – Smadouce (FR) (Smadoun (FR)) [2017/18 h16.3v* h15.7v* h16.7s* h16.7s Feb 18] compact gelding: dam sister to smart hurdler/chaser (stays 21f) Theinval: 15f winner on Flat for D. Sourdeau de Beauregard: fairly useful form over hurdles: won juveniles at Newbury in December and Ascot in January. *Alan King* h119

NEACHELLS BRIDGE (IRE) 6 ch.g. Getaway (GER) – Strawberry Lane (IRE) (Moscow Society (USA)) [2017/18 b16.7g² b16.7s⁴ h19.4s⁵ h16.7s³ Mar 24] second foal: half-brother to a winning pointer by Westerner: dam, winning pointer, half-sister to winning hurdler/useful chaser (winner up to 2½m) Deans Road: fairly useful form when in frame in bumpers at Bangor: fair form over hurdles: better effort when fifth in novice at Doncaster in February: remains with potential. *Neil Mulholland* h108 p
b97

NEAREST THE PIN (IRE) 13 b.g. Court Cave (IRE) – Carnbelle (IRE) (Electric) [2017/18 c100§, h–: c20g c16.5g^pu Aug 1] lengthy gelding: winning hurdler: useful chaser at best, no form in 2017/18: stays 2½m: acts on soft and good to firm going: usually wears headgear/tongue tie: unreliable. *Oliver Greenall* c– §
h–

NEARLY NAMA'D (IRE) 10 b.g. Millenary – Coca's Well (IRE) (Religiously (USA)) [2017/18 c134, h–: c20.5g c16.7v⁴ c16.5s* c17s Feb 3] winning hurdler: useful handicap chaser: returned to best when won at Fairyhouse in December: best form up to 2½m: acts on good to firm and heavy going: has worn hood: in tongue tie last 2 starts. *Augustine Leahy, Ireland* c141
h–

NEARLY PERFECT 4 b.g. Malinas (GER) – The Lyme Volunteer (IRE) (Zaffaran (USA)) [2017/18 b16d Apr 26] €44,000 3-y-o, £100,000 4-y-o: useful-looking gelding: fifth foal: half-brother to useful hurdler Crucial Role (19f-3m winner, by Westerner): dam (c105/h108) 3m/3¼m hurdle/chase winner: runner-up in Irish point: 33/1, pulled hard when ninth in bumper at Warwick (6½ lengths behind Emitom). *Neil King* b85

NEAR TO TEARS (IRE) 8 br.m. Robin des Pres (FR) – Tears of Jade (IRE) (Presenting) [2017/18 h82: c20.1g² c22.5d^pu h23.9d³ Aug 2] poor maiden hurdler: poor form over fences: stayed 3m: acted on soft going: tried in tongue tie: dead. *Lucinda Russell* c83
h84

NEBUKA (IRE) 4 b.f. So You Think (NZ) – Nicea (GER) (Lando (GER)) [2017/18 b12.6s Dec 20] lengthy filly: second foal: half-sister to a Flat winner abroad by Rock of Gibraltar: dam, useful German performer up to 11f, half-sister to useful hurdler/chaser (stayed 2½m) Nexius: tailed off in fillies junior bumper (tongue tied). *Jean-Rene Auvray* b–

NEEDLESS SHOUTING (IRE) 7 b.g. Footstepsinthesand – Ring The Relatives (Bering) [2017/18 c–, h82: c16.4g^pu c17.3d⁴ h21.6m Jul 7] rather leggy gelding: winning hurdler: little form over fences: left Joanne Foster after second start: tried in visor: in tongue tie last 3 starts. *Alexandra Dunn* c67
h–

NEEDS FURTHER (IRE) 5 ch.g. Doyen (IRE) – My Linda (IRE) (Bob Back (USA)) [2017/18 b16v⁶ Dec 9] tailed off in bumper (tongue tied). *Tom George* b–

NEED TO KNOW (IRE) 10 b.g. Definite Article – Desperado Queen (IRE) (Un Desperado (FR)) [2017/18 c22.4d* c24.9g c30.2g^pu Nov 17] workmanlike gelding: fairly useful chaser: won cross-country event at Le Lion-d'Angers in May: fatally injured in similar event at Cheltenham: stayed 25f: acted on soft and good to firm going: tried in cheekpieces: usually tongue tied: front runner/raced prominently: unreliable. *John Paul Brennan, Ireland* c115 §

NEE

NEETSIDE (IRE) 6 b.m. Getaway (GER) – Lady Wagtail (IRE) (Milan) [2017/18 b16.8m² b16d⁵ h18.5v^F h18.5v⁵ h16v⁴ h21.4s⁴ h20.7s h21.2d⁴ h23.9m⁵ Apr 25] modest form in bumpers: modest maiden hurdler: stays 21f: acts on soft going: in tongue tie last 4 starts: often travels strongly. *David Dennis*   **h98 b83**

NEFYN BAY 9 b.g. Overbury (IRE) – So Cloudy (Cloudings (IRE)) [2017/18 c112, h–: h17d h15.8d⁵ c19.2s² c19.9s* h23.8d* c19.9d* c19.3g⁴ Apr 23] smallish gelding: fair handicap hurdler: won at Musselburgh in February: fairly useful handicap chaser: won at same course in January and March: stays 3m: acts on soft and good to firm going: has worn cheekpieces, including in 2017/18: wears tongue tie: often races prominently. *Donald McCain*   **c115 h108**

NEFYN POINT 4 gr.g. Overbury (IRE) – So Cloudy (Cloudings (IRE)) [2017/18 b16.2s³ Apr 27] fifth foal: brother to fair hurdler/fairly useful chaser Nefyn Bay (2m-3m winner): dam (h95), 2m-2½m hurdle winner, out of half-sister to very smart chaser Cloudy Lane (stayed 3¼m): 33/1, third in bumper at Perth (4¼ lengths behind Jarveys Plate). *Donald McCain*   **b97**

NELLEMANI 6 ch.m. Sulamani (IRE) – Send Me An Angel (IRE) (Lycius (USA)) [2017/18 b16.7v⁶ b16.7d Apr 21] sixth foal: sister to bumper winner/fair hurdler Jonny Delta (2m-19f winner) and half-sister to bumper winner Absolute Angel (by Primo Valentino): dam, ran once over hurdles, 1¼m-1¾m winner on Flat, half-sister to fairly useful hurdler (best up to 2½m) Clear Riposte: no form in bumpers. *John Groucott*   **b–**

NELLY LA RUE (IRE) 11 b.m. Flemensfirth (USA) – Desperately Hoping (IRE) (Un Desperado (FR)) [2017/18 c73, h–: c23.4g⁵ c24.2s^{pu} c26.3s⁵ c19.3s⁴ c19.3s⁶ c23.8s^{ur} c23.8d⁶ c23.9s² c24.1v³ c24.2v* c26.3v³ c26.3v⁴ c23.4v⁵ c24.2d^{pu} Apr 23] no form over hurdles: poor handicap chaser: won novice event at Hexham in March: stayed 3¼m: acted on good to firm and heavy going: wore cheekpieces: front runner/raced prominently: dead. *Victor Thompson*   **c69 h–**

NELSON'S TOUCH 5 gr.g. Mount Nelson – Lady Friend (Environment Friend) [2017/18 b99: h16.3s⁵ h16.3v h16.5v* h16s³ Apr 9] angular gelding: fair form over hurdles: won maiden at Taunton in March. *Seamus Mullins*   **h108**

NEMEAN LION (IRE) 6 b.g. Mahler – Sandy Desert (Selkirk (USA)) [2017/18 b16s⁴ b16g h20.5d⁶ b18.8g⁴ h19.9g* h19.9g² h24d* h20g h25.8g⁵ h24.4d⁵ h19.7s⁵ Dec 26] €23,000 3-y-o: tall, rather unfurnished gelding: eighth foal: dam unraced half-sister to fairly useful hurdler/fair chaser (2m winner) Dealing River: unplaced in point: fair bumper performer: fair hurdler: won novices at Sedgefield in August and Southwell in October: left Joseph Patrick O'Brien after fourth start: stays 3m: acts on good to soft going: wears tongue tie. *Philip Kirby*   **h107 b92**

NENDRUM (IRE) 9 br.g. Westerner – Westgrove Berry (IRE) (Presenting) [2017/18 h18.1g h20.9d h15.6g³ h15.6s* h15.7s² h15.6d⁶ h16.4d Mar 16] pulled up in point: fair handicap hurdler: won at Musselburgh in January and February (novice): stays 2½m: acts on heavy going: has worn hood: has worn tongue tie, including last 5 starts: front runner. *Sandy Thomson*   **h104**

NENERGY'S QUEST 7 b.m. Pasternak – Coolers Quest (Saddlers' Hall (IRE)) [2017/18 b–: h16.8g^{ur} h15.9g h16.8m⁴ h18.5d⁴ h16.8d h21.7d Nov 19] of no account: in hood last 5 starts. *Richenda Ford*   **h–**

NESTERENKO (GER) 9 b.g. Doyen (IRE) – Nordwahl (GER) (Waajib) [2017/18 c–, h122: h19.2s h20.5s³ Apr 15] sturdy gelding: fairly useful handicap hurdler: little aptitude for chasing: stays 21f: acts on soft going: has worn hood: often races prominently. *Venetia Williams*   **c– h118**

NESTOR PARK (FR) 5 b.g. Walk In The Park (IRE) – Cila (FR) (Saint Preuil (FR)) [2017/18 b16.7g² b15.7d* b16.3v⁵ b16.4s Mar 14] €70,000 3-y-o: tall, useful-looking gelding: second foal: dam, French 15f-2¼m hurdle/chase winner, sister to fairly useful hurdler/chaser (stayed 3m) Preuty Boy: fairly useful form in bumpers: won at Ascot in November. *Ben Pauling*   **b101**

NET DE TREVE (FR) 5 b.g. Network (GER) – Dame de Treve (FR) (Cadoudal (FR)) [2017/18 b16.6d³ Dec 1] €100,000 4-y-o: brother to fairly useful French cross-country chaser Net Lady (2¼m-2¾m winner) and half-brother to 3 winners in France, including fairly useful hurdler/useful chaser Roi de Treve (17f/2¼m winner, by Martaline): dam once-raced sister to Welsh National winner Le Beau Bai: runner-up in Irish point: 6/1, third in conditionals/amateur bumper at Doncaster (6 lengths behind Sangha River): will be suited by 2½m+. *Tom George*   **b87**

NEW

NETHERTON BOY 5 b.g. Black Sam Bellamy (IRE) – Simple Glory (IRE) (Simply Great (FR)) [2017/18 b15.7g² Oct 11] third foal: half-brother to fair hurdler Wildmoor Boy (2m-21f winner, by Midnight Legend): dam (c85/h99), 3m hurdle winner, half-sister to useful hurdler/smart chaser (2½m-25f winner) According To John: 11/1, second in maiden bumper at Towcester (length behind Raving Bonkers). *Robin Dickin* b83

NEVADA 5 gr.g. Proclamation (IRE) – La Columbina (Carnival Dancer) [2017/18 b74: b13.7d³ Nov 25] modest form in bumpers. *Steve Gollings* b76

NEVASCA (IRE) 4 gr.g. Invincible Spirit (IRE) – Snowdrops (Gulch (USA)) [2017/18 h16.7gpu Sep 30] no form in Flat maidens/juvenile hurdle. *Lydia Pearce* h–

NEVER A WORD (USA) 4 br.g. Lonhro (AUS) – Janetstickettocats (USA) (Storm Cat (USA)) [2017/18 h16s⁴ h15.8d⁶ h16.7s⁶ h16.2v⁵ Apr 10] fair maiden on Flat, stays 9.5f: modest form over hurdles: wears tongue tie. *Oliver Greenall* h92

NEVER COMPLAIN (IRE) 10 ch.g. Beneficial – Polly Native (IRE) (Be My Native (USA)) [2017/18 c109, h–: c21.1s* c20.3vpu c15.9v³ c21.1s Apr 12] workmanlike gelding: multiple point winner: maiden hurdler: fairly useful chaser: won lady riders' hunter at Fontwell in May: stays 3m: acts on good to firm and heavy going: has worn cheekpieces, including last 5 starts: often races towards rear. *Mrs F. Marshall* c118 h–

NEVER EQUALLED (IRE) 9 br.g. Brian Boru – Broken Thought (IRE) (Broken Hearted) [2017/18 c126, h122: h21.9v⁶ h21.4sur h19.5v³ h20v* h23.9v⁴ Apr 15] lengthy gelding: runner-up in Irish maiden point on debut: fairly useful handicap hurdler: second to Ffos Las in April: maiden chaser: stays 21f: best form on soft/heavy going: wears cheekpieces: usually races close up. *Bernard Llewellyn* c– h126

NEVER GO SHORT 6 ch.m. Midnight Legend – Tulipa (POL) (Jape (USA)) [2017/18 b16s Feb 23] sixth foal: half-sister to modest chaser On The Case (2m winner, by Generous), stayed 2½m: dam (h119), 2m/17f hurdle winner, also winner up to 13f on Flat: well beaten in mares bumper. *Tom George* b–

NEVER LEARN (IRE) 7 b.g. King's Theatre (IRE) – Hamari Gold (IRE) (Priolo (USA)) [2017/18 h105: c20.2gF c23g² c23s⁴ h19s³ c19.2v² Apr 17] workmanlike gelding: maiden hurdler: modest form over fences: stays 3¼m: acts on soft going: in tongue tie last 5 starts. *Colin Tizzard* c98 h88

NEVER UP (GER) 7 b.g. Danehill Dancer (IRE) – Never Green (IRE) (Halling (USA)) [2017/18 c114, h96: c19m² c20v* c15.2s⁴ c20.1spu c20s³ c19.3v² c24.5vpu c20v⁴ Mar 8] sturdy gelding: winning hurdler: fairly useful handicap chaser: won at Carlisle in October: stays 2½m: acts on good to firm and heavy going: usually leads. *Sue Smith* c115 h–

NEVERUSHACON (IRE) 7 b.g. Echo of Light – Lily Beth (IRE) (Desert King (IRE)) [2017/18 c143, h–: c16gF c18.2s* c20.5gpu c17d⁴ c16v⁴ h16s h16.2d² Apr 26] fairly useful handicap hurdler: second to Park Paddocks at Punchestown in April: useful handicap chaser: won at Galway in August: stays 2¼m: acts on soft and good to firm going: usually wore cheekpieces in 2017/18: has worn tongue tie. *Mrs J. Harrington, Ireland* c143 h125

NEW AGENDA 6 b.g. New Approach (IRE) – Prove (Danehill (USA)) [2017/18 h108: h16m² h15.8m* h15.8g³ h15.8g* h16g⁴ c16gpu Nov 9] good-topped gelding: fairly useful hurdler: won maiden at Huntingdon in May and novice there in October: pulled up in novice handicap on chasing debut: raced only at 2m: acts on good to firm going: wears hood: front runner. *Paul Webber* c– h115

NEWBERRY NEW (IRE) 6 b.g. Kodiac – Sunblush (UAE) (Timber Country (USA)) [2017/18 c112, h–: c20.3s³ c21.2s⁵ c20v* c19.4s* c20.2v³ c21.3v² c24v⁵ Apr 7] good-topped gelding: winning hurdler: fair handicap chaser: won at Uttoxeter in December and Wetherby in January: stays 3m: best form on soft/heavy going: wears cheekpieces nowadays: often races towards rear. *Harriet Bethell* c114 h–

NEWERA 6 ch.g. Makfi – Coming Home (Vettori (IRE)) [2017/18 h110: h16d h16.7s³ May 20] fair maiden hurdler: raced around 2m: acts on soft going. *John Groucott* h105

NEW GRANADA 5 b.g. Zamindar (USA) – Costa Rica (IRE) (Sadler's Wells (USA)) [2017/18 b76: b16.4d Mar 16] mid-field at best in bumpers: tried in hood/tongue tie. *George Bewley* b–

NEW KID IN TOWN (IRE) 9 b.g. Gamut (IRE) – Echo Queen (IRE) (Luso) [2017/18 c20vpu h19d c19.4dpu Nov 18] bumper winner: fair hurdler/fairly useful chaser at best, no form in 2017/18: left W. P. Mullins after second start: has worn hood: usually races prominently: temperamental. *Peter Winks* c– § h– §

NEW LIST 5 ch.g. Pivotal – Angel's Tears (Seeking The Gold (USA)) [2017/18 h102, b76: h20.1g² h15.8d⁵ h19.7spu Dec 26] won point bumper: maiden hurdler: standout effort when third in late-2016/17: tried in cheekpieces. *Brian Ellison* h79

NEW

NEW MILLENNIUM (IRE) 5 b.g. Galileo (IRE) – Banquise (IRE) (Last Tycoon) [2017/18 h101p: h16d h15.8g³ h16.5g³ h16.5s³ h16m Apr 26] fair maiden hurdler: raced only at 2m: acts on soft and good to firm going: tried in hood: usually leads, often races freely. *Philip Hobbs* — **h105**

NEW MOON (FR) 4 b.c. Kapgarde (FR) – Not Lost (FR) (Lost World (IRE)) [2017/18 b16g Apr 21] second foal: dam unraced sister to smart hurdler/high-class chaser (15f-21f winner) Nickname: 3/1, ninth in bumper at Ayr (17 lengths behind Sebastopol): likely to improve. *Nicky Henderson* — **b– p**

NEWQUAY CARDS (IRE) 6 gr.g. Tikkanen (USA) – Sanadja (IRE) (Slip Anchor) [2017/18 b–: h15.8d h16s h15.3v⁶ h16.5s h16v⁴ h17.7s^ur Apr 6] big, workmanlike gelding: poor maiden hurdler: usually races close up. *Evan Williams* — **h70**

NEW QUAY (IRE) 5 b.g. Mahler – Beg La Eile (IRE) (Lahib (USA)) [2017/18 h20d h18.6d³ h18.6v³ Jan 17] €14,000 3-y-o, £90,000 4-y-o: second foal: dam (c98) bumper winner/winning pointer: off mark in Irish points at second attempt: fair form over hurdles: best effort when third in novice at Market Rasen in November: should prove suited by 2½m+: in tongue tie last 2 starts: remains with potential. *Dan Skelton* — **h112 p**

NEWS FOR PASCAL (IRE) 10 b.g. Kutub (IRE) – Direction (Lahib (USA)) [2017/18 h20.6v⁴ Apr 14] winning pointer: modest maiden hurdler at best: stays 2½m: acts on good to soft going: usually wears headgear: has worn tongue tie. *Simon West* — **h83**

NEWSTART (IRE) 7 br.g. Stowaway – Joes Annie (IRE) (Norwich) [2017/18 h99, b81: h15.8g² h16.2m² h16.6s⁴ h16.7s² h16v² h16.2d* h17d⁵ ab16g² h16.7s⁶ h21.2g³ Apr 23] fair handicap hurdler: won at Kelso in October: stays 21f: acts on good to firm and heavy going: usually wears cheekpieces nowadays. *Brian Ellison* — **h108**

NEWSWORTHY (IRE) 8 br.g. Presenting – Cousin Jen (IRE) (Oscar (IRE)) [2017/18 c108, h115: c20m^F h20.2m² h16g² c18g⁵ c22g* h24.2s³ c22s⁵ h20.3v⁴ c21.1s^ur c20s^pu Apr 25] lengthy, angular gelding: fair handicap chaser: fairly useful chaser: won maiden at Kilbeggan in July: stays 3m: acts on heavy going: has worn headgear. *Mrs D. A. Love, Ireland* — **c125 h115**

NEWT 4 b.f. Sixties Icon – Froglet (Shaamit (IRE)) [2017/18 h16.8g⁶ h16g³ h17.7d Sep 10] half-sister to fairly useful hurdler The Tiddly Tadpole (17f winner, by Tipsy Creek): fair on Flat, stays 1¾m: modest form over hurdles: best effort when third in juvenile at Worcester in August: flashed tail repeatedly on debut. *David Dennis* — **h88**

NEWTON GERONIMO 9 b.g. Brian Boru – Newton Commanche (IRE) (Commanche Run) [2017/18 c–, h129§: c16.1g* c20g³ c21.4g⁶ c19.4m⁴ c17.8g⁶ Oct 7] fairly useful hurdler: useful chaser: won maiden at Towcester in May: stays 21f: acts on good to firm and good to soft going: has worn hood, including in 2017/18: temperamental (has twice refused to race). *Ben Pauling* — **c130 § h– §**

NEW TO THIS TOWN (IRE) 7 b.g. Milan – Jade River (FR) (Indian River (FR)) [2017/18 h15.8d* h20.5s² Dec 18] well-made gelding: useful hurdler: won maiden at Ludlow in November: second in novice at Plumpton (7 lengths behind Sam Brown) 3 weeks later: stays 21f: acts on soft going: tried in cheekpieces: in tongue tie last 4 starts: usually races close up. *Colin Tizzard* — **h134**

NEWTOWN BELLE 5 b.m. And Beyond (IRE) – Coldwells (IRE) (Presenting) [2017/18 b16.2g b16v Feb 20] second foal: dam (c99/h95) 25f chase winner: last in bumpers: tried in hood. *George Bewley* — **b–**

NEWTOWN BOY (IRE) 5 b.g. Beneficial – Tanit Lady (IRE) (Presenting) [2017/18 b16.5m² Apr 25] €100,000 3-y-o: fifth foal: half-brother to 3 winners, including fairly useful hurdler/useful chaser Tanit River (2m-3m winner, by Indian River) and bumper winner/fairly useful hurdler Lieutenant Gruber (2m/17f winner, by Scorpion): dam, winning pointer, half-sister to useful chaser (stayed 27f) Dance Island: 11/10, second in bumper at Taunton (3 lengths behind Anytime Will Do): will be suited by further than 2m. *Alan King* — **b99**

NEWTOWN LAD (IRE) 8 b.g. Craigsteel – Rocher Lady (IRE) (Phardante (FR)) [2017/18 c124, h109: c24.1s^pu c23.4v² c24.5v^pu c26.2v^pu Apr 16] winning hurdler: fairly useful handicap chaser: second at Newcastle in January: stays 3m: best form on soft/heavy going: wears headgear/tongue tie: front runner/races prominently: unreliable. *Lucinda Russell* — **c124 § h–**

NEXT DESTINATION (IRE) 6 b.g. Dubai Destination (USA) – Liss Alainn (IRE) (Flemensfirth (USA)) [2017/18 b115: h19v* h20v* h20v* h21.1s³ h24s* Apr 25]   **h151 p**

The second day of the Punchestown Festival proved a decisive one in determining the destination of the Irish trainers' title. Six wins on the day for Willie Mullins wiped out Gordon Elliott's lead of more than €400,000 in a matter of hours, with a Grade 1 treble from Next Destination, Bellshill and Tornado Flyer doing the most damage to Elliott's hopes of becoming champion for the first time. Next Destination, who won the War of Attrition Novices' Hurdle (branded as the Irish Daily Mirror), was also a significant winner for his jockey as he formed part of a treble for Paul Townend just twenty-fours after incurring a twenty-one day ban for mistakenly steering Al Boum Photo around the final fence in the Champion Novices' Chase. As for Next Destination himself, he arguably didn't get the recognition he deserved for being his stable's highest-rated novice hurdler. He didn't go to Cheltenham with quite the same reputation as stable-companion Getabird who started a short price for the Supreme or come away from the Festival with an impressive win like Laurina. In the wider scheme of things, Next Destination was overshadowed by Samcro. However, Next Destination won four of his five starts, the War of Attrition being one of two Grade 1 wins, and, had he run in the Spa instead of taking on Samcro in the Baring Bingham, he might well have been unbeaten over hurdles.

Next Destination had been one of the leading bumper performers the previous season, winning at Fairyhouse before finishing fourth in the Champion Bumper at Cheltenham and second at the Punchestown Festival in a race for horses which had not won more than one bumper. He made an impressive hurdling debut at Naas in November in a well-contested maiden in which he stormed clear to win by thirteen lengths, having the Punchestown Champion Bumper runner-up Paloma Blue back in third and the smart Flat stayer Pallasator in fifth, both of whom themselves went on to better things over hurdles. Next Destination's first Grade 1 win came two starts later in the Lawlor's of Naas Novices' Hurdle in January and, like the two previous winners, stable-companion Bellshill and Death Duty, he was following up a win in the Grade 2 Navan Novices' Hurdle three weeks earlier. Mikael d'Haguenet and Briar Hill had been other Mullins-trained novices to win both races, though when Briar Hill did so in 2013/14 it was the final season before Grade 1 status was switched from the Navan race to the longer-established Naas contest which has been known as the Slaney Novices' Hurdle for most of its history. Samcro had been due to run at Naas, but, in his absence, Next Destination landed the odds from Samcro's stable-companion Cracking Smart as he had done at Navan. Next Destination drew clear under just hands and heels after leading at the last to win by five and a half lengths at Navan, but things were closer between them three weeks later. The main feature of Next Destination's Naas win was his fluent jumping, though that probably took him to the front sooner than ideal which resulted in Next Destination—after

Irish Daily Mirror Novices' Hurdle (War of Attrition), Punchestown—the favourite Next Destination just gets the better of Delta Work (right) and Kilbricken Storm (left) in a thrilling three-way finish

NEX

leading on the bridle early in the straight—having to work harder in the closing stages and having only a length to spare from the keeping-on Cracking Smart. The winner's stable-companion Duc des Genievres made a promising debut for Mullins another three lengths back in third—he was second to Samcro next time out—with Jetz, who had finished third at Navan, making the frame again, while Blow By Blow, a well-held sixth, went on to win the Martin Pipe at Cheltenham.

Both Next Destination and Cracking Smart looked as though the Spa would be the ideal race for them at Cheltenham, Next Destination having shaped like a stayer as early as his bumper days and Cracking Smart already a winner over three miles. The pair headed the ante-post betting but a setback, announced early in March, ruled out Cracking Smart for the rest of the season, and Next Destination, who was entered in all three Grade 1 novice hurdles at the Festival, somewhat surprisingly lined up as Samcro's chief rival among four from his yard in the shorter Baring Bingham. Mullins was represented by three outsiders in the Spa instead, with Ballyward faring best of them in fourth at 20/1. Next Destination ran creditably to take third behind Samcro and Black Op in the Baring Bingham, beaten less than eight lengths behind the impressive winner, putting in his best work at the finish after getting outpaced when the tempo quickened and finishing just in front of stable-companions Scarpeta and Duc des Genievres.

The War of Attrition at Punchestown, run each year since it became a Grade 1 in 2012 (after an unseemly fast-tracking to that status) as the Irish Daily Mirror Novices' Hurdle, not only gave Next Destination the chance to show what he could do at three miles but also pitched him against the Spa winner Kilbricken Storm. The betting was fairly unequivocal about the likely outcome, Next Destination sent off at 5/4 and Kilbricken Storm at 5/1, though there was a cracking eleven-runner line-up also featuring a couple of Gordon Elliott's Cheltenham winners. Coral Cup winner Delta Work joined Blow By Blow, while Jetz was another taking on Next Destination again, with Ballyward also representing the Spa form. In a well-run race, Next Destination, Delta Work and Kilbricken Storm served up a tremendous finish, only necks separating the three of them as they pulled twenty lengths clear of Ballyward. Kilbricken Storm led on the home turn, but the two others soon joined issue in the straight before Next Destination just proved the strongest to edge ahead in the last hundred yards. 'That was a great performance from horse and rider,' said Mullins afterwards, especially pleased that Paul Townend had put events the day before firmly behind him. 'I am delighted for him and the crowd are delighted for him, which shows how well thought of he is over here.'

Next Destination (IRE) (b.g. 2012) — Dubai Destination (USA) (b 1999) — Kingmambo (b 1990) — Mr Prospector / Miesque; Mysterial (b or br 1994) — Alleged / Mysteries. Liss Alainn (IRE) (b 2006) — Flemensfirth (b 1992) — Alleged / Etheldreda; Blazing Liss (b 1999) — Supreme Leader / Liss de Paor.

Next Destination is by the high-class miler Dubai Destination who has proven much more of an influence for stamina than might have been deduced from his own racing career. Perhaps it is less of a surprise on breeding, though, as Dubai Destination is out of a mare by the strong influence for stamina Alleged. With his career as a Flat stallion failing to take off at Sheikh Mohammed's Dalham Hall Stud, Dubai Destination was moved on to Ireland to become a jumps sire, though, in the meantime, Dubai Destination's Flat-bred daughters have produced the likes of Golden Horn, Postponed and Thunder Snow to show that his years under the Darley banner weren't so disappointing after all. Next Destination comes from a family in which the mares have been particularly successful. His dam Liss Alainn is an unraced daughter of Blazing Liss who was well fancied for the Champion Bumper at Cheltenham, after winning her first three starts, but clipped heels and fell. Blazing Liss finished second in the equivalent race at Punchestown and ended her career at the same meeting a year later with her fourth success over hurdles in a listed race for mares which has nowadays become the Grade 1 Mares Champion Hurdle. Blazing Liss is the dam of the useful hurdler Kilfenora who won over three miles at Punchestown in February. Next Destination's great grandam Liss de Paor was also successful in bumpers before showing fairly useful form over hurdles for Aidan O'Brien, winning the Slaney in 1997 when it was run at Thurles. The best mare in the family, though, was Liss de Paor's very smart half-sister Liss A Paoraigh. She went one better than Blazing Liss in the Champion Bumper at Punchestown and gained two more Grade 1 wins over hurdles, in the Royal Bond Novices' and the December Festival Hurdle, and she also finished second in the Irish Champion Hurdle, as well once getting the better of Limestone Lad, from several meetings with him, in the Lismullen Hurdle. Liss A Paoraigh's granddaughter Just Janice showed useful form over hurdles in the latest season when her wins included a Grade 3 mares novice hurdle at Down Royal. This is very much a staying family further back, many of whose members carried the 'Shuil' prefix. Shuil Liss, Next Destination's fourth dam, was a half-sister to the Scottish Grand National winner Baronet, while this is also the family of Welsh National winner Jocks Cross and Shuil Ar Aghaidh, the 1993 Stayers' Hurdle winner. Next Destination is his dam's second foal, while her third, Imperial Nemesis (by Stowaway), looks a future winner after finishing second on his hurdling debut at Perth for Nigel Twiston-Davies late in the latest season.

Next Destination is a rather unfurnished gelding who won his only start in points in Ireland and should have a good future over fences, though he would almost certainly be capable of better still if kept to hurdles for the time being. He is likely to prove better at three miles than shorter and he acts on heavy ground, though he doesn't need conditions to be that testing judged on his last couple of starts in bumpers. Next Destination's owner Malcolm Denmark went agonisingly close to winning the Grand National with Pleasant Company in the latest season, but the owner's best jumper remains Monsignor despite that horse never getting the chance to fulfil his potential. Monsignor won the Champion Bumper at Cheltenham and capped an unbeaten season over hurdles in the Royal & SunAlliance Hurdle, but talk

Mr Malcolm C. Denmark's "Next Destination"

of him being a future Gold Cup horse proved no more than that as he never made it to the track again. Eighteen years later, with a horse who finished third in the same race at Cheltenham, Malcolm Denmark might finally have another potentially high-class jumper on his hands. *W. P. Mullins, Ireland*

NEXT EXIT (IRE) 13 b.g. Exit To Nowhere (USA) – Pilgrim Star (IRE) (Marju (IRE)) [2017/18 c73x, h–: c20.9d^{ur} c15.7d^5 c24g^6 c19.4m c23.9g c22.7m c19.9s Dec 26] winning hurdler: poor handicap chaser: stays 2½m: acts on any going: usually wears tongue tie: often let down by jumping. *John Cornwall*   **c61 x**
h–

NEXT HIGHT (IRE) 11 b.g. High Chaparral (IRE) – Night Petticoat (GER) (Petoski) [2017/18 c–§, h65§: h20.1g^{pu} May 23] leggy gelding: poor handicap hurdler nowadays: maiden chaser: stays 3m: acts on heavy going: tried in headgear: front runner/races prominently: unreliable. *Jonathan Haynes*   **c– §**
h– §

NEXT LEVEL (IRE) 7 b.g. Mahler – Molly Be (First Trump) [2017/18 h83: h23.3d^2 h20.7g Nov 14] sturdy gelding: off mark in points at sixth attempt: modest form over hurdles: stays 23f: acts on good to soft going: in tongue tie last 2 starts. *Paul Cowley*   **h87**

NEXT SENSATION (IRE) 11 b.g. Brian Boru – Road Trip (IRE) (Anshan) [2017/18 c131§, h–: c19m^3 c20g^5 May 26] big, rangy gelding: maiden hurdler: useful handicap chaser: best around 2m: acts on good to firm and heavy going: tried in hood: wears tongue tie: front runner, tends to find little: temperamental. *Michael Scudamore*   **c130 §**
h–

NEYJA BLUE (FR) 6 gr.g. Blue Bresil (FR) – Laura's Dream (FR) (Bonnet Rouge (FR)) [2017/18 h20.5s^6 h20.5v^6 Jan 7] placed in Irish points: poor form in novice hurdles. *Chris Gordon*   **h77**

NIBLAWI (IRE) 6 b.g. Vale of York (IRE) – Finnmark (Halling (USA)) [2017/18 h15.7v^2 h16.6s^6 h19.2d^2 Feb 25] useful on Flat, stays 1½m: fairly useful form over hurdles: best effort when second in novice at Fontwell in February: sure to progress further. *Neil Mulholland*   **h123 p**

NICEANDEASY (IRE) 5 b.g. Kalanisi (IRE) – High Priestess (IRE) (Priolo (USA)) [2017/18 b99: h20.1v* h20.1s* h24.3v^{ur} h19.3s^2 h25.3d^5 Feb 2] lengthy, angular gelding: bumper winner: fairly useful form over hurdles: won maiden at Hexham in October and novice there in November: stays 2½m: acts on heavy going. *Keith Dalgleish*   **h115**

NICELY DONE (IRE) 5 b.m. Mahler – Rare Dollar (IRE) (Bob's Return (IRE)) [2017/18 b16m^6 b16.3g^4 b17.7s^5 h15.7g^4 h16g h15.8g h15.7g h16.2v^6 Apr 10] sixth foal: half-sister to bumper winner Nicely Indeed (by Marienbard) and modest hurdler Millen Dollar Man (19f winner, by Millenary): dam unraced half-sister to fair hurdler/fairly useful chaser (2m-21f winner) Shekels: modest form in bumpers: poor form over hurdles: will stay at least 2½m: tried in cheekpieces: usually in tongue tie: often races towards rear. *Seamus Durack*   **h81**
b78

NICELY INDEED (IRE) 8 b.g. Marienbard (IRE) – Rare Dollar (IRE) (Bob's Return (IRE)) [2017/18 h103+: h19d^2 h19.9g^3 h19.9g^2 h20.5s^2 h19.7d^5 h21.3s h16.8s^4 h20.6s h19.9v^{pu} Feb 22] good-topped gelding: unseated in Irish point: dual bumper winner: fair maiden hurdler: left Kim Bailey after second start: stays 2½m: acts on soft going: has worn hood. *Philip Kirby*   **h108**

NICE THOUGHTS (IRE) 6 b.g. Shamardal (USA) – Zacheta (Polish Precedent (USA)) [2017/18 h101: h16.8g h20g^4 h16.8g Aug 16] angular gelding: modest maiden hurdler: left David Pipe after second start: stays 2½m: acts on heavy going: usually wears headgear: tried in tongue tie: often races towards rear: temperament under suspicion. *Mark Shears*   **h88**

NICE VINTAGE (IRE) 6 b.m. Big Bad Bob (IRE) – High Vintage (IRE) (High Chaparral (IRE)) [2017/18 h16.2g^{pu} h17d h15.6s^{pu} Jan 3] fair at best on Flat, stayed 10.5f: maiden hurdler, no form in 2017/18: tried in headgear/tongue tie: dead. *Katie Scott*   **h–**

NICHEINTHEMARKET (IRE) 6 b.m. Oscar (IRE) – Supreme Kellycarra (IRE) (Supreme Leader) [2017/18 h16s^4 h20.7s h15.7v^6 h24v^{pu} h20.3g Apr 20] €8,500 3-y-o, £5,000 5-y-o: closely related to modest chaser Mocho (19f winner, by Accordion), stayed 3m: dam bumper winner: unplaced in Irish points: poor form over hurdles. *Caroline Fryer*   **h84**

NICHOLS CANYON 8 b.g. Authorized (IRE) – Zam Zoom (IRE) (Dalakhani (IRE)) [2017/18 h165: h20s^2 h24s^F Dec 28]   **h156**

The number of fatalities on the racecourse provide a sad but inevitable footnote to every jumps campaign. Around one hundred and twenty-five jumpers die each season on Britain's racecourses, some of them better known than others, and missed more than others, but all of them mourned by those closely associated with them. As in every dangerous sport or activity, accidents happen, like the fall in a hurdle race at Huntingdon in January in which that grand servant Taquin du Seuil broke his neck, or the fatal fall of the high-class Ar Mad in the Celebration Chase at Sandown, or the last-fence fall that did for Sir Valentino in the Tingle Creek Chase. That trio all contested championship races at the Cheltenham Festival at one time or another, and the deaths of North Hill Harvey, Dresden, Sandsend, Some Plan, Report To Base and Mossback at the latest renewal of jumping's showpiece further emphasised the dangers. Their deaths took the total number of fatalities at the Cheltenham Festival over the last three years to seventeen, which has prompted a full review, reportedly covering twenty years of fatalities and serious injuries at the course. The report was due to be completed in time for recommendations to be acted on by the time racing at Cheltenham resumes for the 2018/19 season, with a reduction in the permitted number of runners and changes to the position of some of the starts among areas likely to be examined. After a similar review into the Grand National following the 2012 race, the fences on that course were redesigned and made softer (with many of the drops after the fences levelled out). The modified Grand National course has made it easier to defend the race in a changing society and it has helped that there have been no fatalities in that particular race since the modifications. Cheltenham's fences will come under the microscope—they are among the stiffest in the country—but any moves to reduce the size of them or make them easier will be met with opposition from those who say that such a change could speed up races and make them even more dangerous. The Cheltenham report might make grim reading, but an investigation was needed and the initiative taken by the authorities can only be applauded.

Not all racecourse fatalities occur at the obstacles, of course. The fatal injury in the Caspian Caviar Gold Cup to the smart chaser Starchitect occurred on the flat between the third- and second-last (there is more about that accident in the essay on Elgin), while Cheltenham was also the course on which the useful Dame Rose collapsed and died after a hurdle race on a new all-mares raceday staged in exceptionally warm weather in April (the long-distance chase on the card was abandoned on welfare grounds). The deaths of three horses at a Monday meeting at Hexham in April, by the way, attracted nothing like the publicity of most of the Cheltenham fatalities (a BHA investigation found no links between the three Hexham deaths, two of which involved horses breaking down on the flat). The same applied to the demise of the versatile veteran Jonny Delta who suffered spinal injuries in a fall at Musselburgh in December, and to the fatal fall of the modest Honest Intent when in a clear lead on his chasing debut in a novice handicap at Wetherby on Boxing Day, and to the deaths of other personal favourites whom readers will probably recall for themselves.

The Cheltenham Festival was the scene of some of Irish-trained Nichols Canyon's best performances. He finished third in the Baring Bingham (the only reverse in his novice season on five completed starts) and third in the Champion Hurdle (to stablemate Annie Power) before winning the Stayers' Hurdle in 2017, filling in one of the few remaining blanks in his trainer's record in the Cheltenham Festival's Grade 1s. Nichols Canyon was still only seven when he won the Stayers' Hurdle but it proved to be the final victory of an illustrious career over hurdles in which he won eight Grade 1s. After a creditable second (probably not fully wound up) to Apple's Jade in the Hatton's Grace Hurdle at Fairyhouse, Nichols Canyon met with a sad end in the Christmas Hurdle at Leopardstown (also won by Apple's Jade). Nichols Canyon suffered a fatal shoulder injury when falling at the fifth flight, an obstacle that had been omitted because of low sun in the two preceding races. There was no suggestion from the connections of any of the runners in the Christmas Hurdle that the flight should not have been reinstated, the clerk of the course explaining that the glare wasn't so strong as it had been for the first two races when it was 'very bright and full on'. Ironically, the flight in question had to be bypassed on the final circuit while vets tried to save Nichols Canyon. 'A small horse with a big heart' was how his trainer Willie Mullins described Nichols Canyon afterwards, with regular jockey Ruby Walsh, sidelined by injury for the Christmas Hurdle, calling him 'as tough as nails, a good horse who will be hard to replace.'

NIC

```
                            ┌ Authorized (IRE)   ┌ Montjeu        ┌ Sadler's Wells
                            │    (b 2004)        │   (b 1996)     └ Floripedes
                            │                    └ Funsie         ┌ Saumarez
Nichols Canyon              │                        (b 1999)     └ Vallee Dansante
   (b.g. 2010)              │                    ┌ Dalakhani      ┌ Darshaan
                            │ Zam Zoom (IRE)     │   (gr 2000)    └ Daltawa
                            └    (gr 2005)       └ Mantesera      ┌ In The Wings
                                                    (ch 2000)     └ Lucayan Princess
```

The compact Nichols Canyon was bred for the Flat—he was from the family of those Group 1 middle-distance half-brothers Luso, Warrsan and Needle Gun—and he made his own mark on the Flat before joining the Mullins stable. He was sold privately out of John Gosden's yard after developing into a smart stayer and winning listed races at Ascot and Saint-Cloud at the back end of his three-year-old campaign when he was also runner-up in the St Simon Stakes at Newbury. As well as his victory at the Cheltenham Festival, Nichols Canyon also put his owners Andrea and Graham Wylie in the winner's enclosure after big wins at the Aintree and Punchestown Festivals, both in his novice season when he won four Grade 1s in all. Another of his Grade 1 wins came in the Morgiana Hurdle in his second season over jumps when he pulled off a major shock when inflicting the first defeat on his long-odds-on stablemate Faugheen. The genuine Nichols Canyon won Grade 1s at two miles to three miles and although he acted on heavy going he didn't need the mud, his three Cheltenham Festival performances—over three different distances—among those recorded on good going. *W. P. Mullins, Ireland*

NICKI'S NIPPER 10 b.m. Denounce – Mistress Star (Soldier Rose) [2017/18 c80, h88: c21.2m^{pu} h23.3g^4 h22.1d^{pu} h25.4g* h25.4s h23.3d^6 h20.1d^4 h26.4s^6 c23.8g^{pu} c25.2d^6 h25.8s^{pu} c23.8d Feb 14] modest handicap hurdler: won at Cartmel in July: poor maiden chaser: won point in April: left Sam England after eighth start: stays 27f: acts on soft and good to firm going: wears headgear: tried in tongue tie: unreliable. *Simon Waugh* **c– §**
h96 §

NICKNAME EXIT (FR) 8 b.g. Nickname (FR) – Exit To Fire (FR) (Exit To Nowhere (USA)) [2017/18 c–§, h–: c19.4v^5 c21.7v* Apr 27] winning hurdler: fair handicap chaser: won at Towcester (conditional) in April: stays 3m: acts on heavy going: usually wears headgear: temperamental. *Henry Oliver* **c106 §**
h–

NICOLAS CHAUVIN (IRE) 10 b.g. Saffron Walden (FR) – Kenzie (IRE) (Presenting) [2017/18 c125, h–: c16m^4 h17.2g^5 c17.3s^4 c17.3g^2 c17.1g^4 c15.2d* c16.4d^3 c16d^6 Dec 20] fairly useful hurdler/chaser: won handicap over fences at Wetherby in October: left Nicky Henderson after first start: unproven beyond 17f: acts on good to firm and good to soft going: has worn hood: usually races in rear. *James Moffatt* **c124**
h118

NICOLOSIO (IRE) 8 b.g. Peintre Celebre (USA) – Nicolaia (GER) (Alkalde (GER)) [2017/18 h–: h15.8g Nov 14] sturdy gelding: useful on Flat at one time: no form over hurdles. *Paul Cowley* **h–**

NIETZSCHE 5 ch.g. Poet's Voice – Ganga (IRE) (Generous (IRE)) [2017/18 h129: h16.4s^6 h15.7d h16.3v h16.2v Apr 7] angular gelding: fairly useful handicap hurdler: stays 19f: acts on soft going: has worn hood. *Brian Ellison* **h119**

NIFTY AT FIFTY (IRE) 5 b.g. Gold Well – Tropical Sunset (IRE) (Overbury (IRE)) [2017/18 b15.3v^5 Apr 9] 25/1, fifth in bumper at Wincanton (15½ lengths behind Unwin Vc). *Jeremy Scott* **b76**

NIGH OR NEVER (IRE) 4 b.g. Excelebration (IRE) – Nigh (IRE) (Galileo (IRE)) [2017/18 h16d h15.8v^2 h16.2s^2 h18.8s^4 Mar 24] compact gelding: has reportedly had breathing operation: modest maiden on Flat, stays 8.5f: fair form over hurdles: in blinkers/tongue tie last 3 starts. *Rebecca Curtis* **h110**

NIGHT AT TARA 7 b.m. Kayf Tara – Parthenia (IRE) (Night Shift (USA)) [2017/18 b15.8d^3 h22.2d^3 Jul 11] second foal: dam, maiden (third at 7f in France), half-sister to useful/ungenuine staying chasers Sonevafushi and Celtic Son and to dam of very smart staying chaser Junior: poor form when third in mares bumper/maiden hurdle: last of 4 finishers in mares maiden point in April: wears tongue tie. *Dan Skelton* **h69**
b68

NIGHT COMES IN (IRE) 6 b.g. Definite Article – Couture Daisy (IRE) (Desse Zenny (USA)) [2017/18 h89, b–: h16.2g h20.6s h23.8s^{pu} Jan 19] maiden hurdler, no form in 2017/18. *Donald Whillans* **h–**

582

NOB

NIGHTFLY 7 br.m. Midnight Legend – Whichway Girl (Jupiter Island) [2017/18 h100: h16d² h20.3g^pu c15.7d* c16v² c16.5g² Apr 24] good-topped mare: fair form over hurdles: similar form over fences: won novice handicap at Southwell in December: stays 21f: acts on heavy going: has worn tongue tie, including last 5 starts. *Charlie Longsdon* — **c112 h105**

NIGHT GENERATION (GER) 6 ch.g. Sholokhov (IRE) – Night Woman (GER) (Monsun (GER)) [2017/18 h25.6g³ h25d³ h25g* h24.5d Nov 27] closely related to fair hurdler Norab (19f winner, by Galileo), stays 2¾m: fairly useful at one time on Flat, stays 16.5f: fair handicap hurdler: won at Huntingdon in November: left Noel Meade after final (2016/17) start: stays 25f: acts on heavy going: wears headgear/tongue tie: often races towards rear: temperamental. *Chris Gordon* — **h105 §**

NIGHTLINE 8 b.g. Midnight Legend – Whichway Girl (Jupiter Island) [2017/18 c118, h–: c23.6g⁵ c24d² c24s² c24d^pu c25.3g⁵ Apr 18] tall gelding: winning hurdler: fairly useful maiden chaser: second in novice handicaps at Doncaster in December and January: stays 3m: acts on heavy going: tried in hood: has worn tongue tie: front runner/races prominently. *Charlie Longsdon* — **c119 h–**

NIGHT MANAGER (FR) 4 b.g. Sageburg (IRE) – Pretty Soon (FR) (Zafonic (USA)) [2017/18 b16.2d⁴ Apr 23] 11/4, fourth in bumper at Hexham (10 lengths behind Melekhov). *Micky Hammond* — **b77**

NIGHT OF GLORY 4 b.g. Sea The Stars (IRE) – Kesara (Sadler's Wells (USA)) [2017/18 h16s³ h16s³ h17.7v* Feb 15] lengthy gelding: dam half-sister to useful hurdler (stays 21f) Desoto County: useful on Flat, stays 1½m: fairly useful form over hurdles: won juvenile at Fontwell in February. *Andrew Balding* — **h118**

NIGHT OF SIN (FR) 5 gr.g. Sinndar (IRE) – Natt Musik (FR) (Kendor (FR)) [2017/18 h125: h15.7g h18.5v² h19.3v h15.8d⁵ h19v³ Apr 12] lengthy gelding: fairly useful handicap hurdler: second at Exeter in December: stays 19f: acts on heavy going: tried in headgear: usually races close up. *Nick Williams* — **h125**

NIKAP (FR) 4 b.f. Kapgarde (FR) – Nika Glitters (FR) (Nikos) [2017/18 b16v² Apr 14] seventh foal: half-sister to 2 winners, including useful chaser Elenika (2m-19f winner, by Martaline): dam, French 7f/1m winner, half-sister to useful French 17f/2¼m hurdle winner Glamour Glitters: 14/1, saddle soon slipped when second in bumper at Chepstow (8 lengths behind Garretstown). *Nigel Hawke* — **b85**

NIKKI STEEL (IRE) 8 b.g. Craigsteel – Nikikita (IRE) (Nikos) [2017/18 h117: h20d^pu Apr 7] winning pointer: fairly useful hurdler at best, weakened quickly only start in 2017/18: stays 2¾m: acts on soft going: often races prominently, tends to find little. *Dr Richard Newland* — **h–**

NINE ALTARS (IRE) 9 b.g. Heron Island (IRE) – Tawny Owl (IRE) (Be My Native (USA)) [2017/18 c115, h97: c19.3g² c26.6s⁴ c26.2v⁴ Apr 7] strong gelding: winning hurdler: fair maiden chaser, below best under Rules in 2017/18 (won point in March): left Ann Hamilton after first start: should stay beyond 17f: acts on heavy going. *Mrs E. J. Dun* — **c96 h–**

NINEPOINTSIXTHREE 8 b.g. Bertolini (USA) – Armada Grove (Fleetwood (IRE)) [2017/18 h107§ h107: h16.7g⁵ h20.1g⁵ c16.4d⁴ c15.5v⁶ h16.7s* h15.6s² h16.8v² Feb 22] lengthy gelding: fair handicap hurdler: won selling event at Market Rasen in December: fair form over fences: best effort when third in handicap at Ayr in October: stays 21f: acts on good to firm and heavy going: has worn headgear, including last 4 starts: usually races nearer last than first: ungenuine (refused to race final start in 2016/17). *Sam England* — **c102 § h110 §**

NI SIN E MO AINM (IRE) 10 b.g. Balakheri (IRE) – Bramslam (IRE) (Glacial Storm (USA)) [2017/18 c104, h–: c26.3d⁵ May 5] multiple point winner: winning hurdler: fair form on first of 2 starts in hunter chases: stays 3¼m: acts on good to firm going: has worn cheekpieces. *Miss Alexandra Bell* — **c75 h–**

NJORLS SAGA 7 b.m. Sagamix (FR) – Programme Girl (IRE) (Definite Article) [2017/18 h–, b–: h21.6g⁵ h16.7s^pu h21.6m⁴ May 30] little show in bumpers/over hurdles. *Nigel Hawke* — **h76**

NO ALARM (IRE) 6 b.g. Getaway (GER) – Chapanga (IRE) (Un Desperado (FR)) [2017/18 h20s¹ h16v⁵ h16v⁴ Jan 22] €22,000 3-y-o: half-brother to fair hurdler/fairly useful chaser Lukie Victor (2m-2¼m winner, by Old Vic) and a winning pointer by Scorpion: dam unraced half-sister to high-class chaser (stayed 25f) Bertone: pulled up both starts in points: modest form over hurdles: best effort when fourth in maiden at Fakenham: wears tongue tie. *Olly Murphy* — **h93**

NOBBY 4 b.g. Authorized (IRE) – Magic Music (IRE) (Magic Ring (IRE)) [2017/18 b16v² Mar 11] brother to fair 17f hurdle winner/winning pointer Magic Music Man and half- — **b89 p**

NOB

brother to 3 winners on Flat: dam 6f winner: won point bumper on debut: 3/1, second in bumper at Warwick (length behind Milanstorm): open to improvement. *Alan King*

NOBEL DUKE (IRE) 5 ch.g. Duke of Marmalade (IRE) – Dowager (Groom Dancer (USA)) [2017/18 h16.6s^pu h15.8s Feb 21] maiden on Flat, best effort on debut in 2016: no show over hurdles. *Michael Scudamore* — h–

NOBLE CALL (IRE) 10 b.g. King's Best (USA) – Really (IRE) (Entrepreneur) [2017/18 c90, h91: c17.3d⁶ h20.6g⁶ c21.2s² c21.2d⁴ Aug 26] fair hurdler at best: modest maiden chaser: stays 21f: acts on soft going: has worn headgear: wears tongue tie. *Joanne Foster* — c89 h–

NOBLE FRIEND (IRE) 10 b.g. Presenting – Laragh (IRE) (Oscar (IRE)) [2017/18 c–, h97: c20.3g^F Apr 20] workmanlike gelding: maiden hurdler: fairly useful chaser at best, no longer of any account (races mainly in points nowadays): wears headgear: tried in tongue tie. *Miss Beth Childs* — c– h–

NOBLE GLANCE 5 b.m. Schiaparelli (GER) – Ragdollianna (Kayf Tara) [2017/18 b–: b17.7g⁵ b17.7d Jun 6] no form in bumpers. *Mark Hoad* — b–

NOBLE INN (FR) 8 b.g. Sinndar (IRE) – Nataliana (Surumu (GER)) [2017/18 h19.5d⁵ h20g² h24d^pu Aug 7] useful hurdler: stays 2½m: acts on heavy going: in cheekpieces/tongue tie last 3 starts. *Mark Fahey, Ireland* — h131

NOBLE ROBIN (IRE) 7 b.g. Robin des Champs (FR) – Which Thistle (IRE) (Saddlers' Hall (IRE)) [2017/18 h98p: h20v* h19.7s* h22.8v^pu Feb 17] won Irish point on debut: fairly useful form over hurdles: won maiden at Ffos Las in November and novice at Wetherby in January: went as if amiss final start: should stay further than 2½m. *Jonjo O'Neill* — h122

NOBODYDOESITBETTER 6 b.g. Apple Tree (FR) – Elfailwen (Afzal) [2017/18 b16.8m⁵ Jun 16] maiden Irish pointer: 9/4, fifth in conditionals/amateur bumper at Newton Abbot (10 lengths behind Bubbles Arcade). *Nigel Twiston-Davies* — b71

NO BOUNDARIES (IRE) 6 ch.g. Spadoun (FR) – Dawn Princess (IRE) (Old Vic) [2017/18 b17.3g h16.2v⁶ h21.2g h16.4g h16.4v⁴ h16s^F Dec 26] second foal: half-brother to 2m chase winner Cap'n (by Gamut): dam, placed in point, sister to fairly useful hurdler/useful chaser (stayed 3m) Toby Lerone: little impact in bumpers: modest form over hurdles: left D. Hassett after first start: unproven beyond 2m: acts on heavy going: usually races freely. *Simon Waugh* — h99 b–

NO BUTS 10 b.g. Kayf Tara – Wontcostalotbut (Nicholas Bill) [2017/18 c126, h–: c25.8g^pu c24g h24g² h26d⁴ c22.4g c24s⁵ h25v c25.7s⁵ Apr 15] leggy, lengthy gelding: fair maiden hurdler: useful handicap chaser at best, little impact in 2017/18: stays 3½m: acts on good to firm and heavy going: has worn cheekpieces, including in 2017/18: tried in tongue tie: usually races prominently. *David Bridgwater* — c105 h110

NOBUTTABOY (IRE) 7 b.g. Darsi (FR) – Buckalong (IRE) (Buckskin (FR)) [2017/18 h116§: c25d⁴ c23.5s^pu c23.6s^pu c24g^pu Apr 20] point winner: fairly useful hurdler: some promise when fourth in novice handicap on chasing debut, but looked one with problems subsequently: stays 3m: acts on heavy going: tried in cheekpieces: unreliable. *Ben Pauling* — c109 § h– §

NO CEILING (IRE) 8 b.g. Turtle Island (IRE) – Pyrexie (FR) (Pistolet Bleu (IRE)) [2017/18 c107, h115: c20d⁴ c16.4d* c20.5g^pu c17.4d⁴ Apr 21] rather leggy gelding: fairly useful hurdler: fair handicap chaser: won at Doncaster in December: best around 2m: acts on good to soft going: usually wears hood: usually races in rear, often freely. *Ian Williams* — c114 h–

NOCHE DE REYES (FR) 9 b.g. Early March – Cochinchine (IRE) (Namaqualand (USA)) [2017/18 c129, h–: c16m² c17g² c16g* c18.2s⁶ c18g^F c15.8s Apr 12] lengthy gelding: winning hurdler: useful handicap chaser: won at Perth (by 10 lengths from Muwalla) in July: best around 2m: acts on good to firm and heavy going: tried in tongue tie. *Tom George* — c134 h–

NO COMMENT 7 br.g. Kayf Tara – Dizzy Frizzy (Loup Sauvage (USA)) [2017/18 h143, b–: c20s³ c31.8s⁶ Mar 13] well-made gelding: bumper winner: useful hurdler: fairly useful form over fences: shaped very well when third in Scilly Isles Novices' Chase at Sandown (30¼ lengths behind Terrefort) in February: excused next run: stays 25f: acts on heavy going: wears hood: often races towards rear, usually travels strongly: remains with plenty of potential as a chaser. *Philip Hobbs* — c122 P h–

NOCTURNAL MYTH 5 b.g. Midnight Legend – Gan On (Missed Flight) [2017/18 b16s⁶ b17.7d⁵ Dec 4] first foal: dam (c131/h119) 2½m/21f hurdle/chase winner: fair form in bumpers: better effort when sixth at Chepstow in November: wears tongue tie. *Anthony Honeyball* — b85

NON

NO DICE (IRE) 9 ch.g. Presenting – Roxbury (Overbury (IRE)) [2017/18 c20v[5] c16.5g[pu] Apr 24] sturdy gelding: maiden hurdler: fair maiden chaser at best, no form in 2017/18 after lengthy absence/leaving A. J. Martin: best form at 2m on soft/heavy going: usually wears tongue tie. *Fergal O'Brien* — c– h–

NO DUFFER 11 ch.g. Karinga Bay – Dolly Duff (Alflora (IRE)) [2017/18 c142, h–: c23.6d[pu] c24.2s[pu] c24s[5] c23.8s[2] Mar 25] deep-girthed gelding: maiden hurdler: useful handicap chaser: back near best when second in veterans event at Ascot (2¼ lengths behind Rathlin Rose) in March: stays 3¼m: acts on heavy going: in cheekpieces last 2 starts: wears tongue tie: usually races prominently. *Tom George* — c137 h–

NO GETAWAY (IRE) 5 ch.g. Getaway (GER) – Nonnetia (FR) (Trempolino (USA)) [2017/18 b15.8d[5] b16.6s[5] Feb 21] €75,000 3-y-o: sixth foal: half-brother to 3 winners by Milan, including Grand National winner One For Arthur and useful hurdler Forza Milan (19f winner, stays 25f): dam French 15f hurdle winner: fair form in bumpers: better effort when fifth at Uttoxeter in November. *Dan Skelton* — b85

NO HASSLE HOFF (IRE) 6 b.g. Craigsteel – Endless Patience (IRE) (Miner's Lamp) [2017/18 h133: h23.3s* h22.8v[4] h25s h22.8v[3] h20.3v h24.7s Apr 14] good-topped gelding: runner-up in Irish maiden point on debut: useful handicap hurdler: won at Uttoxeter in October: third in Rendlesham Hurdle at Haydock (6¼ lengths behind Donna's Diamond) in February: stays 3¼m: acts on heavy going: often races towards rear. *Dan Skelton* — h136

NO HIDING PLACE (IRE) 5 b.g. Stowaway – Subtle Gem (IRE) (Subtle Power (IRE)) [2017/18 b86: b16.3g[2] h19.6d[4] h20s[4] h21.2s h16s[2] h16s[2] h20.5s[5] Apr 15] placed in bumpers: fair form over hurdles: should stay beyond 2m: acts on soft going: often races prominently. *Nicky Henderson* — h113 b89

NOISY NEIGHBOUR 4 b.f. Malinas (GER) – Mooreheigh (Sir Harry Lewis (USA)) [2017/18 b15.7g Apr 20] second foal: dam (b79) second from 2 starts in bumpers: in visor, 66/1, in rear in maiden bumper at Southwell. *Louise Allan* — b–

NO LIKEY (IRE) 11 b.g. Helissio (FR) – Money Galore (IRE) (Monksfield) [2017/18 c126, h–: c19.4g[ur] c20g[3] c24.1g c21d[4] c21g[4] c20.5m[6] Apr 26] winning hurdler: fairly useful chaser, below best in 2017/18: left Philip Hobbs after fifth start: stays 21f: acts on good to firm and heavy going: wears headgear: has worn tongue tie, including in 2017/18. *Mrs Julie Mansell* — c104 h–

NOMINATION GAME (IRE) 7 b.g. Oscar (IRE) – Tiarella (IRE) (Supreme Leader) [2017/18 h16.6s[6] Feb 21] pulled up in Irish point: in hood, 100/1, raced freely when sixth in novice at Doncaster (29¼ lengths behind First Drift) on hurdling debut. *Ian Williams* — h79

NOMOREBLACKJACK (IRE) 7 b.g. Robin des Pres (FR) – Hardabout (IRE) (Alderbrook) [2017/18 c130p, h87p: c15.2d[6] Oct 18] angular gelding: maiden hurdler: useful chaser at best, folded only start in 2017/18: stayed 19f: acted on soft going: front runner/raced prominently: dead. *Sue Smith* — c– h–

NONNO GIULIO (IRE) 7 ch.g. Halling (USA) – Contrary (IRE) (Mark of Esteem (IRE)) [2017/18 h15.8g h15.7d[6] Nov 6] modest/unreliable on Flat, stays 1m: well held both starts over hurdles. *Conor Dore* — h–

NO NO CARDINAL (IRE) 9 ch.g. Touch of Land (FR) – Four Moons (IRE) (Cardinal Flower) [2017/18 c86§, h–§: c16.5m[2] c16.3m* c16.3d c15.7d c15.9m[2] c15.7v[4] c17s[4] Apr 15] maiden hurdler: modest handicap chaser: won at Newton Abbot in June: unproven beyond 17f: acts on good to firm going: usually wears headgear: has worn tongue tie: often races prominently but finishes weakly, and isn't one to rely on. *Mark Gillard* — c85 § h– §

NO NO JOLIE (FR) 6 gr.m. Martaline – Virgata (FR) (Turgeon (USA)) [2017/18 b–: h19g[5] h21s[pu] Nov 22] no form in bumpers or over hurdles. *Oliver Sherwood* — h–

NO NO JULIET (IRE) 5 br.m. Scorpion (IRE) – Full Imperatrice (FR) (Dernier Empereur (USA)) [2017/18 ab16g[4] b17.7d[6] h16.5m[5] Apr 25] sixth foal: half-sister to 3 winners, including fair hurdler Ambitious Fan (2m winner, by Loup Solitaire) and modest hurdler/fair chaser Dazzlers Day (21f-3m winner, by Lando): dam, unraced, out of half-sister to dam of Cheltenham Gold Cup winner Long Run: modest form in bumpers: 25/1, fifth in mares novice at Taunton (10½ lengths behind Cockney Wren) on hurdling debut. *Oliver Sherwood* — h98 b77

NO NO LEGEND 5 b.m. Midnight Legend – Karinga Madame (Karinga Bay) [2017/18 b–: b15.8g ab16d h20.7d h15.8g Apr 24] sturdy mare: poor form in bumpers: fair form over hurdles: better effort when seventh in mares novice at Huntingdon in March: has joined Mark Gillard. *Charlie Longsdon* — h100 b74

NON

NO NO MAC (IRE) 9 b.g. Oscar (IRE) – Whatdoyouthinkmac (IRE) (Supreme Leader) [2017/18 c132, h–: c20.5v^5 c24.3v^6 c21.1v^F c21.6s^4 h19.5v Mar 21] sturdy gelding: winning hurdler: useful handicap chaser, below form in 2017/18: left Ian Duncan after fourth start: stays 25f: acts on heavy going: has worn headgear/tongue tie, including in 2017/18. *Tim Vaughan* — **c111 h–**

NO PLANNING 11 b.g. Kayf Tara – Poor Celt (Impecunious) [2017/18 c130, h–: c24d^2 h24.1d^6 c25d c20.1g^{pu} h24d^6 c22.9v^5 c25.2s^{pu} Feb 12] big gelding: useful handicap hurdler/chaser, below form in 2017/18 after first start: stays 25f: acts on heavy going. *Sue Smith* — **c127 h110**

NORAB (GER) 7 b.g. Galileo (IRE) – Night Woman (GER) (Monsun (GER)) [2017/18 h103: h19.1m* h20g^4 h20g^3 Oct 17] fair form over hurdles: won novice at Fontwell in June: stays 2¾m: acts on good to firm going: wears headgear: usually races close up. *Bernard Llewellyn* — **h113**

NO REFUND (IRE) 7 b.g. Invincible Spirit (IRE) – Evangeline (Sadler's Wells (USA)) [2017/18 h15.8s^{pu} Feb 22] modest at best on Flat (stays 1m), no form in 2017: pulled up in novice on hurdling debut. *Martin Smith* — **h–**

NORMAL NORMAN 4 ch.g. Shamardal (USA) – Ambria (GER) (Monsun (GER)) [2017/18 b13.7g^2 b13.1g* b14s ab16g* b17s^{pu} Apr 13] sturdy gelding: third foal: half-brother to 9.5f/1¼m winner Victoriously (by Azamour): dam German 7.5f winner: fairly useful bumper performer: won at Market Rasen (junior) in October and Lingfield in February. *John Ryan* — **b96**

NORMANDY KING (IRE) 7 b.g. King's Theatre (IRE) – Clairefontaine (Alflora (IRE)) [2017/18 c73p, h85: c22.6g^3 c20v^2 c19.8s^6 c20.3v* Feb 25] winning hurdler: modest form over fences: won novice handicap at Southwell in February: stays 23f: acts on heavy going: has worn tongue tie, including last 5 starts. *Tim Vaughan* — **c97 h–**

NORMAN STANLEY (IRE) 6 b.g. Flemensfirth (USA) – Ballerina Laura (IRE) (Riot Helmet) [2017/18 b16.7d^3 b16v^5 b16.7d* Apr 21] €28,000 3-y-o: brother to 2 winners, including fairly useful chaser Glencairn View (3m/25f winner), and half-brother to bumper winner/fairly useful hurdler Werenearlyoutofit (2½m winner, by Asian Heights): dam unraced half-sister to top-class chaser (stayed 29f) Joe Lively (by Flemensfirth): fairly useful form in bumpers: won conditionals/amateur event at Bangor in April. *Graeme McPherson* — **b98**

NORMAN THE RED 8 ch.g. Tobougg (IRE) – Linden Lime (Double Trigger (IRE)) [2017/18 h98: h19.2d^6 h21.7s* Apr 6] lengthy, angular gelding: fair hurdler, lightly raced: won handicap at Fontwell in April: stays 2¾m: acts on heavy going: tried in hood. *John E. Long* — **h110**

NORM THE STORM 5 b.g. Multiplex – Macnance (IRE) (Mandalus) [2017/18 b16.8d^6 b16.3d^5 Sep 9] well held in bumpers. *Evan Williams* — **b–**

NORPHIN 8 b.g. Norse Dancer (IRE) – Orphina (IRE) (Orpen (USA)) [2017/18 c–, h69: c17.5s^{pu} c17.8g^6 c16g^{ur} c19.5v* c17v^5 c16v^5 Feb 19] maiden hurdler: poor handicap chaser: won at Fontwell in December: stays 19f: acts on heavy going: has worn hood: tried in tongue tie: often let down by jumping. *Seamus Mullins* — **c75 x h–**

NORSE CASTLE 5 b.g. Norse Dancer (IRE) – Hursley Hope (IRE) (Baratheo (IRE)) [2017/18 h–: h16.7d^6 h16d h15.5d^5 h15.8v Dec 31] poor maiden hurdler: raced around 2m: tried in cheekpieces. *Martin Bosley* — **h63**

NORSE DA 8 b.g. Norse Dancer (IRE) – End of An Error (Charmer) [2017/18 h–: h21.6g^{pu} h21.6v^{pu} Nov 26] of no account: tried in cheekpieces/tongue tie. *Helen Nelmes* — **h–**

NORSE LEGEND 7 b.g. Norse Dancer (IRE) – Methodical (Lujain (USA)) [2017/18 h23.6s h19s^{pu} h20.5v^3 h19.5v^4 h21.7s^5 h23.1v^3 Apr 17] angular gelding: fair handicap hurdler nowadays: left Chris Gordon after second start: stays 23f: best form on soft/heavy going: in cheekpieces last 3 starts. *Colin Tizzard* — **h108**

NORSE LIGHT 7 ch.g. Norse Dancer (IRE) – Dimelight (Fantastic Light (USA)) [2017/18 c98, h95: c16.5g c20m^{pu} h18.6g^4 h23.3d^6 h16.8s^2 h18.5v* h16.8v^3 c19.9s* c21.2v^2 c16.1v^3 c19.2s h20.6s* c15.7v^4 Apr 9] strong gelding: modest handicap hurdler: won at Exeter in November and Market Rasen in March: modest handicap chaser: won at Huntingdon in December: stays 21f: acts on good to firm and heavy going: wears headgear/tongue tie. *David Dennis* — **c97 h99**

NORTHANDSOUTH (IRE) 8 ch.g. Spadoun (FR) – Ennel Lady (IRE) (Erin's Hope) [2017/18 c101, h97: h22g^6 h15.8d^5 h19.9v^5 h16v^5 h16v* h16s^3 h16v^6 h16v Apr 14] modest handicap hurdler: won at Lingfield in January: maiden chaser: left Nigel Twiston-Davies after second start: stays 21f: acts on heavy going: has worn hood, including usually in 2017/18. *Samuel Drinkwater* — **c– h94**

586

NOT

NORTHERN BEAU (IRE) 5 b.m. Canford Cliffs (IRE) – View (IRE) (Galileo (IRE)) [2017/18 h15.6s² h16v² h18.6s^pu h20.3g Apr 19] no form on Flat: fair form over hurdles: tried in cheekpieces. *Michael Scudamore* — **h105**

NORTHERN GIRL (IRE) 5 b.m. Westerner – Janebailey (Silver Patriarch (IRE)) [2017/18 h67: h16v⁴ h16d h20.6s h16v³ h19.7v^F h15.7v h21.2d Apr 9] leggy mare: modest maiden hurdler: stays 2½m: acts on heavy going. *Philip Kirby* — **h94**

NORTHERN SOUL 5 ch.g. Presenting – Our Ethel (Be My Chief (USA)) [2017/18 b16.7d⁵ b16.7g* Apr 22] half-brother to several winners, including smart hurdler Attaglance (2m-2½m winner, by Passing Glance), stayed 3m, and fairly useful hurdler/useful chaser Hi George (2¼m-21f winner, by Doyen): dam bumper winner: fairly useful form in bumpers: won at Market Rasen in April. *Ruth Jefferson* — **b98**

NORTHGEORGE 10 b.g. Overbury (IRE) – River Treasure (IRE) (Over The River (FR)) [2017/18 c85: c26d c27.5d^pu Jun 9] multiple winning pointer: maiden chaser, no form in 2017/18: tried in cheekpieces. *J. W. Tudor* — **c–**

NORTH HILL HARVEY 7 br.g. Kayf Tara – Ellina (Robellino (USA)) [2017/18 h144: c15.9g* c15.9s* c15.5d² c16.2s³ c16.3v^F Mar 16] useful hurdler: smart form over fences: won novice at Cheltenham (by neck from Sceau Royal) in October and Grade 2 novice there (by 18 lengths from River Wylde) in November: second in Henry VIII Novices' Chase at Sandown (11 lengths behind Sceau Royal) in December: stayed 2½m: acted on soft going: tried in cheekpieces: front runner/raced prominently: dead. *Dan Skelton* — **c146 h–**

NORTH HILL (IRE) 7 b.g. Westerner – Hill Fairy (Monsun (GER)) [2017/18 h104: h21m* h23.1g⁵ h16.8g Apr 18] sturdy gelding: fair handicap hurdler: won at Kempton in May: stays 2¾m: acts on good to firm going: usually wears hood: often races towards rear. *Ian Williams* — **h107**

NORTH WEST WIND 5 b.g. Shirocco (GER) – Crystal Ballerina (IRE) (Sadler's Wells (USA)) [2017/18 h16v⁴ h19.5v³ h15.7v³ h19v h19s^pu Mar 26] £28,000 3-y-o: fourth foal: dam unraced sister to useful hurdler/fairly useful chaser (2½m/21f winner) Sizing Symphony: modest form over hurdles. *Evan Williams* — **h88**

NORTON GROVE 11 gr.g. Presidium – Glenvally (Belfort (FR)) [2017/18 c24.2g⁶ May 6] winning pointer: 40/1, sixth in maiden hunter at Hexham (18¼ lengths behind Tallow Fair) on chasing debut. *J. J. O'Shea* — **c81**

NORTONTHORPELEGEND (IRE) 8 b.g. Midnight Legend – Tanit (Xaar) [2017/18 c119, h–: c20v c24.2s⁴ c24.5s² c24.1v c25.2s³ c24.2d⁴ c23.4v⁴ Apr 14] maiden hurdler: fair handicap chaser: stays 3¼m: acts on soft and good to firm going: tried in cheekpieces: often races prominently. *Rebecca Menzies* — **c114 h–**

NOSPER (FR) 6 b.g. Whipper (USA) – Nostaltir (FR) (Muhtathir) [2017/18 h101: h19.2v^pu h21.7s h19.2v Feb 1] maiden hurdler, little form in 2017/18: in tongue tie last 3 starts. *Bob Buckler* — **h62**

NO SUCH NUMBER 10 b.g. King's Best (USA) – Return (USA) (Sadler's Wells (USA)) [2017/18 c76, h–: c20.1g* c20.1g* c20.1g* c20g* c22.6g⁶ c20.1s⁴ c23.8m³ c19.9g³ Nov 30] winning hurdler: fair handicap chaser: completed 4-timer at Hexham (3) and Uttoxeter early in season, including in 2 novice events: stays 2½m: acts on good to soft going: wears cheekpieces/tongue tie: often leads. *Maurice Barnes* — **c110 h–**

NOT AN OSCAR (IRE) 6 b.g. Wareed (IRE) – High Dough (IRE) (High Roller (IRE)) [2017/18 h16.7g^pu h20.3d^pu Nov 6] placed on completed start in Irish points: no show over hurdles: tried in visor. *Nick Kent* — **h–**

NOT ANOTHER MUDDLE 7 b.g. Kayf Tara – Spatham Rose (Environment Friend) [2017/18 h118: c19.7s* c15.9s* Jan 11] good-topped gelding: fairly useful hurdler: useful form over fences: won novice at Plumpton in December and novice handicap at Leicester in January: stays 21f: best form on soft/heavy going: usually races freely: remains open to improvement as a chaser. *Gary Moore* — **c131 p h–**

NOTARFBAD (IRE) 12 b.g. Alderbrook – Angels Flame (IRE) (Un Desperado (FR)) [2017/18 c131, h–: c20.1m³ c16.5g⁵ c20.1d⁴ c20.2s² c21.7g⁴ c16d³ c21.1s^pu Apr 13] lengthy gelding: winning hurdler: fairly useful handicap chaser: won at Taunton in November: stays 2¾m: acts on good to firm and heavy going: wears hood: usually leads: temperamental. *Jeremy Scott* — **c129 § h–**

NOT A ROLE MODEL (IRE) 6 b.g. Helissio (FR) – Mille Et Une Nuits (FR) (Ecologist) [2017/18 b63: h16g⁴ h15.9s⁵ h19s⁶ c19.4d² Apr 22] fair form over hurdles: best effort when fourth in maiden at Fakenham in November: 11/2, similar form when second in novice handicap at Stratford (8 lengths behind Zamparelli) on chasing debut: will stay beyond 19f: often races prominently. *Sam Thomas* — **c106 h103**

NOT

NOT AT ALL (FR) 5 b.g. Martaline – Not Lost (FR) (Lost World (IRE)) [2017/18 b72: h15.8g⁵ h15.8g⁶ h15.8m h16.3g⁵ h16.3g⁶ h16.3s⁵ h21.6s⁶ Oct 24] poor maiden hurdler on balance: tried in tongue tie: usually races prominently. *Jonjo O'Neill* h66

NOTEBOOK 7 b.g. Invincible Spirit (IRE) – Love Everlasting (Pursuit of Love) [2017/18 h–§: h19.3d⁶ h16s³ h15.7v⁵ h16.4v³ Feb 5] smallish gelding: poor handicap hurdler nowadays: unproven beyond 2m: acts on soft going: has worn cheekpieces: best treated with caution (often proves reluctant). *Simon Waugh* h81 §

NOTHING PERSONAL 11 b.g. Double Trigger (IRE) – Nothings Forever (Oats) [2017/18 c16.3d⁵ May 5] winning pointer: maiden hurdler: well beaten in hunter on chasing debut: in hood last 5 starts: in tongue tie last 3. *S. G. Allen* c71 h–

NO THROUGH ROAD 11 b.g. Grape Tree Road – Pendil's Delight (Scorpio (FR)) [2017/18 c92§, h–: h24g h23g h24g⁴ c23g c25.8d^pu Aug 22] modest maiden hurdler: fair chaser, below best since 2015/16: stays 25f: acts on heavy going: has worn tongue tie, including final start: unreliable. *Michael Scudamore* c85 § h85 §

NOT MANY LEFT (IRE) 5 b.g. Oscar (IRE) – Lasado (IRE) (Jurado (USA)) [2017/18 b16s⁴ b16v³ h20.2s⁵ h20v* h20s³ h20s² Apr 25] £32,000 3-y-o, €150,000 4-y-o: brother to 2 winners, including fairly useful hurdler/useful chaser Coverholder (2m-23f winner), closely related to fairly useful hurdler/chaser Angus Milan (2m-2¾m winner, by Milan) and half-brother to bumper winner Captain Woodie (by Presenting): dam unraced half-sister to top-class chaser (stayed 3¼m) Harbour Pilot: won maiden point on debut: modest form in bumpers: useful form over hurdles: won maiden at Navan in January: second in minor event at Punchestown (8 lengths behind Pravalaguna) in April: will stay at least 2¾m: usually races close up. *Mrs J. Harrington, Ireland* h131 b83

NOT NEVER 6 ch.g. Notnowcato – Watchoverme (Haafhd) [2017/18 h108p: h15.7d² h15.9v* h15.9d* Feb 26] neat gelding: fairly useful handicap hurdler: won at Plumpton in January and February: likely to prove best at 2m: acts on heavy going. *Gary Moore* h120

NOT NORMAL (IRE) 5 b.g. Robin des Champs (FR) – Mardi Roberta (IRE) (Bob Back (USA)) [2017/18 b16.7s³ b16s² Jan 25] £105,000 3-y-o: fourth foal: half-brother to bumper winner/useful hurdler Blood Crazed Tiger (2½m-3m winner, by King's Theatre): dam (b93), 1¾m bumper winner, sister to fair hurdler/fairly useful chaser (stayed 3m) Big Rob: fairly useful form when placed in bumpers at Bangor and Warwick. *Emma Lavelle* b99

NOTNOWDEAR 6 ch.g. Notnowcato – Cup of Love (USA) (Behrens (USA)) [2017/18 h15.8g Oct 5] well held in Flat maidens in 2014: tailed off in novice on hurdling debut. *J. R. Jenkins* h–

NOTNOWSAM 7 ch.g. Notnowcato – First Fantasy (Be My Chief (USA)) [2017/18 c–, h–: h23.3g h22.1s h20.1d³ h20.9d Oct 8] poor handicap hurdler nowadays: winning chaser: stays 2½m: acts on soft going: wears headgear. *Micky Hammond* c– h77

NOTNOW SEAMUS 7 b.g. Notnowcato – Special Beat (Bustino) [2017/18 h91, b86: h22.7g* May 10] fair form over hurdles: won handicap at Kelso in May: likely to prove as effective at 2½m as 2¾m: has worn cheekpieces. *Marjorie Fife* h102

NOTONEBUTTWO (IRE) 11 b.g. Dushyantor (USA) – Daiquiri (IRE) (Houmayoun (FR)) [2017/18 c–, h–: c23.4g⁴ h23.3g^rtr c20.1g* c24.2g c19.2g h23g c15.6v⁴ c23.4g³ c24.2d c20.1v^ur c20.1v⁵ c24.2v^nv c16.4v⁴ c15.6d³ Apr 23] compact gelding: winning hurdler: poor handicap chaser: won at Hexham in June: stays 3¼m: acts on heavy going: wears headgear: has worn tongue tie: temperamental (has refused to race). *Kenny Johnson* c78 § h– §

NOTRE AMI (IRE) 7 br.g. Kalanisi (IRE) – Shuilan (IRE) (Good Thyne (USA)) [2017/18 b96: h16d⁴ h15.7g⁴ h19.3g⁶ h17.7v² h19s² h16v* h19.8v^pu h16s* h16s Apr 28] good-topped gelding: bumper winner: fairly useful hurdler: won novices at Sandown in February and Kempton in April: best form at 2m: acts on heavy going: has worn hood, including last 2 starts. *Nick Gifford* h120

NOT THAT FUISSE (FR) 5 b.g. Fuisse (FR) – Edelmira (FR) (Kahyasi) [2017/18 b103: h16.7g^pu h16s² h16.6s⁴ Jan 9] bumper winner: fair form over hurdles: best effort when fourth in novice at Doncaster in January: open to further improvement. *Dan Skelton* h107 p

NOTWHATIAM (IRE) 8 b.g. Morozov (USA) – Riverfort (IRE) (Over The River (FR)) [2017/18 h20v^pu h23d³ c17.7v^ur h20.5v⁴ Feb 26] fairly useful hurdler: behind when unseated 4 out in novice at Limerick on chasing debut: left R. P. Rath after second start, R. P. McNamara after third: stays 21f: acts on heavy going: has worn hood: tried in tongue tie: front runner/races prominently. *A. P. Keatley, Ireland* c– h118

NUI

NOUAILHAS 12 b.g. Mark of Esteem (IRE) – Barachois Princess (USA) (Barachois (CAN)) [2017/18 c71§, h–§: h15.9g⁵ May 14] leggy gelding: winning hurdler/maiden chaser, no longer of any account (including in points): usually wears headgear: tried in tongue tie: temperamental. *Daniel O'Brien* c– §
h– §

NOVIS ADVENTUS (IRE) 6 b.g. New Approach (IRE) – Tiffed (USA) (Seattle Slew (USA)) [2017/18 h16.2g^ur h16m* h16g² h17.7g⁴ Aug 24] useful on Flat, stays 1¾m: fairly useful form over hurdles: won novice at Worcester in July and handicap at Fontwell in August: will stay 2½m. *Neil Mulholland* h118

NOVO DAWN (IRE) 9 b.g. Gamut (IRE) – Curious Kate (IRE) (Phardante (FR)) [2017/18 h80: c20.1g h16.2g h17.2s³ h16.2g⁵ c21.2d² h23.9v³ h22.5d⁴ Oct 13] point winner: poor maiden hurdler: modest form in chases: better effort when second in handicap at Cartmel in August: barely stays 2¾m: acts on soft going: tried in tongue tie: usually travels strongly. *Stuart Crawford, Ireland* c90
h81

NOW BEN (IRE) 10 ch.g. Beneficial – Bannow Beach (IRE) (Saddlers' Hall (IRE)) [2017/18 c115, h–: c27.5d* Jun 9] prolific point winner: well held only start over hurdles: fairly useful form in chases: won novice hunter at Stratford in June: stays 3½m. *Philip Rowley* c121
h–

NOWHERETOEXIT 4 b.f. Exit To Nowhere (USA) – Lady of Scarvagh (IRE) (Zaffaran (USA)) [2017/18 b13.2s b16.2s Dec 16] fourth foal: sister to a winning pointer and half-sister to another by Desert King: dam (c120/h108) 2lf-3m hurdle/chase winner: little show in bumpers. *David Rees* b–

NOW LISTEN HERE (IRE) 6 b.g. Captain Marvelous (IRE) – Thanks Eileen (Emperor Fountain) [2017/18 h19.1m³ h15.9s h17.7v⁴ h21.7v² h20.7s^ur h21.7g³ Apr 20] €14,000 3-y-o: first foal: dam unraced half-sister to fairly useful chaser (stayed 2½m) Scottish Bambi: modest form over hurdles: stays 2¾m: acts on good to firm going: tried in cheekpieces: often races towards rear. *Gary Moore* h94

NOW MCGINTY (IRE) 7 b.g. Stowaway – Western Whisper (IRE) (Supreme Leader) [2017/18 h19.9d³ h19.5s³ h21g^pu h23.5d h24.4s h21v* h21v* h24.7s² Apr 14] angular gelding: brother to several winners, most at least useful, including smart hurdler/high-class chaser Outlander (2m-3m winner) and useful hurdler/chaser Western Leader (2½m–/2lf winner, stayed 3m): dam (b68) ran twice in bumpers: fair bumper performer for Ronald O'Neill: useful handicap hurdler: won at Warwick (twice) in March: improved again when second in Grade 3 at Aintree (¾ length behind Mr Big Shot) in April: stays 25f: best form on soft/heavy going: in cheekpieces last 3 starts: front runner/races prominently, often travels strongly/finds plenty for pressure. *Stuart Edmunds* h141

NOW VOYAGER 5 b.m. Fair Mix (IRE) – Bleu d'Avril (FR) (Pistolet Bleu (IRE)) [2017/18 b16.8m b17.7s⁶ Sep 10] well clear when fell 2 out in maiden point on debut: no form in bumpers: dead. *Nick Williams* b–

NUBE NEGRA (SPA) 4 br.g. Dink (FR) – Manly Dream (FR) (Highest Honor (FR)) [2017/18 h16.7g⁴ h16.8s² h16.6s* h16.4s³ h17s⁵ Apr 12] good-topped gelding: maiden on Flat in Spain: useful form over hurdles: won juvenile at Market Rasen in November and novice at Doncaster in January: third in Fred Winter Juvenile Handicap at Cheltenham (4 lengths behind Veneer of Charm) in March: likely to prove best around 2m: acts on soft going: usually travels strongly. *Dan Skelton* h131

NUCKY THOMPSON 5 b.g. Cockney Rebel (IRE) – Vino Veritas (USA) (Chief's Crown (USA)) [2017/18 h119: h16.7g Jul 22] compact gelding: fairly useful 2m hurdle winner, has lost his way: wears headgear: tried in tongue tie: usually races freely: sold only £800 in August. *Richard Spencer* h–

NUCLEAR (IRE) 5 b.g. Elusive Pimpernel (USA) – Heroine (Sadler's Wells (USA)) [2017/18 b16g² b16g⁶ h16.8v^pu h15.3v^pu Jan 18] no form in bumpers/over hurdles: fell in point in April: tried in cheekpieces. *Seamus Mullins* h–
b–

NUITS PREMIER CRU (FR) 5 b.g. Buck's Boum (FR) – Fee Magic (FR) (Phantom Breeze) [2017/18 h19.4d⁶ c19.4d⁴ h18.9s⁴ c20.9g⁴ c20.9g* h18.4d³ h25.3s⁴ c22.9v^F c19.9v Jan 16] fifth foal: half-brother to top-class hurdler/very smart chaser Grands Crus (2½m-3m winner) and smart hurdler/useful chaser Gevrey Chambertin (2m-25f winner) (both by Dom Alco): dam unraced half-sister to Scottish Grand National winner Al Co: fairly useful form over hurdles: fourth in listed handicap at Cheltenham in November: fairly useful handicap chaser: won at Vittel in August: likely to prove best up to easy 3m: acts on soft going: wears cheekpieces: has worn tongue tie. *Emmanuel Clayeux, France* c117
h117

NUM

NUMBERCRUNCHER (IRE) 12 b.g. Beneficial – Josie's Turn (IRE) (Kambalda) [2017/18 c17d* c15.9vpu c21s² c20dur Apr 9] good-topped gelding: multiple point winner: maiden hurdler: fair chaser: won hunter at Stratford in June: stays 3m, as effective around 2m: acts on good to firm and heavy going. *David O'Brien* c106 h–

NUMBER ONE LONDON (IRE) 8 b.g. Invincible Spirit (IRE) – Vadorga (Grand Lodge (USA)) [2017/18 h–: h22g¹ h20.3g² h19.6g² h19.3v³ h21.2dpu Nov 27] modest handicap hurdler: stayed 2¾m: acted on good to firm and heavy going: tried in cheekpieces: dead. *Tim Vaughan* h98

NUMERO NEUF (FR) 5 b.g. Saint des Saints (FR) – Aimela (FR) (Sagamix (FR)) [2017/18 b17.7s⁴ Dec 18] 7/1, fourth in bumper at Plumpton (24¼ lengths behind Hideaway Vic). *Gary Moore* b68

NUOVA SCUOLA 5 b.m. Mount Nelson – La Vecchia Scuola (IRE) (Mull of Kintyre (USA)) [2017/18 h16.2d⁶ h20.9g h20.5s⁵ h23.8gpu Dec 18] dam (h137) 2m-2½m hurdle winner (stayed 3m): poor maiden on Flat: little show over hurdles. *Jim Goldie* h–

NUTS WELL 7 b.g. Dylan Thomas (IRE) – Renada (Sinndar (IRE)) [2017/18 h130: c15.9v² c15.9d* Nov 13] useful hurdler: similar form over fences: won graduation event at Carlisle in November: best around 2m: acts on heavy going: usually races prominently, often travels strongly: remains open to improvement as a chaser. *Ann Hamilton* c132 p h–

O

OAKIDOAKI 6 b.g. Sulamani (IRE) – Sweet Robinia (IRE) (Bob Back (USA)) [2017/18 h101, b79: h19.6m⁵ h23.4g⁵ c20s⁶ c21.2s² c21.2v⁴ c21.6dur c19.9d³ Apr 24] sturdy gelding: modest form over hurdles/fences: stays 21f: acts on heavy going: often wears cheekpieces/tongue tie: front runner/races prominently. *Brendan Powell* c94 h61

OAKLEY HALL (IRE) 6 b.g. Milan – Rockwell College (IRE) (Supreme Leader) [2017/18 h19.3g³ h21.6d⁶ h19.4sF h25s² Mar 14] good-topped gelding: fourth foal: brother to fair 2m hurdle winner Miss Tiggy: dam unraced sister to dam of useful hurdler/smart chaser (winner up to 21f) Oscar Rock: bumper winner: fairly useful form over hurdles: stays 25f: tried in cheekpieces: often races prominently. *Jonjo O'Neill* h121

OAKLEY (IRE) 5 b.g. Oscar (IRE) – Tirolean Dance (IRE) (Tirol) [2017/18 b16s³ b16d⁵ Apr 26] £46,000 3-y-o: lengthy gelding: closely related to fairly useful hurdler/fair chaser Tampa Boy (2m-23f winner, by Montjeu) and half-brother to 2 winners on Flat: dam Italian 5f-1m winner: fair form in bumpers: better effort when third in maiden at Kempton in March. *Philip Hobbs* b94

OAKLY (IRE) 6 br.g. Brian Boru – Auntie Bob (Overbury (IRE)) [2017/18 h20.5d* h20.5d⁴ h20.7d* Aug 3] €6,500 3-y-o: half-brother to useful 2m hurdle winner Dani California and bumper winner/fair 2m hurdle winner Beatu (both by Beat All): dam, no form in bumpers, out of half-sister to high-class hurdler (winner up to 21f) Muse: carried out in point: useful form over hurdles: won maiden at Roscommon in June and novice at Galway (by ½ length from Robin des Foret) in August: will stay 3m. *P. G. Fahey, Ireland* h130*

OAK VINTAGE (IRE) 8 b.g. Fruits of Love (USA) – Brandam Supreme (IRE) (Supreme Leader) [2017/18 c82, h103: c15.6v² c17.1g* c19.2d² c16.4s c15.7d* c20v³ c16.4v* c17.1vpu c16.4g* Apr 23] sturdy gelding: fair hurdler: fair handicap chaser: won at Kelso in November, Catterick in February, and Sedgefield in March and April: best at short of 2½m: acts on heavy going: usually leads. *Ann Hamilton* c105 h–

OATH BREAKER (IRE) 6 b.g. Oscar (IRE) – Turtle Lamp (IRE) (Turtle Island (IRE)) [2017/18 b17s h20mbd h16g³ h16.5s⁴ h18.8g h20g h16.3gpu Oct 21] €33,000 3-y-o: fourth foal: closely related to fairly useful chaser The Cobbler Swayne (2½m winner, by Milan): dam unraced half-sister to smart hurdler/very smart chaser (stayed 3m) Colonel Braxton: pulled up in point: modest form in bumpers: similar form over hurdles: left Joseph Patrick O'Brien after sixth start: best effort at 2m: usually wears headgear: wears tongue tie. *Olly Murphy* h93 b–

OBER WATER 7 gr.g. Fair Mix (IRE) – Pougatcheva (FR) (Epervier Bleu) [2017/18 b16.3d Jun 9] placed in points: tongue tied when tailed off in bumper. *J. H. Young* b–

OBORNE LADY (IRE) 5 b.m. Watar (IRE) – Lady Shackleton (IRE) (Zaffaran (USA)) [2017/18 ab16g³ b15.8s ab16g b16s h15.9s h16.5m Apr 25] half-sister to useful hurdlers/chasers Los Amigos (21f/2¾m winner, by Overbury), stays 25f, and Tom Horn (2½m-25f winner, by Beneficial): dam unraced: poor form in bumpers: well held over hurdles: often races towards rear. *Seamus Mullins* h– b73

590

OFF

OCCASIONALLY YOURS (IRE) 14 b.g. Moscow Society (USA) – Kristina's Lady (IRE) (Lafontaine (USA)) [2017/18 c–, h103: h20.3d^5 h20d^5 h20.7g* h20s* h15.8s h21.7s h25d Apr 24] tall gelding: fair handicap hurdler: won at Huntingdon and Fakenham in November: maiden chaser: stays 23f: acts on good to firm and heavy going: has worn headgear: usually races prominently. *Alan Blackmore*   c– h103

OCEAN BENTLEY (IRE) 6 b.g. Amadeus Wolf – Bentley's Bush (IRE) (Barathea (IRE)) [2017/18 h91: h18.7g^2 h23d^5 h18.7g^4 c15.9m^3 Nov 20] modest maiden hurdler: 200/1, third of 4 in maiden at Leicester (34½ lengths behind Tommy Silver) on chasing debut: tried in tongue tie. *Tony Carroll*   c94 h88

OCEAN COVE (IRE) 6 ch.g. Ask – Sand Eel (IRE) (Sandalay) [2017/18 h15.8v^2 h23.1v^2 h23.3v^3 h21v^2 h24.3g* Apr 20] €4,200 3-y-o: tenth foal: dam lightly-raced half-sister to fair hurdler/useful chaser (stayed 25f) Cameron Bridge: third in Irish point: second in conditionals/amateur bumper at Ffos Las: fairly useful form over hurdles: won novice handicap at Ayr in April: tried in tongue tie: often races towards rear. *Fergal O'Brien*   h123 b84

OCEAN ELEVEN 5 b.g. Equiano (FR) – Fittonia (FR) (Ashkalani (IRE)) [2017/18 h16m h16m^5 h16.3g^{su} h18.7g^4 h16.8d Nov 5] fairly useful on Flat, stays 1¼m: modest form over hurdles: tried in cheekpieces: front runner/races prominently: has joined Phillip Berg, Germany. *Martin Keighley*   h98

OCEAN JIVE 5 b.g. Norse Dancer (IRE) – Kaylianni (Kalanisi (IRE)) [2017/18 h15.8g* May 29] fairly useful on Flat, best effort at 1¼m: 11/4, won maiden at Huntingdon (by ¾ length from Jodies Jem) on hurdling debut: should improve. *Charlie Mann*   h105 p

OCEANUS (IRE) 4 b.g. Born To Sea (IRE) – Alkhawarah (USA) (Intidab (USA)) [2017/18 h16s^3 Dec 4] fair on Flat, stays 11f: 33/1, third in juvenile at Fakenham (21 lengths behind Oxford Blu) on hurdling debut. *Julia Feilden*   h99

OCHOS RIOS 5 b.g. Shirocco (GER) – Society Rose (Saddlers' Hall (IRE)) [2017/18 h92: h15.9d^{pu} h21.6v^{pu} Nov 26] fair on Flat, stays 1½m: maiden over hurdles, no form in 2017/18: stays 2½m: acts on soft going: tried in tongue tie: has joined David Evans. *Neil Mulholland*   h–

OCTAGON 8 b.g. Overbury (IRE) – Dusky Dante (IRE) (Phardante (FR)) [2017/18 h123: h15.7d* h15.5s* h19.9s* h16v^{pu} Mar 10] medium-sized gelding: fairly useful hurdler: completed hat-trick when winning sellers at Southwell in November and Leicester in December, and handicap at Sedgefield later in December: stays 21f: acts on heavy going: usually races close up. *Harry Whittington*   h120

ODDS ON DAN (IRE) 12 b.g. Oscar (IRE) – Grange Classic (IRE) (Jurado (USA)) [2017/18 c84: c19.3v^5 Feb 22] poor chaser: stays 2½m: acts on good to soft going: wears cheekpieces/tongue tie: often races towards rear. *Lucinda Egerton*   c–

ODELLO 7 b.m. King's Theatre (IRE) – Isabello (IRE) (Presenting) [2017/18 h87, b92: h19.5d h16g h16.3d h21.7s^2 h23.9s Feb 20] bumper winner: modest form over hurdles: stays 2¾m: acts on soft going: usually wears tongue tie. *Warren Greatrex*   h93

ODEN 4 ch.g. Lope de Vega (IRE) – Dashing (IRE) (Sadler's Wells (USA)) [2017/18 h16.3s^5 Mar 24] good-quartered gelding: fairly useful on Flat, stays 1¼m: well beaten in novice on hurdling debut. *Nick Gifford*   h–

O'FAOLAINS BOY (IRE) 11 b.g. Oscar (IRE) – Lisa's Storm (IRE) (Glacial Storm (USA)) [2017/18 c134, h–: c29.5v^{pu} Jan 6] well-made gelding: winning hurdler: high-class chaser at best: pulled up 4 of last 5 starts, including in Welsh Grand National in January: stays 3m: acts on good to firm and heavy going: tried in cheekpieces: has worn tongue tie. *Rebecca Curtis*   c– h–

OFCOURSEIWILL (IRE) 6 b.g. Publisher (USA) – Camden Princess (IRE) (Alderbrook) [2017/18 b16.7v^3 h21.2s^{pu} h16.2v^6 h16.7s^2 h19.6d^2 Apr 21] £20,000 5-y-o: second foal: dam, ran twice in bumpers, half-sister to fairly useful hurdler/chaser (2½m winner) Bigirononhiship: won Irish point on debut: some encouragement when third in bumper at Bangor (5 lengths behind Passam) in December: modest form over hurdles: often leads. *Donald McCain*   h97 b88

OFFICER HOOLIHAN 8 b.g. Kayf Tara – Major Hoolihan (Soldier Rose) [2017/18 h117: c19.9g* c21.4d^{pu} c20.2s^3 Feb 17] fairly useful hurdler: similar form over fences: won novice handicap at Huntingdon in October, showing clear: stays 2½m: acts on soft and good to firm going: wears hood/tongue tie. *Tim Vaughan*   c121 h–

OFFICERNISI (IRE) 5 b.g. Kalanisi (IRE) – Some Say (IRE) (King's Theatre (IRE)) [2017/18 b15.3v Apr 9] tailed off in bumper. *Seamus Mullins*   b–

OFF

OFF THE BEAT 4 ch.g. Black Sam Bellamy (IRE) – Off By Heart (Royal Applause) [2017/18 b13d Dec 2] 16/1, eighth in junior bumper at Doncaster. *John Mackie* — b–

OFF THE HOOK (IRE) 6 b.m. Getaway (GER) – Call Her Again (IRE) (Old Vic) [2017/18 h86, b–: h16v² h16.2v² h16.4s² Feb 24] fair form over hurdles: will be suited by 2½m+: often races towards rear: remains open to improvement. *N. W. Alexander* — h104 p

OFF THE SCALE (IRE) 6 b.g. Strategic Prince – Vanilla Delight (IRE) (Orpen (USA)) [2017/18 h15.8d^pu h16.5s^pu Jan 20] fair on Flat, stays 6f: shown little over hurdles. *Sarah Robinson* — h–

OFF YOU GO (IRE) 5 b.g. Presenting – Ozzy Oscar (IRE) (Oscar (IRE)) [2017/18 h16.4d⁴ h20s⁶ h16s⁶ h20.1v³ h20v* h16s* Feb 3] second foal: dam unraced close relative of Irish Grand National winner Shutthefrontdoor: useful form over hurdles: won handicap at Limerick in December and Coral Hurdle at Leopardstown (by 1¼ lengths from Deal d'Estruval) in February: stays 2½m: acts on heavy going: open to further improvement. *Charles Byrnes, Ireland* — h131 p

OGBOURNE DOWNS 8 b.g. Royal Applause – Helen Sharp (Pivotal) [2017/18 h16g⁶ h16g Aug 23] fair on Flat, stays 1¼m: poor form over hurdles. *Ben Pauling* — h81

O'HANRAHAN BRIDGE (IRE) 6 b.g. Gold Well – Greenacre Mandalay (IRE) (Mandalus) [2017/18 b15.8s⁴ Oct 21] £24,000 5-y-o: half-brother to fairly useful chaser Kandinski (2½m winner, by Bienamado): dam, well beaten in bumper, half-sister to useful hurdler (stayed 3m) Special Rate: first past the post (subsequently disqualified due to positive sample) in Irish point in June: 10/1, fourth in maiden bumper at Ffos Las (2 lengths behind The Dubai Way): has joined Donald McCain: should improve. *Rebecca Curtis* — b94 p

OH DEAR OH DEAR 10 b.m. Pasternak – Post It (Thowra (FR)) [2017/18 h16d c16.5g^F h21.6d^pu h16v⁴ h18.5v³ h16.5s h18.5v³ Apr 8] poor maiden hurdler: close up when fell heavily 5 out in novice handicap at Worcester on chasing debut: stays 19f: acts on heavy going: tried in blinkers/tongue tie. *Ron Hodges* — c– h68

OH LAND ABLOOM (IRE) 8 b.g. King's Theatre (IRE) – Talinas Rose (IRE) (Definite Article) [2017/18 h126: h22.8m h25d* h20.6d⁴ ab18d⁶ h25.8v² h24g h25d Apr 26] close-coupled gelding: has had breathing operation: fairly useful handicap hurdler: won at Plumpton in October: second at Fontwell in March: stays 3¼m: acts on good to firm and heavy going: has worn cheekpieces/tongue tie. *Neil King* — h129

OH MICHELLE 7 br.m. Kayf Tara – Grenfell (IRE) (Presenting) [2017/18 b95: h20.7s² h19.8v^pu h15.8d² Apr 9] fair form over hurdles: best effort when second in mares maiden at Huntingdon in January: will stay at least 2¾m: tried in tongue tie. *Nigel Twiston-Davies* — h110

OHMS LAW 13 b.g. Overbury (IRE) – Polly Live Wire (El Conquistador) [2017/18 c82, h–: c21.2m³ May 9] maiden hurdler: poor form over fences: stayed 21f: acted on soft and good to firm going: dead. *Anthony Day* — c79 h–

OH SO GIGOLO (IRE) 8 b.g. Milan – Oh So Breezy (IRE) (Be My Native (USA)) [2017/18 h74: h22.1d⁶ h16.2g h22.1g* h22.1d h18.1g c17.2g^ur h23.8g⁶ Nov 30] lengthy gelding: poor handicap hurdler: won novice event at Cartmel in July: unseated rider third on chasing debut: left Kenneth Slack after sixth start: stays 2¾m: acts on good to firm going: wears headgear: often leads. *Andrew Hamilton* — c– h80

OI OI (IRE) 5 b.m. Oscar (IRE) – Mandys Native (IRE) (Be My Native (USA)) [2017/18 h19.6d h21.2g⁶ h21.2g⁵ h21g⁵ Nov 30] €42,000 3-y-o: closely related to 3 winners by Kayf Tara, including useful hurdlers/chasers Alfie Sherrin (2½m-3m winner, stayed 29f) and Hawkes Point (3m-29f winner), and half-sister to 2 winners, including useful hurdler/chaser Kimberlite Candy (19f-3m winner, by Flemensfirth): dam (h92) 21f hurdle winner/winning pointer (stayed 25f): poor form over hurdles. *Jonjo O'Neill* — h70

OISHIN 6 b.g. Paco Boy (IRE) – Roshina (IRE) (Chevalier (IRE)) [2017/18 h95, b70: h16.2v⁴ h19.9g² Oct 3] modest handicap hurdler: probably stays 3m: acts on soft going: wears tongue tie. *Maurice Barnes* — h93

OISTRAKH LE NOIR (FR) 4 b.g. Kentucky Dynamite (USA) – Linares Noire (FR) (Russian Blue (IRE)) [2017/18 h15.9g⁴ h16.9s* h15.7v² h16.7s* h18.8s² h16d³ h16s Apr 28] well-made gelding: twice-raced on Flat in France: fairly useful hurdler: won juveniles at Cholet in September (left D. Sourdeau de Beauregard after) and Market Rasen in February: stays 19f: acts on heavy going. *Ben Pauling* — h126

OK CORRAL (IRE) 8 b.g. Mahler – Acoola (IRE) (Flemensfirth (USA)) [2017/18 h16g* h16.3s² h21s* h24v² h24.7s⁵ Apr 13] lengthy gelding: smart form over hurdles: won novices at Kempton in May (by 12 lengths from Shining Romeo) and February (by 8 — h148

OLD

lengths from Run To Milan): second in Albert Bartlett Novices' Hurdle (Spa) at Cheltenham (3 lengths behind Kilbricken Storm) in March: stays 3m: acts on heavy going: usually races prominently. *Nicky Henderson*

OKEY DOKEY (IRE) 7 b.g. Papal Bull – Allsorts (USA) (Lemon Drop Kid (USA)) [2017/18 h19.4g(pu) h20.6s6 h20.5v(ur) h16v h19.3v h20v Feb 7] third foal: dam maiden on Flat in USA: placed on completed start in Irish points: modest form over hurdles: stays 21f: best form on soft/heavy going: in tongue tie last 2 starts: often races towards rear. *Patrick Griffin, Ireland*   **h91**

OKOTOKS (IRE) 8 b.g. Gamut (IRE) – Whats Another One (IRE) (King's Theatre (IRE)) [2017/18 h16.8s h23.4v h19.2s5 Mar 7] angular gelding: fair handicap hurdler: stays 2½m: acts on soft going: usually races towards rear. *Fergal O'Brien*   **h113**

OKSANA 5 b.m. Midnight Legend – La Harde (FR) (Valanour (IRE)) [2017/18 b15.7d3 b16m3 b16.3g3 h15.7d4 h16.7s5 h20.7d5 Mar 26] sixth foal: half-sister to bumper winner Ilovemints (by Kayf Tara): dam, placed up to 1¼m on Flat/ran twice over hurdles in France, half-sister to fairly useful hurdler/useful chaser (stayed 3m) Kerada: fair form in bumpers: similar form over hurdles: best effort when fifth in mares novice at Huntingdon in March: likely to prove best at around 2m: usually wears hood: usually races towards rear. *Ben Case*   **h102 b85**

OLDGRANGEWOOD 7 b.g. Central Park (IRE) – Top of The Class (IRE) (Rudimentary (USA)) [2017/18 c147, h108+: h16d3 c19.9d3 c19.9g* c20.8s(pu) c25s4 Apr 14] rangy gelding: useful form over hurdles: third in handicap at Chepstow (3¼ lengths behind Misterton) in October: smart handicap chaser: won at Newbury (by ½ length from Jameson) in December: fourth in Grade 3 at Aintree in April: stays 2½m: acts on heavy going: usually wears tongue tie: often travels strongly. *Dan Skelton*   **c145 h133**

OLD GUARD 7 b.g. Notnowcato – Dolma (FR) (Marchand de Sable (USA)) [2017/18 c136p, h149: h19.5d h16g* h16.4s3 h20.5d* h16.8s5 h20.3s4 h19.2d* h24.7s h21.5s4 Apr 28] useful-looking gelding: smart hurdler: won listed event at Kempton (by 4½ lengths from San Benedeto) in October, handicap at Newbury (by 2¾ lengths from Remiluc) in   **c– h151**

The Brooks, Stewart Families & J. Kyle's "Old Guard"

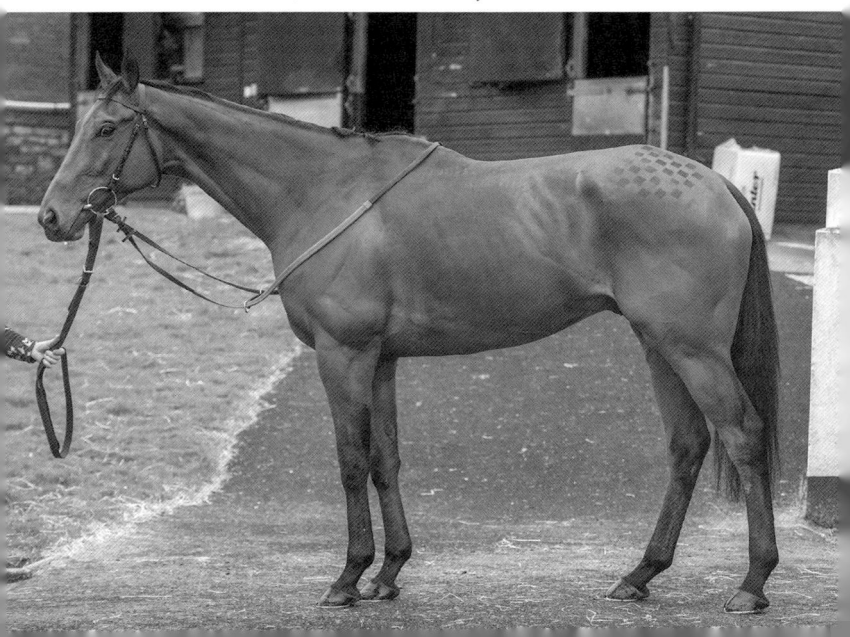

OLD

December and National Spirit Hurdle at Fontwell (by 1½ lengths from Lil Rockerfeller) in February: useful form over fences: stays 21f: acts on heavy going: tried in cheekpieces: often races prominently. *Paul Nicholls*

OLD HARRY ROCKS (IRE) 6 b.g. Milan – Miss Baden (IRE) (Supreme Leader) [2017/18 h112, b98: h20s* h21.6g² h23g² h24g⁶ h20g⁴ h15.5d* h21.4v h19.5s⁶ Apr 27] smallish gelding: fairly useful hurdler: won maiden at Worcester in May and seller at Leicester in November: left Harry Fry after sixth start: stays 23f: acts on soft going: tried in cheekpieces: usually races nearer last than first. *Sophie Leech*   **h118**

OLD SALT (IRE) 6 b.g. Craigsteel – Andrea Gale (IRE) (Presenting) [2017/18 h113: c20.9v^pu c16.4s³ c20s⁴ c19.9s Feb 22] sturdy gelding: third on second of 2 completed starts in Irish points: fair form over hurdles: similar form over fences: unproven beyond 2m: acts on heavy going: tried in tongue tie: often races towards rear. *Evan Williams*   **c107 h–**

OLDTOWN POLLY (IRE) 6 b.m. Publisher (USA) – Oldtown Gill (Robertico) [2017/18 b15.7v Apr 27] £5,500 6-y-o: second foal: dam unraced: off mark in Irish points at fifth attempt: well held in mares bumper. *Brendan Powell*   **b–**

OLIVER JAMES 11 b.g. Kayf Tara – Shuil Tsarina (IRE) (King's Ride) [2017/18 c25.3d^pu May 5] multiple point winner: in cheekpieces, pulled up in hunter on chasing debut. *J. H. Henderson*   **c–**

OLIVER'S GOLD 10 b.g. Danehill Dancer (IRE) – Gemini Gold (IRE) (King's Best (USA)) [2017/18 c124, h117: c17.1g^pu c17.3d* c15.8g⁵ c17.3s² c17.3g³ c17.1g h16g⁶ Apr 20] sturdy gelding: fair handicap hurdler: fairly useful handicap chaser: won at Cartmel in May: unproven beyond 17f: acts on soft and good to firm going: has worn cheekpieces: usually races towards rear. *Mark Walford*   **c125 h103**

OLIVER'S HILL (IRE) 9 b.g. Shantou (USA) – River Rouge (IRE) (Croco Rouge (IRE)) [2017/18 c111, h–: c26m⁵ c19.3g^pu c17g² c17.8g* c18g* c19.4g⁵ Nov 2] lengthy gelding: winning hurdler: fairly useful handicap chaser: won at Fontwell and Kempton in October: has form at 3¼m, effective over much shorter: acts on any going: wears headgear/tongue tie. *Lawney Hill*   **c119 h–**

OLIVER'S ISLAND (IRE) 6 b.g. Milan – Leading Rank (IRE) (Supreme Leader) [2017/18 h85, b77: h25g⁵ May 14] modest form over hurdles: should prove suited by 3m+. *Jamie Snowden*   **h–**

OLIVIA JOAN 7 ch.m. Grape Tree Road – Thorterdykes Lass (IRE) (Zaffaran (USA)) [2017/18 b–: b16.2m h19.3s^pu h20.5s h20.5v^F h20.6s^pu h24.1v h24.3v Feb 11] little show in bumpers: poor form over hurdles. *Alistair Whillans*   **h77 b–**

OLLIE VAAR 6 b.g. Sulamani (IRE) – It's A Discovery (IRE) (Grand Plaisir (IRE)) [2017/18 h16s⁵ h16.6d⁴ h20.3s h16.6d⁶ Feb 8] rather unfurnished gelding: first foal: dam (c81/h102), 21f hurdle winner/winning pointer, half-sister to fair hurdler/fairly useful chaser (2m/17f winner) Practice Match: failed to complete both starts in points: modest form over hurdles: in hood last 2 starts. *Richard Price*   **h97**

OLLISU LAD (IRE) 9 b.g. Westerner – Nick's Jule (IRE) (Perugino (USA)) [2017/18 h20.5s⁶ h19v⁴ h23.3v^F h27v Apr 13] poor maiden hurdler. *Ian Duncan*   **h80**

O MAONLAI (IRE) 10 b.g. Oscar (IRE) – Another Gaye (IRE) (Classic Cliche (IRE)) [2017/18 c140, h–: c22.4g^pu c20.2v² c20.2v⁵ c20.2v⁶ c19.2v² c25.8s² Apr 23] workmanlike gelding: winning hurdler: fairly useful handicap chaser: second at Wincanton in January: left Tom George after fourth start: best form up to 2¾m: acts on heavy going: tried in cheekpieces: wears tongue tie: held up. *Alexandra Dunn*   **c129 h–**

OMID 10 b.g. Dubawi (IRE) – Mille Couleurs (FR) (Spectrum (IRE)) [2017/18 h111§: h25.4g⁶ Jul 2] strong, close-coupled gelding: fair hurdler, well held in 2017/18 (including on Flat): stays 27f: acts on soft and good to firm going: wears headgear/tongue tie: unreliable. *Kenneth Slack*   **h– §**

ONAHANDSHAKE 6 b.m. Victory Note (USA) – Second Bite (Gildoran) [2017/18 b16.2g b16.2s Aug 19] seventh foal: dam winning pointer: no form in bumpers. *Lucinda Russell*   **b–**

ON ALBERTS HEAD (IRE) 8 b.g. Mountain High (IRE) – Dear Money (IRE) (Buckskin (FR)) [2017/18 c87, h97: h19.9d h21.6s⁶ h18.7g⁴ h21.6m² h20g h19.6g² h21.6g² h20.3g⁴ h19.9g h23.9g^pu Nov 16] modest handicap hurdler: maiden chaser: left Richard Woollacott after fifth start: stays 3m: acts on good to firm and good to soft going: wears headgear: usually wears tongue tie. *Neil Mulholland*   **c– h88**

ONE

ON A PROMISE (IRE) 6 gr.g. Definite Article – Silvers Promise (IRE) (Presenting) [2017/18 h58: h21.3s* h23.3s* h24.1s² h23.1s* Mar 29] useful-looking gelding: fair handicap hurdler: won at Wetherby (conditionals novice event) and Hexham in November, and Market Rasen in March: stays 3m: acts on soft going: often races prominently/travels strongly. *Nicky Richards* **h114**

ONCE AN ANGEL (IRE) 6 br.m. Robin des Pres (FR) – Easter Day (IRE) (Simply Great (FR)) [2017/18 b18g h19.3s^pu h20.6g h19.9s⁴ h19.3v² h24.1d⁵ Mar 29] €1,800 4-y-o: half-sister to fairly useful hurdler Dreambrook Lady (2m winner, by Alderbrook) and fair chaser Easter Hunt (25f winner, by Kalanisi): dam unraced: runner-up in point: tailed off in mares maiden bumper: poor form over hurdles: left Brian Jordan after first start: sometimes in tongue tie: usually races towards rear. *Martin Todhunter* **h79 b–**

ONCEUPONATHYME (IRE) 10 b.m. Westerner – Chief Confidant (IRE) (Oscar (IRE)) [2017/18 c19.3g⁵ c25.5s^pu May 18] first foal: dam little sign of ability: point winner: poor form in hunter chases: in headgear last 2 starts. *Miss L. Horsfall* **c69**

ON DEMAND 7 ch.m. Teofilo (IRE) – Mimisel (Selkirk (USA)) [2017/18 h117: h21.2m³ h15.3s* h21.4s⁵ h21.6d c17.5v³ c20.2v⁴ c20v³ h15.8d Apr 9] rather leggy mare: fairly useful handicap hurdler: won at Wincanton in October: similar form over fences: third in handicap at Warwick in March: stays 2¾m: acts on good to firm and heavy going: tried in hood: wears tongue tie: front runner/races prominently. *Colin Tizzard* **c116 h121**

ONDERUN (IRE) 9 b.g. Flemensfirth (USA) – Warts And All (IRE) (Commanche Run) [2017/18 c113, h–: c21.5v c31.9v^pu c26.9v⁵ c26.2d⁵ c26.2v* c30.6s³ Apr 27] well-made gelding: maiden hurdler: fair handicap chaser: won at Carlisle in April: third at Perth next time: stays 31f: acts on heavy going: has worn headgear: front runner/races prominently. *George Bewley* **c103 h–**

ONE CONEMARA (IRE) 10 b.g. Milan – Rose of Kerry (IRE) (Roselier (FR)) [2017/18 c95, h–: c32.5d^pu May 5] useful-looking gelding: multiple point winner: winning hurdler: modest form over fences, pulled up sole start under Rules in 2017/18: should stay beyond 3m: acts on heavy going: tried in headgear. *Mrs C. A. Coward* **c– h–**

ONE COOL BOY (IRE) 9 b.g. One Cool Cat (USA) – Pipewell (IRE) (Lake Coniston (IRE)) [2017/18 h96: h15.8g h19g⁴ Nov 30] lengthy gelding: modest handicap hurdler: stays 19f: acts on soft going: has worn headgear: in tongue tie last 2 starts: often races towards rear. *Tracey Watkins* **h93**

ONEFITZALL (IRE) 8 b.g. Indian Danehill (IRE) – Company Credit (IRE) (Anshan) [2017/18 h134: h24.2d^F h23.5s^pu Mar 25] well-made gelding: useful hurdler at best, no form in 2017/18: stays 21f: acts on soft going. *Philip Hobbs* **h–**

ONE FOR BILLY 6 b.g. Midnight Legend – Saxona (IRE) (Jade Robbery (USA)) [2017/18 h93p, b90: h16.2g* h15.8g h20d³ h16d* h16.6d⁵ h16s⁶ Jan 13] fair hurdler: won novice at Hexham in May and handicap at Warwick in November: unproven beyond 2m: acts on good to soft going: wears tongue tie. *Dan Skelton* **h113**

ONE FOR HARRY (IRE) 10 b.g. Generous (IRE) – Strawberry Fool (FR) (Tel Quel (FR)) [2017/18 h134: h20d⁵ h18.9v* h21.4v² h20.2s⁴ Apr 27] sturdy gelding: useful handicap hurdler: won at Haydock in December: second at Ayr (3 lengths behind Elusive Theatre) in January: stays 3m: acts on heavy going: tried in cheekpieces: front runner/races prominently. *Nicky Richards* **h135**

ONE FOR ROSIE 5 gr.g. Getaway (GER) – Whisky Rose (IRE) (Old Vic) [2017/18 b16.7g* Oct 31] €48,000 3-y-o: second foal: half-brother to bumper winner/useful hurdler Air Horse One (17f-19f winner, by Mountain High): dam, unraced, out of half-sister to dam of Cheltenham Gold Cup winner Native River: 5/2, won 10-runner bumper at Bangor by 3 lengths from Neachells Bridge: sure to progress. *Nigel Twiston-Davies* **b100 p**

ONE FOR THE BOSS (IRE) 11 b.g. Garuda – Tell Nothing (IRE) (Classic Secret (USA)) [2017/18 c124, h–: c19.4g⁶ c23.8g c20d Sep 24] workmanlike gelding: maiden hurdler: fairly useful chaser at best, well below form in 2017/18 (went pointing later in season): stays 3m: acts on heavy going: wears cheekpieces: has worn tongue tie. *Dai Burchell* **c87 h–**

ONEFORTHEROADTOM 5 gr.g. Fair Mix (IRE) – Ifni du Luc (FR) (Chamberlin (FR)) [2017/18 h16.8s³ h16s³ h20.3s⁵ ab18d* h20.3g⁶ Apr 18] €12,500 3-y-o, £100,000 4-y-o: good-topped gelding: fourth foal: half-brother to modest chaser Ifonlyalfie (3m winner, by Alflora): dam (c133/h120) 2m-2¾m hurdle/chase winner: won Irish point on debut: fairly useful form over hurdles: won novice at Exeter in October: also won jumpers bumper at Kempton in March. *Harry Fry* **h125**

ONE

ONE FOR THE TEAM 4 b.g. Shirocco (GER) – One Gulp (Hernando (FR)) [2017/18 **b89 p**
b15.3v* Mar 8] fifth foal: half-brother to fairly useful hurdler/chaser Two Swallows (2½m-
3m winner, by Kayf Tara) and fair hurdler One of Us (23f winner, by Presenting): dam
(h143), bumper/2½m-3m hurdle winner, closely related to Grand National winner Rule
The World: 2/1, won maiden bumper at Wincanton (by 3¼ lengths from Zee Man) on
debut: open to improvement. *Nick Williams*

ONE FORTY SEVEN (IRE) 6 b.g. Beneficial – Still Bubbly (IRE) (Hubbly Bubbly **h114**
(USA)) [2017/18 h119p: h21.1g h19.9v[5] h23.3v[pu] h25d[2] Apr 24] workmanlike gelding:
won Irish maiden point on debut: fair maiden hurdler: stays 25f: acts on good to soft going:
tried in visor. *Nigel Twiston-Davies*

ONEHELLUVATOUCH 5 gr.m. Hellvelyn – Soft Touch (IRE) (Petorius) [2017/18 **h80**
h17.7m[5] h17.7d[6] h17.7m[5] h15.9d[6] h20.7g h21g[3] h21.7g Apr 20] dam (h91) 2m hurdle
winner (stayed 3¼m): fair at best on Flat, stays 1¼m: poor maiden hurdler: stays 21f: often
wears cheekpieces: often races prominently. *Philip Hide*

ONEIDA TRIBE (IRE) 9 b.g. Turtle Island (IRE) – Glory Queen (IRE) (Taipan (IRE)) **c108**
[2017/18 c98p, h–: c21.7s[5] c20.3v[2] c24.5v* c24v[ur] c23.6v[6] Apr 14] winning pointer: **h–**
maiden hurdler: fair handicap chaser: joined on line in novice event at Bangor (subsequently
demoted having edged right run-in) in January, then won similar event at Towcester in
February: stays 3m: acts on heavy going: in blinkers last 3 starts: often races prominently/
travels strongly. *Robin Dickin*

ONE IN A ROW (IRE) 11 ch.g. Saffron Walden (FR) – Rostarr (IRE) (Roselier (FR)) **c– x**
[2017/18 h19.9g h23.3s[4] h19.9s[6] h20.5v[4] h19.7v[3] h19.9v[6] Mar 23] sturdy gelding: poor **h67**
maiden hurdler: maiden chaser: stays 2½m: acts on heavy going: wears headgear: tried in
tongue tie: often let down by jumping. *Julia Brooke*

ONELASTHAND 5 b.m. Haafhd – Miss Molly Be Rude (IRE) (Perugino (USA)) **b–**
[2017/18 b15.8d[6] Jun 7] second foal: dam (h80), 2½m hurdle winner, half-sister to fairly
useful hurdler (stayed 21f) Swift Lord: tailed off in mares bumper: has joined Ruth
Jefferson. *William Kinsey*

ONE LEADER (IRE) 7 b.g. Oscar (IRE) – Be My Leader (IRE) (Supreme Leader) **h62**
[2017/18 b16d h21.2d[5] h19.5v h23.6v[5] Feb 2] little show in bumper/over hurdles. **b–**
Tim Vaughan

ONE MORE BID (IRE) 6 b.g. Grandera (IRE) – Martin's Oscar (IRE) (Oscar (IRE)) **b–**
[2017/18 b16d Oct 31] tailed off in bumper. *Mark Wall*

ONE NIGHT IN MILAN (IRE) 5 b.g. Milan – Native Mo (IRE) (Be My Native **h82 p**
(USA)) [2017/18 b16.5s b15.3v[3] h21.7g[5] Apr 20] €80,000 3-y-o: half-brother to 3 winners, **b76**
notably Cheltenham Gold Cup winner Native River (17f-29f winner, by Indian River),
stays 4m: dam unraced: modest form in bumpers: 8/1, fifth in novice at Fontwell (14
lengths behind Canelo) on hurdling debut: in cheekpieces last 2 starts: has joined Keith
Dalgleish: entitled to do better over hurdles. *Paul Nicholls*

ONE OF US 6 b.g. Presenting – One Gulp (Hernando (FR)) [2017/18 h99: h23.9g[4] **h105**
h23.5d[4] h24.4s Jan 26] well-made gelding: fair handicap hurdler: won novice event at
Ascot in December: stays 3m: acts on soft going: front runner/races prominently.
Nick Williams

ONE STYLE (FR) 8 b.g. Desert Style (IRE) – Arieta (FR) (Pistolet Bleu (IRE)) [2017/18 **c114**
c19.4v[4] c15.7v[3] c20.9v* c21.4d* Apr 22] maiden hurdler: fairly useful handicap chaser: **h–**
won at Hereford (novice) and Market Rasen in April: stays 21f: acts on heavy going.
Venetia Williams

ONE TERM (IRE) 11 b.g. Beneficial – One Edge (IRE) (Welsh Term) [2017/18 c–, h–: **c127**
h20g[4] c20g[4] h20g[6] c20g[3] h19.4m[5] Aug 24] well-made gelding: fair handicap hurdler: fairly **h106**
useful handicap chaser: won at Worcester in May: stays 2½m: acts on soft and good to firm
going: usually wears headgear. *Rebecca Curtis*

ON FIDDLERS GREEN (IRE) 8 b.g. Stowaway – Knockalane (IRE) (Executive Perk) **c139**
[2017/18 c24.9s* c22.5s c24s c25g[pu] c24.5d Dec 27] tall, angular gelding: winning hurdler: **h–**
useful handicap chaser: won Connacht National at Roscommon in June: stays 25f: acts on
good to firm and heavy going: tried in cheekpieces: usually races prominently. *Henry de
Bromhead, Ireland*

ONLYFOOLSOWNHORSES (IRE) 7 br.g. Presenting – Lizzy Langtry (IRE) (King's **c–**
Theatre (IRE)) [2017/18 h88: h19.3m* h20.2g* h23.9g* h23.3d[2] c20v[4] Apr 17] fair **h112**
handicap hurdler: completed hat-trick when winning at Carlisle in May and Perth in May/

July: well beaten in novice handicap on chasing debut: thorough stayer: acts on good to firm and good to soft going: wears tongue tie: usually responds generously to pressure. *Micky Hammond*

ONLY GORGEOUS (IRE) 9 b.g. Vertical Speed (FR) – Pure Beautiful (IRE) (Un Desperado (FR)) [2017/18 c110, h80: c26.1g² c26.1d⁴ c24.2v⁶ c30.7v^pu c19.2v⁴ h21.6v³ Apr 8] lengthy gelding: modest maiden hurdler: fair handicap chaser: stays 31f: acts on good to firm and heavy going. *Susan Gardner* **c109 h90**

ONLY ORSENFOOLSIES 9 b.g. Trade Fair – Desert Gold (IRE) (Desert Prince (IRE)) [2017/18 c–, h121: h16d h19.7s³ h21.3s* h21.4v⁵ h20.1d² Apr 23] fairly useful handicap hurdler: won at Wetherby in December: maiden chaser: stays 21f: acts on heavy going. *Micky Hammond* **c– h126**

ONLY ORVIETO (IRE) 7 b.m. Kayf Tara – Vigna Maggio (FR) (Starborough) [2017/18 h–: h20.1v^pu h20d⁵ h21.3v³ h23.1v⁴ h20.9v^pu Apr 7] modest form over hurdles: in headgear last 2 starts: has joined Mark Walford. *Ruth Jefferson* **h96**

ON PAROLE (IRE) 5 b.g. Kayf Tara – Ain't Misbehavin (IRE) (Trempolino (USA)) [2017/18 b16d Apr 26] good-topped gelding: tailed off in bumper. *Tom George* **b–**

ON THE BLIND SIDE (IRE) 6 b.g. Stowaway – Such A Set Up (IRE) (Supreme Leader) [2017/18 h20d* h21.1d* h19.8s* h20s⁶ Apr 14] good-topped gelding: fifth foal: dam unraced half-sister to smart hurdler/chaser (stayed 27f) Knockara Beau: won Irish point on debut: smart form over hurdles: won maiden at Aintree (by ¾ length from Another Stowaway) in October, Hyde Novices' Hurdle at Cheltenham (by 2½ lengths from Momella) in November and Winter Novices' Hurdle at Sandown (by 9 lengths from Springtown Lake) in December: bad mistake 2 out when down field in Mersey Novices' Hurdle at Aintree: will stay 3m. *Nicky Henderson* **h146**

ON THE FRINGE (IRE) 13 b.g. Exit To Nowhere (USA) – Love And Porter (IRE) (Sheer Grit) [2017/18 c129: c24.3vpu c26.3v c21.1s⁵ c24.5s³ Apr 27] rangy gelding: useful hunter chaser in his prime, not quite the force of old: stays 3¼m: acts on soft going: tried in headgear. *Enda Bolger, Ireland* **c117**

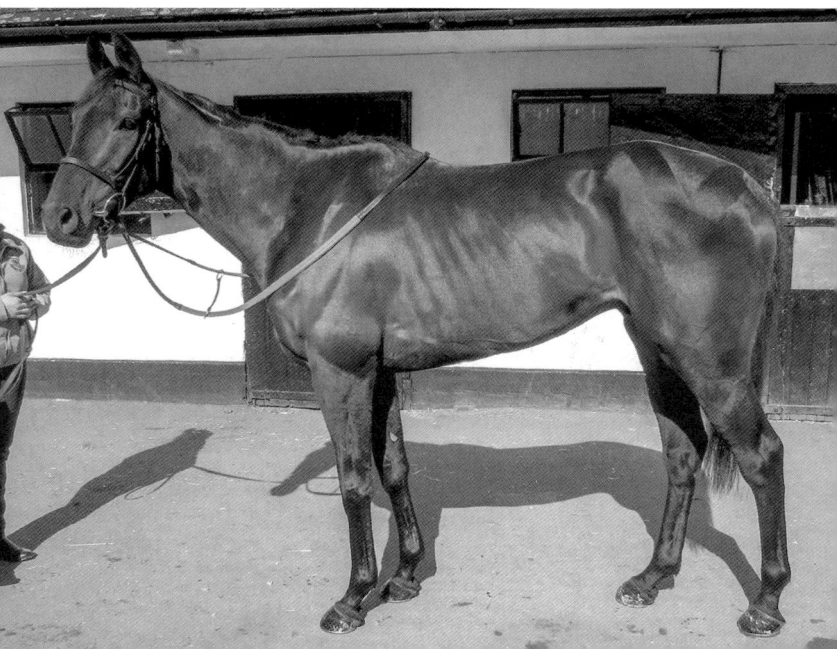

Mr A. D. Spence's "On The Blind Side"

ONT

ON THE ROAD (IRE) 8 b.g. Stowaway – B Greenhill (Gunner B) [2017/18 c130, h104: h21.9v², c29.5v^ur c29.2s^pu h19.8v⁵ Feb 1] sturdy gelding: fairly useful handicap hurdler: second at Ffos Las in November: fairly useful chaser, ran no sort of race third outing in 2017/18: stays 2¾m: acts on heavy going: has worn cheekpieces: in tongue tie last 3 starts. *Evan Williams*   c– h119

ON THE ROX (IRE) 5 b.g. Fastnet Rock (AUS) – Dance Parade (USA) (Gone West (USA)) [2017/18 ab16.3g* ab16.3g Apr 15] 5,500 3-y-o: closely related/half-brother to several winners, including smart hurdler John Constable (2m/17f winner, by Montjeu): dam useful 5f-1m winner: fairly useful form in bumpers: won at Newcastle in February: has joined Evan Williams. *Sally Haynes*   b102

ON TOUR (IRE) 10 b.g. Croco Rouge (IRE) – Galant Tour (IRE) (Riberetto) [2017/18 c137, h–: c19.9s* c22.4g^ur c23.8d c24d^F h19.9v⁶ c25s² Apr 14] workmanlike gelding: winning hurdler: useful handicap chaser: won at Aintree in November: second in Grade 3 at same course (4 lengths behind Thomas Patrick) in April: stays 25f: acts on heavy going: held up. *Evan Williams*   c140 h–

ONURBIKE 10 b.g. Exit To Nowhere (USA) – Lay It Off (IRE) (Strong Gale) [2017/18 c–, h–: c19.8s^pu c20.2s c21.7v² c22.7v² c24.5v² c27.5d⁴ Apr 22] maiden hurdler: poor maiden chaser: stays 3m: best form on heavy going: tried in blinkers. *John O'Neill*   c75 h–

ONYATOES 8 ch.m. Kier Park (IRE) – Sylphide (Ballet Royal (USA)) [2017/18 h21.6g^pu Aug 16] second foal: dam (c93/h77) 2¾m-3¼m hurdle/chase winner: fell in point: pulled up in maiden on hurdling debut. *Deborah Faulkner*   h–

OOLOGIST 7 gr.g. Proclamation (IRE) – Orchid's Silver (Silver Patriarch (IRE)) [2017/18 b82: h20g^pu h19.2g^pu h19.7g^f h16.6s h16.2s h16v^pu h16.5v⁶ Apr 12] poor maiden hurdler: tried in hood. *John Gallagher*   h79

O O SEVEN (IRE) 8 b.g. Flemensfirth (USA) – Kestral Heights (IRE) (Eagle Eyed (USA)) [2017/18 c150, h–: c19.9g³ c23.8d⁴ c20.8v⁵ c25s c21.1s^pu c22.7d³ Apr 28] good sort: winning hurdler: smart handicap chaser: third at Newbury (1¾ lengths behind Oldgrangewood) in December and in Oaksey Chase at Sandown (12¾ lengths behind Top Notch) in April: stays easy 3m, effective at shorter: acts on heavy going. *Nicky Henderson*   c150 h–

OPECHEE (IRE) 7 b.g. Robin des Champs (FR) – Falcons Gift (IRE) (Zaffaran (USA)) [2017/18 c99, h89: c22.6g³ Jul 4] modest form over hurdles/fences: probably stays 23f: acts on firm going: tried in hood. *David Bridgwater*   c91 h–

OPEN HEARTED 11 b.g. Generous (IRE) – Romantic Dream (Bustino) [2017/18 c123, h–: c20.3g² May 16] tall gelding: winning hurdler: useful chaser at best: second in hunter at Southwell in May: won point later in season: stays 3m: acts on soft going: in cheekpieces last 3 starts: wears tongue tie. *Dan Skelton*   c123 h–

OPENING BATSMAN (IRE) 12 b.g. Morozov (USA) – Jolly Signal (IRE) (Torus) [2017/18 c136, h–: c23s⁴ c20.9s⁴ c23.8d³ Mar 22] workmanlike gelding: winning hurdler: smart chaser at best, in frame in hunters in 2017/18: stays 3m: acts on heavy going: has worn headgear, including in 2017/18: wears tongue tie: often races freely. *Harry Fry*   c112 h–

OPERA BUFFA (IRE) 5 b.m. Exceed And Excel (AUS) – Dubai Opera (USA) (Dubai Millennium) [2017/18 h–: c15.9v⁴ Mar 9] no form over hurdles/fences: tried in cheekpieces/tongue tie. *Steve Flook*   c– h–

OPTICAL HIGH 9 b.g. Rainbow High – Forsweets (Forzando) [2017/18 c–, h–: h23.3d^pu Jun 7] modest hurdler at best, no form for long time: well held both starts over fences: stays 27f: acts on heavy going: in cheekpieces last 2 starts: usually races close up. *Tony Forbes*   c– h–

OPTIMA PETAMUS 6 gr.g. Mastercraftsman (IRE) – In A Silent Way (IRE) (Desert Prince (IRE)) [2017/18 h73: h15.6m Nov 8] modest on Flat, stays 10.5f: no form over hurdles: has joined Lawrence Mullaney. *Patrick Holmes*   h–

OPTIMISTIC BIAS (IRE) 9 b.g. Sayarshan (FR) – Dashers Folly (IRE) (Dr Massini (IRE)) [2017/18 c120, h119: c24d* c27.5g* c26.1m c29.2g⁶ Nov 2] fairly useful hurdler: fairly useful handicap chaser: won at Uttoxeter (novice) in May and Stratford in June: best up to 3½m: acts on soft going: tried in tongue tie: front runner/races prominently, usually travels strongly. *James Evans*   c124 h–

OPTIMUS PRIME (FR) 6 b.g. Deportivo – Diluvienne (FR) (Kaldoun (FR)) [2017/18 c119+, h138: h15.7m² h16g⁴ c16.5s* c17d* c15.9s* c16d² Apr 26] well-made gelding: useful hurdler: second in Swinton Handicap at Haydock in May: smart chaser: won small-field novices at Worcester in November, Plumpton (by 12 lengths from Shaama Grise) in December and Leicester in January: second in Ryanair Novices' Chase at Punchestown (12 lengths behind Footpad) in April: unproven beyond 17f: acts on soft going: tried in cheekpieces: wears tongue tie: often leads, usually travels strongly. *Dan Skelton*   c146 h125

ORBASA (FR) 7 b.g. Full of Gold (FR) – Ierbasa de Kerpaul (FR) (Cadoubel (FR)) [2017/18 c129, h–: c21g⁴ c21.2g³ c17.8g⁵ c20.2s* c23.8g⁶ c24.2d⁴ c23s⁴ c24.2v⁵ c20.5s⁴ c19.9s⁴ Mar 31] good-topped gelding: winning hurdler: fairly useful handicap chaser: won at Wincanton in October: stays 3m: acts on soft and good to firm going: wears headgear: has worn tongue tie: one to treat with caution. *Paul Nicholls* — **c128 §** **h–**

ORBIT LIGHT (IRE) 7 b.m. Echo of Light – Niobe (Pivotal) [2017/18 h18.5d^pu h16.8g⁶ h21.6d³ h21.6d h18.5v^pu h18.5v⁵ h16.5s^pu Jan 9] poor maiden hurdler: tried in hood: often wears tongue tie: often races towards rear. *Mark Gillard* — **h65**

ORCHARD LANE (IRE) 6 b.g. Gamut (IRE) – Me No Puppet (Mtoto) [2017/18 b16g³ Jul 10] placed in points: 14/1, third in bumper at Worcester. *Katy Price* — **b73**

ORCHARD MOON 5 b.m. Apple Tree (FR) – Flaviola (IRE) (Moscow Society (USA)) [2017/18 b15.8v⁴ b15.7v Apr 27] third foal: dam, no sign of ability, sister to fairly useful hurdler/fair chaser (stayed 2½m) Hot Port: poor form in bumpers. *Nigel Twiston-Davies* — **b70**

ORCHARDSTOWN CROSS (IRE) 7 b.g. Westerner – Shang A Lang (IRE) (Commander Collins (IRE)) [2017/18 c–, h89: h20.3g⁶ h21.6d² Oct 12] placed in Irish maiden point: fair form over hurdles: second in novice handicap at Exeter in October: well held on chasing debut. *Tim Vaughan* — **c–** **h102**

ORCHESTRATED (IRE) 7 b.g. Mahler – Rose Island (Jupiter Island) [2017/18 h–, b–: c19.4g^pu c21.6g² c21d⁶ c21.6g* c19.7d⁴ Nov 6] compact gelding: poor form over hurdles: modest form over fences: won handicap at Fontwell (conditional) in October: stays 2¾m: best form on good going: often wears cheekpieces. *David Bridgwater* — **c93** **h–**

ORDENSRITTER (GER) 10 ch.g. Samum (GER) – Dramraire Mist (Darshaan) [2017/18 h19.5d h23.9g h19g Nov 30] lengthy gelding: poor maiden hurdler: stays 3m: acts on good going: has worn headgear: has worn tongue tie, including in 2017/18. *Chris Down* — **h60**

ORDER OF SERVICE 8 ch.g. Medicean – Choir Gallery (Pivotal) [2017/18 h–: h16m^pu May 9] fair on Flat, stays 1m: little impact over hurdles. *Shaun Harris* — **h–**

OR DE VASSY (FR) 6 b.g. Assessor (IRE) – Mona Vassy (FR) (Sleeping Car (FR)) [2017/18 b96: h19.9g³ h19.9g* h16.4d h19.9s² h16.7s* Mar 26] compact gelding: fairly useful form over hurdles: won novices at Sedgefield in October and Market Rasen in March: stays 2½m: acts on soft going. *Dan Skelton* — **h117**

ORDINARY WORLD (IRE) 8 br.g. Milan – Saucy Present (IRE) (Presenting) [2017/18 c152, h–: c16v² c17d³ c17s⁴ c15.9s⁵ c16s Apr 24] good-topped gelding: winning chaser: very smart chaser: second in Poplar Square Chase at Naas (5 lengths behind Ball d'Arc) in November and third in Paddy's Rewards Club Chase at Leopardstown (15½ lengths behind Min) in December: raced around 2m: acts on good to firm and heavy going: has worn hood/tongue tie. *Henry de Bromhead, Ireland* — **c155** **h–**

ORDO AB CHAO (IRE) 9 b.g. Heron Island (IRE) – Houldyurwhist (IRE) (Supreme Leader) [2017/18 h110: h20d⁴ h19.8s Apr 28] useful-looking gelding: useful hurdler at best, lightly raced and below that level since 2014/15: stays 21f: acts on soft going. *Olly Murphy* — **h125**

OREGON GOLD (FR) 5 b.g. Confuchias (IRE) – Gold Wine (FR) (Holst (USA)) [2017/18 b86: h20.6g⁶ h16g⁴ h16.7g⁶ h15.5s h25.3d^f h21.2v h20.3g Apr 20] fair maiden hurdler: stays 2½m: best form on good going: often races towards rear. *Nick Kent* — **h102**

ORIENTAL CROSS (IRE) 5 b.m. Cape Cross (IRE) – Orion Girl (GER) (Law Society (USA)) [2017/18 b93: b17d ab16g* ab16.3g² Feb 5] fair form in bumpers: won at Lingfield in December: left Patrick Chamings after second start. *Tim Vaughan* — **b86**

ORIENTAL FIXER (IRE) 9 b.g. Vertical Speed (FR) – Hannah Rose (IRE) (Un Desperado (FR)) [2017/18 h93: h25m² c25.8g* c25.8d² c24.2d² c25.1s^pu Oct 20] modest maiden hurdler: fair form over fences: won novice handicap at Newton Abbot in June: stays 3¼m: acts on good to firm and heavy going: tried in hood. *Michael Scudamore* — **c100** **h92**

ORIENTAL FLAME 5 b.m. Norse Dancer (IRE) – Eastern Paramour (IRE) (Kris Kin (USA)) [2017/18 ab16g⁴ ab16d³ b16.8g Apr 19] first foal: dam, 1½m bumper winner, also 1¼m-1½m winner on Flat: fair form in bumpers: best effort when third in maiden at Kempton in March: tried in hood. *Charlie Mann* — **b91**

ORION D'AUBRELLE (FR) 5 b.g. Saint des Saints (FR) – Erbalunga (FR) (Mansonnien (FR)) [2017/18 h20v⁵ h16s h24d⁴ Apr 26] fifth foal: half-brother to French chasers Olcani (2½m-27f cross-country winner, by Al Namix) and Gritta (17f winner, by Goldneyev): dam French 15f-23f hurdle/cross-country chase winner: useful form over — **h131**

hurdles: in cheekpieces, won juvenile in 2016/17 for A. Adeline de Boisbrunet: fourth in handicap at Punchestown (3 lengths behind A Great View) in April: stays 3m: acts on soft going. *W. P. Mullins, Ireland*

ORIONINVERNESS (IRE) 7 b.g. Brian Boru – Woodville Leader (IRE) (Supreme Leader) [2017/18 c100, h65: c24.1v^F c20.1v^4 c20.1v* c24.2d^3 Apr 23] maiden hurdler: modest handicap chaser: won at Newcastle in April: stays 2½m: best form on heavy going: wears cheekpieces/tongue tie. *Lucinda Russell*   **c96 h–**

ORION'S MIGHT (IRE) 8 b.g. Antonius Pius – Imperial Conquest (IRE) (Imperial Ballet (IRE)) [2017/18 h89§: h15.7m^2 h15.8d* h15.8g h18.7m h16.3g^3 h16.8g h18.7g^{pu} h15.8m Oct 11] sturdy gelding: modest hurdler: won at Uttoxeter in May: stays 2½m: acts on good to firm and good to soft going: wears headgear: tried in tongue tie: temperamental. *Matt Sheppard*   **h92 §**

ORKAN 4 b.g. Shirocco (GER) – Zefooha (FR) (Lomitas) [2017/18 b13.6v^5 b14.6s^5 b16.7g Apr 22] first foal: dam (h111) 2m-2½m hurdle winner, also winner up to 2¼m on Flat: fair form in bumpers. *Mark Walford*   **b88**

ORMSKIRK 5 gr.g. Hellvelyn – River Song (USA) (Siphon (BRZ)) [2017/18 h16.7g^4 h16.2d^4 h16g h15.9v^3 h15.3v^3 Apr 9] modest maiden hurdler: left Gavin Patrick Cromwell after third start: raced around 2m: acts on heavy going: sometimes in blinkers. *Seamus Mullins*   **h99**

ORNUA (IRE) 7 ch.g. Mahler – Merry Heart (IRE) (Broken Hearted) [2017/18 h16m* h16.5g* h16d^{pu} h16s^3 h16.5s Apr 13] €16,000 3-y-o: angular gelding: fifth foal: half-brother to a winning pointer by Moscow Society: dam unraced: off mark in maiden points at second attempt: useful hurdler: won maiden at Down Royal and minor event at Clonmel (by 17 lengths from Morgan) in May: third in minor event at Punchestown (7¼ lengths behind Campeador) in October: unproven beyond 2m: acts on soft and good to firm going: front runner. *Henry de Bromhead, Ireland*   **h131**

ORTENZIA (IRE) 4 b.f. Lawman (FR) – Ondoyante (IRE) (Slickly (FR)) [2017/18 h16g^2 h16.7g^5 h16.7g^4 ab16d^6 h16.7s^{pu} Mar 26] has had breathing operation: fair on Flat, stays 1¼m: fair form over hurdles: tried in tongue tie: front runner/races prominently. *Charlie Longsdon*   **h102**

ORTHODOX LAD 10 ch.g. Monsieur Bond (IRE) – Ashantiana (Ashkalani (IRE)) [2017/18 c96, h83: h16d h15.9m h16d^F Oct 31] angular gelding: fair hurdler at best, no form in 2017/18: maiden chaser: usually wore cheekpieces: dead. *Grace Harris*   **c– h–**

OSCAR BRAVO (IRE) 7 br.g. Oscar (IRE) – Brave Commitment (IRE) (Henbit (USA)) [2017/18 b77: h16.6s h16v h15.8d h20.3g^3 Apr 20] modest form over hurdles: tried in hood: wears tongue tie: usually races towards rear. *Tom George*   **h98**

OSCAR JANE (IRE) 11 b.m. Oscar (IRE) – Turrill House (Charmer) [2017/18 h76: h20.3g^3 h25g^F May 29] modest handicap hurdler: stays 3m: acts on heavy going: wears headgear/tongue tie: front runner/races prominently. *Johnny Farrelly*   **h89**

OSCAR KNIGHT (IRE) 9 b.g. Oscar (IRE) – Cool Supreme (IRE) (Supreme Leader) [2017/18 c138, h114: h16d h20v* c24.5d h24s^2 c29v^{bd} c20s^3 Apr 25] useful handicap hurdler: won at Naas in November: second at Leopardstown (3 lengths behind Total Recall) in February: useful handicap chaser: third in Guinness Handicap Chase at Punchestown (8¼ lengths behind Patricks Park) in April: stays 3m: acts on heavy going: often travels strongly. *Thomas Mullins, Ireland*   **c136 h131**

OSCAR LATEEN (IRE) 10 b.g. Oscar (IRE) – Storm Call (Celestial Storm (USA)) [2017/18 c79x, h–: c23.8g c23g^3 Jul 27] maiden hurdler: poor handicap chaser: left Victor Thompson after first start: stays 27f: acts on heavy going: has worn headgear, including in 2017/18: tried in tongue tie: often races prominently: often let down by jumping. *Dan Skelton*   **c82 x h–**

OSCAR LIGHT (IRE) 5 b.m. Oscar (IRE) – Sound of Light (IRE) (General Monash (USA)) [2017/18 b16.2s^4 Aug 19] fifth foal: dam, lightly raced on Flat, half-sister to useful hurdler/fairly useful chaser (stayed 29f) Golden Storm: in tongue tie, 16/1, fourth in mares bumper at Perth (11¾ lengths behind Secret Escape): third on completed starts in points in 2018. *Noel C. Kelly, Ireland*   **b73**

OSCAR O'SCAR (IRE) 10 b.g. Oscar (IRE) – Shining Lights (IRE) (Moscow Society (USA)) [2017/18 c114§, h–§: c19.3g^{pu} c24.1d^4 c21.1g^4 c20s^5 c19.3s^3 c21.6v^6 Apr 16] maiden hurdler: fair handicap chaser: stays 3m: acts on good to firm and heavy going: wears cheekpieces: often races towards rear: not one to trust. *Micky Hammond*   **c107 § h– §**

OSG

OSCAR ROSE (IRE) 6 b.m. Oscar (IRE) – Ben Roseler (IRE) (Beneficial) [2017/18 **h121** b107: h16d² h19.5d⁴ h15.8g² h20.3s^ur h19.4s⁴ h19s³ h20.5s⁶ h20.3g² Apr 19] lengthy mare: useful bumper performer: fairly useful maiden hurdler: third in listed mares handicap at Cheltenham in April: stays 21f: acts on soft going: often races towards rear. *Fergal O'Brien*

OSCARS BOSS 8 b.g. Norse Dancer (IRE) – Kimmeridge Bay (Karinga Bay) [2017/18 **h100** h104, b106: h19.9g² May 16] bumper winner: fair form over hurdles: tried in cheekpieces: often races towards rear. *Neil Mulholland*

OSCARS LEADER (IRE) 5 b.g. Oscar (IRE) – Lead'er Inn (IRE) (Supreme Leader) **h118** [2017/18 b16.6d⁴ b16s⁴ h15.8s² h20.5s⁴ h21.4d Apr 22] €22,000 3-y-o, £17,000 4-y-o: **b84** unfurnished gelding: seventh foal: closely related to fair hurdler/modest chaser Try It Sometime (2½m-3m winner, by Milan), and half-brother to bumper winner/fairly useful hurdler An Caisteal Nuadh (2m winner) and fairly useful hurdler Casual Approach (19f-2¾m winner) (both by Scorpion): dam unraced: fourth in Irish maiden point on debut: modest form in bumpers: fairly useful form over hurdles: best effort when second in novice at Huntingdon in February: should stay beyond 2m. *Jo Davis*

OSCARS LITTLE ROSE (IRE) 5 b.m. Oscar (IRE) – One Swoop (IRE) (Be My **h88** Native (USA)) [2017/18 b15.8v⁶ h16v³ h21.7v⁶ h15.8d Apr 19] closely related to fair **b–** hurdler Ballyquin Queen (21f winner, by King's Theatre) and half-sister to 2 winners, including fair hurdler One Back For Luck (3m winner, by Bob Back): dam unraced half-sister to useful hurdler/smart chaser Calling Brave, stayed 25f, and smart staying chaser Ottowa: down the field in bumper: modest form over hurdles: bred to stay 21f. *Sam Thomas*

OSCAR'S PROSPECT (IRE) 6 b.m. Oscar (IRE) – Divine Prospect (IRE) **c–** (Namaqualand (USA)) [2017/18 h100: c20.5v^pu h24.1s^pu Dec 9] fair form over hurdles: **h–** pulled up both starts in 2017/18, including on chasing debut: stays 3m: acts on soft going: tried in visor: usually races towards rear. *Jedd O'Keeffe*

OSCAR'S SONG (IRE) 7 b.m. Oscar (IRE) – Bint Bladi (FR) (Garde Royale) [2017/18 **h90** h86p, b80: h19.9m h19.9d^pu h16.7g³ h20g² h16g h15.7g^F h16.5g⁶ h16.5s^pu Dec 14] modest maiden hurdler: left Charlie Longsdon after second start: unproven beyond 17f: best form on good going: usually wears tongue tie: often races in rear. *Dan Skelton*

OSCAR STANLEY (IRE) 11 b.g. Oscar (IRE) – Mujavail (IRE) (Mujadil (USA)) **c91** [2017/18 c19.3g³ May 4] multiple point winner: maiden hurdler: 8/1, third in novice hunter **h–** at Sedgefield (7¾ lengths behind Mr Raj) on chasing debut: stays 19f: best form on good going: tried in headgear/tongue tie. *Mrs D. Walton*

OSCAR STAR (IRE) 5 b.m. Oscar (IRE) – Tucacas (FR) (Highest Honor (FR)) [2017/18 **h114** b83: b16s h15.7g⁵ h20.5d² h24s* h23.4v³ h21v h20.7g³ Apr 24] smallish mare: has had **b–** breathing operation: modest bumper performer: fair form over hurdles: won mares novice at Southwell in December: stays 3m: acts on soft going: often races towards rear. *Jamie Snowden*

OSCAR SUNSET (IRE) 11 b.g. Oscar (IRE) – Derravarra Sunset (IRE) (Supreme **c–** Leader) [2017/18 c103, h124: h20.6g h20.3g^pu Apr 18] lengthy gelding: useful hurdler/ **h107** chaser at best, on downgrade nowadays: stays 2¾m: acts on heavy going. *Evan Williams*

OSCARTEEA (IRE) 9 b.g. Oscar (IRE) – Miss Arteea (IRE) (Flemensfirth (USA)) **c116 §** [2017/18 h122§: h20g h23.1g* h23.1g⁴ c20g⁵ h23.3s² c23.8v⁴ h24.2d Dec 1] well-made **h131 §** gelding: useful handicap hurdler: won at Market Rasen in June: second at Uttoxeter (1¼ lengths behind No Hassle Hoff) in October: fairly useful form over fences: stayed 3m: acted on heavy going: wore headgear/tongue tie: temperamental: dead. *Peter Bowen*

OSCAR WORLD (IRE) 6 b.m. Oscar (IRE) – Maresin (I'm Supposin (IRE)) [2017/18 **h88** b16.4g⁴ b16s² h21v⁵ h19.4s⁶ Feb 21] €7,000 4-y-o, £20,000 5-y-o: lengthy mare: fourth **b85** foal: dam, little form over hurdles, out of sister to high-class hurdler (stayed 25f) Marello: runner-up in Irish point: fair form in bumpers: modest form over hurdles. *Martin Keighley*

OSCATARA (IRE) 11 b.g. Oscar (IRE) – Nethertara (Netherkelly) [2017/18 c117§, h–: **c–** c19.3g^ur May 4] winning hurdler: fairly useful chaser at best, unseated rider sole start in **h–** 2017/18: placed all 4 starts in pointing sphere in 2017/18: stays 19f: acts on heavy going: often wears cheekpieces: often finishes weakly. *Donald McCain*

OSGOOD 11 b.g. Danehill Dancer (IRE) – Sabreon (Caerleon (USA)) [2017/18 c–, h98§: **c–** h15.7m h15.9g⁶ h15.8g* h17.7m h15.9m^ur h19.6g⁵ h16d⁶ Oct 20] rather leggy gelding: **h84 §** poor handicap hurdler: won at Huntingdon in May: well held on chasing debut: stays 19f: acts on soft and good to firm going: often wears headgear: temperamental. *Gary Moore*

OSK

OSKAR DENARIUS (IRE) 7 b.g. Authorized (IRE) – Elizabethan Age (FR) (King's Best (USA)) [2017/18 h78: h15.7g[5] h18.5g h24g[pu] h19.3d* h19.2v* h21v[pu] h15.7g* Apr 20] fair handicap hurdler: won at Catterick (amateur) and Fontwell (conditional) in December, and Southwell in April: left Jennifer Mason after fifth start: stays 19f: acts on heavy going: wears hood/tongue tie: front runner/races prominently. *Ben Pauling* — **h100**

OSKI (IRE) 6 b.g. Oscar (IRE) – Mossville (FR) (Villez (USA)) [2017/18 b95: h19g[3] h19.9d* h21.1s[pu] h24.4d* Dec 15] bumper winner: fair form over hurdles: won conditionals maiden at Uttoxeter in October and novice at Doncaster in December: best effort at 3m: has worn hood: usually races close up. *Ben Case* — **h111**

OSSIE'S DANCER 9 ch.g. Osorio (GER) – Nina Ballerina (Kahyasi) [2017/18 h98: h20.5g[2] h20.6g[2] May 21] fair handicap hurdler: stays 21f: acts on heavy going: tried in tongue tie: often races towards rear. *Martin Smith* — **h109**

OSTUNI (FR) 5 b.g. Great Pretender (IRE) – Mamassita (FR) (Loup Solitaire (USA)) [2017/18 b16s Nov 12] strong gelding: 9/1, in need of experience when eighth in bumper at Sandown (21½ lengths behind Mercy Mercy Me). *Paul Nicholls* — **b–**

OTTER MOON 6 b.g. Midnight Legend – Highland Dawn (Primitive Rising (USA)) [2017/18 h82p, b86: h15.8m[2] h15.8d[3] h20.2g* h19.7s[5] h15.8s[3] h15.8d[3] h16.7g* Apr 22] fairly useful hurdler: won maiden at Perth in July and novice handicap at Market Rasen in April: stays 2½m: acts on soft and good to firm going. *Tom George* — **h126**

OTTO THE GREAT (FR) 10 gr.g. Turgeon (USA) – Hunorisk (FR) (Mansonnien (FR)) [2017/18 c20.8d[pu] May 5] useful-looking gelding: multiple point winner: winning hurdler: fairly useful chaser at best, little impact in hunter chases: stays easy 3m: acts on good to firm and good to soft going: tried in cheekpieces: irresolute. *J. H. Henderson* — **c– §** / **h– §**

OULAMAYO (FR) 7 b.g. Solon (GER) – La Titie du Perche (FR) (Rochesson (FR)) [2017/18 h85: h16.8g[pu] May 10] sturdy gelding: modest form over hurdles, pulled up sole start in 2017/18. *Dan Skelton* — **h–**

OUR BELLE AMIE 6 b.m. Black Sam Bellamy (IRE) – Very Special One (IRE) (Supreme Leader) [2017/18 b88: h16d[2] h24s[4] Dec 17] modest form over hurdles: better effort when second in mares novice at Wetherby in November: should be suited by 2½m+: wears tongue tie. *Kim Bailey* — **h89**

OURCRAZYANNE 9 b.m. Lahib (USA) – Shareef Walk (Shareef Dancer (USA)) [2017/18 h–: h21.6g[pu] May 5] angular mare: no show over hurdles: in hood last 2 starts. *Roger Ingram* — **h–**

OUR DUKE (IRE) 8 b.g. Oscar (IRE) – Good Thyne Jenny (IRE) (Good Thyne (USA)) [2017/18 c167p, h–: c24s c24s[4] c20v* c26.3v[pu] Mar 16] well-made gelding: winning hurdler: top-class chaser: won Irish Grand National (by 14 lengths from Bless The Wings) in 2016/17: also won Red Mills Chase at Gowran (by length from Presenting Percy) in February: stayed 29f: acted on heavy going: front runner/raced prominently: often let down by jumping (including on final start in Cheltenham Gold Cup): died after heart attack at exercise in April. *Mrs J. Harrington, Ireland* — **c167 x** / **h–**

OUR FOLLY 10 b.g. Sakhee (USA) – Regent's Folly (IRE) (Touching Wood (USA)) [2017/18 h105: h23g h26.5g* h26.5m[pu] h26.5d[6] h23.3g[5] h23.1v[pu] Nov 7] rather leggy gelding: fair handicap hurdler: won at Newton Abbot in June: stays 3¼m: acts on good to firm and heavy going: has worn headgear: usually wears tongue tie: usually races prominently. *Stuart Kittow* — **h104**

OUR KAEMPFER (IRE) 9 b.g. Oscar (IRE) – Gra-Bri (IRE) (Rashar (USA)) [2017/18 c145, h–: c23.4v[pu] h21d h25s[6] h21g h25d[6] Apr 26] tall gelding: fairly useful handicap hurdler: smart chaser: stays 3m: acts on good to soft going: tried in cheekpieces: usually wears tongue tie. *Charlie Longsdon* — **c–** / **h124**

OUR KYLIE (IRE) 6 b.m. Jeremy (USA) – Prakara (IRE) (Indian Ridge) [2017/18 h114p: h16.5g h16.8g* h16.8g* h16.4g[5] h16d[4] h21.6d Dec 22] sturdy mare: fairly useful handicap hurdler: won at Sedgefield in September and October: unproven beyond 17f: acts on good to soft going: tried in cheekpieces. *Brian Ellison* — **h121**

OUR LUCAS (IRE) 6 b.g. Jeremy (USA) – Alassio (USA) (Gulch (USA)) [2017/18 h–: h16v[2] h15.6d[2] h16v[3] h16v* h17d[4] h16g[2] h20.2s Apr 27] fair handicap hurdler: won at Ayr and Carlisle in March: second at former course in April: unproven beyond 17f: acts on heavy going. *R. Mike Smith* — **h107**

OUR

OUR MERLIN 6 b.g. Pasternak – Lorgnette (Emperor Fountain) [2017/18 h–p, b88: h20f⁶ h17.7s^F h15.9d* h17.7v* h16.5s* h16.2s h16.8v³ h16.5s⁵ Feb 20] sturdy gelding: fairly useful handicap hurdler: completed hat-trick when winning at Plumpton, Fontwell and Taunton in December: placed at Sandown and Cheltenham in January: stays 2¼m: acts on heavy going: usually races close up, often travels strongly. *Robert Walford* — **h124**

OUR MORRIS (IRE) 7 b.g. Milan – Broken Gale (IRE) (Broken Hearted) [2017/18 h79, b71: h23.3g⁵ h23.3v^pu h20.1v Nov 22] poor maiden hurdler: stays 23f. *George Bewley* — **h80**

OURO BRANCO (FR) 5 b.g. Kapgarde (FR) – Dolce Vita Yug (Emperor Jones (USA)) [2017/18 b95: h15.8d⁴ h19.9d h16.2s⁶ h19.4s⁵ h23.1s Feb 23] bumper winner: fair form over hurdles: may prove best at around 2m: acts on good to soft going: tried in hood: usually races nearer last than first. *Nigel Hawke* — **h107**

OUR PHILLIE LILY 6 b.m. Sulamani (IRE) – Tyre Hill Lilly (Jupiter Island) [2017/18 h–, b–: h21.6g⁶ h16.8d³ h16.8d³ h20g h18.5v Nov 7] lengthy mare: poor maiden hurdler. *Susan Gardner* — **h76**

OUR REWARD (IRE) 8 b.g. Morozov (USA) – Paddyeoin (IRE) (Insan (USA)) [2017/18 h115: c23.8g³ c23.4g² May 28] winning Irish pointer: fairly useful hurdler: fair form over fences: probably stays 23f: acts on soft going. *Jamie Snowden* — **c110 h–**

OUR SIOUX SUE (IRE) 6 b.m. Zagreb (USA) – Wuchowsen (IRE) (King's Ride) [2017/18 b16.2g⁶ May 28] fifth foal: half-sister to bumper winner Helmsley Lad (by Fair Mix): dam, well held in bumpers, half-sister to useful hurdler (2m-2¼m winner) Issaquah: well beaten in mares bumper. *Malcolm Jefferson* — **b–**

OURSON (FR) 11 br.g. Sagacity (FR) – Houri (FR) (Luynes (USA)) [2017/18 c19.4g⁶ Sep 9] point winner: no form under Rules. *Phil York* — **c– h–**

OUR SOX (IRE) 9 b.g. September Storm (GER) – Winning Sally (IRE) (Lancastrian) [2017/18 c112, h101: c20m h24g c26.7g^pu c19.7s^pu Nov 20] angular gelding: fair hurdler/chaser, no form in 2017/18: left A. J. Martin after second start: tried in blinkers: usually wears tongue tie: often races towards rear. *Anthony Honeyball* — **c– h–**

OUR THOMAS (FR) 6 b.g. Dylan Thomas (IRE) – Sinamay (USA) (Saint Ballado (CAN)) [2017/18 h113: h19.9d Sep 24] sturdy gelding: fairly useful hurdler at best, well held sole start in 2017/18: stays 2¼m: acts on good to soft going: often wears cheekpieces/tongue tie: usually races close up. *John Cornwall* — **h–**

Red Mills Chase, Gowran—a final win for the ill-fated Our Duke, who claims the scalp of leading novice Presenting Percy (noseband) despite having to concede that rival 7 lb

OUR

OUR THREE SONS (IRE) 7 b.g. Shantou (USA) – Ballyquinn (IRE) (Anshan) [2017/18 h115: h16m* h16.3g² h16.3m* h17.7g² h16.8g⁴ Oct 3] fairly useful handicap hurdler: won at Kempton (amateur) in May and Stratford in July: second at Fontwell in August: stays 2¼m: acts on good to firm and good to soft going: often wears cheekpieces: front runner. *Jamie Snowden*   **h118**

OUR VALENTINA (IRE) 7 b.m. Shantou (USA) – Par Street (IRE) (Dolphin Street (FR)) [2017/18 h98, b84: h20.5v⁴ h20s* h20.6s⁵ h19.5vᵖᵘ h21.4v⁵ h17d² h24.3g² Apr 20] fair handicap hurdler: won mares event at Carlisle in December: second in similar event at Ayr in April: stays 3m: acts on heavy going: often in headgear. *Stuart Crawford, Ireland*   **h109**

OURVILLE'S MILLION (FR) 5 b.g. Sageburg (IRE) – Madeka (FR) (Kadalko (FR)) [2017/18 b15.8d⁶ b15.7g⁴ h16d⁶ h15.8s Jan 10] €75,000 3-y-o: half-brother to 3 winners in France, including useful hurdler Ladeka (17f winner, by Linda's Lad) and the dam of smart 2m hurdler We Have A Dream: dam ran twice over hurdles in France: modest form in bumpers/over hurdles. *Oliver Sherwood*   **h91 b76**

OUR YOUNG UN 5 b.g. Native Ruler – Dani (IRE) (Modigliani (USA)) [2017/18 b–: ab16g Nov 28] no form in bumpers. *John Gallagher*   **b–**

OUTBACK BLUE 5 gr.g. Aussie Rules (USA) – Beautiful Lady (IRE) (Peintre Celebre (USA)) [2017/18 h16.8s h15.6s⁵ Jan 3] fair on Flat, stays 10.5f: modest form over hurdles: better effort when fifth in maiden at Musselburgh: wears tongue tie. *George Bewley*   **h85**

OUTCROP (IRE) 4 b.g. Rock of Gibraltar (IRE) – Desert Sage (Selkirk (USA)) [2017/18 h15.8s⁵ h16.4v⁶ h15.7d² h15.7s⁵ Jan 11] fairly useful on Flat, stays 11f: fair form when second in juvenile at Catterick, standout effort over hurdles: in hood last 2 starts. *Jennie Candlish*   **h101**

OUT FOR JUSTICE (IRE) 5 b.g. Beneficial – Dustys Delight (IRE) (Oscar (IRE)) [2017/18 b15.8d⁶ Apr 24] runner-up in Irish point on debut: in tongue tie, 10/1, sixth in bumper at Ludlow. *Katy Price*   **b–**

OUTLANDER (IRE) 10 b.g. Stowaway – Western Whisper (IRE) (Supreme Leader) [2017/18 c165, h–: c25d⁶ c24s* c25.6v³ c24d³ c24s² c26.3vᵖᵘ c29vᵖᵘ c24.5s Apr 25] lengthy gelding: winning hurdler: high-class chaser: won JNwine.com Champion Chase at Down Royal (by ½ length from Road To Respect) in November: third in Christmas Chase at Leopardstown (3½ lengths behind Road To Respect) in December and second in Irish Gold Cup there (neck behind Edwulf) in February: well held in Punchestown Gold Cup final outing: stays 25f: acts on heavy going: wears headgear: often races prominently: unreliable. *Gordon Elliott, Ireland*   **c164 § h–**

*JNwine.com Champion Chase, Down Royal—
first-time cheekpieces spark a revival from 16/1-shot Outlander who defeats Road To Respect
(nearest camera) in a race in which Gigginstown has 4 of the first 5 home*

OVE

OUTLAW JACK (IRE) 6 b.g. Mr Dinos (IRE) – Bonus Issue (IRE) (Treasure Hunter) h– [2017/18 h19.6g⁵ Oct 17] won Irish point on debut: tailed off in maiden hurdle. *Alan Jessop*

OUTLAW JOSEY WALES (IRE) 7 b.g. Jeremy (USA) – Trinity Scholar (IRE) h– (Invincible Spirit (IRE)) [2017/18 h71: h16.2g h16.2g h18.1g Sep 20] maiden hurdler, no form in 2017/18. *R. Mike Smith*

OUTNUMBERED (IRE) 5 b.g. Stowaway – Back Market Lass (IRE) (Bob Back **h100** (USA)) [2017/18 h19.7s h20.8d h22.7s⁴ h22.7v h18.9s⁶ Mar 21] €21,000 3-y-o: sixth foal: half-brother to a winning pointer by King's Theatre: dam unraced half-sister to useful hurdler/chaser (stayed 3¼m) Corket and to dam of Midlands Grand National winner Minella Four Star: fair form over hurdles: probably stays 23f: acts on soft going. *Chris Grant*

OUT OF STYLE (IRE) 7 b.g. Court Cave (IRE) – Portanob (IRE) (Be My Native **h84** (USA)) [2017/18 b88p: h19.5d h16.7g⁵ Apr 22] won Irish maiden point on debut: poor form over hurdles: has joined Alastair Ralph. *Fergal O'Brien*

OUT OF THE LOOP 5 b.g. Shantou (USA) – Sparron Hawk (FR) (Hawker's News **h136 p** (IRE)) [2017/18 h18.8v³ h18.8d* h16s⁵ h20s* h20s* Feb 24] fifth foal: half-brother to fairly useful hurdler Some Hawk (2¾m winner) and modest hurdler Uptake (2½m-2¾m winner) (both by Presenting): dam (b98), bumper winner, half-sister to useful chaser (stayed 3m) The Wicketkeeper and to dam of high-class hurdler/smart chaser L'Ami Serge and useful hurdler/very smart chaser Sizing Codelco (both stay 25f): useful form over hurdles: won maiden at Downpatrick in October, and handicaps at Fairyhouse in December and February (by 5½ lengths from Sire du Berlais): should stay further than 2½m: acts on heavy going: will go on improving. *Padraig Roche, Ireland*

OUTOFTHISWORLD (IRE) 5 b.m. Shantou (USA) – Mystic Masie (IRE) (Turgeon b– (USA)) [2017/18 b97P: b15.8s Dec 26] impressive winner of bumper on debut, well held sole outing in 2017/18. *Harry Fry*

OUTRAGEOUS ROMANA (IRE) 7 b.m. Mahler – South West Nine (IRE) (Oscar **h74** (IRE)) [2017/18 h–: h19.9s³ h19.9d* h23.1s³ h19.7s⁵ Mar 27] unseated rider in point: poor handicap hurdler: won mares event at Uttoxeter in November: will stay 3m: acts on soft going: usually races nearer last than first. *John O'Shea*

OUT SAM 9 b.g. Multiplex – Tintera (IRE) (King's Theatre (IRE)) [2017/18 c134§, h111§: **c134 §** c24.5d c25v⁶ c28.7vᵖᵘ c28.5s³ c24.7v³ Apr 2] lengthy gelding: fair hurdler: useful handicap **h– §** chaser: third in Ulster National at Downpatrick in March: stays 29f: acts on heavy going: often wears headgear/tongue tie: usually races towards rear: unreliable. *Gordon Elliott, Ireland*

OVERAWED 7 b.m. Overbury (IRE) – Alleged To Rhyme (IRE) (Leading Counsel **c76** (USA)) [2017/18 h102: h20g h16.5s c19.4d⁵ Apr 22] fair form over hurdles, well held first **h–** 2 starts in 2017/18: 16/1, fifth in novice handicap at Stratford (28¼ lengths behind Zamparelli) on chasing debut: best effort at 2m: acts on heavy going. *Tom George*

OVERLAND FLYER (IRE) 7 b.g. Westerner – Love Train (IRE) (Sadler's Wells h– (USA)) [2017/18 h120: h23.1vᵖᵘ Feb 11] winning pointer: fairly useful hurdler, pulled up sole start in 2017/18: wears tongue tie. *Paul Nicholls*

OVER MY HEAD 10 gr.g. Overbury (IRE) – Altesse de Sou (FR) (Saint Preuil (FR)) **c67** [2017/18 c65, h65: c23.6s² c23.6s⁴ c24.5v c24.5v⁴ c24.5vᴿ c24.5vᵖᵘ Mar 29] tall gelding: **h–** winning hurdler: poor maiden chaser: stays 3m: acts on heavy going: wears tongue tie: front runner/races prominently. *Claire Dyson*

OVERRIDER 8 b.g. Cockney Rebel (IRE) – Fustaan (IRE) (Royal Applause) [2017/18 h– h78: h16g⁵ h15.8g⁶ h16d Sep 3] little form over hurdles: often in tongue tie. *Shaun Lycett*

OVER STATED (IRE) 6 b.g. Shantou (USA) – Mrs Gordi (Classic Cliche (IRE)) **h94** [2017/18 h19.5d⁵ h20.3s⁶ Dec 17] €34,000 3-y-o, £80,000 5-y-o: fifth foal: half-brother to fair hurdler/winning pointer Billy Billy (3m winner, by Darsi): dam, unraced, out of half-sister to Stayers' Hurdle winner Anzum: off mark in Irish points at fourth attempt (first completed start): modest form over hurdles. *Richard Phillips*

OVER THE AIR 10 br.m. Overbury (IRE) – Moonlight Air (Bold Owl) [2017/18 h–: **h106** h23.g³ h20g³ h23g⁴ h20g h20.3d h21.2mᵖᵘ Oct 11] fair handicap hurdler: stays 3m: acts on soft and good to firm going: tried in hood/tongue tie: often races towards rear. *John Spearing*

OVE

OVER THE ARCH (IRE) 6 br.g. Presenting – On The Outside (IRE) (Anshan) [2017/18 h19.3s h21m⁴ Apr 26] has scope: fourth foal: dam (c124/h95), 17f-3m hurdle/chase winner, half-sister to fair hurdler/useful chaser (stayed 2½m) Cruising Katie: placed twice in Irish points: modest form over hurdles: better effort when fourth in novice at Kempton. *Richard Rowe* **h93**

OVERTHEEDGE (IRE) 9 b.g. Morozov (USA) – Ballyroe Hill (IRE) (Over The River (FR)) [2017/18 c–, h108: h20.3g⁶ h22.1d³ h25.4g^pu h23.1g⁴ Aug 19] point winner: fair handicap hurdler: failed to complete both chase starts: stays 23f: acts on soft going: often races in rear. *Simon West* **c– h103**

OVER TO MIDNIGHT 8 b.m. Midnight Legend – Makeover (Priolo (USA)) [2017/18 h–: h19.6d^pu h19.7s⁶ c16d c16d^F Mar 22] little form over hurdles: twice-raced over fences: dead. *Lady Susan Brooke* **c83 h–**

OVERTOUJAY 8 b.g. Overbury (IRE) – Ouh Jay (Karinga Bay) [2017/18 h89, b80: h20.6g⁴ h23.4g² h20.6g* h22g⁶ h18.6g⁴ h24g Aug 20] maiden pointer: modest handicap hurdler: won at Market Rasen in June: stays 3m: acts on good to soft going: often wears cheekpieces: often races freely. *Charles Pogson* **h89**

OVERTOWN EXPRESS (IRE) 10 br.g. Overbury (IRE) – Black Secret (Gildoran) [2017/18 c142, h–: c16.4g* c17.5v^F c15.5s³ c20.5s⁴ c16s² h19.9v⁵ c15.8s Apr 12] workmanlike gelding: fairly useful form over hurdles: smart handicap chaser: won at Newbury (by 10 lengths from Rock On Rocky) in December: second at Chepstow in February: stays 2½m: acts on heavy going: races towards rear. *Harry Fry* **c149 h129**

OVERWORKDUNDERPAID (IRE) 5 b.g. Getaway (GER) – Another Whiparound (IRE) (Saddlers' Hall (IRE)) [2017/18 b15.8s³ h20s h21.3s⁴ h21.6v⁵ h23.1s⁵ h23.1d Apr 21] €20,000 3-y-o, £82,000 4-y-o: useful-looking gelding: third foal: half-brother to a winning pointer by Robin des Pres: dam (c101/h85), winning pointer/maiden under Rules (stayed 3m), closely related to useful hurdler/chaser (stays 3¼m) Call Me Vic and half-sister to useful hurdler/chaser (stayed 3½m) Shoreacres: Irish point winner (finished alone): shaped well when third in maiden bumper at Ffos Las (1½ lengths behind The Dubai Way) in October: fair form over hurdles: stays 23f: acts on soft going: in cheekpieces last 2 starts. *Charlie Longsdon* **h109 b95**

OWEN NA VIEW (IRE) 10 b.g. Presenting – Lady Zephyr (IRE) (Toulon) [2017/18 c124, h–: h17g c16.5g⁴ c15.8g^pu c16gur c20g⁵ c16.5g c17g h16g Nov 1] angular gelding: fairly useful hurdler at best: fairly useful handicap chaser: fourth at Worcester in June, only form in 2017/18: stays 21f: acts on good to firm and good to soft going: often wears headgear: has worn tongue tie: front runner/races prominently, tends to find little. *Fergal O'Brien* **c121 h–**

OWL 7 b.m. Overbury (IRE) – Lady Howe (Lord Americo) [2017/18 b–: h16.2g^F May 28] tailed off in bumper: fell fatally on hurdling debut. *Sandy Forster* **h–**

OWNERS DAY 8 gr.m. Fair Mix (IRE) – Charmeille (FR) (Exit To Nowhere (USA)) [2017/18 h112: h15.7g⁶ h17.2s^pu h20g Aug 30] rather leggy mare: fair hurdler, no form in 2017/18: tried in tongue tie: usually races towards rear. *Neil Mulholland* **h–**

OXFORD BLU 4 b.g. Aqlaam – Blue Zealot (IRE) (Galileo (IRE)) [2017/18 h16s* h17.7v⁴ h16v³ h16.7s² h16.4s^pu h16.8g Apr 18] compact gelding: fairly useful form over hurdles: won juvenile at Fakenham in December: second in handicap at Market Rasen in February: unproven beyond 17f: acts on soft going: in cheekpieces last 3 starts. *Olly Murphy* **h120**

OXWICH BAY (IRE) 6 b.g. Westerner – Rose de Beaufai (FR) (Solon (GER)) [2017/18 h116p, b93: h16d² h16.4d² h20v* h19.3v^F h15.8v² h19.8v^pu h20v⁴ Apr 15] unfurnished gelding: bumper winner: fairly useful hurdler: won maiden at Ffos Las in December: stays 2½m: acts on heavy going. *Evan Williams* **h119**

OYSTER PEARL (IRE) 5 gr.m. Thousand Words – Rectify (IRE) (Mujadil (USA)) [2017/18 h16g h16g h16.8g⁵ Sep 2] poor maiden on Flat: well held in novice hurdles: wears tongue tie. *Carroll Gray* **h–**

OYSTER SHELL 11 br.g. Bollin Eric – Pearly-B (IRE) (Gunner B) [2017/18 c–§, h–§: c22.6g^pu Jun 20] winning pointer: winning hurdler: fairly useful chaser at best, pulled up in handicap only start in 2017/18: in cheekpieces last 2 starts: often wears tongue tie: temperamental. *Oliver Greenall* **c– § h– §**

OZZIE THE OSCAR (IRE) 7 b.g. Oscar (IRE) – Private Official (IRE) (Beneficial) [2017/18 h136: h15.8s⁵ c16.2d* c15.9s³ c16² c16.2g* Apr 26] useful-looking gelding: useful hurdler: smart form over fences: won novice at Warwick (by 2 lengths from Shantou Rock) in November and novice handicap there (by 5 lengths from Sister Sibyl) in April: raced around 2m: acts on soft going. *Philip Hobbs*   c150 + h–

OZZY THOMAS (IRE) 8 b.g. Gold Well – Bramble Leader (IRE) (Supreme Leader) [2017/18 c125, h115: c23.8m* c26.1m^F c24g* c23.8m² c23.9s³ c25.3g^pu Apr 18] rather leggy gelding: fairly useful hurdler: useful chaser: won novice handicap at Ludlow in May and novice at Southwell in September: second in handicap at former course in October: stays 3m: acts on soft and good to firm going: wears cheekpieces: tried in tongue tie. *Henry Oliver*   c139 h–

P

PACHA DU POLDER (FR) 11 b.g. Muhtathir – Ambri Piotta (FR) (Caerwent) [2017/18 c137, h–: c26s³ c26.3v* Mar 16]   c134 h–

The fact that, for the first time in Britain, a racehorse tested positive for the controversial performance-enhancing substance cobalt was big news in itself. Cases involving the substance have been in the limelight in Australia where there has been a spate of positives in recent years, in response to which Britain and Ireland introduced thresholds for the naturally-occurring mineral in April 2016. However, perhaps just as worrying as the cobalt positive itself recorded by Anseanachai Cliste was the fact that the horse was a point-to-point winner running in a hunter chase. Does it indicate a problem with drugs right down at the sport's grassroots? If so, racing is in serious trouble. Although Flat trainer Rebecca Bastiman (£5,000 fine) and her father/assistant Robin (disqualified for three years) were found guilty in August 2018 after retrospective testing relating to a race in 2016, the British Horseracing Authority says it has found no evidence of widespread cobalt use in Britain (in higher doses it produces more red blood cells), while the Irish authorities—Anseanachai Cliste was trained in Northern Ireland—say they 'don't know' whether it is a problem, or not, but have said that more out-of-competition testing and stable inspections are taking place ('two, three or four a week'). It emerged meanwhile, shortly after the test on Anseanachai Cliste, that on a routine inspection of champion trainer Willie Mullins' yard in February 2015, veterinary surgeon Tim Brennan, a long-serving vet for the stable, had his vehicle searched by officials from the special investigations unit of the Department of Agriculture and the Irish Turf Club. Unlicenced substances were found, including catosal (a painkiller used in animals), quinidine sulphate (used to treat atrial fibrillation in horses) and Hemo-15, an injectable supplement that contains cobalt. Brennan faced a number of charges at a 'fitness to practice' veterinary hearing after the judge at Kilkenny District Court in late-2017 decided Brennan's offences, involving fourteen separate charges over animal remedies and issues over their labelling, had been due to 'inadvertence'. Most of the charges were struck out, though Brennan was found guilty at the district court hearing on three counts of possession of unauthorised animal remedies and one of failing to keep records. No conviction was recorded against him on any of the charges but he was ordered to pay €1,150 in witness expenses, though there was no order as to legal costs. Brennan also found himself implicated in a British Horseracing Authority investigation into irregular betting patterns ahead of the withdrawal of the Mullins-trained Faugheen from the 2016 Champion Hurdle, a case discussed in the Introduction.

Anseanachai Cliste, a leading point-to-pointer, was an eleventh hour withdrawal from the 2017 Foxhunter Challenge Cup at Cheltenham, ordered to be taken out by the stewards who were not satisfied that he had been administered only normal feed and water on raceday, as required under the rules. Bloody syringes were found in a bag at the racecourse stables and the horse subsequently tested positive with cobalt levels seven times above the permitted limit. Anseanachai Cliste's trainer Stephen McConville and his son Michael, who owns and rides the horse, admitted before a disciplinary panel in September to giving two injections to the horse on raceday, one of them Hemo-15. The McConvilles lied to Cheltenham stewards

St James's Place Foxhunter Challenge Cup, Cheltenham—Pacha du Polder defies even longer odds than 12 months earlier as he overhauls leader Top Wood (No.16) to repeat his 2017 win; Cousin Pete (left) and 2017 third Barel of Laughs (cheekpieces) dead-heat for third

on the day, saying Anseanachai Cliste had not been injected and that the syringes had mistakenly been left in the bag by another son. Both eventually co-operated with the BHA's investigations and pleaded guilty at the September hearing when they were disqualified from racing for three years (nine days after being prevented from running in the Foxhunter, Anseanachai Cliste had given Stephen McConville his biggest win as a trainer when landing the Ulster National at Downpatrick, the trainer's first win under Rules since 2011). The season's leading Irish hunter chaser Foxrock had also been prevented from running in the 2017 Foxhunter, in his case because he had been placed in a Grade 1 chase the previous season which made him ineligible for the Cheltenham race. Foxrock was again in the news after the latest edition of the Foxhunter when a veterinary officer reported that a kit bag search on the day of the race revealed possession of an oral paste, an electrolyte trace element replacer. The trainer's assurance that Foxrock had received only normal food and water on raceday was accepted, the container for the paste having not been opened. Foxrock was allowed to run but he was routine tested and the substance was confiscated, with the trainer facing an inquiry at a later date.

Foxrock proved the big disappointment of the latest St James's Place Foxhunter, the race immediately after the Gold Cup on the final day of the Festival. Starting second favourite behind fellow Irish challenger Burning Ambition, Foxrock was struggling early on the final circuit and was tailed off when pulled up two out. Both Foxrock (Ms Katie Walsh) and Burning Ambition (Mr J. J. Codd) were partnered by top amateurs, as was the only other runner to start at single-figure odds Wonderful Charm (Mr Sam Waley-Cohen). Wonderful Charm was one of four runners for Manor Farm Stables which also saddled the previous year's winner Pacha du Polder, a 25/1-shot this time ridden by the relatively inexperienced Miss Harriet Tucker, a 7-lb claiming amateur unable to draw her allowance in the Foxhunter, whose only other ride under Rules had been when partnering Pacha du Polder in his preparatory race (weak in the betting when third of five in a hunter chase behind Warden Hill at Doncaster three weeks earlier). Miss Tucker qualified to ride in the Foxhunter (for which amateurs now need a category B permit) by virtue of having had 'at least twenty completed rides in point-to-points and/or under the rules of racing, the majority over obstacles.' The new restrictions would have prevented Olympic cycling champion Victoria Pendleton from completing her year-long 'switching saddles' challenge in the 2016 Foxhunters in which she finished a never-nearer fifth on Pacha du Polder, riding with a category A licence which requires amateurs only to pass a two-day course (Pendleton had competed in more than a dozen points, had five rides on the Flat and two races over fences under Rules in the run up to Cheltenham, but she had not had twenty completions). Pacha du Polder won the Foxhunter twelve months later under the more experienced Miss Bryony Frost, who went on to make an even bigger name for herself in the latest season.

Pacha du Polder's latest victory made him the third horse this decade to retain the Foxhunter (following Salsify in 2012 and 2013) and On The Fringe (2015 and 2016), his jockey belying her relative inexperience and riding a patient race to produce him to lead at the last. Front-running 50/1-shot Top Wood rallied after blundering at the final fence but Pacha du Polder held him by a neck, despite his rider having to cope with a partially dislocated shoulder in the closing stages. Barel of Laughs, third the previous year at 100/1, and Cousin Pete dead-heated for third, with Burning Ambition (subsequently found to be suffering from heat exhaustion) running much better than his final placing of eighth after travelling strongly entering the home straight, and Wonderful Charm, runner-up to Pacha du Polder the year before, proving a big let-down and eventually pulled up. Wonderful Charm had gone on to run in the Grand National after his Foxhunter second but, under new rules introduced by the BHA, horses with licenced trainers will not now be allowed to switch back to handicaps in the same season if they run in a hunter chase (the rule does not apply to permit holders and point-to-point stables campaigning horses in a higher grade). The BHA has made a concession, after meeting resistance from the National Trainers' Federation, and the rules now allow horses which run for licenced trainers in November and December to be eligible for hunter chases after the turn of the year.

The results at the latest Cheltenham Festival, incidentally, featured four winning female jockeys, Ms Katie Walsh being successful in the Champion Bumper on Relegate, while 3-lb claimers Lizzie Kelly (Coo Star Sivola in the Ultima Handicap Chase) and Bridget Andrews (Mohaayed in the County Hurdle) became the first female professionals to win at the Festival. Despite those successes, and those of the British season's most successful female rider Bryony Frost who also claims 3 lb, female jockeys are still not making the significant impact over jumps that perhaps they deserve (Bryony Frost had thirty-eight wins—twice as many as any other female—from 204 rides in 2017/18 when female jockeys as a whole obtained just over five per cent of all rides).

Pacha du Polder (FR) (b.g. 2007)
- Muhtathir (ch 1995)
  - Elmaamul (ch 1987)
    - Diesis
    - Modena
  - Majmu (b 1988)
    - Al Nasr
    - Affirmative Fable
- Ambri Piotta (FR) (b 1991)
  - Caerwent (b 1985)
    - Caerleon
    - Marwell
  - Alkmene (b 1980)
    - Matahawk
    - Astrale

The well-made Pacha du Polder, whose Flat-oriented pedigree was outlined in last year's Annual, never fully lived up to the high hopes held for him when he first joined Paul Nicholls from France (he once had a Timeform 'squiggle'). He has been rejuvenated as a hunter chaser, however, and will attempt to become the first horse to win the Foxhunter three times when he is returned to Cheltenham again in the next season. Pacha du Polder has proved himself an ideal mount for an amateur and, as well as being proven over the trip, is also versatile with regards to ground, having won on going ranging from good to firm to heavy. *Paul Nicholls*

PACIFIC DE BAUNE (FR) 5 gr.g. Al Namix (FR) – Perle de Baune (FR) (En Calcat (FR)) [2017/18 h16.3s* h20.3v h16.3s* h16d² Apr 7] £60,000 4-y-o: rather unfurnished gelding: half-brother to 3 winners, including fair hurdler Sydney de Baune (19f winner, by Califet) and French hurdler/chaser Seville de Baune (15f-17f winner, by Nononito): dam French 15f-17f hurdle/chase winner: runner-up in Irish point on debut: useful form over hurdles: won maiden at Newbury in December and novice there (by 12 lengths from Article Fifty) in March: likely to prove best around 2m. *Nicky Henderson* h133

PAC

PAC IT IN 4 b.f. Paco Boy (IRE) – Bisaat (USA) (Bahri (USA)) [2017/18 ab16d Mar 5] b–
sister to 1¼m winner Ventura Castle and half-sister to several winners, including bumper winner/fair hurdler At First Light (2m-2¾m winner, by Echo of Light) and fair hurdler Khismet (17f winner, by Kheleyf): dam once-raced sister to fairly useful hurdler/fair chaser (stayed 3m) Maraafeq: well beaten in maiden bumper. *David Weston*

PACKETTOTHERAFTERS (IRE) 9 b.g. Craigsteel – Darazari River (IRE) (Darazari (IRE)) [2017/18 c26d^{pu} c21.2d^4 c22.6d^{pu} c24g^4 c24.1g* c25.8d^{pu} c24s^2 c24.2v^{pu} Nov 7] c91
lengthy gelding: winning pointer: modest chaser: won handicap at Bangor in August: left Miss S. Whitehead after third start: stays 3m: acts on soft going: wears cheekpieces: front runner/races prominently. *Gary Hanmer*

PACK IT IN (IRE) 5 br.g. Big Bad Bob (IRE) – Evening Dress (Medicean) [2017/18 h16.8v^{bd} h16v^{pu} Nov 22] fair at one time on Flat, stays 1½m: failed to complete both starts over hurdles. *Alexandra Dunn* h–

PACOFILHA 4 b.f. Paco Boy (IRE) – Seradim (Elnadim (USA)) [2017/18 h16d^6 h20.5v^5 h15.8v h19s Mar 26] half-sister to fair hurdler Excellent Team (2m-2¼m winner, by Teofilo): fair maiden on Flat, stays 1½m: no form over hurdles. *John Flint* h–

PADAWAN (IRE) 9 br.g. Stowaway – Afsana (IRE) (Bluebird (USA)) [2017/18 h60 h16g^6 h23g^4 Jun 14] lengthy gelding: off mark in Irish points at fifth attempt: poor form over hurdles. *David Dennis* h70

PADDLING (FR) 7 b.g. Walk In The Park (IRE) – Sea Mamaille (FR) (Sea Full (FR)) [2017/18 c84, h80, b–: c15.6v^4 c15.7d^3 c19.2d* c20.5v^3 c21.1v^2 c19.3v^3 c16.4v^4 c16.4v^2 Apr 13] close-coupled gelding: maiden hurdler: modest handicap chaser: won at Catterick in December: stays 19f: acts on heavy going. *Micky Hammond* c96 h–

PADDOCKS LOUNGE (IRE) 11 b.g. Oscar (IRE) – Sister Rosza (IRE) (Roselier (FR)) [2017/18 c93, h110: h17.2d^6 c21.2g^4 c25.5d^6 Aug 26] lengthy gelding: Irish point winner: fair hurdler: fair form over fences: stays 21f: acts on good to firm and heavy going: has worn hood: wears tongue tie: front runner. *Aytach Sadik* c102 h–

PADDY BOSS (IRE) 6 ch.g. Gamut (IRE) – Agladora (FR) (Take Risks (FR)) [2017/18 b16g* May 13] fourth foal: dam, French maiden (ran once over hurdles), half-sister to fairly useful French hurdler (15f-17f winner) La Reine Chic: 7/4, looked useful prospect when won bumper at Warwick (by 2¼ lengths from Jersey Bean) on debut. *Alan King* b99 p

PADDY'S FIELD (IRE) 8 b.g. Flemensfirth (USA) – Kittys Oscar (IRE) (Oscar (IRE)) [2017/18 c117, h–: h21m^2 h24g* h23g^3 c23g^4 Aug 30] useful-looking gelding: fairly useful handicap hurdler: won at Southwell in June: fair form over fences: stays 3m: acts on good to firm and heavy going: tried in cheekpieces. *Ben Pauling* c111 h119

PADDYS MOTORBIKE (IRE) 6 ch.g. Fast Company (IRE) – Saffa Garden (IRE) (King's Best (USA)) [2017/18 h111: h20g^2 May 9] fairly useful form over hurdles: second in handicap at Ffos Las (in cheekpieces) only start in 2017/18: likely to stay 3m: acts on heavy going: has joined Sam Thomas. *Christian Williams* h115

PADDY'S POEM 7 b.g. Proclamation (IRE) – Ashleys Petale (IRE) (Ashley Park (IRE)) [2017/18 b92: h16s h15.9s^3 h15.9v^3 h15.9v^2 h16v Feb 16] fair form over hurdles: raced only at 2m on soft/heavy going: usually races close up. *Nick Gifford* h113

PADDYS RUNNER 6 gr.g. Sir Percy – Frosty Welcome (USA) (With Approval (CAN)) [2017/18 h118: h17.7g^6 h20.6g^2 h19.8s^5 h19.4d^6 h16.7s^6 h21.4d Apr 22] close-coupled gelding: fairly useful handicap hurdler: stays 21f: acts on soft going: has worn headgear, including last 2 starts. *Graeme McPherson* h117

PADDY'S YARN (IRE) 8 ch.g. Houmayoun (FR) – Deidamia (USA) (Dayjur (USA)) [2017/18 h78: h23.3g May 23] poor maiden hurdler: failed to complete in points: has worn tongue tie: often races towards rear, usually freely. *Valerie Jackson* h–

PADDY THE OSCAR (IRE) 15 b.g. Oscar (IRE) – Parsonage (The Parson) [2017/18 c110, h–: c24.1d^2 c23.6d^2 c23.6s* c24.2s^2 c24v^2 c23.6v^3 c23.6s^5 Mar 22] maiden hurdler: fairly useful handicap chaser: won at Chepstow in November and February: stays 3¼m: acts on heavy going: tried in cheekpieces/tongue tie: front runner. *Grace Harris* c115 h–

PADDY THE STOUT (IRE) 13 b.g. Oscar Schindler (IRE) – Misty Silks (Scottish Reel) [2017/18 c91§, h–: c20.9s^{pu} Jan 29] strong gelding: maiden hurdler: fair chaser at best, no longer of any account (races mainly in points nowadays): wears tongue tie: temperamental. *L. Humphrey* c– § h–

PADGE (IRE) 9 b.g. Flemensfirth (USA) – Mona Vic (IRE) (Old Vic) [2017/18 h21.4v^{pu} h23.6s^5 h20v^{pu} Apr 1] sturdy gelding: useful hurdler at best, little show in 2017/18 after long absence: winning chaser: stays 23f: acts on heavy going. *Evan Williams* c– h103

610

PAL

PADLEYOUROWNCANOE 4 b.g. Nayef (USA) – Pooka's Daughter (IRE) (Eagle Eyed (USA)) [2017/18 h15.8d³ h16d⁴ h16.8v* h19s* h19s² h16.4s⁴ h17s Apr 12] compact gelding: fair on Flat, stays 1¾m: fairly useful handicap hurdler: won at Exeter (conditional) in November and Taunton in December: left Daniel Loughnane after first start: stays 19f: acts on heavy going: front runner/races prominently. *Colin Tizzard* **h124**

PADS (IRE) 8 b.g. Luso – Augusta Victoria (Callernish) [2017/18 h109, b67: h20m² h16.2g⁵ h15.7g h22.1g^F h23.9d⁴ h22.1d³ h20.2d³ c19.3g⁵ Apr 23] modest maiden hurdler: placed in points before winning first start in novice hunter at Sedgefield on chasing debut: left Iain Jardine after first start, Philip Kirby after fourth, Iain Jardine again after seventh: probably stays easy 3m: acts on soft going: has worn hood: often races prominently. *D. F. Bourke* **c74** **h98**

PAGEBURG (FR) 4 b.g. Sageburg (IRE) – Peace of Oasis (FR) (Oasis Dream) [2017/18 h16.7s Nov 15] dam half-sister to fairly useful French hurdler/chaser (17f-19f winner) Peace of Burg (by Sageburg): won 1¼m maiden only start on Flat for Cedric Rossi: 11/8, too free when well held in juvenile maiden at Bangor on hurdling debut: should do better. *Alan King* **h– p**

PAIN AU CHOCOLAT (FR) 7 b.g. Enrique – Clair Chene (FR) (Solido (FR)) [2017/18 c139, h84: c15.8s c15.2s² c15.2s^ur c15.8s⁴ c19.4v² c19.9s⁵ c20.1v* c20.1s² Apr 26] good-topped gelding: winning hurdler: useful handicap chaser: won at Newcastle in April: stays 2½m: acts on heavy going: has worn hood/tongue tie: front runner/races prominently. *Rebecca Menzies* **c139 h–**

PAINTERS LAD (IRE) 7 b.g. Fruits of Love (USA) – Great Cullen (IRE) (Simply Great (FR)) [2017/18 h–: h16.2g^pu h19.4g⁵ Dec 18] no form in bumper/over hurdles: tried in tongue tie. *Alison Hamilton* **h–**

PAIROFBROWNEYES (IRE) 9 b.g. Luso – Frankly Native (IRE) (Be My Native (USA)) [2017/18 c141, h116: h22.6v c17d c23v* c29v^F Apr 2] workmanlike gelding: fairly useful hurdler: smart handicap chaser: won Leinster National Handicap Chase at Gowran (by 3¾ lengths from Space Cadet) in March: fell fifth in Irish Grand National at Fairyhouse: left Barry John Murphy after second start: stays 23f: acts on heavy going: has worn cheekpieces, including in 2017/18. *W. P. Mullins, Ireland* **c148 h103**

PAIR OF JACKS (IRE) 10 ch.g. Presenting – Halona (Pollerton) [2017/18 c134, h–: c24d^pu May 6] winning hurdler: useful chaser at best, no form in 2017/18 (including in points): stays 25f: acts on good to firm and good to soft going. *Malcolm Jefferson* **c– h–**

PAISLEY PARK (IRE) 6 b.g. Oscar (IRE) – Presenting Shares (IRE) (Presenting) [2017/18 b97: h19.7s* h21s² h20.8d² h24v Mar 16] well-made gelding: useful form over hurdles: won novice at Hereford in December: second in Leamington Novices' Hurdle at Warwick (length behind Mr Whipped) in January: should stay 3m: tried in visor: often races towards rear. *Emma Lavelle* **h137**

PALADIN (IRE) 9 b.g. Dubawi (IRE) – Palwina (FR) (Unfuwain (USA)) [2017/18 h–: h20.3g h16.8d^f Jul 31] fair on Flat, stayed 1½m: maiden hurdler: tried in hood last 3 starts: tried in tongue tie: dead. *Michael Blake* **h–**

PALLASATOR 9 b.g. Motivator – Ela Athena (Ezzoud (IRE)) [2017/18 h19v⁵ h16v⁴ h20s* h20v* h25s* Apr 27] half-brother to modest hurdler Khan Tengri (2m-2¼m winner, by Sadler's Wells): very smart at best on Flat, stays 2¼m: useful form over hurdles: won maiden at Leopardstown in March and Grade 2 novice at Fairyhouse (by 2¼ lengths from Jetz) in April: will stay further than 2½m: raced only on soft/heavy going. *Gordon Elliott, Ireland* **h144**

PALMARIA 8 b.m. Kayf Tara – Ollejess (Scallywag) [2017/18 c24.2v* Apr 17] multiple point winner: maiden hurdler: 5/2, clear when left alone last in novice hunter at Exeter on chasing debut: stays 3m: best form on soft/heavy going: in hood last 2 starts. *Caroline Keevil* **c99 h–**

PALMERS HILL (IRE) 5 b.g. Gold Well – Tosca Shine (IRE) (Topanoora) [2017/18 h15.8d* h21.6d⁴ h19.8v³ Feb 3] £310,000 4-y-o: lengthy gelding: third foal: dam, unraced, out of sister to top-class 2m-2½m hurdler Mighty Mogul: off mark in Irish points at second attempt: fairly useful form over hurdles: won maiden at Uttoxeter in October: should stay beyond 2m. *Jonjo O'Neill* **h116**

PALM GREY (IRE) 10 gr.g. Great Palm (USA) – Lucy Cooper (IRE) (Roselier (FR)) [2017/18 c128, h70: c24.5s Oct 19] workmanlike gelding: winning hurdler: fairly useful chaser, well held only start in 2017/18: stayed 3m: acted on heavy going: dead. *Sue Smith* **c– h–**

PALOMA BLUE (IRE) 6 br.g. Stowaway – Court Leader (IRE) (Supreme Leader) [2017/18 b118: h19v³ h16s² h16d* h16s³ h16.4s⁴ h16.5d Apr 24] lengthy gelding: will make a chaser: smart bumper performer: smart form over hurdles: won maiden at Leopardstown (by 2 lengths from Impact Factor) in December: progressed further when in **h148**

PAL

frame behind Samcro in Deloitte Novices' Hurdle at Leopardstown and Supreme Novices' Hurdle (beaten 3 lengths) at Cheltenham: unproven beyond 2m: acts on soft going: front runner/races prominently. *Henry de Bromhead, Ireland*

PALOMA'S PRINCE (IRE) 9 ch.g. Nayef (USA) – Ma Paloma (FR) (Highest Honor (FR)) [2017/18 h85: h16d* h15.7g^{pu} Jun 13] modest handicap hurdler: won at Warwick in May: stayed 21f: acted on good to firm and good to soft going: tried in blinkers/tongue tie: front runner/raced prominently: dead. *Noel Williams* h87

PANDINUS IMPERATOR (IRE) 5 b.g. Scorpion (IRE) – Casiana (GER) (Acatenango (GER)) [2017/18 b16g^4 b16.7g h20.5s^6 h21.7g Apr 20] close-coupled gelding: little impact in varied events. *Martin Smith* h– b–

PANDY WELLS 9 b.m. Kayf Tara – Alina Rheinberg (GER) (Waky Nao) [2017/18 c69, h–: c19.9s^4 Dec 26] maiden hurdler: modest handicap chaser at one time, faded only start in 2017/18: stays 3m: acts on soft going. *Graeme McPherson* c67 h–

PANIC AND RUN (IRE) 5 b.g. Roderic O'Connor (IRE) – Bolas (Unfuwain (USA)) [2017/18 b16.7g^5 b17.7d^5 Jun 6] modest form in bumpers. *Oliver Sherwood* b77

PANIS ANGELICUS (FR) 9 b.g. Panis (USA) – Pyu (GER) (Surumu (GER)) [2017/18 h92: h20g^6 h18.5d h21.6g* h23.9g^2 h25.3s^F Jan 1] workmanlike gelding: modest handicap hurdler: won at Newton Abbot in September: stays 3m: acts on soft and good to firm going: has worn visor, including last 3 starts. *Tim Vaughan* h97

PANTOMIME (IRE) 6 gr.m. Mastercraftsman (IRE) – Dama'a (IRE) (Green Desert (USA)) [2017/18 h16s ab16.3g^4 Mar 3] modest on Flat, stays 16.5f: tailed off in novice on hurdling debut. *Rebecca Menzies* h–

PANTXOA (FR) 11 b.g. Daliapour (IRE) – Palmeria (FR) (Great Palm (USA)) [2017/18 c120, h–: c32.5d^{pu} c23.8g^5 Jul 5] sturdy gelding: winning hurdler: one-time useful chaser: nothing like force of old, but won point shortly after end of season: stays 27f: acts on soft and good to firm going: front runner/races prominently: inconsistent. *Fergal O'Brien* c94 h–

PAPAGANA 5 b.m. Martaline – New Destiny (FR) (Highest Honor (FR)) [2017/18 b16.7s^4 b15.7g^5 Apr 20] fifth foal: half-sister to 2 winners in France, including fairly useful hurdler/chaser News Reel (2¼m/19f winner, by Vespone): dam, French 10.5f winner, half-sister to smart hurdler/high-class chaser (15f-21f winner) Nickname: modest form in bumpers. *Oliver Sherwood* b83

PAPAGAYO (IRE) 6 b.g. Shirocco (GER) – Jomana (IRE) (Darshaan) [2017/18 h17s h19.7s^{pu} Nov 3] maiden on Flat: no form over hurdles. *Barry Murtagh* h–

PAPER LANTERN (IRE) 9 b.g. Oscar (IRE) – Lantern Lark (IRE) (Be My Native (USA)) [2017/18 c24s^5 c24v^{pu} h21v^4 h23.5v h19.5v^3 h24v^4 c24s^3 c24v^4 c24.7v* c25s^3 c30s^5 Apr 28] angular gelding: fair maiden hurdler: useful handicap chaser: won at Fairyhouse in April: third in Grade 3 at Aintree (8½ lengths behind Thomas Patrick) next time: stays 3¾m: best form on soft/heavy going: has worn headgear, including last 3 starts: has worn tongue tie. *Karl Thornton, Ireland* c132 h107

PAPER PROMISE (IRE) 6 ch.m. Gamut (IRE) – Rose Vic (IRE) (Old Vic) [2017/18 b16.2g^2 b15.6s* b16v* b17s Apr 12] €1,600 4-y-o: good-topped mare: second foal: dam unraced half-sister to useful hurdler (2½m winner) Arrive Sir Clive: fairly useful form in bumpers: won at Musselburgh in January and Wetherby (mares) in February: will stay further than 2m. *Donald Whillans* b99

PAPER ROSES (IRE) 7 b.m. Gamut (IRE) – Rose Vic (IRE) (Old Vic) [2017/18 h109, b76: h20.5v^2 h20s^2 h15.7s^5 h16.8v^4 Mar 23] fair maiden hurdler: stays 2½m: best form on soft/heavy going: often travels strongly. *Donald Whillans* h111

PARDON ME 5 ch.m. Tobougg (IRE) – Andromache (Hector Protector (USA)) [2017/18 b17.5s^3 b16.3s^3 Oct 2] fourth foal: half-sister to modest hurdler Miss Fortywinks (2m winner, by Act One): dam (h75) maiden hurdler: fair form when third in bumpers. *Seamus Mullins* b86

PARISIAN STAR 6 ch.m. Champs Elysees – Cavallo da Corsa (Galileo (IRE)) [2017/18 b–: h21.2g^{pu} Oct 26] leggy mare: no form in bumpers/novice hurdle. *Clare Ellam* h– b–

PARIS PROTOCOL 5 b.g. Champs Elysees – Island Vista (Montjeu (IRE)) [2017/18 h16.6s h19.3v^4 h16.6s Feb 21] useful on Flat, stays 2m: modest form over hurdles: best effort when fourth in novice at Catterick in January: remains capable of better. *Mark Walford* h96 p

PARKER (IRE) 4 b.g. Cape Cross (IRE) – Mount Elbrus (Barathea (IRE)) [2017/18 b15.6s Feb 4] last in bumper. *Lucinda Russell* b–

PAS

PARK HOUSE 9 b.g. Tillerman – Rasin Luck (Primitive Rising (USA)) [2017/18 h88: h23.3d h19.9s^{pu} Dec 26] modest hurdler at best, no form in 2017/18: stays 3m: acts on good to firm going: tried in cheekpieces. *Ray Craggs*   **h–**

PARKWARDEN (IRE) 4 b.g. Bushranger (IRE) – Honour And Obey (IRE) (Hurricane Run (IRE)) [2017/18 h16.2g³ h16.7g^{ur} h16.7g^{pu} h16.2d⁵ Aug 21] modest maiden on Flat, stays 11f: poor form over hurdles. *Chris Grant*   **h78**

PARLOUR MAID 7 gr.m. Dr Massini (IRE) – Charliebob (Nomadic Way (USA)) [2017/18 h–: h15.7g* h16.0d h19.9d^{bd} h21.2g² c20.3v^{pu} Jan 4] winning pointer: fair handicap hurdler: won at Towcester (conditional) in May: soon went wrong on chasing debut: stays 21f: in cheekpieces last 5 starts: wears tongue tie. *Richard Hawker*   **c–** **h100**

PAROLE (IRE) 6 ch.g. Mastercraftsman (IRE) – Leniency (IRE) (Cape Cross (IRE)) [2017/18 h17.2d^{pu} Aug 26] fair on Flat, stays 1¼m: pulled up in novice on hurdling debut (tongue tied). *Tim Easterby*   **h–**

PARSNIP PETE 12 b.g. Pasternak – Bella Coola (Northern State (USA)) [2017/18 c138, h–: c18m^{pu} c15.8g³ Jun 16] sturdy gelding: winning hurdler: useful handicap chaser: unproven beyond 17f: acts on soft and good to firm going: wears tongue tie: strong-travelling sort, has found less than seemed likely. *Tom George*   **c128** **h–**

PARSONAL (IRE) 5 b.g. Oscar (IRE) – Rith Ar Aghaidh (IRE) (Phardante (FR)) [2017/18 b15.7v⁵ h19.9v³ Apr 13] closely related to fairly useful hurdler/useful chaser Tintern Theatre (2m-3m winner, by King's Theatre) and half-brother to several winners, including fair hurdler/fairly useful chaser Rith Bob (2½m-2¾m winner, by Bob Back): dam 2m hurdle winner out of Stayers' Hurdle winner Shuil Ar Aghaidh: placed in Irish points: well beaten in maiden bumper: 20/1, third in novice at Sedgefield (14¾ lengths behind Just Bobby) on hurdling debut. *Sarah Humphrey*   **h97** **b–**

PART AND PARCEL (IRE) 10 b.g. Zerpour (IRE) – Carriacou (Mark of Esteem (IRE)) [2017/18 h85: h23g^{pu} h20g h23g Aug 23] winning pointer: maiden hurdler, no form in 2017/18: tried in cheekpieces/tongue tie. *Hannah James*   **h–**

PARTHENIUS (GER) 5 b.g. Soldier Hollow – Princess Li (GER) (Monsun (GER)) [2017/18 h15.9d* h15.7d³ h16.5s Dec 14] useful on Flat in Germany, stays 9f: fair form over hurdles: won maiden at Plumpton in November. *Dan Skelton*   **h109**

PARWICH LEES 6 ch.g. Pasternak – Barton Dante (Phardante (FR)) [2017/18 b80: h19.9d³ h15.8g⁵ h15.8m⁵ Jul 2] fourth in bumper: poor form over hurdles: should be suited by further than 2m. *Neil Mulholland*   **h82**

PASAKA BOY 8 ch.g. Haafhd – Shesha Bear (Tobougg (IRE)) [2017/18 h16g³ h16.7g³ h15.5s Dec 3] useful at one time on Flat, stays 1½m: fair form over hurdles. *Harry Whittington*   **h102**

PASSAM 6 b.g. Black Sam Bellamy (IRE) – One Wild Night (Rakaposhi King) [2017/18 b75: b16.7v* h15.5v h15.8v⁵ h15.3s³ h15.8d h16v³ Apr 14] fairly useful form in bumpers: won at Bangor in December: fair form over hurdles: will be suited by further than 2m: acts on heavy going: wears tongue tie. *Claire Dyson*   **h104** **b95**

PASSING CALL 5 b.m. Passing Glance – Call Me A Legend (Midnight Legend) [2017/18 b90: h15.8d² h15.7d² h15.8s² h15.8d² h16.3d³ Apr 22] lengthy mare: fairly useful form over hurdles, placed all 5 starts including in handicap: will stay beyond 2m: acts on soft going. *Alan King*   **h116**

PASSING DREAM 5 b.m. Passing Glance – Violet's Walk (Dr Fong (USA)) [2017/18 h16.5m Apr 25] little form on Flat: 66/1, showed more when seventh in mares novice at Taunton (13½ lengths behind Cockney Wren) on hurdling debut: open to improvement. *Seamus Mullins*   **h94 p**

PASSING FIESTA 9 b.m. Passing Glance – Clarice Starling (Saddlers' Hall (IRE)) [2017/18 c–§, h–: c17.4g^{pu} c15.9m^{pu} c20g^{pu} h16.7v⁵ h23.8v^{F} h23.8s^{pu} h20.5v⁵ h24s⁶ Feb 8] winning hurdler/maiden chaser, no form since 2015/16: has worn headgear/tongue tie: temperamental. *Sarah-Jayne Davies*   **c– §** **h– §**

PASSMORE 6 b.m. Passing Glance – Call Me A Legend (Midnight Legend) [2017/18 h107: h18.5s³ h18.7g* Jun 20] fair form at best over hurdles: won mares novice at Stratford in June, finishing lame: stays 19f: acts on good to firm going: tried in hood. *Alan King*   **h84**

PASS ON THE MANTLE 10 b.g. Bollin Eric – Swiss Rose (Michelozzo (USA)) [2017/18 h–§: h20g^{pu} Jul 18] workmanlike gelding: poor/lightly-raced hurdler, no form since 2015/16: tried in cheekpieces: temperamental. *Julian Smith*   **h– §**

*Guinness Handicap Chase, Punchestown—
a day of redemption for Paul Townend as Patricks Park completes a near 54/1 treble for the jockey
with this defeat of Blast of Koeman (right) whose rider is about to lose his irons*

PASTORAL MUSIC 5 b.g. Pastoral Pursuits – Jasmeno (Catcher In The Rye (IRE)) [2017/18 h15.6g² h15.8s h15.8s h17v Apr 17] fairly useful on Flat, stays 17f: modest form over hurdles, standout effort on debut: will stay beyond 2m. *Donald McCain* **h98**

PATGARY (FR) 6 b.g. Ballingarry (IRE) – Maylady Pat (FR) (Saint Cyrien (FR)) [2017/18 h20g h23.9v^{ur} Nov 24] off mark in Irish points at fourth attempt: no form over hurdles. *Warren Greatrex* **h–**

PATH TO FREEDOM (IRE) 6 b.g. Mr Dinos (IRE) – Old Kentucky (IRE) (Mandalus) [2017/18 c22.7v² Feb 15] €6,800 3-y-o, £8,200 4-y-o: sixth foal: half-brother to a winning pointer by Zagreb: dam unraced: multiple point winner: 6/1, second of 4 in hunter at Leicester (10 lengths behind Hazel Hill) on chasing debut. *Mrs C. A. Coward* **c103**

PATIENCE TONY (IRE) 7 b.g. Windsor Knot (IRE) – Johar Jamal (IRE) (Chevalier (IRE)) [2017/18 b79: h16g h16g⁵ h16.7g³ h16.8g⁵ Aug 31] bumper winner: modest form over hurdles: tried in cheekpieces. *Lucinda Egerton* **h85**

PATRICKS PARK (IRE) 7 b.g. Insatiable (IRE) – Rose Gallery (FR) (Gallery of Zurich (IRE)) [2017/18 c16.3g* c16g c20.9s⁴ c20.9s* h23.5v⁶ c17s* c16.7v⁵ c20s* Apr 25] second foal: dam unraced half-sister to Grand Steeple-Chase de Paris winner Remember Rose (by Insatiable): well held only start on Flat: modest form over hurdles: useful chaser: won maiden at Roscommon in May, handicap at Ffos Las in October, Coral Sandyford Handicap Chase at Leopardstown in February and Guinness Handicap Chase at Punchestown (by neck from Blast of Koeman) in April: left David Harry Kelly after second start, Matt Sheppard after fourth: stays 21f: acts on soft and good to firm going: has worn headgear: tried in tongue tie: often travels strongly: open to further improvement over fences. *W. P. Mullins, Ireland* **c141 p h90**

PATRICKTOM BORU (IRE) 11 b.g. Brian Boru – Brehon Law (IRE) (Alphabatim (USA)) [2017/18 c111, h–: c22.6d² c25.8m² c25.8d³ h23.3d⁴ Aug 21] prolific winning pointer: fair handicap hurdler/chaser: left R. W. J. Willcox after first start: stays 3¼m: acts on soft and good to firm going: front runner/races prominently. *Evan Williams* **c114 h106**

PAT'S OSCAR (IRE) 7 b.m. Oscar (IRE) – Coming Home (FR) (Exit To Nowhere (USA)) [2017/18 h16m⁶ h21g h20g⁶ h16.5g h21.8g^{pu} h20.2d² h20.2v* h19.6v² h16v⁴ h16v⁶ h16v² h20.2v³ h16v⁶ h16v* h16v h20s⁶ Apr 19] sixth foal: sister to bumper winner/ **h114**

fairly useful hurdler Kilkishen (2½m-2¾m winner), and half-sister to fair hurdler/chaser Chase The Favorite (19f-2¾m winner, by Hubbly Bubbly) and a winning pointer by Tamayaz: dam French 1½m-15f winner: bumper winner: fair hurdler: won mares novice at Perth in September and novice handicap at Fairyhouse in February: stays 2½m: acts on heavy going. *Gordon Elliott, Ireland*

PAT'S PEARL (IRE) 7 b.m. Kalanisi (IRE) – Seductive Dance (Groom Dancer (USA)) [2017/18 h16g² h18.8g² h18.8g² h22d² h19.6g* h21.8g⁴ h20v h20d Nov 9] seventh foal: half-sister to fairly useful chaser Dancing Art (2½m winner, by Definite Article), stayed 3m, and bumper winner/fairly useful hurdler The Bosses Cousin (2m winner, by King's Theatre): dam once-raced half-sister to Galway Plate winner Dovaly: modest hurdler: won mares maiden at Bangor in August: stays 2¾m: acts on heavy going: has worn headgear, including last 4 starts: wears tongue tie: often races prominently. *John McConnell, Ireland* **h95**

PATSY ORIEL (IRE) 10 b.g. Heron Island (IRE) – James's Princess (IRE) (Toulon) [2017/18 c23g⁴ h21.6g³ c25.8gᵖᵘ Sep 2] winning pointer: well beaten in maiden on hurdling debut: modest form in hunter chases: left Michael Winters after first start: usually in headgear. *Nigel Hawke* **c86 h–**

PATSYS CASTLE (IRE) 11 ch.g. Windsor Castle – Annienoora (IRE) (Topanoora) [2017/18 c96, h114: c26.1g May 28] good-bodied gelding: winning pointer: fairly useful hurdler at best: maiden chaser: stayed 3¼m: acted on good to firm and good to soft going: wore headgear: dead. *Kim Bailey* **c– h–**

PAUL (FR) 7 b.g. Boris de Deauville (IRE) – Bartjack (FR) (Lost World (IRE)) [2017/18 h–: h19.7g⁴ h21.2sᵖᵘ Jan 18] Irish point winner: modest form over hurdles: in tongue tie last 2 starts. *Rebecca Curtis* **h88**

PAULS HILL (IRE) 6 b.g. Marienbard (IRE) – Lunar Star (IRE) (King's Theatre (IRE)) [2017/18 h19.9d h21.6s⁶ h21s* h23.6v³ Feb 2] €19,000 3-y-o: first foal: dam unraced half-sister to smart hurdler (stayed 3m) Make Your Mark: runner-up on completed start in Irish points: fairly useful form over hurdles: standout effort when won novice at Towcester in December: should stay 3m. *Fergal O'Brien* **h115**

PAWN STAR (IRE) 8 b.g. Beneficial – Missindependence (IRE) (Executive Perk) [2017/18 c127, h100: c23.9g* May 12] smallish gelding: fair hurdler: fairly useful form over fences: won handicap at Market Rasen in May: stays 3¼m: acts on soft and good to firm going: usually travels strongly. *Emma Lavelle* **c128 h–**

PC DIXON 5 ch.g. Sixties Icon – Lakaam (Danzero (AUS)) [2017/18 h15.6m h16.4g h19.9s⁶ h19.3v h16.4v² h15.6d⁴ h16v² h17v² h16.2v* h17d² h16.8v³ h16.2s⁴ h20.2s³ Apr 27] half-brother to useful hurdler/chaser Sgt Reckless (2m winner, by Imperial Dancer): fair maiden at best on Flat, stays 1¼m: modest hurdler: won novice at Hexham in March: stays 2½m: acts on heavy going. *Victor Thompson* **h97**

PEACE AND CO (FR) 7 b.g. Falco (USA) – Peace Lina (FR) (Linamix (FR)) [2017/18 h–: h15.7m h15.6g* h15.7g³ Jul 16] good-topped gelding: high-class hurdler, lightly raced and well below best since 2014/15: fairly useful form over fences: won novice at Hexham in June: raced around 2m: acts on soft going: in hood last 4 starts: temperament under suspicion: has joined D. Cottin, France. *Nicky Henderson* **c124 h–**

PEACOCKS SECRET (IRE) 6 b.g. Court Cave (IRE) – Secret Can't Say (IRE) (Jurado (USA)) [2017/18 b16.7g³ b16s² b18.3d⁵ b19.5s* b16v² h16d⁶ b16s⁵ h16s h16d Dec 26] €40,000 3-y-o: brother to bumper winner/smart hurdler Clondaw Court (2¼m-2¾m winner) and fairly useful hurdler Just Cause (2½m-2¾m winner), and half-brother to bumper winner/fair hurdler Pro Pell (2½m winner, by Goldmark): dam (c82/h90) 3m chase winner: pulled up in point: useful bumper performer: won 19f maiden at Kilbeggan in September: modest form over hurdles. *Emmet Mullins, Ireland* **h96 b105**

PEAK OF BEAUTY (IRE) 5 b.m. Mountain High (IRE) – Minoras Return (IRE) (Bob's Return (IRE)) [2017/18 b16.2g b16v⁶ b16v⁶ Jan 31] small mare: fourth foal: sister to fairly useful hurdler/winning pointer Ballymountain Boy (2½m/21f winner), stays 3m: dam, unraced, out of half-sister to high-class chaser Observe: poor form in bumpers: wears hood: temperament under suspicion. *N. W. Alexander* **b64**

PEAK SEASONS (IRE) 15 ch.g. Raise A Grand (IRE) – Teresian Girl (IRE) (Glenstal (USA)) [2017/18 c–x, h–x: c21.2m⁶ c24.2g⁶ Jun 4] leggy, close-coupled gelding: winning hurdler/chaser, no longer of any account: has worn blinkers: often let down by jumping. *Michael Chapman* **c– x h– x**

PEAK STORM 9 b.g. Sleeping Indian – Jitterbug (IRE) (Marju (IRE)) [2017/18 h16d h15.8d Nov 18] maiden hurdler, no form in 2017/18: raced only at 2m: tried in tongue tie. *John O'Shea* **h–**

PEA

PEAK TO PEAK (IRE) 6 br.g. Authorized (IRE) – Bayourida (USA) (Slew O' Gold (USA)) [2017/18 h130: h19.5d³ Oct 14] well-made gelding: useful handicap hurdler: third in Silver Trophy at Chepstow, only start in 2017/18: stays 21f: acts on soft and good to firm going: usually races close up. *Paul Nicholls* — **h123**

PEARLESQUE (FR) 6 gr.m. Martaline – Anazeem (IRE) (Irish River (FR)) [2017/18 b71: h19.5d Nov 14] compact mare: poor form in bumpers: well beaten in novice on hurdling debut: won point in April. *Nicky Henderson* — **h–**

PEARLITA 6 b.m. Milan – Pearl Buttons (Alflora (IRE)) [2017/18 h83: h22g* h23s² h23.3g⁵ h24g* h23g^rr h23.3d* h23.1g⁶ Oct 31] angular mare: fair handicap hurdler: won at Stratford in May, Southwell in July and Uttoxeter in September: stays 3m: acts on soft going: wears headgear: one to treat with caution (has refused to race). *Henry Daly* — **h102 §**

PEARL OF PHOENIX 8 b.m. Phoenix Reach (IRE) – Pearl's Girl (King's Best (USA)) [2017/18 h16s^pu Dec 5] no form on Flat: pulled up in mares novice on hurdling debut. *Seamus Mullins* — **h–**

PEARL OF THE WEST (IRE) 4 b.f. Teofilo (IRE) – Creese (Halling (USA)) [2017/18 h15.8s⁴ h17d* Mar 25] useful on Flat, stays 12.5f: fairly useful form over hurdles: won novice at Carlisle in March: wears tongue tie: open to further improvement. *John McConnell, Ireland* — **h115 p**

PEARL ROYALE (IRE) 6 b.m. Robin des Champs (FR) – Dartmeet (IRE) (Presenting) [2017/18 h118, b90: c20.2v* c24.2v^F Feb 3] workmanlike mare: fairly useful hurdle winner: useful form over fences: won mares novice at Wincanton (by 11 lengths from Jessber's Dream) in December: fell ninth in Towton Novices' Chase at Wetherby: will stay beyond 2½m: acts on heavy going: front runner/races prominently: remains open to improvement as a chaser. *Nigel Hawke* — **c136 p** / **h–**

PEARLS LEGEND 11 b.g. Midnight Legend – Pearl's Choice (IRE) (Deep Run) [2017/18 c128, h–: c17.8g² c18g⁵ c16d² c16.3s^pu Jan 6] rather leggy gelding: winning hurdler: fairly useful handicap chaser: stays 2½m, races mainly over shorter: acts on good to firm and heavy going: has worn cheekpieces. *John Spearing* — **c128** / **h–**

PEARL SWAN (FR) 10 b.g. Gentlewave (IRE) – Swanson (USA) (Diesis) [2017/18 c137, h–: h19.9v c25s c31.8g Apr 21] good-topped gelding: winning hurdler: useful chaser: stays 3m (stamina possibly stretched over 4m): acts on soft going: wears headgear/tongue tie: often leads. *Peter Bowen* — **c128** / **h–**

PECULIAR PLACES (IRE) 6 b.g. Presenting – Blu Louisiana (IRE) (Milan) [2017/18 b112: b16.2g* h21.2v^pu ab18d² h22d^F Apr 22] useful form in bumpers: won at Hereford in November: fair form over hurdles: leading when falling 2 out in novice won by Secret Investor at Stratford in April. *Warren Greatrex* — **h112** / **b86**

PEDULIA ALBA (FR) 5 b.m. Beat Hollow – Parthenia (IRE) (Night Shift (USA)) [2017/18 b15.8d b16.5s b16s Mar 22] €15,000 3-y-o: fourth foal: half-sister to fairly useful hurdler Resolution Bay (2m/17f winner, by Presenting), stayed 3m: dam, maiden (third at 7f in France), half-sister to useful/ungenuine staying chasers Sonevafushi and Celtic Son and to dam of very smart staying chaser Junior: no form in bumpers: left Philip Hobbs after first start. *Susan Gardner* — **b–**

PEGGIES VENTURE 7 b.m. Presenting – Peggies Run (Kayf Tara) [2017/18 h97, b99: h16g² h19g² h19.4d² ab18d³ h18.9v Mar 31] smallish, sturdy mare: dual bumper winner: fair maiden hurdler: bred to stay at least 2½m: acts on good to soft going. *Alan King* — **h114**

PEGGY'S ACRE (IRE) 5 b.m. Yeats (IRE) – Lorraine's Secret (IRE) (Desert King (IRE)) [2017/18 b16.5g b15.8d h16g⁶ h16d h17.3s³ h16g h15.8d^pu Sep 24] well held in bumpers/Flat maidens: ran out in point: poor form over hurdles: tried in hood: in tongue tie last 5 starts. *Gavin Patrick Cromwell, Ireland* — **h80** / **b–**

PEKANHEIM (IRE) 10 b.g. Putra Pekan – Delheim (IRE) (Un Desperado (FR)) [2017/18 c92, h65: c20.1g² c17.3d³ c20.1g⁴ c21.2d^ur Aug 26] winning hurdler: modest handicap chaser: stays 21f: acts on heavy going: has worn cheekpieces: often travels strongly. *Martin Todhunter* — **c91** / **h–**

PEMBA (FR) 6 ch.m. Zanzibari (USA) – Ayaam (IRE) (Danehill (USA)) [2017/18 c107, h113: c19.4g⁴ c16.4g² c16.5g² c20g³ Oct 17] tall mare: fair hurdler/maiden chaser: unproven beyond 17f: acts on heavy going: has worn headgear, including in 2017/18: usually races close up. *Fergal O'Brien* — **c110** / **h–**

PEMBERLEY (IRE) 5 b.g. Darsi (FR) – Eyebright (IRE) (Zaffaran (USA)) [2017/18 b16.2s⁵ b16s Feb 24] mid-field in bumpers. *Emma Lavelle* — **b76**

PEN

PEMBROKE HOUSE 11 gr.g. Terimon – Bon Coeur (Gunner B) [2017/18 c100, h–: c20m² c16.1g⁵ c19.9d³ c20v⁵ c18.9s² c16.1v⁵ c16v² c16v³ c15.2d⁴ c20.9v² c19.9d² Apr 24] sturdy gelding: winning hurdler: modest handicap chaser: stays 21f: acts on good to firm and heavy going: wears headgear: usually races prominently. *Sarah-Jayne Davies*   c95 h–

PENA DORADA (IRE) 11 b.g. Key of Luck (USA) – Uluwatu (IRE) (Unfuwain (USA)) [2017/18 c105, h–: c24.2g⁴ c29.4d c23.9g^pu Aug 6] stocky gelding: winning hurdler: fair chaser, below form in 2017/18: stays 27f: acts on soft and good to firm going: has worn headgear, including in 2017/18: front runner/races prominently. *Alistair Whillans*   c89 h–

PENDRA (IRE) 10 ch.g. Old Vic – Mariah Rollins (IRE) (Over The River (FR)) [2017/18 c148, h–: c26s c34.3s^pu Apr 14] rather plain gelding: winning hurdler: smart chaser at best, very lightly raced nowadays: stays 3¼m: acts on good to firm and heavy going: wears headgear: tried in tongue tie. *Charlie Longsdon*   c– h–

PENGO'S BOY 9 gr.g. Proclamation (IRE) – Homeoftheclassics (Tate Gallery (USA)) [2017/18 h20g h16.3g⁶ h16.8g h16.8d* h18.5d² h19.3g³ h23.9g^F Nov 30] rather leggy gelding: fair handicap hurdler: won novice event at Newton Abbot in September: may prove best short of 3m: acts on good to soft going: wears hood nowadays usually races nearer last than first, often travels strongly. *Stuart Kittow*   h109

PENHILL 7 b.g. Mount Nelson – Serrenia (IRE) (High Chaparral (IRE)) [2017/18 h152: h24s* h24d² Apr 26]   h164

    For the second year running, Willie Mullins won a race at the Cheltenham Festival with a horse making its seasonal debut. Paul Townend had ridden a long-priced double on the final day of the 2017 Cheltenham Festival on Arctic Fire in the County Hurdle and Penhill in the Spa Novices'. Arctic Fire carried top weight to victory on his first run since January the year before while, at the latest Festival, it was Penhill who overcame a lengthy absence since the Punchestown Festival the previous spring when winning the Sun Bets Stayers' Hurdle. As mentioned in the essay on Arctic Fire in last year's Annual, Mullins had produced Quevega to win most of her six David Nicholson Mares' Hurdles after similar absences. It wasn't the first time, either, that a Stayers' Hurdle had been won by a horse having its first run of the season. Martin Pipe won the 1996 edition with Cyborgo who had been kept off the course by the effects of a virus since finishing second in the same race twelve months earlier. Penhill's lengthy absence was also an enforced one. He had been due to be campaigned on the Flat after his novice season but 'lots of niggles' had put paid to that plan and prevented him from seeing any action over hurdles before the Festival. Penhill's readiness evidently came as a surprise to his trainer—'he was way fitter than I thought he was'—not that he was taking much of the credit for his preparation which he attributed instead to Holly Conte 'who leads him up, rides him and does everything with him. She has virtually trained this horse herself.'

    Had all seventeen declared runners gone to post, the latest running of the Stayers' Hurdle would have been contested by the largest field since Inglis Drever beat sixteen others for the last of his three wins in the race in 2008. However, neither Old Guard nor Apple's Jade took part, the latter only left in as a precaution having

Sun Bets Stayers' Hurdle, Cheltenham—
Penhill (hooped cap) becomes the first since 1996 winner Cyborgo to land the Stayers' on his reappearance; fellow Irish raider Supasundae pushes him closest in a falsely-run affair

contested the David Nicholson Mares' Hurdle forty-eight hours earlier which had always been her intended engagement. Among others missing from the line-up was Nichols Canyon, who had given Mullins a first win in the race twelve months earlier but had been fatally injured in a fall in the Christmas Hurdle at Leopardstown which Apple's Jade had won from Supasundae. Despite dropping back to two miles to win the Irish Champion Hurdle in the interim, the previous season's Coral Cup winner Supasundae took his chance as the main Irish hope in the Stayers'. The placed pair from the year before, Lil Rockerfeller and Unowhatimeanharry, were back again, though neither had been a match for Sam Spinner who had emerged as the most likely pretender to the stayers' crown with an impressive win in the Long Walk Hurdle at Ascot. With soft ground looking ideal for strong stayer Sam Spinner, he was sent off the 9/4 favourite, with Supasundae sharing second spot in the betting on 6/1 with Yanworth, who had been unconvincing over fences and was back over hurdles for the first time since beating Supasundae in the Liverpool Hurdle at Aintree the previous spring. At 12/1, Penhill was the shortest odds of four runners from his stable, reunited with Townend who had been successful on all three previous occasions he had ridden him.

Sam Spinner had set a good pace to win his last two races so it came as a surprise, including to the jockeys on his some of his rivals, that his jockey dictated such a sedate gallop. As a result, the field was still well bunched two from home and room was at a premium when the pace finally picked up. A patient ride wouldn't normally pay off in such circumstances but, having travelled well in rear, Penhill was produced wide to avoid trouble turning for home and made smooth headway to take it up from Sam Spinner approaching the final flight. Supasundae made a race of it after the last but, contrary to connections' fears that the lack of a run might find Penhill out in the closing stages, he stayed on the better to win by two lengths. Wholestone kept on well to take third, beaten another three lengths, and filling the same position as he had behind the winner in the Spa twelve months earlier. Sam Spinner was only fifth, a place in front of Yanworth who didn't find much off the bridle, while the likes of Unowhatimeanharry and Lil Rockerfeller, both well beaten, were among those done no favours at all by the steady pace. Penhill's stable-companion Bacardys would likely have finished third had he not fallen at the last, having been among those poorly placed when the pace quickened. In short, the race did little to sort the pecking order among the leading staying hurdlers. Things were not much clearer either after Penhill's only subsequent start when he finished second to Faugheen in the Champion Stayers' Hurdle at Punchestown. While Faugheen stole a march from the off, the race went less well for Penhill who didn't settle fully in mid-division and made only a brief challenge to his stablemate who pulled away again in the straight to win by thirteen lengths, Penhill already held when untidy at the last.

Penhill (b.g. 2011)	Mount Nelson (b 2004)	Rock of Gibraltar (b 1999)	Danehill / Offshore Boom
		Independence (b 1998)	Selkirk / Yukon Hope
	Serrenia (IRE) (b 2005)	High Chaparral (b 1999)	Sadler's Wells / Kasora
		Helvellyn (b 1990)	Gone West / Accredited

The pedigree of the well-made Penhill was covered in last year's Annual. Since then, younger half-brother Sierra Law (by Lawman), a winner on the Flat in Sweden, has opened his account over hurdles in a two-mile handicap at Down Royal. Penhill's unraced dam Serrenia was also represented by two-year-old filly Harbour Rose (by Harbour Watch) in 2017 but she didn't show much ability. Penhill was a useful handicapper on the Flat, firstly for James Bethell and then for Luca Cumani, before going hurdling for Mullins. His trainer's immediate reaction after the Stayers' Hurdle was to put Penhill away to concentrate on Cheltenham again in 2018 but, just a day before he ran at Punchestown, he was listed among the entries for the Gold Cup at Royal Ascot (though, in the end, that engagement was not taken up). Penhill stays three miles and acts on soft going. He travels strongly through his races and is usually patiently ridden. He wore ear plugs once again at Cheltenham.

W. P. Mullins, Ireland

PER

PENNANT LEGEND 5 b.m. Flying Legend (USA) – Pennant Princess (Alflora (IRE)) **b70**
[2017/18 b15.7g⁴ b16.2g Nov 29] fifth foal: dam unraced half-sister to modest hurdler Pennant Dancer (21f-3m winner, by Grape Tree Road) and a winning pointer by Fair Mix: dam unraced: poor form in bumpers. *Debra Hamer*

PENNEYS HUN (IRE) 5 b.g. Arakan (USA) – De Street (IRE) (Sunshine Street (USA)) **h109**
[2017/18 b16.8d⁵ b16.4d b17g⁵ h16g* h16v⁵ h18s² h15.3d Apr 22] first foal: dam unraced **b88**
half-sister to fairly useful hurdler/smart chaser (2m-2½m winner) Hold Fast: mid-field at best in bumpers: fair form over hurdles: won maiden at Tramore in August: left John Halley after sixth start. *Michael Blanshard*

PENNIES AND POUNDS 11 b.m. Sir Harry Lewis (USA) – Sense of Value (Trojan **c–**
Fen) [2017/18 c–, h68: h20gᵖᵘ h18.6gᵖᵘ h21.6g h19.6d⁵ Apr 21] poor hurdler, no form in **h– §**
2017/18: no show only start over fences: tried in cheekpieces: temperamental. *Julian Smith*

PENNINGTON 4 b.g. Poet's Voice – Pryka (ARG) (Southern Halo (USA)) [2017/18 **h–**
h15.7sᵖᵘ h16dᶠ Mar 29] maiden on Flat: no form over hurdles: dead. *Russell Ross*

PENN LANE (IRE) 7 b.g. Scorpion (IRE) – Belsalsa (FR) (Kingsalsa (USA)) [2017/18 **h122**
h118p: h20.7s² Jan 26] bumper winner: fairly useful form over hurdles: second in handicap at Huntingdon, only start in 2017/18: stays 21f. *Warren Greatrex*

PENNY BLAK 5 ch.g. Black Sam Bellamy (IRE) – Pennys Pride (IRE) (Pips Pride) **b89 p**
[2017/18 b16.2d² Apr 23] closely related to fairly useful hurdler/useful chaser Victor Hewgo (2½m-3m winner, by Old Vic) and half-brother to several winners, including bumper winner/useful hurdler Crowning Jewel (2½m-2¾m winner, by Sulamani): dam (b104), bumper winner (also 1¼m winner on Flat), half-sister to top-class chaser (stayed 2½m) Direct Route: 8/1, promise when second in bumper at Hexham (1½ lengths behind Melekhov): sure to progress. *Gillian Boanas*

PENNY JANE (IRE) 6 b.m. King's Theatre (IRE) – Shannon Rose (IRE) (Topanoora) **c111**
[2017/18 b17.5g* b16m³ h16.5m³ h16.5m³ h16.2g* h20d² c16g² c19.9s² c18.2s³ c17.4v* **h111**
Sep 27] €75,000 3-y-o: sixth foal: sister to useful hurdler/chaser Minella Foru (2m-3m **b85**
winner) and bumper winner/fairly useful hurdler Sumkindofking (2m winner, stays 21f), and closely related to bumper winner/fair hurdler Minella Hero (2m-25f winner, by Old Vic): dam (b85) bumper winner: fair form in bumpers: won maiden at Downpatrick in May: fair form over hurdles: won mares maiden at Listowel in June and novice at Perth in July: similar form over fences: won mares maiden at Sligo in September: likely to stay beyond 2½m: acts on heavy going: wears hood. *Gordon Elliott, Ireland*

PENNY RED 4 ch.f. Medicean – Peintre d'Argent (IRE) (Peintre Celebre (USA)) **h83**
[2017/18 h15.8m⁶ h15.5d⁴ h15.8s³ Jan 10] fair maiden on Flat, stayed 1¼m: poor form over hurdles: wore tongue tie: dead. *Nikki Evans*

PENNYWELL (IRE) 8 b.m. Gold Well – Boyne Bridge (IRE) (Lord Americo) [2017/18 **h100**
h102: h23.1g⁵ h15.9g⁴ h19.9dᶠ h23.3v* h23.8s³ h23.8s³ h25s⁴ h23.1vᵖᵘ h26.4dᵖᵘ Apr 22] compact mare: winning Irish pointer: fair handicap hurdler: won mares event at Uttoxeter in November: stays 23f: acts on heavy going: has worn cheekpieces, including last 4 starts. *Warren Greatrex*

PENSION MADNESS (IRE) 5 b.g. Vocalised (USA) – Grinneas (IRE) (Barathea **h82**
(IRE)) [2017/18 h95: h18.5m h16g³ h15.8d h15.8d h18.7m³ h16.8d² h15.8g h18.5s Apr 23] compact gelding: poor maiden hurdler: stays 2¼m: acts on good to firm and good to soft going: has worn headgear. *Johnny Farrelly*

PENTIFFIC (NZ) 15 br.g. Pentire – Sailing High (NZ) (Yachtie (AUS)) [2017/18 c120§: **c– §**
c32.5dᵖᵘ May 5] sturdy gelding: winning pointer: useful chaser at best: stays 33f: acts on soft going: has worn headgear: unreliable. *P. P. C. Turner*

PENTITO RAP (USA) 4 b.g. Smart Strike (CAN) – Sing Like A Bird (USA) (Lawyer **h–**
Ron (USA)) [2017/18 h16.2sᵖᵘ h16.5v Feb 4] poor maiden on Flat: no form over hurdles: tried in cheekpieces. *Rod Millman*

PEPPAY LE PUGH (IRE) 7 b.g. Arakan (USA) – Pinaflore (FR) (Formidable (USA)) **c91 §**
[2017/18 h96§: h16g⁴ h15.8g h16g⁶ h15.3v⁴ h16s² h16.6s² c15.7d² c15.7vᵖ c16.5d² Mar **h91 §**
26] workmanlike gelding: modest maiden hurdler/chaser: unproven beyond 17f: acts on heavy going: has worn headgear: usually wears tongue tie: often travels strongly, but is irresolute. *David Dennis*

PERCY STREET 5 br.g. Sir Percy – Star of Gibraltar (Rock of Gibraltar (IRE)) [2017/18 **h111 §**
h117: h16d⁶ h16.4g⁴ h16.6d h16.3s h15.7s⁴ Mar 31] compact gelding: fair handicap hurdler: raced around 2m: tried in blinkers: ungenuine. *Nicky Henderson*

619

PER

PERCY THROWER (IRE) 4 ch.g. Sir Percy – Dayrose (Daylami (IRE)) [2017/18 h16.2s^{pu} Jan 16] modest maiden on Flat, stays 2m: pulled up in juvenile maiden on hurdling debut. *Sarah-Jayne Davies* — h–

PERCY VERENCE 5 b.g. Sir Percy – Bermondsey Girl (Bertolini (USA)) [2017/18 h16.8g^{pu} Oct 25] modest maiden on Flat, stays 1¾m: pulled up in maiden on hurdling debut. *Tracy Waggott* — h–

PEREGRINE RUN (IRE) 8 b.g. King's Theatre (IRE) – Masriyna's Article (IRE) (Definite Article) [2017/18 h141: c16.1s^2 c16g* c16g* c18.2d^3 c20.5g* c20.5g^{ur} Apr 21] good-topped gelding: useful hurdler: similar form over fences: won maidens at Wexford in June, and novices at Wexford in July and Killarney (by ½ length from Conrad Hastings) in August: stays 21f: acts on soft going: often travels strongly. *Peter Fahey, Ireland* — c141 h–

PERFECT AIM 6 b.m. Kalanisi (IRE) – Long Shot (Sir Harry Lewis (USA)) [2017/18 b16.8g b16.2g Jun 17] second foal: dam (h102) bumper/2m-2¾m hurdle winner: no form in bumpers. *Lynn Siddall* — b–

PERFECT CANDIDATE (IRE) 11 b.g. Winged Love (IRE) – Dansana (IRE) (Insan (USA)) [2017/18 c152, h–: c25g c27.3s* c24.2s c25.3v^5 c34.3s^F Apr 14] strong gelding: winning hurdler: smart handicap chaser: won Grade 3 event at Cheltenham (by neck from Vicente) in November: fell first in Grand National: stays 27f: acts on heavy going: usually wears headgear nowadays: has worn tongue tie: usually races close up. *Fergal O'Brien* — c153 h–

PERFECT HARMONY (IRE) 6 b.g. Definite Article – Brandam Supreme (IRE) (Supreme Leader) [2017/18 b102: h20d^4 h21.6d^2 h19.4s^2 Jan 26] tall gelding: fell in Irish point: bumper winner: fairly useful form when in frame in maiden/novice hurdles. *Alan King* — h116

PERFECTLY WILLING (IRE) 12 b.g. Luso – Dark Nightingale (Strong Gale) [2017/18 c23.8g^4 c24g Jul 19] multiple winning pointer: pulled up only start over hurdles: maiden chaser, modest form at best: stays 3¼m: acts on good to soft going: tried in visor. *Mark Wall* — c73 h–

PERFECT MOMENT (IRE) 5 b.m. Milan – Faucon (Polar Falcon (USA)) [2017/18 b74: b17.7d^4 Feb 26] leggy, lightly-built mare: modest form in bumpers. *Michael Roberts* — b80

PERFECT MYTH 4 b.f. Midnight Legend – Perfect Silence (Dansili) [2017/18 b12.4s^2 b15.6d^3 Feb 14] first foal: dam useful 6f/7f winner: modest form when placed in bumpers. *Harry Whittington* — b81

PERFECT PIRATE 6 b.g. Black Sam Bellamy (IRE) – Supreme Gem (IRE) (Supreme Leader) [2017/18 h123, b–: c19.8g* c20s c20.9s^4 c25d* Apr 26] compact gelding: fairly useful hurdle winner: similar form over fences: won novice at Towcester in November: stays 23f: acts on heavy going: in cheekpieces last 2 starts: temperamental. *Ben Pauling* — c124 § h–

PERFECT SUMMER (IRE) 8 b.m. High Chaparral (IRE) – Power of Future (GER) (Definite Article) [2017/18 h108: h21.1s h24.4d^5 Dec 15] compact mare: fair hurdler, below form in 2017/18: stays 2½m: acts on good to firm and heavy going: usually wears headgear: front runner/races prominently. *Ian Williams* — h95

PERFECT TIMING 10 b.g. Shantou (USA) – Winnetka Gal (IRE) (Phardante (FR)) [2017/18 c118, h–: c19.7g* c20s^6 c18.2s^{pu} Dec 14] strong gelding: maiden hurdler: fairly useful handicap chaser: completed hat-trick (following wins in 2016/17) at Plumpton in May: stays 3m, races over shorter nowadays: acts on good to firm and heavy going: wears headgear: tried in tongue tie: usually races prominently. *Neil Mulholland* — c121 h–

PERFECT TIMING (FR) 8 b.g. Sassanian (USA) – Royale Sulawesie (FR) (Jimble (FR)) [2017/18 h–: h15.7m h18.7g^{pu} May 8] little form over hurdles: has worn headgear, including last 2 starts: sometimes in tongue tie: temperamental. *Andrew Martin* — h– §

PERFORMANCE ART (IRE) 4 b.f. Art Connoisseur (IRE) – Heroic Performer (IRE) (Royal Applause) [2017/18 h16.8d^6 Jul 23] half-sister to useful hurdler MacNicholson (2m winner, by Definite Article), stays 2½m: poor maiden on Flat: tailed off in juvenile on hurdling debut. *Seamus Mullins* — h–

PERFORM (IRE) 9 b.g. King's Theatre (IRE) – Famous Lady (IRE) (Presenting) [2017/18 h126: c25d^F c24.2s^4 Nov 15] strong gelding: useful hurdle winner, lightly raced: well held completed start over fences: stays 2½m: tried in cheekpieces. *Philip Hobbs* — c– h–

PERMISSION GRANTED (IRE) 6 b.g. Oscar (IRE) – Ask The Misses (IRE) (Supreme Leader) [2017/18 b–: h16.7g h15.6m h16.4g h19.3d h19.4s h19.3v Apr 17] modest form over hurdles. *Rose Dobbin* — h88

PET

PERSEID (IRE) 8 br.g. Robin des Pres (FR) – Cowanstown Miss (IRE) (Presenting) [2017/18 h108: c17.1g³ c20g⁴ h20.6g⁴ h23.3d⁵ c16.4g⁴ c19.3d³ c20.1v³ h16s h18.6v³ h19.3d³ h17d⁵ h17v⁵ Apr 17] modest handicap hurdler: fair form over fences: left Sue Smith after tenth start: stays 3m: acts on soft and good to firm going: often races prominently: temperament under suspicion. *Barbara Butterworth*   **c101 h89**

PERSHING 7 gr.g. Mount Nelson – La Gandilie (FR) (Highest Honor (FR)) [2017/18 c–, h77: h15.7g* h16.7g⁴ h16.3g² Oct 21] fair hurdler: won novice seller at Southwell in July, only start for Olly Murphy: well held sole outing over fences: raced around 2m: acts on soft going: usually wears headgear: has worn tongue tie. *Kevin Frost*   **c– h111**

PERSHING MISSILE (IRE) 6 b.g. Milan – Banbury Cross (IRE) (Supreme Leader) [2017/18 b16.5g² h16.2g⁴ h20.5d h16.3g h16.2v² h21.2d² Apr 24] €45,000 3-y-o: seventh foal: brother to useful hurdler/chaser The Paparrazi Kid (19f/2½m winner, stays 3m) and bumper winner/fairly useful hurdler Rourke's Cross (2½m winner): dam ran twice in bumpers: fair form in bumpers/over hurdles: left Noel Meade after fourth start. *Graeme McPherson*   **h102 b89**

PERSIAN DELIGHT 8 b.g. Lucarno (USA) – Persian Walk (FR) (Persian Bold) [2017/18 h123: h16.8s³ h21.4v⁴ c15.7v² Feb 1] fairly useful hurdler: 10/11, second in novice handicap at Wincanton (2½ lengths behind Valhalla) on chasing debut: stays 21f: acts on heavy going: wears tongue tie: often races prominently: has joined Claire Dyson. *Paul Nicholls*   **c128 h113**

PERSIAN SNOW (IRE) 12 b.g. Anshan – Alpine Message (Tirol) [2017/18 c128, h–: c20s⁶ c20vᵘʳ c19.2vᵖᵘ Apr 8] good-topped gelding: winning hurdler: useful chaser at best, no form in 2017/18: wears tongue tie: front runner/races prominently. *Philip Hobbs*   **c– h–**

PERSISTANTPRINCESS (IRE) 6 b.m. Scorpion (IRE) – Classy Conflict (IRE) (Close Conflict (USA)) [2017/18 h20gᵖᵘ h19.6g⁵ h20g⁵ Aug 23] first foal: dam, maiden (placed in points), half-sister to fair hurdler/fairly useful chaser (stays 21f) De Benno: twice-raced in Irish maiden points, runner-up on completed start: no form over hurdles. *David Rees*   **h–**

PERSONAL COACH (FR) 5 b.g. Motivator – Castellina (USA) (Danzig Connection (USA)) [2017/18 b16.5g³ b15.8s Dec 26] brother to 2 winners on Flat in France and half-brother to several winners, including modest hurdlers Castle River (2m winner, by Irish River) and Blaise Hollow (2½m winner, by Woodman): dam US 8.5f winner: fair form in bumpers: better effort when third in maiden at Taunton in November. *Robert Stephens*   **b91**

PERTUIS (IRE) 12 gr.g. Verglas (IRE) – Lady Killeen (IRE) (Marju (IRE)) [2017/18 h–: h16.8s³ h19.3d Dec 19] leggy gelding: maiden hurdler, fair at best: best around 2m: acted on heavy going: sometimes in headgear: dead. *Micky Hammond*   **h69**

PERUVIEN BLEU (FR) 6 b.g. Fuisse (FR) – Edelmira (FR) (Kahyasi) [2017/18 h123: h15.8m* h16.8d² h16.8g⁴ h15.8g* h15.7g h16.5v⁶ h15.8d³ Apr 9] rather unfurnished gelding: fairly useful handicap hurdler: won at Ludlow in May and October: raced around 2m: acts on soft and good to firm going: has worn tongue tie: usually races towards rear. *Nick Williams*   **h122**

PETAPENKO 7 b.g. Archipenko (USA) – Tricoteuse (Kris) [2017/18 h92: c17.1g h15.6d⁵ Feb 14] workmanlike gelding: bumper winner: modest maiden hurdler: well held in novice handicap on chasing debut: unproven beyond 17f: acts on good to soft going: has worn blinkers, including in 2017/18. *Pauline Robson*   **c– h91**

PETERBOROUGH (FR) 7 b.g. Fuisse (FR) – Peony Girl (FR) (Phantom Breeze) [2017/18 b15.3s Nov 11] won Irish point on debut: tailed off in bumper. *Evan Williams*   **b–**

PETERBROWN (IRE) 10 b.g. Shantou (USA) – Grove Juliet (IRE) (Moscow Society (USA)) [2017/18 c106, h98: c25.8g^R h23m Jul 5] maiden hurdler: fair chaser: showed nothing when returned to points in 2017/18: stays 3¼m: acts on good to firm and heavy going: tried in cheekpieces: usually races prominently: hinted at temperament. *Philip Hobbs*   **c95 h77**

PETERS COUSIN (IRE) 5 b.m. Presenting – Sunwake (GER) (Tiger Hill (IRE)) [2017/18 b16.8v* b16.8v² b16g Apr 21] €20,000 3-y-o: first foal: dam (c97/h112) 2m hurdle winner (stayed 3m): fair form in bumpers: won mares event at Carlisle in October: bred to stay beyond 2m. *Nicky Richards*   **b90**

PETERS GREY (IRE) 8 gr.g. Aussie Rules (USA) – Aliyshan (IRE) (Darshaan) [2017/18 h–: h16v⁵ h16vᵖᵘ h16.4d h16.2sᵖᵘ Apr 26] maiden hurdler, little form since 2015/16: raced around 2m: acts on heavy going. *R. Mike Smith*   **h–**

PET

PETER THE MAYO MAN (IRE) 8 ch.g. Dylan Thomas (IRE) – Mommkin (Royal Academy (USA)) [2017/18 h132: h15.7g c19.1d* c19.9s^F ab18d^5 c15.7g* Apr 20] strong gelding: useful hurdler: smart form over fences: won novices at Doncaster (by 6 lengths from Stowaway Magic) in December and Southwell (by 6 lengths from Western Miller) in April: stays 19f: acts on good to soft going. *Paul Nicholls* — c145 h–

PETE THE FEAT (IRE) 14 b.g. King's Theatre (IRE) – Tourist Attraction (IRE) (Pollerton) [2017/18 c128, h–: c24.2s^4 c24.2d* c24.2s^2 c24.2v^{pu} c24.2v* Mar 10] angular gelding: winning hurdler: useful handicap chaser: won at Sandown in December (amateur) and March (by neck from Horatio Hornblower): stays 29f: acts on heavy going: wears tongue tie: often travels strongly. *Charlie Longsdon* — c133 h–

PETITE GANACHE (IRE) 6 ch.g. Presenting – Ain't Misbehavin (IRE) (Trempolino (USA)) [2017/18 h–: h20.2g May 18] good-topped gelding: poor form over hurdles: signs of temperament. *Nicky Richards* — h69

PETITE POWER (IRE) 9 b.g. Subtle Power (IRE) – Little Serena (Primitive Rising (USA)) [2017/18 c125, h113: c25g^4 c25.6g^5 c27.6s^5 c28.8v^2 c30.6s Apr 27] smallish gelding: fair hurdler: fairly useful handicap chaser: second at Lingfield in February: stays 29f: acts on heavy going: has worn cheekpieces: wears tongue tie. *Fergal O'Brien* — c123 h–

PETIT FILOUS 4 b.g. Equiano (FR) – Haiti Dancer (Josr Algarhoud (IRE)) [2017/18 h15.5d^4 Nov 20] fair maiden on Flat, stayed 1m: in tongue strap, fourth in selling hurdle at Leicester: dead. *Michael Wigham* — h65

PETIT MOUCHOIR (FR) 7 gr.g. Al Namix (FR) – Arnette (FR) (Denham Red (FR)) [2017/18 h162: c16.2d* c17s^2 c15.9s^3 c15.8s^2 c16d^4 Apr 26] good-topped gelding: high-class hurdler: very smart form over fences: won maiden at Punchestown in October: second in Frank Ward Solicitors Arkle Novices' Chase at Leopardstown (5 lengths behind Footpad) in February, third in Arkle Chase at Cheltenham (14¾ lengths behind Footpad) in March and second in Maghull Novices' Chase at Aintree (2½ lengths behind Diego du Charmil) in April: unproven beyond 17f: acts on heavy going: has worn hood (wore ear plugs which were removed at start in Arkle Chase): front runner/races prominently, often travels strongly. *Henry de Bromhead, Ireland* — c159 + h–

PETIVILLE (FR) 6 gr.g. Montmartre (FR) – Aegle (IRE) (Night Shift (USA)) [2017/18 h113, b71: h20s^3 h25.4d^2 h23.3g* Jun 17] fairly useful form over hurdles: won novice at Hexham in June: stays 25f: acts on good to soft going: tried in tongue tie. *Richard Hobson* — h117

PETRIFY 8 b.g. Rock of Gibraltar (IRE) – Frigid (Indian Ridge) [2017/18 h62: h15.8m^6 h17.7m^4 h18.5v^5 Oct 2] poor maiden hurdler: stays 2¼m: acts on good to firm and heavy going: wears cheekpieces/tongue tie. *Bernard Llewellyn* — h59

PETRONELLA MANNERS 5 b.m. Shirocco (GER) – Last of Her Line (Silver Patriarch (IRE)) [2017/18 h74 bd h15.8g^6 h20.5s^{bd} h15.7v^5 h20.7d^2 h20.3g Apr 19] fourth foal: half-sister to fairly useful hurdler Lord Grantham (2½m-2¾m winner, by Definite Article) and fairly useful/temperamental hurdler Go West Young Man (21f winner, by Westerner), stays 3m: dam unraced half-sister to fairly useful hurdler/useful chaser (19f-3¼m winner) Sail By The Stars: modest form in bumpers: fair form over hurdles: standout effort when second in mares novice at Huntingdon: will stay 2¾m. *Henry Daly* — h108 b76

PETROU (IRE) 8 b.g. Mountain High (IRE) – Evnelu (IRE) (Old Vic) [2017/18 h104: h22d* h20.3g* h20g* c22.5g* h22.1s^{pu} c20d^2 c23.6d^2 c20.5g^4 c24.1g^4 Apr 21] fairly useful handicap hurdler: completed hat-trick when winning at Stratford, Southwell and Aintree (conditional) in May/June: useful form over fences: won novice handicap at Uttoxeter later in June: in frame all 3 starts in handicaps after: stays 3m: acts on heavy going: has worn headgear. *Dan Skelton* — c136 h118

PETRUCCI (IRE) 6 b.g. Azamour (IRE) – Spring Symphony (IRE) (Darshaan) [2017/18 h84: h15.8d^3 h15.8g^3 h15.7g Apr 20] modest maiden hurdler: unproven beyond 2m: acts on good to soft going: races towards rear. *Derek Shaw* — h91

PETTICOAT TAILS 6 b.m. Presenting – Theatre Girl (King's Theatre (IRE)) [2017/18 b107: h21.4v^3 h19.7s* h20.6v* h20.5s^5 h20.3g^5 Apr 19] good-topped mare: useful bumper performer: fairly useful form over hurdles: won mares novices at Wetherby in December and Newcastle in January, idling both times: will stay 2¾m: acts on heavy going: tried in cheekpieces. *Warren Greatrex* — h121

PEUR DE RIEN (FR) 5 b.g. Kapgarde (FR) – Tango Princess (FR) (Fabulous Dancer (USA)) [2017/18 b16g h16.3d h15.8s^4 Feb 22] £85,000 3-y-o: sturdy gelding: half-brother to fairly useful French hurdler Summer Tango (2m winner, by Polish Summer): dam unraced: showed a bit in bumper: fairly useful form over hurdles: better effort when fourth in novice at Huntingdon. *Oliver Sherwood* — h115 b–

PHANGIO (USA) 9 ch.g. Invasor (ARG) – Muneera (USA) (Green Dancer (USA)) [2017/18 c104§, h–: h21.2m³ h23g³ h23m h26.4s^pu c23.6d⁶ h21.2g h23.8d⁴ h23.8s h26s² h23.6v³ c29.2g* Apr 26] sturdy gelding: poor handicap hurdler: modest handicap chaser: won at Warwick in April: stays 29f: acts on good to firm and heavy going: wears headgear: in tongue tie last 5 starts: sometimes let down by attitude. *Matt Sheppard* — c99 h83

PHANTOM ISLE 5 b.g. Teofilo (IRE) – Antillia (Red Ransom (USA)) [2017/18 b–: b16.8g² b15.7d h16.8v⁴ h19.9v⁶ h19.9v⁵ Apr 13] runner-up on second of 3 starts in bumpers: poor form over hurdles. *Chris Grant* — h82 b77

PHANTOM PRINCE (IRE) 9 b.g. Jeremy (USA) – Phantom Waters (Pharly (FR)) [2017/18 c–, h112: h16.8g May 10] leggy gelding: fairly useful hurdler at best, offered little only start in 2017/18: winning chaser: stays 2½m: acts on heavy going: has worn cheekpieces/tongue tie. *Jimmy Frost* — c– h–

PHARAWAY VIEW 4 br.f. Beat All (USA) – High Park Lady (IRE) (Phardante (FR)) [2017/18 b13.7g Apr 20] half-sister to useful hurdler/winning pointer Clean Sheet (2m-2½m winner) and bumper winner/useful hurdler Nelson's Bridge (19f winner) (both by Oscar): dam winning pointer: tailed off in bumper. *David Bridgwater* — b–

PHARE ISLE (IRE) 13 b.g. Turtle Island (IRE) – Pharenna (Phardante (FR)) [2017/18 c–x, h100: h25g³ h23g⁵ h20.7g^bd h23.4s⁵ h24s h23.4v⁵ h23.8s⁵ h20.7s h25d⁶ Mar 26] sturdy gelding: modest handicap hurdler nowadays: winning chaser, often let down by jumping: stays 3¼m: acts on good to firm and heavy going: wears cheekpieces/tongue tie: often races prominently. *Ben Case* — c– x h88

PHIL'S MAGIC 8 b.g. Fruits of Love (USA) – Inch Rose (IRE) (Eurobus) [2017/18 c26s⁴ c25g⁴ c22.5g³ c25g* c22.5s² c24s³ c25d⁵ c24.5d⁶ h24s⁶ Feb 4] useful hurdler at best: useful handicap chaser: won Midlands National Handicap Chase at Kilbeggan by head from Mr Boss Man) in July: left Ms Sandra Hughes after first start: stays 25f: acts on heavy going: wears headgear/tongue tie. *A. J. Martin, Ireland* — c131 h113

PHOBIAPHILIAC (IRE) 7 b.g. Beneficial – Denys Eyre (IRE) (Eurobus) [2017/18 h127: c17.5s⁴ c16g⁶ c17.5v² h16.8v^pu Apr 8] sturdy gelding: fairly useful hurdler at best: fair form over fences: best effort when fourth in maiden at Exeter: stays 2½m: acts on good to firm going: has worn hood, including in 2017/18. *Nicky Martin* — c109 h–

PHOEBUS LESCRIBAA (FR) 6 b.g. Policy Maker (IRE) – Mia Lescribaa (FR) (Saint des Saints (FR)) [2017/18 b85: h20d h19m³ h25.5g⁴ h21.7v^pu c19.4d³ Apr 22] sturdy gelding: won Irish maiden point on debut: modest form over hurdles: 4/1, third in novice handicap at Stratford (10¼ lengths behind Zamparelli) on chasing debut: left Rebecca Curtis after third start: stays 19f: acts on good to firm and good to soft going: tried in hood. *Fergal O'Brien* — c98 h98

PHOENICIANA 7 b.m. Phoenix Reach (IRE) – Viciana (Sir Harry Lewis (USA)) [2017/18 h106, b75: h15.8d⁵ h20.6d^pu h23.4v³ c19.2s² c24s h15.7v* c19.8v^pu Apr 27] fair hurdler: won mares maiden at Towcester in March: similar form over fences: best effort when second in novice handicap at Market Rasen: stays 23f: best form on soft/heavy going. *Lucy Wadham* — c106 h107

PHOENIX DAWN 4 b.g. Phoenix Reach (IRE) – Comtesse Noire (CAN) (Woodman (USA)) [2017/18 h16.3m² h16.8d³ h16.7g⁶ h15.8m² h15.8g* h16s² ab16d h18.8s³ h16s Apr 27] lengthy gelding: brother to fair hurdler/modest chaser Xenophon (2m-3m winner): fair on Flat, stays 1¾m: fairly useful hurdler: won juvenile at Ludlow in November: unproven beyond 2m: acts on soft and good to firm going: wears headgear: tried in tongue tie: usually races close up. *Brendan Powell* — h119

PHOENIX FIREBIRD 5 b.m. Flying Legend (USA) – Flamebird (IRE) (Mukaddamah (USA)) [2017/18 h–, b–: h21.6g⁴ May 10] poor form over hurdles. *Nigel Hawke* — h81

PHOENIX PARK (GER) 6 b.g. Sholokhov (IRE) – Piercetown (IRE) (Germany (USA)) [2017/18 h18.7g h23g³ h20d^pu h21.6s^pu h16.6d⁶ Dec 2] third on sole start in Irish points: no form over hurdles: tried in tongue tie. *David Dennis* — h–

PHOENIX ROCK (IRE) 6 b.g. Winged Love (IRE) – Guillaume Rock (IRE) (Definite Article) [2017/18 h16g⁴ h15.7d h15.7s h16.6s h20.7s Feb 22] first foal: dam unraced half-sister to useful hurdler/chaser Rock Gone (by Winged Love): challenging when fell last in Irish point on debut: poor form over hurdles. *Jonjo O'Neill* — h74

PHYSICIST (IRE) 4 b.g. Galileo (IRE) – Impressionist Art (USA) (Giant's Causeway (USA)) [2017/18 h16s h15.6d⁶ h16v h16v⁵ Feb 10] fair form in Flat maidens: little impact over hurdles: wears tongue tie. *Patrick Griffin, Ireland* — h–

PICCOLORO 4 b.g. Piccolo – Spanish Gold (Vettori (IRE)) [2017/18 h16.3m^pu Jul 16] no form in Flat maidens/juvenile hurdle. *Jonathan Portman* — h–

PIC

PICKAMIX 7 gr.g. Sagamix (FR) – Star of Wonder (FR) (The Wonder (FR)) [2017/18 h118, b99: h23.1g* c21.6g² c23g² c25d³ c24.2d⁶ c24.1g⁵ Apr 21] rather leggy gelding: bumper winner: fairly useful form over hurdles: won handicap at Market Rasen in May: useful form over fences: best effort when second in novice handicap at Worcester (2½ lengths behind Remind Me Later) in October: stays 23f: acts on good to firm and good to soft going: wears tongue tie. *Charlie Mann* **c131 h120**

PICKNICK PARK 6 b.g. Sulamani (IRE) – Eva's Edge (IRE) (Good Thyne (USA)) [2017/18 h105?, b–: h21.3sᶠ h16.7d⁴ h20.6s⁶ Dec 26] modest maiden hurdler: often races towards rear. *Nick Kent* **h92**

PICTURE PAINTER (IRE) 5 gr.g. Zoffany (IRE) – Sisceal (Dalakhani (IRE)) [2017/18 h80: h20.2g² h20.2m⁴ h16.2d* h16.2g Oct 28] fair form over hurdles: won handicap at Kelso in October: left Jim Goldie after second start: stays 2½m: acts on good to soft going: has worn headgear: often races prominently: has joined David Pipe. *Keith Dalgleish* **h104**

PIECEOFTHEACTION (IRE) 5 br.g. Oscar (IRE) – Homebird (IRE) (Be My Native (USA)) [2017/18 b17v³ Apr 17] half-brother to several winners, including fairly useful hurdler/useful chaser Brackloon High (2m-25f winner, by Bob Back) and fairly useful hurdler/chaser Bon Chic (19f-25f winner, by Presenting): dam bumper winner: multiple point winner: 13/2, third in bumper at Carlisle (14½ lengths behind Lily's Gem). *Chris Grant* **b84**

PIETRALUNGA (FR) 5 b.m. Soldier of Fortune (IRE) – Ascot One (FR) (Septieme Ciel (USA)) [2017/18 h16v* h16.8s h20v h16.5d Apr 24] angular mare: 17f winner on only Flat start in France: fair form over hurdles: won mares maiden at Clonmel in January: little impact in face of much stiffer tasks after: in tongue tie last 3 starts. *W. P. Mullins, Ireland* **h104**

PIKARNIA 8 b.g. Authorized (IRE) – Kartuzy (JPN) (Polish Precedent (USA)) [2017/18 h105, b–: h22.7g³ h20.2d² h23.9s² h23.9d⁴ Sep 11] fair handicap hurdler: stays 3m: acts on soft and good to firm going: wears tongue tie. *Rebecca Menzies* **h98**

PILGRIMS BAY (IRE) 8 b.g. Turtle Island (IRE) – Lady Ariadna (IRE) (Supreme Leader) [2017/18 c135§, h–: c25.1s⁶ c26g⁵ c24s² Dec 27] workmanlike gelding: winning hurdler: useful handicap chaser: second at Kempton (2¾ lengths behind Tintern Theatre) in December: stays 3m: acts on heavy going: wears headgear: often races in rear, usually travels strongly: irresolute. *Neil Mulholland* **c136 § h–**

PILLARD (FR) 6 b.g. Muhaymin (USA) – Ultime Moment (IRE) (Anabaa (USA)) [2017/18 h119: h24g³ h24s Dec 28] lengthy, sparely-made gelding: fairly useful hurdler at best: left Jonjo O'Neill after first start: best short of 3m: acts on heavy going: has worn headgear, including in 2017/18: usually in tongue tie. *Paul Hennessy, Ireland* **h110**

PINCH OF GINGER (IRE) 7 ch.g. Golden Lariat (USA) – Espiritu Santo (IRE) (Trans Island) [2017/18 h87, b69: h23.3g³ c26.3sᶠ c20.3v* c25.2v⁵ c20.9v⁴ h21v⁴ Apr 27] modest form over hurdles: fair form over fences: won novice handicap at Bangor (awarded race after dead-heating with Oneida Tribe) in January: stays 23f: acts on heavy going: sometimes in headgear: usually races close up. *Donald McCain* **c100 h90**

PINEAPPLE CRUSH (IRE) 6 b.m. Milan – Katie Snurge (IRE) (Snurge) [2017/18 h–: h19.3m⁴ h22.1d c20.1g⁵ c21.2gpᵘ h24.1s Dec 27] poor maiden hurdler: no form over fences: left Martin Todhunter after fourth start: in cheekpieces/tongue tie last 2 starts. *Philip Kirby* **c– h72**

PINEAPPLE RUSH 5 b.m. Kayf Tara – Celtic Native (IRE) (Be My Native (USA)) [2017/18 b16.4s³ b15.7s² h19.9v* h20.1d* Apr 23] €42,000 3-y-o: tall mare: sister to 3 winners, including useful chaser Ace High (3m winner, stayed 29f) and useful hurdler/chaser Premier Bond (2m-25f winner), and half-sister to 3 winners: dam (c116/h145) 2m-2¾m hurdle/chase winner: fairly useful form when placed in bumpers: fairly useful form over hurdles: won mares novices at Sedgefield in March and Hexham in April: will be suited by 3m. *Philip Hobbs* **h120 b100**

PINE WARBLER 9 b.g. Pilsudski (IRE) – Cetti's Warbler (Sir Harry Lewis (USA)) [2017/18 h116: c19.8gᵘʳ c21.7s c23.6v⁴ c24v³ c23.6s⁴ Mar 22] maiden hurdler: modest form over fences: stays 3m: best form on soft/heavy going: has worn cheekpieces, including last 3 starts: wears tongue tie. *Stuart Edmunds* **c99 h–**

PINK CHAMPERS 5 b.m. Malinas (GER) – Shady Olive (Terimon) [2017/18 h16.7dpᵘ h16g⁵ h15.8m h16g Jul 10] first foal: dam no form: no form over hurdles. *Dan Skelton* **h–**

PINK COAT 11 gr.g. Alhaarth (IRE) – In The Pink (IRE) (Indian Ridge) [2017/18 c–, h101: h22.1gpᵘ h23.3d pᵘ Jul 11] winning hurdler, no show in 2017/18 after 12-month absence: maiden chaser: has worn headgear/tongue tie. *Sam England* **c– h–**

624

PINK EYED PEDRO 7 b.g. Dr Massini (IRE) – Poacher's Paddy (IRE) (Jurado (USA))   **c96**
[2017/18 c72: c23.6s⁴ Apr 27] multiple winning pointer: modest form when fourth in
novice hunter at Chepstow on second start in chases: wears hood: tried in tongue tie.
David Brace

PINK GIN 10 ch.g. Alflora (IRE) – Miss Mailmit (Rakaposhi King) [2017/18 c110, h109:   **c107**
c23.8v² c25.1v² c21.7s^F c23.6s c25.1v^pu h24v⁵ Apr 27] workmanlike gelding: winning   **h–**
hurdler: fair maiden chaser: stays 25f: raced mainly on soft/heavy going: wears tongue tie:
front runner/races prominently. *Nigel Twiston-Davies*

PINKIE BROWN (FR) 6 gr.g. Gentlewave (IRE) – Natt Musik (FR) (Kendor (FR))   **c–**
[2017/18 c134, h125: h20m⁶ Jul 5] rather leggy gelding: fairly useful hurdler, well held   **h–**
only start in 2017/18: useful form over fences: ran on Flat in France in 2018 for Mme
G. Rarick: unproven beyond 17f: acts on good to firm and heavy going: wears hood.
Johnny Farrelly

PINK TARA 7 b.m. Kayf Tara – Red And White (IRE) (Red Ransom (USA)) [2017/18   **h97**
h21.2s⁵ h19.7s* Mar 27] modest handicap hurdler: won at Hereford in March: stays 2½m:
raced mainly on soft/heavy going. *Venetia Williams*

PINOTAGE 10 br.g. Danbird (AUS) – Keen Melody (USA) (Sharpen Up) [2017/18   **h90**
h16.2g⁶ h20.6v⁴ h18.8v² h20v^pu Sep 29] modest maiden hurdler: stays 19f: acts on heavy
going: has worn cheekpieces: in tongue tie last 3 starts. *Gordon Elliott, Ireland*

PIQUE ROCK 6 b.m. King's Theatre (IRE) – Flutter Bye (IRE) (Alflora (IRE)) [2017/18   **h–**
b82: h16d May 1] close-coupled mare: modest form in bumpers: little show in maiden
hurdle: successful in points subsequently: tried in hood. *Alan King*

PIQUE SOUS (FR) 11 gr.g. Martaline – Six Fois Sept (FR) (Epervier Bleu) [2017/18   **h132**
h135: h20g² Jul 14] good-topped gelding: useful hurdler: second in minor event at Cork
(2¼ lengths behind Rashaan) on only start in 2017/18: stays 2½m: acts on soft going: wears
tongue tie. *W. P. Mullins, Ireland*

PIRATE LOOK (IRE) 4 b.g. Canford Cliffs (IRE) – Gerika (FR) (Galileo (IRE))   **h104**
[2017/18 h15.8s² h16d² Mar 29] fairly useful form when second in
maiden hurdles at Huntingdon and Wetherby (juvenile). *Martin Keighley*

PIRI MASSINI (IRE) 7 b.g. Pierre – Lady Doctor (IRE) (Dr Massini (IRE)) [2017/18   **h117**
h23.4v* h22.8v⁵ h23.3v³ h24v² Apr 15] £36,000 4-y-o: third foal: dam unraced: off mark
in Irish points at second attempt: fairly useful form over hurdles: won novice at Fakenham
in January. *Olly Murphy*

PIROLO (IRE) 6 ch.g. Teofilo (IRE) – Zavaleta (IRE) (Kahyasi) [2017/18 h19s^pu h15.3d   **h–**
Apr 22] fair on Flat, stays 2m: no show in novice hurdles: tried in tongue tie. *Nigel Hawke*

PISTOL (IRE) 9 b.g. High Chaparral (IRE) – Alinea (USA) (Kingmambo (USA))   **c–**
[2017/18 c–, h111§: h17.2m⁶ h22.1d⁶ h17d h16.2v² h16.8s h17v* h19.3d³ h20.6v³ h20.1d   **h107 §**
Apr 23] useful-looking gelding: fair handicap hurdler: won at Carlisle in February: maiden
chaser: stays 25f, as effective over much shorter: acts on heavy going: has worn headgear:
usually races prominently: temperamental. *John Dixon*

PISTOL PARK (FR) 7 b.g. Poliglote – Pistolera (GER) (Monsun (GER)) [2017/18 c137,   **c133**
h–: c20.5v^F c15.2s² c15.7v⁴ c15.2v⁴ c15.9d³ c20d² c15.9v* Apr 17] winning hurdler: useful   **h–**
handicap chaser: won at Carlisle (by 1¼ lengths from Wolf Sword) in April: stays 2½m:
acts on heavy going: has worn cheekpieces: in tongue tie last 4 starts. *Brian Ellison*

PISTOL SHOOT (IRE) 6 b.g. Milan – Emesions Lady (IRE) (Bigstone (IRE)) [2017/18   **c–**
b17g⁵ b16.3d* h23f² h21.4g h21.6s⁴ h23.9s h21.7v^pu c24.1d^pu Apr 21] €18,000 3-y-o: **h97**
closely related to bumper winner/winning pointer Tim Henry (by Sonus): dam unraced: **b86**
placed in points: fair form in bumpers: won conditionals/amateur event at Stratford in June:
modest form over hurdles: pulled up in novice handicap on chasing debut: stays 2¾m: acts
on soft going: usually wears headgear: front runner/races prominently. *Nicky Martin*

PITCH PINE (IRE) 4 b.g. Lilbourne Lad (IRE) – Timber Tops (UAE) (Timber Country   **b–**
(USA)) [2017/18 b13.1g b14d Nov 5] well held in bumpers. *Giles Bravery*

PITON PETE (IRE) 7 b.g. Westerner – Glenair Lucy (IRE) (Luso) [2017/18 h101p: **h118**
h19.6g² h20.5d³ h19.7s³ h15.7s* h16v* h19.2v² h16s Apr 28] fairly useful hurdler: won
maiden at Towcester in February and novice at Warwick in March: stays 2½m: acts on
heavy going. *Oliver Sherwood*

PIVOTAL FLAME (IRE) 5 b.m. Pivotal – Saadiah (IRE) (Dubai Destination (USA))   **h91**
[2017/18 h95: h15.8g⁴ h15.9d⁴ h16.4d h16s Dec 8] sparely-made mare: modest maiden
hurdler: raced only at 2m: acts on good to firm and good to soft going: usually races
towards rear. *Pat Phelan*

PIX

PIXIEPOT 8 b.m. Alflora (IRE) – Folly Foster (Relkino) [2017/18 h95: h16.8g h16.7d² h19.9s³ h18.6v² h17d* Mar 31] modest handicap hurdler: won mares event at Carlisle in March: stays 21f: acts on good to firm and heavy going: tried in cheekpieces: front runner/races prominently. *Peter Niven* — **h99**

PLACEDELA CONCORDE 5 b.g. Champs Elysees – Kasakiya (IRE) (Zafonic (USA)) [2017/18 h–: h16.8v h17d^pu Mar 25] lightly raced on Flat: no form in novice hurdles: wears tongue tie. *Maurice Barnes* — **h–**

PLAISIR D'AMOUR (FR) 6 b.m. Linngari (IRE) – Analfabeta (FR) (Anabaa (USA)) [2017/18 c137, h–: c20.4s^pu c19.9s⁶ c23.8s³ Apr 27] good-topped mare: winning hurdler: useful chaser: easily best effort in 2017/18 when third in listed mares event at Perth (7¼ lengths behind Rons Dream) in April: stays 3m: acts on heavy going. *Venetia Williams* — **c129 h–**

PLANET NINE (IRE) 6 b.g. Flemensfirth (USA) – Old Moon (IRE) (Old Vic) [2017/18 b108: h19.7s⁴ h20s⁵ h19.3s³ h25.3d* h22s* h22.8v⁴ Mar 31] useful bumper performer: fairly useful form over hurdles: won handicap at Catterick and 3-runner novice at Newcastle in February: stays 25f: acts on soft going: has worn hood: often races prominently: remains capable of better. *Rose Dobbin* — **h122 p**

PLANTAGENET 6 b.g. Midnight Legend – Marsh Court (Overbury (IRE)) [2017/18 h77, b–: h23.1g* h23g* h21g* h23g* c25.7d² c25.2g^w h23.5d⁶ h25v³ h25.5v⁴ h21.6v⁴ Apr 8] rangy, rather unfurnished gelding: fair handicap hurdler: completed 4-timer at Bangor (conditional), Worcester, Towcester (novice) and Worcester again in first half of season: fair form over fences: better effort when second in novice handicap at Plumpton: stays 3¼m: acts on heavy going: tried in hood. *Seamus Mullins* — **c107 h104**

PLATO'S KODE (IRE) 4 b.g. Kodiac – Speedy Sonata (USA) (Stravinsky (USA)) [2017/18 h16.7g* h16g* h15.8g² h16d³ h16.4d Nov 17] compact gelding: fair on Flat, stayed 1¾m: fairly useful form over hurdles: won juveniles at Market Rasen and Worcester in August: raced around 2m: acted on good to soft going: wore cheekpieces/tongue tie: dead. *Seamus Durack* — **h116**

PLAYFUL PRINCE 7 gr.g. Act One – Princess Angelique (FR) (Sagacity (FR)) [2017/18 h20v^pu h24d^pu Nov 21] failed to complete in points/over hurdles: tried in blinkers. *Michael Scudamore* — **h–**

PLAY PRACTICE 8 b.m. Josr Algarhoud (IRE) – More Flair (Alflora (IRE)) [2017/18 h16.4s h16.2v³ h17d^pu h24v⁴ h23.9s^pu Apr 25] point winner: poor maiden hurdler. *James Walton* — **h78**

PLAY THE ACE (IRE) 9 b.g. Scorpion (IRE) – Henris Blaze (IRE) (Be My Native (USA)) [2017/18 c113: c25.5m^pu c22.6g* c22.6m² c21.1g³ c22.6g* c21.4g⁴ c20.2s³ c22.6g* c20.2s* c20.5d* c19.9v* c19.4v^pu Jan 6] useful handicap chaser: won at Stratford in June, September and November, Wincanton (conditional) and Kempton later in November, and Aintree (by nose from Katachenko) in December: stays 23f: acts on good to firm and heavy going: wears cheekpieces/tongue tie: usually races close up. *Peter Bowen* — **c136**

PLAY THE GAME (IRE) 5 b.g. Lawman (FR) – Neutral (Beat Hollow) [2017/18 h16.2m² h16.7g^f h16s⁴ h16d⁵ h16v* h16s Apr 17] useful on Flat, stays 1¼m: fairly useful form over hurdles: won maiden at Fairyhouse in January: left John McConnell after second start: raced around 2m: acts on heavy and good to firm going: front runner/races prominently. *T. Gibney, Ireland* — **h118**

PLEASANT COMPANY (IRE) 10 b.g. Presenting – Katie Flame (IRE) (Alderbrook) [2017/18 c151, h–: c24.5d c25v^pu c34.3s² Apr 14] tall gelding: maiden hurdler: smart handicap chaser: handy all the way, and jumped superbly in main when second in Grand National at Aintree (head behind Tiger Roll after looking held early on run-in) in April: stays 4¼m: acts on heavy going: has worn hood, including in 2017/18: tried in tongue tie. *W. P. Mullins, Ireland* — **c152 h–**

PLEASURE DOME 5 b.m. Makfi – Nouvelle Lune (Fantastic Light (USA)) [2017/18 h91p: h21g² May 15] good-topped mare: fairly useful on Flat, stays 1¾m: fair form over hurdles: second in mares maiden at Kempton (in cheekpieces) on sole outing in 2017/18: has joined W. P. Mullins: likely to progress further. *Jonjo O'Neill* — **h105 p**

PLENTY OF BUTTY (IRE) 5 b.g. Germany (USA) – Jump For Joy (IRE) (Liboi (USA)) [2017/18 b15.7d b17d h19.5s Apr 27] no form in bumpers/novice hurdle. *Michael Scudamore* — **h– b–**

PLINTH 8 b.g. Montjeu (IRE) – Crazy Volume (IRE) (Machiavellian (USA)) [2017/18 c–p, h137: h20s* h20m³ h16g* h16d h17g⁵ h16v h24v Sep 30] rather leggy gelding: useful hurdler: won minor event at Killarney in May and Grimes Hurdle at — **c– h143**

Tipperary (by 3½ lengths from Kitten Rock) in July: once-raced chaser: stays 2¾m, effective at much shorter: acts on soft and good to firm going: wears headgear/tongue tie. *Joseph Patrick O'Brien, Ireland*

PLUS JAMAIS (FR) 11 b.g. Caballo Raptor (CAN) – Branceilles (FR) (Satin Wood) [2017/18 c117, h113: c20.1v* h21.4v[6] c20.1s* c34v[pu] c20.1v[ur] Apr 14] sturdy gelding: fair handicap hurdler: fairly useful handicap chaser: won at Newcastle in December and February: stays 3m: acts on heavy going: has worn headgear, including usually in 2017/18. *Iain Jardine*   **c125 h96**

PLUS ONE (IRE) 6 b.g. Winged Love (IRE) – Balwaney (FR) (Exit To Nowhere (USA)) [2017/18 h114p: h19.5s[6] h24d[3] Dec 5] off mark in Irish maiden points at second attempt: fairly useful form over hurdles: better effort in 2017/18 when third in novice at Southwell: has joined Ben Pauling. *Jonjo O'Neill*   **h115**

POBBLES BAY (IRE) 8 b.g. Oscar (IRE) – Rose de Beaufai (FR) (Solon (GER)) [2017/18 c144, h–: c19.9s c29.5v c24.2v[4] c27.9v[pu] Apr 1] good-topped gelding: winning hurdler: useful chaser, below best in 2017/18: stays 3¼m: raced only on soft/heavy going: often races in rear. *Evan Williams*   **c119 h–**

PODILI ROAD (IRE) 6 b.g. Darsi (FR) – Geray Lady (IRE) (Roselier (FR)) [2017/18 h15.3s h16.5g[4] h16.3s h19.2v h19.2v c20.9s[pu] Apr 8] no form over hurdles/fences: in headgear last 2 starts. *Evan Williams*   **c– h–**

POETIC LADY (IRE) 7 b.m. Yeats (IRE) – Apollo Lady (Alflora (IRE)) [2017/18 h17.7m[2] h20m[2] h16g[4] h20g* h21.7d* h21.2m[4] Oct 11] third foal: dam (h112) bumper/2m hurdle winner (stayed 2½m): fair hurdler: won mares maiden at Worcester in August and mares handicap at Fontwell in September: left P. J. Colville after final (2016/17) start: stays 2¾m: acts on soft and good to firm going: wears headgear/tongue tie. *Neil Mulholland*   **h108**

POETIC LICENSE (IRE) 6 b.g. Dylan Thomas (IRE) – Bright Bank (IRE) (Sadler's Wells (USA)) [2017/18 h58: h19d May 1] little form: wears tongue tie. *James Grassick*   **h–**

POETIC PRESENCE (IRE) 8 b.m. Presenting – Johnston's Crest (IRE) (Be My Native (USA)) [2017/18 h22g[2] h22.1g[pu] h23.3s h24.3s[5] h23.3s[3] h23.1s[4] h24.1s[6] h25.8s[6] c21.6v[3] c23.4v[4] Feb 15] winning pointer: poor maiden hurdler: similar form in chases: stays 3m: acts on soft going: has worn visor: tried in tongue tie: usually races close up: temperamental. *Stuart Coltherd*   **c71 § h71 §**

POETIC RHYTHM (IRE) 7 ch.g. Flemensfirth (USA) – Sommer Sonnet (IRE) (Taipan (IRE)) [2017/18 h131, b107: h19.5d* h21.1d* h20.5v* h24v h20.3g Apr 18] strong gelding: winning pointer: useful bumper performer: useful hurdler: won Persian War Novices'   **h138**

Betfred Challow Novices' Hurdle, Newbury—second-season novice Poetic Rhythm wears down long-time leader Mulcahys Hill (noseband) in a gruelling finish

The Yes No Wait Sorries' "Poetic Rhythm"

Hurdle at Chepstow (by 1¼ lengths from Amour de Nuit) in October and Challow Novices' Hurdle at Newbury (by short head from Mulcahys Hill) in December: third in Hyde Novices' Hurdle at Cheltenham (2½ lengths behind On The Blind Side) in between: should be suited by 3m: acts on heavy going: races prominently. *Fergal O'Brien*

POET'S CHARM (IRE) 4 b.g. Poet's Voice – Antillia (Red Ransom (USA)) [2017/18 h16d^F h16.8v^F h16.8s^6 Apr 23] modest maiden on Flat: poor form over hurdles: wears hood. *Martin Hill* — **h78**

POINTED AND SHARP (IRE) 6 b.g. Scorpion (IRE) – Leamybe (IRE) (Religiously (USA)) [2017/18 b70: h16.8g^6 h16s h16s* h16s^6 h16.5s^3 h17.7g^2 Apr 20] has scope: fair form over hurdles: won novice at Worcester in November: stays 2¼m: acts on soft going: in hood last 5 starts: races freely. *Philip Hobbs* — **h113**

POINT N SHOOT (IRE) 7 b.g. Broadway Flyer (USA) – Ali's Dipper (IRE) (Orchestra) [2017/18 h95, b63: c20s^{ur} c23.5s^F h21.6v^6 h25v^5 h25.8v^2 h21.9v^3 h23.1v^2 h23.1d* Apr 24] fair handicap hurdler: won at Exeter in April: let down by jumping over fences: stays 3¼m: acts on heavy going: wears headgear: in tongue tie last 4 starts: front runner/races prominently. *Nigel Hawke* — **c– x / h100**

POINT OF PRINCIPLE (IRE) 5 b.g. Rip Van Winkle (IRE) – L'Ancresse (IRE) (Darshaan) [2017/18 b107: h16.8d^2 h16.4g^2 h19.4g^2 h19.3s* h24.7s h19.5s^5 Apr 27] sturdy gelding: bumper winner: useful form over hurdles: won novice at Ascot (by nose from Dame de Compagnie) in February: stays 19f: acts on soft going: often races prominently. *Tim Vaughan* — **h133 / b89**

POINT THE WAY (IRE) 7 br.g. Brian Boru – Caslain Og (IRE) (Supreme Leader) [2017/18 h125: c23.4d* c23.4v^3 c23.4s^5 c30s^3 c24.5v^4 c31.9v^{ur} Mar 15] good-topped gelding: fairly useful hurdler: similar form over fences: won novice at Kelso in October: thorough stayer: acts on heavy going: has worn cheekpieces, including last 3 starts. *Brian Ellison* — **c120 / h–**

POKARI (FR) 6 ch.g. Bonbon Rose (FR) – Pokara (FR) (Kutub (IRE)) [2017/18 b94: h16.5m^6 Nov 1] angular gelding: bumper winner: 7/1, sixth in maiden at Taunton (9 lengths behind Dentley De Mee) on hurdling debut after 14-month absence: entitled to do better. *Alan Jones* — **h85 p**

POL

POKER PLAY (FR) 5 ch.g. Martaline – Becquarette (FR) (Nombre Premier) [2017/18 h122: h21.1s⁵ h21.4v^pu h23.1v³ h23.6s³ Feb 24] good-topped, attractive gelding: fairly useful handicap hurdler: in cheekpieces, third at Chepstow in February: may prove best short of 3m: acts on heavy going: has worn tongue tie. *David Pipe*   **h123**

POKER SCHOOL (IRE) 8 b.g. Gold Well – Frozen Pockets (IRE) (Broken Hearted) [2017/18 c136, h122: c21.3m⁶ c21.4g⁴ c16.5g² c21.4g⁵ c15.9g⁴ c19.4d² c19.1d^ur c18.8d⁴ c16d² Apr 24] lengthy gelding: fairly useful hurdler: useful handicap chaser: second at Worcester in August and Wetherby (nose behind Wolf Sword) in November: stays easy 21f: acts on soft going: tried in tongue tie: usually races towards rear. *Ian Williams*   **c132 h–**

POKORA DU LYS (FR) 7 b.g. Saint des Saints (FR) – Shailann (FR) (Gaspard de La Nuit (FR)) [2017/18 h111: h15.5d h25.3d³ h19.3s h25v^F Feb 19] fair maiden hurdler: left Dan Skelton after third start: barely stays 25f: acts on soft going: tried in tongue tie: usually races prominently, tends to find little. *Rebecca Menzies*   **h102**

POLARBROOK (IRE) 11 br.g. Alderbrook – Frozen Cello (IRE) (Arctic Lord) [2017/18 c57, h77: h20.3g⁴ h20.3g³ h24g* h22g⁴ h20.3g³ h19.9d⁴ h23.1g⁵ h16.8g⁶ h20.7g⁵ h23.4s² Dec 4] angular gelding: modest handicap hurdler: won at Southwell in June and Stratford in July: winning chaser: stays 3m: acts on good to firm and heavy going: wears headgear: has worn tongue tie: often races towards rear. *Derek Shaw*   **c– h91**

POLAR PRESENT (IRE) 7 b.m. Presenting – Sleepless Eye (Supreme Leader) [2017/18 h20m² h24g* h20v² h23d² h20s⁵ h18s h24d⁶ Apr 26] third foal: half-sister to bumper winner/useful hurdler Foryourinformation (2½m winner, by Kayf Tara) and fairly useful hurdler/chaser Tonvadosa (2¾m-3m winner, by Flemensfirth): dam, ran once over hurdles, half-sister to fairly useful hurdlers/useful chasers Wee Robbie and Isn't That Lucky (both stayed 3m): bumper winner: useful hurdler: won handicap at Gowran in June: stays 3m: acts on good to firm and heavy going: wears cheekpieces: usually races close up. *Seamus Fahey, Ireland*   **h132**

POLICY BREACH (IRE) 7 b.g. Kayf Tara – Just Stunning (IRE) (Presenting) [2017/18 h120: c23g⁵ h26.4g⁴ Jul 23] fairly useful handicap hurdler: 12/1, fifth in novice at Worcester (16½ lengths behind Work du Breteau) on chasing debut: should stay beyond 23f: acts on good to firm going: wears tongue tie. *Kim Bailey*   **c116 h88**

POLIDAM (FR) 9 b.g. Trempolino (USA) – Eladame (FR) (Snurge) [2017/18 c134, h116: c20s* c24.5d c21s⁵ c21.1s c20s⁴ Apr 25] good-topped gelding: has had breathing operation: winning hurdler: smart handicap chaser: won at Navan (by 9 lengths from Acapella Bourgeoisi) in December: should stay 3m: acts on heavy going: wears headgear. *W. P. Mullins, Ireland*   **c148 h–**

POLISHED ROCK (IRE) 8 ch.g. Rock of Gibraltar (IRE) – Where We Left Off (Dr Devious (IRE)) [2017/18 h20.3d h15.8g h19.2d Nov 19] fairly useful hurdler at best, lightly raced and no form since 2014/15: tried in cheekpieces: in tongue tie last 2 starts. *Johnny Farrelly*   **h–**

POLITENESS (FR) 9 b.g. Poliglote – Martiniquaise (FR) (Anabaa (USA)) [2017/18 h–: h16.2g² May 28] fair handicap hurdler: stays easy 2½m: acts on soft and good to firm going: usually wears hood. *Rose Dobbin*   **h99**

POLITOLOGUE (FR) 7 gr.g. Poliglote – Scarlet Row (FR) (Turgeon (USA)) [2017/18 c153, h–: c17.5v* c15.5d* c16s* c16.4s² c15.9s⁴ c19.9s* Apr 13]   **c166 h–**

Consolation doesn't always come to unlucky losers in such abundance, but Lady Luck has repaid the connections of Politologue in spades. Politologue was a smart novice chaser, a winner three times before an unexpected stumble denied him what would have been a deserved victory in a Grade 1, after he had jumped the last cleanly with a narrow lead in the Maghull Chase at Aintree. Politologue came down just a stride or two after the final fence, looking a most unlucky loser (his stablemate San Benedeto, who looked booked for third at the final fence, was the beneficiary in the end of Politologue's misfortune). When Politologue returned to action in the autumn, in the 188Bet Haldon Gold Cup at Exeter, he set the record straight by beating San Benedeto (who had the benefit of a run), idling in front before being ridden out to win by two and a quarter lengths, the pair twenty-five lengths and more clear of the remainder (the Maghull runner-up Forest Bihan was pulled up). Politologue's performance was at least as good as anything he had produced as a novice but it remained to be seen how far he could go in his second season.

Betfair Tingle Creek Chase, Sandown—a tenth Tingle Creek win for trainer Paul Nicholls as the grey Politologue beats Fox Norton (noseband) and the ill-fated Ar Mad (chevrons)

Even after his Haldon Gold Cup victory, Politologue looked a far from obvious candidate to develop into a top contender for the season's two-mile championship events. 'We'll get back to winning those big races, I'm incredibly lucky to have had all the good ones I had and it doesn't frustrate me that I haven't got the top horses any more, you just have to rebuild,' Paul Nicholls said at the start of the season. 'We'll get the maximum out of the horses we train and the really good horses will turn up again. When we had Denman and he went novice hurdling, there was no way you'd have known he was a Gold Cup horse. Horses improve.' Those remarks were borne out time and time again at Manor Farm Stables in the latest season, there being no better example than Politologue from whom the maximum was certainly extracted by Nicholls, who is on the verge of becoming only the third trainer to have 3,000 jumps winners in Britain (following Martin Pipe and Nicky Henderson who reached that milestone in August 2018).

The Tingle Creek Chase at Sandown, the season's first Grade 1 for the established two-milers, had been won on nine occasions by ten-times champion trainer Nicholls, and both Politologue and San Benedeto were in the line-up for the latest edition. The preamble was marred by stars dropping out. Firstly, Altior was sidelined by the need for a breathing operation, and worse followed for race sponsors Betfair and the Sandown management with the eleventh-hour withdrawal of both of the Willie Mullins-trained pair Douvan and Un de Sceaux. Connections of Douvan had also sidestepped the previous year's Tingle Creek at a very late stage and there was again a kerfuffle in the ante-post market as a result of six-day entry Douvan's unexpected absence from the final list of declarations. It was said that he was not ready to return to action after his golden run had been brought to an end when he trailed home only seventh in the Queen Mother Champion Chase at the Cheltenham Festival (afterwards found to have suffered a hairline stress fracture to his pelvis). As for Un de Sceaux, winner of the Tingle Creek twelve months earlier, it was thought he had been entered as cover for Douvan but he too was missing, redirected to easier pickings in the Hilly Way Chase at Cork the next day (the same event Douvan had won the year before after being 7/4-on for the Tingle Creek four days before that race).

Even the absence of Altior, Douvan and Un de Sceaux couldn't make it appear as if the Tingle Creek was there for Politologue's taking. It clearly wasn't anything like so strong a field as it might have been—Queen Mother Champion

Chase winner Special Tiara was another absentee—and Politologue started 7/2 second favourite in the field of six. Fox Norton, narrowly beaten by Special Tiara in the Queen Mother Champion Chase and winner of the Champion Chase over the distance at Punchestown (from Un de Sceaux), looked a worthy 13/8-on favourite on the day. He had been warmed up when landing the odds in the Shloer Chase at Cheltenham in November, looking as good as ever. Manor Farm Stables had moved past the million-pound mark in seasonal earnings earlier on Tingle Creek afternoon and Politologue's hard-fought victory over Fox Norton in the day's feature consolidated Paul Nicholls' lead in the seasonal trainers' championship (he eventually finished runner-up to Nicky Henderson). Despite sweating up beforehand (on a cold afternoon), Politologue put up an almost faultless performance, jumping fluently and travelling well until moving to the front after the second last and keeping on strongly to hold off Fox Norton by half a length. Front-running Ar Mad finished five lengths behind Fox Norton, with Charbel fourth, on his first outing in open company over fences, and San Benedeto fifth. Sadly, the sixth runner Sir Valentino, third in the previous season's Queen Mother Champion Chase, suffered a fatal fall at the final fence.

Winning a Tingle Creek raised the profile of Politologue considerably, as it had done for the last Nicholls-trained winner of the race, Dodging Bullets, in the 2014/15 season. Dodging Bullets, a surprise winner of the Tingle Creek, went on to add two further Grade 1s to his record, winning the Clarence House at Ascot (overturning the odds laid on Sprinter Sacre on that horse's much-awaited comeback) and the Queen Mother Champion Chase itself (in which Sprinter Sacre was pulled up). Politologue's next target, though, was partly decided by his owner's post-Christmas holiday plans and he took in the Grade 2 Desert Orchid Chase at Kempton's Christmas meeting instead of the Clarence House. Sent off at odds on himself this time, Politologue was left with a straightforward task after his main rival Special Tiara (twice a winner of the race) fell at the eighth. The Desert Orchid was just two and a half weeks after the Tingle Creek and Politologue won in no more than workmanlike fashion (though he did win by thirteen lengths from Vaniteux), eventually having to be ridden out after being left in front and being well clear in the

JLT Melling Chase, Aintree—
an emotional win for owner John Hales as Politologue battles back to beat Min in the race which the owner's One Man was killed 20 years earlier

Mr J. Hales's "Politologue"

home straight. Paul Nicholls explained that he had been 'quite hard' on Politologue in the run up to Sandown in order to have him at his peak for the Tingle Creek. Having taken full advantage of Altior's absence in the autumn, Politologue came up against him, after a break, in his first two races in the spring proving no match when beaten four lengths in the three-runner Game Spirit at Newbury by a returning Altior, and then managing fourth behind Altior, Min and God's Own in the Queen Mother Champion Chase. Left in front when Douvan fell at the tenth at Cheltenham, Politologue was headed before two out and found no extra from the last, finishing twenty-three lengths behind Altior.

One footnote to Politologue's appearance in the Queen Mother Champion Chase was that his jockey was fined £1,000 by the Cheltenham stewards for breaking out of the pre-race parade too early. The fine didn't go down well with Paul Nicholls' assistant Harry Derham who said 'It's wrong that in the build-up to the most important race of a horse's life, the parade should be considered more important than the horse.' It transpired that Politologue had become unruly and had kicked and broken the wrist of one of his handlers. His jockey Sam Twiston-Davies successfully appealed the fine, saying he had been given permission by one of the officials to leave the parade, a submission which the appeal panel accepted. Parades before championship races help to create a sense of occasion but they are not popular with some trainers and discretion should be exercised if a horse becomes upset or unruly. Politologue wore a hood in his last three races in his novice season and he was re-equipped with one (in addition to a first-time tongue tie) when he lined up for the JLT Melling Chase—with Altior again missing—at Aintree over two and a half miles against Min, the Ryanair Chase winner Balko des Flos and three others.

There was no repeat in the Melling Chase of Politologue's pre-race behaviour at Cheltenham (he was allowed by the Aintree stewards to lead the parade which enabled him to leave the paddock first). An 11/1 underdog in betting dominated by

Min (11/10) and Balko des Flos (2/1), Politologue produced his best performance yet to land his second Grade 1 of the season, fighting out a thrilling duel in the home straight with Min and beating him in very game fashion by a neck after edging ahead on the run-in. Sizing Granite was twenty lengths back in third and Balko des Flos only fourth after leading for a long way. It was a first-class performance from Politologue who saw the trip out well, which gives his connections a wider choice of races to aim at in the next season. 'He blew his brains at Cheltenham and was more relaxed here, I also think a flat track suits him best,' said Paul Nicholls. As well as making up for his loss in the Maghull on the same course twelve months earlier, Politologue also won the Melling on the twentieth anniversary of the death of his owner's One Man, also a grey, in the same race. One Man was a dual winner of the King George VI Chase, a race connections mentioned as a possible target for Politologue after he had won at Aintree.

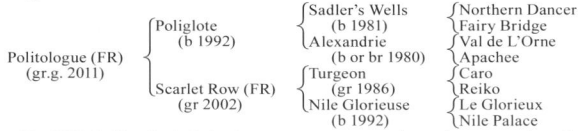

Politologue (FR) (gr.g. 2011)
- Poliglote (b 1992)
  - Sadler's Wells (b 1981)
    - Northern Dancer
    - Fairy Bridge
  - Alexandrie (b or br 1980)
    - Val de L'Orne
    - Apachee
- Scarlet Row (FR) (gr 2002)
  - Turgeon (gr 1986)
    - Caro
    - Reiko
  - Nile Glorieuse (b 1992)
    - Le Glorieux
    - Nile Palace

Paul Nicholls alluded, in the same pre-season interview quoted earlier, to the changes that have taken place in the jumps bloodstock market since the days of Kauto Star, Big Buck's and the like. 'They'd had half a dozen runs and you knew the form was there, but you never get that now. There are more people trying to buy nowadays so you have to purchase the French horses after one or two runs. It's not that I'm being priced out of the market, but I try to get value for money for my clients and don't like taking a big gamble for a lot of money.' The good-bodied Politologue had raced twice for Etienne Leenders, winning a four-year-old event over hurdles at Auteuil, before being bought privately for John Hales, one of the long-standing patrons at Manor Farm Stables (though he has horses in other yards as well, including that of Nicholls' former assistant Dan Skelton). Politologue is by the now-deceased top French sire Poliglote out of the stoutly-bred Scarlet Row who won ten times over jumps in France at up to two and a half miles, being successful in listed company over hurdles and showing useful form over fences (second in the Prix Maurice Gillois). Politologue is Scarlet Row's third foal, her first being the winning French hurdler over seventeen furlongs Scarlett du Mesnil (by Muhtathir). Politologue's grandam Nile Glorieuse won over hurdles and fences, and is a half-sister to the grandam of the Prix des Drags winner Princesse Kap. Politologue, who travels strongly in his races, is fully effective at around two miles and will probably stay three. He acts on heavy going but doesn't need the mud. *Paul Nicholls*

POLKARENIX (FR) 6 b.g. Policy Maker (IRE) – Arenix (FR) (Fragrant Mix (IRE)) [2017/18 c89, h–: c19.4d⁴ c17.3g⁵ c20.2g^F Oct 29] winning hurdler: maiden chaser: often wore headgear: in tongue tie last 2 starts: dead. *Brendan Powell*   c–
h–

POLLY'S PURSUIT (IRE) 6 br.m. Westerner – Miss Denman (IRE) (Presenting) [2017/18 b96: h15.7g² h20.3g* h16g² h19s h19.4s³ h18.5s⁵ h16d⁵ h16m Apr 26] sturdy mare: bumper winner: fair hurdler: won mares maiden at Southwell in June: stays 2½m: acts on soft going: wears hood: often races rear. *Nicky Henderson*   h106

POLO THE MUMM (FR) 8 b.g. Great Journey (JPN) – Maido (FR) (French Glory) [2017/18 c95, h102: h19m³ c20g⁴ h21s⁶ h21.7v^{pu} Mar 10] workmanlike gelding: point winner: fair handicap hurdler: modest maiden chaser: stays 2¾m: acts on soft and good to firm going: wears tongue tie. *Jackie du Plessis*   c84
h97

POLYDORA (IRE) 6 b.g. Milan – Mandysway (IRE) (Mandalus) [2017/18 b78: h19.5d* h21.6d⁶ h23.1v* h26s^{ur} Jan 25] unfurnished gelding: close up when unseated 2 out in maiden point: fairly useful form over hurdles: won maiden at Chepstow in October and novice at Exeter in December: will stay 3m: acts on heavy going: often races prominently. *Tom Lacey*   h118

POLYMATH (IRE) 7 ch.g. Stowaway – Godlylady (IRE) (Old Vic) [2017/18 h21.8g² h21.5g³ h21.3g³ h21.8g h20.5g⁴ h21.7g* c23g³ c23.6s^{pu} Mar 22] €70,000 3-y-o: third foal: dam unraced half-sister to top-class chaser up to 3m Flemenstar: winning pointer: fair   c107
h100

POL

hurdler: won maiden at Downpatrick in August: similar form on completed chase start: left Gordon Elliott after sixth start: stays 3m: best form on good going: tried in cheekpieces. *Deborah Faulkner*

POMME 7 b.m. Observatory (USA) – Mirthful (USA) (Miswaki (USA)) [2017/18 h110: h21.6g^{pu} h20.6g* h20.6g^2 c24.2d^4 Oct 12] fair form over hurdles: won novice at Market Rasen in July: tailed off in maiden on chasing debut: stays 21f: best form on good going: usually leads. *Nigel Hawke* — c– h110

POMME DE NUIT 5 b.m. Midnight Legend – Apple Days (Sovereign Water (FR)) [2017/18 b15.7s Feb 17] second foal: sister to bumper winner Rosemary Russet: dam, winning pointer, half-sister to useful chaser (stayed 29f) Strongbows Legend (by Midnight Legend): well held in bumper. *Martin Keighley* — b–

PONGO TWISTLETON 5 b.g. Champs Elysees – Pretty Girl (IRE) (Polish Precedent (USA)) [2017/18 h104p: h19.6m* h21.9g^F h19.9m h19.9d^6 Jul 28] fair handicap hurdler: won at Huntingdon in May: stayed 2½m: acted on soft and good to firm going: in headgear last 2 starts: in tongue tie last 4: dead. *Jonjo O'Neill* — h112

PONTRESINA (IRE) 5 b.g. Milan – Gilt Benefit (IRE) (Beneficial) [2017/18 h19.5s h20.3s^{pu} h21m^3 Apr 26] €13,500 3-y-o, £40,000 4-y-o: fourth foal: dam (c88/h105) 19f/2½m hurdle winner: won point on debut: fair form over hurdles: best effort when third in novice at Kempton in April. *Oliver Sherwood* — h109

POOKIE PEKAN (IRE) 5 b.g. Putra Pekan – Shii-Take's Girl (Deploy) [2017/18 h16.2g^4 h16.8s^4 h16.2s h19.7v* h22.8s^6 Mar 21] €5,000 3-y-o: sixth foal: half-brother to fair hurdler/winning pointer Nicks Power (2m winner, by Luso): dam, lightly raced over hurdles, 1¼m winner on Flat: placed on last of 3 starts in Irish points: modest form over hurdles: won handicap at Wetherby in February: stays 2½m: acts on heavy going: front runner/races prominently. *Stuart Colthred* — h94

POOLE MASTER 13 ch.g. Fleetwood (IRE) – Juste Belle (FR) (Mansonnien (FR)) [2017/18 c121, h–: c20.8d^F c20d^3 c24s^F Jan 25] tall gelding: winning hurdler: fairly useful hunter chaser nowadays: stays 3m: acts on heavy going: has worn headgear, including final start: has worn tongue tie: races prominently. *Chris Honour* — c114 h–

POPAWAY 13 b.m. Nomadic Way (USA) – Sea Poppy (Baron Blakeney) [2017/18 c109: c25.3d^3 c22.6d^{pu} Jun 9] prolific point winner: fair hunter chaser: out of sorts in early-2017/18: stays 25f: acts on soft and good to firm going: wears tongue tie. *Mrs Pauline Harkin* — c–

POPELYS GULL (IRE) 6 ch.g. Recharge (IRE) – Circus Rose (Most Welcome) [2017/18 h113, b72: h23.1g^{pu} c19.4d* c20.3d^4 c21.2s^2 c24.2v^F c23.8d^6 c24.2s^3 Mar 16] maiden hurdler: fairly useful form over fences: won novice at Wetherby in October: stays 3m: acts on heavy going: often races in rear. *Pam Sly* — c127 h–

POPERINGHE GINGER (IRE) 5 ch.m. Beneficial – Masamor (IRE) (Saddlers' Hall (IRE)) [2017/18 b15.7g^4 Apr 20] €10,000 3-y-o: third foal: dam, unraced, closely related/ half-sister to useful hurdlers/chasers Holly Bush Henry (stays 25f) and Corkage (stayed 3¼m): 25/1, fourth in conditional/amateur maiden bumper at Southwell (4½ lengths behind dead-heaters Indefatigable and Sweet Adare). *Graeme McPherson* — b84

POPPING ALONG 9 ch.m. Volochine (IRE) – So Long (Nomadic Way (USA)) [2017/18 h104: h20g^6 h20.2v h16s Feb 22] brood mare: fair handicap hurdler: with Jeremy Scott/fit from points, well beaten last 2 starts: stays 2½m: acts on soft and good to firm going: usually wears cheekpieces: wears tongue tie: often races towards rear. *Turlough O'Connor, Ireland* — h98

POPPY HILL 6 b.m. Black Sam Bellamy (IRE) – Talk The Talk (Terimon) [2017/18 h19.5s^{pu} h16s Dec 5] £11,000 3-y-o, £11,000 5-y-o: fourth foal: closely related to bumper winner Troyan (by King's Theatre) and half-sister to modest chaser Longueville Flier (3m winner, by Definite Article): dam, maiden pointer/ran once over hurdles, half-sister to useful hurdler/fairly useful chaser (stayed 2¾m) Over Sixty: Irish point winner: no show over hurdles. *Gary Moore* — h–

POPPY KAY 8 b.m. Kayf Tara – Double Red (IRE) (Thatching) [2017/18 h126: h16.3d* h16.3d^3 h19.8s* h16.3v h20.3v^{pu} h16.8g^4 Apr 18] sturdy mare: useful hurdler: won conditional handicap at Newbury in November and listed mares event at Sandown (by ½ length from Midnight Jazz) in January: stays 2½m: acts on heavy going: often races towards rear. *Philip Hobbs* — h134

POR

POP ROCKSTAR (IRE) 6 b.g. Flemensfirth (USA) – Special Ballot (IRE) (Perugino (USA)) [2017/18 h108p, b78: h16.7d h20s² h22.8v* h24.1s* h23.5s h25v⁶ Mar 12] fair handicap hurdler: won at Haydock (conditional) and Wetherby in December: stays 3m: best form on soft/heavy going: in tongue tie last 4 starts: usually travels strongly. *Jonjo O'Neill*   **h114**

POP THE CHAMPERS (IRE) 7 b.g. Scorpion (IRE) – Manesbil (IRE) (Fourstars Allstar (USA)) [2017/18 h20.6g⁴ Jul 22] won last 2 starts in Irish points: tailed off in novice on hurdling debut. *Nick Kent*   **h54**

PORTASH 6 b.m. Tobougg (IRE) – Circadian Rhythm (Lujain (USA)) [2017/18 b15.7d Nov 21] second foal: dam 1m-1¼m winner: tailed off in mares bumper. *Geoffrey Deacon*   **b–**

PORTERS LANE 7 ch.g. Generous (IRE) – Private Company (IRE) (Great Marquess) [2017/18 c–:, h–, b–: c20.9g^{pu} c23g⁴ Jul 10] maiden pointer: once-raced hurdler: poor maiden chaser: wears cheekpieces. *Henry Oliver*   **c62 h–**

PORT LAIRGE 8 b.g. Pastoral Pursuits – Stylish Clare (IRE) (Desert Style (IRE)) [2017/18 h83: h16.7g⁵ h25g⁴ h20.6s Dec 26] poor maiden hurdler: tried in blinkers: races well off pace. *Michael Chapman*   **h–**

PORT MELON (IRE) 10 br.g. Presenting – Omyn Supreme (IRE) (Supreme Leader) [2017/18 c130, h–: c20.5m* Apr 26] tall, good sort: has reportedly had breathing operation: winning hurdler: useful chaser at best: won hunter at Kempton in April after 12-month absence: stays 3m: acts on soft and good to firm going: has worn headgear: tried in tongue tie. *Paul Nicholls*   **c113 h–**

PORTO DU SUD (FR) 5 gr.g. Lord du Sud (FR) – Queen du Vallon (FR) (Jeune Homme (USA)) [2017/18 b–: b16.2g⁵ h16.8g³ h17d⁶ h16.8s² Nov 28] needed experience in bumpers: fair form over hurdles: best effort when second in novice at Sedgefield in November: left James Ewart after first start: will stay further than 17f: in hood last 4 starts. *Rebecca Menzies*   **h101 b–**

PORTRAIT KING (IRE) 13 gr.g. Portrait Gallery (IRE) – Storm Queen (IRE) (Le Bavard (FR)) [2017/18 c126, h111: h23.3s² h24.7d^{pu} c25.9v⁵ h24v⁶ c23.5v⁴ c32.6s³ c31.9v³ Mar 15] sturdy gelding: fair maiden hurdler: fairly useful handicap chaser: fifth in Becher Chase at Aintree in December: stays 33f: acts on heavy going: has worn headgear, including in 2017/18. *Patrick Griffin, Ireland*   **c123 h99**

PORT ROYALE 6 b.m. King's Theatre (IRE) – Easibrook Jane (Alderbrook) [2017/18 b17.7d Feb 26] fourth foal: half-sister to useful hurdler Draco (2m/17f winner, by Hernando): dam (c98/h109) 19f-21f hurdle/chase winner: tailed off in mares bumper. *Anthony Honeyball*   **b–**

PORTRUSH TED (IRE) 6 b.g. Shantou (USA) – Village Queen (IRE) (King's Theatre (IRE)) [2017/18 b103: b15.7d² b15.7d^{pu} b16.2s² b17s* Apr 13] well-made gelding: useful bumper performer: in tongue tie, 25/1, won Grade 2 event at Aintree (by 3¼ lengths from Kateson) in April: will stay 2½m. *Warren Greatrex*   **b112**

Weatherbys Racing Bank Standard Open National Hunt Flat, Aintree—
Portrush Ted (second right) is driven home to beat the grey Kateson in a finish dominated by outsiders in rain-softened conditions

POS

POSH TOTTY 11 ch.m. Midnight Legend – Well Bred (Rakaposhi King) [2017/18 h20.5d² h23.8d² c24g* Apr 26] angular mare: prolific point winner: poor maiden hurdler: 2/1, won novice handicap at Warwick (by 3 lengths from Goodnight Charlie with plenty in hand) on chasing debut: stays 3m: acts on good to soft going: capable of better over fences. *Jack R. Barber* — **c82 p h75**

POSH TRISH (IRE) 5 b.m. Stowaway – Moscow Demon (IRE) (Moscow Society (USA)) [2017/18 b17d* b16.4s* b15.7d b16v³ b17s Apr 12] £135,000 4-y-o: rangy mare: first foal: dam well beaten in bumpers/over hurdles: winning Irish pointer: useful bumper performer: won mares events at Aintree (awarded race) in October and Cheltenham (listed, by 3¼ lengths from Grageelagh Girl) in November: also third in listed mares event at Sandown (3¼ lengths behind Queenohearts) in March. *Paul Nicholls* — **b107**

POSITIVELY DYLAN 7 b.g. Multiplex – Wou Oodd (Barathea (IRE)) [2017/18 h106: h20g* h21.9d* h21.6d³ c16.2g³ c16.2d³ c15.7v^{ur} c15.2s* c19.9v^F c16.3s² Feb 16] poor mover: fairly useful hurdler: won handicap and novice at Ffos Las in May: useful form over fences: won handicap at Wetherby (by 6 lengths from Kayf Blanco) in January: stays 2¾m: acts on heavy going: often races prominently: room for improvement in jumping over fences. *Evan Williams* — **c137 h121**

POSTBRIDGE (IRE) 7 b.rm. Robin des Pres (FR) – Dartmeet (IRE) (Presenting) [2017/18 h110: h23.3d c17.2g^{pu} h19.2g⁶ c19.9d⁴ c21.2s^{pu} h20.7s^{pu} h23.4v⁶ h16v Jan 22] fair hurdler at best: no form in 2017/18, including over fences: left Warren Greatrex after first start: stays 2¾m: acts on good to firm and heavy going: has worn headgear, including last 5 starts: in tongue tie last 2 starts: usually leads. *Sarah Humphrey* — **c– h–**

POT COMMITTED (IRE) 7 b.g. Presenting – Keats Dream (Turtle Island (IRE)) [2017/18 h116, b78: h16.2g^{pu} h19.4d^{pu} c19.9s^F Jan 3] fairly useful hurdler at best: no form in 2017/18, including on chasing debut/in point. *Iain Jardine* — **c– h–**

POTTERMAN 5 b.g. Sulamani (IRE) – Polly Potter (Kayf Tara) [2017/18 b15.8g* h16d³ h16.3s² h16.7v³ Feb 9] rather unfurnished gelding: second foal: dam (b97), placed in bumpers, sister to smart bumper winner/useful hurdler around 2m Kayf Grace out of half-sister to Cheltenham Gold Cup winner Denman: won bumper at Huntingdon (by 10 lengths from Raising The Bar) in May: fair form over hurdles: best effort when second in maiden at Newbury in December: remains open to improvement. *Alan King* — **h113 p b101**

POTTERS APPROACH (IRE) 7 b.g. Scorpion (IRE) – Moon Approach (IRE) (Shernazar) [2017/18 h114, b90: h25g⁵ May 25] sturdy gelding: winning pointer: fair hurdler: well held only start in 2017/18: stays 3¼m: acts on good to soft going: front runner/races prominently: has joined Dan Skelton. *Warren Greatrex* — **h–**

POTTERS CROSS 11 b.g. Alflora (IRE) – Teeno Nell (Teenoso (USA)) [2017/18 c135§, h–: c23.6d⁵ c25d⁵ c22.4g^{pu} Dec 2] big gelding: winning hurdler: useful chaser: stays 3¼m: acts on heavy going: tried in cheekpieces: has worn tongue tie: often races prominently: untrustworthy. *Rebecca Curtis* — **c128 § h–**

POTTERS HEDGER 6 b.g. Midnight Legend – Loose Morals (IRE) (Luso) [2017/18 b91: h19.5d⁴ h21g⁴ h20s² h20.7s h20.6v² Apr 11] has had breathing operation: fair form over hurdles: stays 21f: acts on heavy going: tried in cheekpieces. *Lucy Wadham* — **h110**

POTTERS LEGEND 8 b.g. Midnight Legend – Loose Morals (IRE) (Luso) [2017/18 c141p, h–: c23.6d c24.1s⁴ c26g c26v^{pu} c20.8v⁶ c24.2v⁴ c24.2s^F c25.6v* Mar 31] well-made gelding: winning hurdler: useful handicap chaser: won at Haydock (by 11 lengths from Horatio Hornblower) in March: will stay 3½m+: acts on heavy going: wears headgear: often let down by jumping. *Lucy Wadham* — **c139 x h–**

POTTERS MIDNIGHT 8 b.m. Midnight Legend – Craughwell Suas (IRE) (Turtle Island (IRE)) [2017/18 h15.7g⁴ h16s³ h16v* h15.8v³ h16s* h18.9v Mar 31] fairly useful hurdler: won maiden at Fakenham in January and handicap there in March: stays 21f: acts on heavy going. *Lucy Wadham* — **h116**

POTTERS POINT (IRE) 8 b.g. Robin des Champs (FR) – Tango Lady (IRE) (King's Theatre (IRE)) [2017/18 c131p, h118p: c16g² c16.1s³ c19.9s³ c22.7g² c18.2d² c22s* c24v* c20v⁴ c24v c24.5d⁴ Dec 27] winning hurdler: smart chaser: won minor event at Tramore (by 8 lengths from Bentelimar) in August and Kerry National Handicap Chase at Listowel (by ½ length from Arkwrisht) in September: fourth in Paddy Power Chase at Leopardstown (10½ lengths behind Anibale Fly) final start: will stay further than 3m: acts on heavy going: wears tongue tie: often races prominently. *Gordon Elliott, Ireland* — **c148 h–**

POTTERS SAPPHIRE 5 gr.m. Aussie Rules (USA) – Arabescato (UAE) (Gone West (USA)) [2017/18 b83: h21s⁵ h20.7s³ h16.7s² h21.7v^{pu} Mar 17] compact mare: fair form over hurdles: should prove suited by further than 17f: usually wears headgear. *Lucy Wadham* — **h104**

POTTERS STORY 6 b.g. Kayf Tara – Lily Potter (Karinga Bay) [2017/18 h114, b98: h21.1g h21.1s h15.8v* Dec 18] good-bodied gelding: bumper winner: useful form over hurdles: improved when won handicap at Ffos Las (in tongue strap, by 21 lengths from Rayvin Black) in December: should be suited by at least 2½m: best form on soft/heavy going: often races prominently. *Peter Bowen*   **h134**

POTTERS TALE 5 b.g. Kayf Tara – Lily Potter (Karinga Bay) [2017/18 b15.8v² b16g⁶ b16g⁴ Apr 21] fifth foal: brother to bumper winner/useful 2m hurdle winner Potters Story: dam unraced half-sister to useful hurdler/winning chaser (2m-19f winner) Missis Potts and smart bumper winner/useful hurdler around 2m Kayf Grace (by Kayf Tara) out of half-sister to Cheltenham Gold Cup winner Denman: fair form in bumpers: best effort when fourth at Ayr (tongue tied) in April: tried in hood. *Peter Bowen*   **b91**

POUGNE BOBBI (FR) 7 b.g. Protektor (GER) – Amicus (Xaar) [2017/18 c140, h–: c21d⁴ c18.8d⁵ c19.9s* c20.8s Mar 15] well-made gelding: winning hurdler: useful handicap chaser: won at Huntingdon in January: stays 2½m: best form on soft/heavy going: races towards rear: has joined Donald McCain. *Nicky Henderson*   **c141 h–**

POWDERONTHEBONNET (IRE) 10 b.g. Definite Article – Zuhal (Busted) [2017/18 c–, c–, h90: h24g² h15.8g* h15.7g Jun 13] sturdy gelding: modest handicap hurdler: won at Ffos Las in June: pulled up only chase start: stays 3m, as effective at much shorter: acts on good to firm and heavy going: in cheekpieces last 3 starts. *Sam Thomas*   **c– h96**

POWERFUL SYMBOL (IRE) 8 b.g. Robin des Champs (FR) – Be My Rainbow (IRE) (Be My Native (USA)) [2017/18 c114, h98: c24d⁶ c24d* c24d* c24dᶠ h23.9vᵖᵘ Apr 15] maiden hurdler: fairly useful handicap chaser: won novice events at Southwell in November and Doncaster in December: left Jonjo O'Neill after third start: stays 3m: acts on heavy going: has worn cheekpieces, including in 2017/18: often in tongue tie: usually races prominently. *Ben Pauling*   **c122 h–**

POWERSTOWN PARK (IRE) 5 b.g. Craigsteel – Smiths Lady (IRE) (Anshan) [2017/18 b16.8v h17.7s⁴ h19.9v h21d Apr 26] rather unfurnished gelding: off mark in points at second attempt: tailed off in bumper: poor form over hurdles: usually in cheekpieces. *Sam Thomas*   **h81 b–**

POYNTZPASS (IRE) 8 ch.g. Gamut (IRE) – Play Trix (IRE) (Saddlers' Hall (IRE)) [2017/18 h21.6g⁵ h18.5d³ h19.2v⁴ h19.2v⁵ h25d⁴ Feb 26] dual point winner: poor form over hurdles: signs of temperament. *Richard Harper*   **h64**

PRAIRIE IMPULSE 5 b.m. Major Cadeaux – Prairie Sun (GER) (Law Society (USA)) [2017/18 h70p: h16.8g* h16.7g² h16.8g⁴ h15.8d Sep 24] modest handicap hurdler: won at Sedgefield in May: raced around 2m: best form on good going: often races towards rear. *Rebecca Menzies*   **h86**

PRAIRIE TOWN (IRE) 7 b.g. High Chaparral (IRE) – Lake Baino (Highest Honor (FR)) [2017/18 c125, h121: h15.7g h16d³ c16.8d⁴ h16.3s c16.4v* c16.1v² c16.5g³ Apr 20] rather leggy gelding: fairly useful handicap hurdler: similar standard over fences: won novice handicap at Sedgefield in January: unproven beyond 2m: acts on heavy going: usually wears headgear: often races towards rear. *Tony Carroll*   **c119 h113**

Guinness Kerry National Handicap Chase, Listowel—
a second successive victory in the race for amateur Lisa O'Neill as Potters Point (second right)
beats fellow Gigginstown representative Arkwright (centre) and Bay of Freedom (noseband)

PRA

PRAVALAGUNA (FR) 6 b.m. Great Pretender (IRE) – Arnette (FR) (Denham Red (FR)) [2017/18 h133: h17.9s³ h17.9d^F h20.2v⁴ h19.9s^pu h16s⁴ h20s* Apr 25] smallish mare: useful hurdler: won minor event at Punchestown in April: had improved when fourth on handicap debut at Fairyhouse (5¾ lengths behind Low Sun) 8 days earlier: likely to prove best up to 2½m: acts on heavy going: has worn hood, including last 4 starts. *W. P. Mullins, Ireland* — **h136**

PRAY FOR A RAINBOW 7 b.g. Rainbow High – Blackchurch Lass (IRE) (Taum Go Leor (IRE)) [2017/18 c–, h74: h19.9s⁵ h23v* h19.5v³ Apr 14] winning pointer: modest hurdler: won handicap at Lingfield in March: pulled up only chase start: stays 23f: acts on heavy going: tried in cheekpieces: usually races prominently. *Samuel Drinkwater* — **c– h88**

PREACHER'S BELLE 9 ch.m. Courteous – Moonshine Malt (Superlative) [2017/18 c19.3g⁴ c21.2d May 29] maiden pointer: poor form in chases: usually in hood. *Graeme Scantlebury* — **c78**

PRECIOUS CARGO (IRE) 5 b.g. Yeats (IRE) – Kilbarry Classic (IRE) (Classic Cliche (IRE)) [2017/18 b16v* b16v² b16g Apr 21] £35,000 3-y-o: first foal: dam (b101) bumper winner: fairly useful form in bumpers: won at Ayr in January: wears tongue tie. *Lucinda Russell* — **b96**

PRECIOUS ROCK (IRE) 4 b.g. Fastnet Rock (AUS) – Attasliyah (IRE) (Marju (IRE)) [2017/18 h16.7g Nov 9] little show in Flat maidens: tailed off in juvenile on hurdling debut. *Jedd O'Keeffe* — **h–**

PREDICT A RIOT (IRE) 7 ch.g. Flemensfirth (USA) – Ballerina Laura (IRE) (Riot Helmet) [2017/18 h101: h24.4d h25s^pu h26s h21.2d^pu Apr 24] won completed start in Irish maiden points: maiden hurdler, no form in 2017/18: tried in cheekpieces: often races prominently. *Ian Williams* — **h–**

PREMIER BOND 8 b.g. Kayf Tara – Celtic Native (IRE) (Be My Native (USA)) [2017/18 c138, h–: c27.3s^pu h21g h24g Apr 18] rangy gelding: winning hurdler/chaser at best, no form in 2017/18: wears cheekpieces: tried in tongue tie: lazy. *Nicky Henderson* — **c– h–**

PREMIER PORTRAIT (IRE) 11 b.g. Portrait Gallery (IRE) – Shesnotthelast (IRE) (Mandalus) [2017/18 c111§, h–§: c23s* c24.2s^ur c26.3v^pu Mar 16] useful-looking gelding: prolific winning pointer: winning hurdler: fairly useful chaser: won hunter at Taunton in January: stays 23f: acts on heavy going: wears headgear: temperamental. *Dr Charles Levinson* — **c118 § h– §**

PREMIER ROSE (IRE) 9 b.m. Westerner – Alltoplayfor (IRE) (Broken Hearted) [2017/18 h80: h20g⁵ h20g² h24g* h21.6m* h26g³ Sep 26] winning Irish pointer: modest handicap hurdler: won at Southwell and Newton Abbot in August: left Katy Price after second start: may prove best at shorter than 3¼m: acts on good to firm going: tried in cheekpieces: in tongue tie last 3 starts: front runner/races prominently. *Dan Skelton* — **h92**

PRENDERGAST HILL (IRE) 6 b.g. Raven's Pass (USA) – Daraliya (IRE) (Kahyasi) [2017/18 h16g^R Sep 18] fairly useful on Flat, stayed 1½m: in blinkers, clear when refused third in maiden on hurdling debut, having jumped erratically: dead. *Ed de Giles* — **h–**

PREROGATIVE (IRE) 4 b.g. Rock of Gibraltar (IRE) – Tedarshana (Darshaan) [2017/18 h16s^F Nov 29] fair maiden on Flat, stays 13.5f: fell first on hurdling debut. *Tony Carroll* — **h–**

PRESENCE FELT (IRE) 10 br.g. Heron Island (IRE) – Faeroe Isle (IRE) (Erins Isle) [2017/18 c89§, h114: h21.3s Dec 26] good-topped gelding: fairly useful hurdler at best, well held only start in 2017/18: fair form over fences (generally let down by jumping/attitude): stays 25f: acts on good to firm and heavy going: has worn headgear: usually races prominently. *John Dixon* — **c– § h–**

PRESENT DESTINY (IRE) 6 b.g. Dubai Destination (USA) – Anns Present (IRE) (Presenting) [2017/18 b86: h16.7s⁴ h19.1m^F h19g⁴ h16s⁵ Jan 13] lengthy gelding: fair form in bumpers/over hurdles: stays 19f: acts on soft going. *Seamus Mullins* — **h103**

PRESENTED (IRE) 11 ch.g. Presenting – Rustic Court (IRE) (Quayside) [2017/18 c111§, h–§: h23.9g c29.4d⁶ c24.2g⁵ h23.9g c23.8s⁴ c25.5d⁴ c24.2v² c23.8v² c24d^pu c26.2v² c26.2d³ c24.3v³ c24.5s³ c24.1v⁴ c24.1v⁶ c23.4v⁶ c24.1v⁴ c26.9v* Feb 26] rather leggy gelding: maiden hurdler: fair handicap chaser: won at Ayr in February: stays 33f: acts on good to firm and heavy going: has worn headgear: tried in tongue tie: usually races close up: temperamental. *Lisa Harrison* — **c101 § h– §**

PRESENTEDWITHWINGS (IRE) 4 br.g. Presenting – Rosa Rugosa (IRE) (In The Wings) [2017/18 b15.8d⁴ Apr 24] 6/1, showed a bit when fourth in bumper at Ludlow. *Tom Symonds* — **b77**

PRE

PRESENT FLIGHT (IRE) 9 ch.g. Presenting – Grangeclare Flight (IRE) (Old Vic) [2017/18 c20.5v² c26.9v³ c20v⁴ c20s^pu Apr 8] maiden hurdler: fair handicap chaser nowadays, off 22 months before return: stays 27f: acts on good to firm and heavy going: wears tongue tie: inconsistent. *Lucinda Russell* c114 h–

PRESENT FROM DUBAI (IRE) 5 b.g. Dubai Destination (USA) – Inch Promise (IRE) (Presenting) [2017/18 b14d h16.6s² Jan 26] €10,000 3-y-o, £35,000 4-y-o: fourth foal: half-brother to bumper winner/fair hurdler Presentingoscar (2½m winner, by Oscar), stays 23f: dam winning pointer: placed both starts in Irish points: showed a bit in bumper: 33/1, second in novice at Doncaster (8 lengths behind Nube Negra) on hurdling debut. *Richard Phillips* h99 b–

PRESENTING BERKLEY (IRE) 8 br.g. Presenting – Tynelucy (IRE) (Good Thyne (USA)) [2017/18 h84: h22g² h23.4g³ c18.2m^pu Apr 25] modest maiden hurdler: pulled up in novice handicap on chasing debut: stays 2¾m: best form on good going: often in headgear. *Tim Vaughan* c– h85

PRESENTING JULIO (IRE) 10 b.g. Presenting – Ouro Preto (Definite Article) [2017/18 c100, h101: h21.8g* h24.6g² h24.7d* h24g* h22d⁵ c20.5g* c25g⁵ Oct 27] lengthy gelding: fair handicap hurdler: won at Downpatrick in May, and Roscommon and Limerick in July: fair form over fences: won handicap at Killarney in August: stays 25f: acts on good to firm and good to soft going: wears headgear/tongue tie: often travels strongly. *Gordon Elliott, Ireland* c114 h113

PRESENTING JUNIOR (IRE) 11 b.g. Presenting – Dr Alice (IRE) (Dr Massini (IRE)) [2017/18 c123, h–: c21.2d⁴ c24.2g² c25.5g* c20s^pu Apr 8] maiden hurdler: fair handicap chaser: won at Cartmel in July: stayed 3¼m: acted on soft and good to firm going: occasionally wore headgear: dead. *Martin Todhunter* c105 h–

PRESENTING LUCINA (IRE) 6 b.m. Presenting – Lucina (GER) (Groom Dancer (USA)) [2017/18 h71: h16.8v⁶ Apr 17] little show over hurdles. *Neil Mulholland* h–

PRESENTING PEARL (IRE) 5 b.m. Presenting – Asigh Pearl (IRE) (Lord of Appeal) [2017/18 b87: b15.8m* b16.4s⁵ h20.7d* h20.3g Apr 19] lengthy mare: fairly useful form in bumpers: won mares event at Ludlow in October: fair form over hurdles: won mares novice at Huntingdon in March: will stay beyond 21f: front runner/races prominently. *Jamie Snowden* h110 b96

PRESENTING PERCY 7 b.g. Sir Percy – Hunca Munca (IRE) (Presenting) [2017/18 h152, b–: c22.5s* c22.6s³ c29s* h24v* c20v² c24.4s* Mar 14] c164 p h152 +

Samcro has been hailed in some quarters as 'the new Messiah of Irish racing'—as if Irish racing is short of top horses—but there is another candidate for the fulsome title, one who has so far largely avoided the hyperbole which has attended Samcro's rise. While Samcro is owned by Ireland's champion owners Gigginstown House Stud and is trained at one of the powerhouses of Irish jumping, Cullentra House stables, the very exciting chaser Presenting Percy by contrast hails from the small yard of Patrick G. Kelly who has just a handful of horses in his care in County Galway. Kelly might have been a peripheral figure in Irish racing for most of his twenty or so years with a licence, but his name has been up in lights in each of the last three seasons when saddling a winner at the Cheltenham Festival. Presenting Percy has been responsible for the last two wins, in the Pertemps Network Final at the 2017 Festival and the RSA Insurance Chase (the 'novices' Gold Cup') at the latest one.

Not many performances in recent times at British racing's most prestigious jumps meeting have made such an impression. Presenting Percy looked the proverbial 'graded horse in a handicap' when successful as a novice in the Pertemps, recording a performance that would have been good enough to have won every running bar one of the three-mile novices' championship at the Festival, the Spa Hurdle, which was introduced in 2005. Presenting Percy looked even better in the RSA Chase at the latest Festival, turning in a flawless display, jumping well and travelling strongly, and looking every inch a Cheltenham Gold Cup horse in the making as he spreadeagled his field without seeming to have to perform right to the limit of his ability, the patient Davy Russell producing him to lead in eye-catching style approaching the second last, after which he drew away comfortably to put up one of the best performances in the race in the last twenty years or more. If Presenting Percy continues to progress as anticipated, by the way, it should make the

639

build-up to the next Gold Cup interesting for those who comment on the sport, as Pat Kelly is a man of few words who very much prefers to let his horses do the talking. He rarely speaks to the media and has not done so either before or after Presenting Percy's two Festival wins, leaving the horse's owner Philip Reynolds and jockey Davy Russell to field the questions.

Presenting Percy took a rather unorthodox route to the RSA Chase after getting off the mark over fences at the first time of asking in a maiden chase at Galway in October. His accurate jumping was one of the features of his debut but, stepped up in class on his second start, he made a mistake at an inopportune time, when closing at the second last, from which he could not recover when third to Jury Duty and Shattered Love in the Florida Pearl Novices' Chase at Punchestown. Connections took the unusual step, for his third start over fences, of running Presenting Percy under 11-10 in the Bar One Racing Porterstown Handicap Chase over three miles five furlongs at Fairyhouse. He won the race off an Irish Turf Club mark of 145, 11 lb below his hurdle rating at the time, jumping impeccably and cruising to the front, after being waited with, to win by eleven lengths and eight lengths from Forever Gold and He Rock's, with his stablemate Mall Dini (who had won the 2016 Pertemps Final for Pat Kelly) in fourth.

Presenting Percy's fine performance at Fairyhouse was more than good enough to confirm that he would be able to hold his own in Grade 1 novice company and it came as a surprise to see him switched back to hurdling for the John Mulhern Galmoy Hurdle, a Grade 2 over three miles at Gowran towards the end of January. Presenting Percy took the opportunity to open his account in graded races, winning impressively by five and a half lengths from Augusta Kate and the rest of an up-to-scratch field, showing smart form in the process, his owner saying afterwards that the idea of running Presenting Percy over hurdles had been 'to save the horse a bit for Cheltenham'. It was confirmed that he was being aimed at the RSA Chase for which he was cut generally to 4/1 favourite. Presenting Percy took on four seasoned chasers in his final preparatory race for Cheltenham in the Red Mills Chase over two and a half miles at Gowran in February. He pulled a long way clear with Gold Cup-

*Bar One Racing Porterstown Handicap Chase Fairyhouse—
an impressive weight-carrying performance by the novice Presenting Percy*

RSA Insurance Novices' Chase, Cheltenham—Irish novices are already in control two out, where Presenting Percy (noseband) stretches clear of Monalee as Al Boum Photo (left) falls

bound Our Duke, going down by a length in receipt of 7 lb but noticeably not being given an unduly hard time by Davy Russell. On form, it represented a career best by Presenting Percy and it looked as if he would take plenty of beating in the RSA.

Davy Russell had ridden Monalee to victory in the Grade 1 Flogas Novices' Chase at Leopardstown but he remained loyal to Presenting Percy at Cheltenham, Presenting Percy starting 5/2 favourite and Monalee 100/30 second favourite respectively in a field of ten, split evenly between the home defence and Irish-trained challengers. The Irish challenge also included two of those who had made the frame behind Monalee at Leopardstown, runner-up Al Boum Photo and close fourth Dounikos. The standard of the graded staying novice chases in Ireland had been higher than in Britain and the RSA Chase looked set to produce an Irish one, two, three before Al Boum Photo departed at the second last when held in third behind Presenting Percy and Monalee. Monalee did all he could, barely putting a foot wrong and keeping on well after being handy from the start, but Presenting Percy swept him aside in the home straight to win in clear-cut fashion by seven lengths, looking to have something in hand. The smart Elegant Escape, the Towton Chase winner Ballyoptic and the prolific Reynoldstown Chase winner Black Corton, who ensured there was a good gallop, were the only other finishers, with Dounikos well beaten when he was pulled up.

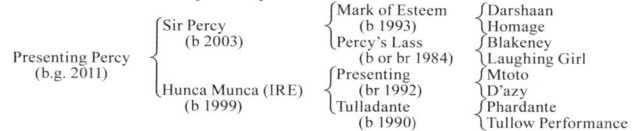

Presenting Percy (b.g. 2011)	Sir Percy (b 2003)	Mark of Esteem (b 1993)	Darshaan
			Homage
		Percy's Lass (b or br 1984)	Blakeney
			Laughing Girl
	Hunca Munca (IRE) (b 1999)	Presenting (br 1992)	Mtoto
			D'azy
		Tulladante (b 1990)	Phardante
			Tullow Performance

The good-topped Presenting Percy is British bred and had his pedigree examined in *Chasers & Hurdlers 2016/17*. The distaff side of his family has produced a number of good performers including two others who won at the Cheltenham Festival, the 2006 Gold Cup winner War of Attrition and the first winner of the novices' handicap chase at the meeting King Harald, both of whom are descended from Presenting Percy's great grandam Tullow Performance. The smart staying hurdler Emotional Moment is out of another of Tullow Performance's daughters. Presenting Percy's dam Hunca Munca, winner of two points in Britain after being purchased in Ireland, is a half-sister to the useful Western Charmer who was runner-up in the 2011 Irish National while still a novice. Hunca Munca has also produced a couple of winning pointers. Presenting Percy, who wears a tongue tie, stays twenty-nine furlongs and acts on heavy ground, though connections think he is at his best on less testing going (it was good when he won the Pertemps). A strong traveller, he is usually waited with. Festival form is a valuable asset for any big-race contender at Cheltenham and the stamina-laden Presenting Percy looks sure to give a very good account in the Gold Cup. *Patrick G. Kelly, Ireland*

Badger Ales Trophy Handicap Chase, Wincanton—
Present Man (noseband) just holds off Final Nudge in a race that has taken over the mantle from the Hennessy Gold Cup as jumping's longest-running commercial sponsorship

PRESENTING ROSE (IRE) 8 b.m. Presenting – Berkeley House (IRE) (Beneficial) [2017/18 h100: h20.5v⁶ h16v⁶ Jan 15] fair hurdler, well below best both starts in 2017/18 after long absence: stays 21f: acts on heavy going. *N. W. Alexander* **h83**

PRESENTING WILLIAM (IRE) 10 b.g. Presenting – Clanwilliam Source (IRE) (Eurobus) [2017/18 c15.9g⁶ c16.5s⁵ c20d³ c19.8s^pu Dec 21] strong gelding: multiple point winner: no form in chases. *Alan Phillips* **c–**

PRESENT MAN (IRE) 8 b.g. Presenting – Glen's Gale (IRE) (Strong Gale) [2017/18 c142, h–: h21g* c25.1s* c26g h23.8s⁴ c28.8d³ Apr 28] rangy gelding: fairly useful hurdler at best: won novice at Kempton in October: useful handicap chaser: won Badger Ales Trophy Handicap Chase at Wincanton (by head from Final Nudge) in November: back to form when 27 lengths third to Step Back in bet365 Gold Cup at Sandown, tying up late on: barely stays 29f: acts on good to firm and heavy going: tried in headgear: wears tongue tie: front runner/races prominently. *Paul Nicholls* **c143 h106**

PRESENT RANGER (IRE) 5 b.g. Presenting – Papoose (IRE) (Little Bighorn) [2017/18 h16.3d⁵ h16.3v³ h19.4s³ Jan 26] £40,000 3-y-o: sturdy gelding: brother to Grand National winner Ballabriggs and fairly useful hurdler/chaser Letterman (2½m-2¾m winner), and half-brother to fair hurdler/modest chaser Queen of Mantua (19f-21f winner, by Old Vic): dam winning pointer: runner-up in point on debut: fair form over hurdles: easily best effort when third in maiden at Doncaster: will be suited by 2½m+: open to further improvement. *Dan Skelton* **h114 p**

PRESENT TIMES (IRE) 7 b.g. Kalanisi (IRE) – Beguiling (IRE) (Dr Massini (IRE)) [2017/18 h110: h23.1s* h23.6v² h23.1v^pu h21.7s⁴ Apr 6] sturdy gelding: fairly useful handicap hurdler: won at Exeter in November: stays 3m: best form on soft/heavy going: often races towards rear. *Evan Williams* **h117**

PRESENT TREND (IRE) 9 br.m. Presenting – Trendy Attire (IRE) (Luso) [2017/18 h81: h19.3m⁶ h20g⁵ h20g⁵ h23.1g⁴ Aug 4] poor handicap hurdler: stays 23f: tried in tongue tie: usually races close up. *Richard Ford* **h72**

PRESSURIZE (IRE) 12 b.g. Witness Box (USA) – Cockpit Rose (IRE) (Be My Native (USA)) [2017/18 c100, h–: c19.4v* c20.8v^pu c20s⁵ c26s c27.9v⁶ c23.8v⁵ Apr 15] sturdy gelding: twice-raced hurdler: useful handicap chaser: won at Chepstow (by 15 lengths from Templehills) in January: below form after: stays 21f: best form on heavy going: tried in blinkers. *Venetia Williams* **c131 d h–**

PRI

PRETTYLITTLETHING (IRE) 8 b.m. Tajraasi (USA) – Cloncunny Girl (IRE) (Roselier (FR)) [2017/18 c99p, h90p: c20.9g⁴ c21g* c23m⁵ c21.2s⁴ c20g⁵ c21.2g⁵ h21g h19.6s h19.2v⁵ Feb 15] modest handicap hurdler, below form last 3 starts in 2017/18: fair handicap chaser: won at Newton Abbot in June: stays 25f: acts on soft and good to firm going: in headgear last 4 starts: often races towards rear. *Neil Mulholland*   **c104** **h76**

PRETTY MISS MAHLER (IRE) 7 b.m. Mahler – So Pretty (IRE) (Presenting) [2017/18 h99: h20.2g h22.1g⁴ h25.4s* h21.2d³ c20.1v³ c21.1v² Apr 13] runner-up on completed start in Irish points: modest handicap hurdler: won at Cartmel in July: similar form in chases: better effort when second in mares handicap at Sedgefield: stays 25f: acts on heavy going: has worn cheekpieces. *Martin Todhunter*   **c100** **h98**

PRETTY OBVIOUS (FR) 5 b.g. Montmartre (FR) – Societe (FR) (Panis (USA)) [2017/18 b16.7g⁶ May 12] first foal: dam, lightly raced on Flat in France, half-sister to very smart French performer up to 1½m Silver Pond: 13/8, sixth in bumper at Market Rasen: fair form on Flat. *Jonjo O'Neill*   **b–**

PRETTY RECKLESS (IRE) 5 b.m. Scorpion (IRE) – Deep Supreme (IRE) (Supreme Leader) [2017/18 h97, b64: h19.6g c16.4g³ c20g* c19.2g* c20.3d³ h18.6s h21.2d c20.8g¹ Apr 19] maiden hurdler, no form in 2017/18: fair form over fences: won handicaps at Warwick in September and Market Rasen in November: stays 21f: acts on good to soft going: tried in cheekpieces: usually races nearer last than first, often travels strongly. *Dan Skelton*   **c106** **h–**

PRETTY ROSE (IRE) 8 b.m. King's Theatre (IRE) – Rosies All The Way (Robellino (USA)) [2017/18 h98: h20m² h20g² h23.3d^pu Sep 24] modest handicap hurdler: stayed 21f: acted on soft and good to firm going: often wore cheekpieces: dead. *Ben Case*   **h91**

PRIDE OF PARISH (IRE) 8 br.g. Indian Danehill (IRE) – Inchneedlequinn (IRE) (Needle Gun (IRE)) [2017/18 c107: c26d^pu c24.2s^F Feb 16] has had breathing operation: multiple point winner: fair form when won novice hunter on chasing debut, failed to complete both starts under Rules in 2017/18. *Alan Hill*   **c–**

PRIME VENTURE (IRE) 7 br.g. Primary (USA) – Next Venture (IRE) (Zaffaran (USA)) [2017/18 h127: h22.8m² h23.9v* h25s⁴ h23.4v h24s h24.7s⁶ Apr 14] useful-looking gelding: useful handicap hurdler: won at Ffos Las in November: stays 25f: acts on good to firm and heavy going: often races towards rear. *Evan Williams*   **h135**

PRIMO BLUE 8 b.g. Primo Valentino (IRE) – Flintwood (Gunner B) [2017/18 c–, h104: h21.2g h20.5s⁵ h16.5s^pu Dec 14] fair maiden hurdler: fell first only start over fences: stays 2½m: acts on soft going: in hood last 2 starts: often races towards rear. *Noel Williams*   **c–** **h97**

PRIMOGENITURE (IRE) 7 b.g. Glory of Dancer – Jacqueline (IND) (King Charlemagne (USA)) [2017/18 h15.7v³ Apr 27] sturdy gelding: fairly useful on Flat, stays 2m: poor form over hurdles. *Martin Keighley*   **h83**

PRIMO ROSSI 9 b.g. Primo Valentino (IRE) – Flaming Rose (IRE) (Roselier (FR)) [2017/18 h75: h20.6g³ c16.5g³ c20g^ur h19.6g h27g^F h23.3d Sep 24] smallish gelding: poor handicap hurdler: similar form over fences: stays 19f: best form on good going: wears cheekpieces/tongue tie. *Tom Gretton*   **c70** **h67**

PRIMO TIME 7 b.g. Primo Valentino (IRE) – Eva's Edge (IRE) (Good Thyne (USA)) [2017/18 b97: h16.7d^pu Oct 4] bumper winner: pulled up in novice hurdle: dead. *Sam England*   **h–**

PRINCE CARN 7 b.g. Lucarno (USA) – Broadbrook Lass (Broadsword (USA)) [2017/18 h21.7s^pu h21.2d^pu Apr 9] no show in novice hurdles: tried in cheekpieces. *Steve Flook*   **h–**

PRINCE DUNDEE (IRE) 5 b.g. Stowaway – Miss Dundee (IRE) (Bob Back (USA)) [2017/18 h16.2s⁵ h16v⁶ Dec 22] €15,000 3-y-o: good-topped gelding: third foal: half-brother to useful hurdler Ben Dundee (2m-2½m winner, by Beneficial): dam, unraced, out of sister to very smart chaser Nick Dundee (stayed 3m): pulled up in Irish point: poor form in maiden hurdles: will be suited by further than 2m. *Lucinda Russell*   **h84**

PRINCE FLORBURY 5 b.g. Prince Flori (GER) – Lady Sambury (Overbury (IRE)) [2017/18 b–: b15.6g h16.7s^ur Mar 26] no form in bumpers: unseated first on hurdling debut: in tongue tie last 2 starts. *Maurice Barnes*   **h–** **b–**

PRINCE GARYANTLE (IRE) 8 b.g. Exit To Nowhere (USA) – Last Sunrise (IRE) (Shahanndeh) [2017/18 c19.9d² h21.5g² h20g⁴ h24g⁶ h24g h20s* h20d h21s* h20s Apr 28] useful handicap hurdler: won at Clonmel (novice) in September and Punchestown (conditional, by 8½ lengths from Man of Plenty) in April: 5/1, second in maiden at Kilbeggan (6½ lengths behind Black Zambezi) on chasing debut: stays 25f: acts on soft going: usually in headgear: wears tongue tie: front runner/races prominently: should do better over fences. *Matthew J. Smith, Ireland*   **c111 p** **h134**

PRINCE KHURRAM 8 b.g. Nayef (USA) – Saree (Barathea (IRE)) [2017/18 c119, h98: h16.8g³ h20g² h19.6g* h19.2g* h16.7g* h16.2g³ h16.2d⁵ h20.9g³ c15.8g⁵ h16.8s⁵ h16.8vᵖᵘ Jan 28] useful-looking gelding: fair handicap hurdler: completed hat-trick with wins at Bangor (2) and Fontwell in August/September: fairly useful chaser at best, made bad mistake only start over fences in 2017/18: stays 21f: acts on any going: often in cheekpieces: wears tongue tie. *Donald McCain* — c–, h108

PRINCE KUP (IRE) 7 ch.g. High Rock (IRE) – Lockup (IRE) (Inchinor) [2017/18 h20.3g h19.9d h23.3gᵖᵘ c19.7dᵖᵘ h20.5d⁵ h19.9v⁶ h23.1vᵖᵘ h15.8s³ Mar 14] fair hurdler at best when trained in Ireland, little form in 2017/18: no show over fences: left Laura Hurley after seventh start: stays 2½m: acts on heavy going: usually wears headgear. *Dan Skelton* — c–, h70

PRINCELY PLAYER (IRE) 11 b.g. King's Theatre (IRE) – Temptation (FR) (Lando (GER)) [2017/18 c23s⁵ Jan 9] sturdy gelding: point winner: useful hurdler/chaser at one time: never a threat on hunter debut: stays 23f: acts on soft and good to firm going: tried in tongue tie. *Mrs K. Hobbs* — c98, h–

PRINCE MAHLER (IRE) 8 b.g. Mahler – Strokestown Queen (IRE) (Presenting) [2017/18 c–, h95: h21.6g⁶ h25g² h21.9g⁵ h20g⁶ h23g h19.8s² h19s h21.4s² h23.9s³ h21s Apr 9] modest handicap hurdler: well held completed start over fences: stays 25f: acts on soft and good to firm going: tried in headgear: often wears tongue tie. *Kayley Woollacott* — c–, h98

PRINCE OF POETS 7 gr.g. Byron – Princess Maud (USA) (Irish River (FR)) [2017/18 c22.6d Jun 9] point/bumper winner: maiden hurdler: well held in novice hunter on chasing debut: unproven beyond 17f: acts on soft going: often wears headgear: has worn tongue tie. *J. Heard* — c75, h–

PRINCESSE FLEUR 10 b.m. Grape Tree Road – Princesse Grec (FR) (Grand Tresor (FR)) [2017/18 c89, h–: c20.9d⁵ h20g³ h23g³ h24g³ h24g⁶ Aug 20] poor handicap hurdler/chaser nowadays: stays 3m: acts on soft and good to firm going: has worn headgear, including in 2017/18: often races towards rear. *Michael Scudamore* — c60, h76

PRINCESS MIDNIGHT 4 ch.f. Midnight Legend – Setter's Princess (Generous (IRE)) [2017/18 b16.5vᵖᵘ Apr 12] first foal: dam (h99), maiden hurdler, 1½m winner on Flat: pulled up in bumper. *Ron Hodges* — b–

PRINCESS MONONOKE (IRE) 7 b.m. Oscar (IRE) – Grande Solitaire (FR) (Loup Solitaire (USA)) [2017/18 h97, b77: h16.2gᵖᵘ h19.3v⁵ h16.2s h16.7v³ h16.8v* h16v⁴ h16.2v² h16.8v* h20.2s* Apr 25] Irish maiden point winner: fair handicap hurdler: won at Sedgefield in January (mares) and April, and at Perth (mares) later in April: stays 2½m: best form on soft/heavy going. *Donald McCain* — h104

PRINCESS ROANIA (IRE) 7 b.m. Dubai Destination (USA) – Lady Roania (IRE) (Saddlers' Hall (IRE)) [2017/18 h105: h20g h23.1d³ h20g⁵ h18.5m⁴ h21.7d⁵ h20g⁴ h16d² h15.8v³ h19gᵖᵘ h20v³ h17.7v⁵ h15.8v Feb 18] modest maiden hurdler: stays 2½m: acts on heavy going: wears headgear: has worn tongue tie. *Peter Bowen* — h92

PRINCESS ROXY 5 ch.m. Midnight Legend – Royal Roxy (IRE) (Exit To Nowhere (USA)) [2017/18 b16.6s* b16v b17s Apr 12] £5,000 3-y-o, £115,000 4-y-o: rather unfurnished mare: fourth foal: dam unraced half-sister to useful hurdler/smart chaser (2m/17f winner) Crossbow Creek and useful hurdler/chaser (2m-21f winner) Mwaleshi: won Irish point on debut: fair form in bumpers: won mares event at Doncaster in January: wears tongue tie. *Ben Case* — b94

PRINCESS TARA (IRE) 8 b.m. Kayf Tara – Oscars Vision (IRE) (Oscar Schindler (IRE)) [2017/18 c20.1g² c20.1s⁵ c21.4sᵖᵘ h19.4sᶠ h20.6s h24v⁵ Mar 5] fairly useful hurdler at best, no form in 2017/18: promise on chasing debut, but went wrong way over fences after: stays 2¾m: acts on heavy going: tried in blinkers. *Ruth Jefferson* — c112, h–

PRINCETON ROYALE (IRE) 9 br.g. Royal Anthem (USA) – Shelikesitstraight (IRE) (Rising) [2017/18 c131, h–: c21.7gᵖᵘ c21.2s³ c19.9s² c21.2s² c21.2d² c19.4d* Apr 22] lengthy gelding: winning hurdler: useful handicap chaser: won at Stratford (by 5 lengths from Champagne At Tara) in April: stays 3m: acts on good to firm and heavy going: wears headgear: front runner. *Neil King* — c131, h–

PRIVATE MALONE (IRE) 9 b.g. Darsi (FR) – Native Artist (IRE) (Be My Native (USA)) [2017/18 c122, h–: c20d⁵ c21.6d² c20.5d⁵ c23.4s⁴ c23s² c22.4s² c25.6v⁶ Mar 31] rangy gelding: winning hurdler: fairly useful maiden chaser: stays 23f: acts on heavy going: wears headgear: usually races close up. *Emma Lavelle* — c125, h–

PRODUCT OF LOVE (IRE) 7 b.g. Fruits of Love (USA) – Annshoon (IRE) (Jurado (USA)) [2017/18 b107: h16.5m* h20.5d c17g* Aug 26] useful bumper performer: fairly useful form over hurdles: won maiden at Ballinrobe in May: 6/1, also won maiden at Killarney (by length from Roconga) on chasing debut: should stay beyond 17f: front runner/races prominently: open to improvement over fences. *Alan Fleming, Ireland* — c133 p h118

PROFESSOR PLUM (IRE) 8 b.g. Kalanisi (IRE) – Miss Plum (Ardross) [2017/18 h–: h22.7g⁶ h23.8g³ h25.3d^pu h23.8d Feb 14] modest maiden hurdler: stays 25f: acts on good to soft going: in visor last 3 starts. *Rose Dobbin* — h97

PROGRESS DRIVE (IRE) 7 b.g. Stowaway – Dolphins View (IRE) (Dolphin Street (FR)) [2017/18 h123: c20d⁴ c20.5v² c24.1v* c24.2v² c24.1g Apr 21] fairly useful hurdler: useful form over fences: won 3-runner novice handicap at Ayr (by 17 lengths from Lochnell) in February: stays 3m: acts on heavy going: tried in cheekpieces: usually races close up. *Nicky Richards* — c132 h–

PROJECT BLUEBOOK (FR) 5 bl.g. Sinndar (IRE) – Apperella (Rainbow Quest (USA)) [2017/18 h136: h16d⁶ h16.4s h16.3v h20s⁶ Apr 13] workmanlike gelding: useful handicap hurdler: sixth in Grade 3 at Aintree (4¼ lengths behind Jester Jet) in April: barely stays 2½m, at least when conditions are testing: acts on heavy going. *John Quinn* — h133

PROJECT MARS (IRE) 6 b.g. Presenting – Molly Massini (IRE) (Dr Massini (IRE)) [2017/18 h109, b83: h15.7m^F h19.2g⁵ h16.8s h21.7d⁶ h19.2v² h20.5v h19.5v⁶ h21.7g² Apr 20] modest maiden hurdler: stays 2¾m: acts on good to firm and heavy going: often in headgear. *Nick Gifford* — h97

PRONOUNCED (IRE) 4 b.g. Power – Le Montrachet (Nashwan (USA)) [2017/18 h17.3s* h17g² h16v h16s⁵ h16s^F h16v^pu h16s⁴ Mar 16] half-brother to fairly useful 2m hurdle winner Zig Zag (by Zoffany), stays 19f: modest maiden on Flat, barely stays 1¼m: fair hurdler: won juvenile maiden at Ballinrobe in August: left Joseph Patrick O'Brien after sixth start: raced around 2m: acts on soft going. *Michael Roberts* — h107

PRONTO TONTO (IRE) 5 b.g. Thousand Words – Island Sun (IRE) (Trans Island) [2017/18 h16s h18.6v h20.6s h16.8v⁴ Mar 13] first foal: dam (h80), lightly raced over hurdles, 9f winner on Flat: poor form over hurdles. *Tim Easterby* — h82

PROSPECTUS 5 b.g. Sakhee (USA) – Some Sunny Day (Where Or When (IRE)) [2017/18 h126: h16v⁴ h16.1s² h20v h16v³ h17.8v² Apr 13] angular gelding: useful handicap hurdler: 6 days on from Flat win, second at Ballinrobe (2½ lengths behind Carrig Cathal) in April: stays 2¼m: best form on soft/heavy going: tried in cheekpieces. *Gavin Patrick Cromwell, Ireland* — h137

PROSPERA PASCHA 5 br.m. Robin des Champs (FR) – Easter Legend (Midnight Legend) [2017/18 b66: h21.6g³ h19.9g³ h23.3g^pu Jun 15] modest form over hurdles: best effort when third in mares maiden at Uttoxeter in May: wears headgear/tongue tie. *David Pipe* — h86

PROTEK DES FLOS (FR) 6 b.g. Protektor (GER) – Flore de Chantenay (FR) (Smadoun (FR)) [2017/18 c73p, h129: c20dp^u h21.4v* h25s³ h24s Mar 15] useful-looking gelding: useful handicap hurdler: won at Wincanton (by 2¼ lengths from Boite) in December: little aptitude for chasing: stays 25f: best form on soft/heavy going. *Nicky Henderson* — c– h133

PROTEST (IRE) 5 b.g. Fastnet Rock (AUS) – Phrase (Royal Anthem (USA)) [2017/18 h16.8m^F May 9] fair on Flat, stayed 9.5f: weakening when fell fatally last in maiden at Exeter on hurdling debut. *Dan Skelton* — h–

PROUTS PUB (IRE) 9 b.g. Catcher In The Rye (IRE) – A Woman In Love (Muhtarram (USA)) [2017/18 c–, h117: h20.5g^pu h19.1m^F h19.2m⁶ h21.7g³ Aug 24] angular gelding: fair handicap hurdler: no form over fences: stays 2¾m: acts on heavy going: has worn headgear: usually races close up, often travels strongly: temperamental. *Nick Gifford* — c– h112 §

PROXIMO (FR) 10 b.g. Maille Pistol (FR) – La Curieuse (FR) (Robin des Champs (FR)) [2017/18 c23.6m³ c15.9v^pu Mar 9] multiple winning pointer: lightly-raced maiden hurdler: poor form in hunter chases: stays 2½m: acts on soft going: in cheekpieces last 2 starts. *Stuart Morris* — c79 h–

PRUSSIAN EAGLE (IRE) 7 br.g. Jeremy (USA) – Absolutely Cool (IRE) (Indian Ridge) [2017/18 c75, h–: h15.8g⁴ h15.8g⁸ h18.5d⁴ h16g³ h15.5d⁵ h15.8d² h15.8v^F Jan 27] fair handicap hurdler: won at Ffos Las in June: little show over fences: unproven beyond 2m: acted on heavy going: tried in cheekpieces: front runner/raced prominently: dead. *Evan Williams* — c– h109

PSY

PSYCHEDELIC ROCK 7 b.g. Yeats (IRE) – Gemini Lucy (IRE) (Glacial Storm (USA)) [2017/18 b16.7g h16g* h17.7m² h19.6g² h19.9d⁶ h20g* h20.6d² h19.8s⁶ Apr 28] €50,000 3-y-o: second foal: half-brother to useful hurdler Dadsintrouble (15f-23f winner, by Presenting): dam (c140/h117) 2m-2½m hurdle/chase winner: well held in bumpers: fairly useful hurdler: won maiden at Worcester in July and novice handicap there in October: left M. M. Lynch after first start: stays 21f: acts on good to firm and good to soft going: in cheekpieces last 4 starts. *Ian Williams*   h126 b–

PSYCHOCANDY (IRE) 6 b.m. Oscar (IRE) – Derrigra Sublime (IRE) (Flemensfirth (USA)) [2017/18 h84, b–: h25d⁵ h21.3s^F h19.9d³ h24.1s^pu h20.5v^F c20.2v^pu h21.2d Apr 9] poor maiden hurdler: pulled up in novice handicap on chasing debut: stays 25f: acts on good to soft going: wears cheekpieces. *Ian Williams*   c– h83

PTIT ZIG (FR) 9 b.g. Great Pretender (IRE) – Red Rym (FR) (Denham Red (FR)) [2017/18 c–, h161: h25.4s h24.1s⁴ c21.7s³ c23.8d c25.6v^pu h23.6s^pu Feb 24] strong gelding: high-class hurdler/chaser at best, went wrong way temperamentally in 2017/18: stays 25f: acts on good to firm and heavy going: wears blinkers: one to leave alone. *Paul Nicholls*   c139 § h136 §

PULLING POWER 8 br.m. Erhaab (USA) – Pulling Strings (IRE) (Accordion) [2017/18 h112: h23.3d^pu May 6] good-bodied mare: fair hurdler at best, ran poorly only start in 2017/18: should stay 3m: acts on heavy going: wears tongue tie: front runner/races prominently. *Kim Bailey*   h–

PULL THE CHORD (IRE) 8 b.g. St Jovite (USA) – Gold Chord (IRE) (Accordion) [2017/18 c133, h–: c21.6g^F Oct 6] useful-looking gelding: winning hurdler: useful maiden chaser: stayed 2¾m: acted on good to firm and heavy going: often raced towards rear: dead. *Philip Hobbs*   c– h–

PULL THE TRIGGER 7 b.g. Double Trigger (IRE) – Soloism (Sulaafah (USA)) [2017/18 h–, b–: h20g⁶ h20g Jul 10] maiden pointer: no form under Rules: in tongue tie last 2 starts. *Tim Vaughan*   h–

PULL TOGETHER (IRE) 6 b.g. Curtain Time (IRE) – Whos To Know (IRE) (Bravefoot) [2017/18 b15.3s h20.5v⁴ h20.5v¹ h15.7s³ h19.5v² h15.9v* Apr 11] €9,500 3-y-o: first foal: dam (h101), 2¼m hurdle winner, half-sister to useful chaser (2m-19f winner) Lord Maizey: tailed off in bumper: fair form over hurdles: won maiden at Plumpton in April: stays 21f: acts on heavy going: front runner. *Stuart Edmunds*   h112 b–

PULP FICTION (IRE) 6 b.g. Robin des Champs (FR) – Bean Ki Moon (IRE) (King's Theatre (IRE)) [2017/18 b94: h16s² h16.7s³ h19.4d⁵ Dec 15] third in Irish point on debut: fair form over hurdles: placed in novices at Worcester and Bangor: wears hood: in tongue tie last 3 starts. *Ben Case*   h109

PULPITARIAN (USA) 10 b.g. Pulpit (USA) – Bedanken (USA) (Geri (USA)) [2017/18 h95: h22.7g^pu h23.9g⁶ Jul 5] small gelding: modest handicap hurdler, below form in 2017/18: stays 3m: acts on soft going: wears headgear: usually races prominently. *Lucinda Russell*   h77

PUMAFLOR (IRE) 6 b.g. Aussie Rules (USA) – Krasotka (IRE) (Soviet Star (USA)) [2017/18 h15.8g³ h15.6m h16.4g⁶ h16.6d h15.7s^pu Jan 1] close-coupled gelding: fairly useful at best on Flat, stays 9f: modest form over hurdles: raced around 2m: tried in cheekpieces/tongue tie. *Philip Kirby*   h92

PUPPET WARRIOR 6 ch.g. Black Sam Bellamy (IRE) – Rakajack (Rakaposhi King) [2017/18 b95: h20.5d² h21.6d h19.2v² h20.5v³ h19.2d³ h24.2s⁴ h20.5s⁴ Apr 15] sturdy gelding: fair maiden hurdler: stays 3m: acts on soft going: tried in cheekpieces. *Nick Gifford*   h113

PURCELL'S BRIDGE (FR) 11 b.g. Trempolino (USA) – Theatrical Lady (USA) (Theatrical) [2017/18 c115, h–: c24.2v^pu c24.2s⁵ c24.5s Dec 3] winning hurdler: fairly useful handicap chaser, below form in 2017/18: stays 3¼m: acts on good to firm and heavy going: wears hood. *Rose Dobbin*   c93 h–

PURE AFFECTION (IRE) 7 b.m. Beneficial – Regents Dancer (IRE) (Flemensfirth (USA)) [2017/18 b16m⁴ b16.3g² b16.4g Oct 28] sturdy mare: fourth foal: half-sister to bumper winner Mrs Jordan (by King's Theatre) and modest hurdler/fair chaser Mrsrobin (23f-3¼m winner, by Robin des Pres): dam, winning pointer, half-sister to fairly useful chaser (stayed 25f) Just For Men: winning Irish pointer: fair form in bumpers: best effort when second in mares event at Stratford in July: will be suited by further than 2m. *Ian Williams*   b86

PURE VISION (IRE) 7 b.g. Milan – Distillery Lane (IRE) (Exit To Nowhere (USA)) [2017/18 h117: c24.2s^F c20.9v* c23.6v⁴ c24.2s^pu c25.3g² Apr 18] useful-looking gelding: fairly useful hurdler: useful form over fences: won novice handicap at Ffos Las in   c131 h–

QUA

November: second in novice handicap at Cheltenham (½ length behind Winter Lion) in April: will be suited by 3½m+: acts on heavy going: wears tongue tie: usually races towards rear. *Anthony Honeyball*

PURPLE HARRY 10 gr.g. Sir Harry Lewis (USA) – Ellfiedick (Alfie Dickins) [2017/18 c97, h–: c22.9v^{pu} c24.2v^{ro} c24.1v^{pu} c24.2v^6 c23.4v^2 c24.2d^4 Apr 23] winning novice chaser: modest handicap chaser: stays 25f: acts on heavy going: tried in cheekpieces: has run out. *Tina Jackson*   **c88 h–**

PURPLE 'N GOLD (IRE) 9 b.g. Strategic Prince – Golden Dew (IRE) (Montjeu (IRE)) [2017/18 c134, h118: c19m c20.3g^4 h18.6g^5 c17.4m* c16m^5 h16g c16.5g^5 c17.8g h16.8s h19m^4 h20s^{ur} Nov 14] compact gelding: fair handicap hurdler: fairly useful handicap chaser: won at Fontwell in June: stays 2½m: acts on good to firm and good to soft going: wears headgear: has worn tongue tie: unreliable. *David Pipe*   **c122 § h104 §**

PUT THE BOOT IN (IRE) 6 ch.g. Duke of Marmalade (IRE) – Mubkera (IRE) (Nashwan (USA)) [2017/18 h–: h23.3d^{pu} Sep 24] sturdy gelding: little form over hurdles: tried in cheekpieces. *Nikki Evans*   **h–**

PUZZLE CACHE 4 b.f. Phoenix Reach (IRE) – Secret Queen (Zafeen (FR)) [2017/18 b15.3v b16.5m Apr 25] first foal: dam 6f winner: no form in bumpers: tried in blinkers. *Martin Hill*   **b–**

PYLONTHEPRESSURE (IRE) 8 b.g. Darsi (FR) – Minnie O'Grady (IRE) (Welsh Term) [2017/18 h124: c21.2v^4 c16v* c31.8s^5 c21.2v^{pu} c21s^{pu} Apr 27] workmanlike gelding: fairly useful hurdler: useful form over fences: won maiden at Thurles in February: lost way after, jumping poorly: stays 2½m: raced only on soft/heavy going. *W. P. Mullins, Ireland*   **c134 x h–**

PYM (IRE) 5 b.g. Stowaway – Liss Rua (IRE) (Bob Back (USA)) [2017/18 b106: b16g^2 b17s Apr 13] compact gelding: fairly useful form in bumpers: better effort in 2017/18 when second at Kempton in February. *Nicky Henderson*   **b102**

PYRIOS (FR) 5 b.g. Heliostatic (IRE) – Nuance Tartare (FR) (Nononito (FR)) [2017/18 b–: b16g^4 h15.8d^4 h15.8s h15.3v^F h15.3s^4 Feb 17] modest form in bumpers: fair form over hurdles: will stay beyond 2m: often races towards rear. *Philip Hobbs*   **h104 b83**

Q

QALINAS (FR) 11 gr.g. Malinas (GER) – Tabletiere (FR) (Kaldounevees (FR)) [2017/18 c20.9p^{u} Jun 1] tall, angular gelding: multiple winner in points, including in 2018: winning hurdler: twice-raced chaser, pulled up on hunter debut in June: stays 3m: acts on heavy going: usually wears blinkers: wears tongue tie. *David Rees*   **c– h–**

QASR 4 b.g. Excelebration (IRE) – Blur (Oasis Dream) [2017/18 b14d^3 b13.6v^2 Nov 15] fifth foal: half-brother to 2 winners on Flat, including 7f winner Everleigh (by Bahamian Bounty): dam maiden (stayed 1¼m): fair form in bumpers: better effort when second in junior event at Ayr (hooded) in November: poor form on Flat debut. *Keith Dalgleish*   **b88**

QAVIY CASH 4 b.g. Oasis Dream – Neartica (FR) (Sadler's Wells (USA)) [2017/18 h16.6s^{pu} Feb 21] fairly useful on Flat, stays 1½m: pulled up in novice on hurdling debut (tongue tied). *Dan Skelton*   **h–**

QUADRIGA (IRE) 8 b.g. Acclamation – Turning Light (GER) (Fantastic Light (USA)) [2017/18 h19.9v^6 h16.8v^{pu} Feb 22] poor on Flat nowadays: no show over hurdles: wears hood. *Chris Grant*   **h–**

QUADRILLER (FR) 11 b.g. Lando (GER) – Tabachines (FR) (Art Francais (USA)) [2017/18 c117, h–: h16.8g* h18.5d^6 Sep 11] fairly useful hurdler: won handicap at Newton Abbot in September after 15-month absence: disappointed in seller soon after: fairly useful chaser: stays 2¼m: acts on soft and good to firm going: wears tongue tie. *Philip Hobbs*   **c– h115**

QUALANDO (FR) 7 b.g. Lando (GER) – Qualite Controlee (FR) (Poliglote) [2017/18 c130, h206: c20d^2 c20s^{pu} h16.8s h20.3g^4 Apr 18] good-topped gelding: useful handicap hurdler: fourth at Cheltenham (1½ lengths behind Champagne Express) in April: similar form over fences: second in maiden at Uttoxeter (3 lengths behind Aqua Dude) in October: stays 2½m: acts on heavy going: wears headgear: held up. *Alan Jones*   **c133 h133**

QUANTUM OF SOLACE 8 b.m. Kayf Tara – Fashion House (Homo Sapien) [2017/18 c87, h91: h15.7g Apr 20] modest handicap hurdler at best, never a threat only start in 2017/18: lightly-raced chaser: unproven beyond 2m: acts on good to firm and good to soft going: wears hood: tried in tongue tie. *Fergal O'Brien*   **c– h–**

QUA

QUARENTA (FR) 6 b.g. Voix du Nord (FR) – Negresse de Cuta (FR) (Baroud d'Honneur (FR)) [2017/18 h110: h21m² h21g³ h23g² h21g* h23.9g h21.1s h19s Dec 14] compact gelding: fairly useful handicap hurdler: won at Warwick in October: stays 23f: best form on good going: tried in cheekpieces: signs of temperament. *Jonjo O'Neill* **h115**

QUARRY LAMI (IRE) 7 gr.g. Daylami (IRE) – Lady Leila (IRE) (Taipan (IRE)) [2017/18 h–, b–: h15.8d h23.9m* Nov 1] leggy gelding: runner-up on second of 2 starts in Irish maiden points: modest form over hurdles: much improved in first-time cheekpieces when won handicap at Taunton in November, but finished lame: stays 3m: acts on good to firm going: in tongue tie last 2 starts. *Oliver Greenall* **h92**

QUARRY LEADER (IRE) 7 b.g. Darsi (FR) – Pollys Leader (IRE) (Supreme Leader) [2017/18 h21.6v⁴ h20.3g Apr 18] €7,800 3-y-o, £46,000 5-y-o: sturdy gelding: ninth foal: dam unraced sister to useful hurdler/modest chaser (2m/17f winner) Gatflax and half-sister to fair hurdler/useful chaser (2¼m-2½m winner) In The Blood: won Irish point on debut: fair form over hurdles: better effort when fourth in novice at Ascot in January: remains open to improvement. *Alex Hales* **h112 p**

QUARRY WIZARD (IRE) 8 b.g. Trans Island – Hazel Green (IRE) (Teamster) [2017/18 h87: h19.5v⁴ Apr 14] strong gelding: Irish point winner: poor maiden hurdler on balance: should stay further than 19f: acts on heavy going: usually wears hood: often races towards rear. *Oliver Greenall* **h71**

QUASHA 5 b.m. Black Sam Bellamy (IRE) – Gloriana (Formidable (USA)) [2017/18 b16v⁶ b16v⁵ Feb 20] half-sister to 3 winners, including bumper winner/fair hurdler Brook No Argument (2m-19f winner, by Alderbrook) and fair hurdler/winning pointer Sackett (2½m winner, by Midnight Legend): dam (h82), 2¼m hurdle winner, also 1m/9f winner on Flat: well held in bumpers. *John Wainwright* **b–**

QUASI (IRE) 6 ch.g. Presenting – Pink Mist (IRE) (Montelimar (USA)) [2017/18 h19.6s^pu h20.8s^pu Jan 9] no show in novice/maiden hurdles. *Tim Vaughan* **h–**

QUAY QUEST 4 ch.g. Shami – Quay Four (IRE) (Barathea (IRE)) [2017/18 ab16.3g Apr 15] 66/1, eighth in bumper at Newcastle (4½ lengths behind Summer Lightening). *Ray Craggs* **b79**

QUEBEC 7 b.g. Dansili – Milford Sound (Barathea (IRE)) [2017/18 c–, h104: h17.2d³ h15.8m h21.4s⁶ Oct 20] good-topped gelding: fair handicap hurdler: well held only chase start: stays 2½m: acts on soft going: has worn cheekpieces, including last 3 starts: in tongue tie last 4 starts: unreliable. *Matt Sheppard* **c–** **h97 §**

QUEEN MONTOYA 4 b.f. High Chaparral (IRE) – Rainbow Queen (FR) (Spectrum (IRE)) [2017/18 b13.7g b14s b16.6s ab16g Feb 19] half-sister to 2 winners on Flat, including useful 1¼m-1½m winner (stayed 2m) Quixote (by Singspiel): dam, 6.5f-1m winner in France/Belgium, half-sister to useful French hurdler/fairly useful chaser (15f-17f winner) Libranous: little show in bumpers. *James Eustace* **b–**

QUEEN OF AVALON (IRE) 7 b.m. Westerner – Courtain (USA) (Diesis) [2017/18 h83, b–: h20.1g^pu h20.2m^pu h16.2g³ h16.2g h17.2d^pu Aug 26] poor maiden hurdler: tried in hood. *N. W. Alexander* **h77**

QUEEN OF EPIRUS 10 ch.m. Kirkwall – Andromache (Hector Protector (USA)) [2017/18 h81: h16.3d² May 21] poor maiden hurdler: stays 19f: acts on soft going: tried in tongue tie. *Nigel Hawke* **h80**

QUEEN OF THE WIND 5 b.m. Shirocco (GER) – Kaydee Queen (IRE) (Bob's Return (IRE)) [2017/18 b16.3s h15.8s^ur h20.5d⁵ h19.5s⁴ h21v^pu h15.7v* h15.8d⁶ Apr 9] half-sister to fairly useful hurdlers/useful chasers Royal Player (21f-3m winner, by King's Theatre) and Pires (2m/17f winner, by Generous): dam unraced half-sister to fairly useful hurdler/useful chaser (2m/17f winner) Queen of Spades: well held in bumper: modest form over hurdles: won mares handicap at Southwell in March: best effort at 2m: acts on heavy going. *Colin Tizzard* **h96** **b–**

QUEENOHEARTS (IRE) 5 ch.m. Flemensfirth (USA) – Chars (IRE) (Old Vic) [2017/18 b16s⁴ b15.7s* b16v* Mar 10] £13,000 3-y-o: lengthy, rather unfurnished mare: first foal: dam unraced sister to useful hurdler/chaser (stayed 3m) Sea of Thunder and half-sister to top-class hurdler (2m-2¼m winner) Macs Joy: useful form in bumpers: won mares events at Towcester (by 5 lengths from Pineapple Rush) in December and Sandown (listed, by neck from Queens Cave) in March: will be suited by further than 2m. *Stuart Edmunds* **b107**

QUEEN OLIVIA 10 b.m. King's Theatre (IRE) – Queen's Leader (Supreme Leader) [2017/18 c–, h–: c25.5s* c20d² c23.8d² Apr 24] winning hurdler/pointer: fair form in chases: won mares hunter at Fontwell in May: stays 25f: acts on soft going: usually wears hood: tried in tongue tie. *Miss V. Collins* **c113** **h–**

QUEENS CAVE (IRE) 5 b.m. Court Cave (IRE) – Shuilan (IRE) (Good Thyne (USA)) [2017/18 b15.8v* b16v² Mar 10] €8,000 3-y-o, £175,000 4-y-o: lengthy mare: sixth foal: half-sister to 3 winners, including fairly useful hurdler Shuilamach (2½m winner, by Presenting) and bumper winner/fairly useful hurdler Notre Ami (2m winner, by Kalanisi): dam (h113), bumper/19f hurdle winner, out of half-sister to Welsh Grand National winner Jocks Cross: won Irish point on debut: useful form in bumpers: won mares maiden at Uttoxeter (by 5 lengths from Shapiro) in March: improved when second in listed mares event at Sandown (neck behind Queenohearts) in March. *David Pipe* — **b107**

QUEENS CLOAK (IRE) 5 b.m. Definite Article – Love Divided (IRE) (King's Ride) [2017/18 – : h16g Oct 25] no show in mares bumper/novice hurdle. *Jamie Snowden* — **h–**

QUEEN'S MAGIC (IRE) 6 b.m. Kalanisi (IRE) – Black Queen (IRE) (Bob Back (USA)) [2017/18 b17.7d* b16.8g³ Apr 19] half-sister to useful hurdler/smart chaser Bold Sir Brian (2m-3m winner, by Brian Boru) and fair chaser Mumgos Debut (2m-2½m winner, by Royal Anthem): dam (c92/h131) 2m-2¼m hurdle winner: placed in Irish point on debut: fairly useful form in bumpers: won mares event at Plumpton in February. *Neil Mulholland* — **b101**

QUEEN SPUD 9 b.m. Multiplex – Hurtebise (FR) (Groom Dancer (USA)) [2017/18 c112x, h–: c29.1m⁶ c22.6g⁴ Jun 20] compact mare: winning hurdler: fair handicap chaser: last of 3 in point in April: stays 3m: acts on soft going: wears headgear: often let down by jumping. *Henry Daly* — **c100 x / h–**

QUERRY HORSE (FR) 6 b.g. Equerry (USA) – La Richelandiere (FR) (Garde Royale) [2017/18 c125, h–: h20g⁶ h19.7s h19.4d^pu Dec 15] fairly useful chaser at best, largely disappointing in 2017/18: fairly useful chaser: should stay beyond 19f: tried in headgear: usually races close up. *Oliver Sherwood* — **c– / h115 ?**

QUEST FOR LIFE 6 b.g. Dapper – Lewesdon Duchess (Alhaatmi) [2017/18 b16.7g² b16.2g³ h16.7g² h16s² h19.7s h16.6s³ h16v² h20.6s² h20.5g³ Apr 21] second foal: dam winning pointer: placed in bumpers: fairly useful maiden hurdler: will probably stay 3m: acts on heavy going. *Mark Walford* — **h117 / b94**

QUICK BREW 10 b.g. Denounce – Darjeeling (IRE) (Presenting) [2017/18 c103, h103: c19.3g² c20.3g c20.1g³ c23.8s² c15.6d⁵ Sep 5] fair fairly useful hurdler: fair handicap chaser: stays 3m: acts on soft going: has worn headgear: wears tongue tie: often races towards rear. *Maurice Barnes* — **c102 / h–**

QUICK N' EASY (IRE) 8 ch.g. Vertical Speed (FR) – Tarmons Duchess (IRE) (The Parson) [2017/18 c25.8g² c25.8m² c25.8d² Sep 11] maiden hurdler: modest form over fences: will stay beyond 3¼m: acts on good to firm and good to soft going: wears hood. *Susan Gardner* — **c91 / h–**

QUICK PICK (IRE) 7 b.g. Vinnie Roe (IRE) – Oscars Arrow (IRE) (Oscar (IRE)) [2017/18 b91: h16s² h20.5s³ h19.9s* h19.9s* h19.8v h19.9v³ h24.3g Apr 20] Irish point winner: fairly useful hurdler: won novices at Sedgefield in December and January: stays 2½m: best form on soft/heavy going. *Jennie Candlish* — **h120**

QUICK WAVE (FR) 5 b.m. Gentlewave (IRE) – Magicaldoun (FR) (Kaldoun (FR)) [2017/18 h16.9s⁵ c17.9v⁴ c17.9s² c17.9s² c17.4s⁴ h15.7s⁴ Mar 7] second foal: half-sister to 3 winners in France, including fairly useful chaser Quick Dream (21f winner, by Dream Well): dam French 1½m winner: fair form over hurdles: fairly useful form over fences: best effort when second in 4-y-o event at Compiegne in October: left Y. Fouin after fourth start: stays 2¼m: acts on soft going. *Venetia Williams* — **c116 / h102 +**

QUIDS IN (IRE) 5 b.g. Pour Moi (IRE) – Quixotic (Pivotal) [2017/18 h115: h15.8g⁴ h15.5d² h18.9v³ h15.7v⁴ h19.5v⁵ h19.9v h19.8s⁴ May 9] useful-looking gelding: fair handicap hurdler: stays 19f: acts on heavy going: tried in cheekpieces: wears tongue tie: often races towards rear. *Oliver Greenall* — **h114**

QUIETLY (IRE) 7 b.g. Oscar (IRE) – Gimme Peace (IRE) (Aristocracy) [2017/18 h115: h19.3s⁴ h26.3g^ro c19.4s³ c24v^pu c20.5v^pu h19.9g⁵ Apr 23] sturdy gelding: maiden hurdler, well below best in 2017/18: fair form only completed start over fences (ran out on debut): stays 3m: acts on soft and good to firm going: usually races close up. *Sue Smith* — **c112 / h94**

QUIETO SOL (FR) 7 ch.g. Loup Solitaire (USA) – First Wonder (FR) (Mansonnien (FR)) [2017/18 h112: h21.2g⁵ h24.4d⁶ Dec 1] angular gelding: fair handicap hurdler: stays 2½m: acts on good to firm and good to soft going: tried in cheekpieces: has joined Kerry Lee. *Charlie Longsdon* — **h102**

QUIET WEEKEND 4 b.g. Mawatheeq (USA) – Maid of Perth (Mark of Esteem (IRE)) [2017/18 h16d^pu Oct 18] poor maiden on Flat: pulled up in juvenile on hurdling debut (wore hood). *James Bethell* — **h–**

QUI

QUILL ART 6 b.g. Excellent Art – Featherweight (IRE) (Fantastic Light (USA)) [2017/18 h96: h16.8g^F h16.6d h15.7v^6 Jan 24] fair hurdler at best, no form in 2017/18: has worn headgear. *Richard Fahey* — h–

QUIMBA (SPA) 4 b.f. Dink (FR) – Die Beste (SPA) (Spartacus (IRE)) [2017/18 b12.6s h15.8s Jan 10] sturdy filly: third foal: half-sister to a Flat winner in Spain by Palamoss: dam Spanish maiden on Flat: well held in fillies junior bumper/juvenile hurdle. *Nigel Twiston-Davies* — h– b–

QUINE DES CHAMPS 6 b.m. Midnight Legend – Quine de Sivola (FR) (Robin des Champs (FR)) [2017/18 b61: b15.7d^3 h15.8s h20.8d^6 Feb 8] modest form in bumpers: best effort when third in mares event at Southwell in November: well held in novice hurdles: in tongue tie last 3 starts. *Alastair Ralph* — h– b82

QUINNSBOROTEMPTRES (IRE) 6 ch.m. Gamut (IRE) – Quinnsboro Native (IRE) (Be My Native (USA)) [2017/18 h16.8d h21g c19.4d Apr 22] half-sister to fair chaser Troy Tempest (3¼m winner, by Old Vic) and fair hurdler Oscar Vespasian (2m winner, by Oscar): dam unraced: placed in bumper: no form over hurdles/on chasing debut: won point in February: left Gordon Elliott after second start. *Aytach Sadik* — c– h–

QUINTO 8 ch.g. Desideratum – Cruz Santa (Lord Bud) [2017/18 c101, h101: c21g^{pu} c23g^{pu} h16.8s h23.1v^1 h23.1v^3 h23.9v^5 h23.1v^3 h26.4d Apr 22] medium-sized gelding: winning pointer: modest handicap hurdler: maiden chaser: should stay beyond 25f: acts on heavy going: has worn cheekpieces, including final start: in tongue tie last 5 starts. *Jimmy Frost* — c– h92

QUITE BY CHANCE 9 b.g. Midnight Legend – Hop Fair (Gildoran) [2017/18 c148, h–: c16.8g^2 c16.8d^3 c20.8s^5 c24.2s^{pu} c20.8s c20.8g Apr 18] sturdy gelding: has had breathing operation: maiden hurdler: useful handicap chaser: second in listed event at Ascot (7 lengths behind Exitas) in November: below form after next outing: stays 23f, races mainly over shorter: acts on good to firm and heavy going: tried in blinkers: in tongue tie last 3 starts. *Colin Tizzard* — c144 h–

QUITE RIGHT 7 b.m. Lucarno (USA) – Thebelloftheball (Classic Cliche (IRE)) [2017/18 h18.5v^{pu} h21s Mar 17] well-made mare: first foal: dam (h102), 19f hurdle winner, half-sister to useful hurdler/chaser (2m-21f winner) Poole Master: unplaced in maiden point: no show over hurdles. *Polly Gundry* — h–

QUIZ MASTER (IRE) 6 b.g. Ask – Good Bye Dolly (IRE) (Buckskin (FR)) [2017/18 h84p, b73: h21.6v^4 h20.5d^4 h21.7d^2 h16.2s^2 h15.3v^5 h19.5v^3 h21.7d* h21.4v^2 h21.6s^2 Apr 23] fairly useful handicap hurdler: won at Fontwell in February: second at Newton Abbot in April: likely to stay 3m: acts on heavy going: wears tongue tie: front runner/races prominently. *Colin Tizzard* — h115

QUOTHQUAN (FR) 4 b.g. Myboycharlie (IRE) – Lonestar Spirit (IRE) (Invincible Spirit (IRE)) [2017/18 h17.7d^3 h16s^2 h17.7v^3 h16v^3 Mar 10] compact gelding: fairly useful on Flat, stays 2m: fair form over hurdles. *Michael Madgwick* — h108

R

RABUNDA (IRE) 8 b.g. Milan – Cush Ramani (IRE) (Pistolet Bleu (IRE)) [2017/18 h83: h22g^F May 8] useful-looking gelding: runner-up in Irish maiden point: fair form over hurdles, fell sole start in 2017/18: should stay 2¾m: tried in tongue tie. *Tom George* — h–

RACING EUROPE (IRE) 9 b.g. Kayf Tara – Titanic Quarter (IRE) (Turgeon (USA)) [2017/18 c31.8g^{pu} Apr 21] tall gelding: point winner: winning hurdler: useful form over fences in 2015/16, showed nothing on first start since in Scottish Grand National at Ayr: stays 27f: acts on heavy going. *Brian Ellison* — c– h–

RACING PULSE (IRE) 9 b.g. Garuda (IRE) – Jacks Sister (IRE) (Entitled) [2017/18 c113, h–: c24d^{pu} c28s^{pu} h20v h24s h23.1v Mar 8] sturdy gelding: useful hurdler/chaser at best, little show in handicaps in 2017/18: left Richard Hobson after first start, W. P. Mullins after fourth: stays 3m: acts on heavy going: tried in cheekpieces: has worn tongue tie: often races towards rear. *Turlough O'Connor, Ireland* — c– h103

RACING SPIRIT 6 ch.g. Sir Percy – Suertuda (Domedriver (IRE)) [2017/18 h87: h23.3d^3 h20.6g h19.6g h20g^3 h23g^2 Oct 17] modest maiden hurdler: stays 23f: acts on good to firm and good to soft going: has worn headgear, including final start: tried in tongue tie. *Dave Roberts* — h93

650

RAI

RADICAL ARCHIE 7 ch.g. Prince Arch (USA) – Radical Gunner (Gunner B) [2017/18 h101p, b90: h16.7s h15.5d^{pu} h19.2v^{pu} h15.8v* Apr 7] fair form over hurdles: won handicap at Uttoxeter (conditional) in April: unproven beyond 2m: acts on heavy going: front runner/races prominently. *Evan Williams*   **h105**

RAFAFIE 10 b.g. Kayf Tara – Florie (Alflora) (IRE) [2017/18 h102: h23.6s^5 h21.9v^3 h17.7v^{pu} h19.5v^{pu} Feb 2] modest handicap hurdler: stays 3m: acts on heavy going: races towards rear. *Susan Gardner*   **h97**

RAGGED DREAM (FR) 5 b.g. Ragmar (FR) – Birdream (FR) (Lucky Dream (FR)) [2017/18 b16.8m b16.8d^6 Sep 22] no form in bumpers: placed in points. *Jackie du Plessis*   **b–**

RAGGED WOOD (IRE) 6 b.g. Yeats (IRE) – She's All That (IRE) (Bob Back (USA)) [2017/18 b95: b16d^{pu} May 16] maiden pointer: fair form on bumper debut: went wrong and pulled up sole outing in 2017/18: dead. *Nigel Twiston-Davies*   **b–**

RAID STANE (IRE) 12 b.g. Morozov (USA) – Rashhattan (IRE) (Rashar (USA)) [2017/18 c–, h103: h21.2g^{pu} Apr 23] winning pointer: fair hurdler, pulled up sole start in 2017/18: maiden chaser: stays 3¼m: acts on good to firm and heavy going: wears headgear: has worn tongue tie. *Lucinda Egerton*   **c–**   **h–**

RAIFTEIRI (IRE) 11 b.g. Galileo (IRE) – Naziriya (FR) (Darshaan) [2017/18 c–x, h–: h16.2g^{pu} h16.2g h17.2g h20.2g h22.1s^4 h23.9d h22.1d^{ur} h20.2d^5 h20.9d h22.7g h16.2s h23.8g Nov 30] rather leggy gelding: winning hurdler/maiden chaser, no longer of much account: has worn headgear/tongue tie. *William Young Jnr*   **c– x**   **h–**

RAILROAD JUNKIE (IRE) 5 b.g. Thousand Words – Eckbeag (USA) (Trempolino (USA)) [2017/18 b17.7g^2 b16s Nov 12] €9,000 3-y-o: sturdy gelding: fourth foal: half-brother to bumper winner/fair hurdler Fourni (2m winner, by Rakti): dam, modest maiden hurdler, 1½m winner on Flat: fell both starts in points: fair form in bumpers: better effort when second at Fontwell in August: wears tongue tie. *Evan Williams*   **b86**

RAILWAY ICON (IRE) 11 b.g. Flemensfirth (USA) – Dorans Glen (Over The River (FR)) [2017/18 h25.4g^{pu} Jul 2] placed in points: fair hurdler, pulled up sole start under Rules in 2017/18: maiden chaser: stays 3m: acts on good to firm going. *Kevin Bishop*   **c–**   **h–**

RAILWAY STORM (IRE) 13 ch.g. Snurge – Stormy Bee (IRE) (Glacial Storm (USA)) [2017/18 c95, h–: c29.1m c25.8s^2 c25.8m^F c25.8s^4 Apr 23] tall gelding: point winner: maiden hurdler: modest handicap chaser: left Jimmy Frost after fourth start: stays 31f: acts on good to firm and heavy going: has worn cheekpieces/tongue tie. *C. White*   **c94**   **h–**

RAINBOW HAZE 12 b.g. Rainbow High – Kristal Haze (Krisinsky (USA)) [2017/18 c–, h90: h23m* h21.6s* h26.5d^{pu} Aug 22] multiple point winner: modest handicap hurdler: won at Worcester in May and Newton Abbot in June: maiden chaser: stays 3m: acts on good to firm and heavy going: tried in blinkers/tongue tie. *Phillip Dando*   **c–**   **h92**

RAINBOW LEGEND 5 b.g. Midnight Legend – Princess Rainbow (FR) (Raintrap) [2017/18 b17d b14s Jan 18] no form in bumpers. *Jennie Candlish*   **b–**

RAIN IN THE FACE 5 b.g. Naaqoos – Makaaseb (USA) (Pulpit (USA)) [2017/18 h–: h16.8g^{pu} c15.7v^6 c16.4v^{pu} Mar 23] fair at best on Flat, stays 1m: no form over hurdles/fences: tried in tongue tie. *Sam England*   **c–**   **h–**

RAINY CITY (IRE) 8 b.g. Kalanisi (IRE) – Erintante (IRE) (Denel (FR)) [2017/18 c126p, h133: c23.8g^2 c21.4g^2 h20.6g^6 h16.8g^6 h19.4g^4 h23.8d^5 c19.9s^2 c24.1v^{pu} c24.5d^2 c23.8s* Apr 25] lengthy, useful-looking gelding: fairly useful handicap hurdler: fairly useful handicap chaser: won novice event at Perth in April: left Paul Nicholls after third start: stays 3m: acts on firm and soft going: wears headgear: has worn blinkers: often races towards rear: temperamental. *Iain Jardine*   **c119 §**   **h117 §**

RAINY DAY DYLAN (IRE) 7 br.g. Spadoun (FR) – Honeyed (IRE) (Persian Mews) [2017/18 h95, b96: h16g^4 h20s^{pu} h16s h15.3v* h15.3v^4 h20.3v^2 h18.5v* Apr 17] workmanlike gelding: bumper winner: fairly useful handicap hurdler: won at Wincanton (novice) in January and Exeter in April: stays 2½m: best form on heavy going: often wears hood: usually wears tongue tie: front runner. *Neil Mulholland*   **h118**

RAISE A SPARK 8 b.g. Multiplex – Reem Two (Mtoto) [2017/18 h120: h16.2g^F h15.8d^6 Apr 9] fairly useful handicap hurdler: stays 2½m: acts on heavy going: wears hood. *Donald McCain*   **h122**

RAISED ON GRAZEON 7 ch.m. Lucky Story (USA) – Graze On And On (Elmaamul (USA)) [2017/18 b75: h16.0g^3 h15.6g^2 h15.7s* h16v^2 h16.4s* Mar 23] fairly useful hurdler: won mares novices at Catterick in January and Newcastle in February: unproven beyond 17f: acts on heavy going: usually travels strongly. *John Quinn*   **h120**

RAI

RAISING HOPE (IRE) 9 b.m. Turtle Island (IRE) – Jurado It Is (IRE) (Jurado (USA)) [2017/18 c–, h71: h21g⁴ h25.6d³ h21.6m* c25.8g² c22.6m⁵ c21.6g⁵ h23.4g^pu Nov 1] point winner: poor handicap hurdler: won mares event at Newton Abbot in June: similar form over fences: stays 3¼m: acts on soft and good to firm going: wears tongue tie. *Paul Henderson* c76 h75

RAISING THE BAR (IRE) 6 b.g. Kalanisi (IRE) – Cool Quest (IRE) (Turtle Island (IRE)) [2017/18 b79: b15.8g² May 29] rather unfurnished gelding: fair form in bumpers: second at Huntingdon on sole start in 2017/18: will be suited by 2½m. *Nicky Henderson* b89

RAJAPUR 5 gr.g. Dalakhani (IRE) – A Beautiful Mind (GER) (Winged Love (IRE)) [2017/18 h93: h16v⁴ h19.3v³ h21.3d h19.3v⁵ Apr 17] fair form over hurdles: stays 19f: acts on heavy going: wears cheekpieces. *David Thompson* h105

RAKAIA ROSA (IRE) 9 b.m. Balakheri (IRE) – Ashanti's Dream (IRE) (Right Win (IRE)) [2017/18 c19.8m* c20g³ c19.8g^pu c17g³ c23g⁶ c17.8d³ c15.7d⁵ c20g⁶ c20g⁴ c15.9m⁶ Nov 20] third foal: dam, pulled up both starts in points, half-sister to dam of smart chaser (best around 2m) Fix The Rib: maiden hurdler: modest handicap chaser: won mares event at Towcester in May: stays 2½m: acts on good to firm going: has worn headgear/ tongue tie: usually leads. *Dai Williams* c91 h–

RAKTIMAN (IRE) 11 ch.g. Rakti – Wish List (IRE) (Mujadil (USA)) [2017/18 c124, h–: c24.2d³ c25.2d^pu Nov 24] quite good-topped gelding: winning hurdler: fairly useful handicap chaser, well below form both starts in 2017/18: stays 3¼m: acts on good to firm and heavy going: has worn cheekpieces: wears tongue tie: often races towards rear. *Sam England* c83 h–

RALEAGH MOUNTAIN (IRE) 7 b.g. Mountain High (IRE) – Culmore Lady (IRE) (Insan (USA)) [2017/18 h87: c17.4g² c20.3g³ h18.7g⁵ Sep 9] modest form over hurdles: fair form over fences: better effort when second in novice handicap at Bangor in August: placed in points: unproven beyond 17f: acts on good to soft going: tried in cheekpieces: usually wears tongue tie. *Dan Skelton* c103 h–

RALLY 9 b.g. Rail Link – Waki Music (USA) (Miswaki (USA)) [2017/18 c32.5d^pu May 5] good-topped gelding: maiden pointer: winning hurdler: fairly useful form at best in chases, pulled up in hunter sole start in 2017/18: stays 3m: acts on soft and good to firm going: wears headgear/tongue tie: temperamental. *Mrs Jo Paynter* h– § c– §

RAMBLING QUEEN (IRE) 5 gr.m. Mastercraftsman (IRE) – Dos Lunas (IRE) (Galileo (IRE)) [2017/18 b–: b16.2g May 28] no form in bumpers/Flat maidens: tried in tongue tie. *Brian Rothwell* b–

RAMBLING RECTOR (FR) 6 ch.g. Bonbon Rose (FR) – Califea (FR) (Nikos) [2017/18 b–: h21.7s⁴ h23.6s^pu Mar 22] won Irish point on debut: fair form over hurdles: better effort when fourth in maiden at Hereford in January. *Warren Greatrex* h100

RAMBLING RIVER 7 b.g. Revoque (IRE) – Just Beth (Carlingford Castle) [2017/18 b16g Sep 18] well beaten in bumper. *Giuseppe Fierro* b–

RAMONEX (GER) 7 b.g. Saddex – Ramondia (GER) (Monsun (GER)) [2017/18 h107, b88: h17g² c16.2d⁵ c19.2d³ c19.2s* c21.6s² c24.1g c20d^pu Apr 28] workmanlike gelding: fairly useful form over hurdles: second in novice at Aintree in May: useful form over fences: won handicap at Catterick in January: stays 2¾m: acts on soft going: tried in cheekpieces/tongue tie: usually leads. *Richard Hobson* c130 h115

RAMORE WILL (IRE) 7 gr.g. Tikkanen (USA) – Gill Hall Lady (Silver Patriarch (IRE)) [2017/18 h96, b–: h18.7m³ h19.2m² h21.7g* c19.7m* c24g³ c18d⁴ c20d⁴ c19.7v³ c17v³ c19.7v^ur h20.5v* h21s* Apr 9] tall, angular gelding: fair handicap hurdler: won at Fontwell in August, and Plumpton (conditional) and Kempton in April: fair handicap chaser: won novice event at Plumpton in September: stays 3m: acts on good to firm and heavy going: wears headgear. *Chris Gordon* c107 h106

RAMSES DE TEILLEE (FR) 6 gr.g. Martaline – Princesse d'Orton (FR) (Saint Cyrien (FR)) [2017/18 h112: h19.2d³ h21.6v² h23.6d² c23.6v* c26v² c23.6v* c24.2v² c25s c20.8g Apr 18] leggy gelding: fairly useful maiden hurdler: placed first 3 starts in 2017/18: useful form over fences: won novice handicap at Chepstow in November and novice there (by 7 lengths from Rons Dream) in January: stays 3¼m: acts on heavy going: wears tongue tie: usually travels strongly. *David Pipe* c144 h119

RANCHER LASS (IRE) 7 gr.m. Tikkanen (USA) – Belledornie (IRE) (Buckskin (FR)) [2017/18 c21d^F c25d h19.8s c23.8g* c21.3s^F Mar 9] third foal: dam, winning pointer, half-sister to fairly useful hurdler/chaser (stayed 21f) Ajar: point winner: little form over c93 x h–

hurdles: modest handicap chaser: won at Musselburgh in December: stays 3m: best form on good going: has worn hood: wears tongue tie: often races towards rear: often let down by jumping. *Karl Thornton, Ireland*

RANDY PIKE (IRE) 8 b.g. Mahler – Niamh's Leader (IRE) (Supreme Leader) [2017/18 **h117** h19.7s h19.7d h16.8s h20.6s* h23.8s⁶ h21.2v^{pu} h18.9s* h22v³ h20.1d* Apr 23] has had breathing operation: fairly useful handicap hurdler: won at Market Rasen (novice) in December, Haydock (novice) in March and Hexham in April: stays 2¾m: acts on heavy going: in tongue tie last 3 starts. *Tim Easterby*

RAPANUI (IRE) 6 ch.g. Flemensfirth (USA) – Beautiful Night (FR) (Sleeping Car (FR)) **h–** [2017/18 h63: h25d^{pu} May 1] little form over hurdles: in headgear last 2 starts. *Jonjo O'Neill*

RAPID ESCAPE (IRE) 5 ch.g. Doyen (IRE) – Kenzie (IRE) (Presenting) [2017/18 **b113** b16s* b16s* b16v* b16s⁵ b16.3s⁴ Apr 25] €46,000 3-y-o, £240,000 4-y-o: seventh foal: closely related to fairly useful hurdler/chaser Nicolas Chauvin (winner around 2m, by Saffron Walden) and half-brother to a winning pointer by Gamut: dam unraced half-sister to useful hurdler/chaser (stayed 2½m) Chauvinist: won point by 10 lengths on debut: useful bumper performer: won at Down Royal (maiden) and Punchestown in November, and Navan (listed event, by 11 lengths from Lady Ischia) in December: fourth in Champion INH Flat Race at Punchestown (16 lengths behind Tornado Flyer) in April. *Gordon Elliott, Ireland*

RAPID FRITZ (IRE) 9 ch.g. Kutub (IRE) – Another Pet (IRE) (Un Desperado (FR)) **c–** [2017/18 h16.5g³ h16.5m² h16.5d h18.8g h16.2d^{pu} h16.2v⁵ h16.2v h16.2s⁶ c15.2d^F h16.4v **h90** h16.4v⁶ c16.4v^{pu} h16.8v⁵ c16.4v³ Apr 13] modest maiden hurdler: no form over fences: left Gerard Keane after second start, John G. Carr after fourth: best efforts around 2m: acts on soft and good to firm going: wears tongue tie: often races towards rear. *Victor Thompson*

RARE LEGEND (IRE) 11 b.g. Stowaway – Shambala (IRE) (Imperial Ballet (IRE)) **c82** [2017/18 h25d* h22.3s³ c30.7v^{pu} c19.7v⁵ h23.5v h24v Feb 11] winning pointer: modest **h95** handicap hurdler: won at Huntingdon in November: poor maiden chaser: stays 25f: acts on heavy going: wears cheekpieces: often races prominently. *John Joseph Hanlon, Ireland*

RASASEE (IRE) 5 gr.g. Rip Van Winkle (IRE) – Gleaming Silver (IRE) (Dalakhani **h107** (IRE)) [2017/18 h64: h15.9g³ h16.7g* h15.8m⁴ h19.2g h19m² h19.7g⁵ Nov 29] sturdy gelding: fair hurdler: won 3-runner novice at Market Rasen in June: stays 19f: acts on good to firm going: wears hood: often races towards rear. *Tim Vaughan*

RASHAAN (IRE) 6 ch.g. Manduro (GER) – Rayyana (IRE) (Rainbow Quest (USA)) **h144** [2017/18 h146: h16g* h16g h20g* h24.4g* Sep 1] useful hurdler: won minor events at Down Royal in June, Cork (by 2¼ lengths from Pique Sous) in July and Down Royal again in September: stays easy 3m: acts on good to firm and heavy going. *Colin Thomas Kidd, Ireland*

RASHEE (IRE) 6 gr.m. Daylami (IRE) – Celtic Angel (IRE) (Bob Back (USA)) [2017/18 **b85** b16.2g⁴ Nov 11] €6,500 4-y-o: rather leggy mare: seventh foal: half-sister to bumper winner/fair hurdler Hayes Princess (2m winner, by King's Theatre): dam of little account over hurdles: 7/2, some encouragement when fourth in mares bumper at Kelso (6 lengths behind Strike The Pose). *Stuart Crawford, Ireland*

RAT A TAT TAT 6 b.g. Getaway (GER) – Knock Down (IRE) (Oscar (IRE)) [2017/18 b–: **h–** h19g⁶ May 13] tailed off in bumper/novice hurdle: dead. *Tim Vaughan*

RATHCORMAC INN (IRE) 5 b.m. Flemensfirth (USA) – Tiarella (IRE) (Supreme **h–** Leader) [2017/18 h20d^{pu} Sep 29] third foal: dam (c118/h108), 2m-2½m hurdle/chase winner, half-sister to dam of smart hurdler/chaser (stayed 3m) Fox Appeal: pulled up in novice hurdle. *Dan Skelton*

RATHEALY (IRE) 7 b.g. Baltic King – Baltic Belle (IRE) (Redback) [2017/18 h106: **h–** h16g^{pu} Nov 1] rather leggy gelding: fair hurdler, pulled up sole start in 2017/18: stays 2½m: acts on heavy going: wears headgear/tongue tie: usually leads. *Christine Dunnett*

RATHER BE (IRE) 7 b.g. Oscar (IRE) – Irish Wedding (IRE) (Bob Back (USA)) **c152 p** [2017/18 h143: c16.1s* c17v^{ur} c16.3s* c20.4s² Mar 13] good-topped gelding: useful form **h–** over hurdles: smart form over fences: won novices at Towcester (by 19 lengths from War Sound) in December and Fakenham (by 17 lengths from Positively Dylan) in February: second in Close Brothers Novices' Handicap Chase at Cheltenham (head behind Mister Whitaker) in March: stays 2½m: acts on heavy going: tried in hood: front runner/races prominently: open to further improvement as a chaser. *Nicky Henderson*

National Hunt Challenge Cup, Cheltenham—a second win in the race for Mr Patrick Mullins as the ten-year-old Rathvinden (diamonds) gamely holds off the mare Ms Parfois

RATHLIN 13 b.g. Kayf Tara – Princess Timon (Terimon) [2017/18 c111, h–: c19.4d Nov 18] strong, deep-girthed gelding: has had breathing operation: winning hurdler: smart chaser at best, on downgrade nowadays: stays 2¾m: acts on good to firm and heavy going: often in cheekpieces: wears tongue tie: often races freely. *Micky Hammond*   c– h–

RATHLIN ROSE (IRE) 10 b.g. Bonbon Rose (FR) – A Plus Ma Puce (FR) (Turgeon (USA)) [2017/18 c136, h–: c27.7d³ c21.1v^{pu} c29.5v⁶ c26.7v^{pu} c24.2v* c24.2s² c23.8s* c21.1s^F c28.8d^{pu} Apr 28] good-topped gelding: winning hurdler: useful chaser: won Royal Artillery Gold Cup (Amateur Riders) at Sandown in February for second year running and veterans handicap at Ascot in March: stays 25f: acts on good to firm and heavy going: wears headgear. *David Pipe*   c131 h–

RATHVINDEN (IRE) 10 b.g. Heron Island (IRE) – Peggy Cullen (IRE) (Presenting) [2017/18 c–, h–: c19.5m² c25.1g* c18.2d* c20.5g³ c20v* c20v* c20s² c24s^{bd} c21s^{ur} c31.8s* c24.5s⁴ Apr 24] sturdy gelding: winning hurdler: smart chaser: won maiden at Wexford in July, novices at Galway (Grade 3, by 5 lengths from Potters Point) in August, Listowel in September and Tipperary (another Grade 3, by 18 lengths from Ask Nile) in October, and National Hunt Chase at Cheltenham (by ½ length from Ms Parfois, having hard race) in March: stays 4m: acts on good to firm and heavy going. *W. P. Mullins, Ireland*   c153 h–

RATIFY 14 br.g. Rakaposhi King – Sea Sky (Oats) [2017/18 c99, h–: c17d^{pu} c20.2v* c18.9s⁴ c19.9s* h16s* c19.9d⁴ Apr 24] sturdy, good-bodied gelding: fair handicap hurdler: won at Sandown (amateur) in March: fairly useful handicap chaser: won at Wincanton (amateur) in December, and Huntingdon in February and April: left Dai Burchell after first start: stays 25f: acts on heavy going: tried in visor: has worn tongue tie: usually leads. *Fergal O'Brien*   c117 h102

RAVENHILL ROAD (IRE) 7 ch.g. Exit To Nowhere (USA) – Zaffarella (IRE) (Zaffaran (USA)) [2017/18 b110: h16.8g* h16.6s³ h23.8s^{pu} Feb 4] won Irish maiden point on debut: useful bumper performer: fairly useful form over hurdles: won maiden at Sedgefield (impressively, by 23 lengths from Inniscastle Lad) in October: front runner/races prominently. *Brian Ellison*   h123

RAVENSDALE (IRE) 6 ch.g. Flemensfirth (USA) – Thunder Belle (IRE) (Glacial Storm (USA)) [2017/18 b15.7g² h18.9v* h15.7v⁴ Dec 30] third foal: dam maiden half-sister to top-class hurdler/very smart chaser (stayed 3¼m) Time For Rupert (by Flemensfirth): off   h116 b93 mark in Irish points at sixth attempt: shaped well when second in maiden bumper at Southwell (2 lengths behind Hidden Glen): fairly useful form over hurdles: won novice at Haydock in December. *Nigel Twiston-Davies*

RAVENS HILL (IRE) 5 ch.g. Raven's Pass (USA) – Sister Red (IRE) (Diamond Green (FR)) [2017/18 h108p: h16.8g* h15.8g* h17.2s⁵ c20s³ c17m³ c20g^pu c18.9s^F c15.9d² Mar 25] fair hurdler: won maiden at Sedgefield in May and novice at Uttoxeter in June: modest form over fences: left Dan Skelton after sixth start: unproven beyond 17f: acts on soft and good to firm going: tried in cheekpieces/tongue tie. *C. von der Recke, Germany* **c95 h110**

RAVEN'S TOWER (USA) 8 b.g. Raven's Pass (USA) – Tizdubai (USA) (Cee's Tizzy (USA)) [2017/18 c130, h119: h15.7g² h19.7s² h17.7d* h16.8s h16s h16.3s Mar 23] compact gelding: fairly useful handicap hurdler: won at Fontwell in November: useful chaser: stays 2½m: acts on good to firm and heavy going: tried in blinkers/tongue tie. *Ben Pauling* **c– h125**

RAVING BONKERS 5 ch.g. Notnowcato – Harriet's Girl (Choisir (AUS)) [2017/18 b15.7g* b15.7d⁵ Dec 19] second foal: half-brother to 7f winner Mallymkun (by Kheleyf): dam 6f-1m winner: modest form in bumpers: won maiden at Towcester in October. *Martin Keighley* **b84**

RAVISHED (IRE) 10 b.g. Oscar (IRE) – Fair Present (IRE) (Presenting) [2017/18 c19.9v⁵ c23.8s^pu c23.8d⁶ Apr 24] winning hurdler: useful chaser at best, below that level in 2017/18: stays 25f: acts on heavy going: has worn headgear: has worn tongue tie, including in 2017/18. *Charlie Longsdon* **c114 h–**

RAY'S THE MONEY (IRE) 4 b.g. Dragon Pulse (IRE) – Riymaisa (IRE) (Traditionally (USA)) [2017/18 h16s⁶ ab16d⁵ h16m^pu Apr 26] fairly useful but temperamental on Flat, stays 11f: folded quickly both starts over hurdles: tried in cheekpieces: has joined Amy Murphy. *Charlie Mann* **h–**

Mr R. A. Bartlett's "Rathvinden"

RAY

RAYVIN BLACK 9 b.g. Halling (USA) – Optimistic (Reprimand) [2017/18 c86p, h143: h16g[5] h19.7s[2] h15.8v[2] h20.3s c15.9s[2] c19.2v[ur] c20d* c20v[3] c20.2v* c20d[5] Apr 28] good-topped gelding: useful hurdler: second in handicap at Hereford (2 lengths behind Stamp Your Feet) in December: useful chaser: won small-field novices at Ludlow (by 4 lengths from Coastal Tiep) in February and Wincanton in April: stays 2½m: acts on good to firm and heavy going: usually wears headgear: usually leads. *Oliver Sherwood*   **c132 h130**

RAZ DE MAREE (FR) 13 ch.g. Shaanmer (IRE) – Diyala III (FR) (Quart de Vin (FR)) [2017/18 c141x, h118: c24s[F] c28s[2] h24d[2] c29.5v* c34.3s Apr 14]   **c144 x h118**

    Age is only a number. On the same day as a memorable final of the Veterans' Handicap Chase series at Sandown, two thirteen-year-olds filled the first two places in the rescheduled Coral Welsh National at Chepstow. For the winner Raz de Maree, a sprightly veteran of the long-distance chasing scene who had won two Cork Nationals and a Munster National in his time, the Welsh National represented the best win of his career. Runner-up to Native River in the race the previous season, Raz de Maree hadn't won since and, after a creditable second in the latest edition of the Cork National in November, he ran over hurdles on his only other appearance before Chepstow, finishing second (off a much lower mark than his chasing mark) to Red Rising at Southwell in early-December, confirming he was still in good heart. Chepstow's Christmas fixture was claimed by the weather after torrential rain left the course waterlogged and Raz de Maree and his groom Jenny Murphy had to spend Christmas Day at Chepstow after travelling over from Ireland on Christmas Eve (they returned home the day after Boxing Day).

    The Welsh National reverted to the original entries made back in November and a maximum field of twenty—the race shaping up much as the original—went to post for the rescheduled running on the first Saturday in January, the fourth time since the 2010/11 season that the race has had to be postponed until the New Year. Four inches of rain had fallen since Christmas Day and, although the Chepstow ground staff did really well to avoid the meeting being called off for a second time, the conditions for the Welsh National were demanding even by the usual traditions of the race. The raceday crowd was understandably smaller, the official attendance of 5,711 around half the number expected on the original date, but the race itself did not disappoint. Raz de Maree teamed up for the first time with Welsh-born sixteen-

Coral Welsh Grand National Handicap Chase, Chepstow—teenagers dominate in desperate conditions as James Bowen helps Raz de Maree (right) go one place better than twelve months earlier, fellow thirteen-year-old Alfie Spinner (cheekpieces) taking second

year-old James Bowen, a very promising 5-lb claimer (went on to be champion conditional) who had yet to have his first ride under Rules when Raz de Maree had finished runner-up twelve months earlier. Raz de Maree was sent off at 16/1 in a betting market in which only the gambled-on 7/1 favourite, the novice Vintage Clouds, and 9/1-shot Bishops Road, runner-up in the Rehearsal Chase at Newcastle, started at single-figure odds. Dual Scottish National winner Vicente was top weight, ahead of the penalised Rehearsal Chase winner Beware The Bear (a rare runner in the race for Nicky Henderson) and the Haydock winner Chase The Spud who had won the previous season's Midlands National. Final Nudge, still in with a chance when falling four out in that Midlands National, had just been touched off in the Badger Ales Trophy at Wincanton on his reappearance.

A furious early gallop made for a particularly attritional running of the Welsh National, in which, because of the conditions, a handful of fences had to be omitted (there were eighteen instead of the usual twenty-two). Raz de Maree was well back early on, his jockey reportedly thinking at one stage that the partnership would do well to get round, but he began to make headway from four out and passed the leader, the other teenager in the line-up Alfie Spinner, at the second last. Alfie Spinner had been in the firing line all the way and kept on well to finish clear second. Alfie Spinner's claiming rider dropped his whip as Raz de Maree challenged but it made no difference to the result, Raz de Maree winning by six lengths with Alfie Spinner nine lengths in front of third-placed Final Nudge, and Vintage Clouds far from disgraced in fourth, rallying after looking to be struggling approaching the home turn and then suffering interference four out. Only seven of the twenty completed the course. Raz de Maree, just three years younger than his jockey, was the oldest winner of the Welsh National since World War II (a thirteen-year-old won the race in 1927 when it was run at Cardiff). The only previous Welsh National winner who had been trained in Ireland was Notre Pere in 2008.

Raz de Maree (FR) (ch.g. 2005)	Shaanmer (IRE) (b 1999)	Darshaan (br 1981)	Shirley Heights / Delsy
		Fee des Mers (b 1991)	Alzao / Nordica
	Diyala III (FR) (b 1991)	Quart de Vin (b 1972)	Devon / Quartelette
		Judy (b 1975)	Laniste / Upsala III

The sturdy Raz de Maree was seen out only once after his Welsh National triumph, contesting his third Grand National at Aintree. He got round for the second time, though never landing a blow (reportedly found to be suffering from heat stress) before finishing tenth, two places lower than when also well held in 2014 (he was an unlucky early casualty in 2017). Raz de Maree's French sire Shaanmer was also represented in the latest Grand National field by the smart Tenor Nivernais. Raz de Maree's dam Diyala III, a maiden over fences who was placed twice in non-thoroughbred contests on the Flat in France, is a sister to the outstanding French chaser Ucello II, and his grandam Judy was a sister to the 1987 King George VI Chase winner Nupsala. When 25/1-shot Nupsala won the King George the letters (FR), denoting a French-bred, were rarely seen on jumps race cards in Britain and Ireland. Nupsala was trained by Francois Doumen and the successful challenge started a lucrative Boxing Day tradition for the trainer at Kempton, which eventually opened the floodgates for a booming cross-Channel trade in French jumpers.

Ucello II, also trained by Doumen, never raced in Britain but, along with stablemates Ubu III and The Fellow, dominated French steeplechasing in the 'nineties. All three were owned by the Marquesa de Moratalla—they became known as the three musketeers—and they won four editions of the Grand Steeple-Chase de Paris (a race all three won), two editions of the Grande Course de Haies and most of the other major events at Auteuil. In addition, The Fellow twice won the King George VI Chase and also took the Cheltenham Gold Cup (after two short-head defeats and a fourth in that race). The Marquesa de Moratalla died in November, aged eighty-seven, and she will be remembered in Britain mainly for her bold, unorthodox decision to campaign The Fellow in Britain's top races (she won a third King George with First Gold, another winner of the Grand Steeple-Chase de Paris). There was no finer advertisement for French-bred jumpers than The Fellow who left a legacy that is still yielding rich dividends for the jumping arm of the French breeding industry. The Marquesa, incidentally, also had horses trained in Britain by Jimmy FitzGerald at Malton, among them the notable performers Sybillin and Trainglot. Ucello II and Nupsala, like The Fellow and Ubu III, were both non-thoroughbred selle francais (French saddle-breds). The French saddle-breds and anglo-arabs are all registered simply as AQPS horses nowadays, the inclusive AQPS stud-book having rendered the other terms redundant. Raz de Maree, who was bought by his original trainer Dessie Hughes as a store for £16,000 at Doncaster Sales, is the best of his dam's offspring, though she also bred three other winners, the pick of them the fairly useful staying handicap chaser Latitude (by Kadalko) who is the dam of the useful chasers Casablanca Mix and Arkwrisht, winners for Nicky Henderson and Joseph O'Brien respectively in the latest season; the latter was challenging when badly hampered at the last in the Irish Grand National. Raz de Maree, who has worn headgear and has sometimes been let down by his jumping, stays very long distances and acts on heavy going. *Gavin Patrick Cromwell, Ireland*

R BREN (IRE) 5 b.m. Curtain Time (IRE) – Bramblehill Dream (Presenting) [2017/18 b16v b15.8v h18.5d⁶ Apr 24] €2,500 3-y-o: tenth foal: dam unraced half-sister to high-class chaser (stayed 3¼m) Senor El Betrutti: no form in bumpers/maiden hurdle. *Tracey Barfoot-Saunt* **h–** **b–**

READ'EM AND WEEP (IRE) 8 b.g. Kutub (IRE) – Amalita (IRE) (Brief Truce (USA)) [2017/18 h20.5s h20.5v h16v⁴ h20.5v^pu h16.8v^pu h16.4d h17d^ur h16.2s^F Apr 26] in frame completed start in Irish points: modest maiden hurdler: best effort at 2m: acts on heavy going: tried in cheekpieces. *R. Mike Smith* **h87**

READY AND ABLE (IRE) 5 b.g. Flemensfirth (USA) – Gypsy Mo Chara (IRE) (Oscar (IRE)) [2017/18 h16.7d⁴ h16.8s h16s⁶ h15.7s Dec 17] €115,000 3-y-o: third foal: brother to fair 2m hurdle winner Usurp: dam unraced half-sister to fair hurdler/fairly useful chaser (2m-2½m winner) Bohemian Lass: modest form over hurdles. *Jonjo O'Neill* **h95**

READY TOKEN (IRE) 10 gr.g. Flemensfirth (USA) – Ceol Tire (IRE) (Roselier (FR)) [2017/18 c125, h–: c23.9g h23.5d^pu c25.6s^bd c26.6s⁶ c23.9d⁶ Apr 22] workmanlike gelding: maiden hurdler: fairly useful handicap chaser, below best in 2017/18: stays 25f: acts on soft and good to firm going: has worn headgear: wears tongue tie: front runner/races prominently. *Charlie Longsdon* **c113** **h–**

REALLY SUPER 4 b.f. Cacique (IRE) – Sensationally (Montjeu (IRE)) [2017/18 h16g² h15.5d⁵ h17v^pu Dec 9] fairly useful maiden on Flat, stays 1¾m: modest form over hurdles: best effort when second in fillies juvenile at Fakenham in November. *Amy Murphy* **h90**

REAL MILAN (IRE) 13 b.g. Milan – The Real Athlete (IRE) (Presenting) [2017/18 c112, h–: c26.3d³ c23.8s² c23.9s^ur c26d² c23.8d² Mar 22] useful-looking gelding: multiple point winner: winning hurdler: fair hunter chaser: stays 25f: acts on heavy going: wears headgear: has worn tongue tie: signs of temperament. *Nick J. Jones* **c112** **h–**

REALMS OF FIRE 5 ch.g. Malinas (GER) – Realms of Gold (USA) (Gulch (USA)) [2017/18 b16d⁶ Apr 26] rather unfurnished gelding: half-brother to several winners, including fairly useful hurdlers Kenai Peninsula (19f-21f winner, by Tikkanen) and Board of Trade (21f winner, Black Sam Bellamy), latter also bumper winner: dam of little account on Flat: 14/1, sixth in bumper at Warwick (6 lengths behind Emitom): has joined Dan Skelton. *Alan King* **b87**

REAL STEEL (FR) 5 b.g. Loup Breton (IRE) – Kalimina (FR) (Monsun (GER)) [2017/18 h16s* h16s^F h16s⁵ h24v h20v^pu h20s⁴ Apr 27] rather unfurnished gelding: half-brother to French 2¼m hurdle winner Sunny Wells (by Falco): fairly useful maiden on Flat, stays 10.5f: useful hurdler: won maiden at Thurles in November: upsides but under pressure when fell last in Future Champions Novices' Hurdle at Leopardstown in December: likely to prove best at around 2m: acts on soft going. *W. P. Mullins, Ireland* **h136**

REAL WARRIOR (IRE) 7 b.g. Tikkanen (USA) – Muffin Top (IRE) (Synefos (USA)) [2017/18 h18.6d^pu c20.3v³ Feb 5] £15,000 6-y-o: third foal: dam, winning pointer, out of half-sister to useful staying chaser On The Other Hand: off mark in Irish points at fourth attempt: pulled up in novice on hurdling debut: 150/1, pulled hard when third in novice at Southwell (15½ lengths behind Two Swallows) on chasing debut. *Charles Pogson* **c112** **h–**

RED

REAPLEE 5 ch.g. Recharge (IRE) – Chant de L'Aube (FR) (Bon Sang (FR)) [2017/18 b15.6s ab16.3g Feb 24] no form in bumpers. *Chris Grant* — b–

REAR ADMIRAL (IRE) 12 b.g. Dushyantor (USA) – Ciaras Charm (IRE) (Phardante (FR)) [2017/18 c118§, h–: c20.1g* c19.3g^3 Apr 23] big, lengthy gelding: winning hurdler: fairly useful handicap chaser: won veterans event at Newcastle in November: stays 21f: acts on soft going: wears tongue tie: usually races nearer last than first: consistent, but irresolute. *Michael Easterby* — c121 § h–

REBEL BEAT 7 b.g. Lucarno (USA) – Callitwhatyalike (Tamure (IRE)) [2017/18 h94: h20g^4 h20g^4 h19.9s^{pu} h19.6s^{pu} Jan 26] modest maiden hurdler: left David Dennis after third start: probably stays 2½m: acts on good to soft going: tried in tongue tie: often races in rear. *Ian Williams* — h89

REBEL COLLINS (IRE) 7 gr.g. Jeremy (USA) – Million All Day (IRE) (Daylami (IRE)) [2017/18 h16s h15.9s h15.9v^5 h16.7v^2 h16.7s^2 h17.7g^4 Apr 20] angular gelding: fair form over hurdles: should stay beyond 17f: acts on heavy going: tried in cheekpieces: usually races nearer last than first. *Neil Mulholland* — h109

REBEL COMMANDER (IRE) 6 b.g. Flemensfirth (USA) – Pharney Fox (IRE) (Phardante (FR)) [2017/18 b–: b17.7g^2 b15.7d^2 b20.7s Feb 22] useful-looking gelding: fairly useful form in bumpers: best effort when second in conditionals/amateur event at Southwell in December: tailed off in maiden on hurdling debut. *Nicky Henderson* — h– b98

REBEL REBELLION (IRE) 13 b.g. Lord Americo – Tourmaline Girl (IRE) (Toulon) [2017/18 c122, h–: c20d* c25.8m* c27.5d^4 c23g^3 c24.1g^3 c25.5g^2 Aug 28] big, strong gelding: winning hurdler: fairly useful chaser: won hunters at Warwick and Newton Abbot in May: second in handicap chase at Cartmel in August: stays 3¼m: acts on good to firm and heavy going: has worn headgear, including in 2017/18: wears tongue tie: front runner/races prominently. *Paul Nicholls* — c125 h–

REBEL ROYAL (IRE) 5 b.g. Getaway (GER) – Molly Duffy (IRE) (Oscar (IRE)) [2017/18 b13.7s h19.4s h16m* Apr 20] €45,000 3-y-o: second foal: half-brother to bumper winner/winning pointer Monbeg Worldwide (by Lucarno): dam, unraced, out of half-sister to Champion Hurdle winners Morley Street and Granville Again: seventh in bumper at Huntingdon: fairly useful form over hurdles: won novice at Kempton in April: should stay beyond 2m: likely to progress further. *Dan Skelton* — h115 p b76

REBEL YEATS (IRE) 6 b.m. Yeats (IRE) – Sorivera (Irish River (FR)) [2017/18 h16d* h20.6g^2 h16.3m^2 h15.8d^2 h20g^4 h19g^4 h19.3g^5 h21.1s Nov 19] £26,000 4-y-o: workmanlike mare: closely related to smart hurdler/useful chaser Mossley (2m-3m winner, by Old Vic) and half-sister to several winners, including fairly useful hurdler Credo Star (2m-2½m winner, by Presenting): dam, useful German 6f-1m winner, half-sister to Irish Grand National winner Commanche Court: runner-up completed start in points: fairly useful hurdler: won mares maiden at Warwick in May and mares handicap there in September: stays 21f: acts on good to firm and good to soft going. *Ian Williams* — h115

REBOUND (IRE) 5 b.g. Big Bad Bob (IRE) – Shine Silently (IRE) (Bering) [2017/18 b94: b14s* Jan 18] fairly useful form in bumpers: tongue tied when won at Ludlow on sole start in 2017/18. *Anthony Honeyball* — b102

RECKLESS BEHAVIOUR (IRE) 6 b.g. Gold Well – Wee Wallis (Windsor Castle) [2017/18 h20g^6 h18.7m^3 h16.3g^2 h20.3d^5 h25g^4 h20.3v^6 h20.6v* h25d Apr 24] €10,000 3-y-o, £27,000 4-y-o: lengthy gelding: third foal: dam unraced half-sister to fair hurdler/useful chaser (stayed 4m) Leading Man: runner-up sole start in Irish point: fair handicap hurdler: won at Market Rasen in April: should be suited by 3m: acts on heavy going: usually races close up. *Caroline Bailey* — h112

RECOGNITION (IRE) 5 g.g. Rip Van Winkle (IRE) – Bali Breeze (IRE) (Common Grounds) [2017/18 h100: h15.8g^{pu} Jun 15] fair on Flat, stays 1½m: modest hurdler, pulled up sole start in sphere in 2017/18: unproven beyond 17f: best form on good going: sometimes wears cheekpieces. *Barry Murtagh* — h–

RED ADMIRABLE (IRE) 12 b.g. Shantou (USA) – Eimears Pet (IRE) (Lord Americo) [2017/18 c–x, h94: h19.9s^2 h23.9g* h24s^6 h20.7s* h25d Mar 26] modest handicap hurdler: won at Taunton in November and Huntingdon in February: winning chaser (often let down by jumping): stays 3m: acts on heavy going: wears cheekpieces/tongue tie: often races towards rear. *Graeme McPherson* — c– x h96

REDBRIDGE MILLER (IRE) 6 b.g. Milan – Definite Miller (IRE) (Definite Article) [2017/18 h100: h23m^3 May 11] placed in Irish maiden points: modest form over hurdles: stayed 19f: acted on good to firm going: tried in tongue tie: dead. *Chris Down* — h89

Mrs D. Thompson's "Redicean"

RED COSSACK (CAN) 7 ch.g. Rebellion – Locata (USA) (Stravinsky (USA)) [2017/18 h16g⁶ May 15] fair on Flat, stays 1¼m: in hood/tongue tie, tailed off in novice on hurdling debut. *Paul Webber*   **h–**

RED DANAHER (IRE) 11 ch.g. Shantou (USA) – Red Rover (Infantry) [2017/18 c20.1v⁴ c24.2d³ c26.3s² c25.2d⁵ h25.3s* h23.1v c20.3v⁴ h19.3v* h22.8s² c26.3v⁵ Apr 13] sturdy gelding: fair handicap hurdler: won at Catterick in January and conditionals/amateur event at Carlisle in March: modest maiden chaser: stays 25f: acts on heavy going: front runner/races prominently: temperamental. *Sue Smith*   **c89 §** / **h104 §**

RED DEVIL LADS (IRE) 9 b.g. Beneficial – Welsh Sitara (IRE) (Welsh Term) [2017/18 c–, h121: h24d⁶ h22.6v* h24s c28.7v c20d^pu Apr 9] useful handicap hurdler: won at Navan (by 2½ lengths from Glenloe) in November: useful chaser at best, let down by jumping both starts over fences in 2017/18: left Emmet Mullins after fourth start: stays 25f: acts on heavy going: wears hood: often wears tongue tie: front runner/races prominently. *Mrs Sherree Lean*   **c86 x** / **h132**

RED DEVIL STAR (IRE) 8 b.g. Beneficial – Gortbofearna (IRE) (Accordion) [2017/18 c121, h–: c20d c16d³ c15.5d² c18.8d⁶ c18.8v³ c17.2v* c17.4d³ Apr 21] lengthy gelding: winning hurdler: fairly useful handicap chaser: won at Market Rasen in April: stays 19f: acts on heavy going: wears tongue tie. *Suzy Smith*   **c123** / **h–**

REDDINGTON (IRE) 6 b.g. Getaway (GER) – Nikkis Alstar (IRE) (Fourstars Allstar (USA)) [2017/18 h57, b–: h18.5v^pu Nov 7] good-topped gelding: little form over hurdles. *Tim Vaughan*   **h–**

REDEMPTION SONG (IRE) 6 gr.m. Mastercraftsman (IRE) – Humilis (IRE) (Sadler's Wells (USA)) [2017/18 b100: h20.6g* h19.4d³ h21v³ h19.8v⁵ Feb 16] workmanlike mare: off mark in Irish points at second attempt: bumper winner: fair form over hurdles: won mares maiden at Market Rasen in November: will be suited by 2¾m+: tried in cheekpieces: usually races prominently. *Kevin Frost*   **h110**

RED

RED FOUR 8 ch.m. Singspiel (IRE) – Protectorate (Hector Protector (USA)) [2017/18 h16.2v[5] Apr 10] fairly useful hurdler at best, showed some ability remains on return from long absence in 2017/18: unproven beyond 17f: acts on good to firm and heavy going: often wears headgear. *Sarah-Jayne Davies*   **h94**

RED GIANT (IRE) 7 ch.g. Beneficial – Barrack Star (IRE) (Overbury (IRE)) [2017/18 c23g[5] c15.7g[6] c16g[5] c16d[6] c21.6g* c24.1d c23.9g Oct 21] €32,000 3-y-o: fourth foal: dam, unraced, out of half-sister to useful hurdler/chaser (stayed 19f) Crack On: fairly useful form over hurdles: fair handicap chaser: won at Kelso in September: left Noel Meade after first start: stays 25f: acts on soft going: has worn headgear. *Jennie Candlish*   **c105 h–**

RED HANRAHAN (IRE) 7 b.g. Yeats (IRE) – Monty's Sister (IRE) (Montelimar (USA)) [2017/18 h114p, h–§: c20g[2] c21m[5] c24.2s[2] Nov 21] sturdy gelding: winning hurdler: fairly useful form over fences: second in novice handicap at Warwick in May: stays 3m: acts on good to soft: tried in cheekpieces: wears tongue tie: often races towards rear: has joined Suzi Best: one to treat with caution. *Paul Nicholls*   **c123 § h– §**

RED HOT CHILLY (IRE) 5 ch.g. Frozen Power (IRE) – She's Got The Look (Sulamani (IRE)) [2017/18 h98: h16.3s Dec 20] rather leggy gelding: fairly useful on Flat, stays 1½m: lightly raced over hurdles. *Fergal O'Brien*   **h–**

RED HOUSE HILL (IRE) 8 b.g. Ad Valorem (USA) – Laetitia (IRE) (Priolo (USA)) [2017/18 h16dpu Oct 20] bumper winner: fair on Flat, stayed 15f: twice-raced over hurdles: dead. *Olly Murphy*   **h76**

REDICEAN 4 b.g. Medicean – Red Halo (IRE) (Galileo (IRE)) [2017/18 h16v* h16s* h16g* h16.8v[6] Mar 16] compact gelding: useful on Flat, stays 1¾m: useful form over hurdles: won juvenile events at Kempton in December and January, and Adonis Juvenile Hurdle there (by 7 lengths from Malaya) in February: sixth in Triumph Hurdle at Cheltenham. *Alan King*   **h141**

RED INCA 10 ch.g. Pivotal – Magicalmysterykate (USA) (Woodman (USA)) [2017/18 c16.3dpu May 5] close-coupled gelding: maiden pointer: winning hurdler: pulled up in hunter on chasing debut: raced around 2m: acts on heavy going: usually in cheekpieces: often wears tongue tie. *Con Rutledge*   **c– h–**

RED INDIAN 6 b.g. Sulamani (IRE) – Rafiya (Halling (USA)) [2017/18 h126, b86: h19g[2] h21.1s[3] h21s[3] h19.2s[2] h21.1s[6] h24.7s Apr 14] sturdy gelding: bumper winner: useful handicap hurdler: placed 4 times in 2017/18, including at Warwick in May and in Lanzarote Hurdle (2¾ lengths behind William Henry) at Kempton in January: stays 25f: acts on heavy going. *Ben Pauling*   **h136**

RED INFANTRY (IRE) 8 ch.g. Indian River (FR) – Red Rover (Infantry) [2017/18 h114: c23.9g[4] c24.7d[3] c24d[3] c24s* c25.2s[2] c24v* c25.3gF Apr 18] stocky gelding: fairly useful handicap hurdler: third at Aintree (conditional) in October: fairly useful form over fences: won novice handicaps at Doncaster in January and Warwick in March: stays 25f: acts on heavy going: usually wears headgear: front runner/races prominently. *Ian Williams*   **c126 h116**

REDKALANI (IRE) 10 b.g. Ashkalani (IRE) – La Femme En Rouge (Slip Anchor) [2017/18 c–, h102: h22.7g[5] May 10] tall gelding: fair handicap hurdler, well held sole start in 2017/18: maiden chaser: stays 25f: acts on heavy going: often wears blinkers: front runner/races prominently. *Gillian Boanas*   **c– h67**

REDMOND (IRE) 8 b.g. Tikkanen (USA) – Medal Quest (FR) (Medaaly) [2017/18 c89p, h84: c25.6s[2] c21.6v[2] c22.7v[3] c21.7m[3] Apr 25] rangy gelding: maiden hurdler: modest form over fences: won handicap at Fontwell in February: stays 3¼m: acts on good to firm and heavy going: tried in blinkers: often wears tongue tie. *Jack R. Barber*   **c98 h–**

RED OCHRE 5 b.g. Virtual – Red Hibiscus (Manduro (GER)) [2017/18 b87: h16.4g h16.8s[5] h16.8s[3] h19.7s[6] h16.8v[3] h15.7s[5] h16.7s[2] Mar 26] fair maiden hurdler: should stay at least 2½m: acts on heavy going. *Chris Grant*   **h103**

RED PENNY (IRE) 11 b.m. Definite Article – Hurricane Dawn (IRE) (Strong Gale) [2017/18 c103, h–: c19.5s[4] Apr 6] winning pointer: maiden hurdler: fair maiden chaser, well held sole start in 2017/18: stays 3¼m: acts on good to firm and heavy going: tried in tongue tie. *Jimmy Frost*   **c– h–**

RED RISING (IRE) 7 ch.g. Flemensfirth (USA) – Fugal Maid (IRE) (Winged Love (IRE)) [2017/18 h125p: h23.6s[3] h24d* h24s[2] h24.1v* h22.8vpu Mar 31] well-made gelding: off mark in Irish maiden points at second attempt: useful form over hurdles: won handicaps at Southwell in December and Wetherby (by 7 lengths from Bryden Boy) in February: sure to stay long distances: acts on heavy going: often races prominently. *Dan Skelton*   **h134**

*Keltbray Swinley Chase (Limited Handicap), Ascot—
another valuable Ascot prize for Regal Encore (hoops) who swoops late to catch Minella Daddy*

RED RIVER (IRE) 5 ch.g. Beneficial – Socker Toppen (IRE) (Great Palm (USA)) **h139 p**
[2017/18 h21.4g* h19.8s³ h23.8s* Feb 4] €16,500 3-y-o, £58,000 4-y-o: rangy gelding: has had breathing operation: second foal: dam, maiden pointer, out of half-sister to useful hurdler/winning chaser (stayed 3m) Big Strand: runner-up on sole outing in Irish points: useful form over hurdles: won novices at Wincanton in October and Musselburgh (by 2¼ lengths from Mr Whipped, despite bad mistake last) in February: in tongue tie last 2 starts: should improve further. *Kim Bailey*

RED RIVERMAN 10 b.g. Haafhd – Mocca (IRE) (Sri Pekan (USA)) [2017/18 c17.3g² **c122** c16g* c17g* c19.2g³ c19.4s² c16.3g⁵ c16.4s² Dec 20] lengthy gelding: winning hurdler: **h–** fairly useful handicap chaser: won at Uttoxeter and Stratford in July: stays 19f: acts on good to firm and heavy going: wears headgear. *Nigel Twiston-Davies*

RED SPINNER (IRE) 8 b.g. Redback – Massalia (IRE) (Montjeu (IRE)) [2017/18 c140, **c128** h–: c20.1d² Aug 2] sturdy gelding: winning hurdler: useful handicap chaser: stays 2½m: **h–** acts on good to firm and heavy going: tried in cheekpieces. *Kim Bailey*

RED SQUARE REVIVAL (IRE) 7 b.g. Presenting – Alder Flower (IRE) (Alderbrook) **c107** [2017/18 h83, b96: c25.8g⁵ c20g³ c25.1s³ c19.7d* c22.7m⁴ c20g* Dec 6] bumper winner: **h–** poor form over hurdles: fair form over fences: won handicap at Plumpton in November and novice handicap at Ludlow in December: seems best at around 2½m: acts on good to soft going: wears headgear/tongue tie: front runner/races prominently. *David Pipe*

RED TORNADO (FR) 6 ch.g. Dr Fong (USA) – Encircle (USA) (Spinning World **h127** (USA)) [2017/18 h133: h15.7m h16g³ h16.3g h16.7g² h16.7g h16.5m⁴ h20.3g Apr 18] smallish, good-bodied gelding: fairly useful handicap hurdler: second in Summer Hurdle at Market Rasen in July: raced mainly around 2m: acts on soft and good to firm going. *Dan Skelton*

RED TORTUE (IRE) 9 b.g. Turtle Island (IRE) – Howrwedoin (IRE) (Flemensfirth **c64** (USA)) [2017/18 c–, h–: h19s⁵ h24s^pu h19.9s⁵ c19.1s c15.9v³ Feb 15] sturdy gelding: point **h64** winner: fair hurdler at best, little form in 2017/18: poor form over fences: stays 2½m: acts on heavy going: often wears cheekpieces: tried in tongue tie: usually leads. *Jennie Candlish*

RED WHISPER 14 ch.g. Midnight Legend – Secret Whisper (Infantry) [2017/18 c–§, h–: **c– §** c16.1g^pu May 22] modest hurdler/chaser at best, no form for long while: tried in **h–** cheekpieces: wears tongue tie: temperamental. *Rob Summers*

662

REELINGINTHEYEARS (IRE) 6 b.g. Flemensfirth (USA) – Savitha (IRE) (King's Theatre (IRE)) [2017/18 b16.7g h16.3v² h16v⁶ h19.5v* h21.4v⁴ Apr 9] €55,000 3-y-o: third foal: half-brother to bumper winner Presavita (by Presenting): dam (c124/h126) 2m/2¼m hurdle/chase winner: no form in bumpers: fair form over hurdles: won maiden at Chepstow in March: left Paul Nolan after third start: often travels strongly. *Emma Lavelle* — h110 b–

REFUSED A NAME 11 b.g. Montjeu (IRE) – Dixielake (IRE) (Lake Coniston (IRE)) [2017/18 c99, h–: c20vᵖᵘ c19.4vᵖᵘ Jan 19] maiden hurdler: modest chaser at best, pulled up both starts in 2017/18: stays 21f: acts on heavy going: wears headgear/tongue tie. *Kevin Bishop* — c– h–

REGAL ENCORE (IRE) 10 b.g. King's Theatre (IRE) – Go On Eileen (IRE) (Bob Back (USA)) [2017/18 c147, h–: c23.8g c26g³ c23.8dᵖᵘ c23.8s* c28.8dᵖᵘ Apr 28] compact gelding: winning hurdler: smart handicap chaser: won listed event at Ascot (by 1½ lengths from Minella Daddy) in February: pulled up in bet365 Gold Cup in April: stays 3¼m: acts on soft going: has worn hood: often wears tongue tie: usually races towards rear: unreliable. *Anthony Honeyball* — c152 § h–

REGAL FLOW 11 b.g. Erhaab (USA) – Flow (Over The River (FR)) [2017/18 c123, h–: c25g³ c25d c25.1v* c25.2s² c28.4v* c34v* c31.8g Apr 21] sturdy gelding: winning hurdler: useful handicap chaser: won at Wincanton in December, and at Taunton and Uttoxeter (Midlands Grand National, by 10 lengths from Milansbar) in March: stays 4¼m: acts on any going: tried in cheekpieces: often travels strongly. *Bob Buckler* — c139 h–

REGARDING RUTH (IRE) 4 b.f. Flemensfirth (USA) – May's June (IRE) (Oscar (IRE)) [2017/18 b16.7s³ b15.7v Apr 27] £12,000 3-y-o: first foal: dam unraced half-sister to useful hurdler/chaser (stays 3m) Fagan and useful chaser (stayed 25f) Creevytennant: fair form in bumpers: better effort when third in mares maiden at Market Rasen in March. *Lucy Wadham* — b88

REGGIE B 5 ch.g. Midshipman – Dot Up (Weld) [2017/18 b16d Apr 26] workmanlike gelding: tailed off in bumper. *Roy Brotherton* — b–

REGISTAN (IRE) 6 b.g. Darsi (FR) – Hannabelle (IRE) (Rudimentary (USA)) [2017/18 b–: h20.2gᵖᵘ May 17] no impact in bumper/maiden hurdle: wears tongue tie. *George Charlton* — h–

REGULATION (IRE) 9 br.g. Danehill Dancer (IRE) – Source of Life (IRE) (Fasliyev (USA)) [2017/18 h124: h19.9g³ h18.6g⁴ h18.5g⁶ h15.9m⁴ h16m* Apr 26] fairly useful handicap hurdler: won at Kempton (conditional) in April: unproven beyond 17f: acts on good to firm and good to soft going: sometimes wears headgear: often races freely. *Neil King* — h119

REIGNING SUPREME (IRE) 7 b.g. Presenting – Gli Gli (IRE) (Supreme Leader) [2017/18 h128p; c20.5dᵘʳ c23.4v² c31.8sᵖᵘ Mar 13] strong gelding: fairly useful form over hurdles: useful form when second in novice handicap at Newbury (12 lengths behind Indy Five) on completed start over fences: stays 23f: acts on heavy going. *Nicky Henderson* — c132 h–

REIKERS ISLAND (IRE) 5 b.g. Yeats (IRE) – Moricana (GER) (Konigsstuhl (GER)) [2017/18 h18.5sᶠ h21.7s* h24.6s⁵ Apr 9] €28,000 3-y-o, £60,000 4-y-o: closely related to modest hurdler Mexican Border (17f winner, by Sholokhov) and half-brother to numerous winners, including hurdler Modesto (winner up to 21f in Europe, by Platini): dam German 9.5f/1¼m winner: off mark at fourth attempt in Irish points: fair form over hurdles: won novice at Fontwell in March. *Philip Hobbs* — h114

*Betfred Midlands Grand National Handicap Chase, Uttoxeter—
the much improved Regal Flow records a wide-margin win over 2016 runner-up Milansbar*

REI

REILLY'S MINOR (IRE) 7 b.g. Westerner – Ringzar (IRE) (Shernazar) [2017/18 h114: h20g⁶ c23gᵘʳ c24d⁵ c19.4m⁶ c19.4g⁴ Sep 9] sturdy gelding: late faller (looked likely winner) in Irish maiden point on debut: fair handicap hurdler: poor form in chases: stays 25f: acts on soft going: wears headgear: front runner/races prominently. *Warren Greatrex*   **c75 h103**

REINE DES MIRACLES 5 br.m. Poet's Voice – Cheerleader (Singspiel (IRE)) [2017/18 b81: h16g h16g h16.5g h24.4sᵖᵘ Jan 9] smallish mare: modest form in bumpers: no form over hurdles: modest maiden on Flat: in tongue tie last 2 starts: usually races towards rear. *Jonjo O'Neill*   **h–**

REIVERS LODGE 6 b.m. Black Sam Bellamy (IRE) – Crystal Princess (IRE) (Definite Article) [2017/18 b–: h16.2g² h20.2g h16.7g⁵ h18.6gᵖᵘ h20.1d⁵ h16.2d² h16.2v³ h20.9d² h22.7g* h24.3v³ h24.6s⁵ h20.6s⁴ h18.9v h22.7v⁵ h20.2s⁴ Apr 26] modest handicap hurdler: won at Kelso (conditional) in October: stays 3m: acts on heavy going: wears hood/tongue tie: often races towards rear/travels strongly. *Susan Corbett*   **h99**

REJAAH 6 b.m. Authorized (IRE) – Dhan Dhana (IRE) (Dubawi (IRE)) [2017/18 c114, h128: h19s h18.5s⁶ h20.3g* Apr 19] fairly useful handicap hurdler: won listed mares event at Cheltenham (by ½ length from Whatzdjazz) in April: fair form over fences: stays 2½m: acts on good to firm and good to soft going: wears tongue tie. *Nigel Hawke*   **c– h126**

RELEGATE (IRE) 5 b.m. Flemensfirth (USA) – Last of The Bunch (Silver Patriarch (IRE)) [2017/18 b16v* b16s* b16.4s* b16.3s Apr 25]   **b116**

Willie Mullins could have been forgiven for thinking he'd unwittingly walked under a ladder on the way to the weighing room before the SalesSense International Novices' Hurdle on the fourth day of the Punchestown Festival. Noel Fehily, the jockey originally booked for Antey (one of three Mullins-trained runners in a seventeen-strong field), had suffered a neck fracture in a fall earlier on the card, and a subsequent spill for first-choice replacement Danny Mullins (the trainer's nephew) had led to his joining Fehily in hospital. The trainer then searched for Rachael Blackmore, only to be told that she had been sent to hospital too, albeit to keep another injured rider company. Mullins eventually booked leading amateur Katie Walsh (youngest sister of the trainer's stable jockey Ruby) with just minutes to spare. She has developed a reputation as something of a 'super sub' for the Closutton yard over the years and was on the up-and-coming Antey for the first time in public. Walsh made the most of her opportunity, swooping late on the outside as Antey got up in the dying strides to land the €15,375 first prize by a neck. It turned out to be the final time Mullins would be able to call on the services of Walsh who announced her retirement from the saddle immediately after the race. 'It's been on my mind, but I just wanted to go out on a winner, and I had decided that whenever I rode the next winner that that would be it,' the thirty-three-year-old explained afterwards, adding that children are likely to feature as part of the 'next chapter' for her and husband Ross O'Sullivan, himself a trainer. Irish racing lost another of its star names to retirement less than twenty-four hours later when Walsh's sister-in-law Nina Carberry (who had only returned to the saddle in September after the birth of her first child Rosie) bowed out after partnering Josies Orders to victory in a cross-country chase. 'I think either way I would have stopped today. Today was the day and it was just nice to have Josie bring me home in front,' Carberry revealed afterwards.

The now-retired duo have been at the forefront of raising the profile of female jumps jockeys, particularly with the betting public. Walsh, for example, twice partnered the favourite for the Grand National, while Carberry had a strong following with punters on short-priced runners in bumpers, races which are still confined to amateurs in Ireland. The careers of Ms Walsh and Miss Carberry were closely matched long before they became related (Carberry married Walsh's other brother Ted Jr in 2012). Walsh's father Ted was champion amateur in Ireland eleven times in his riding days and has also enjoyed big-race highlights as a trainer, notably Papillon's win (under Ruby) in the 2000 Grand National and Katie's third on Seabass in the same race twelve years later. Carberry is also the daughter of a Grand National-winning trainer in Tommy Carberry, who died at the age of seventy-five in July 2017, a month after one of his sons Philip (now based in France) had himself retired from the saddle—another of Carberry's sons Paul (twice Irish champion and rider of the family's 1999 Grand National winner Bobbyjo) had hung up his boots in the summer of 2016. Paul, Philip and Nina Carberry all emulated their father by winning the Irish Grand National in their riding days, the most recent of those successes coming in 2011 when Nina partnered Organisedconfusion (trained by her uncle Arthur Moore). Katie Walsh also won the Easter Monday showpiece, her win aboard 20/1-shot Thunder And Roses in 2015 proving to be the biggest success of her career—fifteen years after her father and brother had teamed up to win the same race with Commanche Court. Ruby Walsh has enjoyed plenty of other high profile wins and has won twelve Irish jockeys titles, and is also the most successful jockey in Cheltenham Festival history, two wins at the latest meeting taking his tally to fifty-six. He was forced to miss his intended mount on Carefully Selected in the latest renewal of the Weatherbys Champion Bumper, however, which deprived the Welsh family of a famous one, two as that horse filled the runner-up spot behind his sister's mount Relegate.

Relegate and Carefully Selected were part of a five-strong challenge from the Willie Mullins stable, which has now won the Champion Bumper for a remarkable nine times, the Mullins quintet filling five of the first seven places in the latest edition, an ominous sign for rival trainers with their eyes on the novice hurdling ranks for 2018/19. As the jockey bookings suggested, the mare Relegate wasn't the Mullins stable's first string—she was actually fourth choice of the Mullins runners in the betting, though odds of 25/1 clearly underestimated her chance. Walsh had previous experience of riding Relegate in the Grade 2 Coolmore NH Sires Irish EBF Mares INH Flat Race at Leopardstown in February, when she provided her stable with its seventh and final winner at the inaugural two-day Dublin Racing Festival. Despite having created a good impression when winning a mares maiden at Punchestown on her debut the previous month, Relegate started at 16/1 behind odds-on stable-companion Colreevy. In the race itself, Relegate could be named the winner some way out, with the Nina Carberry-ridden Getaway Katie Mai emerging as the biggest threat in the end. Relegate had a length and a half to spare at the line, with Colreevy a further two and a half lengths away in third, that trio pulling fifteen lengths clear of the remainder. The form of the race worked out very well, with Getaway Katie Mai winning the Grade 2 Nickel Coin Mares' National Hunt Flat Race at Aintree on her only subsequent start, while the next two home Colreevy and Tintangle also went on to land good bumper prizes (Grade 3 and listed company respectively). Relegate did her own bit for the form on the biggest stage of all, coming from much further back than at Leopardstown and producing a remarkably strong finish. She was still only fourteenth with just over a furlong to run and, despite drifting left under pressure (which she had also done at Leopardstown), managed to

Coolmore NH Sires Irish European Breeders Fund Mares INH Flat, Leopardstown—
Ms Katie Walsh drives home Relegate (No.6) to beat sister-in-law Miss Nina Carberry aboard
Getaway Katie Mai in what was to prove the final season in the saddle for both

Weatherbys Champion Bumper, Cheltenham—a third Festival winner for Ms Katie Walsh as Relegate (star on cap) swoops late to deny stable-companion Carefully Selected

reel in the enterprisingly-ridden Carefully Selected (with Danny Mullins deputising for Ruby Walsh) close home. Katie Walsh's riding of Relegate attracted the attention of the Cheltenham stewards who banned her for six days for using her whip in an incorrect place. Relegate was a third Cheltenham Festival win for Walsh, eight years after her double on Poker de Sivola in the National Hunt Chase (which she won from the Nina Carberry-ridden Becauseicouldntsee, both jockeys incurring whip bans on that occasion) and Thousand Stars in the County Hurdle. The fact that Carefully Selected was ridden in starkly contrasting fashion to Relegate suggests that tactics played no significant role in the result of the Champion Bumper and Relegate was a worthy winner of a competitive, if not vintage, renewal (just over fifteen lengths covered the first dozen home). Relegate came a disappointing seventh behind stable-companion Tornado Flyer (third at Cheltenham) in Punchestown's Grade 1 bumper on her only subsequent outing, the fact that she finished behind four horses she had beaten previously underlining that she clearly didn't give her running.

Relegate (IRE) (b.m. 2013)
- Flemensfirth (USA) (b 1992)
  - Alleged (b 1974): Hoist The Flag / Princess Pout
  - Etheldreda (ch 1985): Diesis / Royal Bund
- Last of The Bunch (ch 2005)
  - Silver Patriarch (gr 1994): Saddlers' Hall / Early Rising
  - Elegant City (ch 1994): Scallywag / City's Sister

Like Walsh and Carberry, Relegate is also a member of a very successful jumping family. She is the first foal of Last of The Bunch, a bumper winner and dual winning hurdler who showed fair form at up to three miles, being a sister to two winners including the listed bumper winner Funny Games who is now a broodmare too and the dam of the fairly useful winning two and a half mile hurdler Flementime (by Relegate's sire Flemensfirth). Relegate's grandam Elegant City was also successful in bumpers and over hurdles during a brief racing career, the decision to fast track her to the paddocks no doubt influenced by the fact that she is a sister to the smart staying hurdler/useful chaser Better Times Ahead, who showed versatility and durability in equal measure to win twenty-three races for Gordon and Nicky Richards during a terrific career. Relegate's great grandam City's Sister was a winner at up to thirteen furlongs on the Flat, but is perhaps best known for being a half-sister to the smart above-average jumps mare in Another City who showed useful form at up to three miles for Gordon Richards in the mid-'eighties. All of which made Relegate look well bought for €35,000 as a three-year-old, having previously changed hands for €10,000 as a foal and €14,000 as a yearling. Relegate's exploits on the track in the interim presumably helped to take the bidding to €100,000 when her three-year-old brother (as yet unnamed) went under the hammer at the Derby Sale in June. Their four-year-old half-brother Glenduff (by Gold Well) has yet to reach the racecourse, while Last of The Bunch has since visited Ocovango three times, producing two fillies (in 2016 and 2018) and a colt (2017).

The compact Relegate will clearly make a promising broodmare herself in time, though the enhanced programme for mares over both hurdles and fences suggests that she will be extending her racing career for a while longer yet. It is to be hoped she enjoys more luck than the previous Champion Bumper winners of her sex. The 2017 winner Fayonagh suffered a fatal injury on the gallops in late-October after opening her account over hurdles earlier in the month, while the 2004 winner Total Enjoyment had to be put down after developing laminitis at the end of an injury-curtailed novice hurdling campaign (won once from three starts). The 1994 winner Mucklemeg had just two starts over hurdles (placed in Grade 2 novice company) and died after producing only one foal (which never ran). As things stand, Relegate holds a lofty position in Closutton's sizeable collection of novice hurdle hopefuls for the next season, when it would be no surprise to see Mullins turn to the aforementioned Rachael Blackmore should he have a multiple entry in a big race. Ireland's new female riding star Blackmore is already developing her own 'super sub' reputation, having landed three valuable handicaps for Mullins in the second half of the latest season, notably the Ballymore Handicap Hurdle at Punchestown just twenty-four hours after Katie Walsh's retirement. *W. P. Mullins, Ireland*

RELENTLESS DREAMER (IRE) 9 br.g. Kayf Tara – Full of Elegance (FR) (Cadoudal (FR)) [2017/18 c133, h–: c23.6d^6 c25.1s^{pu} c25.6g^2 c23.8d* c23s^6 c32.8s^3 c24g^6 c28.8d^4 Apr 28] tall gelding: winning hurdler: useful handicap chaser: won at Ludlow (by neck from Marcilhac) in December: stays 3¼m: acts on good to firm and heavy going: wears headgear/tongue tie: often races towards rear. *Rebecca Curtis* c137
h–

RELIGHT THE FIRE 7 ch.g. Firebreak – Alula (In The Wings) [2017/18 h–: h15.8d h16d^5 Apr 7] placed in bumpers: no form over hurdles: tried in cheekpieces/tongue tie. *Denis Quinn* h–

REMASTERED 5 ch.g. Network (GER) – Cathodine Cayras (FR) (Martaline) [2017/18 b16s^2 b16v* Feb 2] first foal: dam (c120/h120), French 2½m chase winner, sister to smart hurdler/chaser (winner up to 2½m) Le Vent d'Antan: fairly useful form in bumpers: won at Chepstow in February: left Miss Elizabeth Doyle after first start. *David Pipe* b102

REMEMBER FOREVER (IRE) 8 b.g. Indian River (FR) – Running Wild (IRE) (Anshan) [2017/18 c93, h73: c19.7d^4 c20d^5 c20.2g^3 c19.7s^3 Apr 15] lengthy gelding: maiden hurdler: modest handicap chaser, below form in 2017/18: stays 2½m: acts on good to firm and heavy going: usually leads. *Richard Rowe* c76
h–

REMEMBER ME WELL (IRE) 5 b.m. Doyen (IRE) – Creidim (IRE) (Erins Isle) [2017/18 b17.7s^6 h17.7v^{pu} h20.7g Apr 24] sturdy mare: closely related to fairly useful chaser Fight Commander (3m winner, by Oscar), stays 29f: dam (h80), maiden hurdler, 1m-9.5f winner on Flat: tailed off in bumper: no form over hurdles. *Richard Rowe* h–
b–

REMILUC (FR) 9 b.g. Mister Sacha (FR) – Markene de Durtal (FR) (Sharken (FR)) [2017/18 c120+, h135: h19.2g^4 h15.8^{sur} h17.7d^3 h20.5d^2 h16.8s^2 c16.4v^2 h16.8v* h16.3v^5 h19.5v^2 h16.8v^2 h15.9v^{ur} Apr 1] strong gelding: smart handicap hurdler: won at Cheltenham (by 2 lengths from Huntsman Son) in January; second in County Hurdle there (2¾ lengths behind Mohaayed) in March: useful form over fences: second in novice handicap at Newbury (9 lengths behind Saint Calvados) in December: stays 21f: acts on heavy going: usually wears tongue tie: usually races prominently. *Chris Gordon* c131
h147

REMIND ME LATER (IRE) 9 b.g. Zerpour (IRE) – Two T'three Weeks (Silver Patriarch (IRE)) [2017/18 c118, h–: c17.4d^2 c17.4m^2 c19.5g^5 c23g* c23.8d^3 c21.4v^2 c24m^2 Apr 26] sturdy gelding: winning hurdler: fairly useful handicap chaser: won novice event at Worcester in October: stays 3m: acts on any going: usually races towards rear/travels strongly. *Gary Moore* c126
h–

RENARD (FR) 13 b.g. Discover d'Auteuil (FR) – Kirmelia (FR) (Chamberlin (FR)) [2017/18 c117, h–: c25.5d^5 c24.2v^3 c23.6v^4 Apr 14] good-topped gelding: winning hurdler: fairly useful chaser: third in Royal Artillery Gold Cup (Amateur Riders) at Sandown in February: stays 3¼m: acts on good to firm and heavy going: wears headgear: usually leads. *Venetia Williams* c115
h–

RENDEZVOUS PEAK 9 b.g. High-Rise (IRE) – Jurado Park (IRE) (Jurado (USA)) [2017/18 c16g^2 Aug 1] winning hurdler: fair form in chases: won twice in points soon after end of season: stays 3m: acts on soft going: usually wears hood. *Gordon Elliott, Ireland*   c105 h–

RENE'S GIRL (IRE) 8 b.m. Presenting – Brogella (IRE) (King's Theatre (IRE)) [2017/18 h127: h25g^2 h20g^F c20f* c17.4s^3 c20.5s* c19.9s* c19.9s^2 Apr 12] tall mare: fairly useful handicap hurdler: second at Warwick in May: useful form over fences: won mares novice at Worcester in October, and listed mares events at Doncaster (by 10 lengths from Song Saa) in January and Huntingdon (by 2 lengths from Happy Diva) in February: second in Manifesto Novices' Chase at Aintree (2 lengths behind Finian's Oscar) in April: stays 25f: acts on any going: usually leads/travels strongly: sound jumper. *Dan Skelton*   c144 h128

RENEWING 7 b.g. Halling (USA) – Electric Society (IRE) (Law Society (USA)) [2017/18 h97: h20g^6 h23g^5 Jun 14] sturdy gelding: modest maiden hurdler, below form both starts in 2017/18: stays 23f: acts on good to soft going: wears headgear: one to treat with caution. *Roy Brotherton*   h78 §

RENWICK (IRE) 5 b.g. Milan – Come In Moscow (IRE) (Over The River (FR)) [2017/18 b16s^6 Feb 9] €140,000 3-y-o: fifth foal: half-brother to fair chaser Wood Pigeon (21f winner, by Presenting), stays 25f: dam (c112/h89), 2m-2½m hurdle/chase winner, half-sister to dam of smart chaser (stayed 3m) Rolling Aces: 8/1, some encouragement when sixth in maiden bumper at Kempton (14½ lengths behind Sevarano): will do better. *Dan Skelton*   b80 p

REPEAT BUSINESS (IRE) 10 b.g. Croco Rouge (IRE) – Bay Pearl (FR) (Broadway Flyer (USA)) [2017/18 c114, h–: c27.5d^{pu} c23.6s^6 Mar 22] multiple point winner: maiden hurdler: fair hunter chaser, below best in 2017/18: stays 25f: acts on good to firm and good to soft going: tried in cheekpieces. *J. W. Tudor*   c– h–

REPEAT THE FEAT (FR) 7 br.g. Kingsalsa (USA) – Sharon du Berlais (FR) (Lute Antique (FR)) [2017/18 h59: c22.6g^6 c24.2g^4 c25.8g^{pu} Jun 27] good-topped gelding: poor form over hurdles/fences: tried in cheekpieces: in tongue tie last 2 starts. *Charlie Longsdon*   c67 h–

REPLACEMENT PLAN (IRE) 9 b.g. Flemensfirth (USA) – Shannon Pearl (IRE) (Oscar (IRE)) [2017/18 c84§, h84§: c23g Sep 18] winning hurdler: poor maiden chaser: placed in points: stays 25f: acts on heavy going: usually wears headgear: wears tongue tie: usually races close up: temperamental. *Richard Woollacott*   c– § h– §

REPORT TO BASE (IRE) 6 b.g. Westerner – Marina du Berlais (FR) (Mister Sicy (FR)) [2017/18 h132: c15.9s c19.2v^2 c17.5v*^{d} c16s* c20.4s^F Mar 13] useful form over hurdles: similar form over fences: first past post in 3-runner maiden at Exeter (disqualified after rider mistakenly bypassed fence) and similar event at Hereford (10 lengths ahead of Shear Rock) in January: stayed 2½m: acted on heavy going: front runner/raced prominently: dead. *Evan Williams*   c136 h–

REPRESENTED (IRE) 5 b.g. Presenting – Lunar Path (IRE) (Night Shift (USA)) [2017/18 b16.5g* Nov 16] €10,000 3-y-o, resold £34,000 3-y-o: third foal: dam (h108), French 2¼m hurdle winner, also 9f winner on Flat, half-sister to useful/unreliable staying chasers Celtic Son and Sonevafushi: 5/2, won maiden bumper at Taunton (by neck from Gwalia) on debut: better to come. *Anthony Honeyball*   b92 p

REPUTATIONAL RISK (IRE) 4 b.g. Watar (IRE) – She's All There (IRE) (Tragic Role (USA)) [2017/18 b16v h16s Apr 27] tailed off in bumper/on hurdling debut. *Matt Sheppard*   h– b–

RESIDENCE AND SPA (IRE) 10 b.g. Dubai Destination (USA) – Toffee Nosed (Selkirk (USA)) [2017/18 c26.7v^{pu} c23.5v^{pu} h23.9v Mar 12] sturdy gelding: poor hurdler: modest form over fences, pulled up first 2 starts in 2017/18 after long absence: has worn headgear: has worn tongue tie, including last 2 starts. *Helen Rees*   c– h–

RESILIENCY (IRE) 7 ch.g. Mastercraftsman (IRE) – Euroceleb (IRE) (Peintre Celebre (USA)) [2017/18 h19.9d h20g^5 h16s^3 h15.7s h16sp^{pu} Jan 13] good-bodied gelding: dam half-sister to useful hurdler (2m-2½m winner) Tervel: fairly useful on Flat, stays 1¾m: modest form over hurdles: best effort at 2m: acts on soft going: wears tongue tie. *Dan Skelton*   h99

RESOLUTE REFORMER (IRE) 9 b.g. Arcadio (GER) – Booking Note (IRE) (Brush Aside (USA)) [2017/18 c95, h–: c20.1g c20.1g Jun 3] maiden hurdler: modest chaser, below form both starts in 2017/18: stayed 25f: acted on good to firm and good to soft going: temperamental: dead. *Stuart Coltherd*   c– § h–

RESOLUTION BAY 6 br.g. Presenting – Parthenia (IRE) (Night Shift (USA)) [2017/18 h121: h19g5 h19.2d2 h21g3 c19.7d2 c21.7g2 c23.8g2 Dec 6] well-made gelding: fairly useful handicap hurdler: second at Fontwell in September: useful form over fences, runner-up all 3 starts: stays 3m: acts on good to firm and good to soft going. *Philip Hobbs* **c131 h122**

RESPECTABILITY 6 b.m. Echo of Light – Respectfully (Mark of Esteem (IRE)) [2017/18 h15.5vpu h16.6sF h15.7sro Feb 8] no form on Flat/over hurdles: tried in eyeshields. *Michael Mullineaux* **h–**

RESTRAINT OF TRADE (IRE) 8 br.g. Authorized (IRE) – Zivania (IRE) (Shernazar) [2017/18 c207, h106: h17.2m2 h21.5d* h17.2g3 h20.3g* Jul 16] sturdy gelding: fair handicap hurdler: won at Uttoxeter in June and Southwell in July: maiden chaser: stays 21f: acts on good to firm and heavy going: has worn headgear/tongue tie. *Jennie Candlish* **c– h113**

RETAIN THAT MAHLER (IRE) 5 b.m. Mahler – Retain That Magic (IRE) (Presenting) [2017/18 b16g4 May 25] tailed off in bumper: dead. *Alastair Ralph* **b–**

RETRACE (FR) 4 b.f. Rob Roy (USA) – Puerta Grande (FR) (Lesotho (USA)) [2017/18 b16.2s Apr 27] €3,000 3-y-o: half-sister to several winners, including French 17f winners Role Model (hurdler, by Malinas) and Puerto Saves (chaser, by Nononito): dam, French 17f hurdle winner, half-sister to useful French hurdler up to 2½m Elling: fell in point: tailed off in bumper. *Stuart Crawford, Ireland* **b–**

RETRIEVE (IRE) 11 b.g. Rahy (USA) – Hold To Ransom (USA) (Red Ransom (USA)) [2017/18 h18.5d6 h21.6s Apr 23] sturdy gelding: fairly useful hurdler at best, no form in 2017/18: left Carroll Gray after first start: unproven beyond 2m: acts on good to firm going: tried in cheekpieces/tongue tie. *Johnny Farrelly* **h–**

RETURN FLIGHT 7 b.g. Kayf Tara – Molly Flight (FR) (Saint Cyrien (FR)) [2017/18 c129p, h102: h20d ab16.3g3 c23.9d5 Apr 22] lengthy gelding: fair hurdler: fairly useful chaser: left Dan Skelton after first start: stays 21f: acts on soft going: tried in hood/tongue tie: front runner/races prominently. *Rebecca Menzies* **c118 h–**

RETURN TICKET (IRE) 5 b.g. Getaway (GER) – Capelvenere (IRE) (Baratheа (IRE)) [2017/18 b15.7d3 b15.7d* Dec 19] €20,000 3-y-o: third foal: dam, Italian 1m/8.5f winner, half-sister to Italian 17f-19f hurdle/chase winner Corpus Iuris: fairly useful form in bumpers: won at Catterick in December. *Malcolm Jefferson* **b100**

REVERANT CUST (IRE) 7 gr.g. Daylami (IRE) – Flame Supreme (IRE) (Saddlers' Hall (IRE)) [2017/18 h108, b–: h19.7s h19.7s6 h15.7v2 h16.8v6 h15.7s* h16.4s2 h16.2v2 h21.4g6 Apr 21] fairly useful handicap hurdler: won at Catterick in February: stays 2½m: acts on heavy going: wears tongue tie: often races towards rear. *Peter Atkinson* **h120**

REVERSE THE CHARGE (IRE) 11 b.g. Bishop of Cashel – Academy Jane (IRE) (Satco (FR)) [2017/18 c80, h–: c16.4g4 c20.1g4 c24.2g c15.6gpu c19.2d3 c19.3vpu Feb 22] winning pointer: maiden hurdler: poor maiden chaser: stays 2½m: acts on good to soft going: usually wears cheekpieces: tried in tongue tie: front runner/races prominently: temperamental. *Jane Walton* **c70 § h–**

RGB THE ARCHITECT 5 b.g. Mount Nelson – Dialma (USA) (Songandaprayer (USA)) [2017/18 b–: b16s b13.7g Apr 20] no form in bumpers: in tongue tie both 2017/18 starts. *Fergal O'Brien* **b–**

RHAEGAR (IRE) 7 b.g. Milan – Green Star (FR) (Green Tune (USA)) [2017/18 b16d* h21.6s2 h23.6v* h21.4v4 h24.1d3 h19d Apr 26] €110,000 3-y-o: tall, good-topped gelding: fourth foal: half-brother to fairly useful hurdler/useful chaser Stellar Notion (2m-2½m winner, by Presenting), stays 3m: dam French maiden (third at 9.5f): fairly useful form when won bumper at Warwick (comfortably by 3¼ lengths from Diva du Maquis) in May: similar form over hurdles: won conditionals novice at Chepstow (dead-heated with Bill And Barn, 27 lengths clear of rest) in December: stays 3m: acts on heavy going. *Kim Bailey* **h115 b95**

RHINESTONE (IRE) 5 b.g. Montjeu (IRE) – Apticanti (USA) (Aptitude (USA)) [2017/18 b16s2 b16v* b16s2 b16.4s Mar 14] smallish gelding: first foal: dam, ran twice on Flat, half-sister to Dewhurst Stakes winner Distant Music: smart form in bumpers: won maiden at Thurles in December: second in Grade 2 at Leopardstown (1½ lengths behind Blackbow) in February: wears tongue tie. *Joseph Patrick O'Brien, Ireland* **b119**

RHYMERS STONE 10 b.g. Desideratum – Salu (Ardross) [2017/18 h111: h17d* h21.4v h19.3d4 h20.1d5 Apr 23] fairly useful handicap hurdler: won at Carlisle in November: stays 21f: acts on heavy going: often wears cheekpieces. *Harriet Graham* **h115**

RHY

RHYTHM IS A DANCER 5 b.g. Norse Dancer (IRE) – Fascinatin Rhythm (Fantastic Light (USA)) [2017/18 b16s² b16s⁴ Mar 17] useful-looking gelding: third foal: half-brother to 11.5f winner Da Do Run Run (by Sixties Icon): dam maiden on Flat (stayed 1¾m): fair form in bumpers: better effort when second in maiden at Kempton in February: wears tongue tie. *Paul Nicholls* — **b91**

RHYTHM OF SOUND (IRE) 8 ch.g. Mahler – Oscarvail (IRE) (Oscar (IRE)) [2017/18 c–, h–: c23.4g^pu c20.1g c24.2g^pu c15.6g⁴ c15.7g² c17.3s⁵ c15.6g^F c15.9m* c16.4s* h15.6s Jan 31] no form over hurdles: poor handicap chaser: won at Leicester (conditional) and Sedgefield in November: stays 19f: acts on soft and good to firm going: wears headgear: in tongue tie last 3 starts: unreliable. *Micky Hammond* — **c80 §**, **h– §**

RICHARDOFDOCCOMBE (IRE) 12 b.g. Heron Island (IRE) – Strike Again (IRE) (Phardante (FR)) [2017/18 c–, h–: h19.8s³ h15.8v² h19.5v⁴ c18.2s^F h21.6s Apr 23] poor handicap hurdler/maiden chaser: stays 2½m: acts on heavy going: usually wears tongue tie. *Gail Haywood* — **c–**, **h83**

RICHARD STRAUSS (IRE) 4 b.g. Kheleyf (USA) – Symfony (IRE) (Monsun (GER)) [2017/18 h16d³ h17.3s h16g⁶ h16s⁵ h15.6g⁴ Dec 18] fair on Flat, stays 1½m: modest form over hurdles: left Joseph Patrick O'Brien after third start: raced around 2m: acts on good to soft going: tried in tongue tie. *Philip Kirby* — **h99**

RICHIE VALENTINE 4 b.g. Native Ruler – Karmest (Best of The Bests (IRE)) [2017/18 b15.7v Feb 25] tailed off in bumper. *Martin Keighley* — **b–**

RICHMOND (FR) 13 b.g. Assessor (IRE) – Hirondel de Serley (FR) (Royal Charter (FR)) [2017/18 c101, h–: c23.6s⁴ Mar 22] sturdy gelding: point winner: maiden hurdler: fair hunter chaser: stays 3m: acts on good to firm and heavy going: usually wears cheekpieces. *P. P. C. Turner* — **c107**, **h–**

RIDDLESTOWN (IRE) 11 b.g. Cloudings (IRE) – Gandi's Dream (IRE) (Commanche Run) [2017/18 c111§, h107§: h24m* c24.5g* c24.5g³ c20.3g⁴ c25.7s^pu c24s^pu c19.8v³ c24g³ c21.7v^pu Apr 27] strong gelding: fair handicap hurdler/chaser: won at Towcester (twice) in May: stays 3¼m: acts on good to firm and heavy going: usually wears headgear. *Caroline Fryer* — **c115**, **h114**

RIDERS ONTHE STORM (IRE) 5 br.g. Scorpion (IRE) – Endless Moments (IRE) (Saddlers' Hall (IRE)) [2017/18 h16s⁵ h16v* h16v* h16v² h20v⁶ h16s Apr 27] second foal: dam unraced half-sister to smart hurdler/useful chaser (stayed 3m) Emotional Moment: useful form over hurdles: won novice at Navan in January: second in listed novice at Punchestown (2¼ lengths behind Hardline) in February: unproven beyond 2m: acts on heavy going: usually races prominently. *Tom J. Taaffe, Ireland* — **h133**

RIDGEWAY FLYER 7 b.g. Tobougg (IRE) – Running For Annie (Gunner B) [2017/18 h124p: c19.7d* c23g* c19.9g Dec 1] good-topped gelding: fairly useful form over hurdles: useful form over fences: won novice handicap at Plumpton in October and 2-runner novice at Taunton in November: stays 23f: acts on soft and good to firm going: wore hood in 2017/18: wears tongue tie: usually races towards rear: temperament under suspicion. *Paul Nicholls* — **c134**, **h–**

RIDGEWAY PEARL 5 b.m. Malinas (GER) – Sparkling Jewel (Bijou d'Inde) [2017/18 b16m⁵ b16.8g Oct 3] half-sister to fairly useful/untrustworthy hurdler/chaser Tara Road (19f-21f winner, by Kayf Tara): dam, 5f winner, half-sister to fair hurdler/useful staying chaser Classic Capers: modest form in bumpers: left Tom Lacey after first start. *Mike Sowersby* — **b80**

RIF RAFTOU (IRE) 8 b.m. Shantou (USA) – Sanadja (IRE) (Slip Anchor) [2017/18 h20g³ h20g² h17.7m⁵ h20g³ h16d h20.3d* h24s Dec 21] €15,000 4-y-o: third foal: half-sister to useful hurdler/smart chaser Art of Logistics (2m-2¼m winner, by Exit To Nowhere) and fair chaser Butlergrove King (2½m-3m winner, by King's Theatre): dam (h92), 2½m-3m hurdle winner, also 1¾m winner on Flat: poor handicap hurdler: won at Southwell in December: stays 2½m: acts on good to soft going: in hood last 2 starts: tried in tongue tie. *Samuel Drinkwater* — **h81**

RIGADIN DE BEAUCHENE (FR) 13 b.g. Visionary (FR) – Chipie d'Angron (FR) (Grand Tresor (FR)) [2017/18 c121, h–: c26.1v³ c30.7v^pu c29.6v^ur c29.2v Mar 11] useful-looking gelding: maiden hurdler: smart handicap chaser at best, on downgrade nowadays: stays 29f: acts on heavy going: wears headgear: front runner/races prominently. *Venetia Williams* — **c105**, **h–**

RIP

RIGHTDOWNTHEMIDDLE (IRE) 10 b.g. Oscar (IRE) – Alternative Route (IRE) (Needle Gun (IRE)) [2017/18 c138, h115: c23.8m^{pu} h20v h22.5s h21.1g h22.6v^{pu} h24s^6 h20v h20.3v h22v^{pu} h22.4v Apr 13] compact gelding: fair handicap hurdler: useful chaser: stays 25f: acts on good to firm and heavy going. *Gordon Elliott, Ireland* c– h106

RIGHTEOUS RIVER 4 b.f. Bahri (USA) – Marie Louise (Helissio (FR)) [2017/18 b14s^5 b13.7g^6 b16.8v^5 b14s^5 b15.5v^{pu} h16.2s Mar 27] second foal: dam maiden on Flat (best efforts at 1¼m): modest form in bumpers: no form over hurdles: tried in tongue tie: often races towards rear. *Bill Turner* h– b76

RIGHT OF REPLY (IRE) 7 b.g. Presenting – Baliya (IRE) (Robellino (USA)) [2017/18 h91: h23.3g* h24.5d^5 c20d^6 c20.3v^4 Feb 9] strong gelding: maiden Irish pointer: fair form over hurdles: won maiden at Hexham in May for Alistair Whillans: fair form over fences: better effort when fourth in hunter at Bangor in February: stays 23f. *Dan Skelton* c105 h103

RIGHT ON ROY 8 b.g. Double Trigger (IRE) – One Wild Night (Rakaposhi King) [2017/18 h15.8s h24s^{pu} Feb 8] placed in points: no form under Rules. *Samuel Drinkwater* h–

RINGA DING DING 5 b.g. Shirocco (GER) – Blue Dante (IRE) (Phardante (FR)) [2017/18 b16.5g^4 b15.3v h19m^3 Apr 25] fifth foal: half-brother to bumper winner Dantes Firth (by Flemensfirth) and fairly useful hurdler Duke Debarry (19f winner, by Presenting): dam (b115), won both starts in bumpers, out of sister to high-class staying chaser Marlborough: fair form in bumpers: better effort when fourth in maiden at Taunton in November: 8/1, third of 4 in novice at same course (2¼ lengths behind Don't Ask) on hurdling debut: tried in tongue tie. *Paul Nicholls* h117 b90

RING BEN (IRE) 12 b.g. Beneficial – Ringzar (IRE) (Shernazar) [2017/18 c17d^3 Jun 9] point winner: maiden hurdler/chaser: tried in cheekpieces: often wears tongue tie. *Philip Rowley* c83 h–

RING EYE (IRE) 10 b.g. Definite Article – Erins Lass (IRE) (Erins Isle) [2017/18 h20.3d^{ur} c16g^6 h21.2g^3 h16.2s h16s h19.7s Mar 27] maiden hurdler: little form in 2017/18 (including on chasing debut): has worn tongue tie, including final start: often races freely. *Sarah-Jayne Davies* c– h75

RING MINELLA (IRE) 7 b.g. King's Theatre (IRE) – Ring of Water (USA) (Northern Baby (CAN)) [2017/18 h16s^F h16s h20.5s h21.7s^3 h19.9v^{pu} h19.8v^5 h26v^{pu} h23.1d Apr 24] poor maiden hurdler: best effort at 2¾m: acts on soft going: in tongue tie last 3 starts: often races towards rear. *Paul Henderson* h80

RINGMOYLAN (IRE) 6 b.g. Mahler – La Speziana (IRE) (Perugino (USA)) [2017/18 h19.9m^2 h24d^2 c24g^{pu} Oct 26] €42,000 3-y-o: half-brother to fair hurdler Bobby John (2m-2¼m winner, by Bob Back) and a winning pointer by Flemensfirth: dam, ran twice over hurdles, 7f winner on Flat, sister to useful hurdler/chaser (stayed 3m) First Ballot: runner-up twice in Irish maiden points: fair form over hurdles: better effort when second in maiden at Uttoxeter: pulled up in novice handicap on chasing debut. *Jonjo O'Neill* c– h108

RINNAGREE ROSIE 12 gr.m. Silver Patriarch (IRE) – Gretton (Terimon) [2017/18 h83: h23.3s^{pu} h19v h23.3v^3 h22.7v^6 Apr 16] compact mare: poor handicap hurdler: stays 21f: acts on heavy going: wears cheekpieces. *Lucy Normile* h66

RIO BRAVO (IRE) 7 b.g. Westerner – Diaconate (IRE) (Cape Cross (IRE)) [2017/18 h92, b70: h20d^2 h23.1v^{pu} h19.4d^5 h16.5s^2 h24.1v^6 Feb 3] maiden pointer: fair maiden hurdler: best up to 2½m: acts on soft going: wears tongue tie: often leads. *Graeme McPherson* h107

RIO QUINTO (FR) 5 b.g. Loup Breton (IRE) – Seal of Cause (IRE) (Royal Academy (USA)) [2017/18 b16.4s h20s* h23.4v^2 h21s^2 h20.6v^2 h19.5s^4 Apr 27] €42,000 3-y-o, £130,000 4-y-o: good-topped gelding: seventh foal: half-brother to French 9.5f-1½m winner Seldom Found (by Nombre Premier): dam unraced: placed both starts in Irish points: well beaten in listed bumper: fairly useful form over hurdles: won maiden at Fakenham in December: stays 23f: raced only on soft/heavy going: tried in cheekpieces. *Olly Murphy* h123 b–

RIPPLING WATERS (FR) 4 b.f. Areion (GER) – Pepples Beach (GER) (Lomitas) [2017/18 b13.1g^5 b16.7s Mar 26] sister to useful German 7f/1m winner Prakasa and half-sister to 3 winners in France, including fairly useful hurdler/chaser Provokator (17f-19f winner, by Trempolino): dam German 1¼m/11f winner: poor form in bumpers. *Mick Channon* b69

RIP

RIPSTICK 7 b.g. Lucarno (USA) – Posh Stick (Rakaposhi King)[2] [2017/18 h20.1g[pu] h16.2g[4] h16.2g[3] c19.3g Apr 23] third foal: dam (c102/h94) 2m-21f chase winner: point winner: modest form over hurdles: best effort when third in novice at Hexham in June: well held in novice hunter on chasing debut. *James Walton*   c– h85

RISE OF AN EMPIRE (IRE) 8 br.g. Stowaway – Kymin (IRE) (Kahyasi) [2017/18 c20m[3] c19.9d[5] c22g[6] c23.8d[3] Apr 24] €50,000 3-y-o: seventh foal: brother to bumper winner Kymin's Way and half-brother to a winner on Flat abroad by Mark of Esteem: dam (h98) 19f-2¾m hurdle winner: fairly useful hurdler: fair form over fences: left Noel Meade after third start: stays 3m: acts on soft going: tried in cheekpieces: wears tongue tie: usually races prominently. *Harry Fry*   c114 h–

RISING MARIENBARD (IRE) 6 b.g. Marienbard (IRE) – Dromkeen Wood (Primitive Rising (USA)) [2017/18 h74, b–: h20.6s h22.7s h23.8d[4] h24.1d[4] Mar 29] won Irish maiden point on debut: modest form over hurdles: best effort at 3m: acts on good to soft going: usually in tongue tie. *Lucinda Russell*   h99

RISING TIDE (IRE) 7 b.g. Dubai Destination (USA) – Erins Love (IRE) (Double Bed (FR)) [2017/18 h73: h15.9d c20s[pu] c19.9d Apr 24] poor form over hurdles: no form over fences: tried in hood/tongue tie. *Laura Morgan*   c– h–

RISK AND CO (FR) 4 b.g. No Risk At All (FR) – Chin'ba (FR) (Take Risks (FR)) [2017/18 b16d[4] Apr 7] 5/1, fourth in bumper at Fakenham (14½ lengths behind Before Midnight). *Jamie Snowden*   b74

RISK AND ROLL (FR) 4 b.g. No Risk At All (FR) – Rolie de Vindecy (FR) (Roli Abi (FR)) [2017/18 h17.7g[5] h16g* h15.3g[3] h19v* h17.7g[5] Apr 20] useful-looking gelding: second foal: dam (c124/h141) French 2m-19f hurdle/chase winner: fairly useful form over hurdles: won juvenile at Kempton in October and handicap at Taunton in April: stays 19f: acts on heavy going: in cheekpieces last 3 starts: usually wears tongue tie: often travels strongly. *Paul Nicholls*   h125

RITAS BID (IRE) 5 b.m. Oscar (IRE) – Present Bid (IRE) (Presenting) [2017/18 b16.6s ab16d h19.8d Apr 22] £30,000 3-y-o: first foal: dam unraced sister to useful hurdler (stayed 3m) Mayfair Music and half-sister to fairly useful hurdler/smart chaser (stays 3m) Beware The Bear: modest form in bumpers: well beaten in novice on hurdling debut: tried in tongue tie. *Harry Fry*   h– b75

RITASUN (FR) 5 b.g. Monsun (GER) – Baselga (GER) (Second Set (IRE)) [2017/18 h16g[3] h16.3g[5] h16.7g[3] h16.7g[4] h16g Nov 1] fairly useful on Flat, stays 8.5f: fair form over hurdles: raced around 2m: in hood last 2 starts: tried in tongue tie: has joined Frau M. Rotering, Germany. *Harry Whittington*   h100

RIVABODIVA (IRE) 8 ch.m. Flemensfirth (USA) – Sheebadiva (IRE) (Norwich) [2017/18 c100, h97: h23.9g h20.1s[3] h24.3s* h23.3s[2] h24.3v[2] h24v* h26.6s[5] Apr 26] compact mare: winning Irish pointer: fair handicap hurdler: won at Ayr (conditional) in October and Newcastle (novice) in April: similar form over fences: stays 3m: acts on heavy going: tried in cheekpieces: wears tongue tie: front runner/races prominently. *Lucinda Russell*   c– h110

RIVER ARROW 7 b.m. Kayf Tara – Supreme Gem (IRE) (Supreme Leader) [2017/18 h118: h21.6d[5] h20.3s[2] Dec 16] sturdy mare: fairly useful form over hurdles: second in mares handicap at Cheltenham in December: will stay 3m: acts on heavy going: signs of temperament. *Tom Symonds*   h124

RIVER BLUE (IRE) 6 b.g. Flemensfirth (USA) – Tracker (Bustino) [2017/18 h20.6g[pu] Aug 19] pulled up on point/hurdling debut (tongue tied): dead. *Richard Hobson*   h–

RIVER BRAY (IRE) 5 ch.g. Arakan (USA) – Cill Fhearga (IRE) (Lahib (USA)) [2017/18 b89: b16.8g[2] h19.9d h15.7d[5] h19s[2] Dec 30] fair form in bumpers: second at Newton Abbot in October: fairly useful form over hurdles: best effort when second in novice at Taunton in December: in hood last 3 starts. *Victor Dartnall*   h117 b93

RIVER DUN 8 br.m. Indian River (FR) – Sight'n Sound (Chief Singer) [2017/18 h91, b75: h19.2v[2] h23.3v[5] h19v[pu] h23.9s[4] h23.9s[4] h23.9m[3] Apr 25] modest maiden hurdler: stays 3m: acts on good to firm and heavy going: wears headgear: tried in tongue tie. *David Pipe*   h89

RIVER FROST 6 b.g. Silver Frost (IRE) – River Test (Beat Hollow) [2017/18 h140: h19.5d[5] h21.1s Mar 14] good-topped gelding: useful handicap hurdler: fifth in Silver Trophy at Chepstow (2 lengths behind Court Minstrel) in October: stays 21f: acts on good to soft going. *Alan King*   h139

RIVER ICON 6 b.m. Sixties Icon – River Alder (Alderbrook) [2017/18 h87p, b81: h22.1d* h24.7g² h23.9g² h22.1d* h24.3g⁶ Apr 20] fairly useful hurdler: won mares maiden at Cartmel in May and mares handicap there in August: stays 25f: acts on good to soft going: often races in rear. *Iain Jardine*   **h119**

RIVER OF INTRIGUE (IRE) 8 b.g. Indian River (FR) – Molly Hussey (IRE) (Flemensfirth (USA)) [2017/18 h105: c24d⁴ c22.5g² c21.4g³ c24.2d⁵ c20g⁶ Sep 13] fair hurdler: similar form over fences: left Nicky Henderson after third start: stays 2¾m: best form on good going: in headgear last 3 starts: tried in tongue tie: usually leads. *Fergal O'Brien*   **c112 h–**

RIVER PURPLE 11 b.g. Bollin Eric – Cerise Bleue (FR) (Port Lyautey (FR)) [2017/18 c103, h–: c16.5mᵖᵘ c16.5gᵖᵘ c16dᵖᵘ Nov 27] maiden hurdler: fair handicap chaser, no form in 2017/18: wears tongue tie: unreliable. *Lady Susan Brooke*   **c– § h–**

RIVERSIDE BRIDGE (IRE) 6 gr.g. Rugby (USA) – Sahara Gold (IRE) (Desert Prince (IRE)) [2017/18 h16gᵖᵘ h16.2v⁶ h15.8d⁶ h16.8g h16.7dᵖᵘ Nov 23] modest maiden on Flat, best effort at 1m: poor maiden hurdler: left W. J. Burke after first start: raced around 2m: tried in hood: often in tongue tie: usually races towards rear. *Brian Ellison*   **h69**

RIVERSIDE CITY (IRE) 9 ch.g. Presenting – Blazing Sky (IRE) (Beneficial) [2017/18 c23g⁵ c20.9spᵘ c20d c23.6sᵖᵘ Jan 12] winning hurdler: fair handicap chaser: stays 29f: left Gordon Elliott after final start in 2016/17: tried in blinkers: has worn tongue tie: usually races nearer last than first: unreliable. *Jonjo O'Neill*   **c107 § h–**

RIVER WYLDE (IRE) 7 b.g. Oscar (IRE) – Clarin River (IRE) (Mandalus) [2017/18 h149, b96: c16d* c15.9s² Nov 19] strong, compact gelding: bumper winner: smart form over hurdles: useful form over fences: won maiden at Uttoxeter in November: second in 3-runner Grade 2 novice at Cheltenham (18 lengths behind North Hill Harvey) next time: raced only at 2m: acts on soft going: remains capable of better as a chaser. *Nicky Henderson*   **c140 p h–**

RIZZARDO 6 gr.g. Tikkanen (USA) – Last Spruce (USA) (Big Spruce (USA)) [2017/18 b15.7d h20vᵖᵘ Dec 18] fifth in Irish point: well beaten in bumper: stopped quickly in maiden on hurdling debut. *Nigel Twiston-Davies*   **h– b–**

ROAD TO GOLD (IRE) 9 b.g. Gold Well – Haut de Gamme (IRE) (Carmelite House (USA)) [2017/18 c–, h–: c20.5vᵖᵘ c20v⁵ h20.9v² h22.7v⁴ Apr 16] Irish point winner: fairly useful handicap hurdler: second at Kelso in April: little show in chases: stays 23f: acts on heavy going: often races in rear. *N. W. Alexander*   **c– h118**

ROAD TO RESPECT (IRE) 7 ch.g. Gamut (IRE) – Lora Lady (IRE) (Lord Americo) [2017/18 c156+, h–: c25d⁵ c24s² c24d* c26.3v⁴ c24.5s³ Apr 25]   **c167 h–**

    A well-known name disappeared from the racing calendar in the latest season after car company Lexus ended its sponsorship of the Grade 1 chase that is Ireland's mid-season championship chase for stayers. Lexus sponsored the race that is Ireland's closest equivalent to the King George VI Chase for thirteen years, taking over from former sponsors Ericsson who supported the race for almost as long. Leopardstown has been fortunate to enjoy the continuity of such loyal sponsors, which has undoubtedly helped to establish the Ericsson Chase/Lexus Chase as one of the most significant chases run in Ireland, not far, in terms of quality, behind what is now the Irish Gold Cup (for most of its existence known simply as the Hennessy Gold Cup, thanks to a sponsorship that lasted for a quarter of a century). The last three editions of the Irish Gold Cup, since Hennessy pulled out, have been run under three different titles, the first unsponsored as the 'Irish Gold Cup' and the second and third with the added tag of sponsors Stan James and Unibet respectively. It is to be hoped that Leopardstown's new sponsor, the international property firm Savills which has signed a three-year deal for the course's Christmas feature, will be around for the long run. In the latest season, the 'Lexus' was run as the Leopardstown Christmas Chase and that title would have made a good permanent one, with a sponsor's handle added, but the race will be known simply as the Savills Chase. It can irritate sponsors when their races are constantly referred to by their historical or colloquial name (not a problem, of course, for Hennessy, Ericsson or Lexus in their time), but turnover of sponsors is becoming more regular than it used to be and a permanent title helps those who follow the sport, particularly those with an interest in its history and traditions. Nearly all the major graded races have a permanent registered title which needs to be displayed prominently, not merely in brackets at the end of the branded name, as if it was something of an afterthought.

*Leopardstown Christmas Chase, Leopardstown—
Gigginstown-owned runners dominate for the second year running as Road To Respect (No.8)
beats outsider Balko des Flos (No.2) and 2016 winner Outlander*

British stables enjoyed plenty of success in the Leopardstown Christmas Chase in the early part of the century, both as the Ericsson and the Lexus, with Best Mate, Denman and Synchronised all winning it in the same season that they went on to land the Cheltenham Gold Cup. There hasn't been a British-trained winner, though, since Bobs Worth took it in the 2013/14 season following his Cheltenham Gold Cup success, on the way to an unsuccessful attempt to retain his crown in March. A future winner of the Gold Cup, Lord Windermere, finished down in seventh in that Lexus; his trainer Jim Culloty, who rode Best Mate to his three Gold Cup wins, had a much less successful career as a trainer—Lord Windermere's best achievements apart—and he announced in July that he would not be renewing his licence. One of Ireland's jumping superpowers, Gigginstown House Stud, has taken the four runnings since Bobs Worth's success, reflecting the strength of Irish jumping in general nowadays, and of Gigginstown House Stud in particular. The latest running produced a one, two, three carrying Gigginstown's maroon, white star and armlets, though, at the time, the running of the reigning Cheltenham Gold Cup winner Sizing John, odds-on at Leopardstown, made just as many headlines. Attempting to stretch his winning sequence in Grade 1 chases to five, and running at Leopardstown in preference to Kempton, Sizing John beat only one home and was found to be 'post-race abnormal' afterwards. As Sizing John's ante-post Gold Cup odds drifted to 8/1, those of the Leopardstown Christmas Chase winner Road To Respect halved from 20/1 to 10/1 (with King George winner Might Bite replacing Sizing John as favourite).

Road To Respect, still only six at the time of the Christmas Chase, had enjoyed a fine season as a novice in 2016/17, winning at the Cheltenham Festival (in the two and a half mile handicap, the Plate) and following up in the Ryanair Gold Cup for novices at Fairyhouse (a race which Yorkhill threw away by jumping repeatedly left and almost running out at the final fence). Road To Respect had seven Gigginstown performers rated above him at the end of that season and had ground to make up if he was to hold his own in Grade 1 company. He picked up where he left off by winning the Irish Daily Star Chase on his reappearance at Punchestown in October, though not many of his opponents gave their running on the day. One of them, the previous year's Lexus winner Outlander, turned the tables on Road To Respect in the JNwine.com Champion Chase at Down Royal, the first of Ireland's four open Grade 1s for staying chasers. Road To Respect ran well, looming up and leading briefly at the last before going down by half a length, with a fourteen-length gap back to third-placed Zabana, who also improved from the Irish Daily Star Chase.

When the same trio met again in the Christmas Chase, the progressive Road To Respect was sent off at much shorter odds than Outlander and Zabana, starting joint third favourite with Djakadam behind Sizing John and the enigmatic Yorkhill. In a hood for the first time, Road To Respect continued his rise through the chasing ranks, making steady headway and recovering from a stumble between the third- and second-last to collar 66/1-shot Balko des Flos at the final fence and win, driven out, by a length and a quarter, with Outlander a further two and a quarter lengths back in third, and the only British raider, the Cheltenham Gold Cup runner-up Minella Rocco (a 25/1-shot at Leopardstown), completing the frame. Sizing John was already beaten before an untidy jump at the last, while Yorkhill, who made the running until blundering five out, faded to finish a tired last of eight finishers. The race was marred by the fatal fall of Zabana, though his demise tended to be overshadowed on the day by the news of the loss of reigning Stayers' Hurdle winner Nichols Canyon after a fall in the Christmas Hurdle on the same card.

Road To Respect wasn't seen out between Christmas and the Cheltenham Festival where he showed that he had come a long way since his handicap win at the meeting twelve months earlier. He travelled well in the Cheltenham Gold Cup, going third behind Native River and Might Bite at the fourth last and just briefly threatening to close the gap on the first two before finishing a one-paced fourth, twelve and a half lengths behind the winner Native River. Road To Respect ran to a similar level of form with third, starting 7/2 favourite, in the Punchestown Gold Cup on his only start after Cheltenham. A couple of late mistakes didn't help his cause and he was beaten by Bellshill and Djakadam (runner-up for the fourth time) in a field that included the winners of the three earlier open Grade 1 staying chases in Ireland, but none of the first three from Cheltenham. With time on his side, Road To Respect should remain a force in Grade 1 staying chases for some time to come, all being well.

```
                                 ┌Spectrum       ┌Rainbow Quest
                    ┌Gamut (IRE) │ (b 1992)      └River Dancer
                    │ (b 1999)   └Greektown      ┌Ela-Mana-Mou
Road To Respect (IRE)│            (ch 1985)      └Edinburgh
(ch.g. 2011)        │            ┌Lord Americo   ┌Lord Gayle
                    │Lora Lady (IRE)│ (b 1984)   └Hynictus
                    └(b 2001)    └Bellora        ┌Over The River
                                  (br 1991)      └Chorabelle
```

Road To Respect, a strong gelding, embodies the Gigginstown policy of concentrating on the recruitment of potential staying chasers. He first ran for Gigginstown when winning a maiden point as a four-year-old and his close relative Road To Riches, also a Gigginstown performer, was another who started in points (though before Gigginstown acquired him). Both Road To Respect and Road To Riches are by Gamut, and Road To Respect's dam the unraced Lora Lady is a half-sister to Road To Riches. Road To Riches also won the Lexus Chase before going one better than Road To Respect when finishing third in the Cheltenham Gold Cup. Grandam Bellora was unraced but is a sister to the Leopardstown Chase winner Sullane River and a half-sister to the dam of another notable jumper in the family, the smart hurdler Davenport Milenium. Road To Respect, who retained his hood at Cheltenham and Punchestown (has also been tried in a tongue tie), stays twenty-five furlongs and acts on heavy going, though he doesn't need the mud. *Noel Meade, Ireland*

ROAD TO RICHES (IRE) 11 b.g. Gamut (IRE) – Bellora (IRE) (Over The River (FR)) **c133** [2017/18 c152, h–: c22.5g c24v c24.5d c28.7vpu c34.3s6 Apr 14] rangy gelding: winning **h–** hurdler: top-class chaser at best, on decline since 2015/16: stays 3¼m: acts on heavy going: sometimes in headgear: usually in tongue tie in 2017/18. *Noel Meade, Ireland*

ROAD TO ROME (IRE) 8 b.g. Choisir (AUS) – Tibbie (Slip Anchor) [2017/18 h112: **c111** h19.7s5 h20.7s c16d2 c19.9d4 c20.3d3 Apr 21] has had breathing operation: fair form over **h93** hurdles: similar form over fences: best effort when second in novice handicap at Ludlow in February: best up to 2½m: acts on good to soft going: tried in hood: often races in rear. *Oliver Sherwood*

ROB

ROBBING THE PREY (IRE) 7 b.g. Robin des Pres (FR) – Derravarra Lady (IRE) (Flemensfirth (USA)) [2017/18 h115: c16.4g² c16.4s* c15.9d⁶ c15.7g³ Apr 20] fairly useful form over hurdles: useful form over fences: won novice handicap at Sedgefield in November: unproven beyond 2m: acts on soft going: tried in hood: usually races prominently. *Ruth Jefferson*   **c128 h–**

ROBBIN'HANNON (IRE) 7 ch.g. Robin des Champs (FR) – Culleen Lady (IRE) (Presenting) [2017/18 h131p: h23g* h23.9g² h22.8v c24s⁴ Jan 26] sturdy gelding: won Irish maiden point on debut: useful form over hurdles: won 3-runner novice at Worcester in September: second in similar event at Cheltenham (4½ lengths behind Calett Mad) in October: well beaten in novice on chasing debut: stays 3m: acts on heavy going: front runner/races prominently. *Philip Hobbs*   **c– h134**

ROBERT DE BRUCE (IRE) 7 b.g. Brian Boru – Have At It (IRE) (Supreme Leader) [2017/18 h–, b67: h15.8d⁴ h16.7v⁵ h19.6d^pu Apr 21] little impact in Irish maiden points: poor form over hurdles: should be suited by further than 2m: in tongue tie last 2 starts. *Donald McCain*   **h79**

ROBERT'S STAR (IRE) 8 b.g. Oscar (IRE) – Halona (Pollerton) [2017/18 c109p, h110: h21.7g⁵ h23g h20.5s⁴ h23.1v³ h23.1s* h23.9v² Apr 12] fairly useful handicap hurdler: won at Exeter in February: second at Taunton in April: similar form over fences: stays 3m: acts on heavy going: often wears headgear. *Mark Bradstock*   **c– h120**

ROBERTTOWN ROSE (IRE) 5 b.m. Milan – Windfola (FR) (Bonbon Rose (FR)) [2017/18 b16s ab16.3g b16.8g Apr 23] £4,000 3-y-o: first foal: dam, unraced, closely related to useful hurdler/very smart chaser (stayed 2½m) Mansony: no form in bumpers. *Andrew Crook*   **b–**

ROBIN DE BOSS (IRE) 8 b.g. Robin des Pres (FR) – Gevity (Kris) [2017/18 b83: c26d⁶ May 5] multiple point winner: in visor, 20/1, showed a bit when sixth in hunter at Cheltenham (37¾ lengths behind Woodfleet) on chasing debut. *Tommy Morgan*   **c83**

ROBIN DE BROOME (IRE) 6 b.g. Robin des Pres (FR) – Croghan Lass (IRE) (Vestris Abu) [2017/18 b17.7d h23.1v^pu h23.9s h15.3v⁵ h19.2v Feb 1] fourth foal: half-brother to a winning pointer by Quws: dam, third in a point, half-sister to fair hurdler/useful chaser (stayed 3m) Light On The Broom: placed twice in Irish points: well beaten in bumper: modest form on standout effort over hurdles: races prominently. *Brian Barr*   **h85 b–**

ROBINDENEST (IRE) 6 br.g. Robin des Pres (IRE) – Baby Harriet (IRE) (Cape Cross (IRE)) [2017/18 h80, b–: h17.7d^pu May 28] little form over hurdles. *Seamus Mullins*   **h–**

ROBIN DES FORET (IRE) 8 br.g. Robin des Pres (FR) – Omyn Supreme (IRE) (Supreme Leader) [2017/18 h24.8d* h20.5d² h20.5d* h20.7d² h22g* h21s* h24s² Nov 5] second foal: half-brother to fairly useful hurdler/useful chaser Port Melon (19f-3m winner, by Presenting): dam unraced: bumper winner: useful novice hurdler: won at Kilbeggan in May, Roscommon in July and Killarney in August. and listed event at Limerick (by 7 lengths from Fabulous Saga) in October: has won over 25f, likely to prove best at shorter: acts on soft going: front runner/races prominently, strong traveller. *W. P. Mullins, Ireland*   **h142**

ROBIN DES PEOPLE (IRE) 8 br.g. Robin des Pres (FR) – Zelea (USA) (Be My Guest (USA)) [2017/18 c22.6d c23.6s³ Apr 27] multiple point winner: maiden hurdler: fair maiden chaser: left Mrs Amber Mathias after first start: stays 3m: acts on good to firm and heavy going: sometimes in headgear: in tongue tie both 2017/18 starts. *David Brace*   **c102 h–**

ROBIN DEUZ POIS (IRE) 6 ch.m. Robin des Champs (FR) – Native Wood (IRE) (Be My Native (USA)) [2017/18 h80: h15.5d⁵ h20.5d h19.6s h23.9m⁶ Apr 25] runner-up in Irish point: poor form over hurdles. *Paul Webber*   **h80**

ROBINESSE (IRE) 7 ch.m. Robin des Champs (FR) – Jennifers Diary (IRE) (Supreme Leader) [2017/18 h106: h23.3d⁴ May 20] good-topped mare: modest maiden hurdler: should stay 2½m: acts on heavy going. *Oliver Sherwood*   **h99**

ROBIN OF LOCKSLEY (IRE) 8 b.g. Robin des Pres (IRE) – Duggary Dancer (IRE) (Sadlers' Hall (IRE)) [2017/18 h130: c22.5s² c21.6d^pu c20.6v³ h19.9v⁴ h20.5v* h16.8v c23.6s^R c31.8s^R h20v^R Apr 1] good-topped gelding: fair hurdler: won seller at Leicester in January: fairly useful form over fences: second in novice handicap at Uttoxeter in October: left Caroline Bailey after fifth start: stays 21f: acts on good to soft going: often wears headgear: has worn tongue tie: behind when refused last 3 starts: unreliable. *Sophie Leech*   **c129 § h104 §**

ROBINROYALE (IRE) 7 b.g. Robin des Champs (FR) – Rosafi (IRE) (Roselier (FR)) [2017/18 c–, h114: h24.3g Apr 20] strong gelding: Irish point winner: fair hurdler: maiden chaser: stays 3m: acts on good to soft going: tried in cheekpieces: often races prominently. *Seamus Mullins*   **c– h103**

ROBINSFIRTH (IRE) 9 b.g. Flemensfirth (USA) – Phardester (IRE) (Phardante (FR)) [2017/18 c144p, h–: c25g⁴ c25.6v² c26s* Dec 15] rangy gelding: winning hurdler: useful form over fences: won Grade 3 handicap at Cheltenham (by 2 lengths from Shanroe Santos) in December: stays 3¼m: acts on heavy going: in tongue tie last 2 starts: strong traveller. *Colin Tizzard*   c144 h–

ROBINSHILL (IRE) 7 ch.g. Robin des Champs (FR) – I Remember It Well (IRE) (Don't Forget Me) [2017/18 h132: c21vᵖᵘ c16gᵘʳ c16g* c16d* c21vᵖᵘ c15.9s⁵ c15.8sᵖᵘ Apr 12] sturdy gelding: useful hurdler: useful handicap chaser: won at Ludlow (twice, by 5 lengths from Pearls Legend second occasion) in November: stays 19f: acts on heavy going: often wears tongue tie: often races prominently. *Nigel Twiston-Davies*   c137 h–

ROBINS LEGEND (IRE) 6 b.g. Robin des Pres (FR) – Lemons Legend (Midnight Legend) [2017/18 h85, b–: c20.1vᵖᵘ c21.1g c23.8d⁴ c23.8d² Mar 16] sturdy gelding: maiden hurdler: poor form over fences: stays 3m: acts on good to soft going: wears headgear: front runner/races prominently. *Chris Grant*   c79 h–

ROBINSSON (IRE) 8 b.g. Robin des Champs (FR) – Silver Proverb (Silver Patriarch (IRE)) [2017/18 h21.7d³ h21.7sᵖᵘ Apr 6] sturdy gelding: fair maiden hurdler: stays 2¾m: acts on heavy going: in cheekpieces both starts in 2017/18. *Oliver Sherwood*   h107

ROBINTHEAULAD (IRE) 7 b.g. Robin des Champs (FR) – Brotenstown (IRE) (Presenting) [2017/18 h98: c23.4d^F c20.5s^F h17s⁶ Apr 8] third on completed start in Irish points: fair form over hurdles: showed aptitude despite falling both starts over fences: stays 2½m: acts on good to soft going: wears tongue tie: front runner/races prominently. *Sandy Thomson*   c96 h75

ROBIN THE RAVEN (IRE) 6 b.g. Robin des Pres (FR) – Omyn Supreme (IRE) (Supreme Leader) [2017/18 b99: h21.2m* h23.3d³ h20d³ h20g^F h21.2d* Nov 27] good-topped gelding: bumper winner: useful form over hurdles: won novices at Ludlow in May, Uttoxeter in June and again at Ludlow (by 8 lengths from Crucial Role) in November: will stay 3m: acts on good to firm and good to soft going: wears cheekpieces: tried in tongue tie: front runner/races prominently. *Kim Bailey*   h135

ROBIN WATERS (FR) 5 b.g. Irish Wells (FR) – Skandia (FR) (Robin des Champs (FR)) [2017/18 h20.5d³ h21.6d³ h21.3v* h24v⁶ Mar 16] tall, good-topped gelding: will make a chaser: fifth foal: dam French 17f/2¼m hurdle/chase winner: easy winner of point on debut: useful form over hurdles: won novice at Wetherby in February: sixth in Albert Bartlett Novices' Hurdle (Spa) at Cheltenham in March: sure to go on to better things. *Dan Skelton*   h140 p

ROBIN WHY NOT (IRE) 6 b.g. Robin des Pres (FR) – Lady Mariah (IRE) (Moonax (IRE)) [2017/18 h77: h20g h21.6dᵖᵘ c16gᵖᵘ Nov 16] little form over hurdles: pulled up in novice handicap on chasing debut: placed in points: sometimes in headgear: tried in tongue tie. *Nigel Hawke*   c– h–

ROBIN WILL (FR) 13 bl.g. Dark Moondancer – Gleep Will (FR) (Cadoudal (FR)) [2017/18 c–, h–: c22.5d May 20] tall, useful-looking gelding: maiden hurdler: fairly useful chaser at best, retains little ability: usually wears headgear. *Gemma Anderson*   c– h–

ROB ROBIN (IRE) 8 b.g. Robin des Champs (FR) – Ashwell Lady (IRE) (Presenting) [2017/18 h19.1m⁴ h16g⁵ h19.2g³ h15.9m* h15.9d Oct 23] useful-looking gelding: modest handicap hurdler: won at Plumpton in September: stays 19f: acts on good to firm going: usually races prominently. *Chris Gordon*   h92

ROB ROYAL (IRE) 10 b.g. Royal Anthem (USA) – Shamble Street (IRE) (Bob Back (USA)) [2017/18 h–: h19.6sᵖᵘ h17sᵖᵘ Apr 8] no form over hurdles: tried in hood. *Mike Hammond*   h–

ROB'S LEGACY 5 ch.g. Phoenix Reach (IRE) – Clumber Pursuits (Pastoral Pursuits) [2017/18 h15.7g⁶ h20.3g h20.3d⁵ Nov 6] modest maiden on Flat, stays 13f: well held all 3 starts over hurdles. *Shaun Harris*   h–

ROCCO (IRE) 5 b.g. Shantou (USA) – Navaro (IRE) (Be My Native (USA)) [2017/18 b14d⁶ h23.6v² h19.4s Feb 21] £90,000 4-y-o: half-brother to 3 winners, including useful hurdler/fairly useful chaser Line Ball (2m-21f winner, by Good Thyne): dam unraced half-sister to top-class hurdler (2m-2½m winner) Mighty Mogul: won completed start in Irish maiden points: sixth in bumper at Ludlow: modest form over hurdles: better effort when second in maiden at Chepstow in January. *Nigel Twiston-Davies*   h89 b77

ROC

ROC D'APSIS (FR) 9 gr.g. Apsis – Rocapina (FR) (Solon (GER)) [2017/18 c129x, h–: c24m* c23.8m⁵ Jun 4] well-made gelding: maiden hurdler: useful handicap chaser: won at Kempton in May: stays 3m: acts on soft and good to firm going: wears cheekpieces: often let down by jumping. *Tom George* — **c130 x / h–**

ROCHES POINT (IRE) 6 b.g. Yeats (IRE) – She's A Venture (IRE) (Supreme Leader) [2017/18 b16.2m⁶ Jul 16] tailed off in bumper. *James Ewart* — **b–**

ROCKABILLY RIOT (IRE) 8 br.g. Footstepsinthesand – Zawariq (IRE) (Marju (IRE)) [2017/18 b84: h16.2g³ h17.2g² h17.2s h17.2d Aug 26] poor handicap hurdler: best effort at 2m: acts on soft going: has worn hood: often races towards rear. *Martin Todhunter* — **h80**

ROCKALZARO (FR) 6 gr.g. Balko (FR) – Royale Wheeler (FR) (Rusticaro (FR)) [2017/18 b83: b17m* h16.2g³ h15.7d³ h16.8s³ h19.3s Feb 12] fair form in bumpers: won at Carlisle in May: similar form over hurdles: won novice at Catterick in November. *Donald McCain* — **h108 / b88**

ROCK AND ROLL KING (IRE) 6 b.g. King's Theatre (IRE) – Lunar Path (IRE) (Night Shift (USA)) [2017/18 h102, b–: h15.8v⁴ h16.2s h20.5v^pu h19.2v^pu Feb 14] modest maiden hurdler: best effort at 2½m: acts on heavy going: tried in cheekpieces. *Evan Williams* — **h98**

ROCKCHASEBULLETT (IRE) 10 b.g. Catcher In The Rye (IRE) – Last Chance Lady (IRE) (Mister Lord (USA)) [2017/18 c103, h–: h23m⁵ h23.3g² h23.3d⁵ h20m⁵ c26m² c21.6s* Sep 10] fair maiden hurdler: fair handicap chaser: won at Fontwell in September: stays 3¼m: acts on soft and good to firm going: wears headgear: has worn tongue tie: often races prominently/travels strongly. *Fergal O'Brien* — **c114 / h100**

ROCKERY GARDEN (IRE) 5 b.g. Wareed (IRE) – Rock Garden (IRE) (Bigstone (IRE)) [2017/18 b16.8d³ b16.7g Apr 22] brother to 2 winners, including fairly useful/unreliable hurdler/chaser Victor Leudorum (19f-3½m winner), and half-brother to 2 winners by Carlo Bank, including fairly useful hurdler Miss Maiden Over (19f/2½m winner): dam (h107) bumper/21f hurdle winner: modest form in bumpers: better effort when third in maiden at Newton Abbot in July. *Fergal O'Brien* — **b84**

ROCKET MAN RODNEY 5 b.g. Black Sam Bellamy (IRE) – Miss Quickly (IRE) (Anshan) [2017/18 b16.2v⁶ Oct 14] tailed off in bumper. *Harriet Graham* — **b–**

ROCKET RONNIE 8 b.g. Antonius Pius (USA) – Ctesiphon (USA) (Arch (USA)) [2017/18 h16.8d⁴ h18.5d² h19m⁴ h19g h19.3d⁵ h19.3d⁵ h20.5v⁶ h19.5v h19.6d³ Apr 21] compact gelding: modest on Flat, stays 1¼m: modest maiden hurdler: left Brian Barr after seventh start, then had one run for Ben Pauling: stays 2¼m: acts on good to soft going: sometimes in headgear: often wears tongue tie. *Adrian Wintle* — **h96**

ROCK GONE (IRE) 10 b.g. Winged Love (IRE) – Guillem (USA) (Nijinsky (CAN)) [2017/18 c138, h–: c23.8g² Nov 4] winning hurdler: useful chaser: second in Sodexo Gold Cup (Handicap Chase) at Ascot (4½ lengths behind Go Conquer) sole outing in 2017/18: stays 3m: acts on heavy going. *Dr Richard Newland* — **c137 / h–**

ROCKLANDER (IRE) 9 b.g. Oscar (IRE) – Rua Lass (IRE) (Beau Sher) [2017/18 h135: c20d* c24d^ur c22.4v* c20.4s³ c25s^F Apr 14] sturdy gelding: useful hurdler: smart form over fences: won maiden at Ludlow (left clear in straight) in November and novice handicap at Newbury (by 3¼ lengths from Duke des Champs) in December: third in Close Brothers Novices' Handicap Chase at Cheltenham (3¼ lengths behind Mister Whitaker) in March: stays 3m: acts on good to firm and heavy going. *Tom George* — **c147 / h–**

ROCKLIFFE 5 b.g. Notnowcato – Hope Island (IRE) (Titus Livius (FR)) [2017/18 h84: h16.2d h16.2s h16.8s⁶ h15.6d* h16.8g* Apr 23] modest handicap hurdler: won at Musselburgh in February and Sedgefield in April: raced around 2m: acts on good to soft going. *Micky Hammond* — **h91**

ROCK ME ZIPPO (IRE) 10 b.g. Millenary – Babylonia (IRE) (Be My Guest (USA)) [2017/18 c–, h–: c21.7m^pu May 4] placed in points: little form under Rules. *Gary Moore* — **c– / h–**

ROCK MY STYLE (IRE) 6 b.g. Marienbard (IRE) – Meara Trasna (IRE) (Rock Hopper) [2017/18 h118, b80: h19.7s* h23.6v* Feb 2] runner-up in Irish maiden point on debut: fairly useful form over hurdles: won maiden at Hereford in January and novice at Chepstow in February: will stay 3m+: acts on heavy going: tried in cheekpieces. *Warren Greatrex* — **h121**

ROCKNROLLRAMBO (IRE) 11 b.g. Winged Love (IRE) – Lady Padivor (IRE) (Zaffaran (USA)) [2017/18 c112, h–: c23.9g² c25.5d² c19.4v Dec 9] winning hurdler: fair handicap chaser: stays 3m: acts on heavy going: usually in cheekpieces: often wears tongue tie: usually races towards rear. *Ian Williams* — **c109 / h–**

ROC

ROCK N'STONES (IRE) 7 b.g. Stowaway – Rock Abbey (IRE) (College Chapel) [2017/18 h16.2g³ h20.6g³ h20.6g⁵ h22.1g^pu h19.9g h24g^pu h20.3d^pu h15.7d h20.6s⁶ Mar 26] sixth foal: half-brother to a winning pointer by Gamut and 2 winners on Flat: dam unraced: placed in points: poor maiden hurdler: left Mark Walford after fourth start: stays 21f: best form on good going: usually wears headgear: tried in tongue tie: often let down by jumping. *Gillian Boanas*   **h82 x**

ROCK OF LEON 7 b.g. Rock of Gibraltar (IRE) – Leonica (Lion Cavern (USA)) [2017/18 c121x, h108: c29.2g^pu c24.3v h19.9v² h19.9v³ h21.3v⁴ h19.7d* h21.2g² Apr 23] sturdy gelding: fair hurdler: won seller at Wetherby in March: fairly useful chaser, below best over fences in 2017/18: stays 3m: acts on good to firm and heavy going: wears headgear: has worn tongue tie, including last 3 starts: front runner/races prominently: usually let down by jumping/attitude. *Philip Kirby*   **c– x** / **h104 §**

ROCK ON OSCAR (IRE) 8 b.g. Oscar (IRE) – Brogeen Lady (IRE) (Phardante (FR)) [2017/18 c125, h–: c23.6d³ c21.6g^ur Apr 20] rangy gelding: has had breathing operation: won sole start in points: winning hurdler: fairly useful form over fences: third in novice at Chepstow in October: stays 3m: acts on soft going: wears hood/tongue tie: carries head awkwardly. *Paul Nicholls*   **c116 p** / **h–**

ROCK ON ROCKY 10 b.g. Overbury (IRE) – Tachometer (IRE) (Jurado (USA)) [2017/18 c126, h92: c17.1d⁴ c16.5v c15.9d⁴ c16.4g² c18.8d² c19.4v³ c16s⁴ c20.2v⁴ c16.4s* c16d* c20.8g^pu Apr 18] lengthy gelding: winning hurdler: useful handicap chaser: won at Newbury (by 11 lengths from Imperial Presence) in March and Ludlow (by 1¼ lengths from Colin's Brother) in April: stays 2½m: acts on heavy going: wears cheekpieces/tongue tie: often races towards rear. *Matt Sheppard*   **c132** / **h–**

ROCK ON ROY 6 b.g. Revoque (IRE) – Pistol Dawn (Primo Valentino (IRE)) [2017/18 b16.4g Nov 17] well beaten in bumper (tongue tied): dead. *John Dixon*   **b–**

ROCKPOINT 5 b.g. Shirocco (GER) – Tinagoodnight (FR) (Sleeping Car (FR)) [2017/18 b72: h16.8g⁴ h15.7g³ h19.3g⁵ h18.5v³ h16.3v² h16g Feb 24] stocky gelding: fairly useful form over hurdles: third in handicap at Exeter in December: stays 19f: acts on heavy going. *Colin Tizzard*   **h118**

ROCK SOLID (IRE) 9 b.m. Beneficial – Gaelic (IRE) (Strong Gale) [2017/18 h89: h16.2g⁵ h16.4d Jun 13] point winner: modest form at best over hurdles: tried in tongue tie. *Paul Stafford, Ireland*   **h71**

ROCK THE KASBAH (IRE) 8 ch.g. Shirocco (GER) – Impudent (IRE) (In The Wings) [2017/18 c144, h–: c23.6d* c25.6v^pu c28.8d² Apr 28] useful-looking gelding: winning hurdler: smart handicap chaser: won at Chepstow (by 2 lengths from Petrou) in October: second in bet365 Gold Cup at Sandown (13 lengths behind Step Back) in April: stays 29f: acts on heavy going: tried in cheekpieces. *Philip Hobbs*   **c150** / **h–**

ROCK THE WORLD (IRE) 10 b.g. Orpen (USA) – Sue N Win (IRE) (Beneficial) [2017/18 c157, h–: c20.5s² c17g² c22.5g c17s⁴ c16.3v Mar 16] sturdy gelding: winning hurdler: very smart chaser, below best in 2017/18: stays 2½m: acts on heavy going: tried in cheekpieces: wears tongue tie: usually races towards rear. *Mrs J. Harrington, Ireland*   **c136** / **h–**

ROCKY'S TREASURE (IRE) 7 b.g. Westerner – Fiddlers Bar (IRE) (Un Desperado (FR)) [2017/18 h126p: h25.3s³ h24s^pu h24v^pu h24g⁵ Apr 18] sturdy gelding: won Irish maiden point on debut: fairly useful handicap hurdler: third in listed event at Cheltenham in November: stays 25f: acts on heavy going: usually races towards rear: temperament under suspicion. *Kim Bailey*   **h128**

ROC MERLE (IRE) 6 b.g. Milan – Me Grannys Endoors (IRE) (Tremblant) [2017/18 b15.7d h19.5v⁴ Feb 19] good-topped gelding: well beaten in bumper/novice hurdle. *Venetia Williams*   **h–** / **b–**

ROCOCO RIVER 4 b.g. Shirocco (GER) – Noun de La Thinte (FR) (Oblat (FR)) [2017/18 h16.2s^F Mar 27] second foal: dam (c123/h96), 2¼m-2½m winner (stayed 3¼m), half-sister to useful chaser (stayed 3m) Royal de La Thinte: chasing leaders and yet to be asked for effort when fell 3 out in juvenile maiden hurdle won by Broughtons Admiral at Hereford on debut. *Nick Williams*   **h– p**

ROCOCO STYLE 5 b.m. Shirocco (GER) – Akdara (IRE) (Sadler's Wells (USA)) [2017/18 b15.7g⁷ b16.3s b16.7v⁶ b17s Apr 12] sturdy mare: half-sister to several winners, including useful hurdler Aklan (2m winner, by Dalakhani), stayed 2½m, and fairly useful hurdler/chaser Akarshan (2m/17f winner, by Intikhab), stayed 21f: dam 1½m winner: fair form in bumpers: won maiden at Southwell in September. *Steve Gollings*   **b85**

ROC

ROCONGA (IRE) 8 b.g. Rakti – Nafzira (IRE) (Darshaan) [2017/18 c17g³ c19.5m³ c16g² c16g⁴ c17.4d² c17g² c17v^F h19v^pu Apr 1] fairly useful hurdler, pulled up final start in 2017/18: useful maiden chaser: second in maiden at Killarney (length behind Product of Love) in August: stays 19f: acts on soft and good to firm going. *E. J. O'Grady, Ireland* — **c132 h–**

RODEO DODO (IRE) 8 b.g. Milan – Laney Mary (IRE) (Mister Lord (USA)) [2017/18 h63: h19d h16.3g Oct 21] point winner: little form over hurdles. *Dan Skelton* — **h–**

ROD OF IRON 5 br.g. Alkaased (USA) – Leading Star (Motivator) [2017/18 h17.7d^pu Sep 10] poor maiden on Flat: pulled up in novice on hurdling debut. *Michael Madgwick* — **h–**

ROD'S DREAM 5 ch.g. Midnight Legend – Norton Sapphire (Karinga Bay) [2017/18 b16.8m³ May 30] third foal: brother to fair hurdler Midnight Sapphire (21f winner, stayed 3¼m): dam (c122/h117) 2m-23f hurdle/chase winner: 3/1, shaped better than distance beaten suggests when third in bumper at Newton Abbot (21½ lengths behind Horse Force One) on debut: should improve. *David Pipe* — **b66 p**

ROGUE ANGEL (IRE) 10 b.g. Presenting – Carrigeen Kohleria (IRE) (Luso) [2017/18 c132, h–: c24s c28s⁶ c24v^pu c25.9v^pu c23v⁵ c24.7v^pu c21.1s^pu c24.5s² Apr 28] workmanlike gelding: winning hurdler: fairly useful handicap chaser nowadays: stays 4m: acts on good to firm and heavy going: wears headgear/tongue tie: unreliable. *M. F. Morris, Ireland* — **c126 § h–**

ROJA DOVE (IRE) 9 b.m. Jeremy (USA) – Knight's Place (IRE) (Hamas (IRE)) [2017/18 h84: h16.8g h20g³ h19.9g⁴ h18.7m⁴ h16s* h16v* h21v⁶ h16v⁶ Feb 10] angular mare: fair handicap hurdler: won at Fairyhouse and Gowran (mares) in November: left David Thompson after fourth start: stays 21f: acts on heavy going: has worn headgear. *Peter Fahey, Ireland* — **h96**

ROKSANA (IRE) 6 b.m. Dubai Destination (USA) – Talktothetail (IRE) (Flemensfirth (USA)) [2017/18 b75p: h19.5d³ h20.5d* h19.2v* h20.5s* h24.7s² Apr 13] good-topped mare: useful form over hurdles: won mares novices at Plumpton in November and Fontwell in December, and Mares 'National Hunt' Novices' Hurdle Finale at Newbury (by 2¾ lengths from Kalahari Queen) in March: improved again when second in Sefton Novices' Hurdle at Aintree (1½ lengths behind Santini) in April: stays 25f: acts on heavy going: tried in hood: often races towards rear, usually travels strongly. *Dan Skelton* — **h142**

ROLLERBALL ROCCO (IRE) 6 b.g. Ask – Jamica Ginger (IRE) (Flemensfirth (USA)) [2017/18 h24d⁴ h15.7d h20.8s Jan 9] placed in Irish points: no form over hurdles. *Charles Pogson* — **h–**

ROLLING ALONG 5 b.g. Bollin Eric – Brychan (IRE) (Un Desperado (FR)) [2017/18 b16.2g Nov 29] 25/1, tenth in bumper at Hereford. *David Rees* — **b–**

ROLLING DICE 7 b.g. Rail Link – Breathing Space (USA) (Expelled (USA)) [2017/18 h16.3g⁴ h15.7g⁴ Jul 16] modest maiden hurdler: raced only at 2m: acts on soft going. *Dominic Ffrench Davis* — **h87**

EBF TBA Mares' 'National Hunt' Novices' Hurdle Finale (Limited Handicap), Newbury—Roksana (right) completes a hat-trick by defeating Kalahari Queen (white breastgirth)

ROM

ROLLING DYLAN (IRE) 7 ch.g. Indian River (FR) – Easter Saturday (IRE) (Grand Plaisir (IRE)) [2017/18 h128: c23g5 c20s* c20.6vpu c23s2 c23.6v3 c23.6s* c25.2s2 Mar 27] sturdy gelding: fairly useful hurdler: useful chaser: won handicap at Worcester in November and novice at Chepstow (3-runner event, by 18 lengths from Flintham) in February: stays 3¼m: acts on heavy going: has worn cheekpieces, including last 3 starts. *Philip Hobbs*   **c138 h–**

ROLLING MAUL (IRE) 10 b.g. Oscar (IRE) – Water Sports (IRE) (Marju (IRE)) [2017/18 c133§, h128§: h24.7g4 h23g5 h23.9g h25.3s h24d Dec 5] good-topped gelding: fairly useful handicap hurdler: winning chaser: stays 25f: acts on good to firm and heavy going: usually wears headgear: has worn tongue tie: often races prominently: temperamental. *Peter Bowen*   **c– § h118 §**

ROLLING THUNDER (IRE) 8 gr.g. Cloudings (IRE) – Peazar (IRE) (Inzar (USA)) [2017/18 c116, h–: c24.2g4 May 6] maiden hurdler: fair chaser, well held sole start under Rules in 2017/18: should stay further than 3m: acts on heavy going: usually wears headgear: in tongue tie last 2 starts: usually leads: unreliable. *Donald McCain*   **c– § h–**

ROLL OF THE DICE (IRE) 6 b.g. Publisher (USA) – Dinah B (IRE) (Yashgan) [2017/18 b17g4 h15.9d5 h19.3g h20.5d h17.7v5 h21.7d4 Feb 25] €3,500 3-y-o: useful-looking gelding: half-brother to fair/unreliable chaser Tim The Chair (23f-3¼m winner) and a winning pointer (both by Pierre): dam winning pointer: off mark in points at fourth attempt: fourth in conditionals/amateur bumper at Aintree for Dan Skelton: fair form over hurdles: stays 2¾m: acts on good to soft going. *Gary Moore*   **h103 b79**

ROLL OF THUNDER 9 b.g. Antonius Pius (USA) – Ischia (Lion Cavern (USA)) [2017/18 h90: c19.3gpu c16.4spu Nov 28] winning hurdler: little impact in chases/points: stays 21f: acts on good to firm and good to soft going: tried in tongue tie. *James Walton*   **c– h–**

ROLLO'S REFLECTION (IRE) 8 b.g. Shantou (USA) – Lola's Reflection (Presenting) [2017/18 h–: h23s2 h20.3d5 h23gpu h23.3gpu Sep 13] runner-up sole start in maiden points: fair form over hurdles: stays 23f: acts on soft going: tried in blinkers. *Ben Case*   **h109**

ROLL THE DOUGH (IRE) 9 b.g. Definite Article – High Dough (IRE) (High Roller (IRE)) [2017/18 c117, h–: c20d3 c20.2s4 c23.6s c25.2g4 c23s5 c24s6 c24g3 Apr 26] sturdy gelding: winning hurdler: fair maiden chaser: may prove best up to 21f: acts on soft going: often wears tongue tie. *Philip Hobbs*   **c109 h–**

ROMAIN DE SENAM (FR) 6 b.g. Saint des Saints (FR) – Salvatrixe (FR) (Housamix (FR)) [2017/18 c133, h–: c19.4d* c20.9g* c20.4s5 c20.8s5 c20.8s c20.5g Apr 20] well-made gelding: winning hurdler: useful handicap chaser: won at Chepstow and Stratford in October: stays 21f: acts on soft going: wears hood/tongue tie. *Paul Nicholls*   **c144 h–**

ROMAN DE BRUT (IRE) 6 ch.g. Rock of Gibraltar (IRE) – Nesmeh (USA) (More Than Ready (USA)) [2017/18 h15.8d Nov 25] fairly useful on Flat, stays 1¼m: in hood, tailed off in maiden on hurdling debut. *Denis Quinn*   **h–**

ROMANN ANGEL 9 b.m. Sir Harry Lewis (USA) – Roman Gospel (Roi de Rome (USA)) [2017/18 h80: h16.7g5 h18.7m4 h19.6g h20.6g h23.1s6 Dec 2] poor maiden hurdler: stays 2½m: best form on good going: sometimes in headgear: usually leads, often races freely. *Michael Mullineaux*   **h76**

ROMAN NUMERAL (IRE) 10 b.g. King's Best (USA) – Trespass (Entrepreneur) [2017/18 c–, h91: h20.3g c20.1g c20.1g2 c15.7g* c20.1gpu c17.4g c16.4g4 c15.6v2 c15.7d6 c15.6v3 c16.3gF c19.2dF h15.7d2 h20vpu h19.9v4 h16.8v6 Apr 13] poor handicap hurdler/chaser: won over fences at Southwell in July: stays 2¾m: acts on good to firm and heavy going: has worn headgear/tongue tie. *David Thompson*   **c82 h81**

ROMANOR 4 b.g. Holy Roman Emperor (IRE) – Salinia (IRE) (Rainbow Quest (USA)) [2017/18 h16.2spu h16.2s h15.8s h16.2s2 Mar 27] dam half-sister to useful hurdler/very smart chaser (2m-2½m winner) French Opera: fairly useful on Flat, stays 11.5f: fair form over hurdles: in hood last 3 starts. *Seamus Mullins*   **h101**

ROMEO AMERICO (IRE) 11 b.g. Lord Americo – Crazy Falcon (IRE) (Polar Falcon (USA)) [2017/18 c–, h92: h25g6 h21.6mur h21.6m5 Jul 7] modest handicap hurdler: maiden chaser: barely stays 3¼m: acts on good to firm and heavy going: has worn hood, including last 2 starts: often races towards rear. *Seamus Mullins*   **c– h69**

ROMEO BROWN 4 br.g. Yeats (IRE) – Santia (Kahyasi) [2017/18 b14s3 Jan 1] £16,000 3-y-o: lengthy, rather unfurnished gelding: fourth foal: dam (h134) bumper/2m-2¼m hurdle winner: 14/1, promise when third in listed bumper at Cheltenham (11¾ lengths behind Acey Milan) on debut: should improve. *Nick Williams*   **b93 p**

ROM

ROMEO IS BLEEDING (IRE) 12 b.g. Carroll House – Ean Eile (IRE) (Callernish) [2017/18 c–, h–: c16.5g² c20g² c20g^pu c20g* Aug 23] maiden hurdler: fair form over fences: won handicap at Worcester in August: stays 2¾m: acts on good to firm and good to soft going: has worn cheekpieces: wears tongue tie: has joined Kevin Bishop. *Ronald Harris* — c100 h–

ROMULUS DU DONJON (IRE) 7 gr.g. Stormy River (FR) – Spring Stroll (USA) (Skywalker (USA)) [2017/18 h–: h18.1g⁴ h20.9d⁴ h16.2g⁵ h19.3d* h19.4g h19.3s⁴ c21.1v⁵ c24.5d³ c20.9s² c20v³ Apr 17] lengthy gelding: fair handicap hurdler: won at Catterick (conditional) in November: similar form over fences: barely stays 3m: acts on soft going: has worn headgear. *Rose Dobbin* — c110 h103

RONALDINHO (IRE) 8 b.g. Jeremy (USA) – Spring Glory (Dr Fong (USA)) [2017/18 h88: h20.2g h22.1d^pu h20.2g⁶ h22.1s³ h20.2d⁵ h22.1d Aug 28] rather leggy gelding: poor maiden hurdler: stays 2½m: acts on heavy going: has worn headgear/tongue tie, including in 2017/18: often races towards rear: ungenuine. *Dianne Sayer* — h69 §

RONNIE LAWSON (IRE) 9 b.g. King's Theatre (IRE) – Sarahs Quay (IRE) (Witness Box (USA)) [2017/18 h20d^pu h23.3g⁶ h19.5d⁴ c24d² c25.2v⁴ Jan 24] rangy gelding: multiple point winner: poor form over hurdles: modest form over fences: better effort when second in handicap at Southwell in December: stays 3m: acts on good to soft going: tried in tongue tie: usually leads. *Tim Vaughan* — c88 h76

RONN THE CONN (IRE) 6 ch.g. Whitmore's Conn (USA) – Speedy Fairy (IRE) (Speedmaster (GER)) [2017/18 h109: c24.2s² c20.1v² Dec 2] good-topped gelding: fair form over hurdles: similar form over fences: stays 25f: acts on heavy going: remains capable of better as a chaser. *Rebecca Menzies* — c113 p h–

RONS DREAM 8 b.m. Kayf Tara – Empress of Light (Emperor Jones (USA)) [2017/18 c–p, h137: h15.8s⁴ h24.5d⁵ h20.3s h24.6v² c23.6v² c20.3v² c23.4v* c24.1s² c22.2v* c24.1g^bd c23.8s* Apr 27] workmanlike mare: useful handicap hurdler: second in mares event at Kempton (4 lengths behind Midnight Tune) in December: useful chaser: won mares novice at Kelso in February, valuable mares handicap at Haydock in March and listed mares event at Perth (by 1¼ lengths from Jennys Surprise) in April: stays 25f: acts on heavy going: tried in tongue tie: usually races towards rear: tough and reliable. *Peter Bowen* — c137 h133

ROO ROO (IRE) 4 b.g. Court Cave (IRE) – Shuil Sionnach (IRE) (Mandalus) [2017/18 ab16.3g⁵ Apr 15] £25,000 3-y-o: closely related to fairly useful hurdler Kings Walk (2½m/21f winner, by King's Theatre) and half-brother to 3 winners, including fairly useful hurdler/useful chaser Shuil Aris (2m-2½m winner, by Anshan), stayed 25f: dam unraced: 6/1, fifth in bumper at Newcastle (3½ lengths behind Summer Lightening). *Iain Jardine* — b81

ROOSTER COGBURN (IRE) 5 b.g. Westerner – Hollygrove (IRE) (Commander Collins (IRE)) [2017/18 b–: b16.8g⁶ b16.6s⁴ h16.8s⁴ Apr 23] tall gelding: fair form in bumpers: better effort when fourth at Doncaster in February: 9/2, fourth in novice at Newton Abbot (37¾ lengths behind Higgs) on hurdling debut: should do better. *Emma Lavelle* — h62 p b87

Smarkets Challenger Series Mares' Final Handicap Chase, Haydock—
a valuable prize for Rons Dream (left) on Finals day of the Challenger series (geared towards
middle-ranking jumpers) in late-March, which attracted some decent-sized fields

ROOSTER SPIRIT (IRE) 5 gr.g. Craigsteel – Turlututu (FR) (Turgeon (USA)) [2017/18 b85§: h16.2g^{ur} h16.2d h16.2g h15.6m h19.4g h15.6g h20.5v^6 Jan 15] no form over hurdles: tried in hood: has refused to race. *R. Mike Smith* — h– §

ROPARTA AVENUE 11 b.g. Nomadic Way (USA) – Miss Fizz (Charmer) [2017/18 c72§, h–: c25.7g^2 h25.8g^4 h25.8g* h25s^4 Nov 20] poor handicap hurdler: won at Fontwell in November: poor handicap chaser: left Diana Grissell after first start: stays 3¼m: acts on heavy going: often in headgear: unreliable. *Chris Gordon* — c72 § h77 §

RORY'S VALENTINE (IRE) 7 br.m. Windsor Knot (IRE) – Housekeeping (Dansili) [2017/18 c–, h77: h22.7g^4 h25.3s^3 h25.8s^{pu} Jan 14] poor maiden hurdler: pulled up both starts over fences: usually wears tongue tie: often races towards rear. *Katie Scott* — c– h65

ROSA DAMASCENA (FR) 5 b.m. Kalanisi (IRE) – Rosewater (GER) (Winged Love (IRE)) [2017/18 h–: h16.3d^6 h16s^{pu} Dec 19] fairly useful on Flat, stays 11.5f: no form over hurdles. *Alan King* — h–

ROSEMARY RUSSET 6 b.m. Midnight Legend – Apple Days (Sovereign Water (FR)) [2017/18 b93: h18.5s h19.2v^5 h21.4v^2 Feb 1] bumper winner: fair form over hurdles: best effort when second in novice at Wincanton in February: tried in tongue tie: often races prominently. *Harry Fry* — h103

ROSE OF CIMARRON (IRE) 5 b.m. Westerner – Sharp Single (IRE) (Supreme Leader) [2017/18 b16.7s^5 b15.8d^4 b16.4s h16s h20.7g Apr 24] sturdy mare: sixth foal: half-sister to fairly useful hurdler/chaser The Nipper (2m-2½m winner, by Scorpion) and fair chaser Milly Malone (23f-3½m winner, by Milan): dam (c90/h76) 2m chase winner (stayed 2½m): fair form in bumpers: won mares event at Uttoxeter in June: mid-field in 2 mares novice hurdles. *Warren Greatrex* — h90 b94

ROSE TO FAME 4 b.f. Fame And Glory – Cinderella Rose (Midnight Legend) [2017/18 ab16d Mar 5] first foal: dam (h120), bumper/2m-2¾m hurdle winner, sister to useful hurdler/chaser (stayed 24m) Twelve Roses: well beaten in maiden bumper. *Kim Bailey* — b–

ROSE TREE (IRE) 5 b.m. Yeats (IRE) – Isabellareine (GER) (Goofalik (USA)) [2017/18 b85: b15.7m^3 b16.2d^3 h20.2v^6 h20.9d h19.3v^5 h19.4g^3 h19.4d h20.2s^6 Apr 27] modest form in bumpers: poor form over hurdles: left Pam Sly after first start: stays 19f: acts on heavy going: in cheekpieces last 2 starts: wears tongue tie. *Susan Corbett* — h81 b83

ROSEY 4 b.f. Multiplex – Rose Street (IRE) (Noverre (USA)) [2017/18 b17d Mar 31] third foal: dam (h108), placed over hurdles, useful 1¼m winner on Flat: tailed off in mares bumper. *Rose Dobbin* — b–

ROSIE HALL (IRE) 8 ch.m. Lion Heart (USA) – Baltic Dip (IRE) (Benny The Dip (USA)) [2017/18 h16.7s^{pu} Dec 26] poor maiden handicapper on Flat: no show in novice hurdles. *John Wainwright* — h–

ROSIE LEA (FR) 5 b.m. Manduro (GER) – Saralea (FR) (Sillery (USA)) [2017/18 b55p: b16.8g* b16.3s Oct 2] compact mare: fair form in bumpers: won at Newton Abbot in August. *Stuart Kittow* — b85

ROSIE MCQUEEN (IRE) 6 b.m. Milan – Royal Rosy (IRE) (Dominion Royale) [2017/18 h112p: h19.5d h20.6g^F h20.6d^4 h19.4s^2 Jan 9] good-topped mare: off mark in Irish points at second attempt: fair maiden hurdler: will stay 2¾m+: acts on soft going: tried in cheekpieces/tongue tie. *Jonjo O'Neill* — h105

ROSMUC RELAY (IRE) 6 br.g. Presenting – Aughrim Vic (IRE) (Old Vic) [2017/18 h20.5v* h19.7v* h23.1s^{pu} Mar 24] €26,000 3-y-o, £42,000 5-y-o: second foal: dam unraced sister to useful hurdler (stayed 25f) Bygones Sovereign out of sister to top-class hurdler/useful chaser (2m-2½m winner) Mister Morose: off mark in Irish points at second attempt: fairly useful form over hurdles: won novices at Leicester in January and Wetherby in February: should be suited by 3m+. *Kim Bailey* — h121

ROSQUERO (FR) 13 ch.g. Blushing Flame (USA) – Kingsgirl (FR) (Dom Alco (FR)) [2017/18 c105§, h–§: c24.2g^2 c21.6g c22.5d^5 c21.1g c21s c20s c16.5v* c20.1v^{pu} Feb 5] tall gelding: winning hurdler: modest handicap chaser: won at Ayr in January: stays 23f, effective at much shorter: acts on heavy going: wears headgear: has worn tongue tie: usually races close up: unreliable. *Kenny Johnson* — c93 § h– §

ROSSAMILAN (IRE) 7 b.g. Milan – Beautiful Blue (IRE) (Xaar) [2017/18 h16.2v h16.2v^6 h16.2v c15.9v^4 Oct 26] £18,000 6-y-o: third foal: half-brother to fairly useful hurdler/useful chaser Bernardelli (2m-2¾m winner, by Golan), stays 3m: dam unraced half-sister to useful hurdler/fairly useful chaser (2m-2¾m winner) Premier Dane: Irish point winner: poor form over hurdles/on chasing debut: bred to be suited by 2½m+. *Lucinda Russell* — c82 h80

ROS

ROSSETTI 10 gr.g. Dansili – Snowdrops (Gulch (USA)) [2017/18 h130: h16g* h16.3g* h15.8m[5] h16.7g h16.7g h16d[ur] Oct 15] compact gelding: useful handicap hurdler: won at Warwick in May and Stratford (by 2 lengths from Court Minstrel) in June: unproven beyond 17f: acts on good to firm and good to soft going: wears hood: usually races close up. *Neil Mulholland* — **h134**

ROSSINGTON 9 b.g. Gentleman's Deal (IRE) – Ettrbee (IRE) (Lujain (USA)) [2017/18 h98: h16.7g[2] h16.7g[4] h16.7g h18.6g[F] h16.7g Aug 19] poor maiden hurdler: unproven beyond 17f: best form on good going: has worn hood: front runner/races prominently. *John Wainwright* — **h69**

ROSSINI'S DANCER 13 b.g. Rossini (USA) – Bint Alhabib (Nashwan (USA)) [2017/18 c23.8g[pu] May 17] multiple point winner: maiden hurdler: fairly useful chaser at best, pulled up in hunter in May: stays 25f: acts on heavy going: usually wears headgear: best treated with caution (has been reluctant at start). *N. W. Alexander* — **c– § h–**

ROSY WORLD 5 b.m. Shirocco (GER) – Material World (Karinga Bay) [2017/18 b15.7s[2] b16.5v[3] b15.8v* Apr 7] fourth foal: dam (h146) bumper/2¾m-3m hurdle winner: fair form in bumpers: won mares event at Uttoxeter in April. *Suzy Smith* — **b94**

ROTHMAN (FR) 8 b.g. Michel Georges – Bravecentadj (FR) (True Brave (USA)) [2017/18 c115, h109: c21.6s[3] h22s[su] h20.5d[2] h20.5[2] h21d c20.5d[2] c17.8v[2] c20.5g[5] c17.8v[2] h20.5s* Apr 15] rather leggy gelding: fairly useful handicap hurdler: won at Plumpton in April: fair handicap chaser: stays 21f: acts on heavy going: wears headgear/tongue tie: usually races close up. *Chris Gordon* — **c109 h115**

ROUERGATE (FR) 5 b.m. Sageburg (IRE) – Rouge des Champs (FR) (Robin des Champs (FR)) [2017/18 b87: b16.3s[5] h15.8d[3] h15.8s[F] h16.7s* h16.8s h15.3v[pu] h20.6g[4] Apr 22] sturdy mare: fair form in bumpers: similar form over hurdles: won mares novice at Market Rasen in February: should stay 2½m: acts on soft going. *Venetia Williams* — **h109 b85**

ROUGE DEVILS (IRE) 7 b.g. Scorpion (IRE) – Penny's Dream (IRE) (Saddlers' Hall (IRE)) [2017/18 h115: c23.8m[su] c23g[4] c21.4g[pu] Jul 22] point winner: fairly useful form over hurdles: no form in chases: wears headgear: usually leads. *Paul Nicholls* — **c– h–**

ROUGE ET BLANC (FR) 13 ch.g. Mansonnien (FR) – Fidelety (FR) (Villez (USA)) [2017/18 c–, h–: c20.9s[6] c20v* c15.9v[2] c21.1s[pu] Apr 12] good-topped gelding: maiden hurdler: fair chaser: won hunter at Lingfield in February: stays 21f: acts on heavy going: usually wears cheekpieces: tried in tongue tie. *Oliver Sherwood* — **c110 h–**

ROUGE ET SAGE (FR) 8 b.g. Sageburg (IRE) – Rouge Amour (FR) (Cadoudal (FR)) [2017/18 c99, h124: h16.2g h20.6g[pu] h16.2d c20v c20.1v[F] Dec 2] fairly useful hurdler/chaser at best in France, no form in 2017/18: tried in headgear/tongue tie: often raced towards rear: dead. *Susan Corbett* — **c– h–**

ROUGE VIF (FR) 4 b.g. Sageburg (IRE) – Rouge Amour (FR) (Cadoudal (FR)) [2017/18 b15.8d* Mar 22] brother to 2 winners, including fairly useful French hurdler/chaser Rouge Et Sage (2¼m/19f winner), and half-brother to 2 winners by Robin des Champs, including fairly useful French hurdler/useful chaser Ruthenoise (17f-19f winner): dam lightly raced in France (third in 15f hurdle): 9/2, won bumper at Ludlow (by 1¼ lengths from Ballinahinch) on debut, responding well. *Harry Whittington* — **b95**

ROUGH JUSTICE (IRE) 10 b.g. Beneficial – Ringzar (IRE) (Shernazar) [2017/18 c101§, h–: c26.2g[pu] c23.9g[4] c23.9g* c21.1g[4] c23.9g[5] c24.2d[pu] Nov 18] winning hurdler: fair handicap chaser: won at Market Rasen in August: left Alan Brown after first start: stays 3m: acts on good to firm and good to soft going: has worn headgear/tongue tie: unreliable. *John Wainwright* — **c101 § h–**

ROUND TOWER (IRE) 9 br.g. Presenting – Cash Customer (IRE) (Bob Back (USA)) [2017/18 c122, h114: c24.9s[4] c24g[pu] c20d c17.4d[6] h20d c20.3s[5] c23.8d Nov 25] rather sparely-made gelding: fair hurdler: fairly useful maiden chaser: stays 25f: acts on soft going: often wears hood: wears tongue tie: front runner/races prominently. *Karl Thornton, Ireland* — **c117 h–**

ROWDY ROBIN 6 b.g. Revoque (IRE) – Youamazeme (Kayf Tara) [2017/18 h24.1d[6] h16.2d[6] Apr 23] placed in points: well held in 2 novice hurdles. *Ruth Jefferson* — **h–**

ROWDY ROCHER (IRE) 12 br.g. Winged Love (IRE) – Madam Rocher (IRE) (Roselier (FR)) [2017/18 c119, h117: c20v h24.3v[pu] h25.8v[4] h22.7v Feb 15] rather lightly-built gelding: fair handicap hurdler: fairly useful handicap chaser: stays 3¼m: acts on heavy going: has worn cheekpieces, including last 2 starts. *Sandy Thomson* — **c– h112**

ROWLEY PARK (IRE) 5 b.g. Golan (IRE) – Atomic Winner (IRE) (Poliglote) [2017/18 b58: b15.3v Dec 26] well held in 2 bumpers. *Linda Blackford* — **b–**

ROXYFET (FR) 8 b.g. Califet (FR) – Roxalamour (FR) (Valanour (IRE)) [2017/18 c92§, h–: c16.4g⁶ c15.6v c21.1g c16.4s² h16.7d³ c16.4s* c16.5v² c16.4v² c17.2v* c16.4v⁵ h19.9v⁵ c15.2d³ c17.2v³ c16.4g⁶ Apr 23] modest handicap hurdler: fair handicap chaser: won at Sedgefield in December and Market Rasen in March: best at around 2m: acts on heavy going: has worn headgear/tongue tie: has looked ungenuine. *Micky Hammond* **c103 h85**

ROYAL ACT 6 br.g. Royal Anthem (USA) – Native's Return (IRE) (Presenting) [2017/18 b74: h16.2g^F h16.2g⁴ h15.8s h15.8d c16.2v² c16s⁴ c15.7v³ c16.1v* c18.2s* c18.2m^{pu} Apr 25] poor form over hurdles: modest form over fences: won handicaps at Taunton (twice, novice event second occasion) in March: left Sam England after second start: stays 2¼m: acts on heavy going: sometimes wears headgear. *Sarah-Jayne Davies* **c91 h58**

ROYAL BATTALION 7 b.g. Sea The Stars (IRE) – Yummy Mummy (Montjeu (IRE)) [2017/18 h105: h19.6m³ h19.1m² h21.7g^F h19.2d⁵ h21.4g Oct 29] sturdy gelding: modest handicap hurdler: stays 2¾m: acts on soft and good to firm going: usually wears headgear. *Gary Moore* **h93**

ROYAL BEEKEEPER 5 ch.g. Champs Elysees – Lasso (Indian Ridge) [2017/18 h15.7d⁵ h20g⁴ h18.7g* h20.3d⁵ h15.8g^F h16s³ h18.6v h15.8s ab16g⁴ h16v^{pu} h16.7s^{pu} Mar 26] won both completed starts in points: fair hurdler: won conditionals seller at Stratford in November and novice claimer at Ludlow in December: left Dan Skelton after fifth start: stays 2½m: acts on good to soft going: wears cheekpieces: often races towards rear. *Conor Dore* **h106**

ROYAL CHIEF (IRE) 9 gr.g. Royal Anthem (USA) – Help Yourself (IRE) (Roselier (FR)) [2017/18 c67, h95: h20g h23g⁴ h20f⁴ c23m⁴ h23.9g⁶ Nov 16] sturdy gelding: winning pointer: modest handicap hurdler: poor maiden chaser: stays 3m, effective at shorter: acts on any going: usually races prominently. *Alexandra Dunn* **c66 h87**

ROYAL CLARET 6 b.m. Yeats (IRE) – Kerada (FR) (Astarabad (USA)) [2017/18 b86: h18.5s⁴ h16s⁴ h21.7v^{pu} h25.5s* h23.9v³ Apr 15] fair form over hurdles: won mares handicap at Hereford in March: stays 3¼m: acts on heavy going: often wears tongue tie. *Tom Symonds* **h101**

ROYAL DEBUTANTE (IRE) 7 b.m. Presenting – Chinatownqueen (IRE) (Westerner) [2017/18 h114: h20.3g² c18g^F h19.2g^{pu} h16.3d^{pu} Apr 22] fair handicap hurdler: weakening when fell heavily 2 out in novice handicap won by Exitas at Kempton on chasing debut: stays 21f: acts on good to soft going: usually wears tongue tie. *Paul Webber* **c102 h112**

ROYALE CHAMP (IRE) 6 b.m. Robin des Champs (FR) – Rosafi (IRE) (Roselier (FR)) [2017/18 h73, b65: h25.8g h20g Oct 17] third in Irish mares maiden point on debut: poor form over hurdles: bred to be suited by 3m+: tried in tongue tie. *Seamus Mullins* **h–**

ROYALE DJANGO (IRE) 9 b.g. Kayf Tara – Royale Boja (FR) (Kadalko (FR)) [2017/18 c–, h–: h23.1m^{pu} h23.3g⁵ h23.3g³ h25g³ h23.6d^{pu} c26.6s^F c23.6v^{pu} Apr 14] has had breathing operation: fair handicap hurdler: fairly useful handicap chaser: stays 3m: acts on good to firm and heavy going: usually wears cheekpieces: in tongue tie last 2 starts: unreliable. *Tim Vaughan* **c115 § h102 §**

ROYALE KNIGHT 12 b.g. King's Theatre (IRE) – Gardana (FR) (Garde Royale) [2017/18 c128, h110: h24d⁴ c28.4v^{pu} c26d^{pu} Dec 15] winning hurdler: smart chaser at best, no form in 2017/18: stays 35f: acts on good to firm and heavy going: often wears headgear. *Dr Richard Newland* **c– h–**

ROYAL ESCAPE (IRE) 6 b.g. Getaway (GER) – Echo Queen (IRE) (Luso) [2017/18 b88: h19.9g^{bd} h19.9d⁵ h19.7d⁴ Oct 18] modest form over hurdles. *Jonjo O'Neill* **h90**

ROYAL ETIQUETTE (IRE) 11 b.g. Royal Applause – Alpine Gold (IRE) (Montjeu (IRE)) [2017/18 h88: h18.7m⁵ h16.2d⁴ h15.9m h15.5v³ h16s^{ur} h15.9v⁴ h21s³ Apr 9] angular gelding: poor maiden hurdler: stays 2½m: acts on good to firm and heavy going: wears headgear/tongue tie: often races towards rear. *Lawney Hill* **h84**

ROYALEWHIT 5 b.m. Robin des Champs (FR) – Tosca Bella (CZE) (Tauchsport (EG)) [2017/18 ab16g Nov 14] second foal: dam, 15f-2½m hurdle/chase winner in Belgium/Germany (also 1¾m winner on Flat), half-sister to high-class hurdler (stayed 25f) Solwhit: in hood/tongue tie, tailed off in mares bumper. *Anthony Honeyball* **b–**

ROYALE ZANZIBAR (FR) 4 gr.g. Blue Bresil (FR) – Royale Punta Cana (FR) (Verbier (FR)) [2017/18 h16.9s³ h16.9g² h16.3s h16.2s* h16v⁴ Mar 10] tall gelding: fair hurdler: won juvenile maiden at Hereford in January: left Guillaume Macaire after second start: would have stayed beyond 2m: acted on soft going: dead. *Tom Symonds* **h114**

ROY

ROYAL FLAG 8 b.g. New Approach (IRE) – Gonbarda (GER) (Lando (GER)) [2017/18 h16.2v⁵ Oct 14] fair on Flat, stays 16.5f: 13/2, fifth in novice at Hexham (28¾ lengths behind Dame Rose) on hurdling debut. *Brian Ellison* — **h86**

ROYAL ICON 4 b.f. Sixties Icon – Gillstown Great (Royal Applause) [2017/18 h15.5d Nov 20] fair maiden on Flat, stays 11f: considerate ride when well beaten in fillies juvenile on hurdling debut: open to improvement. *Kevin Ryan* — **h– p**

ROYAL IRISH HUSSAR (IRE) 8 b.g. Galileo (IRE) – Adjalisa (IRE) (Darshaan) [2017/18 h124: h18.7g h15.8s^F h21m² Apr 26] close-coupled gelding: fairly useful handicap hurdler: second at Kempton in April: stays 21f: acts on soft and good to firm going: has worn cheekpieces: front runner/races prominently. *Nicky Henderson* — **h120**

ROYAL MAGIC (IRE) 6 b.g. Whitmore's Conn (USA) – Room To Room Magic (IRE) (Casteddu) [2017/18 b16.3d⁶ h21g* h24.6s⁵ h22d Apr 22] £5,500 5-y-o: eighth foal: half-brother to a winning pointer by Dushyantor: dam 11.5f winner: unplaced both completed starts in Irish points: sixth in bumper at Newbury: fairly useful form over hurdles: won novice at Towcester in November: should stay 3m: wears tongue tie. *Sam Thomas* — **h120 b75**

ROYAL MANDATE (IRE) 6 ch.g. Manduro (GER) – Hesperia (Slip Anchor) [2017/18 h–: h16.7g³ h15.6m⁴ h15.6g h19.4s³ h23.8d⁵ ab16.3g⁶ h20.2s⁶ Apr 26] modest maiden hurdler: stays 3m: acts on soft going: often wears cheekpieces: front runner/races prominently. *Rebecca Menzies* — **h95**

ROYAL MARSKELL 9 b.g. Multiplex – Socialise (Groom Dancer (USA)) [2017/18 h16.7g³ h15.9d⁵ h15.8d h15.8g Apr 24] fairly useful on Flat, stays 16.5f: fair form over hurdles. *Gay Kelleway* — **h107**

ROYAL PALLADIUM (FR) 10 gr.g. King's Theatre (IRE) – Dent Sucree (FR) (Turgeon (USA)) [2017/18 c123§, h–: c24.2v³ c26.7vᵖᵘ c30.7vᵖᵘ Apr 17] useful-looking gelding: maiden hurdler: fairly useful handicap chaser: third at Exeter in November: stays 3¼m: acts on heavy going: tried in cheekpieces: front runner/races prominently: unreliable. *Venetia Williams* — **c125 § h–**

ROYAL PLAZA 7 b.g. King's Theatre (IRE) – Friendly Craic (IRE) (Mister Lord (USA)) [2017/18 h119: c20.3g² c19.4g² c17.2g⁴ c19.9g² c20.5s³ c25.6g^F c21.2s⁶ c17.2s³ Dec 26] fairly useful hurdler: fairly useful maiden chaser: second in handicap at Huntingdon in October: left Alan King after third start: stays 2½m: acts on soft and good to firm going: wears headgear/tongue tie: often races in rear/travels strongly (has found little). *Olly Murphy* — **c118 h–**

ROYALRAISE (IRE) 9 b.g. Royal Anthem (USA) – Raise The Issue (IRE) (Galileo (IRE)) [2017/18 c125, h–: h24.5d c23s³ c23s^F c20.3g³ Apr 20] lengthy gelding: fairly useful hurdler at best: fairly useful chaser: third in hunter at Southwell in April: stays 3m: acts on soft and good to firm going: usually wears blinkers. *Oliver Sherwood* — **c119 h–**

ROYAL REGATTA (IRE) 10 b.g. King's Theatre (IRE) – Friendly Craic (IRE) (Mister Lord (USA)) [2017/18 c157, h–: c19.9dᵖᵘ c21dᵖᵘ Nov 25] useful-looking gelding: winning hurdler: very smart chaser, pulled up both starts in 2017/18: stays 21f: acts on soft going: wears headgear/tongue tie: usually leads: has hinted at temperament. *Philip Hobbs* — **c– h–**

ROYAL RUBY 6 b.g. Yeats (IRE) – Close Harmony (Bustino) [2017/18 h86: h16g³ h16.3v⁴ h15.9d² h15.8d Mar 26] rather unfurnished gelding: bumper winner: fair form over hurdles: wears hood: often races prominently/freely. *Nicky Henderson* — **h110**

ROYAL SALUTE 8 br.g. Flemensfirth (USA) – Loxhill Lady (Supreme Leader) [2017/18 c116, h–: h24.3v^F h24.3vᵖᵘ h25.3dᵖᵘ h25d⁴ c26.2vᵖᵘ Apr 16] well-made gelding: has had breathing operation: fair handicap hurdler: fairly useful chaser: stays 3¼m: acts on heavy going: has worn blinkers/tongue tie, including in 2017/18: usually leads. *George Bewley* — **c– h109**

ROYALS AND REBELS (IRE) 8 b.g. Robin des Pres (FR) – Native Deal (IRE) (Be My Native (USA)) [2017/18 c99, h103: c25.7g* c26.1gᵖᵘ c25.8mᵖᵘ c25.8dᵖᵘ h23.1v c21.6v³ c24v³ c21.2d⁴ Apr 7] fair form over hurdles: fair handicap chaser: won at Plumpton in May: stays 3¼m: acts on heavy going: wears headgear/tongue tie: often races towards rear: ungenuine. *Charlie Mann* — **c106 § h– §**

ROYAL SUMMIT 7 b.g. Kayf Tara – Nas Na Riogh (IRE) (King's Theatre (IRE)) [2017/18 b16.2m h19.4g h16vᵖᵘ h22.7sᵖᵘ h19.3vᵖᵘ Apr 17] no form in bumper/over hurdles: tried in tongue tie. *Alison Hamilton* — **h– b–**

ROYAL SUNDAY (FR) 4 gr.g. Never On Sunday (FR) – Royale Malaisie (FR) (Villez (USA)) [2017/18 h16.2v² h15.7v^F Apr 27] half-brother to French hurdler Nicea Bella (2m-19f winner, by Great Pretender): dam lightly-raced sister to fairly useful French hurdler (2¼m/19f winner) Question de Chance: fair maiden on Flat, stays 8.5f: fair form over hurdles: won juvenile maiden at Hereford in April: remains with potential. *Alex Hales* — **h108 p**

ROYAL SUPREMO (IRE) 7 b.g. Beneficial – Slaney Athlete (IRE) (Warcraft (USA)) **h102**
[2017/18 h111, b92: h21.2m² May 14] runner-up in Irish maiden point: bumper winner: fair hurdler: stays 21f: acts on good to firm going. *Kim Bailey*

ROYAL TARA (IRE) 9 b.g. Kayf Tara – The Irish Whip (Presenting) [2017/18 c23g* **c119** h21s⁶ h18.5s⁵ c19.9d c24.2d² Apr 24] €20,000 3-y-o, resold €25,000 3-y-o: has had **h65** breathing operation: third foal: half-brother to a winning pointer by Revoque: dam (h81), lightly raced (second over 2½m only start over hurdles), half-sister to fairly useful hurdler/chaser (stayed 21f) Keepthedreamalive: winning pointer: poor form over hurdles: fairly useful form over fences: won novice hunter at Tipperary in May with plenty in hand: left J. L. Hassett after that: stays 3m: acts on good to soft going. *Venetia Williams*

ROYAL VACATION (IRE) 8 b.g. King's Theatre (IRE) – Summer Break (IRE) **c131** (Foxhound (USA)) [2017/18 c146, h–: c19.4s³ c26g^pu h20.3s⁵ h21.1s c28.8d^pu Apr 28] **h136** useful-looking gelding: useful hurdler: useful handicap chaser: third in listed event at Wetherby (23 lengths behind Guitar Pete) in November: stays 3m: acts on heavy going: wears headgear: usually wears tongue tie: usually races prominently. *Colin Tizzard*

ROYAL VILLAGE (IRE) 6 b.g. Scorpion (IRE) – Etoile Margot (FR) (Garde Royale) **h122**
[2017/18 h116, b106: h23g* h22.1s⁵ Jul 22] fell in Irish maiden point: useful bumper performer: fairly useful form over hurdles: won novice at Worcester in May: stays 23f: acts on good to firm and heavy going. *Philip Hobbs*

ROYBUOY 11 b.g. Royal Applause – Wavy Up (IRE) (Brustolon) [2017/18 h21.6d⁶ Sep **c– §** 22] maiden hurdler/chaser, well beaten on sole start in 2017/18 after 41-month absence: **h–** has worn headgear: often wears tongue tie: temperamental. *Derrick Scott*

ROYCANO 8 ch.g. Lucarno (USA) – Royal Distant (USA) (Distant View (USA)) **h116**
[2017/18 h24.1v³ Mar 20] workmanlike gelding: multiple point winner: fairly useful handicap hurdler: off 23 months, third at Wetherby on sole start in 2017/18: stays 3m: acts on heavy going. *Michael Easterby*

RUACANA 9 b.g. Cape Cross (IRE) – Farrfesheena (USA) (Rahy (USA)) [2017/18 c–, **c–** h129: h21.1g Oct 27] smallish, sturdy gelding: useful hurdler, well below form sole start in **h–** 2017/18: jumped sketchily only chase outing: stays 21f: acts on heavy going: has worn headgear, including last 3 starts. *Tim Vaughan*

RUARAIDH HUGH (IRE) 9 b.g. Craigsteel – Decent Shower (Decent Fellow) **h–** [2017/18 h111: h19.4s h23.9s Apr 25] fair hurdler, below form in 2017/18: stays 23f: acts on good to firm and good to soft going: wears headgear: often races towards rear. *Julia Brooke*

RUBBING SHOULDERS (IRE) 6 b.m. Saint des Saints (FR) – Saine d'Esprit (FR) **b80** (Dom Alco (FR)) [2017/18 b17.3g⁶ b16.2m² b16.2d⁴ Aug 2] first foal: dam, French maiden (failed to complete both starts over fences), half-sister to useful hurdler/high-class chaser (2¼m-3m winner) Quel Esprit (by Saint des Saints): modest form in bumpers: best effort when second at Perth in July. *Gordon Elliott, Ireland*

RUBYDOOBS (IRE) 5 b.m. Beneficial – Time In Milan (IRE) (Milan) [2017/18 b16.2m **b72** b16.2g⁶ b15.6g b15.6d Feb 14] rather unfurnished mare: second foal: half-sister to fair 2m hurdle winner Western Ruler (by Westerner): dam, unraced, closely related to Grand National runner-up Oscar Time: poor form in bumpers: wears tongue tie. *Lucinda Russell*

RUBY FOOL 8 b.m. Apple Tree (FR) – Westbourne (IRE) (King's Ride) [2017/18 h19v⁴ **h–** h21.6s Apr 23] third foal: half-sister to a winning pointer by Milan: dam winning pointer: point winner: well held in 2 novice hurdles: wears cheekpieces. *Richard Mitford-Slade*

RUBY RAMBLER 8 b.m. Notnowcato – Arruhan (IRE) (Mujtahid (USA)) [2017/18 **c72** c16.1s⁴ c15.9s c16v⁴ Jan 30] strong mare: winning hurdler: poor form over fences: **h–** unproven beyond 2m: acts on heavy going. *Lucy Wadham*

RUBY RUSSET 6 b.m. Apple Tree (FR) – Fair Coppelia (Saddlers' Hall (IRE)) [2017/18 **h79** h92, b75: h21.4s^pu h16.5v^pu h16.5s^pu h18.5s⁴ Apr 23] poor maiden hurdler: usually in tongue tie. *Colin Tizzard*

RUBYS CUBE 5 b.m. Multiplex – Cresswell Ruby (IRE) (Rashar (USA)) [2017/18 b–: **h58** h15.8g⁴ h20g⁴ h16g⁶ h20g^F Aug 23] little form in bumper/over hurdles: should be suited by at least 2½m. *Debra Hamer*

RUBY TIGER (IRE) 4 b.f. Sulamani (IRE) – Fenney Spring (Polish Precedent (USA)) **b73**
[2017/18 b17d³ Mar 31] sixth foal: half-sister to 3 winners, including bumper winner/useful hurdler Knight Bachelor (2½m-2¾m winner, by Midnight Legend), stayed 25f, and

bumper winner/fair hurdler Tearsofclewbay (2m winner, by Kayf Tara): dam (h69) bumper/2m hurdle winner (stayed 2½m): 4/1, third in mares bumper at Carlisle (18½ lengths behind Derriana Spirit): will be suited by 2½m. *Henry Daly*

RUBYTWO 6 b.m. Sulamani (IRE) – Miss Nellie (IRE) (Presenting) [2017/18 b16.2g³ b16.2g⁵ b16.2s² Aug 19] first foal: dam unraced half-sister to fairly useful hurdler/chaser (stayed 3½m) Aldertune: fair form in bumpers: best effort when second in mares event at Perth in August. *Nicky Richards* **b85**

RUBY WHO (IRE) 6 gr.g. Daylami (IRE) – Lelepa (IRE) (Inchinor) [2017/18 h–, b–: c20.1vᵖᵘ Oct 14] maiden hurdler: pulled up in novice handicap on chasing debut. *Rose Dobbin* **c–**
h–

RUBY YEATS 7 b.m. Yeats (IRE) – Newbay Lady (Terimon) [2017/18 h114: h19.4s c18.2s² c24sᵖᵘ h25.5sᵖᵘ h16v Apr 14] workmanlike mare: maiden pointer: fair handicap hurdler: fairly useful form over fences: better effort when second in novice handicap at Taunton in February: should stay beyond 2¼m: acts on heavy going: usually wears headgear: usually races prominently. *Harry Whittington* **c117**
h93

RUDE AND CRUDE (IRE) 9 b.g. Rudimentary (USA) – Sorry Sarah (IRE) (Good Thyne (USA)) [2017/18 c95, h–: c16.5mᵖᵘ May 11] tall gelding: point winner: maiden hurdler: modest form in chases: stayed 2½m: acted on good to firm and heavy going: tried in tongue tie: dead. *Gary Moore* **c–**
h–

RUFFLING FEATHERS (IRE) 4 b.g. Presenting – Oilily (IRE) (Dr Massini (IRE)) [2017/18 b16s b15.3d⁴ Apr 22] €60,000 3-y-o: first foal: dam (h143), bumper/2m-2½m hurdle winner, also 1¾m winner on Flat: fair form in bumpers: better effort when fourth at Wincanton in April, needing stiffer test. *Colin Tizzard* **b85**

RUGGIERO (IRE) 5 ch.g. Robin des Champs (FR) – Kayf Vera (IRE) (Kayf Tara) [2017/18 b15.8d h21.7vᵖᵘ Jan 21] seventh in bumper at Uttoxeter (19¼ lengths behind Article Fifty) in November: pulled up in novice on hurdling debut. *Emma Lavelle* **h–**
b70

RULER OF THE NILE 6 b.g. Exceed And Excel (AUS) – Dinka Raja (USA) (Woodman (USA)) [2017/18 h90: h21.6g May 10] fair on Flat, stays 2¼m: modest maiden hurdler: tried in cheekpieces. *Robert Stephens* **h–**

RUMOR 5 ch.g. Windsor Castle – Whispering Wind (IRE) (Sunshine Street (USA)) [2017/18 b16g⁴ h16d h15.7g h19.5v h20.5vᵖᵘ Jan 23] smallish gelding: fourth in bumper at Worcester (16¼ lengths behind Hatcher): no form over hurdles. *John Flint* **h–**
b69

RUMSDEN RAH RAH 5 b.m. Multiplex – Scottish Heights (IRE) (Selkirk (USA)) [2017/18 b16g³ May 25] seventh foal: half-sister to 3 winners on Flat, including 1¼m-1½m winner Turnbury (by Azamour): dam ran once on Flat: in tongue tie, tailed off in bumper. *Chris Gordon* **b–**

RUM SWIZZLE 6 b.m. Mawatheeq (USA) – Port Providence (Red Ransom (USA)) [2017/18 h20mᵖᵘ May 11] fair on Flat, stays 13f: pulled up in mares maiden on hurdling debut. *Harry Dunlop* **h–**

RUNASIMI RIVER 5 ch.m. Generous (IRE) – Zaffaranni (IRE) (Zaffaran (USA)) [2017/18 b83: b15.7g h15.7g* h16.8g^F h16.7g⁴ Sep 30] modest form in bumpers: fair form over hurdles: won mares novice at Southwell in August: often let down by jumping. *Neil Mulholland* **h102 x**
b–

RUN DON'T HIDE (IRE) 7 b.g. High Chaparral (IRE) – Right Key (IRE) (Key of Luck (USA)) [2017/18 h20.7m h20g h20g h22s h24s h15.3v³ h19.6sᵖᵘ c20.3v³ c20.9vᵖᵘ Apr 10] poor maiden hurdler: similar form over fences: better effort when third in novice handicap at Southwell in February: left J. D. Motherway after fourth start: stays 2½m: acts on heavy going: tried in cheekpieces: wears tongue tie. *Paul Henderson* **c81**
h78

RUN FOR EVA 5 b.m. Westerner – Glorybe (GER) (Monsun (GER)) [2017/18 b–: b15.7g⁵ h15.7vᵖᵘ h16.7s³ h15.8g Apr 24] leggy mare: poor form in bumpers/over hurdles: left Olly Williams after first start: wore hood in 2017/18. *Laura Morgan* **h69**
b68

RUNNING IN HEELS (IRE) 9 br.m. September Storm (GER) – Ceo Draiochta (IRE) (Erins Isle) [2017/18 c71: c26.2g⁶ h16.7g* h17.2g⁶ c19.9m² c19.9g³ Dec 18] won 3 times in points: modest form over hurdles: won mares handicap at Market Rasen in June: similar form in chases: left Miss L. V. Horner after first start: stays 2½m: acts on good to firm going: wears headgear: often wears tongue tie: has joined Gavin Patrick Cromwell. *Rebecca Menzies* **c93**
h90

RUNNING WOLF (IRE) 7 b.g. Amadeus Wolf – Monet's Lady (IRE) (Daylami (IRE)) [2017/18 c94§, h82§: c21.4g* c22.5d⁴ c23.8g² c22.7m* c21.4s^ur Dec 26] lengthy, workmanlike gelding: winning hurdler: fair handicap chaser: won at Market Rasen (novice) in May and Leicester in November: stays 3m: acts on soft and good to firm going: wears tongue tie: unreliable. *Alex Hales* c108 §
h– §

RUN ROCKY RUN (IRE) 5 b.g. Vertical Speed (FR) – Marlatara (IRE) (Marju (IRE)) [2017/18 b16s b16v Dec 22] no form in bumpers. *Lucinda Russell* b–

RUNSWICK ROYAL (IRE) 9 ch.g. Excellent Art – Renada (Sinndar (IRE)) [2017/18 c–, h136: h22.8m h20.1g Jun 17] good-topped gelding: useful hurdler, well below best both starts in 2017/18: winning chaser: probably stays 25f, effective at much shorter: acts on good to firm and heavy going. *Ann Hamilton* c–
h–

RUN TO MILAN (IRE) 6 b.g. Milan – Run Supreme (IRE) (Supreme Leader) [2017/18 b105: h16.8v² h18.5v* h21s² h19.8v^pu h21.4v² Mar 28] rather unfurnished gelding: useful bumper performer: fairly useful form over hurdles: won maiden at Exeter in January: second in novice at Kempton in February: stays 21f: acts on heavy going: often in hood: often races prominently. *Victor Dartnall* h125

RUNYON RATTLER (IRE) 8 b.g. Runyon (IRE) – Lake Majestic (IRE) (Mister Majestic) [2017/18 h117: h16g² h20.2g* h20d⁵ h21.1s^ur h24s^F Dec 28] sturdy gelding: fairly useful handicap hurdler: won at Bellewstown in August: stays 2½m: acts on soft going: tried in hood: usually leads. *P. J. Rothwell, Ireland* h125

RUPERRA TOM 10 b.g. Kayf Tara – Cathy's Dream (IRE) (Husyan (USA)) [2017/18 c–p, h–: c22.6d² Jun 9] multiple point winner: maiden hurdler: fair form in hunter chases: second in novice at Stratford in June: stays 23f: acts on good to soft going: wears hood: in tongue tie last 2 starts: open to further improvement over fences. *N. Williams* c109 p
h–

RUPERT VALENTINO 5 b.g. Schiaparelli (GER) – Magic Valentine (Magic Ring (IRE)) [2017/18 b16.8s Feb 23] in hood, tailed off in bumper. *Jackie du Plessis* b–

RUSSBOROUGH (FR) 9 b.g. Turgeon (USA) – Heritage River (FR) (Kaldounevees (FR)) [2017/18 c110§, h–: c18.8v² c19.9s⁵ c24s⁴ c23.9v⁵ Apr 11] strong gelding: maiden hurdler: fair handicap chaser: stays 2½m: acts on heavy going: has worn cheekpieces, including last 2 starts: often races prominently: unreliable. *Venetia Williams* c114 §
h–

RUSSE BLANC (FR) 11 wh.g. Machiavellian Tsar (FR) – Fleur de Mad (FR) (Maiymad) [2017/18 c129, h–: c26.2d⁴ c28.4v^ur c26.3s⁴ c29.2s^pu c29.2v^pu c34u^ur Mar 17] angular gelding: maiden hurdler: fairly useful handicap chaser: fourth at Carlisle in November: stays 29f: acts on heavy going: wears headgear: often races towards rear. *Kerry Lee* c121
h–

RUSSIAN HAWK 4 b.g. Malinas (GER) – Sparron Hawk (FR) (Hawker's News (IRE)) [2017/18 b15.3d³ Apr 22] €90,000 3-y-o: sixth foal: half-brother to 3 winners, including useful hurdler Out of The Loop (19f/2½m winner, by Shantou) and fairly useful hurdler Some Hawk (2¾m winner, by Presenting): dam (b98), bumper winner, half-sister to useful chaser (stayed 3m) The Wicketkeeper and to dam of high-class hurdler/smart chaser L'Ami Serge and useful hurdler/very smart chaser Sizing Codelco (both stay 25f): 20/1, shaped like stayer when third in bumper at Wincanton (6¼ lengths behind Samarquand). *Colin Tizzard* b94

RUSSIAN RASCAL 5 b.g. Kyllachy – Russian Ruby (FR) (Vettori (IRE)) [2017/18 h–: h16.8g⁴ h16.8g³ h16.2g h16.8g h19.7d h19.9v^pu h16.7g⁶ Apr 22] modest maiden hurdler: wears tongue tie. *Maurice Barnes* h89

RUSSIAN REGENT (IRE) 14 b.g. Moscow Society (USA) – Micro Villa (IRE) (Electric) [2017/18 c133, h92: h22.5g⁵ c23.8g³ c23.8g c29.2g h22s^pu Dec 9] tall gelding: modest maiden hurdler: fairly useful handicap chaser: third at Perth in July: stays 25f: acts on good to firm and heavy going: has worn cheekpieces. *Gordon Elliott, Ireland* c126
h86

RUSSIAN ROYALE 8 b.m. Royal Applause – Russian Ruby (FR) (Vettori (IRE)) [2017/18 h95: h16.8g h16.7d h16.8v⁵ h16.8v³ h21.2g⁴ Apr 23] smallish mare: modest handicap hurdler: stays 21f: acts on good to firm and heavy going: in cheekpieces last 2 starts. *Micky Hammond* h89

RUSSIAN SERVICE 6 b.g. Robin des Champs (FR) – Just Kate (Bob's Return (IRE)) [2017/18 h119, b76: h21g h21g h24s⁴ h26v^pu c20.9v³ Mar 10] rather unfurnished gelding: won only start in maiden points: fair handicap hurdler: 14/1, third in novice handicap at Hereford (11¼ lengths behind Lord Bryan) on chasing debut: should stay 3m+: acts on heavy going: tried in cheekpieces: often races towards rear: should improve over fences. *Samuel Drinkwater* c107 p
h102

RUS

RUSSIAN SPY (IRE) 5 b.g. Sholokhov (IRE) – Elle Desert (GER) (Next Desert (IRE)) [2017/18 b17s⁴ b14d h19.7s h16v h17.7v⁵ h19.8vᵖᵘ Mar 8] poor form in bumpers: no form over hurdles: tried in cheekpieces. *Evan Williams*   h– b72

RUSSIANTOM (IRE) 7 b.m. Dylan Thomas (IRE) – Russian Roubles (IRE) (Sadler's Wells (USA)) [2017/18 b16.4g b16s⁶ h20.6vᵖᵘ h20.2s⁶ Apr 25] fourth foal: closely related/half-sister to winners on Flat in Italy by Duke of Marmalade and Dubai Destination: dam, lightly raced on Flat, half-sister to fairly useful hurdler/fair chaser (stayed 3m) Lorenzino: no form in bumpers/over hurdles: in tongue tie last 2 starts. *Susan Corbett*   h– b–

RUWASI 7 b.g. Authorized (IRE) – Circle of Love (Sakhee (USA)) [2017/18 h109: h16gᵘʳ May 15] sturdy gelding: fair form over hurdles: every chance when unseated rider 2 out in novice won by Ok Corral at Kempton: dead. *Gary Moore*   h107

RUZEIZ (USA) 9 b.g. Muhtathir – Saraama (USA) (Bahri (USA)) [2017/18 h–: h18.5gᵖᵘ Jun 27] no form over hurdles: sometimes in headgear: tried in tongue tie. *Peter Hedger*   h–

RYALEX (IRE) 7 b.g. Arcadio (GER) – Lady Ramona (IRE) (Lord Americo) [2017/18 c102, h102: c20.1g² May 17] point winner: maiden hurdler: modest form over fences: stays 2½m: acts on soft and good to firm going: usually wears hood: usually leads. *Lucinda Russell*   c97 h–

RYE CROSS (IRE) 11 b.g. Catcher In The Rye (IRE) – Jeanette Hall (IRE) (Saddlers' Hall (IRE)) [2017/18 c25.3dᵖᵘ c23g* May 26] tall gelding: multiple point winner: modest form in hunter chases: won at Worcester in May: tried in cheekpieces/tongue tie. *Miss E. Alvis*   c95

RYEDALE RACER 7 b.g. Indian Danehill (IRE) – Jontys'lass (Tamure (IRE)) [2017/18 h118: h20.1s² h21.3s⁴ h22.7v³ h20.1d³ Apr 23] fairly useful handicap hurdler: third at Kelso in February: stays 3lf: acts on heavy going. *Ruth Jefferson*   h119

RYLESTONE 7 ch.m. Presenting – Silver Monument (Silver Patriarch (IRE)) [2017/18 h20.6v h16.4s h20.5vᵖᵘ Mar 10] first foal: dam winning pointer: no form over hurdles. *Stuart Coltherd*   h–

S

SABLE ISLAND (IRE) 4 b.g. New Approach (IRE) – Ratukidul (FR) (Danehill (USA)) [2017/18 h16.2s⁶ h15.8sᵖᵘ Mar 14] lightly raced on Flat, stays 1¾m: only poor form on hurdling debut: fatally injured next time. *Olly Murphy*   h77

SACKETT 7 b.g. Midnight Legend – Gloriana (Formidable (USA)) [2017/18 h23.3d² h25sᵖᵘ h19.9vᵖᵘ h20.7s³ h21.7v² h19.7s* h19.9v² h25d³ Apr 24] strong gelding: winning pointer: fair handicap hurdler: won at Hereford in March: left Mark Walford after first start: stays 25f: acts on heavy going: front runner/races prominently. *Neil King*   h109

SACKFULLOFDREAMS (IRE) 5 b.g. Rock of Gibraltar (IRE) – Nymphaea Alba (IRE) (Monsun (GER)) [2017/18 h16d h16g h16g⁶ h16g h16.5gᵖᵘ h15.8g h19.2dᵖᵘ Nov 19] fair at best on Flat in France, has become disappointing: modest maiden hurdler: left E. J. O'Grady after fifth start: unproven beyond 2m: acts on good to soft going: often in headgear: has worn tongue tie, including last 5 starts. *Mike Hammond*   h89

SACRAMENTO KING (IRE) 9 gr.g. Desert King (IRE) – Kindle Ball (FR) (Kaldounevees (FR)) [2017/18 h87: c23.6g⁴ May 29] workmanlike gelding: modest maiden hurdler, very lightly raced: well beaten in novice handicap on chasing debut: probably stays 3m: best efforts on good going: in tongue tie last 2 starts. *Jonathan Geake*   c– h–

SADDLERS ENCORE (IRE) 9 br.g. Presenting – Saddlers Leader (IRE) (Saddlers' Hall (IRE)) [2017/18 c109p, h–: c20v² c26.3vᶠ Mar 16] big gelding: point winner: useful hurdler in 2015/16: very lightly raced and only fair form in chases (not a fluent jumper): should stay beyond 23f: acts on soft going. *Miss Chloe Newman*   c102 x h–

SADLER'S GOLD (IRE) 8 b.g. Gold Well – Mrs Quigley (IRE) (Mandalus) [2017/18 h–: h19.9g² May 28] fair hurdler, lightly raced: should stay beyond 2½m: tried in cheekpieces: in tongue tie last 3 starts. *David Pipe*   h109

SADLER'S RISK (IRE) 10 b.g. Sadler's Wells (USA) – Riskaverse (USA) (Dynaformer (USA)) [2017/18 c150§, h129§: c21g³ h24g c22.5g c22.7dᵖᵘ Apr 28] strong, sturdy gelding: smart hurdler/chaser at best: disappointing in 2017/18 after reappearance (left Henry de Bromhead after third start): stays 25f: acts on heavy going: tried in headgear/tongue tie: often races towards rear: moody. *Tom George*   c129 § h– §

690

SADMA 9 gr.g. Street Cry (IRE) – Blue Dress (USA) (Danzig (USA)) [2017/18 c–, h75: c19.2v^{pu} Apr 8] pulled up in point: fair hurdler at best: little form in chases: unproven beyond 2m: acts on soft and good to firm going. *Nick Lampard*   c–
h–

SAFARI JOURNEY (USA) 14 ch.g. Johannesburg (USA) – Alvernia (USA) (Alydar (USA)) [2017/18 c103§, h–: c15.6g⁶ May 13] tall, good-topped gelding: winning hurdler: fair handicap chaser nowadays: unplaced in points in 2018: stays 2½m: acts on soft and good to firm going: wears headgear: often races in rear: unreliable. *Lucinda Egerton*   c– §
h–

SAFE HARBOUR (FR) 6 b.g. Stowaway – Beharista (FR) (Sendawar (IRE)) [2017/18 h92: h19.4d h21s^F h19.7s^{pu} Mar 27] has had breathing operation: modest maiden hurdler at best, little show in 2017/18: stays 19f: acts on heavy going: tried in blinkers. *Oliver Sherwood*   h75

SAFFRON PRINCE 10 b.g. Kayf Tara – Jan's Dream (IRE) (Executive Perk) [2017/18 c–, h–: c16.5m⁴ c15.7g⁴ c16.3m⁴ c15.7g⁶ c16.3d* c17.8m³ c17.8d² c15.7d² c17d* Oct 23] winning hurdler: fair handicap chaser: won at Newton Abbot in July and Plumpton (novice) in October: stays 2¼m: acts on heavy going: tried in cheekpieces. *David Bridgwater*   c101
h–

SAFFRON WELLS (IRE) 10 b.g. Saffron Walden (FR) – Angel's Folly (Wesaam (USA)) [2017/18 c120, h125: h23.1g³ h20g⁴ c15.7s⁴ h21.6v³ h21.4v⁶ Dec 26] good-topped gelding: fairly useful handicap hurdler: not quite so good over fences: left Neil King after second start: stays easy 23f: acts on good to firm and heavy going: in cheekpieces 6 of last 7 outings. *Colin Tizzard*   c113
h118

SAGE MONKEY (IRE) 9 br.g. Craigsteel – Braw Lass (Alflora (IRE)) [2017/18 c–: c20.9d^{pu} c19.4g³ c17.4g* c16.5g^F c17.4d⁵ h21.2g^{ur} c16g² c16s³ Dec 16] unseated early only start over hurdles: modest handicap chaser: won novice event at Bangor in August: stays 19f: acts on good to firm going: tried in cheekpieces/tongue tie: often races towards rear: has found little. *Kerry Lee*   c94
h–

SAGLAWY (FR) 4 b.g. Youmzain (IRE) – Spasha (Shamardal (USA)) [2017/18 h16v³ h16v* h16s* h16s³ Apr 28] useful on Flat, stays 1¼m: useful form over hurdles: won maiden at Gowran in March and Grade 2 juvenile at Fairyhouse (by 2½ lengths from Mitchouka) in April: third in AES Champion Four Year Old Hurdle at Punchestown (6½ lengths behind Saldier) final start. *W. P. Mullins, Ireland*   h138

SAHALIN 5 b.m. Red Rocks (IRE) – Tamathea (IRE) (Barathea (IRE)) [2017/18 h–: h15.8d h20g⁵ h16g^{ur} h16g h19.6g⁶ h18.5d Sep 22] formerly fair on Flat (unproven beyond 8.5f): poor maiden hurdler: stays 2½m. *John Flint*   h77

SAHARA HAZE 9 b.m. Rainbow High – Gypsy Haze (Romany Rye) [2017/18 h93: h21.6g h23.6d⁴ h23.6v³ h23.9s⁴ h23.8s h26s* h23.3v⁴ h25.5s² h23.9v Apr 15] placed twice from 3 starts in points: modest handicap hurdler: won conditionals/amateur event at Warwick in February: stays 3¼m: acts on heavy going. *Phillip Dando*   h99

SAI KUNG SING (IRE) 4 b.g. Finsceal Fior (IRE) – Sanan Dancer (IRE) (Danehill Dancer (IRE)) [2017/18 b13d⁶ b14.6s ab16.3g^{pu} Feb 24] modest form in bumpers only on debut: tried in tongue tie. *Nigel Tinkler*   b77

SAILING AWAY (IRE) 5 ch.m. Stowaway – Drama Chick (Riverwise (USA)) [2017/18 b17d ab16.3g Apr 15] €8,000 3-y-o: fifth foal: dam unraced sister to Champion Hurdle winner Rooster Booster: no form in bumpers. *Sheena Walton*   b–

SAILOR SAM 5 b.g. Sulamani (IRE) – Lago d'Oro (Slip Anchor) [2017/18 b–: h19.5d Oct 31] tailed off in bumper and maiden hurdle (tongue tied). *Tim Vaughan*   h–

SAILORS WARN (IRE) 11 b.g. Redback – Coral Dawn (IRE) (Trempolino (USA)) [2017/18 h111: h16.3g* h17.2g⁶ h15.7g³ h16s³ Nov 3] small, stocky gelding: fairly useful handicap hurdler: won at Stratford in June: stayed 2¼m: acted on heavy going: often wore cheekpieces/tongue tie: raced towards rear: dead. *Ian Williams*   h116

SAINT ARE (FR) 12 b.g. Network (GER) – Fortanea (FR) (Video Rock (FR)) [2017/18 c148, h–: h24v^{pu} c30.2s^{pu} c34.3s^{bd} Apr 14] workmanlike gelding: winning hurdler: smart chaser at best, placed twice in Grand National at Aintree: failed to complete in 2017/18: stays 35f: acts on heavy going: usually in headgear nowadays: wears tongue tie: front runner/races prominently. *Tom George*   c–
h–

SAINT BREIZ (FR) 12 b.g. Saint des Saints (FR) – Balladina (FR) (Saint Cyrien (FR)) [2017/18 c85, h84: c25.2s⁴ Mar 7] lengthy gelding: point/hurdle winner: fair maiden chaser: stays 25f: acts on heavy going: has worn headgear: usually tongue tied. *Mrs G. B. Walford*   c97
h–

SAINT CAJETAN (FR) 6 b.g. Saint des Saints (FR) – Erivieve (FR) (Marchand de Sable (USA)) [2017/18 h106, b–: h19.4s Jan 27] fair maiden hurdler: tailed off only outing in 2017/18: stays 2½m: probably acts on soft going. *Charlie Longsdon*   h–

Betfred 'Racing's Biggest Supporter' Novices' Handicap Chase, Newbury—the first of three hugely impressive wins by the bold-jumping front runner Saint Calvados

SAINT CALVADOS (FR) 5 b.g. Saint des Saints (FR) – Lamorrese (FR) (Pistolet Bleu (IRE)) [2017/18 c16.4v* c16.4s* c16.2s* c15.9s⁴ Mar 13] lengthy gelding: useful juvenile hurdler in France for S.Culin: quickly developed into even better chaser, winning novice handicaps at Newbury in December/January and Kingmaker Novices' Chase at Warwick (by 22 lengths from Diego du Charmil) in February: possibly amiss in Arkle Chase at Cheltenham final outing: stays 2¼m: acts on heavy going: bold-jumping front runner. *Harry Whittington*   c157 + h–

SAINT CONTEST (FR) 5 b.g. Air Chief Marshal (IRE) – Sainte Adresse (Elusive City (USA)) [2017/18 h106: h16.7g² c18g^ur c19.7s^F Nov 20] good-topped gelding: fair form over hurdles: failed to complete both outings over fences: unproven beyond 17f: acts on good to soft going: remains with potential as a chaser. *Alan King*   c– p h105

SAINT DE REVE (FR) 4 b.g. Saint des Saints (FR) – Ty Mat (FR) (Panoramic) [2017/18 b15.3d Apr 22] 4/1, very green when ninth in bumper at Wincanton (12 lengths behind Ebony Gale). *Paul Nicholls*   b–

SAINTE LADYLIME (FR) 7 b.m. Saint des Saints (FR) – Lady Pauline (FR) (Hamas (IRE)) [2017/18 c133, h125: c24d* c20.6v^ur h23.8v² h23.5v² h23.6s² c24.2v* Mar 20] workmanlike mare: useful hurdler: runner-up all 3 starts in 2017/18, 2¼ lengths behind Carnspindle in handicap at Chepstow third occasion: useful form over fences: won novices at Uttoxeter (mares) in November and Wetherby in March: stays 3m: acts on heavy going. *Kim Bailey*   c134 h132

SAINT FREULE (FR) 5 br.g. Saint des Saints (FR) – Topsy Blue (FR) (Anabaa Blue) [2017/18 h20.1v² h16s⁶ h15.7v⁵ h16v⁵ h20.5v⁴ h17s² h20.2s^rr Apr 27] €15,000 3-y-o: second foal: dam French maiden on Flat: winning Irish pointer: fair maiden hurdler: stays 2½m: raced on soft/heavy going: in hood last 5 starts: tongue tied 4 of 7 outings: usually races freely: one to treat with caution (refused to race final start). *Lucinda Russell*   h108 §

SAINT JOHN HENRY (FR) 8 b.g. Saint des Saints (FR) – Noceane (FR) (Pistolet Bleu (IRE)) [2017/18 h118x: c26.2d* c24.2s^pu c25.5s³ c27.6s^pu c23.4s^pu c28.8v^pu c24v^pu Apr 7] angular gelding: winning hurdler: fairly useful handicap chaser: won novice event at Chepstow on return in October: disappointing after: stays 3¼m: acts on heavy going: wears headgear: normally tongue tied nowadays: often let down by jumping over hurdles. *David Pipe*   c125 d h– x

SAINTS AND SINNERS (IRE) 10 b.g. Gold Well – How Provincial (IRE) (Be My Native (USA)) [2017/18 c20.1s* Dec 23] strong gelding: winning hurdler: useful handicap chaser: won at Newcastle (by 7 lengths from Chidswell) only outing in 2017/18: stays 2½m: acts on heavy going: wears tongue tie. *Michael Easterby*   c134 h–

SAKHEE'S CITY (FR) 7 b.g. Sakhee (USA) – A Lulu Ofa Menifee (USA) (Menifee (USA)) [2017/18 h126§: h16d⁴ h16s² h19.3v* h19.3v⁵ h16.4s⁴ h19.9v h16.4v* Apr 14] rangy gelding: useful handicap hurdler: won at Catterick in January and Newcastle (by 9 lengths from Bulls Head) in April: stays 19f: acts on heavy going: wears cheekpieces: temperamental. *Philip Kirby*   h130 §

SALDIER (FR) 4 b.g. Soldier Hollow – Salve Evita (Monsun (GER)) [2017/18 h16v* h16.8v⁵ h16s³ h16s* Apr 28]   h145

Following early successes over jumps with Scotsirish, who ran under the banner of the Double R Stables Syndicate, Susannah and Rich Ricci had horses registered in their own name for the first time in 2007/08—carrying the pink, light green spots, pink sleeves and cap with which they have become synonymous. The Ricci-owned novice chaser Pomme Tiepy was the leading money-earner for Mullins during that campaign with her four wins including successive Grade 2 wins at Leopardstown and Navan. Mullins has now won the trainers' championship in Ireland eleven years running and, though not the only reason for his domination, the support of the Riccis has undoubtedly been a catalyst, with the partnership having quickly blossomed into one of the most formidable owner-trainer combinations of modern times. From just a handful in training with Mullins in 2007/08, the Riccis have more than sixty in training nowadays in Ireland. In 2015/16, they won a record-equalling (at the time) five races at the Cheltenham Festival courtesy of Douvan (Arkle), Annie Power (Champion Hurdle), Vroum Vroum Mag (Mares' Hurdle), Vautour (Ryanair Chase) and Limini (Dawn Run Mares' Novices' Hurdle). That took the owners' tally at the meeting to thirteen in just nine years, and further wins at each of the last two Festivals have seen that rise to fifteen, which could easily have been more but for the misfortune that has befallen some of their stable stars. Their five winners at the 2016 meeting all missed out on repeat successes for one reason or another the following year. Douvan was only seventh, suffering a stress fracture of the pelvis, when sent off at 9/2-on for the Champion Chase; Annie Power was forced to miss the Champion Hurdle through injury, as did, for the second year in succession, the 2015 winner Faugheen; Vroum Vroum Mag and Limini were only second and third, respectively, behind Apple's Jade in the Mares' Hurdle; and, saddest of all, Vautour broke a leg in a freak accident at Mullins' Closutton stables in the autumn.

Whilst Mullins was crowned Ireland's champion jumps trainer again in 2017/18, the Riccis endured mixed fortunes once more. The campaign started well with Faugheen making a winning return after twenty-two months off in the Morgiana Hurdle at Punchestown in November, but the Christmas Festival at Leopardstown, a meeting which has traditionally been dominated by Mullins in recent years, was in Rich Ricci's words 'an exceptionally challenging week', with many of the stable's more high-profile runners performing below expectations. Min, who was another Ricci-owned horse to miss Cheltenham in 2017 through injury, just about managed to scramble home from the veteran Simply Ned in the Paddy's Rewards Club Chase, only to lose the race in the stewards' room after causing interference to his rival on the run-in; Sharjah looked set to win the Paddy Power Future Champions Novices' Hurdle when he fell at the last, along with stablemate Real Steel; Djakadam ran no sort of race when pulled up in the Christmas Chase; and, five weeks on from his impressive comeback, Faugheen shaped as if amiss when pulled up behind Mick Jazz in the Ryanair Hurdle, with the alarm bells starting to ring before the fourth flight when Cilaos Emery passed him for the lead. Ricci summed up his emotions in an interview with *At The Races* following Faugheen's reversal. 'If you had told me that this season would be worse than last season I would have said absolutely not, but my god it's proving to be so,' he said. The inaugural Dublin Racing Festival at Leopardstown in February was more fruitful for the Riccis, with Min winning the Dublin Chase and Faugheen (second in the Irish Champion Hurdle) and Djakadam (third in the Irish Gold Cup) posting more encouraging efforts in their respective

*AES Champion Four Year Old Hurdle, Punchestown—
total domination by the Willie Mullins-trained runners, though they don't finish in the expected
order with Saldier proving too strong for Mr Adjudicator (dark colours) and Saglawy (No.5)*

races, but the sole win at the Cheltenham Festival, courtesy of Benie des Dieux in the Mares' Hurdle, will have come as something of a disappointing return given the success that the Riccis have become accustomed to. Notable reverses included that of 7/4 favourite Getabird, who was well held when attempting to provide connections with a fourth win in six years in the Supreme Novices' Hurdle, while Min simply found Altior too strong in the Champion Chase, the same race in which Douvan, making his first start since the previous year's renewal, fell when travelling strongly at the head of affairs four out.

The Punchestown Festival also got off to a frustrating start for the Riccis. Douvan ran just respectably when second to stablemate Un de Sceaux in the Boylesports Champion Chase, with Min perhaps feeling the effects of a long season back in fourth, while Djakadam also hit the crossbar in the Punchestown Gold Cup, filling the runner-up spot in the race for the fourth year in succession (he was subsequently retired after reportedly finishing lame when well held in the Grand Steeple-Chase de Paris at Auteuil after the end of the British jumps season). The relief from Rich Ricci after Faugheen (only sixth in the Champion Hurdle at Cheltenham) bounced back to win the Champion Stayers' Hurdle on the third day of Punchestown was palpable. 'I am emotional, as you would expect from me, but absolutely delighted,' he said. 'It has been a tough old season for Faugheen and for us. It is nice to have a change of luck.' The Riccis ended the week with four winners, with Antey giving Ms Katie Walsh a final winner before retirement in Friday's two-mile novice hurdle, and Benie des Dieux and Saldier both winning Grade 1s on the final day of the meeting.

A fairly useful performer on the Flat for Tony Castanheira in France, Saldier looked a good prospect right from the start when he made a winning debut for Mullins over hurdles at Gowran in February, hitting the front on the approach to two out and quickly forging clear. The following month's Triumph Hurdle at Cheltenham perhaps came a bit too soon in Saldier's development and he was beaten over twenty-four lengths by Farclas into fifth. He showed the benefit of that experience with a much improved effort when three and three quarter lengths third behind stablemate Saglawy and Mitchouka in the Grade 2 Boylesports Juvenile Hurdle at Fairyhouse a month later, still not looking the finished article but running on late, after being left behind briefly by the leading pair from two out, and finishing with running left. All seven runners that day were trained by either Mullins or Gordon Elliott and it was a similar story for the AES Champion Four Year Old Hurdle at Punchestown, with the betting dominated by Stormy Ireland, who unseated her rider at the last when already beaten in the Triumph, and the first two from that race, Farclas (5/2) and Mr Adjudicator (100/30). The field was completed by four of the first five home at Fairyhouse, with Saglawy (8/1) expected to confirm his superiority over Saldier (10/1), Mitchouka (20/1) and Msassa (33/1). As she had at Cheltenham, Stormy Ireland raced keenly, although a stop-start pace resulted in a sprint for home, with all seven runners still closely bunched in the back straight. Saldier showed the best turn of foot to lead on the approach to the last and never looked in any danger of defeat, for all that Mr Adjudicator, who met trouble in running, closed to within three lengths at the line. Saglawy was three and a half lengths further back in third, with Msassa taking fourth to complete a one, two, three, four for their trainer. Mullins also won the last two races on the card to make it a record eighteen winners for the week, and he ended the season with first-three prize money of €5,546,771. The result also meant that the three juvenile Grade 1 events at the spring festivals were won by different horses, highlighting the fact that there was no outstanding performer in the division in the latest season. Saldier will certainly have to raise his game a good deal further to be considered Champion Hurdle material, though it would be no surprise if there was more to come from him, as he has had just four starts over hurdles.

Saldier (FR) (b.g. 2014)	Soldier Hollow (br 2000)	In The Wings (b 1986)	Sadler's Wells
			High Hawk
		Island Race (b 1995)	Common Grounds
			Lake Isle
	Salve Evita (b 2004)	Monsun (br 1990)	Konigsstuhl
			Mosella
		Wendylina (ch 1999)	In The Wings
			Dinalina

The angular Saldier is by the very smart German mile and a quarter performer Soldier Hollow, who stands at Gestut Auenquelle at a fee of €25,000. His best progeny on the Flat include the Grosser Preis von Berlin and Prix Foy winner Dschingis Secret, and the Grosser Preis von Baden winner Ivanhowe, a half-brother to the very smart hurdler Irving. Soldier Hollow's other good hurdlers so far include Arctic Fire, who was second behind Faugheen in the Champion Hurdle in 2015, and the West Yorkshire Hurdle winner Silsol. Saldier is the fourth foal, but only runner to date, out of Salve Evita who ran once on the Flat in Germany. Salve Evita is a half-sister to the very smart mile and a quarter performer Sri Putra and Duty, a useful stayer on the Flat who ran to a similar level as a juvenile hurdler and himself

Mrs S. Ricci's "Saldier"

SAL

finished fifth in the Champion Four Year Old Hurdle. This is a very good Flat family, as Saldier's unraced grandam Wendylina is a half-sister to the Prix de Diane winner Caerlina, now the grandam of Prix Jacques le Marois winner Al Wukair. Saldier wore ear plugs at Cheltenham. *W. P. Mullins, Ireland*

SALIX (FR) 4 gr.g. Grey Risk (FR) – Yes Mate (FR) (Lord of Men) [2017/18 h16v⁴ h16.2s⁶ h16s⁴ Apr 9] sturdy gelding: 1½m winner on only start on Flat in France for Mlle C. Courtade: easily best effort over hurdles when fourth in novice at Kempton final start: still unexposed. *Ben Pauling* — **h90 p**

SALLY PARK (IRE) 7 b.g. Flemensfirth (USA) – They Call Me Molly (CAN) (Charlie Barley (USA)) [2017/18 b16s* b19d* b19v⁶ Nov 11] fifth foal: half-brother to useful bumper winner Owen Mc (by Oscar) and bumper winner/fair chaser Call Me Mulligan (winner up to 3¼m, by Bach): dam fair bumper winner: won bumpers at Navan (maiden) in September and Cork (useful form) in October: better for experience when mid-field in maiden at Naas on hurdling debut: will stay at least 2½m: front runner. *Paul W. Flynn, Ireland* — **h100 p / b106**

SALMANAZAR 10 b.g. Classic Cliche (IRE) – Leroy's Sister (FR) (Phantom Breeze) [2017/18 h25s h23.6s⁴ h23.5s² h25d³ Apr 26] good-topped gelding: fairly useful handicap hurdler: winning chaser: stays 25f: acts on heavy going: tried in hood: temperament under suspicion. *Alan King* — **c– / h120**

SALSARETTA (FR) 5 b.m. Kingsalsa (USA) – Kendoretta (FR) (Kendor (FR)) [2017/18 h16.8s^F h20v⁵ Apr 1] angular mare: first foal: dam maiden on Flat in France: useful form over hurdles in France for Francois Nicolle: folded on completed start in 2017/18: should stay beyond 2¼m: acts on soft going. *W. P. Mullins, Ireland* — **h117**

SALTO CHISCO (IRE) 10 b.g. Presenting – Dato Fairy (IRE) (Accordion) [2017/18 c111, h97: h16g* h16.2m² h15.8g h16.8m* h16.7d⁴ c16.5g* h16d⁴ Nov 13] fair handicap hurdler: won at Kempton in May and Newton Abbot in August: fairly useful handicap chaser: won at Huntingdon in November: unproven beyond 17f: acts on soft and good to firm going. *Harry Whittington* — **c120 / h108**

SALUBRIOUS (IRE) 11 b.g. Beneficial – Who Tells Jan (Royal Fountain) [2017/18 c19.2v* Apr 8] useful-looking gelding: winning hurdler: useful chaser at one time: left Paul Nicholls/off 25 months, won hunter at Exeter (by 16 lengths from O Maonlai) in April: stays 25f: acts on heavy going: tried in headgear. *Miss Chloe Roddick* — **c121 / h–**

SAMARAYIA 6 b.m. Black Sam Bellamy (IRE) – Samrana (FR) (Tagula (IRE)) [2017/18 b16s³ b16d h18.5v² h15.5v³ h18.6s⁵ h16.2v* Mar 15] fifth foal: dam unraced half-sister to useful hurdler/winning chaser (stayed 2½m) Samapour: poor form in bumpers: fair form over hurdles: won handicap at Hexham (conditionals) in March: likely to stay 2½m: tracks pace. *Henry Oliver* — **h110 / b74**

SAMARQUAND 4 b.g. Malinas (GER) – Samandara (FR) (Kris) [2017/18 b15.3d* Apr 22] £38,000 3-y-o: seventh foal: half-brother to useful hurdler/smart chaser Warriors Tale (2½m-3m winner, by Midnight Legend): dam (h102), maiden hurdler (stayed 21f), French 1m-11f winner: 5/1 and hooded, looked good prospect when winning bumper at Wincanton (by neck from Bold Plan, pair clear) on debut: sure to go on to better things. *Harry Fry* — **b103 p**

SAMBA TIME 6 gr.m. Black Sam Bellamy (IRE) – Tikk Tokk (IRE) (Tikkanen (USA)) [2017/18 b–: b17v Apr 17] well beaten in bumpers: tried in hood. *George Bewley* — **b–**

SAM BROWN 6 b.g. Black Sam Bellamy (IRE) – Cream Cracker (Sir Harry Lewis (USA)) [2017/18 b113: h21.4g⁴ h20.5s* Dec 18] rather unfurnished gelding: useful form when winning both starts in bumpers: much better effort in novice hurdles (useful form) when winning at Plumpton by 7 lengths from New To This Town, staying on well: should stay at least 21f: will go on improving. *Anthony Honeyball* — **h135 p**

SAMBURU SHUJAA (FR) 5 b.g. Poliglote – Girelle (FR) (Le Nain Jaune (FR)) [2017/18 b95: h19s³ h18.5v³ h19.8v³ h19.5v⁴ Mar 21] fairly useful form when placed over hurdles, though didn't progress: bred to be suited by 2½m+. *Philip Hobbs* — **h120**

SAM CAVALLARO (IRE) 12 b.g. Oscar Schindler (IRE) – Gaelic Holly (IRE) (Scenic) [2017/18 c112: c16.3d² c20.9d² Jun 9] good-topped gelding: multiple winning pointer: fair hunter chaser: stays 21f: acts on good to soft going: has worn headgear/tongue tie: usually races nearer last than first. *Miss H. Brookshaw* — **c101**

SAMCRO (IRE) 6 ch.g. Germany (USA) – Dun Dun (IRE) (Saddlers' Hall (IRE))   **h163 p**
[2017/18 b115p: h16d* h20v* h16s* h21.1s* h16s^F Apr 27]

It should be well worth the wait, but a little more patience will be needed before seeing how jumping's most exciting prospect properly measures up against the best around. Samcro has already gone a long way to fulfilling early promise, proving himself the top novice hurdler, firstly in Ireland, and then, by winning at Cheltenham, extending his bragging rights over the best of the British novices as well. But that was never going to be enough for a horse whose unbeaten record kept setting the bar of expectation ever higher. Beating fellow novices was one thing, but Samcro would only properly lose his 'hype horse' tag—one way or another—when taking on the best around. The opportunity looked like it would come sooner rather than later as Samcro was tested in open company in the final week of the season in the Punchestown Champion Hurdle. Sent off at odds on against the Champion Hurdle runner-up Melon and the Irish Champion Hurdle winner Supasundae, Samcro went tantalisingly close to ending his novice season with a performance that could well have made him the season's best hurdler. But a fall three out when still hard on the bridle, and about to make his move, means Samcro will begin his second season over jumps with his huge potential yet to be fully realised.

Samcro was on his feet straight away after his fall—rather an odd one as he appeared to jump the hurdle cleanly but knuckled over on landing. Not so fortunate was another Irish novice with a big reputation whose campaign forty years earlier bore close similarities to Samcro's. Golden Cygnet, winner of all four of his races over hurdles in Ireland beforehand for Edward O'Grady, was sent off the 5/4-on favourite for the Supreme Novices' at Cheltenham which he won impressively by fifteen lengths. After taking his unbeaten record to six at Fairyhouse later in March, Golden Cygnet was then tested against some of the best established hurdlers, in handicap company, in the Scottish Champion Hurdle. Like Samcro at Punchestown, Golden Cygnet had the Champion Hurdle runner-up to beat at Ayr, but as well as Sea Pigeon, from whom he was receiving just 1 lb, Golden Cygnet was set to concede 5 lb and 7 lb respectively to former dual Champion Hurdle winner Night Nurse and Beacon Light, the pair who had finished third and fourth in the latest Champion Hurdle. Golden Cygnet had made enough of an impression at Cheltenham to share favouritism with Sea Pigeon at 7/4 and he looked the likely winner when challenging leader Night Nurse at the last, two lengths up on Sea Pigeon at the time. Golden Cygnet fell heavily, slightly hampering Sea Pigeon who nonetheless caught Night Nurse near the line. Sea Pigeon's connections didn't dispute the general feeling that Golden Cygnet had his measure at the time of his exit, leading *Chasers & Hurdlers 1977/78* to conclude that 'for a novice to have defeated a seasoned campaigner of Sea Pigeon's calibre at a difference of only 1 lb would have been a staggering achievement.' Sadly, Golden Cygnet never got the opportunity to confirm his outstanding rating for a novice of 176 as two days after the race he succumbed to an injury sustained in the fall.

Another outstanding Irish novice who did go on to enjoy a top-class career, achieving huge popularity in the process, was Danoli. Having lived up to his billing as an Irish banker when winning the 1994 Sun Alliance Novices' Hurdle, he too was pitched into open company for the final start of his novice season when taking on Champion Hurdle winner Flakey Dove and Fortune And Fame (who had already beaten him in the Irish Champion Hurdle) in the Aintree Hurdle. Putting up a performance that had been bettered only by Golden Cygnet among novices in the *Chasers & Hurdlers* era, Danoli ran out an eight-length winner from the Champion Hurdle fourth Mole Board, with Fortune And Fame third and Flakey Dove fifth, his rating of 172p making him Timeform's Champion Jumper that season. Danoli won the Aintree Hurdle again a year later and made the frame in both Champion Hurdles he contested, while he proved top-class in his novice season over fences as well, despite his jumping often letting him down. Danoli fell in the Cheltenham Gold Cup but had beaten two former winners of that race, Jodami and Imperial Call, in the Hennessy Cognac Gold Cup at Leopardstown on his previous start.

Deloitte Novices' Hurdle, Leopardstown—
Samcro looks a horse of rare potential as he passes this test with flying colours again

Speaking after his win at Cheltenham, Danoli's trainer Tom Foley had memorably said 'He's too good for me to say how good he is.' Samcro's connections, on the other hand, were at pains all along not to fuel the hype surrounding their horse, though, frankly, they had their work cut out to keep expectations in check even before Samcro had first jumped a hurdle in public. By then, Samcro had won his only start in Irish points (from Elegant Escape, third in the latest RSA Chase) as a four-year-old before being bought by Gigginstown for a sale-topping £335,000 at the inaugural Aintree Sales at the Grand National meeting and had then proceeded to win all three of his bumpers, the last of them by seventeen lengths at Fairyhouse, showing form which put him among the best bumper performers of 2016/17. After cruising to a fifteen-length win in a maiden hurdle at Punchestown in October, Samcro was installed as ante-post favourite for both the Supreme and the Baring Bingham at Cheltenham, and he strengthened his credentials for the Baring Bingham when stepping up to two and a half miles for the first time to record another impressive win in the Monksfield Novices' Hurdle at Navan the following month, this time by twelve lengths from the useful Jetz. For his final start before Cheltenham, Samcro had options in both Grade 1 novice hurdles at the new Dublin Racing Festival at Leopardstown at the beginning of February and was dropped back to two miles for the Deloitte Novices' Hurdle, a race which had been won by future Champion Hurdle winners Istabraq and Brave Inca, as well as by Danoli. Samcro was sent off at odds on again despite his ten rivals including several useful and progressive novices. A falsely-run race put the emphasis on speed, but that didn't inconvenience Samcro in the slightest as he readily went clear approaching the last and pulled further ahead on the run-in, Duc des Genievres emerging from the pack to chase him home five and a half lengths back in second.

Despite impressing back at two miles, Samcro's Cheltenham target was confirmed as the Baring Bingham a few weeks later, a race which reverted to being branded as the Ballymore Novices' Hurdle for the first time since 2009. Sent off at 11/8-on, Samcro was bidding to become only the second odds-on winner of the race after Mr Kildare who won at the same odds in 1978, another Irish banker during a

*Ballymore Novices' Hurdle (Baring Bingham), Cheltenham—
Jack Kennedy has already made his winning move on Samcro; Black Op (right) takes second*

period when eight of the ten 'Sun Alliance' winners between 1973 and 1982 were trained in Ireland. Duc des Genievres re-opposed Samcro from the Deloitte, though Willie Mullins' main hope was 4/1-chance Next Destination who was himself unbeaten in three races over hurdles, including the Grade 1 Lawlor's of Naas Novices' Hurdle in January which Samcro had been due to contest. The only other runner in a field of fourteen at single-figure odds was the main British hope Black Op (8/1) who had finished second in the Classic Novices' Hurdle at Cheltenham's Trials meeting. The first three in the betting duly came to the fore, though Samcro (who lost a front shoe) simply proved too good for all his rivals, travelling strongly as usual, improving to lead after two out and keeping on well to beat Black Op and Next Destination by two and three quarter lengths and five. Black Op went on to win the Mersey at Aintree, while Next Destination was suited by the step up to three miles when also winning in Grade 1 company next time at Punchestown. The decision to run Samcro in the Punchestown Champion Hurdle rather than one of the less valuable Grade 1 novice events was probably partly influenced by his trainer's title bid, but Samcro's fall made it mathematically impossible for Gordon Elliott to peg back Willie Mullins.

    By all accounts, Samcro was creating a buzz in Ireland well before he made his debut under Rules in the Gigginstown colours. In an interview with his breeder Douglas Taylor, it was revealed that in pre-training, before first going through the ring as a three-year-old store, he had been 'killing everything, even seasoned handicappers'. Samcro had originally fetched €95,000 at the Land Rover Sale, appearing there principally to qualify for valuable bumpers, and, whether it was a genuine sale or not, he still carried Taylor's colours when winning his point a year later, after which 'everybody in the country was ringing me wanting the horse. I was only slightly interested in selling him, but the sales companies were offering free flights and all sorts to let them have him.' Samcro's first appearance in a sale-ring had come just months after Faugheen had done plenty to advertise the merits of his sire Germany by winning the Champion Hurdle and then following up in the Punchestown version. Apart from the 2008 Supreme Novices' winner Captain Cee

SAM

Bee, Germany sired few others of real note in a lengthy but not always prolific stud career, Samcro being one of just four registered foals in his 2012 crop. Germany died a year later, but was survived by his own sire Trempolino, the 1987 Arc winner, who died in March at the venerable age of thirty-four. Samcro's career has begun in remarkably similar fashion to fellow Baring Bingham winner Faugheen's, their pointing background being an unlikely one for horses who have proven, or promised to be, effective at the top level over two miles as hurdlers.

Samcro (IRE) (ch.g. 2012)	Germany (USA) (b 1991)	Trempolino (ch 1984)	Sharpen Up / Trephine
		Inca Princess (b 1983)	Big Spruce / Inca Queen
	Dun Dun (IRE) (b 2002)	Saddlers' Hall (b 1988)	Sadler's Wells / Sunny Valley
		Frankly Native (ch 1994)	Be My Native / Frankford Run

Samcro's female family is a highly successful one, though neither his dam Dun Dun nor grandam Frankly Native ever raced. Dun Dun's only other winner to date is the fairly useful hurdler Cocacobana (by Snurge), a winner at up to three miles who was also successful in points. Samcro's four-year-old half-brother Think Positive (by Jeremy) showed promise in a bumper at Towcester on his debut for Peter Hedger in the latest season but finished lame on his only other start when favourite for the Goffs Land Rover Bumper at the Punchestown Festival, by which time he had joined Willie Mullins. Dun Dun is a sister to a couple of smart winners in Master of The Hall, whose biggest win came in the Reynoldstown Novices' Chase, and hurdler Featherbed Lane who was beaten a nose in the Lanzarote. Dun Dun's other winning siblings include Pairofbrowneyes, winner of the Leinster National in the latest season on his first start for Willie Mullins and an early faller when favourite for the Irish Grand National. The family's best horse, though, is the top-class chaser at up to two and a half miles Sound Man, a son of Samcro's great grandam Frankford

Gigginstown House Stud's "Samcro"

Run who was placed in a bumper and maiden hurdle in Ireland. Another of the best horses trained by Edward O'Grady, Sound Man recorded fifteen career wins including two editions of the Tingle Creek.

At the time of writing, Samcro is ante-post favourite in at least one place for each of the Arkle, the Golden Miller and the RSA, at Cheltenham, as well as being prominent in the Champion Hurdle betting, while, a year too soon surely, he is in the lists for the Gold Cup as well. Discussions over the summer between Gordon Elliott and the Gigginstown team will need to establish first whether Samcro stays over hurdles or is sent chasing. His trainer is on record as saying he would like to train him for the Champion Hurdle, but hurdling is only a means to an end so far as his owners are concerned and they would no doubt, all other things being equal, be keen to get Samcro's chasing career under way. He is a strong, chasing type on looks. The strong-travelling Samcro is effective at two miles and is bred to stay further than the twenty-one furlongs of the Baring Bingham, the longest trip he has tackled so far. He has done all his racing on ground softer than good. Samcro is the highest-rated novice hurdler of the season, though the fall at Punchestown (too far out to suggest where he would have finished) undoubtedly robbed him of the opportunity to run to a higher rating. Ratings, of course, are a measure of what a horse *has* achieved on form. As for what Samcro might *go on* to achieve, with the usual provisos regarding health and soundness, he looks to have the potential to go right to the top. For those closest to Samcro, the 'hype' and weight of expectation surrounding him may well be something they could do without though, as their fellow Irishman Oscar Wilde wrote, 'There is only one thing in life worse than being talked about, and that is not being talked about.' For racing's followers, newsworthy budding champions like Samcro are the ones that undoubtedly generate the most excitement and anticipation.
Gordon Elliott, Ireland

SAMDIBIEN (FR) 6 b.g. Day Flight – Sambirane (FR) (Apeldoorn (FR)) [2017/18 h107: h21.9g⁶ h20.3g⁶ h25s³ Dec 26] fair maiden hurdler: stays 25f: acts on heavy going: wears tongue tie. *Sam Thomas*   **h100**

SAME CIRCUS (IRE) 7 b.m. Brian Boru – Curragh Orpen (IRE) (Orpen (USA)) [2017/18 h115: h19.3s⁶ c20s² c24.2s³ c20.5s⁴ c25.2d* c24.1s* c23.8s⁴ Apr 27] smallish mare: fairly useful hurdler: better form in mares events over fences, winning handicaps at Catterick in February and Bangor in March: will stay extreme distances: acts on soft going: in cheekpieces last 3 starts: usually leads. *Donald McCain*   **c127 h–**

SAMETEGAL (FR) 9 b.g. Saint des Saints (FR) – Loya Lescribaa (FR) (Robin des Champs (FR)) [2017/18 c19.4s² c21.1v³ c20.8s³ c24.2s Feb 3] tall gelding: winning hurdler: useful handicap chaser: off further 20 months, placed first 3 starts in 2017/18, including third in Grand Sefton Chase at Aintree (7 lengths behind Gas Line Boy) in December: stays 21f (seemingly failed to stay 3m final outing): acts on good to firm and heavy going: has worn tongue tie, including last 5 outings. *Paul Nicholls*   **c141 h–**

SAM I (FR) 5 gr.g. Lord du Sud (FR) – Blue Girl Star (FR) (Anabaa Blue) [2017/18 b15.8s² Mar 14] first foal: dam unraced half-sister to smart 2m hurdler Ivan Grozny: 4/1, shaped with promise when second in bumper at Huntingdon (1½ lengths behind That's A Given, best work finish). *Harry Fry*   **b97**

SAMMAMISH (IRE) 5 b.m. Oscar (IRE) – Issaquah (IRE) (Supreme Leader) [2017/18 b16s⁴ b16.8s Dec 26] second foal: dam (h141) bumper/2m-2¼m hurdle winner: well beaten in bumpers (9/4 on debut). *Malcolm Jefferson*   **b–**

SAMMY B 8 br.g. Overbury (IRE) – This Thyne (Good Thyne (USA)) [2017/18 h119: c20d Nov 5] fairly useful hurdler: well held in novice handicap at Carlisle on chasing debut: stays 3m: acts on heavy going. *Lucinda Russell*   **c– h–**

SAMMYLOU (IRE) 5 b.g. Beneficial – Carrigeen Diamond (IRE) (Old Vic) [2017/18 b16g b16s⁴ b16.6s h21v^pu h21d Apr 26] €1,200 3-y-o, £15,000 4-y-o: good-topped gelding: second foal: half-brother to fairly useful hurdler/chaser Gray Day (2½m-23f winner, by Daylami): dam unraced half-sister to useful hurdler/smart chaser Benatar (19f-21f winner, by Beneficial): in frame on completed start in Irish points: form (fair) in bumpers only when fourth at Sandown in November: tongue tied, better effort in maiden hurdles at Warwick when eighth to Minella Warrior: open to further improvement. *Graeme McPherson*   **h91 p b90**

European Breeders' Fund Matchbook VIP 'National Hunt' Novices' Handicap Hurdle Final, Sandown—northern raider Sam's Gunner (noseband) copes best with the very testing conditions

SAM NOIR 6 ch.g. Black Sam Bellamy (IRE) – United (GER) (Desert King (IRE)) [2017/18 h91p, b89: h20s* h20g h20.6g³ h26.5d³ h23g⁵ h21.2g h22.8v h23.4s⁵ c24vᶠ h23.1s³ h26.4d Apr 22] fair handicap hurdler: won at Worcester in May: tailed off when fell 2 out in novice handicap at Uttoxeter on chasing debut: stays 3¼m: acts on soft going: usually in cheekpieces: wears tongue tie. *Peter Bowen*   **c–** **h105**

SAMOSET 8 b.g. Sir Percy – Great Quest (IRE) (Montjeu (IRE)) [2017/18 h105: h16.7g⁶ May 12] sturdy gelding: fair handicap hurdler: stays 19f: acts on soft and good to firm going: has worn cheekpieces: wears tongue tie: usually races close up. *Graeme McPherson*   **h86**

SAM RED (FR) 7 b.g. Denham Red (FR) – Call Me Nana (FR) (Call Me Sam (FR)) [2017/18 c107p, h135: c21.7m³ c22.6s* c24.2d* c23.4vᶠ h23.4s⁴ c19.1s² c19.4vᵖᵘ h24v⁵ c24.2d² c25.3g Apr 18] lengthy gelding: useful handicap hurdler: similar form over fences: won small-field novices at Stratford and Fakenham in October: stays 3m: acts on good to firm and heavy going: has worn headgear: wears tongue tie. *Dan Skelton*   **c133** **h125**

SAM'S A DIAMOND 6 b.g. What A Caper (IRE) – Barlin Bay (Karinga Bay) [2017/18 h80, b–: h15.8g⁶ h15.8gᵖᵘ Jun 21] little form in bumpers/maiden hurdles: dead. *J. R. Jenkins*   **h–**

SAM'S GUNNER 5 ch.g. Black Sam Bellamy (IRE) – Falcon's Gunner (Gunner B) [2017/18 h93, b74: h19.3s² h19.3d* h16.2v² h19.8v* h24.7sᵖᵘ Apr 13] rangy gelding: useful form over hurdles: won novice at Catterick in February and EBF 'National Hunt' Novices' Handicap Hurdle Final at Sandown (by 7 lengths from Dentley de Mee) in March: should be well suited by 3m: acts on heavy going. *Michael Easterby*   **h132**

SAMSON 7 ch.g. Black Sam Bellamy (IRE) – Riverine (Risk Me (FR)) [2017/18 h92: h22gᵖᵘ h19.9d h22g* h22g⁴ h20g³ h15.8d* h18.5d⁵ h16.4d h20.5s c15.7v³ Apr 9] angular gelding: fair handicap hurdler: won novice events at Stratford in June and Uttoxeter in September: inadequate test when 7¼ lengths third to The Last But One in novice handicap at Wincanton on chasing debut (open to improvement): stays 2¾m: acts on heavy going: often in headgear. *Sophie Leech*   **c101 p** **h102**

SAMSON'S REACH 5 b.g. Phoenix Reach (IRE) – Court Wing (IRE) (Hawk Wing (USA)) [2017/18 b82: h16.3g⁶ h16v⁶ h15.7v³ h19v* h19.9vᵖᵘ h21.2sᵖᵘ h21.7vᵖᵘ h21.2d* Apr 24] unfurnished gelding: bumper winner: fair handicap hurdler: won novice events at Warwick in December and Ludlow in April: stays 21f: acts on heavy going. *Richard Price*   **h103**

SAMSON THE MAN 5 b.g. Black Sam Bellamy (IRE) – Princess Cara (Rakaposhi King) [2017/18 b15.7g² b16.4g b17.7d⁶ h19s⁵ h15.3v⁵ h16.5s⁵ h19.2v⁶ Mar 17] angular gelding: first foal: dam unraced: fair form in bumpers only on debut: modest form over hurdles: wears hood. *Noel Williams*   **h98** **b89**

SAM SPINNER 6 b.g. Black Sam Bellamy (IRE) – Dawn Spinner (Arctic Lord) [2017/18 h139p: h19.5d² h22.8v* h24.4d* h24s⁵ h24.7s³ Apr 14]   **h158**

    Unusually testing conditions at the Cheltenham Festival made it difficult to win races from the front. Native River was a notable exception in the Gold Cup, of course, and Missed Approach made all in the Fulke Walwyn Kim Muir, but the only other front runner to be successful was Blow By Blow who took up the running soon after the second hurdle in the Martin Pipe. Thorough stayers Native River and Missed Approach received excellently-judged rides which exploited their proven stamina (they had finished runner-up in the National Hunt Chase at previous Festivals). Both jockeys maintained gallops that drew the finish out of their rivals without harming their own prospects of seeing the races out. As an aside, both Richard Johnson on Native River and Mr Noel McParlan on Missed Approach infringed the whip rules, Johnson being suspended for seven days and fined £6,550 (around a fifth of his prize money) and the amateur picking up a nine-day ban and a £400 fine. Getabird, Apple's Jade and Un de Sceaux were Festival favourites who tried and failed to make all, along with the likes of Saint Calvados, Black Corton and Maria's Benefit who were leading contenders for their races. The Stayers' Hurdle favourite Sam Spinner was another front runner who came unstuck, but not because he went off too quickly, failed to settle or was taken on for the lead. A proven stayer, Sam Spinner had his downfall exacerbated by his jockey dictating too steady a pace to make the most of his prime asset—his stamina. Headed before the final flight, he was unable to quicken and wound up being beaten just over six lengths into fifth behind the winner Penhill. Aintree looked to be a good opportunity for Sam Spinner to put the record straight and he started an even shorter-priced favourite to make amends in the Liverpool Hurdle. There was another confirmed front runner in the field this time and Sam Spinner tracked the pace set by outsider Coole Cody, but he simply seemed to run below form on this occasion, despite again having underfoot conditions to suit and he managed only a well-held third behind Identity Thief and the Stayers' Hurdle third Wholestone.

The staying hurdling scene in Britain had had a dominant leader the previous season in Unowhatimeanharry (who had met his only defeat in the Stayers' Hurdle), as it had in 2015/16 with Thistlecrack who had gone unbeaten through his campaign which he had ended by winning at Cheltenham and then Aintree. Sam Spinner had looked the likely successor to that pair when he joined them on the roll of honour of the Long Walk Hurdle at Ascot two days before Christmas, the JLT-sponsored contest commemorating Reve de Sivola, fatally injured at Kelso earlier in the year, after contesting the five previous editions of the Long Walk and completing a hat-

Betfair Stayers' Handicap Hurdle, Haydock—
Sam Spinner relishes the step up in trip as he runs out a clear winner

SAM

trick of wins in 2014. Unowhatimeanharry still looked the one to beat in the staying hurdle division before the latest Long Walk, sent off the 6/4 favourite despite his defeat at the hands of shock winner Beer Goggles who had denied him a second win in Newbury's Long Distance Hurdle earlier in December. Lil Rockerfeller, runner-up to Unowhatimeanharry in the 2016 Long Walk and then a place ahead of him when second in the Stayers' Hurdle, was another of the established stayers in the Long Walk line-up, along with L'Ami Serge who had won the Grande Course de Haies d'Auteuil in the summer and had been beaten by Lil Rockerfeller, conceding him weight, in the Ascot Hurdle the previous month. Of the other leading contenders, L'Ami Serge's stable-companion Thomas Campbell and Sam Spinner were both stepping up from handicap company. Thomas Campbell had won both his starts at Cheltenham in the autumn, while Sam Spinner had begun his second season over hurdles with a couple of excellent performances in competitive events. He had shaped like the best horse when beaten half a length by Court Minstrel in the Silver Trophy at Chepstow in October, taking a keen hold and then rallying after losing momentum when wandering approaching the final flight. That form worked out well, and Sam Spinner made no mistake when stepping up in trip for the following month's Betfair Stayers' Handicap Hurdle. The race was run over conventional hurdles for the first time, instead of the fixed brush obstacles but, on form, it looked as competitive as ever. In the event, the extreme conditions played their part in rendering it anything but, Sam Spinner setting an end-to-end gallop, going with enthusiasm and staying on strongly to draw seventeen lengths clear of runner-up The Dutchman at the line.

Conditions for the Long Walk at Ascot weren't so testing as they had been at Haydock, but the slightly longer trip played to Sam Spinner's strengths, as did a good ride from Joe Colliver who partnered him in all his races in the latest season, his ride at Ascot making full use of Sam Spinner's abundant stamina and again highlighting his very willing attitude. Jumping well in the main, Sam Spinner again went with enthusiasm out in front and sealed matters with a prodigious jump at the last where he was being strongly pressed by the much more patiently-ridden L'Ami Serge. While that rival made a mistake, Sam Spinner stayed on strongly to win by two and three quarter lengths, with Unowhatimeanharry beaten another eight lengths into third, while Thomas Campbell and Lil Rockerfeller finished fifth and sixth of the eight runners. Sam Spinner's performance was backed up by an excellent timefigure and augured well for the Stayers' Hurdle, in which he even had the bonus of underfoot conditions being ideal, though, for reasons already outlined, he wasn't seen to best effect.

JLT Reve de Sivola Long Walk Hurdle, Ascot—a first Grade 1 winner for trainer Jedd O'Keeffe and jockey Joe Colliver as Sam Spinner defeats L'Ami Serge (left)

SAM

While his Cheltenham performance was disappointing, Sam Spinner had come a long way since starting his career with a win in a bumper at Catterick. He went on to win three of his four starts in novice hurdles the following season, one at Newcastle and the two others back at Catterick, though he ran his best race in defeat, finishing second at Kelso when trying to concede weight to the useful Mount Mews. Sam Spinner's rapid rise through the hurdling ranks captured media attention all the more as he hailed from a small dual-purpose yard which sent out just two other winning jumpers in the latest season. Trained by Jedd (real names John Eamon Declan Dunderdale) O'Keeffe near Middleham, Sam Spinner was one of the success stories of the season for a smaller stable and, in the fairly late, but expected, absence of Waiting Patiently from the Ryanair Chase, he looked the North's big hope at Cheltenham. O'Keeffe spent nine years working for Micky Hammond, eventually becoming assistant trainer, before taking out his own licence with three horses in 2000. A combination of serious illness and financial pressures very nearly forced O'Keeffe to call it a day in 2011 but support from Sam Spinner's owners, among others, was instrumental in enabling him to continue training. It wasn't just his trainer's career which hung in the balance at one time, either. Colliver had to set about rebuilding his riding career after serving three months of a ten-month jail sentence in 2016 for perverting the course of justice after lying about the circumstances of crashing a car when over the drink-drive limit.

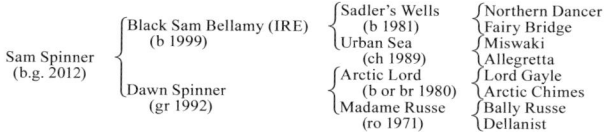

Sam Spinner (b.g. 2012)
- Black Sam Bellamy (IRE) (b 1999)
  - Sadler's Wells (b 1981)
    - Northern Dancer
    - Fairy Bridge
  - Urban Sea (ch 1989)
    - Miswaki
    - Allegretta
- Dawn Spinner (gr 1992)
  - Arctic Lord (b or br 1980)
    - Lord Gayle
    - Arctic Chimes
  - Madame Russe (ro 1971)
    - Bally Russe
    - Dellanist

Sam Spinner was one of two store horses O'Keeffe bought on the Chapmans' behalf at Doncaster May Sales in 2015 when the owners decided to branch out into jumping for the first time. Sam Spinner was bought for just £12,000, having no more than what his trainer described as a 'solid' pedigree, but making plenty of appeal as an individual. As it has turned out, only the Cheltenham Gold Cup runner-up The Giant Bolster has earned a higher rating among the progeny of Sam Spinner's sire Black Sam Bellamy, a brother to Galileo and half-brother to Sea The Stars. Sam Spinner's dam Dawn Spinner won a bumper at Hereford for Nicky Henderson before running just twice over hurdles, finishing second in a novice at Exeter on her only completed start. Dawn Spinner was twenty when she foaled Sam Spinner who was her final foal and she had produced nothing remotely as good before. Her other winners comprised Floral Spinner (by Alflora), a bumper winner and flat hurdler at up to three miles, the two and a half mile hurdle winner Carys's Lad (by Exit To Nowhere) and Misty Dawn (by King's Ride) who won a bumper on his only start. In addition, Dawn Spinner produced the winning pointer It Just Aint Right (by Dr Massini) and the mare Halfway Home (by Presenting) who never ran but became dam of the useful Irish chaser Balbriggan, winner of the Troytown Handicap Chase. Henderson also trained Dawn Spinner's much better known half-brother The Tsarevich. In a long career during the 'eighties, he eventually shrugged off a Timeform 'squiggle' early in his career to win fifteen races in all, including two editions of the Mildmay of Flete at the Festival, and, although by top-class sprinter Mummy's Pet, went close to giving his trainer a win in the Grand National when runner-up to Maori Venture in 1987. The Tsarevich's sister Tsarella, fairly useful over both hurdles and fences, produced the very smart chaser Gungadu whose wins for Paul Nicholls included the Reynoldstown Novices' and the Racing Post Chase. The angular Sam Spinner stays three miles well and has raced only on ground softer than good—his win at Haydock came on a day when he and Betfair Chase winner Bristol de Mai were among the few horses who coped well with the heavy ground. Sam Spinner will be very fortunate if the ground comes up soft again in any future visits to the Cheltenham Festival, but his genuine attitude will always stand him in good stead and he seems sure to win more good races when stamina is at a premium either over hurdles or if sent chasing. *Jedd O'Keeffe*

SAM

SAMSTOWN 11 b.g. Kingsalsa (USA) – Red Peony (Montjeu (IRE)) [2017/18 c26.2v^{pu} c23.8s Apr 25] winning hurdler: useful chaser at best: off 3 years, possibly needed both outings in 2017/18: stays 27f: acts on good to firm and heavy going: has worn cheekpieces. *Alistair Whillans*   c– h–

SAM'S TREASURE 6 ch.m. Black Sam Bellamy (IRE) – Poppy Day (Bal Harbour) [2017/18 b–: c19.3g Apr 23] dual point winner: well held in bumper/novice hunter chase. *I. M. Mason*   c–

SAMTU (IRE) 7 b.g. Teofilo (IRE) – Samdaniya (Machiavellian (USA)) [2017/18 h117: h20.5g Apr 21] fairly useful on Flat (stays 14.5f): fairly useful handicap hurdler: possibly amiss only outing in 2017/18: stays easy 2½m: acts on good to firm going: in cheekpieces last 2 starts: wears tongue tie. *Marjorie Fife*   h–

SAMUEL JACKSON 6 b.g. Alflora (IRE) – Primitive Quest (Commanche Run) [2017/18 h23.9s* h23.1v* h24.4s³ h23.5s⁵ Mar 25] good-topped gelding: second foal: half-brother to bumper winner/winning pointer Winter Soldier (by Apple Tree): dam winning pointer: winning pointer: useful form over hurdles: won novices at Taunton (100/1) in December and Bangor in January: not discredited in River Don Novices' Hurdle at Doncaster (9 lengths third to Enniscoffey Oscar) and conditionals handicap at Ascot (beaten 6¼ lengths into fifth behind Sir Will). *Richard Mitford-Slade*   h132

SAMURAI SAM 5 b.g. Black Sam Bellamy (IRE) – Aspra (FR) (Green Tune (USA)) [2017/18 b16s Feb 9] in cheekpieces/tongue tie, looked awkward when well beaten in maiden bumper at Kempton. *Lawney Hill*   b–

SAN BENEDETO (FR) 7 ch.g. Layman (USA) – Cinco Baidy (FR) (Lure (USA)) [2017/18 c153, h–: h16g² c17.5v² c16.8d⁴ c15.5d⁵ c16.8v⁴ c15.5d² Apr 28] tall gelding: useful hurdler: very smart chaser: second in Haldon Gold Cup at Exeter (2¼ lengths behind Politologue) in November and Celebration Chase at Sandown (3¼ lengths behind Altior) in April: has won at 2½m, but best form at shorter: acts on good to firm and heavy going: wears headgear/tongue tie. *Paul Nicholls*   c158 h128

SAND BLAST 7 b.g. Oasis Dream – New Orchid (USA) (Quest For Fame) [2017/18 h110: c19.4d³ h15.8g⁴ Jun 21] maiden pointer: formerly fair hurdler: remote third in novice handicap on chasing debut: stays 2½m: acts on good to firm and good to soft going: wears cheekpieces/tongue tie: front runner/races prominently. *Dan Skelton*   c77 h84

SANDFORD CASTLE (IRE) 8 b.g. Norwich – Pegs Polly (IRE) (Phardante (FR)) [2017/18 h16s Apr 9] point winner: fair maiden hurdler in 2015/16: off 2 years, always behind in novice sole outing since: should prove suited by 2½m+: acts on heavy going. *Johnny Farrelly*   h–

SANDGATE 6 ch.g. Compton Place – Jump Ship (Night Shift (USA)) [2017/18 h97: h16.8g^{pu} May 16] modest hurdler at best: little form since autumn 2016 (including on Flat): unproven beyond 17f: acts on good to firm and good to soft going: has worn headgear/tongue tie. *Kenny Johnson*   h–

SANDHURST LAD (IRE) 7 b.g. Presenting – Off She Goes (IRE) (Sadler's Wells (USA)) [2017/18 h96, b74: h20.5s* h24.1s h25v² h25v² h25v⁴ h23.1v^{pu} Apr 17] strong gelding: fair handicap hurdler: won at Plumpton (amateur) on return in November: runner-up twice after: stays 25f: acts on heavy going: in cheekpieces/tongue tie last 4 starts: often races prominently. *Warren Greatrex*   h109

SANDRO BOTTICELLI (IRE) 6 b.g. Galileo (IRE) – Ask For The Moon (FR) (Dr Fong (USA)) [2017/18 h16.5v⁶ Mar 12] fairly useful on Flat (stays 16.5f) nowadays: in cheekpieces, 36¼ lengths sixth to Nelson's Touch in maiden at Taunton on hurdling debut. *Alexandra Dunn*   h63

SANDS COVE (IRE) 11 b.g. Flemensfirth (USA) – Lillies Bordello (IRE) (Danehill Dancer (IRE)) [2017/18 c24s⁵ c24g Apr 20] good-topped gelding: winning hurdler: fairly useful handicap chaser at best: off 2 years, signs of retaining ability both outings in 2017/18: stays 3m: acts on good to firm and heavy going: tried in headgear: formerly tongue tied. *James Evans*   c96 h–

SANDSEND (FR) 5 gr.g. Turgeon (USA) – Sans Rien (FR) (Poliglote) [2017/18 h20v³ h16v* h16.8v^{ur} Mar 16] useful form over hurdles: won Limestone Lad Hurdle at Naas (by neck from Forge Meadow) in January: closing when broke down before last in County Hurdle won by Mohaayed at Cheltenham: dead. *W. P. Mullins, Ireland*   h142

SANDY BEACH 8 b.g. Notnowcato – Picacho (IRE) (Sinndar (IRE)) [2017/18 c135, h–: c23s³ c16.1s³ c24s³ c19.5s² Mar 7] good-topped gelding: maiden hurdler: fairly useful handicap chaser nowadays: stays easy 23f: acts on heavy going: has worn tongue tie, including last 2 starts (when also in cheekpieces): often leads. *Colin Tizzard*   c118 h–

SANDY COVE 7 br.g. Oasis Dream – Maganda (IRE) (Sadler's Wells (USA)) [2017/18 h16m h15.8m⁴ h16.3g³ h19.9m⁴ h16.3g h15.7d⁴ h15.8g⁵ Dec 6] fair on Flat (stays 1¾m) at best: modest maiden hurdler: left James Eustace after fourth start: stays 2½m: acts on good to firm going: in blinkers last 2 starts. *Olly Murphy* **h87**

SANDYMOUNT DUKE (IRE) 9 b.g. Hernando (FR) – Joleah (IRE) (Ela-Mana-Mou) [2017/18 c136, h–: c21g* c20m* c22.5g⁵ c24.5s Apr 25] strong, lengthy gelding: winning hurdler: very smart chaser: won minor event at Punchestown (by 9½ lengths from Hidden Cyclone) in May and handicap at Down Royal (by head from Net d'Ecosse) in June: also won on Flat following month: stays 25f: acts on good to firm and good to soft going: tried in cheekpieces: front runner/races prominently. *Mrs J. Harrington, Ireland* **c155 h–**

SANDYMOUNT (IRE) 7 b.g. Yeats (IRE) – Flaiha (FR) (Esprit du Nord (USA)) [2017/18 h111, b94: h20.6g* h25.4d h23.1g² Jul 9] fairly useful form over hurdles: won handicap at Market Rasen in May: second in similar event there in July: stays 23f: acts on heavy going. *Tom George* **h123**

SANGHA RIVER (IRE) 5 br.g. Arcadio (GER) – Hidden Reserve (IRE) (Heron Island (IRE)) [2017/18 b16.6d* ab16g² Feb 19] fourth foal: brother to bumper winner Hardline, and half-brother to fair hurdler Wolfslair (2¾m winner, by Yeats): dam (b103), bumper winner, sister to fairly useful hurdler/chaser (stayed 2½m) Crocodiles Rock: unseated 2 out in point: promising start in bumpers, winning conditionals/amateur event at Doncaster (by head from Kingsplace) in December: should have followed up when ¾-length second to Normal Norman at Lingfield, finishing strongly from poor position: remains open to progress. *Olly Murphy* **b103 p**

SANOK (POL) 6 b.g. Jape (USA) – Sun Queen (POL) (Don Corleone) [2017/18 h15.5vᵖᵘ h16v⁶ h16s⁴ h16sᶠ Apr 27] fair form over hurdles: raced only at 2m: acted on soft going: dead. *Paul Cowley* **h100**

SAN PEDRO DE SENAM (FR) 5 br.g. Saint des Saints (FR) – Tetiaroa (FR) (Poliglote) [2017/18 h16s c16.2s² c17d³ c17v* c15.7v³ c19.7vᵘʳ c16.1v⁴ c16.5g⁶ Apr 24] good-topped gelding: first foal: dam unraced half-sister to dam of useful French hurdler/chaser (stays 3¼m) Gorvello: fairly useful hurdler at best in France: fairly useful form over fences: won novice at Plumpton (left with simple task after odds-on favourite unseated early) in January: little form in handicaps after: stays 2¼m: best form on soft/heavy going: tried in blinkers: has worn tongue tie: front runner/races prominently. *Gary Moore* **c122 h–**

SAN PIETRO (FR) 10 b.g. Poliglote – Sainte Berinne (FR) (Bering) [2017/18 c108, h105: c22.7s⁴ c24.2v⁴ c24.1sᵖᵘ c21.4d³ Apr 22] fair maiden hurdler: modest handicap chaser nowadays: stays 3¼m: acts on heavy going: tried in blinkers. *Donald McCain* **c94 h–**

SAN QUENTIN (IRE) 7 gr.g. Lawman (FR) – In The Soup (USA) (Alphabet Soup (USA)) [2017/18 h15.7g⁴ h15.8g⁵ Jul 19] fair on Flat (stays 13.5f): only poor form over hurdles: in cheekpieces last 2 starts. *Dr Richard Newland* **h60**

SAN SATIRO (IRE) 7 b.g. Milan – Longueville Quest (IRE) (Witness Box (USA)) [2017/18 h119: h22.8mᵖᵘ May 13] well-made gelding: should make a chaser: won both completed starts in points: fairly useful novice hurdler in 2016/17: pulled up only outing since: stays 23f: acts on firm going. *Paul Nicholls* **h–**

SANTA'S SECRET (IRE) 10 b.g. Basanta (IRE) – Rivers Town Rosie (IRE) (Roselier (FR)) [2017/18 c15.9vᵖᵘ Mar 9] maiden hurdler: fairly useful form over fences in 2015/16 (for Oliver Sherwood): pulled up in hunter only Rules appearance since (won point soon after end of season): should stay beyond 2m: acts on heavy going: tried in cheekpieces/ tongue tie. *Miss Chloe Boxall* **c– h–**

SANTIAGO DE CUBA (IRE) 5 b.g. Pour Moi (IRE) – Marjalina (IRE) (Marju (IRE)) [2017/18 b17g* b17g² b16s⁵ Sep 23] first foal: dam, useful 1m winner, half-sister to very smart hurdler/smart chaser (stayed 19f) Australia Day and useful 2m hurdler Gwafa: useful form in bumpers: won maiden at Killarney (by 3¾ lengths from Chess Grand Master) on debut in July: 7/2, fifth in maiden at Navan (12¼ lengths behind Mengli Khan) on hurdling debut: wears tongue tie: should do better. *Joseph Patrick O'Brien, Ireland* **h99 p b110**

SANTINI 6 b.g. Milan – Tinagoodnight (FR) (Sleeping Car (FR)) [2017/18 h20.5d* h20.3v* h24v³ h24.7s* Apr 13] **h150**

Seven Barrows was home to a particularly strong crop of novice hurdlers in the latest season among whom Claimantakinforgan, Ok Corral, On The Blind Side and Santini were the pick, with little to choose between any of the quartet. Claimantakinforgan finished second in the Scottish Champion Hurdle and Ok Corral was runner-up in the Spa at Cheltenham, while On The Blind Side met with his first defeat when sixth in the Mersey at Aintree, but Santini, a smashing prospect for staying novice chases, was the only one of the four to end his season with a big win when successful in the Sefton Novices' Hurdle at Aintree. With Willie Mullins and Gordon Elliott concentrating their firepower largely on Cheltenham and Punchestown instead, for all that they dominated the Grand National itself, Henderson enjoyed a hugely successful Aintree where Santini was his fifth Grade 1 winner over the three days. Like Gold Cup runner-up Might Bite, L'Ami Serge and Terrefort, Santini had been beaten beforehand at Cheltenham where Henderson's other big Aintree winner We Have A Dream had been an absentee.

Santini might well have been a third winner, to go with Altior and Buveur d'Air, for his stable at Cheltenham in different circumstances. As it was, he finished only third behind outsider Kilbricken Storm and stable-companion Ok Corral when sent off favourite for the Spa. Santini's inexperience—it was only his third start under Rules—may have been a factor in a big field, but he was also taken widest of all virtually throughout under a patient ride and could only stay on late to take third on the run-in. Conditions were heavy at Cheltenham, and the emphasis was firmly on stamina again three weeks later in the Doom Bar-sponsored Sefton in which Santini confirmed earlier promise. Only seven of the thirteen completed, the rest being pulled up in a gruelling contest in which those who did finish were well strung out. While the Spa winner Kilbricken Storm was an absentee (a narrowly beaten third when running at Punchestown later in the month instead), the placed horses re-opposed, with Santini the 6/4 favourite to turn the tables on Ok Corral at 7/2. Henderson saddled the first three in the betting as Chef des Obeaux (6/1) also took his chance, though he had more to prove after being pulled up in the Spa. Being ridden handily this time definitely helped Santini and he stayed on strongly once leading three out where he took over from outsider Dans Le Vent whom he had pressed throughout. The mare Roksana, bidding for a four-timer, came from much further back to tackle Santini on the run-in, but he found plenty to beat her by a length and half. Tower Bridge was a further six lengths back in third (he'd been beaten a similar distance when fifth in the Spa) ahead of Uppertown Prince who fared best of the outsiders, while Ok Corral failed to repeat his Cheltenham form in fifth and Chef des Obeaux was again among those pulled up. Santini was Henderson's second

Ballymore Classic Novices' Hurdle, Cheltenham—Santini (right) shows plenty of stamina and resolution to reel in the leader Black Op under very testing conditions

Doom Bar Sefton Novices' Hurdle, Aintree—a gruelling affair is won by Santini (breastgirth) who finds plenty on the run-in to hold off the mare Roksana; Tower Bridge (partly hidden) and Uppertown Prince come next

winner of the Sefton since it became a Grade 1 contest, following Might Bite's half-brother Beat That (another by Santini's sire Milan) who was successful in 2014 but had been seen seldomly since then before the latest season.

Santini had won both his first two starts over two and a half miles whilst shaping as though more of a test would suit him ideally. Along with Chef des Obeaux he made his hurdling debut in a novice at Newbury at the beginning of December and beat his shorter-priced stable companion in good style by four and a half lengths. The runner-up went on to win his next three starts before those disappointing efforts at Cheltenham and Aintree, while Santini went straight into graded company and followed up in the Ballymore Classic Novices' Hurdle on Cheltenham's Trials day. Santini stayed on strongly to beat Black Op by three quarters of a length, the pair pulling twenty-nine lengths clear of the third. The runner-up did his bit for the form afterwards, finding only Samcro too good in the Baring Bingham at the Festival before he won the Mersey at Aintree.

Santini (b.g. 2012)	Milan (b 1998)	Sadler's Wells (b 1981)	Northern Dancer
			Fairy Bridge
		Kithanga (b 1990)	Darshaan
			Kalata
	Tinagoodnight (FR) (b 2004)	Sleeping Car (b or br 1988)	Dunphy
			Lorelta
		Tinarctica (ch 1995)	Arctic Tern
			Tinopasa

Santini is a graduate from the pointing field but, unlike most of the good jumpers from that background, he won his point in Britain, not Ireland, at Didmarton in the Cotswolds to be precise. He's British-bred too, and a first home-bred Grade 1 winner for his owners Richard and Lizzie Kelvin-Hughes whose other good winners with Henderson have included the bet365 Gold Cup winner Hadrian's Approach. Although he races in his breeders' colours, Santini went through the ring at the 2017 Cheltenham Festival Sales shortly after winning his point and was recorded as having been bought by Dan Skelton for £150,000. The Kelvin-Hughes Trull House Stud sponsors the Dawn Run Mares' Novices' Hurdle at the Festival, a race in which Santini's useful half-sister Dusky Legend (by Midnight Legend), a faller in the Coral Cup at the latest Festival, has twice been placed. Santini's year-younger half-brother Rockpoint (by Shirocco) has shown fairly useful form over hurdles but also a degree of temperament which has prevented him getting his head in front so far. That is something he has inherited from the dam Tinagoodnight who won a mile and a half newcomers race at Clairefontaine on her only start on the Flat and a juvenile hurdle at Kempton on her first start for Nicky Henderson. She made only one other appearance on a racecourse back at Kempton over a year after that successful hurdling debut but refused to race after being reluctant to go to the start. Santini's grandam Tinarctica also had a rather disconcerting racing record in France, where a couple of fourth places was the best she could manage from a dozen starts on the Flat, while she failed to complete in both tries over hurdles. Great grandam Tinopasa, on the other hand, had a lot more ability as she won eight of her twelve starts over jumps, most of those wins coming at Auteuil where she won over both hurdles and fences. Tinopasa did very well as a broodmare too, producing ten winners, among them Gem Daly and Que Pasa who both showed useful form in novice hurdles in Ireland.

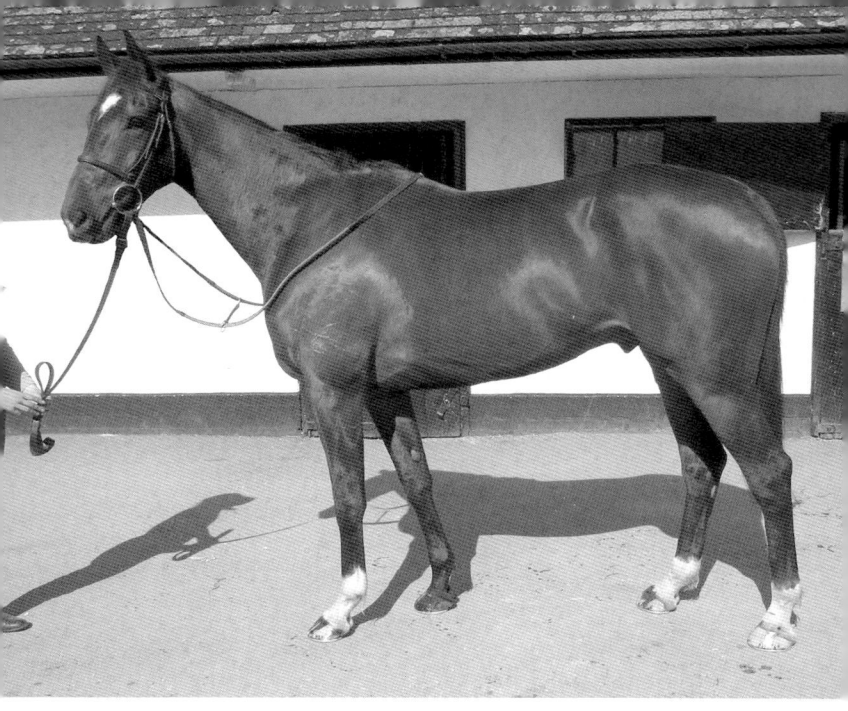

Mr & Mrs R. Kelvin-Hughes' "Santini"

Tinopasa's other winners include fairly useful staying hurdler Sir Will who won a couple of races for Kerry Lee in the latest season. Just days before Santini won on Cheltenham's Trials day, his dam Tinagoodnight was among a draft of twenty-five fillies and mares from Trull House Stud put up for dispersal at Doncaster. In foal to Derby winner Pour Moi, Tinagoodnight was sold for £32,000, while her three-year-old filly by High Chaparral made £62,000 and her yearling filly by Walk In The Park £22,000. The top-priced mare in the dispersal was Hora who was sold for £95,000; three of her first four foals were successful during the latest season, notably smart staying hurdler Thomas Campbell who won a couple of handicaps at Cheltenham in the autumn for Santini's connections, while another of her sons, Coeur de Lion, a useful hurdler, won on the Flat at Southwell in February. Santini is a strong gelding who should take high rank as a novice chaser in 2018/19. He will stay further than three miles given the chance and acts on heavy ground, having raced only on going softer than good so far. *Nicky Henderson*

SANTO DE LUNE (FR) 8 gr.g. Saint des Saints (FR) – Tikidoun (FR) (Kaldoun (FR)) **h109**
[2017/18 h119p: h16s³ Nov 22] lightly-raced maiden hurdler: fair form when third in novice at Warwick on sole outing in 2017/18. *Dan Skelton*

SAO (FR) 4 b.g. Great Pretender (IRE) – Miss Country (FR) (Country Reel (USA)) **h124**
[2017/18 h15.9s* h15.3s² h16s⁴ h16.8s² Apr 23] useful-looking gelding: third foal: half-brother to useful hurdler/high-class chaser Frodon (15f-21f winner, by Nickname), stays 3m, and French hurdler Tidjy (15f winner, by Slickly): dam, French 2¼m hurdle winner, half-sister to very smart hurdler/top-class chaser (stayed 25f) Medermit: fairly useful form

over hurdles: won minor event at Compiegne in May, then left Guillaume Macaire: headstrong sort, needs to settle to stay beyond 2m: raced only on soft going: in hood last 3 starts, also tongue tied final one. *Paul Nicholls*

SAO MAXENCE (FR) 5 b.g. Saint des Saints (FR) – Primadona (FR) (Dernier Empereur (USA)) [2017/18 b16v* b16v² Jan 31] sixth foal: brother to French chaser Saintedonalime (2¼m winner) and half-brother to 2 winners in France, including hurdler Limouline (17f winner, by Martaline): dam French 15f-2½m hurdle/chase winner: fairly useful form in bumpers at Ayr, winning on debut in December before clear second to impressive Precious Cargo: wears hood. *James Ewart*   **b102**

SAPHIR DU RHEU (FR) 9 gr.g. Al Namix (FR) – Dona du Rheu (FR) (Dom Pasquini (FR)) [2017/18 c161, h–: c23.4s³ c26.3v^pu Mar 16] robust gelding: winning hurdler: high-class chaser at best, fifth to Sizing John in Cheltenham Gold Cup in 2017: just twice-raced in 2017/18, pulled up in latest renewal of race: stays 3¼m: acts on heavy going: tried in blinkers: in tongue tie last 2 starts. *Paul Nicholls*   **c129 h–**

SAPPHIRE NOIRE (IRE) 5 b.m. Shantou (USA) – Cool Cool (FR) (Anabaa (USA)) [2017/18 h84, b–: h19.3s h19.9d^pu h19v^pu Feb 4] disappointing maiden hurdler: tried in cheekpieces. *Nigel Hawke*   **h–**

SAQIL (USA) 10 b.g. El Prado (IRE) – Rumansy (USA) (Theatrical) [2017/18 c17.4s⁴ May 18] tall gelding: maiden pointer: winning hurdler: tailed off in hunter on chasing debut: unproven beyond 2m: acts on good to firm going: tried in visor: wears tongue tie: temperamental. *Mrs L. J. Varnham*   **c– § h– §**

SARAKOVA (IRE) 5 b.g. Iffraaj – Mary Pickford (USA) (Speightstown (USA)) [2017/18 h15.7g^pu Jul 16] modest maiden on Flat, stays 9.5f: blinkered, pulled up in novice seller on hurdling debut. *Kevin Frost*   **h–**

SAROQUE (IRE) 11 b.g. Revoque (IRE) – Sarakin (IRE) (Buckskin (FR)) [2017/18 c115, h–: c25.5d c25.1v⁶ c23.6s^pu c26.7v* Apr 9] workmanlike gelding: winning hurdler: fair handicap chaser: blinkered, won at Wincanton in April: stays 27f: acts on heavy going. *Venetia Williams*   **c102 h–**

SARPECH (IRE) 7 b.g. Sea The Stars (IRE) – Sadima (IRE) (Sadler's Wells (USA)) [2017/18 h105: c16.2g^ur c16.5s⁴ c16.5g⁵ Jun 3] sturdy gelding: fair hurdler: similar form in novice handicap chases only when fourth at Worcester in May: raced around 2m: acts on soft and good to firm going: in cheekpieces last 2 starts: has pulled hard. *Charlie Longsdon*   **c102 h–**

SARTENE'S SON (FR) 5 ch.g. Linda's Lad – Sartene (FR) (Bakharoff (USA)) [2017/18 b15.8s h26d^pu h16.8s h19.5v h21s³ h24v³ h20v³ Apr 1] rather unfurnished gelding: sixth foal: half-brother to 3 winners in France, including hurdler/chaser Sacre Tsar (17f-19f winner, by Stormy River): dam, French 1m-1¼m winner, half-sister to fairly useful hurdler/chaser (stayed 3¼m) Sarde: well beaten in maiden bumper: fair form over hurdles: probably stays 3m: acts on heavy going. *Nigel Twiston-Davies*   **h110 b–**

SARTORIAL ELEGANCE 7 b.g. Kayf Tara – Blue Ride (IRE) (King's Ride) [2017/18 c126, h–: c24.2s^pu h23.1s h23.6v h26v^pu h25v⁴ h23.1s³ Feb 23] strong gelding: has had breathing operation: modest handicap hurdler: fairly useful chaser at best, pulled up on return: stays 3¼m: acts on heavy going: regularly wears blinkers: tongue tied 4 of last 5 outings: front runner/races prominently. *Colin Tizzard*   **c– h94**

SASHEEDA 4 br.f. Putra Sas (IRE) – Majeeda (IRE) (Jeremy (USA)) [2017/18 b13.7g b12.4s Dec 9] smallish filly: second foal: dam unraced: little form in 3-y-o bumpers/on Flat. *Lisa Williamson*   **b56**

SATELLITE (IRE) 7 b.g. Danehill Dancer (IRE) – Perihelion (IRE) (Galileo (IRE)) [2017/18 h94+: h21.4g h18.6s Dec 26] useful-looking gelding: fairly useful hurdler at best: little show in 2017/18 (virtually refused to race final outing): stays 2¼m: acts on soft going: tried in visor: in tongue tie last 2 starts. *Tim Vaughan*   **h–**

SATIS HOUSE 4 b.f. Bahri (USA) – Ex Mill Lady (Bishop of Cashel) [2017/18 h16.7g² h16.2d² h16d⁵ h16.7g³ h16s⁶ Nov 29] half-sister to fairly useful hurdler Scoglio (2m winner, by Monsieur Bond): little form on Flat: modest form over hurdles: raced around 2m: wears tongue tie. *Susan Corbett*   **h99**

SATURDAYNIGHTFEVER 6 b.g. King's Theatre (IRE) – Get Me Home (IRE) (Alderbrook) [2017/18 b16d⁴ b15.7g⁵ b16g Feb 24] compact gelding: first foal: dam unraced half-sister to high-class hurdler (stayed 21f) Get Me Out of Here: fair form first 2 starts in bumpers. *Fergal O'Brien*   **b93**

SAT

SATURNAS (FR) 7 b.g. Davidoff (GER) – Sayuri (GER) (Acatenango (GER)) [2017/18 h145: c16v² c17s* c20v c16d⁶ Apr 26] smart hurdler: useful form over fences: won maiden at Fairyhouse (by 1¼ lengths from De Plotting Shed) in January: let down by jumping in stronger company after: should prove suited by further than 2m: acts on heavy going: tried in tongue tie. *W. P. Mullins, Ireland* **c141 h–**

SAUCYSIOUX 8 b.m. Tobougg (IRE) – Mohican Pass (Commanche Run) [2017/18 h–: h18.6g⁵ h22.1d² h23.4s* h23.8d* h23.4s* h25v^pu h23v h16s² h21.3v² c19.8v^pu Apr 27] fair handicap hurdler: won at Fakenham (mares) and Ludlow (conditional) in November, and at Fakenham again in December: left Olly Murphy, pulled up in mares novice handicap on chasing debut: stays 3m: acts on heavy going: wears headgear/tongue tie. *Barry Brennan* **c– h107**

SAUVIGNON 7 b.m. Yeats (IRE) – Dalriath (Fraam) [2017/18 h86, b–: h23.1g⁴ h20.3d^F Dec 5] modest maiden hurdler: should stay beyond 2½m: acts on soft going. *Dan Skelton* **h89**

SAVA BRIDGE (IRE) 11 b.g. Zagreb (USA) – Myglass (IRE) (Strong Gale) [2017/18 c26d^pu May 5] little form outside points (dual winner). *Ben Durrell* **c– h–**

SAVANNA ROAR (IRE) 5 b.g. Let The Lion Roar – Addie's Choice (IRE) (Norwich) [2017/18 b16.3d b15.8s b16s Mar 17] modest form in bumpers. *Ben Pauling* **b75**

SAVELLO (IRE) 12 ch.g. Anshan – Fontaine Frances (IRE) (Lafontaine (USA)) [2017/18 c69, h115: c16s³ c16v^pu c15.8s c19.4d³ Apr 22] lengthy gelding: winning hurdler: fairly useful handicap chaser nowadays: best around 2m: acts on heavy going: wears headgear/tongue tie: usually races in rear. *Dan Skelton* **c119 h–**

SAVE THE PENNIES (IRE) 7 ch.m. Shantou (USA) – Penny Fiction (IRE) (Welsh Term) [2017/18 b16.8v³ Dec 8] €5,000 3-y-o, £18,500 5-y-o: fifth foal: sister to useful hurdler/chaser Carriganog (2m-2¾m winner) and bumper winner/fairly useful hurdler Eyesontheprize (2m winner), stayed 2½m: dam (h95): bumper winner, second only start over hurdles: runner-up on completed start in Irish maiden points: 66/1, third in bumper at Exeter (10½ lengths behind Time To Move On). *Grant Cann* **b84**

SAVOY COURT (IRE) 7 b.g. Robin des Champs (FR) – North Star Poly (IRE) (Presenting) [2017/18 h111: h20v⁵ h21.4v* h21.4s^pu h21.9v³ Apr 1] fairly useful hurdler: form in 2017/18 only when winning handicap at Wincanton in January: stays 21f: acts on heavy going: tried in cheekpieces: front runner/races prominently. *Warren Greatrex* **h123**

SAXO JACK (FR) 8 b.g. King's Best (USA) – Gamma (FR) (Sadler's Wells (USA)) [2017/18 h16.7g⁴ h16g² h16.8g* h16.7d² h16g⁵ h16.4s h16.8g h15.8d³ Apr 24] workmanlike gelding: fairly useful on Flat, stays 1½m: fair hurdler: won novice at Newton Abbot in September: raced around 2m: acts on good to soft going: sometimes in hood: wears tongue tie. *Sophie Leech* **h114**

SAYAR (IRE) 5 b.g. Azamour (IRE) – Seraya (FR) (Danehill (USA)) [2017/18 h16d* h16v* h16v Apr 2] half-brother to modest hurdler/chaser Sendiym (2m-21f winner, by Rainbow Quest) and modest hurdler Sarwistan (2¼m winner, by Nayef): fair form both starts on Flat: fairly useful form over hurdles, winning maiden at Kilbeggan in August and Joe Mac Novices' Hurdle at Tipperary (by 2¾ lengths from Morgan) in October: off 6 months, shaped better than result (raced too freely) in Rathbarry & Glenview Studs Novices' Hurdle at Fairyhouse final outing: may do better. *W. P. Mullins, Ireland* **h126**

SAY MY NAME (IRE) 7 ch.g. Fleetwood (IRE) – River Reine (IRE) (Lahib (USA)) [2017/18 c112, h112: h23.6s c30.7v c21.7s c23.6v⁶ Feb 2] sturdy gelding: winning hurdler: maiden chaser, just modest form in 2017/18: stays 3¼m: acts on heavy going: often in headgear. *Bob Buckler* **c87 h–**

SAYO 4 gr.g. Dalakhani (IRE) – Tiyi (FR) (Fairy King (USA)) [2017/18 h17.4d² h16v* h16.8v³ Mar 16] good-topped gelding: half-brother to fair hurdler Takendo (2m winner, by Acatenango) and French hurdler Tiyikaan (17f-19f winner, by Nashwan): fair on Flat (stays 12.5f) in France for Y. Durepaire: smart form over hurdles: left F. Matzinger, won maiden at Naas (by ¾ length from Les Arceaux) in January: much improved when third in Triumph Hurdle at Cheltenham (5¼ lengths behind Farclas) final outing. *W. P. Mullins, Ireland* **h142**

SAYYESTOTHEDRESS (IRE) 5 b.m. Stowaway – Cordially (AUS) (Galileo (IRE)) [2017/18 b15.6g Nov 30] first foal: dam, unraced, out of half-sister to very smart hurdler/ useful chaser (best around 2m) Desert Quest: well beaten in maiden bumper. *Paul Stafford, Ireland* **b–**

SCALES (IRE) 12 b.g. Bob Back (USA) – Mrs Avery (IRE) (Supreme Leader) [2017/18 c–, h92: h19d h22d² h18.5v* h21.2d⁶ h19s^F h19v^pu h19.7s² h19.3v⁴ Apr 17] has had breathing operation: fair handicap hurdler: won conditionals selling event at Newton Abbot in October: let down by jumping in novice handicap only start over fences: stays 2¾m: acts on heavy going: has worn headgear/tongue tie. *Kerry Lee*   **c–** **h102**

SCAPPATO 4 b.g. Librettist (USA) – Rhetorique (FR) (Smadoun (FR)) [2017/18 b16.7s⁵ b15.8d Apr 24] no form in bumpers. *Oliver Greenall*   **b–**

SCARBOROUGH BOY (IRE) 7 b.g. Kalanisi (IRE) – Turgeon L'Imprevue (FR) (Turgeon (USA)) [2017/18 h21.2d Nov 27] runner-up in point: tailed off in novice on hurdling debut. *Charlie Mann*   **h–**

SCARLET COUTURE 5 b.m. Schiaparelli (GER) – Little Red Spider (Bustino) [2017/18 b15.7s Feb 17] half-sister to 3 winners, including useful hurdler/chaser Alfie Spinner (17f-27f winner, by Alflora), stays 4m, and fairly useful hurdler/chaser Cousin Nicky (19f-16m winner, by Bob Back): dam bumper winner: last of 9 in mares bumper at Ascot. *Gary Moore*   **b–**

SCARLET DRAGON 5 b.g. Sir Percy – Welsh Angel (Dubai Destination (USA)) [2017/18 h16g² h16.5s Apr 13] sturdy gelding: smart on Flat, stays 1½m: better effort over hurdles (useful form) when never-nearer 9 lengths second to Global Citizen in Dovecote Novices' Hurdle at Kempton: wears hood. *Alan King*   **h132**

SCARLET FIRE (IRE) 11 b.g. Helissio (FR) – Ross Dana (IRE) (Topanoora) [2017/18 c–, h–: c24.2g^pu Jun 25] good-topped gelding: multiple winning pointer: winning hurdler: fair chaser at best: lightly raced and no form since early 2015/16: stays 3¼m: acts on soft going: usually tongue tied. *Nicky Richards*   **c– h–**

SCARLETT OF TARA 5 b.m. Kayf Tara – Late For Class (IRE) (Bob's Return (IRE)) [2017/18 b16s Feb 23] £13,000 4-y-o: third foal: half-sister to useful hurdler Midnight Stroll (2m-2½m winner, by Midnight Legend): dam (b72), lightly raced in bumpers/over hurdles, half-sister to fairly useful hurdler/useful chaser (stays 29f) Tulsa Jack: badly needed experience in mares bumper. *Nigel Twiston-Davies*   **b–**

SCARPETA (FR) 5 b.g. Soldier of Fortune (IRE) – Sanada (IRE) (Priolo (USA)) [2017/18 h16s³ h16v⁴ h21.1s⁴ h20v³ h20s^pu Apr 27] compact gelding: fairly useful on Flat, stays 2m: smart form over hurdles: won maiden at Gowran (by 17 lengths from Cartwright) in January: best effort when third in Grade 2 novice at Fairyhouse (10¼ lengths behind Pallasator) in April: stays 21f: raced on soft/heavy going: races prominently. *W. P. Mullins, Ireland*   **h146**

SCARTARE (IRE) 7 br.g. Trans Island – La Speziana (IRE) (Perugino (USA)) [2017/18 h72: h20.3d³ h19.5v² h19.2v² h19.7s⁴ h23.3v⁵ Apr 7] sturdy gelding: poor maiden hurdler: stays 2½m: acts on heavy going: has worn hood. *Rosemary Gasson*   **h81**

SCEAU ROYAL (FR) 6 b.g. Doctor Dino (FR) – Sandside (FR) (Marchand de Sable (USA)) [2017/18 h151: c16.2g* c15.9g² c16.2s* c15.5d* c16.4s* Jan 27]   **c157 h–**

'To win two races within a week over the Christmas period was a tremendous thrill. Hopefully, in time, I may be lucky enough to win some of the bigger trophies. That's the ambition.' So said asset manager Simon Munir after the Nicky Henderson-trained Radium had won the opening novice event at Cheltenham on New Year's Day 2010, three days on from Be There In Five's winning debut in a similar event at Chepstow on Welsh Grand National day. Munir, who had only recently begun buying National Hunt horses with bloodstock agent Anthony Bromley, didn't have to wait long for his first 'big trophy', with Soldatino following up his Adonis win to take the Triumph Hurdle at the Cheltenham Festival less than three months later, a day when Radium finished second in the Martin Pipe. That early success seemingly only buoyed Munir's interest in racing—which reportedly began through school friend William Haggas—and he brought fellow city colleague Isaac Souede into partnership with him not long after. Success in the pair's now-familiar emerald green, dark green sleeves, quartered cap has been on an exponential scale, with Munir and Souede finishing runner-up to J. P. McManus in the leading owners' table in Britain for the first time in the most recent season. Their jumpers in Britain are spread between Nicky Henderson, Nigel Twiston-Davies, Alan King and most recently Ben Pauling and the Munir/Souede horses won forty-three races at an impressive 32% win ratio. Their prize money haul (£1,484,998 in first-three money) included sums earned by other horses based with leading Irish trainer Willie

randoxhealth.com Henry VIII Novices' Chase, Sandown—
Sceau Royal already has the measure of Brain Power who is about to unseat at the last

Mullins (they also have horses with Gordon Elliott) and with Guillaume Macaire, who trains the pair's substantial French contingent, which often acts as a feeder of sorts for the owners' main operation. Eight Grade 1 wins in Britain and Ireland between 2014/15 and 2016/17 wasn't bad going, but Munir and Souede beat that total in the most recent season alone, with established performers such as Bristol de Mai (Betfair Chase), L'Ami Serge (Aintree Hurdle) and Footpad (unbeaten in four Grade 1 novice chases, including the Arkle) combining with more recent acquisitions We Have A Dream (Finale Juvenile Hurdle and Anniversary Hurdle) and Terrefort (Scilly Isles Novices' Chase and Mildmay Novices' Chase) to help the owners to reach a total of eleven Grade 1s in Britain and Ireland.

Like all the above, Sceau Royal began his career in France, winning a three-year-old hurdle at Bordeaux in March 2015 for Macaire before being sent to Alan King for the 2015/16 season. Sceau Royal was first past the post on four of his first five outings for King, but came up short in the Grade 1 juvenile events at the Cheltenham and Aintree Festivals, and it was something of a similar story during 2016/17 as well, with Sceau Royal winning his first two starts, including the Elite Hurdle at Wincanton, before falling short at the very highest level when managing only sixth in the Champion Hurdle behind Buveur d'Air. Sceau Royal started the most recent season in now-typical style, impressing with his jumping when readily winning on his chasing debut at Warwick in early-October and then just being edged out by North Hill Harvey in a similar event at Cheltenham later that month. Sceau Royal justified very short odds in a match at Warwick on his next start and then started as the outsider of the quintet that lined up for the Henry VIII Novices' Chase at Sandown. The betting revolved around dual Grade 1-winning hurdler Finian's Oscar, with Brain Power—impressive when winning on his chasing debut at Kempton—sent off second favourite in a race that also attracted unbeaten chaser Capitaine and Sceau Royal's old adversary North Hill Harvey. One by one, Sceau Royal's rivals fell by the wayside, Finian's Oscar jumping poorly from the outset as Brain Power and North Hill Harvey took each other on for the lead down the back straight in a battle that did neither any favours. Sceau Royal made smooth progress in behind the front pair and loomed up two out before taking up the running approaching the final fence and recording an eleven-length win from North Hill Harvey (Brain Power unseated at the last when looking like being a five-length second) in a time that compared very favourably with the Tingle Creek won by Politilogue later on the card.

After falling short of Grade 1 level over hurdles, Sceau Royal had bridged the gap switched to chasing, Alan King saying after the race: 'I'd always said to Daryl [Jacob] he's probably 6 lb or 7 lb shy of the very top, but fences look to have pulled that out of him. I wouldn't mind if he went straight to the Arkle.' Sceau Royal's Sandown win meant that Munir and Souede were responsible for the top two in the ante-post betting for the Arkle, Sceau Royal promoted to second favourite behind Footpad, who had been extremely impressive on his chasing debut at Navan in November. Sceau Royal had one more race before his intended Festival target, landing the odds in the Lightning Novices' Chase at Doncaster in late-January, needing only to be shaken up briefly to keep tabs on Shantou Rock but then taking time to master that rival after hitting the front between the last two fences. Unfortunately, that was the last time Sceau Royal was seen in 2017/18, King revealing just over a week before the Arkle that he had met with a setback 'It's very slight and he's perfectly sound but there was just a little bit of filling there. It's minute but it's there and we can't kick on.'

Sceau Royal (FR) (b.g. 2012)	Doctor Dino (FR) (ch 2002)	Muhtathir (ch 1995)	Elmaamul / Majmu
		Logica (b 1994)	Priolo / Salagangai
	Sandside (FR) (b 2005)	Marchand de Sable (b or br 1990)	Theatrical / Mercantile
		Moi (b 1993)	Al Nasr / Oui Papa

Sceau Royal cost €14,000 as a yearling and ran once on the Flat (third in a two-year-old newcomers race at Fontainebleau in November 2014) before being sent hurdling. His dam Sandside began her career in Spain before winning four times at up to a mile in France in handicap/claiming company, while his elder half-brother Sandoside (by Palace Episode) has winning form at up to a mile and a quarter in France. Sandside is out of the French mile winner Moi, a half-sister to The Little Thief, a smart French stayer who broke down contesting the Gold Cup at Royal Ascot. Sceau Royal is by dual Hong Kong Vase winner Doctor Dino, who stands at Haras du Mesnil in France at €8,000 and, though now sixteen years of age, is something of an emerging National Hunt sire (his fee has gone up from €4,500

Mr Simon Munir & Mr Isaac Souede's "Sceau Royal"

SCE

in 2017). Among his progeny are the Warren Greatrex-trained La Bague Au Roi, who won three of her five starts in the most recent season including the Grade 2 Warfield Hurdle at Ascot, and the Willie Mullins-trained Sharjah who won twice in the colours of Mrs Susannah Ricci. The good-topped Sceau Royal is a strong traveller in his races and will prove best at around two miles. He has made a fine start to his chasing career, winning four of his five starts, with his jumping often an asset, and it is to be hoped he makes a full recovery from the leg injury that kept him out of the Arkle. *Alan King*

SCENIC STAR (IRE) 8 b.g. Erewhon (USA) – African Scene (IRE) (Scenic) [2017/18 c26.2g^3 c23.5g^{ur} c21.7g^{ur} c22.5d* c24g^3 c22.6m^4 h23.9g^4 c21d^4 c21s^{pu} Apr 23] poor handicap hurdler: modest handicap chaser: won novice event at Uttoxeter in June: left Gavin Patrick Cromwell, ran badly final start: stays 3m: acts on good to firm and good to soft going: tried in hood: wears tongue tie. *Mark Shears* — c97 h81

SCENTED LILY (IRE) 5 b.m. Presenting – Wood Lily (IRE) (Definite Article) [2017/18 b16.3s h15.8d h15.8g h15.7g ab18d^5 h20.6s^2 Mar 26] first foal: dam (h114) 2m hurdle winner out of half-sister to triple Cheltenham Gold Cup winner Best Mate: seventh in mares bumper at Stratford: improved form (fair) over hurdles when runner-up in handicap at Market Rasen final outing: stays 2½m: tried in hood. *Charlie Longsdon* — h104 b80

SCHAP 6 ch.m. Schiaparelli (GER) – Royal Keel (Long Leave) [2017/18 b93: h16g^6 h16s^3 h15.7v^{pu} h21d Apr 26] stocky mare: placed in bumpers: modest form over hurdles: tried in hood. *Caroline Fryer* — h95

SCHEU TIME (IRE) 5 br.g. Arakan (USA) – Time Limit (IRE) (Alzao (USA)) [2017/18 b99: b16m^4 b16.4d^2 b17g^4 h19.3d^2 h16.5v^4 h16s* h16.5s^F Apr 14] fairly useful bumper performer: useful form over hurdles: won maiden at Thurles in March: looked set to follow up when falling last in conditionals/amateur handicap at Aintree: tried in hood. *James A. Nash, Ireland* — h131 b100

SCHIAPARANNIE 6 b.m. Schiaparelli (GER) – Annie's Answer (IRE) (Flemensfirth (USA)) [2017/18 b91p: b16.7s^3 b17d^6 h16d* h19.7s^2 Mar 26] fairly useful bumper winner: fair form over hurdles: won mares novice at Wetherby in November: placed in similar events both starts after: wears hood: races prominently. *Ruth Jefferson* — h111 b97

SCHIEHALLION MUNRO 5 ch.g. Schiaparelli (GER) – Mrs Fawlty (Kayf Tara) [2017/18 b16.2v^4 b16.8s^3 Jan 12] first foal: dam (c101/h103), 19f hurdle winner, half-sister to fairly useful hurdler (2m-2¾m winner) Leave At Dawn: fair form when third at Sedgefield (still green) on second of 2 starts in bumpers. *Micky Hammond* — b85

SCHINDLER'S PRINCE (IRE) 13 ch.g. Oscar Schindler (IRE) – Coppeen Storm (IRE) (Glacial Storm (USA)) [2017/18 c105: c20.3s^4 c26.1d* c26.1g^4 Jun 21] workmanlike gelding: multiple point winner: fair handicap chaser: won at Uttoxeter in June: stays 3¼m: acts on good to firm and heavy going: wears cheekpieces/tongue tie. *Katy Price* — c103

SCHLIPF 5 b.g. Supreme Sound – Zahara Joy (Cayman Kai (IRE)) [2017/18 b–: b17m^2 h16.2g^4 h16.2g^3 h22.1g^3 h23.9m^4 h23.9s Aug 19] modest form on second of 2 starts in bumpers: similar form over hurdles: stays 2¾m. *Iain Jardine* — h88 b78

SCHNABEL (IRE) 6 b.g. Ask – Velsatis (IRE) (Commanche Run) [2017/18 h100, b82: h21g^4 h21.3s h19.7g^2 h21.2g* h19.4d^3 Dec 15] fourth in Irish point: fair handicap hurdler: won conditionals novice event at Ludlow in December: should stay 23f+: acts on good to soft going: open to further improvement. *David Dennis* — h106 p

SCOOBY (IRE) 7 b.g. Dubai Destination (USA) – Maggie Howard (IRE) (Good Thyne (USA)) [2017/18 h106: h21.4g^5 h20.3d^3 h23.4s^3 h25d Apr 24] well-made gelding: fair handicap hurdler: stays 3m: acts on soft going: tried in hood. *Graeme McPherson* — h105

SCOOP THE POT (IRE) 8 b.g. Mahler – Miss Brecknell (IRE) (Supreme Leader) [2017/18 h108: h23g* h25.8g^3 h23g* c16.5g^3 Nov 14] good-topped gelding: fairly useful handicap hurdler: won at Worcester in August and October: 5/2, third in novice handicap at Huntingdon (16 lengths behind Cyrname) on chasing debut: barely stays 3¼m: acts on soft going: wears tongue tie: usually races towards rear: open to improvement over fences. *Philip Hobbs* — c121 p h126

SCORPION HAZE (IRE) 5 b.g. Scorpion (IRE) – Sea Maiden (IRE) (Presenting) [2017/18 b15.7g^4 b15.8v^2 b13.7v^3 b17.7s^2 Apr 15] £16,000 3-y-o: tall, useful-looking gelding: second foal: dam lightly-raced sister to fair hurdler/fairly useful chaser (stayed 3m) Calusa Caldera: fairly useful form in bumpers: tried in cheekpieces. *Ali Stronge* — b95

SCORPION PRINCESS (IRE) 7 b.m. Scorpion (IRE) – Cailin's Princess (IRE) (Luso) [2017/18 b–: h15.7d h15.8d³ h17.7v⁴ h15.6s h16.3d^pu Apr 22] lengthy mare: bumper winner: fair form over hurdles: should stay beyond 2m: acts on good to soft going: tried in tongue tie. *Charlie Longsdon* — **h100**

SCORPION SID (IRE) 6 b.g. Scorpion (IRE) – Gaye Lady (IRE) (Pistolet Bleu (IRE)) [2017/18 h19.5v* h15.8v* h23.9s² Apr 25] €7,500 3-y-o, £50,000 5-y-o: fourth foal: half-brother to a winning jumper in USA by Soviet Star: dam unraced half-sister to fairly useful hurdler (stayed 3m) Minella Humour out of half-sister to high-class staying chaser Kingsmark: runner-up in Irish point on debut: useful form over hurdles: won novices at Chepstow in January and Ffos Las in February: stays 19f well, though didn't get home at 3m final outing. *Jamie Snowden* — **h130**

SCORPIONS SOUND (IRE) 6 b.g. Scorpion (IRE) – Sounds Attractive (IRE) (Rudimentary (USA)) [2017/18 b15.8m h15.8s^pu h19.7s^pu Nov 3] no promise in maiden bumper (for Dominic Ffrench Davis) or novice hurdles. *Sam England* — **h–** / **b–**

SCORPION STAR (IRE) 9 b.g. Scorpion (IRE) – Chapanga (IRE) (Un Desperado (FR)) [2017/18 c21.9g² c21m^pu h16.8g⁵ h16.8d h16.5v h18.5s^pu Apr 23] multiple point winner: modest maiden hurdler: trained by A Pennock, similar form when second in novice hunter at Sedgefield on first of 2 starts in chases: stays 19f: acts on good to firm going: in cheekpieces last 4 starts: tried in tongue tie. *Martin Hill* — **c97** / **h84**

SCORPO (IRE) 7 b.g. Scorpion (IRE) – Malteste (IRE) (Never So Bold) [2017/18 c15.7v^pu c16.5v^ur c20.5v³ c19.2s⁵ c16.9d⁴ c16.4v⁶ c26.2d^pu c20.1v^pu Apr 15] €9,000 3-y-o, £6,800 5-y-o: seventh foal: half-brother to 2 winners by Germany, including fairly useful hurdler/chaser Malt Gem (2¼m-3m winner): dam (h93), 2½m hurdle winner, also 1¼m-2m winner on Flat: maiden pointer: maiden chaser, probably flattered on second outing. *Victor Thompson* — **c–**

SCOTCHTOWN (IRE) 6 ch.g. Beneficial – Always Present (IRE) (Presenting) [2017/18 h132, b96: c23g⁴ c23.6v² c23.6v⁵ c24.5v² c26g^ur Apr 18] tall gelding: useful hurdler: fairly useful maiden chaser: stays 3¼m: acts on heavy going: front runner/races prominently: not a fluent jumper of fences. *Nigel Twiston-Davies* — **c127 x** / **h–**

SCOTSBROOK NIGHT 5 b.m. Midnight Legend – Won More Night (Kayf Tara) [2017/18 b70: h20g h16g⁴ h16g⁴ h18.7m⁶ h16g⁵ h16g^ur hp Oct 17] angular mare: poor maiden hurdler: unproven beyond 2m: tried in hood: wears tongue tie. *Shaun Lycett* — **h81**

SCOTS SONNET 4 b.g. Poet's Voice – Jabbara (IRE) (Kingmambo (USA)) [2017/18 b13d ab16.3g⁵ b16.4d⁶ Mar 16] poor form in bumpers: tried in hood. *Jim Goldie* — **b71**

SCOTSWELL 12 b.g. Endoli (USA) – Tofino Swell (Primitive Rising (USA)) [2017/18 c119§, h–§: h25.8g h25.8v^pu c26.2v Apr 16] plain gelding: fairly useful handicap hurdler/chaser at best: little form in 2017/18: stays 4m: acts on good to firm and heavy going: forces pace: unreliable. *Harriet Graham* — **c– §** / **h– §**

SCOTTSDALE 5 b.g. Cape Cross (IRE) – High Praise (USA) (Quest For Fame) [2017/18 b84: b16.7g* Jul 16] fairly useful form in bumpers: won at Market Rasen in June and Perth in July: only modest form on Flat subsequently. *Brian Ellison* — **b100**

SCOTTSHILL (IRE) 6 ch.g. Flemensfirth (USA) – Loch Lomond (IRE) (Dry Dock) [2017/18 b16.8s² h19.9v h21d Apr 26] sturdy gelding: brother to several winners, including bumper winner/useful hurdler Highland Valley (19f-21f winner) and fairly useful hurdler Dunlough Bay (19f-3m winner), and half-brother to 2 winners: dam maiden pointer: placed in Irish points: second in bumper at Sedgefield (9 lengths behind Windsor Avenue), then left Mrs Caroline McCaldin: better effort in maiden hurdles when tenth at Warwick final outing: type to do better in time. *Jonjo O'Neill* — **h83 p** / **b92**

SCRAFTON 7 b.g. Leporello (IRE) – Some Diva (Dr Fong (USA)) [2017/18 h19.4s h16s Mar 9] fairly useful hurdler for John Quinn: folded both starts in handicaps in 2017/18: won on Flat in April for Tony Carroll: stays 2¼m: acts on heavy going: tried in blinkers. *Ben Pauling* — **h–**

SCRIPTURIENT (IRE) 6 ch.g. Arakan (USA) – Kelso Magic (USA) (Distant View (USA)) [2017/18 c22.1g h21g⁶ h21.3g c22.6m²* c21d⁶ c22.6m^pu Aug 24] €800 3-y-o: half-brother to several winners on Flat: dam useful 5f winner: unplaced in point: poor form over hurdles: fair form over fences: won handicap at Stratford in July: stays 23f: acts on good to firm going: in blinkers last 5 starts: wears tongue tie: often leads: temperamental. *Gavin Patrick Cromwell, Ireland* — **c105 §** / **h81**

SCRUMPY BOY 6 b.g. Apple Tree (FR) – Presuming (Mtoto) [2017/18 h80: h16.8g h23.3d h21.6s⁵ h19.8s⁶ h19v^pu h21s Apr 9] poor maiden hurdler: left Kayley Woollacott after fifth start: stays 23f: acts on heavy going: tried in tongue tie. *Brian Barr* — **h81**

SCR

SCRUPULEUX (FR) 7 b.g. Laveron – Rouge Folie (FR) (Agent Bleu (FR)) [2017/18 h21.4g^{pu} h20s^{pu} h21.6v c17.5d^{pu} Apr 24] maiden hurdler/chaser: little form in 2017/18: tried in tongue tie. *Chris Down* — c–, h–

SCRUTINISE 6 b.g. Intense Focus (USA) – Tetravella (IRE) (Groom Dancer (USA)) [2017/18 h102p: h16d^{pu} h16.8s^{pu} h15.6g^{6} h16.6s Jan 26] useful-looking gelding: formerly useful on Flat (stays 1¾m): disappointing maiden hurdler: tried in cheekpieces. *Tim Vaughan* — h84

SEABOARD (IRE) 7 b.g. Pivotal – Ocean Silk (USA) (Dynaformer (USA)) [2017/18 h16.8d^{4} h20d h16g h16.5g h16.5g h18.5v^{pu} Dec 8] fifth foal: half-brother to 2 winners, including bumper winner/fair hurdler Plain Sailing (19f winner, by Manduro): dam smart 1¼m winner: modest form only outing on Flat: modest maiden hurdler: barely stays 2½m: acts on soft going: sometimes in headgear: tongue tied last 2 outings. *John Joseph Hanlon, Ireland* — h91

SEABORN (IRE) 4 b.g. Born To Sea (IRE) – Next To The Top (Hurricane Run (IRE)) [2017/18 h15.8g h16.4v^{4} h17.7v^{5} Dec 11] modest on Flat, stays 1¼m: little form in juvenile hurdles. *Tim Vaughan* — h–

SEACON BEG (IRE) 9 b.g. Generous (IRE) – Moon Storm (IRE) (Strong Gale) [2017/18 c–, h70: h18.7m^{pu} Jul 16] modest hurdler at best: lightly raced and little form since 2015/16: pulled up only start over fences: stays 19f: acts on good to firm and good to soft going: wears tongue tie. *Nikki Evans* — c–, h–

SEAMOUR (IRE) 7 b.g. Azamour (IRE) – Chifney Rush (IRE) (Grand Lodge (USA)) [2017/18 h16d^{3} Oct 18] smart stayer on Flat at best: lightly-raced hurdler, fairly useful form when third in handicap at Wetherby on sole outing in 2017/18: will be well suited by 2½m. *Brian Ellison* — h125

SEAN O'CASEY (IRE) 5 b.g. Galileo (IRE) – Lahinch (IRE) (Danehill Dancer (IRE)) [2017/18 h15.8s Jan 10] fairly useful on Flat, stays 1½m: 40/1, tired when well held in maiden at Ludlow on hurdling debut. *Michael Appleby* — h–

SEA OF MYSTERY (IRE) 5 b.g. Sea The Stars (IRE) – Sassenach (IRE) (Night Shift (USA)) [2017/18 h16.5s h17.7s^{6} h17s h15.7v^{4} Apr 27] has had breathing operation: fairly useful maiden on Flat, stays 15f: well held in novice/maiden hurdles. *Dan Skelton* — h78

SEARCHING (IRE) 6 ro.g. Mastercraftsman (IRE) – Miracolia (IRE) (Montjeu (IRE)) [2017/18 h111: h20.5d h15.5d^{3} h21s h20.5s Apr 15] sturdy gelding: fair hurdler at best: disappointing in 2017/18: stays 2¼m: acts on heavy going: wears headgear. *Gary Moore* — h84

SEA SOVEREIGN (IRE) 5 b.g. Sea The Stars (IRE) – Lidakiya (IRE) (Kahyasi) [2017/18 b94: h17.7m^{4} Sep 24] leggy, close-coupled gelding: fair form in bumpers/fairly useful form on Flat: 9/2, fourth in novice at Plumpton (23½ lengths behind Arthington) on hurdling debut: should improve. *Mark Pitman* — h91 p

SEASTON SPIRIT 5 b.g. Kayf Tara – Aphrodisias (FR) (Double Bed (FR)) [2017/18 b15.7g^{3} b17.7d^{2} h19.2v* h21s^{4} h20.5v^{2} Mar 12] £34,000 3-y-o: well-made gelding: closely related to a winning pointer by Dr Massini and half-brother to 3 winners, including modest hurdler Solitairy Girl (19f winner, by Loup Solitaire): dam unraced sister to high-class French chaser (stayed 27f) Matinee Lover: fair form in bumpers: similar form over hurdles: won maiden at Fontwell in January. *Oliver Sherwood* — h113, b94

SEA STORY 5 b.m. Black Sam Bellamy (IRE) – Charlottes Webb (IRE) (Luso) [2017/18 b15.8g^{ur} b15.8v* b15.8s^{4} b15.7s* b17s Apr 12] sturdy mare: second foal: sister to fairly useful hurdler General Consensus (21f winner, stays 3m): dam (h90), winning pointer, half-sister to useful hurdler (stayed 3m) Kilcrea Kim: fairly useful bumper performer: won mares events at Ludlow in January and Catterick (conditionals/amateur) in March: will stay at least 2½m. *Kim Bailey* — b98

SEA THE SPRINGS (FR) 7 gr.g. Slickly (FR) – Cristal Springs (FR) (Loup Solitaire (USA)) [2017/18 h85: h24g^{pu} h20.5d^{pu} Oct 23] good-topped gelding: poor maiden hurdler: stayed 19f: acted on heavy going: wore headgear: dead. *Michael Roberts* — h57

SEA WALL (FR) 10 b.g. Turgeon (USA) – Si Parfaite (FR) (Solon (GER)) [2017/18 c121, h116: h16.3d^{2} h16s^{2} h16.8s^{6} h15.3v* c15.7s* h15.3v^{2} Mar 8] tall gelding: fairly useful handicap hurdler: won at Wincanton in January: useful handicap chaser: won at same track in February: best around 2m: acts on heavy going: wears hood: often races prominently/travels strongly. *Chris Gordon* — c131, h124

SED

SEBASTIAN BEACH (IRE) 7 b.g. Yeats (IRE) – Night Club (Mozart (IRE)) [2017/18 h111: h21g⁴ h25m⁵ h20.3g⁵ c24d* c24.1g⁴ Sep 1] rather leggy gelding: fair handicap hurdler: similar form both starts over fences, winning novice handicap at Uttoxeter in July: stays 3m: acts on soft and good to firm going: tried in cheekpieces: has worn tongue tie: front runner/races prominently. *Jonjo O'Neill* **c112 h108**

SEBASTOPOL (IRE) 4 b.g. Fame And Glory – Knockcroghery (IRE) (Pelder (IRE)) [2017/18 b16g* Apr 21] €52,000 3-y-o: first foal: dam (c98/h119), 2m hurdle winner (stayed 2½m), also 1¼m winner on Flat, half-sister to fairly useful hurdler (2m winner) The Brock Inn: easy winner on only outing in points: 3/1, looked smart prospect when also won bumper at Ayr by 3¾ lengths from Black Pirate: sure to progress. *Tom Lacey* **b101 p**

SEBS SENSEI (IRE) 7 ch.g. Art Connoisseur (IRE) – Capetown Girl (Danzero (AUS)) [2017/18 h–: h21.6d⁹ h21.6m Jun 15] modest maiden hurdler at best: little form since 2015/16: unproven beyond 2m: acts on firm and good to soft going: tried in tongue tie. *Mark Hoad* **h–**

SECOND TIME AROUND 6 b.g. Midnight Legend – Silk Rope (IRE) (Presenting) [2017/18 b85: b16.7g* h16s⁴ h16.3d⁶ h18.6v h19d⁵ Apr 26] lengthy gelding: fair form in bumpers: won at Market Rasen in May: modest form over hurdles: patiently ridden. *Alan King* **h99 b91**

SECRET APPROACH (IRE) 7 b.g. Gamut (IRE) – No Time At All (IRE) (Saddlers' Hall (IRE)) [2017/18 h–, b75: h16.8d h20.4s h16.2g⁶ h20.8s⁴ h23.3v h21.5v³ h24.3v⁶ h19.3v Dec 7] pulled up both starts in points: poor maiden hurdler: stays 21f: acts on soft going: often leads. *Neil McKnight, Ireland* **h80**

SECRET DOOR (IRE) 7 b.m. Stowaway – Cellar Door (IRE) (Saddlers' Hall (IRE)) [2017/18 h118p: h20.6g³ h23.3s³ h21.4s h19.8s⁵ c20s c22.5v⁵ c25.2v⁹ h21.4d² Apr 22] good-topped mare: runner-up in Irish point on debut: fairly useful handicap hurdler: little show in handicap chases: stays 23f: acts on heavy going: sometimes in cheekpieces. *Harry Fry* **c– h118**

SECRET ESCAPE (IRE) 6 ch.m. Getaway (GER) – Portorosa (USA) (Irish River (FR)) [2017/18 b16.3g* b16.2s* b17d⁴ b16.4s⁴ b17s⁶ Apr 12] €9,000 3-y-o: sturdy mare: half-sister to several winners, including fairly useful hurdler (Grade 1 winner in USA) Portrade (2m-19f winner, by Trade Fair) and fair hurdler Kind Heart (2m winner, by Red Ransom): dam French 9f winner: fairly useful bumper performer: won mares events at Stratford in July and Perth in August. *Donald McCain* **b100**

SECRET STREAM (IRE) 9 ch.g. Fruits of Love (USA) – Bonny River (IRE) (Exit To Nowhere (USA)) [2017/18 h128: c20d⁵ c24.2s³ c20d⁵ h20.2s³ Apr 27] close-coupled gelding: fairly useful handicap hurdler: similar form when fifth in novice handicap at Carlisle on chasing debut: let down by jumping at chases: stays 2½m: acts on heavy going: tried in blinkers: usually races prominently. *Ruth Jefferson* **c127 h123**

SECRET INVESTOR 6 b.g. Kayf Tara – Silver Charmer (Charmer) [2017/18 h122p: h21d² h24.6s² h20.8d h19.8v² h22d* Apr 22] good-topped gelding: won Irish point on debut: fairly useful form over hurdles: won at Stratford in April: should stay 3m: probably acts on heavy going: in tongue tie last 5 starts: front runner/races prominently. *Paul Nicholls* **h129**

SECRET LEGACY (IRE) 7 b.g. Flemensfirth (USA) – Wingfield Lady (IRE) (Erdelistan (FR)) [2017/18 b20s* b19d³ h16v³ h20.5v⁹ h19.3v³ h18.9s³ h19.9v* Apr 7] €40,000 3-y-o: half-brother to winning pointers by Deploy and Tikkanen: dam unraced half-sister to useful staying chaser Kinburn: fairly useful form in bumpers, winning maiden at Tipperary in October before third at Cork: fairly useful form over hurdles (left Gordon Elliott after hurdling debut): won maiden at Uttoxeter in April: stays 2½m: acts on heavy going: usually travels strongly. *Ian Williams* **h117 b102**

SECRET MELODY 5 b.g. Sakhee's Secret – Montjeu's Melody (IRE) (Montjeu (IRE)) [2017/18 h18.6d⁹ h16.8s⁵ h19.3s h16v⁴ h15.8d Apr 24] compact gelding: second foal: dam maiden on Flat (barely stayed 1¾m): modest form over hurdles: unproven beyond 17f: acts on heavy going. *Tim Easterby* **h91**

SECRET PASSENGER (IRE) 5 ch.g. Stowaway – Mtpockets (IRE) (Deploy) [2017/18 b60: h20.1v⁶ h19.3v h19.9s³ h25.3d⁶ Dec 28] mid-field in bumper: modest form over hurdles: bred to be suited by further than 2½m. *Brian Ellison* **h95**

SEDDON (IRE) 5 b.g. Stowaway – Andreas Benefit (IRE) (Beneficial) [2017/18 b15.6s* b16.4s Mar 14] €30,000 3-y-o: good-topped gelding: fourth foal: dam unraced half-sister to fairly useful hurdler (stays 2½m) Destiny's Gold: useful form in bumpers: won at **b107 p**

SED

Musselburgh (by 5 lengths from Chanceanotherfive) on debut in February: shaped well when mid-field in 23-runner Champion Bumper won by Relegate at Cheltenham, threatening long way: remains with potential. *Tom George*

SEEANYTHINGYOULIKE (IRE) 7 b.g. Fruits of Love (USA) – California Dreamin (Slip Anchor) [2017/18 h16d h18.5m³ h18.5g³ h20g⁶ c21.6g⁴ c23g⁴ Sep 18] modest maiden hurdler: similar form in handicap chases at Fontwell (novice) and Worcester (plenty to do): stays 23f: acts on good to firm going: wears hood: usually races freely in rear: temperamental. *Jeremy Scott*   c94 § h93 §

SEE DOUBLE YOU (IRE) 15 b.g. Saddlers' Hall (IRE) – Mandy's Treasure (IRE) (Mandalus) [2017/18 c121, h106: h23.3g h23.3g⁵ c20.1g³ h22.1s² h23.9d² c22s Aug 18] angular gelding: modest handicap hurdler nowadays: formerly fairly useful handicap chaser: little show over fences in 2017/18: stays 25f: acts on heavy going: has worn cheekpieces, including last 3 starts. *Ronan M. P. McNally, Ireland*   c79 h91

SEE IT IN 6 ch.m. Black Sam Bellamy (IRE) – Lucky Arrow (Indian Ridge) [2017/18 b–: b13.6g⁵ May 5] well held in bumpers 5 months apart. *Oliver Sherwood*   b–

SEELATERALLIGATOR (IRE) 6 b.m. Getaway (GER) – Charming Present (IRE) (Presenting) [2017/18 b94: h16d³ h15.7g^pu May 15] fair bumper winner: modest form on hurdling debut: fatally injured next time. *Dan Skelton*   h90

SEE THE ROCK (IRE) 8 b.g. Shirocco (GER) – Samara (IRE) (Polish Patriot (USA)) [2017/18 h18.6s Dec 26] fairly useful on Flat: fairly useful novice hurdler in 2015/16: well held in handicap only start since: stayed 19f: acted on soft going: in hood 4 of last 5 outings: dead. *Jonjo O'Neill*   h–

SEE THE WORLD 8 b.g. Kayf Tara – My World (FR) (Lost World (IRE)) [2017/18 h101: c16.2g³ c20.3g^pu Jun 13] tall gelding: bumper winner: lightly raced and disappointing over jumps. *Emma Lavelle*   c82 h–

SEEYOUATMIDNIGHT 10 b.g. Midnight Legend – Morsky Baloo (Morpeth) [2017/18 c159, h149: c19.9s³ c34.3s Apr 14] strong, rangy gelding: smart hurdler/chaser in prime: signs of retaining ability when 20 lengths third to Tiquer in handicap Newbury on belated return: prominent long way (finished lame) in Grand National at Aintree after: stays 4m: acts on heavy going: front runner/races prominently. *Sandy Thomson*   c132 h–

SEGO SUCCESS (IRE) 10 b.g. Beneficial – The West Road (Mister Lord (USA)) [2017/18 c139, h–: c24g² c24d c23.8s³ c24s³ c23.8s Mar 25] good-topped gelding: winning hurdler: useful handicap chaser nowadays, on long losing run: stays 25f: acts on good to firm and heavy going: wears headgear: often let down by jumping. *Alan King*   c134 x h–

SELDOM INN 10 ch.g. Double Trigger (IRE) – Portland Row (IRE) (Zaffaran (USA)) [2017/18 c145, h–: c21.6v⁵ h21.4v³ h25.8v² c23.4v³ c26.2v⁵ c23.8s³ Apr 25] workmanlike gelding: useful handicap chaser/hurdler: stays 3¼m: acts on heavy going: often in headgear: temperamental. *Sandy Thomson*   c131 § h131 §

SELFCONTROL (FR) 7 b.g. Al Namix (FR) – L'Ascension (FR) (River Sand (FR)) [2017/18 h–: h19.8v⁶ h19.8d Apr 22] lightly raced and little form over hurdles. *Paul Nicholls*   h–

SENDIYM (FR) 11 b.g. Rainbow Quest (USA) – Seraya (FR) (Danehill (USA)) [2017/18 c76x, h85: h21.2g⁸ c16.4g² h22.1d² c21.2g³ h22.1s^ur h23.9d⁶ h21.2g⁴ c21.6g⁵ c19.3d Oct 3] modest handicap hurdler: won at Sedgefield in May: modest handicap chaser: stays 23f, effective at shorter: acts on soft and good to firm going: has worn headgear/tongue tie: often races prominently. *Dianne Sayer*   c89 h86

SENIERGUES 6 ch.g. Midnight Legend – Lady Samantha (Fraam) [2017/18 h–, b87: h21.7s⁵ h16v² Apr 14] better effort in novice hurdles (fair form) when second at Chepstow: bred to prove best at 2½m+. *Robert Stephens*   h101

SENIOR CITIZEN 5 b.g. Tobougg (IRE) – Mothers Help (Relief Pitcher) [2017/18 b15.7v³ b16g³ Apr 21] €25,000 3-y-o: seventh foal: dam (c117/h106) 2m-3½m hurdle/chase winner: runner-up in Irish point: fair form when third in bumpers at Towcester and Ayr. *Alan King*   b92

SENIOR COUNSEL (IRE) 7 b.g. Galileo (IRE) – Discreet Brief (IRE) (Darshaan) [2017/18 h15.8m⁶ May 23] fair maiden on Flat, stays 1½m: no form in maiden hurdles. *Anabel K. Murphy*   h–

SENOR ALCO (FR) 12 gr.g. Dom Alco (FR) – Alconea (FR) (Brezzo (FR)) [2017/18 c84, h–: c24.2g May 6] multiple point winner: poor maiden hurdler/chaser: stays 3¼m: acts on good to firm and heavy going: usually in headgear nowadays: tried in tongue tie. *Victor Thompson*   c– h–

SENOR LOMBARDY (IRE) 5 b.g. Milan – Killoughey Babe (IRE) (Alderbrook) [2017/18 b16.2g² b16.2v* h22.7g* h22v² Dec 2] €34,000 3-y-o, €125,000 4-y-o: rather unfurnished gelding: sixth foal: dam twice-raced half-sister to Irish Grand National winner Glebe Lad: won sole start in Irish maiden points: fairly useful form in bumpers: won conditionals/amateur event at Hexham in October: also won novice at Kelso on hurdling debut in November: better form (useful) when 1¼ lengths second to Coole Hall in similar event at Newcastle: will stay 3m: open to further progress. *Keith Dalgleish* — **h131 p b103**

SENSE OF URGENCY (IRE) 6 ch.m. Captain Rio – Itsallaracket (IRE) (Rudimentary (USA)) [2017/18 b80: b16.2g² h16.2m⁴ h16.2g² h16.2s⁴ h18.1g Sep 20] modest form in bumpers: similar form over hurdles: should prove suited by further than 2m. *Lucy Normile* — **h98 b82**

SENSIBLE FRIEND (GR) 5 b.g. Reel Buddy (USA) – Senseansensibility (USA) (Capote (USA)) [2017/18 b86: h16g h15.3g h17.7g⁴ Nov 10] modest form over hurdles: best effort when fourth in conditionals novice at Fontwell: open to further improvement. *Amanda Perrett* — **h98 p**

SENSULANO (IRE) 5 b.m. Milan – Espresso Lady (IRE) (Shantou (USA)) [2017/18 b79: b16.2g² b16d³ h21v² h21s* h19.8v³ h20.5s h21.6s² Apr 23] useful-looking mare: in frame in bumpers: fairly useful form over hurdles: won mares novice at Warwick in January: good placed efforts 2 of 3 starts after: stays 21f: acts on heavy going: front runner/races prominently. *Noel Williams* — **h122 b88**

SENTIMENTALJOURNEY (IRE) 11 ch.g. Portrait Gallery (IRE) – Hazy Rose (IRE) (Roselier (FR)) [2017/18 c24.2v c24.2s⁶ Mar 9] point winner: winning hurdler: fair chaser: stays 3½m: acts on soft and good to firm going: has worn headgear. *R. W. Varnham* — **c108 h–**

SEQUINSATDAWN 6 ch.m. Tobougg (IRE) – Two Aye Em (Double Trigger (IRE)) [2017/18 h21s⁵ Jan 25] fifth foal: dam unraced sister to fair hurdler/fairly useful chaser (stayed 3¼m) Twelve Paces and half-sister to useful hurdler/chaser (stayed 23f) Crocadee: hooded, tailed off in mares novice hurdle on debut. *Sarah-Jayne Davies* — **h–**

SERENITY NOW (IRE) 10 b.g. Key of Luck (USA) – Imdina (IRE) (Soviet Star (USA)) [2017/18 h108: h20.6g⁶ᵘ h15.8g² h20s² h20.5d⁴ Dec 7] fair hurdler: won on Flat in December/January: stays 2½m: acts on heavy going: has worn headgear: usually races towards rear. *Brian Ellison* — **h111**

SERGEANT BRODY 7 ch.g. Black Sam Bellamy (IRE) – Ardent Bride (Ardross) [2017/18 h104p: h21s² h21v³ᵘ h25d Apr 26] lengthy gelding: winning pointer: fair form over hurdles: stays 25f: tried in tongue tie. *Samuel Drinkwater* — **h106**

SERGEANT PINK (IRE) 12 b.g. Fasliyev (USA) – Ring Pink (USA) (Bering) [2017/18 c–, h–: c20.1g* c20.1g c21.2sᵖᵘ Jul 22] good-topped gelding: winning hurdler: modest handicap chaser nowadays: won at Perth in May: stays 3m, effective at shorter: acts on good to firm and heavy going: sometimes wears headgear: tried in tongue tie: temperamental. *Dianne Sayer* — **c89 § h–**

SERGIO (IRE) 6 b.g. Flemensfirth (USA) – Aventia (IRE) (Bob Back (USA)) [2017/18 h–, b74: h20.6s³ h20.7sᵖᵘ Feb 22] sturdy gelding: modest form over hurdles: likely to stay beyond 21f: acts on soft going: in tongue tie last 2 starts. *Tim Vaughan* — **h87**

SERIENSCHOCK (GER) 10 br.g. Sholokhov (IRE) – Saldenehre (GER) (Highest Honor (FR)) [2017/18 h21.4s² h20.4v⁵ h24.7s⁵ Apr 14] sturdy gelding: useful hurdler: stiff task when fifth to Identity Thief in Stayers Hurdle (Liverpool) at Aintree final start: winning chaser: stays 25f: acts on heavy going: has worn headgear/tongue tie. *Mlle A. Rosa, France* — **c– h136**

SEROSEVSKY (IRE) 5 b.g. Morozov (USA) – Be My Rainbow (IRE) (Be My Native (USA)) [2017/18 b16.5s⁵ b15.8d⁵ h15.3d⁵ Apr 22] €20,000 3-y-o, £60,000 4-y-o: closely related to 2 winners, including fairly useful hurdler Memories of Milan (2m-3m winner, by Milan), and half-brother to 2 winners, including fairly useful chaser Powerful Symbol (3m winner, by Robin des Champs): dam unraced: won maiden point at second attempt: fair form on second of 2 starts in bumpers: 16/1, fifth in novice at Wincanton (16¼ lengths behind Diamond Guy) on hurdling debut: will be suited by 2½m+: wears tongue tie. *Harry Fry* — **h91 b86**

SERPICO (IRE) 7 br.g. Scorpion (IRE) – Call Her Again (IRE) (Old Vic) [2017/18 h99, b93: h24dᵖᵘ h24.1s⁵ h26.4d⁴ Apr 22] fair maiden hurdler: stays 3¼m: acts on soft going: tried in blinkers: in tongue tie last 3 starts: temperament under suspicion. *Graeme McPherson* — **h105**

SERVEONTIME (IRE) 7 b.g. Echo of Light – Little Lovely (IRE) (Mizzen Mast (USA)) [2017/18 h90, b–: h16.8gᵘʳ h17.7d h16.8d⁵ h16.5m² h16.5g² h16.5g⁶ Nov 30] rather leggy gelding: modest maiden hurdler: unproven beyond 2m: acts on good to firm going: wears cheekpieces/tongue tie. *Helen Nelmes* — **h96**

SET

SET LIST (IRE) 9 b.g. Heron Island (IRE) – Copper Magic (IRE) (Zaffaran (USA)) [2017/18 c130, h–: c24d c25.5d[4] c22.6m[pu] h24.3g[5] Apr 20] sturdy gelding: fair maiden hurdler: fairly useful handicap chaser: left Emma Lavelle after third start: stays 3¼m: acts on good to firm and good to soft going: wears headgear: not straightforward. *Dan Skelton* — **c113 h109**

SETTIE HILL (USA) 5 b.g. Cape Blanco (IRE) – Claire Soleil (USA) (Syncline (USA)) [2017/18 b111: h19.3g h21.6d[2] Dec 22] rather leggy gelding: useful bumper winner: much better effort in maiden hurdles (fairly useful form) at Ascot when close second to Clondaw Native: open to further improvement. *Nicky Henderson* — **h128 p**

SEVARANO (IRE) 5 b.g. Shantou (USA) – Eva La Diva (IRE) (Azamour (IRE)) [2017/18 b16s[*] b17s[5] Apr 13] €110,000 3-y-o: good-topped gelding: first foal: dam (b92), placed in bumpers (including at 2½m), half-sister to fairly useful hurdler (2m winner) First Trim: fairly useful form in bumpers: forged clear when winning maiden at Kempton on debut, then 14¼ lengths fifth of 20 to Portrush Ted in Grade 2 at Aintree 2 months later. *Oliver Sherwood* — **b101**

SEVENBALLS OF FIRE (IRE) 9 b.g. Milan – Leadamurraydance (IRE) (Supreme Leader) [2017/18 c109§, h119§: h25.8v[5] Jan 25] fairly useful hurdler at best: left Iain Jardine, little show only start in 2017/18: fair maiden chaser: stays 4m: raced on going softer than good (acts on heavy): has worn cheekpieces: hard ride. *George Bewley* — **c– h95**

SEVEN DEVILS (IRE) 8 b.g. Definite Article – Top Lot (IRE) (Topanoora) [2017/18 c107x, h–: c20.1g[2] May 6] maiden hurdler: fair handicap chaser: stays 2½m: acts on soft and good to firm going: wears tongue tie: usually races in rear: often let down by jumping. *Lucinda Russell* — **c97 x h–**

SEVEN KINGDOMS (IRE) 6 b.g. Yeats (IRE) – Valrhona (IRE) (Spectrum (IRE)) [2017/18 c101, h87: c20.5g[6] c19.2d[ur] c23.8g[pu] h20.3d h20.7s h21s Apr 9] rather leggy gelding: winning hurdler/chaser: no form in 2017/18: usually in headgear: wears tongue tie: often let down by jumping over fences. *David Dennis* — **c– x h–**

SEVEN NATION ARMY (IRE) 9 gr.g. Rock of Gibraltar (IRE) – Crepe Ginger (IRE) (Sadler's Wells (USA)) [2017/18 c95, h110: c16.3g[3] h17.7d[3] May 28] rather leggy gelding: disappointing maiden hurdler/chaser: regularly wears headgear: tongue tied. *Alexandra Dunn* — **c92 h70**

SEYMOUR LEGEND 12 b.g. Midnight Legend – Rosehall (Ardross) [2017/18 c–, h73: h22g[pu] h20g[6] h23.1g[6] h23g[5] c23g c23.6g[pu] Oct 17] bad handicap hurdler: mistakes and no form over fences: stays 2¾m: acts on good to soft going: wears headgear. *Jim Wilson* — **c– x h57**

SEYMOUR STAR 10 b.g. Alflora (IRE) – Seymour Chance (Seymour Hicks (FR)) [2017/18 h126: h21.1s h19.7s[3] c20d[3] h23.1s Mar 24] good-topped gelding: fairly useful handicap hurdler: 3/1, last of 3 in novice at Ludlow (8½ lengths behind Rayvin Black) on chasing debut: stays 23f: acts on soft and good to soft going: usually races prominently. *Alastair Ralph* — **c124 h123**

SGROPPINO (IRE) 6 b.g. Getaway (GER) – Boadicea (Celtic Swing) [2017/18 b98: h15.8g h16.8v[pu] Apr 17] useful-looking gelding: fair form on first of 2 starts in bumpers: better effort over hurdles when eighth in novice at Ludlow. *Philip Hobbs* — **h85**

SGT BULL BERRY 11 b.g. Alflora (IRE) – Cede Nullis (Primitive Rising (USA)) [2017/18 c83, h–: c26.2g[pu] c24g[pu] c22.6m[pu] h23.1g Aug 4] of little account nowadays: tried in cheekpieces/tongue tie. *Peter Maddison* — **c– h–**

SHAAMA GRISE (FR) 6 gr.m. Montmartre (FR) – Shaama Rose (FR) (Verglas (IRE)) [2017/18 h131: c17d[2] c17.5v[2] c20s[3] Jan 18] useful hurdler: not so good over fences, best effort when 12 lengths second to Optimus Prime in novice at Plumpton: stays 21f: acts on soft going: usually wears hood: tried in tongue tie: usually races close up. *David Pipe* — **c119 h–**

SHACKLETON (IRE) 6 b.g. Stowaway – Art of Survival (IRE) (Saddlers' Hall (IRE)) [2017/18 h16g[bd] Oct 5] in frame once from 3 starts in Irish maiden points: brought down third in novice on hurdling debut: dead. *Jonjo O'Neill* — **h–**

SHADARPOUR (IRE) 9 b.g. Dr Fong (USA) – Shamadara (IRE) (Kahyasi) [2017/18 h–: h21.4d Apr 22] sturdy gelding: fairly useful hurdler at best: lightly raced and disappointing since 2015/16: should stay beyond 2¾m: acts on soft and good to firm going: regularly wears headgear. *Katie Stephens* — **h–**

SHADDAII (FR) 12 gr.g. April Night (FR) – Gypsie d'Artois (FR) (Mistigri) [2017/18 h80: h21.6g[pu] May 5] poor handicap hurdler: stayed 2½m: acted on soft going: wore tongue tie: usually raced close up: dead. *Robert Walford* — **h–**

SHA

SHADES OF MIDNIGHT 8 b.g. Midnight Legend – Hannah Park (IRE) (Lycius (USA)) [2017/18 h132: c20d^5 c19v^R c24.2v^3 c31.8s^{ur} c24.1g Apr 21] good-topped gelding: useful hurdler: similar form over fences only when third in Towton Novices' Chase at Wetherby (9¾ lengths behind Ballyoptic) in February: left Donald Whillans after second start: stays 3¼m: best form on soft/heavy going: tried in cheekpieces: tongue tied for former stable. *Sandy Thomson* c137 h–

SHADES OF SILVER 8 b.g. Dansili – Silver Pivotal (IRE) (Pivotal) [2017/18 h20.5d^{pu} Dec 1] fairly useful on Flat, stays 2m: little aptitude when pulled up in novice on hurdling debut. *Ed de Giles* h–

SHADOW BLUE (IRE) 9 br.g. Blueprint (IRE) – Rosie Belle (IRE) (Roselier (FR)) [2017/18 h85: h16d^4 h19.2d^5 h21.6v Dec 21] well held only completed start in points: poor maiden hurdler: stays 19f: acts on good to firm and good to soft going: front runner. *Steven Dixon* h82

SHADOW'S BOY 9 gr.g. Norse Dancer (IRE) – Inspired Role VII (Damsire Unregistered) [2017/18 h18.5m^3 h18.5d^3 h21.2m^2 h21.2g^3 h21.4v* Dec 7] sturdy gelding: maiden pointer: fair form over hurdles: won novice handicap at Wincanton in December: stays 21f: acts on good to firm and heavy going. *Bernard Llewellyn* h112

SHADOW'S GIRL 6 gr.m. Fair Mix (IRE) – Special Beat (Bustino) [2017/18 b16.8m^4 b16g^3 b15.8m Oct 11] half-sister to several winners, including fairly useful hurdler/winning pointer Special Occasion (2m-19f winner, by Inchinor) and fairly useful hurdler/chaser Gee Dee Nen (21f-3m winner, by Mister Baileys), both unreliable: dam (h119), 19f/2½m hurdle winner, also 17f winner on Flat: failed to complete in points: poor form in bumpers/on Flat. *Bernard Llewellyn* b69

SHADY GLEN (IRE) 9 br.g. Dr Massini (IRE) – Poppins (IRE) (Invited (USA)) [2017/18 c111, h–: c20m^4 c24.2g^2 c23.8g^3 c21.4g* c21.2s^2 c21d^2 c22.6g^4 h21g^4 c23.9g^3 c23.9g* Nov 9] maiden hurdler: fairly useful handicap chaser: won at Market Rasen in July and November: stays 3m: acts on soft and good to firm going: wears headgear/tongue tie: tends to find little. *Graeme McPherson* c115 h74

SHADY OPERATOR (IRE) 5 b.g. Court Cave (IRE) – Native Artist (IRE) (Be My Native (USA)) [2017/18 h20s^2 h16s^2 h16v^2 h16s^2 Apr 27] €115,000 3-y-o: brother/close relative to bumper winners/fairly useful 2½m hurdle winners Court Artist and Araucaria (latter by Accordion) and half-brother to useful hurdler Private Malone (2½m-2¾m winner, by Darsi): dam (h104), placed all 3 starts in bumpers/over hurdles, out of half-sister to Grand National winner Corbiere: successful only outing in bumper: useful form over hurdles: won maiden at Cork in November: runner-up in novices at Gowran and Punchestown (nose behind Antey) after: travels strongly: remains open to improvement. *Joseph Patrick O'Brien, Ireland* h135 p

SHAELLA (IRE) 4 ch.f. Casamento (IRE) – Mouriyana (IRE) (Akarad (FR)) [2017/18 b13.7g^3 b13.7g^5 Nov 14] lengthy filly: closely related/half-sister to several winners, including French hurdler Golden Thai (15f winner, by Red Ransom): dam French 2-y-o 1m winner: modest form in bumpers, and on first of 2 starts on Flat (for Jane Chapple-Hyam): wears hood. *Amy Murphy* b77

SHAIYZAR (IRE) 9 b.g. Azamour (IRE) – Shaiyzima (IRE) (Polish Precedent (USA)) [2017/18 c89, h93: c23.8g^2 c24.2g^2 c24g^5 c22.6m^2 c24.1g c24d^3 c24d^2 Nov 6] winning hurdler: modest maiden chaser: stays 3m: acts on soft and good to firm going: wears headgear: has worn tongue tie. *David Thompson* c85 h–

SHAKABULA (IRE) 4 b.g. Kheleyf (USA) – Tinaar (USA) (Giant's Causeway (USA)) [2017/18 h15.8s^{pu} Oct 19] modest maiden on Flat, stays 1½m: blinkered, pulled up in juvenile on hurdling debut. *Brian Ellison* h–

SHAKE IT UP (IRE) 9 br.g. Presenting – Miss Fresher (FR) (Pampabird) [2017/18 c106, h–: c23.5g^3 c25.5d* c23.9g^4 c31.9v^3 ab16.3g^3 Mar 3] maiden hurdler: fairly useful handicap chaser: left J. T. R. Dreaper, won at Cartmel (only outing for Richard Ford) in August: stays 3¼m: acts on heavy going: tried in hood. *Micky Hammond* c117 h–

SHALAKAR (FR) 5 b.g. Cape Cross (IRE) – Shalanaya (IRE) (Lomitas) [2017/18 h15.8v^{pu} h15.8d^3 h15.8s^3 h15.7s^3 h15.8s^3 h21.2d* Apr 9] useful on Flat (stays 15.5f) in France for M. Delzangles: fairly useful form over hurdles: won novice at Ludlow in April: stays 21f: acts on soft going: front runner/races prominently: remains open to improvement. *Venetia Williams* h121 p

SHA

SHALAMAN (IRE) 9 b.g. Oratorio (IRE) – Shalama (IRE) (Kahyasi) [2017/18 h16m^F h17g h17d Nov 13] fairly useful on Flat, stays 1½m: running best race over hurdles when falling 2 out in maiden won by Ornua at Down Royal on hurdling debut: tried in cheekpieces: wears tongue tie. *Matthew J. Smith, Ireland* **h99**

SHALAMZAR (FR) 9 ch.g. Selkirk (USA) – Shamalana (IRE) (Sinndar (IRE)) [2017/18 h70§: h19.3d h15.7d* h15.7s^6 h19.9v^{pu} Mar 13] close-coupled gelding: poor handicap hurdler: won selling event at Catterick in December: best around 2m: acts on good to soft going: in headgear 6 of last 7 outings, also tongue tied last 3. *Micky Hammond* **h76**

SHALL WE GO NOW 5 b.g. Midnight Legend – Suave Shot (Suave Dancer (USA)) [2017/18 b16g^3 b16.7d^6 h15.8s ab16d^2 Mar 5] £37,000 3-y-o: brother to fairly useful hurdler/useful chaser Midnight Shot (2m-2¾m winner) and half-brother to 2 winners, including bumper winner Gagas Horse (by Kayf Tara): dam once-raced half-sister to very smart hurdler/smart chaser (2m-19f winner) Grey Shot: fair form in bumpers: mistakes when well beaten in maiden on hurdling debut. *Harry Fry* **h– b90**

SHAMAN DU BERLAIS (FR) 5 b.g. Saint des Saints (FR) – Shinca (FR) (Port Lyautey (FR)) [2017/18 b16.8d^3 Apr 24] runner-up on completed outing in points (in front when unseating 2 out starts either side): 27¾ lengths third of 8 to Billygwyn Too in maiden bumper at Exeter. *Mrs Abbi Vaughan* **b64**

SHAMASH (IRE) 6 b.g. Oasis Dream – Shareen (IRE) (Bahri (USA)) [2017/18 h16.7g^4 h18.8g^3 h16.7g^2 Aug 4] dam half-sister to fairly useful hurdler (stayed 2¾m) Shariyan: fairly useful on Flat, stays 1¾m: fair form over hurdles: unproven beyond 17f: acts on good to soft going: wears tongue tie. *John McConnell, Ireland* **h102**

SHAMBRA (IRE) 4 b.f. Clodovil (IRE) – Shambodia (IRE) (Petardia) [2017/18 h15.8s* h16v* h15.7v^4 h16v^5 Mar 10] neat filly: fair to fair, stays 11f: similar form over hurdles: won fillies juvenile at Ludlow in January and mares novice at Wetherby in February: struggled in stronger races after: wears hood. *Lucy Wadham* **h113**

SHAMILAN (IRE) 5 b.g. Milan – Shatani (IRE) (Shahrastani (USA)) [2017/18 b17d^3 Nov 13] €32,000 3-y-o: fifth foal: brother to a winning pointer and half-brother to fairly useful hurdler/chaser Guiding George (19f-3m winner, by Flemensfirth): dam, placed in points, half-sister to useful hurdler/smart chaser (stayed 4m) Measureofmydreams: 10/3, some encouragement when third in bumper at Carlisle (11¼ lengths behind Aye Right): bred to stay at least 2½m. *Ronald O'Leary, Ireland* **b90**

SHAMITSAR 4 b.g. Shami – Tsarina Louise (Red Ransom (USA)) [2017/18 ab16.3g^3 Apr 15] second foal: dam showed little on Flat: third in bumper at Newcastle on debut. *Ray Craggs* **b84**

SHANAHAN'S TURN (IRE) 10 b.g. Indian Danehill (IRE) – Chanson Indienne (FR) (Indian River (FR)) [2017/18 c15.9d c20.8s c21.1s^2 c20s^{pu} Apr 25] well-made gelding: winning hurdler: useful handicap chaser: second in Topham Chase at Aintree (3¾ lengths behind Ultragold) in April: stays easy 23f: acts on soft and good to firm going: tried in cheekpieces: in tongue tie last 3 starts: unreliable. *Colin Tizzard* **c137 § h–**

SHANANN STAR (IRE) 12 br.m. Anshan – Baile An Droichid (IRE) (King's Ride) [2017/18 c93, h–: c25.1s^4 c26.7v^3 c26v^5 c25.1s^3 c25.2v^3 c29.2v^4 c26.7v^2 c25.1d^6 Apr 22] workmanlike mare: maiden hurdler: poor handicap chaser: stays 27f: acts on heavy going: wears headgear. *Gordon Edwards* **c82 h–**

SHANAWAY (IRE) 7 b.g. Stowaway – Shannagh Run (IRE) (Denel (FR)) [2017/18 h92: h16v^F h17v^4 h17d^4 h17s^5 h20.2s^2 Apr 27] pulled up in point: modest maiden hurdler: should be suited by further than 2½m: acts on soft going: has worn headgear: tried in tongue tie. *Stuart Coltherd* **h90**

SHANESHILL (IRE) 9 b.g. King's Theatre (IRE) – Darabaka (IRE) (Doyoun) [2017/18 c–, h154: h21.4s* h25.4s^3 c22.5g^2 c22.5s^2 c20v^4 c20.2v^{pu} h24d^3 Apr 26] sturdy gelding: smart hurdler: won Prix La Barka at Auteuil (by ¾ length from L'Ami Serge) in May: third after in Grande Course de Haies d'Auteuil (11½ lengths behind same rival) and Champion Stayers' Hurdle at Punchestown (17¾ lengths behind Faugheen): smart chaser: second in Galway Plate (4¾ lengths behind Balko des Flos) in August: stays 25f: acts on heavy going. *W. P. Mullins, Ireland* **c152 h154**

SHANKILL CASTLE 5 b.g. Lord Shanakill (USA) – Sagina (Shernazar) [2017/18 b16g^3 b17.8v^{6d} b16g^6 b16g Apr 21] half-brother to 2 winners, including fair hurdler/ winning pointer To Begin (21f winner, by Tobougg), stays 27f: dam French maiden (third **b84**

at 1½m): form in bumpers only when 7¼ lengths sixth of 9 to Kaloci at Fakenham third outing (left John Joseph Hanlon after): should stay at least 2¼m. *R. Mike Smith*

SHANKLYS DAWN (IRE) 7 gr.m. Mountain High (IRE) – Sika Trix (IRE) (Try Prospect (USA)) [2017/18 c23.5g c21.7g^{ur} c20.6s^{pu} c20.5g c24.4d^{4} c25.2g^{ur} c23.5v^{4} c23.5d c21v^{2} c21v^{3} c20v^{F} c23.6v c25.2v^{5} c19.2s* c21.2v^{4} Apr 16] maiden hurdler: poor handicap chaser: won at Downpatrick in March: stays 25f, effective at shorter: acts on heavy going: wears cheekpieces/tongue tie. *P. J. Rothwell, Ireland* — c73 h–

SHANKSFORAMILLION 9 b.g. Needle Gun (IRE) – Cool Connie (IRE) (Commanche Run) [2017/18 h20g* h20g^{8} h21g^{2} h19.3g Nov 4] workmanlike gelding: modest handicap hurdler: won at Worcester in July (2) and August (novice): stays 21f: best form on good going: often travels strongly. *Debra Hamer* — h99

SHANMULLAGH (IRE) 6 b.g. Royal Anthem (USA) – Next Best Thing (IRE) (Taipan (IRE)) [2017/18 h17s Oct 19] placed on completed starts in Irish points: showed nothing in novice on hurdling debut. *Noel C. Kelly, Ireland* — h–

SHANNON BRIDGE (IRE) 5 ch.g. Flemensfirth (USA) – Bridgequarter Lady (IRE) (King's Ride) [2017/18 h23.1s* h20.3s^{2} h24.4s^{2} h22.8v^{pu} h24.7s Apr 14] good-topped gelding: half-brother to several winners, including fair hurdler/fairly useful chaser Ballyvesey (2¾m-3m winner, by Anshan), stayed 3½m, and fairly useful hurdler Bridgequarter Girl (2m winner, by Presenting): dam, unraced, out of half-sister to Grand National winner Royal Athlete: unplaced on both starts in Irish points: useful form over hurdles: won maiden at Bangor in November: much improved when second in River Don Novices' Hurdle at Doncaster (short head behind Enniscoffey Oscar, moving smoothly into contention only to be edged out late after drifting left run-in) next time: excuses last 2 outings: stays 3m: acts on soft going: patiently ridden. *Dan Skelton* — h135

SHANNON LIGHT (IRE) 6 ch.g. Ask – Shannon Mist (IRE) (Perugino (USA)) [2017/18 b17.7s^{5} Apr 15] runner-up both starts in Irish points: 11/1, fifth in bumper at Plumpton (23½ lengths behind Baddesley Knight). *Brett Johnson* — b75

SHANNON SILVER 9 b.g. Grape Tree Road – Pinch Me Silver (Silver Patriarch (IRE)) [2017/18 c–: c24.2g^{F} May 6] multiple winning pointer: lightly raced and no form in hunter chases: in cheekpieces last 2 starts. *Mrs Anthea Morshead* — c–

SHANPALLAS (IRE) 10 b.g. Golan (IRE) – Evnelu (IRE) (Old Vic) [2017/18 c–, h133: c16g^{4} h24g^{4} c22.5g c24v^{pu} c24s h23d^{6} Oct 26] workmanlike gelding: fairly useful handicap hurdler/useful handicap chaser nowadays: stays 3m: acts on soft and good to firm going: ran out once. *Charles Byrnes, Ireland* — c132 h122

SHANROE IN MILAN (IRE) 6 b.g. Milan – Shanroe Scenario (IRE) (Presenting) [2017/18 h111: h22g^{3} c20d^{ur} c20d^{5} c24s* c25.6v^{5} c24.1g^{6} Apr 21] fair maiden hurdler: fairly useful form over fences: won handicap at Doncaster in January: stays 3m well: acts on soft going: front runner/races prominently. *Charlie Longsdon* — c123 h110

SHANROE SAINT 6 b.g. Saint des Saints (FR) – Aconit (FR) (Shining Steel) [2017/18 h16.3g^{3} h19.9d^{6} h16s^{2} h16s^{5} h21d h15.5v^{3} h16v h15.7v^{2} Apr 27] €11,000 3-y-o, £13,000 5-y-o: sturdy gelding: half-brother to 3 winners in France, including useful hurdler Brighter Later (2¼m/19f winner, by Turgeon): dam, French 15f-2¼m hurdle winner, also 1m-9.5f winner on Flat: placed in Irish maiden point: fairly useful maiden hurdler: should be suited by 2½m: acts on heavy going. *Ben Case* — h118

SHANROE SANTOS (IRE) 9 b.g. Definite Article – Jane Hall (IRE) (Saddlers' Hall (IRE)) [2017/18 c129, h–: c24g^{6} c26.2v^{3} c26.1d^{3} c24.2d^{m} c26s^{2} c28.5v^{2} c24.2s^{pu} c24.5v* c24.2v^{ur} c26s^{6} Mar 24] lengthy gelding: winning hurdler: useful handicap chaser: won at Carlisle in February: stays 3½m: acts on heavy going: wears headgear: usually races towards rear: usually makes mistakes. *Lucy Wadham* — c135 x h–

SHANROE STREET (IRE) 8 b.g. Mustameet (USA) – Zaffran Lady (IRE) (Zaffaran (USA)) [2017/18 c105, h–: c24.1v^{2} c24.1v^{3} c24.5d^{2} c23.8s^{F} Apr 25] Irish point winner: winning hurdler: fair handicap chaser: won novice event at Carlisle in March: probably stays 31f: acts on heavy going: front runner/races prominently. *Lucinda Russell* — c110 h–

SHANROE TIC TEC (IRE) 6 b.g. Flemensfirth (USA) – Bonny Hall (IRE) (Saddlers' Hall (IRE)) [2017/18 h25s^{3} h24.1d^{5} Mar 29] €18,000 3-y-o, £10,500 5-y-o: sixth foal: brother to fair chaser Surrogate Lad (2¼m winner) and fair/unreliable chaser Allerton — h107

SHA

(2½m-2¾m winner): dam unraced half-sister to smart French hurdler/high-class chaser (stayed 25f) Boca Boca: placed once in points: better effort over hurdles (fair form) when third in maiden at Huntingdon. *Jennifer Mason*

SHANTALUZE (IRE) 6 b.g. Shantou (USA) – Nut Touluze (IRE) (Toulon) [2017/18 b16.2v* b17v³ Mar 8] £40,000 5-y-o: seventh foal: brother to fair hurdler Cochinillo (2½m winner) and half-brother to 2 winners, including fair hurdler/chaser Kid Kalanisi (25f winner, by Kalanisi): dam, winning pointer, half-sister to fairly useful hurdler/chaser (stayed 3m) Lochan Lacha: off mark in Irish points at second attempt: much better effort in bumpers (fairly useful form) when winning at Kelso in January: found far less next time: will stay at least 2½m. *Donald McCain* — **b100**

SHANTOU BOB (IRE) 10 b.g. Shantou (USA) – Bobset Leader (IRE) (Bob Back (USA)) [2017/18 h142: h20d h24s⁴ h23.6v² h24s h22.8v⁶ Feb 17] sturdy gelding: has had breathing operation: winning pointer: useful handicap hurdler: second at Chepstow (½ length behind Flemcara) in January: stays 3m: acts on heavy going: usually in headgear: wears tongue tie: front runner/races prominently. *Warren Greatrex* — **h141**

SHANTOU FLYER (IRE) 8 b.g. Shantou (USA) – Carrigmorna Flyer (IRE) (Bob Back (USA)) [2017/18 c155, h–: c24.2s⁵ c25.6vᵖᵘ c24.2sᵖᵘ c20.8s² c20.8v² c23.4v² c25s² c34.3sᵖᵘ Apr 14] workmanlike gelding: winning hurdler: very smart handicap chaser: closing second in Ultima Handicap Chase at Cheltenham (neck behind Coo Star Sivola) in March: should stay further than 25f: acts on soft and good to firm going: in headgear last 5 starts: wears tongue tie. *Richard Hobson* — **c155 h–**

SHANTOU MAGIC (IRE) 11 b.g. Shantou (USA) – Supreme Magical (Supreme Leader) [2017/18 c124, h–: c26.3vᵖᵘ c24.2d² Apr 23] sturdy gelding: multiple winning pointer: winning hurdler: useful novice chaser in 2014/15: mostly disappointing since: stays 3m: acts on heavy going: tried in cheekpieces/tongue tie. *Will Ramsay* — **c70 h–**

SHANTOU PRINCE (IRE) 9 b.g. Shantou (USA) – Princess Nina (IRE) (King's Theatre (IRE)) [2017/18 c110: c26d⁴ c25.2s⁶ c19.3g² Apr 23] multiple point winner: fair maiden hunter chaser: stays 3¼m: acts on good to soft going: tried in tongue tie. *Mrs G. B. Walford* — **c106**

SHANTOU ROCK (IRE) 6 b.g. Shantou (USA) – Cool Cool (FR) (Anabaa (USA)) [2017/18 h140: c16.3g* c16.2d² c16s² c16.4s² c15.8s³ Apr 14] angular gelding: useful hurdler: smart novice chaser: won at Newton Abbot in October on chasing debut: placed all starts after, including when second in Lightning Novices' Chase at Doncaster (2 lengths behind Sceau Royal) in January and third in Maghull Novices' Chase at Aintree (8½ lengths behind Diego du Charmil) in April: will prove best around 2m: acts on soft going: wears tongue tie: usually leads: travels strongly/jumps boldly. *Dan Skelton* — **c146 h–**

SHANTOU TIGER (IRE) 9 b.g. Shantou (USA) – Opus One (Slip Anchor) [2017/18 c–, h111: h24m⁴ c21.2d² h23.1d⁴ h25.4g³ h25.4s² h23g⁴ h26gᵘʳ h24.7d⁶ Oct 29] close-coupled gelding: fair handicap hurdler: maiden chaser: won point in April: stays 25f: acts on soft and good to firm going: usually wears headgear: front runner/races prominently: moody. *Donald McCain* — **c65 § h107 §**

SHANTOU VILLAGE (IRE) 8 b.g. Shantou (USA) – Village Queen (IRE) (King's Theatre (IRE)) [2017/18 c149p, h–: c19.9dᵖᵘ c20.8g Apr 18] sturdy gelding: winning hurdler: smart novice chaser in 2016/17: seen out only twice in 2017/18 6 months apart, well below form both times: stays 21f: acts on good to firm and good to soft going: often leads. *Neil Mulholland* — **c– h–**

SHANTUNG (IRE) 5 ch.m. Shantou (USA) – Sarah's Cottage (IRE) (Topanoora) [2017/18 b16s⁴ b15.7s⁶ b16.6s⁵ b16s³ Feb 23] €15,000 3-y-o: sister to several winners, including useful hurdler/smart chaser Super Duty (17f-21f winner), stayed 29f, and fairly useful hurdler Howaboutnever (2½m-3¼m winner): dam unraced: fair form in bumpers. *Lucy Wadham* — **b90**

SHANTY ALLEY 4 b.g. Shantou (USA) – Alexander Road (IRE) (Kaldounevees (FR)) [2017/18 b16d Apr 26] good-topped gelding: 40/1, shaped as if needed experience when seventh in bumper at Warwick (15¾ lengths behind Umndeni). *Ben Case* — **b78**

SHANTY TOWN (IRE) 9 b.g. Zagreb (USA) – Rapsan (IRE) (Insan (USA)) [2017/18 h112: c22.5s c20d² c20.9s² c24.1v³ c21.4v* c24vᵖᵘ Mar 28] tall gelding: maiden hurdler: fair form over fences: won handicap at Market Rasen in March: stays 21f: acts on good to firm and heavy going: in cheekpieces last 4 starts: has worn tongue tie. *David Dennis* — **c109 h–**

SHA

SHAPIRO 5 b.m. Schiaparelli (GER) – Lady Turk (FR) (Baby Turk) [2017/18 b15.8v⁶ b15.8v² b17.7d³ b16s⁵ Mar 22] seventh foal: half-sister to 3 winners, including bumper winner/fairly useful hurdler Alphabetical Order (2m-21f winner, by Alflora) and bumper winner/fair hurdler Act Now (25f winner, by Act One): dam (c93/h108) 17f-2¾m hurdle/chase winner (stayed 25f): modest form in bumpers. *Anthony Honeyball* — **b84**

SHARJAH (FR) 5 b.g. Doctor Dino (FR) – Saaryeh (Royal Academy (USA)) [2017/18 h16v* h16v* h16s^F h16s h16.4s h16v⁴ h16.5d⁶ Apr 24] well-made gelding: useful on Flat (stays 12.5f) for H-F. Devin: useful novice hurdler: won at Gowran in September (maiden) and November: upsides and going best when falling last in Future Champions Novices' Hurdle won by Whiskey Sour at Leopardstown next time: raced only at 2m: acts on heavy going: tried in tongue tie. *W. P. Mullins, Ireland* — **h137**

SHARNEY SIKE 12 ch.g. And Beyond (IRE) – Squeeze Box (IRE) (Accordion) [2017/18 c109, h–: c20v⁴ c24.2d⁵ c22.9v^pu c16.3v³ c24.1v^pu c20.1v³ Apr 15] tall, lengthy, angular gelding: maiden handicap chaser nowadays: stays 3m: acts on heavy going: in headgear last 3 starts: front runner/races prominently: often let down by jumping. *Stuart Coltherd* — **c102 x h–**

SHARP GETAWAY (IRE) 6 b.g. Getaway (GER) – Thanks Noel (IRE) (Tel Quel (FR)) [2017/18 b16.6s⁶ b15.8d h21d Apr 26] tall gelding: poor form in bumpers: 100/1, well held in maiden on hurdling debut. *Ben Case* — **h– b71**

SHARP RESPONSE (IRE) 7 b.g. Oscar (IRE) – Lambourne Lace (IRE) (Un Desperado (FR)) [2017/18 h116, b81: c22.5s c20d³ c24.2s² c25.2s* Feb 12] fairly useful hurdler: similar form over fences: improved again when winning novice handicap at Catterick in February: stays 25f: acts on heavy going: usually races close up. *Sue Smith* — **c120 h–**

SHATTERED LOVE (IRE) 7 b.m. Yeats (IRE) – Tracker (Bustino) [2017/18 h131: c21d* c18s* c22.6s² c16.7v² c24s* c20v² c24.5s⁵ Apr 24] — **c154 h–**

Championing the cause of jump-bred fillies and mares has seemed a more worthwhile task in recent times, with steady progress being made in providing greater opportunities for jumping mares to race against their own sex. However, there is still a very long way to go to get anywhere near the expansive programme of pattern races that exists for fillies on the Flat. The first two Grade 1 hurdles in the British Isles restricted to mares were introduced in Ireland in the 2012/13 season and, in Britain, the David Nicholson Mares' Hurdle at the Cheltenham Festival became a Grade 1 in 2014/15. The Mares' Hurdle had been won six times by a genuine Grade 1 performer in Quevega, though she rarely had to run within a stone of her best to win it, with the race distinctly short of strength in depth. The upgrading of the programme of mares races, not really justified by the usual standards set for such upgrading, has to be seen in the wider context of encouraging owners and trainers to buy and race more jump-bred fillies. At a time when jumping is looking for more runners to make its programmes competitive, it seems folly that half the potential jumping population should be virtually ignored (some National Hunt breeders don't even bother offering fillies for sale because of the low returns). The Cheltenham Festival now has a second race restricted to fillies and mares, the Dawn Run Novices' Hurdle which has Grade 2 status. There are also plans for a mares chase to be introduced at the Festival in the next few years, probably at the expense of one of the existing races, as the Festival already comprises four seven-race cards and it is unlikely Cheltenham will want to create an eight-race programme on one of the days (a mares chase would be definite if Cheltenham were to add a fifth day, as has been mooted).

How competitive a new mares chase at the Cheltenham Festival would prove to be is a matter for conjecture. At present, there is no Grade 1 chase in Britain and Ireland restricted to mares, which suggests the demand is not there (though two-thirds of owners and trainers with mares who ran in 'black-type' races over hurdles indicated in a fairly recent BHA questionnaire that they would send their mares chasing if there was a more lucrative programme over fences). With Cheltenham's two existing mares races often under fire because of the relatively low standard of many of the runners, it hardly seems the time to introduce a third one, even though promoting prestigious contests for fillies and mares on jumping's biggest stage is undoubtedly one of the best ways to fuel demand for them at the sales. Benie des

SHA

Dieux, who reverted to hurdling to run in the David Nicholson Mares' Hurdle, would almost certainly have contested a mares chase had there been one, as would the novice Shattered Love who took on male counterparts in the Grade 1 Golden Miller Novices' Chase (branded as the JLT). Shattered Love's owners Gigginstown House Stud stick to a policy of running their horses in the races they are most likely to win, as they did with another of their mares, Apple's Jade, who was always bound for the Mares' Hurdle, which she had won the previous year, even though she could have been a leading contender for the Stayers' Hurdle. Benie des Dieux was also given a Cheltenham Festival entry in the Ryanair Chase before it was finally decided to run her in the Mares' Hurdle (which she won, with odds-on Apple's Jade only third). The well-bred Shattered Love, a mare with plenty of scope, was always going to make a chaser and, after a very promising start in points and then bumpers (finishing third in the Grade 2 Nickel Coin at Aintree's Grand National meeting), she progressed into a useful performer in her only season over hurdles, though running below form in Grade 1 novice company at Cheltenham and Fairyhouse (she was pitched into the Baring Bingham at the Festival, with her connections having Barra that year for the Dawn Run Mares' Novices' Hurdle).

Sent over fences in the latest season, Shattered Love was in her element and won four of her five races before the Cheltenham Festival, easily winning a mares maiden chase at Fairyhouse in October and following up in a mares chase at Clonmel in November (long odds-on both times). She improved further, stepped up to two and three quarter miles in the Grade 2 Florida Pearl Novices' Chase at Punchestown, where she went down narrowly to her stablemate Jury Duty (Presenting Percy, who made a mistake at a crucial time, was a dozen lengths behind in third). After trotting up in a Grade 3 mares novice at Cork in December, Shattered Love turned the tables on Jury Duty over three miles in the Fort Leney Novices' Chase (branded as the Neville Hotels) at Leopardstown's Christmas meeting, gaining the biggest victory of her career up to that point, owing her success to a good round of jumping and a willingness to battle when tackled by Jury Duty, after she had been sent on some way from home after the fall of the favourite Monalee, who brought down another of the leading fancies Rathvinden. Shattered Love wasn't seen out between the Fort Leney and the Golden Miller at Cheltenham where Dounikos represented connections in the 'novices' Gold Cup', the RSA Insurance Chase, which had looked an appealing target for Shattered Love. The RSA is a stiff test of stamina and jumping prowess, and it has been won only twice by a mare since it was inaugurated in 1964 as the Totalisator Champion Chase. Lesley Ann won in 1981 and Brief Gale was successful in 1995, both in the days of the three-day Festival and Lesley Ann in the days when there was no weight-for-sex allowance (mares received 5 lb when Brief Gale won).

Neville Hotels Novices' Chase (Fort Leney), Leopardstown—
the last fence has to be bypassed as the mare Shattered Love reverses form with stable-companion
Jury Duty from earlier in the campaign

JLT Novices' Chase (Golden Miller), Cheltenham—Shattered Love survives a mistake at the last to become the first mare to win a Festival novice chase in 23 years; the grey Terrefort takes second

The choice of the Golden Miller Chase as the Cheltenham Festival target for Shattered Love proved the right one in hindsight. Even with the 7-lb mares allowance, she wouldn't have beaten the very impressive Presenting Percy in the RSA Chase. Shattered Love was nevertheless one of the best winners of the Golden Miller in its short history (the race was inaugurated in 2011 and fast-tracked to Grade 1 status after just three editions). Irish-trained horses have won all bar one of the runnings of the Golden Miller, though it was the Nicky Henderson-trained, ex-French Terrefort, the only other runner who had already won a Grade 1, who started favourite for the latest edition. He had won the Scilly Isles Novices' at Sandown from Cyrname who had gone on to win his second Grade 2 novice chase, the Pendil Novices' at Kempton, on his next start. Second and third favourites were Shattered Love and Invitation Only, the close third in the Flogas Novices' at Leopardstown's two-day Dublin Racing Festival. Among the others to attract support were Invitation Only's stablemate Kemboy and Finian's Oscar, a big money purchase from Irish points who had done very well as a novice hurdler but wasn't making the smoothest of transitions to chasing. The only unbeaten runner over fences was 10/1-shot Benatar who had won three out of three, including the Noel Novices' Chase at Ascot where he had beaten Finian's Oscar by a short head, receiving 5 lb. The unusually testing conditions at the latest Festival suited Shattered Love (the going had been good when she disappointed in the Baring Bingham the previous year). She jumped soundly as usual and travelled well before taking over in front soon after the second last. Despite jinking on the run-in, Shattered Love kept on well to win by seven lengths and five lengths from Terrefort and Benatar, with Kemboy and Finian's Oscar the only others in the field of nine to finish within twenty lengths of the winner (Invitation Only was pulled up after all but coming down at the fourth last at the top of the hill when still going well).

Shattered Love was one of only two mares to contest any of the five races for novice chasers at the Festival. Ms Parfois had gone close to winning the National Hunt Chase on the opening day and Shattered Love became the first of her sex to win a novice chase at Britain's most prestigious jumps meeting since Brief Gale twenty-three years earlier. Shattered Love shaped as if she would benefit from a return to three miles but she was kept at two and a half for the Ryanair Gold Cup Novices' Chase at Fairyhouse on her next start. She looked likely to follow up for most of that race, jumping well and travelling best until losing momentum when steadied into the last. Al Boum Photo, who would have finished third in the RSA Chase had he not fallen late on, got up on the run-in to beat Shattered Love by a length, with Invitation Only seven lengths further back in third. That trio met again in the Growise Champion Novices' Chase over three miles at the Punchestown Festival where a rather one-paced Shattered Love managed only fifth in a bizarre running in which the leader Al Boum Photo took the wrong course at the last, carrying out the challenging Finian's Oscar in the process. Shattered Love was among a number of runners from her stable who didn't show their form at the Punchestown Festival and she should be forgiven her rare below-par effort there. Her Golden Miller form was franked on a number of occasions by the performances of some of those she beat.

Shattered Love (IRE) (b.m. 2011)	Yeats (IRE) (b 2001)	Sadler's Wells (b 1981)	Northern Dancer / Fairy Bridge
		Lyndonville (b 1988)	Top Ville / Diamond Land
	Tracker (b 1995)	Bustino (b 1971)	Busted / Ship Yard
		Make A Signal (ch 1973)	Royal Gunner / Look Out

The tall Shattered Love made €50,000 at the Derby Sale as an unbroken three-year-old by virtue of her physique and her pedigree. Her sire Yeats, winner of the Gold Cup at Royal Ascot on four occasions, has since made a good start to his career as a sire of jumpers. Shattered Love is from his first crop which also includes another Grade 1-winning mare in Augusta Kate, while his second crop includes the smart staying hurdler Thomas Campbell, among others. The family of Shattered Love on the distaff side is no stranger to Cheltenham Festival success, her half-brother Irish Cavalier (by Aussie Rules), who had to be put down in December after suffering complications from a leg injury, having won the novices' handicap chase

Gigginstown House Stud's "Shattered Love"

SHE

at the 2015 Festival (he went on to win the Charlie Hall Chase at Wetherby and was also fifth in Don Cossack's Gold Cup). Another half-brother, the ill-fated Make A Track (by Hernando), was also a smart chaser. Their dam, the Bustino mare Tracker, didn't race but is a half-sister to the 1997 Champion Hurdle winner Make A Stand. Shattered Love's grandam Make A Signal was a fair handicapper on the Flat who won seven times from eleven furlongs to two miles. Shattered Love's great grandam Look Out also has a connection with the Cheltenham Festival in that she was a half-sister to the Goodwood and Doncaster Cup winner Raise You Ten who sired the 1975 Cheltenham Gold Cup winner Ten Up. With so much stamina in her pedigree, it is little wonder that the strong-travelling Shattered Love stays so well, though she is also effective at around two and a half miles. She acts on heavy going and probably needs some give in the ground to be seen at her best. She wears a tongue tie. *Gordon Elliott, Ireland*

SHAUGHNESSY 5 b.g. Shantou (USA) – Sudden Beat (Beat All (USA)) [2017/18 b15.8s² b17.7d² Feb 25] €105,000 3-y-o: second foal: dam (b94), placed in bumpers, sister to fair hurdler/useful chaser (2m-27f winner) Gentleman Jon: fairly useful form in bumpers, runner-up both outings: will prove suited by 2½m+. *Oliver Sherwood*   **b102**

SHAZZAMATAZ (IRE) 6 br.m. Presenting – Dame O'Neill (IRE) (Dr Massini (IRE)) [2017/18 b18g h20.7d⁴ h20.7g⁴ Apr 24] smallish mare: fifth foal: sister to bumper winner/ fairly useful hurdler Templeross (21f-3m winner) and half-sister to fair hurdler/fairly useful hurdler Wolf Sword (19f-3m winner, by Flemensfirth): dam unraced sister to smart hurdler/useful chaser around 2m Clopf: placed in points: always behind in mares maiden bumper (for James G. Sheehan): fair form on first of 2 starts in mares novice hurdles: remains with potential. *Alex Hales*   **h104 p**
b–

SHEAR ROCK (IRE) 8 b.g. Spadoun (FR) – Sleeping Diva (FR) (Sleeping Car (FR)) [2017/18 c123, h–: c16s² Jan 29] useful-looking gelding: fairly useful hurdler: similar form when second both starts over fences: stays 21f: has form on heavy ground, all wins on good or firmer: hooded prior to sole start in 2017/18. *Kerry Lee*   **c121**
h–

SHEELBEWHATSHEELBE (IRE) 8 b.m. Oscar (IRE) – Cheerymount (IRE) (Oscar Schindler (IRE)) [2017/18 h83, b67: h19d⁴ h19.9d² h23.9s⁶ h19.2v* h20.5d⁴ h19.2v⁵ h21s⁶ Apr 9] modest handicap hurdler: won at Towcester in February: should stay further than 2½m: acts on heavy going. *Richard Phillips*   **h87**

SHEER POETRY (IRE) 7 b.m. Yeats (IRE) – Sassari (IRE) (Darshaan) [2017/18 h103: h16.8g h23m² h23g c21m³ c20g* h21.1s³ c20.8sᵖᵘ Apr 19] sturdy mare: fair handicap hurdler: fair form over fences: won mares handicap at Worcester in October: trained until final outing by Richard Woollacott: stays 23f: acts on soft and good to firm going: wears tongue tie: often races towards rear. *Nigel Hawke*   **c114**
h106

SHEE'S LUCKY 4 b.f. Yorgunnabelucky (USA) – She's The Lady (Unfuwain (USA)) [2017/18 h15.5d² h15.8s² h15.3v⁵ Mar 28] half-sister to useful hurdler Twobeelucky (2m/17f winner, by Tobougg): dam, bumper winner, half-sister to useful hurdler/smart chaser (stayed 21f) I'm So Lucky: modest maiden on Flat, stays 8.5f: fair form over hurdles: best effort when second in fillies juvenile at Ludlow. *Neil Mulholland*   **h103**

SHELFORD (IRE) 9 b.g. Galileo (IRE) – Lyrical (Shirley Heights) [2017/18 c127, h145: c25.5d² c26.1m² c21.4g³ c27.7d⁵ h22.8v³ h24.7s⁶ Apr 14] compact gelding: useful hurdler: not quite so good over fences, though placed in competitive handicaps at Uttoxeter (Summer Cup) and Market Rasen (Summer Plate) in July: stays 3¼m: acts on good to firm and heavy going: often in headgear. *Dan Skelton*   **c129**
h130

SHELL CRYSTAL 4 b.f. Schiaparelli (GER) – Solent Crystal (Generous (IRE)) [2017/18 b13.2s Oct 24] first foal: dam, unraced, out of fairly useful hurdler/chaser (2m/17f winner) Laser Crystal: tongue tied, well held in junior bumper. *David Pipe*   **b–**

SHENEEDEDTHERUN (IRE) 8 b.m. Kayf Tara – Lady Moon (FR) (Monsun (GER)) [2017/18 h104: h23.3d h23gᵖᵘ c21.6g⁵ c20sᵖᵘ c24.2s* c25.2d² c24s* c22.2v³ Mar 31] lightly-raced winning hurdler: fair form over fences: won mares handicaps at Wetherby in December and Warwick in February: stays 25f: acts on heavy going: in tongue tie last 4 starts. *Michael Scudamore*   **c107**
h–

SHEPHERD'S BIGHT (IRE) 6 b.g. Court Cave (IRE) – Orador Sur Glane (IRE) (Shernazar) [2017/18 h89, b–: h16.2g⁶ h20.5vᵖᵘ h22.7s⁵ Jan 14] modest form over hurdles: left George Charlton after first start. *Malcolm Jefferson*   **h90**

SHE

SHES A GANGSTER (IRE) 9 ch.m. Flemensfirth (USA) – Pataya (IRE) (Bravefoot) [2017/18 c21.1s⁴ c21g⁶ h21.6g Sep 2] point winner: poor maiden hurdler/chaser: trained on reappearance only by D. C. Gibbs: stays 2¾m: acts on soft going: usually in headgear: has worn tongue tie: temperamental. *Tim Vaughan* — **c74 § h–**

SHE'S GINA (GER) 5 b.m. It's Gino (GER) – Song of Night (GER) (Tiger Hill (IRE)) [2017/18 h17.9s h16.5s⁵ h20.7s h16v* h17.7v^F h15.3v² h16.2v Apr 10] half-sister to French 15f hurdle winner Songaron (by Nicaron): useful on Flat (stays 11f) for Markus Klug: fair hurdler: won mares novice at Lingfield in January: left C. von der Recke after first start: unproven beyond 2m: acts on heavy going. *Seamus Mullins* — **h105**

SHESTHEBUSINESS 7 b.m. Midnight Legend – Sabreflight (Sabrehill (USA)) [2017/18 b16.2g⁶ b16.2g⁶ b16.2d³ b16.2s h20.9g^ur h16.2g h16.4v h19.7d⁵ Mar 29] smallish, lengthy mare: first foal: dam (c89/h103) 2m-3¼m hurdle/chase winner: placed once in bumpers: little form over hurdles: hooded second to eighth starts: wears tongue tie. *Susan Corbett* — **h– b72**

SHILLELAGH TIARA (IRE) 7 b.m. Kayf Tara – Deploy Or Die (IRE) (Deploy) [2017/18 b16d b16.2s⁶ Aug 19] first foal: dam unraced sister to smart hurdler (stayed 3m) Shinrock Paddy: shaped like a stayer in bumpers at Warwick and Perth. *Gordon Elliott, Ireland* — **b78**

SHILLINGSWORTH (IRE) 5 b.g. Presenting – Miss Bobs Worth (IRE) (Bob Back (USA)) [2017/18 b–: b16d⁵ h16s h16.5g⁵ h16.3s Dec 20] well-made gelding: well held in bumpers: fair form over hurdles: will stay 2¼m+. *Colin Tizzard* — **h104 b71**

SHIMBA HILLS 7 b.g. Sixties Icon – Search Party (Rainbow Quest (USA)) [2017/18 h103: h17.7g Apr 20] fair hurdler: possibly needed race only outing in 2017/18: best around 2m: acts on good to firm and heavy going: wears cheekpieces/tongue tie. *Lawney Hill* — **h–**

SHIMLA DAWN (IRE) 10 b.g. Indian Danehill (IRE) – Tina Thyne (IRE) (Good Thyne (USA)) [2017/18 c128, h–: h20.6g⁶ c20.3g⁵ Apr 20] rather leggy, lengthy gelding: point winner: useful handicap hurdler/chaser at best: just fair form both starts in 2017/18 (left Mark Walford in between): stays 2¾m: acts on heavy going: tried in hood. *Mrs C. Drury* — **c109 h106**

SHINE A DIAMOND (IRE) 10 gr.g. St Jovite (USA) – Mossy Grey (USA) (Step Together (USA)) [2017/18 c79, h68: c23.8g⁴ May 18] maiden hurdler: poor handicap chaser: stays 3m: acts on soft and good to firm going: wears headgear/tongue tie: held up: hard to win with. *Lucinda Russell* — **c71 § h–**

SHINE AWAY (IRE) 8 b.m. Robin des Pres (FR) – Bramble Bree (IRE) (Rashar (USA)) [2017/18 c–, h–: h20.3g⁴ c15.6g c21.2d* c20.1s² c22.5d^pu Nov 3] placed in Irish points: fair maiden hurdler: similar form over fences: won handicap at Cartmel in August: may prove best at shorter than 2¾m: acts on soft going. *Sue Smith* — **c100 h70**

SHINE BABY SHINE 4 b.f. Aqlaam – Rosewood Belle (USA) (Woodman (USA)) [2017/18 h16.4v⁵ h15.7s³ ab16g² h15.7s* h15.7s h16.8g⁴ Apr 19] leggy filly: fair on Flat (stays 16.5f) similar form over hurdles: won mares novice at Catterick in March: likely to stay beyond 17f: acts on soft going. *Philip Kirby* — **h108**

SHINE'S BAR (IRE) 5 b.g. Darsi (FR) – Ninty Annie (Winged Love (IRE)) [2017/18 b16.3d³ b17.7g h16g⁵ h16.3g⁶ h19.7g h19v^pu Dec 31] first foal: dam unraced: well held in bumpers: poor form over hurdles: tried in blinkers. *Fergal O'Brien* — **h84 b57**

SHINGHARI (IRE) 6 b.g. Cape Cross (IRE) – Sindiyma (IRE) (Kalanisi (IRE)) [2017/18 h16.7s³ h16g⁴ h16.7g⁵ h15.8g Oct 26] fairly useful on Flat, stays 17f: fair form over hurdles: left Denis Hogan after third start: in cheekpieces first 3 outings. *Alexandra Dunn* — **h101**

SHINING ROMEO 6 b.g. Royal Applause – Silver Pivotal (IRE) (Pivotal) [2017/18 h112p: h16g² h16.3g³ h19.9g⁴ h19.9d h19s³ h18.6s⁵ h19.6s⁵ h16s h15.5s* h16s⁶ h16m² Apr 26] fairly useful handicap hurdler: won at Huntingdon in February: stays 2½m: acts on soft and good to firm going: patiently ridden. *Denis Quinn* — **h120**

SHININSTAR (IRE) 9 b.g. Westerner – Shiny Button (Bob's Return (IRE)) [2017/18 h–: h16.7g h16.7v c16d c16.5d³ c16.5g⁵ Apr 24] poor maiden hurdler: similar form over fences: likely to stay beyond 2m: acts on good to soft going: has worn hood, including last 2 starts. *John Groucott* — **c80 h–**

SHINOOKI (IRE) 11 br.g. Blueprint (IRE) – Rapid Response (IRE) (Be My Native (USA)) [2017/18 c–, h108: h23.5s⁵ h23.4g³ c25.2g² h23.4s⁶ c22.7s⁵ c24g^pu Apr 20] fair handicap hurdler/chaser: will stay long distances: acts on heavy going: has worn headgear: front runner/races prominently. *Alex Hales* — **c109 h105**

SHINTORI (FR) 6 b.g. Enrique – La Masai (FR) (Bernebeau (FR)) [2017/18 c94, h62: c16.5mpu h18.5m⁴ h20gpu h16.8dpu Sep 11] lengthy, workmanlike gelding: maiden hurdler, fair at best (in France): modest maiden chaser: stays 2¼m: acts on soft and good to firm going: has worn headgear/tongue tie. *Richard Woollacott*   c– h83

SHIROCCAN ROLL 4 b.g. Shirocco (GER) – Folie Dancer (Exit To Nowhere (USA)) [2017/18 b13d⁵ Dec 2] 9/2, fifth in junior bumper at Doncaster (5 lengths behind Ettila de Sivola, shaping as if needing run). *Emma Lavelle*   b77

SHIROCCODEE 5 b.m. Shirocco (GER) – La Marianne (Supreme Leader) [2017/18 b–: b16s b16m h19.4d⁶ h20.3spu h15.8s h20.3g Apr 20] no form in bumpers: little show over hurdles: left Brian Barr after second start: races freely. *Alex Hales*   h– b–

SHIVERMETIMBERS (IRE) 6 br.g. Black Sam Bellamy (IRE) – Kimouna (FR) (Round Sovereign (FR)) [2017/18 b96: h15.7vur h16.8v h15.8s² h16vpu Apr 14] bumper winner: fair form over hurdles: easily best effort when second in maiden at Ludlow in January: 11/10-on, downed tools final start: will stay further than 2m: usually races close up: one to be wary of. *Venetia Williams*   h111 §

SHOAL BAY (IRE) 5 b.g. Gold Well – Ring Hill (Bering) [2017/18 b16f* h19g* h16.8s⁴ h16g⁶ h16.4spu h15.3d² Apr 22] €58,000 3-y-o: well-made gelding: will make a chaser: fourth foal: dam (1m, 2m hurdle winner, also 9f-1½m winner on Flat: won at Worcester (by 2½ lengths from The Go Tou Man) only start in bumpers: fairly useful form over hurdles: won maiden at Taunton in November: best effort when second in novice at Wincanton final outing: stays 19f: acts on soft going: in tongue tie last 3 starts: usually races prominently. *Colin Tizzard*   h118 b90

SHOCKINGTIMES (IRE) 11 b.g. Wareed (IRE) – Jolly Lady (IRE) (Jolly Jake (NZ)) [2017/18 c26gF c25.1vR c22.7s² c22.6vur c22.9s* c23.9v² Apr 11] strong gelding: maiden hurdler: fairly useful handicap chaser: won veterans event at Haydock in March: stays 25f: acts on heavy going: usually wears headgear: tongue tied: often races towards rear/travels strongly: often let down by jumping. *Jamie Snowden*   c118 x h–

SHOOFLY MILLY (IRE) 9 b.m. Milan – Jacksister (IRE) (Flemensfirth (USA)) [2017/18 h107: h23.1spu h23.1spu h21.7v⁶ h21.2s h25v⁵ h25.8v³ h23.1v* Apr 8] fair handicap hurdler: won at Exeter in April: stays 25f: acts on heavy going: wears headgear/tongue tie: front runner/races prominently: quirky sort. *Jeremy Scott*   h100

SHORELINE (FR) 5 b.m. Coastal Path – Bahamas (FR) (Pistolet Bleu (IRE)) [2017/18 b15.7d h20.7g Apr 24] £4,000 3-y-o: close-coupled mare: sixth foal: half-sister to 2 winners, including bumper winner/fair hurdler Fort Montagu (2m winner, by Fuisse): dam, French 1m/9f winner, half-sister to dam of Champion Hurdle winner Binocular: last of 4 finishers in point: hinted at ability in mares bumper at Southwell (raced too keenly): also showed up long way in mares novice on hurdling debut: wears hood: should improve. *Jack R. Barber*   h– p b72

SHORT FLIGHT (IRE) 6 b.g. Trans Island – Surricate (FR) (True Brave (USA)) [2017/18 h70: h20.3g⁴ h16.4s⁶ h19.9s Jan 12] third in Irish maiden point on debut: poor maiden hurdler: stays 2½m: acts on heavy going. *Julia Brooke*   h59

SHOTAVODKA (IRE) 12 ch.g. Alderbrook – Another Vodka (IRE) (Moscow Society (USA)) [2017/18 c120, h121: c20.9s* c22.2v² c26.3v c20.3g² Apr 20] stocky gelding: winning hurdler: fairly useful chaser nowadays: won hunter at Hereford in January: stays 3¼m: acts on heavy going: used to wear headgear: tried in tongue tie: races towards rear. *Miss H. Brookshaw*   c129 h–

SHOTGUN PADDY (IRE) 11 b.g. Brian Boru – Awesome Miracle (IRE) (Supreme Leader) [2017/18 c136x, h–: c27.3s⁵ c23.6v⁵ c26vpu c28.5v⁶ c30.7s² c27.9v³ Apr 1] well-made gelding: winning hurdler: formerly smart handicap chaser: just fairly useful form in 2017/18, though placed last 2 outings: stays 31f: acts on heavy going: has worn headgear: prone to mistakes over fences: not one to trust (often races lazily). *Emma Lavelle*   c128 § h–

SHOTOFWINE 9 b.g. Grape Tree Road – Icy Gunner (Gunner B) [2017/18 h91: h25g* May 29] modest handicap hurdler: won at Huntingdon (conditional) only outing in 2017/18: stays 25f: acts on soft going: in tongue tie last 4 starts: front runner/races prominently. *Nicky Richards*   h98

SHOULDAGONETOVEGAS (IRE) 6 b.g. Whitmore's Conn (USA) – Jennifers Guest (IRE) (Be My Guest (USA)) [2017/18 b15.8s b16s h16s⁶ Mar 16] well held in bumpers/conditionals maiden hurdle. *Neil King*   h– b–

SHO

SHOUTING HILL (IRE) 8 br.g. Golan (IRE) – Brook Queen (IRE) (Lafontaine (USA)) [2017/18 c62§, h74: h24g* May 16] winning Irish pointer: poor handicap hurdler: won novice event at Southwell only start in 2017/18: little enthusiasm for chasing: stayed 3m: best efforts on good going: often wore headgear: tried in tongue tie: dead. *Johnny Farrelly*   c– § h77

SHOW ON THE ROAD 7 b.g. Flemensfirth (USA) – Roses of Picardy (IRE) (Roselier (FR)) [2017/18 h15.3s[6] h16.5g[2] h16.5s[2] h16.8v* h15.3v[3] h15.3v[3] h16.8v* h16s Apr 28] lengthy, useful-looking gelding: fairly useful hurdler: won novice in January and handicap in April, both at Exeter: will stay 2½m: acts on heavy going: wears hood: often travels strongly. *Philip Hobbs*   h128

SHOW'S OVER (IRE) 7 b.g. Curtain Time (IRE) – Sailors Run (IRE) (Roselier (FR)) [2017/18 c88, h–: c20.9d[3] c16.3m c20g[3] c16v[pu] h23.8s[pu] c16.1v[2] c17s[5] Apr 15] poor maiden hurdler/handicap chaser: stays 23f: acts on heavy going: wears headgear/tongue tie. *Tim Vaughan*   c78 h–

SHREWD 8 b.g. Street Sense (USA) – Cala (FR) (Desert Prince (IRE)) [2017/18 h16d Aug 3] useful stayer on Flat: similar form over hurdles: mid-field in Galway Hurdle, only outing in 2017/18: should stay beyond 17f: acts on soft and good to firm going. *Iain Jardine*   h108

SHROUGHMORE LASS (IRE) 7 b.m. Flemensfirth (IRE) – Smokey Bandit (IRE) (Oscar (IRE)) [2017/18 h16d h15.8s[6] h16g h16v* h16s[3] h20.5v[4] h20.5d[2] h16.2v[2] Apr 10] €3,500 4-y-o: sturdy mare: third foal: dam (b82), lightly raced in bumpers/over hurdles, half-sister to useful hurdler/chaser (2m winner) in Irish mares maiden points: Dylan Ross: runner-up all 3 starts in Irish mares maiden points: fair handicap hurdler: won mares event at Chepstow in November: should stay beyond 2m: acts on heavy going: usually races prominently. *Henry Oliver*   h100

SHRUBLAND 5 b.g. High Chaparral (IRE) – Ratukidul (FR) (Danehill (USA)) [2017/18 h96: h15.7m h16d h20d[pu] h15.8d* h16.8g* h19.6g[2] h20.6g* h18.6g[3] Nov 9] sturdy gelding: fair handicap hurdler: won at Uttoxeter in July, Sedgefield in August and Market Rasen in October: left Alexandra Dunn after third start: stays 21f: acts on good to soft going: wears headgear: often races towards rear. *Dan Skelton*   h106

SHTAN ON (IRE) 7 b.g. Generous (IRE) – Lady Oakwell (IRE) (King's Ride) [2017/18 h20.5v[4] h20s h20.5v[3] Dec 22] £9,000 4-y-o: half-brother to fair hurdler/fairly useful chaser Posh Bird (2½m-3¼m winner, by Winged Love) and bumper winner/fair hurdler Ballykelly (19f winner, by Insan): dam failed to complete both starts in points: runner-up in Irish point: fair form over hurdles: best effort when third in novice at Ayr: will stay 3m. *Alistair Whillans*   h101

SHUFOOG 5 b.m. Mawatheeq (USA) – Hamloola (Red Ransom (USA)) [2017/18 h16.3s h15.8s h16v[4] Apr 14] leggy mare: fairly useful on Flat (stays 1¼m): promise all 3 starts over hurdles: type to do better in handicaps. *Mark Usher*   h76 p

SHUIL ROYALE (IRE) 13 b.g. King's Theatre (IRE) – Shuil Na Lee (IRE) (Phardante (FR)) [2017/18 c145, h–: c24d[pu] c23.6d c25d[ur] Oct 29] tall, useful-looking gelding: winning hurdler: smart handicap chaser at best: little show in 2017/18: stays 3¼m: acts on good to firm and heavy going: wears headgear/tongue tie. *Harry Fry*   c124 h–

SHULAMMITE MAN (IRE) 5 ch.g. Arcano (IRE) – Shulammite Woman (IRE) (Desert Sun) [2017/18 h16.7g[pu] May 21] modest maiden on Flat, stays 16.5f: pulled up in novice on hurdling debut. *Sally Haynes*   h–

SHUTSCOMBE HILL 6 b.g. Arvico (FR) – Storm Kitten (IRE) (Catrail (USA)) [2017/18 b15.3d Apr 22] tailed off in bumper. *Victor Dartnall*   b–

SHUT THE BOX (IRE) 4 ch.g. Doyen (IRE) – Bond Holder (IRE) (Hawkeye (IRE)) [2017/18 b15.7g[3] Apr 20] second foal: dam unraced half-sister to fair hurdler/useful chaser (stayed 31f) Sizing Australia and useful hurdler/fairly useful chaser (stayed 3m) Frontier Dancer: 13/2, encouraging third in bumper at Fontwell (4½ lengths behind Kalinihta). *Chris Gordon*   b89

SIANNES STAR (IRE) 5 b.g. Arakan (USA) – Musical Madam (IRE) (Musical Pursuit) [2017/18 b16.7g b16.8g[4] b17d[6] ab16.3g Apr 15] modest form in bumpers. *Brian Ellison*   b79

SIDBURY FAIR 7 br.m. Fair Mix (IRE) – Manque Pas d'Air (FR) (Kadalko (FR)) [2017/18 h67: h16m h16v h21.6v[pu] Dec 21] little form in bumpers/over hurdles: tried in cheekpieces. *Victor Dartnall*   h–

SIDE OF THE ROAD (IRE) 6 b.m. Beneficial – Roses And Wine (IRE) (Roselier (FR)) [2017/18 h–, b–: h20.5v[5] h20s h20.6s[6] h19v[pu] Jan 31] modest form over hurdles: stays 21f: acts on soft going. *Donald Whillans*   h85

SIDSTEEL (IRE) 7 b.g. Craigsteel – Clare Hogan (IRE) (Moscow Society (USA)) [2017/18 h74, b–: h19.6s h23.1g² h19.7g Nov 29] poor maiden hurdler: stays 23f: best form on good going: in tongue tie last 2 starts: usually races close up. *John Groucott* **h75**

SIEMPRE AMIGOS (IRE) 5 gr.m. Fast Company (IRE) – Zamiyla (IRE) (Daylami (IRE)) [2017/18 h20s h16v h16d h20.2v⁶ h15.8v Feb 10] fair maiden on Flat (should stay beyond 1½m): modest form over hurdles: barely stays testing 2½m: acts on good to soft going. *Gavin Patrick Cromwell, Ireland* **h85**

SIENNA ROYALE (IRE) 4 b.f. Sholokhov (IRE) – Dartmeet (IRE) (Presenting) [2017/18 b16.5v h18.5d⁴ Apr 24] £10,000 3-y-o: sixth foal: half-sister to 3 winners, including fairly useful hurdler/useful chaser Pearl Royale (2½m winner, by Robin des Champs) and fair hurdler Postbridge (2m-19f winner, by Robin des Pres): dam, winning pointer, sister to smart hurdler/chaser (stayed 25f) Bear's Affair: little show in mares bumper: 50/1, showed aptitude when fourth in maiden at Exeter (27 lengths behind Whitley Neill) on hurdling debut. *Nigel Hawke* **h77 b–**

SIERRA OSCAR (IRE) 6 b.g. Robin des Champs (FR) – John's Eliza (IRE) (Dr Massini (IRE)) [2017/18 h98p, b54: h23.3d⁴ h20g² h23.9dF h16.2d⁶ h20.9g h18.1vF Apr 16] compact gelding: modest handicap hurdler: left Dan Skelton after second start: barely stays 23f: best form on good going: often races towards rear. *Jean McGregor* **h94**

SIGNED AND SEALED 5 b.g. Authorized (IRE) – Broken Peace (USA) (Devil's Bag (USA)) [2017/18 h15.7d^pu Dec 5] fair maiden on Flat, stays 1¼m: off 17 months and in cheekpieces, pulled up in maiden on hurdling debut. *Neil Mulholland* **h–**

SIGURD (GER) 6 ch.g. Sholokhov (IRE) – Sky News (GER) (Highest Honor (FR)) [2017/18 h115: h20.6g May 21] fairly useful hurdler at best: tailed off sole outing in 2017/18 (placed on Flat after): stays 21f: acts on good to firm going: tried in cheekpieces. *Jonjo O'Neill* **h–**

SIKANDAR (IRE) 6 ch.g. Medicean – Siniyya (IRE) (Grand Lodge (USA)) [2017/18 h15.7d⁵ Jun 6] close-coupled gelding: fair on Flat (stays 1½m): similar merit in juvenile hurdles: last in handicap at Southwell only outing in 2017/18: raced around 2m: acts on heavy going: has worn headgear: in tongue tie last 2 starts. *Brian Ellison* **h–**

SILENT ACCOUNT (IRE) 7 b.g. Jimble (FR) – Mary Money (Vettori (IRE)) [2017/18 h–, b–: h16g^pu h17g^pu h19.2g² h19.8g⁶ c18g⁴ c18s⁶ Nov 30] third on completed start in Irish maiden points: modest maiden hurdler: similar form on second of 2 starts in maiden chases: stays 19f: acts on soft going: tried in blinkers. *Des Donovan, Ireland* **c89 h88**

SILENT DOCTOR (IRE) 8 br.g. Dr Massini (IRE) – Wild Noble (IRE) (Aristocracy) [2017/18 h–: h20.5v h19.2v⁴ h24s^pu Apr 18] runner-up completed start in points: little form over hurdles: in cheekpieces last 2 starts: tried in tongue tie. *Alan Phillips* **h61**

SILENT ENCORE (IRE) 6 ch.g. Curtain Time (IRE) – What Can I Say (IRE) (Mister Lord (USA)) [2017/18 h104, b–: h21d³ May 16] workmanlike gelding: fair form over hurdles: likely to stay 3m: acts on good to soft going: wears tongue tie: waited with. *Ben Case* **h107**

SILENT MAN (IRE) 8 br.g. Morozov (USA) – Outdoor Heather (IRE) (Presenting) [2017/18 h72: h23.3d⁴ h23g c17.4d^pu c23.6g* c23.8d^pu c25.6s* c26v³ c23.6d⁴ Apr 24] good-topped gelding: poor handicap hurdler: won novice event at Uttoxeter in May: better form over fences: won handicaps at Huntingdon (novice) in November and Southwell in December: stays 3¼m: probably acts on heavy going: in tongue tie last 3 starts. *Tom Weston* **c97 h72**

SILENT STEPS (IRE) 7 b.m. Milan – Taking Silk (IRE) (Mister Lord (USA)) [2017/18 h105: h23.9g² c23s² c23s⁴ h24.3g Apr 20] won completed start in Irish points: fair maiden hurdler: better effort in novice handicap chases at Taunton when second to Kelvingrove: stays 3m: acts on soft and good to firm going: tried in cheekpieces: usually leads. *Paul Nicholls* **c111 h107**

SILENT WARRIOR 6 br.g. Yeats (IRE) – Zariyka (IRE) (Kalanisi (IRE)) [2017/18 h75: h20.3g⁵ Jun 15] poor maiden hurdler: stays 2½m: acts on good to soft going: tried in cheekpieces: in tongue tie last 2 starts. *Charlie Longsdon* **h68**

SILK OR SCARLET (IRE) 6 ch.g. Mahler – Spirit of Clanagh (IRE) (Zagreb (USA)) [2017/18 h82: h16.2s⁶ h15.7v⁴ h16.2s h16v⁶ h20.2s² Apr 27] compact gelding: placed in bumper for Tim Fitzgerald: fair form over hurdles: will stay further than 2½m: acts on soft going: patiently ridden. *N. W. Alexander* **h100**

SIL

SILK RUN (IRE) 5 b.m. Oscar (IRE) – Asian Alliance (IRE) (Soviet Star (USA)) [2017/18 b16.2s⁵ b16f³ h15.8g⁶ h15.5d⁶ h16.7s h15.5v⁴ Jan 23] €4,000 3-y-o: sixth foal: half-sister to fair hurdler Empty The Tank (2m winner, by Lawman) and fair chaser Asian Prince (2½m winner, by Strategic Prince): dam (h86) 2m hurdle winner (stayed 19f): modest form in bumpers/over hurdles. *Tom Lacey* — h86 b80

SILSOL (GER) 9 b.g. Soldier Hollow – Silveria (GER) (Groom Dancer (USA)) [2017/18 c–, h156: h22.8v c29.5v⁵ c28.4vᵘʳ c34v⁴ c31.8g Apr 21] sturdy gelding: very smart hurdler at best: useful handicap chaser: fifth in Welsh Grand National at Chepstow (16¾ lengths behind Raz de Maree) in January and fourth in Midlands Grand National at Uttoxeter (15 lengths behind Regal Flow) in March: stays 4¼m: acts on heavy going: wears headgear/tongue tie. *Paul Nicholls* — c138 h–

SILVA ECLIPSE 5 gr.g. Multiplex – Linen Line (Double Eclipse (IRE)) [2017/18 h16.2v* h20.6s² h19.7s² h19.3v Jan 24] dam half-sister to fairly useful hurdler/chaser (stayed 25f) Rattlin: fairly useful on Flat, stays 16.5f: fairly useful form over hurdles: won novice at Hexham in September (then left Jedd O'Keeffe). *Sue Smith* — h120

SILVA SAMOURAI 9 gr.g. Proclamation (IRE) – Ladykirk (Slip Anchor) [2017/18 h–: h19.6g³ h18.5v h19.7g Nov 29] lengthy gelding: poor maiden hurdler: has worn hood: tongue tied last 3 starts. *Graeme McPherson* — h75

SILVER BULLION 7 br.g. Three Valleys (USA) – Silver Yen (USA) (Silver Hawk (USA)) [2017/18 b92: h16.2g⁵ h16.4vᵖᵘ h15.6s h15.6s Feb 3] bumper winner: form (modest) over hurdles only when fifth in maiden at Kelso: hooded once: dead. *Pauline Robson* — h93

SILVER CONCORDE 10 b.g. Dansili – Sacred Pearl (IRE) (Daylami (IRE)) [2017/18 h16.5g⁵ h20.2g² h20s³ h19.4g* h15.6g* h15.6d² h19.4d² h20sᵖᵘ Apr 14] smallish gelding: useful hurdler: left D. K. Weld, won maiden in November and novices in December and February, all at Musselburgh: stays 2½m: acts on good to soft going: often travels strongly. *Keith Dalgleish* — h137

SILVER DRAGON 10 gr.g. Silver Patriarch (IRE) – Gotogeton (Le Moss) [2017/18 c–§, h96§: h24.1d h24.1s h25.3s⁴ h23.3vᵖᵘ h27v³ Apr 13] poor handicap hurdler: maiden chaser: stays 4m: acts on heavy going: wears headgear: tried in tongue tie: often leads: most temperamental. *Mike Sowersby* — c– § h74 §

SILVER DUKE (IRE) 7 gr.g. Papal Bull – Dumaani's Dream (USA) (Dumaani (USA)) [2017/18 h16.2dᵖᵘ h20.2s⁶ Aug 19] leggy gelding: fairly useful hurdler at best: out of sorts in 2017/18 (including on Flat): best around 2m: acts on soft going: tried in hood. *Jim Goldie* — h–

SILVER HOLLOW 6 g.g. Beat Hollow – Onemix (Fair Mix (IRE)) [2017/18 b–: h16.6sᵖᵘ Feb 21] showed little in bumper (3/1) and novice hurdle. *Ben Pauling* — h–

SILVERHOW (IRE) 7 br.g. Yeats (IRE) – Monte Solaro (IRE) (Key of Luck (USA)) [2017/18 h121, b99: c19.7sᶠ c20.2v⁴ c20.9s² c20.2s* c20v² c19.2v³ c20d* Apr 28] good-topped gelding: fairly useful hurdler: fairly useful handicap chaser: won at Wincanton in February and Sandown (novice) in April: stays 21f: acts on heavy going. *Colin Tizzard* — c129 h–

SILVER KAYF 6 gr.g. Kayf Tara – Silver Spinner (Silver Patriarch (IRE)) [2017/18 b100: h21gᶠ h21.6v⁴ h19.6d* h20.3s³ h21.2d* h20.3g Apr 18] well-made gelding: fairly useful form over hurdles: won novices at Huntingdon in November and Ludlow in March: will stay beyond 21f: acts on soft going: front runner/races prominently. *Kim Bailey* — h127

SILVER MAN 11 gr.g. Silver Patriarch (IRE) – Another Mans Cause (FR) (Highest Honor (FR)) [2017/18 c136, h115: c24d⁶ c29.4d² c26.1m Jul 2] lengthy gelding: maiden hurdler: useful handicap chaser: won veterans event at Cartmel in May: stays 29f: acts on good to firm and good to soft going: wears headgear: front runner/races prominently. *Jo Hughes* — c130 h–

SILVER QUAY (IRE) 6 gr.g. Dark Angel (IRE) – She Runs (FR) (Sheyrann) [2017/18 h21.6d² h21.6d⁴ h19.8s h16.8v⁵ Nov 26] fairly useful on Flat, stays 16.5f: modest form on hurdling debut, went wrong way after: tried in hood. *Jimmy Frost* — h91

SILVER ROQUE (FR) 12 b.g. Laveron – Bible Gun (FR) (Pistolet Bleu (IRE)) [2017/18 c–, c20.3vᵖᵘ Feb 9] good-topped gelding: maiden hurdler: smart chaser at best: failed to complete since autumn 2015: stays 21f: acts on heavy going: has worn cheekpieces/tongue tie. *Mary Vestey* — c– h–

SILVER SHUFFLE (IRE) 11 ch.g. Big Shuffle (USA) – Silvetta (Lando (GER)) [2017/18 c–§, h92§: h22.12d² h20g Jun 16] modest handicap hurdler: lightly-raced maiden chaser: stays 25f: acts on good to firm and heavy going: tried in headgear: often tongue tied: patiently ridden: temperamental. *Dianne Sayer* — c– § h90 §

SILVER STREAK (IRE) 5 gr.g. Dark Angel (IRE) – Happy Talk (IRE) (Hamas (IRE)) [2017/18 h117: h16d* h15.7d² h16.3vᵘʳ h16v⁶ Mar 10] rather leggy gelding: fairly useful handicap hurdler: impressive winner at Chepstow on return in October: further progress when second in Racing Welfare Handicap Hurdle at Ascot in December: raced around 2m: acts on good to soft going (unsuitable conditions last 2 outings): strong-travelling sort with turn of foot. *Evan Williams*   **h128**

SILVER TASSIE (IRE) 10 b.g. Shantou (USA) – Silver Castor (IRE) (Indian Ridge) [2017/18 c130, h–: c24.5s⁶ c24.3v⁵ c23.4s⁶ c23.4v² c32.6sᵖᵘ c24.2d³ c26.2v² Apr 16] winning hurdler: useful handicap chaser: stays 3¼m: acts on good to firm and heavy going: tried in hood/tongue tie: races in rear. *Micky Hammond*   **c130 h–**

SILVER TICKET (IRE) 7 gr.g. Tikkanen (USA) – Windmill View (IRE) (Glacial Storm (USA)) [2017/18 h69: h19.2v⁶ h21.7g⁶ Apr 20] sturdy gelding: poor maiden hurdler on balance: stays 19f: probably acts on heavy going: usually races close up. *Laura Mongan*   **h67**

SILVERTON 11 gr.m. Silver Patriarch (IRE) – Gretton (Terimon) [2017/18 c–, h–: c24.1v c20.1v³ c20.1v² Mar 15] maiden hurdler: poor handicap chaser nowadays: stays 23f: acts on heavy going: tried in cheekpieces. *Lucy Normile*   **c81 h–**

SILVER TRIX (IRE) 8 gr.m. Mahler – Sika Trix (IRE) (Try Prospect (USA)) [2017/18 c–, h–: c20.1gᵖᵘ May 6] little form in varied company: has worn tongue tie. *George Bewley*   **c– h–**

SIMAFAR (IRE) 4 b.g. Makfi – Simawa (IRE) (Anabaa (USA)) [2017/18 h16.7s⁶ h16s³ h16v Mar 11] dam half-sister to fairly useful 2m hurdle winner Sinntaran: fair maiden hurdler on Flat, stays 1¼m: form (modest) over hurdles only when third in juvenile at Warwick in February. *Olly Murphy*   **h97**

SIMMPLY SAM 11 b.m. Nomadic Way (USA) – Priceless Sam (Silly Prices) [2017/18 c–, h82: c19.3g⁶ Apr 23] maiden pointer: winning hurdler: well held both outings over fences: stays 21f: acts on heavy going: has worn cheekpieces. *Miss J. I. Bedi*   **c64 h–**

SIMONE (IRE) 6 b.m. Presenting – Dusty Too (Terimon) [2017/18 b16.7g* h20.2v³ h15.6g² h15.6sᵖᵘ Jan 19] €15,000 3-y-o: seventh foal: sister to bumper winner/useful chaser (2m-19f winner) Drumcliff and half-sister to 2 winners, including high-class hurdler/top-class chaser Simonsig (2m-21f winner, by Fair Mix): dam (h112) bumper/2¼m-21f hurdle winner: fair bumper performer: won maiden at Punchestown in May (then left Shane Nolan): modest form over hurdles. *Lucinda Russell*   **h97 b94**

SIMONIA (IRE) 5 gr.m. Yeats (IRE) – Dusty Too (Terimon) [2017/18 b15.8v² ab16g⁶ ab16d h15.8d³ h20.7g Apr 24] compact mare: half-sister to several winners, including high-class hurdler/top-class chaser Simonsig (2m-21f winner, by Fair Mix) and bumper winner/useful chaser Drumcliff (2m-19f winner, by Presenting): dam (h112) bumper/2¼m-21f hurdle winner: fair form on debut in bumpers: failed to progress: only modest form in mares novice hurdles: should stay 2½m. *Nicky Henderson*   **h91 b94**

SIMPLE AS THAT (IRE) 7 b.g. Stowaway – Suzy Q (IRE) (King's Ride) [2017/18 h99: h16.8g⁴ h25g⁶ h18.6gᵖᵘ Nov 9] modest maiden hurdler, lightly raced: often wore tongue tie: made running/raced prominently: dead. *Jonjo O'Neill*   **h–**

SIMPLY BLESSED (IRE) 7 ch.m. Flemensfirth (USA) – Simply Joyful (Idiot's Delight) [2017/18 h70§, b81: h23.1g h25.8mᵘʳ Aug 17] sturdy mare: poor maiden hurdler: stays 27f: acts on soft going: in headgear last 4 starts: temperamental. *Peter Bowen*   **h62 §**

SIMPLY BUSINESS (FR) 5 b.m. Maresca Sorrento (FR) – Fabulous Darling (FR) (Freedom Cry) [2017/18 h16d h15.7g⁴ h16.3g⁴ h16g h16.3gᵖᵘ h16.8v⁶ h16.8vᵖᵘ h15.7v⁴ h16.8v² c16.4vᵖᵘ Mar 23] €14,000 3-y-o: sixth foal: sister to useful French hurdler/chaser Rescato de L'Oust (2¼m-23f winner) and French chaser Darling Oust (19f winner, by Early March): dam French maiden (placed up to 1½m): poor maiden hurdler: pulled up quickly after blunder seventh in novice handicap on chasing debut: left Charlie Longsdon after fifth start: raced around 2m: acts on heavy going: has worn hood: tongue tied 3 of last 4 starts. *Sam England*   **c– h76**

SIMPLY LOVELEH 5 b.m. Beneficial – Pippedatthepost (Exit To Nowhere (USA)) [2017/18 b16.7v⁴ Jan 17] second foal: dam unraced: 16/1, fourth in listed mares bumper at Market Rasen (11½ lengths behind Dissavril). *Robert Stephens*   **b89**

SIMPLY MANI 6 ch.g. Sulamani (IRE) – Simply Mystic (Simply Great (FR)) [2017/18 b15.7d³ ab16.3g h16.7g Apr 22] poor form in bumpers: 50/1, last in maiden at Market Rasen on hurdling debut. *Peter Niven*   **h– b72**

Paddy's Rewards Club Chase, Leopardstown—fourth time lucky in this race for Simply Ned who is led by Min over the last; the win comes via the stewards' room after Min causes interference on the run-in (Simply Ned was the only British-trained winner of a Grade 1 in Ireland)

SIMPLY NED (IRE) 11 ch.g. Fruits of Love (USA) – Bishops Lass (IRE) (Marju (IRE)) [2017/18 c154, h–: c17.1d² c15.9s⁴ c17d* c17s² Feb 3] tall, rather sparely-made gelding: winning hurdler: very smart chaser: awarded Paddy's Rewards Club Chase at Leopardstown in December having been beaten ½ length by Min but badly hampered run-in: respectable 12 lengths second of 7 to same rival in Dublin Chase there after: unproven beyond 17f: acts on good to firm and heavy going. *Nicky Richards* **c157 h–**

SIMPLY THE BETTS (IRE) 5 b.g. Arcadio (GER) – Crimson Flower (IRE) (Soviet Lad (USA)) [2017/18 b16.7g* h16.3d³ h16d⁴ h15.6s² h16.4s Mar 13] €18,000 3-y-o: sturdy gelding: fifth foal: brother to useful hurdler/winning pointer Crimson Ark (19f-21f winner): dam (c96/h115), 2m-2¼m hurdle winner, also 1¾m-2m winner on Flat: won at Market Rasen (by 1¾ lengths from Theclockisticking) on sole outing in bumpers: fairly useful form over hurdles: best effort when second in novice at Musselburgh in February: stiff task next time. *Harry Whittington* **h129 b98**

SIMPLY THE WEST (IRE) 9 b.g. Westerner – Back To Stay (IRE) (Supreme Leader) [2017/18 c24d^pu h24s^pu h20.7s^pu Jan 26] sturdy gelding: winning Irish pointer: fairly useful hurdler/maiden chaser at best: pulled up all 3 outings in 2017/18: in cheekpieces last 2 starts: normally tongue tied: none too resolute. *Charlie Longsdon* **c– h–**

SINDARBAN (IRE) 7 ch.g. Teofilo (IRE) – Sinndiya (IRE) (Pharly (FR)) [2017/18 h16.7g⁶ h15.6m Nov 8] fair handicap hurdler: raced around 2m: acts on good to firm going: tongue tied prior to 2017/18: often makes mistakes/finishes weakly. *Keith Dalgleish* **h91 x**

SINGLEFARMPAYMENT 8 b.g. Milan – Crevamoy (IRE) (Shardari) [2017/18 c149, h–: c25g² c26g^F c23.8d⁵ c25.3v^pu c25s⁵ c26g² Apr 18] good-topped gelding: winning hurdler: smart handicap chaser: second at Cheltenham in October and April (short head behind Another Hero): stays 3¼m: acts on heavy going: wears hood: travels well held up. *Tom George* **c147 h–**

SINOUR (IRE) 8 b.g. Observatory (USA) – Siniyya (IRE) (Grand Lodge (USA)) [2017/18 h79: c19.2g⁵ c20.1g h22.1g³ Jul 2] poor maiden hurdler: modest form on first of 2 starts in chases: off mark in points soon after end of season: stays 19f: acts on good to soft going: normally hooded/tongue tied. *Aaron Stronge, Ireland* **c94 h64**

SIN SIN (IRE) 4 b.f. Intense Focus (USA) – Saor Sinn (IRE) (Galileo (IRE)) [2017/18 h16.5s⁴ h15.8s³ h15.7d⁵ Feb 2] sister to Italian hurdler/chaser Solar Focus (2m-19f winner): fairly useful maiden on Flat, stays 1½m: some promise over hurdles. *Nigel Hawke* **h83**

SIR

SIOUX CHIEFTAIN (IRE) 8 b.g. Mount Nelson – Lady Gin (USA) (Saint Ballado (CAN)) [2017/18 h–: h15.8g³ h15.8g⁶ h15.8m Oct 11] fair hurdler: raced only at 2m: acts on soft going: in tongue tie last 2 starts. *Dr Richard Newland*   **h102**

SIR ANTONY BROWNE 6 ch.g. Black Sam Bellamy (IRE) – Shayaza (Generous (IRE)) [2017/18 h134: h20.5v^pu Dec 30] good-topped gelding: bumper winner: useful novice hurdler in 2016/17: pulled up in handicap at Newbury only outing since: stays 2½m: acts on heavy going. *Alan King*   **h–**

SIR CHAUVELIN 6 b.g. Authorized (IRE) – Jabbara (IRE) (Kingmambo (USA)) [2017/18 h15.6d* h15.6k⁴ h16g Apr 21] useful stayer on Flat: useful handicap hurdler: won at Musselburgh (by 1¼ lengths from Silver Concorde) in January: will be suited by further than 2m: acts on good to soft going: hooded in 2015/16. *Jim Goldie*   **h131**

SIR DYLAN 9 b.g. Dylan Thomas (IRE) – Monteleone (IRE) (Montjeu (IRE)) [2017/18 h104: h16.8g h20g² h17.7g² h21.4s⁵ Oct 20] fair handicap hurdler: stays 2½m: acts on good to firm going: hooded prior to final start: temperamental. *Polly Gundry*   **h106 §**

SIRE DE GRUGY (FR) 12 b.g. My Risk (FR) – Hirlish (FR) (Passing Sale (FR)) [2017/18 c165, h–: h15.8s³ c16.8d c16.3s⁶ Dec 16] rangy gelding: winning hurdler: top-class chaser at best: won 5 Grade 1 events, including Tingle Creek (twice) at Sandown and Queen Mother Champion Chase at Cheltenham: well below form in 2017/18: best around 2m: acted on good to firm and heavy going: retired. *Gary Moore*   **c–** / **h118**

SIRE DU BERLAIS (FR) 6 b.g. Poliglote – Royale Athenia (FR) (Garde Royale) [2017/18 h131: h20s² h20.3v⁴ h20s Apr 25] useful handicap hurdler: again shaped well when fourth in Martin Pipe Conditional Jockeys' Handicap Hurdle at Cheltenham (7½ lengths behind Blow By Blow) in March: likely to stay 3m: acts on heavy going: in tongue tie last 2 starts: waited with. *Gordon Elliott, Ireland*   **h141**

SIR EGBERT 5 b.g. Kayf Tara – Little Miss Flora (Alflora (IRE)) [2017/18 h90: h15.8v³ h15.7d⁶ h15.8s³ h16s^ur h15.8s⁴ h16.5s^v Mar 26] fairly useful form over hurdles: won handicap at Taunton in March: raced around 2m: acts on soft going: wears hood (races freely). *Tom Lacey*   **h117**

SIR GEORGE SOMERS (USA) 5 ch.g. Cape Blanco (IRE) – Sense of Class (USA) (Fusaichi Pegasus (USA)) [2017/18 h16m⁴ h15.8d³ h16g Nov 1] fair maiden on Flat, stays 1¼m: best effort over hurdles (modest form) when third in novice at Ffos Las in May: in tongue tie last 2 starts. *Nigel Twiston-Davies*   **h90**

SIR HUBERT 8 b.g. Multiplex – Lacounsel (FR) (Leading Counsel (USA)) [2017/18 h91: c20s³ c19.7v⁴ c17v³ c17v* c19.7v^F Mar 12] sturdy gelding: maiden hurdler: modest form over fences: won novice handicap at Plumpton in February: stayed 2½m: acted on heavy going: dead. *Richard Rowe*   **c89** / **h–**

SIRIUS STAR 9 b.g. Beat All (USA) – Miss Sirius (Royal Vulcan) [2017/18 c101, h–: h20.6g c23g^F c23.9g^pu c21.6g^pu c21.4g³ c24.5g⁵ c23.6g⁵ Oct 17] workmanlike gelding: maiden hurdler: poor handicap chaser nowadays: stays 3m: acts on soft going: has worn hood: usually races in rear. *Brian Ellison*   **c81** / **h–**

SIR IVAN 8 b.g. Midnight Legend – Tisho (Sir Harry Lewis (USA)) [2017/18 c136, h126: c23.8g* c22.5s* c23.4g³ c24s^pu c24s^pu ab18d* c23.8d^F Apr 9] angular gelding: winning hurdler: useful chaser: won maiden at Ffos Las in May and novice handicap at Uttoxeter in October: also won jumpers bumper at Kempton in March: stays 3m: acts on heavy going: tried in hood: wears tongue tie. *Harry Fry*   **c137** / **h–**

SIR JACK YEATS (IRE) 7 b.g. Yeats (IRE) – Quadrennial (IRE) (Un Desperado (FR)) [2017/18 h20g⁶ h21g² h20.4s* h24g² c22.7g* c22.5s⁵ c22d* c20v⁴ c24v^pu h24v c20s⁵ c20.9s³ c23.9s* c23.4v* c26.3v c21.1s Apr 12] €55,000 3-y-o: sixth foal: closely related to smart bumper winner Mono Man and bumper winner/modest hurdler (2m-19f winner) Act Four (both by Old Vic): dam unraced half-sister to fairly useful hurdler (stayed 3m) Turtle Dubh: fair handicap hurdler: won at Wexford in June: fairly useful chaser: won handicaps at Killarney in July and Tramore in August, and hunters at Market Rasen and Kelso in February: left Ellmarie Holden after eleventh start: stays 3m: acts on heavy going: wears headgear: races prominently: sometimes idles, he is tough. *Richard Spencer*   **c128** / **h109**

SIR MANGAN (IRE) 10 b.g. Darsi (FR) – Lady Pep (IRE) (Cajetano (USA)) [2017/18 c–, h132: h22.8m⁵ h26.5g² c24.1s* c29.2s⁶ c28.4v^pu h19.9v⁶ h23.5s⁶ h20d² h24.7s Apr 14] sturdy gelding: useful handicap hurdler: useful handicap chaser: won at Bangor (by 1¼ lengths from Actinpieces) in November: stays 27f: acts on heavy going: has worn cheekpieces. *Dan Skelton*   **c134** / **h132**

SIR

SIR MIX 5 gr.g. Fair Mix (IRE) – Highland Cherry (Milan) [2017/18 h23.9s Jan 9] tailed off in maiden hurdle on debut. *Nigel Hawke*   **h–**

SIROBBIE (IRE) 4 br.g. Arakan (USA) – Presentbreeze (IRE) (Presenting) [2017/18 b16s⁴ b15.3d Apr 22] €8,000 3-y-o: fourth foal: half-brother to modest/unreliable chaser Breezy Kin (23f winner, by Kris Kin): dam lightly-raced half-sister to useful hurdler/smart chaser (2½m-27f winner) Ballycassidy: fair form on first of 2 starts in bumpers. *Sam Thomas*   **b85**

SIROP DE MENTHE (FR) 8 ch.g. Discover d'Auteuil (FR) – Jolie Menthe (FR) (Bateau Rouge) [2017/18 h124: h19.5d⁵ Nov 14] angular gelding: fairly useful handicap hurdler at best: weakened late on only appearance in 2017/18: stays 2¾m: acts on good to firm and heavy going: tried in headgear: usually races nearer last than first: has looked hard ride. *Susan Gardner*   **h–**

SIR TOMMY 9 ch.g. Sir Harry Lewis (USA) – Rose of Overbury (Overbury (IRE)) [2017/18 h–: h16.2g⁵ h15.8g⁴ h20.2m⁴ h16.2g^pu h16.2d* h20.9d⁶ h19.7s^pu Nov 29] fair hurdler: won novice at Perth in September: should stay further than 2m: acts on good to soft going: wears tongue tie. *Maurice Barnes*   **h100**

SIRUH DU LAC (FR) 5 b.g. Turgeon (USA) – Margerie (FR) (Le Balafre (FR)) [2017/18 h109: c18g^pu c20.3s* c19.2v* c20.2v³ Feb 1] tall gelding: has scope: fair form over hurdles: much better form over fences: won handicaps at Bangor in November and Exeter in December: also shaped well long way final outing: stays 2½m: acts on heavy going: usually races close up. *Nick Williams*   **c123 h–**

SIR VALENTINO (FR) 9 b.g. Early March – Valentine (FR) (Double Bed (FR)) [2017/18 c159, h130: c17.5v^pu c16.8d* c15.5d^F Dec 9] strong gelding: winning hurdler: very smart handicap chaser: won Shawbrook Handicap Chase at Ascot (by ½ length from Cepage) in November: stayed 2½m: acted on good to firm and heavy going: wore tongue tie: often raced towards rear: dead. *Tom George*   **c158 h–**

SIR VINCENT (IRE) 15 b.g. Norwich – Another Partner (Le Bavard (FR)) [2017/18 h22d h23.1g^pu h19.8g^pu h22.5d^pu Oct 13] fairly useful hurdler at best for W. P. Mullins, no form in 2017/18: winning chaser: stays 3m. *Hugh Beggs, Ireland*   **c– h–**

Shawbrook Handicap Chase, Ascot—final win for the ill-fated Sir Valentino who springs a surprise

SIZ

SIR WILL (IRE) 7 b.g. Yeats (IRE) – Tinopasa (FR) (No Pass No Sale) [2017/18 h114: h19.9d⁵ c21.7s^F h23.3v* h26s³ h23.5s* h24.3g⁴ Apr 20] good-topped gelding: useful hurdler: won maiden at Uttoxeter in December and handicap at Ascot (conditional) in March: fell heavily first in novice handicap on chasing debut: stays 3¼m: acts on heavy going: wears cheekpieces/tongue tie: usually races close up. *Kerry Lee*   **c–** **h130**

SISANIA (IRE) 5 gr.m. Mastercraftsman (IRE) – Avril Rose (IRE) (Xaar) [2017/18 h89: h18.7g^pu h15.8m⁵ h21.6d⁴ h20.5d⁴ h25.8g h20.7s h21.7g⁴ Apr 20] poor handicap hurdler: left Gary Moore after sixth start: stays 2¾m: often in headgear in 2017/18. *Suzy Smith*   **h84**

SISSINGHURST (IRE) 8 b.g. Kalanisi (IRE) – Sissinghurst Storm (IRE) (Good Thyne (USA)) [2017/18 c–, h95, b80: h19.6g* h20f* Oct 12] workmanlike gelding: fair form over hurdles: won handicaps at Huntingdon and Worcester in October: pulled up only chase start: stays 2½m: acts on firm going: tried in cheekpieces: in tongue tie last 2 starts: open to further improvement. *Fergal O'Brien*   **c–** **h105 p**

SISTER DUDE 5 ch.m. Notnowcato – Inaminute (IRE) (Spectrum (IRE)) [2017/18 h15.7g⁵ Aug 20] raced on Flat, stays 1m: 20/1, fifth in mares novice at Southwell (24 lengths behind Runasimi River) on hurdling debut. *Jonathan Portman*   **h67**

SISTER SIBYL (IRE) 7 br.m. King's Theatre (IRE) – Rose of The Erne (IRE) (Presenting) [2017/18 h111: c20s³ c19.1d⁴ c16v^F c20v² c16.2g² Apr 26] lengthy mare: winning hurdler: fairly useful form over fences: won mares handicap at Cheltenham in April: stays 2½m: acts on heavy going: often races towards rear. *Hughie Morrison*   **c122** **h–**

SIVOLA DE SIVOLA (FR) 12 gr.g. Martaline – Kerrana (FR) (Cadoudal (FR)) [2017/18 c20.8d⁶ May 5] sturdy, compact gelding: maiden pointer: winning hurdler: fairly useful chaser at best, behind only outing under Rules since 2013/14: has worn headgear: temperamental. *S. J. Gilmore*   **c– §** **h– §**

SIX A SIDE (IRE) 10 b.g. St Jovite (USA) – Persian Leader (IRE) (Supreme Leader) [2017/18 c102: c20.8d³ May 5] multiple point winner: fair form in hunter chases. *Miss E. L. Todd*   **c106**

SIX GUN SERENADE (IRE) 7 b.g. Kalanisi (IRE) – Zenaide (IRE) (Zaffaran (USA)) [2017/18 b15.8s h15.9v⁵ h15.9s* Apr 15] €120,000 4-y-o: third foal: half-brother to bumper winner/useful hurdler Myska (2m-2¾m winner, by Presenting) and bumper winner Daring Carlotta (by Kayf Tara): dam, bumper winner, half-sister to fair hurdler/fairly useful chaser (stayed 3m) Very Stylish: won completed start in Irish points: tailed off in bumper: fair form over hurdles: won maiden at Plumpton in April: likely to progress further. *Suzi Best*   **h104 p** **b–**

SIXTIES IDOL 5 b.m. Sixties Icon – Fading Away (Fraam) [2017/18 h82: h16m³ h15.9g⁴ h17.7d⁵ h17.7m⁵ h15.9m h20f⁶ h15.9d h19.2d² h19.2v⁵ h15.9v³ h15.9v⁵ h20.5d* h20.7s⁵ Mar 14] modest handicap hurdler: won mares event at Plumpton in February: stays 21f: acts on heavy going: wears blinkers/tongue tie. *Sheena West*   **h85**

SIXTIES STAR 4 b.g. Sixties Icon – Songbook (Singspiel (IRE)) [2017/18 b16.6s⁶ ab16.3g² Apr 15] £1,000 3-y-o: eighth foal: dam unraced: modest form in bumpers: in tongue tie, better effort when second at Newcastle in April. *Chris Fairhurst*   **b84**

SIXTY'S BELLE 4 b.f. Gold Well – Over Sixty (Overbury (IRE)) [2017/18 ab16g⁵ Jan 30] third foal: closely related to bumper winner/useful hurdler Spirit of Kayf (2m-2¾m winner, by Kayf Tara): dam (c128/h135), 2m-2¾m hurdle/chase winner, half-sister to useful hurdler (stayed 3m) Diamant Noir: 13/2, fifth in mares bumper at Lingfield (4¼ lengths behind Ceara Be). *Alan King*   **b76**

SIZING CODELCO (IRE) 9 b.g. Flemensfirth (USA) – La Zingarella (IRE) (Phardante (FR)) [2017/18 c157, h–: c23.6d^pu c27.3s⁶ c25.9v^pu c25s^pu c25s⁴ c31.8g Apr 21] useful-looking gelding: winning hurdler: high-class chaser: career-best effort when fourth to Might Bite in Bowl Chase at Aintree, though jumped none too fluently and never on terms: stays 25f: acts on heavy going: has worn headgear: tried in tongue tie: inconsistent. *Colin Tizzard*   **c160 ?** **h–**

SIZING CUSIMANO 5 b.g. Midnight Legend – Combe Florey (Alflora (IRE)) [2017/18 b16.4s⁶ h16.5s⁶ h18.5v⁶ h16.7v² Mar 11] €100,000 3-y-o: sturdy gelding: fifth foal: brother to bumper winner/useful hurdler Meet The Legend (2m winner) and half-brother to 2 winners, including fairly useful hurdler/chaser Kayfleur (2½m-3m winner, by Kayf Tara): dam (h87), lightly raced over hurdles, half-sister to smart hurdler/chaser (stayed 25f) Young Spartacus: very green when sixth in listed bumper at Cheltenham: fair form over hurdles: best effort when second in novice at Market Rasen in March. *Colin Tizzard*   **h101** **b77**

SIZ

SIZING GRANITE (IRE) 10 br.g. Milan – Hazel's Tisrara (IRE) (Mandalus) [2017/18 c157, h127: c19.4d^{pu} c21d h16.3s* c19.9s³ c24.5s⁶ Apr 25] tall, angular gelding: has had breathing operation: useful handicap hurdler: won at Newbury (by 3½ lengths from Early du Lemo) in March: very smart chaser: third in Melling Chase at Aintree (20¼ lengths behind Politologue) in April: stays 2½m: acts on soft going: has worn cheekpieces, including in 2017/18: wears tongue tie. *Colin Tizzard*   **c157 h139**

SIZING JOHN 8 b.g. Midnight Legend – La Perrotine (FR) (Northern Crystal) [2017/18 c170, h–: c20.2v* c24d Dec 28]   **c171 h–**

    What a difference a year makes. The main part of the new season had barely got under way when the news came through that Alan Potts had died at the age of eighty from a heart attack, barely three months after his wife Ann had lost a long battle with illness. The couple's major breakthrough into the league of jumping's big owners was all too short-lived but had been capped by a magnificent season in 2016/17 when their best-known horse Sizing John completed the Irish Gold Cup/Cheltenham Gold Cup/Punchestown Gold Cup treble, an unprecedented achievement that perhaps deserved to be celebrated more than it actually was at the time. It was announced that Sizing John would be aimed at the 'Classic Triple Crown' in the latest season, attempting to land the million-pound bonus offered by Jockey Club Racecourses for any horse that wins the Betfair Chase, the King George VI Chase and the Cheltenham Gold Cup in the same season. The Betfair Chase was just a fortnight away when the Grim Reaper took Alan Potts, who was the driving force behind the idea of trying to land a second historic treble in as many seasons with Sizing John. Potts and his wife were passionate supporters of jumping and they were not afraid to ring the changes with their trainers and jockeys in pursuit of success. One of the last of those changes by Alan Potts had been to appoint Bryan Cooper as first jockey for the Potts horses trained in Britain and the owner had been all booked to see the partnership in action at Cheltenham's November meeting. Cooper carried the emerald green, yellow chevron and sleeves to victory on Fox Norton in the Shloer Chase at the fixture where he also won the Steel Plate and Sections Novices' Chase on Finian's Oscar on the first day (Cooper wore a black armband in that race, before which an image of Alan Potts was shown on the big screen). Fox Norton and Finian's Oscar were among fifteen horses that had been sent by the Potts's to trainer Colin Tizzard at the start of the previous season. Fox Norton was a private purchase from Neil Mulholland's stable and Finian's Oscar was a big money buy (£250,000) from Irish points. Money, it seemed, was no object to Alan Potts who spent vast sums on top prospects at the upper end of the market. Tizzard also took delivery of Flemenshill who set a new auction record for a pointer of £480,000 at Cheltenham's January Sales in 2017. Alas, Flemenshill never saw a racecourse for Potts and Tizzard, suffering a heart attack on the gallops in light pre-season training. For mining tycoon Alan Potts, covering the costs of his hobby was not a priority; he memorably described racing as 'how we spend the money, not how we earn it.' The horses in training continued to race in the name of Ann & Alan Potts Limited after his death but there are said to be no plans by the Potts family to maintain an ownership connection with the sport once the present crop of jumpers have finished their careers.

    Irish-trained Sizing John had been another of the Potts-owned horses to move stables at the start of the 2016/17 season when he was transferred from Henry de Bromhead to Jessica Harrington, along with others including Supasundae (who went on to win the Coral Cup at the Cheltenham Festival in his first season with Harrington). Plans for an assault on the 'Classic Triple Crown' fell at the first hurdle when, after Alan Potts's death, it was decided Sizing John would miss the Betfair Chase at Haydock because of the prevailing very heavy going (underfoot conditions were deplorable on the day for a championship event). Sizing John's absence took some of the gloss off the Betfair Chase but Haydock's loss was Punchestown's gain when he was rerouted to the John Durkan Memorial Punchestown Chase a fortnight later. Djakadam, who had finished fourth to Sizing John in the Cheltenham Gold Cup and runner-up to him in the Punchestown Gold Cup, started favourite for the Punchestown Chase which he had won in the two previous years. But Sizing John got the better of Djakadam for the third time, surviving an uncharacteristic early

John Durkan Memorial Punchestown Chase, Punchestown—an impressive winning return by Sizing John, who is far too strong for the 2015 and 2016 winner Djakadam (third right)

blunder before asserting himself from the second last to beat his old rival by seven lengths, with Sub Lieutenant (runner-up in the Ryanair Chase at the Cheltenham Festival) filling third in the Punchestown Chase for the second successive year. Sizing John, at the head of the ante-post betting (at a general 4/1) for the Cheltenham Gold Cup, looked at least as good as ever and seemed set to take plenty of beating if he got to the Cheltenham Festival fit and in top form. It is rare, incidentally, to see a Gold Cup winner dropped back in trip (the Punchestown Chase is over two and a half miles) and Sizing John was the first reigning Gold Cup winner to win a race over two and three quarter miles or shorter since Kauto Star who won the Ascot Chase in the season after his first Gold Cup win (Best Mate had twice enjoyed victories in the Peterborough Chase as part of his Gold Cup warm-up).

Sizing John's regular jockey Robbie Power (who regained the rides on the Potts-owned Tizzard horses from Bryan Cooper after the turn of the year) sung Sizing John's praises after the John Durkan, saying he had all the attributes for the King George VI Chase at Kempton. But Sizing John's trainer was keen to stress that there were now other options on the road to Cheltenham and Sizing John lined up instead in the Leopardstown Christmas Chase (formerly the Lexus). His attempt to stretch his winning run to five in Grade 1 chases ended with a disappointing seventh (beating only one other finisher) behind Road To Respect, after which Sizing John was found to be 'post-race abnormal'. It was the first time Sizing John had finished out of the places in his career and the first time he had been beaten for twelve months, since finishing second to Douvan over two miles and a furlong in the Paddy Power Cashcard Chase at the same Leopardstown Christmas meeting (Sizing John had done nearly all his racing at around two miles up to that point). The Christmas Chase turned out to be Sizing John's final outing of the campaign. He was reported to be 'in top shape' for a Cheltenham Gold Cup challenge at the end of February (at which time he was third favourite in most books behind Might Bite and Native River) but he was ruled out a week before the race after suffering a hairline fracture of his pelvis.

Sizing John became the third successive Gold Cup winner to be thwarted by injury from defending his Cheltenham title. Interestingly, seven-year-old Gold Cup winners have a decidedly mixed record in adding substantially to their reputations in later seasons. Like Arkle, Best Mate won his first Gold Cup at seven and followed up at both eight and nine, and Kauto Star regained the Gold Cup after losing it as an eight-year-old, but, of the other seven-year-old winners in the *Chasers & Hurdlers* era, Royal Frolic missed the season after his Gold Cup win with injury before making a successful return, only to come a cropper when looking set to finish in the frame in Midnight Court's Gold Cup; Davy Lad had a disappointing campaign, and didn't manage to win, in the season after his Gold Cup win; Midnight Court missed the following season with a leg injury and never recovered his best form; misfortune dogged Little Owl for the rest of his career after his win in 1981; Imperial Call failed fully to recapture his best form, becoming injury prone, though he did win an Ericsson Chase and a Punchestown Gold Cup later in his career; Kicking King followed up his Gold Cup win by winning a second King George but suffered

SIZ

a tendon injury at Kempton, which kept him off the course for a year, and he was a long way below his best in subsequent seasons; War of Attrition had a setback the following season which kept him out of the Gold Cup, and he was never the same again after having stem-cell regeneration treatment for a tendon injury. All of which illustrates the fragility of many of the top jumpers and reinforces the wisdom of the saying about racehorses being like strawberries—'Enjoy them while they're here.'

Sizing John (b.g. 2010)
- Midnight Legend (b 1991)
  - Night Shift (b 1980)
    - Northern Dancer
    - Ciboulette
  - Myth (b 1983)
    - Troy
    - Hay Reef
- La Perrotine (FR) (b 2000)
  - Northern Crystal (b 1988)
    - Crystal Glitters
    - North Cliff
  - Haratiyna (b 1986)
    - Top Ville
    - Halwah

The pedigree of the useful-looking Sizing John was covered in detail in *Chasers & Hurdlers 2016/17* and there is nothing to add, the ill-fated mare Scholastica (by Old Vic), who was a fairly useful hurdler, being the dam's only other winner so far. The normally reliable Sizing John, who travels strongly in his races, stays three and a quarter miles, and is fully effective at around two and a half miles. He acts on heavy going but doesn't need the mud. Still only eight, he has time on his side—in theory at least—and it is to be hoped he makes a full recovery from injury and returns as good as ever. *Mrs J. Harrington, Ireland*

SIZING PLATINUM (IRE) 10 b.g. Definite Article – Quest of Passion (FR) (Saumarez) [2017/18 c142, h–: c16.3v* c15.9g³ c16.3v c15.8s⁶ c20.5g² Apr 20] workmanlike gelding: winning hurdler: smart handicap chaser: won at Newton Abbot (by 14 lengths from Ut Majeur Aulmes) in October: second in listed event at Ayr (length behind Value At Risk) in April: stays 2½m: acts on good to firm and heavy going: wears tongue tie. *Colin Tizzard* c148 h–

SIZING SAHARA 10 gr.g. Shirocco (GER) – Aristocratique (Cadeaux Genereux) [2017/18 c–, h78: h21.6s³ h26.5g⁴ h20.7s Feb 22] angular gelding: poor handicap hurdler: maiden chaser: stays 3¼m: acts on soft going. *Paul Henderson* c– h80

SIZING TARA 5 b.g. Kayf Tara – As Was (Epalo (GER)) [2017/18 b16.5s⁶ h16.5v h19.7vᵖᵘ Mar 10] second foal: half-brother to a winning pointer by Midnight Legend: dam unraced half-sister to useful French hurdler/fairly useful chaser (17f-21f winner) Line Salsa: sixth in bumper at Taunton: poor form over hurdles. *Colin Tizzard* h79 b71

SIZING TENNESSEE (IRE) 10 ch.g. Robin des Champs (FR) – Jolivia (FR) (Dernier Empereur (USA)) [2017/18 c133, h–: c21g² c24.4gᶠ c18.8dᵘʳ c25.3s* c20.8s² c20.8v³ c31.8s³ c31.8gᵖᵘ Apr 21] strong gelding: winning hurdler: smart chaser: won novice at Cheltenham (by 6 lengths from Duel At Dawn) in December: placed in Dipper Novices' Chase (neck behind Yanworth) in January and National Hunt Chase (21½ lengths behind Rathvinden) in March, both at same course: probably stays 4m: acts on heavy going: tried in blinkers: usually leads. *Colin Tizzard* c148 h–

SIZING TITANIUM (IRE) 10 b.g. Flemensfirth (USA) – White On Red (GER) (Konigsstuhl (GER)) [2017/18 c17v* c16v⁴ c16.5v² Feb 11] point winner: winning hurdler: fairly useful form over fences: won handicap at Navan in December: unproven beyond 17f: best form on heavy going: tried in cheekpieces. *J. T. R. Dreaper, Ireland* c118 h–

SKANDIBURG (FR) 4 b.g. Sageburg (IRE) – Skandia (FR) (Robin des Champs (FR)) [2017/18 b16d⁴ Apr 26] good-topped gelding: sixth foal: half-brother to useful hurdler/winning pointer Robin Waters (21f winner, by Irish Wells), stays 3m: dam French 17f/2¼m hurdle/chase winner: 14/1, fourth in bumper at Warwick (8 lengths behind Umndeni). *Dan Skelton* b89

SKA RIDGE 6 b.g. Distant Peak (IRE) – Tandawizi (Relief Pitcher) [2017/18 b16v b17d Mar 25] no form in bumpers. *Rebecca Menzies* b–

SKEAPING 5 b.g. Excellent Art – Gale Green (Galileo (IRE)) [2017/18 h99: h16.8d h17.6d² h20.2g² h18.8g⁴ h16g² h16g⁶ h16.2d⁴ Sep 11] fair maiden hurdler: stays 19f: acts on good to soft going: wears headgear/tongue tie. *Gordon Elliott, Ireland* h105

SKEWIFF 6 b.m. Doyen (IRE) – Skew (Niniski (USA)) [2017/18 b82: h15.8g* h19.5dᶠ h21.2g³ h19.5v⁵ h23.5s⁶ h22.8s* Mar 21] lengthy, angular mare: bumper winner: fair form over hurdles: won mares novices at Ffos Las in June and Haydock in March: stays 3m: acts on soft going. *Evan Williams* h112

SKY

SKIDOOSH 5 b.g. Midnight Legend – Southern Exit (Poliglote) [2017/18 b16g* b16.4s[5] b16.6s[2] b17s Apr 13] rangy gelding: second foal: dam (h86) ungenuine maiden hurdler (best at 2m): fairly useful form in bumpers: won at Worcester in October. *Ben Pauling* — **b97**

SKILFUL LORD (IRE) 4 ch.g. Lord Shanakill (USA) – Monsusu (IRE) (Montjeu (IRE)) [2017/18 h16.8g h15.8m h15.8s Oct 19] poor maiden on Flat: no form over hurdles: wears tongue tie. *David Pipe* — **h–**

SKILLED 7 b.g. Mastercraftsman (IRE) – Treacle (USA) (Seeking The Gold (USA)) [2017/18 h16d h16g c20g[2] c19.4g* c20.3g* c20g[4] h20.3d Oct 3] fair hurdler at best, no form in 2017/18: fairly useful form over fences: won novice handicap at Stratford in July and handicap at Southwell in August: left Anabel K. Murphy after second start: stays 2½m: acts on soft going: in hood last 5 starts: often races in rear. *Olly Murphy* — **c115 h–**

SKINFLINT (IRE) 6 b.g. Scorpion (IRE) – Gales Hill (IRE) (Beau Sher) [2017/18 h19s[pu] h16.5v h16.3v[6] h16s[6] h19s h23.1v[pu] Apr 17] £30,000 4-y-o: half-brother to useful hurdler/smart chaser Ballybolley (2m-21f winner, by Kayf Tara) and fair hurdler Meitheamh (2m winner, by Beneficial), stayed 2½m: dam, of little account, half-sister to smart hurdlers up to 3m Sweet Kiln and Earth Magic and to dam of Limestone Lad: runner-up in Irish point: fair form over hurdles: tried in cheekpieces/tongue tie. *David Pipe* — **h101**

SKINT 12 b.g. King's Theatre (IRE) – No More Money (Alflora) (IRE)) [2017/18 c103§, h87§: c20.3g c20m[5] c20g[5] c20.3d[5] c19.9s[6] c20.3v[7] c19.9s* c17.8g* Apr 20] well-made gelding: winning hurdler: fair handicap chaser: won at Huntingdon in March and Fontwell in April: stays 2¾m: acts on good to firm and heavy going: has worn headgear, including last 2 starts: has worn tongue tie, including last 3 starts: temperamental. *Michael Scudamore* — **c98 § h– §**

SKIP 5 ch.g. Peintre Celebre (USA) – Fluffy (Efisio) [2017/18 b83: b17m[3] May 11] modest form in bumpers. *Kevin Ryan* — **b64**

SKIPPING ON (IRE) 9 b.g. Westerner – Skipping Along (IRE) (Anshan) [2017/18 h15.7d c15.9s[5] c16.1v* c19.8s[ur] c15.9v[3d] c20.3v* c16.1v* c15.9s[2] c20v* Apr 17] maiden hurdler: fairly useful handicap chaser: won at Towcester (conditional) in February, Southwell and Towcester (novice) in March, and Carlisle (novice) in April: stays 2½m: acts on heavy going: wears hood. *Laura Morgan* — **c117 h–**

SKIPTHECUDDLES (IRE) 7 b.g. Westerner – Autumn Sky (IRE) (Roselier (FR)) [2017/18 h128, b86: h24.3v[pu] h24d[5] h24s[5] h23.1v h23.8d* h19.8s[F] Apr 28] sturdy gelding: bumper winner: useful handicap hurdler: won at Ludlow (by 12 lengths from Call To Order) in April: stays 3m: acts on soft going: in cheekpieces/tongue tie last 2 starts. *Graeme McPherson* — **h132**

SKIPTHESCALES (IRE) 6 b.g. Winged Love (IRE) – Waterland Gale (IRE) (Fourstars Allstar (USA)) [2017/18 h92: h20.1s[6] h21.3s[3] h24.1d* h24.1s[4] h24.3v[3] h24v* h24.3v[4] h25d* h26.6s[3] Apr 26] placed in Irish points: fairly useful handicap hurdler: won at Wetherby in November, Newcastle in January and Carlisle in March: will stay long distances: acts on heavy going: wears headgear. *Philip Kirby* — **h115**

SKYE CHIEF 6 b.g. Sulamani (IRE) – Isle of Skye (Terimon) [2017/18 b15.6s[2] b16.2v[5] h20.2s[2] Apr 25] first foal: dam winning pointer: fair form in bumpers: 28/1, second in maiden at Perth (9 lengths behind Blue Flight) on hurdling debut. *Simon Waugh* — **h103 b92**

SKY FULL OF STARS (IRE) 8 b.g. Mahler – Gold Flo (IRE) (Fourstars Allstar (USA)) [2017/18 c97, h99: h16.2s[ur] c16.4s[3] c16.4s[6] c16.5v* c16.4v[2] h16v[4] c15.6d[2] Apr 23] workmanlike gelding: modest handicap hurdler: modest handicap chaser: won at Ayr in January: raced mainly around 2m: acts on heavy going: wears headgear. *James Ewart* — **c99 h90**

SKY KHAN 9 b.g. Cape Cross (IRE) – Starlit Sky (Galileo (IRE)) [2017/18 h127: h20.6g h20.1g[ur] h20g[3] h23.9v[6] h20d h21.4g[2] Apr 21] good-topped gelding: fairly useful handicap hurdler: stays 3m: acts on good to firm and heavy going: usually in headgear: wears tongue tie: usually races nearer last than first. *Lucinda Russell* — **h129**

SKYLINE 4 b.g. Stimulation (IRE) – Yonder (And Beyond (IRE)) [2017/18 b13d[2] b14s[6] ab16g[3] Mar 5] lengthy, unfurnished gelding: third foal: half-brother to 8.6f winner Kissy Suzuki (by Sakhee's Secret): dam (h95), 13f bumper winner (placed up to 21f over hurdles), also 1½m-1¾m winner on Flat: fair form in bumpers. *Hughie Morrison* — **b85**

SKY OF STARS (IRE) 5 b.g. Frozen Power (IRE) – So So Lucky (IRE) (Danehill (USA)) [2017/18 h–: h15.8d[2] h18.7m* h18.6g* h17.7m h20.3d[3] h16.3g[5] h20.5d[5] h15.5d[2] h15.3s[5] Nov 23] rather leggy gelding: modest handicap hurdler: won at Stratford (conditional) in July and Market Rasen in August: left Olly Murphy after seventh start: stays 2½m: acts on good to firm and good to soft going: wears headgear. *Barry Brennan* — **h97**

SKY

SKY PIRATE 5 b.g. Midnight Legend – Dancingwithbubbles (IRE) (Supreme Leader) [2017/18 h20g* h20.3d² h21.6d³ Dec 22] €34,000 3-y-o, £150,000 4-y-o: good-topped gelding: third foal: dam (h124), bumper/2m-21f hurdle winner, half-sister to useful hurdler (stays 23f) Theo's Charm out of smart hurdler/fairly useful chaser (stayed 3m) Kates Charm: point winner: fairly useful form over hurdles: won novice at Worcester in October: likely to stay 3m. *Jonjo O'Neill* — h118

SKYWARDS REWARD (IRE) 7 b.g. Dubawi (IRE) – Russian Society (Darshaan) [2017/18 h88, b72: h21.3s^{ur} h20.1v⁶ h16s h16v* h20.5v² h17s* h17v* h20.1d^{pu} Apr 23] fairly useful handicap hurdler: won at Wetherby (conditional) in February and Carlisle (twice, conditional first occasion) in April: stayed 2½m: best form on soft/heavy going: often raced prominently: dead. *Micky Hammond* — h119

SLAINE 4 b.f. Brian Boru – Flowing On (Alflora (IRE)) [2017/18 b15.8v³ b15.7v Apr 27] fourth foal: dam (b89), bumper winner, half-sister to useful hurdler/chaser (stayed 19f) Crack On: poor form in bumpers. *G. C. Maundrell* — b74

SLANELOUGH (IRE) 6 b.g. Westerner – Tango Lady (IRE) (King's Theatre (IRE)) [2017/18 h110p: h17s* h16.4d h19.4d² h19.7s³ h19.4s* h19.3v² h19.3d⁶ Mar 25] workmanlike gelding: runner-up in Irish point: fairly useful hurdler: won novice at Carlisle in October and handicap at Doncaster in January: stays 2½m: acts on heavy going: wears hood. *Rose Dobbin* — h126

SLATE HOUSE (IRE) 6 b.g. Presenting – Bay Pearl (FR) (Broadway Flyer (USA)) [2017/18 h16.4g* h16.4s* h15.7d⁴ h20.3v⁵ h16.4s^F h16.5s Apr 13] €44,000 3-y-o, £260,000 5-y-o: strong, good sort: fourth foal: brother to fairly useful hurdler/chaser Touch Kick (19f/2½m winner) and half-brother to fair chaser Repeat Business (3m winner, by Croco Rouge): dam (b77), placed in bumpers, half-sister to dam of Big Buck's: Irish point winner: useful form over hurdles: won maiden in October and Sharp Novices' Hurdle (by ¾ length from Summerville Boy) in November, both at Cheltenham: seems best around 2m: acts on soft going: in tongue tie last 2 starts. *Colin Tizzard* — h138

SLAYING THE DRAGON (IRE) 5 ch.g. Notnowcato – Empress Charlotte (Holy Roman Emperor (IRE)) [2017/18 b–: h16.8v^{bd} h19g h23.9s^{pu} h16.8s Apr 23] stocky gelding: no form over hurdles. *Martin Hill* — h–

SLEEP EASY 6 b.g. Rip Van Winkle (IRE) – Strictly Lambada (Red Ransom (USA)) [2017/18 h130: h20g h18.5d³ h19.8s³ Mar 9] compact gelding: useful handicap hurdler: third at Sandown (6½ lengths behind Soul Emotion) in March: stays 21f: acts on soft going: wears cheekpieces: tried in tongue tie. *Neil Mulholland* — h131

SLEEP IN FIRST (FR) 12 b.g. Sleeping Car (FR) – First Union (FR) (Shafoun (FR)) [2017/18 c102, h105: h16.8s² h15.6s⁵ h15.6d Feb 14] fair handicap hurdler/chaser nowadays: best form around 2m: acts on soft and good to firm going: has worn headgear, including last 2 starts: has worn tongue tie: front runner/races prominently. *James Ewart* — c– / h95

SLEEPY HAVEN (IRE) 8 b.g. Indian Haven – High Society Girl (IRE) (Key of Luck (USA)) [2017/18 c–x, h125: h16v⁵ h16s³ h15.7v² h15.5v⁶ h19.9v³ h19.2s⁵ h15.7s Mar 31] sturdy gelding: fairly useful handicap hurdler: maiden chaser (often let down by jumping): best up to 2½m: acts on heavy going: has worn headgear, including final start: has worn tongue tie. *Jennie Candlish* — c– x / h119

SLICE OF LEMON 6 b.m. Dr Massini (IRE) – Lady Maranzi (Teenoso (USA)) [2017/18 h16s⁶ h15.8v^{pu} Apr 1] second foal: dam (h94) 2m-19f hurdle winner: no form over hurdles. *Debra Hamer* — h–

SLIDING DOORS (IRE) 5 b.g. Ask – Reseda (GER) (Lavirco (GER)) [2017/18 b92: h20.5s h16.6s h16.7v h19s⁴ Feb 23] placed in bumpers: fair form over hurdles: often races towards rear. *Ian Williams* — h103

SLIM PICKENS (IRE) 10 b.g. Craigsteel – Couleurs d'Automne (FR) (Galant Vert (FR)) [2017/18 h16.2g* h20g² h20g² h20m² h23g* c22.6m³ h24g³ Apr 18] workmanlike gelding: useful hurdler: won seller at Hexham in May and handicap at Worcester in July: 9/4, third in novice at Stratford (3¾ lengths behind Ballinure) on chasing debut: stays 3m: acts on good to firm and good to soft going: entitled to do better as a chaser. *Dr Richard Newland* — c118 p / h130

SLOWMOTION (FR) 6 b.m. Soldier of Fortune (IRE) – Second Emotion (FR) (Medaaly) [2017/18 c138, h137: c22.5g³ c24v c24s^{pu} c20.6v³ c21s⁶ Apr 27] useful chaser: useful handicap chaser: third in Galway Plate (5½ lengths behind Balko des Flos) in August: best up to 3m: acts on heavy going: tried in cheekpieces. *Joseph Patrick O'Brien, Ireland* — c139 / h–

SLUMBER PARTY 5 gr.g. Hellvelyn – In Some Style (IRE) (Grand Lodge (USA)) [2017/18 b15.8v[6] Dec 18] tailed off in maiden bumper. *Matthew Salaman* — b–

SMACKWATER JACK (IRE) 4 b.g. Flemensfirth (USA) – Malachy's Attic (IRE) (Old Vic) [2017/18 b16d[2] Apr 7] sixth foal: half-brother to fair chaser Das Mooser (2½m winner, by Definite Article): dam (h118), 19f hurdle winner, half-sister to fair hurdler/fairly useful chaser (stayed 3m) Fresh Air And Fun: 12/1, second in bumper at Fakenham (nose behind Before Midnight). *Olly Murphy* — b94

SMAD PLACE (FR) 11 gr.g. Smadoun (FR) – Bienna Star (FR) (Village Star (FR)) [2017/18 c161, h–: c19.9d* c21d[5] c20.5d[4] Jan 13] sturdy gelding: had breathing operation: winning hurdler: high-class chaser, successful in Hennessy Gold Cup at Newbury and Cotswold Chase at Cheltenham in 2015/16: final win in Old Roan Chase at Aintree (by ¾ length from Cloudy Dream) in October: stayed 3¼m: acted on good to firm and heavy going: front runner/raced prominently: retired. *Alan King* — c161 h–

SMADYNIUM (FR) 10 gr.g. Smadoun (FR) – Sea Music (FR) (Bering) [2017/18 c130, h98: c25.2g[pu] c19.9d[2] h24g c23.5g[F] c17.3s[3] h16.6s c19.9g[pu] Aug 12] rather leggy gelding: fairly useful hurdler at best, no form in 2017/18: fairly useful handicap chaser: stays 3m: acts on heavy going: has worn headgear, including in 2017/18: wears tongue tie: usually races close up: unreliable. *John Joseph Hanlon, Ireland* — c124 § h– §

SMAOINEAMH ALAINN (IRE) 6 b.m. Shantou (USA) – Dathuil (IRE) (Royal Academy (USA)) [2017/18 h109p, b83: h15.3g* h16.8s* h16.8v[pu] Mar 16] good-topped mare: useful form over hurdles: won novice at Wincanton in October and handicap at Cheltenham (by 2 lengths from Remiluc) in December: in hood last 4 starts: usually races close up, often travels strongly. *Robert Walford* — h130

SMART BOY (IRE) 7 b.g. Mahler – Supreme Style (IRE) (Supreme Leader) [2017/18 h76: h20.5d* h19.5d[2] h20.7s[3] h21s[2] h19s* Mar 26] runner-up in point: fair handicap hurdler: won at Plumpton in October and Taunton in March: stays 21f: acts on heavy going: usually races close up. *Jack R. Barber* — h112

SMART CATCH (IRE) 12 b.g. Pivotal – Zafaraniya (IRE) (Doyoun) [2017/18 c86x, h94§: c25.7g[pu] May 14] lengthy, angular gelding: fair hurdler/chaser at best, pulled up in handicap chase sole outing in 2017/18: stays 25f: acts on soft going: in tongue tie last 4 starts: held up: often let down by jumping over fences: temperamental. *Tony Carroll* — c– x h– §

SMART GETAWAY (IRE) 6 b.m. Getaway (GER) – Legendsofthefall (IRE) (Arctic Lord) [2017/18 b16d[6] b15.8g[4] Dec 6] €1,000 4-y-o: fifth foal: half-sister to a winning pointer by Milan: dam (h79), 2½m hurdle winner, half-sister to fairly useful/ungenuine hurdler/chaser (stayed 23f) Craven: modest form in bumpers: will stay at least 2¼m. *Dominic Ffrench Davis* — b82

SMART PACO 4 ch.g. Paco Boy (IRE) – La Gifted (Fraam) [2017/18 ab16.3g b17d Mar 25] no form in bumpers: wears tongue tie. *Maurice Barnes* — b–

SMART RULER (IRE) 12 ch.g. Viking Ruler (AUS) – Celebrated Smile (IRE) (Cadeaux Genereux) [2017/18 h109: h22.1d[4] c21.2g[3] c21.2s[3] c21.2d[4] h17d Nov 13] fair handicap hurdler: similar form over fences: stays 21f: acts on good to firm and good to soft going: tried in eyeshields. *James Moffatt* — c103 h100

SMART TALK (IRE) 8 b.m. Hubbly Bubbly (USA) – Belon Breeze (IRE) (Strong Gale) [2017/18 h16.6s[6] h16.4s[3] h16s h24.3g Apr 20] big, good-topped mare: Irish point winner: useful hurdler, not at best in 2017/18 after long absence: stays 2¾m, effective at shorter: acts on heavy going. *Brian Ellison* — h120

SMILEY (FR) 5 b.g. Blue Bresil (FR) – Loving Smile (FR) (Sillery (USA)) [2017/18 b–: b15.7g[5] May 15] compact gelding: no form in bumpers: tried in hood. *Seamus Mullins* — b–

SMILING JESSICA (IRE) 8 ch.m. Golden Tornado (IRE) – Charlie's Mary (IRE) (Daar Alzamaan (IRE)) [2017/18 b20g h19.8g h23.3d[4] h23.9v[pu] c24d[2] c26d[2] c26.3s[F] c23.8d* c23.8s[pu] Jan 19] second foal: half-sister to modest hurdler/chaser The Bishop (21f-3m winner, by Winged Love): dam unraced: no form in bumpers: little show over hurdles: poor form over fences: won novice handicap at Musselburgh in January: left Christian Delcros after second start: stays 3¼m: acts on good to soft going: in headgear last 5 starts: front runner/races prominently. *Rebecca Menzies* — c83 h64 b–

SMITH'S BAY 5 b.g. Midnight Legend – Takotna (IRE) (Bering) [2017/18 b16.5s* b16.6s[5] Feb 21] second foal: dam (h98) 19f hurdle winner: fair form in bumpers: won at Taunton in January. *Alan King* — b91

SMI

SMITHS CROSS (IRE) 6 b.g. Westerner – Blue Supreme (IRE) (Pistolet Bleu (IRE)) [2017/18 b15.8v* b15.8v² Apr 15] €13,000 3-y-o, £50,000 6-y-o: smallish, strong gelding: second foal: dam, winning pointer, half-sister to fairly useful hurdler/fair chaser (winner up to 23f) Luckymilman: Irish point winner: fairly useful form in bumpers: won at Uttoxeter in March. *Michael Scudamore* — **b101**

SMOKEY JOE JOE (IRE) 12 b.g. Snurge – Goldens Monkey (Monksfield) [2017/18 h20d c24.9s^{pu} c22.5s c22.5v^F c20v* h20v⁶ h20v² h23.1s² h22.4v³ h21s Apr 25] fairly useful handicap hurdler: useful handicap chaser: won at Cork in January: stays 23f: acts on heavy going: tried in cheekpieces: wears tongue tie: often races towards rear. *S. J. Mahon, Ireland* — **c132 h124**

SMOKING DIXIE (IRE) 7 ch.g. Beneficial – Jacksister (IRE) (Flemensfirth (USA)) [2017/18 h91: c23.6v^{pu} c18.2v³ c18.2m⁵ Apr 25] maiden hurdler: modest form over fences: left Ben Pauling after first start: tried in hood. *John Groucott* — **c93 h–**

SMOKING JACKET (IRE) 8 b.g. Beneficial – Unalaska (IRE) (High Estate) [2017/18 c114, h–: c20.3d^{pu} Jun 6] sturdy gelding: maiden hurdler: fair chaser, pulled up sole start in 2017/18: unproven beyond 17f: acts on good to soft going. *Tom George* — **c– h–**

SMOOTH OPERATOR 6 b.g. Azamour (IRE) – Teggiano (IRE) (Mujtahid (USA)) [2017/18 h15.8g h15.8g⁵ Oct 17] half-brother to fair hurdler Minneapolis (2m winner, by Sadler's Wells): fair maiden on Flat, stays 1¾m: modest form over hurdles: best effort when fifth in novice at Huntingdon. *Mark Pitman* — **h86**

SMOOTH STEPPER 9 b.g. Alflora (IRE) – Jazzy Refrain (IRE) (Jareer (USA)) [2017/18 c131, h–: h24.1d⁵ c29.2g c26.1d² c23.4v* c32.6s⁶ c26.2v* c26g Apr 18] workmanlike gelding: winning hurdler: useful handicap chaser: won at Newcastle in February and Kelso (by 8 lengths from Baywing) in April: stays 3¼m: acts on heavy going: usually races close up. *Sue Smith* — **c142 h–**

SMUGGLER'S BLUES (IRE) 6 b.g. Yeats (IRE) – Rosy de Cyborg (FR) (Cyborg (FR)) [2017/18 b16g⁶ h19.7s⁴ h15.3d³ Apr 22] €40,000 3-y-o, £50,000 5-y-o: second foal: half-brother to French hurdler/chaser Une Lapin Rouge (17f-19f winner, by Martaline): dam (c108/h137), French 2¼m/19f hurdle winner, half-sister to fairly useful hurdler/useful chaser (stayed 3m) No Full: Irish point winner: sixth in bumper at Worcester: fair form over hurdles: better effort when third in novice at Wincanton in April: should be suited by 2½m. *Tom George* — **h109 b89**

SMUGGLER'S STASH (IRE) 8 ch.g. Stowaway – Sweetasanu (IRE) (Sri Pekan (USA)) [2017/18 c98§, h–: c24.2v^{pu} c24.2s² c24.5s⁶ c26.3s³ c25.2v² c24.1v* c24.1v¹ c26.2d⁴ c26.2v³ Apr 16] tall gelding: maiden hurdler: fair handicap chaser: won at Ayr in February and March: should stay extreme distances: acts on heavy going: wears headgear: front runner/races prominently. *Rose Dobbin* — **c106 h–**

SNAPDRAGON FIRE (IRE) 5 b.g. Getaway (GER) – Global Diamond (IRE) (Classic Music (USA)) [2017/18 b15.7g² b16.7g⁴ h16.8s h16.5g² h20.6s³ h16.2s² h19.8v⁴ Feb 16] £32,000 3-y-o: half-brother to fair hurdler Global Fert (2m winner, by Flemensfirth), stays 2½m: dam (c95/h94), 2m hurdle winner, also 13f winner on Flat: fair form in bumpers: similar form over hurdles: stays 21f: acts on soft going. *Tom Lacey* — **h113 b87**

SNATCHITBACK 7 b.g. Overbury (IRE) – Talk The Talk (Terimon) [2017/18 h19.5s^{pu} Nov 8] fourth only start in points: poor form in bumpers: pulled up in maiden on hurdling debut. *Michael Scudamore* — **h–**

SNAZZ MAN 8 b.g. Beat All (USA) – Ela d'Argent (IRE) (Ela-Mana-Mou) [2017/18 h18.5d h20v h23.1v^{pu} h19.5v⁵ h19.5v Apr 14] poor form over hurdles. *Susan Gardner* — **h59**

SNEAKING BUDGE 6 b.g. Nayef (USA) – Ikat (IRE) (Pivotal) [2017/18 h–: h15.5d⁴ h20.7s⁵ h15.5v⁶ h16s⁶ h15.7g Apr 20] sturdy gelding: modest handicap hurdler: stays 21f: best form on soft/heavy going: in cheekpieces last 2 starts. *Stuart Edmunds* — **h92**

SNEAKY FEELING (IRE) 6 b.g. Oscar (IRE) – Shuil Aris (IRE) (Anshan) [2017/18 h133p, b91: h20d h21d Nov 13] lengthy, rather unfurnished gelding: in frame in Irish point: useful hurdler at best, disappointing both starts in 2017/18: stays 2½m: acts on soft going. *Philip Hobbs* — **h–**

SNIPPETYDOODAH 10 b.m. King's Theatre (IRE) – Kimpour (FR) (Hawker's News (IRE)) [2017/18 h92: h19.2d h20.5v h20.5v* Mar 12] modest handicap hurdler: won mares event at Plumpton in March: stays 2¾m: acts on heavy going: wears hood/tongue tie: front runner. *Michael Roberts* — **h97**

SNOBBERY 5 b.g. Duke of Marmalade (IRE) – Boast (Most Welcome) [2017/18 h16.2v⁵ h20g⁵ h15.7d h23.3v^{pu} Dec 31] fairly useful on Flat, stays 1½m: poor form over hurdles: tried in tongue tie. *Nigel Twiston-Davies* — **h83**

SNOOKERED (IRE) 4 b.g. Born To Sea (IRE) – Secret Quest (Pivotal) [2017/18 h16.7s³ Nov 15] fair on Flat, stays 1½m: 4/1, third in juvenile maiden at Bangor (24 lengths behind Born Legend) on hurdling debut: should do better. *Brian Ellison* — **h62 p**

SNOUGAR (IRE) 5 b.g. Arakan (USA) – Thorbella (Deploy) [2017/18 b16.7s h16v³ h16v* h18.9s⁴ h16.4v^F Apr 15] half-brother to several winners on Flat, including 7f/1m winner Goodison Glory (by Tout Seul): dam French maiden (stayed 1¼m): last in bumper: fair form over hurdles: won maiden at Ayr in March: usually races prominently. *Donald McCain* — **h109 b—**

SNOWBALL (IRE) 11 gr.g. Alderbrook – Rosafi (IRE) (Roselier (FR)) [2017/18 c76, h75: c24.5g⁴ c25.5d⁴ c26.7v^pu c26v c24.5v⁴ Feb 1] rather leggy gelding: winning hurdler: poor handicap chaser: stays 25f: acts on heavy going. *David Arbuthnot* — **c75 h—**

SNOW CASTLE (IRE) 6 b.g. Oscar (IRE) – Scartara (FR) (Linamix (FR)) [2017/18 h95, b79: h20g⁴ h21.6g⁴ h18.5m^pu Aug 29] fair form over hurdles: in headgear last 3 starts: usually races close up: temperament under suspicion. *Evan Williams* — **h106**

SNOWED IN (IRE) 9 gr.g. Dark Angel (IRE) – Spinning Gold (Spinning World (USA)) [2017/18 c—, h94: h17.2d h17.2g³ h17.2s⁴ h17.2d² h18.1g³ h19.3v h20.1v^pu h15.7s* h15.7s⁵ h15.7s⁴ h17v h16v⁶ Mar 20] modest handicap hurdler: won at Catterick in January: twice-raced chaser: stays 21f: acts on good to firm and heavy going: wears cheekpieces. *Barbara Butterworth* — **c— h89**

SNOW FALCON (IRE) 8 b.g. Presenting – Flocon de Neige (IRE) (Kahyasi) [2017/18 h153: c19v² c20s³ c21d* c21s⁵ c29v^ur c25s^pu Apr 13] sturdy gelding: smart hurdler: similar form over fences: won maiden at Leopardstown (by 28 lengths from Wishmoor) in December: third in Drinmore Novices' Chase at Fairyhouse (6 lengths behind Death Duty) earlier in month: stays 25f: acts on heavy going: has worn headgear. *Noel Meade, Ireland* — **c149 + h—**

SNOW RESCUE (IRE) 6 gr.g. Stowaway – Annilogs Palm (IRE) (Great Palm (USA)) [2017/18 h67, b58: h20g c15.7g⁵ Oct 26] modest maiden hurdler: well held in novice handicap on chasing debut: in tongue tie last 2 starts. *Tom Gretton* — **c— h—**

SNOWY OSCAR (IRE) 5 b.g. Oscar (IRE) – Reedsbuck (FR) (Cyborg (FR)) [2017/18 b17.7d h16.3v⁶ h17.7v^F h15.9d⁴ h15.9v Apr 1] smallish, plain gelding: fifth foal: dam, unraced, out of half-sister to top-class chaser up to 25f Cyfor Malta: eighth in bumper at Plumpton: modest form over hurdles: tried in hood/tongue tie. *Nick Gifford* — **h94 b63**

SNUFF BOX (IRE) 7 b.g. Witness Box (USA) – Dara Supreme (IRE) (Darazari (IRE)) [2017/18 h26.8v h19.5v² h19.5s^F h19.8v* Apr 9] £9,000 5-y-o: first foal: dam winning pointer: point winner: tailed off in bumper: fair form over hurdles: won maiden at Wincanton in April. *Venetia Williams* — **h108 b—**

SOBRE TRESOR (FR) 12 b.g. Grand Tresor (FR) – Gaie Anna (FR) (Art Bleu) [2017/18 c24.5v³ Mar 15] multiple point winner: maiden hurdler: fair hunter chaser, well below form sole outing in 2017/18: stays 3¼m: best form on good going or softer. *Miss Chloe Newman* — **c75 h—**

SO CELEBRE (GER) 5 ch.g. Peintre Celebre (USA) – Saldennahe (GER) (Next Desert (IRE)) [2017/18 h125: h15.8g⁴ Nov 14] good-topped gelding: fairly useful hurdler: will prove best at 2m: acts on soft and good to firm going: in cheekpieces sole outing in 2017/18. *Ian Williams* — **h116**

SOCKSY (IRE) 7 ch.m. Flemensfirth (USA) – Bachello (IRE) (Bach (IRE)) [2017/18 h115, b—: c20.5s* c23.6v³ c24s⁴ c22.2v² c20.8g Apr 19] fairly useful hurdler: similar form over fences: won novice handicap at Ayr in October: stays 3m: best form on soft/heavy going: tried in blinkers: wears tongue tie: races prominently. *Fergal O'Brien* — **c121 h—**

SODOI 5 b.m. Millkom – Island Path (IRE) (Jupiter Island) [2017/18 b16.2d b16.4d Mar 16] sixth foal: sister to bumper winner/fair hurdler Ten Trees (17f-21f winner) and half-sister to bumper winner/fairly useful hurdler Turbo Island (2m winner, by Turbo Speed): dam unraced half-sister to fairly useful hurdler/fair chaser (stayed 25f) Hand Woven: in tongue tie, well beaten in bumpers. *Susan Corbett* — **b—**

SO HOITY TOITY 4 ch.f. Harbour Watch (IRE) – Dignify (IRE) (Rainbow Quest (USA)) [2017/18 h15.5d⁶ h16.3s^pu Dec 20] sparely-made filly: fair maiden on Flat, stays 1m: no form over hurdles: wears hood. *Robin Mathew* — **h—**

SOIESAUVAGE (FR) 7 b.m. Lauro (GER) – Taffetas (FR) (Nikos) [2017/18 h81: h16g⁶ h16.8g h15.8d* h20.1s² h16v⁵ h16.2s⁵ h18.6s⁴ Dec 26] sturdy mare: modest handicap hurdler: won mares event at Uttoxeter in September: stays 2½m: acts on soft going: wears hood/tongue tie: usually races in rear. *Sophie Leech* — **h91**

SOJ

SOJOURN (IRE) 5 b.g. Getaway (GER) – Toscar (IRE) (Oscar (IRE)) [2017/18 b16.3d⁴ Nov 9] second foal: dam unraced half-sister to fairly useful hurdler/smart chaser (stayed 25f) Exmoor Ranger: in tongue tie, 33/1, fourth in bumper at Newbury (13½ lengths behind Tidal Flow). *Anthony Honeyball* **b85**

SOLAR IMPULSE (FR) 8 b.g. Westerner – Moon Glow (FR) (Solar One (FR)) [2017/18 c124, h–: c19m⁴ c15.8g⁶ c15.7g² c16g² c16d⁵ c15.8s² c15.8s⁴ Feb 3] good-topped gelding: has had breathing operation: winning hurdler: fairly useful handicap chaser: best around 2m: acts on good to firm and heavy going: has worn headgear, including last 3 starts: has worn tongue tie, including in 2017/18: often races freely: unreliable. *Christopher Kellett* **c121 §** **h–**

SOLATENTIF (FR) 8 b.g. Solon (GER) – Indian Mist (FR) (River Mist (USA)) [2017/18 c134, h129: c20s² c16.5g³ h26.5d² h26.5g⁴ h23.9g h25.3s⁶ h16.5s⁶ Apr 14] sturdy gelding: fairly useful handicap hurdler/maiden chaser: stays 3¼m: acts on soft and good to firm going: often in headgear in 2017/18: wears tongue tie: temperamental. *Colin Tizzard* **c124 §** **h126 §**

SOLDIER BOY (IRE) 6 b.g. Millenary – Oscar Mary (IRE) (Oscar (IRE)) [2017/18 b80: h16.3g^pu h15.7g h16v Nov 22] big gelding: modest form in bumpers: no form over hurdles. *Barry Brennan* **h–**

SOLDIER OF LOVE 5 b.g. Yeats (IRE) – Monsignorita (IRE) (Classic Cliche (IRE)) [2017/18 b15.7g² b16s Mar 17] good-topped gelding: third foal: closely related to a winning pointer by Kayf Tara and half-brother to bumper winner Mercy Mercy Me (by Shirocco): dam (h77), ungenuine maiden hurdler (stayed 2½m), out of sister to Champion Bumper winner/very smart hurdler (stayed 21f) Monsignor: fairly useful form in bumpers: better effort when second at Ascot on debut for Mark Pitman. *Fergal O'Brien* **b95**

SOLEGLAD (IRE) 6 b.g. Scorpion (IRE) – Tilaiya (IRE) (Fantastic Light (USA)) [2017/18 b16.3g* b16.7g² b17g⁴ h16s h18.9v h16.1s⁵ h20s Apr 19] €7,500 3-y-o: first foal: dam unraced half-sister to fairly useful hurdler (stayed 2½m) Tilabay: fairly useful form in bumpers: won conditionals/amateur event at Stratford in July: modest form over hurdles. *Gavin Patrick Cromwell, Ireland* **h92** **b104**

SOLID JUSTICE (IRE) 7 b.g. Rock of Gibraltar (IRE) – Burnin' Memories (USA) (Lit de Justice (USA)) [2017/18 h17.7m⁶ Sep 24] modest on Flat, stays 13.5f: well beaten in novice on hurdling debut. *Mark Pattinson* **h–**

SOLID STRIKE 10 b.g. Sir Harry Lewis (USA) – Solid Land (FR) (Solid Illusion (USA)) [2017/18 c100: c20.3v⁵ c19.2s³ c22.9s⁶ c26.2v³ Apr 17] multiple point winner: fair form in chases: stays 3¼m: acts on heavy going. *Paul Collins* **c107**

SOLIGHOSTER (FR) 6 ch.g. Loup Solitaire (USA) – Miss Martine (FR) (Waki River (FR)) [2017/18 h126, b101: c23.8v* c23.9d³ c22.4v^pu c24s* c24v⁵ c20d^F Apr 28] well-made gelding: fairly useful hurdler: useful form over fences: won novices at Ffos Las in November and Warwick in February: stays 3m: best form on soft/heavy going. *Neil Mulholland* **c135** **h–**

SOLOMN GRUNDY (IRE) 8 b.g. Westerner – Marika's King (IRE) (King's Ride) [2017/18 h130: c23g^pu c20d⁶ c23.4v² c24.2v² h23.1v² h21s h23.9v* Apr 15] lengthy gelding: useful handicap hurdler: won at Ffos Las (by 2½ lengths from Laugharne) in April: fairly useful form over fences: stays 3m: acts on heavy going: often races towards rear/travels strongly. *Neil Mulholland* **c126** **h134**

SOLOMON GREY (FR) 6 gr.g. Sulamani (IRE) – Sardagna (FR) (Medaaly) [2017/18 b96: b17.7g² h16.7s² h15.9d* h16d³ h16.7s* Feb 18] fairly useful form in bumpers: useful form over hurdles: won novice at Plumpton (by 11 lengths from Knocknanuss) in December and handicap at Market Rasen (by neck from Oxford Blu) in February: often travels strongly. *Dan Skelton* **h133** **b101**

SO LONELY (IRE) 4 b.f. So You Think (NZ) – Via Aurelia (IRE) (Antonius Pius (USA)) [2017/18 b14s⁶ b12.6s² b12.4s² b16v Apr 1] smallish filly: third foal: half-sister to 1¼m-1½m winner Street Art (by Excellent Art): dam maiden on Flat (stayed 1m): fair form in bumpers: left John Butler after third start: tried in hood. *Charles O'Brien, Ireland* **b87**

SOLO SAXOPHONE (IRE) 4 b.g. Frankel – Society Hostess (USA) (Seeking The Gold (USA)) [2017/18 h15.7d* h16v* h16.8v³ h16.4s⁶ Mar 14] rather leggy gelding: fairly useful maiden on Flat, stays 12.5f: fair form over hurdles: won juveniles at Catterick in December and Wetherby in January: will be suited by further than 2m: tried in blinkers: wears tongue tie. *Dan Skelton* **h113**

SOM

SOLSTALLA 6 b.m. Halling (USA) – Solstice (Dubawi (IRE)) [2017/18 h107: h16g⁴ h16g³ h16g² h16g² h19.2m⁴ h16g³ h16g⁵ h16g⁴ Oct 5] fair handicap hurdler: stays 2¼m: acts on good to firm and good to soft going: tried in cheekpieces. *David Weston* **h105**

SOLSTICE SON 9 b.g. Haafhd – Karasta (IRE) (Lake Coniston (IRE)) [2017/18 c113, h–: c24d² c25d^pu c24d Dec 16] sturdy gelding: winning hurdler: fairly useful handicap chaser: stays 27f: acts on soft going: wears blinkers/tongue tie: front runner/races prominently. *Anthony Honeyball* **c129 h–**

SOLSTICE STAR 8 b.g. Kayf Tara – Clover Green (IRE) (Presenting) [2017/18 c–, h131: c20d³ c20d² c23.5s⁴ h15.8v⁵ c20.8v⁶ h19.3s⁶ h16.3s⁴ Mar 23] well-made gelding: has had breathing operation: useful hurdler, below form in 2017/18: fairly useful maiden chaser: stays 2½m: acts on heavy going: often in headgear: wears tongue tie: often races prominently. *Martin Keighley* **c126 h100**

SOLSTICE TWILIGHT 6 b.m. Milan – Twilight Eclipse (IRE) (Presenting) [2017/18 b16.3d⁴ b15.8g⁶ b15.3s⁴ h19.2v h21.4v h19s h20.5v³ h23.1d³ Apr 24] £10,000 3-y-o: first foal: dam unraced half-sister to useful hurdler/chaser (17f-23f winner) Tagrita out of half-sister to top-class staying chaser Grey Abbey: modest form in bumpers: similar form over hurdles: left Hugo Froud after second start. *Anthony Honeyball* **h89 b78**

SOLWAY BERRY 7 b.m. Overbury (IRE) – Solway Rose (Minster Son) [2017/18 b16.2s³ b16.2d⁶ Sep 11] poor form in bumpers: will be suited by further than 2m. *Lisa Harrison* **b74**

SOLWAY DANDY 11 b.g. Danroad (AUS) – Solway Rose (Minster Son) [2017/18 h111+: h23.9g² h20.6g³ h20.2s³ h23.3d⁶ h24.7d h25.8g⁴ Nov 11] sturdy gelding: fair handicap hurdler: stays 3m: acts on heavy going: races towards rear. *Lisa Harrison* **h114**

SOLWAY LARK 7 b.g. Beat All (USA) – Solway Larkin (IRE) (Supreme Leader) [2017/18 b16.2d⁶ Aug 2] little impression in bumpers nearly 2 years apart. *Lisa Harrison* **b–**

SOLWAY LIZZIE 6 ch.m. Tobougg (IRE) – Solway Rose (Minster Son) [2017/18 b16.2m⁵ Jul 16] seventh foal: half-sister to 3 winners, including fairly useful hurdler Solway Dandy (2½m winner, by Danroad), stays 3m: dam (c103/h93) 3m/3¼m hurdle/chase winner: fifth of 7 in bumper at Perth. *Lisa Harrison* **b–**

SOLWAY PALM 8 gr.g. Great Palm (USA) – Solway Donal (IRE) (Celio Rufo) [2017/18 h20.2m³ h23.9d³ h23.3d Aug 21] poor form over hurdles: best effort when third in novice at Perth in August. *Lisa Harrison* **h83**

SOLWAY PRINCE 9 ch.g. Double Trigger (IRE) – Solway Rose (Minster Son) [2017/18 h–: h23.9m h23.9m⁴ h23.9d^pu Aug 2] modest handicap hurdler: won at Perth in July: stays 3m: acts on soft and good to firm going: has worn cheekpieces, including last 2 starts. *Lisa Harrison* **h88**

SOLWAY SUNNY 6 b.m. Double Trigger (IRE) – Solway Sunset (Primitive Rising (USA)) [2017/18 b15.8g² Jul 19] second foal: dam (c83/h106) 2½m-3¼m hurdle/chase winner: 6/1, second in bumper at Uttoxeter (18 lengths behind Arizona Bound): will stay at least 2½m. *Lisa Harrison* **b66**

SOLWAY TRIGGER 9 b.g. Double Trigger (IRE) – Double Flight (Mtoto) [2017/18 h59: h23.9g c20.1g c23.8g² c24g² h23.9d c15.6v⁶ c22.5d^pu Oct 8] poor maiden hurdler: similar form over fences. *Lisa Harrison* **c66 h–**

SOMCHINE 10 b.g. Volochine (IRE) – Seem of Gold (Gold Dust) [2017/18 c136, h–: c16.8g c15.7v^pu c16.2s⁵ c15.5s⁵ c16v³ c20.2v* Mar 28] lengthy gelding: maiden hurdler: fairly useful handicap chaser: won at Wincanton in March: stays 21f, effective at shorter: acts on heavy going: has worn hood, including in 2017/18: tried in tongue tie: usually races towards rear. *Seamus Mullins* **c126 h–**

SOME AMBITION (IRE) 5 b.g. Westerner – Heath Heaven (Alflora (IRE)) [2017/18 b15.7g h20.5s⁴ h19s h15.7s⁵ Feb 8] £22,000 4-y-o: third foal: dam, lightly raced in points, half-sister to useful hurdler (stays 2½m) That's A Wrap out of half-sister to dam of Cheltenham Gold Cup winner Long Run: placed in point: faded in maiden bumper: modest form over hurdles: in tongue tie last 3 starts. *Charlie Longsdon* **h99 b–**

SOME ARE LUCKY (IRE) 7 b.g. Gold Well – Foreign Estates (IRE) (Be My Native (USA)) [2017/18 c131, h123: c22.6s² c25d c26d^pu c22.7v* c20.2v³ c23.8s² c20.1s⁵ Apr 26] well-made gelding: winning hurdler: fairly useful handicap chaser: won 3-runner novice event at Leicester in January: stays 23f: acts on heavy going: in cheekpieces last 5 starts: front runner/races prominently. *Tom George* **c122 h–**

SOM

SOME BOY MCCOY (FR) 4 b.g. Enrique – Khaylama (IRE) (Dr Devious (IRE)) [2017/18 b16d Apr 26] useful-looking gelding: 33/1, shaped as if needed experience when eleventh in bumper at Warwick (14¾ lengths behind Emitom). *Olly Murphy* — b–

SOME BUCKLE (IRE) 9 b.g. Milan – Miss Moppit (IRE) (Torus) [2017/18 c143, h–: c21s* Apr 23] useful-looking gelding: winning hurdler: useful handicap chaser: won at Newton Abbot after year off: stays 2¾m, effective at shorter: acts on soft going: wears tongue tie. *Tom George* — c142 h–

SOME DAY SOON (IRE) 5 b.g. Robin des Champs (FR) – Creative Approach (IRE) (Toulon) [2017/18 b16s³ b16.1v² b16.6v b15.8d² Mar 26] €29,000 3-y-o: half-brother to several winners, including fair hurdler/fairly useful chaser Swingbridge (2¾m-25f winner, by Milan): dam unraced half-sister to smart hurdler/chaser (stayed 3m) Adamant Approach: fairly useful form in bumpers: second in conditionals/amateur event at Huntingdon in March: left Patrick J. Flynn after third start. *Jamie Snowden* — b96

SOME FINISH (IRE) 9 b.g. Kayf Tara – Kylie Kaprice (GER) (Big Shuffle (USA)) [2017/18 c94§, h–§: c19.2d⁵ c23.8g⁵ c21.7g⁴ c19.8⁵ c21.7v^pu c20.2v⁴ c21.7v³ Apr 27] maiden hurdler: poor handicap chaser: won at Towcester in November: stays 3m: acts on good to firm and heavy going: often in headgear: temperamental. *Robin Dickin* — c82 § h– §

SOME INVITATION (IRE) 7 b.g. Presenting – Bolly (IRE) (Jolly Jake (NZ)) [2017/18 h132p: c24.2s* c24d^pu c26g⁵ Apr 18] well-made gelding: useful hurdler: similar form over fences: won novice at Wetherby in November: stays 3¼m: acts on soft going: tried in cheekpieces: in tongue tie last 5 starts. *Dan Skelton* — c134 h–

SOME KINDA LAMA (IRE) 7 gr.g. Daylami (IRE) – Last Sunrise (IRE) (Shahannde) [2017/18 h128: c23d⁵ c25d h24d h26.1s Feb 4] fairly useful hurdler at best: no form in 2017/18, including over fences: in cheekpieces last 3 starts: in tongue tie last 5. *Charlie Mann* — c– h–

SOME MAN (IRE) 5 b.g. Beat Hollow – Miss Denman (IRE) (Presenting) [2017/18 h16s⁴ h16.8s⁵ Dec 15] €36,000 3-y-o, £165,000 4-y-o: good-topped gelding: seventh foal: half-brother to 3 winners, including bumper winner/smart hurdler Polly Peachum (2m-2¾m winner, by Shantou) and fairly useful hurdler Le Dauphin (21f winner, by Robin des Champs): dam unraced sister to Cheltenham Gold Cup winner Denman: Irish point winner: fair form over hurdles: remains with potential. *Paul Nicholls* — h109 p

SOME NECK (FR) 7 gr.g. Yeats (IRE) – Maternelle (FR) (Machiavellian (USA)) [2017/18 c20v* c24v⁴ c24.5s^ur Apr 28] €100,000 3-y-o: fifth foal: dam once-raced half-sister to Irish St Leger winner Jukebox Jury: winning hurdler: useful form in chases: won maiden at Gowran in February: stays 2¾m: best form on heavy going. *W. P. Mullins, Ireland* — c144 h–

SOME PLAN (IRE) 10 b.g. Winged Love (IRE) – Lough Hyne (Classic Cliche (IRE)) [2017/18 c143, h–: c19.5s⁴ c15.9g c16.5s³ c17s^F c16.3v^F Mar 16] good-topped gelding: winning hurdler: useful handicap chaser: third at Fairyhouse (6¼ lengths behind Nearly Nama'd) in December: raced mainly around 2m: acted on soft going: tried in hood: wore tongue tie: front runner/raced prominently: dead. *Henry de Bromhead, Ireland* — c143 h–

SOME REIGN (IRE) 7 b.g. Kayf Tara – Bridge Love (FR) (Astarabad (USA)) [2017/18 b97: h16.2d² h16.2g* h19.4g^rr h16s³ h16.2s³ Jan 14] third in Irish point: bumper winner: fairly useful form over hurdles: won maiden at Kelso in October: will stay further than 2m: acts on good to soft going: refused to race on third outing. *Rose Dobbin* — h124

SOMERSET JEM 9 b.g. Sir Harry Lewis (USA) – Monger Lane (Karinga Bay) [2017/18 c92, h68: h19.8s^pu h19s³ h23.1v⁴ h23.9v² h25v⁶ Feb 12] modest handicap chaser: twice-raced chaser: stays 3m: best form on soft/heavy going. *Kevin Bishop* — c– h93

SOMETHING BREWING (FR) 4 gr.g. Clodovil (IRE) – Talwin (IRE) (Alhaarth (IRE)) [2017/18 h16.2d* h16d⁴ h16s^pu ab16.3g* Mar 3] dam half-sister to useful hurdler/fair chaser (stayed 2¼m) Lethal Weapon: fair on Flat, stays 12.5f: fair form over hurdles: won juvenile at Hexham in August: also successful in jumpers bumper at Newcastle final outing. *Iain Jardine* — h102

SOMEWHERE TO BE (IRE) 6 ch.g. Golan (IRE) – Somethinaboutmolly (IRE) (Choisir (AUS)) [2017/18 h108, b87: h15.8d h19.2g⁴ c20d* c21.7s⁶ c19.2v* c23.4s^pu Mar 23] workmanlike gelding: maiden hurdler: fairly useful form over fences: won novice handicaps at Lingfield in November and Catterick in January: stays 2½m: acts on heavy going: in headgear last 5 starts: usually races prominently. *Martin Keighley* — c116 h67

752

SOMMERVIEU (FR) 4 gr.g. Rajsaman (FR) – Simple Solution (USA) (Dynaformer (USA)) [2017/18 h16.4s h14.9d² h17.4s⁵ h17.4d² h16.9s³ h16.6d^pu h15.8v⁴ h19.4s Jan 27] fair maiden on Flat, stays 9.5f: fair maiden hurdler: left Francois-Marie Cottin after fifth start: unproven beyond 17f: acts on soft going: usually wears blinkers. *Charlie Longsdon*   **h113**

SONG LIGHT 8 b.g. Echo of Light – Blue Lullaby (IRE) (Fasliyev (USA)) [2017/18 h130: h15.7m^rr h15.7g h19.5s^rr Nov 28] useful handicap hurdler at best: refused/virtually refused to race all 3 outings in 2017/18: in headgear last 4 starts: one to avoid. *Seamus Mullins*   **h §§**

SONG SAA 8 b.m. Midnight Legend – Mystere (IRE) (Montelimar (USA)) [2017/18 c124, h–: c20g² c20s² c20.8s³ c20.5s² c23.8s^pu Apr 27] sturdy mare: winning hurdler: fairly useful handicap chaser: second in listed mares event at Doncaster (10 lengths behind Rene's Girl) in January: stays 23f: acts on heavy going: wears tongue tie. *Tom George*   **c123 h–**

SONIC (IRE) 5 b.g. Vinnie Roe (IRE) – Bella's Bury (Overbury (IRE)) [2017/18 b15.8g³ b15.6g² h19.4g⁴ h19.3s⁴ Jan 11] €6,000 3-y-o, £24,000 4-y-o: third foal: dam showed little in bumpers/over hurdles: runner-up on second of 2 starts in Irish points: fair form in bumpers: similar form over hurdles: in control when fell 2 out in novice won by Ballycrystal Court at Musselburgh in December. *Donald McCain*   **h112 b92**

SONIC WIND (IRE) 4 ch.f. Windsor Knot (IRE) – Tarziyma (IRE) (Kalanisi (IRE)) [2017/18 h17.3s⁶ h16g⁵ h15.8m⁵ h16v Nov 25] fair maiden on Flat, stays 1¼m: poor form over hurdles: tried in cheekpieces. *Sabrina J. Harty, Ireland*   **h83**

SONNEOFPRESENTING (IRE) 8 b.g. Presenting – Sonne Cinq (IRE) (Old Vic) [2017/18 c112, h92: c21.1d* c20g* c23.8g³ c23g* c25.5g² c25g⁶ c23.8d^pu Apr 9] lengthy gelding: winning hurdler: useful handicap chaser: won at Fontwell in June, and Worcester in July and August: stays 25f: acts on soft going: usually leads. *Kim Bailey*   **c132 h–**

SON OF FEYAN (IRE) 7 ch.g. Nayef (USA) – Miss Penton (Primo Dominie) [2017/18 h80: h23.9g h20.2g h23.8g⁵ h25.8s Jan 14] maiden hurdler, no form in 2017/18: has worn tongue tie, including in 2017/18. *Lucy Normile*   **h–**

SONOFTHEKING (IRE) 10 b.g. King's Theatre (IRE) – Nikadora (FR) (Nikos) [2017/18 c106, h–: c23.6d c24.2s* c25.2s² c21.6d⁴ c25.1v⁴ Mar 28] useful-looking gelding: maiden hurdler: fair handicap chaser: won at Exeter in November: stays 25f: acts on good to firm and heavy going: has worn cheekpieces, including in 2017/18: wears tongue tie. *Nicky Martin*   **c106 h–**

SOPHIE OLIVIA (IRE) 6 gr.m. Ask – Gill's Honey (IRE) (Celio Rufo) [2017/18 h97, b79: h16.2d* h16.2v² h19.9g Nov 2] fair form over hurdles: won novice at Hexham in September: should stay 2½m+: acts on heavy going: usually leads. *Martin Todhunter*   **h108**

SORT IT OUT (IRE) 9 b.g. Milan – Snowbelle (IRE) (Flemensfirth (USA)) [2017/18 c16.2d⁶ c17v⁵ c17v c16v h24v³ h24s Mar 15] sturdy gelding: useful handicap hurdler: third at Punchestown (3½ lengths behind Kilfenora) in February: little impact over fences: stays 2½m: acts on soft going: tried in hood. *Edward P. Harty, Ireland*   **c– h136**

SORY 11 b.g. Sakhee (USA) – Rule Britannia (Night Shift (USA)) [2017/18 h19.9s h19.9s² h24.3v³ h19.3v⁴ h19.9v Mar 23] poor maiden hurdler: stays 3m: acts on heavy going. *Tina Jackson*   **h71**

SO SATISFIED 7 b.g. Aqlaam – Pirouetting (Pivotal) [2017/18 c110, h–: c20.1g⁵ c20.1g c23g⁶ c23.8s² c25.2v* c23.8d⁴ c21.6v Apr 16] winning hurdler: fair handicap chaser: won at Catterick in January: stays 25f: acts on heavy going: wears cheekpieces: often races in rear. *Iain Jardine*   **c103 h–**

SOUL EMOTION (FR) 5 b.g. Martaline – Second Emotion (FR) (Medaaly) [2017/18 c17.9v^pu c18.9s^F h19.8s* h19.8s* Apr 28] good second foal: half-brother to useful hurdler/chaser Slowmotion (2m-2½m winner, by Soldier of Fortune): dam French 17f hurdle/chase winner: useful form over hurdles: won handicaps at Sandown in March and April (by 4 lengths from Wolf of Windlesham): failed to complete both starts over fences: left Guillaume Macaire after second start: stays 2½m: acts on soft going: likely to progress further. *Nicky Henderson*   **c– h146 p**

SOUL MAN 5 ch.g. Sulamani (IRE) – Present Your Case (IRE) (Presenting) [2017/18 b15.7d h19.6d⁶ Nov 25] well held in bumper/novice hurdle: dead. *Lucy Wadham*   **h– b–**

SOULSAVER 6 ch.g. Recharge (IRE) – Lapina (IRE) (Fath (USA)) [2017/18 h88: h21.6g³ h19.2d* h19g² h15.9v³ h25d⁶ h21.7g* Apr 20] fair handicap hurdler: won at Fontwell in November and April: stays 2¾m: acts on good to soft going: has worn tongue tie, including last 5 starts: often travels strongly. *Anthony Honeyball*   **h101**

SOU

SOUNDS OF ITALY (IRE) 9 b.g. Milan – Sound Hill (FR) (Green Tune (USA)) [2017/18 c–: h19.5d h16.7s h16v h24.1v⁴ h20v³ c25.7v² c23.8v³ Apr 15] point winner: poor form over hurdles/fences: stays 3m: acts on heavy going: in headgear last 4 starts. *Michael Scudamore* — c70 h70

SOUND THE BUGLE 8 b.g. Overbury (IRE) – Fusion of Tunes (Mr Confusion (IRE)) [2017/18 h60: c19.8g^pu c22.5d^pu Jun 7] maiden hurdler: no form over fences: tried in hood. *Anthony Day* — c– h–

SOUPY SOUPS (IRE) 7 ch.g. Stowaway – Near Dunleer (IRE) (Soviet Lad (USA)) [2017/18 h123: c23.6g⁶ c23.8d c21.4s^F Dec 26] good-topped gelding: Irish point winner: fairly useful hurdler: similar form in chases: yet to be asked for effort when fell 2 out in novice handicap won by Kimberlite Candy at Market Rasen: stays 3m: acts on good to firm and good to soft going. *Neil Mulholland* — c119 h–

SOURIYAN (FR) 7 b.g. Alhaarth (IRE) – Serasana (Red Ransom (USA)) [2017/18 c–, h102: h23.3g* h22s* h19.5d h23.6v⁴ c23.6v² c23.6v⁵ h23.1s^F h23.8d^pu Apr 24] rather leggy gelding: fairly useful handicap hurdler: won at Uttoxeter in September and Stratford in October: fairly useful maiden chaser: stays 3m: acts on heavy going: wears headgear: tried in tongue tie. *Peter Bowen* — c123 h126

SOUTHFIELD ROYALE 8 b.g. Presenting – Chamoss Royale (FR) (Garde Royale) [2017/18 c122, h–: c25.1s^pu c26g^pu h22.8v² h22.8v⁴ h24.4d⁶ h22.8v Mar 31] good sort: fairly useful handicap hurdler nowadays: useful chaser at best, no form over fences in 2017/18: stays 4m: acts on heavy going: has worn headgear: tried in tongue tie: races prominently. *Neil Mulholland* — c– h122

SOUTHFIELD STONE 5 gr.g. Fair Mix (IRE) – Laureldean Belle (IRE) (Supreme Leader) [2017/18 b16.8s³ Feb 23] fourth foal: dam (b89), 2½m bumper winner, out of half-sister to high-class staying chaser Chatam: 6/1, third in bumper at Exeter (8¼ lengths behind Unwin Vc). *Paul Nicholls* — b88

SOUTHFIELD THEATRE (IRE) 10 b.g. King's Theatre (IRE) – Chamoss Royale (FR) (Garde Royale) [2017/18 c150, h–: c25.1s⁴ c28.8d c26s³ c26.3s^pu c32.8s^pu c24m³ Apr 26] good-topped gelding: winning hurdler: useful handicap chaser nowadays: fourth in Badger Ales Trophy Handicap Chase at Wincanton (11¾ lengths behind Present Man) in November: stays 25f: acts on soft going: wears headgear: has worn tongue tie, including in 2017/18: temperamental. *Paul Nicholls* — c139 § h–

SOUTHFIELD TORR 5 gr.g. Fair Mix (IRE) – Chamoss Royale (FR) (Garde Royale) [2017/18 b17.7d³ b16.5m⁴ Apr 25] fifth foal: half-brother to smart hurdler/chaser Southfield Theatre (19f-23f winner, by King's Theatre) and useful hurdlers/chasers Southfield Vic (2½m-3¼m winner, by Old Vic) and Southfield Royale (2½m-3m winner, by Presenting): dam (c134/h134) 17f-25f hurdle/chase winner: fair form in bumpers. *Paul Nicholls* — b94

SOUTHFIELD VIC (IRE) 9 ch.g. Old Vic – Chamoss Royale (FR) (Garde Royale) [2017/18 c145, h132: c25.8g* c26.1m c25g Oct 28] leggy gelding: winning hurdler: useful handicap chaser: won at Newton Abbot by 24 lengths from Wadswick Court) in May: stays 3¼m: acts on soft and good to firm going: wears headgear: often races prominently. *Paul Nicholls* — c143 h–

SOUTHPORT 6 b.g. Robin des Pres (FR) – First Katoune (FR) (Poliglote) [2017/18 h114: h23.1g⁶ c19.9g^pu c24s^pu Apr 9] fair hurdler at best: no form in 2017/18, including in chases. *Nigel Twiston-Davies* — c– h–

SOUTHSEA ISLAND (IRE) 10 b.g. Heron Island (IRE) – Southsea Lady (IRE) (Kemal (FR)) [2017/18 h16.2v h17s h24.3v⁵ Nov 15] maiden hurdler, little impact after long absence in 2017/18: in hood last 5 starts. *Andrew Hamilton* — h80

SOVINNIE (IRE) 9 ch.g. Vinnie Roe (IRE) – Sohapara (Arapahos (FR)) [2017/18 h94?: h23.1g h25.5v⁴ Mar 10] maiden hurdler, no form in 2017/18: has worn tongue tie, including last 5 starts (when also in cheekpieces). *Jane Mathias* — h–

SO YOU WIN AGAIN (IRE) 4 b.g. Requinto (IRE) – Vintage Allure (IRE) (Barathea (IRE)) [2017/18 b14d Nov 5] tailed off in junior bumper. *Tim Easterby* — b–

SPACE CADET (IRE) 8 b.g. Flemensfirth (USA) – Shuil A Hocht (IRE) (Mohaajir (USA)) [2017/18 c132, h–: c24v⁶ c24.5d c25v³ c28.7v⁴ c23v² h22v^pu c30s^pu Apr 28] maiden hurdler: useful handicap chaser: second in Leinster National Handicap Chase at Gowran (3¾ lengths behind Pairofbrowneyes) in March: stays 25f: acts on heavy going: tried in cheekpieces. *Gordon Elliott, Ireland* — c136 h–

754

SPACE ODDITY (FR) 7 b.g. Al Namix (FR) – Schoune (FR) (Majorien) [2017/18 h127: c16d* c16.3g⁴ c18.8g² c19.9g c16.1s² c17.8d^ur c16d⁵ c16.2g⁴ Apr 26] compact gelding: winning hurdler: useful chaser: won maiden at Uttoxeter in May: second in novice handicap at Ascot (3¾ lengths behind Benatar) in November: stays 19f: acts on good to firm and heavy going: wears hood: front runner/races prominently. *Harry Fry* **c136** **h–**

SPACE SHIP 8 ch.g. Galileo (IRE) – Angara (Alzao (USA)) [2017/18 h121: c17.3g^pu h17.2g^F Jun 30] fairly useful hurdler: pulled up in maiden on chasing debut: unproven beyond 2m: acts on heavy going: usually wears tongue tie: has rejoined Robert Hennessy, Ireland. *James Moffatt* **c–** **h–**

SPADER (IRE) 5 b.g. Jeremy (USA) – Poulkovo (IRE) (Sadler's Wells (USA)) [2017/18 h104p: h16g² h16.2g⁴ h16s h15.8s h16v^pu h16.7s h15.7g Apr 20] compact gelding: modest maiden hurdler: stays 19f: acts on good to soft going: wears tongue tie: often races towards rear. *Dan Skelton* **h94**

SPANISH ARCH (IRE) 11 b.g. Westerner – Piepowder (In The Wings) [2017/18 c24.2v⁴ c24.2s Mar 9] compact gelding: point winner: winning hurdler: fair chaser: stays 3m: acts on heavy going: has worn headgear: has worn tongue tie, including in 2017/18: temperamental. *Mrs V. Sollitt* **c109 §** **h–**

SPANISH FLEET 10 b.g. Cadeaux Genereux – Santisima Trinidad (IRE) (Definite Article) [2017/18 c122, h–: c20d c20.1v c20.5v⁴ Dec 22] winning hurdler: fairly useful maiden chaser, well below form in 2017/18: stays 2¾m: acts on heavy going: has worn headgear: often races in rear/lazily. *George Bewley* **c73** **h–**

SPANISH OPTIMIST (IRE) 12 b.g. Indian Danehill (IRE) – La Traviata (Spectrum (IRE)) [2017/18 c81§, h–: c25.5d^pu c21.1m^pu c23g c24s⁵ Oct 19] winning hurdler: fair chaser at best, little form since 2014/15: has worn visor, including last 2 starts: has worn tongue tie: one to leave alone. *Sarah Robinson* **c– §** **h–**

SPANISH QUEEN 5 b.m. Fantastic Spain (USA) – Smart Cassie (Allied Forces (USA)) [2017/18 h68: h16.8m² h21.6g^ur h21.6d^pu Jul 23] little form: tried in cheekpieces: temperamental. *Mark Gillard* **h– §**

SPARKLEANDSHINE (IRE) 5 b.g. Olden Times – Little Flower (IRE) (Talkin Man (CAN)) [2017/18 h15.8d* Mar 26] second foal: dam unraced: little impact in Irish points: 28/1, won maiden at Huntingdon (by 5 lengths from Passing Call) on hurdling debut: likely to improve. *Sam Thomas* **h113 p**

SPARKLING DAWN 6 gr.m. Sulamani (IRE) – Clotted Cream (USA) (Eagle Eyed (USA)) [2017/18 b92: b15.8s* b17s Apr 12] sturdy mare: fairly useful form in bumpers: won mares event at Huntingdon in February. *Johnny Farrelly* **b98**

SPARKLING ICE (IRE) 7 gr.m. Verglas (IRE) – Sand Crystal (IRE) (Singspiel (IRE)) [2017/18 h74: h24g⁵ May 16] poor maiden hurdler: stays 3m: best form on good going: tried in blinkers. *Laura Young* **h71**

SPARKLING RIVER (IRE) 8 gr.m. Indian River (FR) – Full Deck (IRE) (Roselier (FR)) [2017/18 h114: c23g c20s* c20.8s⁴ c22.5v* c24s³ c24.1s^pu Mar 24] angular mare: fair hurdler: fairly useful form over fences: won handicaps at Warwick in November and Uttoxeter in January: stays 3m: acts on heavy going: front runner: signs of temperament. *Henry Oliver* **c125** **h–**

SPARKY'S SPIRIT (IRE) 9 ch.g. Flemensfirth (USA) – Pretty In Pink (IRE) (Teamster) [2017/18 h19.5v h19s^pu h15.9v h15.3s c20.2v² c21s⁴ Apr 23] maiden pointer: no form over hurdles: poor form in chases: races prominently. *Colin Tizzard* **c81** **h–**

SPEAK EASY 5 b.g. Beneficial – For Bill (IRE) (Presenting) [2017/18 h16s* h20v⁵ h16s³ h24s² Apr 17] £40,000 3-y-o, £220,000 4-y-o: first foal: dam (c140/h141) 2m-2¾m hurdle/ chase winner: point winner: useful form over hurdles: won maiden at Navan in December: improved upped to 3m when second in novice handicap at Fairyhouse (3 lengths behind Agent Boru) in April. *Joseph Patrick O'Brien, Ireland* **h141 p**

SPECIAL ACCEPTANCE 5 b.g. Malinas (GER) – Doubly Guest (Barathea Guest) [2017/18 b13.7s² b16g⁴ Feb 24] £16,000 3-y-o: second foal: half-brother to bumper winner/fair hurdler Glanvilles Guest (21f winner, by Sulamani): dam (h123) unreliable 2m hurdle winner (stayed 19f): fairly useful form when in frame in bumpers. *Paul Webber* **b95**

SPECIAL CATCH (IRE) 11 b.g. Catcher In The Rye (IRE) – Top Quality (Simply Great (FR)) [2017/18 c142, h–: c16.5v⁶ c19.4s² c19.4v^pu c20.1v^pu Apr 14] winning hurdler: useful handicap chaser: second at Wetherby (9 lengths behind Caraline) in December: stays 2½m: acts on heavy going. *Ruth Jefferson* **c131** **h–**

SPE

SPECIALIST (IRE) 4 b.g. Mastercraftsman (IRE) – My Lass (Elmaamul (USA)) [2017/18 h16v⁶ h16v⁵ h16d³ Mar 29] fairly useful on Flat for Mark Johnston, stays 1½m: poor form over hurdles. *William Young Jnr* h80

SPECIAL PREP (IRE) 6 b.g. Brian Boru – Schindler's Dame (IRE) (Oscar Schindler (IRE)) [2017/18 b16.2m³ h20.2g⁴ h20.2g³ h19.9g⁴ h24d* Oct 3] €27,000 3-y-o: first foal: dam, little impact in bumpers/over hurdles, sister to fairly useful hurdler/useful chaser (stayed 2¾m) Schindler's Gold: point winner: third in bumper at Perth (3¼ lengths behind Mighty Thunder): fair form over hurdles: won handicap at Southwell (conditional) in October: in tongue tie last 3 starts: front runner/races prominently. *Pauline Robson* h113 b88

SPECIAL PRINCESS (IRE) 8 br.m. Cloudings (IRE) – Cockpit Rose (IRE) (Be My Native (USA)) [2017/18 h24s⁴ h19.3v³ h23.3v⁵ Mar 17] sixth foal: sister to a winning pointer and half-sister to 3 winners, including useful chaser Pressurize (2m-19f winner, by Witness Box): dam lightly raced in bumpers/over hurdles: maiden hurdler, no form in 2017/18: twice-raced chaser for J. P. O'Keeffe: has worn cheekpieces, including final start: has worn tongue tie, including in 2017/18. *Mike Hammond* c– h–

SPECIAL RELATION (IRE) 4 b.g. Casamento (IRE) – Sindiyma (IRE) (Kalanisi (IRE)) [2017/18 h16.7d² h16.3v⁴ h15.7v³ Jan 20] rather leggy gelding: useful on Flat, stays 1½m: fair form over hurdles: tried in cheekpieces. *Hughie Morrison* h102

SPECIAL TIARA 11 b.g. Kayf Tara – Special Choice (IRE) (Bob Back (USA)) [2017/18 c166, h–: c15.9s³ c16sᶠ c17s³ c15.9sᵖᵘ c15.5d⁴ Apr 28] big gelding: winning chaser: top-class chaser: below best in 2017/18, even when third in Shloer Chase at Cheltenham (8¼ lengths behind Fox Norton) in November and Dublin Chase at Leopardstown (12¼ lengths behind Min) in February: stays 2¼m: acts on heavy going: tried in hood: usually leads. *Henry de Bromhead, Ireland* c155 d h–

SPECIAL WELLS 9 ch.g. Alflora (IRE) – Oso Special (Teenoso (USA)) [2017/18 c120, h–: c19.4s⁵ c20v⁶ Jan 27] big gelding: winning hurdler: fairly useful chaser at best, no form in 2017/18: stays 2½m: acts on heavy going. *Sue Smith* c– h–

SPECIAL YOU 4 b.f. Arabian Gleam – Mighty Flyer (IRE) (Mujtahid (USA)) [2017/18 b12.4s b14.6s Dec 23] half-sister to several winners, including fairly useful hurdler Lady Pilot (2m-21f winner, by Dansili): dam French 9f winner: no form in bumpers. *Tracy Waggott* b–

SPECTATOR 7 br.g. Passing Glance – Averami (Averti (IRE)) [2017/18 h105: h17v² h16d⁵ h19.4s⁸ h19.9v⁴ h15.7s³ Mar 31] fair handicap hurdler: won at Musselburgh in January: stays 2½m: acts on good to firm and heavy going: tried in headgear/tongue tie: often travels strongly. *Tim Vaughan* h110

SPEEDALONG (IRE) 7 b.g. Vertical Speed (FR) – Emily's Bracelet (IRE) (Priolo (USA)) [2017/18 h102: h21.4v² c19.9s⁶ c20.2v* c23s⁴ c22.4sᵖᵘ Mar 23] sturdy gelding: fair form over hurdles: similar form over fences: won novice handicap at Wincanton in January: stays 21f: acts on heavy going: has worn hood, including in 2017/18: wears tongue tie. *Jeremy Scott* c113 h107

SPEEDBIRD ONE 7 ch.m. Mount Nelson – Good Girl (IRE) (College Chapel) [2017/18 h16g h20dᶠ h16v h15.6g⁶ Nov 30] modest maiden on Flat, stays 1¼m: poor form over hurdles: tried in tongue tie. *Stuart Crawford, Ireland* h68

SPEED COMPANY (IRE) 5 b.g. Fast Company (IRE) – Trentini (IRE) (Singspiel (IRE)) [2017/18 h15.5d⁴ h16.6d⁶ Dec 16] useful on Flat, stays 10.5f: modest form over hurdles: wears hood. *John Quinn* h95

SPEED DEMON (IRE) 9 b.g. Beneficial – Brierfield Lady (IRE) (Montelimar (USA)) [2017/18 c91, h–: c22.6g² c24.2g³ c20.9g* c21g⁴ Jun 27] lengthy gelding: winning hurdler: fair handicap chaser: won novice event at Stratford in June: stays 25f: acts on good to firm and heavy going: has worn blinkers: in tongue tie last 4 starts: often travels strongly, tends to find little. *Dan Skelton* c109 h–

SPEEDO BOY (FR) 4 ch.g. Vision d'Etat (FR) – Shamardanse (IRE) (Shamardal (USA)) [2017/18 h16d³ h15.8g* h16.4s⁵ Nov 18] sturdy gelding: dam half-sister to fairly useful French hurdler/chaser (winner up to 3m) Magic Mambo: useful on Flat, stays 1½m: fair form over hurdles: won juvenile at Huntingdon in November. *Ian Williams* h110

SPEEDY GONZALEZ 4 b.g. Josr Algarhoud (IRE) – Tellmethings (Distant Music (USA)) [2017/18 b13.7g b13.2s⁴ b16.5s Jan 9] first foal: dam well beaten in bumper: modest form in bumpers. *William Muir* b84

SPI

SPENCER MOON (IRE) 10 b.g. Dr Massini (IRE) – Nana Moon (IRE) (Flemensfirth (USA)) [2017/18 c106, h–: c21.1s* c22.6d⁴ Jun 9] multiple point winner: maiden hurdler: fair form in chases: won maiden hunter at Fontwell in May: stays 3m: acts on soft and good to firm going: in cheekpieces last 3 starts. *Kieran Price*   c106 h–

SPENDAJENNIE (IRE) 9 b.m. Old Vic – American Jennie (IRE) (Lord Americo) [2017/18 h24v^{pu} h20.6s Mar 26] point winner: maiden hurdler, no form in 2017/18 after long absence: tried in cheekpieces. *Nick Kent*   h–

SPENVIA 7 b.g. Fair Mix (IRE) – Wannaplantatree (Niniski (USA)) [2017/18 b16v⁶ Dec 31] tailed off in bumper. *John O'Shea*   b–

SPEREDEK (FR) 7 b.g. Kapgarde (FR) – Sendamagic (FR) (Sendawar (IRE)) [2017/18 c135, h–: h16.8s* h15.7g² c15.5s* c16.8v² c16d Apr 26] good-topped gelding: useful handicap hurdler: won at Exeter (by 15 lengths from Brave Eagle) in November: smart chaser: won handicap at Sandown (by 8 lengths from Gino Trail) in January: second in Clarence House Chase at Ascot (7 lengths behind Un de Sceaux) in January: best around 2m nowadays: acts on heavy going: wears cheekpieces: has worn tongue tie: front runner/races prominently. *Nigel Hawke*   c153 h136

SPERONIMO (FR) 6 b.g. Diamond Green (FR) – Spepita (FR) (Marathon (USA)) [2017/18 h–: c20d^{pu} h23.3s^{pu} Nov 10] tall, rather unfurnished gelding: little form: tried in cheekpieces: often in tongue tie. *Nigel Hawke*   c– h–

SPESSARTINE (IRE) 8 b.g. Duke of Marmalade (IRE) – Lasting Chance (USA) (American Chance (USA)) [2017/18 c23.6m⁵ May 23] point winner: little form under Rules: usually wears hood: tried in tongue tie. *Steve Barry*   c– h–

SPICE BOAT 6 ch.g. Shamardal (USA) – Frizzante (Efisio) [2017/18 h–: h15.9v^{pu} h15.9s h16m^{pu} Apr 26] no form over hurdles: tried in cheekpieces/tongue tie. *Paddy Butler*   h–

SPICE GIRL 5 ch.m. Black Sam Bellamy (IRE) – Karmest (Best of The Bests (IRE)) [2017/18 b69: b16.3g* b16m* b15.8d* h15.7g² h16.8s⁵ h15.7v* h16.8s h20.3g^{pu} Apr 19] sturdy mare: fairly useful form in bumpers: won at Stratford (maiden) in June, and Worcester (mares) and Uttoxeter in July: fair form over hurdles: won maiden at Towcester in November and novice there in February: unproven beyond 2m: acts on heavy going: tried in cheekpieces: wears tongue tie: often races prominently. *Martin Keighley*   h114 b100

SPIDER'S BITE (IRE) 6 b.g. Scorpion (IRE) – Model Girl (Classic Cliche (IRE)) [2017/18 b86: h20s³ h18.9v³ h21.2v⁶ h23.8s* h24.3g^{pu} Apr 20] rangy, useful-looking gelding: bumper winner: fair form over hurdles: won maiden at Ludlow in February: stays 3m: best form on soft/heavy going: usually races nearer last than first. *Henry Daly*   h113

SPILLERS DREAM (IRE) 9 b.g. Shantou (USA) – Eibhlinarun (IRE) (Charnwood Forest (IRE)) [2017/18 c94§, h94§: h16d^{pu} Oct 31] point winner: maiden hurdler/chaser: has worn headgear: temperamental. *Hannah James*   c– § h– §

SPINNING SCOOTER 8 b.g. Sleeping Indian – Spinning Coin (Mujahid (USA)) [2017/18 h79: h16.2g⁴ h16.2g⁶ h20.1v^{pu} h19.9g⁴ Apr 23] modest maiden hurdler: stays 2½m: best form on good going: tried in visor: wears tongue tie. *Maurice Barnes*   h95

SPIN POINT (IRE) 6 b.g. Pivotal – Daneleta (IRE) (Danehill (USA)) [2017/18 h–: h16m⁵ h23.4g^{pu} Nov 1] fair on Flat: poor form over hurdles: tried in cheekpieces. *Ian Williams*   h65

SPIN THE BEAT 8 b.g. Beat All (USA) – Little Red Spider (Bustino) [2017/18 h18.5v^{pu} Apr 8] no form in bumpers/over hurdles. *Deborah Faulkner*   h–

SPIN THE COIN (IRE) 5 b.g. Witness Box (USA) – Kempinski (IRE) (Moscow Society (USA)) [2017/18 h17d⁵ h19.3d⁴ h21.2s h19.3v^F Mar 8] £27,000 4-y-o: second foal: dam winning pointer out of useful hurdler/fairly useful chaser (stayed 21f) Image de Marque II: runner-up in point: fair form over hurdles: should stay 2½m: will go on improving. *Donald McCain*   h105 p

SPINY NORMAN 5 ch.m. Malinas (GER) – Helen Wood (Lahib (USA)) [2017/18 b15.8m May 14] tailed off in maiden bumper. *Alexandra Dunn*   b–

SPIRITOFCHARTWELL 10 ch.g. Clerkenwell (USA) – Rollin Rock (Rock Hopper) [2017/18 c17.8d* c17.8g² c21.6d* c19.5v² c17.8s* c17.8g³ Apr 20] maiden hurdler: modest handicap chaser: won at Fontwell in September, November and March: stays 2¾m: acts on soft and good to firm going: usually races towards rear. *Phil York*   c93 h–

SPIRIT OF HALE (IRE) 7 ch.g. Stowaway – Roseboreen (IRE) (Roselier (FR)) [2017/18 h–: c23.8d⁴ c20.3v⁴ c25.2v³ c21.7v⁴ c24.1d² Apr 21] tall gelding: maiden hurdler: modest form over fences: won handicap at Bangor in March: stays 25f: acts on heavy going: in cheekpieces last 5 starts. *Jennie Candlish*   c95 h–

SPI

SPIRIT OF MENDIP (IRE) 5 b.m. Arakan (USA) – Afdale (IRE) (Old Vic) [2017/18 b15.8g b16s h16.5m Apr 25] €16,500 3-y-o: first foal: dam, unraced, closely related to useful hurdler/smart staying chaser Balthazar King: down the field in bumpers/mares novice hurdle: tried in hood. *Philip Hobbs*   h– b–

SPIRIT OF ROME (IRE) 4 ch.f. Mastercraftsman (IRE) – Zagreb Flyer (Old Vic) [2017/18 h17.7v² h16.2s³ h15.7d⁴ h15.8d⁵ Apr 24] half-sister to useful hurdler Joe Jo Star (2m winner, by Piccolo): modest maiden on Flat, stays 1½m: modest form over hurdles. *Harry Whittington*   h98

SPIRITOFTHEGAMES (IRE) 6 b.g. Darsi (FR) – Lucy Walters (IRE) (King's Ride) [2017/18 h126p: h19.5s⁸ h21s² h16.3v³ h16.8v⁵ h20s Apr 13] lengthy gelding: Irish point winner: useful handicap hurdler: won at Lingfield in November: placed in Lanzarote Hurdle at Kempton and Betfair Hurdle at Newbury: fifth in County Hurdle at Cheltenham (5½ lengths behind Mohaayed) in March: stays 21f: acts on heavy going: in cheekpieces last 3 starts. *Dan Skelton*   h139

SPIRIT OF WATERLOO 4 b.g. Malinas (GER) – Warm Front (Bustino) [2017/18 b17s⁶ Apr 8] half-brother to fair hurdler/winning pointer Great Gusto (3m winner, by Moscow Society): dam, lightly raced in bumpers, half-sister to useful hurdler/chaser (stayed 25f) Tarablaze: 66/1, sixth in bumper at Carlisle (11¾ lengths behind Largy Glory). *Oliver Greenall*   b84

SPIRITUAL MAN (IRE) 6 b.g. Lawman (FR) – Vee Gita (IRE) (Vettori (IRE)) [2017/18 h108: h16d⁶ h16d h16.4d h21.2d⁴ c19.1s^{pu} Jan 26] angular gelding: modest maiden hurdler: pulled up in novice handicap on chasing debut: unproven beyond 2m: acts on soft going: tried in cheekpieces. *Jonjo O'Neill*   c– h91

SPITFIRE REGGIE 5 b.g. Flying Legend (USA) – Angie Marinie (Sabrehill (USA)) [2017/18 b15.8d^{pu} May 20] pulled up in bumper. *Samuel Drinkwater*   b–

SPLASH OF GINGE 10 b.g. Oscar (IRE) – Land of Honour (Supreme Leader) [2017/18 c131§, h134§: c19.4s⁴ c20.4s⁴ c20.8s c20.8s^{pu} h22.8v c20.8s² Mar 15] lengthy gelding: winning hurdler: useful handicap chaser: won BetVictor Gold Cup at Cheltenham (by neck from Starchitect) in November: second in Brown Advisory & Merriebelle Stable Plate at same course (1¾ lengths behind The Storyteller) in March: stays 23f: acts on heavy going: has worn visor: usually races close up: not one to trust. *Nigel Twiston-Davies*   c140 § h– §

SPOCK (FR) 13 b.g. Lost World (IRE) – Quark Top (FR) (Perrault) [2017/18 c89§, h–: c20m^{pu} c17.4d* c15.7g c16.5g⁶ c21g⁴ c20g c16v² c20.9s* c18.9s⁵ c21.6d³ c16d⁴ c19.4v⁴ c16v⁴ c21.7m⁵ Apr 25] winning hurdler: modest handicap chaser: won at Fontwell in May and Hereford in December: stays 2¾m: acts on good to firm and heavy going: has worn headgear: tried in tongue tie: front runner/races prominently: unreliable. *Lady Susan Brooke*   c91 § h–

BetVictor Gold Cup Handicap Chase, Cheltenham—
Splash of Ginge holds off the blinkered Starchitect to spring a 25/1 surprise

SPR

SPOILS OF WAR (IRE) 9 b.g. Craigsteel – Mooreshill Lady (IRE) (King's Ride) [2017/18 c93, h73: h23.9g* h23.9g³ h23.9s^pu h23.9v² h24.3s⁴ h24.3v^F h24.1s h27v* Apr 13] modest handicap hurdler: won at Perth (novice) in May and Sedgefield in April: maiden chaser: stays 27f: acts on heavy going: has worn headgear, including in 2017/18: front runner/races prominently: temperament under suspicion. *Lucinda Russell*   c– h95

SPOILT ROTTEN 9 b.g. Kayf Tara – Rosita Bay (Hernando (FR)) [2017/18 c111, h–: c17.4d³ c16.5g² c17g^F c16.5g³ c18.2m^pu Apr 25] twice-raced hurdler: fair maiden chaser: left Mark Pitman after fourth start: raced mainly around 2m: acts on soft going: wears hood: often races freely. *Fergal O'Brien*   c108 h–

SPOOKYDOOKY (IRE) 10 b.g. Winged Love (IRE) – Kiora Lady (IRE) (King's Ride) [2017/18 c128, h–: c25.2s⁵ c30.7s c22.9s⁴ c30.7v* Apr 17] workmanlike gelding: has had breathing operation: winning hurdler: fairly useful handicap chaser nowadays: won at Exeter in April: stays 31f: acts on heavy going: has worn cheekpieces, including final start: wears tongue tie: usually races towards rear. *Jonjo O'Neill*   c126 h–

SPORTING BOY (IRE) 10 b.g. Baratheo (IRE) – Sportsticketing (IRE) (Spectrum (IRE)) [2017/18 h23g h26.5d² h23.3d² c23.9g* c25g c21.7g⁴ Nov 16] quite good-topped gelding: fairly useful handicap hurdler: second at Uttoxeter in October: useful handicap chaser: won at Market Rasen in October: best up to 3m: acts on firm and good to soft going: usually in headgear, has worn tongue tie, including last 4 starts: usually races prominently/travels strongly. *Johnny Farrelly*   c133 h124

SPORTING MILAN (IRE) 7 b.g. Milan – Sports Leader (IRE) (Supreme Leader) [2017/18 h99: h20.5v h23.9s⁶ Apr 25] runner-up in Irish point: modest hurdle winner, excuses after long absence in 2017/18: should be suited by 3m+: acts on good to soft going: tried in cheekpieces. *Stuart Coltherd*   h75

SPORTING PRESS (IRE) 5 b.g. Flemensfirth (USA) – Rudy Renata (IRE) (Rudimentary (USA)) [2017/18 b16v³ b16.4d⁴ b16g Apr 21] €40,000 3-y-o: fifth foal: dam, ran twice, out of sister to useful staying chaser Rust Never Sleeps: maiden Irish pointer: fair form in bumpers: won at Musselburgh in March: will stay 2½m. *Keith Dalgleish*   b91

SPORTS BARROW (IRE) 6 b.g. Windsor Knot (IRE) – Liberty Grace (IRE) (Statue of Liberty (USA)) [2017/18 h100: h17.3g⁶ h16.2m⁵ Jul 16] modest handicap hurdler: best around 2m: best form on good going: has worn cheekpieces: tried in tongue tie. *Colin A. McBratney, Ireland*   h90

SPORTY YANKEE (USA) 5 gr.g. Paddy O'Prado (USA) – I Insist (USA) (Green Dancer (USA)) [2017/18 h96: h16g⁶ h20.5d³ h15.5v h15.5v² h23v Feb 19] tall gelding: fair handicap hurdler: stays 2½m: acts on heavy going: usually in cheekpieces, in tongue tie last 4 starts. *Martin Keighley*   h105

SPOSALIZIO (IRE) 11 ch.g. Dr Fong (USA) – Wedding Cake (IRE) (Groom Dancer (USA)) [2017/18 c–, h–: c20.1g^F Jun 17] multiple point winner: maiden hurdler: fair chaser at best, fell sole outing under Rules in 2017/18: stays 21f: acts on good to firm going: has worn headgear: wears tongue tie. *Chris Grant*   c– h–

SPRING BOK (FR) 5 b.g. Turtle Bowl (IRE) – Rock Harmonie (FR) (Rock of Gibraltar (IRE)) [2017/18 h16.3g^pu Jun 10] fairly useful on Flat for P. Bary, stayed 1¼m: in hood, fatally injured on hurdling debut. *Dr Richard Newland*   h–

SPRINGCOMBE JOE 6 b.g. Kayf Tara – Dissolve (Sharrood (USA)) [2017/18 b16.8v² b16s Jan 25] brother to fairly useful hurdler Bianco Fuji (2½m winner) and closely related/half-brother to several winners, including bumper winner/fairly useful hurdler Argento Luna (2m-21f winner, by Mtoto) and useful hurdler/fairly useful chaser Lyes Green (19f-25f winner, by Bien Bien), stayed 4m: dam (h78) 2m/17f hurdle winner (stayed 2¾m): modest form in bumpers: better effort when second in maiden at Exeter in January. *Bill Turner*   b83

SPRING OVER (IRE) 12 ch.m. Samraan (USA) – Superswap (IRE) (Gone Fishin') [2017/18 c–, h79: c19.3s^F h23.3v⁴ h27v⁴ Apr 13] poor handicap hurdler nowadays: maiden chaser: stays 3m: acts on heavy going: wears tongue tie. *Ian Duncan*   c– h64

SPRING STEEL (IRE) 9 b.g. Dushyantor (USA) – Fieldtown (Anshan) [2017/18 c102, h103: c20m⁵ c16.5g² c19.4g c17.2g² Jul 22] close-coupled gelding: maiden hurdler: fair handicap chaser: stays 21f: acts on good to firm and good to soft going: has worn hood: wears tongue tie. *Alexandra Dunn*   c108 h–

SPRINGTOWN LAKE (IRE) 6 b.g. Gamut (IRE) – Sprightly Gal (IRE) (Old Vic) [2017/18 h118p, b–: h20g² h19.8s^F h19.8s² h20.3s³ h20.5v* h21.1s Mar 14] good-topped gelding: runner-up in Irish maiden point: useful hurdler: won maiden at Worcester in October and novice at Leicester (by 38 lengths from I'm Always Trying) in January: placed   h132

SPR

in between in Winter Novices' Hurdle at Sandown (9 lengths behind On The Blind Side) and listed novice at Cheltenham (4¾ lengths behind Tikkanbar): stays 2½m: acts on heavy going: usually leads. *Philip Hobbs*

SPROGZILLA 9 gr.m. Fair Mix (IRE) – Gentle Approach (Rakaposhi King) [2017/18 h89: h15.7g⁶ h15.7g³ h19.5d Oct 31] pulled up in mares maiden point: modest maiden hurdler: unproven beyond 2m: acts on good to firm going: has worn hood, including in 2017/18: usually leads. *Hannah James* — **h90**

SPYDER 10 b.g. Resplendent Glory (IRE) – Collect (Vettori (IRE)) [2017/18 h–: h20.3g⁵ May 24] fairly useful hurdler at best, little form since 2013/14: stays 2½m: acts on heavy going. *Tracey Leeson* — **h69**

SPY IN THE SKY 9 b.m. Generous (IRE) – Lady Deploy (Deploy) [2017/18 h86: h20g² h25g^pu Nov 5] sturdy mare: fair form over hurdles: stays 2½m: acts on soft going: in tongue tie last 3 starts. *Fergal O'Brien* — **h100**

SQUARE VIVIANI (FR) 7 b.g. Satri (IRE) – Idria (GER) (Kings Lake (USA)) [2017/18 h18.9s³ c21.9sF c19.9s^pu c22.9v⁴ c15.7s⁴ c21.3v³ c23.9v⁴ Apr 11] seventh foal: half-brother to 2 winners on Flat in Germany by Banyumanik: dam German 1m-1½m winner: winning hurdler: fair handicap chaser: left David Cottin after fourth start: stays 21f: acts on heavy going: tried in headgear. *Micky Hammond* — **c102 h94**

SQUEEZE ME 11 b.m. Grape Tree Road – Ask Me Not (IRE) (Shernazar) [2017/18 h95: h19.9d² h22.1d⁴ May 29] modest handicap hurdler: stays 23f: acts on good to firm and good to soft going: has worn cheekpieces: tried in tongue tie. *Gary Hanmer* — **h96**

SQUOUATEUR (FR) 7 gr.g. Martaline – Samansonnienne (FR) (Mansonnien (FR)) [2017/18 c132, h–: c16.5s⁶ c24.5d³ c17s c26s³ c29v^bd c21s^pu Apr 27] strong, lengthy gelding: winning hurdler: useful maiden chaser: third in Fulke Walwyn Kim Muir Handicap (amateurs), 5½ lengths behind Missed Approach): stays 3¼m: acts on heavy going: wears tongue tie: often races towards rear. *Gordon Elliott, Ireland* — **c136 h–**

STAFF COLLEGE (FR) 4 b.g. Slickly (FR) – School of Music (FR) (Green Tune (USA)) [2017/18 h15.8g³ h16s² h16s^F h17.9v h17.6s² Apr 24] dam half-sister to very smart hurdler (stayed 2½m) Sentry Duty: fair maiden on Flat, stays 1¼m: fair form over hurdles: left Henry Spiller after third start: stays 2¼m: acts on soft going. *David Cottin, France* — **h103**

STAGECOACH JASPER 12 b.g. Sir Harry Lewis (USA) – Flintwood (Gunner B) [2017/18 c–x, h–: c21.2d May 29] big gelding: multiple point winner: maiden hurdler/chaser: in cheekpieces last 3 starts: often let down by jumping. *R. Tate* — **c64 x h–**

STAGED ENGAGEMENT (IRE) 5 b.g. Darsi (FR) – Katishna (IRE) (Heron Island (IRE)) [2017/18 b16.7d⁴ Apr 21] 8/1, fourth in conditionals/amateur bumper at Bangor (16¼ lengths behind Stoney Mountain). *P. E. Collins, Ireland* — **b71**

STAGE SUMMIT (IRE) 5 gr.g. Tikkanen (USA) – Summittotalkabout (IRE) (Lahib (USA)) [2017/18 b20d⁵ b16d* h19.7g² h21.6d⁵ h21.2d³ Mar 22] €1,500 3-y-o: rangy gelding: second foal: dam, unraced, out of half-sister to Grand National winner Earth Summit: pulled up only start in points: fair form in bumpers: won maiden at Limerick in July: fair form over hurdles: best effort when second in novice at Hereford in November: left Roger McGrath after second start: stays 2½m. *Ben Pauling* — **h112 b87**

STAGS LEAP (IRE) 11 b.g. Refuse To Bend (IRE) – Swingsky (IRE) (Indian Ridge) [2017/18 h114: h15.6s h16.2s Apr 26] fair hurdler at best, little impact after long absence in 2017/18: wears headgear. *Julia Brooke* — **h62**

STAIGUE FORT 10 b.g. Kirkwall – Mulberry Wine (Benny The Dip (USA)) [2017/18 c–, c–, h104: h19.7s^pu h19.4d^pu h23.8d^ur h19.4d⁵ Mar 16] lengthy, good-bodied gelding: fairly useful hurdler at best, little form in 2017/18: maiden chaser: stays 3m: acts on good to firm going: tried in tongue tie: often races in rear. *Susan Corbett* — **c– h73**

STAMP YOUR FEET (IRE) 6 b.g. Galileo (IRE) – Nausicaa (USA) (Diesis) [2017/18 h118, b100: h21.6g⁴ h20d² h21.1s^pu h19.7s* h23.8d² h26.1s⁴ h19.8s^pu Apr 28] sturdy gelding: bumper winner: useful handicap hurdler: won at Hereford in December: second at Musselburgh in January: stays 3¼m: acts on soft going: wears tongue tie: usually races towards rear, often travels strongly. *Tom George* — **h131**

STAND BY ME (FR) 8 b.g. Dream Well (FR) – In Love New (FR) (Perrault) [2017/18 b94: h15.3g Oct 29] bumper winner: tailed off in novice after long absence on hurdling debut. *Alan Jones* — **h–**

STA

ST ANDREWS (IRE) 5 ch.g. Rip Van Winkle (IRE) – Stellavera (FR) (Anabaa (USA)) [2017/18 h66: h20f³ h23.9m³ Nov 1] modest form over hurdles: stays 3m: acts on firm going: in visor last 2 starts: tried in tongue tie. *Ian Williams* **h96**

STANS BLACK FIVE 5 b.g. Multiplex – Globe Dream (IRE) (Eagle Eyed (USA)) [2017/18 b16v Jan 2] tailed off in bumper. *Barry Murtagh* **b–**

STANZA BOY (IRE) 6 b.g. Stowaway – Lisa Bleu (IRE) (Pistolet Bleu (IRE)) [2017/18 b–: h16s h16v⁶ h19.5s Apr 27] no form. *Deborah Faulkner* **h–**

STARCHITECT (IRE) 7 b.g. Sea The Stars (IRE) – Humilis (IRE) (Sadler's Wells (USA)) [2017/18 c141+, h147: c19.4g* c20.4s² c20.8s^pu Dec 16] compact gelding: smart hurdler: very smart handicap chaser: won at Stratford (by 3 lengths from Cut The Corner) in November: clear when suffering fatal injury in Caspian Caviar Gold Cup at Cheltenham: stayed 2¾m: acted on heavy going: often wore blinkers: wore tongue tie: raced prominently, strong traveller. *David Pipe* **c156 h–**

STARCROSSED 6 b.g. Cape Cross (IRE) – Gretna (Groom Dancer (USA)) [2017/18 h16.6d h15.8s* Feb 22] fair on Flat, stays 2m: fairly useful form over hurdles: won novice at Huntingdon in February: will stay beyond 2m: likely to progress further. *Dan Skelton* **h119 p**

STAR FOOT (IRE) 7 b.g. Soviet Star (USA) – On The Backfoot (IRE) (Bob Back (USA)) [2017/18 h110: h16.7g* h18.6g* h16.7g⁵ h20g h15.8d* h16.6d h15.8d⁵ h21m³ Apr 26] sturdy gelding: fairly useful handicap hurdler: won at Market Rasen in May and June, and lady riders event at Huntingdon in November: stays 21f: acts on soft and good to firm going: has worn headgear: wears tongue tie. *Jo Davis* **h120**

STARJAC (FR) 4 gr.g. Linda's Lad – Star's Mixa (FR) (Linamix (FR)) [2017/18 b16s⁵ Mar 17] rather unfurnished gelding: 50/1, fifth in maiden bumper at Kempton (17½ lengths behind Mister Fisher). *Paul Webber* **b71**

STARKIE 11 b.g. Putra Sandhurst (IRE) – Lysways (Gildoran) [2017/18 c113, h–: c20.5m³ Apr 26] good-topped gelding: placed in points: winning hurdler: fair chaser: stays 2¼m: acts on heavy going: has worn headgear: tried in tongue tie. *Anthony Ward-Thomas* **c108 h–**

STARLETTE 7 b.m. Winker Watson – Imaginemysurprise (Mujadil (USA)) [2017/18 ab18d Mar 5] second foal: dam maiden, stayed 8.5f: 66/1, tailed off in jumpers bumper. *Jo Hughes*

STARLIGHT COURT (IRE) 7 b.g. Court Cave (IRE) – Marie The (FR) (Exit To Nowhere (USA)) [2017/18 h106: c21.4g^F h20.3d⁴ h15.3g Oct 29] modest maiden hurdler: fell fifth in novice handicap on chasing debut: won point in February: left Dan Skelton after first start: unproven beyond 17f: acts on heavy going: has worn hood: often in tongue tie: front runner/races prominently. *Charlie Longsdon* **c– p h99**

STARLIT NIGHT 6 b.m. Nayef (USA) – Perfect Night (Danzig Connection (USA)) [2017/18 h61: h18.5m h21.6m² h18.5g² h22g* h21.6g h23.9m h18.5v^pu Dec 8] rather leggy mare: poor handicap hurdler: won novice event at Stratford in August: stays 2¾m: best form on good going: has worn hood: tried in tongue tie: front runner/races prominently. *Chris Down* **h74**

STAR OF LANKA (IRE) 4 b.g. Zoffany (IRE) – Indian Bounty (Indian Ridge) [2017/18 b14.6s* b15.6s³ b16.6s³ Feb 21] £800 3-y-o: sixth foal: closely related/half-brother to winners on Flat in Italy by Strategic Prince and Intikhab: dam maiden (stayed 1m): fair form in bumpers: won junior event at Newcastle in December: has joined Warren Greatrex. *Sally Haynes* **b92**

STAR OF MILAN 5 b.g. Milan – Innovate (IRE) (Posen (USA)) [2017/18 h16.2g h16.4g Nov 17] tailed off both starts over hurdles. *Lucinda Russell* **h–**

STAR OF NAMIBIA (IRE) 8 b.g. Cape Cross (IRE) – Sparkle of Stones (FR) (Sadler's Wells (USA)) [2017/18 h82: h19.9d h23.1d² h22.1g³ h19.7v h22.8s Mar 21] poor maiden hurdler: stays 23f: acts on good to soft going: sometimes in cheekpieces: front runner/races prominently. *Michael Mullineaux* **h84**

STARPLEX 8 b.g. Multiplex – Turtle Bay (Dr Fong (USA)) [2017/18 h103: h15.6s⁵ Feb 3] fairly useful on Flat, stays 13f: fair hurdler: stays 21f: best form on good going: usually races close up. *Keith Dalgleish* **h91**

STARSHELL (IRE) 4 b.g. Sea The Stars (IRE) – Aquarelle Bleue (Sadler's Wells (USA)) [2017/18 h15.7d Dec 19] fair but temperamental maiden on Flat, stays 1½m: 66/1, well held in juvenile at Catterick on hurdling debut. *Barry Murtagh* **h–**

STA

STAR TACKLE (IRE) 7 b.g. Milan – Grangebridge (IRE) (Strong Gale) [2017/18 h101: c20.5s^{ur} c20.9v^2 c19.3s^{pu} Dec 26] off mark in Irish points at fifth attempt: fair form over hurdles: similar form over fences: best effort when ninth in novice handicap at Ffos Las in November: stayed 21f: acted on heavy going: dead. *Harry Whittington*   **c112 h–**

STAR TROUPER (IRE) 8 b.g. King's Theatre (IRE) – Wyndham Sweetmarie (IRE) (Mister Lord (USA)) [2017/18 c–, h101: h20.6g^6 h23.3g^4 h21.6m^6 c21g^3 c21d^{pu} h23d^4 c19.2d^{pu} Oct 12] sturdy gelding: modest maiden hurdler: similar form over fences: left Sophie Leech after third start: likely to prove best up to 21f: best form on good going: has worn hood, including final start: wears tongue tie: often races in rear. *Grace Harris*   **c91 h92**

STATE SOVEREIGNTY 6 b.m. Authorized (IRE) – Sovereign's Honour (USA) (Kingmambo (USA)) [2017/18 b89: b15.8d^2 h15.7s^6 h16.5m^6 Apr 25] has had breathing operation: fairly useful on Flat, stays 1½m: placed in bumpers: modest form over hurdles: better effort when sixth in mares novice at Taunton in April, though reportedly bled: in tongue tie last 2 starts: usually races nearer last than first. *Michael Scudamore*   **h96 b76**

STATE THE OBVIOUS (IRE) 6 ch.g. Presenting – New Vega (FR) (Blushing Flame (USA)) [2017/18 h72p: h15.8g^5 h20g^2 h20g^2 h20g* h20f^2 h19.7g^3 Nov 29] fair handicap hurdler: won novice event at Worcester in August: stays 2½m: best form on good going. *Jonjo O'Neill*   **h101**

STATION CLOSED (IRE) 10 b.m. Kutub (IRE) – Laser Supreme (IRE) (Supreme Leader) [2017/18 h83: h16m h21.5g* h19.5m* h21.3g* h21.3g* h24g^{pu} h24.8g h19g h23.4s^6 h23v^{pu} Feb 19] modest handicap hurdler: won at Downpatrick and Down Royal in May, and again at Downpatrick in June: left Gordon Elliott after seventh start: stays 21f: acts on good to firm and good to soft going: wears headgear/tongue tie: often races towards rear. *Michael Attwater*   **h96**

STATION MASTER (IRE) 7 b.g. Scorpion (IRE) – Gastounette (IRE) (Presenting) [2017/18 b17g* h18.5d^3 h26d* h24d* h24.4s^6 h24g Apr 18] €37,000 3-y-o: first foal: dam, little form over hurdles, out of sister to top-class hurdler Rhinestone Cowboy and half-sister to smart hurdler/chaser Wichita Lineman (both stayed 3m): point winner: also won conditionals/amateur bumper at Aintree (by 11 lengths from Aptly Put) in May for Peter Fahey: useful form over hurdles: won novices at Warwick in November and Southwell (by 4 lengths from Aloomomo) in December: stays 3¼m: acts on good to soft going: tried in cheekpieces: usually races prominently. *Kim Bailey*   **h131 b95**

STATUS QUO (IRE) 5 b.g. Thewayyouare (USA) – Again Royale (IRE) (Royal Academy (USA)) [2017/18 h89: h15.8m h16.5g^5 h16.5s^F h18.6v^{pu} Mar 11] lengthy gelding: modest maiden hurdler: unproven beyond 2m: acts on firm going: wears hood: in tongue tie in 2017/18: usually races nearer last than first. *Harry Fry*   **h96**

STAUNTON 7 b.m. Kayf Tara – Aranga (IRE) (Supreme Leader) [2017/18 h69: c26v^4 h23.9s^3 Feb 20] lengthy mare: poor maiden hurdler: 5/4, last of 4 in novice handicap at Fontwell on chasing debut, not jumping fluently: stays 3m: acts on soft going. *Tim Vaughan*   **c58 h71**

STAY IN TOUCH (IRE) 7 b.g. Touch of Land (FR) – Supreme Dancer (IRE) (Supreme Leader) [2017/18 h15.8d^{ur} h17s h16s h15.8d^4 h19.9s^3 ab16.3g^2 h21.3d h19.9g^2 Apr 23] €1,200 3-y-o, £17,000 6-y-o: third foal: half-brother to 2½m bumper winner Baltimore Buzz (by Beneficial): dam, unraced, out of half-sister to top-class 2m hurdler Classical Charm: off mark in Irish points at sixth attempt: fair maiden hurdler: stays 2½m: acts on soft going: in cheekpieces last 2 starts: front runner/races prominently. *Donald McCain*   **h105**

STAY OUT OF COURT (IRE) 7 b.g. Court Cave (IRE) – Lucky To Live (IRE) (Salluceva) [2017/18 h119, b79: h26.4d^5 May 21] fair maiden hurdler: won point in April: stays 25f: acts on heavy going: in cheekpieces last 3 starts: front runner/races prominently. *David Pipe*   **h92**

STEADY MAJOR (IRE) 6 b.g. Invincible Spirit (IRE) – Combust (USA) (Aptitude (USA)) [2017/18 h74: h16.7g Jul 9] poor maiden hurdler: often in blinkers: usually wears tongue tie: usually races nearer last than first. *Mark Brisbourne*   **h–**

STEALING MIX 8 b.g. Fair Mix (IRE) – Minimum (Terimon) [2017/18 h103, b–: h20g c17g^2 c15.7g^2 c16.4g^F Aug 31] good-topped gelding: Irish point winner: fair handicap hurdler: similar form over fences: best effort when second in novice at Southwell in August: stays 2½m: acts on firm going: wears tongue tie. *Neil Mulholland*   **c106 h94**

STEEL BOB (IRE) 6 b.g. Craigsteel – Lady Kamando (Hernando (FR)) [2017/18 h–p, b101: h24.5m^4 h23s* h21.6d^2 Jun 6] point/bumper winner: fair form over hurdles: won novice at Worcester in May: stays 23f: tried in cheekpieces. *Harry Fry*   **h111**

STEEL CITY 10 gr.g. Act One – Serraval (FR) (Sanglamore (USA)) [2017/18 c–x, h99x: h16d h15.7s* h16.7v⁶ h16.7sᵖᵘ Mar 26] useful-looking gelding: fair handicap hurdler: won at Catterick in January: maiden chaser: left Seamus Mullins after first start: unproven beyond 17f: acts on heavy going: has worn headgear, including in 2017/18: usually races prominently: often let down by jumping. *Michael Easterby*   c– x
 h101 x

STEEL EXPRESS (IRE) 6 b.g. Craigsteel – Assidua (IRE) (Anshan) [2017/18 h97, b91: h19.5d h21.6v³ h21.7s h21.4s h23.6v² h23.1vᵖᵘ Apr 8] bumper winner: modest maiden hurdler: stays 3m: acts on good to firm and heavy going. *Linda Blackford*   h97

STEEL HELMET (IRE) 4 ch.g. Helmet (AUS) – Marine City (JPN) (Carnegie (IRE)) [2017/18 h16.7g h16d h16.7sᵖᵘ Nov 15] modest on Flat, stays 1¼m: no form over hurdles: left Brian Ellison after second start. *Harriet Bethell*   h–

STEEL NATIVE (IRE) 7 b.g. Craigsteel – Princess Gloria (IRE) (Prince Rupert (FR)) [2017/18 h98: h23.3d⁶ c25.8mᶠ c23.8gᵖᵘ c23.8v* c23.8v⁵ h20v* c25.2sᵖᵘ c23.6vᶠ h20v⁵ h21.9v⁵ c23.8v⁵ Apr 15] modest handicap hurdler: won at Ffos Las (conditional) in December: modest handicap chaser: won at same course in November: stays 3m: acts on heavy going: often wears hood: often races towards rear: often let down by jumping. *David Rees*   c96 x
 h94 x

STEEL RUN 6 gr.g. Sagamix (FR) – Safari Run (IRE) (Supreme Leader) [2017/18 h19.9sᵖᵘ Jan 12] pulled up all 3 starts in points/on hurdling debut. *Neil Mechie*   h–

STEEL'S COTTON 9 b.m. Tikkanen (USA) – Last Spruce (USA) (Big Spruce (USA)) [2017/18 h78: c20m⁴ c19.9d c26.2v⁴ Apr 16] placed in points: maiden hurdler: modest form over fences: left Ian Ferguson after second start: stays 21f: acts on good to firm and good to soft going: usually wears cheekpieces: often in tongue tie. *Jane Clark*   c94
 h–

STEEL SUMMIT (IRE) 9 b.g. Craigsteel – B Greenhill (Gunner B) [2017/18 h23.6vᵖᵘ c24.2vᵖᵘ c24sᵖᵘ Jan 26] rather leggy gelding: fairly useful hurdler/useful chaser at best, off 31 months and pulled up all 3 starts in 2017/18: has worn cheekpieces. *David Dennis*   c–
 h–

STEELY ADDITION (IRE) 6 b.g. Craigsteel – Blond's Addition (IRE) (Lord Americo) [2017/18 h110: h18.5dᶠ h21.4g* h23.6s* h24g Apr 18] won maiden point on debut: fairly useful handicap hurdler: won at Wincanton in October and Chepstow in November: stays 3m: acts on soft going: remains with potential. *Philip Hobbs*   h128 p

STELLAR NOTION (IRE) 10 b.g. Presenting – Green Star (FR) (Green Tune (USA)) [2017/18 c143, h–: c24vᵖᵘ c24s c24m⁴ Apr 26] well-made gelding: winning hurdler: useful handicap chaser, below form in 2017/18: left Henry de Bromhead after second start: stays 3m: acts on heavy going: tried in cheekpieces: has worn tongue tie, including final start: front runner/races prominently, tends to find little. *Tom George*   c122
 h–

STEP BACK (IRE) 8 ch.g. Indian River (FR) – Stepitoutmary (IRE) (Roselier (FR)) [2017/18 h107+: c23.6v² c24.2v³ c24.2d* c28.8d* Apr 28]   c146 p
 h–

    The latest bet365 Gold Cup, the big handicap that is the traditional highlight of the last day of the season, was unusual in one major respect. There was no trademark dramatic finish up the Sandown hill, no rousing climax and no confusion over the right winning post. The well-backed 7/1-shot Step Back, a novice with just three steeplechases under his belt, turned the race into a rout, making most of the running and jumping superbly to record the sort of dominant performance that is rarely seen in a competitive major handicap. Step Back's nineteen opponents never saw the way he went as he scored a thirteen-length victory over the previous year's close sixth Rock The Kasbah, the only one to keep tabs on him over the final circuit. Rock The Kasbah, recording a career-best, beat the rest by upwards of fourteen lengths. The Badger Ales Trophy winner Present Man, the consistent Relentless Dreamer and the previous season's Hennessy runner-up Carole's Destrier finished third, fourth and fifth, all running respectably but never threatening Step Back or Rock The Kasbah. The field was made up largely of seasoned thorough stayers, some of them probably 'over the top' at the end of a long campaign, but they also included the Becher Chase winner Blaklion, who started 6/1 favourite under top weight, the Fulke Walwyn Kim Muir winner Missed Approach, the first two in the valuable Keltbray Swinley Chase at Ascot, Regal Encore and Minella Daddy, the third and fourth from the previous year Theatre Guide and Benbens, the 2016 winner

*bet365 Gold Cup Handicap Chase, Sandown—
the novice Step Back belies his inexperience with a dominant display; Rock The Kasbah comes in a distant second after being the only one to give the winner a race*

The Young Master (who had gone at the first fence seven days earlier in the Scottish National), and Sugar Baron, a leading fancy the year before, when he finished a close seventh in a bunched finish behind 40/1 winner Henllan Harri, who missed the cut for the latest edition.

Step Back was the first novice to win the Sandown Gold Cup since Hennessy in 2009 (unlike the Scottish National, for example, it is not a race that attracts many novices, possibly because of the eccentric layout of Sandown's steeplechasing course which tests a horse's jumping technique). Step Back's zestful, front-running display was a revelation and his splendid jumping will continue to stand him in good stead as he makes his way through the chasing ranks. The Ladbrokes Trophy (formerly the Hennessy Gold Cup) looks sure to be his first port of call in the next season and he would be a splendid sight, out in front forcing the pace, in the Grand National if he were to get there. He has the potential to make a name for himself eventually in open graded company and looks ready to take over from the 2015 Cheltenham Gold Cup winner Coneygree as the star of his small stable (injury-prone Coneygree was pulled up on his two appearances in the latest season and his trainer says they will have one final try with him in the next season).

While Coneygree, who won the Cheltenham Gold Cup as a novice, was bred by Lord Oaksey, the father of the trainer's wife Sara Bradstock, and owned by a family partnership, Step Back was bought by his trainer Mark Bradstock for £47,000 as a six-year-old at the Cheltenham Premier Sales in May 2016. He had won three times in points in Ireland that spring and finally made his debut over hurdles in a maiden at Ludlow for his new stable as a seven-year-old. After making all and winning in the style of a promising recruit, Step Back was thrown in at the deep end in the Spa Hurdle at the Cheltenham Festival where, starting at 100/1, he seemed to show fairly useful form in finishing ninth to Penhill, weakening from two out after showing up from the start.

Step Back's future, though, was clearly going to be over fences and he made his first appearance over the larger obstacles when shaping well in second behind the promising Thomas Patrick, after eleven months off, in a three-mile novice event at Chepstow in February. Step Back raced with plenty of zest that day and he looked to have been let in on a handy weight (BHA mark of 124) on his handicap debut in a useful contest at Sandown two weeks later. He started favourite but, in finishing a staying-on third to Tanit River and Aubusson, he ran as if needing further than three miles. The form of Step Back's first two runs over fences was franked in the weeks that followed, particularly by the progressive Thomas Patrick (the fourth in the Sandown race, Potters Legend, also went on to win in good style at Haydock).

The bet365 Gold Cup is an early-closing race and there are no penalties after the publication of the weights. Step Back got off the mark over fences three weeks before the Sandown feature with an impressive, all-the-way win in a small novice event at Fakenham. He showed improved form to beat Sam Red by sixteen lengths, in the process looking a potential force to be reckoned with in better company.

Step Back's triumph in the bet365 Gold Cup brought back memories of the days when the late Lord Oaksey was riding as an amateur. As Mr John Lawrence, he rode Taxidermist to victory in the 1958 Whitbread Gold Cup (as the race was then known), beating stablemate Mandarin. Taxidermist and Mr Lawrence also won the following autumn's Hennessy Gold Cup (run at Cheltenham), producing a fine turn of foot after landing fifth over the final fence. Mr Lawrence was also first past the post on Proud Tarquin in the 1974 Whitbread Gold Cup. Proud Tarquin had finished second to Red Rum in the Scottish Grand National seven days earlier and it looked as if victory in the Whitbread was going to provide handsome consolation until the stewards, after a twenty-minute inquiry into interference caused by Proud Tarquin to runner-up The Dikler, reversed the placings. Proud Tarquin, who had scrambled home by a head, was shown on the head-on camera patrol film (whose flickering images were in their infancy) to have hung across towards The Dikler just after the last. There was no contact but The Dikler veered away, which was enough to convince the stewards that he would have won but for the interference, a decision, it should be said, that was controversial.

```
                         ┌ Indian River (FR)    ┌ Cadoudal      ┌ Green Dancer
                         │    (b 1994)          │   (br 1979)   └ Come To Sea
Step Back (IRE)          │                      └ The Fun       ┌ Funny Hobby
   (ch.g. 2010)          │                          (b 1979)    └ The Lark
                         │                      ┌ Roselier      ┌ Misti Iv
                         └ Stepitoutmary (IRE)  │   (gr 1973)   └ Peace Rose
                              (b 1995)          └ Strong Mary   ┌ Strong Gale
                                                    (b 1989)    └ The Wren's Nest
```

Step Back, a sturdy gelding, is by Native River's sire Indian River, a son of Cadoudal who won six times over hurdles and fences in France and, in 2005, was among the first of the influx of ex-French jumps stallions that have been imported to Ireland in the last dozen years or so. Step Back is a half-brother to three winners including the fairly useful staying chaser Prince of Leisure (by Hushang) and the fair hurdler Declan's Lad (by Mister Mat) who stayed three miles. Step Back's dam Stepitoutmary was unraced and his grandam Strong Mary was a winning pointer who bred little of note. Step Back's great grandam The Wren's Nest was a winner on the Flat and over hurdles, and was a half-sister to the Hennessy Gold Cup winner Arctic Call who was runner-up in the 1992 Whitbread Gold Cup. Another of The Wren's Nest's half-brothers Polar Nomad won an Eider Chase. Step Back's strong suit is stamina too—he relished the step up in trip at Sandown—and he stays twenty-nine furlongs well. A front runner, he acts on heavy going (the going was good to soft for the Sandown Gold Cup). He looks sure to go on improving over fences. *Mark Bradstock*

STEPOVER 7 b.m. Midnight Legend – Ring Back (IRE) (Bob Back (USA)) [2017/18 h98: h16d h15.7g* h15.7g^2 h15.7d^2 h16.2g* Nov 29] workmanlike mare: fair handicap hurdler: won at Southwell in June and mares event at Hereford in November: stays 2½m: acts on good to soft going: has worn hood: wears tongue tie: usually races nearer last than first, often travels strongly. *Alex Hales*   **h106**

STEPS AND STAIRS (IRE) 8 b.g. Robin des Pres (FR) – Be Mine Tonight (IRE) (Carroll House) [2017/18 c103, h–: c19.3v* c24.1s^3 c24g* Apr 20] winning hurdler: fair handicap chaser: won at Sedgefield in February and Southwell in April: stays 3m: acts on heavy going: has worn cheekpieces. *Henry Oliver*   **c111 h–**

STEP YOU GAILY 5 b.m. Crosspeace (IRE) – Khadija (Kadastrof (FR)) [2017/18 b16s Feb 23] second foal: dam (h83) 3m hurdle winner: tailed off in mares bumper. *Ben Pauling*   **b–**

STERNRUBIN (GER) 7 b.g. Authorized (IRE) – Sworn Mum (GER) (Samum (GER)) [2017/18 h142: c17.5s^2 c18.8d^2 h16.8v h16.5s^3 Apr 14] tall gelding: useful handicap hurdler: third in conditionals/amateur event at Aintree (10¾ lengths behind Havana Beat)   **c138 h131**

STE

in April: similar form over fences: better effort when second in maiden at Exeter (2 lengths behind Yanworth) in October: raced mainly around 2m: acts on good to firm and heavy going: has worn hood: front runner. *Philip Hobbs*

STETCHWORTH (IRE) 7 ch.g. New Approach (IRE) – Hallowed Park (IRE) (Barathea (IRE)) [2017/18 h68: h19.9s^{pu} Jan 12] fairly useful on Flat for Mark Johnston, stays 10.5f: no form over hurdles. *Russell Ross* — h–

STETSONSNSTILETTOS (IRE) 6 ch.m. Presenting – Clonogan (IRE) (Bob Back (USA)) [2017/18 h22.1g^5 h16g^6 h19.9d^4 h20.1d h27g^{pu} Sep 7] fifth foal: dam twice-raced half-sister to Grande Course de Haies d'Auteuil winner Nobody Told Me: placed in Irish maiden points: poor form over hurdles: tried in tongue tie. *Donald McCain* — h76

STEVE MEQUINE 5 ch.g. Native Ruler – Rabbit (Muhtarram (USA)) [2017/18 b–: b16.2v^6 Apr 10] no form in bumpers: in hood/tongue tie sole 2017/18 start. *Sophie Leech* — b–

STEVE PRESCOTT 6 gr.g. Dutch Art – Toy Top (USA) (Tactical Cat (USA)) [2017/18 h15.8g^{pu} Jun 15] useful on Flat, stays 6f: pulled up in novice on hurdling debut. *Ian Williams* — h–

ST GEORGE'S OVAL (IRE) 5 b.g. Milan – Lisselton Lady (IRE) (Anshan) [2017/18 b16.3g^4 b14s h15.7v h15.8s h15.8s^5 Mar 14] €10,000 4-y-o: fourth foal: dam unraced half-sister to useful hurdler/very smart chaser (2m-3m winner) Scotsirish: modest form in bumpers: similar form over hurdles: usually races towards rear. *Daniel Loughnane* — h92 b81

STICK TO THE PLAN (IRE) 6 b.g. Gold Well – Chloes Choice (IRE) (Presenting) [2017/18 h122p: h24d^{ur} h23.9g^5 h20.6d^2 h21s^4 h20.3g Apr 18] well-made gelding: will make a chaser: fairly useful handicap hurdler: stays 3m: acts on good to soft going: tried in cheekpieces: wears tongue tie: waited with. *Dan Skelton* — h121

STIFF UPPER LIP (IRE) 8 b.g. Sakhee's Secret – Just In Love (FR) (Highest Honor (FR)) [2017/18 h99: h24m^5 May 4] strong, compact gelding: modest hurdler, well held sole start in 2017/18: stays 2½m: acts on heavy going: usually in headgear. *Oliver Sherwood* — h–

STILL BELIEVING (IRE) 10 ch.m. Blueprint (IRE) – Im A Believer (IRE) (Erins Isle) [2017/18 c130, h102: h23.9d^2 c26.1m^{pu} h23.3d* h21.2m* c23.8g c25.6g c23.8d^{pu} c24s^6 c22.2v Mar 31] angular mare: fairly useful handicap hurdler: won at Uttoxeter in July and mares event at Ludlow in October: fair handicap chaser: stays 3¼m: acts on good to firm and heavy going: often races towards rear. *Evan Williams* — c104 h127

STILL WILLIAM 6 b.g. Overbury (IRE) – Romany Dream (Nomadic Way (USA)) [2017/18 b81: h21.6d^{pu} Jul 31] modest bumper performer: pulled up in novice on hurdling debut. *Jo Davis* — h–

STING IN HIS TAIL (IRE) 5 b.g. Scorpion (IRE) – Glory Queen (IRE) (Taipan (IRE)) [2017/18 h19.7v^5 h24.1d^{pu} Mar 29] little impact both starts over hurdles. *Tim Easterby* — h72

STIPULATE 9 b.g. Dansili – Indication (Sadler's Wells (USA)) [2017/18 h110: ab16.3g^4 Mar 3] smart at one time on Flat: fair form over hurdles: fourth of 6 in jumpers bumper at Newcastle in March. *Sam England* — h–

ST JOHN'S 5 b.g. Aqlaam – Diam Queen (GER) (Lando (GER)) [2017/18 b88: b16.8m^3 h15.8g h15.8d^6 h15.8s Jan 10] sturdy gelding: fair form in bumpers: third at Exeter in May: modest form over hurdles: left Rod Millman after first start: will prove suited by sharp 2m: usually races towards rear. *Evan Williams* — h91 b93

ST MERRYN (IRE) 7 b.g. Oscar (IRE) – Kigali (IRE) (Torus) [2017/18 b–: h16s h19.9v^6 h15.3v c15.9v^3 c20.3v^{pu} c17.5d^3 Apr 24] third in maiden point on debut: no form over hurdles: poor form over fences: should stay at least 2½m: tried in hood: in tongue tie last 3 starts. *Rob Summers* — c80 h–

STOCKBURN (IRE) 5 b.g. Scorpion (IRE) – Hayabusa (Sir Harry Lewis (USA)) [2017/18 b16g b15.7d h19s^6 h21s^5 h21.7s^4 h24.6s^4 Apr 9] £28,000 3-y-o: workmanlike gelding: third foal: half-brother to fairly useful chaser Coeur Joyeux (21f-23f winner, by Beneficial): dam (b93), placed in bumpers, half-sister to useful chaser (21f-3¼m winner) Gunner Welburn: modest form in bumpers: fair form over hurdles: stays 3m: usually races towards rear. *Alan King* — h110 b80

STOICAL PATIENT (IRE) 9 b.m. Shantou (USA) – Dust Gale (IRE) (Strong Gale) [2017/18 c84, h–: c19.7d* c17.8g* c19.7s^F c19.2s* c20v^{pu} Mar 10] good-topped mare: maiden hurdler: fair handicap chaser: won at Plumpton in October, Fontwell in November and Market Rasen (mares) in February: stays 2½m: acts on soft and good to firm going: wears headgear: usually leads. *Gary Moore* — c103 h–

STO

STOLBERG (IRE) 10 br.g. Vinnie Roe (IRE) – Givehertthewhistle (IRE) (Supreme Leader) [2017/18 h16s h15.7g h23.6v h20.5v^F h19.5v* h21.4s^{pu} h16s^4 h19.5v c19.4v^4 c21.7v^3 Apr 27] workmanlike gelding: fair handicap hurdler: won at Lingfield in January: poor form over fences: stays 2¾m: acts on heavy going: often wears cheekpieces: has worn tongue tie, including final start. *Dai Williams* — c73 h102

STONEBOAT BILL 6 ch.g. Virtual – Applauding (IRE) (Royal Applause) [2017/18 h15.7d^6 h16.7g^5 h16s h16.4g^4 h16.8s Nov 28] fair on Flat, stays 2m: modest form over hurdles: raced around 2m: acts on good to soft going: usually races freely. *Declan Carroll* — h97

STONEBRIGG LEGEND 6 b.m. Midnight Legend – Forget The Ref (IRE) (Dr Massini (IRE)) [2017/18 h69p, b83: h20s^4 h20.7s h25.6v^3 h25d h23.9m Apr 25] poor form over hurdles: best effort at 3¼m: acts on heavy going. *Sarah Humphrey* — h72

STONECOLDSOBA 5 b.g. Aqlaam – Aswaaq (IRE) (Peintre Celebre (USA)) [2017/18 h15.7m^4 h15.7g^5 h15.8m^3 h20g* h15.8g* h16d h19.4d h20.7s^{ur} h15.5v h21s h15.8s h15.8d* Apr 24] leggy gelding: fair handicap hurdler: won at Worcester and Uttoxeter in July, and Huntingdon in April: stays 2½m: acts on good to soft going: tried in cheekpieces. *Denis Quinn* — h107

STONEHAM 7 b.m. Sixties Icon – Cibenze (Owington) [2017/18 h118: h20.2s^4 Aug 19] leggy mare: fair handicap hurdler: seemingly stays 3¼m: acts on good to firm and heavy going: wears hood: usually races in rear. *Iain Jardine* — h88

STONEMADFORSPEED (IRE) 10 b.g. Fruits of Love (USA) – Diamond Forever (Teenoso (USA)) [2017/18 h95§: h20g^3 h20.3g^3 h23.3d^3 h20f* h21.4s* h23.3d^3 h20s^4 ab18d h21.4v^{pu} Mar 28] point winner: fair handicap hurdler: won at Worcester and Wincanton in October: stays 23f: acts on firm and soft going: tried in headgear/tongue tie: usually leads: temperamental. *Roger Teal* — h108 §

STONEY MOUNTAIN (IRE) 5 ch.g. Mountain High (IRE) – Cherry Pie (FR) (Dolpour) [2017/18 b16.8v^5 b16s* b16.4s b16.7d* Apr 21] medium-sized gelding: seventh foal: half-brother to bumper winner/fairly useful hurdler Great Try (17f winner, by Scorpion): dam, French maiden (second at 1½m), half-sister to useful hurdler/high-class chaser (2m-2½m winner) The Nightingale: fairly useful form in bumpers: won at Warwick in January and Bangor (conditionals/amateur) in April: will stay 2½m. *Henry Daly* — b100

STOP THE WORLD (IRE) 5 b.g. Oscar (IRE) – Coolsilver (IRE) (Good Thyne (USA)) [2017/18 b16s^4 b16.7d^3 Apr 21] €40,000 3-y-o: fourth foal: half-brother to useful hurdler/chaser Up For Review (2½m-3m winner, by Presenting): dam unraced half-sister to high-class but ungenuine chaser (stayed 4m) Turpin Green: runner-up in Irish maiden point: fair form in bumpers: better effort when third in conditionals/amateur event at Bangor. *Tom George* — b89

STORM ALERT 11 ch.g. Karinga Bay – Rash-Gale (IRE) (Rashar (USA)) [2017/18 c–, h73: h19.2g^4 h25.6d* Jun 6] good-topped gelding: poor handicap hurdler: maiden chaser: stays 25f: acts on good to firm and heavy going: has worn cheekpieces: usually races close up. *Susan Gardner* — c– h57

STORMBAY BOMBER (IRE) 9 b.g. September Storm (GER) – Top Tottie (IRE) (Alzao (USA)) [2017/18 c100, h–: c15.7d^4 c15.7g^5 c17.4g c20.3g^{pu} c15.8m c19.2d^{pu} Nov 24] winning hurdler: modest handicap chaser: won at Southwell in June: unproven beyond 17f: acts on heavy going: tried in cheekpieces/tongue tie: usually races close up: has joined Rebecca Menzies: unreliable. *Patrick Holmes* — c99 § h–

STORM CONTROL (IRE) 5 b.g. September Storm (GER) – Double Dream (IRE) (Double Eclipse (IRE)) [2017/18 h19.3g^4 h18.5v^1 h19.3s^2 Mar 25] €27,000 3-y-o, £130,000 4-y-o: tall, unfurnished gelding: sixth foal: brother to fair hurdler Atlantic Storm (17f winner) and half-brother to useful hurdler/chaser Tagrita (17f-23f winner, by King's Theatre): dam unraced half-sister to top-class staying chaser Grey Abbey: easy winner of Irish point on debut: fairly useful form in maiden hurdles: will stay beyond 19f. *Kerry Lee* — h117

STORM FIRE 5 b.g. Fair Mix (IRE) – Tara Gale (Kayf Tara) [2017/18 b13.7g Apr 20] tailed off in bumper. *Brian Barr* — b–

STORM HOME (IRE) 6 br.g. King's Theatre (IRE) – Miss Mayberry (IRE) (Bob Back (USA)) [2017/18 h15.3g^2 h21.4s^5 h16d^F h16.5v* h15.3v^1 h20s Apr 13] €40,000 3-y-o, £130,000 4-y-o: rather unfurnished gelding: seventh foal: closely related to a winning pointer by Milan: dam unraced sister to dam of useful hurdler/smart chaser (stayed 3¼m) The Romford Pele: leading when fell 2 out in point: fairly useful form over hurdles: won novices at Taunton in February and Wincanton in March: should stay at least 2½m: acts on heavy going: front runner/races prominently, often travels strongly. *Colin Tizzard* — h127

STO

STORMINGIN (IRE) 5 gr.g. Clodovil (IRE) – Magadar (USA)(Lujain (USA)) [2017/18 h15.8s Jan 26] fair on Flat, stays 1¼m: 9/1, tenth in novice at Huntingdon on hurdling debut: has joined Gary Moore. *Don Cantillon* — h–

STORM NELSON (IRE) 5 b.g. Gold Well – Dabiyra (IRE) (Linamix (FR)) [2017/18 b76: b16v⁴ b16v⁴ h20.1v^pu h20.2s⁴ Apr 25] poor form in bumpers/over hurdles: likely to stay 2¾m+. *Lucy Normile* — h83 b74

STORM OF INTRIGUE (IRE) 6 b.g. Oscar (IRE) – Storminoora (IRE) (Topanoora) [2017/18 b15.8g* h19.3g Nov 24] €52,000 3-y-o: tall gelding: third foal: dam unraced half-sister to fairly useful hurdler/useful chaser (stayed 3¼m) Chill Factor (by Oscar): won conditional/amateur maiden bumper at Ffos Las (by 4 lengths from Angels Antics) on debut in May: 9/2, twelfth in maiden at Ascot (23¼ lengths behind Kildisart) on hurdling debut: should do better. *Nicky Henderson* — h– p b90

STORM PATROL 7 b.m. Shirocco (GER) – Material World (Karinga Bay) [2017/18 b92: h20.7d h21.6s⁶ Apr 23] lengthy mare: placed in bumpers: down the field in 2 mares novice hurdles: wears tongue tie. *Suzy Smith* — h–

STORM SALLY (IRE) 5 br.m. September Storm (GER) – Gaelic River (IRE) (Deploy) [2017/18 b16.8g Apr 19] first foal: dam unraced: 100/1, well held in mares bumper. *Tim Dennis* — b–

STORM WARNING (IRE) 6 b.g. September Storm (GER) – Ceo Draiochta (IRE) (Erins Isle) [2017/18 h–, b85: h19d^pu h20.1s⁵ h16.2v Nov 22] compact gelding: runner-up in point on debut: no form over hurdles: left Warren Greatrex after first start: tried in cheekpieces. *Tim Reed* — h–

STORMY IRELAND (FR) 4 b.f. Motivator – Like A Storm (IRE) (Ultimately Lucky (IRE)) [2017/18 h15.9s² h16v⁴ h16.8v^F h16s^ur Apr 28] neat filly: dam (c128/h127) French 2m/17f hurdle/chase winner: once-raced on Flat: useful form over hurdles: won juvenile maiden at Fairyhouse (by 58 lengths) in December: raced freely and weakening when departing last in Grade 1 juveniles at Cheltenham and Punchestown: left D. Bressou after first start: raced around 2m only on soft/heavy going. *W. P. Mullins, Ireland* — h137

STORMY MILAN (IRE) 5 b.g. Milan – Socialite Girl (Glacial Storm (USA)) [2017/18 b16.3d h20.8d⁵ h21d Apr 26] €30,000 3-y-o: tall, useful-looking gelding: has had breathing operation: fourth foal: half-brother to fairly useful 2m hurdle winner Lisdoonvarna Lad (by Westerner): dam, little form, half-sister to fairly useful hurdler/useful chaser (stays 3¼m) Wizards Bridge: well held in bumper: fair form over hurdles: will be suited by 3m: remains with potential. *Charlie Longsdon* — h102 p b69

STOWAWAY MAGIC (IRE) 7 b.g. Stowaway – Irish Mystics (IRE) (Ali-Royal (IRE)) [2017/18 h136: c20.3d² c19.1d² h19.3s⁴ h21.1s h19.8s Apr 28] good-topped gelding: point winner: useful handicap hurdler: similar form in novice chases: stays 21f: acts on soft and good to firm going: often races prominently: has joined Dan Skelton: should do better as a chaser. *Nicky Henderson* — c132 p h135

ST PATRICK'S DAY (IRE) 6 b.g. Fastnet Rock (AUS) – Race For The Stars (USA) (Fusaichi Pegasus (USA)) [2017/18 h16d³ h15.8s^F h16s⁴ h15.8g⁵ Apr 24] tall gelding: modest on Flat, stays 8.5f: modest form over hurdles: wears headgear. *J. R. Jenkins* — h99

ST PETER'S SQUARE (IRE) 7 b.g. Danehill Dancer (IRE) – Glamour (IRE) (Sadler's Wells (USA)) [2017/18 h16g⁵ h16g^pu h16g h16.7g h15.8g h18.5v^pu h16.8d Oct 12] modest handicap hurdler: pulled up only chase outing: left Eoin Doyle after third start, Alexandra Dunn after fifth: stays 2½m: acts on good to firm and heavy going: has worn headgear: sometimes wears tongue tie. *Katie Stephens* — c– h93

STRADIVARIUS DAVIS (FR) 5 b.g. Turgeon (USA) – Trumpet Davis (FR) (Rose Laurel) [2017/18 h24.4d⁵ h23.1d⁵ Apr 24] won maiden point on debut: well held in 2 novice hurdles: wears tongue tie. *Paul Nicholls* — h–

STRAIDNAHANNA (IRE) 9 gr.g. Medaaly – Sue's Song (Alflora (IRE)) [2017/18 c136, h–: c19.4d⁶ c24.1s⁵ c25.9v^pu c25.2s* c31.8g^pu Apr 21] big, strong, close-coupled gelding: maiden hurdler: useful handicap chaser: won at Catterick (by 3¼ lengths from Boric) in February: stays 3¾m: acts on heavy going: front runner/races prominently: temperamental. *Sue Smith* — c132 § h–

STRAIGHT RED (IRE) 5 b.g. Westerner – Stratosphere (Selkirk (USA)) [2017/18 b16s Feb 9] won Irish point on debut: tailed off in maiden bumper. *Jonjo O'Neill* — b–

STRAIT OF MAGELLAN (IRE) 6 ch.g. Captain Rio – Golden (FR) (Sanglamore (USA)) [2017/18 h105: h16.2d⁵ h19.4d h16.6s Jan 26] maiden hurdler, modest form at best: in tongue tie last 3 starts. *Nicky Richards*   h–

STRAIT RUN (IRE) 7 ch.g. Rock of Gibraltar (IRE) – Gentlemen's Guest (USA) (Gentlemen (ARG)) [2017/18 h82: h15.7d h16.8v* h17v³ h16.8v h16.8g Apr 23] neat gelding: poor handicap hurdler: won at Sedgefield in February: unproven beyond 17f: acts on heavy going: often wears headgear: wears tongue tie. *Micky Hammond*   h82

STRAITS OF MESSINA (IRE) 9 b.g. Mountain High (IRE) – Scylla (Rock City) [2017/18 h97: c23d⁴ c15.7d⁶ c20g⁶ Jul 27] winning hurdler: poor form over fences: stays 2¼m: acts on heavy going: tried in cheekpieces/tongue tie. *Tom Symonds*   c73 h–

STRANGSMILL (IRE) 9 b.m. Beneficial – Sweet Vale (IRE) (Supreme Leader) [2017/18 h96: h20g³ h21.6m^pu h16g Sep 3] Irish point winner: fair maiden hurdler: should stay beyond 2½m: best form on good going: usually races close up. *Sheila Lewis*   h100

STRATHY 5 b.g. Mount Nelson – Rose Street (IRE) (Noverre (USA)) [2017/18 ab16.3g b16.4d Mar 16] no form in bumpers. *Jim Goldie*   b–

STRATUM 5 b.g. Dansili – Lunar Phase (IRE) (Galileo (IRE)) [2017/18 h16.5s* h16v² Nov 12] useful on Flat, stays 1½m: useful form over hurdles: won maiden at Galway in September: second in For Auction Novices' Hurdle at Navan (4 lengths behind Mengli Khan): should improve further. *W. P. Mullins, Ireland*   h131 p

STRAVINSKYS FLAME 5 b.m. Motivator – Firebird Rising (USA) (Stravinsky (USA)) [2017/18 b15.7s b16.2s Jan 16] second foal: dam, ungenuine maiden on Flat, lightly raced over hurdles: tailed off in 2 bumpers: in hood first start. *Grace Harris*   b–

STRAWBERRY SPIRIT (IRE) 5 b.m. Saint des Saints (FR) – Strawberry (IRE) (Beneficial) [2017/18 b16s⁵ b15.8v h20.7s^ur h23.4v⁴ h20s⁵ h21.7v⁵ h21.2d Apr 9] second foal: dam (c137/h135) 2m-3m hurdle/chase winner: poor form over hurdles: modest form over hurdles: best effort at 2¾m: acts on heavy going: in headgear last 2 starts: tried in tongue tie: often races prominently. *Amy Murphy*   h87 b67

STREETS OF PROMISE (IRE) 9 b.m. Westerner – Miracle Lady (Bob's Return (IRE)) [2017/18 c124, h–: c23.6v c27.3v⁴ c25.2s⁶ c23.8v c23.6s³ c28.4v² c26.2v⁵ Apr 16] sturdy mare: winning hurdler: fair handicap chaser: stays 3½m: acts on heavy going: wears cheekpieces: front runner/races prominently. *Michael Scudamore*   c114 h–

STRIKE AGAIN 7 b.g. Misu Bond (IRE) – Mrs Quince (Mark of Esteem (IRE)) [2017/18 b16.2g May 10] tailed off in bumper. *Fred Watson*   b–

STRIKE FEAR (IRE) 6 b.g. Scorpion (IRE) – Skatey Kate (IRE) (Oscar (IRE)) [2017/18 h–, b–: h19.9g⁶ h20g⁶ h15.8g Jul 19] no form over hurdles: tried in hood. *Rebecca Menzies*   h–

STRIKE IN MILAN (IRE) 6 b.g. Milan – Great Days (IRE) (Magical Strike (USA)) [2017/18 b15.7v³ Feb 25] €36,000 3-y-o, £105,000 5-y-o: half-brother to 3 winners, including bumper winner/useful hurdler Kerb Appeal (2m-3m winner, by Needle Gun) and useful hurdler Fly Vinnie (2½m-3m winner, by Vinnie Roe): dam bumper/fair 2m-2½m hurdle winner: runner-up on debut in Irish point: in tongue tie, 11/4, third in bumper at Southwell (13 lengths behind Katahdin): will stay further than 2m: should improve. *Tom George*   b84 p

STRIKE THE POSE (FR) 6 b.m. Saint des Saints (FR) – Royale Sulawesie (FR) (Jimble (FR)) [2017/18 b16.2g* b15.8s b16.2v⁴ ab16.3g Feb 5] compact mare: fifth foal: dam, French maiden (placed up to 19f over hurdles), half-sister to fairly useful French hurdler (2¼m/19f winner) Question de Chance: fair form in bumpers: won mares event at Kelso in November. *James Ewart*   b93

STRIKE WEST (IRE) 6 b.g. Westerner – Fuel Queen (IRE) (Flemensfirth (USA)) [2017/18 h78, b–: h19.7s h16.2v⁶ h16s^ur h16s⁴ h16v h16.8v³ h19.3v* Apr 17] modest handicap hurdler: won at Carlisle (conditional) in April: stays 19f: acts on heavy going. *Micky Hammond*   h96

STRIKING NIGELLA 8 b.m. Striking Ambition – Fiona Fox (Foxhound (USA)) [2017/18 h16.8g³ Sep 7] of no account. *Michael Chapman*   h–

STROLLAWAYNOW (IRE) 11 b.g. Oscar (IRE) – Rose of Salome (IRE) (Roselier (FR)) [2017/18 c–, h–: c25.8s^pu c24.5v² Mar 15] rangy gelding: point winner: winning hurdler: fair chaser: stays 3m: acts on heavy going: has worn headgear/tongue tie, not in 2017/18: often let down by jumping. *David Arbuthnot*   c102 x h–

STR

STRONG CONVICTION 8 ch.g. Piccolo – Keeping The Faith (IRE) (Ajraas (USA)) [2017/18 h63: c24.2v^{pu} Apr 17] angular gelding: placed in points: maiden hurdler: pulled up in novice hunter on chasing debut: tried in tongue tie. *J. Cole*   c– h–

STRONG ECONOMY (IRE) 6 ch.g. Sandmason – Odd Decision (IRE) (Little Bighorn) [2017/18 h113, b65: h16.2v^3 c20.5v^3 c20.5v^4 c24.1v^4 h20.5v^2 c21.5v^3 h24.3g^{bd} Apr 20] maiden pointer: fair handicap hurdler: similar form over fences: should be suited by 3m: acts on heavy going: has joined Ian Duncan. *R. Mike Smith*   c109 h112

STRONG GLANCE 5 bl.g. Passing Glance – Strong Westerner (IRE) (Westerner) [2017/18 b15.7d* b15.7d^5 Dec 22] lengthy gelding: first foal: dam unraced half-sister to Hennessy Gold Cup winner Strong Flow: useful form in bumpers: won maiden at Southwell (by 3½ lengths from Doctor Dex) in November: fifth in listed event at Ascot (4¼ lengths behind Didtheyleaveuoutto) in December: bred to stay at least 2½m. *Fergal O'Brien*   b105

STRONGLY SUGGESTED 11 b.g. Kayf Tara – Branston Lily (Cadeaux Genereux) [2017/18 c120§, h–: c20.3g^3 c19.4g^6 c20g^5 c24.1g c21d^6 c24g* c23g^2 c25.2d^3 c27.6s^{pu} Dec 26] compact gelding: winning hurdler: fairly useful handicap chaser: won at Warwick in September: stays 25f: acts on good to firm and heavy going: tried in cheekpieces: has worn tongue tie: often races towards rear: untrustworthy. *Jonjo O'Neill*   c123 § h–

STRONGPOINT (IRE) 14 b.g. Bob Back (USA) – Ceo Draiochta (IRE) (Erins Isle) [2017/18 c17d^4 Jun 9] multiple point winner: winning hurdler: useful chaser at best, well held sole start (tongue tied) under Rules in 2017/18: stays 3m: acts on any going: has worn hood. *Miss S. Coward*   c74 h–

STRONG PURSUIT (IRE) 8 ch.g. Flemensfirth (USA) – Loughaderra (IRE) (Strong Gale) [2017/18 h130: c22.4d* Nov 9] rangy gelding: useful hurdler: 4/1, won maiden at Newbury (by 2¾ lengths from Morello Royale, with bit in hand) on chasing debut: should be suited by 3m+: acts on soft going: usually leads: remains a smart chaser in making. *Philip Hobbs*   c139 p h–

STRONG RESEMBLANCE (IRE) 7 b.g. Tikkanen (USA) – Shenamar (IRE) (Beneficial) [2017/18 h22.1m^5 h22.1g^2 h22.1s^4 h22.1d^3 h21.3s^6 c23.8s^F Apr 25] first foal: dam, unraced, closely related to fairly useful hurdler/useful chaser (stayed 21f) Laganbank: placed on second of 2 starts in points: fair form over hurdles: fell heavily fourth on chasing debut: should stay 3m: acts on soft going: front runner/races prominently. *James Moffatt*   c– h103

STRONG TEAM (IRE) 5 b.g. Exceed And Excel (AUS) – Star Blossom (USA) (Good Reward (USA)) [2017/18 b–: b16.8g^4 b16.2g^3 b16.7g h16.8g^6 h16.2d h16.8g Oct 25] modest form in bumpers: no form over hurdles: tried in hood. *Chris Grant*   h– b79

STRUMBLE HEAD (IRE) 13 b.g. Anshan – Milan Moss (Le Moss) [2017/18 c113, h–: c23.8g c19.4g c25.8d* c23.9g^5 c22.6m* c25.8d^2 c26g^3 c25.8s* Apr 23] winning hurdler: fairly useful chaser: won handicaps at Newton Abbot in July and Stratford in August, and hunter at Newton Abbot in April: stays 3¼m: acts on any going: wears headgear: tried in tongue tie: usually leads: temperamental. *Mickey Bowen*   c119 § h–

STRUMMER (IRE) 5 b.g. Frozen Power (IRE) – Question (USA) (Coronado's Quest (USA)) [2017/18 h16.8g^3 Aug 31] fair on Flat (not one to trust), stays 1¼m: 10/1, third in novice at Sedgefield (29 lengths behind Gibson Park) on hurdling debut. *Kevin Ryan*   h77

ST SAVIOUR 6 b.g. Danehill Dancer (IRE) – Titivation (Montjeu (IRE)) [2017/18 h126x: h16.3g^2 h16.3m^3 h16.8d^3 h16.3g^5 h16.4g^{bd} Oct 27] lengthy, sparely-made gelding: fairly useful handicap hurdler: third at Newton Abbot in August: unproven beyond 17f: acts on heavy going: wears headgear: usually races prominently: often let down by jumping. *Philip Hobbs*   h125 x

STUCCODOR (IRE) 9 b.g. Modigliani (USA) – Armilina (FR) (Linamix (FR)) [2017/18 h16.4g h16.4d^{pu} h20v^5 h15.8g^3 h15.8d h16s^4 h15.5v^4 h15.7v* h15.7g Apr 20] angular gelding: fairly useful on Flat, stays 1½m: modest handicap hurdler: won selling event at Southwell in February: left Sophie Leech after that: unproven beyond 2m: acts on heavy going: wears headgear: has worn tongue tie. *Conor Dore*   h98

STUN GUN 8 b.g. Medicean – Tapas En Bal (FR) (Mille Balles (FR)) [2017/18 h16.7g^6 h16.7g h18.7m^5 h20.3g Sep 6] fair but unreliable on Flat, stays 1¼m: poor form over hurdles. *Derek Shaw*   h70

STUPID CUPID (IRE) 7 b.m. Beneficial – Supreme Arrow (IRE) (Supreme Leader) [2017/18 b71: h20m^{pu} h15.8d h23.1d Apr 21] won Irish mares maiden point on debut: no form over hurdles. *Sheila Lewis*   h–

SUG

STURDY DAWN 8 br.m. Striking Ambition – Lucky Find (IRE) (Key of Luck (USA)) [2017/18 h19.6g^F Aug 4] poor form over hurdles: tried in headgear: dead. *Michael Mullineaux* — **h72**

STYLE DE GARDE (FR) 4 b.g. Kapgarde (FR) – Anowe de Jelois (FR) (Red Guest (IRE)) [2017/18 h17.4d* h16.3s* h15.8s⁴ h16.5s^pu Apr 13] good-topped gelding: first foal: dam (c124/h125) French 17f-2½m hurdle/chase winner: useful form over hurdles: won juveniles at Strasbourg in October (left Y. Fouin after) and Newbury in December: second in Fred Winter Juvenile Handicap Hurdle at Cheltenham (3 lengths behind Veneer of Charm) in March: raced around 2m: acts on soft going: often wears hood. *Nicky Henderson* — **h134**

STYLISH DANCER 4 b.f. Nathaniel (IRE) – Hazy Dancer (Oasis Dream) [2017/18 h15.7s h16s h15.8d⁶ h16.8g* Apr 19] rather leggy filly: fair maiden on Flat, stays 2m: fair form over hurdles: won handicap at Cheltenham in April: should stay 2½m. *Dan Skelton* — **h103**

STYLISH MOMENT (IRE) 5 b.g. Milan – Up The Style (IRE) (Ashkalani (IRE)) [2017/18 b16.7g³ b16.7s⁶ h20.8d³ h19.8d¹ Apr 22] €42,000 3-y-o: second foal: dam (h83), lightly raced in bumpers/over hurdles, half-sister to useful hurdler/chaser (2¼m-2¾m winner) Aura About You and fairly useful hurdler/chaser (stayed 3m) Comehomequietly: fairly useful form in bumpers: better effort when third at Bangor in October: fair form over hurdles: better effort when third in novice at Doncaster in February: will be suited by further than 21f: remains open to improvement. *Alan King* — **h106 p / b96**

STYNES (IRE) 8 b.g. Aussie Rules (USA) – Magic Princess (Bahhare (USA)) [2017/18 h115: c16.5s* c16.3g² c15.7g* c20d^pu Apr 28] rather leggy gelding: useful hurdler: similar form over fences: won handicaps at Worcester (novice) in May and Southwell in June: stays 19f: acts on soft and good to firm going: tried in cheekpieces: wears tongue tie. *Graeme McPherson* — **c126 / h–**

SUBCONTINENT (IRE) 6 b.g. Dubawi (IRE) – Saree (Barathea (IRE)) [2017/18 h76p: h15.8d^pu h19.5v⁴ h19.5v⁶ h16v h18.9s² h15.8d⁵ h21d² Apr 26] compact gelding: fair maiden hurdler: stays 21f: acts on heavy going: usually races close up. *Venetia Williams* — **h114**

SUB LIEUTENANT (IRE) 9 b.g. Brian Boru – Satellite Dancer (IRE) (Satco (FR)) [2017/18 c167, h–: c25d³ c24s⁵ c20.2v³ c20.8s⁴ c25s⁵ c24.5s⁴ Apr 25] strong gelding: winning hurdler: very smart chaser: third in John Durkan Memorial Punchestown Chase (9¾ lengths behind Sizing John) in December and fourth in Punchestown Gold Cup in April: stays 25f: acts on heavy going: has worn headgear: wears tongue tie: usually races close up. *Henry de Bromhead, Ireland* — **c159 / h–**

SUBTLE SOLDIER (IRE) 6 b.g. Subtle Power (IRE) – Killeen Queen (IRE) (Beneficial) [2017/18 h–, b–: h16.8d h16.7d c20d^pu Nov 14] rather leggy gelding: no form: has worn tongue tie. *Evan Williams* — **c– / h–**

SUCH A LEGEND 10 ch.g. Midnight Legend – Mrs Fizziwig (Petoski) [2017/18 c124, h–: c20.3g² c20g^pu c23.8d^ur c20.5m⁵ Apr 26] strong gelding: has had breathing operation: winning hurdler: fairly useful chaser: second in novice handicap at Southwell in May: stays 2½m: acts on soft and good to firm going: often wears tongue tie: front runner/races prominently. *Tracey L. Bailey* — **c123 / h–**

SUDSKI STAR (IRE) 10 br.g. Pilsudski (IRE) – Mogen's Star (IRE) (Be My Native (USA)) [2017/18 c–, h106: h16.2g⁴ h16.2g⁶ c17.1g* h16.2d c21.6g³ c15.9d* Mar 25] fair handicap hurdler: won at Kelso (conditional) in May: fairly useful handicap chaser: won at same course in September and Carlisle in March: stays 2¾m: acts on heavy going: wears headgear/tongue tie. *Harriet Graham* — **c120 / h106**

SUE BE IT (IRE) 7 b.m. Presenting – Runaround Sue (IRE) (Among Men (USA)) [2017/18 h99, b–: h20g h19.9m^ur h19.9d² h16.2s⁵ h20.5d⁵ h16.2v³ Apr 10] modest maiden hurdler: stays 21f: acts on heavy going: usually wears tongue tie. *Nikki Evans* — **h98**

SUENO TOMS 5 b.m. Oscar (IRE) – Smooth Technology (IRE) (Astronef) [2017/18 ab16.3g b17d Mar 31] half-sister to a winning sprinter in Italy by Mull of Kintyre: dam modest 2m hurdle winner: last in bumpers. *N. W. Alexander* — **b–**

SUFFICE (IRE) 9 b.g. Iffraaj – Shallat (Pennekamp (USA)) [2017/18 h81: h16.3s h25g Nov 5] poor hurdler: stays 2½m: acts on good to firm and heavy going: has worn headgear: in tongue tie last 2 starts. *Laura Young* — **h–**

SUGAR BARON (IRE) 8 b.g. Presenting – Shuil Oilean (IRE) (Be My Native (USA)) [2017/18 c136, h–: c25d² c28.8d² c26s c28.8d^pu Apr 28] rangy gelding: winning hurdler: useful handicap chaser: second at Cheltenham (amateur/½ length behind What A Moment) — **c133 § / h–**

SUG

in November and in Betfair London National at Sandown (neck behind Benbens) in December: stays 29f: acts on good to firm and heavy going: wears headgear: often let down by jumping/attitude. *Nicky Henderson*

SUGAR GLIDER 6 b.m. Morpeth – Definite Lynn (IRE) (Definite Article) [2017/18 h16.8d^{pu} h16.8v^{pu} Oct 2] second foal: dam, little sign of ability in bumpers/over hurdles, out of half-sister to high-class hurdler/top-class chaser (stayed 25f) Jair du Cochet: tailed off on completed start in points: pulled up in novice hurdles. *Jimmy Frost*   h–

SUGAR MIX 7 gr.g. Sagamix (FR) – Bruley (Weld) [2017/18 h57: h16g h21.6m Jun 15] little form over hurdles: sometimes in cheekpieces. *Charlie Longsdon*   h–

SUGAR STORM 7 b.m. Kayf Tara – Golden Buck (Golden Snake (USA)) [2017/18 h76, b–: h20m^{pu} h20.3d h17v^2 Mar 11] well-made mare: poor form over hurdles: left Fergal O'Brien after first start: sometimes in tongue tie. *Martin Keighley*   h–

SUGGESTION 6 gr.g. Dansili – Jibboom (USA) (Mizzen Mast (USA)) [2017/18 h99, b77: h15.6m h20.3d h17v^2 Apr 17] bumper winner: fair handicap hurdler: may prove best at around 2m: acts on heavy going. *Philip Kirby*   h103

SUIT HER (IRE) 6 ch.m. Shantou (USA) – Spanker (Suave Dancer (USA)) [2017/18 b17.7g h16g h20s Nov 7] sister to a winning pointer and half-sister to 3 winners, including fairly useful hurdler First Trim (2m winner, by Acclamation): dam irresolute maiden (stayed 1½m): tailed off in bumper/maiden hurdles. *John Joseph Hanlon, Ireland*   h– b–

SULAMANI THE LATE (FR) 6 b.g. Sulamani (IRE) – Delayed (FR) (Fijar Tango (FR)) [2017/18 h98§: h15.7m^3 h19.9d^3 May 20] modest maiden hurdler: stays 2½m: acts on good to firm and good to soft going: often wears cheekpieces: often travels strongly: temperamental. *Dan Skelton*   h98 §

SULLIVAN (IRE) 6 b.g. Oscar (IRE) – Courtain (USA) (Diesis) [2017/18 b16.2d Apr 23] tailed off in bumper. *Donald McCain*   b–

SULTANA BELLE (IRE) 10 b.m. Black Sam Bellamy (IRE) – Sultana (GER) (Law Society (USA)) [2017/18 c–, h82: h19.3m h22.1d^{pu} h20.2g^{pu} h16.3g^4 c19.3s^3 c16.5v^3 h19v^{pu} Jan 31] poor handicap hurdler: poor chaser: left R. Mike Smith after third start: stays 21f: acts on soft and good to firm going: has worn headgear, including in 2017/18: temperamental. *Ronan M. P. McNally, Ireland*   c76 § h57 §

SULTANS PRIDE 6 b.g. Sulamani (IRE) – Pennys Pride (IRE) (Pips Pride) [2017/18 b89: b16.4g^5 h20.6s h16.2s h22v^4 h23.1s Mar 26] modest form in bumpers/over hurdles: often races in rear. *Gillian Boanas*   h99 b84

SUM FUN NOW (IRE) 4 b.g. Jeremy (USA) – Blond's Addition (IRE) (Lord Americo) [2017/18 b16.3s Mar 24] rather unfurnished gelding: tailed off in Goffs UK Spring Sales Bumper. *Ali Stronge*   b–

SUMKINDOFKING (IRE) 7 br.g. King's Theatre (IRE) – Shannon Rose (IRE) (Topanoora) [2017/18 h123, b104: h19.5d h21d^6 h19.4d^4 h20s Apr 13] well-made gelding: has had breathing operation: winning Irish pointer: bumper winner: fairly useful handicap hurdler: stays 21f: acts on good to soft going: in tongue tie last 2 starts: often travels strongly: temperament under suspicion. *Tom George*   h119

SUMMER GETAWAY (IRE) 6 b.g. Getaway (GER) – Summer Crush (USA) (Summer Squall (USA)) [2017/18 h105, b–: h19.3g h19.5v^{pu} h15.3s h16.5m^5 Apr 25] workmanlike gelding: placed in point: modest maiden hurdler: seemingly stays 2½m: acts on good to soft going. *Nick Mitchell*   h93

SUMMER LIGHTENING 4 gr.f. Fair Mix (IRE) – Kristineau (Cadeaux Genereux) [2017/18 ab16.3g* Apr 15] third foal: dam (h83) maiden hurdler (stayed 2½m): 20/1, won bumper at Newcastle (by 1¼ lengths from Sixties Star) on debut. *Kenneth Slack*   b79

SUMMER STORM 8 b.g. Lucarno (USA) – Midsummer Magic (Muhtarram (USA)) [2017/18 c68, h104: c17d^3 c16d^{pu} h16.7g^3 h17.7g^2 c19.5g^4 h16g^6 Nov 1] fair handicap hurdler: similar form over fences: stays 19f: acts on good to soft going: tried in cheekpieces: wears tongue tie. *John Joseph Hanlon, Ireland*   c102 h107

SUMMERVILLE BOY (IRE) 6 b.g. Sandmason – Suny House (Carroll House) [2017/18 b17s* h16.3g^2 h16.4s^2 h16.8s^3 h16s* h16.4s* Mar 13]   h156 p b98

The winner's enclosure at the Cheltenham Festival is a hard place to get into, even, it seems, if you're fortunate enough to have trained the winning horse. 'They didn't want me to come in,' said Tom George after Summerville Boy had won the Supreme Novices' Hurdle. 'I nearly had fisticuffs with the gateman. They probably didn't know who I was, that's probably understandable.' Indeed, it had

32Red Tolworth Novices' Hurdle, Sandown—a much improved performance by Summerville Boy (right) who comprehensively defeats Kalashnikov (second left) and Mont des Avaloirs (left)

been sixteen years since the trainer had last been in the winner's enclosure at the Festival when Galileo won the 2002 Royal & SunAlliance Novices' Hurdle. George has trained Grade 1 winners at both Aintree and Punchestown in the meantime, but success at his local festival—he trains only a dozen or so miles away—has been much more elusive. Twelve months earlier, The Worlds End had held every chance when falling two out in the Spa at Cheltenham before gaining compensation in the Sefton at Aintree. God's Own finished second in the Arkle as a novice and made the frame in the Queen Mother Champion Chase for the second time when third in the latest edition, whereas he has won twice in Grade 1 company at the Punchestown Festival as well as winning the Melling Chase at Aintree. Tom George was among the top ten trainers by prize money for the second season running and has gone close to winning some of the biggest races in recent years. Double Shuffle was beaten a length by Might Bite in the latest King George VI Chase, while Saint Are has been placed twice in the Grand National.

  The George stable's first Festival winner had been sourced from Poland as the trainer cast his net wider in search of cheaper alternatives to the usual market places for jumpers of Ireland and France. Like his more famous Irish namesake, Galileo had been a classic winner, successful in the Polish St Leger, and had cost the equivalent of around £22,000. These days, with backing from owners like Roger Brookhouse, George's Festival runners come from more conventional backgrounds, with price tags to match; Summerville Boy had been bought by Brookhouse for £130,000 and Black Op, who carried his colours into second in the Baring Bingham twenty-four hours later, cost £210,000. Summerville Boy was bought to join his current connections after landing a gamble (backed down from 33/1 to 7/2) on his debut in a lady riders bumper at Killarney in May for Sam Curling. It took four races for Summerville Boy to get his head in front over hurdles for his new stable, but, when he did, it came in the Grade 1 Tolworth Hurdle at Sandown in January. Summerville Boy raced freely on his hurdling debut at Stratford when beaten by another promising bumper winner, Mr One More, and he then showed plenty of improvement, starting as the outsider of five, when running Slate House to three quarters of a length in a Grade 2 novice at Cheltenham in November, coming from last in a slowly-run race in which the flights in the home straight were omitted because of the low sun. Summerville Boy was returned to Cheltenham the following

Sky Bet Supreme Novices' Hurdle, Cheltenham—Summerville Boy (far side) overcomes late mistakes to confirm Sandown superiority over Kalashnikov (in front at the last); Mengli Khan, in between them, fares best of the Irish in third

month but, in another slowly-run race, was unable to repeat his previous effort, finishing third this time, though the pair that beat him, Western Ryder and Lalor, went on to prove themselves smart performers later in the season.

Summerville Boy was therefore only fourth in the betting in a five-runner Tolworth sponsored by 32Red, behind Western Ryder, the unbeaten Kalashnikov and Mont des Avaloirs, who had beaten the Tolworth outsider The Russian Doyen in a bumper and would have won both his starts over hurdles had he not fallen in the first of them. Despite the small field and quite testing conditions, the race was run at a strong gallop set by Mont des Avaloirs, and Summerville Boy showed improved form, really appreciating contesting his first well-run race over hurdles. Taking over in front soon after the leader hit the second last, Summerville Boy ran green before making a mistake of his own at the final flight which allowed Kalashnikov to get on terms. However, Summerville Boy found extra on the run-in and was going away at the finish to beat Kalashnikov by four lengths, with Mont des Avaloirs another nine lengths back in third and a disappointing Western Ryder a well-beaten fourth.

While Summerville Boy went to Cheltenham without another run, Kalashnikov went on to win the Betfair Hurdle before opposing Summerville Boy again in a nineteen-runner Sky Bet Supreme Novices' at the Festival. Unbeaten Getabird started 7/4 favourite to give Willie Mullins a fourth win in the last six runnings, and Kalashnikov and Summerville Boy were the only others at single-figure odds, sent off at 5/1 and 9/1 respectively in contradiction of the Tolworth form. 'I had to keep my mouth shut about that,' said George afterwards. 'Inside I thought it was ridiculous.' In fact, it looked a much more competitive race all round than the betting suggested, with Summerville Boy's conquerors from earlier in the season Slate House and Western Ryder also in the line-up, along with Grade 2 winners Claimantakinforgan and First Flow, while Mengli Khan and Paloma Blue were others with good form in Ireland. Patiently ridden by Noel Fehily who had also partnered him in his last couple of starts, Summerville Boy had improved to track the leading pair Getabird and Kalashnikov as they ran down the hill to the second last. From then on, his trainer must have been wishing this was another Cheltenham race where the final flights had been omitted. Impeded slightly by Getabird, Summerville Boy momentarily lost his hind legs on landing and immediately lost several places, turning for home only seventh as a result. With Kalashnikov now clear, Summerville Boy rallied to go third on the run to the last only to make another mistake there, but he still wasn't done with and clawed his way back into the race, overhauling

SUM

first Mengli Khan and then Kalashnikov in the closing stages to beat that pair by a neck and a length and three quarters. Paloma Blue rallied for fourth, ahead of Claimantakinforgan and Western Ryder, while Getabird was soon done with after two out and finished well held.

Summerville Boy (IRE) (b.g. 2012)	Sandmason (ch 1997)	Grand Lodge (ch 1991)	Chief's Crown / La Papagena
		Sandy Island (b 1981)	Mill Reef / Sayonara
	Suny House (b 1998)	Carroll House (ch 1985)	Lord Gayle / Tuna
		Mulloch Brae (b 1984)	Sunyboy / Stella Roma

There is more about Summerville Boy's sire in the essay on his stable-companion Black Op, also by Sandmason, who went on to win the Mersey Novices' at Aintree after finishing second to Samcro in the Baring Bingham. The success of that pair has led to a dramatic increase in demand for the twenty-one-year-old Sandmason's services in the spring, when he was reported to have covered more than two hundred mares. Summerville Boy changed hands for only €4,000 when he first went through the ring as a three-year-old at the Fairyhouse August National Hunt Sale. His dam Suny House was unraced and she had yet to have a runner, although Summerville Boy is her sixth foal. Suny House has since been represented by Summerville Boy's ungenuine year-older brother Desert Retreat who has been placed numerous times in bumpers, over hurdles and in points but still hasn't won. The wider family is no stranger to success at Cheltenham, though. Summerville Boy's grandam Mulloch Brae won once over hurdles and ran up a four-timer over fences at up to twenty-five furlongs before going on to become dam of the cross-

Mr R. S. Brookhouse's "Summerville Boy"

SUM

country chaser Wonderkid, who was runner-up in the La Touche Cup at Punchestown but gained his only win over Cheltenham's cross-country course. Mulloch Brae's other winner, the fairly useful staying hurdler Mini Moo Min, is the dam of the Paddy Power Gold Cup and Kauto Star Novices' Chase winner Annacotty. Mulloch Brae is herself a sister to Bigsun, a Festival winner in the Ritz Club National Hunt Handicap Chase, and a half-sister to dual Scottish Grand National winner Androma. Bigsun also won the four-mile handicap that used to be run at Cheltenham on New Year's Day and finished sixth when a leading fancy for the 1990 Grand National. As well as coming from a family of staying chasers, the lengthy Summerville Boy is very much the type for fences on looks but, with Black Op earmarked to go chasing, it looks as though Summerville Boy will remain over hurdles instead for the time being. He is sure to stay further than two miles and, while not short of speed, he will have to brush up his jumping if he is to improve enough to trouble the best two-mile hurdlers. He has raced only on soft ground apart from on his hurdling debut when the going was good. *Tom George*

SUMMIT LIKE HERBIE 6 ch.g. Sulamani (IRE) – Colline de Fleurs (Alflora (IRE)) [2017/18 b16.8v* b16.8s⁵ b15.8v⁶ Apr 15] first foal: dam (c92/h119), bumper/21f hurdle winner, half-sister to fairly useful hurdlers/useful chasers Steel Summit (stays 25f) and On The Road (stays 2¾m): fair form in bumpers: won maiden at Exeter in January: temperamental. *Nigel Twiston-Davies* — **b91 §**

SUMMONED (IRE) 7 b.g. Kris Kin (USA) – Technohead (IRE) (Distinctly North (USA)) [2017/18 c19.3g⁴ Apr 23] multiple point winner: in cheekpieces, 5/1, fourth in novice hunter at Sedgefield (25¼ lengths behind Mantou) on chasing debut. *Mrs S. E. Grant* — **c74**

SUMOS NOVIOS (IRE) 10 b.g. Flemensfirth (USA) – Gaelic Million (IRE) (Strong Gale) [2017/18 c139: c22.6s² c19.5v² c25v c22v* c24v* c24.5sᵖᵘ Apr 25] smart chaser: won veterans handicap at Wexford (by ¾ length from Undressed) in March and Imperial Call Chase at Cork (by 2¼ lengths from Mala Beach) in April: stays 3m: acts on heavy going: tried in tongue tie. *W. J. Burke, Ireland* — **c150**

SUNADER (FR) 5 ch.g. Creachadoir (IRE) – Suerte Loca (IRE) (Peintre Celebre (USA)) [2017/18 b16g⁶ h15.8gᵖᵘ h15.8d Mar 26] no form in bumper/over hurdles. *Charlie Longsdon* — **h–** / **b–**

SUN CLOUD (IRE) 11 b.g. Cloudings (IRE) – Miss Melrose (Bob Back (USA)) [2017/18 c125, h115: h26.4d⁴ h23.9v* h27g* c30s⁶ h26.6s Apr 26] smallish, good-topped gelding: fairly useful handicap hurdler: won at Perth in September and Sedgefield in November: fairly useful handicap chaser: stays 3¾m: acts on heavy going: usually wears headgear: tried in tongue tie: front runner/races prominently. *Ruth Jefferson* — **c104** / **h127**

SUNDANCE BOY 9 gr.g. Proclamation (IRE) – Just Beth (Carlingford Castle) [2017/18 h–: h18.7m h23.3d h19.6d⁴ Apr 21] no form over hurdles: wore blinkers in 2017/18. *Giuseppe Fierro* — **h–**

SUNDAY CENTRAL 7 ch.g. Central Park (IRE) – Sunday News'n'echo (USA) (Trempolino (USA)) [2017/18 h96, b99: h19.9v* Dec 22] sturdy gelding: fair handicap hurdler: won at Uttoxeter only start in 2017/18: stays 23f: acts on heavy going: often races towards rear. *Tom Weston* — **h102**

SUNDAY IN THE PARK 5 gr.m. Fair Mix (IRE) – Just Smokie (Cloudings (IRE)) [2017/18 h15.9d h15.9d⁶ h16s² h19.7s⁶ h20.5d h15.7v¹ h15.9s⁴ Apr 15] £3,200 3-y-o: second foal: dam (h90), maiden hurdler (stayed 3m), half-sister to fairly useful/temperamental chaser (stayed 2½m) Greywell Boy (by Fair Mix): modest maiden hurdler: unproven beyond 2m: acts on soft going: sometimes wears hood. *David Bridgwater* — **h93**

SUNDIAL STORM 5 ch.m. Shantou (USA) – Shadow Line (FR) (Ballingarry (IRE)) [2017/18 b15.8d⁴ b16m² Jul 5] £1,500 3-y-o: first foal: dam unraced half-sister to useful hurdler/chaser (17f-19f winner) Granit Jack: fair form in bumpers: better effort when second in mares event at Worcester. *Seamus Mullins* — **b85**

SUNNY DESTINATION (IRE) 6 b.g. Dubai Destination (USA) – Railway House (IRE) (Ashkalani (IRE)) [2017/18 b90: b17d⁶ b16v⁵ h20.5v⁴ h18.1v² Apr 16] poor form in bumpers: modest form over hurdles: better effort when second in novice at Kelso: front runner/races prominently. *George Bewley* — **h96** / **b74**

SUNNY LEDGEND 13 b.g. Midnight Legend – Swordella (Broadsword (USA)) [2017/18 c120, h–: c23.9d^{pu} c20v^3 c24.1v^{pu} c19.2s^4 c29.2v^5 c27.5d^5 Apr 22] tall gelding: winning hurdler: fair handicap chaser nowadays: best up to 3m: acts on good to firm and heavy going: often in cheekpieces in 2017/18: tried in tongue tie: front runner/races prominently. *Andrew Martin*   c106 h–

SUNNYTAHLIATEIGAN (IRE) 6 b.g. Robin des Pres (FR) – Wavering Bee (IRE) (Oscar (IRE)) [2017/18 h108, b81: h20.5g^4 h16.4g^6 h19.8s^2 h19.6s Jan 12] useful-looking gelding: fair handicap hurdler: stays 2½m: acts on soft going: often races prominently. *Ian Williams*   h111

SUNSET MARQUIS (IRE) 7 b.m. Kayf Tara – Miss Abrahmovic (IRE) (Deploy) [2017/18 h97, b62: h16.2g^4 h20.1s^{pu} Oct 6] maiden hurdler, standout effort on debut in 2016/17: tried in cheekpieces. *Alison Hamilton*   h69

SUNSET SHOWDOWN (IRE) 5 b.g. Flemensfirth (USA) – Sunset Queen (IRE) (King's Theatre (IRE)) [2017/18 b16s^5 h19.7s^2 h19.3s^4 Mar 25] €58,000 3-y-o: good-topped gelding: sixth foal: half-brother to fairly useful hurdler/useful chaser Definite Ruby (2¼m-23f winner, by Definite Article): dam unraced: won Irish point on debut: fifth in bumper at Chepstow (5½ lengths behind Good Boy Bobby): fairly useful form over hurdles: better effort when second in maiden at Hereford in January: will be suited by 2¾m+: should still improve. *Rebecca Curtis*   h119 p b93

SUNSET SKYE 5 b.m. Sea Freedom – Money Central (Central Park (IRE)) [2017/18 b17.7d h15.7v^{ur} h19.2s^{pu} h21.6s^{pu} Apr 23] first foal: dam placed in point: no form in bumper/over hurdles: tried in visor. *Lydia Richards*   h– b–

SUNSHADE 5 b.m. Sulamani (IRE) – Spring Flight (Groom Dancer (USA)) [2017/18 b95p: h15.8g* h18.6d* h16.5s^3 h20.5s Mar 24] bumper winner: fairly useful form over hurdles: won mares maiden at Ludlow in November and novice at Market Rasen in December: should stay 2½m: often in hood. *Nicky Henderson*   h121

SUN SPIDER (IRE) 7 br.g. Scorpion (IRE) – Benedicta Rose (IRE) (Beneficial) [2017/18 h–: h23.3g^{pu} Jun 25] placed both starts in Irish maiden points: no form over hurdles. *Brian Ellison*   h–

SUPAKALANISTIC (IRE) 5 b.g. Kalanisi (IRE) – Keys Hope (IRE) (Luso) [2017/18 b88: b16g^3 b16g^5 h21.2g^{pu} h15.8d h15.8s^6 h20.3v* h23.1v^{pu} Mar 11] fair form in bumpers: fairly useful form over hurdles: won handicap at Southwell in February: best effort at 2½m: acts on heavy going. *Nigel Twiston-Davies*   h115 b91

SUPAPOWERS (IRE) 12 ch.m. Subtle Power (IRE) – Hi Sheree (IRE) (Beau Sher) [2017/18 c–, h86: c24g^{pu} h25.6d^5 h23g h20g Sep 12] angular mare: winning Irish pointer: maiden hurdler/chaser: in cheekpieces last 3 starts: wears tongue tie. *Robert Stephens*   c– h–

SUPASUNDAE 8 b.g. Galileo (IRE) – Distinctive Look (IRE) (Danehill (USA)) [2017/18 h154: h20s^3 h24s^2 h16s* h24s^2 h20s^2 h16s* Apr 27]   h162

Either Sizing John or Our Duke might have been expected to be the flagship horse for Jessica Harrington's stable in the latest season. But both of those high-class chasers experienced mixed fortunes, with injury ruling Sizing John out of a defence of his Gold Cup title and the ill-fated Our Duke coming up short in his bid to follow in his stablemate's footsteps. Instead, it was hurdler Supasundae who provided the highlights of his stable's season, winning twice in Grade 1 company. A step up in trip had paid dividends for a couple of Ireland's other leading hurdlers after they were beaten in the Champion Hurdle. Identity Thief, who was fourth at Cheltenham, won the Liverpool Hurdle at Aintree on his first try at three miles, while former two-mile champion Faugheen, only sixth in the latest Champion Hurdle, won the Champion Stayers' Hurdle at Punchestown on a return to three miles for the first time since his novice days. Supasundae, on the other hand, has now been beaten in all three of his races over three miles, albeit running well and finishing second each time, and it was a drop in distance which worked best for him, both of his wins and his two very best efforts in the latest season coming when returned to the minimum trip.

Supasundae's first big win had come in the Coral Cup at Cheltenham in 2017, a victory that served as a springboard for his first tilt at three miles at Aintree where he confirmed his improvement, stepped up in grade as well as trip, to run Yanworth a length in the Liverpool Hurdle. That run not only showed that Supasundae was able to hold his own in Grade 1 company (he had finished only seventh in the Supreme as a novice), but it also suggested that his future over hurdles was going

BHP Insurance Irish Champion Hurdle, Leopardstown—Supasundae (nearest camera) copes with the marked drop in trip and lowers the colours of 2016 winner Faugheen

to be as a stayer. He was campaigned accordingly at the outset of the latest season, looking ring-rusty on his return behind Apple's Jade and Nichols Canyon in the Hatton's Grace Hurdle at Fairyhouse, but making Apple's Jade work much harder for her half-length win in the Christmas Hurdle at Leopardstown, headed only close home after making much of the running back at three miles. Faugheen's shock defeat at the same meeting left Ireland's two-mile hurdling division suddenly looking a lot more open and, with no big staying hurdle to go for, Supasundae was returned to two miles for the first time in just over a year for the BHP Insurance Irish Champion Hurdle, highlight of the first day of the new two-day Dublin Racing Festival at Leopardstown at the beginning of February. One way or another, each member of the eight-runner field had something to prove, though none more than Faugheen, whose abject performance at the track in December was still a mystery. Supasundae's well-being wasn't in doubt, but he clearly faced a very different test, taking on top two-milers. Mick Jazz had to show that the form of his win in the Ryanair Hurdle, in which Faugheen had flopped, was all that it had seemed, while the up-and-coming Melon had fallen short against some of the best British hurdlers when third in the International Hurdle at Cheltenham. The only British-trained visitor in the field was the previous season's top juvenile hurdler Defi du Seuil, though he too needed to make amends after disappointing on his reappearance. Bapaume had been beaten nearly five lengths behind Supasundae when third in the Christmas Hurdle, while Supasundae's stable-companion Jezki had been well beaten in the same race. Identity Thief completed the line-up, starting the rank outsider on his first start since running poorly when reverting to hurdles from fences the previous spring. Supasundae was sent off at 8/1 along with Mick Jazz, while enough faith was retained in Faugheen (such an impressive winner of the race two years earlier) for him to start 10/9-on, with stable-companion Melon at 7/2. Supasundae's jumping has sometimes let him down but an impressive round of hurdling on this occasion helped him keep tabs on Faugheen. After travelling well close up, Supasundae gamely stuck to his task in the straight to head Faugheen on the run-in and stayed on strongly to win by two and a quarter lengths, with Mick Jazz beaten a total of seven lengths into third without managing to land a blow at the first two. Jezki and Melon were next, with the rest well beaten, Melon disappointing for the first time, tried in headgear.

Having run a new career-best over two miles, the Champion Hurdle at Cheltenham might have looked a tempting option for Supasundae but he had not been given an entry and, instead of being supplemented, he took his chance instead in the Stayers' Hurdle which had been the long-term plan. Even so, with Melon (beaten a neck), Mick Jazz and Identity Thief (sixth at Leopardstown) filling the frame behind Buveur d'Air in the Champion Hurdle, it would have been interesting to see how Supasundae might have fared in the shorter race. On the other hand, there probably weren't too many regrets about Supasundae taking up the staying option after he had given a good account in a race that played to his strengths. Supasundae was disadvantaged much less than some others by the lack of pace, something which proved the undoing of the favourite Sam Spinner in particular. Supasundae improved to hold every chance at the last and kept on to be beaten two lengths into second behind Penhill. Instead of taking the three-mile option at Aintree again where conditions were also testing, connections decided that the intermediate trip of the Aintree Hurdle presented a better opportunity for Supasundae who was sent off the 11/10 favourite but, running creditably once again, he went down by three lengths to the stronger stayer L'Ami Serge who had finished only eighth in the Stayers' Hurdle.

A longer gap than usual between Cheltenham and Aintree meant a shorter one between Aintree and Punchestown and it was to Supasundae's credit, as one of the few horses to run at all three major spring festivals, that he was able to bounce back from two defeats to end his season with another win back at two miles in the Betdaq 2% Commission Punchestown Champion Hurdle. Willie Mullins had dominated the race in recent years, winning seven of the eight previous renewals (four of those with Hurricane Fly), and Jessica Harrington is the only other trainer to have won it more than once, doing so with Moscow Flyer, Macs Joy and most recently in 2014 with Jezki who beat Hurricane Fly in a three-runner contest to supplement his Champion Hurdle win at Cheltenham. The 2006 winner Macs Joy, who had won the Irish Champion Hurdle the previous season, had finished second to Brave Inca in the Champion Hurdle at Cheltenham before turning the tables on his old rival at Punchestown. In the aftermath of a dramatic race, the victory of 7/1 favourite Supasundae wasn't the only topic of conversation, or even the major one, but he ran just about his best race yet in beating the previous year's winner Wicklow Brave, becoming his stable's fourth Punchestown Champion Hurdle winner. Inevitably, the biggest headlines were made by events at the third-last hurdle where the first two in the betting Samcro and Melon came down in independent falls when poised to take a hand in the finish. That robbed the race of its main point of interest, that of seeing how the season's star novice would fare on his first start against some of the established top two-milers. Wicklow Brave and Supasundae were left clear with Supasundae taking over in front early in the straight and then asserting before the final flight to win by three and a quarter lengths with the three other finishers, Bleu Berry, Coquin Mans and The Game Changer, coming home at wide intervals.

Supasundae has one of the choicest Flat pedigrees of any jumper currently in training and is one of the best sons of Galileo to end up over hurdles, along with Celestial Halo (another who proved effective at a range of trips, runner-up in

Betdaq 2% Commission Punchestown Champion Hurdle, Punchestown—
Supasundae takes full advantage of some earlier carnage as he defeats 2017 winner Wicklow Brave
for his second Grade 1 win of the campaign

SUP

both a Champion Hurdle and a Stayers' Hurdle during his career) and the Baring Bingham winner Windsor Park. Supasundae was evidently too big and backward to be given a chance on the Flat as a young horse. He was entered in, but ultimately withdrawn from, the Autumn Horses in Training Sales as a two-year-old when in training with Ed Dunlop under the name of War Horse, but, still unraced a year later and now nameless (and gelded), he changed hands privately for just £9,500 at Doncaster where the catalogue described him as 'a fine individual whose looks and appearance clearly indicate that he has needed time.' Supasundae finally made his debut, a successful one, as a four-year-old in a bumper at Wetherby for North Yorkshire trainer Tim Fitzgerald in the spring of 2014. His next appearance, another win, came late the same year when springing a 16/1 surprise in a listed bumper at Ascot (impressively beating Yanworth, with Thistlecrack back in fifth) by which time he had joined Andrew Balding. That was only briefly, as it turned out, because he changed ownership again, having his third start for as many different trainers when finishing sixth for Henry de Bromhead and Ann & Alan Potts in the Champion Bumper at Cheltenham after making most of the running. Supasundae (along with Sizing John, among others) eventually joined his current stable when the Potts horses with de Bromhead were moved elsewhere in the autumn of 2016.

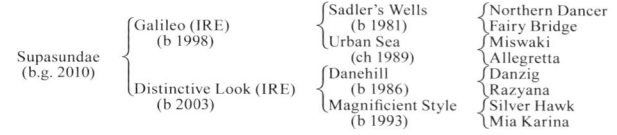

Supasundae (b.g. 2010)
- Galileo (IRE) (b 1998)
  - Sadler's Wells (b 1981)
    - Northern Dancer
    - Fairy Bridge
  - Urban Sea (ch 1989)
    - Miswaki
    - Allegretta
- Distinctive Look (IRE) (b 2003)
  - Danehill (b 1986)
    - Danzig
    - Razyana
  - Magnificent Style (b 1993)
    - Silver Hawk
    - Mia Karina

Supasundae's grandam Magnificent Style won the Musidora Stakes in a brief career for Sir Henry Cecil and has earned greater fame as an outstanding broodmare, with her ten winners including the Eclipse and King George winner Nathaniel, as well as his Irish Oaks-winning sister Great Heavens, both of those by Galileo. Great Heavens also won the Lancashire Oaks, a race won by another of Magnificent Style's daughters Playful Act who also won the Fillies' Mile. Magnificent Style is also dam of the Sun Chariot and Park Hill Stakes winner Echoes In Eternity and Percussionist who finished fourth in the Derby and gained his biggest win on the Flat in the Yorkshire Cup. Percussionist also had a successful and varied jumping career, which included a win over fences, two successes at Ovrevoll in Norway (including their Champion Hurdle) and the Grade 1 Grand National Hurdle at Far Hills in New Jersey. Supasundae's dam Distinctive Look was no better than fairly useful, her only win coming in a nine-furlong maiden at Goodwood. Her first foal, Royal Peculiar, also by Galileo, won over a mile and a half on the Flat, while she has produced two more winners since Supasundae. Posing (by Medicean) won a maiden at Dundalk over an extended ten furlongs, while Distingo (by Smart Strike) showed fairly useful form over hurdles, winning twice, for Gary Moore in the latest season, having won at around a mile and a half on the Flat in France. There were few better hurdlers than Supasundae in the latest season and he coped admirably with a campaign that tested both his versatility and his toughness, the very best of his form coming at two miles for all that he stays three. He has raced only on good going or softer and acts on heavy. *Mrs J. Harrington, Ireland*

SUPER CHARGE 6 ch.g. Recharge (IRE) – Arctic Ring (Karinga Bay) [2017/18 h77: h19.7s h16.4g Nov 17] won point on debut: modest form over hurdles: best effort at 2m. *Chris Fairhurst* **h87**

SUPERIOR COMMAND (IRE) 9 b.g. Lahib (USA) – Decent Dime (IRE) (Insan (USA)) [2017/18 c–, h103: h16.2d⁴ h15.6m* Nov 8] fair handicap hurdler: won at Musselburgh in November: winning chaser: stays 2¾m: acts on soft and good to firm going: wears headgear: often wears tongue tie: usually races nearer last than first. *Lucinda Russell* **c–** **h110**

SUPERMAN DE LA RUE (FR) 12 b.g. Akhdari (USA) – Impala de La Rue (FR) (Brugnon (FR)) [2017/18 c–, h–: h26.5d³ Jul 23] multiple point winner: fairly useful hurdler at best: maiden chaser: stayed 3¼m: acted on soft and good to firm going: tried in headgear: dead. *Mary Evans*   c–
h94

SUPER SCORPION (IRE) 8 b.g. Scorpion (IRE) – Nolagh Supreme (IRE) (Supreme Leader) [2017/18 c114, h–: c23.8g* c23.8g* c23g⁵ c24.1g⁴ c23.8m³ c23.8g⁵ Nov 9] maiden hurdler: fairly useful handicap chaser: won at Ffos Las in May and June: stays 3m: acts on good to soft going: wears headgear: usually races nearer last than first. *Debra Hamer*   c129
h–

SUPER SID (IRE) 6 b.g. Westerner – Super Sammy (Mesleh) [2017/18 b77p: h15.7s* h18.6v⁴ h16s h15.7s h21.4d Apr 22] runner-up in Irish maiden point: fairly useful form over hurdles: won maiden at Southwell in December: stays 19f: acts on heavy going. *Tom George*   h117

SUPREME AMBITION (IRE) 6 gr.g. Acambaro (GER) – Supreme Argument (IRE) (Supreme Leader) [2017/18 h18.8g⁵ h18.8g^bd h16g h16g h16.7g c25.8g^pu Sep 2] failed to complete all 4 starts in points: poor form over hurdles: pulled up in novice handicap on chasing debut: left P. J. Rothwell after third start: sometimes in blinkers. *Katy Price*   c–
h73

SUPREME DANEHILL (IRE) 10 b.g. Indian Danehill (IRE) – Monte Rosa (IRE) (Supreme Leader) [2017/18 c96: c25.5s* c27.5d³ c25.1v³ Feb 1] multiple point winner: fairly useful chaser: won novice hunter at Fontwell in May: stays 25f: acts on soft and good to firm going: wears cheekpieces: usually leads. *Alan Hill*   c117

SUPREMELY LUCKY (IRE) 6 b.g. Milan – Lucky Supreme (IRE) (Supreme Leader) [2017/18 b16s* Feb 24] £34,000 5-y-o: seventh foal: brother to fairly useful chaser Luckyinmilan (2m-23f winner) and half-brother to 2 winners, including fair hurdler Supreme Benefit (2m winner, by Beneficial), stayed 2½m: dam, winning pointer, half-sister to fair hurdler/fairly useful chaser (stayed 3m) Seafield Bogie: runner-up on second of 2 starts in Irish points: 7/1, won conditional/amateur maiden bumper at Chepstow by 2 lengths from Kapgarry: sure to stay beyond 2m. *Dan Skelton*   b99

SUPREME STEEL (IRE) 7 b.g. Craigsteel – Tubber Gael Holly (IRE) (Arctic Cider (USA)) [2017/18 h23.3g² h23.3g* h23.1g² h23.6v⁵ h24s⁶ Jan 1] €6,000 3-y-o: rather leggy gelding: first foal: dam (c100/h100) 2½m hurdle/chase winner: fairly useful handicap hurdler: won at Uttoxeter in July: second at Market Rasen in August: stays 23f: acts on heavy going: wears headgear: strong traveller. *Dr Richard Newland*   h117

SUPRISE VENDOR (IRE) 12 ch.g. Fath (USA) – Dispol Jazz (Alhijaz) [2017/18 c–§, h103§: h16.2g⁴ h16.2v³ c16.5v^pu h16.4v³ h15.6d h16v h17s Apr 8] close-coupled gelding: modest handicap hurdler: winning chaser: stays 19f: acts on heavy going: often let down by jumping/attitude. *Stuart Coltherd*   c– x
h93 x

SURENESS (IRE) 8 ch.m. Hurricane Run (IRE) – Silk Dress (IRE) (Gulch (USA)) [2017/18 c–, h109: h20m³ h20.3g⁴ h16.8d^pu h19g Nov 16] workmanlike mare: modest handicap hurdler: maiden chaser: stays 21f: acts on good to firm and good to soft going: often wears cheekpieces: wears tongue tie: front runner/races prominently: has joined Tony Newcombe. *Charlie Mann*   c–
h98

SURE REEF (IRE) 9 ch.g. Choisir (AUS) – Cutting Reef (IRE) (Kris) [2017/18 h134: h20m⁵ c24.9s^pu Jun 12] big, workmanlike gelding: useful handicap hurdler: fifth at Ballinrobe (5 lengths behind Swamp Fox) in May: didn't take to chasing at first attempt: stays 3m: acts on good to firm and heavy going. *W. P. Mullins, Ireland*   c–
h133

SURF AND TURF (IRE) 12 ch.g. Beneficial – Clear Top Waltz (IRE) (Topanoora) [2017/18 c125x, h98: h20.1g⁴ h20g⁴ c20.3g⁴ c22.6g^pu h15.7g⁴ Oct 11] workmanlike gelding: fairly useful handicap chaser: won at Hexham in June: fairly useful handicap hurdler: stays 2½m: acts on good to firm and good to soft going: has worn cheekpieces, including final start: tried in tongue tie: often let down by jumping over fences. *Richard Hobson*   c116 x
h119

SURTEE DU BERLAIS (IRE) 8 b.m. High Chaparral (IRE) – Marina du Berlais (FR) (Mister Sicy (FR)) [2017/18 h130: c21.6g⁴ c23.4s⁵ c23.6v⁶ c23.6v⁴ c24.2s^F h25.5v⁴ Apr 10] good-bodied mare: fairly useful handicap hurdler: fair form over fences: stays 3m: acts on heavy going: usually wears headgear: often held back by attitude nowadays. *Oliver Sherwood*   c111 §
h95 §

SURTEES 5 b.m. Native Ruler – Royalty (IRE) (Fairy King (USA)) [2017/18 b15.7d⁵ Jun 6] well beaten in mares bumper: dead. *Philip Kirby*   b–

SUSSEX RANGER (USA) 4 b.g. Hat Trick (JPN) – Purple (USA) (Royal Academy (USA)) [2017/18 h17.7g* h16s* h16v² h16.8v Mar 16] tall gelding: half-brother to a winner over hurdles in Italy by Henrythenavigator: fairly useful on Flat, stays 2m: useful   h131

SUS

form over hurdles: won juveniles at Fontwell in October and Sandown (by 14 lengths from Quothquan) in December: second in Finale Juvenile Hurdle at Chepstow (1½ lengths behind We Have A Dream) in January: likely to stay further than 2m. *Gary Moore*

SUSSEX ROAD (IRE) 8 b.g. Mahler – Rose Island (Jupiter Island) [2017/18 c80§, h–§: c21.7m³ c16.1g^{pu} c21.2d³ h15.8g⁵ c21.2g c21.2d^{pu} c16.5g⁵ c16.1g⁵ c19.9g^{pu} c15.9m^{pu} c16.2v³ c19.1s³ c23.6v⁴ c15.9s^{pu} c15.9v^{pu} c21.7v^R Apr 27] angular gelding: of little account: wears headgear: temperamental. *Aytach Sadik* **c– §** **h– §**

SUSTAINABLE STAR (IRE) 7 gr.g. Winged Love (IRE) – Fooling Around (IRE) (Medaille Militaire) [2017/18 b16.8g h15.3g h16.8v h19.8v⁴ h16s h19.5v Apr 14] €20,000 3-y-o, £16,000 5-y-o: lengthy gelding: second foal: dam unraced half-sister to smart hurdler/very smart chaser (stayed 21f) Barker: tailed off in bumper: little form over hurdles. *Richenda Ford* **h–** **b–**

SUTOOR (IRE) 4 b.g. Cape Cross (IRE) – Yanabeeaa (USA) (Street Cry (IRE)) [2017/18 b13.1g^{ur} b13.7g Nov 14] sparely-made gelding: no form in bumpers/Flat maidens. *Mark Brisbourne* **b–**

SUTTER'S MILL (IRE) 7 b.g. Gold Well – Shamriyna (IRE) (Darshaan) [2017/18 h103: h25d² h26.5d* h21g² h23.1s h20.3d c20.9v⁴ c23.6v⁵ c19.4v² c25.1v^{pu} c24.2v^{pu} Apr 8] fair handicap hurdler: won at Newton Abbot in July: similar form over fences: stays 3¼m: acts on heavy going: sometimes wears cheekpieces: often races in rear. *Evan Williams* **c102** **h104**

SUTTON MANOR (IRE) 7 b.g. Gold Well – Nighty Bless (IRE) (Executive Perk) [2017/18 h140: c22.5s⁴ c20s³ c21.2s² c19.7v* c21s c20s⁶ c23v^F c29v^{pu} c24.5s^{pu} Apr 28] rangy gelding: useful hurdler: useful chaser: won maiden at Down Royal in December: stays 3m: acts on heavy going: in cheekpieces last 3 starts. *Gordon Elliott, Ireland* **c133** **h–**

SUTTON PLACE (IRE) 7 b.g. Mahler – Glebe Beauty (IRE) (Good Thyne (USA)) [2017/18 h160: c21.2v* c21s^{pu} Feb 4] high-class hurdler: smart form over fences: won maiden at Fairyhouse (readily, by 3¼ lengths from Kemboy) in January: made mistakes when pulled up in Flogas Novices' Chase at Leopardstown: stays 21f: acts on heavy going: usually wears tongue tie: should still do better as a chaser. *Gordon Elliott, Ireland* **c145 p** **h–**

SUZIE STAPLES 4 ch.f. Black Sam Bellamy (IRE) – Dawn Breaker (Rakaposhi King) [2017/18 b12.6s Dec 20] leggy filly: eleventh foal: dam unraced half-sister to dam of very smart chaser (stayed 3¼m) Planet of Sound: tailed off in fillies junior bumper. *Richard Price* **b–**

SWAFFHAM BULBECK (IRE) 4 b.g. Jeremy (USA) – Ballygologue (IRE) (Montjeu (IRE)) [2017/18 h16s² h15.7v⁵ Feb 17] fair on Flat, stays 8.5f: fairly useful form over hurdles: better effort when second in juvenile at Warwick in January. *Olly Murphy* **h115**

SWALEDALE LAD (IRE) 11 b.g. Arakan (USA) – Tadjnama (USA) (Exceller (USA)) [2017/18 c100§, h97§: h16.8s⁴ h16.2g² h18.7m⁴ c17.4g⁵ h16.3m^{ur} Aug 24] tall, narrow gelding: poor handicap hurdler/handicap chaser nowadays: stays 19f: acts on good to firm and heavy going: often wears cheekpieces: weak finisher. *Graeme McPherson* **c82 §** **h82 §**

SWALLOWSHIDE 9 b.g. Hernando (FR) – Kentford Grebe (Teenoso (USA)) [2017/18 c81, h–: c21.1s² c20.9d³ c20v⁴ c22.6d⁴ Apr 22] point winner: winning hurdler: modest form in hunter chases: should stay 3m: acts on soft going: tried in hood. *J. H. Young* **c97** **h–**

SWAMP FOX (IRE) 6 br.g. Windsor Knot (IRE) – Brogella (IRE) (King's Theatre (IRE)) [2017/18 h133: h17g⁴ h20m* h17g* h16d² h16v⁴ h16.2s³ h20s h20s Apr 28] smart handicap hurdler: won at Ballinrobe (by short head from Polar Present) in May and Killarney (by 2½ lengths from Is She Diesel) in July: second in Galway Hurdle in August: stays 2½m: acts on good to firm and heavy going: wears blinkers: usually races prominently. *Joseph G. Murphy, Ireland* **h152**

SWANTYKAY (IRE) 9 b.g. Darsi (FR) – Glamorous Leader (IRE) (Supreme Leader) [2017/18 c20m* c20.1m^{ur} c21.2g⁶ c20.1v⁴ c15.9s^{pu} c23.8m^{ur} h25.3d h19.9s^{pu} Jan 12] fair hurdler at best: fairly useful handicap chaser: won at Down Royal in May on final start for Ellmarie Holden: little form after: stays 3m: acts on good to firm and good to soft going: tried in cheekpieces. *Barry Murtagh* **c117 d** **h–**

SWASHBUCKLE 5 b.g. Dashing Blade – Inhibition (Nayef (USA)) [2017/18 h15.7d³ h16.2s⁴ ab16g* Mar 2] dam half-sister to Imperial Cup winner Scorned: useful on Flat, stays 16.5f: fair form over hurdles: better effort when third in maiden at Catterick in December: won jumpers bumper at Southwell in March: will be suited by 2½m+: should still improve. *Donald McCain* **h106 p**

SWATOW 6 b.m. Shantou (USA) – Sudden Beat (Beat All (USA)) [2017/18 h110, b–: h18.5m² h20.7g^{ur} Apr 24] good-topped mare: fair form over hurdles: tried in hood. *Emma Lavelle* **h102**

SWEEPING ROCK (IRE) 8 b.g. Rock of Gibraltar (IRE) – Sweeping Story (USA) (End Sweep (USA)) [2017/18 h94: h20.6g h16g* h15.8m² h15.8g h16d³ h19.6g⁴ h18.5v⁶ h19g³ Nov 30] modest handicap hurdler: won novice event at Worcester in June: stays 2½m: acts on good to soft going: has worn cheekpieces: tried in tongue tie. *John Spearing* **h98**

SWEET ADARE (IRE) 5 b.m. Getaway (GER) – The Adare Woman (IRE) (Oscar (IRE)) [2017/18 b16.7s⁴ b15.7g* Apr 20] first foal: dam, promoted third in bumper on only start, sister to useful hurdler/smart chaser (stayed 2½m) William's Wishes and smart bumper winner Acey Milan: fair form in bumpers: dead-heated with Indefatigable in conditional/amateur maiden at Southwell in April. *Victor Dartnall* **b89**

SWEET AS CANDY (IRE) 6 b.g. Morozov (USA) – Sweet Nancy (IRE) (Moscow Society (USA)) [2017/18 b16.4g b20.6s⁴ h24.3v³ Feb 26] £42,000 5-y-o: second foal: dam, third from 2 starts in points, half-sister to fairly useful hurdler/useful chaser (stayed 3m) Duers: won Irish point on debut: modest form in bumper: fair form over hurdles: won maiden at Ayr in January: stays 3m. *Rose Dobbin* **h114 b83**

SWEET BELLE 8 b.m. Black Sam Bellamy (IRE) – Phildante (IRE) (Phardante (FR)) [2017/18 c90, h–: c24.2g² c26.2g h20.3d c21.1gᵖᵘ Oct 25] little impact over hurdles: modest handicap chaser: stays 3¼m: acts on good to firm going: usually in cheekpieces: tried in tongue tie. *David Thompson* **c91 h–**

SWEET HOLLY 7 b.m. Kayf Tara – Presuming (Mtoto) [2017/18 h97: h15.7g³ h20.3g* h19.9d⁴ h18.6g* h20.9g* h20.6gᶠ Apr 22] fair hurdler: won handicaps at Southwell (conditional) in June and Market Rasen in August, and novice at Kelso in September: stays 21f: acts on soft and good to firm going: tried in tongue tie: usually races towards rear. *Ruth Jefferson* **h108**

SWEET MIDNIGHT 6 b.m. Mawatheeq (USA) – Sweet Reply (Opening Verse (USA)) [2017/18 h–: h16.7g h24g Jul 16] lengthy mare: little form over hurdles: sometimes in cheekpieces. *Laura Morgan* **h–**

SWEET'N'CHIC (IRE) 8 b.m. Midnight Legend – Sweetbitter (FR) (Turgeon (USA)) [2017/18 h80: h15.9vᵖᵘ h25s² Apr 15] poor maiden hurdler: stays 25f: acts on soft going. *Richard Rowe* **h80**

SWEET SHIRLEEN (IRE) 8 br.m. Kris Kin (USA) – Dashers Folly (IRE) (Dr Massini (IRE)) [2017/18 h19.5d⁴ c21.7g h24g⁵ h24g h21.8g h27g h20.5d⁵ h24s Dec 21] third foal: half-sister to fairly useful hurdler/chaser Optimistic Bias (2½m-27f winner, by Sayarshan): dam showed little over hurdles/maiden pointer: poor maiden hurdler: well held in maiden on chasing debut: left Ms Margaret Mullins after fifth start: stays 19f: acts on good to soft going: sometimes wears headgear: often races towards rear. *James Evans* **c– h81**

SWEETOOTHTOMMY (IRE) 8 b.g. Definite Article – My Linda (IRE) (Bob Back (USA)) [2017/18 c100§, h97: c25.8m³ May 30] tall gelding: maiden hurdler: modest maiden chaser: stays 3¼m: acts on good to soft going: wears headgear: often in tongue tie: temperamental. *David Pipe* **c76 § h–**

SWEET VINETTA 4 b.f. Fair Mix (IRE) – Vinetta (Grape Tree Road) [2017/18 ab16.3g³ b16.7s Mar 26] first foal: dam (h105) 19f hurdle winner: modest form in bumpers. *Gillian Boanas* **b75**

SWIFT CRUSADOR 7 b.g. Kayf Tara – Goldenswift (IRE) (Meneval (USA)) [2017/18 h111p: c16s² c19.9v³ c16.2s⁴ c15.2v Feb 20] rangy gelding: Irish point winner: fair form when winning sole start over hurdles in 2016/17: fairly useful form over fences: second in novice handicap at Chepstow in November: should stay further than 2½m: raced only on soft/heavy going. *Evan Williams* **c124 h–**

SWIFT NATIVE (IRE) 6 b.m. Mahler – Hasty Native (IRE) (Be My Native (USA)) [2017/18 h20.5dᵖᵘ h21.7gᵖᵘ Apr 20] £20,000 5-y-o: seventh foal: half-sister to winning pointers by Accordion and Bob Back: dam (h125) 2m-3m hurdle winner: Irish point winner: no form over hurdles. *Nick Gifford* **h–**

SWINCOMBE SCORCHIO 8 b.g. Scorpion (IRE) – Lady Felix (Batshoof) [2017/18 c127: c24.2vᵖᵘ c24.2vᶠ c25.5s c24s Mar 17] long-backed gelding: has had breathing operation: fairly useful chaser, no form in 2017/18: wears tongue tie. *Polly Gundry* **c–**

SWINGBRIDGE (IRE) 10 b.g. Milan – Creative Approach (IRE) (Toulon) [2017/18 c25.5s³ h23.9d* c22g* c25d* h22.9g² h24s⁴ h22v⁶ c25v³ h20v² c23.5v³ h24v² c24sᶠ Feb 25] fair handicap hurdler: won at Perth in August: useful chaser: won maiden at Tramore and handicap at Kilbeggan later in August: left Miss L. Thomas after first start: stays 25f: acts on heavy going: wears headgear/tongue tie. *Gordon Elliott, Ireland* **c119 h111**

SWI

SWING HARD (IRE) 10 br.g. Zagreb (USA) – Hurricane Jane (IRE) (Strong Gale) [2017/18 c112, h–: c20.6v³ c19.9s³ c20v^{pu} c22.9s^{pu} c20s² c20.1v³ Apr 15] maiden hurdler: fair handicap chaser: stays 25f: acts on heavy going: front runner/races prominently: temperamental. *Sue Smith*   **c108 §**
h–

SWINITHWAITE LADY 4 b.f. Josr Algarhoud (IRE) – Happy Mood (Piccolo) [2017/18 b12.4s Dec 9] second foal: dam, lightly raced on Flat, half-sister to useful hurdler/chaser (stayed 3m) How's Business (by Josr Algarhoud): well beaten in junior bumper. *Mark Weatherer*   **b–**

SWINTON DIAMOND (IRE) 7 b.g. Dubai Destination (USA) – Absent Beauty (IRE) (Dancing Dissident (USA)) [2017/18 h88: h20.6g* h22.1g² Jul 2] fair handicap hurdler: won at Market Rasen in May: stays 2¾m: acts on soft going: has worn hood: tail flasher. *Micky Hammond*   **h101**

SWORD OF FATE (IRE) 5 b.g. Beneficial – Beann Ard (IRE) (Mandalus) [2017/18 b98: h16g² h16f* h16g* h16s h16.6d h15.5v Jan 11] completed start in points: bumper winner: fairly useful form over hurdles: won novices at Worcester (twice) in October: raced around 2m: acts on firm going: front runner/races prominently. *Tom Lacey*   **h118**

SYBARITE (FR) 12 b.g. Dark Moondancer – Haida III (FR) (Video Rock (FR)) [2017/18 c115§, h–§: c32.5d² c25.5s⁵ c22.7v⁴ Feb 15] rangy, well-made gelding: prolific point winner: winning hurdler: fairly useful maiden hunter chaser: stays 4m: has worn headgear/tongue tie: usually races towards rear: most temperamental. *Miss V. Collins*   **h115 §**

SYBIL GREY 9 gr.m. Fair Mix (IRE) – Gimme Shelter (IRE) (Glacial Storm (USA)) [2017/18 h86: h23.3g^{pu} h23.3v^{pu} h22.7g h20.6g⁶ h23.8g Nov 30] poor maiden hurdler: sometimes in headgear. *George Bewley*   **h66**

SYDNEY DE BAUNE (FR) 7 b.g. Califet (FR) – Perle de Baune (FR) (En Calcat (FR)) [2017/18 h60p: h19.5d* c16g⁵ c23s³ Dec 30] sturdy gelding: modest form over hurdles: won handicap at Chepstow in October: similar form over fences: better effort when third in novice handicap at Taunton: stays 23f: acts on soft going. *Robert Walford*   **c99**
h96

SYKES (IRE) 9 b.g. Mountain High (IRE) – Our Trick (IRE) (Flemensfirth (USA)) [2017/18 c127, h–: h23g⁴ h21.9v* h24s² h25s² h24s h24.7s Apr 14] compact gelding: useful handicap hurdler: won at Ffos Las in November: second at Warwick (1¼ lengths behind Black Ivory) in January: fairly useful form over fences: stays 25f: acts on heavy going: front runner/races prominently. *Nicky Martin*   **c–**
h137

SYLVAN LEGEND 10 b.g. Midnight Legend – Sylvan Warbler (USA) (Blushing Groom (FR)) [2017/18 c76, h–: h15.8g c21.1m⁴ c20m⁶ c16.5g⁵ Aug 1] winning hurdler: poor chaser: wears headgear/tongue tie. *Matt Sheppard*   **c–**
h–

SYMPHONY OF ANGELS 6 b.g. Sulamani (IRE) – Flying Lion (Hunting Lion (IRE)) [2017/18 b85: b16.8m² h15.7d* h16.2g⁴ h20.6g³ h16.8g Apr 18] fair form in bumpers: fairly useful form over hurdles: won novices at Southwell and Hexham in June: may prove best at 2m: has joined Dan Skelton: may yet do better. *Graeme McPherson*   **h117**
b88

SYRACUSE'S DREAM (FR) 7 gr.g. Lord du Sud (FR) – Laura's Dream (FR) (Bonnet Rouge (FR)) [2017/18 c–, h–: h23g h16.3m Aug 24] point winner: maiden hurdler/chaser: has worn cheekpieces. *Jackie du Plessis*   **c–**
h68

SYRINGA POWER (IRE) 6 ch.m. Subtle Power (IRE) – Shes Silver (IRE) (Shantou (USA)) [2017/18 b16v Nov 4] €500 3-y-o: first foal: dam, unraced, out of half-sister to dam of top-class chaser (stayed 25f) The Listener: departed early both starts (refused second one) in points: well beaten in bumper. *Jim Goldie*   **b–**

T

TAB HOGARTH (IRE) 5 b.g. Westerner – Vintage Vic (IRE) (Old Vic) [2017/18 b16.8s⁵ h15.7d^{ur} h19.9s^{rr} Jan 12] small gelding: first foal: dam winning pointer: well held in bumper: reluctant/unseated start on hurdling debut, then refused to race next time: one to avoid. *Kenneth Slack*   **h– §**
b–

TABLE BLUFF (IRE) 9 ch.g. Indian Haven – Double Deal (Keen) [2017/18 c–, h–: c20g^{pu} h22g h24g² h20g³ h24g² Aug 20] modest maiden hurdler: modest chaser at best: stays 3m, effective at shorter: acts on good to soft going: tried in cheekpieces: front runner/races prominently. *David Drinkwater*   **c–**
h86

TACENDA (IRE) 6 b.m. Flemensfirth (USA) – Tordasia (IRE) (Dr Devious (IRE)) [2017/18 c108p, b93: c21.6g* c20s² c23.4s⁴ c20.2v² Jan 18] sturdy mare: fairly useful form over fences: won mares maiden at Fontwell in November: failed to progress: stays 2¾m: acts on heavy going: usually leads. *Anthony Honeyball* c127

TACTICAL MANOEUVRE (IRE) 7 b.g. Marienbard (IRE) – Pride O'Fleet (IRE) (Bob's Return (IRE)) [2017/18 c–, h92: h21.6v⁴ h19v* h19.2v³ c17.8s² c17v³ c21.7m^bd Apr 25] maiden pointer: fair handicap hurdler: won at Taunton (conditionals) in February: modest form over fences: stays 23f, effective at shorter: acts on heavy going: wears tongue tie. *Alexandra Dunn* c89 h101

TAEL O' GOLD 4 ch.f. Zoffany (IRE) – Wedding Dream (Oasis Dream) [2017/18 h15.7d^pu h16.7s⁵ ab16.3g⁵ Mar 3] regressive maiden on Flat: well held on completed start over hurdles: tongue tied. *Lucinda Egerton* h–

TAILOR TOM (IRE) 6 b.g. Fruits of Love (USA) – Anfield Lady (IRE) (Safety Catch (USA)) [2017/18 h20d h19.9d h19.9v⁴ h23.1v* h25.3s² h24v h22.8s⁴ Mar 21] £16,000 5-y-o: sixth foal: half-brother to a winning pointer by Bienamado: dam unraced: placed on last of 3 starts in Irish points: fair handicap hurdler: won at Bangor in January: stays 25f: acts on heavy going: in cheekpieces last 2 starts. *Donald McCain* h103

TAJ BADALANDABAD (IRE) 8 ch.g. Shantou (USA) – Last Chance Lady (IRE) (Mister Lord (USA)) [2017/18 h–: h24s h21.4v^pu h25s* h23.4v h24s⁴ h24g⁴ Apr 18] smallish, sparely-made gelding: runner-up in Irish maiden point: useful handicap hurdler: won at Huntingdon in January: good fourth in Pertemps Final at Cheltenham (5¼ lengths behind Delta Work) in March: stays 25f: acts on heavy going: wears headgear: in tongue tie last 4 starts: patiently ridden. *David Pipe* h138

TAKE A BREAK (FR) 7 b.g. Sunday Break (JPN) – Popee (FR) (Take Risks (FR)) [2017/18 h16.2v* h21.6v^pu c16.5g⁵ c20.2s^pu h16.5g⁵ h23.9v⁶ h17v³ h16.8v² h18.5v^pu Apr 17] compact gelding: fair handicap hurdler: won at Hexham in September: maiden chaser, only modest form in 2017/18: stays 19f: acts on good to firm and heavy going: has worn headgear/tongue tie (in latter last 3 starts): temperamental. *Nigel Hawke* c96 § h113 §

TAKE EM OUT (IRE) 6 b.g. Amadeus Wolf – Toorah Laura La (USA) (Black Minnaloushe (USA)) [2017/18 b95: b16d h16.5g⁴ h19.3s^F h15.8v² h19.5v^pu Mar 21] runner-up both starts in Irish points: also placed on bumper debut: fair form over hurdles: in tongue tie last 5 starts: front runner/races prominently. *Tim Vaughan* h105 b65

TAKEITFROMALADY (IRE) 9 b.g. Intikhab (USA) – Pinheiros (IRE) (Rock of Gibraltar (IRE)) [2017/18 h20.5s^pu Apr 15] of little account nowadays: wears headgear. *Daniel Steele* h–

TAKEN BY FORCE (IRE) 5 b.g. Millenary – Along Came Polly (IRE) (Old Vic) [2017/18 b–: h21.2d^pu h15.8g⁶ h15.8d h20.5v^pu h16.6d⁴ h21.7v^pu h19.7s^pu Mar 27] placed both starts in points: poor maiden hurdler: best effort at 17f on good to soft going. *Tom Weston* h64

TAKE THE HIGH ROAD 4 b.g. Kyllachy – China Tea (USA) (High Chaparral (IRE)) [2017/18 h15.7s⁴ h16v⁵ h16v⁶ Feb 26] half-brother to very smart hurdler Elgin (winner around 2m, by Duke of Marmalade) and fair maiden Clemency (2m-21f winner, by Halling): fairly useful maiden on Flat, stays 1½m: modest form over hurdles (remains capable of better). *Keith Dalgleish* h85 p

TAKE TO HEART 6 b.g. Sakhee (USA) – Romantic Dream (Bustino) [2017/18 h–p, b95: h21.2m² h20g* h20g* h21.6d h21g h21m⁴ Apr 26] tall, useful-looking gelding: fairly useful hurdler: won maiden at Worcester and novice at Ffos Las, both in June: lightly raced and below form after: stays 21f: acts on good to firm going: tried in cheekpieces: front runner/races prominently. *Nicky Henderson* h126

TAKING A CHANCE (IRE) 5 b.m. Flemensfirth (USA) – Northern Mill (IRE) (Distinctly North (USA)) [2017/18 h16s^pu h15.8s⁵ h16v h16v⁵ Mar 28] eighth foal: sister to a winning pointer: dam, 2m-2½m hurdle winner, also 1½m winner who stayed 2m on Flat: runner-up in Irish maiden point on debut: fair form (modest) over hurdles only when 12¼ lengths fifth to Comrade Conrad in maiden at Ludlow in January. *Ian Williams* h91

TAKING AIM (IRE) 6 b.g. Acambaro (GER) – Sharp Missile (IRE) (Son of Sharp Shot (IRE)) [2017/18 b16v Jan 31] failed to complete in 2 Irish points: heavily eased when tailed off in bumper. *Chris Grant* b–

TAKINGRISKS (IRE) 9 b.g. Golden Tornado (IRE) – Downtown Rosie (IRE) (Good Thyne (USA)) [2017/18 c129, h–: c19.1d² c21.6s^F c19.4v⁴ c20.1s² c24.1v* h25.8v³ Apr 7] winning hurdler: fairly useful handicap chaser: won at Ayr in March: stays 25f: acts on heavy going. *Nicky Richards* c127 h101

TAK

TAKING THE MICKEY (IRE) 5 b.g. Primary (USA) – Bid To Win (IRE) (Old Vic) [2017/18 b17g May 19] won maiden in 2017, only completed start in points: well beaten in conditionals/amateur bumper at Aintree. *Miss A. M. Bacon*   **b–**

TALENT TO AMUSE (IRE) 5 b.m. Manduro (GER) – Burn Baby Burn (IRE) (King's Theatre (IRE)) [2017/18 h114p: h16.8g* h16d^F Oct 14] fairly useful form over hurdles: further progress when completing hat-trick in novice at Newton Abbot in May: fell first in handicap only subsequent outing: tongue tied. *Emma Lavelle*   **h124**

TALES OF THE TWEED (IRE) 6 b.g. Robin des Champs (FR) – Dancer Privado (IRE) (Alderbrook) [2017/18 h119p, b91: h20m* May 9] good-topped gelding: has reportedly had breathing operation: fairly useful form over hurdles: easy winner of novice at Fakenham in May: should stay beyond 2½m: looked capable of better but not seen out again. *Nicky Henderson*   **h123**

TALKISCHEAP (IRE) 6 b.g. Getaway (GER) – Carrigmoorna Oak (IRE) (Milan) [2017/18 b92: h19.1g* h19g* h20.8d^4 h24.2v* h24v^{pu} Mar 16] sturdy gelding: unbeaten in points: useful form over hurdles: won maiden at Fontwell and novice at Warwick in May, and handicap at Newbury (resumed progress, beating King Uther 2¼ lengths) in February: stiff task final outing: stays 3m: acts on heavy going. *Alan King*   **h131**

TALKOFGOLD (IRE) 6 gr.m. Gold Well – Talk of Rain (FR) (Turgeon (USA)) [2017/18 h20.1g* h23.3g^3 h20.1d^2 h20.2v^4 Sep 27] £5,000 3-y-o: fourth foal: half-sister to fair hurdler Captainofindustry (19f-3m winner, by Definite Article): dam French maiden sister to useful French hurdler (2¼m/19f winner) Brighter Later: Irish maiden point winner: fair form over hurdles: won maiden at Hexham in May on hurdling debut: in frame in novices after. *Martin Todhunter*   **h103**

TALK OF MONTY 5 b.g. Fair Mix (IRE) – Talk The Talk (Terimon) [2017/18 b15.8s b16s b15.8s b15.8g Apr 24] neat gelding: well held in bumpers/maiden hurdle: pulls hard. *Lucy Wadham*   **h76 b–**

TALK OF THE SOUTH (IRE) 9 b.g. Milan – Smalltowntalk (IRE) (Carroll House) [2017/18 c115, h109: c29.1m^3 c24.2s^{pu} c24.2s^3 c25.7d^{ur} c25.7s^3 c25.1v^{pu} c25.5s^2 c25.5s* c29.2v* c28.4v^{pu} Mar 31] sturdy gelding: winning hurdler: fair handicap chaser: won at Warwick in February and March: barely stays testing 29f: acts on heavy going: temperamental. *Paul Henderson*   **c108 § h–**

TALKONTHESTREET (IRE) 11 b.g. Milan – Super Size (IRE) (Shernazar) [2017/18 c26.3d^{pu} May 5] well-made gelding: winning hurdler: fairly useful chaser at best for Philip Hobbs: pulled up sole outing in 2017/18: stays 3½m: acts on soft going: often in cheekpieces. *Chris McSharry*   **c– h–**

TALLOW FAIR (IRE) 13 b.g. Busy Flight – Carrigeen Wood (IRE) (Buckskin (FR)) [2017/18 c108: c24.2g* c26.2g^{ur} c26d^{ro} Feb 25] multiple point winner: lightly-raced hunter chaser: won maiden event at Hexham in May: ran out final outing: one to be wary of. *Miss L. V. Horner*   **c97 §**

TAMARILLO GROVE (IRE) 11 b.g. Cape Cross (IRE) – Tamarillo (Daylami (IRE)) [2017/18 h94: h18.5m^2 h16.3g^F h16.8g* h16.8g^5 h15.8m h19m h15.7g Apr 20] smallish gelding: modest handicap hurdler: won at Newton Abbot (fourth course success) in August: best around 2m: acts on good to firm and good to soft going: tried in cheekpieces: wears tongue tie. *Sophie Leech*   **h95**

TAMAYEF (IRE) 4 b.g. Sir Prancealot (IRE) – Miss Glitters (IRE) (Chevalier (IRE)) [2017/18 h15.8g^4 h16.8s^4 Dec 16] compact gelding: fairly useful on Flat, stays 1¼m: modest form in juvenile hurdles: in tongue tie final start. *Matt Sheppard*   **h85**

TAMBOUR MAJOR (FR) 11 b.g. Myrakalu (FR) – Joaillere (FR) (Silver Rainbow) [2017/18 c69, h–: c16g^3 May 17] multiple point winner: maiden hurdler: poor maiden chaser: best around 2m: acts on good to soft going: wears headgear: normally tongue tied. *Alison Hamilton*   **c59 h–**

TAMBURA 8 b.m. Tamure (IRE) – Singing Cottage (Greensmith) [2017/18 h115: h23.6v^4 h25d^4 h23.8v^5 h25v^5 h24v* h25v* h23.9v^{pu} Apr 15] strong, sturdy mare: fairly useful handicap hurdler: won at Towcester (mares) in February and Plumpton in March: thorough stayer: acts on heavy going. *G. C. Maundrell*   **h120**

TANACANDO (FR) 6 b.g. Ballingarry (IRE) – Tamaziya (IRE) (Law Society (USA)) [2017/18 b–: h21g^6 h16s h16.8v h19v^2 h19.9v^3 Feb 10] modest form over hurdles: will be suited by 2¾m+. *Tim Vaughan*   **h94**

TANARPINO 7 ch.g. Tobougg (IRE) – Got Tune (FR) (Green Tune (USA)) [2017/18 c123, h–: h21g⁵ h19.6g⁵ h24.4d³ h25.3d² h22.8v h24.4s³ h23.1s³ c25.3g³ Apr 18] workmanlike gelding: fairly useful handicap hurdler/maiden chaser: placed 5 times in 2017/18: stays 25f: acts on heavy going: in cheekpieces last 5 starts. *Jennie Candlish* **c126 h126**

TANGLEY 6 b.m. Black Sam Bellamy (IRE) – All Rise (GER) (Goofalik (USA)) [2017/18 h94p, b–: h19.6d⁵ h16g⁶ h16v h20.7sᴾᵘ Mar 14] won mares maiden point on debut: modest form over hurdles: should stay beyond 2m: acts on soft going. *Harry Fry* **h94**

TANGO DU ROY (IRE) 5 b.g. Court Cave (IRE) – Hamari Gold (IRE) (Priolo (USA)) [2017/18 b15.8d h15.5v h18.5vᴾᵘ h15.8v⁴ h16sᴾᵘ Apr 27] little show in bumper/over hurdles. *Evan Williams* **h69 b–**

TANGOED (IRE) 5 ch.m. Papal Bull – Dainty Steps (IRE) (Xaar) [2017/18 b15.7g³ b16.8m² h15.8d h15.8g h15.7g h20.6s h16.5m Apr 25] £10,000 4-y-o: second foal: sister to fairly useful hurdler Walkabout (2m/17f winner): dam maiden on Flat: won point on debut: placed both starts in bumpers: no form over hurdles, including in handicaps: should stay 2¼m+: tried in cheekpieces. *Harry Whittington* **h– b91**

TANGOLAN (IRE) 10 ch.g. Golan (IRE) – Classic Note (IRE) (Classic Secret (USA)) [2017/18 c117, h107: h23.1g h23.9g⁴ c20.1g* c20.1m* h20.6gᶠ c20.1d⁴ h25g⁶ Oct 5] fair handicap hurdler: fairly useful handicap chaser: won at Perth (2) in July: stays 3m: acts on good to firm and good to soft going: has worn headgear: wears tongue tie: often races prominently. *Fergal O'Brien* **c126 h103**

TANIT RIVER (IRE) 8 br.g. Indian River (FR) – Tanit Lady (IRE) (Presenting) [2017/18 c131, h–: h22s⁶ c25gᴾᵘ c26v⁵ c24.2v* c24.2v⁴ Mar 10] tall gelding: winning hurdler: fairly useful handicap chaser: won at Sandown in February: stays 3m: acts on heavy going: has worn hood: wears tongue tie. *Tim Vaughan* **c125 h102**

TANKERTON BOY (IRE) 5 br.g. Marienbard (IRE) – Smashing Leader (IRE) (Supreme Leader) [2017/18 b16.7g³ b16.7d b16s b16d Apr 7] €38,000 3-y-o: sixth foal: brother to bumper winner My Liege and half-brother to useful hurdler/chaser Blakemount (2½m-3¼m winner, by Presenting), stays 3½m: dam unraced half-sister to fairly useful hurdler/useful chaser (stays 3¼m) Lamb Or Cod: modest form in bumper on debut: regressed after. *Neil King* **b82**

TANTAMOUNT 9 b.g. Observatory (USA) – Cantanta (Top Ville) [2017/18 h122: h23.8d⁶ h26.1sᴾᵘ Feb 4] good-bodied gelding: fairly useful handicap hurdler: stays 25f: acts on soft and good to firm going: tried in hood: wears tongue tie: patiently ridden. *Lucinda Russell* **h116**

TAP NIGHT (USA) 11 ch.g. Pleasant Tap (USA) – Day Mate (USA) (Dayjur (USA)) [2017/18 c92, h108§: h22.1g h23.8s³ h21.3dᴾᵘ Mar 29] close-coupled gelding: useful handicap hurdler/smart handicap chaser in prime: only modest form over hurdles in 2017/18: stays 21f: acts on heavy going: usually in headgear: tried in tongue tie: unreliable. *Lucinda Russell* **c– § h88 §**

TAQUIN DU SEUIL (FR) 11 b.g. Voix du Nord (FR) – Sweet Laly (FR) (Marchand de Sable (USA)) [2017/18 c158, h152: h24.2d³ h24.4d h25sᶠ Jan 26] good sort: smart hurdler: fell fatally at Huntingdon: high-class chaser at best, won BetVictor Gold Cup Handicap Chase at Cheltenham in 2016/17: stayed 25f: acted on heavy going: tried in cheekpieces. *Jonjo O'Neill* **c– h144**

TARA BRIDGE 10 b.g. Kayf Tara – Annie Greenlaw (Petoski) [2017/18 c113, h–: h15.9v² c16v⁴ c15.5v* c15.5sᶠ Mar 9] well-made gelding: fairly useful maiden hurdler: fairly useful handicap chaser: won at Lingfield in January and Sandown in February: stays 2¾m: acts well on heavy going: usually leads. *Chris Gordon* **c121 h117**

TARA FORCE 4 b.f. Kayf Tara – Whizz Back (IRE) (Bob Back (USA)) [2017/18 b12.4s⁶ Jan 13] fourth foal: dam (b84), ran twice in bumpers, half-sister to fairly useful hurdler (stayed 3m) Beluckyagain out of half-sister to smart hurdler/top-class chaser (stayed 25f) Tiutchev: 5/1, well-held sixth in bumper at Wetherby. *Tim Easterby* **b–**

TARA MAC 9 b.m. Kayf Tara – Macklette (IRE) (Buckskin (FR)) [2017/18 c96, h–: c22.6g* c20d² c20.8sᶠ h24vᵘʳ h21.9vᴾᵘ h20.6v* Apr 14] angular mare: modest handicap hurdler/chaser: won over fences at Stratford in October and over hurdles at Newcastle in April: stays 3m: acts on heavy going: tried in cheekpieces. *Tim Vaughan* **c91 h98**

TARA MIST 9 gr.m. Kayf Tara – Island Mist (Jupiter Island) [2017/18 h115: c23.8g³ c22.5d* c23.4sᴾᵘ c22.7v* c22.2v⁵ c20.8g⁴ Apr 19] good-topped mare: winning hurdler: fairly useful form over fences: won mares handicaps at Uttoxeter in November and Leicester in February: stays 23f: acts on heavy going: often races towards rear. *Henry Daly* **c127 h–**

TAR

TARAS DAY 5 b.m. Kayf Tara – One of Those Days (Soviet Lad (USA)) [2017/18 b16d h21.2d h16.7s h20.7d Mar 26] sister to fairly useful hurdler Orangeaday (2½m/21f winner) and half-sister to fairly useful/ungenuine hurdler/chaser Carnival Town (2½m-3¼m winner, by Classic Cliche): dam unraced half-sister to high-class hurdlers Anzum (stayed 25f) and Jazilah (best at 2m): well beaten in mares bumper/novice hurdles. *Harry Whittington* — h– b–

TARA'S RAINBOW 8 b.m. Kayf Tara – Nile Cristale (FR) (Northern Crystal) [2017/18 h71: h15.8m^3 h19.9g^4 h18.7g^2 h19.9d^5 h19.6g^3 h20g^3 h20g c20f Oct 12] well-made mare: poor maiden hurdler: stiff task on chasing debut: stays 2½m: acts on good to firm going: wears tongue tie. *Trevor Wall* — c– h84

TARA VIEW 7 b.m. Kayf Tara – Temptation (FR) (Lando (GER)) [2017/18 h127, b97: h21.4s^{pu} h24d^3 h24.3g Apr 20] angular mare: bumper winner: fairly useful handicap hurdler: stays 3m: acts on soft going: has hinted at temperament. *Alan King* — h125

TARA WELL (IRE) 8 b.m. Kayf Tara – Miss Baden (IRE) (Supreme Leader) [2017/18 h–: h20.5d h19.9d^4 h23.1s^2 h19.9v^2 h21.2s^3 h20.5v* h25.6v^4 h21.7v h23.3v^2 h23.1d^5 Apr 24] off mark in Irish points at seventh attempt: modest handicap hurdler: won at Leicester (conditionals mares) in January: stays 23f: acts on heavy going: wears cheekpieces: in tongue tie last 2 starts. *Robin Dickin* — h86

TAROUM (IRE) 11 b.g. Refuse To Bend (IRE) – Taraza (IRE) (Darshaan) [2017/18 c90§, h90§: h20g h19.2g^4 h19.6g h18.5d^4 h19.9s Oct 19] dipped-backed gelding: poor handicap hurdler: maiden chaser: stays 2½m: acts on soft and good to firm going: wears headgear/tongue tie: front runner/races prominently: temperamental. *John Flint* — c– § h76 §

TARRONA 9 b.g. Kayf Tara – Lisrona (IRE) (Presenting) [2017/18 h115: h21.1s h21.7s Jan 29] fairly useful maiden hurdler in 2016/17: just twice-raced since, last both times: stays 2¾m: acts on heavy going. *Alan Phillips* — h–

TASHUNKA (IRE) 5 b.m. Flemensfirth (USA) – Las Palmas (IRE) (Brian Boru) [2017/18 b16.7s^2 b16.8g^6 Apr 19] first foal: dam unraced half-sister to useful hurdler/staying chaser Control Man: little impact in Irish points: fair form in mares bumpers at Market Rasen and Cheltenham (again plenty to do). *Fergal O'Brien* — b94

TASTE THE WINE (IRE) 12 gr.g. Verglas (IRE) – Azia (IRE) (Desert Story (IRE)) [2017/18 h82: h21.9g^2 h21.6m^4 h21.6m* h20g^F h21.6g Sep 2] close-coupled gelding: modest handicap hurdler: won selling event at Newton Abbot in July: stays 2¾m: acts on soft and good to firm going: regularly wears cheekpieces/tongue tie. *Bernard Llewellyn* — h88

TAURIAN 7 b.m. Central Park (IRE) – Emma-Lyne (Emarati (USA)) [2017/18 h88: h15.9g^3 h15.7g^5 May 22] modest handicap hurdler: raced around 2m: acts on good to firm going: has worn cheekpieces, including last 3 starts in 2017/18. *Ian Williams* — h86

TAWS 7 b.m. Hernando (FR) – Reaf (In The Wings) [2017/18 h111: h16g* Jul 18] fair form over hurdles: won mares maiden at Worcester in July: also successful twice back on Flat subsequently (useful staying handicapper): should stay 3m: acts on soft going: has worn cheekpieces. *Rod Millman* — h110

TAWSEEF (IRE) 10 b.g. Monsun (GER) – Sahool (Unfuwain (USA)) [2017/18 h24g h24g h24.8d h22.1g^2 h25.4d* h27g^2 h23.9v^3 h25.8g* h18.9v^2 h23.1v* Dec 15] smallish gelding: fair on Flat (stays 17f), successful twice in 2017: useful handicap hurdler: won at Cartmel in August, Kelso (by 13 lengths) in November and Bangor in December: left Colin Bowe after third start: stays 27f: acts on heavy going: has worn headgear. *Donald McCain* — h133

TAXMEIFYOUCAN (IRE) 4 b.g. Beat Hollow – Accounting (Sillery (USA)) [2017/18 h16.3m* h16.2d^{ur} h16.2v* h16.2v^3 h16s Apr 28] good-topped gelding: half-brother to fair hurdler Full Success (15f winner in France, by Acclamation): dam, sister to fairly useful hurdler/chaser (stayed 3¼m) Double Account: useful on Flat, stays 1¾m: fairly useful form over hurdles: won juvenile at Stratford in July and novice at Kelso (by 2¼ lengths from Sam's Gunner) in February: will stay beyond 2m: acts on good to firm and heavy going: in cheekpieces last 3 starts. *Keith Dalgleish* — h127

TAYAAR (IRE) 5 b.g. High Chaparral (IRE) – Ursula Minor (IRE) (Footstepsinthesand) [2017/18 h15.8g^{pu} Oct 5] modest maiden on Flat, stays 2m: pulled up in novice on hurdling debut. *John Ryan* — h–

TAYARAT (IRE) 13 b.g. Noverre (USA) – Sincere (IRE) (Bahhare (USA)) [2017/18 c–§, h–§: c15.7d^{pu} Jun 6] rather leggy gelding: of little account nowadays: has worn headgear/tongue tie: temperamental. *Michael Chapman* — c– § h– §

TAYLOR (IRE) 9 b.m. Presenting – Britway Lady (IRE) (Norwich) [2017/18 c–, h88: c20.1g^{pu} c20.1g Jun 3] winning hurdler: little form in handicap chases: stays 2½m: acts on firm going: has worn cheekpieces, including last 3 starts. *Micky Hammond* — c– h–

TEE

TAYLORMADE BOY 6 b.g. Josr Algarhoud (IRE) – Bula Rose (IRE) (Alphabatim (USA)) [2017/18 b16.3d⁶ Jun 9] winning pointer: tongue tied, well held in bumper. *M. V. Coglan* — **b–**

TAYZAR 7 b.g. Kayf Tara – Matilda Too (IRE) (Definite Article) [2017/18 b72: b16.2v h18.6d² h16.6d⁴ h20.6g² Apr 22] never dangerous in bumpers: fair form over hurdles: should stay 2½m. *Ruth Jefferson* — **h112, b–**

TB BROKE HER (IRE) 8 br.m. Indian River (FR) – Catch Ball (Prince Sabo) [2017/18 c19.2g⁶ c16g c19.2g² h21.8g⁶ c22s c25.2g² c18.4s⁶ c23.5d⁵ c20g³ c25.2s* c25.6s* Jan 10] poor handicap hurdler: fair handicap chaser: left A. L. T. Moore after eighth start and much improved subsequently, winning at Hereford in December and Ludlow in January: stays 3¼m: acts on soft going: wears cheekpieces: tried in tongue tie. *Matt Sheppard* — **c100, h77**

TEA FOR TWO 9 b.g. Kayf Tara – One For Me (Tragic Role (USA)) [2017/18 c166, h–: c19.9d c25.6v⁴ c24d³ c25.3vᵖᵘ c26.3v c25s⁶ Apr 12] strong gelding: winning hurdler: high-class chaser: third in King George VI Chase at Kempton (3 lengths behind Might Bite) in December, easily best effort in 2017/18: stays 25f: has won on heavy ground, but very best form under less testing conditions: tried in hood. *Nick Williams* — **c160, h–**

TEA IN TRANSVAAL (IRE) 7 b.m. Teofilo (IRE) – Mpumalanga (Observatory (USA)) [2017/18 h123: h18.5f Jun 5] rather leggy mare: useful hurdler at best: best around 2m: acted on heavy going: enthusiastic front runner: dead. *Evan Williams* — **h–**

TEAK (IRE) 11 b.g. Barathea (IRE) – Szabo (IRE) (Anabaa (USA)) [2017/18 c–, h103: h25g⁴ h24.5d⁴ Nov 27] smallish gelding: fair handicap hurdler: lightly-raced chaser, placed twice: stays 3¼m: acts on good to firm going: wears headgear: has worn tongue tie, including last 3 starts: usually races close up. *Ian Williams* — **c–, h101**

TEA TIME FRED 9 b.g. Kayf Tara – Darjeeling (IRE) (Presenting) [2017/18 c–, h110: h26.4dᵖᵘ c26.2dᵘʳ c24.2sᵖᵘ c25.2g⁵ h21.4v³ h23.1s⁶ h19.2vᵘʳ h18.5vᵖᵘ Apr 17] lengthy gelding: fair handicap hurdler: let down by jumping over fences: stays 3¼m: acts on good to firm and heavy going: in cheekpieces last 4 starts. *Susan Gardner* — **c87 x, h106**

TEA TIME ON MARS 6 ch.g. Schiaparelli (GER) – Darjeeling (IRE) (Presenting) [2017/18 b15.8d⁴ b15.7d Nov 25] rangy gelding: modest form on first of 2 outings in bumpers: will be suited by 2½m. *Susan Gardner* — **b79**

TECTONIC (IRE) 9 b.g. Dylan Thomas (IRE) – Pine Chip (USA) (Nureyev (USA)) [2017/18 h16.2d h20.5sᵖᵘ Oct 30] fair on Flat, stays 2m: little promise both starts over hurdles, pulling hard. *Keith Dalgleish* — **h–**

TEDDIEMOY 9 ch.g. And Beyond (IRE) – Crevamoy (IRE) (Shardari) [2017/18 c21.6gᵖᵘ May 10] pulled up in points/novice hunter chase (tongue tied). *Mrs L. A. Coltherd* — **c–**

TEDDY TEE (IRE) 9 b.g. Mountain High (IRE) – Knocksouna Lady (IRE) (Oscar (IRE)) [2017/18 c–, h100: c24.2s³ c23.4s² c26.9v² c23.4vᵖᵘ c23.8s³ Apr 25] tall, lengthy gelding: winning hurdler: fairly useful but error-prone maiden chaser: placed in handicaps first 3 starts in 2017/18: stays 27f: acts on heavy going. *Nicky Richards* — **c122 x, h–**

TEDHAM 4 b.g. Shirocco (GER) – Alegralil (King's Theatre (IRE)) [2017/18 b16d³ Apr 26] €50,000 3-y-o: good-topped gelding: second foal: dam (h128), bumper/2m-19f hurdle winner, sister to fairly useful staying chaser Theatrical Star: 5/1, third in bumper at Warwick (6½ lengths behind Umndeni). *Jonjo O'Neill* — **b91**

TED'S BROTHER (IRE) 10 b.g. Fath (USA) – Estertide (IRE) (Tagula (IRE)) [2017/18 h16.7g Apr 22] fair on Flat, stays 13f: well-held seventh in maiden on belated hurdling debut. *Laura Morgan* — **h–**

TED THISTLE (IRE) 6 b.g. Getaway (GER) – Which Thistle (IRE) (Saddlers' Hall (IRE)) [2017/18 h20g⁵ Oct 25] runner-up on completed start in Irish maiden points: last in bumper for Eoghan O'Grady: mid-field in maiden on hurdling debut. *Stuart Edmunds* — **h73**

TED VEALE (IRE) 11 b.g. Revoque (IRE) – Rose Tanner (IRE) (Roselier (FR)) [2017/18 c–x, h139+: h16.3g* c17d² h16s h16s c17s⁶ Feb 3] medium-sized gelding: useful hurdler: won minor event at Sligo in August: useful chaser: best around 2m: acts on heavy going: has worn hood: usually races towards rear: prone to mistakes over fences. *A. J. Martin, Ireland* — **c137 x, h125**

TEE IT UP TOMMO (IRE) 9 gr.g. Clodovil (IRE) – Lamh Eile (IRE) (Lend A Hand) [2017/18 h–: h15.9v Jan 7] fair on Flat (stayed 8.5f): no form over hurdles: tongue tied 3 of last 4 outings: dead. *Daniel Steele* — **h–**

TEE

TEESCOMPONENTS LAD 5 b.g. Midnight Legend – Northern Native (IRE) (Be My Native (USA)) [2017/18 b90: b16.2v³ h16.2v² h15.7d² h19.3v* h19.7v³ h16.2v³ h19.3v⁴ Apr 17] placed 3 times in bumpers: fairly useful form over hurdles: dead-heated with Jaunty Flyer in novice at Catterick in January: stays 2½m: acts on heavy going: usually races prominently. *Gillian Boanas* — h115 b95

TEESCOMPONENTS MAX 9 b.g. Grape Tree Road – Our Tees Component (IRE) (Saddlers' Hall (IRE)) [2017/18 c81, h–: h15.8d⁶ h15.8d³ h16.7d² h16.8s h16.6d² Feb 8] poor maiden hurdler/chaser: raced around 2m: acts on soft and good to firm going. *Gillian Boanas* — c– h78

TEKAP (FR) 5 ch.g. Kapgarde (FR) – Textuelle (FR) (Roakarad) [2017/18 b–: b17d Nov 13] tall gelding: well held both outings in bumpers. *Henry Daly* — b–

TEKIBLUE DE L'ORME (FR) 5 b.g. Blue Bresil (FR) – Tekila de L'Orme (FR) (Ultimately Lucky (IRE)) [2017/18 b–: h16d h19.5s h19.3v⁴ h19.7d⁶ h17s h16.8g Apr 23] good-bodied gelding: well held in bumper (for Paul Morgan)/over hurdles: left Christian Williams after second start. *Philip Kirby* — h–

TEKTHELOT (IRE) 12 b.g. Shantou (USA) – Bryna (IRE) (Ezzoud (IRE)) [2017/18 h105: h20.2g⁶ h20.2d⁶ h16.8g Aug 31] modest handicap hurdler nowadays: stays 3m: acts on soft and good to firm going: has worn headgear. *Nicky Richards* — h88

TELEGRAPH PLACE (IRE) 5 br.g. Yeats (IRE) – Sea Skate (USA) (Gilded Time (USA)) [2017/18 ab16g h16s² Mar 16] second foal: dam (h101), 2m hurdle winner, also 1½m winner on Flat: pulled up in Irish point: seventh in bumper at Lingfield: 25/1, 6 lengths second to Weebill in conditionals maiden at Fakenham on hurdling debut: open to improvement. *Olly Murphy* — h99 p b–

TELL IT TO ME 6 b.m. Kayf Tara – Liberthine (FR) (Chamberlin (FR)) [2017/18 b15.8m³ b15.7d⁴ h21.2d Dec 20] fourth foal: half-sister to bumper winner/fairly useful hurdler Free Thinking (2m winner, by Hernando), stayed 19f: dam (c139/h119), 15f-21f hurdle/chase winner (best up to 29f), closely related to Cheltenham Gold Cup winner Long Run: fairly useful form in bumpers: won mares event at Southwell (stormed clear) in June: 5/1, seventh in novice at Ludlow on hurdling debut: should do better. *Nicky Henderson* — h73 p b98

TELLTHEMNUTTIN (IRE) 7 b.m. Shantou (USA) – Peggy Maddock (IRE) (Oscar (IRE)) [2017/18 h24g* h24.5m* h22.8s^pu h20v^pu h16s⁶ h24v⁵ h16s⁵ Nov 30] fourth foal: half-sister to useful hurdler/chaser Marinero (2¼m-3m winner, by Presenting) and a winning pointer by Publisher: dam, half-sister to useful hurdler/chaser (stayed 29f) Feathered Leader: useful handicap hurdler: won at Wexford and Down Royal in May: stays 25f: acts on good to firm and heavy going: in cheekpieces last 3 starts: usually races nearer last than first. *W. F. Codd, Ireland* — h134

TELL THE TALE (IRE) 8 b.g. Craigsteel – Club Member (IRE) (Flemensfirth (USA)) [2017/18 h103, b84: h20.1g^pu h20g⁵ h16.8g h15.8m⁵ h16.7d⁵ Nov 23] sturdy gelding: maiden pointer: modest maiden hurdler: stays 19f: acts on good to firm and good to soft going: in cheekpieces last 5 starts: tried in tongue tie: temperamental. *Neil Mulholland* — h91 §

TELMADELA (IRE) 8 b.g. Definite Article – Miss Pickering (IRE) (Accordion) [2017/18 h–, b–: h15.8d h16.3g h16.3g⁵ h23m^pu h21.6g⁶ h21.6d³ h23.9m⁴ h23.9g^F Nov 16] lengthy, rather sparely-made gelding: point winner: poor maiden hurdler: stays 3m: acts on good to firm going: has worn tongue tie, including last 4 starts. *Richenda Ford* — h73

TELSON BARLEY (IRE) 5 b.g. Scorpion (IRE) – El Monica (IRE) (Kahyasi) [2017/18 b16s h19s⁵ Jan 20] tailed off in bumper: 125/1, showed bit more when fifth of 6 in novice at Taunton on hurdling debut. *Graeme McPherson* — h86 b–

TEMIR KAZYK 4 b.g. Oasis Dream – Tingling (USA) (Storm Cat (USA)) [2017/18 h15.8m h16d^pu h15.8d h16.5m Apr 25] fair maiden on Flat, stays 1½m: little promise over hurdles. *Henry Oliver* — h–

TEMPESTATEFLORESCO 10 b.g. Storming Home – Empress Dagmar (Selkirk (USA)) [2017/18 c131: c19.2m* h21.6d² c26.1m* h16.8g² c24v^pu h21.2m* h23.9g c25.1s^pu Nov 11] fairly useful form over hurdles: won novices at Fontwell in June and Ludlow in October: useful handicap chaser: won at Exeter in May and Summer Cup at Uttoxeter (career-best effort, by 6 lengths from Shelford) in July: stays 3¼m: acts on good to firm and good to soft going: wears tongue tie. *Colin Tizzard* — c142 h117

TEQ

TEMPLEHILLS (IRE) 7 b.g. Kalanisi (IRE) – Sissinghurst Storm (IRE) (Good Thyne (USA)) [2017/18 c136x, h120: c19.4v² c20s⁴ c21.2d* Apr 7] tall gelding: fairly useful hurdler: useful but error-prone handicap chaser: won at Fakenham (by 1½ lengths from Princeton Royale) in April: stays 21f: acts on good to firm and heavy going: wears hood: in tongue tie last 3 starts: front runner/races prominently. *Nigel Twiston-Davies*   c136 x h–

TEMPLE MAN 6 b.g. Sulamani (IRE) – Altogether Now (IRE) (Step Together (USA)) [2017/18 b86: h16.2d⁵ h16.2g* h19.7d^F Nov 18] in frame in bumpers: modest form over hurdles: won maiden at Kelso in October: should stay beyond 2m: remains with potential. *Malcolm Jefferson*   h95 p

TEMPLENABOE (IRE) 6 b.g. Milan – Pretty Impressive (IRE) (Presenting) [2017/18 b68: h20.5s^F h16.2s^pu Jan 14] point winner: well held in bumper: little show over hurdles, showed some ability before falling last on debut. *Lucinda Russell*   h75

TEMPLEPOINT 7 b.g. Fair Mix (IRE) – Flamebird (IRE) (Mukaddamah (USA)) [2017/18 b16g h22.2d⁶ h20g⁵ Jul 27] well held in bumper: poor form over hurdles: finally off mark in points in April. *Nigel Twiston-Davies*   h72 b–

TEMPLEROSS (IRE) 7 b.g. Presenting – Dame O'Neill (IRE) (Dr Massini (IRE)) [2017/18 h129: c20d⁴ c26.2d⁵ h22.8v^pu h25s h23.5s Feb 17] well-made gelding: fell in Irish maiden point: fairly useful handicap hurdler at best: similar form both starts over fences: probably stays 3¼m: acts on soft going: tried in visor. *Nigel Twiston-Davies*   c122 h98

TEMPLIER (IRE) 5 b.g. Mastercraftsman (IRE) – Tigertail (FR) (Priolo (USA)) [2017/18 h118: h17.7g h15.3g² h16d³ h16s^F Feb 9] well-made gelding: fair handicap hurdler: best around 2m: acts on good to soft going, probably on soft: usually in cheekpieces: front runner/races prominently. *Gary Moore*   h110

TEMPURAN 9 b.g. Unbridled's Song (USA) – Tenderly (IRE) (Danehill (USA)) [2017/18 c–, h106: h15.7g³ h15.8g⁴ h19m² h21.2g* h21g^F Nov 30] sturdy gelding: fair handicap hurdler: won at Ludlow in November: winning chaser: left Dr Richard Newland after first start: stays 21f: acts on good to firm going: tried in cheekpieces: front runner/races prominently. *Alastair Ralph*   c– h114

TEN IN THE HAT (IRE) 4 b.g. Sir Prancealot (IRE) – Vampire Queen (IRE) (General Monash (USA)) [2017/18 h16.7g⁶ Nov 9] little form on Flat: tailed off in juvenile on hurdling debut. *Tom Gretton*   h–

TENNEWROW (IRE) 6 b.m. Stowaway – Silent Supreme (IRE) (Supreme Leader) [2017/18 h21v^pu h20.7d Mar 26] £25,000 5-y-o: half-sister to fairly useful hurdler/useful chaser Have You Seen Me (2m-2½m winner, by Beneficial) and fair hurdler/chaser Millers Reef (2m-25f winner, by Bob Back): dam unraced sister to very smart chaser up to 3m Nick Dundee and high-class hurdler/smart chaser (2m-2½m winner) Ned Kelly: off mark in Irish points at second attempt: some promise on second of 2 starts in mares novice hurdles. *Ben Pauling*   h90 ?

TENOR NIVERNAIS (FR) 11 b.g. Shaanmer (IRE) – Hosanna II (FR) (Marasali) [2017/18 c156, h–: c24s^pu c23.8s⁶ c34.3s^pu Apr 14] rangy, useful-looking gelding: winning hurdler: very smart chaser at best: no form in 2017/18: tried in cheekpieces: normally ridden positively: not one to trust (all taken off for lead). *Venetia Williams*   c– § h– §

TEN TIMES BETTER (IRE) 8 ch.m. Beneficial – Allaboveboard (IRE) (Alphabatim (USA)) [2017/18 h18.5s^pu h19.5v h16.3d^pu Apr 22] second foal: sister to bumper winner Stack The Deck: dam (h99) 2m-23f hurdle winner: fairly useful hurdler at best: left P. A. Fahy and off 22 months, no form in handicaps in 2017/18: stays 2½m: acts on good to soft going: tried in cheekpieces/tongue tie. *Matt Sheppard*   h–

TEN TREES 8 b.m. Millkom – Island Path (IRE) (Jupiter Island) [2017/18 h105: h20.1d⁶ Apr 23] fair handicap hurdler: off 17 months, in need of race only appearance in 2017/18: should stay beyond 21f: acts on soft going. *Sally Haynes*   h93

TEQUILA SECRET (IRE) 7 b.m. Kayf Tara – Jubilee Queen (IRE) (Exit To Nowhere (USA)) [2017/18 h15.7g⁴ h16.8m h17s³ h20.5d^pu h19s h19s c19.8v^pu Apr 27] €14,000 3-y-o: first foal: dam (b94), bumper winner, half-sister to smart hurdler/chaser (stayed 25f) Fundamentalist and to dam of useful hurdler (stays 3m) Barters Hill: modest form on first of 2 outings in bumpers (left Henry Oliver after second one): similar form on hurdling debut: none after, including in mares novice handicap chase: should stay beyond 17f: acts on soft going: tried in tongue tie. *Nigel Hawke*   c– h95 b76

TER

TEREZAZ NIMROD 4 b.g. Arvico (FR) – Anynearexit (IRE) (Exit To Nowhere (USA)) b–
[2017/18 b15.8d b15.8d Apr 24] last of 8 in bumpers at Ludlow. *Roy Brotherton*

TERMINAL ONE (IRE) 4 b.f. Stowaway – Kalyfa Royale (IRE) (Blueprint (IRE)) b67
[2017/18 b16.8v³ Mar 13] second foal: dam (h81) maiden hurdler: 7/2, third in mares bumper at Sedgefield (11 lengths behind Jaxlight). *Stuart Crawford, Ireland*

TERREFORT (FR) 5 gr.g. Martaline – Vie de Reine (FR) (Mansonnien (FR)) c156 p
[2017/18 c19.4s* c17.4d³ h17.9v* c21.9s³ c19.9s* c20s* c19.9s² c25s* Apr 13] h124

In a season when Nicky Henderson was crowned the champion jumps trainer in Britain for a fifth time, it is fair to say that few horses surprised him quite so much as Terrefort. 'When he arrived at Seven Barrows if you'd have said to me he'd be contesting a Grade 1, let alone winning one, I'd be sending you to a psychiatrist,' Henderson joked in his blog before the horse's run in the Betfred TV Scilly Isles Novices' Chase at Sandown in February. 'I have to admit I'll be absolutely staggered if he's good enough to win this, certainly on what I've seen at home anyway.' Terrefort had shown fairly useful form in ten starts for Guillaume Macaire in France, winning a couple of four-year-old events at Clairefontaine, firstly over fences in August and then back over hurdles in September. He made his British debut in a novices limited handicap chase at Huntingdon in January—sent off the well-backed 6/4 favourite in a field of seven—and his supporters never had a moment's worry. Terrefort created a very good impression, beating Bentelimar by ten lengths, after jumping well towards the head of affairs and quickly asserting after two out. A 14-lb hike in the weights for that win, raising him to a BHA mark of 151 left connections with little choice but to try their hand in graded company on Terrefort's next start, despite his trainer's obvious misgivings. Henderson's comments before the Scilly Isles possibly played a part in Terrefort's market weakness on the day, as he drifted from an opening show of 6/4 to an SP of 15/8. Jumping assuredly from the outset, Terrefort took turns in the lead with chief market rival Cyrname (9/4), who had won the Wayward Lad Novices' Chase at Kempton on his previous start. The pair drew clear of their toiling rivals on the run to three out, at which point Terrefort appeared to be getting the better of the argument. Cyrname rallied after the last, however, and Terrefort was ultimately all out to hold on by a neck. The form was well up to standard for the race (Cyrname came out best at the weights conceding 3 lb to the year-younger winner). Terrefort gave his owners Simon Munir and Isaac Souede a fourth consecutive Scilly Isles victory, following those of Gitane du Berlais, Bristol de Mai and Top Notch, and Terrefort looked a leading contender for the Golden Miller Novices' Chase at Cheltenham.

Henderson stressed in the build up to Cheltenham that Terrefort would not run unless the ground was soft, but his participation was never really in doubt given the prolonged wet spell that resulted in the softest ground at the meeting for over

Betfred TV Scilly Isles Novices' Chase, Sandown—
the grey Terrefort gets the better of a race-long duel with Cyrname

Betway Mildmay Novices' Chase, Aintree—
a second Grade 1 success for Terrefort, this time over a longer trip as he defeats Ms Parfois

twenty years. Bristol de Mai and Top Notch both finished second in the Golden Miller after winning the Scilly Isles, and Terrefort fully confirmed the form he had shown at Sandown when doing the same, keeping on well to be beaten seven lengths by Shattered Love, simply finding the concession of 7 lb to the mare beyond him. Terrefort was stepped up to three miles on his final start, in the Betway Mildmay Novices' Chase at Aintree for which he was sent off 3/1 favourite after his form had been well advertised in the preceding twenty-four hours—Golden Miller fifth Finian's Oscar and Bentelimar both won on the opening day of the Aintree Festival, while Kemboy, who had finished one place ahead of Finian's Oscar at Cheltenham, won a Grade 3 at Limerick on the same afternoon. Held up in mid-division in the early stages and again jumping well in the main, Terrefort was produced to lead on the run to the last and saw out the longer trip really well to win by three and three quarter lengths from National Hunt Chase runner-up Ms Parfois, with another nine lengths back to the third Elegant Escape, who had filled the same position on his previous start in the RSA. The last two winners of the Mildmay before Terrefort, Native River and Might Bite, filled the first two places in the Gold Cup in the latest season, and it would be no surprise if that race were to feature prominently on the agenda for Terrefort in 2018/19, although it is unlikely that conditions will prove quite so testing as they were for the latest Festival. Indeed, a race in the first half of the season such as the Betfair Chase, when Terrefort is more likely to get his favoured soft going, would possibly offer the best chance of further Grade 1 success in the short term, although his owners also have Bristol de Mai, who won the Haydock event by fifty-seven lengths in the latest campaign.

Terrefort (FR) (gr.g. 2013)	Martaline (gr 1999)	Linamix (gr 1987)	Mendez / Lunadix
		Coraline (b 1994)	Sadler's Wells / Bahamian
	Vie de Reine (FR) (b 1998)	Mansonnien (ch 1984)	Tip Moss / Association
		Synecure (b 1988)	Synefos / Cartune

The tall Terrefort is out of Vie de Reine, a six-times winner over jumps in France for Guillaume Macaire, including in the Group 3 Prix Edmond Barrachin as a four-year-old over fences. Terrefort is his dam's fifth winner, the best of the others being the smart but unreliable chaser Vino Griego (by Kahyasi) and the useful juvenile hurdler Las Ventas (by Poliglote). Terrefort's brother Taruma showed useful form in France before winning a three-mile hurdle in Britain. An unraced three-year-old half-brother Mont Segur (by French Fifteen) was sold to Anthony Honeyball for

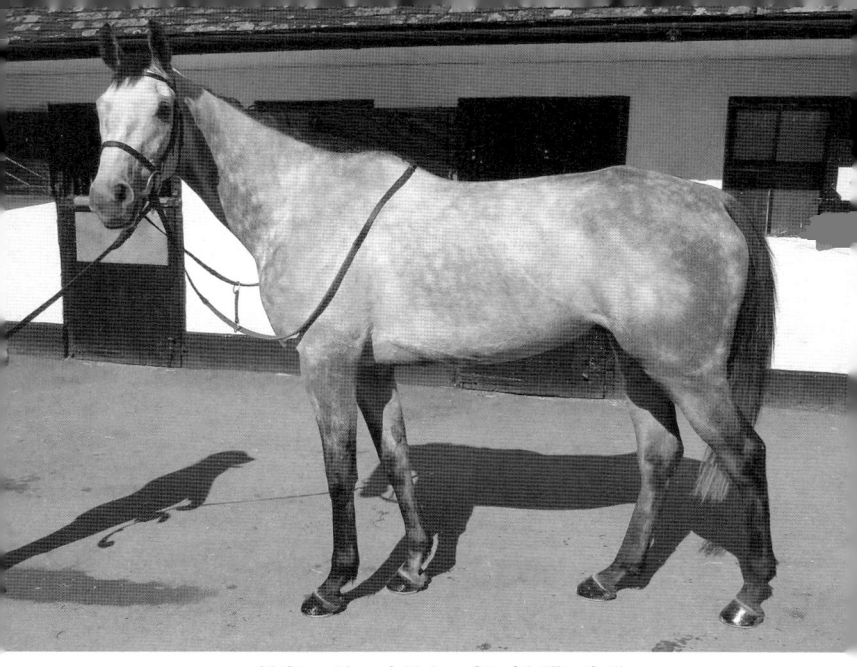

Mr Simon Munir & Mr Isaac Souede's "Terrefort"

£58,000 at the Doncaster Sales in May. Terrefort is by one of the leading jumping sires in France, Martaline, standing at a fee of €15,000 in 2018. His first crop, bred when his fee was just €3,500, included the 2014 Ryanair winner Dynaste and the Spa Novices' Hurdle winner Very Wood. Other noteworthy offspring currently in training include Terrefort's stablemates Soul Emotion, who produced a smart performance when winning a handicap hurdle on the final day of the British jumps season at Sandown, and leading juvenile hurdler We Have A Dream. Terrefort and We Have A Dream were in good company as two of five multiple Grade 1 winners for Seven Barrows in the latest campaign—the remaining trio was made up of the top-class Altior, Buveur d'Air and Might Bite! Terrefort still needs to improve the best part of a stone to be considered in that class, but he remains capable of better over fences, especially over staying trips. Terrefort reportedly shows very little on the gallops at Seven Barrows ('You couldn't watch anything slower,' reiterated Henderson after his Sandown win), but he usually travels strongly in his races, and his jumping has looked assured for one so inexperienced. He acts on heavy going, but has raced only on soft on his four starts in Britain so far. *Nicky Henderson*

TERRY THE FISH (IRE) 6 b.g. Milan – Have More (Haafhd) [2017/18 h93, b–: h23.3d* h23.3g* h23.3d* h23g² h24.2d⁴ h23.4s^pu h24g Apr 18] strong gelding: useful handicap hurdler: completed hat-trick when winning at Uttoxeter in May (novice), June and July: looks a thorough stayer: acts on soft going: front runner/races prominently. *Jonjo O'Neill*   **h131**

TESTIFY (IRE) 7 b.g. Witness Box (USA) – Tanya Thyne (IRE) (Good Thyne (USA)) [2017/18 h124: c17.4s* c15.7v* c19.9v* c20.4s c25s^pu Apr 13] strong gelding: fairly useful hurdler: useful form over fences: won small-field novices at Bangor and Haydock in December, and Grade 2 novice also at Haydock (by 7 lengths from other finisher Lake View Lad) in January: much stiffer tasks last 2 outings: stays 23f, fully effective over shorter: acts well on heavy going: front runner/races prominently. *Donald McCain*   **c142 h–**

TEST RIDE (IRE) 4 b.g. Rip Van Winkle (IRE) – Easter Fairy (USA) (Fusaichi Pegasus (USA)) [2017/18 b14d b13.7g Nov 30] well held in bumpers. *John Butler* — b–

TETRAITES STYLE (IRE) 6 b.g. Court Cave (IRE) – Kilmessan (IRE) (Flemensfirth (USA)) [2017/18 h66p: h16.2v² h16.2s h18.1v⁶ Apr 16] rather unfurnished gelding: fair form over hurdles: off 5 months and left Nicky Richards, well beaten in handicap (tongue tied) final outing: should be suited by further than 2m. *Gillian Boanas* — h106

TEXAN NOMAD 6 ch.g. Nomadic Way (USA) – Texas Belle (IRE) (Glacial Storm (USA)) [2017/18 b15.8d⁴ b16g⁶ b16f⁵ Oct 12] ran out in point: modest form in bumpers: tried in hood. *Ronald Harris* — b76

TEXAS FOREVER (IRE) 9 b.g. Heron Island (IRE) – Gravinis (FR) (Grape Tree Road) [2017/18 c100, h97: h15.8d Oct 8] point winner: modest maiden hurdler: fair maiden chaser (has made mistakes): stays 2½m: acts on soft going: wears headgear: usually races prominently. *Kim Bailey* — c–, h–

THADY QUIL (IRE) 8 ch.g. Stowaway – Aunt Sue (IRE) (Shahanndeh) [2017/18 c83, h103: c20.9d⁶ h23g⁴ h21.6s⁵ c20m⁴ h24g⁴ c23g⁶ h26.4s c25g Oct 27] workmanlike gelding: poor maiden hurdler: modest handicap chaser: won at Worcester in July: stays 3m: acts on good to firm going: wears headgear/tongue tie: ungenuine. *Martin Keighley* — c92 §, h76 §

THAHAB IFRAJ (IRE) 5 ch.g. Frozen Power (IRE) – Penny Rouge (IRE) (Pennekamp (USA)) [2017/18 h62: h15.8d⁴ h16.3g² h18.7m* Aug 24] fair form over hurdles: won novice at Stratford in August. *Alexandra Dunn* — h107

THAMES KNIGHT 6 b.g. Sir Percy – Bermondsey Girl (Bertolini (USA)) [2017/18 h15.9d h15.9s h16.3s h15.9vᵘʳ h16v h15.8d Apr 24] small, close-coupled gelding: useful on Flat (stays 1½m): little form over hurdles. *Jim Boyle* — h–

THANK YOU BEFORE (FR) 5 b.m. Saddler Maker (IRE) – Before Royale (FR) (Dauphin du Bourg (FR)) [2017/18 b13.7v⁵ ab16d⁴ b15.7v⁴ Mar 29] half-sister to useful hurdler/very smart chaser Module (2m-2¼m winner, by Panoramic) and 1¾m bumper winner Ambition Royal (by Cyborg): dam, French 15f hurdle winner (also 11.5f winner on Flat), sister to very smart 2m hurdler Blue Royal: modest form in bumpers. *Gary Moore* — b75

THANKYOU VERY MUCH 8 b.m. Lucky Story (USA) – Maid of Perth (Mark of Esteem (IRE)) [2017/18 c114, h94: c16m⁵ c15.7g⁴ h20.3d⁶ c15.8g² c15.9d ab16.3g⁴ Mar 3] modest handicap hurdler: fair handicap chaser: stays 2½m, at least as effective at 2m: acts on firm and good to soft going: wears headgear/tongue tie. *James Bethell* — c107, h91

THAT MAN OF MINE (IRE) 6 ch.g. Thewayyouare (USA) – Do The Deal (IRE) (Halling (USA)) [2017/18 h80: h24g h20.6g² h20.6g³ Jun 23] poor maiden hurdler: stays 21f: acts on good to firm going: races towards rear. *Mike Sowersby* — h71

THAT'S A GIVEN (FR) 4 b.g. Great Pretender (IRE) – Aulne River (FR) (River Mist (USA)) [2017/18 b15.8s* b16.5d Apr 24] half-brother to 3 winners, including useful hurdler/chaser Wait For Me (2m-2½m winner, by Saint des Saints) and French 2¼m-3¼m hurdle/chase winner Yoneti (by Irish Wells): dam French 12.5f/13.5f winner: fairly useful form when winning bumper at Huntingdon on debut in March: stiffer task next time. *Philip Hobbs* — b96

THAT'S GONNA STING (IRE) 7 b.g. Scorpion (IRE) – Creme d'Arblay (IRE) (Singspiel (IRE)) [2017/18 h95: c26.3mᶠ c23g⁵ c26.2sᵖᵘ Apr 27] strong gelding: winning hurdler: little form over fences: stays 3m: acts on good to soft going: wears tongue tie. *Jeremy Scott* — c69, h–

THAT'S LIFE (IRE) 6 b.g. Presenting – Leader's Hall (IRE) (Saddlers' Hall (IRE)) [2017/18 b16.6d h19.4s h16.2v h19.6sᵖᵘ h16.2sᶠ Apr 26] little sign of ability in bumper/over hurdles. *Nicky Richards* — h–, b–

THATS MY RABBIT (IRE) 9 b.g. Heron Island (IRE) – Minnie Turbo (IRE) (General View) [2017/18 h15.7v h15.7v⁶ h17.7g Apr 20] fairly useful handicap hurdler at best: off 27 months, limited impact in 2017/18: stays 21f: acts on heavy going. *Suzi Best* — h62

THAT'S THE DEAL (IRE) 14 b.g. Turtle Island (IRE) – Sister Swing (Arctic Lord) [2017/18 c77§, h–: c21.2m² c20.3g³ c19.9m² c24.2g⁸ c20.3g² c15.7g⁴ c22.6m³ c20g⁵ c24d⁶ c23.6g⁴ c21.2g⁴ c21.2s⁴ c20.3s⁶ c23.6sᵖᵘ c19.9d Apr 24] well-made gelding: maiden hurdler: modest handicap chaser: won at Fakenham in May and June, and at Huntingdon in October: stays 25f: acts on good to firm and heavy going: races prominently. *John Cornwall* — c93, h–

THAT'STHESCOOP 5 ch.g. Dabbers Ridge (IRE) – Artemise (FR) (Cyborg (FR)) [2017/18 b16s b15.7v⁵ Feb 25] workmanlike gelding: has had breathing operation: well beaten in bumpers. *Dan Skelton* — b–

THE

THE ABSENT MARE 10 gr.m. Fair Mix (IRE) – Precious Lucy (FR) (Kadrou (FR)) [2017/18 c–, h–: h16.7g c16.5g Aug 1] of little account nowadays: in headgear last 3 starts: normally tongue tied: often races in rear/finishes weakly. *Sarah-Jayne Davies* c– §
h– §

THE ARTFUL COBBLER 7 gr.g. Saint des Saints (FR) – Serhaaphim (Erhaab (USA)) [2017/18 h97: c23.6g³ c23.8d* c25.5s* c28.8v* c34v^{pu} Mar 17] sturdy gelding: winning hurdler: fairly useful form over fences: won handicaps at Ludlow (novice) in November, Warwick in January and Lingfield in February: stays 29f: acts on heavy going: has worn cheekpieces: usually leads. *Henry Daly* c118
h–

THEATRE ACT 7 ch.m. Act One – Theatre Belle (King's Theatre (IRE)) [2017/18 h103: h20g^{pu} h20.1s⁵ h19.9g h20.5v^{pu} h20s⁵ h19.9s^{pu} h16.8v² h15.7v Mar 5] leggy, close-coupled mare: formerly fair handicap hurdler: only poor form in 2017/18: stays 21f: acts on heavy going: wears headgear: usually races prominently. *Chris Grant* h84

THEATREBAR 10 b.g. King's Theatre (IRE) – Ardenbar (Ardross) [2017/18 c–, h124: h19.9g² h20d⁶ h23.8d³ Apr 24] good-topped gelding: fairly useful handicap hurdler: runner-up both starts in novice handicap chases in 2014/15: stays 3m: acts on heavy going: wears tongue tie: patiently ridden. *Dan Skelton* c–
h117

THEATRE GUIDE (IRE) 11 b.g. King's Theatre (IRE) – Erintante (IRE) (Denel (FR)) [2017/18 c153, h–: c25.1s³ c25.3v⁶ c24g^{pu} c23.8s^F c28.8d Apr 28] tall gelding: winning hurdler: smart handicap chaser: third in Badger Ales Trophy at Wincanton (8 lengths behind Present Man) in November, easily best effort in 2017/18: stays 29f when conditions aren't testing: acts on soft going: wears headgear/tongue tie. *Colin Tizzard* c147
h–

THEATRE LEGEND 5 b.g. Midnight Legend – Theatre Belle (King's Theatre (IRE)) [2017/18 b–: b16.8g* b16.8s* b15.6s b17s Apr 13] useful-looking gelding: fairly useful bumper performer: won at Sedgefield in October and December. *Chris Grant* b98

THEATRE MILL (IRE) 10 b.g. King's Theatre (IRE) – River Mill (IRE) (Supreme Leader) [2017/18 c118, h96: c21d³ c21g⁵ c17.8g c24g⁶ c19.4d Apr 22] workmanlike gelding: winning hurdler: fairly useful handicap chaser: disappointing after reappearance: stays 21f: acts on soft and good to firm going: has worn hood: wears tongue tie: races towards rear. *Richenda Ford* c115 d
h–

THEATRE MIX 5 gr.m. Fair Mix (IRE) – Theatre Diva (IRE) (King's Theatre (IRE)) [2017/18 b16.5v⁶ Mar 12] first foal: dam (c119/h123) 2m-3¼m hurdle/chase winner: fourth in point: well beaten in bumper. *Jackie du Plessis* b–

THEATRE ROUGE (IRE) 6 b.m. King's Theatre (IRE) – Toulon Rouge (IRE) (Toulon) [2017/18 h100, b78: h23s^{pu} h23g^F Jun 3] fair hurdler at best: failed to complete in 2017/18: stays 2¾m: acts on good to firm going: hooded prior to final outing: usually races freely. *Philip Hobbs* h–

THEATRE ROYALE 6 ch.m. Sulamani (IRE) – Theatre Belle (King's Theatre (IRE)) [2017/18 h–, b–: h16.8d^F Sep 22] no form in bumper/novice hurdles: tried in tongue tie. *Brian Barr* h–

THEATRE STAGE (IRE) 6 b.g. Gamut (IRE) – Castletown Girl (Bob Back (USA)) [2017/18 h101p: h20d⁵ h16.8s³ h15.8v⁵ h21.7s⁵ Jan 16] modest maiden hurdler: probably stays 2½m: acts on soft going. *Evan Williams* h87

THEATRE TERRITORY (IRE) 8 b.m. King's Theatre (IRE) – Specifiedrisk (IRE) (Turtle Island (IRE)) [2017/18 h121: c19.9d² c20.8s² c20.2v³ c20.8v² c24g³ c21.1s³ Apr 13] useful-looking mare: fairly useful hurdler: useful maiden over fences: placed all starts including second in Timeform Novices' Handicap at Cheltenham (1¾ lengths behind Mister Whitaker) in January and third in Topham Chase at Aintree (9¾ lengths behind Ultragold): stays 3m: acts on heavy going: in cheekpieces last 2 starts: sound jumper: tough and genuine. *Warren Greatrex* c136
h–

THEATRICAL STAR 12 b.g. King's Theatre (IRE) – Lucy Glitters (Ardross) [2017/18 c130x, h117: c23.6d⁶ c25d^F c21.7g³ c24.2d³ c24.2s c23s⁴ c28.4v² c28.4s⁵ Mar 26] angular gelding: fairly useful hurdler: fairly useful handicap chaser: stays 31f: acts on heavy going: has worn headgear/tongue tie: front runner/races prominently: often let down by jumping over fences. *Colin Tizzard* c125 x
h–

THEATRICAL STYLE (IRE) 9 b.g. Alhaarth (IRE) – Little Theatre (IRE) (Old Vic) [2017/18 h81: h16.7g h22.1d⁵ Aug 28] in frame in Irish maiden points: fair handicap hurdler: unproven beyond 17f: acts on heavy going: wears headgear. *Donald McCain* h95

THE BANASTOIR (IRE) 9 b.g. Presenting – Kimouna (IRE) (Round Sovereign (FR)) [2017/18 c95, h–: h16.2s⁶ Apr 26] maiden pointer: lightly-raced hurdler, fair at best: modest form in chases: stays 2½m: acts on good to firm going. *Lucinda Russell* c–
h58

THE

THEBANNERKINGREBEL (IRE) 5 b.g. Arakan (USA) – One Love (IRE) (Bravefoot) [2017/18 b16s* b16.7v* b16.4s]pu Mar 14] €2,700 3-y-o: sturdy gelding: fifth foal: half-brother to fairly useful hurdler/chaser Gold Patrol (21f-23f winner, by Gold Well): dam winning pointer: useful form in bumpers: won at Warwick (maiden event, by 12 lengths) in January and Bangor (by 3¾ lengths from Harambe) in February: pulled up in Champion Bumper at Cheltenham. *Jamie Snowden* — **b105**

THEBARROWMAN (IRE) 8 b.g. Mahler – Pixie Dust (IRE) (Desert King (IRE)) [2017/18 h134: c19.5s² c21s² c24s⁴ c25v c32.6s^F Feb 24] useful hurdler: fairly useful form over fences: stayed 2¾m: acted on heavy going: tried in cheekpieces/tongue tie: made running/raced prominently: dead. *A. P. Keatley, Ireland* — **c126 h–**

THE BATHAM BOY (IRE) 4 b.g. Thewayyouare (USA) – Margaux Dancer (IRE) (Danehill Dancer (IRE)) [2017/18 h16.3s⁵ h15.8s⁴ h16.7s⁶ h20.3d^pu Dec 5] poor maiden on Flat: similar form over hurdles: tried in cheekpieces. *Daniel Loughnane* — **h80**

THE BAY BIRCH (IRE) 7 b.m. Beneficial – Tournant Vic (Old Vic) [2017/18 c16g c16g h21.8g⁵ h24d⁶ c22s c25.2g⁴ c23.5v⁵ c25d² c21s³ c23.5s⁵ c22.6s c20.2v² c19.8s* c19.4v² c19.8v* c19.2v² c20.8g² Apr 19] third foal: half-sister to fairly useful hurdler/useful chaser The Bay Oak (2½m-3½m winner, by Vinnie Roe): dam ran once in bumper: maiden hurdler: fairly useful handicap chaser: left F. Flood after eleventh start and much improved after, winning at Towcester in February (novice) and March, and at Exeter (another novice) in April: stays 25f, effective at much shorter: acts on heavy going: usually travels strongly towards rear. *Matt Sheppard* — **c125 h77**

THE BIG BITE (IRE) 5 b.g. Scorpion (IRE) – Thanks Noel (IRE) (Tel Quel (FR)) [2017/18 b89: b15.8s* b16.4s Mar 14] well-made gelding: useful form in bumpers: won at Huntingdon (by 2½ lengths from Shaughnessy) on return in December: raced too freely in Champion Bumper at Cheltenham. *Tom George* — **b107**

THE BISHOP (IRE) 10 b.g. Winged Love (IRE) – Charlie's Mary (IRE) (Daar Alzamaan (IRE)) [2017/18 c82, h94§: h24.3s c24.2s⁵ Nov 10] sturdy gelding: modest handicap hurdler/chaser: stays 3m: acts on heavy going: tried in cheekpieces: temperamental. *N. W. Alexander* — **c76 § h– §**

THE BLACK SQUIRREL (IRE) 5 br.g. Craigsteel – Terra Lucida (IRE) (Alderbrook) [2017/18 b16.3g³ b15.8d² b16.3d* h19.2g⁶ h16.3g⁵ h15.3g Oct 29] €1,500 3-y-o, £13,500 4-y-o: first foal: dam, pulled up all 3 starts in points, sister to fairly useful hurdler/fair chaser (stayed 3m) Clashnabrook and half-sister to fairly useful chaser (25f/3¼m winner) Duhallow Tornado: runner-up in maiden point: fairly useful form in bumpers: won at Stratford in September: just modest form over hurdles: should stay well beyond 2m. *Warren Greatrex* — **h97 b96**

THE BLUE BOMBER 6 b.g. Stimulation (IRE) – Mar Blue (FR) (Marju (IRE)) [2017/18 h105, b87: h16d h15.5s h16s⁶ h19.6s⁶ h15.5v⁶ h20.7s⁶ h15.7s* h15.8d² Apr 24] lengthy gelding: modest handicap hurdler: won at Market Rasen in March: unproven beyond 17f: acts on soft going: tried in hood. *Caroline Fryer* — **h94**

THE BLUES MASTER (IRE) 4 gr.g. Mastercraftsman (IRE) – Catch The Blues (IRE) (Bluebird (USA)) [2017/18 h16s h16.3s³ h15.8s² Jan 26] compact gelding: fair on Flat, stays 1¾m: similar form when placed last 2 starts over hurdles. *Alan King* — **h111**

THE BOOM IS BACK (IRE) 6 b.g. Publisher (USA) – Wild Coast (IRE) (Gothland (FR)) [2017/18 h16s Apr 27] off mark in Irish points at second attempt: 16/1, well-held seventh in maiden at Chepstow on hurdling debut. *Christian Williams* — **h–**

THEBOSS ON THEHILL (IRE) 10 ch.g. Bach (IRE) – Consproblem (IRE) (Mazaad) [2017/18 h68: c23.6s^pu Apr 27] point winner: modest maiden hurdler in 2013/14: little form under Rules since (pulled up on chasing debut) for various trainers: tried in headgear. *Miss C. Heelay* — **c– h–**

THE BOSS'S DREAM (IRE) 10 b.g. Luso – Mrs Kick (IRE) (Supreme Leader) [2017/18 h23.6v⁶ c19.9s³ c24.2v⁵ c28.8v³ c29.2v⁶ c23.6s⁵ Apr 14] workmanlike gelding: formerly useful handicap hurdler: only fair form over fences: best up to 3¼m: acts on heavy going: tried in cheekpieces: in tongue tie last 2 starts: front runner/races prominently. *Neil King* — **c114 h83**

THE BOTTOM BAR (IRE) 6 br.g. Stowaway – Serenade Leader (IRE) (Supreme Leader) [2017/18 b16.7g² h15.7s² h20.6s* Apr 11] fair form on second of 2 outings in bumpers (then left Paul Webber): fairly useful form in maiden hurdles: won at Market Rasen in April: open to further improvement. *Nicky Henderson* — **h122 p b91**

THE

THE BROTHERS (IRE) 5 b.g. Flemensfirth (USA) – Laboc (Rymer) [2017/18 b17.7g h15.3s h16.5g^{ur} h16.8v⁵ h15.3v³ h16s h18.5v⁴ Apr 17] €36,000 3-y-o: brother to 2¾m hurdle winner McGinty's Dream and half-brother to fairly useful hurdler/winning pointer Abnaki (2¾m-27f winner, by Milan): dam, third in bumper, half-sister to Cheltenham Gold Cup winner See More Business: shaped like a stayer in bumper: fair form over hurdles: likely to prove best at 2½m+: acts on heavy going. *Colin Tizzard* — **h109 b73**

THE BUNNYMAN 4 b.g. Authorized (IRE) – Linnet (GER) (Dr Fong (USA)) [2017/18 b16.7v⁵ Apr 11] €70,000 3-y-o: fifth foal: half-brother to modest hurdler/chaser Etania (21f-23f winner, by King's Theatre): dam (h107), 2m hurdle winner (stayed 2¾m), also 1m/1¼m winner on Flat, half-sister to smart hurdler/useful chaser (2m winner) Zamdy Man (by Authorized) and smart hurdler (2m-2½m winner) Clyne: 8/1, fifth in bumper at Market Rasen (12¾ lengths behind Dorking Boy). *Emma Lavelle* — **b83**

THE BUTCHER SAID (IRE) 5 b.g. Robin des Champs (FR) – Georgina Valleya (IRE) (King's Theatre (IRE)) [2017/18 b16s³ h20.5s⁶ Dec 3] rangy gelding: first foal: dam, unraced, half-sister to fairly useful hurdler (stayed 2½m) Meetmeatthemoon: trained by Emmet Mullins, fairly useful form when second of 23 in bumper (4-y-o maiden) at Punchestown on debut: favourite, only third at Sandown on reappearance: found little when remote sixth to Vinndication in novice at Leicester on hurdling debut (should do better). *Warren Greatrex* — **h80 p b91**

THE CALLER 7 b.g. Yeats (IRE) – Wyldello (Supreme Leader) [2017/18 h115, b101: h23.9m* h23g c22.6d⁵ Apr 22] compact gelding: bumper winner: fairly useful handicap hurdler: won at Perth in June: left Warren Greatrex and fit from points (maiden), tailed off in hunter on chasing debut: stays 3m: acts on good to firm and heavy going: in headgear last 2 starts. *Mary Vestey* — **c– h117**

THE CANNISTER MAN (IRE) 6 b.g. Arakan (USA) – Ladyrosaro (IRE) (Roselier (FR)) [2017/18 b16v^{su} h19.6s^{pu} h20.3v⁴ h17.7s² h16.8v* Apr 17] £2,000 3-y-o, £13,000 5-y-o: sixth foal: half-brother to a winning pointer by Lahib: dam (b65), ran twice in bumpers, sister to fair hurdler/useful chaser (stayed 4m) Kinburn: runner-up on second start in Irish points: slipped up after 2f in bumper: fair form over hurdles: improved when winning maiden at Exeter in April: in hood last 3 starts: acts well on heavy going. *Sam Thomas* — **h114 b–**

THE CAPTAIN (IRE) 5 b.g. Millenary – Quilt (Terimon) [2017/18 h15.8g⁶ Apr 24] £8,000 3-y-o, £15,000 5-y-o: sturdy gelding: half-brother to several winners, including fairly useful hurdler/winning pointer Quarrymount (2½m winner, by Polar Falcon), stayed 27f: dam, maiden on Flat (stayed 1¼m), half-sister to smart hurdler/useful chaser (stayed 2¾m) Quinze: runner-up completed start in points: 28/1, some encouragement when sixth in maiden at Huntingdon (13¼ lengths behind Movie Set) on hurdling debut: will be suited by at least 2½m: entitled to progress. *Caroline Bailey* — **h97 p**

THE CIDER MAKER 8 b.g. Kayf Tara – Dame Fonteyn (Suave Dancer (USA)) [2017/18 c19.4v⁵ c19.2v³ h23.9v^{pu} h25.5v² c25.1v^{pu} Apr 12] fair maiden hurdler: fair handicap chaser: stays 3¼m: acts on good to firm and heavy going: wears tongue tie. *Colin Tizzard* — **c106 h110**

THECLOCKISTICKING (IRE) 6 br.g. Gamut (IRE) – Curragheen (IRE) (Sadler's Wells (USA)) [2017/18 b16.7g² h16d* h15.8g² h15.7d³ h19.6s³ h20.3g² Apr 18] tall gelding: second foal: dam unraced sister to Cheltenham Gold Cup winner Synchronised: placed in 2 Irish points: second in bumper at Market Rasen (1¾ lengths behind Simply The Betts): useful novice hurdler: won at Fakenham (by 32 lengths) in October and Huntingdon in November: placed all 3 starts after, notably when third in Kennel Gate Novices' Hurdle at Ascot (4¼ lengths behind Claimantakinforgan) in December: stays 2½m: acts on good to soft going. *Stuart Edmunds* — **h137 b94**

THE CLOCK LEARY (IRE) 10 b.g. Helissio (FR) – Kiwi Babe (Karinga Bay) [2017/18 c109, h–: c20.3s* c21.4g² c24.1g* c25.5g⁴ c23.8d* c21.4g^{pu} c26.2g⁵ c20d^{pu} Mar 31] sturdy gelding: winning hurdler: fairly useful handicap chaser: won at Bangor in May and August, and at Perth in September: stays 3m: acts on heavy going: has worn headgear: often leads. *Donald McCain* — **c128 h–**

THE COBBLER SWAYNE (IRE) 9 b.g. Milan – Turtle Lamp (IRE) (Turtle Island (IRE)) [2017/18 c113, h–: c21.5v* Nov 4] sturdy gelding: winning pointer: maiden hurdler: fair handicap chaser: stayed 2¾m: acted on heavy going: dead. *Pauline Robson* — **c103 h–**

THE COFFEE HUNTER (FR) 6 gr.g. Doctor Dino (FR) – Mamamia (FR) (Linamix (FR)) [2017/18 c105, h86: c20g^{pu} h20g⁵ Jun 3] rather unfurnished gelding: maiden hurdler: fair form on chasing debut, disappointing under Rules since (won point soon after end of season): should stay beyond 2m: acts on soft going: often tongue tied. *Nick Williams* — **c– h79**

THE COMPELLER (IRE) 6 b.g. Lawman (FR) – Mark Too (IRE) (Mark of Esteem (IRE)) [2017/18 h75: h16.4s^{pu} h15.6d h16.4d^2 h16.2s* Apr 26] modest handicap hurdler: won at Perth in April: best form at 2m: acts on soft going: tried in cheekpieces: in tongue tie last 4 starts. *Lucinda Russell*   h91

THE CONN (IRE) 8 b.g. Milan – Grandy Invader (IRE) (Presenting) [2017/18 h–: h23.3g^{pu} h20.2g h22.1s^5 h23.9s^3 h23.3v^4 h23.3s^5 h24g^5 Nov 17] poor maiden hurdler: will stay long distances: acts on soft going: tried in headgear/tongue tie: usually races nearer last than first. *Sheena Walton*   h76

THECORRUPTOR (IRE) 8 b.g. Robin des Pres (FR) – Cappard View (IRE) (Rudimentary (USA)) [2017/18 h20.3d^{pu} Nov 21] useful-looking gelding: Irish maiden point winner: lightly-raced hurdler, form only when placed in maiden at Fakenham in 2014/15: best effort at 2½m on soft going: hooded once: dead. *Paul Webber*   h–

THE CRAZED MOON (IRE) 6 b.m. Yeats (IRE) – Rose Gallery (FR) (Gallery of Zurich (IRE)) [2017/18 h16s^4 h15.7g^2 h19.4s h15.7s^5 h15.7v^5 Mar 29] €18,500 3-y-o, £37,000 5-y-o: third foal: half-sister to useful chaser Patricks Park (2m-21f winner, by Insatiable): dam unraced half-sister to Grand Steeple-Chase de Paris winner Remember Rose: off mark in Irish maiden points at fourth attempt: fair form over hurdles: should stay beyond 2m: acts on soft going. *Henry Oliver*   h101

THE CRAZY CRAB (IRE) 12 b.g. Heron Island (IRE) – Smiths Lady (IRE) (Anshan) [2017/18 c–: c21.7g^4 c15.7g^6 Apr 20] winning pointer: lightly raced and no form in chases. *Daniel O'Brien*   c–

THE DAWN BANDIT (IRE) 5 gr.m. Daylami (IRE) – Queen of The Dawn (IRE) (Royal Anthem (USA)) [2017/18 b16.2g b16v h16.2s^6 h17d^4 Mar 25] first foal: dam unraced half-sister to useful hurdler (stayed 2m) On Raglan Road: well held in bumpers: some promise in novice hurdles at Kelso and Carlisle: will be suited by 2½m+. *Katie Scott*   h81 b–

THE DAWN MAN (IRE) 7 b.g. Milan – Calling Classy (IRE) (Good Thyne (USA)) [2017/18 h20g^3 h16s^4 h19.7s^3 h19.3s^5 c20.9v^5 c20.3g^{pu} Apr 20] £30,000 6-y-o: fifth foal: brother to fair hurdler/fairly useful chaser Goodthynemilan (2½m-3m winner) and closely related to fair chaser The Rockies (3m winner, by Oscar): dam (h101) 2m-2½m hurdle winner: won on completed start in Irish points: fair form over hurdles: little promise in handicap chases: bred to stay further than 2½m: acts on soft going: usually races close up. *Henry Oliver*   c70 h107

THE DELLERCHECKOUT (IRE) 5 b.g. Getaway (GER) – Loreley (IRE) (Oscar (IRE)) [2017/18 h20s^6 h19.6s^2 h21.2v^5 h19.8v^4 Apr 9] €27,000 3-y-o, £260,000 4-y-o: second foal: dam unraced sister to fair hurdlers/fairly useful chasers Avoca Promise (stayed 2½m) and Point Blank (stayed 3m) out of half-sister to Champion Hurdle winners Granville Again and Morley Street: finished alone in Irish point: fair form first 2 starts over hurdles, but folded tamely both outings after (tongue tied final one). *Paul Nicholls*   h114

THE DELRAY MUNKY 6 b.m. Overbury (IRE) – Delray Beach (FR) (Saint Preuil (FR)) [2017/18 h96, b74: h16.2g h16.2v h19.4g^3 h25.8s h19v* h19.5v* h24.3v* h18.9v* h20.3g Apr 19] fairly useful handicap hurdler: won at Ayr in January (mares), twice there in February (first one another mares race) and also at Haydock (awarded race after hampered late on when finishing well) in March: stays 3m: revels in the mud: in cheekpieces last 5 starts. *Iain Jardine*   h119

THE DETAINEE 5 b.g. Aqlaam – Jakarta Jade (IRE) (Royal Abjar (USA)) [2017/18 h17.7d^4 h19.2g^3 Oct 7] dam half-sister to useful hurdler/chaser Dubai Prince and fairly useful hurdler Authorship, both winners around 2m: fair on Flat (stays 1½m): similar form when placed on second of 2 starts in novice hurdles at Fontwell: wears cheekpieces. *Neil Mulholland*   h109

THE DEVILS DROP (IRE) 5 b.g. Court Cave (IRE) – Concernforkillen (IRE) (Anshan) [2017/18 h19.5s^4 h21g^3 h24.6s^3 h23.8s^3 h23.8d^5 Apr 24] €3,500 3-y-o, £36,000 4-y-o: second foal: dam pulled up over hurdles on only start: runner-up in Irish maiden point on debut: fair form over hurdles: stays 3m: acts on soft going. *Alan King*   h111

THEDFACTOR (IRE) 9 b.g. Kalanisi (IRE) – Insan Magic (IRE) (Insan (USA)) [2017/18 c–: c20.1g^4 c23.4g c16.4s^{pu} c23.8d c26.2d c24.2d^{pu} Apr 23] maiden pointer: no solid form in chases: in cheekpieces last 3 starts: tried in tongue tie. *Jane Walton*   c84 ?

THE

THE DOORMAN (IRE) 9 b.g. King's Theatre (IRE) – Amber Light (IRE) (Anshan) [2017/18 c113x, h108: h19.3m* h19.9g* h20.1g³ c20.3g⁶ c21.4g² c23.9g c21.1g* c21.4g⁵ c23.9d⁶ c21.4v^pu c19.3g⁶ Apr 23] fair hurdler: won novices at Carlisle and Sedgefield in May: fair handicap chaser: won at latter course in September: barely stays 25f: acts on soft and good to firm going: wears cheekpieces/tongue tie: held up: often let down by jumping over fences. *Ben Haslam* — c107 x / h109 §

THE DRACONIAN (IRE) 7 b.g. Kalanisi (IRE) – Lucky Hand (IRE) (Shernazar) [2017/18 b81: h15.3s h15.8d h16.7v⁵ h15.8d h26s⁵ Feb 23] poor form over hurdles: tried in cheekpieces. *David Pipe* — h75

THEDRINKYMEISTER (IRE) 9 b.g. Heron Island (IRE) – Keel Row (Relkino) [2017/18 c118§, h–: c24.3v^F c24.1v² c23.6v² c25.1v c23.9v* Apr 11] rangy gelding: winning hurdler: fairly useful handicap chaser: left Kim Bailey, better than ever when winning at Market Rasen in April: stays 3m: acts on heavy going: wears headgear: usually races close up: ungenuine. *Henry Daly* — c127 § / h–

THE DUBAI WAY (IRE) 6 b.g. Dubai Destination (USA) – Britway Lady (IRE) (Norwich) [2017/18 h15.8s* h16.2v^F h16.8s* h16s* h19.8v Mar 10] good-topped gelding: second foal: half-brother to fair hurdler Taylor (19f winner, by Presenting): dam, pulled up only start over hurdles, half-sister to fairly useful hurdler/very smart chaser (stayed 2¾m) Thyne Again: Irish point winner: won maiden bumper at Ffos Las (by ½ length from Al Dancer) in October: fairly useful form over hurdles: won novices at Hexham in November and Sedgefield in December, and handicap at Warwick in February: should prove suited by 2½m+. *Harry Whittington* — h123 / b97

THE DUTCHMAN (IRE) 8 b.g. King's Theatre (IRE) – Shivermetimber (IRE) (Arctic Lord) [2017/18 c142, h129+: h22.8v² h24s⁶ c25.6v* c28.4v^pu c34.3s^ur Apr 14] sturdy gelding: useful handicap hurdler: second in Betfair Stayers' Handicap Hurdle at Haydock (17 lengths behind Sam Spinner) in November: smart handicap chaser: won Peter Marsh Chase there (by 13 lengths from Captain Redbeard) in January: stays 3¼m: acts on heavy going: tried in cheekpieces: in tongue tie last 5 starts: often travels strongly. *Colin Tizzard* — c147 / h132

THE EAGLEHASLANDED (IRE) 8 b.g. Milan – Vallee Doree (FR) (Neverneyev (USA)) [2017/18 h135: h24.2v^pu Feb 10] useful-looking gelding: winning pointer: useful handicap hurdler: pulled up only appearance in 2017/18: stays 25f: acts on heavy going: wears headgear/tongue tie. *Paul Nicholls* — h–

THE FERICK (IRE) 12 b.g. Kris Kin (USA) – Minaun Heights (Doyoun) [2017/18 h20^pu h16.7g^pu Jul 9] maiden hurdler: off 49 months, pulled up both starts in 2017/18: tried in hood: has worn tongue tie, including last 3 outings. *Ben Case* — h–

THE FINAL WHISTLE (IRE) 5 ch.g. Approve (IRE) – Fairnilee (Selkirk (USA)) [2017/18 b16d b15.8g h20v h19.7s h19.7s Jan 16] no form in bumpers: well held over hurdles. *Sheila Lewis* — h– / b–

THE FLAME (IRE) 5 b.g. Flemensfirth (USA) – Molly Round (IRE) (Old Vic) [2017/18 b96: h16.7d h15.8s h16.3g³ h19.6s⁶ h21.4s Feb 17] won maiden point on debut: modest form over hurdles: should stay 21f: acts on soft going: in hood last 4 starts. *Jonjo O'Neill* — h93

THEFLYINGPORTRAIT (IRE) 9 gr.g. Portrait Gallery (IRE) – Skule Hill Lass (IRE) (Close Conflict) [2017/18 c129, h102: c17.3d⁵ c15.8g* c16m⁴ h16.2s⁵ c17.1d³ c15.9g c15.8s Apr 12] winning hurdler: useful handicap chaser: won at Aintree (by 2¼ lengths from Lofgren) in June: stays 2½m: acts on good to firm and heavy going: tried in cheekpieces: wears tongue tie: front runner/races prominently. *Jennie Candlish* — c136

THE FLYING SOFA (FR) 5 b.g. Sholokhov (IRE) – La Julie (IRE) (Peintre Celebre (USA)) [2017/18 b15.7d³ b17.3v⁵ b17.7d* b16.4s Mar 14] £45,000 3-y-o: compact gelding: first foal: dam German 1¼m winner: useful form in bumpers: won maiden at Fontwell in February: had been third in listed event at Ascot (3 lengths behind Didtheyleaveuoutto) on debut. *Gary Moore* — b107

THE FRESH PRINCE (IRE) 8 b.g. Robin des Pres (FR) – Hayley Cometh (IRE) (Supreme Leader) [2017/18 c122, h–: c19.9s^pu c19.1d⁴ c24g⁶ Apr 20] rangy gelding: winning hurdler: fairly useful handicap chaser: best short of 3m: acts on good going: front runner/races prominently: has idled/made mistakes. *Oliver Sherwood* — c113 / h–

THEFRIENDLYGREMLIN 10 b.g. Vinnie Roe (IRE) – Queens Fantasy (Grand Lodge (USA)) [2017/18 c–, h–§: h19d^pu h21.7g^pu Apr 20] of little account nowadays: has worn headgear: ungenuine. *Tracey Leeson* — c– / h– §

THE GAME CHANGER (IRE) 9 b.g. Arcadio (GER) – Gilt Ridden (IRE) (Heron Island (IRE)) [2017/18 c150, h144: h16d h16.3g² c17d* h16v* h16s^pu c16v⁴ c17s c16s h16s⁵ Apr 27] tall gelding: useful hurdler/chaser: won minor events over fences at — c140 / h134

Ballinrobe (by 2¼ lengths from Ted Veale) in August and over hurdles at Listowel (by head from Ballycasey) in September: stays 2½m: acts on good to firm and heavy going: has worn headgear: wears tongue tie: often races prominently: has finished weakly. *Gordon Elliott, Ireland*

THE GAME IS A FOOT (IRE) 11 b.g. Oscar (IRE) – Cooksgrove Rosie (IRE) (Mandalus) [2017/18 h95: h25g⁴ h20.5d* h16d* h19.5s* h16v⁴ h15.7v* Feb 1] tall gelding: placed in points: fair handicap hurdler: won at Plumpton (conditional) and Lingfield in November, Lingfield again in December and Towcester in February: stays 25f: acts on heavy going: tried in blinkers: held up: tough. *Zoe Davison* h110

THE GEEGEEZ GEEGEE (IRE) 9 b.g. Beneficial – Shanann Lady (IRE) (Anshan) [2017/18 c102, h–: c17.4gᵘʳ c20.3gᵖᵘ c21g* c20g³ c20.9s* c19.4g⁴ Nov 2] winning hurdler: fairly useful handicap chaser: left Anthony Honeyball, won at Newton Abbot in August and Stratford in October: stays 3m, effective at shorter: acts on heavy going: wears headgear: has worn tongue tie, including last 4 starts. *Olly Murphy* c121 h–

THE GINGER NINJER 5 ch.m. Malinas (GER) – Atabaas Allure (FR) (Alhaarth (IRE)) [2017/18 b17.7g ab16g Nov 14] second foal: dam (h68), maiden hurdler (placed up to 2½m), 7f/1m winner on Flat: no promise in bumpers. *Suzy Smith* b–

THE GIPPER (IRE) 8 b.g. King's Theatre (IRE) – Merrill Gaye (IRE) (Roselier (FR)) [2017/18 h126: c16.3g² c16mᶠ h16.8s⁵ h15.3v⁵ h15.7v⁶ c16.1s³ c18.2s⁴ c19.2v⁴ Apr 8] sturdy gelding: useful hurdler at best, below form in 2017/18: easily best effort over fences (fairly useful hurdler) when third in novice handicap at Taunton in January: unproven beyond 2m: acts on heavy going: usually races close up. *Evan Williams* c118 h–

THEGIRLFROMMILAN (IRE) 8 b.m. Milan – Legendsofthefall (IRE) (Arctic Lord) [2017/18 h101, b83: c25.8gᵖᵘ c22.5d⁴ c23.8vᵖᵘ c23g Nov 30] good-topped mare: multiple point winner: maiden hurdler: modest form in chases: stays 3m: acts on heavy going: tried in cheekpieces. *Rebecca Curtis* c91 h–

THE GOLDEN HOUR (IRE) 8 b.m. Gold Well – Kirktonmoor Katie (IRE) (Rich Charlie) [2017/18 h70: h23.4s³ h20.5d⁶ h20.5v³ h25v* Feb 12] has had breathing operation: runner-up in Irish mares maiden point: modest handicap hurdler: won at Plumpton in February: stays 25f: acts on heavy going. *Zoe Davison* h86

THE GO TOU MAN (IRE) 5 b.g. Shantou (USA) – Golan Lady (IRE) (Golan (IRE)) [2017/18 b16f² b17.7g⁴ h15.7s h15.8s⁴ h16.5v⁴ Mar 12] €34,000 3-y-o: first foal: dam unraced half-sister to fairly useful hurdler/smart chaser (stayed 29f) Same Difference and useful hurdler/chaser (stays 21f) Forever Field: fair form on first of 2 outings in bumpers: easily best effort over hurdles when fourth in novice at Huntingdon in January: will be suited by 2½m. *Harry Whittington* h105 b87

THE GREAT GETAWAY (IRE) 6 b.g. Getaway (GER) – Park Mist (IRE) (Great Palm (USA)) [2017/18 b16v⁴ h20.6s* Dec 23] €35,000 3-y-o: fourth foal: dam unraced half-sister to useful hurdler/smart chaser (stayed 25f) Gallant Oscar: off mark in Irish points at fourth attempt: fourth in maiden bumper at Ayr: 9/1, won novice at Newcastle (by 1½ lengths from Silva Eclipse) on hurdling debut, staying on well: will be suited by further than 2½m: open to improvement. *Donald McCain* h114 p b76

THE GREEDY BOY 5 b.g. Atlantic Sport (USA) – Indian Girl (Erhaab (USA)) [2017/18 h–: h22.2d⁴ h16g Aug 11] modest maiden on Flat (stays 9.5f): poor form over hurdles: in tongue tie last 2 starts. *Steve Flook* h77

THEGREENDALEROCKET (IRE) 9 b.g. Oscar (IRE) – Classy Society (IRE) (Moscow Society (USA)) [2017/18 c113, h–: c23.6dᵖᵘ c23.6s c25.1ᵖᵘ Nov 23] maiden hurdler: fair chaser at best: out of sorts in 2017/18, finishing weakly: in headgear 3 of last 4 outings: tried in tongue tie: usually races prominently. *Richard Woollacott* c– h–

THE GREEN OGRE 8 b.g. Dubai Destination (USA) – Takegawa (Giant's Causeway (USA)) [2017/18 c16d c15.5dᵖᵘ h19s⁵ h16.3s⁵ h19.2v² h15.7vᵖᵘ Mar 29] workmanlike gelding: fair handicap hurdler nowadays: fairly useful chaser at best: off 21 months, let down by jumping first 2 starts in 2017/18: stays 19f: acts on heavy going: wears blinkers: front runner/races prominently. *Gary Moore* c– h109

THE GREENVET (IRE) 8 b.g. Acrobat (IRE) – Glacial Air (IRE) (Glacial Storm (USA)) [2017/18 c–, h91: h19.9s⁵ h23.1vᵖᵘ h23.9g⁵ h21.4s Feb 17] winning pointer: poor maiden hurdler: struggling when unseating only chase outing: stays 3m: best form on good going: wears cheekpieces: tried in tongue tie. *Laura Young* c– h84

THE

THE GREY ENFORCER (FR) 4 gr.g. Gris de Gris (IRE) – Bleue Et Bleue (FR) (Loup Solitaire (USA)) [2017/18 b16.7g⁴ Apr 22] second foal: half-brother to French hurdler Lutin des Taillons (2m-19f winner, by Robin des Champs): dam lightly raced in France: 7/1, green when fourth in bumper at Market Rasen (4¼ lengths behind Northern Soul). *Harry Whittington* — **b91**

THE GREY TAYLOR (IRE) 9 gr.g. Royal Anthem (USA) – Penny Tan (IRE) (Roselier (FR)) [2017/18 c–, h–: c16.5g c24.2g^pu c20g^pu Jul 19] tall, close-coupled gelding: winning hurdler: useful novice chaser in 2015/16: disappointing since, including over hurdles: has worn tongue tie, including last 4 starts: usually races close up. *Brian Ellison* — **c– h–**

THE GRINDER (IRE) 6 b.g. Arcadio (GER) – Bincas Beauty (IRE) (Kayf Tara) [2017/18 h106, b–: h21d h19.4d h15.6⁶ h16.7g² Apr 22] in frame completed start in Irish maiden points: fair maiden hurdler: stays 21f: best form on good going. *Nick Kent* — **h102**

THE GROOVE 5 b.g. Azamour (IRE) – Dance East (Shamardal (USA)) [2017/18 h76, b–: h15.8g h16g^pu Jun 25] little promise in bumper/over hurdles: in headgear last 2 starts: tried in tongue tie: has bled. *Fergal O'Brien* — **h–**

THE GROOVY HOOVY 6 b.g. Sulamani (IRE) – Kingennie (Dunbeath (USA)) [2017/18 b16g² h20.3s h16.5v⁵ h16.5s⁴ h22d Apr 22] £10,000 4-y-o: seventh foal: half-brother to bumper winner/useful hurdler Clova Island (17f-21f winner, by Turtle Island) and fair hurdler Rev Up Ruby (2½m-25f winner, by Revoque): dam (h89) 2½m hurdle winner: rallying second in bumper at Worcester (head behind Mcnamaras Band): only modest form in novice hurdles: should be suited by 2½m+. *Oliver Sherwood* — **h96 b90**

THE GUNNER MURPHY (IRE) 5 br.g. Oscar (IRE) – River Finn (IRE) (Luso) [2017/18 b16.6v* b16s² h16v^pu Apr 2] first foal: dam, ran once over hurdles/failed to complete in points, half-sister to fairly useful hurdler/smart chaser (stayed 3¼m) Treacle: useful form in bumpers: won maiden at Galway (by ½ length from First Approach) in October before runner-up at Leopardstown (1¾ lengths behind Minella Encore): 28/1, pulled up in Rathbarry & Glenview Studs Novices' Hurdle at Fairyhouse on hurdling debut (open to plenty of improvement): will stay further than 2m: wears tongue tie. *Joseph Patrick O'Brien, Ireland* — **h– p b106**

THE HAPPY CHAPPY (IRE) 7 b.g. Flemensfirth (USA) – Native Design (IRE) (Be My Native (USA)) [2017/18 h105: h25m* c23g² c26.3g* c25.6g* c28.8d c23.8d⁴ Apr 24] lengthy, angular gelding: fair form over hurdles: won handicap at Huntingdon in May: fairly useful form over fences: won handicaps at Sedgefield (novice) and Ludlow in November: suited by 3m+: acts on soft and good to firm going: wears tongue tie. *Sarah Humphrey* — **c120 h108**

THE HARD SHOULDER (IRE) 5 gr.g. Cloudings (IRE) – Our Witness (IRE) (Witness Box (USA)) [2017/18 b–: b16.4g b16.2v⁶ h16v Mar 9] well held in bumpers/maiden hurdle: tried in tongue tie. *Chris Grant* — **h– b–**

THE HERDS GARDEN 9 b.g. Multiplex – Eternal Legacy (IRE) (Monashee Mountain (USA)) [2017/18 c120, h–: h20.1g⁴ c21.2g⁶ Jun 30] fair hurdler/fairly useful maiden chaser at best: disappointing both outings in 2017/18: stays 2½m: acts on soft and good to firm going: has worn headgear/tongue tie. *Donald McCain* — **c– h92**

THE HIKING VIKING 5 b.g. Beat Hollow – Swaythe (USA) (Swain (IRE)) [2017/18 b–: h16.6d Dec 2] little show in bumper/novice hurdle (hooded). *Paul Webber* — **h–**

THE HOLLOW GINGE (IRE) 5 b.g. Oscar (IRE) – Some Gem (IRE) (Flemensfirth (USA)) [2017/18 b92: h21.6v* h24g³ h19.7s³ h22.8v h19.5v⁶ Mar 5] fairly useful form over hurdles: won novice at Newton Abbot in October: stays 3m well: acts on heavy going: signs of temperament. *Nigel Twiston-Davies* — **h118**

THE HORSECHESNUT (IRE) 10 ch.g. Definite Article – Ballinahowliss (IRE) (Supreme Leader) [2017/18 c–, h–: c20v^pu c26.3s^pu c24v^pu Dec 31] winning pointer: fairly useful novice hurdler in 2014/15: raced over fences since, completing only once: wears cheekpieces/tongue tie. *Jennie Candlish* — **c– h–**

THE IBBSTER (IRE) 8 b.g. Shantou (USA) – Annalisa (IRE) (Rhoman Rule (USA)) [2017/18 h18.5d Oct 12] dual point winner: well held in novice on hurdling debut. *Brian Forsey* — **h–**

THE ICE FACTOR 10 b.g. Iceman – Kiruna (Northern Park (USA)) [2017/18 c74§, h55§: c15.6g h16.2s Nov 10] poor hurdler/maiden chaser: stays 2½m: acts on good to firm and good to soft going: wears cheekpieces: has worn tongue tie: temperamental. *Alison Hamilton* — **c– § h– §**

THE

THE IMITATION GAME 5 b.m. Yeats (IRE) – Katmai (IRE) (Bob Back (USA)) [2017/18 b–: b13.7v⁴ b15.7s h16.5v h19s^ur Mar 26] modest form in bumpers: let down by jumping both outings over hurdles. *Susan Gardner*   h– b78

THEINVAL (FR) 8 b.g. Smadoun (FR) – Kinevees (FR) (Hard Leaf (FR)) [2017/18 c149, h–: c16.8g⁴ c20.4s^F c16.4g³ c20.8s⁶ c16.3v⁴ c15.8s² c20.5g⁴ c16.5g* Apr 21] sturdy gelding: winning hurdler: smart handicap chaser: second run in as many days, won listed event at Ayr (by ½ length from Dolos) in April: stays 21f: acts on soft going: wears cheekpieces: strong-travelling sort. *Nicky Henderson*   c148 h–

THE JAM MAN (IRE) 5 br.g. Papal Bull – Kathy Jet (USA) (Singspiel (IRE)) [2017/18 h19.5s h16v h18.8d h16s h16.3v h16v^pu h24.3v⁶ h25.3s* h21.4v* h19.9v* h23.9s³ Apr 25] seventh foal: half-brother to 3 winners on Flat, including 5f-1m winner He's Got Rhythm (by Invincible Spirit): dam Italian 10.5f winner: unplaced in points: fair handicap hurdler: won at Catterick, Ayr and Sedgefield (left R. A. Curran after), all in March: stays 25f: acts on heavy going: travels strongly held up. *Ronan M. P. McNally, Ireland*   h107

THE JAZZ SINGER 7 ch.g. Tobougg (IRE) – Ridgeway Jazz (Kalanisi (IRE)) [2017/18 h108: c20m* c20m⁴ c20.1m⁴ h22g Sep 1] fair hurdler: immediately better over fences: won novice at Down Royal in May on chasing debut: stays 23f: acts on good to firm and heavy going: tried in tongue tie: usually races towards rear. *Colin A. McBratney, Ireland*   c127 h–

THE JUGOPOLIST (IRE) 11 b.g. Oscar (IRE) – Chance My Native (IRE) (Be My Native (USA)) [2017/18 c88§, h–: c16.5g⁶ c20.3d^pu c25.6s^pu c23.6d⁶ Apr 24] lengthy, angular gelding: winning hurdler: poor handicap chaser: stays 3¼m: acts on heavy going: wears headgear: temperamental. *John Cornwall*   c56 § h–

THE JUNIOR MAN (IRE) 7 b.g. Darsi (FR) – Pear Tart (IRE) (Rock Hopper) [2017/18 h–, b–: h20.1v^pu h24.1s^pu Dec 27] third on completed start in Irish points: little show in bumper/over hurdles: tried in cheekpieces. *John Norton*   h–

THE KID 7 b.g. High Chaparral (IRE) – Shine Like A Star (Fantastic Light (USA)) [2017/18 h85: h16d* h16d³ h15.8m³ h19m h17s⁶ Apr 8] sturdy gelding: modest handicap hurdler: won at Worcester in September: left Alexandra Dunn after fourth start: unproven beyond 2m: acts on soft going: wears headgear: has worn tongue tie, including last 5 starts. *Kevin Bishop*   h87

THE KING OF MAY (FR) 4 b.g. High Rock (IRE) – Waltzing (IRE) (Cadeaux Genereux) [2017/18 h16.4s⁶ h15.9g* h15.9g* h15.6s³ h16.4s h16.7s² Apr 11] good-topped gelding: once-raced on Flat: fairly useful hurdler: won juveniles at Saint-Malo in June and August, then left A. Lefeuvre: placed twice after, including when third in listed juvenile at Musselburgh (6¾ lengths behind We Have A Dream) in February: raced around 2m: acts on soft going. *Brian Ellison*   h121

THE KING'S STEED 5 b.g. Equiano (FR) – King's Siren (IRE) (King's Best (USA)) [2017/18 h16.2g⁴ Aug 1] fair on Flat, stays 8.5f: tailed off in novice on hurdling debut. *Micky Hammond*   h–

THE KINGS WRIT (IRE) 7 b.g. Brian Boru – Letterwoman (IRE) (Fourstars Allstar (USA)) [2017/18 h100: c20.3v^F c25.2s² c23s² c24.2v* Apr 8] maiden hurdler: fair form over fences: won handicap at Exeter in April: stays 25f: acts on heavy going: tried in tongue tie. *Kayley Woollacott*   c113 h–

THE KVILLEKEN 10 b.g. Fair Mix (IRE) – Wannaplantatree (Niniski (USA)) [2017/18 c81§, h96§: c16.8s h16.8g⁶ h24g^pu h16.8g⁵ h17.7m³ h16.3m h20g³ h16.3s³ h16.8d h23.9m Nov 1] tall gelding: poor handicap hurdler: maiden chaser: stays 2¾m: acts on good to firm and good to soft going: wears headgear: usually in tongue tie: ungenuine. *Martin Keighley*   c– § h66 §

THE LADY RULES 4 ch.f. Native Ruler – Lady Author (Authorized (IRE)) [2017/18 h16.7g⁵ h16.2v⁴ h16.7d³ h16.4s³ h15.7d³ h20.7s^pu h21s⁴ h16.8g⁵ Apr 19] modest form on Flat: modest maiden hurdler: left Mark Walford after fourth start: stays 21f: acts on heavy going. *Sarah Humphrey*   h91

THE LAMPO GENIE 6 b.g. Champs Elysees – Samar Qand (Selkirk (USA)) [2017/18 h99: h22g Jul 4] small gelding: modest maiden hurdler: will stay beyond 23f: acts on good to soft going: has worn headgear. *Johnny Farrelly*   h–

THE LAND AGENT (IRE) 7 b.g. Touch of Land (FR) – La Carlota (Starborough) [2017/18 b16.8m² b16.8m⁵ c20s⁴ h17.7m h16g⁶ c19.4g^pu c23g^pu c21.6g^pu Oct 7] maiden pointer: modest form on debut in bumpers (for Henry Tett): no form in varied company after: has worn cheekpieces/tongue tie. *Dai Williams*   c– h– b80

803

THE

THE LAST BAR 8 b.m. Kayf Tara – Ardenbar (Ardross) [2017/18 h–: h19g^5 h23.4s^4 h21.2s h26.4d Apr 22] angular mare: modest maiden hurdler: stays 23f: acts on soft going. *Dan Skelton* — **h97**

THE LAST BRIDGE 11 b.g. Milan – Celtic Bridge (Celtic Cone) [2017/18 c82§, h–§: c24g* c24.1s^2 c24g c23.9s* c29.2v^3 c27.5d^{pu} Apr 22] winning hurdler: modest handicap chaser: won at Warwick (conditionals) in May, and at Market Rasen in January and February: stays 29f: acts on heavy going: wears headgear/tongue tie: front runner/races prominently: lazy and unreliable. *Susan Johnson* — **c97 §**, **h– §**

THE LAST BUT ONE (IRE) 6 b.g. Kutub (IRE) – Last Hope (IRE) (Jurado (USA)) [2017/18 h99, b89: h21.4s^{pu} h25.5g^2 c19.9s* c21.6d* c20v^F c15.7v* c20.2d^F Apr 22] rangy gelding: lightly-raced maiden hurdler: vastly better form over fences: won handicaps at Musselburgh (novice) and Fontwell in February, and at Wincanton (another novice) in April: in front when falling last final outing: stays 3m: acts on heavy going: tried in tongue tie: front runner/races prominently: will go on improving. *Paul Nicholls* — **c132 p**, **h96**

THE LAST DAY (IRE) 6 b.g. Oscar (IRE) – The Last Bank (IRE) (Phardante (FR)) [2017/18 b92: h16s* h17v^3 h19.3d^4 h16v* Mar 21] bumper winner: fairly useful form over hurdles: won maiden in November and novice in March, both at Chepstow: likely to be suited by further than 19f: usually travels strongly close up. *Evan Williams* — **h121**

THE LAST LEG (IRE) 9 b.g. Old Vic – Raphuca (IRE) (Be My Native (USA)) [2017/18 h–: h20.2g^{pu} h20.9d Oct 8] maiden hurdler, lightly raced and little form since 2015/16: should stay 3m: normally in headgear: in tongue tie last 2 starts. *Alison Hamilton* — **h–**

THE LAST LETTY 6 ch.m. Desideratum – Let's Hang On (IRE) (Petorius) [2017/18 b16.2g b16.7g Jun 23] half-sister to a winning pointer by Keen and a winner on Flat in Italy by Totem: dam lightly-raced half-sister to fairly useful staying hurdler Aahsaylad: failed to complete all 4 starts in points: no form in bumpers. *John Quinn* — **b–**

THE LAST OF THEM 6 b.g. Kayf Tara – Marello (Supreme Leader) [2017/18 b16.3d h19.5v^{pu} h16.6s Jan 9] no show in bumper/novice hurdles. *Tom Lacey* — **h–**, **b–**

THE LAST SAMURI (IRE) 10 ch.g. Flemensfirth (USA) – Howaboutthis (IRE) (Oscar (IRE)) [2017/18 c161, h–: h21d^2 c25.9v^2 c25.3v^4 c30.2s^3 c34.3s^{pu} Apr 14] sturdy gelding: winning hurdler: very smart handicap chaser: good effort when 9 lengths second of 15 to Blaklion in Becher Chase at Aintree in December: in tongue strap, very edgy in paddock before pulled up in Grand National (runner-up in race in 2016) final outing: thorough stayer: acts on good to firm and heavy going: has worn hood: has joined Harry Fry. *Kim Bailey* — **c156**, **h154**

THE LAWLEY 7 b.m. Alflora (IRE) – La Bella Villa (Relkino) [2017/18 b15.7s h21d^{pu} Apr 26] sparely-made mare: sister to bumper winner/fair chaser Amroth Bay (23f-3¾m winner): dam (b84) bumper winner: no promise in mares bumper/maiden hurdle. *Michael Appleby* — **h–**, **b–**

THELIGNY (FR) 7 gr.g. Martaline – Romilly (FR) (Subotica (FR)) [2017/18 h128: h20d h20.5v^2 h19.9v^{pu} Mar 17] angular gelding: useful handicap hurdler, lightly raced: second at Newbury (½ length behind Brave Eagle) in December, best effort in 2017/18: stays 21f: acts on good to firm and heavy going: front runner/races prominently. *Tim Vaughan* — **h131**

THE LINKSMAN (IRE) 6 b.g. Westerner – Lost Link (IRE) (Shernazar) [2017/18 h97: h16.2v^4 h16s h16.2s h16.6d^{ro} h16.7v^2 h16v* h16.7v* Feb 9] workmanlike gelding: bumper winner: fairly useful hurdler: much improved when winning maiden at Fakenham in January and novice at Bangor in February: raced around 2m: acts on heavy going: tried in hood. *Sam England* — **h123**

THE LION DANCER (IRE) 6 b.g. Let The Lion Roar – Shesadoll (IRE) (Naheez (USA)) [2017/18 c23.6d^5 c24.2s^{pu} h23.9s^6 h24.6s^6 c19.8s^{ro} h25d^3 c25.7v* c25.7v* c23.8v* Apr 15] €10,500 4-y-o, £30,000 5-y-o: first foal: dam ungenuine 2¾m hurdle winner/winning pointer: Irish point winner: poor form over hurdles: fairly useful form over fences: much improved in spring, winning handicaps at Plumpton in March and April (novice) and Ffos Las later in April: stays 3¼m: acts on heavy going: wears headgear: seems best ridden forcefully: has shown temperament. *Charlie Mann* — **c116**, **h78**

THE LION MAN (IRE) 8 b.g. Let The Lion Roar – Just Smart (IRE) (Anshan) [2017/18 c–, h74: h23.3d h18.7m^5 h20g^4 h21.2g^F h24s Dec 21] poor maiden hurdler: failed to complete both starts in handicap chases: stays 3m: acts on soft and good to firm going: wears headgear. *Robin Dickin* — **c–**, **h65**

THE LIZARD KING (IRE) 9 b.g. Indian River (FR) – Norwich Breeze (IRE) (Norwich) [2017/18 c23s c23v^{pu} Apr 12] dual point winner: seemingly modest form on first of 2 outings in hunter chases: in cheekpieces last 2 starts. *Nicky Martin* — **c92 ?**, **h–**

THE

THELOBSTERCATCHER 14 gr.g. Silver Patriarch (IRE) – Everything's Rosy (Ardross) [2017/18 c101§, h–: h26.5g^{pu} Jun 27] workmanlike gelding: winning hurdler: fairly useful chaser at best: stays 29f: acts on good to firm and heavy going: wears headgear: has worn tongue tie, including last 5 starts: unreliable. *Matt Sheppard*   c– §
h– §

THELUNARSCHOONER (IRE) 5 b.m. Milan – Garden City (IRE) (Shernazar) [2017/18 b16d b16.8m* h16.7g^6 h15.7g^2 Oct 11] sister to smart hurdler/useful chaser Raya Star (2m winner, stayed 2½m) and fair 2¼m hurdle winner Jojabean: dam unraced half-sister to useful hurdler/smart chaser (stayed 3m) Risk Accessor: fair form in bumpers: left David Harry Kelly, won mares event at Newton Abbot in August: modest form both outings in mares events over hurdles. *Warren Greatrex*   h95
b94

THE MAD WELL (IRE) 9 b.g. Milan – Silverfortprincess (IRE) (Mull of Kintyre (USA)) [2017/18 h16.2s h21.4v^{pu} Jan 18] fair hurdler: little show both outings in 2017/18: stays 21f: acts on heavy going: regularly in cheekpieces/tongue tie: races in rear. *Kevin Bishop*   h–

THE MAJOR 5 b.g. Major Cadeaux – Ballerina Suprema (IRE) (Sadler's Wells (USA)) [2017/18 h15.8d^{ro} h15.9d h16.8v^5 h16.5s h19s^4 h18.5s^6 Apr 23] fairly useful hurdler, stays 1¼m: poor form over hurdles: may prove best around 2m: acts on soft going: in hood last 2 starts: free-going sort, usually held up. *Kayley Woollacott*   h79

THEMANFROM MINELLA (IRE) 9 b.g. Shantou (USA) – Bobomy (IRE) (Bob Back (USA)) [2017/18 c119§, h–: c29.1m^{pu} c23.9g^{pu} c24.2v^2 c24v* c26.7v* c32.6s^{pu} c34v^{pu} c23.8v^{pu} Apr 15] rangy gelding: winning hurdler: fairly useful handicap chaser: won at Warwick in December and Wincanton in January: pulled up 5 of 6 other outings: stays 27f: acts on heavy going: wears headgear/tongue tie: unreliable. *Ben Case*   c123 §
h–

THE MANUSCRIPT (IRE) 5 b.g. Mahler – Limavady (IRE) (Executive Perk) [2017/18 h15.8s h16.3d h16.3d Dec 1] good-topped gelding: well held over hurdles. *Jonjo O'Neill*   h–

THE MIGHTY ASH (GER) 8 b.g. Arcadio (GER) – She's Got To Go (IRE) (Glacial Storm (USA)) [2017/18 h104, b–: h19.3g h17.7v^5 h21s^3 h18.5v^2 Apr 17] maiden Irish pointer: fair maiden hurdler: stays 21f: acts on heavy going: in headgear last 2 starts: usually makes running/races close up. *Fiona Shaw*   h104

THE MIGHTY DON (IRE) 6 ch.g. Shantou (USA) – Flying Answer (IRE) (Anshan) [2017/18 h121, b95: h21.1g h21.1s h21.6d^2 h25s^2 h21g^2 h24s h24.7s^5 Apr 14] useful-looking gelding: bumper winner: useful handicap hurdler: reliable in 2017/18 (runner-up 3 times): stays 25f: acts on soft going: tried in cheekpieces. *Nick Gifford*   h132

THE MISSUS 7 b.m. Presenting – Violet Express (FR) (Cadoudal (FR)) [2017/18 h104: h16.5s^{pu} h16.3d Apr 22] leggy, angular mare: fair hurdler at best: off 23 months, folded tamely both starts in 2017/18: formerly hooded: tried in tongue tie. *Warren Greatrex*   h–

THE MISTRESS (IRE) 7 b.m. Kalanisi (IRE) – Sonnerschien (IRE) (Be My Native (USA)) [2017/18 b80: b16s^3 h19.7s h15.8s^6 h15.8s h19v^{pu} Feb 4] placed twice in bumpers: poor form over hurdles: bred to stay at least 2½m: wears tongue tie. *Dan Skelton*   h79
b77

THE MODEL COUNTY (IRE) 8 b.m. Robin des Champs (FR) – Ware It Vic (IRE) (Old Vic) [2017/18 h86: h23.3v^{pu} h26v^{pu} h26.6v* h25v^{pu} h26v^{pu} h23.1v^5 Apr 8] sturdy mare: winning pointer: modest handicap hurdler: form in 2017/18 only when winning mares event at Southwell in February: stays 3¼m: acts on heavy going: tried in cheekpieces: front runner/races prominently. *Alan Phillips*   h86

THE MUMPER (IRE) 11 br.g. Craigsteel – Na Moilltear (IRE) (Miner's Lamp) [2017/18 c114, h–: c20g^6 May 1] winning hurdler: fair chaser at best: stays 3m: acts on heavy going: in headgear last 3 starts: tried in tongue tie. *Neil King*   c–
h–

THE MYTHOLOGIST (IRE) 10 ch.g. Motivator – Dilemma (Generous (IRE)) [2017/18 c94, h–: c20.9g^4 c25.8g^5 Jun 27] lengthy gelding: multiple point winner: maiden hurdler: modest handicap chaser: stays 3¼m: acts on firm and soft going: usually races towards rear: often let down by jumping. *Tim Vaughan*   c86 x
h–

THE NEW ONE (IRE) 10 b.g. King's Theatre (IRE) – Thuringe (FR) (Turgeon (USA)) [2017/18 h158x: h15.8s* h16.4s^4 h16.8s^2 h16d^2 h15.7v* h24s h20s^{pu} Apr 12] sturdy gelding: very smart hurdler: won Welsh Champion Hurdle (Limited Handicap) at Ffos Las in October and Champion Hurdle Trial at Haydock (for fourth successive season, by ½ length from Ch'tibello) in January for fourth time: in frame 3 other times in 2017/18,   h157

*Unibet Champion Hurdle Trial, Haydock—
a fourth win in the race for The New One (left) as he rallies to beat Ch'tibello*

including second (also for fourth occasion) in Christmas Hurdle at Kempton (2¼ lengths behind easy winner Buveur d'Air): stays 21f: acts on heavy going: front runner/races prominently: often makes mistakes. *Nigel Twiston-Davies*

THE NEW PHARAOH (IRE) 7 b.g. Montjeu (IRE) – Out West (USA) (Gone West (USA)) [2017/18 h19.9v³ h15.5v* h16.8v⁵ h16s Apr 28] compact gelding: brother to fair/ungenuine hurdler/winning pointer Macarthur (2½m winner): fairly useful on Flat, stays 2m: similar form over hurdles: won novice at Leicester in January: stays 2½m: acts on heavy going: in headgear last 3 starts. *Laura Morgan* h116

THE NIPPER (IRE) 7 b.m. Scorpion (IRE) – Sharp Single (IRE) (Supreme Leader) [2017/18 h127, b–§: c15.2s² c17.4s⁴ c17.5v* c20.2v* h16.6s⁵ c20.3v³ c22.2vᵖᵘ c16.3g⁴ Apr 19] lengthy mare: bumper winner: fairly useful hurdler: similar form over fences: won mares novice at Exeter in December and mares handicap at Wincanton (match) in January: stays 2½m: acts on heavy going: has worn tongue tie: not straightforward (ran out once). *Warren Greatrex* c127 h–

THE OGLE GOGLE MAN (IRE) 6 b.g. Yeats (IRE) – Miss Otis Regrets (IRE) (Bob Back (USA)) [2017/18 h21.4g³ h21gᶠ h24.4d⁴ h20.8s³ c23.6s³ c21.4v³ c20.5s⁶ Apr 9] £36,000 5-y-o: rangy gelding: third foal: half-brother to fairly useful hurdler/chaser Marquis of Carabas (19f winner, by Hurricane Run): dam (b81), bumper winner on only start, half-sister to fairly useful hurdler/chaser (stayed 3m) Aneyeforaneye: Irish point winner: fair form over hurdles: similar form when third in novice handicap at Huntingdon on chasing debut: went wrong way subsequently: stays 3m: acts on soft going: in headgear last 2 starts: temperament under suspicion. *Charlie Mann* c102 h102

THEO (IRE) 8 b.g. Westerner – Jemima Jay (IRE) (Supreme Leader) [2017/18 h102: h20g h16g* h19.9m* h18.5d* c19.4g* c16.3g* c20.1dᵘʳ c16.4s³ Jan 27] sturdy gelding: fairly useful handicap hurdler: left Shane Donohoe, vastly improved when winning at Worcester (conditional) in June and Uttoxeter and Newton Abbot in July: useful form over fences: won handicaps at Stratford (novice) in August and Newton Abbot in September: best up to 2½m: acts on good to firm and heavy going: wears headgear: usually travels strongly held up. *Dr Richard Newland* c134 h115

THE ORANGE ROGUE (IRE) 11 br.g. Alderbrook – Classic Enough (Classic Cliche (IRE)) [2017/18 c113, h–: c21.5v³ c20.1vᵖᵘ c24.2vᵖᵘ c21.5vᶠ c23.4vᵖᵘ Apr 14] maiden hurdler: fair handicap chaser: failed to complete in 2017/18 after reappearance: stays 3m: acts on heavy going: has worn headgear: wears tongue tie: signs of temperament. *N. W. Alexander* c99 h–

THE ORGANIST (IRE) 7 b.m. Alkaadhem – Go On Eileen (IRE) (Bob Back (USA)) [2017/18 c125, h132: h21.4s h24.2d* h25s⁵ h21.1s⁵ h20.3g Apr 19] compact mare: useful handicap hurdler: won at Newbury in December: also good fifth in Coral Cup at Cheltenham (5½ lengths behind Bleu Berry) in March: runner-up on chasing debut, but let down by jumping since: stays 3m: acts on heavy going: patiently ridden. *Oliver Sherwood* c– h137

THEO'S CHARM (IRE) 8 b.g. Presenting – Kates Charm (IRE) (Glacial Storm (USA)) [2017/18 c133, h133: c19.7d³ h22.8v³ c18.8dᵇᵈ c20s h21.7v² h22.8v² h24s c19.4d⁴ Apr 22] medium-sized gelding: useful handicap hurdler: runner-up at Fontwell and Haydock (neck c129 h134 behind Tommy Rapper in valuable event) in 2017/18: fairly useful maiden chaser: stays 23f: acts on heavy going: has worn headgear. *Nick Gifford*

THE OTMOOR POET 5 b.g. Yeats (IRE) – Kristalette (IRE) (Leporello (IRE)) [2017/18 h94: h18.7g⁴ h16.7g³ Sep 1] lengthy, rather sparely-made gelding: fairly useful maiden on Flat (stays 1¾m): modest maiden hurdler: should stay further than 2m: acts on heavy going: in cheekpieces last 2 starts. *Alex Hales* **h84**

THE PADDY PIE (IRE) 5 b.g. Beneficial – Salsita (FR) (Fijar Tango (FR)) [2017/18 b16g b16d h19.9v^pu Apr 13] maiden pointer: no form in bumpers (for John Paul Brennan): pulled up in novice on hurdling debut. *Sue Smith* **h–**
b–

THEPARTYSOVER 13 gr.g. Cloudings (IRE) – Just A Tipple (IRE) (Roselier (FR)) [2017/18 c64, h84: c25.5g³ c25.5m⁵ Jun 15] winning hurdler: poor maiden chaser: stays 25f: acts on heavy going: has worn headgear: wears tongue tie: usually races towards rear: unreliable. *Paul Henderson* **c72 §**
h–

THEPENSIONFUND (IRE) 6 b.g. Big Bad Bob (IRE) – Whizz (Salse (USA)) [2017/18 b16v³ Jan 2] €15,000 3-y-o: closely related to fair hurdler/chaser Inthejungle (2¼m-2½m winner, by Bob Back) and half-brother to bumper winner/fairly useful hurdler Beluckyagain (2m winner, by Old Vic), stayed 3m: dam, lightly raced on Flat, half-sister to smart hurdler/top-class chaser (stayed 25f) Tiutchev: 6/1, third in bumper at Ayr (8 lengths behind Idee de Garde): should improve. *Lucinda Russell* **b91 p**

THE PIERRE LARK (IRE) 8 b.g. Pierre – Kyle Lark (Miner's Lamp) [2017/18 h94: c16g² May 17] winning Irish pointer: modest maiden hurdler: second in novice handicap at Perth (8 lengths behind Welcome Ben) on chasing debut: stays 2½m: acts on heavy going: in tongue tie last 4 starts. *Donald McCain* **c94**
h–

THE PINE MARTIN (IRE) 8 b.g. Kalanisi (IRE) – Regal Holly (Gildoran) [2017/18 h16.2g* h16.2g² Jun 3] modest handicap hurdler: won amateur novice event at Hexham in May: unproven beyond 2m: acts on heavy going: has worn headgear. *Micky Hammond* **h88**

THE POODLE FAKER 7 b.g. Pastoral Pursuits – Flirtatious (Generous (IRE)) [2017/18 h97: h21m⁴ h25m^pu May 23] strong gelding: modest maiden hurdler: stays 21f: acts on good to firm going, probably on good to soft: tried in blinkers: temperament under suspicion. *Hughie Morrison* **h86**

THE POOLER (IRE) 6 b.g. Kalanisi (IRE) – Bakiya (USA) (Trempolino (USA)) [2017/18 b–: h21.4g h21d^F h16.5g⁶ Nov 30] placed in point: no form under Rules: in visor last 2 starts. *Robert Walford* **h–**

THEPREMIERBROKER (IRE) 7 b.g. Sandmason – Neelia Nayr (IRE) (Boyne Valley) [2017/18 h–: h17m⁶ h23.3g³ h20.3g Sep 6] poor maiden hurdler on balance: left Jennie Candlish after second start: won point in March: tried in tongue tie. *Ian O'Connor, Ireland* **h63**

THE PREMIER CELTIC 5 b.g. Black Sam Bellamy (IRE) – Maria Antonia (IRE) (King's Best (USA)) [2017/18 b17.7g h16d h16.3v⁵ h15.9d* h16s⁶ h20.5s^F Apr 15] £7,000 3-y-o: workmanlike gelding: first foal: dam (h113), 17f hurdle winner, also 1¼m-1½m winner on Flat, half-sister to fairly useful 2m hurdler Dal Cais: seventh in bumper: fair form over hurdles: won maiden at Plumpton in February: should stay at least 2½m: acts on heavy going. *Pat Phelan* **h111**
b81

THE RAVEN MASTER (IRE) 4 b.g. Raven's Pass (USA) – Rainbow Desert (USA) (Dynaformer (USA)) [2017/18 h16.3m³ h16.8g* h16g⁴ h15.9m² Sep 24] fair maiden on Flat, stays 1½m: fair juvenile hurdler: won at Newton Abbot in August: in tongue tie last 3 starts: possibly best forcing pace. *Dan Skelton* **h108**

THE RAVEN'S RETURN 5 b.g. Scorpion (IRE) – Mimis Bonnet (FR) (Bonnet Rouge (FR)) [2017/18 b15.7d⁴ b15.7d Dec 22] €7,000 3-y-o: unfurnished gelding: fourth foal: half-brother to fairly useful hurdler/chaser Moss On The Mill (2¾m-3¼m winner, by Overbury): dam unraced: much better effort in bumpers at Ascot (fair form) when never-nearer fourth on debut: stiff task in listed event next time. *Seamus Mullins* **b91**

THE REAL SCORPION (IRE) 7 b.g. Scorpion (IRE) – Italian Belle (IRE) (Milan) [2017/18 b16g⁶ May 13] runner-up on completed start in points: 20/1, well-held sixth in bumper at Warwick. *Anna Newton-Smith* **b–**

THE REAL SNOOPY (IRE) 6 b.g. Presenting – Senora Snoopy (IRE) (Un Desperado (FR)) [2017/18 h23g² h24d³ h20g⁶ Oct 25] £25,000 5-y-o: second foal: brother to fairly useful hurdler/chaser Ten Sixty (2½m-2¾m winner): dam (h100), bumper winner/maiden hurdler (stayed 21f), half-sister to useful hurdler/high-class chaser (stayed 3¼m) Snoopy **h105**

THE

Loopy and useful hurdler/fairly useful chaser (stayed 3m) Sam Adams (by Presenting): won Irish maiden point at third attempt: fair form when second in novice at Worcester on hurdling debut: disappointing after. *Charlie Longsdon*

THE RESDEV WAY 5 b.g. Multiplex – Lady Duxyana (Most Welcome) [2017/18 h20g h15.8g⁶ h19.3d h19.3d ab16.3g² Mar 3] sturdy gelding: fairly useful on Flat, stays 2m: no form over hurdles, making mistakes. *Philip Kirby* h–

THERE'S NO PANIC (IRE) 13 ch.g. Presenting – Out Ranking (FR) (Le Glorieux) [2017/18 c32.5d⁶ May 5] strong gelding: winning hurdler: useful chaser at best: well held in hunter in May: reverted to pointing subsequently, winning 3 times: stays 29f: acts on good to firm and heavy going: in cheekpieces last 4 starts: tried in tongue tie. *M. Biddick* c103 h–

THEREYARSEE 9 b.g. Fair Mix (IRE) – Sea Laughter (IRE) (Presenting) [2017/18 c–: c24.2vᵖᵘ Apr 17] prolific winner in points: tongue tied, failed to complete in hunter chases. *Mrs S. Alner* c–

THE ROAD AHEAD 11 b.m. Grape Tree Road – Althrey Flame (IRE) (Torus) [2017/18 h114: h24.7g May 19] fairly useful hurdler at best: tailed off only outing in 2017/18: stays 3m: acts on good to soft going: has worn headgear. *Gary Hanmer* h–

THE ROAD HOME (IRE) 6 b.g. Oscar (IRE) – In Fact (IRE) (Classic Cliche (IRE)) [2017/18 b16.4g⁵ h16s h15.6s* h19.4d²ᵈ h19.4d³ h20.5g Apr 21] €13,500 3-y-o: lengthy gelding: fifth foal: dam unraced out of useful French hurdler/chaser (stayed 2¼m) Soupinette: off mark in Irish points at fourth attempt: fair form over hurdles: won maiden at Musselburgh in January: stays 19f: acts on soft going: wears tongue tie: usually leads. *Lucinda Russell* h110 b90

THE RODEO CLOWN (IRE) 13 b.g. Luso – Reuben Jane (IRE) (Toulon) [2017/18 c–, h–: c26.3dᵖᵘ c24.5g⁶ May 15] multiple winning pointer: no form in novice hurdles/hunter chases: tried in blinkers. *G. E. Burton* c– h–

THE ROESTONE (IRE) 4 ch.g. Vinnie Roe (IRE) – Pidgeon Bay (IRE) (Perugino (USA)) [2017/18 b16.8d⁵ Apr 24] won point on debut: well beaten in maiden bumper. *R. B. Chanin* b54

THE ROMFORD PELE (IRE) 11 b.g. Accordion – Back And Fore (IRE) (Bob Back (USA)) [2017/18 c–, h144: c25d² c22.7g* Dec 3] rather leggy gelding: useful hurdler: smart handicap chaser: left Rebecca Curtis, won veterans events at Aintree in October and Leicester (by 3½ lengths from Fox Appeal) in December: stays 3¼m: acts on good to firm and heavy going: wore headgear for former yard. *Tom George* c148 h–

THE ROOF HUB 5 b.g. Dick Turpin (IRE) – Glen Molly (IRE) (Danetime (IRE)) [2017/18 b15.7d⁶ Dec 19] well held in bumper/on Flat. *Micky Hammond* b–

THE RUSSIAN DOYEN (IRE) 5 b.g. Doyen (IRE) – Namloc (IRE) (Phardante (FR)) [2017/18 b16d² b15.3s³ h16.8v* h16s⁵ h16.5s* h19.8v⁶ Mar 10] €58,000 3-y-o: lengthy, useful-looking gelding: half-brother to fair hurdler New Horizons (21f-3m winner, by Presenting) and 3 winning pointers: dam unraced half-sister to Cheltenham Gold Cup winner Denman: fairly useful form in bumpers: similar form over hurdles: won novices at Exeter in December and Taunton in February: should stay 2½m: front runner/races prominently: remains open to improvement. *Colin Tizzard* h123 p b96

THE SALMON MAN 6 b.g. Showcasing – Donna Vita (Vettori (IRE)) [2017/18 h15.8g h15.9d h19.5 Nov 1] angular gelding: fair but unginuine maiden on Flat (stays 1½m): never dangerous over hurdles. *Brendan Powell* h–

THE SHEPHERD KING (IRE) 14 b.g. Marignan (USA) – Boolavogue (IRE) (Torus) [2017/18 c17m⁵ c17g c17.4d c15.6g⁴ c16.5g³ c16.5s² c16v⁵ Nov 12] winning hurdler: modest handicap chaser: best around 2m: acts on heavy going: has worn headgear, including last 5 starts: wears tongue tie: usually races close up: temperamental. *R. K. Watson, Ireland* c99 § h–

THE SOCIETY MAN (IRE) 11 ch.g. Moscow Society (USA) – Redruth (IRE) (Sri Pekan (USA)) [2017/18 c95§, h–: c22.6g c23.6gᵖᵘ c19.2g⁵ c15.7g⁴ c17.3s⁴ c21.4g⁴ c21.2d⁵ c16.4g⁶ c16.1g⁴ c24.2d³ c21.2g⁶ c15.7dᵘʳ c23.6g⁵ c21.7g⁵ c21.4d³ c21.4sᵖᵘ c23.9sᵘʳ ab16g² c21.2s⁴ c15.7g Apr 20] workmanlike gelding: winning hurdler: poor maiden chaser: stays 25f: acts on good to firm and heavy going: temperamental. *Michael Chapman* c83 § h–

THE SOME DANCE KID (IRE) 5 b.g. Shantou (USA) – River Rouge (IRE) (Croco Rouge (IRE)) [2017/18 b15.7s* b17v² Apr 17] €17,500 3-y-o, £30,000 4-y-o: fourth foal: brother to fairly useful hurdler/chaser Oliver's Hill (2m-2½m winner): dam unraced: runner-up on second of 2 outings in Irish points: fairly useful form in bumpers: won conditionals/amateur maiden event at Catterick in February: shaped like a stayer next time: will be suited by at least 2½m. *Donald McCain* b97

Brown Advisory & Merriebelle Stable Plate Handicap Chase, Cheltenham—The Storyteller (No.6) completes a red letter day for jockey Davy Russell as he overhauls the leader Splash of Ginge; King's Odyssey (noseband) and Ballyalton (hooped sleeves) complete the frame

THE STATESMAN 4 b.g. Zoffany (IRE) – Chelsey Jayne (IRE) (Galileo (IRE)) [2017/18 h15.8m* Oct 11] useful on Flat, stays 1¼m: 4/7, created good impression when winning juvenile maiden at Ludlow (by 16 lengths from Phoenix Dawn with plenty in hand) on hurdling debut: looked sure to progress but not seen out again. *Ian Williams* **h127 p**

THE STEWARD (USA) 7 b.g. Street Cry (IRE) – Candlelight (USA) (Kingmambo (USA)) [2017/18 h15.7d² Nov 24] useful on Flat, stays 16.5f: 16/1, second in novice at Catterick (3½ lengths behind Rockalzaro) on hurdling debut: likely to stay further than 2m. *James Moffatt* **h103**

THE STINGING BEE 7 b.g. Striking Ambition – Queen of The Bees (IRE) (Bob Back (USA)) [2017/18 b16.3d May 21] tailed off in bumper. *Geoffrey Deacon* **b–**

THE STORYTELLER (IRE) 7 ch.g. Shantou (USA) – Bally Bolshoi (IRE) (Bob Back (USA)) [2017/18 h144p, b99: h20s² c21.2s* c20v³ c21s c20.8s* c20v⁵ c24.5s* Apr 24] sturdy gelding: useful hurdler: smart form over fences: won maiden at Fairyhouse (by 4¾ lengths from Sutton Manor) in December, Brown Advisory & Merriebelle Stable Plate at Cheltenham (by 1¾ lengths from Splash of Ginge) in March and Champion Novices' Chase at Punchestown (held in third when left clear, by 6 lengths from Monbeg Notorious) in April: stays 25f, effective at shorter: acts on heavy going. *Gordon Elliott, Ireland* **c153 h136**

Growise Champion Novices' Chase, Punchestown—16/1-shot The Storyteller takes full advantage of the bizarre last-fence exits of Al Boum Photo (riderless) and Finian's Oscar

THE

THE SWEENEY (IRE) 6 b.g. Oscar (IRE) – Banningham Blaze (Averti (IRE)) [2017/18 b95: h19.9d^6 h19.5v^3 h19.5v h23.8s^4 h19.8v^3 h21.4d* Apr 22] fairly useful form over hurdles: won handicap at Wincanton in April: stays 21f: acts on heavy going. *Emma Lavelle*   **h115**

THE TAILGATER (IRE) 7 b.g. Oscar (IRE) – Zaffaran Express (IRE) (Zaffaran (USA)) [2017/18 h117: h20.3g* c20g^3 c19.2g^4 c19.1d* c20.5d^4 Jan 13] good-topped gelding: fairly useful handicap hurdler: won at Southwell in May: similar form over fences: won handicap at Doncaster in December: stays 21f: acts on soft going: often races towards rear/travels strongly. *Jonjo O'Neill*   **c124 h119**

THE TIN MINER (IRE) 8 br.g. Presenting – Sidalcea (IRE) (Oscar (IRE)) [2017/18 h93: c19.7m^{ur} Sep 24] maiden hurdler: upsides when unseated rider last in novice handicap won by Ramore Will at Plumpton on chasing debut, probably would have won: tried in cheekpieces: open to improvement as a chaser. *David Bridgwater*   **c109 p h–**

THE TOOJUMPA 5 b.m. Midnight Legend – Sunnyland (Sovereign Water (FR)) [2017/18 b15.7s b16.2s^5 b15.8s h19.7v^4 h16s^5 h15.8d^5 Apr 9] third foal: half-sister to poor hurdler East Hill (2½m winner, by Lucarno): dam (h104), 2m hurdle winner, half-sister to fair hurdler/fairly useful chaser (stayed 2½m) Brown Teddy: well held in bumpers: poor form over hurdles: tried in hood. *John Groucott*   **h77 b–**

THE TOURARD MAN (IRE) 12 b.g. Shantou (USA) – Small Iron (General Ironside) [2017/18 c131^4, h138: h22.8m^6 h23.1g* h23.9g h24g^{ur} Apr 18] compact gelding: useful handicap hurdler: won at Market Rasen in July: useful chaser: stays 3¼m: acts on good to firm and heavy going. *Alan King*   **c– h141**

THE TRIGGER (IRE) 9 ch.g. Beneficial – Ardrom (Ardross) [2017/18 h86: h20g c16.8s^5 h20.6g^4 c20.5g* c22.6g* h19.5g^2 h16s h22s h20d h16.3g Oct 21] modest maiden hurdler: fair form over fences: won handicaps at Killarney in July and Stratford in August: stays 23f: best form on good going: tried in cheekpieces/tongue tie. *Ronan M. P. McNally, Ireland*   **c101 h88**

THE TWISLER 6 b.g. Motivator – Panna (Polish Precedent (USA)) [2017/18 h19.9d h15.8g^3 Oct 26] half-brother to fairly useful hurdler Hot Diamond (2m winner, by Desert Prince): fairly useful on Flat, stays 2m: fair form over hurdles: better effort when third in novice at Ludlow: wears cheekpieces. *Neil Mulholland*   **h106**

THE TWO AMIGOS 6 b.g. Midnight Legend – As Was (Epalo (GER)) [2017/18 h106, b–: h25m^6 May 23] prolific point winner, mostly in 2018: fair maiden hurdler: stays 3m: best form on good going: wears tongue tie. *David Pipe*   **h93**

THE UNIT (IRE) 7 b.g. Gold Well – Sovana (FR) (Kadounor (FR)) [2017/18 h138: c16.3g^2 c19.9g^3 c20.5g^2 h16g Apr 21] sturdy gelding: useful hurdler: similar form over fences: placed in novice at Huntingdon (1¾ lengths behind Willoughby Court) in November and Pendil Novices' Chase at Kempton (11 lengths behind Cyrname) in February: stays 2½m: best form on good going. *Alan King*   **c143 h137**

THE VENERABLE BEDE (IRE) 7 b.g. Kalanisi (IRE) – Feedthegoodmare (IRE) (Heron Island (IRE)) [2017/18 h19.3g Nov 24] workmanlike gelding: limited impact in novice/maiden hurdles. *Paul Webber*   **h–**

THE VERY THING (IRE) 4 b.g. Getaway (GER) – Katie Quinn (IRE) (Glacial Storm (USA)) [2017/18 ab16.3g^4 Apr 15] €62,000 3-y-o: eighth foal: dam, winning pointer, sister to useful hurdler/staying chaser Control Man: 8/13, fourth in bumper at Newcastle (1½ lengths behind Summer Lightening): should improve. *Olly Murphy*   **b84 p**

THE VOCALIST 6 b.m. Recharge (IRE) – Ivy Edith (Blakeney) [2017/18 b94: h19.2v^2 h20.7s* h15.7v^2 Feb 1] bumper winner: fairly useful form over hurdles: won mares maiden at Huntingdon in January: front runner/races prominently: remains with potential. *Nicky Henderson*   **h115 p**

THE WALLACE LINE (IRE) 7 b.g. Mastercraftsman (IRE) – Surval (IRE) (Sadler's Wells (USA)) [2017/18 h120: c23g^6 Oct 25] sturdy gelding: fairly useful hurdler: well beaten in novice handicap on chasing debut: thorough stayer: acts on heavy going: tried in cheekpieces. *Tim Vaughan*   **c85 h–**

THE WAY YOU DANCE (IRE) 6 b.g. Thewayyouare (USA) – Beautiful Dancer (IRE) (Danehill Dancer (IRE)) [2017/18 h108: c16.5s^{pu} c16.5g^4 c15.7g h23.4g* Nov 1] fair handicap hurdler: won at Fakenham in November: poor form over fences: stays 23f: acts on good to firm going: wears headgear: temperament under suspicion. *Neil Mulholland*   **c75 h105**

THE WEALERDEALER (IRE) 11 b.g. Vinnie Roe (IRE) – Lantern Liz (IRE) (Montelimar (USA)) [2017/18 c110, h112: c26.3d^2 c27.5d Jun 9] lengthy gelding: multiple point winner: fair hurdler: fairly useful form in chases: second in hunter at Cheltenham in May: stays 3¼m: acts on good to firm and heavy going: has worn headgear. *I. Chanin*   **c122 h–**

THE WELSH PADDIES (IRE) 6 b.g. Court Cave (IRE) – Masiana (IRE) (Daylami (IRE)) [2017/18 h5: h19.9g² h21g* h19s⁵ h20.3g Apr 18] rather unfurnished gelding: bumper winner: fair form over hurdles: won maiden at Warwick in October: left Christian Williams after third start. *Kerry Lee*   **h111**

THE WEST'S AWAKE (IRE) 7 b.g. Yeats (IRE) – Bilboa (FR) (Phantom Breeze) [2017/18 h16g³ c19.5g* c19.5s* c20v³ c20s* c19.5v⁵ c16.7v⁶ c21s Apr 27] closely related to bumper winner/fair hurdler Glorious Twelfth (21f winner, by Old Vic), and half-brother to fairly useful hurdler/useful chaser Three Wise Men (2m-2¼m winner, by Presenting) and fairly useful chaser Doctor Pat (2½m-2¾m winner, by Definite Article): dam (c128/h154), French 2m-2¼m hurdle winner, also 1½m winner on Flat: fairly useful form over hurdles: won maiden at Fairyhouse in 2016/17: useful chaser: won maiden and novice at Limerick in July, and novice at Punchestown (by 3¾ lengths from Woods Well) in November: stays 2½m: acts on soft going: tried in hood. *E. J. O'Grady, Ireland*   **c138 h119**

THE WEXFORDIAN (IRE) 9 b.g. Shantou (USA) – Going My Way (Henbit (USA)) [2017/18 c101§, h101§: c25.8m^pu May 30] well-made gelding: point winner: fair maiden hurdler/chaser, pulled up sole outing in 2017/18: stays 2½m: acts on heavy going: usually wears headgear: temperamental. *Martin Hill*   **c– § h– §**

THE WHITE MOUSE (IRE) 4 br.f. Stowaway – Maxwells Demon (IRE) (King's Theatre (IRE)) [2017/18 b15.7g Apr 20] €50,000 3-y-o: first foal: dam, winning pointer, sister to smart hurdler (stayed 3m) African Gold: 4/1, ninth in conditional/amateur maiden bumper at Southwell. *Lucy Wadham*   **b–**

THE WICKET CHICKEN (IRE) 6 b.m. Milan – Soniadoir (IRE) (Presenting) [2017/18 b83: b16.2g* h17.7d* h17.2g² h20.3g* h19.8s⁶ Dec 9] Irish point winner: fair form in bumpers: won mares event at Hexham in May: fair form over hurdles: won maiden at Fontwell in May and mares novice at Southwell in July: will be suited by further than 2½m: often races towards rear. *Neil Mulholland*   **h112 b88**

THE WINNINGTIPSTER 5 ch.g. Kheleyf (USA) – Freedom Song (Singspiel (IRE)) [2017/18 h21.7g^ur Apr 20] no form in Flat maidens: hampered and unseated first on hurdling debut. *Paul Henderson*   **h–**

THE WISE ONE (IRE) 7 b.g. Tikkanen (USA) – Mary Mac Swiney (IRE) (Flemensfirth (USA)) [2017/18 h97: h23.8m h23.8g² Nov 30] Irish point winner: modest handicap hurdler: stays 3m: acts on heavy going: often races prominently. *James Ewart*   **h99**

THE WORLDS END (IRE) 7 b.g. Stowaway – Bright Sprite (IRE) (Beneficial) [2017/18 h146p: h22.8v h24.4d⁴ h24v⁴ h24s h24.7s⁴ Apr 14] good-topped gelding: fell in Irish point: smart hurdler: stays 25f: acts on soft going. *Tom George*   **h153**

THE YANK 9 b.g. Trade Fair – Silver Gyre (IRE) (Silver Hawk (USA)) [2017/18 c112, h–: c17d⁴ c16.3s² c16g³ c16d⁴ c17.8g³ c17g⁴ c16.5f² c17.4g⁵ Oct 31] compact gelding: maiden hurdler: fair handicap chaser: raced mainly around 2m: acts on firm and good to soft going: wears headgear: has worn tongue tie: usually leads: temperamental. *David Bridgwater*   **c106 § h–**

THEYDON PARK 5 b.g. Royal Applause – Velvet Waters (Unfuwain (USA)) [2017/18 h105, b80: h16.5g⁵ h21g² h17.3g² h24g² h24.2s^ur h21d⁴ h24g⁶ h20v h16s^pu h19.5s⁵ h20.5v⁴ h15.7v^pu Mar 29] bumper winner: fair maiden hurdler: left Joseph Patrick O'Brien after ninth start: stays 3m: acts on soft going: wears headgear. *Michael Roberts*   **h109**

THE YOUNG MASTER 9 b.g. Echo of Light – Fine Frenzy (IRE) (Great Commotion (USA)) [2017/18 c138, h–: c23.8g^ur c25.9v⁶ c24d³ c23.4v^pu c26s⁶ c31.8g^ur c28.8d Apr 28] workmanlike gelding: winning bumper hurdler: useful handicap chaser nowadays: stays 29f: acts on heavy going: usually wears cheekpieces: has worn tongue tie, including in 2017/18: usually races close up: often let down by jumping. *Neil Mulholland*   **c130 x h–**

THIBAULT 5 b.g. Kayf Tara – Seemarye (Romany Rye) [2017/18 b14d³ b15.7v⁴ Feb 25] €53,000 3-y-o, resold £95,000 3-y-o: third foal: dam, little impact in bumpers/over hurdles, half-sister to useful hurdler/chaser (stayed 25f) See You Sometime: fair form in bumpers: much better effort when third at Ludlow in December. *Kim Bailey*   **b90**

THINK AHEAD 7 b.g. Shamardal (USA) – Moonshadow (Diesis) [2017/18 h–p: h17.2s* h15.7s² h16.2s³ Apr 25] fair form over hurdles: won maiden at Cartmel in July: in cheekpieces last 3 starts. *James Moffatt*   **h114**

THINK POSITIVE (IRE) 4 br.g. Jeremy (USA) – Dun Dun (IRE) (Saddlers' Hall (IRE)) [2017/18 b13.7g⁴ b16.5d Apr 24] €30,000 3-y-o: fifth foal: half-brother to high-class hurdler/winning pointer Samcro (2m-21f winner, by Germany) and fairly useful hurdler Cocacobana (2½m-3m winner, by Snurge): dam unraced sister to useful hurdler/very smart chaser (stayed 25f) Master of The Hall and smart hurdler (stayed 21f)   **b85**

THI

Featherbed Lane: fair form in bumpers: better effort when fourth in junior event at Towcester (trained by Peter Hedger): reportedly lame when well held in Goffs Land Rover Bumper at Punchestown. *W. P. Mullins, Ireland*

THIRD ACT (IRE) 9 b.g. King's Theatre (IRE) – Starry Lady (IRE) (Marju (IRE)) [2017/18 c102§, h113§: h20.6g^5 c16.3d^2 c16.3m^3 c21d^4 c19.2d^F c20.2v^{pu} h15.9v c16s^{pu} Feb 24] lengthy, useful-looking gelding: winning hurdler: fair maiden chaser: stays 2¾m: acts on soft and good to firm going: has worn headgear, including in 2017/18: wears tongue tie: temperamental. *Colin Tizzard* — c102 § h– §

THIRD ESTATE (IRE) 6 b.g. Suleiman (IRE) – Fizanni (IRE) (Arzanni) [2017/18 h105p, b88: h20.6g^4 h18.5d^5 h21.2d^3 Apr 24] bumper winner: fair maiden hurdler: has worn hood, including in 2017/18. *Neil King* — h103

THIRD INTENTION (IRE) 11 b.g. Azamour (IRE) – Third Dimension (FR) (Suave Dancer (USA)) [2017/18 c148§, h–: c19.9d c24.2s^2 c24.2s^{pu} Jan 6] tall gelding: has had breathing operation: winning hurdler: smart handicap chaser: second in veterans event at Sandown (½ length behind Houblon des Obeaux) in November: stays 25f: acts on heavy going: has worn headgear, including in 2017/18: wears tongue tie: temperamental. *Colin Tizzard* — c145 § h–

THIRD OF THE THIRD 11 b.g. Presenting – Gavotte du Cochet (FR) (Urbain Minotiere (FR)) [2017/18 c22.7v^3 Feb 15] point winner: maiden hurdler: modest form in hunter chases: stays 25f: acts on soft going: tried in cheekpieces. *Miss S. Whitehead* — c93 h–

THIRD WIND 4 b.g. Shirocco (GER) – Act Three (Beat Hollow) [2017/18 b15.8d^3 b16d Apr 26] well-made gelding: third foal: dam ran once over hurdles/ungenuine maiden on Flat (stayed 1¾m): fair form in bumpers: better effort when third in conditionals/amateur event at Huntingdon. *Hughie Morrison* — b93

THIS IS IT (IRE) 6 b.g. Milan – Riviera Sands (IRE) (Mister Lord (USA)) [2017/18 h114, b85: h23.1v* h24.2d^6 h23.5d h23.6v^2 h23.6s^{pu} h23.6s^2 Mar 22] workmanlike gelding: fairly useful handicap hurdler: won at Exeter in November: stays 3m: acts on heavy going: tried in cheekpieces: front runner/races prominently. *Nick Mitchell* — h119

THIS IS WENDY 5 b.m. Multiplex – This Is Us (IRE) (Kheleyf (USA)) [2017/18 b15.7g Sep 6] first foal: dam, ran twice on Flat, half-sister to fairly useful hurdler (2m/17f winner) Russian George: well beaten in maiden bumper. *Julie Camacho* — b–

THISONETIME (IRE) 7 br.g. Kalanisi (IRE) – Dizzy's Whisper (IRE) (Supreme Leader) [2017/18 h107: h17.7d^2 h19.2g^4 c16s^3 c19.4v^4 c15.7d^{pu} h21v^4 h25d Apr 24] angular gelding: fair maiden hurdler: similar form over fences: left Dan Skelton after fifth start: stays 2¼m: acts on heavy going: has worn headgear, including in 2017/18: often wears tongue tie: often races towards rear. *Andrew Martin* — c111 h107

THIS THYNE JUDE 10 gr.m. Silver Patriarch (IRE) – This Thyne (Good Thyne (USA)) [2017/18 h102: h23.9g h23.9m Jun 4] fair hurdler, beaten by form in 2017/18: will stay beyond 3m: acts on heavy going: usually races towards rear. *Lucy Normile* — h93

THISTIMENEXTYEAR 4 gr.g. New Approach (IRE) – Scarlet Empire (IRE) (Red Ransom (USA)) [2017/18 h16s^F h15.8d^2 h16.7g^2 Apr 22] fairly useful on Flat, stays 11.5f: fair form over hurdles: wears hood: tried in tongue tie: remains open to improvement. *Richard Spencer* — h107 p

THISTLECRACK 10 b.g. Kayf Tara – Ardstown (Ardross) [2017/18 c174, h–: h24.2d^5 c24d^4 Dec 26] sturdy gelding: top-class hurdler/chaser, below best in 2017/18 after injury: stays 25f: acts on heavy going: tracks pace, races enthusiastically. *Colin Tizzard* — c158 + h–

THISTLE DO NICELY (IRE) 4 b.g. Arcadio (GER) – April Thistle (IRE) (Alphabatim (USA)) [2017/18 b13.7g* b16.3v Feb 10] €17,000 3-y-o: sixth foal: half-brother to fairly useful hurdler/smart chaser Croco Bay (2m-19f winner, by Croco Rouge): dam unraced half-sister to fairly useful hurdler/chaser up to 3m Cottage Oak: fair form in bumpers: won junior event at Towcester in November: left Tom Lacey before next start. *Jamie Snowden* — b94

THOMAS BLOSSOM (IRE) 8 b.g. Dylan Thomas (IRE) – Woman Secret (IRE) (Sadler's Wells (USA)) [2017/18 h100: h19.7g^4 c19.1s^6 c19.9s^3 Mar 14] close-coupled gelding: has had breathing operation: modest handicap hurdler: similar form over fences: seems to stay 2½m, at least when conditions aren't testing: acts on soft going: usually wears tongue tie. *Ali Stronge* — c90 h98

THOMAS BROWN 9 b.g. Sir Harry Lewis (USA) – Tentsmuir (Arctic Lord) [2017/18 c138, h–: c23.8g^6 c21d^{ur} c23.8d^{pu} Dec 20] rangy gelding: winning hurdler: useful handicap chaser: stayed 3m: acted on soft going: wore headgear: often raced prominently: dead. *Harry Fry* — c130 h–

THO

THOMAS CAMPBELL 6 b.g. Yeats (IRE) – Hora (Hernando (FR)) [2017/18 h138p, **h149** b108: h23.9g* h25.3s* h24.4d⁵ h24v⁶ h24s h24.7sᵖᵘ Apr 14] good-topped gelding: smart hurdler: won handicap at Cheltenham (by 2¼ lengths from Milrow) in October and listed handicap there (by 2½ lengths from Anteros) following month: stays 25f: acts on soft going: in headgear last 2 starts. *Nicky Henderson*

THOMAS CRAPPER 11 b.g. Tamure (IRE) – Mollycarrs Gambul (General Gambul) **c–** [2017/18 c138, h–: c20sᵖᵘ c20.5s Mar 17] tall gelding: winning hurdler: useful chaser at **h–** best, no form in 2017/18: stays 21f: acts on heavy going: usually in headgear: wears tongue tie. *Robin Dickin*

THOMAS PATRICK (IRE) 6 b.g. Winged Love (IRE) – Huncheon Siss (IRE) **c147 p** (Phardante (FR)) [2017/18 h15.7d h16.8s h16.8v² h23.1v* h22.8v² h22.8v c23.6v* **h123** c30.7s⁴ c26s* c25s* Apr 14]

'Everybody says he's a Grand National horse—well, maybe further down the line he will be, but he won't be next year.' That was the post-race verdict of Garth Broom, part-owner of Native River, when seemingly ruling out the newly-crowned Cheltenham Gold Cup winner from a tilt at the Aintree showpiece in 2019. Whether regular partner Richard Johnson will still be in the saddle when Native River eventually makes his debut over those famous Aintree obstacles is another matter, though, as the rider turned forty-one in July and will presumably hang up his boots before too long. The three-times champion jockey holds the dubious distinction of the most losing rides (twenty) without winning in Grand National history, that lack of success possibly a factor in why he has opted, in the end, to sit out the two most recent renewals. However, on closer inspection, Johnson's Aintree record isn't quite so bad as the drought might imply—he's twice been runner-up (on What's Up Boys in 2002 and Balthazar King in 2014) in the National, and rode Gower-Slave to victory in the 2001 Topham Chase (the final renewal as the John Hughes Trophy before reverting to its original title) and he has been placed on a further five occasions in races over the National fences. Johnson has been instrumental in Native River's rise to the top of the staying chase division and the combination of his forcing riding style and Native River's bold front-running make them look tailor-made for the Grand National. The same comments apply to another strong front-running performer who has been much improved since teaming up with Johnson.

Betway Handicap Chase, Aintree—
another fine front-running display by the novice Thomas Patrick; On Tour takes second

THO

Thomas Patrick made tremendous strides (in every sense of that phrase) during the closing months of 2017/18, culminating in victory in the Betway Handicap Chase at Aintree on Grand National day, and it would be no surprise at all to see him develop into a leading contender for the big race itself.

The Betway Handicap was just Thomas Patrick's fourth start over fences and he belied his relative lack of experience with a dominant display to justify well-backed favouritism in a field of sixteen. The Grade 3 staying handicap traditionally isn't quite so strong as other races of its type at the big spring festivals—with the Grand National, naturally, attracting a sizeable chunk of potential runners—but Thomas Patrick's convincing four-length victory over course specialist On Tour looked solid form and underlined that he was still very much on the upgrade. In style, it was a carbon copy of his two previous chase wins, in a novice at Chepstow in February and a handicap at Newbury in March, giving a largely fluent display of jumping at the head of affairs before staying on very strongly in the closing stages. The latter trait was particularly evident on that chasing debut success at Chepstow, where he rallied very strongly after briefly looking in trouble early in the straight, eventually winning by four and a half lengths from clear runner-up Step Back, who went on to land a valuable handicap of his own in the bet365 Gold Cup at Sandown. Stamina was also Thomas Patrick's strong suit over hurdles earlier in the season, his form in that sphere only really improving once he was stepped up in trip, his win in a twenty-three-furlong handicap hurdle at Exeter in November coming off a BHA mark 25 lb lower than for his Aintree win just over four months later, which illustrates how much he has progressed since switching to the larger obstacles. Thomas Patrick's record suggests long distances should suit him down to the ground, so it's probably best to ignore his one defeat to date over fences when he managed only fourth in the Devon National back at Exeter in February, particularly as he returned with a nasty cut that day.

Thomas Patrick (IRE) (b.g. 2012)
- Winged Love (IRE) (b 1992)
  - In The Wings (b 1986)
    - Sadler's Wells
    - High Hawk
  - J'ai Deux Amours (b 1986)
    - Top Ville
    - Pollenka
- Huncheon Siss (IRE) (b 1997)
  - Phardante (b 1982)
    - Pharly
    - Pallante
  - Parsons Term (b 1988)
    - The Parson
    - Zozimus

Thomas Patrick isn't the only member of his family to have enjoyed success at Aintree's three-day Grand National meeting, as both God's Own and Blitzkreig enjoyed big days there. High-class chaser God's Own is out of a sister to Thomas Patrick's dam Huncheon Siss and the 2016 Melling Chase was his biggest prize on home soil, while Blitzkreig, out of a half-sister to Thomas Patrick's third dam Zozimus, won the Captain Morgan Aintree Chase Limited Handicap (now the Red Rum) in 1991, having also won the Victor Chandler Chase at Ascot earlier that season. That pair made their name over shorter distances, but there is plenty of stamina to be found elsewhere in the pedigree. Huncheon Siss is a half-sister to useful chasers Work In Progress and Moonshine Lad, who both showed their form over staying trips, while seeming ideally suited by around two and a half miles. That sort of trip also yielded the best form from Huncheon Siss herself during a brief career under Rules, when she was placed over hurdles for both Ian Ferguson and Howard Johnson. However, she had been a winning pointer before that and her offspring seem more at home over further. The fact that she has had five foals by Winged Love might have something to do with that, as the late sire has proved a strong influence for stamina, his two biggest earners in 2017/18 other than Thomas Patrick being Grand National third Bless The Wings and Eider Chase winner Baywing. All three of Thomas Patrick's brothers are winning chasers too, notably the ill-fated hunter Walden (who stayed well) and Wings Attract, who showed fairly useful form at up to three miles for Chris Bealby in 2015/16 but has rather lost his way since that trainer relinquished his licence. Their sister Roughandtumble was a lightly-raced maiden in Irish points and is now a broodmare, producing her first foal in 2018, a colt by Conduit. Huncheon Siss, meanwhile, has since produced a 2015 filly by Frammassone and a 2016 colt by Watar, both as yet unnamed.

The tall Thomas Patrick, who cost €30,000 as an unbroken three-year-old, is one of the chief flag-bearers for the up-and-coming Herefordshire yard of Tom Lacey, who himself enjoyed a fine second half to 2017/18 on the way to a career-best seasonal tally of thirty-nine wins, which included another one at the Aintree Festival thanks to Jester Jet's 20/1 success in the Alder Hey Children's Charity Handicap Hurdle on the Friday. Lacey describes himself as an old school trainer and Thomas Patrick is certainly in the old-fashioned mould for a chasing type, having begun his career in the pointing ranks (where his only win in six starts came in a walkover). 'He enjoys bowling along and jumps well. There are lots of valuable staying chases that will really suit him in 2018/19,' is Johnson's verdict, with the likes of the Ladbrokes Trophy at Newbury and Welsh Grand National at Chepstow (both races that Native River won in his second season over fences) appealing as likely targets, particularly if there is another wet winter—all four of Thomas Patrick's wins under Rules have come on soft/heavy going. Johnson was already in his car outside the course when the 2018 Grand National was under way, but he could enjoy a Rolls Royce ride over those famous fences in the next season if Thomas Patrick continues his progression between now and then. His ante-post odds of 40/1 for the 2019 Grand National, at the time of writing, certainly looks on the generous side. *Tom Lacey*

THOMAS SHELBY (IRE) 7 b.g. Witness Box (USA) – Deemiss (IRE) (Buckskin (FR)) [2017/18 h110: c24g³ Oct 26] fair maiden hurdler: 7/4, third in novice handicap at Southwell (20 lengths behind Miami Present) on chasing debut: should be suited by 3m: acts on soft going: open to improvement as a chaser. *Alan King* — c103 p h–

THOMAS TODD 8 b.g. Passing Glance – Miss Danbys (Charmer) [2017/18 h96, b81: h15.8d May 6] maiden hurdler, well held sole outing in 2017/18: in hood last 3 starts: often races in rear. *Laura Morgan* — h–

THOMOND (IRE) 10 b.g. Definite Article – Hushaby (IRE) (Eurobus) [2017/18 c125, h–: c25.2g² c25g⁶ c19.9g⁶ c25d⁵ c23.4s⁴ c26.6g⁶ Feb 3] strong gelding: winning hurdler: fairly useful chaser, on decline in 2017/18: left Noel Meade after fourth start: stays 29f: acts on firm and soft going: tried in cheekpieces: wears tongue tie. *N. W. Alexander* — c113 h–

THOONAVOLLA (IRE) 10 ch.g. Beneficial – Another Partner (Le Bavard (FR)) [2017/18 c106, h93: c20.3s⁵ h23g^pu c24d c21.7m⁶ Apr 25] winning hurdler: fair chaser at best, no form in 2017/18: has worn cheekpieces. *Tom Weston* — c– h–

THORPE (IRE) 8 b.g. Danehill Dancer (IRE) – Minkova (IRE) (Sadler's Wells (USA)) [2017/18 h120: h20.2g⁴ h23.9m⁴ h20.2g* h20.2d* h20.2s² h19.7s h19.4d* h19.3v^pu h20.2s* Apr 27] sturdy gelding: fairly useful handicap hurdler: won at Perth (conditional events) in July and August, Musselburgh in January and Perth again in April: stays 2½m: acts on soft going: wears cheekpieces/tongue tie. *Lucinda Russell* — h120

THOSEDAYSAREGONE (IRE) 5 b.g. Getaway (GER) – Gonearethedays (IRE) (Be My Native (USA)) [2017/18 b16s³ b16v³ b20v* b16v³ b17s Apr 13] lengthy gelding: half-brother to bumper winner/fair hurdler Lord Adare (2¼m winner, by Moscow Society) and fair hurdler Beabus Jack (2½m winner, by Lord Americo): dam unraced half-sister to useful hurdler/smart cross-country chaser (stayed 33f) Uncle Junior: fairly useful bumper performer: won maiden at Wexford in March: likely to stay beyond 2½m. *Charles Byrnes, Ireland* — b99

THOUNDER (FR) 4 ch.g. Hurricane Cat (USA) – Meldown (FR) (Until Sundown (USA)) [2017/18 h15.8g* h15.3g* h17.7d⁴ Nov 19] first foal: dam unraced: fairly useful form over hurdles: won juveniles at Huntingdon and Wincanton in October. *Gary Moore* — h117

THREE COLOURS RED (IRE) 6 b.g. Camacho – Colour's Red (IRE) (Red Ransom (USA)) [2017/18 h103: h19.2g² h23g* h23g² h19.5v⁶ Apr 14] rather leggy gelding: modest handicap hurdler: won at Worcester in June: stays 23f: acts on good to soft going: has worn headgear, including last 4 starts: has worn tongue tie. *Robert Stephens* — h92

THREE FACES WEST (IRE) 10 b.g. Dr Massini (IRE) – Ardnataggle (IRE) (Aristocracy) [2017/18 c151, h–: c27.3s³ c22.9v^F c28.4v^F h25.8v^pu Mar 17] workmanlike gelding: winning hurdler: smart handicap chaser, shaped as if better for run only completed start in 2017/18: stays 3m: acts on heavy going: wears cheekpieces: front runner/races prominently. *Philip Hobbs* — c133 h–

THREE MUSKETEERS (IRE) 8 b.g. Flemensfirth (USA) – Friendly Craic (IRE) (Mister Lord (USA)) [2017/18 c152, h–: h19.5d h20d^5 h22.8v c21.4v^2 h20s Apr 13] strong, workmanlike gelding: useful but unreliable handicap hurdler: smart chaser: second in graduation event at Market Rasen (1¼ lengths behind Le Rocher) in January: stays 2¾m: acts on heavy going: has worn cheekpieces, including last 2 starts. *Dan Skelton* — c144 h134 §

THREE STAR GENERAL 5 b.g. Montjeu (IRE) – Honorlina (FR) (Linamix (FR)) [2017/18 h110: h21.9d^2 h20g* h20g^2 h23.1g h26.5d^{pu} h23.8s h23.5s^2 h19.8s^3 Mar 9] rather leggy gelding: fairly useful hurdler: won maiden at Worcester in June: stays 3m: acts on soft going: wears headgear: tried in tongue tie. *David Pipe* — h115

THREE STARS (IRE) 8 b.g. Westerner – Hapeney (IRE) (Saddlers' Hall (IRE)) [2017/18 c141, h–: c20v^3 c17d^5 c19.9s^5 c24.5d c17s^2 c16.3v^5 c16d Apr 26] lengthy gelding: winning hurdler: useful handicap chaser: second in Coral Sandyford Handicap Chase at Leopardstown (2¾ lengths behind Patricks Park) in February: stays 2¼m: acts on good to firm and heavy going: in cheekpieces last 3 starts: front runner/races prominently. *Henry de Bromhead, Ireland* — c140 h–

THREE WAYS 7 b.g. Flemensfirth (USA) – Serenique (Good Thyne (USA)) [2017/18 h130: c24d^2 c24.2s^2 c25.2s* c23.4v^F c25.2s^3 Mar 27] sturdy gelding: useful hurdler: similar form over fences: won novice at Catterick in January: stays 25f: acts on soft going: in headgear last 4 starts: wears tongue tie: front runner/races prominently. *Jamie Snowden* — c134 h–

THREE WISE MEN (IRE) 8 b.g. Presenting – Bilboa (FR) (Phantom Breeze) [2017/18 c138, h128: c16g^F c18.2g* c20v^2 c18d^{pu} c18v^3 c16.7v Apr 1] winning hurdler: useful chaser: won maiden at Galway in August: stays 2½m: acts on heavy going: often leads. *Henry de Bromhead, Ireland* — c131 h–

THROTHETHATCH (IRE) 9 b.g. Beneficial – Castletownroche (IRE) (Saddlers' Hall (IRE)) [2017/18 c114, h110: c15.9v^4 Mar 9] point winner: winning hurdler: fair chaser: likely to stay beyond 2½m: acts on heavy going: in tongue tie last 3 starts. *Miss Jennifer Pidgeon* — c101 h–

THUMB STONE BLUES (IRE) 8 b.g. High Chaparral (IRE) – Jade River (FR) (Indian River (FR)) [2017/18 h129, b94: c23d^3 c24.2d^2 c25.2d^2 c24s Jan 27] bumper winner: fairly useful hurdler: useful form over fences: second in handicap at Catterick in November: stays 25f: acts on good to firm and heavy going: in cheekpieces last 2 starts: wears tongue tie: front runner/races prominently. *Kim Bailey* — c130 h–

THUNDER AND ROSES (IRE) 10 b.g. Presenting – Glen Empress (IRE) (Lancastrian) [2017/18 c147, h–: c29s^{pu} c24.5d c25v^4 c28.7v^{pu} c23v^F c29v^F c34.3s^{pu} c30s Apr 28] sturdy gelding: winning hurdler: smart handicap chaser, largely disappointing in 2017/18: stays 3¾m: acts on heavy going: wears headgear/tongue tie: races prominently. *M. F. Morris, Ireland* — c133 h–

THUNDERING HOME 11 gr.g. Storming Home – Citrine Spirit (IRE) (Soviet Star (USA)) [2017/18 h104: h16.8g^5 h15.8g^4 h16g h18.5d^{pu} h15.3s h15.3g^4 h16.8v^4 h15.9s h17.7v^6 h16.6d^3 h17.7s h16.5m Apr 25] smallish gelding: fair handicap hurdler, below best in 2017/18: stays 19f: acts on good to firm and heavy going: wears headgear/tongue tie. *Richard Mitchell* — h91

THUNDER SHEIK (IRE) 10 b.g. Green Tune (USA) – Realy Queen (USA) (Thunder Gulch (USA)) [2017/18 c–, h108: h16.2v^2 h16.4g h19.7s^5 Dec 11] compact gelding: fairly useful handicap hurdler: second at Perth in September: twice-raced chaser: best around 2m: acts on good to firm and heavy going: wears headgear: often tongue tied: often races prominently. *Nigel Twiston-Davies* — c– h116

THYNE FOR GOLD (IRE) 7 b.g. Robin des Pres (FR) – My Name's Not Bin (IRE) (Good Thyne (USA)) [2017/18 c–, h111: c19.3g^3 c23.4g^4 c25.5g^4 c20g* Jul 27] useful-looking gelding: fair hurdler: similar form over fences: won handicap at Worcester in July: stays 23f: acts on good to firm and heavy going: tried in hood. *Donald McCain* — c107 h–

TIBBIE TAMSON 7 b.m. Josr Algarhoud (IRE) – Midlem Melody (Syrtos) [2017/18 b16.2g h17d Mar 25] fifth foal: dam (c90/h60) 2m-2½m hurdle/chase winner: tailed off in mares bumper/novice hurdle. *Stuart Coltherd* — h– b–

TICKANRUN (IRE) 8 gr.g. Tikkanen (USA) – Dusty Lane (IRE) (Electric) [2017/18 h93: h24.1s^2 h24v^2 h25.3s^{pu} h19.3v^5 Apr 17] modest maiden hurdler: stays 3m: acts on heavy going: has worn headgear, including in 2017/18. *Micky Hammond* — h91

816

TICKENWOLF (IRE) 8 gr.g. Tikkanen (USA) – Emma's Choice (IRE) (Indian Danehill (IRE)) [2017/18 c118, h116: c26.2g⁴ c24.2g⁴ c23.8gᵘʳ c24.2v* c23.9gʳᵒ c24.2sᶠ c24.5sᶠ Dec 3] big, lengthy gelding: winning hurdler: fairly useful handicap chaser: won at Hexham in September: stays 3¼m: acts on heavy going: often races towards rear. *Micky Hammond* — c122 h–

TICKERTY BOO (IRE) 6 gr.m. Tikkanen (USA) – La Fille d'Or (IRE) (Goldmark (USA)) [2017/18 b–: b16.8s⁴ b16.7v Jan 17] modest form in bumpers. *Brian Ellison* — b78

TICKET TO RIDE (FR) 5 b.g. Al Namix (FR) – Eightdaysaweek (Montjeu (IRE)) [2017/18 b–p: h16.5s h19.7s⁴ c19.9s² c19.7d² c24g Apr 26] workmanlike gelding: point winner: poor form over hurdles: modest form in chases: in hood last 5 starts. *Polly Gundry* — c91 h81

TIDAL FLOW 5 b.g. Black Sam Bellamy (IRE) – Mrs Philip (Puissance) [2017/18 b16.3d* b15.3d⁴ Apr 22] £35,000 3-y-o: fourth foal: closely related to bumper winner/fairly useful hurdler Kayf Willow (2m-2¾m winner, by Kayf Tara) and poor hurdler Millie O'Brien (2¾m winner, by Milan): dam (h93), 19f-2¾m hurdle winner, half-sister to fairly useful hurdler/chaser (stayed 3m) Cabochon and fairly useful hurdler (2m/17f winner) Lawahik: useful form in bumpers: won at Newbury (by 5 lengths from Burrows Edge) in November. *Philip Hobbs* — b105

TIDAL WATCH (IRE) 4 b.g. Harbour Watch (IRE) – Najmati (Green Desert (USA)) [2017/18 h16g⁵ h17.7d³ h16.3s⁴ Oct 2] fairly useful maiden on Flat, stays 1½m: modest form over hurdles. *Jonjo O'Neill* — h98

TIDESTREAM 8 b.g. Galileo (IRE) – Sweet Stream (ITY) (Shantou (USA)) [2017/18 c–, h88: c20.9g⁶ h24g² h24g Aug 20] good-topped gelding: modest handicap hurdler: little impact in chases: stays 3m: acts on soft going: often in visor nowadays: wears tongue tie. *Tim Vaughan* — c– h90

TIERRA VERDE 7 b.m. Josr Algarhoud (IRE) – La Corujera (Case Law) [2017/18 b86: b15.7d h17.7v⁵ h15.9v³ h16.5v³ h16.5v² Apr 12] placed in bumper: fair form over hurdles: will be suited by 2¼m+: often races prominently. *Harry Whittington* — h100 b74

TIGER MOUNTAIN (IRE) 7 b.g. Mountain High (IRE) – Our Trick (IRE) (Flemensfirth (USA)) [2017/18 h105, b–: h21.3s Nov 3] maiden hurdler, fair form at best: tried in visor. *Malcolm Jefferson* — h–

TIGER ROLL (IRE) 8 b.g. Authorized (IRE) – Swiss Roll (IRE) (Entrepreneur) [2017/18 c151§, h–: c23s² c20.6vᵖᵘ c30.2d⁵ c30.2s* c34.3s* Apr 14] — c155 h–

Amid all the changes made to the Grand National course in recent times, the four-hundred-and-ninety-four-yard run-in with its famous elbow has remained a constant, untouched so far by the modernisers. The Aintree fences are less of a test than they used to be, but the same cannot be said of the unique run-in (the longest in Britain with the exception of Cartmel's) which has been the scene of some heartbreaking incidents in the Grand National. The rather awkward elbow was created in 1888 because of the need to steer the runners round the Chair; the three flights of hurdles in the original straight in which the National used to finish were replaced by two fences built at a tangent on adjoining ground on the inside (the last of the hurdles used to be between the adjacent Chair and the water, giving a run-in of around a hundred yards). Likely victory has been turned into defeat on numerous occasions as the long run-in, after more than four miles and thirty fences, has tested endurance and courage to the limit. For some of the last-fence leaders in the extensive period since the end of World War II, the writing was on the wall as they jumped. Young Driver, Moorcroft Boy, Encore Un Peu and The Last Samuri, for example, were sitting ducks in their years for West Tip, Miinnehoma, Rough Quest and Rule The World, whose jockeys were only biding their time.

In the first post-war National, though, Prince Regent, carrying 12-5, looked home and hosed at the final fence, only to slow dramatically on the run-in where he was passed by lightweights Lovely Cottage and Jack Finlay. Prince Regent had won the Cheltenham Gold Cup on his previous outing and a similar fate befell another Gold Cup winner Garrison Savannah forty-five years later when he opened up a three- to four-length lead over Seagram between the last two fences. With his jockey riding confidently, it looked as if Garrison Savannah only had to jump the last to win; he actually increased his advantage over Seagram to half a dozen lengths early on the run-in, only to falter at the elbow which allowed his rallying rival to collar him about a hundred yards out. The most dramatic such collapse in the period between

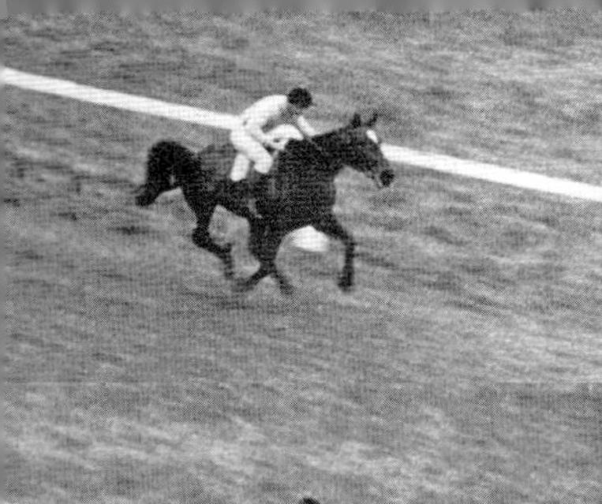

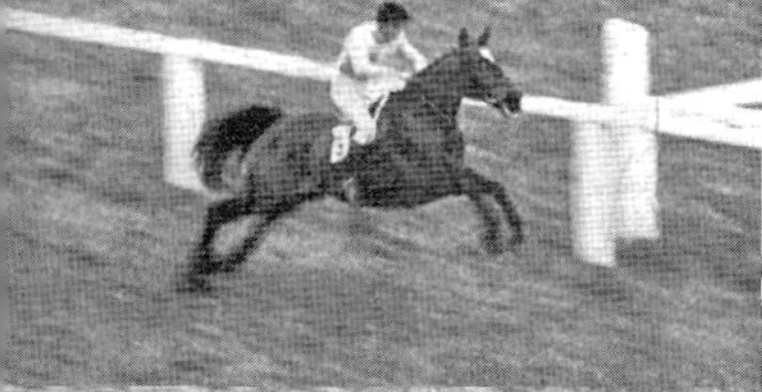

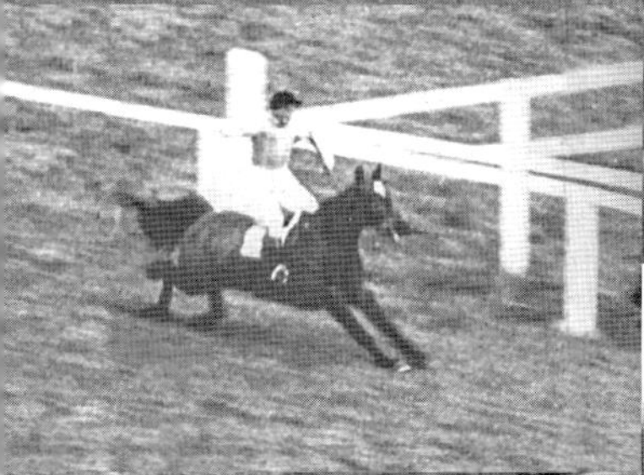

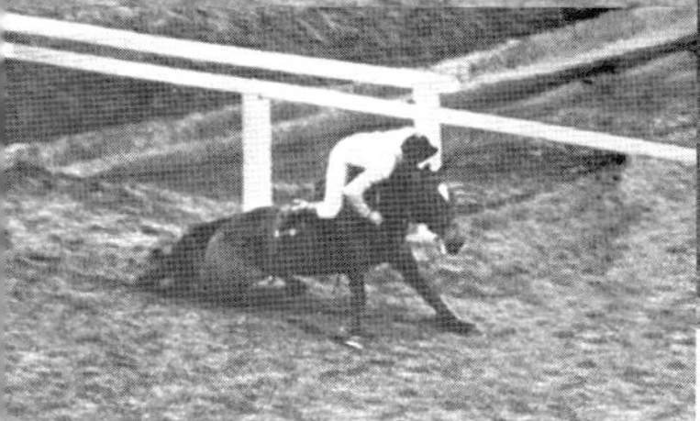

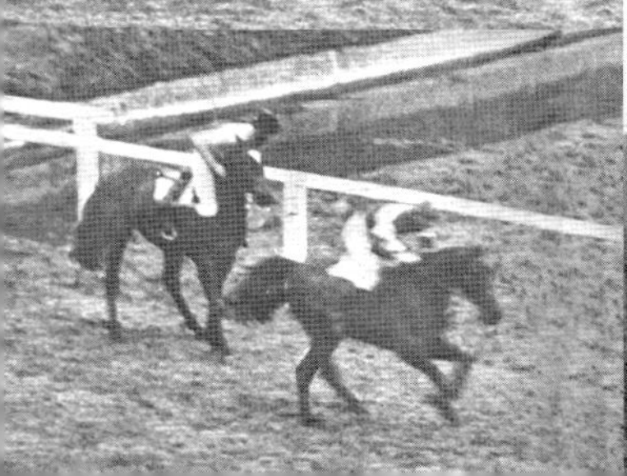

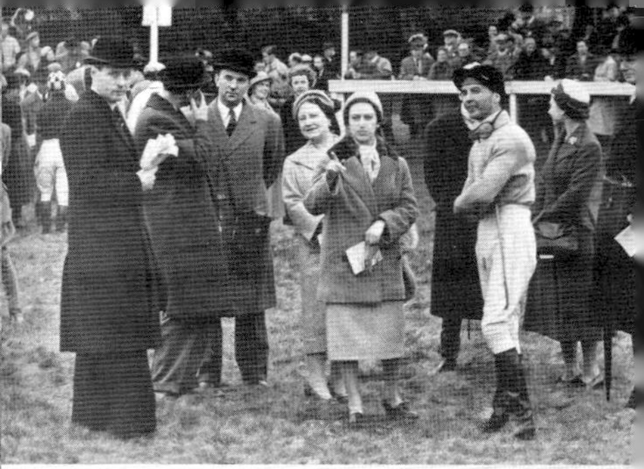

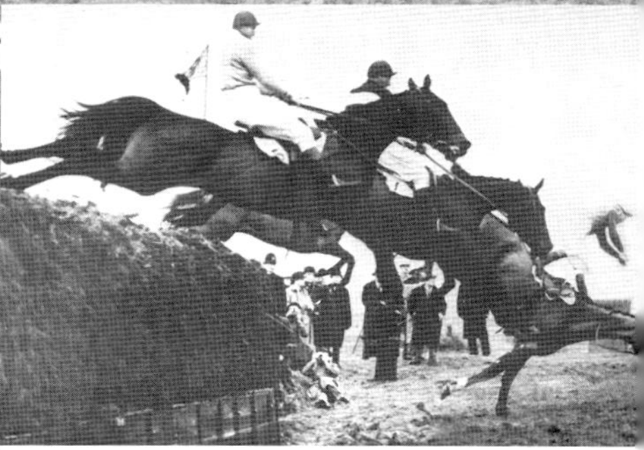

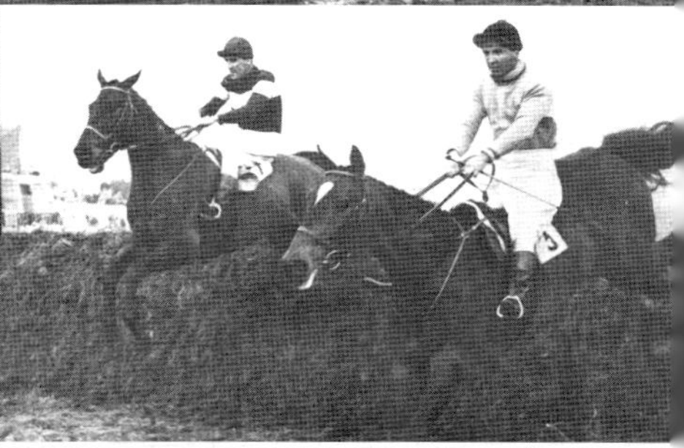

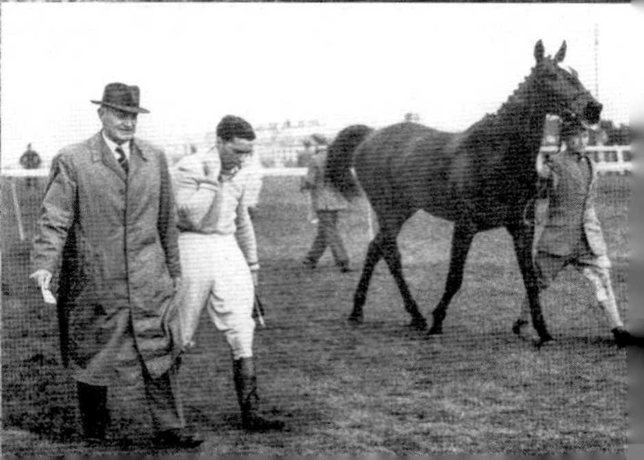

Prince Regent and Garrison Savannah (when First of the Dandies, Carrickbeg, Mr Snugfit, Lean Ar Aghaidh and Durham Edition were others caught on the run-in) was undoubtedly that of another top-class performer Crisp (carried 12-0) who was fifteen lengths in front at the last in 1973, only to be pegged back by Red Rum in one of the most famous Grand National finishes. Crisp's defeat, after one of the finest displays of bold jumping and front running ever seen over the big fences at Aintree, was even more dramatic than those of Prince Regent and Garrison Savannah (the last-named ridden by Mark Pitman, son of Crisp's rider Richard Pitman who became a broadcaster and witnessed Garrison Savannah's collapse from the television commentary box).

Others since Garrison Savannah have seen the prospect of victory dashed after leading over the last. Hennessy winner What's Up Boys passed the elbow still in a three-length lead in 2002 only to be collared fifty yards from the line by the rallying Bindaree (it was twenty-seven lengths back to the third); a desperately-tired Clan Royal had a lead of two and a half lengths at the final fence in 2004 and had to be wrenched to the right on the run-in after briefly looking as if he might run off the course, only for him and Lord Atterbury to be passed by Amberleigh House inside the final furlong; the last-fence leader in 2012, Sunnyhillboy, was still just over a length in front of Seabass at the elbow, where Neptune Collonges was two to three lengths away in third before staying on strongly to prevail in the closest finish in the history of the race (the verdict involving Neptune Collonges and Sunnyhillboy could have gone either way and the result would have been a dead heat before the age of pixels). Sunnyhillboy's jockey had felt his mount become a little unbalanced after rounding the elbow and it transpired that his off-fore had been struck into, causing a tendon injury.

If Sunnyhillboy was unlucky in what was, not only the closest, but also one of the most dramatic finishes in Grand National history, there is no doubt about the most dramatic climax of them all. Devon Loch's mysterious and never-to-be-forgotten bellyflop on the run-in, perhaps the most sensational climax to any race in living memory, guaranteed the 1956 Grand National a place in racing folklore. Devon Loch's sudden sprawling fifty yards from the line, when holding a lead of half a dozen lengths and with the race in the bag, will be debated for as long as the National is discussed. The story of his collapse, which was all over in a matter of seconds, is too widely known to need re-telling here in full (a comprehensive account appeared in the essay on Numbersixvalverde in *Chasers & Hurdlers 2005/06* on the fiftieth anniversary of the race). However, there is not much doubt that Devon Loch was the unluckiest loser in the Grand National's long history (the jockey on the eventual winner E.S.B. had accepted defeat with a hundred yards to go). The Grand National was the last of the really big sporting events to be signed up by television—largely because of the obstinacy of Aintree's owners over copyright—and, with the first live TV coverage still four years away, the only record was cinema newsreel footage. Movietone put out a special newsreel showing the incident in slow motion and speculating about why Devon Loch had suddenly lost his footing. The newsreel film seemed to suggest that Devon Loch tried to jump an imaginary fence, perhaps misled by a shadow of the water jump. He stopped dead in his tracks before slithering, his jockey Dick Francis sinking to the ground with him. Francis appeared on the newsreel footage and was asked what had happened, to which he replied, 'It's something I will never know and I don't think anyone else will.' Devon Loch's owner the Queen Mother, who also had M'As Tu Vu making a second attempt at the race, was philosophical, reportedly saying 'That's racing, I suppose' when E.S.B.'s owner Mrs Stella Carver commiserated with her.

The 1956 Grand National produced arguably the most sensational climax to any race in living memory when the clear leader Devon Loch, in the royal colours, suddenly skidded and slithered to the ground with only fifty yards to go; the slow motion newsreel film seemed to suggest that Devon Loch had attempted to jump a fence that wasn't there, but the bizarre incident remains an unsolved mystery that is still talked about; the Queen Mother and the Queen, among those in the paddock beforehand, never attended the race again (Devon Loch is also pictured jumping second Becher's and the last)

Glenfarclas Chase (Cross Country), Cheltenham—Tiger Roll (star on cap) tracks early leader Beeves on his way to a third Cheltenham Festival win

Neither the Queen Mother, a great jumping supporter, nor the Queen attended the Grand National after Devon Loch's puzzling mishap and some argue that the race only emphasised the National's unpredictability and actually contributed to the decline of Aintree in the quarter of a century or so that followed, when the course's very future was sometimes in doubt. The fact that Devon Loch was owned by royalty undoubtedly added to the fascination. A similar thing had happened, without the attendant hysteria, to 25/1-shot Drumree who 'stopped and fell with the staggers' approaching the final fence in 1903 when seemingly going well and about to take up the running. It is idle to speculate about whether a royal victory in 1956 would have changed the course of Aintree history, but the huge noise of the crowd as they cheered on Devon Loch up the run-in, contrasting with the near-silence in the aftermath of the race, was testament to how popular a result it would have been (there was a theory that the crescendo of cheering had startled Devon Loch). As with Drumree, Devon Loch seemed none the worse afterwards, quickly regaining his feet and then walking normally from the course. The vets could find nothing wrong with him and he continued racing, winning twice with Francis in the saddle the next season, when he was also runner-up in the King George VI Chase. He was entered in the 1957 National but suffered a recurrence of tendon trouble when fourth under 12-1 in the Mildmay Memorial Handicap Chase in January and never ran again. Dick Francis himself retired shortly afterwards and went on to become a best-selling writer of racing thrillers, once admitting that he would have regarded the story of Devon Loch's collapse as too fanciful for one of his novels.

Among the final-fence leaders who narrowly avoided joining the ranks of the last-gasp Grand National losers was the 2007 winner Silver Birch who was one of eight in the parade of former Grand National winners (led by Bindaree) before the latest National. Silver Birch's three-length lead on the run-in in his National was whittled down to three quarters of a length by McKelvey who was still closing gradually on the winner as the line was reached (the runner-up was afterwards found to have sustained a tendon injury). Silver Birch, a former winner of the Welsh National, had been weeded out of Paul Nicholls' stable and bought for 20,000 guineas to join a new young trainer in Ireland called Gordon Elliott who was operating from a small rented yard with mostly moderate horses and point-to-pointers. The aim had been to campaign Silver Birch in cross country races but he staked his claim as a plausible Grand National outsider by running a good second in the Cross Country Handicap Chase at the Cheltenham Festival (he had also won a Becher Chase over the National fences in his earlier days). Elliott hadn't trained a winner under Rules in his native country (he had had three in Britain earlier in the season) and Silver Birch's Grand National triumph was the start of a meteoric rise that has seen his Cullentra House yard in County Meath grow into one of the juggernauts of jumps racing.

Gordon Elliott's second Grand National winner came in the latest season with Tiger Roll whose amazing career already included three wins at the Cheltenham Festival, in the 2014 Triumph Hurdle, the 2017 National Hunt Chase over four miles and the latest Cross Country Chase (not a handicap these days), sponsored by Glenfarclas. A relative youngster by cross country standards at only eight, Tiger Roll had had a sighter on the unconventional course in December when he had never really figured behind veteran stablemate Bless The Wings. Bless The Wings was a faller in the Cross Country Chase at the Festival in which Elliott also ran the previous season's Grand National runner-up Cause of Causes who had won the Cross Country twelve months earlier on his way to Aintree. If Cause of Causes proved a disappointment in his bid for a fourth successive victory at the Festival (he had won the National Hunt Chase, the Kim Muir and the Cross Country), the Elliott stable found a new Grand National contender in Tiger Roll who matched the best of his conventional chase form, travelling strongly, taking the lead before the fifth last and winning by two lengths and eleven lengths from French challenger Urgent de Gregaine and the 2016 Grand National runner-up The Last Samuri who also had the Grand National as his main target again (he had been second in the Becher Chase in December). On veterinary advice, Tiger Roll and The Last Samuri were not taken to the unsaddling area for the first four after the Cross Country when both were found to be suffering from mild heatstroke. Tiger Roll's trainer also faced a stewards' inquiry into the horse's improvement in form. He hadn't run since the Cross Country Handicap at Cheltenham's December meeting, before which he had been pulled up when well held Alpha des Obeaux in the Clonmel Oil Chase in November. Tiger Roll certainly has his 'non-going days', sometimes let down by his jumping as well as his resolve, and he has had a Timeform squiggle over fences (which was removed only after his National win) to denote that he is unreliable and cannot be trusted. Gordon Elliott's representative told the Cheltenham stewards that Tiger Roll had jumped slowly at Cheltenham in December and had benefited from subsequent schooling at home. The stewards 'noted' the explanation and had Tiger Roll routine tested.

The section mark '§', or 'the dreaded Timeform squiggle' as it has become known, was used in Timeform's early days to identify 'a horse who is either a rogue, ungenerous, faint-hearted or which for other reasons we do not think should ever be relied upon: one which, though it may have the ability signified by its rating, cannot be trusted to run up to it.' The definition is more utilitarian nowadays—denoting a horse that is 'unreliable for temperamental or other reasons'—but the symbol is one that has made the hackles rise sometimes when an owner or trainer has found his or her horse's rating accompanied by a squiggle. Josh Gifford told us that after seeing the symbol against one of his stable stars, Royal Judgement, he had thrown his copy of *Chasers & Hurdlers 1982/83* into the fire, while Noel Meade took exception to the squiggle on Harchibald, saying 'If he's a rogue or a thief, I wish to God they'd send me ten more like him.' Only two hurdlers in the *Chasers & Hurdlers* era have been rated higher than Harchibald and also given a squiggle, Bird's Nest (the best horse never to win the Champion Hurdle) and Morley Street (winner of the 1991 Champion Hurdle and four successive Aintree Hurdles). Mercy Rimell was another trainer who was outspoken when a squiggle was given to her Champion Hurdle winner Gaye Brief. Brilliant but exasperatingly erratic horses—recent examples include the quirky Tidal Bay, the weak-finishing Wishfull Thinking and the reluctant starters Sanctuaire and Wicklow Brave—are treated no differently to horses at the lower end of the ratings scale and, whatever the horse, a squiggle is awarded only after the most careful consideration of the facts. Where there may be a valid explanation for a horse's in-and-out form, that horse is always given the benefit of the doubt.

The '§' symbol was an obvious requirement from the very start of Timeform ratings to warn punters about the severe unreliability of certain horses as betting propositions. That Grand National legend The Pilgarlic (a half-brother to L'Escargot) took little interest in races away from Aintree and had a squiggle on each of the three occasions he finished in the frame in the big race; Last Suspect, who produced an amazing finishing burst, making up more ground than any Grand National winner

*Randox Health Grand National Handicap Chase, Aintree—
on the 25th anniversary of the infamous void National, a first-time start for the thirty-eight runners
in front of the Saturday tea-time packed stands*

since Red Rum, to catch Mr Snugfit on the run-in in 1985, was always teetering on the brink of a squiggle, finally being awarded one the season after his Aintree success. Tiger Roll, though, is the only Grand National winner to have carried the Timeform squiggle alongside his name going into the race. By coincidence, another squiggle horse, Ultragold, has won the last two editions of the Topham Chase over the big fences at the Grand National meeting. The successful jumps sire Shantou, represented by the very smart Shantou Flyer in the latest National, remains, incidentally, the only winner of a British classic to carry a squiggle when successful in the race (he won the 1996 St Leger).

The enigmatic Tiger Roll clearly has two ways of running but he had never raced over the Grand National fences before and he may have been stimulated by doing something different. He had reverted to type after producing his best effort over fences, up to that time, to win the previous season's Munster National at Limerick, going with plenty of zest stepped up in trip, and had then seemed to have his interest sparked again after some lacklustre efforts by the unusual demands of the National Hunt Chase at Cheltenham (surviving three notable errors and putting his best foot forward on the day). Since the Grand National course was remodelled in 2013, the race has arguably placed slightly more emphasis on stamina than jumping ability, with the easier fences causing relatively fewer problems (the percentage who fall, unseat or are brought down has been around fifty per cent lower than previously). There is still plenty of attention focussed beforehand on the pick of the runners who have shown form over the National fences, particularly in the National itself. The previous year's winner One For Arthur missed the latest season with a tendon injury and runner-up Cause of Causes had been retired after returning lame from the Cheltenham Festival. But nine of those who had finished the course in the first Randox Health-sponsored Grand National in 2017 were back again, chief among them Saint Are (third) who was running in his fifth National and looking to reach the first three for the third time, Blaklion (fourth) who had since won the Becher Chase over the big fences, the Grand Sefton winner Gas Line Boy (fifth) and another Becher winner Vieux Lion Rouge (sixth), the two last-named in their third National. The former Cheltenham Gold Cup winner Lord Windermere (seventh behind One For Arthur) was also contesting his third Grand National, while Pleasant Company had looked one to be interested in another year when running ninth behind One For Arthur, after making a bad mistake. The 2016 runner-up The Last Samuri (sixteenth behind One For Arthur) was back again, while others with experience of the National fences were Ucello Conti, sixth in Rule The World's National and travelling well when unseating his jockey at second Becher's in One For Arthur's edition, Double Ross, who had got round in a Topham and a Grand Sefton in his time, and Tiger Roll's stablemate Bless The Wings, whose form figures had more letters than numbers but included a ninth in the Topham back in 2015.

In an unusually wet winter, the latest Grand National was always going to prove an extreme test and, after the official going became 'heavy, soft in places' after further rain the day before, there were a number of late changes to the field. Top weight Minella Rocco, the dual Scottish Grand National winner Vicente and the useful Beeves (seventh behind Tiger Roll in the Cross Country) were taken out, giving three of the nominated four reserves the chance to run. One of those reserves Walk In The Mill was, in the end, also a non-runner, along with late absentee Regal Encore (eighth the previous year), leaving a field of thirty-eight, two short of the maximum permitted nowadays. The biggest field for the Grand National—and the biggest field for any event in racing's history— was the line-up of sixty-six in 1929, in an era when there was no concept of placing safety limits on the number of runners in a race. Minella Rocco's defection from the latest National resulted in the weights being raised by 1 1b, with Blaklion becoming top weight on 11-10 (the official race card carried the old weights) in a field in which the bottom weights (including reserves Thunder And Roses and Delusionofgrandeur) were on 10-5, equivalent to a BHA mark of 142. The full permitted weight range in the National has been only 24 1b since 2009 (11-10 to 10-0), a far cry from the days when Cloister, Manifesto, Jerry M and Poethlyn won the race carrying 12-7 (Easter Hero was runner-up under 12-7 in the sixty-six-runner 1929 edition after leading most of the way). The latest National was the last for which the weights were compiled by Phil Smith who retired as the BHA's Head of Handicapping at the end of the season. Mr Smith's practice of favouring the top horses when framing the Grand National handicap has not been apparent in the most recent runnings. Neptune Collonges and Many Clouds were the last such 'leniently-treated' winners, given marks in the National that were 2 1b and 5 1b respectively lower than they would have been allotted at the time in handicaps away from Aintree. Since the course was modified, incidentally, Many Clouds, successful under 11-9, is the only Grand National winner to have carried 11-0 or more and only four others have made the frame under 11-0 or more.

The Grand National weights launch has been staged at glitzy London venues in the past two years (the latest at BAFTA's Piccadilly headquarters plagued by the effects of a power cut). There is talk that the occasion might return to Liverpool in 2019 which will be the hundredth anniversary of Poethlyn's weight-carrying feat in

First Becher's—I Just Know crashes out, leaving Milansbar (No.37) and Double Ross (No.39) at the head of affairs; Tiger Roll (No.13) is already handy

The Chair—a heavy fall for Rachael Blackmore, one of three female jockeys in the race, as Alpha des Obeaux exits just ahead of fellow Gigginstown runner Tiger Roll (cheekpieces)

the year when the race returned to Aintree after three World War I substitutes held at Gatwick. The weights launch in 2017 had featured a clash between Phil Smith and the millionaire owner of Gigginstown House Stud, Michael O'Leary, who took exception to what he saw as unfair treatment of three of his horses (three of the four top weights) who were allotted marks that were higher than their current Irish Turf Club marks. Gigginstown had eleven original entries in the latest Grand National but O'Leary and his brother Eddie had no issue with the weights allotted this time ('All our entries are there with a fair weight'). Tiger Roll's weight put him in the top forty, therefore guaranteeing he would make the field, and he was immediately earmarked as one of the likely Gigginstown runners. The Grand National handicap came out before Tiger Roll won the Cross Country Chase and there are no penalties in the National after the publication of the weights.

The make-up of jumping's most valuable races, including the biggest handicaps, has become increasingly dominated by a small group of big owners and by the top stables, and Gigginstown had five runners in the latest National, trained by four different trainers (Tiger Roll was the only one of them trained by Gordon Elliott who also saddled Ucello Conti and Bless The Wings). Ireland's other superpower jumps owner J. P. McManus had three runners (he also owned the late defectors Minella Rocco and Regal Encore) and the McManus horses included the seemingly well handicapped Anibale Fly who had shown improved form to finish third in the Cheltenham Gold Cup since the National weights had been issued. Willie Mullins, facing what looked a stiff task at the time to retain his Irish trainers' title in the face of Gordon Elliott's fine run of success, saddled three Grand National runners, the Ladbrokes Trophy (former Hennessy) winner Total Recall, who had been running a good race in the Cheltenham Gold Cup until falling at the third last, Pleasant Company ('It was always the plan to have another tilt … he could go close') and Childrens List. Total Recall was sent off the 7/1 favourite in a market headed by three Irish horses who had not run over the big fences before. Tiger Roll and Anibale Fly were joint second favourites at 10/1, ahead of Scotland's big hope the 11/1-shot Seeyouatmidnight, who had needed a recent comeback run at Newbury to qualify and was another who had yet to encounter the National fences. Yet another first-timer the Yorkshire-trained I Just Know, a notably fluent jumper of conventional fences, and top weight Blaklion, came next at 14/1.

The runners got away to a trouble-free start on the twenty-fifth anniversary of the infamous void race in which there were two false starts and seven horses completed the course, their jockeys ignoring, or unaware of, attempts to stop the race after the second false start. Backers of Blaklion knew their fate at the first in the latest National when he was brought down, simply having nowhere to go when outsider Perfect Candidate fell in front of him. I Just Know made the running over the early fences and there were no more casualties until he himself came down at first Becher's, along with Houblon des Obeaux (tenth in 2017) and Virgilio. Lord Windermere, short of room when unseating his jockey at the Canal Turn, was also a notable casualty on the first circuit, failing to complete for the third time in four appearances in all over the National fences. The Chair, the biggest fence on the course, claimed the close-up Alpha des Obeaux, who fell heavily and brought down Saint Are. Ucello Conti had taken over in front when I Just Know fell and he led twenty-six survivors out into the country for the final time, followed by Pleasant Company, who was jumping superbly, The Dutchman, Double Ross, Milansbar, Seeyouatmidnight, Valseur Lido, Bless The Wings, Childrens List and Tiger Roll. Tiger Roll's jumping had been accurate and he made his only mistake (his jockey briefly lost a stirrup) at the nineteenth, the first on the final circuit.

The field was whittled down further, mostly through stragglers being pulled up, on the run to second Becher's which had to be bypassed with Charlie Deutsch, the rider of Houblon des Obeaux, still being tended to by medical staff after his fall. Pleasant Company and Ucello Conti led the runners round the outside of the fence where I Just Know's jockey Danny Cook was helping to direct the runners (something to which the Aintree stewards took exception, calling Cook to a subsequent inquiry where he was told of his 'responsibilities not to get involved', though no such reprimand had been given to Ruby Walsh when he did a similar thing at the Canal Turn in the 2015 National). Crossing the Melling Road and coming back on to the main racecourse with two left to jump, Pleasant Company led from the improving Tiger Roll, with ten others still more or less in touch, though they did not include Ucello Conti, who parted company with his jockey four out, or Total Recall who wasn't being persevered with after being badly let down by his jumping. The wheat was sorted from the chaff rounding the home turn and approaching the second last, with Pleasant Company, Tiger Roll, Bless The Wings, Valseur Lido and Anibale Fly opening up a gap on the others. Pleasant Company wasn't fluent at the second last where Tiger Roll went on.

Quickening clear soon after jumping the final fence, Tiger Roll looked in complete control as he rounded the elbow with a five-length lead, his jockey not even having had to draw his stick in earnest up to that point. The gap between Tiger Roll and Pleasant Company still seemed wide enough when the wilting Tiger Roll suddenly began to tire inside the final furlong, his stride shortening dramatically. Now under strong driving, Tiger Roll still had a three-length advantage passing the water with fifty yards to go but he had reached the end of his tether and his lead over

Second Canal Turn—leader Pleasant Company is just out of shot as Ucello Conti (noseband) blunders; Tiger Roll (No.13) is poised to challenge, jumping alongside Milansbar (blinkers), eventual third Bless The Wings and Double Ross (outside)

The last—Davy Russell has made his move on Tiger Roll, who leads from Pleasant Company (right), Bless The Wings (second left) and Anibale Fly (left)

Pleasant Company was diminishing rapidly with the winning post in sight, the Elliott and Mullins stables fighting it out in a storyline repeated time and again in the latest season. As Tiger Roll and Pleasant Company passed the post together, not everyone was sure who had won. In two more strides the result would definitely have been different but the photo-finish—rarely called upon to decide a National—showed that Tiger Roll had held on by a head to avoid his name joining the lengthy list of Grand National losers undone on the long run-in.

Eleven lengths behind the first two came Bless The Wings (only twelve days earlier a runner in the Irish National) who gamely held on to finish just ahead of Anibale Fly (one of three runners treated afterwards for heat stress) who kept on well after being taken wide most of the way, a manoeuvre that led to his conceding plenty of ground to the other principals. It was a one, two, three, four for Irish stables with Milansbar, prominent for a long way, beaten a further twenty-one lengths into fifth, finishing lame but giving his rider Bryony Frost the distinction of achieving the best result by a British female jockey in the history of the race. Female jockeys attract plenty of media attention nowadays before a Grand National, the two others in the latest running being Irish amateur Katie Walsh who rode the last of the twelve finishers, the gambled-on Baie des Isles, and her compatriot Rachael Blackmore, the first female to win the conditional jump jockeys' title in Ireland, who crashed out on Alpha des Obeaux. Sixth-placed Road To Riches was never dangerous and, of the others, Aintree regulars Gas Line Boy and Vieux Lion Rouge finished seventh and ninth respectively, separated by the weakening Valseur Lido. The Welsh National winner Raz de Maree (eighth back in 2014) never landed a blow, coming tenth (treated for heat stress afterwards), with Seeyouatmidnight finishing lame and running better than his eleventh placing. Half of the twenty-six who failed to finish were pulled up when out of contention. All thirty-eight runners came back safely— for the sixth year in a row—though Saint Are had to be taken from the course by horse ambulance after his unfortunate exit at the Chair, and he was retired some days later. Charlie Deutsch eventually limped back to the weighing room and won a race at Plumpton the following day. Gavin Sheehan, the rider of Final Nudge, another who fell when short of room at the first Canal Turn, reportedly suffered a broken arm.

The fact that stamina was the biggest virtue for the runners in the 2018 Grand National was illustrated by the winner's time of 9m 40.10sec which was the slowest since Numbersixvalverde recorded 9m 41.00sec in the stamina-sapping renewal of 2006. The Grand National start was moved closer to the first fence in 2013, shortening the distance of the National which has made six to seven seconds difference—under normal conditions—to the overall time of the race. That would make Tiger Roll's time, when adjusted, the slowest since Red Marauder's year (2001) when he completed an infamous victory in barely raceable conditions—one of only two to complete without incident—in 11m 00.06sec.

The victory of Tiger Roll was the second in the Grand National for his owners Gigginstown House Stud who had another magnificent season, dominating the leading owners' table in Ireland (leading owner there for the fifth time in the last six seasons). All the Gigginstown horses are trained in Ireland and the maroon, white star and armlets is always well represented at the Cheltenham Festival where the colours were carried to a record-breaking seven victories (no owner had previously had more than five, which had been achieved twice by J. P. McManus and once by the Riccis). Gigginstown had won the Grand National two years earlier with Rule The World (ridden by David Mullins, rider of Pleasant Company) whose trainer Mouse Morris completed a National double for the same owners after a win in the Irish Grand National, as did Gordon Elliott, still only forty, in the latest season with another Gigginstown horse General Principle (who won narrowly from the Willie Mullins-trained Isleofhopendreams). Michael O'Leary, who took sixty Gigginstown horses away from Willie Mullins early in the 2016/17 season in a disagreement over training fees, took pleasure in the wider achievements of Ireland's two superpower stables, saying 'We're in a golden age in Ireland, keeping our best horses, but our luck may turn in a few years, so while we are winning we should enjoy it.' O'Leary praised Gordon Elliott for his handling of Tiger Roll. 'He's a master trainer, taking this horse from winning a test of speed in the Triumph Hurdle to victory in the Grand National four years later. The horse is a little rat of a thing and I didn't think he would handle those fences.' Elliott himself pulled no punches about Tiger Roll, saying 'He can be in great form one day, terrible form the next. He's allowed to be in bad form whenever he wants, though, because, when he's good, he's very very good!'

Keith Donoghue had ridden Tiger Roll in the Cross Country Chase at Cheltenham but he couldn't make the weight for the Grand National. The mount went to Davy Russell, who hadn't ridden Tiger Roll since he was a juvenile hurdler (he had won the Triumph on him as a late replacement for injured Bryan Cooper). Russell had been sacked three months before the Triumph by Michael O'Leary while having what became a notorious cup of tea at the races. At thirty-eight, Russell was the oldest jockey with a mount in the National and he was having his fourteenth ride in the race, never previously having won it (his best placing had been third on Saint Are the previous year). Apart from losing that job as first jockey for Gigginstown, from which, after a couple of tough years, he has rebounded and now rides regularly

The elbow—Tiger Roll looks to have the race in the bag having opened up a lead over Pleasant Company with the other survivors well held

The line—desperate stuff by now, though, as Pleasant Company (checks) just fails with a late rally; twelve complete the course

for the O'Learys again, Davy Russell has enjoyed a career with plenty of ups and downs. In the latest season, for example, as well as winning the National and being leading jockey at the Cheltenham Festival, in addition to being champion in Ireland for the third time, he found himself in the eye of a social media storm in early-September when TV coverage showed him punching one of his mounts in a race at Tramore in mid-August. The raceday stewards did not see the incident but an investigation subsequently took place and Russell was given only a caution, which inflamed some of his critics even further. The Irish Turf Club re-opened the case, seeming to bow to the backlash from public opinion, and Russell's punishment was increased to a four-day ban. What seemed a relatively minor transgression had been allowed to escalate out of all proportion: with the RSPCA—'If someone loses their temper, they must not take it out on the horse'—becoming involved as the case dragged on for three weeks, with attendant bad publicity for racing. Russell, by the way, denied that 'anger' was involved. 'It was a matter of trying to get back control and trying to get the mare to pay attention.'

By contrast, Davy Russell was feted as a hero after his victory on Tiger Roll, after which he made his trademark idiosyncratic double-handed wave to the crowd. Asked what the run-in had been like, he replied 'Long … very long. Tiger Roll has a reputation for being a bit of a monkey and it was early enough to send him on, for sure, but I needed to wake him up. I didn't really get stuck into him until after the elbow and just had enough to get home, though I did fear we'd been beaten.' Russell reflected on his childhood days when he would watch the National on TV and used to collect up the grass, while his father mowed the lawn, to make his own Aintree fences around the garden. 'I've won this race thousands of times but I've never won it quite like I have today! There would probably have been no consoling me if I'd lost.' Russell was riding at Tramore the day after the Grand National—he had a double—and wasn't at the homecoming parade held in Summerhill, County Meath, for Tiger Roll who was accompanied by Bless The Wings and the Irish Grand National winner General Principle.

The headlines in Britain's Sunday newspapers the day after the National were about a surprise allied missile strike on chemical weapons stockpiles in Syria. There was little room for anything else on the front pages which traditionally carry a Grand National story. The coverage in the inside news pages of the 'red tops' was largely of the television celebrities and footballers' wives who were at Aintree. The story of the National itself was confined to the sports pages where it was, without exception, the day's main story. A quarter of Britain's population have a bet on the Grand National which remains far and away the biggest attraction in British racing as the TV viewing figures illustrate every year. The National's figures dwarf those for any other race, the latest running attracting a peak audience of 8.5m viewers, a sixty per cent share of the total terrestrial audience watching at the time. ITV has a policy of not commenting on audience figures but the broadcaster has continued the practice of Channel 4 which in its final year (2016) calculated its Grand National audience using a five-minute peak. Before that, the figure had always been for a fifteen-minute peak, which has traditionally been quoted in *Chasers & Hurdlers*. The fifteen-minute peak figure is 'no longer available' and the figures quoted for the last three Nationals have been for the five-minute peak, which would always be higher. Using that measure, the last Grand National shown by Channel 4 attracted an audience of 10.1m, compared to the first two years of ITV's coverage which have yielded 8.2m and 8.5m respectively. The weather may have had some bearing on the figures. It rained on the day of Channel 4's final National and the weather round the country has been good on the day of both renewals since (viewing figures tend to be higher when the weather is poor). That said, Aintree's management had been hoping that audience figures would, by now, have hit at least 12m, given that ITV has a much greater audience base than Channel 4.

The last three Grand Nationals have been run at 5.15 (back by an hour), in a tea-time slot—described by ITV as the 'sweet spot'—intended to boost the TV audience, but it is a time that creates difficulties for early editions of the Sunday newspapers, not to mention making it a long day for the Aintree crowd (the National is now the second-last race). The on-course crowd was slightly larger than for the two preceding years, despite a clash with Liverpool's match against Bournemouth which kicked off at Anfield as Tiger Roll was on his way back to the winner's enclosure. The official attendances for the last three Nationals—63,648, 64,300 and 64,716—are, however, among the lowest this century (the highest peak in that time was reached in 2004, Amberleigh House's year, when a final audited figure of 71,293 was credited). Taken together, the size of the TV audience and the crowd figures probably reflect a gentle slide in the Grand National's popularity as the wider public begins to recognise that the National's unique character has been diluted by the changes made to the course. As has been said before in these pages, the modifications have made the Grand National more defensible in a changing society, but the race no longer produces quite the same number of thrilling and dramatic moments as it used to. That remark applies less to the latest edition than to some of the others since 2013. There were thrills and spills, and the famous run-in—untouched by the changes, as has been said—conjured up one of the most compelling conclusions to the Grand National in the modern era, one that deserves to take its place in the race's rich legacy and will be recalled for years to come.

Many different types have won the Grand National, from giants such as Moifaa, Troytown and Party Politics to small horses including those dual winners in the nineteenth century, Abd-el-Kader and The Lamb, and the likes of Battleship, Team Spirit and Amberleigh House, all of whom were around 15.2 hands. Size matters less in a Grand National candidate than whether the horse takes to the National fences. Amberleigh House, for example, made eleven appearances over the fences—five Grand Nationals, five Becher Chases and a Topham—and he got round each time, except for being put out of the race at the first Canal Turn in the 2001 National and being pulled up on his last appearance in the big race as a fourteen-year-old. The lengthy, leggy Tiger Roll hasn't grown since his early days as a hurdler and is only 15.3 hands and, with his rather low jumping technique, it is easy to see why his owner might have had doubts about his being a Grand National type (though he has never fallen). He wasn't bred for jumping either, having been purchased by John Ferguson on behalf of Sheikh Mohammed for 70,000 guineas as a foal at the December Sales, He never went into training for Darley and was discarded and bought by Nigel Hawke as an unraced three-year-old at Doncaster Sales for only

TIG

£10,000. Gigginstown acquired Tiger Roll for £80,000 at the Cheltenham Sales that December after he had made a winning debut for Hawke in a juvenile hurdle at Market Rasen. After moving to Gordon Elliott, he won the Triumph Hurdle on his second start for the yard.

```
                                ┌ Authorized (IRE)   ┌ Montjeu         ┌ Sadler's Wells
                                │ (b 2004)           │ (b 1996)        └ Floripedes
                                │                    └ Funsie          ┌ Saumarez
Tiger Roll (IRE)  ┤                                    (b 1999)        └ Vallee Dansante
  (b.g. 2010)                   │                    ┌ Entrepreneur    ┌ Sadler's Wells
                                │ Swiss Roll (IRE)   │ (b 1994)        └ Exclusive Order
                                └ (b 2000)           └ On Air          ┌ Chief Singer
                                                       (b 1988)        └ Green Light
```

It hadn't been the intention to breed a Triumph Hurdle winner, let alone a Grand National winner, when the fairly useful Flat mare Swiss Roll was sent to the Derby winner Authorized. Swiss Roll, a sister to the National Stakes runner-up Berenson and a half-sister to Pollen (by Orpen) who won the Park Express Stakes at the Curragh, showed her form at up to two miles (second in the Vintage Crop Stakes) and was one of four winners produced by the mile and a quarter winner On Air. On Air stayed a mile and a half and she supplemented her three wins on the Flat with a win in a Haydock novice hurdle and a fourth in graded company in the Kennel Gate Castle Novices' Hurdle at Ascot. On Air's winners also include the Flat winner turned useful hurdler/chaser Khachaturian who was ungenuine and had a Timeform squiggle. Swiss Roll has already matched On Air's four winners, also producing the Godolphin-owned Lonsdale Cup winner and Irish St Leger and Goodwood Cup runner-up Ahzeemah (by Dubawi) who is much the best of the three others. Swiss Roll's three-year-old Austrian School (by Teofilo) is a smart staying handicapper for Mark Johnston.

Swiss Roll and Authorized have the same grandsire, the phenomenal Sadler's Wells whose record-breaking achievements on the Flat have tended to overshadow his significant influence on jumping. Four of the top six sires of jumpers in Britain and Ireland in the latest season are sons of Sadler's Wells who was responsible for eleven of the top twenty-five in all in the *Racing Post* table (three of the fourteen others are grandsons of Sadler's Wells, those being Authorized and Scorpion, the sire of the King George winner Might Bite, both by Montjeu, and Mahler a son of Galileo). Tiger Roll, incidentally, is the first Grand National winner to be sired by an Epsom Derby winner since the 1884 winner Voluptuary (by Cremorne) who had run in the 1881 Derby and won the Grand National on his first start over fences. The sisters Emblem and Emblematic, who won in 1863 and 1864, were sired by the Derby winner Teddington. Much more recently, the Irish Derby and Prix du Jockey Club winner Old Vic sired two Grand National winners, Comply Or Die and Don't Push It. Tiger Roll stays four and a quarter miles and acts on good to firm and heavy going. He is usually in headgear (wore cheekpieces at Aintree) and races in a tongue tie. *Gordon Elliott, Ireland*

TIGER SKY (IRE) 5 br.m. Milan – Standfast (IRE) (Supreme Leader) [2017/18 b14d Dec 20] £16,000 3-y-o: sister to useful hurdler/chaser Ceasar Milan (19f winner, stayed 3m): dam (h91), maiden on Flat/over hurdles, half-sister to fairly useful hurdler/chaser (stayed 2½m) Native Endurance: 20/1, ninth in bumper at Ludlow (18¼ lengths behind Harambe). *Harry Fry*   b–

TIGER TIME (IRE) 4 b.g. Scorpion (IRE) – Summertime Girl (IRE) (Glacial Storm (USA)) [2017/18 b16v⁶ ab16.3g Apr 15] down the field in bumpers. *Philip Kirby*   b–

TIGER TREK (IRE) 9 b.g. Tiger Hill (IRE) – Zayana (IRE) (Darshaan) [2017/18 c118, h114: c16.2g⁴ c15.7g² c16.5g³ c16g⁴ Jun 22] winning chaser: fairly useful maiden chaser: stays 2½m, usually raced over shorter: acts on good to soft going: in headgear last 4 starts: often let down by jumping. *Dr Richard Newland*   c114 x   h–

TIGER TWENTY TWO 7 b.g. Authorized (IRE) – Collette's Choice (Royal Applause) [2017/18 h95§: h20.6v⁵ Apr 11] modest maiden hurdler: stays 19f: acts on good to firm temperamental. *Brian Rothwell*   h85 §

TIGGER TWO (IRE) 6 b.g. Getaway (GER) – Anne Hathaway (IRE) (Definite Article) [2017/18 b16s b17.7d h16.8v Jan 1] poor form in bumpers: tailed off in novice on hurdling debut. *David Pipe*   h–   b68

Guinness Galway Hurdle Handicap, Galway—
a first win in the race for Barry Geraghty as Tigris River (hoops) finds plenty on the run-in to deprive the blinkered Swamp Fox; the mare Airlie Beach (star) takes third

TIGRIS RIVER (IRE) 7 b.g. Montjeu (IRE) – Hula Angel (USA) (Woodman (USA)) **h144**
[2017/18 h137: h17g h20g* h16d* h16.4s h16s h20v⁶ h16s h16.8vᵖᵘ h16s h16.5d⁶ Apr 24] compact gelding: useful hurdler: won minor event at Bellewstown in July and Galway Hurdle (by neck from Swamp Fox) in August: stays 2½m: acts on heavy going: tried in cheekpieces: wears tongue tie. *Joseph Patrick O'Brien, Ireland*

TIKANITE (IRE) 7 b.g. Tikkanen (USA) – Scented Night (IRE) (Mandalus) [2017/18 **b85** b83: b16g³ Jun 3] fair form in bumpers. *Shaun Lycett*

TIKKANBAR (IRE) 7 b.g. Tikkanen (USA) – Fields of Barley (IRE) (Zaffaran (USA)) **h137 x**
[2017/18 b104: h20.5s* h20.3s* h20.3v⁶ h24.7s Apr 14] tall gelding: bumper winner: useful form over hurdles: won novice at Plumpton in November and listed novice at Cheltenham (by 1¼ lengths from Ainchea) in January: bred to stay 3m: tried in hood: often leads, travels strongly: not a fluent jumper. *Neil Mulholland*

TIKKANDEMICKEY (IRE) 12 gr.g. Tikkanen (USA) – Miss Vikki (IRE) (Needle **c100** Gun (IRE)) [2017/18 c111, h–: c20.1s⁵ c20v⁵ c20d⁴ c20s³ c21.6v Apr 16] winning hurdler: **h–** fair handicap chaser: stays 3m: acts on heavy going: usually wears headgear. *Raymond Shiels*

TIKKEN AWAY (IRE) 7 gr.g. Tikkanen (USA) – Lady Goldilocks (IRE) (Mister Lord **c–**
(USA)) [2017/18 h15.3g h16.5g⁶ h19.2v h16.3s⁶ h16s⁵ c20.5mᵖᵘ Apr 26] €11,000 3-y-o: **h102** fourth foal: half-brother to useful hurdler Sir Scorpion (2m-2½m winner, by Scorpion): dam unraced: fair maiden hurdler: pulled up in novice handicap on chasing debut: should stay beyond 2m: acts on soft going. *Robert Walford*

TIKKINTHEBOX (IRE) 6 b.g. Tikkanen (USA) – Surfing France (FR) (Art Francais **c102**
(USA)) [2017/18 h102, b–: h19.8sᵖᵘ c16gᶠ c20g⁶ c16.1v³ c18.2sᵖᵘ c18.2m* Apr 25] **h–** maiden hurdler: fair form over fences: won novice handicap at Taunton in April: stays 2¼m: acts on soft and good to firm going: has worn hood, including in 2017/18: wears tongue tie. *Jeremy Scott*

TIK

TIKK TOCK BOOM (IRE) 6 gr.m. Tikkanen (USA) – Henrietta (IRE) (Hushang (IRE)) [2017/18 b16.8v h21v⁴ h20.7d^ur h23.1d Apr 21] £20,000 5-y-o: second foal: dam (c88/h102), 2m-21f hurdle winner/winning pointer, half-sister to smart chasers (stayed 3¼m) An Accordion and Horus: Irish point winner: well beaten in bumper: modest form over hurdles: best effort when fourth in mares novice at Warwick in December: should still improve. *Ian Williams* **h96 p / b–**

TILDAS ICON (IRE) 4 b.f. Sixties Icon – I Tilda (IRE) (Kris Kin (USA)) [2017/18 h16v³ h16v⁶ h16v^ur h16v³ h20.1d⁵ Apr 23] fair maiden on Flat, stays 13f: modest form over hurdles: left Thomas Mullins after fourth start: raced mainly at 2m: acts on heavy going: tried in hood. *Patrick Griffin, Ireland* **h89**

TILLYTHETANK (IRE) 5 b.m. Stowaway – All Heart (Alhaarth (IRE)) [2017/18 h18.5s⁶ Nov 15] €18,000 3-y-o, £30,000 4-y-o: second foal: dam (c102/h113), 2m hurdle/chase winner (stayed 2½m), also 2m winner on Flat: placed both starts in Irish points: 8/1, sixth in mares novice at Exeter (20¾ lengths behind Waiheke) on hurdling debut: likely to improve. *Alan King* **h80 p**

TIME AND AGAIN (FR) 8 b.g. Sassanian (USA) – Petillante Royale (FR) (Vertical Speed (FR)) [2017/18 c97x, h79: h22g⁶ c20g h21.7d⁵ h19.9v h19.6d⁶ Apr 21] sturdy gelding: poor maiden hurdler nowadays: maiden chaser, well held sole outing over fences in 2017/18: best up to 2¼m: acts on soft going: often in hood: has worn tongue tie, including final start. *Tim Vaughan* **c– / h80**

TIME FOR ANOTHER (IRE) 5 ch.g. Shantou (USA) – Borleagh Blonde (IRE) (Zaffaran (USA)) [2017/18 b15.8s³ Mar 14] €78,000 3-y-o: fourth foal: half-brother to fair hurdler What A Jewel (21f winner) and a winning pointer (both by Presenting): dam (h85), lightly-raced maiden hurdler, half-sister to dams of very smart hurdler/smart chaser around 2m Brain Power and very smart staying chaser Vics Canvas: 5/1, third in bumper at Huntingdon (3¼ lengths behind That's A Given). *Kim Bailey* **b95**

TIMEFORASPIN 4 b.g. Librettist (USA) – Timeforagin (Pasternak) [2017/18 b16v⁶ Apr 14] 20/1, sixth in bumper at Chepstow (21¼ lengths behind Garrettstown). *Brian Eckley* **b75**

TIMEFORBEN (IRE) 6 ch.m. Beneficial – Shokalocka Baby (IRE) (Accordion) [2017/18 b16.8g³ h18.5s³ h15.7g h16.8v⁶ h21.4s h24.6s* Apr 9] £28,000 4-y-o: second foal: sister to a winning pointer: dam, winning pointer, half-sister to fairly useful hurdler/fair chaser (stayed 3¼m) Mr Supreme (by Beneficial): Irish point winner: third in bumper at Newton Abbot (8¾ lengths behind Crooks Peak): fair form over hurdles: won mares handicap at Kempton in April: stays 25f: acts on soft going: tried in cheekpieces/tongue tie. *David Pipe* **h106 / b82**

TIME FOR CHAMPERS (IRE) 8 b.m. Robin des Champs (FR) – Someone Told Me (IRE) (Saddlers' Hall (IRE)) [2017/18 h62: h15.7g² May 22] poor maiden hurdler: wears hood: has worn tongue tie. *Nikki Evans* **h76**

TIMEFORWEST (IRE) 6 b.m. Westerner – Shang A Lang (IRE) (Commander Collins (IRE)) [2017/18 h118, b–: c20f⁶ c24.2s⁵ c20.8s^bd c23s c22.5v⁶ c20v* c22.2v Mar 31] sturdy mare: winning hurdler: fairly useful handicap chaser: won at Warwick in March: stays 3m: acts on good to firm and heavy going: usually races towards rear. *Jonjo O'Neill* **c120 / h–**

TIME IS MONEY 9 b.m. Presenting – No More Money (Alflora (IRE)) [2017/18 h99: h25m May 23] modest hurdler, well beaten sole outing in 2017/18: stays 2½m: best form on good going. *Emma Lavelle* **h–**

TIMELY GIFT (IRE) 5 b.g. Presenting – Give It Time (Kayf Tara) [2017/18 h64: h16.3s h15.8v* h18.5v^pu Dec 8] poor form over hurdles: won handicap at Ffos Las (conditional) in November: unproven beyond 2m: acts on heavy going: usually races towards rear. *Tim Vaughan* **h84**

TIMESAWAITING (IRE) 5 b.g. Arakan (USA) – Princess Nicole (IRE) (Alhaarth (IRE)) [2017/18 b15.6s⁶ Feb 4] runner-up in Irish point: in tongue strap, 25/1, sixth in bumper at Musselburgh (12¼ lengths behind Seddon). *Lucinda Russell* **b83**

TIMETOBENEFIT (IRE) 7 b.m. Beneficial – Shokalocka Baby (IRE) (Accordion) [2017/18 h68, b–: h15.8g h15.8d h16.6s h21s⁶ Apr 9] Irish point winner: modest form over hurdles: stays 21f: acts on soft going: usually races towards rear. *Richard Phillips* **h86**

TIME TO MOVE ON (IRE) 5 ch.g. Flemensfirth (USA) – Kapricia Speed (FR) (Vertical Speed (FR)) [2017/18 b16.8v* b16.8v* Feb 11] £52,000 3-y-o: brother to fairly useful hurdler/winning pointer Cadeyrn (2¾m/23f winner) and half-brother to 3 winners, including smart hurdler/chaser Barney Dwan (17f-3m winner, by Vinnie Roe): dam (c88/h104), French maiden hurdler/chaser, half-sister to high-class hurdler/smart chaser (stayed **b107 p**

TIR

2½m) Geos and useful French hurdler/chaser (15f-2¼m winner) Kapgarde: useful form in bumpers: won at Exeter in December (by 10 lengths from Caribert) and February (by 3¼ lengths from Bang On): exciting prospect. *Fergal O'Brien*

TIMIYAN (USA) 7 b.g. Ghostzapper (USA) – Timarwa (IRE) (Daylami (IRE)) [2017/18 h16.4d* h16.7g* h16d h17g⁴ h16v c20v^{pu} c20v⁵ c17.5s⁵ c17v⁶ c16d^F Apr 26] smart on Flat, stays 1½m: useful handicap hurdler: won maiden at Listowel in 2016/17: also won at Roscommon in June and Bellewstown (by 2¼ lengths from Top Othe Ra) in July: well below that level over fences: unproven beyond 17f: acts on heavy going: wears tongue tie. *Gordon Elliott, Ireland*   **c94 h136**

TIMON'S TARA 9 gr.m. Kayf Tara – Princess Timon (Terimon) [2017/18 c112, h–: c24g^{pu} c22.5d² c24.2s^{pu} c20v⁴ c20v² c25.2d³ c22.7v⁴ c25.2v⁶ Mar 10] well-made mare: winning hurdler: fair handicap chaser: stays 3m: acts on heavy going: wears headgear: front runner/races prominently. *Robin Dickin*   **c107 h–**

TINDARO (FR) 11 gr.g. Kingsalsa (USA) – Star's Mixa (FR) (Linamix (FR)) [2017/18 c127, h–: c19.4g⁴ h15.8d h23.8s Jan 10] tall gelding: fairly useful hurdler/useful chaser at best, little impact in 2017/18: stays 21f: acts on good to firm and good to soft going: has worn headgear, including in 2017/18: wears tongue tie. *Paul Webber*   **c101 h–**

TINKERS HILL TOMMY (IRE) 7 b.g. King's Theatre (IRE) – Satco Street (IRE) (Satco (FR)) [2017/18 c108, h–: c27.5d² c23.6s² c19.2v³ c23.6s* Apr 27] multiple point winner: once-raced hurdler: fairly useful form in hunter chases: won novice event at Chepstow in April: stays 3½m: acts on soft and good to firm going: in tongue tie last 4 starts: usually travels strongly. *Mrs Bridget Lewis*   **c120 h–**

TINKER TIME (IRE) 10 b.g. Turtle Island (IRE) – Gypsys Girl (IRE) (Husyan (USA)) [2017/18 c128, h–: c25.8g⁴ c23.8g⁶ c23g^{pu} Jun 28] workmanlike gelding: winning hurdler: fairly useful handicap chaser: stays 3½m: acts on heavy going: tried in cheekpieces: temperamental. *Bob Buckler*   **c118 § h–**

TIN POT MAN (IRE) 12 br.g. Tillerman – White-Wash (Final Straw) [2017/18 c80, h–: c32.5d May 5] multiple point winner: winning hurdler: one-time fair chaser, lightly raced under Rules nowadays: stays easy 3m: acts on any going: has worn headgear, including sole outing in 2017/18: wears tongue tie. *G. Hiscock*   **c84 h–**

TINSELTOWN GIRL 6 b.m. Josr Algarhoud (IRE) – Festive Chimes (IRE) (Efisio) [2017/18 b16m b15.7g h15.7g h24g^{pu} Oct 26] second foal: dam (h124) ungenuine 2m-2½m hurdle winner: no form in bumpers/over hurdles: tried in cheekpieces. *Clare Hobson*   **h– b–**

TIN SOLDIER (FR) 7 b.g. Soldier of Fortune (IRE) – Everlast (IRE) (Anabaa (USA)) [2017/18 h143: c20v^F Nov 25] sturdy gelding: useful hurdler: still finding when fell 2 out in maiden won by Dounikos at Gowran on chasing debut, looking sure to be placed: stays 3m: acts on heavy going: has worn headgear: remains with potential as a chaser. *W. P. Mullins, Ireland*   **c135 p h–**

TINTED ROSE 6 ch.m. Black Sam Bellamy (IRE) – Miniature Rose (Anshan) [2017/18 h104, b87: h18.5d Oct 12] bumper winner: fair maiden hurdler, excuses sole outing in 2017/18: stays 21f: acts on soft going. *Charlie Longsdon*   **h64**

TINTERN THEATRE (IRE) 7 b.g. King's Theatre (IRE) – Rith Ar Aghaidh (IRE) (Phardante (FR)) [2017/18 h125: c19.4d² c19.8g^f c25d⁴ c25.3s^{ur} c24s* c25.6v^{ur} c24g c26s c25.3g Apr 18] sturdy gelding: winning hurdler: useful handicap chaser: won at Kempton in December: stays 25f: acts on heavy going. *Nigel Twiston-Davies*   **c139 h–**

TINY DANCER (IRE) 10 b.g. Darsi (FR) – Taipans Girl (IRE) (Taipan (IRE)) [2017/18 c–, c–, h–: c20.1g⁶ Jun 3] workmanlike gelding: maiden hurdler: fair chaser at best, behind sole outing in 2017/18: stays 25f: acts on heavy going: has worn visor. *Chris Grant*   **c– h–**

TIQUER (FR) 10 b.g. Equerry (USA) – Tirenna (FR) (Sleeping Car (FR)) [2017/18 c121, h–: c19.9s c19.9s* c20.1s⁴ Apr 26] maiden hurdler: fairly useful handicap chaser: won at Newbury in March: stays 2½m: acts on heavy going: tried in cheekpieces. *Alan Jones*   **c128 h–**

TIRADIA (FR) 11 b.g. Without Connexion (IRE) – Jimanji (FR) (Kadalko (FR)) [2017/18 h91: h15.8m⁴ h15.8g h16.7g³ h18.6g* h19.6g^{pu} Oct 5] sturdy gelding: modest handicap hurdler: won at Market Rasen in August: stayed 2½m: acted on soft and good to firm going: in cheekpieces last 3 starts: usually raced towards rear: dead. *J. R. Jenkins*   **h89**

TIR DUBH (IRE) 9 br.m. Sandmason – Turbine Hill (IRE) (Hubbly Bubbly (USA)) [2017/18 h94: h23.9s⁵ h23.9m⁴ Apr 25] modest handicap hurdler: stays 23f: acts on good to soft going: wears cheekpieces. *Robert Stephens*   **h82**

TIS

TISFREETDREAM (IRE) 17 b.g. Oscar (IRE) – Gayley Gale (IRE) (Strong Gale) [2017/18 c–, h66§: h22g⁴ May 8] small gelding: poor handicap hurdler: winning chaser: stays 25f: acts on good to firm and heavy going: wears headgear: has worn tongue tie: ungenuine. *Peter Pritchard*   c–
h– §

TIS WHAT IT IS (IRE) 5 b.g. Gold Well – Justines Joy (IRE) (Taipan (IRE)) [2017/18 b15.8d³ b16g⁴ h19g⁶ h16.5g h16.7v h15.8d h23.8sᵖᵘ h23.1dᵖᵘ Apr 24] modest form in bumpers: no form over hurdles: in headgear last 2 starts. *David Pipe*   h–
b77

TITAN 4 b.g. Lawman (FR) – Dragonera (Doyen (IRE)) [2017/18 h15.8gᵖᵘ h16.3s h16v² h16.8v⁵ h16.2s⁴ Mar 27] rather leggy gelding: fair maiden on Flat, stayed 1¼m: poor form over hurdles: tried in blinkers: in tongue tie last 4 starts: usually raced close up: dead. *Oliver Greenall*   h81

TITIAN BOY (IRE) 9 ch.g. Spadoun (FR) – Leodotcom (IRE) (Safety Catch (USA)) [2017/18 c101, h–: c21.5v c16.5v⁴ c20.1v⁴ c16.3v⁴ Apr 14] maiden hurdler: modest handicap chaser: stays 2½m: raced only on soft/heavy going: usually in tongue tie. *N. W. Alexander*   c93
h–

TITUS BOLT (IRE) 9 b.g. Titus Livius (FR) – Megan's Bay (Muhtarram (USA)) [2017/18 h15.6g⁵ h19.4d h15.6s h15.6d⁶ h16.4d⁵ Mar 16] fair handicap hurdler, below form in 2017/18: stays 2½m: acts on heavy going: tried in visor: often races towards rear. *Jim Goldie*   h94

TJONGEJONGE (FR) 7 b.g. Blue Bresil (FR) – Vavea (FR) (Saint des Saints (FR)) [2017/18 c125, h93: c23.9g⁵ May 12] sturdy gelding: winning hurdler: fairly useful chaser, behind sole outing in 2017/18: stays 3m: acts on good to firm going: tried in cheekpieces: often let down by jumping. *Charlie Longsdon*   c– x
h–

TOARMANDOWITHLOVE (IRE) 10 ch.m. Choisir (AUS) – Deadly Buzz (IRE) (Darshaan) [2017/18 h80: h17.2d² h18.6g⁴ h20.1v⁵ h19.3d⁴ h15.6s⁴ h19.3d* h15.6d Feb 14] poor handicap hurdler: won at Catterick (conditional) in February: stays 25f: acts on heavy going: has worn blinkers, including last 2 starts: wears tongue tie. *Susan Corbett*   h78

TOBACCO ROAD (IRE) 8 b.g. Westerner – Virginias Best (King's Best (USA)) [2017/18 h100: h16.5g* h16.5s⁶ h16s h16.5s⁴ Mar 26] fair handicap hurdler: won at Taunton in November: raced mainly around 2m: best form on good going: usually in headgear: in tongue tie last 4 starts: often races freely. *David Pipe*   h100

TOBEFAIR 8 b.g. Central Park (IRE) – Nan (Buckley) [2017/18 h137: c20.9s⁴ h24.2d h25s³ Jan 13] sturdy gelding: useful handicap hurdler: third at Warwick (2½ lengths behind Black Ivory) in January: fourth in maiden at Ffos Las (31 lengths behind West Approach) on chasing debut: stays 3¼m: acts on soft and good to firm going: has worn cheekpieces, including in 2017/18. *Debra Hamer*   c110
h134

TOBERDOWNEY (IRE) 6 br.m. Stowaway – Velsheda (IRE) (Royal Vulcan) [2017/18 h114, b90: h23.3d⁴ h21.7vᵖᵘ Dec 26] bumper winner: fair handicap hurdler: stays 23f: acts on soft going. *Oliver Sherwood*   h109

TOBOGGAN'S FIRE 5 b.m. Firebreak – Toboggan Lady (Tobougg (IRE)) [2017/18 h15.6s* h16.4s⁴ Feb 24] fairly useful on Flat, stays 8.5f: fair form over hurdles: won mares novice at Musselburgh in January: will prove best at sharp 2m. *Donald McCain*   h106

TOBOGGAN'S GIFT 6 b.m. Major Cadeaux – Toboggan Lady (Tobougg (IRE)) [2017/18 h88: h16.8vᵖᵘ Jan 28] lengthy mare: maiden hurdler: modest form at best: tried in cheekpieces. *Donald McCain*   h–

TOBY LERONE (IRE) 11 b.g. Old Vic – Dawn's Double (IRE) (King's Ride) [2017/18 c128, h–: c20.9sᵖᵘ c23.9sᵖᵘ Feb 6] rangy gelding: winning hurdler: useful chaser at best, no form in 2017/18: stays 3m: acts on heavy going: has worn headgear: usually races close up: temperamental. *Dan Skelton*   c– §
h–

TODAY PLEASE (IRE) 8 b.g. Westerner – Casiana (GER) (Acatenango (GER)) [2017/18 c114, h111: c16.5m² c15.2d h15.5d h15.7s⁵ c15.7v² c16dᵖᵘ Apr 24] fair handicap hurdler, below form in 2017/18: fairly useful form over fences: raced around 2m nowadays: acts on good to firm and heavy going: has worn tongue tie: often races prominently. *Henry Oliver*   c117
h88

TOE TO TOE (IRE) 10 br.g. Presenting – Tavildara (IRE) (Kahyasi) [2017/18 c64, h–: h23.1g³ c20g⁴ c16.5g² c15.7d h23g⁶ Oct 17] poor handicap hurdler/maiden chaser: stays 23f: best form on good going: has worn headgear/tongue tie: usually races towards rear: unreliable. *Debra Hamer*   c75 §
h72 §

TOGETHERNESS (IRE) 5 b.g. Pour Moi (IRE) – Madeira Mist (IRE) (Grand Lodge (USA)) [2017/18 h16v h16.3s h16.3s h16.5m Apr 25] sturdy gelding: fairly useful maiden on Flat, stays 1¾m: poor form over hurdles. *Patrick Chamings*   h77

TOKARAMORE 6 b.m. Sulamani (IRE) – More Likely (Shambo) [2017/18 b95: h20.6g⁵ h15.6s³ h19.4s³ h19.9v^pu Mar 13] small mare: bumper winner: modest form over hurdles: should be suited by 2½m+: wears hood. *Iain Jardine* — **h98**

TOLEDO GOLD (IRE) 12 ch.g. Needwood Blade – Eman's Joy (Lion Cavern (USA)) [2017/18 c100, h73: c16.4g⁵ c16g⁵ c15.6g^pu Aug 21] medium-sized gelding: winning hurdler: fairly useful chaser at best, no form in 2017/18: has worn headgear: wears tongue tie: usually leads. *Maurice Barnes* — **c– h–**

TOMAHAWK WOOD 9 ch.g. Courteous – Meda's Song (Master Willie) [2017/18 c–, h93: h16.2v^pu h16.8s h20.5v³ h20.6v³ Apr 14] modest handicap hurdler: maiden chaser: stays 2¾m: best form on soft/heavy going: tried in tongue tie. *Donald Whillans* — **c– h87**

TOM BARTON 8 b.g. Lucky Story (USA) – Chiddingfold Chick (Zaffaran (USA)) [2017/18 c20.5m^ur Apr 26] multiple point winner: behind when unseated 4 out in hunter at Kempton on chasing debut: tried in cheekpieces. *Mrs S. Alner* — **c–**

TOMBSTONE (IRE) 8 ch.g. Robin des Champs (FR) – Connaught Hall (IRE) (Un Desperado (FR)) [2017/18 h148: c16d² c19.5s* c16.2s² c17s* c19.5v² c21s⁶ c18s³ c20v⁶ c24v² c21s⁶ Apr 27] strong gelding: smart hurdler: smart chaser: won maiden at Down Royal in November and Grade 3 novice at Navan (by 3¾ lengths from Jett) in December: also second in Craddockstown Novices' Chase at Punchestown, Grade 2 novice at Limerick and Grade 3 novice at Limerick (8 lengths behind Kemboy): stays 3m: acts on heavy going: tried in hood: in tongue tie last 2 starts. *Gordon Elliott, Ireland* — **c147 h–**

TOMKEVI (FR) 7 b.g. Khalkevi (IRE) – Tamsna (FR) (Smadoun (FR)) [2017/18 c118, h111: c24.2g* h19.9g⁵ c26.2d c25.2d^ur h22.8v⁵ h22.8v⁵ h25.3d³ h24v* h19.3d⁵ Mar 25] fairly useful handicap hurdler: won at Southwell in March: fairly useful handicap chaser: won at Hexham in May: stays 3m: acts on heavy going: wears headgear: has worn tongue tie, including last 3 starts: often let down by jumping over fences. *Rebecca Menzies* — **c122 x h115**

TOMMY HALLINAN (IRE) 4 b.g. Intense Focus (USA) – Bowstring (IRE) (Sadler's Wells (USA)) [2017/18 h16s^pu Dec 8] sturdy gelding: fairly useful on Flat, stays 1¼m: in tongue strap, pulled up in juvenile on hurdling debut. *Paul Nicholls* — **h–**

TOMMY O'DWYER (IRE) 9 b.g. Milan – Always Present (IRE) (Presenting) [2017/18 c88, h80: c24.2g c24.2g⁶ c24.2g³ c25.5g⁵ Jun 30] multiple point winner: maiden hurdler: poor maiden chaser: stays 3m: acts on good to soft going: often wears cheekpieces: temperamental. *Neil Mechie* — **c79 § h–**

TOMMY RAPPER (IRE) 7 b.g. Milan – Supreme Evening (IRE) (Supreme Leader) [2017/18 h137: h19.5d h21s² h20.8s* h21s* h22.8v* h20.3v Mar 16] useful-looking gelding: useful hurdler: won maiden at Doncaster in January, and novice at Towcester and handicap at Haydock (by neck from Theo's Charm) in February: should stay 3m: acts on heavy going: in tongue tie last 5 starts: often races towards rear/travels strongly. *Dan Skelton* — **h132**

TOMMY SILVER (FR) 6 b.g. Silver Cross (FR) – Sainte Mante (FR) (Saint des Saints (FR)) [2017/18 h143: c16.5s² c15.9m* c17.4s² c16s¹ ab18d² c15.8s^pu c16.2g³ Apr 26] tall, good-topped gelding: useful hurdler: similar form over fences: won maiden at Leicester in November: third in Wayward Lad Novices' Chase at Kempton (7½ lengths behind Cyrname) in December: raced mainly around 2m: acts on soft and good to firm going: wears tongue tie: usually races close up. *Paul Nicholls* — **c141 h–**

TOMMY THE RASCAL 8 b.g. Multiplex – Tina Gee (Orchestra) [2017/18 c83, h68: c21.2m⁵ c24d⁵ c25.5s⁵ c21.2s³ c23.6s³ c23.9s^F h25d Mar 26] sturdy gelding: winning hurdler: poor maiden chaser: stays 25f: acts on soft going: wears headgear: front runner/races prominently: temperamental. *Jennie Candlish* — **c71 § h–**

TOM NEARY (IRE) 11 b.g. Atraf – La Fandango (IRE) (Taufan (USA)) [2017/18 c111, h–: c24.5g⁴ May 15] lightly-raced hurdler: fair handicap chaser, behind sole outing in 2017/18: barely stays 3m: acts on good to firm going: wears tongue tie. *Robert Walford* — **c61 h–**

TOMNGERRY (IRE) 8 b.g. Craigsteel – Lady Vic (IRE) (Old Vic) [2017/18 h20d² c25.2d^F c21.4v⁴ h19.3v⁴ ab16g⁴ h21.4g^ur Apr 21] useful-looking gelding: won jumpers bumper at Southwell in March: useful hurdler: second in handicap at Carlisle (¾ length behind Desert Cry) in November: last of 4 in graduation event on completed start over fences: should stay 3m: acts on heavy going: often races prominently: should improve as a chaser.. *Brian Ellison* — **c108 p h132**

TOMOROZ MAN (IRE) 6 b.g. Morozov (USA) – Outdoor Heather (IRE) (Presenting) [2017/18 c23.6s^pu Apr 27] placed in points: in blinkers/tongue tie, pulled up in novice hunter on chasing debut. *Paul Morgan* — **c–**

TOM

TOMORROW'S LEGEND 8 b.g. Midnight Legend – Colvada (North Col) [2017/18 c17.1g⁶ c15.7d² c19.9s⁶ Jan 19] good-topped gelding: maiden hurdler: fair handicap chaser: stays 2½m: acts on heavy going. *Patrick Holmes*   c109 h–

TONGANUI (IRE) 7 ch.g. Stowaway – Murrosie (IRE) (Anshan) [2017/18 h94: h16.8g May 10] modest maiden hurdler, below form sole outing in 2017/18: stays 2¼m: acts on soft going: in cheekpieces last 2 starts: tried in tongue tie. *Harry Fry*   h81

TONTO'S SPIRIT 6 b.g. Authorized (IRE) – Desert Royalty (IRE) (Alhaarth (IRE)) [2017/18 h123: h17.2g h16s³ h19.9s³ h16.8v⁴ h19.3d² Mar 25] fairly useful handicap hurdler: stays 19f: acts on good to firm and heavy going: in hood last 5 starts: front runner/races prominently. *Kenneth Slack*   h119

TONY STAR (FR) 11 b.g. Lone Bid (FR) – Effet de Star (FR) (Grand Tresor (FR)) [2017/18 c117, h118: h21.9g⁴ Jun 1] sturdy gelding: point winner: fair handicap hurdler, below form sole outing in 2017/18: fairly useful chaser: best at 3m+ nowadays: acts on heavy going: has worn cheekpieces: tried in tongue tie. *Peter Bowen*   c– h86

TOOLA BOOLA 8 b.m. Tobougg (IRE) – Forsythia (Most Welcome) [2017/18 h75: c17.1g⁶ Nov 11] smallish mare: poor hurdler: 25/1, sixth in novice handicap at Kelso on chasing debut: unproven beyond 17f: best form on soft/heavy going: tried in visor: temperament under suspicion. *Jedd O'Keeffe*   c54 h–

TOO LATE TO SELL (IRE) 12 b.g. Oscar (IRE) – Native Monk (IRE) (Be My Native (USA)) [2017/18 c25.8s⁵ Apr 23] modest point winner: maiden hurdler: fair chaser at best, well held sole outing under Rules in 2017/18: stays 3¾m: acts on good to firm and heavy going: tried in cheekpieces. *Mrs E. Scott*   c– h–

TOO MANY CHIEFS (IRE) 7 br.g. Indian River (FR) – Wahiba Hall (IRE) (Saddlers' Hall (IRE)) [2017/18 c–, h101: h23.3s h22.7g² h24.3v* h24.6s⁴ h24.3v* h24.3v* h25s Apr 8] fairly useful handicap hurdler: won at Ayr in November and twice there in January: twice-raced chaser: stays 3m: acts on heavy going: tried in cheekpieces: front runner/races prominently. *Sharon Watt*   c– h119

TOO MANY DIAMONDS (IRE) 7 br.g. Diamond Green (FR) – Too Much Color (USA) (Spectrum (IRE)) [2017/18 h61: h15.9g⁴ h16.8g⁴ h19.6s* h16.2g² h16g³ h16.8d c19.4g² h15.9m⁴ Sep 24] modest handicap hurdler: completed 4-timer at Plumpton, Sedgefield, Bangor and Market Rasen, all in May: 12/1, second in novice at Stratford (23 lengths behind Western Miller) on chasing debut: stays 2½m: acts on soft going: has worn cheekpieces/tongue tie: often travels strongly. *Dan Skelton*   c102 h97

TOOSEY 7 b.g. Lucarno (USA) – Quiz Night (Kayf Tara) [2017/18 h16.7s⁶ h16.6d⁵ h19.7s⁵ h21s^pu Feb 9] point winner: modest form over hurdles: should stay at least 2½m: in tongue tie last 4 starts. *Tom Symonds*   h96

TOP BILLING 9 br.g. Monsun (GER) – La Gandilie (FR) (Highest Honor (FR)) [2017/18 c–, h108§: h24.4s h25v⁶ h25s⁴ Apr 8] leggy gelding: modest handicap hurdler nowadays: maiden chaser: stays 3¼m: acts on heavy going: has worn headgear: temperamental. *Nicky Richards*   c– § h91 §

TOP CAT DJ (IRE) 10 ch.g. St Jovite (USA) – Lady Coldunell (Deploy) [2017/18 c65§, h–: c23.4g^pu h22.1d^pu c20.1g^pu c23.4g c19.9m⁴ c19.2d⁵ Nov 24] maiden hurdler: poor maiden chaser: left Chris Grant after third start: stays 3m: acts on heavy going: has worn headgear/tongue tie, including in 2017/18: temperamental. *Maurice Barnes*   c63 § h–

TOP CAT HENRY (IRE) 10 b.g. Dr Massini (IRE) – Bells Chance (IRE) (Needle Gun (IRE)) [2017/18 c125, h–: c21.6s⁵ c20v^pu c22.9s^pu h20.1d Apr 23] useful-looking gelding: winning hurdler: fairly useful chaser at best, no form in 2017/18: wears headgear/tongue tie. *N. W. Alexander*   c– h–

TOP DECISION (IRE) 5 ch.g. Beneficial – Great Decision (IRE) (Simply Great (FR)) [2017/18 h16.4g b14s h15.8v h16s² h16.3s⁴ Mar 24] £42,000 4-y-o: rather unfurnished gelding: fourth foal: brother to useful hurdler/winning pointer Top Ville Ben (2m-23f winner): dam, failed to complete in points, out of half-sister to Champion Hurdle winner For Auction: third on sole outing in Irish points: no form in bumpers: modest form over hurdles: hooded first 3 starts. *Samuel Drinkwater*   h93 b–

TOP GAMBLE (IRE) 10 ch.g. Presenting – Zeferina (IRE) (Sadler's Wells (USA)) [2017/18 c159, h–: c21d c16.7v² c20.8s⁴ c15.5s⁴ c16.3v³ c21.1s Apr 13] rangy gelding: winning hurdler: smart handicap chaser: placed in Hilly Way Chase at Cork (25 lengths behind Un de Sceaux) in December and Grand Annual at Cheltenham (4¾ lengths behind Le Prezien) in March: stays 21f, effective over shorter: acts on good to firm and heavy going: tried in cheekpieces: wears tongue tie. *Kerry Lee*   c152 h–

TOP GARRY (FR) 5 ch.g. Ballingarry (IRE) – Top Fleur (FR) (Mansonnien (FR)) [2017/18 b–: b16d Oct 31] poor form in bumpers, looking temperamental. *Stuart Edmunds* **b63 §**

TOPHAM BAY (IRE) 6 b.m. Milan – Topham Gale (IRE) (Topanoora) [2017/18 h86, b–: h18.1g⁶ h20.9d⁵ h20.1v^pu h25.8s⁵ h19v^pu Jan 31] poor maiden hurdler: should stay 3¼m: acts on soft going: has worn headgear, including in 2017/18: in tongue tie last 4 starts: often races in rear. *Lucinda Russell* **h80**

TOPLINE DIVA 6 b.m. Top Line Dancer (IRE) – Sita (IRE) (Indian Ridge) [2017/18 b13.7d Nov 25] seventh foal: half-sister to 2 winners abroad on Flat, including French 9.5f-10.5f winner Witty (by Singspiel): dam smart 1m-1¼m winner: in hood, tailed off in maiden bumper. *Jose Santos* **b–**

TOP NOTCH (FR) 7 b.g. Poliglote – Topira (FR) (Pistolet Bleu (IRE)) [2017/18 c157, h–: h20s³ c21d* c21.7s* c21s⁴ c22.7d* Apr 28] **c166 h139**

Concerns over Britain's impending withdrawal from the European Union continue to make the racing news, with the prospect of the ending of free movement, both of horses and people, at the top of the list. The British Government says it recognises 'the importance of movement of people across borders to maintain a thriving horse racing sector' and is aware of the need for an immigration system that 'addresses concerns around the shortage of work riders'. There has, however, been no detail forthcoming about preparations to ensure that racing is ready for the new situation (the European Commission has ruled out Britain, Ireland and France continuing with a tripartite agreement—predating the European Union—which allows the free movement of thoroughbreds between the countries). The return of border controls, with inspection of horses and more red tape, would be a costly inconvenience, but arguably even more serious would be immigration restrictions in Britain on the recruitment of stable staff, more of whom nowadays come from overseas. Good stable staff are essential and they play a key role, not only in preserving high standards of horse welfare, but also in advising trainers on the well-being of horses and making sure the horses are at the top of their game when racing. Ireland's champion trainer Willie Mullins went out of his way at the Cheltenham Festival to give the credit for the fragile Penhill's successful preparation for the

Christy 1965 Chase, Ascot—an impressive winning return to chasing by Top Notch

bet365 Oaksey Chase, Sandown—Top Notch gains compensation for missing both Cheltenham and Aintree with a victory over Art Mauresque (noseband) and O O Seven (right)

Stayers' Hurdle to Holly Conte, the girl who looks after him, and when jockey Daryl Jacob returned victorious on Top Notch at Sandown's Finale meeting he gave a good mention to Sarah Shreeve, long-serving travelling head girl at Nicky Henderson's, for strongly advising connections that Top Notch hadn't been 'right' and recommending that he bypassed the big spring meetings at Cheltenham and Aintree (by all accounts, blood tests and veterinary checks revealed nothing physically or clinically untoward but the stable went with the judgement of Shreeve who rides Top Notch every day and 'knows the horse inside out').

Top Notch finished fourth in a very good edition of the Ascot Chase in mid-February. The race was strongly-run and developed into a thorough test, both of stamina and jumping, which left its mark on some of the runners (the second and third, Cue Card and Frodon, were both big disappointments at Cheltenham). The Ascot Chase winner Waiting Patiently wasn't seen out again and Top Notch, who was given ten weeks off, was the only one of the principals to win again before the end of the season (66/1-shot Traffic Fluide, outpaced on the final circuit at Ascot and not persevered with from a long way out, made no impression at the Cheltenham Festival but won a novice hurdle at Plumpton and a good handicap at Cheltenham in April). Top Notch had been a very smart hurdler, touched off in a Triumph Hurdle and a 'Fighting Fifth' and fifth in a Champion Hurdle, and he has become an even better performer over fences, despite not having the size and physique usually associated with the good chaser (Un de Sceaux is another notable chaser who belies the stereotype). Top Notch won the Scilly Isles Novices' Chase at Sandown and finished second in the Golden Miller at the Cheltenham Festival and third in the Manifesto at Aintree in his first season over the bigger obstacles.

After a warm-up over hurdles on his reappearance in the latest season, Top Notch picked up the winning thread over fences in the Christy 1965 Chase, over the Ascot Chase course and distance in November, and then followed up in the Peterborough Chase which was saved by the BHA, following the abandonment of

TOP

Huntingdon's December meeting, and rearranged a few days later at Taunton. Top Notch started joint favourite for the nine-runner 1965 Chase with Smad Place, in a line-up in which the Manifesto winner Flying Angel and Frodon were the only others sent off at single-figure odds. Top Notch was impressive, quickening clear early in the home straight and keeping on well to win by eight lengths from Double Shuffle, with Frodon two and a quarter lengths further back in third, and Flying Angel completing the frame. The rescheduled Peterborough Chase looked another good opportunity for Top Notch and he duly landed the odds by three and a quarter lengths from stablemate Josses Hill (who had won the previous year's renewal), firmly in control when putting in an untidy jump at the final fence, his only mistake in an otherwise polished round.

Top Notch's trainer had had one eye on running Top Notch in the King George VI Chase at Kempton, but the same owners had the Betfair Chase winner Bristol de Mai for that race, while Seven Barrows had the short-priced favourite Might Bite. Top Notch certainly looked capable of better things, and seemed a likely candidate for Grade 1 honours in open company over fences. However, his below-form effort in the Ascot Chase (in which he started second favourite to Waiting Patiently), and his subsequent absence from the big spring meetings, means he will have to wait until the next season for another opportunity. The bet365 Oaksey Chase at Sandown—before which Cue Card and the winner of the four previous runnings Menorah were paraded—provided Top Notch with the perfect chance to end his second season over fences on a high note. He landed the odds by two and three quarter lengths from Art Mauresque, travelling well and jumping soundly in the main before leading on the bridle after the third last and keeping on. Top Notch was one of four winners for his stable—including the winners of all three graded

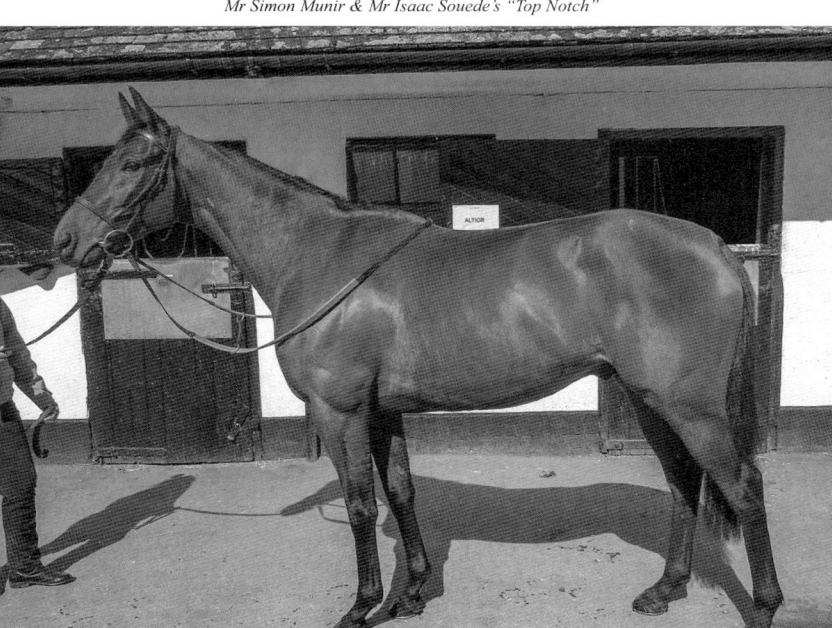

Mr Simon Munir & Mr Isaac Souede's "Top Notch"

TOP

events—at Sandown's Finale meeting where Nicky Henderson also received his end-of-season award for winning his fifth trainers' championship, and his second in a row.

```
                        ┌Poliglote      ┌Sadler's Wells    ┌Northern Dancer
                        │ (b 1981)      │ (b 1981)         \Fairy Bridge
                        │               \Alexandrie        ┌Val de L'Orne
Top Notch (FR)          │                 (b 1980)         \Apachee
   (b.g. 2011)          │               ┌Pistolet Bleu     ┌Top Ville
                        \Topira (FR)    │ (b 1988)         \Pampa Bella
                         (b 1996)       \El Quahirah       ┌Cadoudal
                                          (b 1987)         \Belgaum
```

The compact Top Notch may not be the biggest for fences but that hasn't held him back and, still only seven, he should continue to pay his way in good races (he has won seven of his eleven starts over fences and has yet to finish out of the frame). This is the third essay on him in *Chasers & Hurdlers* and there is nothing to add to the details about his pedigree which have appeared previously. His sire Poliglote, who died in March at the age of twenty-six, had the distinction of being the leading sire (by prize money) in France in 2012 both on the Flat (thanks to Prix de l'Arc winner Solemia) and over jumps. Top Notch's dam Topira, a winner at up to a mile and a half, was a half-sister, among other winners, to the fair hurdler and fairly useful chaser Monte Cristo who showed his best form at up to two and a half miles but seemed to get three and a quarter miles when sent hunter chasing late in his career. Top Notch has done most of his racing over fences at around two and a half miles but the Oaksey Chase is over an extended two and three quarters and Top Notch, who often travels strongly in his races, should get three miles. He acts on heavy going but has shown his form under much less testing conditions. A thoroughly genuine racehorse, he is a great credit to those who work with him at Seven Barrows where he is said to be a firm favourite. *Nicky Henderson*

TOPOFTHECOTSWOLDS (IRE) 4 b.g. Arcadio (GER) – Bambootcha (IRE) (Saddlers' Hall (IRE)) [2017/18 b13.7g³ b16.2s² b15.8d⁵ Mar 22] €16,000 3-y-o: fourth foal: half-brother to modest hurdler Anna Hotly (19f winner, by Beneficial): dam (h121), 2m hurdle winner/winning pointer, half-sister to useful chaser (2m-19f winner) Lord Maizey: fair form when placed in bumpers. *Nigel Twiston-Davies* **b86**

TOPOFTHEGAME (IRE) 6 ch.g. Flemensfirth (USA) – Derry Vale (USA) (Mister Lord (USA)) [2017/18 h138p: c22.4d^F h21s⁴ h23.4v* h21.1s² Mar 14] tall, raw-boned gelding: won maiden point on debut: smart form over hurdles: won handicap at Sandown (by 1½ lengths from Golan Fortune) in February: second in Coral Cup at Cheltenham (neck behind Bleu Berry) in March: yet to be asked for effort when fell 5 out in maiden won by Strong Pursuit at Newbury on chasing debut: stays 23f: acts on heavy going: often wears tongue tie: usually races prominently/travels strongly. *Paul Nicholls* **c– p h154**

TOP OF THE MORNING (IRE) 6 b.g. Kalanisi (IRE) – Lady of The Mill (IRE) (Woods of Windsor (USA)) [2017/18 h20.3d^pu Jun 6] reportedly bled when pulled up in maiden hurdle. *David Arbuthnot* **h–**

TOP OF THE ROCKS (FR) 5 b.g. Rock of Gibraltar (IRE) – Runaway Top (Rainbow Quest (USA)) [2017/18 h–: h18.5m² h18.7g h18.5g⁵ h23g h21.6m Aug 29] sturdy gelding: poor maiden hurdler: best effort at 2¼m: acts on good to firm going: wears headgear/tongue tie: often races prominently. *Katie Stephens* **h74**

TOP OTHE RA (IRE) 10 ch.g. Whitmore's Conn (USA) – The Top Road (IRE) (Toulon) [2017/18 h16.5g⁴ h16.7g² h17.6d* h16s* h17g² h16v⁶ h16s* h16.2s* h16s h15.7d h16v⁵ h16s Feb 4] workmanlike gelding: useful hurdler: won maiden at Ballinrobe in July, and handicaps at Galway in August and Down Royal and Punchestown (by length from Yaha Fizz) in November: stays 2¼m: acts on heavy going: tried in hood. *Thomas Mullins, Ireland* **h133**

TOPPER THORNTON (IRE) 9 ch.g. Double Eclipse (IRE) – Gailybay Ellen (IRE) (Supreme Leader) [2017/18 c20m c26.2d² c28.8d⁵ c29.2s^pu c24.2v^pu Mar 10] sturdy gelding: winning hurdler: fairly useful handicap chaser: second at Carlisle in November: left Colin A. McBratney after first start: stays 29f: acts on good to firm and heavy going: has worn headgear: often races in rear: unreliable. *Alex Hales* **c129 § h–**

TOR

TOP VILLE BEN (IRE) 6 b.g. Beneficial – Great Decision (IRE) (Simply Great (FR)) [2017/18 h130, b101: h16d[6] h20d[3] h19.4d[2] h22.8v* h21s[pu] h22.8v[F] h23.5s h21.4g[F] Apr 21] useful-looking gelding: point/bumper winner: useful handicap hurdler: won at Haydock in December: stays 23f: acts on heavy going: wears hood: front runner. *Philip Kirby*   **h136**

TOP WOOD (FR) 11 ch.g. Kotky Bleu (FR) – Heure Bleu (FR) (Grand Tresor (FR)) [2017/18 c127§, h–: c26.3v[2] c24.5s[pu] Apr 27] lengthy gelding: won both starts in points: winning hurdler: useful chaser: second in Foxhunter Chase at Cheltenham (beaten neck by Pacha du Polder) in March: stays 3¼m: acts on good to firm and heavy going: wears headgear/tongue tie: front runner/races prominently: moody and can't be relied on. *Mrs Katie Morgan*   **c133 §** / **h–**

TOR 4 ch.g. Orientor – Dance In The Sun (Halling (USA)) [2017/18 h16.8g[6] Oct 25] useful on Flat, stays 14.5f: 4/9, only sixth in juvenile at Sedgefield (10½ lengths behind Level of Intensity) on hurdling debut: should do better. *Iain Jardine*   **h86 p**

TOREADOR (FR) 11 b.g. Epalo (GER) – Etoile d'Or II (FR) (Lute Antique (FR)) [2017/18 c62, h–: c23.4g[pu] c24.2g[pu] Jun 3] point winner: little form under Rules: tried in blinkers: has worn tongue tie. *Andrew Hamilton*   **c–** / **h–**

TORERO 9 b.g. Hernando (FR) – After You (Pursuit of Love) [2017/18 h73§: h16.2g h22.1d h23g Aug 23] sturdy gelding: poor hurdler: left Joanne Foster after second start: wears headgear/tongue tie: unreliable. *Alan Phillips*   **h– §**

TORHOUSEMUIR 7 b.g. Sagamix (FR) – Royal Musical (Royal Abjar (USA)) [2017/18 h99, b–: h15.8m[F] c16g[3] c19.9s c17s[3] Apr 15] modest form over hurdles: poor form over fences: stays 19f: acts on soft going: has worn hood: usually races towards rear. *Sam Thomas*   **c81** / **h–**

Chris Giles & Mr & Mrs P K Barber's "Topofthegame"

Racing Post Champion INH Flat, Punchestown—Tornado Flyer (diamonds) pulls out all the stops to defeat stable-companions Blackbow (hooped sleeves) and Carefully Selected (rail)

TORNADO FLYER (IRE) 5 b.g. Flemensfirth (USA) – Mucho Macabi (IRE) (Exceed And Excel (AUS)) [2017/18 b16s* b16.4s³ b16.3s* Apr 25] €63,000 3-y-o: sturdy gelding: first foal: dam, Italian maiden (placed at 6f), half-sister to dual Champion Hurdle winner Hurricane Fly: smart form in bumpers: won maiden at Fairyhouse (by head from Getaway John) in January and Champion INH Flat Race at Punchestown (by 1¼ lengths from Blackbow) in April: third in Champion Bumper at Cheltenham (3½ lengths behind Relegate) in between: excellent hurdling prospect. *W. P. Mullins, Ireland* **b125**

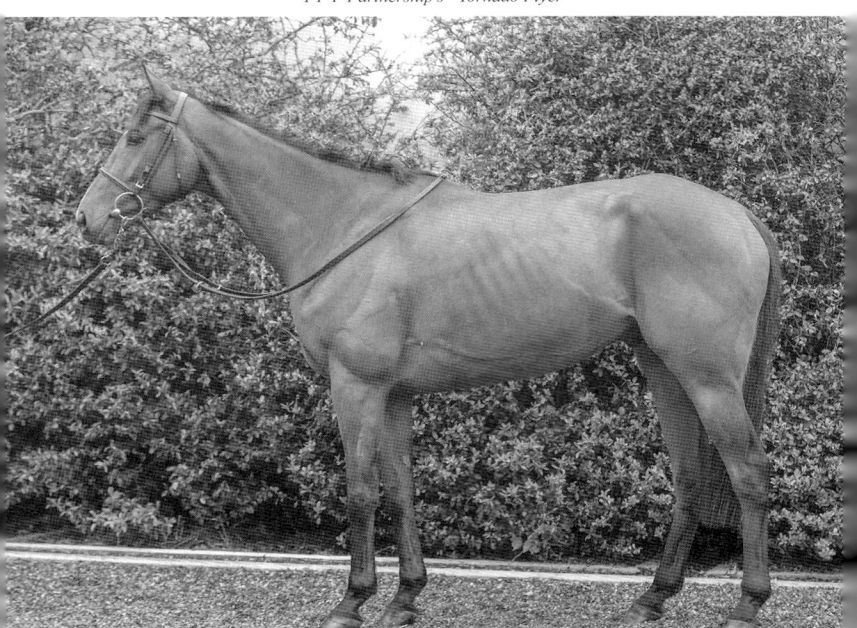

T F P Partnership's "Tornado Flyer"

TOT

TORNADO IN MILAN (IRE) 12 b.g. Milan – Julika (GER) (Nebos (GER)) [2017/18 c134, h136: c20.1m c16d⁴ h15.8v³ c16.3v² c19.3v⁴ c16s* c16d* Mar 22] sturdy gelding: useful handicap hurdler: useful handicap chaser: won at Chepstow in February and Ludlow (by 3¼ lengths from Just Cameron) in March: stays 2½m: acts on heavy going: has worn hood. *Evan Williams*   **c137 h112**

TORNADO WATCH (IRE) 9 ch.g. Selkirk (USA) – Pattimech (USA) (Nureyev (USA)) [2017/18 h104: h17.2d² h20.1d² h20v h16v h16v* Apr 16] fair handicap hurdler: won at Tramore in April: left David Loughnane after second start: stays 2½m: acts on heavy going: often races prominently. *Emmet Mullins, Ireland*   **h114**

TORRENT DES MOTTES (FR) 7 gr.g. Montmartre (FR) – Wavy (FR) (Lavirco (GER)) [2017/18 b20g² h16.8s^pu Apr 23] €46,000 3-y-o: first foal: dam, French 1¼m-11.5f winner, half-sister to smart French hurdler/chaser (winner up to 2½m) Sandcreek: second in maiden bumper at Roscommon (4 lengths behind Mr Showtime) for W. P. Mullins: fair form on first of 2 starts over hurdles. *Alexandra Dunn*   **h– b94**

TOSSAPENNY (IRE) 5 b.g. Presenting – Blueanna (IRE) (Blueprint (IRE)) [2017/18 b16s² h15.7s² h21.7s² h21v⁴ Mar 28] €31,000 3-y-o, £170,000 4-y-o: fourth foal: dam (h88), maiden hurdler, half-sister to smart hurdle chaser (stayed 19f) Kilcash: won Irish point on debut: promise when promoted second in bumper at Chepstow (¾ length behind Good Boy Bobby) in November: fairly useful form over hurdles: best effort when second in maiden at Hereford. *Evan Williams*   **h122 b100**

TOTAL ASSETS 10 b.m. Alflora (IRE) – Maid Equal (Pragmatic) [2017/18 c110, h116: h23.3v² c25.2d⁵ h25.8v³ h22.7v² Feb 15] rather leggy mare: fairly useful handicap hurdler: second at Kelso in February: fair handicap chaser: stays 27f: acts on good to firm and heavy going: has worn cheekpieces. *Simon Waugh*   **c111 h120**

TOTALIZE 9 b.g. Authorized (IRE) – You Too (Monsun (GER)) [2017/18 h142: c15.7v* Jan 24] useful hurdler: 11/4, won novice at Catterick (by 9 lengths from Kelka) on chasing debut: stayed 23f: acted on heavy going: tried in hood: dead. *Brian Ellison*   **c142 h–**

TOTAL REBELLION (IRE) 12 b.g. Craigsteel – Hil Rhapsody (Anshan) [2017/18 c–, h–: c32.5d^pu May 5] lengthy gelding: multiple point winner: winning hurdler: no form in hunter chases: has worn headgear/tongue tie. *B. V. Lund*   **c– h–**

TOTAL RECALL (IRE) 9 b.g. Westerner – Auegst Weekend (IRE) (Dr Massini (IRE)) [2017/18 c130, h–: c24s* c26g* h24s* c26.3v^F c34.3s^pu c24.5s^pu Apr 25]   **c163 + h143 p**

A new name but the same great race. The inaugural Ladbrokes Trophy, with a first prize boosted to £142,375 (making it the second most valuable handicap over jumps in Britain by some way), attracted a field worthy of its status. The 2015 Cheltenham Gold Cup winner Coneygree was top weight with 11-12, racing off a BHA handicap mark of 165, the highest for a top weight in the race since Tidal Bay ran second five years earlier off a mark of 166 behind Bobs Worth who went on to win the same season's Cheltenham Gold Cup. Bobs Worth had won the previous season's RSA Chase and had ended his novice chasing campaign quoted at a best-priced 8/1 for the Cheltenham Gold Cup. He carried 11-6, racing off a BHA mark of 160 in the Hennessy (the forerunner of the Ladbrokes Trophy), and his stable saddled the RSA runner-up Whisper in the latest edition of Newbury's autumn showpiece. Whisper's weight and mark (11-8, BHA 161) included a 4-lb penalty for winning a graduation event at Kempton on his reappearance, in which he beat a sole opponent, an unfortunate miscalculation, in hindsight, on the part of Seven Barrows, as the particular graduation chase fell inside the period when penalties applied (Smad Place, the 2015 Hennessy winner and also an RSA Chase runner-up, had won the same race as Whisper but it had been run ten days earlier and did not attract a penalty). The Henderson stable also saddled the previous year's sixth Vyta du Roc, who had been narrowly beaten in the bet365 Gold Cup at Sandown and had had his warm-up race for the Ladbrokes Trophy over hurdles. Second-season chasers, particularly those relatively lightly raced and not fully exposed, were always among the types to watch out for in the Hennessy, and among those fitting the credentials in the first Ladbrokes Trophy, were the two Irish-trained challengers, Total Recall who had won the Munster National at Limerick in October, and A Genie In Abottle who had shown smart form in his novice season culminating in a third in the Champion Novices' Chase at Punchestown on his final start. There was plenty of money too for the Harry Fry-trained American who had won all three of his starts in his first season

TOT

over fences (all three wins below graded company) and looked open to significant improvement. Total Recall, under 10-8 and representing perennial Irish champion trainer Willie Mullins, was a strong favourite at 9/2 in the twenty-runner field, with American at 5/1, ahead of another second-season chaser Singlefarmpayment at 13/2, Whisper and Coneygree at 8/1, and A Genie In Abottle and Vyta du Roc at 10/1, 14/1 bar.

Total Recall had been having his first start for Willie Mullins when he won the JT McNamara Ladbrokes Munster National at Limerick in early-October (starting 2/1 favourite in a field of sixteen and beating Alpha des Obeaux impressively by seven lengths). A winning pointer and hurdler before showing useful form over fences for Sandra Hughes (who retired at the end of the 2016/17 season), Total Recall had done most of his racing at up to two and a half miles. He showed in the Munster National that he stayed three miles well and he improved again, stepped up further in trip, in the Ladbrokes Trophy (in which the British handicappers raised him 18 lb from his Limerick mark). Total Recall moved through the race at Newbury like a horse who was still ahead of his handicap mark, travelling strongly before making smooth headway to challenge at the third last. Total Recall's jumping hadn't been particularly fluent, though, and a slow jump at the second last, where the leader Whisper (who had taken over on the bridle three out) came across him, cost Total Recall some ground and momentum. The keeping-on Whisper looked the more likely winner at the last, and he edged further ahead straight after the fence before Total Recall rallied strongly and gradually wore down Whisper in the closing stages, finding plenty to get his head in front very late and win by a neck, the first two pulling nine lengths clear of the third, 66/1-shot Regal Encore. Singlefarmpayment had looked in with a good chance of taking third when he fell three out, and neither Coneygree nor American completed, both pulled up in the home straight after being beaten quickly. Coneygree, who led for a long way, was afterwards found to have

JT McNamara Ladbrokes Munster National Handicap Chase, Limerick—Total Recall is a revelation on his debut for the Willie Mullins stable as he cruises clear of top weight Alpha des Obeaux (right)

Ladbrokes Trophy Chase (Handicap), Newbury—belated compensation for Be My Royal's disqualification in 2002 as Total Recall rallies to pip Whisper (No.2) in the first running of Newbury's autumn showpiece under the Ladbrokes banner

suffered a recurrence of a breathing problem, while American was found by the course vet to have suffered an overreach. Total Recall's jockey Paul Townend picked up a four-day ban for using his whip on Total Recall above the permitted limit.

It was the first time Willie Mullins had had the winner of Newbury's historic handicap, Be My Royal having been disqualified after passing the post first in the 2002 edition when traces of a prohibited substance, morphine, were found in a post-race sample. Be My Royal was one of thirty-seven horses which were tested positive in Britain in an infamous case in which contaminated feed produced by an Irish feed stuffs supplier was established as the source of the morphine. The connections of Be My Royal, supported by Connolly Red Mills, challenged the disqualification and, after a three-year battle, the case eventually reached the High Court before the outcome of the race was confirmed, in favour of Gingembre as the promoted winner. Until Total Recall's victory, the 1980 victor Bright Highway had remained the only Irish-trained winner since Arkle's two wins under 12-7 in 1964 and 1965.

The race run as the Hennessy between 1957 and 2016 has often had a bearing on the rest of the season, with some of its winners going on to make their mark in graded company. In the last twenty runnings, only two horses older than eight have won, emphasising the influence of the second-season novices, while, in the last fifteen runnings, Total Recall is only the fourth winner to carry less than 11-0, emphasising the quality of the winners. Whisper's performance in the first edition under the Ladbrokes banner was the best in the race since that 2011 running featuring Bobs Worth and Tidal Bay, and he looked a genuine Cheltenham Gold Cup candidate. Injury kept Whisper out of that race and the Grand National, which became his main target, though Total Recall did make the line-up in both races and was running well when he came down at the third last in the Gold Cup, in sixth place and only around a length behind the eventual third Anibale Fly. Total Recall's connections had capitalised on his lower handicap mark over hurdles to stretch his unbeaten record for the Mullins stable in the valuable William Fry Handicap Hurdle at the new Dublin Racing Festival at Leopardstown in February. Odds-on Total Recall pulled his way to the front some way from home and won readily from Oscar Knight, Flawless Escape and Delta Work, the last-named going on to win the Pertemps Final at the Cheltenham Festival.

Total Recall's BHA mark over fences had been raised to 156 and he appealed as still being well handicapped in the Grand National which he contested four weeks after falling in the Gold Cup. Sent off the 7/1 favourite at Aintree, Total Recall was badly let down by his jumping over the big, unusual fences, almost coming down at the third, then blundering at first Valentine's and generally not being fluent after that. He was dropping back and not being persevered with as the runners came back on to the main racecourse for the last time and he was eventually pulled up before the second last. The anti-climactic end to Total Recall's campaign was completed when

TOT

he was again pulled up, well held, in the Punchestown Gold Cup only eleven days after the Grand National. Notwithstanding his last three performances, Total Recall made great strides over the season and there are probably more good races to be won with him. Along with the likes of Pairofbrowneyes and Patricks Park, he was a good advertisement for the skill of his trainer at improving horses he gets from other yards, though he didn't win a race with Acapella Bourgeois, the runaway winner of the previous season's Ten Up Novices' Chase who was also sent to him by Total Recall's owners when Sandra Hughes handed in her licence.

Total Recall (IRE) (b.g. 2009)	Westerner (b 1999)	Danehill (b 1986)	Danzig / Razyana
		Walensee (b 1982)	Troy / Warsaw
	Augest Weekend (IRE) (b 2003)	Dr Massini (b 1993)	Sadler's Wells / Argon Laser
		Cut It Out (ch 1986)	Cut Above / Riberta

The lengthy Total Recall is by the Gold Cup winner Westerner (who was himself from a stout family) out of the unraced Augest Weekend who has yet to breed another winner. Augest Weekend is, however, a half-sister to the Aintree Hurdle winner Bimsey who stayed well. Total Recall's grandam Cut It Out was also unraced but was by the St Leger winner Cut Above out of the Ribblesdale Stakes third Riberta. Riberta was a half-sister to Fair Filly, the great grandam of Fair Along, who enjoyed a varied career, finishing second in the Triumph Hurdle, going back on the Flat after his first season over fences (when he was second in the Arkle) to be placed in the Chester Cup and the Cesarewitch, and winning successive editions of the West Yorkshire Hurdle, while combining a career over fences in which he went on to finish in the frame in good races including a Hennessy Gold Cup at Newbury.

Slaneyville Syndicate's "Total Recall"

Another of Riberta's half-sisters became the grandam of the most notable member of this family, the Irish Two Thousand Guineas winner Turtle Island. Total Recall should stay beyond three and a quarter miles. He acts on heavy going but doesn't need the mud (the Ladbrokes Trophy was run on good). He wore ear plugs in the Grand National. *W. P. Mullins, Ireland*

TOTTERDOWN 7 b.g. Pasternak – Yeldham Lady (Mujahid (USA)) [2017/18 b15.8g[5] b16.2g[2] b15.8s h15.8s h16v h16.2v* h15.7v[F] Apr 27] second foal: half-brother to unreliable 7f-1¼m winner Nifty Kier (by Kier Park): dam, lightly raced over hurdles, 8.6f winner on Flat: fair form in bumpers: similar form over hurdles: won maiden at Hereford in April: wears hood: usually leads. *Richard Phillips* — **h112 b87**

TOUCH KICK (IRE) 7 b.g. Presenting – Bay Pearl (FR) (Broadway Flyer (USA)) [2017/18 h120, b88: c20s c20d* c20.5d[3] Dec 26] good-topped gelding: bumper winner: fairly useful hurdler: similar form over fences: won novice handicap at Sandown in December: stays 2½m: acts on soft going: wears hood/tongue tie. *Paul Nicholls* — **c125 h–**

TOUCH OF STEEL (IRE) 9 b.g. Craigsteel – Tourmaline Girl (IRE) (Toulon) [2017/18 c–p, h88: c23.4g c24.2g[pu] c24.5v c19.9s[pu] c24.1d[pu] Apr 21] winning hurdler: poor form over fences: left James Ewart after second start: stays 25f: acts on good and to firm going: has worn headgear, including last 3 starts: tried in tongue tie. *Oliver Greenall* — **c78 h–**

TOUCH OF VELVETT 6 gr.m. Proclamation (IRE) – Rose Bien (Bien Bien (USA)) [2017/18 b16s[5] b15.8g h19.7s[5] h20.7s[5] h22.8s[5] Mar 21] second foal: dam, ran once over hurdles, 1½m-17f winner on Flat: pulled up in maiden point on debut: poor form in bumpers: modest form over hurdles. *Graeme McPherson* — **h94 b63**

TOUCH SCREEN (IRE) 8 b.g. Touch of Land (FR) – Capard Lady (IRE) (Supreme Leader) [2017/18 c78, h77, b–: c21.2m[pu] c21.7g[3] c23g[3] h21.4s[6] c20d* c20s[4] c21.2v[ur] c24.5v c23.5v[3] c19.7v[ur] Apr 1] maiden pointer: poor maiden hurdler: poor handicap chaser: won at Lingfield in November: stays 2½m: acts on heavy going: often let down by jumping over fences. *Mark Gillard* — **c81 x h–**

TOUCHY SUBJECT (IRE) 5 br.g. Tikkanen (USA) – Legal Lodge (IRE) (Carroll House) [2017/18 b16.3d h20.5s h21.2d[3] Apr 9] £24,000 4-y-o: second foal: dam, placed in points, out of half-sister to useful/smart staying chasers Into The Red, Over The Road and Planetman: runner-up in Irish point on debut: tailed off in bumper: fair form over hurdles: better effort when third in novice at Ludlow: tried in tongue tie. *Jo Davis* — **h111 b–**

TOULOUSE THE PLOT 6 b.g. Tamure (IRE) – Red Reef (King's Best (USA)) [2017/18 b–: b15.8d May 20] no show in bumpers or points. *Ben Pauling* — **b–**

TOVIERE (IRE) 7 ch.g. Presenting – Aventia (IRE) (Bob Back (USA)) [2017/18 h115: h21g* c21.6g[4] c19.9g[4] c23.8d* c26g[2] Apr 20] fairly useful handicap hurdler: won novice event at Kempton in May: useful form over fences: won novice handicap at Ascot in November: stays 3¼m: acts on good to firm and good to soft going: often leads: remains with potential as a chaser. *Oliver Sherwood* — **c130 p h118**

TOWER BRIDGE (IRE) 5 b.g. High Chaparral (IRE) – Walkamia (FR) (Linamix (FR)) [2017/18 b16.4m* b16.7g[4] h16s b20.2s[4] h22s[4] h24v[5] h24.7s[3] Apr 13] compact gelding: closely related/half-brother to several winners on Flat, including smart French winner around 1¼m War Is War (by Galileo): dam, smart French 1m-10.5f winner, sister to useful 2m hurdle winner Walk On Mix: useful form in bumpers: won at Ballinrobe (maiden) in May and Bellewstown (by 7½ lengths from Dalouga) in July: similar form over hurdles: won Nathaniel Lacy & Partners Solicitors Novices' Hurdle at Leopardstown (by head from Jetz) in February: third in Sefton Novices' Hurdle at Aintree (7½ lengths behind Santini) in April: stays 25f: acts on heavy going, bumper winner on good to firm: wears tongue tie. *Joseph Patrick O'Brien, Ireland* — **h143 b109**

TOWERBURN (IRE) 9 b.g. Cloudings (IRE) – Lady Newmill (IRE) (Taipan (IRE)) [2017/18 h70: c24.2g[5] c21.2d[F] h19.9v[pu] h18.1v[4] Apr 16] point winner: poor maiden hurdler: modest form in chases: stays 3m: acts on good to soft going: tried in cheekpieces: often wears tongue tie. *Alison Hamilton* — **c85 h74**

TOWERING (IRE) 9 b.g. Catcher In The Rye (IRE) – Bobs Article (IRE) (Definite Article) [2017/18 c121§, h111§: h16.2g* h23.3g[4] h18.5d[4] h16.7g[2] h16g[6] h16d h19.9s* h19.3v[2] h20.3d[4] h20.6d[5] h16s[5] h18.6v[6] h20.6s* h21v h20.6v Apr 11] good-topped gelding: fair hurdler: won seller at Hexham in June, and handicaps at Uttoxeter in October and Market Rasen in February: fairly useful form completed start over fences: left Alexandra Dunn after fourth start: stays 3m: acts on good to firm and heavy going: wears headgear: tried in tongue tie: usually races nearer last than first: temperamental. *Conor Dore* — **c– § h104 §**

TOW

TOWER OF ALLEN (IRE) 7 b.g. Beneficial – Baile An Droichid (IRE) (King's Ride) [2017/18 h98: c20.5g[5] c19.2g[3] c20.2g[4] c21.2v[F] c19.8s[F] h20.6s[3] Mar 26] modest maiden hurdler: poor form over fences: left Nicky Henderson after first start: stays 2½m: acts on good to soft going: sometimes in tongue tie. *Alex Hales* — c72 h88

TOWIE (IRE) 4 br.c. Sea The Stars (IRE) – Epping (Charnwood Forest (IRE)) [2017/18 h16v[5] Dec 27] good-topped colt: fair maiden on Flat, stays 11.5f: tailed off in juvenile on hurdling debut. *Gary Moore* — h–

TOWN HEAD 5 ch.g. Archipenko (USA) – Forever Loved (Deploy) [2017/18 b95: b15.6g* Nov 30] fairly useful form in bumpers: won maiden event at Musselburgh only start in 2017/18 by 5 lengths from Sonic. *Michael Easterby* — b97

TOWN PARKS (IRE) 7 b.g. Morozov (USA) – Outdoor Heather (IRE) (Presenting) [2017/18 h123: c15.9s[4] c20s[4] c17.4s[ur] c20v* c20.9s* c20d[F] c20v[4] Apr 7] angular gelding: fairly useful form over hurdles: useful handicap chaser: won novice events at Uttoxeter in December and Hereford (by 4½ lengths from Silverhow) in January: stays 21f: acts on heavy going. *Kerry Lee* — c133 h–

TOWNSHEND (GER) 7 b.g. Lord of England (GER) – Trikolore (GER) (Konigsstuhl (GER)) [2017/18 c146p, h–: c16g* c16.1s* c18.2d[4] c20s[5] c17s[ur] c17s c16.3v[pu] c16d Apr 26] winning hurdler: smart chaser: won novices at Punchestown (by 7 lengths from Potters Point) in May and Roscommon (by 4½ lengths from Peregrine Run) in June: disappointing after: stays 2½m: acts on heavy going: tried in hood: in tongue tie last 3 starts: usually races towards rear. *W. P. Mullins, Ireland* — c146 h–

TRADITIONAL DANCER (IRE) 6 b.g. Danehill Dancer (IRE) – Cote Quest (USA) (Green Desert (USA)) [2017/18 h129: h15.7m h16.2d[4] h15.6d[4] h15.6s[4] h19.4d[3] Mar 16] tall gelding: fairly useful handicap hurdler: fourth at Musselburgh in January: stays 21f: acts on good to firm and heavy going: has worn headgear: tried in tongue tie: often races prominently: no easy ride. *Iain Jardine* — h119 §

TRAFALGAR (FR) 11 b.g. Laveron – Dzaoudzie (FR) (El Badr) [2017/18 c82§, h–: c22.5d[3] c26.1g[4] May 28] lengthy gelding: maiden pointer: winning hurdler: poor handicap chaser: stays 3m: acts on soft and good to firm going: wears headgear: has worn tongue tie, including final start: often races towards rear: temperamental. *Sarah-Jayne Davies* — c68 § h–

TRAFALGAR ROCK 7 b.g. Mount Nelson – Helter Helter (USA) (Seeking The Gold (USA)) [2017/18 h120: h17m[2] h15.7d* c20g[2] c20g[3] c19.2g[6] c15.9v[pu] Mar 9] fairly useful form over hurdles: won handicap at Southwell in June: similar form over fences: second in novice handicap at Uttoxeter later in month: left Dr Richard Newland after fifth start and little impact in points/hunter subsequently: stays 2½m: acts on good to firm and good to soft going: tried in cheekpieces: often let down by jumping over fences. *Alexandra Dunn* — c120 x h120

TRAFFIC FLUIDE (FR) 8 b.g. Astarabad (USA) – Petale Rouge (FR) (Bonnet Rouge (FR)) [2017/18 c156, h–: c19.9d[2] c25.6v[5] c24d c21s[5] c20.8s h20.5v* c20.8g[4] Apr 18] lengthy gelding: fair form over hurdles: won novice at Plumpton in April: smart chaser: won Silver Trophy Chase (Limited Handicap) at Cheltenham (by 1½ lengths from Art of Payroll) final start: stays 23f: acts on heavy going: often wears headgear nowadays. *Gary Moore* — c145 h110

TRAINWRECK (IRE) 6 b.g. Stowaway – Trail Storm (IRE) (Supreme Leader) [2017/18 h18.9v[6] h16.6s* h16v[2] h16s* h16s Feb 4] £78,000 3-y-o: fifth foal: half-brother to bumper winner Lucca Lady (by Milan): dam (h104), 2½m hurdle winner/winning pointer, half-sister to fairly useful hurdler (winner up to 21f) Lady Zephyr: point winner: useful form over hurdles: won maiden at Clonmel in November and handicap at Leopardstown in December: should prove suited by further than 2m: acts on heavy going: usually races prominently. *Henry de Bromhead, Ireland* — h138

TRALEE HILLS 4 b.g. Mount Nelson – Distant Waters (Lomitas) [2017/18 b13.7s b13.7v[4] b15.8d Mar 26] modest form in bumpers. *Peter Hedger* — b77

TRAMPLING DUST 8 gr.m. Proclamation (IRE) – Scisciabubu (IRE) (Danehill (USA)) [2017/18 h16g[6] h16g h20d[pu] Sep 29] half-sister to several winners on Flat in Italy: dam Italian 5f/6f winner: no form over hurdles: wears hood. *Mark Wall* — h–

TRANS EXPRESS (IRE) 8 br.g. Trans Island – Hazel Fastrack (Shambo) [2017/18 h106: h20s[5] h18.5d* h21.1g[5] h23.1s[6] h18.5v* h19.7s[6] h16.8v[2] Apr 8] close-coupled gelding: fair handicap hurdler: won at Exeter in October and December: stays 19f: acts on heavy going: in cheekpieces last 2 starts: often races prominently. *Susan Gardner* — h112

TRANSIENT BAY (IRE) 8 b.g. Trans Island – Boarding Pass (IRE) (Accordion) [2017/18 c–, h110: h19v h24.3v^{pu} h19.9v* h24.3v^{pu} h19.9v^{pu} Apr 7] fair handicap hurdler: won at Uttoxeter in February: maiden chaser: stays 23f: acts on heavy going: wears cheekpieces: tried in tongue tie: untrustworthy. *Philip Kirby* — c– h106 §

TRANSPENNINE STAR 5 ch.g. Mount Nelson – Brave Mave (Daylami (IRE)) [2017/18 h20.5v^3 h21s^3 h21.3d^3 h24v^2 Apr 27] half-brother to fairly useful hurdler Ryeolliean (2m-2½m winner, by Haafhd): fairly useful on Flat, stays 17f: fair form over hurdles: stays 3m. *Jonjo O'Neill* — h108

TRAPPER PEAK (IRE) 9 b.g. Westerner – Banningham Blaze (Averti (IRE)) [2017/18 c103§, h105§: h16.7g h16.7g^6 h15.7g^3 h15.8m^3 h18.7m^6 h16d h15.7g^6 Oct 26] sturdy gelding: poor handicap hurdler nowadays: winning chaser: has form at 23f, usually races over much shorter: acts on heavy going: wears headgear: has worn tongue tie: front runner/races prominently: temperamental. *Conor Dore* — c– § h84 §

TRAVERTINE (IRE) 8 b.g. Danehill Dancer (IRE) – Mer de Corail (IRE) (Sadler's Wells (USA)) [2017/18 h24d* h24.2s h24g h18.5v h19.6s^2 Jan 12] rather leggy gelding: fair handicap hurdler: won at Listowel in June: left N. Madden after third start: stays 3m: acts on heavy going: tried in hood: often races towards rear. *Jonjo O'Neill* — h114

TREACKLE TART (IRE) 6 b.m. Winged Love (IRE) – Battle Over (FR) (Sillery (USA)) [2017/18 h114, b77: h20d^4 h21.1g^2 h24.5d^6 h24.6v^{pu} h21s^5 h24.3g Apr 20] workmanlike mare: fairly useful hurdler: won novice at Worcester in September: stays 2¾m: acts on soft going. *Charlie Longsdon* — h124

TREACYSWESTCOUNTY (IRE) 10 b.g. Urban Ocean (FR) – Bridge Hotel Lilly (IRE) (Roselier (FR)) [2017/18 c78, h–: c16.3d^3 May 5] multiple point winner: maiden hurdler: modest form in hunter chases: in cheekpieces last 2 starts. *Miss L. Horsfall* — c92 h–

TREAD LIGHTLY 4 b.g. Canford Cliffs (IRE) – Step Lightly (IRE) (Danehill Dancer (IRE)) [2017/18 h16d Oct 18] fair maiden on Flat, stays 1¼m: well held in juvenile on hurdling debut. *Tim Easterby* — h56

TREASURE THE RIDGE (IRE) 9 b.g. Galileo (IRE) – Treasure The Lady (IRE) (Indian Ridge) [2017/18 h99: h16.8g^6 h16.3g^4 h18.5d^2 h16.8d^5 h16.8d^5 h19.8s h21.6s Apr 23] fair handicap hurdler: won at Newton Abbot in July: stays 2¼m: acts on good to soft going: usually wears headgear: has worn tongue tie. *Martin Hill* — h108

TREATY GIRL (IRE) 7 b.m. Milan – Back To Cloghoge (IRE) (Bob Back (USA)) [2017/18 c126, h–: c23.9g^{pu} c24.1s^2 Dec 2] sturdy mare: point winner: winning hurdler: fair maiden chaser: stays 3¼m: acts on soft going: tried in tongue tie: often races prominently. *Ben Pauling* — c110 h–

TREAT YOURSELF (IRE) 11 b.g. Beat Hollow – Cartesian (Shirley Heights) [2017/18 c111§, h–: c24.2g^5 c20.1g^4 c20.5m^2 Apr 26] winning hurdler: fairly useful chaser: second in hunter at Kempton in April: left Micky Hammond after second start: probably stays 3¼m: acts on good to firm and heavy going: usually wears headgear: often wears tongue tie: temperamental. *Miss Michelle Bentham* — c116 § h–

TRED SOFTLY (IRE) 5 b.g. Yeats (IRE) – Elayoon (USA) (Danzig (USA)) [2017/18 h16.7g^4 Jul 22] modest on Flat, stays 1¾m: 7/1, fourth in novice at Market Rasen (38¼ lengths behind Hestina) on hurdling debut. *John Quinn* — h66

TREE OF LIBERTY (IRE) 6 ch.g. Stowaway – The Wrens Nest (IRE) (Shernazar) [2017/18 h123, b95: c16v* c16.4s^2 c15.9v* c16d^2 c16.2g^5 Apr 26] well-made gelding: fairly useful form over hurdles: useful form over fences: won novice handicaps at Ludlow (by 11 lengths from Nightfly) in January and Leicester (3-runner event, by 20 lengths from Chirico Vallis) in February: stays 21f: acts on heavy going: front runner/races prominently. *Kerry Lee* — c141 h–

TREMENDOUS (IRE) 4 b.f. Kodiac – Clockwise (Pivotal) [2017/18 h16.2v^{pu} h16v^{ur} h16v^{ur} h16v^{pu} Feb 14] modest maiden on Flat, stays 7f: failed to complete all 4 starts over hurdles. *Liam Lennon, Ireland* — h–

TRENDSETTER (IRE) 7 b.g. Mastercraftsman (IRE) – Fashion Trade (Dansili) [2017/18 h15.7d^4 Nov 6] sturdy gelding: fair on Flat nowadays, stays 16.5f: maiden hurdler: tried in cheekpieces: has joined Brian Francis Cawley. *Micky Hammond* — h75

TRENDY NURSE (IRE) 10 b.g. Gold Well – Rotoruasprings (IRE) (Jurado (USA)) [2017/18 h16.3m^5 h15.8g^5 h15.8g Nov 9] poor maiden hurdler: raced around 2m: best form on good going: in headgear last 4 starts: wears tongue tie. *Ken Wingrove* — h60

TRENTMAN 6 ch.g. Denounce – Sharabosky (Shahrastani (USA)) [2017/18 b–: b13.7s Jan 26] no form in bumpers: tried in blinkers. *John Mackie* — b–

TRE

TREPUCO WARRIOR (IRE) 6 b.g. Mahler – Monas Run (IRE) (Commanche Run) [2017/18 h21g[5] Nov 30] pulled up both starts in Irish maiden points: tailed off in novice on hurdling debut. *Phil Middleton* — h–

TRESHNISH (FR) 5 ch.g. Gold Away (IRE) – Didn't I Tell You (IRE) (Docksider (USA)) [2017/18 h76: h16.2g[2] h16.4v* h15.7v[3] h15.6s* h16.2v Apr 7] fairly useful form over hurdles: won maiden at Newcastle in December and handicap at Musselburgh in January: raced around 2m: acts on heavy going. *Sue Smith* — h123

TREVISANI (IRE) 6 b.g. Dubawi (IRE) – Geminiani (IRE) (King of Kings (IRE)) [2017/18 h105p: h20m[3] h21.6m* h21.6g* h21.6g Sep 2] good-topped gelding: fairly useful form over hurdles: won novices at Newton Abbot (twice) in June: stays easy 2¾m: acts on good to firm going: often in headgear: races prominently. *Paul Nicholls* — h120

TRIBAL DANCE (IRE) 12 br.g. Flemensfirth (USA) – Native Sparkle (IRE) (Be My Native (USA)) [2017/18 c62§, h54§: h23.1d[5] c22.6g c24.1g c25.8m[pu] c20.3d[pu] h23.1g Oct 31] smallish gelding: fair handicap hurdler/chaser at best, little form since 2015/16: wears headgear: tried in tongue tie: usually races nearer last than first: unreliable. *John O'Shea* — c– §, h– §

TRICKY (IRE) 9 br.g. Indian Danehill (IRE) – Amelia Island (IRE) (Supreme Leader) [2017/18 c83p, h106: h16.8g Jun 27] Irish maiden point winner: fair form over hurdles at best, well held sole start in 2017/18: not fluent only chase outing: unproven beyond 17f: acts on good to soft going. *Philip Hobbs* — c–, h–

TRICKY ISSUE (IRE) 6 b.m. Manduro (GER) – Tricky Situation (Mark of Esteem (IRE)) [2017/18 h94: h21.6g May 5] modest form over hurdles, well held sole start in 2017/18: best effort at 2¾m: acts on soft going. *Seamus Mullins* — h–

TRICKY SILENCE (IRE) 6 br.g. Whitmore's Conn (USA) – No Sound (FR) (Exit To Nowhere (USA)) [2017/18 h66: h23.3d[5] May 6] well held over hurdles: won point in 2018: tried in cheekpieces. *Stuart Edmunds* — h59

TRIGGER NICHOL (IRE) 6 b.g. Dubai Destination (USA) – Run For Cover (IRE) (Lafontaine (USA)) [2017/18 b77: h15.7d h15.8d h16.7v[3] h15.8v[4] Jan 27] modest form in bumpers: similar form over hurdles. *Dr Richard Newland* — h91, b–

TRIGGITAS 8 b.g. Double Trigger (IRE) – Suntas (IRE) (Riberetto) [2017/18 h15.8g[3] h16g[2] Jul 10] fair form over hurdles: second in maiden at Worcester in July: bred to be suited by 2½m+: tried in hood. *Paul Webber* — h105

TRIGGYWINKLE (FR) 9 b.m. Le Triton (USA) – Periwinkle (FR) (Perrault) [2017/18 c91§: c16.5m[3] c16.1g[2] c16.3m[2] h16.8g* h18.5m c16.3m[ur] c17g[5] c16d[3] Sep 24] poor form over hurdles: poor handicap chaser: joined Bob Buckler after fifth start and rejoined former trainer after next: stays 21f: acts on soft and good to firm going: wears headgear/tongue tie: unreliable. *Laura Young* — c77 §, h73 §

TRILLERIN MINELLA (IRE) 10 b.g. King's Theatre (IRE) – Eva Fay (IRE) (Fayruz) [2017/18 c94§, h–: c25.5g[6] c19.3d[pu] c24s[pu] c24d c24.2d[pu] c26d[pu] Dec 2] lengthy gelding: maiden hurdler: fair chaser at best, no form in 2017/18: wears headgear: temperamental. *Kevin Hunter* — c– §, h–

TRIOLET (IRE) 8 b.g. Westerner – Trinity Belle (FR) (Tel Quel (FR)) [2017/18 h16m[2] h20.4d[3] h20m* h20.5d h20.2m[2] h24g h21.6v[F] Mar 19] fair handicap hurdler: won at Down Royal in June: stays 2½m: acts on good to firm and good to soft going: tried in cheekpieces/tongue tie. *Colin A. McBratney, Ireland* — h111

TRIOPAS 6 b.g. Stowaway – Aine Dubh (IRE) (Bob Back (USA)) [2017/18 h80, b72: h23.3d h23g[3] h23.6s* h24g[3] h23.1d* h24s* h25.3d* c20.2v[3] h26s h24v[pu] Mar 15] fair handicap hurdler: won at Chepstow (conditional) in November, and Market Rasen, Towcester and Catterick (conditional) in December: evens, third in novice handicap at Wincanton (1¼ lengths behind Speedalong) on chasing debut: stays 25f: acts on heavy going: usually leads: should do better over fences. *Tom Lacey* — c110 p, h104

TRIPLE CHIEF (IRE) 7 b.g. High Chaparral (IRE) – Trebles (IRE) (Kenmare (FR)) [2017/18 c101, h87: c20.5g[2] c19.2d[2] c20.2s[4] h19g* c19.2v[2] c20.2v[6] c18.2s* h19v[6] Mar 12] workmanlike gelding: fair handicap hurdler: won at Taunton in November: fair handicap chaser: won at same course in February: left Chris Down after first start: stays 2½m: acts on heavy going: wears headgear: has worn tongue tie: often races prominently. *Jimmy Frost* — c113, h101

TRIPTICO (FR) 12 gr.g. Turgeon (USA) – Al Kicks (FR) (Al Nasr (FR)) [2017/18 c90, h–: c24g[3] c22.5d* c20g[pu] c25.1s[pu] c21.2v[5] Jan 1] winning hurdler: modest handicap chaser: won at Uttoxeter in May: stays 2¾m: acts on heavy going: often wears headgear: tried in tongue tie: temperamental. *Alexandra Dunn* — c89 §, h–

850

TRISTRAM 4 b.g. Sinndar (IRE) – Treasured Dream (Oasis Dream) [2017/18 h16.7d[pu] Dec 7] fair maiden on Flat, best effort at 1½m: pulled up in juvenile on hurdling debut. *John Mackie* — h–

TRIXSTER (IRE) 5 b.g. Beneficial – Our Trick (IRE) (Flemensfirth (USA)) [2017/18 h16g[6] h20v[4] h21.3s[5] h23.6v[F] h22v[5] Apr 14] €27,000 3-y-o: third foal: half-brother to useful hurdler/fairly useful chaser Sykes (2¾m-25f winner, by Mountain High): dam unraced sister to useful staying chaser Emperor's Choice: fair form over hurdles: stays 3m: acts on heavy going: often races towards rear. *Tim Vaughan* — h113

TROJAN LASS (IRE) 6 b.m. Robin des Champs (FR) – Berties Sister (IRE) (Golden Tornado (IRE)) [2017/18 b18g b20v h19.8s h15.8s Jan 18] first foal: dam unraced sister to smart hurdler/fairly useful chaser (stayed 3m) Berties Dream: no form in bumper/over hurdles: left Henry de Bromhead after third start. *Henry Oliver* — h– b–

TROJAN STAR (IRE) 8 b.g. Tikkanen (USA) – Mystical Queen (IRE) (Dr Devious (IRE)) [2017/18 c105§, h–: c23.6g[4] c22.7m[3] c19.9s[3] c15.9v[5] c17.5d Apr 24] maiden hurdler: fair handicap chaser, below best in 2017/18: stays 3m: acts on good to firm and good to soft going: wears headgear: usually wears tongue tie: one to treat with caution. *Kim Bailey* — c89 § h–

TRONGATE (IRE) 6 b.g. Dansant – Val Eile (IRE) (Aahsaylad) [2017/18 h106, b93: h16.2v[4] h17s h23.8m[4] h19v* h24.3v[4] h16v[3] h16v[3] h24.3g Apr 20] fair handicap hurdler: won at Ayr in December: likely to prove best at short of 3m when conditions are testing: acts on heavy going. *R. Mike Smith* — h104

TROOBLUE 6 gr.m. Great Palm (USA) – Touch of Ivory (IRE) (Rossini (USA)) [2017/18 b17d b16.8s[3] h16v[4] h16.7s[3] h16.8v[3] h20.1d[4] Apr 23] £800 5-y-o: second foal: dam (h90), ungenuine 2m/17f hurdle winner, also 7.5f-1¼m winner on Flat: modest form in bumpers: fair form over hurdles: should be suited by 2¼m+. *Sue Smith* — h104 b81

TROUBLE IN PARIS (IRE) 11 ch.g. Great Palm (USA) – Ten Dollar Bill (IRE) (Accordion) [2017/18 c69§, h–: c20.1g c20.1g[5] c25.5s[5] Jul 22] lightly-raced hurdler: poor maiden chaser: has worn headgear, including in 2017/18: has worn tongue tie: usually races away: temperamental. *Barry Murtagh* — c– § h–

TROY DEE KNEE 6 b.g. Rainbow High – Matthew's Bridey (El Conquistador) [2017/18 b13.7s Jan 26] tailed off in bumper. *Shaun Lycett* — b–

TRUCKERS HIGHWAY (IRE) 9 b.g. Rudimentary (USA) – Countessdee (IRE) (Arctic Lord) [2017/18 c116, h–: c24d[pu] c16.5g* c20.3s[4] c17.4s[3] c16d[5] c18.9s[pu] c16v[5] c17.4d[2] Apr 21] maiden hurdler: fairly useful handicap chaser: won at Worcester in October: stays 2½m: acts on heavy going: often wears hood: wears tongue tie. *John Groucott* — c118 h–

TRUCKERS LODGE (IRE) 6 b.g. Westerner – Galeacord (IRE) (Accordion) [2017/18 b105: h19.7s[4] h19.3v[2] Feb 19] off mark in Irish maiden points at second attempt: useful bumper performer: fair form over hurdles: better effort when second in novice at Carlisle in February: bred to stay 3m: will go on improving. *Tom George* — h111 p

TRUCKERS TANGLE (IRE) 6 b.g. Tajraasi (USA) – Lodge Tangle (IRE) (Well Chosen) [2017/18 b16.3g[6] h15.8g[4] h17.2d[6] h18.5d[5] h16.8d[5] h15.9d h18.5v[pu] Nov 7] maiden Irish pointer: last in bumper: no form over hurdles. *Alexandra Dunn* — h– b–

TRUE BALLEW (IRE) 4 b.f. Equiano (FR) – Hula Ballew (Weldnaas (USA)) [2017/18 b12.4s[6] b12.4s[4] anb16.3g Feb 5] third foal: dam 1m winner: unplaced in bumpers and on Flat debut. *Philip Kirby* — b67

TRUE SELF (IRE) 5 b.m. Oscar (IRE) – Good Thought (IRE) (Mukaddamah (USA)) [2017/18 b93p: b16s* b16g* h16.1d* h16v[2] h18v[4] h16s[F] h16.5d* Apr 24] fairly useful form in bumpers: won mares maiden at Galway in August and mares event at Down Royal in September: useful form over hurdles: won mares maiden at Thurles in November and handicap at Punchestown (by 2½ lengths from Joey Sasa) in April: stays 2¼m: acts on heavy going. *W. P. Mullins, Ireland* — h131 b102

TRULY AMAZING (IRE) 5 br.m. Presenting – Asian Maze (IRE) (Anshan) [2017/18 b16.6s[6] b16.7s Mar 26] fifth foal: sister to useful hurdler/fairly useful chaser Cup Final (2m-3¼m winner) and a winning pointer: dam (h162), 2¼m-3m hurdle winner, sister to very smart chaser (stayed 33f) Quantitativeeasing: modest form in bumpers. *Emma Lavelle* — b81

TRUST ME I'M A DR (IRE) 9 b.g. Dr Massini (IRE) – Friendly Flick (IRE) (Anshan) [2017/18 h22v[pu] h20.5v[pu] c23.9s[pu] h20.1v[pu] h16.7s[4] h19.9v[pu] h20.6g[6] Apr 22] maiden pointer: modest form over hurdles: pulled up in novice on chasing debut. *Victor Thompson* — c– h94

TRU

TRUST THE MAN (IRE) 5 br.g. Manduro (GER) – Saree (Barathea (IRE)) [2017/18 h15.9d³ h16s² h19.6d³ h19.8v⁵ Feb 16] angular gelding: half-brother to fair hurdler/fairly useful chaser Prince Khurram (2m-2½m winner, by Nayef): modest maiden on Flat, stays 1¾m: fair form over hurdles: wears tongue tie. *Adam West*   h107

TRUST THOMAS 10 ch.g. Erhaab (USA) – Yota (FR) (Galetto (FR)) [2017/18 c120, h–: h17s^pu c17.1g³ c15.8g* c15.7d⁵ c16.5v³ c17.1v^pu c19.3g^pu Apr 23] good-bodied gelding: winning hurdler: fair handicap chaser: won at Musselburgh in November: stays 2¾m: acts on heavy going: tried in headgear/tongue tie: usually races towards rear. *Ann Hamilton*   c107 h–

TRY CATCH ME (IRE) 13 b.g. Commander Collins – Misty River (IRE) (Over The River (FR)) [2017/18 c19.5s^pu c19.7s⁵ Apr 15] tall, close-coupled gelding: maiden hurdler: fair chaser at best, retains little ability: sometimes wears headgear: tried in tongue tie. *Zoe Davison*   c– h–

TRY IT SOMETIME (IRE) 10 b.g. Milan – Lead'er Inn (IRE) (Supreme Leader) [2017/18 c76§, h–: c23.8v^pu c24.5v c24v^pu c24.5v² c24.5v⁴ Mar 29] winning hurdler: poor handicap chaser: stays 25f: acts on heavy going: wears headgear/tongue tie: temperamental. *Sheila Lewis*   c70 § h–

TRYSOR YNYS (IRE) 5 b.m. Beat Hollow – Brave Betsy (IRE) (Pistolet Bleu (IRE)) [2017/18 h16s h19.5s^pu Apr 27] second foal: closely related to bumper winner/fair hurdler Arian (2m winner, by King's Theatre): dam (h123) bumper/2m hurdle winner (stayed 2½m): no show in bumper/novice hurdle. *John Flint*   h– b–

TSUNDOKU (IRE) 7 ch.m. Medicean – Toberanthawn (IRE) (Danehill Dancer (IRE)) [2017/18 h103: h19.9d* h21.6g Oct 13] modest handicap hurdler: won mares event at Uttoxeter in July: stays 2½m: acts on soft going: usually races close up. *Alexandra Dunn*   h99

TUCKS BERGIN (IRE) 6 b.g. Getaway (GER) – Dr Sandra (IRE) (Dr Massini (IRE)) [2017/18 h19.5s^pu Apr 27] point winner: in tongue tie, pulled up in novice on hurdling debut. *Adrian Wintle*   h–

TUDORS TREASURE 7 b.g. Dr Massini (IRE) – Rude Health (Rudimentary (USA)) [2017/18 h105: h23.1v h21.4v^pu h20v² h24.2s⁵ h23.9v⁵ Apr 15] lengthy gelding: fair handicap hurdler: stays 2¾m: acts on good to firm and heavy going: in cheekpieces last 2 starts: often races prominently. *Robert Stephens*   h102

TUGBOAT (IRE) 10 b.g. Galileo (IRE) – Alleluia (Caerleon (USA)) [2017/18 c–, h–: c24.2m³ c27.2s⁴ c20.9d c23.8s³ c20.9v⁴ c23.8d⁵ Mar 22] angular gelding: point winner: winning hurdler: fair hunter chaser: stays 3m: acts on good to firm and heavy going: often races towards rear. *G. Slade-Jones*   c105 h–

TULLY EAST (IRE) 8 b.g. Shantou (USA) – Ghillie's Bay (IRE) (King's Ride) [2017/18 c147, h–: h16s⁴ c20.4s⁶ c17s³ Feb 3] good-topped gelding: fair hurdler: useful handicap chaser: third in Coral Sandyford Handicap Chase at Leopardstown (8¼ lengths behind Patricks Park) in February: stays 2½m: acts on heavy going: races towards rear, often travels strongly. *Alan Fleming, Ireland*   c140 h112

TULSA JACK (IRE) 9 b.g. Urban Ocean (FR) – Jessica's Pet (IRE) (King's Ride) [2017/18 c135, h112: c26s⁶ c25g⁴ h24.2s² h24g³ c24s⁴ c28s h24v c28.5s² c30s^ur Apr 28] rather leggy gelding: fairly useful handicap hurdler: third at Bellewstown in August: useful handicap chaser: fourth in Munster National at Limerick (18 lengths behind Total Recall) in October and second in Ulster National at Downpatrick (6½ lengths behind Poormans Hill) in March: stays 29f: acts on soft and good to firm going: wears blinkers: often races towards rear. *Noel Meade, Ireland*   c135 h118

TUNNEL CREEK 6 b.g. Tobougg (IRE) – Free Offer (Generous (IRE)) [2017/18 h20g⁵ h20d⁶ h16g h20g h20g* h15.8m⁴ h19m⁵ h20.3d⁶ Nov 21] angular gelding: fair handicap hurdler: won conditionals/amateur event at Worcester in September: left Thomas Cooper after fourth start: stays 2½m: acts on good to soft going: wears headgear: usually races towards rear. *Olly Murphy*   h101

TUPOLEV (IRE) 5 b.g. Black Sam Bellamy (IRE) – Mariah Rollins (IRE) (Over The River (FR)) [2017/18 b16v³ Feb 3] 10/3, third in bumper at Wetherby (9¼ lengths behind Black Pirate): dead. *Amy Murphy*   b92

TUPPENCE COLOURED 4 br.f. Oasis Dream – No Frills (IRE) (Darshaan) [2017/18 b13.7g⁵ b15.8d Mar 26] half-sister to several winners, including fairly useful hurdler Ephorus (2m-2¼m winner, by Galileo): dam ran twice on Flat: modest form in bumpers: wears hood. *Jo Davis*   b77

TURANGI 6 b.g. King's Theatre (IRE) – Bold Fire (Bold Edge) [2017/18 h19.3g h18.5v h21d Apr 26] sturdy gelding: third foal: dam (c122/h133) 2m-2¾m hurdle/chase winner: fair form over hurdles: capable of better. *Philip Hobbs* **h109 p**

TURBAN (FR) 11 b.g. Dom Alco (FR) – Indianabelle (FR) (Useful (FR)) [2017/18 c118x, h–: c25.8g^{pu} c21.2g c20.2s^2 c17.5v^5 c20.5d^5 c21.6v^5 c19.5s^3 c20.5s^4 c20.2d^2 Apr 22] sturdy gelding: winning hunter chaser: fair handicap chaser: stays 3m: acts on heavy going: has worn headgear: often let down by jumping over fences. *Paul Henderson* **c102 x h–**

TURBOTIM (IRE) 5 b.g. Arakan (USA) – Katy McKay (IRE) (Milan) [2017/18 b16s b16v^4 h15.3v h15.8v^6 Feb 18] no form in bumpers/novice hurdles. *Michael Scudamore* **h– b–**

TURCAGUA (FR) 8 gr.g. Turgeon (USA) – Acancagua (FR) (Subotica (FR)) [2017/18 h135, b–: c20v^2 c16v^F c22s^F h20s Apr 28] well-made gelding: useful form over hurdles: similar form when second in maiden at Navan (11 lengths behind Bonbon Au Miel) on completed start over fences: stays 2½m: acts on heavy going: tried in hood: remains with potential as a chaser. *W. P. Mullins, Ireland* **c133 p h–**

TURKEY CREEK (IRE) 9 b.g. Scorpion (IRE) – Emesions Lady (IRE) (Bigstone (IRE)) [2017/18 h–: h20.6g^4 h20.6g^2 h20g^4 c21.4g^2 Aug 19] poor form over hurdles: 4/1, second in novice handicap at Market Rasen (6 lengths behind Miami Present) on chasing debut: stays 21f: best form on good going: tried in tongue tie: races towards rear. *Paul Webber* **c85 h80**

TURNBURY 7 b.g. Azamour (IRE) – Scottish Heights (IRE) (Selkirk (USA)) [2017/18 h61: h19.6s^5 h15.8g^4 h15.8m Jul 2] poor maiden hurdler: often wears cheekpieces: tried in tongue tie. *Nikki Evans* **h74**

TURNING GOLD 4 ch.g. Pivotal – Illusion (Anabaa (USA)) [2017/18 h16s^2 h15.7s^2 h16.6d^4 h15.7v* h16.4s^5 h15.7s Mar 25] tall gelding: fairly useful on Flat, stays 1m: fairly useful form over hurdles: won Victor Ludorum Juvenile Hurdle at Haydock (by nose from Cornerstone Lad) in February: raced around 2m: acts on heavy going: front runner/races prominently. *Nigel Twiston-Davies* **h117**

TURN TURK (IRE) 7 gr.m. Robin des Champs (FR) – Revelate (IRE) (Great Palm (USA)) [2017/18 b94: h19.9g* h21.6m^2 h20g* Aug 30] bumper winner: fairly useful form over hurdles: won mares maiden at Uttoxeter in May and mares handicap at Worcester in August: likely to stay at least 3m: will go on improving. *Nicky Henderson* **h116 p**

TURTLE CASK (IRE) 9 b.g. Turtle Island (IRE) – Sayce (IRE) (Supreme Leader) [2017/18 c–§, h90: h25.4g^5 h24g h27g^5 h23.3v* h23.3s^6 h19.3v h23.1d^3 h24.1s h25.8s^4 h25.3s h23.3v^2 h27v^v Mar 23] strong gelding: modest handicap hurdler: won at Hexham in September: maiden chaser: stays 3¼m: acts on heavy going: wears headgear: unreliable. *Mike Sowersby* **c– § h89 §**

TURTLE WARS (FR) 5 b.g. Turtle Bowl (IRE) – Forces Sweetheart (Allied Forces (USA)) [2017/18 h16.7g^3 h19.3g h15.8s* h19.8v^5 Mar 10] €20,000 3-y-o: well-made gelding: fourth foal: half-brother to 2 winners in France, including fair hurdler Force Aliee (2¼m/19f winner, by Muhtathir): dam 5f/6f winner: third in Irish point: fairly useful form over hurdles: won maiden at Huntingdon in January: remains capable of better. *Nicky Henderson* **h116 p**

TUSCAN GOLD 11 ch.g. Medicean – Louella (USA) (El Gran Senor (USA)) [2017/18 h101: h25.4g^4 h25.4s^6 Jul 24] well-made gelding: fair on Flat, stays 21.5f: fair handicap hurdler, well below best both starts in 2017/18: stays 25f: acts on soft and good to firm going: has worn cheekpieces: front runner/races prominently. *Micky Hammond* **h82**

TWENTY EIGHT GUNS 8 b.m. Black Sam Bellamy (IRE) – Glory Be (Gunner B) [2017/18 c127, h114: c20g^{pu} c19.4d^4 c20.8s^{ur} c20.5s^5 c21.2s* c21.2s^4 c19.9s Mar 31] sturdy mare: maiden hurdler: fairly useful handicap chaser: won at Fakenham in February: stays 2¾m: acts on heavy going: wears cheekpieces: in tongue tie last 3 starts. *Michael Scudamore* **c124 h–**

TWENTYONEBLACKJACK (IRE) 6 b.g. Robin des Pres (FR) – Grove Juliet (IRE) (Moscow Society (USA)) [2017/18 b16g h21s^{pu} h23.9s^{pu} Jan 9] no show in bumper/over hurdles. *Martin Keighley* **h– b–**

TWISTER MIX 7 gr.g. Fair Mix (IRE) – Reverse Swing (Charmer) [2017/18 c–, h–: c16.5g c20m Jul 5] point winner: maiden hurdler: no form in chases: often in hood: sometimes in tongue tie: front runner/races prominently. *Katy Price* **c– h–**

TWI

TWIST ON GINGE (IRE) 6 b.g. Craigsteel – Miss Top (IRE) (Tremblant) [2017/18 h104§, b90: c25.8g³ c24g² c20v^pu Nov 26] tall, rather unfurnished gelding: fair form over hurdles: similar form over fences: best effort when second in novice handicap at Southwell in October: stays 3¼m: acts on heavy going: often wears cheekpieces: temperamental. *Nigel Twiston-Davies* — c101 § h– §

TWOBEELUCKY 5 b.g. Tobougg (IRE) – She's The Lady (Unfuwain (USA)) [2017/18 h16.4d* h16.7g* h16.6s² h16.4g* Oct 28] good-topped gelding: dam, bumper winner, half-sister to useful hurdler/smart chaser (stayed 21f) I'm So Lucky: fairly useful maiden on Flat, stays 10.5f: useful form over hurdles: won maiden at Roscommon in June, novice at Bellewstown in July and minor event at Cheltenham (by 5 lengths from Arthington) in October: open to further improvement. *Henry de Bromhead, Ireland* — h134 p

TWO FOR GOLD (IRE) 5 b.g. Gold Well – Two of Each (IRE) (Shernazar) [2017/18 b15.7d* b15.7d⁶ b16.6s* Feb 21] tall gelding: third foal: half-brother to bumper winner/fairly useful hurdler Westendorf (2½m winner, by Coroner): dam, maiden hurdler, half-sister to useful hurdler (stayed 3m) Free To Dream: useful form in bumpers: won at Southwell (conditionals/amateur, by 4½ lengths from Rebel Commander) in December and Doncaster (by ¾ length from Finalshot) in February: will be suited by further than 2m. *Kim Bailey* — b108

TWO HOOTS (IRE) 7 gr.g. Tikkanen (USA) – Supreme Beneficial (IRE) (Beneficial) [2017/18 h82p, b61: h19v⁵ c17v⁴ c17v^ur c19.4v⁵ c25.7v³ Apr 1] poor form over hurdles/fences. *Jeremy Scott* — c82 h80

TWOJAYSLAD 9 b.g. Kayf Tara – Fulwell Hill (Anshan) [2017/18 c114, h–: c24d c25.5s^pu c25.1d³ Apr 22] maiden hurdler: fair handicap chaser: stays 3m: acts on heavy going: tried in cheekpieces. *Ian Williams* — c104 h–

TWO SMOKIN BARRELS 9 b.m. Kayf Tara – Coldabri (IRE) (Husyan (USA)) [2017/18 c126, h104: c26.2d c23.5s² c27.6s^F c23.4s³ c22.7v² c25.1v* c22.2v c23.8s⁵ Apr 27] workmanlike mare: fair hurdler: fairly useful handicap chaser: won at Wincanton in March: stays 25f: acts on heavy going. *Michael Scudamore* — c127 h–

TWO SWALLOWS 8 b.m. Kayf Tara – One Gulp (Hernando (FR)) [2017/18 h121: c21.6g² c23.4s³ c20.3v* Feb 5] lengthy mare: fairly useful hurdler: similar form over fences: won novice at Southwell in February: stays 3m: acts on heavy going. *Ben Pauling* — c125 h–

TWO TAFFS (IRE) 8 b.g. Flemensfirth – Richs Mermaid (IRE) (Saddlers' Hall (IRE)) [2017/18 c147, h116+: c19.8g² Oct 28] well-made gelding: fairly useful hurdler: smart form over fences: second in novice at Cheltenham (3¾ lengths behind Double Treasure) on sole start in 2017/18: stays 21f: acts on soft going: in cheekpieces/tongue tie last 3 starts: strong traveller. *Dan Skelton* — c138 h–

TWOTWOTHREE (IRE) 5 b.g. Shantou (USA) – Sibury (IRE) (Overbury (IRE)) [2017/18 b15.7s² b17v² b16.7d^p Apr 21] €4,000 3-y-o: sixth foal: dam unraced half-sister to fair hurdler/useful chaser (stayed 3½m) Mattock Ranger: off mark in points at second attempt: fair form when in frame all 3 starts in bumpers: tried in hood/tongue tie. *Oliver Greenall* — b90

TYCOON PRINCE (IRE) 8 b.g. Trans Island – Downtown Train (IRE) (Glacial Storm (USA)) [2017/18 h133: c17v² c17d* c17s^F c20.4s^pu c20v c16d^pu Apr 26] strong gelding: has had breathing operation: useful form over hurdles: similar form over fences: won maiden at Leopardstown in December, but became disappointing: stays 2½m: acts on heavy going: tried in hood: wears tongue tie. *Gordon Elliott, Ireland* — c141 h–

TYNECASTLE PARK 5 b.g. Sea The Stars (IRE) – So Silk (Rainbow Quest (USA)) [2017/18 h104: h20.3g² h21g² h21.1s^pu h20.7s^pu Jan 26] fair form over hurdles: stays 21f: best form on good going. *Robert Eddery* — h107

TYRELL (IRE) 5 b.g. Teofilo (IRE) – Sleeveless (USA) (Fusaichi Pegasus (USA)) [2017/18 h117p: h16d h16s⁴ h15.8d h18.6s h19.3s* ab16.3g⁴ h23.1s⁴ Mar 26] fairly useful handicap hurdler: won at Catterick in February: stays 19f: acts on soft going: usually wears headgear/tongue tie. *Micky Hammond* — h119

TYROLEAN 5 b.g. Raven's Pass (USA) – Alessandria (Sunday Silence (USA)) [2017/18 h15.8d⁵ Oct 8] fair maiden on Flat, stays 1¾m: 9/1, fifth in maiden at Uttoxeter (27½ lengths behind Palmers Hill) on hurdling debut: has joined Dai Burchell: should do better. *Seamus Durack* — h73 p

ULT

TYRRELL'S SUCCES (FR) 7 br.g. Forestier (FR) – Irish Succes (FR) (Turgeon (USA)) [2017/18 h107, b96: h20g² h20.3g⁴ h22g⁴ c22d^F c21s⁴ c21s c23.5v⁶ Jan 30] runner-up both starts in maiden points: bumper winner: fair handicap hurdler: fairly useful form over fences: left Aaron Stronge after third start: stays 2¾m: acts on soft going: in tongue tie last 3 starts. *Dermot Anthony McLoughlin, Ireland*   c115 h110

TZAR DE L'ELFE (FR) 8 b.g. Satri (IRE) – Rue Tournefort (FR) (Marchand de Sable (USA)) [2017/18 c–, h88: c20d³ c23.5s^F h20.5v³ h21.7d h19.8s* h26v⁴ h25d Apr 24] sturdy gelding: fair handicap hurdler: won novice event at Sandown in March: fair maiden chaser: stays 25f: acts on heavy going: has worn headgear/tongue tie. *Richard Rowe*   c103 h101

U

UBAK (FR) 10 b.g. Kapgarde (FR) – Gesse Parade (FR) (Dress Parade) [2017/18 c–, h145: h24.4d h23.4v⁶ h19.2d^{pu} Feb 25] good-topped gelding: smart hurdler at best: useful form over fences (jumped sketchily): stayed 25f: acted on heavy going: often raced prominently: dead. *Gary Moore*   c– h138

UBALTIQUE (FR) 10 b.g. Balko – Ode Antique (FR) (Subotica (FR)) [2017/18 c125§, h–§: c21.2d^{pu} c16.5v⁵ c17.5v³ c15.7v* c16.3v* c15.5v³ c16.5v⁴ h16.2v Apr 7] good-topped gelding: winning hurdler: fairly useful handicap chaser: won at Haydock in December and January: stays 19f: acts on heavy going: wears blinkers/tongue tie: races towards rear: temperamental. *Donald McCain*   c123 § h– §

UCELLO CONTI (FR) 10 b.g. Martaline – Gazelle Lulu (FR) (Altayan) [2017/18 c149, h–: c24.5d² c25v^{pu} c34.3s^{ur} Apr 14] sturdy gelding: winning hurdler: smart handicap chaser: second in Paddy Power Chase at Leopardstown (7 lengths behind Anibale Fly) in December: prominent long way and still close up when unseating (for second year) 4 out in Grand National: stays 3¼m: acts on good to firm and heavy going: wears tongue tie: often travels strongly. *Gordon Elliott, Ireland*   c149 h–

UDOGO 7 b.g. Lucky Story (USA) – Welanga (Dansili) [2017/18 h17.7d h18.6g h15.3g⁶ h21s Apr 9] fair on Flat, stays 13f: maiden hurdler, no form in 2017/18. *Brendan Powell*   h–

UEUETEOTL (FR) 10 gr.g. Tikkanen (USA) – Azturk (FR) (Baby Turk) [2017/18 c118§, h115§: h25.8g³ h24.4d c23.4s³ Jan 14] big gelding: fair handicap hurdler/chaser nowadays: stays 25f: acts on soft going: wears headgear: usually leads: unreliable. *James Ewart*   c109 § h111 §

UGOLIN DE BEAUMONT (FR) 10 b.g. Alberto Giacometti (IRE) – Okarina de Beaumont (FR) (Ragmar (FR)) [2017/18 c113, h–: c23.8g² May 9] winning hurdler: fairly useful form over fences: second in handicap at Ffos Las sole outing in 2017/18: stayed 3½m: acted on heavy going: dead. *Bob Buckler*   c120 h–

UHLAN BUTE (FR) 10 ch.g. Brier Creek (USA) – Jonquiere (FR) (Trebrook (FR)) [2017/18 c125§, h–: c20.2v³ c18.8v⁶ c23.8d⁴ c23.8d* c23.8s⁵ Apr 25] workmanlike gelding: winning hurdler: fairly useful handicap chaser: won at Ludlow in April: stays 3m: acts on good to firm and heavy going: usually wears headgear: unreliable. *Venetia Williams*   c121 h–

UJAGAR (IRE) 7 gr.g. Dalakhani (IRE) – No Secrets (USA) (El Corredor (USA)) [2017/18 h76: h16d h15.8g h16.3m³ h16.8g h19.6g h23g^{pu} h16d^F h15.9v^{pu} Nov 7] rather leggy gelding: poor handicap hurdler: unproven beyond 2m: has worn headgear, including last 3 starts: tried in tongue tie: unreliable. *Kevin Bishop*   h66 §

ULIS DE VASSY (FR) 10 b.g. Voix du Nord (FR) – Helathou (FR) (Video Rock (FR)) [2017/18 c126, h–: c20.9d^{pu} c16.4s⁵ c16.3s^F c16.4s² c15.7v* c16v³ c15.7v* c16.5d⁴ c15.9v⁴ c20.3g* Apr 20] tall gelding: winning hurdler: fair handicap chaser nowadays: won at Southwell in February (twice) and April: stays 2½m: acts on good to firm and heavy going: wears headgear: has worn tongue tie: temperamental. *Laura Morgan*   c102 § h–

ULSTERMAN 6 b.g. Apple Tree (FR) – Lady Blade (IRE) (Daggers Drawn (USA)) [2017/18 b16s³ b17d Nov 13] placed on first of 2 starts in bumpers: wore tongue tie: dead. *Ian Duncan*   b68

ULTIMATE CLIMAX (IRE) 4 ch.g. Casamento (IRE) – Intricate Design (Zafonic (USA)) [2017/18 b16s^{pu} Feb 16] no show in bumper/Flat maiden. *Derek Shaw*   b–

ULTIMATE DREAM (FR) 7 b.g. Ultimately Lucky (IRE) – Carazia (FR) (Labus (FR)) [2017/18 h91: h25d c23.6g⁶ c23.8g⁶ h23.1g Aug 4] modest hurdler at best: no form in 2017/18, including over fences: has worn blinkers, including final start. *Jonjo O'Neill*   c– h–

ULT

ULTIMATUM DU ROY (FR) 10 b.g. Brier Creek (USA) – La Fleur du Roy (FR) (Sleeping Car (FR)) [2017/18 c117, h–: c23.9g³ c23.9g³ c23.9d⁵ Nov 23] good-bodied gelding: maiden hurdler: fairly useful handicap chaser: stays 3¼m: acts on heavy going: has worn cheekpieces: wears tongue tie. *Alex Hales* c117 h–

ULTRAGOLD (FR) 10 b.g. Kapgarde (FR) – Hot d'Or (FR) (Shafoun (FR)) [2017/18 c138§, h–: c19.4d³ c23.8g c21.1v² c20.8v^{pu} c20.8s c21.1s* Apr 13] c148 § h–

There are only five races a year over the Grand National course—the Grand National itself, the Foxhunters' and three other valuable handicaps, the Becher and the Grand Sefton, both run in December, and the Topham which, like the Foxhunters', is run at the Grand National meeting. The National, the Becher and the Topham all feature among the top eight most valuable handicaps run over fences in Britain, with the Grand Sefton (run over the Topham course and distance of a circuit and a bit) just outside the top twenty-five. All five races usually feature a quota of Aintree regulars, some of whom tend to reserve their best efforts for races over the unusual spruce fences which, although modified significantly in 2013, still provide a tough test for horse and rider. It is hard to say exactly why some horses cope much better than others in races over the National fences but Ultragold is one of those for whom the Grand National course is proving the perfect stage. A chaser who has sometimes promised more than he has delivered, Ultragold deserves his Timeform squiggle for the number of times he has tamely surrendered or finished weakly in races in which he should have found more. But he can be thoroughly relied on at Aintree where his record over the National fences is now two wins and a second from three starts. He has won the last two editions of the Topham Chase, becoming only the fourth horse to win the race more than once, and, in the twelve months between his two wins, he put up his best performance when runner-up in the Grand Sefton to another proven over the course Gas Line Boy.

Ultragold joined his present stable from France (where he was already a winner over fences) as a six-year-old and he took a while to find his feet, finally getting off the mark in Britain in a handicap at Exeter during his second season with Colin Tizzard. Further wins followed at Wincanton and Newbury—both at two miles—in his third season, and he won again over two at Newbury in the campaign which culminated in his first victory in the Topham, which he won at 50/1 running over the longest distance he had encountered since his first season in Britain. Ultragold started the latest season off a BHA mark 6 lb higher than the one from which he had won the Topham but, after a creditable third at Chepstow on his reappearance, he was below form and never involved on his other appearances, apart from his good effort in the Grand Sefton (in which he kept on after taking second to Gas Line Boy on the run-in before going down by four and a half lengths). Returned to Aintree still on a BHA mark 5 lb higher than in his first Topham, Ultragold started a 14/1-shot in a typically competitive field containing its share of seasoned, exposed performers (the Topham has been an open handicap since 2007 and always attracts a maximum, or near maximum field, three late withdrawals on account of the prevailing heavy going resulting in twenty-seven going to post for the latest edition). One of the less exposed Irish challengers Polidam was sent off 9/1 favourite, ahead of three 10/1-shots: Flying Angel, who had won the previous year's Manifesto Novices' Chase on the Mildmay course and was running in the Topham in preference to the Grade 1 Melling; the previous year's fourth O O Seven, attempting to give trainer Nicky Henderson a sixth Topham winner; and the useful mare Theatre Territory, a novice with several good placed efforts to her name in competitive handicaps who was ridden by 3-lb claiming amateur Mr Sam Waley-Cohen who has a fine record in races over the National fences.

The start of the Topham was unsatisfactory, with part of the tape failing to spring clear, which caused several of the jockeys to have to duck under it (Richard Johnson on Village Vic seemed to become caught up in the tape, though none of the jockeys interviewed afterwards at a stewards' inquiry reported that they had suffered any disadvantage as a result of the malfunction). Despite attritional conditions which produced the slowest time for the race since the infamous mud bath Grand National meeting of 2001, more than half the field got round in the latest Topham.

Randox Health Topham Handicap Chase, Aintree—
Ultragold takes over the lead at the Canal Turn on his way to a second successive Topham win;
stablemate and eventual runner-up Shanahan's Turn (No.19) isn't far away

In all honesty, though, only a handful were ever seriously involved, Ultragold racing prominently from the start and being in front from a long way out, shaken up only after the last, his jockey having to switch him left to avoid a loose horse before he came home three and three quarter lengths ahead of Shanahan's Turn who gave his stable a one, two (the runner-up had won the 2015 Galway Plate when trained in Ireland and had not long been with the Tizzards). Theatre Territory finished six lengths behind Shanahan's Turn in third, with the Henderson second string Kilcrea Vale completing the frame, ahead of Ballyalton and Clarcam (Polidam and Flying Angel came ninth and tenth, while O O Seven shaped as if amiss and was eventually pulled up). The three horses to have won the Topham or its equivalent on more than one occasion before Ultragold (the race commemorated former Aintree clerk of the course John Hughes for a number of years) were Culworth (1950 and 1951), Roughan (1957 and 1958) and Always Waining (2010, 2011 and 2012). Topham winners have gone on to be placed in the Grand National, but none has ever won it. It remains to be seen whether Ultragold attempts to emulate, or better, the feats of Churchtown Boy, Clan Royal (Topham winners who were runner-up in the National, the first-named only two days after his Topham victory), and Irish Lizard (one of the early Topham winners who was twice third in the big one). One thing is certain though: if Ultragold is fit and well, he will be back at Aintree in April for either the National itself or for a third tilt at the Topham, and will be one for the short-list whichever is chosen for him. All eight of his career wins so far have come over fences and it is worth noting that he is still eligible for novice hurdles should connections wish to run him over the smaller obstacles in preparation for Aintree.

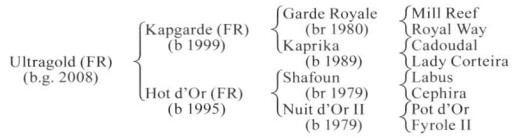

	Kapgarde (FR) (b 1999)	Garde Royale (br 1980)	Mill Reef
Ultragold (FR) (b.g. 2008)			Royal Way
		Kaprika (b 1989)	Cadoudal
			Lady Corteira
	Hot d'Or (FR) (b 1995)	Shafoun (br 1979)	Labus
			Cephira
		Nuit d'Or II (b 1979)	Pot d'Or
			Fyrole II

The sturdy Ultragold is by the French sire Kapgarde, a half-brother to the Nicky Henderson-trained very smart hurdler/chaser Geos. Kapgarde was a useful juvenile hurdler for Guillaume Macaire and was also runner-up over fences in the Group 1 Prix Ferdinand Dufaure for four-year-olds before his racing career was cut short. Ultragold's unraced dam Hot d'Or is a sister to the Grand Steeple-Chase de

ULU

Paris and King George VI Chase winner First Gold, and the family on the distaff side is steeped in jumping. Ultragold's grandam Nuit d'Or II was a high-class performer in cross country races in France and his great grandam Fyrole II, also a successful racemare in France, became the grandam of Galway Hurdle winner Rebel Fitz and the Mersey Novices' Hurdle winner Ubak. Ultragold's dam Hot d'Or has bred numerous other winners including the fairly useful French chaser at up to twenty-one furlongs Steeple d'Or and the fair two and a half mile chaser Quell The Storm (both by Sleeping Car), as well as the useful seven-year-old chaser Braqueur d'Or (by Epalo) who won three times in the latest season at up to three miles. Ultragold, who wears a tongue tie, stays three miles and acts on heavy going. *Colin Tizzard*

ULUROO (FR) 6 b.g. Centennial (IRE) – Kica (FR) (Noir Et Or) [2017/18 h87, b–: h16.2g^6 h16.2g^2 May 28] modest form over hurdles: best effort when second in novice at Kelso in May: will prove suited by 2¼m+. *Pauline Robson* — **h92**

ULVA FERRY (IRE) 6 ch.g. Stowaway – Lisacul Queen (IRE) (Old Vic) [2017/18 h84: h19.5d c23.5s^5 c25.1v^{pu} c25.7v^{pu} Apr 1] little form over hurdles/fences. *Chris Gordon* — **c57 h–**

ULYSSES (GER) 4 b.g. Sinndar (IRE) – Ungarin (GER) (Goofalik (USA)) [2017/18 h17.7d^4 h20v^2 h16.8v^3 h18.8s^5 Mar 24] good-topped gelding: half-brother to bumper winner/fairly useful hurdler Utility (2m winner, by Yeats): fair maiden on Flat, should stay beyond 1½m: fair form over hurdles: left Ralph Beckett after first start, Stuart Edmunds after second: in cheekpieces last 3 starts. *Barry Brennan* — **h107**

UMBERTO D'OLIVATE (FR) 10 b.g. Alberto Giacometti (IRE) – Komunion (FR) (Luchiroverte (IRE)) [2017/18 c120§, h–: c24.2s c24.2v^3 c30.7v c25.1v^{pu} c23.6v^{bd} c23.6v^3 Apr 14] lengthy gelding: maiden hurdler: fairly useful handicap chaser, below form in 2017/18: stays 31f: acts on heavy going: has worn headgear: temperamental. *Robert Walford* — **c107 § h– §**

U ME AND THEM (IRE) 9 ch.g. Vertical Speed (FR) – Bodies Pride (IRE) (John French) [2017/18 c–: c25.3d^{pu} c24.5g^4 c24.5g^{pu} c23s^{pu} Jan 9] point winner: modest form on completed start in chases: trained by Alan Phillips third start only: often let down by jumping. *Miss Hannah Taylor* — **c91 x**

UMNDENI (FR) 4 b.g. Balko (FR) – Marie Royale (FR) (Turgeon (USA)) [2017/18 b16d* Apr 26] £175,000 3-y-o: sturdy gelding: second foal: brother to bumper winner/ smart hurdler Vision des Flos (17f winner, stays 21f): dam, lightly raced in France, half-sister to Galway Plate/Ryanair Chase winner Balko des Flos (by Balko): 3/1, won bumper at Warwick (by 2¾ lengths from Morning Vicar) on debut: sure to go on to better things. *Philip Hobbs* — **b101 p**

U NAME IT (IRE) 10 b.g. Gold Well – Bypharthebest (IRE) (Phardante (FR)) [2017/18 h24.7d^{pu} h19.7s^{pu} h25.3d^{pu} h18.1v^4 h20.5v^5 Mar 9] fairly useful handicap hurdler at best, little impact after long absence in 2017/18: no form in chases: stays 3m: acts on good to soft going. *R. Mike Smith* — **c– h89**

UN BEAU ROMAN (FR) 10 bl.g. Roman Saddle (IRE) – Koukie (FR) (Lute Antique (FR)) [2017/18 c133§, h–: c16mp^{pu} c16.3v^5 c15.9g c15.9d^5 c18.8d c15.5v^4 Feb 16] lengthy gelding: winning hurdler: useful handicap chaser, below form in 2017/18: stays 2¼m: acts on heavy going: wears hood: often races towards rear: unreliable. *Paul Henderson* — **c116 § h–**

UNBLINKING 5 b.g. Cacique (IRE) – Deliberate (King's Best (USA)) [2017/18 h95: h20.6v^6 h19.5s^2 Apr 27] angular gelding: fair form over hurdles: stays 19f: acts on soft going: often races towards rear. *Nigel Twiston-Davies* — **h103**

UNCLE ALASTAIR 6 b.g. Midnight Legend – Cyd Charisse (Kayf Tara) [2017/18 b98: h20.5v^F h20s* h20.5v* h16v* h22s^3 h24.3g^3 Apr 20] unbeaten in 2 bumpers: useful form over hurdles: won novices at Carlisle and Ayr in December, and again at Ayr in January: will stay further than 3m: acts on heavy going: tried in tongue tie. *Nicky Richards* — **h131**

UNCLE DANNY (IRE) 9 b.g. Catcher In The Rye (IRE) – Bobset Leader (IRE) (Bob Back (USA)) [2017/18 c136, h–: c16v^5 c20v^3 c19.5v c21s^3 c21.3s^2 Mar 9] well-made gelding: winning hurdler: useful handicap chaser: second at Leopardstown (1¾ lengths behind Spider Web) in March: stays 21f: best form on soft/heavy going: tried in blinkers: has worn tongue tie, including in 2017/18. *John Queally, Ireland* — **c139 h–**

UNCLE JIMMY (IRE) 11 b.g. Alderbrook – Carrabawn (Buckskin (FR)) [2017/18 c–, h137: c23.4s^3 c24.2v^{pu} Apr 17] useful hurdler for Philip Hobbs: lightly raced in chases, modest form in hunters in 2017/18: stays 3¼m: acts on heavy going. *Miss Beth Childs* — **c97 h–**

UNCLE PERCY 6 b.g. Sir Percy – Forsythia (Most Welcome) [2017/18 h84, b87: h20f^3 h20.7g^F h21s Apr 9] workmanlike gelding: modest form over hurdles: stays 2½m: acts on firm going: tried in cheekpieces. *Ben Pauling* — **h96**

UND

UNCLE PETTIT (IRE) 10 b.g. Heron Island (IRE) – Special Ballot (IRE) (Perugino (USA)) [2017/18 c76x, h–: c24g^{pu} May 13] workmanlike gelding: maiden hurdler: poor handicap chaser: stays 25f: acts on heavy going: has worn cheekpieces, including in 2017/18: wears tongue tie. *Jonathan Portman*   c–
h–

UNCLE TONE (IRE) 9 b.g. Pelder (IRE) – Daisy A Day (IRE) (Asir) [2017/18 h105: h23g h23.3d^4 h23.1g^6 Aug 6] useful-looking gelding: fair handicap hurdler, below form in 2017/18: stays 23f: acts on good to firm and heavy going: in cheekpieces last 2 starts. *Michael Appleby*   h95

UNDEFINED BEAUTY (IRE) 9 gr.m. Kayf Tara – Lorna (IRE) (Roselier (FR)) [2017/18 h20.5g h20g h19d h16g^2 h15.7g* h19.9g* h16.2g^3 h21.7v^2 h16.4v^2 Feb 5] sixth foal: half-sister to fair hurdler/chaser Maid of Malabar (2m-2½m winner, by Oscar Schindler): dam unraced half-sister to fairly useful hurdlers Curvaceous (2m winner) and Knighton Lad (stayed 3¼m): fair handicap hurdler: won at Southwell (conditional) in October and Sedgefield (mares) in November: left Edward Stanners after third start: stays 2¾m: acts on heavy going: has worn hood. *Olly Murphy*   h113

UNDER THE PHONE (IRE) 9 b.g. Heron Island (IRE) – Theo On The Bench (IRE) (Mister Lord (USA)) [2017/18 c85, h–: c19.9s^5 c20.5s^3 Apr 9] winning hurdler: fair handicap chaser: stays 3m, effective over shorter: acts on good to soft going: has worn headgear, including in 2017/18. *Robin Dickin*   c107
h–

UNDER THE RED SKY (IRE) 11 ch.g. Insatiable (IRE) – Official Secret (Polish Patriot (USA)) [2017/18 c81§: c20.1v^{pu} c23.4g^3 c24.2d c20v^4 c19.2d c23.8s c20v^3 c20.1v^2 c16.3s^5 c20.9v^6 c23.4v^3 c24.2d^{pu} Apr 23] modest maiden chaser: stays 3m: acts on heavy going: wears headgear: no battler. *Kenny Johnson*   c85 §

UNDER THE WOODS 6 b.g. Kayf Tara – Palmito (IRE) (Great Palm (USA)) [2017/18 h16s h15.8v^3 h15.8v^3 h16s^2 h18.5v* Apr 8] first foal: dam (h104), 2m hurdle winner, half-sister to useful hurdler/smart but temperamental chaser (2m-2½m winner) Crescent Island: fair form over hurdles: in cheekpieces/tongue tie, won novice seller at Exeter in April: will be suited by 2½m: raced only on soft/heavy going. *Evan Williams*   h100

UN DE SCEAUX (FR) 10 b.g. Denham Red (FR) – Hotesse de Sceaux (FR) (April Night (FR)) [2017/18 c169, h–: c16.7v* c16.8v* c20.8s^2 c20v* c16s* Apr 24]   c169
h–

'It is better to sell and regret, than to keep and regret,' is usually the best advice for any small owner who finds himself or herself being offered good money for a promising young performer. So many horses thought to have the potential to become high-class performers end up falling by the wayside, particularly over jumps, and knowing there can be no guarantees in racing usually results in the cheque book winning the day. That didn't happen with Un de Sceaux, though, whose owner Edward O'Connell was offered 'mad stuff, crazy money' for ex-French Un de Sceaux after two runaway wins in novice hurdles in his first season with the Willie Mullins stable as a five-year-old. Colm O'Connell, son of the owner, says there was 'a brief temptation to take the money, but my dad reckoned that no-one had made an offer to buy any of the other horses he had had over the years and he thought this was the one we needed to hold on to.' The decision has certainly paid off and must have provided unbridled joy for the O'Connell family, who are typically accompanied on racedays by plenty of friends and Un de Sceaux supporters all wearing scarves in the pale blue and orange of Edward O'Connell's racing colours. Those colours have now been carried to victory by Un de Sceaux in twenty of his twenty-five completed starts for the Mullins stable, for which he has won prize money well in excess of £1m. Un de Sceaux's record over fences—twelve wins (nine of them Grade 1s) and four seconds from sixteen completed starts—is a remarkable testament to his reliability and consistency. Consistency with knobs on. There have been only a handful of occasions in the last four seasons when Un de Sceaux has failed to run up to, or very close to, his Timeform rating, and he must be an absolute pleasure to own.

After that short first season at Closutton, Un de Sceaux added five more wins from five starts in his second season with Willie Mullins adopting a lower-key approach than he usually does with his best horses (Un de Sceaux missed the big championship events at Cheltenham and Punchestown in favour of a return to France for two easier graded races over hurdles). Un de Sceaux was therefore sent chasing without ever having been tested against the very best hurdlers in Britain and

Ireland, though he had shown himself a top-class hurdler without actually meeting any tip-top opposition. As a free-going front runner, typically bowling along in front and opening up a big lead, Un de Sceaux put up straightforward performances that made it easy for the handicappers to assess him. Apart from falling when an 8/1-on shot on his debut over fences (with the race at his mercy), Un de Sceaux recorded clear-cut victories in the Arkle at both Leopardstown and Cheltenham, and in the Ryanair Novices' Chase at Punchestown, to establish himself as the Timeform top-rated two-mile chaser while still a novice (his performance in the Arkle being better than the one recorded by Dodging Bullets in the Queen Mother Champion Chase).

Starting odds on for the Queen Mother Champion Chase in his second season over fences, Un de Sceaux came up short against a resurgent Sprinter Sacre (he also won the Prix La Barka at Auteuil, reverting to hurdling after being beaten again by Sprinter Sacre in the Celebration Chase at Sandown). The two defeats by Sprinter Sacre, together with the emergence of the imperious Douvan who scarcely put a foot wrong in his unbeaten novice chasing campaign, saw Un de Sceaux slip down the pecking order at Closutton. In the last two seasons, he has been aimed at the Ryanair Chase at the Cheltenham Festival while firstly Douvan, and then Min and Douvan, have been the Closutton contenders in the Queen Mother Champion Chase. Douvan started at 9/2-on in 2017 but he was beaten a long way from home and was afterwards found to have suffered a hairline stress fracture of the pelvis. In the end, Douvan didn't race again for twelve months and he was a faller in the latest Queen Mother Champion Chase, in which Min finished second to Altior (Willie Mullins has yet to saddle a winner of the race).

Douvan was originally pencilled in to return in the Tingle Creek Chase at Sandown in December, a race Un de Sceaux had won the year before, when doing duty for Closutton in place of Douvan. In the end, the latest Tingle Creek went by without either Un de Sceaux or Douvan (shortly afterwards said to be suffering from intermittent lameness and to be 'missing the rest of the season'). Un de Sceaux reappeared instead in the Kerry Group Hilly Way Chase at Cork (his owner's local track) where he beat British raider Top Gamble unchallenged by twenty-five lengths, another wide-margin rout to add to his impressive record. Un de Sceaux appeared next in the Royal Salute Whisky Clarence House Chase at Ascot in January, a race in which he had landed the odds in each of the two previous seasons, the 2017 renewal taking place at Cheltenham. It was the eleventh running of Ascot's big January feature since it became a Grade 1 conditions event (previously staged as a very valuable handicap which often attracted a leading two-mile chaser conceding lumps of weight to smart rivals). Un de Sceaux, starting at 9/4-on, made the most of a good opportunity and didn't need to be at his best to win by seven lengths and

Royal Salute Whisky Clarence House Chase, Ascot—
a third successive win in the race for Un de Sceaux who lands the odds from outsider Speredek (cheekpieces); Brain Power (centre) is about to fall two out

Boylesports Champion Chase, Punchestown—a dashing front-running ride from Mr Patrick Mullins as Un de Sceaux lowers the colours of odds-on stable-companion Douvan

fourteen lengths from Speredek and Kylemore Lough, after his main rival Brain Power fell heavily when just in second at the penultimate fence (looking unlikely to threaten Un de Sceaux).

Un de Sceaux's three odds-on victories in the Clarence House, which had a first prize in the latest season of £85,425, were fairly typical of the race since it was turned into a conditions event. Eight of the eleven runnings have had an odds-on favourite and only one favourite has been sent off at longer than 11/8. There were, incidentally, four other Grade 1 or Grade 2 non-handicaps in Britain on the same afternoon and, just like the Clarence House, three of them were virtually one-horse contests and all four were won by the favourite (La Bague Au Roi won the Warfield Mares' Hurdle at 11/8-on, First Flow the Rossington Main Novices' hurdle at 9/4, The New One the Champion Hurdle Trial at evens, and Testify the Altcar Novices' Chase at 15/8-on). Field sizes in what were the day's most important races averaged less than five and the margin of victory averaged around eight lengths. If the race planners had set out with the deliberate intention of creating the dreariest shop window for the sport, on the biggest day of the sporting week, they could hardly have done a better job!

The original entries for the big championship races at the Cheltenham Festival were made after the turn of the year and Douvan was among them after 'surprising with his progress'. Willie Mullins tends to keep his star performers apart and Un de Sceaux, in particular, has come up against very few of his stablemates in his career. There was some surprise, therefore, when, on the Sunday before the Festival, it was announced that Douvan was likely to be redirected to the Ryanair Chase—'which looks to be cutting up'—instead of lining up with the same owner's Min in the Queen Mother Champion Chase. In the end, though, Un de Sceaux carried the banner for Closutton alone in the Ryanair in which he met only five rivals, among them the 2013 winner Cue Card and the runner-up in the Christmas Chase at Leopardstown and Galway Plate winner Balko des Flos. The latest Ryanair Chase provided a rare hiccup in Un de Sceaux's career. Starting at 11/8-on, he wasn't able to produce his best on the day, capitulating pretty tamely to Balko des Flos who left him standing entering the home straight and eventually beat him by four and a half lengths.

Un de Sceaux was out again two and a half weeks later in the inaugural Devenish Chase over two and a half miles at Fairyhouse on Irish Grand National day (the race has been transferred from Navan, where it was run as the Webster Cup Chase, and the aim is for it to eventually become a Grade 1 as there isn't a chase of that type over two and a half miles at the Punchestown Festival). Un de

Sceaux resumed winning ways at Fairyhouse, winning by eighteen lengths from A Toi Phil after the outcome looked in the balance when the challenging Doctor Phoenix (receiving 5 lb) tipped up at the second last when alongside Un de Sceaux and seemingly travelling just as well.

The result of the Devenish Chase had little effect on the ante-post betting for the Boylesports Champion Chase, the two-mile championship at Punchestown, in which Un de Sceaux had been beaten by Fox Norton when odds-on twelve months earlier. The four horses at the head of the ante-post betting for the latest running were all trained by Willie Mullins. They were Great Field, Min, Douvan and, fourth choice at 6/1, Un de Sceaux. The odds against them all turning up looked much longer, but one of the consequences of the battle between Willie Mullins and Gordon Elliott for the trainers' championship in Ireland was that both stables were mob-handed in many of the races at the Punchestown Festival, as Elliott tried to hold on to a sizeable lead (he started the meeting even further ahead than he had been at the same stage the previous year when Mullins had overtaken him on the final two days of Punchestown). Racegoers and armchair viewers were treated to some tremendously competitive-looking races, including Douvan, Min and Un de Sceaux taking on each other on the opening day in the Champion Chase in which the Mullins and Elliott stables were responsible for four runners apiece in the nine-runner line-up (Doctor Phoenix and A Toi Phil were among the Elliott-trained quartet). In truth, the Champion Chase turned into more of a procession than the blood-and-thunder encounter that many hoped for. 'Team tactics' are not allowed in horse racing but it was certainly possible to argue that Un de Sceaux was allowed too easy a lead in the first part of the race by the other Mullins runners. Un de Sceaux went with plenty of enthusiasm out in front, and he jumped superbly all the way. By halfway, he had begun to draw further clear of odds-on Douvan who had followed him from the start, also travelling strongly, and, when Douvan was far from fluent at both the third last and the second last, it was clear that he was going to come out second best. Un de Sceaux kept on well under pressure to win by two and three quarter lengths, with A Toi Phil a further seven lengths behind Douvan in third. There was another four and a half lengths to the close finishers Min and Doctor Phoenix, with Ballycasey picking up sixth prize money of €2,750 for the Mullins stable. Ballycasey, incidentally, was one of only five different stablemates whom Un de Sceaux had come up against in the course of his twenty-six previous starts for Closutton. It is interesting to reflect that it took a knife-edge situation in a trainers' championship—for which only prestige is at stake—to produce a clash between three of the best two-mile chasers in training that might well have taken place in the Queen Mother Champion Chase back in the days of a three-day, eighteen-race Cheltenham Festival. Un de Sceaux's victory, incidentally, was his third at the Punchestown Festival.

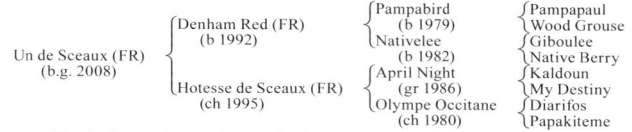

Un de Sceaux (FR) (b.g. 2008)	Denham Red (FR) (b 1992)	Pampabird (b 1979)	Pampapaul
			Wood Grouse
		Nativelee (b 1982)	Giboulee
			Native Berry
	Hotesse de Sceaux (FR) (ch 1995)	April Night (gr 1986)	Kaldoun
			My Destiny
		Olympe Occitane (ch 1980)	Diarifos
			Papakiteme

Un de Sceaux's physique—he is strong and compact but not the biggest for fences—was reportedly one of the reasons Willie Mullins was able to fulfil the O'Connells' order to buy them 'a good horse for small money'. Un de Sceaux's breeder sent Un de Sceaux's undistinguished dam Hotesse de Sceau to the sparely-used Denham Red because the stallion was 'only about ten kilometres away'. There were reportedly 'several trainers who came to look at Un de Sceaux before he had run, but they didn't like him physically. He wasn't a colt who really took the eye.' Un de Sceaux's breeder leased him to his first trainer Fabrice Foucher but he was always quite headstrong and difficult and won his first race at Machecoul 'by miles with the jockey just a passenger.' It was a similar story some months later at Saint-Brieuc and Mullins is said to have warned the O'Connells that the horse took too much out of himself and 'might only last a year or two, but you'll have some fun.' Un de Sceaux can thankfully be ridden with a little more restraint these days but he

UNO

is suited by forcing the pace. A strong traveller, Un de Sceaux failed to stay twenty-five furlongs the only time he was tried over further than twenty-one furlongs (he is fully effective at the minimum trip). He used to make the odd bad mistake over fences—he has fallen twice in his career—but is more consistently fluent nowadays and gave a foot-perfect display in the Champion Chase at Punchestown where he was ridden for the first time by Mr Patrick Mullins who was champion amateur in Ireland for the tenth time (one short of the record held by Mr Ted Walsh whose record total for an amateur of 545 wins passed shortly after the end of the latest season). Un de Sceaux, as genuine and consistent a horse as you'll find, wore ear plugs before the latest Ryanair Chase but they were removed at the start. *W. P. Mullins, Ireland*

UNDISPUTED (IRE) 7 b.m. King's Theatre (IRE) – Gleanntan (IRE) (Lil's Boy (USA)) [2017/18 h106p: h20g h18.5s* h20.6d^2 h21.7v h20.7s^4 h15.7v^3 Mar 29] fair hurdler: won mares maiden at Newton Abbot in June: stays 21f: acts on soft going: wears hood. *Noel Williams* **h106**

UNEX PICASSO 10 b.g. Galileo (IRE) – Ruff Shod (USA) (Storm Boot (USA)) [2017/18 c–, h–: h23.3g^{pu} Jun 3] good-topped gelding: fair hurdler at best, very lightly raced and no form since 2013/14: pulled up only start over fences: has worn cheekpieces/tongue tie. *Barry Murtagh* **c– h–**

UN GUET APENS (FR) 10 b.g. Enrique – Belisama (FR) (Mansonnien (FR)) [2017/18 c–, h107: c20d* h22.8v^6 c20.1s^4 c21.6s* h18.1v^2 c24.5v^5 c20d^6 c20.1v^2 Apr 14] fair handicap hurdler: fairly useful handicap chaser: won at Carlisle in November and Kelso in January: stays 2¾m: acts on heavy going: wears headgear: no easy ride. *James Ewart* **c121 § h108 §**

UNIONISTE (FR) 10 gr.g. Dom Alco (FR) – Gleep Will (FR) (Cadoudal (FR)) [2017/18 c128, h–: c23s^2 c25.1v* c26d* c26.3v c25.1v* c21.1s Apr 12] tall, useful-looking gelding: winning hurdler: useful hunter chaser: won at Wincanton and Fontwell in February, and again at Wincanton (finished alone) in March: stays 3¼m: acts on heavy going: has worn cheekpieces: tried in tongue tie. *Paul Nicholls* **c130 h–**

UNION JACK D'YCY (FR) 10 b.g. Bonnet Rouge (FR) – Jacady (FR) (Fill My Hopes (FR)) [2017/18 c–, h92: c23.8g c25g^5 h26g^{pu} c24.2s^{pu} Nov 15] maiden hurdler/fairly useful chaser, no form in 2017/18: has worn cheekpieces, including final start: often let down by jumping over fences. *Deborah Faulkner* **c– x h–**

UNISON (IRE) 8 b.g. Jeremy (USA) – Easter Song (USA) (Rubiano (USA)) [2017/18 h128: h15.8g* h16s h16v^5 h15.7v^3 h16.5v* h16.5s* h16.5s^{pu} Apr 14] sturdy gelding: useful handicap hurdler: won at Huntingdon in November and Taunton (twice, by 4½ lengths from Caid du Lin second occasion) in February: third in Champion Hurdle Trial at Haydock (11½ lengths behind The New One) in January: raced mainly around 2m: acts on good to firm and heavy going: usually races close up. *Jeremy Scott* **h141**

UNIVERSAL SOLDIER (IRE) 13 b.g. Winged Love (IRE) – Waterland Gale (IRE) (Fourstars Allstar (USA)) [2017/18 c25.5s^4 c25.5g^{pu} Aug 28] big gelding: winning hurdler: useful handicap chaser, below form after long absence in 2017/18: stays 33f: acts on heavy going: has worn headgear: unreliable. *Peter Bowen* **c118 § h–**

UN NOBLE (FR) 8 gr.g. Near Honor (GER) – Noble Gary (FR) (Loup Solitaire (USA)) [2017/18 c100, h–: h23.9g c24.1v^{pu} c20.5v^{pu} Jan 31] fair hurdler/fairly useful chaser at best, no form in 2017/18: in tongue tie last 3 starts. *Nicky Richards* **c– h–**

U NO LIKE (IRE) 6 b.g. Daylami (IRE) – Bee-Hive Queen (IRE) (King's Ride) [2017/18 h19.5s Feb 24] placed twice from 4 starts in points: well beaten in maiden hurdle. *Grace Harris* **h–**

UNO VALOROSO (FR) 10 b.g. Voix du Nord (FR) – Danse d'Avril (FR) (Quart de Vin (FR)) [2017/18 c107§, h–: h16.2s^5 c17.4s* c15.7v^2 c17.1v^3 c15.2v^3 c15.7s^2 c15.2d^5 Mar 29] close-coupled gelding: maiden hurdler: fair handicap chaser: won at Bangor in December: stays 2½m: acts on heavy going: tried in cheekpieces: front runner/races prominently: untrustworthy. *Mark Walford* **c112 § h85**

UNOWHATIMEANHARRY 10 b.g. Sir Harry Lewis (USA) – Red Nose Lady (Teenoso (USA)) [2017/18 h165: h20s* h24.2d^2 h24.4d^3 h24s Mar 15] leggy gelding: high-class hurdler at best, smart nowadays: won 3-runner minor event at Aintree (by 1½ lengths from Value At Risk) in November: placed in Long Distance Hurdle at Newbury (2¼ lengths behind Beer Goggles) and Long Walk Hurdle at Ascot (10¾ lengths behind Sam Spinner) following month: stays 3m: acts on heavy going: wears tongue tie. *Harry Fry* **h154**

UNP

UN PROPHETE (FR) 7 gr.g. Carlotamix (FR) – Pollita (FR) (Nombre Premier) [2017/18 c128, h–07: c16.3g⁴ c16d^F c17.5v* c15.7s^{pu} Jan 11] big gelding: maiden hurdler: fairly useful handicap chaser: won at Exeter in November: raced mainly around 2m: acts on heavy going. *Venetia Williams*   c129 h–

UNSAFE CONDUCT 5 ch.g. Pasternak – Symbiosis (Bien Bien (USA)) [2017/18 h90, b–: h16g^F h15.3g⁶ h16.8v⁶ h16.2s h16.7s⁵ Mar 24] rather unfurnished gelding: well held in bumpers: modest form over hurdles: raced around 2m: acts on soft going: often races towards rear, usually freely. *Colin Tizzard*   h91

UNTIL WINNING (FR) 10 b.g. Kapgarde (FR) – Fripperie (FR) (Bojador (FR)) [2017/18 c19.4√⁵ c21.4v* c20v² c22.9s⁵ c23.9d⁴ Apr 22] useful-looking gelding: maiden hurdler: fairly useful handicap chaser: won at Market Rasen in January: stays 3m: acts on heavy going: usually races towards rear. *Tom George*   c120 h–

UNWIN VC 4 b.g. Black Sam Bellamy (IRE) – Becky B (Alflora (IRE)) [2017/18 b16.8s* b15.3v* Apr 9] £47,000 3-y-o: first foal: dam unraced half-sister to useful hurdler (stayed 25f) Lord Generous out of top-class 2½m-3m hurdle winner Lady Rebecca: useful form in bumpers: won both starts, at Exeter (by 2¼ lengths from Come On Teddy) in February and Wincanton (by 1¼ lengths from Lamanver Pippin) in April: good prospect. *Bob Buckler*   b106 p

UPBEAT COBBLER (FR) 10 gr.m. Brier Creek (USA) – Jade de Chalamont (FR) (Royal Charter (FR)) [2017/18 c109, h–: c24.5g³ c24g c27.6s^{pu} c23.6s² c27.5d⁶ Apr 22] good-topped mare: winning hurdler: fair handicap chaser, below form in 2017/18: stays 3m: acts on heavy going: has worn cheekpieces, including last 3 starts: front runner/races prominently: often let down by jumping. *Henry Daly*   c94 x h–

UP FOR REVIEW (IRE) 9 br.g. Presenting – Coolsilver (IRE) (Good Thyne (USA)) [2017/18 c29v² c20v* c20v⁴ c21s Apr 27] strong, rather plain gelding: useful hurdler: similar form over fences: won maiden at Gowran in March: fourth in Ryanair Gold Cup Novices' Chase at Fairyhouse (16 lengths behind Al Boum Photo) following month: stays 3m: acts on heavy going. *W. P. Mullins, Ireland*   c144 h–

UPHAM RUNNING (IRE) 10 b.g. Definite Article – Tara Brooch (IRE) (Supreme Leader) [2017/18 h–: h19.2v^{pu} h15.9v² h15.9v⁴ h19.8v⁶ h16.5v⁴ Apr 12] angular gelding: has had breathing operation: little impact in points: poor handicap hurdler: stays 2½m: acts on heavy going: tried in blinkers. *Kate Buckett*   h76

UP HELLY AA KING 7 ch.g. And Beyond (IRE) – Gretton (Terimon) [2017/18 b85: h16v^{pu} h16v h16v⁴ h22.8s⁵ h18.1v⁵ Apr 16] modest form over hurdles: should stay further than 2m: acts on heavy going: in tongue tie last 3 starts: often races towards rear. *N. W. Alexander*   h95

UPPERTOWN PRINCE (IRE) 6 b.g. Strategic Prince – Tarrawarra (IRE) (Kayf Tara) [2017/18 h19.6s* h23.1v² h22.8v² h20.5v* h24.7s⁴ Apr 13] £35,000 5-y-o: useful-looking gelding: first foal: dam (c96), placed in points/2½m chase, half-sister to fairly useful hurdler/chaser (stayed 2½m) Ballybogey out of half-sister to smart hurdler/top-class chaser Native Upmanship (best around 2½m): point winner: useful form over hurdles: won novices at Bangor in December and Ayr in March: improved when fourth in Sefton Novices' Hurdle at Aintree: Stays 25f: raced only on soft/heavy going. *Donald McCain*   h140

UPSETTHEODDS (IRE) 6 b.g. Oscar (IRE) – Cruella de Vil (Overbury (IRE)) [2017/18 b16.7v⁴ Jan 4] point winner: 5/1, fourth in bumper at Bangor (17¾ lengths behind Before Midnight). *Donald McCain*   b71

UPSILON BLEU (FR) 10 b.g. Panoramic – Glycine Bleue (FR) (Le Nain Jaune (FR)) [2017/13 c144, h–: c16.5v² c16.8d⁵ c19.9d² c16.4s c16.5g⁵ Apr 21] strong gelding: winning hurdler: useful handicap chaser: second at Ayr (3 lengths behind Archive) in November and Musselburgh (1¼ lengths behind Knockgraffon) in January: stays 23f: acts on heavy going: tried in hood: often races prominently. *Pauline Robson*   c139 h–

UPSWING (IRE) 10 b.g. Beneficial – Native Country (IRE) (Be My Native (USA)) [2017/18 c138x, h–: c23.8m c26.1m c24s⁶ Feb 21] strong gelding: winning hurdler: useful handicap chaser, below form in 2017/18: stays 27f: acts on heavy going: wears headgear: often races towards rear: often let down by jumping. *Jonjo O'Neill*   c120 x h–

UP TO AL (IRE) 10 b.g. Heron Island (IRE) – Pretonic (Precocious) [2017/18 h68: c21.2d^{pu} May 29] point winner: little form over hurdles: pulled up in maiden hunter on chasing debut: has worn headgear. *R. D. Potter*   c– h–

UTM

UP TO NO GOOD (IRE) 5 b.g. Oscar (IRE) – You Take Care (IRE) (Definite Article) [2017/18 b16.3s⁵ b16v⁴ Mar 20] €50,000 3-y-o: third foal: half-brother to useful hurdler/chaser Keeper Hill (2½m-3m winner, by Westerner) and a winning pointer by St Jovite: dam (h92), maiden hurdler (stayed 19f), half-sister to useful hurdler/top-class chaser Irish Cavalier (stayed 3¼m) and useful hurdler/smart chaser Shattered Love (stays 3m): fair form in bumpers. *Warren Greatrex* **b87**

UPTOWN FUNK (IRE) 4 b.g. Galileo (IRE) – All's Forgotten (USA) (Darshaan) [2017/18 h15.6d* h15.6s⁴ h19.4d^F Mar 16] closely related to fairly useful hurdler Rae's Creek (17f/2¼m winner, by New Approach) and fair hurdler Exulto (2m winner, by Barathea): fairly useful maiden on Flat, stays 16.5f: fairly useful form over hurdles: won juvenile at Musselburgh (by 1½ lengths from Je Suis Charlie) in January. *Keith Dalgleish* **h119**

URADEL (GER) 7 b.g. Kallisto (GER) – Unavita (GER) (Vettori (IRE)) [2017/18 h16d* h19s* h16s Apr 17] dam half-sister to fairly useful 2m hurdler Utility: fairly useful on Flat, stays 1¾m: fairly useful form over hurdles: won maiden at Listowel in June and novice at Naas in February: stays 19f: acts on soft going: tried in hood. *W. P. Mullins, Ireland* **h129**

URBAN KODE (IRE) 10 b.g. Kodiac – Urbanize (USA) (Chester House (USA)) [2017/18 h92: h20.2g⁵ h20.2g³ h20.2d¹ h18.6g² h16.4d⁴ Mar 16] modest handicap hurdler: stays 2½m: acts on good to firm and heavy going: wears headgear. *Lucinda Russell* **h86**

URCA DE LIMA 5 b.m. Black Sam Bellamy (IRE) – Dame Fonteyn (Suave Dancer (USA)) [2017/18 h98: b16v¹ b16.2d⁵ Apr 23] good-topped mare: modest form in bumpers. *Anthony Honeyball* **b76**

URGENT DE GREGAINE (FR) 10 b.g. Truth Or Dare – Hispanie (FR) (Bad Conduct (USA)) [2017/18 c132, h88: c34.5s² c30.2g³ c30.2s² Mar 14] lengthy gelding: twice-raced hurdler: smart cross-country chaser: placed all 3 starts in 2017/18, including in Glenfarclas Chase at Cheltenham (2 lengths behind Tiger Roll) in March: stays 4¼m: acts on soft going: in cheekpieces/tongue tie last 5 starts. *Emmanuel Clayeux, France* **c148 h–**

URIAH HEEP (FR) 9 b.g. Danehill Dancer (IRE) – Canasita (Zafonic (USA)) [2017/18 c–, h91: h17m⁵ h20.2d h20.9d^bd Oct 8] sturdy gelding: fairly useful hurdler at best, no form in 2017/18: winning chaser: has worn cheekpieces. *R. Mike Smith* **c– h–**

URTHEONEIWANT (FR) 8 b.m. Kayf Tara – Mascareigne (FR) (Subotica (FR)) [2017/18 c–, h115: c20m⁶ c19.9d c19.5g⁴ c20g^bd c19.2g⁵ c20.1g³ c23.8m* c25.5d³ c23.8s⁵ c23.8d² c23.8v⁴ Sep 27] winning hurdler: fairly useful handicap chaser: won novice event at Perth in July: stays 3¼m: acts on good to firm and good to soft going: often wears hood: in tongue tie last 2 starts: held up. *Gordon Elliott, Ireland* **c117 h–**

URTHEONETHATIWANT (IRE) 5 ch.g. Shantou (USA) – Roberta Supreme (IRE) (Bob's Return (IRE)) [2017/18 h19.5d h15.8d h16.8v^pu h19.8v Apr 9] no form over hurdles. *Jeremy Scott* **h–**

URUMQI (FR) 7 b.g. Soldier of Fortune (IRE) – Love In Paradise (Dalakhani (IRE)) [2017/18 c19.9s* c22.9v³ c26.4v^pu c22.9v² c19.9v² c30.2s^pu Mar 14] lengthy gelding: maiden on Flat: maiden hurdler: fairly useful novice chaser: won minor event at Pau in December: stiff task when pulled up in Glenfarclas Chase (Cross Country) at Cheltenham final outing: stays 21f: acts on heavy going: has worn headgear/tongue tie, including in 2017/18. *David Cottin, France* **c128 h–**

US AND THEM (IRE) 5 b.g. Stowaway – Manorville (IRE) (Flemensfirth (USA)) [2017/18 b16d³ h16v* h16v* h16.4s Mar 13] €28,000 3-y-o: rather unfurnished gelding: second foal: dam fair hurdler/chaser (2½m-2¾m winner): made frame in bumpers: useful form over hurdles: won maiden at Cork in November and novice at Punchestown (by ½ length from Trainwreck) in December: second in Irish Independent Hurdle at Limerick (2½ lengths behind Duca de Thaix) later in December. *Joseph Patrick O'Brien, Ireland* **h136 b92**

UTILITY (GER) 7 b.g. Yeats (IRE) – Ungarin (GER) (Goofalik (USA)) [2017/18 h109: h16m^F h16g* h16g* h16d h16.3d⁶ h19.4d Dec 2] useful-looking gelding: fairly useful handicap hurdler: won at Worcester (twice) in July: unproven beyond 2m: acts on good to soft going: wears tongue tie. *Jonjo O'Neill* **h127**

UT MAJEUR AULMES (FR) 10 ch.g. Northern Park (USA) – My Wish Aulmes (FR) (Lyphard's Wish (FR)) [2017/18 c133, h–: c16.3v² c15.8s² c15.8s³ c16.1s⁴ c16.4s⁴ c16d⁴ Apr 24] rangy gelding: winning hurdler: useful handicap chaser: second at Aintree (neck behind Baby King) in November: unproven beyond 2m: acts on heavy going: has worn cheekpieces, including in 2017/18: wears tongue tie. *Victor Dartnall* **c134 h–**

V

VADO FORTE (FR) 5 b.g. Walk In The Park (IRE) – Gloire (FR) (Sillery (USA)) [2017/18 b–p: h16g h15.8g⁶ h16s h15.7d² h16s* h16s² h19v* h15.9v* Apr 1] tall gelding: fairly useful handicap hurdler: won at Warwick (novice) in January, Taunton in March and Plumpton in April: stays 19f: acts on heavy going: in hood last 5 starts: usually races nearer last than first, often travels strongly. *Tom Lacey* — **h127**

VALADOM (FR) 9 gr.g. Dadarissime (FR) – Laurana (FR) (Badolato (USA)) [2017/18 c137, h115: h23s⁴ c20g^{ur} c23.8m⁴ Jun 4] workmanlike gelding: maiden hurdler: useful handicap chaser: stays 25f: acts on good to firm and heavy going: has worn cheekpieces, including in 2017/18: wears tongue tie: front runner/races prominently. *Richard Hobson* — **c116 h74**

VALDAS PRINCESS 6 b.m. King's Theatre (IRE) – Valdas Queen (GER) (Platini (GER)) [2017/18 b74p: b17.7d⁴ h21.2d^F h16.6d h20.7d h16.3d Apr 22] modest form in bumpers/over hurdles: will be suited by 2¾m+: often races towards rear. *Oliver Sherwood* — **h96 b70**

VAL DE FERBET (FR) 9 b.g. Voix du Nord (FR) – Intrigue Deferbet (FR) (Lights Out (FR)) [2017/18 c143, h138: c20v⁵ c22v² h24v³ c25s³ c26.2v⁴ c24v³ Apr 1] useful hurdler/chaser: stays 25f: acts on heavy going: wears tongue tie: usually leads. *Andrew McNamara, Ireland* — **c140 h113**

VALDEZ 11 ch.g. Doyen (IRE) – Skew (Niniski (USA)) [2017/18 c16.4s² c16.3v^{ur} Mar 16] good-topped gelding: winning hurdler: high-class chaser at one time: last of 3 in Game Spirit Chase (17 lengths behind Altior) at Newbury after very long lay-off, completed start in 2017/18: stays 2½m: acts on good to firm and heavy going. *Alan King* — **c141 h–**

VALGOR DU RONCERAY (FR) 9 gr.g. Al Namix (FR) – Malta de Ronceray (FR) (Dress Parade) [2017/18 h19.5d⁵ h16g³ h16.5m³ c16.8s^F c18g² c20d^{ur} c17.4d³ h16.2d* c15.2d^{ur} c19.2d⁴ c15.7d^F h19.9v⁴ ab16.3g⁵ Mar 3] fairly useful hurdler: won conditionals maiden at Ballinrobe in August: fairly useful maiden chaser: left Joseph Patrick O'Brien after eighth start: stays 19f: acts on soft and good to firm going: has worn hood: often in tongue tie in 2017/18: often let down by jumping. *Micky Hammond* — **c116 x h116**

VALHALLA (IRE) 8 b.g. Scorpion (IRE) – Fox Theatre (IRE) (King's Theatre (IRE)) [2017/18 c112p, h134: c22.6s³ c16g³ c20.2s^F c17.5v* c15.7v* c21s³ c16.5g⁵ Apr 20] good-topped gelding: useful hurdler: useful chaser: won maiden at Exeter (awarded race) in January and novice handicap at Wincanton (by 2½ lengths from Persian Delight) in February, both 3-runner events: stays 3¼m, effective at much shorter: acts on heavy going: wears tongue tie: front runner/races prominently. *Colin Tizzard* — **c130 h–**

VALLEYOFMILAN (IRE) 11 b.g. Milan – Ikdam Valley (IRE) (Ikdam) [2017/18 c116, h–: c29.4d² c26.1g³ c25.5s³ c23.8s* c24.1g⁵ Sep 1] winning hurdler: fairly useful handicap chaser: won at Perth in August: stays 29f: acts on soft and good to firm going: wears cheekpieces: usually races close up. *Donald McCain* — **c118 h–**

VALSEUR DU GRANVAL (FR) 9 b.g. Della Francesca (USA) – La Grande Vallee (FR) (Chef de Clan (FR)) [2017/18 c129, h–: c20g² c20.1m⁵ c16.4d⁵ c20.5g c16d* Apr 24] tall, useful-looking gelding: maiden hurdler: fairly useful handicap chaser: won at Ludlow in April: stays 2½m: acts on soft and good to firm going: wears tongue tie: often travels strongly. *Tom George* — **c129 h–**

VALSEUR LIDO (FR) 9 b.g. Anzillero (GER) – Libido Rock (FR) (Video Rock (FR)) [2017/18 c168, h–: c24d⁵ c24s⁵ c20v⁵ c20v³ c34.3s Apr 14] compact gelding: winning hurdler: top-class chaser, below best in 2017/18 after missing a year: stays 25f: acts on good to firm and heavy going. *Henry de Bromhead, Ireland* — **c154 h–**

VALSHAN TIME (IRE) 6 b.g. Atraf – Valshan (IRE) (Anshan) [2017/18 c16.3m³ c20g⁴ c17g^{ur} c16.3d⁴ c15.7g⁵ c19.2v^{pu} Apr 17] Irish maiden pointer: no form in chases: tried in blinkers. *Laura Young* — **c– h–**

VALUE AT RISK 9 b.g. Kayf Tara – Miss Orchestra (IRE) (Orchestra) [2017/18 c133, h–: h20s² h18.9v h19.4d² c20s⁶ h19.2d⁵ c20.5g* Apr 20] strong gelding: useful hurdler: won handicap at Doncaster (by ½ length from Cake de L'Isle) in December: useful handicap chaser: won listed event at Ayr (by length from Sizing Platinum) in April: stays 2½m: acts on heavy going: has worn headgear: tried in tongue tie: unreliable. *Dan Skelton* — **c135 § h141 §**

VALZAN (FR) 6 b.g. Zanzibari (USA) – Victory Road (FR) (Grape Tree Road) [2017/18 c20.4g² h19.3s⁵ h20d c24.1v c24.1v c20.5v^{pu} c20.1v^{pu} c24.2d Apr 23] lightly raced on Flat: maiden hurdler: fair chaser at best, little show in Britain: left G. Cherel after first start: stays 2½m: acts on heavy going: usually wears headgear: often races prominently. *Rebecca Menzies* — **c109 d h–**

VEL

VAMANOS (IRE) 4 b.g. Fame And Glory – Bean Ki Moon (IRE) (King's Theatre (IRE)) [2017/18 b16.7g Apr 22] fourth foal: dam unraced out of useful 2m hurdle winner Titled Dancer: 6/1, seventh in bumper at Market Rasen (5½ lengths behind Northern Soul). *Olly Murphy* **b89**

VANCOUVER 6 ch.g. Generous (IRE) – All Told (IRE) (Valanjou (FR)) [2017/18 h106, b84: h16.8g³ h15.8g* h18.5d⁴ h17.7m³ h19.9g* Oct 25] lengthy gelding: fairly useful handicap hurdler: won at Uttoxeter in May and Sedgefield in October: stays 21f: acts on good to soft going: often travels strongly. *Neil Mulholland* **h122**

VANGO DE VAIGE (FR) 5 b.g. Great Pretender (IRE) – Yellow Park (FR) (Northern Park (USA)) [2017/18 h16d h15.3s² h16s⁶ h19.5vᵖᵘ h19.8s⁶ h23.1vᵖᵘ Apr 17] £14,000 3-y-o: strong gelding: fourth foal: half-brother to French chaser Elival de Sanson (21f winner, by Martillo): dam, lightly raced over hurdles, winner around 1½m on Flat in France: fair form over hurdles: should stay further than 2m. *Philip Hobbs* **h101**

VAN GROGAN (IRE) 4 ch.g. Rip Van Winkle (IRE) – Metaphor (USA) (Woodman (USA)) [2017/18 b13.1g b13.7g Nov 14] smallish, leggy gelding: little show in bumpers. *Denis Quinn* **b–**

VANITEUX (FR) 9 br.g. Voix du Nord (FR) – Expoville (FR) (Video Rock (FR)) [2017/18 c159, h–: c15.9g c15.9s⁵ c16.8d c21.7s⁴ c16s² c16.3v c16.5g Apr 21] well-made gelding: winning hurdler: very smart chaser, below best in 2017/18: stays 2½m: acts on soft and good to firm going: wears headgear: has worn tongue tie: races towards rear. *David Pipe* **c144 h–**

VARENE DE VAUZELLE (FR) 9 b.g. Assessor (IRE) – Laureine (FR) (Sleeping Car (FR)) [2017/18 h24g² h23g³ h24g³ h26.4s h23.1d⁴ c24.2vᵖᵘ Apr 17] modest maiden hurdler: lightly-raced chaser: runner-up in point in February: left M. Hourigan after final 2016/17 start, Olly Murphy after fifth one in 2017/18: stays 3m: acts on soft going: wears headgear: has worn tongue tie, including in 2017/18: usually races towards rear: ungenuine. *B. V. Lund* **c– § h94 §**

VASCO DU MEE (FR) 9 b.g. Goldneyev (USA) – British Nellerie (FR) (Le Pontet (FR)) [2017/18 c129, h–: c23.6s³ Mar 22] winning pointer/hurdler: fairly useful hunter chaser: stays 33f: acts on heavy going: wears headgear/tongue tie: often races prominently. *Martin Weston* **c116 h–**

VAZIANI (FR) 4 b.g. Sinndar (IRE) – Visinova (FR) (Anabaa (USA)) [2017/18 h16.5s* h16s² Jan 13] dam half-sister to fairly useful/ungenuine hurdler/chaser (2m-19f winner) Visibility: fair form on Flat for A. de Royer Dupre: similar form over hurdles: won juvenile at Taunton in December: will stay 2½m. *Robert Walford* **h110**

VBADGE TREAT (FR) 5 b.m. My Risk (FR) – Peutiot (FR) (Valanour (IRE)) [2017/18 b–p: b17d b16s⁶ Dec 19] well held in bumpers/novice hurdle. *Harry Whittington* **h– b–**

VEAUCE DE SIVOLA (FR) 9 b.g. Assessor (IRE) – Eva de Chalamont (FR) (Iron Duke (FR)) [2017/18 c83§, h–: c24gᵖᵘ c23.8v³ c23.5v c23.5v⁶ Mar 5] lengthy gelding: winning hurdler: poor handicap chaser: stays 3m: acts on heavy going: tried in cheekpieces: wears tongue tie: front runner/races prominently: unreliable. *Brian Barr* **c71 § h–**

VEILED SECRET (IRE) 4 b.g. Teofilo (IRE) – Seven Veils (IRE) (Danehill Dancer (IRE)) [2017/18 h16.6s⁵ h15.8d² h15.8d⁴ Apr 24] fairly useful on Flat, stays 2m: fair form over hurdles: best effort when second in novice at Ludlow in March: wears tongue tie. *David Dennis* **h104**

VEINARD (FR) 9 ch.g. Shaanmer (IRE) – Ombline (FR) (Subotica (FR)) [2017/18 h128: h16g⁴ h16s h16s h15.7d h16s c17.5s² h16.5d Apr 24] good-bodied gelding: fairly useful handicap hurdler: 5/2, second in maiden at Fairyhouse (5½ lengths behind Cadmium) on chasing debut: stays 2½m: acts on heavy going: has worn hood: wears tongue tie: usually races nearer last than first, often travels strongly: open to improvement over fences. *Gordon Elliott, Ireland* **c127 p h125**

VELVET COGNAC 10 b.g. Grape Tree Road – Scandalous Affair (Alflora (IRE)) [2017/18 c21.6m³ c24.2d⁴ c26g² c25.7d⁴ c23.5s⁴ c25.7s⁵ Dec 18] winning pointer: maiden hurdler: fair form in chases: stays 3¼m: acts on good to soft going: in headgear last 5 starts: wears tongue tie: often races prominently. *Lawney Hill* **c102 h–**

VELVET MAKER (FR) 9 b.g. Policy Maker (IRE) – Evasion de L'Orne (FR) (Beyssac (FR)) [2017/18 c–, h131: h17g c15.9vᵘʳ Mar 9] angular gelding: useful hurdler/chaser at best: left Alan Fleming when unseated on hunter debut: stays 2¼m: acts on heavy going: has worn hood. *David Christie, Ireland* **c– h117**

867

*Boodles Fred Winter Juvenile Handicap Hurdle, Cheltenham—
a second long-priced winner of this race for Gordon Elliott as 33/1-shot Veneer of Charm (hoops)
defeats Style de Garde (hood, third left)*

VENDREDI TROIS (FR) 9 b.g. Shaanmer (IRE) – Legende Sacree (FR) (Hawker's News (IRE)) [2017/18 c–, h96: h19.6m⁴ h23g* h26.5g⁶ h23g³ h21.4s³ ab18d⁵ Mar 5] fair handicap hurdler: won at Worcester in June: winning chaser: has form at 3¼m, effective at much shorter: acts on soft and good to firm going: often wears headgear: front runner/races prominently. *Emma Lavelle*   c–
h102

VENEER OF CHARM (IRE) 4 b.g. Fast Company (IRE) – Nova Tor (IRE) (Trans Island) [2017/18 h16v* h16s² h16v h16.4s* h16v⁶ h16s⁴ Apr 17] compact gelding: fairly useful on Flat, stays 1½m: useful form over hurdles: won juvenile maiden at Punchestown in December and Fred Winter Juvenile Handicap Hurdle at Cheltenham (by 3 lengths from Style de Garde) in March: raced only at 2m on soft/heavy going: often races towards rear. *Gordon Elliott, Ireland*   h130

VENETIAN LAD 13 ro.g. Midnight Legend – Henrietta Holmes (IRE) (Persian Bold) [2017/18 c100§, h–: c25.5d³ c21.6g⁴ c19.7d³ c25.7d⁶ Dec 4] compact gelding: maiden hurdler: modest handicap chaser: stays 3¼m, effective at shorter: acts on heavy going: tried in headgear: unreliable. *Lydia Richards*   c98 §
h–

VENETIAN PROPOSAL (IRE) 4 b.f. Fast Company (IRE) – Ide Say (IRE) (Grand Lodge (USA)) [2017/18 h16.2s^pu h15.9s⁵ Apr 15] modest on Flat, stays 1¼m: poor form over hurdles: better effort when fifth in maiden at Plumpton. *Zoe Davison*   h83

VENGEUR DE GUYE (FR) 9 b.g. Dom Alco (FR) – Mascotte de Guye (FR) (Video Rock (FR)) [2017/18 c122, h120: c17.3d³ c17.1g⁶ c16.5s* c17.1g⁴ c15.7s⁶ c17.1v² c15.2v⁵ c17.1v² Apr 7] good-topped gelding: fairly useful hurdler: fairly useful handicap chaser: won at Ayr in October: stays 2½m: acts on heavy going: has worn headgear: wears tongue tie: often flatters to deceive. *Lucinda Russell*   c118 §
h–

VENTUREPREDEMENTIA 7 b.g. Indian Danehill (IRE) – Sounds Familiar (IRE) (Orchestra) [2017/18 h–, b–: h19.7d^pu Nov 18] little show in bumpers/novice hurdles. *Andrew Crook*   h–

VERANO (GER) 9 ch.g. Lord of England (GER) – Vive La Vie (GER) (Big Shuffle (USA)) [2017/18 h19.6g h21.2g h21g h16.7v⁴ h19.7v Jan 23] maiden pointer: fairly useful hurdler at best, no form in 2017/18: lightly-raced maiden chaser: sometimes in headgear nowadays: wears tongue tie. *Oliver Greenall*   c–
h–

VERCINGETORIX (IRE) 7 b.g. Dylan Thomas (IRE) – Great Artist (FR) (Desert Prince (IRE)) [2017/18 c–§, h96: h16.2m⁴ h20.1g* h20.2g² h19.5s c20.1s⁴ h17s² h15.6m³ c19.9g² Nov 30] lengthy gelding: fairly useful handicap hurdler: won at Hexham in June: fairly useful maiden chaser: left Iain Jardine after third start, Patrick Griffin after sixth: stayed 2½m: acted on good to firm and heavy going: usually wore headgear: retried in tongue tie in 2017/18: temperamental: dead. *Iain Jardine* c115 §
h117 §

VERDANA BLUE (IRE) 6 b.m. Getaway (GER) – Blue Gallery (IRE) (Bluebird (USA)) [2017/18 h133, b93: h15.7g⁵ h15.7g* h15.7d³ h16.3v h16g Apr 21] angular mare: bumper winner: useful handicap hurdler: won at Ascot in November: third in Racing Welfare Handicap Hurdle there (4½ lengths behind Hunters Call) next time: successful at 19f, but seems best at 2m: acts on soft going: waited with, travels strongly. *Nicky Henderson* h140

VERING (FR) 12 b.g. Bering – Forcia (FR) (Homme de Loi (IRE)) [2017/18 c–§, h–§: c17.4s³ May 18] winning pointer: maiden hurdler/chaser, of little account nowadays: often wears headgear/tongue tie: temperamental. *Mrs Linda Pile* c– §
h– §

VERKO (FR) 9 br.g. Lavirco (GER) – Lady Vernizy (FR) (Video Rock (FR)) [2017/18 c90, h–: c24.2gᵘʳ May 13] maiden hurdler: fair chaser at best, unseated early only start in 2017/18: stayed 25f: best form on soft/heavy going: in cheekpieces last 2 starts: often raced towards rear: dead. *Micky Hammond* c–
h–

VERNI (FR) 9 ch.g. Sabrehill (USA) – Nobless d'Aron (FR) (Ragmar (FR)) [2017/18 h138: h18.9v⁵ c19.2v² c19.2s² h20.3g⁶ Apr 18] useful handicap hurdler: similar form over fences: better effort when second in novice at Exeter (2½ lengths behind Allysson Monterg) in February: stays 2½m: acts on heavy going: often races prominently, strong traveller but no battler. *Philip Hobbs* c131 §
h136 §

VERONA OPERA (IRE) 7 b.m. King's Theatre (IRE) – Timissa (IRE) (Kahyasi) [2017/18 h100: h16.2g² h16.2g³ c21.2g* h17.5g³ h20.2s h19.3s* h16s c20s³ h20.5v⁴ c20d⁴ Mar 31] fair handicap hurdler: won mares event at Carlisle in October: fairly useful form over fences: won maiden at Cartmel in June: best effort when third in listed mares event at Carlisle (10½ lengths behind Benie des Dieux) in December: stays 21f: acts on heavy going: has worn hood. *Stuart Crawford, Ireland* c117
h113

VERSIFIER 6 b.m. Yeats (IRE) – Daprika (FR) (Epervier Bleu) [2017/18 h93, b81: h20mᵖᵘ h16.8d h20.5d h20.7s² h24.6s⁶ Apr 9] modest maiden hurdler: stays 21f: best form on soft/heavy going: tried in cheekpieces. *Oliver Sherwood* h96

VERTIGO (IRE) 6 b.g. Jeremy (USA) – Lady Coquette (SWE) (Mujadil (USA)) [2017/18 h107, b90: h20.1gᵖᵘ h20.2v² h24.7d h16.2vᵖᵘ h19v h16.7sᵖᵘ Mar 24] placed on completed start in Irish points: fair handicap hurdler, largely out of form in 2017/18: stays 21f: best form on soft/heavy going: often in tongue tie nowadays: usually races close up. *Lucinda Russell* h105

VERY EXTRAVAGANT (IRE) 9 ch.m. Touch of Land (FR) – Raveleen Rose (IRE) (Norwich) [2017/18 h118: h23.1g⁶ c22.5gᵖᵘ Jun 21] sturdy mare: fairly useful hurdler at best, below form on return in 2017/18: pulled up in novice handicap on chasing debut: stays 3¼m: acts on soft going: wears cheekpieces. *Neil Mulholland* c–
h–

VERY FIRST TIME 6 b.g. Champs Elysees – Like A Virgin (IRE) (Iron Mask (USA)) [2017/18 h124: c24.2sᶠ c24.2v* c23.4s* c21.6v² c26s c25s Apr 14] sturdy gelding: fairly useful hurdler: useful form over fences: won 3-runner novice at Hexham in November and novice handicap at Newcastle (by 6 lengths from Teddy Tee) in December: stays 25f: acts on heavy going: front runner/races prominently. *Tim Easterby* c130
h–

VERYGOODVERYGOOD (FR) 7 b.g. Yeats (IRE) – Rose d'Or (IRE) (Polish Precedent (USA)) [2017/18 h121: h20gᵖᵘ c23g⁴ h23g⁴ h24.7dᵖᵘ h23.9v Nov 12] fairly useful handicap hurdler: tailed off in novice on chasing debut: stays 3m: acts on good to firm and heavy going: usually wears headgear, including in 2017/18: usually races towards rear: unreliable. *Nigel Twiston-Davies* c–
h116 §

VERY LIVE (FR) 9 b.g. Secret Singer (FR) – Iona Will (FR) (Kadalko (FR)) [2017/18 c93, h–: c19.8s² c20v² c23.5vᵖᵘ c19.5s² Apr 6] well-made gelding: maiden hurdler: modest handicap chaser: stays 2½m: best form on soft/heavy going: wears headgear: tried in tongue tie. *Paul Webber* c95
h–

VESUVHILL (FR) 9 ch.g. Sabrehill (USA) – L'Orchidee (FR) (Gunboat Diplomacy (FR)) [2017/18 c79, h–: c20.1gᶠ c20.1gᵖᵘ Jun 3] sturdy gelding: winning hurdler: maiden chaser, failed to complete both starts in 2017/18: stayed easy 25f: acted on good to firm and heavy going: usually wore hood: tried in tongue tie: dead. *Gemma Anderson* c–
h–

VET

VET CERT (IRE) 10 b.g. Dr Massini (IRE) – Fernhill Queen (IRE) (Strong Gale) [2017/18 h19.9m⁴ h21.6d⁴ h23d⁴ h23.3d h20f Oct 12] maiden pointer: modest form over hurdles: tried in cheekpieces. *Ronald Harris*   h90 ?

VETONCALL (IRE) 6 b.g. Well Chosen – Miss Audacious (IRE) (Supreme Leader) [2017/18 h21.2dᵖᵘ Apr 9] off mark in Irish points at fourth attempt: pulled up in novice on hurdling debut. *Alan Jones*   h–

VEXILLUM (IRE) 9 br.g. Mujadil (USA) – Common Cause (Polish Patriot (USA)) [2017/18 c107, h–: c19.2g h19m Nov 1] stocky gelding: fair hurdler/chaser at best, no form in 2017/18: stays 21f: acts on firm going: usually wears headgear: has worn tongue tie: often races towards rear. *Neil Mulholland*   c– h–

VIACOMETTI (FR) 9 gr.g. Alberto Giacometti (IRE) – L'Epi (FR) (Great Palm (USA)) [2017/18 c24.2g May 6] close-coupled gelding: multiple point winner: maiden hurdler: well beaten in maiden hunter on chasing debut: should stay 2½m: acts on good to soft going: tried in cheekpieces. *Mrs K. Lynn*   c– h–

VIBRATO VALTAT (FR) 9 gr.g. Voix du Nord (FR) – La Tosca Valtat (FR) (Dom Alco (FR)) [2017/18 c154§, h–: c17.5v⁵ c19.9g⁴ c24d² c24s c24g c21s³ Apr 23] sturdy gelding: winning hurdler: smart handicap chaser: second at Doncaster (neck behind Mustmeetalady) in December: stays 3m: acts on good to firm and heavy going: has worn headgear: usually tongue tied. *Emma Lavelle*   c146 h–

VIC DE TOUZAINE (FR) 9 gr.g. Dom Alco (FR) – Diana de Vonnas (FR) (El Badr) [2017/18 c136, h–: c24.5s* c25.1sᵖᵘ c22.9v c20.2vᵖᵘ c25sᵖᵘ c26g⁶ Apr 18] sturdy gelding: maiden hurdler: useful handicap chaser: won at Carlisle in October: mainly disappointing after: stays 3m: best form on soft/heavy going. *Venetia Williams*   c137 h–

VICE ET VERTU (FR) 9 b.g. Network (GER) – Duchesse du Cochet (FR) (Native Guile (USA)) [2017/18 c111, h–: c24.5g* c30.7vᵖᵘ c24.1v* c23s³ c29.2vᵖᵘ Mar 11] tall gelding: winning hurdler: fairly useful handicap chaser: won at Towcester in May and Bangor in January: stays 3m: acts on heavy going: wears headgear: tried in tongue tie. *Henry Daly*   c116 h–

VICENTE (FR) 9 b.g. Dom Alco (FR) – Ireland (FR) (Kadalko (FR)) [2017/18 c151, h–: c27.3s² c29.5vᵘʳ c25sᵖᵘ c31.8g⁵ Apr 21] tall gelding: winning hurdler: smart handicap chaser: dual Scottish Grand National winner: best effort in 2017/18 when second in Grade 3 at Cheltenham (neck behind Perfect Candidate) in November: stays 4m: acts on good to firm and heavy going: wears hood: often travels strongly: often let down by jumping. *Paul Nicholls*   c151 x h–

VICENZO MIO (FR) 8 b.g. Corri Piano (FR) – Sweet Valrose (FR) (Cadoudal (FR)) [2017/18 c121, h119: h19.8s h20.5d⁶ h17.7v⁴ h21.4v⁴ h16v⁵ h16v² c16v² c19.4v³ c16v² Apr 15] well-made gelding: fair handicap hurdler nowadays: fairly useful form over fences: second in handicap at Ffos Las in April: stays 2¾m: acts on heavy going: wears cheekpieces/tongue tie. *Chris Gordon*   c121 h111

VICOMTE DU SEUIL (FR) 9 b.g. Special Kaldoun (IRE) – Marie du Seuil (FR) (Video Rock (FR)) [2017/18 h18.9s c21.4g* c21.4d* c20.9m c21.4m* h18.9d³ c23.9d* c30.2g² c30.2sᵖᵘ c26.8s² c20.9dᵖᵘ Apr 20] leggy gelding: winning hurdler: fairly useful chaser: won minor events at Lignieres in May and July, and cross-country event at same course in October: second in cross-country handicap at Cheltenham in November: stays 3¾m: acts on good to firm and heavy going: wears headgear: has worn tongue tie. *Emmanuel Clayeux, France*   c129 h106

VICONTE DU NOYER (FR) 9 gr.g. Martaline – Zouk Wood (USA) (Woodman (USA)) [2017/18 c150, h–: c25g c20.4s c20.8sᵖᵘ c20.8sᵖᵘ c20s⁶ Apr 25] lengthy, rather sparely-made gelding: has had breathing operation: winning hurdler: smart handicap chaser, below best in 2017/18: stays 27f: acts on soft and good to firm going: tried in cheekpieces: often wears tongue tie. *Colin Tizzard*   c139 h–

VIC'S LAST STAND (IRE) 8 b.m. Old Vic – Misleain (IRE) (Un Desperado (FR)) [2017/18 h110: h20g⁴ h23.3g⁴ c15.6g³ c19.2g Jul 9] workmanlike mare: fair handicap hurdler: modest form over fences: barely stays 23f: acts on good to soft going. *Gillian Boanas*   c92 h102

VICTARION (IRE) 6 b.g. Scorpion (IRE) – Gaye Preskina (IRE) (Presenting) [2017/18 b99: h21.2v h21s⁴ Feb 10] in frame in bumpers: fair form over hurdles: better effort when fourth in novice at Warwick. *Philip Hobbs*   h103

VICTORIAN TEO (FR) 8 b.g. Teofilo (IRE) – Chalouchi (USA) (Mt Livermore (USA)) [2017/18 h15.8dᵖᵘ h15.8v h19v Feb 4] no form over hurdles: in headgear last 2 starts: tried in tongue tie. *Tom Symonds*   h–

870

VICTORIA SAYS (IRE) 6 b.m. Shantou (USA) – Ballestra (IRE) (Alflora (IRE)) [2017/18 h97, b–: h18.8d⁴ h20.5v* h19.5v^pu Jan 31] modest hurdler: won maiden at Ayr in November: stays 23f: acts on heavy going. *Stuart Crawford, Ireland* — h95

VIDE CAVE (FR) 9 b.g. Secret Singer (FR) – Kenna (FR) (Epervier Bleu) [2017/18 c66, h–: c17d Jun 9] maiden pointer: winning hurdler/chaser, retains little ability: has worn tongue tie. *Mrs N. White* — c– h–

VIENS CHERCHER (IRE) 7 b.g. Milan – La Zingarella (IRE) (Phardante (FR)) [2017/18 c134, h–: c21.4g⁴ c21.4g c25.5g⁶ c19.3v³ c20.1s^pu Feb 24] workmanlike gelding: winning hurdler: useful handicap chaser, below best in 2017/18: stays 3m: acts on heavy and good to firm going: has worn cheekpieces, including last 4 starts. *Brian Ellison* — c124 h–

VIEUX LILLE (IRE) 8 b.g. Robin des Champs (FR) – Park Athlete (IRE) (Supreme Leader) [2017/18 c131x, h–: c24.2s⁶ c26v⁴ c25.1v⁵ h25.5v^pu Apr 10] strong gelding: useful hurdler/maiden chaser at best, disappointing in 2017/18: stays 3m: acts on heavy going: tried in headgear: often let down by jumping over fences. *Philip Hobbs* — c114 x h–

VIEUX LION ROUGE (FR) 9 ch.g. Sabiango (GER) – Indecise (FR) (Cyborg (FR)) [2017/18 c155, h–: c24.2s⁴ c25.9v c23.8s⁴ c34.3s Apr 14] lengthy gelding: winning hurdler: very smart handicap chaser, below best in 2017/18: stays 3½m: acts on heavy going: wears headgear: tried in tongue tie. *David Pipe* — c140 h–

VIEUX MORVAN (FR) 9 bl.g. Voix du Nord (FR) – Moskoville (FR) (Kadalko (FR)) [2017/18 c24.5d⁵ c21s² Feb 4] winning hurdler: useful handicap chaser: second in Leopardstown Handicap Chase (9 lengths behind Last Goodbye) in February: trained in France before 2017/18, mainly by G. Cherel: stays 3¼m: best form on soft/heavy going: wears headgear. *Joseph Patrick O'Brien, Ireland* — c143 h–

VIKEKHAL (FR) 9 b.g. Khalkevi (IRE) – Gesse Parade (FR) (Dress Parade) [2017/18 c119, h–: c21.1d³ c22.6m³ c16.5g* c20.3g³ c22.6g⁵ c20d c23.8m^F h20.3g⁶ c17.4d⁶ Apr 21] tall gelding: winning hurdler: fairly useful handicap chaser: won at Worcester in August: left Gary Moore after second start: stays 25f, effective at much shorter: acts on good to firm and heavy going: has worn headgear: wears tongue tie. *Steve Flook* — c122 h–

VIKING MISTRESS 10 b.m. Bollin Eric – Mistress Caramore (IRE) (Moscow Society (USA)) [2017/18 c84, h93: h20g⁴ h20.3d* c16.5g² h20g⁶ c23g² c20g⁴ c20.8s⁵ Dec 15] workmanlike mare: fair handicap hurdler: won mares events at Worcester in May and Southwell in June: similar form over fences: stays 3m: acts on soft going: wears cheekpieces/tongue tie. *Martin Keighley* — c104 h109

VIKING QUEEN 7 b.m. Presenting – Swaythe (USA) (Swain (IRE)) [2017/18 h19.4d⁴ h19.8v^pu Feb 17] placed in bumper: modest form when fourth in mares novice at Doncaster on hurdling debut: out of depth next time. *Paul Webber* — h90

VIKING RIDGE (IRE) 11 gr.g. Cloudings (IRE) – Lady Newmill (IRE) (Taipan (IRE)) [2017/18 c19.2g c23g Jul 27] well-made gelding: winning pointer: winning hurdler: fairly useful chaser at best, well held in handicaps in early-2017/18: stays 2½m: acts on good to soft going: has worn headgear: often let down by jumping over fences. *Stuart Edmunds* — c– x h–

VIKING RUBY 5 ch.m. Sulamani (IRE) – Viking Torch (Loup Sauvage (USA)) [2017/18 b15.7v⁶ Apr 27] first foal: dam, pulled up in point, half-sister to fairly useful hurdler/useful staying chaser Harry The Viking: 25/1, sixth in mares bumper at Towcester. *Neil Mulholland* — b57

VILLAGE VIC (IRE) 11 b.g. Old Vic – Etoile Margot (FR) (Garde Royale) [2017/18 c159, h–: c19.4d^F c24.2s^pu c20.8s c21.1s^pu Apr 21] rather sparely-made gelding: has had breathing operation: winning hurdler: very smart chaser at best, no form in 2017/18. *Philip Hobbs* — c– h–

VINCENT'S FOREVER 5 b.g. Pour Moi (IRE) – Glen Rosie (IRE) (Mujtahid (USA)) [2017/18 h89: h19.6d Jun 8] sturdy gelding: fairly useful at best on Flat, stays 1½m: maiden hurdler, well held in handicap only start in 2017/18: should stay further than 2m: in headgear/tongue tie last 4 starts: has joined Ed de Giles. *David Pipe* — h–

VINCITORE (FR) 12 b.g. Starborough – Viva Vodka (FR) (Crystal Glitters (USA)) [2017/18 c107, h–: c26.3d⁴ c23s⁶ c25.1v² c26.3v^ur c23.4s^ur Mar 23] leggy gelding: winning hurdler: modest hunter chaser nowadays: stays 3¼m: acts on soft and good to firm going: has worn headgear: wears tongue tie. *Miss Sarah Rippon* — c95 h–

VINEGAR HILL 9 b.g. Kayf Tara – Broughton Melody (Alhijaz) [2017/18 c101p, h112: c26.2d c23.9d* c27.6s^pu h23.8s⁵ Jan 18] fair handicap hurdler: fairly useful form over fences: won handicap at Market Rasen in November: stays 3m: acts on heavy going: tried in visor: in tongue tie last 3 starts: front runner/races prominently. *Stuart Edmunds* — c122 h85

VIN

VINNDICATION (IRE) 5 b.g. Vinnie Roe (IRE) – Pawnee Trail (IRE) (Taipan (IRE)) [2017/18 b15.8g* h20.5s* h21.6v* h19.6s* Feb 8] £28,000 3-y-o: lengthy gelding: fourth foal: dam, unraced, out of half-sister to Irish Grand National winner Insure: won bumper at Ludlow on debut in November: smart form over hurdles: maintained unbeaten record in novices at Leicester in December, Ascot in January and Huntingdon (beat Western Ryder by 3¼ lengths in listed event) in February: will stay 3m: open to further improvement. *Kim Bailey* — h146 p b96

VINNIE LEWIS (IRE) 7 b.g. Vinnie Roe (IRE) – Ballyann Lewis (IRE) (Sir Harry Lewis (USA)) [2017/18 h110, b84: c24.1d³ c26.2d⁴ c26.3s* c28.5v* c32.6s^pu Feb 24] winning pointer: maiden hurdler: useful form in chases: won handicaps at Sedgefield in November and Plumpton (by 6 lengths from Shanroe Santos) in January: should stay 4m: acts on heavy going: front runner/races prominently. *Harry Whittington* — c134 h–

VINO GRIEGO (FR) 13 b.g. Kahyasi – Vie de Reine (FR) (Mansonnien (FR)) [2017/18 c24.2s⁵ c20s⁴ c24.2s^ur c24.2s⁶ c24.2v⁵ Feb 16] tall gelding: winning hurdler: fairly useful handicap chaser nowadays: stays 25f: acts on heavy going: has worn headgear, including final start: tried in tongue tie: often let down by temperament. *Gary Moore* — c119 § h–

VINO'S CHOICE (IRE) 6 b.g. Kalanisi (IRE) – Ard's Pet (IRE) (Among Men (USA)) [2017/18 b16.2d* h16.2g⁶ h17d h19.4g⁴ h15.6s Feb 3] fifth foal: dam maiden on Flat (placed up to 1m): pulled up in Irish maiden point: won bumper at Perth in August: modest form over hurdles: left Gavin Patrick Cromwell after first start: wears tongue tie: often races in rear. *Lucinda Russell* — h94 b96

VINTAGE CLOUDS (IRE) 8 gr.g. Cloudings (IRE) – Rare Vintage (IRE) (Germany (USA)) [2017/18 c132, h–: c25d* c21.6v² c29.5v⁴ c24.2v² c25s³ c31.8g³ Apr 21] compact gelding: winning hurdler: useful handicap chaser: won novice event at Aintree (by 18 lengths from Lovely Job) in October: placed 4 times after, including in Towton Novices' Chase at Wetherby (2¾ lengths behind Ballyoptic), Ultima Handicap Chase at Cheltenham and Scottish Grand National at Ayr (4 lengths third to Joe Farrell): stays 4m: acts on heavy going: usually leads but has raced lazily. *Sue Smith* — c143 h–

VINTAGE GLEN (IRE) 6 b.g. Ask – Rare Vintage (IRE) (Germany (USA)) [2017/18 b15.7v⁵ b16.2v⁴ Feb 15] poor form in bumpers. *Rose Dobbin* — b69

VINTAGE PARADISE (IRE) 5 b.g. Pour Moi (IRE) – Cru Paradis (FR) (Kendor (FR)) [2017/18 b16.8g⁶ b16g⁵ Sep 18] poor form in bumpers. *Fergal O'Brien* — b66

VINTAGE SALON (IRE) 7 b.m. King's Theatre (IRE) – Lounaos (FR) (Limnos (JPN)) [2017/18 h97, b60: h17.5g c19.2g h15.8g² c16d Oct 5] modest handicap hurdler: no form over fences: unproven beyond 2m: acts on good to soft going: has worn headgear, including in 2017/18: often in tongue tie: often races towards rear. *James A. Nash, Ireland* — c– h86

VINTAGE VINNIE (IRE) 9 b.g. Vinnie Roe (IRE) – Bobby's Jet (IRE) (Bob's Return (IRE)) [2017/18 c135, h119: c25g* c26.1m⁶ c22.5g c24f² Apr 14] tall, useful-looking gelding: fairly useful hurdler: useful handicap chaser: won at Aintree (by 22 lengths from Buachaill Alainn) in June: left Rebecca Curtis after third start: stays 25f: acts on heavy going: has worn hood/tongue tie: free-going sort. *Joseph G. Davies, USA* — c138 h–

VIOGNIER 6 ch.m. Black Sam Bellamy (IRE) – Noun de La Thinte (FR) (Oblat (FR)) [2017/18 b16.7g⁴ b16.7g³ b15.7g b16.7g⁴ h15.7g³ h16.8g^ur h20.1v² h20.1s^pu h20.6d^pu Nov 23] first foal: dam (c123/h96), 2¼m-2½m hurdle/chase winner (stayed 3¼m), half-sister to useful chaser (stayed 3m) Royal de La Thinte: pulled up all 3 starts in points: poor form in bumpers: modest form over hurdles: stays 2½m: acts on heavy going: wears tongue tie. *Susan Corbett* — h91 b74

VIRAK (FR) 9 b.g. Bernebeau (FR) – Nosika d'Airy (FR) (Oblat (FR)) [2017/18 c142d, h–: c23.8s* c22.2v* c26.3v c25.8s³ Apr 23] sturdy gelding: winning hurdler: fairly useful hunter chaser nowadays: won at Ludlow and Haydock in February: should stay beyond 3m: acts on heavy going: has worn cheekpieces, including in 2017/18: tried in tongue tie: usually races prominently. *Paul Nicholls* — c126 h–

VIRGILIO (FR) 9 b.g. Denham Red (FR) – Liesse de Marbeuf (FR) (Cyborg (FR)) [2017/18 c144, h–: c25g* c19.9s c24d^pu c34.3s^F Apr 14] sturdy gelding: winning hurdler: smart handicap chaser: won at Aintree (by 7 lengths from Minellacelebration) in May: fell sixth in Grand National final start: stays 25f: acts on heavy going: wears tongue tie. *Dan Skelton* — c146 h–

VIRGINIA CHICK (FR) 6 b.g. Nickname (FR) – Sweet Jaune (FR) (Le Nain Jaune (FR)) [2017/18 h–, b85: h18.5d⁶ h18.5d h18.5v* h16.7v* h23.8s* h21v² h19.5v* Mar 21] fairly useful handicap hurdler: won conditional events at Exeter (novice) and Bangor in — h119

VIV

December, amateur contest at Ludlow (dead-heated) in January and 14-runner race at Chepstow in March: stays 3m: best form on soft/heavy going: has worn headgear/tongue tie: often races towards rear. *Evan Williams*

VIRNON 7 b.g. Virtual – Freedom Song (Singspiel (IRE)) [2017/18 c117, h–: c15.7g[F] c16g[4] Jul 11] lengthy gelding: winning hurdler: fairly useful handicap chaser, well held completed start in 2017/18: stays 2¼m: acts on heavy going: has joined Sarah Humphrey. *Sally Haynes*   **c92** / **h–**

VIRTUEL D'OUDON (FR) 9 b.g. Network (GER) – La Belle Illusion (FR) (Turgeon (USA)) [2017/18 c–, h–: h23.3v[pu] Nov 26] angular gelding: point winner: useful hurdler at best, no show only 2 starts since 2014/15: lightly-raced maiden chaser: stays 25f: acts on heavy going: usually wears headgear. *David Pipe*   **c–** / **h–**

VISAGE BLANC 5 b.m. Champs Elysees – Russian Empress (IRE) (Trans Island) [2017/18 h98: h19.9g h15.5d h16.3d[5] Apr 22] fairly useful on Flat, stays 1½m: maiden hurdler, modest form at best: in tongue tie last 4 starts. *Graeme McPherson*   **h81**

VISERION 6 ch.g. Tamayuz – Frivolity (Pivotal) [2017/18 h121: h20.6g[pu] h18.7g h17d[6] h16.8s* h16s[4] h19.6s[6] h17d[2] h16.8g Apr 18] fairly useful handicap hurdler: won at Sedgefield in December: unproven beyond 17f: acts on soft going: in cheekpieces last 4 starts. *Donald McCain*   **h121**

VISION D'AUTEUIL (FR) 6 b.g. Vision d'Etat (FR) – Pharistella (FR) (Double Bed (FR)) [2017/18 b–: b15.8g[3] May 9] modest form in bumpers: better effort when third in conditional/amateur maiden at Ffos Las: wears tongue tie. *Harry Fry*   **b80**

VISION DE GLOIRE (FR) 4 b.g. Vision d'Etat (FR) – Rose Paola (FR) (Cadoudal (FR)) [2017/18 h20.5d[5] h16g[6] Aug 30] modest form on first of 2 starts in juvenile hurdles: tried in tongue tie. *Nick Williams*   **h82**

VISION DES CHAMPS (FR) 9 b.g. Saint des Saints (FR) – Manita des Champs (FR) (Fabulous Dancer (USA)) [2017/18 c–, h–: c17d[pu] h16g h20g Jul 10] good-topped gelding: fair hurdler/fairly useful chaser at best, no form since 2015/16: in cheekpieces last 2 starts: wears tongue tie. *Roy Brotherton*   **c–** / **h–**

VISION DES FLOS (FR) 5 b.g. Balko (FR) – Marie Royale (FR) (Turgeon (USA)) [2017/18 h19.5d[3] h21.1d[4] h19.7s[2] h16.8v* h21.1s[6] h16.5s[2] h16.5d[2] Apr 24] €25,000 3-y-o: good sort: has had breathing operation: first foal: dam, lightly raced in France, half-sister to Galway Plate/Ryanair Chase winner Balko des Flos (by Balko): won only start in bumpers for Robert Tyner: useful hurdler: won listed novice at Exeter (by 31 lengths from Mercenaire) in February: second in Top Novices' Hurdle at Aintree (2½ lengths behind Lalor) and Champion Novices' Hurdle at Punchestown (2¼ lengths behind Draconien) in April: stays 21f: acts on heavy going: in tongue tie last 4 starts. *Colin Tizzard*   **h146**

VITAL EVIDENCE (USA) 8 b.g. Empire Maker (USA) – Promising Lead (Danehill (USA)) [2017/18 c104, h102: h18.7g[6] c19.7m[pu] Sep 24] quite good-topped gelding: maiden hurdler/chaser, no form in 2017/18: unproven beyond 17f: acts on soft going: wears headgear: has worn tongue tie, including in 2017/18. *Neil Mulholland*   **c–** / **h–**

VITARRA 9 b.m. Kayf Tara – Vivante (IRE) (Toulon) [2017/18 h–: h20g[6] Aug 23] chunky mare: no form in bumpers/over hurdles: tried in cheekpieces/tongue tie: dead. *Jim Wilson*   **h–**

VIVACCIO (FR) 9 b.g. Antarctique (IRE) – Cybelle (FR) (Saint Cyrien (FR)) [2017/18 c16d[3] c16.2s[3] c19.9s[3] c20.9v[4] c23.8d[5] Apr 24] sturdy gelding: winning hurdler: fairly useful handicap chaser: stays 2½m: acts on heavy going: often races towards rear. *Venetia Williams*   **c115** / **h–**

VIVALDI COLLONGES (FR) 9 b.g. Dom Alco (FR) – Diane Collonges (FR) (El Badr) [2017/18 c90, h–: c23.4s[pu] c23.4s* Mar 23] sturdy gelding: winning hurdler: smart chaser at best: in cheekpieces, won hunter at Newbury in March: stays 25f: acts on heavy going: wears tongue tie. *Paul Nicholls*   **c123 +** / **h–**

VIVANT 5 gr.m. Shirocco (GER) – Sisella (IRE) (Bob Back (USA)) [2017/18 h18.6s h21.4v[pu] Mar 28] second foal: dam (h103), placed in bumper/2m hurdle on only 2 outings, out of half-sister to useful staying chaser Ackzo: maiden hurdler, fair form at best when trained in France: should stay beyond 17f: acts on soft going: has worn cheekpieces/tongue tie. *Harry Fry*   **h–**

VIVA RAFA (IRE) 8 b.g. Scorpion (IRE) – Back To Stay (IRE) (Supreme Leader) [2017/18 h104: h21m h21s c20.9v[2] Apr 10] maiden hurdler, well held in handicaps first 2 starts in 2017/18: 9/2, second in novice handicap at Hereford (3¼ lengths behind One Style) on chasing debut: stays 21f: acts on heavy going: has worn hood, including in 2017/18: usually in tongue tie nowadays. *Richard Phillips*   **c107** / **h–**

VIV

VIVAS (FR) 7 b.g. Davidoff (GER) – Lavircas (FR) (Lavirco (GER)) [2017/18 h112: h19.9d* h21.1g² h21.1s h18.6s³ h19.3v⁵ h19.3s³ h20.3g³ Apr 18] sturdy gelding: fairly useful handicap hurdler: won at Uttoxeter in September: third at Cheltenham in April: stays 21f: acts on soft going: in cheekpieces last 2 starts: wears tongue tie. *Charlie Longsdon* — h123

VIVA STEVE (IRE) 10 b.g. Flemensfirth (USA) – Eluna (Unfuwain (USA)) [2017/18 c139, h–: c24v⁴ c25.9vᵖᵘ Dec 9] lengthy gelding: winning hurdler: useful handicap chaser: fourth in Kerry National Handicap Chase at Listowel (6 lengths behind Potters Point) in September: reportedly bled next time: stays 3m: acts on heavy going: in tongue tie last 5 starts. *Fergal O'Brien* — c135 h–

VIVA VITTORIA (IRE) 4 b.f. Stowaway – La Fisarmonica (IRE) (Accordion) [2017/18 b16s² Mar 22] €32,000 3-y-o: fifth foal: half-sister to 3 winners by Flemensfirth, including bumper winner Coolanly and fairly useful hurdler/fair chaser Bronco Billy (3m/25f winner): dam (h108), 2½m hurdle winner, half-sister to fairly useful hurdler/winning chaser (stayed 2½m) Joe Cullen: 5/2, second in mares bumper at Chepstow (3¾ lengths behind Meep Meep) on debut. *Emma Lavelle* — b84

VIVE LE ROI (IRE) 7 b.g. Robin des Pres (FR) – Cappard View (IRE) (Rudimentary (USA)) [2017/18 h120: h18.7g⁴ h20.5d⁵ h20vᵖᵘ h15.8d h16mᶠ Apr 26] useful-looking gelding: fairly useful hurdler, below best in 2017/18: left Charlie Longsdon after third start: stays 21f: acts on good going: front runner/races prominently. *Tony Carroll* — h104

VOCALISER (IRE) 6 b.g. Vocalised (USA) – Bring Back Matron (IRE) (Rock of Gibraltar (IRE)) [2017/18 h96: c16.2g² c15.9d* c15.9s² c16.1s* c18.2s* c16d³ c16s* c16.8s⁵ c20.5mᵖᵘ Apr 26] good-topped gelding: maiden hurdler: fairly useful handicap chaser: won at Leicester in December, Taunton in January and February, and Kempton in March, last 3 novice events: stays 2¼m: acts on soft going: has worn cheekpieces, including last 3 starts: tried in tongue tie: often races prominently. *Robin Dickin* — c119 h–

VOCARIUM (IRE) 5 b.g. Poet's Voice – Vituisa (Bering) [2017/18 b105: b16.8d² b16s² b16.4s Nov 19] lengthy gelding: useful form in bumpers: best effort in 2017/18 when second at Galway in August. *Peter Fahey, Ireland* — b104

VODKA ALL THE WAY 6 b.g. Oscar (IRE) – Fully Focused (IRE) (Rudimentary (USA)) [2017/18 b86: h21.4s⁶ h23.9s h19s² h21.6v² h23.1d* Apr 24] big, workmanlike gelding: fairly useful form over hurdles: won novice at Exeter in April: stays 23f: acts on heavy going. *Philip Hobbs* — h119

VODKA ISLAND (IRE) 9 b.m. Turtle Island (IRE) – Fromrussiawithlove (Moscow Society (USA)) [2017/18 h23.3g³ h24g h19.9dᵖᵘ Nov 18] runner-up in Irish maiden point: poor handicap hurdler: stays 3m: acts on soft going: tried in cheekpieces. *Michael Appleby* — h74

VODKA RED (IRE) 10 b.g. Ivan Denisovich (IRE) – Begine (IRE) (Germany (USA)) [2017/18 h71: h19.3v⁴ h24g h16.4s c19.3sᶠ Jan 12] poor handicap hurdler: 3 lengths down when fell heavily last in novice handicap won by Instant Replay at Sedgefield on chasing debut: stayed 3m: acted on good to firm and heavy going: wore headgear: refitted with tongue tie last 4 starts: dead. *Kenny Johnson* — c84 h81

VODKA WELLS (FR) 8 b.g. Irish Wells (FR) – Kahipiroska (FR) (Mansonnien (FR)) [2017/18 c122, h111: c16.4g² c15.6g* c16.5g³ c16g³ Jul 6] good-topped gelding: has reportedly had breathing operation: fair hurdler: fairly useful handicap chaser: won at Hexham (conditional) in May: unproven beyond 17f: acts on heavy going: wears headgear: often races prominently. *Rebecca Menzies* — c115 h–

VOIE DANS VOIE (FR) 5 br.g. Coastal Path – Peggy Pierji (FR) (Cadoudal (FR)) [2017/18 h19.5d³ h20.5s⁵ h19.2v² h20.7s² h19.3s³ h24.3g⁶ Apr 20] £95,000 4-y-o: good-topped gelding: seventh foal: brother to French chaser Double Voie (21f winner) and half-brother to 2 winners in France, including smart hurdler Ambroise (15f-19f winner, by Epalo): dam unraced: placed both starts in Irish maiden points: fairly useful form over hurdles: second in novice at Towcester in February: should stay beyond 21f: best form on soft/heavy going. *Alan King* — h120

VOIX D'EAU (FR) 8 b.g. Voix du Nord (FR) – Eau de Chesne (FR) (R B Chesne) [2017/18 c146, h–: c19.2g² c20.3gᵖᵘ c20.9g³ c19.9s⁶ c21d⁵ c20.8g Apr 18] big, lengthy gelding: winning hurdler: useful handicap chaser: stays 21f: acts on good to firm and good to soft going: tried in cheekpieces: wears tongue tie. *Harry Fry* — c140 h–

VOIX DES TIEP (FR) 6 b.g. Voix du Nord (FR) – Tiepataxe (FR) (Mad Tax (USA)) [2017/18 b105p: b16s³ b19v³ b16v* b16v⁵ b16.2d² Apr 26] useful bumper performer: won maiden at Thurles in March: second at Punchestown (1¾ lengths behind Dunvegan) in April. *W. P. Mullins, Ireland* — b110

VOIX DU REVE (FR) 6 br.g. Voix du Nord (FR) – Pommbelle (FR) (Apple Tree (FR)) [2017/18 h24s h24s h21.1s h16s h20s Apr 28] neat gelding: useful hurdler, below best in 2017/18 after long lay-off: should stay beyond 17f: acts on heavy going: wears hood. *W. P. Mullins, Ireland* — h129

VOLCANIC (FR) 9 br.g. Al Namix (FR) – Queen of Rock (FR) (Video Rock (FR)) [2017/18 c–, h121: h24.5d³ h23.8d³ ab16g² h23.1v⁵ h25d³ Mar 31] leggy gelding: fairly useful handicap hurdler: winning chaser: stays 27f: acts on good to firm and heavy going: tried in cheekpieces: wears tongue tie. *Donald McCain* — c– h116

VOLCANIC JACK (IRE) 10 b.g. Kodiac – Rosaria Panatta (IRE) (Mujtahid (USA)) [2017/18 c75§, h–§: c21.2g c25.5s c19.4g^{pu} h16.7g⁴ c21.2d^{pu} h16.2d^{pu} h20g⁵ Sep 12] sturdy gelding: winning hurdler/chaser, little form in 2017/18: stays 2¾m: acts on soft and good to firm going: unreliable. *Michael Chapman* — c– § h73 §

VOLCANO (FR) 4 gr.g. Martaline – Lyli Rose (FR) (Lyphard's Wish (FR)) [2017/18 b13.2s* b14s⁵ b16.4s Mar 14] smallish gelding: sixth foal: half-brother to 3 winners, including smart hurdler Rolling Star (2m-2¼m winner, by Smadoun): dam French maiden on Flat (placed at 11.5f): fairly useful form when won junior event at Exeter in October, standout effort in bumpers: left Christian Williams after second start. *Nigel Twiston-Davies* — b101

VOLCAN SURPRISE (FR) 10 b.g. Dom Alco (FR) – Invitee Surprise (FR) (April Night (FR)) [2017/18 h26.4d^{pu} Apr 22] neat gelding: multiple winning pointer: maiden hurdler/chaser: stays 2¾m: acts on soft going: has worn headgear, including last 4 starts. *Caroline Fryer* — c– h–

VOLNAY DE THAIX (FR) 9 ch.g. Secret Singer (FR) – Mange de Thaix (FR) (Mont Basile (FR)) [2017/18 c–, h147: h22.8m c23.8m³ h23.1g³ c26.3v Mar 16] tall, useful-looking gelding: useful hurdler/chaser nowadays: left Nicky Henderson after third start: easily won both starts in points in 2018: stays 3m: acts on soft and good to firm going: tried in cheekpieces. *Stuart Morris* — c144 h136

VOLPONE JELOIS (FR) 5 gr.g. Vol de Nuit – Jenne Jelois (FR) (My Risk (FR)) [2017/18 h120: h18.5m⁴ h16.3d⁴ h19.8s⁵ ab16d* h19.8d⁴ Apr 22] fair handicap hurdler: won jumpers bumper at Kempton in March: stays 19f: acts on soft and good to firm going: wears cheekpieces. *Paul Nicholls* — h114

VOLT FACE (FR) 9 ch.g. Kapgarde (FR) – Jourenuit (FR) (Chamberlin (FR)) [2017/18 c118, h110: c18g² c16.4g³ c20.5d⁴ c18.8d^{pu} c20s⁵ h24.4s³ Jan 26] rather leggy gelding: fair handicap hurdler: fairly useful maiden chaser: stays 3m: acts on good to firm and heavy going: has worn headgear: wears tongue tie. *Charlie Longsdon* — c119 h112

VOLVALIEN (FR) 9 b.g. Network (GER) – Josvalie (FR) (Panoramic) [2017/18 c118, h99: h15.7d c16.5g² Oct 25] rather leggy gelding: maiden hurdler: fairly useful handicap chaser: stays 2½m, at least as effective at 2m: acts on soft going: has worn headgear: wears tongue tie: front runner/races prominently. *Brian Ellison* — c116 h–

VOODOO DOLL (IRE) 5 b.g. Getaway (IRE) – Voodoo Magic (GER) (Platini (GER)) [2017/18 h15.5d h16.5g h16.5s⁴ h15.8s² h18.6v⁶ Mar 11] €28,000 3-y-o: fourth foal: half-brother to bumper winners Mystical Dreamer (by Flemensfirth) and Wylde Magic (by Oscar): dam once-raced close relative of fairly useful hurdler (stayed 2¾m) Val de Fleurie: fair form over hurdles. *Evan Williams* — h103

VOSNE ROMANEE (FR) 7 ch.g. Arakan (USA) – Vento Del Oreno (FR) (Lando (GER)) [2017/18 h131: h15.7m^{pu} c16m⁴ c17g⁴ c16.3d² c16.5g³ c16.5g* h19.6s⁴ ab16d⁵ c15.8s c16s³ Apr 26] smallish gelding: useful handicap hurdler, shaped better than result at Huntingdon on seventh outing: useful chaser: won novices at Perth in June and Stratford in July, and handicap at Worcester in September: stays 2¼m: acts on good to firm and good to soft going: wears headgear/tongue tie. *Dr Richard Newland* — c138 h114

VOTE OF CONFIDENCE (USA) 8 ch.g. Pleasantly Perfect (USA) – Sogna di Me (Danehill (USA)) [2017/18 c95, h120: c25.5d^{pu} h23g^{pu} h19.6g c20g⁶ c20g c19.9s⁴ Mar 14] fairly useful hurdler at best, no form in 2017/18: little show over fences: left Laura Hurley after fifth start: usually in headgear: wears tongue tie: often races towards rear. *Dan Skelton* — c– h–

VOUVRAY (FR) 7 b.g. Califet (FR) – Cartzagrouas (FR) (Esprit du Nord (USA)) [2017/18 h–: c20.9v^{ur} c23.8d^F Mar 22] won Irish maiden point on debut, only sign of ability. *G. M. Davies* — c– h–

VOYAGE A NEW YORK (FR) 9 b.g. Kapgarde (FR) – Pennsylvanie (FR) (Dadarissime (FR)) [2017/18 c116, h–: c24.2g^{pu} c21.6g⁴ c21.5v³ c20s c20.6v⁶ c24.2v^{pu} c21.6v Apr 16] tall gelding: winning hurdler: fairly useful handicap chaser at best, has become disappointing: stays 25f: acts on heavy going: wears tongue tie: often races towards rear. *Lucinda Russell* — c101 h–

VOY

VOYAGE DE RETOUR (IRE) 6 b.g. Craigsteel – Taipers (IRE) (Taipan (IRE)) [2017/18 b17.7s[6] Apr 15] off mark in Irish points at third attempt: tailed off in bumper. *Nicky Henderson* — b–

VYTA DU ROC (FR) 9 gr.g. Lion Noir – Dolce Vyta (FR) (Grand Tresor (FR)) [2017/18 c140, h124+: h24.7s[5] c26g c26.3s* Jan 1] good-topped gelding: smart hurdler at best: smart handicap chaser: in cheekpieces, won at Cheltenham (by 22 lengths from Lamb Or Cod) in January: stays 4m: acts on heavy going: tried in tongue tie. *Nicky Henderson* — c146 h136

W

WADE HARPER (IRE) 8 b.g. Westerner – Nosie Betty (IRE) (Alphabatim (USA)) [2017/18 c113, h–: c24d[2] c22.6m[2] c23.6d[3] c21.2g h20v h20v h16v[5] h16s[5] h17.8v[5] Apr 13] close-coupled gelding: fair handicap hurdler: fair maiden chaser: left David Dennis after fourth start: stays 3m: acts on heavy going: tried in cheekpieces: regularly tongue tied: races towards rear. *P. J. Rothwell, Ireland* — c107 h106

WADSWICK COURT (IRE) 10 b.g. Court Cave (IRE) – Tarasandy (IRE) (Arapahos (FR)) [2017/18 c128, h–: c25.8g[2] c21.2d[5] c23g[2] c20g[2] c21.4g[2] c20s* c21.4g[6] c19.4d[5] c20.1s* Apr 26] useful-looking gelding: winning hurdler: useful handicap chaser: won at Uttoxeter in July and Perth in April: stays 3m: acts on heavy going: wears headgear: has worn tongue tie, including last 5 starts: often races prominently/travels strongly. *Peter Bowen* — c135 h–

WAGNER KLASS (FR) 6 ch.g. Prince Kirk (FR) – Bartjack (FR) (Lost World (IRE)) [2017/18 b–: ab16.3g[6] Apr 15] twice-raced in bumpers at Newcastle: off 16 months and left Kenny Johnson, seemingly better effort when sixth in April. *Rebecca Menzies* — b82

WAHWONAISA 6 b.g. Kalanisi (IRE) – Clandestine (Saddlers' Hall (IRE)) [2017/18 h15.8[dur] h15.8s h15.9d h19.5v Mar 21] little form over hurdles: tried in cheekpieces. *David Bridgwater* — h–

WAIHEKE 5 ch.m. Black Sam Bellamy (IRE) – Its Meant To Be (Gunner B) [2017/18 h15.8s[5] h18.5s* h18.5v[4] h16.8s[2] h19.2s[4] Mar 7] £2,500 3-y-o: half-sister to fair chaser Todareistodo (2m-19f winner, by Fair Mix): dam (b85), lightly raced in bumpers/over hurdles, half-sister to dam of very smart chaser (stayed 3¼m) Planet of Sound: fair form over hurdles: won mares novice at Exeter in November: stays 19f: acts on soft going. *Philip Hobbs* — h112

WAIKIKI WAVES (FR) 5 b.g. Alexandros – Lulabelle Spar (IRE) (Milan) [2017/18 b69: b17.7g[4] h15.9d[6] h20.5s h19.2v[4] h19.6s h21s Apr 9] poor form in bumpers: modest form over hurdles: should stay beyond 19f: acts on heavy going. *Gary Moore* — h92 b68

WAIT FOR ME (FR) 8 b.g. Saint des Saints (FR) – Aulne River (FR) (River Mist (USA)) [2017/18 h138: h21.6g[2] c20g* c23.6d[F] c23.4g[4] h21.4v[3] h24s Mar 15] robust gelding: useful handicap hurdler: landed odds in maiden at Worcester in September on chasing debut: running better race after when falling 4 out in novice won by Knight of Noir at Chepstow: may prove best short of 3m when conditions are testing: acts on heavy going: wears hood/tongue tie: travels strongly well off pace. *Philip Hobbs* — c141 h138

WAITING PATIENTLY (IRE) 7 b.g. Flemensfirth (USA) – Rossavon (IRE) (Beneficial) [2017/18 c150p, h–: c20d* c20.5d* c21s* Feb 17] — c168 p h– p

Memories can be short. The much discussed decline of northern jumping can be exaggerated. It is only six years since northern trainers outscored even Ireland's large raiding party with six winners at the Cheltenham Festival. The fact that Cheltenham went by in the latest season without a northern-trained winner— for the fourth year in succession—may be an indicator that jumping in the North is short of star material at present, but the outlook is nowhere near so gloomy as some make it out to be. Even the big southern stables have had their work cut out in recent seasons to compete with Ireland's best at jumping's most prestigious meeting which is dominated nowadays by the powerhouse stables of Willie Mullins and Gordon Elliott. Northern racing lost one of its own stalwarts in the latest season when Malcolm Jefferson died, age seventy-one, in early-February after a lengthy battle with cancer. Jefferson trained a string of around fifty (a long way short of the numbers trained at the big southern yards) at Newstead Cottage Stables at Malton, from where his flow of winners (he had forty in his best season, 2016/17) included two of those six Cheltenham Festival winners for the North in 2012, Cape Tribulation in the Pertemps Final and Attaglance in the Martin Pipe Conditional Jockeys' Handicap Hurdle, both of whom followed up in handicaps (under top weight) at the Grand National meeting. Those winners came seventeen years after Jefferson's best horse Dato Star (later the winner of the Christmas Hurdle at Kempton and two editions of the 'Fighting Fifth' at Newcastle) had won the Champion Bumper at the Festival, and eighteen years after he had saddled his first Festival winner, Tindari, to win the Gold Card Final (now the Pertemps).

Jefferson first took out a licence in the early-'eighties after spending his formative years as travelling head man to Gordon Richards (he drove Lucius to Aintree when he won the 1978 National). Gordon Richards was part of the last golden era for northern jumping, thirty or forty years ago, when his was one of several powerful yards which really put the North on the map, along with those run by such as Peter Easterby, the Dickinsons, Arthur Stephenson and Jimmy FitzGerald. Gordon Richards' son Nicky, who took over the famous Greystoke yard, flew the flag for the North in the latest season when Simply Ned, something of a regular in the big two-mile chases, became the only overseas raider to win a Grade 1 in Ireland in the latest season when he was awarded the Paddy's Rewards Club Chase at Leopardstown's Christmas meeting (promoted at the expense of Mullins-trained Min). The Richards-trained Guitar Pete became the first northern-based winner—albeit in tragic circumstances—of Cheltenham's big December handicap (now run as the Caspian Caviar Gold Cup) since Legal Right (trained by Jonjo O'Neill when he was Cumbria-based). Another of those northern trainers who were on the scoreboard at the 2012 Cheltenham Festival, Scottish-based Lucinda Russell, had the misfortune to lose the 2017 Grand National winner One For Arthur through injury for the latest campaign and she slipped outside the top thirty trainers in the end-of-season tables.

Donald McCain, who had two of those winners at the Festival in 2012, has bounced back from a difficult few years to regain his position as the leading northern-based trainer, chalking up ninety-eight wins and finishing tenth in the overall prize-money table in the latest season. McCain's new link-up in the 2018/19 season with the North's top jockey and Waiting Patiently's regular partner Brian Hughes, who rode regularly for Malcolm Jefferson over the years and has finished runner-up in the overall table in the last two seasons, should see McCain regaining further lost ground on the leading southern yards. Sue Smith and Nicky Richards completed the trio of northern trainers to end the season in the top thirty in the trainers' table, while Jedd O'Keefe, Brian Ellison and Chris Grant were others who won pattern races with, respectively, Sam Spinner (Long Walk Hurdle), Definitly Red (Many Clouds Chase, Cotswold Chase) and Donna's Diamond (Rendlesham Hurdle).

Sam Spinner shaped in the Long Walk Hurdle as if he might be the champion that the North has been looking for to take on the best. He started favourite for the Stayers' Hurdle at the Cheltenham Festival but finished fifth behind the Mullins-trained Penhill and then managed only third, behind another Irish-trained horse Identity Thief, when favourite again in the Liverpool Hurdle at Aintree. Unfortunately, the best horse trained in the North in the latest season, the unbeaten chaser Waiting Patiently, missed both the Cheltenham Festival and the Grand National meeting and wasn't seen out at all after extending his winning run over fences to six in the Betfair Ascot Chase in February, a race his trainer didn't live to see, Ruth Jefferson having taken over the stable after the death of her father. Waiting Patiently's hard-fought victory over the veteran Cue Card was one of the races of the season and his success was a poignant one, coming only a day after five hundred had attended Malcolm Jefferson's funeral.

Waiting Patiently, a €16,000 three-year-old at the 2014 Derby Sale, began his racing career at four with Keith Reveley (finishing second in a maiden hurdle at Hexham on his racecourse debut, with the Jefferson-trained dual bumper winner Cloudy Dream—who, along with another owned by Trevor Hemmings, Mount Mews, will be with Donald McCain in 2018/19—beaten into third at odds-on). Waiting Patiently won a novice hurdle at Sedgefield, showing useful form, on the last of his three starts for Saltburn trainer Keith Reveley before being transferred

Betfair Ascot Chase, Ascot—Waiting Patiently (right) is produced late to beat dual winner Cue Card in a vintage renewal; Frodon (hooped sleeves) comes third ahead of Top Notch

to the Jefferson stable in the summer of 2016 shortly before Reveley's retirement. Keith Reveley's son James is a top jockey in France and the trainer's retirement ended the long association of the Reveley name with northern racing. Only a year after Keith Reveley left the training ranks, his mother Mary passed away at the age of seventy-seven, just three months before Malcolm Jefferson. Mary Reveley's training achievements were remarkable, her career record of just over two thousand wins exceeding the number achieved by any other woman trainer in British racing history. She started off in that vintage period for northern jumping in the 'eighties competing against Easterby, Stephenson, the Dickinsons and the like, before enjoying her greatest successes in the 'nineties. Two-thirds of Mary Reveley's winners came over jumps but she also had nearly seven hundred winners on the Flat which puts her among the leading dual-purpose trainers of recent times. Young Flat horses or veteran jumpers, it made no difference to Mary Reveley. None of her winners, however, came at the Cheltenham Festival, her illness- and injury-prone best jumper Cab On Target finally making it there when second as an eleven-year-old in the Foxhunter (he also ran in the Fulke Walwyn Kim Muir as a thirteen-year-old). Whether Waiting Patiently will ever run at the Cheltenham Festival may be in some doubt. He was ante-post second favourite, behind Un de Sceaux, for the latest Ryanair Chase after his success at Ascot but punters were urged by connections to hold their bets, with Ruth Jefferson saying: 'Everyone else is obsessed by Cheltenham but we're not fussed and won't be risking him for the sake of it. This could have been his Cheltenham and, in any case, there are plenty of other races, and other places we can go.' A chip of the old block! As it happened, Waiting Patiently took some time to get over his race in the Ascot Chase—he was finally ruled out of the Ryanair Chase a week before, said to be 'short of peak form'—and he then suffered a slight setback which ended his campaign altogether.

    Connections and followers of Waiting Patiently have already become used to doing just that. He ran only three times in his first season over fences, completing a hat-trick in various novice events at Sedgefield, Newcastle and Haydock, the last-named success coming in a Grade 2 contest in which he beat Politologue. A small setback meant that Waiting Patiently was on the sidelines that season for the major spring festivals, and he made light of a ten-month absence when landing the odds from three opponents in the Colin Parker Memorial Intermediate Chase at Carlisle in November, confirming himself a very promising prospect with a smooth two-and-a-half-length victory over southern raider Belami des Pictons. After his training had been interrupted by a 'a bit of a head cold', Waiting Patiently was cast in the role of 'northern raider' on his two other starts, which took him first to Kempton in mid-January for another listed event, the 32Red Casino Chase, in which he was the youngest horse in the field and came up against three regulars in Grade 1 company over the years, God's Own, Smad Place and Josses Hill, as well as the very smart Art Mauresque. Waiting Patiently started 13/8 favourite and put up a performance bordering on top class to win by eight lengths and four lengths from Art Mauresque and God's Own, travelling and jumping well before quickening clear in the home straight.

Waiting Patiently was again favourite in an up-to-scratch renewal of the Grade 1 Betfair Ascot Chase in which the opposition included Top Notch, winner on his last two starts of the 1965 Chase over the course and distance in November and the Peterborough Chase (which had had to be transferred from its usual venue Huntingdon to Taunton) in December. Irish challenger Coney Island was another course and distance winner, having been impressive in a graduation event on his reappearance in December, while the veteran Cue Card had won the Ascot Chase twice before, in 2013 and 2017. Frodon was fresh from running away with a valuable handicap at Cheltenham's Trials meeting at the end of January. Cue Card and Waiting Patiently had the Ascot Chase between them over the last two fences after the race had been run at a strong pace from the outset, making for a searching test of both jumping technique and stamina at the trip. As usual, Brian Hughes rode Waiting Patiently with restraint and didn't produce him to lead until the last ('Malcolm would be bollocking me because I got there too soon'). Driven out on the run-in to beat Cue Card by two and three quarter lengths, Waiting Patiently passed his most demanding test to date with flying colours. Frodon was a further fifteen lengths back in third, with Top Notch completing the frame. Top Notch, like Waiting Patiently, bypassed Cheltenham and Aintree, for reasons explained in the essay on him, and, perhaps tellingly, Frodon and Cue Card, who both contested the Ryanair Chase at the Festival, figured among the biggest Cheltenham disappointments.

Waiting Patiently (IRE) (b.g. 2011)
- Flemensfirth (USA) (b 1992)
  - Alleged (b 1974)
    - Hoist The Flag
    - Princess Pout
  - Etheldreda (ch 1985)
    - Diesis
    - Royal Bund
- Rossavon (IRE) (b 2005)
  - Beneficial (b 1990)
    - Top Ville
    - Youthful
  - Sparkling Opera (ch 1984)
    - Orchestra
    - Shining Jug

Waiting Patiently is the latest in a long line of good performers—headed by such as Imperial Commander, Tidal Bay and Flemenstar—for Flemensfirth who is one of the elder statesmen in the ranks of the jumping sires. Now twenty-six, and still going strongly at Coolmore's Beeches Stud in Ireland, Flemensfirth has consistently figured highly in the end-of-season sires' tables and he became champion for the first time in the latest season, according to the *Racing Post*'s combined table of the leading sires in Britain and Ireland, his progeny earning £2,623,164 with King's Theatre (champion in five of the six previous seasons) runner-up with total earnings of £2,554,076, and Presenting (£2,264,229), Milan (£2,008,072), Kayf Tara (£1,918,707) and Oscar (£1,904,280) completing the top six. Flemensfirth's progeny also gave him more individual winners (114) and more wins (173) than any of his rivals. Flemensfirth and the now-deceased Presenting, incidentally, were contemporaries with John Gosden in the mid-'nineties, though the pair never met in racecourse competition, Flemensfirth finishing fifth in Celtic Swing's Prix du Jockey Club and Presenting third in Lammtarra's Derby in the same year.

On the distaff side, Waiting Patiently is from a family which boasts a Supreme Novices' Hurdle winner in Miller Hill and another top hurdler in the ill-fated Mighty Mogul who won the Christmas Hurdle at Kempton and was ante-post favourite for the Champion Hurdle when suffering a fatal injury at what is now known as Cheltenham's Trials meeting. Mighty Mogul was out of a half-sister to Miller Hill, who was also a half-brother to Waiting Patiently's great grandam Shining Jug. Mighty Mogul's dam Deep Shine also became the great grandam of another Cheltenham Festival winner in the family, Ballynagour, who won the Byrne Group Plate in 2014 before going on to be placed after that in the Melling Chase at Aintree and the Champion Chase at Punchestown (he was also runner-up in the 2015 Aintree Bowl before landing a big win over hurdles in the Prix La Barka at Auteuil). Waiting Patiently's dam Rossavon and his grandam Sparkling Opera were both unraced, but Sparkling Opera bred several winners including the fairly useful hurdler/fair chaser Ciara's Prince. Rossavon's only other winner so far is Waiting Patiently's ill-fated, year-older brother Walking In The Air, a fairly useful hurdler who was fatally injured in a novice handicap at Market Rasen on his chasing debut. Waiting Patiently has yet to race over further than two miles five furlongs, the distance of the Ascot Chase, but, judged on the way he finished that strongly-run race, it should not be an issue if and when he is eventually stepped up to three miles (the King George VI Chase has been mentioned as a target by connections). Waiting Patiently acts on soft going and is a strong traveller who is held up to make the best use of his turn of foot. He is open to further improvement and, provided all remains well with him, he will be a major contender wherever connections opt to run him. *Ruth Jefferson*

WAITINONASUNNYDAY (IRE) 5 gr.g. Tikkanen (USA) – Coppenagh Lady (IRE) (Tawrrific (NZ)) [2017/18 h19.5s h21.4s^{pu} h16.8v^{pu} h19.8v^5 h21v^2 Apr 27] unplaced in Irish point on debut: poor form over hurdles: best effort at 21f on heavy going: tried in hood/tongue tie. *Michael Blake*   **h75**

WAKANDA (IRE) 9 b.g. Westerner – Chanson Indienne (FR) (Indian River (FR)) [2017/18 c150, h–: c26.2g^2 c23.4v^5 c24.2s^2 c24s* c25s^{pu} c25s Apr 14] sturdy gelding: winning hurdler: smart handicap chaser: won Sky Bet Chase at Doncaster (by head from Warriors Tale) in January: stays 3m: acts on good to firm and heavy going: tough and genuine. *Sue Smith*   **c146 h–**

WAKEA (USA) 7 b.g. Cape Cross (IRE) – Imiloa (USA) (Kingmambo (USA)) [2017/18 h141: h16.7g^f h24.4g^2 h16s^2 h16s^4 h19.3d^3 Nov 25] smart hurdler: in frame all 4 completed starts in 2017/18, third behind Lil Rockerfeller in Coral Hurdle at Ascot final one: beaten only narrowly over easy 3m, but better at much shorter: acts on soft going: wears hood/tongue tie: front runner/races prominently. *Karl Thornton, Ireland*   **h145**

WALDEN PRINCE (IRE) 11 b.g. Saffron Walden (FR) – Kahyasi Princess (IRE) (Kahyasi) [2017/18 c129§, h60§: c17.4g c16.5g^6 c16.3g^4 c16d^2 c15.7d^4 c25g^{pu} c20d^6 c16d^3 c15.9d^6 c16d^3 Apr 24] leggy gelding: winning hurdler: fair handicap chaser nowadays: best around 2m: acts on good to firm and heavy going: normally in headgear: wears tongue tie: waited with: unreliable. *Sophie Leech*   **c100 § h– §**

WALDORF SALAD 10 b.g. Millenary – Ismene (USA) (Bad Conduct (USA)) [2017/18 c121, h–: c26.2d^{pu} c24.1s^4 c24v^5 c23.6v c23.6v^{pu} Apr 14] tall gelding: winning hurdler: useful handicap chaser at best: lightly raced and mostly out of sorts since 2015/16: stays 3m: best form on soft/heavy going: has worn headgear, including last 4 starts: usually races close up. *Venetia Williams*   **c100 h–**

WALKABOUT (IRE) 6 b.g. Papal Bull – Dainty Steps (IRE) (Xaar) [2017/18 h16.4d^6 h17.3s* h16.7g Sep 30] modest maiden on Flat, stays 1½m: fairly useful handicap hurdler: won at Ballinrobe in August: raced around 2m: acts on heavy going: in cheekpieces last 3 starts: front runner/races prominently. *Gordon Elliott, Ireland*   **h121**

WALKAMI (FR) 7 b.g. Walk In The Park (IRE) – Ominneha (FR) (Exit To Nowhere (USA)) [2017/18 c–, h102: c20m* c26.1g^5 May 28] good-topped gelding: fair maiden hurdler: form (fair) over fences only when winning handicap at Worcester in May: best around 2½m: acts on good to firm going: has worn headgear, including last 4 starts: races prominently. *Jonjo O'Neill*   **c102 h–**

WALKERS POINT (IRE) 7 b.g. Golan (IRE) – Don't Wait (IRE) (Oscar (IRE)) [2017/18 h20.7m h19.4g^4 h21d^{pu} h20.2g h24s^4 h24s h20s h21.2g Apr 23] €10,500 3-y-o: second foal: dam, winning pointer, sister to fairly useful hurdler/useful chaser (winner up to 2½m) Arteea: modest maiden hurdler: left David M. O'Brien after fifth start: stays 3m: acts on soft going: has worn headgear/tongue tie. *Sean McParlan, Ireland*   **h95**

WAR

WALK IN THE MILL (FR) 8 b.g. Walk In The Park (IRE) – Libre Amour (FR) (Lost **c140**
World (IRE)) [2017/18 c137: c20.9g⁵ c23.8d* c23.8d³ c25.6v^pu Jan 20] sturdy gelding:
useful handicap chaser: won at Ascot in November: also third in Silver Cup there (4 lengths
behind Gold Present) following month: stays 3m: acts on soft going. *Robert Walford*

WALK OF GLEAMS 9 b.m. Gleaming (IRE) – Harlequin Walk (IRE) (Pennine Walk) **h80**
[2017/18 h74: h20.5d^pu h20.5d⁶ h19.2v⁶ h15.9v⁶ h20.5d h21.7g^pu Apr 20] poor maiden
hurdler: stays 21f: acts on heavy going. *Anna Newton-Smith*

WALK WATERFORD 7 bl.g. Fair Mix (IRE) – Woore Lass (IRE) (Persian Bold) **h86**
[2017/18 h96: h16g⁴ h16.3g^pu h20.3g Jul 16] last in Irish maiden point: modest form over
hurdles: tried in tongue tie. *Jonjo O'Neill*

WALLACE SPIRIT (FR) 5 gr.g. Le Havre (IRE) – In Love New (FR) (Perrault) **h114**
[2017/18 b15.7d h20.5s^pu h21s h20.5s^F h16m² Apr 26] €44,000 3-y-o: good-topped **b82**
gelding: seventh foal: half-brother to 3 winners, including French chasers Champagne
Ariston (19f-21f winner) and New Raptor (2¼m winner) (both by Caballo Raptor): dam
unraced: badly needed experience in bumper at Ascot: fair form last 2 starts in novice
hurdles: tried in cheekpieces: temperament under suspicion. *Nicky Henderson*

WALSINGHAM GRANGE (USA) 5 b.g. Paddy O'Prado (USA) – Mambo Queen **h111**
(USA) (Kingmambo (USA)) [2017/18 h106: h20.3d h16s³ h16s² h16.7v* h15.8s⁵ h15.7v³
h16d⁴ Apr 7] fair handicap hurdler: won at Bangor in February: unproven beyond 17f: acts
on heavy going: wears headgear: front runner/races prominently. *Pam Sly*

WALTER ONEEIGHTONE (IRE) 6 b.g. Morozov (USA) – Matinee Show (IRE) **h90**
(Carroll House) [2017/18 h–: h20g⁵ h23.3d h23.1g* h23.9g⁴ h23.4s³ Dec 4] modest
handicap hurdler: won at Bangor in October: best form on good going: tried in
cheekpieces: in tongue tie last 3 starts: front runner/races prominently. *Jonjo O'Neill*

WALT (IRE) 7 b.g. King's Theatre (IRE) – Allee Sarthoise (FR) (Pampabird) [2017/18 **c123**
h126: c21.6d⁴ c23.6v³ c20.2v³ c24.2s^pu Feb 23] fairly useful hurdler: similar form in **h–**
novice handicap chases: stays 3m: acts on heavy going. *Neil Mulholland*

WALTZ DARLING (IRE) 10 b.g. Iffraaj – Aljafliyah (Halling (USA)) [2017/18 c–, h–: **c–**
h20.3g h22.1g⁶ h23.3d h23.1g³ h23.1g² h23.3g h23.1g² h23.8m³ h24s⁵ h23.8s⁵ Jan 19] fair **h106**
handicap hurdler: winning chaser: stays 3m: acts on soft and good to firm going: wears
cheekpieces. *Gillian Boanas*

WANDAOVER 6 b.m. Overbury (IRE) – Programme Girl (IRE) (Definite Article) **h–**
[2017/18 b–: b16.7g h23.3d^pu h19.9g h20.1d⁴ Sep 5] of no account: tried in cheekpieces. **b–**
Neil Mechie

WANDRIN STAR (IRE) 7 b.g. Flemensfirth (USA) – Keralba (USA) (Sheikh Albadou) **c113**
[2017/18 h20v⁵ c19.8g⁴ c20d⁴ c20s c19.9s⁴ c24s² Apr 9] £52,000 6-y-o: half-brother to 3 **h80 p**
winners, including useful hurdler/chaser Hash Brown (2½m-2¾m winner, by Vinnie Roe)
and bumper winner/fair hurdler Dingaling (2½m winner, by Milan): dam, ran once on Flat,
half-sister to fairly useful hurdler (2m winner) Soothfast: won Irish maiden point on debut:
better for run sole outing over hurdles, fair form over fences: stays 3m: acts on soft going:
tried in tongue tie. *Kim Bailey*

WAR AT SEA (IRE) 4 gr.g. Mastercraftsman (IRE) – Swirling (IRE) (Galileo (IRE)) **h73**
[2017/18 h16s⁵ h16.6s h17.7s Mar 7] fairly useful maiden on Flat (stays 1½m) at best:
never dangerous over hurdles: in hood last 2 starts. *Ali Stronge*

WAR CREATION (IRE) 6 b.m. Scorpion (IRE) – Creation (IRE) (Definite Article) **h112**
[2017/18 h101, b98: h19.6g⁴ h18.9v* h21.2s^pu h20.6g⁶ Apr 22] bumper winner: fair
handicap hurdler: won at Haydock (conditionals) in December: should stay at least 2½m:
acts on good to firm and heavy going: front runner/races prominently. *Nicky Henderson*

WARDEN HILL (IRE) 10 br.g. Presenting – Moon Storm (IRE) (Strong Gale) [2017/18 **c119**
c118, h–: h29.3s³ c26s* c26.3v c21.1s^ur Apr 12] workmanlike gelding: multiple point **h–**
winner: winning hurdler: fairly useful hunter chaser nowadays: won at Doncaster in
February: stays 3¼m: acts on heavy going: in cheekpieces last 4 starts. *Mrs H. Connors*

WAR JOEY (IRE) 5 b.g. Primary (USA) – Wake Me Gently (IRE) (Be My Native **h87**
(USA)) [2017/18 b–: h15.7g h16.2g⁵ h16.2s^pu h16.2v h17v⁴ h17d h20.6v⁵ Apr 14] **b–**
workmanlike gelding: well beaten in bumpers: modest maiden hurdler: left Philip Kirby
after second start: stays 17f: acts on heavy going: in tongue tie last 4 starts. *Ann Hamilton*

WARKSBURN BOY 8 b.g. Kayf Tara – Bonchester Bridge (Shambo) [2017/18 c65, h–: **c–**
c20.1g⁴ c15.6g^pu Jun 17] maiden hurdler/chaser: tried in cheekpieces: has worn tongue tie, **h–**
including last 5 starts. *Sheena Walton*

WAR

WAR ON THE ROCKS (IRE) 9 b.g. Wareed (IRE) – Rock Garden (IRE) (Bigstone (IRE)) [2017/18 h19.8s³ h16.4d Nov 17] bumper winner: fair maiden hurdler: probably stays 2½m: acts on soft going: strong-travelling sort. *Fergal O'Brien* — **h104**

WAR PATH (FR) 9 b.g. Walk In The Park (IRE) – Childermas (IRE) (Darshaan) [2017/18 c–, h–: c24s⁵ Jan 25] multiple winning pointer: first form under Rules when fifth in 3m hunter chase at Warwick: tried in cheekpieces. *Miss Hannah Lewis* — **c86 h–**

WARRIORS TALE 9 b.g. Midnight Legend – Samandara (FR) (Kris) [2017/18 c141, h–: c19.9sᵘʳ c22.4g² c24s² c34.3sᵖᵘ Apr 14] workmanlike gelding: winning hurdler: smart handicap chaser: runner-up twice in 2017/18, including in Sky Bet Chase at Doncaster (head behind Wakanda) in January: stays 3m: acts on good to firm and heavy going: tried in hood: wears tongue tie: strong-travelling sort who can finish weakly. *Paul Nicholls* — **c148 h–**

WAR SINGER (USA) 11 b.g. War Chant (USA) – Sister Marilyn (USA) (Saint Ballado (CAN)) [2017/18 c129, h–: c16.5g⁶ h15.8m⁴ Jul 2] sturdy gelding: fairly useful hurdler/chaser: raced around 2m: acts on soft and good to firm going: wears headgear/tongue tie: patiently ridden: has found little. *Johnny Farrelly* — **c– h121**

WAR SOUND 9 b.g. Kayf Tara – Come The Dawn (Gunner B) [2017/18 c16d³ c18d² c16.1s² c16.4s³ c20.8v⁴ c15.7s² c20v² c20d² Apr 22] well-made gelding: smart hurdler: useful maiden chaser: runner-up 5 times in 2017/18, in handicaps last 3 outings: stays 2½m: acts on heavy going. *Philip Hobbs* — **c136 h–**

WARTHOG (FR) 6 gr.g. Martaline – Shekira (FR) (Medaaly) [2017/18 b97: h16.8v³ h20.5sᵖᵘ h19.3s³ h24.1v² h23.1d Apr 21] useful-looking gelding: point winner in Ireland: fairly useful form in bumpers: similar form over hurdles: stays 3m: acts on heavy going: tried in cheekpieces: wears tongue tie: travels strongly towards rear. *David Pipe* — **h123**

WASHED ASHORE (IRE) 7 ch.g. Presenting – Give It Time (Kayf Tara) [2017/18 h111, b71: c20.3g⁵ c19.2g⁵ c23.9g² c23.9g⁴ c23g² c29.2g c24d⁴ Feb 8] compact gelding: winning hurdler: fairly useful handicap chaser: won at Market Rasen in August: stays 3m: acts on good to soft going: often travels strongly. *Jonjo O'Neill* — **c122 h–**

WATCOMBE HEIGHTS (IRE) 8 b.g. Scorpion (IRE) – Golden Bay (Karinga Bay) [2017/18 h21.6g² h18.5m* h19.3gᶠ h21.6s³ h21.6v² h21.4s² h15.3v⁶ h19.8d⁴ Apr 22] lengthy, angular gelding: fairly useful hurdler: won maiden at Newton Abbot in August: left Martin Hill after fifth start: stays 2¾m: acts on good to firm and heavy going: has worn hood. *Colin Tizzard* — **h121**

WATERCLOCK (IRE) 9 ch.g. Notnowcato – Waterfall One (Nashwan (USA)) [2017/18 h–: h23.3g⁵ May 13] sturdy gelding: fair handicap hurdler: won at Hexham only start in 2017/18: stayed 23f: acted on good to firm and heavy going: wore headgear: dead. *Micky Hammond* — **h108**

WATERLOO WARRIOR (IRE) 6 b.g. Kalanisi (IRE) – Vindonissa (IRE) (Definite Article) [2017/18 h113, b95: h21.6v⁴ h23.1s² h23.6s² h23.6vᵖᵘ h21.4v⁶ h21.4d⁴ Apr 22] good-topped gelding: fair maiden hurdler: stays 3m: acts on soft going: wears headgear: usually in tongue tie: temperamental. *Colin Tizzard* — **h112 §**

WATERLORD 7 b.g. Cape Cross (IRE) – Shell Garland (USA) (Sadler's Wells (USA)) [2017/18 h15.7v⁶ h16.7v* h15.7v* h15.7v⁴ h16.3vᵖᵘ h16.7sᶠ Mar 24] sturdy gelding: useful hurdler: won novices at Bangor and Haydock in December: raced around 2m: acted on heavy going: made running/raced prominently: dead. *Donald McCain* — **h132**

WATERVILLE ROCK (IRE) 8 b.g. Diamond Green (FR) – Sandy Fitzgerald (IRE) (Last Tycoon) [2017/18 h20.4d³ h24.5m h19.9gᵖᵘ Jul 19] maiden hurdler, no form in 2017/18: has worn headgear/tongue tie, including last 2 starts. *James A. Nash, Ireland* — **h–**

WATER WAGTAIL 11 b.g. Kahyasi – Kentford Grebe (Teenoso (USA)) [2017/18 c99², h–: c25.5d* c25.1s³ c25.1vᴿ c25.1d Apr 22] maiden hurdler: fair handicap chaser: won at Warwick on reappearance in November: stays 3¼m: acts on heavy going: wears cheekpieces: unreliable. *Emma Lavelle* — **c100 § h–**

WATER WILLOW 6 b.m. Tobougg (IRE) – Water Flower (Environment Friend) [2017/18 h70: h15.9g² h15.7gᶠ h15.8g h21.6m³ h18.5d h16.3s h21.6dᵖᵘ Oct 12] smallish mare: poor maiden hurdler: stays easy 2¾m: acts on good to firm going: tried in tongue tie. *Bill Turner* — **h81**

WAY BACK THEN (IRE) 7 b.g. Robin des Champs (FR) – Ashwell Lady (IRE) (Presenting) [2017/18 b106: h21d* h20.5v⁴ Dec 30] useful-looking gelding: runner-up in Irish point on debut: useful bumper winner: created good impression when winning novice at Kempton in November on hurdling debut: disappointed in face of stiffer task next time. *Ben Pauling* — **h129**

WAY OF THE WORLD (IRE) 7 b.g. Flemensfirth (USA) – Night Heron (IRE) (St Jovite (USA)) [2017/18 h99, b83: h23m^{pu} h20s^F h19.7g h20v^5 h23.8s h19.2v^3 h20v h21.7v^4 h19.7s^3 h19.6d^4 Apr 21] fourth in maiden point: modest handicap hurdler: stays 2½m: acts on heavy going: has worn cheekpieces: front runner/races prominently. *Sheila Lewis* **h86**

WAY OUT WEST (IRE) 5 b.g. Westerner – Rose Vic (IRE) (Old Vic) [2017/18 b16.8g* b16.4g h15.8d^5 h16.3s h16.6d h16s^6 Apr 27] €9,000 3-y-o: sturdy gelding: third foal: half-brother to bumper winner Paper Promise (by Gamut): dam unraced half-sister to useful hurdler (2½m winner) Arrive Sir Clive: trained by Stuart Crawford, landed odds in conditionals/amateur maiden bumper at Sedgefield in May on debut: in hood/tongue tie, modest form over hurdles: likely to stay 2¼m+: often races freely. *Charlie Longsdon* **h95 b85**

WAYSIDE MAGIC 5 b.g. Thewayyouare (USA) – Poppy's Rose (Diktat) [2017/18 h16.7d^{pu} h16.3g^{pu} Oct 21] regressive maiden on Flat: pulled up both outings over hurdles. *Henry Oliver* **h–**

WAYUPINTHESKY (IRE) 11 gr.g. Cloudings (IRE) – Riancoir Alainn (Strong Gale) [2017/18 c101: c23.8g^3 c25.5d^3 May 31] multiple winning pointer: modest hunter chaser: stays 3¼m: acts on good to soft going. *Alison Hamilton* **c93**

WAZOWSKI 9 b.g. Overbury (IRE) – Malay (Karinga Bay) [2017/18 h103: h22.1d^3 h17s^3 h20.1v^4 h16.7v^2 h19.9s* h21.2v^6 Jan 28] fair handicap hurdler: won at Sedgefield in January: stays 2¾m: acts on heavy going. *Donald McCain* **h100**

WEAPON OF CHOICE (IRE) 10 b.g. Iffraaj – Tullawadgeen (IRE) (Sinndar (IRE)) [2017/18 h100: h16.2g^2 h16.2g^5 h16.2g^4 h16.2d^5 Oct 8] modest handicap hurdler: won at Perth in July: raced around 2m: acts on good to soft going: wears headgear: usually tongue tied. *Dianne Sayer* **h98**

WEARDIDITALLGORONG 6 b.m. Fast Company (IRE) – Little Oz (IRE) (Red Ransom (USA)) [2017/18 h15.8d Nov 3] regressive on Flat: blinkered, tailed off in mares maiden on hurdling debut. *Des Donovan, Ireland* **h–**

WEATHER FRONT (USA) 5 ch.g. Stormy Atlantic (USA) – Kiswahili (Selkirk (USA)) [2017/18 h15.6s Jan 3] fair on Flat (stays 1¼m): well beaten in maiden on hurdling debut. *Karen McLintock* **h–**

WEEBILL 6 b.g. Schiaparelli (GER) – Wee Dinns (IRE) (Marju (IRE)) [2017/18 b15.7d^4 h16.7s^3 h15.9v^3 h19s^2 h15h* h21.2d^2 Apr 9] £14,000 3-y-o: second foal: dam (h132), 2¼m/19f hurdle winner, also 1¼m winner on Flat: shaped well when fourth in conditionals/amateur bumper at Southwell: fairly useful form over hurdles: won conditionals maiden at Fakenham in March: stays 21f: acts on heavy going: remains with potential. *Olly Murphy* **h116 p b96**

WEE BOGUS 5 b.g. Multiplex – Silver Gyre (IRE) (Silver Hawk (USA)) [2017/18 b72: b16.8g^4 May 16] modest form in bumpers: poor form on Flat subsequently. *Alistair Whillans* **b76**

WE HAVE A DREAM (FR) 4 b.g. Martaline – Sweet Dance (FR) (Kingsalsa (USA)) [2017/18 h15.9s^4 h14.9d^4 h16d* h16.6d* h16v* h15.6s* h17s* Apr 12] **h150 p**

The top juvenile hurdler turned out to be among the many good horses in Nicky Henderson's stable but, for much of the season, it was a stablemate that many thought was destined for that honour. The filly Apple's Shakira shaped like the best four-year-old through the winter, taking an unbeaten record into the Triumph Hurdle after winning all three of her starts at Cheltenham after being imported from France. Finding only Irish-trained rivals too good when fourth behind Farclas in the Triumph, Apple's Shakira still had claims to being Britain's top juvenile when sent off favourite again for the Anniversary Hurdle at Aintree but, in finishing a well-held third to We Have A Dream, who had to miss Cheltenham, it was clear that she had met her match, not just among the British four-year-olds, but even within her own stable.

Not that We Have A Dream's win at Aintree came as too much of a surprise. He too had run up an unbeaten sequence since joining Seven Barrows and, in the absence of the Triumph principals, the two stable companions dominated the betting for the ten-runner Doom Bar Anniversary 4-Y-O Juvenile Hurdle, Apple's Shakira sent off at 13/8 and We Have A Dream at 2/1. Apple's Shakira had shaped very much like a stayer in the Triumph, which raised concerns about Aintree providing enough of a test for her, even on soft ground. She was fitted with a hood for the first time and was bidding to emulate her sister Apple's Jade who had won the same race two years earlier by an astonishing forty-one lengths, also on soft ground, when turning the tables on the Triumph winner Ivanovich Gorbatov who had beaten her into second at Cheltenham. We Have A Dream had landed the odds in each of his four races in Britain before Aintree and would have been a serious Triumph Hurdle candidate himself had he not been forced to miss Cheltenham through illness. He more than made up for that in the Anniversary, however, putting up an impressive performance and running his best race. We Have A Dream could be named the winner from a long way out after jumping into the lead at the final flight in the back straight and was never really threatened once in line for home, before staying on particularly strongly on the run-in to win by seven lengths. Gumball, who had been pulled up in the Triumph and had been trounced by Apple's Shakira in an earlier meeting at Cheltenham, was no match for the winner but belatedly fulfilled early promise (he had won his first two starts for Philip Hobbs in October). Gumball pulled ten lengths clear of Apple's Shakira who ran below even her Triumph form, her lack of acceleration again evident.

Each of the first three in the Anniversary had begun their hurdling careers in France where We Have A Dream had three runs for Tatiana Puitg, finishing fourth at Auteuil in the last of them in May. He looked a good prospect right from his British debut when making all to win by ten lengths at Warwick in November, before he then followed up by the same margin, and in similar style, in the bet365 Summit Juvenile Hurdle at Doncaster in December. We Have A Dream had less to spare when completing his hat-trick in the Coral Future Champions Finale Juvenile Hurdle on the postponed Welsh National card at Chepstow in January, but he was well on top in beating main market rival Sussex Ranger, winner of both his starts beforehand, by a length and a half. For his final start before an intended run at Cheltenham, We Have A Dream was sent to Musselburgh for the bet365 Scottish Triumph Hurdle Trial. Back to making the running, We Have A Dream was joined briefly by second

Coral Future Champions Finale Juvenile Hurdle, Chepstow—
We Have A Dream (nearest camera) lands the odds from Sussex Ranger

Doom Bar Anniversary 4-Y-O Juvenile Hurdle, Aintree—
We Have A Dream bounces back in fine style, after being forced to miss Cheltenham, with this very impressive defeat of Gumball (checked cap)

favourite Act of Valour when not fluent three out. He ultimately asserted himself approaching the final flight to beat that rival by four and a half lengths, the runner-up having his first run since disappointing in the Summit.

We Have A Dream (FR) (b.g. 2014)	Martaline (gr 1999)	Linamix (gr 1987)	Mendez / Lunadix
		Coraline (b 1994)	Sadler's Wells / Bahamian
	Sweet Dance (FR) (bl 2005)	Kingsalsa (br 1996)	Kingmambo / Caretta
		Madeka (b 1996)	Kadalko / Made To Win

We Have A Dream's dam Sweet Dance ran only on the Flat in France. Her two wins over middle distances at Nort-sur-Erdre and Les Sables d'Olonne were not particularly noteworthy, except that at the latter track the horse she beat into second was Zaynar, then owned by the Aga Khan, but who later won the 2009 Triumph Hurdle for Nicky Henderson. Sweet Dance's half-brother Ourville's Million showed just modest form for Oliver Sherwood in the latest season, but a couple of her half-sisters, Miss Lino and Ladeka, won over hurdles at three in France, the latter going on to show useful form at Auteuil. We Have A Dream's grandam Madeka completed once from just two starts over hurdles in France but she comes from a successful Flat family. Her half-sister Femme de Fer produced the American Grade 2 winners Jaunatxo and Iron Deputy as well as the dam of Gabrial who has enjoyed a long and successful career, mostly at a mile, for Richard Fahey. We Have A Dream is

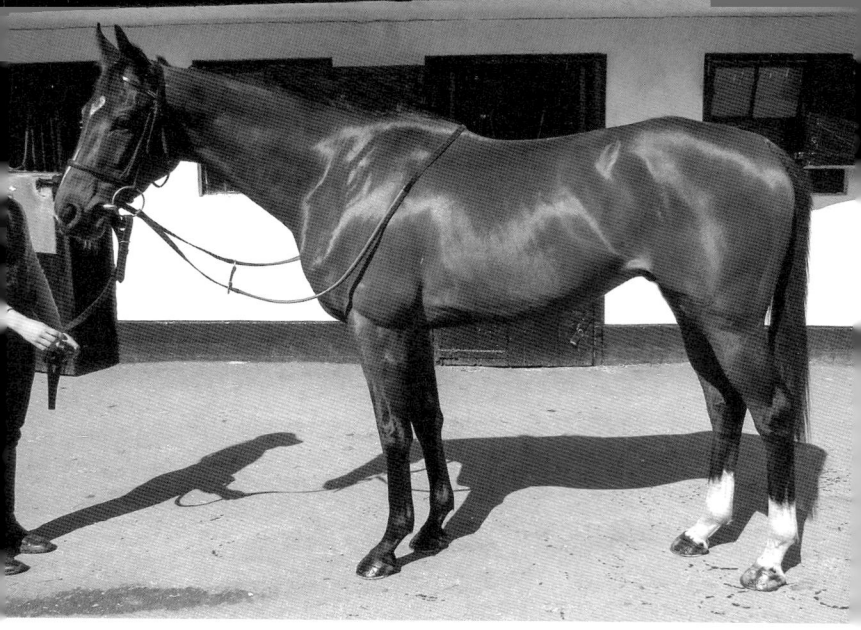

Mr Simon Munir & Mr Isaac Souede's "We Have A Dream"

his dam's second foal after Mystic Dancer (by Namid) who was pulled up over hurdles on his only start in France. We Have A Dream shares his sire Martaline with Terrefort, another French recruit for We Have A Dream's owners Simon Munir and Isaac Souede who enjoyed their third Grade 1 win—following a first-day double completed by L'Ami Serge—at the Grand National meeting in Friday's Mildmay Novices' Chase. The same emerald green, dark green sleeves, quartered cap was carried by the 2015 Triumph Hurdle winner Peace And Co, who has largely disappointed since, but the likes of Footpad, Bristol de Mai and Top Notch have all gone on to very successful jumping careers for the same owners after first making names for themselves as juvenile hurdlers. Footpad was third in the Triumph, Bristol de Mai won the Finale at Chepstow, as We Have A Dream did, while Top Notch was beaten a neck by Peace And Co in the Triumph and has outshone his stable companion since. We Have A Dream is still rather unfurnished at present and looks the type to go on improving, though his future may well be over further than two miles, rather than as a Champion Hurdle contender. Raced only on ground softer than good so far, he acts on heavy, and looks a straightforward ride, usually making the running or being ridden prominently. *Nicky Henderson*

WELCOME BEN (IRE) 9 b.g. High Roller (IRE) – Bramble Cottage (IRE) (Eurobus) [2017/18 c92, h86: c16g* c16g* c16d² c17.1g² c16.4d⁶ Dec 1] lengthy gelding: winning hurdler: fair handicap chaser: won novice events at Perth in May and July: stays 21f: acts on soft and good to firm going: wears headgear: has worn tongue tie: usually leads. *Jackie Stephen*   **c110 h–**

WELCOME POLLY (IRE) 6 br.m. Milan – Culmore Lady (IRE) (Insan (USA)) [2017/18 h20.5d^pu h21.2d h20.5s⁶ h21.7v^pu h23.9m^pu Apr 25] £14,000 4-y-o: fourth foal: dam (h80) bumper winner/maiden hurdler (stayed 2½m): well beaten in point: shown more temperament than ability over hurdles: in cheekpieces last 3 starts: one to leave alone. *Charlie Mann*   **h69 §**

WELD ARAB (IRE) 7 b.g. Shamardal (USA) – Itqaan (USA) (Danzig (USA)) [2017/18 h97: h15.7g² h16g⁴ h16.8d⁵ h15.8g Sep 13] modest maiden hurdler: raced around 2m: best form on good going. *Michael Blake* — **h90**

WELL ABOVE PAR (IRE) 6 b.g. Gold Well – Glynn Glory (IRE) (Presenting) [2017/18 h102, b74: c16v² c20.5sᶠ c20.1v⁶ Dec 2] in frame completed starts in Irish maiden points: twice-raced hurdler: fair form in handicap chases, going best when falling 3 out at Ayr second outing: should stay beyond 2m: acts on heavy going. *Lucinda Russell* — **c111 h–**

WE'LL BE THERE 9 b.m. Kayf Tara – Teachmetotango (Mister Baileys) [2017/18 h97: h21.6v h21.7s h19.5v h23.6v⁴ h23.9m Apr 25] unplaced in point: poor maiden hurdler: stays 3m: acts on heavy going: in cheekpieces last 3 starts: wears tongue tie. *Stuart Kittow* — **h73**

WELL END GIRL (IRE) 6 b.m. Yeats (IRE) – Ginandit (IRE) (Definite Article) [2017/18 b–: b16.3d May 21] well beaten in bumpers 7 weeks apart. *John Butler* — **b–**

WELL METT (IRE) 11 b.g. Gold Well – Beit Millat (USA) (Alleged (USA)) [2017/18 c96, h–: c25.3d⁵ May 5] compact gelding: multiple point winner: winning hurdler: modest hunter chaser nowadays: stays 3½m: acts on firm and soft going: wears headgear/tongue tie: often let down by jumping. *Mrs C. Banks* — **c84 x h–**

WELLS DE LUNE (FR) 7 b.g. Irish Wells (FR) – Pepite de Lune (FR) (Mansonnien (FR)) [2017/18 c129, h–: c20.3v² c20.9v* c26.3vᵖᵘ c21.1sᵘʳ Apr 12] good-topped gelding: winning hurdler: useful chaser, left Charlie Longsdon before reappearance: won hunter at Ffos Las in February: has won at 21f, but very best form at shorter: acts on heavy going: wears headgear/tongue tie: free-going sort, best when forcing pace. *Mickey Bowen* — **c129 h–**

WELLS GOLD (IRE) 7 b.g. Gold Well – Exit Baby (IRE) (Exit To Nowhere (USA)) [2017/18 h16.3m⁶ h20g⁴ h20.6g⁵ h16.8g h21.6s h23.1dᵖᵘ Dec 7] €16,000 3-y-o: second foal: dam unraced half-sister to fairly useful 2½m hurdle winner Bayross out of half-sister to smart French hurdler (stayed 25f) Vic Toto: Irish maiden point winner: poor handicap hurdler: won novice event at Fontwell in November: best effort at 2¾m on good to soft going: in cheekpieces last 3 starts: patiently ridden. *Fergal O'Brien* — **h83**

WELL SMITTEN (IRE) 6 b.g. Gold Well – The Dark One (IRE) (Mandalus) [2017/18 b88: h19.5dᵘʳ h16v h19.7v² Feb 20] placed once in bumpers: fair form over hurdles: likely to stay beyond 2½m: front runner/races prominently. *Warren Greatrex* — **h110**

WELLUPTOSCRATCH (FR) 7 b.g. Irish Wells (FR) – Aulne River (FR) (River Mist (USA)) [2017/18 h93: h17.7d² ab16d h17.7s⁶ h16.5m Apr 25] lengthy gelding: modest maiden hurdler: should stay 2½m: acts on good to soft going: tried in cheekpieces: wears tongue tie. *David Arbuthnot* — **h97**

WELSBY (IRE) 6 b.g. Gold Well – Stonehouse (IRE) (Snurge) [2017/18 b17.5s* Nov 11] €44,000 3-y-o: second foal: dam (c109/h105) 19f/2½m hurdle/chase winner: evens, won 4-runner bumper at Aintree (by 3½ lengths from Henry's Joy, readily) on debut. *Nicky Henderson* — **b92**

WELSH BARD (IRE) 9 ch.g. Dylan Thomas (IRE) – Delphinium (IRE) (Dr Massini (IRE)) [2017/18 c24.1d³ c25.5g⁵ c24s⁵ c25.5d³ h27g* h26.5d⁴ Sep 22] fair handicap hurdler: won at Sedgefield in September: fair handicap chaser: stays 27f: acts on good to firm and heavy going: wears headgear: temperamental. *Donald McCain* — **c109 § h107 §**

WELSH DESIGNE 10 ch.g. Midnight Legend – Barton Dante (Phardante (FR)) [2017/18 c76, h–: c20.9d⁵ c20.9g⁵ Jun 1] winning pointer: twice-raced hurdler: poor maiden chaser: probably stays 3m: acts on good to firm going: wears tongue tie. *Sirrell Griffiths* — **c– h–**

WELSH RAREBIT 5 b.g. Dylan Thomas (IRE) – Chelsey Jayne (IRE) (Galileo (IRE)) [2017/18 b15.7s⁶ ab16.3g³ Mar 3] modest form in bumpers. *Lucinda Egerton* — **b79**

WEMYSS POINT 6 b.g. Champs Elysees – Wemyss Bay (Sadler's Wells (USA)) [2017/18 b96: h19.7s⁵ h19.7d* h21.3s¹ Dec 9] fair form in novice hurdles at Wetherby, winning in November: also won on Flat in April: likely to stay beyond 21f: front runner/races prominently. *Philip Kirby* — **h114**

WENCESLAUS (GER) 6 b.g. Tiger Hill (IRE) – Warrior Czarina (USA) (Pleasantly Perfect (USA)) [2017/18 b15.8d⁵ h16.8g h20.3g⁴ h16gᵘʳ h16.3g³ h15.7d h16.2s⁶ h15.8s⁶ h19.5v h19.5v Apr 14] first foal: dam ran twice on Flat in USA: ran once on Flat: well held in bumpers: modest maiden hurdler: may prove best around 2m. *David Bridgwater* — **h99 b–**

WENYERREADYFREDDIE (IRE) 7 ch.g. Beneficial – Ware It Vic (IRE) (Old Vic) [2017/18 h125p: h16s⁴ c20.5dᵖᵘ Dec 26] strong gelding: fairly useful hurdler: none too fluent when pulled up in novice handicap at Kempton on chasing debut: should stay beyond 19f: acts on soft going. *Nicky Henderson* — **c– h103**

WERENEARLYOUTOFIT (IRE) 10 b.g. Asian Heights – Ballerina Laura (IRE) (Riot Helmet) [2017/18 h23g^{pu} Sep 18] runner-up in Irish maiden point: very lightly-raced winning hurdler, fairly useful at best: off further 26 months, pulled up only outing in 2017/18. *Graeme McPherson* — h–

WEST APPROACH 8 b.g. Westerner – Ardstown (Ardross) [2017/18 h143: c20.9s* c24.4s^3 c19.2v* c24d^3 c20s^5 c19.9s^6 c31.8g^{pu} Apr 21] workmanlike gelding: winning hurdler: useful chaser: won maiden at Ffos Las in October and novice at Exeter (by 3¼ lengths from Report To Base) in December: stays 3m: acts on heavy going: in blinkers last 2 starts: tried in tongue tie: inconsistent. *Colin Tizzard* — c142 h–

WEST CLASS (IRE) 7 b.g. Westerner – Catch The Class (IRE) (Flemensfirth (USA)) [2017/18 h78, b78: h16.8g^3 h15.7g^3 h20.3d^2 h19.9m^6 c17.4g^{pu} Aug 16] Irish point winner: modest form over hurdles: pulled up in novice handicap on chasing debut: stays 2½m: acts on good to soft going: in visor last 2 starts. *Peter Winks* — c– h98

WEST COAST LASS (IRE) 5 br.m. Westerner – Afairs (IRE) (Old Vic) [2017/18 b16.7s h16.2s^6 Apr 27] €3,700 3-y-o: second foal: dam, unraced, closely related to useful hurdler (stayed 3m) Younevercall and half-sister to dam of smart hurdler (2½m/21f winner) Black Op: well beaten in mares maiden bumper: 80/1, sixth in mares novice at Perth (15¼ lengths behind Floral Bouquet) on hurdling debut. *R. Mike Smith* — h79 b–

WESTELLO (IRE) 7 b.m. Westerner – The Keane Edge (IRE) (Definite Article) [2017/18 h–, b–: h20m^{pu} May 11] little show in bumpers/over hurdles. *Graeme McPherson* — h–

WESTEND STORY (IRE) 7 b.g. Westerner – Sarahall (IRE) (Saddlers' Hall (IRE)) [2017/18 h113: h20d^4 h19.7s* h19.8s^2 h21.7s* Mar 27] lengthy gelding: fell both starts in Irish points: useful hurdler: won handicap at Wetherby in January and novice at Hereford in March: good second in handicap at Sandown (6 lengths behind Soul Emotion) in between: should stay at least 3m: acts on soft going: front runner/races prominently. *Philip Hobbs* — h131

WESTEND THEATRE (IRE) 9 b.g. Darsi (FR) – Ballyvelig Lady (IRE) (Project Manager) [2017/18 c67, h–: c24.2g^4 c23.4d^3 Oct 8] poor maiden hurdler/chaser: stays 3m: acts on heavy going. *Jane Walton* — c80 h–

WESTERBEE (IRE) 7 b.m. Westerner – Pass The Honey (IRE) (Snurge) [2017/18 h101: h19s h21.2s^F h16.5v^6 h17.7s Apr 6] small, angular mare: fair novice hurdler in 2016/17: disappointing since: should stay beyond 2m: acts on good to soft going and good to firm going: tried in headgear. *Seamus Mullins* — h–

WESTERBERRY (IRE) 6 b.m. Westerner – Casiana (GER) (Acatenango (GER)) [2017/18 b16.8g h18.5s h21.4v^{pu} h20.5s h19s^6 h19.7s^{pu} Mar 27] has had breathing operation: fifth foal: sister to fair hurdler/fairly useful chaser Today Please (2m winner): dam German maiden (placed up to 11f): down field in bumper: poor form over hurdles. *Seamus Mullins* — h79 b–

WESTERLY BREEZE (IRE) 10 b.g. Westerner – Sup A Whiskey (IRE) (Commanche Run) [2017/18 c–, h94: h23g h23g Jun 14] modest maiden hurdler at best, no form in 2017/18: little form over fences (including in points): wears headgear: usually races prominently. *Sheila Lewis* — c– h–

WESTERN CLIMATE (IRE) 9 b.g. Westerner – Jo Peeks (IRE) (Be My Native (USA)) [2017/18 h116: h23.3d^3 h23.6s^{pu} c23.8g* c24.2v* c24s^4 c34v c23.8d^{pu} h25d^4 Apr 26] angular gelding: fairly useful handicap hurdler: better form over fences: won novice at Ludlow in December and handicap at Exeter (by 28 lengths) in January: stays 3m: acts on heavy going: in cheekpieces last 2 starts. *Tom Weston* — c133 h122

WESTERN DREAM 10 b.g. Westerner – Simiola (Shaamit (IRE)) [2017/18 c16.3d^{pu} h16.3g^6 h20g^F h20g^5 h16.3s h21g^{pu} Oct 11] lengthy gelding: of no account: tried in hood. *Alan Phillips* — c– h–

WESTERNER POINT (IRE) 9 b.g. Westerner – Its Only Gossip (IRE) (Lear Fan (USA)) [2017/18 c131, h115: h21.6s h24v^2 c25.9v h20v c23.5v* c18s^3 c29v^{pu} c24.5s^6 Apr 28] fairly useful handicap chaser: useful chaser: form in 2017/18 only when winning minor event at Fairyhouse (by nose from Drumacoo) in February: unproven beyond 3m: acts on heavy going: tried in hood. *Eoghan O'Grady, Ireland* — c134 h119

WESTERN HONOUR (IRE) 6 b.g. Westerner – Cailins Honour (IRE) (City Honours (USA)) [2017/18 h19.5s h16.2v^4 h20.1v^4 Mar 15] £18,000 3-y-o, £120,000 5-y-o: fifth foal: dam (h74), maiden hurdler (stayed 2¾m), half-sister to smart hurdler (stayed 3m) Castlekellyleader and useful hurdler (stayed 2½m) Cailin Supreme, latter dam of very smart staying hurdler Black Jack Ketchum: won Irish point on debut: fair form over hurdles: left Paul Nicholls after debut: will stay beyond 2½m. *James Moffatt* — h111

WESTERN JO (IRE) 10 b.g. Westerner – Jenny's Jewel (IRE) (Be My Native (USA)) [2017/18 c114§, h–: c23.9g⁴ h23.3g h23.3v² h23.3d⁴ c20.1v* c20v³ c24.2s* Nov 10] sturdy gelding: winning hurdler: fairly useful handicap chaser: left Alan Brown after second start and back near best subsequently, winning novice events at Hexham in October and November: stays 3m: acts on heavy going: has worn headgear: in tongue tie last 5 starts: often leads: has looked far from straightforward (has been reluctant to race) but done little wrong for current stable. *Sam England* — **c126 h99**

WESTERN LASS (IRE) 5 br.m. Westerner – Lady Roania (IRE) (Saddlers' Hall (IRE)) [2017/18 b72: b16.2g⁴ b16.2g⁵ h16v³ Nov 4] poor form in bumpers: 16/1, third in mares maiden at Ayr (7¼ lengths behind Miss Tiggy) on hurdling debut: likely to be suited by 2½m+. *Katie Scott* — **h91 b70**

WESTERN MILLER (IRE) 7 b.g. Westerner – Definite Miller (IRE) (Definite Article) [2017/18 h100: h21.2m⁴ h19.6d* h20.6g* h20.3g⁵ h20g⁴ c19.4g* c16.4d^F c17.2g² c20s² c19.9g⁴ c20.4s c15.7g² Apr 20] good-topped gelding: fairly useful handicap hurdler: made all at Bangor in June and Market Rasen (conditional) in July: useful novice chaser: won at Stratford in September: effective at 2m to 2¾m: acts on heavy going: wears tongue tie: front runner/races prominently. *Charlie Longsdon* — **c138 h124**

WESTERN MORNING (IRE) 5 b.g. Westerner – Gweedara (IRE) (Saddlers' Hall (IRE)) [2017/18 h19.5d h19.7g h16.7v h15.7v h16v³ h20.3g⁵ Apr 20] £24,000 3-y-o: third foal: half-brother to fair hurdler/fairly useful chaser Bright Tomorrow (2½m winner, by Robin des Pres): dam unraced half-sister to very smart staying chaser Hey Big Spender: winning pointer: modest form over hurdles: stays 2½m: acts on heavy going: in cheekpieces last 2 starts: usually tongue tied. *Oliver Greenall* — **h88**

WESTERN RULES (IRE) 8 b.g. Westerner – Ryehill Lady (IRE) (Accordion) [2017/18 h24.1d⁴ h23.1v³ h24.4s⁴ ab16.3g² h24.3v* h25.8v^pu Apr 7] fairly useful handicap hurdler: won at Ayr (amateur) in March: stays 3m: acts on heavy going: in cheekpieces last 2 starts: tried in tongue tie. *Nicky Richards* — **h116**

WESTERN RYDER (IRE) 6 b.g. Westerner – Seesea (IRE) (Dr Massini (IRE)) [2017/18 b116: h16.3g^ur h16v* h16.8s* h16s⁴ h19.6s² h16.4s⁶ h20s⁵ Apr 14] well-made gelding: smart bumper performer: similar merit in novice hurdles: won at Chepstow in November and Cheltenham (by 2 lengths from Lalor) in December: better form after, including when 7½ lengths sixth of 19 to Summerville Boy in Supreme Novices' Hurdle at latter track: stays 2½m: acts on heavy going. *Warren Greatrex* — **h145**

WESTERN SUNRISE (IRE) 9 b.m. Westerner – Presenting Gayle (IRE) (Presenting) [2017/18 h105: h23.3d⁵ h21.9g³ h19.5s⁶ h23.9s⁶ c19.7v^ur Mar 12] fair handicap hurdler: unseated early on chasing debut: stays 3m: acts on soft and good to firm going. *Johnny Farrelly* — **c– h91**

WESTERN WAVE (FR) 6 b.g. Westerner – Kaprissima (FR) (Epervier Bleu) [2017/18 h107: h23.9g⁴ h23.1v⁶ h20.5s² h19s⁴ h21v³ Mar 11] fair handicap hurdler: stays easy 3m: acts on soft going: has finished weakly. *Tom George* — **h109**

WEST LAKE (FR) 8 b.g. Michel Georges – Darnaway (FR) (Pelder (IRE)) [2017/18 c25.5s^pu c24.2s² Feb 16] multiple point winner: poor form on second of 2 starts in hunter chases: wears cheekpieces: tried in tongue tie. *David Phelan* — **c79**

WEST OF THE EDGE (IRE) 10 b.g. Westerner – Bermuda Bay (IRE) (Be My Native (USA)) [2017/18 c127, h106: h27g³ h25.3d c27.3v² c32.6s² c34v^pu Mar 17] fair handicap hurdler: useful handicap chaser: second in Betfred Eider at Newcastle (4 lengths behind Baywing) in February: thorough stayer: acts on heavy going: has worn headgear, including last 3 outings: tough. *Dr Richard Newland* — **c131 h114**

WEST TO CROSSGALES (IRE) 7 b.g. Westerner – Mooreshill Bay (IRE) (Lord Americo) [2017/18 h–: h15.8d h15.7g⁴ h20.7g h23.1d⁵ h15.7v^pu Feb 25] point winner: poor maiden hurdler: should stay beyond 2m: tried in hood/tongue tie. *Charles Pogson* — **h81**

WEST TORR (IRE) 7 br.g. Scorpion (IRE) – Native Craft (IRE) (Be My Native (USA)) [2017/18 h112, h91: c19.4d³ c19.4g³ Jun 22] fair hurdler: better effort in handicap chases (fair form) when third at Ffos Las in June: should be suited by further than 2½m: acts on heavy and good to firm going: in cheekpieces last 3 starts: often races prominently. *Nigel Twiston-Davies* — **c104 h–**

WEST TO THE BRIDGE (IRE) 5 b.g. Flemensfirth (USA) – Godlylady (IRE) (Old Vic) [2017/18 b16s³ b15.7d b16.2s² b15.8s⁵ Mar 14] good-topped gelding: fourth foal: half-brother to fair hurdler/winning pointer Polymath (2¾m winner, by Stowaway), stays 3m: dam unraced half-sister to top-class chaser up to 3m Flemenstar (by Flemensfirth): fairly useful form in bumpers: demoted from second (hung right and impeded rival) at — **b100**

WES

Chepstow on debut: failed to progress after, looking less than straightforward: wears hood: in tongue tie last 2 starts. *Dan Skelton*

WEST WIZARD (FR) 9 b.g. King's Theatre (IRE) – Queen's Diamond (GER) (Konigsstuhl (GER)) [2017/18 c129, h–: c26.1m c24.1g² c23g⁶ c25g^pu c19.9d⁶ c22.9v⁵ c20v⁴ c25.5s³ c26s c27.9v^pu Apr 1] good sort: winning hurdler: fairly useful handicap chaser: largely disappointing in 2017/18: stays 25f: acts on heavy going: has worn headgear: wears tongue tie. *Sophie Leech*   **c128 h–**

WEYBURN (IRE) 7 gr.g. September Storm (GER) – Saffron Pride (IRE) (Be My Native (USA)) [2017/18 c109, h109: h23.3d⁶ c20.3s* c19.2s³ c16v³ c15.7v⁴ Feb 25] fair hurdler: similar form over fences: won handicap at Southwell in December: probably stays easy 23f: acts on soft going: tried in headgear: usually in tongue tie. *Martin Keighley*   **c110 h–**

WHAT A DIVA 7 b.m. Kayf Tara – Land of Glory (Supreme Leader) [2017/18 h112: h23.1s h25d⁵ h24.4d⁶ h23.1v² h23.1v⁵ Mar 11] sturdy mare: fair handicap hurdler: stays 3m: acts on heavy going: wears tongue tie. *Peter Bowen*   **h105**

WHAT A DREAM 12 ch.g. Supreme Sound – Ben Roseler (IRE) (Beneficial) [2017/18 c77, h–: h20.5v* c20.1v⁶ c19.3v³ h21.4v⁵ c20.1v^pu Apr 15] poor handicap hurdler: won at Ayr in January: poor handicap chaser: stays 3m: acts on heavy going: wears headgear/tongue tie: usually races prominently. *Alison Hamilton*   **c68 h68**

WHAT A GAME (IRE) 7 ch.g. Milan – Moscow Mo Chuisle (IRE) (Moscow Society (USA)) [2017/18 c70, h91: c23.4g^pu h22.1d* h25.4g² Jul 2] modest handicap hurdler: won at Cartmel (both wins there) in May: little promise over fences: stays 25f: acts on soft and good to firm going: wears blinkers: tried in tongue tie. *Tim Easterby*   **c– h90**

WHATAKNIGHT 9 b.g. Midnight Legend – What A Mover (Jupiter Island) [2017/18 c133+, h138: h22.8m h26.5g³ h23.9g h24.2d² h24.2d h24s h24s h24g² Apr 18] good-topped gelding: useful handicap hurdler: second at Cheltenham (3¼ lengths behind Monbeg Theatre) final outing: winning chaser but not a fluent jumper: stays 25f: acts on soft and good to firm going: wears tongue tie. *Harry Fry*   **c– h137**

WHAT A LAUGH 13 b.g. Kayf Tara – Just For A Laugh (Idiot's Delight) [2017/18 c112, h–: c20.3s^ur c24.1d^pu c23.6d^R Apr 24] sturdy gelding: prolific winning pointer: maiden hurdler: fairly useful chaser at best: failed to complete in 2017/18: stays 25f: acts on soft and good to firm going: usually travels strongly. *Gary Hanmer*   **c– h–**

WHATALOVE 4 ch.f. Arcano (IRE) – Secret Happiness (Cape Cross (IRE)) [2017/18 h16d^pu Nov 10] modest maiden on Flat (stayed 1m): hooded, pulled up in juvenile hurdle: dead. *Martin Keighley*   **h–**

WHAT A MOMENT (IRE) 8 b.g. Milan – Cuiloge Lady (IRE) (Beneficial) [2017/18 c132, h103: c25d* Nov 17] workmanlike gelding: maiden handicap chaser: useful handicap chaser: won at Cheltenham (amateur event, for second successive year) only outing in 2017/18: stays 25f: acts on soft going: tried in headgear/tongue tie. *David Pipe*   **c136 h–**

WHAT A SCORCHER 7 b.m. Authorized (IRE) – Street Fire (IRE) (Street Cry (IRE)) [2017/18 h114: h18.5d⁵ h19g Sep 26] fair handicap hurdler at best: poor efforts in 2017/18: stays easy 19f: acts on heavy and good to firm going: tried in tongue tie. *Nikki Evans*   **h81**

WHATDUHAVTOGET (IRE) 6 b.m. Presenting – Smooching (IRE) (Saddlers' Hall (IRE)) [2017/18 h127: h19.5d c15.2d^F h19.8s⁴ h21d h21.4g³ Apr 21] good-topped mare: won Irish maiden point on debut: fairly useful handicap hurdler: running below that level when falling 2 out in novice won by Ami Desbois at Wetherby on chasing debut: stays 21f: acts on soft going: tried in hood: keen sort. *Dan Skelton*   **c111 h124**

WHAT HAPPENS NOW (IRE) 9 b.g. Dr Massini (IRE) – Euro Burden (IRE) (Good Thyne (USA)) [2017/18 c119, h–: h20g³ h22.1s* h23.9d* h23.3d* c24.1g² c25.8d³ c25g* c25d c24d³ c24.2s² c26g Apr 18] medium-sized gelding: fair novice hurdler: won at Cartmel in July, and Perth and Hexham in August: fairly useful handicap chaser: won at Cheltenham (amateur) in October: stays 25f: acts on good to firm and heavy going: tried in hood: front runner/races prominently. *Donald McCain*   **c125 h113**

WHAT LARKS (IRE) 10 b.g. Pierre – Bint Rosie (Exit To Nowhere (USA)) [2017/18 c101, h61: c20.9d^pu c25.2s^pu c26v⁴ c23.6s^pu c23.5v⁴ c26v² c24.5v^pu c26.7v³ c25.1d⁵ Apr 22] sturdy gelding: maiden hurdler: poor handicap chaser nowadays: left Hugo Froud after first start: stays 3¼m: acts on heavy going: wears headgear. *Dr Jeremy Naylor*   **c76 h–**

WHATMORE 6 b.g. Schiaparelli (GER) – Polymiss (FR) (Poliglote) [2017/18 h114, b83: h17g* h16.7g* h15.7v⁴ h20.3s⁶ h19.3v h16v* Mar 28] well-made gelding: chasing type: fairly useful novice hurdler: won at Aintree in May, Bangor in October and Warwick in March: bred to be suited by 2½m but usually races freely: acts on heavy going: tried in hood. *Henry Daly*   **h127**

WHI

WHATS HAPPENING (IRE) 11 b.g. Lahib (USA) – Rebeccas Star (IRE) (Camden Town) [2017/18 c134, h–: c29.4d³ May 29] lengthy gelding: winning hurdler: useful handicap chaser: stays 3½m: acts on good to firm and heavy going: has worn cheekpieces, including only start in 2017/18: wears tongue tie. *Tom George*   c123 h–

WHAT'S OCCURRING (IRE) 5 b.g. Rail Link – Lovely Origny (FR) (Robin des Champs (FR)) [2017/18 b16.3d⁵ h15.9d³ h16.3s³ h20.6s⁵ Feb 6] fourth foal: half-brother to fair hurdler/winning pointer Is Love Alive (2½m winner, by Presenting) and a winning pointer by Black Sam Bellamy: dam unraced half-sister to fair hurdler/useful chaser (stayed 3m) Forzy Origny out of half-sister to top-class chaser (stayed 25f) Cyfor Malta: left poorly placed when fifth in bumper at Newbury (14¾ lengths behind Tidal Flow): fair form when third first 2 starts in novice hurdles: should stay beyond 2m. *Oliver Sherwood*   h111 b84

WHATSTHATALLABOUT (IRE) 7 b.m. Milan – Peinture Francaise (FR) (Pistolet Bleu (IRE)) [2017/18 h115p: h21.6d h18.5s h18.9vᶠ Mar 31] lengthy mare: fairly useful hurdler at best: off 14 months, failed to show form in 2017/18: stays 2½m: best form on good going: tried in tongue tie: patiently ridden. *Neil Mulholland*   h–

WHAT'S THE SCOOP (IRE) 8 ch.g. Presenting – Dame d'Harvard (USA) (Quest For Fame) [2017/18 c–, h–§: h19.3d³ Feb 2] well-made gelding: fair maiden hurdler: left Nicky Henderson before sole start in 2017/18: well held both outings in novice handicap chases: stays 19f: acts on heavy going: signs of temperament. *Sue Smith*   c– h106

WHATSTHESTORYMAN (IRE) 10 b.g. Alderbrook – Express Way Lady (IRE) (Camden Town) [2017/18 c88, h–: h20.9dᵖᵘ c23.4g c24.2dᵖᵘ Nov 18] poor maiden hurdler: modest handicap chaser: failed to show form in 2017/18: stays 21f: acts on good to firm and good to soft going: wears tongue tie. *Katie Scott*   c62 h–

WHAT'S UP RORY (IRE) 7 b.g. Craigsteel – Clifton Four (USA) (Forest Wildcat (USA)) [2017/18 c92, h–: c16d c20.3v⁵ h15.5v c16s c16v⁵ Mar 21] well held both starts over hurdles: modest chaser at best: lost way in 2017/18: probably stays 2½m: acts on heavy going: regularly in headgear/tongue tie: held up. *Richard Price*   c– h–

WHATSWRONGWITHYOU (IRE) 7 ch.g. Bienamado (USA) – Greenfield Noora (IRE) (Topanoora) [2017/18 b104: h16s² h16.3s* h16.3v* h16v³ Mar 10] sturdy gelding: Irish point winner: fairly useful bumper winner: similar sort form over hurdles: won novices at Newbury in January and February: 10/3, also shaped well when 9¼ lengths third of 17 to Mr Antolini in Imperial Cup (Handicap) at Sandown final start: wears hood: enthusiastic sort, still open to improvement. *Nicky Henderson*   h128 p

WHATTHEBUTLERSAW (IRE) 9 br.g. Arcadio (GER) – Phar From Men (IRE) (Phardante (FR)) [2017/18 h106: h21.2m* May 14] lengthy gelding: fair handicap hurdler: won at Ludlow in May: stays 21f: acts on good to firm and heavy going: tried in tongue tie: held up. *Dominic Ffrench Davis*   h99

WHATZDJAZZ (IRE) 6 b.m. Yeats (IRE) – What A Mewsment (IRE) (Persian Mews) [2017/18 b92: h20m* h21.6m³ h20g* h21.6gᶠ h16.7s⁵ h15.8d h20.3g² Apr 19] useful-looking mare: bumper winner: fairly useful hurdler: won mares maiden in May and novice in July, both at Worcester, and handicap at Market Rasen later in July: stays easy 2¾m: acts on good to firm going: patiently ridden. *Dan Skelton*   h126

WHEREDIDHECOMEFROM (IRE) 7 ch.g. Royal Anthem (USA) – Grand Missy (IRE) (Grand Plaisir (IRE)) [2017/18 b16g⁶ Jul 10] no sign of ability in points/bumper. *Tracey Barfoot-Saunt*   b–

WHERE'S CHERRY (IRE) 7 b.m. King's Theatre (IRE) – I'm Grand (IRE) (Raise A Grand (IRE)) [2017/18 h98p: c19.9dᵖᵘ h21.2sᵖᵘ Jan 10] sturdy mare: modest maiden hurdler: pulled up both starts in 2017/18, including on chasing debut: stays easy 2¾m: acts on soft and good to firm going: tried in cheekpieces. *Neil Mulholland*   c– h–

WHERE'S TIGER 7 b.g. Tiger Hill (IRE) – Where's Broughton (Cadeaux Genereux) [2017/18 h101: c16.3s² c15.7d³ Feb 2] fair hurdler: modest form in novice handicap chases (lame second outing): unproven beyond 17f: acts on soft going: tried in tongue tie. *Lucinda Russell*   c99 h–

WHILE YOU WAIT (IRE) 9 b.g. Whipper (USA) – Azra (IRE) (Danehill (USA)) [2017/18 h96: h15.7g* h19.9m⁶ c19.4g⁶ c21g c21dᵖᵘ Sep 11] good-bodied gelding: fair handicap hurdler: won at Towcester in May: no form over fences: best form around 2m: acts on soft and good to firm going. *Susan Gardner*   c– h100

WHIN PARK 6 b.g. Great Pretender (IRE) – Pocahontas (FR) (Nikos) [2017/18 h99, b–: h20.3g⁴ h20.3d h16.5sᵖᵘ c19.9s⁵ Dec 26] rather unfurnished gelding: fair form over hurdles: well held in novice handicap on chasing debut (should improve): stays 2½m: acts on good to soft going: tried in blinkers. *Ben Pauling*   c79 p h102

WHI

WHIPCORD (IRE) 7 gr.g. Tikkanen (USA) – Dapples (IRE) (Accordion) [2017/18 h94: h15.8g^{pu} h20g c21.6g^F Aug 24] Irish maiden point winner: disappointing maiden hurdler: beaten when fell heavily 3 out on chasing debut: in headgear last 2 starts: wears tongue tie. *Johnny Farrelly* — c– h–

WHIPCRACKAWAY (IRE) 9 b.g. Whipper (USA) – Former Drama (USA) (Dynaformer (USA)) [2017/18 h68: h15.8d^{ur} Jul 30] good-topped gelding: fairly useful juvenile in 2012/13: little form over hurdles since: wears headgear. *Peter Hedger* — h–

WHISKEY BARON (IRE) 6 b.g. Darsi (FR) – Roupolino (IRE) (Trempolino (USA)) [2017/18 b16.3d^5 h19.9m h19.6g^3 h21.6d^5 h23.9m Nov 1] workmanlike gelding: runner-up on second of 2 starts in points: fifth in conditionals/amateur bumper at Stratford (for A. J. Rhead): poor form over hurdles: tried in tongue tie. *Adrian Wintle* — h54 b67

WHISKEY CHASER (IRE) 10 br.g. Flemensfirth (USA) – Cregane Lass (IRE) (Oscar (IRE)) [2017/18 c109, h–: c22.9v* c27.3v^5 c25.5s^6 c29.6v^6 c22.9s^3 c23.4v^2 Apr 14] maiden hurdler: fair handicap chaser: won at Haydock in December: not at best after: stays 3m: raced almost exclusively on soft/heavy going: wears headgear. *Donald McCain* — c110 h–

WHISKEY IN THE JAR (IRE) 6 b.g. Oscar (IRE) – Baie Barbara (IRE) (Heron Island (IRE)) [2017/18 b107p: h16.7s^2 h21.6d^6 h15.8v* h20s* h19.9v^2 Mar 17] lengthy gelding: useful bumper performer: fairly useful form over hurdles: landed odds in conditionals maiden at Uttoxeter in January and novice at Fakenham in February: stays 2½m: acts on heavy going. *Olly Murphy* — h123

WHISKEY JOHN 8 b.g. Westerner – Cherry Lane (Buckley) [2017/18 h69: h19.5d^{ur} h18.5v^3 h21.6v^6 h18.5v^{pu} h23.9v Mar 12] lengthy, dipped-backed gelding: poor maiden hurdler: should stay 3m: acts on heavy going: has worn cheekpieces. *Laura Young* — h69

WHISKEY MOON 6 b.g. Erhaab (USA) – Flaviola (IRE) (Moscow Society (USA)) [2017/18 b–: h15.8g Oct 17] little show in bumpers/novice hurdle. *Nigel Twiston-Davies* — h–

WHISKEY SOUR (IRE) 5 b.g. Jeremy (USA) – Swizzle Stick (IRE) (Sadler's Wells (USA)) [2017/18 h16g* h16s* h16s^4 h16.8v^3 h16.5d^4 h20s^2 Apr 27] compact gelding: useful stayer on Flat: similar form over hurdles: won maiden at Tramore in June and Future Champions Novices' Hurdle at Leopardstown (by 19 lengths from Le Richebourg, left clear when both leaders fell at last) in December: also shaped well when third in County Hurdle (Handicap) at Cheltenham (3½ lengths behind Mohaayed) in March: may prove best around 2m: acts on heavy going: tried in tongue tie: held up. *W. P. Mullins, Ireland* — h141

WHISPERDALE 10 ch.g. Supreme Sound – Tarbolton Moss (Le Moss) [2017/18 c26.2v^F Apr 16] multiple point winner: blinkered, fell 2 out in maiden hunter on chasing debut: dead. *Mrs L. A. Colthred* — c–

WHISPER (FR) 10 b.g. Astarabad (USA) – Belle Yepa (FR) (Mansonnien (FR)) [2017/18 c159, h–: c20.5d* c26g^2 c24d^5 Dec 26] tall, useful-looking gelding: winning hurdler: top-class chaser: won graduation event at Kempton in November: easily better effort after when second of 20 in Ladbrokes Trophy Chase (Handicap) at Newbury (neck behind Total Recall) following month: stays 3¼m: acts on good to firm and heavy going: has run well when sweating. *Nicky Henderson* — c165 h–

WHISPERING AFFAIR 7 b.m. Black Sam Bellamy (IRE) – City of Angels (Woodman (USA)) [2017/18 h83: h20.2g^3 h22.1s^2 h22.1d^5 h22g h22.5d^2 h22s^5 Nov 3] pulled up in maiden point: fair maiden hurdler: likely to stay 3m: acts on soft going: tried in cheekpieces. *Stuart Crawford, Ireland* — h101

WHISPERING HARRY 9 b.g. Sir Harry Lewis (USA) – Welsh Whisper (Overbury (IRE)) [2017/18 c–§, h112§: c19.4g c17.4s^{ur} c16.4s^6 c19.7v^2 c19.4v^{pu} h19.2v^3 h15.8v Apr 7] sturdy gelding: modest handicap hurdler: fair handicap chaser nowadays: stays 2½m: acts on heavy going: has worn tongue tie, including last 2 starts: usually races close up: temperamental. *Henry Oliver* — c108 § h96 §

WHISPERING NICK 8 b.g. Kayf Tara – Dalriath (Fraam) [2017/18 h–, b81: h23g^6 Jun 14] good-topped gelding: modest form in bumpers: little show over hurdles: in cheekpieces/tongue tie last 4 starts. *Robin Dickin* — h–

WHITE MOON (GER) 6 gr.g. Sholokhov (IRE) – Westalin (GER) (Sternkoenig (IRE)) [2017/18 h21.4s* h21.6s* h19.8s Dec 8] big gelding: fourth foal: brother to a winner on Flat in Poland: dam German 9f winner: maiden point winner in Ireland: looked good prospect when winning maiden at Wincanton in October and novice at Exeter in November first 2 starts over hurdles: 7/2, possibly amiss in Winter Novices' Hurdle at Sandown: in tongue tie last 2 starts: remains open to improvement. *Colin Tizzard* — h127 p

WHO

WHITEOAK FLEUR 5 b.m. Black Sam Bellamy (IRE) – Harringay (Sir Harry Lewis (USA)) [2017/18 b16.8g³ Apr 23] €10,000 3-y-o: fourth foal: closely related to fair hurdler Playhara (2m-2½m winner, by King's Theatre) and half-sister to bumper winner/fair hurdler Danielle's Journey (2m winner, by Presenting), stayed 2¾m: dam (c109/h120) 19f-21f hurdle/chase winner: 6/1, running-on third in mares bumper at Sedgefield (length behind It's O Kay). *Donald McCain* **b86**

WHITEOAK STROLLER 5 b.m. Shirocco (GER) – Whiteoak (IRE) (Oscar (IRE)) [2017/18 b63: b17s⁴ h15.6g⁴ Nov 30] well-made mare: well held in bumpers: showed more when fourth in mares maiden at Musselburgh (9¾ lengths behind Canny Style) on hurdling debut. *Donald McCain* **h87 b–**

WHITE VALIANT (FR) 5 gr.g. Youmzain (IRE) – Minnie's Mystery (FR) (Highest Honor (FR)) [2017/18 b97: b17.7d² h17.7d⁵ Sep 10] small, close-coupled gelding: fairly useful bumper winner: 5/1, better than result when fifth in novice at Fontwell (13 lengths behind Jackblack) on hurdling debut: should improve. *John Berry* **h94 p b96**

WHITLEY NEILL (IRE) 6 b.g. Shantou (USA) – Maidrin Rua (IRE) (Zaffaran (USA)) [2017/18 b62: b18.5d* Apr 24] well held in bumpers: tongue tied and 20/1, won maiden at Exeter (easily by 13 lengths from Darling Maltaix) on hurdling debut: tried in hood: open to improvement. *David Pipe* **h112 p**

WHITMEL 5 b.g. Sulamani (IRE) – My Valentina (Royal Academy (USA)) [2017/18 b15.7g³ b16.8g b15.7g Oct 26] form (including on Flat) only when third of 7 in maiden bumper at Southwell on debut. *Michael Appleby* **b77**

WHITSUNDAYS (IRE) 9 b.g. Kutub (IRE) – Urdite's Vic (IRE) (Old Vic) [2017/18 c105, h–: c21.4g³ c17.4s² c19.3s² c17.1v* c16.3v⁵ c20v⁵ c20.1v⁴ Apr 15] winning hurdler: fair handicap chaser: won at Kelso in January: stays 2¾m: acts on heavy going: tried in headgear: wears tongue tie: temperamental. *Donald McCain* **c112 § h–**

WHO AM I 12 b.g. Tamayaz (CAN) – Short Fuse (IRE) (Zaffaran (USA)) [2017/18 c–x, h93: c23.8g^pu h23g⁴ h23g³ c23g⁵ c23.6d^pu Oct 14] modest handicap hurdler: error-prone maiden chaser: stays 23f: acts on soft and good to firm going: wears headgear. *Debra Hamer* **c77 x h92**

WHO DARES WINS (IRE) 6 b.g. Jeremy (USA) – Savignano (Polish Precedent (USA)) [2017/18 h147: h21d³ h24s⁵ h20s³ Apr 13] compact gelding: smart handicap hurdler: third in Grade 3 event at Aintree (1½ lengths behind Jester Jet) in April: barely stays testing 3m: acts on heavy going: usually races prominently: tough and consistent. *Alan King* **h146**

WHOLESTONE (IRE) 7 br.g. Craigsteel – Last Theatre (IRE) (King's Theatre (IRE)) [2017/18 h147: h19.5d⁴ h24.1s² h24.2d⁶ h20.3s* h24v² h24s³ h24.7s² h21.5s³ Apr 28] sturdy gelding: very smart hurdler: won Relkeel Hurdle at Cheltenham (by 3¼ lengths from Agrapart) in January: held form well until below par final outing, placed in Stayers' **h159**

*Dornan Engineering Relkeel Hurdle, Cheltenham—
a deserved success for the consistent Wholestone; 2017 winner Agrapart (left) rallies for second*

WHO

Hurdle at Cheltenham (5 lengths third to Penhill) in March and Liverpool Hurdle at Aintree (5 lengths second to Identity Thief) in April: effective at 2½m to 25f: acts on heavy going: often travels strongly: likeable type. *Nigel Twiston-Davies*

WHO'S CROSS (IRE) 10 b.g. Runyon (IRE) – Mystery Escort (Sir Harry Lewis (USA)) [2017/18 c19.9s^{pu} h20g h16.4g h16.3g h16s^3 c21v^3 h16.2s c20.5v^{pu} Dec 7] good-topped gelding: modest handicap hurdler: no solid form over fences: unproven beyond 2m: acts on soft going: wears headgear/tongue tie: usually races prominently. *John Patrick Ryan, Ireland*   c– h88

WHOS DE BABY (IRE) 10 gr.g. Bienamado (USA) – Beaus Rose (IRE) (Roselier (FR)) [2017/18 c88, h–: c19.4d^2 c20.3d* c20.9g^3 c21.4g^{pu} c21d^2 c20.3d^6 Oct 4] maiden hurdler: modest handicap chaser: won novice event at Bangor in June: stays 23f: acts on good to firm and heavy going: wears headgear: front runner: temperamental. *Sarah-Jayne Davies*   c96 § h–

WHO'S FOR TEA (IRE) 5 ch.m. Beat Hollow – Ring of Water (USA) (Northern Baby (CAN)) [2017/18 b73p: h17.2s^4 b16.7g Aug 31] poor form on first of 2 starts in bumpers: well beaten in maiden on hurdling debut: tried in hood. *John Joseph Hanlon, Ireland*   h– b–

WHOSHOTWHO (IRE) 7 br.g. Beneficial – Inishbeg House (IRE) (Glacial Storm (USA)) [2017/18 b–: h15.7g* h15.8m^3 h21.6d* h18.5d^2 h21.6g h19.9d^2 h21.6v^3 h16.8v^2 h16.2d^2 Apr 23] fair form in bumpers: won at Southwell in May: fairly useful hurdler: won maiden at Newton Abbot (left Nicky Henderson after) in July: placed 4 times after: stays 2¾m: acts on heavy going: wears hood: front runner/races prominently. *Dr Richard Newland*   h121 b91

WHO'S MY JOCKEY (IRE) 5 b.g. Yeats (IRE) – Scandisk (IRE) (Kenmare (FR)) [2017/18 b94: h15.8d^3 h19.9d* h21g^2 h23.1v^3 h21m* Apr 26] bumper winner: fairly useful form over hurdles: won novices at Uttoxeter in November and Kempton in April: should stay beyond 21f (let down by jumping when tried at 23f): acts on good to firm and good to soft going. *Philip Hobbs*   h128

WHOSTOSAY (IRE) 6 br.g. Witness Box (USA) – Black N Amber (IRE) (Alderbrook) [2017/18 b16v Feb 3] little form in points: no promise in bumpers: wears hood, also tongue tied sole start in 2017/18. *Micky Hammond*   b–

WHO YOU FOR (IRE) 8 b.g. Craigsteel – Knappogue Honey (IRE) (Anshan) [2017/18 h95: h24.4d c21.2s^4 Dec 19] workmanlike gelding: point/bumper winner: fair form when second in maiden on hurdling debut: lightly raced and largely disappointing since, including in novice handicap on chasing debut: likely to stay beyond 3m: acts on soft and good to firm going. *Sarah Humphrey*   c66 h–

WHY BUT WHY (USA) 10 b.g. Whywhywhy (USA) – Miss Orah (Unfuwain (USA)) [2017/18 h17s^{pu} h16.2s h16v c16.5v^{pu} Jan 2] maiden hurdler/chaser, little form since 2014/15: used to regularly wear headgear. *William Young Jnr*   c– h–

WICKED SPICE (IRE) 9 b.g. Old Vic – Afdala (IRE) (Hernando (FR)) [2017/18 c112, h–: h24.4s^5 h24.4s^{pu} Feb 21] formerly fairly useful handicap hurdler: off 19 months, well below form in 2017/18: winning chaser: stays 3m: acts on soft going: tried in cheekpieces. *Nicky Richards*   c– h89

WICKED WILLY (IRE) 7 br.g. Arcadio (GER) – How Provincial (IRE) (Be My Native (USA)) [2017/18 h118: c23.6g* c24.2s^{pu} c25.6g^4 c23s* c24.2s^4 c25.6v^F c24.5s^{pu} Apr 28] fairly useful hurdler: fairly useful handicap chaser: won at Huntingdon (novice) in October and Taunton in January: stays 27f: acts on soft going. *Nigel Twiston-Davies*   c129 h–

WICKLOW BRAVE 9 b.g. Beat Hollow – Moraine (Rainbow Quest (USA)) [2017/18 h161§: h16.4s h16s^2 Apr 27] smallish, strong gelding: high-class hurdler: much better effort in 2017/18 when second in Punchestown Champion Hurdle (3¼ lengths behind Supasundae): raced around 2m: acts on heavy going: in blinkers last 3 starts: not one to trust (has given trouble at start). *W. P. Mullins, Ireland*   h161 §

WICKLOW LAD 14 gr.g. Silver Patriarch (IRE) – Marina Bird (Julio Mariner) [2017/18 c110, h–: c25.5d^4 May 31] quite good-topped gelding: winning hurdler: fair hunter chaser nowadays: stays 25f: acts on heavy going: wears headgear. *N. W. Alexander*   c88 h–

WIDE AWAKE 9 b.m. And Beyond (IRE) – Quonarose (Feelings (FR)) [2017/18 h–: h20.2v^5 h20.9d^4 h19.9g^2 h20.5v^3 Nov 15] fair form over hurdles: will be well suited by 3m: acts on heavy going: has looked tricky ride. *Sandy Thomson*   h109

WIESENTRAUM (GER) 12 ch.g. Next Desert (IRE) – Wiesenblute (GER) (Big Shuffle (USA)) [2017/18 c–, h–: c29.1m^{pu} May 9] good-topped gelding: winning hurdler: useful chaser at best: stayed 3¼m: acted on soft going: wore headgear: dead. *Lucy Wadham*   c– h–

WIG WAM WIGGLE (IRE) 6 b.g. Mahler – Last Sunrise (IRE) (Shahanndeh) **h84**
[2017/18 b88: h17.2s[5] h20.2g h23.3d h16.8d h20.1v* Nov 22] failed to progress in bumpers: first form over hurdles when winning handicap at Hexham in November: should stay beyond 2½m: acts on heavy going. *Micky Hammond*

WILBERDRAGON 8 b.g. Kayf Tara – Swaythe (USA) (Swain (IRE)) [2017/18 c118, **c122** h–: c19.5g[3] c20.2g* c21.4d[3] c20d[5] c23.4s[5] c20.2d[5] Apr 22] good-topped gelding: winning **h–** hurdler: fairly useful handicap chaser: won novice event at Wincanton in October: barely stays 2¾m: acts on heavy going: in cheekpieces last 5 starts: wears tongue tie: front runner/races prominently. *Charlie Longsdon*

WILD BILL (IRE) 9 b.g. Westerner – Sarahall (IRE) (Saddlers' Hall (IRE)) [2017/18 c–, **c109** h–: c27.5d[5] c23.8s[5] Jan 18] won all 3 completed starts in points: lightly-raced maiden **h–** hurdler: fairly useful novice chaser in 2015/16: lightly raced and disappointing since (trained on reappearance only by Sally Randell): stays 3m: acts on heavy going. *Mrs A. Rucker*

WILDE BLUE YONDER (IRE) 9 b.g. Oscar (IRE) – Blue Gallery (IRE) (Bluebird **h132** (USA)) [2017/18 h20.5v[3] h19.6s[3] h19.8s[F] Apr 28] useful-looking gelding: useful handicap hurdler: not quite at best in 2017/18 following long absence, though still in frame all 3 completed outings (1½ lengths fourth of 19 to Jester Jet in Grade 3 event at Aintree final one): stays 21f: acts on good to firm and heavy going. *Alan King*

WILDE SPIRIT (IRE) 4 b.f. Oscar (IRE) – Full of Spirit (IRE) (Exit To Nowhere **b59** (USA)) [2017/18 b14s b12.6s[4] b16.5v[5] Mar 12] second foal: dam (b89), bumper winner, half-sister to high-class hurdler (stayed 3m) Prince of Scars and useful staying chaser/smart staying chaser Folsom Blue: poor form in bumpers. *Alan King*

WILD GINGER 7 ch.g. Presenting – Diamant Noir (Sir Harry Lewis (USA)) [2017/18 **c–** h76p: c25.1s[pu] Oct 20] lightly raced: point winner: poor form in novice hurdles: pulled up **h–** in novice handicap on chasing debut. *Jonjo O'Neill*

WILDMOOR BOY 7 b.g. Midnight Legend – Simple Glory (IRE) (Simply Great (FR)) **h–** [2017/18 h108: h15.8s[pu] Feb 21] sturdy gelding: fair hurdler at best: off a year, pulled up only outing in 2017/18: stays 21f: acts on good to firm and heavy going: wears headgear/tongue tie: front runner. *Robin Dickin*

WILD MURPHY (IRE) 7 b.g. Winged Love (IRE) – Yolande (IRE) (King Persian) **h92** [2017/18 h–: h18.7g[6] h18.5m[4] h20.3d Oct 3] winning pointer: modest form over hurdles: should stay 2½m: acts on good to firm going: tried in cheekpieces. *Noel Williams*

WILD WEST WIND (IRE) 9 b.g. Westerner – Mhuire Na Gale (IRE) (Norwich) **c142** [2017/18 c138, h–: c23.6v* c29.5v[F] c28.4v[R] c26s[ur] c26.2v[pu] Apr 7] winning hurdler: useful **h–** handicap chaser: won at Chepstow in December with something in hand: failed to complete subsequently: stays 3¼m (went best long way but exhausted when refused 2 out at testing 3½m): acts on heavy going: wears tongue tie. *Tom George*

WILLEM (FR) 8 b.g. Turtle Bowl (IRE) – Zita Blues (IRE) (Zieten (USA)) [2017/18 **c60** c123, h116: c16.3d[6] May 5] lengthy gelding: winning pointer: fairly useful hurdler: **h–** disappointing over fences since runner-up on chasing debut: stays easy 21f: acts on soft and good to firm going: usually in headgear: has worn tongue tie. *Mrs Teresa Clark*

WILLIAM H BONNEY 7 b.g. Midnight Legend – Calamintha (Mtoto) [2017/18 h130: **h130** h15.7m[6] h16.4s[5] h16s[6] h16.3v h16.8v Mar 16] compact gelding: useful handicap hurdler: shaped well when fifth in Greatwood Hurdle at Cheltenham (6¾ lengths behind Elgin) in November: unproven beyond 17f: acts on heavy going: travels strongly but often finds less than seems likely (did so last 3 outings). *Alan King*

WILLIAM HENRY (IRE) 8 b.g. King's Theatre (IRE) – Cincuenta (IRE) (Bob Back **c–** (USA)) [2017/18 h143p: c20.4d[pu] h21s* h21.1s[4] h21.4g[4] Apr 21] good-topped gelding: **h150** smart handicap hurdler: won Lanzarote Hurdle at Kempton (by ¾ length from Spiritofthegames) in January: fourth after at Cheltenham (2¾ lengths behind Bleu Berry in 26-runner Coral Cup) and Ayr: not fluent/saddle slipped when pulled up in novice on chasing debut: likely to stay 3m: acts on soft going: in cheekpieces last 2 starts. *Nicky Henderson*

WILLIAM HUNTER 6 b.g. Mawatheeq (USA) – Cosmea (Compton Place) [2017/18 **h105** h15.9d[2] h15.7g[4] h20s[pu] Dec 19] workmanlike gelding: down field in bumpers: fairly useful on Flat (stays 1½m): fair form first 2 outings over hurdles. *Alan King*

WILLIAM MONEY (IRE) 11 b.g. Cloudings (IRE) – All of A Kind (IRE) (Orchestra) **c111** [2017/18 c112, h98: c23.9g[2] May 21] workmanlike, close-coupled gelding: winning **h–** hurdler: fair handicap chaser: stays 3½m: acts on heavy going: has worn headgear: wears tongue tie: front runner. *Tim Vaughan*

WILLIAM OF ORANGE 7 b.g. Duke of Marmalade (IRE) – Critical Acclaim (Peintre Celebre (USA)) [2017/18 h110: h17.2m^{pu} h16.7d^5 h16d* h16.6d^2 h16.6d^5 ab16.3g^3 h15.7s* h16.5s^{pu} Apr 14] strong gelding: fairly useful handicap hurdler: won at Wetherby in November and Haydock in March: will stay beyond 2½m: acts on heavy going: wears headgear/tongue tie: probably best ridden positively. *Donald McCain* — h123

WILLIE BOY (IRE) 7 b.g. Tikkanen (USA) – Pandora's Moon (IRE) (Tamayaz (CAN)) [2017/18 c129p, h107p: c19.9d* c19.9g^6 c20.8s^F Mar 15] good-topped gelding: lightly-raced maiden hurdler: useful form over fences: won handicap at Newbury in November, easily best effort in 2017/18: stays 2½m: acts on soft going: usually ridden positively. *Venetia Williams* — c136 h–

WILLIE MCLOVIN 6 b.g. Apple Tree (FR) – Kiss Me du Cochet (FR) (Orival (FR)) [2017/18 b16.8v h18.5v h15.3v^6 h18.5v h23.1d Apr 24] well beaten in bumper/over hurdles. *Carroll Gray* — h– b–

WILLIES DREAM 5 b.g. Dream Eater (IRE) – Willies Witch (Bandmaster (USA)) [2017/18 b16.8v Dec 8] no promise in bumper. *Jess Westwood* — b–

WILL O'THE WEST (IRE) 7 b.g. Westerner – Simply Divine (IRE) (Be My Native (USA)) [2017/18 h126: h25g^4 c22.5s^4 c23.8d c23.8d^6 c23s^{pu} h23.8d^6 Apr 24] good-topped gelding: fairly useful hurdler at best: similar form when fourth in novice handicap at Uttoxeter on chasing debut: went wrong way subsequently: should stay beyond 21f: acts on heavy going: waited with. *Henry Daly* — c118 h113

WILLOUGHBY COURT (IRE) 7 br.g. Court Cave (IRE) – Willoughby Sue (IRE) (Dabali (IRE)) [2017/18 h151p: c19.9g* c19.9g* c20.8s^3 Jan 1] lengthy gelding: smart hurdler: similar form over fences: won novice at Huntingdon in November and Berkshire Novices' Chase at Newbury (by 3 lengths from Yanworth) in December: ridden less positively when only third in Dipper Novices' Chase at Cheltenham sole subsequent outing: will stay beyond 21f: acts on soft going: tried in tongue tie: front runner/races prominently: remains open to improvement as a chaser. *Ben Pauling* — c149 p h–

WILLOW GRANGE (IRE) 10 b.g. Turtle Island (IRE) – Rainbow Times (IRE) (Jareer (USA)) [2017/18 c22.1g^2 c21.7g^6 c25.3g h24g c24.4d c22s c23s^3 h23.3s^{pu} h21v^{pu} c21v^{pu} c19.7v^{pu} Dec 26] sturdy gelding: poor maiden hurdler: modest handicap chaser: stays 3m: acts on heavy going: wears headgear/tongue tie. *John Patrick Ryan, Ireland* — c86 h–

WILLOW MAY 4 b.f. Sakhee (USA) – Cerise Bleue (FR) (Port Lyautey (FR)) [2017/18 b16.5v^3 Apr 12] half-sister to 3 winners, including bumper winner/useful hurdler Knight In Purple (2m/17f winner, by Sir Harry Lewis) and fairly useful chaser River Purple (2m-21f winner, by Bollin Eric): dam, French 17f hurdle winner, half-sister to useful hurdler around 2m Dibea Times: 11/4, shaped as if needing run when third in mares maiden bumper at Taunton. *Nick Williams* — b67

WILLSHEBETRYING 7 b.m. Act One – Precedence (IRE) (Polish Precedent (USA)) [2017/18 h82: h19.2v* h19.2v^{pu} h19.2v h23v^6 h20.5v Apr 1] poor handicap hurdler: won at Fontwell in December: stays 19f: acts on heavy going: tried in visor. *Mark Hoad* — h82

WILLYEGOLASSIEGO 5 br.m. Kheleyf (USA) – Kryena (Kris) [2017/18 h–: h21.6d^2 h19.9g* h20g h19g^5 Nov 30] rather leggy mare: poor handicap hurdler: won mares event at Uttoxeter in June: also won on Flat in December/January: stays 2¾m: acts on good to soft going: waited with. *Neil Mulholland* — h84

WILSPA'S MAGIC (IRE) 5 gr.m. Zebedee – Triple Zero (IRE) (Raise A Grand (IRE)) [2017/18 h16.5m h18.5s^{pu} Nov 15] regressive maiden on Flat: no promise over hurdles. *Ron Hodges* — h–

WIMPOLE 5 b.g. Zamindar (USA) – Proportional (Beat Hollow) [2017/18 b16.8g^4 b16.2g b15.6s Jan 19] fourth in bumper on debut: no form after, including on Flat: tried in tongue tie. *Michael Scudamore* — b81

WIND OF HOPE (IRE) 9 b.g. September Storm (GER) – Ciara's Run (IRE) (Topanoora) [2017/18 c99, h–: c23.8g^{pu} h25.8g^6 h24.1s h19.9s^2 h19.9s^4 h23.8d Feb 14] lengthy gelding: modest handicap hurdler: first past post at Sedgefield in December but demoted after hanging left and hampering rival: maiden chaser, modest at best: left Alan J. Brown after first start: stays 23f: acts on heavy going: has worn cheekpieces, including last 3 starts. *Alistair Whillans* — c– h95

WIND PLACE AND SHO 6 b.g. Shirocco (GER) – Coh Sho No (Old Vic) [2017/18 h99: h16g^4 h15.5s^2 h15.5v h15.8d^6 Mar 26] fair maiden hurdler: should be well suited by 2½m: acts on soft going. *James Eustace* — h108

WIN

WINDSHEAR 7 b.g. Hurricane Run (IRE) – Portal (Hernando (FR)) [2017/18 h–: h16.4g h16.3d³ h15.7v^pu h16s h23.8s h20.6s⁴ Apr 11] lengthy gelding: smart at one time on Flat (stayed 14.5f): fair maiden hurdler: in tongue tie last 2 starts: usually raced nearer last than first: dead. *Sophie Leech* — **h103**

WINDSOR AVENUE (IRE) 6 b.g. Winged Love (IRE) – Zaffarella (IRE) (Zaffaran (USA)) [2017/18 b16.8s* b17v* Feb 19] £65,000 5-y-o: second foal: half-brother to fairly useful hurdler/winning pointer Ravenhill Road (17f winner, by Exit To Nowhere): dam (h112), 2m-3m hurdle winner, half-sister to fair hurdler/fairly useful chaser (stayed 2½m) Prosecco: off mark in Irish points at second attempt: looked useful prospect when winning small-field bumpers at Sedgefield in January and Carlisle (unchallenged) in February. *Brian Ellison* — **b104 p**

WINDSPIEL (FR) 5 b.g. Sholokhov (IRE) – Wildlife (GER) (Waky Nao) [2017/18 h–, b–: h16d³ h16s^su h15.3v h19.6s Jan 26] good-topped gelding: modest maiden hurdler: unproven beyond 2m: acts on good to soft going: tried in tongue tie. *David Arbuthnot* — **h93**

WIND TURBINE (IRE) 4 b.g. Power – First Breeze (USA) (Woodman (USA)) [2017/18 h15.7d Dec 19] little promise on Flat/in juvenile hurdle. *Tim Easterby* — **h–**

WINDY WRITER (IRE) 8 br.g. Rudimentary (USA) – Hardabout (IRE) (Alderbrook) [2017/18 c–, h98: c16.5m^pu h19.9g h15.7d⁵ h20.3d⁴ h24.1s^pu Dec 27] maiden hurdler, just poor form in 2017/18: no aptitude for chasing: left Shaun Lycett after first start: unproven beyond 2m: acts on soft going: has worn cheekpieces: in tongue tie last 3 starts. *Sam England* — **c – x**, **h69**

WINGED CRUSADER (IRE) 10 b.g. Winged Love (IRE) – Reine Berengere (FR) (Esprit du Nord (USA)) [2017/18 c114§, h–: c23.4s³ c26.6s² c23.4v⁵ c21.1s^ur Apr 12] useful-looking gelding: winning hurdler: fair handicap chaser nowadays: stays 27f: acts on heavy going: has worn visor: unreliable. *Miss A. Waugh* — **c114 §**, **h–**

WINGS ATTRACT (IRE) 9 b.g. Winged Love (IRE) – Huncheon Siss (IRE) (Phardante (FR)) [2017/18 c124, h–: c23.9g^pu c24.2d Mar 29] strong gelding: winning hurdler: fairly useful chaser at best: ran badly both starts in 2017/18 (left Olly Williams in between): stays 3m: acts on good to soft going: usually in headgear: tried in tongue tie: front runner/races prominently: untrustworthy. *Dan Skelton* — **c – §**, **h–**

WINGS OF DARKNESS (IRE) 4 b.g. Winged Love (IRE) – Night Therapy (IRE) (Mandalus) [2017/18 b16.3s Mar 24] good-topped gelding: tongue tied, tailed off in Goffs UK Spring Sales Bumper at Newbury. *Paul Webber* — **b–**

WINGS OF SMOKE (IRE) 13 gr.g. King's Theatre (IRE) – Grey Mo (IRE) (Roselier (FR)) [2017/18 c124§, h–: c21.2g c20s³ c19.9s⁴ c20v³ Mar 17] winning hurdler: fair handicap chaser nowadays: stays 2¾m: acts on good to firm and heavy going: has worn visor: wears tongue tie: often races in rear: weak finisher. *Tim Vaughan* — **c107 §**, **h–**

WINIDO 6 b.g. Sulamani (IRE) – Princess Claudia (IRE) (Kahyasi) [2017/18 h–, b65: h19d³ h19.6g^f h16d^F h21.2g^pu Dec 6] modest maiden hurdler: should stay beyond 19f: acts on good to soft going: in tongue tie last 4 starts. *Tim Vaughan* — **h93**

WINNING SPARK (USA) 11 b.g. Theatrical – Spark Sept (FR) (Septieme Ciel (USA)) [2017/18 h121: h19.8s² h19.7s⁴ h21.4v^pu h19.8s⁶ Mar 9] good-topped gelding: fairly useful handicap hurdler: stays 2½m: acts on good to firm and heavy going: tried in tongue tie: usually races towards rear. *Jackie du Plessis* — **h118**

WINNINGTRY (IRE) 7 br.g. Flemensfirth (USA) – Jeruflo (IRE) (Glacial Storm (USA)) [2017/18 h121: h26.5g⁶ h24.7s Nov 11] type to make a chaser: fairly useful handicap hurdler: stays 3m: acts on good to soft going: travels strongly. *Paul Nicholls* — **h115**

WINTER ESCAPE (IRE) 7 b.g. Robin des Pres (FR) – Saddleeruppat (IRE) (Saddlers' Hall (IRE)) [2017/18 h138: c18d³ Nov 27] lengthy gelding: useful form over hurdles: very considerately handled when well beaten in novice on chasing debut on sole start in 2017/18: unproven beyond 17f: acts on good to soft going: has joined Aidan Anthony Howard: will prove different proposition in time over fences. *Alan King* — **c89 P**, **h–**

WINTERFELL (FR) 6 b.g. Voix du Nord (FR) – Goldville (FR) (Gold And Steel (FR)) [2017/18 h23.3d⁵ h18.9s³ h18.9v^pu h20.4d² Apr 20] strong, compact gelding: fair hurdler, off nearly 2 years before reappearance: left Jonjo O'Neill after second start: stays 2½m: acts on soft going. *L. Baudron, France* — **h115**

WINTER LION (IRE) 8 ch.g. Galileo (IRE) – Hill of Snow (Reference Point) [2017/18 h123: c20m² c22.5g⁴ h20.5g c20d³ c25.5v³ c20.3v⁴ c24.2s⁴ c25.3g* Apr 18] fairly useful hurdler: fairly useful chaser: won novice handicap at Cheltenham in April: left Matthew J. Smith after sixth start: stays 25f: acts on good to firm and heavy going: sometimes wears headgear: wears tongue tie. *Fergal O'Brien* — **c125**, **h–**

WIN

WINTERLUDE (IRE) 8 b.g. Street Cry (IRE) – New Morning (IRE) (Sadler's Wells (USA)) [2017/18 h114: h19.6g³ Aug 4] useful on Flat, stays 2m: fairly useful form over hurdles: stays 2½m. *Jennie Candlish*   **h117**

WINTER SQUAW 6 b.m. Indian Danehill (IRE) – Briery Breeze (IRE) (Anshan) [2017/18 h18.5d^pu h16.8s h16.8v h18.5s Nov 15] lengthy mare: second foal: dam, lightly raced over hurdles, half-sister to useful hurdler/chaser (stays 21f) Briery Queen and useful staying chaser Briery Fox: maiden pointer: no form over hurdles. *Susan Gardner*   **h–**

WINTOUR LEAP 7 b.m. Nayef (USA) – Mountain Leap (IRE) (Sadler's Wells (USA)) [2017/18 h19.9d Jul 11] fair hurdler at best, well held sole start in 2017/18: stays 21f: acts on soft going. *Robert Stephens*   **h–**

WISE COCO 5 b.m. Shirocco (GER) – Sensible (Almutawakel) [2017/18 b16.2g b16v b15.6d Feb 14] rather unfurnished mare: second foal: half-sister to 1m winner Wekeyll (by Exceed And Excel): dam maiden on Flat (stayed 13f): little impact in bumpers/on Flat. *Alistair Whillans*   **b66**

WISECRACKER 5 br.g. Sageburg (IRE) – Folie Lointaine (FR) (Poliglote) [2017/18 h–, b–: h16.7g h16g⁵ h15.9d⁵ h16.6s³ h16s⁵ Mar 16] modest form over hurdles: raced around 2m: acts on soft going: tried in hood: in tongue tie in 2017/18. *Ben Case*   **h90**

WISHFULL DREAMING 7 ch.g. Alflora (IRE) – Poussetiere Deux (FR) (Garde Royale) [2017/18 h133: h15.8m⁴ h18.5s^sur h20g^pu h21s Jan 13] lengthy gelding: fairly useful handicap hurdler: left Philip Hobbs after third start: unproven beyond 2m: acts on soft going: tried in tongue tie: often let down by jumping. *Olly Murphy*   **h115 x**

WISH IN A WELL (IRE) 9 b.g. Gamut (IRE) – Lady Bellingham (IRE) (Montelimar (USA)) [2017/18 c75, h–: c21.2m c22.6g⁶ c21.6d⁴ c26.7v^pu c23.6s^pu c21.2v² c21.2v³ c24.5s⁶ c19.5s³ Apr 6] workmanlike gelding: maiden hurdler: poor handicap chaser: stays 21f: acts on heavy going: wears headgear: has worn tongue tie: usually races prominently: often let down by jumping. *Ben Case*   **c64 x / h–**

WISHING AND HOPING (IRE) 8 b.g. Beneficial – Desperately Hoping (IRE) (Un Desperado (FR)) [2017/18 c130, h126: h19.5d^F Oct 14] useful-looking gelding: fairly useful hurdler: running creditably when falling 2 out in Silver Trophy Handicap at Chepstow sole start in 2017/18: useful form completed start over fences in 2016/17: stays 21f: acts on good to soft going. *Alan King*   **c– / h125**

WISHMAKER 4 b.g. Raven's Pass (USA) – Wedding March (IRE) (Dalakhani (IRE)) [2017/18 b13.1g³ b13.7g⁶ h16.4v⁴ h16s⁵ Dec 27] workmanlike gelding: third foal: dam useful French 1m winner: fair form in bumpers: well held in 2 juvenile hurdles: has joined Rebecca Menzies. *Tony Coyle*   **h71 / b86**

WISTY (IRE) 9 gr.g. Cloudings (IRE) – Alpine Message (Tirol) [2017/18 h125: c17.3g* c17.3s* c17.3g* c17.1d c15.8s^pu Apr 12] fairly useful hurdler: useful form over fences: won maiden in May and handicaps in July and August (by 17 lengths from Nicolas Chauvin), all at Cartmel: unproven beyond 17f: acts on soft and good to firm going: has worn hood: usually leads. *Martin Todhunter*   **c137 / h–**

WITHAM 5 b.m. Beat Hollow – Wistow (Sir Harry Lewis (USA)) [2017/18 b83: b16.7g⁴ May 12] fourth in bumpers, modest form at best on debut. *Pam Sly*   **b66**

WITH DISCRETION (IRE) 7 b.m. Tiger Hill (IRE) – Discreet (Kahyasi) [2017/18 h21v* h21.6s* Apr 23] second foal: dam, ran once in bumper, half-sister to fairly useful hurdlers Tengo Ambro (2m winner) and Marcus (2¾m winner) out of National Hunt Chase winner Loving Around: maiden pointer: fairly useful form over hurdles: won mares novices at Towcester in March and Newton Abbot in April: will go on improving. *Nicky Henderson*   **h128 p**

WITHOUTDEFAVOURITE (IRE) 10 b.g. Oscar (IRE) – Camden Confusion (IRE) (Camden Town) [2017/18 h24g^pu c23g c22.5d⁶ c24.2d⁴ c25.1v³ c26.7v⁴ Apr 9] rangy gelding: winning pointer: maiden hurdler: fair maiden chaser at best, below form in 2017/18: stays 25f: acts on heavy going: often wears cheekpieces: ungenerous. *Tim Vaughan*   **c74 § / h–**

WITHOUT FRONTIER (IRE) 6 b.g. Stowaway – Hollygrove Samba (IRE) (Accordion) [2017/18 h92§, b–: h21.6s³ h19.8s^pu Nov 23] poor maiden hurdler: stays 2½m: acts on good to soft going: tried in cheekpieces: wears tongue tie: temperamental. *Tim Vaughan*   **h75 §**

WITH PLEASURE 5 b.g. Poet's Voice – With Fascination (USA) (Dayjur (USA)) [2017/18 h98: h15.8g³ h15.8g² h19.3g^su h19.5v² h16s h19.5v Feb 2] close-coupled gelding: modest maiden hurdler: stays 19f: acts on good to firm and heavy going: often races in rear. *John Flint*   **h99**

WON

WITNESS (FR) 9 b.g. Astarabad (USA) – Belle Yepa (FR) (Mansonnien (FR)) [2017/18 c105, h–: c20d⁶ c20.1v³ c19.2s⁴ h23.8d⁶ h24.1d* Mar 29] close-coupled gelding: modest handicap hurdler: won at Wetherby in March: modest handicap chaser: stays 3m: acts on heavy going: sometimes wears headgear: tried in tongue tie: often races towards rear. *Micky Hammond* — **c99 h94**

WITNESS IN COURT (IRE) 11 b.g. Witness Box (USA) – Inter Alia (IRE) (Dr Massini (IRE)) [2017/18 c138§, h–: c17.1g³ c20.1m c19.9g c16.5g⁴ Oct 25] tall, angular gelding: winning hurdler: useful handicap chaser, well below best in 2017/18: stays 21f: acts on good to firm and heavy going: unreliable. *Donald McCain* — **c100 § h–**

WITNESS TIME (IRE) 6 b.g. Witness Box (USA) – Emotional Melody (IRE) (Saddlers' Hall (IRE)) [2017/18 h58p, b82: h16.2g h16.2vᵖᵘ h19.7sᵘʳ h19.9s h16.8g Apr 23] modest maiden hurdler: left Rose Dobbin after fourth start: best effort at 2m: wears hood: tried in tongue tie. *Tristan Davidson* — **h86**

WIXFORD (IRE) 7 b.g. Westerner – Chirouble (IRE) (High Roller (IRE)) [2017/18 b–: b16.3dᵖᵘ May 21] no form in bumpers. *Johnny Farrelly* — **b–**

WIZADORA 10 b.m. Alflora (IRE) – Moor Spring (Primitive Rising (USA)) [2017/18 c24.2g May 6] multiple point winner: little impact in hunter chases. *Miss S. Coward* — **c–**

WIZARDS BRIDGE 9 b.g. Alflora (IRE) – Island Hopper (Be My Native (USA)) [2017/18 c115§, h117: c26g* c24.2v⁴ c25.1v³ c25.1vᵖᵘ c19.4v⁴ c26s* c30.7vᵖᵘ Apr 17] rangy gelding: fairly useful hurdler: fairly useful handicap chaser: won at Fontwell (conditional) in October, Chepstow in March and Fontwell again in April: stays 3¼m: acts on good to firm and heavy going: wears headgear: tried in tongue tie: temperamental. *Colin Tizzard* — **c120 § h–**

WIZARD'S SLIABH (IRE) 7 b.m. King's Theatre (IRE) – Darling Smile (IRE) (Darshaan) [2017/18 h122, b81: h23.3s⁴ h21.4s⁴ Nov 11] bumper winner: fairly useful form over hurdles: stays 23f: acts on good to soft going: in cheekpieces last 3 starts: wears tongue tie: often races towards rear. *Fergal O'Brien* — **h119**

WOLFCATCHER (IRE) 6 b.g. King's Best (USA) – Miss Particular (IRE) (Sadler's Wells (USA)) [2017/18 h–: h20g⁶ h16s⁵ h19.4d³ h21d h21g³ h15.7s⁶ h20.5s⁶ Apr 15] compact gelding: fairly useful handicap hurdler: stays 21f: acts on heavy going: wears headgear/tongue tie. *Ian Williams* — **h116**

WOLF OF WINDLESHAM (IRE) 6 ch.g. Mastercraftsman (IRE) – Al Amlah (USA) (Riverman (USA)) [2017/18 h113: h19.8s² Apr 28] workmanlike gelding: useful handicap hurdler: fitter for run on Flat, second at Sandown (4 lengths behind Soul Emotion) in April: stays 2½m: acts on soft going. *Stuart Edmunds* — **h135**

WOLFSLAIR (IRE) 7 b.g. Yeats (IRE) – Hidden Reserve (IRE) (Heron Island (IRE)) [2017/18 h20d h24g h15.7dᵖᵘ h19.3d h24s⁶ h25.3sᵘʳ Jan 1] €85,000 3-y-o: second foal: dam (b103), bumper winner on only start, sister to fairly useful hurdler/chaser (stayed 2½m) Crocodiles Rock: fair handicap hurdler: left Gordon Elliott after second start: stays 2¾m: acts on good to soft going: tried in cheekpieces: has worn tongue tie, including in 2017/18. *David Thompson* — **h100**

WOLF SWORD (IRE) 9 b.g. Flemensfirth (USA) – Dame O'Neill (IRE) (Dr Massini (IRE)) [2017/18 c127, h–: c16.5v⁴ c19.4d* c20.6vᵖᵘ c19.4v⁴ c20.1s⁴ c20d c15.9v² c23.9d* Apr 22] strong gelding: winning hurdler: fairly useful handicap chaser: won at Wetherby in November and Market Rasen in April: stays 3m: acts on good to firm and heavy going. *Sue Smith* — **c123 h–**

WOLFTRAP (IRE) 9 b.g. Mountain High (IRE) – Dear Money (IRE) (Buckskin (FR)) [2017/18 h112: h20g⁵ c19.4d⁵ h19.1m⁵ h23.3d h21.6m⁴ h23.3g² h21.4sᵖᵘ c19.2vᵖᵘ Apr 8] rather leggy gelding: fair handicap hurdler: no form over fences: left Philip Hobbs after seventh start: stays 21f: acts on heavy going: usually wears headgear: tried in tongue tie. *Mrs K. Heard* — **c– h106**

WONDERFUL CHARM (FR) 10 b.g. Poliglote – Victoria Royale (FR) (Garde Royale) [2017/18 c136, h–: c27.5d³ c26.6s* c26.3vᵖᵘ c21.1s Apr 12] rangy gelding: has had breathing operation: winning hurdler: fairly useful hunter chaser nowadays: won at Musselburgh in February: had been third in Stratford Champion Hunters' Chase: stays 27f: acts on soft going: wears headgear/tongue tie: races towards rear: temperamental. *Paul Nicholls* — **c123 § h–**

WONDEROFTHEWORLD (IRE) 6 b.g. Beneficial – Our Lucky Supreme (IRE) (Supreme Leader) [2017/18 h24.8g* h22gᶠ h21s⁶ h23.8s³ Feb 4] €10,000 3-y-o, £80,000 4-y-o: seventh foal: half-brother to a winning pointer by Dr Massini: dam unraced out of — **h133**

WON

sister to smart hurdler/chaser (stayed 3m) Mutare: runner-up in point: useful form over hurdles: won maiden at Kilbeggan in August: third in novice at Musselburgh in February: wears tongue tie. *Alan Fleming, Ireland*

WONGA SWINGER 8 b.g. Lucky Story (USA) – Chippewa (FR) (Cricket Ball (USA)) [2017/18 h90: h15.8m h18.7m^{pu} c16.4g^{pu} Sep 7] placed twice in points: modest hurdler at best: no form in 2017/18, including in novice handicap on chasing debut: wears headgear: front runner/races prominently: temperament under suspicion. *Sam Thomas* c–
h–

WONTSTOPMENOW (IRE) 5 b.g. Scorpion (IRE) – Jodi (IRE) (Phardante (FR)) [2017/18 b17.7s b17.7d^5 h21.7g^6 Apr 20] no form in bumpers: 200/1, sixth in novice at Fontwell (40 lengths behind Canelo) on hurdling debut. *Linda Jewell* h77
b–

WOOD BREIZH (FR) 8 gr.g. Stormy River (FR) – Polynevees (FR) (Poliglote) [2017/18 h22.4d^4 h20d^{pu} Oct 29] fair handicap hurdler: left W. P. Mullins after first start in 2017/18: stays 3m: acts on heavy going: has worn cheekpieces. *James Moffatt* h109

WOODFIELD ROBIN (IRE) 7 ch.m. Robin des Champs (FR) – Ticket To Mars (IRE) (Sabrehill (USA)) [2017/18 h23g^4 Jul 18] half-sister to a winning pointer by Black Sam Bellamy: dam, 2m-2¼m hurdles winner in Germany/Italy, half-sister to fair hurdler/fairly useful chaser (stayed 3m) Prince of Persia: last of 3 finishers in Irish mares maiden on completed start in points: in tongue tie, tailed off in novice on hurdling debut. *Katy Price* h–

WOODFLEET (IRE) 7 b.g. Fleetwood (IRE) – Norwer (IRE) (Norwich) [2017/18 c26d* May 5] €2,500 3-y-o, £12,000 4-y-o: fifth foal: half-brother to fairly useful hurdler/chaser Lilly The Lioness (2m/17f winner, by Welsh Lion): dam unraced: multiple point winner: 12/1, won hunter at Cheltenham (by 5 lengths from Excitable Island, finding extra) on chasing debut. *Richard J. Bandey* c111

WOODFORT 6 gr.g. Dalakhani (IRE) – Akdara (IRE) (Sadler's Wells (USA)) [2017/18 h111, b98: h23.9v h20.3g^2 Oct 26] well-made gelding: fourth in Irish maiden point: bumper winner: fair maiden hurdler: may prove best at around 2½m: acts on good to soft going: often races prominently: temperamental. *Nigel Twiston-Davies* h113 §

WOODLAND OPERA (IRE) 8 br.g. Robin des Champs (FR) – Opera Hat (IRE) (Strong Gale) [2017/18 c151, h–: c20.5s^F c18d^3 c20s^3 c16.2s* c17d^4 c20v^3 c20s Apr 25] winning hurdler: smart chaser: won Craddockstown Novices' Chase at Punchestown (by ½ length from Tombstone) in November: third in Buck House Novices' Chase at Punchestown (15¾ lengths behind Death Duty) previous month: stays 21f, effective at shorter: acts on soft going: wears tongue tie: temperament under suspicion. *Mrs J. Harrington, Ireland* c145
h–

WOOD PIGEON (IRE) 9 b.g. Presenting – Come In Moscow (IRE) (Over The River (FR)) [2017/18 c101, h–: h24.3s^6 c26.3s^4 c20v^{ur} c21.2v* c19.8s^{ur} c19.3v^2 c20.3vp^u c21.2s^2 c20.9v^4 Apr 10] poor form over hurdles: fair handicap chaser: won at Fakenham in January: stays 25f: acts on heavy going: wears headgear: front runner/races prominently. *Olly Murphy* c101
h80

WOODS WELL (IRE) 7 ch.g. Fleetwood (IRE) – Millbrook Marble (IRE) (Rudimentary (USA)) [2017/18 h133, b101: c21s* c20s^2 c24.5d^{pu} c25v^5 c28.7v^{pu} c24v^5 c29v^{pu} c30s^6 Apr 28] useful form over hurdles: useful chaser: won maiden at Fairyhouse in November: stays 3¾m: acts on heavy going. *Gordon Elliott, Ireland* c135
h–

WOOD YER (IRE) 12 ch.g. Anshan – Glenasheen (IRE) (Presenting) [2017/18 c115, h–: c25g^{pu} c26.1v^4 c25.3v^5 c23.6v^F c28.8v^{pu} Feb 19] lengthy, angular gelding: maiden hurdler: fair handicap chaser, below form in 2017/18: stays 3¾m: acts on heavy going: wears headgear: usually wears tongue tie: temperamental. *Nigel Twiston-Davies* c98 §
h–

WOOLSTONE ONE 6 b.m. Authorized (IRE) – Saralea (FR) (Sillery (USA)) [2017/18 h16g^6 h15.8s* h15.8v^2 h19.4s* h21s* h20v^6 Apr 1] rather leggy mare: useful form over hurdles: won mares maiden at Ffos Las in October, mares handicap at Doncaster in January and listed mares event at Warwick (by 2¾ lengths from Jester Jet) in February: left Harry Whittington after first start: stays 21f: acts on soft going: usually wears hood. *Emma Lavelle* h131

WORKBENCH (FR) 10 b.g. Network (GER) – Danhelis (FR) (Hellios (USA)) [2017/18 c131, h113: h20.3g^4 h16.3g^5 h19.2d* c21.6g^5 c18g^3 c15.8s^4 c15.5d* c15.7s^4 Jan 11] good-topped gelding: fair handicap hurdler: won at Fontwell in September: fairly useful handicap chaser: won at Sandown in December: stays 2½m: acts on heavy going: has worn headgear, including last 3 starts: wears tongue tie: usually races nearer last than first. *Dan Skelton* c125
h114

WORK DU BRETEAU (FR) 8 ch.g. Network (GER) – Salinka (FR) (Green Tune (USA)) [2017/18 c107, h112, b65: h20.2g^3 h23.9m^3 c23g* c19.4d^F c24.2s^2 h19.4g^6 h24.4s c31.8g Apr 21] fair handicap hurdler: fairly useful form over fences: won novice at c128
h113

WOU

Worcester in June: left Tim Reed after sixth start: stays 3m: acts on good to firm and heavy going: has worn hood, including in 2017/18: has worn tongue tie, including last 3 starts. *Dan Skelton*

WORKING CLASS 4 b.g. Bahri (USA) – Louise d'Arzens (Anabaa (USA)) [2017/18 h16.7s³ h16s^bd h16s⁵ h15.8g^ur Apr 24] workmanlike gelding: fairly useful on Flat, stays 1¼m: fair form over hurdles. *Oliver Sherwood*   **h103**

WORKING LEATHER (IRE) 5 b.g. Teofilo (IRE) – Masnada (IRE) (Erins Isle) [2017/18 b15.8d b16.7g² Jun 23] modest form in bumpers: dead. *Mark Walford*   **b81**

WORK IN PROGRESS (IRE) 8 b.g. Westerner – Parsons Term (IRE) (The Parson) [2017/18 c125, h–: h19.1g⁴ h20.6g⁵ c19.2g* c19.2g* c20s* c21.4g^ur c20.3d^ur c16s* Dec 16] fairly useful handicap hurdler: won 3-runner event at Fontwell (in control when left alone last) in May: useful chaser: won small-field novices at Market Rasen (2) and Uttoxeter in June/July, and Hereford in December: stays 21f: acts on soft going: wears tongue tie: front runner/races prominently. *Dan Skelton*   **c143 h121**

WORK (IRE) 5 b.m. Mastercraftsman (IRE) – Abbeyleix Lady (IRE) (Montjeu (IRE)) [2017/18 h89: h19d h20g⁶ h21.6d⁶ h18.5v^pu Oct 2] rather leggy mare: poor maiden hurdler: unproven beyond 2m: acts on heavy going: in headgear last 3 starts: often wears tongue tie: weak finisher. *David Pipe*   **h79 §**

WORLD PREMIER (FR) 5 gr.g. Montmartre (FR) – Kelbelange (FR) (Ganges (USA)) [2017/18 b101: h16.3d h15.8s³ h15.8s Mar 14] good-topped gelding: bumper winner: fairly useful form over hurdles: best effort when third in novice at Huntingdon in February. *Ben Pauling*   **h115**

WORTHABOBORTWO 6 gr.g. Proclamation (IRE) – Bobs Bay (IRE) (Bob's Return (IRE)) [2017/18 b16.7g b16.3g⁵ b16v Mar 11] pulled up in 2 maiden points: no form in bumpers: tried in hood. *Andrew Martin*   **b–**

WORTHY FARM (IRE) 5 b.g. Beneficial – Muckle Flugga (IRE) (Karinga Bay) [2017/18 h23.1d³ Apr 21] €60,000 3-y-o: fourth foal: half-brother to useful hurdler/chaser Mister Miyagi (2m-2½m winner, by Zagreb): dam (h104), 2½m-3m hurdle winner, half-sister to fairly useful hurdler/useful chaser Cootehill (stayed 25f): easy winner of point on debut: 3/1, third in maiden at Bangor (½ length behind Merry Milan) on hurdling debut: will improve. *Paul Nicholls*   **h113 p**

WOR VERGE 5 b.g. Virtual – Hanover Gate (Motivator) [2017/18 b15.6g b16v ab16.3g³ h17d⁵ h20.6v^pu Apr 14] modest form in bumpers: poor form over hurdles: often races towards rear. *Susan Corbett*   **h80 b80**

WOTABREEZE (IRE) 5 ch.g. Excellent Art – Sparkling Crystal (IRE) (Danehill Dancer (IRE)) [2017/18 h16.7g⁴ h15.6m⁶ Nov 8] fair on Flat, stays 1½m: modest form over hurdles: remains with potential. *John Quinn*   **h93 p**

WOT A SHOT (IRE) 9 b.g. Refuse To Bend (IRE) – Ashdali (IRE) (Grand Lodge (USA)) [2017/18 c101, h–: h15.8g⁴ c15.6g h16.2g² h16.7g^pu h18.1g h15.8g² h15.6m² h15.6g* h16g⁴ Apr 20] fair handicap hurdler: won at Perth (novice) in July and Musselburgh in December: fair chaser: best at 2m: acts on soft and good to firm going: has worn hood: tried in tongue tie: waited with, strong traveller. *Nicky Richards*   **c– h100**

WOTZIZNAME (IRE) 8 b.g. Fruits of Love (USA) – Native Beau (IRE) (Be My Native (USA)) [2017/18 c132p, h136: c24.2d² c24.2s* c26s⁴ c24s* c26s⁵ c26g³ Apr 20] useful-looking gelding: useful form over hurdles: useful chaser: won novice handicap at Exeter (by 3¼ lengths from Another Venture) in November and novice at Doncaster (by ½ length from Mount Mews) in January: stays 3¼m: acts on soft going: wears tongue tie. *Harry Fry*   **c138 h–**

WOULDUADAMANDEVEIT (IRE) 5 b.g. Stowaway – Figlette (Darshaan) [2017/18 b16.3d² b16.4s³ b15.7d b13.v² Feb 10] €15,000 3-y-o: compact gelding: half-brother to several winners, including fairly useful hurdler Act Alone (19f winner, by Act One): dam unraced half-sister to Champion Hurdle winner Sublimity: fairly useful form in bumpers: placed in listed events at Cheltenham (2¾ lengths behind Crooks Peak) in November and Newbury (11 lengths behind Acey Milan) in February. *Susan Gardner*   **b103**

WOUNDED WARRIOR (IRE) 9 b.g. Shantou (USA) – Sparkling Sword (Broadsword (USA)) [2017/18 c139, h–: c28s^pu c24v c29s c25v² c28.7v c23v c28.5s⁶ c30s* Apr 28] tall, lengthy gelding: winning hurdler: useful handicap chaser: won at Punchestown (by 7 lengths from Isleofhopendreams) in April: stays 3¾m: acts on heavy going: usually wears headgear: usually races close up: temperamental. *Noel Meade, Ireland*   **c136 § h–**

Betfred Grand National Trial Handicap Chase, Haydock—
Yala Enki copes best with the gruelling conditions and draws well clear of 2017 runner-up Blaklion;
Wild West Wind has refused in the background

WUFF (IRE) 10 b.g. Beneficial – Dummy Run (IRE) (Glacial Storm (USA)) [2017/18 c130, h–: c24.1v² c26v⁽ᵖᵘ⁾ c26.7v⁽ᵖᵘ⁾ Jan 18] strong gelding: winning hurdler: fairly useful handicap chaser: second at Bangor in December: stays 3m: acts on heavy going: usually wears cheekpieces: wears tongue tie: often races towards rear: temperamental. *Tom George*   **c126 §**
h–

WYFIELD ROSE 9 b.m. Kayf Tara – Miniature Rose (Anshan) [2017/18 c–, h114: c23.4g⁽ᵘʳ⁾ c20.1g⁴ c23.8m⁵ h23.9g⁵ h19.3d h20.2s⁴ Apr 25] smallish, workmanlike mare: has had breathing operation: modest handicap hurdler: similar form over fences: stays 27f: acts on good to soft going: wears cheekpieces: tried in tongue tie: temperamental. *Alistair Whillans*   **c89 §**
h95 §

WYLDE MAGIC (IRE) 7 b.g. Oscar (IRE) – Voodoo Magic (GER) (Platini (GER)) [2017/18 h115: h23.6d³ h21.1s⁶ Nov 19] compact gelding: fair maiden hurdler: stays 3m: acts on good to soft going: tried in tongue tie: usually races prominently. *Evan Williams*   **h114**

WYNFORD (IRE) 5 ch.g. Dylan Thomas (IRE) – Wishing Chair (USA) (Giant's Causeway (USA)) [2017/18 h83: h16.2g⁵ h16.8g h15.8g* h18.7g² h19.6g* h20g² Sep 3] fairly useful handicap hurdler: won at Uttoxeter in June and Bangor in August: left David Loughnane after second start: stays 2½m: best form on good going: tried in cheekpieces: often wears tongue tie. *Dan Skelton*   **h121**

X

XENOPHON 10 b.g. Phoenix Reach (IRE) – Comtesse Noire (CAN) (Woodman (USA)) [2017/18 h20g⁽ᵖᵘ⁾ c23.9g³ c23g⁽ʳᵘ⁾ Sep 18] leggy gelding: winning hurdler: poor handicap chaser nowadays: stays 25f: acts on good to firm and heavy going: has worn headgear/tongue tie: often let down by jumping well over fences. *Nick Kent*   **c75 x**
h–

XHALE (FR) 6 br.g. Halling (USA) – Xanadu Bliss (FR) (Xaar) [2017/18 h80: h20.7g⁶ h19v⁽ᵖᵘ⁾ h16.6s⁵ Jan 26] angular gelding: poor maiden hurdler: best effort at 2m: acts on good to soft going. *Ian Williams*   **h68**

XIN CHAO 5 b.m. Showcasing – Nelly's Glen (Efisio) [2017/18 b–: b16.8g³ May 16] poor form in bumpers: dead. *Brian Ellison*   **b70**

XPO UNIVERSEL (FR) 9 b.g. Poliglote – Xanadu Bliss (FR) (Xaar) [2017/18 c20.9s⁶ h19.4s h20.4d⁴ h19.4s⁽ᵖᵘ⁾ h18.9g⁶ c23.9v⁶ h19.4v h19.9v³ h20.9v⁵ h16.4v³ Apr 15] modest maiden hurdler nowadays: well held over fences: left Ferdy Murphy after seventh start: stays 2½m: acts on heavy going: wears headgear: tried in tongue tie: often races prominently. *Rebecca Menzies*   **c–**
h92

Y

YAHA FIZZ (IRE) 8 b.g. Zagreb (USA) – Ross Dana (IRE) (Topanoora) [2017/18 h16.2s² h16s³ h16s⁶ h20v h16s² h20s Apr 28] useful handicap hurdler: second at Fairyhouse (2¼ lengths behind Low Sun) in April: failed to complete both starts over fences: left E. D. Delany after fourth start: unproven beyond 2m: acts on soft going: front runner. *Gordon Elliott, Ireland*   **c–**
h138

YEA

YALA ENKI (FR) 8 b.g. Nickname (FR) – Cadiane (FR) (Cadoudal (FR)) [2017/18 c152, h134: c25.1s^{pu} c23.4v^3 c23.8d^6 c25.6v^4 c24.2s^F c28.4v* c25s^6 c26.2v^6 Apr 7] useful-looking gelding: useful hurdler: smart handicap chaser: won 3-finisher Grand National Trial at Haydock (by 54 lengths from Blaklion) in February: stays 3½m: acts on heavy going: tried in cheekpieces: front runner/races prominently. *Venetia Williams* **c150 h–**

YALLA HABIBTI 5 b.m. Kayf Tara – Majeeda (IRE) (Jeremy (USA)) [2017/18 b–: b16.8m b16.8g^5 Apr 23] poor form in bumpers: left Lisa Williamson after first start. *Michael Mullineaux* **b75**

YALLTARI 7 gr.g. Kayf Tara – Lily Grey (FR) (Kadalko (FR)) [2017/18 h100: h16.2s* h18.5v* h19.9v* Jan 27] fairly useful form over hurdles: unbeaten in 2017/18, winning handicaps at Hereford in December, and Exeter and Uttoxeter (by ½ length from Applesandpierres) in January: stays 2½m: raced only on soft/heavy going: front runner/races prominently. *Venetia Williams* **h125**

YANMARE (IRE) 8 b.g. Soapy Danger – Bell Walks Caroll (IRE) (Carroll House) [2017/18 c105x, h–: c24.2s^F c30.7v* c25.5s^5 c30.7s c30.7v^{pu} Apr 17] big, workmanlike gelding: twice-raced hurdler: fair handicap chaser: won at Exeter in December: thorough stayer: acts on heavy going: has worn headgear, including last 3 starts: wears tongue tie. *Nigel Twiston-Davies* **c109 h–**

YANWORTH 8 ch.g. Norse Dancer (IRE) – Yota (FR) (Galetto (FR)) [2017/18 h164: c17.5s* c19.2s^F c19.9g^2 c20.8s* h24s^6 Mar 15] compact gelding: high-class hurdler: smart form but didn't convince over fences despite winning maiden at Exeter in October and Dipper Novices' Chase at Cheltenham (by neck from Sizing Tennessee) in January: stays 25f, effective at much shorter: acts on heavy going: tried in cheekpieces: not straightforward. *Alan King* **c150 + h153**

YASIR (USA) 10 b.g. Dynaformer (USA) – Khazayin (USA) (Bahri (USA)) [2017/18 h–§: h15.8d* h15.8d^2 h20.3d^2 h19.9v^4 h16s^5 Feb 16] close-coupled gelding: modest handicap hurdler: won at Uttoxeter in November: stays 21f: acts on heavy going: has worn headgear, including final start: tried in tongue tie: races towards rear: moody. *Conor Dore* **h88 §**

YEATS BABY (IRE) 6 b.m. Yeats (IRE) – Cabo (FR) (Sagamix (FR)) [2017/18 h–: h19d^2 h19.3s^5 h20.5v^F h16s Apr 19] fourth in Irish mares maiden point: modest maiden hurdler: standout effort on return: left Ian Williams after that, Martin Todhunter after third start: should be suited by at least 2½m: acts on good to soft going: has worn cheekpieces: tried in tongue tie. *F. Flood, Ireland* **h95**

BetBright Dipper Novices' Chase, Cheltenham—Yanworth reverses Newbury form with Willoughby Court (striped sleeves), but is still pushed close by Sizing Tennessee (white face)

YEL

YELLOW DOCKETS (IRE) 6 ch.m. Getaway (GER) – Soft Skin (IRE) (Rudimentary (USA)) [2017/18 b15.7v^3 Apr 27] €2,700 3-y-o, £30,000 5-y-o: fourth foal: half-sister to a winning pointer by Gamut: dam unraced: runner-up in Irish point on debut: in hood, 5/1, third in mares bumper at Towcester (¾ length behind Destinee Royale). *Nicky Henderson* **b88**

YELLOW KANGAROO (IRE) 6 b.g. Aussie Rules (USA) – Sue N Win (IRE) (Beneficial) [2017/18 b81: h16g h15.5d h16.5g^5 h19v^5 h20.7s Feb 22] little form over hurdles. *Evan Williams* **h57**

YESANDNO (IRE) 5 b.g. Scorpion (IRE) – In Fact (IRE) (Classic Cliche (IRE)) [2017/18 b15.7v^3 Mar 29] €15,000 3-y-o, £50,000 4-y-o: sixth foal: half-brother to fair hurdler/winning pointer The Road Home (2m winner, by Oscar): dam unraced out of useful French hurdler/chaser (stayed 2¼m) Soupinette: third when unseated rider last in Irish point on debut: 5/1, green when third in maiden bumper at Towcester (23¾ lengths behind Captain Drake): should improve. *Alan King* **b65 p**

YES DADDY (IRE) 10 b.g. Golan (IRE) – Hollygrove Samba (IRE) (Accordion) [2017/18 c108, h108: c15.7g^3 h20g^2 c20.3g^{pu} h19m^{pu} Nov 1] lengthy, useful-looking gelding: fair handicap hurdler: fair form over fences: stays 2½m: acts on good to firm and good to soft going: has worn headgear, including usually in 2017/18: in tongue tie last 3 starts. *Robert Stephens* **c108 h103**

YES TOM (IRE) 13 gr.g. Tikkanen (USA) – Ammieanne (IRE) (Zaffaran (USA)) [2017/18 c133, h–: c24.9s^{pu} c20m^{bd} c23.8g^6 c16d^6 c19.2g Aug 28] lengthy gelding: maiden pointer: winning hurdler: useful chaser at best, no form in 2017/18: has worn headgear, including in 2017/18: tried in tongue tie. *Stuart Crawford, Ireland* **c– h–**

YOREDOINGWELL (IRE) 5 b.g. Mount Nelson – Local Abbey (IRE) (Primo Dominie) [2017/18 b16.8g^6 b16.2g b16.7g Aug 6] no form in bumpers: tried in blinkers. *Andrew Crook* **b–**

YORGONNAHEARMEROAR (IRE) 7 b.g. Scorpion (IRE) – Etoile Margot (FR) (Garde Royale) [2017/18 h115, b72: c15.9s c16s^{pu} h19.5s^4 c18.9s* Jan 16] fair handicap hurdler: fair form over fences: won handicap at Hereford in January: stays 19f: acts on heavy going: usually wears headgear: often races prominently. *Henry Oliver* **c113 h109**

YORKHILL (IRE) 8 ch.g. Presenting – Lightning Breeze (IRE) (Saddlers' Hall (IRE)) [2017/18 c161p, h–: c24d c17s^6 h16.4s^{pu} h24d Apr 26] rangy gelding: high-class hurdler/chaser at best, very disappointing in 2017/18: stays 21f. *W. P. Mullins, Ireland* **c– h–**

YORKIST (IRE) 10 ch.g. Urban Ocean (FR) – Kilbarry Demon (IRE) (Bob's Return (IRE)) [2017/18 c133, h–: c19.4g^2 c19.2g^3 May 21] workmanlike gelding: winning hurdler: useful handicap chaser: second at Stratford (4½ lengths behind Days of Heaven) in May: stays 19f: acts on good to firm and heavy going: has worn headgear/tongue tie: usually travels strongly. *Dan Skelton* **c133 h–**

YORKSHIRE MONARCH (IRE) 7 b.g. Montjeu (IRE) – Inkling (USA) (Seeking The Gold (USA)) [2017/18 h16.7d Oct 4] little show on Flat: tailed off in novice on hurdling debut. *Sarah Hollinshead* **h–**

YORKSHIRE STAR (IRE) 4 ch.g. Fast Company (IRE) – March Star (IRE) (Mac's Imp (USA)) [2017/18 h16.3m^4 h16.8d^4 h15.8m^4 h15.9d^{pu} Oct 23] poor maiden on Flat: modest form over hurdles: in cheekpieces last 2 starts. *Bill Turner* **h91**

YOUCANTCALLHERTHAT (IRE) 7 b.m. Brian Boru – Fruitful Venture (IRE) (Fruits of Love (USA)) [2017/18 c18g^2 c20s^F c21v* c20s* c19.5v c20v^3 c16v^4 c24.1s* c22.5v* c20s* c24.5s^6 Apr 24] first foal: dam (b89) bumper winner: maiden hurdler: useful chaser: won maiden at Cork in November, mares handicap at Fairyhouse in December, mares novice at Thurles in February, Grade 2 mares novice at Limerick (by ½ length from Dinaria des Obeaux) in March and Grade 3 mares event at Fairyhouse (by 6 lengths from Asthuria) in April: stays 3m: raced mainly on soft/heavy going: tried in cheekpieces. *Denis Hogan, Ireland* **c141 h–**

YOUKNOWELL (IRE) 5 b.m. Gold Well – Islands Sister (IRE) (Turtle Island (IRE)) [2017/18 h15.7g^F h20.7s h16.7s^6 h15.7v Mar 29] £8,000 3-y-o, £52,000 4-y-o: first foal: half-sister to bumper winner/fairly useful hurdler Tuzo (23f winner, by Flemensfirth): dam unraced sister to fairly useful hurdler/chaser (stayed 21f) Island Life: runner-up on second of 2 starts in Irish points: no form over hurdles. *Paul Webber* **h–**

YOU NEVER KNOW 7 ch.m. Apple Tree (FR) – Capricorn Princess (Nicholas Bill) [2017/18 b16.7v^4 Dec 15] third foal: dam (c80/h114), 2m/17f hurdle winner, half-sister to useful hurdler/high-class chaser (2m-27f winner) Midnight Chase: tailed off in bumper. *Claire Dyson* **b–**

YOU

YOUNG CHEDDAR (IRE) 11 b.m. Croco Rouge (IRE) – Sin Ceist Eile (IRE) (Simply Great (FR)) [2017/18 c–, h–: c25.5m⁴ Jun 15] smallish mare: maiden pointer/hurdler: fair hunter chaser at best: stays 3¼m: acts on heavy going: tried in tongue tie. *Robin Dickin* — c93 h–

YOUNG DILLON (IRE) 9 b.g. Vinnie Roe (IRE) – Rongai (IRE) (Commanche Run) [2017/18 h131: h22.8m c23g³ c24g³ h25.8g² h26.5g^pu Oct 13] useful handicap hurdler: second at Fontwell in October: well held in novice chases: placed in points in 2018: stays 3¼m: acts on soft going: wears headgear: front runner/races prominently. *Dr Richard Newland* — c– h129

YOUNG HURRICANE (IRE) 12 b.g. Oscar (IRE) – Georgia On My Mind (FR) (Belmez (USA)) [2017/18 c111, h–: c26.2g* c27.5d* c26.3v^pu Mar 16] multiple winning pointer: winning hurdler: fairly useful chaser: won hunter at Kelso in May and Stratford Champion Hunters' Chase (by 2 lengths from Balnaslow) in June: stays 3½m: acts on heavy going: has worn blinkers/tongue tie: often races towards rear/travels strongly. *G. C. Brewer* — c126 h–

YOUNG LOU 9 b.m. Kadastrof (FR) – Wanna Shout (Missed Flight) [2017/18 h89: h24s h23.1v^pu h24v⁶ h26v* Mar 28] modest handicap hurdler: won at Warwick in March: stays 3¼m: acts on heavy going: usually wears headgear: tried in tongue tie: usually races close up. *Robin Dickin* — h93

YOUNGOCONNOR (IRE) 5 b.m. Kalanisi (IRE) – Strike Three (IRE) (Presenting) [2017/18 h16.5v⁵ h19s^bd h16.2v⁵ h21.6s⁵ Apr 23] second foal: half-sister to a winning pointer by Court Cave: dam (h96) lightly raced in bumpers/over hurdles: placed both completed starts in Irish points: poor form over hurdles. *Christian Williams* — h66

YOUNG PHOENIX (IRE) 6 b.g. Robin des Pres (FR) – Lady Phoenix (IRE) (Erins Isle) [2017/18 h16.3d³ h18.5d h25.5g³ h21.2v h26.4d⁶ Apr 22] €4,000 3-y-o, £1,000 4-y-o: second foal: dam, maiden pointer, sister to fair hurdler/fairly useful chaser (stayed 21f) Compostello: third in bumper at Stratford: modest form over hurdles: tried in cheekpieces. *Martin Keighley* — h95 b81

YOUNG SUNSHINE (IRE) 5 b.m. Pour Moi (IRE) – Garra Molly (IRE) (Nayef (USA)) [2017/18 b16.7g b15.7g⁵ Jul 16] third foal: half-sister to 2 winners on Flat, including useful 7f/1m performer Molly Dolly (by Exceed And Excel): dam maiden on Flat (stayed 1¾m): poor form in bumpers. *Sally Haynes* — b64

YOUNG TOM 5 b.g. Sir Percy – Enford Princess (Pivotal) [2017/18 h15.7d⁴ h15.7d⁵ h19.3v⁶ h15.7s² h15.7s Apr 8] fair on Flat, stays 1½m: modest form over hurdles: has joined Mandy Rowland. *Sue Smith* — h98

YOUNOSO 7 b.g. Alflora (IRE) – Teeno Nell (Teenoso (USA)) [2017/18 b16.8s h20.6s^pu h19.3s h19.7v h19.7v h20.6v Apr 14] of no account. *Tina Jackson* — h– b–

YOUNOYOUNOYOUNO 5 b.g. Overbury (IRE) – Ceiriog Valley (In The Wings) [2017/18 b16v h19.3d⁴ h24v^pu Apr 15] sixth foal: dam, ran once over hurdles, 7f-1½m winner on Flat: well beaten in bumper: poor form over hurdles: better effort when fourth in novice at Carlisle in March. *Iain Jardine* — h83 b–

YOU RAISED ME UP (IRE) 5 b.g. Presenting – Morning Supreme (IRE) (Supreme Leader) [2017/18 ab16g³ b18s⁴ Apr 27] €45,000 3-y-o: first foal: dam (c130/h133), 2m-2½m hurdle/chase winner, half-sister to useful hurdler (stayed 2¼m) Morning Run: fairly useful form in bumpers: best effort when fourth in maiden at Punchestown in April: will be suited by further than 2¼m: in tongue tie last 2 starts. *Martin Brassil, Ireland* — b103

YOU'RE A LADY 6 b.m. Midnight Legend – Pulling Strings (Accordion) [2017/18 b–: b15.7m² b16s⁵ b15.8d Jun 7] modest form in bumpers, standout effort when second in mares event at Towcester: refused early in point in 2018: tried in tongue tie. *Kim Bailey* — b82

YOU'RE SO RIGHT (IRE) 5 b.g. Presenting – Miss Brandywell (IRE) (Sadler's Wells (USA)) [2017/18 b15.7g³ h21d h21.2v^pu h21m⁶ Apr 26] €65,000 3-y-o: seventh foal: half-brother to fairly useful hurdler/useful chaser Killer Miller (19f-21f winner, by Flemensfirth): dam unraced sister to fairly useful hurdler/very smart chaser (stayed 3½m) Cane Brake and fairly useful hurdler/useful chaser (stayed 3m) Bob Hall: third in maiden bumper at Southwell: poor form over hurdles. *Jonjo O'Neill* — h81 b78

YOURHOLIDAYISOVER (IRE) 11 ch.g. Sulamani (IRE) – Whitehaven (Top Ville) [2017/18 c87§, h70§: h16d⁶ c15.7d² c17.3s² h17.2d⁶ c16d⁶ h16.3g⁶ h16d⁵ c16v³ c16.3s² c16.1s⁴ h16v³ c15.7v⁶ c17.2v⁴ c17s Apr 15] rather leggy gelding: poor handicap hurdler: modest handicap chaser: stays 2½m: acts on heavy going: wears headgear/tongue tie: often races towards rear: irresolute. *Tom Gretton* — c89 § h69 §

905

YOU

YOUR PREFERENCE 9 b.g. Dolpour – Royal Reference (Royal Fountain) [2017/18 h–: h20.1g^{pu} h20.2m^{pu} Jun 4] no form, including in points: tried in cheekpieces. *Lisa Harrison* — **h–**

YOUR TURN (IRE) 7 b.m. Milan – Pop Princess (Compton Place) [2017/18 h95: h19.2g^3 May 15] third on completed start in Irish points: maiden hurdler, modest at best: has worn headgear: tried in tongue tie. *Tom Gretton* — **h61**

YOUR WAN (IRE) 5 b.m. Galileo (IRE) – Mayasta (IRE) (Bob Back (USA)) [2017/18 b16.3s^4 h15.7g h16.6s h16.6s^3 h20.7s Mar 14] closely related to 2 winners by Sadler's Wells, notably Cheltenham Gold Cup winner Synchronised (stayed 33f), and half-sister to useful hurdler Cross The Flags (21f/2¾m winner, by Flemensfirth): dam (c106/h139), 2m-2½m hurdle/chase winner, also 1¼m-13f winner on Flat: fourth in mares bumper at Stratford: modest form over hurdles. *Jonjo O'Neill* — **h88 b85**

YOU SAY WHAT (IRE) 8 b.g. Milan – Wave Back (IRE) (Bob Back (USA)) [2017/18 c–, h109: c24.2v^5 c24.2v* c30.7v^2 c24.2v^{pu} c23.4s^{pu} Jan 17] workmanlike gelding: winning hurdler: fairly useful handicap chaser: won at Exeter in November: stays 31f: best form on soft/heavy going: wears cheekpieces/tongue tie nowadays: often travels strongly. *David Pipe* — **c128 h–**

YUKON DELTA (IRE) 11 ch.g. Old Vic – Red Fern (IRE) (Mister Lord (USA)) [2017/18 c97§, h96§: h21.6g h21.6d^5 h25.6d^6 h19.2v^4 h20.5v h25s Apr 15] modest handicap hurdler: winning chaser: stays 3¼m: acts on heavy going: usually wears headgear: temperamental. *Gary Moore* — **c– § h85 §**

YUR NEXT (IRE) 10 br.m. Definite Article – Listen Up (Good Thyne (USA)) [2017/18 h103: h20.3g h16.7g h23.1g h23.3g Sep 13] Irish point winner: fair hurdler at best, no form in 2017/18: stays 3m: has worn blinkers/tongue tie, including in 2017/18. *Johnny Farrelly* — **h–**

Z

ZABANA (IRE) 9 ch.g. Halling (USA) – Gandia (IRE) (Danehill (USA)) [2017/18 c161, h–: c25d^5 c24s^3 c24d^F Dec 28] well-made gelding: winning hurdler: very smart chaser at best: third in JNwine.com Champion Chase at Down Royal (14½ lengths behind Outlander) in November: fell fatally in Leopardstown Christmas Chase: stayed 25f: acted on good to firm and heavy going: in tongue tie last 3 starts: often raced prominently. *Andrew Lynch, Ireland* — **c149 h–**

ZAIDIYN (FR) 8 b.g. Zamindar (USA) – Zainta (IRE) (Kahyasi) [2017/18 h19.7s^5 h16.8v Jan 27] good-topped gelding: useful handicap hurdler at best: fell only chase start: raced mainly around 2m: acts on heavy going: has worn headgear. *Brian Ellison* — **c– h124**

ZAKHAROVA 4 ch.f. Beat Hollow – Tcherina (IRE) (Danehill Dancer (IRE)) [2017/18 b15.6d* b17s Apr 12] rather unfurnished filly: third foal: half-sister to bumper winner/fairly useful hurdler Balmusette (19f-3m winner) and bumper winner Tolethorpe (both by Halling): dam (h85), lightly raced over hurdles, 1m-1½m winner on Flat: fair form in bumpers: won maiden event at Musselburgh in February. *Laura Morgan* — **b94**

ZALGARRY (FR) 11 b.g. Ballingarry (IRE) – Spleen (FR) (Sillery (USA)) [2017/18 c–, h116: c20.9v^4 c19.4v^4 Dec 9] fairly useful hurdler: fair form over fences: stays 3m: acts on good to firm and heavy going: tried in cheekpieces: often races towards rear. *Arthur Whitehead* — **c103 h–**

ZALVADOS (FR) 5 ch.g. Soldier of Fortune (IRE) – Zariyana (IRE) (Desert Prince (IRE)) [2017/18 h118: h20g^5 h16.7g^2 h16.4d^4 h18.9v^2 h15.8s* h16.3v h15.8d^2 Apr 24] rather sparely-made gelding: fairly useful hurdler: won maiden at Ludlow in January: stays 19f: acts on heavy going: often in headgear: wears tongue tie: often races towards rear/travels strongly. *Oliver Greenall* — **h124**

ZAMALIGHT 4 ch.f. Zamindar (USA) – Mountain Chain (USA) (Royal Academy (USA)) [2017/18 h16s h16v h16v^6 Mar 28] fair maiden on Flat, stays 1¼m: no form over hurdles: tried in hood. *Olly Murphy* — **h–**

ZAMARKHAN (FR) 5 b.g. Great Journey (JPN) – Zannkiya (Sendawar (IRE)) [2017/18 b73: b16.2g^5 h16.2g Oct 28] pulled up in point: placed on first start in bumpers: well beaten on hurdling debut. *Lucy Normile* — **h– b–**

ZAMA ZAMA 11 b.g. Sakhee (USA) – Insinuation (IRE) (Danehill (USA)) [2017/18 c96, h–: c20g^{pu} c22.6m^{pu} Jul 16] good-topped gelding: winning hurdler: fair chaser at best, no form in 2017/18: stays 25f: acts on good to firm and heavy going: usually wears headgear: tried in tongue tie: temperamental. *Evan Williams* — **c– § h–**

ZEE

ZAMBEZI TIGER (IRE) 9 b.g. Tiger Hill (IRE) – Johannesburg Cat (USA) (Johannesburg (USA)) [2017/18 h24g^F h20.2s Apr 27] little form over hurdles: left Garry Bernard Caldwell after first start: tried in hood/tongue tie. *Hugh Burns* — h–

ZAMDY MAN 9 b.g. Authorized (IRE) – Lauderdale (GER) (Nebos (GER)) [2017/18 c143, h–: c19.4s^5 Nov 3] strong, good-topped gelding: winning hurdler: useful chaser, well held sole outing in 2017/18: unproven beyond 2m: acts on heavy going. *Venetia Williams* — c– h–

ZAMOYSKI 8 ch.g. Dutch Art – Speech (Red Ransom (USA)) [2017/18 h89: h23.3d^6 h20.3g* h20.3d* Oct 3] fair handicap hurdler: won at Southwell in September and October: stays 2½m: acts on soft going: wears cheekpieces. *Steve Gollings* — h104

ZAMPARELLI (IRE) 6 b.g. Mahler – Goulburn Bridge (IRE) (Rock Hopper) [2017/18 h97: h15.3s^5 c15.7v^3 h24.1d^6 c19.4d* Apr 22] workmanlike gelding: has had breathing operation: maiden hurdler, modest form at best: fair form over fences: won novice handicap at Stratford in April: stays 3m: acts on heavy going: tried in cheekpieces: wears tongue tie: often races towards rear: open to further improvement as a chaser. *Dan Skelton* — c111 p h76

ZAMPERINI (IRE) 6 ch.g. Fast Company (IRE) – Lucky Date (IRE) (Halling (USA)) [2017/18 h17.7g^3 Aug 24] fairly useful on Flat, stays 11.5f: 5/2, third in novice at Fontwell (15 lengths behind Jackback) on hurdling debut. *Mike Murphy* — h80

ZANSTRA (IRE) 8 b.g. Morozov (USA) – Enistar (IRE) (Synefos (USA)) [2017/18 c118, h–: h22s c24.2s^{ur} h23.6v^3 h23.1s^2 h23.1v c23.6v^2 Apr 14] lengthy gelding: fairly useful handicap hurdler: fair maiden chaser: stays 3m: acts on heavy going: tried in blinkers/tongue tie. *Colin Tizzard* — c109 h115

ZANTE (FR) 6 ch.g. Zanzibari (USA) – Calling All Angels (FR) (Ange Gabriel (FR)) [2017/18 h100: h16g h17.7d May 28] angular gelding: fair hurdler at best, no form in 2017/18: unproven beyond 2m: acts on good to soft going: in cheekpieces last 3 starts: often races prominently. *Gary Moore* — h–

ZARA'S REFLECTION 5 b.m. Midnight Legend – Twoy's Reflection (Presenting) [2017/18 h15.7m^5 b16.7s b15.7g b15.7d h15.7v h19s Feb 23] first foal: dam unraced: poor form in bumpers: no form over hurdles: tried in hood: in tongue tie last 3 starts. *Ben Case* — h– b73

ZARIB (IRE) 7 b.g. Azamour (IRE) – Zariziyna (IRE) (Dalakhani (IRE)) [2017/18 c131, h131: h20.1g^4 c19.4s^4 c15.2s^5 Jan 13] lengthy gelding: useful hurdler/chaser, below form in 2017/18: stays 21f: acts on good to firm and heavy going: has worn headgear/tongue tie. *Dianne Sayer* — c98 h118

ZARKANDAR (IRE) 11 b.g. Azamour (IRE) – Zarkasha (IRE) (Kahyasi) [2017/18 h147: h22.8v^{pu} h22.8v^4 Feb 17] rather leggy gelding: top-class hurdler at best: stayed 25f: acted on heavy going: wore headgear/tongue tie: retired. *Paul Nicholls* — h125

ZARLIMAN (IRE) 8 ch.g. Zamindar (USA) – Zarlana (IRE) (Darshaan) [2017/18 h78: h15.9d^6 Dec 4] little form over hurdles: wears cheekpieces: has worn tongue tie. *Roger Ingram* — h–

ZAROCCO 5 b.m. Shirocco (GER) – Zariyka (IRE) (Kalanisi (IRE)) [2017/18 b71p: b16.8g Apr 19] placed on first of 2 starts in bumpers. *Tom Lacey* — b–

ZARU (FR) 12 b.g. Laveron – Zianini (FR) (Dom Pasquini (FR)) [2017/18 c113, h90: h22.7g^6 May 10] strong gelding: one-time fairly useful hurdler/chaser, below best since 2013/14: stays 3m: acts on heavy going: wears cheekpieces. *James Ewart* — c– h–

ZAYDANIDES (FR) 6 bl.g. American Post – Ouarzazate (IRE) (Enrique) [2017/18 b16.5g b13.7s^4 b16d Apr 26] good-topped gelding: third foal: dam French 1¼m winner: fair form in bumpers. *Tim Pinfield* — b91

ZAYFIRE ARAMIS 9 ch.g. Zafeen (FR) – Kaylifa Aramis (Kayf Tara) [2017/18 c103, h–: c20.3d^4 c20g^4 c20d^3 c20.2v^{ur} c20.2s* c19.9s^3 c20s^4 Apr 8] lengthy, angular gelding: maiden hurdler: fair handicap chaser: won at Leicester in January: stays 2½m: acts on heavy going: often travels strongly. *Michael Scudamore* — c108 h–

ZEBI BOY 7 b.g. Multiplex – Atlantic Jane (Tamure (IRE)) [2017/18 h21.2s^{pu} h15.8v h21s h19s h20.6s Mar 26] no form over hurdles. *Dan Skelton* — h–

ZEE MAN (FR) 4 b.g. Soldier of Fortune (IRE) – Sky High Flyer (Anabaa (USA)) [2017/18 b16.2s^3 b16s^5 b15.3v^2 b16d Apr 26] tall, unfurnished gelding: fifth foal: half-brother to French 10.5f winner Sainte Suzanne (by Speightstown): dam, useful 6f-8.5f winner, half-sister to useful hurdler (stayed 21f) Dansimar: fair form in bumpers. *David Dennis* — b85

ZEN

ZENAFIRE 9 b.g. Firebreak – Zen Garden (Alzao (USA)) [2017/18 h112: h16.7s* h17v⁵ Oct 26] compact gelding: fair handicap hurdler: won at Bangor in May: likely to stay beyond 2m: acts on soft going: often races towards rear. *Sarah Hollinshead* — **h104**

ZEN MASTER (IRE) 6 b.g. Shantou (USA) – Back Log (IRE) (Bob Back (USA)) [2017/18 h15.7d³ h16.7g* h16d h15.5s⁶ h15.9d⁵ h19s² h20.6v Apr 11] €50,000 3-y-o: seventh foal: brother to 3 winners, including bumper winner/fairly useful hurdler Touch Back (2¼m-3m winner): dam 1¼m winner: fair hurdler: won maiden at Market Rasen in October: stays 19f: acts on soft going: usually wears hood. *Charlie Mann* — **h109**

ZEPHYR 7 ch.g. Shirocco (GER) – Pelagia (IRE) (Lycius (USA)) [2017/18 h100: h23.3g^pu h26.5d h27g* Sep 7] sturdy gelding: point winner: fair handicap hurdler: won at Sedgefield in September: stays 27f: acts on good to firm and heavy going: has worn headgear, including in 2017/18. *Nick Williams* — **h105**

ZEPHYROS BLEU (IRE) 8 b.g. Westerner – Quel Bleu (IRE) (Tel Quel (FR)) [2017/18 c124, h–: c24.2s c26.1v^F Nov 26] maiden hurdler: fairly useful chaser: stays 3m: best form on heavy going: wears cheekpieces. *Harry Whittington* — **c110 h–**

ZEPHYROS (GER) 7 br.g. Areion (GER) – Zandra (GER) (Lagunas (GER)) [2017/18 h103: h16g⁴ h16.3g⁶ Jul 4] fair on Flat: modest form over hurdles: tried in hood. *David Bridgwater* — **h95**

ZERACHIEL (IRE) 8 b.g. Winged Love (IRE) – At Dawn (IRE) (Lashkari) [2017/18 c112, h108: c25.5d² c30.7v^pu c29.6v² c29.2v⁴ c28.4v* Mar 31] sturdy gelding: maiden hurdler: fairly useful handicap chaser: won at Haydock in March: stays 3¾m: acts on heavy going: wears headgear: often races prominently. *Ian Williams* — **c117 h–**

ZEROESHADESOFGREY (IRE) 9 gr.g. Portrait Gallery (IRE) – Hazy Rose (IRE) (Roselier (FR)) [2017/18 c131, h–: h19.7s⁵ h23.3v⁶ h21.4v³ h19.3v² h16s⁴ h22.8v c23.8v⁴ Apr 15] big, workmanlike gelding: has had breathing operation: fairly useful handicap hurdler: winning chaser: stays 3m: acts on heavy going: has worn headgear, including last 5 starts: tried in tongue tie: usually leads: no battler. *Neil King* — **c113 § h126 §**

ZERO GRAND (IRE) 7 b.g. Thousand Words – Ellistown Lady (IRE) (Red Sunset) [2017/18 h125: h24d h21.4v^pu h21.4s^ur h21.4v Apr 9] fairly useful handicap hurdler: stays 3¼m: acts on heavy going. *Johnny Farrelly* — **h117**

ZIGGER ZAGGER (IRE) 9 b.g. Mountain High (IRE) – Main Suspect (IRE) (Be My Native (USA)) [2017/18 c92x, h–x: c22.7d⁴ c20.2s⁶ Jan 11] workmanlike gelding: maiden hurdler: modest maiden chaser: stays 2½m: acts on soft going: has worn hood: usually races in rear: often let down by jumping. *Richard Rowe* — **c88 x h– x**

ZIG ZAG (IRE) 5 b.g. Zoffany (IRE) – Le Montrachet (Nashwan (USA)) [2017/18 h118: h19.4g² h16.5m² h19.5d⁶ h16g h20.5g⁴ h20.2g h19.9d² Sep 24] compact gelding: fairly useful handicap hurdler: left Joseph Patrick O'Brien after sixth start: stays 2½m: acts on soft going: tried in cheekpieces: often wears tongue tie: usually races towards rear. *Philip Kirby* — **h122**

ZILLA 4 ch.f. Zamindar (USA) – Caesarea (GER) (Generous (IRE)) [2017/18 b13.1g^ur b14d Nov 5] 3,000 3-y-o: sister to smart 1¼m-1½m winner Corriolanus and half-sister to several winners, including fairly useful hurdler Ashbrittle (2m-21f winner, by Rainbow Quest): dam German 11f/1½m winner: well held completed start in bumpers. *John Wainwright* — **b–**

ZILLION (IRE) 4 b.g. Zebedee – Redelusion (IRE) (Hernando (FR)) [2017/18 h16d h16.8s⁵ Apr 23] down the field in 2 maidens on Flat: no form over hurdles. *Susan Gardner* — **h–**

ZIPPLE BACK (IRE) 6 b.g. Sendawar (IRE) – With Conviction (IRE) (Barathea (IRE)) [2017/18 h114: h18.7g* h19.9d* h19.6s^pu Feb 8] fairly useful hurdler: won novices at Stratford and Uttoxeter in May: left Alan King after second start: stayed 2½m: acted on good to soft going: in hood last 3 starts: tried in tongue tie: dead. *Harry Fry* — **h121**

ZOLFO (IRE) 6 gr.g. Cloudings (IRE) – Hardy Lamb (IRE) (Witness Box (USA)) [2017/18 h82: c19.3g³ c20.3d^F c22.5g^F c20g⁶ c17.4g⁴ Aug 4] big, rangy gelding: maiden hurdler: modest form over fences: should prove suited by further than 2½m. *Jennie Candlish* — **c93 h–**

ZOLTAN VARGA 4 b.g. Sayif (IRE) – Mar Blue (FR) (Marju (IRE)) [2017/18 b13.7g⁶ b14d b13d⁴ b16.2s⁴ h15.8s h16.7s⁴ h16.5v h21.2d⁴ Apr 24] half-brother to bumper winner/fair hurdler Mr Kite (2m winner, by Sixties Icon) and fair hurdler The Blue Bomber (17f winner, by Stimulation): dam 9f winner: modest form in bumpers/over hurdles: tried in hood. *Mick Channon* — **h91 b84**

ZUBAYR (IRE) 6 b.g. Authorized (IRE) – Zaziyra (IRE) (Dalakhani (IRE)) [2017/18 h138: h15.7m⁵ h15.3s⁶ h16s ab16d² h21s² h20s h19.8s Apr 28] neat gelding: useful handicap hurdler: second at Kempton (2¼ lengths behind Kildisart) in March: stays 21f: acts on soft going. *Paul Nicholls* — **h137**

ZYO

ZULU OSCAR 9 b.g. Oscar (IRE) – Loxhill Lady (Supreme Leader) [2017/18 h129: h15.7m h16d h16s h19.4d h18.5v⁴ h15.7s h19.8d⁵ Apr 22] well-made gelding: fairly useful hurdler, largely out of sorts in 2017/18: stays 2¾m: acts on soft going: tried in blinkers: has worn tongue tie. *Jeremy Scott*   **h108**

ZYON 4 gr.g. Martaline – Temptation (FR) (Lando (GER)) [2017/18 b15.3d Apr 22] green, well held in bumper. *Paul Nicholls*   **b–**

PROMISING HORSES

Selected British- and Irish-trained horses in *Chasers & Hurdlers* thought capable of noteworthy improvement are listed under the trainers for whom they last ran.

N. W. ALEXANDER
Off The Hook (IRE) 6 b.m h104p

G. T. H. BAILEY
Thomas Shelby (IRE) 7 b.g c103p

KIM BAILEY
Cloone Lady (IRE) 6 b.m h113p
Diva Reconce (FR) 5 b.m h105p
Red River (IRE) 5 ch.g h139p
Vinndication (IRE) 5 b.g h146p b96
Wandrin Star (IRE) 7 b.g h80p c113

RALPH BECKETT
Dolphin Vista (IRE) 5 b.g h102p

SUZI BEST
Six Gun Serenade (IRE) 7 b.g h104p

GILLIAN BOANAS
Crixus's Escape (IRE) 5 ch.g h121p
Just Call Me Al (IRE) 5 br.g b90p
Penny Blak 5 ch.g b89p

MARK BRADSTOCK
Step Back (IRE) 8 ch.g c146p

DAVID BRIDGWATER
Cohesion 5 b.g h99p
Dame du Soir (FR) 5 br.m h98p
The Tin Miner (IRE) 7 br.g c109p

HENRY DE BROMHEAD, IRELAND
Monalee (IRE) 7 b.g c157p
Twobeelucky 5 b.g h134p

LADY SUSAN BROOKE
Starcrossed 6 b.g h119p

DAI BURCHELL
Tyrolean 5 b.g h73p

CHARLES BYRNES, IRELAND
Off You Go (IRE) 5 b.g h131p

BEN CASE
Kings Temptation 6 b.g h104 c103p

MICK CHANNON
Mister Whitaker (IRE) 6 b.g c146p

REBECCA CURTIS
Geordie des Champs (IRE) 7 br.g c135p
Sunset Showdown (IRE) 5 b.g h119p b93

KEITH DALGLEISH
One Night In Milan (IRE) 5 b.g h82p b76
Senor Lombardy (IRE) 5 b.g h131p b103
The Vocalist 6 b.m h115p

HENRY DALY
Back To The Thatch (IRE) 6 b.g c127p
Honest Vic (IRE) 5 b.g h122p b90

JO DAVIS
Ken's Well (IRE) 7 b.g h108p c100p b95

DAVID DENNIS
Brunel Woods (IRE) 6 b.g h85p
Schnabel (IRE) 6 b.g h106p

ROSE DOBBIN
Planet Nine (IRE) 6 b.g h122p

SEAN THOMAS DOYLE, IRELAND
Crosshue Boy (IRE) 8 b.g h122 c141p

J. T. R. DREAPER, IRELAND
Mullaghmurphy Blue (IRE) 7 br.g h95p c110

SAMUEL DRINKWATER
Maximus Maridius 7 br.g h105 c96p
Russian Service 6 b.g h102 c107p

MICHAEL EASTERBY
Albert's Back 4 b.g h128p

STUART EDMUNDS
Klare Castle 6 b.g h99p b100

GORDON ELLIOTT, IRELAND
Commander of Fleet (IRE) 4 b.g h107p
Cracking Smart (FR) 6 b. or br.g h150p
Flawless Escape 5 gr.g h131p b99
Master of Tara (FR) 5 b.g h106p
Minellafordollars (IRE) 6 b.g h129p
Monbeg Worldwide (IRE) 6 b.g h130p
Samcro (IRE) 6 ch.g h163p
Sutton Place (IRE) 7 b.g c145p
Veinard (FR) 9 ch.g h125 c127p

BRIAN ELLISON
Bowban 4 b.c h58p
Snookered (IRE) 4 b.g h62p
Tomngerry (IRE) 8 b.g h132 c108p
Windsor Avenue (IRE) 6 b.g b104p

DAVID ELSWORTH
Miss Heritage (IRE) 4 b.f b95p

SAM ENGLAND
Ask Paddy (IRE) 6 ch.g c103p

P. A. FAHY, IRELAND
Castlegrace Paddy (IRE) 7 b.g c145p
Dunvegan (FR) 5 gr.g h122p b112

ALAN FLEMING, IRELAND
Product of Love (IRE) 7 b.g h118 c133p

PAUL W. FLYNN, IRELAND
Sally Park (IRE) 7 b.g h100p b106

HARRY FRY
Acting Lass (IRE) 7 b.g c149p
Chalonnial (FR) 6 ch.g c124P
If The Cap Fits (IRE) 6 b.g h149p
Samarquand 6 b. or br.g h103p

TOM GEORGE
Boyhood (IRE) 7 b.g h135p
Cuirassier Dempire (FR) 6 ch.g c134p
Drill Baby Drill 7 b.m h92p
Espoir de Teiliee (FR) 6 b.g h124p
Forgot To Ask (IRE) 6 b.g h109p
Mzuzu (IRE) 6 b.g h117p b66p
Seddon (IRE) 5 b.g h107p
Strike In Milan (IRE) 6 b.g h84p
Summerville Boy (IRE) 6 b.g h156p b98

CHRIS GORDON
Telegraph Place (IRE) 5 br.g h99p
CHRIS GRANT
Colby (IRE) 5 b.g h101p b90
Jacks Last Hope 9 b.g h139 c115p
WARREN GREATREX
Another Emotion (FR) 6 gr.g h113p
Don des Fosses (FR) 5 b.g h71p b94
The Butcher Said (IRE) 5 b.g h80p b91
ALEX HALES
Quarry Leader (IRE) 7 b.g h112p
Royal Sunday (FR) 4 gr.g h108p
Shazzamataz (IRE) 6 br.m h104p
ANN HAMILTON
Nuts Well 7 b.g c132p
MRS WENDY HAMILTON
Diamond Brig 6 b.g c107p
NIGEL HAWKE
Pearl Royale (IRE) 6 b.m c136p
NICKY HENDERSON
Casablanca Mix (FR) 6 ch.m c141p
Champ (IRE) 6 b.g h134p
Dame de Compagnie (FR) 5 b.m h131p
Diese des Bieffes (FR) 5 gr.g h136p
Divine Spear (IRE) 7 b.g c143p
Du Destin (FR) 5 gr.g h73p
Fixe Le Kap (FR) 6 gr.g h138 c126p
French Crusader (FR) 5 b.g h122p b95
Lust For Glory (IRE) 5 b.m b86p
Rather Be (IRE) 7 b.g c152p
River Wylde (IRE) 7 b.g c140p
Settie Hill (USA) 5 b.g h128p
Soul Emotion (FR) 5 b.g h146p
Tell It To Me 6 b.m h73p b98
Terrefort (FR) 5 gr.g h124 c156p
The Bottom Bar (IRE) 6 br.g h122p b91
Turn Turk (IRE) 7 gr.m h116p
Turtle Wars (FR) 5 b.g h116p
We Have A Dream (FR) 4 b.g h150p
Whatswrongwithyou (IRE) 7 ch.g h128p
With Discretion (IRE) 7 b.m h128p
LAWNEY HILL
Clondaw Westie (IRE) 7 b.g h88 c122p
CHARLES HILLS
Grapevine (IRE) 5 b.g h106p
PHILIP HOBBS
Dostal Phil (FR) 5 b.g h107p
Festival Dawn 6 b.m h112p
For Good Measure (IRE) 7 b.g c132p
Gosheven (IRE) 5 b.g h125p b72
Horse Force One (IRE) 7 b.g h91p b96
Little Rory Mac (IRE) 4 b.g h91p
Longtown (IRE) 7 b.g c122p
Lord Duveen (IRE) 5 br.g h116p
No Comment 7 br.g c122P
Scoop The Pot (IRE) 8 b.g h126 c121p
Steely Addition (IRE) 6 b.g h128p
Strong Pursuit (IRE) 8 ch.g c139p
Turangi 6 b.g h109p
Umndeni (FR) 4 b. or br.g b101p

HENRY HOGARTH
Gris de Pron (FR) 5 b.g h79 c112p
ANTHONY HONEYBALL
My Dance 6 b.m h114p b78
Represented (IRE) 5 b.g h92p
Sam Brown 6 b.g h135p
SARAH HUMPHREY
Brecon Hill (IRE) 5 b.g h107p b102
IAIN JARDINE
L'Inganno Felice (FR) 8 br.g h109p
Tor 4 ch.g h86p
RUTH JEFFERSON
Temple Man 6 b.g h95p
Waiting Patiently (IRE) 7 b.g c168p
ALAN JONES
Duhallow Lad (IRE) 6 b.g h100 c114p
Pokari (FR) 6 ch.g h85p
PATRICK G. KELLY, IRELAND
Presenting Percy 7 b.g h152 c164p
JOHN E. KIELY, IRELAND
Dont Tell No One (IRE) 10 b.g c134p
ALAN KING
Ballywhim (FR) 4 b.g h121 c117p
Cosmeapolitan 5 b.g h119p
Deyrann de Carjac (FR) 5 b.g h119p b97
Dingo Dollar (IRE) 6 ch.g c147p
Dusky Legend 8 b.m h123 c143p
Full Glass (FR) 5 b.g h124 c141p
Kozier (GER) 4 ch.g h111p
Nobby 4 b.g b89p
Paddy Boss (IRE) 6 ch.g b99p
Potterman 5 b.g h113p b101
Stylish Moment (IRE) 5 b.g h106p b96
Tillythetank (IRE) 5 b.m h80p
Yesandno (IRE) 5 b.g h65p
TOM LACEY
Mary Eleanor 6 b.m h101p b86
Sebastopol (IRE) 4 b.g b101p
Thomas Patrick (IRE) 6 b.g h123 c147p
Triopas (IRE) 6 b.g h104 c110p
EMMA LAVELLE
Gunfleet (IRE) 6 b.g h130p
Majestic Moll (IRE) 6 b.m h112p
KERRY LEE
Matchaway (IRE) 9 b.g h117 c103p
SOPHIE LEECH
Samson 7 ch.g h102 c101p
CHARLIE LONGSDON
Ballydine (IRE) 8 ch.g c133p
Braddan Head 5 br.g h97p
Djarkevi (FR) 5 b.g h98p
Midnight Sonata (IRE) 4 b.g b90p
Stormy Milan (IRE) 5 b.g h102p b69
CHARLIE MANN
Ocean Jive 5 b.g h105p
DONALD MCCAIN
Gray Day (IRE) 7 gr.g c122p
Mount Mews (IRE) 7 b.g h138 c138p
O'Hanrahan Bridge (IRE) 6 b.g b94p

Spin The Coin (IRE) 5 b.g h105p
Swashbuckle 5 b.g h106p
The Great Getaway (IRE) 6 b.g h114p b76

JOHN MCCONNELL, IRELAND
Fred The Foot (IRE) 6 b.g h99p b98
Pearl of The West (IRE) 4 b.f h115p

OLIVER MCKIERNAN, IRELAND
All For Joy (IRE) 6 b.g h109p b106

DERMOT ANTHONY MCLOUGHLIN, IRELAND
Canardier (FR) 6 b.g h130p

NOEL MEADE, IRELAND
De Name Escapes Me (IRE) 8 ch.g h133 c112p
Dream Conti (FR) 5 br.g h107p

REBECCA MENZIES
All Hail Caesar (IRE) 4 b.g b86p
Ronn The Conn (IRE) 6 ch.g c113p

GARY MOORE
Age of Wisdom (IRE) 5 ch.g h66p
Altaayil (IRE) 7 br.g h83p
Benatar (IRE) 6 b.g c150p
Bridle Loanan (IRE) 5 b.g b77p
Iballisticvin 5 b.g h91p
Not Another Muddle 7 b.g c131p

M. F. MORRIS, IRELAND
Grotesque 7 b.g h114p

HUGHIE MORRISON
Apres Le Deluge (FR) 4 gr.g h91p
Brother Brian (IRE) 10 b.g c107p

NEIL MULHOLLAND
Better News 7 b.m h81p
Inaminna (IRE) 7 b.g h116p b68
Kalondra (IRE) 7 b.g c147p
Meribel Millie 7 b.m c83p
Milkwood (IRE) 4 b.g b86p
Mind Your Back (IRE) 5 b.g b84p
Neachells Bridge (IRE) 6 ch.g h108p b97
Niblawi (IRE) 6 b.g h123p

W. P. MULLINS, IRELAND
Bacardys (IRE) 7 b. or br.g h155 c136p
Bachasson (FR) 7 gr.g c159p
Benie des Dieux (FR) 7 b.m h151p c148P
Blazer (FR) 7 ch.g c137p
Brahma Bull (IRE) 7 ch.g h126p b111
Bunk Off Early (IRE) 6 ro.g h145 c138p
Cadmium (FR) 6 b.g c148p
Childrens List (IRE) 8 b.g c146p
Deal d'Estruval (FR) 5 b.g h134p
Footpad (FR) 6 b.g c174p
Great Field (FR) 7 b.g c170p
Kemboy (FR) 6 b.g c157p
Laurina (FR) 5 b.m h150p
Mystic Theatre (IRE) 7 b.m h135p b103
Next Destination (IRE) 6 b.g h151p
Patricks Park (IRE) 7 b.g h90 c141p
Pleasure Dome 5 b.m h105p
Stratum 5 b.g h131p
Tin Soldier (FR) 7 b.g c135p
Total Recall (IRE) 9 b.g h143p c163+
Turcagua (FR) 8 gr.g c133p

AMY MURPHY
Kalashnikov (IRE) 5 br.g h152p

OLLY MURPHY
Ballinslea Bridge (IRE) 6 b.g h125p b94p
Brewin'upastorm (IRE) 5 b.g b112p
General Bux 7 b.g h94p
Sangha River (IRE) 5 br.g b103p
The Very Thing (IRE) 4 b.g b84p
Weebill 6 b.g h116p b96

DR RICHARD NEWLAND
Capitoul (FR) 6 b.g h109 c126p
Competition 6 b.g h103p
Slim Pickens (IRE) 10 b.g h130 c118p

PAUL NICHOLLS
Bill And Barn (IRE) 7 br.g h111 c121p
Brio Conti (FR) 7 gr.g c129P
Chameron (FR) 5 b.g c132p
Danny Kirwan (IRE) 5 b.g b103P
Diamond Guy (FR) 5 b.g h115p
Diego du Charmil (FR) 5 b.g c155p
El Bandit (IRE) 7 b. or br.g c141p
Emerging Talent (IRE) 9 b.g c126p
Give Me A Copper (IRE) 8 ch.g c140p
Jessber's Dream (IRE) 8 b.m h135 c125p
Kapcorse (FR) 5 br.g h103 c125p
Magoo (IRE) 6 gr.g h121p
Master Tommytucker 7 b.g h129p
Rock On Oscar (IRE) 8 b.g c116p
Some Man (IRE) 5 b.g h109p
The Last But One (IRE) 6 b.g h96 c132p
Truckers Lodge (IRE) 6 b.g h111p
Worthy Farm (IRE) 5 b.g h113p

PAUL NOLAN, IRELAND
Fitzhenry (IRE) 6 b.g h121 c131p

FERGAL O'BRIEN
De Name Evades Me (IRE) 6 b.g h115p
Jarveys Plate (IRE) 5 ch.g b104p
Sissinghurst (IRE) 5 b.g h105p
Time To Move On (IRE) 5 ch.g b107p

JOSEPH PATRICK O'BRIEN, IRELAND
Lone Wolf (IRE) 5 b.g h126p b106
Los Alamos (IRE) 5 b.g h103p b111
Shady Operator (IRE) 5 b.g h135p
Speak Easy 5 b.g h141p

JONJO O'NEILL
Call To Order 8 b.g h118 c117p
Fleminport (IRE) 5 b.g h124p
For Instance (IRE) 8 b.g h119 c125p
Minotaur (IRE) 6 b.g h121p
Santiago de Cuba (IRE) 5 b.g h99p b110
Scottshill (IRE) 6 ch.g h83p b92

HENRY OLIVER
Megabucks (IRE) 7 b.g h108 c115p

JAMIE OSBORNE
Battalion (IRE) 8 b.g h114p

BEN PAULING
Brave Dancing 4 b.g h115 c101p
My Turgeon (FR) 5 gr.g b66p
Whin Park 6 b.g h102 c79p
Willoughby Court (IRE) 7 br.g c149p

C. C. PIMLOTT
Duhallow Tornado (IRE) 6 b.g c125p

DAVID PIPE
Buster Edwards (IRE) 5 b.g h104p
Crawfords Mill (IRE) 6 br.m h96 c96p
Mr Big Shot (IRE) 7 br.g h142p
Rod's Dream 5 ch.g b66p
Take The High Road 4 b.g h85p
Whitley Neill (IRE) 6 b.g h112p

BRENDAN POWELL
Ballyhome (IRE) 7 b.g h104p
Sea Sovereign (IRE) 5 b.g h91p

PIERCE MICHAEL POWER, IRELAND
Burning Ambition (IRE) 7 b.g c132p

ALASTAIR RALPH
Billingsley (IRE) 6 b.g h113p

PADRAIG ROCHE, IRELAND
Out of The Loop 5 b.g h136p

PHILIP ROWLEY
Hazel Hill (IRE) 10 b.g c116p

LUCINDA RUSSELL
Grand Morning 6 b.g h123p
Thepensionfund (IRE) 6 b.g h91p

OLIVER SHERWOOD
Dominateur (FR) 5 b.g b93p
Toviere (IRE) 7 ch.g h118 c130p

DAN SKELTON
Aintree My Dream (FR) 8 b. or br.g c132p
Anytime Will Do (IRE) 5 b.g b103p
Beakstown (IRE) 5 b.g b95p
Cosy Club (IRE) 4 br.g b101p
Elton des Mottes (FR) 4 b.g b91p
Etamine du Cochet (FR) 4 gr.f h103p
Ferrobin (FR) 4 br.g b87p
Finley's Eyes (IRE) 5 b.g b87p
Floki 4 b.g b86p
Idee de Garde (FR) 5 b.g b93p
Kereman (IRE) 4 b.g h94p
Must Havea Flutter (IRE) 6 b.g h93 c124p
New Quay (IRE) 5 b.g h112p
Not That Fuisse (FR) 5 b.g h107p
Present Ranger (IRE) 5 b.g h114p
Rebel Royal (IRE) 5 b.g h115p b76
Renwick (IRE) 5 b.g b80p
Robin Waters (FR) 5 b.g h140p
Stowaway Magic (IRE) 7 b.g h135 c132p
Zamparelli (IRE) 6 b.g h76 c111p

MATTHEW J. SMITH, IRELAND
Prince Garyantle (IRE) 8 b.g h134 c111p

SUE SMITH
Informateur (FR) 5 b.g h100p b87

JAMIE SNOWDEN
Alrightjack (IRE) 4 b.g b95p
Kalahari Queen 5 br.m h125p

RICHARD SPENCER
Movie Set (USA) 6 b. or br.g h115p

Thistimenextyear 4 gr.g h107p

JONATHAN SWEENEY, IRELAND
Lighthouse Warrier (IRE) 8 b.g h114p b105

TOM J. TAAFFE, IRELAND
Goose Man (IRE) 6 b.g h104 c132p

SAM THOMAS
Dancing Doug (IRE) 5 br.g h103p b87
Sparkleandshine (IRE) 5 b.g h113p

SANDY THOMSON
Caventara 6 b.g h115p

COLIN TIZZARD
Ainchea (IRE) 5 b.g h136p b104
Kings Walk (IRE) 7 b.g h120 c106p
The Russian Doyen (IRE) 5 b.g h123p b96
White Moon (GER) 6 gr.g h127p

NIGEL TWISTON-DAVIES
Ballymoy (IRE) 5 b.g h136p b92p
Chase Me (IRE) 7 b.g h81 c74p
Imperial Acolyte 4 b.g b64p
Imperial Nemesis (IRE) 5 b.g h104p b86
Luckofthedraw (FR) 5 gr.g h118p b95
One For Rosie 5 gr.g b100p

JOHN J. WALSH, IRELAND
Davids Charm (IRE) 7 b.g h137p

HARRY WHITTINGTON
Carole's Vigilante (IRE) 7 ch.g h110p
Court Liability (IRE) 5 b.g h120p b102
Djin Conti (FR) 5 b.g h99p
Jumbo Davis (IRE) 5 b.m b63p

CHRISTIAN WILLIAMS
Ebonys Encore (IRE) 6 b.m h96p
Fifty Shades (IRE) 5 gr.g c77p

EVAN WILLIAMS
Billy Bronco 7 ch.g c116p
Bold Plan (IRE) 4 b.g b103p
Clyne 8 b.g h145x c134p
Court Royale (IRE) 5 b.g b95p

IAN WILLIAMS
Almost Gold (IRE) 5 b.g h87p
Cause Toujours (FR) 6 b.g h114p
Don't Act Up 7 gr.g h89p
King of Realms (IRE) 6 b.g h126p
The Statesman 4 b.g h127p
Tikk Tock Boom (IRE) 6 gr.m h96p

NOEL WILLIAMS
Breaking Waves (IRE) 4 b.g b102p
Briery Express 5 b.m b86p
Briery Queen 9 b.m c140p
Drunken Pirate 5 b.g b94p

VENETIA WILLIAMS
Belami des Pictons (FR) 7 b.g c150p
Dark Force (FR) 5 gr.g h76p
Shalakar (FR) 5 b.g h121p

KAYLEY WOOLLACOTT
Floresco (GER) 8 ch.g h109 c98p

2017/18 IRISH STATISTICS

The following tables show the leading owners, trainers, jockeys, sires of winners and horses over jumps in Ireland during 2017/18 (April 30-April 28). The prize money statistics are in euros and have been compiled by *Timeform*. They relate to first-three prize money (prize money used to be converted to sterling at the prevailing rate at the time but that is no longer the case, though the prize money for individual races that appear in *'Selected Big Races'* has been converted to sterling).

OWNERS (1,2,3 earnings)

		Horses	Wnrs	Indiv'l Races Won	Runs	%	Stakes €
1	Gigginstown House Stud	220	97	151	940	16.1	3,974,344
2	Mr John P. McManus	260	82	123	996	12.3	2,539,035
3	Mrs S. Ricci	44	26	41	185	22.2	1,224,494
4	Andrea Wylie/Graham Wylie	14	7	10	47	21.3	475,175
5	Ann & Alan Potts Limited	27	11	14	79	17.7	417,124
6	Sullivan Bloodstock Limited	15	10	17	50	34.0	316,285
7	Mr Edward O'Connell	3	3	6	7	85.7	297,885
8	Mrs Patricia Hunt	22	9	16	82	19.5	224,542
9	Barry Connell	42	14	18	115	15.7	212,011
10	Mr C. Jones	15	4	5	45	11.1	174,608
11	Mr Simon Munir/Mr Isaac Souede	3	1	2	5	40.0	159,399
12	Luke McMahon	8	3	5	21	23.8	157,493

TRAINERS (1,2,3 earnings)

		Horses	Wnrs	Indiv'l Races Won	Runs	%	Stakes €
1	W. P. Mullins, Ireland	243	131	212	797	26.6	5,546,771
2	Gordon Elliott, Ireland	310	125	210	1,255	16.7	4,690,241
3	Joseph Patrick O'Brien, Ireland	121	48	67	473	14.2	1,307,529
4	Henry de Bromhead, Ireland	127	42	60	473	12.7	1,210,618
5	Mrs J. Harrington, Ireland	96	28	38	408	9.3	1,149,305
6	Noel Meade, Ireland	118	43	57	448	12.7	1,072,547
7	Charles Byrnes, Ireland	37	17	22	157	14.0	361,706
8	Denis Hogan, Ireland	51	13	21	219	9.6	318,216
9	John Patrick Ryan, Ireland	31	6	12	234	5.1	291,707
10	Thomas Mullins, Ireland	22	6	10	125	8.0	259,193
11	Peter Fahey, Ireland	38	12	18	120	15.0	242,341
12	John J. Walsh, Ireland	44	8	12	180	6.7	241,034

JOCKEYS (by winners)

		1st	2nd	3rd	Unpl	Mts	%
1	Davy Russell	119	125	94	253	591	20.1
2	P. Townend	84	71	57	212	424	19.8
3	R. Walsh	63	33	17	106	219	28.8
4	J. W. Kennedy	63	48	32	184	327	19.3
5	Sean Flanagan	59	51	53	356	519	11.4
6	Mr P. W. Mullins	54	27	25	49	155	34.8
7	M. P. Walsh	51	51	36	241	379	13.5
8	A. E. Lynch	38	49	65	440	592	6.4
9	Robbie Power	38	48	35	187	308	12.3
10	D. E. Mullins	35	41	29	327	432	8.1
11	D. J. McInerney	34	20	22	226	302	11.3
12	Rachael Blackmore	34	27	44	270	375	9.1

		Races Won	Runs	%	Stakes €
SIRES OF WINNERS (1,2,3 earnings)					
1	Flemensfirth (by Alleged)	72	454	15.9	1,393,026
2	Beneficial (by Top Ville)	58	699	8.3	1,002,797
3	King's Theatre (by Sadler's Wells)	48	350	13.7	903,076
4	Milan (by Sadler's Wells)	50	472	10.6	860,012
5	Oscar (by Sadler's Wells)	40	441	9.1	699,694
6	Presenting (by Mtoto)	36	493	7.3	674,660
7	Stowaway (by Slip Anchor)	36	360	10.0	671,119
8	Westerner (by Danehill)	43	385	11.2	643,002
9	Shantou (by Alleged)	34	220	15.5	634,308
10	Gold Well (by Sadler's Wells)	18	196	9.2	557,971
11	Galileo (by Sadler's Wells)	20	147	13.6	489,355
12	Yeats (by Sadler's Wells)	31	238	13.0	467,313

	LEADING HORSES	Won	Runs	€
1	Supasundae 8 b.g Galileo–Distinctive Look	2	4	274,900
2	General Principle 9 b.g Gold Well–How Provincial	1	6	270,000
3	Un de Sceaux 10 b.g Denham Red–Hotesse de Sceaux	3	3	249,050
4	Faugheen 10 b.g Germany–Miss Pickering	2	4	246,849
5	Footpad 6 b.g Creachadoir–Willamina	4	4	199,721
6	Bellshill 8 b.g King's Theatre–Fairy Native	2	3	191,949
7	Balko des Flos 7 ch.g Balko–Royale Marie	1	4	189,050
8	Tigris River 7 b.g Montjeu–Hula Angel	2	8	185,007
9	Road To Respect 7 ch.g Gamut–Lora Lady	2	4	163,450
10	Next Destination 6 b.g Dubai Destination–Liss Alainn	4	4	145,607
11	Apple's Jade 6 b.f Saddler Maker–Apple's For Ever	3	4	145,348
12	Potters Point 8 b.g Robin des Champs–Tango Lady	2	10	134,966

TIMEFORM TOP 20 IRISH CHASERS		**TIMEFORM TOP 20 IRISH HURDLERS**	
174p	Footpad	166	Melon
171	Sizing John	165	Faugheen
170p	Great Field	164	Penhill
169	Un de Sceaux	163p	Samcro
169	Min	162	Bapaume
168	Bellshill	162	Supasundae
167	Road To Respect	161	Identity Thief
167x	Our Duke	161	Mick Jazz
166	Balko des Flos	161§	Wicklow Brave
165+	Douvan	157	Cilaos Emery
165	Djakadam	156	Nichols Canyon
164+	Disko	156	Apple's Jade
164p	Presenting Percy	155	Bacardys
164	Anibale Fly	154	Shaneshill
164§	Outlander	153	Coquin Mans
163+	Total Recall	152	Presenting Percy
163x	Killultagh Vic	152	Swamp Fox
162	Doctor Phoenix	151p	Benie des Dieux
161+	Al Boum Photo	151p	Next Destination
161	Edwulf	151	Bleu Et Rouge
		151	Campeador
		151	Diamond Cauchois

SELECTED BIG RACES 2017/18

Prize money for racing abroad has been converted to £ sterling at the exchange rate current at the time of the race. The figures are correct to the nearest £.

HAYDOCK Saturday, May 13   GOOD to FIRM

1 Pertemps Network Swinton Handicap Hurdle (Gr 3) (1) (4yo+) £34,170   1m7f144y (9)
```
JOHN CONSTABLE (IRE) EvanWilliams 6-11-2¹³⁴ (t) DavyRussell ............... 5/1f      1
OPTIMUS PRIME (FR) DanSkelton 5-11-8¹⁴⁰ (t) NoelFehily ..................... 12/1    14  2
GREAT FIGHTER JimGoldie 7-10-13¹³¹ (v) CallumBewley(3) ..................... 25/1    nk  3
Court Minstrel (IRE) EvanWilliams 10-11-12¹⁴⁴ AdamWedge .................... 20/1    nk  4
Zubayr (IRE) PaulNicholls 5-11-10¹⁴² SamTwiston-Davies ....................... 8/1    1¼  5
William H Bonney AlanKing 6-11-1¹³³ WayneHutchinson ......................... 14/1    3¾  6
Zulu Oscar JeremyScott 8-10-13¹³¹ MattGriffiths ............................. 14/1    hd  7
London Prize IanWilliams 6-11-3¹³⁵ TomO'Brien ................................. 8/1    2¾  8
Holly Bush Henry (IRE) GraemeMcPherson 6-11-2¹³⁴ (s+t) PaddyBrennan ....... 33/1     2  9
Red Tornado (IRE) DanSkelton 5-11-5¹³⁷ BridgetAndrews(3) ................... 11/1    nk 10
Traditional Dancer (IRE) IainJardine 5-10-13¹³¹ HenryBrooke ................ 40/1    10 11
Multiculture (IRE) PhilipHobbs 5-10-12¹³⁰ RichardJohnson ..................... 7/1     5 12
Peace And Co (FR) NickyHenderson 6-11-12¹⁴⁴ (h) DarylJacob ................ 11/2    1¼ 13
High Secret (IRE) PaulNicholls 6-11-9¹⁴¹ HarryCobden ....................... 16/1    38 14
Fergall (IRE) SeamusMullins 10-11-8¹⁴⁰ (s) KevinJones(5) ................... 22/1       F
Vosne Romanee DrRichardNewland 6-11-4¹³⁶ (b+t) AidanColeman ............... 25/1       pu
Song Light SeamusMullins 7-11-0¹³² (s) DanielSansom(7) ..................... 12/1       rr
```
Walters Plant Hire Ltd 17ran 3m43.70

STRATFORD Friday, Jun 9   GOOD to SOFT

2 Pertemps Network Stratford Foxhunters Champion Hunters' Chase (2) (5yo+) £14,990   3m3f119y (17)

The ditch in the back straight was omitted due to being damaged
```
YOUNG HURRICANE (IRE) G.C.Brewer 11-12-0 MrJohnDawson ................... 16/1        1
BALNASLOW (IRE) GrahamMcKeever,Ireland 10-12-0 MrDerekO'Connor ...... 5/2      2  2
WONDERFUL CHARM (FR) PaulNicholls 9-12-0 (s+t) MrSamWaley-Cohen ... 11/8f    1½  3
Rebel Rebellion (IRE) PaulNicholls 12-12-0 (t) BryonyFrost .................. 16/1    10  4
Wild Bill (IRE) SallyRandell 8-12-0 MrConorOrr ............................... 33/1     7  5
Bear's Affair (IRE) PhilipRowley 11-12-0 MrAlexEdwards ...................... 16/1     7  6
The Wealerdealer (IRE) I.Chanin 10-12-0 MrLorcanWilliams ..................... 9/1     6  7
Master Workman (IRE) DavidKemp 11-12-0 (s) MrSamuelDavies-Thomas ... 20/1    24  8
Mr Mercurial (IRE) MrsSheilaCrow 9-12-0 (t) MrWilliamBiddick ............... 16/1       pu
Man of Steel (IRE) AlanHill 8-12-0 (s+t) MrJoeHill ........................... 16/1       pu
```
Mr C. Helfferich 10ran 7m07.90

MARKET RASEN Saturday, Jul 22   GOOD

3 Betfred Summer Plate Handicap Chase (L) (1) (4yo+) £28,475   2m5f89y (14)
```
ALCALA (FR) PaulNicholls 7-11-7¹⁴⁷ (t) SamTwiston-Davies ................... 9/1       1
WADSWICK COURT (IRE) PeterBowen 9-10-0¹²⁶ (b+t) AdamWedge ........... 20/1    ¾  2
SHELFORD (IRE) DanSkelton 8-10-3¹²⁹ (b) HarrySkelton ...................... 5/1f   4½  3
Poker School IanWilliams 7-10-5¹³¹ TomO'Brien ................................. 7/1     1  4
Lofgren DonaldMcCain 6-10-4¹³⁰ (t) WillKennedy .............................. 33/1    3¼  5
Newton Geronimo BenPauling 8-10-6¹³² (h) A.P.Heskin ....................... 33/1     3  6
Days of Heaven (FR) NickyHenderson 7-11-11¹⁵¹ (h) NicodeBoinville ........ 8/1     ¾  7
Viens Chercher (IRE) BrianEllison 6-10-6¹³² (s) TomScudamore ............... 8/1    ½  8
Earthmoves (FR) PeterBowen 7-10-7¹³³ (s+t) SeanBowen ....................... 10/1     5  9
It's A Gimme (IRE) JonjoO'Neill 10-10-8¹³⁴ AidanColeman ..................... 10/1     6 10
Cup Final (IRE) BenHaslam 8-10-6¹³² (t) RichieMcLernon ..................... 16/1     2 11
Midnight Shot CharlieLongsdon 7-10-13¹³⁹ JonathanBurke ................... 12/1    ½ 12
I'dliketheoption (IRE) JonjoO'Neill 6-10-6¹³² (t) KillianMoore(3) ........... 12/1    ½ 13
Henryville HarryFry 9-11-12¹⁵² (h+t) NiallMadden ............................ 14/1    13 14
Casino Markets (IRE) EmmaLavelle 9-10-11¹³⁷ LeightonAspell ................. 12/1    1½ 15
```
Owners Group 016 15ran 5m21.10

GALWAY Wednesday, Aug 2   GOOD

4 thetote.com Galway Plate (Handicap Chase) (Gr A) (4yo+) £131,696   2¾m111y (14)
```
BALKO DES FLOS (FR) HenrydeBromhead 6-10-10¹⁴⁶ DavyRussell ............. 6/1        1
SHANESHILL (IRE) W.P.Mullins 8-11-3¹⁵³ R.Walsh .............................. 3/1f    4¾  2
SLOWMOTION (FR) JosephPatrickO'Brien 5-10-6¹⁴² J.S.McGarvey ........... 14/1     ¾  3
A Toi Phil (FR) GordonElliott 7-10-13¹⁴⁹ (t) B.J.Cooper ....................... 9/1     ¾  4
```

	Sandymount Duke (IRE) *Mrs.J.Harrington* 8-11-6[156] D.E.Mullins 12/1	1¼	5
	Arbre de Vie (FR) *W.P.Mullins* 7-10-9[145] D.J.Mullins 14/1	11	6
	Shanpallas (IRE) *Charles Byrnes* 9-10-5[141] NiallMadden 20/1	1¼	7
	Lord Scoundrel (IRE) *GordonElliott* 8-11-6[156] (t) JamesBowen(7) 25/1	3½	8
	Ballybolley (IRE) *NigelTwiston-Davies,GB* 8-10-6[142] (t) DarylJacob 16/1	2½	9
	Road To Riches (IRE) *NoelMeade* 10-11-6[156] (b) SeanFlanagan 12/1	hd	10
	Ballycasey (IRE) *W.P.Mullins* 10-11-10[160] MrP.W.Mullins 20/1	8½	11
	Sadler's Risk (IRE) *HenrydeBromhead* 9-11-3[153] A.E.Lynch 33/1	4¼	12
	Vintage Vinnie (IRE) *RebeccaCurtis,GB* 8-10-4[140] (t) JonathanMoore 25/1	2½	13
	Deans Road (IRE) *HenrydeBromhead* 8-10-2[138] DonaghMeyler 16/1	4½	14
	Rock The World (IRE) *Mrs.J.Harrington* 9-11-5[155] (t) BarryGeraghty 25/1	15	15
	Heron Heights (IRE) *HenrydeBromhead* 8-10-2[138] (t) PhilipEnright 25/1	26	16
	Devils Bride (IRE) *HenrydeBromhead* 10-11-4[154] (s+t) MsL.O'Neill(5) 33/1	F	
	Bentelimar (IRE) *J.R.Barry* 8-10-1[137] RachaelBlackmore 12/1	ur	
	Marinero (IRE) *HenrydeBromhead* 8-10-5[141] (b) J.J.Slevin(3) 33/1	ur	
	Three Kingdoms (IRE) *D.K.Weld* 8-10-7[143] JonathanBurke 25/1	pu	
	Haymount (IRE) *W.P.Mullins* 8-10-9[145] P.Townend 10/1	pu	
	Alelchi Inois (FR) *W.P.Mullins* 9-11-6[156] (t) B.Hayes 33/1	pu	

Gigginstown House Stud 22ran 5m22.80

GALWAY Thursday, Aug 3 GOOD to SOFT

5 Guinness Galway Hurdle Handicap (Gr A) (4yo+) £158,036   2m1y (8)

	TIGRIS RIVER (IRE) *JosephPatrickO'Brien* 6-10-9[140] (t) BarryGeraghty 5/1		1
	SWAMP FOX (IRE) *JosephG.Murphy* 5-11-3[148] (b) B.Browne(7) 8/1	nk	2
	AIRLIE BEACH (IRE) *W.P.Mullins* 7-10-10[141] P.Townend 9/1	5	3
	Joey Sasa (IRE) *NoelMeade* 8-10-7[138] SeanFlanagan 25/1	3¼	4
	Morga (IRE) *DesmondMcDonogh* 7-10-0[131] B.R.Dalton 33/1	hd	5
	Project Bluebook (FR) *JohnQuinn,GB* 4-10-5[141] B.S.Hughes 16/1	4¾	6
1	Fergall (IRE) *SeamusMullins,GB* 10-10-10[141] (s) KevinJones(5) 25/1	½	7
	Plinth (IRE) *JosephPatrickO'Brien* 7-10-11[142] (b+t) J.J.Slevin(3) 20/1	2½	8
	Max Dynamite (FR) *W.P.Mullins* 7-10-10[141] R.Walsh 7/2f	1	9
	Shrewd *IainJardine,GB* 7-10-1[132] HenryBrooke 20/1	4¾	10
	Thomas Edison (IRE) *A.J.Martin* 10-10-13[144] (h+t) DavyRussell 16/1	nk	11
	Clondaw Warrior (IRE) *W.P.Mullins* 10-11-10[155] (b) MsK.Walsh 25/1	3¾	12
	The Game Changer (IRE) *GordonElliott* 8-10-9[140] (t) JamesBowen(7) 40/1	5½	13
	Timiyan (USA) *GordonElliott* 6-10-4[135] (t) AidanColeman 8/1	4½	14
	Ancient Sands (IRE) *JohnE.Kiely* 9-10-4[135] RachaelBlackmore 25/1	F	
1	Court Minstrel (IRE) *EvanWilliams,GB* 10-11-0[145] MitchellBastyan(7) 33/1	F	
	Ivan Grozny (FR) *W.P.Mullins* 7-11-5[150] (h) D.E.Mullins 20/1	bd	
	All The Answers *JosephPatrickO'Brien* 6-10-11[7] (t) NiallMadden 25/1	pu	
	Western Boy (IRE) *P.A.Fahy* 8-10-6[137] J.S.McGarvey 11/1	pu	
	Ornua (IRE) *HenrydeBromhead* 6-10-7[138] BrianO'Connell 20/1	pu	

Mr John P. McManus 20ran 3m42.50

GALWAY Saturday, Aug 5 SOFT

6 Galway Shopping Centre Handicap Hurdle (Gr B) (4yo+) £52,679   2¾m168y (13)

	BALLYEGAN HERO (IRE) *JohnJ.Walsh* 6-9-11[122] RachaelBlackmore 16/1		1
	MINE NOW (IRE) *PeterFahey* 9-10-3[130] MrR.Deegan(7) 11/1	ns	2
	LAGOSTOVEGAS (IRE) *W.P.Mullins* 5-9-13[124] D.E.Mullins 7/2f	2¼	3
	Mr Showtime (IRE) *NoelMeade* 5-10-0[125] JonathanMoore 16/1	2¾	4
	Ah Littleluck (IRE) *T.Gibney* 7-10-1[127] (t) P.E.Corbett(3) 25/1	1½	5
	After Rain (FR) *J.R.Barry* 7-10-5[130] (h) J.S.McGarvey 8/1	8	6
	The Crafty Butcher (IRE) *W.P.Mullins* 10-10-3[128] R.Walsh 11/2	nk	7
	Aussie Reigns (IRE) *W.P.Mullins* 7-10-4[129] D.J.Mullins 14/1	½	8
	Hidden Cyclone (IRE) *JohnJosephHanlon* 12-11-9[148] (s) DavyRussell 14/1	3½	9
	Showem Silver (IRE) *NoelMeade* 6-9-13[124] SeanFlanagan 10/1	4	10
	Westland Row (IRE) *GordonElliott* 5-9-13[124] (t) JamesBowen(7) 20/1	2	11
	Whatsforuwontgobyu (IRE) *A.J.Martin* 7-9-11[122] NiallMadden 25/1	5½	12
	Madurai (GER) *W.P.Mullins* 6-9-10[121] MsK.Walsh 33/1	5½	13
	Jimmy Two Times (IRE) *B.R.Hamilton* 8-10-8[133] A.E.Lynch 16/1	2¼	14
	Phil The Flyer (IRE) *RayHackett* 10-10-1[126] (t) RogerLoughran 50/1	4½	15
	Cap d'Aubois (FR) *W.P.Mullins* 5-11-1[140] P.Townend 16/1	2¼	16
	Prince Charmin' (IRE) *A.J.Martin* 4-9-10[127] (s+t) M.A.Enright 20/1	F	
	Sea Light (IRE) *CharlesByrnes* 9-10-3[128] (s) PhilipEnright 20/1	ur	
	Sang Tiger (GER) *MissNicoleMcKenna* 9-9-10[123] (s) JonathanBurke 40/1	pu	
	Tellthemnuttin (IRE) *W.F.Codd* 6-10-9[134] J.J.Slevin(3) 20/1	pu	

Mr T. A. O'Brien 20ran 5m47.70

LISTOWEL Wednesday, Sep 13 HEAVY

7 Guinness Kerry National Handicap Chase (Gr A) (4yo+) £93,864 3m (17)

POTTERS POINT (IRE) *GordonElliott* 7-10-5[139] (t) MsL.O'Neill(5) 8/1		1
ARKWRISHT (FR) *JosephPatrickO'Brien* 7-9-11[131] (t) AndrewRing(3) 8/1	½	2
BAY OF FREEDOM (IRE) *PeterFahey* 8-9-13[133] K.C.Sexton 12/1	¾	3
Viva Steve (IRE) *FergalO'Brien,GB* 9-10-2[136] (t) PaddyBrennan 12/1	4¾	4
4 A Toi Phil (FR) *GordonElliott* 7-11-3[151] (t) DavyRussell 6/1jf	1¼	5
4 Bentelimar (IRE) *J.R.Barry* 8-10-2[136] P.Townend 10/1	6	6
4 Arbre de Vie (FR) *W.P.Mullins* 7-11-2[150] R.Walsh 6/1jf	sh	7
4 Slowmotion (FR) *JosephPatrickO'Brien* 5-10-11[145] M.P.Walsh 9/1	5½	8
4 Road To Riches (IRE) *NoelMeade* 10-11-6[154] (s+t) A.W.Short(7) 20/1	25	9
6 Sea Light (IRE) *CharlesByrnes* 9-9-10[130] PhilipEnright 20/1		pu
Sir Jack Yeats (IRE) *EllmarieHolden* 6-9-11[131] (b) RachaelBlackmore 16/1		pu
King Leon (IRE) *JosephPatrickO'Brien* 8-9-13[133] M.A.Enright 33/1		pu
Kilcarry Bridge (IRE) *JohnPatrickRyan* 10-10-4[138] (t) DonaghMeyler 33/1		pu
Kylecrue (IRE) *JohnPatrickRyan* 10-10-5[139] (b) D.E.Mullins 8/1		pu
4 Shanpallas (IRE) *CharlesByrnes* 9-10-6[140] J.S.McGarvey 20/1		pu
Stellar Notion (IRE) *HenrydeBromhead* 9-10-8[142] A.E.Lynch 20/1		pu
Tempestatefloresco *ColinTizzard,GB* 9-10-11[145] (t) RobbiePower 20/1		pu
4 Lord Scoundrel (IRE) *GordonElliott* 8-11-7[155] (t) ChrisMeehan(7) 20/1		pu

Gigginstown House Stud 18ran 6m21.80

MARKET RASEN Saturday, Sep 30 GOOD

8 188Bet.co.uk Prelude Handicap Chase (L) (1) (4yo+) £28,475 2m5f89y (14)

4 BALLYBOLLEY (IRE) *NigelTwiston-Davies* 8-11-9[143] (t) DarylJacob 10/1		1
GUITAR PETE (IRE) *NickyRichards* 7-10-5[125] RyanDay(3) 9/2	4	2
MASTER DEE (IRE) *FergalO'Brien* 8-11-10[144] (t) PaddyBrennan 8/1	1½	3
Play The Ace (IRE) *PeterBowen* 8-10-0[120] (s+t) JamesBowen(7) 14/1	6	4
3 Poker School (IRE) *IanWilliams* 7-10-13[133] TomO'Brien 5/1	3¾	5
3 Wadswick Court (IRE) *PeterBowen* 9-11-0[134] (b+t) SeanBowen 14/1	1½	6
Catamaran du Seuil (FR) *DrRichardNewland* 5-10-10[130] (b) SamTwiston-Davies ..6/1	24	7
Work In Progress (IRE) *DanSkelton* 7-11-6[140] (t) HarrySkelton 4/1f		ur
The Clock Leary (IRE) *DonaldMcCain* 9-10-11[131] WillKennedy 25/1		pu
Brave Spartacus (IRE) *GillianBoanas* 11-10-13[133] MissEmmaTodd(7) 25/1		pu
Its'afreebee (IRE) *DanSkelton* 7-11-3[137] BridgetAndrews(3) 12/1		pu
Germany Calling (IRE) *CharlieLongsdon* 8-11-11[145] (s+t) JonathanBurke 25/1		pu
Junction Fourteen (IRE) *EmmaLavelle* 8-11-12[146] (t) NickScholfield 20/1		pu

Mr Simon Munir & Mr Isaac Souede 13ran 5m23.70

GOWRAN Saturday, Sep 30 HEAVY

9 PWC Champion Chase (Gr 2) (5yo+) £23,894 2½m (14)

7 A TOI PHIL (FR) *GordonElliott* 7-11-8 (t) J.W.Kennedy 6/1		1
4 BALKO DES FLOS (FR) *HenrydeBromhead* 6-11-3 DavyRussell 11/8f	6½	2
4 BALLYCASEY (IRE) *W.P.Mullins* 10-11-8 P.Townend 11/2	22	3
4 Shaneshill (IRE) *W.P.Mullins* 8-11-3 R.Walsh 15/8	8	4
7 Kylecrue (IRE) *JohnPatrickRyan* 10-11-3 (b) D.E.Mullins 40/1	52	5

Gigginstown House Stud 5ran 5m07.00

LIMERICK Sunday, Oct 8 SOFT

10 JT McNamara Ladbrokes Munster National Handicap Chase (Gr A) (4yo+) 3m (16)
£52,212

TOTAL RECALL (IRE) *W.P.Mullins* 8-10-5[129] R.Walsh 2/1f		1
ALPHA DES OBEAUX (FR) *M.F.Morris* 7-11-7[145] DavyRussell 4/1	7	2
PHIL'S MAGIC (FR) *A.J.Martin* 7-10-5[129] (s+t) DonaghMeyler 14/1	11	3
Tulsa Jack (IRE) *NoelMeade* 8-10-10[134] (b) SeanFlanagan 20/1	hd	4
Net d'Ecosse (FR) *NoelMeade* 7-10-5[129] (b+t) JonathanMoore 20/1	6	5
Dromnea (IRE) *M.F.Morris* 10-10-13[137] M.A.Enright 14/1	11	6
7 Shanpallas (IRE) *CharlesByrnes* 9-10-13[137] L.P.Dempsey 33/1	6½	7
On Fiddlers Green (IRE) *HenrydeBromhead* 7-10-12[136] D.J.Mullins 18/1	4¾	8
Rogue Angel (IRE) *M.F.Morris* 9-11-2[140] (b+t) ChrisMeehan(7) 25/1	3	9
7 Stellar Notion (IRE) *HenrydeBromhead* 9-11-2[140] (s) A.E.Lynch 25/1	68	10
7 Arkwrisht (IRE) *JosephPatrickO'Brien* 7-11-0[138] (t) J.J.Slevin(3) 7/1		F
Raz de Maree (FR) *GavinPatrickCromwell* 12-11-0[138] B.J.Cooper 25/1		F
Rock On Fruity (IRE) *CharlesByrnes* 8-10-4[128] D.J.McInerney(7) 8/1		ur
Auvergnat (FR) *EndaBolger* 7-10-6[130] M.P.Walsh 8/1		bd
7 King Leon (IRE) *JosephPatrickO'Brien* 8-10-8[132] ShaneShortall(3) 50/1		bd
7 Slowmotion (FR) *JosephPatrickO'Brien* 5-11-6[144] BarryGeraghty 12/1		pu

Slaneyville Syndicate 16ran 6m22.90

CHEPSTOW Saturday, Oct 14   GOOD to SOFT

11 Totepool Silver Trophy Handicap Hurdle (Gr 3) (1) (4yo+) £28,475   2m3f100y (8)

5	COURT MINSTREL (IRE) *EvanWilliams* 10-11-4[142] MitchellBastyan(7) 14/1		1
	SAM SPINNER *JeddO'Keeffe* 5-10-12[136] JoeColliver 8/1	½	2
	PEAK TO PEAK (IRE) *PaulNicholls* 5-10-1[125] HarryCobden 10/1	nk	3
	Wholestone (IRE) *NigelTwiston-Davies* 6-11-7[145] DarylJacob 4/1f	¾	4
	River Frost *AlanKing* 5-11-4[142] BarryGeraghty 16/1	½	5
	Louis' Vac Pouch (IRE) *PhilipHobbs* 5-10-8[132] (h) RichardJohnson 25/1	ns	6
	Old Guard *PaulNicholls* 6-11-12[150] BryonyFrost(5) 22/1	1½	7
	Bags Groove (IRE) *HarryFry* 6-10-9[133] (t) NoelFehily 7/1	hd	8
	Sumkindofking (IRE) *TomGeorge* 6-10-5[129] A.P.Heskin 8/1	4	9
	Drumcliff (IRE) *HarryFry* 6-10-1[125] (t) NiallMadden 10/1	1¼	10
	Le Rocher (FR) *NickWilliams* 7-11-5[143] TomScudamore 20/1	ns	11
	Milrow (IRE) *SophieLeech* 4-10-1[125] (t) SeanHoulihan(7) 66/1	4	12
	Souriyan (FR) *PeterBowen* 6-10-7[131] (b) SeanBowen 25/1	1½	13
	Three Musketeers (IRE) *DanSkelton* 7-11-7[145] BridgetAndrews(3) 33/1	7	14
	Whatduhavtoget (IRE) *DanSkelton* 5-10-6[130] HarrySkelton 12/1	1½	15
	Doesyourdogbite (IRE) *JonjoO'Neill* 5-10-9[133] AidanColeman 25/1	29	16
	Alary (FR) *ColinTizzard* 7-11-8[146] (t) B.J.Cooper 20/1	14	17
	Wishing And Hoping (IRE) *AlanKing* 7-10-4[128] WayneHutchinson 16/1		F

Mrs Janet Davies 18ran 4m48.90

CHEPSTOW Sunday, Oct 15   GOOD to SOFT

12 Totepool Persian War Novices' Hurdle (Gr 2) (1) (4yo+) £19,932   2m3f100y (11)

	POETIC RHYTHM (IRE) *FergalO'Brien* 6-11-0 PaddyBrennan 3/1		1
	AMOUR DE NUIT (IRE) *PaulNicholls* 5-11-0 SamTwiston-Davies 7/1	1¼	2
	VISION DES FLOS (FR) *ColinTizzard* 4-11-0 B.J.Cooper 13/2	5	3
	Dear Sire (FR) *DonaldMcCain* 5-11-0 (h) WillKennedy 14/1	3¼	4
	Black Mischief *HarryFry* 5-11-0 NoelFehily 13/2	9	5
	Ballymountain Boy (IRE) *MartinKeighley* 6-11-0 (s) AndrewTinkler 20/1	3	6
	Tommy Rapper (IRE) *DanSkelton* 6-11-0 HarrySkelton 9/4f	33	7
	Equus Amadeus (IRE) *TomLacey* 4-11-0 RichardJohnson 25/1		pu
	Gustave Mahler (IRE) *AlastairRalph* 7-11-0 AidanColeman 33/1		pu

The Yes No Wait Sorries 9ran 4m47.30

PUNCHESTOWN Thursday, Oct 19   GOOD to SOFT

13 Irish Daily Star Chase (Gr 3) (5yo+) £21,071   3m1f (18)

	ROAD TO RESPECT (IRE) *NoelMeade* 6-11-10 SeanFlanagan 7/2		1
7	KILCARRY BRIDGE (IRE) *JohnPatrickRyan* 10-11-0 (t) D.E.Mullins 25/1	1½	2
	SUB LIEUTENANT (IRE) *HenrydeBromhead* 8-11-8 (t) B.J.Cooper 3/1	4¼	3
	Minella Rocco (IRE) *JonjoO'Neill,GB* 7-11-0 (t) BarryGeraghty 7/4f	4½	4
	Zabana (IRE) *AndrewLynch* 8-11-10 (t) DavyRussell 8/1	17	5
	Outlander (IRE) *GordonElliott* 9-11-10 J.W.Kennedy 8/1	15	6
	Carlingford Lough (IRE) *JohnE.Kiely* 11-11-10 M.P.Walsh 16/1	4¼	7

Gigginstown House Stud 7ran 6m52.10

AINTREE Sunday, Oct 29   GOOD to SOFT

14 188Bet Monet's Garden Old Roan Limited Handicap Chase (Gr 2) (1) (4yo+) £39,389   2m3f200y (16)

	SMAD PLACE (FR) *AlanKing* 10-11-3[159] WayneHutchinson 12/1		1
	CLOUDY DREAM (IRE) *MalcolmJefferson* 7-10-13[155] BrianHughes 9/2	¾	2
	OLDGRANGEWOOD *DanSkelton* 6-10-5[147] (t) HarrySkelton 9/1	9	3
	Traffic Fluide (FR) *GaryMoore* 7-11-0[156] JamieMoore 8/1	4½	4
	Aso (FR) *VenetiaWilliams* 7-11-0[156] CharlieDeutsch(3) 16/1	5	5
	God's Own (IRE) *TomGeorge* 9-11-10[166] A.P.Heskin 12/1	1¼	6
	Bouvreuil (FR) *PaulNicholls* 6-10-4[146] (h+t) SamTwiston-Davies 13/2	5	7
	Third Intention (FR) *ColinTizzard* 10-10-8[150] (t) AidanColeman 12/1	7	8
	Tea For Two *NickWilliams* 8-11-8[164] LizzieKelly(3) 12/1	8	9
4	Devils Bride (IRE) *HenrydeBromhead,Ireland* 10-10-12[154] (s+t) JonathanMoore ..50/1	42	10
	Shantou Village (IRE) *NeilMulholland* 7-10-7[149] NoelFehily 7/2f		pu
	Royal Regatta (IRE) *PhilipHobbs* 9-10-12[154] (b+t) RichardJohnson 28/1		pu

Mrs Peter Andrews 12ran 5m01.40

DOWN ROYAL Friday, Nov 3   SOFT

15 WKD Hurdle (Gr 2) (5yo+) £26,106   2m (8)

	MELON *W.P.Mullins* 5-11-2 R.Walsh 2/5f		1
	COQUIN MANS (FR) *W.P.Mullins* 5-11-5 (h) P.Townend 9/2	4½	2
	MICK JAZZ (FR) *GordonElliott* 6-11-2 (h) DavyRussell 7/1	¾	3
	Wakea (USA) *KarlThornton* 6-11-2 (h+t) Mr.J.C.Barry 16/1	2¼	4

	Forge Meadow (IRE) *MrsJ.Harrington* 5-11-1 RobbiePower 50/1	13	5
6	Tellthemnuttin (IRE) *W.F.Codd* 6-10-9 (s) D.Robinson 66/1	19	6

Mrs J. Donnelly 6ran 4m00.70

DOWN ROYAL Saturday, Nov 4   SOFT

16   JNwine.com Champion Chase (Gr 1) (5yo+) £73,097   3m (17)

13	OUTLANDER (IRE) *GordonElliott* 9-11-10 (s) J.W.Kennedy 16/1		1
13	ROAD TO RESPECT (IRE) *NoelMeade* 6-11-10 SeanFlanagan 7/2	½	2
13	ZABANA (IRE) *AndrewLynch* 8-11-10 (t) DavyRussell 25/1	14	3
10	Alpha des Obeaux (FR) *M.F.Morris* 7-11-10 M.A.Enright 12/1	2¾	4
13	Sub Lieutenant (IRE) *HenrydeBromhead* 8-11-10 (t) R.Walsh 6/1	11	5
	More of That (IRE) *JonjoO'Neill,GB* 9-11-10 BarryGeraghty 14/1	12	6
	Our Duke (IRE) *MrsJ.Harrington* 7-11-10 RobbiePower 5/6f	11	7
13	Carlingford Lough (IRE) *JohnE.Kiely* 11-11-10 (t) M.P.Walsh 33/1		ur

Gigginstown House Stud 8ran 6m16.70

17   mycarneedsa.com Chase (Skymas) (Gr 2) (4yo+) £26,106   2m3f120y (13)

	DISKO (FR) *NoelMeade* 6-11-12 (h) SeanFlanagan 5/4f		1
	BALLYOISIN (IRE) *EndaBolger* 6-11-5 BarryGeraghty 4/1	½	2
	BALL D'ARC (FR) *GordonElliott* 6-11-5 KeithDonoghue 16/1	8	3
9	A Toi Phil (FR) *GordonElliott* 7-11-10 (t) J.W.Kennedy 3/1	1½	4
	Anibale Fly (FR) *A.J.Martin* 7-11-8 (t) M.P.Walsh 10/1	18	5
	Neverushacon (IRE) *MrsJ.Harrington* 6-11-5 (s) RobbiePower 33/1	2¼	6
	Tout Est Permis (FR) *M.F.Morris* 4-10-7 M.A.Enright 12/1	12	7

Gigginstown House Stud 7ran 4m55.90

ASCOT Saturday, Nov 4   GOOD

18   Byrne Group Handicap Chase (L) (1) (150) (4yo+) £34,170   2m167y (13)

	EXITAS (IRE) *PhilMiddleton* 9-10-1[123] JamesBowen(7) 11/2		1
	QUITE BY CHANCE *ColinTizzard* 8-11-8[144] TomO'Brien 7/1	7	2
	MARRACUDJA (FR) *PaulNicholls* 6-11-5[141] (h+t) SamTwiston-Davies 4/1f	13	3
	Theinval (FR) *NickyHenderson* 7-11-12[148] (s) JeremiahMcGrath 6/1	1	4
	Calipto (FR) *VenetiaWilliams* 7-11-2[138] B.J.Cooper 5/1	7	5
	Max Ward (IRE) *TomGeorge* 8-11-11[147] NoelFehily 7/1	13	6
	Festive Affair (IRE) *JonjoO'Neill* 9-11-14[140] (s+t) AidanColeman 20/1	18	7
	Somchine *SeamusMullins* 9-11-0[136] AndrewThornton 16/1	13	8
	Chris Pea Green *GaryMoore* 8-10-9[131] JamieMoore 10/1	16	9
	Little Hope *NigelTwiston-Davies* 9-10-3[125] (h+t) JamieBargary(3) 16/1		pu

Mr P. W. Middleton 10ran 4m02.90

19   William Hill Handicap Hurdle (L) (1) (4yo+) £34,170   1m7f152y (8)

	ELGIN *AlanKing* 5-11-11[140] TomCannon 6/1jf		1
	LIMITED RESERVE (IRE) *ChristianWilliams* 5-10-8[123] DenisO'Regan 8/1	1¼	2
	HIGH BRIDGE *BenPauling* 6-11-12[141] MrAlexFerguson(7) 7/1	¾	3
	Air Horse One *HarryFry* 6-11-12[141] NoelFehily 8/1	hd	4
	Verdana Blue (IRE) *NickyHenderson* 5-11-7[136] JeremiahMcGrath 6/1jf	4½	5
	Midnight Maestro *AlanKing* 5-10-11[126] BrendanPowell 9/1	nk	6
	Caid du Lin (FR) *DrRichardNewland* 5-11-4[133] (s+t) SamTwiston-Davies ..12/1	3	7
	Fou Et Sage (FR) *HarryWhittington* 6-11-2[131] B.J.Cooper 40/1	1¾	8
	East Indies *GaryMoore* 4-10-6[121] JamieMoore 25/1	nk	9
	Dolos (FR) *PaulNicholls* 4-11-6[135] (t) StanSheppard(3) 7/1	7	10
	Peruvien Bleu (FR) *NickWilliams* 5-11-1[130] MrC.Williams(7) 16/1	4	11
1	Song Light *SeamusMullins* 7-11-3[132] (b) KevinJones(5) 8/1	10	12
	Clayton *GaryMoore* 8-10-7[122] AndrewGlassonbury 20/1	14	13
	Prairie Town (FR) *TonyCarroll* 6-10-10[125] LeeEdwards 66/1	4½	14

Elite Racing Club 14ran 3m40.70

20   Sodexo Gold Cup Handicap Chase (Gr 3) (1) (4yo+) £56,950   2m7f180y (20)

	GO CONQUER (IRE) *JonjoO'Neill* 8-11-0[142] AidanColeman 7/1		1
	ROCK GONE *DrRichardNewland* 9-10-8[136] BrendanPowell 20/1	4½	2
	BRAQUEUR D'OR (FR) *PaulNicholls* 6-10-11[139] SamTwiston-Davies 7/1	3	3
	Dark Flame (FR) *RichardRowe* 8-10-5[133] AndrewGlassonbury 10/1	3	4
	Antony (FR) *GaryMoore* 7-10-4[132] JamieMoore 4/1f	4	5
	Thomas Brown *HarryFry* 8-10-10[138] D NiallMadden 9/1	1	6
	Fourth Act (IRE) *ColinTizzard* 8-10-1[129] SeanBowen 10/1	nk	7
	Emerging Force (IRE) *HarryWhittington* 9-10-11[139] HarryBannister 11/2	¾	8
	Ultragold (FR) *ColinTizzard* 9-10-13[141] (t) TomO'Brien 25/1	6	9
	Ballykan *NigelTwiston-Davies* 7-10-9[137] (t) JamieBargary(3) 16/1	3½	10
8	Junction Fourteen (IRE) *EmmaLavelle* 8-10-13[141] (v+t) LeightonAspell ..16/1	24	11
	Regal Encore (IRE) *AnthonyHoneyball* 9-11-8[150] (t) RichieMcLernon ..33/1	2	12

920

	Meldrum Lad (IRE) *SeamusDurack* 8-10-0[128] (t) ConorO'Farrell	50/1	15	13
	Art Mauresque (FR) *PaulNicholls* 7-11-8[150] BryonyFrost(5)	20/1		F
	The Young Master *NeilMulholland* 8-11-3[145] (s) MrJamesKing(5)	16/1		ur
	Ballycross *NigelTwiston-Davies* 6-10-5[133] AlainCawley	11/1		pu

Paul & Clare Rooney 16ran 6m03.40

WETHERBY Saturday, Nov 4   SOFT

21   Bet365 Hurdle (West Yorkshire) (Gr 2) (1) (4yo+) £22,780   3m26y (12)

	COLIN'S SISTER *FergalO'Brien* 6-10-10 PaddyBrennan	10/1		1
11	WHOLESTONE (IRE) *NigelTwiston-Davies* 6-11-3 DarylJacob	2/1jf	2	2
	LIL ROCKEFELLER (USA) *NeilKing* 6-11-0 (s) TrevorWhelan	2/1jf	12	3
	Ptit Zig (FR) *PaulNicholls* 8-11-0 (b) HarryCobden	4/1	4	4
	Fountains Windfall *AnthonyHoneyball* 7-11-4 DavidNoonan	14/1	11	5
	Missed Approach (IRE) *WarrenGreatrex* 7-11-0 RichardJohnson	20/1		pu
	Gayebury *EvanWilliams* 7-11-2 AdamWedge	14/1		pu

Mrs Caroline Beresford-Wylie 7ran 6m15.30

22   Bet365 Charlie Hall Chase (Gr 2) (1) (5yo+) £56,950   3m45y (19)

	BRISTOL DE MAI (FR) *NigelTwiston-Davies* 6-11-0 DarylJacob	6/1		1
	BLAKLION *NigelTwiston-Davies* 8-11-0 GavinSheehan	5/1	½	2
	DEFINITLY RED (IRE) *BrianEllison* 8-11-4 DannyCook	8/1	23	3
	Vieux Lion Rouge (FR) *DavidPipe* 8-11-4 (s) TomScudamore	25/1	20	4
	Shantou Flyer (IRE) *RichardHobson* 7-11-4 (t) AdamWedge	40/1	15	5
	Cue Card *ColinTizzard* 11-11-6 (t) PaddyBrennan	5/2		F
	Coneygree *MarkBradstock* 10-11-0 NicodeBoinville	7/4f		
	Village Vic (IRE) *PhilipHobbs* 9-11-0 RichardJohnson	33/1		pu

Mr Simon Munir & Mr Isaac Souede 8ran 6m28.30

AINTREE Saturday, Nov 11   SOFT

23   Rugby Betting At 188Bet Handicap Chase (2) (150) (4yo+) £46,425   2m3f200y (16)

	ON TOUR (IRE) *EvanWilliams* 9-10-11[135] MitchellBastyan(5)	4/1		1
8	MASTER DEE (IRE) *FergalO'Brien* 8-11-7[145] (t) JonathanBurke	8/1	3	2
8	BALLYBOLLEY (IRE) *NigelTwiston-Davies* 8-11-2[150] (t) DarylJacob	6/1	6	3
	Gardefort (FR) *VenetiaWilliams* 8-11-7[145] B.J.Cooper	12/1	1½	4
	Three Stars (IRE) *HenrydeBromhead,Ireland* 7-11-3[141] J.J.Slevin(3)	16/1	½	5
	Voix d'Eau (FR) *HarryFry* 7-11-7[145] (t) MrM.Legg(5)	8/1	½	6
	Tiquer (FR) *AlanJones* 9-10-0[124] BrendanPowell	40/1	6	7
	Virgilio (FR) *DanSkelton* 8-11-11[149] (t) HarrySkelton	11/4f	½	8
	Pobbles Bay (IRE) *EvanWilliams* 7-11-7[145] AdamWedge	9/1	5	9
	Warriors Tale *PaulNicholls* 8-11-5[143] (t) SeanBowen	11/1		ur
	The Fresh Prince (IRE) *OliverSherwood* 7-10-3[127] HarrisonBeswick(7)	20/1		pu
	Matorico (FR) *JonjoO'Neill* 6-10-5[129] (t) RichieMcLernon	50/1		pu

Mr T. Hywel Jones 12ran 5m12.70

WINCANTON Saturday, Nov 11   SOFT

24   John Romans Park Homes 'Rising Stars' Novices' Chase (Gr 2) (1) (4yo+) £18,224   2½m35y (17)

	MODUS *PaulNicholls* 7-11-2 SamTwiston-Davies	4/6f		1
	KALONDRA (IRE) *NeilMulholland* 6-11-2 (t) NoelFehily	15/8	9	2
	VALHALLA (IRE) *ColinTizzard* 7-11-2 (t) HarryCobden	7/1		F

Mr John P. McManus 3ran 5m27.80

25   Unibet Elite Hurdle (Limited Handicap) (Gr 2) (1) (4yo+) £34,170   1m7f65y (7)

1	LONDON PRIZE *IanWilliams* 6-10-9[134] (s) TomO'Brien	4/1		1
	LOUGH DERG SPIRIT (IRE) *NickyHenderson* 5-10-12[137] NicodeBoinville	5/2f	3	2
	FLYING TIGER (IRE) *NickWilliams* 4-11-2[141] NoelFehily	4/1	1¾	3
	Charbel (IRE) *KimBailey* 6-11-10[149] (t) DavidBass	5/1	6	4
	Coeur de Lion *AlanKing* 4-11-5[144] KevinDowling(10)	12/1	1	5
1	Zubayr (IRE) *PaulNicholls* 5-11-3[142] SamTwiston-Davies	9/2	7	6
	Melodic Rendezvous *JeremyScott* 11-10-10[137] (s) MattGriffiths	20/1	65	7

Mrs Margaret Forsyth 7ran 3m48.70

26   Badger Ales Trophy Handicap Chase (L) (1) (155) (4yo+) £34,170   3m1f30y (21)

	PRESENT MAN (IRE) *PaulNicholls* 7-11-0[142] (t) BryonyFrost(5)	8/1		1
	FINAL NUDGE (IRE) *DavidDennis* 8-10-11[139] LeightonAspell	12/1	hd	2
	THEATRE GUIDE (IRE) *ColinTizzard* 10-11-12[154] (b+t) PaddyBrennan	16/1	8	3
	Southfield Theatre (IRE) *PaulNicholls* 9-11-8[150] (s) SamTwiston-Davies	12/1	3¾	4
	Fox Appeal (IRE) *EmmaLavelle* 10-11-0[142] (v+t) NickScholfield	25/1	6	5
	Pilgrims Bay (IRE) *NeilMulholland* 7-10-9[137] (s+h) JamesBest	20/1	nk	6
	Henllan Harri (IRE) *PeterBowen* 9-10-2[130] (b) JamesBowen(7)	8/1		pu

	Fact of The Matter (IRE) *JamieSnowden* 7-10-2[130] (t) GavinSheehan 25/1	pu
	Relentless Dreamer (IRE) *RebeccaCurtis* 8-10-4[132] (s+t) JonathanMoore 25/1	pu
	Alfie Spinner (IRE) *KerryLee* 12-10-7[135] (s+t) JamieMoore 33/1	pu
	Southfield Royale *NeilMulholland* 7-10-10[138] (s) TomScudamore 8/1	pu
	Vic de Touzaine (FR) *VenetiaWilliams* 8-10-11[139] WayneHutchinson 7/1	pu
	Fletchers Flyer (IRE) *HarryFry* 9-11-1[143] (t) NoelFehily 6/1f	pu
	Mr Mix (FR) *PaulNicholls* 6-11-2[144] HarryCobden 7/1	pu
7	Tempestatefloresco *ColinTizzard* 9-11-3[145] (t) SeanHoulihan(7) 33/1	pu
	Yala Enki (FR) *VenetiaWilliams* 7-11-9[151] LiamTreadwell 8/1	pu

Woodhouse & Sutton 16ran 6m49.00

SANDOWN Sunday, Nov 12 SOFT

27 188Bet Future Stars Intermediate Chase (L) (1) (4yo+) £17,085   3m37y (22)

	MIGHT BITE (IRE) *NickyHenderson* 8-11-0 NicodeBoinville 4/9f		1
	FRODON (FR) *PaulNicholls* 5-11-7 (t) SamTwiston-Davies 16/1	8	2
	LABEL DES OBEAUX (FR) *AlanKing* 6-11-1 WayneHutchinson 8/1	½	3
	As de Mee (FR) *PaulNicholls* 7-11-1 HarryCobden 4/1	6	4

The Knot Again Partnership 4ran 6m29.80

NAVAN Sunday, Nov 12 HEAVY

28 Lismullen Hurdle (Gr 2) (4yo+) £23,318   2½m (12)

	APPLE'S JADE (FR) *GordonElliott* 5-11-5 (t) J.W.Kennedy 8/15f		1
	JER'S GIRL (IRE) *GavinPatrickCromwell* 5-10-12 BarryGeraghty 9/4	2	2
	FLAXEN FLARE (IRE) *GordonElliott* 8-11-5 (s) DavyRussell 33/1	9½	3
	Monksland (IRE) *NoelMeade* 10-11-5 SeanFlanagan 9/1	1¾	4

Gigginstown House Stud 4ran 5m18.90

29 thetote.com Fortria Chase (Gr 2) (5yo+) £23,496   2m (11)

	CLARCAM (FR) *GordonElliott* 7-11-7 (s+t) J.W.Kennedy 7/2		1
	ALISIER D'IRLANDE (FR) *HenrydeBromhead* 7-11-7 (t) A.E.Lynch 2/1jf	½	2
	FINE RIGHTLY (IRE) *StuartCrawford* 9-11-4 P.Townend 5/1	2	3
5	The Game Changer (IRE) *GordonElliott* 8-11-4 (t) DavyRussell 2/1jf	30	4
	The Shepherd King (IRE) *R.K.Watson* 13-11-4 (s+t) M.A.Enright 100/1	26	5
	Draycott Place (IRE) *JohnPatrickRyan* 8-11-4 (t) D.E.Mullins 16/1	sh	6

Gigginstown House Stud 6ran 4m18.90

CLONMEL Thursday, Nov 16 HEAVY

30 Clonmel Oil Chase (Gr 2) (4yo+) £26,549   2½m132y (14)

16	ALPHA DES OBEAUX (FR) *M.F.Morris* 7-11-4 (s) SeanFlanagan 7/1		1
17	A TOI PHIL (FR) *GordonElliott* 7-11-6 (t) J.W.Kennedy 3/1	5½	2
9	BALKO DES FLOS (FR) *HenrydeBromhead* 6-11-1 DavyRussell 11/10f	10	3
	Realt Mor (IRE) *GordonElliott* 12-11-5 DenisO'Regan 80/1	39	4
	Champagne West (IRE) *HenrydeBromhead* 9-11-5 A.E.Lynch 7/2	11	5
	Tiger Roll (IRE) *GordonElliott* 7-11-6 (b+t) KeithDonoghue 20/1		pu

Gigginstown House Stud 6ran 5m37.50

CHELTENHAM Friday, Nov 17 GOOD to SOFT

31 Ballymore Novices' Hurdle (Hyde) (Gr 2) (1) (4yo+) £17,085   2m5f26y (10)

	ON THE BLIND SIDE (IRE) *NickyHenderson* 5-11-0 NicodeBoinville 9/2		1
	MOMELLA (IRE) *DanSkelton* 5-10-7 HarrySkelton 9/2	2½	2
12	POETIC RHYTHM (IRE) *FergalO'Brien* 6-11-5 PaddyBrennan 9/2	ns	3
12	Vision des Flos (FR) *ColinTizzard* 4-11-0 B.J.Cooper 3/1	22	4
	Calett Mad (FR) *NigelTwiston-Davies* 5-11-0 (t) DarylJacob 7/4f	2¾	5
	Aye Aye Charlie *FergalO'Brien* 5-11-0 ConorShoemark 40/1		F

Mr A. D. Spence 6ran 5m13.50

CHELTENHAM Saturday, Nov 18 SOFT

32 JCB Triumph Trial Juvenile Hurdle (Prestbury) (Gr 2) (1) (3yo) £17,085   2m87y (8)

	APPLE'S SHAKIRA (FR) *NickyHenderson* 3-10-5 BarryGeraghty .... evsf		1
	GUMBALL (FR) *PhilipHobbs* 3-10-12 RichardJohnson 5/4	17	2
	ERAGON DE CHANAY (FR) *GaryMoore* 3-10-12 JoshuaMoore 28/1	5	3
	Eh Georges (FR) *EmmanuelClayeux,France* 3-10-12 (t) FelixdeGiles 40/1	1¼	4
	Speedo Boy (FR) *IanWilliams* 3-10-12 TomO'Brien 14/1	2	5
	Apparition (IRE) *JosephPatrickO'Brien,Ireland* 3-10-12 J.J.Slevin 25/1	74	6

Mr John P. McManus 6ran 4m09.60

33 betvictor.com Handicap Chase (Gr 3) (1) (4yo+) £28,475   3m3f71y (22)

	PERFECT CANDIDATE (IRE) *FergalO'Brien* 10-10-12[152] (s) PaddyBrennan 7/1		1
	VICENTE (FR) *PaulNicholls* 8-10-10[150] (h) HarryCobden 9/2	nk	2
	THREE FACES WEST (IRE) *PhilipHobbs* 9-10-7[147] (s) RichardJohnson 5/1	17	3

Benbens (IRE) *NigelTwiston-Davies* 12-10-0^{140} JamieBargary(3) 16/1 1½ 4
Shotgun Paddy (IRE) *EmmaLavelle* 10-10-0^{140} AidanColeman 13/2 4½ 5
Sizing Codelco (IRE) *ColinTizzard* 8-11-4^{158} B.J.Cooper 14/1 7 6
Premier Bond *NickyHenderson* 7-10-0^{140} (s) NicodeBoinville .... 4/1f pu
13 Minella Rocco (IRE) *JonjoO'Neill* 7-11-12^{166} (t) BarryGeraghty ....9/2 pu
ISL Recruitment 8ran 7m29.70

34 BetVictor Gold Cup Handicap Chase (Gr 3) (1) (4yo+) £91,120 2½m78y (16)
SPLASH OF GINGE *NigelTwiston-Davies* 9-10-6^{134} TomBellamy 25/1 1
STARCHITECT (IRE) *DavidPipe* 6-11-2^{144} (b+t) TomScudamore ....10/1 nk 2
LE PREZIEN (FR) *PaulNicholls* 6-11-8^{150} (t) BarryGeraghty 6/1 2½ 3
Ballyalton (IRE) *IanWilliams* 10-11-1^{143} (s) TomO'Brien 8/1 3¾ 4
Romain de Senam (FR) *PaulNicholls* 5-11-3^{145} (h+t) HarryCobden 10/1 6 5
Tully East (IRE) *AlanFleming,Ireland* 7-11-6^{148} DenisO'Regan ....8/1 nk 6
Double Treasure *JamieSnowden* 6-11-8^{150} (t) GavinSheehan 25/1 10 7
Foxtail Hill (IRE) *NigelTwiston-Davies* 8-11-5^{147} JamieBargary(3) 9/1 2¼ 8
8 Guitar Pete (IRE) *NickyRichards* 7-10-6^{134} RyanDay(3) ....11/1 nk 9
7 Bentelimar (IRE) *CharlieLongsdon* 8-10-11^{139} JonathanBurke 25/1 2 10
Viconte du Noyer (FR) *ColinTizzard* 8-11-8^{150} (t) B.J.Cooper 20/1 33 11
18 Theinval (FR) *NickyHenderson* 7-11-4^{146} (s) JeremiahMcGrath ....20/1 F
Lake Takapuna (IRE) *J.Culloty,Ireland* 6-10-1^{129} PaddyBrennan ....20/1 pu
Plaisir d'Amour (FR) *VenetiaWilliams* 5-10-10^{138} AidanColeman ....20/1 pu
Aqua Dude (IRE) *EvanWilliams* 7-10-11^{139} AdamWedge ....16/1 pu
3 Days of Heaven (FR) *NickyHenderson* 7-11-7^{149} (h) NicodeBoinville ....33/1 pu
Kylemore Lough *HarryFry* 8-11-12^{154} (t) NoelFehily .... 4/1f pu
Mr J. D. Neild 17ran 5m24.40

35 Regulatory Finance Solutions Handicap Hurdle (L) (1) (4yo+) £17,085 3m1f67y (12)
THOMAS CAMPBELL *NickyHenderson* 5-11-10^{148} JamesBowen(7) 13/8f 1
ANTEROS (IRE) *SophieLeech* 9-10-4^{128} (s+t) PaddyBrennan 8/1 2½ 2
ROCKY'S TREASURE (IRE) *KimBailey* 6-10-10^{134} DavidBass 13/2 5 3
Nuits Premier Cru (FR) *EmmanuelClayeux,France* 5-10-3^{127} (s+t) FelixdeGiles ...20/1 4½ 4
Connetable (FR) *PaulNicholls* 5-10-9^{133} BryonyFrost(5) 10/1 2¾ 5
Solatentif (FR) *ColinTizzard* 7-10-8^{132} (b+t) B.J.Cooper 14/1 7 6
Rolling Maul (IRE) *PeterBowen* 9-10-5^{129} (b) RichardJohnson 16/1 9 7
Kk Lexion (IRE) *TomGeorge* 6-10-7^{131} A.P.Heskin 5/1 2 8
Dell' Arca (IRE) *DavidPipe* 8-11-12^{150} (b+t) TomScudamore ....10/1 pu
Mrs Van Geest & Mrs Kelvin Hughes 9ran 6m49.50

CHELTENHAM Sunday, Nov 19 SOFT

36 Racing Post Arkle Trophy Trial Novices' Chase (November) (Gr 2) (1) (4yo+) £19,932 1m7f199y (13)
NORTH HILL HARVEY *DanSkelton* 6-11-5 HarrySkelton 6/4 1
RIVER WYLDE (IRE) *NickyHenderson* 6-11-2 NicodeBoinville .... evsf 18 2
OZZIE THE OSCAR (IRE) *PhilipHobbs* 6-11-2 RichardJohnson 5/1 1¼ 3
Mrs G. Widdowson & Mrs R. Kelvin-Hughes 3ran 4m05.60

37 Shloer Chase (Cheltenham) (Gr 2) (1) (4yo+) £42,712 1m7f199y (13)
FOX NORTON (FR) *ColinTizzard* 7-11-6 (h) B.J.Cooper 4/5f 1
14 CLOUDY DREAM (IRE) *MalcolmJefferson* 7-11-3 BrianHughes 9/4 8 2
SPECIAL TIARA *HenrydeBromhead,Ireland* 10-11-6 NoelFehily ....8/1 nk 3
Simply Ned (IRE) *NickyRichards* 10-11-0 WayneHutchinson 14/1 1¼ 4
Vaniteux (FR) *DavidPipe* 8-11-4 (s+t) TomScudamore 20/1 42 5
Ann & Alan Potts Limited 5ran 4m04.40

38 Unibet Greatwood Handicap Hurdle (Gr 3) (1) (4yo+) £56,950 2m87y (8)
19 ELGIN *AlanKing* 5-10-8^{145} WayneHutchinson 10/1 1
MISTERTON *HarryFry* 6-10-0^{137} TomScudamore ....10/1 nk 2
11 OLD GUARD *PaulNicholls* 6-10-12^{149} BryonyFrost(5) 8/1 4½ 3
The New One (IRE) *NigelTwiston-Davies* 9-11-12^{163} RichardJohnson 7/1 1 4
1 William H Bonney *AlanKing* 6-10-0^{137} MitchellBastyan(5) 12/1 1 5
Nietzsche *BrianEllison* 4-10-0^{137} (h) JamesBowen(5) 12/1 8 6
Jenkins (IRE) *NickyHenderson* 5-10-0^{137} DavidBass ....5/1 ½ 7
5 Project Bluebook (FR) *JohnQuinn* 4-10-6^{143} BrianHughes ....40/1 ½ 8
5 Tigris River (IRE) *JosephPatrickO'Brien,Ireland* 6-10-13^{150} (t) BarryGeraghty ...14/1 6 9
Chesterfield (IRE) *SeamusMullins* 7-10-11^{148} DanielSansom(7) 25/1 2½ 10
Mohaayed *DanSkelton* 5-10-0^{137} (t) HarrySkelton 9/1 30 11
Ivanovich Gorbatov (IRE) *JosephPatrickO'Brien,Ireland* 5-11-0^{151} (t) AidanColeman 20/1 3¾ 12
25 London Prize *IanWilliams* 6-10-2^{139} (s) TomO'Brien .... 9/2f F
Elite Racing Club 13ran 4m03.10

39 Sky Bet Supreme Trial Novices' Hurdle (Sharp) (Gr 2) (1) (4yo+) £17,085 2m87y (5)
Both flights in the home straight were omitted due to the low trajectory of the sun
SLATE HOUSE (IRE) *ColinTizzard* 5-11-0 HarryCobden 5/2 1
SUMMERVILLE BOY (IRE) *TomGeorge* 5-11-0 A.P.Heskin ....16/1 ¾ 2
BETTER GETALONG (IRE) *NickyRichards* 6-11-0 NoelFehily 7/1 3¾ 3
Bedrock *DanSkelton* 4-11-0 (t) HarrySkelton 8/1 3 4
Dame de Compagnie (FR) *NickyHenderson* 4-10-7 (h) BarryGeraghty 10/11f 1¾ 5
Eric Jones, Geoff Nicholas, John Romans 5ran 4m07.90

PUNCHESTOWN Sunday, Nov 19 SOFT

40 Ryans Cleaning Craddockstown Novices' Chase (Gr 2) (4yo+) £24,416 2m40y (12)
WOODLAND OPERA (IRE) *MrsJ.Harrington* 7-11-4 (t) RobbiePower 11/2 1
TOMBSTONE (IRE) *GordonElliott* 7-11-4 DavyRussell ....10/11f ½ 2
CALINO D'AIRY (FR) *HenrydeBromhead* 5-11-4 SeanFlanagan 10/3 15 3
Brelade *GordonElliott* 5-11-4 DenisO'Regan 4/1 4½ 4
Mrs T K Cooper/D Cooper/C A Waters 4ran 4m17.10

41 Liam & Valerie Brennan Memorial Florida Pearl Novices' Chase (Gr 2) 2¾m140y (17)
(5yo+) £23,628
JURY DUTY (IRE) *GordonElliott* 6-11-3 RobbiePower 6/1 1
SHATTERED LOVE (IRE) *GordonElliott* 6-10-10 (t) SeanFlanagan .... 11/4 ¾ 2
PRESENTING PERCY *PatrickG.Kelly* 6-11-3 (t) DavyRussell .... evsf 12 3
7 Arbre de Vie (FR) *W.P.Mullins* 7-11-3 P.Townend 13/2 11 4
Call The Taxie (IRE) *EllmarieHolden* 6-11-3 RachaelBlackmore 12/1 34 5
Sideways Syndicate 5ran 6m08.50

42 Unibet Morgiana Hurdle (Gr 1) (4yo+) £49,645 2m40y (8)
FAUGHEEN (IRE) *W.P.Mullins* 9-11-10 P.Townend 4/11f 1
JEZKI (IRE) *MrsJ.Harrington* 9-11-10 M.P.Walsh 6/1 16 2
5 SWAMP FOX (IRE) *JosephG.Murphy* 5-11-10 (b) D.J.Mullins 20/1 37 3
Campeador (FR) *GordonElliott* 5-11-10 (h) DavyRussell ....9/2 F
Mrs S. Ricci 4ran 3m59.90

ASCOT Saturday, Nov 25 GOOD to SOFT

43 Christy 1965 Chase (Gr 2) (1) (4yo+) £39,865 2m5f8y (17)
TOP NOTCH (FR) *NickyHenderson* 6-11-4 NicodeBoinville 5/2jf 1
DOUBLE SHUFFLE (IRE) *TomGeorge* 7-11-1 (h) JonathanBurke 12/1 8 2
27 FRODON (FR) *PaulNicholls* 5-11-5 (t) SeanBowen 8/1 2¼ 3
Flying Angel (IRE) *NigelTwiston-Davies* 7-11-1 (t) TomBellamy 7/1 1¾ 4
14 Smad Place (FR) *AlanKing* 10-11-7 WayneHutchinson 5/2jf 15 5
Josses Hill (IRE) *NickyHenderson* 9-11-7 (s) AidanColeman 10/1 32 6
Top Gamble (IRE) *KerryLee* 9-11-1 (t) JamieMoore 10/1 7
Sizing Granite (IRE) *ColinTizzard* 9-11-5 (s+t) RobertDunne 33/1 8
14 Royal Regatta (IRE) *PhilipHobbs* 9-11-7 (b+t) TomO'Brien 20/1 9
Mr Simon Munir & Mr Isaac Souede 9ran 5m15.40

44 Coral Hurdle (Ascot) (Gr 2) (1) (4yo+) £56,950 2m3f58y (10)
21 LIL ROCKERFELLER (USA) *NeilKing* 6-11-0 (s) TrevorWhelan 9/4 1
L'AMI SERGE (IRE) *NickyHenderson* 7-11-6 (h) NicodeBoinville 7/2 1½ 2
15 WAKEA (USA) *KarlThornton,Ireland* 6-11-4 (h+t) MrJ.C.Barry ....50/1 hd 3
Defi du Seuil (FR) *PhilipHobbs* 4-11-3 BarryGeraghty 10/11f 16 4
Dicosimo (FR) *WarrenGreatrex* 6-11-0 (h) GavinSheehan 50/1 88 5
Davies Smith Govier & Brown 5ran 4m42.20

45 Shawbrook Handicap Chase (2) (4yo+) £62,560 2m167y (13)
SIR VALENTINO (FR) *TomGeorge* 8-11-5[159] (t) JonathanBurke 16/1 1
CEPAGE (FR) *VenetiaWilliams* 5-10-0[139] LiamTreadwell .... 11/2 ½ 2
18 QUITE BY CHANCE *ColinTizzard* 8-10-7[146] TomO'Brien 7/2 1½ 3
San Benedeto (FR) *PaulNicholls* 6-11-4[157] (s+t) BryonyFrost(5) .... 2/1f ns 4
Upsilon Bleu (FR) *PaulineRobson* 9-10-3[142] CraigNichol 11/1 1¼ 5
Dandridge *A.L.T.Moore,Ireland* 8-10-1[140] (t) AidanColeman 10/1 16 6
37 Vaniteux (FR) *DavidPipe* 8-11-5[158] (s+t) DavidNoonan 20/1 1¾ 7
Sire de Grugy (FR) *GaryMoore* 11-11-12[165] JamieMoore 6/1 1¾ 8
Doone Hollow Susie Saunders & Lady Cobham 8ran 4m12.00

HAYDOCK Saturday, Nov 25 HEAVY

46 Betfair Stayers' Handicap Hurdle (Gr 3) (1) (4yo+) £56,950 2¾m177y (12)
11 SAM SPINNER *JeddO'Keeffe* 5-10-9[139] JoeColliver 6/1 1
THE DUTCHMAN (IRE) *ColinTizzard* 7-10-5[135] (t) RobbiePower 12/1 17 2
THEO'S CHARM (IRE) *NickGifford* 7-10-7[137] (b) DarylJacob 16/1 5 3

	No Hassle Hoff (IRE) *DanSkelton* 5-10-11[141] HarrySkelton	8/1	2¾	4
	Champers On Ice (IRE) *DavidPipe* 7-10-13[143] (b) TomScudamore	13/2	3½	5
	Fingerontheswitch (IRE) *NeilMulholland* 7-10-0[130] (s+t) JamesBowen(5)	40/1	hd	6
11	Le Rocher (FR) *NickWilliams* 7-10-11[141] LizzieKelly(3)	8/1	3	7
	The Worlds End (IRE) *TomGeorge* 6-11-5[149] A.P.Heskin	5/1f	2	8
11	Three Musketeers (IRE) *DanSkelton* 7-10-10[140] BridgetAndrews(3)	16/1	16	9
	Ibsen (IRE) *GordonElliott,Ireland* 8-10-0[130] (s+t) J.W.Kennedy	25/1	1¼	10
21	Gayebury *EvanWilliams* 7-11-4[148] (s) MitchellBastyan(5)	25/1	8	11
	Robbin'hannon (IRE) *PhilipHobbs* 6-10-12[142] RichardJohnson	16/1	nk	12
	Silsol (GER) *PaulNicholls* 8-11-12[156] (b+t) HenryMorshead(7)	25/1	3½	13
	Templeross (IRE) *NigelTwiston-Davies* 6-10-1[131] JamieBargary(3)	14/1		pu
	Minella Awards (IRE) *HarryFry* 6-11-1[145] (t) NoelFehily	6/1		pu
	Zarkandar (IRE) *PaulNicholls* 10-11-6[150] (b+t) HarryCobden	20/1		pu

Caron & Paul Chapman 16ran 5m47.60

47 Betfair Chase (Lancashire) (Gr 1) (1) (5yo+) £112,540 3m1f125y (19)

22	BRISTOL DE MAI (FR) *NigelTwiston-Davies* 6-11-7 DarylJacob	11/10f		1
22	CUE CARD *ColinTizzard* 11-11-7 (t) HarryCobden	2/1	57	2
16	OUTLANDER (IRE) *GordonElliott,Ireland* 9-11-7 (s) J.W.Kennedy	5/1	9	3
14	Tea For Two *NickWilliams* 8-11-7 LizzieKelly	9/1	½	4
14	Traffic Fluide (FR) *GaryMoore* 7-11-7 (s) JoshuaMoore	28/1	¾	5
22	Shantou Flyer (IRE) *RichardHobson* 7-11-7 (t) AdamWedge	50/1		pu

Mr Simon Munir & Mr Isaac Souede 6ran 7m00.60

NAVAN Sunday, Nov 26 HEAVY

48 'Monksfield' Novices' Hurdle (Gr 3) (4yo+) £22,388 2½m (11)

	SAMCRO (IRE) *GordonElliott* 5-11-2 J.W.Kennedy	1/4f		1
	JETZ (IRE) *MrsJ.Harrington* 5-11-2 RobbiePower	6/1	12	2
	DELTA WORK (FR) *GordonElliott* 4-10-12 (h+t) DavyRussell	20/1	¾	3
	Half The Odds (IRE) *NoelMeade* 5-10-9 SeanFlanagan	10/1	3¾	4
	Good Thyne Tara *W.P.Mullins* 7-10-9 P.Townend	8/1	2	5
	Turbojet *DermotAnthonyMcLoughlin* 6-11-2 M.A.Enright	20/1	15	6
	Cosmo's Moon (IRE) *R.P.McNamara* 4-10-12 A.E.Lynch	66/1	4½	7
	Creation (FR) *HenrydeBromhead* 5-10-9 D.J.Mullins	25/1	40	8

Gigginstown House Stud 8ran 5m11.50

49 Ladbrokes Troytown Handicap Chase (Gr B) (150) (4yo+) £52,679 3m (17)

	MALA BEACH (IRE) *GordonElliott* 9-11-9[148] DavyRussell	12/1		1
	DONT TELL NO ONE (IRE) *JohnE.Kiely* 9-10-5[130] A.E.Lynch	12/1	2¾	2
	BONNY KATE (IRE) *NoelMeade* 7-10-13[138] SeanFlanagan	16/1	8	3
	Poormans Hill (IRE) *GordonElliott* 6-9-10[121] AndrewRing(3)	16/1	½	4
	Tesseract (IRE) *JosephPatrickO'Brien* 6-10-4[129] J.J.Slevin(3)	25/1	13	5
	Space Cadet (IRE) *GordonElliott* 7-10-7[132] B.Hayes	33/1	nk	6
	General Principle (IRE) *GordonElliott* 8-11-1[140] J.W.Kennedy	6/1	6½	7
	He Rock's (IRE) *S.J.Mahon* 8-10-1[126] (b+t) JonathanMoore	33/1	3¼	8
	Whatareudoingtome (IRE) *J.P.Dempsey* 7-9-10[121] L.P.Dempsey	14/1	2	9
7	Potters Point (IRE) *GordonElliott* 7-11-9[148] (t) MsL.O'Neill(5)	20/1	3½	10
	Icantsay (IRE) *JohnPatrickRyan* 7-9-13[124] JonathanBurke	25/1	4¾	11
	Last Goodbye (IRE) *MissElizabethDoyle* 6-10-11[136] M.P.Walsh	12/1	2	12
	Hurricane Darwin (IRE) *AlanFleming* 7-10-8[133] (t) DenisO'Regan	12/1	7	13
	Wounded Warrior (IRE) *NoelMeade* 8-11-3[142] A.W.Short(7)	25/1	9½	14
10	Arkwrisht (FR) *JosephPatrickO'Brien* 7-10-13[138] (t) ShaneShortall(3)	20/1	18	15
	Acapella Bourgeois (FR) *W.P.Mullins* 7-11-10[149] P.Townend	7/4f		F
	Paper Lantern (IRE) *KarlThornton* 8-9-10[121] (t) R.C.Colgan	40/1		pu
	Don Vincenzo (IRE) *ColinBowe* 8-9-11[122] (t) RachaelBlackmore	33/1		pu
	As de Pique (IRE) *GavinPatrickCromwell* 12-9-13[124] (t) PhilipEnright	33/1		pu
	The Winkler (IRE) *EoinDoyle* 8-10-4[130] (b+t) D.J.McInerney(5)	25/1		pu
10	Rogue Angel (IRE) *M.F.Morris* 9-10-10[135] (b+t) ChrisMeehan(5)	33/1		pu

Mr C. Jones 21ran 6m34.30

NEWBURY Friday, Dec 1 Chase course: GOOD, Hurdles course: GOOD to SOFT

50 Ladbrokes Novices' Chase (Berkshire) (Gr 2) (1) (4yo+) £22,780 2m3f187y (16)

	WILLOUGHBY COURT (IRE) *BenPauling* 6-11-1 NicodeBoinville	15/8		1
	YANWORTH *AlanKing* 7-11-1 BarryGeraghty	5/6f	3	2
	ADRIEN DU PONT (FR) *PaulNicholls* 5-11-1 (t) HarryCobden	11/2	3½	3
	Western Miller (IRE) *CharlieLongsdon* 6-11-1 (t) RichardJohnson	25/1	43	4
	Battle Anthem (IRE) *RichardRowe* 6-11-1 LeightonAspell	150/1		pu

Paul & Clare Rooney 5ran 4m57.90

51 Ladbrokes Long Distance Hurdle (Gr 2) (1) (4yo+) £28,475 3m52y (12)
BEER GOGGLES (IRE) *RichardWoollacott* 6-11-0 RichardJohnson 40/1 1
UNOWHATIMEANHARRY *HarryFry* 9-11-6 (t) BarryGeraghty 7/4 2¼ 2
TAQUIN DU SEUIL (FR) *JonjoO'Neill* 10-11-0 AidanColeman 33/1 3¾ 3
21 Colin's Sister *FergalO'Brien* 6-10-13 PaddyBrennan 8/1 3 4
Thistlecrack *ColinTizzard* 9-11-0 TomScudamore 11/10f 4 5
21 Wholestone (IRE) *NigelTwiston-Davies* 6-11-3 DarylJacob ....10/1 ½ 6
Bradley Partnership 6ran 6m01.50

NEWBURY Saturday, Dec 2 GOOD
52 Ladbrokes John Francome Novices' Chase (Gr 2) (1) (4yo+) £22,780 2m7f86y (18)
ELEGANT ESCAPE (IRE) *ColinTizzard* 5-11-2 HarryCobden 5/1 1
BLACK CORTON (FR) *PaulNicholls* 6-11-5 (t) BryonyFrost ....9/4 ¾ 2
SIR IVAN *HarryFry* 7-11-2 (t) NoelFehily 6/1 13 3
Wait For Me (FR) *PhilipHobbs* 7-11-2 (h+t) RichardJohnson 8/1 2¼ 4
21 Fountains Windfall *AnthonyHoneyball* 7-11-2 AidanColeman .... 7/4f F
Mr J. P. Romans 5ran 5m52.70

53 Ladbrokes Trophy Chase (Handicap) (Gr 3) (1) (4yo+) £142,375 3m1f214y (21)
10 TOTAL RECALL (IRE) *W.P.Mullins,Ireland* 8-10-8^{147} P.Townend 9/2f 1
WHISPER (FR) *NickyHenderson* 9-11-8^{161} DavyRussell ....8/1 nk 2
20 REGAL ENCORE (IRE) *AnthonyHoneyball* 9-10-11^{150} (t) RichieMcLernon 66/1 9 3
20 Braqueur d'Or (FR) *PaulNicholls* 6-10-0^{139} HarryCobden 33/1 3¾ 4
26 Pilgrims Bay (IRE) *NeilMulholland* 7-10-0^{139} (s+h) JamesBest 33/1 4 5
21 Missed Approach (IRE) *WarrenGreatrex* 7-10-6^{145} (b) RichardJohnson 20/1 10 6
Potters Legend *LucyWadham* 7-10-0^{139} (b) BrianHughes 20/1 4½ 7
Carole's Destrier *NeilMulholland* 9-11-1^{154} RobertDunne 33/1 7 8
A Genie In Abottle (IRE) *NoelMeade,Ireland* 6-10-13^{152} SeanFlanagan ....10/1 ¾ 9
Bigbadjohn (IRE) *RebeccaCurtis* 8-10-5^{144} AdamWedge 50/1 3½ 10
Vyta du Roc (FR) *NickyHenderson* 8-10-1^{140} AidanColeman ....10/1 ¾ 11
26 Present Man (IRE) *PaulNicholls* 7-10-7^{146} (t) BryonyFrost(5) 16/1 3½ 12
Singlefarmpayment *TomGeorge* 7-10-8^{147} (h) A.P.Heskin ....13/2 F
26 Southfield Royale *NeilMulholland* 7-10-0^{139} (b) BrendanPowell ....33/1 pu
Cogry *NigelTwiston-Davies* 8-10-0^{139} (s) JamieBargary(3) ....14/1 pu
Double Ross (IRE) *NigelTwiston-Davies* 11-10-8^{147} TomBellamy ....33/1 pu
Royal Vacation (IRE) *ColinTizzard* 7-10-10^{149} (b+t) PaddyBrennan ....20/1 pu
27 Label des Obeaux (FR) *AlanKing* 6-11-0^{153} (s) D.J.Mullins ....33/1 pu
American (FR) *HarryFry* 7-11-4^{157} NoelFehily ....5/1 pu
22 Coneygree *MarkBradstock* 10-11-12^{165} NicodeBoinville ....8/1 pu
Slaneyville Syndicate 20ran 6m29.80

NEWCASTLE Saturday, Dec 2 HEAVY
54 Unibet 'Fighting Fifth' Hurdle (Gr 1) (1) (4yo+) £61,897 2m98y (9)
BUVEUR D'AIR (FR) *NickyHenderson* 6-11-7 BarryGeraghty 1/6f 1
IRVING *PaulNicholls* 9-11-7 SeanBowen 9/2 3½ 2
25 FLYING TIGER (IRE) *NickWilliams* 4-11-7 TomScudamore 9/1 1 3
Katgary (FR) *PaulineRobson* 7-11-7 (s) CraigNichol 66/1 8 4
Mirsaale *KeithDalgleish* 7-11-7 CallumBewley 33/1 17 5
Mr John P. McManus 5ran 4m07.40

55 At The Races Rehearsal Handicap Chase (L) (1) (4yo+) £39,865 2m7f91y (16)
The second fence in the home straight was omitted on both circuits due to being damaged from the previous chase
BEWARE THE BEAR (IRE) *NickyHenderson* 7-11-7^{145} SeanBowen 11/4f 1
BISHOPS ROAD (IRE) *KerryLee* 9-11-6^{144} JamieMoore 9/2 2¼ 2
26 YALA ENKI (FR) *VenetiaWilliams* 7-11-12^{150} LiamTreadwell 9/2 5 3
Boric *SimonWaugh* 9-10-2^{126} (s) CallumBewley(3) 14/1 6 4
Wakanda (IRE) *SueSmith* 8-11-9^{147} DannyCook 7/2 20 5
Sam Red (FR) *DanSkelton* 6-10-13^{137} (t) HarrySkelton ....6/1 F
Dedigout (IRE) *MickyHammond* 11-11-2^{140} (t) FinianO'Toole(5) ....50/1 pu
Our Kaempfer (IRE) *CharlieLongsdon* 8-11-8^{146} (t) BarryGeraghty ....14/1 pu
Mr G. B. Barlow 8ran 6m15.80

FAIRYHOUSE Sunday, Dec 3 SOFT
56 Bar One Racing Royal Bond Novices' Hurdle (Gr 1) (4yo+) £44,777 2m (9)
MENGLI KHAN (IRE) *GordonElliott* 4-11-7 J.W.Kennedy .... evsf 1
EARLY DOORS (FR) *JosephPatrickO'Brien* 4-11-7 M.P.Walsh 7/1 5½ 2
HARDLINE (IRE) *GordonElliott* 5-11-10 (h) DavyRussell 14/1 15 3
Morgan (IRE) *GordonElliott* 5-11-10 KeithDonoghue ....20/1 ¾ 4
Red Jack (IRE) *NoelMeade* 4-11-7 SeanFlanagan ....13/2 ½ 5

Le Richebourg (FR) *JosephPatrickO'Brien* 4-11-7 BarryGeraghty ... 5/1 1½ 6
Makitorix (FR) *W.P.Mullins* 4-11-7 P.Townend ... 7/1 pu
Gigginstown House Stud 7ran 4m01.30

57 Bar One Racing Hatton's Grace Hurdle (Gr 1) (4yo+) £52,679 2½m (11)
28 APPLE'S JADE (FR) *GordonElliott* 5-11-3 (t) J.W.Kennedy ... evsf 1
NICHOLS CANYON *W.P.Mullins* 7-11-10 P.Townend ... 2/1 9 2
SUPASUNDAE *MrsJ.Harrington* 7-11-10 RobbiePower ... 14/1 1¾ 3
Cilaos Emery (FR) *W.P.Mullins* 5-11-10 (h) MrP.W.Mullins ... 8/1 sh 4
15 Mick Jazz (FR) *GordonElliott* 6-11-10 (h) DavyRussell ... 25/1 2½ 5
Augusta Kate *W.P.Mullins* 6-11-3 D.E.Mullins ... 16/1 21 6
42 Swamp Fox (IRE) *JosephG.Murphy* 5-11-10 (b) SeanFlanagan ... 50/1 6 7
Gigginstown House Stud 7ran 5m07.00

58 Bar One Racing Handicap Hurdle (Gr A) (4yo+) £52,679 2m (9)
DAVIDS CHARM (IRE) *JohnJ.Walsh* 6-10-8^{134} (h) RachaelBlackmore ... 10/1 1
MERI DEVIE (FR) *W.P.Mullins* 4-10-7^{136} (h) P.Townend ... 13/2 2¾ 2
SHE'S A STAR (IRE) *NoelMeade* 5-10-2^{128} SeanFlanagan ... 14/1 ½ 3
YAHA FIZZ (IRE) *E.D.Delany* 7-10-9^{135} R.P.Treacy(5) ... 12/1 dh 3
Agent Boru (IRE) *T.Gibney* 6-9-10^{122} JonathanMoore ... 33/1 hd 5
Ben Dundee (IRE) *GordonElliott* 5-10-4^{130} J.W.Kennedy ... 7/2f 1½ 6
Charlie Stout (IRE) *ShaneNolan* 6-10-4^{130} (t) R.C.Colgan ... 16/1 ½ 7
Veinard (FR) *GordonElliott* 8-9-13^{128} (t) DenisO'Regan ... 14/1 ¾ 8
Highland Fling (IRE) *GavinPatrickCromwell* 5-10-3^{129} A.E.Lynch ... 12/1 ¾ 9
Ted Veale (IRE) *A.J.Martin* 10-11-0^{140} E.O'Connell(7) ... 20/1 8½ 10
38 Tigris River (IRE) *JosephPatrickO'Brien* 6-11-9^{149} (t) J.S.McGarvey ... 25/1 ½ 11
Housesofparliament (IRE) *JosephPatrickO'Brien* 4-10-3^{132} (t) M.P.Walsh ... 20/1 nk 12
Laverteen (FR) *NoelMeade* 6-9-10^{120} A.W.Short(7) ... 20/1 1¾ 13
Chateau Conti (FR) *W.P.Mullins* 5-11-2^{142} D.E.Mullins ... 8/1 2 14
Bleu Et Rouge (FR) *W.P.Mullins* 6-11-5^{145} BarryGeraghty ... 6/1 6½ 15
Timi Roli (FR) *W.P.Mullins* 5-10-0^{126} B.Hayes ... 33/1 3¼ 16
Top Othe Ra (IRE) *ThomasMullins* 9-10-10^{136} RobbiePower ... 16/1 14 17
Time For Mabel (FR) *E.J.O'Grady* 6-10-4^{130} (s) PhilipEnright ... 66/1 1 18
West Coast Time (IRE) *JosephPatrickO'Brien* 5-9-10^{122} (t) AndrewRing(3) ... 16/1 hd 19
38 Ivanovich Gorbatov (IRE) *JosephPatrickO'Brien* 5-11-10^{150} (t) L.P.Dempsey ... 40/1 ½ 20
T A O'Brien Partnership 20ran 4m03.00

59 Bar One Racing Drinmore Novices' Chase (Gr 1) (4yo+) £45,535 2½m (14)
DEATH DUTY (IRE) *GordonElliott* 6-11-10 DavyRussell ... 8/11f 1
RATHVINDEN (IRE) *W.P.Mullins* 9-11-10 P.Townend ... 3/1 3¼ 2
SNOW FALCON (IRE) *NoelMeade* 7-11-10 SeanFlanagan ... 16/1 2¾ 3
Dinaria des Obeaux (FR) *GordonElliott* 4-10-9 (t) J.W.Kennedy ... 4/1 3¾ 4
Townshend (GER) *W.P.Mullins* 6-11-10 D.E.Mullins ... 33/1 23 5
Gigginstown House Stud 5ran 5m20.90

60 Bar One Racing Porterstown Handicap Chase (Gr B) (5yo+) £26,339 3m5f (22)
41 PRESENTING PERCY *PatrickG.Kelly* 6-11-10^{145} (t) DavyRussell ... 7/2jf 1
FOREVER GOLD (IRE) *EdwardCawley* 10-10-13^{134} (s) C.D.Timmons(3) ... 10/1 11 2
49 HE ROCK'S (IRE) *S.J.Mahon* 8-10-4^{125} (b+t) DenisO'Regan ... 20/1 8 3
Mall Dini (IRE) *PatrickG.Kelly* 7-11-8^{143} (t) M.P.Walsh ... 9/1 1¾ 4
49 Poormans Hill (IRE) *GordonElliott* 6-10-0^{121} J.W.Kennedy ... 7/2jf 8½ 5
Une Lavandiere (FR) *NoelMeade* 6-9-10^{117} JonathanMoore ... 10/1 8 6
Anseanachai Cliste (IRE) *RonanM.P.McNally* 9-9-10^{117} (s) D.Robinson(5) ... 8/1 1 7
49 Wounded Warrior (IRE) *NoelMeade* 8-11-3^{138} (b) SeanFlanagan ... 14/1 31 8
Carrigeen Acebo (IRE) *R.H.Lalor* 9-9-10^{117} (s+h) MissLizLalor(5) ... 33/1 20 9
Some Drama (IRE) *DermotAnthonyMcLoughlin* 10-9-10^{117} (s+t) R.C.Colgan ... 25/1 ur
49 Icantsay (IRE) *JohnPatrickRyan* 7-10-2^{123} D.E.Mullins ... 20/1 pu
Undressed (FR) *M.Hourigan* 9-10-2^{123} (t) PhilipEnright ... 20/1 pu
Bless The Wings (IRE) *GordonElliott* 12-11-4^{139} (s+t) KeithDonoghue ... 14/1 pu
Thunder And Roses (IRE) *M.F.Morris* 9-11-10^{145} (s+t) MsL.O'Neill(5) ... 12/1 pu
Philip J. Reynolds 14ran 7m55.60

SANDOWN Friday, Dec 8 SOFT

61 Ballymore Novices' Hurdle (Winter) (Gr 2) (1) (4yo+) £17,085 2m3f173y (9)
31 ON THE BLIND SIDE (IRE) *NickyHenderson* 5-11-5 NicodeBoinville ... 6/5f 1
SPRINGTOWN LAKE (IRE) *PhilipHobbs* 5-11-0 RichardJohnson ... 10/1 9 2
RED RIVER (IRE) *KimBailey* 4-11-0 (t) DavidBass ... 4/1 11 3
Marley Firth (IRE) *DanSkelton* 5-11-0 HarrySkelton ... 14/1 5 4
Dynamite Dollars (FR) *PaulNicholls* 4-11-0 HarryCobden ... 12/1 6 5
Diamant Bleu (FR) *NickWilliams* 4-11-5 LizzieKelly ... 66/1 7 6

White Moon (GER) *ColinTizzard* 5-11-0 (t) AidanColeman 7/2 13 7
Mr A. D. Spence 7ran 4m59.50

AINTREE Saturday, Dec 9 HEAVY

62 Randox Health Becher Handicap Chase (Gr 3) (1) (6yo+) £81,388   3m1f188y (21)
  22 BLAKLION *NigelTwiston-Davies* 8-11-6[153] GavinSheehan 7/4f 1
      THE LAST SAMURI (IRE) *KimBailey* 9-11-12[170] DavidBass 7/1 9 2
      HIGHLAND LODGE (IRE) *JamesMoffatt* 11-10-5[138] (s) HenryBrooke 12/1 5 3
      Federici *DonaldMcCain* 8-10-0[133] (s) WillKennedy 33/1 2¾ 4
      Portrait King (IRE) *PatrickGriffin,Ireland* 12-10-0[133] (s) ConorO'Farrell 33/1 4½ 5
  20 The Young Master *NeilMulholland* 8-10-12[145] MrSamWaley-Cohen(3) 28/1 6 6
  22 Vieux Lion Rouge (FR) *DavidPipe* 8-11-5[152] (s) TomScudamore 7/1 38 7
      Westerner Point (IRE) *EoghanO'Grady,Ireland* 8-10-1[134] PhilipEnright 12/1 6 8
      Lord Windermere (IRE) *J.Culloty,Ireland* 11-10-11[144] BrianHughes ...... 25/1 F
  27 As de Mee (FR) *PaulNicholls* 7-11-2[149] SeanBowen .... 14/1 ur
      Straidnahanna (IRE) *SueSmith* 8-10-0[133] SeanQuinlan .... 40/1 pu
  49 Rogue Angel (IRE) *M.F.Morris,Ireland* 9-10-2[135] (b+t) RichieMcLernon ... 20/1 pu
  7   Viva Steve (IRE) *FergalO'Brien* 9-10-5[138] (s) JonathanBurke .... 12/1 pu
      Goodtoknow *KerryLee* 9-10-9[142] (b) JamieMoore .... 14/1 pu
  33 Sizing Codelco (IRE) *ColinTizzard* 8-11-9[156] TomO'Brien .... 25/1 pu
S Such & CG Paletta 15ran 7m18.10

63 188Bet.co.uk Many Clouds Chase (Gr 2) (1) (4yo+) £28,135   3m210y (19)
  22 DEFINITLY RED (IRE) *BrianEllison* 8-11-4 DannyCook 9/4jf 1
  37 CLOUDY DREAM (IRE) *MalcolmJefferson* 7-11-3 BrianHughes 9/4jf 7 2
  43 FLYING ANGEL (IRE) *NigelTwiston-Davies* 6-11-3 TomBellamy 4/1 8 3
  30 Alpha des Obeaux (FR) *M.F.Morris,Ireland* 7-11-6 (b) JonathanBurke 5/2 5 4
Mr P. J. Martin 4ran 7m12.20

64 188Bet Grand Sefton Handicap Chase (2) (6yo+) £43,330   2m5f19y (18)
      GAS LINE BOY (IRE) *IanWilliams* 11-11-10[142] (v) RobertDunne 9/2f 1
  20 ULTRAGOLD (FR) *ColinTizzard* 9-11-9[141] (t) TomO'Brien 16/1 4½ 2
      SAMETEGAL (FR) *PaulNicholls* 8-11-12[144] (t) SeanBowen 5/1 2½ 3
      Mystifiable *FergalO'Brien* 9-10-12[130] (t) PaddyBrennan 8/1 17 4
      Imjoeking (IRE) *LucindaRussell* 10-10-11[129] (t) DerekFox 20/1 5 5
      Captain Redbeard (IRE) *StuartColtherd* 8-11-5[137] SamColtherd(5) 9/1 11 6
      Dresden (IRE) *HenryOliver* 9-11-5[137] LiamTreadwell 14/1 24 7
      Mercian Prince (IRE) *AmyMurphy* 6-11-3[135] JackQuinlan 6/1 49 8
      No No Mac (IRE) *IanDuncan* 8-10-9[127] (b+t) HenryBrooke .... 33/1 F
      Arctic Gold (IRE) *NigelTwiston-Davies* 6-11-0[132] TomBellamy .... 5/1 F
      Rathlin Rose (IRE) *DavidPipe* 9-11-0[132] (b) TomScudamore .... 8/1 pu
The Three Graces 11ran 6m05.50

SANDOWN Saturday, Dec 9 Chase course: GOOD to SOFT, Hurdles course: SOFT

65 randoxhealth.com Henry VIII Novices' Chase (Gr 1) (1) (4yo+) £28,475   1m7f119y (12)
      SCEAU ROYAL (FR) *AlanKing* 5-11-2 DarylJacob 11/1 1
  36 NORTH HILL HARVEY *DanSkelton* 6-11-2 HarrySkelton 11/2 11 2
      FINIAN'S OSCAR (IRE) *ColinTizzard* 5-11-2 RobbiePower 13/8f 50 3
      Capitaine *PaulNicholls* 5-11-2 HarryCobden .... 8/1 F
      Brain Power (IRE) *NickyHenderson* 6-11-2 D.J.Mullins .... 15/8 ur
Mr Simon Munir & Mr Isaac Souede 5ran 3m53.80

66 Jumeirah Hotels And Resorts December Handicap Hurdle (L) (1) (4yo+) £33,762   1m7f216y (8)
      A HARE BREATH (IRE) *BenPauling* 9-11-11[139] DarylJacob 8/1 1
  19 CAÏD DU LIN (FR) *DrRichardNewland* 5-11-4[132] (s+t) CharlieHammond(7) .. 20/1 ½ 2
      CROSSED MY MIND (IRE) *A.L.T.Moore,Ireland* 5-10-9[123] BarryGeraghty .. 10/3f 4 3
      Fidux (FR) *AlanKing* 4-11-5[133] KevinDowling(7) .... 8/1 nk 4
      Man of Plenty *SophieLeech* 8-10-9[123] (v+t) AidanColeman 18/1 2¾ 5
  38 William H Bonney *AlanKing* 6-11-7[135] WayneHutchinson 9/2 4½ 6
  38 Jenkins (IRE) *NickyHenderson* 5-11-7[135] NicodeBoinville 9/2 1¼ 7
  18 Exitas (IRE) *PhilMiddleton* 9-10-11[125] DanielSansom(7) 11/1 2¾ 8
      Unison (IRE) *JeremyScott* 7-11-10[138] MattGriffiths 25/1 4 9
      Evening Hush (IRE) *EvanWilliams* 4-11-5[133] MitchellBastyan(5) 25/1 3 10
  25 Zubayr (IRE) *PaulNicholls* 5-11-12[140] MrLorcanWilliams(7) 10/1 16 11
MrsS.N.J.Embiricos/MrS.N.J.Embiricos 11ran 4m00.30

67 Betfair Tingle Creek Chase (Gr 1) (1) (4yo+) £85,425   1m7f119y (13)
      POLITOLOGUE (FR) *PaulNicholls* 6-11-7 HarryCobden 7/2 1
  37 FOX NORTON (FR) *ColinTizzard* 7-11-7 (h) RobbiePower .... 8/13f ½ 2
      AR MAD (FR) *GaryMoore* 7-11-7 JoshuaMoore 8/1 5 3

25	Charbel (IRE) *KimBailey* 6-11-7 (s) NoelFehily	12/1	hd	4
45	San Benedeto (FR) *PaulNicholls* 6-11-2 (s+t) NickScholfield	33/1	7	5
45	Sir Valentino (FR) *TomGeorge* 8-11-7 (t) A.P.Heskin	20/1		F
	Mr J. Hales 6ran 3m54.50			
68	**Betfair London National Handicap Chase (2) (150) (5yo+) £30,950**		3½m166y (21)	
	The final fence was omitted all three circuits due to an injured horse from the previous race			
33	BENBENS (IRE) *NigelTwiston-Davies* 12-10-13[135] MrZacBaker(5)	14/1		1
	SUGAR BARON (IRE) *NickyHenderson* 7-10-13[135] (b) NicodeBoinville	3/1f	nk	2
	CRESSWELL BREEZE *AnthonyHoneyball* 7-11-1[137] (t) AidanColeman	8/1	2¾	3
	Doing Fine (IRE) *NeilMulholland* 9-11-1[137] (s+t) BarryGeraghty	11/2	2¼	4
	Topper Thornton (IRE) *AlexHales* 8-10-10[132] DarylJacob	20/1	1¼	5
	Houblon des Obeaux (FR) *VenetiaWilliams* 10-11-7[143] (s) CharlieDeutsch(3)	7/1	2¼	6
26	Fletchers Flyer (IRE) *HarryFry* 9-11-4[140] (s+t) NoelFehily	7/1	3½	7
	The Happy Chappy (IRE) *SarahHumphrey* 6-10-0[122] (t) HarryCobden	7/1	5	8
26	Southfield Theatre (IRE) *PaulNicholls* 9-11-12[148] (s) MrLorcanWilliams(7)	8/1	22	9
	Dancing Shadow (IRE) *VictorDartnall* 8-11-2[138] (s) NickScholfield	16/1	5	10
	S Such & CG Paletta 10ran 7m39.20			
	CORK Sunday, Dec 10 HEAVY			
69	**Kerry Group Hilly Way Chase (Gr 2) (5yo+) £32,920**		2m160y (12)	
	UN DE SCEAUX (FR) *W.P.Mullins* 9-11-12 D.J.Mullins	4/6f		1
43	TOP GAMBLE (IRE) *KerryLee,GB* 9-11-4 (t) M.A.Enright	7/1	25	2
29	ALISIER D'IRLANDE (FR) *HenrydeBromhead* 7-11-7 (t) A.E.Lynch	25/1	50	3
29	Clarcam (FR) *GordonElliott* 7-11-10 (s+t) J.W.Kennedy	28/1	15	4
17	Ballyoisin (IRE) *EndaBolger* 6-11-4 BarryGeraghty	9/4		F
	Mr Edward O'Connell 5ran 4m54.30			
	PUNCHESTOWN Sunday, Dec 10 HEAVY			
70	**John Durkan Memorial Punchestown Chase (Gr 1) (5yo+) £45,132**		2½m40y (15)	
	SIZING JOHN *MrsJ.Harrington* 7-11-10 RobbiePower	2/1		1
	DJAKADAM (FR) *W.P.Mullins* 8-11-10 P.Townend	5/4f	7	2
16	SUB LIEUTENANT (IRE) *HenrydeBromhead* 8-11-10 (t) DavyRussell	7/1	2¾	3
30	A Toi Phil (FR) *GordonElliott* 7-11-10 (t) KeithDonoghue	10/1	4	4
16	Carlingford Lough (IRE) *JohnE.Kiely* 11-11-10 (t) M.P.Walsh	33/1	5½	5
9	Shaneshill (IRE) *W.P.Mullins* 8-11-10 MrP.W.Mullins	14/1		pu
	Ann & Alan Potts Limited 6ran 5m32.50			
	TAUNTON Thursday, Dec 14 SOFT			
71	**Peterborough Chase (Gr 2) (1) (4yo+) £28,475**		2m5f150y (15)	
43	TOP NOTCH (FR) *NickyHenderson* 6-11-6 DarylJacob	4/9f		1
43	JOSSES HILL (IRE) *NickyHenderson* 9-11-6 (s) NicodeBoinville	9/1	3¼	2
21	PTIT ZIG (FR) *PaulNicholls* 8-11-0 (b) HarryCobden	11/4	4½	3
45	Vaniteux (FR) *DavidPipe* 8-11-4 (b) TomScudamore	33/1	5	4
	Mr Simon Munir & Mr Isaac Souede 4ran 5m43.40			
	DONCASTER Saturday, Dec 16 GOOD to SOFT			
72	**Bet365 December Novices' Chase (Gr 2) (1) (4yo+) £19,932**		2m7f214y (18)	
	KEEPER HILL (IRE) *WarrenGreatrex* 6-11-1 GavinSheehan	5/2		1
53	BRAQUEUR D'OR (FR) *PaulNicholls* 6-11-1 (h) BryonyFrost	7/4jf	8	2
	BALLYCRYSTAL (IRE) *BrianEllison* 6-11-1 DannyCook	16/1	1¾	3
	Rocklander (IRE) *TomGeorge* 8-11-1 A.P.Heskin	7/4jf		ur
	McNeill Family 4ran 6m05.90			
73	**Bet365 Summit Juvenile Hurdle (Gr 2) (1) (3yo) £25,628**		2m128y (8)	
	WE HAVE A DREAM (FR) *NickyHenderson* 3-10-12 DarylJacob	5/6f		1
	CITY DREAMER (IRE) *AlanKing* 3-11-1 WayneHutchinson	16/1	10	2
	JE SUIS CHARLIE *JohnQuinn* 3-10-12 BrianHughes	14/1	17	3
32	Eragon de Chanay (FR) *GaryMoore* 3-10-12 JoshuaMoore	25/1	14	4
	Act of Valour *PaulNicholls* 3-11-1 A.P.Heskin	7/4	22	5
	Sommervieu (FR) *CharlieLongsdon* 3-10-12 (b) NicodeBoinville	66/1		pu
	Mr Simon Munir & Mr Isaac Souede 6ran 4m00.30			
	CHELTENHAM Saturday, Dec 16 SOFT			
74	**Caspian Caviar Gold Cup Handicap Chase (Gr 3) (1) (4yo+) £68,340**		2½m166y (17)	
34	GUITAR PETE (IRE) *NickyRichards* 7-10-5[134] RyanDay(3)	9/1		1
	CLAN DES OBEAUX (FR) *PaulNicholls* 5-11-12[155] HarryCobden	3/1f	2¾	2
	KING'S ODYSSEY (IRE) *EvanWilliams* 8-10-11[140] AdamWedge	9/1	5	3
34	Ballyalton (IRE) *IanWilliams* 10-11-0[143] (t) TomO'Brien	15/2	1¾	4
34	Romain de Senam (FR) *PaulNicholls* 5-11-2[145] (h+t) NoelFehily	14/1	¾	5

34	Foxtail Hill (IRE) *NigelTwiston-Davies* 8-11-4[147] JamieBargary(3)	12/1	6	6
34	Splash of Ginge *NigelTwiston-Davies* 9-10-10[139] TomBellamy	11/1	4½	7
34	Le Prezien (FR) *PaulNicholls* 6-11-9[152] BarryGeraghty	9/2	15	8
	Deauville Dancer (IRE) *DavidDennis* 6-10-8[137] (t) AidanColeman	28/1	7	9
34	Starchitect (IRE) *DavidPipe* 6-11-5[148] (b+t) TomScudamore	13/2		pu

Mrs Pat Sloan 10ran 5m17.10

75 Albert Bartlett Novices' Hurdle (Bristol) (Gr 2) (1) (4yo+) £17,085   2m7f213y (12)

	KILBRICKEN STORM (IRE) *ColinTizzard* 6-12-0 (t) HarryCobden	3/1		1
	COUNT MERIBEL *NigelTwiston-Davies* 5-11-1 MarkGrant	7/4f	2¾	2
	EQUUS SECRETUS (IRE) *BenPauling* 5-10-12 DavidBass	9/4	54	3
	Global Stage *FergalO'Brien* 6-10-12 PaddyBrennan	11/2	15	4

Mr A. Selway 4ran 6m02.30

76 Unibet International Hurdle (Gr 2) (1) (4yo+) £74,035   2m179y (8)

	MY TENT OR YOURS (IRE) *NickyHenderson* 10-11-0 (h) BarryGeraghty	5/1		1
38	THE NEW ONE (IRE) *NigelTwiston-Davies* 9-11-6 SamTwiston-Davies	5/2	1¼	2
15	MELON *W.P.Mullins,Ireland* 5-11-6 D.J.Mullins	7/4f	1	3
	Ch'tibello (FR) *DanSkelton* 6-11-0 HarrySkelton	15/2	¾	4
38	Old Guard *PaulNicholls* 6-11-4 HarryCobden	9/1	¾	5
1	John Constable (IRE) *EvanWilliams* 6-11-4 (t) DavyRussell	25/1	½	6
35	Dell' Arca (IRE) *DavidPipe* 8-11-0 (b+t) TomScudamore	66/1	18	7

Mr John P. McManus 7ran 4m08.10

NAVAN Sunday, Dec 17   HEAVY

77 Navan Novices' Hurdle (Gr 2) (4yo+) £22,368   2½m (11)

	NEXT DESTINATION (IRE) *W.P.Mullins* 5-11-3 D.J.Mullins	10/11f		1
	CRACKING SMART (FR) *GordonElliott* 5-11-3 J.W.Kennedy	7/4	5½	2
48	JETZ (IRE) *MrsJ.Harrington* 5-11-3 RobbiePower	16/1	1¾	3
48	Half The Odds (IRE) *NoelMeade* 5-10-10 SeanFlanagan	25/1	2¼	4
	Poli Roi (FR) *GordonElliott* 5-11-3 DavyRussell	7/1	5	5

Mr Malcolm C. Denmark 5ran 5m26.10

ASCOT Friday, Dec 22   GOOD to SOFT

78 Sky Bet Supreme Trial Novices' Hurdle (Kennel Gate) (Gr 2) (1) (4yo+) £19,932   1m7f152y (8)

	CLAIMANTAKINFORGAN (FR) *NickyHenderson* 5-11-0 NicoDeBoinville	6/4f		1
	DR DES (IRE) *HenryOliver* 6-11-0 TomO'Brien	16/1	2¼	2
	THECLOCKISTICKING (IRE) *StuartEdmunds* 5-11-0 CiaranGethings	7/1	2	3
39	Slate House (IRE) *ColinTizzard* 5-11-5 HarryCobden	4/1	3½	4
	Coeur Blimey (IRE) *SusanGardner* 6-11-0 LucyGardner	5/1	½	5
	Mr One More (IRE) *HarryFry* 5-11-0 BarryGeraghty	5/1	2½	6

Grech & Parkin 6ran 3m48.00

79 Mitie Noel Novices' Chase (Gr 2) (1) (4yo+) £19,932   2m5f8y (17)

	BENATAR *GaryMoore* 5-11-0 JamieMoore	7/4		1
65	FINIAN'S OSCAR (IRE) *ColinTizzard* 5-11-5 B.J.Cooper	6/5f	sh	2
19	DOLOS (FR) *PaulNicholls* 4-10-8 (t) SamTwiston-Davies	7/2	35	3

Mr Ashley Head 3ran 5m25.40

ASCOT Saturday, Dec 23   GOOD to SOFT

80 JLT Reve de Sivola Long Walk Hurdle (Gr 1) (1) (4yo+) £56,950   3m97y (12)

46	SAM SPINNER *JeddO'Keeffe* 5-11-7 JoeColliver	9/2		1
44	L'AMI SERGE (IRE) *NickyHenderson* 7-11-7 DarylJacob	5/1	2¾	2
51	UNOWHATIMEANHARRY *HarryFry* 9-11-7 (t) BarryGeraghty	6/4f	8	3
46	The Worlds End (IRE) *TomGeorge* 6-11-7 A.P.Heskin	10/1	nk	4
35	Thomas Campbell *NickyHenderson* 5-11-7 NicoDeBoinville	15/2	2¼	5
44	Lil Rockerfeller (USA) *NeilKing* 6-11-7 (s) TrevorWhelan	7/1	10	6
	Ubak (FR) *GaryMoore* 9-11-7 JoshuaMoore	66/1	9	7
51	Taquin du Seuil (FR) *JonjoO'Neill* 10-11-7 AidanColeman	20/1	9	8

Caron & Paul Chapman 8ran 6m03.90

81 Lavazza Silver Cup Handicap Chase (L) (1) (4yo+) £56,950   2m7f180y (20)

	GOLD PRESENT (IRE) *NickyHenderson* 7-11-3[147] NicoDeBoinville	17/2		1
43	FRODON (FR) *PaulNicholls* 5-11-7[151] (t) BryonyFrost(5)	8/1	3	2
	WALK IN THE MILL (FR) *RobertWalford* 7-10-9[139] JamesBest	9/1	1	3
	O O Seven (IRE) *NickyHenderson* 7-11-9[153] DarylJacob	11/1	7	4
53	Singlefarmpayment *TomGeorge* 7-11-3[147] (h) A.P.Heskin	5/1f	¾	5
55	Yala Enki (FR) *VenetiaWilliams* 7-11-5[149] (s) CharlieDeutsch(3)	12/1	11	6
	Fortunate George (IRE) *EmmaLavelle* 7-10-3[133] (v) JonathanBurke	8/1	3½	7
53	Bigbadjohn (IRE) *RebeccaCurtis* 8-10-9[139] SeanBowen	20/1	17	8

930

23 On Tour (IRE) *EvanWilliams* 9-10-10^{140} MitchellBastyan(5) 8/1 1¾ 9
Icing On The Cake (IRE) *OliverSherwood* 7-10-0^{132} LeightonAspell 20/1 8 10
71 Ptit Zig (FR) *PaulNicholls* 8-11-12^{156} (b) SamTwiston-Davies 25/1 7 11
20 Go Conquer (IRE) *JonjoO'Neill* 8-11-7^{151} AidanColeman ....11/1 F
Clondaw Cian (IRE) *SuzySmith* 7-10-6^{136} (s) GavinSheehan ....16/1 pu
53 Regal Encore (IRE) *AnthonyHoneyball* 9-11-6^{150} (t) BarryGeraghty ....9/1 pu
Mr and Mrs J. D. Cotton 14ran 6m09.60

82 Racing Welfare Handicap Hurdle (Gr 3) (1) (4yo+) £85,425 1m7f152y (8)
HUNTERS CALL (IRE) *OllyMurphy* 7-10-3^{128} J.W.Kennedy 9/1 1
SILVER STREAK (IRE) *EvanWilliams* 4-10-5^{130} MitchellBastyan(5) 8/1 3 2
19 VERDANA BLUE (IRE) *NickyHenderson* 5-11-5^{144} NicodeBoinville 5/1f 1½ 3
58 Bleu Et Rouge (FR) *W.P.Mullins,Ireland* 6-11-7^{146} BarryGeraghty 7/1 1½ 4
66 Man of Plenty *SophieLeech* 8-10-0^{125} (v+t) SeanHoulihan(7) 40/1 1 5
38 Elgin *AlanKing* 5-11-12^{151} WayneHutchinson 13/2 2¾ 6
Magic Dancer *KerryLee* 5-10-0^{125} (s+t) RichardPatrick(5) ....9/1 ½ 7
58 Top Othe Ra (IRE) *ThomasMullins,Ireland* 9-10-12^{137} D.J.Mullins 33/1 1 8
58 Veinard (FR) *GordonElliott,Ireland* 8-10-4^{129} (t) DenisO'Regan ....14/1 ns 9
38 Nietzsche *BrianEllison* 4-10-10^{135} (h) HenryBrooke 28/1 2 10
Charli Parcs (FR) *NickyHenderson* 4-11-7^{146} AidanColeman ....7/1 ¾ 11
66 Caid du Lin (FR) *DrRichardNewland* 5-10-12^{137} (s+t) CharlieHammond(7) ....25/1 ½ 12
38 Chesterfield (IRE) *SeamusMullins* 7-11-7^{146} DanielSansom(7) 16/1 6 13
Divin Bere (FR) *PaulNicholls* 4-11-9^{148} BryonyFrost(5) 16/1 10 14
19 Air Horse One *HarryFry* 6-11-8^{147} NoelFehily 10/1 13 15
5 Fergall (IRE) *SeamusMullins* 10-11-1^{140} (s) KevinJones(5) ....25/1 nk 16
66 Evening Hush (IRE) *EvanWilliams* 4-10-3^{128} ConorRing(3) ....50/1 F
Holloway,Clarke,Black 17ran 3m49.60

KEMPTON Tuesday, Dec 26 GOOD to SOFT

83 32Red Kauto Star Novices' Chase (Gr 1) (1) (4yo+) £42,712 3m (18)
52 BLACK CORTON (FR) *PaulNicholls* 6-11-7 (t) BryonyFrost 4/1 1
52 ELEGANT ESCAPE (IRE) *ColinTizzard* 5-11-7 TomO'Brien 11/2 1½ 2
WEST APPROACH *ColinTizzard* 7-11-7 TomScudamore 11/1 21 3
Ballyoptic (IRE) *NigelTwiston-Davies* 7-11-7 (t) SamTwiston-Davies 11/4 4½ 4
Mia's Storm (IRE) *AlanKing* 7-11-0 WayneHutchinson .... 5/2f F
52 Fountains Windfall *AnthonyHoneyball* 7-11-7 AidanColeman ....13/2 F
Some Invitation (IRE) *DanSkelton* 6-11-7 (t) HarrySkelton ....40/1 pu
The Brooks, Stewart Families & J. Kyle 7ran 6m08.20

84 Unibet Christmas Hurdle (Gr 1) (1) (4yo+) £68,340 2m (8)
54 BUVEUR D'AIR (FR) *NickyHenderson* 6-11-7 BarryGeraghty 2/11f 1
76 THE NEW ONE (IRE) *NigelTwiston-Davies* 9-11-7 SamTwiston-Davies 5/1 2¼ 2
38 MOHAAYED *DanSkelton* 5-11-7 (t) HarrySkelton 20/1 3¾ 3
82 Chesterfield (IRE) *SeamusMullins* 7-11-7 NoelFehily 33/1 4 4
Mr John P. McManus 4ran 3m57.70

85 32Red King George VI Chase (Gr 1) (1) (4yo+) £128,137 3m (18)
27 MIGHT BITE (IRE) *NickyHenderson* 8-11-10 NicodeBoinville 6/4f 1
43 DOUBLE SHUFFLE (IRE) *TomGeorge* 7-11-10 (h) A.P.Heskin 50/1 1 2
47 TEA FOR TWO *NickWilliams* 8-11-10 LizzieKelly 20/1 2 3
51 Thistlecrack *ColinTizzard* 9-11-10 TomScudamore 5/1 2¾ 4
53 Whisper (FR) *NickyHenderson* 9-11-10 AidanColeman 7/1 16 5
47 Bristol de Mai (FR) *NigelTwiston-Davies* 6-11-10 DarylJacob 3/1 4 6
47 Traffic Fluide (FR) *GaryMoore* 7-11-10 (v) JoshuaMoore 66/1 27 7
67 Fox Norton (FR) *ColinTizzard* 7-11-10 (h) B.J.Cooper ....7/1 pu
The Knot Again Partnership 8ran 6m06.20

LEOPARDSTOWN Tuesday, Dec 26 GOOD to SOFT

86 Knight Frank Juvenile Hurdle (Gr 2) (3yo) £23,496 2m (8)
ESPOIR D'ALLEN (FR) *GavinPatrickCromwell* 3-11-1 M.P.Walsh 1/2f 1
FARCLAS (FR) *GordonElliott* 3-10-12 J.W.Kennedy 10/1 1¼ 2
MITCHOUKA (FR) *GordonElliott* 3-10-12 DavyRussell 7/2 1¼ 3
Grey Waters (IRE) *JosephPatrickO'Brien* 3-10-5 ShaneShortall 25/1 5 4
Tenth Amendment (IRE) *KeithHenryClarke* 3-10-12 (h) R.C.Colgan 33/1 3¾ 5
Mastermind (IRE) *CharlesO'Brien* 3-10-12 (h) DenisO'Regan ....10/1 ¾ 6
Minnie Dahill (IRE) *T.M.Walsh* 3-10-5 MsK.Walsh 25/1 13 7
Mr John P. McManus 7ran 4m07.20

87 Racing Post Novices' Chase (Christmas) (Gr 1) (4yo+) £52,565 2m1f (11)
FOOTPAD (FR) *W.P.Mullins* 5-11-12 P.Townend 4/6f 1
ANY SECOND NOW (IRE) *T.M.Walsh* 5-11-12 M.P.Walsh 12/1 11 2

        JETT (IRE) *Mrs.J.Harrington* 6-11-12 RobbiePower 25/1   13   3
59 Death Duty (IRE) *GordonElliott* 6-11-12 DavyRussell ....7/4   F
        Avenir d'Une Vie (FR) *HenrydeBromhead* 7-11-12 J.W.Kennedy ....25/1   ur
        Mr Simon Munir/Mr Isaac Souede 5ran 4m13.00

LIMERICK Tuesday, Dec 26 HEAVY

88 **McMahons Builders Providers - New Online Store Just Launched**   2m3f120y (14)
     Novices' Chase (Gr 2) (4yo+) £24,416
        DOUNIKOS (FR) *GordonElliott* 6-11-4 AndrewRing 14/1   1
40 TOMBSTONE (IRE) *GordonElliott* 7-11-7 KeithDonoghue 7/2   4½ 2
41 ARBRE DE VIE (FR) *W.P.Mullins* 7-11-4 AlexisPoirier 10/1   4½ 3
        Inis Meain (USA) *DenisHogan* 10-11-4 D.G.Hogan 33/1   61   4
17 Tout Est Permis (FR) *M.F.Morris* 4-10-11 RachaelBlackmore ....11/1   F
        Al Boum Photo (FR) *W.P.Mullins* 5-11-4 D.J.Mullins .... 1/2f   F
        Gigginstown House Stud 6ran 5m54.50

WETHERBY Tuesday, Dec 26 SOFT

89 **188Bet Rowland Meyrick Handicap Chase (Gr 3) (1) (4yo+) £22,780**   3m45y (19)
        GET ON THE YAGER *DanSkelton* 7-10-7[133] HenryBrooke 10/3f   1
55 WAKANDA (IRE) *SueSmith* 8-11-4[144] DannyCook ....7/2   hd 2
        DELUSIONOFGRANDEUR (IRE) *SueSmith* 7-11-2[142] SeanQuinlan ....7/1   nk 3
        Actinpieces *PamSly* 6-10-13[139] MissGinaAndrews(3) ....8/1   hd 4
        Baywing (IRE) *NickyRichards* 8-11-4[144] RyanDay(3) 7/1   1½ 5
        Aloomomo (FR) *WarrenGreatrex* 7-10-7[133] BrianHughes ....4/1   pu
55 Dedigout (IRE) *MickyHammond* 11-10-9[135] (t) JoeColliver ....50/1   pu
47 Shantou Flyer (IRE) *RichardHobson* 7-11-12[152] (t) JamesReveley ....10/1   pu
        Dick and Mandy Higgins 8ran 6m48.50

KEMPTON Wednesday, Dec 27 SOFT

90 **32Red.com Wayward Lad Novices' Chase (Gr 2) (1) (4yo+) £22,780**   2m (12)
        CYRNAME (FR) *PaulNicholls* 5-11-2 (h+t) SeanBowen 7/4   1
        SHANTOU ROCK (IRE) *DanSkelton* 5-11-2 (t) HarrySkelton 6/4f   7   2
        TOMMY SILVER (FR) *PaulNicholls* 5-11-2 (t) SamTwiston-Davies ....9/4   ½   3
        Kostaquarta (IRE) *MarkGillard* 10-11-2 (s+t) JamesBanks ....100/1   pu
        Mrs Johnny de la Hey 4ran 4m04.40

91 **Unibet Desert Orchid Chase (Gr 2) (1) (4yo+) £51,255**   2m (12)
67 POLITOLOGUE (FR) *PaulNicholls* 6-11-6 SamTwiston-Davies 8/15f   1
71 VANITEUX (FR) *DavidPipe* 8-11-4 (s) TomScudamore 25/1   13   2
        FOREST BIHAN (FR) *BrianEllison* 6-11-3 DarylJacob 6/1   14   3
37 Special Tiara *HenrydeBromhead,Ireland* 10-11-6 NoelFehily ....3/1   F
        Mr J. Hales 4ran 4m06.50

LEOPARDSTOWN Wednesday, Dec 27 Chase: GOOD to SOFT, Hurdles: SOFT

92 **Paddy's Rewards Club Chase (Gr 1) (4yo+) £53,097**   2m1f (11)
     Order as they passed the post (after stewards' inquiry Simply Ned was promoted)
        MIN (FR) *W.P.Mullins* 6-11-12 P.Townend 2/7f   2
37 SIMPLY NED (IRE) *NickyRichards,GB* 10-11-12 M.P.Walsh ....16/1   ½   1
        ORDINARY WORLD (IRE) *HenrydeBromhead* 7-11-12 DavyRussell 12/1   15   3
40 Woodland Opera (IRE) *Mrs.J.Harrington* 7-11-12 (t) RobbiePower 14/1   31   4
        Tell Us More (IRE) *GordonElliott* 8-11-12 (b) SeanFlanagan 50/1   45   5
17 Ball d'Arc (FR) *GordonElliott* 6-11-12 J.W.Kennedy .... 11/2   ur
        Mrs S. Ricci 6ran 4m10.10

93 **Paddy Power Future Champions Novices' Hurdle (Gr 1) (4yo+) £46,636**   2m (8)
        WHISKEY SOUR (IRE) *W.P.Mullins* 4-11-7 D.J.Mullins 9/1   1
56 LE RICHEBOURG (FR) *JosephPatrickO'Brien* 4-11-7 BarryGeraghty 8/1   19   2
56 HARDLINE (IRE) *GordonElliott* 5-11-10 (h) DavyRussell 25/1   1   3
56 Makitorix (FR) *W.P.Mullins* 4-11-7 AlexisPoirier 33/1   52   4
        Real Steel (IRE) *W.P.Mullins* 4-11-7 P.Townend ....11/4   F
        Sharjah (FR) *W.P.Mullins* 4-11-7 MrP.W.Mullins ....8/1   F
56 Mengli Khan (IRE) *GordonElliott* 4-11-7 J.W.Kennedy .... evsf   ro
        Luke McMahon 7ran 4m02.20

94 **Paddy Power Chase (Extended Handicap) (Gr B) (150) (5yo+) £97,345**   3m100y (17)
17 ANIBALE FLY (FR) *A.J.Martin* 7-11-8[148] (t) DonaghMeyler 14/1   1
        UCELLO CONTI (FR) *GordonElliott* 9-11-5[145] (t) L.A.McKenna(7) 25/1   7   2
        SQUOUATEUR (FR) *GordonElliott* 6-10-7[133] (t) BarryGeraghty 4/1   1¼ 3
49 Potters Point (IRE) *GordonElliott* 7-11-7[147] (t) ChrisMeehan(5) 33/1   2¼ 4
        Vieux Morvan (FR) *JosephPatrickO'Brien* 8-10-7[133] (b) ShaneShortall(3) 40/1   3   5

10	Phil's Magic (IRE) *A.J.Martin* 7-10-3[129] (s+t) DenisO'Regan 20/1	4	6
	Full Cry (IRE) *HenrydeBromhead* 7-10-6[132] (s+t) RogerLoughran 40/1	hd	7
60	Thunder And Roses (IRE) *M.F.Morris* 9-11-3[143] (v+t) MsL.O'Neill(3) 40/1	5	8
49	Space Cadet (IRE) *GordonElliott* 7-10-6[132] B.Hayes 25/1	¾	9
	Out Sam *GordonElliott* 8-10-6[132] L.P.Dempsey 20/1	¾	10
	Polidam (FR) *W.P.Mullins* 8-11-6[146] (h) P.Townend 6/1	4¼	11
49	General Principle (IRE) *GordonElliott* 7-10-6[140] (t) J.W.Kennedy 16/1	1½	12
	Apache Stronghold (IRE) *NoelMeade* 9-11-4[144] (t) JonathanMoore 33/1	½	13
	Pleasant Company (IRE) *W.P.Mullins* 9-11-7[147] (h) D.J.Mullins 16/1	5	14
	Texas Jack (IRE) *NoelMeade* 11-10-8[134] M.A.Cooper 50/1	3¼	15
10	On Fiddlers Green (IRE) *HenrydeBromhead* 7-10-9[135] D.Robinson(5) 33/1	3¾	16
7	Road To Riches (IRE) *NoelMeade* 10-11-10[150] (t) A.W.Short(7) 33/1	2½	17
28	Flaxen Flare (IRE) *GordonElliott* 8-10-12[138] (s) DavyRussell 16/1	20	18
7	Bay of Freedom (IRE) *PeterFahey* 8-10-12[138] K.C.Sexton 20/1	14	19
	Oscar Knight (IRE) *ThomasMullins* 8-10-10[136] M.P.Walsh 7/1	5	20
23	Three Stars (IRE) *HenrydeBromhead* 7-10-13[139] RobbiePower 33/1	23	21
	Teacher's Pet (IRE) *J.P.Dempsey* 6-10-0[127] (t) M.J.Bolger 25/1		F
10	Dromnea (IRE) *M.F.Morris* 10-10-8[134] (s+t) M.A.Enright 33/1		F
41	Call The Taxie (IRE) *EllmarieHolden* 6-10-9[135] RachaelBlackmore 16/1		F
60	Forever Gold (IRE) *EdwardCawley* 10-10-8[134] (b) C.D.Timmons(3) 20/1		ur
49	Tesseract (IRE) *JosephPatrickO'Brien* 6-10-2[128] R.C.Colgan 28/1		pu
	Woods Well (IRE) *GordonElliott* 6-10-9[135] AndrewRing(3) 25/1		pu
49	Bonny Kate (IRE) *NoelMeade* 7-10-12[138] SeanFlanagan 10/1		pu

Mr John P. McManus 28ran 6m19.60

LEOPARDSTOWN Thursday, Dec 28   Chase course: GOOD to SOFT, Hurdles course: SOFT

95 Squared Financial Christmas Hurdle (Gr 1) (4yo+) £45,132   3m (11)

What should have been the final flight was omitted due to a stricken horse

57	APPLE'S JADE (IRE) *GordonElliott* 5-11-3 (t) DavyRussell 4/6f		1
57	SUPASUNDAE (IRE) *Mrs.J.Harrington* 7-11-10 RobbiePower 7/1	½	2
	BAPAUME (FR) *W.P.Mullins* 4-11-5 NoelFehily 20/1	4¾	3
57	Augusta Kate *W.P.Mullins* 6-11-3 D.J.Mullins 25/1	8	4
42	Jezki (IRE) *Mrs.J.Harrington* 9-11-10 BarryGeraghty 9/1	12	5
57	Nichols Canyon *W.P.Mullins* 7-11-10 P.Townend 7/2		F

Gigginstown House Stud 6ran 6m16.80

96 Leopardstown Christmas Chase (Gr 1) (5yo+) £78,319   3m (16)

16	ROAD TO RESPECT (IRE) *NoelMeade* 6-11-10 (h) SeanFlanagan 8/1		1
30	BALKO DES FLOS (FR) *HenrydeBromhead* 6-11-10 DenisO'Regan 66/1	1¼	2
47	OUTLANDER (IRE) *GordonElliott* 9-11-10 (s) RachaelBlackmore 16/1	2¼	3
33	Minella Rocco (IRE) *JonjoO'Neill,GB* 7-11-10 (h) M.P.Walsh 25/1	5½	4
	Valseur Lido (FR) *HenrydeBromhead* 8-11-10 NoelFehily 16/1	5	5
63	Alpha des Obeaux (FR) *M.F.Morris* 7-11-10 (s+t) B.J.Cooper 66/1	¾	6
70	Sizing John *Mrs.J.Harrington* 7-11-10 RobbiePower 9/10f	17	7
	Yorkhill (IRE) *W.P.Mullins* 7-11-10 P.Townend 7/2	27	8
16	Zabana *AndrewLynch* 8-11-10 DavyRussell 28/1		F
70	Carlingford Lough (IRE) *JohnE.Kiely* 11-11-10 (t) BarryGeraghty 33/1		pu
70	Djakadam (FR) *W.P.Mullins* 8-11-10 (h) D.J.Mullins 8/1		pu
	Edwulf *JosephPatrickO'Brien* 8-11-10 (t) MrD.O'Connor 66/1		pu

Gigginstown House Stud 12ran 6m08.90

LEOPARDSTOWN Friday, Dec 29   SOFT

97 Neville Hotels Novices' Chase (Fort Leney) (Gr 1) (4yo+) £44,381   3m (15)

The fence before the winning post was omitted due to the low trajectory of the sun

41	SHATTERED LOVE (IRE) *GordonElliott* 6-11-3 (t) M.P.Walsh 10/1		1
41	JURY DUTY (IRE) *GordonElliott* 6-11-10 RobbiePower 6/1	1¾	2
	BON PAPA (FR) *W.P.Mullins* 6-11-10 BarryGeraghty 12/1	16	3
	Thebarrowman (IRE) *A.P.Keatley* 7-11-10 RogerLoughran 66/1	19	4
	Moulin A Vent *NoelMeade* 5-11-10 SeanFlanagan 8/1	2½	5
59	Dinaria des Obeaux (FR) *GordonElliott* 4-10-8 (t) DenisO'Regan 9/1	23	6
	Monalee (IRE) *HenrydeBromhead* 6-11-10 DavyRussell		evsf F
59	Rathvinden (IRE) *W.P.Mullins* 9-11-10 P.Townend 6/1		bd

Gigginstown House Stud 8ran 6m19.40

98 Ryanair Hurdle (December) (Gr 1) (4yo+) £54,867   2m (8)

57	MICK JAZZ (FR) *GordonElliott* 6-11-10 (h) DavyRussell 14/1		1
57	CILAOS EMERY (FR) *W.P.Mullins* 5-11-10 (h) D.J.Mullins 6/1	1¾	2
42	CAMPEADOR (FR) *GordonElliott* 5-11-10 (h+t) BarryGeraghty 12/1	21	3
29	The Game Changer (IRE) *GordonElliott* 8-11-10 (t) SeanFlanagan 33/1	40	4

	42	Faugheen (IRE) *W.P.Mullins* 9-11-10 P.Townend	2/11f	pu
		Mr G. P. Mahoney 5ran 4m04.50		

LIMERICK Friday, Dec 29 HEAVY

99 Guinness Novices' Hurdle (Dorans Pride) (Gr 2) (4yo+) £23,628 3m (14)
		FABULOUS SAGA (FR) *W.P.Mullins* 5-11-6 (t) D.E.Mullins	8/13f	1
	48	DELTA WORK (IRE) *GordonElliott* 4-10-12 (h+t) B.J.Cooper	8/1	3¾ 2
		BURREN LIFE (IRE) *GordonElliott* 5-11-3 KeithDonoghue	16/1	2½ 3
		Ainsi Va La Vie (FR) *W.P.Mullins* 7-10-10 B.Hayes	5/1	10 4
		Minella Fair (IRE) *NoelMeade* 6-11-3 (t) JonathanMoore	5/1	4¾ 5
		Sullivan Bloodstock Limited 5ran 6m39.40		

NEWBURY Saturday, Dec 30 HEAVY

100 Betfred Challow Novices' Hurdle (Gr 1) (1) (4yo+) £22,780 2½m118y (10)
		POETIC RHYTHM (IRE) *FergalO'Brien* 6-11-7 PaddyBrennan	15/8f	1
	31	MULCAHYS HILL (IRE) *WarrenGreatrex* 5-11-7 A.P.Heskin	16/1	sh 2
	75	KILBRICKEN STORM (IRE) *ColinTizzard* 6-11-7 (t) HarryCobden	11/4	23 3
		Way Back Then (IRE) *BenPauling* 6-11-7 NicoBoinville	7/1	2½ 4
		Dans Le Vent (FR) *JamieSnowden* 4-11-7 GavinSheehan	16/1	30 5
		Dame Rose (FR) *RichardHobson* 4-11-0 HarrySkelton	3/1	pu
		The Yes No Wait Sorries 6ran 5m24.90		

CHELTENHAM Monday, Jan 1 SOFT

101 Betbright Dipper Novices' Chase (Gr 2) (1) (5yo+) £19,932 2½m166y (17)
		YANWORTH *AlanKing* 8-11-0 BarryGeraghty	15/8jf	1
	50	SIZING TENNESSEE (IRE) *ColinTizzard* 10-11-3 B.J.Cooper	12/1	nk 2
	50	WILLOUGHBY COURT (IRE) *BenPauling* 7-11-5 NicodeBoinville	15/8jf	8 3
		Ballyandy *NigelTwiston-Davies* 7-11-0 SamTwiston-Davies	10/3	3½ 4
		Ami Desbois (FR) *GraemeMcPherson* 8-11-0 (t) PaddyBrennan	12/1	pu
		Mr John P. McManus 5ran 5m34.20		

102 Betbright Best For Festival Betting Handicap Chase (Gr 3) (1) (5yo+) £42,712 2½m166y (17)
		BALLYHILL (FR) *NigelTwiston-Davies* 7-10-5[133] JamieBargary(3)	9/1	1
	89	SHANTOU FLYER (IRE) *RichardHobson* 8-11-0[152] (s+t) MitchellBastyan(5)	8/1	1¾ 2
	64	SAMETEGAL (FR) *PaulNicholls* 9-11-2[144] (t) SamTwiston-Davies	5/1	6 3
	69	Top Gamble (IRE) *KerryLee* 10-11-12[154] (t) JamesBowen(5)	7/2jf	½ 4
	45	Quite By Chance *ColinTizzard* 9-11-4[146] TomO'Brien	14/1	8 5
	34	Theinval (FR) *NickyHenderson* 8-11-2[144] (s) JeremiahMcGrath	11/1	4½ 6
		Burtons Well (IRE) *VeneticaWilliams* 9-10-12[140] AidanColeman	7/2jf	2¼ 7
	74	Splash of Ginge *NigelTwiston-Davies* 10-10-11[139] TomHumphries(7)	6/1	pu
	34	Viconte du Noyer (FR) *ColinTizzard* 9-11-6[148] (t) B.J.Cooper	18/1	pu
		S Such & CG Paletta 9ran 5m36.10		

103 Dornan Engineering Relkeel Hurdle (Gr 2) (1) (5yo+) £28,475 2½m56y (10)
		WHOLESTONE (IRE) *NigelTwiston-Davies* 7-11-3 DarylJacob	9/4jf	1
	51	AGRAPART (FR) *NickWilliams* 7-11-6 LizzieKelly	4/1	3¼ 2
	51	COLIN'S SISTER *FergalO'Brien* 7-10-13 PaddyBrennan	9/4jf	3¼ 3
	76	Old Guard *PaulNicholls* 7-11-4 BryonyFrost	9/2	2½ 4
	53	Royal Vacation *ColinTizzard* 8-11-0 (b+t) HarryCobden	12/1	8 5
	35	Anteros (IRE) *SophieLeech* 10-11-4 (v+t) AidanColeman	40/1	18 6
		Rayvin Black *OliverSherwood* 9-11-0 (v) ThomasGarner	28/1	61 7
		Qualando (FR) *AlanJones* 7-11-2 (s) HarrySkelton	66/1	pu
		Mr Simon Munir & Mr Isaac Souede 8ran 5m16.40		

CHEPSTOW Saturday, Jan 6 HEAVY

104 Coral Future Champions Finale Juvenile Hurdle (Gr 1) (1) (4yo) £28,475 2m11y (6)
	73	WE HAVE A DREAM (FR) *NickyHenderson* 4-11-0 DarylJacob	8/11f	1
		SUSSEX RANGER (USA) *GaryMoore* 4-11-0 JamieMoore	3/1	1½ 2
		MERCENAIRE (FR) *NickWilliams* 4-11-0 LizzieKelly	10/1	11 3
		Staff College (FR) *HenrySpiller* 4-11-0 AidanColeman	100/1	73 4
		Famous Milly (IRE) *GavinPatrickCromwell,Ireland* 4-10-7 (t) RobertDunne	9/2	F
		Mr Simon Munir & Mr Isaac Souede 5ran 4m08.70		

105 Coral Welsh Grand National Handicap Chase (Gr 3) (1) (5yo+) £85,425 3m5f110y (18)
	10	RAZ DE MAREE (FR) *GavinPatrickCromwell,Ireland* 11-10-5 JamesBowen(5)	16/1	1
	26	ALFIE SPINNER (IRE) *KerryLee* 13-10-7[132] (s+t) RichardPatrick(5)	33/1	6 2
	26	FINAL NUDGE (IRE) *DavidDennis* 9-11-6[145] AidanColeman	12/1	9 3
		Vintage Clouds (IRE) *SueSmith* 8-11-1[140] DannyCook	7/1f	1½ 4
	46	Silsol (GER) *PaulNicholls* 9-11-8[147] (b+t) BryonyFrost(5)	28/1	nk 5

64	Rathlin Rose (IRE) *DavidPipe* 10-10-7[132] (b) TomScudamore 50/1	1	6
23	Pobbles Bay (IRE) *EvanWilliams* 8-11-5[144] AdamWedge 20/1	25	7
	Emperor's Choice (IRE) *VenetiaWilliams* 11-10-3[128] (s) CharlieDeutsch(3) 10/1		F
	Firebird Flyer (IRE) *EvanWilliams* 11-10-5[130] ConorRing(3) 33/1		F
	Wild West Wind (IRE) *TomGeorge* 9-11-3[142] (t) A.P.Heskin 10/1		F
	On The Road (IRE) *EvanWilliams* 8-10-5[130] (t) MitchellBastyan(5) 20/1		ur
	Milansbar (IRE) *NeilKing* 11-10-9[134] (s) TrevorWhelan 14/1		ur
33	Vicente (FR) *PaulNicholls* 9-11-12[151] (h) SamTwiston-Davies 22/1		ur
	O'Faolains Boy (IRE) *RebeccaCurtis* 11-10-12[137] BarryGeraghty 25/1		pu
	Buckhorn Timothy *ColinTizzard* 9-10-12[137] DarylJacob 20/1		pu
	Ask The Weatherman *JackR.Barber* 9-10-13[138] (s) NickScholfield 12/1		pu
	Mysteree (IRE) *MichaelScudamore* 10-10-13[138] RobertDunne 12/1		pu
55	Bishops Road (IRE) *KerryLee* 10-11-5[144] JamieMoore 9/1		pu
	Chase The Spud *FergalO'Brien* 10-11-9[148] PaddyBrennan 11/1		pu
55	Beware The Bear (IRE) *NickyHenderson* 8-11-10[149] JeremiahMcGrath 11/1		pu

Mr James J. Swan 20ran 8m13.00

SANDOWN Saturday, Jan 6 SOFT

106 32Red Tolworth Novices' Hurdle (Gr 1) (1) (4yo+) £28,475   1m7f216y (8)
39	SUMMERVILLE BOY (IRE) *TomGeorge* 6-11-7 NoelFehily 8/1		1
	KALASHNIKOV (IRE) *AmyMurphy* 5-11-7 JackQuinlan 2/1	4	2
	MONT DES AVALOIRS (FR) *PaulNicholls* 5-11-7 SeanBowen 4/1	9	3
	Western Ryder (IRE) *WarrenGreatrex* 6-11-7 RichardJohnson 7/4f	18	4
	The Russian Doyen (IRE) *ColinTizzard* 5-11-7 RobbiePower 10/1	36	5

Mr R. S. Brookhouse 5ran 4m03.30

107 32Red Veterans' Handicap Chase (Series Final) (2) (10yo+) £61,900   3m37y (22)
	BUYWISE *EvanWilliams* 11-10-8[138] LeightonAspell 12/1		1
	PETE THE FEAT (IRE) *CharlieLongsdon* 14-10-0[130] (t) JonathanBurke ...12/1	2	2
64	GAS LINE BOY (IRE) *AmyMurphy* 12-11-4[148] (v) BrianHughes 11/2	3	3
	Cloudy Too *SueSmith* 12-10-0[130] HenryBrooke 8/1	sh	4
	Loose Chips *CharlieLongsdon* 12-10-0[140] (b) PaulO'Brien(3) 16/1	4½	5
68	Houblon des Obeaux (FR) *VenetiaWilliams* 11-10-13[143] (s) NoelFehily 5/1f	2	6
	Theatrical Star *ColinTizzard* 12-10-0[130] BrendanPowell 10/1	10	7
53	Double Ross (IRE) *NigelTwiston-Davies* 12-11-2[146] MrZacBaker(5) 10/1	¾	8
68	Benbens (IRE) *NigelTwiston-Davies* 13-10-8[138] JamieBargary(3) 10/1	6	9
33	Perfect Candidate (IRE) *FergalO'Brien* 11-10-12[156] (s) ConorShoemark ...16/1	29	10
26	Fox Appeal (IRE) *EmmaLavelle* 11-10-10[140] (v+t) RichardJohnson 12/1		F
	Vino Griego (FR) *GaryMoore* 13-10-0[130] JonjoO'Neill(7) 14/1		ur
	No Duffer *TomGeorge* 11-10-12[142] (t) CiaranGethings(3) 25/1		pu
14	Third Intention (IRE) *ColinTizzard* 11-11-1[145] (b+t) RobbiePower 14/1		pu

Mr T. Hywel Jones 14ran 6m36.40

NAAS Sunday, Jan 7 HEAVY

108 Lawlor's of Naas Novices' Hurdle (Gr 1) (5yo+) £46,991   2½m (10)
77	NEXT DESTINATION (IRE) *W.P.Mullins* 6-11-10 P.Townend 8/15f		1
77	CRACKING SMART (FR) *GordonElliott* 6-11-10 (s+t) DavyRussell 9/2	1	2
	DUC DES GENIEVRES (FR) *W.P.Mullins* 5-11-7 D.J.Mullins 25/1	3	3
77	Jetz (IRE) *MrsJ.Harrington* 6-11-10 RobbiePower 14/1	4¾	4
	Speak Easy *JosephPatrickO'Brien* 5-11-7 BarryGeraghty 7/1	13	5
	Blow By Blow (IRE) *GordonElliott* 7-11-10 (b+t) J.W.Kennedy 14/1	11	6
	Moyross *NoelMeade* 7-11-10 JonathanMoore 28/1	3	7
	Athenean (IRE) *NoelMeade* 5-11-7 SeanFlanagan 16/1	½	8

Mr Malcolm C. Denmark 8ran 5m09.90

PUNCHESTOWN Saturday, Jan 13 HEAVY

109 Sky Bet Moscow Flyer Novices' Hurdle (Gr 2) (5yo+) £23,235   2m (9)
	GETABIRD (IRE) *W.P.Mullins* 6-11-2 MrP.W.Mullins ....evsf		1
93	MENGLI KHAN (IRE) *GordonElliott* 5-11-8 DavyRussell 7/4	9	2
	CARTER MCKAY *W.P.Mullins* 7-11-2 D.J.Mullins 7/1	4½	3
	High School Days (USA) *HenrydeBromhead* 5-11-2 DenisO'Regan 12/1	3¼	4
82	Top Othe Ra (IRE) *ThomasMullins* 10-11-2 B.J.Cooper 50/1	4	5
93	Makitorix (FR) *W.P.Mullins* 5-11-0 RachaelBlackmore 33/1	12	6

Mrs S. Ricci 6ran 4m05.00

WARWICK Saturday, Jan 13 SOFT

110 Ballymore Leamington Novices' Hurdle (Gr 2) (1) (5yo+) £19,932   2m5f (11)
	MR WHIPPED (IRE) *NickyHenderson* 5-11-0 NicodeBoinville 6/4f		1
	PAISLEY PARK (IRE) *EmmaLavelle* 6-11-0 NickScholfield 9/2	1	2
	KNIGHT IN DUBAI (IRE) *DanSkelton* 5-11-0 HarrySkelton 16/1	6	3

	Chooseyourweapon (IRE) *EvanWilliams* 5-11-0 AdamWedge 9/2	7	4
	Cave Top (IRE) *OliverGreenall* 6-11-0 DavidEngland 20/1	3¼	5
75	Count Meribel (IRE) *NigelTwiston-Davies* 6-11-3 MarkGrant 3/1	1¾	6
	Grech & Parkin 6ran 5m13.40		

111	**Betfred Classic Handicap Chase (Gr 3) (5) (5yo+) £42,712**	3m5f54y (22)
105	MILANSBAR (IRE) *NeilKing* 11-11-7[134] (b) BryonyFrost(5) 12/1	1
53	COGRY *NigelTwiston-Davies* 9-11-11[138] (s) JamieBargary(3) 14/1	11 2
53	MISSED APPROACH (IRE) *WarrenGreatrex* 8-11-12[139] (s) GavinSheehan ..9/2f	12 3
	Crosspark *CarolineBailey* 8-11-9[136] MissGinaAndrews(3) 14/1	4½ 4
68	Cresswell Breeze *AnthonyHoneyball* 8-11-10[137] (t) SeanBowen 6/1	2 5
	Sir Mangan (IRE) *DanSkelton* 10-11-11[138] HarrySkelton 8/1	1¼ 6
	Indian Castle (IRE) *IanWilliams* 10-11-0[127] (v) RobertDunne 9/1	4 7
	Krackatoa King *KerryLee* 10-11-0[127] (v) RichardPatrick(5) 5/1	40 8
	Russe Blanc (FR) *KerryLee* 11-10-12[125] (s) CharliePoste 25/1	pu
	On The Road (IRE) *EvanWilliams* 8-11-3[130] (t) AdamWedge 16/1	pu
20	Ballycross *NigelTwiston-Davies* 7-11-4[131] (s) MrZacBaker(5) 9/1	pu
68	Topper Thornton (IRE) *AlexHales* 9-11-4[131] HarryBannister 18/1	pu
62	Goodtoknow *KerryLee* 10-11-11[138] (b) JamieMoore 18/1	pu
	Mr Robert Bothway 13ran 7m41.30	

KEMPTON Saturday, Jan 13   Chase course: GOOD to SOFT   Hurdles course: SOFT

112	**32Red Casino Chase (L) (1) (5yo+) £22,780**	2½m110y (16)
	WAITING PATIENTLY (IRE) *MalcolmJefferson* 7-11-4 BrianHughes 13/8f	1
20	ART MAURESQUE (FR) *PaulNicholls* 8-11-0 HarryCobden 16/1	8 2
14	GOD'S OWN (IRE) *TomGeorge* 10-11-0 PaddyBrennan 5/2	4 3
43	Smad Place (FR) *AlanKing* 11-11-6 WayneHutchinson 9/2	nk 4
71	Josses Hill (IRE) *NickyHenderson* 10-11-6 (s) AidanColeman 8/1	9 5
23	Ballybolley (IRE) *NigelTwiston-Davies* 9-11-4 (t) DarylJacob 16/1	3¼ 6
	Mr Richard Collins 6ran 5m09.10	

113	**32Red Lanzarote Handicap Hurdle (L) (1) (4yo+) £25,628**	2m5f (10)
	WILLIAM HENRY (IRE) *NickyHenderson* 8-11-12[145] JamesBowen(5) 7/1	1
	SPIRITOFTHEGAMES (IRE) *DanSkelton* 6-11-1[134] BridgetAndrews(3) 16/1	¾ 2
	RED INDIAN *BenPauling* 8-11-1[134] DavidBass 8/1	2 3
	Topofthegame (IRE) *PaulNicholls* 6-11-6[139] (t) SamTwiston-Davies 11/1	sh 4
	Diese des Bieffes (FR) *NickyHenderson* 5-11-2[135] MitchellBastyan(5) 5/1f	1 5
78	Coeur Blimey (IRE) *SusanGardner* 7-10-13[132] LucyGardner(5) 8/1	4½ 6
	Le Patriote (FR) *DrRichardNewland* 6-10-8[127] BrianHughes 10/1	1½ 7
	Dentley de Mee (FR) *NickWilliams* 5-10-6[126] LizzieKelly(3) 25/1	2¼ 8
	Man From Mars *NickWilliams* 6-10-3[122] HarryCobden 25/1	4 9
11	Bags Groove (IRE) *HarryFry* 7-11-12[145] (v) NoelFehily 10/1	2 10
	Wishfull Dreaming *OllyMurphy* 7-10-8[127] (v) AidanColeman 14/1	1 11
	Dino Velvet (FR) *AlanKing* 5-10-4[123] WayneHutchinson 16/1	1¼ 12
	El Terremoto (FR) *NigelTwiston-Davies* 6-11-9[142] DarylJacob 66/1	47 13
	I Shot The Sheriff (IRE) *FergalO'Brien* 11-11-4[137] PaddyBrennan 33/1	pu
	Top Ville Ben (IRE) *PhilipKirby* 6-11-9[142] (h) AdamNicol 16/1	pu
11	River Frost *AlanKing* 6-11-12[145] BarryGeraghty 8/1	pu
	Walters Plant Hire Ltd 16ran 5m11.40	

FAIRYHOUSE Sunday, Jan 14   SOFT

114	**Bar One Racing Dan Moore Memorial Handicap Chase (Gr A) (4yo+) £52,212**	2m1f (12)
	DOCTOR PHOENIX (IRE) *GordonElliott* 10-11-3[146] (s+t) DavyRussell 13/2	1
13	KILCARRY BRIDGE (IRE) *JohnPatrickRyan* 11-10-8[137] (t) DonaghMeyler 20/1	9 2
	DYSIOS (IRE) *DenisW.Cullen* 10-10-3[132] (t) RachaelBlackmore 20/1	1 3
4	Rock The World (IRE) *MrsJ.Harrington* 10-11-10[153] (t) D.J.McInerney(5) ..25/1	15 4
	Mallowney (IRE) *TimothyDoyle* 12-11-2[145] B.J.Cooper 16/1	3½ 5
	Don't Touch It (IRE) *MrsJ.Harrington* 8-11-7[150] BarryGeraghty 14/1	13 6
98	The Game Changer (IRE) *GordonElliott* 9-11-1[144] (t) J.W.Kennedy 14/1	6 7
	Elusive Ivy (IRE) *GavinPatrickCromwell* 8-10-3[132] J.B.Kane(5) 16/1	10 8
59	Townshend (GER) *W.P.Mullins* 7-11-2[145] D.J.Mullins 5/1	ur
49	Acapella Bourgeois (FR) *W.P.Mullins* 8-11-7[150] P.Townend 9/10f	pu
	Nick Bradley Racing Club 10ran 4m27.00	

ASCOT Saturday, Jan 20   HEAVY

115	**OLBG.com Mares' Hurdle (Warfield) (Gr 2) (1) (4yo+) £28,475**	2m7f118y (12)
	LA BAGUE AU ROI (FR) *WarrenGreatrex* 7-11-4 NoelFehily 8/11f	1
	SAINTE LADYLIME (FR) *KimBailey* 8-11-0 SeanBowen 8/1	16 2
	GRACEFUL LEGEND *BenCase* 7-11-0 (s) KielanWoods 6/1	13 3
	Midnight Tune *AnthonyHoneyball* 7-11-0 (t) AidanColeman 4/1	73 4

      Hitherjacques Lady (IRE) *OliverSherwood* 6-11-0 LeightonAspell ....20/1   pu
      Mrs Julien Turner & Mr Andrew Merriam 5ran 6m14.00

116 Ascot Spring Garden Show Holloway's Handicap Hurdle (Gr 3) (1) (4yo+)   2m3f58y (10)
    £28,475

66	JENKINS (IRE) *NickyHenderson* 6-11-8[143] (b) JamesBowen(5) 5/1		1
82	AIR HORSE ONE *HarryFry* 7-11-12[147] NoelFehily 14/1	2¼	2
	BURBANK (IRE) *NickyHenderson* 6-11-7[142] (s) JeremiahMcGrath 16/1	2	3
82	Man of Plenty *SophieLeech* 9-10-12[123] (v+t) SeanHoulihan(7) 16/1	2¼	4
	Vivas (FR) *CharlieLongsdon* 7-10-0[121] (h) AidanColeman 25/1	11	5
66	Crossed My Mind (IRE) *A.L.T.Moore,Ireland* 6-10-3[124] JonjoO'Neill(7) 3/1f	13	6
	Jabulani (FR) *NigelTwiston-Davies* 5-10-6[127] TomHumphries(7) 14/1	3¼	7
	Whatmore *HenryDaly* 6-10-11[132] (h) AndrewTinkler 25/1	10	8
	Night of Sin (FR) *NickWilliams* 5-10-11[132] LizzieKelly(3) 7/1	7	9
	Oxwich Bay (IRE) *EvanWilliams* 6-10-3[124] MitchellBastyan(5) 10/3		F
	Monty's Award (IRE) *CharlieLongsdon* 6-10-0[121] (h) RichardPatrick(5) 33/1		pu
	Thorpe (IRE) *LucindaRussell* 8-10-3[124] (s+t) BlairCampbell(5) 50/1		pu
82	Caid du Lin (FR) *DrRichardNewland* 6-11-0[135] (s+t) CharlieHammond(7) 20/1		pu

    Pump & Plant Services Ltd 13ran 4m59.90

117 Bet365 Handicap Chase (2) (5yo+) £46,920   2m5f8y (17)

	ACTING LASS (IRE) *HarryFry* 7-10-12[143] (t) NoelFehily 7/4f		1
	KILCREA VALE (IRE) *NickyHenderson* 8-10-6[137] JeremiahMcGrath 5/1	2¼	2
81	FORTUNATE GEORGE (IRE) *EmmaLavelle* 8-10-2[133] (v) LeightonAspell 9/2	17	3
	Minella Daddy (IRE) *PeterBowen* 8-10-8[139] (b) SeanBowen 6/1	42	4
74	Guitar Pete (IRE) *NickyRichards* 8-10-8[139] RyanDay(3) 4/1		ur
	Robinshill (IRE) *NigelTwiston-Davies* 7-10-12[143] (t) MrZacBaker(5) 16/1		pu

    Nigel & Barbara Collison 6ran 5m46.50

118 Royal Salute Whisky Clarence House Chase (Gr 1) (1) (5yo+) £85,425   2m167y (13)

69	UN DE SCEAUX (FR) *W.P.Mullins,Ireland* 10-11-7 P.Townend 4/9f		1
	SPEREDEK (FR) *NigelHawke* 7-11-7 (s) SeanBowen 16/1	7	2
34	KYLEMORE LOUGH *HarryFry* 9-11-7 NoelFehily 8/1	14	3
67	San Benedeto (FR) *PaulNicholls* 7-11-7 (s+t) NickScholfield 25/1	50	4
65	Brain Power (IRE) *NickyHenderson* 7-11-7 NicodeBoinville 7/2		F

    E. O'Connell 5ran 4m26.80

HAYDOCK Saturday, Jan 20   HEAVY

119 Sky Bet Supreme Trial Rossington Main Novices' Hurdle (Gr 2) (1) (4yo+)   1m7f144y (9)
    £17,085

	FIRST FLOW (IRE) *KimBailey* 6-11-4 DavidBass 9/4f		1
	MIDNIGHT SHADOW *SueSmith* 5-11-4 DannyCook 5/1	10	2
	LISDOONVARNA LAD (IRE) *CharlieLongsdon* 6-11-4 JonathanBurke 12/1	1½	3
	Waterlord *DonaldMcCain* 7-11-4 WillKennedy 11/4	¾	4
	Mcgowan's Pass *SandyThomson* 7-11-4 HenryBrooke 14/1	12	5
	Lostintranslation *ColinTizzard* 6-11-4 HarryCobden 7/2	11	6

    Mr A. N. Solomons 6ran 4m11.20

120 Unibet Champion Hurdle Trial Hurdle (Gr 2) (1) (4yo+) £42,712   1m7f144y (9)

84	THE NEW ONE (IRE) *NigelTwiston-Davies* 10-11-10 SamTwiston-Davies ......evsf		1
76	CH'TIBELLO (FR) *DanSkelton* 7-11-4 HarrySkelton 15/8	½	2
66	UNISON (IRE) *JeremyScott* 8-11-4 MattGriffiths 50/1	11	3
	Clyne *EvanWilliams* 8-11-4 RichardJohnson 7/2	1¾	4

    S Such & CG Paletta 4ran 4m12.00

121 Peter Marsh Handicap Chase (Limited Handicap) (Gr 2) (1) (5yo+) £42,712   3m1f125y (17)

46	THE DUTCHMAN (IRE) *ColinTizzard* 8-10-6[135] (t) HarryCobden 13/2		1
64	CAPTAIN REDBEARD (IRE) *StuartColthred* 9-11-1[144] SamColtherd(5) 12/1	13	2
	HAINAN (IRE) *SueSmith* 7-10-11[140] DannyCook 6/1	¾	3
81	Yala Enki (FR) *VenetiaWilliams* 8-11-4[147] CharlieDeutsch(3) 5/1f	2¼	4
29	Fine Rightly (IRE) *StuartCrawford,Ireland* 10-11-0[143] (h) A.E.Lynch 22/1	6	5
	Tintern Theatre (IRE) *NigelTwiston-Davies* 7-10-9[138] JamieBargary(3) 13/2		ur
	Forest des Aigles (FR) *LucindaRussell* 7-10-4[133] (t) DerekFox 14/1		pu
	Knockanrawley (IRE) *KimBailey* 10-10-4[133] (s) DavidBass 12/1		pu
62	Highland Lodge (IRE) *JamesMoffatt* 12-10-9[138] (s) HenryBrooke 25/1		pu
81	Walk In The Mill (FR) *RobertWalford* 8-10-12[141] JamesBest 9/1		pu
53	Carole's Destrier *NeilMulholland* 10-11-6[149] TomScudamore 16/1		pu
	Rock The Kasbah (IRE) *PhilipHobbs* 8-11-6[149] RichardJohnson 7/1		pu
81	Ptit Zig (FR) *PaulNicholls* 9-11-10[153] (b) SamTwiston-Davies 33/1		pu

    Sprayclad UK 13ran 7m22.40

GOWRAN Thursday, Jan 25 HEAVY

122 John Mulhern Galmoy Hurdle (Gr 2) (5yo+) £23,496 3m (13)
60 PRESENTING PERCY *PatrickG.Kelly* 7-11-3 (t) DavyRussell 9/4jf 1
95 AUGUSTA KATE *W.P.Mullins* 7-11-3 D.J.Mullins 8/1 5½ 2
     DIAMOND CAUCHOIS (FR) *GordonElliott* 7-11-3 (t) DenisO'Regan 5/1 1 3
96 Alpha des Obeaux (FR) *M.F.Morris* 8-11-3 (s+t) SeanFlanagan 9/2 2¼ 4
     Let's Dance (FR) *W.P.Mullins* 6-11-1 P.Townend 9/4jf 24 5
     Admiral Brian (IRE) *EamonO'Connell* 9-11-3 (h+t) E.O'Connell 66/1 30 6
     Lieutenant Colonel *GordonElliott* 9-11-3 (s+t) J.W.Kennedy ....16/1 pu
Philip J. Reynolds 7ran 7m09.50

123 Goffs Thyestes Handicap Chase (Gr A) (5yo+) £52,212 3m1f (15)
     MONBEG NOTORIOUS (IRE) *GordonElliott* 7-10-2[137] (v) J.W.Kennedy 7/2f 1
60 WOUNDED WARRIOR (IRE) *NoelMeade* 9-9-13[134] (s) A.W.Short(7) 25/1 11 2
94 SPACE CADET (IRE) *GordonElliott* 8-9-10[131] M.A.Enright ....16/1 hd 3
94 Thunder And Roses (IRE) *M.F.Morris* 10-10-7[142] (v+t) MsL.O'Neill(3) 20/1 5½ 4
94 Woods Well (IRE) *HenryDeBromhead* 7-10-0[135] ChrisMeehan(5) ....14/1 ½ 5
94 Out Sam *GordonElliott* 9-10-10[131] (s+t) JamesBowen(3) 6/1 1 6
     Fine Theatre (IRE) *PaulNolan* 8-9-12[134] (b) K.C.Sexton 16/1 18 7
     Sumos Novios (IRE) *W.J.Burke* 10-10-10[145] RobbiePower 8/1 24 8
53 A Genie In Abottle (IRE) *NoelMeade* 7-11-1[150] SeanFlanagan 7/1 13 9
94 Call The Taxie (IRE) *EllmarieHolden* 7-10-0[135] (v) RachaelBlackmore ....9/1 pu
     Isleofhopendreams *W.P.Mullins* 11-10-1[136] D.J.Mullins ....10/1 pu
94 Flaxen Flare (IRE) *GordonElliott* 9-10-2[137] (s) DenisO'Regan ....40/1 pu
94 Pleasant Company (IRE) *W.P.Mullins* 10-10-11[146] (h) P.Townend ....8/1 pu
94 Ucello Conti (FR) *GordonElliott* 10-10-13[148] (t) L.A.McKenna(7) ....7/1 pu
30 Champagne West (IRE) *HenryeBromhead* 10-11-10[159] (s) D.Robinson(5) ....20/1 pu
Gigginstown House Stud 15ran 6m55.20

CHELTENHAM Saturday, Jan 27 HEAVY

124 JCB Triumph Trial Juvenile Hurdle (Finesse) (Gr 2) (1) (4yo) £18,224 2m179y (8)
32 APPLE'S SHAKIRA (FR) *NickyHenderson* 4-10-12 BarryGeraghty 1/7f 1
     LOOK MY WAY *JohnQuinn* 4-11-0 TomScudamore 5/1 8 2
     ULYSSES (GER) *BarryBrennan* 4-11-0 (t) BarryCobden 100/1 13 3
     Broughtons Admiral *AlastairRalph* 4-11-0 LeeEdwards 50/1 8 4
     Erick Le Rouge (FR) *NickWilliams* 4-11-0 LizzieKelly 25/1 12 5
     Elixir de Nutz (FR) *PhilipHobbs* 4-11-0 RichardJohnson 10/1 46 6
Mr John P. McManus 6ran 4m25.50

125 Timeform Novices' Handicap Chase (2) (5yo+) £17,204 2½m166y (17)
     MISTER WHITAKER (IRE) *MickChannon* 6-10-8[129] A.P.Heskin 6/1 1
     THEATRE TERRITORY (IRE) *WarrenGreatrex* 8-10-7[128] MrSamWaley-Cohen(3) ..8/1 1¾ 2
101 SIZING TENNESSEE (IRE) *ColinTizzard* 10-12[147] B.J.Cooper 11/4jf 15 3
     War Sound *PhilipHobbs* 9-10-11[132] RichardJohnson ....5/1 hd 4
     Full Irish (IRE) *EmmaLavelle* 7-11-2[137] (t) NickScholfield 8/1 28 5
     Solstice Star *MartinKeighley* 8-10-9[130] (s+t) TomBellamy 16/1 21 6
101 Ballyandy *NigelTwiston-Davies* 7-11-9[145] NoelFehily ....11/4jf pu
Mr T. P. Radford 7ran 5m28.80

126 Crest Nicholson Handicap Chase (Gr 3) (1) (5yo+) £42,712 2½m166y (17)
81 FRODON (FR) *PaulNicholls* 6-11-12[154] (t) BryonyFrost(5) 13/2 1
102 SHANTOU FLYER (IRE) *RichardHobson* 8-11-11[153] JamesBowen(3) 10/1 17 2
74 KING'S ODYSSEY (IRE) *EvanWilliams* 9-10-11[139] BarryGeraghty 7/1 2 3
     Coo Star Sivola (FR) *NickWilliams* 6-10-7[135] LizzieKelly(3) 3/1f 1½ 4
81 O O Seven (IRE) *NickyHenderson* 8-11-10[152] NicodeBoinville ....7/1 hd 5
53 Potters Legend *LucyWadham* 8-10-5[133] (s) DavidNoonan 10/1 14 6
     Casse Tete (FR) *GaryMoore* 6-10-9[137] JoshuaMoore 25/1 1¼ 7
64 Arctic Gold (IRE) *NigelTwiston-Davies* 7-10-4[132] TomHumphries(7) 9/1 1¼ 8
     Drumlee Sunset (IRE) *TomGeorge* 8-10-6[134] TomScudamore 33/1 24 9
102 Ballyhill (FR) *NigelTwiston-Davies* 7-10-10[138] JamieBargary(3) 10/1 16 10
     Dream Bolt (IRE) *DavidRees* 10-10-3[131] PaddyBrennan ....33/1 pu
     Bally Longford (IRE) *ColinTizzard* 10-10-6[134] (t) NicodeBoinville ....16/1 pu
     Pressurize (IRE) *VenetiaWilliams* 12-10-8[136] CharlieDeutsch(3) ....20/1 pu
64 Ultragold (IRE) *ColinTizzard* 10-11-0[142] (t) HarryCobden ....33/1 pu
Mr P. J. Vogt 14ran 5m28.40

127 Betbright Trial Cotswold Chase (Gr 2) (1) (5yo+) £56,950 3m1f56y (21)
63 DEFINITELY RED (IRE) *BrianEllison* 9-11-6 DannyCook 7/1 1
53 AMERICAN (FR) *HarryFry* 8-11-2 NoelFehily 9/2 8 2
85 BRISTOL DE MAI (FR) *NigelTwiston-Davies* 7-11-6 DarylJacob 7/4f 2¼ 3

938

62	The Last Samuri (IRE) *KimBailey* 10-11-0 DavidBass	9/2	½	4
107	Perfect Candidate (IRE) *FergalO'Brien* 11-11-4 (b) PaddyBrennan	33/1	38	5
26	Theatre Guide (IRE) *ColinTizzard* 11-11-4 (b+t) HarryCobden	33/1	19	6
81	Singlefarmpayment *TomGeorge* 8-11-0 (h) A.P.Heskin	15/2		pu
85	Tea For Two *NickWilliams* 9-11-6 LizzieKelly	17/2		pu

Mr P. J. Martin 8ran 6m52.70

128 Ballymore Classic Novices' Hurdle (Gr 2) (1) (4yo+) £18,224 2½m56y (10)

	SANTINI *NickyHenderson* 6-11-5 JeremiahMcGrath	4/1		1
	BLACK OP (IRE) *TomGeorge* 7-11-5 (t) TomScudamore	8/1	¾	2
31	AYE AYE CHARLIE *FergalO'Brien* 6-11-5 PaddyBrennan	16/1	29	3
100	Mulcahys Hill (IRE) *WarrenGreatrex* 6-11-5 A.P.Heskin	11/4f	1¾	4
78	Slate House (IRE) *ColinTizzard* 6-11-10 HarryCobden	9/1	2¾	5
	Tikkanbar (IRE) *NeilMulholland* 7-11-10 NoelFehily	6/1	14	6
	Pacific de Baune (FR) *NickyHenderson* 5-11-5 NicodeBoinville	4/1	9	7
	De Rasher Counter *EmmaLavelle* 6-11-5 NickScholfield	20/1		F
	Fairmount *MartinKeighley* 7-11-5 RichardJohnson	50/1		pu

Mr & Mrs R. Kelvin-Hughes 9ran 5m22.20

129 galliardhomes.com Cleeve Hurdle (Gr 2) (1) (5yo+) £34,170 2m7f213y (12)

103	AGRAPART *NickWilliams* 7-11-6 LizzieKelly	9/1		1
103	WHOLESTONE (IRE) *NigelTwiston-Davies* 7-11-6 DarylJacob	9/2	3	2
103	COLIN'S SISTER *FergalO'Brien* 7-10-13 PaddyBrennan	10/1	8	3
80	The Worlds End (IRE) *TomGeorge* 7-11-3 A.P.Heskin	5/1	5	4
51	Beer Goggles (IRE) *KayleyWoollacott* 7-11-6 RichardJohnson	11/2	6	5
80	Thomas Campbell *NickyHenderson* 6-11-4 JamesBowen	7/1	4	6
80	Ex Patriot (IRE) *EllmarieHolden,Ireland* 5-11-0 RachaelBlackmore	20/1	7	7
	Saint Are (IRE) *TomGeorge* 12-11-0 (t) MrNoelGeorge	100/1		pu
79	Finian's Oscar (IRE) *ColinTizzard* 6-11-3 B.J.Cooper	11/4f		pu

The Gascoigne Brookes Partnership III 9ran 6m25.60

DONCASTER Saturday, Jan 27 SOFT

130 Napoleons Casino & Restaurant Owlerton Sheffield Lightning Novices' Chase 2m78y (12)
(Gr 2) (1) (5yo+) £19,932

65	SCEAU ROYAL (FR) *AlanKing* 6-11-5 WayneHutchinson	1/2f		1
90	SHANTOU ROCK (IRE) *DanSkelton* 6-11-0 (t) HarrySkelton	4/1	2	2
50	ADRIEN DU PONT (FR) *PaulNicholls* 6-11-0 (t) SamTwiston-Davies	4/1	11	3
	Ballycamp (IRE) *CharlesPogson* 9-11-00 (t) AdamPogson	100/1	76	4

Mr Simon Munir & Mr Isaac Souede 4ran 4m05.50

131 Albert Bartlett River Don Novices' Hurdle (Gr 2) (1) (5yo+) £17,085 3m84y (10)

	ENNISCOFFEY OSCAR (IRE) *EmmaLavelle* 6-10-12 LeightonAspell	9/2		1
	SHANNON BRIDGE (IRE) *DanSkelton* 5-10-12 HarrySkelton	16/1	sh	2
	SAMUEL JACKSON *RichardMitford-Slade* 6-10-12 MichealNolan	5/1	9	3
31	Calett Mad (FR) *NigelTwiston-Davies* 6-10-12 (s) SamTwiston-Davies	5/1	19	4
	Linenhall (IRE) *BenPauling* 6-10-12 (s) AidanColeman	33/1	11	5
	Station Master *KimBailey* 7-10-12 BrianHughes	9/1	3½	6
	Classic Ben *StuartEdmunds* 5-10-12 CiaranGethings	16/1	13	7
	Indian Hawk (IRE) *NickyHenderson* 6-10-12 DavyRussell	15/8f	43	8

The Pick 'N' Mix Partnership 8ran 6m08.80

132 OLBG.com Yorkshire Rose Mares' Hurdle (Gr 2) (1) (4yo+) £28,475 2m128y (8)

	MARIA'S BENEFIT (IRE) *StuartEdmunds* 6-11-2 CiaranGethings	10/11f		1
	IRISH ROE (IRE) *PeterAtkinson* 7-11-0 HenryBrooke	5/1	¾	2
	DUSKY LEGEND *AlanKing* 8-11-0 WayneHutchinson	5/1	7	3
100	Dame Rose (IRE) *RichardHobson* 5-11-2 DavyRussell	11/2	1¼	4
	The Nipper (IRE) *WarrenGreatrex* 7-11-0 GavinSheehan	20/1	24	5
	Smart Talk *BrianEllison* 8-11-0 ConnorKing	33/1	43	6

Mr P. D. Wells 6ran 4m03.80

133 Sky Bet Handicap Chase (L) (1) (5yo+) £45,560 2m7f214y (18)

89	WAKANDA *SueSmith* 9-11-0[145] HenryBrooke	8/1		1
23	WARRIORS TALE *PaulNicholls* 9-11-2[147] (t) SeanBowen	12/1	hd	2
80	L'AMI SERGE (IRE) *NickyHenderson* 8-11-7[152] (h) DavyRussell	13/8f	½	3
	Long House Hall (IRE) *DanSkelton* 10-11-0[145] (h+t) HarrySkelton	18/1	nk	4
62	Federici *DonaldMcCain* 9-10-0[131] (b) BrianHughes	25/1	1¾	5
53	Label des Obeaux (FR) *AlanKing* 7-11-6[151] (s) WayneHutchinson	20/1	9	6
	Minella On Line (IRE) *OliverSherwood* 9-10-3[134] ConorShoemark	33/1	9	7
63	Flying Angel (IRE) *NigelTwiston-Davies* 7-11-7[152] SamTwiston-Davies	6/1	7	8
	Vibrato Valtat (FR) *EmmaLavelle* 9-11-4[149] (t) LeightonAspell	16/1	½	9
	Mustmeetalady (IRE) *JonjoO'Neill* 8-10-3[134] (s) RichieMcLernon	20/1	2¼	10

	Thumb Stone Blues (IRE) *KimBailey* 8-10-1[132] (s+t) CiaranGethings(3) 7/1	12	11
	Coologue (IRE) *CharlieLongsdon* 9-10-6[137] JonathanBurke 16/1		pu
	Tenor Nivernais (FR) *VenetiaWilliams* 11-11-12[157] AidanColeman 33/1		pu
	M. B. Scholey & The Late R. H. Scholey 13ran 6m07.70		

FAIRYHOUSE Saturday, Jan 27 HEAVY

134 Solerina Mares Novices' Hurdle (Gr 3) (4yo+) £17,688 2¼m (9)

	LAURINA (FR) *W.P.Mullins* 5-10-11 P.Townend 13/8f		1
	ALLETRIX (IRE) *Mrs.J.Harrington* 5-10-11 (h) RobbiePower 25/1	11	2
	DAWN SHADOW (IRE) *MrsD.A.Love* 6-11-3 M.P.Walsh 14/1	8	3
	True Self (IRE) *W.P.Mullins* 5-10-11 B.Hayes 8/1	5½	4
	Minnies Secret (IRE) *CharlesByrnes* 6-10-13 (s) PhilipEnright 12/1	3¼	5
99	Ainsi Va La Vie (FR) *W.P.Mullins* 8-10-13 D.J.Mullins 6/1	¾	6
	Just Janice (IRE) *JohnE.Kiely* 6-11-6 DenisO'Regan 20/1	4¼	7
	The Birdie Crowe (IRE) *Mrs.J.Harrington* 7-10-13 (s+t) M.J.Bolger 66/1	1¼	8
	Gracemount (IRE) *SeanThomasDoyle* 7-10-13 (h) J.J.Slevin 33/1	4	9
	Killahara Castle (IRE) *JohnMichaelBurke* 7-10-13 M.P.Burke 50/1	24	10
	Crackerdancer (IRE) *RayHackett* 8-10-13 (t) MrE.P.O'Brien 9/4		F
	Sullivan Bloodstock Limited 11ran 4m50.60		

LEOPARDSTOWN Saturday, Feb 3 SOFT

135 Nathaniel Lacy & Partners Solicitors Novices' Hurdle (Golden Cygnet) (Gr 1) (5yo+) £51,754 2¾m (12)

	TOWER BRIDGE (IRE) *JosephPatrickO'Brien* 5-11-8 (t) J.J.Slevin 25/1		1
108	JETZ (IRE) *Mrs.J.Harrington* 6-11-10 RobbiePower 5/1	hd	2
109	CARTER MCKAY (IRE) *W.P.Mullins* 7-11-10 D.J.Mullins 9/2	2½	3
	Dortmund Park (FR) *GordonElliott* 5-11-8 (t) DavyRussell 5/2	3½	4
	Dicey O'Reilly (IRE) *HenrydeBromhead* 6-11-10 (t) D.Robinson 14/1	3	5
108	Moyross *NoelMeade* 7-11-10 SeanFlanagan 16/1	½	6
99	Fabulous Saga (FR) *W.P.Mullins* 6-11-10 (t) P.Townend 7/4f	14	7
	Mr John P. McManus 7ran 5m47.80		

136 Coral Dublin Chase (Gr 2) (5yo+) £51,754 2m1f (11)

92	MIN (FR) *W.P.Mullins* 7-11-10 D.J.Mullins 11/8f		1
92	SIMPLY NED (IRE) *NickyRichards,GB* 11-11-10 M.P.Walsh 12/1	12	2
91	SPECIAL TIARA *HenrydeBromhead* 11-11-10 RobbiePower 12/1	nk	3
92	Ordinary World (IRE) *HenrydeBromhead* 8-11-7 DavyRussell 10/1	18	4
9	Ballycasey (IRE) *W.P.Mullins* 11-11-7 MsK.Walsh 12/1	4½	5
96	Yorkhill (IRE) *W.P.Mullins* 8-11-10 P.Townend 7/4	46	6
69	Alisier d'Irlande (FR) *HenrydeBromhead* 8-11-7 (t) A.E.Lynch 20/1	2¼	7
	Mrs S. Ricci 7ran 4m13.20		

137 Frank Ward Solicitors Arkle Novices' Chase (Gr 1) (5yo+) £54,386 2m1f (11)

87	FOOTPAD (FR) *W.P.Mullins* 6-11-10 P.Townend 4/9f		1
	PETIT MOUCHOIR (FR) *HenrydeBromhead* 7-11-10 DavyRussell 3/1	5	2
87	ANY SECOND NOW (IRE) *T.M.Walsh* 6-11-10 M.P.Walsh 8/1	19	3
	Demi Sang (FR) *W.P.Mullins* 5-11-5 D.J.Mullins 16/1	22	4
	Tycoon Prince (IRE) *GordonElliott* 8-11-10 (t) J.W.Kennedy 28/1		F
	Mr Simon Munir/Mr Isaac Souede 5ran 4m13.20		

138 Coral Sandyford Handicap Chase (Gr B) (150) (5yo+) £38,816 2m1f (11)

	PATRICKS PARK (IRE) *W.P.Mullins* 7-9-12[123] RachaelBlackmore 6/1		1
94	THREE STARS (IRE) *HenrydeBromhead* 8-10-12[137] (s) J.J.Slevin 25/1	2¾	2
34	TULLY EAST (IRE) *AlanFleming* 8-11-5[144] DenisO'Regan 7/1	5½	3
	Blast of Koeman (IRE) *RobertTyner* 7-10-0[125] (t) PhilipEnright 8/1	¾	4
114	Dysios (IRE) *DenisW.Cullen* 10-10-5[130] (t) RogerLoughran 25/1	10	5
58	Ted Veale (IRE) *A.J.Martin* 11-11-1[140] MrL.Quinlan(7) 33/1	nk	6
114	Townshend (GER) *W.P.Mullins* 7-11-6[145] (t) P.Townend 16/1	1¼	7
	Bel Ami de Sivola (FR) *NoelMeade* 7-10-5[130] SeanFlanagan 7/1	¾	8
114	Kilcarry Bridge (IRE) *JohnPatrickRyan* 11-10-12[137] (t) DonaghMeyler 20/1	12	9
92	Tell Us More (IRE) *GordonElliott* 9-11-6[145] (b) KeithDonoghue 33/1	11	10
	Presenting Mahler (IRE) *JohnPatrickRyan* 8-9-10[121] C.A.Landers(7) 50/1	6	11
114	Conrad Hastings (IRE) *HenrydeBromhead* 7-11-4[143] DavyRussell 16/1	nk	12
94	Squouateur (FR) *GordonElliott* 7-10-10[135] (t) M.P.Walsh 11/2f	14	13
114	Mallowney (IRE) *TimothyDoyle* 12-11-5[144] B.J.Cooper 33/1	4½	14
	Nearly Nama'd (IRE) *AugustineLeahy* 10-10-0[139] (t) L.P.Dempsey 20/1	4½	15
	That's A Wrap *ThomasMullins* 7-9-12[123] M.A.Enright 12/1		F
	Some Plan (IRE) *HenrydeBromhead* 10-11-4[143] (t) D.Robinson(5) 12/1		F
114	Don't Touch It (IRE) *Mrs.J.Harrington* 8-11-10[149] D.J.McInerney(5) 28/1		ur
	Kilfenora (IRE) *EdwardP.Harty* 6-9-10[121] NiallMadden 8/1		pu

940

Hurricane Ben (IRE) *JamesG.Sheehan* 9-11-6[145] (t) RobbiePower ....33/1 pu
Bowes Lodge Stables Partnership 20ran 4m14.90

139 BHP Insurance Irish Champion Hurdle (Gr 1) (4yo+) £74,342 2m (8)
95 SUPASUNDAE *MrsJ.Harrington* 8-11-10 RobbiePower 8/1 1
98 FAUGHEEN (IRE) *W.P.Mullins* 10-11-10 P.Townend 9/10f 2¼ 2
98 MICK JAZZ (FR) *GordonElliott* 7-11-10 (h) DavyRussell 8/1 4¾ 3
95 Jezki (IRE) *MrsJ.Harrington* 10-11-10 (b) M.P.Walsh 25/1 4½ 4
76 Melon *W.P.Mullins* 6-11-10 (h) D.J.Mullins ....7/2 nk 5
Identity Thief (IRE) *HenrydeBromhead* 8-11-10 SeanFlanagan 40/1 14 6
44 Defi du Seuil (FR) *PhilipHobbs,GB* 5-11-10 RichardJohnson ....9/1 ¾ 7
95 Bapaume (FR) *W.P.Mullins* 5-11-9 MsK.Walsh 9/1 4½ 8
Ann & Alan Potts Partnership 8ran 4m02.10

140 Coral Hurdle (Extended Handicap) (Liffey) (Gr B) (150) (4yo+) £51,754 2m (8)
OFF YOU GO (IRE) *CharlesByrnes* 5-9-10[122] M.A.Enright 6/1 1
DEAL D'ESTRUVAL (FR) *W.P.Mullins* 5-10-0[126] MsK.Walsh 9/1 1¼ 2
GRAND PARTNER (IRE) *ThomasMullins* 10-10-2[128] (v) B.J.Cooper ..33/1 2½ 3
109 Makitorix (IRE) *W.P.Mullins* 5-10-1[127] (h+t) B.Hayes 25/1 1¼ 4
Tudor City (IRE) *A.J.Martin* 6-10-3[129] (t) DonaghMeyler 25/1 2¾ 5
Miles To Memphis (IRE) *MrsDeniseFoster* 9-10-0[126] (t) L.P.Dempsey ...20/1 ½ 6
82 Veinard (FR) *GordonElliott* 9-10-0[126] (t) DenisO'Regan ....20/1 ½ 7
58 Agent Boru (IRE) *T.Gibney* 5-9-10[122] JonathanMoore 33/1 1½ 8
On The Go Again (IRE) *MichaelMulvany* 5-10-7[134] (t) MrR.E.O'Sullivan(7) ...20/1 2½ 9
58 Ben Dundee (IRE) *GordonElliott* 6-10-8[134] J.W.Kennedy ....7/1 nk 10
Mind's Eye (IRE) *HenrydeBromhead* 6-10-7[133] D.Robinson(5) 11/2f 1¼ 11
58 Highland Fling (IRE) *GavinPatrickCromwell* 6-10-2[128] (t) A.E.Lynch ...25/1 1¾ 12
58 Charlie Stout (IRE) *ShaneNolan* 7-10-3[129] (s+t) P.E.Corbett(3) ....20/1 ¾ 13
Midnight Stroll *RobertTyner* 6-10-3[129] PhilipEnright 8/1 1¼ 14
Cliff House (IRE) *JohnJ.Walsh* 8-10-8[134] RachaelBlackmore ....33/1 sh 15
Deor (IRE) *JohnE.Kiely* 7-9-12[124] R.C.Colgan ....50/1 ½ 16
Bleu Berry (FR) *W.P.Mullins* 7-11-2[142] P.Townend 12/1 2¼ 17
Tandem *D.K.Weld* 9-10-0[126] ChrisMeehan(5) ....25/1 ¾ 18
58 Tigris River (IRE) *JosephPatrickO'Brien* 7-11-7[147] (t) J.J.Slevin 33/1 4¼ 19
Low Sun *W.P.Mullins* 5-9-11[123] (s) D.G.Hogan 14/1 11 20
58 Ivanovich Gorbatov (IRE) *JosephPatrickO'Brien* 6-11-7[147] (t) D.J.McInerney(5) ...33/1 6 21
Boherbuoy (IRE) *N.Madden* 6-10-4[130] NiallMadden 16/1 5½ 22
Ice Cold Soul (IRE) *NoelMeade* 8-10-2[128] (t) SeanFlanagan 20/1 5½ 23
Peace News (GER) *HenrydeBromhead* 6-10-7[133] MrDanielHolden(7) ...25/1 19 24
Indian Monsoon (IRE) *CharlesByrnes* 6-10-7[133] (s) RobbiePower ...20/1 17 25
De Name Escapes Me (IRE) *NoelMeade* 8-10-4[130] (h+t) M.P.Walsh ...20/1 pu
Karalee (FR) *W.P.Mullins* 7-10-12[138] (t) D.J.Mullins ....25/1 pu
Quick Jack (IRE) *A.J.Martin* 9-11-3[143] E.O'Connell(7) ....33/1 pu
Mr John P. McManus 28ran 4m02.30

141 Goffs Future Stars (C & G) INH Flat (Gr 2) (4, 5, 6 and 7yo) £38,816 2m
BLACKBOW (IRE) *W.P.Mullins* 5-11-10 MrP.W.Mullins 11/4f 1
RHINESTONE (IRE) *JosephPatrickO'Brien* 5-11-10 (t) MrD.O'Connor ...4/1 1½ 2
BRACE YOURSELF (IRE) *NoelMeade* 5-11-10 MissN.Carberry 7/2 15 3
Minella Encore (IRE) *W.P.Mullins* 6-12-0 MsK.Walsh 7/1 3¼ 4
Rapid Escape (IRE) *GordonElliott* 5-11-13 MsL.O'Neill 3/1 1¼ 5
Dunvegan (FR) *P.A.Fahy* 5-11-10 MrC.Fahy 20/1 30 6
The Shunter (IRE) *JohnO.Clifford* 5-11-6 MrsF.O'Keeffe 66/1 27 7
Village Mystic (FR) *NoelMeade* 7-11-11 MrB.O'Neill ....20/1 ¾ 8
Empire Burleque (IRE) *GordonElliott* 6-11-11 MrD.G.Lavery ....20/1 ds 9
Roaringwater Syndicate 9ran 4m00.60

SANDOWN Saturday, Feb 3   Chase course: SOFT, Hurdles course: HEAVY

142 Betfred 'Supports Jack Berry House' Contenders Hurdle (L) (1) (4yo+) 1m7f216y (8)
£17,085
84 BUVEUR D'AIR (FR) *NickyHenderson* 7-11-6 BarryGeraghty 1/16f 1
76 JOHN CONSTABLE (IRE) *EvanWilliams* 7-11-6 LeightonAspell 10/1 1¾ 2
CAP'N (IRE) *ClaireDyson* 7-11-0 (t) BrendanPowell 100/1 39 3
Mr John P. McManus 3ran 4m14.80

143 Betfred TV Scilly Isles Novices' Chase (Gr 1) (1) (5yo+) £31,322 2½m10y (17)
TERREFORT (IRE) *NickyHenderson* 5-11-1 DarylJacob 15/8f 1
90 CYRNAME (FR) *PaulNicholls* 6-11-4 (h+t) SeanBowen ....9/4 nk 2
NO COMMENT *PhilipHobbs* 7-11-4 (h) TomO'Brien 8/1 30 3
24 Kalondra (IRE) *NeilMulholland* 7-11-4 (h) NoelFehily 9/2 20 4

941

83 West Approach *ColinTizzard* 8-11-4 TomScudamore 6/1   1¼   5
Mr Simon Munir & Mr Isaac Souede 5ran 5m17.70

144 Betfred Heroes Handicap Hurdle (Gr 3) (1) (4yo+) £56,270   2m7f98y (12)
113 TOPOFTHEGAME (IRE) *PaulNicholls* 6-11-7[142] (t) SamTwiston-Davies 11/2f   1
     GOLAN FORTUNE (IRE) *PhilMiddleton* 6-11-2[137] (s) DanielSansom(7) 9/1   1½   2
     MELROSE BOY (FR) *HarryFry* 6-11-0[135] NoelFehily 7/1   2   3
     Folsom Blue (IRE) *GordonElliott,Ireland* 11-10-11[132] (s+t) BarryGeraghty 14/1   1½   4
 11 Doesyourdogbite (IRE) *JonjoO'Neill* 6-10-2[123] (s) RichieMcLernon 40/1   2½   5
 80 Ubak (FR) *GaryMoore* 10-11-11[146] JoshuaMoore .... 25/1   ½   6
116 Man of Plenty *SophieLeech* 9-10-2[123] (t) SeanHoulihan(7) 16/1   1½   7
     Dashing Perk *DrRichardNewland* 7-10-6[127] JamieMoore 7/1   2   8
     Flemcara (IRE) *EmmaLavelle* 6-11-4[139] (t) PatrickCowley(7) 16/1   1   9
     Kris Spin (IRE) *KerryLee* 10-11-0[135] JamesBowen(3) 33/1   1½ 10
107 Buywise (IRE) *EvanWilliams* 11-10-12[133] LeightonAspell .... 22/1   ¾   11
 20 Fourth Act (IRE) *ColinTizzard* 9-10-3[124] (t) HarryCobden 12/1   5   12
     Prime Venture (IRE) *EvanWilliams* 7-11-7[142] TomO'Brien .... 12/1   ¾   13
     Beat That (IRE) *NickyHenderson* 10-11-12[147] NicodeBoinville .... 20/1   ¾   14
     Taj Badalandabad (IRE) *DavidPipe* 8-11-3[138] (v+t) TomScudamore 20/1   18 15
     Okotoks (IRE) *FergalO'Brien* 8-10-9[130] SeanBowen 20/1   4½ 16
     King of Fashion (IRE) *KerryLee* 8-10-8[129] (t) RichardPatrick(5) .... 7/1   pu
Mr Chris Giles & Mr&Mrs P K Barber 17ran 6m20.20

WETHERBY Saturday, Feb 3   HEAVY
145 totesport.com Towton Novices' Chase (Gr 2) (1) (5yo+) £19,932   3m45y (17)
 83 BALLYOPTIC (IRE) *NigelTwiston-Davies* 8-11-3 TomBellamy 5/2jf   1
105 VINTAGE CLOUDS (IRE) *SueSmith* 8-11-0 DannyCook 5/2jf   2¾   2
     SHADES OF MIDNIGHT *SandyThomson* 8-11-0 HarryBannister 9/1   7   3
     Captain Chaos (IRE) *DanSkelton* 7-11-0 HarrySkelton 4/1   27   4
     Pearl Royale (IRE) *NigelHawke* 6-10-7 TomCannon .... 6/1   F
101 Ami Desbois (FR) *GraemeMcPherson* 6-11-0 (t) KielanWoods .... 8/1   pu
Mills & Mason Partnership 6ran 6m52.30

LEOPARDSTOWN Sunday, Feb 4   SOFT
146 Tattersalls Ireland Spring Juvenile Hurdle (Gr 1) (4yo) £52,632   2m (8)
     MR ADJUDICATOR *W.P.Mullins* 4-11-0 P.Townend 3/1   1
 86 FARCLAS (FR) *GordonElliott* 4-11-0 J.W.Kennedy 3/1   1¼   2
 86 GREY WATERS (IRE) *JosephPatrickO'Brien* 4-10-7 ShaneShortall 33/1   16   3
 86 Espoir d'Allen (FR) *GavinPatrickCromwell* 4-11-0 BarryGeraghty 4/5f   5½   4
 86 Tenth Amendment (IRE) *KeithHenryClarke* 4-11-0 (t) R.C.Colgan .... 66/1   ds   5
Mr David Bobbett 5ran 4m06.80

147 Deloitte Novices' Hurdle (Brave Inca) (Gr 1) (5yo+) £51,754   2m (8)
 48 SAMCRO (IRE) *GordonElliott* 6-11-10 J.W.Kennedy 4/6f   1
108 DUC DES GENIEVRES (FR) *W.P.Mullins* 5-11-9 NoelFehily 9/1   5½   2
     PALOMA BLUE (IRE) *HenrydeBromhead* 6-11-10 DavyRussell 16/1   3¾   3
 93 Whiskey Sour (IRE) *W.P.Mullins* 5-11-9 (t) D.J.Mullins 25/1   3¼   4
 93 Real Steel *W.P.Mullins* 5-11-9 MrP.W.Mullins .... 14/1   ½   5
     Debuchet (FR) *MsMargaretMullins* 5-11-9 RobbiePower .... 16/1   ¾   6
 93 Sharjah (FR) *W.P.Mullins* 5-11-9 P.Townend .... 4/1   ½   7
 93 Le Richebourg (FR) *JosephPatrickO'Brien* 5-11-9 BarryGeraghty 50/1   6   8
 56 Early Doors (FR) *JosephPatrickO'Brien* 5-11-9 M.P.Walsh .... 20/1   nk   9
     Trainwreck (IRE) *HenrydeBromhead* 6-11-10 SeanFlanagan 50/1   7½ 10
109 Top Othe Ra (IRE) *ThomasMullins* 10-11-10 B.J.Cooper 66/1   3½ 11
Gigginstown House Stud 11ran 4m08.10

148 William Fry Handicap Hurdle (Glencullen) (Gr B) (150) (4yo+) £38,816   3m (12)
 53 TOTAL RECALL (IRE) *W.P.Mullins* 9-10-4[125] P.Townend 5/6f   1
 94 OSCAR KNIGHT (IRE) *ThomasMullins* 4[125] M.P.Walsh 14/1   3   2
     FLAWLESS ESCAPE *GordonElliott* 5-10-4[125] RogerLoughran .... 7/1   ¾   3
 99 Delta Work (FR) *GordonElliott* 5-10-12[113] (h+t) DavyRussell .... 10/1   sh   4
     A Great View (IRE) *DenisW.Cullen* 7-10-10[131] (s) BarryGeraghty 11/2   19   5
 94 Phil's Magic (IRE) *A.J.Martin* 8-10-2[123] (s+t) DonaghMeyler 20/1   1¼   6
     Giant Spirit (USA) *W.P.Mullins* 6-10-1[122] RachaelBlackmore 16/1   11   7
     Racing Pulse (IRE) *W.P.Mullins* 9-10-2[123] (t) B.Hayes 33/1   2   8
     Voix du Reve (FR) *W.P.Mullins* 6-11-9[144] (h) N.M.Kelly(5) 16/1   44   9
     Shantou Bob (IRE) *WarrenGreatrex,GB* 10-11-10[145] (s+t) RobbiePower .... 20/1   hd 10
     Waaheb (USA) *PadraigRoche* 11-9-10[117] (s) K.J.Brouder(7) 33/1   2¼ 11
     Balzac Turgot (FR) *HenrydeBromhead* 7-10-3[124] (t) D.Robinson(5) .... 33/1   ½   12
     Massini's Trap (IRE) *JamesA.Nash* 9-10-11[132] (b) C.A.Landers(7) 40/1   1   13

Lite Duties (IRE) *CharlesByrnes* 9-10-13[134] D.J.McInerney(5) 8/1	3½	14
Rathpatrick (IRE) *EoinGriffin* 10-10-6[127] (s) J.P.Dempsey 33/1	2½	15
Taglietelle *GordonElliott* 9-11-3[138] (b) J.W.Kennedy 33/1		pu
Slaneyville Syndicate 16ran 6m29.90		

149 Flogas Novices' Chase (Scalp) (Gr 1) (5yo+) £51,754 2m5f (14)

97	MONALEE (IRE) *HenrydeBromhead* 7-11-10 NoelFehily 11/4jf		1
88	AL BOUM PHOTO (FR) *W.P.Mullins* 6-11-10 D.J.Mullins 9/1	¾	2
	INVITATION ONLY (IRE) *W.P.Mullins* 7-11-10 P.Townend 7/2	hd	3
88	Dounikos (FR) *GordonElliott* 7-11-10 J.W.Kennedy 25/1	¾	4
59	Snow Falcon (IRE) *NoelMeade* 8-11-10 SeanFlanagan 12/1	3¾	5
88	Tombstone (IRE) *GordonElliott* 8-11-10 DavyRussell 25/1	1¾	6
	The Storyteller (IRE) *GordonElliott* 7-11-10 KeithDonoghue 20/1	sh	7
97	Bon Papa (FR) *W.P.Mullins* 7-11-10 (t) M.P.Walsh 25/1	8	8
97	Rathvinden (IRE) *W.P.Mullins* 10-11-10 MrP.W.Mullins 12/1		ur
	Koshari (FR) *W.P.Mullins* 6-11-10 RobbiePower 25/1		pu
	Sutton Place (IRE) *GordonElliott* 7-11-10 (t) BarryGeraghty 11/4jf		pu

Mr Barry Maloney 11ran 5m35.20

150 Unibet Irish Gold Cup (Gr 1) (5yo+) £100,000 3m (17)

96	EDWULF (IRE) *JosephPatrickO'Brien* 9-11-10 (t) MrD.O'Connor 33/1		1
96	OUTLANDER (IRE) *GordonElliott* 10-11-10 (s) J.W.Kennedy 6/1	nk	2
96	DJAKADAM (FR) *W.P.Mullins* 9-11-10 MrP.W.Mullins 13/2	10	3
16	Our Duke (IRE) *Mrs.J.Harrington* 8-11-10 RobbiePower 9/4f	5½	4
96	Valseur Lido (FR) *HenrydeBromhead* 9-11-10 SeanFlanagan 8/1	12	5
122	Alpha des Obeaux (FR) *M.F.Morris* 8-11-10 (s+t) RachaelBlackmore 25/1	7½	6
94	Anibale Fly (FR) *A.J.Martin* 8-11-10 (t) BarryGeraghty 7/1		F
	Killultagh Vic (IRE) *W.P.Mullins* 9-11-10 P.Townend 5/1		F
96	Minella Rocco (IRE) *JonjoO'Neill,GB* 8-11-10 (s) M.P.Walsh 12/1		F
49	Mala Beach (IRE) *GordonElliott* 10-11-10 DavyRussell 14/1		pu

Mr John P. McManus 10ran 6m24.20

151 Chanelle Pharma Handicap Chase (Leopardstown) (Gr A) (5yo+) £51,754 2m5f (14)

49	LAST GOODBYE (IRE) *MissElizabethDoyle* 7-10-7[135] (b+t) A.W.Short(7) 12/1		1
94	VIEUX MORVAN (FR) *JosephPatrickO'Brien* 9-10-5[133] (b) J.J.Slevin 5/1	9	2
	UNCLE DANNY (IRE) *JohnQueally* 9-10-7[135] A.E.Lynch 33/1	9½	3
94	General Principle (IRE) *GordonElliott* 10-11-11[139] (t) DavyRussell 10/1	¾	4
94	Polidam (FR) *W.P.Mullins* 9-11-4[146] (h) NoelFehily 8/1	5½	5
	Coeur Joyeux (IRE) *J.P.Dempsey* 7-9-13[127] (h+t) L.P.Dempsey 16/1	1½	6
	Colms Dream (IRE) *KarlThornton* 9-10-12[140] (h+t) DonaghMeyler 40/1	6	7
	De Benno (IRE) *JamesGrace* 13-9-13[127] (t) C.A.Landers(7) 14/1	hd	8
87	Jett (IRE) *Mrs.J.Harrington* 9-10-7[142] RobbiePower 8/1	1¼	9
	Goulane Davina (IRE) *SeamusSpillane* 9-9-10[124] D.Robinson(5) 50/1	1¼	10
94	Dromnea (IRE) *M.F.Morris* 11-10-5[133] (v+t) RachaelBlackmore 33/1	1½	11
	Magic of Light (IRE) *Mrs.J.Harrington* 7-10-1[129] B.J.Cooper 16/1	3¾	12
4	Heron Heights (IRE) *HenrydeBromhead* 9-10-9[137] (s+t) PhilipEnright 40/1	5	13
	Sutton Manor (IRE) *GordonElliott* 7-10-10[138] J.W.Kennedy 7/1	4½	14
	Cause of Causes (USA) *GordonElliott* 10-11-10[152] (s+t) M.P.Walsh 33/1	1¾	15
94	Apache Stronghold (IRE) *NoelMeade* 10-10-13[141] (b+t) SeanFlanagan 28/1		F
	Landofhopeandglory (IRE) *JosephPatrickO'Brien* 5-9-12[132] (s+t) M.A.Enright ..14/1		ur
	Gwencily Berbas (FR) *AlanFleming* 7-10-5[133] (s+t) DenisO'Regan 12/1		ur
34	Lake Takapuna (IRE) *J.Culloty* 7-9-12[126] JonathanMoore 25/1		pu
9	Kylecrue (IRE) *JohnPatrickRyan* 11-10-9[137] (b) D.J.McInerney(5) 50/1		pu
88	Arbre de Vie (FR) *W.P.Mullins* 8-11-0[142] D.J.Mullins 25/1		pu
	Hell's Kitchen *HarryFry,GB* 7-11-1[143] (h+t) BarryGeraghty 9/2f		pu

Last Goodbye Syndicate 22ran 5m32.20

152 Coolmore NH Sires Irish European Breeders Fund Mares INH Flat (Deep Run) (Gr 2) (4, 5, 6 and 7yo) £38,816 2m

RELEGATE (IRE) *W.P.Mullins* 5-11-5 MsK.Walsh 16/1		1
GETAWAY KATIE MAI (IRE) *JohnQueally* 5-11-5 MissN.Carberry 8/1	1½	2
COLREEVY (IRE) *W.P.Mullins* 5-11-5 MrP.W.Mullins 5/6f	2½	3
Tintangle (IRE) *GordonElliott* 5-11-1 MsL.O'Neill 12/1	15	4
Chisholm Trail (IRE) *PaulNolan* 5-11-1 MrD.G.Lavery 50/1	10	5
The Princetonian (IRE) *Mrs.J.Harrington* 5-11-1 MissK.Harrington 40/1	hd	6
Lady Ischia (IRE) *GavinPatrickCromwell* 6-11-6 MrD.O'Connor 14/1	2¾	7
Fiveaftermidnight (IRE) *P.J.Rothwell* 5-11-1 (h) MrN.McParlan 66/1	nk	8
Hazy Shadow (IRE) *MrsD.A.Love* 5-11-1 MrA.Murphy 66/1	26	9
Motown Girl (IRE) *MsMargaretMullins* 5-11-5 MrR.Deegan 12/1	56	10
Welsh Pearl (IRE) *JohnPatrickRyan* 4-10-2 MissG.Ryan 80/1	nk	11

Cordovan Brown (IRE) *MissElizabethDoyle* 5-11-5 MrF.Maguire ....3/1 pu
Mr Paul McKeon 12ran 4m10.40

NEWBURY Saturday, Feb 10 Chase course: SOFT, Hurdles course: HEAVY

153 Betfair Denman Chase (Gr 2) (1) (5yo+) £28,475   2m7f86y (18)
    NATIVE RIVER (IRE) *ColinTizzard* 8-11-6 (s) RichardJohnson 8/11f 1
 63 CLOUDY DREAM (IRE) *RuthJefferson* 8-11-3 BrianHughes 11/4 12 2
    SAPHIR DU RHEU (FR) *PaulNicholls* 9-11-0 (t) SamTwiston-Davies 10/3 24 3
Brocade Racing 3ran 6m12.70

154 Betfair Exchange Chase (Game Spirit) (Gr 2) (1) (5yo+) £28,475   2m92y (13)
    ALTIOR (IRE) *NickyHenderson* 8-11-6 NicodeBoinville 1/3f 1
 91 POLITOLOGUE (FR) *PaulNicholls* 7-11-6 SamTwiston-Davies 5/2 4 2
    VALDEZ *AlanKing* 11-11-0 WayneHutchinson 25/1 13 3
Mrs Patricia Pugh 3ran 4m20.70

155 Betfair Hurdle (Handicap) (Gr 3) (1) (4yo+) £88,272   2m69y (8)
106 KALASHNIKOV (IRE) *AmyMurphy* 5-11-5[141] JackQuinlan 8/1cf 1
 82 BLEU ET ROUGE (FR) *W.P.Mullins,Ireland* 7-11-10[146] (t) BarryGeraghty 10/1 4½ 2
113 SPIRITOFTHEGAMES (FR) *DanSkelton* 6-11-3[139] (t) BridgetAndrews(3) 20/1 8 3
113 Coeur Blimey (IRE) *SusanGardner* 7-10-10[132] (s) LucyGardner(3) 14/1 9 4
    Remiluc (FR) *ChrisGordon* 9-11-8[144] HarryReed(7) 33/1 1¼ 5
 25 Lough Derg Spirit (IRE) *NickyHenderson* 6-11-2[138] JeremiahMcGrath 20/1 1 6
    Zalvados (FR) *OliverGreenall* 5-10-7[129] (b+t) RossTurner(5) ....25/1 hd 7
 66 William H Bonney *AlanKing* 7-10-12[134] WayneHutchinson ....20/1 ½ 8
 38 Misterton *HarryFry* 7-11-6[142] NickScholfield 20/1 1¾ 9
 82 Verdana Blue (IRE) *NickyHenderson* 6-11-9[145] DavyRussell 14/1 3¾ 10
    Moon Racer (IRE) *DavidPipe* 9-11-6[142] (t) TomScudamore 25/1 3½ 11
    Kayf Grace *NickyHenderson* 8-11-4[140] NicodeBoinville ....8/1cf ½ 12
    Lalor (GER) *KayleyWoollacott* 6-11-1[137] DarylJacob 14/1 5 13
 82 Charli Parcs (FR) *NickyHenderson* 5-11-9[145] NedCurtis(5) 33/1 4 14
 82 Nietzsche *BrianEllison* 5-10-10[132] JamesBest 20/1 2¾ 15
116 Jenkins (IRE) *NickyHenderson* 6-11-12[148] (b) JamesBowen(3) 8/1cf 2½ 16
 19 High Bridge *BenPauling* 7-11-12[148] MrAlexFerguson(7) 12/1 4½ 17
 38 Project Bluebook (FR) *JohnQuinn* 5-11-5[141] BrianHughes 50/1 17 18
    Poppy Kay *PhilipHobbs* 8-11-1[137] RichardJohnson 25/1 29 19
 82 Divin Bere (FR) *PaulNicholls* 5-11-8[144] SamTwiston-Davies 50/1 23 20
 82 Silver Streak (IRE) *EvanWilliams* 5-10-11[133] MitchellBastyan(5) ....16/1 ur
132 Irish Roe (IRE) *PeterAtkinson* 7-10-12[134] HenryBrooke ....10/1 pu
    Knocknanuss (IRE) *GaryMoore* 8-10-13[135] JamieMoore ....14/1 pu
119 Waterlord *DonaldMcCain* 7-10-13[135] WillKennedy ....25/1 pu
Mr Paul Murphy 24ran 4m09.30

WARWICK Saturday, Feb 10 SOFT

156 Betway Kingmaker Novices' Chase (Gr 2) (1) (5yo+) £22,780   2m54y (12)
    SAINT CALVADOS (FR) *HarryWhittington* 5-10-12 AidanColeman 4/9f 1
    DIEGO DU CHARMIL (FR) *PaulNicholls* 6-11-0 (t) BryonyFrost 11/1 22 2
 65 NORTH HILL HARVEY *DanSkelton* 7-11-5 HarrySkelton 11/4 17 3
 11 Drumcliff *HarryFry* 7-11-0 (t) NiallMadden 14/1 13 4
Mr A. Brooks 4ran 4m07.10

PUNCHESTOWN Sunday, Feb 11 HEAVY

157 Boylesports Grand National Trial Handicap Chase (Gr B) (5yo+) £52,212   3½m150y (20)
144 FOLSOM BLUE (IRE) *GordonElliott* 11-10-11[133] (s+t) J.W.Kennedy 5/1f 1
123 ISLEOFHOPENDREAMS *W.P.Mullins* 11-10-13[135] RobbiePower 16/1 1½ 2
    BAIE DES ILES (FR) *RossO'Sullivan* 7-11-9[145] (s) MsK.Walsh 12/1 13 3
123 Space Cadet (IRE) *GordonElliott* 8-10-10[132] DavyRussell 10/1 5 4
    Mick The Jiver *EoghanO'Grady* 8-10-7[129] D.E.Splaine 33/1 13 5
    Spider Web (IRE) *ThomasMullins* 7-9-10[118] M.A.Enright 10/1 1¼ 6
    Toubaloo (IRE) *AndrewLee* 10-10-0[122] J.J.Slevin ....10/1 ¾ 7
    Cappacurry Zak (IRE) *L.Young* 9-9-10[118] (s) D.Robinson(5) 33/1 4½ 8
    Red Devil Lads (IRE) *EmmetMullins* 9-10-8[130] (h+t) D.J.McInerney(5) 14/1 32 9
123 Wounded Warrior (IRE) *NoelMeade* 9-11-0[136] (s) A.W.Short(5) 14/1 89 10
    Without Limites (FR) *MissElizabethDoyle* 6-10-7[129] DonaghMeyler ....8/1 F
    White Arm (FR) *A.J.Martin* 9-10-2[124] (s+t) M.P.Walsh ....16/1 pu
 94 Teacher's Pet (IRE) *J.P.Dempsey* 7-10-6[128] (t) L.P.Dempsey ....20/1 pu
123 Out Sam *GordonElliott* 9-10-9[131] (s+t) DenisO'Regan ....12/1 pu
 94 Forever Gold (IRE) *EdwardCawley* 11-10-12[134] (s) C.D.Timmons(3) ....16/1 pu
123 Woods Well (IRE) *GordonElliott* 7-10-13[135] ChrisMeehan(5) ....12/1 pu
123 Thunder And Roses (IRE) *M.F.Morris* 10-11-5[141] (v+t) MsL.O'Neill(3) ....14/1 pu

	Childrens List (IRE) *W.P.Mullins* 8-11-9[145] D.J.Mullins	12/1	pu
94	Road To Riches (IRE) *NoelMeade* 11-11-10[146] (t) SeanFlanagan	25/1	pu

Core Partnership 19ran 8m08.70

ASCOT Saturday, Feb 17 SOFT

158 Sodexo Reynoldstown Novices' Chase (Gr 2) (1) (5yo+) £22,780 2m7f180y (20)

	BLACK CORTON (FR) *PaulNicholls* 7-11-5 (t) BryonyFrost	10/11f		1
83				
	MS PARFOIS (IRE) *AnthonyHoneyball* 7-10-12 (t) SeanBowen	7/4	8	2
	MOUNT MEWS (IRE) *RuthJefferson* 7-11-0 BrianHughes	5/1	4	3
	Crystal Lad (FR) *GaryMoore* 6-11-0 JoshuaMoore	25/1	24	4

The Brooks, Stewart Families & J. Kyle 4ran 6m22.90

159 Keltbray Swinley Chase (Limited Handicap) (L) (1) (5yo+) £42,712 2m7f180y (20)

81	REGAL ENCORE (IRE) *AnthonyHoneyball* 10-11-5[150] RichieMcLernon	6/1		1
117	MINELLA DADDY (IRE) *PeterBowen* 8-10-6[137] (s) SeanBowen	4/1	1½	2
	ANOTHER VENTURE (IRE) *KimBailey* 7-10-4[135] (s) MikeyHamill(5)	11/4jf	10	3
62	Vieux Lion Rouge (FR) *DavidPipe* 9-11-5[150] (b) TomScudamore	13/2	nk	4
1	Holly Bush Henry (IRE) *PhilMiddleton* 7-10-4[135] (s) JamesBowen(3)	11/4jf	6	5
133	Tenor Nivernais (FR) *VenetiaWilliams* 11-11-7[152] BrianHughes	9/1	23	6

Mr John P. McManus 6ran 6m15.90

160 Betfair Ascot Chase (Gr 1) (1) (5yo+) £85,425 2m5f8y (17)

112	WAITING PATIENTLY (IRE) *RuthJefferson* 7-11-7 BrianHughes	2/1f		1
47	CUE CARD *ColinTizzard* 12-11-7 (t) PaddyBrennan	9/1	2¾	2
126	FRODON (FR) *PaulNicholls* 6-11-7 (t) BryonyFrost	9/1	15	3
71	Top Notch (FR) *NickyHenderson* 7-11-7 DarylJacob	9/4	2½	4
85	Traffic Fluide (FR) *GaryMoore* 8-11-7 JoshuaMoore	66/1	16	5
	Coney Island (IRE) *EdwardP.Harty,Ireland* 7-11-7 BarryGeraghty	10/3		pu
118	Speredek (FR) *NigelHawke* 7-11-7 (s) SeanBowen	22/1		pu

Mr Richard Collins 7ran 5m24.80

GOWRAN Saturday, Feb 17 HEAVY

161 Red Mills Chase (Gr 2) (5yo+) £23,894 2½m (14)

150	OUR DUKE (IRE) *MrsJ.Harrington* 8-11-10 RobbiePower	5/2		1
122	PRESENTING PERCY *PatrickG.Kelly* 7-11-3 (t) DavyRussell	evsf	1	2
136	BALLYCASEY (IRE) *W.P.Mullins* 11-11-8 D.J.Mullins	16/1	16	3
70	A Toi Phil (FR) *GordonElliott* 8-11-8 (t) J.W.Kennedy	7/2	1	4
150	Valseur Lido (FR) *HenrydeBromhead* 9-11-10 SeanFlanagan	12/1	28	5

Cooper Family Syndicate 5ran 5m35.90

162 Red Mills Trial Hurdle (Gr 3) (4yo+) £23,496 2m (9)

15	FORGE MEADOW (IRE) *MrsJ.Harrington* 6-11-3 RobbiePower	7/4		1
139	IDENTITY THIEF (IRE) *HenrydeBromhead* 8-11-1 SeanFlanagan	9/2	1½	2
6	LAGOSTOVEGAS (IRE) *W.P.Mullins* 6-10-8 D.J.Mullins	6/4f	3	3
	Abbyssial (IRE) *W.P.Mullins* 8-11-1 D.E.Mullins	12/1	3½	4
140	On The Go Again (IRE) *MichaelMulvany* 5-11-0 (t) A.E.Lynch	14/1	30	5
	Arcenfete (IRE) *HenrydeBromhead* 6-11-1 J.W.Kennedy	33/1	12	6

Mr Joseph M. Doyle 6ran 4m22.40

HAYDOCK Saturday, Feb 17

163 Betfred Rendlesham Hurdle (Gr 2) (1) (4yo+) £22,780 2¾m177y (12)

	DONNA'S DIAMOND (IRE) *ChrisGrant* 9-11-2 CallumBewley	7/1		1
129	AGRAPART (FR) *NickWilliams* 7-11-8 LizzieKelly	4/7f	2¼	2
46	NO HASSLE HOFF (IRE) *DanSkelton* 6-11-2 BridgetAndrews	10/1	4	3
46	Zarkandar (IRE) *PaulNicholls* 11-11-8 (b+t) SamTwiston-Davies	20/1	16	4
	Boite (IRE) *WarrenGreatrex* 8-11-2 GavinSheehan	4/1		F

D&D Armstrong Ltd 5ran 5m58.80

164 Betfred Grand National Trial Handicap Chase (Gr 3) (5yo+) £56,950 3½m97y (22)

121	YALA ENKI (FR) *VenetiaWilliams* 8-10-11[146] CharlieDeutsch	8/1		1
62	BLAKLION *NigelTwiston-Davies* 9-11-12[161] SamTwiston-Davies	9/4f	54	2
105	MYSTEREE (IRE) *MichaelScudamore* 10-10-3[138] RobertDunne	9/1	74	3
33	Three Faces West (IRE) *PhilipHobbs* 10-10-9[144] (s) TomO'Brien	16/1		F
105	Wild West Wind (IRE) *TomGeorge* 9-10-9[144] A.P.Heskin	9/2		R
105	Silsol (GER) *PaulNicholls* 9-10-9[144] (b+t) NoelFehily	5/1		ur
111	Sir Mangan (IRE) *DanSkelton* 10-10-3[138] HenryBrooke	20/1		pu
121	The Dutchman (IRE) *ColinTizzard* 8-10-13[148] (t) DannyCook	9/2		pu

Hills of Ledbury (Aga) 8ran 8m17.80

165 Albert Bartlett Novices' Hurdle (Prestige) (Gr 2) (1) (5yo+) £16,938 2¾m177y (12)

	CHEF DES OBEAUX (FR) *NickyHenderson* 6-11-0 NoelFehily	13/8f	1

	UPPERTOWN PRINCE (IRE) *DonaldMcCain* 6-11-0 WillKennedy 12/1	15	2
144	GOLAN FORTUNE (IRE) *PhilMiddleton* 6-11-0 (s) JamieMoore 7/2	1¼	3
	Just Your Type (IRE) *CharlieLongsdon* 6-11-0 JonathanBurke 25/1	1¼	4
	Piri Massini (IRE) *OllyMurphy* 7-11-0 FergusGregory 33/1	5	5
	Coole Hall (IRE) *RoseDobbin* 6-11-3 CraigNichol 6/1	3¾	6
75	Global Stage *FergalO'Brien* 7-11-0 (s) AlainCawley 33/1		pu
131	Shannon Bridge (IRE) *DanSkelton* 7-11-0 (t) BridgetAndrews 7/2		pu
	Sullivan Bloodstock Limited 8ran 6m00.50		

WINCANTON Saturday, Feb 17 SOFT

166 Betway Kingwell Hurdle (Gr 2) (1) (4yo+) £34,170 1m7f65y (7)

82	ELGIN *AlanKing* 6-11-6 WayneHutchinson 5/1		1
120	CH'TIBELLO (FR) *DanSkelton* 7-11-2 (t) HarrySkelton 6/4f	2½	2
	CALL ME LORD (FR) *NickyHenderson* 5-11-2 AidanColeman 13/8	2	3
54	Flying Tiger (IRE) *NickWilliams* 5-11-4 RichardJohnson 8/1	½	4
142	Cap'n (IRE) *ClaireDyson* 7-11-2 JackQuinlan 250/1	61	5
	Cliffs of Dover *PaulNicholls* 5-11-5 HarryCobden 16/1		pu
	Elite Racing Club 6ran 3m55.90		

NAVAN Sunday, Feb 18 HEAVY

167 Ten Up Novices' Chase (Gr 2) (5yo+) £24,823 3m (17)

123	MONBEG NOTORIOUS (IRE) *GordonElliott* 7-11-3 (v) J.W.Kennedy 5/4f		1
	MOSSBACK (IRE) *GordonElliott* 6-11-3 DavyRussell 5/2	½	2
97	MOULIN A VENT *NoelMeade* 6-11-3 (b) SeanFlanagan 4/1	19	3
	C'est Jersey (FR) *W.P.Mullins* 6-11-3 DarylJacob 5/1		pu
	Gigginstown House Stud 4ran 6m51.50		

FAIRYHOUSE Saturday, Feb 24 SOFT

168 At The Races Bobbyjo Chase (Gr 3) (5yo+) £26,282 3m1f (18)

	BELLSHILL (IRE) *W.P.Mullins* 8-11-8 D.J.Mullins 8/13f		1
123	A GENIE IN ABOTTLE (IRE) *NoelMeade* 7-11-6 SeanFlanagan 11/4	4¾	2
	VAL DE FERBET (FR) *AndrewMcNamara* 9-11-6 (t) RobbiePower 14/1	8½	3
7	Lord Scoundrel (IRE) *GordonElliott* 9-11-0 (t) RachaelBlackmore 8/1		ur
	Champagne Harmony (IRE) *S.J.Mahon* 8-11-3 DenisO'Regan 33/1		pu
	Andrea Wylie/Graham Wylie 5ran 6m58.00		

KEMPTON Saturday, Feb 24 GOOD

169 Betdaq Now 2% Commission Pendil Novices' Chase (Gr 2) (1) (5yo+) £18,224 2½m110y (16)

143	CYRNAME (FR) *PaulNicholls* 6-11-5 (h+t) SeanBowen 2/5f		1
	THE UNIT (IRE) *AlanKing* 7-11-0 WayneHutchinson 7/2	11	2
	FOR GOOD MEASURE (IRE) *PhilipHobbs* 7-11-0 TomO'Brien 20/1	5	3
	Petrou (IRE) *DanSkelton* 8-11-0 HarrySkelton 14/1	94	4
	Mrs Johnny de la Hey 4ran 5m06.00		

170 Betdaq #Changingforthebettor Adonis Juvenile Hurdle (Gr 2) (1) (4yo) £17,085 2m (8)

	REDICEAN *AlanKing* 4-11-1 WayneHutchinson 10/11f		1
	MALAYA (FR) *PaulNicholls* 4-10-10 SamTwiston-Davies 4/1	7	2
	BEAU GOSSE (FR) *GuillaumeMacaire,France* 4-11-3 (t) DarylJacob 4/1	10	3
	Grand Sancy (FR) *PaulNicholls* 4-10-12 (h) HarryCobden 10/1	½	4
	Harmonise *SheenaWest* 4-10-5 (h) MarcGoldstein 20/1	25	5
	Kasperenko *BrendanPowell* 4-10-12 (t) BrendanPowell 40/1	17	6
	Bid Adieu (IRE) *VenetiaWilliams* 4-10-12 (h) SeanBowen 33/1		pu
	Apple Tree Stud 7ran 3m49.90		

171 Sky Bet Dovecote Novices' Hurdle (Gr 2) (1) (4yo+) £17,085 2m (8)

	GLOBAL CITIZEN (IRE) *BenPauling* 6-11-2 DarylJacob 5/1		1
	SCARLET DRAGON *AlanKing* 5-11-2 (h) WayneHutchinson 13/2	9	2
	MICHAEL'S MOUNT *IanWilliams* 5-11-2 TomO'Brien 7/1	3¾	3
106	Mont des Avaloirs (FR) *PaulNicholls* 5-11-2 (h) SeanBowen 2/1f	¾	4
	Destrier (FR) *DanSkelton* 5-11-2 HarrySkelton 16/1	4½	5
	Shoal Bay (IRE) *ColinTizzard* 5-11-2 (t) HarryCobden 10/1	9	6
	Rockpoint *ColinTizzard* 5-11-2 AidanColeman 25/1	2¾	7
	Humphrey Bogart (IRE) *NickyHenderson* 5-11-2 (h) NicodeBoinville 7/1	19	8
	Carntop *JamieSnowden* 5-11-2 GavinSheehan 40/1	3¼	9
	Ballywood (FR) *AlanKing* 4-10-12 TomCannon 25/1	5	10
	The Megsons 10ran 3m47.00		

172 Betdaq Handicap Chase (Gr 3) (1) (5yo+) £56,950 3m (18)

23	MASTER DEE (IRE) *FergalO'Brien* 9-11-5[145] (t) BarryGeraghty 8/1		1

20	BALLYKAN *NigelTwiston-Davies* 8-10-7^{133} (s+t) DarylJacob	14/1	3¾	2
125	THEATRE TERRITORY (IRE) *WarrenGreatrex* 8-10-6^{132} (s) MrSamWaley-Cohen(3)	10/1	4	3
112	Art Mauresque (FR) *PaulNicholls* 8-11-10^{150} HarryCobden	10/1	1¼	4
81	Go Conquer (IRE) *JonjoO'Neill* 9-11-11^{151} AidanColeman	16/1	1½	5
26	Relentless Dreamer (IRE) *RebeccaCurtis* 9-10-11^{137} (s+t) CiaranGethings	33/1	3¾	6
133	Vibrato Valtat (FR) *EmmaLavelle* 9-11-7^{147} (t) LeightonAspell	33/1	¾	7
133	Label des Obeaux (FR) *AlanKing* 7-11-9^{149} (s) WayneHutchinson	14/1	10	8
117	Acting Lass (IRE) *HarryFry* 7-11-9^{149} (t) NoelFehily	7/2f	ns	9
62	As de Mee (FR) *PaulNicholls* 8-11-9^{149} SeanBowen	20/1	6	10
121	Tintern Theatre (IRE) *NigelTwiston-Davies* 7-10-12^{138} SamTwiston-Davies	5/1	16	11
107	Loose Chips *CharlieLongsdon* 12-10-13^{139} (b) PaulO'Brien(5)	20/1	20	12
	Monbeg Charmer (IRE) *CharlieLongsdon* 7-10-8^{134} (h+t) JonathanBurke	16/1		pu
112	Josses Hill (IRE) *NickyHenderson* 10-11-10^{150} (b) NicodeBoinville	12/1		pu
127	Theatre Guide (IRE) *ColinTizzard* 11-11-12^{152} (b+t) TomO'Brien	20/1		pu

Paul & Clare Rooney 15ran 6m01.30

NEWCASTLE Saturday, Feb 24 SOFT

173 Betfred Eider Handicap Chase (2) (5yo+) £50,048 — 4m122y (25)

89	BAYWING (IRE) *NickyRichards* 9-11-3^{140} RyanDay(3)	8/1		1
	WEST OF THE EDGE (IRE) *DrRichardNewland* 10-10-5^{128} (s) WillKennedy	11/1	4	2
62	PORTRAIT KING (IRE) *PatrickGriffin,Ireland* 13-10-4^{127} (v) A.W.Short(5)	33/1	16	3
121	Hainan (FR) *SueSmith* 7-11-3^{140} DannyCook	11/2	ns	4
111	Milansbar (IRE) *NeilKing* 11-11-6^{143} (b) JamieMoore	11/1	13	5
	Smooth Stepper *SueSmith* 9-11-1^{138} SeanQuinlan	20/1	22	6
	Back To The Thatch (IRE) *HenryDaly* 6-10-6^{129} RichardJohnson	6/1		F
97	Thebarrowman (IRE) *A.P.Keatley,Ireland* 8-10-8^{131} (s+t) RogerLoughran	14/1		F
	Millicent Silver *NigelTwiston-Davies* 9-10-0^{123} (v) MrJ.Nailor(7)	50/1		ur
	Lochnell (IRE) *IanDuncan* 9-10-0^{123} HenryBrooke	50/1		pu
55	Boric *SimonWaugh* 10-10-0^{123} (s) CallumBewley(3)	14/1		pu
	Milborough (IRE) *IanDuncan* 12-10-1^{124} DerekFox	14/1		pu
	Silver Tassie (IRE) *MickyHammond* 10-10-4^{127} AlainCawley	33/1		pu
	Themanfrom Minella (IRE) *BenCase* 9-10-5^{128} (b+t) MaxKendrick(5)	20/1		pu
	Vinnie Lewis (IRE) *HarryWhittington* 7-10-13^{136} HarryBannister	5/1f		pu
107	Houblon des Obeaux (FR) *VenetiaWilliams* 11-11-7^{144} (s) CharlieDeutsch	16/1		pu
105	Chase The Spud *FergalO'Brien* 10-11-12^{149} PaddyBrennan	16/1		pu

David & Nicky Robinson 17ran 8m58.80

FONTWELL Sunday, Feb 25 GOOD to SOFT

174 totepool National Spirit Hurdle (Gr 2) (1) (4yo+) £45,560 — 2m3f49y (10)

103	OLD GUARD *PaulNicholls* 7-11-7 HarryCobden	11/4		1
80	LIL ROCKERFELLER (USA) *NeilKing* 7-11-9 (b) TrevorWhelan	5/2f	1½	2
116	AIR HORSE ONE *HarryFry* 7-11-3 NoelFehily	10/3	11	3
120	Clyne *EvanWilliams* 8-11-3 AdamWedge	12/1	2½	4
	Value At Risk *DanSkelton* 9-11-3 BridgetAndrews	28/1	5	5
	Norman The Red *JohnE.Long* 8-11-3 MattieBatchelor	200/1	5	6
78	Dr Des (IRE) *HenryOliver* 7-11-3 JamesDavies	13/2	nk	7
144	Ubak (FR) *GaryMoore* 10-11-3 JoshuaMoore	8/1		pu

The Brooks, Stewart Families & J. Kyle 8ran 4m48.50

SANDOWN Saturday, Mar 10 HEAVY

175 European Breeders' Fund Matchbook VIP 'National Hunt' Novices' Handicap Hurdle Final (Gr 3) (1) (4, 5, 6 and 7yo) £42,202 — 2m3f173y (9)

	SAM'S GUNNER *MichaelEasterby* 5-10-12^{125} WillKennedy	12/1		1
113	DENTLEY DE MEE (FR) *NickWilliams* 5-10-11^{124} (s) MrChesterWilliams(7)	16/1	7	2
	FIRST ASSIGNMENT (IRE) *IanWilliams* 5-10-12^{125} TomScudamore	10/1	6	3
	Canelo (IRE) *AlanKing* 5-11-1^{128} WayneHutchinson	10/1	1¾	4
	Turtle Wars (FR) *NickyHenderson* 5-10-11^{124} JamesBowen(3)	12/1	2¼	5
106	The Russian Doyen (IRE) *ColinTizzard* 5-11-12^{139} HarryCobden	18/1	5	6
	Game On (IRE) *LucyWadham* 6-11-3^{130} LeightonAspell	16/1	6	7
	The Dubai Way (IRE) *HarryWhittington* 6-10-13^{126} HarryBannister	8/1	1¾	8
	Quick Pick (IRE) *JennieCandlish* 7-10-9^{122} SeanQuinlan	16/1	6	9
	Midnight Chill *JamieSnowden* 6-10-9^{122} GavinSheehan	33/1		pu
116	Oxwich Bay (IRE) *EvanWilliams* 6-10-11^{124} AdamWedge	14/1		pu
116	Jabulani (FR) *NigelTwiston-Davies* 5-10-11^{124} JamieBargary(3)	25/1		pu
	Notre Ami (IRE) *NickGifford* 7-10-12^{125} TomCannon	40/1		pu
144	Dashing Perk *DrRichardNewland* 7-10-12^{125} (s) SamTwiston-Davies	12/1		pu
	Al Shahir (IRE) *DanSkelton* 6-11-0^{127} HarrySkelton	11/2f		pu
	Run To Milan (IRE) *VictorDartnall* 6-11-5^{132} (h) ConorShoemark	12/1		pu

131	Indian Hawk (IRE) *NickyHenderson* 6-11-9[136] DarylJacob 13/2		pu
	Falcon's Line Ltd 17ran 5m11.40		

176	**Matchbook Imperial Cup Handicap Hurdle (Gr 3) (1) (4yo+) £42,202**	1m7f216y (8)	
	MR ANTOLINI (IRE) *NigelTwiston-Davies* 8-10-4[130] JamieBargary(3) 20/1		1
166	CALL ME LORD (FR) *NickyHenderson* 5-11-12[152] DarylJacob 8/1	nk	2
	WHATSWRONGWITHYOU (IRE) *NickyHenderson* 7-10-13[139] (h)		
	NicodeBoinville 10/3f	9	3
	Huntsman Son (IRE) *AlexHales* 8-10-9[135] JamesBowen(3) 9/1	hd	4
144	Man of Plenty *SophieLeech* 9-10-0[126] (t) SeanHoulihan(5) 25/1	1¾	5
155	Silver Streak (IRE) *EvanWilliams* 5-10-7[133] TomO'Brien 16/1	hd	6
66	Fidux (FR) *AlanKing* 5-10-8[134] WayneHutchinson 20/1	6	7
	Castafiore (USA) *CharlieLongsdon* 5-10-4[130] (s+h) PaulO'Brien(5) 25/1	1¼	8
	Chti Balko (FR) *DonaldMcCain* 6-11-0[140] WillKennedy 25/1	2¾	9
	Highway One O One (IRE) *ChrisGordon* 6-10-7[133] TomCannon 12/1	1¼	10
	Gassin Golf *KerryLee* 9-10-0[126] (b+t) RichardPatrick(5) 16/1	2¼	11
	Shanroe Saint *BenCase* 6-10-0[126] JonathanBurke 40/1	13	12
	Birch Hill (IRE) *SophieLeech* 8-10-0[126] (t) JamesBest 28/1		ur
	Friday Night Light (FR) *DavidPipe* 5-10-2[128] (v+t) TomScudamore 8/1		pu
	Octagon *HarryWhittington* 6-10-3[129] HarryBannister 20/1		pu
	Master of Irony (IRE) *JohnQuinn* 6-10-7[133] (s) RichardJohnson 12/1		pu
113	Le Patriote (FR) *DrRichardNewland* 6-10-9[135] (s) SamTwiston-Davies 7/1		pu
	Alan & Sally Coney 17ran 4m09.70		

GOWRAN Saturday, Mar 10   HEAVY

177	**toals.com Bookmakers Leinster National Handicap Chase (Gr A) (5yo+)**	2m7f (14)	
	£52,679		
	PAIROFBROWNEYES (IRE) *W.P.Mullins* 9-11-4[137] P.Townend 9/2		1
157	SPACE CADET (IRE) *GordonElliott* 8-10-12[131] DavyRussell 11/2	3¾	2
	GLENCAIRN VIEW (IRE) *AnthonyMullins* 8-10-1[120] D.E.Mullins 8/1	3¼	3
123	Fine Theatre (IRE) *PaulNolan* 8-11-0[133] (b) D.Robinson(5) 16/1	8½	4
62	Rogue Angel (IRE) *M.F.Morris* 10-10-12[131] (s+t) RachaelBlackmore 25/1	3½	5
60	Poormans Hill (IRE) *GordonElliott* 7-10-2[121] J.W.Kennedy 4/1f	½	6
157	Wounded Warrior (IRE) *NoelMeade* 9-11-2[135] (s) A.W.Short(5) 20/1	9	7
157	Mick The Jiver *EoghanO'Grady* 8-10-8[127] D.E.Splaine 25/1	¾	8
151	Sutton Manor (IRE) *GordonElliott* 7-11-3[136] (s) ChrisMeehan(5) 20/1		F
157	Thunder And Roses (IRE) *M.F.Morris* 10-11-7[140] (v+t) MsL.O'Neill(3) 25/1		F
	Routes Choice (IRE) *J.P.Dempsey* 7-10-3[124] B.Browne(5) 28/1		pu
151	Coeur Joyeux (IRE) *J.P.Dempsey* 7-10-8[127] (h+t) L.P.Dempsey 14/1		pu
	Close Shave *Mrs.J.Harrington* 7-10-12[131] BarryGeraghty 12/1		pu
	Scoir Mear (IRE) *ThomasMullins* 8-10-12[131] M.P.Walsh 10/1		pu
94	Bonny Kate (IRE) *NoelMeade* 8-11-5[138] SeanFlanagan 12/1		pu
	Fibbage Syndicate 15ran 6m40.20		

CHELTENHAM Tuesday, Mar 13   SOFT

178	**Sky Bet Supreme Novices' Hurdle (Gr 1) (1) (4yo+) £71,187**	2m87y (8)	
106	SUMMERVILLE BOY (IRE) *TomGeorge* 6-11-7 NoelFehily 9/1		1
155	KALASHNIKOV (IRE) *AmyMurphy* 5-11-7 JackQuinlan 5/1	nk	2
109	MENGLI KHAN (IRE) *GordonElliott,Ireland* 5-11-7 (t) J.W.Kennedy 14/1	1¾	3
147	Paloma Blue (IRE) *HenrydeBromhead,Ireland* 5-11-7 DavyRussell 14/1	1	4
78	Claimantakinforgan (FR) *NickyHenderson* 6-11-7 NicodeBoinville 16/1	2¼	5
106	Western Ryder (IRE) *WarrenGreatrex* 6-11-7 RichardJohnson 20/1	2¼	6
119	Lostintranslation (IRE) *ColinTizzard* 6-11-7 RobbiePower 40/1	¾	7
147	Sharjah (IRE) *W.P.Mullins,Ireland* 5-11-7 P.Townend 20/1	2¼	8
147	Debuchet (FR) *MsMargaretMullins,Ireland* 5-11-7 D.E.Mullins 20/1	1¾	9
	Simply The Betts (IRE) *HarryWhittington* 5-11-7 SeanBowen 40/1	22	10
109	Getabird (IRE) *W.P.Mullins,Ireland* 6-11-7 R.Walsh 7/4f	9	11
	Us And Them (IRE) *JosephPatrickO'Brien,Ireland* 5-11-7 J.J.Slevin 28/1	19	12
	Khudha (IRE) *AlanFleming,Ireland* 4-10-13 (s) DenisO'Regan 200/1	½	13
	Saxo Jack (FR) *SophieLeech* 8-11-7 (t) SeanHoulihan 200/1	1	14
	Golden Jeffrey (SWI) *IainJardine* 5-11-7 ConorO'Farrell 150/1	2¼	15
128	Slate House (IRE) *ColinTizzard* 6-11-7 (t) HarryCobden 20/1		F
132	Dame Rose (FR) *RichardHobson* 5-11-0 (t) JonathanBurke 40/1		pu
119	First Flow (IRE) *KimBailey* 6-11-7 DavidBass 12/1		pu
171	Shoal Bay (IRE) *ColinTizzard* 5-11-7 (t) TomScudamore 80/1		pu
	Mr R. S. Brookhouse 19ran 4m05.60		

179	**Racing Post Arkle Challenge Trophy Novices' Chase (Gr 1) (1) (5yo+)**	1m7f199y (13)	
	£99,662		
137	FOOTPAD (FR) *W.P.Mullins,Ireland* 6-11-4 R.Walsh 5/6f		1

118	BRAIN POWER (IRE) *NickyHenderson* 7-11-4 NicodeBoinville 14/1	14	2
137	PETIT MOUCHOIR (FR) *HenrydeBromhead,Ireland* 7-11-4 DavyRussell 4/1	¾	3
156	Saint Calvados (FR) *HarryWhittington* 5-11-4 AidanColeman 11/4	38	4
117	Robinshill (IRE) *NigelTwiston-Davies* 7-11-4 SamTwiston-Davies 66/1	71	5

Mr Simon Munir/Mr Isaac Souede 5ran 4m02.30

180	**Ultima Handicap Chase (Gr 3) (1) (5yo+)** £62,645		3m1f (20)
126	COO STAR SIVOLA (FR) *NickWilliams* 6-10-13[142] LizzieKelly(3) 5/1f		1
126	SHANTOU FLYER (IRE) *RichardHobson* 8-11-9[152] (v+t) JamesBowen(3) 14/1	nk	2
145	VINTAGE CLOUDS (IRE) *SueSmith* 8-10-12[141] DannyCook 7/1	6	3
105	Beware The Bear (IRE) *NickyHenderson* 8-11-7[150] JeremiahMcGrath 14/1	2¾	4
127	Singlefarmpayment *TomGeorge* 8-11-2[145] (h) A.P.Heskin 8/1	3	5
164	Yala Enki (FR) *VenetiaWilliams* 8-11-9[152] CharlieDeutsch 12/1	2½	6
	Ramses de Teillee (FR) *DavidPipe* 6-11-2[145] (t) TomScudamore 12/1	4	7
126	Casse Tete (FR) *GaryMoore* 6-10-9[138] JoshuaMoore 16/1	8	8
	Eamon An Cnoic (IRE) *DavidPipe* 7-10-8[137] (s) DavidNoonan 28/1	hd	9
126	O O Seven (IRE) *NickyHenderson* 8-11-9[152] AidanColeman 20/1	7	10
111	Cogry *NigelTwiston-Davies* 9-10-9[138] JamieBargary(3) 11/1	1	11
159	Minella Daddy (IRE) *PeterBowen* 8-10-10[139] (s) SeanBowen 14/1	14	12
26	Vic de Touzaine (FR) *VenetiaWilliams* 9-10-10[139] B.J.Cooper 40/1		pu
	Knight of Noir (IRE) *MichaelBlake* 9-10-13[142] (t) NickScholfield 33/1		pu
133	Wakanda (IRE) *SueSmith* 9-11-5[148] SeanQuinlan 25/1		pu
105	Vicente (FR) *PaulNicholls* 9-11-8[151] (h) SamTwiston-Davies 20/1		pu
62	Sizing Codelco (IRE) *ColinTizzard* 9-11-11[154] RobbiePower 50/1		pu
81	Gold Present (FR) *NickyHenderson* 8-11-12[155] NicodeBoinville 10/1		pu

Babbit Racing 18ran 6m48.30

181	**Unibet Champion Hurdle Challenge Trophy (Gr 1) (1) (4yo+)** £266,384		2m87y (8)
142	BUVEUR D'AIR (FR) *NickyHenderson* 7-11-10 BarryGeraghty 4/6f		1
139	MELON (IRE) *W.P.Mullins,Ireland* 6-11-10 P.Townend 7/1	nk	2
139	MICK JAZZ (FR) *GordonElliott,Ireland* 7-11-10 (h+t) DavyRussell 25/1	3	3
162	Identity Thief (IRE) *HenrydeBromhead,Ireland* 8-11-10 SeanFlanagan 50/1	9	4
166	Elgin *AlanKing* 6-11-10 WayneHutchinson 12/1	1¾	5
139	Faugheen (IRE) *W.P.Mullins,Ireland* 10-11-10 (s) R.Walsh 4/1	8	6
	Wicklow Brave (IRE) *W.P.Mullins,Ireland* 9-11-10 (b) MrP.W.Mullins 14/1	½	7
166	Ch'tibello (FR) *DanSkelton* 7-11-10 HarrySkelton 33/1	1¼	8
142	John Constable (IRE) *EvanWilliams* 7-11-10 (t) LeightonAspell 66/1	17	9
155	Charli Parcs (FR) *NickyHenderson* 5-11-10 NoelFehily 100/1		pu
136	Yorkhill (IRE) *W.P.Mullins,Ireland* 8-11-10 D.J.Mullins 14/1		pu

Mr John P. McManus 11ran 4m05.10

182	**OLBG Mares' Hurdle (David Nicholson) (Gr 1) (1) (4yo+)** £67,524		2m3f200y (10)
	BENIE DES DIEUX (FR) *W.P.Mullins,Ireland* 7-11-5 R.Walsh 9/2		1
	MIDNIGHT TOUR *AlanKing* 8-11-5 DavyRussell 33/1	½	2
95	APPLE'S JADE (FR) *GordonElliott,Ireland* 6-11-5 (t) J.W.Kennedy 1/2f	1	3
	Indian Stream *NeilMulholland* 9-11-5 (t) TomScudamore 66/1	7	4
28	Jer's Girl (IRE) *GavinPatrickCromwell,Ireland* 6-11-5 BarryGeraghty 10/1	2½	5
	Midnight Jazz *BenCase* 8-11-5 (s) DarylJacob 66/1	¾	6
115	La Bague Au Roi (FR) *WarrenGreatrex* 7-11-5 RichardJohnson 5/1	¾	7
155	Kayf Grace *NickyHenderson* 8-11-5 NicodeBoinville 25/1		F
	Pravalaguna (FR) *W.P.Mullins,Ireland* 6-11-5 (h) D.E.Mullins 50/1		pu

Mrs S. Ricci 9ran 5m10.00

183	**National Hunt Challenge Cup Amateur Riders' Novices' Chase (Gr 2) (1) (5yo+)** £74,950		3m7f170y (25)
149	RATHVINDEN (IRE) *W.P.Mullins,Ireland* 10-11-6 MrP.W.Mullins 9/2		1
158	MS PARFOIS (IRE) *AnthonyHoneyball* 7-10-13 (t) MrWilliamBiddick ..11/2	½	2
125	SIZING TENNESSEE (IRE) *ColinTizzard* 10-11-6 MrBarryO'Neill 8/1	21	3
	Impulsive Star (IRE) *NeilMulholland* 8-11-6 (t) MrSamWaley-Cohen 25/1	2½	4
	Pylonthepressure (IRE) *W.P.Mullins,Ireland* 8-11-6 MsK.Walsh 16/1	11	5
143	No Comment *PhilipHobbs* 7-11-6 (h) MrDerekO'Connor 9/1	23	6
72	Keeper Hill *WarrenGreatrex* 7-11-6 MrRichardDeegan 25/1		F
167	Mossback (IRE) *GordonElliott,Ireland* 6-11-6 MsL.O'Neill 6/1		F
	Robin of Locksley (IRE) *SophieLeech* 8-11-6 (s+t) MrD.Skehan 100/1		R
97	Jury Duty (IRE) *GordonElliott,Ireland* 7-11-6 (t) MrJ.J.Codd 4/1f		ur
145	Shades of Midnight *SandyThomson* 8-11-6 MrT.Hamilton 20/1		ur
	All Kings *BobBuckler* 9-11-6 MrJoshuaNewman 200/1		pu
81	Clondaw Cian (IRE) *SuzySmith* 8-11-6 (b) ShaneFitzgerald 66/1		pu
	Duel At Dawn (IRE) *AlexHales* 6-11-6 (s) MrTommieM.O'Brien 16/1		pu
3	Lofgren *DonaldMcCain* 7-11-6 (t) MrTheoGillard 150/1		pu

Reigning Supreme (IRE) *NickyHenderson* 7-11-6 MrJamesKing ....33/1   pu
Mr R. A. Bartlett 16ran 8m50.30

184 Close Brothers Novices' Handicap Chase (L) (1) (145) (5yo+) £39,865   2½m78y (16)
125 MISTER WHITAKER (IRE) *MickChannon* 6-11-2[137] BrianHughes 13/2   1
      RATHER BE (IRE) *NickyHenderson* 7-11-8[143] JeremiahMcGrath ....12/1   hd 2
 72 ROCKLANDER (IRE) *TomGeorge* 9-11-7[142] A.P.Heskin 25/1   3¼ 3
      Barney Dwan (IRE) *FergalO'Brien* 8-11-8[143] NoelFehily 15/2   8 4
      Ibis du Rheu (IRE) *PaulNicholls* 7-11-6[141] (t) SamTwiston-Davies 25/1   3½ 5
      Jameson *NigelTwiston-Davies* 6-11-5[140] TomBellamy 40/1   2 6
      Kayf Adventure *PhilipHobbs* 7-11-3[138] RichardJohnson ....25/1   sh 7
137 Any Second Now (IRE) *T.M.Walsh,Ireland* 6-11-10[145] MarkWalsh 5/1f 1½ 8
126 Ballyhill (FR) *NigelTwiston-Davies* 7-11-3[138] JamieBargary(3) 25/1 14 9
 50 Western Miller (IRE) *CharlieLongsdon* 7-11-6[141] (t) JonathanBurke ....100/1 ¾ 10
      Testify (IRE) *DonaldMcCain* 7-11-10[145] WillKennedy ....11/1 hd 11
      Report To Base (IRE) *EvanWilliams* 6-11-4[139] AdamWedge ....14/1   F
      Livelovelaugh (IRE) *W.P.Mullins,Ireland* 8-11-4[139] R.Walsh ....10/1   F
 46 Le Rocher (FR) *NickWilliams* 8-11-9[144] TomScudamore ....14/1   bd
      Markov (IRE) *BenPauling* 8-11-3[138] DarylJacob ....66/1   pu
138 Conrad Hastings (IRE) *HenrydeBromhead,Ireland* 7-11-8[143] DylanRobinson(5) ...66/1 pu
      De Plotting Shed (IRE) *GordonElliott,Ireland* 8-11-8[143] (t) DavyRussell ....11/2 pu
137 Tycoon Prince (IRE) *GordonElliott,Ireland* 8-11-9[144] (t) J.W.Kennedy ....25/1 pu
137 Demi Sang (FR) *W.P.Mullins,Ireland* 5-11-9[145] BarryGeraghty ....20/1 pu
Mr T. P. Radford 19ran 5m29.00

CHELTENHAM Wednesday, Mar 14 SOFT

185 Ballymore Novices' Hurdle (Baring Bingham) (Gr 1) (1) (4yo+) £71,187   2m5f26y (10)
147 SAMCRO (IRE) *GordonElliott,Ireland* 7-11-7 J.W.Kennedy 8/11f   1
128 BLACK OP (IRE) *TomGeorge* 7-11-7 (t) NoelFehily 8/1 2¾ 2
108 NEXT DESTINATION (IRE) *W.P.Mullins,Ireland* 6-11-7 R.Walsh 4/1   5 3
      Scarpeta (FR) *W.P.Mullins,Ireland* 5-11-7 D.E.Mullins ....33/1 nk 4
147 Duc des Genievres (FR) *W.P.Mullins,Ireland* 5-11-7 P.Townend 10/1   1 5
 31 Vision des Flos (FR) *ColinTizzard* 5-11-7 (t) RobbiePower ....14/1 ¾ 6
128 Aye Aye Charlie *FergalO'Brien* 6-11-7 ConorShoemark 100/1 14 7
      Gowiththeflow (FR) *W.P.Mullins,Ireland* 5-11-7 DarylJacob ....40/1 sh 8
      Brahma Bull (IRE) *W.P.Mullins,Ireland* 7-11-7 D.J.Mullins 25/1 2¼ 9
140 Mind's Eye (IRE) *HenrydeBromhead,Ireland* 6-11-7 DavyRussell 66/1   9 10
      Diablo de Rouhet (FR) *JoHughes* 5-11-7 MarkGrant 200/1 2¼ 11
      Coolanly (IRE) *FergalO'Brien* 6-11-7 PaddyBrennan 100/1 2½ 12
110 Knight In Dubai (IRE) *DanSkelton* 5-11-7 (t) HarrySkelton 100/1 16 13
      Ahead of The Curve (FR) *SusanCorbett* 6-11-7 (s+t) JamesCorbett ....200/1 pu
Gigginstown House Stud 14ran 5m18.70

186 RSA Insurance Novices' Chase (Gr 1) (1) (5yo+) £99,662   3m80y (20)
161 PRESENTING PERCY *PatrickG.Kelly,Ireland* 7-11-4 (t) DavyRussell 5/2f   1
149 MONALEE (IRE) *HenrydeBromhead,Ireland* 7-11-4 NoelFehily 10/3   7 2
 83 ELEGANT ESCAPE (IRE) *ColinTizzard* 6-11-4 HarryCobden 9/1   7 3
145 Ballyoptic (IRE) *NigelTwiston-Davies* 8-11-4 SamTwiston-Davies 9/1 1½ 4
158 Black Corton (FR) *PaulNicholls* 7-11-4 (t) BryonyFrost 5/1 1¾ 5
149 Al Boum Photo (FR) *W.P.Mullins,Ireland* 6-11-4 R.Walsh ....8/1   F
      Bonbon Au Miel (FR) *W.P.Mullins,Ireland* 7-11-4 (t) P.Townend ....33/1   F
      Allysson Monterey (FR) *RichardHobson* 8-11-4 (t) JonathanBurke ....50/1   pu
149 Dounikos (FR) *GordonElliott,Ireland* 7-11-4 (t) J.W.Kennedy ....12/1   pu
125 Full Irish (IRE) *EmmaLavelle* 7-11-4 (s+t) LeightonAspell ....100/1 pu
Philip J. Reynolds 10ran 6m32.10

187 Coral Cup Handicap Hurdle (Gr 3) (1) (4yo+) £56,950   2m5f26y (10)
140 BLEU BERRY (FR) *W.P.Mullins,Ireland* 7-11-2[143] M.P.Walsh 20/1   1
144 TOPOFTHEGAME (IRE) *PaulNicholls* 6-11-9[150] (t) SamTwiston-Davies ....9/1   nk 2
      BARRA (IRE) *GordonElliott,Ireland* 7-10-10[137] (t) J.W.Kennedy 16/1 1¼ 3
113 William Henry (IRE) *NickyHenderson* 8-11-10[151] (s) JamesBowen(3) 8/1jf 1¼ 4
      The Organist (IRE) *OliverSherwood* 7-10-12[139] LeightonAspell 25/1 2¾ 5
113 Red Indian *BenPauling* 6-10-12[139] DavidBass 14/1   1 6
116 Burbank (IRE) *NickyHenderson* 6-11-2[143] (s) JeremiahMcGrath ....18/1 ½ 7
      Stowaway Magic (IRE) *NickyHenderson* 7-10-13[140] NicodeBoinville ....33/1 ½ 8
      Mischievious Max (IRE) *JosephPatrickO'Brien,Ireland* 5-10-8[135] J.J.Slevin(3) ...25/1 4½ 9
158 Mount Mews (IRE) *RuthJefferson* 7-11-1[142] BrianHughes 12/1 3¾ 10
144 Flemcara (IRE) *EmmaLavelle* 6-10-11[138] (t) PatrickCowley(5) 66/1   3 11
      Fixe Le Kap (FR) *NickyHenderson* 6-11-0[141] DarylJacob ....16/1 ½ 12
      Jeannot de Nonant (FR) *PeterBowen* 6-10-12[139] (s) SeanBowen ....40/1 ½ 13
148 Voix du Reve (FR) *W.P.Mullins,Ireland* 6-11-1[142] (h) D.J.Mullins 10/1   1 14

950

113	River Frost *AlanKing* 6-11-4[145] BarryGeraghty 25/1	½	15
	Le Breuil (FR) *BenPauling* 6-10-12[139] AidanColeman 14/1	nk	16
	Bastien (FR) *AlanKing* 7-10-10[137] TomCannon 50/1	1½	17
103	Royal Vacation (IRE) *ColinTizzard* 8-11-1[142] (b+t) HarryCobden 22/1	2	18
61	Springtown Lake (IRE) *PhilipHobbs* 6-10-12[139] RichardJohnson 20/1	2	19
115	Graceful Legend *BenCase* 7-10-9[136] (s) MaxKendrick(5) 66/1	2¼	20
167	C'est Jersey (FR) *W.P.Mullins,Ireland* 6-10-12[139] (b) NoelFehily 33/1	12	21
5	Max Dynamite (FR) *W.P.Mullins,Ireland* 8-10-12[141] P.Townend 8/1jf	hd	22
132	Dusky Legend *AlanKing* 8-10-12[139] WayneHutchinson 33/1		F
	As You Were (FR) *AlanFleming,Ireland* 6-10-13[140] (s+t) DenisO'Regan 20/1		pu
162	Abbyssial (IRE) *W.P.Mullins,Ireland* 8-11-6[147] D.E.Mullins 33/1		pu
	Diamond King (IRE) *GordonElliott,Ireland* 10-11-12[153] (t) DavyRussell ...33/1		pu
	Luke McMahon 26ran 5m22.00		

188	**Betway Queen Mother Champion Chase (Gr 1) (1) (5yo+) £227,800**	1m7f199y (13)	
154	ALTIOR (IRE) *NickyHenderson* 8-11-10 NicodeBoinville .... evsf		1
136	MIN (FR) *W.P.Mullins,Ireland* 7-11-10 P.Townend 5/2	7	2
112	GOD'S OWN (IRE) *TomGeorge* 10-11-10 PaddyBrennan 40/1	11	3
154	Politologue (FR) *PaulNicholls* 7-11-10 SamTwiston-Davies 12/1	5	4
136	Ordinary World (IRE) *HenrydeBromhead,Ireland* 10-11-10 DavyRussell ...40/1	12	5
67	Charbel (IRE) *KimBailey* 7-11-10 (s) DavidBass 28/1		F
	Douvan (FR) *W.P.Mullins,Ireland* 8-11-10 MrP.W.Mullins 9/2		F
67	Ar Mad (FR) *GaryMoore* 8-11-10 (s) JoshuaMoore 50/1		pu
136	Special Tiara *HenrydeBromhead,Ireland* 11-11-10 NoelFehily 25/1		pu
	Mrs Patricia Pugh 9ran 4m06.00		

189	**Glenfarclas Chase (Cross Country) (2) (5yo+) £40,235**	3¾m37y (30)	
	The Aintree fence was omitted due to waterlogging		
30	TIGER ROLL (IRE) *GordonElliott,Ireland* 8-11-4 (s+t) KeithDonoghue 7/1		1
	URGENT DE GREGAINE (FR) *EmmanuelClayeux,France* 10-11-4 (s+t)		
	FelixdeGiles 12/1	2	2
127	THE LAST SAMURI (IRE) *KimBailey* 10-11-4 DavidBass 11/4f	11	3
10	Auvergnat (FR) *EndaBolger,Ireland* 8-11-4 MarkWalsh 10/1	4½	4
	Chic Name (FR) *RichardHobson* 6-11-4 (h) JonathanBurke 100/1	nk	5
	Josies Orders (IRE) *EndaBolger,Ireland* 10-11-4 (s) MissN.Carberry 7/1	25	6
	Beeves (IRE) *JennieCandlish* 11-11-4 (b) SeanQuinlan 50/1	1½	7
60	Bless The Wings (IRE) *GordonElliott,Ireland* 13-11-4 (s) DavyRussell 9/1		F
	Belamix Dor (FR) *PatriceQuinton,France* 7-10-11 (t) ThomasBeaurain ...100/1		pu
	Cantlow (IRE) *EndaBolger,Ireland* 13-11-4 (s) D.J.McInerney 25/1		pu
151	Cause of Causes (USA) *GordonElliott,Ireland* 10-11-4 (s+t) Mr.J.J.Codd ...10/3		pu
133	Federici *DonaldMcCain* 9-11-4 (s) WillKennedy 66/1		pu
49	Hurricane Darwin (IRE) *AlanFleming,Ireland* 8-11-4 (t) DenisO'Regan ...25/1		pu
129	Saint Are (FR) *TomGeorge* 12-11-4 (s+t) A.P.Heskin 33/1		pu
	Urumqi (FR) *DavidCottin,France* 7-11-4 (t) JonathanPlouganou 33/1		pu
	Vicomte du Seuil (FR) *EmmanuelClayeux,France* 9-11-4 (s+t) CharlieDeutsch ...50/1		pu
	Gigginstown House Stud 16ran 8m51.50		

190	**Boodles Fred Winter Juvenile Handicap Hurdle (Gr 3) (1) (4yo) £45,560**	2m87y (8)	
	VENEER OF CHARM (IRE) *GordonElliott,Ireland* 4-11-0[129] J.W.Kennedy 33/1		1
	STYLE DE GARDE (FR) *NickyHenderson* 4-11-8[137] (h) NicodeBoinville 12/1	3	2
	NUBE NEGRA (SPA) *DanSkelton* 4-11-6[135] HarrySkelton 15/2f	1	3
	Padleyourowncanoe *ColinTizzard* 4-11-3[132] TomScudamore 33/1	2¾	4
	Turning Gold *NigelTwiston-Davies* 4-10-12[127] TomBellamy 20/1	4	5
	Solo Saxophone (IRE) *DanSkelton* 4-10-13[128] (b+t) P.Townend 40/1	¾	6
73	Eragon de Chanay (FR) *GaryMoore* 4-10-11[126] JoshuaMoore 8/1	1½	7
124	Look My Way *JohnQuinn* 4-11-6[135] BrianHughes 8/1	½	8
73	Act of Valour *PaulNicholls* 4-11-7[136] A.P.Heskin 14/1	2¼	9
	The King of May (FR) *BrianEllison* 4-10-13[128] DannyCook 12/1	6	10
86	Mastermind (IRE) *CharlesO'Brien,Ireland* 4-10-12[127] RobbiePower 25/1	1	11
	Embole (FR) *DanSkelton* 4-11-0[129] (h+t) DarylJacob 33/1	1¼	12
	Casa Tall (FR) *TomGeorge* 4-11-10[139] JamesBowen(3) 25/1	15	13
	Esprit de Somoza (FR) *NickWilliams* 4-11-6[135] LizzieKelly(3) 16/1	11	14
	Knight Destroyer (IRE) *JonjoO'Neill* 4-10-12[127] AidanColeman 20/1		F
	Lisp (IRE) *AlanKing* 4-11-3[132] WayneHutchinson 10/1		F
170	Grand Sancy (FR) *PaulNicholls* 4-10-12[127] (h) SamTwiston-Davies 16/1		pu
	Oxford Blu *OllyMurphy* 4-10-13[128] (s) RichardJohnson 14/1		pu
	Eureu du Boulay (FR) *RichardHobson* 4-11-0[129] (t) JonathanBurke 50/1		pu
	Brave Dancing *DavidCottin,France* 4-11-5[134] (t) FelixdeGiles 33/1		pu
104	Mercenaire (FR) *NickWilliams* 4-11-6[135] MrChesterWilliams(7) 25/1		pu

86 Mitchouka (FR) *GordonElliott,Ireland* 4-11-10^{139} M.P.Walsh ....8/1 pu
Mr M. Wasylocha 22ran 4m10.80

191 Weatherbys Champion Bumper (Standard Open National Hunt Flat) (Gr 1) (1) (4, 5 and 6yo) £42,712 2m87y

152 RELEGATE (IRE) *W.P.Mullins,Ireland* 5-10-12 MsK.Walsh 25/1 1
CAREFULLY SELECTED (IRE) *W.P.Mullins,Ireland* 6-11-5 D.E.Mullins ....6/1 nk 2
TORNADO FLYER (IRE) *W.P.Mullins,Ireland* 5-11-5 P.Townend 14/1 3¼ 3
Acey Milan (IRE) *AnthonyHoneyball* 4-10-11 (t) AidanColeman 9/2f 1¾ 4
141 Blackbow (IRE) *W.P.Mullins,Ireland* 5-11-5 MrP.W.Mullins ....5/1 ½ 5
Felix Desjy (FR) *GordonElliott,Ireland* 5-11-5 (h) KeithDonoghue 8/1 1¾ 6
152 Colreevy (IRE) *W.P.Mullins,Ireland* 5-10-12 D.J.Mullins ....50/1 ½ 7
Mercy Mercy Me *FergalO'Brien* 6-11-5 PaddyBrennan 25/1 1½ 8
141 Rhinestone (IRE) *JosephPatrickO'Brien,Ireland* 5-11-5 (t) BarryGeraghty 5/1 1¼ 9
Didtheyleaveuoutto (IRE) *NickGifford* 5-11-5 MarkWalsh 12/1 3¼ 10
The Big Bite (IRE) *TomGeorge* 5-11-5 NoelFehily ....20/1 hd 11
Seddon (IRE) *TomGeorge* 5-11-5 A.P.Heskin 33/1 1¼ 12
Dashel Drasher *JeremyScott* 5-11-5 MattGriffiths 100/1 3¾ 13
Know The Score (IRE) *DavidPipe* 5-11-5 TomScudamore 20/1 9 14
Arch My Boy *MartinSmith* 4-10-11 LeightonAspell ....100/1 nk 15
Stoney Mountain (IRE) *HenryDaly* 5-11-5 AndrewTinkler 100/1 1½ 16
Jaytrack Parkhomes *ColinTizzard* 4-10-11 HarryCobden 80/1 1 17
Volcano (FR) *NigelTwiston-Davies* 4-10-11 SamTwiston-Davies 50/1 3¾ 18
Nestor Park (FR) *BenPauling* 5-11-5 DarylJacob 100/1 3 19
The Flying Sofa (FR) *GaryMoore* 5-11-5 JamieMoore 66/1 1½ 20
Doc Penfro *KevinFrost* 6-11-5 BrianHughes 200/1 9 21
Crooks Peak *PhilipHobbs* 5-11-5 RichardJohnson 25/1 48 22
Thebannerkingrebel (IRE) *JamieSnowden* 5-11-5 GavinSheehan ....33/1 pu
Mr Paul McKeon 23ran 4m04.60

CHELTENHAM Thursday, Mar 15 SOFT

192 JLT Novices' Chase (Golden Miller) (Gr 1) (1) (5yo+) £85,425 2m3f198y (16)

97 SHATTERED LOVE (IRE) *GordonElliott,Ireland* 7-10-11 (t) J.W.Kennedy 4/1 1
143 TERREFORT (FR) *NickyHenderson* 5-11-3 DarylJacob 3/1f 7 2
79 BENATAR (IRE) *GaryMoore* 6-11-4 JamieMoore 10/1 5 3
Kemboy (FR) *W.P.Mullins,Ireland* 6-11-4 D.J.Mullins 15/2 2½ 4
129 Finian's Oscar (IRE) *ColinTizzard* 6-11-4 (s+t) RobbiePower ....11/2 ¾ 5
143 West Approach *ColinTizzard* 8-11-4 (b) TomScudamore 33/1 6 6
Bigmartre (FR) *HarryWhittington* 7-11-4 HarryBannister 20/1 4 7
24 Modus *PaulNicholls* 8-11-4 BarryGeraghty 12/1 14 8
149 Invitation Only (IRE) *W.P.Mullins,Ireland* 7-11-4 P.Townend ....9/2 pu
Gigginstown House Stud 9ran 5m12.20

193 Pertemps Network Final Handicap Hurdle (Gr 3) (1) (5yo+) £56,950 2m7f213y (12)

148 DELTA WORK (FR) *GordonElliott,Ireland* 5-10-10^{139} (h+t) DavyRussell 6/1 1
GLENLOE (IRE) *GordonElliott,Ireland* 7-10-8^{137} BarryGeraghty .... 9/2f ns 2
35 CONNETABLE (FR) *PaulNicholls* 6-10-7^{136} (b) HarryCobden 33/1 2¾ 3
144 Taj Badalandabad (IRE) *DavidPipe* 8-10-9^{138} (v+t) TomScudamore 40/1 2½ 4
Who Dares Wins (IRE) *AlanKing* 6-11-6^{149} WayneHutchinson 14/1 2¾ 5
148 A Great View (IRE) *DenisW.Cullen,Ireland* 7-10-6^{135} (s) JodyMcGarvey ....12/1 hd 6
Whataknight *HarryFry* 9-10-9^{138} (t) NoelFehily ....33/1 ½ 7
144 Prime Venture (IRE) *EvanWilliams* 7-10-12^{141} AdamWedge 40/1 2¼ 8
The Mighty Don (IRE) *NickGifford* 6-10-8^{137} LeightonAspell 33/1 2½ 9
52 Wait For Me (FR) *PhilipHobbs* 8-10-13^{142} (h+t) TomO'Brien 25/1 2¼ 10
46 Theo's Charm (IRE) *NickGifford* 8-10-9^{138} TomCannon 33/1 2 11
11 Louis' Vac Pouch (IRE) *PhilipHobbs* 6-11-2^{145} (h) RichardJohnson ....10/1 ¾ 12
Kansas City Chief (IRE) *NeilMulholland* 9-10-8^{137} (s) SamTwiston-Davies ....25/1 nk 13
129 Thomas Campbell *NickyHenderson* 6-11-12^{155} (b) JamesBowen(3) ....20/1 sh 14
6 Mine Now (IRE) *PeterFahey,Ireland* 10-11-2^{145} MrRichardDeegan(5) ....25/1 hd 15
Lovenormoney (IRE) *WarrenGreatrex* 7-10-13^{142} (v) AndrewTinkler ....22/1 ¾ 16
Protek des Flos (FR) *NickyHenderson* 6-10-8^{137} AidanColeman 14/1 14 17
76 Dell' Arca (IRE) *DavidPipe* 9-11-2^{145} (b+t) MichaelHeard(5) 50/1 2¼ 18
Sort It Out (IRE) *EdwardP.Harty,Ireland* 9-10-12^{141} MarkWalsh 10/1 3 19
163 Boite (IRE) *WarrenGreatrex* 8-11-5^{148} GavinSheehan 33/1 5 20
Sykes (IRE) *NickyMartin* 9-10-13^{142} MattGriffiths 28/1 18 21
Dadsintrouble (IRE) *TimVaughan* 8-10-7^{136} AlanJohns 40/1 29 22
Forza Milan (IRE) *JonjoO'Neill* 6-10-9^{138} (t) KillianMoore(3) ....15/2 pu
Gigginstown House Stud 23ran 6m09.10

194 Ryanair Chase (Festival Trophy) (Gr 1) (1) (5yo+) £199,325 2½m166y (17)

96 BALKO DES FLOS (FR) *HenrydeBromhead,Ireland* 7-11-10 DavyRussell 8/1 1

118	UN DE SCEAUX (FR) *W.P.Mullins,Ireland* 10-11-10 P.Townend	8/11f	4½	2
153	CLOUDY DREAM (IRE) *RuthJefferson* 8-11-10 BrianHughes	10/1	8	3
70	Sub Lieutenant (IRE) *HenrydeBromhead,Ireland* 9-11-10 (t) SeanFlanagan	18/1	15	4
160	Frodon (FR) *PaulNicholls* 6-11-10 (t) SamTwiston-Davies	9/1	9	5
160	Cue Card *ColinTizzard* 12-11-10 (t) PaddyBrennan	9/2		pu

Gigginstown House Stud 6ran 5m23.20

195 Sun Bets Stayers' Hurdle (Gr 1) (1) (4yo+) £192,707   2m7f213y (12)

	PENHILL *W.P.Mullins,Ireland* 7-11-10 P.Townend	12/1		1
139	SUPASUNDAE (*MrsJ.Harrington,Ireland* 8-11-10 RobbiePower	6/1	2	2
129	WHOLESTONE (IRE) *NigelTwiston-Davies* 7-11-10 AidanColeman	14/1	3	3
129	Colin's Sister *FergalO'Brien* 7-11-3 PaddyBrennan	33/1	1	4
80	Sam Spinner *JeddO'Keeffe* 6-11-10 JoeColliver	9/4f	nk	5
101	Yanworth *AlanKing* 8-11-10 BarryGeraghty	6/1	½	6
129	The Worlds End (IRE) *TomGeorge* 7-11-10 A.P.Heskin	33/1	¾	7
133	L'Ami Serge (IRE) *NickyHenderson* 8-11-10 (h) DarylJacob	14/1	½	8
122	Augusta Kate *W.P.Mullins,Ireland* 7-11-3 D.J.Mullins	20/1	6	9
80	Unowhatimeanharry *HarryFry* 10-11-10 (t) NoelFehily	8/1	1¾	10
163	Donna's Diamond (IRE) *ChrisGrant* 9-11-10 (t) CallumBewley	66/1	2¼	11
120	The New One (IRE) *NigelTwiston-Davies* 10-11-10 SamTwiston-Davies	18/1	hd	12
174	Lil Rockerfeller (USA) *NeilKing* 7-11-10 (s) TrevorWhelan	33/1	1	13
122	Let's Dance (FR) *W.P.Mullins,Ireland* 6-11-3 (s) D.E.Mullins	33/1		F
	Bacardys (FR) *W.P.Mullins,Ireland* 7-11-10 MrP.W.Mullins	14/1		F

Mr Tony Bloom 15ran 6m20.50

196 Brown Advisory & Merriebelle Stable Plate Handicap Chase (Gr 3) (1)   2½m166y (17)
(5yo+) £62,645

149	THE STORYTELLER (IRE) *GordonElliott,Ireland* 7-11-4[147] DavyRussell	5/1f		1
102	SPLASH OF GINGE *NigelTwiston-Davies* 10-10-8[137] JamieBargary(3)	25/1	1¾	2
126	KING'S ODYSSEY (IRE) *EvanWilliams* 9-10-10[139] AdamWedge	14/1	5	3
74	Ballyalton *IanWilliams* 11-10-9[138] (t) TomO'Brien	16/1	1	4
	King's Socks (FR) *DavidPipe* 6-10-11[140] TomScudamore	7/1	¾	5
117	Guitar Pete (IRE) *NickyRichards* 8-10-10[139] RyanDay(3)	10/1	1¼	6
	Pougne Bobbi (FR) *NickyHenderson* 7-10-11[140] JeremiahMcGrath	16/1	9	7
3	Midnight Shot *CharlieLongsdon* 8-10-11[140] JonathanBurke	50/1	3¼	8
	Shanahan's Turn (IRE) *ColinTizzard* 10-10-8[137] (t) PaulO'Brien(5)	50/1	¾	9
151	Last Goodbye (IRE) *MissElizabethDoyle,Ireland* 7-11-6[149] (b+t) SeanFlanagan	8/1	1¼	10
160	Traffic Fluide (FR) *GaryMoore* 8-11-2[145] (v) JoshuaMoore	16/1	6	11
74	Romain de Senam (FR) *PaulNicholls* 6-10-13[142] (h+t) SamTwiston-Davies	20/1	6	12
126	Ultragold (FR) *ColinTizzard* 10-10-13[142] (t) HarryCobden	66/1	10	13
112	Ballybolley (IRE) *NigelTwiston-Davies* 9-11-4[147] (t) DarylJacob	40/1	16	14
22	Village Vic (IRE) *PhilipHobbs* 11-11-12[155] RichardJohnson	33/1	10	15
102	Quite By Chance *ColinTizzard* 9-11-0[143] (b+t) PaddyBrennan	33/1	nk	16
64	Mercian Prince *AmyMurphy* 7-11-1[144] JackQuinlan	25/1	17	17
	Willie Boy *VenetiaWilliams* 7-10-9[138] B.J.Cooper	14/1		F
156	Drumcliff (IRE) *HarryFry* 7-10-12[141] (t) NiallMadden	25/1		pu
	Movewiththetimes (IRE) *PaulNicholls* 7-10-13[142] BarryGeraghty	8/1		pu
14	Oldgrangewood *DanSkelton* 7-11-4[147] (t) HarrySkelton	20/1		pu
102	Viconte du Noyer (FR) *ColinTizzard* 9-11-4[147] (t) RobbiePower	33/1		pu

Mrs Pat Sloan 22ran 5m29.50

197 Trull House Stud Mares' Novices' Hurdle (Dawn Run) (Gr 2) (1) (4yo+)   2m179y (8)
£51,255

134	LAURINA (FR) *W.P.Mullins,Ireland* 5-11-7 P.Townend	4/7f		1
	CAP SOLEIL (FR) *FergalO'Brien* 5-11-7 PaddyBrennan	10/1	18	2
	CHAMPAYNE LADY (FR) *AlanFleming,Ireland* 6-11-2 (t) DenisO'Regan	80/1	sh	3
132	Maria's Benefit (IRE) *StuartEdmunds* 6-11-7 CiaranGethings	9/2	1¾	4
	Countister (FR) *NickyHenderson* 6-11-2 BarryGeraghty	16/1	8	5
	Cut The Mustard (FR) *W.P.Mullins,Ireland* 6-11-2 NoelFehily	20/1	8	6
	Pietralunga (FR) *W.P.Mullins,Ireland* 5-11-2 (t) D.J.Mullins	40/1	7	7
	Spice Girl *MartinKeighley* 5-11-2 (t) RichardJohnson	66/1	4	8
	Rouergate (FR) *VenetiaWilliams* 5-11-2 AidanColeman	100/1	7	9
	Ellie Mac (IRE) *HenrydeBromhead,Ireland* 5-11-2 MrDanielHolden	100/1	2¼	10
	Salsaretta (FR) *W.P.Mullins,Ireland* 5-11-2 RobbiePower	18/1		F
134	Dawn Shadow (IRE) *MrsD.A.Love,Ireland* 6-11-5 RachaelBlackmore	50/1		F
	Angels Antics *NigelTwiston-Davies* 5-11-2 SamTwiston-Davies	66/1		pu
109	High School Days (USA) *HenrydeBromhead,Ireland* 5-11-2 DavyRussell	9/1		pu

Sullivan Bloodstock Limited 14ran 4m14.80

953

198 Fulke Walwyn Kim Muir Challenge Cup Amateur Riders' Handicap Chase (2) 3¼m (22) **(145) (5yo+) £41,972**

111	MISSED APPROACH (IRE) *WarrenGreatrex* 8-11-5[138] (b) MrN.McParlan 8/1		1
60	MALL DINI (IRE) *PatrickG.Kelly,Ireland* 8-11-10[143] (b+t) MrP.W.Mullins 4/1f	½	2
138	SQUOUATEUR (FR) *GordonElliott,Ireland* 7-11-2[135] (t) MrJ.J.Codd 5/1	5	3
107	Double Ross (IRE) *NigelTwiston-Davies* 12-11-10[143] MrZacBaker 40/1	9	4
89	Actinpieces *PamSly* 7-11-12[145] MissGinaAndrews 33/1	1	5
62	The Young Master *NeilMulholland* 9-11-2[135] (s) MrSamWaley-Cohen 16/1	3	6
126	Pressurize (IRE) *VenetiaWilliams* 12-11-0[133] MissLucyTurner(7) 80/1	6	7
	West Wizard (FR) *SophieLeech* 9-10-0[119] (t) MissA.B.O'Connor(3) 50/1	1¼	8
105	Final Nudge (IRE) *DavidDennis* 9-11-10[143] MrBarryO'Neill 12/1	7	9
	Aubusson (FR) *NickWilliams* 9-11-2[135] MrChesterWilliams(3) 12/1	¾	10
172	Tintern Theatre (IRE) *NigelTwiston-Davies* 7-11-5[138] MrJordanNailor(5) 25/1	nk	11
	Band of Blood (IRE) *DrRichardNewland* 10-11-0[133] (b) MrJamesKing 10/1	2	12
	Very First Time *TimEasterby* 6-11-2[135] MrWilliamEasterby(3) 40/1	9	13
68	Sugar Baron (IRE) *NickyHenderson* 8-11-4[137] (b) MsK.Walsh 8/1	7	14
	Pendra (FR) *CharlieLongsdon* 10-11-12[145] (b) MrDerekO'Connor 14/1	3¾	15
	Captain Buck's (FR) *PaulNicholls* 6-10-8[127] (s+t) MrLorcanWilliams(5) 20/1	1¾	16
164	Wild West Wind (IRE) *TomGeorge* 9-11-1[144] (t) MrNoelGeorge(5) 25/1		ur
126	Arctic Gold (IRE) *NigelTwiston-Davies* 7-10-13[132] MissLillyPinchin(7) 25/1		F
	Millanisi Boy *KayleyWoollacott* 9-10-7[126] (s) MrMichaelLegg 16/1		pu
4	Marinero (IRE) *DavidChristie,Ireland* 9-11-1[134] MrDavidMaxwell(3) 100/1		pu

Alan & Andrew Turner 20ran 7m08.10

CHELTENHAM Friday, Mar 16 HEAVY

199 JCB Triumph Hurdle (Gr 1) (1) (4yo) £71,187 2m179y (8)

146	FARCLAS (FR) *GordonElliott,Ireland* 4-11-0 (t) J.W.Kennedy 9/1		1
146	MR ADJUDICATOR *W.P.Mullins,Ireland* 4-11-0 P.Townend 8/1	1¾	2
	SAYO *W.P.Mullins,Ireland* 4-11-0 D.E.Mullins 33/1	3½	3
124	Apple's Shakira (FR) *NickyHenderson* 4-10-7 BarryGeraghty 6/5f	1½	4
	Saldier (FR) *W.P.Mullins,Ireland* 4-11-0 D.J.Mullins 14/1	18	5
170	Redicean *AlanKing* 4-11-0 WayneHutchinson 7/1	2	6
104	Sussex Ranger (USA) *GaryMoore* 4-11-0 JamieMoore 28/1	36	7
	Stormy Ireland (FR) *W.P.Mullins,Ireland* 4-10-7 NoelFehily 9/2		F
32	Gumball (FR) *PhilipHobbs* 4-11-0 (t) RichardJohnson 40/1		pu

Gigginstown House Stud 9ran 4m17.00

200 Randox Health County Handicap Hurdle (Gr 3) (1) (5yo+) £56,950 2m179y (8)

84	MOHAAYED *DanSkelton* 6-10-11[139] (t) BridgetAndrews(3) 33/1		1
155	REMILUC (FR) *ChrisGordon* 9-11-2[144] (t) HarryReed(5) 50/1	2¾	2
147	WHISKEY SOUR (IRE) *W.P.Mullins,Ireland* 5-10-13[141] D.J.Mullins 7/1	¾	3
84	Chesterfield (IRE) *SeamusMullins* 8-10-12[140] DanielSansom(5) 16/1	1½	4
155	Spiritofthegames *DanSkelton* 6-10-11[139] (t) HarrySkelton 12/1	½	5
162	Lagostovegas (IRE) *W.P.Mullins,Ireland* 6-11-4[146] D.E.Mullins 20/1	dh	5
40	Brelade *GordonElliott,Ireland* 6-10-13[141] (t) MarkEnright 25/1	7	7
66	A Hare Breath (IRE) *BenPauling* 10-11-3[145] DarylJacob 20/1	1	8
155	Moon Racer (IRE) *DavidPipe* 9-11-0[142] (t) TomScudamore 20/1	1¼	9
	Sternrubin (GER) *PhilipHobbs* 7-11-1[143] RichardJohnson 40/1	½	10
140	Ben Dundee (IRE) *GordonElliott,Ireland* 6-10-11[139] DavyRussell 12/1	1¾	11
155	William H Bonney *AlanKing* 7-10-5[133] WayneHutchinson 16/1	1½	12
58	Meri Devie (FR) *W.P.Mullins,Ireland* 5-10-13[141] P.Townend 12/1	hd	13
155	Bleu Et Rouge (FR) *W.P.Mullins,Ireland* 7-11-12[154] (t) BarryGeraghty 10/1	¾	14
147	Le Richebourg (FR) *JosephPatrickO'Brien,Ireland* 5-11-3[145] MarkWalsh 33/1	2¾	15
166	Flying Tiger (IRE) *NickWilliams* 5-10-13[141] (t) NoelFehily 6/1f	4½	16
140	Ivanovich Gorbatov (IRE) *JosephPatrickO'Brien,Ireland* 6-11-6[148] (t) J.J.Slevin(3) ...25/1	11	17
	All Set To Go (IRE) *KevinFrost* 7-10-12[140] JamieBargary(3) 100/1	3½	18
	Duca de Thaix (FR) *GordonElliott,Ireland* 5-10-8[136] (t) J.W.Kennedy 10/1	19	19
	Sandsend (FR) *W.P.Mullins,Ireland* 5-11-3[145] MsK.Walsh 11/1		ur
	Smaoineamh Alainn (IRE) *RobertWalford* 6-10-9[137] (h) JamesBest 16/1		pu
155	Divin Bere (FR) *PaulNicholls* 5-10-13[141] (t) SamTwiston-Davies 33/1		pu
140	Tigris River (IRE) *JosephPatrickO'Brien,Ireland* 7-11-5[147] (t) JodyMcGarvey ...50/1		pu
155	Jenkins (IRE) *NickyHenderson* 6-11-9[151] (b) JamesBowen(3) 33/1		pu

Mrs June Watts 24ran 4m19.10

201 Albert Bartlett Novices' Hurdle (Spa) (Gr 1) (1) (4yo+) £77,600 2m7f213y (12)

100	KILBRICKEN STORM (IRE) *ColinTizzard* 7-11-5 (t) HarryCobden 33/1		1
	OK CORRAL (IRE) *NickyHenderson* 8-11-5 BarryGeraghty 16/1	3	2
128	SANTINI *NickyHenderson* 6-11-5 NicodeBoinville 11/4f	1½	3
	Ballyward (IRE) *W.P.Mullins,Ireland* 6-11-5 P.Townend 20/1	1½	4
135	Tower Bridge (IRE) *JosephPatrickO'Brien,Ireland* 5-11-5 (t) J.J.Slevin 33/1	1¾	5

	Robin Waters (FR) *DanSkelton* 5-11-5 HarrySkelton	50/1	2¾	6
135	Fabulous Saga (FR) *W.P.Mullins,Ireland* 6-11-5 (t) D.E.Mullins	20/1	1¼	7
135	Dortmund Park (FR) *GordonElliott,Ireland* 5-11-5 (t) DavyRussell	12/1	14	8
	Chris's Dream (IRE) *HenrydeBromhead,Ireland* 6-11-5 MarkWalsh	6/1	13	9
100	Poetic Rhythm (IRE) *FergalO'Brien* 7-11-5 PaddyBrennan	10/1	2¾	10
147	Real Steel (FR) *W.P.Mullins,Ireland* 5-11-5 D.J.Mullins	33/1	9	11
131	Enniscoffey Oscar (IRE) *EmmaLavelle* 6-11-5 LeightonAspell	25/1	3	12
110	Paisley Park (IRE) *EmmaLavelle* 6-11-5 (v) NickScholfield	33/1	hd	13
	Beyond The Law (IRE) *M.F.Morris,Ireland* 6-11-5 (t) RobbiePower	50/1		pu
131	Calett Mad (FR) *NigelTwiston-Davies* 6-11-5 (t) DarylJacob	16/1		pu
165	Chef des Obeaux (FR) *NickyHenderson* 6-11-5 NoelFehily	6/1		pu
	Crucial Role *HenryDaly* 6-11-5 RichardJohnson	66/1		pu
110	Mr Whipped (IRE) *NickyHenderson* 5-11-5 JeremiahMcGrath	16/1		pu
128	Mulcahys Hill (IRE) *WarrenGreatrex* 6-11-5 A.P.Heskin	50/1		pu
	Talkischeap (IRE) *AlanKing* 6-11-5 WayneHutchinson	25/1		pu

A Selway & P Wavish 20ran 6m13.70

202 Timico Cheltenham Gold Cup Chase (Gr 1) (1) (5yo+) £369,822 3¼m70y (22)

153	NATIVE RIVER (IRE) *ColinTizzard* 8-11-10 (s) RichardJohnson	5/1		1
85	MIGHT BITE (IRE) *NickyHenderson* 9-11-10 NicodeBoinville	4/1f	4½	2
150	ANIBALE FLY (FR) *A.J.Martin,Ireland* 8-11-10 (t) BarryGeraghty	33/1	4	3
96	Road To Respect (IRE) *NoelMeade,Ireland* 7-11-10 (h) SeanFlanagan	9/1	4	4
150	Djakadam (FR) *W.P.Mullins,Ireland* 9-11-10 MrP.W.Mullins	25/1	8	5
127	Definitly Red (IRE) *BrianEllison* 9-11-10 DannyCook	8/1	18	6
127	Tea For Two *NickWilliams* 9-11-10 LizzieKelly	50/1	1½	7
150	Edwulf *JosephPatrickO'Brien,Ireland* 9-11-10 (t) MrDerekO'Connor	20/1	7	8
127	American (FR) *HarryFry* 8-11-10 NoelFehily	25/1	18	9
	Bachasson (FR) *W.P.Mullins,Ireland* 7-11-10 D.E.Mullins	33/1		F
148	Total Recall (IRE) *W.P.Mullins,Ireland* 9-11-10 D.J.Mullins	14/1		F
150	Killultagh Vic (IRE) *W.P.Mullins,Ireland* 9-11-10 P.Townend	8/1		pu
161	Our Duke (IRE) *MrsJ.Harrington,Ireland* 8-11-10 RobbiePower	9/2		pu
150	Outlander (IRE) *GordonElliott,Ireland* 10-11-10 (s) J.W.Kennedy	20/1		pu
153	Saphir du Rheu (FR) *PaulNicholls* 9-11-10 (t) SamTwiston-Davies	66/1		pu

Brocade Racing 15ran 7m02.60

203 St James's Place Foxhunter Challenge Cup Open Hunters' Chase (2) (5yo+) £26,982 3¼m70y (22)

	PACHA DU POLDER (FR) *PaulNicholls* 11-12-0 MissHarrietTucker	25/1		1
	TOP WOOD (FR) *MissKellyMorgan* 11-12-0 (v+t) MrSamuelDavies-Thomas	50/1	nk	2
	BAREL OF LAUGHS (IRE) *PhilipRowley* 12-12-0 (s) MrAlexEdwards	14/1	3¼	3
	COUSIN PETE *MrsElizabethBrown* 10-12-0 (t) MrNickPhillips	66/1	dh	3
	Caid du Berlais (FR) *MrsRoseLoxton* 9-12-0 (t) MrWilliamBiddick	12/1	hd	5
	Grand Vision (IRE) *ColinTizzard* 12-12-0 MrBarryO'Neill	14/1	3	6
2	Balnaslow (IRE) *GrahamMcKeever,Ireland* 11-12-0 MrDerekO'Connor	28/1	½	7
	Burning Ambition (IRE) *PierceMichaelPower,Ireland* 7-12-0 MrJ.J.Codd	4/1f	9	8
	On The Fringe (IRE) *EndaBolger,Ireland* 13-12-0 MissN.Carberry	14/1	1¾	9
	Unioniste (FR) *PaulNicholls* 10-12-0 MrDavidMaxwell	12/1	4	10
	Volnay de Thaix (FR) *StuartMorris* 9-12-0 (s) MrJackAndrews	33/1	3½	11
7	Sir Jack Yeats (IRE) *RichardSpencer* 7-12-0 (b) MrJamesKing	20/1	16	12
	Virak (FR) *PaulNicholls* 9-12-0 MrLorcanWilliams	14/1	1	13
	Shotavodka (IRE) *MissH.Bradshaw* 12-12-0 MrHughNugent	33/1	63	14
	Warden Hill (IRE) *MrsH.Connors* 10-12-0 (s) MrTomChatfeild-Roberts	100/1	38	15
	Saddlers Encore (IRE) *MissChloeNewman* 9-12-0 MrJoshuaNewman	100/1		F
	Vincitore (IRE) *MissSarahRippon* 12-12-0 (t) MissSarahRippon	200/1		ur
	Foxrock (IRE) *AlanFleming,Ireland* 10-12-0 (b+t) MsK.Walsh	9/2		pu
	Minella For Value (IRE) *DeclanQueally,Ireland* 9-12-0 MrD.Queally	25/1		pu
	Premier Portrait (IRE) *DrCharlesLevinson* 11-12-0 (v) MrGusLevinson	100/1		pu
	Shantou Magic (IRE) *WillRamsay* 11-12-0 MrWillRamsay	100/1		pu
	Wells de Lune (FR) *MickeyBowen* 7-12-0 (h+t) MrPeterBryan	50/1		pu
2	Wonderful Charm (FR) *PaulNicholls* 10-12-0 (s+t) MrSamWaley-Cohen	11/2		pu
2	Young Hurricane (IRE) *G.C.Brewer* 12-12-0 MrJohnDawson	50/1		pu

The Stewart Family 24ran 7m17.50

204 Martin Pipe Conditional Jockeys' Handicap Hurdle (2) (145) (4yo+) £43,792 2½m56y (10)

108	BLOW BY BLOW (IRE) *GordonElliott,Ireland* 7-11-10[144] (b+t) DonaghMeyler	11/1		1
	DISCORAMA (FR) *PaulNolan,Ireland* 5-11-2[136] DylanRobinson	33/1	5	2
147	EARLY DOORS (FR) *JosephPatrickO'Brien,Ireland* 5-11-8[142] J.J.Slevin	9/1	1¼	3
	Sire du Berlais (FR) *GordonElliott,Ireland* 6-11-10[144] (t) D.J.McInerney	10/1	1¼	4
113	Diese des Bieffes (FR) *NickyHenderson* 5-11-3[137] JamesBowen	17/2	1½	5
155	Lough Derg Spirit (IRE) *NickyHenderson* 6-11-3[137] NedCurtis	20/1	¾	6
	Dream Berry (FR) *JonjoO'Neill* 7-11-9[143] (tp) JonjoO'Neill(3)	33/1	½	7

	Brillare Momento (IRE) *MartinKeighley* 7-11-5[139] (s) HarryStock(3) 25/1	hd	8
12	Tommy Rapper (IRE) *DanSkelton* 7-11-6[140] (t) BridgetAndrews 25/1	1¾	9
	Mr Big Shot (IRE) *DavidPipe* 7-11-4[138] MichaelHeard 14/1	1	10
135	Carter McKay *W.P.Mullins,Ireland* 7-11-4[138] JamieBargary 12/1	4	11
148	Flawless Escape *GordonElliott,Ireland* 5-11-3[137] JonathanMoore 13/2f	2½	12
	Brave Eagle (IRE) *NickyHenderson* 6-11-2[136] AlanDoyle(5) 20/1	3¾	13
163	No Hassle Hoff (IRE) *DanSkelton* 6-11-6[140] FergusGregory(3) 33/1	2½	14
25	Coeur de Lion *AlanKing* 5-11-5[139] KevinDowling(5) 33/1	1¼	15
	Delire d'Estruval (FR) *BenPauling* 5-11-4[138] RichardPatrick 50/1	¾	16
	Brelan d'As (FR) *PaulNicholls* 7-11-6[140] (h+t) BryonyFrost 50/1	½	17
	Arthington *SeamusMullins* 5-11-3[137] DanielSansom(3) 80/1	½	18
144	Melrose Boy (FR) *HarryFry* 6-11-3[137] KieronEdgar 12/1	1¼	19
123	Flaxen Flare (IRE) *GordonElliott,Ireland* 9-11-9[143] (b) CiaranGethings 50/1	4	20
140	Deal d'Estruval (FR) *W.P.Mullins,Ireland* 5-11-3[137] L.P.Gilligan(5) 7/1	3½	21
	Burrows Saint (FR) *W.P.Mullins,Ireland* 5-11-3[137] (t) LizzieKelly 16/1	18	22
155	Poppy Kay *PhilipHobbs* 8-11-2[136] SeanHoulihan 66/1		pu

Gigginstown House Stud 23ran 5m23.00

205 Johnny Henderson Grand Annual Challenge Cup Handicap Chase (Gr 3) (1)   2m62y (14) (5yo+) £62,645

74	LE PREZIEN (FR) *PaulNicholls* 7-11-8[150] (t) BarryGeraghty 15/2		1
	GINO TRAIL (IRE) *KerryLee* 11-11-10[152] (s) JamieMoore 25/1	4½	2
102	TOP GAMBLE (IRE) *KerryLee* 10-11-7[149] (s+t) DavyRussell 8/1	nk	3
102	Theinval (FR) *NickyHenderson* 8-10-13[141] (s) JeremiahMcGrath 16/1	½	4
138	Three Stars (FR) *HenrydeBromhead,Ireland* 11-11-2[144] (s) J.J.Slevin(3) 12/1	6	5
	Doitforthevillage (IRE) *PaulHenderson* 9-10-11[139] (t) PaddyBrennan 20/1	4½	6
79	Dolos (FR) *PaulNicholls* 5-11-5[147] (t) HarryCobden 16/1	3¾	7
	Born Survivor (IRE) *DanSkelton* 7-10-13[141] (t) BridgetAndrews(3) 25/1	1	8
114	Rock The World (IRE) *Mrs.J.Harrington,Ireland* 10-11-11[153] (t) RobbiePower 20/1	½	9
	Bright New Dawn (IRE) *VenetiaWilliams* 11-10-11[139] AlainCawley 66/1	7	10
74	Foxtail Hill (IRE) *NigelTwiston-Davies* 9-11-1[143] JamieBargary(3) 20/1	3½	11
	Sizing Platinum (IRE) *ColinTizzard* 11-11-5[147] (t) TomO'Brien 50/1	3	12
	Garde La Victoire (FR) *PhilipHobbs* 9-11-12[154] RichardJohnson 25/1	14	13
91	Vaniteux (FR) *DavidPipe* 9-11-9[151] (b) TomScudamore 16/1	23	14
	Eastlake (IRE) *JonjoO'Neill* 12-11-5[147] (s+t) JonjoO'Neill(7) 33/1	16	15
138	Some Plan (IRE) *HenrydeBromhead,Ireland* 10-11-2[144] (t) NoelFehily 20/1		F
64	Dresden (FR) *HenryOliver* 10-11-2[144] JamesDavies 16/1		F
156	North Hill Harvey *DanSkelton* 7-11-8[150] (s) HarrySkelton 7/1f		F
154	Valdez *AlanKing* 11-11-7[149] WayneHutchinson 25/1		ur
14	Bouvreuil (FR) *PaulNicholls* 7-11-0[142] (t) SamTwiston-Davies 10/1		bd
138	Townshend (GER) *W.P.Mullins,Ireland* 7-11-2[144] (t) P.Townend 16/1		pu
138	Don't Touch It (IRE) *Mrs.J.Harrington,Ireland* 8-11-7[149] (s) MarkWalsh 11/1		pu

Mr John P. McManus 22ran 4m21.20

UTTOXETER Saturday, Mar 17   HEAVY

206 Betfred Midlands Grand National (Open Handicap Chase) (L) (1) (5yo+)   4¼m8y (19) £70,337

	REGAL FLOW *BobBuckler* 11-11-3[135] SeanHoulihan(5) 16/1		1
173	MILANSBAR (IRE) *NeilKing* 11-11-10[142] (v) MrJackAndrews(7) 16/1	10	2
	BALLYMALIN (IRE) *NigelTwiston-Davies* 8-10-12[130] TomBellamy 14/1	4½	3
164	Silsol (GER) *PaulNicholls* 9-11-12[144] (b+t) BryonyFrost(3) 10/1	½	4
105	Alfie Spinner (IRE) *KerryLee* 13-11-11[137] (s+t) RichardPatrick(5) 16/1	1¾	5
111	Krackatoa King *KerryLee* 10-10-8[126] (v) LeightonAspell 14/1	2¼	6
	Western Climate (IRE) *TomWeston* 9-11-5[137] JamesBowen(3) 10/1	6	7
	Billy Bronco *EvanWilliams* 7-10-4[122] AdamWedge 14/1	3¾	8
89	Get On The Yager *DanSkelton* 8-11-8[140] HenryBrooke 9/1	½	9
111	Russe Blanc (FR) *KerryLee* 10-10-5[123] (s) DerekFox 33/1		ur
	The Artful Cobbler *HenryDaly* 7-10-3[121] AndrewTinkler 7/1f		pu
	Plus Jamais (FR) *IainJardine* 11-10-9[127] RossChapman(3) 33/1		pu
173	Themanfrom Minella (IRE) *BenCase* 9-10-10[128] (b+t) MaxKendrick(5) 40/1		pu
173	Back To The Thatch (IRE) *HenryDaly* 6-10-11[129] TomO'Brien 15/2		pu
	Bob Ford (IRE) *DrRichardNewland* 11-10-12[130] (h) SeanBowen 12/1		pu
173	West of The Edge (IRE) *DrRichardNewland* 10-10-13[131] (s) WillKennedy 8/1		pu
107	Benbens (IRE) *NigelTwiston-Davies* 13-11-6[138] MrZacBaker(5) 33/1		pu
173	Hainan (FR) *SueSmith* 7-11-7[139] DannyCook 10/1		pu

Mrs C. J. Dunn 18ran 9m43.80

NAVAN Friday, Mar 23   HEAVY

207 toals.com Bookmakers Webster Cup Chase (Gr 2) (5yo+) £26,550   2m (11)

| | GREAT FIELD (FR) *W.P.Mullins* 7-11-12 J.S.McGarvey ....11/8jf | | 1 |

	114	DOCTOR PHOENIX (IRE) *GordonElliott* 10-11-8 (s+t) DavyRussell	11/8jf	1¾	2
	136	ALISIER D'IRLANDE (FR) *HenrydeBromhead* 8-11-8 (t) A.E.Lynch	9/1	18	3
	138	Kilcarry Bridge (IRE) *JohnPatrickRyan* 11-11-5 (t) D.E.Mullins	40/1	10	4
	138	Tell Us More (IRE) *GordonElliott* 9-11-8 (b) KeithDonoghue	33/1	½	5
		American Tom (FR) *W.P.Mullins* 7-11-5 (t) P.Townend	6/1	2¼	6

Mr John P. McManus 6ran 4m20.80

NEWBURY Saturday, Mar 24 SOFT

208 EBF & TBA Mares' 'National Hunt' Novices' Hurdle Finale 2½m118y (10)
(Limited Handicap) (Gr 2) (1) (4yo+) £22,780

		ROKSANA (IRE) *DanSkelton* 6-11-5[130] BridgetAndrews(3)	8/1		1
		KALAHARI QUEEN *JamieSnowden* 5-11-1[126] GavinSheehan	12/1	2¾	2
		JUBILYMPICS *SeamusMullins* 6-10-4[115] DanielSansom(5)	50/1	½	3
		Just A Thought (IRE) *RebeccaCurtis* 6-10-11[122] AdamWedge	7/1	2	4
		Petticoat Tails *WarrenGreatrex* 6-10-11[122] RichardJohnson	3/1	ns	5
		Oscar Rose (IRE) *FergalO'Brien* 6-10-8[119] PaddyBrennan	6/1f	½	6
		Bee Crossing *SeamusMullins* 7-10-4[115] KevinJones(5)	25/1	5	7
		Black Tulip *HenryDaly* 6-10-7[118] TomO'Brien	20/1	2	8
		Sunshade *NickyHenderson* 5-11-9[134] JamesBowen(3)	10/1	6	9
		Sensulano (IRE) *NoelWilliams* 5-11-2[127] WayneHutchinson	12/1	14	10
	115	Midnight Tune *AnthonyHoneyball* 7-11-10[135] (t) AidanColeman	11/1	9	11
		Jet Set (IRE) *CharlieLongsdon* 6-10-9[120] JonathanBurke	16/1	20	12
		Kaloci (IRE) *StuartEdmunds* 6-10-8[119] CiaranGethings	20/1	7	13
		Lostnfound *JamieSnowden* 5-10-4[115] MichealNolan	33/1	pu	
		Lady of Lamanver *HarryFry* 8-11-0[125] (t) NoelFehily	9/1	pu	
		If You Say Run (IRE) *PaulNicholls* 6-11-7[132] (t) SamTwiston-Davies	8/1	pu	

Mrs Sarah Faulks 16ran 5m18.30

FAIRYHOUSE Sunday, Apr 1 HEAVY

209 Irish Stallion Farms European Breeders Fund Mares Novices' Hurdle 2½m (10)
Championship Final (Gr 1) (4yo+) £51,754

	197	LAURINA (FR) *W.P.Mullins* 5-11-7 P.Townend	2/11f		1
		LACKANEEN LEADER (IRE) *GordonElliott* 6-11-7 DavyRussell	8/1	8½	2
	134	ALLETRIX (FR) *MrsJ.Harrington* 5-11-7 (h) RobbiePower	20/1	3¾	3
	197	Dawn Shadow (IRE) *MrsD.A.Love* 6-11-7 RachaelBlackmore	25/1	6	4
	197	Salsaretta (FR) *W.P.Mullins* 5-11-7 M.P.Walsh	20/1	3¾	5
		Woolstone One *EmmaLavelle,GB* 6-11-7 (h) G.Sheehan	10/1	25	6
	197	Cut The Mustard (FR) *W.P.Mullins* 6-11-7 D.J.Mullins	25/1		7
		Pietralunga (FR) *W.P.Mullins* 5-11-7 (t) D.E.Mullins	40/1		8
		Redhotfillypeppers (IRE) *W.P.Mullins* 6-11-7 (h) MrDavidDunsdon	33/1		9
	197	High School Days (USA) *HenrydeBromhead* 5-11-7 SeanFlanagan	20/1		10
		Tara Dylan (FR) *ThomasMullins* 6-11-7 A.E.Lynch	40/1		11

Sullivan Bloodstock Limited 11ran 5m29.60

210 Underwriting Exchange Novices' Hurdle (Gr 2) (4yo+) £25,877 2½m (10)

		PALLASATOR *GordonElliott* 9-11-5 DavyRussell	12/1		1
	135	JETZ (IRE) *MrsJ.Harrington* 6-11-5 (h) RobbiePower	5/1	2¼	2
	185	SCARPETA (FR) *W.P.Mullins* 5-11-5 D.E.Mullins	10/3	8	3
	204	Blow By Blow (IRE) *GordonElliott* 7-11-8 (b+t) J.W.Kennedy	9/2	3	4
	185	Duc des Genievres (FR) *W.P.Mullins* 5-11-5 P.Townend	2/1f	9½	5
		Riders Onthe Storm (IRE) *TomJ.Taaffe* 5-11-5 J.J.Slevin	20/1	13	6
		Mount Hanover *HenrydeBromhead* 7-11-5 D.Robinson	50/1	pu	
	201	Real Steel (FR) *W.P.Mullins* 5-11-5 D.J.Mullins	10/1	pu	

Qatar Racing Limited 8ran 5m26.70

211 Boylesports Novices' Handicap Chase (Gr B) (5yo+) £25,877 2m150y (13)

	138	BEL AMI DE SIVOLA (FR) *NoelMeade* 7-10-12[129] SeanFlanagan	7/1		1
	149	BON PAPA (FR) *W.P.Mullins* 7-11-8[139] (t) M.P.Walsh	3/1	1½	2
		CROSSHUE BOY (IRE) *SeanThomasDoyle* 8-11-1[132] (t) MrH.D.Dunne(5)	20/1	½	3
		Blazer (IRE) *W.P.Mullins* 7-11-4[135] J.S.McGarvey	8/1	2¼	4
	138	Patricks Park (IRE) *W.P.Mullins* 7-11-2[133] P.Townend	2/1f	10	5
		The West's Awake (IRE) *E.J.O'Grady* 7-11-9[140] A.E.Lynch	20/1	1	6
		Ask Nile (IRE) *SeamusNeville* 6-11-1[132] B.Hayes	25/1	1	7
		Our Dougal (IRE) *HenrydeBromhead* 8-10-11[128] RobbiePower	33/1	1¾	8
		The Irregular (IRE) *DenisHogan* 6-10-3[120] (t) AndrewRing(3)	28/1	7½	9
		Three Wise Men (IRE) *HenrydeBromhead* 8-11-5[136] D.Robinson(5)	14/1	3	10
	177	Coeur Joyeux (IRE) *J.P.Dempsey* 7-10-9[126] (h+t) L.P.Dempsey	12/1	¾	11
		Robin des Mana (IRE) *GordonElliott* 7-11-1[132] (t) DavyRussell	12/1	pu	

Gigginstown House Stud 12ran 4m36.80

212	**Ryanair Gold Cup Novices' Chase (Gr 1) (5yo+) £51,754**		2½m (16)
186	AL BOUM PHOTO (FR) *W.P.Mullins* 6-11-10 D.J.Mullins 11/2		1
192	SHATTERED LOVE (IRE) *GordonElliott* 7-11-3 (t) J.W.Kennedy 13/8f	1	2
192	INVITATION ONLY (IRE) *W.P.Mullins* 7-11-10 P.Townend 5/1	7	3
	Up For Review (IRE) *W.P.Mullins* 9-11-10 D.E.Mullins 8/1	8	4
196	The Storyteller (IRE) *GordonElliott* 7-11-10 DavyRussell 5/1	1¾	5
149	Tombstone (IRE) *GordonElliott* 8-11-10 RachaelBlackmore 25/1	4¼	6
	Montalbano *W.P.Mullins* 6-11-10 (h) RobbiePower 33/1	11	7
	Saturnas (FR) *W.P.Mullins* 7-11-10 M.P.Walsh 14/1	½	8
184	Tycoon Prince (IRE) *GordonElliott* 8-11-10 (t) SeanFlanagan 50/1	23	9
	Mrs J. Donnelly 9ran 5m35.90		

FAIRYHOUSE Monday, Apr 2 HEAVY

213	**Rathbarry & Glenview Studs Novices' Hurdle (Gr 2) (4yo+) £25,877**		2m (9)
178	GETABIRD (IRE) *W.P.Mullins* 6-11-10 P.Townend .... evsf		1
	DRACONIEN (FR) *W.P.Mullins* 5-11-4 NoelFehily 16/1	12	2
93	HARDLINE (IRE) *GordonElliott* 6-11-10 (h) DavyRussell 6/1	1¾	3
178	Sharjah (FR) *W.P.Mullins* 5-11-4 D.J.Mullins 9/2	½	4
	Or Jaune de Somoza (FR) *HenrydeBromhead* 6-11-4 SeanFlanagan 50/1	13	5
190	Veneer of Charm (FR) *GordonElliott* 4-10-10 J.W.Kennedy 8/1	13	6
	Sayar (IRE) *W.P.Mullins* 5-11-7 D.E.Mullins 12/1	3	7
	Damalisque (FR) *EdwardP.Harty* 5-11-4 BarryGeraghty 25/1	54	8
	The Gunner Murphy (IRE) *JosephPatrickO'Brien* 5-11-4 (t) M.P.Walsh 28/1		pu
	Mrs S. Ricci 9ran 4m37.80		

214	**Keelings Irish Strawberry Hurdle (Gr 2) (5yo+) £36,228**		2½m (11)
15	COQUIN MANS (FR) *W.P.Mullins* 6-11-6 (h) P.Townend 7/1		1
122	DIAMOND CAUCHOIS (FR) *GordonElliott* 7-11-8 (t) DavyRussell 7/2f	5½	2
195	LET'S DANCE (FR) *W.P.Mullins* 6-11-1 (s) B.J.Cooper 12/1	8	3
187	Bleu Berry (FR) *W.P.Mullins* 7-11-8 M.P.Walsh 8/1	18	4
195	Augusta Kate (FR) *W.P.Mullins* 7-11-3 D.J.Mullins 8/1	24	5
187	Barra (FR) *GordonElliott* 7-10-10 (t) J.W.Kennedy 9/1	ns	6
162	Forge Meadow (IRE) *Mrs.J.Harrington* 6-11-1 RobbiePower 5/1		pu
122	Lieutenant Colonel *GordonElliott* 9-11-3 (b+t) RachaelBlackmore 33/1		pu
139	Jezki (IRE) *Mrs.J.Harrington* 10-11-6 (b) BarryGeraghty 6/1		pu
139	Bapaume (FR) *W.P.Mullins* 5-11-10 NoelFehily 20/1		pu
	Renneti (FR) *W.P.Mullins* 9-11-8 (b) D.E.Mullins 16/1		rr
	George Creighton 11ran 5m59.10		

215	**Devenish Chase (Gr 2) (5yo+) £43,509**		2½m (16)
194	UN DE SCEAUX (FR) *W.P.Mullins* 10-11-12 P.Townend 5/6f		1
161	A TOI PHIL (FR) *GordonElliott* 8-11-10 (t) J.W.Kennedy 12/1	18	2
161	BALLYCASEY (IRE) *W.P.Mullins* 11-11-10 D.J.Mullins 25/1	23	3
121	Fine Rightly (IRE) *StuartCrawford* 10-11-4 (h+t) J.J.Slevin 40/1	ds	4
207	Doctor Phoenix (IRE) *GordonElliott* 10-11-7 (s+t) DavyRussell 5/1		F
118	Kylemore Lough *HarryFry,GB* 9-11-4 NoelFehily 13/2		pu
160	Coney Island (IRE) *EdwardP.Harty* 7-11-12 BarryGeraghty 11/2		pu
	Mr Edward O'Connell 7ran 5m57.10		

216	**Boylesports Irish Grand National Chase (Extended Handicap) (Gr A) (5yo+)** **£236,842**		3m5f (24)
	Order as they passed the post (after stewards' inquiry Folsom Blue was promoted to 4th)		
151	GENERAL PRINCIPLE (IRE) *GordonElliott* 9-10-0[139] (t) J.J.Slevin 20/1		1
157	ISLEOFHOPENDREAMS (IRE) *W.P.Mullins* 6-10-1[140] RobbiePower 16/1	hd	2
157	FOREVER GOLD (IRE) *EdwardCawley* 11-9-10[135] (s+t) A.W.Short(5) 20/1	½	3
168	Bellshill (IRE) *W.P.Mullins* 8-11-5[158] D.J.Mullins 12/1	hd	5
157	Folsom Blue (IRE) *GordonElliott* 11-10-3[142] (s+t) RobbiePower 11/1	¾	4
49	Arkwright (FR) *JosephPatrickO'Brien* 8-9-12[137] (t) RachaelBlackmore 25/1	10	6
	Call It Magic (IRE) *RossO'Sullivan* 8-10-0[139] (b) A.E.Lynch 33/1	2½	7
167	Monbeg Notorious (IRE) *GordonElliott* 7-10-13[152] (v) J.W.Kennedy 8/1	41	8
207	Kilcarry Bridge (IRE) *JohnPatrickRyan* 11-9-11[136] (t) D.Robinson(5) 50/1		F
	The Paparrazi Kid (IRE) *GordonElliott* 11-10-1[140] (t) B.Hayes 50/1		F
177	Thunder And Roses (IRE) *M.F.Morris* 10-10-1[140] (v+t) MsLisaO'Neill(3) 25/1		F
192	Kemboy (FR) *W.P.Mullins* 6-10-6[145] B.J.Cooper 14/1		F
177	Pairofbrowneyes (IRE) *W.P.Mullins* 9-10-7[146] P.Townend 13/2f		F
	Moulin A Vent *NoelMeade* 6-10-6[145] JonathanMoore 25/1		ur
149	Snow Falcon (IRE) *NoelMeade* 8-10-10[149] SeanFlanagan 16/1		ur
	Killaro Boy (IRE) *AdrianMurray* 9-9-10[135] (h) R.C.Colgan 33/1		bd
177	Fine Theatre (IRE) *PaulNolan* 8-9-10[135] (b+t) C.A.Landers(7) 33/1		bd
198	Squouateur (FR) *GordonElliott* 7-9-10[135] (t) M.A.Enright 10/1		bd

148	Oscar Knight (IRE) *ThomasMullins* 9-9-11[136] L.P.Dempsey 16/1		bd
168	Champagne Harmony (IRE) *S.J.Mahon* 8-9-10[135] (b) ChrisMeehan(5) 66/1		pu
157	Woods Well (IRE) *GordonElliott* 7-9-10[135] AndrewRing(3) 33/1		pu
189	Bless The Wings (IRE) *GordonElliott* 13-9-12[137] (s) BrianHughes 25/1		pu
177	Sutton Manor (IRE) *GordonElliott* 7-9-12[137] (s) DonaghMeyler 33/1		pu
62	Westerner Point (IRE) *EoghanO'Grady* 9-9-12[137] PhilipEnright 33/1		pu
	Jetstream Jack (IRE) *GordonElliott* 8-10-1[140] (b+t) DenisO'Regan 33/1		pu
207	Tell Us More (IRE) *GordonElliott* 9-10-3[142] (p) J.S.McGarvey 66/1		pu
198	Mall Dini (IRE) *PatrickG.Kelly* 8-10-4[143] (v) M.P.Walsh 8/1		pu
168	Lord Scoundrel (IRE) *GordonElliott* 9-10-11[150] (b+t) BarryGeraghty 33/1		pu
186	Dounikos (FR) *GordonElliott* 7-10-12[151] DavyRussell 20/1		pu
202	Outlander (IRE) *GordonElliott* 10-11-10[163] (b) MrR.James(7) 33/1		pu

Gigginstown House Stud 30ran 9m01.40

AINTREE Thursday, Apr 12 SOFT

217 Big Buck's Celebration Manifesto Novices' Chase (Gr 1) (1) (5yo+) £56,130 2m3f200y (16)

192	FINIAN'S OSCAR (IRE) *ColinTizzard* 6-11-4 (s) RobbiePower 5/2		1
	RENE'S GIRL (IRE) *DanSkelton* 8-10-11 HarrySkelton 8/1	2	2
40	CALINO D'AIRY (FR) *HenrydeBromhead,Ireland* 6-11-4 SeanFlanagan 33/1	3¼	3
169	Cyrname (FR) *PaulNicholls* 6-11-4 (h+t) SeanBowen 2/1f	1¾	4
192	Modus *PaulNicholls* 8-11-4 BarryGeraghty 14/1	9	5
179	Brain Power (IRE) *NickyHenderson* 7-11-4 (t) NicodeBoinville 5/2		F

Ann & Alan Potts Limited 6ran 5m14.90

218 Doom Bar Anniversary 4-Y-O Juvenile Hurdle (Gr 1) (1) (4yo) £56,130 2m209y (9)

104	WE HAVE A DREAM (FR) *NickyHenderson* 4-11-0 DarylJacob 2/1		1
199	GUMBALL (FR) *PhilipHobbs* 4-11-0 RichardJohnson 20/1	7	2
199	APPLE'S SHAKIRA (FR) *NickyHenderson* 4-10-7 (h) BarryGeraghty 13/8f	10	3
	Cristal Icon (IRE) *ThomasMullins,Ireland* 4-10-7 D.J.Mullins 50/1	3¾	4
190	Nube Negra (SPA) *DanSkelton* 4-11-0 HarrySkelton 10/1	nk	5
	Et Moi Alors *GaryMoore* 4-11-0 JoshuaMoore 28/1	4	6
170	Beau Gosse (FR) *GuillaumeMacaire,France* 4-11-0 (t) JamesReveley 20/1	14	7
170	Malaya (FR) *PaulNicholls* 4-10-7 SamTwiston-Davies 8/1	¾	8
190	Padleyourowncanoe *ColinTizzard* 4-11-0 TomScudamore 25/1	4	9
	Les Arceaux (FR) *HenrydeBromhead,Ireland* 4-10-7 (h) SeanFlanagan 50/1		pu

Mr Simon Munir & Mr Isaac Souede 10ran 4m15.20

219 Betway Bowl Chase (Gr 1) (1) (5yo+) £106,647 3m210y (19)

202	MIGHT BITE (IRE) *NickyHenderson* 9-11-7 NicodeBoinville 4/5f		1
127	BRISTOL DE MAI (FR) *NigelTwiston-Davies* 7-11-7 DarylJacob 5/1	7	2
74	CLAN DES OBEAUX (FR) *PaulNicholls* 6-11-7 HarryCobden 8/1	3¼	3
180	Sizing Codelco (IRE) *ColinTizzard* 9-11-7 RobbiePower 33/1	3	4
194	Sub Lieutenant (IRE) *HenrydeBromhead,Ireland* 9-11-7 (t) SeanFlanagan 25/1	¾	5
202	Tea For Two *NickWilliams* 9-11-7 LizzieKelly 12/1	23	6
85	Double Shuffle (IRE) *TomGeorge* 8-11-7 (h) A.P.Heskin 11/1	3	7
202	Definitly Red (IRE) *BrianEllison* 9-11-7 DannyCook 8/1		ur

The Knot Again Partnership 8ran 6m39.40

220 Betway Aintree Hurdle (Gr 1) (1) (4yo+) £140,325 2½m (12)

195	L'AMI SERGE (IRE) *NickyHenderson* 8-11-7 (h) DarylJacob 5/1		1
195	SUPASUNDAE (*Mrs*J.Harrington,Ireland* 8-11-7 RobbiePower 11/10f	3	2
174	CLYNE *EvanWilliams* 8-11-7 AdamWedge 25/1	3¾	3
76	My Tent Or Yours (IRE) *NickyHenderson* 11-11-7 (h) BarryGeraghty 9/2	6	4
	Cyrus Darius *RuthJefferson* 9-11-7 BrianHughes 12/1	9	5
	Diakali *GaryMoore* 8-11-7 (b) JoshuaMoore 25/1	23	6
	Izzo (GER) *MlleC.Fey,France* 5-11-7 (h) RichardJohnson 50/1	46	7
174	Air Horse One *HarryFry* 7-11-7 NoelFehily 20/1		pu
195	The New One (IRE) *NigelTwiston-Davies* 10-11-7 SamTwiston-Davies 8/1		pu

Mr Simon Munir & Mr Isaac Souede 9ran 5m05.30

221 Randox Health Foxhunters' Open Hunters' Chase (2) (6yo+) £26,685 2m5f19y (18)

203	BALNASLOW (IRE) *GrahamMcKeever,Ireland* 11-12-0 MrDerekO'Connor 11/2		1
2	BEAR'S AFFAIR (IRE) *PhilipRowley* 12-12-0 MrAlexEdwards 20/1	2½	2
	GREENSALT (IRE) *W.H.Easterby* 10-12-0 (t) MrWilliamEasterby 66/1	4	3
	Barrakilla (IRE) *FergalO'Brien* 11-12-0 MrZacBaker 8/1	4	4
203	On The Fringe (IRE) *EndaBolger,Ireland* 13-12-0 MissN.Carberry 8/1	¾	5
	Bound For Glory (IRE) *D.M.G.Fitch-Peyton* 12-12-0 (t) MissHannahLewis 100/1	2½	6
203	Unioniste (FR) *PaulNicholls* 10-12-0 MrDavidMaxwell 8/1	5	7
	Distime (IRE) *MrsD.J.Ralph* 12-12-0 MrWilliamBiddick 14/1	6	8
203	Sir Jack Yeats (IRE) *RichardSpencer* 7-12-0 (b) MrJamesKing 16/1	7	9
	Never Complain (IRE) *MrsF.Marshall* 10-12-0 (s) MrCharlieMarshall 66/1	21	10

203	Wonderful Charm (FR) *PaulNicholls* 10-12-0 (b+t) MrSamWaley-Cohen	8/1	nk	11
	Gallery Exhibition (IRE) *KimBailey* 11-12-0 (t) MrGuyDisney	40/1	2¾	12
203	Grand Vision (IRE) *ColinTizzard* 12-12-0 MrJ.J.Codd	7/2f		F
	Lilbitluso (IRE) *J.J.O'Shea* 10-12-0 MrGillonCrow	100/1		F
	Eddies Miracle (IRE) *DavidChristie,Ireland* 10-12-0 MrBarryO'Neill	16/1		ur
203	Warden Hill (IRE) *MrsH.Connors* 10-12-0 (s) MrTomChatfeild-Roberts	50/1		ur
203	Wells de Lune (FR) *MickeyBowen* 7-12-0 (h+t) MrPeterBryan	16/1		ur
	Winged Crusader (IRE) *MissA.Waugh* 10-12-0 MissAmieWaugh	66/1		ur
	Curraigflemens (IRE) *DavidKemp* 10-12-0 (s) MrRichardCollinson	66/1		pu
	Mon Parrain (FR) *MrsKimSmyly* 12-12-0 (b+t) MissPageFuller	40/1		pu
	Rouge Et Blanc (FR) *OliverSherwood* 13-12-0 (s) MissPippaGlanville	66/1		pu
	Exors of the Late Mrs M. E. Hagan 21ran 5m48.20			

222 Zut Media Red Rum Handicap Chase (Gr 3) (1) (5yo+) £50,517   1m7f176y (12)

34	BENTELIMAR (IRE) *CharlieLongsdon* 9-10-8[135] (s) JonathanBurke	10/1		1
205	THEINVAL (FR) *NickyHenderson* 8-11-0[141] (s) JeremiahMcGrath	5/1	3¼	2
205	GINO TRAIL (IRE) *KerryLee* 11-11-12[153] (s) JamieMoore	10/1	18	3
205	Doitforthevillage (IRE) *PaulHenderson* 9-10-12[139] (t) TomO'Brien	10/1	3¼	4
	Bun Doran (IRE) *TomGeorge* 7-10-12[139] PaddyBrennan	11/2	4½	5
205	Sizing Platinum (IRE) *ColinTizzard* 10-11-3[144] (t) RobbiePower	20/1	3½	6
	Noche de Reyes (FR) *PaulNicholls* 9-10-10[137] CiaranGethings	66/1	5	7
1	Vosne Romanee *DrRichardNewland* 7-10-11[138] (s+t) BrianHughes	25/1	3½	8
	Overtown Express (IRE) *HarryFry* 10-11-6[147] NoelFehily	14/1	nk	9
	Savello (IRE) *DanSkelton* 12-10-2[129] (s+t) BridgetAndrews(3)	33/1	3¼	10
	Theflyingportrait (IRE) *JennieCandlish* 9-10-12[139] (t) SeanQuinlan	25/1	23	11
	Baby King (IRE) *TomGeorge* 9-10-10[137] (t) A.P.Heskin	20/1		pu
179	Robinshill (IRE) *NigelTwiston-Davies* 7-10-13[140] TomBellamy	33/1		pu
196	King's Socks (IRE) *DavidPipe* 6-10-13[140] TomScudamore	7/2f		pu
	Wisty (IRE) *MartinTodhunter* 9-11-0[141] HenryBrooke	33/1		pu
90	Tommy Silver (FR) *PaulNicholls* 6-11-3[144] (s) SamTwiston-Davies	8/1		pu
	Swanee River Partnership 16ran 4m04.80			

223 Goffs Nickel Coin Mares' Standard Open National Hunt Flat (Gr 2) (1)   2m209y
(4, 5 and 6yo) £25,322

152	GETAWAY KATIE MAI (IRE) *JohnQueally,Ireland* 5-11-0 MrJ.J.Codd	15/8f		1
	MIDNIGHTREFERENDUM *AlanKing* 5-11-0 WayneHutchinson	25/1	1¼	2
	DUHALLOW GESTURE (IRE) *AnthonyHoneyball* 6-11-0 RichieMcLernon	10/1	2¾	3
	Meep Meep (IRE) *TomLacey* 5-11-0 TomScudamore	9/1	nk	4
	Buildmeupbuttercup *MickChannon* 4-10-8 (h) GrahamLee	20/1	½	5
	Secret Escape (IRE) *DonaldMcCain* 6-11-0 BrianHughes	25/1	1½	6
	Paper Promise (IRE) *DonaldWhillans* 6-11-0 CallumWhillans	33/1	hd	7
	Sparkling Dawn *JohnnyFarrelly* 6-11-0 TomCannon	33/1	3	8
	Cedar Valley (IRE) *PhilipHobbs* 4-10-8 RichardJohnson	12/1	¾	9
	Posh Trish (IRE) *PaulNicholls* 5-11-0 SamTwiston-Davies	5/1	¾	10
	Ceara Be (IRE) *AlexHales* 5-11-0 PaddyBrennan	100/1	2	11
	Zakharova *LauraMorgan* 4-10-8 PatrickCowley	25/1	1½	12
	Maebh (IRE) *SeamusMullins* 4-10-8 DanielSansom	100/1	7	13
	Princess Roxy *BenCase* 5-11-0 (t) KielanWoods	33/1	2¾	14
	Darling du Large (FR) *TomGeorge* 5-11-0 CiaranGethings	50/1	1	15
	Sea Story *KimBailey* 5-11-0 DavidBass	28/1	7	16
	Rococo Style *SteveGollings* 5-11-0 JamieMoore	100/1	2¾	17
	Kuragina (IRE) *KennethSlack* 4-10-8 RobertHogg	33/1	25	18
	Jaxlight *AndrewCrook* 6-11-0 FinianO'Toole	100/1	4	19
	Dissavril (FR) *EmmaLavelle* 5-11-0 GavinSheehan	7/1	17	20
	Michael Owen Daly 20ran 4m21.70			

LIMERICK Thursday, Apr 12   HEAVY

224 Hugh McMahon Memorial Novices' Chase (Gr 3) (5yo+) £22,368   3m (16)

216	KEMBOY (FR) *W.P.Mullins* 6-11-0 P.Townend	5/4f		1
212	TOMBSTONE (IRE) *GordonElliott* 8-11-6 (t) DavyRussell	7/1	8	2
	TWISS'S HILL (IRE) *DavidHarryKelly* 9-11-6 P.E.Corbett	33/1	19	3
	Some Neck (FR) *W.P.Mullins* 7-11-0 M.P.Walsh	13/8	1¼	4
216	Moulin A Vent *NoelMeade* 6-11-6 JonathanMoore	6/1	7½	5
	SupremeHorseRacingClub/BTGraham/KSharpe 5ran 6m54.50			

AINTREE Friday, Apr 13   HEAVY

225 Alder Hey Children's Charity Handicap Hurdle (Gr 3) (1) (4yo+) £42,202   2½m (11)

	JESTER JET *TomLacey* 8-10-9[133] RobertDunne	20/1		1
	EATON HILL (IRE) *KerryLee* 6-9-12[124] (t) JamieMoore	20/1	¾	2
193	WHO DARES WINS (IRE) *AlanKing* 6-11-11[149] WayneHutchinson	13/2f	¾	3

960

	Wilde Blue Yonder (IRE) *AlanKing* 9-10-8[132] TomCannon 14/1	hd	4
140	Grand Partner (IRE) *ThomasMullins,Ireland* 10-10-12[136] D.J.Mullins 20/1	¾	5
155	Project Bluebook (FR) *JohnQuinn* 5-10-12[136] BrianHughes 25/1	2	6
200	Spiritofthegames (IRE) *DanSkelton* 6-11-1[139] (s) BridgetAndrews(3) 15/2	nk	7
	Cyrius Moriviere (FR) *BenPauling* 8-10-4[128] (t) NicodeBoinville 20/1	7	8
148	Massini's Trap (IRE) *JamesA.Nash,Ireland* 9-10-12[136] (b) MarkWalsh 16/1	2¼	9
	Storm Home (IRE) *ColinTizzard* 6-11-0[138] HarryCobden 7/1	1¾	10
11	Court Minstrel (IRE) *EvanWilliams* 11-11-9[147] MissIsabelWilliams(7) 33/1	nk	11
46	Three Musketeers (IRE) *DanSkelton* 8-11-0[138] (s) HarrySkelton 10/1	21	12
66	Zubayr (IRE) *PaulNicholls* 6-11-0[138] MrLorcanWilliams(7) 8/1	2	13
200	Jenkins (IRE) *NickyHenderson* 6-11-12[150] (s) JamesBowen(3) 20/1	1¼	14
11	Sumkindofking (IRE) *TomGeorge* 7-10-12[126] (t) CiaranGethings 12/1	2½	15
	Cornborough *MarkWalford* 7-10-1[125] JamieHamilton 66/1	18	16
180	Eamon An Cnoic (IRE) *DavidPipe* 7-10-8[132] (t) TomScudamore 16/1		pu
	Landin (GER) *SeamusMullins* 5-10-8[132] DanielSansom(5) 10/1		pu
200	Ivanovich Gorbatov (IRE) *JosephPatrickO'Brien,Ireland* 6-11-7[145] (h+t) BarryGeraghty 25/1		pu

Mrs T. P. James 19ran 5m11.50

226 Betway Top Novices' Hurdle (Gr 1) (1) (4yo+) £56,130   2m103y (9)

155	LALOR (GER) *KayleyWoollacott* 6-11-4 RichardJohnson 14/1		1
185	VISION DES FLOS (FR) *ColinTizzard* 5-11-4 (t) RobbiePower 11/4	2½	2
39	BEDROCK *IainJardine* 5-11-4 (t) RossChapman 33/1	¾	3
185	Mind's Eye (IRE) *HenrydeBromhead,Ireland* 6-11-4 DavyRussell 16/1	9	4
185	Coolanly (IRE) *FergalO'Brien* 6-11-4 PaddyBrennan 40/1	nk	5
171	Global Citizen (IRE) *BenPauling* 6-11-4 DarylJacob 5/2f	nk	6
119	Midnight Shadow *SueSmith* 5-11-4 DannyCook 25/1	hd	7
178	Slate House (IRE) *ColinTizzard* 6-11-4 (t) HarryCobden 10/1	14	8
171	Scarlet Dragon *AlanKing* 5-11-4 (h) WayneHutchinson 11/1	6	9
5	Ornua (IRE) *HenrydeBromhead,Ireland* 7-11-4 NoelFehily 33/1	9	10
	Impact Factor (IRE) *Mrs.J.Harrington,Ireland* 6-11-4 MarkWalsh 8/1	11	11
190	Style de Garde (FR) *NickyHenderson* 4-10-12 (h) NicodeBoinville 8/1		pu
	Distingo (IRE) *GaryMoore* 5-11-4 (v) JoshuaMoore 40/1		pu

Mr D. G. Staddon 13ran 4m15.50

227 Betway Mildmay Novices' Chase (Gr 1) (1) (5yo+) £56,130   3m210y (19)

192	TERREFORT (FR) *NickyHenderson* 5-11-4 DarylJacob 3/1f		1
183	MS PARFOIS (IRE) *AnthonyHoneyball* 7-10-11 (t) NoelFehily 9/2	3¾	2
186	ELEGANT ESCAPE (IRE) *ColinTizzard* 6-11-4 (t) HarryCobden 4/1	9	3
186	Black Corton (FR) *PaulNicholls* 7-11-4 (t) BryonyFrost 6/1	18	4
145	Captain Chaos (IRE) *DanSkelton* 7-11-4 (b) HarrySkelton 25/1	6	5
	Hogan's Height (IRE) *JamieSnowden* 7-11-4 (t) GavinSheehan 33/1	57	6
180	Coo Star Sivola (FR) *NickWilliams* 6-11-4 LizzieKelly 7/1		pu
216	Snow Falcon (IRE) *NoelMeade,Ireland* 8-11-4 SeanFlanagan 7/1		pu
184	Testify (IRE) *DonaldMcCain* 7-11-4 BrianHughes 16/1		pu

Mr Simon Munir & Mr Isaac Souede 9ran 6m47.70

228 JLT Melling Chase (Gr 1) (1) (5yo+) £140,325   2m3f200y (16)

188	POLITOLOGUE (FR) *PaulNicholls* 7-11-7 (h+t) SamTwiston-Davies 11/1		1
188	MIN (FR) *W.P.Mullins,Ireland* 7-11-7 P.Townend 11/10f	nk	2
43	SIZING GRANITE (IRE) *ColinTizzard* 10-11-7 (t) RobbiePower 20/1	20	3
194	Balko des Flos (FR) *HenrydeBromhead,Ireland* 7-11-7 DavyRussell 2/1	13	4
194	Cloudy Dream (IRE) *RuthJefferson* 8-11-7 BrianHughes 10/1	8	5
205	Le Prezien (FR) *PaulNicholls* 7-11-7 (t) BarryGeraghty 11/1		pu

Mr J. Hales 6ran 5m18.60

229 Randox Health Topham Handicap Chase (Gr 3) (1) (5yo+) £78,582   2m5f19y (18)

196	ULTRAGOLD (FR) *ColinTizzard* 10-11-1[141] HarryCobden 14/1		1
196	SHANAHAN'S TURN (IRE) *ColinTizzard* 10-10-8[134] (t) RobbiePower 14/1	3¾	2
172	THEATRE TERRITORY (IRE) *WarrenGreatrex* 8-10-6[132] (s) MrSamWaley-Cohen(3) 10/1	6	3
117	Kilcrea Vale (IRE) *NickyHenderson* 8-10-9[135] JeremiahMcGrath 12/1	8	4
196	Ballyalton (IRE) *IanWilliams* 11-10-12[138] TomO'Brien 11/1	2½	5
69	Clarcam (FR) *GordonElliott,Ireland* 8-11-9[149] (s+t) DavyRussell 16/1	1½	6
	Indian Temple (IRE) *TimReed* 9-10-6[132] HarryReed(4) 50/1	ns	7
205	Top Gamble (IRE) *KerryLee* 10-11-10[150] (t) JamesBowen(3) 12/1	7	8
151	Polidam (FR) *W.P.Mullins,Ireland* 9-11-6[146] (h) DarylJacob 9/1f	9	9
133	Flying Angel (IRE) *NigelTwiston-Davies* 7-11-8[148] TomBellamy 10/1	3¼	10
64	Mystifiable (IRE) *N.Meade* 10-11-0[126] (t) PaddyBrennan 12/1	16	11
74	Deauville Dancer (IRE) *DavidDennis* 7-10-10[136] (t) BrianHughes 50/1	5	12
205	Eastlake (IRE) *JonjoO'Neill* 12-11-1[141] (t) BarryGeraghty 33/1	49	13

961

14	Devils Bride (IRE) *HenrydeBromhead,Ireland* 11-11-12¹⁵² (s+t) J.J.Slevin(3)	......66/1	71	14
105	Rathlin Rose (IRE) *DavidPipe* 10-10-7¹³³ (b) TomScudamore	............16/1		F
	Flying Eagle (IRE) *PeterBowen* 10-9-12¹²⁶ (b+t) SeanBowen	............40/1		ur
133	Minella On Line (IRE) *OliverSherwood* 9-10-4¹³⁰ (s) ConorShoemark	......33/1		ur
	Newsworthy (IRE) *MrsD.A.Love,Ireland* 8-10-4¹³⁰ JonathanMoore	......66/1		ur
	Beau Bay (FR) *DrRichardNewland* 7-10-8¹³⁴ (h+t) WillKennedy	............33/1		ur
81	Bigbadjohn (IRE) *NigelTwiston-Davies* 9-10-12¹³⁸ JamieBargary	............14/1		ur
	Greybougg *NigelHawke* 9-10-0¹²⁶ ConorO'Farrell	............66/1		pu
177	Rogue Angel (IRE) *M.F.Morris,Ireland* 10-10-4¹³⁰ (s+t) RachaelBlackmore	........20/1		pu
	Notarfbad (IRE) *JeremyScott* 12-10-5¹³¹ (h) MattGriffiths	............66/1		pu
196	Midnight Shot *CharlieLongsdon* 8-10-13¹³⁹ JonathanBurke	............33/1		pu
205	Bouvreuil (FR) *PaulNicholls* 7-11-2¹⁴² (t) SamTwiston-Davies	............14/1		pu
180	O O Seven (IRE) *NickyHenderson* 8-11-10¹⁵⁰ AidanColeman	............10/1		pu
196	Village Vic (IRE) *PhilipHobbs* 11-11-10¹⁵⁰ RichardJohnson	............40/1		pu

Brocade Racing J P Romans Terry Warner 27ran 5m50.10

230	**Doom Bar Sefton Novices' Hurdle (Gr 1) (1) (4yo+) £56,130**		3m149y (13)	
201	SANTINI *NickyHenderson* 6-11-4 NicodeBoinville	............6/4f		1
208	ROKSANA (IRE) *DanSkelton* 6-10-11 HarrySkelton	............9/1	1½	2
201	TOWER BRIDGE (IRE) *JosephPatrickO'Brien,Ireland* 5-11-4 (t) J.J.Slevin	............8/1	6	3
165	Uppertown Prince (IRE) *DonaldMcCain* 6-11-4 AdamHughes	............40/1	2¾	4
201	Ok Corral (IRE) *NickyHenderson* 8-11-4 BarryGeraghty	............7/2	8	5
100	Dans Le Vent (FR) *JamieSnowden* 5-11-4 (s) GavinSheehan	............66/1	3¼	6
	Point of Principle (IRE) *TimVaughan* 5-11-4 AlanJohns	............66/1	14	7
	Another Stowaway (IRE) *TomGeorge* 6-11-4 (t) A.P.Heskin	............50/1		pu
201	Chef des Obeaux (FR) *NickyHenderson* 6-11-4 NoelFehily	............66/1		pu
110	Count Meribel *NigelTwiston-Davies* 6-11-4 MarkGrant	............25/1		pu
	Good Man Pat (IRE) *AlanKing* 5-11-4 TomBellamy	............25/1		pu
	Louse Talk (IRE) *CharlieLongsdon* 6-11-4 PaulO'Brien	............66/1		pu
175	Sam's Gunner *MichaelEasterby* 5-11-4 WillKennedy	............12/1		pu

Mr & Mrs R. Kelvin-Hughes 13ran 6m41.30

231	**Weatherbys Racing Bank Standard Open National Hunt Flat (Gr 2) (1)**		2m209y	
	(4, 5 and 6yo) £25,322			
	PORTRUSH TED (IRE) *WarrenGreatrex* 6-11-4 (t) GavinSheehan	............25/1		1
	KATESON *TomLacey* 5-11-4 TomScudamore	............16/1	3¼	2
	HARAMBE *AlanKing* 5-11-4 TomBellamy	............33/1	ns	3
	Al Dancer (FR) *NigelTwiston-Davies* 5-11-4 (h) JamieBargary	............28/1	4	4
	Sevarano (IRE) *OliverSherwood* 5-11-4 NoelFehily	............8/1	7	5
	Commanche Red (IRE) *ChrisGordon* 5-11-4 TomCannon	............20/1	1¼	6
191	Mercy Mercy Me *FergalO'Brien* 6-11-4 PaddyBrennan	............4/1	¾	7
	Thosedaysaregone (IRE) *CharlesByrnes,Ireland* 5-11-4 DavyRussell	............14/1	1½	8
	Pym (IRE) *NickyHenderson* 5-11-4 JeremiahMcGrath	............8/1	sh	9
	Highland Hunter (IRE) *LucindaRussell* 5-11-4 DerekFox	............50/1	4½	10
	Arthur Mac (IRE) *PhilipHobbs* 5-11-4 RichardJohnson	............20/1	hd	11
	Amoola Gold (GER) *DanSkelton* 5-11-4 HarrySkelton	............50/1	hd	12
	Mister Fisher (IRE) *NickyHenderson* 4-10-12 NicodeBoinville	............6/1	¾	13
	Chanceanotherfive (IRE) *KeithDalgleish* 6-11-4 BrianHughes	............33/1	5	14
	Dali Mail (FR) *DonaldWhillans* 5-11-4 (t) CallumWhillans	............66/1	3	15
	Theatre Legend *ChrisGrant* 5-11-4 JamieMoore	............100/1	26	16
	Danny Kirwan (IRE) *PaulNicholls* 5-11-4 SamTwiston-Davies	............11/4f	1¾	17
	Skidoosh *BenPauling* 5-11-4 DarylJacob	............50/1	13	18
	Dazibao (FR) *GeorgeBaker* 5-11-4 AndrewTinkler	............66/1	47	19
	Normal Norman *JohnRyan* 4-10-12 ThomasGarner	............100/1		pu

McNeill Family 20ran 4m26.80

AINTREE Saturday, Apr 14   SOFT

232	**Gaskells Handicap Hurdle (Gr 3) (1) (4yo+) £42,202**		3m149y (13)	
204	MR BIG SHOT (IRE) *DavidPipe* 7-11-5¹³⁸ TomScudamore	............7/1f		1
	NOW MCGINTY (IRE) *StuartEdmunds* 7-11-2¹³⁵ (s) TomO'Brien	............12/1	¾	2
6	AH LITTLELUCK (IRE) *T.Gibney,Ireland* 8-11-2¹³⁵ (t) A.E.Lynch	............10/1	10	3
	Debece *TimVaughan* 7-11-8¹⁴¹ AlanJohns	............8/1	nk	4
193	The Mighty Don (IRE) *NickGifford* 6-11-2¹³⁵ TomCannon	............25/1	nk	5
193	Prime Venture (IRE) *EvanWilliams* 7-11-7¹⁴⁰ MissIsabelWilliams(7)	............14/1	2	6
187	Red Indian *BenPauling* 6-11-6¹³⁹ DavidBass	............8/1	nk	7
187	Fixe Le Kap (FR) *NickyHenderson* 6-11-5¹³⁸ (s) DarylJacob	............16/1	1¼	8
	Jaleo (GER) *BenPauling* 6-11-4¹³⁷ MrAlexFerguson(7)	............40/1	3	9
187	Jeannot de Nonant (FR) *PeterBowen* 6-11-6¹³⁹ (s) SeanBowen	............33/1	6	10
204	No Hassle Hoff (IRE) *DanSkelton* 6-11-5¹³⁸ BridgetAndrews(3)	............12/1	nk	11
165	Shannon Bridge (IRE) *DanSkelton* 5-11-7¹⁴⁰ HarrySkelton	............10/1	1¼	12

180	Knight of Noir (IRE) *MichaelBlake* 9-11-12[145] TomBellamy	50/1	2 13
193	Sykes (IRE) *NickyMartin* 9-11-9[142] MattGriffiths	33/1	1½ 14
128	Tikkanbar (IRE) *NeilMulholland* 7-11-9[142] (h) NoelFehily	14/1	3½ 15
164	Sir Mangan (IRE) *DanSkelton* 10-11-1[134] FergusGregory(5)	33/1	3½ 16
193	Louis' Vac Pouch (IRE) *PhilipHobbs* 6-11-12[145] (h) RichardJohnson	11/1	4½ 17
165	Golan Fortune (IRE) *PhilMiddleton* 6-11-8[141] (s) RichardPatrick(5)	14/1	17 18
193	Connetable (FR) *PaulNicholls* 6-11-5[138] (b) AidanColeman	12/1	¾ 19
117	Fortunate George (IRE) *EmmaLavelle* 8-11-2[135] (v) AdamWedge	33/1	¾ 20

Prof. Caroline Tisdall 20ran 6m19.20

233 Betway Mersey Novices' Hurdle (Gr 1) (1) (4yo+) £56,130 2½m (11)

185	BLACK OP (IRE) *TomGeorge* 7-11-4 (t) NoelFehily	3/1	1
178	LOSTINTRANSLATION (IRE) *ColinTizzard* 6-11-4 RobbiePower	12/1	½ 2
31	MOMELLA (IRE) *DanSkelton* 6-10-11 HarrySkelton	10/1	3 3
185	Aye Aye Charlie *FergalO'Brien* 6-11-4 PaddyBrennan	25/1	1 4
178	Western Ryder (IRE) *WarrenGreatrex* 6-11-4 RichardJohnson	13/2	1¾ 5
61	On The Blind Side (IRE) *NickyHenderson* 6-11-4 NicodeBoinville	11/8f	2¾ 6
	Euxton Lane (IRE) *OliverSherwood* 6-11-4 AidanColeman	28/1	2½ 7
	Chosen Path (IRE) *AlanKing* 5-11-4 WayneHutchinson	20/1	22 8
	Kildisart (IRE) *BenPauling* 6-11-4 DarylJacob	25/1	22 9
39	Better Getalong (IRE) *NickyRichards* 7-11-4 DavyRussell	40/1	pu
	Brianstorm (IRE) *WarrenGreatrex* 6-11-4 (h) GavinSheehan	33/1	pu
	Silver Concorde *KeithDalgleish* 10-11-4 BrianHughes	50/1	pu

Mr R. S. Brookhouse 12ran 5m03.80

234 Doom Bar Maghull Novices' Chase (Gr 1) (1) (5yo+) £56,130 1m7f176y (12)

156	DIEGO DU CHARMIL (FR) *PaulNicholls* 6-11-4 (t) HarryCobden	5/1	1
179	PETIT MOUCHOIR (FR) *HenrydeBromhead,Ireland* 7-11-4 DavyRussell	4/5f	2½ 2
130	SHANTOU ROCK (IRE) *DanSkelton* 6-11-4 (t) HarrySkelton	13/2	6 3
	Lady Buttons *PhilipKirby* 6-10-11 AdamNicol	4/1	nk 4
	Kauto Riko (FR) *TomGretton* 7-11-4 RobertDunne	25/1	24 5
	Delegate *KeithDalgleish* 8-11-4 (t) BrianHughes	33/1	24 6

Mrs Johnny de la Hey 6ran 4m02.40

235 Betway Handicap Chase (Gr 3) (1) (5yo+) £42,202 3m210y (19)

	THOMAS PATRICK (IRE) *TomLacey* 6-10-10[139] RichardJohnson	3/1f	1
81	ON TOUR (IRE) *EvanWilliams* 10-10-8[137] AdamWedge	14/1	4 2
49	PAPER LANTERN (IRE) *KarlThornton,Ireland* 9-10-4[133] (b) DonaghMeyler(3)	10/1	4½ 3
196	Oldgrangewood *DanSkelton* 7-11-3[146] (t) HarrySkelton	14/1	5 4
184	Ibis du Rheu (FR) *PaulNicholls* 7-10-11[140] (h) SamTwiston-Davies	7/1	nk 5
159	Holly Bush Henry (FR) *PhilMiddleton* 7-10-6[135] (s) JamesBowen(3)	14/1	3¾ 6
	Heist (IRE) *PatrickGriffin,Ireland* 8-10-4[133] (s+t) A.W.Short(7)	33/1	4 7
	Pearl Swan (IRE) *PeterBowen* 10-10-5[134] (v+t) SeanBowen	14/1	1 8
180	Casse Tete (FR) *GaryMoore* 6-10-9[138] JoshuaMoore	9/1	2½ 9
198	Very First Time *TimEasterby* 6-10-3[132] DannyCook	14/1	7 10
180	Wakanda (IRE) *SueSmith* 9-11-5[148] HenryBrooke	14/1	6 11
	Bearly Legal (IRE) *KarlThornton,Ireland* 12-10-0[129] (t) A.E.Lynch	50/1	6 12
184	Rocklander (IRE) *TomGeorge* 9-11-2[145] A.P.Heskin	7/1	F
183	Clondaw Cian (IRE) *SuzySmith* 8-10-2[131] (h) GavinSheehan	14/1	pu
	Bells of Ailsworth (IRE) *TimVaughan* 8-10-3[132] (t) AlanJohns	12/1	pu
	Hammersly Lake (FR) *CharlieLongsdon* 10-11-12[155] BrianHughes	33/1	pu

Mr David Kellett 16ran 6m44.70

236 Ryanair Stayers' Hurdle (Liverpool) (Gr 1) (1) (4yo+) £101,034 3m149y (13)

181	IDENTITY THIEF (IRE) *HenrydeBromhead,Ireland* 8-11-7 SeanFlanagan	14/1	1
195	WHOLESTONE (IRE) *NigelTwiston-Davies* 7-11-7 DarylJacob	7/2	5 2
195	SAM SPINNER *JeddO'Keeffe* 6-11-7 JoeColliver	6/5f	10 3
195	The Worlds End (IRE) *TomGeorge* 7-11-7 PaddyBrennan	6/1	8 4
	Serienschock (GER) *MlleA.Rosa,France* 10-11-7 (t) LudovicPhilipperon	66/1	nk 5
3	Shelford (IRE) *DanSkelton* 9-11-7 HarrySkelton	80/1	6 6
174	Old Guard *PaulNicholls* 7-11-7 HarryCobden	12/1	50 7
	Coole Cody (IRE) *MichaelBlake* 7-11-7 (h+t) TomScudamore	25/1	pu
195	Lil Rockerfeller (USA) *NeilKing* 7-11-7 (t) TrevorWhelan	12/1	pu
193	Thomas Campbell *NickyHenderson* 6-11-7 (s) NicodeBoinville	16/1	pu

Gigginstown House Stud 10ran 6m20.10

237 Randox Health Grand National Handicap Chase (Gr 3) (1) (7yo+) £500,000 4¼m74y (29)

Becher's on the second circuit was omitted due to a stricken jockey

189	TIGER ROLL (IRE) *GordonElliott,Ireland* 8-10-13[150] (s+t) DavyRussell	10/1	1
123	PLEASANT COMPANY (IRE) *W.P.Mullins,Ireland* 10-10-11[148] D.J.Mullins	25/1	hd 2
216	BLESS THE WINGS (IRE) *GordonElliott,Ireland* 13-10-6[143] (s) J.W.Kennedy	40/1	11 3

202	Anibale Fly (FR) *A.J.Martin,Ireland* 8-11-8[159] (t) BarryGeraghty 10/1		nk	4
206	Milansbar (IRE) *NeilKing* 11-10-6[143] (b) BryonyFrost 25/1		21	5
157	Road To Riches (IRE) *NoelMeade,Ireland* 11-10-5[142] (t) SeanFlanagan 33/1		12	6
107	Gas Line Boy (IRE) *IanWilliams* 12-10-11[148] (v) RobertDunne 25/1		7	7
161	Valseur Lido (FR) *HenrydeBromhead,Ireland* 9-11-7[158] KeithDonoghue 66/1		4	8
159	Vieux Lion Rouge (FR) *DavidPipe* 9-10-13[150] (s) TomScudamore 25/1		¾	9
105	Raz de Maree (FR) *GavinPatrickCromwell,Ireland* 13-10-9[146] RobbiePower 20/1		¾	10
	Seeyouatmidnight *SandyThomson* 10-10-12[149] BrianHughes 11/1		29	11
157	Baie des Iles (FR) *RossO'Sullivan,Ireland* 7-10-8[145] (s) MsK.Walsh 16/1		2¾	12
198	Final Nudge (FR) *DavidDennis* 9-10-6[143] (s) GavinSheehan 33/1			F
173	Houblon des Obeaux (FR) *VenetiaWilliams* 11-10-7[144] (b) CharlieDeutsch 25/1			F
	I Just Know (IRE) *SueSmith* 8-10-8[145] DannyCook 14/1			F
23	Virgilio (FR) *DanSkelton* 9-10-8[145] (t) HarrySkelton 50/1			F
127	Perfect Candidate (IRE) *FergalO'Brien* 11-11-3[154] AlainCawley 50/1			F
150	Alpha des Obeaux (FR) *M.F.Morris,Ireland* 8-11-4[155] (s) RachaelBlackmore 33/1			F
62	Lord Windermere (IRE) *J.Culloty,Ireland* 12-10-7[144] A.E.Lynch 50/1			ur
121	Captain Redbeard (IRE) *StuartColtherd* 9-10-7[144] SamColtherd 20/1			ur
144	Buywise (IRE) *EvanWilliams* 11-10-8[145] AdamWedge 50/1			ur
123	Ucello Conti (FR) *GordonElliott,Ireland* 10-10-10[147] (t) DarylJacob 16/1			ur
164	The Dutchman (IRE) *ColinTizzard* 8-10-11[148] (t) HarryCobden 20/1			ur
189	Saint Are (FR) *TomGeorge* 12-10-10[147] (b+t) CiaranGethings 50/1			bd
164	Blaklion *NigelTwiston-Davies* 9-11-10[161] SamTwiston-Davies 14/1			bd
216	Thunder And Roses (IRE) *M.F.Morris,Ireland* 10-10-5[142] (s+t) J.J.Slevin 33/1			pu
89	Delusionofgrandeur (IRE) *SueSmith* 8-10-5[142] HenryBrooke 50/1			pu
198	Double Ross (IRE) *NigelTwiston-Davies* 12-10-6[143] TomBellamy 66/1			pu
	Maggio (FR) *PatrickGriffin,Ireland* 13-10-8[145] (b) BrendanPowell 66/1			pu
198	Pendra (IRE) *CharlieLongsdon* 10-10-8[145] (b+t) AidanColeman 80/1			pu
157	Childrens List (IRE) *W.P.Mullins,Ireland* 8-10-8[145] JonathanBurke 66/1			pu
173	Chase The Spud *FergalO'Brien* 10-10-12[149] PaddyBrennan 25/1			pu
133	Warriors Tale *PaulNicholls* 9-10-12[149] (t) SeanBowen 33/1			pu
159	Tenor Nivernais (FR) *VenetiaWilliams* 11-11-1[152] TomO'Brien 66/1			pu
96	Carlingford Lough (IRE) *JohnE.Kiely,Ireland* 12-11-1[152] MarkWalsh 33/1			pu
180	Shantou Flyer (IRE) *RichardHobson* 8-11-2[153] (v+t) JamesBowen 20/1			pu
202	Total Recall (IRE) *W.P.Mullins,Ireland* 9-11-5[156] P.Townend 7/1f			pu
189	The Last Samuri (IRE) *KimBailey* 10-11-8[159] (t) DavidBass 16/1			pu

Gigginstown House Stud 38ran 9m40.20

238 Pinsent Masons Handicap Hurdle (Conditional Jockeys' And Amateur Riders') (2) (4yo+) £30,950 2m103y (9)

	HAVANA BEAT (IRE) *TonyCarroll* 8-10-4[124] JamesNixon(7) 12/1			1
12	DEAR SIRE (FR) *DonaldMcCain* 6-11-6[140] (h) LorcanMurtagh(5) 12/1		10	2
200	STERNRUBIN (GER) *PhilipHobbs* 7-11-6[140] SeanHoulihan(5) 7/1		¾	3
200	All Set To Go (IRE) *KevinFrost* 7-11-2[136] SamColtherd(5) 25/1		2½	4
124	Broughtons Admiral *AlastairRalph* 4-10-0[126] (s) CharlieHammond(7) 20/1		sh	5
35	Solatentif (FR) *ColinTizzard* 8-10-12[132] (b+t) RichardPatrick(5) 20/1		1¼	6
	Final Choice *WarrenGreatrex* 5-10-3[123] (s) BenHicks(7) 16/1		1¾	7
171	Michael's Mount *IanWilliams* 5-11-0[134] JamesBowen(3) 4/1f		nk	8
	Colwinston (IRE) *MissSuzyBarkley,Ireland* 8-10-0[120] (t) A.W.Short(5) 66/1		20	9
176	Birch Hill (IRE) *SophieLeech* 8-10-5[125] (s+t) CiaranGethings 25/1		7	10
	Scheu Time (IRE) *JamesA.Nash,Ireland* 5-10-4[124] (h) MsK.Walsh 9/2			F
	Maquisard (FR) *GaryMoore* 6-10-5[125] HarryTeal(7) 14/1			F
	William of Orange *DonaldMcCain* 7-10-6[126] (b+t) RyanDay(3) 13/2			pu
	High Expectations (IRE) *GordonElliott,Ireland* 7-10-7[127] DonaghMeyler(3) 15/2			pu
120	Unison (IRE) *JeremyScott* 8-11-12[146] RobertHawker(5) 20/1			pu

Northway Lodge Racing 15ran 4m11.10

FAIRYHOUSE Tuesday, Apr 17 SOFT

239 Rybo Handicap Hurdle (Glascarn) (Gr A) (4yo+) £51,304 2m (10)

140	LOW SUN *W.P.Mullins* 5-10-2[123] (s) KatieO'Farrell(7) 25/1			1
58	YAHA FIZZ (IRE) *GordonElliott* 8-11-0[135] J.W.Kennedy 6/1		2¼	2
140	CHARLIE STOUT (IRE) *ShaneNolan* 7-10-5[126] (t) P.E.Corbett(3) 33/1		3½	3
182	Pravalaguna (FR) *W.P.Mullins* 6-11-2[137] (h) B.Hayes 33/1		ns	4
140	Karalee (FR) *W.P.Mullins* 7-11-1[136] (t) RobbiePower 20/1		1¾	5
200	Meri Devie (FR) *W.P.Mullins* 5-11-4[139] D.J.Mullins 11/1		1¼	6
	Uradel (GER) *W.P.Mullins* 7-10-11[132] P.Townend 4/1f		5½	7
56	Morgan (FR) *GordonElliott* 6-11-3[138] SeanFlanagan 12/1		1	8
200	Duca de Thaix (FR) *GordonElliott* 5-11-0[135] (t) DavyRussell 14/1		16	9
	Destin d'Ajonc (FR) *GordonElliott* 5-10-13[134] (t) BarryGeraghty 20/1		½	10
187	Voix du Reve (FR) *W.P.Mullins* 6-11-6[141] (h) N.M.Kelly(5) 10/1		1½	11
	Gran Geste (FR) *MissElizabethDoyle* 5-10-5[126] M.P.Walsh 10/1		9½	12

187	Abbyssial (IRE) *W.P.Mullins* 8-11-8[143] MrW.J.Gleeson(7) 20/1	6	13
	Orion d'Aubrelle (FR) *W.P.Mullins* 5-10-8[129] JonathanBurke 33/1	28	14
	Play The Game (IRE) *T.Gibney* 5-10-4[125] A.E.Lynch 9/1	28	15
151	Landofhopeandglory (IRE) *JosephPatrickO'Brien* 5-11-10[145] (b+t) J.S.McGarvey ..33/1	2½	16
200	Tigris River (IRE) *JosephPatrickO'Brien* 7-11-10[145] (t) L.P.Dempsey 50/1	2½	17
134	True Self (IRE) *W.P.Mullins* 5-10-2[123] RachaelBlackmore 12/1		F
	Nessun Dorma (IRE) *W.P.Mullins* 5-10-11[132] B.J.Cooper 14/1		F

Mrs S. Ricci 19ran 4m04.90

CHELTENHAM Wednesday, Apr 18   GOOD

240 Barchester Healthcare Silver Trophy Chase (Limited Handicap) (Gr 2) (1) 2½m166y (17) **(5yo+)** £34,170

196	TRAFFIC FLUIDE (FR) *GaryMoore* 8-10-4[140] (s) JoshuaMoore 13/2f		1
	ART OF PAYROLL (GER) *HarryFry* 9-10-6[142] (t) B.J.Cooper 20/1	1½	2
143	KALONDRA (IRE) *NeilMulholland* 7-10-9[145] (t) NoelFehily 7/1	1¼	3
45	Cepage (FR) *VenetiaWilliams* 6-10-7[143] CharlieDeutsch 8/1	7	4
184	Jameson *NigelTwiston-Davies* 6-10-4[140] SamTwiston-Davies 7/1	1½	5
	Knockgraffon (IRE) *OllyMurphy* 8-10-7[143] (s+t) BrianHughes 14/1	2	6
196	Quite By Chance *ColinTizzard* 9-10-5[141] (t) HarryCobden 14/1	1½	7
172	Go Conquer (IRE) *JonjoO'Neill* 9-11-0[150] AidanColeman 11/1	sh	8
180	Ramses de Teillee (FR) *DavidPipe* 6-10-6[142] (t) TomScudamore 10/1	¾	9
23	Voix d'Eau (FR) *HarryFry* 5-10-5[141] (t) MrMichaelLegg(5) 14/1	ns	10
3	Casino Markets (IRE) *EmmaLavelle* 10-10-4[140] NickScholfield 50/1	9	11
34	Days of Heaven (IRE) *NickyHenderson* 6-10-12[148] (h) NicodeBoinville 25/1	2¼	12
194	Frodon (FR) *PaulNicholls* 6-11-10[160] (t) BryonyFrost(3) 7/1	1¾	13
	Enjoy Responsibly (IRE) *OliverSherwood* 9-10-4[140] HarrisonBeswick(7) 66/1	1¾	14
	Shantou Village (IRE) *NeilMulholland* 8-10-12[148] RobertDunne 10/1	3	15
14	Rock On Rocky *MattSheppard* 10-10-4[140] (s+t) StanSheppard(3) 25/1		pu

Galloping On The South Downs Partnership 16ran 5m09.80

AYR Saturday, Apr 21   GOOD

241 Dawn Homes Novices' Championship Handicap Chase (2) (5yo+) £64,980   3m20y (19)

211	CROSSHUE BOY (IRE) *SeanThomasDoyle,Ireland* 8-11-5[136] (t) MrH.D.Dunne(5) ..22/1		1
	DINGO DOLLAR (IRE) *AlanKing* 6-11-12[143] (s) WayneHutchinson 13/2	1	2
	ACDC (IRE) *ChrisGrant* 8-10-8[125] (h+t) MrLiamQuinlan(7) 10/1	2	3
169	Petrou (IRE) *DanSkelton* 8-11-3[134] BridgetAndrews(3) 33/1	3¼	4
	Pickamix *CharlieMann* 7-10-13[130] HarryBannister 9/1	5	5
	Shanroe In Milan (IRE) *CharlieLongsdon* 6-10-7[124] AidanColeman 20/1	½	6
	Progress Drive (IRE) *NickyRichards* 7-11-3[134] BrianHughes 20/1	1¾	7
183	Shades of Midnight *SandyThomson* 8-11-4[135] (s) HenryBrooke 12/1	1½	8
26	Mr Mix (FR) *PaulNicholls* 7-11-12[143] (s) HarryCobden 20/1	11	9
205	Born Survivor (IRE) *DanSkelton* 7-11-8[139] HarrySkelton 7/1	5	10
72	Braqueur d'Or (FR) *PaulNicholls* 7-11-6[137] SamTwiston-Davies 7/1	5	11
	Ramonex (GER) *RichardHobson* 7-10-11[128] (s) JamesBowen(3) 25/1	64	12
184	Barney Dwan (IRE) *FergalO'Brien* 8-11-12[143] NoelFehily 4/1f		F
	Rons Dream *PeterBowen* 8-11-8[139] SeanBowen 16/1		bd
72	Ballycrystal (IRE) *BrianEllison* 7-10-13[130] DannyCook 25/1		pu
183	Keeper Hill (IRE) *WarrenGreatrex* 7-11-12[143] RichardJohnson 9/1		pu

Mr N. J. Heffernan 16ran 5m58.30

242 QTS Scottish Champion Hurdle (Limited Handicap) (Gr 2) (1) (4yo+) £59,797   2m (9)

226	MIDNIGHT SHADOW *SueSmith* 5-10-4[134] DannyCook 25/1		1
178	CLAIMANTAKINFORGAN (FR) *NickyHenderson* 6-11-3[147] NicodeBoinville ..11/2f	1¼	2
200	CHESTERFIELD (IRE) *SeamusMullins* 8-10-11[141] DanielSansom(5) 6/1	½	3
181	Charli Parcs (FR) *NickyHenderson* 5-10-10[144] BarryGeraghty 14/1	2	4
200	Brelade *GordonElliott,Ireland* 6-10-10[140] (t) DavyRussell 12/1	1	5
155	Irish Roe (IRE) *PeterAtkinson* 7-10-10[140] HenryBrooke 20/1	½	6
169	The Unit (IRE) *AlanKing* 7-10-12[142] WayneHutchinson 20/1	nk	7
200	A Hare Breath (IRE) *BenPauling* 10-10-12[142] DarylJacob 33/1	2	8
	I'm A Game Changer (IRE) *PhilipHobbs* 6-10-8[138] RichardJohnson 10/1	hd	9
200	Flying Tiger (IRE) *NickWilliams* 5-10-10[140] MrChesterWilliams(7) 17/2	1¾	10
155	Verdana Blue (IRE) *NickyHenderson* 6-11-1[145] JamesBowen(3) 6/1	9	11
	Beyond The Clouds *KevinRyan* 5-10-12[142] BrianHughes 13/2	½	12
181	Ch'tibello (FR) *DanSkelton* 7-11-10[154] HarrySkelton 20/1	½	13
	Sir Chauvelin *JimGoldie* 6-10-4[134] CallumBewley(3) 20/1	11	14
	Attest *WarrenGreatrex* 5-10-4[134] (s) HarryBannister 40/1	58	15
	Flashing Glance *TomLacey* 5-10-4[134] (h) RobertDunne 12/1		pu

Mrs Aafke Clarke 16ran 3m41.60

243 Jordan Electrics Ltd Future Champion Novices' Chase (Gr 2) (1) (5yo+) 2½m110y (18) £25,978

192	BIGMARTRE (FR) *HarryWhittington* 7-11-0 HarryBannister 4/1		1
	COBRA DE MAI (FR) *DanSkelton* 6-11-0 (s+t) HarrySkelton 7/1	1¾	2
83	MIA'S STORM (IRE) *AlanKing* 8-10-12 WayneHutchinson 15/8f		F
130	Adrien du Pont (FR) *PaulNicholls* 6-11-0 (h+t) HarryCobden 7/2		F
	Peregrine Run (IRE) *PeterFahey,Ireland* 8-11-0 RogerLoughran 7/2		ur

Mr P. J. Dixon 5ran 5m03.10

244 Coral Scottish Grand National Handicap Chase (Gr 3) (1) (5yo+) £122,442 3m7f176y (27)

	JOE FARRELL (IRE) *RebeccaCurtis* 9-10-6[135] AdamWedge 33/1		1
186	BALLYOPTIC (IRE) *NigelTwiston-Davies* 8-11-6[149] TomBellamy 9/1	ns	2
180	VINTAGE CLOUDS (IRE) *SueSmith* 8-10-12[141] DannyCook 12/1	4	3
68	Doing Fine (IRE) *NeilMulholland* 10-10-6[135] (s+t) NoelFehily 12/1	7	4
180	Vicente (FR) *PaulNicholls* 9-11-7[150] (h) SamTwiston-Davies 8/1	1¾	5
172	Label des Obeaux (FR) *AlanKing* 7-11-4[147] (s) WayneHutchinson 20/1	ns	6
235	Pearl Swan (FR) *PeterBowen* 10-10-5[134] (b+t) JamesBowen(3) 66/1	3	7
219	Sizing Codelco (FR) *ColinTizzard* 9-11-7[150] PaulO'Brien(5) 28/1	4½	8
26	Fact of The Matter (IRE) *JamieSnowden* 8-10-0[129] (t) HarryBannister 50/1	10	9
206	Regal Flow *BobBuckler* 11-11-2[145] SeanHoulihan(5) 25/1	7	10
	Alzammaar (USA) *SamEngland* 7-10-1[130] CallumBewley(3) 50/1	3½	11
206	Silsol (GER) *PaulNicholls* 9-10-13[142] (b+t) HarryCobden 14/1	1	12
	Work du Breteau (FR) *DanSkelton* 8-10-6[135] (t) BridgetAndrews(3) 100/1	20	13
	Indy Five (IRE) *DavidDennis* 8-10-7[136] BrianHughes		F
198	The Young Master *NeilMulholland* 9-10-3[132] (s) MrSamWaley-Cohen(3) 12/1		ur
	Racing Europe (IRE) *NigelTwiston-Davies* 9-10-0[129] DerekFox 100/1		pu
	Boa Island (IRE) *JamesMoffatt* 8-10-1[130] (s) ConorO'Farrell 100/1		pu
177	Glencairn View (IRE) *AnthonyMullins,Ireland* 8-10-4[133] D.E.Mullins 11/1		pu
62	Straidnahanna (IRE) *SueSmith* 9-10-7[136] HenryBrooke 66/1		pu
	Looking Well (IRE) *NickyRichards* 9-10-8[137] RyanDay(3) 16/1		pu
180	Cogry *NigelTwiston-Davies* 9-10-8[137] (s) JamieBargary 25/1		pu
206	Benbens (IRE) *NigelTwiston-Davies* 13-10-9[138] AidanColeman 40/1		pu
	Henri Parry Morgan *PeterBowen* 10-10-10[139] (b+t) SeanBowen 18/1		pu
206	Get On The Yager *DanSkelton* 8-10-11[140] HarrySkelton 28/1		pu
192	West Approach *ColinTizzard* 8-11-1[144] (b) TomScudamore 33/1		pu
183	Sizing Tennessee (IRE) *ColinTizzard* 10-11-2[145] RobbiePower 10/1		pu
	Fagan *GordonElliott,Ireland* 8-11-4[147] DavyRussell 7/1f		pu
180	Beware The Bear (IRE) *NickyHenderson* 8-11-6[149] JeremiahMcGrath 14/1		pu
180	Gold Present (IRE) *NickyHenderson* 8-11-12[155] NicodeBoinville 20/1		pu

M Sherwood, N Morris & R Curtis 29ran 8m02.30

PUNCHESTOWN Tuesday, Apr 24 Chase course: SOFT, Hurdles course: GOOD to SOFT

245 Herald Champion Novices' Hurdle (Gr 1) (5yo+) £51,754 2m100y (9)

213	DRACONIEN (FR) *W.P.Mullins* 5-11-12 NoelFehily 25/1		1
226	VISION DES FLOS (FR) *ColinTizzard,GB* 5-11-12 (t) RobbiePower 11/1	2¼	2
178	MENGLI KHAN (IRE) *GordonElliott* 5-11-12 (t) J.W.Kennedy 11/2	7	3
200	Whiskey Sour (IRE) *W.P.Mullins* 5-11-12 D.J.Mullins 10/1	4	4
	Cartwright *GordonElliott* 5-11-12 M.P.Walsh 33/1	2	5
213	Sharjah (FR) *W.P.Mullins* 5-11-12 (t) MrP.W.Mullins 11/1	4¾	6
213	Getabird (IRE) *W.P.Mullins* 6-11-12 P.Townend 11/10f	1¾	7
213	Hardline (IRE) *GordonElliott* 6-11-12 (bh) SeanFlanagan 25/1	5½	8
201	Beyond The Law (IRE) *M.F.Morris* 6-11-12 (t) B.J.Cooper 66/1	24	9
178	Paloma Blue (IRE) *HenrydeBromhead* 6-11-12 DavyRussell 11/2	8	10

Clipper Logistics Group Ltd 10ran 4m03.10

246 Boylesports Champion Chase (Drogheda) (Gr 1) (5yo+) £142,325 2m (11)

215	UN DE SCEAUX (FR) *W.P.Mullins* 8-11-12 MrP.W.Mullins 9/2		1
188	DOUVAN (FR) *W.P.Mullins* 8-11-12 P.Townend 4/5f	2¾	2
215	A TOI PHIL (FR) *GordonElliott* 8-11-12 (t) J.W.Kennedy 33/1	7	3
228	Min (FR) *W.P.Mullins* 7-11-12 D.J.Mullins 3/1	4½	4
215	Doctor Phoenix (IRE) *GordonElliott* 10-11-12 (s+t) M.P.Walsh 12/1	nk	5
215	Ballycasey (IRE) *W.P.Mullins* 11-11-12 D.E.Mullins 66/1	8	6
188	Ordinary World (IRE) *HenrydeBromhead* 8-11-12 DavyRussell 16/1	3¾	7
114	The Game Changer (IRE) *GordonElliott* 10-11-12 (t) M.A.Enright 66/1	3	8
216	Tell Us More (IRE) *GordonElliott* 9-11-12 (b) KeithDonoghue 100/1	15	9

Mr Edward O'Connell 9ran 4m16.10

247 Goffs Land Rover Bumper (4 and 5yo) £8,772 2m100y

	COMMANDER OF FLEET (IRE) *GordonElliott* 4-11-4 MrB.O'Neill 5/1		1
	COLUMN OF FIRE (IRE) *GordonElliott* 4-11-4 MrM.J.O'Hare(5) 12/1	8½	2

	SANTANA PLESSIS (FR) *GordonElliott* 4-11-4 MrA.J.Fox(7) 20/1	3¾	3
	Design Matters *RobertTyner* 4-11-4 MrR.W.Barron(7) 12/1	2¼	4
	Whatucallher (IRE) *EdwardP.Harty* 4-10-11 (h) MrF.Maguire(3) 33/1	4¾	5
	Glocca Mora *JosephPatrickO'Brien* 4-11-4 (t) MrD.O'Connor 6/1	½	6
	Wolfofallstreets (IRE) *P.J.Rothwell* 4-11-4 MrH.D.Dunne(5) 25/1	hd	7
	Seeyouinvinnys (IRE) *NoelMeade* 4-11-4 (h) MissN.Carberry 11/1	1	8
	Kerrkenny Gold (IRE) *MsMargaretMullins* 4-11-4 MsK.Walsh 13/2	nk	9
	Foxy Jacks (IRE) *M.F.Morris* 4-11-4 MrJ.C.Barry(5) 16/1	hd	10
	That's A Given (FR) *PhilipHobbs,GB* 4-11-4 MrR.Deegan(5) 6/1	1½	11
	Cap'tain Youm (FR) *JohnJosephHanlon* 4-11-4 MrR.O.Harding(3) 33/1	10	12
	A Dos No Bueno *ConorO'Dwyer* 4-11-4 MrR.P.Quinlan(3) 25/1	3	13
	Tashinny (IRE) *DenisHogan* 4-11-4 MrJ.Hogan(7) 33/1	2¾	14
	Think Positive (IRE) *W.P.Mullins* 4-11-4 MrP.W.Mullins 9/2f	31	15
	Tobias Lochlan (IRE) *MadeleineTylicki* 4-11-4 MrL.Quinlan(7) 66/1	28	16
	Gigginstown House Stud 16ran 4m18.70		
248	**Growise Champion Novices' Chase (Ellier) (Gr 1) (5yo+) £51,754**	3m120y (17)	
212	THE STORYTELLER (IRE) *GordonElliott* 7-11-10 DavyRussell 16/1		1
216	MONBEG NOTORIOUS (IRE) *GordonElliott* 7-11-10 (v) DenisO'Regan 33/1	6	2
183	JURY DUTY (IRE) *GordonElliott* 7-11-10 (t) M.P.Walsh 16/1	1¼	3
183	Rathvinden (IRE) *W.P.Mullins* 10-11-10 MrP.W.Mullins 10/1	hd	4
212	Shattered Love (IRE) *GordonElliott* 7-11-3 (t) J.W.Kennedy 4/1	¾	5
	Youcantcallherthat (IRE) *DenisHogan* 7-11-3 D.G.Hogan 33/1	9½	6
186	Monalee (IRE) *HenrydeBromhead* 7-11-10 NoelFehily 2/1f		F
212	Invitation Only (IRE) *W.P.Mullins* 7-11-10 D.J.Mullins 10/1		ur
217	Finian's Oscar (IRE) *ColinTizzard,GB* 7-11-10 (s) RobbiePower 13/2		co
212	Al Boum Photo (FR) *W.P.Mullins* 6-11-10 P.Townend 11/2		ro
216	Dounikos (FR) *GordonElliott* 7-11-10 KeithDonoghue 33/1		pu
	Mrs P. Sloan 11ran 6m41.40		
	PUNCHESTOWN Wednesday, Apr 25 SOFT		
249	**Irish Daily Mirror Novices' Hurdle (War of Attrition) (Gr 1) (4yo+) £51,754**	3m (13)	
185	NEXT DESTINATION (IRE) *W.P.Mullins* 6-11-10 P.Townend 5/4f		1
193	DELTA WORK (FR) *GordonElliott* 5-11-9 (h+t) DavyRussell 7/1	nk	2
201	KILBRICKEN STORM (IRE) *ColinTizzard,GB* 7-11-10 (t) HarryCobden 5/1	nk	3
201	Ballyward (IRE) *W.P.Mullins* 6-11-10 D.J.Mullins 8/1	20	4
204	Discorama (FR) *PaulNolan* 5-11-9 K.C.Sexton 20/1	4½	5
185	Brahma Bull (IRE) *W.P.Mullins* 7-11-10 NoelFehily 16/1	3½	6
210	Blow By Blow (IRE) *GordonElliott* 7-11-10 (b+t) J.W.Kennedy 12/1	nk	7
210	Jetz (IRE) *MrsJ.Harrington* 6-11-10 (h) RobbiePower 10/1	2½	8
	General Consensus *SamuelDrinkwater,GB* 6-11-10 MrJosephDrinkwater 100/1	½	9
	The Conditional (IRE) *MartinHassett* 6-11-10 A.E.Lynch 100/1	½	10
209	Lackaneen Leader (IRE) *GordonElliott* 6-11-3 M.P.Walsh 25/1		pu
	Mr Malcolm C. Denmark 11ran 6m14.20		
250	**Coral Punchestown Gold Cup Chase (Gr 1) (5yo+) £142,325**	3m120y (17)	
216	BELLSHILL (IRE) *W.P.Mullins* 8-11-10 D.J.Mullins 4/1		1
202	DJAKADAM (FR) *W.P.Mullins* 9-11-10 MrP.W.Mullins 5/1	¾	2
202	ROAD TO RESPECT (IRE) *NoelMeade* 7-11-10 (h) SeanFlanagan 7/2f	8	3
219	Sub Lieutenant (IRE) *HenrydeBromhead* 9-11-10 (t) DavyRussell 12/1	hd	4
202	Killultagh Vic (IRE) *W.P.Mullins* 9-11-10 P.Townend 11/2	2	5
228	Sizing Granite (IRE) *ColinTizzard,GB* 10-11-10 (t) RobbiePower 16/1	sh	6
202	Edwulf *JosephPatrickO'Brien* 9-11-10 (t) MrD.O'Connor 8/1	6	7
216	Outlander (IRE) *GordonElliott* 10-11-10 (s) J.W.Kennedy 18/1	24	8
	Arctic Skipper (IRE) *VincentLaurenceHalley* 9-11-10 (s+t) A.E.Lynch 100/1	hd	9
4	Sandymount Duke (IRE) *MrsJ.Harrington* 9-11-10 (s) BarryGeraghty 25/1	32	10
123	Sumos Novios (IRE) *W.J.Burke* 10-11-10 JonathanBurke 33/1		pu
237	Total Recall (IRE) *W.P.Mullins* 9-11-10 NoelFehily 10/1		pu
	Andrea Wylie/Graham Wylie 12ran 6m41.90		
251	**Racing Post Champion INH Flat (Gr 1) (4, 5, 6 and 7yo) £51,754**	2m70y	
191	TORNADO FLYER (IRE) *W.P.Mullins* 5-12-0 MrR.Deegan 12/1		1
191	BLACKBOW (IRE) *W.P.Mullins* 5-12-0 MrP.W.Mullins 9/4f	1¼	2
191	CAREFULLY SELECTED (IRE) *W.P.Mullins* 6-12-0 MrD.O'Connor 4/1	1¾	3
141	Rapid Escape (IRE) *GordonElliott* 5-12-0 MsLisaO'Neill 12/1	13	4
191	Felix Desjy (FR) *GordonElliott* 5-12-0 MrB.O'Neill 8/1	2¾	5
	Young Ted (IRE) *NoelMeade* 4-11-4 MissN.Carberry 18/1	½	6
191	Relegate (IRE) *W.P.Mullins* 5-11-7 MsK.Walsh 9/2	5½	7
	Dorking Boy *TomLacey,GB* 4-11-4 (t) MrTommieM.O'Brien 16/1	2	8
	Where Eagles Dare (IRE) *NoelMeade* 5-12-0 MrM.J.O'Hare 40/1	18	9

      Getaway John (IRE) *GordonElliott* 5-12-0 MrF.Maguire 6/1   43 10
T. F. P. Partnership 10ran 4m00.50

252	**Guinness Handicap Chase (Gr A) (5yo+) £51,754**		2½m (14)

211 PATRICKS PARK (IRE) *W.P.Mullins* 7-10-1[133] P.Townend 11/2   1
138 BLAST OF KOEMAN (IRE) *RobertTyner* 7-9-10[128] (s+t) PhilipEnright ....6/1   nk 2
216 OSCAR KNIGHT (IRE) *ThomasMullins* 9-10-4[136] M.P.Walsh 7/1   8   3
229 Polidam (FR) *W.P.Mullins* 9-10-13[145] (h) D.J.Mullins 12/1   12 4
216 Jetstream Jack (IRE) *GordonElliott* 8-10-6[138] (b+t) DenisO'Regan 20/1   9   5
196 Viconte du Noyer (FR) *ColinTizzard,GB* 9-10-1[143] (h) JonathanBurke ....16/1   ½   6
123 Champagne West (IRE) *HenrydeBromhead* 10-11-10[156] NoelFehily ....25/1   ¾   7
88 Tout Est Permis (FR) *M.F.Morris* 5-9-10[131] RachaelBlackmore 16/1   1¾ 8
92 Woodland Opera (IRE) *Mrs.J.Harrington* 8-11-2[148] (t) RobbiePower 7/1   16 9
      Cold March (FR) *HarryWhittington,GB* 8-10-10[142] (s) B.J.Cooper 33/1   4¾ 10
229 Clarcam (FR) *GordonElliott* 8-11-2[148] (s+t) DavyRussell 14/1   1¼ 11
216 Lord Scoundrel (IRE) *GordonElliott* 9-11-1[147] (b+t) J.W.Kennedy 25/1   8½ 12
216 The Paparazzi Kid (IRE) *GordonElliott* 11-10-8[140] (t) DonaghMeyler 25/1   24 13
229 Devils Bride (IRE) *HenrydeBromhead* 11-11-4[150] (s+t) D.Robinson(5) ....33/1   sh 14
      Goulane Chosen (IRE) *SeamusSpillane* 9-10-5[137] D.J.McInerney(5) ....16/1   F
229 Newsworthy (IRE) *MrsD.A.Love* 8-9-10[128] JonathanMoore ....50/1   pu
229 Shanahan's Turn (IRE) *ColinTizzard,GB* 10-10-4[136] (t) HarryCobden .... 9/2f   pu
184 Demi Sang (FR) *W.P.Mullins* 5-10-8[144] BarryGeraghty ....12/1   pu
Bowes Lodge Stables Partnership 18ran 5m25.60

PUNCHESTOWN Thursday, Apr 26 GOOD to SOFT

253	**pigsback.com Handicap Chase (Gr B) (4yo+) £33,640**		2m (11)

      CADMIUM (FR) *W.P.Mullins* 6-10-7[133] D.E.Mullins 12/1   1
211 COEUR JOYEUX (IRE) *J.P.Dempsey* 7-9-13[125] (s) L.P.Dempsey 25/1   8   2
211 BON PAPA (FR) *W.P.Mullins* 7-11-3[143] (t) BarryGeraghty 7/2f   2   3
      Mr Fiftyone (IRE) *Mrs.J.Harrington* 9-10-11[137] (s) RobbiePower ....25/1   ½   4
      Sunsetstorise (IRE) *GordonElliott* 10-9-12[124] (s+t) J.W.Kennedy ....7/1   ¾   5
      Just Get Cracking (IRE) *JamesDanielDullea* 8-9-10[122] (t) PhilipEnright 25/1   3½ 6
207 American Tom (FR) *W.P.Mullins* 7-11-2[142] (t) P.Townend 12/1   2¾ 7
160 Speredek (FR) *NigelHawke,GB* 7-11-10[150] (s) DavidNoonan 8/1   3¼ 8
205 Townshend (GER) *W.P.Mullins* 7-11-2[142] (t) D.J.Mullins 12/1   7   9
      Balbir du Mathan (FR) *S.J.Mahon* 9-10-1[127] (s) DenisO'Regan 11/1   1¼ 10
151 Lake Takapuna (IRE) *J.Culloty* 7-9-13[125] A.E.Lynch ....25/1   nk 11
151 De Benno (IRE) *JamesGrace* 13-9-12[124] (t) C.A.Landers(7) 25/1   4½ 12
      Tongie (IRE) *P.A.Fahy* 8-9-10[122] RachaelBlackmore 50/1   1¼ 13
      Shadow Catcher (GordonElliott) 10-10-11[137] (b+t) B.Hayes 50/1   6 14
205 Three Stars (IRE) *HenrydeBromhead* 8-11-1[141] (s) SeanFlanagan 12/1   6 15
  5 Timiyan (USA) *GordonElliott* 7-9-10[122] (t) M.A.Enright ....40/1   F
      Tisamystery (IRE) *HenrydeBromhead* 10-9-10[122] (s) MrL.Quinlan(7) ....25/1   F
      Lean And Keen (IRE) *SeanByrne* 8-9-11[125] K.C.Sexton ....50/1   F
      Powersbomb (IRE) *BrianM.McMahon* 8-10-8[134] (h) R.C.Colgan ....12/1   F
211 Our Dougal (IRE) *HenrydeBromhead* 8-10-1[127] D.Robinson(5) ....33/1   ur
138 Hurricane Ben (IRE) *JamesG.Sheehan* 9-11-4[144] (t) NoelFehily ....50/1   bd
      Eight Till Late (IRE) *FrancisCasey* 10-9-11[123] AndrewRing(3) ....22/1   pu
211 Robin des Mana (IRE) *GordonElliott* 7-10-5[131] (t) M.P.Walsh ....33/1   pu
212 Tycoon Prince (IRE) *GordonElliott* 8-11-2[142] (t) DavyRussell ....16/1   pu
Supreme Horse Racing Club/K. Sharp 24ran 4m11.40

254	**Ladbrokes Champion Stayers Hurdle (Tipperkevin) (Gr 1) (4yo+) £142,323**		3m (13)

181 FAUGHEEN (IRE) *W.P.Mullins* 10-11-10 D.J.Mullins 11/2   1
195 PENHILL *W.P.Mullins* 7-11-10 P.Townend 2/1f   13 2
 70 SHANESHILL (IRE) *W.P.Mullins* 9-11-10 D.E.Mullins 33/1   4¾ 3
236 Identity Thief (IRE) *HenrydeBromhead* 8-11-10 SeanFlanagan 6/1   12 4
214 Bapaume (FR) *W.P.Mullins* 5-11-9 NoelFehily ....25/1   ½   5
214 Diamond Cauchois (FR) *GordonElliott* 7-11-10 (t) DavyRussell ....14/1   ¾   6
182 La Bague Au Roi (FR) *WarrenGreatrex,GB* 7-11-3 HarryBannister 14/1   2¾ 7
181 Yorkhill (IRE) *W.P.Mullins* 8-11-10 RobbiePower 14/1   7½ 8
200 Bleu Et Rouge (FR) *W.P.Mullins* 7-11-10 (t) M.P.Walsh 33/1   32 9
195 Bacardys (FR) *W.P.Mullins* 7-11-10 MrP.W.Mullins ....4/1   hd 10
214 Jezki (IRE) *Mrs.J.Harrington* 10-11-10 (b) BarryGeraghty ....20/1   hd 11
214 Lieutenant Colonel *GordonElliott* 9-11-10 (b+t) J.W.Kennedy ....66/1   pu
Mrs S. Ricci 12ran 6m05.60

255	**Ryanair Novices' Chase (Colliers) (Gr 1) (5yo+) £59,518**		2m (12)

179 FOOTPAD (FR) *W.P.Mullins* 6-11-10 DarylJacob 2/5f   1
  1 OPTIMUS PRIME (FR) *DanSkelton,GB* 6-11-10 (t) NoelFehily 25/1   12 2
      ASTHURIA (FR) *W.P.Mullins* 7-11-3 (h) D.J.Mullins 20/1   5   3

234 Petit Mouchoir (FR) *HenrydeBromhead* 7-11-10 DavyRussell ... 4/1 6½ 4
Castlegrace Paddy (IRE) *P.A.Fahy* 7-11-10 A.E.Lynch ... 9/1 7 5
212 Saturnas (FR) *W.P.Mullins* 7-11-10 (t) P.Townend ... 20/1 12 6
Mr Simon Munir & Mr Isaac Souede 6ran 4m14.10

PUNCHESTOWN Friday, Apr 27 SOFT

256 EMS Copiers Novices' Handicap Chase (Gr A) (5yo+) £51,754 2m5f (15)
224 KEMBOY (FR) *W.P.Mullins* 6-11-10^{147} P.Townend ... 11/4f 1
A RATED (IRE) *HenrydeBromhead* 7-10-12^{135} D.Robinson(5) ... 20/1 5 2
211 BEL AMI DE SIVOLA (FR) *NoelMeade* 7-10-13^{136} SeanFlanagan ... 8/1 8 3
A Sizing Network (FR) *MrsJ.Harrington* 8-10-10^{133} RobbiePower ... 14/1 11 4
Bravissimo (FR) *W.P.Mullins* 7-10-3^{126} (t) KatieO'Farrell(7) ... 16/1 14 5
224 Tombstone (IRE) *GordonElliott* 8-11-8^{145} (t) J.W.Kennedy ... 14/1 2¾ 6
177 Scoir Mear (IRE) *ThomasMullins* 8-10-8^{131} M.P.Walsh ... 10/1 4¼ 7
212 Up For Review (IRE) *W.P.Mullins* 9-11-10^{147} D.J.Mullins ... 13/2 4½ 8
212 Montalbano *W.P.Mullins* 6-11-6^{143} (h) MrR.Deegan ... 25/1 2 9
211 The West's Awake (IRE) *E.J.O'Grady* 7-11-2^{139} A.E.Lynch ... 16/1 1½ 10
211 Ask Nile (IRE) *SeamusNeville* 6-10-8^{131} B.Hayes ... 25/1 F
149 Koshari (FR) *W.P.Mullins* 6-11-10^{147} RachaelBlackmore ... 11/1 F
Surf Instructor (IRE) *HenrydeBromhead* 6-10-4^{127} PhilipEnright ... 50/1 bd
177 Close Shave *MrsJ.Harrington* 7-10-7^{130} J.S.McGarvey ... 33/1 pu
183 Pylonthepressure (IRE) *W.P.Mullins* 8-10-12^{135} D.E.Mullins ... 20/1 pu
216 Squouateur (FR) *GordonElliott* 7-11-1^{138} (t) BarryGeraghty ... 10/1 pu
184 Conrad Hastings (IRE) *HenrydeBromhead* 7-11-4^{141} NoelFehily ... 25/1 pu
184 De Plotting Shed (IRE) *GordonElliott* 8-11-5^{142} (t) DavyRussell ... 16/1 pu
SupremeHorseRacingClub/BTGraham/KSharpe 18ran 5m42.30

257 Betdaq 2% Commission Punchestown Champion Hurdle (Gr 1) (4yo+) £144,737 2m (9)
220 SUPASUNDAE *MrsJ.Harrington* 8-11-12 RobbiePower ... 7/1 1
181 WICKLOW BRAVE *W.P.Mullins* 9-11-12 (b) MrP.W.Mullins ... 12/1 3¼ 2
214 BLEU BERRY (FR) *W.P.Mullins* 7-11-12 M.P.Walsh ... 40/1 19 3
214 Coquin Mans (FR) *W.P.Mullins* 6-11-12 D.J.Mullins ... 14/1 33 4
246 The Game Changer (IRE) *GordonElliott* 9-11-12 (t) DavyRussell ... 66/1 46 5
181 Melon *W.P.Mullins* 6-11-12 P.Townend ... 11/4 F
185 Samcro (IRE) *GordonElliott* 6-11-12 J.W.Kennedy ... 5/6f F
Ann & Alan Potts Limited 7ran 3m56.60

258 Profile Systems Champion Novices' Hurdle (Tickell) (Gr 1) (4yo+) £51,754 2½m (11)
201 DORTMUND PARK (FR) *GordonElliott* 5-11-10 (t) J.W.Kennedy ... 16/1 1
245 WHISKEY SOUR (IRE) *W.P.Mullins* 5-11-10 D.J.Mullins ... 11/2 10 2
204 BURROWS SAINT (FR) *W.P.Mullins* 5-11-10 (t) RobbiePower ... 33/1 2 3
210 Real Steel (FR) *W.P.Mullins* 5-11-10 BarryGeraghty ... 25/1 8½ 4
210 Pallasator *GordonElliott* 9-11-10 DavyRussell ... 11/4jf 6 5
210 Duc des Genievres (FR) *W.P.Mullins* 5-11-10 M.P.Walsh ... 7/1 26 6
178 Debuchet (FR) *MsMargaretMullins* 5-11-10 D.E.Mullins ... 8/1 F
245 Getabird (IRE) *W.P.Mullins* 6-11-10 MrP.W.Mullins ... 11/4jf pu
210 Scarpeta (FR) *W.P.Mullins* 5-11-10 P.Townend ... 11/2 pu
Gigginstown House Stud 9ran 5m11.20

SANDOWN Saturday, Apr 28 Chase course: GOOD to SOFT, Hurdles course: SOFT

259 Bet365 Novices' Championship Final Handicap Hurdle (2) (4yo+) £61,900 1m7f216y (8)
BALLYMOY (IRE) *NigelTwiston-Davies* 5-11-7^{132} DarylJacob ... 13/2jf 1
176 HIGHWAY ONE O ONE (IRE) *ChrisGordon* 6-11-10^{135} HarryReed(5) ... 10/1 1¼ 2
12 EQUUS AMADEUS (IRE) *TomLacey* 5-10-13^{124} RobertDunne ... 12/1 ¾ 3
171 Mont des Avaloirs (FR) *PaulNicholls* 5-11-12^{137} (h) HarryCobden ... 15/2 1½ 4
190 Act of Valour *PaulNicholls* 4-11-3^{133} SamTwiston-Davies ... 11/1 ns 5
Burrows Edge (FR) *NickyHenderson* 5-11-5^{130} JamesBowen(3) ... 9/1 2½ 6
Oistrakh Le Noir (FR) *BenPauling* 4-11-1^{131} TomBellamy ... 20/1 hd 7
Show On The Road *PhilipHobbs* 7-11-2^{127} (h) RichardJohnson ... 13/2jf 4½ 8
Django Django (FR) *JonjoO'Neill* 5-10-13^{124} AidanColeman ... 20/1 5 9
Kelpies Myth *LucindaRussell* 5-11-0^{125} BlairCampbell(5) ... 25/1 ½ 10
Piton Pete (IRE) *OliverSherwood* 7-11-7^{132} ConorShoemark ... 50/1 nk 11
176 Friday Night Light (FR) *DavidPipe* 5-11-3^{128} (s+t) DavidNoonan ... 25/1 hd 12
Going Gold (IRE) *RichardHobson* 6-11-0^{125} RichardPatrick(5) ... 20/1 nk 13
The New Pharaoh (IRE) *LauraMorgan* 7-10-8^{119} (v) PatrickCowley(5) ... 25/1 2½ 14
175 Notre Ami (IRE) *NickGifford* 7-10-12^{123} (h) TomCannon ... 20/1 ns 15
Grapevine (IRE) *NickyHenderson* 5-10-7^{118} NicodeBoinville ... 20/1 2 16
Taxmeifyoucan (IRE) *KeithDalgleish* 4-11-6^{136} (s) BrianHughes ... 16/1 11 17
Jaisalmer (IRE) *MarkBradstock* 6-11-7^{132} BryonyFrost ... 40/1 1 18
Ar Mest (FR) *GaryMoore* 5-10-10^{121} JamieMoore ... 16/1 ¾ 19

		Enola Gay (FR) *VenetiaWilliams* 5-10-8[119] WayneHutchinson	33/1	11	20
		Mr Simon Munir & Mr Isaac Souede 20ran 4m00.10			
260		**Bet365 Oaksey Chase (Gr 2) (1) (5yo+)** £31,322	2¾m164y (17)		
	160	TOP NOTCH (FR) *NickyHenderson* 7-11-6 DarylJacob	4/5f		1
	172	ART MAURESQUE (FR) *PaulNicholls* 8-11-0 HarryCobden	6/1	2¾	2
	229	O O SEVEN (IRE) *PaulNicholls* 8-11-0 NicodeBoinville	6/1	10	3
	219	Double Shuffle (IRE) *TomGeorge* 8-11-0 (h) JonathanBurke	9/2	ns	4
	3	Alcala (FR) *PaulNicholls* 8-11-4 (t) SamTwiston-Davies	16/1	6	5
	4	Sadler's Risk (IRE) *TomGeorge* 10-11-4 BrianHughes	33/1		pu
		Mr Simon Munir & Mr Isaac Souede 6ran 6m00.30			
261		**Bet365 Celebration Chase (Gr 1) (1) (5yo+)** £74,035	1m7f119y (13)		
	188	ALTIOR (IRE) *NickyHenderson* 8-11-7 NicodeBoinville	2/11f		1
	118	SAN BENEDETO (FR) *PaulNicholls* 7-11-7 (s+t) SamTwiston-Davies	33/1	3¼	2
	188	GOD'S OWN (FR) *TomGeorge* 10-11-7 PaddyBrennan	11/1	3¾	3
	188	Special Tiara *HenrydeBromhead,Ireland* 11-11-7 DarylJacob	12/1	3¾	4
	234	Diego du Charmil (FR) *PaulNicholls* 6-11-7 (t) HarryCobden	10/1	5	5
	188	Ar Mad (FR) *GaryMoore* 8-11-7 JoshuaMoore	16/1		F
		Mrs Patricia Pugh 6ran 3m57.90			
262		**Bet365 Gold Cup Handicap Chase (Gr 3) (1) (5yo+)** £84,405	3½m166y (24)		
		STEP BACK (IRE) *MarkBradstock* 8-10-0[135] (s) JamieMoore	7/1		1
	121	ROCK THE KASBAH (IRE) *PhilipHobbs* 8-11-0[149] (s) RichardJohnson	12/1	13	2
	53	PRESENT MAN (IRE) *PaulNicholls* 8-10-12[147] (t) BryonyFrost(3)	25/1	14	3
	172	Relentless Dreamer (IRE) *RebeccaCurtis* 9-10-1[136] (s+t) AdamWedge	33/1	½	4
	121	Carole's Destrier *NeilMulholland* 10-10-3[138] (s) RobertDunne	14/1	½	5
		Dawson City *PollyGundry* 9-10-0[136] TomO'Brien	14/1	5	6
	172	Theatre Guide (IRE) *ColinTizzard* 11-11-0[149] (b+t) PaddyBrennan	25/1	6	7
	244	The Young Master *NeilMulholland* 9-10-0[135] (s) ConorShoemark	12/1	3	8
	237	Houblon des Obeaux (FR) *VenetiaWilliams* 11-10-7[142] (b) CharlieDeutsch	25/1	6	9
	198	Band of Blood (IRE) *DrRichardNewland* 10-10-0[135] (t) BrianHughes	25/1	24	10
	244	Benbens (IRE) *NigelTwiston-Davies* 13-10-3[138] AidanColeman	50/1	19	11
	229	Rathlin Rose (IRE) *DavidPipe* 10-10-0[135] (s) DavidNoonan	16/1		pu
	180	Minella Daddy (IRE) *PeterBowen* 8-10-2[137] (b) JamesBowen(3)	8/1		pu
	198	Sugar Baron (IRE) *NickyHenderson* 8-10-2[137] (b) NicodeBoinville	12/1		pu
	229	Bigbadjohn (IRE) *NigelTwiston-Davies* 9-10-3[138] JamieBargary	12/1		pu
		Domesday Book (USA) *StuartEdmunds* 8-10-5[140] (b) MissGinaAndrews(3)	25/1		pu
	187	Royal Vacation (IRE) *ColinTizzard* 8-10-10[145] (b) HarryCobden	20/1		pu
	198	Missed Approach (IRE) *WarrenGreatrex* 8-10-11[146] (b) MrN.McParlan(3)	8/1		pu
	159	Regal Encore (IRE) *AnthonyHoneyball* 10-11-5[154] RichieMcLernon	16/1		pu
	237	Blaklion *NigelTwiston-Davies* 9-11-12[161] SamTwiston-Davies	6/1f		pu
		Cracker and Smodge Partnership 20ran 7m38.40			
263		**Bet365 Select Hurdle (Gr 2) (1) (4yo+)** £31,322	2m5f110y (11)		
	176	CALL ME LORD (FR) *NickyHenderson* 5-11-0 NicodeBoinville	6/4jf		1
	236	LIL ROCKERFELLER (USA) *NeilKing* 7-11-0 WayneHutchinson	8/1	16	2
	236	WHOLESTONE (IRE) *NigelTwiston-Davies* 7-11-6 DarylJacob	6/4jf	6	3
	236	Old Guard *PaulNicholls* 7-11-6 HarryCobden	10/1	8	4
	193	Boite (IRE) *WarrenGreatrex* 8-11-0 (s+t) RichardJohnson	20/1	33	5
	220	Diakali (FR) *GaryMoore* 9-11-0 (b) JamieMoore	16/1	33	6
		Mr Simon Munir & Mr Isaac Souede 6ran 5m30.90			
		PUNCHESTOWN Saturday, Apr 28 SOFT			
264		**European Breeders Fund Annie Power Mares Champion Hurdle (Gr 1) (4yo+)** £51,754	2½m (11)		
	182	BENIE DES DIEUX (FR) *W.P.Mullins* 7-11-7 P.Townend	3/1		1
	214	AUGUSTA KATE *W.P.Mullins* 7-11-7 D.J.Mullins	16/1	3	2
	182	APPLE'S JADE (FR) *GordonElliott* 6-11-7 (t) J.W.Kennedy	5/6f	2½	3
	214	Let's Dance (FR) *W.P.Mullins* 6-11-7 (s) RachaelBlackmore	9/1	2¼	4
	214	Barra (FR) *GordonElliott* 7-11-7 (t) M.P.Walsh	33/1	11	5
	182	Midnight Tour *AlanKing,GB* 8-11-7 DavyRussell	12/1	7	6
	182	Jer's Girl (IRE) *GavinPatrickCromwell* 6-11-7 BarryGeraghty	12/1	6½	7
	214	Forge Meadow (IRE) *MrsJ.Harrington* 6-11-7 RobbiePower	14/1		pu
		Mrs S. Ricci 8ran 4m54.70			
265		**AES Champion Four Year Old Hurdle (Gr 1) (4yo)** £51,754	2m (9)		
	199	SALDIER (FR) *W.P.Mullins* 4-11-0 RobbiePower	10/1		1
	199	MR ADJUDICATOR *W.P.Mullins* 4-11-0 P.Townend	10/3	3	2
		SAGLAWY (FR) *W.P.Mullins* 4-11-0 RachaelBlackmore	8/1	3½	3
		Msassa (FR) *W.P.Mullins* 4-11-0 D.E.Mullins	33/1	2	4

199	Farclas (FR) *GordonElliott* 4-11-0 (t) J.W.Kennedy 5/2	hd	5
190	Mitchouka (FR) *GordonElliott* 4-11-0 DavyRussell 20/1	22	6
199	Stormy Ireland (FR) *W.P.Mullins* 4-10-7 D.J.Mullins 15/8f		ur

Mrs S. Ricci 7ran 3m55.50

266 Ballymore Handicap Hurdle (Gr B) (4yo+) £51,754   2½m (11)

239	MERI DEVIE (FR) *W.P.Mullins* 5-10-13[139] RachaelBlackmore 14/1		1
187	C'EST JERSEY (FR) *W.P.Mullins* 6-10-10[136] (b) A.E.Lynch 33/1	1¾	2
	BENKEI (IRE) *HarryRogers* 8-9-10[122] PhilipEnright 25/1	nk	3
	Bunk Off Early (IRE) *W.P.Mullins* 6-11-1[141] N.M.Kelly(5) 28/1	½	4
239	Low Sun *W.P.Mullins* 5-10-5[131] (s) KatieO'Farrell(7) 9/1	¾	5
204	Dream Berry (FR) *JonjoO'Neill,GB* 7-11-2[142] (t) J.S.McGarvey 11/1	2¾	6
239	Karalee (FR) *W.P.Mullins* 7-10-10[136] (t) P.Townend 12/1	3	7
5	Joey Sasa (FR) *NoelMeade* 9-10-12[138] SeanFlanagan 8/1	nk	8
239	Yaha Fizz (IRE) *GordonElliott* 8-10-9[135] J.W.Kennedy 8/1	¾	9
204	Early Doors (FR) *JosephPatrickO'Brien* 5-11-3[143] BarryGeraghty 6/1f	1	10
	Prince Garyantle (IRE) *MatthewJ.Smith* 8-10-7[133] (s+t) A.W.Short(5) 14/1	4	11
	Bargy Lady (IRE) *W.P.Mullins* 6-9-12[124] (h) M.A.Enright 20/1	4¾	12
239	Voix du Reve (FR) *W.P.Mullins* 6-11-1[141] (h) L.P.Gilligan(7) 16/1	2¾	13
140	Agent Boru (IRE) *T.Gibney* 7-10-1[127] JonathanMoore 16/1	2¼	14
	Allblak des Places (FR) *W.P.Mullins* 6-10-7[133] MrR.Deegan(5) 33/1	3¼	15
57	Swamp Fox (IRE) *JosephG.Murphy* 6-11-12[152] (b) B.Browne(5) 28/1	10	16
	Carrig Cathal *S.J.Mahon* 7-10-10[136] (s+t) MrS.P.Byrne 66/1	1½	17
	Turcagua (FR) *W.P.Mullins* 8-10-11[137] RobbiePower 20/1	2¼	18
239	Abbyssial (FR) *W.P.Mullins* 8-11-3[143] RogerLoughran 33/1	1¾	19
	Minella Beau (FR) *W.P.Mullins* 7-10-3[129] D.E.Mullins 16/1	¾	20
	Spades Are Trumps (IRE) *GavinPatrickCromwell* 5-10-3[129] M.P.Walsh 11/1	35	21
	Court Artist (IRE) *W.P.Mullins* 7-10-2[128] JohnJ.Fitzpatrick(7) 33/1		pu
187	Max Dynamite (FR) *W.P.Mullins* 8-11-0[140] D.J.Mullins 16/1		pu
187	Diamond King (IRE) *GordonElliott* 10-11-8[148] (t) DavyRussell 25/1		pu

Andrea Wylie/Graham Wylie 24ran 4m59.80

AUTEUIL Sunday, May 20   SOFT

267 Grand Steeple-Chase de Paris (Gr 1) (5yo+) £326,549   3m5f182y

	ON THE GO (FR) *GuillaumeMacaire,France* 5-10-6 JamesReveley 12/1		1
	PERFECT IMPULSE (FR) *A.Chaille-Chaille,France* 6-10-6 TristanLemagnen .. 23/10f	hd	2
	EDWARD D'ARGENT (FR) *GuillaumeMacaire,France* 5-10-6 KevinNabet ... 38/10	7	3
	Milord Thomas (FR) *D.Bressou,France* 9-10-10 JacquesRicou 9/1	5	4
	Balkan du Pecos (FR) *FrancoisNicolle,France* 7-10-10 TheoChevillard 25/1	14	5
	Valtor (FR) *E.Leray,France* 9-10-10 ThomasBeaurain 62/1	18	6
	Borice (FR) *FrancoisNicolle,France* 7-10-10 (s) DavidGallon 34/1	20	7
250	Djakadam (FR) *W.P.Mullins,Ireland* 9-10-10 D.J.Mullins 11/1	ds	8
	Punch Nantais (FR) *GuillaumeMacaire,France* 6-10-10 (s) KilianDubourg 30/1		ur
	So French (FR) *GuillaumeMacaire,France* 7-10-10 BertrandLestrade 15/1		bd
	Roi Mage (FR) *FrancoisNicolle,France* 6-10-10 StevenColas 25/1		bd
	Bipolaire (FR) *FrancoisNicolle,France* 7-10-10 ThomasGueguen 48/10		F
	Sainte Turgeon (FR) *PatriceQuinton,France* 6-10-10 JordanDuchene 31/1		ur
	Geluroni (FR) *DavidCottin,France* 8-10-10 JonathanPlouganou 65/1		pu

Mme Patrick Papot 14ran 7m09.77

268 Grande Course de Haies d'Auteuil Hurdle (Gr 1) (5yo+) £139,381   3m1f77y

	DE BON COEUR (FR) *FrancoisNicolle,France* 5-10-1 KevinNabet 18/10f		1
254	BAPAUME (FR) *W.P.Mullins,Ireland* 5-10-5 JacquesRicou 35/1	16	2
	DALIA GRANDCHAMP (FR) *FrancoisNicolle,France* 5-10-3 StevenColas ... 10/1	sh	3
	Alex de Larredya (FR) *FrancoisNicolle,France* 8-10-10 TheoChevillard 28/10	1¾	4
	Galop Marin (IRE) *D.Bressou,France* 6-10-10 MorganRegairaz 30/1	3	5
254	Yorkhill (IRE) *W.P.Mullins,Ireland* 8-10-10 D.E.Mullins 73/1	5	6
220	L'Ami Serge (IRE) *NickyHenderson,GB* 6-10-10 (h) DarylJacob 35/10	¾	7
	Pop Art du Berlais (FR) *P.Lenogue,France* 5-10-5 (b) LudovicPhilipperon 35/1	12	8
	Alti Plano (FR) *AlainCouetil,France* 8-10-10 (s) AlexisPoirier 48/1		pu
257	Coquin Mans (FR) *W.P.Mullins,Ireland* 6-10-10 JamesReveley 22/1		pu
	Plumeur (FR) *G.Chaignon,France* 11-10-10 ThomasBeaurain 116/1		pu
219	Tea For Two *NickWilliams,GB* 9-10-10 LizzieKelly 78/1		pu
250	Killultagh Vic (IRE) *W.P.Mullins,Ireland* 9-10-10 D.J.Mullins 13/1		pu

Jacques Detre & Haras De Saint-Voir 13ran 5m51.62

INDEX TO SELECTED BIG RACES

Abbyssial (IRE) 162⁴, 187ᵖᵘ, 239, 266
Acapella Bourgeois (FR) 49ᶠ, 114ᵖᵘ
Acdc (IRE) 241³
Acey Milan (IRE) 191⁴
Acting Lass (IRE) 117*, 172
Actinpieces 89⁴, 198⁵
Act of Valour 73⁵, 190, 259⁵
Admiral Brian (IRE) 122⁶
A Dos No Bueno 247
Adrien du Pont (FR) 50³, 130³, 243ᶠ
After Rain (FR) 6⁶
A Genie In Abottle (IRE) 53, 123, 168³
Agent Boru (IRE) 58⁵, 140, 266
Agrapart (FR) 103², 129*, 163²
A Great View (IRE) 148⁵, 193⁶
A Hare Breath (IRE) 66*, 200, 242
Ahead of The Curve (FR) 185ᵖᵘ
Ah Littleluck (IRE) 6⁵, 232³
Ainsi Va La Vie (FR) 99⁴, 134⁶
Air Horse One (IRE) 19⁴, 82, 116², 174³, 220ᵖᵘ
Airlie Beach (IRE) 5³
Alary (FR) 11
Al Boum Photo (FR) 88ᶠ, 149², 186ᶠ, 212*, 248ʳᵒ
Alcala (FR) 3*, 260⁵
Al Dancer (FR) 231⁴
Alex de Larredya (FR) 268⁴
Alfie Spinner (IRE) 26ᵖᵘ, 105², 206⁵
Alisier d'Irlande (FR) 29², 69³, 136, 207³
Allblak des Places (FR) 266
Alletrix (IRE) 134², 209³
All Kings (IRE) 183ᵖᵘ
All Set To Go (IRE) 200, 238⁴
All The Answers 5ᵖᵘ
Allysson Monterg (FR) 186ᵖᵘ
Aloomomo (FR) 89ᵖᵘ
Alpha des Obeaux (FR) 102, 16⁴, 30⁴, 63⁴, 96⁶, 122⁴, 150⁶, 237ᶠ
Al Shahir (IRE) 175ᵖᵘ
Altior (IRE) 154*, 188³, 261*
Alti Plano (FR) 268ᵖᵘ
Alzammaar (USA) 244
American (FR) 53ᵖᵘ, 127², 202
American Tom (FR) 207⁶, 253
Ami Desbois (FR) 101ᵖᵘ, 145⁶
Amoola Gold (GER) 231
Amour de Nuit (IRE) 12²
Ancient Sands (IRE) 5ᶠ
Angels Antics 197ᵖᵘ
Anibale Fly (FR) 17⁵, 94*, 150ᵖᵘ, 202³, 237⁴
Another Stowaway (IRE) 230ᵖᵘ
Another Venture (IRE) 159³
Anseanachai Cliste (IRE) 60
Anteros (IRE) 35², 103⁶

Antony (FR) 20⁵
Any Second Now (IRE) 87², 137³, 184
Apache Stronghold (IRE) 94, 151ᶠ
Apparition (IRE) 32⁶
Apple's Jade (FR) 28*, 57*, 95*, 182³, 264³
Apple's Shakira (FR) 32*, 124*, 199⁴, 218³
Aqua Dude (IRE) 34ᵖᵘ
A Rated (IRE) 256ᶠ
Arbre de Vie (FR) 4⁶, 7, 41⁴, 88³, 151ᵖᵘ
Arcenfete (IRE) 162⁶
Arch My Boy 191
Arctic Gold (FR) 64ᶠ, 126, 198ᶠ
Arctic Skipper (IRE) 250
Arkwright (FR) 7², 10ᶠ, 49, 216⁶
Ar Mad (FR) 67³, 188ᵖᵘ, 261ᶠ
Ar Mest (FR) 259
Arthington 204
Arthur Mac (IRE) 231
Art Mauresque (FR) 20ᶠ, 112², 172⁴, 260²
Art of Payroll (GER) 240²
As de Mee (FR) 27⁴, 62ʷ, 172
As de Pique (IRE) 49ᵖᵘ
A Sizing Network (FR) 256⁴
Ask Nile (IRE) 211, 256ᶠ
Ask The Weatherman 105ᵖᵘ
Aso (FR) 14⁵
As You Were (FR) 187ᵖᵘ
Asthuria (FR) 255³
Athenean (IRE) 108
A Toi Phil (FR) 4⁴, 7⁵, 9*, 17⁴, 30², 70⁴, 161⁴, 215², 246³
Attest 242
Aubusson (FR) 198
Augusta Kate 57⁶, 95⁴, 122², 195, 214⁵, 264²
Aussie Reigns (IRE) 6
Auvergnat (FR) 10ᵇᵈ, 189⁴
Avenir d'Une Vie (FR) 87ᵘʳ
Aye Aye Charlie 31ᶠ, 128³, 185, 234⁴
Baby King (IRE) 222ᵖᵘ
Bacardys (FR) 195ᶠ, 254
Bachasson (FR) 202ᶠ
Back To The Thatch (IRE) 173ᶠ, 206ᵖᵘ
Bags Groove (IRE) 11, 113
Baie des Iles (FR) 157³, 237
Balbir du Mathan (FR) 253
Balkan du Pecos (FR) 267⁵
Balko des Flos (FR) 4⁴, 9², 30³, 96², 194⁴, 228⁴
Ball d'Arc (FR) 17³, 92ᵘʳ
Ballyalton (IRE) 34⁴, 74⁴, 196⁴, 229⁵
Ballyandy 101⁴, 125⁶
Ballybolley (IRE) 4, 8*, 23³, 112⁶, 196
Ballycamp (IRE) 130⁴

Ballycasey (IRE) 4, 9³, 136⁵, 161³, 215³, 246⁶
Ballycross 20ᵖᵘ, 111ᵖʷ
Ballycrystal (IRE) 72³, 241ᵖᵘ
Ballyegan Hero (IRE) 6*
Ballyhill (FR) 102*, 126, 184
Ballykan 20, 172²
Bally Longford (IRE) 126ᵖʷ
Ballymalin (IRE) 206³
Ballymountain Boy (IRE) 12⁶
Ballymoy (IRE) 259*
Ballyoisin (IRE) 17², 69ᶠ
Ballyoptic (IRE) 83⁴, 145*, 186⁴, 244²
Ballyward (IRE) 201⁴, 249⁴
Ballywood (FR) 171
Balnaslow (IRE) 2², 203, 221*
Balzac Turgot (FR) 148
Band of Blood (IRE) 198, 262
Bapaume (FR) 95³, 139, 214ᵖᵘ, 254⁵, 268²
Barel of Laughs (IRE) 203³
Bargy Lady (IRE) 266
Barney Dwan (IRE) 184⁴, 241ᶠ
Barra (FR) 187³, 214⁶, 264⁵
Barrakilla (IRE) 221⁴
Bastien (FR) 187
Battle Anthem (IRE) 50ᵖᵘ
Bay of Freedom (FR) 7³, 94
Baywing (IRE) 89⁵, 173*
Bear's Affair (IRE) 2⁶, 221²
Bearly Legal (IRE) 235
Beat That (IRE) 144
Beau Bay (FR) 229ᵘʳ
Beau Gosse (FR) 170³, 218
Bedrock 39⁴, 226³
Bee Crossing 208
Beer Goggles (IRE) 51*, 129⁵
Beeves (IRE) 189
Bel Ami de Sivola (FR) 138, 211*, 256³
Belamix Dor (FR) 189ᵖᵘ
Bellshill (IRE) 168⁵, 216⁵, 250*
Bells of Ailsworth (IRE) 235ᵖᵘ
Benatar (IRE) 79*, 192³
Benbens (FR) 33⁴, 68*, 107, 206ᵖᵘ, 244ᵖᵘ, 262
Ben Dundee (IRE) 58⁶, 140, 200
Benie des Dieux (FR) 182*, 264*
Benkei (IRE) 266³
Bentelimar (IRE) 4ᵘʳ, 7⁶, 34, 222*
Better Getalong (IRE) 39³, 233ᵖᵘ
Beware The Bear (IRE) 55*, 105ᵖᵘ, 180⁴, 244ᵖᵘ
Beyond The Clouds 242
Beyond The Law (IRE) 201ᵖᵘ, 245
Bid Adieu (IRE) 170ᵖᵘ
Bigbadjohn (IRE) 53, 81, 229ᵘʳ, 262ᵖᵘ
Bigmartre (FR) 192, 243*
Billy Bronco 206
Bipolaire (FR) 267ᶠ

Birch Hill (IRE) 176ur, 238
Bishops Road (IRE) 55², 105pu
Blackbow (IRE) 141*, 191⁵, 251²
Black Corton (FR) 52², 83*, 158², 186⁵, 227⁴
Black Mischief 12⁵
Black Op (IRE) 128², 185², 233*
Black Tulip 208
Blaklion 22², 62², 164², 237ᵇᵈ, 262ᵖᵘ
Blast of Koeman (IRE) 138⁴, 252²
Blazer (FR) 211⁴
Bless The Wings (IRE) 60ᵖᵘ, 189ᶠ, 216ᵖᵘ, 237³
Bleu Berry (FR) 140, 187*, 214⁴, 257³
Bleu Et Rouge (FR) 58, 82⁴, 155², 200, 254
Blow By Blow (IRE) 108⁶, 204*, 210⁴, 249
Boa Island (IRE) 244ᵖᵘ
Bob Ford (IRE) 206ᵖᵘ
Boherbuoy (IRE) 140
Boite (IRE) 163ᶠ, 193, 263⁵
Bonbon Au Miel (FR) 186ᶠ
Bonny Kate (IRE) 49³, 94ᵖᵘ, 177ᵖᵘ
Bon Papa (FR) 97³, 149, 211², 253³
Boric 55⁴, 173ᵖᵘ
Borice (FR) 267
Born Survivor (IRE) 205, 241
Bound For Glory (IRE) 221⁶
Bouvreuil (FR) 14, 205ᵇᵈ, 229ᵖᵘ
Brace Yourself (IRE) 141³
Brahma Bull (IRE) 185, 249⁶
Brain Power (IRE) 65ᵘʳ, 118ᶠ, 179², 217ᶠ
Braqueur d'Or (FR) 20³, 53⁴, 72², 241
Brave Dancing 190ᵖᵘ
Brave Eagle (IRE) 204
Brave Spartacus (IRE) 8ᵖᵘ
Bravissimo (FR) 256⁵
Brelade 40⁴, 200, 242⁵
Brelan d'As (FR) 204
Brianstorm (IRE) 233ᵖᵘ
Bright New Dawn (IRE) 205
Brillare Momento (IRE) 204
Bristol de Mai (FR) 22², 47*, 85⁶, 127³, 219²
Broughtons Admiral 124⁴, 238⁵
Buckhorn Timothy 105ᵖᵘ
Buildmeupbuttercup 223⁵
Bun Doran (IRE) 222⁵
Bunk Off Early (IRE) 266⁴
Burbank (IRE) 116³, 187
Burning Ambition (IRE) 203
Burren Life (IRE) 99³
Burrows Edge (FR) 259⁶
Burrows Saint (FR) 204, 258³
Burtons Well (IRE) 102
Buveur D'Air (FR) 54*, 84*, 142*, 181*
Buywise (IRE) 107*, 144, 237ᵘʳ
C'est Jersey (FR) 167ᵖᵘ, 187, 266²

Cadmium (FR) 253*
Caid du Berlais (FR) 203⁵
Caid du Lin (FR) 19, 66², 82, 116ᵖᵘ
Calett Mad (FR) 31⁵, 131⁴, 201ᵖᵘ
Calino d'Airy (FR) 40³, 217³
Calipto (FR) 18⁵
Call It Magic (IRE) 216
Call Me Lord (FR) 166³, 176², 263*
Call The Taxie (IRE) 41⁵, 94ᶠ, 123ᵖᵘ
Campeador (FR) 42ᶠ, 98³
Canelo (IRE) 175⁴
Cantlow (IRE) 189ᵖᵘ
Cap'n (IRE) 142³, 166⁵
Cap'tain Youm (FR) 247
Cap d'Aubois (FR) 6
Capitaine (FR) 65ᶠ
Cappacurry Zak (IRE) 157
Cap Soleil (FR) 197²
Captain Buck's (FR) 198
Captain Chaos (IRE) 145⁴, 227⁵
Captain Redbeard (IRE) 64⁶, 121², 237ᵘʳ
Carefully Selected (IRE) 191², 251³
Carlingford Lough (IRE) 13, 16ᵘʳ, 70⁵, 96ᵖᵘ, 237ᵖᵘ
Carntop 171
Carole's Destrier 53, 121ᵖᵘ, 262⁵
Carrig Cathal 266
Carrigeen Acebo (IRE) 60
Carter McKay 109³, 135³, 204
Cartwright 245⁵
Casa Tall 190
Casino Markets (IRE) 3, 240
Casse Tete (FR) 126, 180, 235
Castafiore (USA) 176
Castlegrace Paddy (IRE) 255⁵
Catamaran du Seuil (FR) 8
Cause of Causes (USA) 151, 189ᵖᵘ
Cave Top (IRE) 110⁵
Ceara Be (IRE) 223
Cedar Valley (IRE) 223
Cepage (FR) 45², 240⁴
Ch'tibello (FR) 76⁴, 120², 166², 181, 242
Champagne Harmony (IRE) 168ᵖᵘ, 216ᵖᵘ
Champagne West (IRE) 30⁵, 123ᵖᵘ, 252
Champayne Lady (IRE) 197³
Champers On Ice (IRE) 46⁵
Chanceanotherfive (IRE) 231
Charbel (IRE) 25⁴, 67⁴, 188ᶠ
Charlie Stout (IRE) 58, 140, 239³
Charli Parcs (FR) 82, 155, 181ᵖᵘ, 242⁴
Chase The Spud 105ᵖᵘ, 173ᵖᵘ, 237ᵖᵘ
Chateau Conti (FR) 58
Chef des Obeaux (IRE) 165*, 201ᵖᵘ, 230ᵖᵘ

Chesterfield (IRE) 38, 82, 84⁴, 200⁴, 242³
Chic Name (FR) 189⁵
Childrens List (IRE) 157ᵖᵘ, 237ᵖᵘ
Chisholm Trail (IRE) 152⁵
Chooseyourweapon (IRE) 110⁴
Chosen Path (FR) 233
Chris's Dream (IRE) 201
Chris Pea Green 18
Chti Balko (FR) 176
Cilaos Emery (FR) 57⁴, 98²
City Dreamer (IRE) 73²
Claimantakinforgan (FR) 78*, 178⁵, 242²
Clan des Obeaux (FR) 74², 219³
Clarcam (FR) 29⁴, 69⁴, 229⁶, 252
Classic Ben (IRE) 131
Clayton 19
Cliff House (IRE) 140
Cliffs of Dover 166⁷
Clondaw Cian (IRE) 81ᵖᵘ, 183ᵖᵘ, 235ᵖᵘ
Clondaw Warrior (IRE) 5
Close Shave 177ᵖᵘ, 256ᵖᵘ
Cloudy Dream (IRE) 14², 37², 63², 153², 194³, 228⁵
Cloudy Too (IRE) 107⁴
Clyne 120⁴, 174⁴, 220³
Cobra de Mai (FR) 243²
Coeur Blimey (FR) 78⁵, 113⁶, 154⁴
Coeur de Lion 25⁵, 204
Coeur Joyeux (IRE) 151⁶, 177ᵖᵘ, 211, 253²
Cogry 53ᵖᵘ, 111², 180, 244ᵖᵘ
Cold March (FR) 252
Colin's Sister 21*, 51⁴, 103³, 129³, 195⁴
Colms Dream (IRE) 151
Colreevy (IRE) 152³, 191
Column of Fire (IRE) 247²
Colwinston (IRE) 238
Commanche Red (IRE) 231⁶
Commander of Fleet (IRE) 247*
Coneygree 22ᵖᵘ, 53²
Coney Island (IRE) 160ᵖᵘ, 215ᵖᵘ
Connetable (FR) 35⁵, 193³, 232
Conrad Hastings (FR) 138, 184ᵖᵘ, 256ᵖᵘ
Coolanly (IRE) 185, 226⁵
Coole Cody (IRE) 236ᵖᵘ
Coole Hall (IRE) 165⁶
Coologue (IRE) 133ᵖᵘ
Coo Star Sivola (FR) 126⁴, 180*, 227ᵖᵘ
Coquin Mans (FR) 15², 214*, 257⁴, 268ᵖᵘ
Cordovan Brown (IRE) 152⁵
Cornborough 225
Cosmo's Moon (IRE) 48
Countister (FR) 197⁵
Count Meribel 75², 110⁶, 230ᵖᵘ
Court Artist (IRE) 266ᵖᵘ
Court Minstrel (IRE) 1⁴, 5ᶠ, 11*, 225

Cousin Pete 203[3]
Crackerdancer (IRE) 134[F]
Cracking Smart (FR) 77[2], 108[2]
Creation (FR) 48
Cresswell Breeze 68[3], 111[5]
Cristal Icon (IRE) 218[4]
Crooks Peak 191
Crossed My Mind (IRE) 66[3], 116[6]
Crosshue Boy (IRE) 211[3], 241[*]
Crosspark 111[4]
Crucial Role 201[pu]
Crystal Lad (IRE) 158[4]
Cue Card 22[F], 47[2], 160[2], 194[pu]
Cup Final (IRE) 3
Curraigflemens (IRE) 221[pu]
Cut The Mustard (FR) 197[6], 209
Cyrius Moriviere (FR) 225
Cyrname (FR) 90[*], 143[2], 169[*], 217[4]
Cyrus Darius 220[5]
Dadsintrouble (IRE) 193
Dalia Grandchamp (FR) 268[3]
Dali Mail (FR) 231
Damalisque (FR) 213
Dame de Compagnie (FR) 39[5]
Dame Rose (FR) 100[pu], 132[4], 178[pu]
Dancing Shadow (IRE) 68
Dandridge 45[6]
Danny Kirwan (IRE) 231
Dans Le Vent (FR) 100[5], 230[6]
Dark Flame (IRE) 20[4]
Darling du Large (FR) 223
Dashel Drasher 191
Dashing Perk 144, 175[pu]
Davids Charm (IRE) 58[*]
Dawn Shadow (IRE) 134[3], 197[F], 209[4]
Dawson City 262[6]
Days of Heaven (FR) 3, 34[pu], 240
Dazibao (FR) 231
Deal d'Estruval (FR) 140[2], 204
Deans Road (IRE) 4
Dear Sire (FR) 12[4], 238[2]
Death Duty (FR) 59[2], 87[F]
Deauville Dancer (IRE) 74, 229
Debece 232[4]
De Benno (IRE) 151, 253
De Bon Coeur (FR) 268[*]
Debuchet (FR) 147[6], 178, 258[F]
Dedigout (IRE) 55[pu], 89[pu]
Defi du Seuil (FR) 44[4], 139
Definitly Red (IRE) 22[3], 63[*], 127[2], 202[6], 219[ur]
Delegate 234[6]
Delire d'Estruval (FR) 204
Dell' Arca (IRE) 35[pu], 76, 193
Delta Work (FR) 48[3], 99[2], 148[3], 193[*], 249[2]
Delusionofgrandeur (IRE) 89[3], 237[pu]
Demi Sang (FR) 137[4], 184[pu], 252[pu]
De Name Escapes Me (IRE) 140[pu]
Dentley de Mee (FR) 113, 175[2]

Deor (IRE) 140
De Plotting Shed (IRE) 184[pu], 256[pu]
De Rasher Counter 128[F]
Design Matters 247[4]
Destin d'Ajonc (FR) 239
Destrier (FR) 171[*]
Devils Bride (IRE) 4[F], 14, 229, 252
Diablo de Rouhet (FR) 185
Diakali (FR) 220[6], 263[6]
Diamant Bleu (FR) 61[F]
Diamond Cauchois (FR) 122[3], 214[2], 254[6]
Diamond King (IRE) 187[pu], 266[pu]
Dicey O'Reilly (IRE) 135[5]
Dicosimo (FR) 44[5]
Didtheyleaveuoutto (IRE) 191
Diego du Charmil (FR) 156[2], 234[*], 261[5]
Diese des Bieffes (FR) 113[5], 204[5]
Dinaria des Obeaux (FR) 59[4], 97[6]
Dingo Dollar (FR) 241[2]
Dino Velvet (FR) 113
Discorama (FR) 204[2], 249[5]
Disko (FR) 17[*]
Dissavril (FR) 223
Distime (IRE) 221
Distingo (FR) 226[pu]
Divin Bere (FR) 82, 155, 200[pu]
Djakadam (FR) 70[2], 96[pu], 150[3], 202[5], 250[2], 267
Django Django (FR) 259
Doc Penfro 191
Doctor Phoenix (IRE) 114[*], 207[2], 215[F], 246[5]
Doesyourdogbite (IRE) 11, 144[5]
Doing Fine (IRE) 68[4], 244[4]
Doitforthevillage (IRE) 205[6], 222[4]
Dolos (FR) 19, 79[3], 205
Domesday Book (USA) 262[pu]
Don't Touch It (IRE) 114[6], 138[pu], 205[pu]
Donna's Diamond (IRE) 163[*], 195
Dont Tell No One (IRE) 49[2]
Don Vincenzo (IRE) 49[pu]
Dorking Boy 251
Dortmund Park (FR) 135[4], 201, 258[*]
Double Ross (IRE) 53[pu], 107, 198[4], 237[pu]
Double Shuffle (FR) 43[2], 85[2], 219, 260[4]
Double Treasure 34
Dounikos (FR) 88[3], 149[4], 186[pu], 216[pu], 248[pu]
Douvan (FR) 188[2], 246[2]
Draconien (FR) 213[2], 245[*]
Draycott Place (IRE) 29[6]
Dr Des (IRE) 78[2], 174
Dream Berry (FR) 204, 266[6]
Dream Bolt (FR) 126[pu]
Dromnea (IRE) 10[6], 94[F], 151

Drumcliff (IRE) 11, 156[4], 196[pu]
Drumlee Sunset (FR) 126
Duca de Thaix (FR) 200, 239
Duc des Genievres (FR) 108[3], 147[2], 185[3], 210[5], 258[6]
Duel At Dawn (IRE) 183[pu]
Duhallow Gesture (IRE) 223[3]
Dunvegan (FR) 141[6]
Dusky Legend 132[3], 187[F]
Dynamite Dollars (FR) 61[5]
Dysios (IRE) 114[3], 138[5]
Eamon An Cnoic (IRE) 180, 225[pu]
Early Doors (FR) 56[2], 147, 204[3], 266
Earthmoves (FR) 3
East Indies 19
Eastlake (IRE) 205, 229
Eaton Hill (IRE) 225[2]
Eddies Miracle (IRE) 221[ur]
Edward d'Argent (FR) 267[3]
Edwulf 96[pu], 150[4], 202, 250
Eh Georges (FR) 32[4]
Eight Till Late (IRE) 253[pu]
Elegant Escape (IRE) 52[*], 83[2], 186[3], 227[3]
Elgin 19[*], 38[*], 82[6], 166[*], 181[5]
Elixir de Nutz (FR) 124[6]
Ellie Mac (IRE) 197
El Terremoto (FR) 113
Elusive Ivy (IRE) 114
Embole (FR) 190
Emerging Force (IRE) 20
Emperor's Choice (IRE) 105[F]
Empire Burleque (IRE) 141
Enjoy Responsibly (IRE) 240
Enniscoffey Oscar (IRE) 131[*], 207
Enola Gay (FR) 259
Equus Amadeus (IRE) 12[pu], 259[3]
Equus Secretus (IRE) 75[3]
Eragon de Chanay (FR) 32[3], 73[4], 190
Erick Le Rouge (FR) 124[5]
Espoir d'Allen (FR) 86[*], 146[4]
Esprit de Somoza (FR) 190
Et Moi Alors (FR) 218[6]
Eureu du Boulay (FR) 190[pu]
Euxton Lane (IRE) 233
Evening Hush (IRE) 66, 82[F]
Exitas (IRE) 18[*], 66
Ex Patriot (IRE) 129
Fabulous Saga (FR) 99[*], 135, 201
Fact of The Matter (IRE) 26[pu], 244
Fagan 244[pu]
Fairmount 128[pu]
Famous Milly (IRE) 104[F]
Farclas (FR) 86[2], 146[2], 199[*], 265[5]
Faugheen (IRE) 42[*], 98[pu], 139[2], 181[6], 254[F]
Federici 62[4], 133[5], 189[pu]
Felix Desjy (FR) 191[6], 251[5]
Fergall (IRE) 1[F], 5, 82
Festive Affair (IRE) 18
Fidux (FR) 66[4], 176
Final Choice 238

974

Final Nudge (IRE) 26², 105³, 198, 237ᶠ
Fine Rightly (IRE) 29³, 121⁵, 215⁴
Fine Theatre (IRE) 123, 177⁴, 216ᵇᵈ
Fingeronthesswitch (IRE) 46⁶
Finian's Oscar (IRE) 65³, 79², 129ᵖᵘ, 192⁵, 217², 248ᶜᵒ
Firebird Flyer (IRE) 105ᶠ
First Assignment (IRE) 175³
First Flow (IRE) 119ˣ, 178ᵖᵘ
Fiveaftermidnight (IRE) 152
Fixe Le Kap (FR) 187, 232
Flashing Glance 242ᵖᵘ
Flawless Escape 148³, 204
Flaxen Flare (IRE) 28³, 94, 123ᵖᵘ, 204
Flemcara (IRE) 144, 187
Fletchers Flyer (IRE) 26ᵖᵘ, 68
Flying Angel (IRE) 43⁴, 63³, 133, 229
Flying Eagle (IRE) 229ᵘʳ
Flying Tiger (IRE) 25³, 54³, 166⁴, 200, 242
Folsom Blue (IRE) 144⁴, 157³, 216⁴
Footpad (FR) 87*, 137*, 179*, 255*
Forest Bihan (FR) 91³
Forest des Aigles (FR) 121ᵖᵘ
Forever Gold (IRE) 60², 94ᵘʳ, 157ᵖᵘ, 216³
Forge Meadow (IRE) 15⁵, 162⁵, 214ᵖᵘ, 264ᵖᵘ
For Good Measure (IRE) 169³
Fortunate George (IRE) 81, 117³, 232
Forza Milan (IRE) 193ᵖᵘ
Fou Et Sage (FR) 19
Fountains Windfall 21⁵, 52ᶠ, 83ᶠ
Fourth Act (IRE) 20, 144
Fox Appeal (IRE) 26⁵, 107ᶠ
Fox Norton (FR) 37*, 67², 85ᵖᵘ
Foxrock (IRE) 203ᵖᵘ
Foxtail Hill (IRE) 34, 74⁶, 205
Foxy Jacks (IRE) 247
Friday Night Light (FR) 176ᵖᵘ, 259
Frodon (FR) 27², 43³, 81², 126⁵, 160³, 194⁵, 240
Full Cry (IRE) 94
Full Irish (IRE) 125⁵, 186ᵖᵘ
Gallery Exhibition (IRE) 221
Galop Marin (IRE) 268⁵
Game On (IRE) 175
Gardefort (FR) 23⁴
Garde La Victoire (FR) 205
Gas Line Boy (IRE) 64*, 107³, 237
Gassin Golf 176
Gayebury 21ᵖᵘ, 46
Geluroni (FR) 267ᵖᵘ
General Consensus 249
General Principle (IRE) 49, 94, 151⁴, 216*
Germany Calling (IRE) 8ᵖᵘ
Getabird (IRE) 109*, 178, 213³, 245, 258ᵖᵘ

Getaway John (IRE) 251
Getaway Katie Mai (IRE) 152², 223*
Get On The Yager 89*, 206, 244ᵖᵘ
Giant Spirit (USA) 148
Gino Trail (IRE) 205², 222³
Glencairn View (IRE) 177³, 244ᵖᵘ
Glenloe (IRE) 193²
Global Citizen (IRE) 171*, 226⁶
Global Stage 75⁴, 165ᵖᵘ
Glocca Mora 247⁶
Go Conquer (IRE) 20*, 81ᶠ, 172⁵, 240
God's Own (IRE) 14⁶, 112³, 188³, 261³
Going Gold (IRE) 259
Golan Fortune (IRE) 144², 165³, 232
Golden Jeffrey (SWI) 178
Gold Present (IRE) 81*, 180ᵖᵘ, 244ᵖᵘ
Good Man Pat (IRE) 230ᵖᵘ
Good Thyne Tara 48⁵
Goodtoknow 62ᵖᵘ, 111ᵖᵘ
Goulane Chosen (IRE) 252ᶠ
Goulane Davina (IRE) 151
Gowiththeflow (IRE) 185
Graceful Legend 115³, 187
Gracemount (IRE) 134
Grand Partner (IRE) 140³, 225⁵
Grand Sancy (FR) 170⁴, 190ᵖᵘ
Grand Vision (IRE) 203⁶, 221ᶠ
Gran Geste (FR) 239
Grapevine (IRE) 259
Great Field (FR) 207*
Great Fighter 1³
Greensalt (IRE) 221³
Greybougg 229ᵖᵘ
Grey Waters (IRE) 86⁴, 146³
Guitar Pete (IRE) 8², 34, 74*, 117ᵘʳ, 196⁶
Gumball (FR) 32², 199ᵖᵘ, 218²
Gustave Mahler (IRE) 12ᵖᵘ
Gwencily Berbas (FR) 151ᵘʳ
Hainan (FR) 121³, 173⁴, 206ᵖᵘ
Half The Odds (IRE) 48⁴, 77⁴
Hammersly Lake (FR) 235ᵖᵘ
Harambe 231³
Hardline (FR) 56³, 93³, 213³, 245
Harmonise 170⁵
Havana Beat (IRE) 238*
Haymount (IRE) 4ᵖᵘ
Hazy Shadow (IRE) 152
Heist (IRE) 235
Hell's Kitchen 151ᵖᵘ
Henllan Harri (IRE) 26ᵖᵘ
Henri Parry Morgan 244ᵖᵘ
Henryville 3
He Rock's (IRE) 49, 60³
Heron Heights (IRE) 4, 151
Hidden Cyclone (IRE) 6
High Bridge 19³, 155
High Expectations (FR) 238ᵖᵘ
Highland Fling (IRE) 58, 140
Highland Hunter (IRE) 231

Highland Lodge (IRE) 62³, 121ᵖᵘ
High School Days (USA) 109⁴, 197ᵖᵘ, 209
High Secret (IRE) 1
Highway One O One (IRE) 176, 259²
Hitherjacques Lady (IRE) 115ᵖᵘ
Hogan's Height (IRE) 227⁶
Holly Bush Henry (IRE) 1, 159⁵, 235⁶
Houblon des Obeaux (FR) 68⁶, 107⁶, 173ᵖᵘ, 237ᶠ, 262
Housesofparliament (IRE) 58
Humphrey Bogart (IRE) 171
Hunters Call (IRE) 82*
Huntsman Son (IRE) 174
Hurricane Ben (IRE) 138ᵖᵘ, 253ᵇᵈ
Hurricane Darwin (IRE) 49, 189ᵖᵘ
I'dliketheoption (IRE) 3
I'm A Game Changer (IRE) 242
Ibis du Rheu (FR) 184⁵, 235⁵
Ibsen (IRE) 46
Icantsay (IRE) 49, 60ᵖᵘ
Ice Cold Soul (IRE) 140
Icing On The Cake (IRE) 81
Identity Thief (IRE) 139⁶, 162², 181⁴, 236², 254⁴
If You Say Run (IRE) 208ᵖᵘ
I Just Know (IRE) 237ᶠ
Imjoeking (IRE) 64⁵
Impact Factor (IRE) 226
Impulsive Star (IRE) 183⁴
Indian Castle (IRE) 111
Indian Hawk (IRE) 131, 175ᵖᵘ
Indian Monsoon (IRE) 140
Indian Stream 182⁴
Indian Temple (IRE) 229
Indy Five (IRE) 244ᵖᵘ
Inis Meain (USA) 88⁴
Invitation Only (IRE) 149³, 192ᵖᵘ, 212³, 248ᵘʳ
Irish Roe (IRE) 132², 155ᵖᵘ, 242⁶
Irving 54²
I Shot The Sheriff (IRE) 113ᵖᵘ
Isleofhopendreams 123ᵖᵘ, 157², 216²
It's A Gimme (IRE) 3
Its'afreebee (IRE) 8ᵖᵘ
Ivan Grozny (FR) 5ᵇᵈ
Ivanovich Gorbatov (IRE) 38, 58, 140, 200, 225ᵖᵘ
Izzo (GER) 220
Jabulani (FR) 116, 175ᵖᵘ
Jaisalmer (IRE) 259
Jaleo (GER) 232
Jameson 184⁶, 240⁵
Jaxlight 223
Jaytrack Parkhomes 191
Jeannot de Nonant (FR) 187, 232
Jenkins (IRE) 38, 66, 116*, 155, 200ᵖᵘ, 225
Jer's Girl (IRE) 28², 182⁵, 264
Jester Jet 225*

975

Je Suis Charlie 73[3]
Jet Set (IRE) 208
Jetstream Jack (IRE) 216[pu], 252[5]
Jett (IRE) 87[3], 151
Jetz (IRE) 48[2], 77[3], 108[4], 135[2], 210[2], 249
Jezki (IRE) 42[2], 95[5], 139[4], 214[pu], 254
Jimmy Two Times (IRE) 6
Joe Farrell (IRE) 244[*]
Joey Sasa (IRE) 5[4], 266
John Constable (IRE) 1[*], 76[6], 142[2], 181
Josies Orders (IRE) 189[6]
Josses Hill (IRE) 43[6], 71[2], 112[5], 172[pu]
Jubilympics 208[3]
Junction Fourteen (IRE) 8[pu], 20
Jury Duty (IRE) 41[*], 97[2], 183[ur], 248[3]
Just A Thought (IRE) 208[4]
Just Get Cracking (IRE) 253[6]
Just Janice (IRE) 134
Just Your Type (IRE) 165[4]
Kalahari Queen 208[2]
Kalashnikov (IRE) 106[2], 155[*], 178[2]
Kaloci (IRE) 208
Kalondra (IRE) 24[2], 143[4], 240[3]
Kansas City Chief (IRE) 193
Karalee (FR) 140[pu], 239[5], 266
Kasperenko 170[6]
Kateson 231[2]
Katgary (FR) 54[*]
Kauto Riko (FR) 234[5]
Kayf Adventure 184
Kayf Grace 155, 182[F]
Keeper Hill (IRE) 72[*], 183[F], 241[pu]
Kelpies Myth 259
Kemboy (FR) 192[4], 216[F], 224[*], 256[*]
Kerrkenny Gold (IRE) 247
Khudha (IRE) 178
Kilbricken Storm (IRE) 75[*], 100[3], 201[*], 249[3]
Kilcarry Bridge (IRE) 7[pu], 13[2], 114[2], 138, 207[4], 216[F]
Kilcrea Vale (IRE) 117[2], 229[4]
Kildisart (IRE) 233
Kilfenora (IRE) 138[pu]
Killahara Castle (IRE) 134
Killaro Boy (IRE) 216[bd]
Killultagh Vic (IRE) 150[F], 202[pu], 250[3], 268[pu]
King's Odyssey (IRE) 74[3], 126[3], 196[2]
King's Socks (FR) 196[5], 222[pu]
King Leon (IRE) 7[pu], 10[bd]
King of Fashion (IRE) 144[pu]
Kk Lexion (IRE) 35
Knight Destroyer (IRE) 190[F]
Knight In Dubai (IRE) 110[3], 185
Knight of Noir (IRE) 180[pu], 232
Knockanrawley (IRE) 121[pu]
Knockgraffon (IRE) 240[6]
Knocknanuss (IRE) 155[pu]

Know The Score (IRE) 191
Koshari (FR) 149[pu], 256[F]
Kostaquarta (IRE) 90[pu]
Krackatoa King 111, 206[6]
Kris Spin (IRE) 144
Kuragina (IRE) 223
Kylecrue (IRE) 7[pu], 9[5], 151[pu]
Kylemore Lough 34[pu], 118[3], 215[pu]
L'Ami Serge (IRE) 44[2], 80[2], 133[3], 195, 220[*], 268
La Bague Au Roi (FR) 115[*], 182, 254
Label des Obeaux (FR) 27[3], 53[pu], 133[6], 172, 244[6]
Lackaneen Leader (IRE) 209[2], 249[pu]
Lady Buttons 234[4]
Lady Ischia (IRE) 152
Lady of Lamanver 208[pu]
Lagostovegas (IRE) 6[3], 162[3], 200[5]
Lake Takapuna (IRE) 34[pu], 151[pu], 253
Lalor (GER) 155, 226[*]
Landin (GER) 225[pu]
Landofhopeandglory (IRE) 151[ur], 239
Last Goodbye (IRE) 49, 151[*], 196
Laurina (FR) 134[*], 197[*], 209[*]
Laverteen (FR) 58
Lean And Keen (IRE) 253[F]
Le Breuil (FR) 187
Le Patriote (FR) 113, 176[pu]
Le Prezien (FR) 34[3], 74, 205[*], 228[pu]
Le Richebourg (FR) 56[6], 93[2], 147, 200
Le Rocher (FR) 11, 46, 184[bd]
Les Arceaux (IRE) 218[pu]
Let's Dance (FR) 122[5], 195[F], 214[3], 264[4]
Lieutenant Colonel 122[pu], 214[pu], 254[pu]
Lilbitluso (IRE) 221[F]
Lil Rockerfeller (USA) 21[3], 44[4], 80[6], 174[2], 195, 236[pu], 263[2]
Limited Reserve (IRE) 19[2]
Linenhall (IRE) 131[5]
Lisdoonvarna Lad (IRE) 119[3]
Lisp (IRE) 190[F]
Lite Duties (IRE) 148
Little Pop 18[pu]
Livelovelaugh (IRE) 184[F]
Lochnell (IRE) 173[pu]
Lofgren 3[5], 183[pu]
London Prize 1, 25[*], 38[F]
Long House Hall (IRE) 133[4]
Looking Well (IRE) 244[pu]
Look My Way 124[2], 190
Loose Chips 107[5], 172
Lord Scoundrel (IRE) 4, 7[pu], 168[ur], 216[pu], 252
Lord Windermere (IRE) 62[F], 237[ur]
Lostintranslation (IRE) 119[6], 178, 233[2]
Lostnfound 208[pu]

Lough Derg Spirit (IRE) 25[2], 155[6], 204[6]
Louis' Vac Pouch (IRE) 11[6], 193, 232
Louse Talk (IRE) 230[pu]
Lovenormoney (IRE) 193
Low Sun 140, 239[*], 266[5]
Madurai (GER) 6
Maebh (IRE) 223
Maggio (FR) 237[pu]
Magic Dancer 82
Magic of Light (IRE) 151
Makitorix (FR) 56[pu], 93[4], 109[6], 140[4]
Mala Beach (IRE) 49[*], 150[F]
Malaya (FR) 170[2], 218
Mall Dini (IRE) 60[4], 198[2], 216[pu]
Mallowney (IRE) 114[5], 138
Man From Mars 113
Man of Plenty 66[5], 82[5], 116[4], 144, 176[5]
Man of Steel (IRE) 2[pu]
Maquisard (FR) 238[F]
Maria's Benefit (IRE) 132[*], 197[4]
Marinero (IRE) 4[ur], 198[pu]
Markov (IRE) 184[pu]
Marley Firth (IRE) 61[4]
Marracudja (FR) 18[3]
Massini's Trap (IRE) 148, 225
Master Dee (IRE) 8[3], 23[2], 172[*]
Mastermind (IRE) 86[6], 190
Master of Irony (IRE) 176[pu]
Master Workman (IRE) 2
Matorico (IRE) 23[pu]
Max Dynamite (FR) 5, 187, 266[pu]
Max Ward (IRE) 18[6]
Mcgowan's Pass 119[5]
Meep Meep (IRE) 223[*]
Meldrum Lad (IRE) 20
Melodic Rendezvous 25
Melon 15[*], 76[3], 139[5], 181[2], 257[F]
Melrose Boy (FR) 144[3], 204
Mengli Khan (IRE) 56[*], 93[ro], 109[2], 178[3], 245[3]
Mercenaire (FR) 104[3], 190[pu]
Mercian Prince (IRE) 64, 196
Mercy Mercy Me 191, 231
Meri Devie (FR) 58[2], 200, 239[6], 266[*]
Mia's Storm (IRE) 83[F], 243[F]
Michael's Mount 171[3], 238
Mick Jazz (FR) 15[3], 57[5], 98[*], 139[3], 181[3]
Mick The Jiver 157[5], 177
Midnight Chill 175[pu]
Midnight Jazz 182[6]
Midnight Maestro 19[6]
Midnightreferendum 223[2]
Midnight Shadow 119[2], 226, 242[*]
Midnight Shot 3[6], 229[pu]
Midnight Stroll 140
Midnight Tour 182[2], 264[6]
Midnight Tune 115[4], 208
Might Bite (IRE) 27[*], 85[*], 202[2], 219[*]

Milansbar (IRE) 105ur, 111*, 173⁵, 206², 237⁵
Milborough (IRE) 173ᵖᵘ
Miles To Memphis (IRE) 140⁶
Millanisi Boy 198ᵖᵘ
Millicent Silver 173ᵘʳ
Milord Thomas (FR) 267⁴
Milrow (IRE) 11
Min (FR) 92², 136*, 188², 228², 246⁴
Mind's Eye (IRE) 140, 185, 226⁴
Minella Awards (IRE) 46ᵖᵘ
Minella Beau (IRE) 266
Minella Daddy (IRE) 117⁴, 159², 180, 262ᵖᵘ
Minella Encore (IRE) 141⁴
Minella Fair (IRE) 99⁵
Minella For Value (IRE) 203ᵖᵘ
Minella On Line (IRE) 133, 229ᵘʳ
Minella Rocco (IRE) 13⁴, 33ᵖᵘ, 96⁴, 150ᶠ
Mine Now (IRE) 6², 193
Minnie Dahill (IRE) 86
Minnies Secret (IRE) 134⁵
Mirsaale 54⁵
Mischievious Max (IRE) 187
Missed Approach (IRE) 21ᵖᵘ, 53⁶, 111³, 198, 262ᵖᵘ
Mister Fisher (IRE) 231
Misterton 38², 155
Mister Whitaker (IRE) 125*, 184*
Mitchouka (FR) 86³, 190ᵖᵘ, 265⁴
Modus 24*, 192, 217⁵
Mohaayed 38, 84³, 200*
Momella (IRE) 31², 233³
Monalee (IRE) 97ᶠ, 149², 186², 248ᶠ
Monbeg Charmer (IRE) 172ᵖᵘ
Monbeg Notorious (IRE) 123*, 167*, 216, 248²
Monksland (IRE) 28⁴
Mon Parrain (FR) 221ᵖᵘ
Montalbano 212, 256
Mont des Avaloirs (FR) 106³, 171⁴, 259⁴
Monty's Award (IRE) 116ᵖᵘ
Moon Racer (IRE) 155, 200
More of That (IRE) 16⁶
Morga (IRE) 5⁵
Morgan (IRE) 56⁴, 239
Mossback (IRE) 167², 183ᶠ
Motown Girl (IRE) 152
Moulin A Vent 97⁵, 167³, 216ᵘ, 224⁵
Mount Hanover 210ᵖᵘ
Mount Mews (IRE) 158³, 187
Movewiththetimes (IRE) 196ᵖᵘ
Moyross 108, 135⁶
Mr Adjudicator 146*, 199², 265²
Mr Antolini (IRE) 176*
Mr Big Shot (IRE) 204, 232*
Mr Fiftyone (IRE) 253⁴
Mr Mercurial (IRE) 2ᵖᵘ
Mr Mix (FR) 26ᵖᵘ, 241
Mr One More (IRE) 78⁶

Mr Showtime (IRE) 6⁴
Mr Whipped (IRE) 110*, 201ᵖᵘ
Msassa (FR) 265⁴
Ms Parfois (IRE) 158², 183², 227²
Mulcahys Hill (IRE) 100², 128⁴, 201ᵖᵘ
Multiculture (IRE) 1
Mustmeetalady (IRE) 133
Mysteree (IRE) 105ᵖᵘ, 164³
Mystifiable 64⁴, 229
My Tent Or Yours (IRE) 76*, 220⁴
Native River (IRE) 153*, 202*
Nearly Nama'd (IRE) 138
Nessun Dorma (IRE) 239ᶠ
Nestor Park (FR) 191
Net d'Ecosse (FR) 10⁵
Never Complain (IRE) 221
Neverushacon (IRE) 17⁶
Newsworthy (IRE) 229ᵘʳ, 252ᵖᵘ
Newton Geronimo 3⁶
Next Destination (IRE) 77*, 108*, 185³, 249*
Nichols Canyon 57², 95ᶠ
Nietzsche 38⁶, 82, 155
Night of Sin (FR) 116
Noche de Reyes (FR) 222
No Comment 143³, 183⁶
No Duffer 107ᵖᵘ
No Hassle Hoff (IRE) 46⁴, 163³, 204, 232
No No Mac (IRE) 64ᶠ
Normal Norman 231ᵖᵘ
Norman The Red 174⁶
North Hill Harvey 36³, 65², 156³, 205ᶠ
Notarfbad (IRE) 229ᵖᵘ
Notre Ami (IRE) 175ᵖᵘ, 259
Now McGinty (IRE) 232²
Nube Negra (SPA) 190³, 218⁵
Nuits Premier Cru (FR) 35⁴
O'Faolains Boy (IRE) 105ᵖᵘ
Octagon 176ᵖᵘ
Off You Go (IRE) 140*
Oistrakh Le Noir (FR) 259
Ok Corral (IRE) 201², 230⁵
Okotoks (IRE) 144
Oldgrangewood 14³, 196ᵖᵘ, 235⁴
Old Guard 11, 38³, 76⁵, 103⁴, 174*, 236, 263⁴
On Fiddlers Green (IRE) 10, 94
On The Blind Side (IRE) 31*, 61*, 233⁶
On The Fringe (IRE) 203, 221⁵
On The Go (IRE) 267*
On The Go Again (IRE) 140, 162⁵
On The Road (IRE) 105ᵘʳ, 111ᵖᵘ
On Tour (IRE) 23*, 81, 235²
O O Seven (IRE) 81⁴, 126⁵, 180, 229ᵖᵘ, 260³
Optimus Prime (FR) 1², 255²
Ordinary World (IRE) 92³, 136⁴, 185⁵, 246
Orion d'Aubrelle (FR) 239
Or Jaune de Somoza (FR) 213⁵

Ornua (IRE) 5ᵖᵘ, 226
Oscar Knight (IRE) 94, 148², 216ᵇᵈ, 252³
Oscar Rose (IRE) 208⁶
Our Dougal (IRE) 211, 253ᵘʳ
Our Duke (IRE) 16, 150⁴, 161*, 202ᵖᵘ
Our Kaempfer (IRE) 55ᵖᵘ
Outlander (IRE) 13⁶, 16*, 47³, 96³, 150², 202ᵖᵘ, 216ᵖᵘ, 250
Out Sam 94, 123⁶, 157ᵖᵘ
Overtown Express (IRE) 222
Oxford Blu 190ᵖᵘ
Oxwich Bay (IRE) 116ᶠ, 175ᵖᵘ
Ozzie The Oscar (IRE) 36³
Pacha du Polder (FR) 203*
Pacific de Baune (FR) 128
Padleyourowncanoe (IRE) 190⁴, 218
Pairofbrowneyes (IRE) 177*, 216ᶠ
Paisley Park (IRE) 110², 201
Pallasator 210*, 258⁵
Paloma Blue (IRE) 147³, 178⁴, 245
Paper Lantern (IRE) 49ᵖᵘ, 235³
Paper Promise (IRE) 223
Patricks Park (IRE) 138*, 211⁵, 252*
Peace And Co (FR) 1
Peace News (GER) 140
Peak To Peak (IRE) 11³
Pearl Royale (IRE) 145ᶠ
Pearl Swan (FR) 235, 244
Pendra (IRE) 198, 237ᵖᵘ
Penhill 195*, 254²
Peregrine Run (IRE) 243ᵘʳ
Perfect Candidate (IRE) 33*, 107, 127⁵, 237ᶠ
Perfect Impulse (FR) 267²
Peruvien Bleu (FR) 19
Pete The Feat (IRE) 107²
Petit Mouchoir (FR) 137², 179³, 234², 255*
Petrou (IRE) 169⁴, 241⁴
Petticoat Tails 208⁵
Phil's Magic (IRE) 10³, 94⁶, 148⁶
Phil The Flyer (IRE) 6
Pickamix 241⁵
Pietralunga (FR) 197, 209
Pilgrims Bay (IRE) 26⁶, 53⁵
Piri Massini (IRE) 165⁵
Piton Pete (IRE) 259
Plaisir d'Amour (FR) 34ᵖᵘ
Play The Ace (IRE) 8⁴
Play The Game (IRE) 239
Pleasant Company (IRE) 94, 123ᵖᵘ, 237²
Plinth (IRE) 5
Plumeur (FR) 268ᵖᵘ
Plus Jamais (FR) 206ᵖᵘ
Pobbles Bay (IRE) 23, 105
Poetic Rhythm (IRE) 12*, 31³, 100*, 201
Point of Principle (IRE) 230
Poker School (IRE) 3⁴, 8⁵
Polidam (FR) 94, 151⁵, 229, 252⁴
Poli Roi (FR) 77⁵

977

Politologue (FR) 67*, 91*, 154², 188⁴, 228*
Poormans Hill (IRE) 49⁴, 60⁵, 177⁶
Pop Art du Berlais (FR) 268
Poppy Kay 155, 204ᵖᵘ
Portrait King (IRE) 62⁵, 173³
Portrush Ted (IRE) 231*
Posh Trish (IRE) 223
Potters Legend 53, 126⁶
Potters Point (IRE) 7*, 49, 94⁴
Pougne Bobbi (FR) 196
Powersbomb (IRE) 253ᶠ
Prairie Town (IRE) 19
Pravalaguna (FR) 182ᵖᵘ, 239⁴
Premier Bond 33ᵖᵘ
Premier Portrait (IRE) 203ᵖᵘ
Presenting Mahler (IRE) 138
Presenting Percy 41³, 60*, 122*, 161², 186*
Present Man (IRE) 26*, 53, 262³
Pressurize (IRE) 126ᵖᵘ, 198
Prime Venture (IRE) 144, 193, 232²
Prince Charmin' (IRE) 6ᶠ
Prince Garyantle (IRE) 266
Princess Roxy 223
Progress Drive (IRE) 241
Project Bluebook (FR) 5⁶, 38, 155, 225⁶
Protek des Flos (FR) 193
Ptit Zig (FR) 21⁴, 71³, 121ᵖᵘ
Punch Nantais (FR) 267ᵘʳ
Pylonthepressure (IRE) 183⁵, 256ᵖᵘ
Pym (IRE) 231
Qualando (FR) 103ᵖᵘ
Quick Jack (IRE) 140ᵖᵘ
Quick Pick (IRE) 175
Quite By Chance 18², 45³, 102⁵, 196, 240
Racing Europe (IRE) 244ᵖᵘ
Racing Pulse (IRE) 148
Ramonex (GER) 241
Ramses de Teillee (FR) 180, 240
Rapid Escape (IRE) 141⁵, 251⁴
Rather Be (IRE) 184²
Rathlin Rose (IRE) 64ᵖᵘ, 105⁶, 229ᶠ, 262ᵖᵘ
Rathpatrick (IRE) 148
Rathvinden (IRE) 59², 97ᵇᵈ, 149ᵘʳ, 183*, 248⁴
Rayvin Black 103
Raz de Maree (FR) 10ᶠ, 105*, 237
Real Steel (FR) 93ᶠ, 147⁵, 201, 210ᵖᵘ, 258⁴
Realt Mor (IRE) 30⁴
Rebel Rebellion (IRE) 2⁴
Red Devil Lads (IRE) 157
Redhotfillypeppers (IRE) 209
Redicean 170*, 199⁶
Red Indian 113³, 187⁶, 232
Red Jack (IRE) 56⁵
Red River (IRE) 61³
Red Tornado (FR) 1
Regal Encore (IRE) 20, 53³, 81ᵖᵘ, 159*, 262ᵖᵘ

Regal Flow 206*, 244
Reigning Supreme (IRE) 183ᵖᵘ
Relegate (IRE) 152*, 191*, 251
Relentless Dreamer (IRE) 26ᵖᵘ, 172⁶, 264²
Remiluc (FR) 155⁵, 200²
Rene's Girl (IRE) 217²
Renneti (FR) 214ᵖʳ
Report To Base (IRE) 184ᶠ
Rhinestone (IRE) 141², 191
Riders Onthe Storm (IRE) 210⁶
River Frost 11⁵, 113ᵖᵘ, 187
River Wylde (IRE) 36²
Road To Respect (IRE) 13*, 16², 96*, 202⁴, 250³
Road To Riches (IRE) 4, 7, 94, 157ᵖᵘ, 237⁵
Robbin'hannon (IRE) 46
Robin des Mana (IRE) 211ᵖᵘ, 253ᵖᵘ
Robin of Locksley (IRE) 183ᴿ
Robinshill (IRE) 117ᵖᵘ, 179⁵, 222ᵖᵘ
Robin Waters (FR) 201⁶
Rock Gone (IRE) 20²
Rocklander (IRE) 72ᵘʳ, 184³, 235ᶠ
Rock On Fruity (IRE) 10ᵖʳ
Rock On Rocky 240ᵖᵘ
Rockpoint 171
Rock The Kasbah (IRE) 121ᵖᵘ, 262²
Rock The World (IRE) 4, 114⁴, 205
Rocky's Treasure (IRE) 35³
Rococo Style 223
Rogue Angel (IRE) 10, 49ᵖᵘ, 62ᵖᵘ, 177⁵, 229ᵖᵘ
Roi Mage (FR) 267ᵇᵈ
Roksana (FR) 208*, 230²
Rolling Maul (IRE) 35
Romain de Senam (FR) 34⁵, 74⁵, 196
Rons Dream 241ᵇᵈ
Rouergate (FR) 197
Rouge Et Blanc (FR) 221ᵖᵘ
Routes Choice (IRE) 177ᵖᵘ
Royal Regatta (IRE) 14ᵖᵘ, 43
Royal Vacation (FR) 53ᵖᵘ, 103⁵, 187, 262ᵖᵘ
Run To Milan (IRE) 175ᵖᵘ
Russe Blanc (FR) 111ᵖᵘ, 206ᵘʳ
Saddlers Encore (IRE) 203ᶠ
Sadler's Risk (IRE) 4, 260ᵖᵘ
Saglawy (FR) 265³
Saint Are (FR) 129ᵖᵘ, 189ᵖᵘ, 237ᵇᵈ
Saint Calvados (FR) 156*, 179⁴
Sainte Ladylime (FR) 115²
Sainte Turgeon (FR) 267ᵘʳ
Saldier (FR) 199⁵, 265*
Salsaretta (FR) 197², 209⁵
Sam's Gunner 17*, 230ᵖᵘ
Samcro (IRE) 48*, 147*, 185*, 257ᶠ
Sametegal (FR) 64³, 102³
Sam Red (FR) 55ᶠ
Sam Spinner 11², 46*, 80*, 195³, 236³
Samuel Jackson 131³

San Benedeto (FR) 45⁴, 67⁵, 118⁴, 261²
Sandsend (FR) 200ᵘʳ
Sandymount Duke (IRE) 4⁵, 250
Sang Tiger (GER) 6ᵖᵘ
Santana Plessis (FR) 247³
Santini 128*, 201³, 230*
Saphir du Rheu (FR) 153³, 202ᵖᵘ
Saturnas (FR) 212, 255⁶
Savello (IRE) 222
Saxo Jack (FR) 178
Sayar (FR) 213
Sayo 199³
Scarlet Dragon 171², 226
Scarpeta (FR) 185⁴, 210³, 258²
Sceau Royal (FR) 65*, 130*
Scheu Time (IRE) 238ᶠ
Scoir Mear (IRE) 177ᵖᵘ, 256
Sea Light (IRE) 6ᵘʳ, 7ᵖᵘ
Sea Story 223
Secret Escape (IRE) 223⁶
Seddon (IRE) 191
Seeyoutmidnight 237
Seeyouinvinnys (IRE) 247
Sensulano (FR) 208
Serienschock (GER) 236⁵
Sevarano (IRE) 231⁵
Shades of Midnight 145³, 183ᵘʳ, 241
Shadow Catcher 253
Shanahan's Turn (IRE) 196, 229², 252ᵖᵘ
Shaneshill (IRE) 4², 9⁴, 70*, 254³
Shannon Bridge (IRE) 131², 165ᵖᵘ, 232
Shanpallas (IRE) 4, 7ᵖᵘ, 10
Shanroe In Milan (IRE) 241⁶
Shanroe Saint 176
Shantou Bob (IRE) 148
Shantou Flyer (IRE) 22⁵, 47ᵖᵘ, 89ᵖᵘ, 102², 126², 180², 237ᵖᵘ
Shantou Magic (IRE) 203ᵖᵘ
Shantou Rock (IRE) 90², 130², 234³
Shantou Village (IRE) 14ᵖᵘ, 240
Sharjah (FR) 93ᶠ, 147, 178, 213⁴, 245⁵
Shattered Love (IRE) 41², 97*, 192*, 212², 248⁵
She's A Star (IRE) 58³
Shelford (IRE) 3³, 236ᴿ
Shoal Bay (IRE) 171⁶, 178ᵖᵘ
Shotavodka (IRE) 203
Shotgun Paddy (IRE) 33⁵
Showem Silver (IRE) 6
Show On The Road 259
Shrewd 5
Silsol (GER) 46, 105⁵, 164ᵘʳ, 206⁴, 244
Silver Concorde 233ᵖᵘ
Silver Streak (IRE) 82², 155ᵘʳ, 176³
Silver Tassie (IRE) 173ᵖᵘ
Simply Ned (IRE) 37⁴, 92*, 136²
Simply The Betts (IRE) 178

Singlefarmpayment 53^F, 81^5, 127^{pu}, 185^5
Sir Chauvelin 242
Sire de Grugy (FR) 45
Sire du Berlais (FR) 204^4
Sir Ivan 52^3
Sir Jack Yeats (IRE) 7^{pu}, 203, 221
Sir Mangan (IRE) 111^6, 164^{pu}, 232
Sir Valentino (FR) 45*, 67^F
Sizing Codelco (IRE) 33^6, 62^{pu}, 180^{pu}, 219^4, 244
Sizing Granite (IRE) 43, 228^3, 250^6
Sizing John 70*, 96
Sizing Platinum (IRE) 205, 222^6
Sizing Tennessee (IRE) 101^2, 125^3, 183^3, 244^{pu}
Skidoosh 231
Slate House (IRE) 39^5, 78^4, 128^5, 178^F, 226
Slowmotion (FR) 4^3, 7, 10^{pu}
Smad Place (FR) 14*, 43^5, 112^4
Smaoineamh Alainn (IRE) 200^{pu}
Smart Talk (IRE) 132^6
Smooth Stepper 173^6
Snow Falcon (IRE) 59^3, 149^5, 216^{ur}, 227^8
So French (FR) 267^{bd}
Solatentif (FR) 35^6, 238^6
Solo Saxophone (IRE) 190^6
Solstice Star 125^6
Somchine 18
Some Drama (IRE) 60^{ur}
Some Invitation (IRE) 83^{pu}
Some Neck (FR) 224^4
Some Plan (FR) 138^F, 205^F
Sommervieu (FR) 73^{pu}
Song Light 1^{rr}, 19
Sort It Out (IRE) 193
Souriyan (FR) 11
Southfield Royale 26^{pu}, 53^{pu}
Southfield Theatre (IRE) 26^4, 68
Space Cadet (IRE) 49^6, 94, 123^3, 157^4, 177^2
Spades Are Trumps (IRE) 266
Sparkling Dawn 223
Speak Easy 108^5
Special Tiara 37^3, 91^F, 136^3, 188^{pu}, 261^4
Speedo Boy (FR) 32^5
Speredek (FR) 118^2, 160^{pu}, 253
Spice Girl 197
Spider Web (IRE) 157^6
Spiritofthegames (IRE) 113^2, 155^3, 200^5, 225
Splash of Ginge 34^6, 74, 102^{pu}, 196^2
Springtown Lake (IRE) 61^2, 187
Squouateur (FR) 94^3, 138, 198^3, 216^6, 256^{pu}
Staff College (FR) 104^4
Starchitect (FR) 34^2, 74^{pu}
Station Master (IRE) 131^6
Stellar Notion (IRE) 7^{pu}, 10

Step Back (IRE) 262*
Sternrubin (GER) 200, 238^3
Stoney Mountain (IRE) 191
Storm Home (IRE) 225
Stormy Ireland (IRE) 199^F, 265^{ur}
Stowaway Magic (IRE) 187
Straidnahanna (IRE) 62^{pu}, 244^{pu}
Style de Garde (FR) 190^2, 226^{pu}
Sub Lieutenant (IRE) 13^3, 16^5, 70^3, 194^4, 219^5, 250^4
Sugar Baron (IRE) 68^2, 198, 262^{pu}
Sumkindofking (IRE) 11, 225
Summerville Boy (IRE) 39^2, 106^4, 178*
Sumos Novios (IRE) 123, 250^{pu}
Sunsetstorise (IRE) 253^5
Sunshade 208
Supasundaes (IRE) 57^3, 95^2, 139*, 195^2, 220^2, 257*
Surf Instructor (IRE) 256^{bd}
Sussex Ranger (USA) 104^2, 199
Sutton Manor (IRE) 151, 177^F, 216^{pu}
Sutton Place (IRE) 149^{pu}
Swamp Fox (IRE) 5^2, 42^3, 57, 266
Sykes (IRE) 193, 232
Taglietelle 148^{pu}
Taj Badalandabad (IRE) 144, 193^4
Talkischeap (IRE) 201^{pu}
Tandem 140
Taquin du Seuil (FR) 51^3, 80
Tara Dylan (IRE) 209
Tashinny (IRE) 247
Taxmeifyoucan (IRE) 259
Teacher's Pet (IRE) 94^F, 157^{pu}
Tea For Two 14, 47^4, 85^3, 127^{pu}, 202, 219^5, 268^{pu}
Ted Veale (IRE) 58, 138^5
Tellthemnuttin (IRE) 6^{pu}, 15^6
Tell Us More (IRE) 92^5, 138, 207^5, 216^{pu}, 246
Tempestatefloresco 7^{pu}, 26^3
Templeross (IRE) 46^{pu}
Tenor Nivernais (FR) 133^{pu}, 159^5, 237^{pu}
Tenth Amendment (IRE) 86^5, 146^5
Terrefort (IRE) 143*, 192^2, 227*
Tesseract (IRE) 49^3, 94^{pu}
Testify (IRE) 184, 227^{pu}
Texas Jack (IRE) 94
That's A Given (FR) 247
That's A Wrap 138^F
The Artful Cobbler 206^{pu}
Theatre Guide (IRE) 26^3, 127^6, 172^{pu}, 262
Theatre Legend 231
Theatre Territory (IRE) 125^2, 172^3, 229^3
Theatrical Star 107
Thebannerkingrebel (IRE) 191^{pu}

Thebarrowman (IRE) 97^4, 173^F
The Big Bite (IRE) 191
The Birdie Crowe (IRE) 134
Theclockisticking (IRE) 78^3
The Clock Leary (IRE) 8^{pu}
The Conditional (IRE) 249
The Crafty Butcher (IRE) 6
The Dubai Way (IRE) 175
The Dutchman (IRE) 46^2, 121*, 164^{pu}, 237^{ur}
Theflyingportrait (IRE) 222
The Flying Sofa (FR) 191
The Fresh Prince (IRE) 23^{pu}
The Game Changer (IRE) 5, 29^4, 98^4, 114, 246, 257^5
The Gunner Murphy (IRE) 213^{pu}
The Happy Chappy (IRE) 68
Theinval (FR) 18^4, 34^F, 102^2, 205^4, 222^2
The Irregular (IRE) 211
The King of May (FR) 190
The Last Samuri (IRE) 62^2, 127^4, 189^3, 237^{pu}
Themanfrom Minella (IRE) 173^{pu}, 206^{pu}
The Mighty Don (IRE) 193, 232^5
The New One (IRE) 38^4, 76^2, 84^2, 120*, 195, 220^{pu}
The New Pharoah (IRE) 259
The Nipper (IRE) 132^5
Theo's Charm (IRE) 46^3, 193
The Organist (IRE) 187^5
The Paparrazi Kid (IRE) 216^F, 252
The Princetonian (IRE) 152^6
The Russian Doyen (IRE) 106^5, 175^6
The Shepherd King (IRE) 29^5
The Shunter (IRE) 141
The Storyteller (IRE) 149, 196*, 212^5, 248*
The Unit (IRE) 169^2, 242
The Wealerdealer (IRE) 2
The West's Awake (IRE) 211^6, 256
The Winkler (IRE) 49^{pu}
The Worlds End (IRE) 46, 80^4, 129^4, 195, 236^4
The Young Master 20^{ur}, 62^6, 198^2, 244^{ur}, 262
Think Positive (IRE) 247
Third Intention (IRE) 14, 107^{pu}
Thistlecrack 51^5, 85^4
Thomas Brown 20^6
Thomas Campbell 35*, 80^5, 129^6, 193, 236^{pu}
Thomas Edison (IRE) 5
Thomas Patrick (IRE) 235*
Thorpe (IRE) 116^{pu}
Thosedaysaregone (IRE) 231
Three Faces West (IRE) 33^3, 164^F
Three Kingdoms (IRE) 4^{pu}
Three Musketeers (IRE) 11, 46, 225
Three Stars (IRE) 23^5, 94, 138^2, 205^5, 253
Three Wise Men (IRE) 211

Thumb Stone Blues (IRE) 133
Thunder And Roses (IRE) 60[pu], 94, 123[4], 157[pu], 177[F], 216[F], 237[pu]
Tiger Roll (IRE) 30[pu], 189[*], 237[F]
Tigris River (IRE) 5[*], 38, 58, 140, 200[pu], 239
Tikkanbar (IRE) 128[6], 252
Time For Mabel (FR) 58
Timi Roli (FR) 58
Timiyan (IRE) 5, 253[F]
Tintangle (IRE) 152[4]
Tintern Theatre (IRE) 121[ur], 172, 198
Tiquer (FR) 23
Tisamystery (IRE) 253[F]
Tobias Lochlan (IRE) 247
Tombstone (IRE) 40[2], 88[2], 149[6], 212[6], 224[2], 256[6]
Tommy Rapper (IRE) 12, 204
Tommy Silver (FR) 90[3], 222[N]
Tongie (IRE) 253
Top Gamble (IRE) 43, 69[2], 102[4], 205[3], 229
Top Notch (FR) 43[*], 71[*], 160[4], 260[*]
Topofthegame (IRE) 113[4], 144[*], 187[2]
Top Othe Ra (IRE) 58, 82, 109[5], 147
Topper Thornton (IRE) 68[5], 111[pu]
Top Ville Ben (IRE) 113[pu]
Top Wood (FR) 203[2]
Tornado Flyer (IRE) 191[3], 251[*]
Total Recall (IRE) 10[*], 53[*], 148[2], 202[F], 237[pu], 250[2]
Toubaloo (FR) 157
Tout Est Permis (FR) 17, 88[F], 252
Tower Bridge (IRE) 135[*], 201[5], 230[3]
Townshend (GER) 59[5], 114[ur], 138, 205[pu], 253
Traditional Dancer (IRE) 1
Traffic Fluide (FR) 14[4], 47[5], 85, 160[5], 196, 240[*]
Trainwreck (IRE) 147
True Self (IRE) 134[4], 239[F]
Tudor City (IRE) 140[5]
Tully East (IRE) 34[6], 138[3]
Tulsa Jack (IRE) 10[4]
Turbojet 48[6]
Turcagua (FR) 266
Turning Gold 190[5]
Turtle Wars (FR) 175[5]
Twiss's Hill (IRE) 224[3]
Tycoon Prince (IRE) 137[F], 184[pu], 212, 253[pu]

Ubak (FR) 80, 144[6], 174[pu]
Ucello Conti (FR) 94[2], 123[pu], 237[ur]
Ultragold (FR) 20, 64[2], 126[pu], 196, 229[*]
Ulysses (GER) 124[3]
Uncle Danny (IRE) 151[3]
Un de Sceaux (FR) 69[*], 118[*], 194[2], 215[*], 246[*]
Undressed (FR) 60[pu]
Une Lavandiere (FR) 60[6]
Unioniste (FR) 203, 221
Unison (IRE) 66, 120[3], 238[pu]
Unowhatimeanharry 51[2], 80[3], 195
Up For Review (IRE) 212[4], 256
Uppertown Prince (IRE) 165[2], 230[4]
Upsilon Bleu (FR) 45[5]
Uradel (GER) 239
Urgent de Gregaine (FR) 189[2]
Urumqi (FR) 189[pu]
Us And Them (IRE) 178
Val de Ferbet (FR) 168[3]
Valdez 154[3], 205[ur]
Valhalla (IRE) 24[F]
Valseur Lido (FR) 96[5], 150[5], 161[5], 237
Valtor (FR) 267[*]
Value At Risk 174[3]
Vaniteux (FR) 37[5], 45, 71[4], 91[2], 205
Veinard (FR) 58, 82, 140
Veneer of Charm (IRE) 190[*], 213[6]
Verdana Blue (IRE) 19[5], 82[3], 155, 242
Very First Time 198, 235
Vibrato Valtat (FR) 133, 172
Vic de Touzaine (FR) 26[pu], 180[pu]
Vicente (FR) 33[2], 105[ur], 180[pu], 244[3]
Vicomte du Seuil (FR) 189[*]
Viconte du Noyer (FR) 34, 102[pu], 196[pu], 252[pu]
Viens Chercher (IRE) 3
Vieux Lion Rouge (FR) 22[4], 62, 159[4], 230[*]
Vieux Morvan (FR) 94[5], 151[2]
Village Mystic (FR) 141
Village Vic (IRE) 22[pu], 196, 229[*]
Vincitore (FR) 203[ur]
Vinnie Lewis (IRE) 173[pu]
Vino Griego (FR) 107[ur]
Vintage Clouds (IRE) 105[4], 145[2], 180[3], 244[3]
Vintage Vinnie (IRE) 4
Virak (FR) 203
Virgilio (FR) 23, 237[F]
Vision des Flos (FR) 12[3], 31[4], 185[6], 226[2], 245[2]
Vivas (FR) 116[5]
Viva Steve (IRE) 7[4], 62[pu]
Voix d'Eau (FR) 23[6], 240
Voix du Reve (FR) 148, 187, 239, 266
Volcano (FR) 191
Volnay de Thaix (FR) 203
Vosne Romanee 1[pu], 222
Vyta du Roc (FR) 53
Waaheb (USA) 148
Wadswick Court (IRE) 3[2], 8[6]
Wait For Me (FR) 52[4], 193
Waiting Patiently (IRE) 112[*], 160[*]
Wakanda (IRE) 55[5], 89[2], 133[*], 180[pu], 235

Wakea (USA) 15[4], 44[3]
Walk In The Mill (FR) 81[3], 121[pu]
Warden Hill (IRE) 203, 221[ur]
Warriors Tale 23[ur], 133[2], 237[pu]
War Sound 125[4]
Waterlord 119[4], 155[pu]
Way Back Then (IRE) 100[4]
We Have A Dream (FR) 73[*], 104[*], 218[*]
Wells de Lune (FR) 203[pu], 221[ur]
Welsh Pearl (IRE) 152
West Approach 83[3], 143[5], 192[6], 244[pu]
West Coast Time (IRE) 58
Western Boy (IRE) 5[pu]
Western Climate (IRE) 206
Westerner Point (IRE) 62, 216[pu]
Western Miller (IRE) 50[4], 184
Western Ryder (IRE) 106[4], 178[6], 233[5]
Westland Row (IRE) 6
West of The Edge (IRE) 173[2], 206[pu]
West Wizard (FR) 198
Whataknight 193
Whatareudoingtome (IRE) 49
Whatduhavtoget (IRE) 11
Whatmore 116
Whatsforuwontgobyu (IRE) 6
Whatswrongwithyou (IRE) 176[3]
Whatucallher (IRE) 247[5]
Where Eagles Dare (IRE) 251
Whiskey Sour (IRE) 93[5], 147[4], 200[3], 245[4], 258[2]
Whisper (FR) 53[2], 85[5]
White Arm (FR) 157[pu]
White Moon (GER) 61
Who Dares Wins (IRE) 193[5], 225[3]
Wholestone (IRE) 11[4], 21[2], 51[5], 103[*], 129[2], 195[3], 236[2], 263[3]
Wicklow Brave 181, 257[2]
Wild Bill (FR) 2[5]
Wilde Blue Yonder (IRE) 225[4]
Wild West Wind (IRE) 105[F], 164[R], 198[ur]
William H Bonney 1[6], 38[5], 66[2], 155, 200
William Henry (IRE) 113[*], 187[4]
William of Orange 238[pu]
Willie Boy (IRE) 196[F]
Willoughby Court (IRE) 50[*], 101[3]
Winged Crusader (IRE) 221[ur]
Wishfull Dreaming 113
Wishing And Hoping (IRE) 11[F]
Wisty (FR) 222[pu]
Without Limites (FR) 157[F]
Wolfofallstreets (IRE) 247
Wonderful Charm (FR) 2[3], 203[pu], 221
Woodland Opera (IRE) 40[*], 92[4], 252

Woods Well (IRE) 94^{pu}, 123^5, 157^{pu}, 216^{pu}
Woolstone One 209^6
Work du Breteau (FR) 244
Work In Progress (IRE) 8^{ur}
Wounded Warrior (IRE) 49, 60, 123^2, 157, 177
Yaha Fizz (IRE) 58^3, 239^2, 266
Yala Enki (FR) 26^{pu}, 55^3, 81^6, 121^4, 164*, 180^6
Yanworth 50^2, 101*, 195^6
Yorkhill (IRE) 96, 136^6, 181^{pu}, 254, 268^6
Youcantcallherthat (IRE) 248^6
Young Hurricane (IRE) 2*, 203^{pu}
Young Ted (IRE) 251^6
Zabana (IRE) 13^5, 16^3, 96^F
Zakharova 223
Zalvados (FR) 155
Zarkandar (IRE) 46^{pu}, 163^4
Zubayr (IRE) 1^5, 25^6, 66, 225
Zulu Oscar 1

ERRATA & ADDENDA

Chasers & Hurdlers 2008/09

Lyricist's Dream — not a maiden over hurdles

Chasers & Hurdlers 2011/12

Crescent Island — rating should have been '§§'

Chasers & Hurdlers 2015/16

As de Fer — not a maiden over hurdles

Chasers & Hurdlers 2016/17

As de Fer — not a maiden over hurdles

Timeform 'Top 100' — p25, the list of Hunter Chasers should be headed by Foxrock. First Lieutenant and Hurricane Ben did not achieve their ratings in hunter chases.

TIMEFORM 'TOP HORSES IN FRANCE'

Racegoers at Auteuil on the third Sunday of May were treated to some excellent racing, featuring the closest finish to a Grand Steeple-Chase de Paris for decades as well as one of the most impressive performances seen from a winner of the Grande Course de Haies. A change to the calendar brought together France's top hurdle and chase on the same card, one which also featured the Group 1 chase for four-year-olds, the Prix Ferdinand Dufaure, while the Group 1 four-year-old hurdle, the Prix Alain du Breil, was run on the Saturday of the two-day meeting. The Grande Course de Haies and the Alain du Breil were formerly run three weeks later in June but swapped places with the races which formerly served as preparatory contests for those events, the Prix La Barka and Prix Questarabad. It wasn't quite the innovation which some made out, as the Grand Steeple-Chase de Paris and Grande Course de Haies (along with the two big four-year-old events) had all been run on the same day for several years during the 1980's. No horse, incidentally, while the opportunity existed, ever completed the double of the top chase and hurdle in the same year, though Princesse d'Anjou went close in 2006, finishing second in the Grande Course de Haies after the first of her two victories in the Grand Steeple-Chase. The creation of a weekend meeting in early-summer combining the top chase and hurdle was something proposed here in *Chasers & Hurdlers 2005/06* after the inauguration of Auteuil's 'International Jumps Weekend' staged in November; 'this would have the advantages over an autumn date of avoiding a clash with the start of the main jumps season in the British Isles and of succeeding the spring festivals at Cheltenham, Aintree and Punchestown. Rather than trying to generate interest virtually from scratch in November, this would capitalise on the existing practice of some British and Irish trainers who already send horses for the two big races and other events on the respective supporting cards.' Auteuil's weekend of big races in November remains the highlight of the course's autumn season, but the 'international' tag was eventually dropped after the meeting failed to attract sufficient interest from outside France.

The latest Grand Steeple-Chase had a foreign challenger in Djakadam, Willie Mullins' dual Gold Cup runner-up being the most notable challenger from outside France to take his chance since Gold Cup winner Long Run in 2014. However, like Long Run, Djakadam finished well beaten, and returned with what proved a career-ending injury. Instead, the race belonged once again to trainer Guillaume Macaire and jockey James Reveley after **On The Go** had got up on the line to beat the previous year's runner-up **Perfect Impulse**

Grand Steeple-Chase de Paris, Auteuil—On The Go jumps two out just behind eventual runner-up (for the second year) Perfect Impulse before going on to give jockey James Reveley his third win in a row and trainer Guillaume Macaire a record-equalling sixth win in France's most valuable chase. The winner's stable-companion Edward d'Argent (left) is third and 2015 winner Milord Thomas (right) completes the frame

by a head in the closest finish since 1984 when a short head had separated Brodi Dancer and V'la Paramé. Successful for the fifth time in the last six years, Macaire won his sixth Grand Steeple-Chase in all to equal the record set by Bernard Secly whose winners included a couple of Auteuil legends Katko and Al Capone II. Macaire fielded four runners but Reveley was again on the right one for the third year running, partnering On The Go instead of **So French** who'd been successful in the last two renewals but whose bid to become the first since Katko in 1990 to win three consecutive editions of the Grand Steeple-Chase ended at the very first obstacle. Both jockeys involved in the desperate finish picked up twelve-day bans for misuse of the whip, but their fines of €150 each amounted to barely a slap on the wrist given the race is worth €369,000 to the winning owner!

Like So French for the first of his wins and another of Macaire's winners, Storm of Saintly in 2014, On The Go was only a five-year-old and a virtual novice in British terms having had only five runs over fences beforehand. He had topped the three-year-old hurdle rankings in *Chasers & Hurdlers 2015/16* but was off for over a year before returning over hurdles at Auteuil in September, the only occasion to date that he's finished out of the first two. On The Go was runner-up in three of his four chases in the autumn, twice going down to stable-companion **Edward d'Argent** in the Prix Orcada and Prix Morgex, but in between got the better of that rival by a neck to open his account over fences in the Group 1 Prix Maurice Gillois. Edward d'Argent came out on top again, this time conceding weight, when they met again in the Prix Ingre in April which resulted in Edward d'Argent starting much the shorter price of the two five-year-olds in the Grand Steeple-Chase. Once again it was On The Go who fared the better on the big occasion, though Edward d'Argent was a creditable third, seven lengths behind the first two. Edward d'Argent had been the dominant four-year-old chaser for most of 2017 and has a fine career record himself, not having finished worse than third since his debut. On The Go, who was the Papot family's second winner of the Grand Steeple-Chase after Bel La Vie in 2012, and Edward d'Argent, who carries the colours of Simon Munir and Isaac Souede, represent two of France's major owners of jumpers and the ongoing rivalry of these young stable-companions will be interesting to follow in the months ahead.

The mare Perfect Impulse, who had herself been a five-year-old when beaten six lengths by So French in 2017, went much closer to going one better this time after being up with the pace throughout, and looked to have the upper hand on the run-in until the very last stride. Perfect Impulse, coincidentally a half-sister to the dam of the winner, was sent off favourite for the Grand Steeple-Chase after making all to beat a strong field in another of the main prep races, the Prix Murat. She was chased home in the Murat by the 2015 Grand Steeple-Chase de Paris winner **Milord Thomas** who, along with Perfect Impulse, cut much of the running before finishing fourth in the latest renewal. Milord Thomas was off the track with a leg problem for almost a year after winning his third consecutive Prix La Haye Jousselin in November 2016 and showed he retained plenty of ability, finishing second in his bid to win that race for a fourth time and also finishing second in the Prix Georges Courtois later in November and third behind the Macaire five-year-olds in the Ingre.

So French's departure at the first, a simple hurdle, in the Grand Steeple-Chase was the result of being brought down by another of the leading contenders, **Bipolaire**, while the latter's stablemate **Roi Mage** was a third casualty in the incident. An altercation apparently took place in the aftermath involving So French's rider Bertrand Lestrade and the travelling head lad responsible for the other two horses involved, resulting in a four-day ban for the jockey. Bipolaire had finished fifth in the 2017 Grand Steeple-Chase but returned better still to complete a hat-trick in the autumn, including the Prix Heros XII (from **Sainte Turgeon** and Perfect Impulse), before putting up the best performance over fences in the period under review when beating Milord Thomas and Perfect Impulse in the Prix La Haye Jousselin. Bipolaire was third behind the same pair in the Murat in the spring and ran creditably when seeking some consolation for his fall in the Grand Steeple-Chase when second, conceding nearly a stone to the Irish-trained mare Baie des Iles, in the Prix des Drags (Baie des Iles' essay in the main body of the Annual gives more information about this rare exploit for a chaser trained outside France). So French had a torrid six months or so as he had been involved in another three-horse pile-up in

Prix La Haye Jousselin, Auteuil—the grey Bipolaire foils Milord Thomas's (right) bid to win a fourth consecutive edition of the top chase of the autumn. Perfect Impulse (noseband) and Borice are the next two home

the La Haye Jousselin, this time as the culprit, when bringing down **Shannon Rock** and Sainte Turgeon. So French sustained an injury in that incident, and when he finished only fourth of five to **Srelighonn** in the Prix Troytown in March, after nearly coming down when making a bad mistake at the wall, his bid for a hat-trick in the Grand Steeple-Chase initially looked in doubt. Not surprisingly after those experiences, he jumped with little confidence when only sixth in the Drags and he'll reportedly be switched to hurdles in the autumn. Roi Mage was getting plenty of weight from Milord Thomas when beating him in the Prix Georges Courtois and ran creditably either side of his Grand Steeple-Chase mishap, finishing fourth in the Murat and third in the Drags.

Srelighonn, another five-year-old (winner of the Ferdinand Dufaure in Edward d'Argent's absence earlier in 2017), and the Troytown runner-up **Docteur de Ballon**, a wide-margin winner of the listed Prix General Donnio in the autumn, were absentees from the Grand Steeple-Chase. Also missing was another prolific winner from the Macaire yard, **Saint Goustan Blue**. Mixing hurdling and chasing, he has won thirteen of his seventeen career starts and was completing a four-timer when last seen beating Bipolaire, in receipt of weight, in the Prix Robert de Clermont-Tonnerre in March. Saint Goustan Blue was just as good over hurdles as he showed when winning the Prix Leopold d'Orsetti at Compiegne in November. Away from Auteuil, **Paulougas** won twice at Compiegne in the autumn, winning the Grand Steeple-Chase there after successfully conceding plenty of weight all round in a listed contest. **Urgent de Gregaine**, who had been the shock winner of a handicap over Cheltenham's cross-country course early in 2017, twice ran well to be placed over the same course in the latest season, notably when faring much the best of four French runners in the Glenfarclas Chase at the Festival when two lengths second to future Grand National winner Tiger Roll. He also ran well when second in the Velka Pardubicka in the autumn.

The 2017 generation of four-year-olds who turned five in January was clearly a strong one, as besides the Grand Steeple-Chase de Paris winner, it also included the first three home in the Grande Course de Haies d'Auteuil. **De Bon Coeur** had already established herself as the outstanding juvenile hurdler of her generation by the previous summer, a fall when looking sure to win the Prix Alain du Breil being the only blemish on her record. She proved better still on her return in the autumn, winning the Prix Pierre de Lassus before a ten-length victory over outsider **Pop Art du Berlais** in the Prix Renaud du Vivier. Her first two starts against older rivals in the spring resulted in two more easy wins in the Prix Juigne and Prix Hypothese, but she met with her first defeat in completed starts on her last outing before the Grande Course de Haies when beaten three quarters of a length by the Hypothese runner-up, her high-class stable-companion **Alex de Larredya**, in the Prix Leon Rambaud. De Bon Coeur was reportedly in season on that occasion, but she made it eleven wins from thirteen starts when a hugely impressive winner of the Grande Course de Haies, storming clear on the run-in to win by sixteen lengths. It was the best performance

Grande Course de Haies d'Auteuil, Auteuil—seemingly all to play for two out but the mare De Bon Coeur (left) is full of running and records a most impressive success to take her record to eleven wins from twelve completed starts over hurdles. Bapaume (third right) fares best of a Willie Mullins quartet to take second, while the winner's stablemates Dalia Grandchamp (fourth right) and Alex de Larredya (fifth right) complete the frame. 2017 winner L'Ami Serge (breastgirth) is only seventh this time.

by a French filly or mare over jumps since 'Top Horses In France' became part of *Chasers & Hurdlers in 2003/04*. While the French programme caters well for fillies and mares, a female winner of their top hurdle is rare in the extreme. In fact, the last two mares to win the race had been trained in Ireland. When Willie Mullins won the race for the first time in 2003 with Nobody Told Me, he emulated his father Paddy who famously won the 1984 Grande Course de Haies with Dawn Run. Outsider Nobody Told Me, incidentally, upset the long odds-on favourite, and fellow five-year-old mare, Karly Flight. De Bon Coeur was therefore the first French-trained mare to win the Grande Course de Haies since Choute right back in 1961. De Bon Coeur's win was some compensation for Bipolaire's early exit in the Grand Steeple-Chase for the same owners who reported they'd turned down five big offers for the mare earlier in the year, though injury in the Grand Steeple-Chase to her intended rider required a last-minute change of jockey.

Willie Mullins fielded four runners in the latest Grande Course de Haies which was also contested by L'Ami Serge who never looked like repeating his success of twelve months earlier for Nicky Henderson. Bapaume fared best of the Mullins quartet in second and franked the form when becoming his stable's third consecutive winner (and fifth in all) of the Prix La Barka. Otherwise, the Grande Course de Haies was dominated by the Francois Nicolle stable, with De Bon Coeur's stable-companions **Dalia Grandchamp** and Alex de Larredya finishing third and fourth. Dalia Grandchamp, another mare, had raced mainly over fences, showing useful form, but won both her races back over hurdles in the spring prior to the Grande Course de Haies, including a listed contest at Auteuil. The normally consistent Alex de Larredya was a bit below his best in the Grande Course de Haies but returned to form, conceding plenty of weight to the three who beat him, when fourth in the La Barka. As well as the Leon Rambaud, Alex de Larredya also won the Grand Prix d'Automne in November for the second year running, getting the better of **Device** by a short neck, after finishing runner-up to the same rival on worse terms in the Prix de Compiegne and Prix Carmarthen.

Device fell when long odds-on for the Prix Leon Olry-Roederer later in the autumn and had his attentions switched to fences after finishing only fourth to De Bon Coeur in the Prix Juigne on his return in March. Device has won only one of his three races over the larger obstacles to date, the Prix Marechal Foch for amateurs on the Grand Steeple-Chase de Paris card, but it's still early days in the chasing career of the full brother to So French. The Leon Olry-Roederer was won by **Galop Marin** who had finished a long way behind the first two in the Grand Prix d'Automne and proved no match for De Bon Coeur after the

Grand Prix d'Automne, Auteuil—Alex de Larredya wins for the second year running as he and Device (noseband) pull a long way clear of Galop Marin (dark colours) and Curly Basc

turn of the year, finishing runner-up to her in the Juigne and again running up to his best when fifth in the Grande Course de Haies. Bapaume was chased home in the La Barka by the nine-year-old **Le Grand Luce** who had already twice finished runner-up in the race earlier in his career. The 2014 Grande Course de Haies runner-up Le Grand Luce was off the course for almost two years after being pulled up in the 2016 edition but won a minor event at Compiegne on his first start back in April. The other older hurdler worth a mention was **Izzo** who faced a stiff task when tailed off in the Aintree Hurdle but showed smart form on occasions at Auteuil. He won the Prix de Maisons-Laffitte for four-year-olds in September before taking second behind De Bon Coeur in the Prix Pierre de Lassus the following month and bounced back after Aintree to finish a good third in the La Barka.

Back in 2008, Guillaume Macaire trained a couple of the leading four-year-old fillies over fences in Santa Bamba and Westonne, both group winners at Auteuil. Santa Bamba became the dam of De Bon Coeur, while Westonne is compiling an outstanding record as a broodmare, producing not only So French and Device, but also the latest season's dominant four-year-old over fences **Whetstone**, she too trained by Macaire. Whetstone completed a four-timer over hurdles in the autumn against her own sex which was successful in the Prix Bournosienne but it was when switched to fences that she came into her own, easily winning all five of her chases. She became the first since Cyrlight in 2004 to win all four of Auteuil's group contests for four-year-olds over fences in the spring, taking the Prix Duc d'Anjou, Fleuret (a race also won by her dam), Jean Stern and Ferdinand Dufaure. Although taking a few liberties with her jumping, Whetstone was at her most impressive in the last-named contest in which she coasted home by sixteen lengths, with two more fillies, **Evidence Madrik** and **Kapkiline**, filling the places. Kapkiline had the best form in the Prix La Perichole the following month but finished only fifth behind **Ebene du Breuil** who had been a well-held fifth in the Ferdinand Dufaure. Whetstone was herself beaten back over hurdles in June but will take all the beating again in the top four-year-old chases in the autumn. Of her closest rivals, **Spanish One** finished a well-held fourth in the Ferdinand Dufaure but had fared better when second in the Jean Stern, while the Duc d'Anjou runner-up **My Way** wasn't seen out again as he joined Paul Nicholls for whom he looks an exciting recruit for novice chases. Whetstone might not have had things quite so much all her own way in the spring if **Echiquier Royal** had still been in action. He survived a blunder at the last to beat My Way in the Prix Congress, thereby completing a hat-trick at Auteuil in completed starts over fences in the autumn, but wasn't seen out again subsequently.

Macaire also trained a couple of the leading juvenile hurdlers whose sustained rivalry dominated most of the big races in the division. **Master Dino** and the Polish-bred entire **Tunis** had first met in April of their three-year-old season, and when Master Dino beat Tunis into second in the Prix Questarabad the following June it was their eleventh head-to-head in little more than a year! In most of their encounters they finished one-two, with Tunis coming out on top on eight occasions, but their rivalry was much less one-sided than that would suggest and, if anything, Master Dino, who beat Tunis three lengths in the Questarabad, had the upper hand going into the summer break. Master Dino had also come out on top in their two big races in the autumn but there was just a neck in it in the

Prix Ferdinand Dufaure, Auteuil—Whetstone keeps her unbeaten record over fences with another dominant display in the top four-year-old chase of the first half of the year. Two more fillies, Evidence Madrik and the grey Kapkiline, fill the places

*Prix Cambaceres, Auteuil—this round in the season-long rivalry between
Guillaume Macaire's leading juvenile hurdlers goes narrowly to Master Dino ahead of Tunis (right).
Pesk Ebrel (pale colours) is third ahead of Klassical Dream (left)*

Prix Georges de Talhouet-Roy and then a short neck in the Cambaceres, while Tunis had the edge in their spring encounters, including when having Master Dino back in second in the Prix d'Indy and Prix Amadou. However, their duopoly was unexpectedly broken in the Prix de Pepinvast in April when both were beaten by the filly **Wildriver**, making her Auteuil debut after wins at Cagnes-sur-Mer and Compiegne. She showed that win from the front was no fluke, despite Tunis and Master Dino again starting at shorter odds, when beating them again under a more patient ride in the Prix Alain du Breil in May, where a third Macaire representative, **Lou Buck**'s, unbeaten in four starts including a listed contest, completed the frame. Lou Buck's went on to make a winning debut over fences and looks promising in that sphere for the autumn.

Of the other leading juveniles, **Spinozzar** ran up a hat-trick at Compiegne in the autumn which he completed in the Prix General de Saint-Didier (with Tunis a below-form fourth) and was a good third behind Tunis and Master Dino in the Prix d'Indy on his only start in the spring. **Pesk Ebrel** wasn't far behind the big two in the Cambaceres but failed to make much impression later on, though his fifth in the Alain du Breil was a creditable effort. **Beau Gosse**, like Master Dino trained by Macaire and owned by the Munir/Souede partnership, had two runs in Britain but ran well below his best when third in the Adonis at Kempton and seventh in the Anniversary at Aintree. He proved much more at home at Auteuil where he'd begun the previous autumn by beating both Tunis and Master Dino in a listed contest, albeit in receipt of weight. Beau Gosse returned there in fine form after Aintree, making a winning debut over fences and then reverting to hurdles for two more listed wins.

A clear leader has yet to emerge from the latest crop of three-year-old hurdlers, though Francois Nicolle looks well armed after saddling the first two in the Prix Aguado in June. **Pic d'Orhy** was odds on after winning both his starts beforehand but was beaten by stable-companion **Porto Pollo**, winner of his two completed starts over hurdles, while **Beaumec de Houelle**, he too winner of both his starts, including the listed Prix Stanley, was a close third. Nicolle also won the Prix Sagan for fillies with **La Griottiere**, though she was receiving weight from the neck runner-up **Listenmania** who had won the listed Prix d'Iena when herself receiving weight from the second **Vanille du Berlais** who unseated early in the Sagan.

Chasers (5yo+)					
159	Bipolaire 7	156	Perfect Impulse (f) 6	151	Edward d'Argent 5
157	On The Go 5	155	Milord Thomas 9	150d	Paulougas 6
		154	So French 7	149	Saint Goustan Blue 6

149	Srelighonn 5	128	Park Light 8	135	Milord Thomas 9
148	Shannon Rock 12	128	Urumqi 7	135	Prince Philippe 8
148	Urgent de Gregaine 10	127	Adagio des Bordes 8	134p	Edward d'Argent 5
145	Capferret 6	127	Disco du Chenet 9	134	Demain des L'Aube 5
145	Roi Mage 6	127	Fiasco du Pecos 7	134	Titi de Montmartre (f) 5
144	Chinco Star 6	127	Galop Marin 6	133	Achour 7
144	Docteur de Ballon 6	127	Middle 5	133	Danse Avec Jersey 5
144	Forthing 7	127	Virtus d'Estruval 9	133	Les Beaufs 9
143	Balkan du Pecos 7	126	Domiroli 9	133	Melchief 6
143	Polipa 12	126	Le Mans 5	132	A Mi Manera (f) 5
143	Punch Nantais 6	126	London Whale 7	132	Argentier 8
143	Sainte Turgeon (f) 6	126	Tito dela Barriere 11	132	Cantilien 8
143	Taupin Rochelais 11	126d	Amazone du Lemo (f) 8	132	Ci Blue 6
142	Corazones 6	125p	Darasso 5	132	Darasso 5
141	Danseur Jaguen 5	125	Baby Boy 7	132	D'Entree de Jeu (f) 5
140	Farlow des Mottes 10	125	Balk Man 6	132	Forthing 7
140	Monsamou 9	125	*Bialco 7	132	Middle 5
139	Via Dolorosa 6	125	Bucefal 7	132	Miss Salsa Blue (f) 5
138+	Argentier 8	125	Deadheat 5	131+	Protekapril 8
138	Dica de Thaix 5	125	Diamond Charm 9	131	Cobra de Larre 6
138	Tiesto d'Authie 7	125	Follow Me Soldier 5	131	Daryasi 5
137	Dalia Grandchamp (f) 5	125	Intrinseque 6	131	Grand Depart 5
136+	The Stomp 8	125	La Symphonie (f) 6	131	Oumensour 5
136	Brut Imperial 7	125	Le Toiny 7	131	Polygona (f) 8
136	Speed Fire 6	125	Los Banderos 9	131	Turiamix 8
135p	Janika 5	125	Maximo Meridio 7	130	Aragorn d'Alalia 8
135	Crack de Reve 6	125	Miss Salsa Blue (f) 5	130	Arry 8
135	Device 6	125	Quart de Rhum 9	130	Mali Borgia 8
135	Gothatir 6	125	Team Red 9	130	My Maj 9
135	Saint Palois 10			130	Perfect Impulse (f) 6
135	Vauquoise (f) 6	**Hurdlers (5yo+)**		130	So French 7
134	Al Bucq 12	164	De Bon Coeur (f) 5	130	Yosille (f) 6
134	Buck's Bank 10	160	Alex de Larredya 8	130?	Storminator 9
134	Burn Out 5	156	Device 6	129+	On The Go 5
134	Valtor 9	153	Le Grand Luce 9	129	Amirande 8
133	Accentus 8	151	Galop Marin 6	129	Apero Bleu 8
133	Roxinela (f) 5	150	Dalia Grandchamp (f) 5	129	*Djingle 7
132	A Mi Manera (f) 5	149	Saint Goustan Blue 6	129	Foreign Flower 5
132	Aviso d'Estruval 8	148	Bob And Co 7	129	Golden Chop 10
132	Borice 7	148	Pop Art du Berlais 5	129	Invicter 5
132	Calva du Rib 6	147	Izzo 5	129	Lamigo 10
132	Capivari 6	145§	Azucardel 7	129	Lord Prestige 11
132	Parc Monceau 7	144	Corazones 6	129	Mallorca (f) 8
132	Petellat du Rheu 5	144	Jazz In Montreux 5	129	Monsamou 9
132	Prince Philippe 8	143	The Stomp 8	129	Plumeur 11
132	The Reader 9	142	Chris de Beaumont 9	129	Quart de Rhum 9
131	Kaldou Euanas 9	142	Curly Basc (f) 6	129	Rasango 7
131	Vision de Maitre 5	141	Alti Plano 8	129	Roi Mage 6
130	Cobra de Larre 6	141	Capivari 6	129	Ulysse des Pictons 10
130	Fauburg Rosetgri 6	141	Farlow des Mottes 10	128p	Droit Divin 5
130	King Goubert 5	141	Kalifko 5	128p	Maresias (f) 5
130	Vire A Gauche 9	140	D'vina (f) 5	128	Capucine du Chenet (f) 6
129	Chahuteur 6	140	Silver Axe 8	128	Goddess Freja (f) 5
129	Fasimix 8	139	Dalila du Seuil (f) 5	128	Kazarov 5
129	Golden Chop 10	138	Jubilatoire (f) 5	128	L'Aubade (f) 5
129	Grand Depart 5	137	Al Bucq 12	128	Oro d'Allier 6
129	Grand des Landes 5	137	Balk Man 6	128	Sable Gris 6
129	Mallorca (f) 8	137	Bonne Eleve (f) 7	128	Square Beaujon 9
129	Styline (f) 6	137	Buck's Bank 10	128	Starkhov 5
129	Uroquois 10	137	Hurkhan 5	127+	The Reader 9
129	Vezelay 9	137	Song And Whisper 8	127	Cayo de Pail 9
129	Vicomte du Seuil 9	136	Boston Paris (f) 5	127	Crystal Beach 6
128	Babbo Natale 8	136	Serienschock 10	127	Daddy Banbou 5
128	Cafertiti 6	135	Angel's Share (f) 5	127	Natagaima (f) 5
128	Chaouia (f) 6	135	Crack de Reve 6	127	Rasique 7
128	Chestnut Dream 5	135	Hippomene 8	127	Roxinela (f) 5
128	Coastalina (f) 6	135	Le Chateau 9	127	Srelighonn 5

127d	Fracafigura Has (f) 7	120	Ardcross	124	Artemidor (f)
126	Candide 5	120	Electron Bleu	124	Black Luna (f)
126	Fauburg Rosetgri 6	120	Kapeloi	124	Emirat
126	Fyrmyin 7	120	Royale Pagaille	124	Honneur des Obeaux
126	Gothatir 6			123	Eludy (f)
126	Kami Kaze 7	**Hurdlers (4yo)**		123	En Bonne Main (f)
126	Maximo Meridio 7	150	Master Dino	123	Evidence Madrik (f)
126	Mondieu 5	149	Tunis	123	Gryffichop
126	Salam Bombay 9	147p	Wildriver (f)	123	Sucaille (f)
126	Spiderman 5	143	Beau Gosse	122	Aquatique (f)
126	Tiesto d'Authie 7	143	Lou Buck's	122	Ecbatane (f)
126	Via Dolorosa 6	142	Spinozzar	122	Ermontois
125p	Dellysson 5	141	Pesk Ebrel	122	Etat de Grace
125	Bora des Obeaux (f) 7	138	Klassical Dream	122	Hot Motive
125	Celtino 7	138	Whetstone (f)	122	Joie du Net (f)
125	Defi d'Oudairies 5	137	Enfant du Pays	122	Saint Baron
125	Intrinseque 6	137	Tertre	122	Santa Diana (f)
125	Khefyn 8	136	Equemauville	121+	Jean Luc
125	Kingalola 5	136	Nil Dream	121	Briouze
125	Le Mans 5	135	Desaguadero	121	Echo Sacre
125	*Mrs Lovett (f) 5	133	A Plus Tard	121	Epi Sacre
125	Peace of Burg 5	133	Cote de Grace (f)	121	Evidence Allen (f)
125	Saint Palois 10	133	Magic Saint	121	Marlonne (f)
125	Vendure des Obeaux (f) 9	133	Mozo Guapo	121	Santa Adelia (f)
		131+	Candalex	121	Spirit Sun
Chasers (4yo)		131	Ajas	120p	L'Amour du Risk
149p	Whetstone (f)	131	Cicalina (f)	120	Cocolegustachocho
148p	Echiquier Royal	131	Eclipse de Cotte (f)	120	Enfant Roi
142	My Way	131	Energy d'Olivate (f)	120	Equation (f)
140	Spanish One	131	Sainte Gaya (f)	120	Ex Fan des Sixties (f)
136	Evidence Madrik (f)	130	Good Lucky	120	La Percutante (f)
133p	Echiquier	130	Kapkiline (f)	120	Rhodax
133	Cote de Grace (f)	130	Merlin Woods (f)	120	Royale Pagaille
132	Ex Fan des Sixties (f)	130	*Rock de Baune		
132	Good Lucky	129	*Casa Tall	**Hurdlers (3yo)**	
132	Sharock	129	Raffles Sun (f)	138p	Porto Pollo
131	Majurca	128	Valcroix	138	Beaumec de Houelle
130	Confuceen	127p	El Gringo	138	Pic d'Orhy
130	Ebene du Breuil (f)	127p	Eni Light	137	Listenmania (f)
130	Kapkiline (f)	127p	Golden Sage (f)	134	Vanille du Berlais (f)
128p	Gryffichop	127	Bounwell	133	La Griottiere (f)
128	Ajas	127	Caribean Boy	132	Polirico
128	Cat Tiger	127	Ejland (f)	128p	Powder Path
127+	Cicalina (f)	127	Extreme Nouba	128	Goliath du Berlais
127	Aurelio	127	Hell Boy	126p	Rebellio
127	Eurasien	127	Mysterious Boy	126	Enjoy It (f)
127	Magic Saint	127	Sainte Saone (f)	125p	Thrilling (f)
127	Piton des Neiges	127?	Independenceday	125	Etoile du Ficheaux (f)
126	Eddy Blues	126	Alpha Joa (f)	125	Hurkova (f)
126	Royale Maria Has (f)	126	Blasimon	125	Quel Destin
125	Ecume du Large (f)	126	Doctor Rocket	125	Straycat
125	Joie du Net (f)	126	El Atillo	124	Adjali
125	Santa Diana (f)	126	El Martel	124	Bel Apsis
124	Saint Baron	126	Elimay (f)	124	Dogon
123	Bounwell	126	Lake's Maker	124	Fiumicino
123	Calinight	126	Royale Maria Has (f)	124	Last Sparkler
123	El Camila (f)	126	Sugar Crush	123p	Bernardo Bellotto
121	Amafacon	125	Eragone	123	Blue Silver
121	Excel Quiz Tauel	125	Etourneau	123	Twinkling
121	Rhodax	125	Impala du Rheu (f)	122	Farnice
120p	Envoye Special	125	Janidex	121	Festivalier
120p	Lou Buck's	125	Sharock	120	Shahina du Berlais (f)

NB Ratings relate to performances between July 2017 and June 2018. Horses marked with an * were trained in France for only part of the season; horses which were originally trained in France but subsequently showed much better form in Britain/Ireland are not included in the above lists.

INDEX TO PHOTOGRAPHS
PORTRAITS & SNAPSHOTS

Horse	Age & Breeding	Copyright	Page
Acey Milan	4 b.g. Milan – Strong Wishes	Bill Selwyn	36
Altior	8 b.g. High Chaparral – Monte Solaro	Dinah Nicholson	58
Bellshill	8 b.g. King's Theatre – Fairy Native	Caroline Norris	114
Benie des Dieux	7 b.m. Great Pretender – Cana	Caroline Norris	119
Black Corton	7 br.g. Laverock – Pour Le Meilleur	Bill Selwyn	134
Black Op	7 br.g. Sandmason – Afar Story	Bill Selwyn	138
Bleu Berry	7 b.g. Special Kaldoun – Somosierra	Caroline Norris	142
Bristol de Mai	7 gr.g. Saddler Maker – La Bole Night	Dinah Nicholson	159
Carefully Selected	6 b.g. Well Chosen – Knockamullen Girl	Caroline Norris	184
Claimantakinforgan...	6 b.g. Great Pretender – Taquine d'Estrees	Dinah Nicholson	203
Clan des Obeaux	6 b.g. Kapgarde – Nausicaa des Obeaux	Bill Selwyn	205
Cloudy Dream	8 gr.g. Cloudings – Run Away Dream	Francesca Altoft	209
Cue Card	12 b.g. King's Theatre – Wicked Crack	Bill Selwyn	230
Cyrus Darius	9 b.g. Overbury – Barton Belle	Francesca Altoft	234
Delta Work	5 br.g. Network – Robbe	Peter Mooney	250
Diego du Charmil	6 b.g. Ballingarry – Daramour	Bill Selwyn	259
Doctor Phoenix	10 br.g. Dr Massini – Lowroad Cross	Peter Mooney	264
Dortmund Park	5 b.g. Great Pretender – Qena	Peter Mooney	269
Double Shuffle	8 b.g. Milan – Fiddlers Bar	Bill Selwyn	270
Draconien	5 br.g. Linda's Lad – Holding	Caroline Norris	274
Edwulf	9 b.g. Kayf Tara – Valentines Lady	Peter Mooney	289
Elegant Escape	6 b.g. Dubai Destination – Graineuaile	Bill Selwyn	291
Elgin	6 b.g. Duke of Marmalade – China Tea	Dinah Nicholson	293
Espoir d'Allen	4 b.g. Voix du Nord – Quadanse	Peter Mooney	300
Farclas	4 gr.g. Jukebox Jury – Floriana	Peter Mooney	307
Finian's Oscar	6 b.g. Oscar – Trinity Alley	Bill Selwyn	317
Footpad	6 b.g. Creachadoir – Willamina	Caroline Norris	330
Frodon	6 b.g. Nickname – Miss Country	Bill Selwyn	338
General Principle	9 b.g. Gold Well – How Provincial	Peter Mooney	346
Global Citizen	6 b.g. Alkaadhem – Lady Willmurt	Dinah Nicholson	356
Kalashnikov	5 br.g. Kalanisi – Fairy Lane	Laurie Morton	428
Kemboy	6 b.g. Voix du Nord – Vitora	Caroline Norris	435
Kilbricken Storm	7 b.g. Oscar – Kilbricken Leader	Bill Selwyn	439
Killultagh Vic	9 b.g. Old Vic – Killultagh Dawn	Caroline Norris	442
Laurina	5 b.m. Spanish Moon – Lamboghina	Caroline Norris	464
Lostintranslation	6 b.g. Flemensfirth – Falika	Bill Selwyn	482
Mengli Khan	5 b.g. Lope de Vega – Danielli	Peter Mooney	507
Might Bite	9 b.g. Scorpion – Knotted Midge	Dinah Nicholson	521
Mr Adjudicator	4 b.g. Camacho – Attlongglast	Caroline Norris	553
Ms Parfois	7 ch.m. Mahler – Dolly Lewis	Bill Selwyn	559
Native River	8 ch.g. Indian River – Native Mo	Bill Selwyn	572
Next Destination	6 b.g. Dubai Destination – Liss Alainn	Caroline Norris	579
Old Guard	7 b.g. Notnowcato – Dolma	Bill Selwyn	593
On The Blind Side	6 b.g. Stowaway – Such A Set Up	Dinah Nicholson	597
Poetic Rhythm	7 ch.g. Flemensfirth – Sommer Sonnet	Dinah Nicholson	628
Politologue	7 gr.g. Poliglote – Scarlet Row	Bill Selwyn	632
Rathvinden	10 b.g. Heron Island – Peggy Cullen	Caroline Norris	655
Redicean	4 b.g. Medicean – Red Halo	Dinah Nicholson	660
Saldier	4 b.g. Soldier Hollow – Salve Evita	Caroline Norris	695
Samcro	6 ch.g. Germany – Dun Dun	Peter Mooney	700
Santini	6 b.g. Milan – Tinagoodnight	Dinah Nicholson	710
Sceau Royal	6 b.g. Doctor Dino – Sandside	Dinah Nicholson	715
Shattered Love	7 b.m. Yeats – Tracker	Peter Mooney	730
Summerville Boy	6 b.g. Sandmason – Suny House	Bill Selwyn	775
Terrefort	5 gr.g. Martaline – Vie de Reine	Dinah Nicholson	794
Top Notch	7 b.g. Poliglote – Topira	Dinah Nicholson	839

Topofthegame	6 ch.g. Flemensfirth – Derry Vale	*Bill Selwyn*	841
Tornado Flyer	5 b.g. Flemensfirth – Mucho Macabi	*Caroline Norris*	842
Total Recall	9 b.g. Westerner – Augest Weekend	*Caroline Norris*	846
We Have A Dream	4 b.g. Martaline – Sweet Dance	*Dinah Nicholson*	886

RACE PHOTOGRAPHS

Race and Meeting	*Copyright*	*Page*
AES Champion Four Year Old Hurdle (Punchestown)	*Peter Mooney*	694
Albert Bartlett Novices' Hurdle (Spa) (Cheltenham)	*John Crofts*	438
Alder Hey Children's Charity Handicap Hurdle (Aintree)	*Martin Lynch*	414
Ascot Spring Garden Show Holloway's Handicap Hurdle (Ascot)	*Ed Byrne*	412
Badger Ales Trophy Handicap Chase (Wincanton)	*Bill Selwyn*	642
Ballymore Classic Novices' Chase (Cheltenham)	*Bill Selwyn*	708
Ballymore Handicap Hurdle (Punchestown)	*Caroline Norris*	509
Ballymore Novices' Hurdle (Baring Bingham) (Cheltenham)	*Peter Mooney*	699
Bar One Racing Drinmore Novices' Chase (Fairyhouse)	*Peter Mooney*	244
Bar One Racing Hatton's Grace Hurdle (Fairyhouse)	*Peter Mooney*	72
Bar One Racing Porterstown Handicap Chase (Fairyhouse)	*Caroline Norris*	640
BetBright Best For Festival Betting Handicap Chase (Cheltenham)	*Bill Selwyn*	99
BetBright Dipper Novices' Chase (Cheltenham)	*Francesca Altoft*	903
BetBright Trial Cotswold Chase (Cheltenham)	*Ed Byrne*	246
Betdaq Handicap Chase (Kempton)	*Ed Byrne*	499
Betdaq 2% Commission Punchestown Champion Hurdle (Punchestown)	*Peter Mooney*	779
Betfair Ascot Chase (Ascot)	*Ed Byrne*	878
Betfair Chase (Haydock)	*Martin Lynch*	158
Betfair Denman Chase (Newbury)	*Francesca Altoft*	569
Betfair Exchange Chase (Game Spirit) (Newbury)	*Ed Byrne*	54
Betfair Hurdle (Handicap) (Newbury)	*Ed Byrne*	427
Betfair Stayers' Handicap Hurdle (Haydock)	*George Selwyn*	703
Betfair Tingle Creek Chase (Sandown)	*Bill Selwyn*	630
Betfred Challow Novices' Hurdle (Newbury)	*Francesca Altoft*	627
Betfred Classic Handicap Chase (Warwick)	*George Selwyn*	523
Betfred Grand National Trial Handicap Chase (Haydock)	*Martin Lynch*	902
Betfred Midlands Grand National Handicap Chase (Uttoxeter)	*Martin Lynch*	663
Betfred 'Racing's Biggest Supporter' Novices' Handicap Chase (Newbury)	*Bill Selwyn*	692
Betfred Summer Plate Handicap Chase (Market Rasen)	*Martin Lynch*	48
Betfred TV Scilly Isles Novices' Chase (Sandown)	*Ed Byrne*	792
Betfred TV Summer Handicap Hurdle (Market Rasen)	*Martin Lynch*	419
bet365 Celebration Chase (Sandown)	*George Selwyn*	56
bet365 Charlie Hall Chase (Wetherby)	*Martin Lynch*	157
bet365 Gold Cup Handicap Chase (Sandown)	*Bill Selwyn*	764
bet365 Handicap Chase (Ascot)	*Ed Byrne*	37
bet365 Hurdle (West Yorkshire) (Wetherby)	*Martin Lynch*	212
bet365 Oaksey Chase (Sandown)	*Bill Selwyn*	838
BetVictor Gold Cup Handicap Chase (Cheltenham)	*Martin Lynch*	758
Betway Aintree Hurdle (Aintree)	*Bill Selwyn*	458
Betway Bowl Chase (Aintree)	*Bill Selwyn*	519
Betway Handicap Chase (Aintree)	*Bill Selwyn*	813
Betway Mersey Novices' Hurdle (Aintree)	*Martin Lynch*	137
Betway Mildmay Novices' Chase (Aintree)	*Bill Selwyn*	793
Betway Queen Mother Champion Chase (Cheltenham)	*George Selwyn*	55
Betway Top Novices' Hurdle (Aintree)	*Bill Selwyn*	455
BHP Insurance Irish Champion Hurdle (Leopardstown)	*Peter Mooney*	778
Big Buck's Celebration Manifesto Novices' Chase (Aintree)	*John Grossick*	316
Boodles Fred Winter Juvenile Handicap Hurdle (Cheltenham)	*Bill Selwyn*	868
Boylesports Champion Chase (Punchestown)	*Peter Mooney*	861
Boylesports Irish Grand National Chase (Extended Handicap) (Fairyhouse)	*Healy Racing*	345

Race	Photographer	Page
Boylesports Irish Grand National Chase (Extended Handicap) (Fairyhouse)	Healy Racing	345
Brown Advisory & Merriebelle Stable Plate Handicap Chase (Cheltenham)	Bill Selwyn	809
Caspian Caviar Gold Cup Handicap Chase (Cheltenham)	John Crofts	370
Christy 1965 Chase (Ascot)	Francesca Altoft	837
Close Brothers Novices' Handicap Chase (Cheltenham)	John Grossick	537
Coolmore NH Sires Irish European Breeders Fund Mares INH Flat (Leopardstown)	Caroline Norris	665
Coral Cup Handicap Hurdle (Cheltenham)	Ed Byrne	141
Coral Dublin Chase (Leopardstown)	Peter Mooney	529
Coral Future Champions Finale Juvenile Hurdle (Chepstow)	Bill Selwyn	884
Coral Hurdle (Ascot)	Francesca Altoft	473
Coral Punchestown Gold Cup Chase (Punchestown)	Peter Mooney	113
Coral Scottish Grand National Handicap Chase (Ayr)	John Grossick	416
Coral Scottish Grand National Handicap Chase (Ayr)	John Grossick	417
Coral Welsh Grand National Handicap Chase (Chepstow)	Bill Selwyn	656
Dawn Homes Novices' Championship Handicap Chase (Ayr)	John Grossick	226
Deloitte Novices' Hurdle (Leopardstown)	Caroline Norris	698
Doom Bar Anniversary 4-Y-O Juvenile Hurdle (Aintree)	Bill Selwyn	885
Doom Bar Maghull Novices' Chase (Aintree)	John Grossick	258
Doom Bar Sefton Novices' Hurdle (Aintree)	John Grossick	709
Dornan Engineering Relkeel Hurdle (Cheltenham)	Francesca Altoft	893
EBF TBA Mares' 'National Hunt' Novices' Hurdle Finale (Limited Handicap) (Newbury)	Francesca Altoft	680
EMS Copiers Novices' Handicap Chase (Punchestown)	Caroline Norris	434
European Breeders' Fund Annie Power Mares Champion Hurdle (Punchestown)	Peter Mooney	118
European Breeders' Fund Matchbook VIP National Hunt Novices' Handicap Hurdle Final (Sandown)	Ed Byrne	702
Flogas Novices' Chase (Scalp) (Leopardstown)	Caroline Norris	541
Frank Ward Solicitors Arkle Novices' Chase (Leopardstown)	Peter Mooney	327
Fulke Walwyn Kim Muir Challenge Cup Amateur Riders' Handicap Chase (Cheltenham)	Bill Selwyn	532
galliardhomes.com Cleeve Hurdle (Cheltenham)	Ed Byrne	40
Gaskells Handicap Hurdle (Aintree)	George Selwyn	555
Glenfarclas Chase (Cross Country) (Cheltenham)	Bill Selwyn	820
Goffs Land Rover Bumper (Punchestown)	Peter Mooney	214
Goffs Nickel Coin Mares' Standard Open NH Flat Race (Aintree)	George Selwyn	351
Growise Champion Novices' Chase (Punchestown)	Caroline Norris	46
Growise Champion Novices' Chase (Punchestown)	Peter Mooney	46
Growise Champion Novices' Chase (Punchestown)	Bill Selwyn	809
Guinness Galway Hurdle Handicap (Galway)	Caroline Norris	831
Guinness Handicap Chase (Punchestown)	Caroline Norris	614
Guinness Kerry National Handicap Chase (Listowel)	Caroline Norris	637
Herald Champion Novices' Hurdle (Punchestown)	Peter Mooney	273
Huw Stevens, Jo Whiley Afterparty Onsale Mares' Novices' Hurdle (Cheltenham)	Bill Selwyn	236
Irish Daily Mirror Novices' Hurdle (War of Attrition) (Punchestown)	Bill Selwyn	577
Irish Stallion Farms European Breeders Fund Mares Novices' Hurdle Championship (Punchestown)	Peter Mooney	463
JCB Triumph Hurdle (Cheltenham)	John Crofts	306
JCB Triumph Trial Juvenile Hurdle (Cheltenham)	Ed Byrne	74
JLT Melling Chase (Aintree)	George Selwyn	631
JLT Novices' Chase (Golden Miller) (Cheltenham)	Francesca Altoft	729
JLT Reve de Sivola Long Walk Hurdle (Ascot)	George Selwyn	704
JNwine.com Champion Chase (Down Royal)	Healy Racing	604
John Durkan Memorial Punchestown Chase (Punchestown)	Peter Mooney	743
Johnny Henderson Grand Annual Challenge Cup Handicap Chase (Cheltenham)	Bill Selwyn	469

JT McNamara Ladbrokes Munster National Handicap Chase (Limerick)	*Healy Racing*	844
Keltbray Swinley Chase (Limited Handicap) (Ascot)	*Ed Byrne*	662
Knight Frank Juvenile Hurdle (Leopardstown)	*Peter Mooney*	299
Ladbrokes Champion Stayers' Hurdle (Punchestown)	*Peter Mooney*	310
Ladbrokes Long Distance Hurdle (Newbury)	*Francesca Altoft*	110
Ladbrokes Trophy Chase (Handicap) (Newbury)	*John Crofts*	845
Lavazza Silver Cup Handicap Chase (Ascot)	*Francesca Altoft*	360
Leopardstown Christmas Chase (Leopardstown)	*Caroline Norris*	674
Liam & Valerie Brennan Memorial Florida Pearl Novices' Chase (Punchestown)	*Caroline Norris*	422
Martin Pipe Conditional Jockeys' Handicap Hurdle (Cheltenham)	*Ed Byrne*	143
Matchbook Imperial Cup Handicap Hurdle (Sandown)	*Ed Byrne*	554
National Hunt Challenge Cup (Cheltenham)	*George Selwyn*	654
Neville Hotels Novices' Chase (Fort Leney) (Leopardstown)	*Caroline Norris*	728
1956 Grand National (Aintree)	*Movietone and others*	818
1935 Cheltenham Gold Cup	*Central Press Photos*	567
OLBG.com Mares' Hurdle (Wetherby)	*Martin Lynch*	451
OLBG.com Yorkshire Rose Mares' Hurdle (Doncaster)	*Martin Lynch*	495
OLBG Mares' Hurdle (David Nicholson) (Cheltenham)	*Ed Byrne*	117
188Bet Grand Sefton Handicap Chase (Aintree)	*George Selwyn*	343
Paddy Power Chase (Leopardstown)	*Caroline Norris*	66
Paddy's Rewards Club Chase (Leopardstown)	*Peter Mooney*	738
Pertemps Network Final Handicap Hurdle (Cheltenham)	*Peter Mooney*	249
Prix des Drags Chase (Auteuil)	*Bertrand*	90
Prix La Barka Hurdle (Auteuil)	*Bertrand*	104
Profile Systems Champion Novices' Hurdle (Punchestown)	*Peter Mooney*	268
QTS Scottish Champion Hurdle (Limited Handicap) (Ayr)	*John Grossick*	515
Racing Post Arkle Challenge Trophy Novices' Chase (Cheltenham)	*George Selwyn*	328
Racing Post Champion INH Flat (Punchestown)	*Peter Mooney*	842
Racing Post Novices' Chase (Leopardstown)	*Peter Mooney*	326
Racing Welfare Handicap Hurdle (Ascot)	*George Selwyn*	391
Randox Health Becher Handicap Chase (Aintree)	*Martin Lynch*	140
randoxhealth.com Henry VIII Novices' Chase (Sandown)	*Bill Selwyn*	714
Randox Health County Handicap Hurdle (Cheltenham)	*John Crofts*	538
Randox Health Foxhunters' Chase (Aintree)	*Bill Selwyn*	103
Randox Health Grand National Handicap Chase (Aintree)	*Bill Selwyn*	822
Randox Health Grand National Handicap Chase (Aintree)	*John Grossick*	823
Randox Health Grand National Handicap Chase (Aintree)	*Martin Lynch*	824
Randox Health Grand National Handicap Chase (Aintree)	*George Selwyn*	825
Randox Health Grand National Handicap Chase (Aintree)	*Bill Selwyn*	826
Randox Health Grand National Handicap Chase (Aintree)	*John Grossick*	827
Randox Health Grand National Handicap Chase (Aintree)	*George Selwyn*	828
Randox Health Topham Handicap Chase (Aintree)	*Bill Selwyn*	857
Red Mills Chase (Gowran)	*Peter Mooney*	603
Royal Salute Whisky Clarence House Chase (Ascot)	*Ed Byrne*	860
RSA Insurance Novices' Chase (Cheltenham)	*Bill Selwyn*	641
Ryanair Chase (Festival Trophy) (Cheltenham)	*Bill Selwyn*	94
Ryanair Gold Cup Novices' Chase (Fairyhouse)	*Peter Mooney*	44
Ryanair Hurdle (December) (Leopardstown)	*Peter Mooney*	511
Ryanair Novices' Chase (Punchestown)	*Bill Selwyn*	329
Ryanair Stayers' Hurdle (Liverpool) (Aintree)	*George Selwyn*	395
Shawbrook Handicap Chase (Ascot)	*Francesca Altoft*	740
Shloer Chase (Cheltenham)	*John Crofts*	334
Sky Bet Moscow Flyer Novices' Hurdle (Punchestown)	*Caroline Norris*	349
Sky Bet Supreme Novices' Hurdle (Cheltenham)	*Bill Selwyn*	774
Smarkets Challenger Series Mares' Final Handicap Chase (Haydock)	*Martin Lynch*	682
Sodexo Reynoldstown Novices' Chase (Ascot)	*Ed Byrne*	133
Squared Financial Christmas Hurdle (Leopardstown)	*Caroline Norris*	73
Star Best For Racing Coverage Champion Hunters Chase (Punchestown)	*Bill Selwyn*	175

St James's Place Foxhunter Challenge Cup (Cheltenham)	*George Selwyn*	608
Sun Bets Stayers' Hurdle (Cheltenham)	*Ed Byrne*	617
Ten Up Novices' Chase (Navan)	*Peter Mooney*	543
thetote.com Galway Plate (Galway)	*Caroline Norris*	93
32Red.com Wayward Lad Novices' Chase (Kempton)	*Francesca Altoft*	233
32Red Kauto Star Novices' Chase (Kempton)	*Francesca Altoft*	132
32Red King George VI Chase (Kempton)	*George Selwyn*	517
32Red Tolworth Novices' Hurdle (Sandown)	*George Selwyn*	773
32Red Veterans' Handicap Chase (Series Final) (Sandown)	*George Selwyn*	172
Timeform Novices' Handicap Chase (Cheltenham)	*Ed Byrne*	536
Timico Cheltenham Gold Cup Chase (Cheltenham)	*Bill Selwyn*	570
Timico Cheltenham Gold Cup Chase (Cheltenham)	*John Crofts*	570
totepool Silver Trophy Handicap Hurdle (Chepstow)	*Bill Selwyn*	222
totesport.com Towton Novices' Chase (Wetherby)	*Martin Lynch*	100
Trull House Stud Mares' Novices' Hurdle (Dawn Run) (Cheltenham)	*Peter Mooney*	462
Ultima Handicap Chase (Cheltenham)	*Ed Byrne*	217
Unibet Champion Hurdle Challenge Trophy (Cheltenham)	*Ed Byrne*	170
Unibet Champion Hurdle Trial (Haydock)	*Martin Lynch*	806
Unibet Christmas Hurdle (Kempton)	*Francesca Altoft*	169
Unibet Elite Hurdle (Limited Handicap) (Wincanton)	*Bill Selwyn*	478
Unibet 'Fighting Fifth' Hurdle (Newcastle)	*John Grossick*	168
Unibet Greatwood Handicap Hurdle (Cheltenham)	*John Crofts*	292
Unibet International Hurdle (Cheltenham)	*John Crofts*	564
Unibet Irish Gold Cup (Leopardstown)	*Caroline Norris*	288
Weatherbys Champion Bumper (Cheltenham)	*John Grossick*	666
Weatherbys Racing Bank Standard Open National Hunt Flat (Aintree)	*Bill Selwyn*	635
WKD Hurdle (Down Royal)	*Caroline Norris*	504
Worcester Racecourse	*Bernard Parkin & George Selwyn*	131
Zut Media Red Rum Handicap Chase (Aintree)	*George Selwyn*	121

ADDITIONAL PHOTOGRAPHS

The following photos appear in the Introduction:- Native River and Might Bite at the second last in the Gold Cup (taken by Ed Byrne), the Mullins family (Caroline Norris), Un de Sceaux wins the Boylesports Champion Chase (Peter Mooney), Tiger Roll's connections (Bill Selwyn), Nicky Henderson champion trainer (George Selwyn), Altior wins the Queen Mother Champion Chase (Peter Mooney), The 'beast from the east' (George Selwyn), Richard Johnson and James Bowen (George Selwyn), Dan and Harry Skelton (Bill Selwyn), Waiting Patiently wins the Betfair Ascot Chase (Bill Selwyn), Paul Townend/Andrew Thornton (Bill Selwyn and George Selwyn), Nina Carberry and Katie Walsh (Caroline Norris), Alec Russell master photographer (David Harrison, The Press, York).

Timeform Champions of 2017/18:- Altior (taken by Bill Selwyn)

Credits for the photographs in 'Top Horses In France' are as follows:-
Grand Steeple-Chase de Paris, Prix La Haye Jousselin, Grande Course de Haies, Grand Prix d'Automne, Prix Ferdinand Dufaure, Prix Cambaceres (all taken by Bertrand)

CHAMPIONS FROM THE 'CHASERS & HURDLERS' SERIES

HORSE OF THE YEAR

1975/76	Night Nurse	**178**
1976/77	Night Nurse	**182**
1977/78	Monksfield	**177**
1978/79	Monksfield	**180**
1979/80	Sea Pigeon	**175**
1980/81	Little Owl	**176**
1981/82	Silver Buck	**175**
1982/83	Badsworth Boy	**179**
1983/84	Dawn Run	**173**
1984/85	Burrough Hill Lad	**184**
1985/86	Dawn Run	**167**
1986/87	Desert Orchid	**177**
1987/88	Desert Orchid	**177**
1988/89	Desert Orchid	**182**
1989/90	Desert Orchid	**187**
1990/91	Morley Street	**174**
1991/92	Carvill's Hill	**182**
1992/93	Jodami	**174p**
1993/94	Danoli	**172p**
1994/95	Master Oats	**183**
1995/96	One Man	**179**
1996/97	Make A Stand	**165**
1997/98	Istabraq	**172+**
1998/99	Istabraq	**177+**
1999/00	Istabraq	**180**
2000/01	First Gold	**180**
2001/02	Baracouda	**169+**
2002/03	Best Mate	**182**
2003/04	Moscow Flyer	**183**
2004/05	Moscow Flyer	**184+**
2005/06	Brave Inca	**167**
2006/07	Kauto Star	**184+**
2007/08	Denman	**180p**
2008/09	Kauto Star	**184**
2009/10	Kauto Star	**191**
2010/11	Hurricane Fly	**172**
2011/12	Big Buck's	**176+**
2012/13	Sprinter Sacre	**192p**

	2013/14	More of That			**173p**
	2014/15	Don Cossack			**180**
	2015/16	Don Cossack			**183**
	2016/17	Altior			**175p**
	2017/18	Altior			**179p**

Best Two-Mile Chaser

75/76	Lough Inagh	**167**	97/98	One Man	**176**
76/77	Skymas	**156**	98/99	Direct Route	**166**
77/78	Tingle Creek	**154**	99/00	Flagship Uberalles	**175**
78/79	Siberian Sun	**151**	00/01	Flagship Uberalles	**175**
79/80	I'm A Driver	**163**	01/02	Flagship Uberalles	**170**
80/81	Anaglogs Daughter	**171**	02/03	Moscow Flyer	**170p**
81/82	Rathgorman	**170**	03/04	Moscow Flyer	**183**
82/83	Badsworth Boy	**179**	04/05	Moscow Flyer	**184+**
83/84	Badsworth Boy	**177**	05/06	Kauto Star	**166+**
84/85	Bobsline	**164+**	06/07	Kauto Star	**184+**
85/86	Dawn Run	**167**	07/08	Master Minded	**179**
86/87	Pearlyman	**171**	08/09	Master Minded	**179**
87/88	Pearlyman	**174**	09/10	Big Zeb	**169**
88/89	Desert Orchid	**182**	10/11	Big Zeb	**172**
89/90	Desert Orchid	**187**	11/12	Sprinter Sacre	**175p**
90/91	Desert Orchid	**178**	12/13	Sprinter Sacre	**192p**
91/92	Remittance Man	**173**	13/14	Sire de Grugy	**172**
92/93	Katabatic	**161?**	14/15	Un de Sceaux	**169p**
93/94	Viking Flagship	**166**	15/16	Douvan	**180p**
94/95	Viking Flagship	**169**	16/17	Douvan	**182**
95/96	Klairon Davis	**177**	17/18	Altior	**179p**
96/97	Martha's Son	**177**			

Best Staying Chaser

75/76	Captain Christy	**182**	97/98	Cool Dawn	**173**
76/77	Bannow Rambler	**163**	98/99	Suny Bay	**176**
77/78	Midnight Court	**164**	99/00	See More Business	**182**
78/79	Gay Spartan	**166**	00/01	First Gold	**180**
79/80	Silver Buck	**171**	01/02	Best Mate	**173**
80/81	Little Owl	**176**		Florida Pearl	**173**
81/82	Silver Buck	**175**	02/03	Best Mate	**182**
82/83	Bregawn	**177**	03/04	Best Mate	**176+**
83/84	Burrough Hill Lad	**175**	04/05	Kicking King	**182**
	Wayward Lad	**175**	05/06	Beef Or Salmon	**174x**
84/85	Burrough Hill Lad	**184**	06/07	Kauto Star	**184+**
85/86	Burrough Hill Lad	**183**	07/08	Kauto Star	**182**
86/87	Desert Orchid	**177**	08/09	Kauto Star	**184**
87/88	Desert Orchid	**177**	09/10	Kauto Star	**191**
88/89	Desert Orchid	**182**	10/11	Long Run	**184**
89/90	Desert Orchid	**187**	11/12	Kauto Star	**179**
90/91	Desert Orchid	**178**	12/13	Bobs Worth	**179**
91/92	Carvill's Hill	**182**	13/14	Cue Card	**180**
92/93	Jodami	**174p**	14/15	Don Cossack	**180**
93/94	The Fellow	**171**	15/16	Don Cossack	**183**
94/95	Master Oats	**183**	16/17	Cue Card	**174**
95/96	One Man	**179**		Thistlecrack	**174**
96/97	One Man	**176**	17/18	Native River	**172**

Best Novice Chaser

75/76	Bannow Rambler	**152p**	99/00	Gloria Victis	**172**
76/77	Tree Tangle	**159§**	00/01	Bacchanal	**161p**
77/78	The Dealer	**145**		Shotgun Willy	**161**
78/79	Silver Buck	**151**	01/02	Moscow Flyer	**159p**
79/80	Anaglogs Daughter	**156**	02/03	Beef Or Salmon	**165p**
80/81	Clayside	**145**	03/04	Strong Flow	**156p**
81/82	Brown Chamberlin	**147p**	04/05	Ashley Brook	**154+**
82/83	Righthand Man	**150**		Fundamentalist	**154p**
83/84	Bobsline	**161p**		Ollie Magern	**154**
84/85	Drumadowney	**159**	05/06	Monet's Garden	**156p**
85/86	Pearlyman	**150**	06/07	Denman	**161p**
86/87	Kildimo	**151p**	07/08	Tidal Bay	**161+**
87/88	Danish Flight	**156p**	08/09	Cooldine	**158p**
88/89	Carvill's Hill	**169p**	09/10	Tataniano	**158p**
89/90	Celtic Shot	**152p**	10/11	Wishfull Thinking	**165**
90/91	Remittance Man	**153p**	11/12	Sprinter Sacre	**175p**
91/92	Miinnehoma	**152p**	12/13	Simonsig	**166p**
92/93	Sybillin	**156**	13/14	Holywell	**158p**
93/94	Monsieur Le Cure	**156p**		Balder Succes	**158**
94/95	Brief Gale	**159**	14/15	Vautour	**171p**
95/96	Mr Mulligan	**154**	15/16	Douvan	**180p**
96/97	Strong Promise	**171+**	16/17	Altior	**175p**
97/98	Escartefigue	**171p**	17/18	Footpad	**174p**
98/99	Nick Dundee	**164+**			

Best Two-Mile Hurdler

75/76	Night Nurse	**178**	97/98	Istabraq	**172+**
76/77	Night Nurse	**182**	98/99	Istabraq	**177+**
77/78	Monksfield	**177**	99/00	Istabraq	**180**
78/79	Monksfield	**180**	00/01	Istabraq	**180**
79/80	Sea Pigeon	**175**	01/02	Limestone Lad	**167**
80/81	Sea Pigeon	**175**	02/03	Rooster Booster	**170**
81/82	For Auction	**174**	03/04	Hardy Eustace	**167**
82/83	Gaye Brief	**175**	04/05	Hardy Eustace	**165**
83/84	Dawn Run	**173**	05/06	Brave Inca	**167**
84/85	Browne's Gazette	**172**	06/07	Sublimity	**164**
85/86	See You Then	**173**	07/08	Sizing Europe	**165**
86/87	See You Then	**173**	08/09	Binocular	**166**
87/88	Celtic Shot	**170**	09/10	Binocular	**168**
88/89	Beech Road	**172**	10/11	Hurricane Fly	**172**
89/90	Kribensis	**169**	11/12	Hurricane Fly	**173**
90/91	Morley Street	**174**	12/13	Hurricane Fly	**173**
91/92	Granville Again	**165p**	13/14	Jezki	**171**
92/93	Mighty Mogul	**170**	14/15	Faugheen	**171+**
93/94	Danoli	**172p**	15/16	Faugheen	**176**
94/95	Alderbrook	**174p**	16/17	Buveur d'Air	**170**
95/96	Alderbrook	**174**	17/18	Buveur d'Air	**167**
96/97	Make A Stand	**165**			

Best Staying Hurdler

75/76	Comedy of Errors	**170**	79/80	Pollardstown	**167**
76/77	Night Nurse	**182**	80/81	Daring Run	**171+**
77/78	Monksfield	**177**	81/82	Daring Run	**171**
78/79	Monksfield	**180**	82/83	Gaye Brief	**175**

83/84	Dawn Run	173	01/02	Baracouda	169+
84/85	Bajan Sunshine	162	02/03	Baracouda	175
85/86	Gaye Brief	167	03/04	Iris's Gift	172
86/87	Galmoy	165	04/05	Inglis Drever	162
87/88	Galmoy	160	05/06	Mighty Man	166
88/89	Rustle	169	06/07	Mighty Man	172
89/90	Trapper John	159	07/08	Inglis Drever	169
90/91	King's Curate	164	08/09	Big Buck's	174+
91/92	Nomadic Way	162	09/10	Big Buck's	174+
92/93	Sweet Duke	161	10/11	Big Buck's	176+
93/94	Sweet Glow	162	11/12	Big Buck's	176+
94/95	Dorans Pride	167	12/13	Big Buck's	176+
95/96	Pleasure Shared	163p	13/14	More of That	173p
96/97	Paddy's Return	164	14/15	Jezki	168
97/98	Paddy's Return	168	15/16	Thistlecrack	174p
98/99	Deano's Beeno	165	16/17	Nichols Canyon	165
	Princeful	165		Unowhatimeanharry	165
99/00	Limestone Lad	177	17/18	Faugheen	165
00/01	Le Sauvignon	178			

Best Novice Hurdler

75/76	Grand Canyon	159	96/97	Make A Stand	165
76/77	Outpoint	154	97/98	French Holly	151p
77/78	Golden Cygnet	176	98/99	Barton	153p
78/79	Venture To Cognac	162	99/00	Monsignor	158p
79/80	Slaney Idol	143	00/01	Baracouda	172
80/81	Dunaree	159	01/02	Intersky Falcon	152p
81/82	Angelo Salvini	149	02/03	Iris's Gift	172
82/83	Dawn Run	168	03/04	Inglis Drever	152
83/84	Desert Orchid	158	04/05	Ambobo	149+
84/85	Asir	148p	05/06	Black Jack Ketchum	159p
85/86	River Ceiriog	158p	06/07	Wichita Lineman	152p
86/87	The West Awake	153p	07/08	Binocular	156p
87/88	Carvill's Hill	157p	08/09	Hurricane Fly	157p
88/89	Sondrio	152p	09/10	Dunguib	152
	Wishlon	152+	10/11	Al Ferof	158
89/90	Regal Ambition	151	11/12	Simonsig	162p
90/91	Ruling	167	12/13	My Tent Or Yours	167p
91/92	Royal Gait	164p	13/14	Faugheen	166p
92/93	Montelado	150p	14/15	Douvan	168p
93/94	Danoli	172p	15/16	Altior	167p
94/95	Alderbrook	174p	16/17	Labaik	160§
95/96	Pleasure Shared	163p	17/18	Samcro	163p

Best Juvenile Hurdler

75/76	Valmony	157	85/86	Dark Raven	153p
76/77	Meladon	149	86/87	Aldino	154
77/78	Major Thompson	144	87/88	Kribensis	143p
78/79	Pollardstown	141	88/89	Royal Derbi	144
79/80	Hill of Slane	144	89/90	Sybillin	138
80/81	Broadsword	144	90/91	Oh So Risky	149p
81/82	Shiny Copper	141	91/92	Staunch Friend	151p
82/83	Sabin du Loir	147p	92/93	Shawiya	141p
83/84	Northern Game	142	93/94	Mysilv	144p
84/85	Out of The Gloom	151	94/95	Kissair	143p

95/96	Escartefigue	**159**	06/07	Katchit	**151**	
96/97	Grimes	**138p**	07/08	Binocular	**156p**	
97/98	Deep Water	**149p**	08/09	Zaynar	**155p**	
98/99	Hors La Loi III	**162p**	09/10	Soldatino	**147p**	
99/00	Grand Seigneur	**148p**	10/11	Zarkandar	**155p**	
00/01	Jair du Cochet	**163**	11/12	Grumeti	**148**	
01/02	Scolardy	**147**	12/13	Our Conor	**165p**	
02/03	Nickname	**142**	13/14	Le Rocher	**152**	
03/04	Maia Eria	**143**	14/15	Peace And Co	**161P**	
04/05	Faasel	**144p**	15/16	Apple's Jade	**157p**	
	Penzance	**144p**	16/17	Defi du Seuil	**151p**	
05/06	Detroit City	**146p**	17/18	We Have A Dream	**150p**	

Best Bumper Performer

93/94	Aries Girl	**123**	06/07	Theatrical Moment	**124**
94/95	Dato Star	**120**	07/08	Cousin Vinny	**134**
95/96	Wither Or Which	**122**	08/09	Dunguib	**131**
96/97	Florida Pearl	**124**	09/10	Cue Card	**132**
97/98	Alexander Banquet	**126**	10/11	Cheltenian	**128**
98/99	Monsignor	**122**	11/12	Don Cossack	**128**
99/00	Quadco	**129**	12/13	Briar Hill	**130**
00/01	The Bajan Bandit	**128**	13/14	Shaneshill	**124**
01/02	Pizarro	**123**	14/15	Bellshill	**126**
	Rhinestone Cowboy	**123**	15/16	Ballyandy	**123**
02/03	Rhinestone Cowboy	**123**		Blow By Blow	**123**
03/04	Secret Ploy	**122**	16/17	Fayonagh	**118**
04/05	Karanja	**128**		Paloma Blue	**118**
05/06	Leading Run	**123**	17/18	Tornado Flyer	**125**

Best Hunter Chaser

75/76	Otter Way	**143**		Fantus	**136**
76/77	Under Way	**124**	97/98	Earthmover	**140p**
77/78	Spartan Missile	**133**	98/99	Castle Mane	**148p**
78/79	Spartan Missile	**133+**	99/00	Cavalero	**142**
79/80	Rolls Rambler	**132**	00/01	Sheltering	**136**
80/81	Spartan Missile	**169**	01/02	Torduff Express	**130**
81/82	Compton Lad	**142**	02/03	Kingscliff	**137p**
82/83	Eliogarty	**147**	03/04	Earthmover	**133**
83/84	Venture To Cognac	**149**	04/05	Sleeping Night	**148**
84/85	Further Thought	**141**	05/06	Katarino	**133+**
85/86	Ah Whisht	**148**	06/07	Drombeag	**131**
86/87	Observe	**146**	07/08	Christy Beamish	**137**
87/88	Certain Light	**147**	08/09	Cappa Bleu	**139p**
88/89	Call Collect	**142p**	09/10	Baby Run	**135**
89/90	Mystic Music	**143**	10/11	Baby Run	**139**
90/91	Mystic Music	**143?**	11/12	Salsify	**139**
91/92	Rushing Wild	**127p**	12/13	Salsify	**140**
92/93	Double Silk	**122p**	13/14	Tammys Hill	**137**
93/94	Double Silk	**130p**	14/15	Prince de Beauchene	**146**
	Elegant Lord	**130p**	15/16	On The Fringe	**138**
94/95	Fantus	**139p**	16/17	Foxrock	**142**
95/96	Elegant Lord	**138p**	17/18	Gilgamboa	**134+**
96/97	Celtic Abbey	**136p**		Pacha du Polder	**134**

BIG RACE WINNERS

The record, dating back to the 1992/3 season (earlier results can be found in *Chasers & Hurdlers 1991/92* and preceding editions), includes the Timeform Rating recorded by the winner in the race (not its Timeform Annual Rating), the weight carried (usually preceded by age), starting price, trainer, jockey and number of runners. Race conditions, distances and sponsors' names in the race titles are for the 2017/18 runnings. An asterisk prior to a horse's name denotes that it was awarded the race.

Britain

BetVictor GOLD CUP HANDICAP CHASE (Gr 3) (Cheltenham 2½m78y)

Year	TR	Horse	Trainer	Jockey	Ran
1992	153	Tipping Tim 7-10-10: 11/2	N A Twiston-Davies	*C Llewellyn*	16
1993	160	Bradbury Star 8-11-8: 13/2	J T Gifford	*D Murphy*	15
1994	172	Bradbury Star 9-11-11: 5/1	J T Gifford	*P Hide[3]*	14
1995	164	Dublin Flyer 9-11-8: 4/1	T A Forster	*B Powell*	12
1996	154	Challenger du Luc 6-10-2: 7/1	M C Pipe	*R Dunwoody*	12
1997	159	Senor El Betrutti 8-10-0: 33/1	Mrs S Nock	*J Osborne*	9
1998	158	Cyfor Malta 5-11-3: 3/1	M C Pipe	*A P McCoy*	12
1999	152	The Outback Way 9-10-0: 9/1	Miss V Williams	*N Williamson*	14
2000	157	Lady Cricket 6-10-13: 5/1	M C Pipe	*A P McCoy*	15
2001	158	Shooting Light 8-11-3: 9/4	M C Pipe	*A P McCoy*	14
2002	166	Cyfor Malta 9-11-9: 16/1	M C Pipe	*B J Geraghty*	15
2003	161	Fondmort 7-10-13: 3/1	N J Henderson	*M A Fitzgerald*	9
2004	152	Celestial Gold 6-10-2: 12/1	M C Pipe	*T J Murphy*	14
2005	159	Our Vic 7-11-7: 9/2	M C Pipe	*T J Murphy*	18
2006	145	Exotic Dancer 6-11-2: 16/1	J O'Neill	*A P McCoy*	16
2007	149	L'Antartique 7-11-3: 13/2	F Murphy	*G Lee*	20
2008	153	Imperial Commander 7-10-7: 13/2	N A Twiston-Davies	*P J Brennan*	19
2009	155	Tranquil Sea 7-10-13: 11/2	E J O'Grady	*A J McNamara*	16
2010	153	Little Josh 8-10-5: 20/1	N A Twiston-Davies	*S Twiston-Davies[3]*	18
2011	160	Great Endeavour 7-10-3: 8/1	David Pipe	*Timmy Murphy*	20
2012	169	Al Ferof 7-11-8: 8/1	Paul Nicholls	*R Walsh*	18
2013	146	Johns Spirit 6-10-2: 7/1	Jonjo O'Neill	*Richie McLernon*	20
2014	147	Caid du Berlais 5-10-13: 10/1	Paul Nicholls	*Sam Twiston-Davies*	18
2015	149	Annacotty 7-11-0: 12/1	Alan King	*Ian Popham*	20
2016	158	Taquin du Seuil 9-11-11: 8/1	Jonjo O'Neill	*Aidan Coleman*	17
2017	137	Splash of Ginge 9-10-6: 25/1	Nigel Twiston-Davies	*Tom Bellamy*	17

UNIBET GREATWOOD HANDICAP HURDLE (Gr 3)
(Cheltenham 2m87y; listed prior to 2004)

Year	TR	Horse	Trainer	Jockey	Ran
1992	130	Valfinet 5-10-9: 7/2	M C Pipe	*P Scudamore*	9
1993	144	Leotard 6-12-0: 3/1	O Sherwood	*J Osborne*	7
1994	156	Atours 6-11-5: 3/1	D R C Elsworth	*P Holley*	10
1995	135	Lonesome Train 6-9-9: 33/1	C Weedon	*B Fenton[5]*	15
1996	146	Space Trucker 5-11-1: 7/1	Mrs J Harrington (Ir)	*J Osborne*	9
1997	139	Mr Percy 6-10-9: 14/1	J T Gifford	*P Hide*	17
1998	155	Grey Shot 6-11-5: 11/4	I A Balding	*J Osborne*	16
1999	132	Rodock 5-10-0: 11/4	M C Pipe	*A P McCoy*	13
2000	139	Hulysse Royal 5-10-0: 9/1	O Sherwood	*J A McCarthy*	12
2001	166	Westender 5-10-13: 11/8	M C Pipe	*A P McCoy*	13
2002	166	Rooster Booster 8-11-12: 7/1	P J Hobbs	*S Durack*	11
2003	147	Rigmarole 5-11-2: 33/1	P F Nicholls	*R Walsh*	10
2004	148	Accordion Etoile 5-10-6: 10/3	Paul Nolan (Ir)	*J Cullen*	9
2005	146	Lingo 6-10-6: 5/1	J O'Neill	*A P McCoy*	19
2006	150	Detroit City 4-11-12: 6/5	P J Hobbs	*R Johnson*	9
2007	145	Sizing Europe 5-11-6: 5/1	H de Bromhead (Ir)	*T J Murphy*	19
2008	150	Numide 5-10-3: 5/1	G L Moore	*J Moore*	12
2009	154	Khyber Kim 7-11-9: 9/1	N A Twiston-Davies	*P J Brennan*	15
2010	160	Menorah 5-11-12: 6/1	P J Hobbs	*R Johnson*	17
2011	158	Brampour 4-11-4: 12/1	Paul Nicholls	*Harry Derham[7]*	23

1000

2012	138	Olofi 6-10-11: 8/1	Tom George	Paddy Brennan	18
2013	133	Dell' Arca 4-10-5: 12/1	David Pipe	Tom Scudamore	18
2014	151	Garde La Victoire 5-11-9: 10/1	Philip Hobbs	Richard Johnson	15
2015	154	Old Guard 4-11-3: 12/1	Paul Nicholls	Harry Cobden[7]	17
2016	144	North Hill Harvey 5-11-0: 6/1	Dan Skelton	Harry Skelton	16
2017	145	Elgin 5-10-8: 10/1	Alan King	Wayne Hutchinson	13

BETFAIR CHASE (Lancashire) (Gr 1) (Haydock 3m1f125y)

2005	173	Kingscliff 8-11-8: 8/1	R H Alner	R Walford	7
2006	172	Kauto Star 6-11-8: 11/10	P F Nicholls	R Walsh	6
2007	172	Kauto Star 7-11-7: 4/5	P F Nicholls	S Thomas	7
2008	161	Snoopy Loopy 10-11-7: 33/1	P Bowen	S E Durack	6
2009	175	Kauto Star 9-11-7: 4/6	P F Nicholls	R Walsh	7
2010	161	Imperial Commander 9-11-7: 10/11	N A Twiston-Davies	P Brennan	7
2011	174	Kauto Star 11-11-7: 6/1	Paul Nicholls	R Walsh	6
2012	170	Silviniaco Conti 6-11-7: 7/4	Paul Nicholls	R Walsh	5
2013	176	Cue Card 7-11-7: 9/1	Colin Tizzard	Joe Tizzard	8
2014	171	Silviniaco Conti 8-11-7: 10/3	Paul Nicholls	Noel Fehily	9
2015	181	Cue Card 9-11-7: 7/4	Colin Tizzard	Paddy Brennan	5
2016	174	Cue Card 10-11-7: 15/8	Colin Tizzard	Paddy Brennan	6
2017	165	Bristol de Mai 6-11-7: 11/10	Nigel Twiston-Davies	Daryl Jacob	6

LADBROKES TROPHY CHASE (HANDICAP) (Gr 3) (Newbury 3m1f214y)

1992	150	Sibton Abbey 7-10-0: 40/1	F Murphy	A Maguire	13
1993	151	Cogent 9-10-1: 10/1	A Turnell	D Fortt[7]	9
1994	144	One Man 6-10-0: 4/1	G Richards	A Dobbin	16
1995	160	Couldnt Be Better 8-10-8: 15/2	C P E Brooks	D Gallagher	11
1996	147	Coome Hill 7-10-0: 11/2	W W Dennis	J Osborne	11
1997	170	Suny Bay 8-11-8: 9/4	C P E Brooks	G Bradley	14
1998	158	Teeton Mill 9-10-5: 5/1	Miss V Williams	N Williamson	16
1999	148	Ever Blessed 7-10-0: 9/2	M Pitman	T J Murphy	13
2000	158	King's Road 7-10-7: 7/1	N A Twiston-Davies	J Goldstein	17
2001	153	What's Up Boys 7-10-12: 14/1	P J Hobbs	P Flynn	14
2002	157	*Gingembre 8-10-9: 16/1	Mrs L C Taylor	A Thornton	25
2003	154	Strong Flow 6-11-0: 5/1	P F Nicholls	R Walsh	21
2004	150	Celestial Gold 6-10-5: 9/4	M C Pipe	T J Murphy	14
2005	161	Trabolgan 7-11-12: 13/2	N J Henderson	M A Fitzgerald	19
2006	157	State of Play 6-11-4: 10/1	E Williams	P Moloney	16
2007	176	Denman 7-11-12: 5/1	P F Nicholls	S Thomas	18
2008	160	Madison du Berlais 7-11-4: 25/1	D E Pipe	T Scudamore	15
2009	181	Denman 9-11-12: 11/4	P F Nicholls	R Walsh	19
2010	163	Diamond Harry 7-10-0: 6/1	Nick Williams	D Jacob	18
2011	149	Carruthers 8-10-4: 10/1	Mark Bradstock	Mattie Batchelor	18
2012	171	Bobs Worth 7-11-6: 4/1	Nicky Henderson	Barry Geraghty	19
2013	157	Triolo d'Alene 6-11-1: 20/1	Nicky Henderson	Barry Geraghty	21
2014	159	Many Clouds 7-11-6: 8/1	Oliver Sherwood	Leighton Aspell	19
2015	165	Smad Place 8-11-4: 7/1	Alan King	Wayne Hutchinson	15
2016	162	Native River 6-11-1: 7/2	Colin Tizzard	Richard Johnson	19
2017	153	Total Recall 8-10-8: 9/2	W P Mullins (Ir)	P Townend	20

UNIBET 'FIGHTING FIFTH' HURDLE (Gr 1)
(Newcastle 2m98y; Wetherby in 2008 and Newbury in 2010; Gr 2 prior to 2004; handicap prior to 1998)

1992	135	Halkopous 6-11-0: 7/4	M H Tompkins	S Smith Eccles	6
1993		Abandoned			
1994	142	Batabanoo 5-11-0: 6/4	Mrs M Reveley	P Niven	4
1995	151	Padre Mio 7-10-10: 5/1	C P E Brooks	R C Guest	7
1996	151	Space Trucker 5-10-4: 5/2	Mrs J Harrington (Ir)	J Shortt	8
1997	141	Star Rage 7-11-2: 6/1	M Johnston	D Gallagher	8
1998	170	Dato Star 7-11-8: 13/8	J M Jefferson	L Wyer	6
1999	155	Dato Star 8-11-8: 4/9	J M Jefferson	L Wyer	9
2000	155	Barton 7-11-0: 8/13	T D Easterby	A Dobbin	6
2001	147	Landing Light 6-11-8: 4/5	N J Henderson	J R Kavanagh	5
2002	153	Intersky Falcon 5-11-8: 11/10	J O'Neill	L Cooper	6
2003	146	The French Furze 9-11-0: 25/1	N G Richards	B Harding	8
2004	157	Harchibald 5-11-7: 9/4	N Meade (Ir)	P Carberry	8
2005	150	Arcalis 5-11-7: 9/4	J H Johnson	A Dobbin	9
2006	150	Straw Bear 5-11-7: 1/1	N J Gifford	A P McCoy	9
2007	158	Harchibald 8-11-7: 4/1	N Meade (Ir)	P Carberry	8

2008	155	Punjabi 5-11-7: 8/11	N J Henderson	*B J Geraghty*	6
2009	160	Go Native 6-11-7: 25/1	N Meade (Ir)	*D J Condon*	7
2010	157	Peddlers Cross 5-11-7: 9/4	D McCain	*J Maguire*	5
2011	165	Overturn 7-11-7: 7/4	Donald McCain	*Jason Maguire*	5
2012	156	Countrywide Flame 4-11-7: 11/4	John Quinn	*Denis O'Regan*	4
2013	151	My Tent Or Yours 6-11-7: 8/11	Nicky Henderson	*A P McCoy*	8
2014	152	Irving 6-11-7: 6/4	Paul Nicholls	*Nick Scholfield*	6
2015	157	Identity Thief 5-11-7: 6/1	Henry de Bromhead (Ir)	*B J Cooper*	7
2016	153	Irving 8-11-7: 6/1	Paul Nicholls	*Harry Cobden*	6
2017	143	Buveur d'Air 6-11-7: 1/6	Nicky Henderson	*Barry Geraghty*	5

BETFAIR TINGLE CREEK CHASE (Gr 1)
(Sandown 1m7f11 9y, Cheltenham 2m½f in 2000 & 2010)

1992	159	Waterloo Boy 9-12-0: 11/4	D Nicholson	*R Dunwoody*	5
1993	162	Sybillin 7-11-9: 6/1	J G FitzGerald	*P Niven*	7
1994	165	Viking Flagship 7-11-7: 9/2	D Nicholson	*A Maguire*	6
1995	159	Sound Man 7-11-7: 5/6	E J O'Grady (Ir)	*R Dunwoody*	5
1996	160	Sound Man 8-11-7: 10/11	E J O'Grady (Ir)	*R Dunwoody*	4
1997	168	Ask Tom 8-11-7: 6/1	T P Tate	*R Garritty*	7
1998	154	Direct Route 7-11-7: 7/1	J H Johnson	*N Williamson*	10
1999	167	Flagship Uberalles 5-11-7: 10/3	P F Nicholls	*J Tizzard*	6
2000	175	Flagship Uberalles 6-11-7: 3/1	N T Chance	*R Johnson*	7
2001	170	Flagship Uberalles 7-11-7: 7/2	P J Hobbs	*R Widger*	6
2002	163	Cenkos 8-11-7: 6/1	P F Nicholls	*R Walsh*	6
2003	174	Moscow Flyer 9-11-7: 6/4	Mrs J Harrington (Ir)	*B J Geraghty*	7
2004	184	Moscow Flyer 10-11-7: 2/1	Mrs J Harrington (Ir)	*B J Geraghty*	7
2005	164	Kauto Star 5-11-7: 5/2	P F Nicholls	*M A Fitzgerald*	7
2006	166	Kauto Star 6-11-7: 4/9	P F Nicholls	*R Walsh*	7
2007	157	Twist Magic 5-11-7: 5/1	P F Nicholls	*S Thomas*	8
2008	163	Master Minded 5-11-7: 4/7	P F Nicholls	*A P McCoy*	7
2009	168	Twist Magic 7-11-7: 9/4	P F Nicholls	*R Walsh*	5
2010	168	Master Minded 7-11-7: 10/11	P F Nicholls	*N Fehily*	9
2011	171	Sizing Europe 9-11-7: 11/8	H de Bromhead (Ir)	*A E Lynch*	7
2012	169	Sprinter Sacre 6-11-7: 4/11	Nicky Henderson	*Barry Geraghty*	7
2013	166	Sire de Grugy 7-11-7: 7/4	Gary Moore	*Jamie Moore*	9
2014	168	Dodging Bullets 6-11-7: 9/1	Paul Nicholls	*Sam Twiston-Davies*	10
2015	167	Sire de Grugy 8-11-7: 10/3	Gary Moore	*Jamie Moore*	7
2016	169	Un de Sceaux 8-11-7: 5/4	W P Mullins (Ir)	*R Walsh*	6
2017	164	Politologue 6-11-7: 7/2	Paul Nicholls	*Harry Cobden*	6

CASPIAN CAVIAR GOLD CUP (HANDICAP CHASE) (Gr 3) (Cheltenham 2½m166y)

1992	151	Another Coral 9-11-4: 11/2	D Nicholson	*R Dunwoody*	10
1993	146	Fragrant Dawn 9-10-2: 14/1	M C Pipe	*D Murphy*	11
1994	145	Dublin Flyer 8-10-2: 10/3	T A Forster	*B Powell*	11
1995		Abandoned			
1996	156	Addington Boy 8-11-10: 7/4	G Richards	*A Dobbin*	10
1997	160	Senor El Betrutti 8-11-3: 9/1	Mrs S Nock	*G Bradley*	9
1998	141	Northern Starlight 7-10-1: 15/2	M C Pipe	*A P McCoy*	13
1999	162	Legal Right 6-10-13: 6/1	J O'Neill	*R Johnson*	9
2000	139	Go Roger Go 8-11-0: 7/1	E J O'Grady (Ir)	*N Williamson*	12
2001		Abandoned			
2002	151	Fondmort 6-10-5: 5/1	N J Henderson	*M A Fitzgerald*	9
2003	144	Iris Royal 7-10-13: 7/1	N J Henderson	*M A Fitzgerald*	17
2004	143	Monkerhostin 7-10-2: 4/1	P J Hobbs	*R Johnson*	13
2005	139	Sir OJ 8-10-0: 16/1	N Meade (Ir)	*P Carberry*	16
2006	151	Exotic Dancer 6-11-4: 8/1	J O'Neill	*A Dobbin*	12
2007	155	Tamarinbleu 7-11-8: 22/1	D E Pipe	*D O'Regan*	16
2008		Abandoned			
2009	160	Poquelin 6-11-8: 7/2	P F Nicholls	*R Walsh*	17
2010	160	Poquelin 7-11-7: 16/1	P F Nicholls	*I Popham[5]*	16
2011	156	Quantitativeeasing 6-10-7: 6/1	Nicky Henderson	*Barry Geraghty*	16
2012	145	Unioniste 4-9-9: 15/2	Paul Nicholls	*Harry Derham[8]*	14
2013	137	Double Ross 7-10-8: 7/1	Nigel Twiston-Davies	*Sam Twiston-Davies*	13
2014	148	Niceonefrankie 8-11-5: 16/1	Venetia Williams	*Aidan Coleman*	12
2015	144	Village Vic 8-10-0: 8/1	Philip Hobbs	*Richard Johnson*	14
2016	146	Frodon 4-10-10: 14/1	Paul Nicholls	*Sam Twiston-Davies*	16
2017	138	Guitar Pete 7-10-5: 9/1	Nicky Richards	*Ryan Day[3]*	10

UNIBET INTERNATIONAL HURDLE (Gr 2)
(Cheltenham 2m179y, run at Newbury 2m½f in 2001 and at Ascot 2m in 2008)

1992	164	Halkopous 6-11-2: 8/1	M H Tompkins	A Maguire	6
1993	169	Staunch Friend 5-11-8: 6/1	M H Tompkins	D Murphy	7
1994	156	Large Action 6-11-4: 8/11	O Sherwood	J Osborne	8
1995		Abandoned			
1996	160	Large Action 8-11-8: 5/4	O Sherwood	J Osborne	7
1997	155	Relkeel 8-11-0: 8/1	D Nicholson	R Johnson	8
1998	163	Relkeel 9-11-8: 8/1	D Nicholson	A Maguire	5
1999	159	Relkeel 10-11-8: 13/2	A King	R Johnson	7
2000	160	Geos 5-11-4: 14/1	N J Henderson	M A Fitzgerald	8
2001	161	Valiramix 5-11-4: 1/2	M C Pipe	A P McCoy	4
2002	154	Rooster Booster 8-11-4: 11/8	P J Hobbs	R Johnson	9
2003	149	Rigmarole 5-11-4: 25/1	P F Nicholls	R Thornton	7
2004	161	Back In Front 7-11-8: 5/2	E J O'Grady (Ir)	D N Russell	7
2005	160	Harchibald 6-11-8: 10/11	N Meade (Ir)	P Carberry	9
2006	157	Detroit City 4-11-4: 4/6	P J Hobbs	R Johnson	4
2007	158	Osana 5-11-0: 7/1	D E Pipe	P J Brennan	8
2008	165	Binocular 4-11-4: 1/1	N J Henderson	A P McCoy	5
2009	161	Khyber Kim 7-11-4: 12/1	N A Twiston-Davies	P J Brennan	7
2010	157	Menorah 5-11-4: 7/4	P J Hobbs	R Johnson	9
2011	164	Grandouet 4-11-4: 5/2	Nicky Henderson	Barry Geraghty	8
2012	163	Zarkandar 5-11-4: 6/5	Paul Nicholls	R Walsh	7
2013	153	The New One 5-11-8: 2/5	Nigel Twiston-Davies	Sam Twiston-Davies	7
2014	159	The New One 6-11-8: 4/7	Nigel Twiston-Davies	Sam Twiston-Davies	5
2015	154	Old Guard 4-11-4: 7/1	Paul Nicholls	Sam Twiston-Davies	6
2016	158	The New One 8-11-8: 13/8	Nigel Twiston-Davies	Richard Johnson	6
2017	152	My Tent Or Yours 10-11-0: 5/1	Nicky Henderson	Barry Geraghty	7

JLT REVE DE SIVOLA LONG WALK HURDLE (Gr 1)
(Ascot 3m97y; Windsor in 2004, Chepstow in 2005 & Newbury in 2009 & 2010)

1992	156	Vagog 7-11-7: 15/2	M C Pipe	M Foster	9
1993	152	Sweet Duke 6-11-7: 7/2	N Twiston-Davies	C Llewellyn	9
1994	159	Hebridean 7-11-7: 10/3	D Nicholson	A Maguire	8
1995	153	Silver Wedge 4-11-7: 7/1	S Sherwood	J Osborne	11
1996	152	Ocean Hawk 4-11-7: 7/1	N A Twiston-Davies	C Llewellyn	6
1997	168	Paddy's Return 5-11-7: 8/1	F Murphy	N Williamson	7
1998	165	Princeful 7-11-7: 11/4	Mrs J Pitman	R Dunwoody	11
1999	164	Anzum 8-11-7: 4/1	A King	R Johnson	6
2000	172	Baracouda 5-11-7: 11/4	F Doumen (Fr)	T Doumen	9
2001	161	Baracouda 6-11-7: 2/5	F Doumen (Fr)	T Doumen	5
2002	167	Deano's Beeno 10-11-7: 14/1	M C Pipe	A P McCoy	5
2003	169	Baracouda 8-11-7: 2/7	F Doumen (Fr)	T Doumen	6
2004	156	Baracouda 9-11-7: 8/13	F Doumen (Fr)	A P McCoy	8
2005	157	My Way de Solzen 5-11-7: 12/1	A King	R Thornton	8
2006	141	Mighty Man 6-11-7: 8/11	H D Daly	R Johnson	9
2007	153	Lough Derg 7-11-7: 14/1	D E Pipe	T Scudamore	9
2008	161	Punchestowns 5-11-7: 3/1	N J Henderson	B J Geraghty	11
2009	165	Big Buck's 6-11-7: 1/2	P F Nicholls	R Walsh	8
2010	156	Big Buck's 7-11-7: 2/13	Paul Nichols	A P McCoy	6
2011	152	Big Buck's 8-11-7: 3/10	Paul Nicholls	R Walsh	7
2012	162	Reve de Sivola 7-11-7: 9/2	Nick Williams	Richard Johnson	7
2013	162	Reve de Sivola 8-11-7: 9/4	Nick Williams	Richard Johnson	5
2014	159	Reve de Sivola 9-11-7: 13/2	Nick Williams	Daryl Jacob	5
2015	157	Thistlecrack 7-11-7: 2/1	Colin Tizzard	Tom Scudamore	8
2016	155	Unowhatimeanharry 8-11-7: 6/5	Harry Fry	Barry Geraghty	11
2017	158	Sam Spinner 5-11-7: 9/2	Jedd O'Keeffe	Joe Colliver	8

RACING WELFARE HANDICAP HURDLE (Gr 3)
(Ascot 1m7f152y; Sandown in 2005 & 2006 (Jan), Listed until 2012)

2001	142	Marble Arch 5-10-11: 7/1	H Morrison	N Williamson	16
2002	139	Chauvinist 7-10-0: 15/2	N J Henderson	N Williamson	20
2003	138	Thesis 5-11-2: 33/1	Miss V Williams	B J Crowley	17
2004	141	Tamarinbleu 5-10-11: 14/1	M C Pipe	A P McCoy	23
2005	136	Desert Air 7-10-9: 25/1	M C Pipe	T Scudamore	20
2006	142	Acambo 5-11-9: 7/1	D E Pipe	T J Murphy	20
2007	133	Jack The Giant 5-11-0: 9/4	N J Henderson	M A Fitzgerald	17

2008	154	Sentry Duty 6-11-9: 12/1	N J Henderson	*B J Geraghty*	21
2009		Abandoned			
2010		Abandoned			
2011	135	Raya Star 5-10-1: 12/1	Alan King	*Wayne Hutchinson*	16
2012	150	Cause of Causes 4-10-13: 25/1	Gordon Elliott (Ir)	*Davy Condon*	21
2013	139	Willow's Saviour 6-10-5: 10/1	Dan Skelton	*Harry Skelton*	20
2014	150	Bayan 5-11-5: 14/1	Gordon Elliott (Ir)	*Davy Condon*	18
2015	145	Jolly's Cracked It 6-11-3: 7/1	Harry Fry	*Noel Fehily*	21
	138	Sternrubin 4-10-10: 9/1	Philip Hobbs	*Richard Johnson*	21
2016	158	Brain Power 5-11-11: 12/1	Nicky Henderson	*D J Mullins*	19
2017	139	Hunters Call 7-10-3: 9/1	Olly Murphy	*J W Kennedy*	17

CORAL WELSH GRAND NATIONAL (HANDICAP CHASE) (Gr 3)
(Chepstow 3m5f110y, Newbury in 1994, scheduled races in December 2010, 2012, 2015 and 2017 were all postponed until January of the following year)

1992	155	Run For Free 8-10-9: 11/4	M C Pipe	*M Perrett*	11
1993	126	Riverside Boy 10-10-0: 6/4	M C Pipe	*R Dunwoody*	8
1994	168	Master Oats 8-11-6: 5/2	K C Bailey	*N Williamson*	8
1995		Abandoned			
1996		Abandoned			
1997	146	Earth Summit 9-10-13: 25/1	N A Twiston-Davies	*T Jenks*	14
1998	139	Kendal Cavalier 8-10-0: 14/1	N J Hawke	*B Fenton*	14
1999	136	Edmond 7-10-0: 4/1	H D Daly	*R Johnson*	16
2000	149	Jocks Cross 9-10-4: 14/1	Miss V Williams	*B J Crowley*[3]	19
2001	140	Supreme Glory 8-10-0: 10/1	P G Murphy	*L Aspell*	13
2002	137	Mini Sensation 9-10-4: 8/1	J O'Neill	*A Dobbin*	16
2003	157	Bindaree 9-10-9: 10/1	N A Twiston-Davies	*C Llewellyn*	14
2004	135	Silver Birch 7-10-5: 10/3	P F Nicholls	*R Walsh*	17
2005	138	L'Aventure 6-10-4: 14/1	P F Nicholls	*L Aspell*	18
2006	159	Halcon Genelardais 6-11-3: 7/1	A King	*W Hutchinson*	18
2007	144	Miko de Beauchene 7-10-5: 13/2	R H Alner	*A Thornton*	18
2008	158	Notre Pere 7-11-0: 16/1	J Dreaper (Ir)	*A E Lynch*	20
2009	152	Dream Alliance 8-10-8: 20/1	P J Hobbs	*T J O'Brien*	18
2010	155	Synchronised 8-11-6: 5/1	Jonjo O'Neill	*A P McCoy*	18
2011	141	Le Beau Bai 8-10-1: 10/1	Richard Lee	*Charlie Poste*	20
2012	137	Monbeg Dude 8-10-1: 10/1	Michael Scudamore	*P Carberry*	17
2013	139	Mountainous 8-10-0: 20/1	Richard Lee	*Paul Moloney*	20
2014	136	Emperor's Choice 7-10-8: 9/1	Venetia Williams	*Aidan Coleman*	19
2015	139	Mountainous 11-10-6: 9/1	Kerry Lee	*Jamie Moore*	20
2016	162	Native River 6-11-12: 11/4	Colin Tizzard	*Richard Johnson*	20
2017	144	Raz de Maree 13-11-1: 16/1	Gavin P Cromwell (Ir)	*James Bowen*[5]	20

UNIBET CHRISTMAS HURDLE (Gr 1) (Kempton 2m, Sandown 2005)

1992	170	Mighty Mogul 5-11-7: 3/1	D Nicholson	*R Dunwoody*	8
1993	155	Muse 6-11-7: 3/1	D R C Elsworth	*M Richards*	5
1994	158	Absalom's Lady 6-11-2: 9/2	D R C Elsworth	*P Holley*	6
1995		Abandoned			
1996		Abandoned			
1997	153	Kerawi 4-11-7: 4/1	N A Twiston-Davies	*C Llewellyn*	5
1998	165	French Holly 7-11-7: 5/2	F Murphy	*A Thornton*	5
1999	168	Dato Star 8-11-7: 11/8	J M Jefferson	*L Wyer*	4
2000	144	Geos 5-11-7: 9/4	N J Henderson	*M A Fitzgerald*	7
2001	153	Landing Light 6-11-7: 5/4	N J Henderson	*M A Fitzgerald*	5
2002	158	Intersky Falcon 5-11-7: 1/1	J O'Neill	*C F Swan*	6
2003	157	Intersky Falcon 6-11-7: 11/4	J O'Neill	*L Cooper*	6
2004	160	Harchibald 5-11-7: 8/11	N Meade (Ir)	*P Carberry*	7
2005	152	Feathard Lady 5-11-0: 6/4	C A Murphy (Ir)	*R Walsh*	7
2006	155	Jazz Messenger 6-11-7: 10/1	N Meade (Ir)	*N P Madden*	7
2007	153	Straw Bear 6-11-7: 9/2	N J Gifford	*A P McCoy*	6
2008	152	Harchibald 9-11-7: 7/1	N Meade (Ir)	*P Carberry*	7
2009	153	Go Native 6-11-7: 5/2	N Meade (Ir)	*D J Condon*	7
2010	163	Binocular 7-11-7: 13/8	Nicky Henderson	*A P McCoy*	6
2011	164	Binocular 7-11-7: 5/4	Nicky Henderson	*A P McCoy*	5
2012	158	Darlan 5-11-7: 3/1	Nicky Henderson	*A P McCoy*	7
2013	170	My Tent Or Yours 6-11-7: 11/8	Nicky Henderson	*A P McCoy*	6
2014	171	Faugheen 6-11-7: 4/11	W P Mullins (Ir)	*R Walsh*	6
2015	167	Faugheen 7-11-7: 1/4	W P Mullins (Ir)	*R Walsh*	5

| 2016 | 164 | Yanworth 6-11-7: 5/4 | Alan King | *Barry Geraghty* | 5 |
| 2017 | 153 | Buveur d'Air 6-11-7: 2/11 | Nicky Henderson | *Barry Geraghty* | 4 |

32Red KING GEORGE VI CHASE (Gr 1) (Kempton 3m, Sandown 1996 (Jan) and 2005)

1992	161	The Fellow 7-11-10: 1/1	F Doumen (Fr)	*A Kondrat*	8
1993	167	Barton Bank 7-11-10: 9/2	D Nicholson	*A Maguire*	10
1994	158	Algan 6-11-10: 16/1	F Doumen (Fr)	*P Chevalier*	9
1996	179	One Man 8-11-10: 11/4	G Richards	*R Dunwoody*	11
1996	176	One Man 8-11-10: 8/13	G Richards	*R Dunwoody*	5
1997	167	See More Business 7-11-10: 10/1	P F Nicholls	*A Thornton*	8
1998	173	Teeton Mill 9-11-10: 7/2	Miss V Williams	*N Williamson*	9
1999	182	See More Business 9-11-10: 5/2	P F Nicholls	*M A Fitzgerald*	9
2000	180	First Gold 7-11-10: 5/2	F Doumen (Fr)	*T Doumen*	9
2001	172	Florida Pearl 9-11-10: 8/1	W P Mullins (Ir)	*A Maguire*	8
2002	170	Best Mate 7-11-10: 11/8	Miss H C Knight	*A P McCoy*	10
2003	167	Edredon Bleu 11-11-10: 25/1	Miss H C Knight	*J Culloty*	12
2004	177	Kicking King 6-11-10: 3/1	T J Taaffe (Ir)	*B J Geraghty*	13
2005	167	Kicking King 7-11-10: 11/8	T J Taaffe (Ir)	*B J Geraghty*	9
2006	174	Kauto Star 6-11-10: 8/13	P F Nicholls	*R Walsh*	9
2007	176	Kauto Star 7-11-10: 4/6	P F Nicholls	*R Walsh*	7
2008	173	Kauto Star 8-11-10: 10/11	P F Nicholls	*R Walsh*	10
2009	188	Kauto Star 9-11-10: 8/13	P F Nicholls	*R Walsh*	13
2010	178	Long Run 6-11-10: 9/2	Nicky Henderson	*Mr S Waley-Cohen*	9
2011	179	Kauto Star 11-11-10: 3/1	Paul Nicholls	*R Walsh*	7
2012	166	Long Run 7-11-10: 15/8	Nicky Henderson	*Mr S Waley-Cohen*	9
2013	176	Silviniaco Conti 7-11-10: 7/2	Paul Nicholls	*Noel Fehily*	9
2014	172	Silviniaco Conti 8-11-10: 15/8	Paul Nicholls	*Noel Fehily*	10
2015	181	Cue Card 9-11-10: 9/2	Colin Tizzard	*Paddy Brennan*	9
2016	174	Thistlecrack 8-11-10: 11/10	Colin Tizzard	*Tom Scudamore*	5
2017	163	Might Bite 8-11-10: 6/4	Nicky Henderson	*Nico de Boinville*	8

ROYAL SALUTE WHISKY CLARENCE HOUSE CHASE (Gr 1)
(Ascot 2m167y, except Warwick in 1994, Kempton in 1997, 1999 and replacement race in 2003, Cheltenham in 2005, 2013 and 2017; Sandown in 2006 and 2007; Gr 2 Handicap prior to 2008)

1993	156	Sybillin 7-10-10: 9/2	J G FitzGerald	*M Dwyer*	11
1994	151	Viking Flagship 7-10-10: 3/1	D Nicholson	*R Dunwoody*	4
1995	160	Martha's Son 8-11-9: 3/1	T A Forster	*R Farrant*	8
1996	145	Big Matt 8-10-4: 8/1	N J Henderson	*M Fitzgerald*	11
1997	157	Ask Tom 8-10-10: 9/4	T P Tate	*R Garritty*	8
1998	155	Jeffell 8-10-11: 13/2	A L T Moore (Ir)	*C O'Dwyer*	9
1999	153	Call Equiname 9-11-3: 15/2	P F Nicholls	*R Thornton*	7
2000	151	Nordance Prince 9-10-0: 13/8	Miss V Williams	*A P McCoy*	10
2001	160	Function Dream 9-10-11: 2/1	Mrs M Reveley	*A Ross3*	10
2002	136	Turgeonev 7-10-4: 9/2	T D Easterby	*R McGrath*	8
2003	153	Young Devereaux 10-10-4: 9/2	P F Nicholls	*R Walsh*	9
2004	163	Isio 8-10-5: 4/1	N J Henderson	*M A Fitzgerald*	13
2005	179	Well Chief 6-11-10: 5/1	M C Pipe	*T J Murphy*	10
2006	145	Tysou 9-11-2: 10/1	N J Henderson	*M A Fitzgerald*	10
2007		Abandoned (replaced by substitute event of lower value)			
2008	161	Tamarinbleu 8-11-7: 12/1	D E Pipe	*T Scudamore*	6
2009	167	Master Minded 6-11-7: 1/4	P F Nicholls	*R Walsh*	5
2010	168	Twist Magic 8-11-7: 11/8	P F Nicholls	*R Walsh*	7
2011	168	Master Minded 8-11-7: 4/7	Paul Nicholls	*A P McCoy*	9
2012	165	Somersby 8-11-7: 9/2	Henrietta Knight	*Dominic Elsworth*	8
2013	171	Sprinter Sacre 7-11-7: 1/5	Nicky Henderson	*Barry Geraghty*	7
2014	172	Sire de Grugy 8-11-7: 5/4	Gary Moore	*Jamie Moore*	7
2015	167	Dodging Bullets 7-11-7: 7/2	Paul Nicholls	*Noel Fehily*	5
2016	174	Un de Sceaux 8-11-7: 1/2	W P Mullins (Ir)	*R Walsh*	5
2017	167	Un de Sceaux 9-11-7: 1/2	W P Mullins (Ir)	*R Walsh*	7
2018	164	Un de Sceaux 10-11-7: 4/9	W P Mullins (Ir)	*P Townend*	5

BETFAIR HURDLE (HANDICAP) (Gr 3) (Newbury 2m69y)

1993	147	King Credo 8-10-0: 10/1	S Woodman	*A Maguire*	16
1994	149	Large Action 6-10-8: 9/2	O Sherwood	*J Osborne*	11
1995	160	Mysilv 5-10-8: 9/4	C R Egerton	*J Osborne*	8
1996	148	Squire Silk 7-10-12: 13/2	A Turnell	*P Carberry*	18
1997	151	Make A Stand 6-11-7: 6/1	M C Pipe	*C Maude*	18

1998	145	Sharpical 6-11-1: 10/1	N J Henderson	M A Fitzgerald	14
1999	142	Decoupage 7-11-0: 6/1	C R Egerton	J A McCarthy	18
2000	155	Geos 5-11-3: 15/2	N J Henderson	M A Fitzgerald	17
2001	145	Landing Light 6-10-2: 4/1	N J Henderson	M A Fitzgerald	20
2002	157	Copeland 7-11-7: 13/2	M C Pipe	A P McCoy	16
2003	138	Spirit Leader 7-10-0: 14/1	Mrs J Harrington (Ir)	N Williamson	27
2004	149	Geos 9-10-9: 16/1	N J Henderson	M Foley	25
2005	152	Essex 5-11-6: 4/1	M J P O'Brien (Ir)	B J Geraghty	25
2006		Abandoned			
2007	132	Heathcote 5-10-6: 50/1	G L Moore	J E Moore	20
2008	131	Wingman 6-10-0: 14/1	G L Moore	J E Moore	24
2009		Abandoned			
2010	144	Get Me Out of Here 6-10-6: 6/1	J O'Neill	A P McCoy	23
2011	136	Recession Proof 5-10-8: 12/1	John Quinn	Dougie Costello	15
2012	159	Zarkandar 5-11-1: 11/4	Paul Nicholls	R Walsh	20
2013	162	My Tent Or Yours 6-11-2: 5/1	Nicky Henderson	A P McCoy	21
2014	142	Splash of Ginge 6-11-8: 33/1	Nigel Twiston-Davies	Ryan Hatch[7]	20
2015	139	Violet Dancer 5-10-9: 20/1	Gary Moore	Joshua Moore	23
2016	144	Agrapart 5-10-10: 16/1	Nick Williams	Lizzie Kelly[5]	22
2017	145	Ballyandy 6-11-1: 3/1	Nigel Twiston-Davies	Sam Twiston-Davies	16
2018	152	Kalashnikov 5-11-5: 8/1	Amy Murphy	Jack Quinlan	24

BETFAIR ASCOT CHASE (Gr 1)
(Ascot 2m5f8y, 2m3½f prior to 2005, 2m3f in 2007, Lingfield 2m4½f in 2005 and 2006)

1995	158	Martha's Son 8-11-7: 1/1	T A Forster	R Farrant	6
1996	155	Sound Man 8-11-7: 1/2	E O'Grady (Ir)	R Dunwoody	5
1997	171	Strong Promise 6-11-7: 10/1	G A Hubbard	N Williamson	4
1998	176	One Man 10-11-7: 7/4	G Richards	A Dobbin	3
1999	156	Teeton Mill 10-11-7: 6/4	Miss V Williams	N Williamson	7
2000	155	Rockforce 8-11-7: 2/1	P F Nicholls	J Tizzard	5
2001	163	Tiutchev 8-11-7: 11/8	N J Henderson	M A Fitzgerald	4
2002	148	Tresor de Mai 8-11-7: 9/2	M C Pipe	A P McCoy	5
2003	162	Tiutchev 10-11-7: 15/8	M C Pipe	A P McCoy	7
2004	161	Hand Inn Hand 8-11-7: 15/2	H D Daly	M Bradburne	7
2005	154	It Takes Time 11-11-7: 14/1	M C Pipe	J E Moore	7
2006	156	Our Vic 8-11-7: 2/1	M C Pipe	T J Murphy	7
2007	158	Monet's Garden 9-11-7: 11/10	N G Richards	A Dobbin	7
2008	168	Kauto Star 8-11-7: 4/11	P F Nicholls	R Walsh	9
2009	166	Voy Por Ustedes 8-11-7: 6/5	A King	R Thornton	4
2010	153	Monet's Garden 12-11-7: 11/2	N G Richards	B J Geraghty	6
2011	167	Riverside Theatre 7-11-7: 11/10	Nicky Henderson	Barry Geraghty	7
2012	170	Riverside Theatre 8-11-7: 13/8	Nicky Henderson	Barry Geraghty	8
2013	167	Cue Card 7-11-7: 15/8	Colin Tizzard	Joe Tizzard	6
2014	175	Captain Chris 10-11-7: 8/11	Philip Hobbs	Richard Johnson	8
2015	166	Balder Succes 7-11-7: 4/1	Alan King	Wayne Hutchinson	8
2016	169	Silviniaco Conti 10-11-7: 2/1	Paul Nicholls	Noel Fehily	8
2017	174	Cue Card 11-11-7: 4/9	Colin Tizzard	Paddy Brennan	6
2018	168	Waiting Patiently 7-11-7: 2/1	Ruth Jefferson	Brian Hughes	7

SKY BET SUPREME NOVICES' HURDLE (Gr 1) (Cheltenham 2m87y)

1993	150	Montelado 6-11-8: 5/1	P Flynn (Ir)	C F Swan	15
1994	144	Arctic Kinsman 6-11-8: 50/1	N A Twiston-Davies	C Llewellyn	18
1995	137	Tourist Attraction 6-11-3: 25/1	W P Mullins (Ir)	M Dwyer	20
1996	143	Indefence 5-11-8: 25/1	Mrs J Pitman	W Marston	27
1997	138	Shadow Leader 6-11-8: 5/1	C R Egerton	J Osborne	16
1998	144	French Ballerina 5-11-3: 10/1	P J Flynn (Ir)	G Bradley	30
1999	162	Hors La Loi III 4-11-0: 9/2	M C Pipe	A P McCoy	20
2000	143	Sausalito Bay 6-11-8: 14/1	N Meade (Ir)	P Carberry	15
2001		Abandoned			
2002	138	Like-A-Butterfly 8-11-3: 7/4	C Roche (Ir)	C F Swan	28
2003	151	Back In Front 6-11-8: 3/1	E J O'Grady (Ir)	N Williamson	19
2004	147	Brave Inca 6-11-7: 7/2	C A Murphy (Ir)	B M Cash	19
2005	144	Arcalis 5-11-7: 20/1	J H Johnson	G Lee	20
2006	142	Noland 5-11-7: 6/1	P F Nicholls	R Walsh	20
2007	145	Ebaziyan 6-11-7: 40/1	W P Mullins (Ir)	D J Condon	22
2008	149	Captain Cee Bee 7-11-7: 17/2	E P Harty (Ir)	R Thornton	22
2009	145	Go Native 6-11-7: 12/1	N Meade (Ir)	P Carberry	20

2010	145	Menorah 5-11-7: 12/1	P J Hobbs	R Johnson	18
2011	158	Al Ferof 6-11-7: 10/1	Paul Nicholls	R Walsh	15
2012	149	Cinders And Ashes 5-11-7: 10/1	Donald McCain	Jason Maguire	19
2013	165	Champagne Fever 6-11-7: 5/1	W P Mullins (Ir)	R Walsh	12
2014	154	Vautour 5-11-7: 7/2	W P Mullins (Ir)	R Walsh	18
2015	168	Douvan 5-11-7: 2/1	W P Mullins (Ir)	R Walsh	12
2016	164	Altior 6-11-7: 4/1	Nicky Henderson	Nico de Boinville	14
2017	153	Labaik 6-11-7: 25/1	Gordon Elliott (Ir)	J W Kennedy	14
2018	156	Summerville Boy 6-11-7: 9/1	Tom George	Noel Fehily	19

RACING POST ARKLE CHALLENGE TROPHY NOVICES' CHASE (Gr 1)
(Cheltenham 1m7f199y)

1993	158	Travado 7-11-8: 5/1	N J Henderson	J Osborne	8
1994	164	Nakir 6-11-8: 9/1	S Christian	J Osborne	10
1995	147	Klairon Davis 6-11-8: 7/2	A L T Moore (Ir)	F Woods	11
1996	153	Ventana Canyon 7-11-8: 7/1	E J O'Grady (Ir)	R Dunwoody	16
1997	146	Or Royal 6-11-8: 11/2	M C Pipe	A P McCoy	9
1998	137	Champleve 5-11-0: 13/2	M C Pipe	A P McCoy	16
1999	153	Flagship Uberalles 5-11-0: 11/1	P F Nicholls	J Tizzard	14
2000	152	Tiutchev 7-11-8: 8/1	N J Henderson	M A Fitzgerald	12
2001		Abandoned			
2002	159	Moscow Flyer 8-11-8: 11/2	Mrs J Harrington (Ir)	B J Geraghty	12
2003	158	Azertyuiop 6-11-8: 5/4	P F Nicholls	R Walsh	9
2004	146	Well Chief 5-11-3: 9/1	M C Pipe	A P McCoy	16
2005	150	Contraband 7-11-7: 7/1	M C Pipe	T J Murphy	19
2006	151	Voy Por Ustedes 5-11-2: 15/2	A King	R Thornton	14
2007	157	My Way de Solzen 7-11-7: 7/2	A King	R Thornton	13
2008	160	Tidal Bay 7-11-7: 6/1	J H Johnson	D O'Regan	14
2009	151	Forpadydeplasterer 7-11-7: 8/1	T Cooper (Ir)	B J Geraghty	17
2010	154	Sizing Europe 8-11-7: 6/1	H de Bromhead (Ir)	A E Lynch	12
2011	156	Captain Chris 7-11-7: 6/1	Philip Hobbs	Richard Johnson	10
2012	169	Sprinter Sacre 6-11-7: 8/11	Nicky Henderson	Barry Geraghty	6
2013	160	Simonsig 7-11-7: 8/15	Nicky Henderson	Barry Geraghty	7
2014	157	Western Warhorse 6-11-4: 33/1	David Pipe	Tom Scudamore	9
2015	169	Un de Sceaux 7-11-4: 4/6	W P Mullins (Ir)	R Walsh	11
2016	168	Douvan 6-11-4: 1/4	W P Mullins (Ir)	R Walsh	7
2017	161	Altior 7-11-4: 1/4	Nicky Henderson	Nico de Boinville	9
2018	174	Footpad 6-11-4: 5/6	W P Mullins (Ir)	R Walsh	5

UNIBET CHAMPION HURDLE CHALLENGE TROPHY (Gr 1) (Cheltenham 2m87y)

1993	167	Granville Again 7-12-0: 13/2	M C Pipe	P Scudamore	18
1994	166	Flakey Dove 8-11-9: 9/1	R J Price	M Dwyer	15
1995	174	Alderbrook 6-12-0: 11/2	K C Bailey	N Williamson	14
1996	170	Collier Bay 6-12-0: 9/1	J A B Old	G Bradley	16
1997	165	Make A Stand 6-12-0: 7/1	M C Pipe	A P McCoy	17
1998	172	Istabraq 6-12-0: 3/1	A P O'Brien (Ir)	C F Swan	18
1999	164	Istabraq 7-12-0: 4/9	A P O'Brien (Ir)	C F Swan	14
2000	163	Istabraq 8-12-0: 8/15	A P O'Brien (Ir)	C F Swan	12
2001		Abandoned			
2002	161	Hors La Loi III 7-12-0: 10/1	J R Fanshawe	D Gallagher	15
2003	170	Rooster Booster 9-12-0: 9/2	P J Hobbs	R Johnson	17
2004	165	Hardy Eustace 7-11-10: 33/1	D T Hughes (Ir)	C O'Dwyer	14
2005	164	Hardy Eustace 8-11-10: 7/2	D T Hughes (Ir)	C O'Dwyer	14
2006	167	Brave Inca 8-11-10: 7/4	C A Murphy (Ir)	A P McCoy	18
2007	162	Sublimity 7-11-10: 16/1	J G Carr (Ir)	P Carberry	10
2008	163	Katchit 5-11-10: 10/1	A King	R Thornton	15
2009	164	Punjabi 6-11-10: 22/1	N J Henderson	B J Geraghty	23
2010	167	Binocular 6-11-10: 9/1	N J Henderson	A P McCoy	12
2011	168	Hurricane Fly 7-11-10: 11/4	W P Mullins (Ir)	R Walsh	11
2012	171	Rock On Ruby 7-11-10: 11/1	Paul Nicholls	Noel Fehily	10
2013	170	Hurricane Fly 9-11-10: 13/8	W P Mullins (Ir)	R Walsh	9
2014	170	Jezki 6-11-10: 9/1	Mrs John Harrington (Ir)	Barry Geraghty	9
2015	170	Faugheen 7-11-10: 4/5	W P Mullins (Ir)	R Walsh	8
2016	163	Annie Power 8-11-3: 5/2	W P Mullins (Ir)	R Walsh	12
2017	170	Buveur d'Air 6-11-10: 5/1	Nicky Henderson	Noel Fehily	11
2018	167	Buveur d'Air 7-11-10: 4/6	Nicky Henderson	Barry Geraghty	11

OLBG MARES' HURDLE (David Nicholson) (Gr 1) (Cheltenham 2m3f200y, Gr 2 prior to 2015)

2008	137	Whiteoak 5-11-0: 20/1	D McCain Jnr	J Maguire	13
2009	152	Quevega 5-11-3: 2/1	W P Mullins (Ir)	R Walsh	21
2010	148	Quevega 6-11-5: 6/4	W P Mullins (Ir)	R Walsh	17
2011	146	Quevega 7-11-5: 5/6	W P Mullins (Ir)	R Walsh	14
2012	137	Quevega 8-11-5: 4/7	W P Mullins (Ir)	R Walsh	19
2013	142	Quevega 9-11-5: 8/11	W P Mullins (Ir)	R Walsh	19
2014	139	Quevega 10-11-5: 8/11	W P Mullins (Ir)	R Walsh	16
2015	146	Glens Melody 7-11-5: 6/1	W P Mullins (Ir)	P Townend	15
2016	139	Vroum Vroum Mag 7-11-5: 4/6	W P Mullins (Ir)	R Walsh	19
2017	147	Apple's Jade 5-11-5: 7/2	Gordon Elliott (Ir)	B J Cooper	17
2018	143	Benie des Dieux 7-11-5: 9/2	W P Mullins (Ir)	R Walsh	9

BALLYMORE NOVICES' HURDLE (Baring Bingham) (Gr 1) (Cheltenham 2m5f26y)

1993	134	Gaelstrom 6-11-2: 16/1	N A Twiston-Davies	C Llewellyn	19
1994	138	Danoli 6-11-7: 7/4	T Foley (Ir)	C F Swan	23
1995	142	Putty Road 5-11-7: 7/1	D Nicholson	N Williamson	21
1996	142	Urubande 6-11-7: 8/1	A P O'Brien (Ir)	C F Swan	24
1997	144	Istabraq 5-11-7: 6/5	A P O'Brien (Ir)	C F Swan	17
1998	151	French Holly 7-11-7: 2/1	F Murphy	A Thornton	18
1999	153	Barton 6-11-7: 2/1	T D Easterby	L Wyer	18
2000	149	Monsignor 6-11-7: 5/4	M Pitman	N Williamson	14
2001		Abandoned			
2002	148	Galileo 6-11-7: 12/1	T R George	J M Maguire	27
2003	147	Hardy Eustace 6-11-7: 6/1	D T Hughes (Ir)	K A Kelly	19
2004	147	Fundamentalist 6-11-7: 12/1	N A Twiston-Davies	C Llewellyn	15
2005	147	No Refuge 5-11-7: 17/2	J H Johnson	G Lee	20
2006	146	Nicanor 5-11-7: 17/2	N Meade (Ir)	P Carberry	17
2007	147	Massini's Maguire 6-11-7: 20/1	P J Hobbs	R Johnson	15
2008	146	Fiveforthree 6-11-7: 7/1	W P Mullins (Ir)	R Walsh	15
2009	151	Mikael d'Haguenet 5-11-7: 5/2	W P Mullins (Ir)	R Walsh	14
2010	147	Peddlers Cross 5-11-7: 7/1	D McCain Jnr	J Maguire	17
2011	149	First Lieutenant 6-11-7: 7/1	M F Morris (Ir)	Davy Russell	12
2012	157	Simonsig 6-11-7: 2/1	Nicky Henderson	Barry Geraghty	17
2013	155	The New One 5-11-7: 7/2	Nigel Twiston-Davies	Sam Twiston-Davies	8
2014	155	Faugheen 6-11-7: 6/4	W P Mullins (Ir)	R Walsh	15
2015	154	Windsor Park 6-11-7: 9/2	D K Weld (Ir)	D Russell	10
2016	156	Yorkhill 6-11-7: 3/1	W P Mullins (Ir)	R Walsh	11
2017	151	Willoughby Court 6-11-7: 14/1	Ben Pauling	David Bass	15
2018	155	Samcro 6-11-7: 8/11	Gordon Elliott (Ir)	J W Kennedy	14

RSA INSURANCE NOVICES' CHASE (Gr 1) (Cheltenham 3m80y)

1993	136	Young Hustler 6-11-4: 9/4	N A Twiston-Davies	P Scudamore	8
1994	148	Monsieur Le Cure 8-11-4: 15/2	J A C Edwards	P Niven	18
1995	159	Brief Gale 8-10-13: 13/2	J T Gifford	P Hide	13
1996	146	Nahthen Lad 7-11-4: 7/1	Mrs J Pitman	W Marston	12
1997	150	Hanakham 8-11-4: 13/2	R J Hodges	R Dunwoody	14
1998	169	Florida Pearl 6-11-4: 11/8	W P Mullins (Ir)	R Dunwoody	10
1999	161	Looks Like Trouble 7-11-4: 16/1	N T Chance	P Carberry	14
2000	152	Lord Noelie 7-11-4: 9/2	Miss H C Knight	J Culloty	9
2001		Abandoned			
2002	153	Hussard Collonges 7-11-4: 33/1	P Beaumont	R Garritty	19
2003	150	One Knight 7-11-4: 15/2	P J Hobbs	R Johnson	9
2004	149	Rule Supreme 8-11-4: 25/1	W P Mullins (Ir)	D J Casey	10
2005	150	Trabolgan 7-11-4: 5/1	N J Henderson	M A Fitzgerald	9
2006	145	Star de Mohaison 5-10-8: 14/1	P F Nicholls	B J Geraghty	15
2007	156	Denman 7-11-4: 6/5	P F Nicholls	R Walsh	17
2008	148	Albertas Run 7-11-4: 4/1	J O'Neill	A P McCoy	11
2009	158	Cooldine 7-11-4: 9/4	W P Mullins (Ir)	R Walsh	15
2010	152	Weapon's Amnesty 7-11-4: 10/1	C Byrnes (Ir)	D N Russell	9
2011	147	Bostons Angel 7-11-4: 16/1	Mrs J Harrington (Ir)	Robbie Power	12
2012	159	Bobs Worth 7-11-4: 9/2	Nicky Henderson	Barry Geraghty	9
2013	150	Lord Windermere 7-11-4: 8/1	J H Culloty (Ir)	Davy Russell	11
2014	152	O'Faolains Boy 7-11-4: 12/1	Rebecca Curtis	Barry Geraghty	15
2015	161	Don Poli 6-11-4: 13/8	W P Mullins (Ir)	Bryan J Cooper	8
2016	150	Blaklion 7-11-4: 8/1	Nigel Twiston-Davies	Ryan Hatch	8

| 2017 | 166 | Might Bite 8-11-4: 7/2 | Nicky Henderson | *Nico de Boinville* | 12 |
| 2018 | 164 | Presenting Percy 7-11-4: 5/2 | Patrick G Kelly (Ir) | *Davy Russell* | 10 |

BETWAY QUEEN MOTHER CHAMPION CHASE (Gr 1) (Cheltenham 1m7f199y)

1993	148	Deep Sensation 8-12-0: 11/1	J T Gifford	*D Murphy*	9
1994	166	Viking Flagship 7-12-0: 4/1	D Nicholson	*A Maguire*	8
1995	169	Viking Flagship 8-12-0: 5/2	D Nicholson	*C F Swan*	10
1996	172	Klairon Davis 7-12-0: 9/1	A L T Moore (Ir)	*F Woods*	7
1997	171	Martha's Son 10-12-0: 9/1	T A Forster	*R Farrant*	6
1998	163	One Man 10-12-0: 7/2	G Richards	*B Harding*	8
1999	164	Call Equiname 9-12-0: 7/2	P F Nicholls	*M A Fitzgerald*	13
2000	167	Edredon Bleu 8-12-0: 7/2	Miss H C Knight	*A P McCoy*	9
2001		Abandoned			
2002	166	Flagship Uberalles 8-12-0: 7/4	P J Hobbs	*R Johnson*	12
2003	167	Moscow Flyer 9-12-0: 7/4	Mrs J Harrington (Ir)	*B J Geraghty*	11
2004	172	Azertyuiop 7-11-10: 15/8	P F Nicholls	*R Walsh*	8
2005	181	Moscow Flyer 11-11-10: 6/4	Mrs J Harrington (Ir)	*B J Geraghty*	8
2006	165	Newmill 8-11-10: 16/1	J J Murphy (Ir)	*A J McNamara*	12
2007	160	Voy Por Ustedes 6-11-10: 5/1	A King	*R Thornton*	10
2008	179	Master Minded 5-11-10: 3/1	P F Nicholls	*R Walsh*	8
2009	164	Master Minded 6-11-10: 4/11	P F Nicholls	*R Walsh*	12
2010	169	Big Zeb 9-11-10: 10/1	C A Murphy (Ir)	*B J Geraghty*	9
2011	171	Sizing Europe 9-11-10: 10/1	H de Bromhead (Ir)	*A E Lynch*	11
2012	174	Finian's Rainbow 9-11-10: 4/1	Nicky Henderson	*Barry Geraghty*	8
2013	192	Sprinter Sacre 7-11-10: 1/4	Nicky Henderson	*Barry Geraghty*	7
2014	167	Sire de Grugy 8-11-10: 11/4	Gary Moore	*Jamie Moore*	11
2015	167	Dodging Bullets 7-11-10: 9/2	Paul Nicholls	*Sam Twiston-Davies*	9
2016	176	Sprinter Sacre 10-11-10: 5/1	Nicky Henderson	*Nico de Boinville*	10
2017	166	Special Tiara 10-11-10: 11/1	Henry de Bromhead (Ir)	*Noel Fehily*	10
2018	179	Altior 8-11-10: 1/1	Nicky Henderson	*Nico de Boinville*	9

WEATHERBYS CHAMPION BUMPER (STANDARD OPEN NATIONAL HUNT FLAT) (Gr 1) (Cheltenham 2m87y)

1993	109	Rhythm Section 4-10-11: 16/1	H Scott (Ir)	*P Carberry*	24
1994	121	Mucklemeg 6-11-5: 7/2	E O'Grady (Ir)	*C F Swan*	25
1995	120	Dato Star 4-10-12: 7/2	J M Jefferson	*M Dwyer*	21
1996	122	Wither Or Which 5-11-6: 11/4	W P Mullins (Ir)	*W Mullins*	24
1997	124	Florida Pearl 5-11-6: 6/1	W P Mullins (Ir)	*R Dunwoody*	25
1998	126	Alexander Banquet 5-11-6: 9/1	W P Mullins (Ir)	*Mr R Walsh*	25
1999	122	Monsignor 5-11-6: 50/1	M Pitman	*B Powell*	25
2000	122	Joe Cullen 5-11-6: 14/1	W P Mullins (Ir)	*C F Swan*	17
2001		Abandoned			
2002	123	Pizarro 5-11-6: 14/1	E J O'Grady (Ir)	*J P Spencer*	23
2003	119	Liberman 5-11-6: 2/1	M C Pipe	*A P McCoy*	25
2004	118	Total Enjoyment 5-10-2: 7/1	T Cooper (Ir)	*J Culloty*	24
2005	123	Missed That 6-11-5: 7/2	W P Mullins (Ir)	*R Walsh*	24
2006	121	Hairy Molly 6-11-5: 33/1	J Crowley (Ir)	*P Carberry*	23
2007	122	Cork All Star 5-11-5: 11/2	Mrs J Harrington (Ir)	*B J Geraghty*	24
2008	125	Cousin Vinny 5-11-5: 12/1	W P Mullins (Ir)	*Mr P W Mullins*	23
2009	129	Dunguib 6-11-5: 9/2	P Fenton (Ir)	*Mr B T O'Connell*	24
2010	132	Cue Card 4-10-12: 40/1	C L Tizzard	*J Tizzard*	24
2011	128	Cheltenian 5-11-5: 14/1	Philip Hobbs	*Richard Johnson*	24
2012	127	Champagne Fever 5-11-5: 16/1	W P Mullins (Ir)	*Mr P W Mullins*	20
2013	130	Briar Hill 5-11-5: 25/1	W P Mullins (Ir)	*R Walsh*	23
2014	123	Silver Concorde 6-11-5: 16/1	D K Weld (Ir)	*Mr R P McNamara*	22
2015	122	Moon Racer 6-11-5: 9/2	David Pipe	*Tom Scudamore*	23
2016	123	Ballyandy 5-11-5: 5/1	Nigel Twiston-Davies	*Sam Twiston-Davies*	23
2017	115	Fayonagh 6-10-12: 7/1	Gordon Elliott (Ir)	*Mr J J Codd*	22
2018	116	Relegate 5-10-12: 25/1	W P Mullins (Ir)	*Ms K Walsh*	23

RYANAIR CHASE (Festival Trophy) (Gr 1) (Cheltenham 2½m166y, Gr 2 before 2008)

2005	160	Thisthatandtother 9-11-3: 9/2	P F Nicholls	*R Walsh*	12
2006	158	Fondmort 10-11-0: 10/3	N J Henderson	*M A Fitzgerald*	11
2007	157	Taranis 6-11-0: 9/2	P F Nicholls	*R Walsh*	9
2008	163	Our Vic 10-11-0: 4/1	D E Pipe	*T J Murphy*	9
2009	162	Imperial Commander 8-11-10: 6/1	N A Twiston-Davies	*P J Brennan*	10
2010	165	Albertas Run 9-11-10: 14/1	J O'Neill	*A P McCoy*	13
2011	165	Albertas Run 10-11-10: 6/1	Jonjo O'Neill	*A P McCoy*	11

2012	168	Riverside Theatre 8-11-10: 7/2	Nicky Henderson	Barry Geraghty	12
2013	175	Cue Card 7-11-10: 7/2	Colin Tizzard	Joe Tizzard	8
2014	163	Dynaste 8-11-10: 3/1	David Pipe	Tom Scudamore	11
2015	168	Uxizandre 7-11-10: 16/1	Alan King	A P McCoy	14
2016	180	Vautour 7-11-10: 1/1	W P Mullins (Ir)	R Walsh	15
2017	169	Un de Sceaux 9-11-10: 7/4	W P Mullins (Ir)	R Walsh	8
2018	166	Balko des Flos 7-11-10: 8/1	Henry de Bromhead (Ir)	Davy Russell	6

JLT NOVICES' CHASE (Golden Miller) (Gr 1, Gr 2 until 2013) (Cheltenham 2m3f198y)

2011	151	Noble Prince 7-11-4: 4/1	Paul Nolan (Ir)	A P McCoy	11
2012	160	Sir des Champs 6-11-4: 3/1	W P Mullins (Ir)	Davy Russell	10
2013	153	Benefficient 7-11-4: 20/1	A J Martin (Ir)	Bryan Cooper	13
2014	154	Taquin du Seuil 7-11-4: 7/1	Jonjo O'Neill	A P McCoy	12
2015	171	Vautour 6-11-4: 6/4	W P Mullins (Ir)	R Walsh	8
2016	154	Black Hercules 7-11-4: 4/1	W P Mullins (Ir)	R Walsh	9
2017	160	Yorkhill 7-11-4: 6/4	W P Mullins (Ir)	R Walsh	8
2018	154	Shattered Love 7-10-11: 4/1	Gordon Elliott (Ir)	J W Kennedy	9

SUN BETS STAYERS' HURDLE (Gr 1) (Cheltenham 2m7f213y, 3m½f before 2002)

1993	157	Shuil Ar Aghaidh 7-11-5: 20/1	P Kiely (Ir)	C F Swan	12
1994	157	*Balasani 8-11-10: 9/2	M C Pipe	M Perrett	14
1995	167	Dorans Pride 6-11-10: 11/4	M Hourigan (Ir)	J P Broderick	11
1996	158	Cyborgo 6-11-10: 8/1	M C Pipe	D Bridgwater	19
1997	154	Karshi 7-11-10: 20/1	Miss H C Knight	J Osborne	17
1998	161	Princeful 7-11-10: 16/1	Mrs J Pitman	R Farrant	9
1999	162	Anzum 8-11-10: 40/1	D Nicholson	R Johnson	12
2000	161	Bacchanal 6-11-10: 11/2	N J Henderson	M A Fitzgerald	10
2001		Abandoned			
2002	164	Baracouda 7-11-10: 13/8	F Doumen (Fr)	T Doumen	16
2003	173	Baracouda 8-11-10: 9/4	F Doumen (Fr)	T Doumen	11
2004	172	Iris's Gift 7-11-10: 9/2	J O'Neill	B J Geraghty	10
2005	162	Inglis Drever 6-11-10: 5/1	J H Johnson	G Lee	12
2006	163	My Way de Solzen 6-11-10: 8/1	A King	R Thornton	20
2007	164	Inglis Drever 8-11-10: 5/1	J H Johnson	P J Brennan	14
2008	169	Inglis Drever 9-11-10: 11/8	J H Johnson	D O'Regan	17
2009	172	Big Buck's 6-11-10: 6/1	P F Nicholls	R Walsh	14
2010	169	Big Buck's 7-11-10: 5/6	P F Nicholls	R Walsh	14
2011	162	Big Buck's 8-11-10: 10/11	Paul Nicholls	R Walsh	13
2012	168	Big Buck's 9-11-10: 5/6	Paul Nicholls	R Walsh	11
2013	162	Solwhit 9-11-10: 17/2	Charles Byrnes (Ir)	Paul Carberry	13
2014	167	More of That 6-11-10: 15/2	Jonjo O'Neill	Barry Geraghty	10
2015	164	Cole Harden 6-11-10: 14/1	Warren Greatrex	Gavin Sheehan	16
2016	169	Thistlecrack 8-11-10: 1/1	Colin Tizzard	Tom Scudamore	12
2017	163	Nichols Canyon 7-11-10: 10/1	W P Mullins (Ir)	R Walsh	12
2018	164	Penhill 7-11-10: 12/1	W P Mullins (Ir)	P Townend	15

JCB TRIUMPH HURDLE (4-y-o) (Gr 1) (Cheltenham 2m179y)

1993	133	Shawiya 10-9: 12/1	M O'Brien (Ir)	C F Swan	25
1994	133	Mysilv 10-9: 2/1	D Nicholson	A Maguire	28
1995	143	Kissair 11-0: 16/1	M C Pipe	J Lower	26
1996	144	Paddy's Return 11-0: 10/1	F Murphy	R Dunwoody	29
1997	130	Commanche Court 11-0: 9/1	T M Walsh (Ir)	N Williamson	28
1998	145	Upgrade 11-0: 14/1	N A Twiston-Davies	C Llewellyn	25
1999	151	Katarino 11-0: 11/4	N J Henderson	M A Fitzgerald	23
2000	135	Snow Drop 10-9: 7/1	F Doumen (Fr)	T Doumen	28
2001		Abandoned			
2002	147	Scolardy 11-0: 16/1	W P Mullins (Ir)	C F Swan	28
2003	163	Spectroscope 11-0: 20/1	J O'Neill	B J Geraghty	27
2004	134	Made In Japan 11-0: 20/1	P J Hobbs	R Johnson	23
2005	144	Penzance 11-0: 9/1	A King	R Thornton	23
2006	140	Detroit City 11-0: 7/2	P J Hobbs	R Johnson	17
2007	151	Katchit 11-0: 11/2	A King	R Thornton	23
2008	141	Celestial Halo 11-0: 5/1	P F Nicholls	R Walsh	14
2009	149	Zaynar 11-0: 11/2	N J Henderson	B J Geraghty	18
2010	145	Soldatino 11-0: 6/1	N J Henderson	B J Geraghty	17
2011	152	Zarkandar 11-0: 13/2	Paul Nicholls	Daryl Jacob	23
2012	147	Countrywide Flame 11-0: 33/1	John Quinn	Dougie Costello	20
2013	160	Our Conor 11-0: 4/1	D T Hughes (Ir)	Bryan Cooper	17

2014	150	Tiger Roll 11-0: 10/1	Gordon Elliott (Ir)	*Davy Russell*	15
2015	164	Peace And Co 11-0: 2/1	Nicky Henderson	*Barry Geraghty*	16
2016	156	Ivanovich Gorbatov 11-0: 9/2	Aidan O'Brien (Ir)	*Barry Geraghty*	15
2017	146	Defi du Seuil 11-0: 5/2	Philip Hobbs	*Richard Johnson*	15
2018	149	Farclas 11-0: 9/1	Gordon Elliott (Ir)	*J W Kennedy*	9

ALBERT BARTLETT NOVICES' HURDLE (Spa) (Gr 1)
(Cheltenham 2m7f213y, Gr 2 before 2008)

2005	139	Moulin Riche 5-11-7: 9/1	F Doumen (Fr)	*R Thornton*	18
2006	142	Black Jack Ketchum 7-11-7: 1/1	J O'Neill	*A P McCoy*	19
2007	147	Wichita Lineman 6-11-7: 11/8	J O'Neill	*A P McCoy*	20
2008	144	Nenuphar Collonges 7-11-7: 9/1	A King	*R Thornton*	18
2009	147	Weapon's Amnesty 6-11-7: 8/1	C Byrnes (Ir)	*D N Russell*	17
2010	145	Berties Dream 7-11-7: 33/1	P J Gilligan (Ir)	*A E Lynch*	19
2011	152	Bobs Worth 6-11-7: 15/8	Nicky Henderson	*Barry Geraghty*	18
2012	150	Brindisi Breeze 6-11-7: 7/1	Lucinda Russell	*Campbell Gillies*	20
2013	150	At Fishers Cross 6-11-7: 11/8	Rebecca Curtis	*A P McCoy*	13
2014	146	Very Wood 5-11-7: 33/1	Noel Meade (Ir)	*P Carberry*	18
2015	153	Martello Tower 7-11-7: 14/1	Mrs Margaret Mullins (Ir)	*A P Heskin*	19
2016	145	Unowhatimeanharry 8-11-5: 11/1	Harry Fry	*Noel Fehily*	19
2017	152	Penhill 6-11-5: 16/1	W P Mullins (Ir)	*P Townend*	15
2018	151	Kilbricken Storm 7-11-5: 33/1	Colin Tizzard	*Harry Cobden*	20

TIMICO CHELTENHAM GOLD CUP CHASE (Gr 1) (Cheltenham 3¼m70y)

1993	174	Jodami 8-12-0: 8/1	P Beaumont	*M Dwyer*	16
1994	171	The Fellow 9-12-0: 7/1	F Doumen (Fr)	*A Kondrat*	15
1995	183	Master Oats 9-12-0: 10/3	K C Bailey	*N Williamson*	15
1996	178	Imperial Call 7-12-0: 9/2	F Sutherland (Ir)	*C O'Dwyer*	10
1997	169	Mr Mulligan 9-12-0: 20/1	N T Chance	*A P McCoy*	14
1998	173	Cool Dawn 10-12-0: 25/1	R H Alner	*A Thornton*	17
1999	173	See More Business 9-12-0: 16/1	P F Nicholls	*M A Fitzgerald*	12
2000	176	Looks Like Trouble 8-12-0: 9/2	N T Chance	*R Johnson*	12
2001		Abandoned			
2002	173	Best Mate 7-12-0: 7/1	Miss H C Knight	*J Culloty*	18
2003	174	Best Mate 8-12-0: 13/8	Miss H C Knight	*J Culloty*	15
2004	169	Best Mate 9-11-10: 8/11	Miss H C Knight	*J Culloty*	10
2005	167	Kicking King 7-11-10: 4/1	T J Taaffe (Ir)	*B J Geraghty*	15
2006	169	War of Attrition 7-11-10: 15/2	M F Morris (Ir)	*C O'Dwyer*	22
2007	165	Kauto Star 7-11-10: 5/4	P F Nicholls	*R Walsh*	18
2008	176	Denman 8-11-10: 9/4	P F Nicholls	*S Thomas*	12
2009	184	Kauto Star 9-11-10: 7/4	P F Nicholls	*R Walsh*	16
2010	182	Imperial Commander 9-11-10: 7/1	N A Twiston-Davies	*P J Brennan*	11
2011	176	Long Run 6-11-10: 7/2	Nicky Henderson	*Mr S Waley-Cohen*	13
2012	167	Synchronised 9-11-10: 8/1	Jonjo O'Neill	*A P McCoy*	14
2013	179	Bobs Worth 8-11-10: 11/4	Nicky Henderson	*Barry Geraghty*	9
2014	161	Lord Windermere 8-11-10: 20/1	J H Culloty (Ir)	*Davy Russell*	13
2015	170	Coneygree 8-11-10: 7/1	Mark Bradstock	*Nico de Boinville*	16
2016	181	Don Cossack 9-11-10: 9/4	Gordon Elliott (Ir)	*B J Cooper*	9
2017	169	Sizing John 7-11-10: 7/1	Mrs J Harrington (Ir)	*Robbie Power*	13
2018	172	Native River 8-11-10: 5/1	Colin Tizzard	*Richard Johnson*	15

BIG BUCK'S CELEBRATION MANIFESTO NOVICES' CHASE (Gr 1)
(Aintree 2m3f200y, Gr 2 prior to 2012)

2009	152	Tartak 6-11-4: 11/2	T R George	*P J Brennan*	8
2010	151	Mad Max 8-11-4: 4/1	N J Henderson	*B J Geraghty*	6
2011	155	Wishfull Thinking 8-11-4: 9/4	Philip Hobbs	*Richard Johnson*	7
2012	159	Menorah 7-11-4: 3/1	Philip Hobbs	*Richard Johnson*	5
2013	145	Captain Conan 6-11-4: 6/5	Nicky Henderson	*Barry Geraghty*	7
2014	153	Uxizandre 6-11-4: 11/4	Alan King	*A P McCoy*	5
2015	152	Clarcam 5-11-4: 5/1	Gordon Elliott (Ir)	*R Walsh*	6
2016	156	Arzal 6-11-4: 4/1	Harry Whittingham	*Gavin Sheehan*	8
2017	154	Flying Angel 6-11-4: 5/1	Nigel Twiston-Davies	*Noel Fehily*	6
2018	148	Finian's Oscar 6-11-4: 5/2	Colin Tizzard	*Robbie Power*	6

RYANAIR STAYERS' (Liverpool) HURDLE (Gr 1)
(Aintree 3m149y, Ascot 3m before 2004, Gr 2 prior to 2010)

| 1993 | 161 | Sweet Duke 6-11-3: 5/1 | N A Twiston-Davies | *C Llewellyn* | 7 |
| 1994 | 162 | Sweet Glow 7-11-7: 9/2 | M C Pipe | *R Dunwoody* | 12 |

1995	148	Cab On Target 9-11-7: 11/8	Mrs M Reveley	P Niven	6
1996	163	Pleasure Shared 8-11-10: 6/1	P J Hobbs	W Marston	7
1997	123	Trainglot 10-11-10: 1/2	J G FitzGerald	R Dunwoody	5
1998	160	Marello 7-11-5: 11/4	Mrs M Reveley	P Niven	7
1999	151	Galant Moss 5-11-3: 1/1	M C Pipe	A P McCoy	5
2000	160	Teaatral 6-11-7: 4/1	C R Egerton	D Gallagher	10
2001	147	Maid Equal 10-10-12: 14/1	M C Pipe	Mr T Scudamore	8
2002	149	Spendid 10-11-2: 2/1	A King	W Marston	7
2003	154	Deano's Beeno 11-11-10: 5/4	M C Pipe	A P McCoy	7
2004	153	Iris's Gift 7-11-10: 4/7	J O'Neill	B J Geraghty	8
2005	160	Monet's Garden 7-11-10: 11/2	N G Richards	A Dobbin	9
2006	166	Mighty Man 6-11-6: 11/4	H D Daly	R Johnson	12
2007	172	Mighty Man 7-11-10: 15/8	H D Daly	R Johnson	6
2008	157	Blazing Bailey 6-11-10: 5/1	A King	R Thornton	11
2009	173	Big Buck's 6-11-10: 5/6	P F Nicholls	R Walsh	10
2010	149	Big Buck's 7-11-7: 3/10	P F Nicholls	R Walsh	7
2011	166	Big Buck's 8-11-7: 4/6	Paul Nicholls	R Walsh	11
2012	149	Big Buck's 9-11-7: 2/9	Paul Nicholls	R Walsh	8
2013	158	Solwhit 9-11-7: 9/4	Charles Byrnes (Ir)	Paul Carberry	13
2014	158	Whisper 6-11-7: 4/1	Nicky Henderson	Barry Geraghty	7
2015	163	Whisper 7-11-7: 5/1	Nicky Henderson	Nico de Boinville	9
2016	162	Thistlecrack 8-11-7: 2/7	Colin Tizzard	Tom Scudamore	6
2017	155	Yanworth 7-11-7: 9/4	Alan King	Barry Geraghty	11
2018	161	Identity Thief 8-11-7: 14/1	Henry de Bromhead (Ir)	Sean Flanagan	10

BETWAY BOWL CHASE (Gr 1) (Aintree 3m210y, Gr 2 prior to 2010)

1993	165	Docklands Express 11-11-5: 6/4	K C Bailey	J Osborne	4
1994	159	Docklands Express 12-11-5: 5/2	K C Bailey	R Dunwoody	4
1995	170	Merry Gale 7-11-5: 5/2	J T R Dreaper (Ir)	G Bradley	6
1996	161	Scotton Banks 7-11-5: 9/2	T D Easterby	L Wyer	6
1997	162	Barton Bank 11-11-5: 10/3	D Nicholson	D Walsh	5
1998	171	Escartefigue 6-11-13: 11/2	D Nicholson	R Johnson	8
1999	155	Macgeorge 9-11-5: 11/1	R Lee	A Maguire	5
2000	179	See More Business 10-12-0: 5/4	P F Nicholls	M A Fitzgerald	4
2001	173	First Gold 8-12-0: 7/4	F Doumen (Fr)	T Doumen	7
2002	168	Florida Pearl 10-11-12: 5/2	W P Mullins (Ir)	B J Geraghty	6
2003	171	First Gold 10-11-12: 14/1	F Doumen (Fr)	T Doumen	7
2004	168	Tiutchev 11-11-12: 11/2	M C Pipe	A P McCoy	8
2005	168	Grey Abbey 11-11-12: 7/2	J H Johnson	G Lee	8
2006	166	Celestial Gold 8-11-8: 8/1	M C Pipe	T J Murphy	9
2007	175	Exotic Dancer 7-11-12: 6/4	J O'Neill	A P McCoy	5
2008	170	Our Vic 10-11-10: 9/1	D E Pipe	T J Murphy	6
2009	170	Madison du Berlais 8-11-10: 12/1	D E Pipe	T Scudamore	10
2010	170	What A Friend 7-11-7: 5/2	P F Nicholls	R Walsh	5
2011	164	Nacarat 10-11-7: 7/2	Tom George	Paddy Brennan	6
2012	163	Follow The Plan 9-11-7: 50/1	Oliver McKiernan (Ir)	Tom Doyle	11
2013	170	First Lieutenant 8-11-7: 7/2	M F Morris (Ir)	Bryan Cooper	8
2014	165	Silviniaco Conti 8-11-7: 9/4	Paul Nicholls	Noel Fehily	6
2015	165	Silviniaco Conti 9-11-7: 7/4	Paul Nicholls	Noel Fehily	7
2016	181	Cue Card 10-11-7: 6/5	Colin Tizzard	Paddy Brennan	9
2017	166	Tea For Two 8-11-7: 10/1	Nick Williams	Lizzie Kelly	7
2018	171	Might Bite 9-11-7: 4/5	Nicky Henderson	Nico de Boinville	8

DOOM BAR ANNIVERSARY 4-Y-O JUVENILE HURDLE (Gr 1) (Aintree 2m209y)

1993	132	Titled Dancer 10-9: 9/2	J Coogan (Ir)	J Shortt	8
1994	135	Tropical Lake 10-9: 10/1	M Hourigan (Ir)	K O'Brien	12
1995	139	Stompin 11-0: 9/1	Miss H C Knight	J Osborne	18
1996	138	Zabadi 11-0: 8/1	D Nicholson	A P McCoy	11
1997	135	Quakers Field 11-0: 8/1	G L Moore	D Gallagher	12
1998	149	Deep Water 11-0: 8/1	M D Hammond	R Garritty	14
1999	147	Hors La Loi III 11-4: 8/15	M C Pipe	A P McCoy	6
2000	139	Lord Brex 11-0: 15/2	P J Hobbs	R Johnson	12
2001	154	Bilboa 10-13: 7/4	F Doumen (Fr)	T Doumen	14
2002	137	Quazar 11-4: 16/1	J O'Neill	A Dobbin	17
2003	133	Le Duc 11-0: 33/1	P F Nicholls	R Walsh	19
2004	131	Al Eile 11-0: 25/1	J Queally (Ir)	T J Murphy	18
2005	141	Faasel 11-0: 11/4	N G Richards	A Dobbin	12

2006	144	Detroit City 11-0: 3/1	P J Hobbs	R Johnson	13
2007	147	Katchit 11-0: 1/1	A King	R Thornton	12
2008	151	Binocular 11-0: 11/8	N J Henderson	A P McCoy	10
2009	154	Walkon 11-0: 2/1	A King	R Thornton	13
2010	136	Orsippus 11-0: 40/1	Michael Smith	D J Condon	11
2011	145	Zarkandar 11-0: 4/6	Paul Nicholls	R Walsh	9
2012	148	Grumeti 11-0: 11/4	Alan King	Robert Thornton	11
2013	139	L'Unique 10-7: 10/1	Alan King	Wayne Hutchinson	10
2014	144	Guitar Pete 11-0: 13/2	D T Hughes (Ir)	Paul Carberry	15
2015	145	All Yours 11-0: 16/1	Paul Nicholls	Sam Twiston-Davies	10
2016	157	Apple's Jade 10-7: 3/1	W P Mullins (Ir)	B J Cooper	9
2017	141	Defi du Seuil 11-0: 4/11	Philip Hobbs	Barry Geraghty	8
2018	150	We Have A Dream 11-0: 2/1	Nicky Henderson	Daryl Jacob	10

BETWAY MILDMAY NOVICES' CHASE (Gr 1) (Aintree 3m210y, Gr 2 prior to 2014)

1993	148	Cab On Target 7-11-3: 15/8	Mrs M Reveley	P Niven	5
1994	156	Monsieur Le Cure 8-11-9: 7/4	J A C Edwards	P Niven	6
1995	145	Banjo 5-11-0: 6/4	M C Pipe	R Dunwoody	4
1996	145	Addington Boy 8-11-10: 7/2	G Richards	B Harding	7
1997	143	Cyborgo 7-11-4: 13/8	M C Pipe	R Dunwoody	7
1998	148	Boss Doyle 6-11-7: 5/4	M F Morris (Ir)	A P McCoy	8
1999	140	Spendid 7-11-9: 10/3	D Nicholson	R Johnson	7
2000	147	High Game 6-11-4: 9/1	S E H Sherwood	N Williamson	8
2001	?	Whats Up Boys 7-11-4: 12/1	P J Hobbs	R Johnson	7
2002	154	Barton 9-11-9: 3/1	T D Easterby	A Dobbin	9
2003	142	Irish Hussar 7-11-2: 10/1	N J Henderson	M A Fitzgerald	9
2004	138	Simply Supreme 7-11-2: 13/2	Mrs S J Smith	R McGrath	11
2005	134	Like-A-Butterfly 11-11-2: 6/1	C Roche (Ir)	A P McCoy	10
2006	146	Star de Mohaison 5-11-0: 11/4	P F Nicholls	B J Geraghty	15
2007	149	Aces Four 8-11-5: 5/2	F Murphy	G Lee	10
2008	147	Big Buck's 5-11-3: 11/4	P F Nicholls	R Walsh	8
2009	146	Killyglen 7-11-3: 7/1	J H Johnson	D O'Regan	9
2010	139	Burton Port 6-11-4: 9/2	N J Henderson	B J Geraghty	10
2011	142	Quito de La Roque 7-11-4: 6/1	Colm Murphy (Ir)	Davy Russell	8
2012	158	Silviniaco Conti 6-11-4: 7/4	Paul Nicholls	R Walsh	5
2013	153	Dynaste 7-11-4: 9/4	David Pipe	Tom Scudamore	6
2014	158	Holywell 7-11-4: 7/2	Jonjo O'Neill	A P McCoy	6
2015	161	Saphir du Rheu 6-11-4: 13/8	Paul Nicholls	Sam Twiston-Davies	9
2016	152	Native River 6-11-4: 11/2	Colin Tizzard	Richard Johnson	8
2017	161	Might Bite 8-11-4: 8/13	Nicky Henderson	Nico de Boinville	5
2018	156	Terrefort 5-11-4: 3/1	Nicky Henderson	Daryl Jacob	9

DOOM BAR SEFTON NOVICES' HURDLE (Gr 1) (Aintree 3m149y)

1993	136	Cardinal Red 6-11-4: 4/1	Mrs F Walwyn	B de Haan	6
1994	136	Corner Boy 7-11-4: 10/1	D Nicholson	A Maguire	11
1995	135	Morgans Harbour 9-11-4: 6/1	Mrs M Reveley	P Niven	15
1996	146	Pleasure Shared 8-11-6: 14/1	P J Hobbs	P Carberry	16
1997	140	Forest Ivory 6-11-4: 11/2	D Nicholson	R Johnson	12
1998	145	Unsinkable Boxer 9-11-4: 10/11	M C Pipe	A P McCoy	12
1999	141	King's Road 6-11-4: 3/1	N A Twiston-Davies	C Llewellyn	15
2000	148	Sackville 7-11-4: 12/1	Ms F M Crowley (Ir)	B J Geraghty	17
2001	140	Garruth 7-11-4: 16/1	T D Easterby	R Garritty	13
2002	139	Stromness 5-11-4: 8/1	A King	R Thornton	15
2003	159	Iris's Gift 6-11-4: 10/11	J O'Neill	B J Geraghty	9
2004	140	Accipiter 5-11-4: 14/1	G B Balding	T Best	13
2005	142	Asian Maze 6-10-11: 7/1	T Mullins (Ir)	R Walsh	17
2006	151	Black Jack Ketchum 7-11-4: 8/13	J O'Neill	A P McCoy	11
2007	150	Chief Dan George 7-11-4: 20/1	J Moffatt	M A Fitzgerald	10
2008	146	Pettifour 6-11-4: 16/1	N A Twiston-Davies	P J Brennan	13
2009	143	Ogee 6-11-4: 25/1	Mrs P Robeson	J A McCarthy	15
2010	144	Wayward Prince 6-11-4: 9/1	I Williams	D Costello	14
2011	139	Saint Are 5-11-4: 33/1	Tim Vaughan	Richard Johnson	19
2012	149	Lovcen 6-11-4: 8/1	Alan King	Robert Thornton	19
2013	147	At Fishers Cross 6-11-4: 11/8	Rebecca Curtis	A P McCoy	9
2014	153	Beat That 6-11-4: 9/2	Nicky Henderson	Barry Geraghty	18
2015	149	Thistlecrack 7-11-4: 25/1	Colin Tizzard	Tom Scudamore	16
2016	146	Ballyoptic 6-11-4: 9/1	Nigel Twiston-Davies	Ryan Hatch	15

| 2017 | 146 | The Worlds End 6-11-4: 3/1 | Tom George | A P Heskin | 11 |
| 2018 | 150 | Santini 6-11-4: 6/4 | Nicky Henderson | Nico de Boinville | 13 |

JLT MELLING CHASE (Gr 1) (Aintree 2m3f200y)

1993	148	Deep Sensation 8-11-10: 7/4	J T Gifford	D Murphy	4
1994	161	Katabatic 11-11-10: 14/1	J T Gifford	S McNeill	5
1995	164	Viking Flagship 8-11-10: 5/2	D Nicholson	A Maguire	6
1996	172	Viking Flagship 9-11-10: 5/2	D Nicholson	A P McCoy	4
1997	177	Martha's Son 10-11-10: 5/2	T A Forster	C Llewellyn	4
1998	155	Opera Hat 10-11-5: 10/1	J R H Fowler (Ir)	C O'Dwyer	5
1999	166	Direct Route 8-11-10: 7/2	J H Johnson	N Williamson	6
2000	160	Direct Route 9-11-10: 11/8	J H Johnson	N Williamson	5
2001	167	Fadalko 8-11-10: 9/2	P F Nicholls	R Walsh	7
2002	158	Native Upmanship 9-11-10: 10/3	A L T Moore (Ir)	C O'Dwyer	8
2003	168	Native Upmanship 10-11-10: 5/4	A L T Moore (Ir)	C O'Dwyer	6
2004	170	Moscow Flyer 10-11-10: 1/1	Mrs J Harrington (Ir)	B J Geraghty	7
2005	176	Moscow Flyer 11-11-10: 4/9	Mrs J Harrington (Ir)	B J Geraghty	6
2006	156	Hi Cloy 9-11-10: 14/1	M Hourigan (Ir)	A J McNamara	11
2007	160	Monet's Garden 9-11-10: 4/1	N G Richards	A Dobbin	6
2008	170	Voy Por Ustedes 7-11-10: 5/1	A King	R Thornton	6
2009	163	Voy Por Ustedes 8-11-10: 11/8	A King	R Thornton	10
2010	165	Albertas Run 9-11-10: 8/1	J O'Neill	A P McCoy	11
2011	170	Master Minded 8-11-10: 11/2	Paul Nicholls	R Walsh	10
2012	170	Finian's Rainbow 9-11-10: 13/8	Nicky Henderson	Barry Geraghty	8
2013	183	Sprinter Sacre 7-11-10: 1/3	Nicky Henderson	Barry Geraghty	6
2014	159	Boston Bob 9-11-10: 5/1	W P Mullins (Ir)	Paul Townend	10
2015	180	Don Cossack 8-11-10: 3/1	Gordon Elliott (Ir)	A P McCoy	10
2016	168	God's Own 8-11-10: 10/1	Tom George	Paddy Brennan	6
2017	170	Fox Norton 7-11-7: 4/1	Colin Tizzard	Robbie Power	9
2018	166	Politologue 7-11-7: 11/1	Paul Nicholls	Sam Twiston-Davies	6

BETWAY TOP NOVICES' HURDLE (Gr 1) (Aintree 2m103y)

1993	140	Roll A Dollar 7-11-6: 9/4	D R C Elsworth	P Holley	9
1994	141	Jazilah 6-11-6: 7/4	R Akehurst	G McCourt	8
1995	128	Sweet Mignonette 7-10-11: 4/1	Mrs M Reveley	P Niven	15
1996	132	Tragic Hero 4-10-8: 20/1	M C Pipe	J Lower	15
1997	131	Midnight Legend 6-11-0: 11/2	D Nicholson	R Johnson	9
1998	137	Fataliste 4-10-12: 7/2	M C Pipe	A P McCoy	10
1999	142	Joe Mac 5-11-8: 6/4	C Roche (Ir)	C O'Dwyer	9
2000	139	Phardante Flyer 6-11-10: 5/1	P J Hobbs	R Johnson	13
2001	133	Ilico II 5-11-5: 16/1	P J Hobbs	A Maguire	15
2002	144	In Contrast 6-11-5: 5/2	P J Hobbs	R Johnson	11
2003	132	Limerick Boy 5-11-0: 5/1	Miss V Williams	A Dobbin	12
2004	138	Royal Shakespeare 5-11-3: 25/1	S Gollings	R Thornton	12
2005	138	Mighty Man 5-11-0: 3/1	H D Daly	R Johnson	7
2006	127	Straw Bear 5-11-3: 2/1	N J Gifford	A P McCoy	16
2007	144	Blythe Knight 7-11-0: 14/1	J J Quinn	A P McCoy	8
2008	149	Pierrot Lunaire 4-10-8: 5/1	P F Nicholls	R Walsh	14
2009	140	El Dancer 5-11-0: 14/1	Mrs L Wadham	D Elsworth	11
2010	143	General Miller 5-11-4: 7/1	N J Henderson	B J Geraghty	9
2011	143	Topolski 5-11-4: 11/2	David Arbuthnot	Daryl Jacob	13
2012	146	Darlan 5-11-4: 7/4	Nicky Henderson	A P McCoy	12
2013	159	My Tent Or Yours 6-11-4: 4/11	Nicky Henderson	A P McCoy	4
2014	149	Josses Hill 6-11-4: 6/4	Nicky Henderson	Barry Geraghty	10
2015	159	Cyrus Darius 6-11-4: 8/1	Malcolm Jefferson	Brian Hughes	11
2016	151	Buveur d'Air 5-11-4: 11/4	Nicky Henderson	Noel Fehily	11
2017	140	Pingshou 7-11-4: 16/1	Colin Tizzard	Robbie Power	9
2018	147	Lalor 6-11-4: 14/1	Kayley Woollacott	Richard Johnson	13

BETWAY AINTREE HURDLE (Gr 1) (Aintree 2½m)

1993	169	Morley Street 9-11-7: 6/1	G B Balding	G Bradley	6
1994	172	Danoli 6-11-7: 9/2	T Foley (Ir)	C F Swan	8
1995	167	Danoli 7-11-7: 2/1	T Foley (Ir)	C F Swan	6
1996	149	Urubande 6-11-7: 10/3	A P O'Brien (Ir)	C F Swan	8
1997	162	Bimsey 7-11-7: 14/1	R Akehurst	M Fitzgerald	7
1998	168	Pridwell 8-11-7: 6/1	M C Pipe	A P McCoy	6
1999	170	Istabraq 7-11-7: 1/2	A P O'Brien (Ir)	C F Swan	7
2000	159	Mister Morose 10-11-7: 16/1	N A Twiston-Davies	C Llewellyn	10

2001	157	Barton 8-11-7: 9/1	T D Easterby	*A Dobbin*	8
2002	156	Ilnamar 6-11-7: 9/1	M C Pipe	*R Walsh*	14
2003	159	Sacundai 6-11-7: 9/1	E J O'Grady (Ir)	*R Walsh*	11
2004	159	Rhinestone Cowboy 8-11-7: 5/2	J O'Neill	*Mr J P Magnier*	11
2005	159	Al Eile 5-11-7: 11/1	J Queally (Ir)	*T J Murphy*	9
2006	162	Asian Maze 7-11-0: 4/1	T Mullins (Ir)	*R Walsh*	9
2007	156	Al Eile 7-11-7: 12/1	J Queally (Ir)	*T J Murphy*	11
2008	159	Al Eile 8-11-7: 11/4	J Queally (Ir)	*T J Murphy*	9
2009	160	Solwhit 5-11-7: 6/1	C Byrnes (Ir)	*D N Russell*	16
2010	157	Khyber Kim 8-11-7: 7/2	N A Twiston-Davies	*P J Brennan*	7
2011	162	Oscar Whisky 6-11-7: 6/1	Nicky Henderson	*Barry Geraghty*	8
2012	163	Oscar Whisky 7-11-7: 9/4	Nicky Henderson	*Barry Geraghty*	5
2013	160	Zarkandar 6-11-7: 11/2	Paul Nicholls	*R Walsh*	9
2014	159	The New One 6-11-7: 4/9	Nigel Twiston-Davies	*Sam Twiston-Davies*	7
2015	167	Jezki 7-11-7: 3/1	Mrs J Harrington (Ir)	*A P McCoy*	6
2016	170	Annie Power 8-11-0: 4/9	W P Mullins (Ir)	*R Walsh*	6
2017	170	Buveur d'Air 6-11-7: 4/9	Nicky Henderson	*Barry Geraghty*	6
2018	163	L'Ami Serge 8-11-7: 5/1	Nicky Henderson	*Daryl Jacob*	9

DOOM BAR MAGHULL NOVICES' CHASE (Gr 1) (Aintree 1m7f176y)

1993	135	Valiant Boy 7-11-10: 12/1	S Kettlewell	*R Garritty*	7
1994	136	Nakir 6-11-10: 6/5	S Christian	*J Osborne*	6
1995	144	Morceli 7-11-3: 11/4	J H Johnson	*N Williamson*	7
1996	135	Ask Tom 7-11-4: 10/1	T P Tate	*P Niven*	10
1997	145	Squire Silk 8-11-4: 2/1	A Turnell	*J Osborne*	6
1998	140	Direct Route 7-11-4: 9/2	J H Johnson	*P Carberry*	6
1999	141	Flagship Uberalles 5-10-11: 5/2	P F Nicholls	*J Tizzard*	7
2000	146	Cenkos 6-11-4: 7/2	O Sherwood	*D J Casey*	6
2001	139	Ballinclay King 7-11-4: 6/1	F Murphy	*A Maguire*	7
2002	144	Armaturk 5-11-1: 5/2	P F Nicholls	*T J Murphy*	5
2003	156	Le Roi Miguel 5-11-1: 9/4	P F Nicholls	*R Walsh*	5
2004	140	Well Chief 5-11-1: 15/8	M C Pipe	*A P McCoy*	10
2005	154	Ashley Brook 7-11-4: 3/1	K Bishop	*P J Brennan*	10
2006	155	Foreman 8-11-4: 4/1	T Doumen (Fr)	*A P McCoy*	7
2007	147	Twist Magic 5-11-1: 9/4	P F Nicholls	*R Walsh*	6
2008	151	Tidal Bay 7-11-4: 6/4	J H Johnson	*D O'Regan*	8
2009	152	Kalahari King 8-11-4: 9/4	F Murphy	*G Lee*	6
2010	153	Tataniano 6-11-4: 10/3	P F Nicholls	*R Walsh*	10
2011	150	Finian's Rainbow 8-11-4: 10/11	Nicky Henderson	*Barry Geraghty*	7
2012	160	Sprinter Sacre 6-11-4: 1/7	Nicky Henderson	*Barry Geraghty*	4
2013	152	Special Tiara 6-11-4: 28/1	H de Bromhead (Ir)	*Bryan Cooper*	6
2014	158	Balder Succes 6-11-4: 7/2	Alan King	*Wayne Hutchinson*	7
2015	155	Sizing Granite 7-11-4: 9/2	Henry de Bromhead (Ir)	*J J Burke*	6
2016	180	Douvan 6-11-4: 2/13	W P Mullins (Ir)	*P Townend*	5
2017	151	San Benedeto 6-11-4: 4/1	Paul Nicholls	*Nick Scholfield*	5
2018	155	Diego du Charmil 6-11-4: 5/1	Paul Nicholls	*Harry Cobden*	6

RANDOX HEALTH GRAND NATIONAL CHASE (HANDICAP) (Gr 3)
(Aintree 4¼m74y, 4m3½f 2013-15, 4½m before 2013)

1993		Void			
1994	159	Miinnehoma 11-10-8: 16/1	M C Pipe	*R Dunwoody*	36
1995	161	Royal Athlete 12-10-6: 40/1	Mrs J Pitman	*J Titley*	35
1996	157	Rough Quest 10-10-7: 7/1	T Casey	*M Fitzgerald*	27
1997	160	Lord Gyllene 9-10-0: 14/1	S A Brookshaw	*A Dobbin*	36
1998	156	Earth Summit 10-10-5: 7/1	N A Twiston-Davies	*C Llewellyn*	37
1999	152	Bobbyjo 9-10-0: 10/1	T Carberry (Ir)	*P Carberry*	32
2000	154	Papillon 9-10-12: 10/1	T M Walsh (Ir)	*R Walsh*	40
2001	?	Red Marauder 11-10-11: 33/1	N B Mason	*Richard Guest*	40
2002	146	Bindaree 8-10-4: 20/1	N A Twiston-Davies	*J Culloty*	40
2003	149	Monty's Pass 10-10-7: 16/1	J J Mangan (Ir)	*B J Geraghty*	40
2004	146	Amberleigh House 12-10-10: 16/1	D McCain	*G Lee*	39
2005	157	Hedgehunter 9-11-1: 7/1	W P Mullins (Ir)	*R Walsh*	40
2006	149	Numbersixvalverde 10-10-8: 11/1	M Brassil (Ir)	*N P Madden*	40
2007	147	Silver Birch 10-10-6: 33/1	G Elliott (Ir)	*R M Power*	40
2008	155	Comply Or Die 9-10-9: 7/1	D E Pipe	*T J Murphy*	40
2009	159	Mon Mome 9-11-0: 100/1	Miss V Williams	*L Treadwell*	40
2010	162	Don't Push It 10-11-5: 10/1	J O'Neill	*A P McCoy*	40

2011	159	Ballabriggs 10-11-0: 14/1	Donald McCain	*Jason Maguire*	40
2012	166	Neptune Collonges 11-11-6: 33/1	Paul Nicholls	*Daryl Jacob*	40
2013	145	Auroras Encore 11-10-3: 66/1	Sue Smith	*Ryan Mania*	40
2014	151	Pineau de Re 11-10-6: 25/1	Dr Richard Newland	*Leighton Aspell*	40
2015	168	Many Clouds 8-11-9: 25/1	Oliver Sherwood	*Leighton Aspell*	40
2016	156	Rule The World 9-10-7: 33/1	M F Morris (Ir)	*David Mullins*	39
2017	157	One For Arthur 8-10-11: 14/1	Lucinda Russell	*Derek Fox*	40
2018	155	Tiger Roll 8-10-13: 10/1	Gordon Elliott (Ir)	*Davy Russell*	38

CORAL SCOTTISH GRAND NATIONAL HANDICAP CHASE (Gr 3)
(Ayr 3m7f176y, run over 4m1f until 2006)

1993	153	Run For Free 9-11-10: 6/1	M C Pipe	*M Perrett*	21
1994	134	Earth Summit 6-10-0: 16/1	N A Twiston-Davies	*D Bridgwater*	22
1995	144	Willsford 12-10-12: 16/1	Mrs J Pitman	*R Farrant*	22
1996	142	Moorcroft Boy 11-10-2: 20/1	D Nicholson	*M Dwyer*	20
1997	152	Belmont King 9-11-10: 16/1	P F Nicholls	*A P McCoy*	17
1998	137	Baronet 8-10-0: 7/1	D Nicholson	*A Maguire*	18
1999	153	Young Kenny 8-11-10: 5/2	P Beaumont	*B Powell*	15
2000	150	Paris Pike 8-11-0: 5/1	F Murphy	*A Maguire*	18
2001	150	Gingembre 7-11-2: 12/1	Mrs L C Taylor	*A Thornton*	30
2002	145	Take Control 8-10-6: 20/1	M C Pipe	*R Walsh*	18
2003	146	Ryalux 10-10-5: 15/2	A Crook	*R McGrath*	19
2004	159	Grey Abbey 10-11-12: 12/1	J H Johnson	*G Lee*	28
2005	138	Joes Edge 8-9-11: 20/1	F Murphy	*K Mercer³*	20
2006	141	Run For Paddy 10-10-2: 33/1	C Llewellyn	*C Llewellyn*	30
2007	138	Hot Weld 8-9-9: 14/1	F Murphy	*P J McDonald⁵*	23
2008	149	Iris de Balme 8-9-7: 66/1	S Curran	*Mr C Huxley⁷*	24
2009	141	Hello Bud 11-10-9: 12/1	N A Twiston-Davies	*P J Brennan*	17
2010	138	Merigo 9-10-0: 18/1	A Parker	*T J Murphy*	30
2011	149	Beshabar 9-10-4: 15/2	Tim Vaughan	*Richard Johnson*	28
2012	142	Merigo 11-10-2: 15/2	Andrew Parker	*Timmy Murphy*	24
2013	148	Godsmejudge 7-11-3: 12/1	Alan King	*Wayne Hutchinson*	24
2014	144	Al Co 9-10-0: 40/1	Peter Bowen	*Jamie Moore*	29
2015	142	Wayward Prince 11-10-1: 25/1	Hilary Parrott	*Robert Dunne*	29
2016	152	Vicente 7-11-3: 14/1	Paul Nicholls	*Sam Twiston-Davies*	28
2017	151	Vicente 8-11-10: 9/1	Paul Nicholls	*Sam Twiston-Davies*	30
2018	140	Joe Farrell 9-10-6: 33/1	Rebecca Curtis	*Adam Wedge*	29

bet365 CELEBRATION CHASE (Gr 1) (Sandown 1m7f119y; Grade 2 until 2013)

2002	160	Cenkos 8-11-6: 8/1	P F Nicholls	*B J Geraghty*	5
2003	158	Seebald 8-11-6: 11/8	M C Pipe	*A P McCoy*	5
2004	163	Cenkos 10-11-10: 9/2	P F Nicholls	*B J Geraghty*	11
2005	164	Well Chief 6-11-10: 9/4	M C Pipe	*T J Murphy*	9
2006	153	River City 9-11-6: 9/1	N T Chance	*T Doyle*	4
2007	149	Dempsey 9-11-6: 5/4	C Llewellyn	*T J Murphy*	8
2008	157	Andreas 8-11-2: 9/2	P F Nicholls	*R Walsh*	11
2009	158	Twist Magic 7-11-6: 7/2	P F Nicholls	*R Walsh*	7
2010	151	I'm So Lucky 8-11-2: 9/1	D E Pipe	*T Scudamore*	8
2011	154	French Opera 8-11-2: 2/1	Nicky Henderson	*A P McCoy*	6
2012	169	Sanctuaire 6-11-2: 9/2	Paul Nicholls	*Daryl Jacob*	8
2013	166	Sire de Grugy 7-11-2: 6/1	Gary Moore	*Jamie Moore*	10
2014	158	Sire de Grugy 8-11-7: 2/7	Gary Moore	*Jamie Moore*	6
2015	167	Special Tiara 8-11-7: 3/1	Henry de Bromhead (Ir)	*Noel Fehily*	7
2016	179	Sprinter Sacre 10-11-7: 11/10	Nicky Henderson	*Nico de Boinville*	6
2017	175	Altior 7-11-7: 30/100	Nicky Henderson	*Nico de Boinville*	4
2018	162	Altior 8-11-7: 2/11	Nicky Henderson	*Nico de Boinville*	6

bet365 GOLD CUP CHASE (HANDICAP) (Gr 3) (Sandown 3½m166y)

1993	152	*Topsham Bay 10-10-1: 10/1	D H Barons	*R Dunwoody*	13
1994	148	Ushers Island 8-10-0: 25/1	J H Johnston	*C F Swan*	12
1995	145	Cache Fleur 9-10-1: 10/1	M C Pipe	*R Dunwoody*	14
1996	166	Life of A Lord 10-11-10: 12/1	A P O'Brien (Ir)	*C F Swan*	17
1997	139	Harwell Lad 8-10-0: 14/1	R H Alner	*Mr R Nuttall*	9
1998	155	Call It A Day 8-10-10: 8/1	D Nicholson	*A Maguire*	19
1999	144	Eulogy 9-10-0: 14/1	R Rowe	*B Fenton*	19
2000	168	Beau 7-10-9: 6/1	N A Twiston-Davies	*C Llewellyn*	20
2001	149	Ad Hoc 7-10-4: 14/1	P F Nicholls	*R Walsh*	25
2002	155	Bounce Back 6-10-9: 14/1	M C Pipe	*A P McCoy*	20

2003	156	Ad Hoc 8-12-0: 7/1	P F Nicholls	R Walsh	16
2004	147	Puntal 8-11-4: 25/1	M C Pipe	D J Howard[3]	18
2005	134	Jack High 10-10-0: 16/1	T M Walsh (Ir)	G Cotter	19
2006	159	Lacdoudal 7-11-5: 10/1	P J Hobbs	R Johnson	18
2007	141	Hot Weld 8-10-0: 6/1	F Murphy	G Lee	10
2008	154	Monkerhostin 11-10-13: 25/1	P J Hobbs	R Johnson	19
2009	137	Hennessy 8-10-7: 13/2	C Llewellyn	A P McCoy	14
2010	149	Church Island 11-10-5: 20/1	M Hourigan (Ir)	A P Heskin[7]	19
2011	141	Poker de Sivola 8-10-12: 11/1	Ferdy Murphy	Timmy Murphy	18
2012	165	Tidal Bay 11-11-12: 9/1	Paul Nicholls	Daryl Jacob	19
2013	138	Quentin Collonges 9-10-12: 14/1	Henry Daly	Andrew Tinkler	19
2014	152	Hadrian's Approach 7-11-0: 10/1	Nicky Henderson	Barry Geraghty	19
2015	142	Just A Par 8-10-3: 14/1	Paul Nicholls	Sean Bowen[3]	20
2016	152	The Young Master 7-11-1: 8/1	Neil Mulholland	Mr S Waley-Cohen[3]	20
2017	127	Henllan Harri 9-10-0: 40/1	Peter Bowen	Sean Bowen	13
2018	146	Step Back 8-10-0: 7/1	Mark Bradstock	Jamie Moore	20

Ireland

thetote.com GALWAY PLATE (HANDICAP CHASE) (Galway 2¾m111y)

1993	153	General Idea 8-12-0: 9/2	D K Weld	A Maguire	21
1994	123	Feathered Gale 7-9-11: 8/1	A L T Moore	F Woods	22
1995	156	Life of A Lord 9-11-8: 12/1	A P O'Brien	T Horgan	21
1996	171	Life of A Lord 10-12-0: 9/2	A P O'Brien	C F Swan	17
1997	128	Stroll Home 7-9-12: 11/2	J J Mangan	P Carberry	22
1998	142	Amlah 6-9-13: 16/1	P J Hobbs (GB)	B Powell	22
1999	149	Moscow Express 7-11-4: 4/1	Miss F M Crowley	R Walsh	21
2000	118	Dovaly 7-9-13: 20/1	M J P O'Brien	T P Rudd	22
2001	132	Grimes 8-10-1: 4/1	C Roche	C O'Dwyer	14
2002	120	Rockholm Boy 9-10-5: 20/1	M Hourigan	K Hadnett[5]	22
2003	130	Nearly A Moose 7-10-1: 25/1	P Mullins	R M Power[1]	22
2004	130	Ansar 8-10-12: 10/1	D K Weld	D J Casey	22
2005	143	Ansar 9-11-11: 10/1	D K Weld	D F O'Regan[3]	22
2006	135	Far From Trouble 7-10-4: 8/1	C Roche	R Loughran	22
2007	136	Sir Frederick 7-9-10: 12/1	W J Burke	K T Coleman[3]	22
2008	153	Oslot 6-10-13: 11/4	P F Nicholls (GB)	R Walsh	22
2009	142	Ballyholland 8-10-9: 16/1	C A McBratney	A J McNamara	20
2010	143	Finger Onthe Pulse 9-10-12: 22/1	T J Taaffe	A P McCoy	22
2011	151	Blazing Tempo 7-10-4: 5/1	W P Mullins	Paul Townend	22
2012	145	Bob Lingo 10-10-13: 16/1	Thomas Mullins	Mark Walsh	20
2013	141	Carlingford Lough 7-10-7: 7/2	John E Kiely	A P McCoy	22
2014	161	Road To Riches 7-11-4: 14/1	Noel Meade	Shane Shortall[7]	22
2015	149	Shanahan's Turn 7-10-10: 16/1	Henry de Bromhead	J J Burke	22
2016	150	Lord Scoundrel 7-10-7: 10/1	Gordon Elliott	Donagh Meyler[5]	22
2017	153	Balko des Flos 6-10-10: 6/1	Henry de Bromhead	Davy Russell	22

GUINNESS GALWAY HURDLE HANDICAP (Galway 2m11y)

1993	?	Camden Buzz 5-10-12: 4/1	P Mullins	C F Swan	22
1994	128	Oh So Grumpy 6-10-9: 7/1	Mrs J Harrington	M Dwyer	27
1995	130	No Tag 7-10-11: 11/2	P G Kelly	J Titley	23
1996	127	Mystical City 6-10-1: 20/1	W P Mullins	D Casey	21
1997	150	Toast The Spreece 5-10-9: 12/1	A P O'Brien	A P McCoy	20
1998	130	Black Queen 7-10-2: 10/1	J E Kiely	J Barry	24
1999	152	Quinze 6-11-12: 11/1	P Hughes	R Dunwoody	25
2000	137	Perugino Diamond 4-9-8: 14/1	S O'Farrell	J Culloty	20
2001	136	Ansar 5-9-9: 6/1	D K Weld	P Carberry	20
2002	131	Say Again 6-10-7: 16/1	P Nolan	J L Cullen	24
2003	120	Sabadilla 9-9-7: 14/1	P M Verling	P M Verling	24
2004	129	Cloone River 8-10-7: 7/2	P Nolan	J Cullen	24
2005	128	More Rainbows 5-9-10: 33/1	N Meade	N P Madden	17
2006	132	Cuan Na Grai 5-10-9: 7/1	P Nolan	P W Flood	20
2007	143	Farmer Brown 6-10-11: 9/2	P Hughes	D N Russell	20
2008	131	Indian Pace 7-9-10: 7/1	J E Kiely	P Townend[5]	20
2009	152	Bahrain Storm 6-10-12: 20/1	P J Flynn	S J Gray[5]	20

1017

2010	161	Overturn 6-11-6: 6/1	Donald McCain (GB)	*Graham Lee*	19
2011	146	Moon Dice 6-10-0: 20/1	Paul Flynn	*Tom Doyle*	20
2012	156	Rebel Fitz 7-11-5: 11/2	Michael Winters	*Davy Russell*	20
2013	145	Missunited 6-10-8: 7/1	Michael Winters	*Robbie Power*	20
2014	142	Thomas Edison 7-10-6: 7/2	A J Martin	*A P McCoy*	20
2015	143	Quick Jack 6-10-4: 9/2	A J Martin	*Denis O'Regan*	20
2016	145	Clondaw Warrior 9-11-5: 9/2	W P Mullins	*R Walsh*	20
2017	144	Tigris River 6-10-9: 5/1	Joseph Patrick O'Brien	*Barry Geraghty*	20

JNwine.com CHAMPION CHASE (Gr 1) (Down Royal 3m, Gr 1 from 2002)

1999	164	Florida Pearl 7-11-10: 11/10	W P Mullins	*P Carberry*	6
2000	164	Looks Like Trouble 8-11-10: 5/4	N T Chance (GB)	*R Johnson*	5
2001	143	Foxchapel King 8-11-3: 4/1	M F Morris	*D J Casey*	7
2002	144	More Than A Stroll 10-11-10: 20/1	A L T Moore	*C O'Dwyer*	7
2003	143	Glenelly Gale 9-11-10: 7/1	A L T Moore	*C O'Dwyer*	4
2004	171	Beef Or Salmon 8-11-10: 1/1	M Hourigan	*T J Murphy*	8
2005		Abandoned			
2006	155	Beef Or Salmon 10-11-10: 11/4	M Hourigan	*A J McNamara*	7
2007	146	Taranis 6-11-10: 10/11	P F Nicholls (GB)	*R Walsh*	6
2008	149	Kauto Star 8-11-10: 2/5	P F Nicholls (GB)	*R Walsh*	5
2009	164	The Listener 10-11-10: 7/1	N Mitchell	*A J McNamara*	8
2010	162	Kauto Star 10-11-10: 4/7	Paul Nicholls (GB)	*R Walsh*	7
2011	161	Quito de La Roque 7-11-10: 11/4	Colm A Murphy	*Davy Russell*	7
2012	160	Kauto Stone 6-11-10: 4/1	Paul Nicholls (GB)	*Daryl Jacob*	8
2013	159	Roi du Mee 8-11-10: 12/1	Gordon Elliott	*Bryan Cooper*	6
2014	162	Road To Riches 7-11-10: 9/2	Noel Meade	*Paul Carberry*	8
2015	173	Don Cossack 8-11-10: 2/11	Gordon Elliott	*B J Cooper*	4
2016	168	Valseur Lido 7-11-10: 2/1	Henry de Bromhead	*R Walsh*	7
2017	164	Outlander 9-11-10: 16/1	Gordon Elliott	*J W Kennedy*	8

BAR ONE RACING HATTON'S GRACE HURDLE (Gr 1) (Fairyhouse 2½m)

1994	162	Danoli 6-12-0: 4/6	T Foley	*C F Swan*	7
1995	140	Dorans Pride 6-12-0: 1/5	M Hourigan	*J Broderick*	3
1996	160	Large Action 8-12-0: 9/4	O Sherwood (GB)	*J Osborne*	8
1997	136	Istabraq 5-12-0: 1/3	A P O'Brien	*C F Swan*	5
1998	151	Istabraq 6-12-0: 1/5	A P O'Brien	*C F Swan*	6
1999	177	Limestone Lad 7-11-9: 13/2	J Bowe	*S M McGovern*	5
2000	161	Youlneverwalkalone 6-11-12: 5/4	C Roche	*C O'Dwyer*	7
2001	167	Limestone Lad 9-11-12: 9/4	J Bowe	*P Carberry*	7
2002	152	Limestone Lad 10-11-12: 8/15	J Bowe	*B J Geraghty*	5
2003	138	Solerina 6-11-7: 7/4	J Bowe	*G T Hutchinson*	10
2004	157	Solerina 7-11-7: 4/5	J Bowe	*G T Hutchinson*	5
2005	158	Solerina 8-11-7: 6/4	J Bowe	*G T Hutchinson*	5
2006	155	Brave Inca 8-11-12: 10/3	C A Murphy	*A P McCoy*	5
2007	152	Aitmatov 6-11-10: 2/1	N Meade	*P Carberry*	8
2008	156	Catch Me 6-11-10: 7/4	E J O'Grady	*A J McNamara*	8
2009	140	Oscar Dan Dan 7-11-10: 11/2	T Mullins	*D N Russell*	7
2010	155	Hurricane Fly 6-11-10: 11/4	W P Mullins	*Paul Townend*	11
2011	149	Voler La Vedette 7-11-3: 7/4	Colm A Murphy	*A E Lynch*	4
2012	158	Zaidpour 6-11-10: 7/4	W P Mullins	*R Walsh*	5
2013	160	Jezki 5-11-10: 4/6	Mrs John Harrington	*A P McCoy*	5
2014	148	Lieutenant Colonel 5-11-10: 7/2	Ms Sandra Hughes	*Bryan J Cooper*	5
2015	155	Arctic Fire 6-11-10: 4/5	W P Mullins	*R Walsh*	7
2016	148	Apple's Jade 4-10-13: 4/1	Gordon Elliott	*B J Cooper*	7
2017	156	Apple's Jade 5-11-3: 1/1	Gordon Elliott	*J W Kennedy*	7

JOHN DURKAN MEMORIAL PUNCHESTOWN CHASE (Gr 1)
(Punchestown 2½m40y, run at Fairyhouse in 1997 and 2010)

1992	143	Gold Options 10-11-4: 10/1	P McCreery	*M Dwyer*	9
1993	141	Cahervillahow 9-11-4: 3/1	M F Morris	*N Williamson*	11
1994	166	Merry Gale 6-12-0: 9/4	J Dreaper	*K O'Brien*	5
1995	161	Merry Gale 7-12-0: 6/4	J Dreaper	*R Dunwoody*	7
1996	152	Royal Mountbrowne 8-11-8: 7/1	A P O'Brien	*C F Swan*	6
1997	171	Dorans Pride 8-12-0: 2/5	M Hourigan	*R Dunwoody*	5
1998	153	Imperial Call 9-12-0: 13/8	R Hurley	*P Carberry*	8
1999	152	Buck Rogers 8-11-8: 16/1	V Bowens	*K Whelan*	8
2000	157	Native Upmanship 7-11-12: 9/10	A L T Moore	*C O'Dwyer*	4
2001	163	Florida Pearl 9-11-12: 5/1	W P Mullins	*P Carberry*	4

2002	168	Native Upmanship 9-11-12: 5/4	A L T Moore	C O'Dwyer	5
2003	167	Beef Or Salmon 7-11-12: 4/5	M Hourigan	T J Murphy	7
2004	165	Kicking King 6-11-12: 2/1	T J Taaffe	B J Geraghty	6
2005	153	Hi Cloy 8-11-12: 7/1	M Hourigan	A J McNamara	8
2006	149	In Compliance 6-11-12: 5/1	M J P O'Brien	B J Geraghty	8
2007	166	The Listener 8-11-10: 1/1	R H Alner (GB)	D A Jacob	10
2008	165	Noland 7-11-10: 9/4	P F Nicholls (GB)	S Thomas	8
2009	154	Joncol 6-11-10: 9/4	P Nolan	A P Cawley	5
2010	157	Tranquil Sea 8-11-10: 5/2	E J O'Grady	Andrew J McNamara	8
2011	162	Rubi Light 6-11-10: 5/2	Robert Hennessy	A E Lynch	7
2012	174	Flemenstar 7-11-10: 1/1	Peter Casey	A E Lynch	3
2013	162	Arvika Ligeonniere 8-11-10: 4/7	W P Mullins	R Walsh	3
2014	160	Don Cossack 7-11-10: 13/8	Gordon Elliott	Brian O'Connell	6
2015	175	Djakadam 6-11-10: 7/4	W P Mullins	R Walsh	7
2016	169	Djakadam 7-11-10: 4/5	W P Mullins	R Walsh	5
2017	169	Sizing John 7-11-10: 2/1	Mrs J Harrington	Robbie Power	6

PADDY'S REWARDS CLUB CHASE (Gr 1)
(Leopardstown 2m1f, 2¼m 1996-1997, handicap prior to 1999, Grade 1 from 2004)

1992	117	Saraemma 6-10-2: 5/1	J H Scott	C F Swan	9
1993	?	Lasata 8-10-12: 6/1	M F Morris	C O'Dwyer	9
1994	139	Brockley Court 7-11-2: 7/2	Mrs J Harrington	C F Swan	9
1995		Abandoned			
1996	155	Merry Gale 8-10-13: 5/4	J T R Dreaper	R Dunwoody	5
1997	108	MacAllister 7-9-13: 7/1	V Bowens	B Bowens[3]	4
1998	143	Papillon 7-10-11: 11/4	T M Walsh	R Walsh	4
1999	139	Merry Gale 11-11-5: 8/1	J T R Dreaper	P Moloney	10
2000	142	Papillon 9-12-0: 8/1	T M Walsh	R Walsh	4
2001	146	Knife Edge 6-12-0: 1/1	M J P O'Brien	T P Rudd	8
2002	151	Moscow Flyer 8-11-12: 4/9	Mrs J Harrington	B J Geraghty	6
2003	157	Moscow Flyer 9-11-12: 2/7	Mrs J Harrington	B J Geraghty	6
2004	153	Central House 7-11-12: 9/2	D T Hughes	P Carberry	4
2005	155	Hi Cloy 8-11-12: 8/1	M Hourigan	A J McNamara	5
2006	154	Nickname 7-11-12: 5/2	M Brassil	N P Madden	6
2007	153	Mansony 8-11-12: 2/1	A L T Moore	D N Russell	6
2008	155	Big Zeb 7-11-12: 5/1	C A Murphy	M M O'Connor	7
2009	160	Golden Silver 7-11-12: 5/2	W P Mullins	P Townend	7
2010	158	Big Zeb 9-11-12: 1/1	Colm A Murphy	Barry Geraghty	4
2011	159	Big Zeb 10-11-12: 7/10	Colm A Murphy	Robbie Power	5
2012	164	Sizing Europe 10-11-12: 1/3	H de Bromhead	A E Lynch	5
2013	162	Benefficient 7-11-12: 9/1	A J Martin	Bryan Cooper	7
2014	161	Twinlight 7-11-12: 16/1	W P Mullins	R Walsh	9
2015	160	Flemenstar 10-11-12: 16/1	Anthony Curran	A E Lynch	6
2016	182	Douvan 6-11-12: 1/8	W P Mullins	R Walsh	5
2017	157	*Simply Ned 10-11-12: 16/1	Nicky Richards (GB)	M P Walsh	6

PADDY POWER CHASE (EXTENDED HANDICAP) (Leopardstown 3m100y)

1996	137	New Co 8-10-6: 11/4	M F Morris	C O'Dwyer	17
1997	140	Time For A Run 10-11-1: 12/1	E J O'Grady	Mr P Fenton	21
1998	142	Calling Wild 8-11-3: 8/1	P F Nicholls (GB)	J Tizzard	26
1999	135	Inis Cara 7-10-8: 11/1	M Hourigan	R P McNally[3]	20
2000	116	Call Me Dara 7-9-4: 33/1	R Tyner	N P Mulholland[3]	23
2001	112	I Can Imagine 6-9-2: 12/1	R Tyner	J P Elliott[5]	23
2002	115	Coq Hardi Diamond 8-9-11: 14/1	N Meade	G T Hutchinson[3]	21
2003	122	World Wide Web 7-10-1: 8/1	J O'Neill (GB)	L Cooper	28
2004	129	Keepatem 8-10-8: 7/2	M F Morris	C O'Dwyer	30
2005	123	Black Apalachi 6-10-5: 25/1	P J Rothwell	J L Cullen	26
2006	147	Cane Brake 7-11-3: 14/1	T J Taaffe	A B Joyce[7]	28
2007	125	Newbay Prop 8-9-10: 14/1	A J Martin	R Geraghty	29
2008	141	Wheresben 9-10-7: 33/1	S Fahey	Mr J A Fahey[7]	28
2009	138	Oscar Time 8-10-3: 10/1	M M Lynch	R M Power	28
2010	153	Majestic Concorde 7-11-9: 33/1	D K Weld	Mr R P McNamara	28
2011	132	Cross Appeal 5-10-4: 7/1	Noel Meade	Paul Carberry	26
2012	144	Colbert Station 8-10-11: 5/1	T M Walsh	A P McCoy	28
2013	130	Rockyaboya 9-10-3: 7/1	W P Mullins	R Walsh	28
2014	141	Living Next Door 8-10-9: 20/1	A J Martin	Denis O'Regan	26
2015	142	Minella Foru 6-10-8: 7/1	Edward Harty	Barry Geraghty	28

| 2016 | 158 | Noble Endeavor 7-11-3: 6/1 | Gordon Elliott | *Davy Russell* | 28 |
| 2017 | 161 | Anibale Fly 7-11-8: 14/1 | A J Martin | *Donagh Meyler* | 28 |

LEOPARDSTOWN CHRISTMAS CHASE (Gr 1) (Leopardstown 3m, Gr 2 prior to 2002)

1992	153	General Idea 7-11-11: 9/4	D K Weld	*B Sheridan*	10
1993	150	Deep Bramble 6-11-11: 4/1	M Hourigan	*P Niven*	9
1994	151	Commercial Artist 8-12-0: 9/1	V Bowens	*G Bradley*	5
1995		Abandoned			
1996	149	Johnny Setaside 7-12-0: 2/1	N Meade	*R Dunwoody*	7
1997	170	Imperial Call 8-12-0: 4/7	F Sutherland	*C O'Dwyer*	4
1998	?	Dorans Pride 9-12-0: 4/1	M Hourigan	*P Carberry*	6
1999	157	Rince Ri 6-12-0: 9/2	T M Walsh	*C O'Dwyer*	6
2000	162	Rince Ri 7-12-0: 5/1	T M Walsh	*R Walsh*	7
2001	164	Foxchapel King 8-12-0: 9/2	M F Morris	*D J Casey*	8
2002	156	Beef Or Salmon 6-11-9: 5/1	M Hourigan	*T J Murphy*	7
2003	171	Best Mate 8-11-12: 8/11	Miss H C Knight	*J Culloty*	8
2004	171	Beef Or Salmon 8-11-12: 9/4	M Hourigan	*P Carberry*	6
2005	169	Beef Or Salmon 9-11-12: 9/10	M Hourigan	*P Carberry*	5
2006	164	The Listener 7-11-10: 7/1	R H Alner	*D Jacob*	6
2007	162	Denman 7-11-10: 4/9	P F Nicholls (GB)	*R Walsh*	6
2008	168	Exotic Dancer 8-11-10: 4/1	J O'Neill (GB)	*A P McCoy*	9
2009	158	What A Friend 6-11-10: 11/2	P F Nicholls (GB)	*S Thomas*	11
2010	164	Pandorama 7-11-10: 7/2	Noel Meade	*Paul Carberry*	12
2011	165	Synchronised 8-11-10: 8/1	Jonjo O'Neill (GB)	*A P McCoy*	9
2012	170	Tidal Bay 11-11-10: 9/2	Paul Nicholls (GB)	*R Walsh*	9
2013	163	Bobs Worth 8-11-10: 11/4	Nicky Henderson (GB)	*Barry Geraghty*	9
2014	161	Road To Riches 7-11-10: 4/1	Noel Meade	*Bryan J Cooper*	9
2015	160	Don Poli 6-11-10: 4/6	W P Mullins	*B J Cooper*	6
2016	165	Outlander 8-11-10: 11/1	Gordon Elliott	*J W Kennedy*	13
2017	167	Road To Respect 6-11-10: 8/1	Noel Meade	*Sean Flanagan*	12

RYANAIR HURDLE (December) (Gr 1) (Leopardstown 2m, Grade 1 in 1993 and from 2002)

1992	140	Novello Allegro 4-11-2: 6/1	N Meade	*C F Swan*	7
1993	150	Fortune And Fame 6-12-0: 2/1	D K Weld	*B Sheridan*	7
1994	145	Boro Eight 8-11-7: 11/10	P Mullins	*T P Treacy*	4
1995	140	Kharasar 5-11-7: 10/1	A Mullins	*M Dwyer*	10
1996	144	Theatreworld 4-11-2: 2/1	A P O'Brien	*C F Swan*	6
1997	136	Istabraq 5-12-0: 1/6	A P O'Brien	*C F Swan*	5
1998	150	Istabraq 6-12-0: 1/10	A P O'Brien	*C F Swan*	3
1999	161	Istabraq 7-12-0: 1/8	A P O'Brien	*C F Swan*	6
2000	161	Moscow Flyer 6-12-0: 5/1	Mrs J Harrington	*B J Geraghty*	7
2001	157	Istabraq 9-11-12: 4/11	A P O'Brien	*C F Swan*	6
2002	158	Liss A Paoraigh 7-11-7: 11/10	J E Kiely	*B J Geraghty*	5
2003	146	Golden Cross 4-11-7: 66/1	M Halford	*A P Lane*	7
2004	163	Macs Joy 5-11-12: 7/1	Mrs J Harrington	*B J Geraghty*	6
2005	163	Brave Inca 7-11-12: 9/4	C A Murphy	*A P McCoy*	5
2006	160	Brave Inca 8-11-12: 6/4	C A Murphy	*R Walsh*	4
2007	157	Al Eile 7-11-10: 9/2	J Queally	*T J Murphy*	6
2008	167	Sublimity 8-11-10: 3/1	R A Hennessy	*P A Carberry*	9
2009	159	Solwhit 5-11-10: 8/11	C Byrnes	*D N Russell*	6
2010	159	Hurricane Fly 6-11-10: 8/11	W P Mullins	*Paul Townend*	5
2011	153	Unaccompanied 4-11-0: 10/3	D K Weld	*Paul Townend*	7
2012	169	Hurricane Fly 8-11-10: 1/5	W P Mullins	*R Walsh*	5
2013	168	Hurricane Fly 9-11-10: 11/10	W P Mullins	*R Walsh*	5
2014	157	Hurricane Fly 10-11-10: 5/6	W P Mullins	*R Walsh*	7
2015	159	Nicholas Canyon 5-11-10: 2/5	W P Mullins	*R Walsh*	4
2016	162	Petit Mouchoir 5-11-10: 6/1	Henry de Bromhead	*B J Cooper*	5
2017	159	Mick Jazz 6-11-10: 14/1	Gordon Elliott	*Davy Russell*	5

BHP INSURANCE IRISH CHAMPION HURDLE (Gr 1)
(Leopardstown 2m, run at Fairyhouse 1995)

1993	144	Royal Derbi 8-11-10: 14/1	N A Callaghan (GB)	*D Murphy*	11
1994	166	Fortune And Fame 7-11-10: 4/5	D K Weld	*A Maguire*	7
1995	144	Fortune And Fame 8-11-10: 1/2	D K Weld	*M Dwyer*	5
1996	160	Collier Bay 6-11-10: 5/1	J A B Old (GB)	*J Osborne*	11
1997	150	Cockney Lad 8-11-10: 10/1	N Meade	*R Hughes*	7
1998	150	Istabraq 6-11-10: 4/11	A P O'Brien	*C F Swan*	7
1999	165	Istabraq 7-11-10: 8/15	A P O'Brien	*C F Swan*	6

2000	160	Istabraq 8-11-10: 2/9	A P O'Brien	*C F Swan*	6
2001	160	Istabraq 9-11-10: 4/11	A P O'Brien	*C F Swan*	7
2002	143	Ned Kelly 6-11-10: 11/8	E J O'Grady	*N Williamson*	8
2003	152	Like-A-Butterfly 9-11-5: 6/4	C Roche	*C F Swan*	5
2004	151	Foreman 6-11-10: 8/1	T Doumen (Fr)	*T Doumen*	8
2005	160	Macs Joy 6-11-10: 11/8	Mrs J Harrington	*B J Geraghty*	6
2006	164	Brave Inca 8-11-10: 6/5	C A Murphy	*A P McCoy*	7
2007	161	Hardy Eustace 10-11-10: 9/1	D T Hughes	*C O'Dwyer*	8
2008	160	Sizing Europe 6-11-10: 10/3	H de Bromhead	*A J McNamara*	6
2009	155	Brave Inca 11-11-10: 11/4	C A Murphy	*R Walsh*	9
2010	162	Solwhit 6-11-10: 5/6	C Byrnes	*D N Russell*	7
2011	169	Hurricane Fly 7-11-10: 4/9	W P Mullins	*Paul Townend*	5
2012	168	Hurricane Fly 8-11-10: 4/5	W P Mullins	*R Walsh*	5
2013	169	Hurricane Fly 9-11-10: 1/6	W P Mullins	*R Walsh*	5
2014	163	Hurricane Fly 10-11-10: 4/7	W P Mullins	*R Walsh*	4
2015	167	Hurricane Fly 11-11-10: 11/10	W P Mullins	*R Walsh*	6
2016	176	Faugheen 8-11-10: 3/10	W P Mullins	*R Walsh*	5
2017	162	Petit Mouchoir 6-11-10: 9/10	Henry de Bromhead	*D J Mullins*	4
2018	162	Supasundae 8-11-10: 8/1	Mrs J Harrington	*Robbie Power*	8

UNIBET IRISH GOLD CUP (Gr 1) (Leopardstown 3m)

1993	161	Jodami 8-12-0: 11/8	P Beaumont (GB)	*M Dwyer*	7
1994	160	Jodami 9-12-0: 5/4	P Beaumont (GB)	*M Dwyer*	6
1995	162	Jodami 10-12-0: 13/8	P Beaumont (GB)	*M Dwyer*	6
1996	176	Imperial Call 7-12-0: 4/1	F Sutherland	*C O'Dwyer*	8
1997	168	Danoli 9-12-0: 6/1	T Foley	*T Treacy*	8
1998	165	Dorans Pride 9-12-0: 6/4	M Hourigan	*R Dunwoody*	8
1999	166	Florida Pearl 7-12-0: 8/15	W P Mullins	*R Dunwoody*	7
2000	170	Florida Pearl 8-12-0: 8/11	W P Mullins	*P Carberry*	7
2001	169	Florida Pearl 9-12-0: 5/4	W P Mullins	*R Johnson*	7
2002	167	Alexander Banquet 9-12-0: 3/1	W P Mullins	*B J Geraghty*	5
2003	159	Beef Or Salmon 7-12-0: 1/1	M Hourigan	*T J Murphy*	5
2004	166	Florida Pearl 12-11-12: 5/1	W P Mullins	*R Johnson*	7
2005	167	Rule Supreme 9-11-12: 11/2	W P Mullins	*D J Casey*	7
2006	160	Beef Or Salmon 10-11-12: 2/5	M Hourigan	*P Carberry*	7
2007	167	Beef Or Salmon 11-11-12: 11/4	M Hourigan	*A J McNamara*	5
2008	157	The Listener 9-11-10: 2/1	R H Alner (GB)	*D A Jacob*	8
2009	168	Neptune Collonges 8-11-10: 8/13	P F Nicholls (GB)	*R Walsh*	6
2010	159	Joncol 7-11-10: 9/4	P Nolan	*A P Cawley*	7
2011	159	Kempes 8-11-10: 5/1	W P Mullins	*D J Casey*	9
2012	156	Quel Esprit 8-11-10: 5/4	W P Mullins	*R Walsh*	7
2013	167	Sir des Champs 7-11-10: 11/8	W P Mullins	*Davy Russell*	4
2014	161	Last Instalment 9-11-10: 8/1	Philip Fenton	*Brian O'Connell*	7
2015	161	Carlingford Lough 9-11-10: 4/1	John E Kiely	*A P McCoy*	8
2016	167	Carlingford Lough 10-11-10: 20/1	John E Kiely	*Barry Geraghty*	10
2017	164	Sizing John 7-11-10: 100/30	Mrs J Harrington	*Robbie Power*	7
2018	161	Edwulf 9-11-10: 33/1	Joseph Patrick O'Brien	*Mr D O'Connor*	10

BOYLESPORTS IRISH GRAND NATIONAL CHASE (EXTENDED HANDICAP) (Fairyhouse 3m5f)

1993	142	Ebony Jane 8-10-7: 6/1	F Flood	*C F Swan*	27
1994	148	Son of War 7-10-10: 12/1	P McCreery	*F Woods*	18
1995	169	Flashing Steel 10-12-0: 9/1	J Mulhern	*J Osborne*	18
1996	145	Feathered Gale 9-10-0: 8/1	A L T Moore	*F Woods*	17
1997	142	Mudahim 11-10-3: 13/2	Mrs J Pitman (GB)	*J Titley*	20
1998	143	Bobbyjo 8-11-3: 8/1	T Carberry	*P Carberry*	22
1999	138	Glebe Lad 7-10-0: 8/1	M J P O'Brien	*T P Rudd*	18
2000	150	Commanche Court 7-11-4: 14/1	T M Walsh	*R Walsh*	24
2001	140	Davids Lad 7-10-0: 10/1	A J Martin	*T J Murphy*	19
2002	138	The Bunny Boiler 8-9-9: 12/1	N Meade	*R Geraghty[5]*	17
2003	137	Timbera 9-10-12: 11/1	D T Hughes	*J Culloty*	21
2004	129	Granit d'Estruval 10-10-0: 33/1	F Murphy (GB)	*B Harding*	28
2005	129	Numbersixvalverde 9-10-1: 9/1	M Brassil	*R Walsh*	26
2006	134	Point Barrow 8-10-8: 20/1	P Hughes	*P A Carberry*	26
2007	140	Butler's Cabin 7-10-4: 14/1	J O'Neill (GB)	*A P McCoy*	29
2008	140	Hear The Echo 7-10-0: 33/1	M F Morris	*P W Flood*	23
2009	147	Niche Market 8-10-5: 33/1	R H Buckler (GB)	*H Skelton[1]*	28

2010	142	Bluesea Cracker 8-10-4: 25/1	J Motherway	A J McNamara	26
2011	139	Organisedconfusion 6-9-13: 12/1	A L T Moore	Miss N Carberry	25
2012	147	Lion Na Bearnai 10-10-8: 33/1	Thomas Gibney	A P Thornton[3]	29
2013	135	Liberty Counsel 10-9-5: 50/1	Mrs D A Love	Ben Dalton[s]	28
2014	148	Shuttthefrontdoor 7-10-13: 8/1	Jonjo O'Neill (GB)	Barry Geraghty	26
2015	143	Thunder And Roses 7-10-6: 20/1	Ms Sandra Hughes	Ms K Walsh	28
2016	145	Rogue Angel 8-10-9: 16/1	M F Morris	G N Fox[3]	27
2017	167	Our Duke 7-11-4: 9/2	Mrs J Harrington	Robbie Power	28
2018	142	General Principle 9-10-0: 20/1	Gordon Elliott	J J Slevin	28

BOYLESPORTS CHAMPION CHASE (Drogheda) (Gr 1)
(Punchestown 2m, handicap before 1999, run at Fairyhouse, 2m100y in 2001)

1993	144	Viking Flagship 6-10-7: 5/4	D Nicholson (GB)	R Dunwoody	8
1994	138	Saraemma 8-10-12: 16/1	J H Scott	K F O'Brien	9
1995	148	Strong Platinum 7-11-1: 3/1	P Burke	C O'Dwyer	9
1996	177	Klairon Davis 7-12-0: 5/2	A L T Moore	F Woods	8
1997	171	Klairon Davis 8-12-0: 11/10	A L T Moore	F Woods	7
1998	162	Big Matt 10-10-11: 16/1	N Henderson (GB)	M A Fitzgerald	8
1999	154	Celibate 8-11-9: 7/1	C J Mann (GB)	R Dunwoody	6
2000	157	Get Real 9-11-6: 3/1	N J Henderson (GB)	M A Fitzgerald	7
2001	162	Micko's Dream 9-12-0: 5/1	W P Mullins	R Walsh	9
2002	140	Strong Run 9-12-0: 4/1	N Meade	P Carberry	7
2003	148	Flagship Uberalles 9-12-0: 12/1	P J Hobbs (GB)	R Johnson	7
2004	153	Moscow Flyer 10-11-12: 4/11	Mrs J Harrington	B J Geraghty	7
2005	155	Rathgar Beau 9-11-12: 8/1	E Sheehy	J R Barry	7
2006	159	Newmill 8-11-12: 5/4	J J Murphy	A J McNamara	6
2007	149	Mansony 8-11-12: 13/2	A L T Moore	D N Russell	7
2008	151	Twist Magic 6-11-12: 6/4	P F Nicholls (GB)	R Walsh	9
2009	162	Master Minded 6-11-12: 3/10	P F Nicholls (GB)	R Walsh	6
2010	161	Golden Silver 8-11-12: 12/1	W P Mullins	P Townend	11
2011	172	Big Zeb 10-11-12: 9/4	Colm A Murphy	Barry Geraghty	6
2012	167	Sizing Europe 10-11-12: 8/13	H de Bromhead	A E Lynch	6
2013	178	Sprinter Sacre 7-11-12: 1/9	Nicky Henderson (GB)	Barry Geraghty	5
2014	160	Sizing Europe 12-11-12: 7/1	Henry de Bromhead	A E Lynch	8
2015	157	Felix Yonger 9-11-12: 5/1	W P Mullins	D E Mullins	9
2016	168	God's Own 8-11-12: 9/1	Tom George (GB)	Paddy Brennan	7
2017	168	Fox Norton 7-11-12: 5/2	Mrs J Harrington	Robbie Power	8
2018	168	Un de Sceaux 10-11-12: 9/2	W P Mullins	Mr P W Mullins	9

CORAL PUNCHESTOWN GOLD CUP CHASE (Gr 1)
(Punchestown 3m120y, run at Fairyhouse in 2001)

1999	175	Imperial Call 9-11-9: 8/1	R Hurley	R Walsh	5
2000	157	Commanche Court 7-11-9: 10/3	T M Walsh	R Walsh	11
2001	158	Moscow Express 9-12-0: 14/1	Ms F M Crowley	B J Geraghty	6
2002	173	Florida Pearl 10-12-0: 13/8	W P Mullins	B J Geraghty	7
2003	170	First Gold 10-12-0: 7/4	F Doumen (Fr)	T Doumen	7
2004	170	Beef Or Salmon 8-11-12: 5/4	M Hourigan	T J Murphy	6
2005	169	Kicking King 7-11-12: 8/11	T J Taaffe	B J Geraghty	6
2006	160	War of Attrition 7-11-12: 4/5	M F Morris	C O'Dwyer	6
2007	161	Neptune Collonges 6-11-12: 8/1	P F Nicholls (GB)	R Walsh	10
2008	166	Neptune Collonges 7-11-10: 9/10	P F Nicholls (GB)	R Walsh	9
2009	167	Notre Pere 8-11-10: 15/8	J T R Dreaper	A E Lynch	12
2010	159	Planet of Sound 8-11-10: 14/1	P J Hobbs	R Johnson	11
2011	151	Follow The Plan 8-11-10: 20/1	Oliver McKiernan	T J Doyle	8
2012	164	China Rock 9-11-10: 20/1	M F Morris	Barry Geraghty	8
2013	171	Sir Des Champs 7-11-10: 2/1	W P Mullins	Davy Russell	8
2014	165	Boston Bob 9-11-10: 5/2	W P Mullins	R Walsh	9
2015	180	Don Cossack 8-11-10: 5/2	Gordon Elliott	Paul Carberry	8
2016	167	Carlingford Lough 10-11-10: 12/1	John E Kiely	Barry Geraghty	6
2017	168	Sizing John 7-11-10: 9/10	Mrs J Harrington	Robbie Power	8
2018	168	Bellshill 8-11-10: 4/1	W P Mullins	D J Mullins	12

LADBROKES CHAMPION STAYERS HURDLE (Tipperkevin) (Gr 1)
(Punchestown 3m, run at Fairyhouse in 2001)

1995	146	Derrymoyle 6-11-11: 8/1	M Cunningham	M Dwyer	8
1996	154	Derrymoyle 7-12-0: 10/3	M Cunningham	M Dwyer	10
1997	164	Paddy's Return 5-11-12: 10/3	F Murphy (GB)	N Williamson	8

1998	157	Derrymoyle 9-12-0: 10/1	M Cunningham	*A P McCoy*	8
1999	164	Anzum 8-12-0: 7/1	D Nicholson (GB)	*R Johnson*	6
2000	159	Rubhahunish 9-11-11: 5/1	N A Twiston-Davies (GB)	*C Llewellyn*	9
2001	141	Bannow Bay 6-11-12: 11/8	C Roche	*C F Swan*	9
2002	144	Limestone Lad 10-11-12: 4/6	J Bowe	*P Carberry*	9
2003	144	Holy Orders 6-11-12: 6/1	W P Mullins	*J R Barry*	6
2004	163	Rhinestone Cowboy 8-11-12: 5/2	J O'Neill (GB)	*Mr J P Magnier*	8
2005	137	Carlys Quest 11-11-12: 25/1	F Murphy (GB)	*K J Mercer*	9
2006	151	Asian Maze 7-11-7: 8/13	T Mullins	*R Walsh*	12
2007	150	Refinement 8-11-7: 16/1	J O'Neill (GB)	*A P McCoy*	9
2008	163	Blazing Bailey 6-11-10: 10/3	A King (GB)	*R Thornton*	12
2009	163	Fiveforthree 7-11-10: 5/4	W P Mullins	*R Walsh*	10
2010	152	Quevega 6-11-5: 5/2	W P Mullins	*P Townend*	13
2011	154	Quevega 7-11-5: 8/11	W P Mullins	*R Walsh*	10
2012	157	Quevega 8-11-3: 11/10	W P Mullins	*R Walsh*	7
2013	159	Quevega 9-11-3: 6/4	W P Mullins	*R Walsh*	6
2014	149	Jetson 9-11-10: 20/1	Mrs John Harrington	*Davy Russell*	9
2015	158	Jezki 7-11-10: 5/2	Mrs John Harrington	*M P Walsh*	11
2016	160	One Track Mind 6-11-10: 10/1	Warren Greatrex (GB)	*Gavin Sheehan*	9
2017	165	Unowhatimeanharry 9-11-10: 4/1	Harry Fry (GB)	*Noel Fehily*	12
2018	165	Faugheen 10-11-10: 11/2	W P Mullins	*D J Mullins*	12

BETDAQ PUNCHESTOWN CHAMPION HURDLE (Gr 1)
(Punchestown 2m, run at Leopardstown in 2001)

1999	177	Istabraq 7-12-0: 1/4	A P O'Brien	*C F Swan*	7
2000	161	Grimes 7-11-9: 6/1	C Roche	*C F Swan*	9
2001	168	Moscow Flyer 7-12-0: 6/1	Mrs J Harrington	*B J Gerraghty*	7
2002	145	Davenport Milenium 6-12-0: 11/2	W P Mullins	*R Walsh*	6
2003	151	Quazar 5-11-13: 7/2	J O'Neill (GB)	*A Dobbin*	6
2004	149	Hardy Eustace 7-11-12: 3/1	D T Hughes	*C O'Dwyer*	9
2005	163	Brave Inca 7-11-12: 2/1	C A Murphy	*A P McCoy*	5
2006	166	Macs Joy 7-11-12: 11/4	Mrs J Harrington	*B J Gerraghty*	4
2007	156	Silent Oscar 8-11-12: 20/1	H Rogers	*R M Power*	8
2008	161	Punjabi 5-11-12: 2/1	N J Henderson (GB)	*B J Gerraghty*	6
2009	164	Solwhit 5-11-12: 2/1	C Byrnes	*D N Russell*	9
2010	161	Hurricane Fly 6-11-12: 3/1	W P Mullins	*P Townend*	11
2011	168	Hurricane Fly 7-11-12: 1/2	W P Mullins	*R Walsh*	6
2012	163	Hurricane Fly 8-11-12: 4/11	W P Mullins	*R Walsh*	4
2013	170	Hurricane Fly 9-11-12: 1/4	W P Mullins	*R Walsh*	6
2014	162	Jezki 6-11-12: 4/5	Mrs John Harrington	*A P McCoy*	3
2015	160	Faugheen 7-11-12: 1/6	W P Mullins	*R Walsh*	4
2016	151	Vroum Vroum Mag 7-11-5: 4/6	W P Mullins	*R Walsh*	6
2017	161	Wicklow Brave 8-11-12: 12/1	W P Mullins	*Mr P W Mullins*	10
2018	162	Supasundae 8-11-12: 7/1	Mrs J Harrington	*Robbie Power*	7

International

GRAND STEEPLE-CHASE DE PARIS (Gr 1) (Auteuil 3m6f, 3m5f prior to 2014)

1993	163	Ucello II 7-10-1	F Doumen	*C Aubert*	9
1994	164	Ucello II 8-10-1	F Doumen	*C Aubert*	9
1995	169	Ubu III 9-10-1	F Doumen	*P Chevalier*	13
1996	164	Arenice 8-10-1	G Macaire	*P Sourzac*	7
1997	173	Al Capone II 9-10-1	B Secly	*J-Y Beaurain*	6
1998	161	First Gold 5-9-11	F Doumen	*Mr T Doumen*	11
1999	168	Mandarino 6-10-1	M Rolland	*P Chevalier*	11
2000	165	Vieux Beaufai 7-10-3	F Danloux	*P Bigot*	12
2001	169	Kotkijet 6-10-5	J-P Gallorini	*T Majorcryk*	11
2002	153	*El Paso III 10-10-8	B Secly	*L Metais*	14
2003	155	Line Marine 6-10-3	C Aubert	*C Pieux*	11
2004	145	Kotkijet 9-10-8	J-P Gallorini	*T Majorcryk*	16
2005	144	Sleeping Jack 6-10-8	J Ortet	*C Pieux*	18
2006	149	Princesse d'Anjou 5-9-13	F M Cottin	*P Carberry*	16
2007	151	Mid Dancer 6-10-8	A Chaille-Chaille	*C Gombeau*	12
2008	147	Princesse d'Anjou 7-10-4	F M Cottin	*P Carberry*	16

1023

2009	161	Remember Rose 6-10-8	J-P Gallorini	*C Pieux*	13
2010	162	Polar Rochelais 7-10-8	P Quinton	*J Zuliani*	13
2011	162	Mid Dancer 10-10-8	C Aubert	*Sylvain Dehez*	14
2012	160	Mid Dancer 11-10-10	C Aubert	*Sylvain Dehez*	19
2013	159	Bel La Vie 7-10-10	G Macaire	*Bertrand Lestrade*	16
2014	155	Storm of Saintly 5-10-6	G Macaire	*Vincent Cheminaud*	15
2015	160	Milord Thomas 6-10-10	D Bressou	*Jacques Ricou*	14
2016	158	So French 5-10-6	G Macaire	*James Reveley*	13
2017	160	So French 6-10-10	G Macaire	*James Reveley*	15
2018	157	On The Go 5-10-6	G Macaire	*James Reveley*	14

GRANDE COURSE DE HAIES D'AUTEUIL (Gr 1) (Auteuil 3m1½f)

1993	?	Ubu III 7-10-5	F Doumen	*A Kondrat*	14
1994	?	Le Roi Thibault 5-10-1	G Doleuze	*Y Fouin*	8
1995	?	Matchou 6-10-5	J Lesbordes	*D Mescam*	12
1996	155	Earl Grant 7-10-5	B Secly	*J Y Beaurain*	10
1997	163	Bog Frog 8-10-5	B Secly	*J Y Beaurain*	15
1998	161	Mantovo 6-10-5	M Rolland	*F Benech*	8
1999	168	Vaporetto 6-10-5	J P Gallorini	*T Majorcryk*	10
2000	164	Le Sauvignon 6-10-5	J Bertran de Balanda	*D Bressou*	7
2001	178	Le Sauvignon 7-10-5	J Bertran de Balanda	*D Bressou*	9
2002	161	Laveron 7-10-8	F Doumen	*T Doumen*	10
2003	140	Nobody Told Me 5-9-13	W P Mullins (Ir)	*D J Casey*	8
2004	149	Rule Supreme 8-10-8	W P Mullins (Ir)	*D J Casey*	7
2005	147	Lycaon de Vauzelle 6-10-8	J Bertran de Balanda	*B Chameraud*	8
2006	154	Mid Dancer 5-10-3	A Chaille-Chaille	*C Pieux*	9
2007	152	Zaiyad 6-10-8	A Chaille-Chaille	*J Ricou*	14
2008	160	Oeil du Maitre 6-10-8	J P Gallorini	*S Colas*	13
2009	151	Questarabad 5-10-3	M Rolland	*R Schmidlin*	7
2010	162	Mandali 6-10-8	J-P Gallorini	*C Soumillon*	8
2011	162	Thousand Stars 7-10-8	W P Mullins (Ir)	*R Walsh*	10
2012	163	Thousand Stars 8-10-10	W P Mullins (Ir)	*R Walsh*	12
2013	165	Gemix 5-10-6	N Bertran de Balanda	*David Cottin*	14
2014	170	Gemix 6-10-10	N Bertran de Balanda	*David Cottin*	13
2015	162	Un Temps Pour Tout 6-10-10	David Pipe (GB)	*James Reveley*	15
2016	162	Ptit Zig 7-10-10	Paul Nicholls (GB)	*Sam Twiston-Davies*	12
2017	161	L'Ami Serge 7-10-10	Nicky Henderson (GB)	*Daryl Jacob*	10
2018	164	De Bon Coeur 5-10-1	Francois Nicolle	*Kevin Nabet*	13

FIND TIMEFORM ONLINE

Desktop: timeform.com
Get the full premium service for Britain and Ireland including Timeform Race Cards, with full commentaries, Flags and ratings for £5 each, Race Passes from less than £2.50 a day, great features from Timeform writers and much more. Register free!

Downloads   Features   Shop

Mobile & Tablet: Download the App
Find winners on the move with the Timeform App. Includes free cards, results and features plus premium tips and Race Passes. Look out for 1-2-3s, Smart Stats and star ratings. **New! Sortable racecards, runners A-Z and free bet Filter**

TF   Download on the App Store   Download for Android

Follow us on Twitter
@Timeform

Find us on Facebook
facebook.com/timeform1948

Get the best advice and analysis, wherever you are.

It's all about winners!

Flags | Ratings | Insight | Analysis

TIMEFORM
PLAY SMARTER